About the Authors

Katherine Barber

Lisa Devries

Heather Fitzgerald

Robert Pontisso

The lexicographers of the Canadian Oxford Dictionary team have collectively over 40 years of experience editing dictionaries and thesauruses. They have lived in seven cities in four provinces, and thus bring a wealth of knowledge of both regional and general Canadian English to the task. Katherine Barber, Editor-in-Chief of Canadian dictionaries since 1991, received the Canadian Booksellers Association's Editor of the Year award in 1999, and is well-known across Canada for frequent appearances on radio and television. In addition to writing Oxford's Canadian dictionaries, the lexicographers are constantly engaged in a reading program to identify new and distinctly Canadian words. They have now read over 9,000 Canadian books, magazines, and newspapers.

Canadian Spelling Bee Dictionary

Edited by
Katherine Barber
Lisa Devries
Heather Fitzgerald
Robert Pontisso

Editor-in-Chief, Canadian Dictionaries
Katherine Barber

OXFORD
UNIVERSITY PRESS

70 Wynford Drive, Don Mills, Ontario M3C 1J9

www.oup.com/ca

Oxford University Press is a department of the University of Oxford. It furthers the University's objective of excellence in research, scholarship, and education by publishing worldwide in

Oxford New York

Auckland Cape Town Dar es Salaam Hong Kong Karachi Kuala Lumpur Madrid Melbourne Mexico City Nairobi New Delhi Shanghai Taipei Toronto

With offices in

Argentina Austria Brazil Chile Czech Republic France Greece Guatemala Hungary Italy Japan Poland Portugal Singapore South Korea Switzerland Thailand Turkey Ukraine Vietnam

Published in Canada by Oxford University Press

First edition 2008

Library and Archives Canada Cataloguing in Publication

Canadian spelling bee dictionary / edited by Katherine Barber... [et al.].

ISBN 978-0-19-542985-5

1. English language--Canada--Orthography and spelling--Dictionaries. 2. English language--Orthography and spelling--Dictionaries. I. Barber, Katherine, 1959- II. Title: Spelling bee dictionary.

PE1153.C36 2008 423'.1 C2008-901709-9

Contents

About this dictionary

Oxford's *Canadian Spelling Bee Dictionary* is unlike any other dictionary. It is designed specifically for those who need help with spelling: students participating in spelling bees, editors needing to check the preferred Canadian spelling of a word, people playing word games, or any of us for whom the English language's notoriously difficult spelling is a challenge.

For this reason, this dictionary includes only the information that is needed to help with spelling difficult words. It includes all the challenging words in the *Canadian Oxford Dictionary* that people need to look up, while leaving out those that most people over the age of eight know how to spell and don't need to check. In contrast, ordinary dictionaries of this size function of necessity in the opposite way, leaving out the more uncommon words and keeping the easier ones.

Since the focus is on spelling, we give only the central definition for each word. Most words have many different meanings, and these take up a lot of the space in a general dictionary. If all you need to do is check a word's spelling, however, these extra definitions are superfluous, so they have been left out. Likewise, this dictionary will not give you information on plurals, conjugations, or different parts of speech for the same word. It does not include proprietary terms, vulgar slang, suffixes, prefixes, abbreviations and acronyms, idioms and phrases, comparatives and superlatives, or compounds written with a space or hyphen. For all such information, you need to consult the larger *Canadian Oxford Dictionary* or *Concise Canadian Oxford Dictionary*. If you are a student and need extra help with how to use words in a sentence, or thorny usage and grammar issues, we recommend the *Student's Oxford Canadian Dictionary*. But if you just need to check a spelling of a troublesome word, or want to improve your vocabulary by learning the spelling and meaning of hard words, you will find it much easier and faster to do so with this dictionary.

Focusing on core information also means that we can have a much more uncluttered layout and larger typeface than in our other dictionaries, though in a more compact and portable book.

On the other hand, this dictionary does include features that are not usually found in dictionaries of this size and price. Etymologies with the language of origin written out in full, plus the root words and their meanings, are provided for every entry. This is an invaluable feature not only for spelling bee participants, but also for any word lovers who are intrigued by the fascinating stories behind our words.

The dictionary has a very easy pronunciation system (see below for more details).

An extra feature is the warnings about confusable words that sound the same but are spelled differently. Some such homophones themselves have entries in the dictionary, but others do not if they are easy to spell. For instance, the entry for the word 'khat' (pronounced "KOT") has the homophones 'cot' and 'caught' listed. Neither 'cot' nor 'caught' has its own entry in the dictionary, the former because it is a common word that is very easy to spell, and the latter because it is a conjugated form of a verb. The pronunciations are those common in general Canadian English; homophones are therefore homophones for speakers of Canadian English, not necessarily for speakers of other varieties of English (for instance, 'khat', 'cot', and 'caught' are all pronounced differently in Southern Standard British English). If the word has more than one pronunciation, homophones are given for all pronunciations as applicable.

We are very grateful for the input of Collene Ferguson, April Andreosso, and Lynne Munro of CanWest CanSpell, whose experience with spelling bees has been invaluable to us.

There is an honourable tradition of 'hard words' dictionaries in the history of lexicography. Oxford's Canadian dictionary editors are proud to revive that tradition with this *Canadian Spelling Bee Dictionary*.

PRONUNCIATIONS

The pronunciations in the Canadian Spelling Bee Dictionary are those of general Canadian English. In transcribing these pronunciations, the editors have put their trust in users' instinctive knowledge of how basic English words are pronounced, and have made no use of foreign characters, distracting accents, or other strange sorts of notation that often confuse more than they clarify. A reader's spontaneous first reading of any given pronunciation should be correct, with proper articulation and natural rhythm:

physiognomy
- "fizzy ONNA mee"

acetylsalicylic
- "a seetle salla SILLIC"

As these examples indicate, words are broken up into natural segments, each with a maximum of two syllables. If a segment has more than one syllable (e.g. "fizzy", "salla"), the stress falls on the first. The segment that takes the strongest stress is printed in capital letters ("ONNA", "SILLIC").

In English it is natural for an unstressed vowel to be pronounced indistinctly. In 'acetylsalicylic', for example, the vowel represented by the first 'y' is not usually enunciated clearly. (The pronunciation "see till" in place of "seetle" would probably strike many as unnaturally persnickety.) Similarly, while the sound of the first 'i' can vary somewhat, it is generally an indistinct "uh". Rather than trying to represent these inherently indefinite sounds with misleadingly precise transcriptions, the editors have relied on English speakers' natural tendency to produce unstressed vowel sounds in certain situations, as when reading a letter 'a' at the end of a word (e.g. 'panda', 'parka', 'soda'). In the sample entries above, the final "a" in "ONNA" and "salla" is automatically pronounced with the indistinct "uh" sound appropriate for the written segments 'ogno' and 'sali'. English speakers will also naturally pronounce the second syllable of "seetle" with suitable fuzziness.

Sometimes an unstressed vowel is so indistinct that it almost disappears altogether. In these cases an apostrophe is often used in the pronunciation:

academician
- "acka duh MISH'n"

Achaean
- "a KEE 'n"

catechetical
- "catta KETTA k'll"

conciliate
- "k'n SILLY ate"

marmoreal
- "mar MORRY 'll"

All pronunciations in general Canadian use are provided for each headword. Words derived from the headword and listed at the end of the entry are given pronunciations only if these differ significantly from that of the headword or any previous derived word, or are likely to be unfamiliar:

indicate *verb*
- "INDA cate"
- **indication** *noun*
- **indicative** *adjective* "in DICKA tiv"
- **indicatively** *adverb*
- **indicator** *noun*

Some other general points:

The letters "zh" are used for the middle sound of 'vision' ("VIZH'n").

The letters "ur" are used for the sound of 'her', 'sir', and 'fur'.

Unless otherwise indicated, "th" represents the sound in 'thin', not the sound in 'this'.

Very common prefixes like 'de-', 'pre-', and 're-', whose vowel can be anything from a short "e" to a long "ee" to a short "i" to an "uh", are often transcribed just as they are spelled, leaving users free to pronounce them as they would instinctively.

A few words in this dictionary have retained their foreign nasal pronunciations (e.g. 'Beauceron', 'chanson', 'embonpoint'). These pronunciations are indicated with a ~ above the nasal vowel and a short explanation:

Beauceron
- "boe suh RÕH" (with a nasal *OH*)

chanson
- "shãh SÕH" (with nasal *ah* and *OH*)

embonpoint
- "ãh bõh PWÃ" (with nasal *ah*, *oh*, and *A*)

When the letter 'n' is followed by a long "oo" sound (as in 'new', 'neutral', and 'nuclear'), some Canadians pronounce a "y" at the beginning of the vowel while others do not. Rather than list both the "noo" and the "nyoo" pronunciations separately in all such cases, the editors have often used "new" to stand for either pronunciation. Whatever pronunciation a user may use for the word 'new' will be acceptable for the words in question.

ETYMOLOGIES

The following conventions are used for etymologies:

If the word is derived from a proper name which is mentioned in the definition, no etymology is given. Thus, there is no etymology at 'Haileyburian' (a resident of Haileybury, Ont.) or 'Hallstatt' (of or relating to the early Iron Age in Europe, as attested by archaeological finds at Hallstatt in Upper Austria). All other types of words have an etymology, which appears in square brackets on a new line after the definition.

The language first mentioned is the language from which the word came directly into English. If the word is ultimately derived from Latin, Greek, Arabic, or Sanskrit, its previous history is often also noted, working backwards from the word's arrival in English.

If the word has exactly the same meaning and form in English as in its original language, just the name of the language is given, in roman letters. Thus, the etymology at 'haiku' is simply

[Japanese]

If the word has the same form in English as in the language of origin, but a different meaning, the name of the language and the meaning of the word in it are given. Thus, the etymology at 'latex' is

[Latin, = liquid]

If the root word in another language has a different form but the same meaning as in English, the foreign word is given in italics but without a translation. Thus, at 'harmattan', the etymology is

[Fanti or Twi *haramata*]

This means that *haramata* designated the same parching dusty land-wind of the West African coast as the English word derived from it does.

If the root word has both a different

form and a different meaning from its English derivative, both are given. Thus, the etymology for 'hadron' (any of a class of subatomic particles) is

[Greek *hadros* bulky]

When the word is traced back through several languages, the same conventions apply. The etymology for 'harmony':

[Old French *harmonie* from Latin *harmonia* from Greek *harmonia* joining, concord, from *harmos* joint]

means that Old French *harmonie* and Latin *harmonia* both meant the same thing as 'harmony' in English, but that the ultimate Greek origin had a different meaning.

When a language of origin is stated followed by two or more foreign words, it is to be understood that all of the words are from the same language (until a different language is mentioned). In the etymology for 'helichrysum'

[Latin from Greek *helikhrusos*, from *helix* spiral + *khrusos* gold]

it is to be understood that the Latin word was also *helichrysum*, derived from the Greek word *helikhrusos* (both Latin and Greek words designating the same plant as the English word), and that the Greek word was itself derived from two other Greek words, *helix* and *khrusos*.

Many etymologies use cross-references to other entries that are in the dictionary, where the full etymological information will be found. These cross-references are in small capital letters.

A few words, usually compounds formed in English from already existing English words, have etymologies which simply specify the base words. Thus 'headdress' has the etymology ['head' + 'dress']. Neither 'head' nor 'dress' is in the dictionary as they are both well-known words that are easy to spell, so they do not appear in the small capital letters of a cross-reference. Words with this kind of etymology should be considered to have English as their language of origin.

FEATURES OF THE DICTIONARY

Headword

ceilidh *noun*
• "CAY lee"
• a party featuring traditional Scottish or Irish music, dancing, songs, and stories.
• [Gaelic, from Old Irish *céilide* visit, visiting, from *céile* companion]

Pronunciation

Headword in italics for foreign borrowings not fully naturalized

censitaire *noun*
• "soncy TARE"
• *Cdn* a tenant on a seigneury.
• [French, from CENS]

Variant spellings (with regions indicated if the variants are regional)

cheque *noun*
ALSO SPELLED: esp. *US* **check**
• "CHECK"
• a written order to a bank to pay the stated sum from the drawer's account to a specified person or company.
• [special use of 'check' to mean 'device for checking the amount of an item']
HOMOPHONES: *check, Czech*

Definition

Warnings about words that sound the same

clamour *noun*
ALSO SPELLED: **clamor**
• "CLAMMER"
• loud or vehement shouting or noise.
• [Old French from Latin *clamor -oris* from *clamare* cry out]
• **clamorous** *adjective*
• **clamorously** *adverb*
• **clamorousness** *noun*
HOMOPHONES: *clammer, clamber*

Part of speech

Derivatives included without their definitions if their meanings can easily be worked out from the meaning of the headword

console[1] *verb*
• "k'n SOLE"
• comfort, esp. in grief or disappointment.
• [French *consoler* from Latin *consolari* (from *com-* with + *solari* soothe)]
• **consolable** *adjective*
• **consolation** *noun*
• **consolatory** *adjective* "k'n SOLLA tory"
• **consoler** *noun*
• **consolingly** *adverb*

Two or more words with the same spelling but different pronunciations are listed as separate entries with different raised numbers

Etymology

Pronunciations for derivatives where necessary

console[2] *noun*
• "CON sole"
• a panel or unit accommodating a set of switches, controls, etc.
• [French, perhaps from *consolider* (as CONSOLIDATE)]

Small capitals indicate cross-references to other entries

Aa

aa *noun*
• "AW aw"
• very rough light-textured lava.
• [Hawaiian *'a-'a*]

aardvark *noun*
• "ARD vark"
• a nocturnal, insectivorous mammal, *Orycteropus afer*, having large ears, a long snout, and a long tongue, native to sub-Saharan Africa.
• [Afrikaans from *aarde* earth + *vark* pig]

aardwolf *noun*
• "ARD wolf"
• an African mammal, *Proteles cristatus*, related to the hyena family, with grey fur and black stripes, that feeds on insects.
• [Afrikaans from *aarde* earth + *wolf* wolf]

abaca *noun*
• "ABBA kuh"
• manila hemp.
• [Spanish *abacá*]

abacus *noun*
• "ABBA cuss"
• an oblong frame with rows of wires or grooves along which beads are slid, used for calculating.
• [Latin from Greek *abax abakos* slab, drawing board, from Hebrew *'āḇāq* dust]

abalone *noun*
• "abba LONE ee"
• any mollusc of the genus *Haliotis*, with a shallow ear-shaped shell having respiratory holes, and lined with mother-of-pearl.
• [Latin American Spanish *abulón*]

abandon
• "a BAN d'n"
• give up completely or before completion.
• [Old French *abandoner* from *à bandon* under control, ultimately from Late Latin *bannus, -um* ban]
• **abandoner** *noun*
• **abandonment** *noun*

abandoned *adjective*
• "a BAN d'nd"
• (of a person) deserted, forsaken.
• [as ABANDON]

abate *verb*
• "a BATE"
• make or become less strong, severe, intense, etc.
• [Old French *abatre* from Latin *batt(u)ere* beat]
• **abatement** *noun*

abatis *noun*
ALSO SPELLED: **abattis**
• "ABBA tiss"
• a defence made of felled trees with the boughs pointing outwards.
• [French from Old French *abatre* fell: see ABATE]

abattoir *noun*
• "ABBA twarr"
• a slaughterhouse.
• [French (as ABATIS)]

abaxial *adjective*
• "a BAXY 'll"
• (esp. of the lower surface of a leaf) facing away from the stem of a plant.
• [Latin *ab-* off, away, from + AXIAL]

abaya *noun*
• "a BAY uh"
• a sleeveless outer garment worn by Arabs.
• [Arabic *'abāya*]

abbacy *noun*
• "ABBA see"
• the office, jurisdiction, or period of office of an abbot or abbess.
• [Church Latin *abbacia* from *abbat-* ABBOT]

abbatial *adjective*
• "a BAY sh'll"
• of an abbey, abbot, or abbess.
• [French *abbatial* or medieval Latin *abbatialis* (as ABBOT)]

abbé *noun*
• "a BAY"
• a francophone priest not belonging to a religious order.
• [French from Church Latin *abbas abbatis* ABBOT]

abbess *noun*
• "AB ess"
• a woman who is the head of certain communities of nuns.

• [Old French *abbesse* from Church Latin *abbatissa* (as ABBOT)]

Abbevillian *noun*
• "ab VILLY 'n"
• the culture of the earliest paleolithic period in Europe, characterized by the production of flint hand axes.
• [French *Abbevillien* from *Abbeville* in N France]

abbey *noun*
• "ABBY"
• the building(s) occupied by a community of monks or nuns, esp. of a Benedictine order.
• [Old French *abbeie* etc. from medieval Latin *abbatia* ABBACY]

abbot *noun*
• "AB it"
• a man who is the head of an abbey of monks.
• [Old English *abbod* from Church Latin *abbas -atis* from Greek *abbas* father, from Aramaic *'abbā*]
• **abbotship** *noun*

Abbotsfordian *noun*
• "ab uts FORDY 'n"
• a resident of Abbotsford, BC.

abbreviate *verb*
• "a BREEVY ate"
• shorten, esp. represent (a word etc.) by a part of it.
• [Latin *abbreviare* shorten, from *brevis* short: compare ABRIDGE]
• **abbreviation** *noun*

abdicate *verb*
• "ABDA cate"
• give up or renounce (the throne).
• [Latin *abdicare abdicat-* (Latin *ab-* off, away, from + *dicare* declare)]
• **abdication** *noun*
• **abdicator** *noun*

abdomen *noun*
• "ABDA m'n"
• the part of the body containing the stomach, bowels, reproductive organs, etc.
• [Latin]
• **abdominal** *adjective* "ab DOMMA n'll"
• **abdominally** *adverb*

abdominoplasty *noun*
• "ab DOMMA no plasty"
• cosmetic surgery in which excess abdominal fat and skin is removed.
• [ABDOMEN + Greek *plastos* formed, moulded]

abduct *verb*
• "ab DUCT"
• carry off or kidnap (a person) illegally by force or deception.
• [Latin *abducere abduct-* (Latin *ab-* off, away, from + *ducere* draw)]
• **abductee** *noun*
• **abduction** *noun*
• **abductor** *noun*

Abegweit *noun*
• "ABBA gwit"
• a member of an Algonquian band living on PEI.
• [Mi'kmaq, = cradled in the waves, a name for Prince Edward Island]

Abelian *adjective*
• "a BEELY 'n"
• designating a group the members of which are related by a commutative operation (i.e. a × b = b × a).
• [N. H. *Abel*, Norwegian mathematician d.1929]

Abenaki *noun*
• "abba NACKY"
• a member of an Algonquian-speaking Aboriginal people of the eastern woodlands of N America, now living mainly in S Quebec and Maine.
• [French *abénaqui* from Eastern Abenaki *wapánahki* lit. 'person of the dawn land']

Aberdonian *adjective*
• "abber DOE nee 'n"
• of Aberdeen in Scotland.
• [medieval Latin *Aberdonia*]

aberration *noun*
• "abba RAY sh'n"
• a departure from what is normal or accepted or regarded as right.
• [Latin *aberratio* from *aberrare aberrant-* (Latin *ab-* off, away, from + *errare* stray)]
• **aberrance** *noun*
• **aberrancy** *noun*
• **aberrant** *adjective* "a BEAR 'nt" or "a BUR 'nt"

abettor *noun*
• "a BETTER"
• a person who encourages or assists (esp. an offender or offence).
• [Old French *abeter* from *à* to + *beter* BAIT]

abeyance *noun*
• "a BAY ince"
• a state of temporary disuse or suspension.
• [Anglo-French *abeiance* from Old French *abeer* from *à* to + *beer* from medieval Latin *batare* gape]
• **abeyant** *adjective*

abhor *verb*
• "ab HORE"
• detest; regard with disgust and hatred.
• [Latin *abhorrēre* (as *ab-* from, *horrēre* shudder)]
• **abhorrence** *noun*
• **abhorrent** *adjective*
• **abhorrer** *noun*

abide *verb*
• "a BIDE"
• tolerate, endure.
• [Old English *ābīdan* from *bidan* stay]
• **abidance** *noun*

abiding *adjective*
• "a BIDE ing"

• enduring, permanent.
• [as ABIDE]
• **abidingly** *adverb*

ability *noun*
• "a BILLA tee"
• capacity or power.
• [from Latin *habilitas -tatis* from *habilis* able]

abiogenesis *noun*
• "ay bio JENNA sis"
• the formation of living organisms from non-living substances.
• [Greek *a-* without + Greek *bios* life + GENESIS]

abiotic *adjective*
• "ay by OTTIC"
• physical rather than biological; not derived from living organisms.
• [Greek *a-* without + Greek *bios* life]

abject *adjective*
• "AB ject"
• miserable, wretched.
• [Latin *abjectus* past participle of *abicere* (Latin *ab-* off, away, from + *jacere* throw)]
• **abjection** *noun*
• **abjectly** *adverb*
• **abjectness** *noun*
HOMOPHONES: *objection*

abjure *verb*
• "ab JURE"
• renounce on oath (an opinion, cause, claim, etc.).
• [Latin *abjurare* (Latin *ab-* off, away, from + *jurare* swear)]
• **abjuration** *noun*

Abkhazian *noun*
• "ab COZZY 'n"
• a native or inhabitant of Abkhazia in the republic of Georgia in SE Europe.

ablation *noun*
• "ab LAY sh'n"
• the surgical removal of body tissue.
• [Latin *ablat-* (Latin *ab-* off, away, from + *lat-* past participle stem of *ferre* carry)]
• **ablate** *verb* "ab LATE"

ablative *noun*
• "ABLA tiv"
• the case (esp. in Latin) of nouns and pronouns (and words in grammatical agreement with them) indicating an agent, instrument, or location.
• [as ABLATION]

ablaut *noun*
• "AB lout"
• a change of vowel in related words or forms, esp. in Indo-European languages, arising from differences of accent and stress in the parent language, e.g. in *sing, sang, sung*.
• [German]

ablution *noun*
• "ab LOO sh'n"
• the ceremonial washing of parts of the body or sacred vessels etc.
• [Latin *ablutio* (Latin *ab-* off, away, from + *lutio* from *luere lut-* wash)]
• **ablutionary** *adjective*

ably *adverb*
• "ABE lee"
• capably, cleverly, competently.
• [Latin *habilis* handy, from *habēre* to hold]

abnegate *verb*
• "ABNA gate"
• give up or deny oneself (a pleasure etc.).
• [Latin *abnegare abnegat-* (*ab-* off, away, from + *negare* deny)]
• **abnegation** *noun*
• **abnegator** *noun*

abnormality *noun*
• "ab nor MALA tee"
• an abnormal quality, occurrence, etc.
• [Latin *ab-* off, away, from + *norma* carpenter's square]

abode *noun*
• "a BODE"
• a dwelling place; one's home.
• [verbal noun of ABIDE]

aboiteau *noun*
• "abwa TOE"
• *Cdn* (*Maritimes*) a sluice gate in a dike, which allows flood water to flow out but does not allow sea water to enter.
• [Acadian French, from Western French dialect *aboteau*, from Old French *bot* dike, influenced by French *bois* wood]

abolish *verb*
• "a BALL ish"
• put an end to the existence or practice of (esp. a custom or institution).
• [Latin *abolēre* destroy]
• **abolishable** *adjective*
• **abolisher** *noun*
• **abolishment** *noun*
• **abolition** *noun*

abolitionist *noun*
• "abba LISHA nist"
• a person who favours the abolition of a practice or institution, esp. of capital punishment or of slavery.
• [as ABOLISH]
• **abolitionism** *noun*

abomasum *noun*
• "abba MAY sum"
• the fourth stomach of a ruminant.
• [modern Latin from Latin *ab-* off, away, from + OMASUM]

abominable *adjective*
• "a BOM 'n a bull"
• detestable; loathsome; morally reprehensible.
• [Latin *abominabilis* from *abominari* deprecate (Latin *ab-* off, away, from + *ominari* from OMEN)]
• **abominably** *adverb*

abominate *verb*
• "a BOMMA nate"
• detest, loathe.
• [as ABOMINABLE]

abomination *noun*
• "a bomma NAY sh'n"
• an object of disgust.
• [as ABOMINABLE]

aboral *adjective*
• "ab OR'll"
• away from or opposite the mouth.
• [Latin *ab-* off, away, from + ORAL]

aboriginal *adjective*
• "abba RIDGE'n 'll"
• (of peoples) inhabiting or existing in a land from the earliest times or from before the arrival of colonists.
• [as ABORIGINE]
• **aboriginality** *noun*
• **aboriginally** *adverb*

aborigine *noun*
• "abba RIDGE 'n ee"
• an Aboriginal inhabitant.
• [back-formation from pl. *aborigines* from Latin, prob. from phrase *ab origine* from the beginning]

aborning *predicative adjective*
• "a BORNING"
• being born or produced.
• [Old English *a* in the process of + 'born']

abortifacient *adjective*
• "a borta FAY sh'nt"
• causing abortion.
• [as ABORTION + Latin *-faciens -entis* participle of *facere* make]

abortion *noun*
• "a BOR sh'n"
• the expulsion of a fetus (naturally or esp. by medical induction) from the womb before it is able to survive independently.
• [Latin *abortion* from *aboriri* miscarry (*ab-* off, away, from + *oriri ort-* be born)]
• **abortionist** *noun*

abortive *adjective*
• "a BORTIV"
• fruitless, unsuccessful, unfinished.
• [as ABORTION]
• **abortively** *adverb*

abracadabra *interjection*
• "abbra kuh DABBRA"
• a supposedly magic word used by conjurors in performing a trick.
• [a mystical word engraved and used as a charm: Latin from Greek]

abrade *verb*
• "a BRAID"
• scrape or wear away (skin, rock, etc.) by rubbing.
• [Latin from *ab-* off, away, from + *radere ras-* scrape]
• **abrader** *noun*
• **abrasion** *noun*
• **abrasive** *adjective*

abreaction *noun*
• "ab ree ACK sh'n"
• the relief of anxiety by the expression and release of a previously repressed emotion, through reliving the experience that caused it.
• [Latin *ab-* off, away, from + 'reaction' after German *Abreagierung*]
• **abreact** *verb*
• **abreactive** *adjective*

abreast *adverb*
• "a BREST"
• side by side and facing the same way.
• [Old English *a* in + *brēost* breast]

abridge *verb*
• "a BRIDGE"
• shorten (a book, film, etc.) by using fewer words or making deletions.
• [Old French *abreg(i)er* from Late Latin *abbreviare* ABBREVIATE]
• **abridgeable** *adjective*
• **abridgement** *noun*
• **abridger** *noun*

abrogate *verb*
• "ABBRA gate"
• repeal or abolish (a law or custom).
• [Latin *abrogare* (*ab-* off, away, from + *rogare* propose a law)]
• **abrogation** *noun*

abscess *noun*
• "AB sess"
• a swollen area accumulating pus within a body tissue.
• [Latin *abscessus* a going away (*ab-* off, away, from + *cedere cess-* go)]
• **abscessed** *adjective*

abscisic *adjective*
• "ab SIZE ick"
• designating a plant hormone which promotes leaf detachment and bud dormancy and inhibits germination.
• [Latin *abscis-* past participle stem of *abscindere* (*ab-* off, away, from + *scindere* to cut)]

abscissa *noun*
• "ab SISSA"
• (in a system of coordinates) the shortest distance from a point to the vertical or *y*-axis, measured parallel to the horizontal or *x*-axis; the Cartesian *x*-coordinate of a point.
• [modern Latin *abscissa (linea)* feminine past participle of *abscindere absciss-* (Latin *ab-* off, away, from + *scindere* cut)]

abscission *noun*
• "ab SIZH'n"
• the act or an instance of cutting off.
• [Latin *abscissio* (as ABSCISSA)]

abscond *verb*
- "ab SKOND"
- depart hurriedly and furtively, esp. unlawfully or to avoid arrest.
- [Latin *abscondere* (*ab-* off, away, from + *condere* stow)]
- **absconder** *noun*

abseil *verb*
- "AB sail"
- descend a steep rock face by using a doubled rope coiled round the body and fixed at a higher point.
- [German *abseilen* from *ab* down + *Seil* rope]

absence *noun*
- "AB since"
- the state of being away from a place or person.
- [Latin *absentia* from *absent-* present participle of *abesse* be absent]

absentee *noun*
- "ab sin TEE"
- a person not present, esp. one who is absent from work or school.
- [as ABSENCE]
- **absenteeism** *noun*

absinth *noun*
- "AB sinth"
- a shrubby plant, *Artemisia absinthium*, or its essence.
- [French *absinthe* from Latin *absinthium* from Greek *apsinthion*]

absolute *adjective*
- "absa LUTE"
- complete, utter, perfect.
- [Latin *absolutus* past participle of *absolvere*: see ABSOLVE]
- **absolutely** *adverb*
- **absoluteness** *noun*

absolutism *noun*
- "absa LUTE izm"
- the acceptance of or belief in absolute principles in political, philosophical, ethical or theological matters.
- [as ABSOLUTE]
- **absolutist** *noun*

absolve *verb*
- "ab ZOLVE"
- set or pronounce free from blame or obligation etc.
- [Latin *absolvere* (*ab-* off, away, from + *solvere solut-* loosen)]
- **absolution** *noun*
- **absolver** *noun*

absorb *verb*
- "ab SORB" or "ab ZORB"
- include or incorporate as part of itself or oneself.
- [Latin *absorbēre absorpt-* (*ab-* off, away, from + *sorbēre* suck in)]
- **absorbability** *noun*
- **absorbable** *adjective*
- **absorbency** *noun*
- **absorbent** *adjective*
- **absorber** *noun*
- **absorption** *noun*
- **absorptive** *adjective*

absorbed *predicative adjective*
- "ab ZORBD"
- intensely engaged or interested.
- [as ABSORB]
- **absorbedly** *adverb* "ab ZORBID lee"

absorbing *adjective*
- "ab ZORBING"
- engrossing; intensely interesting.
- [as ABSORB]
- **absorbingly** *adverb*

abstain *verb*
- "ab STAIN"
- restrain oneself; refrain from indulging in.
- [Latin *abstinēre abstent-* (*ab-* off, away, from + *tenēre* hold)]
- **abstainer** *noun*

abstemious *adjective*
- "ab STEEMY us"
- (of a person, habit, etc.) moderate, not self-indulgent, esp. in eating and drinking.
- [Latin *abstemius* (*ab-* off, away, from + *temetum* strong drink)]
- **abstemiously** *adverb*
- **abstemiousness** *noun*

abstention *noun*
- "ab STEN sh'n"
- the act or an instance of abstaining, esp. from voting.
- [as ABSTAIN]

abstinence *noun*
- "AB stin ince"
- the act of abstaining, esp. from food, drugs, or sexual activity.
- [as ABSTAIN]
- **abstinent** *adjective*
- **abstinently** *adverb*

abstract *adjective*
- "ABS tract"
- to do with or existing in thought rather than matter, or in theory rather than practice; not tangible or concrete.
- [Latin *abstractus* past participle of *abstrahere* (*ab-* off, away, from + *trahere* draw)]
- **abstractly** *adverb*
- **abstractness** *noun*
- **abstractor** *noun*

abstracted *adjective*
- "abs TRACT id"
- inattentive to the matter in hand; preoccupied.
- [as ABSTRACT]
- **abstractedly** *adverb*

abstraction *noun*
- "abs TRACK sh'n"
- the act or an instance of abstracting or taking away.
- [as ABSTRACT]

abstractionism *noun*
- "abs TRACK sh'n izm"
- the principles and practice of abstract art.
- [as ABSTRACT]
- **abstractionist** *noun*

abstruse *adjective*
- "ab STRUCE"
- hard to understand; obscure.
- [Latin *abstrusus* (*ab-* off, away, from + *trusus* past participle of *trudere* push)]
- **abstrusely** *adverb*
- **abstruseness** *noun*

absurd *adjective*
- "ab SURD" or "ab ZURD"
- (of an idea, suggestion, etc.) wildly unreasonable, illogical, or inappropriate.
- [Latin *absurdus* (*ab-* off, away, from + *surdus* deaf, dull)]
- **absurdity** *noun*
- **absurdly** *adverb*

absurdist *adjective*
- "ab SURD ist" or "ab ZURD ist"
- pertaining to or characteristic of the theatre of the absurd.
- [as ABSURD]
- **absurdism** *noun*

abulia *noun*
ALSO SPELLED: **aboulia**
- "a BOOLY uh"
- the loss of willpower as a mental disorder.
- [Greek *a-* not + *boulē* will]
- **abulic** *adjective* (also **aboulic**)

abundant *adjective*
- "a BUN d'nt"
- existing or available in large quantities; plentiful.
- [Old French *abundant* from Latin *abundant* overflowing (*ab-* off, away, from + *undare* from *unda* wave)]
- **abundance** *noun*
- **abundantly** *adverb*

abusive *adjective*
- "a BYOO siv"
- (of a situation) involving maltreatment.
- [Latin *ab-* off, away, from + *ūti, ūsus* use]
- **abusively** *adverb*
- **abusiveness** *noun*

abut *verb*
- "a BUT"
- (of buildings, sites, etc.) be located next to.
- [Old French *abouter* and Anglo-Latin *abuttare* from Old French *but* end]

abutilon *noun*
- "ub YOOTA lon"
- a herbaceous plant or shrub of warm climates, typically bearing showy yellow, red, or mauve flowers and sometimes used for fibre.
- [modern Latin, from Arabic *ūbūṭīlūn* Indian mallow]

abutment *noun*
- "a BUT m'nt"
- the lateral supporting structure of a bridge, arch, etc.
- [as ABUT]

abysm *noun*
- "a BIZ'm"
- an abyss.
- [Old French *abi(s)me* from medieval Latin *abysmus*]

abysmal *adjective*
- "a BIZ m'll"
- extremely bad.
- [as ABYSM]
- **abysmally** *adverb*

abyss *noun*
- "a BISS"
- a deep or seemingly bottomless chasm.
- [Late Latin *abyssus* from Greek *abussos* bottomless (as Greek *a-* without, *bussos* depth)]

abyssal *adjective*
- "a BISS'll"
- at or of the ocean depths or floor.
- [as ABYSS]

Abyssinian *noun*
- "abba SINNY 'n"
- a native or inhabitant of Abyssinia (a former name for Ethiopia).

acacia *noun*
- "a CAY shuh"
- any frequently thorny leguminous tree or shrub of the genus *Acacia* with usu. yellow flowers, esp. *A. senegal* yielding gum arabic.
- [Latin from Greek *akakia*]

academe *noun*
- "acka DEEM"
- the world of learning.
- [Greek *Akadēmos* (see ACADEMY)]

academia *noun*
- "acka DEEMY uh"
- the world of scholarly institutions.
- [modern Latin: see ACADEMY]
- **academic** *adjective* "acka DEMMIC"
- **academically** *adverb*

academicals *plural noun*
- "acka DEMMIC 'lz"
- formal attire as worn in universities.
- [as ACADEMY]

academician *noun*
- "acka duh MISH'n"
- a member of an Academy, e.g. the Royal Academy of Arts.
- [as ACADEMY]

academicism *noun*
- "acka DEMMA sizm"
- academic principles or their application in art, esp. in a conventional or pedantic manner.
- [as ACADEMY]

academics *noun*
- "acka DEMMIX"
- studies in the humanities or sciences.
- [as ACADEMY]

academism *noun*
- "a CADDA mizm"
- academic principles or their application in art, esp. in a conventional or pedantic manner.
- [as ACADEMY]

academy *noun*
- "a CADDA mee"
- a place of study or training in a special field.
- [Greek *akadēmeia* from *Akadēmos* the hero after whom Plato's garden was named]

Acadian *noun*
- "a CAY dee 'n"
- a native or inhabitant of the French colony of Acadia.

HOMOPHONES: *Akkadian*

acanthus *noun*
- "a CANTH us"
- a herbaceous plant or shrub of the genus *Acanthus*, with bold flower spikes and decorative spiny leaves, native to the Mediterranean.
- [Greek *akanthos* from *akantha* thorn, perhaps from *akē* sharp point]

acaricide *noun*
- "a KERRA side"
- a preparation for destroying mites.
- [Greek *akari* mite + Latin *-cida, -cidium* from *caedere* kill]

acarid *noun*
- "ACKA rid"
- any small arachnid of the order Acarina, including mites and ticks.
- [Greek *akari* mite]

accede *verb*
- "ack SEED"
- assent or agree.
- [Latin *accedere* (*ad-* to + *cedere cess-* go)]

HOMOPHONES: *exceed*

accelerando *adjective*
- "ack sella RANDO"
- with a gradual increase of speed.
- [Italian, as ACCELERATE]

accelerant *noun*
- "ack SELLA r'nt"
- a substance used to aid the spread of fire.
- [as ACCELERATE]

accelerate *verb*
- "ack SELLER ate"
- (of a moving body, esp. a vehicle) move or begin to move more quickly; increase speed.
- [Latin *accelerare* (*ad-* to + *celerare* from *celer* swift)]
- **acceleration** *noun*

accelerator *noun*
- "ack SELLA rater"
- a device for increasing speed, esp. the pedal that controls the speed of a vehicle's engine.
- [as ACCELERATE]

accelerometer *noun*
- "ack sella ROMMA tur"
- an instrument for measuring acceleration (esp. of a rocket) or vibrations.
- [as ACCELERATE + Greek *metron* measure]

accent *noun*
- "ACK sent"
- a particular mode of pronunciation, esp. one associated with a particular region or group.
- [Latin *accentus* (*ad-* to + *cantus* song)]
- **accentual** *adjective* "ack SEN choo 'll"

accentor *noun*
- "ack SENTER"
- any bird of the genus *Prunella*, native to Europe and Asia, similar to a sparrow, with greyish-brown plumage.
- [medieval Latin *accentor* from Latin *ad* to + *cantor* singer]

accentuate *verb*
- "ack SEN choo ate"
- emphasize; make prominent.
- [as ACCENT]
- **accentuation** *noun*

accept *verb*
- "ack SEPT"
- consent to receive (a thing offered).
- [Latin *acceptare* from *accipere* (*ad-* to + *capere* take)]
- **acceptability** *noun*
- **acceptable** *adjective*
- **acceptableness** *noun*
- **acceptably** *adverb*
- **acceptance** *noun*

HOMOPHONES: *except*

acceptation *noun*
- "ack sep TAY sh'n"
- a particular sense, or the generally recognized meaning, of a word or phrase.
- [as ACCEPT]

acceptor *noun*
- "ack SEPTER"
- a person who accepts a bill of exchange.
- [as ACCEPT]

access *noun*
- "ACK sess"
- a way of approaching or reaching or entering.
- [Latin *accessus* from *accedere* (*ad-* to + *cedere cess-* go)]
- **accessibility** *noun*
- **accessible** *adjective*
- **accessibly** *adverb*

accession *noun*
• "ack SESH'n"
• entering upon an office (esp. the throne) or a condition (as adulthood).
• [Latin *accessio -onis* (as ACCEDE)]

accessorize *verb*
ALSO SPELLED: esp. *Brit.* **-ise**
• "ack SESSER ize"
• choose or wear accessories to suit (clothing etc.).
• [as ACCESSORY]

accessory *noun*
• "ack SESSER ee"
• an additional or extra thing.
• [medieval Latin *accessorius* (as ACCEDE)]

acciaccatura *noun*
• "a chacka TURA"
• a grace note performed as quickly as possible before an essential note of a melody.
• [Italian, from *acciaccare* to crush, pound]

accidence *noun*
• "ACKSA dince"
• the part of grammar that deals with the variable parts or inflections of words.
• [Late Latin *accidentia* (translation of Greek *parepomena* 'things happening alongside') neuter pl. of *accidere* 'happen']

accipiter *noun*
• "ack SIPPA tur"
• a short-winged, long-legged hawk of the genus *Accipiter*, e.g. a goshawk.
• [Latin, = hawk, bird of prey, from *accipere* (see ACCEPT)]
• **accipitrine** *adjective* "ack SIPPA trine"

acclaim *verb*
• "a CLAIM"
• praise publicly; welcome or applaud enthusiastically.
• [Latin *acclamare* (*ad-* to + *clamare* shout: spelling assimilated to *claim*)]
• **acclaimer** *noun*

acclamation *noun*
• "ackla MAY sh'n"
• *Cdn* the act or an instance of election by virtue of being the sole candidate.
• [Latin *acclamatio* (as ACCLAIM)]
HOMOPHONES: *acclimation*

acclimate *verb*
• "ACKLA mate"
• acclimatize.
• [French *acclimater* from *à* to + *climat* CLIMATE]
• **acclimation** *noun*
HOMOPHONES: *acclamation*

acclimatize *verb*
ALSO SPELLED: esp. *Brit.* **-ise**
• "a CLIME a tize"
• accustom to a new climate or to new conditions.
• [as ACCLIMATE]
• **acclimatization** *noun* (also esp. *Brit.* **-isation**)

acclivity *noun*
• "a CLIVVA tee"
• an upward slope.
• [Latin *acclivitas* from *acclivis* (*ad-* to + *clivis* from *clivus* slope)]
• **acclivitous** *adjective*

accolade *noun*
• "ACKA laid"
• the awarding of praise; an acknowledgement of merit.
• [French from Provençal *acolada* (Latin *ad-* to + *collum* neck)]

accommodate *verb*
• "a COMMA date"
• provide lodging or room for.
• [Latin *accommodare* (*ad-* to + *commodus* fitting)]
• **accommodation** *noun*

accommodating *adjective*
• "a COMMA date ing"
• obliging, compliant.
• [as ACCOMMODATE]
• **accommodatingly** *adverb*

accommodationist *noun*
• "a comma DAY sh'n ist"
• a person who seeks (esp. political) compromise.
• [as ACCOMMODATE]

accompaniment *noun*
• "a CUMPA nee m'nt"
• an instrumental or orchestral part supporting or partnering a solo instrument, voice, or group.
• [as ACCOMPANY]
• **accompanist** *noun*

accompany *verb*
• "a CUMPA nee"
• go with; escort.
• [French *accompagner* from *à* to + Old French *compaing* COMPANION: assimilated to COMPANY]

accomplice *noun*
• "a COM pliss"
• a partner in a crime or wrongdoing.
• [Late Latin *complex complicis* confederate: compare COMPLICATE]

accomplish *verb*
• "a COMP lish"
• perform; complete; succeed in doing.
• [Old French *acomplir* from Latin *complēre* fill up]
• **accomplishment** *noun*

accomplished *adjective*
• "a COM plisht"
• clever, skilled; well trained or educated.
• [as ACCOMPLISH]

accord *verb*
• "a CORD"

• (esp. of a thing) be in harmony; be consistent.
• [Old French *acord*, *acorder* from Latin *cor cordis* heart]
• **accordance** *noun*
• **accordant** *adjective*
• **accordantly** *adverb*

according *adverb*
• "a CORDING"
• as stated by or in.
• [as ACCORD]
• **accordingly** *adverb*

accordion *noun*
• "a CORDY 'n"
• a portable musical instrument played by means of keys, buttons, and pleated bellows, which are expanded and contracted to force air through metal reeds.
• [German *Akkordion* from Italian *accordare* to tune]
• **accordionist** *noun*

accost *verb*
• "a COST"
• approach and address (a person), esp. boldly.
• [French *accoster* from Italian *accostare*, ultimately from Latin *costa* rib]

account *noun*
• "a COUNT"
• a narration or description.
• [Old French *acont*, *aconter* (Latin *ad-* to + Old French *conter* count)]

accountable *adjective*
• "a COUNTA bull"
• responsible; required to account for one's conduct.
• [as ACCOUNT]
• **accountability** *noun*
• **accountably** *adverb*

accountant *noun*
• "a COUNT'nt"
• a person whose profession is to keep or inspect financial accounts.
• [legal French from present participle of Old French *aconter* ACCOUNT]
• **accountancy** *noun*
• **accounting** *noun*

accoutre *verb*
• "a COOTER"
• attire, equip, esp. with a special outfit.
• [Old French *acoustrer* (Latin *ad-* to + *cousture* sewing: compare SUTURE)]

accoutrement *noun*
• "a COOTRA m'nt" or "a COOTER m'nt"
• additional items of dress, equipment, etc., or other items carried or worn by a person or used for a particular activity.
• [as ACCOUTRE]

accredit *verb*
• "a CREDDIT"
• officially recognize as meeting certain standards.
• [French *accréditer* (French *a-* to + *crédit* from Italian *credito* or Latin *creditum* from *credere credit-* believe, trust)]
• **accreditation** *noun*
• **accredited** *adjective*

accrete *verb*
• "a CREET"
• grow together or into one.
• [Latin *accrescere* (*ad-* to + *crescere cret-* grow)]
• **accretion** *noun*
• **accretive** *adjective*

accrue *verb*
• "a CREW"
• come as a natural increase or advantage, esp. financial.
• [Anglo-French *acru(e)*, past participle of *acreistre* increase, from Latin *accrescere* ACCRETE]
• **accrual** *noun* "a CREW 'll"
• **accrued** *adjective*

acculturate *verb*
• "a CULL chur ate"
• adapt to or adopt a different culture.
• [Latin *ad-* to + CULTURE]
• **acculturation** *noun*
• **acculturative** *adjective* "a CULL chur a tiv"

accumulate *verb*
• "a KYOO myoo late"
• acquire an increasing number or quantity of.
• [Latin *accumulare* (*ad-* to + *cumulus* heap)]
• **accumulation** *noun*
• **accumulative** *adjective*
• **accumulatively** *adverb*
• **accumulator** *noun*

accurate *adjective*
• "ACK yur it"
• careful, precise; lacking errors.
• [Latin *accuratus* done carefully, past participle of *accurare* (*ad-* to + *cura* care)]
• **accuracy** *noun*
• **accurately** *adverb*

accursed *adjective*
• "a CUR sed" or "a CURST"
• lying under a curse; ill-fated.
• [past participle of *accurse*, from Old English *a-* adding intensity to verbs of motion + *curs*, *cursian* curse]

accusative *noun*
• "a KYOOZA tiv"
• the case of nouns, pronouns, and adjectives, expressing the object of an action or the goal of motion.
• [Latin (*casus*) *accusativus*, translation of Greek (*ptōsis*) *aitiatikē*]
• **accusatival** *adjective* "a kyooza TIVE 'll"
• **accusatively** *adverb*

accusatorial *adjective*
• "a kyooza TORY 'll"
• (of judicial proceedings) involving accusation

by a prosecutor and a verdict reached by an impartial judge or jury.

• [as ACCUSE]

accusatory *adjective*

• "a KYOOZA tory"

• (of language, manner, etc.) of or implying accusation.

• [as ACCUSE]

accuse *verb*

• "a KYOOZ"

• charge (a person etc.) with a fault or crime; indict.

• [Latin *accusare* (*ad-* to + *cause* cause)]

• **accusal** *noun*

• **accusation** *noun*

• **accuser** *noun*

• **accusing** *adjective*

• **accusingly** *adverb*

accused *noun*

• "a KYOOZD"

• a person charged with a crime.

• [as ACCUSE]

accustom *verb*

• "a CUSS t'm"

• make (a person or thing or oneself) used to.

• [Old French *acostumer* (*a-* to + *costume* CUSTOM)]

• **accustomed** *adjective*

acedia *noun*

• "a SEEDY uh"

• laziness, sloth, apathy.

• [Late Latin *acedia* from Greek *akēdia* listlessness]

acellular *adjective*

• "ay SELL yuh lur"

• having no cells; not consisting of cells.

• [Greek *a-* not + CELL]

acephalous *adjective*

• "ay SEFFA luss"

• headless.

• [Greek *akephalos* headless (as Greek *a-* without, *kephalē* head)]

acerb *adjective*

• "a SURB"

• = ACERBIC.

• [as ACERBIC]

acerbic *adjective*

• "a SUR bick"

• biting in speech, manner, or temper.

• [Latin *acerbus* sour-tasting]

• **acerbically** *adverb*

• **acerbity** *noun* "a SURBA tee"

acerola *noun*

• "assa ROLE uh"

• a plant of tropical America, *Malpighia glabra*, with edible fruit high in vitamin C used to make syrups, jams and vitamins.

• [Latin American Spanish, from Spanish *acerolo*, *azarolla*, a species of hawthorn, from Arabic]

acesulfame *noun*

• "assa SULL fame"

• a white crystalline compound used as a low-calorie artificial sweetener, typically in the form of a potassium salt.

• [20th c.: origin unknown]

acetabulum *noun*

• "assa TAB yuh lum"

• the socket for the head of the thigh bone, or of the leg in insects.

• [Latin, = vinegar cup, from *acetum* vinegar + *-abulum* diminutive of *-abrum* holder]

acetal *noun*

• "ASSA tal"

• any of a class of organic compounds formed by the condensation of two alcohol molecules with an aldehyde molecule.

• [as ACETIC]

acetaldehyde *noun*

• "assa TALDA hide"

• a colourless volatile liquid aldehyde, used in the synthesis of acetic acid and other chemical compounds.

• [ACETIC + ALDEHYDE]

acetaminophen *noun*

• "a seeta MINNA f'n"

• a drug used to relieve pain and reduce fever.

• [ACETYL + AMINO + PHENOL]

acetanilide *noun*

• "assa TANNA lide"

• a crystalline solid obtained by acetylation of aniline, used in dye manufacture.

• [ACETYL + ANILINE]

acetate *noun*

• "ASSA tate"

• a salt or ester of acetic acid, esp. the cellulose ester of acetic acid (cellulose acetate) used to make textiles, plastics, etc.

• [as ACETIC]

acetic *adjective*

• "a SEETIC"

• of or like vinegar.

• [from Latin *acetum* vinegar]

acetone *noun*

• "ASSA tone"

• a colourless volatile liquid ketone valuable as a solvent for paints, varnishes, nail polish, etc.

• [as ACETIC + '-one' forming nouns denoting various compounds, from Greek *-ōnē* feminine patronymic]

acetous *adjective*

• "ASSA tuss"

• having the qualities of vinegar.

• [Late Latin *acetosus* sour (as ACETIC)]

acetyl *noun*

• "ASSA t'll"

- the monovalent radical of acetic acid.
- [as ACETIC]

acetylation *noun*
- "a settle AY sh'n"
- a reaction or process in which one or more acetyl groups are introduced into a molecule.
- [as ACETYL]
- **acetylated** *adjective*

acetylcholine *noun*
- "a seetle CO leen" or "a settle CO leen"
- a compound serving to transmit impulses from nerve fibres.
- [as ACETYL + CHOLINE]

acetylene *noun*
- "a SETTA lean"
- a colourless hydrocarbon gas, burning with a bright flame, used esp. in welding and formerly in lighting.
- [as ACETIC]

acetylide *noun*
- "a SETTLE ide"
- any of a class of salts formed from acetylene and a metal.
- [as ACETIC]

acetylsalicylic *adjective*
- "a seetle salla SILLIC"
- pertaining to an acid used to relieve pain and reduce fever, the active ingredient in Aspirin.
- [as ACETIC + SALICIN]

Achaean *adjective*
- "a KEE 'n"
- of or relating to Achaea, a region of ancient Greece.

ache *noun*
- "AKE"
- a continuous or prolonged dull pain.
- [Old English *æce, acan*]
- **achingly** *adverb* "AKE ing lee"

achene *noun*
- "a KEEN"
- a small dry one-seeded fruit that does not open to liberate the seed, e.g. a strawberry pip.
- [modern Latin *achaenium* (as Greek *a-* without, Greek *khainō* gape)]

Acheulian *adjective*
ALSO SPELLED: **Acheulean**
- "a SHOOLY 'n"
- of the paleolithic period in Europe etc. following the Abbevillian and preceding the Mousterian.
- [French *acheuléen* from St-*Acheul* in N France, where remains of it were found]

achieve *verb*
- "a CHEEVE"
- reach or attain by effort.
- [Old French *achever* from *a chief* to a head]
- **achievable** *adjective*
- **achievement** *noun*
- **achiever** *noun*

achillea *noun*
- "acka LEE uh" or "a KILLY uh"
- any composite herbaceous plant of the genus *Achillea*, with white, purple, or yellow flower heads, esp. the yarrow.
- [Latin from Greek *Akhilleios* a plant supposed to have been used medicinally by ACHILLES]

Achilles *noun*
- "a KILL eez"
- the tendon connecting the heel with the calf muscles.
- [a hero of the Trojan War, killed by an arrow which struck him in the heel, his only vulnerable spot]

achiote *noun*
- "atchy OTTY"
- a paste made from ground annatto seeds.
- [Mexican Spanish, from Nahuatl *achiotl*]

achondroplasia *noun*
- "a condro PLAY zhuh" or "a condro PLAZEY uh"
- a hereditary condition in which the growth of long bones by ossification of cartilage is retarded, resulting in very short limbs and sometimes a face which is small in relation to the (normal sized) skull.
- [Greek *a-* without + *khondros* cartilage + *plasis* moulding]
- **achondroplastic** *adjective* "a condro PLASTIC"

achromat *noun*
- "ACRO mat"
- a lens made achromatic by correction.
- [as ACHROMATIC]

achromatic *adjective*
- "acro MATTIC"
- that transmits light without separating it into constituent colours.
- [as Greek *a-* without + CHROMATIC]
- **achromatically** *adverb*
- **achromaticity** *noun* "a crow muh TISSA tee"
- **achromatism** *noun* "a CROW muh tizm"

achy *adjective*
- "AKE ee"
- full of or suffering from aches.
- [as ACHE]

acidify *verb*
- "a SIDDA fie"
- make or become acid.
- [Latin *acidus* from *acēre* be sour]
- **acidification** *noun*

acidity *noun*
- "a SIDDA tee"
- an acid quality or state.
- [as ACIDIFY]

acidophilic *adjective*
- "assid a FILLIC"
- (of a cell etc.) readily stained with acid dyes.
- [as ACIDOPHILUS]

acidophilus *noun*
• "assid OFFA luss"
• a bacterium, *Lactobacillus acidophilus*, often added to yogourt as being beneficial to the intestinal flora.
• [modern Latin, = acid-loving]

acidosis *noun*
• "assid OH sis"
• an over-acid condition of body fluids or tissues.
• [as ACIDIFY + Greek *-ōsis* suffix of verbal nouns]
• **acidotic** *adjective* "assid OTTIC"

acidulate *verb*
• "a SID yuh late"
• make somewhat acid.
• [Latin *acidulus* diminutive of *acidus* sour]
• **acidulation** *noun*

acidulous *adjective*
• "a SID yoo luss"
• sharp-tongued, sour-tempered.
• [as ACIDULATE]

acinus *noun*
• "ASSIN us"
• any multicellular gland with sac-like secreting ducts.
• [Latin, = berry, kernel]

ackee *noun*
• "ACKY"
• a tropical evergreen tree, *Blighia sapida*.
• [Kru *ākee*]

acknowledge *verb*
• "ack NAW lidge"
• recognize; accept; admit the truth of.
• [as KNOWLEDGE]
• **acknowledgeable** *adjective*
• **acknowledgement** *noun*

acme *noun*
• "ACK mee"
• the highest point or period (of achievement, success, etc.); the peak of perfection.
• [Greek, = highest point]

acne *noun*
• "ACK nee"
• a skin condition, usu. of the face, characterized by red pimples.
• [modern Latin from erroneous Greek *aknas* for *akmas* accusative pl. of *akmē* facial eruption: compare ACME]
• **acned** *adjective* "ACK need"

acolyte *noun*
• "ACKA lite"
• a person assisting a priest in a service or procession.
• [Church Latin *acolytus* from Greek *akolouthos* follower]

aconite *noun*
• "ACKA nite"
• any poisonous herbaceous plant of the genus *Aconitum*, esp. monkshood or wolfsbane.
• [French *aconit* from Greek *akoniton*]

aconitine *noun*
• "a CONNA teen"
• a poisonous alkaloid drug obtained from the aconite plant, esp. from the species *A. napellus*, formerly used as a sedative and for reducing fever.
• [as ACONITE]

acoustic *adjective*
• "a COO stick"
• relating to sound or the sense of hearing.
• [Greek *akoustikos* from *akouō* hear]
• **acoustical** *adjective*
• **acoustically** *adverb*

acoustics *noun*
• "a COO sticks"
• the science of sound.
• [as ACOUSTIC]
• **acoustician** *noun* "ackoo STISH'n"

acquaint *verb*
• "a KWAINT"
• make (a person or oneself) aware of or familiar with.
• [Old French *acointier* from Late Latin *accognitare* (*ad-* to + *cognoscere cognit-* come to know)]

acquaintance *noun*
• "a KWAIN tince"
• a person one knows slightly.
• [as ACQUAINT]
• **acquaintanceship** *noun*

acquiesce *verb*
• "ack wee ESS"
• agree, esp. tacitly; raise no objection.
• [Latin *acquiescere* (*ad-* to + *quiescere* rest)]
• **acquiescence** *noun*
• **acquiescent** *adjective*

acquire *verb*
• "a KWIRE"
• gain by and for oneself; obtain; come to possess.
• [Latin *acquirere* (*ad-* to + *quaerere* seek)]
• **acquirable** *adjective*
• **acquirement** *noun*

acquisition *noun*
• "ackwa ZISH'n"
• the act or an instance of acquiring.
• [Latin *acquisitio* (as ACQUIRE)]

acquisitive *adjective*
• "a KWIZZA tiv"
• keen to acquire things; avaricious; materialistic.
• [French *acquisitive* or Late Latin *acquisitivus* (as ACQUIRE)]
• **acquisitively** *adverb*
• **acquisitiveness** *noun*
• **acquisitor** *noun*

acquit *verb*
- "a KWIT"
- declare (a person) not guilty.
- [Old French *aquiter* from medieval Latin *acquitare* pay a debt (*ad-* to + *quittus* from *quietus* QUIET)]
- **acquittal** *noun*

acquittance *noun*
- "a KWIT ince"
- payment of or release from a debt.
- [as ACQUIT]

acre *noun*
- "AKE ur"
- a measure of land, 4,840 sq. yds., 0.405 hectares.
- [Old English *æcer*, designating the amount of land a yoke of oxen could plow in a day]
- **acred** *adjective* "AY curd"

acreage *noun*
- "AKE ur idge"
- a number of acres.
- [as ACRE]

acrid *adjective*
- "ACK rid"
- bitterly pungent; irritating; corrosive.
- [Latin *acer acris* keen, prob. after *acid*]
- **acridity** *noun* "a CRIDDA tee"
- **acridly** *adverb*

acridine *noun*
- "ACKRA deen"
- a colourless crystalline compound used in the manufacture of dyes and drugs.
- [as ACRID]

acriflavine *noun*
- "ackra FLAY vin"
- a reddish powder used as an antiseptic.
- [ACRIDINE + Latin *flavus* yellow]

acrimony *noun*
- "ACKRA moany"
- extreme bitterness of temper or manner; ill feeling.
- [Latin *acrimonia* pungency (as ACRID)]
- **acrimonious** *adjective*
- **acrimoniously** *adverb*

acro *noun*
- "ACK ro"
- a freestyle skiing event in which competitors perform choreographed acrobatic moves on skis to music.
- [abbreviation of ACROBATICS]

acrobat *noun*
- "ACK ro bat"
- a person who performs feats of agility, esp. in a circus.
- [French *acrobate* from Greek *akrobatēs* from *akron* summit + *bainō* walk]
- **acrobatic** *adjective*
- **acrobatically** *adverb*
- **acrobatics** *noun*

acromegaly *noun*
- "ackra MEGGA lee"
- abnormal enlargement of the hands, feet, and face, caused by excessive activity of the pituitary gland.
- [Greek *akron* extremity + *megas megal-* great]
- **acromegalic** *adjective* "ackra muh GALIC"

acronym *noun*
- "ACKRA nim"
- a word, usu. pronounced as such, formed from the initial letters of other words e.g. *laser*, *NATO*.
- [Greek *akron* end + *-onum-* = *onoma* name]

acropetal *adjective*
- "a CROPPA t'll"
- growing or developing from the base upwards, so that the youngest parts are at the tip.
- [Greek *akron* tip + Latin *petere* seek]
- **acropetally** *adverb* "a CROPPA t'll ee"

acrophobia *noun*
- "ackra FOBEY uh"
- an abnormal dread of heights.
- [Greek *akron* peak + PHOBIA]
- **acrophobic** *adjective*

acropolis *noun*
- "a CROPPA liss"
- a citadel or upper fortified part of an ancient Greek city, esp. that of Athens, site of the Parthenon and other notable buildings.
- [Greek *akropolis* from *akron* summit + *polis* city]

across *preposition*
- "a CROSS"
- to or on the other side of.
- [Old French *a croix*, *en croix*]

acrostic *noun*
- "a CROSS tick"
- a poem or other composition in which certain letters in each line form a word or words.
- [Greek *akrostikhis* from *akron* end + *stikhos* row, line of verse]

acrylamide *noun*
- "a CRILLA mide"
- a colourless crystalline solid which readily forms water-soluble polymers; the amide of acrylic acid.
- [as ACRYLIC]

acrylate *noun*
- "a CRILL ate"
- a salt or ester of acrylic acid.
- [as ACRYLIC]

acrylic *adjective*
- "a CRILLIC"
- of material made with a synthetic polymer.
- [from the liquid aldehyde *acrolein* (from Latin *acer acris* pungent + *olēre* to smell)]

actin *noun*
• "ACK tin"
• a protein which with myosin forms the contractile filaments of muscle fibres.
• [Greek *aktin-, aktis* ray]

actinia *noun*
• "ack TINNY uh"
• any sea anemone, esp. of the genus *Actinia*.
• [modern Latin, as ACTIN]

actinide *noun*
• "ACK tin ide"
• any of the series of 15 radioactive elements having increasing atomic numbers from actinium to lawrencium.
• [as ACTINIUM]

actinism *noun*
• "ACTIN izm"
• the property by which light or other electromagnetic radiation causes chemical changes, as in photography.
• [as ACTIN]
• **actinic** *adjective*

actinium *noun*
• "ack TINNY um"
• a radioactive metallic element of the actinide series, occurring naturally in pitchblende.
• [as ACTIN]

actinolite *noun*
• "ack TINNA lite"
• a green mineral containing calcium, magnesium, and iron silicates, and found esp. in metamorphic rocks.
• [as ACTIN + Greek *lithos* stone]

actinometer *noun*
• "actin OMMA tur"
• an instrument for measuring the intensity of radiation, esp. ultraviolet radiation.
• [as ACTIN + Greek *metron* measure]

actinomorphic *adjective*
• "ack tinna MORFIC"
• radially symmetrical.
• [as ACTIN + Greek *morphē* form]

actinomycete *noun*
• "ack tinna MY seet"
• a filamentous anaerobic bacterium of the order Actinomycetales.
• [as ACTIN + *-mycetes* from Greek *mukēs -etos* mushroom]

activate *verb*
• "ACTIV ate"
• make active; bring into action.
• [ultimately from Latin *agere act-* do]
• **activation** *noun*
• **activator** *noun*

activism *noun*
• "ACTIV izm"
• the policy or action of using vigorous campaigning to bring about social or political change.
• [as ACTIVATE]
• **activist** *noun*

activity *noun*
• "ack TIVVA tee"
• the condition of being active or moving about.
• [as ACTIVATE]

actual *adjective*
• "ACK choo 'll"
• existing in fact; real (often as distinct from ideal).
• [Late Latin *actualis* from *agere* act]
• **actualization** *noun* (also esp. *Brit.* **-isation**)
• **actualize** *verb* (also esp. *Brit.* **-ise**)

actuality *noun*
• "ack choo ALA tee"
• reality; what is the case.
• [Old French *actualité* entity or medieval Latin *actualitas* (as ACTUAL)]

actually *adverb*
• "ACK choo a lee"
• as a fact, really.
• [as ACTUAL]

actuary *noun*
• "ACK choo airy"
• an expert in statistics, esp. one who calculates insurance risks and premiums.
• [Latin *actuarius* bookkeeper, from *actus* past participle of *agere* act]
• **actuarial** *adjective* "ack choo AIRY 'll"
• **actuarially** *adverb*

actuate *verb*
• "ACK choo ate"
• communicate motion to (a machine etc.).
• [medieval Latin *actuare* from Latin *actus*: see ACTUAL]
• **actuation** *noun*
• **actuator** *noun*

acuity *noun*
• "a KYOO a tee"
• (of the mind or the senses, esp. vision) sharpness, acuteness.
• [medieval Latin *acuitas* from *acuere* sharpen, from *acus* needle]

aculeate *adjective*
• "ack YOOLY ate"
• having a sting.
• [Latin *aculeatus* from *aculeus* sting, diminutive of *acus* needle]

acumen *noun*
• "ACK yoo m'n" or "a KYOO m'n"
• the ability to understand and judge things quickly and clearly; shrewdness.
• [Latin *acumen -minis* anything sharp, from *acuere* sharpen, from *acus* needle]

acuminate *adjective*
• "ack YOOMA nate"
• tapering to a point.
• [Latin *acuminatus* pointed (as ACUMEN)]

acupressure *noun*
• "ACK yoo presh ur"
• a kind of therapy, in which pressure is applied with the fingers or palms to certain points of the body.
• [as ACUPUNCTURE + 'pressure']

acupuncture *noun*
• "ACK yoo punk chur"
• a system of complementary medicine in which fine needles are inserted in the skin at specific points along what are considered to be lines of energy (meridians), used in the treatment of various physical and mental conditions.
• [Latin *acu* with a needle + PUNCTURE]
• **acupuncturist** *noun*

acyclovir *noun*
• "ay CYCLO veer"
• an antiviral drug used to combat some types of herpes, esp. genital herpes.
• [as CYCLIC + VIRAL]

acyl *noun*
• "AY sile"
• the monovalent radical of an organic acid.
• [German (as ACIDIFY)]

adage[1] *noun*
• "AD idge"
• a traditional maxim, a proverb.
• [French from Latin *adagium* (*ad-* to + root of *aio* say)]

adage[2] *noun*
• "a DAZH" or "a DOZH"
• slow, flowing movement.
• [French, from ADAGIO]

adagio *adverb*
• "a DAZH ee oh" or "a DADGE ee oh"
• in slow time.
• [Italian, from *ad agio*, 'at ease']

adamant *adjective*
• "ADDA m'nt"
• stubbornly resolute; resistant to persuasion.
• [Latin *adamas adamant-* untameable, from Greek (as Greek *a-* without, *damaō* to tame)]
• **adamantine** *adjective* "adda MAN tine"
• **adamantly** *adverb*

adaptable *adjective*
• "a DAPTA bull"
• able to adapt oneself to new conditions.
• [Latin *adaptare* (*ad-* to, *aptare* from *aptus* fit)]
• **adaptability** *noun*

adaptationism *noun*
• "a dap TAY sh'n izm"
• the axiom or assumption that each feature of an organism is the result of evolutionary adaptation for a particular function.
• [as ADAPTABLE]
• **adaptationist** *noun*

adaptogen *noun*
• "a DAPTA j'n"
• (in herbal medicine) a natural substance considered to help the body adapt to stress and to exert a normalizing effect upon bodily processes. The best-known example is ginseng.
• [as ADAPTABLE + Greek *-genēs* -born, of a specified kind, from *gen-* root of *gignomai* be born, become]
• **adaptogenic** *adjective* "a dapta JENNIC"

adaxial *adjective*
• "a DAXY 'll"
• (esp. of the upper surface of a leaf) facing toward the stem of a plant.
• [Latin *ad-* to + AXIAL]

addax *noun*
• "AD ax"
• a large antelope, *Addax nasomaculatus*, of Northern Africa, with twisted horns.
• [Latin from an African word]

addendum *noun*
• "a DEN dum"
• a thing (usu. something omitted) to be added, esp. as additional matter at the end of a book.
• [Latin, gerundive of *addere* add]

adder *noun*
• "ADDER"
• any of a variety of non-venomous N American snakes, e.g. the hognose snake.
• [Old English *nædre*: *n* lost in Middle English by wrong division of *a naddre*]

addict *noun*
• "AD ict"
• a person addicted to a habit, esp. one dependent on a (specified) drug.
• [Latin *addicere* assign (*ad-* to + *dicere dict-* say)]
• **addicted** *adjective*
• **addiction** *noun*
• **addictive** *adjective*

addition *noun*
• "a DISH'n"
• the act or process of adding or being added.
• [Latin *addere* (*ad-* to + *dare* put)]
• **additional** *adjective*
• **additionally** *adverb*

additive *noun*
• "ADDA tiv"
• a thing added, esp. a substance added to another so as to give it specific qualities.
• [Late Latin *additivus* (as ADDITION)]

addle *verb*
• "ADD'll"
• muddle, confuse.
• [Old English *adela* filth, used as adjective, then as verb]
• **addled** *adjective*

address *noun*
• "AD ress" or "a DRESS"
• the place where a person lives or an organization is situated.
• [Old French *adresse*, *adresser*, ultimately from

Latin (*ad-* to + *directus* past participle of *dirigere direct-* (*di-* indicating completeness + *regere* put straight))]
- **addresser** *noun*

addressable *adjective*
- "a DRESSA bull"
- relating to or denoting a memory unit in which all locations can be separately accessed by a particular program.
- [as ADDRESS]
- **addressability** *noun*

addressee *noun*
- "address EE"
- the person to whom something (esp. a letter) is addressed.
- [as ADDRESS]

adduce *verb*
- "a DYOOSS"
- cite as an instance or as proof or evidence.
- [Latin *adducere adduct-* (*ad-* to + *ducere* lead)]
- **adducible** *adjective*

adductor *noun*
- "a DUCTER"
- any muscle that moves one part of the body towards another or towards the middle line of the body.
- [as ADDUCE]
- **adduct** *verb*
- **adduction** *noun*

adelgid *noun*
- "a DEL jid"
- an insect of the family Adelgidae, which comprises sap-feeding insects resembling aphids and typically covered with white waxy fluff.
- [perhaps from Greek *adelos* unseen + *-gid* of unknown origin]

Adena *noun*
- "a DEENA"
- a prehistoric people living in what is now Kentucky and Ohio from about 500 BC–AD 100.
- [*Adena*, Ohio, near where typical Adena burial mounds were found]

adenine *noun*
- "ADDA neen"
- a purine derivative found in all living tissue as a component base of DNA or RNA.
- [German *Adenin* formed as ADENOIDS]

adenocarcinoma *noun*
- "adda no carsa NOMA"
- a malignant tumour formed from glandular structures in epithelial tissue.
- [Greek *adēn* gland + CARCINOMA]

adenoidal *adjective*
- "adda NOID 'll"
- suffering from enlarged adenoids.
- [as ADENOIDS]
- **adenoidally** *adverb*

adenoids *plural noun*
- "ADDA noids" or "ADD noids"
- a mass of lymphatic tissue between the back of the nose and the throat which, when enlarged, hinders speech and breathing.
- [Greek *adēn -enos* gland]
- **adenoid** *adjective*

adenoma *noun*
- "adda NOMA"
- a gland-like benign tumour.
- [modern Latin from Greek *adēn* gland]

adenosine *noun*
- "a DENNA seen"
- a nucleoside of adenine and ribose present in all living tissue in a combined form.
- [ADENINE + RIBOSE]

adenovirus *noun*
- "ADDA no vie russ"
- any of a group of DNA viruses first discovered in adenoid tissue, most of which cause respiratory diseases.
- [as ADENOID + VIRUS]

adequate *adjective*
- "ADDA kwit"
- sufficient, satisfactory.
- [Latin *adaequatus* past participle of *adaequare* make equal (*ad-* to + *aequus* equal)]
- **adequacy** *noun* "ADDA kwuh see"
- **adequately** *adverb*

adhere *verb*
- "ad HERE"
- (of a substance) stick fast to a surface, another substance, etc.
- [French *adhérer* or Latin *adhaerēre* (*ad-* to + *haerēre haes-* stick)]
- **adhesion** *noun*
- **adhesive** *adjective*
- **adhesively** *adverb*
- **adhesiveness** *noun*

adherent *noun*
- "ad HERE 'nt"
- a supporter of a party, person, etc.
- [as ADHERE]
- **adherence** *noun*

adiabatic *adjective*
- "ay dee a BATTIC" or "ay die a BATTIC"
- impassable to heat.
- [Greek *adiabatos* impassable (as Greek *a-* without, *diabainō* pass)]
- **adiabatically** *adverb*

adieu *interjection*
- "ad DYOO" (with "OO" as in *FOOT*)
- goodbye.
- [Old French from *à* to + *Dieu* God]

adios *interjection*
- "addy OSE" ("OSE" rhymes with *GROSS*)
- goodbye.
- [Spanish *adiós* from *a* to + *Dios* God]

adipocere *noun*
- "ADDA po seer"

• a greyish fatty or soapy substance generated in dead bodies subjected to moisture.
• [French *adipocire* from Latin *adeps adipis* fat + French *cire* wax, from Latin *cera*]

adipose *adjective*
• "ADDA pose" (rhymes with *GROSS*)
• (esp. of body tissue) used for the storage of fat.
• [modern Latin *adiposus* from *adeps adipis* fat]
• **adiposity** *noun* "adda POSSA tee"

adit *noun*
• "AD it"
• a horizontal entrance or passage in a mine.
• [Latin *aditus* (*ad-* to + *itus* from *ire it-* go)]

Adivasi *noun*
• "adda VOSSY"
• a member of any of the aboriginal peoples of India.
• [Hindi *adinivāsī* original inhabitant]

adjacent *adjective*
• "a JAY s'nt"
• lying near or adjoining.
• [Middle English from Latin *adjacēre* (*ad-* to + *jacēre* lie)]
• **adjacency** *noun*

adjective *noun*
• "AD jeck tiv"
• a word or phrase naming an attribute, added to or grammatically related to a noun to modify it or describe it.
• [Old French *adjectif -ive*, ultimately from Latin *adjicere adject-* (*ad-* to + *jacere* throw)]
• **adjectival** *adjective* "ad jeck TIVE'll"
• **adjectivally** *adverb*

adjoin *verb*
• "a JOIN"
• be close to or joined with.
• [Old French *ajoindre, ajoign-* from Latin *adjungere adjunct-* (*ad-* to + *jungere* join)]
• **adjoining** *adjective*

adjourn *verb*
• "a JURN"
• put off; postpone (esp. a court case).
• [Old French *ajorner* (*ad-* to + *jorn* day, ultimately from Latin *diurnus* DIURNAL)]
• **adjournment** *noun*

adjudge *verb*
• "a JUDGE"
• adjudicate (a matter).
• [Old French *ajuger* from Latin *adjudicare*: see ADJUDICATE]
• **adjudgment** *noun* (also **adjudgement**)

adjudicate *verb*
• "a JOODA cate"
• act as judge in a competition, court, tribunal, etc.
• [Latin *adjudicare* (*ad-* to + *judicare* from *judex -icis* judge)]
• **adjudication** *noun*
• **adjudicative** *adjective* "a JOODA kuh tiv"
• **adjudicator** *noun*

adjunct *noun*
• "AD junct"
• something added to something else, and auxiliary to or dependent on it.
• [Latin *adjunctus*: see ADJOIN]
• **adjunctive** *adjective*

adjure *verb*
• "a JURE"
• charge or request (a person) solemnly or earnestly, as if under oath.
• [Latin *adjurare* (*ad-* to + *jurare* swear) in Late Latin sense 'put a person to an oath']
• **adjuration** *noun*
• **adjuratory** *adjective*

adjust *verb*
• "a JUST"
• arrange; put in the correct order or position.
• [French *adjuster*, ultimately from Latin *juxta* near]
• **adjustability** *noun*
• **adjustable** *adjective*
• **adjuster** *noun*
• **adjustment** *noun*

adjutant *noun*
• "ADGE a t'nt"
• an officer who assists superior officers by communicating orders, conducting correspondence, etc.
• [Latin *adjutare* frequentative of *adjuvare*: see ADJUVANT]
• **adjutancy** *noun*

adjuvant *adjective*
• "ADGE a v'nt"
• helpful, auxiliary.
• [French from Latin *adjuvare* (*ad-* to + *juvare jut-* help)]

administer *verb*
• "ad MIN iss tur"
• attend to the running of (business affairs etc.); manage.
• [Latin *administrare* (*ad-* to + MINISTER)]
• **administrate** *verb*
• **administration** *noun*
• **administrative** *adjective*
• **administratively** *adverb*
• **administrator** *noun*
• **administratorship** *noun*

administratrix *noun*
• "ad minna STRAY trix"
• a woman appointed to manage the estate of a person who has died without a will.
• [as ADMINISTER + Latin *-trix* feminine agent noun ending]

admiral *noun*
• "ADMER 'll"
• a naval officer of high rank: (in Canada) the highest rank in the Maritime Command.
• [medieval Latin *a(d)miralis* etc., from Arabic *'amīr* commander (compare EMIR)]
• **admiralship** *noun*

Admiralty *noun*
- "ADMER 'll tee"
- (in the UK) the department administering the Royal Navy.
- [as ADMIRAL]

admire *verb*
- "ad MIRE"
- regard with approval, respect, or satisfaction.
- [Latin *admirari* (*ad-* to + *mirari* wonder at)]
- **admirable** *adjective* "ADMA ruh bull"
- **admirably** *adverb*
- **admiration** *noun* "adma RAY sh'n"
- **admirer** *noun*
- **admiring** *adjective*
- **admiringly** *adverb*

admissible *adjective*
- "ad MISSA bull"
- (of an idea or plan) worth accepting or considering.
- [medieval Latin *admissibilis* (as ADMIT)]
- **admissibility** *noun*

admission *noun*
- "ad MISH'n"
- an acknowledgement or confession.
- [Latin *admissio* (as ADMIT)]

admit *verb*
- "ad MIT"
- acknowledge; recognize as true.
- [Latin *admittere admiss-* (*ad-* to + *mittere* send)]
- **admittedly** *adverb*

admittance *noun*
- "ad MIT ince"
- the right or process of being allowed in, usu. to a place.
- [as ADMIT]
- **admittee** *noun* "ad mit EE"

admixture *noun*
- "ad MIX chur"
- a combination, esp. of disparate elements.
- [Latin *admixtus* past participle of *admiscēre* (*ad-* to + *miscēre* mix)]

admonish *verb*
- "ad MON ish"
- reprove, esp. gently.
- [Latin *admonēre* (*ad-* to + *monēre monit-* warn)]
- **admonishment** *noun*
- **admonition** *noun* "adma NISH'n"
- **admonitory** *adjective* "ad MONNA tory"

adnominal *adjective*
- "ad NOMMA n'll"
- attached to a noun.
- [Latin *adnomen -minis* (added name)]

ado *noun*
- "a DOO"
- fuss, busy activity; trouble, difficulty.
- [originally in *much ado* = much to do, from northern Middle English *at do* (= to do) from Old Norse *at* as sign of infin. + 'do']

adobe *noun*
- "a DOE bee"
- a sun-dried brick made from clay and straw.
- [Spanish, from *adobar* to plaster, from Arabic *aṭ-ṭūb*, from *al* the + *ṭūb* bricks]

adobo *noun*
- "a DOE boe"
- a Filipino dish of chicken or pork stewed in vinegar, garlic, soy sauce, bay leaves, and peppercorns.
- [Spanish, lit. = 'marinade']

adolescent *adjective*
- "adda LESS'nt"
- between childhood and adulthood.
- [Old French from Latin *adolescere* grow up]
- **adolescence** *noun*

Adonis *noun*
- "a DON iss"
- a handsome young man.
- [*Adonis*, a beautiful youth from Greek mythology]

adorable *adjective*
- "a DORA bull"
- delightful, cute.
- [as ADORE]
- **adorably** *adverb*

adore *verb*
- "a DORE"
- regard with honour and deep affection.
- [Latin *adorare* worship (*ad-* to + *orare* speak, pray)]
- **adoration** *noun*
- **adorer** *noun*
- **adoring** *adjective*
- **adoringly** *adverb*

adrenal *adjective*
- "a DREEN 'll"
- of either of two ductless glands above the kidneys, secreting adrenalin.
- [Latin *ad-* to + RENAL]

adrenalin *noun*
ALSO SPELLED: **adrenaline**
- "a DREN'll in"
- a hormone secreted by the adrenal glands, esp. in conditions of stress, increasing rates of blood circulation, breathing, and carbohydrate metabolism and preparing muscles for exertion.
- [as ADRENAL]

adrenalized *adjective*
ALSO SPELLED: esp. *Brit.* **-ised**
- "a DREN'll ized"
- excited, tense, or highly charged.
- [as ADRENAL]

adrenocorticotrophin *noun*
- "a dreeno corta co TRO fin"
- a hormone secreted by the pituitary gland and stimulating the adrenal glands.
- [ADRENAL + CORTEX + *trophē* food]
- **adrenocorticotrophic** *adjective*

Adriatic *adjective*
- "ay dree ATTIC"
- of or relating to the Adriatic Sea between Italy and Greece.

adroit *adjective*
- "a DROIT"
- dexterous, skilful.
- [French from *à droit* according to right]
- ***adroitly*** *adverb*
- ***adroitness*** *noun*

adsorb *verb*
- "ad SORB" or "ad ZORB"
- (usu. of a solid) hold (molecules of a gas or liquid or solute) to its surface, causing a thin film to form.
- [Latin *ad-* to + ABSORB]
- ***adsorbable*** *adjective*
- ***adsorbent*** *adjective* "ad SORB'nt" or "ad ZORB'nt"
- ***adsorption*** *noun* "ad SORP sh'n" or "ad ZORP sh'n"

adsorbate *noun*
- "ad SORE bate"
- a substance adsorbed.
- [as ADSORB]

adulate *verb*
- "AD yuh late" or "ADGE a late"
- flatter or praise obsequiously.
- [Latin *adulari adulat-* fawn on]
- ***adulation*** *noun*
- ***adulator*** *noun*
- ***adulatory*** *adjective* "AD yuh luh tory" or "ADGE a luh tory"

adulterate *verb*
- "a DULLTER ate"
- corrupt or debase (esp. foods) by adding other or inferior ingredients.
- [Latin *adulterare adulterat-* corrupt]
- ***adulterant*** *noun*
- ***adulteration*** *noun*
- ***adulterator*** *noun*

adulterine *adjective*
- "a DULLTER ine"
- illegal, unlicensed.
- [as ADULTERATE]

adultery *noun*
- "a DULLTER ee"
- voluntary sexual intercourse between a married person and a person (married or not) other than his or her spouse.
- [Latin *adulter* adulterer, from *adulterare* corrupt]
- ***adulterer*** *noun*
- ***adulteress*** *noun*
- ***adulterous*** *adjective*
- ***adulterously*** *adverb*

adulticide *noun*
- "a DULLTA side"
- a drug or pesticide that kills the adult forms of a pest or parasite.
- ['adult' + Latin *-cida, -cidium* from *caedere* kill]

adumbrate *verb*
- "ADDUM brate"
- foreshadow, typify.
- [Latin *adumbrare* (*ad-* to + *umbrare* from *umbra* shade)]
- ***adumbration*** *noun*
- ***adumbrative*** *adjective* "a DUMBRA tiv"

advantage *noun*
- "ad VAN tidge"
- a beneficial feature; a favourable circumstance.
- [Old French *avantage, avant* in front, from Late Latin *abante* in front, from Latin *ab* away + *ante* before]
- ***advantageous*** *adjective* "ad v'n TAY juss"
- ***advantageously*** *adverb*

advantaged *adjective*
- "ad VAN tijd"
- having advantages; privileged.
- [as ADVANTAGE]

advection *noun*
- "ad VECK sh'n"
- transfer of heat by the horizontal flow of air.
- [Latin *advectio* from *advehere* (*ad-* to + *vehere* *vect-* carry)]
- ***advective*** *adjective*

adventitious *adjective*
- "adven TISH us"
- accidental, not planned.
- [Latin *adventicius* from *adventus* arrival, from *advenire* (*ad-* to + *venire vent-* come)]
- ***adventitiously*** *adverb*

adventure *noun*
- "ad VEN chur"
- an unusual and exciting experience.
- [Latin *adventurus* about to happen from *adventus* arrival, from *advenire* (as ADVENTITIOUS)]
- ***adventurer*** *noun*
- ***adventuresome*** *adjective*
- ***adventuress*** *noun*
- ***adventurous*** *adjective*
- ***adventurously*** *adverb*
- ***adventurousness*** *noun*

adventurism *noun*
- "ad VEN chur izm"
- a tendency to take risks, often imprudently, esp. in foreign policy.
- [as ADVENTURE]
- ***adventurist*** *noun*

adverb *noun*
- "AD vurb"
- a word or phrase that modifies or qualifies another word (esp. an adjective, verb, or other adverb) or a word group, expressing a relation of place, time, circumstance, manner, cause, degree, etc., e.g. *gently, quite, then, there*.

• [French *adverbe* or Latin *adverbium* (*ad-* to + *verbum* word)]
• **adverbial** *adjective* "ad VURBY 'll"

adversary *noun*
• "AD vur serry"
• an enemy.
• [Latin *adversarius* from *adversus*: see ADVERSE]
• **adversarial** *adjective* "ad vur SERRY 'll"

adversative *adjective*
• "ad VURSA tiv"
• (of words etc.) expressing opposition or antithesis.
• [Late Latin *adversativus*, from *adversari* oppose, from *adversus*: see ADVERSE]
• **adversatively** *adverb*

adverse *adjective*
• "ad VURSE"
• contrary, hostile.
• [Latin *adversus* past participle of *advertere* (*ad-* to + *vertere vers-* turn)]
• **adversely** *adverb*
• **adverseness** *noun*

adversity *noun*
• "ad VURSA tee"
• the condition of adverse fortune.
• [as ADVERSE]

advert *verb*
• "ad VURT"
• refer in speaking or writing.
• [Latin *advertere*: see ADVERSE]

advertise *verb*
• "AD vur tize"
• draw attention to or describe favourably (goods or services) in a public medium to promote sales.
• [Old French *avertir* (stem *advertiss-*) from Latin *advertere*: see ADVERSE]
• **advertisement** *noun* "ad VURT iss m'nt" or "AD vur tize m'nt"
• **advertiser** *noun*

advertorial *noun*
• "ad vur TORY 'll"
• a newspaper or magazine advertisement giving information about a product in the style of an editorial or objective journalistic comment.
• [blend of ADVERTISEMENT + EDITORIAL]

advisable *adjective*
• "ad VIZE a bull"
• (of a course of action etc.) to be recommended, sensible.
• [as ADVISE]
• **advisability** *noun*
• **advisably** *adverb*

advise *verb*
• "ad VIZE"
• give advice to.
• [Latin *ad* to + *visare* frequentative of *vidēre* see]
• **adviser** *noun* (also **advisor**)
• **advisory** *adjective*

advised *adjective*
• "ad VIZED"
• judicious.
• [as ADVISE]
• **advisedly** *adverb* "ad VIZE id lee"

advocaat *noun*
• "adva COT"
• a liqueur of eggs, sugar, and brandy.
• [Dutch, = ADVOCATE (being originally an advocate's drink)]

advocate *noun*
• "ADVA kit"
• a person who supports or speaks in favour.
• [Latin *advocatus* past participle of *advocare* (*ad-* to + *vocare* call)]
• **advocacy** *noun*

advowson *noun*
• "ad VOW z'n"
• (in ecclesiastical law) the right of recommending a member of the clergy for a vacant benefice, or of making the appointment.
• [Anglo-French *a(d)voweson* from Latin *advocatio -onis* (as ADVOCATE)]

adware *noun*
• "AD ware"
• software displaying paid advertisements and distributed free of charge.
• [ADVERTISEMENT + WARE]

adytum *noun*
• "ADDA tum"
• the innermost part of an ancient temple.
• [Latin from Greek *aduton*, impenetrable (as Greek *a-* without, *duō* enter)]

adze *noun*
ALSO SPELLED: *US* also **adz**
• "ADZ"
• a tool for cutting away the surface of wood, like an axe with an arched blade at right angles to the handle.
• [Old English *adesa*]

adzuki *noun*
ALSO SPELLED: **adsuki**, **azuki**
• "ad ZOOKY"
• an annual leguminous plant, *Vigna angularis*, native to China and Japan.
• [Japanese *azuki*]

aedile *noun*
• "EE dile"
• either of a pair of Roman magistrates who administered public works, maintenance of roads, public games, the grain supply, etc.
• [Latin *aedilis* concerned with buildings, from *aedes* building]
• **aedileship** *noun*

Aegean *adjective*
• "a JEE 'n"
• of or relating to the sea or islands between Greece and Asia Minor (Turkey).

aegis *noun*
• "EE jiss"
• auspices; control.
• [Latin from Greek *aigis* mythical shield of Zeus or Athene]

aegrotat *noun*
• "AGRO tat" or "AY grow tat"
• *Cdn & Brit.* a certificate stating that a university student is too ill to attend an examination.
• [Latin, = is sick, from *aeger* sick]

aeolian *adjective*
ALSO SPELLED: **eolian**
• "ay OLEY 'n"
• borne or produced by the wind.
• [Latin *Aeolius* from *Aeolus*, Greek god of the winds]

aepyornis *noun*
• "eepy ORNISS"
• a gigantic flightless extinct bird of the genus *Aepyornis*, resembling a moa, known from remains found in Madagascar.
• [Latin from Greek *aipus* high, *ornis* bird]

aerate *verb*
• "AIR ate"
• charge (a liquid) with a gas, esp. carbon dioxide, e.g. to produce effervescence.
• [Latin *aer* air + *-atus* past participle ending]
• **aeration** *noun*
• **aerator** *noun*

aerenchyma *noun*
• "air 'n KIME uh"
• a soft plant tissue containing air spaces found esp. in many aquatic plants.
• [Greek *aēr* air + *egkhuma* infusion]

aerial *adjective*
• "AIRY 'll"
• by or from or involving aircraft.
• [Latin *aerius* from Greek *aerios* from *aēr* air]
HOMOPHONES: *areal*

aerialist *noun*
• "AIRY 'll ist"
• a high-wire or trapeze artist.
• [as AERIAL]

aerie *noun*
ALSO SPELLED: **eyrie**
• "AIRY" or "EERY"
• a nest of a bird of prey, esp. an eagle, built high up.
• [medieval Latin *aeria*, *aerea*, etc., prob. from Old French *aire* lair, ultimately from Latin *agrum* piece of ground]
HOMOPHONES: *airy*, *eerie*

aero *adjective*
• "AIR oh"
• aerodynamic.
• [abbreviation of AERODYNAMIC]
HOMOPHONES: *arrow*

aerobat *noun*
• "AIR oh bat"
• a pilot who performs feats of expert and usu. spectacular flying and manoeuvring of aircraft.
• [Greek *aero-* from *aēr* air + ACROBAT]
• **aerobatic** *adjective*
• **aerobatically** *adverb*
• **aerobatics** *noun*

aerobe *noun*
• "AIR obe"
• a micro-organism usu. growing in the presence of air, or needing air for growth.
• [French *aérobie* from Greek *aero-* from *aēr* air + *bios* life]

aerobic *adjective*
• "a ROE bick"
• increasing or pertaining to oxygen consumption by the body.
• [as AEROBE]
• **aerobically** *adverb*

aerobicized *adjective*
• "a ROBE a sized"
• (of a person's body) firm, toned, and slender from much aerobic exercise.
• [as AEROBE]

aerobics *plural noun*
• "a ROE bix"
• exercises, esp. those done to music, designed to increase fitness by any maintainable activity that increases oxygen intake and heart rate.
• [as AEROBE]

aerobiology *noun*
• "air oh by OLLA jee"
• the study of airborne micro-organisms, pollen, spores, etc., esp. as agents of infection.
• [as AEROBE]

aerobrake *verb*
• "AIR oh brake"
• cause a spacecraft to slow down by flying through a planet's rarefied atmosphere to produce aerodynamic drag.
• [Greek *aero-* from *aēr* air + 'brake']

aerodrome *noun*
• "AIR oh drome"
• a small airport or airfield.
• [Greek *aero-* from *aēr* air + *dromos* course, running]

aerodynamics *plural noun*
• "air oh die NAMMIX"
• the interaction between the air and solid bodies moving through it.
• [Greek *aero-* from *aēr* air + DYNAMICS (as DYNAMIC)]
• **aerodynamic** *adjective*
• **aerodynamically** *adverb*
• **aerodynamicist** *noun*
"air oh die NAMMA sist"

aerogel *noun*
• "AIR oh jell"
• an extremely light, porous, foam-like

insulating material made from granulated silica.

• [Greek *aero-* from *aēr* air + GEL]

aerogram *noun*

ALSO SPELLED: **aerogramme**

• "AIR oh gram"

• an air letter in the form of a single sheet that is folded and sealed.

• [Greek *aero-* from *aēr* air + *gramma* thing written]

aerolite *noun*

• "AIR oh lite"

• a stony meteorite.

• [Greek *aero-* from *aēr* air + *lithos* stone]

aerology *noun*

• "air OLLA jee"

• the study of the upper levels of the atmosphere.

• [Greek *aero-* from *aēr* air + *logos* word]

• **aerological** *adjective*

aeronautics *plural noun*

• "air oh NOTTIX"

• the science or practice of motion or travel in the air.

• [modern Latin *aeronautica* from *aero* air + NAUTICAL]

• **aeronautic** *adjective*

• **aeronautical** *adjective*

aeronomy *noun*

• "air ONNA mee"

• the science of the upper atmosphere.

• [Greek *aero-* from *aēr* air + ASTRONOMY]

aerosol *noun*

• "AIR a sawl"

• a substance packed under pressure with a device for releasing it as a fine spray.

• [Greek *aéro-* from *aēr* air + SOL]

• **aerosolize** *verb* (also esp. *Brit.* **-ise**)

aerospace *noun*

• "AIR oh space"

• the earth's atmosphere and outer space.

• [Greek *aéro-* from *aēr* air + 'space' from Old French *espace* from Latin *spatium*]

aerostat *noun*

• "AIR oh stat"

• any craft which is sustained in the air by buoyancy, esp. a balloon or dirigible.

• [French *aérostat* from Greek *aéro-* from *aēr* air + *statos* standing]

Aesculapian *adjective*

• "ee skuh LAPEY 'n" or "ess kuh LAPEY 'n"

• of or relating to medicine or physicians.

• [*Aesculapius*, the Roman god of healing]

aesthete *noun*

ALSO SPELLED: esp. *US* **esthete**

• "ESS theet"

• a person who has or professes to have a special appreciation of beauty.

• [Greek *aisthētēs* one who perceives, or from AESTHETIC]

aesthetic *adjective*

ALSO SPELLED: **esthetic**

• "es THETTIC"

• concerned with beauty or the appreciation of beauty.

• [Greek *aisthētikos* from *aisthanomai* perceive]

• **aesthetically** *adverb* (also **esthetically**)

• **aestheticism** *noun* (also **estheticism**) "es THETTA sizm"

aesthetics *noun*

ALSO SPELLED: **esthetics**

• "es THETTIX"

• the philosophy of the beautiful, esp. in art.

• [as AESTHETE]

• **aesthetician** *noun* (also **esthetician**) "estha TISH'n"

aestival *adjective*

ALSO SPELLED: **estival**

• "ESTA v'll"

• belonging to or appearing in summer.

• [Latin *aestivalis* from *aestivus* from *aestus* heat]

aestivate *verb*

ALSO SPELLED: **estivate**

• "ESTA vate" or "EESTA vate"

• spend the summer or dry season in a state of torpor.

• [Latin *aestivare aestivat-* reside during the summer]

aestivation *noun*

ALSO SPELLED: **estivation**

• "esta VAY sh'n" or "eesta VAY sh'n"

• the arrangement of petals in a flower bud before it opens.

• [as AESTIVATE]

affable *adjective*

• "AFFA bull"

• friendly, good-natured.

• [Latin *affabilis* from *affari* (*ad-* to + *fari* speak)]

• **affability** *noun*

• **affably** *adverb*

affect[1] *verb*

• "a FECT"

• produce an effect on; influence.

• [Latin *afficere affect-* influence (*ad-* to + *facere* do)]

• **affecting** *adjective*

• **affectingly** *adverb*

HOMOPHONES: *effect*

affect[2] *verb*

• "a FECT"

• pretend to have or feel.

• [Latin *affectare* aim at, frequentative of *afficere* (as AFFECT[1])]

HOMOPHONES: *effect*

affect[3] *noun*

• "AFF ect"

• an emotion or mood associated with certain ideas.
• [German *Affekt* from Latin *affectus* disposition, from *afficere* (as AFFECT[1])]
• **affectless** *adjective*
• **affectlessness** *noun*

affectation *noun*
• "aff eck TAY sh'n"
• an assumed or contrived manner of behaviour, esp. in order to impress.
• [as AFFECT[2]]
• **affected** *adjective* "a FECTED"
• **affectedly** *adverb*

affection *noun*
• "a FECK sh'n"
• goodwill; fond or kindly feeling.
• [Latin *affectio -onis* (as AFFECT[1])]
• **affectional** *adjective*
• **affectionally** *adverb*
• **affectionate** *adjective*
• **affectionately** *adverb*

affective *adjective*
• "a FECTIV"
• concerning the affections; emotional.
• [Late Latin *affectivus* (as AFFECT[1])]
• **affectivity** *noun*
HOMOPHONES: *effective*, *effectivity*

affenpinscher *noun*
• "AFFEN pinsher"
• a breed of small dog with a short, wiry coat, resembling the griffon.
• [German from *Affe* monkey + *Pinscher* terrier]

afferent *adjective*
• "AFFER 'nt"
• conducting inwards or towards.
• [Latin *afferre* (*ad-* to + *ferre* bring)]

affianced *adjective*
• "affy ONST" or "a FIE inst"
• promised in marriage; betrothed, engaged.
• [Old French *afiancer* from medieval Latin *affidare* (*ad-* to + *fidus* trusty)]

affidavit *noun*
• "affa DAVE it"
• a written statement confirmed by oath (usu. before an authorized official), for use as evidence in court.
• [medieval Latin, = has stated on oath, from *affidare*: see AFFIANCED]

affiliate *verb*
• "a FILLY ate"
• attach or connect (to a larger organization); adopt as a member, branch, etc.
• [medieval Latin *affiliare* adopt (*ad-* to + *filius* son)]
• **affiliated** *adjective*
• **affiliation** *noun*

affinity *noun*
• "a FINNA tee"
• a spontaneous or natural liking for or attraction to a person or thing.
• [Latin *affinitas -tatis* from *affinis* related, lit. 'bordering on' (*ad-* to + *finis* border)]

affirm *verb*
• "a FURM"
• assert strongly; state as a fact.
• [Latin *affirmare* (*ad-* to + *firmus* strong)]
• **affirmation** *noun* "affer MAY sh'n"
• **affirmative** *adjective* "a FURMA tiv"
• **affirmatively** *adverb*

affix *verb*
• "a FIX"
• attach, fasten.
• [French *affixer*, *affixe* or medieval Latin *affixare* frequentative of Latin *affigere* (*ad-* to + *figere fix-* fix)]
• **affixation** *noun*

afflatus *noun*
• "a FLATE us"
• a divine creative impulse; inspiration.
• [Latin from *afflare* (*ad-* to + *flare flat-* to blow)]

afflict *verb*
• "a FLICT"
• distress with bodily or mental suffering.
• [Latin *afflictare*, or *afflict-* past participle stem of *affligere* (*ad-* to + *fligere flict-* dash)]
• **affliction** *noun*

affluent *adjective*
• "AFF loo 'nt"
• wealthy, rich.
• [Old French from Latin *affluere* (*ad-* to + *fluere flux-* flow)]
• **affluence** *noun*

affluenza *noun*
• "aff loo ENZA"
• pursuit of or obsession with wealth, material things, and an affluent lifestyle to a degree that is detrimental to the individual's mental health and to society as a whole.
• [blend of AFFLUENCE + INFLUENZA]

afflux *noun*
• "AFF lucks"
• a flow towards a point; an influx.
• [medieval Latin *affluxus* from Latin *affluere*: see AFFLUENT]

afford *verb*
• "a FORD"
• have enough money, means, time, etc., for; be able to spare.
• [Middle English from Old English *geforthian* promote, assimilated to words in *af-*]
• **affordability** *noun*
• **affordable** *adjective*

afforest *verb*
• "a FOREST"
• convert into forest.
• [medieval Latin *afforestare* (*ad-* to + *foresta* forest)]
• **afforestation** *noun*

affranchise *verb*
- "a FRAN chize"
- release from servitude or an obligation.
- [Old French *afranchir* (as ENFRANCHISE, with prefix *a-* from Latin *ad-* to, at)]

affray *noun*
- "a FRAY"
- a public fight; riot.
- [Anglo-French *afrayer* (v.) from Old French *esfreer* from Romanic]

affricate *noun*
- "AFRIC it"
- a composite speech sound in which a plosive or stopped consonant is gradually released with friction, e.g. *ch* in 'church'.
- [Latin *affricare* (*ad-* to + *fricare* rub)]

affront *noun*
- "a FRUNT"
- an open insult.
- [Old French *afronter* slap in the face, insult, ultimately from Latin *frons frontis* face]

Afghan *noun*
- "AF gan"
- a native or national of Afghanistan in central Asia.
- [Pashto *afghānī*]
- **Afghani** *noun* "af GANNY"

aficionado *noun*
- "a fisha NADDO" or "a fisha NODDO" or "a fish yuh NADDO" or "a fish yuh NODDO"
- a devotee, fan or enthusiast.
- [Spanish, orig. designating a devotee of bullfighting, past participle of *aficioner* 'become fond of', based on Latin *affectio(n-)* 'favourable disposition towards' (as AFFECT[1])]

aflatoxin *noun*
- "AFLA toxin"
- any of several related toxic compounds produced by the fungus *Aspergillus flavus*, which cause tissue damage and cancer.
- [Aspergillus + *flavus* + TOXIN]

aforementioned *adjective*
- "a FOR men chund"
- denoting a thing or person previously mentioned.
- [Old English *a* to + FORE + 'mention' (from Latin *mentio -onis* from the root of *mens* mind)]

aforesaid *adjective*
- "a FOR sed"
- denoting a thing or person previously mentioned.
- [as AFOREMENTIONED + 'said']

aforethought *adjective*
- "a FOR thot"
- premeditated.
- [as AFOREMENTIONED + 'thought']

afoul *adverb*
- "a FOUL"
- into conflict or difficulty with.
- [Old English *a* to + FOUL]

afreet *noun*
ALSO SPELLED: **afrit**
- "AFF reet"
- a powerful, usu. evil jinni in Arabian stories and Islamic mythology.
- [Arabic *'ifrīt*]

African *adjective*
- "AFRA k'n"
- relating to Africa.
- **Africanize** *verb* (also esp. *Brit.* **-ise**)

Africana *plural noun*
- "afra CANNA"
- things connected with Africa.

Afrikaans *noun*
- "affra KONCE"
- the language of the Afrikaner people developed from Dutch, an official language of the Republic of South Africa.
- [Dutch, = African]

Afrikaner *noun*
- "affra CONNER"
- an Afrikaans-speaking white South African, esp. one of Dutch descent.
- [Afrikaans, alteration of Dutch *Afrikaan*, 'an African']

Afrocentric *adjective*
- "afro SENTRIC"
- centred on Africa or on cultures of African origin, esp. N American black culture.
- [Latin *Afer Afr-* African + CENTRIC]
- **Afrocentrism** *noun*
- **Afrocentrist** *noun*

afrormosia *noun*
- "aff roar MOZEY uh"
- an African tree, *Pericopsis* (formerly *Afrormosia*) *elata*, yielding a hard wood resembling teak and used for furniture.
- [modern Latin, from *Afro-* (as AFROCENTRIC) + *Ormosia* genus of trees]

afterthought *noun*
- "AFTER thot"
- an item or thing that is thought of or added later.
- ['after' + 'thought']

afterward *adverb*
- "AFTER wurd"
- later, subsequently.
- [Old English *æftanwearde* adjective from *æftan* toward the stern of a ship + *-weard*, from a Germanic root meaning 'turn']

HOMOPHONES: *afterword*

afterword *noun*
- "AFTER wurd"
- concluding remarks in a book, either by the author or by someone else.
- ['after' + 'word']

HOMOPHONES: *afterward*

aga *noun*
ALSO SPELLED: **agha**
• "OGGA"
• (in Muslim countries, esp. under the Ottoman Empire) a commander, a chief.
• [Turkish *āgā* master]

agamic *adjective*
• "a GAMMIC"
• characterized by the absence of sexual reproduction.
• [Greek *agamos* unmarried]

agapanthus *noun*
• "agga PANTH us"
• any plant of the genus *Agapanthus*, native to Africa, having blue or white funnel-shaped flowers.
• [modern Latin from Greek *agapē* love + *anthos* flower]

agape *noun*
• "AGGA pay"
• a Christian feast in token of fellowship, esp. one held by early Christians in commemoration of the Last Supper.
• [Greek, = brotherly love]

agar *noun*
• "AY gar"
• a gelatinous substance obtained from any of various kinds of red seaweed, and used as a thickener in food, as a culture medium for bacteria, and as a laxative.
• [Malay]

agaric *noun*
• "AGGA rick"
• any fungus of the family Agaricaceae, with cap and stalk, including the common edible mushroom.
• [Latin *agaricum* from Greek *agarikon* 'tree fungus']

agate *noun*
• "AG it"
• any of several varieties of hard usu. streaked chalcedony.
• [French *agate* from Latin *achates* from Greek *akhatēs*]

agave *noun*
• "a GOV ee" or "a GOV ay"
• any plant of the genus *Agave*, with rosettes of succulent spiny leaves, and tall inflorescences, e.g. the century plant.
• [Latin from Greek *Agauē*, proper name in myth, from *agauos* illustrious]

ageism *noun*
ALSO SPELLED: **agism**
• "AGE izm"
• prejudice or discrimination on the grounds of age.
• [from 'age' (from Old French *age*, ultimately from Latin *aetas -atis* age)]
• **ageist** *adjective* (also **agist**)

agency *noun*
• "AGE 'n see"
• an organization or business providing a (usu. specific) service.
• [medieval Latin *agentia* from Latin *agere* do]

agenda *noun*
• "a JENDA"
• a list of items of business to be considered at a meeting.
• [Latin, neuter pl. of gerundive of *agere* do]

agent *noun*
• "AY j'nt"
• a person who provides a specific service etc.
• [Latin *agent-* participle stem of *agere* do]
• **agential** *adjective* "ay JEN sh'll"
• **agenting** *noun*
• **agentry** *noun*

ageratum *noun*
• "adger ATE um" or "adger AT um"
• any of a number of low-growing herbaceous plants of the genus *Ageratum*, bearing clusters of small, long-lasting blue flowers.
• [modern Latin from Latin *ageraton* from Greek *agēratos* from *a-* without + *gērat-*, *gēras* old age, since the plant originally so called had everlasting flowers]

agglomerate *verb*
• "a GLOMMER ate"
• collect into a mass.
• [Latin *agglomerare* (*ad-* to + *glomerare* from *glomus -meris* ball)]
• **agglomeration** *noun*
• **agglomerative** *adjective*

agglutinate *verb*
• "a GLOOT'n ate"
• unite as with glue.
• [Latin *agglutinare* (*ad-* to + *glutinare* from *gluten -tinis* glue)]
• **agglutination** *noun*
• **agglutinative** *adjective*

agglutinin *noun*
• "a GLOOT'n in"
• a substance or antibody causing an unnatural union of surfaces due to inflammation.
• [as AGGLUTINATE]

aggrandize *verb*
ALSO SPELLED: esp. *Brit.* **-ise**
• "a GRAN dize"
• increase the power, rank, or wealth of (a person or nation).
• [French *agrandir* (stem *agrandiss-*), prob. from Italian *aggrandire* from Latin *grandis* large: assimilated to verbs ending in *-ize*]
• **aggrandizement** *noun* (also esp. *Brit.* **-isement**) "a GRAN dize m'nt" or "a GRAN d'z m'nt"
• **aggrandizer** *noun* (also esp. *Brit.* **-iser**)

aggravate *verb*
• "AGRA vate"

• increase the gravity of (an illness, offence, etc.).
• [Latin *aggravare aggravat-* make heavy, from *gravis* heavy]
• **aggravation** *noun*

aggregate *noun*
• "AGRA git"
• a collection of, or the total of, disparate elements.
• [Latin *aggregare aggregat-* herd together (*ad-* to + *grex gregis* flock)]
• **aggregation** *noun*

aggregator *noun*
• "AGRA gater"
• an Internet company that collects information about other companies' products and services and distributes it through a single website.
• [as AGGREGATE]

aggression *noun*
• "a GRESH'n"
• the act or practice of attacking without provocation, esp. beginning a quarrel or war.
• [Latin *aggressio* attack, from *aggredi aggress-* (*ad-* to + *gradi* walk)]
• **aggressive** *adjective* "a GRESSIV"
• **aggressively** *adverb*
• **aggressiveness** *noun*
• **aggressivity** *noun* "a gress IVVA tee"
• **aggressor** *noun*

aggrieved *adjective*
• "a GREEVD"
• wronged; having a grievance.
• [Old French *agrever* make heavier (*ad-* to + GRIEVE)]
• **aggrievedly** *adverb* "a GREEV id lee"

aghast *predicative adjective*
• "a GAST"
• amazed; filled with dismay or consternation.
• [Middle English, past participle of obsolete *agast, gast* frighten: see GHASTLY]

agile *adjective*
• "ADGE ile" or "ADGE'll"
• characterized by ease and grace of movement.
• [Latin *agilis* from *agere* do]
• **agilely** *adverb* "ADGE ile lee"
• **agility** *noun* "a JILLA tee"

agitate *verb*
• "ADGE a tate"
• disturb or excite (a person or feelings).
• [Latin *agitare agitat-* frequentative of *agere* drive]
• **agitated** *adjective*
• **agitatedly** *adverb*
• **agitation** *noun*
• **agitational** *adjective*
• **agitator** *noun*

agitato *adverb*
• "adge ee TOTTO"
• (as a musical direction) in an agitated manner.
• [Italian]

agitprop *noun*
• "ADGE it prop"
• a Soviet agency for the dissemination of Communist political propaganda, esp. in literature, film, etc.
• [Russian *agitpróp*, from *agitátsiya* agitation + *propagánda* propaganda]

aglet *noun*
• "AG lit"
• a plastic or metal tag attached to each end of a shoelace etc.
• [from French *aiguillette* small needle, ultimately from Latin *acus* needle]

agley *adverb*
• "a GLAY" or "a GLEE"
• askew, awry.
• [Old English *an* to + Scots *gley* squint]

agloo *noun*
ALSO SPELLED: **aglu**
• "AG loo"
• *Cdn* (*North*) a breathing hole made by a seal through sea ice.
• [Inuktitut]

agnate *noun*
• "AG nate"
• a person who is descended esp. by male line from the same male ancestor.
• [Latin *agnatus* from *ad* to + *gnasc* be born, from stem *gen-* beget]
• **agnatic** *adjective* "ag NATTIC"
• **agnation** *noun*

agnolotti *noun*
• "anya LOTTY"
• half-moon shaped or triangular pasta filled with meat, cheese, etc.
• [Italian, prob. related to *agnellotto* stuffed meat dumpling, from *agnello* lamb]

agnosia *noun*
• "ag NO see uh"
• the loss of the ability to interpret sensations.
• [modern Latin from Greek *agnōsia* ignorance (as GNOSIS)]

agnostic *noun*
• "ag NOSS tick"
• a person who believes that nothing is known, or can be known, of the existence or nature of God or of anything beyond material phenomena.
• [Greek *a-* without + GNOSTIC]
• **agnosticism** *noun* "ag NOSSTA sizm"

agon *noun*
• "AGGON"
• in literature, a struggle, esp. between protagonist and antagonist.
• [Greek *agōn* contest, struggle]

agonic *adjective*
• "a GONNIC"
• designating a line passing through the two poles, along which a magnetic needle points directly north or south.
• [Greek *agōnios* without angle (*a-* without + *gōnia* angle)]

agonistic *adjective*
• "agga NISTIC"
• polemical, combative.
• [Late Latin *agonisticus* from Greek *agōnistikos* from *agōnistēs* contestant, from *agōn* contest]
• **agonistically** *adverb*

agonize *verb*
ALSO SPELLED: esp. *Brit.* **-ise**
• "AGGA nize"
• undergo (esp. mental) anguish; suffer agony.
• [ultimately from Greek *agōnizomai* contend, from *agōn* contest]
• **agonized** *adjective* (also esp. *Brit.* **-ised**)
• **agonizing** *adjective* (also esp. *Brit.* **-ising**)
• **agonizingly** *adverb* (also esp. *Brit.* **-isingly**)

agony *noun*
• "AGGA nee"
• extreme mental or physical suffering.
• [Greek *agōnia* from *agōn* contest]

agora[1] *noun*
• "AGGA ruh"
• an assembly or place of assembly, esp. a marketplace.
• [Greek]

agora[2] *noun*
• "agga RAW"
• a monetary unit of Israel, equal to one-hundredth of a shekel.
• [Hebrew *agōrāh* 'small coin']

agoraphobia *noun*
• "a gora FOBEY uh"
• an abnormal fear of open spaces or public places.
• [modern Latin from AGORA[1] + PHOBIA]
• **agoraphobe** *noun*
• **agoraphobic** *adjective*

agouti *noun*
• "a GOOTY"
• any burrowing rodent of the genus *Dasyprocta* or *Myoprocta* of Central and S America, related to the guinea pig.
• [Tupi *aguti*]

agrarian *adjective*
• "a GRARE ee 'n"
• of or relating to the land or its cultivation.
• [Latin *agrarius* from *ager agri* field]

agribusiness *noun*
• "AGRA biz niss"
• agriculture conducted on strictly commercial principles, esp. using advanced technology.
• [blend of AGRICULTURE + BUSINESS]

agriculture *noun*
• "AGRA cull chur"
• the science or practice of cultivating the soil and rearing animals.
• [Latin *agricultura* from *ager agri* field + *cultura* CULTURE]
• **agricultural** *adjective*
• **agriculturalist** *noun*
• **agriculturally** *adverb*
• **agriculturist** *noun*

agrimony *noun*
• "AGRA moany"
• any herbaceous plant of the genus *Agrimonia*, with small yellow flowers.
• [Latin *agrimonia* alteration of *argemonia* from Greek *argemōnē* poppy]

agrochemical *noun*
• "agro KEMMA k'll"
• a chemical used in agriculture.
• [Greek *agros* field + CHEMICAL]

agroforestry *noun*
• "agro FORUS tree"
• agriculture in which there is integrated management of trees or shrubs along with conventional crops or livestock.
• [Greek *agros* field + Latin *foresta* forest]

agrology *noun*
• "uh GRAWLA jee"
• *Cdn* the application of science to agriculture.
• [Greek *agros* field + *logos* word]
• **agrologist** *noun*

agronomy *noun*
• "a GRONNA mee"
• the science of soil management and crop production.
• [French *agronomie* from Greek *agros* field + *-nomos* from *nemō* arrange]
• **agronomic** *adjective* "agra NOMMIC"
• **agronomically** *adverb*
• **agronomist** *noun*

ague *noun*
• "AY gyoo"
• a malarial fever, with cold, hot, and sweating stages.
• [from medieval Latin *acuta* (*febris*) acute (fever)]
• **agued** *adjective* "AY gyood"

ahi *noun*
• "AH hee"
• the yellowfin tuna, esp. when caught near Hawaii.
• [Hawaiian]

ahimsa *noun*
• "a HIM saw"
• (in the Hindu, Buddhist, and Jainist tradition) respect for all living things and avoidance of violence towards others both in thought and deed.
• [Sanskrit from *a* without + *himsa* injury]

ahistorical *adjective*
• "ay hiss TORA k'll"
• not historic; unrelated to history.
• [Greek *a* not + Latin *historia* from Greek *historia* finding out, narrative, history, from *histōr* learned, wise man]
• **ahistorically** *adverb*
• **ahistoricism** *noun* "ay hiss TORA sizm"

Ahousaht *noun*
ALSO SPELLED: **Ahousat**
• "a HOWZ it"
• a member of the principal group of Nuu-chah-nulth, living around Clayoquot Sound on the west coast of Vancouver Island.
• [Nuu-chah-nulth, = 'facing opposite from the ocean']

ai *noun*
• "AW ee"
• the three-toed sloth of S America, *Bradypus tridactylus*.
• [Tupi *ai*, representing its cry]

aigrette *noun*
• "AY gret" or "ay GRET"
• a tuft of feathers, esp. one worn as a headdress.
• [French *aigrette* = EGRET]

aiguille *noun*
• "ay GWEEL"
• a sharp peak of rock.
• [French, lit. 'needle']

aiguillette *noun*
• "ay gwee LET"
• a tagged point hanging from the shoulder on the breast of some uniforms.
• [French: see AGLET]

aikido *noun*
• "eye KEE doe" or "EYE kee doe"
• a Japanese form of self-defence and martial art, developed from jiu-jitsu and involving holds and throws.
• [Japanese from *ai* mutual + *ki* mind + *dō* way]

ail *verb*
• "ALE"
• trouble or afflict in mind or body.
• [Old English *egl(i)an* from *egle* troublesome]
HOMOPHONES: *ale*

ailanthus *noun*
• "ay LANTH us"
• an Asian tree, *Ailanthus altissima*, with pinnate leaves, frequently planted as an ornamental for its clusters of winged seeds which turn reddish yellow in the fall.
• [modern Latin *ailantus* from Ambonese *aylanto*]

aileron *noun*
• "AYLA ron"
• a hinged surface in the trailing edge of an airplane wing, used to control lateral balance.
• [French, diminutive of *aile* wing, from Latin *ala*]

Ainu *noun*
• "EYE noo"
• a member of the non-Mongoloid aboriginal inhabitants of the Japanese archipelago.
• [Ainu, = man]

aioli *noun*
• "eye YO lee"
• a garlic mayonnaise, originally a specialty of Provence in SE France.
• [French from Provençal *ai* garlic + *oli* oil]

airborne *adjective*
• "AIR born"
• moving through or carried by the air.
• ['air' + 'borne' (past participle of 'bear')]

Airdrite *noun*
• "AIR drite"
• a resident of Airdrie, Alberta.

Airdronian *noun*
• "air DRONEY 'n"
• a resident of Airdrie, Alberta.

Airedale *noun*
• "AIR dale"
• a large breed of terrier with a rough coat.
• [*Airedale* in Yorkshire, England]

aisle *noun*
• "ILE"
• a passage between rows of pews, seats, etc.
• [Middle English *ele*, *ile* from Old French *ele* from Latin *ala* wing: confused with *island* and French *aile* wing]
• **aisled** *adjective* "ILE'd" (rhymes with *MILD*)
HOMOPHONES: *isle*

aitch *noun*
• "AITCH"
• the name of the letter H.
• [Old French *ache*]

Aivilik *noun*
• "EYE vuh lick"
• the dialect of Inuktitut of the Aivilingmiut.
• [Inuktitut, = 'the place that has walrus']

Aivilingmiut *noun*
• "eye vuh LING mee ut"
• a southern branch of the Iglulik Inuit, occupying the northwestern Hudson Bay area.
• [Inuktitut, = 'people of Aivilik']

Ajacian *noun*
• "a JAY sh'n"
• a resident of Ajax, Ontario.

Akan *noun*
• "OCK'n"
• a member of a people inhabiting Ghana and neighbouring regions of West Africa.
• [the name in Akan]

Akela *noun*
• "a CAYLA"
• the adult leader of a group of Cubs.

• [name of the leader of a wolf pack in *The Jungle Book* by R. Kipling, Indian-born English writer d.1936]

akimbo *adverb*
• "a KIMBO"
• (of the arms) with hands on the hips and elbows turned outwards.
• [Middle English *in kenebowe*, prob. from Old Norse]

Akita *noun*
• "a KEETA"
• a breed of Japanese dog, similar to a spitz.
• [Japanese *Akita* a district in N Japan]

Akkadian *noun*
ALSO SPELLED: **Accadian**
• "a CAY dee 'n"
• the Semitic language of Akkad in ancient Babylonia.
HOMOPHONES: *Acadian*

Alabaman *noun*
• "ala BAM'n"
• a native or inhabitant of Alabama.

alabaster *noun*
• "ALA bast ur"
• a translucent usu. white form of gypsum, often carved into ornaments.
• [Latin *alabaster, -trum*, from Greek *alabastos*]
• **alabastrine** *adjective* "ala BAST rin"

alacrity *noun*
• "a LACKRA tee"
• speed or willingness.
• [Latin *alacritas* from *alacer* brisk]

alanine *noun*
• "ALA neen"
• a hydrophobic amino acid present in proteins.
• [German *Alanin*]

alar *adjective*
• "AIL ur"
• relating to wings.
• [Latin *alaris* from *ala* wing]

alas *interjection*
• "a LASS"
• an expression of regret, sorrow, pity, or concern.
• [Old French *a las(se)* from *a* ah + *las(se)* from Latin *lassus* weary]

Alaskan *noun*
• "a LASK'n"
• a native or inhabitant of Alaska.

alate *adjective*
• "AIL ate"
• having wings or wing-like appendages.
• [Latin *alatus* from *ala* wing]

albacore *noun*
• "ALBA core"
• a long-finned tuna, *Thunnus alalunga*.
• [Portuguese *albacor, -cora*, from Arabic *al* the + *bakr* young camel, or *bakūr* premature, precocious]

Albanian *noun*
• "al BAINY 'n"
• a native or inhabitant of Albania in S Europe.

albatross *noun*
• "ALBA tross"
• any of several large, long-winged, tube-nosed, stout-bodied birds of the family Diomedeidae, which spend most of their lives at sea, coming ashore only to nest.
• [alteration (after Latin *albus* white) of 17th-c. *alcatras*, applied to various seabirds, from Spanish and Portuguese *alcatraz*, var. of Portuguese *alcatruz* from Arabic *alḳādūs* the pitcher]

albedo *noun*
• "al BEE doe"
• the proportion of light or radiation reflected by a surface, esp. of a planet or moon.
• [Church Latin, = whiteness, from Latin *albus* white]

albeit *conjunction*
• "all BEE it"
• though.
• ['all' + 'be' + 'it', = although it be (that)]

albertite *noun*
• "ALBERT ite"
• a jet-black, almost infusible form of bitumen found in New Brunswick.
• [from *Albert* County, New Brunswick + Greek *lithos* stone]

albertosaurus *noun*
• "alberta SORE us"
• a large carnivorous dinosaur resembling *Tyrannosaurus*.
• [from *Alberta* (where its fossilized remains were first discovered) + Greek *sauros* lizard]

Albigensian *noun*
• "alba JENCY 'n"
• a member of a heretical ascetic Christian sect (the Albigenses) in S France in the 12th–13th c.
• [from the Latin name of the town of *Albi* in S France]

albino *noun*
• "al BINE oh"
• a person or animal having a congenital absence of pigment in the skin and hair (which are white), and the eyes (which are usu. pink).
• [Spanish & Portuguese (originally applied to albinos among black Africans) from *albo* Latin from *albus* white + *-inus* of the nature of]
• **albinism** *noun* "ALBIN izm"
• **albinotic** *adjective* "albin OTTIC"

albite *noun*
• "AL bite"
• a feldspar, usu. white, rich in sodium.
• [Latin *albus* white + Greek *lithos* stone]

albumen *noun*
• "al BYOO m'n"
• egg white.
• [Latin *albumen -minis* white of egg, from *albus* white]
HOMOPHONES: *albumin*

albumin *noun*
• "al BYOO m'n"
• any of a class of water-soluble proteins found in egg white, milk, blood, etc.
• [French *albumine* from Latin *albumin-*: see ALBUMEN]
• **albuminous** *adjective* "al BYOO m'n us"
HOMOPHONES: *albumen*

albuminoid *noun*
• "al BYOOMA noid"
• any insoluble structural protein.
• [as ALBUMIN]

albuminuria *noun*
• "al byoomin YURY uh"
• the presence of albumin in the urine, usu. as a symptom of kidney disease.
• [as ALBUMIN + modern Latin *uria* from Greek *-ouria* from *ouron* urine]

alburnum *noun*
• "al BURN um"
• the whiter, soft outer layers of recently formed wood between the heartwood and the bark.
• [Latin from *albus* white]

alcalde *noun*
• "all CALL day"
• a magistrate or mayor in a Spanish, Portuguese, or Latin American city or town.
• [Spanish from Arabic *al-ḳāḍī* the judge: see QADI]

alchemy *noun*
• "ALKA mee"
• the medieval forerunner of chemistry, esp. seeking to turn base metals into gold or silver.
• [medieval Latin *alchimia*, from Arabic *alkīmiyā'* from *al* the + *kīmiyā'* from Greek *khēmia*, *-meia* art of transmuting metals]
• **alchemic** *adjective* "al KEMMIC"
• **alchemical** *adjective*
• **alchemist** *noun*
• **alchemize** *verb* (also esp. *Brit.* **-ise**)

alcid *noun*
• "AL sid"
• a bird of the auk family, Alcidae.
• [modern Latin *Alcidae* from *Alca* genus name (as AUK)]

alcohol *noun*
• "ALKA hawl"
• a colourless volatile inflammable liquid forming the intoxicating element in wine, beer, spirits, etc., and also used as a solvent, as fuel, etc.
• [Arabic *al-kuḥl* from *al* the + *kuḥl* KOHL]
• **alcoholometer** *noun* "alka hawl OMMA tur"
• **alcoholometry** *noun*

alcoholic *noun*
• "alka HAWL ick"
• a person who is addicted to alcohol.
• [as ALCOHOL]
• **alcoholism** *noun* "ALKA hawl izm"

alcool *noun*
• "AL cool"
• *Cdn* (esp. *Que.*) a colourless, unflavoured alcoholic spirit distilled from cereal grains.
• [French, = alcohol]

alcove *noun*
• "AL cove"
• a recess, esp. in the wall of a room.
• [French from Spanish *alcoba* from Arabic *al-ḳubba* from *al* the + *ḳubba* vault]

aldehyde *noun*
• "ALDA hide"
• any of a class of compounds formed by the oxidation of alcohols (and containing the group -CHO).
• [abbreviation of modern Latin *alcohol dehydrogenatum* alcohol deprived of hydrogen]
• **aldehydic** *adjective* "alda HIDDIC"

alder *noun*
• "AWL dur"
• any tree or shrub of the genus *Alnus*, related to the birch, with catkins and toothed leaves.
• [Old English *alor*, *aler*, related to Latin *alnus*, with euphonic *d*]

alderfly *noun*
• "AWL dur fly"
• an insect of the genus *Sialis*, found near streams.
• [as ALDER + Old English *flyge* fly]

alderman *noun*
• "AWL dur m'n"
• a city councillor, esp. the elected representative of a district or ward.
• [Old English *aldor* patriarch, from *ald* old + 'man']
• **aldermanic** *adjective* "awl dur MANNIC"
• **aldermanship** *noun*
• **alderperson** *noun*
• **alderwoman** *noun*

Alderney *noun*
• "AWL dur nee"
• a breed of small dairy cattle.
• [the island of *Alderney* in the English Channel, where the breed originated]

Aldine *adjective*
• "AWL dine"
• of the Italian printer Aldus Manutius (d.1515), or the books printed by him or his family, or certain styles of display types.
• [Latin *Aldinus*, from *Aldus*]

aldosterone *noun*
• "awl doe STAIR own"

• a steroid hormone isolated from the adrenal gland.
• [ALDEHYDE + STEROL + '-one' forming nouns denoting various compounds, from Greek *-ōnē* feminine patronymic]

aldrin *noun*
• "AL drin"
• a white crystalline chlorinated hydrocarbon used as an insecticide, now generally banned.
• [K. *Alder*, German chemist d.1958]

ale *noun*
• "ALE"
• a type of beer fermented rapidly at high temperatures.
• [Old English *alu*, = Old Norse *öl*]
HOMOPHONES: *ail*

aleatoric *adjective*
• "aylee a TORIC"
• involving random choice by a performer or artist.
• [Latin *aleatorius aleator* dice player, from *alea* die]
• **aleatory** *adjective*

alee *adverb*
• "a LEE"
• on the lee or sheltered side of a ship.
• [Old English *a* to + LEE]

alembic *noun*
• "a LEMBICK"
• an apparatus formerly used in distilling.
• [medieval Latin *alembicus* from Arabic *al-'anbīḳ* from *al* the + *'anbīḳ* still, from Greek *ambix, -ikos* cup, cap of a still]

aleph *noun*
• "ALL if"
• the first letter of the Hebrew alphabet.
• [Hebrew *'ālep̱*, lit. 'ox']

aleurone *noun*
• "ALYA rone" or "a LURE own"
• a protein found as granules in the seeds of plants etc.
• [Greek *aleuron* flour]

Aleut *noun*
• "AL yoot" or "a LOOT"
• a member of an Aboriginal people living in the Aleutian Islands and SW Alaska.
• [18th c.: origin unknown]
• **Aleutian** *adjective* "a LOOSH 'n"

alevin *noun*
• "ALA vin"
• a very young fish, esp. a salmon or trout.
• [Old French from Latin *allevare* set up, raise up]

Alexandrian *adjective*
• "al eg ZANDRY 'n"
• of or characteristic of Alexandria, Egypt, founded in 332 BC by Alexander the Great.

alexandrine *adjective*
• "al eg ZAN drin"
• (of a line of verse) having six iambic feet.
• [French *alexandrin* from *Alexandre* Alexander (the Great), the subject of an Old French poem in this metre]

alexandrite *noun*
• "al eg ZAN drite"
• a gem variety of chrysoberyl which appears green in daylight and red in artificial light.
• [Czar *Alexander I* of Russia (d.1825) + Greek *lithos* stone]

alexia *noun*
• "a LEXY uh"
• the inability to understand written words or to read, as a result of brain disorder.
• [modern Latin from Greek *a-* without + Greek *lexis* speech, from *legein* to speak, confused with Latin *legere* to read]
• **alexic** *adjective*

alfredo *adjective*
• "al FRAY doe"
• designating a sauce for pasta made of butter, cream, and Parmesan cheese.
• [*Alfredo* di Lelio, Italian chef (early 20th c.)]

alfresco *adverb*
• "al FRESCO"
• in the open air.
• [Italian *al fresco* in the fresh (air)]

algae *plural noun*
• "AL jee"
• non-vascular, mainly aquatic cryptogams capable of photosynthesis, including seaweeds and many unicellular organisms.
• [Latin]
• **algal** *adjective* "AL g'll"

algebra *noun*
• "AL juh bruh"
• the branch of mathematics that uses letters and other general symbols to represent numbers and quantities in formulae and equations.
• [Italian & Spanish & medieval Latin, from Arabic *al-jabr* from *al* the + *jabr* reunion of broken parts, from *jabara* reunite]
• **algebraic** *adjective* "al juh BRAY ick"
• **algebraically** *adverb*
• **algebraist** *noun* "al juh BRAY ist"

Algerian *noun*
• "al JEERY 'n"
• a native or inhabitant of Algeria in N Africa.

algicide *noun*
• "ALGA side"
• a preparation for destroying algae.
• [as ALGAE + Latin *-cida, -cidium* from *caedere* kill]

alginate *noun*
• "ALJA nate"
• a salt or ester of alginic acid.
• [as ALGAE]

alginic *adjective*
- "al JINNIC"
- designating an acid that is an insoluble carbohydrate found (chiefly as salts) in many brown seaweeds.
- [as ALGAE]

algology *noun*
- "al GOLLA jee"
- the study of algae.
- [as ALGAE + Greek *logos* word]
- **algological** *adjective*
- **algologist** *noun*

Algonquian *noun*
ALSO SPELLED: **Algonkian**
- "al GON kwee 'n" or "al GON kee 'n"
- the largest Aboriginal language group in Canada, including Abenaki, Algonquin, Blackfoot, Cree, Delaware, Maliseet, Mi'kmaq, and Ojibwa.
- [as ALGONQUIN]

Algonquin *noun*
ALSO SPELLED: **Algonkin**
- "al GON kwin" or "al GON kin"
- a member of an Aboriginal people living along the Ottawa River and its tributaries.
- [French from Algonquian, compare Mi'kmaq *algoomeaking* = 'at the place of spearing fish and eels']

algorithm *noun*
- "ALGA rith'm"
- a process or set of rules used for calculation or problem-solving, esp. with a computer.
- [ultimately from Persian *al-Ḵuwārizmī* 9th-c. mathematician: *algorithm* influenced by Greek *arithmos* number]
- **algorithmic** *adjective* "alga RITH mick"

alguacil *noun*
- "al gwuh SILL" or "AL gwuh sill"
- a mounted official at a bullfight.
- [Spanish from Arabic *al-wazīr* from *al* the + *wazir*: see VIZIER]

alias *adverb*
- "AILY us"
- also named or known as.
- [Latin, = at another time, otherwise]

aliasing *noun*
- "AILY us ing"
- the misidentification of a signal frequency, introducing distortion or error, esp. in a computer image.
- [as ALIAS]

alibi *noun*
- "ALA bye"
- a claim, or the evidence supporting it, that when an alleged act took place one was elsewhere.
- [Latin, = elsewhere]

alidade *noun*
- "ALLEY dade"
- an instrument for determining directions or measuring angles.
- [Arabic *al-'iḍāda* the revolving radius, from *'aḍud* upper arm]

alien *adjective*
- "AYLEE 'n"
- unfamiliar; not in accordance or harmony; unfriendly, hostile; unacceptable or repugnant.
- [Latin *alienus* belonging to another (*alius*)]
- **alienness** *noun*

alienable *adjective*
- "AYLEE 'n a bull"
- able to be transferred to new ownership.
- [as ALIEN]
- **alienability** *noun*

alienage *noun*
- "AYLEE 'n idge"
- the state or condition of being a foreigner.
- [as ALIEN]

alienate *verb*
- "AYLEE 'n ate"
- cause (a person) to become unfriendly or hostile.
- [as ALIEN]
- **alienated** *adjective*
- **alienation** *noun*
- **alienator** *noun*

alienist *noun*
- "AYLEE 'n ist"
- a psychiatrist, esp. a legal adviser on psychiatric problems.
- [as ALIEN]

alight *verb*
- "a LITE"
- descend from a vehicle.
- [Old English *ālīhtan* from *a-* implying motion, *līhtan* lighten, dismount (from the idea of relieving a horse of weight)]

align *verb*
- "a LINE"
- put in a straight line or bring into line.
- [French *aligner* from phrase *à ligne* into line: ultimately from Latin *linea* from *linum* flax]
- **alignment** *noun*

aliment *noun*
- "ALA m'nt"
- food.
- [Latin *alimentum* from *alere* nourish]
- **alimentary** *adjective* "ala MENTA ree"
- **alimentation** *noun* "ala m'n TAY sh'n"

alimony *noun*
- "ALA moany"
- a monetary provision for a spouse or former spouse after a separation or divorce.
- [Latin *alimonia* nutriment, from *alere* nourish]

aliphatic *adjective*
- "ala FATTIC"
- of, denoting, or relating to organic

compounds in which carbon atoms form open chains, not aromatic rings.
• [Greek *aleiphar -atos* fat]

aliquot *adjective*
• "ALA kwot"
• (of a part or portion) contained by the whole an integral or whole number of times.
• [Latin *aliquot* some, so many]

aliterate *adjective*
• "ay LITTER it"
• disinclined to read, despite being able to do so.
• [Greek *a-* without + LITERATE]
• **aliteracy** *noun*

aliyah *noun*
• "olly AW"
• the migration of Jews to Israel.
• [Hebrew, lit. 'ascent']

alizarin *noun*
• "a LIZZA rin"
• the red colouring matter of the root of the madder plant, used in dyeing.
• [French *alizarine* from *alizari* madder, from Arabic *al-'iṣara* pressed juice, from *'aṣara* to press fruit]

alkahest *noun*
ALSO SPELLED: **alcahest**
• "ALKA hest"
• the universal solvent sought by alchemists.
• [sham Arabic, prob. invented by Swiss physician Paracelsus (d.1541)]

alkali *noun*
• "ALKA lie"
• any of a class of bases that liberate hydroxide ions in water, usu. form caustic or corrosive solutions, turn litmus blue, and have a pH of more than 7, e.g. caustic soda.
• [Arabic *al-ḳalī* calcined ashes, from *ḳala* fry]
• **alkalimeter** *noun* "alka LIMMA tur"
• **alkalimetry** *noun* "alka LIMMA tree"

alkaline *adjective*
• "ALKA line"
• of, relating to, or having the nature of an alkali; rich in alkali.
• [as ALKALI]
• **alkalinity** *noun* "alka LINNA tee"

alkaloid *noun*
• "ALKA loid"
• any of a series of nitrogenous organic compounds of plant origin, many of which are used as drugs, e.g. morphine, quinine, nicotine.
• [German (as ALKALI)]
• **alkaloidal** *noun*

alkalosis *noun*
• "alka LO sis"
• an excessive alkaline condition of the body fluids or tissues.
• [as ALKALI]

alkane *noun*
• "AL cane"
• any of a series of saturated aliphatic hydrocarbons having the general formula C_nH_{2n+2}, including methane, ethane, and propane.
• [as ALKYL]

alkene *noun*
• "AL keen"
• any of a series of unsaturated aliphatic hydrocarbons containing a double bond and having the general formula C_nH_{2n}, including ethylene and propylene.
• [as ALKYL]

alkyd *noun*
• "AL kid"
• any of the group of synthetic resins derived from various alcohols and acids, commonly used in paints etc.
• [ALKYL + 'acid' from Latin *acidus* from *acēre* be sour]

alkyl *noun*
• "AL kill"
• any radical derived from an alkane by the removal of a hydrogen atom.
• [German *Alkohol* ALCOHOL]
• **alkylate** *verb*

alkyne *noun*
• "AL kine"
• any of a series of unsaturated aliphatic hydrocarbons containing a triple bond and having the general formula C_nH_{2n-2}, including acetylene.
• [as ALKYL]

allantois *noun*
• "a LANTO iss"
• one of several membranes that develop in embryonic reptiles, birds, or mammals.
• [modern Latin from Greek *allantoeidēs* sausage-shaped]
• **allantoic** *adjective* "al an TOE ick"

allay *verb*
• "a LAY"
• diminish (fear, suspicion, etc.).
• [Old English *ālecgan* lay aside]
HOMOPHONES: *allée*

allée *noun*
• "a LAY"
• a walk bordered by trees or clipped hedges in a garden or park.
• [French, past participle of *aller* go]
HOMOPHONES: *allay*

allegation *noun*
• "ala GAY sh'n"
• an assertion or accusation, esp. an unproven one.
• [Latin *allegatio* from *allegare* allege]

allege *verb*
• "a LEDGE"

• declare to be the case, esp. without proof.
• [Anglo-French *alegier*, Old French *esligier* clear at law; confused in sense with Latin *allegare*: see ALLEGATION]
• **alleged** *adjective* "a LEJD" or "a LEJ id"
• **allegedly** *adverb* "a LEDGE id lee"

allegiance *noun*
• "a LEE jince"
• loyalty (to a person or cause etc.).
• [Anglo-French from Old French *ligeance* (as LIEGE): perhaps associated with ALLIANCE]

allegory *noun*
• "ALA gory"
• a story, play, poem, picture, etc., in which the meaning or message is represented symbolically.
• [ultimately from Greek *allēgoria* from *allos* other + *-agoria* speaking]
• **allegorical** *adjective*
• **allegorically** *adverb*
• **allegorist** *noun* "ALA guh rist"
• **allegorization** *noun* (also esp. *Brit.* **-isation**)
• **allegorize** *verb* (also esp. *Brit.* **-ise**)

allegretto *adverb*
• "ala GRETTO"
• in a fairly brisk tempo.
• [Italian, diminutive of ALLEGRO]

allegro *adverb*
• "a LEG roe" or "a LAY groe"
• in a brisk tempo.
• [Italian, = lively, happy]

allele *noun*
• "a LEEL"
• one of the (usu. two) alternative forms of a gene that occupy the same relative position on a chromosome.
• [German *Allel*, abbreviation of ALLELOMORPH]
• **allelic** *adjective*

allelomorph *noun*
• "a LEELA morf"
• = ALLELE.
• [Greek *allēl-* one another + *morphē* form]
• **allelomorphic** *adjective*

alleluia *interjection*
• "ala LOO yuh" or "ollay LOO yuh"
• God be praised.
• [ultimately from Hebrew *hall*[e]*lûyāh* praise ye the Lord]

allemande *noun*
• "al MOND"
• the name of several German dances.
• [French, = German (dance)]

allergen *noun*
• "AL ur j'n"
• any substance that causes an allergic reaction.
• [ALLERGY + Greek *-genēs* -born, of a specified kind, from *gen-* root of *gignomai* be born, become]
• **allergenic** *adjective*

allergy *noun*
• "ALLER jee"
• a condition of reacting adversely to certain substances, esp. particular foods, pollen, fur, or dust.
• [German *Allergie*, after *Energie* ENERGY, from Greek *allos* other]
• **allergic** *adjective*
• **allergist** *noun*

alleviate *verb*
• "a LEEVY ate"
• lessen or make less severe (pain, suffering, a problem, etc.).
• [Late Latin *alleviare* lighten, from Latin *allevare* (*ad-* to + *levare* raise)]
• **alleviation** *noun*
• **alleviative** *adjective* "a LEEVY a tiv"
• **alleviator** *noun*
• **alleviatory** *adjective* "a LEEVY a tory"

alliaceous *adjective*
• "alley AY sh'ss"
• of or relating to the genus *Allium*, including onions, garlic, and leeks.
• [modern Latin *alliaceus* from Latin *allium* garlic]

alliak *noun*
• "ALLEY ack"
• an Inuit sled consisting of two parallel wooden runners connected by wooden slats, usu. pulled by a dog team or snowmobile: a komatik.
• [Inuktitut]

alliance *noun*
• "a LIE ince"
• a formal union or agreement to co-operate, esp. among nations with a specific goal.
• [as ALLY]

allicin *noun*
• "ALA sin"
• a pungent oily liquid with antibacterial properties, present in garlic.
• [Latin *allium* garlic]

alligator *noun*
• "ALA gater"
• a large crocodilian reptile of S America, China, and the southeastern US, with upper teeth that lie outside the lower teeth and a head broader and shorter than that of the crocodile.
• [Spanish *el lagarto* the lizard, from Latin *lacerta*]

alliteration *noun*
• "a litter AY sh'n"
• the occurrence of the same letter or sound at the beginning of adjacent or closely connected words (e.g. *cool, calm, and collected*).
• [modern Latin *alliteratio* (*ad-* to + *littera* letter)]
• **alliterative** *adjective* "a LITTER a tiv"

allium *noun*
• "ALLEY um"

• any plant of the genus *Allium*, usu. bulbous and strong smelling, e.g. onion and garlic.
• [Latin, = garlic]

allocate *verb*
• "ALA cate"
• assign, designate, or set aside for a specific purpose.
• [medieval Latin *allocare* from *locus* place]
• **allocable** *adjective* "ALA kuh bull"
• **allocation** *noun*
• **allocator** *noun*

allochthon *noun*
• "a LOCK th'n" (with "TH" as in *THIN*)
• a body of rock that has been transported a considerable distance to its present position.
• [Greek *allo* other + *khthōn, -onos* earth]
• **allochthonous** *adjective*

allocution *noun*
• "ala KYOO sh'n"
• a formal speech, esp. one that exhorts.
• [Latin *allocutio* from *alloqui allocut-* speak to]

allogamy *noun*
• "a LOGGA mee"
• cross-fertilization in plants.
• [Greek *allo* other + *-gamia* from *gamos* marriage]

allomorph *noun*
• "ALA morf"
• any of two or more alternative forms of a morpheme.
• [Greek *allo* other + MORPHEME]
• **allomorphic** *adjective*

allopath *noun*
• "ALA path"
• a practitioner of allopathy.
• [as ALLOPATHY]
• **allopathic** *adjective*

allopathy *noun*
• "a LOPPA thee" (with "TH" as in *THIN*)
• the treatment of disease by conventional means, i.e. with drugs having opposite effects to the symptoms.
• [German *Allopathie* (Greek *allo* other + *patheia* suffering)]

allopatric *adjective*
• "ala PATRICK"
• occurring in separate geographical areas.
• [Greek *allo* other + *patra* fatherland]

allophone *noun*
• "ALA fone"
• *Cdn* (esp. in Quebec) an immigrant whose first language is neither French nor English.
• [Greek *allo* other + *phōnē* sound]

allot *verb*
• "a LOT"
• give or apportion to (a person) as a share or task; distribute officially to.
• [Old French *aloter* from *a* to + Germanic *lot* portion]
• **allotment** *noun*

allotrope *noun*
• "ALA trope"
• any of two or more different physical forms in which an element can exist.
• [back-formation from ALLOTROPY]

allotropy *noun*
• "a LOTTRA pee"
• the existence of two or more different physical forms of a chemical element.
• [Greek *allotropos* of another form, from *allos* different + *tropos* manner, from *trepō* to turn]
• **allotropic** *adjective* "ala TROPPIC"
• **allotropical** *adjective*

allottee *noun*
• "a lot TEE"
• a person to whom something is allotted.
• [as ALLOT]

allowance *noun*
• "a LOW ince" ("LOW" rhymes with *HOW*)
• an amount or sum given to a person, esp. regularly for a stated purpose.
• [Middle English, from 'allow', originally = 'praise', from Old French *alouer* from Latin *allaudare* to praise, and medieval Latin *allocare* to place]

allowedly *adverb*
• "a LOW id lee" ("LOW" rhymes with *HOW*)
• as is generally allowed or acknowledged.
• [as ALLOWANCE]

alloy *noun*
• "AL oy"
• a metallic substance made by combining two or more elements at least one of which is a metal, e.g. brass (a mixture of copper and zinc).
• [Old French *aloier, aleier* combine, from Latin *alligare* bind]

allude *verb*
• "a LUDE"
• refer, esp. indirectly, covertly, or briefly to.
• [Latin *alludere* (*ad-* to + *ludere lus-* play)]
HOMOPHONES: *elude*

allure *verb*
• "a LURE"
• attract, charm, or fascinate.
• [Old French *alurer* attract (*ad-* to + *luere* lure)]
• **allurement** *noun*
• **alluring** *adjective*
• **alluringly** *adverb*

allusion *noun*
• "a LOO zh'n"
• a reference, esp. a covert, passing, or indirect one.
• [as ALLUDE]
HOMOPHONES: *illusion*

allusive *adjective*
• "a LOO siv"

• containing an allusion.
• [as ALLUDE]
• **allusively** *adverb*
• **allusiveness** *noun*
HOMOPHONES: *elusive, illusive*

alluvion *noun*
• "a LOOVY 'n"
• the formation of new land by the movement of the sea or of a river.
• [Latin *alluvio -onis* from *luere* wash]

alluvium *noun*
• "a LOOVY um"
• a deposit of usu. fine fertile soil left during a time of flood, esp. in a river valley or delta.
• [Latin neuter of *alluvius* adjective, from *luere* wash]
• **alluvial** *adjective*

ally *noun*
• "AL eye"
• a state formally co-operating or united with another for a special purpose, esp. by a treaty.
• [Old French *al(e)ier* from Latin *alligare* bind: compare ALLOY]
• **allied** *adjective*

allyl *noun*
• "AL ill"
• the unsaturated monovalent radical CH_2=CH-CH_2·.
• [Latin *allium* garlic; the substance was first obtained from an oil extracted from garlic]

almanac *noun*
• "AL muh nack" or "AWL muh nack"
• an annual calendar of months and days, usu. with astronomical data and other information.
• [medieval Latin *almanac(h)* from Greek *almenikhiaka*]

almandine *noun*
• "AL m'n deen" or "AL m'n dine"
• a kind of garnet with a violet tint.
• [French, alteration of obsolete *alabandine* from medieval Latin *alabandina* from *Alabanda*, ancient city in Asia Minor]

almighty *adjective*
• "all MITEY"
• having complete power; omnipotent.
• [Old English *ælmihtig*]

almond *noun*
• "OM'nd" or "AWL m'nd"
• the oval nutlike seed (kernel) of the stone fruit from the tree *Prunus dulcis*, of which there are sweet and bitter varieties.
• [medieval Latin *amandula* from Latin *amygdala* from Greek *amugdalē*: associated with words in *al-*]

almoner *noun*
• "OMMA nur"
• an official distributor of alms.
• [Old French *aumonier*, ultimately from medieval Latin *eleēmosynarius* (as ALMS)]

alms *plural noun*
• "OMZ"
• charitable donations of money or food given to the poor.
• [Old English *ælmysse, -messe*, from Germanic, ultimately from Greek *eleēmosunē* from *eleēmōn* (adjective) from *eleos* compassion]
• **almsgiver** *noun*
• **almsgiving** *noun*

almshouse *noun*
• "OMZ house"
• a house for the poor founded by charity.
• [as ALMS + 'house']

almucantar *noun*
ALSO SPELLED: **almacantar**
• "al muh CANTER"
• a line of constant altitude above the horizon.
• [ultimately from Arabic *almuḳanṭarāt* sundial, from *ḳanṭara* arch]

aloe *noun*
• "AL oh"
• any plant of the genus *Aloe*, including succulent herbs, shrubs, and trees.
• [Greek *aloē* denoting the fragrant heartwood of certain oriental trees]

alogical *adjective*
• "ay LODGE a k'll"
• not logical.
• [Greek *a-* without + LOGICAL]

aloha *interjection*
• "a LO haw"
• (in Hawaii and the S Pacific) a greeting or farewell; hello or goodbye.
• [Hawaiian, lit. 'love, affection, pity']

alopecia *noun*
• "ala PEESHA"
• the absence (complete or partial) of hair from areas of the body where it normally grows; baldness.
• [Greek *alōpekia* fox mange, from *alōpēx* fox]

alpaca *noun*
• "al PACKA"
• a S American mammal, *Lama pacos*, related to the llama, with long shaggy hair and usu. brown and white colouring.
• [Spanish from Aymara or Quechua]

alpenglow *noun*
• "ALP'n glow"
• the rosy light of the setting or rising sun seen on high mountains.
• [German *Alpenglühen*, lit. 'Alp-glow']

alpenstock *noun*
• "ALP'n stock"
• a long iron-tipped staff used in mountain climbing.
• [German, lit. 'Alp-stick']

alpha *noun*
• "ALFA"

- the first letter of the Greek alphabet (A, α).
- [Greek]

alphabet *noun*
- "ALFA bet"
- the set of letters used in writing a language.
- [Greek *alpha*, *bēta*, the first two letters of the alphabet]
- **alphabetic** *adjective*
- **alphabetical** *adjective*
- **alphabetically** *adverb*
- **alphabetization** *noun* (also esp. *Brit.* **-isation**)
- **alphabetize** *verb* (also esp. *Brit.* **-ise**)

alphanumeric *adjective*
- "alfa new MARE ick"
- containing both alphabetical and numerical symbols.
- [ALPHABET + NUMERICAL]
- **alphanumerical** *adjective*

alpinist *noun*
- "ALPIN ist"
- a climber of high mountains.
- [from the Alps, a mountain range in Europe]
- **alpinism** *noun*

already *adverb*
- "all REDDY"
- before the time in question.
- ['all' + Old English *rǣde*]

Alsatian *adjective*
- "al SAY sh'n"
- of or relating to Alsace, in NE France.
- [*Alsatia*, Latin name of Alsace]

alsike *noun*
- "AL sike" or "AL sick"
- a species of clover, *Trifolium hybridum*.
- [*Alsike* in Sweden]

alstroemeria *noun*
- "al struh MEERY uh"
- any of various ornamental liliaceous plants of the S American genus *Alstroemeria*, cultivated for their showy flowers.
- [K. von *Alstroemer*, Swedish naturalist d.1796]

Altaic *noun*
- "al TAY ick"
- a family of languages including Turkic and Mongolian.
- [from the *Altai* mountains in central Asia]

altar *noun*
- "ALL tur"
- a table or flat-topped block, often of stone, for sacrifice or offering to a deity.
- [Latin *altaria* (pl.) burnt offerings, altar, prob. related to *adolēre* burn in sacrifice]

HOMOPHONES: *alter*

altarpiece *noun*
- "ALL tur peece"
- a piece of art, esp. a painting, set above or behind an altar.
- [ALTAR + PIECE]

altazimuth *noun*
- "al TAZZA muth"
- an instrument for measuring the altitude and azimuth of celestial bodies.
- [ALTITUDE + AZIMUTH]

alter *verb*
- "ALL tur"
- make or become different; change.
- [Late Latin *alterare* from Latin *alter* other]
- **alterable** *adjective*
- **alteration** *noun*

HOMOPHONES: *altar*

altercation *noun*
- "all tur CAY sh'n"
- a heated argument or dispute; a quarrel.
- [Latin *altercatio* from *altercari* wrangle]

alterity *noun*
- "all TERRA tee"
- the state of being other or different; otherness.
- [Late Latin *alteritas* from *alter* other]

alternate[1] *verb*
- "ALL tur nate"
- (of two things) succeed each other by turns.
- [Latin *alternatus* past participle of *alternare* do things by turns, from *alternus* every other, from *alter* other]
- **alternation** *noun*

alternate[2] *adjective*
- "ALL tur nit"
- (of things of two kinds) each following and succeeded by one of the other kind.
- [as ALTERNATE[1]]
- **alternately** *adverb*

alternative *adjective*
- "all TURNA tiv"
- (of one or more things) available or usable instead of another.
- [as ALTERNATE[1]]
- **alternatively** *adverb*

alternator *noun*
- "ALL tur nater"
- a generator that produces an alternating current.
- [as ALTERNATE[1]]

althorn *noun*
- "ALT horn" (with "A" as in *SHALL*)
- a brass instrument of the saxhorn family, esp. the alto or tenor saxhorn in E flat.
- [German from *alt* high, from Latin *altus* + 'horn' from Old English]

altimeter *noun*
- "al TIMMA tur"
- an instrument for showing height above sea or ground level, esp. one fitted to an aircraft.
- [Latin *altus* high + Greek *metron* measure]

altiplano *noun*
- "alta PLANNO"
- the high tableland of central S America.
- [Spanish, from *alto* high + *plano* flat]

altitude *noun*
- "AL tuh tude"
- the height of an object in relation to a given point, esp. sea level or the horizon.
- [Latin *altitudo* from *altus* high]
- **altitudinal** *adjective* "al tuh TUDE'n 'll"

alto *noun*
- "AWL toe" or "AL toe"
- the lowest female singing voice; contralto.
- [Italian *alto (canto)* high (singing), from Latin *altus* high]

altocumulus *noun*
- "al toe KYOO myoo luss"
- cloud formed at medium altitude as a layer of rounded masses with a level base.
- [Latin *altus* high + CUMULUS]

altogether *adverb*
- "all TOGETHER"
- totally, completely.
- [Middle English from 'all' + 'together']

altoist *noun*
- "AWL toe ist" or "AL toe ist"
- an alto saxophone player.
- [as ALTO]

altostratus *noun*
- "al toe STRAT us"
- cloud formed at medium altitude as a continuous flat greyish sheet.
- [Latin *altus* high + STRATUS]

altruism *noun*
- "AWL true izm" or "AL true izm"
- regard for others as a principle of action.
- [French *altruisme* from Italian *altrui* somebody else (influenced by Latin *alter* other)]
- **altruist** *noun*
- **altruistic** *adjective*
- **altruistically** *adverb*

alum *noun*
- "AL um"
- a double sulphate of aluminum and potassium, having astringent properties.
- [Latin *alumen aluminis*]

alumina *noun*
- "a LOOM 'n uh"
- the compound aluminum oxide occurring naturally as corundum and emery.
- [Latin *alumen* alum, after *soda* etc.]

aluminize *verb*
ALSO SPELLED: esp. *Brit.* **-ise**
- "a LOOM 'n ize"
- coat with aluminum.
- [as ALUMINUM]
- **aluminization** *noun* (also esp. *Brit.* **-isation**)

aluminosilicate *noun*
- "a looma no SILLA cate" or "a looma no SILLA kit"
- a silicate containing aluminum, esp. a rock-forming mineral of this kind, e.g. a feldspar, a clay mineral.
- [as ALUMINUM + SILICATE]

aluminum *noun*
- "a LOOM 'n um"
- a silvery, light, and malleable metallic element resistant to tarnishing by air.
- [alteration (after *sodium* etc.) of *alumium*, from ALUM]

alumna *noun*
- "a LUMNA"
- a female graduate of a specified university or school.
- [as ALUMNUS]

alumnus *noun*
- "a LUM nuss"
- a graduate of a specified university or other school.
- [Latin, = nursling, pupil, from *alere* nourish]

alvar *noun*
- "AL var"
- a low-lying area of flat, exposed limestone with shallow soil, covered with shrubs, native grasses, sedges, or wildflowers. Alvars are found only in a few areas surrounding the Great Lakes, in Estonia, and Sweden.
- [Swedish, from *alv* 'stratum, subsoil', compare German dialect *alben* 'loose chalk soil']

alveolus *noun*
- "alvy OLE us"
- a small cavity, pit, or hollow.
- [Latin diminutive of *alveus* cavity]
- **alveolar** *adjective*
- **alveolate** *adjective* "al VEEA lit"

alyssum *noun*
- "a LISS um"
- a low-growing widely-cultivated plant, *Lobularia maritima*, having very small white or purple flowers.
- [Latin from Greek *alusson*, from *a-* without. + *lussa* rabies (referring to early herbalist use)]

amah *noun*
- "OMMA"
- (in the Far East and India) a nursemaid or maid.
- [Portuguese *ama* nurse]

amalgam *noun*
- "a MAL gum"
- a mixture or blend.
- [medieval Latin *amalgama* from Greek *malagma* an emollient]

amalgamate *verb*
- "a MALGA mate"
- combine or unite to form one structure, organization, etc.
- [medieval Latin *amalgamare amalgamat-* (as AMALGAM)]
- **amalgamation** *noun*

amandine *adjective*
- "AM 'n deen"
- garnished with (usu. sliced) almonds.
- [French]

amanuensis *noun*
• "a man yoo ENSISS"
• a person who writes from dictation or copies manuscripts.
• [Latin from (*servus*) *a manu* secretary + *-ensis* belonging to]

amaranth *noun*
• "AMMA ranth"
• any herbaceous plant of the genus *Amaranthus*, usu. having small green, red, or purple tinted flowers, some species of which are weeds, e.g. pigweed, with other species cultivated as grain crops or ornamentals.
• [modern Latin from Greek *amarantos* everlasting, from *a-* not + *marainō* wither, alteration of *polyanthus* etc.]
• **amaranthine** *adjective* "amma RANTH ine"

amaretti *plural noun*
• "amma RETTY"
• small, dry, Italian macaroons.
• [Italian, diminutive of *amaro* from Latin *amarus* bitter]

amaretto *noun*
• "amma RETTO"
• an almond-flavoured liqueur, often used as a flavouring in desserts, coffee, etc.
• [Italian, as AMARETTI]
HOMOPHONES: *amoretto*

Amarone *noun*
• "amma ROE nay"
• an Italian wine made from dried grapes, with a high alcohol content.
• [Italian, as AMARETTI]

amaryllis *noun*
• "amma RILL iss"
• a plant genus with a single species, *Amaryllis belladonna*, a bulbous lily-like plant native to South Africa with white or rose-pink flowers.
• [Latin from Greek *Amarullis*, name of a country girl]

amateur *noun*
• "AMMA chur" or "AMMA tur"
• a person who engages in a pursuit, e.g. an art or sport as a pastime rather than a profession.
• [French from Latin *amator -oris* lover, from *amare* love]
• **amateurish** *adjective*
• **amateurishly** *adverb*
• **amateurishness** *noun*
• **amateurism** *noun*
HOMOPHONES: *ammeter*

amatory *adjective*
• "AMMA tory"
• of or relating to sexual love or desire.
• [Latin *amatorius* from *amare* love]

amautik *noun*
• "am OW tick"
• *Cdn (North)* an Inuit woman's parka with a large hood in which a child may be carried.
• [Inuktitut]

Amazon *noun*
• "AMMA zon"
• a member of a mythical race of female warriors which appears in many Greek legends.
• [Greek: explained by the Greeks as 'breastless' (as if Greek *a-* without + *mazos* breast), but prob. of foreign origin]

Amazonian *adjective*
• "amma ZONEY 'n"
• of or relating to the Amazon River or the surrounding rainforest.

ambassador *noun*
• "am BASSA dur"
• an accredited diplomat sent by a state on a mission to, or as its permanent representative in, a foreign country.
• [French *ambassadeur* from Italian *ambasciator*, ultimately from Latin *ambactus* servant]
• **ambassadorial** *adjective* "am bassa DORY 'll"
• **ambassadorship** *noun*
• **ambassadress** *noun*

ambergris *noun*
• "AMBER griss" or "AMBER greece"
• a strong-smelling waxlike secretion of the intestine of the sperm whale, found floating in tropical seas and used in perfume manufacture.
• [Old French *ambre gris* grey amber]

ambidextrous *adjective*
• "amby DEX truss"
• (of a person) able to use the right and left hands equally well.
• [Late Latin *ambidexter* from *ambi-* on both sides + *dexter* right-handed]
• **ambidexterity** *noun* "amby dex TERRA tee"
• **ambidextrously** *adverb*
• **ambidextrousness** *noun*

ambience *noun*
ALSO SPELLED: **ambiance**
• "AMBY awnce" or "OMBY awnce" or "AMBY ince"
• the surroundings or atmosphere of a place; mood.
• [as AMBIENT]

ambient *adjective*
• "AMBY 'nt"
• surrounding.
• [Latin *ambiens -entis* present participle of *ambire* go round]

ambiguous *adjective*
• "am BIG yoo us"
• having an obscure or double meaning.
• [Latin *ambiguus* doubtful, from *ambigere* from *ambi-* both ways + *agere* drive]
• **ambiguity** *noun*
• **ambiguously** *adverb*
• **ambiguousness** *noun*

ambisonics *noun*
• "amby SONNIX"
• a system of sound reproduction designed to reproduce the directional and acoustic

properties of the sound source using two or more channels.
• [Latin *ambi-* on both sides + SONIC]

ambit *noun*
• "AM bit"
• the scope, extent, or bounds of something.
• [Latin *ambitus* circuit, from *ambire*: see AMBIENT]

ambition *noun*
• "am BISH'n"
• the determination to achieve success or distinction, usu. in a chosen field.
• [Latin *ambitio -onis* from *ambire ambit-* canvass for votes: see AMBIENT]
• **ambitious** *adjective*
• **ambitiously** *adverb*
• **ambitiousness** *noun*

ambivalence *noun*
• "am BIVVA lince"
• the coexistence in one person of opposing emotions or attitudes towards the same object or situation.
• [German *Ambivalenz* from Latin *ambo* both, after *equivalence*]
• **ambivalent** *adjective*
• **ambivalently** *adverb*

ambivert *noun*
• "AMBY vurt"
• a person who fluctuates between being an introvert and an extrovert.
• [Latin *ambi-* on both sides + *-vert* from Latin *vertere* to turn, after EXTROVERT, INTROVERT]
• **ambiversion** *noun*

amblyopia *noun*
• "ambly OH pee uh"
• impaired vision without obvious defect or change in the eye.
• [Greek from *ambluōpos* (adjective) from *amblus* dull + *ōps, ōpos* eye]
• **amblyopic** *adjective* "ambly OPPIC"

ambo *noun*
• "AM bo"
• a pulpit or reading desk in a Christian church.
• [medieval Latin from Greek *ambōn* rim (in medieval Greek = pulpit)]

Ambonese *noun*
• "ambo NEEZ"
• the language of Ambon, an island of Indonesia.

amboyna *noun*
• "am BOY nuh"
• the decorative wood of the SE Asian tree *Pterocarpus indicus*.
• [*Amboyna* Island in Indonesia, now Ambon]

ambrosia *noun*
• "am BRO zhuh"
• (in Greek and Roman mythology) the food of the gods; the elixir of life.
• [Latin from Greek, = elixir of life, from *ambrotos* immortal]
• **ambrosial** *adjective*
• **ambrosian** *adjective*

ambry *noun*
• "AM bree"
• a small recess in the wall of a church.
• [Old French *almarie, armarie* from Latin *armarium* closet, chest, from *arma* utensils]

ambulacrum *noun*
• "am byoo LACK rum"
• (in an echinoderm) each of the radially arranged bands, together with their underlying structures, through which the double rows of tube feet protrude.
• [Latin, 'avenue', from *ambulare* 'to walk']
• **ambulacral** *adjective*

ambulance *noun*
• "AM byoo lince"
• a vehicle specially equipped for conveying the sick or injured to and from a hospital, esp. in emergencies.
• [French, from *hôpital ambulant* 'mobile (horse-drawn) field hospital' from Latin *ambulant-* 'walking']

ambulant *adjective*
• "AM byoo l'nt"
• able to walk about.
• [Latin *ambulare ambulant-* walk]

ambulatory *adjective*
• "AM byoo luh tory"
• (of a patient) able to walk about; not confined to bed.
• [Latin *ambulatorius* from *ambulare* walk]

ambuscade *noun*
• "amba SKADE"
• an ambush.
• [French *embuscade* from Italian *imboscata* or Spanish *emboscada* from Latin *imboscare* put in a wood]

ameliorate *verb*
• "a MEELY a rate"
• make or become better; improve.
• [alteration of MELIORATE after French *améliorer*]
• **amelioration** *noun*
• **ameliorative** *adjective*

amenable *adjective*
• "a MENNA bull" or "a MEENA bull"
• willing to co-operate; open to suggestion or influence.
• [Anglo-French (Law) from French *amener* bring to, from *a-* to + *mener* bring, from Late Latin *minare* drive animals, from Latin *minari* threaten]
• **amenability** *noun*

amenity *noun*
• "a MENNA tee"
• a pleasant or useful feature.
• [Latin *amoenitas* from *amoenus* pleasant]

amenorrhea *noun*
ALSO SPELLED: **amenorrhoea**
• "ay menna REE uh"
• an abnormal absence of menstruation.
• [Greek *a-* without + Greek *mēnos* month + *-rrhoia* from *rheō* flow]

ament *noun*
• "AY m'nt"
• a catkin.
• [Latin, = thong]

Amerasian *adjective*
• "ammer AY zh'n"
• of mixed American and Asian parentage.
• [blend of 'American' + ASIAN]

americium *noun*
• "ammer ISHY um"
• an artificially made transuranic radioactive metallic element.
• [*America* (where first made)]

Amerindian *adjective*
• "ammer INDY 'n"
• of or relating to American Indians.
• [blend of 'America' and 'Indian']

amethyst *noun*
• "AMMA thist"
• a precious stone of a violet or purple variety of quartz.
• [Greek *amethustos* not drunken, the stone being supposed to prevent intoxication]
• **amethystine** *adjective* "amma THIST een"

Amharic *noun*
• "am HARE ick"
• the official and commercial language of Ethiopia.
• [*Amhara*, Ethiopian province]

Amherstonian *noun*
• "ammer STONEY 'n"
• a resident of Amherst, NS.

amiable *adjective*
• "AIMY a bull"
• friendly and pleasant in temperament; likeable.
• [Old French from Late Latin *amicabilis* amicable: confused with French *aimable* lovable]
• **amiability** *noun*
• **amiableness** *noun*
• **amiably** *adverb*

amianthus *noun*
• "ammy ANTH us"
• any fine silky-fibred variety of asbestos.
• [Latin from Greek *amiantos* undefiled, from *a-* not + *miainō* defile, i.e. purified by fire, being incombustible]

amicable *adjective*
• "AMMIC a bull"
• showing or done in a friendly spirit.
• [Late Latin *amicabilis* from *amicus* friend]
• **amicability** *noun*
• **amicableness** *noun*
• **amicably** *adverb*

amice *noun*
• "AM iss"
• a white linen cloth worn on the neck and shoulders by a priest celebrating the Eucharist.
• [medieval Latin *amicia*, *-sia* from Latin *amictus* outer garment]

amide *noun*
• "AM ide" or "AY mide"
• a compound formed from ammonia by replacement of one (or sometimes more than one) hydrogen atom by a metal or an acyl radical.
• [as AMMONIA]

amigo *noun*
• "a MEE go"
• (often as a form of address) a friend or comrade.
• [Spanish from Latin *amicus* friend]

amine *noun*
• "AM een" or "a MEEN"
• a compound formed from ammonia by replacement of one or more hydrogen atoms by an organic radical or radicals.
• [as AMMONIA]

amino *noun*
• "a MEAN oh"
• of, relating to, or containing the monovalent group $-NH_2$.
• [as AMINE]

Amish *noun*
• "OMM ish" or "AM ish"
• the members of a strict Mennonite group whose communal farms are found in S Ontario and parts of the US, esp. Pennsylvania.
• [prob. from German *Amisch* from J. *Amen* or *Amman* 17th-c. Swiss preacher]
• **Amishman** *noun*

amitosis *noun*
• "amma TOE sis" or "ay my TOE sis"
• a form of cell division that does not involve mitosis.
• [Greek *a-* without + MITOSIS]

amitriptyline *noun*
• "amma TRIPTA leen"
• an antidepressant drug that has a mild tranquilizing action.
• [AMINE + Latin *tri* three + *heptyl* (see HEPTANE)]

amity *noun*
• "AMMA tee"
• friendship; friendly relations.
• [Old French *amitié*, ultimately from Latin *amicus* friend]

ammeter *noun*
• "AMMA tur"
• an instrument for measuring electric current in amperes.
• [AMPERE + Greek *metron* measure]
HOMOPHONES: *amateur*

ammo *noun*
- "AMMO"
- ammunition.
- [abbreviation]

ammolite *noun*
- "AMMA lite"
- the brilliantly coloured opalescent fossilized shell of an ammonite, found only in southern Alberta, used as a precious gem.
- [AMMONITE + Greek *lithos* stone]

ammonia *noun*
- "a MOANY uh"
- a colourless strongly alkaline gas with a characteristic pungent smell.
- [modern Latin from *sal ammoniacus* 'salt of Ammon', associated with the Roman temple of (Jupiter) Ammon in North Africa]
- **ammoniacal** *adjective* "amma NIE a k'll"
- **ammoniated** *adjective* "a MOANY ated"

ammonite *noun*
- "AMMA nite"
- an ammonoid fossil, esp. one of a later type found chiefly in the Jurassic and Cretaceous periods, typically with intricately frilled suture lines.
- [modern Latin *ammonites*, after medieval Latin *cornu Ammonis* horn of Ammon, from the fossil's resemblance to the ram's horn associated with Jupiter Ammon]

ammonium *noun*
- "a MOANY um"
- the monovalent ion NH_4^+, formed from ammonia.
- [modern Latin (as AMMONIA)]

ammonoid *noun*
- "AMMA noid"
- an extinct cephalopod mollusc with a flat coiled spiral shell found commonly as a fossil in marine deposits from the Devonian to the Cretaceous periods.
- [as AMMONITE]

ammunition *noun*
- "am yoo NISH'n"
- a supply of projectiles (esp. bullets, shells, and grenades).
- [obsolete French *amunition*, corruption of (*la*) *munition* (the) MUNITION]

amnesia *noun*
- "am NEE zhuh"
- a partial or total loss of memory.
- [Greek, = forgetfulness]
- **amnesiac** *noun* "am NEEZY ack"
- **amnesic** *adjective* "am NEE zick"

amnesty *noun*
- "AMNA stee"
- a general pardon, esp. for political offences.
- [Greek *amnēstia* oblivion]

amnio *noun*
- "AMNY oh"
- = AMNIOCENTESIS.
- [abbreviation]

amniocentesis *noun*
- "amny oh sen TEE sis"
- the sampling of amniotic fluid by insertion of a hollow needle to determine the condition of an embryo.
- [AMNION + Greek *kentēsis* pricking, from *kentō* to prick]

amnion *noun*
- "AMNY 'n"
- the innermost membrane that encloses the embryo of a reptile, bird, or mammal.
- [Greek, = caul (diminutive of *amnos* lamb)]
- **amniotic** *adjective* "amny OTTIC"

amoeba *noun*

ALSO SPELLED: esp. *US* **ameba**
- "a MEEBA"
- any usu. aquatic protozoan of the genus *Amoeba*, esp. *A. proteus*, capable of changing shape.
- [modern Latin from Greek *amoibē* change]
- **amoebic** *adjective* (also **amebic**)
- **amoeboid** *adjective* (also **ameboid**)

amoebiasis *noun*

ALSO SPELLED: **amebiasis**
- "ammy BY a sis"
- dysentery caused by infection of the intestine with certain amoebae.
- [as AMOEBA]

amok *adverb*

ALSO SPELLED: **amuck**
- "a MUCK" or "a MOCK"
- out of control.
- [Malay *amok* rushing in a frenzy]

amontillado *noun*
- "a monty LODDO" or "a monty ODDO"
- a medium dry sherry.
- [Spanish from *Montilla* in Spain]

amoretto *noun*
- "amma RETTO"
- a cupid.
- [Italian, diminutive of *amore* love, from Latin *amor*]

HOMOPHONES: *amaretto*

Amorite *noun*
- "AMMER ite"
- a member of a group of Semitic peoples whose semi-nomadic culture flourished in Mesopotamia, Palestine, and Syria from *c.*2000 to *c.*1600 BC. They founded the First Dynasty of Babylon, associated with Hammurabi I (d.1750 BC).
- [Hebrew *'emōrī* from Akkadian *'amurrū* west]

amoroso *noun*
- "ammer OH so"
- a full rich type of sherry.
- [Spanish, = amorous]

amorous *adjective*
• "AMMER us"
• showing, feeling, or inclined to sexual love.
• [medieval Latin *amorosus* from Latin *amor* love]
• **amorously** *adverb*
• **amorousness** *noun*

amorphous *adjective*
• "a MORF us"
• shapeless.
• [medieval Latin *amorphus* from Greek *amorphos* shapeless, from *a-* not + *morphē* form]
• **amorphously** *adverb*
• **amorphousness** *noun*

amortize *verb*
ALSO SPELLED: esp. *Brit.* **-ise**
• "AMMER tize"
• gradually pay off (a debt) by money regularly put aside.
• [ultimately from Latin *ad* to + *mors mort-* death]
• **amortization** *noun* (also esp. *Brit.* **-isation**)

amour *noun*
• "a MOOR"
• a love affair, esp. a secret one.
• [French, = love]

amoxicillin *noun*
ALSO SPELLED: **amoxycillin**
• "a moxa SILLIN"
• a broad spectrum semi-synthetic penicillin, closely related to ampicillin but better absorbed when taken orally, used esp. for treating ear and upper respiratory infections.
• [AMINO + OXYGEN + PENICILLIN]

ampelopsis *noun*
• "ampa LOP sis"
• any plant of the genus *Ampelopsis* or *Parthenocissus*, usu. a climber supporting itself by twining tendrils, e.g. Virginia creeper.
• [Greek *ampelos* vine + *opsis* appearance]

amperage *noun*
• "AMPER idge"
• the strength of an electric current in amperes.
• [as AMPERE]

ampere *noun*
• "AM pair"
• the SI base unit of electric current.
• [A.-M. *Ampère*, French physicist d.1836]

ampersand *noun*
• "AMPER sand"
• the sign & (= *and*).
• [corruption of *and per se and* ('&' by itself is 'and')]

amphetamine *noun*
• "am FETTA meen"
• a synthetic drug used esp. as a stimulant.
• [abbreviation of chemical name *a*lpha-*m*ethyl *ph*en*et*hyl*amine*]

amphibian *adjective*
• "am FIBBY 'n"
• living both on land and in water.
• [modern Latin *amphibium* from Greek *amphibion* from *amphi-* both + *bios* life]
• **amphibious** *adjective*
• **amphibiously** *adverb*

amphibole *noun*
• "AMFA bole"
• any of a class of rock-forming silicate and aluminosilicate minerals with fibrous or columnar crystals.
• [French from Latin *amphibolus* ambiguous]

amphimixis *noun*
• "amfa MIX iss"
• true sexual reproduction with the fusion of gametes from two individuals.
• [modern Latin, from Greek *amphi-* both + *mixis* mingling]
• **amphimictic** *adjective* "amfa MICTIC"

amphioxus *noun*
• "amfy OX us"
• any lancelet of the genus *Branchiostoma* (formerly *Amphioxus*).
• [modern Latin, from Greek *amphi-* both + *oxus* sharp]

amphipathic *adjective*
• "amfa PATHIC"
• of a substance or molecule that has both a hydrophilic and a hydrophobic part.
• [Greek *amphi-* both + *pathikos* (as PATHOS)]

amphipod *noun*
• "AMFA pod"
• any crustacean of the largely marine order Amphipoda, having a laterally compressed abdomen with two kinds of limb, e.g. sand hoppers.
• [Greek *amphi-* both + *pous podos* foot]

amphiprostyle *noun*
• "am FIPPRA style"
• a classical building with a portico at each end.
• [Latin *amphiprostylus* from Greek *amphiprostulos* (*amphi-* both *prostulos* having pillars in front)]

amphisbaena *noun*
• "amfiss BEENA"
• any burrowing wormlike lizard of the family Amphisbaena, having no apparent division of head from body, making both ends look similar.
• [Greek *amphisbaina* from *amphis* both ways + *bainō* go]

amphitheatre *noun*
ALSO SPELLED: **amphitheater**
• "AMFA theea tur" (with "TH" as in *THIN*)
• an oval or circular building with seats rising in tiers around a central open space.
• [Greek *amphi-* both + 'theatre' (from Greek *theatron* from *theomai* behold)]

amphora *noun*
• "AMFA ruh"
• a Greek or Roman vessel with two handles and a narrow neck.
• [Latin from Greek *amphoreus*]

amphoteric *adjective*
• "amfa TARE ick"
• able to react as a base and an acid.
• [Greek *amphoteros* comparative of *amphō* both]

ampicillin *noun*
• "ampa SILLIN"
• a semi-synthetic penicillin used esp. in treating infections of the urinary and respiratory tracts.
• [*amino* + *penicillin*]

amplify *verb*
• "AMPLA fie"
• increase the volume or strength of (sound, electrical signals, etc.).
• [Old French *amplifier* from Latin *amplificare* from *amplus* plentiful]
• **amplification** *noun* "ampla fuh CAY sh'n"
• **amplifier** *noun*

amplitude *noun*
• "AMPLA tude"
• the maximum extent of a vibration or oscillation from the position of equilibrium.
• [French *amplitude* or Latin *amplitudo* from *amplus* plentiful]

ampoule *noun*
ALSO SPELLED: esp. *US* **ampul** or **ampule**
• "AMP yool" or "AM pool"
• a small capsule in which measured quantities of liquids or solids, e.g. medications, cosmetics, are sealed ready for use.
• [French from Latin AMPULLA]

ampulla *noun*
• "am PULLA"
• a Roman globular flask with two handles.
• [Latin]

amputate *verb*
• "AM pew tate"
• cut off by surgical operation (a part of the body, esp. a limb), usu. because of injury or disease.
• [Latin *amputare* from *amb-* about + *putare* prune]
• **amputation** *noun*

amputee *noun*
• "am pew TEE"
• a person who has lost a limb etc. by amputation.
• [as AMPUTATE]

amulet *noun*
• "AM yuh lit"
• an ornament or small piece of jewellery worn as a charm against evil.
• [Latin *amuletum*, of unknown origin]

amygdaloid *adjective*
• "a MIGDA loid"
• shaped like an almond.
• [Latin *amygdala* from Greek *amugdalē* almond]

amyl *noun*
• "AMMILL"
• the monovalent group C_5H_{11}-, derived from pentane.
• [Latin *amylum* starch, from which oil containing it was distilled]

amylase *noun*
• "AMMILL ace"
• any of several enzymes that convert starch and glycogen into simple sugars.
• [as AMYL]

amyloid *noun*
• "AMMILL oid"
• a glycoprotein deposited in connective tissue in certain diseases.
• [as AMYL]

amyotrophic *adjective*
• "a my oh TROFFIC"
• pertaining to atrophy of the muscles.
• [Greek *a-* without + *mu-*, *mus* muscle + *trophikos* nourishment]

Anabaptism *noun*
• "anna BAP tizm"
• the doctrine that baptism should only be administered to believing adults.
• [Church Latin *anabaptismus* from Greek *anabaptismos* (*ana-* up + BAPTISM)]
• **Anabaptist** *noun*

anabatic *adjective*
• "anna BATTIC"
• (of a wind) caused by air flowing upwards.
• [Greek *anabatikos* ascending]

anabolism *noun*
• "an AB'll izm"
• the synthesis of complex molecules in living organisms from simpler ones together with the storage of energy; constructive metabolism.
• [Greek *anabolē* ascent (from *ana-* up + *ballō* throw)]
• **anabolic** *adjective*

anachronism *noun*
• "a NACKRA nizm"
• the attribution of a custom, event, etc., to a period to which it does not belong.
• [Greek *anakhronismos* (from *ana-* up + *khronos* time)]
• **anachronistic** *adjective*
• **anachronistically** *adverb*

anacoluthon *noun*
• "anna kuh LOOTH on"
• a sentence or construction which lacks grammatical sequence, e.g. *while in the garden the door banged shut.*

• [Greek *anakolouthon* (from *an-* not + *akolouthos* following)]

anaconda *noun*
• "anna CONDA"
• a S American boa of the genus *Eunectes*, esp. the very large, semi-aquatic *E. murinus*, that kills its prey by constriction.
• [alteration of *anacondaia* from Sinhalese *henakandayā* whip snake, from *hena* lightning + *kanda* stem: originally of a snake in Sri Lanka]

anacrusis *noun*
• "anna CROO sis"
• (in poetry) an unstressed syllable at the beginning of a verse.
• [Greek *anakrousis* (from *ana-* up + *krousis* from *krouō* strike)]

anadromous *adjective*
• "a NADRA muss"
• (of a fish, e.g. the salmon) that swims up a river from the sea to spawn.
• [Greek *anadromos* (from *ana-* up + *dromos* running)]

anaerobe *noun*
• "ANNA robe" or "a NAIR obe"
• an organism that grows without air, or requires oxygen-free conditions to live.
• [Greek *an-* not + AEROBE]
• **anaerobic** *adjective* "anna ROE bick"
• **anaerobically** *adverb*

anaesthesia *noun*
ALSO SPELLED: **anesthesia**
• "anniss THEEZY uh" or "anniss THEE zhuh" (with "TH" as in *THIN*)
• the absence of sensation, esp. artificially induced insensitivity to pain usu. achieved by the administration of gases or the injection of drugs.
• [Greek *an-* without + *aisthēsis* sensation]

anaesthetic *noun*
ALSO SPELLED: **anesthetic**
• "anniss THETTIC"
• a substance that produces insensibility to pain etc.
• [Greek *anaisthētos* insensible (as ANAESTHESIA)]

anaesthetist *noun*
• "a NEECE thuh tist" or "a NESS thuh tist"
• *Cdn & Brit.* a medical doctor specializing in the administration of anaesthetics.
• [as ANAESTHETIC]

anaesthetize *verb*
ALSO SPELLED: **anesthetize**, esp. *Brit.* **anaesthetise**
• "a NEECE thuh tize" or "a NESS thuh tize"
• administer an anaesthetic to.
• [as ANAESTHETIC]
• **anaesthetization** *noun* (also **anesthetization**) (also esp. *Brit.* **anaesthetisation**)

anaglyph *noun*
• "ANNA gliff"
• a composite stereoscopic photograph printed in superimposed complementary colours.
• [Greek *anagluphē* (from *ana-* up + *gluphē* from *gluphō* carve)]

analecta *plural noun*
• "anna LECTA"
• a collection of short literary extracts.
• [Greek *analekta* things gathered, from *analegō* pick up]

analgesia *noun*
• "annal JEE zee uh"
• the absence or relief of pain.
• [modern Latin from Greek, = painlessness]
• **analgesic** *adjective*

analog *noun*
ALSO SPELLED: **analogue**
• "ANNA log"
• (of a watch, clock, etc.) that gives a reading by means of hands or a pointer rather than displayed digits.
• [as ANALOGUE]
HOMOPHONES: *analogue*

analogize *verb*
ALSO SPELLED: esp. *Brit.* **-ise**
• "a NALA jize"
• represent or explain by analogy.
• [as ANALOGOUS]

analogous *adjective*
• "a NALA guss"
• partially similar or parallel; showing analogy.
• [Greek *analogos* proportionate]
• **analogously** *adverb*

analogue *noun*
ALSO SPELLED: *US* **analog**
• "ANNA log"
• an analogous or parallel thing.
• [see ANALOGOUS]
HOMOPHONES: *analog*

analogy *noun*
• "a NALA jee"
• correspondence or partial similarity.
• [as ANALOGOUS]
• **analogical** *adjective* "anna LODGE a k'll"
• **analogically** *adverb*

analysand *noun*
• "a NALA sand"
• a person undergoing psychoanalysis.
• [as ANALYSIS]

analysis *noun*
• "a NALA sis"
• a detailed examination of the elements or structure of a substance etc.
• [Greek *analusis* (from *ana-* up + *luō* set free)]

analyst *noun*
• "ANNA list"
• a person engaged or skilled in analysis.

- [as ANALYSIS]

HOMOPHONES: *annalist*

analytic *adjective*
- "anna LITTIC"
- of, pertaining to, or using analysis.
- [Greek *analutikos* (as ANALYSIS)]
- **analytical** *adjective*
- **analytically** *adverb*

analyze *verb*
ALSO SPELLED: **-yse**
- "ANNA lize"
- examine in detail the constitution or structure of.
- [as ANALYSIS]
- **analyzable** *adjective* (also **-ysable**)
- **analyzer** *noun* (also **-yser**)

anamnesis *noun*
- "annum NEE sis"
- the recalling of things past; reminiscence.
- [Greek, = remembrance]

anamorphosis *noun*
- "anna MORFA sis"
- a distorted projection or drawing which appears normal when viewed from a particular point or by means of a suitable mirror or lens.
- [Greek *anamorphōsis* transformation, from *ana-* back, again + *morphosis* shaping, from *morphoun* to shape, from *morphē* shape, form]
- **anamorphic** *adjective*

anandrous *adjective*
- "a NAN druss"
- having no stamens.
- [Greek *anandros* without males, from *an-* not + *anēr andros* male]

anapest *noun*
ALSO SPELLED: **anapaest**
- "ANNA pest"
- a metrical foot consisting of two short or unstressed syllables followed by one long or stressed syllable.
- [Latin *anapaestus* from Greek *anapaistos* reversed (because the reverse of a dactyl)]
- **anapestic** *adjective* (also **anapaestic**) "anna PESTIC"

anaphase *noun*
- "ANNA faze"
- the stage of meiotic or mitotic cell division when the chromosomes move away from one another to opposite poles of the spindle.
- [from *ana-* up + PHASE]

anaphora *noun*
- "a NAFFA ruh"
- the repetition of a word or phrase at the beginning of successive clauses.
- [Latin from Greek, = repetition (from *ana-* up + *pherō* to bear)]
- **anaphoric** *adjective* "anna FORIC"

anaphrodisiac *adjective*
- "an afro DEEZY ack"
- tending to reduce sexual desire.
- [Greek *an-* without + APHRODISIAC]

anaphylaxis *noun*
- "anna fuh LAX iss"
- an extreme allergic reaction to an antigen, to which the body has become hypersensitive following an earlier exposure.
- [from Greek *ana-* up + *phulaxis* guarding]
- **anaphylactic** *adjective*

anaptyxis *noun*
- "an ap TIX iss"
- the insertion of a vowel between two consonants to aid pronunciation (as in *went thataway*).
- [Greek *anaptuxis* (from *ana-* up + *ptussō* fold)]

anarchism *noun*
- "ANNER kizm"
- the doctrine that all government should be abolished.
- [as ANARCHY]
- **anarchist** *noun*
- **anarchistic** *adjective*

anarchy *noun*
- "ANNER kee"
- disorder, esp. political or social.
- [Greek *anarkhia* (*an-* without + *arkhē* rule)]
- **anarchic** *adjective* "a NARKIC"

Anasazi *noun*
- "anna SOZZY"
- a member of a culture of the southwestern US, dating from about AD 100 to the present, of which the Pueblo culture is a continuation.
- [Navajo *anaasází* 'enemy ancestors', applied by the Navajo to the prehistoric inhabitants of ruined Pueblo villages]

anastigmat *noun*
- "a NASTIG mat"
- a lens or lens system made free from astigmatism by correction.
- [German from *anastigmatisch* ANASTIGMATIC]

anastigmatic *adjective*
- "anna stig MATTIC"
- free from astigmatism.
- [Greek *an-* without + ASTIGMATISM]

anastomose *verb*
- "a NASTA moze"
- link by anastomosis.
- [as ANASTOMOSIS]

anastomosis *noun*
- "a nasta MOE sis"
- a cross-connection of arteries, branches, rivers, etc.
- [Greek from *anastomoō* furnish with a mouth (from *ana-* up + *stoma* mouth)]

anathema *noun*
- "a NATHA muh"
- a detested thing or person.
- [Church Latin, = excommunicated person, excommunication, from Greek *anathema* thing

devoted, (later) accursed thing, from *anatithēmi* set up]

anathematize *verb*
ALSO SPELLED: esp. *Brit.* **-ise**
• "a NATHA muh tize"
• curse.
• [as ANATHEMA]

Anatolian *noun*
• "anna TOLEY 'n"
• a native or inhabitant of Anatolia, the peninsula forming the greater part of Turkey.

anatomist *noun*
• "a NATTA mist"
• a person skilled in anatomy.
• [as ANATOMY]

anatomize *verb*
ALSO SPELLED: esp. *Brit.* **-ise**
• "a NATTA mize"
• examine in detail.
• [as ANATOMY]

anatomy *noun*
• "a NATTA mee"
• the science of the bodily structure of animals and plants.
• [Greek, from *ana* up + *tomia* cutting]
• **anatomic** *adjective* "anna TOMMIC"
• **anatomical** *adjective* "anna TOMMA k'll"
• **anatomically** *adverb*

ancestor *noun*
• "AN sess tur"
• any (esp. remote) person from whom one is descended.
• [Old French *ancestre* from Latin *antecessor -oris* from *antecedere* (from *ante* before + *cedere cess-* go)]
• **ancestral** *adjective*
• **ancestress** *noun*

ancestry *noun*
• "AN sess tree"
• lineage or descent.
• [as ANCESTOR]

anchor *noun*
• "ANKER"
• a heavy metal weight used to moor a ship to the bottom of a river, lake, sea, etc. or a balloon to the ground.
• [Old English *ancor* from Latin *anchora* from Greek *agkura*]

anchorage *noun*
• "ANKER idge"
• a place where a ship may be anchored.
• [as ANCHOR]

anchorite *noun*
• "ANKER ite"
• a hermit; a religious recluse.
• [Church Latin *anchoreta* from ecclesiastical Greek *anakhōrētēs* from *anakhōreō* retire]
• **anchoress** *noun* "ANKER iss"
• **anchoritic** *adjective* "anker ITTIC"

anchorman *noun*
• "ANKER m'n"
• the main announcer on a news or sports broadcast, who introduces the reports of other broadcasters.
• [as ANCHOR]
• **anchorperson** *noun*
• **anchorwoman** *noun*

anchoveta *noun*
• "ancha VETTA"
• a small Pacific anchovy, *Cetengraulis mysticetus*, caught for use as bait or to make fish meal.
• [Spanish, diminutive of *anchova*: compare ANCHOVY]

anchovy *noun*
• "ann CHO vee" or "ANN cho vee" or "ANCHA vee"
• a small, mainly Mediterranean fish of the herring family *Engraulis encrasicholus*, which has a rich flavour and is usu. eaten pickled or in pastes, sauces, etc.
• [Spanish and Portuguese *ancho(v)a*, of uncertain origin]

ancient *adjective*
• "AIN ch'nt"
• of long ago.
• [Old French *ancien*, ultimately from Latin *ante* before]
• **ancientness** *noun*

ancillary *adjective*
• "ann SILLA ree"
• (of a person, activity, or service) providing essential support to a central service or industry.
• [Latin *ancillaris* from *ancilla* maidservant]

ancon *noun*
• "ANK'n"
• a console, usu. of two volutes, supporting or appearing to support a cornice.
• [Latin from Greek *agkōn* elbow]

Andalusian *adjective*
• "anda LUCY 'n"
• of or relating to Andalusia in S Spain.

andante *adverb*
• "on DON tay" or "an DAN tay"
• in a moderately slow tempo.
• [Italian, participle of *andare* go]

andantino *adverb*
• "on don TEENO" or "an dan TEENO"
• somewhat quicker than andante.
• [Italian, diminutive of ANDANTE]

Andean *adjective*
• "an DEE 'n" or "ANDY 'n"
• of or relating to the Andes Mountains of S America.

andesite *noun*
• "ANDEEZ ite"
• a fine-grained brown or greyish intermediate volcanic rock.

• [the *Andes* Mountains of S America + Greek *lithos* stone]
• **andesitic** *adjective* "andeez ITTIC"

andiron *noun*
• "AND iron"
• a metal stand (usu. one of a pair) for supporting burning wood in a fireplace; a firedog.
• [Old French *andier*, of unknown origin: assimilated to 'iron']

Andorran *noun*
• "an DORE 'n"
• a native or inhabitant of the principality of Andorra between France and Spain.

andouille *noun*
• "an DOOEY"
• (in Cajun cuisine) a smoked, spicy, coarse-ground pork sausage.
• [French, from Latin *inductilia* substance introduced (into a casing) from *indūcēre* introduce]

androcentric *adjective*
• "andro SENTRIC"
• male-centred.
• [Greek *anēr andros* male + CENTRIC]
• **androcentrism** *noun*

androecium *noun*
• "an DREECY um" or "an DREESHY um"
• the stamens taken collectively.
• [modern Latin from Greek *anēr andros* male + *oikion* house]

androgen *noun*
• "ANDRA j'n"
• a male sex hormone or other substance capable of developing and maintaining certain male sexual characteristics.
• [Greek *anēr andros* male + *-genēs* -born, of a specified kind]
• **androgenic** *adjective* "andra JENNIC"

androgyne *adjective*
• "ANDRA jine"
• hermaphrodite.
• [Greek *androgunos* (*anēr andros* male, *gunē* woman)]

androgynous *adjective*
• "an DRAW juh nuss"
• partly male and partly female in appearance; of indeterminate sex.
• [as ANDROGYNE]
• **androgyny** *noun* "an DRAW juh nee"

androstenedione *noun*
• "andro STEEN die on"
• a naturally occurring androgenic steroid often taken in concentrated form to elevate blood levels of testosterone.
• [ANDROSTERONE + '-dione' used to form the names of compounds containing two carbonyl groups]

androsterone *noun*
• "andro STAIR own"
• a relatively inactive male sex hormone produced by metabolism of testosterone.
• [Greek *anēr, andr-* 'man' + STEROL + '-one' forming nouns denoting various compounds, from Greek *-ōnē* feminine patronymic]

anecdotage *noun*
• "ANNIC dote idge"
• garrulous old age.
• [blend of ANECDOTE + DOTAGE]

anecdotal *adjective*
• "annick DOTE 'll"
• of, pertaining to, or consisting of anecdotes.
• [as ANECDOTE]
• **anecdotalist** *noun*

anecdote *noun*
• "ANNIC dote"
• a short account of an entertaining or interesting incident.
• [Greek *anekdota* things unpublished (*an-* without + *ekdotos* from *ekdidōmi* publish)]
• **anecdotist** *noun*

anechoic *adjective*
• "anna CO ick"
• free from echo.
• [Greek *an-* without + ECHO]

anemia *noun*
ALSO SPELLED: esp. *Brit.* **anaemia**
• "a NEEMY uh"
• a deficiency in the blood, usu. of red cells or their hemoglobin, resulting in pallor and weariness.
• [modern Latin from Greek *anaimia* (*an-* without + *aimia* from *haima* blood)]

anemic *adjective*
ALSO SPELLED: esp. *Brit.* **anaemic**
• "a NEE mick"
• relating to or suffering from anemia.
• [as ANEMIA]

anemometer *noun*
• "anna MOMMA tur"
• an instrument for measuring the force of the wind.
• [Greek *anemos* wind + *metron* measure]
• **anemometric** *adjective* "anna muh METRIC"
• **anemometry** *noun*

anemone *noun*
• "a NEMMA nee"
• any plant of the genus *Anemone*, related to the buttercup, with flowers of various vivid colours.
• [Greek *anemōnē* windflower, from *anemos* wind]

anemophilous *adjective*
• "anna MOFFA luss"
• wind-pollinated.
• [Greek *anemos* wind + *-philos* loving]

anencephaly *noun*
• "annin SEFFA lee"

• a congenital condition where part or all of the cerebral hemispheres and the rear of the skull are absent.
• [Greek *anenkephalos* 'without brain']
• **anencephalic** *adjective* "annin suh FALIC"

aneroid *adjective*
• "ANNA roid"
• (of a barometer) that measures air pressure by its action on the elastic lid of an evacuated box, not by the height of a column of fluid.
• [French *anéroïde* from Greek *a-* not + *nēros* water]

anesthesiology *noun*
• "anniss theezy OLLA jee"
• the science of administering anaesthetics.
• [as ANAESTHESIA + *logos* word]
• **anesthesiologist** *noun*

aneurysm *noun*
ALSO SPELLED: **aneurism**
• "ANYER izm"
• an excessive localized enlargement of a blood vessel.
• [Greek *aneurusma* from *aneurunō* widen out, from *eurus* wide]
• **aneurysmal** *adjective* (also **aneurismal**)

anfractuosity *noun*
• "an frack choo OSSA tee"
• circuitousness.
• [French *anfractuosité* from Late Latin *anfractuosus* from Latin *anfractus* a bending]
• **anfractuous** *adjective*

angakok *noun*
• "ANG guh coke"
• *Cdn* (*North*) an Inuit shaman or healer.
• [Inuktitut]

angary *noun*
• "ANG guh ree"
• the right of a belligerent (subject to compensation for loss) to seize or destroy neutral property under military necessity.
• [French *angarie*, ultimately from Greek *aggareia* from *aggaros* courier]

Angeleno *noun*
• "anja LEENO"
• a native or inhabitant of Los Angeles.
• [US Spanish *angeleño*]

angelic *adjective*
• "an JELLIC"
• like or relating to angels.
• [Middle English from French *angélique* or Late Latin *angelicus* from Greek *aggelikos* from *aggelos* messenger]
• **angelically** *adverb*

angelica *noun*
• "an JELLIC uh"
• an aromatic umbelliferous plant, *Angelica archangelica*, used in cooking and medicine.
• [medieval Latin (*herba*) *angelica* angelic herb]

angelus *noun*
• "ANJA luss"
• a devotion commemorating the Incarnation and including the recitation of three Hail Marys, traditionally said at morning, noon, and sunset.
• [opening words *Angelus domini* (Latin, = the angel of the Lord)]

Angevin *noun*
• "ANJA vin"
• a native or inhabitant of Anjou in W France.
• [French]

angina *noun*
• "an JINE uh"
• pain in the chest brought on by exertion, owing to an inadequate blood supply to the heart.
• [Latin, = spasm of the chest, from *angina* quinsy, from Greek *agkhonē* strangling]

angiogenesis *noun*
• "anjee oh JENNA sis"
• the development of new blood vessels.
• [as ANGIOMA + GENESIS]

angiogram *noun*
• "ANJEE a gram"
• an X-ray made by angiography.
• [as ANGIOMA + Greek *gramma* thing written]

angiography *noun*
• "anjee OGGRA fee"
• radiography of blood and lymph vessels, carried out after introduction of a radiopaque substance.
• [as ANGIOMA + Greek *graphia* writing]
• **angiographic** *adjective*
• **angiographically** *adverb*

angioma *noun*
• "anjee OH muh"
• a tumour produced by the dilatation or new formation of blood vessels or lymph vessels.
• [modern Latin from Greek *aggeion* vessel]

angioplasty *noun*
• "ANJEE oh plasty"
• surgical repair of a damaged blood vessel.
• [as ANGIOMA + Greek *plastos* formed, moulded]

angiosperm *noun*
• "ANJEE oh spurm"
• any plant producing flowers and reproducing by seeds enclosed within a carpel, including herbaceous plants, herbs, shrubs, grasses and most trees.
• [as ANGIOMA + Latin *sperma* seed]
• **angiospermous** *adjective*

angiotensin *noun*
• "anjee a TENSIN"
• a powerful vasoconstricting polypeptide which stimulates the production of aldosterone and vasopressin and results in an increase in blood pressure.

• [as ANGIOMA + '(hyper)tensin', the former name of the substance, from HYPERTENSION]

anglicism *noun*
• "ANGLA sizm"
• an English word, structure, etc. borrowed into another language.
• [Latin *Anglicus* from *Anglus* Angle (Germanic invaders of England)]

anglicize *verb*
ALSO SPELLED: esp. *Brit.* **-ise**
• "ANGLA size"
• make English in form or character.
• [as ANGLICISM]
• **anglicization** *noun* (also esp. *Brit.* **-isation**)

Anglocentric *adjective*
• "anglo SENTRIC"
• centred on or considered in terms of England.
• [as ANGLICISM + CENTRIC]

anglophile *noun*
• "ANGLO file"
• a person who is fond of or greatly admires England, the English, or English-speaking culture.
• [as ANGLICISM + Greek *philos* dear, loving]
• **anglophilia** *noun* "anglo FILLY uh" or "anglo FEELY uh"

anglophobe *noun*
• "ANGLA fobe"
• a person who greatly hates or fears anglophones, the English or England.
• [as ANGLICISM + PHOBIA]
• **anglophobia** *noun*
• **anglophobic** *adjective*

anglophone *adjective*
• "ANGLA fone"
• esp. *Cdn* English-speaking.
• [as ANGLICISM + Greek *phōnē* voice]

angora *noun*
• "ang GORA"
• a fabric made from the hair of the angora goat or rabbit.
• [*Angora*, the former name for Ankara, Turkey]

angostura *noun*
• "ang guh STURA"
• an aromatic bitter bark used as a flavouring, and formerly used as a tonic and to reduce fever.
• [*Angostura*, a former name for Ciudad Bolívar, Venezuela]

angst *noun*
• "ANGST"
• anxiety.
• [German]
• **angsty** *adjective*

angstrom *noun*
• "ANG strum" or "ONG strum"
• a unit of length equal to 10^{-10} m, used esp. for electromagnetic wavelengths.
• [A. J. *Ångström*, Swedish physicist d.1874]

Anguillan *noun*
• "ang GWEEL'n"
• a native or inhabitant of Anguilla in the W Indies.

anguine *adjective*
• "ANG gwin"
• of or resembling a snake.
• [Latin *anguinus* from *anguis* snake]

anguish *noun*
• "ANG gwish"
• severe misery or mental suffering.
• [Old French *anguisse* choking, from Latin *angustia* tightness, from *angustus* narrow]
• **anguished** *adjective*

angular *adjective*
• "ANG gyuh lur"
• having angles or sharp corners.
• [Latin *angularis* from *angulus* angle]
• **angularity** *noun* "ang gyuh LERRA tee"
• **angularly** *adverb*

anhedonia *noun*
• "an hee DOANY uh"
• inability to feel pleasure in normally pleasurable activities.
• [Greek *an-* without + *hēdonē* pleasure]

anhedral *noun*
• "an HEED rull"
• a downward inclination of an aircraft wing, tailplane, etc.
• [Greek *an-* without + *hedra* base]

anhydride *noun*
• "an HI dride"
• a substance obtained by removing the elements of water from a compound, esp. from an acid.
• [as ANHYDROUS]

anhydrite *noun*
• "an HY drite"
• a naturally occurring, usu. rock-forming, anhydrous mineral form of calcium sulphate.
• [as ANHYDROUS]

anhydrous *adjective*
• "an HY druss"
• without water, esp. water of crystallization.
• [Greek *anudros* (*an-* without + *hudōr* water)]

aniline *noun*
• "ANNA line" or "ANNA lin"
• a colourless oily liquid, used in the manufacture of dyes, drugs, and plastics.
• [German *Anilin* from *Anil* indigo (from which it was originally obtained), ultimately from Arabic *an-nīl*]

anima *noun*
• "ANNA muh"
• the inner personality.
• [Latin, = mind, soul]

animadvert *verb*
• "annim ud VURT"

• criticize, censure (conduct, a fault, etc.).
• [Latin *animadvertere* from *animus* mind + *advertere* (*ad-* to + *vertere vers-* turn)]
• **animadversion** *noun*

animalcule *noun*
• "anna MAL kyool"
• a microscopic animal.
• [modern Latin *animalculum* (from *animalis* having breath, from *anima* breath + *-culus* forming nouns)]
• **animalcular** *adjective*

animality *noun*
• "anna MALA tee"
• the animal world.
• [as ANIMALCULE]

animate *verb*
• "ANNA mate"
• give life to.
• [Latin *animatus* past participle of *animare* give life to, from *anima* life, soul]

animateur *noun*
• "anna muh TUR"
• a person who coordinates, or acts as a driving force behind, a cultural or other activity.
• [French, as ANIMATE]

animator *noun*
• "ANNA mater"
• a person who makes animated films.
• [as ANIMATE]

animatronics *noun*
• "anna muh TRONNIX"
• the technique of constructing robots resembling animals, people, etc. which are programmed to perform lifelike movements to a pre-recorded soundtrack.
• [blend of ANIMATE + ELECTRONICS]
• **animatronic** *adjective*

anime *noun*
• "ANNIE may"
• Japanese film and television animation, typically having a science-fiction theme and sometimes including violent or sexual material.
• [Japanese *anime* from French *animé* animated]

animism *noun*
• "ANNA mizm"
• the attribution of a living soul to plants, inanimate objects, and natural phenomena.
• [Latin *anima* life, soul]
• **animist** *noun*
• **animistic** *adjective*

animosity *noun*
• "anna MOSSA tee"
• a spirit or feeling of strong hostility.
• [Late Latin *animositas* from *animosus* spirited]

animus *noun*
• "ANNA muss"
• a display of animosity.
• [Latin, = spirit, mind]

anion *noun*
• "AN eye 'n"
• a negatively charged ion; an ion that is attracted to the anode in electrolysis.
• [Greek *ana-* without + 'ion' from Greek, neuter present participle of *eimi* go]
• **anionic** *adjective*

anise *noun*
• "ANNISS"
• an umbelliferous plant, *Pimpinella anisum*, having aromatic seeds.
• [Greek *anison* anise, dill]

aniseed *noun*
• "ANNA seed"
• the seed of the anise, used to give liqueurs, candies, etc. a liquorice-like flavour.
• [Middle English from ANISE + 'seed']

anisette *noun*
• "ANNA set"
• a liqueur flavoured with aniseed.
• [French, diminutive of *anis* ANISE]

Anishinabe *noun*
ALSO SPELLED: **Anishnabe**
• "a nish NOBBY"
• the preferred name for the Ojibwa, an Algonquian people living in northern Quebec, northern and central Ontario, Manitoba, and Saskatchewan.
• [Ojibwa, = the people]

anisotropic *adjective*
• "an eye so TROPPIC"
• having physical properties that are different in different directions, e.g. the strength of wood along the grain differing from that across the grain.
• [Greek *an-* without + ISOTROPIC]
• **anisotropically** *adverb*
• **anisotropy** *noun* "anna SOTTRA pee"

ankh *noun*
• "ANK"
• a device consisting of a looped bar with a shorter crossbar, used in ancient Egypt as a symbol of life.
• [Egyptian, = life, soul]

ankylose *verb*
• "ANKY lose" (rhymes with *GROSS*)
• (of bones or a joint) stiffen or unite by ankylosis.
• [back-formation from ANKYLOSIS]

ankylosis *noun*
• "anky LO sis"
• the abnormal stiffening and immobility of a joint by fusion of the bones.
• [modern Latin from Greek *agkulōsis* from *agkuloō* crook]
• **ankylotic** *adjective* "anky LOTTIC"

annalist *noun*
• "ANNA list"
• a writer of annals.

• [as ANNALS]
• **annalistic** *adjective*
HOMOPHONES: *analyst*

annals *plural noun*
• "ANN 'lz"
• a narrative of events year by year.
• [Latin *annales (libri)* yearly (books) from *annus* year]

annates *plural noun*
• "ANN ates"
• the first year's revenue of a see or benefice, paid to the Pope.
• [French *annate* from medieval Latin *annata* year's proceeds, from *annus* year]

annatto *noun*
• "a NATTO"
• a tropical tree, *Bixa orellana*, the coating of the seeds of which is used to produce an orange food colouring.
• [Carib]

anneal *verb*
• "a NEEL"
• heat (metal or glass) and allow it to cool slowly, esp. to toughen it.
• [Old English *onǣlan* from *on* + *ǣlan* burn, bake, from *āl* fire]
• **annealer** *noun*

annelid *noun*
• "ANNA lid"
• an animal of the phylum Annelida, members of which (e.g. marine worms, earthworms, and leeches) have bodies made up of annular segments.
• [ultimately from Latin *anellus* diminutive of *anulus* ring]
• **annelidan** *adjective* "a NELLID 'n"

annex *noun*
ALSO SPELLED: esp. *Brit.* **annexe**
• "ANNEX"
• a separate or added building, esp. for extra accommodation.
• [Old French *annexer* from Latin *annectere* (from *ad-* to + *nectere nex-* bind)]
• **annexation** *noun* "annex AY sh'n"

annexationism *noun*
• "annex AY sh'n izm"
• a policy which favours annexation of territory.
• [as ANNEX]
• **annexationist** *noun*

annihilate *verb*
• "a NIGH a late"
• completely destroy.
• [Late Latin *annihilare* (from *ad-* to + *nihil* nothing)]
• **annihilation** *noun*
• **annihilator** *noun*

anniversary *noun*
• "anna VURSA ree"
• the yearly return of a date on which an event took place in a previous year.
• [Latin *anniversarius* from *annus* year + *versus* turned]

annotate *verb*
• "ANNO tate"
• add explanatory notes to (a book, document, etc.).
• [Latin *annotare* (*ad-* to + *nota* mark)]
• **annotation** *noun*
• **annotator** *noun*

announce *verb*
• "a NOUNCE"
• make publicly known.
• [Old French *annoncer* from Latin *annuntiare* (*ad* to, *nuntius* messenger)]
• **announcement** *noun*
• **announcer** *noun*

annual *adjective*
• "AN yoo 'll"
• reckoned by the year.
• [Late Latin *annualis* from Latin *annalis* from *annus* year]
• **annually** *adverb*

annualized *adjective*
ALSO SPELLED: esp. *Brit.* **-ised**
• "AN yoo 'll ized"
• (of rates of interest, inflation, etc.) calculated on an annual basis, as a projection from figures obtained for a shorter period.
• [as ANNUAL]

annuitant *noun*
• "a NEW a t'nt"
• a person who holds or receives an annuity.
• [as ANNUITY]

annuity *noun*
• "a NEW a tee"
• a yearly grant or allowance.
• [medieval Latin *annuitas -tatis* from Latin *annuus* yearly (as ANNUAL)]
• **annuitize** *verb* (also esp. *Brit.* **-ise**)

annul *verb*
• "a NULL"
• declare (a marriage etc.) invalid.
• [Late Latin *annullare* (*ad-* to + *nullus* none)]
• **annulment** *noun*

annular *adjective*
• "ANYA lur"
• ring-shaped; forming a ring.
• [Latin *annularis* from *an(n)ulus* ring]

annulate *adjective*
• "ANYA lit"
• having rings; marked with or formed of rings.
• [Latin *annulatus* (as ANNULUS)]
• **annulation** *noun*
HOMOPHONES: *annulet*

annulet *noun*
• "ANYA lit"
• a small fillet or band encircling a column.

• [Latin *annulus* ring]
HOMOPHONES: *annulate*

annulus *noun*
• "ANYA luss"
• a ring; a ring-shaped part.
• [Latin *an(n)ulus*]

annunciation *noun*
• "a nuncy AY sh'n"
• the announcing of the Incarnation, made by the angel Gabriel to Mary, related in Luke 1:26–38.
• [Late Latin *annuntiatio -onis* from *annuntiare* announce]

annunciator *noun*
• "a NUNCY ater"
• a device giving an audible or visible indication of which of several electrical circuits has been activated, of the position of a train, etc.
• [as ANNUNCIATION]

anoa *noun*
• "a NOAH"
• any of several small deer-like water buffalo of the genus *Bubalus*, native to the Indonesian island of Sulawesi.
• [the name in Sulawesi]

anode *noun*
• "AN ode"
• the positive electrode in an electrolytic cell or electronic valve or tube.
• [Greek *anodos* way up, from *ana* up + *hodos* way]
• **anodal** *adjective* "a NODE 'll"
• **anodic** *adjective* "a NODDIC"

anodize *verb*
ALSO SPELLED: esp. *Brit.* **-ise**
• "ANNA dize"
• coat (a metal, esp. aluminum) with a protective oxide layer by electrolysis.
• [as ANODE]
• **anodizer** *noun* (also esp. *Brit.* **-iser**)

anodyne *adjective*
• "ANNA dine"
• not likely to cause offence or disagreement and somewhat dull.
• [Latin *anodynus* from Greek *anōdunos* painless (from *an-* without + *odunē* pain)]

anoint *verb*
• "a NOINT"
• apply oil or ointment to, esp. as a religious ceremony, e.g. at baptism, or the consecration of a priest or king, or in ministering to the sick.
• [Old French *enoint* past participle of *enoindre* from Latin *inungere* from *ungere unct-* smear with oil]
• **anointer** *noun*

anomalistic *adjective*
• "a nomma LISTIC"
• of the anomaly or angular distance of a planet from its perihelion.
• [as ANOMALOUS]

anomalous *adjective*
• "a NOMMA luss"
• having an irregular or deviant feature; abnormal.
• [Late Latin *anomalus* from Greek *anōmalos* (*an-* without + *homalos* even)]
• **anomalously** *adverb*
• **anomalousness** *noun*

anomaly *noun*
• "a NOMMA lee"
• an anomalous circumstance or thing; an irregularity.
• [Greek *anōmalia* from *anōmalos* ANOMALOUS]

anomie *noun*
ALSO SPELLED: **anomy**
• "ANNA mee"
• lack of the usual social or ethical standards in an individual or group.
• [Greek *anomia* from *anomos* lawless]
• **anomic** *adjective* "a NOMMIC"

anonymous *adjective*
• "a NONNA muss"
• of unknown name.
• [Late Latin *anonymus* from Greek *anōnumos* nameless (*an-* without + *onoma* name)]
• **anonymity** *noun* "anna NIMMA tee"
• **anonymously** *adverb*

anopheles *noun*
• "a NOFFA leez"
• any of various mosquitoes of the genus *Anopheles*, many of which are carriers of the malarial parasite.
• [Greek *anōphelēs* unprofitable]

anorak *noun*
• "ANNA rack"
• a waterproof jacket of cloth or plastic, usu. with a hood and with drawstrings at the waist, cuffs, and hood.
• [Greenlandic *anoraq*]

anorectic *adjective*
• "anna RECTIC"
• lacking appetite.
• [Greek *anorektos* without appetite (as ANOREXIA)]

anorexia *noun*
• "anna REXY uh"
• a lack or loss of appetite for food.
• [Late Latin from Greek from *an-* not + *orexis* appetite]
• **anorexic** *adjective*

anorthosite *noun*
• "a NORTH a site"
• a granular igneous rock composed largely of plagioclase (usu. labradorite).
• [French from *anorthose* plagioclase, ultimately from Greek *an-* not + *orthos* straight]

anosmia *noun*
• "an OZ mee uh"
• the loss of the sense of smell.

• [Late Latin from Greek from *an-* not + *osmē* smell]
• **anosmic** *adjective*

anovulant *noun*
• "an OVYA l'nt"
• a drug preventing ovulation.
• [*an-* not + OVULE]

anovulatory *adjective*
• "an OVYA luh tory"
• (of a menstrual cycle etc.) not accompanied by ovulation.
• [as ANOVULANT]

anoxia *noun*
• "a NOXY uh"
• an absence or deficiency of oxygen.
• [Greek *an-* without + OXYGEN]
• **anoxic** *adjective*

antagonism *noun*
• "an TAGGA nizm"
• active opposition or hostility.
• [as ANTAGONIZE]
• **antagonist** *noun*
• **antagonistic** *adjective*
• **antagonistically** *adverb*

antagonize *verb*
ALSO SPELLED: esp. *Brit.* **-ise**
• "an TAGGA nize"
• evoke hostility or opposition or enmity in.
• [Greek *antagōnizomai* (as ANTI, *agōnizomai* from *agōn* contest)]
• **antagonization** *noun* (also esp. *Brit.* **-isation**)

antalkali *noun*
• "ant ALKA lie"
• any substance that counteracts an alkali.
• [as ANTI + ALKALI]

Antarctic *adjective*
• "ant ARK tick" or "ant AR tick"
• of, relating to, or denoting the south polar region or Antarctica.
• [Old French *antartique* or Latin *antarcticus* from Greek *antarktikos* (as ANTI, *arktikos* ARCTIC)]

ante *noun*
• "ANTY"
• a stake put up by a player in poker etc. before receiving cards.
• [Latin, = before]
HOMOPHONES: *anti*, *auntie*

antebellum *adjective*
• "anty BELLUM"
• occurring or existing before a particular war, esp. the American Civil War (1861–65).
• [Latin from *ante* before + *bellum* war]

antecedent *noun*
• "anta SEED'nt"
• a preceding thing or circumstance.
• [French *antecedent* from Latin *antecedere* (as ANTE, *cedere* go)]
• **antecedence** *noun*
• **antecedently** *adverb*

antechamber *noun*
• "anty CHAME bur"
• a small room leading to a main one.
• [as ANTE + 'chamber' (Old French *chambre* from Latin *camera* room)]

antedate *verb*
• "anty DATE"
• exist or occur at a date earlier than.
• [as ANTE + 'date' (as DATUM)]

antediluvian *adjective*
• "anty duh LOOVY 'n"
• of or belonging to the time before the Biblical Flood.
• [ANTE + Latin *diluvium* DELUGE]

antelope *noun*
• "ANTA lope"
• any of various deer-like ruminants of the family Bovidae, esp. abundant in Africa and typically tall, slender, graceful, and swift-moving with smooth hair and upward-pointing horns, e.g. gazelles, gnus, kudus, and impala.
• [medieval Latin *ant(h)alopus* from late Greek *antholops*, of unknown origin]

antenatal *adjective*
• "anty NATE 'll"
• prenatal.
• [as ANTE + NATAL]

antenna *noun*
• "an TENNA"
• a metal rod, wire, or other structure by which signals are transmitted or received as part of a radio or television transmitting or receiving system.
• [Latin, = sail yard]

antenuptial *adjective*
• "anty NUP sh'll"
• pre-nuptial.
• [as ANTE + NUPTIAL]

antependium *noun*
• "anty PENDY um"
• a veil or hanging for the front of an altar.
• [medieval Latin (as ANTE, *pendēre* hang)]

antepenult *noun*
• "anty puh NULT"
• the last syllable but two in a word.
• [abbreviation of Late Latin *antepaenultimus* (as ANTE, *paenultimus* PENULTIMATE)]

antepenultimate *adjective*
• "anty pen ULTA mit"
• last but two.
• [as ANTEPENULT]

anterior *adjective*
• "an TEERY ur"
• nearer the front, esp. situated in the front of the body, or nearer to the head or forepart.
• [Latin *anterior* from *ante* before]

- **anteriority** *noun*
- **anteriorly** *adverb*

anteroom *noun*
- "ANTY room"
- a small room leading to a main one, esp. one used as a waiting room.
- [as ANTE + 'room']

anthelion *noun*
- "an TEELY 'n"
- a luminous halo projected on a cloud or fog bank opposite to the sun.
- [Greek, neuter of *anthēlios* opposite to the sun (as ANTI, *hēlios* sun)]

anthelmintic *noun*
- "anth'll MINTIC"
- any drug or agent used to destroy parasitic, esp. intestinal, worms, e.g. tapeworms, roundworms, and flukes.
- [ANTI + Greek *helmins helminthos* worm]

anthem *noun*
- "ANTH'm"
- a solemn song expressing loyalty etc.
- [Old English *antefn, antifne* from Late Latin *antiphona* ANTIPHON]

anthemic *adjective*
- "anth EMMIC"
- (of a song) like an anthem in being rousing or uplifting.
- [as ANTHEM]

anthemion *noun*
- "an THEEMY 'n"
- a Greek decorative motif with radiating leaves of honeysuckle, lotus, or palmette.
- [Greek, = flower]

antheridium *noun*
- "anth a RIDDY um"
- the male sex organ of algae, mosses, ferns, etc.
- [modern Latin from Latin *anthera* 'medicine extracted from flowers' from Greek *anthēra* flowery, feminine adjective from *anthos* flower + Greek *-idion* diminutive suffix]

anthocyanin *noun*
- "anth oh SYE a nin"
- any of several water-soluble nitrogenous pigments which contribute to the red, blue, or violet colours in some plants.
- [Greek *anthocyan* from *anthos* flower + *kuanos* blue]

anthologize *verb*

ALSO SPELLED: esp. *Brit.* **-ise**
- "ann THOLLA jize"
- compile or include in an anthology.
- [as ANTHOLOGY]

anthology *noun*
- "ann THOLLA jee"
- a published collection of poems, stories, songs, reproductions of paintings, etc.
- [Greek *anthologia* from *anthos* flower + *-logia* collection, from *legō* gather]
- **anthologist** *noun*

anthozoan *noun*
- "anth a ZO 'n"
- any of the sessile marine coelenterates of the class Anthozoa, including sea anemones and corals.
- [modern Latin *Anthozoa* from Greek *anthos* flower + *zōia* animals]

anthracene *noun*
- "AN thruh seen"
- a colourless crystalline aromatic hydrocarbon obtained by the distillation of crude oils and used in the manufacture of chemicals.
- [Greek *anthrax -akos* coal]

anthracite *noun*
- "AN thruh site"
- coal of a hard variety burning with little flame and smoke.
- [Greek *anthrakitis* a kind of coal (as ANTHRACENE)]
- **anthracitic** *adjective* "an thruh SITTIC"

anthracnose *noun*
- "an THRACK nose" (rhymes with *GROSS*)
- a fungal disease of plants, characterized by dark lesions.
- [French from Greek *anthrak-, anthrax* coal + *nosos* disease]

anthrax *noun*
- "ANN thrax"
- a lethal disease of sheep and cattle caused by bacterial spores and transmissible to humans.
- [Greek, = carbuncle]

anthropic *adjective*
- "an THROPPIC"
- of or relating to human beings.
- [Greek *anthrōpos* human being]

anthropocentric *adjective*
- "anthra puh SENTRIC"
- regarding human beings as the centre of existence.
- [as ANTHROPIC + CENTRIC]
- **anthropocentrically** *adverb*
- **anthropocentrism** *noun*

anthropogenic *adjective*
- "anthra puh JENNIC"
- caused by human activity.
- [as ANTHROPIC + GENESIS]
- **anthropogenically** *adjective*

anthropoid *adjective*
- "ANTHRA poid"
- of or relating to the primate suborder Anthropoidea (including humans, apes, and monkeys), esp. designating the larger apes.
- [Greek *anthrōpoeidēs* (as ANTHROPIC)]

anthropology *noun*
- "anthra POLLA jee"

• the study of human beings, esp. of their societies and customs.
• [as ANTHROPIC + *logos* word]
• **anthropological** *adjective*
"anthra puh LODGE a k'll"
• **anthropologist** *noun*

anthropomorphism *noun*
• "anthra puh MORF izm"
• the attribution of human characteristics to a god, animal, or thing.
• [Greek *anthrōpomorphos* (as ANTHROPIC + *morphē* form)]
• **anthropomorphic** *adjective*
• **anthropomorphically** *adverb*
• **anthropomorphize** *verb* (also esp. *Brit.* **-ise**)

anthropophagy *noun*
• "anthra POFFA jee"
• cannibalism.
• [Greek *anthrōpophagia* (as ANTHROPIC, *phagō* eat)]
• **anthropophagous** *adjective*
"anthra POFFA guss"

anthroposophy *noun*
• "anthra POSSA fee"
• the knowledge of the nature of humans; human wisdom.
• [ANTHROPIC + Greek *sophos* wise]
• **anthroposophical** *adjective*

anthurium *noun*
• "an THURRY um"
• any of various tropical American plants of the arum family, often grown as a houseplant, with colourful, leathery foliage surrounding a spike that bears several flowers.
• [modern Latin from Greek *anthos* flower + *oura* tail]

anti *preposition*
• "AN tee" or "AN tie"
• opposed to.
• [Greek *anti-* against]
HOMOPHONES: *ante*, *auntie*

antialiasing *noun*
• "anty AILY us ing"
• the reduction or prevention of aliasing, esp. the smoothing of curved or inclined lines that appear artificially jagged in a computer image.
• [as ANTI + ALIASING]

antibacterial *adjective*
• "anty back TEERY 'll"
• active against bacteria, esp. containing an antibiotic that kills bacteria and prevents them from re-establishing themselves.
• [as ANTI + BACTERIA]

antibiosis *noun*
• "anty by OH sis"
• an antagonistic association between two organisms (esp. micro-organisms), in which one is adversely affected.
• [as ANTI, SYMBIOSIS]

antibiotic *noun*
• "anty by OTTIC"
• any of various substances, e.g. penicillin, produced by micro-organisms or made synthetically, that can inhibit or destroy susceptible micro-organisms, esp. disease-producing bacteria and fungi.
• [French *antibiotique* (as ANTI, Greek *biōtikos* fit for life, from *bios* life)]

antic *noun*
• "ANTIC"
• absurd or foolish behaviour.
• [Italian *antico* ANTIQUE, used as meaning 'grotesque']

anticathode *noun*
• "anty CATH ode"
• the target (or anode) of an X-ray tube on which the electrons from the cathode impinge and from which X-rays are emitted.
• [as ANTI + CATHODE]

anticholinergic *adjective*
• "anty cole 'n UR jick"
• (chiefly of a drug) inhibiting the physiological action of acetylcholine, esp. as a neurotransmitter.
• [as ANTI + CHOLINERGIC]

anticipate *verb*
• "an TISSA pate"
• foresee and deal with ahead of time.
• [Latin *anticipare* from *anti* for ANTE + *-cipare* from *capere* take]
• **anticipation** *noun*
• **anticipator** *noun*
• **anticipatory** *adjective* "an TISSA puh tory"

anticlerical *adjective*
• "anty CLERRA k'll"
• opposed to the influence of the clergy, esp. in politics.
• [as ANTI + CLERIC]
• **anticlericalism** *noun*

anticlimax *noun*
• "anty CLY max"
• a trivial conclusion to something significant or impressive, esp. where a climax was expected.
• [as ANTI + CLIMAX]
• **anticlimactic** *adjective* "anty clime ACTIC"
• **anticlimactically** *adverb*

anticline *noun*
• "ANTY cline"
• an arch-shaped fold of stratified rock in which the strata slope down from the crest.
• [ANTI + Greek *klinō* lean]
• **anticlinal** *adjective*

anticoagulant *noun*
• "anty co AG yoo l'nt"
• any drug or agent that retards or inhibits coagulation, esp. of the blood.
• [as ANTI + COAGULATE]

anticodon *noun*
• "anty CO don"
• a sequence of three nucleotides forming a unit of genetic code in a transfer RNA molecule that corresponds to a complementary codon in messenger RNA.
• [as ANTI + CODON]

anticonvulsant *noun*
• "anty k'n VULSE 'nt"
• any drug or agent that prevents or reduces the severity of convulsions, esp. epileptic fits.
• [as ANTI + CONVULSE]

anticyclone *noun*
• "anty SYE clone"
• a pressure system characterized by a high central barometric pressure, usu. resulting in dry conditions.
• [as ANTI + CYCLONE]
• **anticyclonic** *adjective* "anty sye CLONNIC"

antidepressant *noun*
• "anty de PRESS'nt"
• any drug or agent that alleviates depression.
• [as ANTI + DEPRESS]

antidiarrheal *adjective*
• "anty die a REE 'll"
• (of a drug) used to alleviate diarrhea.
• [as ANTI + DIARRHEA]

antidiuretic *adjective*
• "anty die ur ETTIC"
• inhibiting the production of urine.
• [as ANTI + DIURETIC]

antifouling *noun*
• "anty FOULING"
• treatment of a boat's hull with a paint or similar substance designed to prevent fouling.
• [as ANTI + FOUL]

antifungal *adjective*
• "anty FUNG g'll"
• preventing fungal growth.
• [as ANTI + FUNGUS]

antigen *noun*
• "ANTY j'n"
• a foreign substance, e.g. a toxin, which causes the body to produce antibodies.
• [German (as 'antibody', GENESIS)]
• **antigenic** *adjective* "anty JENNIC"

antiglobalization *noun*
• "anty globe'll ize AY sh'n"
• a political movement opposed to the policies of the International Monetary Fund, the World Bank, and the World Trade Organization, esp. increased free trade and open markets, and to the increasing international dominance of multinational corporations and financial institutions to the perceived detriment of the environment and to living standards and human rights in poor countries.
• [as ANTI + GLOBALIZATION]

Antigonisher *noun*
• "an tigga NISHER"
• a resident of Antigonish, NS.

antigravity *noun*
• "anty GRAVVA tee"
• a hypothetical force opposing gravity.
• [as ANTI + GRAVITY]

Antiguan *noun*
• "an TEE g'n"
• a native or inhabitant of Antigua and Barbuda in the W Indies.

antihistamine *noun*
• "anty HISTA min" or "anty HISTA meen"
• a substance that counteracts the effects of histamine, used esp. in the treatment of allergies.
• [as ANTI + HISTAMINE]

antihypertensive *adjective*
• "anty hyper TENSIV"
• designating or relating to the treatment of (esp. arterial) hypertension.
• [as ANTI + HYPERTENSION]

Antillean *adjective*
• "an TILLY 'n" or "anta LEE 'n"
• of or relating to the Antilles in the W Indies.

antilogarithm *noun*
• "anty LOGGA rith'm"
• the number to which a logarithm belongs.
• [as ANTI + LOGARITHM]

antimacassar *noun*
• "anty muh CASSER"
• a covering put over furniture, esp. over the back of a chair, as a protection from grease in the hair or as an ornament.
• [ANTI + MACASSAR]

antimetabolite *noun*
• "anty muh TABBA lite"
• a drug that interferes with the normal metabolic processes within cells, usu. by combining with enzymes, and used esp. in cancer treatment.
• [as ANTI + METABOLITE]

antimicrobial *adjective*
• "anty my CROW bee 'll"
• active against microbes.
• [as ANTI + MICROBE]

antimony *noun*
• "ANTA moany"
• a brittle silvery-white metallic element used esp. in alloys.
• [medieval Latin *antimonium* (11th c.), of unknown origin]

antinode *noun*
• "ANTY node"
• the position of maximum displacement in a standing wave system.
• [as ANTI + NODAL]

antinomian *adjective*
• "anty NOAMY 'n"
• of or relating to the view that Christians are released by grace from the obligation of observing the moral law.
• [medieval Latin *Antinomi*, name of a sect in Germany (1535) alleged to hold this view (as ANTI, Greek *nomos* law)]
• **antinomianism** *noun*

antinomy *noun*
• "an TINNA mee"
• a contradiction between two beliefs or conclusions that are in themselves reasonable; a paradox.
• [Greek ANTI + *nomos* law]

antioxidant *noun*
• "anty OXA d'nt"
• a substance (e.g. vitamins C and E) that removes potentially damaging oxidizing agents in a living organism.
• [as ANTI + OXYGEN]

antiparticle *noun*
• "ANTY parta k'll"
• an elementary particle having the same mass as a given particle but opposite electric or magnetic properties.
• [as ANTI + PARTICLE]

antipasto *noun*
• "anty PASS toe"
• a cold appetizer preceding an Italian meal, usu. consisting of meat or fish and vegetables or fruit.
• [Italian, from *anti* before + *pasto* from Latin *pastus* food]

antipathetic *adjective*
• "an tippa THETTIC"
• having a strong aversion or natural opposition.
• [as ANTIPATHY]

antipathy *noun*
• "an TIP uth ee"
• a strong or deep-seated aversion or dislike.
• [Greek *antipatheia* from *antipathēs* opposed in feeling (as ANTI, *pathos -eos* feeling)]

antiperspirant *noun*
• "anty PERSPER 'nt"
• a substance applied to the skin to prevent or reduce perspiration.
• [as ANTI + PERSPIRE]

antiphlogistic *noun*
• "anty fluh JISTIC"
• any drug or agent that alleviates or reduces inflammation.
• [ANTI + Greek *phlogistos* flammable]

antiphon *noun*
• "ANTA fon"
• a hymn or psalm, the parts of which are sung or recited alternately by two groups.
• [Church Latin *antiphona* from Greek (as ANTI, *phōnē* sound)]
• **antiphonal** *adjective* "an TIFFA n'll"
• **antiphonally** *adverb*

antiphonary *noun*
• "an TIFFA nerry"
• a book of antiphons.
• [as ANTIPHON]

antiphony *noun*
• "an TIFFA nee"
• antiphonal singing or chanting.
• [as ANTIPHON]

antipode *noun*
• "ANTY pode"
• the exact opposite.
• [as ANTIPODES]

antipodes *plural noun*
• "an TIPPA deez"
• places on opposite sides of the earth to each other.
• [Greek *antipodes* having the feet opposite (as ANTI, *pous podos* foot)]
• **antipodal** *adjective* "an TIPPA d'll"
• **antipodean** *adjective* "an tippa DEE 'n"

antipruritic *adjective*
• "anty prur ITTIC"
• relieving itching.
• [ANTI + PRURITUS]

antipsychotic *adjective*
• "anty sye COTTIC"
• (chiefly of a drug) used to treat psychotic disorders.
• [as ANTI + PSYCHOSIS]

antipyretic *adjective*
• "anty pie RETTIC"
• preventing or reducing fever.
• [as ANTI + PYRETIC]

antiquarian *adjective*
• "anta KWERRY 'n"
• of or dealing in antiques or rare books.
• [as ANTIQUARY]
• **antiquarianism** *noun*

antiquark *noun*
• "anty KWARK" or "anty KWORK"
• the antiparticle of a quark.
• [as ANTI + QUARK]

antiquary *noun*
• "ANTA kwerry"
• a student or collector of antiques or antiquities.
• [Latin *antiquarius* from *antiquus* ancient]

antiquated *adjective*
• "ANTA kwated"
• old-fashioned; out of date.
• [Church Latin *antiquare antiquat-* make old, as ANTIQUE]

antique *noun*
• "an TEEK"

• an object of considerable age, esp. an item of furniture or the decorative arts having a high value.
• [Latin *antiquus*, *anticus* former, ancient, from *ante* before]

antiquity *noun*
• “ann TICKWA tee”
• ancient times, esp. the period before the Middle Ages.
• [as ANTIQUE]

antiretroviral *adjective*
• “anty retro VIE rull”
• (of a drug) active against retroviruses.
• [as ANTI + RETROVIRUS]

antirrhinum *noun*
• “anty RYE num”
• any flowering plant of the genus *Antirrhinum*, esp. the snapdragon.
• [Latin from Greek *antirrhinon* from *anti* counterfeiting + *rhis rhinos* nose, from the resemblance of the flower to an animal’s snout]

antiscorbutic *adjective*
• “anty score BYOO tick”
• preventing or curing scurvy.
• [as ANTI + SCORBUTIC]

antisepsis *noun*
• “anty SEP sis”
• the process of using antiseptics to eliminate undesirable micro-organisms such as bacteria, viruses, and fungi that cause disease.
• [modern Latin (as ANTI, SEPSIS)]

antiseptic *adjective*
• “anta SEPTIC”
• counteracting sepsis esp. by preventing the growth of disease-causing micro-organisms.
• [as ANTISEPSIS]
• **antiseptically** *adverb*

antiserum *noun*
• “ANTY seerum”
• a blood serum containing antibodies against specific antigens, injected to treat or protect against specific diseases.
• [as ANTI + SERUM]

antispasmodic *adjective*
• “anty spazz MODDIC”
• (chiefly of a drug) used to relieve spasm of an involuntary muscle.
• [as ANTI + SPASMODIC]

antistrophe *noun*
• “an TISSTRA fee”
• the second section of an ancient Greek choral ode or of one division of it.
• [Late Latin from Greek *antistrophē* from *antistrephō* turn against]

antithesis *noun*
• “an TITH a sis”
• the direct opposite.
• [Late Latin from Greek *antitithēmi* set against (as ANTI, *tithēmi* place)]

antithetical *adjective*
• “anta THETTA k’ll”
• contrasted, opposite.
• [Greek *antithetikos* (as ANTITHESIS)]
• **antithetically** *adverb*

antitoxin *noun*
• “ANTY toxin”
• an antibody that counteracts a toxin.
• [as ANTI + TOXIC]
• **antitoxic** *adjective*

antitussive *adjective*
• “anty TUSSIV”
• suppressing coughing.
• [as ANTI + TUSSIVE]

antivenin *noun*
• “ANTY vennin”
• an antiserum containing antibodies against specific poisons in the venom of esp. snakes, spiders, scorpions, etc.
• [ANTI + Latin *venenum* poison]

antivivisectionism *noun*
• “anty viv a SECK sh’n izm”
• opposition to vivisection.
• [as ANTI + VIVISECTION]
• **antivivisectionist** *noun*

Antonine *adjective*
• “ANTA nine”
• of the Roman emperors Antoninus Pius and Marcus Aurelius or their rules (AD 137–180).

antonomasia *noun*
• “anta nuh MAY zhuh”
• the substitution of an epithet or title etc. for a proper name, e.g. *the Maid of Orleans* for Joan of Arc, *his Grace* for an archbishop.
• [Latin from Greek from *antonomazō* name instead (as ANTI, + *onoma* name)]

antonym *noun*
• “ANTA nim”
• a word opposite in meaning to another, e.g. *bad* and *good*.
• [French *antonyme* (as ANTI, SYNONYM)]
• **antonymous** *adjective* “an TONNA muss”
• **antonymy** *noun* “an TONNA mee”

antrum *noun*
• “AN trum”
• a natural chamber or cavity in the body, esp. one with bony walls.
• [Latin from Greek *antron* cave]
• **antral** *adjective* “AN trull”

anuran *noun*
• “a NURE ’n”
• any tailless amphibian of the order Anura, including frogs and toads.
• [modern Latin *Anura* (Greek *an-* without + *oura* tail)]

anvil *noun*
• “AN v’ll”
• a block (usu. of iron) with a flat top, concave

sides, and often a pointed end, on which metals are worked in forging.
• [Old English *anfilte*]

anxiety *noun*
• "ang ZYE a tee"
• the state of being anxious.
• [French *anxieté* or Latin *anxietas -tatis* (as ANXIOUS)]

anxious *adjective*
• "ANK sh'ss"
• worried or troubled; uneasy in the mind.
• [Latin *anxius* from *angere* choke]
• **anxiously** *adverb*
• **anxiousness** *noun*

Anzac *noun*
• "ANZACK"
• a soldier in the Australian and New Zealand Army Corps (1914–18).
• [acronym]

aorist *noun*
• "AY ur ist"
• an unqualified past tense of a verb (esp. in ancient Greek), without reference to duration or completion.
• [Greek *aoristos* indefinite, from *a-* not + *horizō* define, limit]
• **aoristic** *adjective*

aorta *noun*
• "ay ORTA"
• the main artery, giving rise to the arterial network through which oxygenated blood is supplied to the body from the heart.
• [Greek *aortē* from *a(e)irō* raise]
• **aortic** *adjective*

Apache *noun*
• "a PATCH ee"
• a member of an Aboriginal people living in the southwestern US, primarily in Arizona and New Mexico.
• [Latin American Spanish, prob. from Zuñi *Apachu*, lit. 'enemy']

apartheid *noun*
• "a PAR tite" or "a PAR tide"
• the South African policy of segregation and discrimination against non-whites.
• [Afrikaans, = 'apartness']

apathy *noun*
• "AP uth ee"
• lack of interest or feeling; indifference.
• [Greek *apatheia* from *apathēs* without feeling, from *a-* not + *pathos* suffering]
• **apathetic** *adjective* "appa THETTIC"
• **apathetically** *adverb*

apatite *noun*
• "APPA tite"
• a naturally occurring crystalline mineral of calcium phosphate and fluoride, used in the manufacture of fertilizers.
• [German *Apatit* from Greek *apatē* deceit (from its deceptive forms)]
HOMOPHONES: *appetite*

apatosaurus *noun*
• "uh patta SORE us"
• a huge herbivorous dinosaur of the late Jurassic period, with a long neck and tail. Formerly called BRONTOSAURUS.
• [modern Latin from Greek *apatē* deceit + *sauros* lizard]

aperçu *noun*
• "apper SUE"
• a comment or brief reference which makes an illuminating or entertaining point.
• [French, past participle of *apercevoir* perceive]

aperiodic *adjective*
• "ay peery ODDIC"
• not periodic; irregular.
• [Greek *a-* without + PERIODIC]
• **aperiodicity** *noun* "ay peery a DISSA tee"

aperitif *noun*
• "a perra TEEF"
• an alcoholic drink taken before a meal to stimulate the appetite.
• [French *apéritif* from medieval Latin *aperitivus* from Latin *aperire* to open]

aperture *noun*
• "APPER chur"
• an opening; a gap.
• [Latin *apertura* (as APERITIF)]

apetalous *adjective*
• "ay PETTA luss"
• (of flowers) having no petals.
• [Greek *apetalos* leafless, from *a-* not + *petalon* leaf]

apex *noun*
• "AY pecks"
• the highest point.
• [Latin, = peak, tip]

aphasia *noun*
• "a FAY zhuh" or "a FAZEY uh"
• the loss of ability to understand or express speech, owing to brain damage.
• [modern Latin from Greek from *aphatos* speechless, from *a-* not + *pha-* speak]
• **aphasic** *adjective* "a FAY zick"

aphelion *noun*
• "ap HEELY 'n" or "a FEELY 'n"
• the point in a body's orbit where it is furthest from the sun.
• [Greek *aph' hēliou* from the sun]

apheresis *noun*
ALSO SPELLED: **aphaeresis**
• "a FEERA sis" or "a FERRA sis"
• the omission of a letter or syllable at the beginning of a word as a morphological development, e.g. in the derivation of *adder*.
• [Greek *aphairesis* (*apo* from, away, un-, quite + *haireō* take)]

aphesis *noun*
• "AFFA sis"
• the gradual loss of an unstressed vowel at the beginning of a word (e.g. of *e* from *esquire* to form *squire*).
• [Greek, = letting go (*apo* from, away, un-, quite + *hiēmi* send)]
• **aphetic** *adjective* "a FETTIC"
• **aphetically** *adverb*

aphid *noun*
• "AY fid" or "AFF id"
• any small homopterous insect which feeds by sucking sap from leaves, stems, or roots of plants.
• [back-formation from *aphides*, plural of APHIS]

aphis *noun*
• "AY fiss" or "AFF iss"
• an aphid, esp. of the genus *Aphis*.
• [modern Latin from Greek (1523), perhaps a misreading of *koris* bug]

aphorism *noun*
• "AFFER izm"
• a short pithy maxim.
• [Greek *aphorismos* definition, from *aphorizō* (*apo* from, away, un-, quite + *horos* boundary)]
• **aphorist** *noun*
• **aphoristic** *adjective*
• **aphoristically** *adverb*
• **aphorize** *verb* (also esp. *Brit.* **-ise**)

aphrodisiac *adjective*
• "afro DEEZY ack" or "afro DIZZY ack"
• that arouses sexual desire.
• [Greek *aphrodisiakos* from *aphrodisios* from *Aphrodite*, goddess of beauty, fertility, and sexual love]

aphyllous *adjective*
• "a FILLUS"
• (of plants) having no leaves.
• [modern Latin from Greek *aphullos* from *a-* not + *phullon* leaf]

apian *adjective*
• "APE ee 'n"
• of or relating to bees.
• [Latin *apianus* from *apis* bee]

apiary *noun*
• "APE ee airy"
• a place where bees are kept.
• [Latin *apiarium* from *apis* bee]
• **apiarist** *noun* "APE ee a rist"

apical *adjective*
• "APE ick 'll" or "APP ick 'll"
• of, at, or forming an apex.
• [Latin *apex apicis*: see APEX]
• **apically** *adverb*

apiculture *noun*
• "AYPA cull chur"
• beekeeping.
• [Latin *apis* bee, after AGRICULTURE]
• **apicultural** *adjective*
• **apiculturist** *noun*

aplasia *noun*
• "a PLAY zhuh" or "a PLAZEY uh"
• total or partial failure of development of an organ or tissue.
• [modern Latin from Greek from *a-* not + *plasis* formation]
• **aplastic** *adjective* "a PLASTIC"

aplomb *noun*
• "a PLOM"
• assurance; self-confidence.
• [French, = perpendicularity, from *à plomb* according to a plumb line]

apnea *noun*
ALSO SPELLED: esp. *Brit.* **apnoea**
• "AP nee uh"
• a temporary cessation of breathing.
• [Greek *apnoia* from *apnous* breathless]

apocalypse *noun*
• "a POCKA lips"
• catastrophic destruction, esp. the end of the world.
• [Greek *apokalupsis* from *apokaluptō* uncover, reveal]
• **apocalyptic** *adjective*
• **apocalyptically** *adverb*

apocarpous *adjective*
• "appa CARP us"
• (of the ovaries of flowering plants) having distinct carpels not joined together.
• [Greek *apo* from, away, un-, quite + *karpos* fruit]

apochromat *noun*
• "APPA cruh mat"
• a lens or lens system that reduces spherical and chromatic aberrations.
• [Greek *apo* from, away, un-, quite + CHROMATIC]
• **apochromatic** *adjective*

apocope *noun*
• "a POCKA pee"
• the omission of a letter or letters at the end of a word as a morphological development, e.g. in the derivation of *curio*.
• [Greek *apokopē* (*apo* from, away, un-, quite + *koptō* cut)]

apocrine *adjective*
• "APPA crine" or "APPA crin"
• designating or pertaining to glands which lose some of their cytoplasm during secretion, esp. sweat glands opening into hair follicles (as in the armpits and pubic region).
• [Greek *apo* from, away, un-, quite + *krinō* to separate]

apocrypha *plural noun*
• "a POCKRA fuh"
• writings or reports not considered genuine.
• [Church Latin *apocrypha* (*scripta*) hidden writings, from Greek *apokruphos* from *apokruptō* hide away]
• **apocryphal** *adjective*

apodictic *adjective*
• "appa DICTIC"
• clearly demonstrated or established.
• [Latin *apodicticus* from Greek *apodeiktikos* (*apo* from, away, un-, quite + *deiknumi* show)]

apodosis *noun*
• "a PODDA sis"
• the main (consequent) clause of a conditional sentence, e.g. *I would agree* in *if you asked me I would agree.*
• [Late Latin from Greek from *apodidōmi* give back (*apo* from, away, un-, quite + *didōmi* give)]

apogee *noun*
• "APPA jee"
• the point in a celestial body's orbit where it is furthest from the earth.
• [French *apogée* or modern Latin *apogaeum* from Greek *apogeion* away from earth (*apo* from, away, un-, quite + *gē* earth)]
• **apogean** *adjective* "appa JEE 'n"

apolitical *adjective*
• "ay puh LITTA k'll"
• not interested in or concerned with politics.
• [Greek *a-* not + POLITIC]

Apollonian *adjective*
• "appa LONEY 'n"
• of, relating to, or typical of Apollo, the Greek and Roman sun god, patron of music and poetry, esp. as being orderly and rational.

apologia *noun*
• "appa LO jee uh"
• a formal defence of one's opinions or conduct.
• [Latin: see APOLOGY]

apologist *noun*
• "a POLLA jist"
• a person who defends something by argument.
• [French *apologiste* from Greek *apologizomai* render account, from *apologos* account]

apology *noun*
• "a POLLA jee"
• a regretful acknowledgement of an offence or failure.
• [French *apologie* or Late Latin *apologia* from Greek *apologeomai* speak in defence]
• **apologetic** *adjective*
• **apologetically** *adverb*
• **apologize** *verb* (also esp. *Brit.* **-ise**)

apolune *noun*
• "APPA lune"
• the point in a body's lunar orbit where it is furthest from the moon's centre.
• [Greek *apo* from, away, un-, quite + Latin *luna* moon]

apomixis *noun*
• "appa MIX iss"
• asexual reproduction, esp. in a form outwardly resembling a sexual process.
• [modern Latin, formed as Greek *apo* from, away, un-, quite + *mixis* mingling]
• **apomictic** *adjective* "appa MICTIC"

apophthegm *noun*
ALSO SPELLED: **apothegm**
• "APPA themm" (with "TH" as in *THICK*)
• a terse saying or maxim, an aphorism.
• [Greek *apophthegma -matos* from *apophtheggomai* speak out]
• **apophthegmatic** *adjective* (also **apothegmatic**) "appa theg MATTIC"
HOMOPHONES: *apothem*

apoplexy *noun*
• "APPA plexy"
• a sudden loss of consciousness, voluntary movement, and sensation caused by blockage or rupture of a brain artery; a stroke.
• [Old French *apoplexie* from Late Latin *apoplexia* from Greek *apoplēxia* from *apoplēssō* strike completely (*apo* from, away, un-, quite + *plēssō* strike)]
• **apoplectic** *adjective*
• **apoplectically** *adverb*

apoptosis *noun*
• "appa TOE sis" or "ap up TOE sis"
• the death of cells which occurs as a normal and controlled part of an organism's growth or development.
• [Greek *apoptōsis* 'falling off' from *apo* 'from' + *ptōsis* 'falling, a fall']

aporia *noun*
• "a PORY uh"
• the expression of doubt.
• [Late Latin from Greek, from *aporos* impassable]

aposematic *adjective*
• "appa suh MATTIC"
• (of coloration, markings, etc.) serving to warn or repel.
• [Greek *apo* from, away, un-, quite + *sēma sēmatos* sign]

apostasy *noun*
• "a POSSTA see"
• renunciation of a belief or faith, esp. religious.
• [New Testament Greek *apostasia* from *apostasis* defection (*apo* from, away, un-, quite + *stat-* stand)]

apostate *noun*
• "a POSS tate"
• a person who renounces a former belief, adherence, etc.
• [Greek *apostatēs* deserter (as APOSTASY)]
• **apostatize** *verb* (also esp. *Brit.* **-ise**) "a POSSTA tize"

apostle *noun*
• "a POSS'll"
• any of a group of followers of Christ made up of the twelve disciples and Paul and Barnabas,

sent out to preach the gospel after the Resurrection.
• [Greek *apostolos* messenger (*apo* from, away, un-, quite + *stellō* send forth)]
• **apostleship** *noun*
• **apostolate** *noun*
• **apostolic** *adjective* "appa STAW lick"

apostrophe *noun*
• "a POSSTRA fee"
• a punctuation mark used to indicate the omission of letters or numbers, e.g. *can't*; *he's*; *1 Jan. '97.*
• [Greek *apostrophos* accent of elision, from *apostrephō* turn away (*apo* from, away, un-, quite + *strephō* turn)]

apostrophize *verb*
ALSO SPELLED: esp. *Brit.* **-ise**
• "a POSSTRA fize"
• address an exclamatory passage in a speech or poem to a person.
• [as APOSTROPHE]

apothecary *noun*
• "a PAWTH a carry"
• (historically) a person licensed to dispense medicines and drugs.
• [Late Latin *apothecarius* from Latin *apotheca* from Greek *apothēkē* storehouse]

apothem *noun*
• "APPA themm" (with "TH" as in *THICK*)
• a line from the centre of a regular polygon at right angles to any of its sides.
• [Greek *apotithēmi* put aside (*apo* from, away, un-, quite + *tithēmi* place)]
HOMOPHONES: *apophthegm*

apotheosis *noun*
• "a pothy OH sis"
• elevation to divine status; deification.
• [Church Latin from Greek *apotheoō* make a god of (*apo* from, away, un-, quite + *theos* god)]

apotheosize *verb*
ALSO SPELLED: esp. *Brit.* **-ise**
• "a POTHY a size"
• make divine; deify.
• [as APOTHEOSIS]

Appalachian *adjective*
• "appa LAY sh'n"
• of or relating to the Appalachian Mountains in eastern N America, esp. to the upland region extending from Alabama to Pennsylvania.
HOMOPHONES: *appellation*

appall *verb*
ALSO SPELLED: **appal**
• "a PAUL"
• greatly dismay or horrify.
• [Old French *apalir* grow pale]
• **appalling** *adjective*
• **appallingly** *adverb*

Appaloosa *noun*
• "appa LOOSSA"
• a N American breed of horse, having dark spots on a light background.
• [*Opelousas* in Louisiana, or *Palouse*, a river in Idaho]

appanage *noun*
ALSO SPELLED: **apanage**
• "APPA nidge"
• provision for the maintenance of the younger children of kings etc.
• [French, ultimately from medieval Latin *appanare* endow with the means of subsistence (Greek *apo* from, away, un-, quite + Latin *panis* bread)]

apparat *noun*
• "appa RAT"
• the administrative system of a Communist party, esp. in a Communist country.
• [Russian from German, = apparatus]

apparatchik *noun*
• "appa RAT chick"
• a member of a Communist apparat.
• [Russian: see APPARAT]

apparatus *noun*
• "appa RAT us" or "appa RATE us"
• the equipment needed for a particular purpose or function, esp. scientific or technical.
• [Latin from *apparare apparat-* make ready for]

apparel *noun*
• "a PAIR'll"
• clothing, dress.
• [Old French *apareillier* (v.) from Romanic *appariculare* (unrecorded) make equal or fit, ultimately from Latin *par* equal]

apparent *adjective*
• "a PARE 'nt"
• readily visible or perceivable.
• [Old French *aparant* from Latin (as APPEAR)]

apparently *adverb*
• "a PARENT lee"
• clearly, plainly.
• [as APPARENT]

apparition *noun*
• "appa RISH'n"
• a sudden or dramatic appearance, esp. of a ghost or phantom.
• [Latin *apparitio* attendance (as APPEAR)]

appeal *verb*
• "a PEEL"
• make an earnest or formal request; plead.
• [Old French *apel*, *apeler* from Latin *appellare* to address]

appealable *adjective*
• "a PEELA bull"
• (of a case) that can be referred to a higher court for review.
• [as APPEAL]

appealing *adjective*
• "a PEELING"
• attractive, likeable.

- [as APPEAL]
- **appealingly** *adverb*

appear *verb*
- "a PEER"
- become or be visible.
- [Latin *apparēre* to come in sight]
- **appearance** *noun*

appease *verb*
- "a PEEZ"
- make calm or quiet, esp. conciliate (a potential aggressor) by making concessions.
- [Old French *apaisier* from *à* to + *pais* peace]
- **appeasement** *noun*
- **appeaser** *noun*

appellant *noun*
- "a PELL'nt"
- a person who appeals to a higher court.
- [French (as APPEAL)]

appellate *adjective*
- "a PELLET"
- (esp. of a court) concerned with or dealing with appeals.
- [Latin *appellatus* (as APPEAL)]

appellation *noun*
- "appa LAY sh'n"
- a name or title; nomenclature.
- [Latin *appellatio -onis* (as APPEAL)]

HOMOPHONES: *Appalachian*

appellative *adjective*
- "a PELLA tiv"
- naming.
- [Late Latin *appellativus* (as APPEAL)]

append *verb*
- "a PEND"
- attach, affix, add, esp. to a written document etc.
- [Latin *appendere* hang]

appendage *noun*
- "a PEN didge"
- a thing that is added or attached to something larger or more important.
- [as APPEND]

appendectomy *noun*
- "appen DECTA mee"
- the surgical removal of the appendix.
- [as APPENDIX + Greek *ektomē* excision, from *ek* out + *temnō* cut]

appendicitis *noun*
- "a penda SITE iss"
- inflammation of the appendix.
- [as APPENDIX + Greek *-itis*, forming feminine of adjectives in *-itēs* (with *nosos* 'disease' implied)]

appendix *noun*
- "a PENDIX"
- a small outgrowth of tissue forming a tube-shaped sac attached to the lower end of the large intestine.
- [Latin *appendix -icis* from *appendere* APPEND]

apperceive *verb*
- "apper SEEVE"
- be conscious of perceiving.
- [Old French *aperceveir*, ultimately from Latin *percipere* PERCEIVE]
- **apperception** *noun* "apper SEP sh'n"
- **apperceptive** *adjective* "apper SEPTIV"

appertain *verb*
- "apper TANE"
- pertain.
- [Old French *apertenir* from Late Latin *appertinēre* from *pertinēre* PERTAIN]

appetite *noun*
- "APPA tite"
- a desire for food.
- [Latin *appetitus* from *appetere* seek after]
- **appetitive** *adjective* "a PETTA tiv"

HOMOPHONES: *apatite*

appetizer *noun*

ALSO SPELLED: esp. *Brit.* **-iser**
- "APPA tizer"
- a small amount of food or drink which stimulates the appetite before a meal.
- [as APPETITE]

appetizing *adjective*

ALSO SPELLED: esp. *Brit.* **-ising**
- "APPA tize ing"
- pleasing; stimulating an appetite, esp. for food.
- [French *appétissant* from *appétit*, formed as APPETITE]
- **appetizingly** *adverb* (also esp. *Brit.* **-isingly**)

applaud *verb*
- "a PLOD"
- to clap as an expression of strong approval or praise.
- [Latin *applaudere applaus-* clap hands]

applause *noun*
- "a PLOZZ"
- clapping etc. as an expression of approbation.
- [medieval Latin *applausus* (as APPLAUD)]

applet *noun*
- "APP let"
- a very small application, esp. a utility program performing one or a few simple functions within a larger program.
- [blend of APPLICATION + diminutive suffix '-let']

appliance *noun*
- "a PLY ince"
- an electrical or gas-powered device or piece of equipment used for a specific task, esp. for domestic tasks such as washing dishes etc.
- [as APPLY]

applicable *adjective*
- "a PLICKA bull" or "APPLA kuh bull"
- that may be applied.
- [medieval Latin *applicabilis* (as APPLY)]

- **applicability** *noun*
- **applicably** *adverb*

applicator *noun*
- "APP lick ater"
- a device for applying a substance to a surface.
- [as APPLY]

applied *adjective*
- "a PLIDE"
- (of a subject of study) put to practical use as opposed to being theoretical.
- [as APPLY]

appliqué *noun*
- "APPLA cay"
- ornamental work in which fabric is cut out and attached, usu. sewn, to the surface of another fabric to form pictures or patterns.
- [French, past participle of *appliquer* apply, from Latin *applicare*: see APPLY]

apply *verb*
- "a PLY"
- make a formal request for something to be done.
- [Old French *aplier* from Latin *applicare* fold, fasten to]
- **applicant** *noun*
- **application** *noun*

appoggiatura *noun*
- "a podge a TURA"
- a grace note performed before, and normally taking half the time value of, an essential note of a melody.
- [Italian, from *appoggiare* lean upon, rest]

appoint *verb*
- "a POINT"
- assign a post or office to.
- [Old French *apointer* from *à point* to a point]
- **appointee** *noun*
- **appointer** *noun*

appointed *adjective*
- "a POINTED"
- equipped, furnished.
- [as APPOINT]

appointive *adjective*
- "a POINT iv"
- depending on or filled by appointment.
- [as APPOINT]

appointment *noun*
- "a POINT m'nt"
- an arrangement to meet at a specific time and place.
- [as APPOINT]

apportion *verb*
- "a POR sh'n"
- share out; assign as a share.
- [medieval Latin *apportionare* (*ad-* to + *portio -onis* portion)]
- **apportionable** *adjective*
- **apportionment** *noun*

apposite *adjective*
- "APPA zit"
- apt; well chosen.
- [Latin *appositus* past participle of *apponere* (*ad-* to + *ponere* put)]
- **appositely** *adverb*
- **appositeness** *noun*

apposition *noun*
- "appa ZISH'n"
- placing side by side; juxtaposition.
- [as APPOSITE]
- **appositive** *adjective* "a POZZA tiv"

appraise *verb*
- "a PRAZE"
- estimate the quality or worth of.
- [Old French *aprisier* from *à* to + *pris* price, by assimilation to 'praise']
- **appraisable** *adjective*
- **appraisal** *noun*
- **appraiser** *noun*
- **appraisingly** *adverb*

appreciable *adjective*
- "a PREESHA bull"
- large enough to be noticed; significant; considerable.
- [as APPRECIATE]
- **appreciably** *adverb*

appreciate *verb*
- "a PREESHY ate"
- esteem highly; be grateful for.
- [Late Latin *appretiare* appraise (*ad-* to + *pretium* price)]
- **appreciation** *noun*
- **appreciative** *adjective* "a PREESHA tiv"
- **appreciatively** *adverb*
- **appreciator** *noun*
- **appreciatory** *adjective* "a PREESHY a tory"

apprehend *verb*
- "appree HEND"
- understand, perceive.
- [French *appréhender* or Latin *apprehendere* (*ad-* to + *prehendere prehens-* lay hold of)]
- **apprehensible** *adjective*

apprehension *noun*
- "appree HEN sh'n"
- uneasiness; dread.
- [as APPREHEND]
- **apprehensive** *adjective*
- **apprehensively** *adverb*
- **apprehensiveness** *noun*

apprentice *noun*
- "a PRENTISS"
- a person who is learning a trade by being employed in it for an agreed period, usu. at lower wages than is normal for that trade.
- [Old French *aprentis* from *apprendre* learn (as APPREHEND)]
- **apprenticeship** *noun*

apprise *verb*
- "a PRIZE"
- inform.

• [French *appris -ise* past participle of *apprendre* learn, teach (as APPREHEND)]
HOMOPHONES: *apprize*

approach *verb*
• "a PROACH"
• come near or nearer to (a place or time).
• [Old French *aproch(i)er* from Church Latin *appropiare* draw near (*ad-* to + *propius* comparative of *prope* near)]

approachable *adjective*
• "a PROACH a bull"
• friendly; easy to talk to.
• [as APPROACH]
• **approachability** *noun*

approbation *noun*
• "appro BAY sh'n"
• approval, consent.
• [Latin *approbatio -onis* (*ad-* to + *probare* test from *probus* good)]
• **approbatory** *adjective* "a PROBE a tory"

appropriate[1] *adjective*
• "a PRO pree it"
• suitable or proper.
• [Late Latin *appropriatus* past participle of *appropriare* (*ad-* to + *proprius* own)]
• **appropriately** *adverb*
• **appropriateness** *noun*

appropriate[2] *verb*
• "a PRO pree ate"
• take possession of, esp. without authority.
• [Late Latin *appropriatus* past participle of *appropriare* (*ad-* to + *proprius* own)]
• **appropriation** *noun*
• **appropriator** *noun*

approve *verb*
• "a PROOVE"
• confirm; declare acceptable.
• [Old French *aprover* from Latin (as APPROBATION)]
• **approval** *noun*
• **approving** *adjective*
• **approvingly** *adverb*

approximate[1] *adjective*
• "a PROXA mit"
• fairly correct or accurate; near to the actual.
• [Late Latin *approximatus* past participle of *approximare* (*ad-* to + *proximus* very near)]
• **approximately** *adverb*

approximate[2] *verb*
• "a proxa MATE"
• estimate.
• [as APPROXIMATE[1]]
• **approximation** *noun*

appurtenance *noun*
• "a PURT'n ince"
• a belonging; an appendage; an accessory.
• [Old French *apertenance* (as APPERTAIN)]

appurtenant *adjective*
• "a PURT'n 'nt"
• belonging or appertaining; pertinent.
• [Old French *apartenant* present participle (as APPERTAIN)]

apricot *noun*
• "APPRA cot"
• a juicy soft fruit, similar to but smaller than a peach, of an orange-yellow colour.
• [Portuguese *albricoque* or Spanish *albaricoque* from Arabic *al* the + *barkuk* from late Greek *praikokion* from Latin *praecoquum* var. of *praecox* early-ripe: *apri-* after Latin *apricus* ripe, *-cot* by assimilation to French *abricot*]

apropos *adjective*
• "appra POE"
• to the point or purpose; appropriate.
• [French *à propos* from *à* to + *propos* PURPOSE]

apse *noun*
• "APS"
• a large semicircular or polygonal recess, arched or with a domed roof, esp. at the eastern end of a church.
• [Latin APSIS]

apsis *noun*
• "AP sis"
• a point in the orbit of a planet or other satellite which is either closest to or farthest from the object around which it moves.
• [Latin from Greek *(h)apsis, -idos* arch, vault]
• **apsidal** *adjective* "APP sid 'll"

apterous *adjective*
• "APTER us"
• (of insects) without wings.
• [Greek *apteros* from *a-* not + *pteron* wing]

apteryx *noun*
• "APTER ix"
• the former name for the kiwi.
• [Greek *a-* not + *pterux* wing]

aptitude *noun*
• "APTA tude"
• a natural propensity or talent.
• [Late Latin *aptitudo -inis* from *aptus* fitted, past participle of *apere* fasten]

aqua *noun*
• "ACKWA" or "OCKWA"
• the colour aquamarine.
• [abbreviation]

aquaculture *noun*
• "ACKWA cull chur" or "OCKWA cull chur"
• the cultivation or rearing of fish or aquatic plants for human consumption.
• [Latin *aqua* water + CULTURE, after *agriculture*]
• **aquaculturist** *noun*

aquafit *noun*
• "ACKWA fit" or "OCKWA fit"
• an exercise class conducted in water, often to music.
• [Latin *aqua* water + 'fit']

aquamarine *noun*
- "ackwa muh REEN" or "ockwa muh REEN"
- a light bluish-green.
- [Latin *aqua marina* sea water]

aquanaut *noun*
- "ACKWA not" or "OCKWA not"
- an underwater swimmer or explorer, esp. one working for an extended period in a bathysphere.
- [Latin *aqua* water + Greek *nautēs* sailor]

aquaplane *noun*
- "ACKWA plane" or "OCKWA plane"
- a board for riding on the water, pulled by a speedboat.
- [Latin *aqua* water + *planum* flat surface]

aquarelle *noun*
- "ackwa RELL" or "ockwa RELL"
- a painting in thin, usu. transparent watercolours.
- [French from Italian *acquarella* watercolour, diminutive of *acqua* from Latin *aqua* water]

aquarist *noun*
- "a KWARE ist"
- a person who keeps an aquarium.
- [as AQUARIUM]

aquarium *noun*
- "a KWERRY um"
- a tank of water with transparent sides containing fish or other live aquatic animals and plants.
- [neuter of Latin *aquarius* of water (*aqua*)]

Aquarius *noun*
- "a KWERRY us"
- the eleventh sign of the zodiac.
- [Latin *aquarius* of water (*aqua*)]
- **Aquarian** *adjective*

aquatic *adjective*
- "a KWOTTIC"
- of or relating to water.
- [Latin *aquaticus* from *aqua* water]

aquatint *noun*
- "ACKWA tint" or "OCKWA tint"
- a print resembling a watercolour, produced from a copper plate etched with nitric acid.
- [Italian *acqua tinta* coloured water]

aquavit *noun*
- "ACKWA vit" or "OCKWA vit" or "ACKWA veet"
- an alcoholic spirit made from potatoes etc., usu. flavoured with caraway seeds.
- [Scandinavian *akvavit* from Latin *aqua vitae* water of life]

aqueduct *noun*
- "ACKWA duct"
- an artificial channel for conveying water, esp. in the form of a bridge supported by tall columns across a valley.
- [Latin *aquae ductus* conduit, from *aqua* water + *ducere duct-* to lead]

aqueous *adjective*
- "AKE wee us" or "ACK wee us"
- of, containing, or like water.
- [medieval Latin *aqueus* from Latin *aqua* water]

aquifer *noun*
- "ACKWA fur"
- a layer of permeable rock able to store significant quantities of water, through which groundwater moves.
- [Latin *aqui-* from *aqua* water + *-fer* bearing, from *ferre* bear]

aquilegia *noun*
- "ackwa LEE juh"
- the columbine flower.
- [modern use of a medieval Latin word: origin unknown]

aquiline *adjective*
- "ACKWA line"
- of or like an eagle.
- [Latin *aquilinus* from *aquila* eagle]

aquiver *adverb*
- "a KWIVVER"
- trembling, quivering with excitement.
- [as QUIVER]

arabesque *noun*
- "air a BESK"
- a posture in dance and figure skating with one leg extended straight backwards and usu. elevated.
- [French from Italian *arabesco* from *arabo* Arab]

Arabian *adjective*
- "a RAY bee 'n"
- of or relating to Arabia, a large peninsula of SW Asia.

arabica *noun*
- "a RABBA kuh"
- coffee or coffee beans from the most widely grown species of coffee plant, *Coffea arabica*.
- [modern Latin from Latin *arabicus* Arabic]

arabidopsis *noun*
- "a rabba DOP sis"
- a cruciferous plant much used in genetic research.
- [from ARABIS + Greek *opsis* appearance]

arabis *noun*
- "AIR a biss"
- any plant of the genus *Arabis*, often mat-forming and grown in rock gardens.
- [medieval Latin from Greek, = Arabian]

arable *adjective*
- "AIR a bull"
- (of land) plowed, or suitable for plowing and crop production.
- [Latin *arabilis* from *arare* to plow]

arachidonic *adjective*
- "a racka DONNIC"
- designating a polyunsaturated fatty acid present in animal fats. It is important in

metabolism, esp. in the synthesis of prostaglandins and leukotrienes, and is an essential constituent of the diet.
• [formed irregularly from *arachidic* (a saturated fatty acid) from modern Latin *arachis*, from Greek *arak(h)os*, *-kis*, a leguminous plant]

arachnid *noun*
• "a RACK nid"
• any arthropod of the class Arachnida, having four pairs of walking legs and characterized by simple eyes, e.g. spiders, scorpions, mites, and ticks.
• [modern Latin *arachnida* from Greek *arakhnē* spider]
• **arachnidan** *adjective*

arachnoid *noun*
• "a RACK noid"
• one of the three membranes that surround the brain and spinal cord of vertebrates.
• [modern Latin *arachnoides* from Greek *arakhnoeidēs* like a cobweb, from *arakhnē*: see ARACHNID]

arachnophobia *noun*
• "a rackna FOBEY uh"
• an abnormal fear of spiders.
• [modern Latin from Greek *arakhne* spider + PHOBIA]
• **arachnophobe** *noun*

Aragonese *noun*
• "air a guh NEEZ"
• a native or inhabitant of Aragon in NE Spain.

aragonite *noun*
• "a RAGGA nite"
• a form of calcium carbonate, harder and denser than calcite, occurring around hot springs and geysers, in pearls, and in the shells of molluscs.
• [*Aragon* in NE Spain, where first found, + Greek *lithos* stone]

arak *noun*
ALSO SPELLED: **arrack**
• "a RACK" or "ERRIC"
• a Middle Eastern alcoholic spirit, esp. distilled from coco sap or rice.
• [Arabic *'araḳ* sweat, alcoholic spirit from grapes or dates]

Aramaic *noun*
• "air a MAY ick"
• a branch of the Semitic family of languages, esp. the language of Syria used as a lingua franca in the Near East from the 6th c. BC, later dividing into varieties one of which included Syriac and Mandaean.
• [Latin *Aramaeus* from Greek *Aramaios* of Aram (Biblical name of Syria)]

Aran *adjective*
• "AIR 'n"
• designating a type of thick knitwear with cable patterns and large diamond designs.
• [the *Aran* Islands off the west coast of Ireland, where the design was first devised]

Arapaho *noun*
ALSO SPELLED: **Arapahoe**
• "a RAPPA hoe"
• a member of an Aboriginal people of the Great Plains, now living mainly in Wyoming and Oklahoma.
• [Crow *alappahó*, lit. 'many tattoo marks']

Araucanian *noun*
• "air a CAY nee 'n"
• a member of an Aboriginal people of central Chile and adjacent regions of Argentina.
• [*Araucanía*, a region of Chile]

araucaria *noun*
• "air a KERRY uh"
• any evergreen conifer of the genus *Araucaria*, e.g. the Norfolk Island pine and the monkey-puzzle tree, originally from S America and Australasia.
• [*Arauco* a province in Chile]

Arawak *noun*
• "AIR a wack"
• a member of the Aboriginal peoples of the Greater Antilles and northern and western S America, speaking languages of the same linguistic family, forced out of the Antilles by the Carib Indians shortly before the Spanish expansion into the Caribbean.
• [Carib *aruac*]
• **Arawakan** *adjective* "air a WACK 'n"

arbalest *noun*
• "ARBA lest"
• a large, powerful medieval crossbow with a winch and pulley mechanism for drawing the string, capable of firing stones or bolts.
• [Old French *arbaleste* from Late Latin *arcubalista* from *arcus* bow + BALLISTA]

arbiter *noun*
• "ARBA tur"
• a person who settles a dispute or has ultimate authority in a matter.
• [Latin, = judge]

arbitrage *noun*
• "ARBA trozh" or "ARBA tridge"
• the buying and selling of stocks or bills of exchange to take advantage of varying prices in different markets.
• [French from *arbitrer* (as ARBITER)]
• **arbitrageur** *noun* "arba truh ZHUR"

arbitrament *noun*
• "ar BITTRA m'nt"
• the deciding of a dispute by an arbitrator.
• [medieval Latin *arbitramentum* (as ARBITER)]

arbitrary *adjective*
• "ARBA trerry"
• based on the unrestricted will of a person, not according to a scheme or plan; capricious.

• [Latin *arbitrarius* or French *arbitraire* (as ARBITER)]
• **arbitrarily** *adverb*
• **arbitrariness** *noun*

arbitration *noun*
• “arba TRAY sh’n”
• the hearing and resolution of a dispute by a referee, usu. chosen and agreed upon by all disputants, who has the power to impose a settlement.
• [Latin *arbitratio -onis* (as ARBITER)]
• **arbitral** *adjective*
• **arbitrate** *verb*
• **arbitrator** *noun*
• **arbitratorship** *noun*

arbor *noun*
• “ARBER”
• an axle or spindle on which something rotates, e.g. one holding a cutter in machine tooling.
• [French *arbre* tree, axis, from Latin *arbor*: refashioned on Latin]
HOMOPHONES: *arbour*

arboreal *adjective*
• “ar BORRY ’ll”
• of, living in, or pertaining to trees.
• [Latin *arboreus* from *arbor* tree]

arboreous *adjective*
• “ar BORRY us”
• wooded.
• [as ARBOREAL]

arborescent *adjective*
• “arber ESS’nt”
• treelike in growth or general appearance.
• [Latin *arborescere* grow into a tree (*arbor*)]
• **arborescence** *noun*

arboretum *noun*
• “arber EAT’m”
• a botanical garden devoted to trees.
• [Latin from *arbor* tree]

arboriculture *noun*
• “ar BORA cull chur”
• the cultivation of trees and shrubs.
• [Latin *arbor -oris* tree, after *agriculture*]
• **arboricultural** *adjective*
• **arboriculturist** *noun*

arborio *noun*
• “ar BORY oh”
• a plump, short-grained rice, sticky when cooked, often used in risotto and other Italian dishes.
• [Italian]

arborist *noun*
• “ARBER ist”
• a person who studies or cultivates trees.
• [Latin *arbor* tree]

arborization *noun*
ALSO SPELLED: esp. *Brit.* **-isation**
• “arber ize AY sh’n”
• a treelike arrangement, esp. in anatomy or geology.
• [Latin *arbor* tree]

arborvitae *noun*
• “arber VEE tie” or “arber VITE ee”
• any of the evergreen conifers of the genus *Thuja*, including the eastern white cedar and the western red cedar, native to N America and N Asia, usu. of columnar habit with flattened shoots bearing scale leaves.
• [Latin, = tree of life]

arbour *noun*
ALSO SPELLED: **arbor**
• “ARBER”
• a shady garden alcove with the sides and roof formed by trees or climbing plants; a bower.
• [Anglo-French *erber* from Old French *erbier* from *erbe* herb, from Latin *herba*: phonetic change to *ar-* assisted by association with Latin *arbor* tree]
• **arboured** *adjective* (also **arbored**)
HOMOPHONES: *arbor*

arbutus *noun*
• “ar BYOO tuss”
• any evergreen tree or shrub of the genus *Arbutus*, having dark green leaves and clusters of small, fragrant, bell-shaped flowers, esp.: *A. menziesii*, native to the Pacific coast of N America, with peeling red bark, the only broadleaf evergreen tree native to Canada.
• [Latin]

arc *noun*
• “ARK”
• part of the circumference of a circle or any other curve.
• [Latin *arcus* bow, curve]
HOMOPHONES: *ark*

arcade *noun*
• “ar CADE”
• a series of arches supporting or set along a wall.
• [French from Provençal *arcada* or Italian *arcata* from Romanic: related to ARC]
• **arcaded** *adjective*

Arcadian *noun*
• “ar CAY dee ’n”
• an idealized peasant or country dweller, esp. in poetry.
• [*Arcadia* a mountainous district in southern Greece, representing in poetry a pastoral paradise]
• **Arcadianism** *noun*

arcana *noun*
• “ar CAY nuh”
• mysteries or secrets.
• [Latin neuter plural of *arcanus*: see ARCANE]

arcane *adjective*
• “ar CANE”
• mysterious, secret; understood by few.

• [Latin *arcanus* from *arcēre* shut up, from *arca* chest]
• **arcanely** *adverb*

archaeology *noun*
ALSO SPELLED: **archeology**
• "arky OLLA jee"
• the study of human history and prehistory through the excavation of sites and the analysis of physical remains.
• [modern Latin *archaeologia* from Greek *arkhaiologia* ancient history, from Greek *arkhaios* ancient, from *arkhē* beginning + *logos* word]
• **archaeologic** *adjective* (also **archeologic**) "arky a LODGE ick"
• **archaeological** *adjective* (also **archeological**)
• **archaeologist** *noun* (also **archeologist**)
• **archaeologize** *verb* (also **archeologize**) (also esp. *Brit.* **archaeologise**)

archaeopteryx *noun*
• "arky OPTER ix"
• the oldest known fossil bird, *Archaeopteryx lithographica*, from the Jurassic period, with teeth, feathers, and a reptilian tail.
• [Greek *arkhaios* ancient + *pterux* wing]

archaic *adjective*
• "ar CAY ick"
• antiquated.
• [French *archaïque* from Greek *arkhaïkos* from *arkhaios* ancient, from *arkhē* beginning]
• **archaically** *adverb*

archaism *noun*
• "AR cay izm"
• the retention or imitation of the old or obsolete, esp. in language or art.
• [as ARCHAIC]
• **archaistic** *adjective*

archaize *verb*
ALSO SPELLED: esp. *Brit.* **-ise**
• "AR cay ize"
• imitate the archaic.
• [Greek *arkhaïzō* be old-fashioned, from *arkhaios* ancient]

archangel *noun*
• "ARK ane j'll"
• an angel of the highest rank.
• [Church Latin *archangelus* from ecclesiastical Greek *arkhaggelos* (from *arkhos* chief + *aggelos* messenger)]
• **archangelic** *adjective* "ark an JELLIC"

archbishopric *noun*
• "arch BISHOP rick"
• the office or diocese of an archbishop.
• [Church Latin *arch-* (from Greek *arkhos* chief) + BISHOPRIC]

archdeacon *noun*
• "ARCH deek'n"
• an Anglican cleric ranking below a bishop, or a member of the clergy of similar rank in other Churches.
• [Church Latin *arch-* (from Greek *arkhos* chief) + DEACON]
• **archdeaconry** *noun*
• **archdeaconship** *noun*
• **archidiaconal** *adjective* "arka die ACKA n'll"

archdiocese *noun*
• "arch DIE a sis" or "arch DIE a seez" or "arch DIE a seece"
• the diocese of an archbishop.
• [Church Latin *arch-* (from Greek *arkhos* chief) + DIOCESE]
• **archdiocesan** *adjective* "arch die OSSA s'n" or "arch die OSSA z'n"

archduchess *noun*
• "arch DUTCH iss"
• (historically) a daughter or daughter-in-law of the Emperor of Austria.
• [*arch-* (via Latin from Greek *arkhos* chief) + DUCHESS]

Archean *adjective*
ALSO SPELLED: **Archaean**
• "ar KEE 'n"
• of or relating to the earlier part of the Precambrian era, from about 4 billion to 2.5 billion years ago.
• [Greek *arkhaios* ancient, from *arkhē* beginning]

archegonium *noun*
• "arka GO nee um"
• the female sex organ in mosses, ferns, conifers, etc.
• [Latin, diminutive of Greek *arkhegonos* from *arkhe-* chief + *gonos* race]

Archeozoic *adjective*
ALSO SPELLED: **Archaeozoic**
• "arky a ZO ick"
• of or relating to the earlier part of the Precambrian era, from about 4 billion to 2.5 billion years ago.
• [as ARCHEAN + Greek *zōion* animal]

archeparch *noun*
• "arch EPP ark"
• an archbishop in an Eastern-rite Church.
• [Greek *arkhe-* chief + EPARCH]
• **archeparchy** *noun* "arch EPPER kee"

archetype *noun*
• "ARKA tipe"
• an original model; a prototype.
• [Latin *archetypum* from Greek *arkhetupon* (*arkhe-* chief + *tupos* stamp)]
• **archetypal** *adjective*
• **archetypical** *adjective*

archiepiscopal *adjective*
• "arky ep PISKA p'll"
• of or relating to an archbishop.
• [Church Latin *archiepiscopus* from Greek *arkhiepiskopos* archbishop]
• **archiepiscopate** *noun* "arky ep PISKA pit" or "arky ep PISSKA pate"

archimandrite *noun*
• "arka MAN drite"
• the superior of a large monastery or group of monasteries in the Orthodox Church.
• [ecclesiastical Greek *arkhimandritēs* (*arkhe-* chief + *mandra* monastery)]

Archimedean *adjective*
• "arka MEEDY 'n"
• of or relating to the Greek mathematician and inventor Archimedes (*c.*287–212 BC).

archipelago *noun*
• "arka PELLA go"
• a group of islands.
• [Italian *arcipelago* from Greek *arkhi-* chief + *pelagos* sea (originally = the Aegean Sea)]

architect *noun*
• "ARKA tect"
• a person who designs buildings and supervises their construction.
• [Latin *architectus* from Greek *arkhitektōn* (*arkhe-* chief + *tektōn* builder)]

architectonic *adjective*
• "arka teck TONNIC"
• of or relating to architecture; suggesting architectural design or structure.
• [Greek *arkhitektonikos* (as ARCHITECT)]

architecture *noun*
• "ARKA teck chur"
• the art or science of designing and constructing buildings.
• [Latin *architectura* from *architectus* ARCHITECT]
• **architectural** *adjective*
• **architecturally** *adverb*

architrave *noun*
• "ARKA trave"
• (in classical architecture) a main beam resting across the tops of columns.
• [French from Italian (Greek *arkhe-* chief + Latin *trabs trabis* beam)]

archive *noun*
• "AR kive"
• a collection of public, corporate or institutional documents or records.
• [French *archives* (pl.) from Latin *archi(v)a* from Greek *arkheia* public records, from *arkhē* government]
• **archival** *adjective*
• **archivist** *noun* "ARKA vist"

archivolt *noun*
• "ARKA volt"
• a band of mouldings around the lower curve of an arch.
• [French *archivolte* or Italian *archivolto* (as ARC, VAULT)]

archon *noun*
• "AR con" or "ARK'n"
• each of the nine chief magistrates in ancient Athens.
• [Greek *arkhōn* ruler, = present participle of *arkhō* rule]
• **archonship** *noun*

arco *adverb*
• "ARCO"
• using a bow to sound the strings of a violin, double bass, etc.
• [Italian *arco* bow]

Arctic *noun*
• "ARK tick" or "AR tick"
• the area north of the Arctic Circle.
• [Old French *artique* from Latin *ar(c)ticus* from Greek *arktikos* from *arktos* bear, the Big Dipper]

arcuate *adjective*
• "AR kyoo it" or "AR kyoo ate"
• shaped like a bow; curved.
• [Latin *arcuatus* past participle of *arcuare* curve, from *arcus* bow, curve]

ardent *adjective*
• "ARD'nt"
• zealous, eager; (of persons or feelings) fervent, passionate.
• [Old French *ardant* from Latin *ardens -entis* from *ardēre* burn]
• **ardently** *adverb*

ardour *noun*
ALSO SPELLED: **ardor**
• "ARDER"
• zeal, burning enthusiasm, passion.
• [Latin *ardor -oris* from *ardēre* burn]

arduous *adjective*
• "AR joo us" or "ARD yoo us"
• hard to achieve, overcome or endure; laborious, strenuous.
• [Latin *arduus* steep, difficult]
• **arduously** *adverb*
• **arduousness** *noun*

are *noun*
• "AIR"
• a metric unit of measure, one-hundredth of a hectare, equal to 100 square metres.
• [French from Latin AREA]
HOMOPHONES: *air, err, ere, heir*

area *noun*
• "AIRY uh"
• a region.
• [Latin *area*]
HOMOPHONES: *aria*

areal *noun*
• "AIRY 'll"
• pertaining to an area.
• [as AREA]
HOMOPHONES: *aerial*

areca *noun*
• "A ruh kuh" or "a REEKA"
• any tropical palm of the genus *Areca*, native to Asia.
• [Portuguese from Malayalam *áḍekka*]

arenaceous *adjective*
- "air a NAY sh'ss"
- (of rocks) containing sand; having a sandy texture.
- [Latin *arenaceus* from *arena* sand + adjective suffix *-aceus* of the nature of]

areola *noun*
- "a REE a luh"
- a circular pigmented area, esp. that surrounding a nipple.
- [Latin, diminutive of *area* AREA]
- **areolar** *adjective*

arête *noun*
- "a RET"
- a sharp narrow mountain ridge formed by the meeting of adjacent glacial valleys.
- [French from Latin *arista* ear of corn, fishbone, spine]

argali *noun*
- "ARGA lee"
- a large Asiatic wild sheep, *Ovis ammon*, with massive horns.
- [Mongol]

argent *noun*
- "AR j'nt"
- silver; silvery white.
- [French from Latin *argentum*]

argentiferous *adjective*
- "arj'n TIFFER us"
- containing natural deposits of silver.
- [Latin *argentum* + *-fer* producing, from *ferre* bear]

argentine *adjective*
- "ARJ'n tine" or "ARJ'n teen"
- of silver; silvery.
- [French *argentin* from *argent* silver]

Argentinian *noun*
- "arj'n TINNY 'n"
- a native or inhabitant of Argentina.

argil *noun*
- "ARJ'll"
- clay, esp. that used in pottery.
- [ultimately from Greek *argillos* from *argos* white]
- **argillaceous** *adjective* "arj a LAY sh'ss"

argillite *noun*
- "ARJA lite"
- a metamorphic rock of a softness between shale and slate, used in Haida sculpture.
- [Latin *argilla* clay + Greek *lithos* stone]

arginine *noun*
- "ARJA neen" or "ARJA nine"
- an amino acid present in many animal proteins and an essential nutrient in the vertebrate diet.
- [German *Arginin*, of uncertain origin]

Argive *adjective*
- "ARG ive"
- of Argos in ancient Greece.
- [Latin *Argivus* from Greek *Argeios*]

argosy *noun*
- "ARGA see"
- a large merchant ship.
- [prob. from Italian *Ragusea (nave)* vessel from Ragusa (now Dubrovnik, Croatia) or Venice]

argot *noun*
- "ARGO" or "AR git"
- the jargon of a group or class, formerly esp. of criminals.
- [French: origin unknown]

arguable *adjective*
- "ARG yoo a bull"
- capable of being argued.
- [Old French *arguer* from Latin *argutari* prattle, frequentative of *arguere* make clear, prove, accuse]
- **arguably** *adverb*

argument *noun*
- "ARG yoo m'nt"
- an exchange of views, esp. a contentious or prolonged one.
- [as ARGUABLE]
- **argumentative** *adjective* "arg yoo MENTA tiv"
- **argumentatively** *adverb*
- **argumentativeness** *noun*

argumentation *noun*
- "arg yoo m'n TAY sh'n"
- methodical reasoning.
- [as ARGUABLE]

argus *noun*
- "AR guss"
- a watchful guardian.
- [Latin from Greek *Argos*, the name of a mythological watchman with many eyes]

argyle *adjective*
ALSO SPELLED: **argyll**
- "ARG ile"
- designating a knitting pattern with diamonds of various colours on a single background colour.
- [*Argyll* branch of the Campbell clan (in Scotland), on whose tartan the pattern is based]

aria *noun*
- "ARRY uh" or "AIRY uh"
- a long, accompanied song for solo voice in an opera, oratorio, etc.
- [Italian, from Latin *aer* air]

HOMOPHONES: *area*

Arian *noun*
- "AIRY 'n"
- an adherent of the doctrines of Arius (4th c.), who denied the divinity of Christ.
- **Arianism** *noun*

HOMOPHONES: *Aryan*

arietta *noun*
- "arry ETTA" or "airy ETTA"
- a shorter and simpler aria.
- [Italian]

Arikara *noun*
- "a RICKA ruh"
- a member of an Aboriginal people of the Great Plains, living mainly in N and S Dakota.
- [origin uncertain, possibly = 'horn', referring to a traditional hairstyle]

aril *noun*
- "A rill"
- an extra seed covering, often coloured and hairy or fleshy, e.g. the outer covering of the nutmeg which yields mace.
- [modern Latin *arillus*: compare medieval Latin *arilli* dried grape pits]
- **arillate** *adjective* "A rill it" or "A rill ate"

HOMOPHONES: *aryl*

arioso *noun*
- "arry OH so" or "airy OH so"
- a recitative with expressive qualities similar to those of an aria.
- [Italian]

aristocracy *noun*
- "air iss TOCKRA see"
- the highest class in society; the nobility.
- [Greek *aristokratia* from *aristos* best + *kratia* from *kratos* strength, power]
- **aristocrat** *noun* "a RISTA crat"
- **aristocratic** *adjective* "a rista CRATTIC" or "air iss tuh CRATTIC"
- **aristocratically** *adverb*

Aristotelian *noun*
- "erra stuh TEELY 'n"
- a disciple or student of the Greek philosopher Aristotle (d.322 BC).
- **Aristotelianism** *noun*

Arita *noun*
- "a REETA"
- a type of Japanese porcelain characterized by asymmetric decoration.
- [*Arita* in Japan]

arithmetic *noun*
- "a RITH muh tick"
- the science of numbers.
- [Greek *arithmētikē* (*tekhnē*) art of counting, from *arithmos* number]
- **arithmetician** *noun* "a rith muh TISH'n"

Arizonan *noun*
- "air a ZONE 'n"
- a native or inhabitant of Arizona.

ark *noun*
- "ARK"
- (in the Bible) the ship in which Noah, his family, and the animals were saved.
- [Old English *ærc* from Latin *arca* chest]

HOMOPHONES: *arc*

Arkansan *noun*
- "ar CAN s'n"
- a native or inhabitant of Arkansas.

armada *noun*
- "ar MODDA"
- a fleet of warships, esp. that sent unsuccessfully by Spain to invade England in 1588.
- [Spanish from Romanic *armata* army]

armadillo *noun*
- "arma DILLO"
- any nocturnal insect-eating mammal of the family Dasypodidae, native to S America and southern N America, with large claws for digging and a body covered in bony plates, often rolling itself into a ball when threatened.
- [Spanish diminutive of *armado* armed man, from Latin *armatus* past participle of *armare* provide with weapons]

Armageddon *noun*
- "arma GED'n"
- the last battle between good and evil before the Day of Judgment.
- [Greek from Hebrew *har megiddōn* hill of Megiddo: see Rev. 16:16]

Armagnac *noun*
- "ARMA nyack"
- a brandy from the region of Armagnac in SW France.

armament *noun*
- "ARMA m'nt"
- military weapons and equipment, esp. guns on a warship or missiles on an airplane.
- [Latin *armamentum* from *armare* provide with weapons]

armamentarium *noun*
- "arma m'n TERRY um"
- the instruments, drugs, etc. available for medical use.
- [Latin, = arsenal, from *armare* provide with weapons]

armature *noun*
- "ARMA chur"
- the rotating coil or coils of an electric motor or generator.
- [French from Latin *armatura* armour, from *armare* provide with weapons]

Armenian *noun*
- "ar MEENY 'n"
- a native of the region or the republic of Armenia.

Arminian *adjective*
- "ar MINNY 'n"
- relating to the doctrine of the Dutch Protestant theologian Jacobus Arminius (d.1609).
- **Arminianism** *noun*

armistice *noun*
- "ARMA stiss"
- a cessation of hostilities by common agreement of the opposing sides; a truce.
- [French *armistice* or modern Latin *armistitium*, from *arma* arms, weapons + *-stitium* stoppage]

armoire *noun*
• "arm WARR" ("WARR" rhymes with *FAR*)
• a large wardrobe or cupboard, esp. one that is ornate or antique.
• [French, as AMBRY]

armorial *adjective*
• "ar MORRY 'll"
• of or relating to heraldry or heraldic arms.
• [from *armory* heraldry, from Old French *armoierie* from *armoier* to blazon, from *arme* (from Latin *arma* weapons, assimilated to 'armour')]

arnica *noun*
• "ARNA kuh"
• any composite plant of the genus *Arnica*, having erect stems bearing yellow daisy-like flower heads.
• [modern Latin: origin unknown]

Arnpriorite *noun*
• "ARN pryer ite"
• a resident of Arnprior, Ont.

aroid *adjective*
• "AIR oid"
• of or relating to the family Araceae, including arums.
• [as ARUM]

aroma *noun*
• "a ROME uh"
• a fragrance; a distinctive and pleasing smell, often of food.
• [Latin from Greek *arōma -atos* spice]
• **aromatic** *adjective* "erra MATTIC"
• **aromatically** *adverb*

aromatherapy *noun*
• "a rome a THERRA pee"
• the use of aromatic plant extracts and essential oils, esp. for relief of stress-related symptoms.
• [as AROMA + THERAPY]
• **aromatherapeutic** *adjective* "a rome a therra PYOOTIC"
• **aromatherapist** *noun*

aromatize *verb*
• "a ROME a tize"
• convert (a chemical compound) into an aromatic structure.
• [as AROMA]
• **aromatization** *noun*

arpeggio *noun*
• "ar PEDGY oh"
• the notes of a chord played or sung in succession, either ascending or descending.
• [Italian from *arpeggiare* play the harp, from *arpa* harp]
• **arpeggiated** *adjective* "ar PEDGY ated"

arpent *noun*
• "ARP'nt"
• *Cdn* an old French unit of land area equivalent to 3 420 square metres (about 1 acre), the standard measure of land in those areas settled during the French regime, in use until the 1970s.
• [French]

arrabbiata *adjective*
• "ah rabby ATTA"
• designating a pasta sauce of tomatoes, garlic, bell peppers and hot peppers.
• [Italian, = 'enraged' alluding to the spiciness of the sauce]

arraign *verb*
• "a RAIN"
• call on (a person) to answer a criminal charge before a court; indict; accuse.
• [Anglo-French *arainer* from Old French *araisnier* (ultimately Latin *ad-ratio -onis* reason, discourse)]
• **arraignment** *noun*

arrange *verb*
• "a RANGE"
• put into the required order; classify.
• [Old French *arangier* from *à* to + *rangier* from Old French *range* row, rank, via *ranger* from *rang* rank]
• **arrangeable** *noun*
• **arrangement** *noun*
• **arranger** *noun*

arrant *adjective*
• "AIR 'nt"
• downright, utter, notorious.
• [Middle English, var. of ERRANT, originally in phrases like *arrant* (= outlawed, roving) *thief*]
• **arrantly** *adverb*
HOMOPHONES: *errant*

arras *noun*
• "A russ"
• a rich tapestry, often hung on the walls of a room, or to conceal an alcove.
• [*Arras* in NE France, an important medieval centre of tapestry manufacturing]
HOMOPHONES: *arris*

array *noun*
• "a RAY"
• an imposing or well-ordered series or display.
• [Anglo-French *araier*, Old French *areer*, ultimately from a Germanic root, = prepare]

arrears *plural noun*
• "a REERZ"
• an amount still outstanding or uncompleted, esp. work undone or a debt unpaid.
• [Old French *arere* from medieval Latin *adretro* (*ad-* to + *retro* backwards): first used in phrase *in arrear*]
• **arrearage** *noun* "a REER idge"

arrest *verb*
• "a REST"
• seize (a person) and take into custody, esp. by legal authority.
• [Old French *arester*, ultimately from Latin *restare* remain, stop]
• **arrestee** *noun*

arresting *adjective*
• "a RESTING"
• attracting attention; striking.
• [as ARREST]
• **arrestingly** *adverb*

arrestor *noun*
ALSO SPELLED: **arrester**
• "a RESTER"
• something which arrests, esp. a device on an aircraft carrier for slowing an aircraft by means of a hook and cable after landing.
• [as ARREST]

arrhythmia *noun*
• "a RITH mee uh" (with "TH" as in *THEM*)
• deviation from the normal rhythm of the heart.
• [Greek *arruthmia* lack of rhythm]
• **arrhythmic** *adjective*

arris *noun*
• "A riss"
• a sharp edge formed by the meeting of two flat or curved surfaces.
• [corruption from French *areste*, modern ARÊTE]
HOMOPHONES: *arras*

arriviste *noun*
• "a ree VEEST"
• an ambitious or ruthlessly self-seeking person.
• [French from *arriver*, ultimately from Latin *ad-* to + *ripa* shore]

arrogant *adjective*
• "AIR a g'nt"
• unduly appropriating authority or importance; aggressively conceited or presumptuous; overbearing.
• [Old French (as ARROGATE)]
• **arrogance** *noun*
• **arrogantly** *adverb*

arrogate *verb*
• "AIR a gate"
• claim (power, responsibility, etc.) without justification.
• [Latin *arrogare arrogat-* (*ad-* to + *rogare* ask)]
• **arrogation** *noun*

arrondissement *noun*
• "a rondiss MÃH" (with a nasal *AH*)
• an administrative district of some large cities in France, esp. Paris.
• [French, from *arrondir*, from *rond* round, from Latin *rotundus* (see ROTUND)]

arroyo *noun*
• "a ROY oh"
• a usu. dry channel or gully cut by a stream, esp. in arid regions.
• [Spanish]

arsenal *noun*
• "ARSA n'll"
• a store of weapons.
• [obsolete French *arsenal* or Italian *arzanale* from Arabic *dārṣināʻa* from *dār* house + *sināʻa* art, industry, from *ṣanaʻa* fabricate]

arsenic *noun*
• "ARSA nick" or "AR snick"
• a non-scientific name for arsenic trioxide, a highly poisonous white powdery substance used in weed killers, rat poison, etc.
• [Old French from Latin *arsenicum* from Greek *arsenikon* yellow orpiment, identified with *arsenikos* male, but in fact from Arabic *al-zarnīḵ* from *al* the + *zarnīḵ* orpiment, from Persian from *zar* gold]
• **arsenical** *adjective* "ar SENNA k'll"

arsis *noun*
• "AR sis"
• a stressed syllable or part of a metrical foot in Greek or Latin verse.
• [Late Latin from Greek, = lifting, from *airō* raise]

arson *noun*
• "AR s'n"
• the act of maliciously setting fire to property.
• [legal Anglo-French, Old French, from medieval Latin *arsio -onis* from Latin *ardēre ars-* burn]
• **arsonist** *noun*

artemisia *noun*
• "arta MEE zhuh"
• any of numerous aromatic or bitter-tasting plants of the genus *Artemisia*, of the composite family, which includes silver mound, wormwood, mugwort, sagebrush, etc.
• [Latin from Greek, = wormwood, from *Artemis*, the goddess to whom it was sacred]

arterialize *verb*
ALSO SPELLED: esp. *Brit.* **-ise**
• "ar TEERY'll ize"
• convert venous into arterial (blood) by oxygenation esp. in the lungs.
• [as ARTERY]
• **arterialization** *noun* (also esp. *Brit.* **-isation**)

arteriole *noun*
• "ar TEERY ole"
• a small branch of an artery leading into capillaries.
• [French *artériole*, diminutive of *artère* ARTERY]

arteriosclerosis *noun*
• "ar teery oh skluh ROE sis"
• abnormal thickening and hardening of the walls of the arteries.
• [ARTERY + SCLEROSIS]
• **arteriosclerotic** *adjective*
"ar teery oh skluh ROTTIC"

artery *noun*
• "ARTER ee"
• any of the muscular-walled tubes forming part of the blood circulation system of the body, carrying oxygen-enriched blood from the heart.

• [Latin *arteria* from Greek *artēria* prob. from *airō* raise]
• **arterial** *adjective* "ar TEERY 'll"
• **arteritis** *noun* "arter ITE iss"

artesian *adjective*
• "ar TEE zh'n"
• designating a well bored perpendicularly, esp. through rock, into water-bearing strata lying at an angle, so that natural pressure produces a constant supply of water with little or no pumping.
• [French *artésien* from *Artois* in NW France, where the first such well was sunk in the 12th c.]

arthralgia *noun*
• "arth RAL juh"
• pain in a joint.
• [Latin from Greek from *arthron* joint + *algia* from *algos* pain]

arthritis *noun*
• "ar THRITE iss"
• inflammation of a joint or joints.
• [Latin from Greek from *arthron* joint + *-itis*, forming feminine of adjectives in *-itēs* (with *nosos* 'disease' implied)]
• **arthritic** *adjective* "ar THRITTIC"

arthropod *noun*
• "ARTHRA pod"
• any invertebrate animal of the phylum Arthropoda, with a segmented body, jointed limbs, and an external skeleton, e.g. an insect, spider, or crustacean.
• [Greek *arthron* joint + *pous podos* foot]

arthroscopy *noun*
• "ar THROSCA pee"
• examination of, or surgery on, the interior of a joint by the insertion of an instrument called an arthroscope through a small incision.
• [Greek *arthron* joint + *skopos* target, from *skeptomai* look at]
• **arthroscope** *noun* "ARTHRA scope"
• **arthroscopic** *adjective* "arthra SCOPPIC"

Arthurian *adjective*
• "ar THURRY 'n"
• relating to or associated with Arthur, a legendary king of Britain, or his court.

artichoke *noun*
• "ARTA choke"
• a plant native to the Mediterranean, *Cynara scolymus*, allied to the thistle.
• [Italian *articiocco* from Arabic *al-ḵaršūfa*]

article *noun*
• "ARTA k'll"
• a particular or separate thing, esp. one of a set.
• [Old French from Latin *articulus* diminutive of *artus* joint]

articular *adjective*
• "ar TICK yuh lur"
• of or relating to the joints.
• [Latin *articularis* (as ARTICLE)]

articulate *adjective*
• "ar TICK yuh lit"
• able to speak fluently and coherently.
• [Latin *articulatus* (as ARTICLE)]
• **articulacy** *noun*
• **articulately** *adverb*
• **articulateness** *noun*
• **articulation** *noun*
• **articulator** *noun*

articulated *adjective*
• "ar TICK yuh lated"
• designating a vehicle consisting of two or more sections connected by a flexible joint.
• [as ARTICLE]

artifact *noun*
ALSO SPELLED: **artefact**
• "ARTA fact"
• a product of human art and workmanship.
• [Latin *arte* (ablative of *ars* art) + *factum* (neuter past participle of *facere* make)]
• **artifactual** *adjective* (also **artefactual**) "arta FACK choo 'll"

artifice *noun*
• "ARTA fiss"
• clever or cunning devices or expedients, esp. as used to trick or deceive others.
• [French from Latin *artificium* from *ars artis* art, *-ficium* making, from *facere* make]

artificer *noun*
• "ar TIFFA sur"
• an inventor.
• [as ARTIFICE]

artificial *adjective*
• "arta FISH'll"
• produced by human skill or effort rather than originating naturally.
• [as ARTIFICE]
• **artificiality** *noun* "arta fishy ALA tee"
• **artificially** *adverb*

artillery *noun*
• "ar TILLER ee"
• large-calibre guns used in warfare on land.
• [Old French *artillerie* from *artiller* alteration of *atillier*, *atirier* equip, arm]
• **artilleryman** *noun*

artisan *noun*
• "ARTA zan" or "ARTA san"
• a craftsperson specializing in decorative arts, esp. pottery, weaving, etc.
• [French from Italian *artigiano*, ultimately from Latin *artitus* past participle of *artire* instruct in the arts]
• **artisanal** *adjective*
• **artisanship** *noun*

artiste *noun*
• "ar TEEST"

• a professional performer, esp. a singer or dancer.
• [French from Italian *artista* from Latin *ars artis* art]

arugula *noun*
• "a ROOGA luh"
• a cruciferous plant, *Eruca vesicaria sativa*, having purple-veined pale yellow or white flowers and bitter leaves which are used in salads.
• [Italian dialect, ultimately diminutive of Latin *eruca*]

arum *noun*
• "AIR um"
• any plant of the European genus *Arum*, typically having a white spathe and arrow-shaped leaves, esp. cuckoo pint, *Arum maculatum*.
• [Latin from Greek *aron*]

Arviaqmiut *noun*
• "arvy ACKMY ut"
• a resident of Arviat, Nunavut.
• [Inuktitut]

Aryan *noun*
• "AIRY 'n"
• a member of a people speaking an Indo-European language who invaded N India in the 2nd millennium BC, displacing the Dravidian and other aboriginal peoples.
• [Sanskrit *āryas* noble]
HOMOPHONES: *Arian*

aryl *noun*
• "A rile" or "A rill"
• any radical derived from or related to an aromatic hydrocarbon by removal of a hydrogen atom.
• [German *Aryl* (as AROMA)]
HOMOPHONES: *aril*

asafetida *noun*
ALSO SPELLED: **asafoetida**
• "assa FEETA duh" or "assa FETTA duh"
• an acrid gum resin with a strong smell like that of garlic, obtained from certain Asian plants of the umbelliferous genus *Ferula*, and used in condiments.
• [medieval Latin from *asa* from Persian *azā* mastic + *fetida* (as FETID)]

asana *noun*
• "OSSA nuh"
• any of various postures used in yoga.
• [Sanskrit]

asbestos *noun*
• "az BEST us"
• a fibrous silicate mineral that is incombustible.
• [ultimately from Greek *asbestos* unquenchable, from *a-* not + *sbestos* from *sbennumi* quench]

asbestosis *noun*
• "az bess TOE sis"
• a lung disease resulting from the inhalation of asbestos particles.
• [as ASBESTOS]

ascarid *noun*
• "ASSKA rid"
• a parasitic nematode worm of the genus *Ascaris*, e.g. the intestinal roundworm of mankind and other vertebrates.
• [modern Latin *ascaris* from Greek *askaris* intestinal worm]

ascend *verb*
• "a SEND"
• move upwards; rise.
• [Latin *ascendere* (*ad-* to + *scandere* climb)]
• **ascendant** *adjective*
• **ascension** *noun*
• **ascensional** *adjective*

ascendancy *noun*
ALSO SPELLED: **ascendency**
• "a SEND'n see"
• a superior or dominant condition or position.
• [as ASCEND]

ascender *noun*
• "a SENDER"
• a part of a letter that extends above the main part (as in *b* and *d*).
• [as ASCEND]

Ascensiontide *noun*
• "a SEN sh'n tide"
• the period between Ascension Day, the day on which Christians annually celebrate the ascent of Christ into heaven on the fortieth day after the Resurrection, and the eve of Pentecost.
• [as ASCEND]

ascent *noun*
• "a SENT"
• the act or an instance of ascending.
• [as ASCEND]
HOMOPHONES: *assent*

ascertain *verb*
• "asser TANE"
• find out as a definite fact.
• [Old French *acertener*, stem *acertain-* from *à* to + CERTAIN]
• **ascertainable** *adjective*
• **ascertainment** *noun*

ascetic *noun*
• "a SETTIC"
• a person who practises severe self-discipline and abstains from all forms of pleasure, esp. for religious or spiritual reasons.
• [medieval Latin *asceticus* or Greek *askētikos* from *askētēs* monk, from *askeō* exercise]
• **ascetically** *adverb*
• **asceticism** *noun* "a SETTA sizm"

ascidian *noun*
• "a SIDDY 'n"
• any tunicate animal of the class Ascidiacea,

often found in colonies, the adults sedentary on rocks or seaweeds, e.g. the sea squirt.
• [modern Latin *Ascidia* from Greek *askidion* diminutive of *askos* wineskin]

ASCII *noun*
• "ASKY"
• a standard code for storing and transmitting information in and between computer systems.
• [acronym from American Standard Code for Information Interchange]

ascites *noun*
• "a SITE eez"
• abnormal accumulation of fluid in the abdomen causing swelling.
• [Late Latin from Greek from *askitēs* from *askos* wineskin]

ascorbic *adjective*
• "a SCORE bick"
• designating an acid (vitamin C) found in citrus fruits and green vegetables, essential in maintaining healthy connective tissue, a deficiency of which results in scurvy.
• [Greek *a-* without + medieval Latin *scorbutus* scurvy]

ascot *noun*
• "ASSCOT"
• a broad necktie or scarf covering the area of an open neck or waistcoat.
• [*Ascot* in S England]

ascribe *verb*
• "a SCRIBE"
• attribute or impute.
• [Latin *ascribere* (*ad-* to + *scribere script-* write)]
• **ascribable** *adjective*
• **ascription** *noun* "a SCRIP sh'n"

asdic *noun*
• "AZ dic"
• an early form of sonar used to detect submarines.
• [initials of Allied Submarine Detection Investigation Committee]

asepsis *noun*
• "ay SEP sis"
• the absence of harmful bacteria, viruses, or other micro-organisms.
• [Greek *a-* not + SEPSIS]
• **aseptic** *adjective*

asexual *adjective*
• "ay SECK shoo 'll"
• without sex or sexual organs.
• [Greek *a-* not + Latin *sexus* sex]
• **asexuality** *noun*
• **asexually** *adverb*

Ashanti *noun*
• "a SHANTY"
• a member of the people of the Ashanti region of Ghana in W Africa, one of the country's principal ethnic groups.
• [Twi *Asante*]

Ashkenazi *noun*
• "ashka NOZZY"
• a Jew of central, northern, or eastern Europe, or of such ancestry.
• [modern Hebrew, from *Ashkenaz* a descendant of Japheth (Gen. 10:3)]
• **Ashkenazic** *adjective*

ashlar *noun*
• "ASH lur"
• a large square-cut stone used in building.
• [Old French *aisselier* from Latin *axilla* diminutive of *axis* board]

ashram *noun*
• "ASH rum"
• (in India) a place of religious retreat for Hindus; a hermitage.
• [Sanskrit *āshrama* hermitage]

ashrama *noun*
• "ASH ruh muh"
• any of the four stages of an ideal life, ascending from the status of pupil to the total renunciation of the world.
• [Sanskrit]

Ashtanga *noun*
• "ash TANGA"
• a type of yoga consisting of a series of poses executed in swift succession, combined with deep, controlled breathing.
• [Sanskrit *ashṭaṅga* having eight parts, from *ashtán* eight, because it is based on eight principles]

Asiago *noun*
• "ozzy OGGO"
• a hard light yellow cheese made from cow's milk.
• [*Asiago* in N Italy]

Asian *noun*
• "AY zh'n"
• a native of Asia.

Asiatic *adjective*
• "ay zhee ATTIC"
• Asian.

asinine *adjective*
• "ASSA nine"
• extremely stupid.
• [Latin *asininus* from *asinus* ass]
• **asininity** *noun* "assa NINNA tee"

askance *adverb*
• "a SKANCE"
• sideways or squinting.
• [16th c.: origin unknown]

askari *noun*
• "a SCARRY"
• a soldier or police officer in E Africa.
• [Arabic *'askarī* soldier]

asparagus *noun*
• "a SPARE a guss"
• any plant of the genus *Asparagus*, esp. *A.*

officinalis with edible young shoots used as a vegetable.
• [Latin from Greek *asparagos*]

aspartame *noun*
• "ASPER tame"
• a very sweet low-calorie sugar substitute derived from amino acids.
• [ASPARTIC + -ame, prob. from phenyl*a*lanine + *m*ethyl + *e*ster]

aspartic *adjective*
• "a SPAR tick"
• designating an acidic amino acid present in proteins and important in animal metabolism.
• [French *aspartique*, formed arbitrarily from ASPARAGUS]

aspen *noun*
• "ASP'n"
• any of several poplars characterized by leaves which tremble in the slightest wind, esp. *Populus tremuloides*, widely distributed across N America, and *P. tremula*, found in Europe.
• [earlier name *asp* from Old English *æspe*]

asperity *noun*
• "ass PERRA tee"
• harshness or sharpness of temper or tone.
• [Latin *asperitas* from *asper* rough]

asperse *verb*
• "a SPURSE"
• attack the reputation of; calumniate.
• [Middle English, = besprinkle, from Latin *aspergere aspers-* (*ad-* to + *spargere* sprinkle)]

aspersion *noun*
• "a SPUR zh'n"
• a disparaging remark.
• [as ASPERSE]

asphalt *noun*
• "ASH fault" or "ASS fault"
• a dark bituminous pitch occurring naturally or made from petroleum.
• [Greek *asphalton*]
• **asphalter** *noun*
• **asphaltic** *adjective* "ash FAWL tick" or "ass FAWL tick"

aspherical *adjective*
• "ay SFEERA k'll" or "ay SFERRA k'll"
• (esp. of an optical lens) not spherical.
• [Greek *a-* not + SPHERE]

asphodel *noun*
• "ASSFA dell"
• any liliaceous plant of the genus *Asphodelus*, native to the Mediterranean.
• [Greek *asphodelos*: compare DAFFODIL]

asphyxia *noun*
• "ass FIXY uh"
• a lack of oxygen in the blood, causing unconsciousness or death; suffocation.
• [modern Latin from Greek *asphuxia* from *a-* not + *sphuxis* pulse]
• **asphyxial** *adjective*
• **asphyxiant** *adjective*

asphyxiate *verb*
• "ass FIXY ate"
• cause (a person) to have asphyxia, smother; suffocate.
• [as ASPHYXIA]
• **asphyxiation** *noun*
• **asphyxiator** *noun*

aspic *noun*
• "ASS pick"
• a clear savoury jelly prepared from meat or fish stock, used as a garnish or glaze or combined with meat, vegetables, etc. in moulded dishes.
• [French, from the colours of the jelly (compared to those of a type of snake called an asp)]

aspidistra *noun*
• "aspa DISTRA"
• any liliaceous foliage plant of the genus *Aspidistra*, with broad tapering leaves, native to E Asia, esp. *A. lurida*, often grown as a houseplant.
• [modern Latin from Greek *aspis -idos* shield (from the shape of the leaves)]

aspirant *noun*
• "ASPER 'nt" or "a SPY r'nt"
• a person who aspires.
• [as ASPIRATE]

aspirate *adjective*
• "ASPER it"
• draw (fluid) by suction from a vessel or cavity.
• [Latin *aspiratus* past participle of *aspirare* from *ad* to + *spirare* breathe]
• **aspirator** *noun*

aspiration *noun*
• "aspa RAY sh'n"
• a strong desire to achieve an end; an ambition.
• [as ASPIRATE]
• **aspirational** *adjective*

asquint *adjective*
• "a SKWINT"
• to one side; from the corner of an eye.
• [perhaps from Dutch *schuinte* slant]

assai *adverb*
• "a SYE"
• (as a musical direction) very.
• [Italian]

assail *verb*
• "a SAIL"
• make a strong or concerted attack on.
• [Old French *asaill-* stressed stem of *asalir* from medieval Latin *assalire* from Latin *assilire* (*ad-* to + *salire salt-* leap)]
• **assailable** *adjective*
• **assailant** *noun*

Assam *noun*
• "a SAM"
• a strong, dark brown tea from Assam in NE India.

Assamese *noun*
• "assa MEEZ"
• a native or inhabitant of Assam in NE India.

assassin *noun*
• "a SASSIN"
• a killer, esp. of a political or religious leader.
• [medieval Latin *assassinus* from Arabic *ḥaššāš* hashish-eater, since the medieval Assassins were reputed to consume hashish to fortify themselves for action]
• **assassinate** *verb*
• **assassination** *noun*

assault *noun*
• "a SALT"
• a violent physical or verbal attack.
• [Old French *asaut* ultimately from Latin (*salire salt-* leap)]
• **assaulter** *noun*
• **assaultive** *adjective*

assay *noun*
• "a SAY" or "ASS ay"
• a test to determine the composition of a substance, esp. the analysis of an ore or metal to determine its purity.
• [Old French *assaier*, *assai*, var. of *essayer*, *essai*, ultimately from Late Latin *exagium* weighing, from *exigere* weigh]
• **assayer** *noun*

assegai *noun*
ALSO SPELLED: **assagai**
• "ASSA guy"
• a slender iron-tipped spear made from hardwood, used esp. by southern African peoples.
• [obsolete French *azagaie* or Portuguese *azagaia* from Arabic *az-zaġāyah* from *al* the + *zaġāyah* spear]

assemble *verb*
• "a SEMBLE"
• gather together; collect.
• [Old French *asembler*, ultimately from Latin *ad* to + *simul* together]
• **assemblage** *noun*
• **assembler** *noun*
• **assembly** *noun*

assemblyman *noun*
• "a SEMBLY m'n"
• a member of an (esp. legislative) assembly.
• [as ASSEMBLE]

assent *verb*
• "a SENT"
• consent.
• [ultimately from Latin *assentire* (*ad* to, *sentire* think)]
• **assenter** *noun* (also **assentor**)
HOMOPHONES: *ascent*

assert *verb*
• "a SURT"
• declare; state clearly.
• [Latin *asserere* (*ad-* to + *serere sert-* join)]
• **assertion** *noun*
• **assertor** *noun* (also **asserter**) "a SURT ur"

assertive *adjective*
• "a SURTIV"
• tending to assert oneself; forthright, positive.
• [as ASSERT]
• **assertively** *adverb*
• **assertiveness** *noun*

assess *verb*
• "a SESS"
• determine or estimate the size, quality, or extent of.
• [French *assesser* from Latin *assidēre* (*ad-* to + *sedēre* sit)]
• **assessable** *adjective*
• **assessment** *noun*

assessor *noun*
• "a SESSER"
• a person who makes assessments, esp. one who assesses taxes or estimates the value of property for taxation or insurance purposes.
• [Latin *assessor -oris* assistant judge (as ASSESS)]
• **assessorial** *adjective* "ass ess ORRY 'll"

asseverate *verb*
• "a SEVVER ate"
• declare solemnly.
• [Latin *asseverare* (*ad-* to + *severus* serious)]
• **asseveration** *noun*

assibilate *verb*
• "a SIBBLE ate"
• pronounce (a sound) as a sibilant or affricate ending in a sibilant.
• [Latin *assibilare* (*ad-* to + *sibilare* hiss)]
• **assibilation** *noun*

assiduity *noun*
• "assa JUE a tee" or "ass id YOO a tee"
• constant or close attention to what one is doing.
• [Latin *assiduitas* (as ASSIDUOUS)]

assiduous *adjective*
• "a SIDGE oo us" or "a SID yoo us"
• persevering, hard-working.
• [Latin *assiduus* (as ASSESS)]
• **assiduously** *adverb*
• **assiduousness** *noun*

assign *verb*
• "a SINE"
• allot as a share, responsibility, task, etc.
• [Latin *assignare* mark out to (*ad-* to + *signum* sign)]
• **assignable** *adjective*
• **assignee** *noun*
• **assignment** *noun*

assimilate *verb*
• "a SIM'll ate"
• absorb and digest (food etc.) into the body.
• [Middle English from Latin *assimilare* (*ad-* to + *similis* like)]
• **assimilable** *adjective*

- **assimilation** *noun*
- **assimilationism** *noun*
- **assimilationist** *noun*
- **assimilative** *adjective* "a SIMMLE a tiv"
- **assimilator** *noun*
- **assimilatory** *adjective* "a SIMMLE a tory"

Assiniboine *noun*
- "a SINNA boin"
- a member of an Aboriginal people living in S Saskatchewan and NE Montana.
- [Canadian French from Ojibwa *assini-pwan*, lit. 'stone Sioux', from their practice of cooking by placing heated stones in water]

assize *noun*
- "a SIZE"
- *Cdn* a session of a court.
- [Old French *as(s)ise*, feminine past participle of *aseeir* sit at, from Latin *assidēre*: compare ASSESS]

associate *verb*
- "a SO see ate" or "a SO shee ate"
- connect in the mind.
- [Latin *associatus* past participle of *associare* (*ad-* to + *socius* sharing, allied)]
- **associateship** *noun*
- **associator** *noun*
- **associatory** *adjective* "a SO see a tory" or "a SO shee a tory"

association *noun*
- "a so see AY sh'n" or "a so shee AY sh'n"
- a group of people or organizations united for a joint purpose.
- [as ASSOCIATE]
- **associational** *adjective*
- **associative** *adjective* "a SO see a tiv" or "a SO shee a tiv"

assonance *noun*
- "ASSA nince"
- the resemblance of sound between two syllables in nearby words, arising from the rhyming of two or more accented vowels, but not consonants, or the use of identical consonants with different vowels, e.g. *face*, *mail*, and *killed*, *cold*, *culled*.
- [Latin *assonare* respond to (*ad-* to + *sonus* sound)]
- **assonant** *adjective*
- **assonate** *verb*

assort *verb*
- "a SORT"
- classify or arrange in groups.
- [Old French *assorter* from *à* to + *sorte* sort]
- **assortment** *noun*

assortative *adjective*
- "a SORTA tiv"
- selective.
- [as ASSORT]

assuage *verb*
- "a SWAGE" ("SWAGE" rhymes with *STAGE*)
- calm or soothe (a person, pain, etc.).
- [Old French *as(s)ouagier*, ultimately from Latin *suavis* sweet]
- **assuagement** *noun*
- **assuager** *noun*

assume *verb*
- "a SUME"
- take or accept as being true, without proof, for the purpose of argument or action.
- [Latin *assumere* (*ad-* to + *sumere sumpt-* take)]
- **assumable** *adjective*

assumption *noun*
- "a SUMP sh'n"
- the act or an instance of assuming.
- [Latin *assumptio* (as ASSUME)]

assumptive *adjective*
- "a SUMP tiv"
- taken for granted.
- [Latin *assumptivus* (as ASSUME)]

assure *verb*
- "a SHUR"
- make (a person) sure; convince.
- [Old French *aseürer*, ultimately from Latin *securus* safe, from *cura* care]
- **assurable** *adjective*
- **assurance** *noun*
- **assurer** *noun*

assured *adjective*
- "a SHURD"
- certain, guaranteed.
- [as ASSURE]
- **assuredly** *adverb* "a SHUR id lee"

Assyrian *noun*
- "a SEERY 'n"
- an inhabitant of the ancient country of Assyria, in what is now N Iraq.

Assyriology *noun*
- "a seery OLLA jee"
- the study of the language, history, and antiquities of Assyria.
- [as ASSYRIAN + Greek *logos* word]
- **Assyriologist** *noun*

astatic *adjective*
- "ay STATTIC" or "a STATTIC"
- not static; unstable or unsteady.
- [Greek *astatos* unstable, from *a-* not + *sta-* stand]

astatine *noun*
- "ASTA teen"
- a radioactive element, the heaviest of the halogens, which occurs naturally and can be artificially made by nuclear bombardment of bismuth.
- [as ASTATIC]

asterisk *noun*
- "ASTER isk"
- a symbol (*) used to mark printed or written text, typically as a reference to an annotation or to stand for omitted matter, etc.
- [Greek *asteriskos* diminutive of *astēr* star]

asterism *noun*
- "ASTER izm"
- a cluster of stars.
- [Greek *asterismos* from *astēr* star]

asteroid *noun*
- "ASTER oid"
- any of the small planetary bodies revolving around the sun, mainly between the orbits of Mars and Jupiter.
- [Greek *asteroeidēs* from *astēr* star]
- **asteroidal** *adjective*

asthenia *noun*
- "ass THEENY uh"
- loss of strength; debility.
- [Greek *astheneia* from *asthenēs* weak]

asthenic *adjective*
- "ass THENNIC" (with "TH" as in *THIN*)
- of lean or long-limbed build.
- [as ASTHENIA]

asthenosphere *noun*
- "ass THENNA sfeer" (with "TH" as in *THIN*)
- the upper layer of the earth's mantle, whose capacity for gradual flow is thought to give rise to continental drift.
- [Greek *asthenēs* weak + SPHERE]

asthma *noun*
- "AZMA"
- a respiratory disorder, often provoked by allergy, causing wheezing and paroxysms of difficult breathing.
- [Greek *asthma -matos* from *azō* breathe hard]
- **asthmatic** *adjective* "azz MATTIC"
- **asthmatically** *adverb*

Asti *noun*
- "ASTY"
- a sparkling white wine from the province of Asti or neighbouring provinces in NW Italy, south of Turin.

astigmatism *noun*
- "a STIGMA tizm"
- a defect in the eye or in a lens resulting in distorted images, as light rays are prevented from meeting at a common focus.
- [Greek *a-* without + Greek *stigma -matos* point]
- **astigmatic** *adjective* "astig MATTIC"

astilbe *noun*
- "a STILL bee"
- any plant of the genus *Astilbe*, with plumelike heads of tiny white, red, orange, or pink flowers.
- [modern Latin from Greek *a-* not + *stilbē* feminine of *stilbos* glittering, from the inconspicuous (individual) flowers]

astonish *verb*
- "a STON ish"
- amaze; surprise greatly.
- [obsolete *astone* from Old French *estoner* from Gallo-Roman]
- **astonishing** *adjective*
- **astonishingly** *adverb*
- **astonishment** *noun*

astragal *noun*
- "ASTRA g'll"
- a small semicircular moulding round the top or bottom of a column, often decorated with a bead pattern.
- [as ASTRAGALUS]

astragalus *noun*
- "a STRAGGA luss"
- a small bone in the foot, articulating with the tibia to form the ankle joint.
- [Latin from Greek *astragalos* ankle bone, moulding, a plant]

astrakhan *noun*
- "ASTRA can"
- the dark curly fleece of young lambs from the region of Astrakhan in S Russia.
- [*Astrakhan*, on the Volga delta]

astral *adjective*
- "ASS trull"
- of or connected with the stars.
- [Late Latin *astralis* from *astrum* star]
- **astrally** *adverb*

astringent *adjective*
- "a STRIN j'nt"
- causing the contraction of body tissues.
- [Latin *astringere* (*ad-* to + *stringere* bind)]
- **astringency** *noun*
- **astringently** *adverb*

astrochemistry *noun*
- "astro KEMMA stree"
- the study of molecules and radicals in interstellar space.
- [as ASTRAL + CHEMIST]

astrolabe *noun*
- "ASTRO labe"
- an instrument, usu. consisting of a graduated disc and a pointer, formerly used to make astronomical measurements, esp. of the altitudes of celestial bodies, and as an aid in navigation.
- [Greek *astrolabon*, neuter of *astrolabos* 'star-taking']

astrology *noun*
- "a STRAW luh jee"
- the study of the movements and relative positions of celestial bodies interpreted as an influence on human affairs.
- [Latin *astrologia* from Greek (as ASTRAL + *logos* word)]
- **astrologer** *noun*
- **astrological** *adjective*
- **astrologist** *noun*

astrometry *noun*
- "a STRAW muh tree"
- the measurement of the positions, motions, and magnitudes of stars.
- [as ASTRAL + Greek *metron* measure]

astronaut *noun*
- "ASTRA not"

• a person who is trained to travel in a spacecraft.
• [as ASTRAL + NAUTICAL]

astronautics *noun*
• "astra NOTTIX"
• the science of space travel.
• [as ASTRAL + NAUTICAL]

astronomy *noun*
• "a STRAW nuh mee"
• the study of the universe and its contents beyond the bounds of the earth's atmosphere.
• [Greek *astronomia* from *astronomos* (adjective) 'star-arranging', from *astēr* star + *nemō* arrange]
• **astronomer** *noun*
• **astronomic** *adjective* "astra NOMMIC"
• **astronomical** *adjective*
• **astronomically** *adverb*

astrophotography *noun*
• "astro fuh TOGGRA fee"
• the use of photography in astronomy; the photographing of celestial objects and phenomena.
• [as ASTRAL + PHOTOGRAPH]

astrophysics *noun*
• "astro FIZZIX"
• a branch of astronomy concerned with the physics and chemistry of celestial bodies.
• [as ASTRAL + PHYSICS]
• **astrophysical** *adjective*
• **astrophysicist** *noun* "astro FIZZA sist"

astute *adjective*
• "a STUTE"
• shrewd; clever.
• [obsolete French *astut* or Latin *astutus* from *astus* craft]
• **astutely** *adverb*
• **astuteness** *noun*

asunder *adverb*
• "a SUNDER"
• apart.
• [Old English *on sundran* into pieces]

asura *noun*
• "USSER uh"
• a member of a class of divine beings in the Vedic period, which in Indian mythology tend to be evil (opposed to the devas) and in Zoroastrianism are benevolent.
• [Sanskrit]

asylum *noun*
• "a SYE lum"
• sanctuary; protection, esp. for those pursued by the law.
• [Latin from Greek *asulon* refuge, from *a-* not + *sulon* right of seizure]

asymmetry *noun*
• "ay SIMMA tree" or "a SIMMA tree"
• lack of symmetry.
• [Greek *a-* not + SYMMETRY]
• **asymmetric** *adjective* "ay suh METRIC"
• **asymmetrical** *adjective*
• **asymmetrically** *adverb*

asymptomatic *adjective*
• "ay simpta MATTIC"
• producing or showing no symptoms.
• [Greek *a-* not + SYMPTOM]

asymptote *noun*
• "ASSIM tote" or "ASSIMP tote"
• a line that continually approaches a given curve but does not meet it at a finite distance.
• [modern Latin *asymptota* (*linea* line) from Greek *asumptōtos* not falling together, from *a-* not + *sun* together + *ptōtos* falling, from *piptō* fall]
• **asymptotic** *adjective* "assim TOTTIC" or "assimp TOTTIC"
• **asymptotically** *adverb*

asynchronous *adjective*
• "ay SINK ruh nuss"
• (of equipment or methods of working) making use of pulses to control the timing of operations that are sent when the previous operation is completed, rather than at regular intervals.
• [Greek *a-* not + SYNCHRONOUS]
• **asynchronously** *adverb*

asyndeton *noun*
• "a SINDA t'n"
• the omission or absence of a conjunction between parts of a sentence, as in *I came, I saw, I conquered*.
• [modern Latin from Greek *asundeton* (neuter adjective) from *a-* not + *sundetos* bound together]
• **asyndetic** *adjective* "assin DETTIC"

atavistic *adjective*
• "atta VISTIC"
• related to or characterized by reversion to something ancient or ancestral.
• [from Latin *atavus* forefather]
• **atavism** *noun*
• **atavistically** *adverb*

ataxia *noun*
• "a TAXY uh"
• the loss of full control of bodily movements.
• [modern Latin *ataxia* from Greek from *a-* not + *taxis* order]
• **ataxic** *adjective*

atelier *noun*
• "attle YAY" or "a TELL yay"
• a workshop or studio, esp. of an artist or designer.
• [French from Old French *astelle* splinter of wood, from Latin *astula*]

Athanasian *adjective*
• "atha NAY sh'n"
• designating an affirmation of Christian faith formerly attributed to St. Athanasius (bishop of Alexandria d.373).

Athapaskan *noun*
ALSO SPELLED: **Athapascan**
• "ath a PASK'n"
• an Aboriginal language group, including the Beaver, Carrier, Tsilhqot'in, Chipewyan, Dogrib, Han, Hare, Kaska, Gwich'in, Sarcee, Sekani, Slave, Tagish, Tahltan, and Tutchone, of the subarctic regions of the NWT, Nunavut, Yukon, northern BC, and the northern Prairie provinces.
• [the *Athabasca* River in Alberta, from Cree *athapaskaw*, lit. 'there are reeds here and there']

atheism *noun*
• "AY thee izm" (with "TH" as in *THICK*)
• disbelief in the existence of God or gods.
• [French *athéisme* from Greek *atheos* without God, from *a-* not + *theos* god]
• **atheist** *noun*
• **atheistic** *adjective*
• **atheistical** *adjective*

atheling *noun*
• "ATHA ling"
• a prince or lord in Anglo-Saxon England.
• [Old English *ætheling* from West Germanic, from a base meaning 'race, family']

athenaeum *noun*
ALSO SPELLED: **atheneum**
• "ath a NEE um"
• an institution for literary or scientific study.
• [Late Latin *Athenaeum* from Greek *Athēnaion* temple of Athene (used as a place of teaching)]

Athenian *noun*
• "a THEENY 'n"
• a native or inhabitant of ancient or modern Athens in Greece.

atherosclerosis *noun*
• "atha roe skluh ROE sis"
• a form of arteriosclerosis characterized by the degeneration of the arteries because of the buildup of fatty deposits.
• [German *Atherosklerose* from Greek *athērē* groats + SCLEROSIS]
• **atherosclerotic** *adjective* "atha roe skluh ROTTIC"

athlete *noun*
• "ATH leet"
• a person who trains to compete in sports and other exercises requiring physical skill, strength, and endurance.
• [Greek *athlētēs* from *athleō* contend for a prize (*athlon*)]
• **athletic** *adjective* "ath LETTIC"
• **athletically** *adverb*
• **athleticism** *noun* "ath LETTA sizm"

athwart *preposition*
• "a THWORT"
• from side to side of.
• [as THWART]

atigi *noun*
• "ATTA gee" or "a TEE gee" (with a hard "G" as in *GEEK*)
• *Cdn* (*North*) a type of Inuit parka, made esp. from caribou skin, with the fur on the inside, worn either on its own or as the inner layer of a double-layered parka.
• [Inuktitut, from *attike* covering]

Atlantean *adjective*
• "at LANTY 'n"
• having physical strength like that of Atlas, a Titan made to support the weight of the heavens.
• [as ATLANTES]

atlantes *plural noun*
• "at LANT eez"
• male figures carved in stone and used as columns to support the entablature of a Greek or Greek-style building.
• [Greek, pl. of *Atlas*, a Titan made to support the weight of the heavens]

Atlanticist *adjective*
• "at LANTA sist"
• advocating or favouring a close relationship between N America and Europe.
• [from the *Atlantic Ocean*]

atlatl *noun*
• "AT latt'll"
• a device consisting of a wooden rod, used historically by N American Aboriginal peoples as a spear thrower.
• [Nahuatl *ahtlatl*]

atman *noun*
• "OT m'n"
• the real self.
• [Sanskrit *ātmán* essence, breath]

atmosphere *noun*
• "ATMA sfeer"
• the envelope of gases surrounding the earth, any other planet, or any substance.
• [modern Latin *atmosphaera* from Greek *atmos* vapour: see SPHERE]
• **atmospheric** *adjective*
• **atmospherically** *adverb*

atmospherics *noun*
• "atma SFEER icks" or "atma SFAIR icks"
• electrical disturbance in the atmosphere, esp. caused by lightning.
• [as ATMOSPHERE]

atoll *noun*
• "AT all"
• a ring-shaped coral reef enclosing a lagoon.
• [Maldivian *atolu*]

atomicity *noun*
• "attum ISSA tee"
• the number of atoms in the molecules of an element.
• [Greek *atomos* indivisible]

atomism *noun*
• "ATTUM izm"
• the theory that all matter consists of tiny individual particles.
• [as ATOMICITY]
• **atomist** *noun*
• **atomistic** *adjective*

atomize *verb*
ALSO SPELLED: esp. *Brit.* **-ise**
• "ATTUM ize"
• reduce to atoms or fine particles.
• [as ATOMICITY]
• **atomization** *noun* (also esp. *Brit.* **-isation**)

atomizer *noun*
ALSO SPELLED: esp. *Brit.* **-iser**
• "ATTUM izer"
• a device for emitting water, perfume, or other liquids as a fine spray.
• [as ATOMICITY]

atonic *adjective*
• "a TONNIC"
• without accent or stress.
• [Greek *a-* without + *tonos* tension, tone, from *teinō* stretch]
• **atony** *noun* "ATTA nee"

atopy *noun*
• "ATTA pee"
• an allergic reaction which is associated with a hereditary predisposition to allergy in some form.
• [Greek *atopia* unusualness, from *atopos* unusual, from Greek *a-* without + *topos* place]
• **atopic** *adjective* "a TOPPIC"

atrabilious *adjective*
• "atra BILL yuss" or "atra BILLY us"
• melancholy; ill-tempered.
• [Latin *atra bilis* black bile, translation of Greek *melagkholia* MELANCHOLY]

atrazine *noun*
• "ATTRA zeen"
• a selective, highly persistent herbicide, used alone and with other herbicides to control esp. annual weeds in a wide range of crops.
• [AMINO + TRIAZINE]

atrium *noun*
• "AY tree um"
• a usu. skylit central hall or court, often rising through several storeys, with galleries and rooms opening off it.
• [Latin, = the central court of an ancient Roman house]
• **atrial** *adjective*

atrocious *adjective*
• "a TRO sh'ss"
• very bad or unpleasant.
• [Latin *atrox -ocis* cruel]
• **atrociously** *adverb*
• **atrociousness** *noun*

atrocity *noun*
• "a TROSSA tee"
• an extremely wicked or cruel act, esp. one involving physical violence or injury.
• [as ATROCIOUS]

atrophy *verb*
• "ATRA fee"
• waste away through undernourishment, aging, or lack of use; become emaciated.
• [Late Latin *atrophia* from Greek from *a-* not + *trophē* food]
• **atrophic** *adjective* "a TROFFIC"

atropine *noun*
• "ATRA peen" or "ATRA pin"
• a poisonous alkaloid found in deadly nightshade and other plants, used medicinally esp. to relax muscles and inhibit secretion.
• [modern Latin *Atropa belladonna* deadly nightshade, from Greek *Atropos*, one of the three Fates]

Atsina *noun*
• "at SEENA"
• a member of an Aboriginal people living in Montana and (formerly) in S Saskatchewan, also called Gros Ventre.
• [Blackfoot *ăt-sé-na* 'gut people']

attach *verb*
• "a TATCH"
• fasten, affix, join.
• [Old French *estachier* fasten, from Germanic]
• **attachable** *adjective*
• **attached** *adjective*
• **attacher** *noun*
• **attachment** *noun*

attaché *noun*
• "atta SHAY"
• a person appointed to an ambassador's staff, usu. with a special sphere of activity.
• [French, as ATTACH]

attain *verb*
• "a TANE"
• arrive at; reach (a goal etc.).
• [Old French *ataindre* from Latin *attingere* (*ad-* to + *tangere* touch)]
• **attainability** *noun*
• **attainable** *adjective*

attainder *noun*
• "a TANE dur"
• the forfeiture of land and civil rights suffered as a consequence of a sentence of death for treason or felony.
• [Old French *ateindre* ATTAIN used as noun]

attainment *noun*
• "a TANE m'nt"
• something attained or achieved; an accomplishment.
• [as ATTAIN]

attaint *verb*
• "a TAINT"
• subject to attainder; condemn (for treason).

• [Old French *ataint, ateint* past participle formed as ATTAIN]

attar *noun*
• "AT ar"
• a fragrant essential oil, esp. from rose petals.
• [Persian *'atar* from Arabic from *'iṭr* perfume]

attempt *verb*
• "a TEMPT"
• seek to achieve or complete (a task or action).
• [Latin *attemptare* (*ad-* to + *temptare* TEMPT)]

attend *verb*
• "a TEND"
• be present.
• [Latin *attendere* (*ad* to, *tendere tent-* stretch)]
• **attendance** *noun*
• **attendant** *noun*
• **attendee** *noun*

attention *noun*
• "a TEN sh'n"
• the act or faculty of applying one's mind.
• [Latin *attentio* (as ATTEND)]
• **attentional** *adjective*
• **attentive** *adjective*
• **attentively** *adverb*
• **attentiveness** *noun*

attenuate *verb*
• "a TEN yoo ate"
• reduce in force, value, or virulence.
• [Latin *attenuare* (*ad-* to + *tenuis* thin)]
• **attenuated** *adjective*
• **attenuation** *noun*
• **attenuator** *noun*

attest *verb*
• "a TEST"
• confirm the validity or truth of.
• [French *attester* from Latin *attestari* (*ad-* to + *testis* witness)]
• **attestable** *adjective*
• **attestation** *noun*
• **attestor** *noun*

Attikamek *noun*
• "a TICKA meck"
• a member of an Aboriginal people living in the upper St. Maurice River valley in Quebec.
• [French *Attikameg* from Cree (Montagnais dialect) *atihkame:kw* = whitefish]

attired *adjective*
• "a TIRED"
• dressed, esp. in fine clothes or formal wear.
• [Old French *atir(i)er* equip, from *à tire* in order, of unknown origin]

attitude *noun*
• "ATTA tude"
• a settled opinion or way of thinking.
• [French from Italian *attitudine* fitness, posture, from Late Latin *aptitudo -dinis* from *aptus* fit]
• **attitudinal** *adjective* "atta TUDE'n 'll"

attitudinize *verb*
ALSO SPELLED: esp. *Brit.* **-ise**
• "atta TUDE 'n ize"
• practise or adopt attitudes, esp. for effect.
• [as ATTITUDE]

attorney *noun*
• "a TURN ee"
• a person, esp. a lawyer, appointed to act for another in business or legal matters.
• [Old French *atorné* past participle of *atorner* assign, from *à* to + *torner* turn]
• **attorneyship** *noun*

attract *verb*
• "a TRACT"
• draw or bring to oneself or itself.
• [Latin *attrahere* (*ad-* to + *trahere tract-* draw)]
• **attraction** *noun*
• **attractor** *noun*

attractant *noun*
• "a TRACK t'nt"
• a substance which attracts something.
• [as ATTRACT]

attractive *adjective*
• "a TRACTIV"
• attracting or capable of attracting; interesting.
• [as ATTRACT]
• **attractively** *adverb*
• **attractiveness** *noun*

attribute *verb*
• "a TRIB yoot"
• regard as belonging or appropriate to.
• [Latin *attribuere attribut-* (*ad-* to + *tribuere* assign)]
• **attributable** *adjective*
• **attribution** *noun*

attributive *adjective*
• "a TRIB yoo tiv"
• (of an adjective or noun) preceding the word described and expressing an attribute, as *old* in *the old dog* (but not in *the dog is old*) and *expiry* in *expiry date*.
• [as ATTRIBUTE]
• **attributively** *adverb*

attrition *noun*
• "a TRISH'n"
• reduction of a workforce by processes other than firing, as by non-replacement of employees who retire, die, etc.
• [Late Latin *attritio* from *atterere attrit-* rub]
• **attritional** *adjective*

attune *verb*
• "a TUNE"
• make receptive or aware.
• [from 'tune', unexplained variant of 'tone' (as ATONIC)]

atypical *adjective*
• "ay TIPPA k'll"
• not typical; not conforming to a type.

• [Greek *a-* not + TYPICAL]
• **atypically** *adverb*

aubade *noun*
• "oh BOD"
• a poem or piece of music appropriate to the dawn or early morning.
• [French from Spanish *albada* from *alba* dawn]

auberge *noun*
• "oh BAIRZH"
• an inn.
• [French from Provençal *alberga* lodging]

aubergine *noun*
• "oh bur ZHEEN"
• a dark purple colour.
• [French, = 'eggplant', from Catalan *alberginia* from Arabic *al-bādinjān* from Persian *bādingān* from Sanskrit *vātiṃgaṇa*]

aubrietia *noun*
ALSO SPELLED: **aubretia**
• "aw BREESHA"
• any dwarf perennial rock plant of the genus *Aubrieta*, having purple or pink flowers in spring.
• [Claude *Aubriet*, French botanist d.1743]

auburn *adjective*
• "AW burn"
• reddish brown (usu. of a person's hair).
• [Middle English, originally = yellowish white, from Old French *auborne*, *alborne*, from Latin *alburnus* whitish, from *albus* white]

Aubusson *noun*
• "OH boo sõh" (with a nasal *oh*)
• a kind of tapestry depicting esp. pastoral or chinoiserie designs.
• [*Aubusson* in central France]

auction *noun*
• "OCK sh'n"
• a sale of goods, usu. in public, in which articles are sold to the highest bidder.
• [Latin *auctio* increase, auction, from *augēre auct-* increase]
• **auctioneer** *noun*
• **auctioneering** *noun*

audacious *adjective*
• "aw DAY sh'ss"
• daring, bold.
• [Latin *audax -acis* bold, from *audēre* dare]
• **audaciously** *adverb*
• **audaciousness** *noun*
• **audacity** *noun* "aw DASSA tee"

audible *adjective*
• "ODDA bull"
• capable of being heard.
• [Late Latin *audibilis* from *audire* hear]
• **audibility** *noun*
• **audibleness** *noun*
• **audibly** *adverb*

audience *noun*
• "ODDY ince"
• the assembled listeners or spectators at an event, esp. a stage performance, concert, etc.
• [Latin *audientia* from *audire* hear]

audile *adjective*
• "ODD ile"
• of or referring to the sense of hearing.
• [Latin *audire* hear]

audio *noun*
• "ODDY oh"
• sound or its (esp. electrical) reproduction.
• [Latin *audire* hear]

audiobook *noun*
• "ODDY oh book"
• a recording on audio cassette or CD of a reading of a book, usu. a work of fiction.
• [as AUDIO + 'book']

audioconference *noun*
• "ODDY oh confer ince"
• a meeting that is conducted by telephone or other audio telecommunications device.
• [as AUDIO + CONFERENCE]
• **audioconferencing** *noun*

audiogram *noun*
• "ODDY oh gram"
• a graphic record of a measurement of the range and sensitivity of a person's hearing.
• [as AUDIO + Greek *gramma* thing written]

audiology *noun*
• "oddy OLLA jee"
• the scientific study of hearing, including the treatment of hearing disorders.
• [as AUDIO + Greek *logos* word]
• **audiologist** *noun*

audiometer *noun*
• "oddy OMMA tur"
• an instrument for testing hearing.
• [as AUDIO + Greek *metron* measure]
• **audiometry** *noun*

audiophile *noun*
• "ODDY oh file"
• a person who has a particularly strong interest in high-fidelity sound reproduction.
• [as AUDIO + Greek *philos* dear, loving]

audiotape *noun*
• "ODDY oh tape"
• a magnetic tape on which sound can be recorded.
• [as AUDIO + 'tape']

audiovisual *adjective*
• "oddy oh VIZH oo 'll" or "oddy oh VIZH yoo 'll"
• (esp. of teaching methods) using electrical equipment, e.g. projectors, tape recorders, etc. that are directed at the senses of sight and hearing.
• [as AUDIO + VISUAL]

audit *noun*
• "ODDIT"
• an official examination and verification of accounts.

- [Latin *auditus* hearing, from *audire audit-* hear]
- **auditor** *noun*
- **auditorial** *adjective*

audition *noun*
- "aw DISH'n"
- a practical demonstration of one's abilities as a singer, actor, dancer, etc., with the aim of winning a role or a position.
- [Latin *auditio* from *audire audit-* hear]

auditorium *noun*
- "odda TORY um"
- the part of a theatre etc. in which the audience sits.
- [Latin neuter of *auditorius* (adjective), as AUDIT]

auditory *adjective*
- "ODDA tory"
- concerned with hearing.
- [Latin *auditorius* (as AUDIT)]

Augean *adjective*
- "aw JEE 'n"
- filthy.
- [from Latin *Augeas*, legendary king whose vast stables were cleaned by Hercules]

auger *noun*
- "OGGER"
- a tool resembling a large corkscrew, for boring holes in wood, the ground, ice, etc.
- [Old English *nafogār* from *nafu* the hub of a wheel + *gār* pierce]

HOMOPHONES: *augur*

augite *noun*
- "OGG ite" or "ODGE ite"
- a complex silicate mineral, chiefly of calcium, magnesium, and aluminum, occurring in many igneous rocks.
- [Greek *augitēs* from *augē* lustre]

augment *verb*
- "og MENT"
- make or become greater; increase or enhance.
- [Late Latin *augmentum*, *augmentare* from Latin *augēre* increase]
- **augmentation** *noun*
- **augmentative** *adjective*
- **augmenter** *noun*

augur *verb*
- "OGGER"
- (of an event, circumstance, etc.) suggest a specified outcome.
- [Latin, = a religious official who observed natural signs, esp. the behaviour of birds, interpreting these as an indication of divine approval or disapproval of a proposed action]

HOMOPHONES: *auger*

augury *noun*
- "OG yur ee"
- an omen; a portent.
- [as AUGUR]
- **augural** *adjective*

august *adjective*
- "awe GUST"
- inspiring reverence and admiration; venerable, impressive.
- [Latin *augustus* consecrated, venerable]
- **augustly** *adverb*
- **augustness** *noun*

Augustan *adjective*
- "a GUST'n"
- connected with, occurring during, or influenced by the reign of the Roman emperor Augustus (d.14 AD), esp. as an outstanding period of Latin literature.

Augustinian *adjective*
- "ogga STINNY 'n"
- of or relating to St. Augustine of Hippo (d.430) or his doctrines.

auk *noun*
- "OCK"
- any of various marine diving birds of the family Alcidae, with a heavy body, short wings, and black and white plumage, e.g. the guillemot, puffin, and razorbill.
- [Old Norse *álka*]

auklet *noun*
- "OCK lit"
- any of various small auks, chiefly of the N Pacific.
- [as AUK]

aura *noun*
- "ORA"
- the distinctive atmosphere diffused by or attending a person, place, etc.
- [Greek, = breeze, breath]
- **auric** *adjective*

aural *adjective*
- "OR'll"
- of or relating to or received by the ear.
- [Latin *auris* ear]
- **aurally** *adverb*

HOMOPHONES: *oral*, *orally*

aureate *adjective*
- "ORRY it"
- golden, gold-coloured.
- [Late Latin *aureatus* from Latin *aureus* golden, from *aurum* gold]

aureole *noun*
- "ORY ole"
- a halo or circle of light, esp. around the head or body of a portrayed religious figure.
- [Latin *aureola (corona)*, = golden (crown) from *aurum* gold]

HOMOPHONES: *oriole*

auricle *noun*
- "ORRA k'll"
- a small muscular pouch on the surface of each atrium of the heart.

• [as AURICULA]
HOMOPHONES: *oracle*

auricula *noun*
• "or ICK yoo luh"
• a primula, *Primula auricula*, with a dark purple outer ring and pale yellow centre.
• [Latin, diminutive of *auris* ear, from its ear-shaped leaves]

auricular *adjective*
• "or ICK yuh lur"
• of or relating to the ear or hearing.
• [as AURICULA]

auriculate *adjective*
• "or ICK yuh lit"
• having one or more auricles or ear-shaped appendages.
• [as AURICULA]

auriferous *adjective*
• "or IFFER us"
• containing or yielding gold.
• [Latin *aurifer* from *aurum* gold + *-fer* producing, from *ferre* bear]

Aurignacian *noun*
• "or ig NAY sh'n"
• a culture of the early stages of the upper paleolithic period in Europe and the near East, dating from about 34,000–29,000 years ago. It is associated with Cro-Magnon man and witnessed the first appearance of cave paintings.
• [French *Aurignacien* from *Aurignac* in SW France, where remains of it were found]

aurochs *noun*
• "OR ox"
• an extinct wild ox, *Bos primigenius*, ancestor of domestic cattle and formerly native to many parts of the world.
• [German from Old High German *ūrohso* from *ūr-* urus + *ohso* ox]

aurora *noun*
• "a RORA"
• a luminous phenomenon, usu. of shimmering colours, seen in the upper atmosphere in high northern or southern latitudes, and caused by the interaction of charged solar particles with atmospheric gases, under the influence of the earth's magnetic field; the northern or southern lights.
• [Latin, = dawn]
• **auroral** *adjective*

Auroran *noun*
• "a ROR 'n"
• a resident of Aurora, Ont.

auscultation *noun*
• "oss cull TAY sh'n"
• the act of listening, esp. to sounds from the heart, lungs, etc., as a part of medical diagnosis.
• [Latin *auscultatio* from *auscultare* listen to]
• **auscultatory** *adjective* "oss CULTA tory"

Auslese *noun*
• "OW slay zuh"
• a white wine made esp. in Germany from selected bunches of grapes picked later than the general harvest.
• [German from *aus* out + *lese* picking, vintage]

auspice *noun*
• "OSS piss"
• patronage, support.
• [originally 'observation of bird flight in divination': Latin *auspicium* from *auspex* observer of birds, from *avis* bird]

auspicious *adjective*
• "oss PISH us"
• of good omen; favourable.
• [as AUSPICE]
• **auspiciously** *adverb*
• **auspiciousness** *noun*

Aussie *noun*
ALSO SPELLED: **Ossie**, **Ozzie**
• "OZZY" or "OSSY"
• an Australian.
• [abbreviation]
HOMOPHONES: *Ossi*

austere *adjective*
• "oss TEER"
• severely simple.
• [Greek *austēros* severe]
• **austerely** *adverb*
• **austerity** *noun* "oss TERRA tee"

Austin *noun*
• "OSSTIN"
• an Augustinian friar.
• [contraction of *Augustine*]

austral *adjective*
• "OSS trull"
• southern.
• [Latin *australis* from *Auster* south wind]

Australasian *adjective*
• "osstra LAY zh'n"
• of or relating to Australasia, a region consisting of Australia, New Zealand, New Guinea, and the neighbouring islands of the Pacific.

Australian *noun*
• "oss TRAILY 'n"
• a native or inhabitant of Australia.
• **Australianism** *noun*

Australoid *adjective*
• "OSSTRA loid"
• of or relating to the broad division of humankind represented by Australian Aboriginal peoples.

Australopithecus *noun*
• "osstra lo PITHA cuss"
• any extinct bipedal primate of the genus *Australopithecus* having apelike and human characteristics, or its fossilized remains.

• [modern Latin from Latin *australis* southern + Greek *pithēkos* ape]
• **australopithecine** *noun* "osstra lo PITHA seen"

Austrian *noun*
• "OSS tree 'n"
• a native or inhabitant of Austria.

Austronesian *noun*
• "osstro NEE zh'n"
• a family of languages spoken widely in Malaysia, Indonesia, and other parts of SE Asia, and in the islands of the central and S Pacific.
• [German *austronesisch*, from Latin *australis* southern + Greek *nēsos* island]

autarchy *noun*
• "AW tarky"
• absolute sovereignty.
• [modern Latin *autarchia* (Greek *auto-* from *autos* self + *-arkhia* from *arkhō* rule)]
• **autarchic** *adjective* "aw TARKIC"
• **autarchical** *adjective*
HOMOPHONES: *autarky, autarkic, autarkical*

autarky *noun*
• "AW tarky"
• self-sufficiency, esp. as an economic system.
• [Greek *autarkeia* (*auto-* from *autos* self + *arkeō* suffice)]
• **autarkic** *adjective* "aw TARKIC"
• **autarkical** *adjective*
• **autarkist** *noun*
HOMOPHONES: *autarchy, autarchic, autarchical*

auteur *noun*
• "oh TUR"
• a director who so greatly influences the films directed as to be able to rank as their author.
• [French, = author]
HOMOPHONES: *hauteur*

authentic *adjective*
• "aw THENTIC" (with "TH" as in *THIN*)
• of undisputed origin; genuine.
• [Greek *authentikos* principal, genuine]
• **authentically** *adverb*
• **authenticity** *noun* "oth en TISSA tee"

authenticate *verb*
• "aw THENTA cate" (with "TH" as in *THIN*)
• establish the truth or genuineness of.
• [as AUTHENTIC]
• **authentication** *noun*
• **authenticator** *noun*

author *noun*
• "OTH ur"
• a writer, esp. of books.
• [Old French *autor* from Latin *auctor* from *augēre auct-* increase, originate, promote]
• **authorial** *adjective* "oth ORRY 'll"

authoress *noun*
• "OTH ur ess" (with "TH" as in *THIN*)
• a female writer, esp. of books.
• [as AUTHOR]

authoritarian *adjective*
• "a thora TERRY 'n"
• favouring, encouraging, or enforcing strict obedience to authority, as opposed to individual freedom.
• [as AUTHORITY]
• **authoritarianism** *noun*

authoritative *adjective*
• "a THORA tay tiv"
• recognized as true or dependable.
• [as AUTHORITY]
• **authoritatively** *adverb*
• **authoritativeness** *noun*

authority *noun*
• "a THORA tee"
• the power or right to enforce obedience.
• [Old French *autorité* from Latin *auctoritas* from *auctor*: see AUTHOR]

authorize *verb*
ALSO SPELLED: esp. *Brit.* **-ise**
• "OTH ur ize"
• give official permission for or approval to (an undertaking or agent).
• [Old French *autoriser* from medieval Latin *auctorizare* from *auctor*: see AUTHOR]
• **authorization** *noun* (also esp. *Brit.* **-isation**)

authorship *noun*
• "OTH ur ship"
• the origin of a book or other written work.
• [as AUTHOR]

autism *noun*
• "OTT izm"
• a mental condition, usu. present from childhood, characterized by complete self-absorption and a reduced ability to respond to or communicate with the outside world.
• [modern Latin *autismus* from Greek *auto-* from *autos* self]
• **autistic** *adjective* "ott ISTIC"

autoantibody *noun*
• "OTTO anty body"
• an antibody produced by an organism in response to a constituent of its own tissues.
• [Greek *auto-* from *autos* self + ANTI + 'body' from Old English *bodig*]

autobahn *noun*
• "OTTO bonn"
• an expressway in Germany, Austria, or other German-speaking region.
• [German from *Auto* automobile + *Bahn* path, road]

autobiography *noun*
• "otto by OGGRA fee"
• a personal account of one's own life, esp. for publication.
• [Greek *auto-* from *autos* self + BIOGRAPHY]
• **autobiographer** *noun*
• **autobiographic** *adjective*
• **autobiographical** *adjective*

autocephalous *adjective*
• "otto SEFFA luss"
• (esp. of an Eastern church) appointing its own head.
• [Greek *autokephalos* (*auto-* from *autos* self + *kephalē* head)]

autochthon *noun*
• "aw TOCK t'n"
• the original or earliest known inhabitants of a country; aboriginals.
• [Greek, = sprung from the earth (*auto-* from *autos* self + *khthōn*, *-onos* earth)]

autochthonous *adjective*
• "aw TOCK t'n us"
• (of a rock formation) originating in the place in which it is found.
• [as AUTOCHTHON]

autoclave *noun*
• "OTTO clave"
• a sterilizer using high-pressure steam.
• [Greek *auto-* from *autos* self + Latin *clavus* nail or *clavis* key]

autocracy *noun*
• "aw TOCKRA see"
• absolute government by one person.
• [Greek *autokrateia* (as AUTOCRAT)]

autocrat *noun*
• "OTTO crat"
• an absolute ruler.
• [French *autocrate* from Greek *autokratēs* (*auto-* from *autos* self + *kratos* power)]
• **autocratic** *adjective*
• **autocratically** *adverb*

autodidact *noun*
• "otto DIE dact"
• a self-taught person.
• [Greek *auto-* from *autos* self + DIDACTIC]
• **autodidactic** *adjective*

autogamy *noun*
• "aw TOGGA mee"
• self-fertilization in plants.
• [Greek *auto-* from *autos* self + *-gamia* from *gamos* marriage]
• **autogamous** *adjective*

autogenic *adjective*
• "otto JENNIC"
• self-produced; originating within one's own body.
• [Greek *auto-* from *autos* self + GENESIS]

autogenous *adjective*
• "aw TODGE a nuss"
• self-produced; originating within one's own body.
• [Greek *auto-* from *autos* self + GENESIS]

autograph *noun*
• "OTTA graff"
• a signature, esp. that of a celebrity.
• [Greek *auto-* from *autos* self + *graphia* writing]

autography *noun*
• "aw TOGGRA fee"
• writing done with one's own hand.
• [as AUTOGRAPH]
• **autographic** *adjective*

autogyro *noun*
ALSO SPELLED: **autogiro**
• "otto JYE roe"
• an early form of helicopter with a frontal propeller and freely rotating horizontal vanes which provide lift.
• [Spanish (as Greek *auto-* from *autos* self + *giro* gyration)]

autoimmune *adjective*
• "otto im YOON"
• (of a disease) caused by antibodies produced against substances naturally present in the body.
• [Greek *auto-* from *autos* self + IMMUNE]
• **autoimmunity** *noun*

autointoxication *noun*
• "otto in toxa CAY sh'n"
• poisoning by a toxin formed within the body itself.
• [Greek *auto-* from *autos* self + INTOXICATE]

autologous *adjective*
• "aw TOLLA guss"
• (of a graft, transfusion, etc.) obtained from the same individual who receives it.
• [Greek *auto-* from *autos* self + *-logos* proportional]

autolysis *noun*
• "aw TOLLA sis"
• the destruction of cells by their own enzymes.
• [German *Autolyse* (from Greek *auto-* from *autos* self + LYSIS)]
• **autolytic** *adjective* "otta LITTIC"

automate *verb*
• "OTTA mate"
• convert to or operate by automation.
• [as AUTOMATON]
• **automation** *noun*

automatic *adjective*
• "otta MATTIC"
• (of a machine, device, etc., or its function) working by itself, without direct human intervention.
• [as AUTOMATON]
• **automatically** *adverb*
• **automaticity** *noun* "otta muh TISSA tee"

automatism *noun*
• "a TOMMA tizm"
• the performance of actions unconsciously or subconsciously.
• [French *automatisme* from *automate* AUTOMATON]

automatize *verb*
ALSO SPELLED: esp. *Brit.* **-ise**

- "a TOMMA tize"
- make (a process etc.) automatic.
- [as AUTOMATON]
- **automatization** *noun* (also esp. *Brit.* **-isation**)

automaton *noun*
- "a TOMMA tawn"
- a mechanism which operates with concealed motive power, esp. one simulating a living being.
- [Latin from Greek, neuter of *automatos* acting of itself, from *autos* self]

automobile *noun*
- "OTTA moe beel"
- a car.
- [French from Greek *auto-* from *autos* self + Latin *mobilis* from *movere* move]

automotive *adjective*
- "otta MOE tiv"
- concerned with motor vehicles.
- [Greek *auto-* from *autos* self + Latin *motivus* from *movere* move]

autonomic *adjective*
- "otta NOMMIC"
- functioning involuntarily, esp. designating the part of the nervous system responsible for control of the bodily functions not consciously directed, e.g. heartbeat.
- [as AUTONOMY]

autonomy *noun*
- "aw TONNA mee"
- the right of self-government.
- [Greek *autonomia* from *autos* self + *nomos* law]
- **autonomist** *noun*
- **autonomous** *adjective*
- **autonomously** *adverb*

autopsy *noun*
- "AW topsy"
- a post-mortem examination conducted to determine the cause of death.
- [modern Latin *autopsia* from Greek from *autoptēs* eyewitness]

autoradiograph *noun*
- "otto RADIO graff"
- a photograph of an object produced by radiation from radioactive material in the object.
- [Greek *auto-* from *autos* self + RADIOGRAPH]
- **autoradiographic** *adjective*
- **autoradiography** *noun*

autoroute *noun*
- "OTTO root"
- an expressway in Quebec, France, or other French-speaking region.
- [French (as AUTOMOBILE, ROUTE)]

autostrada *noun*
- "OTTO stradda"
- an expressway in Italy.
- [Italian (as AUTOMOBILE, *strada* road)]

autosuggestion *noun*
- "otto suh JESS ch'n"
- a hypnotic or subconscious suggestion made to oneself which affects behaviour.
- [Greek *auto-* from *autos* self + SUGGEST]

autotelic *adjective*
- "otta TELLIC"
- having or being a purpose in itself.
- [Greek *auto-* from *autos* self + Greek *telos* end]

autotomy *noun*
- "aw TOTTA mee"
- the voluntary severance of a body part, e.g. the tail of a lizard, to escape a predator.
- [Greek *auto-* from *autos* self + *-tomia* cutting, from *temnō* cut]

autotoxin *noun*
- "OTTO toxin"
- a product of an organism's metabolism which is poisonous to the organism itself.
- [Greek *auto-* from *autos* self + TOXIN]
- **autotoxic** *adjective*

autotrophic *adjective*
- "otta TROFFIC"
- able to form complex nutritional organic substances from simple inorganic substances such as carbon dioxide.
- [Greek *auto-* from *autos* self + *trophos* feeder]

autoxidation *noun*
- "aw toxa DAY sh'n"
- oxidation by exposure to air at room temperature.
- [Greek *auto-* from *autos* self + OXIDIZE]

autumn *noun*
- "OTTUM"
- the third season of the year, associated with harvests and falling leaves, in the northern hemisphere from September to November and in the southern hemisphere from March to May.
- [Latin *autumnus*]
- **autumnal** *adjective* "aw TUM n'll"

auxiliary *adjective*
- "og ZILLYA ree" or "og ZILLER ee"
- (of a person or thing) helpful, giving support.
- [Latin *auxiliarius* from *auxilium* help]

auxin *noun*
- "OX 'n"
- a plant hormone that regulates growth.
- [German from Greek *auxō* increase]

avail *verb*
- "a VALE"
- help, benefit.
- [Middle English from obsolete *vail* (v.) from Old French *valoir* be worth, from Latin *valēre*]

available *adjective*
- "a VALE a bull"
- capable of being used; at one's disposal; obtainable.
- [as AVAIL]
- **availability** *noun*

- **availableness** *noun*
- **availably** *adverb*

avalanche *noun*
- "AVVA lanch"
- a mass of snow, ice, rock, etc. tumbling rapidly down a mountainside.
- [French, alteration of dialect *lavanche* after *avaler* descend]

avarice *noun*
- "AVVA riss"
- extreme greed for money or gain; cupidity.
- [Latin *avaritia* from *avarus* greedy]
- **avaricious** *adjective* "avva RISH iss"
- **avariciously** *adverb*
- **avariciousness** *noun*

avatar *noun*
- "AVVA tar"
- a manifestation of a deity or released soul in bodily form on earth; an incarnate divine teacher.
- [Sanskrit *avatāra* descent, from *áva* down + *tṛ-* pass over]

avaunt *interjection*
- "a VONT"
- begone.
- [Old French *avant*, ultimately from Latin *ab* from + *ante* before]

ave *noun*
- "AW vay"
- the prayer starting 'Hail Mary' ('Ave Maria' in Latin).
- [Latin, 2nd sing. imperative of *avēre* fare well]

avenge *verb*
- "a VENGE"
- inflict retribution on behalf of (a person, a violated right, etc.).
- [Old French *avengier* from *à* to + *vengier* from Latin *vindicare* vindicate]
- **avenger** *noun*

avens *noun*
- "AV 'nz"
- any of various rosaceous plants of the genus *Geum*.
- [Old French *avence* (medieval Latin *avencia*), of unknown origin]

aventurine *noun*
- "a VEN chur een"
- brownish ornamental glass containing sparkling gold-coloured particles usu. of copper or gold.
- [French from Italian *avventurino* from *avventura* chance (because of its accidental discovery)]

avenue *noun*
- "AVVA new"
- an urban road or street.
- [French, feminine past participle of *avenir* from Latin *advenire* come to]

aver *verb*
- "a VUR"
- assert or affirm.
- [Old French *averer* (*ad-* to + Latin *verus* true)]
- **averment** *noun*

average *noun*
- "AV ridge"
- the usual amount, extent, or rate.
- [French *avarie* damage to ship or cargo, from Italian *avaria* from Arabic *'awārīya* damaged goods, from *'awār* damage at sea, loss: *-age* after *damage*]
- **averagely** *adverb*

averse *adjective*
- "a VURSE"
- opposed, disinclined.
- [Latin *aversus* (as AVERT)]

aversion *noun*
- "a VUR zh'n"
- a dislike or unwillingness.
- [Latin *aversio* (as AVERT)]

avert *verb*
- "a VURT"
- turn away (one's eyes or thoughts).
- [Latin *avertere* (*ab-* from + *vertere vers-* turn)]

HOMOPHONES: *evert*

Avesta *noun*
- "a VESTA"
- the sacred writings of Zoroastrianism.
- [Persian]
- **Avestan** *adjective*

avgolemono *noun*
- "avgo LEMMA no"
- (in Greek cuisine) a sauce or soup made with eggs and lemon juice.
- [Greek, from *avgo* egg + *lemon* lemon]

avian *adjective*
- "AY vee 'n"
- of or relating to birds.
- [Latin *avis* bird]

aviary *noun*
- "AY vee airy"
- a large enclosure or building for keeping birds.
- [Latin *aviarium* (as AVIAN)]

aviation *noun*
- "ay vee AY sh'n"
- the skill or practice of operating aircraft.
- [French from Latin *avis* bird]

aviator *noun*
- "AY vee ater"
- an aircraft pilot.
- [French *aviateur* from Latin *avis* bird]

aviatrix *noun*
- "ay vee AY trix"
- a female aircraft pilot, esp. in the early days of flying.

• [as AVIATOR + Latin *-trix* feminine agent noun ending]

aviculture *noun*
• "AY vuh cull chur"
• the rearing and keeping of birds.
• [Latin *avis* bird, after AGRICULTURE]
• **aviculturist** *noun*

avifauna *noun*
• "AY vuh fonna"
• birds of a region or country collectively.
• [Latin *avis* bird + FAUNA]

avionics *noun*
• "ay vee ONNIX"
• electronics as applied to aviation.
• [blend of AVIATION + ELECTRONICS]
• **avionic** *adjective*

avitaminosis *noun*
• "ay vite a min OH sis"
• a condition resulting from a deficiency of one or more vitamins.
• [Greek *a-* without + VITAMIN]

avocado *noun*
• "ovva CODDO" or "avva CODDO" or "avva CADDO"
• a pear-shaped fruit with rough leathery skin, a smooth oily edible flesh, and a large pit.
• [Spanish, = advocate (substituted for Aztec *ahuacatl*)]

avocation *noun*
• "avva CAY sh'n"
• a secondary activity undertaken in addition to one's main work.
• [Latin *avocatio* from *avocare* call away]

avocet *noun*
• "AVVA set"
• any wading bird of the genus *Recurvirostra* with long legs and a long slender upward-curved bill and usu. black and white plumage.
• [French *avocette* from Italian *avosetta*]

avoirdupois *noun*
• "avver duh POYZ"
• a system of weights based on a pound of 16 ounces or 7,000 grains.
• [Middle English from Old French *aveir de peis* goods of weight, from *aveir* from Latin *habēre* have + *peis* weight from *pensum* weight, from *pendere pens-* weigh]

avouch *verb*
• "a VOUCH"
• guarantee, affirm, confess.
• [Old French *avochier* from Latin *advocare* (*ad-* to + *vocare* call)]
• **avouchment** *noun*

avowed *adjective*
• "a VOWD"
• admitted.
• [Old French *vo(u)* from Latin *vovēre* vow]
• **avowedly** *adverb* "a VOW id lee"

avulsion *noun*
• "a VULL sh'n"
• a forcible separation or detachment.
• [Latin *avulsio* from *avellere avuls-* pluck away]
• **avulse** *verb* "a VULSE"

avuncular *adjective*
• "a VUNK yuh lur"
• (of an older man, esp. in relation to younger people) benevolent and friendly.
• [Latin *avunculus* maternal uncle, diminutive of *avus* grandfather]

aweigh *predicative adjective*
• "a WAY"
• (of an anchor) clear of the bed of a body of water; hanging.
• [as WEIGH]
HOMOPHONES: *away*

awful *adjective*
• "AW full"
• unpleasant or horrible.
• ['awe' from Middle English *age* from Old Norse *agi* from Germanic]
• **awfully** *adverb*
• **awfulness** *noun*
HOMOPHONES: *offal*

awhile *adverb*
• "a WILE"
• for an unspecified length of time.
• [Old English]

awkward *adjective*
• "OCK wurd"
• ill-adapted for use; unwieldy.
• [obsolete *awk* backhanded, untoward, from Old Norse *afugr* turned the wrong way + *-weard*, from a Germanic root meaning 'turn']
• **awkwardly** *adverb*
• **awkwardness** *noun*

awl *noun*
• "ALL"
• a small pointed tool used for piercing holes, esp. in leather or wood.
• [Old English *æl*]
HOMOPHONES: *all*

awn *noun*
• "ON"
• a bristle-like projection growing from the grain sheath of barley, oats, and other grasses, or terminating a leaf etc.
• [Old Norse *ögn*]
• **awned** *adjective* "OND" (rhymes with *BLOND*)
HOMOPHONES: *on*

awning *noun*
• "ONNING"
• a sheet of canvas, plastic, etc. sloping outward from the top of a window, storefront, or doorway or suspended above a ship's deck or other area to provide protection from the sun or rain.
• [17th c. (Naut.): origin uncertain]
• **awninged** *adjective*

awry *adverb*
• "a RYE"
• crookedly or askew.
• [as WRY]

Axel *noun*
• "AX'll"
• a one-and-a-half-turn jump from the front outside edge of one skate to the back outside edge of the other.
• [*Axel* R. Paulsen, Norwegian figure skater d.1938]
HOMOPHONES: *axle, axil*

axil *noun*
• "AX 'll"
• the upper angle between a leaf and the stem it springs from, or between a branch and the trunk.
• [Latin *axilla*: see AXILLA]
HOMOPHONES: *Axel, axle*

axilla *noun*
• "ack SILLA"
• the armpit.
• [Latin, = armpit, diminutive of *ala* wing]
• **axillary** *adjective*

axiology *noun*
• "axy OLLA jee"
• the theory of values, esp. as they apply to ethics and aesthetics.
• [Greek *axia* value + *logos* word]

axiom *noun*
• "AXY um"
• an established or widely accepted principle.
• [Greek *axiōma axiōmat-* from *axios* worthy]

axiomatic *adjective*
• "axy a MATTIC"
• self-evident.
• [as AXIOM]
• **axiomatically** *adverb*

axis *noun*
• "AX iss"
• an imaginary line about which a body rotates or about which a plane figure is conceived as generating a solid.
• [Latin, = axle, pivot]
• **axial** *adjective*
• **axiality** *noun* "axy ALA tee"
• **axially** *adverb*

axle *noun*
• "AX'll"
• a rod or spindle (either fixed or rotating) on which a wheel or group of wheels is fixed.
• [originally *axle-tree* from Middle English *axel-tre* from Old Norse *öxull-tré*]
HOMOPHONES: *Axel, axil*

Axminster *noun*
• "AX minster"
• a kind of machine-woven patterned carpet with a cut pile.
• [*Axminster* in S England]

axolotl *noun*
• "AXA lot'll"
• any of a number of Central American salamanders of the genus *Ambystoma* (esp. *A. Mexicanum*), which live in lakes and retain many larval characteristics, including external gills, throughout life, although capable in certain conditions of developing full adult form.
• [Nahuatl from *atl* water + *xolotl* servant]

axon *noun*
• "AX on"
• a long threadlike part of a nerve cell, conducting impulses from the cell body.
• [Greek *axōn* axis]

ayah *noun*
• "EYE uh"
• a nursemaid or female servant esp. in India and other former British territories in Asia.
• [Anglo-Indian from Portuguese *aia* nurse]

ayahuasca *noun*
• "eye a WASKA"
• a tropical vine of the Amazon region, noted for its hallucinogenic properties.
• [Quechua *ayawáskha*, from *aya* corpse + *waskha* rope]

ayatollah *noun*
• "eye a TOLE uh"
• a Shiite religious leader in Iran.
• [Persian from Arabic, = token of God]

ayaya *noun*
• "ah yah YAH"
• singing, typically among the Inuit, in which the sounds *ay-ay-a* are used rather than words.
• [imitative]

aye *noun*
• Sounds like *EYE*
• an affirmative answer or assent, esp. in voting.
• [prob. from the pronoun *I* expressing assent]
HOMOPHONES: *eye, I*

Aymara *noun*
• "eye muh RAW"
• a member of an Aboriginal people of modern Bolivia and Peru, mainly inhabiting the plateaus near Lake Titicaca.
• [Bolivian Spanish]

Ayrshire *noun*
• "AIR sheer"
• a hardy breed of dairy cattle, mainly white with spots of red or brown, originating in Ayrshire, Scotland.

Ayurveda *noun*
• "eye yur VAY duh"
• a form of traditional Hindu medicine based on the idea of balance in bodily systems and using diet, herbal treatment, and yogic breathing.
• [Sanskrit *āyur-veda* = science of life, medicine]
• **Ayurvedic** *adjective*

azalea *noun*
- "a ZAILY uh"
- any of various flowering deciduous shrubs of the genus *Rhododendron*, with pink, purple, white, or yellow flowers.
- [Greek, feminine of *azaleos* dry (from the dry soil in which it was believed to flourish)]

azeotrope *noun*
- "a ZEE a trope"
- a mixture of liquids in which the boiling point remains constant during distillation, at a given pressure, without change in composition.
- [Greek *a-* without + Greek *zeō* boil + *tropos* turning]
- **azeotropic** *adjective* "a zee a TROPPIC"

Azerbaijani *noun*
- "azzer by JOHNNY"
- a native or inhabitant of Azerbaijan in the Caucasus of SE Europe.

Azeri *noun*
- "a ZERRY"
- a member of a Turkic people forming the majority population of Azerbaijan, and also living in Armenia and northern Iran.
- [Turkish *azeri*]

Azilian *adjective*
- "a ZILLY 'n"
- of an early mesolithic industry in S France and N Spain, dating to 10,000–8,000 BC.
- [Mas d'*Azil* in the French Pyrenees, where remains of the industry were found]

azimuth *noun*
- "AZZA muth"
- the angle between the most northerly point of the horizon and the point directly below a given celestial body, usu. measured clockwise using due north as the zero point.
- [Old French *azimut* from Arabic *as-sumūt* from *al* the + *sumūt* pl. of *samt* way, direction]
- **azimuthal** *adjective* "azza MOOTH 'll"

azine *noun*
- "AY zeen"
- an organic compound with at least one nitrogen atom in a six-membered ring.
- [French *azote* nitrogen, from Greek *azōos* without life]

azoic *adjective*
- "a ZO ick"
- having no trace of life.
- [Greek *azōos* without life]

Aztec *noun*
- "AZZ teck"
- a member of the Aboriginal people dominant in central and southern Mexico before the Spanish conquest of 1519.
- [Nahuatl *aztecatl* men of the north]

azure *noun*
- "AZH ur" or "AZZ yur"
- a deep sky-blue colour.
- [Old French *azur*, from medieval Latin *azzurum* from Arabic *al* the + *lāzaward* from Persian *lāžward* lapis lazuli]

azygous *adjective*
- "ay ZYE guss"
- (of any organic structure) single, not existing in pairs.
- [Greek *azugos* unyoked, from *a-* not + *zugon* yoke]

Bb

baasskap *noun*
• "BOSS cop"
• (in South Africa) domination, esp. of non-whites by whites.
• [Afrikaans from *baas* master + *-skap* condition]

baba *noun*
• "BOBBA"
• (among people of E European descent) grandmother.
• [Ukrainian]

Babbitt *noun*
• "BABBIT"
• any of a group of soft alloys of tin, antimony, copper, and usu. lead, used for lining bearings etc., to diminish friction.
• [I. *Babbitt*, US inventor d.1862]

babel *noun*
• "BAY bull" or "BABBLE"
• a confused noise, esp. of voices.
• [from *Babel*, where, according to the Biblical story (Gen. 11), God confused the language of the builders of a tower]
HOMOPHONES: *babble*

Babi *noun*
• "BABBY"
• a member of a Persian eclectic sect founded in 1844 by Mirza Ali Muhammad of Shiraz (called *the Bab*), emphasizing the coming of a new prophet or messenger of God. The Baha'i faith is derived from Babism.
• [Persian *Bab*-ed-Din, gate (= intermediary) of the Faith]
• **Babism** *noun*

babiche *noun*
• "ba BEESH"
• strips of rawhide or sinew used as laces, thread, webbing, etc., e.g. in snowshoes.
• [Canadian French from Mi'kmaq *a:papi:č*]

babka *noun*
• "BOB kuh"
• a sweet E European yeast cake flavoured with rum.
• [Polish, lit. 'old woman, grandmother']

babushka *noun*
• "ba BOOSH kuh"
• a kerchief tied under the chin.
• [Russian, = grandmother]

Babylonian *noun*
• "babba LONEY 'n"
• an inhabitant of Babylonia in ancient Mesopotamia, or of Babylon, its capital.

baccala *noun*
• "backa LAW" or "bocka LAW"
• cod, esp. dried and salted.
• [Italian *baccalá*]

baccalaureate *noun*
• "backa LORRY it"
• the university degree of bachelor.
• [French *baccalauréat* or medieval Latin *baccalaureatus* from *baccalaureus* bachelor]

baccarat *noun*
• "BACKA raw" or "BOCKA raw"
• a card game similar to blackjack, in which players take turns betting against the dealer.
• [French]

baccate *adjective*
• "BACK ate"
• bearing berries.
• [Latin *baccatus* berried, from *bacca* berry]

bacchanal *noun*
• "backa NAWL" or "bocka NAWL"
• a wild and drunken revelry.
• [Latin *bacchanalis* from *Bacchus* god of wine]

Bacchanalia *plural noun*
• "backa NAILY uh" or "bocka NAILY uh"
• the Roman festival of Bacchus, the god of wine.
• [Latin, neuter pl. of *bacchanalis*: see BACCHANAL]
• **bacchanalian** *adjective*

bacchant *noun*
• "BACK'nt"
• a priest, worshipper, or follower of Bacchus, the god of wine.
• [French *bacchante* from Latin *bacchari* celebrate Bacchanal rites]
• **bacchantic** *adjective*

bacchante *noun*
• "buh CANTY"
• a female bacchant.
• [as BACCHANT]

Bacchic *adjective*
- "BACKIC" or "BOCKIC"
- pertaining to or characteristic of Bacchus (the god of wine) or his cult.
- [Latin *bacchicus* of Bacchus]

bachelor *noun*
- "BATCH lur"
- an unmarried man.
- [Old French *bacheler* aspirant to knighthood, of uncertain origin]
- **bachelorhood** *noun*

bachelorette *noun*
- "batch lur ET"
- a young unmarried woman.
- [as BACHELOR]

bacilliform *adjective*
- "buh SILLA form"
- rod-shaped.
- [as BACILLUS]

bacillus *noun*
- "buh SILL us"
- any rod-shaped bacterium.
- [Late Latin, diminutive of Latin *baculus* stick]
- **bacillary** *adjective* "buh SILLER ee" or "BASSA lerry"

backgammon *noun*
- "BACK gam 'n"
- a game for two played on a board with pieces moved according to throws of the dice.
- ['back' + Middle English *gamen* game]

backwardation *noun*
- "backward AY sh'n"
- the percentage paid by a person selling stock for the right of delaying the delivery of it.
- [from 'backward']

Baconian *adjective*
- "bay CONEY 'n"
- of or relating to the English philosopher Sir Francis Bacon (d. 1626), or to his inductive method of reasoning and philosophy.

bacteremia *noun*
ALSO SPELLED: esp. *Brit.* **bacteraemia**
- "backter EEMY uh"
- the presence of bacteria in the blood.
- [from BACTERIA + *aimia* from Greek *haima* blood]

bacteria *plural noun*
- "back TEERY uh"
- any of various groups of unicellular micro-organisms lacking organelles and an organized nucleus, some of which can cause disease.
- [Greek *baktērion* diminutive of *baktron* stick]
- **bacterial** *adjective*
- **bacteriological** *adjective*
- **bacteriologically** *adverb*
- **bacteriologist** *noun*
- **bacteriology** *noun*

bactericide *noun*
- "back TEERA side"
- a substance capable of destroying bacteria.
- [as BACTERIA + Latin *-cida, -cidium* from *caedere* kill]
- **bactericidal** *adjective*

bacteriolysis *noun*
- "back teery OLLA sis"
- the rupture of bacterial cells.
- [BACTERIA + LYSIS]
- **bacteriolytic** *adjective* "back teery a LITTIC"

bacteriophage *noun*
- "back TEERY a fage"
- a virus parasitic on a bacterium, by infecting it and reproducing inside it.
- [BACTERIA + Greek *phagein* eat]

bacteriostat *noun*
- "back TEERY oh stat"
- a substance which inhibits the multiplying of bacteria without destroying them.
- [BACTERIA + Greek *statos* standing]
- **bacteriostatic** *adjective* "back teery a STATTIC"

bacteriuria *noun*
- "back teery YURY uh"
- the presence of bacteria in the urine.
- [as BACTERIA + Greek *-ouria* urine]

Bactrian *adjective*
- "BACK tree 'n"
- designating a camel, *Camelus bactrianus*, native to central Asia, with two humps.
- [*Bactria*, an ancient country in central Asia]

Baddecker *noun*
- "buh DECKER"
- a native or inhabitant of Baddeck, NS.

Badian *noun*
- "BAY dee 'n"
- a Barbadian.
- [abbreviation]

badinage *noun*
- "BADDA nozh"
- humorous or playful ridicule.
- [French from *badiner* to joke]

Baedeker *noun*
- "BAY duh kur"
- any of various travel guidebooks published by the firm founded by the German Karl *Baedeker* (d.1859).

bagasse *noun*
- "buh GAS"
- the dry pulpy residue left after the extraction of juice from sugar cane, usable as fuel or to make paper etc.
- [French from Spanish *bagazo*]

bagatelle *noun*
- "bagga TELL"
- a mere trifle; a negligible amount.
- [French from Italian *bagatella*, perhaps from *baga* baggage]

bagel *noun*
• "BAY g'll"
• a chewy, ring-shaped bread roll that is simmered before baking.
• [Yiddish *beygel*]

baggataway *noun*
• "buh GATTA way"
• a forerunner of lacrosse played by the Aboriginal peoples of eastern N America, in which opposing teams attempt to propel a ball into the other's goal using a mesh attached to a curved stick.
• [Ojibwa *paka'atowe* he plays lacrosse]

bagnio *noun*
• "BAN yo"
• a brothel.
• [Italian *bagno* from Latin *balneum* bath]

baguette *noun*
• "ba GET"
• a long narrow loaf of bread.
• [French from Italian *bacchetto* diminutive of *bacchio* from Latin *baculum* staff]

Bahamian *noun*
• "buh HAY mee 'n"
• a native or national of the Bahamas in the W Indies.

Bahasa *noun*
• "buh HOSSA"
• the form of Malay spoken as the official language of Indonesia.
• [from Malay *bahasa* language]

Bahraini *noun*
• "baw RAINY"
• a native or inhabitant of Bahrain in the Persian Gulf.

baht *noun*
• "BOT"
• the basic monetary unit of Thailand, equal to 100 stangs.
• [Thai *bāt*]
HOMOPHONES: *bot*

baidarka *noun*
• "by DARKA"
• a long, kayak-like boat for two or more people, used around the Aleutian Islands of Alaska.
• [Russian, diminutive of *baidara*, from Aleut]

bail *noun*
• "BALE"
• money etc. required as security against the temporary release of a prisoner pending trial.
• [Old French *bail* custody, *bailler* take charge of, from Latin *bajulare* bear a burden]
• **bailsman** *noun*
HOMOPHONES: *bale*

bailer *noun*
• "BAILER"
• a scoop for removing water from a boat.
• [obsolete *bail* (n.) bucket, from French *baille*, ultimately from Latin *bajulus* carrier]
HOMOPHONES: *bailor, baler*

bailey *noun*
• "BAILY"
• the outer wall of a castle.
• [Old French *bail(e)*, perhaps from *bailler* enclose]
HOMOPHONES: *bailie, bailee*

bailie *noun*
• "BAILY"
• a municipal officer and magistrate in Scotland.
• [Old French *bailli(s)* BAILIFF]
HOMOPHONES: *bailey, bailee*

bailiff *noun*
• "BAIL iff"
• an officer of the court who serves processes and enforces orders, esp. warrants authorizing the seizure of a debtor's goods.
• [Old French *baillif*, ultimately from Latin *bajulus* carrier, manager]

bailiwick *noun*
• "BALE a wick"
• the district or jurisdiction of a sheriff or bailiff.
• [BAILIE + Old English *wīc*, prob. from Germanic from Latin *vicus* street, village]

bailor *noun*
• "BAILER"
• a person or party who transfers the possession of goods for a specified purpose, e.g. custody or repair, without transfer of ownership.
• [as BAIL]
• **bailee** *noun*
• **bailment** *noun*
HOMOPHONES: *bailer, baler*

bailout *noun*
• "BAIL out"
• a financial rescue.
• [as BAIL + 'out']

Bairam *noun*
• "by RAM" or "BY ram"
• either of two annual Muslim festivals, the Lesser Bairam, lasting one day, which follows the fast of Ramadan, and the Greater Bairam, lasting three days, seventy days later.
• [Turkish & Persian]

bairn *noun*
• "BAIRN"
• a child.
• [Old English *bearn*]

bait *noun*
• "BATE"
• food used to entice prey.
• [Old Norse *beita* hunt or chase]
• **baited** *adjective*
HOMOPHONES: *bated*

baiza *noun*
• "BY zuh"
• a monetary unit of Oman, equal to one thousandth of a rial.
• [Arabic]

baize *noun*
• "BAZE"
• a coarse usu. green woollen material resembling felt used as a covering or lining, esp. on the tops of billiard tables and card tables.
• [French *baies* (pl.) feminine of *bai* chestnut-coloured, treated as sing.]

Bajan *noun*
• "BAY j'n"
• a Barbadian.
• [representative of a certain pronunciation of BADIAN]

bakeware *noun*
• "BAKE ware"
• pans, pie plates, etc., used in baking.
• ['bake' + WARE]

baklava *noun*
• "BACKLA vuh" or "backla VAW"
• a rich sweet dessert of flaky pastry, honey, and nuts.
• [Turkish]

baksheesh *noun*
ALSO SPELLED: **backsheesh**
• "BACK sheesh"
• (in parts of the Middle East, Far East, and the Indian subcontinent) a small sum of money given as a gratuity or as alms.
• [ultimately from Persian *bak̲šīš* from *bak̲šīdan* give]

balaclava *noun*
• "bala CLAVA"
• a tight knitted garment covering the whole head and neck with holes for the eyes and mouth.
• [*Balaklava* in the Crimea, where soldiers first wore them]

balafon *noun*
• "BALA fon"
• a wooden musical instrument from Africa, precursor of the xylophone.
• [French *balafon* from Manding *bala* xylophone + *fo* play]

balalaika *noun*
• "bala LIKE uh"
• a guitar-like musical instrument having a triangular body and 2 to 4 strings, popular in Russia and other Slavic countries.
• [Russian]

balata *noun*
• "BALA tuh"
• any of several latex-yielding trees of Central America, esp. *Manilkara bidentata*.
• [ultimately from Carib]

balboa *noun*
• "bal BOA"
• the basic monetary unit of Panama, equal to 100 cents.
• [V. N. de *Balboa*, Spanish explorer d.1517]

Balbriggan *noun*
• "bal BRIG'n"
• a knitted cotton fabric used for underwear etc.
• [*Balbriggan* in Ireland, where it was originally made]

balcony *noun*
• "BAL kuh nee"
• a usu. balustraded platform on the outside of a building, with access from an upper-floor window or door.
• [Italian *balcone* from *balco* scaffold]
• **balconied** *adjective* "BAL kuh need"

baldachin *noun*
ALSO SPELLED: **baldaquin**
• "BAWLDA kin"
• an ornamental canopy of cloth or stone over an altar, throne, etc.
• [Italian *baldacchino* from *Baldacco* Baghdad, Iraq, its place of origin]

balderdash *noun*
• "BAWLDER dash"
• senseless talk or writing; nonsense.
• [17th c., earlier = 'mixture of drinks': origin unknown]

baldric *noun*
• "BAWLD rick"
• a belt for a sword, bugle, etc., hung from the shoulder across the body to the opposite hip.
• [Old French *baudrei*: compare Middle High German *balderich*, of unknown origin]

bale *noun*
• "BALE"
• a bundle of material tightly wrapped or bound.
• [Middle English prob. from Middle Dutch, ultimately identical with 'ball']
HOMOPHONES: *bail*

baleen *noun*
• "buh LEEN"
• whalebone.
• [Old French *baleine* from Latin *balaena* whale]

baleful *adjective*
• "BALE full"
• (esp. of a manner, look, etc.) gloomy, menacing.
• [Old English *b(e)alu* evil, destruction, woe, pain, misery]
• **balefully** *adverb*
• **balefulness** *noun*

baler *noun*
• "BAILER"
• a machine for making bales of hay, straw, or other material.

• [as BALE]
HOMOPHONES: *bailer, bailor*

Balinese *noun*
• "bala NEEZ"
• a native or inhabitant of Bali, an island of Indonesia.

balk *verb*
ALSO SPELLED: esp. *Brit.* **baulk**
• "BOCK"
• refuse to go on.
• [Old English *balc* from Old Norse *bálkr* from Germanic]
• **balker** *noun* (also esp. *Brit.* **baulker**)
HOMOPHONES: *bawk, bock*

Balkan *adjective*
• "BAWL k'n"
• of or relating to the people or nations of the Balkan Peninsula in SE Europe.
• [Turkish *balkan* chain of wooded mountains]

balkanize *verb*
ALSO SPELLED: esp. *Brit.* **-ise**
• "BAWLKA nize"
• divide (a country etc.) into smaller mutually hostile units.
• [the Balkan Peninsula, which was divided into quarrelsome units in the late 19th and early 20th c.]
• **balkanization** *noun* (also esp. *Brit.* **-isation**)
• **balkanized** *adjective* (also esp. *Brit.* **-ised**)

balky *adjective*
ALSO SPELLED: esp. *Brit.* **baulky**
• "BOCKY"
• reluctant, perverse.
• [as BALK]
• **balkiness** *noun* (also esp. *Brit.* **baulkiness**)

ballad *noun*
• "BAL id"
• a poem or song narrating a popular story.
• [Old French *balade* from Provençal *balada* dancing song, from *balar* to dance]
• **balladeer** *noun*
• **balladry** *noun*

ballade *noun*
• "buh LOD"
• a poem of one or more triplets of stanzas with a repeated refrain and an envoy.
• [earlier spelling and pronunciation of BALLAD]

ballast *noun*
• "BAL ist"
• any heavy material carried by a ship or balloon etc. to secure stability.
• [16th c.: from Low German or Scandinavian, of uncertain origin]

ballerina *noun*
• "bala REENA"
• a female ballet dancer.
• [Italian, from *ballare* dance, from Late Latin *ballare* dance]

ballet *noun*
• "BAL ay" or "bal AY"
• a theatrical style of dancing using set steps and techniques and characterized esp. by movement with the legs turned out in the hip sockets and by the women dancing on pointe.
• [French from Italian *balletto* diminutive of *ballo* from Late Latin *ballare* dance]
• **balletic** *adjective* "buh LETTIC"

balletomane *noun*
• "buh LETTO mane"
• a devotee of ballet.
• [BALLET + French *-mane*, = MANIAC]
• **balletomania** *noun*

ballicatter *noun*
• "BALA catter"
• *Cdn* (*Nfld*) ice formed along a shoreline from waves and freezing spray.
• [alteration of BARRICADE]

ballista *noun*
• "buh LISTA"
• an ancient weapon resembling a catapult or large crossbow used for hurling stones or other missiles.
• [Latin from Greek *ballō* throw]

ballistic *adjective*
• "buh LISTIC"
• of or relating to projectiles.
• [as BALLISTA]
• **ballistically** *adverb*
• **ballistics** *noun*

ballon *noun*
• "bal ÕH" (with a nasal *OH*)
• a ballet dancer's ability to prolong a jump by appearing to pause in mid-air.
• [French, = balloon]

balloon *noun*
• "buh LOON"
• a small inflatable rubber pouch with a neck, used as a toy or as decoration.
• [French *ballon* or Italian *ballone* large ball]
• **ballooning** *noun*
• **balloonist** *noun*

ballot *noun*
• "BAL it"
• a system of secret voting, usu. by marking a paper with one's choice of candidate etc.
• [Italian *ballotta* diminutive of *balla* ball]

ballyhoo *noun*
• "BALEE hoo"
• extravagant or brash publicity; hype.
• [19th or 20th c., origin unknown]
• **ballyhooed** *adjective*

balm *noun*
• "BOM" or "BAWLM"
• an aromatic ointment for anointing, soothing, or healing.
• [Old French *ba(s)me* from Latin *balsamum* BALSAM]
HOMOPHONES: *bomb, bombe*

balmoral *noun*
• "bal MOR'll"
• a brimless hat with a cockade or ribbons attached.
• [*Balmoral* Castle in Scotland]

balmy *adjective*
• "BOMMY" or "BAWLMY"
• (of weather) warm.
• [as BALM]
• **balmily** *adverb*
• **balminess** *noun*

balneology *noun*
• "bal nee OLLA jee"
• the scientific study of bathing and medicinal springs.
• [Latin *balneum* bath + *logos* word]
• **balneologist** *noun*

baloney *noun*
• "buh LONEY"
• nonsensical or absurd ideas.
• [corruption of BOLOGNA]
HOMOPHONES: *bologna*

balsa *noun*
• "BAWL suh"
• a tough lightweight wood used for making boats, model airplanes, etc.
• [Spanish, = raft]

balsam *noun*
• "BAWL sum"
• any of several aromatic resins, such as balm, obtained from various trees and shrubs and used as a base for certain fragrances and medical preparations.
• [Old English from Latin *balsamum*]
• **balsamic** *adjective* "bawl SAMMIC"

balsamroot *noun*
• "BAWL sum root"
• any of several herbaceous plants of the genus *Balsamorhiza* of western N America, esp. *B. sagittata*, with yellow sunflower-like flowers and arrow-shaped leaves.
• [as BALSAM + 'root']

Balt *noun*
• "BAWLT"
• a native or inhabitant of one of the states surrounding the Baltic Sea, esp. Estonia, Latvia, and Lithuania.
• [Late Latin *Balthae*]
• **Baltic** *adjective*

balti *noun*
• "BAWL tee"
• a type of Pakistani cuisine in which the food is cooked in a small two-handled pan.
• [Urdu *bāltī*, literally 'pail']

Baltimorean *noun*
• "bawl tuh MORY 'n"
• a resident of Baltimore, Maryland.

baluster *noun*
• "BALA stur"
• each of a series of often ornamental short posts supporting a railing etc.
• [French *balustre* from Italian *balaustro* from Latin from Greek *balaustion* wild pomegranate flower]

balustrade *noun*
• "BALA strade"
• a railing supported by balusters, esp. forming an ornamental parapet to a balcony, bridge, or terrace.
• [French (as BALUSTER)]
• **balustraded** *adjective*

bambino *noun*
• "bam BEENO"
• a young (esp. Italian) child.
• [Italian, diminutive of *bambo* silly]

bamboozle *verb*
• "bam BOOZLE"
• cheat, deceive, swindle.
• [*c.*1700: prob. of cant origin]
• **bamboozlement** *noun*
• **bamboozler** *noun*

banal *adjective*
• "buh NAL"
• trite, trivial, commonplace.
• [originally in sense 'compulsory', hence 'common to all', from French from *ban* from a Germanic word meaning 'summon']
• **banality** *noun*
• **banally** *adverb*

banausic *adjective*
• "buh NOSSIC"
• uncultivated, unsophisticated.
• [Greek *banausikos* 'for artisans']

bandana *noun*
ALSO SPELLED: **bandanna**
• "ban DANNA"
• a coloured handkerchief or head scarf, usu. of cotton, and often having a figured design.
• [prob. Portuguese from Hindi]

bandeau *noun*
• "BANDO" or "ban DOE"
• a strapless band of material worn around the breasts, esp. as part of a swimsuit.
• [French]

banderilla *noun*
• "bander EEYA" or "bander EELYA"
• a decorated dart thrust into a bull's neck or shoulders during a bullfight.
• [Spanish]

banderole *noun*
ALSO SPELLED: **banderol**
• "BANDER ole"
• a long narrow flag with a cleft end, flown from the masthead of a ship.
• [French *banderole* from Italian *banderuola* diminutive of *bandiera* banner]

bandicoot *noun*
• "BANDA coot"

• any of the small insect- and plant-eating marsupials of the family Peramelidae, found in Australasia.
• [Telugu *pandikokku* pig-rat]

bandolier *noun*
ALSO SPELLED: **bandoleer**
• "banda LEER"
• a belt or strap worn diagonally across the chest with loops or pockets for ammunition.
• [Dutch *bandelier* or French *bandoulière*, prob. formed as BANDEROLE]

bandura *noun*
• "ban DURA"
• a Ukrainian stringed instrument resembling a large lopsided lute and held almost vertically on the lap when played.
• [Ukrainian]
• **bandurist** *noun*

bane *noun*
• "BANE"
• the cause of ruin or trouble.
• [Old English *bana* from Germanic]
• **baneful** *adjective*
• **banefully** *adverb*

baneberry *noun*
• "BANE berry"
• a plant of the genus *Actaea*, related to the buttercup.
• [as BANE, because its berry is poisonous]

Banffite *noun*
• "BANF ite"
• a resident of Banff, Alberta.

Bangladeshi *noun*
• "bang gla DESHY"
• a native or inhabitant of Bangladesh.

banish *verb*
• "BANNISH"
• formally expel (a person), esp. from a country.
• [Old English *banir*, ultimately from Germanic]
• **banishment** *noun*

banister *noun*
ALSO SPELLED: **bannister**
• "BAN iss tur"
• the handrail at the side a staircase.
• [earlier *barrister*, corruption of BALUSTER]

banjax *verb*
• "BAN jacks"
• ruin, incapacitate.
• [20th c.: orig. Anglo-Irish, of unknown origin]

banjo *noun*
• "BAN joe"
• a four- or five-stringed musical instrument with a neck and head like a guitar and an open-backed body consisting of parchment stretched over a metal hoop.
• [US southern corruption of earlier *bandore*, ultimately from Greek *pandoura* three-stringed lute]
• **banjoist** *noun*

banksia *noun*
• "BANKSY uh"
• any evergreen flowering shrub of the genus *Banksia*, native to Australia.
• [Sir J. *Banks*, English naturalist d.1820]

banneret *noun*
• "BANNER it" or "banner ET"
• a knight who commanded his own troops in battle under his own banner.
• [Old French *baneret*, lit. 'bannered', from *baniere* banner]

bannock *noun*
• "BAN uck"
• *Cdn* a bread similar to tea biscuits, made of flour, water, and fat, sometimes leavened with baking powder, and cooked on a griddle or over a fire.
• [Old English *bannuc*, perhaps from Celtic]

banns *plural noun*
• "BANZ"
• an oral or published notice announcing an intended marriage and giving the opportunity for objections, esp. one repeated on three successive Sundays in a church.
• [Old English *bannan* summon, from Germanic]

banquet *noun*
• "BANG kwit"
• an elaborate and extensive feast.
• [French, diminutive of *banc* bench]
• **banqueter** *noun*

banquette *noun*
• "bang KET"
• an upholstered bench along a wall, esp. in a restaurant or bar.
• [French from Italian *banchetta* diminutive of *banca* bench]

banshee *noun*
• "BANSHY"
• (in Gaelic mythology) a female spirit whose wailing warns of imminent death in a family.
• [Irish *bean sídhe* from Old Irish *ben síde* woman of the fairies]

bantam *noun*
• "BANT'm"
• any of several small breeds of domestic fowl, of which the rooster is very aggressive.
• [apparently from *Bāntān* in Java, although the fowl is not native there]

bantamweight *noun*
• "BAN t'm wate"
• a weight class in certain sports between flyweight and featherweight, in the professional boxing scale not more than 118 lbs. (53 kg) but differing for amateur boxers and wrestlers.
• [as BANTAM (applied to a person who is small but aggressive like the bantam rooster) + 'weight']

Bantu *noun*
- "BAN too"
- a group of Niger-Congo languages spoken in equatorial and southern Africa, including Swahili, Xhosa, and Zulu.
- [in certain Bantu languages, pl. of *-ntu* person]

banyan *noun*
- "BAN y'n"
- an Indian fig tree, *Ficus benghalensis*, the branches of which produce aerial roots to form new trunks.
- [Portuguese *banian* from Gujarati *vāṇiyo* man of trading caste, from Sanskrit: applied originally by Europeans to one such tree under which merchants had built a pagoda]

banzai *interjection*
- "bon ZYE" or "BON zye"
- a Japanese battle cry.
- [Japanese, = ten thousand years (of life to you)]

HOMOPHONES: *bonsai*

baobab *noun*
- "BAY oh bab"
- an African tree, *Adansonia digitata*, with an enormously thick trunk and large fruit containing edible pulp.
- [Latin, prob. from a central African language]

baptism *noun*
- "BAP tizm"
- a religious rite symbolizing admission to the Christian Church, involving sprinkling the forehead with water or total immersion and generally accompanied by naming.
- [ecclesiastical Greek *baptismos* from *baptizō* immerse, baptize]
- **baptismal** *adjective* "bap TIZZ m'll"
- **baptize** *verb* (also esp. *Brit.* **-ise**)

baptistery *noun*
ALSO SPELLED: **baptistry**
- "BAP tiss tree"
- the part of a church used for baptism.
- [as BAPTISM]

barachois *noun*
- "BAR a shwah"
- *Cdn* (*Nfld* & *Maritimes*) a shallow coastal lagoon or pond created by the formation of a sandbar a short distance offshore from a beach.
- [Canadian French]

barathea *noun*
- "bar a THEE uh" (with "TH" as in *THIN*)
- a fine woollen cloth, sometimes mixed with silk or cotton, used esp. for coats, suits, etc.
- [19th c.: origin unknown]

Barbadian *noun*
- "bar BAY dee 'n"
- a native or inhabitant of Barbados in the Caribbean.

barbarian *noun*
- "bar BERRY 'n"
- an uncultured or brutish person.
- [originally of any foreigner with a different language or customs: French *barbarien* from *barbare* from Latin from Greek *barbaros* foreign]

barbaric *adjective*
- "bar BARE ick"
- brutal; cruel.
- [Greek *barbarikos* from *barbaros* foreign]
- **barbarically** *adverb*
- **barbarity** *noun*

barbarism *noun*
- "BARBER izm"
- the absence of culture and civilized standards; ignorance and rudeness.
- [Greek *barbarismos* from *barbarizō* speak like a foreigner, from *barbaros* foreign]
- **barbarization** *noun* (also esp. *Brit.* **-isation**)
- **barbarize** *verb* (also esp. *Brit.* **-ise**)
- **barbarous** *adjective*
- **barbarously** *adverb*
- **barbarousness** *noun*

barbecue *noun*
ALSO SPELLED: **barbeque**
- "BARBA kyoo"
- a meal, esp. of meat, cooked on an open fire or grill out of doors.
- [Spanish *barbacoa* from Arawak *barbacòa* wooden frame on posts]

barbel *noun*
- "BARBLE"
- any large European freshwater fish of the genus *Barbus*, with fleshy filaments hanging from its mouth.
- [Old French from Late Latin *barbellus* diminutive of *barbus* barbel, from *barba* beard]

HOMOPHONES: *barbell*

barbet *noun*
- "BAR bit"
- any small brightly coloured tropical bird of the family Capitonidae, with bristles at the base of its beak.
- [French from *barbe* beard]

HOMOPHONES: *barbotte*

barbette *noun*
- "bar BET"
- a platform in a fort from which guns can be fired over a parapet etc. and not through an embrasure.
- [French, diminutive of *barbe* beard]

barbican *noun*
- "BARBICK 'n"
- the outer defence of a city, castle, etc., esp. a double tower above a gate or drawbridge.
- [Old French *barbacane*, of unknown origin]

barbital *noun*
- "BARBA tawl"
- a long-acting hypnotic and sedative drug.
- [as BARBITURIC + *-al* as in VERONAL]

barbiturate *noun*
- "bar BITCH ur it" or "bar BITCH ur ate"
- any derivative of barbituric acid used in the preparation of sedative and sleep-inducing drugs.
- [as BARBITURIC]

barbituric *adjective*
- "barba CHURIC"
- designating an organic acid from which various sedatives and sleep-inducing drugs are derived.
- [French *barbiturique* from German *Barbitursäure* (*Säure* acid) from the name *Barbara*]

barbotte *noun*
ALSO SPELLED: **barbot**
- "BAR but"
- *Cdn* (*Que.* & *Ont.*) a large catfish, esp. *Ictalurus punctatus*.
- [Canadian French]

HOMOPHONES: *barbet*

barbule *noun*
- "BARB yool"
- a minute filament projecting from the barb of a feather.
- [Latin *barbula*, diminutive of *barba* beard]

barcarole *noun*
ALSO SPELLED: **barcarolle**
- "BARKA role"
- a song sung by Venetian gondoliers.
- [French *barcarolle* from Venetian Italian *barcarola* boatman's song, from *barca* boat]

barège *noun*
- "buh REZH"
- a silky gauze made from wool or other material.
- [French from *Barèges* in SW France, where it was originally made]

bargain *noun*
- "BARG'n"
- an agreement on the terms of a transaction or sale.
- [Old French *bargaine*, *bargaignier*, prob. from Germanic]
- **bargainer** *noun*

bariatric *adjective*
- "berry ATTRIC"
- (of medical care etc.) aimed at treating obesity.
- [Greek *barus* heavy + *iatreia* healing]

barista *noun*
- "bar EESTA"
- a person who makes and serves coffee in a specialty coffee shop.
- [Italian, = bartender]

barite *noun*
ALSO SPELLED: **baryte**
- "BARE ite"
- a mineral form of barium sulphate.
- [Greek *barus* heavy, partly assimilated to mineral names in *-ites*]

baritone *noun*
- "BERRA tone"
- the second-lowest adult male singing voice.
- [Italian *baritono* from Greek *barutonos* from *barus* heavy + *tonos* tone]

barium *noun*
- "BERRY um"
- a white reactive soft metallic element of the alkaline-earth group.
- [as BARYTA]

barley *noun*
- "BARLY"
- any of various hardy awned cereals of the genus *Hordeum*, widely used as food and in malt liquors and spirits such as whisky.
- [Old English *bærlic* (adjective) from *bære*, *bere* barley]

barleycorn *noun*
- "BARLY corn"
- the grain of barley.
- [as BARLEY + 'corn' from Old English from Germanic: related to Latin *granum* grain]

Barmecide *adjective*
- "BARMA side"
- illusory, imaginary; such as to disappoint.
- [the name of a wealthy man in the *Arabian Nights' Entertainments* who gave a beggar a feast consisting of ornate but empty dishes]

barnacle *noun*
- "BARNA k'll"
- any of various species of small marine crustaceans of the class Cirripedia which in adult form cling to rocks, ships' bottoms, etc.
- [Middle English *bernak* (= medieval Latin *bernaca*), of unknown origin]
- **barnacled** *adjective*

barograph *noun*
- "BERRA graff"
- a barometer equipped to record its readings.
- [Greek *baros* weight + *graphia* writing]

Barolo *noun*
- "buh ROLL oh"
- a full-bodied red Italian wine from the Barolo region of Piedmont in N Italy.

barometer *noun*
- "ba ROMMA tur"
- an instrument measuring atmospheric pressure, esp. in forecasting the weather and determining altitude.
- [Greek *baros* weight + *metron* measure]
- **barometric** *adjective* "berra METRIC"

baron *noun*
- "BARE 'n"
- a member of the lowest order of nobility in the United Kingdom or other countries.
- [Old French *baron* from medieval Latin *baro*, *-onis* man, of unknown origin]

• **baronial** *adjective* "buh ROANY 'll"
HOMOPHONES: *barren*

baronage *noun*
• "BARE 'n idge"
• barons or nobles collectively.
• [as BARON]

baroness *noun*
• "BARE 'n ess"
• a woman holding the rank of baron either as a life peerage or as a hereditary rank.
• [as BARON]
HOMOPHONES: *barrenness*

baronet *noun*
• "BARE 'n et"
• a member of the lowest hereditary titled British order, below a baron but above a knight.
• [Anglo-Latin *baronettus* (as BARON)]
• **baronetcy** *noun*

baronetage *noun*
• "BARE 'n ut idge"
• baronets collectively.
• [as BARONET]

barony *noun*
• "BERRA nee"
• the domain, rank, or tenure of a baron.
• [as BARON]

baroque *noun*
• "buh ROKE"
• a style of architecture and decorative art of the late 16th to early 18th c., characterized by extensive ornamentation.
• [French (originally = 'irregular pearl') from Portuguese *barroco*, of unknown origin]

barouche *noun*
• "buh ROOSH"
• a horse-drawn carriage with four wheels and a collapsible hood over the rear half, used esp. in the 19th c.
• [German (dialect) *Barutsche* from Italian *baroccio*, ultimately from Latin *birotus* two-wheeled]

barque *noun*
• "BARK"
• a sailing ship with the rear mast fore-and-aft-rigged and the remaining (usu. two) masts square-rigged.
• [French prob. from Provençal *barca* from Latin *barca* ship's boat]
HOMOPHONES: *bark*

barquentine *noun*
ALSO SPELLED: esp. *US* **barkentine**
• "BARK'n teen"
• a sailing ship with the foremast square-rigged and the remaining (usu. two) masts fore-and-aft-rigged.
• [BARQUE after *brigantine*]

barrack *noun*
• "BARE uck"
• a building or building complex used to house soldiers.
• [French *baraque* from Italian *baracca* or Spanish *barraca* soldier's tent, of unknown origin]

barracuda *noun*
• "berra COODA"
• a large and voracious tropical marine fish of the family Sphyraenidae.
• [Latin American Spanish *barracuda*]

barrage *noun*
• "buh ROZH"
• a concentrated artillery bombardment over a wide area.
• [French from *barrer* from *barre* bar]

barramundi *noun*
• "berra MUNDY"
• any of various edible Australian freshwater fishes, esp. *Lates calcarifer*.
• [prob. Aboriginal (Queensland)]

barratry *noun*
• "BA ruh tree"
• fraud or gross negligence of a ship's master or crew at the expense of its owners or users.
• [Old French *baraterie* deceit, from *barat* deceit, fraud, trouble, etc.]
• **barrator** *noun* "BA ruh tur"
• **barratrous** *adjective*

barre *noun*
• "BAR"
• a waist-level horizontal bar to help dancers keep their balance during some exercises.
• [French]
HOMOPHONES: *bar*

barré *noun*
• "BAR ay"
• a method of playing a chord on the guitar etc. with a finger laid across the strings at a particular fret, raising their pitch.
• [French, past participle of *barrer* bar]

barren *adjective*
• "BARE 'n"
• unable to bear young.
• [Anglo-French *barai(g)ne*, Old French *barhaine* etc., of unknown origin]
• **barrenly** *adverb*
• **barrenness** *noun*
HOMOPHONES: *baron, baroness*

barrette *noun*
• "buh RET"
• a bar-shaped clip or ornament for a woman's or girl's hair.
• [French]

barricade *noun*
• "BERRA cade"
• a barrier, esp. one improvised across a street etc.
• [French from *barrique* cask, from Spanish *barrica*]

barrier *noun*
- "BERRY ur"
- a fence or other obstacle that bars advance or access.
- [Old French *barriere*]

barrio *noun*
- "BAR ee oh"
- a ward or quarter of town in Spain and Spanish-speaking countries.
- [Spanish, = district of a town]

barrique *noun*
- "buh REEK"
- a wine barrel, varying in size according to place of origin, esp. that of Bordeaux in SW France.
- [French]

barrister *noun*
- "BERRA stur"
- *Cdn* a lawyer who pleads cases before the courts.
- [16th c.: from 'bar' (a rail in a law court separating the space occupied by the judge, lawyers, and parties to a case from the general public), perhaps after *minister*]

Barsac *noun*
- "BAR sack"
- a sweet white wine from the district of Barsac, department of Gironde, in SW France.

bartizan *noun*
- "BARTA zan"
- a battlemented parapet or an overhanging corner turret at the top of a castle or church tower.
- [var. of *bertisene*, erroneous spelling of *bratticing*: see BRATTICE]
- **bartizaned** *adjective*

Bartlett *noun*
- "BART let"
- a large, yellow, juicy variety of pear.
- [E. *Bartlett*, US merchant d.1860]

baryon *noun*
- "BERRY on"
- any of the heavier elementary particles (protons, neutrons, hyperons).
- [Greek *barus* heavy]
- **baryonic** *adjective*

barysphere *noun*
- "BERRIS feer"
- the dense interior of the earth, including the mantle and core, enclosed by the lithosphere.
- [Greek *barus* heavy + *sphaira* sphere]

baryta *noun*
- "buh RITE uh"
- barium oxide or hydroxide.
- [BARITE, after *soda* etc.]
- **barytic** *adjective* "buh RITTIC"

basal *adjective*
- "BASE 'll"
- of, at, or forming a base.
- [from 'base', from French *base* or Latin *basis* stepping, from Greek]

basalt *noun*
- "BA salt"
- a dark basic volcanic rock whose strata sometimes form columns.
- [Latin *basaltes* var. of *basanites* from Greek from *basanos* touchstone]
- **basaltic** *adjective* "ba SAUL tick"

bascule *noun*
- "BASK yool"
- a type of drawbridge which is raised and lowered using counterweights.
- [French, earlier *bacule* see-saw, from *battre* bump + *cul* buttocks]

basenji *noun*
- "buh SEN jee"
- a smallish hunting dog of a central African breed, which growls and yelps but does not bark.
- [Bantu]

basicity *noun*
- "bay SISSA tee"
- the number of hydrogen atoms replaceable by a base in a particular acid.
- [from 'base', from French *base* or Latin *basis* stepping, from Greek]

basidium *noun*
- "buh SIDDY um"
- a microscopic spore-bearing structure produced by certain fungi.
- [modern Latin from Greek *basidion* diminutive of *basis* stepping]

basil *noun*
- "BAZZ'Il" or "BAYZ'Il"
- an aromatic herb of the genus *Ocimum*, esp. *O. basilicum* , whose leaves are used as a flavouring in savoury dishes.
- [Old French *basile* from medieval Latin *basilicus* from Greek *basilikos* royal]

basilar *adjective*
- "BAZZ'Il ur"
- of or at the base (esp. of the skull).
- [modern Latin *basilaris* (as BASAL)]

Basilian *noun*
- "buh ZILL y'n"
- a member of the Congregation of St. Basil (Basilian Fathers), an esp. teaching order of Roman Catholic priests.
- [St. *Basil*, Doctor of the Church d.379]

HOMOPHONES: *bazillion*

basilica *noun*
- "ba SILLA kuh" or "buh ZILLA kuh"
- an ancient Roman public hall with an apse and colonnades, used as a law court and place of assembly.
- [Latin from Greek *basilikē* (*oikia*, *stoa*) royal (house, portico) from *basileus* king]
- **basilican** *adjective*

basilisk *noun*
- "BAZZ'll isk"
- a mythical reptile with a lethal gaze and breath.
- [Latin *basiliscus* from Greek *basiliskos* kinglet, serpent]

basipetal *adjective*
- "bay SIPPA t'll"
- (of each new part produced) growing or developing nearer the base than the previous one did.
- [BASAL + Latin *petere* seek]
- **basipetally** *adverb*

basmati *noun*
- "bazz MATTY"
- a kind of rice with very long thin grains and a delicate fragrance.
- [Hindi, = fragrant]

Basque *noun*
- "BASK" or "BOSK"
- a member of a people inhabiting the western Pyrenees in central northern Spain and the extreme southwest of France.
- [French from Latin *Vasco -onis*]

HOMOPHONES: *bask*

bass *noun*
- "BASE"
- the lowest adult male singing voice.
- [alteration of 'base', from French *bas* from medieval Latin *bassus* short after BASSO]

HOMOPHONES: *base*

bassinet *noun*
- "bassa NET"
- a portable basket-like bed for a young baby, often with a hood.
- [French, diminutive of *bassin* basin, from medieval Latin *ba(s)cinus*, perhaps from Gaulish]

bassist *noun*
- "BASE ist"
- a person who plays a bass guitar or a double bass.
- [as BASS]

basso *noun*
- "BASS oh" ("BASS" rhymes with *PASS*)
- a singer with a bass voice.
- [Italian, = BASS]

bassoon *noun*
- "buh SOON"
- a bass instrument of the oboe family, with a double reed.
- [French *basson* from *bas* BASS]
- **bassoonist** *noun*

bastard *noun*
- "BAS turd"
- a person born of parents not married to each other.
- [Old French from medieval Latin *bastardus*, perhaps from *bastum* packsaddle]
- **bastardy** *noun*

bastardize *verb*

ALSO SPELLED: esp. *Brit.* **-ise**
- "BAS turd ize"
- corrupt, debase.
- [as BASTARD]
- **bastardization** *noun* (also esp. *Brit.* **-isation**)

baste *verb*
- "BAYST"
- moisten (meat) with gravy, melted fat, etc. during cooking.
- [16th c.: origin unknown]
- **baster** *noun*

bastinado *noun*
- "bas tee NAY doe"
- punishment by beating with a stick on the soles of the feet.
- [Spanish *bastonada* from *baston* BATON]

bastion *noun*
- "BAS ch'n"
- a projecting part of a fortification built at an angle to, or against the line of, a wall.
- [French from Italian *bastione* from *bastire* build]

batard *noun*
- "buh TAR"
- *Cdn* a birchbark canoe used in the fur trade, about 9 m (30 ft.) long and capable of carrying about 2 000 kg (two tons) of freight.
- [Canadian French *canot bâtard*, as BASTARD]

bateau *noun*

ALSO SPELLED: **batteau**
- "ba TOE"
- *Cdn* a light, shallow-draft, flat-bottomed boat with pointed bow and stern, esp. of the kind used by fur traders, propelled by oars, poles, or sails, or drawn by horses.
- [French, = boat]

bated *adjective*
- "BATED"
- (of the breath) held in anxiety.
- [past participle of obsolete *bate* (v.) restrain, from ABATE]

HOMOPHONES: *baited*

batholith *noun*
- "BATH a lith"
- a dome of igneous rock extending inwards to an unknown depth.
- [German from Greek *bathos* depth + Greek *lithos* stone]

bathos *noun*
- "BAY thoss"
- an unintentional lapse in mood from the sublime to the absurd or trivial; a commonplace or ridiculous feature offsetting an otherwise sublime situation; an anticlimax.
- [Greek, = depth]
- **bathetic** *adjective* "ba THETTIC"

Bathurstonian *noun*
- "bath ur STONEY 'n"
- a resident of Bathurst, NB.

bathymetry *noun*
• "buh THIMMA tree"
• the measurement of depth of water in seas, lakes, etc.
• [Greek *bathus* deep + *metron* measure]
• **bathymeter** *noun*
• **bathymetric** *adjective* "bathy METRIC"

bathyscaphe *noun*
• "BATH a skaff"
• a self-propelled vessel for deep-sea diving.
• [Greek *bathus* deep + *skaphos* ship]

bathysphere *noun*
• "BATH a sfeer"
• a spherical vessel for deep-sea observation, lowered on cables from the surface.
• [Greek *bathus* deep + SPHERE]

batik *noun*
• "ba TEEK"
• a method (originally used in Java) of producing coloured designs on textiles by waxing the parts not to be dyed.
• [Javanese, = painted]

batiste *noun*
• "ba TEEST"
• a fine linen or cotton cloth.
• [French (earlier *batiche*), perhaps related to *battre* beat]

baton *noun*
• "buh TAWN"
• a thin stick used by a conductor to direct an orchestra, choir, etc.
• [French *bâton*, *baston*, ultimately from Late Latin *bastum* stick]

bâtonnier *noun*
• "ba tawn YAY"
• (in Quebec) a president of a Bar Association.
• [French, lit. 'staff bearer', from *bâton* staff]

batrachian *noun*
• "buh TRAY kee 'n"
• a frog or toad.
• [from modern Latin *Batrachia* former name (now Anura) from Greek *batrakhos* frog]

batt *noun*
• "BAT"
• a sheet of usu. fibreglass insulation sized to fit between studs, joists, or rafters.
• [var. of 'bat' (club) from Old English *batt* club, perhaps partly from Old French *batte* club, from *battre* strike]
HOMOPHONES: *bat*

battalion *noun*
• "buh TAL y'n"
• a large body of soldiers ready for battle, esp. an infantry unit forming part of a brigade.
• [French *bataillon* from Italian *battaglione* from *battaglia* battle]

batten *noun*
• "BAT'n"
• a long flat strip of wood or metal used to hold something in place.
• [Old French *batant* participle of *batre* beat, from Latin *battuere*]

battledore *noun*
• "BATTLE dore"
• a game played with a shuttlecock and racquets.
• [15th c., perhaps from Provençal *batedor* beater, from *batre* beat]

battlement *noun*
• "BATTLE m'nt"
• an alternately high and low parapet along the top of a wall, as part of a fortification.
• [Old French *bataillier* furnish with ramparts]
• **battlemented** *adjective*

battue *noun*
• "ba TYOO" or "ba TOO"
• the driving of game towards hunters by beaters.
• [French, feminine past participle of *battre* beat, from Latin *battuere*]

bauble *noun*
• "BOBBLE"
• a showy trinket or toy of little value.
• [Old French *ba(u)bel* child's toy, of unknown origin]
HOMOPHONES: *bobble*

baud *noun*
• "BOD"
• a unit used to express the speed of electronic code signals, corresponding to one information unit per second.
• [J. M. E. *Baudot*, French engineer d.1903]
HOMOPHONES: *bawd*, *bod*

Bauhaus *noun*
• "BOW house" ("BOW" rhymes with *HOW*)
• a German school of architectural design (1919–33).
• [German from *Bau* building + *Haus* house]

bauxite *noun*
• "BOX ite"
• a claylike mineral containing varying proportions of alumina, the chief source of aluminum.
• [French from *Les Baux* near Arles in S France + Greek *lithos* stone]
• **bauxitic** *adjective* "box ITTIC"

Bavarian *noun*
• "buh VERRY 'n"
• a native or inhabitant of Bavaria in SE Germany.

bawd *noun*
• "BOD"
• a woman who runs a brothel.
• [Middle English *bawdstrot* from Old French *baudetrot*, *baudestroyt* procuress, from *baude* shameless]
HOMOPHONES: *baud*, *bod*

bawdy *adjective*
- "BODY"
- humorously indecent.
- [as BAWD]
- **bawdily** *adverb*
- **bawdiness** *noun*

HOMOPHONES: *body*

bawk *noun*
- "BOCK"
- *Cdn* (*Nfld*) an Atlantic white-bellied shearwater, *Puffinus gravis*, common in summer in the Strait of Belle Isle and along the Atlantic coast.
- [origin unknown]

HOMOPHONES: *bock, balk*

bawl *verb*
- Sounds like *BALL*
- speak or call out noisily.
- [imitative: compare medieval Latin *baulare* bark, Icelandic *baula* (Swedish *böla*) to low]
- **bawler** *noun*

HOMOPHONES: *ball*

bawn *noun*
- "BON"
- *Cdn* (*Nfld*) a meadow near a house etc.
- [Irish *badún*, perhaps from *ba* cows + *dún* fortress]

bayonet *noun*
- "bay a NET"
- a stabbing blade attachable to the muzzle of a rifle.
- [French *baïonnette*, perhaps from *Bayonne* in SW France, where they were first made]

bayou *noun*
- "BY oo"
- a marshy offshoot of a river etc. in the southern US.
- [Louisiana French from Choctaw]

bazaar *noun*
- "buh ZAR"
- (esp. in the Middle East) a marketplace or shopping quarter.
- [Persian *bāzār*, prob. through Turkish and Italian]

HOMOPHONES: *bizarre*

bazillion *noun*
- "buh ZILL y'n"
- an exaggeratedly large number.
- [alteration of 'billion' after GAZILLION]

HOMOPHONES: *Basilian*

bazooka *noun*
- "buh ZOOKA"
- a tubular short-range rocket launcher used against tanks.
- [apparently from *bazoo* mouth, of unknown origin]

bdellium *noun*
- "DELLY um"
- any of various trees, esp. of the genus *Commiphora*, yielding resin.
- [Latin from Greek *bdellion* from Hebrew *bᵉdhōlaḥ*]

beacon *noun*
- "BEEK'n"
- a fire or light set up in a high or prominent position as a warning etc.
- [Old English *bēacn* from West Germanic]

beagle *noun*
- "BEEGLE"
- a short-legged breed of dog with a short black and white or brown and white coat.
- [Old French *beegueule* noisy person, prob. from *beer* open wide + *gueule* throat]
- **beagler** *noun*

beaker *noun*
- "BEEKER"
- a lipped cylindrical glass vessel for scientific experiments.
- [Old Norse *bikarr*, perhaps from Greek *bikos* drinking bowl]

bealing *adjective*
- "BEELING"
- (of a part of the body) infected.
- [alteration of 'boil' an inflamed pus-filled swelling, from Old English *bȳl(e)* from West Germanic]

Béarnaise *noun*
- "bay ar NAZE"
- a rich sauce containing egg yolks, butter, vinegar and tarragon.
- [French, feminine of *béarnais* of *Béarn* in SW France]

beatific *adjective*
- "bee a TIFFIC"
- blissful.
- [Latin *beatificus* from *beatus* blessed]
- **beatifically** *adverb*

beatify *verb*
- "bee ATTA fie"
- formally declare a dead person 'blessed', often a step towards sainthood in the Catholic Church.
- [Church Latin *beatificare* from Latin *beatus* blessed]
- **beatification** *noun*

beatitude *noun*
- "bee ATTA tude"
- blessedness.
- [Latin *beatitudo* from *beatus* blessed]

beatnik *noun*
- "BEET nick"
- a member of the beat generation, a movement of young people esp. in the 1950s who rejected conventional society in their dress, habits, and beliefs.
- ['beat' + *-nik* after *Sputnik*, the first artificial satellite, perhaps influenced by use of Yiddish *-nik* agent-suffix]

beau *noun*
- "BOE"
- an admirer; a boyfriend.
- [French, = handsome, from Latin *bellus*]

HOMOPHONES: *bow*

Beauceron *noun*
- "boe suh RÕH" (with a nasal *OH*)
- (in Canada) a native or inhabitant of the Beauce region along the Chaudière river in SE Quebec.

Beaufort *adjective*
- "BOE fort"
- designating a scale of wind speed ranging from 0 (calm) to 12 (hurricane).
- [Sir F. *Beaufort*, English admiral d.1857]

Beaujolais *noun*
- "BOE zhuh lay" or "boe zhuh LAY"
- a red or white burgundy wine from the Beaujolais district of France.

Beaune *noun*
- "BONE"
- a red burgundy wine from the region around the town of Beaune in east central France.

HOMOPHONES: *bone*

beaut *noun*
- "BYOOT"
- an excellent or beautiful person or thing.
- [abbreviation of BEAUTY]

HOMOPHONES: *butte*

beauteous *adjective*
- "BYOOTY us"
- beautiful.
- [as BEAUTY]

beautician *noun*
- "byoo TISH'n"
- a person who gives beauty treatment.
- [as BEAUTY]

beautify *verb*
- "BYOOTA fie"
- make beautiful; adorn.
- [as BEAUTY]
- **beautification** *noun*
- **beautifier** *noun*

beauty *noun*
- "BYOOTY"
- a combination of qualities such as shape, colour, etc., that pleases the aesthetic senses, esp. the sight.
- [Old French *beauté*, ultimately from Latin (as BEAU)]
- **beautiful** *adjective*
- **beautifully** *adverb*

beautybush *noun*
- "BYOOTY bush"
- a shrub, *Kolkwitzia amabilis*, with pink and white flowers, planted as an ornamental.
- [as BEAUTY + 'bush']

béchamel *noun*
- "baysha MELL"
- a sauce made with flour, melted butter, and milk or cream.
- [Louis (Marquis de) *Béchamel*, French courtier who invented it, d.1703]

becket *noun*
- "BECKIT"
- a contrivance such as a hook, bracket, or looped rope, for securing loose lines, tackle, or spars.
- [18th c.: origin unknown]

becquerel *noun*
- "BECKA rell"
- the SI unit of radioactivity, corresponding to one disintegration per second.
- [A.-H. *Becquerel*, French physicist d.1908]

bedaub *verb*
- "be DOB"
- smear or daub with paint etc.
- [as DAUB]

bedizen *verb*
- "be DIZE'n" or "be DIZZ'n"
- deck out gaudily.
- [obsolete *dizen* deck out]

bedlam *noun*
- "BEDLUM"
- a scene of uproar and confusion.
- [alteration of Hospital of St. Mary of *Bethlehem*, an asylum in medieval London]

bedlamer *noun*
- "BEDLUM ur"
- *Cdn* (*Nfld*) a young harp seal.
- [possibly from BEDLAM, reflecting the apparently manic behaviour of the seals]

bedlamite *noun*
- "BEDLUM ite"
- a mentally ill person.
- [as BEDLAM]

Bedouin *noun*

ALSO SPELLED: **Beduin**
- "BED oo in"
- a member of an Arabic-speaking nomadic people inhabiting the desert regions of the Middle East, traditionally herders of camels, goats, and sheep.
- [ultimately from Arabic *badwiyyīn* dwellers in the desert, from *badw* desert]

bedraggled *adjective*
- "be DRAGGLED"
- untidy; dishevelled.
- [from 'drag', from Old English *dragan* or Old Norse *draga* 'draw']

beech *noun*
- "BEECH"
- any large deciduous tree of the genus *Fagus*, growing in temperate regions and having smooth grey bark and glossy leaves.

• [Old English *bēce* from Germanic]
HOMOPHONES: *beach*

beechmast *noun*
• "BEECH mast"
• the beechnut, esp. used as food for animals.
• [as BEECH + Old English *mæst* from West Germanic, prob. related to 'meat']

beechnut *noun*
• "BEECH nut"
• the small rough-skinned fruit of the beech tree.
• [as BEECH + 'nut']

beefalo *noun*
• "BEEFA lo"
• a hybrid breed of bovine, usu. five-eighths buffalo and three-eighths domestic cow, raised for its meat.
• [blend of 'beef' + BUFFALO]

beetle *noun*
• "BEETLE"
• any insect of the order Coleoptera, with modified front wings forming hard protective cases closing over the back wings.
• [Old English *bitula* biter from *bītan* bite]
HOMOPHONES: *betel*, *beadle*

beetling *adjective*
• "BEET'll ing"
• (of brows, cliffs, etc.) projecting; overhanging threateningly.
• [Middle English: origin unknown]

beggar *noun*
• "BEGGER"
• a person who begs, esp. one who lives by begging.
• [Middle English *beg*, prob. from Old English *bedecian* from Germanic: related to 'bid']
• **beggarliness** *noun*
• **beggarly** *adjective*

beggary *noun*
• "BEGGA ree"
• extreme poverty.
• [as BEGGAR]

begonia *noun*
• "buh GO nee uh" or "buh GO nyuh"
• any plant of the genus *Begonia* with brightly coloured flowers, and often having brilliant glossy foliage.
• [M. *Bégon*, French patron of science d.1710]

begorra *interjection*
• "buh GORA"
• by God!
• [corruption]

beguile *verb*
• "be GILE" (with "G" as in *GIVE*)
• charm; amuse.
• [as GUILE]
• **beguilement** *noun*
• **beguiler** *noun*
• **beguiling** *adjective*
• **beguilingly** *adverb*

beguine *noun*
ALSO SPELLED: **biguine**
• "buh GEEN" (with "G" as in *GEAR*)
• a dance of W Indian origin, similar to the foxtrot.
• [West Indian French from French *béguin* infatuation]

begum *noun*
• "BAY gum"
• (in the Indian subcontinent) a Muslim woman of high rank.
• [Urdu *begam* from Eastern Turkish *bīgam* princess, feminine of *big* prince: compare BEY]

behaviour *noun*
ALSO SPELLED: **behavior**
• "be HAY vyur"
• the way one conducts oneself; manners.
• [from 'behave' from *be-* thoroughly + 'have' in the sense 'have or bear (oneself) in a particular way']
• **behavioural** *adjective* (also **behavioral**)
• **behaviouralist** *noun* (also **behavioralist**)
• **behaviourally** *adverb* (also **behaviorally**)

behaviourism *noun*
ALSO SPELLED: **behaviorism**
• "be HAY vyur izm"
• the theory that objective investigation of stimuli and responses is the only valid psychological method, and that psychological disorders are best treated by altering behaviour patterns.
• [as BEHAVIOUR]
• **behaviourist** *noun* (also **behaviorist**)
• **behaviouristic** *adjective* (also **behavioristic**)

behemoth *noun*
• "buh HEE muth" or "BEE a muth"
• an enormous creature or thing.
• [Hebrew *bᵉhēmôṯ* intensive pl. of *bᵉhēmāh* beast (see Job 40:15), perhaps from Egyptian *p-ehe-mau* water ox]

behest *noun*
• "be HEST"
• a command; a request.
• [Old English *behǣs* from Germanic]

beige *noun*
• "BAYZH"
• a very pale yellowish brown.
• [French: origin unknown]

beignet *noun*
• "bay NYAY"
• a fritter.
• [French, from archaic *buyne* bump, a fritter being round and puffy]

Beijinger *noun*
• "bay ZHING ur"
• a resident of Beijing, China.

bejewelled *adjective*
ALSO SPELLED: esp. *US* **bejeweled**

• "buh JOOLD"
• adorned with jewels.
• [from 'jewel' from Anglo-French *juel*, *jeuel*, Old French *joel*, of uncertain origin]

bel *noun*
• "BELL"
• a unit used in the comparison of power levels in electrical communication or intensities of sound, corresponding to an intensity ratio of 10 to 1 (compare DECIBEL).
• [A. G. *Bell*, Scottish-born inventor of the telephone and gramophone d.1922]
HOMOPHONES: *bell*, *belle*

Belarusian *noun*
• "bella ROO see 'n"
• a native or national of Belarus in E Europe.

beleaguer *verb*
• "buh LEE gur"
• vex, harass, beset with difficulties.
• [Dutch *belegeren* camp around, from *leger* a camp]
• **beleaguered** *adjective*

belemnite *noun*
• "BELL'm nite"
• any extinct cephalopod of the order Belemnoidea, having a bullet-shaped internal shell often found in fossilized form.
• [modern Latin *belemnites* from Greek *belemnon* dart + Greek *lithos* stone]

belfry *noun*
• "BELL free"
• a bell tower or steeple housing bells, esp. forming part of a church.
• [Old French *berfrei* from Frankish: altered by association with *bell*]

Belgian *noun*
• "BELL j'n"
• a native or national of Belgium.

Belgic *adjective*
• "BELL jick"
• of or relating to the Belgae, an ancient Celtic people of northern Gaul.
• [Latin *Belgicus*]

belief *noun*
• "buh LEEF"
• a firm opinion or conviction.
• [as BELIEVE]

believe *verb*
• "buh LEEVE"
• accept as true or as conveying the truth.
• [Old English *belȳfan*, *belēfan*, with change of prefix from *gelēfan* from Germanic]
• **believability** *noun*
• **believable** *adjective*
• **believably** *adverb*

believer *noun*
• "buh LEEVER"
• an adherent of a specified religion.
• [as BELIEVE]

Belizean *noun*
• "bell EEZY 'n"
• a native or inhabitant of Belize in Central America.

belladonna *noun*
• "bella DONNA"
• a poisonous plant, *Atropa belladonna*, with purple flowers and purple-black berries.
• [modern Latin from Italian, = fair lady, perhaps from its use as a cosmetic]

belle *noun*
• "BELL"
• a beautiful woman.
• [French from Latin *bella* feminine of *bellus* beautiful]
HOMOPHONES: *bell*, *bel*

Bellevillian *noun*
• "bell VILLY 'n"
• a resident of Belleville, Ont.

bellicose *adjective*
• "BELLA cose" ("COSE" rhymes with *GROSS*)
• inclined to war or fighting; warlike.
• [Latin *bellicosus* from *bellum* war]
• **bellicosity** *noun* "bella COSSA tee"

belligerence *noun*
• "buh LIDGE ur ince"
• aggressive or warlike behaviour.
• [Latin *belligerare* wage war, from *bellum* war + *gerere* wage]
• **belligerent** *adjective*
• **belligerently** *adverb*

bellow *verb*
• "BELLO"
• emit a deep loud roar.
• [Middle English: perhaps related to 'bell' the cry of a stag at rutting time, from Old English *bellan* bark, bellow]

bellows *plural noun*
• "BELL ohs"
• a device with an air bag that emits a stream of air when squeezed, esp.: a kind with two handles used for blowing air onto a fire.
• [Middle English prob. from Old English *belga* pl. of *belig* belly]

bellwether *noun*
• "BELL wether"
• an indicator or predictor of something.
• ['bell' + WETHER, the leading sheep of a flock wearing a bell around its neck]

bellwort *noun*
• "BELL wurt" or "BELL wort"
• any of various liliaceous plants of the genus *Uvularia* of eastern N America, with yellow bell-shaped flowers.
• ['bell' + WORT]

belsnickle *noun*
• "BELL snickle"
• (in Nova Scotia, Virginia, and areas of German settlement) a person in disguise who

seeks admission to the homes of neighbours and relatives, esp. during Christmas.

- [corruption of German *Pelz* fur + *Nickel* diminutive of (Saint) *Nicholas*, from the German custom of a person disguised in furs visiting children on the eve of St. Nicholas's day (6th December) to dispense warnings and gifts]

Beltane *noun*
- "BELL tane"
- an ancient Celtic festival celebrated on May Day.
- [Gaelic *bealltainn*]

beluga *noun*
- "buh LOOGA"
- a whale, *Delphinapterus leucas*, of the Arctic Ocean which is found as far south as the St. Lawrence estuary, and is white when adult.
- [Russian *beluga* from *belyi* white]

belvedere *noun*
- "BELVA dare"
- a raised turret or summer house commanding a fine view.
- [Italian from *bel* beautiful + *vedere* see]

Bembo *noun*
- "BEMBO"
- a typeface modelled on that used in the Aldine edition of the tract *De Aetna* by Pietro Bembo.
- [P. *Bembo*, Italian scholar d.1547]

bemedalled *adjective*
- "be MED'ld"
- adorned with medals.
- [as MEDAL]

benedicite *noun*
- "benna DEE see tay"
- a blessing, esp. a grace said at table in religious communities.
- [Latin, = bless ye: see BENEDICTION]

Benedictine *noun*
- "benna DICK teen"
- a monk or nun of an order following the rule of St. Benedict (d. *c.*547).
- [French *bénédictine* or modern Latin *benedictinus* from *Benedictus* Benedict]

benediction *noun*
- "benna DICK sh'n"
- the utterance of a blessing, esp. at the end of a religious service.
- [Latin *benedictio -onis* from *benedicere -dict-* bless]

Benedictus *noun*
- "bennay DICT us"
- the section of the Mass beginning *Benedictus qui venit in nomine Domini* (Blessed is he who comes in the name of the Lord).
- [Latin, = blessed: see BENEDICTION]

benefactor *noun*
- "BENNA facter"
- a person who gives support (esp. financial) to a person or cause.
- [as BENEFIT]
- **benefaction** *noun*
- **benefactress** *noun*

benefice *noun*
- "BENNA fiss"
- a position held by a member of the clergy that ensures an income or a specified property.
- [Latin *beneficium* favour, from *bene* well + *facere* do]
- **beneficed** *adjective* "BENNA fist"

beneficent *adjective*
- "buh NEFFA s'nt"
- doing good; generous, actively kind.
- [Latin *beneficent-* (as BENEFICE)]
- **beneficence** *noun*
- **beneficently** *adverb*

beneficial *adjective*
- "benna FISH'll"
- advantageous; having benefits.
- [Late Latin *beneficialis* (as BENEFICE)]
- **beneficially** *adverb*

beneficiary *noun*
- "benna FISHY airy" or "benna FISHER ee"
- a person who receives or is entitled to receive benefits, esp. under a will or life insurance policy.
- [Latin *beneficiarius* (as BENEFICE)]

benefit *noun*
- "BENNA fit"
- a favourable or helpful factor or circumstance; advantage, profit.
- [Anglo-French *benfet*, Old French *bienfet*, from Latin *benefactum* from *bene facere* do well]

benevolent *adjective*
- "buh NEVVA l'nt"
- wishing to do good; actively friendly and helpful.
- [Latin *bene volens -entis* well wishing, from *velle* wish]
- **benevolence** *noun*
- **benevolently** *adverb*

Bengali *noun*
- "ben GAL ee" or "ben GOLLY"
- a native of Bengal in NE India and Bangladesh.

bengaline *noun*
- "benga LEEN"
- a lustrous fabric with the weft of a thicker, coarser thread than the warp.
- [French, from *Bengal* in NE India and Bangladesh, whence striped fabrics were imported to Europe]

benighted *adjective*
- "buh NITE id"
- intellectually or morally ignorant.
- [obsolete *benight* (v.) in sense 'cover in the darkness of night']
- **benightedness** *noun*

benign *adjective*
- "buh NINE"
- gentle, mild, kindly.
- [Old French *benigne* from Latin *benignus* from *bene* well + *-genus* born]
- **benignly** *adverb*

benignant *adjective*
- "buh NIG n'nt"
- kindly, gracious.
- [BENIGN or Latin *benignus*, after *malignant*]
- **benignancy** *noun*
- **benignantly** *adverb*
- **benignity** *noun* "buh NIG nit ee"

Beninese *noun*
- "benna NEEZ"
- a native or inhabitant of Benin in W Africa.

benison *noun*
- "BENNA z'n"
- a blessing.
- [Old French *beneiçun* from Latin *benedictio -onis*]

benomyl *noun*
- "BENNA mill"
- a systemic fungicide used on fruit and vegetable crops.
- [*ben(z)o(ic) + m(eth)yl*]

Benthamite *noun*
- "BENTH um ite"
- a proponent of the utilitarian philosophy of Jeremy Bentham, English philosopher d.1832.

benthos *noun*
- "BENTH oss"
- the flora and fauna at the bottom of a sea or lake.
- [Greek, = depth of the sea]
- **benthic** *adjective*

bento *noun*
- "BENTO"
- a lunch of Japanese food, typically rice, vegetables, sashimi, etc. served in a decorated lacquered wood box divided into compartments.
- [Japanese *bento* lunch]

bentonite *noun*
- "BENTA nite"
- a kind of highly absorbent clay having numerous uses, esp. as a filler.
- [Fort *Benton* in Montana]

benumb *verb*
- "be NUM"
- make numb; deaden.
- [originally = deprived, as past participle of Middle English *benimen* from Old English *beniman* from *niman* take]

benzene *noun*
- "BEN zeen"
- a colourless carcinogenic volatile liquid found in coal tar, petroleum, etc., and used as a solvent and in the manufacture of plastics etc.
- [as BENZOIC]
- **benzenoid** *adjective* "BEN zen oid"

HOMOPHONES: *benzine*

benzine *noun*
- "BEN zeen"
- a mixture of liquid hydrocarbons obtained from petroleum, used as a solvent and fuel.
- [as BENZOIN]

HOMOPHONES: *benzene*

benzodiazepine *noun*
- "benzo die AZZA peen"
- any of a class of heterocyclic compounds used as tranquilizers, including Librium and Valium.
- [BENZOIC + Greek *di-* from *dis* twice + French *azote* nitrogen (from Greek *azōos* without life) + Greek *epi* upon, near to, in addition]

benzoin *noun*
- "BENZO in"
- a fragrant gum resin obtained from various E Asian trees of the genus *Styrax*, used in the manufacture of perfumes and incense, and containing a white crystalline aromatic ketone.
- [earlier *benjoin*, ultimately from Arabic *lubān jāwī* incense of Java]
- **benzoic** *adjective* "ben ZO ick"

benzol *noun*
- "BEN zawl"
- benzene, esp. unrefined and used as a fuel.
- [as BENZOIN]

benzoquinone *noun*
- "benzo KWIN own"
- a yellow crystalline compound related to benzene but having two hydrogen atoms replaced by oxygen.
- [as BENZOIN + QUINONE]

benzoyl *noun*
- "BEN zoil"
- the radical C_6H_5CO.
- [as BENZOIN]

benzyl *noun*
- "BEN zill"
- the radical $C_6H_5CH_2$.
- [as BENZOIN]

Beothuk *noun*

ALSO SPELLED: **Beothuck**
- "bee OTH uck"
- a member of an Aboriginal people formerly inhabiting Newfoundland but extinct since the early 19th c.
- [Beothuk, = people]

bequeath *verb*
- "bee KWEETH"
- leave (an estate or piece of property) to a person by will.
- [Old English *becwethan* (from *cwethan* say: compare QUOTH)]
- **bequeathable** *adjective*
- **bequeathal** *noun*
- **bequeather** *noun*

bequest *noun*
• "be KWEST"
• the act or an instance of bequeathing.
• [Middle English from obsolete *quiste* from Old English *-cwiss*, *cwide* saying]

Berber *noun*
• "BURBER"
• a member of the indigenous mainly Muslim Caucasian peoples of N Africa (now mainly in Morocco and Algeria) speaking related languages.
• [Arabic *barbar*]

berberis *noun*
• "BURBER iss"
• any shrub of the genus *Berberis*, esp. one grown for ornament.
• [medieval Latin from Arabic *berberys*, the name of the fruit]

berceuse *noun*
• "bare SOOZ" (with "OO" as in *BOOK*)
• a lullaby.
• [French]

berdache *noun*
ALSO SPELLED: **berdash**
• "BIRD ash"
• a N American Aboriginal male, either celibate or homosexual, who assumes an intermediate social role between that of men and women in Aboriginal society.
• [French *bardache* boy prostitute, from Italian *bardascia* perhaps from Arabic *bardaj* slave]
• **berdachism** *noun* (also **berdashism**) "BIRD ash izm"

bereave *verb*
• "be REEVE"
• deprive of a relation, friend, etc., esp. by death.
• [Old English *berēafian* deprive]
• **bereaved** *adjective*
• **bereavement** *noun*

beret *noun*
• "buh RAY"
• a round brimless cap of felt or cloth that is close-fitting and lies flat on the head.
• [French *béret* Basque cap, from Provençal *berret*]

berg *noun*
• "BURG"
• an iceberg.
• [abbreviation]
HOMOPHONES: *burg*

bergamot *noun*
• "BURGA mot"
• a citrus tree, *Citrus bergamia*, bearing fruit similar to an orange, from the rind of which a fragrant essential oil is extracted.
• [*Bergamo* in N Italy]

bergenia *noun*
• "bur GEENY uh" (with "G" as in *GEEK*)
• any of various perennial plants of the genus *Bergenia*, of the saxifrage family, having large, thick leaves and usu. pink, red or purple flowers.
• [K. A. von *Bergen*, German botanist d.1760]

bergschrund *noun*
• "BAIRK shrunt"
• a crevasse or gap at the head of a glacier or névé.
• [German, from *Berg* mountain + *Schrund* crevice]

beribboned *adjective*
• "be RIB'nd"
• decorated with ribbons.
• [as RIBAND]

beriberi *noun*
• "berry BERRY"
• a disease causing inflammation of the nerves due to a deficiency of vitamin B_1 (thiamine), and mainly associated with rice-based diets.
• [Sinhalese, from *beri* weakness]

Beringian *adjective*
• "buh RINJY 'n"
• of or relating to the land mass formerly linking Alaska with Siberia at what is now the Bering Strait.

berkelium *noun*
• "bur KEELY um" or "BURKLY um"
• a transuranic radioactive metallic element produced by bombardment of americium.
• [*Berkeley*, California (where first made)]

berm *noun*
• "BURM"
• a flat strip of land, raised bank, or terrace bordering a river etc.
• [French *berme* from Dutch *berm*, prob. related to Old Norse *barmr* brim]
• **bermed** *adjective* "BURMD"

Bernese *noun*
• "bur NEEZ"
• a resident of Berne, Switzerland.

berserk *adjective*
• "buh ZURK" or "bur ZURK"
• wild, frenzied; in a violent rage.
• [Icelandic *berserkr* (n.) prob. from *bern-* bear (the animal) + *serkr* coat]

berth *noun*
• "BURTH"
• a fixed bunk on a ship, train, etc., for sleeping in.
• [prob. from naut. use of 'bear']
HOMOPHONES: *birth*

bertha *noun*
• "BURTHA"
• a deep falling collar (often of lace) or small cape on a dress.
• [French *berthe* from *Berthe* Bertha]

beryl *noun*
- "BARE 'll"
- a kind of transparent precious stone, esp. pale green, blue, or yellow, and consisting of beryllium aluminum silicate in a hexagonal form.
- [Latin *beryllus* from Greek *bērullos*]

HOMOPHONES: *barrel*

beryllium *noun*
- "buh RILLY um"
- a hard white metallic element used in the manufacture of light corrosion-resistant alloys.
- [as BERYL]

beseech *verb*
- "be SEECH"
- entreat, implore.
- [Middle English from Old English *secan* seek]
- **beseeching** *adjective*
- **beseechingly** *adverb*

besiege *verb*
- "be SEEDGE"
- lay siege to.
- [Middle English from *assiege* from Old French *asegier* from Romanic]
- **besieger** *noun*

besmirch *verb*
- "be SMURCH"
- soil, discolour.
- [as SMIRCH]

besom *noun*
- "BEEZUM"
- a broom made of twigs tied around a stick.
- [Old English *besema*]

besotted *adjective*
- "be SOTTED"
- infatuated.
- [*besot* (v.) from Old English *sott* & Old French *sot* foolish, from medieval Latin *sottus*]

bespectacled *adjective*
- "be SPECTA k'ld"
- wearing eyeglasses.
- [as SPECTACLE]

Bessarabian *adjective*
- "bessa RAY bee 'n"
- of or relating to the region of Bessarabia in E Europe, most of which is now in Moldova.

bestial *adjective*
- "BEESTY 'll" or "BESTY 'll"
- brutish, cruel, savage.
- [Late Latin *bestialis* from *bestia* beast]
- **bestiality** *noun*
- **bestially** *adverb*

bestiary *noun*
- "BEESTY airy" or "BESTY airy"
- a moralizing medieval treatise on real and imaginary animals.
- [medieval Latin *bestiarium* from Latin *bestia* beast]

bestow *verb*
- "be STOE"
- confer (a gift, right, etc.).
- [Middle English from Old English *stow* a place]
- **bestowal** *noun* "be STOE 'll"
- **bestower** *noun*

bestrew *verb*
- "be STROO"
- cover or partly cover (a surface).
- [as STREW]

beta *noun*
- "BAY tuh"
- the second letter of the Greek alphabet (Β, β).
- [Greek]

betatron *noun*
- "BAYTA tron"
- an apparatus for accelerating electrons in a circular path by magnetic induction.
- [BETA + ELECTRON]

betel *noun*
- "BEETLE"
- the leaf of the Asian evergreen climbing plant *Piper betle*, commonly chewed with parings of the areca nut in SE Asia.
- [Portuguese from Malayalam *veṭṭila*]

HOMOPHONES: *beetle, beadle*

bêtise *noun*
- "bay TEEZ"
- a foolish or ill-timed remark or action.
- [French, from *bête* (lit. = beast) foolish]

betony *noun*
- "BETTA nee"
- a purple-flowered herbaceous plant of the mint family, *Stachys officinalis*.
- [Old French *betoine* from Latin *betonica*]

betroth *verb*
- "be TROTHE" (with "TH" as in *BATHE*)
- bind with a promise to marry.
- [Middle English from *trouthe, treuthe* truth, later assimilated to 'troth' loyalty, truth]
- **betrothal** *noun*

betrothed *noun*
- "be TROTHED" ("TROTHED" rhymes with *CLOTHED*)
- the person to whom one is betrothed; one's fiancé or fiancée.
- [as BETROTH]

bettor *noun*
- "BETTER"
- a person who bets.
- [16th c.: perhaps a shortened form of ABETTOR]

HOMOPHONES: *better, bedder*

betwixt *preposition*
- "be TWIXT"
- between.
- [Old English *betwēox* from Germanic]

bevel *noun*
• "BEV'll"
• a sloping surface or edge; a slope from the horizontal or vertical in carpentry, stonework, etc.
• [Old French *bevel* (unrecorded) from *baïf* from *baer* gape]

beverage *noun*
• "BEVVER idge"
• a drink.
• [Old French *be(u)vrage*, ultimately from Latin *bibere* drink]

bevy *noun*
• "BEVVY"
• a group or company of any kind.
• [15th c.: origin unknown]

bewhiskered *adjective*
• "be WISS kurd"
• having whiskers.
• [as WHISKER]

bewilder *verb*
• "be WILL dur"
• utterly perplex or confuse.
• [obsolete *wilder* lose one's way]
• **bewildered** *adjective*
• **bewilderedly** *adverb*
• **bewildering** *adjective*
• **bewilderingly** *adverb*
• **bewilderment** *noun*

bey *noun*
• "BAY"
• the governor of a district or province in the Ottoman Empire.
• [Turkish]
HOMOPHONES: *bay*

bezant *noun*
• "BEZZ'nt" or "buh ZANT"
• a gold or silver coin originally minted at Byzantium, widely used in the currency of medieval Europe.
• [Old French *besanz -ant* from Latin *Byzantius* Byzantine]

bezel *noun*
• "BEZZ'll"
• the sloped edge of a chisel.
• [Old French *besel* (unrecorded: compare French *béseau, bizeau*) of unknown origin]

Bézier *noun*
• "BAY zee ay"
• designating a polynomial curve expressed in such a way that its shape and curvature is specified by the position of two or more control points, which do not themselves lie on the curve.
• [P. *Bézier*, French mathematician]

bezique *noun*
• "buh ZEEK"
• a card game for two with a double pack of 64 cards, including the seven to ace only in each suit.
• [French *bésigue*, perhaps from Persian *bāzīgar* juggler]

bezoar *noun*
• "BEE zore" or "BEZZO ar"
• a small stone which may form in the stomachs of certain animals, esp. ruminants, and which was once used as an antidote for various ills.
• [ultimately from Persian *pādzahr* antidote, Arabic *bāzahr*]

bhajan *noun*
• "BODGE 'n"
• a Hindu devotional song.
• [Sanskrit *bhajana*]

bhaji *noun*
• "BAWJY"
• an Indian dish of fried vegetables.
• [Hindi *bhājī* fried vegetables]

bhakti *noun*
• "BUCK tee"
• religious devotion or piety as a means of salvation, the most common form of Hinduism.
• [Sanskrit]

bhang *noun*
• "BANG"
• the leaves and flower tops of Indian hemp used as a narcotic.
• [Portuguese *bangue*, Persian & Urdu *bang* later assimilated to Hindi *bhāṅ*, from Sanskrit *bhaṅgā*]
HOMOPHONES: *bang*

bhangra *noun*
• "BANG gra"
• a style of popular (esp. dance) music combining Punjabi folk music with rock or disco elements.
• [Punjabi *bhāngrā* a traditional harvest dance]

bharal *noun*
• "BUH rull"
• a Himalayan wild sheep, *Pseudois nayaur*, with a blue-black coat and horns curved rearward.
• [Hindi]

bhelpuri *noun*
• "BAIL purry"
• an Indian dish of puffed rice, onions, spices, and hot chutney.
• [Hindi *bhel* mixture + *pūrī* deep-fried bread]

Bhutanese *noun*
• "boota NEEZ"
• a native or inhabitant of Bhutan in the Himalayas.

bi *adjective*
• "by"
• bisexual.
• [abbreviation of 'bisexual']
HOMOPHONES: *by, buy, bye*

biannual *adjective*
• "by AN yoo 'll"
• occurring, appearing, etc., twice a year.
• [Latin *bi-* twice + ANNUAL]
• **biannually** *adverb*

bias *noun*
• "BY us"
• a predisposition or prejudice.
• [French *biais*, of unknown origin]
• **biased** *adjective*

biathlon *noun*
• "by ATH lon"
• an athletic contest in cross-country skiing and shooting or in cycling and running.
• [Latin *bi-* twice, after PENTATHLON]
• **biathlete** *noun* "by ATH leet"

biaxial *adjective*
• "by AXY 'll"
• having two axes.
• [Latin *bi-* twice + AXIAL]

bibb *noun*
• "BIBB"
• a mild and tender head lettuce with loose, dark green leaves.
• [John *Bibb*, US horticulturalist d.1884, who developed it]
HOMOPHONES: *bib*

bibelot *noun*
• "BEE blow"
• a small curio or artistic trinket.
• [French]

bibliography *noun*
• "bibbly OGGRA fee"
• a list of the books referred to in a scholarly work, usu. printed as an appendix.
• [modern Latin *bibliographia* from Greek (from *biblion* book, originally diminutive of *biblos*, *bublos* papyrus + *graphia* writing)]
• **bibliographer** *noun*
• **bibliographic** *adjective*
• **bibliographical** *adjective*
• **bibliographically** *adverb*

bibliomancy *noun*
• "BIBBLY oh mancy"
• foretelling the future by the analysis of a randomly chosen passage from a book, esp. the Bible.
• [Greek *biblion* book + *manteia* divination]

bibliomania *noun*
• "bibbly oh MAINY uh"
• an extreme enthusiasm for collecting and possessing books.
• [Greek *biblion* book + MANIA]
• **bibliomaniac** *noun*

bibliophile *noun*
• "BIBBLY oh file"
• a person who collects or is fond of books.
• [Greek *biblion* book + *philos* dear, loving]
• **bibliophilic** *adjective* "bibbly oh FILLIC"

bibliopole *noun*
• "BIBBLY oh pole"
• a seller of (esp. rare) books.
• [Greek *bibliopōlēs* from *biblion* book + *pōlēs* seller]

bibulous *adjective*
• "BIBYOO luss"
• fond of drinking alcoholic liquor.
• [Latin *bibulus* freely drinking, from *bibere* drink]
• **bibulously** *adverb*
• **bibulousness** *noun*

bicameral *adjective*
• "by CAMMER 'll"
• (esp. of a parliament or legislative body) having two chambers.
• [Latin *bi-* twice + *camera* chamber]
• **bicameralism** *noun*

bicarbonate *noun*
• "by CARB'n ate" or "by CARB'n it"
• any acid salt of carbonic acid.
• [Latin *bi-* twice + CARBONATE]

bicentenary *noun*
• "by sen TENNER ee" or "by sen TEENER ee"
• a bicentennial.
• [Latin *bi-* twice + CENTENARY]

bicentennial *noun*
• "by sen TENNY 'll"
• a two-hundredth anniversary.
• [Latin *bi-* twice + CENTENNIAL]

bicephalous *adjective*
• "by SEFFA luss"
• having two heads.
• [Latin *bi-* twice + CEPHALIC]

biceps *noun*
• "BY seps"
• the flexor muscle at the front of the upper arm or at the back of the thigh.
• [Latin, = two-headed, (because the muscle has two attachments at one end) formed as Latin *bi-* twice + *-ceps* from *caput* head]

bichon *noun*
• "BEESH õh" (with a nasal *oh*)
• a small dog of a breed with a fine, curly white coat.
• [French *barbichon* little water spaniel]

bicuspid *adjective*
• "by CUSS pid"
• having two cusps or points.
• [Latin *bi-* twice + *cuspis -idis* sharp point]
• **bicuspidate** *adjective* "by CUSS pid ate"

bicycle *noun*
• "BICE a k'll"
• a vehicle with two wheels held in a frame one behind the other, propelled by pedals and steered with handlebars attached to the front wheel.
• [French from Latin *bi-* twice + Greek *kuklos* wheel]
• **bicyclist** *noun* "BICE a clist"

bicyclic *adjective*
- "by SIKE lick" or "by SICK lick"
- having two (usu. fused) rings of atoms in the molecular structure.
- [as BICYCLE]

bidet *noun*
- "bid AY"
- a low oval bathroom fixture used for washing the genital and anal regions.
- [French, originally = pony]

Biedermeier *adjective*
- "BEEDER my ur"
- denoting or relating to a style of furniture and interior design current in Germany in the period 1815–48, characterized by restraint, conventionality, and utilitarianism.
- [*Biedermaier* a fictitious German poet (1854)]

biennale *noun*
- "bee a NOLLY"
- a large (esp. biennial) art exhibition or music festival, esp. the one held biennially in Venice, Italy.
- [Italian (as BIENNIAL)]

biennial *adjective*
- "by ENNY 'll"
- recurring every two years.
- [Latin *biennis* (*bi-* twice + *annus* year)]
- **biennially** *adverb*

biennium *noun*
- "by ENNY um"
- a period of two years.
- [Latin (as BIENNIAL)]

bier *noun*
- "BEER"
- a movable frame on which a coffin or a corpse is placed, or taken to a grave.
- [Old English *bēr* from Germanic]

HOMOPHONES: *beer*

bierwurst *noun*
- "BEER wurst"
- a cooked, smoked salami of ground beef and pork seasoned with mustard, garlic, onion, and pepper.
- [German, = beer sausage, because traditionally served with beer]

biffin *noun*
- "BIFFIN"
- a deep red cooking apple.
- [corruption of *beefing* from 'beef', with reference to the colour]

bifid *adjective*
- "BY fid"
- divided by a deep cleft into two parts.
- [Latin *bifidus* (*bi-* twice + *fidus* from stem of *findere* cleave)]

bifidum *noun*
- "BIFFID um"
- a bacterium, *Lactobacillus bifidum*, often added to yogourt as being beneficial to the intestinal flora.
- [as BIFID]

bifocal *adjective*
- "by FOKE'll"
- having two focuses, esp. of a lens with a part for distant vision and a part for near vision.
- [Latin *bi-* twice + *focus* hearth]

bifurcate *verb*
- "BY fur cate"
- divide into two branches; fork.
- [medieval Latin *bifurcare* from Latin *bifurcus* two-forked (as Latin *bi-* twice + *furca* fork)]
- **bifurcation** *noun*

bigamy *noun*
- "BIGGA mee"
- the crime of marrying when one is lawfully married to another person.
- [Old French *bigamie* from *bigame* bigamous, from Late Latin *bigamus* (as Latin *bi-* twice + Greek *gamos* marriage)]
- **bigamist** *noun*
- **bigamous** *adjective*

bight *noun*
- "BITE"
- a curve or recess in a coastline, river, etc.
- [Old English *byht*, Middle Low German *bucht* from Germanic]

HOMOPHONES: *bite, byte*

bigot *noun*
- "BIG it"
- a person intolerant of another's beliefs, race, politics, etc.
- [16th c. from French: origin unknown]
- **bigoted** *adjective*
- **bigotry** *noun* "BIGGA tree"

Bihari *noun*
- "be HAR ee"
- a native of Bihar in NE India.

bijou *noun*
- "BEE zhoo" or "bee ZHOO"
- a jewel; a trinket.
- [French, from Breton *bizou* finger ring, from *biz* finger]

bijuralism *noun*
- "by JUR'll izm"
- *Cdn* the existence of two legal systems within a single jurisdiction.
- [Latin *bi-* twice + *jus juris* law]
- **bijural** *adjective* "by JUR 'll"

bikini *noun*
- "be KEENY"
- a two-piece bathing suit for women, the bottom half of which consists of skimpy briefs which do not extend above the top of the pelvis.
- [*Bikini*, an atoll in the Marshall Islands in the W Pacific where nuclear weapons were tested, from the supposed 'explosive' effect]
- **bikinied** *adjective* "be KEE need"

bilabial *adjective*
- "by LAY bee 'll"
- (of a sound etc.) made with closed or nearly closed lips.
- [Latin *bi-* twice + LABIAL]

bilateral *adjective*
- "by LATTER'll"
- of, on, or with two sides.
- [Latin *bi-* twice + LATERAL]
- **bilaterally** *adverb*

bilberry *noun*
- "BILL berry"
- any of several shrubs of the genus *Vaccinium*, with single, edible, blue or black berries.
- [origin uncertain: compare Danish *böllebær*]

bilbo *noun*
- "BILBO"
- a sword noted for the temper and elasticity of its blade.
- [*Bilboa* = Bilbao in N Spain, noted for its manufacture of fine blades]

bilboes *plural noun*
- "BILL boze"
- an iron bar with sliding shackles for a prisoner's ankles.
- [16th c.: origin unknown]

Bildungsroman *noun*
- "BILL dungz roe monn"
- a novel dealing with one person's early life and development.
- [German, from *Bildung* education + *Roman* novel]

bilharzia *noun*
- "bill HARTSY uh"
- a tropical flatworm of the genus *Schistosoma* (formerly *Bilharzia*) which is parasitic in blood vessels in the human pelvic region.
- [modern Latin from T. *Bilharz*, German physician d.1862]

biliary *adjective*
- "BILLY airy" or "BILL yuh ree"
- of the bile.
- [French *biliaire* from Latin *bilis*]

bilingual *adjective*
- "by LING gwul" or "by LING gyoo 'll"
- able to speak two languages, esp. fluently.
- [Latin *bilinguis* (as Latin *bi-* twice + *lingua* tongue)]
- **bilingualism** *noun*
- **bilingualize** *Cdn verb* (also **-ise**)
- **bilingually** *adverb*

bilious *adjective*
- "BILL yuss" or "BILLY us"
- affected by a disorder of the bile.
- [Latin *biliosus* from *bilis* bile]
- **biliously** *adverb*
- **biliousness** *noun*

bilirubin *noun*
- "BILLY roobin"
- the orange-yellow pigment occurring in bile.
- [German from Latin *bilis* bile + *ruber* red]

billabong *noun*
- "BILLA bong"
- a branch of a river forming a backwater or a stagnant pool.
- [Wiradhuri *bilabang* (originally as the name of the Bell River, New South Wales)]

billet *noun*
- "BILLIT"
- a place, esp. a private home, where a student, travelling athlete, soldier, etc. is provided with accommodation, usu. without charge.
- [Anglo-French *billette*, Anglo-Latin *billetta*, diminutive of *billa* bill]
- **billetee** *noun* "billit EE"
- **billeter** *noun*

billiards *noun*
- "BILL yurds"
- any of various games played on an oblong cloth-covered table, with a cue used to strike a number of balls.
- [originally pl., from French *billard* billiards, cue, diminutive of *bille* log]

billionaire *noun*
- "bill yuh NAIR"
- a person possessing over a billion dollars, pounds, etc.
- [French from Latin *bi-* twice + 'million' (from Old French, prob. from Italian *millione* from *mille* thousand + *-one* augmentative suffix)]

billon *noun*
- "BILL 'n"
- an alloy of gold or silver with a predominating admixture of a base metal.
- [French from *bille* log]

bilobate *adjective*
- "by LO bate"
- having or consisting of two lobes.
- [Latin *bi-* twice + LOBATE]

bimah *noun*
ALSO SPELLED: **bima**
- "BEEMA"
- a raised platform for readers in a synagogue.
- [Greek *bēma* step, raised place]

bimetallic *adjective*
- "by muh TALIC"
- made of two metals.
- [Latin *bi-* twice + METAL]

bimetallism *noun*
- "by METTLE izm"
- a system using gold and silver as legal tender to any amount at a fixed ratio to each other.
- [Latin *bi-* twice + METAL]

bimillenary *adjective*
- "by muh LENNER ee"
- of or relating to a two-thousandth anniversary.
- [Latin *bi-* twice + MILLENARY]

bimini *noun*
• “BIMMA nee”
• (on a yacht or other vessel of similar size) an awning attached to the bridge.
• [the *Bimini* Islands in the western Bahamas]

bimodal *adjective*
• “by MODE’ll”
• having two modes.
• [Latin *bi-* twice + ‘mode’ from French *mode* and Latin *modus* measure]
• **bimodality** *noun* “by mo DALA tee”

bimolecular *adjective*
• “by muh LECK yuh lur”
• involving two molecules.
• [Latin *bi-* twice + MOLECULAR]

binary *adjective*
• “BY na ree” or “BY nairy”
• dual.
• [Late Latin *binarius* from *bini* two together]

binate *adjective*
• “BY nate”
• growing in pairs.
• [modern Latin *binatus* from Latin *bini* two together]

binational *adjective*
• “by NASH’n ’ll”
• involving two nations.
• [Latin *bi-* twice + *natio -onis* from *nasci nat-* be born]

binaural *adjective*
• “by NORE’ll”
• of or used with both ears.
• [Latin *bin-* twice + AURAL]

bindi *noun*
• “BINDY”
• a decorative mark worn in the middle of the forehead by South Asian women, esp. Hindus.
• [Hindi]

binnacle *noun*
• “BINNA k’ll”
• a built-in housing for a ship’s compass.
• [earlier *bittacle*, ultimately from Latin *habitaculum* habitation, from *habitare* inhabit]

binocular *adjective*
• “bin OCK yuh lur”
• adapted for or using both eyes.
• [Latin *bin-* twice + *oculus* eye]

binoculars *plural noun*
• “bin OCK yuh lurz”
• an optical instrument with lenses for each eye, for viewing distant objects.
• [as BINOCULAR]

binomial *noun*
• “by NO mee ’ll”
• an algebraic expression of the sum or the difference of two terms.
• [French *binôme* or modern Latin *binomium* (as Latin *bi-* twice + Greek *nomos* part, portion)]
• **binomially** *adverb*

binucleate *adjective*
• “by NEW clee it”
• having two nuclei.
• [Latin *bi-* twice + NUCLEATE]

bioaccumulate *verb*
• “bio a KYOO myoo late”
• (of poisons, chemicals, etc.) collect in animal tissue in progressively higher concentrations towards the top of the food chain.
• [Greek *bios* (course of) human life + ACCUMULATE]

bioassay *noun*
• “bio a SAY”
• a measurement of the concentration or strength of a substance by means of its effect on a living organism.
• [Greek *bios* (course of) human life + ASSAY]

bioavailability *noun*
• “bio a vale a BILLA tee”
• the rate at which a drug etc. is absorbed by the body or exerts an effect after absorption.
• [Greek *bios* (course of) human life + AVAILABLE]
• **bioavailable** *adjective*

biocentrism *noun*
• “bio SEN trizm”
• the belief or view that all life is important, and that no single species should occupy a privileged position.
• [Greek *bios* (course of) human life + CENTRE]
• **biocentric** *adjective*
• **biocentrist** *noun*

biochemistry *noun*
• “bio KEMMA stree”
• the study of the chemical and physicochemical processes of living organisms.
• [Greek *bios* (course of) human life + CHEMISTRY]
• **biochemical** *adjective*
• **biochemically** *adverb*
• **biochemist** *noun*

biocide *noun*
• “BY a side”
• a poisonous substance, esp. a pesticide, herbicide, etc.
• [Greek *bios* (course of) human life + Latin *-cida, -cidium* from *caedere* kill]

biocompatible *adjective*
• “bio k’m PATTA bull”
• not harmful or toxic to living tissue.
• [Greek *bios* (course of) human life + COMPATIBLE]
• **biocompatibility** *noun*

biodegrade *verb*
• “bio de GRADE”
• decompose through the action of bacteria or other living organisms.
• [Greek *bios* (course of) human life + DEGRADE]
• **biodegradability** *noun*

• **biodegradable** *adjective*
• **biodegradation** *noun*

biodiesel *noun*
• "BIO deez'll"
• a biofuel intended as a substitute for diesel.
• [Greek *bios* (course of) human life + DIESEL]

biodiversity *noun*
• "bio die VURSA tee"
• variety of species.
• [Greek *bios* (course of) human life + DIVERSE]

biodynamic *adjective*
• "bio die NAMMIC"
• (of farming) using only organic fertilizers etc.
• [Greek *bios* (course of) human life + DYNAMIC]
• **biodynamics** *noun*

bioenergetics *noun*
• "bio enner JETTIX"
• the study of the transformation of energy in living organisms.
• [Greek *bios* (course of) human life + ENERGETIC]

bioengineering *noun*
• "bio enja NEERING"
• the application of engineering techniques to biological processes.
• [Greek *bios* (course of) human life + Old French *engin* from Latin *ingenium* talent, device]
• **bioengineer** *noun*

bioethics *noun*
• "bio ETHIX"
• the ethics of medical and biological research and practice.
• [Greek *bios* (course of) human life + ETHIC]
• **bioethical** *adjective*
• **bioethicist** *noun* "bio ETH a sist"

bioflavonoid *noun*
• "bio FLAY vuh noid"
• any of a group of substances occurring mainly in citrus fruits and blackcurrants, and formerly thought to be a vitamin.
• [Greek *bios* (course of) human life + FLAVONOID]

biogenesis *noun*
• "bio JENNA sis"
• the synthesis of substances by living organisms.
• [Greek *bios* (course of) human life + GENESIS]
• **biogenetic** *adjective* "bio juh NETTIC"

biogenic *adjective*
• "bio JENNIC"
• produced by living organisms.
• [Greek *bios* (course of) human life + GENESIS]

biogeography *noun*
• "bio jee OGGRA fee"
• the scientific study of the geographical distribution of plants and animals.
• [Greek *bios* (course of) human life + GEOGRAPHY]
• **biogeographic** *adjective*
• **biogeographical** *adjective*

biographee *noun*
• "by oggra FEE"
• a person who is the subject of a biography.
• [as BIOGRAPHY]

biography *noun*
• "by OGGRA fee"
• a written account of a person's life, usu. by another.
• [modern Latin *biographia* from medieval Greek *bios* (course of) human life + GRAPH]
• **biographer** *noun*
• **biographic** *adjective*
• **biographical** *adjective*

biohazard *noun*
• "BIO hazz'rd"
• a risk to human health or the environment arising from biological work, esp. with micro-organisms.
• [Greek *bios* (course of) human life + HAZARD]

bioinformatics *noun*
• "bio in for MATTIX"
• the science of collecting and analysing complex biological data such as genetic codes.
• [Greek *bios* (course of) human life + 'informatics', translation of Russian *informatika* (from Latin *informare* give shape to, fashion, describe (*in* in, *forma* form))]

biology *noun*
• "by OLLA jee"
• the study of living organisms.
• [Greek *bios* (course of) human life + *logos* word]
• **biologic** *adjective*
• **biological** *adjective*
• **biologically** *adverb*
• **biologist** *noun*

bioluminescence *noun*
• "bio loomin ESS ince"
• the emission of light by living organisms such as the firefly and glow-worm.
• [Greek *bios* (course of) human life + LUMINESCENCE]
• **bioluminescent** *adjective*

biome *noun*
• "BY ome"
• a large, naturally occurring community of flora and fauna adapted to the particular conditions in which they occur, e.g. tundra.
• [Greek *bios* (course of) human life]

biomechanics *noun*
• "bio muh CANNIX"
• the study of the mechanical laws relating to the movement or structure of living organisms.
• [Greek *bios* (course of) human life + MECHANIC]
• **biomechanical** *adjective*
• **biomechanically** *adverb*

biomedicine *noun*
• "bio MEDDA sin"
• the application of biology to clinical medicine.

- [Greek *bios* (course of) human life + MEDICINE]
- **biomedical** *adjective* "bio MEDDA k'll"

biometrics *noun*
- "bio METRIX"
- the application of statistical analysis to biological investigation.
- [Greek *bios* (course of) human life + Greek *metron* measure]
- **biometric** *adjective*
- **biometrical** *adjective*
- **biometrician** *noun* "bio muh TRISH'n"

biomimetic *adjective*
- "bio muh METTIC"
- designating synthetic techniques that mimic naturally occurring biological processes.
- [Greek *bios* (course of) human life + MIMESIS]

biomorph *noun*
- "BIO morf"
- a decorative form based on a living organism.
- [Greek *bios* (course of) human life + *morphē* form]
- **biomorphic** *adjective*

bionic *adjective*
- "by ONNIC"
- having artificial body parts or the superhuman powers resulting from these.
- [Greek *bios* (course of) human life + ELECTRONIC]
- **bionically** *adverb*
- **bionics** *noun*

biophysics *noun*
- "bio FIZZIX"
- the science of the application of the laws of physics to biological phenomena.
- [Greek *bios* (course of) human life + PHYSICS]
- **biophysical** *adjective*
- **biophysicist** *noun* "bio FIZZA sist"

biopsy *noun*
- "BY op see"
- the removal and examination of tissue taken from a living body to discover the presence, cause, or extent of a disease.
- [Greek *bios* life + *opsis* sight, after NECROPSY]

bioremediation *noun*
- "bio ruh meedy AY sh'n"
- encouragement of the natural microbial degradation of environmental pollutants, e.g. by the introduction of materials such as appropriate micro-organisms (in addition to those present naturally) and substances which promote the microbial metabolism of specific pollutants.
- [Greek *bios* (course of) human life + REMEDIATION]

biorhythm *noun*
- "BIO rith'm" (with "TH" as in *THEM*)
- any of the recurring cycles of biological processes thought to affect a person's emotional, intellectual, and physical activity.
- [Greek *bios* (course of) human life + RHYTHM]
- **biorhythmic** *adjective*

biosensor *noun*
- "BIO senser"
- a device which uses a living organism or active biological molecules, esp. enzymes or antibodies, combined with an electrochemical transducer, to detect the presence of chemicals.
- [Greek *bios* (course of) human life + SENSOR]

biosphere *noun*
- "BIO sfeer"
- the regions of the earth's crust and atmosphere occupied by living organisms.
- [Greek *bios* (course of) human life + SPHERE]

biostatistics *noun*
- "bio stuh TISTIX"
- the branch of statistics that deals with data relating to life.
- [Greek *bios* (course of) human life + STATISTICS]
- **biostatistical** *adjective*
- **biostatistician** *noun* "bio statta STISH'n"

biosynthesis *noun*
- "bio SINTHA sis"
- the production of organic molecules by living organisms.
- [Greek *bios* (course of) human life + SYNTHESIS]
- **biosynthetic** *adjective* "bio sin THETTIC"

biota *noun*
- "by OH tuh"
- the animal and plant life of a region.
- [modern Latin: compare Greek *biotē* life]

biotech *noun*
- "BIO teck"
- biotechnology.
- [abbreviation]

biotechnology *noun*
- "bio teck NOLLA jee"
- the exploitation of biological processes for industrial and other purposes, esp. genetic manipulation of micro-organisms (for the production of antibiotics, hormones, etc.).
- [Greek *bios* (course of) human life + TECHNOLOGY]
- **biotechnological** *adjective*

bioterrorism *noun*
- "bio TARE ur ism"
- the use of harmful biological or biochemical substances as weapons of terrorism.
- [Greek *bios* (course of) human life + TERROR]
- **bioterror** *noun*
- **bioterrorist** *noun*

biotic *adjective*
- "by OTTIC"
- relating to life or to living things.
- [Greek *biōtikos* from *bios* life]

biotin *noun*
- "BIO tin"
- a vitamin of the B complex, found esp. in egg

yolk, liver, and yeast, and involved in the metabolism of carbohydrates, fats, and proteins.
• [German from Greek *bios* life]

biotite *noun*
• "BY a tite"
• a black, dark brown, or green micaceous mineral occurring as a constituent of metamorphic and igneous rocks.
• [J. B. *Biot*, French physicist d.1862]

bipartisan *adjective*
• "by PARTA z'n"
• of or involving two (esp. political) parties.
• [Latin *bi-* twice + PARTISAN]
• **bipartisanship** *noun*

bipartite *adjective*
• "by PAR tite"
• consisting of two parts.
• [Latin *bipartitus* from *bipartire* (as Latin *bi-* twice + *partire* part)]

biphenyl *noun*
• "by FEN'll" or "by FEEN'll"
• a crystalline hydrocarbon containing two benzene rings.
• [Latin *bi-* twice + PHENYL]

bipinnate *adjective*
• "by PINNATE"
• (of a pinnate leaf) having leaflets that are further subdivided in a pinnate arrangement.
• [Latin *bi-* twice + PINNATE]

bipolar *adjective*
• "by POLE ur"
• having two poles or extremities.
• [Latin *bi-* twice + *polus* from Greek *polos* pivot, axis, sky]
• **bipolarity** *noun* "by puh LERRA tee"

biracial *adjective*
• "by RAY sh'll"
• concerning or containing members of two racial groups.
• [Latin *bi-* twice + 'racial' from French from Italian *razza*, of unknown origin]

birefringent *adjective*
• "by ruh FRIN j'nt"
• having two different refractive indices.
• [Latin *bi-* twice + *refringere refract-* (from *re-* again + *frangere* break)]
• **birefringence** *noun*

bireme *noun*
• "BY reem"
• an ancient warship with two tiers of oars on each side.
• [Latin *biremis* (as Latin *bi-* twice + *remus* oar)]

biretta *noun*
• "bir ETTA"
• a square usu. black cap with three flat projections on top, worn (esp. formerly) by (esp. Roman Catholic) clergymen.
• [Italian *berretta* or Spanish *birreta* from Late Latin *birrus* cape]

birl *verb*
• "BURL" (rhymes with *GIRL*)
• cause (a floating log) to rotate by using one's feet; spin.
• [perhaps related to Scots *birr* a whirring sound + WHIRL]
• **birling** *noun*
HOMOPHONES: *burl*

birr *noun*
• "bur"
• the chief monetary unit of Ethiopia, divided into 100 cents.
• [Amharic]
HOMOPHONES: *burr*, *brr*

birthwort *noun*
• "BIRTH wurt" or "BIRTH wort"
• any of several climbing vines of the genus *Aristolochia*, reputed to have medicinal properties.
• ['birth' + WORT]

biryani *noun*
ALSO SPELLED: **biriani**
• "birry ANNY"
• an originally Indian dish made with highly seasoned rice, and meat or fish etc.
• [Urdu]

biscotti *plural noun*
• "biss COTTY"
• hard, dry, Italian cookies, usu. containing ground nuts.
• [Italian, = biscuits]

biscuit *noun*
• "BISKIT"
• a dry, hard, flat, baked foodstuff.
• [Old French *bescoit* etc., ultimately from Latin *bis* twice + *coctus* past participle of *coquere* cook]
• **biscuity** *adjective*

bishop *noun*
• "BISHUP"
• a member of the highest rank of clerical hierarchy in some Christian denominations, usu. in charge of a diocese, and empowered to confer holy orders.
• [Old English *biscop* (ultimately from Greek *episkopos* overseer, as Greek *epi* upon, near to, in addition, *-skopos* -looking)]

bishopric *noun*
• "BISHUP rick"
• the office of a bishop.
• [as BISHOP + Old English *rīce* realm]

Bislama *noun*
• "bissla MAW"
• an English-based pidgin used as a lingua franca in Fiji and as an official language in Vanuatu in the S Pacific.
• [alteration of 'Beach-la-mar', corruption from Portuguese *bicho do mar* sea cucumber (traded as a commodity: the word then applied to the language of trade)]

bismarck *noun*
- "BIZ mark"
- *Alta., Sask., & US Midwest* a sugar-coated jam-filled doughnut.
- [origin unknown, possibly after O. von *Bismarck*, German chancellor d.1898]

bismuth *noun*
- "BIZ muth"
- a brittle reddish-white metallic element, occurring naturally and used in alloys.
- [modern Latin *bisemutum*, Latinization of German *Wismut*, of unknown origin]

bisque *noun*
- "BISK"
- a rich soup usu. made from shellfish but also from game or vegetables.
- [French]

bistre *noun*
ALSO SPELLED: **bister**
- "BISTER"
- a brownish pigment made from the soot of burnt wood.
- [French, of unknown origin]

bistro *noun*
- "BEE stroe" or "BISS troe"
- a small restaurant or bar.
- [French, perhaps related to *bistouille*, a northern colloquial term meaning 'bad alcohol', perhaps from Russian *bystro* rapidly]

bisulphate *noun*
ALSO SPELLED: **bisulfate**
- "by SULL fate"
- a salt or ester of sulphuric acid.
- [Latin *bi-* twice + SULPHATE]

bitts *plural noun*
- "BITS"
- a pair of posts on the deck of a ship, for fastening cables etc.
- [prob. from Low German: compare Low German & Dutch *beting*]

bitumen *noun*
- "bit YOO m'n" or "bit OO m'n"
- any of various tar-like mixtures of hydrocarbons derived from petroleum naturally or by distillation and used for road surfacing and roofing.
- [Latin *bitumen -minis*]
- **bituminous** *adjective*

bivalent *adjective*
- "by VALE 'nt"
- having a valence of two.
- [Latin *bi-* twice + *valent-* present participle stem formed as VALENCE]
- **bivalence** *noun*

bivouac *noun*
- "BIVVA wack"
- a temporary open encampment e.g. of soldiers or mountaineers.
- [French, prob. from Swiss German *Beiwacht* additional guard at night]

bizarre *adjective*
- "biz AR"
- strange in appearance or effect; eccentric; grotesque.
- [French, originally = handsome, brave, from Spanish & Portuguese *bizarro* from Basque *bizarra* beard]
- **bizarrely** *adverb*
- **bizarreness** *noun*

HOMOPHONES: *bazaar*

bizarrerie *noun*
- "biz AR a ree"
- a bizarre quality; bizarreness.
- [French]

bizarro *adjective*
- "biz AR oh"
- bizarre.
- [alteration of BIZARRE]

blackcurrant *noun*
- "BLACK cur 'nt"
- a widely cultivated shrub, *Ribes nigrum*, bearing flowers in racemes.
- ['black' + CURRANT]

blackguard *noun*
- "BLAG ard" or "BLAG'rd" or "BLACK gard"
- a scoundrel; an unscrupulous, unprincipled person.
- ['black' + 'guard': originally applied collectively to menial workers etc.]
- **blackguardly** *adjective*

blacklead *noun*
- "BLACK led"
- graphite.
- ['black' + 'lead']

blackpoll *noun*
- "BLACK pole"
- a N American warbler, *Dendroica striata*, the male of which has a black crown in spring.
- ['black' + POLL]

bladderwort *noun*
- "BLADDER wurt" or "BLADDER wort"
- any insect-consuming aquatic plant of the genus *Utricularia*, with underwater leaves having small bladders for trapping insects.
- ['bladder' + WORT]

bladderwrack *noun*
- "BLADDER rack"
- a common brown seaweed, *Fucus vesiculosus*, with fronds containing air bladders which give buoyancy to the plant.
- ['bladder' + WRACK]

blain *noun*
- "BLANE"
- an inflamed swelling or sore on the skin.
- [Old English *blegen* from West Germanic]

Blakean *adjective*
ALSO SPELLED: **Blakeian**
• "BLAKE ee 'n"
• relating to or characteristic of English poet and artist William Blake (d.1827) or his work, esp. in its visionary aspects.

blanch *verb*
• "BLANCH"
• make white or pale by extracting colour.
• [Old French *blanchir* from *blanc* white, blank]

blancmange *noun*
• "bluh MONJ"
• a sweet opaque gelatinous dessert made with flavoured milk and thickened with cornstarch.
• [Old French *blancmanger* from *blanc* white + *manger* eat, from Latin *manducare* eat]

blanquette *noun*
• "blon KET"
• a stew of light-coloured meat, esp. veal, in a white sauce.
• [Old French *blancquet* from *blanc* white]

blare *verb*
• "BLARE"
• make a loud harsh sound.
• [Middle Dutch *blaren, bleren*, imitative]

blarney *noun*
• "BLARNY"
• cajoling talk; flattery.
• [*Blarney*, a castle near Cork, Ireland, with a stone said to confer a cajoling tongue on whoever kisses it]

blasé *adjective*
• "blaw ZAY"
• unimpressed or indifferent because of overfamiliarity.
• [French, past participle of *blaser* cloy, prob. from Germanic]

blasphemy *noun*
• "BLASSFA mee"
• the action or offence of speaking sacrilegiously about God or sacred things.
• [Greek *blasphēmia* slander, blasphemy]
• **blaspheme** *verb* "blass FEEM"
• **blasphemer** *noun*
• **blasphemous** *adjective* "BLASSFA muss"
• **blasphemously** *adverb*

blastula *noun*
• "BLAST yoo luh"
• an animal embryo at an early stage of development when it is a hollow ball of cells.
• [modern Latin from Greek *blastos* sprout]

blatant *adjective*
• "BLAY t'nt"
• flagrant, unashamed.
• [perhaps after Scots *blatand* = bleating]
• **blatancy** *noun*
• **blatantly** *adverb*

blatherskite *noun*
• "BLATHER skite"
• a person who blathers.
• [Old Norse *blathra* talk nonsense, from *blathr* nonsense *skite*, corruption of 'skate' (as in 'cheapskate'), of unknown origin]

blaxploitation *noun*
• "blax ploy TAY sh'n"
• the exploitation of blacks, esp. as actors in films.
• [blend of 'black' + EXPLOITATION]

blazon *verb*
• "BLAY z'n"
• display prominently or vividly.
• [Old French *blason* shield, of unknown origin]

blazonry *noun*
• "BLAY z'n ree"
• the art of describing or painting heraldic devices or armorial bearings.
• [as BLAZON]

blear *adjective*
• "BLEER"
• (of the eyes or the mind) dim, dull, filmy.
• [Middle English, of uncertain origin]

bleary *adjective*
• "BLEERY"
• (of the eyes or mind) dim; blurred.
• [as BLEAR]
• **blearily** *adverb*
• **bleariness** *noun*

blemish *noun*
• "BLEM ish"
• a flaw or defect.
• [Old French *ble(s)mir* make pale, prob. of Germanic origin]

blende *noun*
• "BLEND"
• any naturally occurring metal sulphide, esp. zinc blende.
• [German from *blenden* deceive, so called because while often resembling galena it yielded no lead]
HOMOPHONES: *blend*

blenny *noun*
• "BLENNY"
• any of various small spiny-finned marine fishes belonging to the Blenniidae or a related family, most of which are bottom-dwelling fishes of intertidal and shallow inshore waters.
• [Latin *blennius* from Greek *blennos* mucus, with reference to its mucous coating]

blepharitis *noun*
• "bleffa RITE iss"
• inflammation of the eyelids.
• [Greek *blepharon* eyelid + *-itis*, forming feminine of adjectives in *-itēs* (with *nosos* 'disease' implied)]

blepharoplasty *noun*
• "BLEFFA roe plasty"
• the surgical repair or reconstruction of an eyelid.

• [Greek *blepharon* eyelid + *plastos* formed, moulded]

blesbok *noun*
• "BLESS bock"
• a white-faced southern African antelope, *Damaliscus dorcas*, having small lyre-shaped horns.
• [Afrikaans from *bles* blaze (from the white mark on its forehead) + *bok* goat]

bleu *noun*
• "BLUH" (with "UH" like the *OO* in *BOOK*)
• *Cdn* a Quebec supporter of a Conservative party.
• [French, = blue]

blewits *noun*
• "BLOO its"
• an edible European mushroom of the genus *Lepista* with a pale buff or mauve cap and a mauve or bluish stem.
• [prob. from 'blue']

blight *noun*
• "BLITE"
• any plant disease caused by mildews, rusts, smuts, fungi, or insects.
• [17th c.: origin unknown]
HOMOPHONES: *blite*

blighter *noun*
• "BLITE ur"
• a person (esp. as a term of contempt or disparagement).
• [as BLIGHT]

blimey *interjection*
• "BLIME ee"
• an expression of surprise, contempt, etc.
• [corruption of *(God) blind me!*]

blini *noun*
• "BLINNY"
• an originally Russian pancake made from buckwheat flour and yeast.
• [pl. of Russian *blin*]

blintz *noun*
ALSO SPELLED: **blintze**
• "BLINTS"
• a thin pancake wrapped around a filling, usu. of cottage or cream cheese.
• [Yiddish *blintse* from Russian *blinets* diminutive of *blin*]

blite *noun*
• "BLITE"
• any of various plants of the Chenopodiaceae family, esp. a goosefoot of eastern Canada and the northern US, *Chenopodium capitatum*, with red berry-like fruits.
• [Latin *blitum* orache, from Greek *bliton*]
HOMOPHONES: *blight*

blithe *adjective*
• "BLYTHE" (with "TH" either as in *BATH* or as in *BATHE*)
• happy, joyous.
• [Old English *blīthe* from Germanic]
• **blithely** *adverb*
• **blitheness** *noun*

blitz *noun*
• "BLITS"
• an intensive or sudden (esp. aerial) attack.
• [abbreviation of BLITZKRIEG]
• **blitzer** *noun*

blitzed *adjective*
• "BLITST"
• drunk.
• [as BLITZ]

blitzkrieg *noun*
• "BLITS creeg"
• an intense military campaign intended to bring about a swift victory.
• [German, = lightning war]

blizzard *noun*
• "BLIZZ'rd"
• a severe snowstorm with high winds.
• [19th c.: origin unknown]
• **blizzardy** *adjective*

bloc *noun*
• "BLOCK"
• a combination of nations, parties, groups, or people, formed to promote a particular purpose.
• [French, = block]
HOMOPHONES: *block*

blockade *noun*
• "block AID"
• the surrounding or blocking of access to a place to prevent entry and exit of supplies etc., as a military tactic or act of protest etc.
• [from 'block', prob. after AMBUSCADE]
• **blockader** *noun*

bloke *noun*
• "BLOKE"
• a man, a fellow.
• [Shelta]

blokeish *adjective*
• "BLOKE ish"
• indulging in or relating to stereotypically male behaviour and interests.
• [as BLOKE]

Bloquiste *noun*
• "block EEST"
• *Cdn* a member of the Bloc Québécois political party.
• [Canadian French]

blouson *noun*
• "BLOO zon"
• a jacket cinched at the waist so that the fabric covering the torso is full.
• [French]

blowsy *adjective*
ALSO SPELLED: **blowzy**
• "BLOWZY" (rhymes with *LOUSY* and *DROWSY*)
• coarse and red-faced.

• [obsolete *blowze* beggar's wench, of unknown origin]
• **blowsily** *adverb* (also **blowzily**)
• **blowsiness** *noun* (also **blowziness**)

bluchers *plural noun*
• "BLOOKERZ" or "BLOOCHERZ"
• laced half-boots or high shoes in which the vamp and tongue are formed from a single piece of strong leather.
• [G. L. von *Blücher*, Prussian general d.1819]

bludgeon *noun*
• "BLUDGE 'n"
• a club with a heavy end.
• [18th c.: origin unknown]

bluet *noun*
• "BLUE it"
• a N American blue-flowered plant of the madder family, *Hedyotis caerulia*.
• [French *bleuet*, diminutive of *bleu* blue]

bluey *adjective*
• "BLUE ee"
• = BLUISH.
• [from 'blue', from Old French *bleu* from Germanic]

bluing *noun*
• "BLUE ing"
• a blue powder or liquid used to prevent white laundry from yellowing.
• [as BLUEY]

bluish *adjective*
• "BLUE ish"
• somewhat blue.
• [as BLUEY]

blunderbuss *noun*
• "BLUNDER buss"
• a short large-bored gun which sprays several balls or slugs simultaneously at close range.
• [alteration of Dutch *donderbus* thunder gun, associated with 'blunder']

blurb *noun*
• "BLURB"
• a promotional (usu. complimentary) description, esp. printed on a book's jacket by its publisher.
• [coined by G. Burgess, US humorist d.1951]

blurt *verb*
• "BLURT"
• utter abruptly, thoughtlessly, or tactlessly.
• [prob. imitative]

boar *noun*
• "BORE"
• a tusked wild pig of Eurasia and Africa, *Sus scrofa*, from which domestic pigs are descended.
• [Old English *bār* from West Germanic]
HOMOPHONES: *bore*, *Boer*

board *noun*
• "BORD"
• a flat thin piece of sawn timber, usu. long and narrow.
• [Old English *bord* from Germanic]
HOMOPHONES: *bored*

boarder *noun*
• "BORDER"
• a person who boards, esp. a lodger or a pupil at a boarding school.
• [as BOARD]
HOMOPHONES: *border*

boarding *noun*
• "BORDING"
• the infraction of bodychecking an opponent into the boards with excessive force.
• [as BOARD]

boatswain *noun*
ALSO SPELLED: **bosun**
• "BOE z'n"
• a ship's officer in charge of equipment and the duties of the crew.
• [Old English *bātswegen* ('boat' + SWAIN)]

bobbin *noun*
• "BOBBIN"
• a cylinder or cone holding thread, yarn, wire, etc., used esp. in weaving and machine sewing.
• [French *bobine*]

bobolink *noun*
• "BOBBA link"
• a N American songbird, *Dolichonyx oryzivorus*, the male of which is black with yellow and white markings, and the female yellowish buff.
• [originally *Bob (o') Lincoln*: imitative of its call]

bocce *noun*
ALSO SPELLED: **boccie**, **bocci**
• "BOTCHY"
• an Italian form of lawn bowling, usu. played on a narrow dirt-covered court.
• [Italian, pl. of *boccia* ball]

bocconcini *noun*
• "bock on CHEENY"
• a mild Italian cheese similar to mozzarella, in the form of a small ball.
• [Italian, pl. of *bocconcino* little mouthful, from *boccone* mouthful]

bock *noun*
• "BOCK"
• a strong dark German beer.
• [French from German abbreviation of *Eimbockbier* from *Einbeck* in Hanover]
HOMOPHONES: *balk*, *bawk*

bodacious *adjective*
• "boe DAY sh'ss"
• outstanding, excellent.
• [blend of 'bold' + AUDACIOUS]

bode *verb*
• "BODE"
• portend, foreshow.
• [Old English *bodian* from *boda* messenger]
• **boding** *noun*

bodega *noun*
- “bo DAY guh”
- a cellar or store selling wine and food, esp. in Spanish-speaking areas.
- [Spanish from Latin *apotheca* from Greek *apothēkē* storehouse]

Bodhisattva *noun*
- “boe dee SATVA”
- in Mahayana Buddhism, a person who is able to reach nirvana but delays doing so through compassion for suffering beings.
- [Sanskrit, = one whose essence is perfect knowledge]

bodhran *noun*
- “baw RAN” or “bo RAN”
- an Irish folk instrument resembling a large, deep tambourine without jingles, played with a wooden beater knobbed at both ends.
- [Gaelic]

bodice *noun*
- “BODDISS”
- the part of a woman’s dress or blouse (excluding sleeves) which is above the waist.
- [originally *pair of bodies* = stays, corsets]

Boeotian *noun*
- “bee OH sh’n”
- a native or inhabitant of Boeotia in central Greece.

Boer *noun*
- “BORE”
- (historically) a South African of Dutch descent.
- [Dutch: see BOOR]

HOMOPHONES: *bore, boar*

bogan *noun*
- “BOAG’n”
- (*Maritimes* & *Maine*) a stagnant backwater adjacent to a river, lake, etc.
- [prob. of Algonquian origin]

bogey *noun*
- “BOE gee” (with a hard “G” as in *GEEK*)
- an evil or mischievous spirit.
- [19th c., originally as a proper name]

HOMOPHONES: *bogie*

bogeyman *noun*

ALSO SPELLED: **bogyman**
- “BOE gee man” (with “G” as in *GEEK*)
- an imaginary evil spirit, esp. invoked to frighten children.
- [as BOGEY]

bogie *noun*
- “BOE gee” (with “G” as in *GEEK*)
- the swivelling assembly containing the wheels on a railway car.
- [19th-c. English dialect word: origin unknown]

HOMOPHONES: *bogey*

bogus *adjective*
- “BOE guss”
- sham, fictitious, spurious.
- [19th-c. US word, originally an apparatus for counterfeiting coins]
- **bogusly** *adverb*
- **bogusness** *noun*

Bohemian *noun*
- “boe HEEMY ’n”
- a native of Bohemia in the W Czech Republic.

Bohemianism *noun*
- “boe HEEMY ’n izm”
- the qualities of people who are socially unconventional, esp. artists or writers.
- [French *bohémien* Gypsy (because Gypsies were thought to come from Bohemia)]

bohrium *noun*
- “BORY um”
- a very unstable chemical element made by high-energy atomic collisions.
- [modern Latin, from N. *Bohr*, Danish physicist d.1962]

boisterous *adjective*
- “BOY stur us”
- (of a person or thing) rough; noisily exuberant.
- [var. of Middle English *boist(u)ous*, of unknown origin]
- **boisterously** *adverb*
- **boisterousness** *noun*

boîte *noun*
- “BWOT”
- a bar or nightclub.
- [French, lit. = ‘box’]

bolas *noun*
- “BO luz”
- (esp. in S America) a hunting weapon consisting of a number of balls connected by strong cord, which when thrown entangles the limbs of an animal.
- [Spanish & Portuguese, pl. of *bola* ball]

HOMOPHONES: *bolus*

bole *noun*
- “BOLE”
- the stem or trunk of a tree.
- [Old Norse *bolr*, perhaps related to BALK]

HOMOPHONES: *boll, bowl*

bolero *noun*
- “buh LAIR oh”
- a Spanish dance in simple triple time.
- [Spanish]

boletus *noun*
- “buh LEE tuss”
- a mushroom or toadstool of the genus *Boletus*, having many pores on the underside of the cap.
- [Latin from Greek *bōlitēs*, perhaps from *bōlos* lump]

bolivar *noun*
- “BOLLA var”
- the basic monetary unit of Venezuela, equal to 100 centimos.
- [S. *Bolívar*, Venezuelan revolutionary d.1830]

Bolivian *noun*
• "buh LIVVY 'n"
• a native or inhabitant of Bolivia in S America.

boliviano *noun*
• "buh livvy ONNO"
• the basic monetary unit of Bolivia (1863–1962 and since 1987), equal to 100 centavos or cents.
• [Spanish]

boll *noun*
• "BOLE"
• a rounded capsule containing seeds, esp. cotton or flax.
• [Middle Dutch *bolle*]
HOMOPHONES: *bole, bowl*

bollard *noun*
• "BAWL ard"
• a short post on a pier or ship for securing a rope.
• [Old Norse *bolr* BOLE]

bologna *noun*
ALSO SPELLED: **baloney**
• "buh LONEY" or "buh LONA"
• a smoked luncheon meat made from finely minced pork and beef.
• [*Bologna* in N Italy]
HOMOPHONES: *baloney*

bolognese *adjective*
• "bolla NAZE"
• (often placed after noun) designating a sauce for pasta made of ground beef, tomatoes, onions, etc.
• [Italian, = of Bologna]

bolometer *noun*
• "buh LOMMA tur"
• an instrument for measuring electromagnetic radiation (esp. infrared and microwaves) electrically.
• [Greek *bolē* ray + *metron* measure]
• **bolometric** *adjective* "bo luh METRIC"
• **bolometry** *noun*

Bolshevik *noun*
• "BOWL shuh vick"
• a member of the radical faction of the Russian socialist party, which became the communist party in 1918.
• [Russian, = a member of the majority, one who (in 1903) favoured extreme measures, from *bol'she* greater]
• **Bolshevism** *noun*
• **Bolshevist** *noun*

Bolshie *adjective*
ALSO SPELLED: **Bolshy**
• "BOWL shee"
• left-wing, socialist.
• [abbreviation]

bolus *noun*
• "BO luss"
• a soft ball, esp. of chewed food.
• [Late Latin from Greek *bōlos* clod]
HOMOPHONES: *bolas*

bombarde *noun*
• "BOM bard"
• a medieval alto-pitched shawm.
• [Old French *bombarde*, medieval Latin *bombarda* prob. from Latin *bombus* bomb from Greek *bombos* hum]

bombardier *noun*
• "bomba DEER"
• a member of a bomber crew responsible for sighting and releasing bombs.
• [French from *bombarder* from *bombarde*, from medieval Latin *bombarda* a stone-throwing engine]

bombardon *noun*
• "bom BARD'n" or "BOM bur d'n"
• a type of valved bass tuba.
• [Italian *bombardone* from *bombardo* bassoon]

bombazine *noun*
• "BOMBA zeen"
• a twilled dress material of worsted, sometimes blended with silk or cotton, esp., when black, formerly used for mourning.
• [French *bombasin* from medieval Latin *bombacinum* from Late Latin *bombycinus* silken, from *bombyx -ycis* silk or silkworm, from Greek *bombux*]

bombe *noun*
• "BOM"
• a dome-shaped frozen dessert, usu. consisting of an outer layer of ice cream filled with custard, cake crumbs, or another type of ice cream.
• [French, = 'bomb']
HOMOPHONES: *bomb, balm*

bombé *adjective*
• "BOM bay"
• (esp. of furniture) rounded; convex.
• [French, past participle of *bomber* swell out]

bomboniere *noun*
• "bom bon YAIR ay"
• a small favour or keepsake, usu. accompanied by sugared almonds, given to guests at an Italian wedding, christening, etc.
• [Italian, from French *bonbonnière* candy dish, from *bonbon* candy, from *bon* good, from Latin *bonus*]

bombora *noun*
• "bom BORA"
• a dangerous sea area where waves break over a submerged reef.
• [Aboriginal, perhaps Dharuk *bumbora*]

Bonapartism *noun*
• "BONE a part izm"
• (in 19th-c. France) attachment to or advocacy of the autocratic style of government of Napoleon Bonaparte and his dynasty.
• **Bonapartist** *noun*

bonce *noun*
• "BONCE"
• the head.
• [19th c.: origin unknown]

bonhomie *noun*
- "bon omm EE"
- geniality; good-natured friendliness.
- [French from *bonhomme* good fellow]
- **bonhomous** *adjective* "BONNA muss"

bonito *noun*
- "buh NEETO"
- any of various striped tuna, esp. *Sarda sarda* of the Atlantic and Mediterranean.
- [Spanish]

bonobo *noun*
- "BONNA bo"
- a chimpanzee, *Pan paniscus*, with a black face and black hair found in the Congo rainforests. It is believed to be the closest living relative of humans.
- [local name]

bonsai *noun*
- "BON zye" or "BON sye"
- the art of cultivating ornamental artificially dwarfed varieties of trees and shrubs.
- [Japanese, from *bon* tray + *sai* planting]

HOMOPHONES: *banzai*

bonspiel *noun*
- "BON speel"
- a curling tournament.
- [16th c.: perhaps from Low German; compare West Flemish *bonespel* a children's game]

bontebok *noun*
- "BONTA buck"
- a large chestnut antelope, *Damaliscus dorcas*, native to southern Africa, having a white tail and a white patch on its head and rump.
- [Afrikaans from *bont* spotted + *bok* buck]

bonus *noun*
- "BO nuss"
- an unsought or unexpected extra benefit.
- [Latin *bonus*, *bonum* good (thing)]

bonusing *noun*
- "BO nuss ing"
- *Cdn* an act of subsidizing something, esp. as an inducement for development etc.
- [as BONUS]

bonze *noun*
- "BONZ"
- a Japanese or Chinese Buddhist priest.
- [French *bonze* or Portuguese *bonzo* perhaps from Japanese *bonzō* from Chinese *fanseng* religious person, or from Japanese *bō-zi* from Chinese *fasi* teacher of the law]

boogie *verb*
- "BOOGY" (with "OO" either as in *GOOD* or as in *GOOF*)
- dance enthusiastically to rock music.
- [shortening of 'boogie-woogie', of unknown origin]

Boolean *adjective*
- "BOOLY 'n"
- pertaining to a system in which logical propositions are manipulated using the operators 'and', 'or', and 'not'.
- [G. *Boole*, English mathematician d.1864]

boor *noun*
- "BOOR"
- a rude, ill-mannered person.
- [Low German *būr* or Dutch *boer* farmer]
- **boorish** *adjective*
- **boorishly** *adverb*
- **boorishness** *noun*

bootie *noun*

ALSO SPELLED: **bootee**
- "BOOTY"
- a soft woollen or cloth shoe.
- [diminutive of 'boot' from Old Norse *bóti* or from Old French *bote*, of unknown origin]

HOMOPHONES: *booty*

booty *noun*
- "BOOTY"
- plunder gained by force or violence.
- [Middle Low German *būte*, *buite* exchange, of uncertain origin]

HOMOPHONES: *bootie*

bora *noun*
- "BORA"
- a strong cold dry NE wind blowing in the upper Adriatic Sea.
- [Italian dialect from Latin *boreas* north wind: see BOREAL]

boracic *adjective*
- "buh RASSIC"
- of, containing, or derived from borax.
- [medieval Latin *borax -acis*]

borage *noun*
- "BORE idge"
- any plant of the genus *Borago*, esp. *Borago officinalis*, which has hairy leaves and bright blue flowers, and is sometimes used in salads etc.
- [Old French *bourrache* from medieval Latin *borrago* from Arabic *'abu 'ārak* father of sweat (from its use as a diaphoretic)]

borane *noun*
- "BORE ane"
- any hydride of boron, a non-metallic brown amorphous or black crystalline element extracted from borax and boric acid and mainly used for hardening steel.
- [ultimately as BORAX]

borate *noun*
- "BORE ate"
- a salt or ester of boric acid.
- [ultimately as BORAX]

borax *noun*
- "BORE ax"
- the mineral salt sodium borate, occurring in alkaline deposits as an efflorescence or as crystals.

• [medieval Latin from Arabic *būraķ* from Persian *būrah*]

borazon *noun*
• "BORA zon"
• a hard form of boron nitride, resistant to oxidation.
• [BORAX + French *azote* nitrogen, from Greek *azōos* without life]

borborygmus *noun*
• "borba RIG muss"
• a rumbling of gas in the intestines.
• [modern Latin from Greek]

Bordeaux *noun*
• "bore DOE"
• any of various red, white, or rosé wines from the district of Bordeaux in SW France.

bordello *noun*
• "bore DELLO"
• a brothel.
• [Italian from Old French *bordel* small farm, diminutive of *borde*]

border *noun*
• "BORDER"
• the edge or boundary of anything, or the part near it.
• [Old French *bordure*]
• **borderless** *adjective*
HOMOPHONES: *boarder*

borderer *noun*
• "BORDER ur"
• a person who lives near the border between Scotland and England.
• [as BORDER]

borderland *noun*
• "BORDER land"
• the district near a border.
• [as BORDER]

borderline *noun*
• "BORDER line"
• a marginal position between two categories or qualities.
• [as BORDER]

bordure *noun*
• "BORD yur"
• a border around the edge of a shield.
• [Middle English form of BORDER]

boreal *adjective*
• "BORRY 'll"
• of the North or northern regions.
• [Late Latin *borealis* from Latin *Boreas* from Greek *Boreas* god of the north wind]

Borgesian *adjective*
• "bor HESSY 'n"
• relating to or characteristic of Argentinian writer Jorge Luis Borges (d.1986) or his work, esp. in its labyrinthine and metaphysical qualities.

boronia *noun*
• "buh RONEY uh"
• any sweet-scented Australian shrub of the genus *Boronia*.
• [F. *Borone*, Italian botanist d.1794]

borosilicate *noun*
• "boro SILLA cate" or "boro SILLA kit"
• any of many substances containing boron, silicon, and oxygen generally used in glazes and enamels and in the production of glass.
• [as BORAX + SILICATE]

borough *noun*
• "BURRO"
• a town (as distinct from a city) with a corporation and privileges granted by a royal charter.
• [Old English *burg, burh* from Germanic]
HOMOPHONES: *burro, burrow*

borscht *noun*
• "BORSHT"
• an originally Eastern European soup with various ingredients including beets and cabbage, and served with sour cream.
• [Russian *borshch*]

Borstal *noun*
• "BORST 'll"
• an institution for reforming and training young offenders.
• [*Borstal* in S England, where the first of these was established]

borzoi *noun*
• "BORE zoy"
• a breed of large Russian wolfhound with a narrow head and silky, usu. white, coat.
• [Russian from *borzyi* swift]

Bosc *noun*
• "BOSK"
• a firm, sweet, fairly elongated russet winter pear.
• [L. A. G. *Bosc*, French naturalist d.1828]

boscage *noun*
ALSO SPELLED: **boskage**
• "BOSK idge"
• masses of trees or shrubs.
• [Old French *boscage* from Germanic: related to 'bush']

Bosnian *noun*
• "BOZ nee 'n"
• a native or inhabitant of Bosnia and Herzegovina in the Balkans.

bosom *noun*
• "BOOZ'm" (with "OO" as in *BOOK*)
• a person's breast or chest, esp. a woman's.
• [Old English *bōsm* from Germanic]
• **bosomed** *adjective*
• **bosomy** *adjective*

boson *noun*
• "BOE zon"
• any of several elementary particles obeying

the relations stated by Bose and Einstein, with a zero or integral spin, e.g. photons.
• [S. N. *Bose*, Indian physicist d.1974]

botany *noun*
• "BOT 'n ee"
• the study of the physiology, structure, genetics, ecology, distribution, and classification of plants.
• [Greek *botanikos* from *botanē* plant]
• **botanical** *adjective* "buh TANNA k'll"
• **botanically** *adverb*
• **botanist** *noun*
• **botanize** *verb* (also esp. *Brit.* **-ise**)

bothy *noun*
• "BOTHY" (rhymes with *FROTHY*)
• a small hut or cottage, esp. one for housing labourers.
• [18th c.: origin unknown: perhaps related to 'booth']

botryoidal *adjective*
• "BOTTREE oid'll"
• (esp. of a mineral) shaped like a cluster of grapes.
• [Greek *botruoeidēs* from *botrus* bunch of grapes]

botrytis *noun*
• "buh TRITE iss"
• a fungus of the genus *Botrytis*, esp. the grey mould *B. cinerea*, deliberately cultivated on the grapes used for certain wines.
• [modern Latin, from Greek *botrus* cluster of grapes]
• **botrytised** *adjective*

Botswanan *noun*
• "bot SWON 'n"
• a native or inhabitant of Botswana in southern Africa.

botulinum *noun*
• "bot yuh LINE um"
• the bacterial toxin involved in botulism.
• [as BOTULISM]

botulism *noun*
• "BOTCHA lizm"
• poisoning caused by a toxin produced by the bacillus *Clostridium botulinum* growing in poorly preserved food.
• [German *Botulismus* from Latin *botulus* sausage]

bouclé *noun*
• "BOO clay"
• yarn (esp. wool) with a looped or curled ply.
• [French, = buckled, curled]

boudoir *noun*
• "BOO dwar" or "boo DWAR" (with the last syllable rhyming with *FAR*)
• a woman's small private room or bedroom.
• [French, lit. 'sulking place' from *bouder* sulk]

bouffant *adjective*
• "boo FONT"
• (of a dress, hair, etc.) puffed out.
• [French, present participle of *bouffer* swell]

bougainvillea *noun*
• "boo gun VILLY uh"
• any widely cultivated tropical plant of the genus *Bougainvillaea*, with large coloured bracts (usu. purple, red, or white) almost concealing the inconspicuous flowers.
• [L. A. de *Bougainville*, French explorer d.1811]

bough *noun*
• "BOW" (rhymes with *HOW*)
• a branch of a tree, esp. a main one.
• [Old English *bōg*, *bōh* from Germanic]
HOMOPHONES: *bow*

boughten *adjective*
• "BOTTEN"
• bought, as opposed to homemade.
• [var. of past participle of 'buy']

bougie *noun*
• "BOO zhee" or "boo ZHEE"
• a thin flexible surgical instrument for exploring, dilating, etc. the passages of the body.
• [French, lit. 'wax candle', from Arabic *Bujiya* Algerian port with a wax trade]

bouillabaisse *noun*
• "BOOYA base"
• a rich, spicy fish stew, originally from Provence in SE France.
• [French]

bouillon *noun*
• "BULL y'n" or "BOOL y'n" or "BOO yon"
• a clear broth made by cooking meat or fish in water.
• [French from *bouillir* to boil]
HOMOPHONES: *bullion*

boulder *noun*
• "BOLE dur"
• a large stone, esp. one worn smooth by erosion.
• [short for *boulderstone*, Middle English from Scandinavian]
• **bouldery** *adjective*
HOMOPHONES: *bolder*

bouldering *noun*
• "BOLDER ing"
• the sport of climbing large boulders.
• [as BOULDER]

boule[1] *noun*
ALSO SPELLED: **boules**
• "BOOL"
• a French form of lawn bowling, played on rough ground with usu. metal balls.
• [French *boule* from Latin *bulla* bubble]
HOMOPHONES: *buhl*

boule[2] *noun*
• "BOOLY"
• a legislative body of ancient or modern Greece.
• [Greek *boulē* senate]

boulevard *noun*
• "BULL a vard"
• a broad urban road.
• [French from German *Bollwerk* BULWARK, originally of a promenade on a demolished fortification]
• **boulevarded** *adjective*

boulevardier *noun*
• "bull a vard YAY"
• a man who lives luxuriously and frequents fashionable places.
• [French, originally referring to those who frequented the theatrical district along the *Grands Boulevards* of Paris]

boundary *noun*
• "BOUND ree" or "BOUND a ree"
• a line marking the limits of an area, territory, etc.
• [dialect *bounder* from Anglo-French *bounde*, Old French *bonde* a limitation or restriction, from medieval Latin *bodina*, earlier *butina*, of unknown origin]

bounden *adjective*
• "BOUND 'n"
• obligatory.
• [archaic past participle of 'bind']

bounteous *adjective*
• "BOUNTY us"
• = BOUNTIFUL.
• [Middle English from Old French *bontif* from *bonté* bounty, from Latin *bonitas -tatis* from *bonus* good, after *plenteous*]
• **bounteously** *adverb*
• **bounteousness** *noun*

bountiful *adjective*
• "BOUNTA full"
• generous, liberal, plentiful.
• [Old French *bonté* from Latin *bonitas -tatis* from *bonus* good]
• **bountifully** *adverb*

bouquet *noun*
• "bo CAY" or "boo CAY"
• an arrangement of cut flowers, esp. bound together for carrying.
• [French from dialect var. of Old French *bos*, *bois* wood]

bourbon *noun*
• "BUR b'n"
• an American whisky distilled from corn mash and rye.
• [*Bourbon* County, Kentucky, where it was first made]

bourdon *noun*
• "BURD'n"
• a low-pitched stop in an organ or harmonium.
• [French, = bagpipe drone, from Romanic, prob. imitative]
HOMOPHONES: *burden*

bourgeois *adjective*
• "boor ZHWAH" or "BOOR zhwah"
• conventionally middle class.
• [French: see BURGESS]
• **bourgeoisification** *noun*
• **bourgeoisify** *verb* "boor ZHWOZZA fie"

bourgeoisie *noun*
• "boor zhwah ZEE"
• the capitalist class.
• [French, as BOURGEOIS]

bourguignon *adjective*
• "BOORG ee nyõh" (with a nasal *oh*)
• designating a sauce, esp. for beef, of red wine, beef stock, mushrooms, and onions.
• [French, 'Burgundian']

bourn *noun*
• "BORN" or "BURN"
• a small stream.
• [Middle English: S English var. of Old English *burna* stream, from Germanic]
HOMOPHONES: *born*, *borne*, *burn*

bourrée *noun*
• "BOOR ay"
• a lively French dance like a gavotte.
• [French]

bourse *noun*
• "BURSE"
• a stock exchange, esp. in Europe.
• [French, = purse, from medieval Latin *bursa*]

boustrophedon *adjective*
• "bow struh FEED'n" or "boo struh FEED'n" ("BOW" rhymes with *COW*)
• (of written words) from right to left and from left to right in alternate lines.
• [Greek (adverb) = as an ox turns in plowing, from *bous* ox + *-strophos* turning]

boutique *noun*
• "boo TEEK"
• a small shop or department of a store selling specialized goods or services, esp. fashionable clothes or accessories.
• [French, = small shop, from Latin (as BODEGA)]
• **boutiquey** *adjective* "boo TEEKY"

boutonniere *noun*
• "boota NEER"
• a flower or spray of flowers worn in a buttonhole or on a lapel.
• [French]

Bouvier *noun*
• "BOOVY ay"
• a large Belgian breed of dog having a shaggy coat, used as a livestock herder or guard dog.
• [French, lit. 'cowherd']

bouzouki *noun*
• "boo ZOOKY"
• a Greek form of mandolin.
• [modern Greek]

bowline *noun*
- "BOE lin"
- a rope attaching the weather side of a square sail to the bow.
- ['bow' + 'line']

bowser *noun*
- "BOW zur" ("BOW" rhymes with *HOW*)
- a truck with a large tank for fuelling aircraft etc., or for supplying water.
- [origin unknown]

bowyer *noun*
- "BOE yur"
- a maker or seller of archers' bows.
- ['bow' (in archery) from Old English *boga* + *-yer* variant spelling of *-er* (as in 'lawyer')]

boyar *noun*
- "BOE yar"
- a member of an order of the Russian aristocracy (abolished by Peter the Great), next in rank to a prince.
- [Russian *boyarin* grandee]

boycott *verb*
- "BOY cot"
- combine to coerce or punish (a person, company, nation, etc.) by a systematic refusal of normal commercial or social relations.
- [Capt. C. C. *Boycott*, Irish land agent d.1897, so treated from 1880]

boysenberry *noun*
- "BOYZ'n berry"
- a hybrid of several species of bramble.
- [R. *Boysen*, 20th-c. US horticulturalist]

brachial *adjective*
- "BRACKY 'll" or "BRAKEY 'll"
- of or relating to the arm.
- [Latin *brachialis* from *bra(c)chium* arm]

brachiate *verb*
- "BRACKY it" or "BRAKEY it" or "BRACKY ate" or "BRAKEY ate"
- (of certain apes and monkeys) move by using the arms to swing from branch to branch.
- [Latin *bra(c)chium* arm]
- **brachiation** *noun*
- **brachiator** *noun*

brachiopod *noun*
- "BRACKY oh pod" or "BRAKEY oh pod"
- any marine invertebrate of the phylum Brachiopoda (esp. a fossil one) having a two-valved chalky shell and a ciliated feeding arm.
- [modern Latin from Greek *brakhiōn* arm + *pous podos* foot]

brachiosaurus *noun*
- "bracky a SORE us" or "brakey a SORE us"
- a sauropod of the genus *Brachiosaurus*, the heaviest of all dinosaurs, with forelegs longer than its hind legs.
- [modern Latin from Greek *brakhiōn* arm + *sauros* lizard]

brachistochrone *noun*
- "bruh KISTA crone"
- a curve joining two points such that a body travelling along it (e.g. under gravity) takes a shorter time than is possible for any other curve between the points.
- [Greek *brakhistos* shortest + *khronos* time]

brachycephalic *adjective*
- "bracky suh FALIC"
- having a broad short head.
- [Greek *brakhus* short + *kephalē* head]
- **brachycephalous** *adjective*

"bracky SEFFA luss"

brachytherapy *noun*
- "bracky THERRA pee"
- the treatment of cancer, esp. prostate cancer, by the insertion of small radioactive implants directly into the cancerous tissue.
- [Greek *brakhus* short + THERAPY]

brackish *adjective*
- "BRACK ish"
- (of water etc.) slightly salty.
- [obsolete *brack* (adjective) from Middle Low German, Middle Dutch *brac*]
- **brackishness** *noun*

bract *noun*
- "BRACT"
- a modified and often brightly coloured leaf, with a flower or an inflorescence in its axil.
- [Latin *bractea* thin plate, gold leaf]
- **bracteal** *adjective*

bradawl *noun*
- "BRAD awl"
- a small tool with a pointed end for making holes in wood for the insertion of brads etc.
- ['brad', a thin flat nail with a head in the form of a slight enlargement at the top, from Middle English *brod* goad, pointed instrument, from Old Norse *broddr* spike + AWL]

bradycardia *noun*
- "bradda CARDY uh"
- abnormally slow heart rate (usually taken as 60 beats per minute or less).
- [Greek *bradus* slow + *kardia* heart]

brae *noun*
- "BRAY"
- a steep bank or hillside.
- [Old Norse *brá* eyelash]

HOMOPHONES: *bray*

Braeburn *noun*
- "BRAY burn"
- a crisp, flavourful, tart-sweet apple with a greenish-gold to red skin.
- [*Braeburn* Valley in Nelson, NZ, the orchard in which it was discovered in 1950]

braggadocio *noun*
- "bragga DOE chee oh" or "bragga DOE shee oh"

• empty boasting; a boastful manner of speech and behaviour.
• [*Braggadochio*, a braggart in the *Faerie Queene* by English poet E. Spenser (d.1599), from 'brag' + Italian augmentative suffix *-occio*]

braggart *noun*
• "BRAG urt"
• a person given to bragging.
• [French *bragard* from *braguer* brag]

brahma *noun*
• "BROMMA"
• a large Asian breed of domestic fowl.
• [the *Brahmaputra* River in S Asia, from where it was brought]

Brahman *noun*
• "BRAW m'n"
• a member of the highest Hindu caste, whose members are traditionally eligible for the priesthood.
• [Sanskrit *brāhmaṇas* from *brahmaṇ* priest]
• **Brahmanic** *adjective* "bruh MANNIC"
• **Brahmanical** *adjective*

Brahmana *noun*
• "BROMMA nuh"
• any of the lengthy commentaries on the Vedas, composed in Sanskrit *c.*900–700 BC, containing exegetical material relating to Vedic sacrificial ritual.
• [as BRAHMAN]

Brahmanism *noun*
• "BRAW m'n izm"
• the complex sacrificial pantheistic religion that emerged in post-Vedic India (*c.*900 BC), characterized by the caste system.
• [as BRAHMAN]

Braille *noun*
• "BRAIL"
• a system of writing and printing for the blind, in which characters are represented by patterns of raised dots.
• [Louis *Braille*, French educator (d.1852) who devised the system]

brainiac *noun*
• "BRAINY ack"
• a very intelligent or clever person; an expert.
• [the name of *Brainiac*, a super-intelligent alien character in Superman comics, from 'brain' + MANIAC]

braise *verb*
• "BRAZE"
• fry lightly and then stew slowly with a little liquid in a closed container.
• [French *braiser* from *braise* live coals]
HOMOPHONES: *braze*

Bramley *noun*
• "BRAMLY"
• a large green variety of cooking apple, popular in Britain.
• [M. *Bramley*, English butcher in whose garden it may have first grown *c.*1850]

branchia *plural noun*
• "BRANKY uh"
• gills.
• [Latin *branchia*, pl. *-ae*, from Greek *bragkhia* pl.]
• **branchial** *adjective*
• **branchiate** *adjective* "BRANKY ate"

brandade *noun*
• "bron DAD"
• a dish made from puréed fish, esp. salted cod.
• [French from modern Provençal *brandado*, lit. 'thing which has been moved or shaken']

brasserie *noun*
• "BRASSER ee"
• a restaurant, originally one serving beer with food.
• [French, = brewery]

brassica *noun*
• "BRASSA kuh"
• any cruciferous plant of the genus *Brassica*, having taproots and erect branched stems, including cabbage, mustard, cauliflower, kohlrabi, broccoli, kale, and turnip.
• [Latin, = cabbage]

brassiere *noun*
• "bruh ZEER"
• a bra.
• [French, = woman's bodice]

brattice *noun*
• "BRATTISS"
• a wooden partition or shaft lining in a mine.
• [Middle English, ultimately from Old English *brittisc* British]

bratwurst *noun*
• "BRAT wurst"
• a type of small German pork sausage.
• [German from *braten* fry, roast + *Wurst* sausage]

brava *interjection*
• "BROVVA"
• expressing approval of a female performer.
• [feminine of BRAVO]

bravado *noun*
• "bruh VODDO" or "bruh VADDO"
• a bold manner or a show of boldness intended to impress.
• [Spanish *bravata* from *bravo*, ultimately from Latin *barbarus* BARBAROUS]

bravo *interjection*
• "BROVVO" or "bra VOE"
• expressing approval of a performer etc.
• [French from Italian]

bravura *adjective*
• "bra VURA"
• requiring or displaying brilliant or virtuosic skill.
• [Italian]

braw *adjective*
• "BRAW"
• fine, good.
• [var. of *brawf* brave, ultimately from Latin *barbarus* BARBAROUS]
HOMOPHONES: *bra*

brawn *noun*
• "BRON"
• muscular strength.
• [Anglo-French *braun*, Old French *braon* from Germanic]
• **brawniness** *noun*
• **brawny** *adjective*

braze *verb*
• "BRAZE"
• solder with an alloy of copper and zinc at a high temperature.
• [French *braser* solder from *braise* live coals]
HOMOPHONES: *braise*

brazen *adjective*
• "BRAY z'n"
• flagrant and shameless; insolent.
• [Old English *bræsen* from *bræs* brass]
• **brazenly** *adverb*
• **brazenness** *noun*

brazier *noun*
• "BRAZE yur" or "BRAY zhur"
• a charcoal grill for cooking.
• [French *brasier* from *braise* hot coals]

Brazilian *noun*
• "bruh ZILL y'n"
• a native or inhabitant of Brazil.

breach *noun*
• "BREECH"
• the breaking of or failure to observe a law, contract, regulations, procedures, etc.
• [Old French *breche*, ultimately from Germanic]
HOMOPHONES: *breech*

breadth *noun*
• "BREDTH"
• the distance or measurement from side to side of a thing; broadness.
• [obsolete *brede*, Old English *brǣdu*, from Germanic]
• **breadthways** *adverb*
• **breadthwise** *adverb*

bream *noun*
• "BREEM"
• a carp-like freshwater fish of Europe, *Abramis brama*, with an arched back.
• [Old French *bre(s)me* from West Germanic]

breaststroke *noun*
• "BREST stroke"
• a stroke performed by a swimmer floating face down, extending the joined hands outward from the chest to above the head and then sweeping them down on either side of the body, while the legs execute a frog kick.
• ['breast' + 'stroke']

breathable *adjective*
• "BREETHE a bull" (with "TH" as in *THIS*)
• (of air) fit to be breathed.
• [from 'breathe' from Old English]
• **breathability** *noun*

breccia *noun*
• "BRETCHY uh"
• a rock of angular stones etc. cemented by finer material.
• [Italian, = gravel, from Germanic, related to 'break']
• **brecciate** *verb*
• **brecciated** *adjective*
• **brecciation** *noun*

Brechtian *adjective*
• "BRECKTY 'n"
• relating to or characteristic of the German dramatist Bertolt Brecht (d.1956).

breech *noun*
• "BREECH"
• the part of a cannon behind the bore.
• [Old English *brōc*, pl. *brēc* (treated as sing. in Middle English), from Germanic]
HOMOPHONES: *breach*

breechblock *noun*
• "BREECH block"
• a metal block which closes the breech aperture in a gun.
• [as BREECH + 'block']

breechcloth *noun*
• "BREECH cloth"
• a loincloth.
• [as BREECH]

breeches *plural noun*
• "BREECH iz"
• short trousers, esp. fastened below the knee, now used esp. for riding or in court costume.
• [pl. of BREECH]

bremsstrahlung *noun*
• "BREMZ straw lung"
• the electromagnetic radiation produced by the acceleration or esp. the deceleration of a charged particle after passing through the electric and magnetic fields of a nucleus.
• [German, = braking radiation]

bresaola *noun*
• "bress OW luh"
• an Italian dish of raw beef cured by salting and air-drying, typically served in slices with an olive oil, lemon juice, and pepper dressing.
• [Italian, from Italian regional *bresada*, past participle of *brasare* braise]

Breton *noun*
• "BRET 'n"
• a native of Brittany, a peninsula of NW France.
• [Old French, = BRITON]

breve *noun*
• "BREEVE"

• a note, now rarely used, having the time value of two semibreves or whole notes.
• [Middle English var. of BRIEF]

brevet *noun*
• "BREV it"
• a document conferring a privilege from a sovereign or government, esp. a rank in the army, without the appropriate pay.
• [Old French diminutive of *bref* BRIEF]

breviary *noun*
• "BREEV yuh ree" or "BREEVY airy"
• a book containing the divine office for each day, to be recited by those in orders.
• [Latin *breviarium* summary from *breviare* abridge: see ABBREVIATE]

brevity *noun*
• "BREVVA tee"
• economy of expression; conciseness.
• [Anglo-French *breveté*, Old French *brieveté* from *bref* BRIEF]

brewis *noun*
• "BROOZ"
• *Cdn* (*Nfld*) a stew made of hardtack soaked in water and boiled.
• [English dialect 'bread soaked in fat or broth' from Old French *bro(u)ez* broth, ultimately from Germanic]
HOMOPHONES: *bruise*

bricolage *noun*
• "bricka LOZH"
• construction or creation from whatever is immediately available for use.
• [French, from *bricoler* do odd jobs, from Provençal *bricola* or Italian *briccola*, of unknown origin]
• **bricoleur** *noun* "bricka LUR"

bridal *adjective*
• "BRIDE 'll"
• of or concerning a bride or a wedding.
• [originally as noun, = wedding feast, from Old English *brȳd-ealu* from *brȳd* bride + *ealu* ale-drinking]
HOMOPHONES: *bridle*

bridie *noun*
• "BRIDE ee"
• an originally Scottish turnover filled with meat and onions.
• [apparently from 'bridie's pie', a large pie traditionally baked by a bride's family or friends for her wedding guests]

bridle *noun*
• "BRIDE 'll"
• the headgear used to control a horse, consisting of buckled leather straps, a metal bit, and reins.
• [Old English *brīdel*]
HOMOPHONES: *bridal*

bridoon *noun*
• "brid OON"
• a small snaffle used in a double bridle.
• [French *bridon* from *bride* bridle]

brie *noun*
• "BREE"
• a kind of ripened soft cheese with a white mould skin.
• [*Brie*, a former province in N France]

brief *adjective*
• "BREEF"
• of short duration.
• [Anglo-French *bref*, Old French *brief*, from Latin *brevis* short]
• **briefer** *noun*
• **briefly** *adverb*
• **briefness** *noun*

briefcase *noun*
• "BREEF case"
• a flat rectangular case for carrying documents etc.
• [as BRIEF (in the sense of a document) + 'case']

briefing *noun*
• "BREEFING"
• a meeting for giving information or instructions.
• [as BRIEF]

brier *noun*
ALSO SPELLED: **briar**
• "BRY ur"
• any prickly bush esp. of a wild rose.
• [Old English *brǣr*, *brēr*, of unknown origin]
• **briery** *adjective* (also **briary**)

brigade *noun*
• "brig ADE"
• a subdivision of an army.
• [French from Italian *brigata* company, from *brigare* be busy with, from *briga* strife]

brigadier *noun*
• "brigga DEER"
• an officer commanding a brigade.
• [French (as BRIGADE)]

brigand *noun*
• "BRIG'nd"
• a member of a robber band living by pillage and ransom, usu. in wild terrain.
• [Old French from Italian *brigante* from *brigare*: see BRIGADE]
• **brigandage** *noun* "BRIG'nd idge"
• **brigandry** *noun* "BRIG'nd ree"

brigantine *noun*
• "BRIG 'n teen"
• a two-masted sailing ship with a square-rigged foremast and a fore-and-aft-rigged mainmast.
• [Old French *brigandine* or Italian *brigantino* from *brigante* BRIGAND]

brilliantine *noun*
• "BRILL y'n teen"
• an oily liquid dressing for making the hair glossy.

• [French *brillantine* from *brillant* participle of *briller* shine, from Italian *brillare*]

brindled *adjective*
• "BRIND'ld" ("BRIND" rhymes with *PINNED*)
• (esp. of domestic animals) brownish or tawny with streaks of other colour.
• [earlier *brinded*, *brended* from *brend*, perhaps of Scandinavian origin]

briny *adjective*
• "BRINE ee"
• of brine or the sea; salty.
• [Old English *brīne* salt water]

brio *noun*
• "BREE oh"
• style, vigour, vivacity.
• [Italian]

brioche *noun*
• "bree OSH" or "BREE osh"
• a sweet roll or small loaf made with a yeast dough rich in eggs.
• [French, from Norman French *brier*, synonym of *broyer*, literally = split up into very small pieces by pressure]

briquette *noun*
ALSO SPELLED: **briquet**
• "brick ET"
• a block of compressed charcoal or coal dust etc. used as fuel.
• [French *briquette*, diminutive of *brique* brick]

bris *noun*
• "BRISS"
• the rite of circumcision in Judaism, usu. performed eight days after birth.
• [Hebrew *b'rīth* covenant]

brisling *noun*
• "BRIZZ ling" or "BRISS ling"
• a small herring or sprat.
• [Norwegian & Danish, = sprat]
HOMOPHONES: *bristling*

bristle *noun*
• "BRISS'll"
• a short stiff hair, esp. one of those on an animal's back.
• [Middle English *bristel*, *brestel* from Old English *byrst*]
• **bristly** *adjective*

bristlecone *noun*
• "BRISS'll cone"
• a very slow-growing, shrubby pine, *Pinus aristata*, native to the southwest US; some specimens are over 4,000 years old.
• [as BRISTLE + 'cone']

Britannic *adjective*
• "bruh TANNIC"
• of Britain.
• [Latin *Britannicus* from Latin *Britannia* Britain]

Briticism *noun*
• "BRITTA sizm"
• a word or idiom used in Britain but not in other English-speaking countries.
• [as BRITISH]

British *adjective*
• "BRIT ish"
• of or relating to Great Britain or the United Kingdom, or to its people or language.
• [Old English *Brettisc* etc. from *Bret* from Latin *Britto* or Old Celtic]
• **Britisher** *noun*
• **Britishness** *noun*

Briton *noun*
• "BRIT'n"
• a native or inhabitant of Great Britain or (formerly) of the British Empire.
• [Latin *Britto -onis* from Old Celtic]

broach *verb*
• "BROACH"
• raise (a subject) for discussion.
• [Old French *brocher* ultimately from Latin *brocc(h)us* projecting]
HOMOPHONES: *brooch*

broadsword *noun*
• "BROD sord"
• a sword with a broad blade, for cutting rather than thrusting.
• ['broad' + SWORD]

Brobdingnagian *adjective*
• "brob ding NAGGY 'n"
• gigantic, colossal.
• [the imaginary land of *Brobdingnag* in *Gulliver's Travels* by Irish satirist J. Swift (d.1745), where everything is on a gigantic scale]

brocade *noun*
• "bro CADE"
• a rich fabric with a silky finish woven with a raised pattern, and often with gold or silver thread.
• [Spanish & Portuguese *brocado* from Italian *broccato* from *brocco* twisted thread]

broccoflower *noun*
• "BROCKA flower"
• a hybrid vegetable, the result of a genetic cross between broccoli and cauliflower, resembling a green cauliflower that tastes like broccoli.
• [blend of BROCCOLI + CAULIFLOWER]

broccoli *noun*
• "BROCKA lee"
• a brassica, related to the cauliflower, with a loose cluster of usu. greenish flower buds.
• [Italian, pl. of *broccolo* diminutive of *brocco* sprout]

broch *noun*
• "BROCK"
• (in Scotland) a prehistoric circular stone tower.
• [Old Norse *borg* castle]
HOMOPHONES: *brock*

brochette *noun*
• "braw SHET" or "bruh SHET"
• a dish consisting of chunks of food, esp. meat, threaded on a skewer and grilled.
• [French, = skewer, as BROACH]

brochure *noun*
• "bro SHUR" or "bro SHOOR"
• a pamphlet or leaflet, esp. one giving descriptive information.
• [French, lit. 'stitching', from *brocher* stitch]

Brockvillian *noun*
• "brock VILLY 'n"
• a resident of Brockville, Ont.

brogan *noun*
• "BRO g'n"
• a coarse leather work shoe reaching to the ankle.
• [Irish *brógán*, Gaelic *brógan* diminutive of *bróg* BROGUE]

brogue *noun*
• "BRO'g"
• a strong outdoor shoe with ornamental perforated bands.
• [Gaelic & Irish *brōg* from Old Norse *brók*]

brolga *noun*
• "BRAWL guh"
• a large Australian crane, *Grus rubicunda*, with a booming call.
• [Kamilaroi (and other Aboriginal languages) *burralga*]

bromate *noun*
• "BRO mate"
• a salt or ester of bromic acid.
• [as BROMINE]

brome *noun*
• "BROME"
• any oatlike grass of the genus *Bromus* of the temperate zone, having slender stems with flowering spikes.
• [modern Latin *Bromus* from Greek *bromos* oat]

bromeliad *noun*
• "bro MEELY ad"
• any tropical plant of the family Bromeliaceae (esp. of the genus *Bromelia*), having short stems with rosettes of stiff usu. spiny leaves, e.g. pineapple.
• [O. *Bromel*, Swedish botanist d.1705]

bromide *noun*
• "BRO mide"
• a compound of bromine with a less electronegative element or radical; a salt or ester of bromic acid.
• [as BROMINE]

bromine *noun*
• "BRO meen"
• a dark fuming liquid element with a choking irritating smell, used in the manufacture of chemicals for photography and medicine.
• [French *brome* from Greek *brōmos* stink]
• **bromic** *adjective*

bronc *noun*
• "BRONK"
• = BRONCO.
• [abbreviation]

bronchiole *noun*
• "BRONKY ole"
• any of the minute divisions of a bronchus.
• [as BRONCHUS]
• **bronchiolar** *adjective* "bronky OH lur"
HOMOPHONES: *bronchial*

bronchitis *noun*
• "bron KITE iss"
• inflammation of the mucous membrane in the bronchial tubes.
• [BRONCHUS + Greek *-itis*, forming feminine of adjectives in *-itēs* (with *nosos* 'disease' implied)]
• **bronchitic** *adjective* "bron KITTIC"

bronchocele *noun*
• "BRONKA seel"
• a goitre.
• [as BRONCHUS + Greek *kēlē* tumour]

bronchodilator *noun*
• "bronco DIE later"
• a substance which causes widening of the bronchi, used esp. to alleviate asthma.
• [as BRONCHUS + Latin *dilatare* spread out, from *latus* wide]

bronchopneumonia *noun*
• "bronco new MOANY uh"
• inflammation of the lungs, arising in the bronchi or bronchioles.
• [as BRONCHUS + PNEUMONIA]

bronchoscope *noun*
• "BRONCO scope"
• a usu. fibre optic instrument for inspecting the bronchi.
• [as BRONCHUS + *skopos* target, from *skeptomai* look at]
• **bronchoscopy** *noun* "bron COSCA pee"

bronchospasm *noun*
• "BRONCO spazm"
• spasm of the bronchial smooth muscle, producing narrowing of the bronchi.
• [as BRONCHUS + SPASM]

bronchus *noun*
• "BRONK us"
• any of the major air passages of the lungs, esp. either of the two main divisions of the windpipe.
• [Late Latin from Greek *brogkhos* windpipe]
• **bronchial** *adjective*

bronco *noun*
• "BRONCO"
• a wild or half-tamed horse.
• [Spanish, = rough]

broncobuster *noun*
• "BRONCO buster"
• a person who breaks in horses.

• [as BRONCO + 'bust', originally a (dial.) pronunciation of 'burst']
• **broncobusting** *noun*

brontosaurus *noun*
• "bronta SORE us"
• the former name for the APATOSAURUS.
• [Greek *brontē* thunder + *sauros* lizard]

brooch *noun*
• "BROACH"
• an ornament fastened to clothing with a hinged pin.
• [Middle English *broche* (as BROACH)]
HOMOPHONES: *broach*

Brooklynese *noun*
• "brooklin EEZ"
• the English accent of the inhabitants of Brooklyn in New York City.

Brooklynite *noun*
• "BROOKLIN ite"
• a native or inhabitant of Brooklyn in New York City.

brougham *noun*
• "BROO um" or "BROOM" or "BRO um"
• a horse-drawn closed carriage with a driver perched outside in front.
• [Lord *Brougham* (d.1868), who designed the carriage]
HOMOPHONES: *brume, broom*

brouhaha *noun*
• "BREW haw haw"
• commotion, sensation; hubbub, uproar.
• [French]

browse *verb*
• "BROWZ" (rhymes with *PLOWS*)
• survey objects superficially and in a leisurely fashion, esp. goods for sale.
• [Old French *broster* eat young shoots]
• **browsability** *noun*
• **browsable** *adjective*
• **browser** *noun*

brucellosis *noun*
• "broossa LO sis"
• a disease caused by bacteria of the genus *Brucella*, causing spontaneous abortion in cattle and other farm animals, and undulant fever in humans.
• [*Brucella* from Sir D. *Bruce*, Scottish physician d.1931 + Greek *-ōsis* suffix of verbal nouns]

brucite *noun*
• "BROO site"
• a mineral form of magnesium hydroxide.
• [A. *Bruce*, US mineralogist d.1818]

bruin *noun*
• "BROOIN"
• a bear.
• [Middle English from Dutch, = 'brown': used as a name in *Reynard the Fox*]

bruit *verb*
• "BROOT"
• spread (a report or rumour).
• [French, = noise from *bruire* roar]
HOMOPHONES: *brut, brute*

brume *noun*
• "BROOM"
• mist, fog.
• [French from Latin *bruma* winter]
HOMOPHONES: *broom, brougham*

Brummagem *adjective*
• "BRUMMA j'm"
• cheap and showy.
• [dialect form of *Birmingham*, England, with reference to counterfeit coins and plated goods once made there]

Bruneian *noun*
• "broo NIE 'n"
• a native or inhabitant of Brunei, a sultanate on the island of Borneo.

brunette *noun*
• "broo NET"
• a woman with dark brown hair.
• [French, feminine of *brunet*, diminutive of *brun* brown]

bruschetta *noun*
• "broo SHETTA" or "broo SKETTA"
• slices of toasted bread drizzled with olive oil and usu. topped with diced tomatoes, garlic, etc.
• [Italian from *bruscare* roast over coals]

brusque *adjective*
• "BRUSK"
• abrupt or offhand in manner or speech.
• [French from Italian *brusco* sour]
• **brusquely** *adverb*
• **brusqueness** *noun*

brut *adjective*
• "BROOT"
• (of wine) unsweetened; very dry.
• [French]
HOMOPHONES: *brute, bruit*

brutal *adjective*
• "BROOT'll"
• savagely or coarsely cruel.
• [French *brutal* or medieval Latin *brutalis* from *brutus* BRUTE]
• **brutality** *noun*
• **brutalization** *noun* (also esp. *Brit.* **-isation**)
• **brutalize** *verb* (also esp. *Brit.* **-ise**)
• **brutally** *adverb*

brutalism *noun*
• "BROOT'll izm"
• a heavy plain style of architecture etc.
• [as BRUTAL]
• **brutalist** *noun*

brute *noun*
• "BROOT"
• a brutal or violent person or animal.
• [French from Latin *brutus* stupid]

- **brutish** *adjective*
- **brutishly** *adverb*
- **brutishness** *noun*

HOMOPHONES: *brut, bruit*

bruxism *noun*
- "BRUCKS izm"
- the involuntary or habitual grinding or clenching of the teeth.
- [Greek *brukhein* gnash the teeth]

bryology *noun*
- "bry OLLA jee"
- the study of bryophytes.
- [Greek *bruon* moss]
- **bryological** *adjective*
- **bryologist** *noun*

bryony *noun*
- "BRY a nee"
- any climbing plant of the genus *Bryonia*, esp. *B. dioica*, bearing greenish-white flowers and red berries.
- [Latin *bryonia* from Greek *bruōnia*]

bryophyte *noun*
- "BRY a fite"
- any plant of the phylum Bryophyta, including mosses and liverworts.
- [modern Latin *Bryophyta* from Greek *bruon* moss + *phuton* plant]
- **bryophytic** *adjective* "bry a FITTIC"

bryozoan *noun*
- "bry a ZO 'n"
- any aquatic invertebrate animal of the group Bryozoa (now regarded as comprising the phyla Ectoprocta and Entoprocta), which form colonies often suggesting mossy growths on rocks, seaweeds, etc.
- [Greek *bruon* moss + *zōia* animals]

Brythonic *noun*
- "brith ONNIC"
- the language group comprising Welsh, Cornish, and Breton.
- [Welsh *Brython* Britons, from Old Celtic]

bubbe *noun*

ALSO SPELLED: **bubbie**
- "BUBBA" or "BUBBY"
- a Jewish grandmother.
- [Yiddish]

bubkes *noun*

ALSO SPELLED: **bupkes**, **bupkis**, **bupkus**
- "BUB kuss"
- nothing; something worthless.
- [Yiddish *bobke* goat or sheep dung]

bubo *noun*
- "BYOO boe" or "BOO boe"
- a swollen inflamed lymph node esp. in the armpit or groin.
- [medieval Latin *bubo -onis* swelling, from Greek *boubōn* groin]

bubonic *adjective*
- "byoo BONNIC" or "boo BONNIC"
- relating to or characterized by buboes.
- [as BUBO]

buccal *adjective*
- "BUCK'll"
- of or relating to the cheek.
- [Latin *bucca* cheek]

HOMOPHONES: *buckle*

buccaneer *noun*
- "bucka NEER"
- a pirate, esp. one who plundered the Spanish colonies of the Caribbean and South American coasts in the late 17th c.
- [French *boucanier* from *boucaner* cure meat on a barbecue, from *boucan* from Tupi *mukem*]
- **buccaneering** *noun*

buccinator *noun*
- "BUCKSIN ater"
- a flat thin cheek muscle.
- [Latin from *buccinare* blow a trumpet (*buccina*)]

buckminsterfullerene *noun*
- "buck minster FULLER een"
- an extremely unstable form of carbon whose molecule consists of 60 carbon atoms forming a structure suggestive of a geodesic dome.
- [R. *Buckminster Fuller*, US designer and architect d.1983, inventor of the geodesic dome]

buckram *noun*
- "BUCK rum"
- a coarse linen or other cloth stiffened with gum or paste, and used as interfacing or in bookbinding.
- [Anglo-French *bukeram*, Old French *boquerant*, perhaps from *Bokhara* in central Asia]

buckyball *noun*
- "BUCKY ball"
- a molecule of buckminsterfullerene, or more generally of any fullerene.
- [abbreviation of BUCKMINSTERFULLERENE + 'ball']

bucolic *adjective*
- "byoo COLLIC"
- of or pertaining to an idyllic life in the countryside.
- [Latin *bucolicus* from Greek *boukolikos* from *boukolos* herdsman, from *bous* ox]
- **bucolically** *adverb*

Buddha *noun*
- "BOODA" (with "OO" either as in *BOOK* or as in *BOOM*)
- a statue or picture of the founder of Buddhism, Siddhartha Gautama (*c.*563–*c.*480 BC).
- [Sanskrit, = enlightened, past participle of *budh* know]

Buddhism *noun*
- "BOOD izm" (with "OO" either as in *BOOK* or as in *BOOM*)
- a widespread Asian religion or philosophy,

founded by Gautama Buddha in India in the 5th c. BC, which teaches that elimination of the self and earthly desires is the highest goal.
• [as BUDDHA]
• **Buddhist** *noun*
• **Buddhistic** *adjective*

buddleia *noun*
• "BUDLY uh"
• any shrub of the genus *Buddleia*, with fragrant lilac, yellow, or white flowers attractive to butterflies.
• [A. *Buddle*, English botanist d.1715]

budgerigar *noun*
• "BUDGE a ree gar"
• a small Australian parakeet, *Melopsittacus undulatus*, green in the wild state, although captive birds are often bred in a variety of colours.
• [Aboriginal, perhaps alteration of Kamilaroi (and related languages) *gijirrigaa*]

buffalo *noun*
• "BUFFA lo"
• the N American bison, *Bison bison*.
• [prob. from Portuguese *bufalo* from Late Latin *bufalus* from Latin *bubalus* from Greek *boubalos* antelope, wild ox]

buffaloed *adjective*
• "BUFFA lode"
• overawed, outwitted.
• [as BUFFALO]

Buffalonian *noun*
• "buffa LONEY 'n"
• a resident of Buffalo, NY.

buffet[1] *noun*
• "buff AY" or "BUFF ay"
• a meal consisting of several dishes set out from which guests serve themselves.
• [French from Old French *bufet* stool, of unknown origin]

buffet[2] *verb*
• "BUFF it"
• strike or knock repeatedly.
• [Old French diminutive of *bufe* blow]
• **buffeting** *noun*

buffo *noun*
• "BOOFO"
• a comic actor, esp. in Italian opera.
• [Italian, as BUFFOON]

buffoon *noun*
• "buh FOON"
• a stupid person.
• [French *bouffon* from Italian *buffone* from medieval Latin *buffo* clown, from Romanic]
• **buffoonery** *noun*
• **buffoonish** *adjective*

bugloss *noun*
• "BYOOG loss"
• any of various bristly plants related to borage, esp. of the genus *Anchusa* with bright blue tubular flowers.
• [Latin *buglossus* from Greek *bouglōssos* ox-tongued]

buhl *noun*
ALSO SPELLED: **boule**, **boulle**
• "BOOL"
• pieces of brass, tortoiseshell, etc., cut to make a pattern and used as decorative inlays esp. on furniture.
• [(*buhl* Germanized) from A. C. *Boule*, French woodcarver d.1732]
HOMOPHONES: *boule*

bulbil *noun*
• "BUL bill" ("BUL" rhymes with *GULL*)
• a small bulb which grows among the leaves or flowers of a plant.
• [modern Latin *bulbillus*, diminutive of *bulbus* bulb]

bulbous *adjective*
• "BULB us" ("BUL" rhymes with *GULL*)
• shaped like a bulb; fat or bulging.
• [Latin *bulbus* bulb]

bulbul *noun*
• "BULL bull"
• any songbird of the family Pycnonotidae, of dull plumage with contrasting bright patches.
• [Persian from Arabic, of imitative origin]

Bulgarian *noun*
• "bul GARE ee 'n" ("BUL" rhymes with *GULL*)
• a native or national of Bulgaria.

bulgur *noun*
ALSO SPELLED: **bulgar**, **bulghur**
• "BUL gur" ("BUL" rhymes with *GULL*)
• a cereal food of whole wheat partially boiled then dried.
• [Turkish]

bulimia *noun*
• "buh LEEMY uh"
• an emotional disorder in which bouts of extreme overeating are followed by self-induced vomiting, purging, or fasting.
• [modern Latin from Greek *boulimia* from *bous* ox + *limos* hunger]
• **bulimic** *adjective*

bullace *noun*
• "BULL us"
• a thorny shrub, *Prunus institia*, bearing globular yellow or purple-black fruits, of which the damson plum is the cultivated form.
• [Old French *buloce*, *beloce*]

bullion *noun*
• "BULL y'n"
• a metal (esp. gold or silver) in bulk before coining, or valued by weight.
• [Anglo-French = mint, var. of Old French *bouillon*, ultimately from Latin *bullire* boil]
HOMOPHONES: *bouillon*

bullock *noun*
• "BULL uck"
• a castrated male of domestic cattle, esp. one raised for beef.
• [Old English *bulluc*, diminutive of 'bull']

bullwhacker *noun*
• "BULL wacker"
• a person driving a team of oxen.
• ['bull' + 'whack']

bulrush *noun*
• "BULL rush"
• any rushlike water plant of the genus *Scirpus*, esp. *S. lacustris*, used for weaving.
• [perhaps from 'bull' = large, coarse, as in *bullfrog*, *bull trout*, etc.]

bulwark *noun*
• "BULL wurk"
• a defensive wall, esp. of earth; a rampart; a mole or breakwater.
• [Middle Low German, Middle Dutch *bolwerk*: see BOLE + 'work']

bummalo *noun*
• "BUMMA lo"
• a small fish, *Harpodon nehereus*, of S Asian coasts, dried and used as food.
• [perhaps from Marathi *bombīl(a)*]

bumptious *adjective*
• "BUMP sh'ss"
• offensively self-assertive or conceited.
• ['bump', after FRACTIOUS]
• **bumptiously** *adverb*
• **bumptiousness** *noun*

bunco *noun*
• "BUNCO"
• a swindle, esp. by card-sharping or a confidence game.
• [perhaps from Spanish *banca* a card game]

Bundesrat *noun*
• "BOOND us rot"
• the Upper House of Parliament in Germany or in Austria.
• [German from *Bund* federation + *Rat* council]

Bundestag *noun*
• "BOOND us tog"
• the Lower House of Parliament in Germany.
• [German from *Bund* federation + *tagen* confer]

bungee *noun*
• "BUN jee"
• a strong elasticized cord or cable, usu. with a hook on each end and used esp. for securing baggage etc.
• [origin unknown]

Bungi *noun*
• "bun GEE" (with "G" as in *GEEK*)
• the Ojibwa living on the plains of Manitoba, North Dakota, and Montana.
• [corruption of Cree *pahki*, Ojibwa *panki* part, thing, a little]

bunion *noun*
• "BUN y'n"
• a swelling on the foot, esp. at the first joint of the big toe.
• [Old French *buignon* from *buigne* bump on the head]

bunkum *noun*
ALSO SPELLED: **buncombe**
• "BUNK'm"
• nonsense; humbug.
• [originally *buncombe* from *Buncombe* County in N Carolina, mentioned in a nonsense speech by its Congressman, *c.*1820]

buoy *noun*
• "BOY" or "BOOEY"
• an anchored float serving as a navigation mark or to show reefs etc.
• [prob. from Middle Dutch *bo(e)ye*, from a Germanic base meaning 'signal']
• **buoyage** *noun*
HOMOPHONES: *boy*

buoyant *adjective*
• "BOY 'nt"
• able or apt to keep afloat or rise to the top of a liquid or gas.
• [French *buoyant* or Spanish *boyante* participle of *boyar* float, from *boya* BUOY]
• **buoyancy** *noun*
• **buoyantly** *adverb*

burbot *noun*
• "BURR bit"
• a freshwater fish, *Lota lota*, of the cod family, with a broad head and barbels.
• [Old French *borbete*, prob. from *borbe* mud, slime]

bureau *noun*
• "BYUR oh"
• *Cdn & Brit.* a writing desk with drawers and usu. an angled top opening downwards to form a writing surface.
• [French, = desk, originally its baize covering, from Old French *burel* from *bure*, *buire* dark brown, ultimately from Greek *purros* red]

bureaucracy *noun*
• "byur OCKRA see"
• the administration of government by civil servants, esp. when regarded as inflexible or inefficient.
• [French *bureaucratie* (BUREAU + Greek *kratia* from *kratos* strength, power)]
• **bureaucrat** *noun* "BYUR a crat"
• **bureaucratic** *adjective*
• **bureaucratically** *adverb*
• **bureaucratization** *noun* (also esp. *Brit.* **-isation**)
• **bureaucratize** *verb* (also esp. *Brit.* **-ise**)

bureaucratese *noun*
• "byur ockra TEEZ"
• a style of language believed to be

characteristic of bureaucrats, marked by jargon, abstractions, circumlocution, etc.
- [as BUREAUCRACY]

burette *noun*
ALSO SPELLED: **buret**
- "byur ET"
- a graduated glass tube with an end tap for measuring small volumes of liquid in chemical analysis.
- [French, from *buire* jug, of Germanic origin]

burfi *noun*
- "BURR fee"
- an Indian dessert made from milk solids and sugar, cut into squares or diamonds, and typically flavoured with cardamom or nuts.
- [Hindi, from Persian *barfi*, literally 'icy, snowy']

burgee *noun*
- "burr JEE"
- a triangular or swallow-tailed flag flown by yachts etc., usu. bearing distinguishing colours or the emblem of a yacht club or sailing club.
- [18th c.: perhaps = (ship)owner, ultimately French *bourgeois*: see BURGESS]

burgeon *verb*
- "BURR j'n"
- begin to grow rapidly; flourish.
- [Old French *burjon* bud, ultimately from Late Latin *burra* wool]
- **burgeoning** *adjective*

burgess *noun*
- "BURR juss"
- an inhabitant of a town or borough, esp. of one with full municipal rights.
- [Old French *burgeis*, ultimately from Late Latin *burgus* BOROUGH]

burgher *noun*
- "BURGER"
- a middle-class inhabitant of a (usu. specified) city or town.
- [German *Burger* or Dutch *burger* from *Burg*, *burg* BOROUGH]

HOMOPHONES: *burger*

burglar *noun*
- "BURR glur"
- a person who commits burglary.
- [legal Anglo-French *burgler*, related to Old French *burgier* pillage]
- **burglarize** *verb* (also esp. *Brit.* **-ise**)

burglary *noun*
- "BURR glur ee"
- entry into a building illegally with intent to commit theft, do bodily harm, or do damage.
- [as BURGLAR]

burgomaster *noun*
- "BURGO master"
- the mayor of a Dutch or Flemish town.
- [Dutch *burgemeester* from *burg* BOROUGH: assimilated to 'master']

burgoo *noun*
- "BURR goo" or "burr GOO"
- a stew or thick soup, typically one made for an outdoor meal.
- [Arabic *burgul*, related to BULGUR]

Burgundian *noun*
- "burr GUNDY 'n"
- a native or inhabitant of Burgundy in east central France.

burgundy *noun*
- "BURG'n dee"
- the wine (usu. red) of Burgundy in east central France.

burin *noun*
- "BYUR in"
- a steel tool for engraving on copper or wood.
- [French, perhaps related to Old High German *bora* boring tool]

burka *noun*
- "BURKA"
- a long enveloping garment traditionally worn in public by Muslim women.
- [Urdu from Arabic *burḳa'*]

Burkinan *noun*
- "burr KEEN'n"
- a native or inhabitant of Burkina Faso in W Africa.

burl *noun*
- "BURL"
- a flattened knotty growth on a tree.
- [Old French *bourle* tuft of wool, diminutive of *bourre* coarse wool, from Late Latin *burra* wool]
- **burled** *adjective*

HOMOPHONES: *birl*

burlap *noun*
- "BURR lap"
- coarse canvas esp. of jute used for sacking etc.
- [17th c.: origin unknown]

burlesque *noun*
- "burr LESK"
- comic imitation, esp. in parody of a dramatic or literary work.
- [French from Italian *burlesco* from *burla* mockery]

Burmese *noun*
- "burr MEEZ"
- a native or national of Burma (now Myanmar) in SE Asia.

burnet *noun*
- "BURR nit"
- any plant of the genus *Sanguisorba* of the rose family, with pink or red flowers.
- [obsolete *burnet* (adjective) dark brown, from Old French *burnete*]

burnish *verb*
- "BURN ish"
- polish by rubbing.
- [Old French *burnir* = *brunir* from *brun* brown]
- **burnisher** *noun*

burnoose *noun*
ALSO SPELLED: **burnous**
• "burr NOOSE"
• a hooded Arab cloak.
• [French from Arabic *burnus* from Greek *birros* cloak]

burpee *noun*
• "BURPY"
• a physical exercise consisting of a squat thrust made from and ending in a standing position.
• [Royal H. *Burpee*, US psychologist b.1897]

burrito *noun*
• "bur EETO"
• a tortilla rolled around a spicy filling of meat, beans, etc.
• [Latin American Spanish, diminutive of *burro* BURRO]

burro *noun*
• "BURR oh"
• a small donkey used as a pack animal.
• [Spanish]
HOMOPHONES: *borough*, *burrow*

bursa *noun*
• "BURSA"
• a fluid-filled sac of fibrous tissue, esp. one serving to lessen friction between moving parts (e.g. at a joint).
• [medieval Latin, = bag]
• **bursal** *adjective*

bursar *noun*
• "BURR sur"
• a treasurer or other financial officer, esp. of a university or college.
• [French *boursier* or medieval Latin *bursarius* from *bursa* bag]
• **bursarship** *noun*

bursary *noun*
• "BURSA ree"
• *Cdn* a financial award to an esp. university student made primarily on the basis of financial need or some other criterion in addition to academic merit.
• [medieval Latin *bursaria* (as BURSAR)]
• **bursarial** *adjective*

bursitis *noun*
• "burr SITE iss"
• inflammation of a bursa.
• [BURSA + Greek *-itis*, forming feminine of adjectives in *-itēs* (with *nosos* 'disease' implied)]

Burundian *noun*
• "buh ROONDY 'n"
• a native or inhabitant of Burundi in central Africa.

bury *verb*
• "BERRY" or "BURRY"
• place (a dead body) in the earth, in a tomb, or in the sea, a large lake, etc.
• [Old English *byrgan* from West Germanic]
• **burial** *noun*
HOMOPHONES: *berry*

busby *noun*
• "BUZZ bee"
• a tall fur hat worn by hussars etc.
• [18th c.: origin unknown]

bushel *noun*
• "BUSH'll"
• (in Canada and other Commonwealth countries) a measure of capacity for grain, fruit, etc., equal to 8 imperial gallons or 36.4 litres.
• [Old French *buissiel* etc., perhaps of Gaulish origin]
• **bushelful** *noun*

bushido *noun*
• "boo SHEE doe"
• the code of honour and morals evolved by the Japanese samurai.
• [Japanese, = military knight's way]

bushwhack *verb*
• "BUSH wack"
• clear a way through underbrush, dense vegetation, etc.
• ['bush' + 'whack']
• **bushwhacker** *noun*

business *noun*
• "BIZ niss"
• one's regular occupation, profession, or trade.
• [Old English *bisignis* (as BUSY)]
• **businesslike** *adjective*
• **businessman** *noun*
• **businesswoman** *noun*

buskin *noun*
• "BUSKIN"
• either of a pair of thick-soled laced boots worn by an ancient Athenian tragic actor to gain height.
• [prob. from Old French *bouzequin*, var. of *bro(u)sequin*, of unknown origin]

buss *noun*
• "BUSS"
• a kiss.
• [earlier *bass* (n. & v.): compare French *baiser* kiss, from Latin *basiare*]
HOMOPHONES: *bus*

bustard *noun*
• "BUSS turd"
• any large terrestrial bird of the family Otididae, with long neck, long legs, and stout tapering body.
• [Old French *bistarde* from Latin *avis tarda* slow bird (? = slow on the ground; but possibly a perversion of a foreign word)]

bustee *noun*
• "BUSTY"
• (in India) a shantytown; a slum.
• [Hindi *bastī* dwelling]
HOMOPHONES: *busty*

bustier *noun*
• "BUSTY ay"
• a woman's form-fitting, sleeveless, and often strapless bodice or top, sometimes laced at the front.
• [French]

bustle *verb*
• "BUSS'll"
• work etc. showily, energetically, and officiously.
• [perhaps from *buskle* frequentative of *busk* prepare]

busy *adjective*
• "BIZZY"
• occupied or engaged in work etc. with the attention concentrated.
• [Old English *bisig*]
• **busily** *adverb*
• **busyness** *noun*

butadiene *noun*
• "byoota DIE een"
• a colourless gaseous hydrocarbon used in the manufacture of synthetic rubbers.
• [BUTANE + Greek *di-* from *dis* twice + '-ene' forming names of unsaturated hydrocarbons containing a double bond]

butane *noun*
• "BYOO tane"
• a gaseous hydrocarbon of the alkane series used in liquefied form as fuel.
• [as BUTYL]

buteo *noun*
• "BYOOTY oh"
• any of several birds of prey of the genus *Buteo*, having a broad wingspan and a wide rounded tail.
• [Latin *buteo* falcon; compare BUZZARD]

butoh *noun*
• "BOO toe"
• a style of Japanese modern dance featuring nude or nearly nude dancers in white body paint, often performing feats such as lowering themselves on ropes from roofs of buildings.
• [Japanese, = 'dance']

butte *noun*
• "BYOOT"
• a high isolated hill with steep sides and a flat top, esp. in western N America.
• [French, = mound]
HOMOPHONES: *beaut*

butterbur *noun*
• "BUTTER burr"
• any of several plants of the genus *Petasites* with large soft leaves and spikes of purple flowers.
• ['butter' + 'burr' a prickly flower head, probably of Scandinavian origin]

butterflied *adjective*
• "BUTTER flide"
• (of shrimp, a steak, etc.) sliced down the centre and spread apart.
• [from 'butterfly']

butterwort *noun*
• "BUTTER wurt" or "BUTTER wort"
• any bog plant of the genus *Pinguicula*, esp. *P. vulgaris* with violet-like flowers and fleshy leaves that secrete a fluid to trap small insects.
• ['butter' + WORT]

buttinsky *noun*
ALSO SPELLED: **buttinski**
• "but IN skee"
• a person who meddles or intrudes, esp. habitually.
• [*butt in* + *-sky* final element in many Slavic names]

buttock *noun*
• "BUT uck"
• each of two fleshy protuberances on the lower rear part of the human trunk.
• [*butt* ridge + *-ock* diminutive suffix]

buttress *noun*
• "BUT triss"
• a projecting support of stone or brick etc. built against a wall.
• [Old French *(ars) bouterez* thrusting (arch) from *bouteret* from *bouter* butt]

butut *noun*
• "BOO toot"
• a monetary unit of Gambia, equal to one-hundredth of a dalasi.
• [a local word]

butyl *noun*
• "BYOOT'll"
• the monovalent alkyl radical C_4H_9.
• [as BUTYRIC]
• **butylated** *adjective*

butyrate *noun*
• "BYOOTER ate"
• a salt or ester of butyric acid.
• [as BUTYRIC]

butyric *adjective*
• "byoo TEERIC"
• designating a colourless syrupy liquid organic acid found in two isomeric forms in rancid butter or arnica oil.
• [Latin *butyrum* butter]

buxom *adjective*
• "BUCKS'm"
• (of a woman) having large breasts.
• [earlier sense *pliant*: Middle English from stem of Old English *būgan* bow]
• **buxomness** *noun*

buzzard *noun*
• "BUZZ'rd"
• any of a group of predatory birds of the hawk family, esp. of the genus *Buteo*, with broad wings well adapted for soaring flight.

• [Old French *busard*, *buson* from Latin *buteo -onis* falcon]

bwana *noun*
• "BWONNA"
• (in Africa) master, sir.
• [Swahili]

bye *noun*
• "BY"
• the status of an unpaired competitor in a tournament, who proceeds to the next round as if having won.
• ['by' ('beside', etc.) as noun]
HOMOPHONES: *by*, *bi*, *buy*

byre *noun*
• "BIRE"
• a cowshed.
• [Old English *bȳre*]
HOMOPHONES: *buyer*

Byronic *adjective*
• "by RONNIC"
• characteristic of Lord Byron, English poet d.1824, or his romantic poetry.

byssus *noun*
• "BISS'ss"
• a fine textile fibre and fabric of flax.
• [Latin from Greek *bussos* fine linen fabric]
• **byssal** *adjective*

byte *noun*
• "BITE"
• a group of usu. eight binary digits, often used to represent one character.
• [20th c.: perhaps based on 'bit' and 'bite']
HOMOPHONES: *bite*, *bight*

Byzantine *adjective*
• "BIZZ'n teen" or "BIZZ'n tine"
• of or relating to Byzantium or the Eastern Roman Empire (4th–15th c.).
• [French *byzantin* or Latin *Byzantinus* from *Byzantium*, the city later called Constantinople and now Istanbul]

Cc

cabal *noun*
• "kuh BAL"
• a secret intrigue or conspiracy.
• [French *cabale* from medieval Latin *cabala* occult lore, from Rabbinical Hebrew *ḳabbālâ* tradition]

caballero *noun*
• "cabble YERRO"
• a Spanish gentleman.
• [Spanish from medieval Latin *caballarius* from Latin *caballus* horse]

cabana *noun*
• "kuh BANNA"
• a cabin or other shelter, esp. at a beach or swimming pool.
• [Spanish *cabaña* from Late Latin *capanna*]

cabaret *noun*
• "cabba RAY"
• a nightclub or restaurant, esp. one in which entertainment is provided while guests eat or drink at tables.
• [French, = wooden structure, tavern]

caber *noun*
• "CAY bur"
• a roughly trimmed tree trunk thrown in a Scottish Highland sport as a test of physical strength.
• [Gaelic *cabar* pole]

Cabernet *noun*
• "cabber NAY"
• a variety of black grape used in winemaking.
• [French]

cabochon *noun*
• "CABBA shon"
• a convex gem polished but not faceted.
• [French, diminutive of Old French (Picard) *caboche* head, Old French *caboce*, of unknown origin]

caboose *noun*
• "kuh BOOSS"
• a railway car, usu. at the end of the train, for housing the crew etc.
• [Dutch *cabuse* or *combuse*, of unknown origin]

cabotage *noun*
• "CABBA tozh" or "CABBA tidge"
• coastal navigation and trade.
• [French from *caboter* to coast, perhaps from Spanish *cabo* cape, headland]

cabriole *noun*
• "CABRY ole"
• a kind of ornamental and curved leg characteristic of 18th-c. furniture.
• [French from *cabrioler, caprioler,* from Italian *capriolare* to leap in the air; from the resemblance to a leaping animal's foreleg: see CAPRIOLE]

cabriolet *noun*
• "cabry oh LAY"
• a light two-wheeled carriage with a hood, drawn by one horse.
• [French from *cabriole* goat's leap (compare CAPRIOLE), applied to its motion]

cacao *noun*
• "kuh KA oh" or "kuh KAY oh"
• a seed pod from which cocoa and chocolate are made.
• [Spanish from Nahuatl *cacauatl* (*uatl* tree)]

cacciatore *adjective*
• "catch a TORY"
• cooked with tomatoes, mushrooms, and herbs.
• [Italian, lit. 'hunter']

cachaca *noun*
• "kuh SHOCKA"
• a Brazilian white rum made from sugar cane.
• [Brazilian Portuguese, from Portuguese *cacaça* (white) rum]

cachalot *noun*
• "CASHA lot" or "CASHA lote"
• a sperm whale.
• [French from Spanish & Portuguese *cachalote*, of unknown origin]

cache *noun*
• "CASH"
• a hiding place.
• [French from *cacher* to hide]
HOMOPHONES: *cash*

cachepot *noun*
• "CASH poe" or "CASH pot"
• an ornamental holder for a flower pot.
• [French *cacher* hide + *pot* pot]

cachet *noun*
- "ca SHAY" or "CASH ay"
- a distinguishing mark or seal.
- [French from *cacher* press, ultimately from Latin *coactare* constrain]

cachexia *noun*
- "kuh KEXY uh"
- a condition of weakness of body or mind associated with chronic disease.
- [French *cachexie* or Late Latin *cachexia* from Greek *kakhexia* from *kakos* bad + *hexis* habit]
- **cachectic** *adjective*

cachucha *noun*
- "kuh CHOOCHA"
- a lively Spanish solo dance with castanets.
- [Spanish]

cacique *noun*
- "kuh SEEK"
- an Aboriginal chief in the W Indies or S America.
- [Spanish, of Carib origin]

cacomistle *noun*
- "CACKO miss'll"
- any raccoon-like animal of several species of the genus *Bassariscus*, native to Central America, having a black and white ringed tail.
- [Latin American Spanish *cacomixtle* from Nahuatl *tlacomiztli*]

cacophony *noun*
- "kuh COFFA nee"
- a harsh discordant mixture of sound.
- [French *cacophonie* from Greek *kakophōnia* from *kakophōnos* from *kakos* bad + *phōnē* sound]
- **cacophonic** *adjective* "cacka FONNIC"
- **cacophonous** *adjective*

cacuminal *adjective*
- "kuh KYOOMIN 'll"
- pronounced with the tip of the tongue curled up towards the hard palate.
- [Latin *cacuminare* make pointed, from *cacumen -minis* summit, top]

cadastral *adjective*
- "kuh DASS trull"
- of or showing the extent, value, and ownership of land, esp. for taxation.
- [French from *cadastre* register of property, via Provençal *cadastro* from Italian *catast(r)o* (earlier *catastico*), from late Greek *katastikhon* list, register, from *kata stikhon* line by line]

cadaver *noun*
- "kuh DAVVER"
- a corpse, esp. used for dissection.
- [Latin from *cadere* fall]
- **cadaveric** *adjective*
- **cadaverous** *adjective*

caddis *noun*
- "CAD iss"
- any small hairy-winged nocturnal insect of the order Trichoptera, living near water.
- [17th c.: origin unknown]

caddisworm *noun*
- "CADDISS wurm"
- a larva of the caddis fly, living in water and making protective cylindrical cases from bits of sand, wood, leaves, etc.
- [CADDIS + 'worm']

Caddo *noun*
- "CADDO"
- a member of an Aboriginal people once inhabiting present-day Louisiana and Arkansas but now living mostly in Oklahoma.
- [Caddo *Kädohädächo* 'Caddo proper, real Caddo']

Caddoan *noun*
- "CADDO 'n"
- a family of N American Aboriginal languages related to Siouan and spoken by indigenous peoples of the central US.
- [as CADDO]

cadence *noun*
- "CAY dince"
- a fall in pitch of the voice, esp. at the end of a phrase or sentence.
- [Old French from Italian *cadenza*, ultimately from Latin *cadere* fall]
- **cadenced** *adjective*

cadential *adjective*
- "kuh DEN sh'll"
- of a cadence or cadenza.
- [as CADENCE]

cadenza *noun*
- "kuh DENZA"
- a virtuosic passage for a solo voice or instrument, usu. near the close of an aria or a concerto movement, sometimes improvised.
- [Italian: see CADENCE]

cadmium *noun*
- "CAD mee um"
- a soft bluish-white metallic element occurring naturally with zinc ores, and used in the manufacture of solders and in electroplating.
- [obsolete *cadmia* calamine, from Latin *cadmia* from Greek *kadm(e)ia (gē)* Cadmean (earth), from *Cadmus*, the legendary founder of the Greek city of Thebes]

cadre *noun*
- "CAD ruh" or "CAD ray" or "COD ruh" or "COD ray"
- a small, usu. exclusive group with a common objective, occupation, etc.
- [French from Italian *quadro* from Latin *quadrus* square]

caduceus *noun*
- "kuh DOOSSY us" or "kuh DYOOSSY us"
- a staff with a winged top and two serpents coiled around it, esp. as carried by Hermes or Mercury, esp. as a symbol of the medical profession.

• [Latin from Doric Greek *karuk(e)ion* from *kērux* herald]

caducous *adjective*
• "kuh DOOK us"
• (of organs and parts) easily detached or shed at an early stage, after serving their purpose.
• [Latin *caducus* falling, from *cadere* fall]

caecilian *noun*
ALSO SPELLED: **coecilian**
• "see SILLY 'n"
• any burrowing wormlike amphibian of the order Gymnophiona, having poorly developed eyes and no limbs.
• [Latin *caecilia* kind of lizard]

Caerphilly *noun*
• "cur FILLY" or "car FILLY"
• a kind of mild white cheese.
• [*Caerphilly* in S Wales where it was originally made]

Caesar *noun*
• "SEE zur"
• a salad of romaine lettuce tossed usu. with Parmesan cheese, garlic croutons, bacon bits, and a dressing of oil, lemon juice, raw egg, and anchovies.
• [*Caesar* Cardini, Mexican restaurateur who created it in 1924]
HOMOPHONES: *seizer*

Caesarean *noun*
ALSO SPELLED: **Caesarian**, **Cesarean**
• "suh ZERRY 'n"
• an operation for delivering a child by cutting through the wall of the abdomen and uterus.
• [from the name of the Roman emperor Julius Caesar, supposedly born this way]

caesious *adjective*
• "SEEZY us"
• bluish or greyish green.
• [Latin *caesius*]

caesura *noun*
• "siz YURA" or "siz OORA"
• (in Greek and Latin verse) a break between words within a metrical foot.
• [Latin from *caedere caes-* cut]
• **caesural** *adjective*

cafard *noun*
• "kuh FAR"
• melancholia.
• [French, lit. 'cockroach', 'hypocrite']

café *noun*
• "caff AY"
• a restaurant serving coffee and other beverages and light meals.
• [French, = coffee, coffee house]

cafeteria *noun*
• "cafa TEERY uh"
• a restaurant in which customers collect their meals on trays at a counter and usu. pay before sitting down to eat.
• [Latin American Spanish *cafetería* coffee shop]

cafetorium *noun*
• "cafa TORY um"
• a large room serving as both a cafeteria and an auditorium, esp. in a school.
• [blend of CAFETERIA + AUDITORIUM]

caffeine *noun*
• "caf EEN"
• an alkaloid drug with stimulant action found in coffee, tea, chocolate, cola beverages, etc.
• [French *caféine* from *café* coffee]
• **caffeinated** *adjective* "CAF 'n ated"

caftan *noun*
ALSO SPELLED: **kaftan**
• "CAF tan"
• a long, loose tunic or dress.
• [Turkish *ḳaftān*, partly through French *cafetan*]

cagoule *noun*
• "kuh GOOL"
• a light hooded waterproof garment pulled over the head and worn in mountaineering etc.
• [French, literally 'cowl' from ecclesiastical Latin *cuculla* from Latin *cucullus* hood of a cloak]

caiman *noun*
ALSO SPELLED: **cayman**
• "CAY m'n"
• any of various Central and S American alligator-like reptiles, esp. of the genus *Caiman*.
• [Spanish & Portuguese *caiman*, from Carib *acayuman*]

caipirinha *noun*
• "kipey REENYA"
• a Brazilian cocktail made with cachaca, lime or lemon juice, sugar, and crushed ice.
• [Brazilian Portuguese, from *caipira* yokel]

caique *noun*
• "kye EEK"
• a light rowboat or skiff used in the area of Istanbul, Turkey.
• [French from Italian *caicco* from Turkish *kayik*]

cairn *noun*
• "CAIRN"
• a mound of rough stones as a monument or landmark.
• [Gaelic *carn*]

cairngorm *noun*
• "CAIRN gorm"
• a yellow or smoky semi-precious form of quartz.
• [the *Cairngorm* Mountains in N Scotland, where it was first found]

caisse *noun*
• "KESS"
• *Cdn* (in Quebec and other francophone

communities) a co-operative financial institution similar to a credit union.
• [French]

caisson *noun*
• "CAY sonn" or "CAY s'n"
• a watertight chamber in which underwater construction work can be done.
• [French (from Italian *cassone*) assimilated to *caisse* case]

caitiff *noun*
• "CAY tiff"
• a base or despicable person; a coward.
• [Old French *caitif*, *chaitif* ultimately from Latin *captivus* captive, from *capere capt-* take]

cajole *verb*
• "kuh JOLE"
• persuade by flattery, deceit, etc.
• [French *cajoler*]
• **cajolery** *noun*

Cajun *noun*
• "CAY j'n"
• a descendant of the French-speaking settlers who were expelled from Acadia in the mid-18th c., living primarily in S Louisiana.
• [alteration of ACADIAN]

calabash *noun*
• "CALA bash"
• an evergreen tree, *Crescentia cujete*, native to tropical America, bearing fruit in the form of large gourds.
• [French *calebasse* from Spanish *calabaza* perhaps from Persian *karbuz* melon]

calaboose *noun*
• "cala BOOSS"
• a jail or prison.
• [Louisiana French *calabouse* from Spanish *calabozo* dungeon]

calabrese *noun*
• "cala BRAY zay"
• esp. *Cdn* a round white crusty Italian bread.
• [Italian, = Calabrian]

Calabrian *noun*
• "kuh LAB ree 'n"
• a native or inhabitant of Calabria in S Italy.

caladium *noun*
• "kuh LAY dee um"
• any of several plants of the tropical American genus *Caladium*, of the arum family, having starchy tubers and colourful leaves.
• [modern Latin from Malay *keladi*]

calamander *noun*
• "CALA mander"
• a fine-grained red-brown ebony streaked with black, from the Asian tree *Diospyros quaesita*, used in furniture.
• [19th c.: origin unknown: perhaps related to Sinhalese word for the tree *kalu-madīriya*]

calamari *noun*
• "cala MAR ee"
• the flesh of the squid when used as food.
• [Italian (as CALAMARY)]

calamary *noun*
• "CALA merry"
• a squid with a long, tapering, horny, internal shell, esp. one of the common genus *Loligo*.
• [medieval Latin *calamarium* pen case, from Latin *calamus* pen (with reference to its inky secretion)]

calamine *noun*
• "CALA mine"
• a pink powder consisting of zinc carbonate and a small quantity of ferric oxide used as a lotion or ointment, e.g. for sunburn, insect bites, or rashes.
• [French from medieval Latin *calamina* alteration of Latin *cadmia*: see CADMIUM]

calamint *noun*
• "CALA mint"
• any aromatic herb or shrub of the genus *Calamintha* (now usu. included in *Clinopodium* or *Satureja*) of the mint family, with purple, lilac, or white flowers.
• [Old French *calament* from medieval Latin *calamentum* from Late Latin *calaminthe* from Greek *kalaminthē*]

calamity *noun*
• "kuh LAMMA tee"
• a disaster, a great misfortune.
• [French *calamité* from Latin *calamitas -tatis*]
• **calamitous** *adjective*
• **calamitously** *adverb*

calamondin *noun*
• "cala MONDIN"
• a small hybrid citrus tree frequently grown as a houseplant.
• [Tagalog *kalamunding*]

calamus *noun*
• "CALA muss"
• a plant of the arum family, *Acorus calamus*, with leaves resembling those of an iris and an aromatic root used medicinally.
• [Greek *kalamos* reed]

calando *adverb*
• "kuh LANDO"
• (in music) gradually decreasing in speed and volume.
• [Italian, = slackening]

calash *noun*
• "kuh LASH"
• a light low-wheeled carriage with a removable folding hood.
• [see CALÈCHE]

calathea *noun*
• "cala THEE uh" (with "TH" as in *THIN*)
• a plant of the genus *Calathea*, with colourful, patterned leaves, often grown as a houseplant.
• [from Latin *calathus* 'flower-shaped basket']

calcaneus *noun*
• "cal CANEY us"
• the bone forming the heel.
• [Latin]

calcareous *adjective*
• "cal KERRY us"
• of or containing calcium carbonate; chalky.
• [Latin *calcarius* (as CALX)]

calceolaria *noun*
• "cal see a LERRY uh"
• any plant of the genus *Calceolaria*, native to Central and S America, with slipper-shaped flowers.
• [modern Latin from Latin *calceolus* diminutive of *calceus* shoe]

calceolate *adjective*
• "CAL see a late"
• slipper-shaped.
• [as CALCEOLARIA]

calciferol *noun*
• "cal SIFFER awl"
• one of the D vitamins, routinely added to dairy products, essential for the deposition of calcium in bones.
• [as CALCIFEROUS]

calciferous *adjective*
• "cal SIFFER us"
• yielding calcium salts, esp. calcium carbonate.
• [as CALCIUM + Latin *-fer* producing, from *ferre* bear]

calcify *verb*
• "CALSA fie"
• harden or become hardened by deposition of calcium salts; petrify.
• [as CALCIUM]
• **calcification** *noun*

calcine *verb*
• "CAL sine" or "CAL sin"
• reduce, oxidize, or desiccate by strong heat.
• [Old French *calciner* or medieval Latin *calcinare* from Late Latin *calcina* lime, from Latin CALX]
• **calcination** *noun*

calcite *noun*
• "CAL site"
• natural crystalline calcium carbonate.
• [German *Calcit* from Latin CALX lime]

calcitonin *noun*
• "cal suh TOE nin"
• a polypeptide hormone secreted by the thyroid, having the effect of lowering blood calcium.
• [as CALCIUM + 'tonic' from Greek *tonos* tension, tone, from *teinō* stretch]

calcium *noun*
• "CAL see um"
• a soft greyish-white metallic element of the alkaline-earth group occurring naturally in limestone, chalk, etc., and in animal bones and teeth, and whose ions and salts are essential to life.
• [Latin CALX lime]

calculate *verb*
• "CAL kyoo late"
• ascertain or determine by using mathematics or one's judgment; estimate.
• [Late Latin *calculare* (as CALCULUS)]
• **calculability** *noun*
• **calculable** *adjective* "CAL kyoo luh bull"
• **calculably** *adverb*
• **calculation** *noun*
• **calculative** *adjective* "CAL kyoo luh tiv"

calculated *adjective*
• "CAL kyoo lated"
• (of an action) done with awareness of the likely consequences.
• [as CALCULATE]
• **calculatedly** *adverb*

calculating *adjective*
• "CAL kyoo late ing"
• (of a person) shrewd, scheming.
• [as CALCULATE]
• **calculatingly** *adverb*

calculator *noun*
• "CAL kyoo later"
• a device (esp. a small electronic one) used for making mathematical calculations.
• [as CALCULATE]

calculus *noun*
• "CAL kyoo luss"
• a particular method of calculation or reasoning.
• [Latin, = small stone used in reckoning on an abacus]

caldera *noun*
• "cal DARE uh" or "cawl DARE uh"
• a large volcanic crater, esp. one whose breadth greatly exceeds that of the vent or vents within it, created by a volcanic explosion.
• [Spanish from Late Latin *caldaria* pot for boiling]

calèche *noun*
• "ca LESH"
• *Cdn* a two-wheeled one-horse vehicle with a seat for the driver on the splashboard, commonly used in tourist areas of Quebec.
• [French from German *Kalesche* from Polish *kolaska* or Czech *kolesa*]

Caledonian *adjective*
• "cala DOE nee 'n"
• of or relating to Scotland.
• [Latin *Caledonia* N Britain]

calendar *noun*
• "CAL 'n dur"
• a system by which the beginning, length, and subdivisions of the year are fixed.
• [Anglo-French *calender*, Old French *calendier*

from Latin *calendarium* account book (as CALENDS)]
• **calendric** *adjective* "kuh LEND rick"
• **calendrical** *adjective*
HOMOPHONES: *calender*

calender *noun*
• "CAL 'n dur"
• a machine in which cloth, paper, etc., is pressed by rollers to glaze or smooth it.
• [French *calendre(r)*, of unknown origin]
HOMOPHONES: *calendar*

calends *plural noun*
ALSO SPELLED: **kalends**
• "CAL ends"
• the first of the month in the ancient Roman calendar.
• [Old French *calendes* from Latin *kalendae*]

calendula *noun*
• "kuh LEND yoo luh"
• any plant of the genus *Calendula*, with large yellow or orange flowers, e.g. marigold.
• [modern Latin, diminutive of *calendae* (as CALENDS), perhaps = little clock]

calenture *noun*
• "CAL en chur"
• a form of delirium formerly supposed to afflict sailors in the tropics, in which the sea is mistaken for green fields.
• [French from Spanish *calentura* fever, from *calentar* be hot, ultimately from Latin *calēre* be warm]

Calgarian *noun*
• "cal GARE ee 'n"
• a resident of Calgary, Alta.

calibrate *verb*
• "CALA brate"
• mark (a gauge) with a standard scale of readings.
• [as CALIBRE]
• **calibration** *noun*
• **calibrator** *noun*

calibre *noun*
ALSO SPELLED: esp. *US* **caliber**
• "CALA bur"
• the internal diameter of a gun or tube.
• [French *calibre*, Italian *calibro*, from Arabic *ḳālib* mould]

caliche *noun*
• "kuh LEECHY"
• a mineral deposit of gravel, sand, and nitrates found in dry areas of N or S America, esp. Chile saltpetre.
• [Latin American Spanish]

calico *noun*
• "CALA co"
• a cotton fabric with a printed pattern.
• [earlier *calicut* from *Calicut* in SW India]

Californian *noun*
• "cala FORNY 'n"
• a native or inhabitant of California.

californium *noun*
• "cala FORNY um"
• a transuranic radioactive metallic element produced artificially from curium.
• [University of *California*, where it was first made]

calipers *plural noun*
ALSO SPELLED: **callipers**
• "CALA purz"
• an instrument with two pivoting bowed legs for measuring external or internal dimensions.
• [apparently var. of CALIBRE]

caliph *noun*
• "CALE if" or "CAL if"
• the chief Muslim civil and religious ruler, regarded as the successor of Muhammad.
• [Old French *caliphe* from Arabic *Ḵalīfa* successor]
• **caliphate** *noun* "CAY lif ate" or "CAL if ate" or "CAY lif it" or "CAL if it"

calisthenics *plural noun*
ALSO SPELLED: **callisthenics**
• "cal iss THENNIX" (with "TH" as in *THIN*)
• gymnastic exercises to achieve bodily fitness and grace of movement.
• [Greek *kallos* beauty + *sthenos* strength]
• **calisthenic** *adjective* (also **callisthenic**)

calla *noun*
• "CALA"
• the arum lily, *Zantedeschia aethiopica*, with an esp. white funnel-shaped spathe and a yellow spadix.
• [modern Latin]

callaloo *noun*
• "cala LOO"
• a West Indian soup or stew containing salt pork, crabmeat, okra, coconut milk, and greens, esp. the leaves of the taro plant.
• [Latin American Spanish *calalú*]

callibogus *noun*
ALSO SPELLED: **calabogus**
• "cala BOE guss"
• *Cdn* (esp. *Nfld*) a beverage made from spruce beer and rum mixed with molasses.
• [18th c.: origin unknown]

calligraphy *noun*
• "kuh LIGGRA fee"
• handwriting, esp. when fine or pleasing.
• [Greek *kalligraphia* from *kallos* beauty + *graphia* writing]
• **calligrapher** *noun*
• **calligraphic** *adjective*
• **calligraphist** *noun*

calliope *noun*
• "kuh LIE a pee"
• a keyboard instrument resembling an organ, with a set of steam whistles producing musical notes.
• [*Calliope*, the Greek muse of epic poetry (literally 'beautiful-voiced')]

callosity *noun*
• "kuh LOSSA tee"
• a hard thick area of skin usu. occurring in parts of the body subject to pressure or friction.
• [French *callosité* or Latin *callositas* (as CALLUS)]

callous *adjective*
• "CAL us"
• unfeeling, insensitive.
• [Latin *callosus* (as CALLUS) or French *calleux*]
• **calloused** *adjective*
• **callously** *adverb*
• **callousness** *noun*
HOMOPHONES: *callus*

callow *adjective*
• "CAL oh"
• inexperienced, immature.
• [Old English *calu*]
• **callowly** *adverb*
• **callowness** *noun*

calluna *noun*
• "kuh LOONA"
• any common heather of the genus *Calluna*, native to Europe and N Africa.
• [modern Latin from Greek *kallunō* beautify, from *kallos* beauty]

callus *noun*
• "CAL us"
• a hard thick area of skin or tissue.
• [Latin]
• **callused** *adjective*
HOMOPHONES: *callous*

calmative *adjective*
• "COMM a tiv" or "CAL muh tiv"
• tending to calm or sedate.
• [ultimately from Late Latin *cauma* from Greek *kauma* heat]

calomel *noun*
• "CALA mel"
• a compound of mercury and chlorine, formerly used medicinally as a purgative.
• [modern Latin, perhaps from Greek *kalos* beautiful + *melas* black]

calorie *noun*
• "CALA ree"
• the amount of heat needed to raise the temperature of 1 kilogram of water through 1°C, often used to measure the energy value of foods.
• [French, arbitrary alteration of Latin *calor* heat]
• **caloric** *adjective* "kuh LORIC"

calorific *adjective*
• "cala RIFFIC"
• high in calories.
• [Latin *calorificus* from *calor* heat]
• **calorifically** *adverb*

calorimeter *noun*
• "cala RIMMA tur"
• any of various instruments for measuring quantity of heat, esp. to find calorific values.
• [Latin *calor* heat + Greek *metron* measure]
• **calorimetric** *adjective* "kuh lora METRIC"
• **calorimetry** *noun* "cala RIMMA tree"

calque *noun*
• "CALC"
• an expression adopted by one language from another in a more or less literally translated form.
• [French, = copy, tracing, from *calquer* trace, ultimately from Latin *calcare* tread]

caltrop *noun*
ALSO SPELLED: **caltrap**
• "CAL trup"
• an iron ball with four spikes placed so that one point always faces upwards, thrown on the ground to impede cavalry horses.
• [Old French *chauchetrape* from *chauchier* tread, *trappe* trap]

calumet *noun*
• "CAL yuh met"
• a N American Aboriginal tobacco pipe with a clay bowl and long reed stem, smoked esp. as a sign of peace.
• [French, ultimately from Latin *calamus* reed]

calumny *noun*
• "CAL um nee"
• slander; malicious representation.
• [Latin *calumnia*]
• **calumniate** *verb* "kuh LUMNY ate"
• **calumniator** *noun*
• **calumnious** *adjective* "kuh LUMNY us"

Calvados *noun*
• "CALVA doss"
• a French apple brandy.
• [*Calvados*, a region in Normandy, France, where it was first distilled]

Calvinism *noun*
• "CALVIN izm"
• the theology of the French Protestant theologian John Calvin (d.1564) or his followers, in which predestination and justification by faith are important elements.
• **Calvinist** *noun*
• **Calvinistic** *adjective*

calx *noun*
• "CALCS"
• a powdery metallic oxide formed when an ore or mineral has been heated.
• [Latin *calx calcis* lime, prob. from Greek *khalix* pebble, limestone]

calypso *noun*
• "kuh LIP so"
• a kind of West Indian music in syncopated African rhythm, usu. improvised on a topical theme.
• [20th c.: origin unknown]
• **calypsonian** *noun*

calyx *noun*
ALSO SPELLED: **calix**
- "CAY lix" or "CAL ix"
- the sepals collectively, forming the protective layer of a flower in bud.
- [Latin from Greek *kalux* case of bud, husk: compare *kaluptō* hide]

calzone *noun*
- "cal ZONAY"
- a type of baked turnover of bread dough filled with tomato sauce, cheese, and vegetables or meat.
- [Italian dialect, prob. related to *calzone* trouser leg]

camaraderie *noun*
- "comma RODDA ree" or "camma RADDA ree"
- mutual trust and sociability among friends.
- [French, as COMRADE]

camarilla *noun*
- "cama RILLA"
- a cabal or clique.
- [Spanish, diminutive of *camara* chamber]

camas *noun*
- "CAM iss"
- any of several N American plants of the lily family, esp. *Camassia quamash*, the edible bulbs of which were a staple of Aboriginal peoples.
- [Chinook Jargon *kamass*, perhaps from Nuu-chah-nulth]

camber *noun*
- "CAM bur"
- the slightly convex or arched shape of the surface of a road, ship's deck, aircraft wing, etc.
- [French *cambre* arched, from Latin *camurus* curved inwards]

cambium *noun*
- "CAMBY um"
- a cellular plant tissue responsible for the increase in girth of stems and roots.
- [medieval Latin, = change, exchange]
- **cambial** *adjective*

Cambodian *noun*
- "cam BOADY 'n"
- a native or national of Cambodia in SE Asia.

Cambrian *adjective*
- "CAME bree 'n" or "CAM bree 'n"
- Welsh.
- [Latin *Cambria* var. of *Cumbria* from Welsh *Cymry* Welshman or *Cymru* Wales]

cambric *noun*
- "CAM brick"
- a fine white linen or cotton fabric.
- [*Kamerijk*, Flemish form of *Cambrai* in N France, where it was originally made]

cameleer *noun*
- "cam'll EER"
- a camel driver.
- [Latin *camelus* from Greek *kamēlos*, of Semitic origin]

camellia *noun*
- "kuh MEELY uh"
- any evergreen shrub of the genus *Camellia*, native to E Asia, with shiny leaves and red, pink, or white roselike flowers.
- [J. *Camellus* or *Kamel*, 17th-c. Moravian botanist]

Camelot *noun*
- "CAMMA lot"
- a period of perceived prosperity and cultural renaissance.
- [legendary location of King Arthur's court]

Camembert *noun*
- "CAM'm bear"
- a kind of soft creamy cheese with a whitish rind, usu. with a strong flavour.
- [*Camembert* in N France, where it was originally made]

cameo *noun*
- "CAMMY oh"
- a piece of jewellery, typically oval in shape, consisting of a portrait in profile carved in relief on a background of a different colour.
- [Old French *camahieu* and medieval Latin *cammaeus*]

camera *noun*
- "CAMRA" or "CAMMER uh"
- an apparatus for taking photographs or for shooting motion picture film or television.
- [originally = chamber, from Latin *camera* from Greek *kamara* vault etc.]

Cameroonian *noun*
- "cammer OONY 'n"
- a native or inhabitant of Cameroon in W Africa.

cami *noun*
- "CAMMY"
- a camisole.
- [abbreviation]

camiknickers *plural noun*
- "CAMMA nickerz"
- a one-piece close-fitting undergarment worn by women.
- [CAMISOLE + KNICKERS]

camisole *noun*
- "CAMMA sole"
- a woman's waist-length sleeveless undergarment with shoulder straps.
- [French from Italian *camiciola* or Spanish *camisola*: see CHEMISE]

camomile *noun*
ALSO SPELLED: **chamomile**
- "CAMMA mile"
- any of various aromatic plants of the composite family, esp. *Chamaemelum nobilis* and plants of the genera *Anthemis* and *Matricaria*, with daisy-like flowers.
- [Old French *camomille* from Late Latin

camomilla or *chamomilla* from Greek *khamaimēlon* earth apple (from the apple smell of its flowers)]

Camorra *noun*
• "kuh MORA"
• a Mafia-like criminal organization, orig. based in Naples, Italy.
• [Italian, perhaps from Spanish *camorra* dispute, quarrel]

camouflage *noun*
• "CAMMA flozh"
• the disguising of military vehicles, aircraft, ships, personnel, artillery, and installations by painting or covering them to make them blend with their surroundings.
• [French from *camoufler* disguise, from Italian *camuffare* disguise, deceive]

campaign *noun*
• "cam PANE"
• an organized course of action for a particular purpose, esp. to arouse public interest (e.g. before a political election).
• [French *campagne* open country, from Italian *campagna* from Late Latin *campania*]
• **campaigner** *noun*

campanile *noun*
• "campa NEE lay"
• a usu. free-standing bell tower, esp. in Italy.
• [Italian from Late Latin *campana* bell]

campanology *noun*
• "campa NOLLA jee"
• the study of bells.
• [modern Latin *campanologia* from Late Latin *campana* bell + Greek *logos* word]
• **campanological** *adjective*
• **campanologist** *noun*

campanula *noun*
• "cam PAN yoo luh"
• any plant of the genus *Campanula*, with usu. blue, purple, or white bell-shaped flowers.
• [modern Latin diminutive of Latin *campana* bell]

campanulate *adjective*
• "cam PAN yoo lut"
• bell-shaped.
• [as CAMPANULA]

Campbelltonian *noun*
• "cam b'll TONY 'n"
• a resident of Campbellton, NB.

campesino *noun*
• "campa SEENO"
• (in Central or S America) a farmer or peasant.
• [Spanish]

camphor *noun*
• "CAM fur"
• a white translucent crystalline volatile substance with an aromatic smell and bitter taste, used to make celluloid and in medicine.
• [Old French *camphore* or medieval Latin *camphora* from Arabic *kāfūr* from Sanskrit *karpūram*]
• **camphoric** *adjective* "cam FORIC"

camphorate *verb*
• "CAMFA rate"
• impregnate or treat with camphor.
• [as CAMPHOR]

campion *noun*
• "CAMPY 'n"
• any plant of the genus *Silene*, with usu. pink or white flowers with notched petals.
• [perhaps from obsolete *campion* from Old French, = 'champion': translation of Greek *lukhnis stephanōmatikē* a plant used for (champions') garlands]

campylobacter *noun*
• "campa lo BACK tur"
• a bacterium of the genus *Campylobacter*, occurring in unpasteurized dairy products, poultry, and other foods, capable of causing food poisoning in humans.
• [Greek *kampulos* bent, twisted + BACTERIA]

Camrosian *noun*
• "cam ROZEY 'n"
• a resident of Camrose, Alta.

Canaanite *noun*
• "CANE 'n ite"
• a native or inhabitant of Canaan, the land west of the River Jordan.

canaille *noun*
• "kuh NIE"
• the rabble.
• [French from Italian *canaglia* pack of dogs, from *cane* dog]

canapé *noun*
• "CANNA pay"
• a cracker or small piece of bread with a savoury food on top, often served as an hors d'oeuvre.
• [French, as CANOPY]

canard *noun*
• "kuh NARD"
• an unfounded rumour or story.
• [French, = duck]

canary *noun*
• "kuh NERRY"
• any of various small finches of the genus *Serinus*, esp. *S. canaria*, a songbird native to the Canary Islands, of which wild varieties are green and the numerous cage varieties usu. bright yellow.
• [the *Canary* Islands off NW Africa, ultimately from Latin *canis* dog, because one of the islands was noted in Roman times for its large dogs]

canasta *noun*
• "kuh NASTA"
• a card game using two decks and resembling rummy, the aim being to collect sets (or melds) of cards.
• [Spanish, = basket]

cancel *verb*
• "CAN s'll"
• announce that (something already arranged and decided upon) will not be done or take place; call off.
• [French *canceller* from Latin *cancellare* from *cancelli* crossbars, lattice]
• **cancellation** *noun*
• **canceller** *noun*

cancellate *adjective*
• "CANSA lut" or "CANSA late"
• marked with crossing lines.
• [Latin *cancelli* lattice]

cancellous *adjective*
• "CANSA luss"
• (of a bone) with pores; spongy.
• [Latin *cancelli* lattice]

candela *noun*
• "can DEELA" or "can DELLA"
• the SI unit of luminous intensity.
• [Latin, = candle]

candelabra *noun*
• "canda LABBRA" or "canda LOBBRA"
• a large branched candlestick holder for several candles or lamps.
• [Latin from *candela* candle]

candida *noun*
• "can DEEDA" or "CANDID uh"
• any yeastlike parasitic fungus of the genus *Candida*, esp. *C. albicans*, causing thrush.
• [modern Latin feminine of Latin *candidus* white]

candidate *noun*
• "CANDID ate" or "CANDID it"
• a person who seeks or is nominated for an office, award, etc.
• [French *candidat* or Latin *candidatus* white-robed, from *candidus* white (Roman candidates wearing white)]
• **candidacy** *noun* "CANDID a see"
• **candidature** *noun* "CANDID a chur"

candidiasis *noun*
• "candid EYE a sis"
• an infection with candida, esp. causing oral or vaginal thrush.
• [as CANDIDA]

Candlemas *noun*
• "CANDLE muss"
• (in some churches) a feast with blessing of candles (2 Feb.), commemorating the Purification of the Virgin Mary and the presentation of Christ in the Temple.
• [Old English *Candelmæsse* from Latin]

Candomblé *noun*
• "can dom BLAY"
• an Afro-Brazilian folk religion or cult based on traditional African religious practices modified by elements of Roman Catholicism and spiritualism.
• [Brazilian Portuguese, ultimate origin obscure]

canebrake *noun*
• "CANE brake"
• a tract of land overgrown with canes.
• ['cane' from Old French *cane* from Latin *canna* from Greek *kanna* + 'brake' a clump of bushes or broken branches, from Middle Low German *brake*, related to 'break']

canid *noun*
• "CANNID"
• an animal of the family Canidae, which includes dogs, wolves, foxes, etc.
• [modern Latin *canidae* from Latin *canis* dog]

canine *adjective*
• "CAY nine"
• of a dog or dogs.
• [Latin *caninus* from *canis* dog]

canister *noun*
• "CAN iss tur"
• a container, often one of a set, for holding flour, sugar, coffee, tea, etc.
• [Latin *canistrum* from Greek *kanastron* wicker basket, from *kanna* cane]

Canmorite *noun*
• "CAN more ite"
• a resident of Canmore, Alta.

canna *noun*
• "CANNA"
• any tropical plant of the genus *Canna* with bright flowers and ornamental leaves.
• [Latin, = 'cane']

cannabinoid *noun*
• "CANNA bin oid"
• any of a group of closely related compounds which include cannabinol and the active constituents of cannabis.
• [as CANNABIS]

cannabinol *noun*
• "CANNA bin awl"
• a crystalline compound whose derivatives, esp. THC, are the active constituents of cannabis.
• [as CANNABIS]

cannabis *noun*
• "CANNA biss"
• any hemp plant of the genus *Cannabis*, esp. Indian hemp.
• [Latin from Greek]

cannellini *noun*
• "canna LEENY"
• a kidney-shaped bean of a medium-sized creamy-white variety.
• [Italian, lit. = 'small tubes']

cannelloni *plural noun*
• "canna LO nee"
• tubes or rolls of pasta stuffed with meat or a vegetable mixture.
• [Italian from *cannello* stalk]

cannelure *noun*
- "CANNA lure"
- the groove around a bullet etc.
- [French from *canneler* from *canne* reed, cane]

cannibal *noun*
- "CANNA bull"
- a person who eats human flesh.
- [originally pl. *Canibales* from Spanish: var. of *Caribes* name of a West Indian nation]
- **cannibalism** *noun*
- **cannibalistic** *adjective*

cannibalize *verb*
ALSO SPELLED: esp. *Brit.* **-ise**
- "CANNA bull ize"
- use (a machine etc.) as a source of spare parts for others.
- [as CANNIBAL]
- **cannibalization** *noun* (also esp. *Brit.* **-isation**)

cannikin *noun*
- "CANNA kin"
- a small drinking cup or can.
- [Dutch *kanneken*]

cannoli *plural noun*
- "kuh NO lee"
- a dessert consisting of small deep-fried pastry tubes filled with sweetened ricotta cheese and pieces of chocolate etc.
- [Italian, from *canna* reed]

cannon *noun*
- "CAN 'n"
- a large heavy gun installed on a carriage or mounting.
- [French *canon* from Italian *cannone* large tube, from *canna* cane]

HOMOPHONES: *canon*

cannonade *noun*
- "can 'n AID"
- a period of continuous heavy gunfire.
- [French from Italian *cannonata*]

cannonball *noun*
- "CAN 'n ball"
- a large usu. metal ball fired by a cannon.
- [as CANNON + 'ball']

cannula *noun*
- "CAN yoo luh"
- a small tube inserted into the body to allow fluid to enter or escape.
- [Latin, diminutive of *canna* cane]

cannulate *verb*
- "CAN yuh late"
- introduce a cannula into.
- [as CANNULA]
- **cannulation** *noun*

canoe *noun*
- "kuh NOO"
- a small narrow boat with pointed upcurved ends usu. propelled by paddling.
- [Spanish and Haitian *canoa*]
- **canoeable** *adjective*
- **canoeing** *noun*
- **canoeist** *noun*

canola *noun*
- "kuh NO luh"
- any of several varieties of rapeseed low in erucic acid, producing an oil used in cooking.
- [*Canada* + -ola (with reference to Latin *oleum* oil)]

canon *noun*
- "CAN 'n"
- a general law, rule, principle, or criterion.
- [Old English from Latin from Greek *kanōn* rule]

HOMOPHONES: *cannon*

canonical *adjective*
- "kuh NONNA k'll"
- according to or ordered by canon (church) law.
- [as CANON]
- **canonically** *adverb*
- **canonicity** *noun* "can 'n ISSA tee"

canonist *noun*
- "CAN 'n ist"
- an expert in canon (church) law.
- [as CANON]

canonize *verb*
ALSO SPELLED: esp. *Brit.* **-ise**
- "CAN 'n ize"
- declare officially to be a saint, usu. with a ceremony.
- [medieval Latin *canonizare*: see CANON]
- **canonization** *noun* (also esp. *Brit.* **-isation**)

canoodle *verb*
- "kuh NOODLE"
- kiss and cuddle amorously.
- [19th c.: origin unknown]

canopy *noun*
- "CANNA pee"
- a covering hung or held up over a throne, bed, person, etc.
- [medieval Latin *canopeum* from Latin *conopeum* from Greek *kōnōpeion* couch with mosquito netting, from *kōnōps* gnat]

cantabile *adverb*
- "can TABBY lay"
- in a smooth singing style.
- [Italian, = singable]

Cantabrian *noun*
- "can TABREE 'n"
- a native or inhabitant of Cantabria in N Spain.

Cantabrigian *adjective*
- "canta BRIDGE ee 'n"
- of Cambridge, England or Cambridge University.
- [Latin *Cantabrigia* Cambridge]

cantaloupe *noun*
ALSO SPELLED: **cantaloup**
• "CANTA lope"
• a small round variety of melon with netted skin and orange flesh.
• [French *cantaloup* from *Cantaluppi* near Rome, where it was first grown in Europe]

cantankerous *adjective*
• "can TANKER us"
• bad-tempered, quarrelsome.
• [perhaps from Irish *cant* outbidding + *rancorous*]
• **cantankerously** *adverb*
• **cantankerousness** *noun*

cantata *noun*
• "can TATTA" or "can TOTTA"
• a short narrative or descriptive composition with vocal solos and usu. chorus and orchestral accompaniment.
• [Italian *cantata (aria)* sung (air), from *cantare* sing]

cantharides *plural noun*
• "can THAIR id eez" (with "TH" as in *THIN*)
• a preparation made from dried bodies of a beetle, *Lytta vesicatoria*, causing blistering of the skin and formerly used in medicine and sometimes taken as an aphrodisiac.
• [Latin from Greek *kantharis*]

canthus *noun*
• "CANTH us"
• the outer or inner corner of the eye, where the upper and lower lids meet.
• [Latin from Greek *kanthos*]

canticle *noun*
• "CANTA k'll"
• a song or chant with a Biblical text.
• [Old French *canticle* (var. of *cantique*) or Latin *canticulum* diminutive of *canticum* from *canere* sing]

cantilena *noun*
• "canta LEENA" or "canta LAYNA"
• a simple or sustained melody.
• [Italian from Latin, = song]

cantilever *noun*
• "CANTA leever"
• a long bracket or beam etc. projecting from a vertical support.
• [17th c.: origin unknown]
• **cantilevered** *adjective*

cantina *noun*
• "can TEENA"
• a bar or wine shop, esp. in a Spanish-speaking area.
• [Spanish & Italian]

cantle *noun*
• "CANT'll"
• the protuberant part at the back of a saddle.
• [Middle Low German *kant*, *kante*, Middle Dutch *cant*, point, side, edge, ultimately from Latin *cant(h)us* corner of the eye]

canto *noun*
• "CANTO"
• a division of a long poem.
• [Italian, = song, from Latin *cantus*]

canton *noun*
• "CANT on"
• a subdivision of a country.
• [Old French, = corner (see CANTLE)]
• **cantonal** *adjective* "CANTA n'll" or "cant ON 'll"

Cantonese *adjective*
• "canta NEEZ"
• of Canton (also called Guangzhou) in SE China or the Cantonese dialect of Chinese.

cantonment *noun*
• "cant ON m'nt"
• a lodging assigned to troops.
• [as CANTON]

cantor *noun*
• "CAN tur" or "CAN tor"
• the leader of the singing in church.
• [Latin, = singer, from *canere* sing]
• **cantorial** *adjective* "can TORY 'll"
HOMOPHONES: *canter*

cantoris *adjective*
• "can TOR iss"
• to be sung by the cantorial side of the choir in antiphonal singing.
• [Latin, genitive of CANTOR precentor]

canvas *noun*
• "CAN vuss"
• a strong coarse kind of cloth usu. made from cotton or other coarse yarn and used for sails, tents, sturdy bags, etc. and as a surface for oil painting.
• [Old Northern French *canevas*, ultimately from Latin *cannabis* hemp]
HOMOPHONES: *canvass*

canvass *verb*
• "CAN vuss"
• solicit votes, charitable donations, support, custom, etc., esp. by going door to door.
• [originally = toss in a sheet, agitate, from CANVAS]
• **canvasser** *noun*
HOMOPHONES: *canvas*

canyon *noun*
• "CAN y'n"
• a deep gorge, often with a stream or river.
• [Spanish *cañón* tube, ultimately from Latin *canna* cane]
• **canyonland** *noun*

canyoning *noun*
• "CAN y'n ing"
• the sport or activity of jumping into a fast-flowing mountain stream and allowing oneself to be carried downstream at high speed.
• [as CANYON]

caoutchouc *noun*
- "COW chook"
- raw rubber.
- [French from Carib *cahuchu*]

capable *adjective*
- "CAY puh bull"
- competent, able, gifted.
- [French from Late Latin *capabilis* from Latin *capere* hold]
- **capability** *noun*
- **capably** *adverb*

capacious *adjective*
- "kuh PAY sh'ss"
- roomy; able to hold much.
- [Latin *capax -acis* from *capere* hold]
- **capaciously** *adverb*
- **capaciousness** *noun*

capacitance *noun*
- "kuh PASSA tince"
- the ability of a system to store an electric charge.
- [as CAPACITY]

capacitor *noun*
- "kuh PASSA tur"
- a device of one or more pairs of conductors separated by insulators used to store an electric charge.
- [as CAPACITY]

capacity *noun*
- "kuh PASSA tee"
- the power of containing, receiving, experiencing, or producing.
- [French from Latin *capacitas -tatis* (as CAPACIOUS)]

caparison *noun*
- "kuh PERRA s'n"
- a horse's trappings.
- [obsolete French *caparasson* from Spanish *caparazón* saddle cloth, from *capa* cape, cloak]

capelin *noun*
ALSO SPELLED: **caplin**
- "CAP lin" or "CAPE lin"
- a small smelt-like fish, *Mallotus villosus*, of the N Atlantic, used as food and as bait for catching cod etc.
- [French from Provençal *capelan*: see CHAPLAIN]

capellini *noun*
- "cappa LEENY"
- very fine spaghetti.
- [Italian, diminutive of *capelli* hair]

capercaillie *noun*
- "capper CAY lee"
- a large European grouse, *Tetrao urogallus*.
- [Gaelic *capull coille* horse of the wood]

Capetonian *noun*
- "cape TONY 'n"
- a resident of Cape Town, South Africa.

capias *noun*
- "CAPPY us" or "CAPEY us"
- a writ ordering the arrest of the person named.
- [Latin, = you are to seize, from *capere* take]

capicollo *noun*
- "cappy CO lo"
- spicy Italian cured pork shoulder butt, usu. served in thin slices.
- [Italian]

capillarity *noun*
- "cappa LERRA tee"
- a phenomenon at liquid boundaries resulting in the rise or depression of liquids in narrow tubes.
- [French *capillarité* (as CAPILLARY)]

capillary *adjective*
- "kuh PILLA ree"
- of or like a hair.
- [Latin *capillaris* from *capillus* hair]

capisce *interjection*
- "kuh PEESH"
- do you understand?
- [Italian *capisce* formal for 'do you understand?']

capital *noun*
- "CAP it 'll"
- the city or town in a country, province, etc. at which the principal government institutions (the legislature, judiciary, the government administrative headquarters) are located.
- [Old French from Latin *capitalis* from *caput -itis* head]

HOMOPHONES: *Capitol*

capitalism *noun*
- "CAP it 'll izm"
- an economic system in which the production and distribution of goods depend on invested private capital and profit-making.
- [as CAPITAL]
- **capitalist** *noun*
- **capitalistic** *adjective*
- **capitalistically** *adverb*

capitalize *verb*
ALSO SPELLED: esp. *Brit.* **-ise**
- "CAPPA t'll ize"
- begin (a word) with a capital letter.
- [as CAPITAL]
- **capitalization** *noun* (also esp. *Brit.* **-isation**)

capitation *noun*
- "cappa TAY sh'n"
- a tax or fee at a set rate per person.
- [French *capitation* or Late Latin *capitatio* poll tax, from *caput* head]

Capitol *noun*
- "CAP it 'll"
- a building housing a legislature in the US, esp. the federal legislative building in Washington.

• [Latin *capitolium* from *caput* head]
HOMOPHONES: *capital*

capitular *adjective*
• "kuh PITCH'll ur"
• of or relating to a cathedral chapter.
• [Late Latin *capitularis* from Latin *capitulum* chapter]

capitulate *verb*
• "kuh PITCH'll ate"
• surrender, esp. on stated conditions.
• [medieval Latin *capitulare* draw up under headings, from Latin *caput* head]
• **capitulation** *noun*
• **capitulator** *noun*
• **capitulatory** *adjective*

capitulum *noun*
• "kuh PITCH'll um"
• an inflorescence with flowers clustered together like a head, as in the daisy family.
• [Latin, diminutive of *caput* head]

capo[1] *noun*
• "CAY poe"
• a device secured across the neck of a fretted instrument to raise equally the tuning of all strings by the required amount.
• [Italian *capo tasto* head stop]

capo[2] *noun*
• "CAPPO"
• the head of a crime syndicate, esp. the Mafia, or one of its branches.
• [Italian, = 'boss' from Latin *caput* head]

capoeira *noun*
• "cappo AIR uh"
• a system of physical discipline and movement emphasizing leg and foot movements and performed inside a circle formed by onlookers, originating among Brazilian slaves, treated as a martial art and dance form.
• [Brazilian Portuguese]
• **capoeirista** *noun* "cappo air EESTA"

capon *noun*
• "CAY pon"
• a cockerel castrated and fattened for eating.
• [Old English from Anglo-French *capun*, Old French *capon*, ultimately from Latin *capo -onis*]
• **caponize** *verb* (also esp. *Brit.* **-ise**)

caponata *noun*
• "cap 'n ATTA"
• a dish of eggplant, olives, and onions in a tomato sauce, seasoned with herbs, served typically as an appetizer.
• [Italian *capponata*]

capote *noun*
ALSO SPELLED: **capot**
• "kuh POT"
• a long coat with a hood, esp. (in Canada) tied with a colourful sash.
• [French, diminutive of *cape* cape]

Cappadocian *adjective*
• "cappa DOE sh'n"
• of or relating to Cappadocia, an ancient region in what is now Turkey.

cappuccino *noun*
• "cappa CHEENO"
• espresso coffee with milk made frothy with pressurized steam.
• [Italian, = CAPUCHIN]

capri *noun*
• "kuh PREE"
• women's close-fitting, tapered pants or leggings extending to just above the ankles.
• [the island of *Capri* south of Naples, Italy]

capriccio *noun*
• "kuh PREECHY oh"
• a lively and usu. short musical composition.
• [Italian, from *capo* head + *riccio* hedgehog, literally 'head with the hair standing on end', hence 'horror', later 'a sudden start' (influenced by *capra* 'goat', associated with frisky movement)]

capriccioso *adverb*
• "kuh preechy OH so"
• in a free and impulsive style.
• [Italian, = capricious]

caprice *noun*
• "kuh PREECE"
• an unaccountable or whimsical change of mind or conduct.
• [French from Italian CAPRICCIO]
• **capricious** *adjective* "kuh PREESH us" or "kuh PRISH us"
• **capriciously** *adverb*
• **capriciousness** *noun*

Capricorn *noun*
• "CAPPRA corn"
• the tenth sign of the zodiac.
• [Old French *capricorne* from Latin *capricornus* from *caper -pri* goat + *cornu* horn]
• **Capricornian** *noun*

caprine *adjective*
• "CAP rine"
• of or like a goat.
• [Latin *caprinus* from *caper -pri* goat]

capriole *noun*
• "CAP ree ole"
• a leap or caper.
• [French from Italian *capriola* leap, ultimately from Latin *caper -pri* goat]

capsaicin *noun*
• "cap SAY a sin"
• a compound responsible for the pungency of capsicums.
• [as CAPSICUM]

Capsian *adjective*
• "CAPSY 'n"
• of or relating to a mesolithic culture

surrounding the salt lakes of Tunisia (8000–2700 BC).
• [Latin *Capsa* = Gafsa in Tunisia]

capsicum *noun*
• "CAP sick 'm"
• any plant of the genus *Capsicum*, having edible capsular fruits containing many seeds, esp. *C. annuum*, varieties of which yield paprikas, green or red peppers, chilies, and cayenne pepper.
• [modern Latin, perhaps from Latin *capsa* box]

capsid *noun*
• "CAP sid"
• the protein coat or shell of a virus.
• [French *capside* from Latin *capsa* box]

capstan *noun*
• "CAPS t'n"
• a thick revolving cylinder with a vertical axis, for winding an anchor cable or a halyard etc.
• [Provençal *cabestan*, ultimately from Latin *capistrum* halter, from *capere* seize]

capsule *noun*
• "CAPS 'll" or "CAPS y'll"
• a small soluble case of gelatin enclosing a dose of medicine and swallowed with it.
• [French from Latin *capsula* from *capsa* case]
• **capsular** *adjective*
• **capsulate** *adjective*
• **capsulated** *adjective*

capsulize *verb*
ALSO SPELLED: esp. *Brit.* **-ise**
• "CAPS 'll ize"
• put (information etc.) in compact form.
• [as CAPSULE]

captain *noun*
• "CAP t'n"
• a chief or leader.
• [Old French *capitain* from Late Latin *capitaneus* chief, from Latin *caput capit-* head]
• **captaincy** *noun*
• **captainship** *noun*

captious *adjective*
• "CAP sh'ss"
• given to finding fault or raising petty objections.
• [Old French *captieux* or Latin *captiosus* from *capere capt-* take]
• **captiously** *adverb*
• **captiousness** *noun*

captor *noun*
• "CAP tor" or "CAPTER"
• a person who takes or holds (a person etc.) captive.
• [Latin from *capere capt-* take]

Capuchin *noun*
• "CAP yoo chin" or "CAP oo shin" or "CAP oo chin"
• a Franciscan friar of a branch established in 1529 to re-emphasize the ideals of poverty and austerity.
• [French from Italian *cappuccino* from *cappuccio* cowl, from *cappa* cape]

capybara *noun*
• "cappy BAR uh"
• a very large semi-aquatic rodent of the genus *Hydrochoerus*, resembling a guinea pig, native to S America.
• [Tupi]

carabineer *noun*
ALSO SPELLED: **carabinier**
• "care a bin EER"
• a soldier whose principal weapon is a carbine.
• [French *carabinier* from *carabine* carbine, weapon of the *carabin* mounted musketeer]

carabiner *noun*
ALSO SPELLED: **karabiner**
• "care a BEENER"
• a clip with a spring latch used for securing a rope in climbing or mountaineering.
• [German *Karabiner* from *Karabinerhaken* carbine hook: as CARABINEER]

carabiniere *noun*
• "kerra bin YARE ay"
• a member of an Italian army corps which serves as one of Italy's three national police forces.
• [Italian]

caracal *noun*
• "CARE a cal"
• a lynx-like feline, *Felis caracal*, native to N Africa and SW Asia, having tufted black ears.
• [French or Spanish from Turkish *karakulak* from *kara* black + *kulak* ear]

caracara *noun*
• "car uh CAR uh"
• any of several mainly tropical American birds of prey related to falcons but resembling vultures.
• [Spanish or Portuguese *caracará*, from Tupi-Guarani (imitative)]

caracole *noun*
• "CARE a cole"
• a horse's half turn to the right or left.
• [French, from *caracol* snail's shell, spiral]

carafe *noun*
• "kuh RAFF"
• a wide-mouthed glass container for beverages, esp. water or wine.
• [French from Italian *caraffa*, ultimately from Arabic *ġarrāfa* drinking vessel]

caragana *noun*
• "care a GANNA"
• any Asian leguminous shrub of the genus *Caragana*, esp. the Siberian pea (*C. arborescens*), widely planted as hedging.
• [of Turkic origin; compare Kyrgyz *karaghan* Siberian pea]

caramba *interjection*
• "kuh RUM buh"
• expressing exasperation, surprise, etc.
• [Spanish]

carambola *noun*
• "care 'm BOLE uh"
• a small tree, *Averrhoa carambola*, native to SE Asia, bearing golden-yellow ribbed fruit.
• [Portuguese, prob. from Marathi *karambal*]

caramel *noun*
• "CARE a mel" or "CAR m'll"
• sugar or syrup heated until it turns brown, then used as a flavouring, garnish, or colour in food or drink.
• [French from Spanish *caramelo*]
• **caramelization** *noun* (also esp. *Brit.* **-isation**)
• **caramelize** *verb* (also esp. *Brit.* **-ise**)

carapace *noun*
• "CARE a pace"
• the hard upper shell of a turtle or a crustacean.
• [French from Spanish *carapacho*]

Caraquet *noun*
• "CAR a ket"
• *Cdn* a small variety of edible oyster found in the waters off New Brunswick.
• [*Caraquet* in NE New Brunswick]

carat *noun*
• "CARE ut"
• a unit of weight for precious stones, now equivalent to 200 milligrams.
• [French from Italian *carato* from Arabic *ķīrāṭ* weight of four grains, from Greek *keration* fruit of the carob (diminutive of *keras* horn)]
HOMOPHONES: *caret, carrot, karat*

caravan *noun*
• "CARE a van"
• a company of people with vehicles or pack animals travelling together, esp. across a desert.
• [French *caravane* from Persian *kārwān*]

caravanserai *noun*
• "care a VANSA rye"
• (in the Middle East) an inn with a central court where caravans may rest.
• [Persian *kārwānsarāy* from *sarāy* palace]

caravel *noun*
• "CAR a vell"
• a small light fast ship, used from the 15th–17th c. chiefly by the Spanish and Portuguese.
• [French *caravelle* from Portuguese *caravela* from Greek *karabos* horned beetle, light ship]

caraway *noun*
• "CARE a way"
• an umbelliferous plant, *Carum carvi*, bearing clusters of tiny white flowers.
• [prob. Old Spanish *alcarahueya* from Arabic *alkarāwiyā*, perhaps from Greek *karon, kareon* cumin]

carbamazepine *noun*
• "carba MAY zuh peen"
• a synthetic compound of the benzodiazepine class, used as an anticonvulsant and analgesic drug.
• [from 'carbon' and AMIDE, on the pattern of *benzodiazepine*]

carbohydrate *noun*
• "carbo HY drate"
• any of a large group of energy-producing organic compounds containing carbon, hydrogen, and oxygen, e.g. starch, glucose, and other sugars.
• ['carbon' + HYDRATE]

carbolic *noun*
• "car BOLLIC"
• phenol, esp. when used as a disinfectant.
• [from 'carbon' from French *carbone* from Latin *carbo -onis* charcoal]

carbonaceous *adjective*
• "carb'n AY sh'ss"
• consisting of or containing carbon.
• [French *carbone* from Latin *carbo -onis* charcoal + adjective suffix *-aceus* of the nature of]

carbonado *noun*
• "carba NAY doe"
• a dark opaque or impure kind of diamond used as an abrasive, for drilling etc.
• [Portuguese]

carbonara *adjective*
• "carba NAR uh"
• designating a sauce for pasta made of eggs, cream, Parmesan cheese, and pieces of bacon.
• [Italian, perhaps from *carbonata* salt pork grilled over a charcoal fire, after *carbonara*, dialect = charcoal burner's wife]

carbonate *noun*
• "CARB'n ate"
• a salt of carbonic acid.
• [French *carbonat* from modern Latin *carbonatum* from *carbo -onis* charcoal]
• **carbonation** *noun*

carbonated *adjective*
• "CARB 'n ated"
• (of a beverage) having an effervescent quality due to the presence of carbon dioxide.
• [as CARBONATE]

carbonic *adjective*
• "car BONNIC"
• containing carbon.
• [as CARBONATE]

carboniferous *adjective*
• "carb'n IFFER us"
• producing carbon or coal.
• [as CARBONATE + Latin *-fer* producing, from *ferre* bear]

carbonnade *noun*
• "carba NAD"

• a Belgian dish of beef and onions braised in beer.
• [French, denoting a piece of meat or fish cooked on hot coals]

carbonyl *noun*
• "CARB'N ill"
• the divalent radical CO.
• [as CARBONATE]

carboxyl *noun*
• "car BOX 'll"
• the monovalent acid radical (-COOH), present in most organic acids.
• [as CARBONATE + OXYGEN]
• **carboxylic** *adjective* "car bock SILLIC"

carboy *noun*
• "CAR boy"
• a large bottle, usu. of coloured glass and protected by a frame, used chiefly for holding acids and other corrosive liquids.
• [Persian *ḳarāba* large glass flagon]

carbuncle *noun*
• "CAR buncle"
• a collection of boils forming a large abscess.
• [Old French *charbucle* etc. from Latin *carbunculus* small coal, from *carbo* coal]
• **carbuncular** *adjective* "car BUNKYA lur"

carburet *verb*
• "CARBER ate"
• charge (air etc.) with a spray of liquid hydrocarbon fuel, esp. in an internal combustion engine.
• [earlier *carbure* from French from Latin *carbo* charcoal]
• **carburation** *noun*

carburetor *noun*
• "CARBER ater"
• an apparatus for controlling the mixture of gasoline and air in an internal combustion engine.
• [as CARBURET]

carcajou *noun*
• "CARCA joo" or "CARCA zhoo"
• a wolverine.
• [Canadian French, prob. of Algonquian origin]

carcass *noun*
ALSO SPELLED: *Brit.* also **carcase**
• "CAR k'ss"
• the dead body of an animal, esp. one slaughtered for its meat.
• [Anglo-French *carcois* (Old French *charcois*) & from French *carcasse*: ultimate origin unknown]

carcinogen *noun*
• "car SINNA j'n"
• any substance that produces cancer.
• [as CARCINOMA + GENESIS]
• **carcinogenic** *adjective*
• **carcinogenicity** *noun*
"car sinna juh NISSA tee"

carcinogenesis *noun*
• "car sinna JENNA sis"
• the production of cancer.
• [as CARCINOGEN]

carcinoma *noun*
• "carsa NOMA"
• a cancer, esp. one arising in epithelial tissue.
• [Latin from Greek *karkinōma* from *karkinos* crab]
• **carcinomatous** *adjective*

cardamom *noun*
• "CARDA mum"
• an aromatic SE Asian plant, *Elettaria cardamomum*.
• [Latin *cardamomum* or French *cardamome* from Greek *kardamōmon* from *kardamon* cress + *amōmon* a spice plant]

cardiac *adjective*
• "CARDY ack"
• of or relating to the heart.
• [French *cardiaque* or Latin *cardiacus* from Greek *kardiakos* from *kardia* heart]

cardigan *noun*
• "CARDA g'n"
• a knitted jacket or sweater fastening down the front, usu. with long sleeves.
• [7th Earl of *Cardigan* d.1868]

cardinal *noun*
• "CAR d'n 'll"
• a leading dignitary of the Roman Catholic Church, one of the college electing the Pope.
• [Old French from Latin *cardinalis* from *cardo -inis* hinge]
• **cardinalate** *noun*
• **cardinalship** *noun*

cardiogram *noun*
• "CARDY oh gram"
• = ELECTROCARDIOGRAM.
• [as CARDIAC + Greek *gramma* thing written]

cardiograph *noun*
• "CARDY oh graff"
• = ELECTROCARDIOGRAPH.
• [as CARDIAC + Greek *graphia* writing]
• **cardiographer** *noun*
• **cardiography** *noun*

cardiology *noun*
• "cardy OLLA jee"
• the branch of medicine concerned with diseases and abnormalities of the heart.
• [as CARDIAC + Greek *logos* word]
• **cardiologist** *noun*

cardiomyopathy *noun*
• "cardy oh my OPPA thee" (with "TH" as in *THIN*)
• chronic disease of the heart muscle.
• [as CARDIAC + Greek *mus, mu-* muscle + *patheia* suffering]

cardiopulmonary *adjective*
• "cardy oh PUL m'n airy"

• of or relating to the heart and the lungs.
• [as CARDIAC + PULMONARY]

cardiovascular *adjective*
• "cardy oh VASS kyuh lur"
• of or relating to the heart and blood vessels.
• [as CARDIAC + VASCULAR]

cardoon *noun*
• "car DOON"
• a thistle-like plant, *Cynara cardunculus*, related to the artichoke, with leaves used as a vegetable.
• [French *cardon*, ultimately from Latin *cardu(u)s* thistle]

caress *verb*
• "kuh RESS"
• touch or stroke gently or lovingly.
• [French *caresse* (n.), *caresser* (v.), from Italian *carezza*, ultimately from Latin *carus* dear]
• **caressingly** *adverb*

caret *noun*
• "CARE it"
• a mark (^) indicating a proposed insertion in printing or writing.
• [Latin, = is lacking]
HOMOPHONES: *carat, carrot, karat*

Carib *noun*
• "CARE ib"
• an aboriginal inhabitant of the southern W Indies or the adjacent coasts.
• [Spanish *Caribe* from Haitian]

Caribbean *noun*
• "care a BEE 'n" or "kuh RIBBY 'n"
• the part of the Atlantic between the southern W Indies and Central America.

caribou *noun*
• "CARE a boo"
• any of several subspecies of reindeer (*Rangifer tarandus*) inhabiting N Canada and Alaska, esp. the woodland or barren ground caribou.
• [Canadian French from Mi'kmaq *γalipu*, lit. 'snow-shoveller']

caricature *noun*
• "CARE ick a chur"
• a grotesque usu. comic representation of a person by exaggeration of characteristic traits, in a picture, writing, or mime.
• [French from Italian *caricatura* from *caricare* load, exaggerate, from Late Latin *car(ri)care* load, from Latin *carrus* car]
• **caricatural** *adjective*
• **caricaturist** *noun*

caries *noun*
• "CARE eez"
• decay and crumbling of a tooth or bone.
• [Latin]

carillon *noun*
• "CARE a lun" or "CARE a lawn"
• a set of bells sounded either from a keyboard or mechanically.
• [French from Old French *quarregnon* peal of four bells, alteration of Romanic *quaternio* from Latin *quattuor* four]
• **carillonneur** *noun* "care a lawn UR"

carina *noun*
• "kuh REENA"
• a keel-shaped structure, esp. the ridge of a bird's breastbone.
• [Latin, = keel]
• **carinal** *adjective*

carinate *adjective*
• "CARE in ate"
• (of a bird) having a deep keel-like ridge on the breastbone for the attachment of flight muscles.
• [Latin *carinatus* having a keel, from *carina* keel]

carioca *noun*
• "kerry OH kuh"
• a Brazilian dance like the samba.
• [Portuguese]

cariogenic *adjective*
• "kerry oh JENNIC"
• causing caries.
• [as CARIES + GENESIS]

carious *adjective*
• "KERRY us"
• (of bones or teeth) decayed.
• [Latin *cariosus* from *caries* decay]

carline *noun*
• "CAR lin"
• a Eurasian plant of the genus *Carlina*, esp. the thistle-like *C. vulgaris*.
• [French from medieval Latin *carlina* perhaps for *cardina* (Latin *carduus* thistle), associated with *Carolus Magnus* Charlemagne, Holy Roman Emperor d.814]

Carlovingian *adjective*
• "car luh VINJY 'n"
• of or relating to the second Frankish dynasty, founded by Charlemagne (d.814).
• [French *carlovingien* from *Karl* Charles, after *mérovingien* (see MEROVINGIAN)]

Carmelite *noun*
• "CARMA lite"
• a member of an order of mendicant friars (also known as the White Friars), founded in the 12th c.
• [French *Carmelite* or medieval Latin *carmelita* from Mount *Carmel* near Haifa, Israel, where the order was founded]

carminative *adjective*
• "car MINNA tiv" or "CARMA nuh tiv"
• relieving flatulence.
• [French *carminatif -ive* or medieval Latin *carminare* heal (by incantation) from Latin *carmen* song]

carmine *adjective*
• "CAR mine"
• of a vivid crimson colour.
• [French *carmin* or medieval Latin *carminium*

perhaps from *carmesinum* crimson + *minium* cinnabar]

carnage *noun*
- "CAR nidge"
- the killing of many people, animals, etc., usu. with much bloodshed.
- [French from Italian *carnaggio* from medieval Latin *carnaticum* from Latin *caro carnis* flesh]

carnal *adjective*
- "CARN'Il"
- of the body or flesh; worldly.
- [Late Latin *carnalis* from *caro carnis* flesh]
- **carnality** *noun* "car NALA tee"
- **carnally** *adverb*

carnassial *adjective*
- "car NASSY 'Il"
- (of a carnivore's upper premolar and lower molar teeth) adapted for shearing flesh.
- [French *carnassier* carnivorous]

carnauba *noun*
- "car NOW buh" or "car NOBBA" or "car NO buh"
- a fan palm, *Copernicia cerifera*, native to NE Brazil.
- [Portuguese]

carnelian *noun*
- "car NEELY 'n"
- a dull red or reddish-white variety of chalcedony.
- [Old French *corneline*; *car-* after Latin *caro carnis* flesh]

carnival *noun*
- "CARNA v'Il"
- the festivities usual during the period before Lent in some countries.
- [Italian *carne-*, *carnovale* from medieval Latin *carnelevarium* etc. Shrovetide, from Latin *caro carnis* flesh + *levare* put away]
- **carnivalesque** *adjective* "carna v'Il ESK"

carnivore *noun*
- "CARNA vore"
- any mammal of the order Carnivora (cats, dogs, bears, seals, etc.) with powerful jaws and teeth adapted for stabbing, tearing, and eating flesh.
- [French from Latin *carnivorus* from *caro carnis* flesh + Latin *-vorus* from *vorare* devour]
- **carnivorous** *adjective* "car NIVVER us"
- **carnivorously** *adverb*
- **carnivorousness** *noun*
- **carnivory** *noun*

carob *noun*
- "CARE ub"
- an evergreen tree, *Ceratonia siliqua*, native to the Mediterranean, bearing edible pods.
- [obsolete French *carobe* from medieval Latin *carrubia*, *-um* from Arabic *ḵarrūba*]

carol *noun*
- "CARE 'Il"
- a joyous song or hymn, esp. one celebrating Christmas.
- [Old French *carole*, *caroler*, of unknown origin]
- **caroller** *noun* (also *US* **caroler**)

HOMOPHONES: *carrel*

Carolingian *adjective*
- "care a LINJY 'n"
- of or relating to the second Frankish dynasty, founded by Charlemagne (d.814).
- [French *carlovingien* from *Karl* Charles, after *mérovingien* (see MEROVINGIAN): re-formed after Latin *Carolus*]

Carolinian *adjective*
- "care a LINNY 'n"
- of or relating to a forest region extending from S Ontario to North and South Carolina, characterized by broadleaf deciduous trees such as the tulip tree, magnolia, and eastern flowering dogwood.

carom *noun*
- "CARE um"
- (in billiards) a shot in which the cue ball strikes two other balls in succession.
- [abbreviation of *carambole* from Spanish *carambola*, apparently from *bola* ball]

carotene *noun*
- "CARE a teen"
- any of several orange-coloured plant pigments found in carrots, tomatoes, etc., acting as a source of vitamin A.
- [German *Carotin* from Latin *carota* carrot, from Greek *karōton*]

carotenoid *noun*
- "kuh ROT'n oid"
- any of a class of mainly yellow, orange, or red fat-soluble pigments, including carotene, giving colour to plant parts, e.g. ripe tomatoes, autumn leaves.
- [as CAROTENE]

carotid *noun*
- "kuh ROTTID"
- each of the two main arteries carrying blood to the head and neck.
- [French *carotide* or modern Latin *carotides* from Greek *karōtides* (pl.) from *karoō* stupefy (compression of these arteries being thought to cause stupor)]

carouse *verb*
- "kuh ROUSE" ("ROUSE" rhymes with *VOWS*)
- participate in a noisy or lively drinking party.
- [originally as adverb = right out, in phrase *drink carouse* from German *gar aus trinken*]
- **carousal** *noun*
- **carouser** *noun*

carousel *noun*
- "care a SELL" or "CARE a sell"
- a large revolving device in a playground, for children to ride on.
- [French *carrousel* from Italian *carosello*]

carpaccio *noun*
• "car PATCHY oh"
• a thin strip of marinated raw meat, esp. beef, as an appetizer.
• [V. *Carpaccio*, Italian painter d. *c.*1525, who used a distinctive red colour like that of raw beef]

carpal *adjective*
• "CARP 'll"
• of or relating to the bones in the wrist.
• [as CARPUS]
HOMOPHONES: *carpel*

carpel *noun*
• "CARP 'll"
• the female reproductive organ of a flower, consisting of a stigma, style, and ovary.
• [French *carpelle* or modern Latin *carpellum* from Greek *karpos* fruit]
• **carpellary** *adjective* "CARP 'll airy"
HOMOPHONES: *carpal*

carpology *noun*
• "car POLLA jee"
• the study of the structure of fruit and seeds.
• [Greek *karpos* fruit + *logos* word]

carpus *noun*
• "CARP us"
• the small bones between the forelimb and metacarpus in terrestrial vertebrates, forming the wrist in humans.
• [modern Latin from Greek *karpos* wrist]

carrack *noun*
• "CARE uck"
• a large armed merchant ship.
• [French *caraque* from Spanish *carraca* from Arabic *ḳarāḳir*]

carrageen *noun*
ALSO SPELLED: **carragheen**
• "CARE a geen" (with "G" as in *GEEK*)
• an edible purplish-red seaweed, *Chondrus crispus*, of the northern hemisphere.
• [origin uncertain: perhaps from Irish *cosáinín carraige* carrageen, lit. 'little stem of the rock']

carrageenan *noun*
ALSO SPELLED: **carrageenin**
• "care a GEEN 'n" (with "G" as in *GEEK*)
• a mixture of polysaccharides extracted from carrageen or similar seaweed and used as a gelling, thickening, and emulsifying agent in food products.
• [as CARRAGEEN]

carrel *noun*
• "CARE 'll"
• a small cubicle or desk with high sides in a library, designed for individual study.
• [Old French *carole*, medieval Latin *carola*, of unknown origin]
HOMOPHONES: *carol*

carriage *noun*
• "CARE idge"
• a wheeled passenger vehicle, esp. one with four wheels and pulled by horses.
• [Old Northern French *cariage* from *carier* carry]

carriageway *noun*
• "CARE idge way"
• the part of a road intended for vehicles.
• [as CARRIAGE + 'way']

carriole *noun*
ALSO SPELLED: **cariole**
• "KERRY ole"
• a small open carriage for one person.
• [French from Italian *carriuola*, diminutive of *carro* car]

carrion *noun*
• "KERRY 'n"
• dead putrefying flesh.
• [Anglo-French & Old Northern French *caroine*, *-oigne*, Old French *charoigne*, ultimately from Latin *caro* flesh]

carroty *adjective*
• "CARE ut ee"
• (of hair) orangey-red.
• [French *carotte* carrot from Latin *carota* from Greek *karōton*]

carspiel *noun*
• "CAR speel"
• *Cdn* a bonspiel in which curlers compete for a car or cars.
• ['car' + BONSPIEL]

cartel *noun*
• "car TELL"
• a group of manufacturers or suppliers who collude to maintain prices at a high level, and control production, marketing arrangements, etc.
• [German *Kartell* from French *cartel* from Italian *cartello* diminutive of *carta* card]
• **cartelize** *verb* (also esp. *Brit.* **-ise**) "CARTA lize"

Cartesian *adjective*
• "car TEE zh'n" or "car TEEZY 'n"
• of or relating to the French philosopher and mathematician René Descartes (d.1650), his philosophy, or his mathematical methods.
• [modern Latin *Cartesianus* from *Cartesius*, Latinized form of *Descartes*]
• **Cartesianism** *noun*

Carthaginian *adjective*
• "cartha JINNY 'n"
• of or relating to the ancient N African city of Carthage.

Carthusian *noun*
• "carth OO zh'n" or "carth YOOZY 'n"
• a Christian monk or nun of a strictly contemplative order founded at Chartreuse in SE France in 1084, leading a hermitic way of life remarkable for its austerity and self-denial.

• [medieval Latin *Carthusianus* from Latin *Cart(h)usia* Chartreuse]

cartilage *noun*
• "CARTA lidge"
• a firm, elastic, semi-opaque connective tissue of the vertebrate body; gristle.
• [French from Latin *cartilago -ginis*]
• **cartilaginous** *adjective* "carta LADGE 'n us"

cartography *noun*
• "car TOGGRA fee"
• the science or practice of map drawing.
• [French *cartographie* from *carte* map, card]
• **cartographer** *noun*
• **cartographic** *adjective*
• **cartographical** *adjective*

cartomancy *noun*
• "CARTA man see"
• fortune-telling by interpreting a random selection of playing cards.
• [French *cartomancie* from *carte* 'card' + Greek *manteia* divination]

cartouche *noun*
• "car TOOSH"
• a scroll-like ornament, e.g. the volute of an Ionic capital.
• [French, = cartridge, from Italian *cartoccio* from *carta* card]

cartwright *noun*
• "CART rite"
• a maker of carts.
• ['cart' + WRIGHT]

caruncle *noun*
• "CARE 'n k'll" or "kuh RUNK'll"
• a fleshy excrescence, e.g. a turkey's wattles or the red prominence at the inner angle of the eye.
• [obsolete French from Latin *caruncula* from *caro carnis* flesh]
• **caruncular** *adjective* "kuh RUNK yuh lur"

caryatid *noun*
• "kerry AT id"
• a pillar in the form of a draped female figure, supporting an entablature.
• [French *caryatide* from Italian *cariatide* or Latin from Greek *karuatis -idos* priestess at Caryae (*Karuai*) in S Greece]

caryopsis *noun*
• "kerry OP sis"
• a dry one-seeded indehiscent fruit, as in wheat and corn.
• [modern Latin from Greek *karuon* nut + *opsis* appearance]

casaba *noun*
• "kuh SOBBA"
• a type of melon, *Cucumis melo inodorus*, having a yellow wrinkled skin and whitish flesh.
• [prob. from *Kasaba*, former name of Turgutlu, a town in W Turkey]

Casanova *noun*
• "cassa NOVA"
• a man notorious for seducing women.
• [G.J. *Casanova* de Seingalt, Italian adventurer d.1798]

casbah *noun*
ALSO SPELLED: **kasbah**
• "CAZZ bah"
• the citadel of a N African city.
• [French from Arabic *kas(a)ba* citadel]

cascade *noun*
• "cass CADE"
• a small waterfall, esp. forming one in a series or part of a large broken waterfall.
• [French from Italian *cascata* from *cascare* to fall, ultimately from Latin *casus* fall]

cascara *noun*
• "cass CAR uh"
• the dried bark of the western N American cascara buckthorn, *Rhamnus purshiana*, used as a purgative.
• [Spanish *cascara (sagrada)*, = (sacred) bark]

casein *noun*
• "CASE een" or "CAY see een"
• the main protein in milk, esp. in coagulated form as in cheese.
• [Latin *caseus* cheese]

cashew *noun*
• "CASH oo" or "ca SHOO"
• a bushy evergreen tree, *Anacardium occidentale*, native to Central and S America, bearing kidney-shaped nuts attached to fleshy fruits.
• [Portuguese from Tupi *(a)caju*]
HOMOPHONES: *cachou*

cashier *noun*
• "cash EER"
• a person handling customer payments in a store.
• [Dutch *cassier* or French *caissier* from obsolete French *casse* box or Italian *cassa* from Latin *capsa* case]

cashmere *noun*
• "CAZH meer" or "CASH meer"
• a fine soft wool, esp. that of a Kashmir goat.
• [*Kashmir* on the border of India and NE Pakistan]

cashspiel *noun*
• "CASH speel"
• *Cdn* a bonspiel in which curlers compete for cash prizes.
• ['cash' + BONSPIEL]

casino *noun*
• "kuh SEENO"
• a public room or building for gambling.
• [Italian, diminutive of *casa* house, from Latin *casa* cottage]

casque *noun*
• "CASK"
• a helmet or helmet-like structure.

• [French from Spanish *casco*]
HOMOPHONES: *cask*

Cassandra *noun*
• "kuh SANDRA"
• a prophet of disaster, esp. one who is disregarded.
• [*Cassandra*, condemned by Apollo to prophesy correctly but not be believed]

cassata *noun*
• "kuh SOTTA"
• a type of ice cream containing candied or dried fruit and nuts.
• [Italian]

cassava *noun*
• "kuh SOVVA"
• the starchy tuberous root of a tropical tree, used as food in tropical countries.
• [earlier *cas(s)avi* etc., from Taino *casavi*, influenced by French *cassave*]

casserole *noun*
• "CASSER ole"
• a covered dish, usu. of earthenware or glass, in which food is cooked, esp. in an oven.
• [French from *cassole* diminutive of *casse* from Provençal *casa* from Late Latin *cattia* ladle, pan, from Greek *kuathion* diminutive of *kuathos* cup]

cassette *noun*
• "kuh SET"
• a sealed case containing a length of tape, ribbon, etc., ready for insertion in a machine.
• [French, diminutive of *casse* case]

cassia *noun*
• "CASSY uh" or "CASHA"
• any plant of the genus *Cassia*, esp. one yielding senna.
• [Latin from Greek *kasia* from Hebrew *ḳᵉṣî'āh* bark like cinnamon]

cassiope *noun*
• "kuh SYE a pee"
• any of several circumboreal heathers of the genus *Cassiope* with small white bell-shaped flowers.
• [from *Cassiopeia* in Greek mythology]

cassis *noun*
• "kuh SEECE"
• a syrupy blackcurrant liqueur.
• [French, = blackcurrant]

cassiterite *noun*
• "kuh SITTER ite"
• a naturally occurring ore of tin dioxide, from which tin is extracted.
• [Greek *kassiteros* tin]

cassock *noun*
• "CASS uck"
• a close-fitting garment with sleeves, fastened at the neck and reaching to the heels, worn under a surplice, alb, or gown by some clerics, members of choirs, etc.
• [French *casaque* long coat, from Italian *casacca* horseman's coat, prob. from Turkic: compare COSSACK]
• **cassocked** *adjective*

cassoulet *noun*
• "CASSOO lay"
• a stew of beans with pork, mutton, and either duck or goose.
• [French, diminutive of dialect *cassolo* stew pan, from Old Provençal *cassa*, related to CASSEROLE]

cassowary *noun*
• "CASSA werry"
• any large flightless Australasian bird of the genus *Casuarius*, with heavy body, stout legs, a wattled neck, and a bony crest on its forehead.
• [Malay *kasuārī*, *kasavārī*]

castanets *plural noun*
• "casta NETS"
• a pair of shell-shaped pieces of wood, plastic, or ivory clicked together with the fingers, esp. as a rhythmic accompaniment to Spanish dance.
• [Spanish *castañeta* diminutive of *castaña* from Latin *castanea* chestnut]

caste *noun*
• "CAST"
• any of the Hindu hereditary classes whose members have no social contact with other classes, but are socially equal with one another and often follow the same occupations.
• [Spanish and Portuguese *casta* lineage, race, breed, feminine of *casto* pure, CHASTE]
• **casteism** *noun*
HOMOPHONES: *cast*

castellan *noun*
• "CASS t'll 'n"
• the governor of a castle.
• [Old Northern French *castelain* from medieval Latin *castellanus* from Latin *castellum* diminutive of *castrum* fort]

castellated *adjective*
• "CASS t'll ated"
• having battlements.
• [medieval Latin *castellatus* from Latin *castellum* diminutive of *castrum* fort]

castigate *verb*
• "CASTA gate"
• rebuke or punish severely.
• [Latin *castigare* reprove, from *castus* pure]
• **castigation** *noun*
• **castigator** *noun*

Castilian *noun*
• "ca STILLY 'n"
• a native of Castile in central Spain.

castor *noun*
• "CASTER"
• a pungent, bitter-tasting, reddish-brown substance obtained from two perineal sacs of the beaver, formerly used in medicine and perfumes.

• [French or Latin from Greek *kastōr* beaver]
HOMOPHONES: *caster*

castoreum *noun*
• "cass TORY um"
• a pungent, bitter-tasting, reddish-brown substance obtained from two perineal sacs of the beaver, formerly used in medicine and perfumes.
• [French or Latin from Greek *kastōr* beaver]

castrato *noun*
• "cass TRATTO" or "cass TROTTO"
• a male singer castrated in boyhood so as to retain a soprano or alto voice.
• [Italian, past participle of *castrare* from Latin *castrare*]

casual *adjective*
• "CAZH oo 'll" or "CAZH yoo 'll"
• accidental; due to chance.
• [Old French *casuel* & Latin *casualis* from *casus* case]
• **casually** *adverb*
• **casualness** *noun*

casualization *noun*
ALSO SPELLED: esp. *Brit.* **-isation**
• "cazh oo 'll ize AY sh'n" or "cazh yoo 'll ize AY sh'n"
• the practice or process of transforming a workforce from one employed chiefly on permanent contracts to one engaged on a short-term temporary basis.
• [as CASUAL]
• **casualized** *adjective* (also esp. *Brit.* **-ised**)

casualty *noun*
• "CAZH oo 'll tee"
• a person killed or injured in a war or accident.
• [as CASUAL]

casualwear *noun*
• "CAZH oo 'll ware"
• casual clothing.
• [as CASUAL + 'wear']

casuarina *noun*
• "cass yoo a REENA"
• any tree of the genus *Casuarina*, native to Australia and the E Indies, with jointed branches resembling gigantic horsetail plants.
• [modern Latin *casuarius* cassowary (from the resemblance of the branches to the bird's feathers)]

casuist *noun*
• "CAZZ yoo ist" or "CAZH oo ist"
• a person, esp. a theologian, who resolves problems of conscience, duty, etc., often with clever but false reasoning.
• [French *casuiste* from Spanish *casuista* from Latin *casus* case]
• **casuistic** *adjective*
• **casuistical** *adjective*
• **casuistically** *adverb*
• **casuistry** *noun*

catabolism *noun*
• "kuh TAB'll izm"
• the breakdown of complex molecules in living organisms to form simpler ones with the release of energy; destructive metabolism.
• [Greek *katabolē* descent, from *kata* down + *bolē* from *ballō* throw]
• **catabolic** *adjective* "catta BOLLIC"

catachresis *noun*
• "catta CREE sis"
• an incorrect use of words.
• [Latin from Greek *katakhrēsis* from *kata* down + *khraomai* use]
• **catachrestic** *adjective* "catta CREE stick" or "catta CRESS tick"

cataclysm *noun*
• "CATTA clizm"
• a violent, esp. social or political, upheaval or disaster.
• [French *cataclysme* from Latin *cataclysmus* from Greek *kataklusmos* from *kata* down + *klusmos* flood, from *kluzō* wash]
• **cataclysmic** *adjective* "catta CLIZZ mick"
• **cataclysmically** *adverb*

catacomb *noun*
• "CATTA coam"
• an underground cemetery, esp. a Roman subterranean gallery with recesses for tombs.
• [French *catacombes* from Late Latin *catacumbas* (name given in the 5th c. to the cemetery of St. Sebastian near Rome), of unknown origin]

catadromous *adjective*
• "kuh TADRA muss"
• (of a fish, e.g. the eel) that swims down rivers to the sea to spawn.
• [Greek *katadromos* from *kata* down + *dromos* running]

catafalque *noun*
• "CATTA fawlk"
• a decorated wooden framework for supporting the coffin of a distinguished person during a funeral or while lying in state.
• [French from Italian *catafalco*, of unknown origin]

Catalan *noun*
• "CATTA lan"
• a native of Catalonia in NE Spain.
• [French from Spanish]

catalase *noun*
• "CATTA lace"
• an enzyme that catalyzes the reduction of hydrogen peroxide.
• [as CATALYSIS]

catalepsy *noun*
• "CATTA lepsy"
• a state of trance or seizure with loss of sensation and consciousness accompanied by rigidity of the body.
• [Greek *katalēpsis* from *kata* down + *lēpsis* seizure]
• **cataleptic** *adjective*

catalogne *noun*
• "catta LON yuh"
• *Cdn (Que.)* a kind of weaving using rags as the weft and widely spaced threads as the warp.
• [Canadian French]

catalogue *noun*
ALSO SPELLED: esp. *US* **catalog**
• "CATTA log"
• a complete list of items (e.g. articles for sale, books held by a library), usu. in alphabetical or other systematic order and often with a description of each.
• [French from Late Latin *catalogus* from Greek *katalogos* from *katalegō* enrol, from *kata* down + *legō* choose]
• **cataloguer** *noun* (also *US* **cataloger**)

Catalonian *noun*
• "catta LONEY 'n"
• a native or inhabitant of Catalonia in NE Spain.

catalpa *noun*
• "kuh TAL puh"
• any tree of the genus *Catalpa*, with heart-shaped leaves, trumpet-shaped flowers, and long pods, planted as ornamentals.
• [Creek]

catalysis *noun*
• "kuh TALA sis"
• the acceleration of a chemical or biochemical reaction by a catalyst.
• [Greek *katalusis* dissolution, from *kata* down + *luō* set free]
• **catalytic** *adjective* "catta LITTIC"
• **catalytically** *adverb*
• **catalyze** *verb* (also **catalyse**) "CATTA lize"

catalyst *noun*
• "CATTA list"
• a substance that, without itself undergoing any permanent chemical change, increases the rate of a reaction.
• [as CATALYSIS after *analyst*]

catamaran *noun*
• "catta muh RAN"
• a boat with twin hulls in parallel.
• [Tamil *kaṭṭumaram* tied wood]

catamount *noun*
• "CATTA mount"
• a lynx, leopard, cougar, or similar cat.
• [Middle English from *cat of the mountain*]

cataplexy *noun*
• "CATTA plexy"
• sudden temporary paralysis due to fright etc.
• [Greek *kataplēxis* stupefaction]
• **cataplectic** *adjective*

catapult *noun*
• "CATTA pult"
• a military machine worked by a lever and ropes for hurling large stones etc.
• [French *catapulte* or Latin *catapulta* from Greek *katapeltēs*, from *kata* down + *pallō* hurl]

cataract *noun*
• "CATTA ract"
• a large waterfall or cascade.
• [Latin *cataracta* from Greek *katarrhaktēs* down-rushing]

catarrh *noun*
• "kuh TAR"
• inflammation of the mucous membrane of the nose, air passages, etc.
• [French *catarrhe* from Late Latin *catarrhus* from Greek *katarrhous* from *katarrheō* flow down]
• **catarrhal** *adjective* "kuh TAR 'll"

catarrhine *noun*
• "CATTA rine"
• any of various primates having nostrils close together and directed downwards, e.g. baboons, chimpanzees, and humans.
• [Greek *kata* down + *rhis rhinos* nose]

catastrophe *noun*
• "kuh TASS truh fee"
• a great and usu. sudden disaster.
• [Greek *katastrophē*, from *kata* down + *strophē* turning, from *strephō* turn]
• **catastrophic** *adjective* "catta STROFFIC"
• **catastrophically** *adverb*

catastrophism *noun*
• "kuh TASS truh fizm"
• the theory that changes in the earth's crust have occurred in sudden violent and unusual events.
• [as CATASTROPHE]
• **catastrophist** *noun*

catatonia *noun*
• "catta TONY uh"
• schizophrenia with intervals of catalepsy and sometimes violence.
• [German *Katatonie*, from *kata* down + *tonos* tension, tone, from *teinō* stretch]
• **catatonic** *adjective* "catta TONNIC"

catawampus *adjective*
• "catta WOMPUS"
• askew, awry.
• [possibly from Scots *wampish* wave or flop about]

catawba *noun*
• "kuh TOBBA"
• a reddish variety of grape grown in the eastern US.
• [*Catawba* River in the Carolinas, from the Catawba native people]

catbrier *noun*
• "CAT brier" ("brier" rhymes with *DRYER*)
• a climbing vine of the genus *Smilax* of the lily family, with dark blue berries.
• ['cat' + BRIER]

catechesis *noun*
- "catta KEE sis"
- religious instruction.
- [as CATECHISM]
- **catechetic** *adjective* "catta KETTIC"
- **catechetical** *adjective* "catta KETTA k'll"
- **catechetically** *adverb*
- **catechetics** *noun*

catechin *noun*
- "CATTA chin"
- a crystalline compound which is the major constituent of catechu.
- [as CATECHU]

catechism *noun*
- "CATTA kizm"
- a summary of the principles of a Christian religion.
- [Church Latin *catechismus* from *catechizare* catechize, from ecclesiastical Greek *katēkhizō* from *katēkheō* make hear, from *kata* down + *ēkheō* sound]
- **catechist** *noun*
- **catechize** *verb* (also esp. *Brit.* **-ise**)
- **catechizer** *noun* (also esp. *Brit.* **-iser**)

catecholamine *noun*
- "catta COLA meen"
- any of various amines that function as neurotransmitters or hormones, e.g. dopamine, adrenalin.
- [CATECHU + AMINE]

catechu *noun*
- "CATTA choo"
- gambier or a similar vegetable extract containing tannin.
- [modern Latin from Malay *kachu*]

catechumen *noun*
- "catta KYOO m'n"
- a Christian convert under instruction before baptism.
- [Old French *catechumene* or Church Latin *catechumenus* from Greek *katēkheō*: see CATECHISM]

categorical *adjective*
- "catta GORRA k'll"
- unconditional, absolute; explicit, direct.
- [French *catégorique* or Late Latin *categoricus* from Greek *katēgorikos*: see CATEGORY]
- **categorically** *adverb*

categorize *verb*
ALSO SPELLED: esp. *Brit.* **-ise**
- "CATTA gur ize"
- place in a category or categories.
- [as CATEGORY]
- **categorization** *noun* (also esp. *Brit.* **-isation**)

category *noun*
- "CATTA gory"
- a class or division.
- [French *catégorie* or Late Latin *categoria* from Greek *katēgoria* statement, from *katēgoros* accuser]
- **categorial** *adjective*

catenary *noun*
- "CAT 'n airy"
- a curve formed by a uniform chain hanging freely from two points not in the same vertical line.
- [Latin *catenarius* from *catena* chain]

catenate *verb*
- "CAT 'n ate"
- connect like links of a chain.
- [Latin *catenare catenat-* (as CATENARY)]
- **catenation** *noun*

cateran *noun*
- "CATTER 'n"
- an irregular fighting man of the Highlands; a marauder.
- [medieval Latin *cateranus* & Gaelic *ceathairne* peasantry]

caterpillar *noun*
- "CATTER piller"
- the larva of a butterfly or moth.
- [perhaps Anglo-French var. of Old French *chatepelose*, lit. 'hairy cat', influenced by obsolete *piller* ravager]

caterwaul *verb*
- "CATTER wall"
- make the shrill howl of a cat.
- ['cat' + imitative *waul*]

Cathar *noun*
- "CATH ar"
- a member of a medieval sect which sought to achieve great spiritual purity.
- [medieval Latin *Cathari* (pl.) from Greek *katharoi* pure]
- **Catharism** *noun*
- **Catharist** *noun*

catharsis *noun*
- "kuh THAR sis" (with "TH" as in *THIN*)
- a release or relieving of emotions, esp. through drama or art.
- [modern Latin from Greek *katharsis* from *kathairō* cleanse]
- **cathartic** *adjective*
- **cathartically** *adverb*

cathedral *noun*
- "kuh THEED rull" (with "TH" as in *THIN*)
- the principal church of a diocese, containing the bishop's throne.
- [Old French *cathedral* or from Late Latin *cathedralis* from Latin from Greek *kathedra* seat]

catheter *noun*
- "CATHA tur"
- a tube for insertion into a body cavity or blood vessel for introducing or removing fluid etc.
- [Late Latin from Greek *kathetēr* from *kathiēmi* send down]
- **catheterization** *noun* (also esp. *Brit.* **-isation**)
- **catheterize** *verb* (also esp. *Brit.* **-ise**) "CATHA tur ize"
- **catheterized** *adjective* (also esp. *Brit.* **-ised**)

cathexis *noun*
• "kuh THEX iss" (with "TH" as in *THIN*)
• concentration of mental energy on a particular object.
• [Greek *kathexis* retention]
• **cathectic** *adjective*

cathode *noun*
• "CATH ode"
• the negative electrode in an electrolytic cell or electronic valve or tube.
• [Greek *kathodos* descent, from *kata* down + *hodos* way]
• **cathodic** *adjective*

Catholic *adjective*
• "CATH lick"
• of or relating to the part of the Christian Church acknowledging the Pope as its head.
• [Old French *catholique* or Late Latin *catholicus* from Greek *katholikos* universal, from *kata* in respect of + *holos* whole]
• **Catholicism** *noun* "kuh THOLLA sizm"

catholicity *noun*
• "cath'll ISSA tee"
• the quality of having sympathies with all or being all-embracing.
• [as CATHOLIC]
• **catholicly** *adverb*

Catholicize *verb*
ALSO SPELLED: esp. *Brit.* **-ise**
• "kuh THOLLA size"
• make or become Roman Catholic.
• [as CATHOLIC]

cation *noun*
• "CAT eye 'n" or "CAT eye on"
• a positively charged ion; an ion that is attracted to the cathode in electrolysis.
• [Greek *kata* down + *ion* neuter present participle of *eimi* go]
• **cationic** *adjective*

catlinite *noun*
• "CAT l'n ite"
• a hard red clay of the central US, used by American Aboriginal peoples to make tobacco pipes.
• [G. *Catlin*, US artist d.1872 + Greek *lithos* stone]

catoptric *adjective*
• "kuh TOP trick"
• of or relating to a mirror, a reflector, or reflection.
• [Greek *katoptrikos* from *katoptron* mirror]
• **catoptrics** *noun*

cattery *noun*
• "CATTER ee"
• a place where cats are boarded or bred.
• [from 'cat']

cattleya *noun*
• "CATLY uh"
• any epiphytic orchid of the genus *Cattleya*, cultivated for its showy flowers.
• [modern Latin from W. *Cattley*, English patron of botany d.1832]

Caucasian *adjective*
• "caw CAY zh'n"
• of or relating to the white or light-skinned race of human beings originally inhabiting Europe, N Africa, and the Middle East.
• [the *Caucasus*, the supposed place of origin of this race]

Caucasoid *adjective*
• "COCKA soid"
• of or relating to the Caucasian division of humankind.
• [as CAUCASIAN]

caucus *noun*
• "CAW cuss"
• the members of a legislative assembly belonging to a particular party.
• [18th-c., perhaps from Algonquian *cau'-cau'-as'u* adviser]
HOMOPHONES: *coccus*

caudal *adjective*
• "CODDLE"
• of or like a tail.
• [modern Latin *caudalis* from Latin *cauda* tail]
• **caudally** *adverb*
HOMOPHONES: *coddle*

caudate *adjective*
• "CAW date"
• having a tail or an appendage resembling a tail.
• [see CAUDAL]

caudillo *noun*
• "cow DEE yo" or "cow DEEL yo"
• (in Spanish-speaking countries) a military or political leader.
• [Spanish from Late Latin *capitellum*, diminutive of *caput* head]

caul *noun*
• Sounds like *CALL*
• the inner membrane enclosing a fetus.
• [perhaps from Old French *cale* small cap]
HOMOPHONES: *col*, *call*

cauldron *noun*
ALSO SPELLED: *US* also **caldron**
• "CALL drun"
• a large deep bowl-shaped vessel for boiling over an open fire.
• [Anglo-French *caudron*, ultimately from Latin *caldarium* hot bath, from *calidus* hot]

cauliflower *noun*
• "COLLY flower"
• a variety of cabbage with a large white flower head of immature buds in its centre.
• [earlier *cole-florie* etc. from obsolete French *chou fleuri* flowered cabbage, assimilated to COLE and 'flower']

caulk *verb*
ALSO SPELLED: esp. *US* **calk**

• "COCK"
• fill (a seam, crack, etc.) with a watertight or airtight material.
• [Old French dialect *cauquer* tread, press with force, from Latin *calcare* tread, from *calx* heel]
• **caulker** *noun* (also esp. *US* **calker**)
HOMOPHONES: *cock*

causal *adjective*
• "COZZ'll"
• of, forming, or expressing a cause or causes.
• [Latin *causa* cause]
• **causally** *adverb*

causality *noun*
• "cozz ALA tee"
• the relation of cause and effect.
• [as CAUSAL]

causation *noun*
• "cozz AY sh'n"
• the act of causing or producing an effect.
• [as CAUSAL]

causative *adjective*
• "COZZA tiv"
• acting as cause.
• [as CAUSAL]
• **causatively** *adverb*

causerie *noun*
• "COZE ur ee"
• an informal article or talk, esp. on a literary subject.
• [French from *causer* talk, from Latin *causari* to plead, dispute, from *causa* cause]

caustic *adjective*
• "COSS tick"
• capable of burning or corroding organic tissue.
• [Latin *causticus* from Greek *kaustikos* from *kaustos* burned, from *kaiō* burn]
• **caustically** *adverb*
• **causticity** *noun* "coss TISSA tee"

cauterize *verb*
ALSO SPELLED: esp. *Brit.* **-ise**
• "COTTER ize"
• burn or coagulate (tissue) with a heated instrument or caustic substance, esp. to stop bleeding.
• [French *cautériser* from Late Latin *cauterizare* from Greek *kautēriazō* from *kautērion* branding iron]
• **cauterization** *noun* (also esp. *Brit.* **-isation**)

cautery *noun*
• "COTTER ee"
• an instrument or caustic for cauterizing.
• [Latin *cauterium* from Greek *kautērion*: see CAUTERIZE]

caution *noun*
• "COSH'n"
• attention to safety; prudence, carefulness.
• [Old French from Latin *cautio -onis* from *cavēre caut-* take heed]
• **cautious** *adjective* "COSH us"
• **cautiously** *adverb*
• **cautiousness** *noun*

cautionary *adjective*
• "COSH'n airy"
• giving or serving as a warning.
• [as CAUTION]

cava *noun*
• "CAVVA"
• a Spanish sparkling wine made in the same way as champagne.
• [Spanish, = 'cellar']

cavalcade *noun*
• "cav'll CADE"
• a procession or formal company of riders, motor vehicles, etc.
• [French from Italian *cavalcata* from *cavalcare* ride, ultimately from Latin *caballus* pack horse]

cavalier *noun*
• "cavva LEER"
• a gallant or fashionable man, esp. escorting a woman.
• [French from Italian *cavaliere*: see CHEVALIER]
• **cavalierly** *adverb*

cavalry *noun*
• "CAV 'll ree"
• soldiers on horseback.
• [French *cavallerie* from Italian *cavalleria* from *cavallo* horse, from Latin *caballus*]
• **cavalryman** *noun* "CAV'll ree m'n"

cavatina *noun*
• "cavva TEENA"
• a short simple song.
• [Italian]

cavern *noun*
• "CAV urn"
• an underground hollow; a vast cave.
• [Old French *caverne* or from Latin *caverna* from *cavus* hollow]

cavernous *adjective*
• "CAV urn us"
• of or resembling a cavern in size or appearance.
• [as CAVERN]
• **cavernously** *adverb*

caviar *noun*
• "CAV ee arr"
• the pickled roe of sturgeon or other large fish, eaten as a delicacy.
• [early forms representing Italian *caviale*, French *caviar*, prob. from medieval Greek *khavíari*, related to Turkish *havyar*]

cavil *verb*
• "CAV 'll"
• make petty objections; carp.
• [French *caviller* from Latin *cavillari* from *cavilla* mockery]
• **caviller** *noun*

cavitation *noun*
• "cavva TAY sh'n"
• the formation and subsequent collapse of air bubbles or cavities in a liquid, caused by the rapid movement of a propeller etc. through it.
• [as CAVITY]

cavity *noun*
• "CAVVA tee"
• a hollow within a solid body.
• [French *cavité* or Late Latin *cavitas* from Latin *cavus* hollow]

cavort *verb*
• "kuh VORT"
• prance; jump, dance, or behave excitedly or happily.
• [perhaps from *curvet* a horse's leap, from Italian *corvetta* diminutive of *corva* curve, from Latin *curvus* bent]

cavy *noun*
• "CAY vee"
• any small rodent of the family Caviidae, native to S America and having a sturdy body and vestigial tail, including guinea pigs.
• [modern Latin *cavia* from Galibi *cabiai*]

cay *noun*
• "CAY"
• a low insular bank or reef of coral, sand, etc.
• [Spanish *cayo* shoal, reef, from French *quai*: see QUAY]

cayenne *noun*
• "kye YEN" or "KYE yen" or "cay EN" or "CAY en"
• a pungent red powder obtained from the ground fruit and seeds of various capsicums, used as a seasoning.
• [Tupi *kyynha* assimilated to *Cayenne*, the capital of French Guiana in northern S America]

Cayuga *noun*
• "cay OOGA" or "kye OOGA"
• a member of an Iroquoian people originally inhabiting central New York State, now living mainly on the Six Nations reserve near Brantford, Ont.
• [*Cayuga* Lake in New York]
• **Cayugan** *adjective*

cayuse *noun*
• "KYE ooss" or "CAY ooss"
• a feral or domesticated mustang or pony in the N American west, esp. one tamed by Aboriginal peoples.
• [*Cayuse*, an Aboriginal people of Washington and Oregon who domesticated horses]

ceanothus *noun*
• "see a NO thuss" (with "TH" as in *THIN*)
• any shrub of the N American genus *Ceanothus*, with small starry blue or white flowers.
• [modern Latin from Greek *keanōthos* kind of thistle]

cease *verb*
• "SEECE"
• stop; bring or come to an end.
• [Old French *cesser*, Latin *cessare* frequentative of *cedere cess-* yield]
• **ceaseless** *adjective*
• **ceaselessly** *adverb*

ceasefire *noun*
• "SEECE fire"
• an order to stop firing.
• [as CEASE + 'fire']

cecum *noun*
ALSO SPELLED: **caecum**
• "SEEK um"
• a pouch-like cavity at the junction of the small and large intestines.
• [Latin for *intestinum caecum* from *caecus* blind, translation of Greek *tuphlon enteron*]
• **cecal** *adjective* (also **caecal**)

cede *verb*
• "SEED"
• give up one's rights to or possession of.
• [French *céder* or Latin *cedere* yield]
HOMOPHONES: *seed*

cedi *noun*
• "SEEDY"
• the chief monetary unit of Ghana, equal to 100 pesewas.
• [Ghanaian]
HOMOPHONES: *seedy*

cedilla *noun*
• "suh DILLA"
• a mark written under the letter *c* in French and Portuguese to show that it is sibilant (as in *garçon*).
• [Spanish *cedilla*, diminutive of *zeda* from Greek *zēta* letter Z]

ceilidh *noun*
• "CAY lee"
• a party featuring traditional Scottish or Irish music, dancing, songs, and stories.
• [Gaelic, from Old Irish *céilide* visit, visiting, from *céile* companion]

ceiling *noun*
• "SEELING"
• the upper interior surface of a room or other similar compartment.
• [Middle English *celynge, siling*, perhaps ultimately from Latin *caelum* heaven or *celare* hide]
• **ceilinged** *adjective*
HOMOPHONES: *sealing*

cel *noun*
• "SELL"
• a transparent sheet of celluloid or cellulose acetate, which can be drawn on and used in combination with others in the production of animated films.
• [abbreviation of CELLULOID]
HOMOPHONES: *sell, cell*

celadon *noun*
• "SELLA don"
• a pale greyish shade of green.
• [French, from the name of a character in d'Urfé's *L'Astrée* (1607–27)]

celandine *noun*
• "SELL'n dine" or "SELL'n deen"
• either of two yellow-flowered plants, the greater celandine, *Chelidonium majus*, and the lesser celandine, *Ranunculus ficaria*.
• [Old French *celidoine*, ultimately from Greek *khelidōn* swallow: the flowering of the plant was associated with the arrival of swallows]

celebrant *noun*
• "SELLA br'nt"
• a person who performs a rite, esp. a priest who officiates at the Eucharist.
• [French *célébrant* or Latin *celebrare celebrant-*: *see* CELEBRATE]

celebrate *verb*
• "SELLA brate"
• mark (a festival or special event) with festivities etc.
• [Latin *celebrare* from *celeber -bris* frequented, honoured]
• **celebration** *noun*
• **celebrator** *noun*
• **celebratory** *adjective* "SEELA bruh tory"

celebrated *adjective*
• "SELLA brated"
• publicly honoured, widely known.
• [as CELEBRATE]

celebrity *noun*
• "suh LEBBRA tee"
• a well-known person.
• [French *célébrité* or Latin *celebritas* from *celeber*: see CELEBRATE]
• **celebrityhood** *noun*

celeriac *noun*
• "suh LERRY ack"
• a variety of celery with a swollen turnip-like root used as a vegetable.
• [as CELERY]

celerity *noun*
• "suh LERRA tee"
• swiftness (esp. of a living creature).
• [French *célérité* from Latin *celeritas -tatis* from *celer* swift]

celery *noun*
• "SELLER ee"
• an umbelliferous plant, *Apium graveolens*, with closely packed succulent leaf stalks used as a vegetable.
• [French *céleri* from Italian dialect *selleri* from Latin *selinum* from Greek *selinon* parsley]

celesta *noun*
• "suh LESTA"
• a small keyboard instrument resembling a glockenspiel, with hammers striking steel plates suspended over wooden resonators, giving an ethereal bell-like sound.
• [French *céleste* heavenly, from Latin *caelestis* from *caelum* heaven]

celestial *adjective*
• "suh LESS ch'll" or "suh LESTY 'll"
• heavenly; divinely good or beautiful; sublime.
• [Old French from medieval Latin *caelestialis* from Latin *caelestis*: see CELESTA]
• **celestially** *adverb*

celiac *adjective*
ALSO SPELLED: **coeliac**
• "SEELY ack"
• of or pertaining to the abdominal cavity.
• [Latin *coeliacus* from Greek *koiliakos* from *koilia* belly]

celibate *adjective*
• "SELLA bit"
• committed to abstention from sexual relations and from marriage, esp. for religious reasons.
• [French *célibat* or Latin *caelibatus* unmarried state, from *caelebs -ibis* unmarried]
• **celibacy** *noun*

cell *noun*
• "SELL"
• a small room, esp. in a prison or monastery.
• [Old French *celle* or from Latin *cella* storeroom etc.]
HOMOPHONES: *cel*, *sell*

cellar *noun*
• "SELLER"
• a room below ground level in a house, often used for storage of food and wine.
• [Anglo-French *celer*, Old French *celier* from Late Latin *cellarium* storehouse]
HOMOPHONES: *seller*

cellarage *noun*
• "SELLER idge"
• space in a cellar.
• [as CELLAR]

cellarer *noun*
• "SELLER ur"
• an officer in a monastery etc. in charge of food and drink.
• [as CELLAR]

cellaret *noun*
• "seller ET"
• a buffet or case for holding wine bottles in a dining room etc.
• [as CELLAR]

cellblock *noun*
• "SELL block"
• one of several sections of cells into which a large prison is divided.
• [as CELL + 'block']

cellmate *noun*
• "SELL mate"
• a prisoner occupying the same cell as another.
• [as CELL + 'mate']

cello *noun*
• "CHELLO"
• the second-largest instrument of the violin family, held upright on the floor between the knees of the seated player.
• [abbreviation of VIOLONCELLO]
• **cellist** *noun*

cellphone *noun*
• "SELL fone"
• a portable telephone which operates by means of a cellular network.
• [blend of CELLULAR + TELEPHONE]

cellular *adjective*
• "SELL yuh lur"
• of or having small compartments or cavities.
• [French *cellulaire* from modern Latin *cellularis*: see CELLULE]

cellule *noun*
• "SELL yool"
• a small cell or cavity.
• [French *cellule* or Latin *cellula* diminutive of *cella* CELL]

cellulite *noun*
• "SELL yuh lite"
• fatty tissue regarded as causing a dimpled or lumpy texture on the hips and thighs (esp. of women).
• [French (as CELLULE)]

cellulitis *noun*
• "sell yuh LITE iss"
• inflammation of cellular tissue.
• [as CELLULE + Greek *-itis*, forming feminine of adjectives in *-itēs* (with *nosos* 'disease' implied)]

celluloid *noun*
• "SELL yuh loid"
• a transparent flammable plastic made from camphor and nitrocellulose.
• [as CELLULOSE]

cellulose *noun*
• "SELL yuh lose" (rhymes with *GROSS*)
• a carbohydrate forming the main constituent of the cell walls of plants, used in the production of textile fibres.
• [French (as CELLULE)]
• **cellulosic** *adjective*

celosia *noun*
• "suh LO see uh"
• a plant of a genus that includes cockscomb.
• [modern Latin, from Greek *kēlos* burnt, dry (from the burnt appearance of the flowers in some species)]

Celsius *adjective*
• "SELL see us"
• of or denoting a temperature on the Celsius scale, in which water freezes at 0° and boils at 100°.
• [A. *Celsius*, Swedish astronomer d.1744]

celt *noun*
• "SELT"
• a stone or metal prehistoric implement with a chisel edge.
• [medieval Latin *celtes* chisel]

cement *noun*
• "suh MENT"
• a powdery substance made by calcining lime and clay, mixed with water to form mortar or used in concrete.
• [Old French *ciment* from Latin *caementum* quarry stone, from *caedere* hew]
• **cementation** *noun*
• **cementitious** *adjective*

cemetery *noun*
• "SEMMA terry" or "SEMMA tree"
• a graveyard.
• [Late Latin *coemeterium* from Greek *koimētērion* dormitory, from *koimaō* put to sleep]

cenobite *noun*
ALSO SPELLED: **coenobite**
• "SENNA bite" or "SEENA bite"
• a member of a monastic community.
• [Old French *cenobite* from Late Latin *coenobium* from Greek *koinobion* convent, from *koinos* common + *bios* life]
• **cenobitic** *adjective* (also **coenobitic**) "senna BITTIC" or "seena BITTIC"
• **cenobitical** *adjective* (also **coenobitical**)

cenotaph *noun*
• "SENNA taff"
• a tomb-like monument, esp. a war memorial, to a person or persons whose bodies are interred elsewhere.
• [French *cénotaphe* from Late Latin *cenotaphium* from Greek *kenos* empty + *taphos* tomb]

Cenozoic *adjective*
• "senna ZO ick" or "seena ZO ick"
• of, relating to, or denoting the most recent geological era, following the Mesozoic and lasting from about 65 million years ago to the present day. The Cenozoic includes the Tertiary and Quaternary periods, and has seen the rapid evolution of mammals.
• [Greek *kainos* new + *zōion* animal]

cens *noun*
• "SAWNCE"
• *Cdn* a token payment made to a seigneur by a habitant, reaffirming the feudal nature of the land tenure.
• [French, as CENSUS]

cense *verb*
• "SENSE"
• direct smoke from burning incense at, esp. as a religious rite.
• [aphetic from Old French *encenser*]
HOMOPHONES: *sense*

censer *noun*
• "SENSER"
• a vessel in which incense is burned, esp. during a religious procession or ceremony.

• [Anglo-French *censer*, Old French *censier* aphetic form of *encensier* from *encens* INCENSE[1]]
HOMOPHONES: *censor*, *sensor*

censitaire *noun*
• "soncy TARE"
• *Cdn* a tenant on a seigneury.
• [French, from CENS]

censor *noun*
• "SENSER"
• an official authorized to examine printed matter, films, news, etc., before public release, and to suppress any parts on the grounds of obscenity, threats to security, etc.
• [Latin from *censēre* assess]
• **censorial** *adjective* "sen SORRY 'll"
• **censorship** *noun*
HOMOPHONES: *censer*, *sensor*

censorious *adjective*
• "sen SORRY us"
• severely critical; fault-finding; quick or eager to criticize.
• [as CENSOR]
• **censoriously** *adverb*
• **censoriousness** *noun*

censorware *noun*
• "SENSER ware"
• filtering software intended to prevent access to websites identified by the software as offensive, unsuitable, or pornographic by the use of criteria (e.g. key words) written into the program.
• [as CENSOR + WARE]

censure *verb*
• "SEN shur"
• criticize harshly; reprove.
• [Old French from Latin *censura* from *censēre* assess]
• **censurable** *adjective*

census *noun*
• "SEN suss"
• an official count of a population or of a class of things, often with various statistics noted.
• [Latin from *censēre* assess]

centaur *noun*
• "SEN tore"
• a creature in Greek mythology with the head, arms, and torso of a man and the body and legs of a horse.
• [Latin *centaurus* from Greek *kentauros*, of unknown origin]

centaury *noun*
• "SEN tory"
• any plant of the genus *Centaurium*, esp. *C. erythraea*, formerly used in medicine.
• [Late Latin *centaurea*, ultimately from Greek *kentauros* CENTAUR: from the legend that it was discovered by the centaur Chiron]

centavo *noun*
• "sen TOVV oh"
• a small coin and monetary unit of some Latin American countries, worth one-hundredth of the standard unit.
• [Spanish from Latin *centum* hundred]

centenarian *noun*
• "sent'n AIRY 'n"
• a person a hundred or more years old.
• [as CENTENARY]

centenary *noun*
• "sen TENNER ee" or "sen TEENER ee"
• a centennial.
• [Latin *centenarius* from *centeni* a hundred each, from *centum* hundred]

centennial *noun*
• "sen TENNY 'll"
• a hundredth anniversary.
• [Latin *centum* hundred, after BIENNIAL]

centesimal *adjective*
• "sen TESS'm 'll"
• reckoning or reckoned by hundredths.
• [Latin *centesimus* hundredth, from *centum* hundred]
• **centesimally** *adverb*

centésimo *noun*
• "sen TESSY moe"
• a monetary unit of Uruguay, equal to one-hundredth of a peso.
• [Spanish, as CENTESIMAL]

centigrade *adjective*
• "SENTA grade"
• = CELSIUS.
• [French from Latin *centum* hundred + *gradus* step]

centigram *noun*
• "SENTA gram"
• a metric unit of mass, equal to one-hundredth of a gram.
• [French from Latin *centum* hundred + Greek *gramma* small weight]

centilitre *noun*
ALSO SPELLED: esp. *US* **centiliter**
• "SENTA leeter"
• a metric unit of capacity, equal to one-hundredth of a litre.
• [French from Latin *centum* hundred + LITRE]

centime *noun*
• "sawn TEEM"
• a monetary unit in various countries, equal to one-hundredth of a franc or other decimal currency unit.
• [French from Latin *centum* a hundred]

centimetre *noun*
ALSO SPELLED: esp. *US* **centimeter**
• "SENTA meeter"
• a metric unit of length, equal to one-hundredth of a metre (0.394 in.).
• [French from Latin *centum* a hundred + METRE]

centimo *noun*
• "SENTY moe"
• a monetary unit of a number of Latin American countries, equal to one-hundredth of the basic unit.
• [Spanish from Latin *centum* a hundred]

centipede *noun*
• "SENTA peed"
• any arthropod of the class Chilopoda, with a wormlike body of many segments each with a pair of legs.
• [French *centipède* or Latin *centipeda* from *centum* hundred + *pes pedis* foot]

cento *noun*
• "SENTO"
• a composition made up of quotations from other authors.
• [Latin, = patchwork garment]

central *adjective*
• "SEN trull"
• of, at, or forming the centre.
• [French *central* or Latin *centralis* from *centrum* centre, from Greek *kentron* sharp point]
• **centrality** *noun*
• **centralization** *noun* (also esp. *Brit.* **-isation**)
• **centralize** *verb* (also esp. *Brit.* **-ise**)
• **centralizer** *noun* (also esp. *Brit.* **-iser**)
• **centrally** *adverb*

centralism *noun*
• "SEN trull izm"
• a system that centralizes (esp. an administration).
• [as CENTRAL]
• **centralist** *noun*

centre *noun*
ALSO SPELLED: **center**
• "SENTER"
• the middle point, esp. of a line, circle, or sphere, equidistant from the ends or from any point on the circumference or surface.
• [Old French *centre* or Latin *centrum* from Greek *kentron* sharp point]
• **centremost** *adjective* (also **centermost**)
• **centric** *adjective*
• **centricity** *noun* "sen TRISSA tee"

centrifugal *adjective*
• "sen TRIFFA g'll" or "sentra FYOO g'll"
• moving or tending to move from a centre.
• [modern Latin *centrifugus* from Latin *centrum* centre + *fugere* flee]
• **centrifugally** *adverb*

centrifuge *noun*
• "SENTRA fyoodge"
• a machine with a rapidly rotating device designed to separate liquids from solids or other liquids (e.g. cream from milk).
• [as CENTRIFUGAL]
• **centrifugation** *noun* "sentra fyoo GAY sh'n"

centriole *noun*
• "SENTRY ole"
• a minute organelle usu. within a centrosome, involved esp. in the development of spindles in cell division.
• [medieval Latin *centriolum* diminutive of *centrum* centre]

centripetal *adjective*
• "sen TRIPPA t'll"
• moving or tending to move towards a centre.
• [modern Latin *centripetus* from Latin *centrum* centre + *petere* seek]
• **centripetally** *adverb*

centrist *noun*
• "SEN trist"
• a person who holds moderate views.
• [Latin *centrum* centre]
• **centrism** *noun*

centroid *noun*
• "SEN troid"
• the point within an area or volume at which the centre of mass would be if the surface or body had a uniform density.
• [Latin *centrum* centre]

centromere *noun*
• "SENTRA meer"
• the point on a chromosome to which the spindle is attached during cell division.
• [Latin *centrum* centre + Greek *meros* part]
• **centromeric** *adjective* "sentra MARE ick"

centrosome *noun*
• "SENTRA soam"
• a distinct part of the cytoplasm in a cell, usu. near the nucleus, that contains the centriole.
• [German *Centrosoma* from Latin *centrum* centre + Greek *sōma* body]

centrum *noun*
• "SENTRUM"
• the solid central part of a vertebra.
• [Latin, = centre]

centuple *verb*
• "sen TUPPLE"
• multiply by a hundred; increase a hundredfold.
• [French *centuple* or Church Latin *centuplus*, *centuplex* from Latin *centum* hundred]

centurion *noun*
• "sen CHURRY 'n"
• the commander of a company in the ancient Roman army, originally of 100 men, called a century.
• [Latin *centurio -onis* (as CENTURY)]

century *noun*
• "SEN chur ee"
• a period of one hundred years.
• [Latin *centuria* from *centum* hundred]

cep *noun*
• "SEP"
• an edible mushroom, *Boletus edulis*, with a stout stalk and brown smooth cap.

• [French *cèpe* from Gascon *cep* from Latin *cippus* stake]

cephalic *adjective*
• "suh FALIC"
• of or in the head.
• [French *céphalique* from Latin *cephalicus* from Greek *kephalikos* from *kephalē* head]

cephalometry *noun*
• "seffa LOMMA tree"
• measurement of the head.
• [Greek *kephalē* head + *metron* measure]
• **cephalometric** *adjective* "seffa lo METRIC"

cephalopod *noun*
• "SEFFA lo pod"
• any mollusc of the class Cephalopoda, having a well-developed head surrounded by tentacles, e.g. octopus, squid, and cuttlefish.
• [Greek *kephalē* head + *pous podos* foot]

cephalosporin *noun*
• "seffa lo SPORE in"
• any of a class of semi-synthetic antibiotics derived from a mould of the genus *Cephalosporium*.
• [from modern Latin *Cephalosporium*]

cephalothorax *noun*
• "seffa lo THOR ax"
• the fused head and thorax of a spider, crab, or other arthropod.
• [Greek *kephalē* head + THORAX]

Cepheid *noun*
• "SEEFY id" or "SEFFY id"
• any of a class of variable stars with regular cycles of brightness, which can be used to measure distances.
• [named after *Delta Cephei*, which typifies the class]

ceramic *adjective*
• "suh RAMMIC"
• designating or pertaining to hard brittle substances produced by the process of strong heating of a non-metallic mineral, esp. clay.
• [Greek *keramikos* from *keramos* pottery]
• **ceramicist** *noun* "suh RAMMA sist"
• **ceramist** *noun* "SERRA mist"

cerastes *noun*
• "suh RASS teez"
• any viper of the genus *Cerastes*, of N Africa, esp. the horned viper *C. cerastes* having a sharp upright spike over each eye and moving forward in a diagonal motion.
• [Latin from Greek *kerastēs* from *keras* horn]

ceratopsian *noun*
• "serra TOPSY 'n"
• a gregarious quadrupedal herbivorous dinosaur of a group found in the Cretaceous period, including triceratops. It had a large beaded and horned head and a bony frill protecting the neck.
• [modern Latin *Ceratopsia* (plural) from Greek *keras, kerat-* horn + *ops* face]

Cerberus *noun*
• "SUR bur us"
• a person who vigorously protects something from all who would attempt to take it.
• [the three-headed dog said to guard the gates of Hades]

cercaria *noun*
• "sur KERRY uh"
• a free-swimming larval stage in which a parasitic fluke passes from an intermediate host (often a snail) to another intermediate host or to the final vertebrate host.
• [modern Latin, formed irregularly from Greek *kerkos* tail]

cercus *noun*
• "SURK us"
• either of a pair of small appendages at the end of the abdomen of some insects and other arthropods.
• [modern Latin, from Greek *kerkos* tail]
HOMOPHONES: *circus*

cere *noun*
• "SEER"
• a waxy fleshy covering at the base of the upper beak in some birds, e.g. parrots, birds of prey.
• [Latin *cera* wax]
HOMOPHONES: *sear, sere, seer*

cereal *noun*
• "SEERY 'll"
• any kind of grain used for food.
• [Latin *cerealis* from *Ceres* goddess of agriculture]
HOMOPHONES: *serial*

cerebellum *noun*
• "serra BELLUM"
• the part of the brain at the back of the skull in vertebrates, which coordinates and regulates muscular activity.
• [Latin diminutive of CEREBRUM]
• **cerebellar** *adjective*

cerebral *adjective*
• "suh REE brull" or "SARE a brull"
• of the brain.
• [Latin *cerebrum* brain]
• **cerebrally** *adverb*

cerebration *noun*
• "serra BRAY sh'n"
• working of the brain.
• [as CEREBRAL]
• **cerebrate** *verb*

cerebrospinal *adjective*
• "suh reebro SPINE'll" or "serra bro SPINE'll"
• of the brain and spine.
• [as CEREBRAL + 'spinal' from Old French *espine* or Latin *spina* thorn, backbone]

cerebrovascular *adjective*
• "suh reebro VASS kyuh lur" or "serra bro VASS kyuh lur"
• of the brain and its blood vessels.
• [as CEREBRAL + VASCULAR]

cerebrum *noun*
• "suh REE brum" or "SARE a brum"
• the principal part of the brain in vertebrates, located in the front area of the skull, which integrates complex sensory and neural functions.
• [Latin, = brain]

cerecloth *noun*
• "SEER cloth"
• waxed cloth used as a waterproof covering or (esp.) as a shroud.
• [earlier *cered cloth* from *cere* to wax, from Latin *cerare* from *cera* wax]

cerement *noun*
• "SEER m'nt"
• grave clothes; cerecloth.
• [first used by Shakespeare in *Hamlet* (1602): apparently from CERECLOTH]

ceremonious *adjective*
• "serra MOANY us"
• behaving or performed in a formal, ritualistic, or elaborate way.
• [as CEREMONY]
• **ceremoniously** *adverb*
• **ceremoniousness** *noun*

ceremony *noun*
• "SERRA moany"
• a formal religious or public rite, observance, or occasion, esp. celebrating a particular event or anniversary.
• [Latin *caerimonia* religious worship]
• **ceremonial** *adjective*
• **ceremonialism** *noun*
• **ceremonialist** *noun*
• **ceremonially** *adverb*

cerise *adjective*
• "suh REEZ" or "suh REECE"
• of a dark clear red.
• [French, = 'cherry']

cerium *noun*
• "SEERY um"
• a silvery metallic element of the lanthanide series occurring naturally in various minerals and used in the manufacture of lighter flints.
• [named after the asteroid *Ceres*, discovered (1801) about the same time as this]

cermet *noun*
• "SUR met"
• a heat-resistant material made of ceramic and sintered metal.
• [*ceramic* + *metal*]

cert *noun*
• "SURT"
• an event or result regarded as certain to happen.
• [abbreviation of CERTAIN, CERTAINTY]

certain *adjective*
• "SUR t'n"
• confident, convinced.
• [Old French, ultimately from Latin *certus* settled]
• **certainly** *adverb*

certainty *noun*
• "SUR t'n tee"
• an undoubted fact.
• [as CERTAIN]

certifiable *adjective*
• "surta FIE a bull"
• able or needing to be certified.
• [as CERTIFY]

certificate *noun*
• "sur TIFFA kit"
• a formal document attesting a fact, esp. birth, marriage, or death, a medical condition, a level of achievement, a fulfillment of requirements, ownership of shares, etc.
• [French *certificat* or medieval Latin *certificatum* from *certificare*: see CERTIFY]
• **certification** *noun*

certify *verb*
• "SURTA fie"
• make a formal statement of; attest; attest to.
• [Old French *certifier* from medieval Latin *certificare* from Latin *certus* certain]
• **certified** *adjective*

certiorari *noun*
• "surshy or AR ee"
• a writ from a higher court requesting the records of a case tried in a lower court for purposes of judicial review.
• [Late Latin passive of *certiorare* inform, from *certior* comparative of *certus* certain]

certitude *noun*
• "SURTA tude"
• a feeling of absolute certainty or conviction.
• [Late Latin *certitudo* from *certus* certain]

cerulean *adjective*
• "suh RULEY 'n"
• deep blue like a clear sky.
• [Latin *caeruleus* sky blue, from *caelum* sky]

cerumen *noun*
• "suh ROO m'n"
• the yellow waxy substance in the outer ear; earwax.
• [modern Latin from Latin *cera* wax]
• **ceruminous** *adjective*

cervine *adjective*
• "SUR vine"
• of or like a deer.
• [Latin *cervinus* from *cervus* deer]

cervix *noun*
- "SUR vix"
- the narrow lower part of the uterus, extending into the vagina.
- [Latin *cervix -icis* neck]
- **cervical** *adjective*

cesium *noun*
ALSO SPELLED: **caesium**
- "SEEZY um"
- a soft silver-white element of the alkali metal group, occurring naturally in a number of minerals, and used in photoelectric cells.
- [as CAESIOUS (from its spectrum lines)]

cessation *noun*
- "suh SAY sh'n"
- a ceasing.
- [Latin *cessatio* from *cessare* CEASE]

cession *noun*
- "SESH'n"
- the ceding or giving up (of rights, property, and esp. of territory).
- [Old French *cession* or Latin *cessio* from *cedere cess-* go away]

HOMOPHONES: *session*

cesspit *noun*
- "SESS pit"
- a pit for the disposal of refuse.
- [*cess* in CESSPOOL + 'pit']

cesspool *noun*
- "SESS pool"
- an underground container for the temporary storage of liquid waste or sewage.
- [perhaps alteration, after 'pool', of earlier *cesperalle*, from *suspiral* vent, water pipe, from Old French *souspirail* air hole, from Latin *suspirare* breathe up, sigh (as *sub-* under, *spirare* breathe)]

cestode *noun*
- "SESS tode"
- any flatworm of the class Cestoda, including tapeworms.
- [Latin *cestus* from Greek *kestos* girdle]

cetacean *noun*
- "suh TAY sh'n"
- any marine mammal of the order Cetacea with a streamlined hairless body and dorsal blowhole for breathing, including whales, dolphins, and porpoises.
- [modern Latin *Cetacea* from Latin *cetus* from Greek *kētos* whale]
- **cetaceous** *adjective*

cetane *noun*
- "SEE tane"
- a colourless liquid hydrocarbon of the alkane series used in standardizing ratings of diesel fuel.
- [Latin *cetus* whale; related compounds were isolated from spermaceti]

cetology *noun*
- "see TOLLA jee"
- the branch of zoology that deals with whales, dolphins, and porpoises.
- [Latin *cetus* whale + Greek *logos* word]
- **cetologist** *noun*

ceviche *noun*
ALSO SPELLED: **seviche**
- "se VEE chay"
- a Latin American dish of raw fish or seafood marinated in lime or lemon juice, usu. garnished and served as an appetizer.
- [Latin American Spanish *seviche, cebiche*]

Ceylonese *adjective*
- "seela NEEZ"
- of or pertaining to the country now called Sri Lanka.
- [*Ceylon*, the former name (until 1972) for Sri Lanka]

Chablis *noun*
- "sha BLEE"
- a dry white wine from N Burgundy, France.
- [*Chablis* in E France]

chaconne *noun*
- "shuh CON"
- a musical form consisting of variations on a ground bass.
- [French from Spanish *chacona*]

chador *noun*
- "CHUDDER"
- a large piece of cloth worn in some countries by Muslim women, wrapped around the body to leave only the face exposed.
- [Persian, Urdu *chador*]

chaebol *noun*
- "CHAY bawl"
- (in South Korea) a large esp. family-owned business conglomerate.
- [Korean, lit. 'money clan']

chaetognath *noun*
- "KEE tug nath"
- any dart-shaped worm of the phylum Chaetognatha, usu. living among marine plankton, and having a head with external thorny teeth.
- [modern Latin *Chaetognatha* from Greek *khaitē* long hair + *gnathos* jaw]

chafe *verb*
- "CHAFE" (rhymes with *SAFE*)
- make or become sore or damaged by rubbing.
- [Old French *chaufer*, ultimately from Latin *calefacere* from *calēre* be hot + *facere* make]

chafer *noun*
- "CHAFE ur"
- any of various large slow-moving beetles of the family Scarabeidae, esp. the cockchafer.
- [Old English *ceafor, cefer* from Germanic]

chagrin *noun*
- "shuh GRIN"

• acute vexation or mortification.
• [French *chagrin(er)*, of uncertain origin]
• **chagrined** *adjective*

chai[1] *noun*
• "CHY" (rhymes with *BY*)
• tea, esp. when made by boiling the tea leaves with milk, sugar, and cardamom.
• [ultimately from Chinese *ch'a* tea, possibly through Russian *tchaī*]

chai[2] *noun*
• "SHAY"
• a shed for aging wine.
• [French, from Poitou dialect for *quai* quay]

chaise *noun*
• "SHAZE"
• a horse-drawn carriage for one or two persons, esp. one with a folding top and two wheels.
• [French var. of *chaire* seat, from Latin *cathedra* from Greek *kathedra*: see CATHEDRAL]

chakra *noun*
• "CHUCK ruh"
• (in yoga) each of the seven centres of spiritual power in the human body.
• [Sanskrit *cakra* wheel]

chalaza *noun*
• "kuh LAYZA"
• each of two twisted membranous strips joining the yolk to the ends of an egg.
• [modern Latin from Greek, = hailstone]

chalcedony *noun*
• "cal SEDDA nee"
• a type of quartz occurring in several different forms, e.g. onyx, agate, tiger's eye, etc.
• [Latin *c(h)alcedonius* from Greek *khalkēdōn*]
• **chalcedonic** *adjective* "calsa DONNIC"

chalcid *noun*
• "CAL sid"
• any insect of the superfamily Chalcidoidea, esp. the parasitic hymenopterous ones of the family Chalcididae.
• [modern Latin *Chalcis* from Greek *khalkos* copper, brass, from their metallic sheen]

chalcolithic *adjective*
• "calca LITHIC"
• of a prehistoric period in which both stone and bronze implements were used.
• [Greek *khalkos* copper + *lithos* stone]

chalcopyrite *noun*
• "calco PIE rite"
• a yellow mineral consisting of a sulphide of copper and iron, which is the principal ore of copper.
• [Greek *khalkos* copper + PYRITE]

Chaldean *noun*
• "cal DEE 'n"
• a native of Chaldea or Babylonia in ancient Mesopotamia.

Chaldee *noun*
• "CAL dee"
• a native of ancient Chaldea.

chalet *noun*
• "shal AY"
• a style of wooden house, typical of the European Alps, having a steeply pitched roof with very deep overhanging eaves.
• [Swiss French, diminutive of Old French *chasel* from Latin *casa* hut, cottage]

chalice *noun*
• "CHAL iss"
• a wine cup used in the Eucharist.
• [Old French from Latin *calix -icis* cup]

chalk *noun*
• "CHOCK"
• a white soft earthy limestone (calcium carbonate) formed from the skeletal remains of sea creatures.
• [Old English *cealc*, ultimately from West Germanic from Latin CALX]
• **chalkiness** *noun*
• **chalklike** *adjective*
• **chalky** *adjective*
HOMOPHONES: *chock*

chalkboard *noun*
• "CHOCK bord"
• a blackboard.
• [CHALK + 'board']

challah *noun*
• "HOLLA"
• a loaf of white leavened egg bread, often braided, traditionally baked to celebrate the Jewish Sabbath.
• [Hebrew *halah*]

challenge *noun*
• "CHAL 'nj"
• a summons to take part in a contest or a trial of strength etc.
• [Old French *c(h)alenge*, *c(h)alenger* from Latin *calumnia calumniari* calumny]
• **challengeable** *adjective*
• **challenger** *noun*

challenging *adjective*
• "CHAL 'n jing"
• demanding; stimulatingly difficult.
• [as CHALLENGE]

challis *noun*
• "SHALLY" or "shall EE"
• a lightweight soft clothing fabric.
• [perhaps from a surname]

chalybeate *adjective*
• "kuh LIBBY ate" or "kuh LEEBY ate"
• (of mineral water etc.) impregnated with iron salts.
• [modern Latin *chalybeatus* from Latin *chalybs* from Greek *khalups -ubos* steel]

chamaephyte *noun*
• "CAMMA fite"
• a plant whose buds are on or near the ground.
• [Greek *khamai* on the ground + *phuton* plant, from *phuō* come into being]

chamberlain *noun*
• "CHAME bur lin"
• an officer managing the household of a sovereign or a great noble.
• [Old French *chamberlain* etc. from Frankish from Latin *camera* CAMERA]
• **chamberlainship** *noun*

chambray *noun*
• "shom BRAY"
• a linen-finished gingham cloth with a white weft and a coloured warp.
• [*Cambrai*: see CAMBRIC]
HOMOPHONES: *chambré*

chambré *adjective*
• "SHOM bray"
• (of red wine) brought to room temperature.
• [French, past participle of *chambrer* from *chambre* room, from Latin *camera*: see CAMERA]
HOMOPHONES: *chambray*

chameleon *noun*
• "kuh MEELY 'n"
• any of a family of small lizards having grasping tails, long tongues, protruding eyes, and the power of changing colour.
• [Latin from Greek *khamaileōn* from *khamai* on the ground + *leōn* lion]
• **chameleonic** *adjective*

chamfer *verb*
• "CHAM fur"
• bevel symmetrically (a right-angled edge or corner).
• [back-formation from *chamfering* from French *chamfrain* from *chant* edge + *fraint* broken, from Old French *fraindre* break, from Latin *frangere*]

chamois[1] *noun*
• "SHAM wah"
• an agile goat-antelope, *Rupicapra rupicapra*, native to the mountains of Europe and Asia.
• [French]

chamois[2] *noun*
• "SHAMMY"
• a soft pliable leather from sheep, goats, etc., often used for polishing.
• [French]
HOMOPHONES: *shammy*

champagne *noun*
• "sham PANE"
• a white sparkling wine from Champagne in NE France.
HOMOPHONES: *champaign*

champaign *noun*
• "sham PANE"
• an expanse of open country.
• [Old French *champagne* from Late Latin *campania*: compare CAMPAIGN]
HOMOPHONES: *champagne*

champers *noun*
• "SHAMPERZ"
• champagne.
• [abbreviation]

champerty *noun*
• "CHAMPER tee"
• an illegal agreement in which a person not naturally interested in a lawsuit finances it with a view to sharing the disputed property.
• [Anglo-French *champartie* from Old French *champart* feudal lord's share of produce, from Latin *campus* field + *pars* part]
• **champertous** *adjective*

champlevé *noun*
• "shãh luh VAY" (with a nasal *ah*)
• a type of enamelwork in which hollows made in a metal surface are filled with coloured enamels.
• [French, = raised field]

chana *noun*
• "CHUNNA"
• (in Indian cuisine) chickpeas, esp. when roasted and prepared as a snack.
• [Hindi *canā*]

chancel *noun*
• "CHANCE 'll"
• a part of some (esp. Anglican) churches, located near the altar, which is usu. separated from the nave by steps or enclosed by a screen.
• [Old French from Latin *cancelli* lattice]

chancellery *noun*
• "CHANCE'll ree" or "CHANCE luh ree"
• the position, office, staff, department, etc., of a chancellor.
• [Old French *chancellerie* (as CHANCELLOR)]

chancellor *noun*
• "CHANCE'll ur"
• a State or legal official of various kinds.
• [Old English from Anglo-French *c(h)anceler*, Old French *-ier* from Late Latin *cancellarius* porter, secretary, from *cancelli* lattice]
• **chancellorship** *noun*

chancery *noun*
• "CHANCE ur ee"
• an office attached to an embassy or consulate.
• [Middle English, contracted from CHANCELLERY]

chancre *noun*
• "SHANKER"
• a hard, painless ulcer developing as the primary lesion of syphilis and certain other infectious diseases.
• [French from Latin *cancer* cancer, crab]

chandelier *noun*
• "shanda LEER"

• an ornamental branched hanging support for several light bulbs or candles.
• [French from *chandelle* from Latin *candela* from *candēre* shine]
• **chandeliered** *adjective*

chandler *noun*
• "CHAND lur"
• a dealer of supplies or goods for a specific purpose, esp. of boating supplies.
• [Anglo-French *chaundeler* candle, from Latin *candela* from *candēre* shine]
• **chandlery** *noun*

changeable *adjective*
• "CHANGE a bull"
• irregular, inconstant.
• [Old French *change, changer* from Late Latin *cambiare*, Latin *cambire* barter, prob. of Celtic origin]
• **changeability** *noun*
• **changeableness** *noun*
• **changeably** *adverb*

chanson *noun*
• "shãh SÕH" (with nasal *ah* and *OH*)
• a French song, usu. sung by a solo singer with minimal accompaniment and characterized by political or social commentary.
• [Old French from Latin *cantio(n-)* singing, from *cant-*, past participle of *canere* sing]

chansonnier *noun*
• "shãh sawn YAY" (with nasal *ah*)
• a singer of chansons.
• [French (see CHANSON)]

chansonnière *noun*
• "shãh sawn YARE" (with nasal *ah*)
• a female singer of chansons.
• [French (see CHANSON)]

chanterelle *noun*
• "shonta RELL" or "chanta RELL"
• an edible fungus, *Cantharellus cibarius*, with a yellow funnel-shaped cap.
• [French from modern Latin *cantharellus* diminutive of *cantharus* from Greek *kantharos* a kind of drinking vessel]

chanteuse *noun*
• "shon TOOZ" (with "OO" as in *TOOK*)
• a female singer of popular songs.
• [French, as CHANSON]

chanticleer *noun*
• "CHANTA cleer" or "CHONTA cleer" or "SHANTA cleer" or "SHONTA cleer"
• a name given to a rooster, esp. in fairy tales etc.
• [Old French *chantecler* (from Old French *chanter* sing, from Latin *cantare* frequentative of *canere cant-* sing + Old French *cler* from Latin *clarus* clear), a name in *Reynard the Fox*]

Chantilly *noun*
• "shan TILLY"
• a delicate kind of bobbin lace.
• [*Chantilly* near Paris]

chantry *noun*
• "CHAN tree"
• an endowment for a priest or priests to celebrate masses for the founder's soul.
• [Old French *chanterie* from *chanter* chant, sing]

chaos *noun*
• "CAY oss"
• utter confusion.
• [French or Latin from Greek *khaos*]
• **chaotic** *adjective*
• **chaotically** *adverb*

chaparajos *plural noun*
• "shappa RAY ose" or "chappa RAY ose" ("OSE" rhymes with *GROSS*)
• thick leather leggings worn by western riders over trousers as protection against thorns etc.
• [Mexican Spanish, from *chaparrerras* from *chaparra* (with reference to protection from thorny vegetation: see CHAPARRAL); probably influenced by Spanish *aparejo* equipment]

chaparral *noun*
• "shappa RAL" or "chappa RAL"
• vegetation consisting chiefly of tangled shrubs and thorny bushes in southwestern North America.
• [Spanish from *chaparra* dwarf evergreen oak]

chapati *noun*
ALSO SPELLED: **chapatti**
• "chuh POTTY" or "chuh PATTY"
• a flat thin Indian cake of unleavened whole wheat bread.
• [Hindi *capāti*]

chape *noun*
• "CHAPE"
• the metal cap of a scabbard point.
• [Old French, = cope, hood, from Late Latin *cappa*, perhaps from Latin *caput* head]

chapeau *noun*
• "sha POE"
• a hat, esp. an extravagant one.
• [French, as CHAPE]

chaperone *noun*
ALSO SPELLED: **chaperon**
• "SHAPPER own"
• a person who supervises young people on trips etc.
• [French, = hood, chaperone, diminutive of *chape* cope, formed as CHAPE]
• **chaperonage** *noun*

chaperonin *noun*
• "shapper OWN in"
• a protein that aids the assembly and folding of other protein molecules in living cells.
• [as CHAPERONE]

chaplain *noun*
• "CHAP lin"
• a member of the clergy attached to a private chapel, institution, ship, regiment, etc.
• [Old French *c(h)apelain* from *chapele* chapel,

from medieval Latin *cappella* diminutive of *cappa* cloak: the first chapel was a sanctuary in which St. Martin's sacred cloak (*cappella*) was preserved]
• **chaplaincy** *noun*

chaplet *noun*
• "CHAP let"
• a garland or circlet for the head.
• [Old French *chapelet*, ultimately from Late Latin *cappa* cap]

Chaplinesque *adjective*
• "chap lin ESK"
• of or characteristic of the English comedic silent-film actor Charlie Chaplin (d.1977).

chappal *noun*
• "CHAP'll"
• an Indian sandal, usu. of leather.
• [Hindi]
HOMOPHONES: *chapel*

chaptalization *noun*
• "chapt'll ize AY sh'n"
• (in winemaking) the correction or improvement of must by the addition of calcium carbonate to neutralize acid or of sugar to increase alcoholic strength.
• [J. A. *Chaptal* d.1832, French naturalist who invented the process]
• **chaptalize** *verb* (also esp. *Brit.* **-ise**)

charabanc *noun*
• "SHAR a bang"
• an early type of bus, used esp. for pleasure trips.
• [French *char à bancs* lit. = 'coach with benches', a seated carriage]

characin *noun*
• "CAR a sin"
• a freshwater fish of the family Characidae, mainly of South and Central America, including piranhas and tetras.
• [modern Latin *Characinus* genus name, from Greek *kharax*, a kind of fish]

character *noun*
• "CARE uck tur"
• the collective qualities or characteristics, esp. mental and moral, that distinguish a person or thing.
• [Latin from Greek *kharaktēr* stamp, impress]
• **characterful** *adjective*
• **characterless** *adjective*

characteristic *adjective*
• "care uck tur ISTIC"
• typical, distinctive.
• [as CHARACTER]
• **characteristically** *adverb*

characterize *verb*
ALSO SPELLED: esp. *Brit.* **-ise**
• "CARE uck tur ize"
• describe or portray the character of.
• [as CHARACTER]
• **characterization** *noun* (also esp. *Brit.* **-isation**)

characterological *adjective*
• "care uck tur a LODGE a k'll"
• of or relating to character or the study of character.
• [as CHARACTER + Greek *logos* word]

charade *noun*
• "shuh RAID"
• a game of guessing a word from a written or acted clue given for each syllable and for the whole.
• [French from modern Provençal *charrado* conversation, from *charra* chatter]

charas *noun*
• "CHAR us"
• hashish.
• [Hindi]

charcuterie *noun*
• "shar COOTER ee"
• assorted meats such as cold cuts, sausages, pâté, etc.
• [French, from obsolete *char* (modern *chair*) *cuite* cooked flesh]

Chardonnay *noun*
• "SHARDA nay"
• a variety of white grape used in winemaking.
• [French]

charette *noun*
• "shuh RET"
• a workshop-like public meeting to brainstorm community design issues.
• [French *charrette*, lit. = 'cart']

chariot *noun*
• "CHERRY it"
• a two-wheeled vehicle drawn by horses, used in ancient warfare and racing.
• [Old French, augmentative of *char* car]
• **charioteer** *noun*

charisma *noun*
• "kuh RIZZMA"
• the ability to inspire followers with devotion and enthusiasm.
• [Church Latin from Greek *kharisma* from *kharis* favour, grace]
• **charismatic** *adjective*
• **charismatically** *adverb*

charitable *adjective*
• "CHAIR it a bull"
• generous in giving to those in need.
• [as CHARITY]
• **charitableness** *noun*
• **charitably** *adverb*

charity *noun*
• "CHAIR it ee"
• voluntary giving to those in need.
• [Old English from Old French *charité* from Latin *caritas -tatis* from *carus* dear]

charivari *noun*
- "shar ee VAR ee"
- a serenade of banging saucepans etc. to a newly married couple.
- [French, = a serenade with pans, trays, etc., to an unpopular person]

charlatan *noun*
- "SHARLA t'n"
- a person falsely claiming a special knowledge or skill.
- [French from Italian *ciarlatano* from *ciarlare* babble]
- **charlatanism** *noun*
- **charlatanry** *noun*

Charleston *noun*
- "CHARLES t'n"
- a fast dance, popular in the 1920s, in which the knees are turned inwards and the legs kicked sideways.
- [*Charleston*, South Carolina]

charlotte *noun*
- "SHAR lut"
- any of various desserts consisting of a filling of fruit, custard, cream, etc. encased in strips of bread, sponge cake, etc.
- [French, from the female name *Charlotte*]

Charlottetonian *noun*
- "shar luh TONY 'n"
- a resident of Charlottetown, PEI.

charmeuse *noun*
- "shar MOOZ" (with "OO" as in *BOOK*)
- a soft smooth silk fabric with a satin-like surface.
- [French, feminine of *charmeur* from Old French *charmer* charm, from Latin *carmen* song]

Charolais *noun*
- "SHARA lay"
- a breed of large white beef cattle.
- [Monts du *Charolais* in E France]

charpoy *noun*
- "CHAR poy"
- (in India) a light bedstead.
- [Urdu, Persian *chārpāi*]

chary *adjective*
- "CHERRY"
- cautious, wary.
- [Old English *cearig*]
- **charily** *adverb*
- **chariness** *noun*

HOMOPHONES: *cherry*

chasm *noun*
- "CAZM"
- a deep fissure or opening in the earth, rock, etc.
- [Latin *chasma* from Greek *khasma* gaping hollow]
- **chasmic** *adjective*

chassé *noun*
- "SHASS ay"
- a sliding step in dance, in which one foot displaces the other as if by chasing it.
- [French, = chased]

chassis *noun*
- "CHASSY" or "SHASSY"
- the basic frame of a motor vehicle, trailer, etc., including the engine, wheels, and other mechanical parts, but not the body.
- [French *châssis*, ultimately from Latin *capsa* case]

chaste *adjective*
- "CHAYST" (rhymes with *PASTE*)
- abstaining from extramarital, or from all, sexual intercourse.
- [Old French from Latin *castus*]
- **chastely** *adverb*
- **chasteness** *noun*
- **chastity** *noun* "CHASTA tee"

chasten *verb*
- "CHASE 'n"
- subdue, humble.
- [obsolete *chaste* (v.) from Old French *chastier* from Latin *castigare* CASTIGATE]
- **chastener** *noun*

chastise *verb*
- "CHASS tize"
- rebuke or reprimand severely.
- [Middle English, apparently from obsolete verbs *chaste*, *chasty*: see CHASTEN]
- **chastisement** *noun*
- **chastiser** *noun*

chasuble *noun*
- "CHAZ a bull" or "CHAZ yuh bull" or "CHASS a bull"
- a loose sleeveless usu. ornate outer vestment worn by some clergy when celebrating the Eucharist.
- [Old French *chesible*, later *-uble*, ultimately from Latin *casula* hooded cloak, little cottage, diminutive of *casa* cottage]

château *noun*
- "sha TOE"
- a large French country house or castle, often giving its name to wine made in its neighbourhood.
- [French from Old French *chastel* castle, as CASTELLAN]

chateaubriand *noun*
- "sha toe bree ÃH" (with a nasal *AH*)
- a thick beef steak from the tenderloin, grilled and served with a sauce or herbs etc.
- [the Vicomte de *Chateaubriand*, French writer and diplomat d.1848]

chatelaine *noun*
- "SHATTA lane"
- the mistress of a large house.
- [French *châtelaine*, feminine of *chatelain* lord of a castle, from medieval Latin *castellanus* CASTELLAN]

Chathamite *noun*
• "CHAT'm ite"
• a resident of Chatham, Ont.

chattel *noun*
• "CHAT'll"
• a movable possession; any possession or piece of property other than real estate or a freehold.
• [Old French *chatel* from medieval Latin *capitale* from Latin *capitalis* from *caput* head; related to CAPITAL and 'cattle']

Chaucerian *adjective*
• "chaw SEERY 'n"
• of or relating to the English poet Geoffrey Chaucer (d.1400) or his style.

chauffeur *noun*
• "show FUR" or "SHOW fur"
• a person employed to drive a limousine or other automobile.
• [French, lit. 'stoker' (by association with steam engines) from *chauffer* to heat]
HOMOPHONES: *shofar*

chaulmoogra *noun*
• "chol MOOGRA"
• any of various tropical Asian trees, esp. *Hydnocarpus kurzii*, with seeds yielding an oil formerly used in the treatment of leprosy.
• [Bengali *cāulmugrā*]

chautauqua *noun*
• "shuh TOCKWA"
• (in Canada and the US) a cultural program for adults combining lectures with music and theatre, popular in the late 19th and early 20th c.
• [*Chautauqua* in New York State, where the movement originated]

chauvinism *noun*
• "SHOW v'n izm"
• exaggerated or aggressive patriotism.
• [*Chauvin*, a Napoleonic veteran noted for his extreme patriotism in the Cogniards' *Cocarde Tricolore* (1831)]
• **chauvinist** *noun*
• **chauvinistic** *adjective*
• **chauvinistically** *adverb*

chayote *noun*
• "chy OH tee"
• a vine, *Sechium edule*, native to tropical America and cultivated elsewhere for its fruit.
• [Spanish from Nahuatl *chayotli*]

Chechen *noun*
• "CHETCH en"
• a member of a Muslim people of the Chechen Republic, an autonomous republic in SE Russia.

checkrein *noun*
• "CHECK rain"
• a rein attaching one horse's rein to another's bit, or preventing a horse from lowering its head.
• ['check' + REIN]

cheddar *noun*
• "CHEDDER"
• any of several firm varieties of cheese ranging in colour from white to orange and becoming increasingly strong with age.
• [*Cheddar* in S England, where it was originally made]

cheder *noun*
ALSO SPELLED: **heder**
• "HEY dur"
• a school for Jewish children in which Hebrew and religious knowledge are taught.
• [Hebrew *ḥeḏer*, lit. 'room']

cheechako *noun*
• "chee CHACK oh"
• a newcomer or tenderfoot, esp. in the Yukon and Alaska.
• [Chinook Jargon]

cheep *noun*
• "CHEEP"
• the weak shrill cry of a young bird.
• [imitative]
HOMOPHONES: *cheap*

cheetah *noun*
• "CHEETA"
• a spotted feline native to the plains of Africa and SW Asia, *Acinonyx jubatus*, the world's fastest-running land animal.
• [Hindi *cītā*, perhaps from Sanskrit *citraka* speckled]

chef *noun*
• "SHEFF"
• a cook, esp. the chief cook in a restaurant.
• [French, = head, from Latin *caput* head]

Chekhovian *adjective*
• "check OH vee 'n"
• of or characteristic of the work of Russian writer Anton Chekhov (d.1904), esp. in attaching dramatic and symbolic significance to detail.

chela[1] *noun*
• "KEELA"
• a prehensile claw of crabs, lobsters, scorpions, etc.
• [modern Latin from Latin *chele*, or Greek *khēlē* claw]

chela[2] *noun*
• "CHAYLA"
• (in Hinduism) a religious disciple or pupil.
• [Hindi, = servant]

chelate *noun*
• "KEE late"
• a chemical compound containing a bonded ring of atoms including a metal atom.
• [as CHELA[1]]
• **chelation** *noun*
• **chelator** *noun*

Chellean *adjective*
• "SHELLY 'n"
• of the culture of the earliest paleolithic

period in Europe, characterized by the production of flint hand axes.
• [French *chelléen* from *Chelles* near Paris]

chelonian *noun*
• "kuh LONEY 'n"
• any reptile of the order Testudines (formerly Chelonia), including turtles, terrapins, and tortoises.
• [modern Latin *Chelonia* from Greek *khelōnē* tortoise]

chem *noun*
• "KEM"
• a chemistry class or course.
• [abbreviation]

chemical *adjective*
• "KEMMA k'll"
• of, made by, or employing chemistry or chemicals.
• [*chemic* alchemic, from French *chimique* or modern Latin *chimicus*, *chymicus*, from medieval Latin *alchymicus*: see ALCHEMY]
• **chemically** *adverb*

chemise *noun*
• "shuh MEEZ"
• a woman's loose-fitting undergarment or dress hanging straight from the shoulders.
• [Old French from Late Latin *camisia* shirt]

chemisorption *noun*
• "kemma SORP sh'n"
• adsorption by chemical bonding.
• [CHEMICAL + ADSORPTION (see ADSORB)]

chemist *noun*
• "KEMMIST"
• a scientist practising or trained in chemistry.
• [French *chimiste* from modern Latin *chimista* from *alchimista* ALCHEMIST (see ALCHEMY)]

chemistry *noun*
• "KEMMA stree"
• the study of the elements, the compounds they form, and the reactions they undergo.
• [as CHEMIST]

chemo *noun*
• "KEEMO"
• = CHEMOTHERAPY.
• [abbreviation]

chemoprevention *noun*
• "keemo pree VEN sh'n"
• the use of pharmaceuticals to prevent disease.
• [as CHEMICAL + 'prevent', in Middle English = anticipate, from Latin *praevenire praevent-* come before, hinder (as Latin *prae-* before, *venire* come)]

chemoreceptor *noun*
• "KEEMO ree septer"
• a sensory cell or organ responsive to chemical stimuli.
• [as CHEMICAL + RECEPTOR]
• **chemoreception** *noun*

chemosynthesis *noun*
• "keemo SINTHA sis"
• the synthesis of organic compounds by energy derived from chemical reactions.
• [as CHEMICAL + SYNTHESIS]

chemotaxis *noun*
• "keemo TAX iss"
• motion of a motile cell, organism, or part towards or away from a chemical stimulus.
• [as CHEMICAL + Greek *taxis* order]
• **chemotactic** *adjective*

chemotherapy *noun*
• "keemo THERRA pee"
• the treatment of disease, esp. cancer, by use of highly toxic chemical substances which target rapidly-dividing cells to slow cell division.
• [as CHEMICAL + THERAPY]
• **chemotherapeutic** *adjective*
• **chemotherapist** *noun*

chenille *noun*
• "shuh NEEL"
• a velvety cord or yarn surrounded with pile, used in trimming furniture, bedspreads, or clothing.
• [French, lit. 'hairy caterpillar' from Latin *canicula* diminutive of *canis* dog]

cheongsam *noun*
• "chong SAM"
• a woman's garment with a high neck and slit skirt, worn in China and E Asia.
• [Cantonese var. of Mandarin *chángshān*, lit. 'long dress']

cheque *noun*
ALSO SPELLED: esp. *US* **check**
• "CHECK"
• a written order to a bank to pay the stated sum from the drawer's account to a specified person or company.
• [special use of 'check' to mean 'device for checking the amount of an item']
HOMOPHONES: *check*, *Czech*

chequebook *noun*
• "CHECK book"
• a book of forms for writing cheques and recording the transactions of a chequing account.
• [as CHEQUE + 'book']

cherimoya *noun*
• "cherry MOYA"
• a kind of custard apple with a pineapple-like flavour and scaly green skin.
• [Spanish, from Quechua, from *chiri* cold or refreshing + *muya* circle]

cherish *verb*
• "CHAIR ish"
• protect or tend to lovingly.
• [Old French *cherir* from *cher* from Latin *carus* dear]

chernozem *noun*
• "CHUR no zem"
• a fertile black soil rich in humus, found in temperate or cool grasslands.
• [Russian from *chernyĭ* black + *zemlya* earth]
• **chernozemic** *adjective*

Cherokee *noun*
• "CHAIR a key"
• a member of an Iroquoian people formerly inhabiting much of the southeastern US, now largely confined to Oklahoma and N Carolina.
• [Cherokee *Tsálăgī*]

cheroot *noun*
• "shuh ROOT"
• a cigar with both ends open.
• [French *cheroute* from Tamil *shuruṭṭu* roll]

chert *noun*
• "CHURT"
• a flint-like form of quartz composed of chalcedony.
• [17th c.: origin unknown]
• **cherty** *adjective*

cherub *noun*
• "CHAIR ub"
• a representation of a winged or innocent child.
• [Old English *cherubin* and from Hebrew *kᶜrūḇ*, pl. *kᶜrūḇîm* winged angelic being]
• **cherubic** *adjective* "chair OO bick" or "chair UBB ick" or "CHAIR a bick"
• **cherubically** *adverb*

chervil *noun*
• "CHUR vill"
• an umbelliferous plant, *Anthriscus cerefolium*, with small white flowers, used as a herb for flavouring soup, salads, etc.
• [Old English *cerfille* from Latin *chaerephylla* from Greek *khairephullon*]

Cheshire *noun*
• "CHESH ear"
• a kind of firm crumbly cheese resembling cheddar.
• [*Cheshire*, in west central England, where it was originally made]

chestnut *noun*
• "CHESS nut"
• any of several trees of the genus *Castanea* of the beech family, bearing flowers in catkins and nuts enclosed in a spiny fruit, esp.: *C. dentata* of N America.
• [obsolete *chesten* from Old French *chastaine* from Latin *castanea* from Greek *kastanea*]

Chetnik *noun*
• "CHET nick"
• a member of a Serbian nationalist and anti-Communist guerrilla force which operated during both World Wars and re-emerged in the late 1980s.
• [Serbo-Croat *četnik* from *četa* band, troop]

chetrum *noun*
• "CHET room"
• a monetary unit of Bhutan, equal to one-hundredth of a ngultrum.
• [Dzongkha]

chevalier *noun*
• "shev a LEER" or "shuh VAL yay"
• a member of certain orders of knighthood or distinction, as the Legion of Honour in France.
• [Old French from medieval Latin *caballarius* from Latin *caballus* horse]

chevet *noun*
• "shuh VAY"
• the apsidal end of a church, sometimes with an attached group of apses.
• [French, = pillow, from Latin *capitium* from *caput* head]

Cheviot *noun*
• "SHEV ee it" or "CHEV ee it"
• a sheep of a hardy and hornless breed with wool of moderate length and thickness.
• [the *Cheviot* Hills on the English-Scottish border]

chèvre *noun*
• "SHEVRA"
• a soft goat's-milk cheese of a kind orig. from France, usu. made in a log shape.
• [French, = goat]

chevron *noun*
• "SHEV run" or "SHEV ron"
• a badge in a V shape on the sleeve of a uniform indicating rank or length of service.
• [Old French, ultimately from Latin *caper* goat: compare Latin *capreoli* pair of rafters]

chevrotain *noun*
• "SHEVRO tane"
• any small hoofed mammal of the family Tragulidae, native to Africa and SE Asia, resembling a rodent with slender legs, reddish-brown fur spotted with white, and tusks in the male.
• [French, diminutive of Old French *chevrot* diminutive of *chèvre* goat]

Cheyenne *noun*
• "shy ANN" or "shy ENN"
• a member of an Algonquian people formerly living between the Missouri and Arkansas rivers, now inhabiting Oklahoma and Montana.
• [Canadian French from Dakota *Sahiyena*]

chez *preposition*
• "SHAY"
• at the house or home of.
• [French from Old French *chiese* from Latin *casa* cottage]

chi *noun*
• "KIE" (rhymes with *PIE*)
• the twenty-second letter of the Greek alphabet (Χ, χ).
• [Greek *khi*]

chia *noun*
• "CHEE uh"
• a plant of the mint family, *Salvia columbaria*, with clusters of small two-lipped purple flowers, common throughout California.
• [Mexican Spanish from Nahuatl]

Chianti *noun*
• "kee ANTY"
• a dry usu. red Italian wine.
• [*Chianti*, an area in Tuscany, Italy]

chiaroscuro *noun*
• "kee ar oh SCURE oh"
• the treatment of light and shade in drawing and painting.
• [Italian from *chiaro* clear + *oscuro* dark, obscure]

chiasma *noun*
• "kye AZMA"
• an intersection or crossing, esp. the point where the two optic nerves are joined.
• [modern Latin from Greek *chiasma* a cross-shaped mark]

chiasmus *noun*
• "kye AZZ muss"
• inversion in the second of two parallel phrases of the order followed in the first (e.g. *to stop too fearful and too faint to go*).
• [modern Latin from Greek *khiasmos* crosswise arrangement, from *khiazō* mark with letter CHI]
• **chiastic** *adjective*

chibouk *noun*
ALSO SPELLED: **chibouque**
• "chuh BOOK" (rhymes with *SPOOK*)
• a long Turkish tobacco pipe.
• [Turkish *çubuk* tube]

chic *adjective*
• "SHEEK"
• stylish, elegant (in dress or appearance).
• [French, prob. from German *Schick* skill]
• **chicly** *adverb*
• **chicness** *noun*
HOMOPHONES: *sheik*

Chicagoan *noun*
• "shih COGGO 'n"
• a resident of Chicago.

Chicana *noun*
• "chick ONNA" or "chick ANNA"
• a female American of Mexican origin.
• [Spanish *mejicana* Mexican female (see CHICANO)]

chicane *noun*
• "shih CANE"
• an artificial barrier or obstacle on an automobile racetrack.
• [French *chicane(r)* quibble]

chicanery *noun*
• "shi CAY nuh ree"
• clever but misleading talk; a false argument.
• [French *chicanerie* (as CHICANE)]

Chicano *noun*
• "chick ONNO" or "chick ANNO"
• an American, esp. a male, of Mexican origin.
• [Spanish *mejicano* Mexican]

chicle *noun*
• "CHICK'll" or "CHICK lee"
• the milky juice of the sapodilla tree, used in the manufacture of chewing gum.
• [Latin American Spanish from Nahuatl *tzietli*]

chicory *noun*
• "CHICKER ee"
• a blue-flowered plant, *Cichorium intybus*, cultivated for its salad leaves and its root.
• [obsolete French *cicorée* endive, from Latin *cichorium* from Greek *kikhorion*]

chicot *noun*
• "shee COE"
• a dead tree or dead part of a tree.
• [French, = 'stump']

chief *noun*
• "CHEEF"
• a leader or ruler.
• [Old French *ch(i)ef*, ultimately from Latin *caput* head]
• **chiefdom** *noun*

chiefly *adverb*
• "CHEEF lee"
• above all; mainly but not exclusively.
• [as CHIEF]

chieftain *noun*
• "CHEEF t'n"
• the leader of a tribe or clan; chief.
• [Old French *chevetaine* from Late Latin *capitaneus* CAPTAIN: assimilated to CHIEF]
• **chieftaincy** *noun*
• **chieftainship** *noun*

chieftainess *noun*
• "CHEEF t'n ess"
• a female leader of a tribe or clan.
• [as CHIEFTAIN]

chiffon *noun*
• "shif FON"
• a light diaphanous fabric of silk, nylon, etc.
• [French from *chiffe* rag]

chiffonier *noun*
• "shiffa NEER"
• a tall and narrow cabinet with drawers or shelves, often having a small mirror on top.
• [French *chiffonnier*, *-ière* ragpicker, chest of drawers for odds and ends]

chignon *noun*
• "SHEEN yõh" (with a nasal *oh*)
• a coil or knot of hair at the back of a woman's head.
• [French, originally = nape of the neck, based on Latin *catena* chain]

chigoe *noun*
• "CHIGGO"
• a tropical flea, *Tunga penetrans*, the pregnant

females of which burrow beneath the skin of humans and animals and cause painful sores.
• [Carib]

chihuahua *noun*
• "chuh WAH wah"
• a very small breed of dog with smooth hair, large eyes, and prominent ears.
• [*Chihuahua* in N Mexico, where this breed originated]

chilblain *noun*
• "CHILL blane"
• an itching swelling of the skin, usu. on the hands or feet, caused by exposure to cold and by poor circulation.
• ['chill' from Old English *cele, ciele* cold, coldness + BLAIN]
• **chilblained** *adjective*

Chilean *noun*
• "CHILLY 'n" or "chill AY 'n"
• a native or inhabitant of Chile.

chili *noun*
ALSO SPELLED: **chile**, *Brit.* **chilli**
• "CHILLY"
• the small hot-tasting red pod of a capsicum, often dried and ground and used as a seasoning and in several spices.
• [Spanish *chile, chili*, from Aztec *chilli*]
HOMOPHONES: *chilly*

chiliad *noun*
• "KILLY ad"
• a thousand.
• [Late Latin *chilias chiliad-* from Greek *khilias -ados*]

chiliasm *noun*
• "KILLY azm"
• the doctrine of or belief in Christ's prophesied reign of one thousand years on earth.
• [Greek *khiliasmos*: see CHILIAD]
• **chiliast** *noun*
• **chiliastic** *adjective*

Chilkat *noun*
• "CHILL cat"
• a member of a subdivision of the Tlingit people inhabiting the Alaskan coast.
• [Tlingit *jilk̲áat*]

Chilliwack *noun*
• "CHILLA wack"
• a member of a Salishan people, a division of the Halq'emeylem, living in part of the Fraser River valley in BC.
• [Salishan, lit. 'quieter water on the head' or 'travel by way of a backwater']

chimera *noun*
ALSO SPELLED: **chimaera**
• "kye MEERA" or "kim EERA"
• a fire-breathing female monster with a lion's head, a goat's body, and a serpent's tail.
• [Latin from Greek *khimaira* she-goat, chimera]
• **chimeric** *adjective* (also **chimaeric**) "kye MARE ick" or "kim ERIC"
• **chimerical** *adjective* (also **chimaerical**)

chimichanga *noun*
• "chimmy CHANG guh"
• a tortilla wrapped around a filling of meat etc. and deep-fried.
• [Mexican Spanish, = 'trinket']

chiminea *noun*
ALSO SPELLED: **chimenea**
• "chimma NAY uh"
• an earthenware outdoor fireplace shaped like a light bulb, with the bulbous end housing the fire and typically supported by a wrought-iron stand.
• [Mexican Spanish]

chimney *noun*
• "CHIM nee"
• a vertical shaft conducting smoke or combustion gases etc. up and away from a fire, furnace, etc.
• [Old French *cheminée* from Late Latin *caminata* having a fireplace, from Latin *caminus* from Greek *kaminos* oven]

chincherinchee *noun*
• "chincher in CHEE"
• a white-flowered bulbous plant, *Ornithogalum thyrsoides*, native to South Africa.
• [imitative of the squeaky sound made by rubbing its stalks together]

chinchilla *noun*
• "chin CHILLA"
• a small rodent of the genus *Chinchilla*, esp. *C. laniger*, native to S America, having soft silver-grey fur and a bushy tail.
• [Spanish prob. from S American Aboriginal name]

chino *noun*
• "CHEENO"
• a cotton twill fabric, usu. khaki coloured.
• [Latin American Spanish, = toasted]

chinoiserie *noun*
• "sheen wah zuh REE"
• the imitation of Chinese motifs and techniques in painting and in decorating furniture.
• [French]

chinook *noun*
• "shin NOOK" (rhymes with *BOOK*)
• a warm dry wind which blows east of the Rocky Mountains, often causing significant temperature increases in winter.
• [Sne Nay Muxw *tsinúk*]

chinquapin *noun*
• "CHINKA pin"
• any of several N American trees of the beech family, of the deciduous genus *Castanea*, esp. *C. pumila*, resembling the chestnut.
• [Algonquian]

chinse *verb*
• "CHINCE"
• (*Maritimes & New England*) fill (the seams or spaces) in a boat, cabin, etc.
• [dialect var. of 'chink', related to 'chine' from Old French *eschine* from Latin *spina* spine]
HOMOPHONES: *chintz*

chintz *noun*
• "CHINCE"
• a cotton fabric, usu. multicoloured and often with a flower pattern, with a glazed finish.
• [earlier *chints* (pl.) from Hindi *chīṇt* from Sanskrit *citra* variegated]
• **chintzily** *adverb*
• **chintziness** *noun*
• **chintzy** *adjective*
HOMOPHONES: *chinse*

chionodoxa *noun*
• "kye 'n a DOXA"
• any liliaceous plant of the Eurasian genus *Chionodoxa*, having early-blooming blue flowers.
• [modern Latin from Greek *khiōn* snow + *doxa* glory]

Chipewyan *noun*
• "chippa WYE 'n"
• a member of an Athapaskan people inhabiting much of the northern Prairie provinces and the subarctic NWT.
• [Cree *ci:pwaya:n*, lit. '(wearing) pointed-skin (garments)' with reference to a style of drying beaver skins that left shirts with points at the bottom]

chipolata *noun*
• "chipple ATTA"
• a small thin sausage.
• [French from Italian *cipollata* a dish of onions, from *cipolla* onion]

chipotle *noun*
• "chih POTE lay"
• a hot red pepper, usu. smoked, commonly used in Mexican cooking.
• [Mexican Spanish, from Nahuatl *chilli* chili pepper + *poctlí* smoke]

Chippendale *adjective*
• "CHIP'n dale"
• (of furniture) designed or made by the English cabinetmaker Thomas Chippendale (d.1779).

Chippewa *noun*
• "CHIPPA wah"
• a member of an Algonquian people living esp. around Lake Superior and certain adjacent areas; an Ojibwa.
• [alteration of OJIBWA]

chiral *adjective*
• "KIRE'll"
• (of an optically active compound) asymmetric and not superimposable on its mirror image.
• [Greek *kheir* hand]
• **chirality** *noun* "kye RALA tee" or "cant ON 'll"

chiromancy *noun*
• "KYE ro mancy"
• supposed divination from lines and other features on the palm of the hand; palmistry.
• [Greek *kheir* hand + *manteia* divination]

chironomid *noun*
• "kye RONNA mid"
• an insect of the family Chironomidae, which includes many midges.
• [modern Latin *Chironomidae* from Greek *kheironomos* pantomime]

chiropody *noun*
• "shih ROPPA dee" or "kih ROPPA dee"
• esp. *Cdn & Brit.* a medical specialty involving the care of the feet and treatment of foot disorders by surgery, manipulation of soft tissue, medication, etc.; podiatry.
• [Greek *kheir* hand + *pous podos* foot]
• **chiropodist** *noun*

chiropractic *noun*
• "kye roe PRACTIC"
• the diagnosis and manipulative treatment of mechanical disorders of the joints, esp. of the spinal column.
• [Greek *kheir* hand + *praktikos*: see PRACTICAL]
• **chiropractor** *noun*

chiropteran *noun*
• "kye ROPTER 'n"
• any member of the order Chiroptera, which comprises the bats.
• [Greek *kheir* hand + *pteron* wing]

chirr *verb*
ALSO SPELLED: **churr**
• "CHUR"
• (esp. of insects) make a prolonged low trilling sound.
• [imitative]

chirrup *verb*
• "CHUR up"
• (esp. of small birds) chirp, esp. repeatedly; twitter.
• [trilled form of 'chirp', imitative]
• **chirrupy** *adjective*

chiru *noun*
• "CHIH roo"
• an endangered sandy-coloured gazelle with black horns, *Pantholops hodgsoni*, found on the Tibetan plateau.
• [probably from Tibetan]

chisel *noun*
• "CHIZZ'll"
• a hand tool with a squared bevelled blade for shaping wood, stone, or metal.
• [Old Northern French, ultimately from Late Latin *cisorium* from Latin *caedere caes-* cut]
• **chiseller** *noun* (also esp. *US* **chiseler**)

chiselled *adjective*
ALSO SPELLED: esp. *US* **chiseled**
• "CHIZZ'ld"

- (of facial features, muscles, etc.) well defined.
- [as CHISEL]

chital *noun*
- "CHEET'll"
- a S Asian deer with a white-spotted coat, *Axis axis*.
- [Hindi *cītal*]

chitin *noun*
- "KITE 'n"
- a polysaccharide forming the major constituent in the exoskeleton of arthropods and in the cell walls of fungi.
- [French *chitine* from Greek *khitōn*: see CHITON]
- **chitinous** *adjective*

HOMOPHONES: *chiton*

chiton *noun*
- "KITE 'n"
- a long woollen tunic worn by ancient Greeks.
- [Greek *khitōn* tunic]

HOMOPHONES: *chitin*

chivalry *noun*
- "SHIV 'll ree"
- the medieval knightly system with its religious, moral, and social code.
- [Old French *chevalerie* etc. from medieval Latin *caballerius* for Late Latin *caballarius* horseman: see CAVALIER]
- **chivalric** *adjective*
- **chivalrous** *adjective*
- **chivalrously** *adverb*

chlamydia *noun*
- "cluh MIDDY uh"
- any parasitic bacterium of the genus *Chlamydia*, some of which cause diseases such as trachoma and psittacosis.
- [modern Latin from Greek *khlamus -udos* cloak]
- **chlamydial** *adjective*

chloracne *noun*
- "clor ACK nee"
- a skin disease resembling severe acne, caused by exposure to chlorinated chemicals.
- [CHLORINE + ACNE]

chloral *noun*
- "CLOR'll"
- a colourless liquid aldehyde used in making DDT.
- [French from *chlore* chlorine + *alcool* alcohol]

chloramphenicol *noun*
- "clor um FENNA coll"
- an antibiotic prepared from *Streptomyces venezuelae* or produced synthetically and used against severe infections such as typhoid fever.
- [CHLORINE + AMIDE + PHENOL + NITROGEN + GLYCOL]

chlorate *noun*
- "CLOR ate"
- any salt of chloric acid.
- [as CHLORINE]

chlordane *noun*
- "CLOR dane"
- a viscous compound of chlorine, carbon, and hydrogen used as an insecticide.
- [CHLORINE + INDENE]

chlorella *noun*
- "clor ELLA"
- any non-motile unicellular green alga of the genus *Chlorella*.
- [modern Latin, diminutive of Greek *khlōros* green]

chloric *adjective*
- "CLORIC"
- designating a colourless liquid acid with strong oxidizing properties.
- [as CHLORINE]

chloride *noun*
- "CLOR ide"
- any compound of chlorine with another element or group.
- [as CHLORINE]

chlorinate *verb*
- "CLOR 'n ate"
- treat (esp. water) with chlorine, esp. to disinfect.
- [as CHLORINE]
- **chlorination** *noun*
- **chlorinator** *noun*

chlorine *noun*
- "clor EEN" or "CLOR een"
- a poisonous greenish-yellow gaseous element of the halogen group occurring naturally esp. as sodium chloride in salt, sea water, rock salt, etc., and used for purifying water, bleaching, and in the manufacture of many organic chemicals.
- [Greek *khlōros* green]

chlorite *noun*
- "CLOR ite"
- a dark green mineral found in many rocks, consisting of a basic aluminosilicate of magnesium, iron, etc.
- [Greek *khlōros* green + *lithos* stone]
- **chloritic** *adjective* "clor ITTIC"

chlorofluorocarbon *noun*
- "cloro FLORO carb'n"
- any of various usu. gaseous compounds of carbon, hydrogen, chlorine, and fluorine, used in refrigerants, aerosol propellants, etc., and thought to be harmful to the ozone layer in the earth's atmosphere.
- [as CHLORINE + FLUORINE + 'carbon']

chloroform *noun*
- "CLORA form"
- a colourless volatile sweet-smelling liquid used as a solvent and formerly used as a general anaesthetic.
- [French *chloroforme* formed as CHLORINE + *formyle* (see FORMICATION)]

chlorophenol *noun*
• "cloro FEE nawl"
• any phenol derivative in which one or more hydrogen atoms have been replaced by chlorine, such compounds being used in antiseptics, disinfectants, insecticides, herbicides, and dyestuffs.
• [as CHLORINE + PHENOL]

chlorophyll *noun*
• "CLORA fill"
• the green pigment found in most plants, responsible for light absorption to provide energy for photosynthesis.
• [French *chlorophylle* from Greek *khlōros* green + *phullon* leaf]
• **chlorophyllous** *adjective*

chloroplast *noun*
• "CLORO plast"
• a plastid containing chlorophyll found in plant cells.
• [German from Greek *khlōros* green + PLASTID]

chloroquine *noun*
• "CLORO kween"
• a drug related to quinoline used esp. against malaria.
• [CHLORINE + QUINOLINE]

chlorosis *noun*
• "clor OH sis"
• a reduction or loss of the normal green coloration of plants.
• [Greek *khlōros* green]
• **chlorotic** *adjective*

chlorous *adjective*
• "CLOR us"
• designating a pale yellow liquid acid with oxidizing properties.
• [Greek *khlōros* green]

chlorpromazine *noun*
• "clor PROMMA zeen"
• a drug used as a sedative and to control nausea and vomiting.
• [French (as CHLORINE, PROMETHAZINE)]

chocoholic *noun*
ALSO SPELLED: **chocaholic**
• "chocka HOLLIC"
• a person very fond of eating chocolate.
• [blend of CHOCOLATE + ALCOHOLIC]

chocolate *noun*
• "CHOCK lit" or "CHOCKA lit"
• an edible paste or solid made from cacao seeds by roasting, grinding, etc., often combined with flavourings, sugar, cream, etc.
• [French *chocolat* or Spanish *chocolate* from Aztec *chocolatl*]
• **chocolatey** *adjective* (also **chocolaty**)

chocolatier *noun*
• "chock'll a TEER" or "shock'll at YAY"
• a maker or seller of chocolate, esp. of fine quality.
• [French]

Choctaw *noun*
• "CHOCK taw"
• a member of a Muskogean people originally resident in Mississippi and Alabama, and subsequently in Oklahoma.
• [Choctaw *čahta*]

choir *noun*
• "KWIRE"
• a group or company of singers, esp. taking part in church services or performing concerts.
• [Old French *quer* from Latin *chorus*: see CHORUS]
• **choirboy** *noun*
• **choirgirl** *noun*
• **choirmaster** *noun*
HOMOPHONES: *quire*

cholangiography *noun*
• "coll'n jee OGGRA fee"
• X-ray examination of the bile ducts, used to find the site and nature of any obstruction.
• [Greek *kholē* gall, bile + *aggeion* vessel + *graphia* writing]

cholecalciferol *noun*
• "colla cal SIFFER awl"
• one of the D vitamins, produced by the action of sunlight on a cholesterol derivative widely distributed in the skin, a deficiency of which results in rickets in children and osteomalacia in adults.
• [Greek *kholē* gall, bile + CALCIFEROL]

cholecystectomy *noun*
• "colla sis TECTA mee"
• surgical removal of the gallbladder.
• [Greek *kholē* gall, bile + CYST + *ektomē* excision, from *ek* out + *temnō* cut]

cholecystography *noun*
• "colla sis TOGGRA fee"
• X-ray examination of the gallbladder, esp. used to detect the presence of any gallstones.
• [Greek *kholē* gall, bile + CYST + *graphia* writing]

cholecystokinin *noun*
• "colla sisto KYE nin"
• a hormone which is secreted by cells in the duodenum and stimulates the release of bile into the intestine and the secretion of enzymes by the pancreas.
• [Greek *kholē* gall, bile + CYST + KININ]

cholent *noun*
• "CHOLL 'nt"
• a Jewish Sabbath dish of slowly baked meat and vegetables, prepared on a Friday and cooked overnight.
• [Yiddish *tscholnt*]

choler *noun*
• "CALL ur"
• bile regarded as one of the four bodily humours.
• [Old French *colere* bile, anger, from Latin *cholera* from Greek *kholera* diarrhea, in Late Latin = bile, anger, from Greek *kholē* bile]
HOMOPHONES: *collar*, *caller*

cholera *noun*
- "COLLER uh"
- an infectious and often fatal disease of the small intestine caused by the bacterium *Vibrio cholerae*, resulting in severe vomiting and diarrhea.
- [see CHOLER]
- **choleraic** *adjective* "coller AY ick"

choleric *adjective*
- "COLLA rick"
- irascible, angry.
- [as CHOLER]

cholesterol *noun*
- "kuh LESTER awl"
- a sterol found in most body tissues, including the blood, where high concentrations promote arteriosclerosis.
- [*cholesterin* from Greek *kholē* bile + *stereos* stiff]

choli *noun*
- "CHOE lee"
- a short-sleeved bodice worn as part of some East Indian women's clothing.
- [Hindi *colī*]

choliamb *noun*
- "COLEY amb"
- a Greek or Latin metre of limping character, esp. a trimeter of two iambs and a spondee or trochee.
- [Late Latin *choliambus* from Greek *khōliambos* from *khōlos* lame: see IAMBUS]
- **choliambic** *adjective*

choline *noun*
- "COE leen"
- a basic nitrogenous organic compound occurring widely in living matter.
- [German *Cholin* from Greek *kholē* bile]

cholinergic *adjective*
- "cole 'n UR jick"
- releasing or involving acetylcholine as a neurotransmitter.
- [CHOLINE + Greek *ergon* work]

cholinesterase *noun*
- "cole 'n ESTER ace"
- an enzyme which hydrolyzes esters of choline.
- [as CHOLINE + ESTER]

cholla *noun*
- "CHOYA"
- any of several cacti of the genus *Opuntia*, native to the southern US and Central America.
- [Latin American Spanish, lit. 'skull, head']

chon *noun*
- "CHON"
- a monetary unit of North and South Korea, equal to one-hundredth of a won.
- [Korean]

chondrite *noun*
- "CON drite"
- a stony meteorite containing small mineral granules.
- [German *Chondrit* from Greek *khondros* granule]
- **chondritic** *adjective* "con DRITTIC"

choral *adjective*
- "CORE 'll"
- of, for, or sung by a choir or chorus.
- [medieval Latin *choralis* from Latin *chorus*: see CHORUS]
- **chorally** *adverb*

HOMOPHONES: *coral*

chorale *noun*

ALSO SPELLED: **choral**
- "core AL"
- a stately and simple hymn tune.
- [German *Choral(gesang)* from medieval Latin *cantus choralis*]

HOMOPHONES: *corral*

chord *noun*
- "CORD"
- a group of (usu. three or more) notes sounded together, as a basis of harmony.
- [originally *cord* from ACCORD: later confused with 'chord' string, from Latin *chorda*]
- **chordal** *adjective*

HOMOPHONES: *cord*

chordate *noun*
- "CORD ate"
- any animal of the phylum Chordata, possessing a notochord at some stage during its development.
- [modern Latin *chordata* from Latin *chorda* string, after *Vertebrata* etc.]

HOMOPHONES: *cordate*

chorea *noun*
- "kuh REE uh"
- a disorder characterized by jerky involuntary movements affecting esp. the shoulders, hips, and face.
- [Latin from Greek *khoreia* (as CHORUS)]

choreograph *verb*
- "COREY a graff"
- compose the choreography for (a ballet etc.).
- [back-formation from CHOREOGRAPHY]

choreography *noun*
- "corey OGGRA fee"
- the design or arrangement of a staged dance, figure skating, etc.
- [Greek *khoreia* dance + *graphia* writing]
- **choreographer** *noun*
- **choreographic** *adjective*
- **choreographically** *adverb*

choreology *noun*
- "corey OLLA jee"
- the description of dance steps by a system of graphic notation.
- [as CHOREOGRAPHY + Greek *logos* word]
- **choreologist** *noun*

choriamb *noun*
• "COREY amb"
• a metrical foot consisting of two short (unstressed) syllables between two long (stressed) ones.
• [Late Latin Greek *khoriambos* from *khoreios* of the dance + IAMBUS]
• **choriambic** *adjective*

choric *adjective*
• "CORIC"
• of, like, or for a chorus in drama or recitation.
• [as CHORUS]

chorine *noun*
• "CORE een"
• a chorus girl.
• [CHORUS + '-ine' French feminine ending from Latin *-ina* from Greek *-inē*]

chorion *noun*
• "COREY 'n"
• the outermost membrane surrounding an embryo of a mammal, reptile, or bird.
• [Greek *khorion*]
• **chorionic** *adjective*

chorister *noun*
• "CORE iss tur"
• a member of a choir.
• [Middle English, ultimately from Old French *cueriste* from *quer* CHOIR]

chorizo *noun*
• "chur EEZO"
• a type of sausage containing pork, garlic, and hot spices.
• [Spanish]

choroid *adjective*
• "CORE oid"
• like a chorion in shape or vascularity.
• [Greek *khoroeidēs* for *khorioeidēs*: see CHORION]

chorus *noun*
• "CORE us"
• a group (esp. a large one) of singers; a choir.
• [Latin from Greek *khoros*]

choucroute *noun*
• "shoo CROOT"
• sauerkraut as prepared in Alsace, France, with bacon and sausages.
• [French, from German dialect *Surkrut* sauerkraut, influenced by French *chou* cabbage]

chough *noun*
• "CHUFF"
• any corvine bird of the genus *Pyrrhocorax*, with a glossy blue-black plumage and red legs.
• [Middle English, prob. originally imitative]
HOMOPHONES: *chuff*

chrism *noun*
• "CRIZZ'm"
• a consecrated mixture of oil and balsam used for anointing in rites of the Catholic and Orthodox Churches.
• [Old English *crisma* from Church Latin from Greek *khrisma* anointing]
HOMOPHONES: *chrisom*

chrisom *noun*
• "CRIZZ'm"
• a white robe put on a child at baptism, and used as its shroud if the child died within the month.
• [Middle English, as popular pronunciation of CHRISM]
HOMOPHONES: *chrism*

Christadelphian *noun*
• "crissta DELFY 'n"
• a member of a Christian denomination founded in the US, rejecting the doctrine of the Trinity and expecting a second coming of Christ on earth.
• ['Christ' + Greek *adelphos* brother]

christen *verb*
• "CRISS'n"
• admit (a person) to the Christian Church by baptism.
• [Old English *crīstnian* make Christian]
• **christener** *noun*
• **christening** *noun*

Christendom *noun*
• "CRISS'n dum"
• Christians worldwide, regarded as a collective body.
• [Old English *cristendōm* from *cristen* Christian]

Christian *adjective*
• "CRISS ch'n",
• pertaining to Christ or his teachings.
• [Latin *Christianus* from *Christus* Christ]
• **Christianization** *noun* (also esp. *Brit.* **-isation**)
• **Christianize** *verb* (also esp. *Brit.* **-ise**)
• **Christianly** *adverb*

Christianity *noun*
• "criss chee ANNA tee" or "crissty ANNA tee"
• the religion based on the doctrines of Christ and his disciples, encompassing the Catholic, Protestant, and Orthodox faiths.
• [as CHRISTIAN]

Christie *noun*
ALSO SPELLED: **Christy**
• "CRISSTY"
• (in skiing) a sudden turn in which the skis are kept parallel, used for changing direction or stopping quickly.
• [abbreviation of *Christiania*, former name of Oslo, Norway]

Christmas *noun*
• "CRISS muss"
• the annual festival of Christ's birth, celebrated by western churches on 25 December, and by most eastern churches on 7 January.
• [Old English *Crīstes mæsse* 'Christ's mass']
• **Christmastide** *noun*
• **Christmastime** *noun*
• **Christmasy** *adjective* (also **Christmassy**)

Christology *noun*
• "criss TOLLA jee"
• the branch of Christian theology relating specifically to the nature, acts, and person of Christ.
• ['Christ' + Greek *logos* word]
• **Christological** *adjective*

chroma *noun*
• "CROW muh"
• purity or intensity of colour.
• [Greek *khrōma* colour]

chromate *noun*
• "CROW mate"
• a salt or ester of chromic acid.
• [as CHROME]

chromatic *adjective*
• "crow MATTIC"
• of or produced by colour; in (esp. bright) colours.
• [French *chromatique* or Latin *chromaticus* from Greek *khrōmatikos* from *khrōma -atos* colour]
• **chromatically** *adverb*
• **chromaticism** *noun* "crow MATTA sizm"

chromaticity *noun*
• "crow muh TISSA tee"
• the quality of colour regarded independently of brightness.
• [as CHROMATIC]

chromatid *noun*
• "CROW muh tid"
• either of two threadlike strands into which a chromosome divides longitudinally during cell division.
• [Greek *khrōma -atos* colour]

chromatin *noun*
• "CROW muh tin"
• the material in a cell nucleus that stains with basic dyes and consists of protein, RNA, and DNA, of which eukaryotic chromosomes are composed.
• [German: see CHROMATID]

chromatography *noun*
• "crow muh TOGGRA fee"
• the separation of the components of a mixture by slow passage through or over a material which adsorbs them differently.
• [German *Chromatographie* (as CHROMATIC, Greek *graphia* writing)]
• **chromatograph** *noun*
• **chromatographic** *adjective*

chromatophore *noun*
• "crow MATTA for"
• a cell or plastid containing pigment.
• [as CHROMATIC + Greek *-phoros -phoron* bearing, bearer, from *pherō* bear]

chrome *noun*
• "CROME"
• chromium, esp. as plating on the trimmings of a car etc.
• [French, = chromium, from Greek *khrōma* colour]
• **chromed** *adjective*

chromic *adjective*
• "CROW mick"
• of or containing trivalent chromium.
• [as CHROME]

chrominance *noun*
• "CROW m'n ince"
• the colorimetric difference between a given colour and a standard colour of equal luminance.
• [from CHROMATIC after LUMINANCE]

chromite *noun*
• "CROME ite"
• a black mineral of chromium and iron oxides, which is the principal ore of chromium.
• [as CHROME]

chromium *noun*
• "CROW mee um"
• a hard white metallic transition element, occurring naturally as chromite and used in alloys and as a shiny decorative electroplated coating.
• [modern Latin from French CHROME]

chromogenic *adjective*
• "crow muh JENNIC"
• colour-producing.
• [as CHROMATIC + GENESIS]

chromolithograph *noun*
• "crow moe LITHA graff"
• a coloured picture printed by lithography.
• [as CHROMATIC + LITHOGRAPH]
• **chromolithographer** *noun*
• **chromolithographic** *adjective*
• **chromolithography** *noun*

chromophore *noun*
• "CROW muh for"
• that part of the molecule that is responsible for a compound's colour.
• [as CHROME + Greek *-phoros -phoron* bearing, bearer, from *pherō* bear]

chromosome *noun*
• "CROW muh soam"
• one of the threadlike structures, usu. found in the cell nucleus, that carry the genetic information in the form of genes.
• [German *Chromosom* (Greek *khrōma -atos* colour, *sōma* body)]
• **chromosomal** *adjective*

chromosphere *noun*
• "CROW muh sfeer"
• a gaseous layer of the sun's atmosphere between the photosphere and the corona.
• [CHROMATIC + SPHERE]
• **chromospheric** *adjective*

chronic *adjective*
• "CRONNIC"
• persisting for a long time (usu. of an illness or a personal or social problem).

• [French *chronique* from Latin *chronicus* (in Late Latin of disease), from Greek *khronikos* from *khronos* time]
• **chronically** *adverb*
• **chronicity** *noun* "cruh NISSA tee"

chronicle *noun*
• "CRONNA k'll"
• a register of events in order of their occurrence.
• [Anglo-French *cronicle*, ultimately from Latin *chronica* from Greek *khronika* annals: see CHRONIC]
• **chronicler** *noun*

chronobiology *noun*
• "crow no by OLLA jee"
• the branch of biology concerned with natural physiological rhythms and other cyclical phenomena.
• [Greek *khronos* time + BIOLOGY]
• **chronobiologist** *noun*

chronograph *noun*
• "CRONNA graff" or "CROW nuh graff"
• an instrument for recording time with great accuracy.
• [Greek *khronos* time + *graphia* writing]
• **chronographic** *adjective*

chronology *noun*
• "cruh NOLLA jee"
• the arrangement of events, dates, etc. in the order of their occurrence.
• [modern Latin *chronologia* from Greek *khronos* time + *logos* word]
• **chronological** *adjective*
• **chronologically** *adverb*
• **chronologist** *noun*
• **chronologize** *verb* (also esp. *Brit.* **-ise**)

chronometer *noun*
• "cruh NOMMA tur"
• a time-measuring instrument, esp. one keeping accurate time at all temperatures and used in navigation.
• [Greek *khronos* time + *metron* measure]

chronometry *noun*
• "cruh NOMMA tree"
• the science of accurate time measurement.
• [as CHRONOMETER]
• **chronometric** *adjective* "crow no METRIC"

chronotherapy *noun*
• "CROW no therra pee"
• the treatment of an illness or disorder by administering a drug at a time of day believed to be in harmony with the body's natural rhythms.
• [Greek *khronos* time + THERAPY]

chrysalis *noun*
• "CRISSA liss"
• a quiescent pupa of a butterfly or moth.
• [Latin from Greek *khrusallis -idos* from *khrusos* gold]

chrysanthemum *noun*
• "cruh SANTHA mum"
• any composite plant of the genus *Chrysanthemum*, having brightly coloured flowers.
• [Latin from Greek *khrusanthemon* from *khrusos* gold + *anthemon* flower]

chryselephantine *adjective*
• "cris ella FAN tine"
• (of ancient Greek sculpture) overlaid with gold and ivory.
• [Greek *khruselephantinos* from *khrusos* gold + *elephas* ivory]

chrysoberyl *noun*
• "CRISSA bare 'll"
• a yellowish-green gem consisting of a beryllium salt.
• [Latin *chrysoberyllus* from Greek *khrusos* gold + *bērullos* beryl]

chrysolite *noun*
• "CRISSA lite"
• a precious stone, a yellowish-green or brownish variety of olivine.
• [Old French *crisolite* from Latin *chrysolithus* from Greek *khrusolithos* from *khrusos* gold + *lithos* stone]

chrysoprase *noun*
• "CRISSA praze"
• an apple green variety of chalcedony containing nickel and used as a gem.
• [Latin *chrysoprasus* from Greek *khrusoprasos* from *khrusos* gold + *prason* leek]

chrysotile *noun*
• "CRISSA tile"
• fibrous serpentine, an important asbestos mineral.
• [Greek *khrūsos* gold + *tilos* fibre]

chthonic *adjective*
• "k'THONNIC" or "THONNIC"
• of, relating to, or inhabiting the underworld.
• [Greek *khthōn* earth]

chuckwalla *noun*
• "CHUCK wolla"
• a large dark-bodied lizard of the iguana family, *Sauromalus obesus*, of Mexico and the southwestern US. When threatened it inflates itself with air to wedge itself into a crevice.
• [Mexican Spanish *chacahuala*]

chukar *noun*
• "chuh CAR"
• a Eurasian red-legged partridge, *Alectoris chukar*, introduced into the Rockies and also domesticated.
• [Hindi *cakor*]

Chukchi *noun*
• "CHUCK chee"
• a member of an Aboriginal people of extreme NE Siberia.
• [Russian]

chuppah *noun*
ALSO SPELLED: ***chuppa***
• "HOOPA" (with "OO" as in *HOOK*)
• a canopy beneath which Jewish marriage ceremonies are performed.
• [Hebrew *ḥuppāh* cover, canopy]

Churchillian *adjective*
• "chur CHILLY 'n"
• of or characteristic of the British prime minister Winston Churchill (d.1965).

churchwarden *noun*
• "CHURCH ward'n"
• either of two elected lay representatives of a parish, assisting with routine administration.
• ['church' (Old English *cirice*, *circe*, etc. from medieval Greek *kurikon* from Greek *kuriakon (dōma)* Lord's (house) from *kurios* Lord) + 'warden' (Old Northern French *wardein* var. of Old French *g(u)arden* guardian)]

churidars *plural noun*
• "CHURRID arz"
• tight trousers worn by people from the Indian subcontinent, typically with a kameez.
• [Hindi *cūṛīdār* 'having a series of gathered rows' (i.e. at the bottom of the trouser leg, traditionally worn too long and tucked up)]

churinga *noun*
• "chuh RING guh"
• a sacred object, esp. an amulet, among the Australian Aboriginals.
• [Aranda *j*[w]*errenge* 'object from the dreaming']

churl *noun*
• "CHURL"
• an ill-mannered person.
• [Old English *ceorl* from a West Germanic root, = man]
• **churlish** *adjective*
• **churlishly** *adverb*
• **churlishness** *noun*

Churrigueresque *adjective*
• "churra guh RESK"
• lavishly ornamented in the late Spanish baroque style.
• [José de *Churriguera*, Spanish architect d.1725]

churro *noun*
• "CHUR oh"
• a deep-fried ring-shaped pastry of Latin America, often sugar-coated.
• [Spanish]

chute *noun*
• "SHOOT"
• a sloping or vertical channel, tube, or slide, with or without water, for conveying things to a lower level.
• [French *chute* fall (of water etc.), from Old French *cheoite* feminine past participle of *cheoir* fall, from Latin *cadere*]
HOMOPHONES: *shoot*

chutney *noun*
• "CHUT nee"
• a spicy, originally Indian, condiment made of fruits or vegetables, vinegar, sugar, etc.
• [Hindi *caṭnī*]

chutzpah *noun*
• "HOOTS puh" (with "OO" as in *HOOK*) or "HUTS puh"
• shameless audacity; cheek.
• [Yiddish]

chyle *noun*
• "KILE"
• a milky fluid consisting of lymph and absorbed food materials from the intestine after digestion.
• [Late Latin *chylus* from Greek *khulos* juice]
• **chylous** *adjective*

chyme *noun*
• "KIME"
• the acidic semi-solid and partly digested food produced by the action of gastric secretion.
• [Late Latin *chymus* from Greek *khumos* juice]
• **chymous** *adjective*

chymotrypsin *noun*
• "kye muh TRIP sin"
• a proteolytic enzyme active in the small intestine.
• [CHYME + TRYPSIN]

chypre *noun*
• "SHEEPRA"
• a heavy perfume made from sandalwood.
• [French, = Cyprus, perhaps where it was first made]

ciabatta *noun*
• "chuh BOTTA"
• a type of flattish, open-textured Italian bread with a floury crust, made with olive oil.
• [Italian, lit. 'slipper' (from its shape)]

ciao *interjection*
• "CHOW"
• goodbye.
• [Italian]
HOMOPHONES: *chow*

ciborium *noun*
• "suh BORY um"
• a vessel with an arched cover used to hold the Eucharist.
• [medieval Latin from Greek *kibōrion* seed vessel of the water lily, a cup made from it]

cicada *noun*
• "suh CAY duh"
• any transparent-winged large insect of the family Cicadidae, the males of which make a loud, shrill chirping sound.
• [Latin *cicada*, Italian from Latin *cicala*, Italian *cigala*]

cicatrice *noun*
• "SICKA triss"
• any mark left by a healed wound; a scar.

• [Old French *cicatrice* or Latin *cicatrix -icis*]
• **cicatricial** *adjective* "sicka TRISH'll"

cicatrize *verb*
ALSO SPELLED: esp. *Brit.* **-ise**
• "SICKA trize"
• heal (a wound) by scar formation.
• [French *cicatriser*: see CICATRICE]
• **cicatrization** *noun* (also esp. *Brit.* **-isation**)

cicely *noun*
• "SISSLE ee"
• an aromatic white-flowered plant of the parsley family, with fern-like leaves.
• [apparently from Latin *seselis* from Greek, assimilated to the woman's name]

cicerone *noun*
• "sisser OWNY"
• a guide who gives information about antiquities, places of interest, etc. to sightseers.
• [Italian, apparently in allusion to Cicero's eloquence and learning: see CICERONIAN]

Ciceronian *adjective*
• "sisser OH nee 'n"
• (of language) eloquent, classical, or rhythmical, in the style of the Roman statesman and writer Marcus Tullius Cicero (d.43 BC).
• [Latin *Ciceronianus* from *Cicero -onis*]

cichlid *noun*
• "SICK lid"
• any tropical freshwater fish of the family Cichlidae, esp. the kinds kept in aquariums.
• [modern Latin *Cichlidae* from Greek *kikhlē* a kind of fish]

cider *noun*
• "SIDE ur"
• an unfermented drink made from apple juice.
• [Old French *sidre*, ultimately from Hebrew *šēkār* strong drink]

cigar *noun*
• "suh GAR"
• a cylinder of tobacco rolled in tobacco leaves for smoking.
• [French *cigare* or Spanish *cigarro*, probably from Mayan *sik'ar* smoking]

cigarette *noun*
• "sigga RET"
• a thin cylinder of finely-cut tobacco rolled in paper for smoking.
• [French, diminutive of *cigare* CIGAR]

cigarillo *noun*
• "sigga RILLO"
• a small cigar.
• [Spanish, diminutive of *cigarro* CIGAR]

cilantro *noun*
• "sill AN tro"
• fresh coriander, used as a herb.
• [Spanish from Late Latin *coliandrum*, alteration of Latin *coriandrum* coriander]

cilia *plural noun*
• "SILLY uh"
• short minute hairlike vibrating structures on the surface of some cells, causing currents in the surrounding fluid.
• [Latin, = eyelash]
• **ciliary** *adjective* "SILLY airy"
• **ciliated** *adjective*
• **ciliation** *noun*

ciliate *adjective*
• "SILLY ate"
• having cilia.
• [as CILIA]

cimbalom *noun*
• "SIMBA lum"
• a dulcimer.
• [Hungarian from Italian *cembalo*]

cimetidine *noun*
• "sye METTA deen"
• an antihistamine drug that reduces secretion of acid in the stomach, used to treat digestive disorders.
• [CYANOGEN + METHYL]

Cimmerian *noun*
• "sim EERY 'n"
• a member of an ancient nomadic people, the earliest known inhabitants of the Crimea, who overran Asia Minor in the 7th century BC.
• [via Latin from Greek *Kimmerios*]

cinch *noun*
• "SINCH"
• a sure thing; a certainty.
• [Spanish *cincha* girth]

cinchona *noun*
• "sing CONE uh"
• any evergreen tree or shrub of the genus *Cinchona*, native to S America, with fragrant flowers and yielding a bark which contains quinine.
• [modern Latin from Countess of Chinchón d.1641, introducer of quinine into Spain]

cincture *noun*
• "SINK chur"
• a girdle, belt, or border.
• [Latin *cinctura* from *cingere cinct-* gird]

cinder *noun*
• "SIN dur"
• the residue of coal or wood etc. that has stopped giving off flames but still has combustible matter in it.
• [Old English *sinder*, assimilated to the unconnected French *cendre* and Latin *cinis* ashes]
• **cindery** *adjective*

cineaste *noun*
• "SINNAY ast" or "SINNY ast"
• a person working in professional filmmaking, esp. a director or producer.
• [French *cinéaste* (as CINEMATOGRAPHY)]

cinema *noun*
- "SINNA muh"
- motion pictures collectively.
- [French *cinéma*: see CINEMATOGRAPHY]

cinematheque *noun*
- "SINNA muh teck"
- a film library or archive.
- [French]

cinematic *adjective*
- "sinna MATTIC"
- having the qualities characteristic of the cinema.
- [as CINEMATOGRAPHY]
- **cinematically** *adverb*

cinematography *noun*
- "sinna muh TOGGRA fee"
- the art or technique of shooting motion pictures, involving the choice of film, camera, lens, lighting, camera angle, etc.
- [French *cinématographe*, an early motion picture projector, from Greek *kinēma -atos* movement, from *kineō* move + *graphia* writing]
- **cinematographer** *noun*
- **cinematographic** *adjective*
- **cinematographically** *adverb*

cinephile *noun*
- "SINNA file"
- a person who is fond of films, the history of cinema, etc.
- [French *cinéphile* (as CINEMATOGRAPHY + Greek *philos* dear, loving)]

cineraria *noun*
- "sinner AIRY uh"
- any of a variety of hybrids of the species *Pericallis cruenta* having bright daisy-like flowers and frequently grown as a houseplant.
- [modern Latin, feminine of Latin *cinerarius* of ashes, from *cinis -eris* ashes, from the ash-coloured down on the leaves]

cinerarium *noun*
- "sinner AIRY um"
- a place where a cinerary urn is deposited.
- [Late Latin, neuter of *cinerarius*: see CINERARIA]

cinerary *adjective*
- "SINNER airy"
- of ashes.
- [Latin *cinerarius*: see CINERARIA]

cinereous *adjective*
- "sin EERY us"
- (esp. of a bird or plumage) ash-grey.
- [Latin *cinereus* from *cinis -eris* ashes]

cingulum *noun*
- "SING gyuh lum"
- a girdle, belt, or analogous structure, esp. a ridge surrounding the base of the crown of a tooth.
- [Latin, = belt]
- **cingulate** *adjective*

cinnabar *noun*
- "SINNA bar"
- a bright red mineral form of mercuric sulphide from which mercury is obtained.
- [Latin *cinnabaris* from Greek *kinnabari*, of oriental origin]

cinnamon *noun*
- "SINNA m'n"
- an aromatic spice from the peeled, dried, and rolled bark of a SE Asian tree.
- [Old French *cinnamome* from Greek *kinnamōmon*, and Latin *cinnamon* from Greek *kinnamon*, from Semitic (compare Hebrew *ḳinnāmôn*)]
- **cinnamony** *adjective*

cinquecento *noun*
- "chin kwuh CHENTO"
- the style of Italian art and literature of the 16th c., with a reversion to classical forms.
- [Italian, = 500, used with reference to the years 1500–99]
- **cinquecentist** *noun*

cinquefoil *noun*
- "SINK foil"
- any plant of the genus *Potentilla*, with compound leaves of usu. five leaflets.
- [Latin *quinquefolium* from *quinque* five + *folium* leaf]

Cinsault *noun*
ALSO SPELLED: **Cinsaut**
- "san SO"
- a red grape variety originally of the Languedoc region in S France, used in rosé wines and blended with other grapes.
- [French]

cipaille *noun*
- "see PIE"
- *Cdn* a deep pie with alternating layers of meat and pastry.
- [Canadian French]

cipher *noun*
ALSO SPELLED: **cypher**
- "SIFE ur"
- a secret or disguised system of writing; a code.
- [Old French *cif(f)re*, ultimately from Arabic *ṣifr* zero]

circa *preposition*
- "SURKA"
- (preceding a date) about, approximately.
- [Latin]

circadian *adjective*
- "sur CAY dee 'n"
- of or pertaining to physiological and psychological processes occurring or recurring about once per day.
- [Latin *circa* about + *dies* day]

Circassian *noun*
- "sur CASSY 'n"

• a native or inhabitant of Circassia, a region in the N Caucasus.
• [*Circassia*, Latinized form of Russian *Cherkes*]

circinate *adjective*
• "SUR s'n ate"
• rolled up with the apex in the centre, e.g. of young fronds of ferns.
• [Latin *circinatus* past participle of *circinare* make round, from *circinus* pair of compasses]

circuit *noun*
• "SUR kit"
• a line or course enclosing an area; the distance around.
• [Old French, from Latin *circuitus* from *circum* prep. = round, about + *ire it-* go]

circuitous *adjective*
• "sur KYOO it us"
• indirect (and usu. long).
• [medieval Latin *circuitosus* from *circuitus* CIRCUIT]
• **circuitously** *adverb*
• **circuitousness** *noun*

circuitry *noun*
• "SURKA tree"
• a system of electric circuits.
• [as CIRCUIT]

circular *adjective*
• "SUR kyuh lur"
• having the form of a circle.
• [Anglo-French *circuler* from Late Latin *circularis* from Latin *circulus* circle]
• **circularity** *noun* "sur kyuh LERRA tee"
• **circularly** *adverb*

circulate *verb*
• "SUR kyoo late"
• go round from one place or person etc. to the next and so on; be in circulation.
• [Latin *circulare circulat-* from *circulus* circle]
• **circulation** *noun*
• **circulator** *noun*

circulatory *adjective*
• "SUR kyoo luh tory"
• of or relating to the circulation of blood or sap.
• [as CIRCULATE]

circumambient *adjective*
• "sur k'm AMBY 'nt"
• (esp. of air or another fluid) surrounding.
• [Latin *circum* around, about + AMBIENT]

circumambulate *verb*
• "sur k'm AM byoo late"
• walk around or about.
• [Latin *circum* around, about + *ambulate* from Latin *ambulare* walk]
• **circumambulation** *noun*
• **circumambulatory** *adjective*

circumboreal *adjective*
• "sur k'm BORRY 'll"
• of or pertaining to boreal regions around the world.
• [Latin *circum* around, about + BOREAL]

circumcise *verb*
• "SUR k'm size"
• cut off the foreskin of, as a Jewish or Muslim rite or a surgical operation.
• [Latin *circumcidere circumcis-* (from *circum* around, about + *caedere* cut)]
• **circumcision** *noun* "sur k'm SIZH'n"

circumference *noun*
• "sur KUM fur ince"
• the enclosing boundary, esp. of a circle or other figure enclosed by a curve.
• [Old French *circonference* from Latin *circumferentia* (from *circum* around, about + *ferre* bear)]
• **circumferential** *adjective*
• **circumferentially** *adverb*

circumflex *noun*
• "SUR k'm flex"
• a mark (ˆ or ˜) placed over a vowel in some languages to indicate a contraction, length, or a special quality.
• [Latin *circumflexus* (from *circum* around, about + *flectere flex-* bend), translation of Greek *perispōmenos* drawn around]

circumlocution *noun*
• "sur k'm luh KYOO sh'n"
• a roundabout expression.
• [Latin *circum* around, about + LOCUTION]
• **circumlocutory** *adjective*
"sur k'm LOCK yoo tory"

circumlunar *adjective*
• "sur k'm LOONER"
• moving or situated around the moon.
• [Latin *circum* around, about + LUNAR]

circumnavigate *verb*
• "sur k'm NAVVA gate"
• sail or fly around (esp. the world).
• [Latin *circum* around, about + NAVIGATE]
• **circumnavigation** *noun*
• **circumnavigator** *noun*

circumpolar *adjective*
• "sur k'm POLE ur"
• around or near one of the earth's poles.
• [Latin *circum* around, about + POLAR]

circumscribe *verb*
• "SUR k'm scribe"
• (of a line etc.) enclose or outline.
• [Latin *circumscribere* (from *circum* around, about + *scribere script-* write)]
• **circumscription** *noun* "sur k'm SCRIP sh'n"

circumsolar *adjective*
• "sur k'm SO lur"
• moving or situated around or near the sun.
• [Latin *circum* around, about + SOLAR]

circumspect *adjective*
• "SUR k'm spect"
• wary, cautious; taking everything into account.

• [Latin *circumspicere circumspect-* (*circum* around, about + *specere spect-* look)]
• **circumspection** *noun*
• **circumspectly** *adverb*

circumstance *noun*
• "SUR k'm stance"
• a fact, occurrence, or condition, esp. the time, place, manner, cause, occasion etc., or surroundings of an act or event.
• [Latin *circumstantia* (from *circum* around, about + *stantia* from *sto* stand)]
• **circumstanced** *adjective*

circumstantial *adjective*
• "sur k'm STAN sh'll"
• given in full detail.
• [as CIRCUMSTANCE]
• **circumstantiality** *noun*
"sur k'm stanshy ALA tee"
• **circumstantially** *adverb*

circumterrestrial *adjective*
• "sur k'm tuh RESS tree 'll"
• moving or situated around the earth.
• [Latin *circum* around, about + TERRESTRIAL]

circumvallate *verb*
• "sur k'm VAL ate"
• surround with or as with a rampart.
• [Latin *circumvallare circumvallat-* (from *circum* around, about + *vallare* from *vallum* rampart)]
• **circumvallation** *noun*

circumvent *verb*
• "sur k'm VENT"
• evade (a difficulty); find a way around.
• [Latin *circumvenire circumvent-* (from *circum* around, about + *venire* come)]
• **circumvention** *noun*

circumvolution *noun*
• "sur k'm vuh LOO sh'n"
• rotation.
• [Latin *circumvolvere circumvolut-* (*circum* around, about + *volvere* roll)]

ciré *noun*
• "SEE ray"
• a fabric with a smooth shiny surface obtained esp. by waxing and heating.
• [French, = waxed]

cirque *noun*
• "SURK"
• a large bowl-shaped hollow of glacial origin at the head of a valley or on a mountainside.
• [French from Latin *circus* ring]

cirrhosis *noun*
• "suh ROE sis"
• a chronic disease of the liver caused by alcoholism, hepatitis, etc. in which much of the liver is replaced by fibrous tissue.
• [modern Latin from Greek *kirrhos* tawny]
• **cirrhotic** *adjective*
HOMOPHONES: *sorosis*

cirriped *noun*
• "SEERA ped"
• any marine crustacean of the class Cirripedia, having a valved shell and usu. sessile when adult, e.g. a barnacle.
• [Latin *cirrus* curl (from the form of the legs) + *pes pedis* foot]

cirrocumulus *noun*
• "seero KYOO myoo luss"
• cloud forming a broken layer of small fleecy clouds at high altitude, as in a mackerel sky.
• [CIRRUS + CUMULUS]

cirrostratus *noun*
• "seero STRAT us"
• cloud forming a thin, fairly uniform layer at high altitude.
• [CIRRUS + STRATUS]

cirrus *noun*
• "SEER us"
• clouds formed at high altitudes as delicate white wisps.
• [Latin, = curl]
HOMOPHONES: *scirrhus, scirrhous*

cisalpine *adjective*
• "sis ALPINE"
• on the southern side of the Alps.
• [Latin *cis* on this side of + 'alpine' after the *Alps* mountain range in central Europe]

cisatlantic *adjective*
• "sis at LANTIC"
• on one's own side of the Atlantic.
• [Latin *cis* on this side of + the *Atlantic* ocean]

cisco *noun*
• "SIS coe"
• any of various freshwater salmonid whitefish of the genus *Coregonus*, native to N America.
• [Canadian French, back-formation from *ciscoette, ciscaouette*, ultimately from Ojibwa]

cislunar *adjective*
• "sis LOONER"
• between the earth and the moon.
• [Latin *cis* on this side of + LUNAR]

cist *noun*
• "SIST"
• a box used for sacred utensils.
• [Latin *cista* from Greek *kistē* box]
HOMOPHONES: *cyst*

Cistercian *noun*
• "sis TUR sh'n"
• a monk or nun of an order founded in 1098 as a stricter branch of the Benedictines.
• [French *cistercien* from Latin *Cistercium* Cîteaux near Dijon in France, where the order was founded]

cistern *noun*
• "SIS turn"
• a tank or reservoir for storing water.
• [Old French *cisterne* from Latin *cisterna* (as CIST)]

cistus *noun*
• "SIS tuss"
• any shrub of the genus *Cistus*, with large white or red flowers, often cultivated as an ornamental.
• [modern Latin from Greek *kistos*]

citadel *noun*
• "SITTA del" or "SITTA d'll"
• a fortress, usu. on high ground protecting or dominating a city.
• [French *citadelle* or Italian *citadella*, ultimately from Latin *civitas -tatis* city]

citation *noun*
• "sye TAY sh'n"
• the act of citing something from a book or other source.
• [as CITE]

cite *verb*
• "SITE"
• mention as an example or to support an argument.
• [French from Latin *citare* from *ciēre* set moving]
• **citable** *adjective*
HOMOPHONES: *site*, *sight*

citizen *noun*
• "SITTA z'n"
• a member of a nation or Commonwealth, either native or naturalized.
• [Anglo-French *citesein* ultimately from Latin *civitas -tatis* city]
• **citizenship** *noun*

citizenry *noun*
• "SITTA z'n ree"
• citizens collectively.
• [as CITIZEN]

citrate *noun*
• "SIT rate"
• a salt or ester of citric acid.
• [as CITRIC]

citric *adjective*
• "SIT rick"
• derived from citrus fruit.
• [French *citrique* from Latin *citrus* citron]

citrine *noun*
• "SIT rin" or "SIT reen"
• a transparent yellow variety of quartz.
• [Old French *citrin* (as CITRUS)]

citron *noun*
• "SIT run"
• a shrubby tree, *Citrus medica*, bearing large lemon-like fruits with thick fragrant peel.
• [French from Latin CITRUS, after *limon* lemon]

citronella *noun*
• "sitra NELLA"
• any fragrant grass of the genus *Cymbopogon*, native to S Asia.
• [modern Latin, formed as CITRON + diminutive suffix]

citrus *noun*
• "SIT russ"
• any tree or shrub of the genus *Citrus*, including citron, lemon, lime, orange, and grapefruit.
• [Latin, = citron tree or thuja]
• **citrusy** *adjective*

cittern *noun*
• "SITTERN"
• a wire-stringed lute-like instrument usu. played with a plectrum.
• [Latin *cithara*, Greek *kithara* a kind of harp, assimilated to GITTERN]

civet *noun*
• "SIVVIT"
• any of several carnivorous mammals of the Asian and African family Viverridae (which also includes the genets and mongooses), esp. *Viverra civetta* of central Africa.
• [French *civette* from Italian *zibetto* from medieval Latin *zibethum* from Arabic *azzabād* from *al* the + *zabād* this perfume]

civic *adjective*
• "SIVVIC"
• of a city; municipal.
• [French *civique* or Latin *civicus* from *civis* citizen]
• **civically** *adverb*

civil *adjective*
• "SIV'll"
• of or belonging to citizens.
• [Old French from Latin *civilis* from *civis* citizen]
• **civilly** *adverb*

civilian *noun*
• "suh VILL y'n"
• a person not in the armed services or the police force.
• [as CIVIL]
• **civilianization** *noun* (also esp. *Brit.* **-isation**)
• **civilianize** *verb* (also esp. *Brit.* **-ise**)

civility *noun*
• "suh VILLA tee"
• politeness.
• [as CIVIL]

civilization *noun*
ALSO SPELLED: esp. *Brit.* **-isation**
• "sivva lie ZAY sh'n" or "sivva luh ZAY sh'n"
• an advanced stage or system of social development.
• [as CIVIL]

civilize *verb*
ALSO SPELLED: esp. *Brit.* **-ise**
• "SIVVA lize"
• bring out of a barbarous or primitive stage of society.
• [as CIVIL]
• **civilized** *adjective* (also esp. *Brit.* **-ised**)
• **civilizer** *noun* (also esp. *Brit.* **-iser**)

civvy *adjective*
• "SIVVY"
• civilian.
• [abbreviation]

clade *noun*
• "CLADE"
• a group of organisms evolved from a common ancestor.
• [Greek *klados* branch]

cladistics *noun*
• "cluh DISTIC"
• a method of classification of animals and plants on the basis of shared characteristics, which are assumed to indicate common ancestry.
• [as CLADE]
• **cladism** *noun* "CLAD izm"
• **cladistic** *adjective*

cladoceran *noun*
• "cluh DOSSER 'n"
• a minute crustacean of an order that includes the water fleas. They typically have a transparent shell enclosing the trunk, and large antennae which are used for swimming.
• [modern Latin from Greek *klados* branch or root + *keras* horn (because of the branched antennae)]

cladode *noun*
• "CLAY dode"
• a flattened leaflike stem.
• [Greek *kladōdēs* having many shoots, from *klados* shoot]

cladogram *noun*
• "CLAY duh gram"
• a branching diagram showing the cladistic relationship between a number of species.
• [as CLADE + Greek *gramma* thing written]

clafoutis *noun*
ALSO SPELLED: **clafouti**
• "cla foo TEE"
• a dessert consisting of fruit, esp. cherries, baked in a dense custard-like batter.
• [French, from Old French *claufir* fasten with nails, whence 'scatter with something']

claimant *noun*
• "CLAIM 'nt"
• a person making a claim, esp. in a lawsuit or for a government benefit.
• [Old French *claime* from *clamer* call out, from Latin *clamare*]
HOMOPHONES: *clamant*

clairvoyance *noun*
• "clair VOY ince"
• the supposed faculty of perceiving things or events in the future or beyond normal sensory contact.
• [French *clairvoyance* from *clair* clear + *voir voy-* see]
• **clairvoyant** *noun*
• **clairvoyantly** *adverb*

clamant *adjective*
• "CLAIM 'nt"
• noisy; insistent, urgent.
• [Latin *clamare clamant-* cry out]
• **clamantly** *adverb*
HOMOPHONES: *claimant*

clamour *noun*
ALSO SPELLED: **clamor**
• "CLAMMER"
• loud or vehement shouting or noise.
• [Old French from Latin *clamor -oris* from *clamare* cry out]
• **clamorous** *adjective*
• **clamorously** *adverb*
• **clamorousness** *noun*
HOMOPHONES: *clammer, clamber*

clandestine *adjective*
• "clan DESS tine" or "clan DESS tin"
• surreptitious, secret.
• [French *clandestin* or Latin *clandestinus* from *clam* secretly]
• **clandestinely** *adverb*
• **clandestinity** *noun* "clan dess TINNA tee"

clanger *noun*
• "CLANG ur"
• a mistake or blunder.
• [from 'clang' imitative of the sound: influenced by Latin *clangere* resound]
HOMOPHONES: *clangour*

clangour *noun*
ALSO SPELLED: **clangor**
• "CLANG ur"
• a prolonged or repeated clanging noise.
• [Latin *clangor* noise of trumpets etc.]
• **clangorous** *adjective*
• **clangorously** *adverb*
HOMOPHONES: *clanger*

claque *noun*
• "CLACK"
• a group of people hired to applaud in a theatre etc.
• [French from *claquer* to clap]
• **claqueur** *noun* "clack UR"
HOMOPHONES: *clack*

clarence *noun*
• "CLAIR ince"
• a four-wheeled closed carriage with seats for four inside and two on the box.
• [Duke of *Clarence*, afterwards William IV, d.1837]

claret *noun*
• "CLAIR it"
• red wine, esp. from Bordeaux in SW France.
• [Old French *(vin) claret* from medieval Latin *claratum (vinum)* from Latin *clarus* clear]

clarify *verb*
• "CLERRA fie"
• make or become clearer.
• [Old French *clarifier* from Latin *clarus* clear]
• **clarification** *noun*
• **clarifier** *noun*

clarinet *noun*
• "clerra NET"
• a woodwind instrument with a single-reed mouthpiece, a cylindrical tube with a flared end, holes, and keys.
• [French *clarinette*, diminutive of *clarine* a kind of bell]
• **clarinetist** *noun* (also esp. *Brit.* **clarinettist**)

clarion *noun*
• "CLERRY 'n"
• a clear rousing sound.
• [medieval Latin *clario -onis* from Latin *clarus* clear]

clarity *noun*
• "CLERRA tee"
• the state or quality of being clear, esp. of sound or expression.
• [Latin *claritas* from *clarus* clear]

clarkia *noun*
• "CLARKY uh"
• any annual herbaceous plant of the genus *Clarkia*, with showy white, pink, or purple flowers.
• [W. *Clark*, US explorer d.1838]

clary *noun*
• "CLERRY"
• any of various aromatic herbs of the genus *Salvia* of the mint family, esp. *S. sclarea*.
• [obsolete French *clarie* representing medieval Latin *sclarea*]

classicism *noun*
• "CLASSA sizm"
• the following of a classic style.
• [from French *classique* or Latin *classicus* from *classis* class]
• **classicist** *noun* "CLASSA sist"

classicize *verb*
ALSO SPELLED: esp. *Brit.* **-ise**
• "CLASSA size"
• make classic.
• [from French *classique* or Latin *classicus* from *classis* class]
• **classicizing** *adjective* (also esp. *Brit.* **-ising**)

classify *verb*
• "CLASSA fie"
• arrange in classes or categories.
• [back-formation from *classification* from French from Latin *classis* class]
• **classifiable** *adjective*
• **classification** *noun*
• **classificatory** *adjective*
• **classified** *adjective*
• **classifier** *noun*

clastic *adjective*
• "CLASS tick"
• designating a rock composed of broken pieces of older rocks.
• [French *clastique* from Greek *klastos* broken in pieces]

clathrate *noun*
• "CLATH rate"
• a solid in which one component is enclosed in the structure of another.
• [Latin *clathratus* from *clathri* lattice bars, from Greek *klēthra*]

claudication *noun*
• "clodda CAY sh'n"
• limping.
• [Latin *claudicare* limp, from *claudus* lame]

clause *noun*
• "CLOZZ"
• a distinct part of a sentence, including a subject and predicate.
• [Old French from Latin *clausula* conclusion, from *claudere claus-* shut]
• **clausal** *adjective*

claustral *adjective*
• "CLOSS trull"
• of or associated with the cloister; monastic.
• [Late Latin *claustralis* from *claustrum* CLOISTER]

claustrophobia *noun*
• "clostra FOBEY uh"
• an abnormal fear of confined places.
• [modern Latin from Latin *claustrum* (see CLOISTER) + PHOBIA]
• **claustrophobic** *adjective*
• **claustrophobically** *adverb*

clavate *adjective*
• "CLAY vate"
• club-shaped; thicker at the apex than at the base.
• [modern Latin *clavatus* from Latin *clava* club]

claves *plural noun*
• "CLAW vayz"
• a pair of hardwood sticks that make a hollow sound when struck together and are used to accompany certain kinds of music, dancing, etc.
• [Latin American Spanish from Spanish, = keystone, from Latin *clavis* key]

clavichord *noun*
• "CLAVVA cord"
• an early keyboard instrument with strings activated by brass blades fixed upright in the key levers, producing a very soft tone.
• [medieval Latin *clavichordium* from Latin *clavis* key, *chorda* string]

clavicle *noun*
• "CLAVVA k'll"
• the collarbone.
• [Latin *clavicula* diminutive of *clavis* key (from its shape)]
• **clavicular** *adjective* "cla VICK yuh lur"

clavier *noun*
• "CLAVVY ur"
• any keyboard instrument.
• [French *clavier* or German *Klavier* from medieval Latin *claviarius*, originally = key bearer, from Latin *clavis* key]

claviform *adjective*
• "CLAVVA form"
• club-shaped; thicker at the apex than at the base.
• [Latin *clava* club]

cleanly *adjective*
• "CLENLY"
• habitually clean; with clean habits.
• [Old English *clǣnlic*]
• **cleanliness** *noun*

cleanse *verb*
• "CLENZ"
• make clean.
• [Old English *clǣnsian*]

cleanser *noun*
• "CLENZER"
• something that cleans, esp. an abrasive or disinfectant product for cleaning the skin, household surfaces, etc.
• [as CLEANSE]

cleat *noun*
• "CLEET"
• a metal or wooden fitting with two projecting horns, fastened to a flagpole, boat, etc., around which a rope may be made fast.
• [Old English]
• **cleated** *adjective*

cleavage *noun*
• "CLEEVE idge"
• the hollow between a woman's breasts, esp. as exposed by a low-cut garment.
• [as CLEAVE]

cleave *verb*
• "CLEEVE"
• chop or break apart, split.
• [Old English *clēofan* from Germanic]
• **cleavable** *adjective*

cleaver *noun*
• "CLEEVER"
• a tool for cleaving, esp. a broad-bladed knife used for cutting meat.
• [as CLEAVE]

cleavers *noun*
• "CLEEVERZ"
• a plant, *Galium aparine*, having hooked bristles on its stem that catch on clothes etc.
• [Old English *clife*]

clef *noun*
• "CLEFF"
• any of several symbols placed at the beginning of a staff, indicating the pitch of the notes written on it.
• [French from Latin *clavis* key]

cleg *noun*
• "CLEG"
• a horsefly.
• [Old Norse *kleggi*]

cleistogamic *adjective*
• "cly stuh GAMMIC"
• (of a flower) permanently closed and self-fertilizing.
• [Greek *kleistos* closed + *gamos* marriage]

clematis *noun*
• "cluh MAT iss" or "CLEMMA tiss"
• any erect or climbing plant of the genus *Clematis*, bearing white, pink, or purple flowers and feathery seeds, e.g. old man's beard.
• [Latin from Greek *klēmatis* from *klēma* vine branch]

clement *adjective*
• "CLEM 'nt"
• merciful.
• [Latin *clemens -entis*]
• **clemency** *noun*

clementine *noun*
• "CLEM 'n tine" or "CLEM 'n teen"
• a small citrus fruit, thought to be a hybrid between a tangerine and sweet orange.
• [French *clémentine* from the male name *Clément*]

clenbuterol *noun*
• "clen BYOOTER awl"
• a synthetic drug used in the treatment of asthma and respiratory diseases and also in veterinary obstetrics. It also promotes the growth of muscle and has been used illegally by athletes to enhance performance.
• *[c(h)l(oro-) + (ph)en(yl) + but(yl)]*

cleome *noun*
• "clee OH mee"
• any plant of the genus *Cleome*, with long stamens, esp. spider flower and bee plant.
• [modern Latin from Greek]

clepsydra *noun*
• "CLEP sid ruh"
• an instrument used in antiquity to measure time by the flow of water.
• [Latin from Greek *klepsudra* from *kleptō* steal + *hudōr* water]

clerestory *noun*
• "CLEAR stuh ree" or "CLEAR story"
• an upper row of windows in a cathedral or large church, above the level of the aisle roofs.
• [Middle English from 'clear' + STOREY]

clergy *noun*
• "CLUR jee"
• the body of all persons ordained for religious duties, esp. in the Christian church.
• [partly from Old French *clergé* from Church Latin *clericatus*, partly from Old French *clergie* from *clerc* clerk (as CLERIC)]
• **clergyman** *noun*
• **clergyperson** *noun*
• **clergywoman** *noun*

cleric *noun*
• "CLARE ick"
• a member of the clergy.

• [(originally adjective) from Church Latin from Greek *klērikos* from *klēros* lot, heritage, as in Acts 1:17: 'he was allotted his share in this ministry']
• **clericalism** *noun*
• **clericalist** *noun*

clerical *adjective*
• "CLERRA k'll"
• of or done by an office clerk or secretary.
• [as CLERIC]
• **clerically** *adverb*

clerihew *noun*
• "CLERRA hyoo"
• a short comic or nonsensical verse, usu. in two rhyming couplets with lines of unequal length and referring to a famous person.
• [E. *Clerihew* Bentley, English writer d.1956, its inventor]

clerisy *noun*
• "CLERRA see"
• a distinct class of learned or literary persons.
• [apparently after German *Klerisei*, formed as CLERIC]

clevis *noun*
• "CLEV iss"
• a U-shaped piece of metal at the end of a beam for attaching tackle etc.
• [16th c.: related to CLEAVE]

clew *noun*
• "CLOO"
• a lower or after corner of a sail.
• [Old English *cliwen, cleowen*]
HOMOPHONES: *clue*

cliché *noun*
• "clee SHAY" or "CLEE shay"
• a hackneyed phrase, opinion, or thing.
• [French from *clicher* to stereotype]
• **clichéd** *adjective*

client *noun*
• "CLYE 'nt"
• a person using the services of a lawyer, architect, social worker, or other professional person.
• [Latin *cliens -entis* from *cluere* hear, obey]

clientele *noun*
• "clye 'n TELL"
• clients collectively.
• [French *clientèle*]

climacteric *noun*
• "clye MACKTER ick" or "clye mack TARE ick"
• the period of life when fertility and sexual activity are in decline.
• [Latin *climactericus* from Greek *klimaktērikos* from *klimaktēr* critical period, from *klimax -akos* ladder]

climate *noun*
• "CLIME it"
• the prevailing weather conditions of an area.
• [Old French *climat* or Late Latin *clima climat-* from Greek *klima* from *klinō* slope]
• **climatic** *adjective*
• **climatically** *adverb*

climatology *noun*
• "clime a TOLLA jee"
• the scientific study of climate.
• [as CLIMATE + Greek *logos* word]
• **climatological** *adjective*
• **climatologist** *noun*

climax *noun*
• "CLYE max"
• the event or point of greatest intensity or interest; a culmination or apex.
• [Late Latin from Greek *klimax -akos* ladder, climax]
• **climactic** *adjective*
• **climactically** *adverb*

clime *noun*
• "CLIME"
• a region.
• [as CLIMATE]
HOMOPHONES: *climb*

cline *noun*
• "CLINE"
• a continuum with an infinite number of gradations.
• [Greek *klinō* to slope]
• **clinal** *adjective*

clinician *noun*
• "clin ISH'n"
• a doctor having direct contact with and responsibility for patients, as opposed to one doing research.
• [from 'clinic' from French *clinique* from Greek *klinikē* (*tekhnē*) clinical, lit. 'bedside (art)', from *klinē* bed]

clinometer *noun*
• "clin OMMA tur"
• an instrument for measuring slopes.
• [Greek *klinō* to slope + *metron* measure]

clintonia *noun*
• "clin TONY uh"
• any liliaceous plant of the chiefly N American genus *Clintonia*, esp. *C. borealis*, with yellow flowers and dark blue berries.
• [named in honour of DeWitt Clinton, US politician d.1828]

cliometrics *noun*
• "clye a METRIX"
• a method of historical research making much use of statistical information and methods.
• [*Clio* (the Muse of history) + METRIC]
• **cliometric** *adjective*
• **cliometrician** *noun*
• **cliometry** *noun*

clique *noun*
• "CLEEK"
• a small exclusive group of people.
• [French from *cliquer* click]
• **cliquey** *adjective*

- **cliquish** *adjective*
- **cliquishness** *noun*

clitic *adjective*
- "CLITTIC"
- enclitic or proclitic.
- [as ENCLITIC]
- **cliticization** *noun* "clittic ize AY sh'n"

cloaca *noun*
- "cloh AY kuh"
- the genital and excretory cavity at the end of the intestinal canal in birds, reptiles, etc.
- [Latin, = sewer]
- **cloacal** *adjective*

cloche *noun*
- "CLOSH"
- a woman's close-fitting bell-shaped hat.
- [French, = bell, from medieval Latin *clocca*]

cloisonné *noun*
- "clwah zon AY"
- a type of enamel finish in which the colours in the pattern are separated by thin strips of metal.
- [French from *cloison* compartment]

cloister *noun*
- "CLOY stur"
- a covered walk, often with a wall on one side and a colonnade open to a quadrangle on the other, esp. in a convent, monastery, or cathedral.
- [Old French *cloistre* from Latin *claustrum*, *clostrum* lock, enclosed place, from *claudere claus-* shut]
- **cloistral** *adjective*

cloistered *adjective*
- "CLOY sturd"
- secluded, sheltered.
- [as CLOISTER]

clone *noun*
- "CLONE"
- a group of organisms produced asexually from one stock or ancestor, to which they are genetically identical.
- [Greek *klōn* twig, slip]
- **clonal** *adjective*

clonus *noun*
- "CLONE us"
- a spasm with alternate muscular contractions and relaxations.
- [Greek *klonos* turmoil]
- **clonic** *adjective*

closet *noun*
- "CLOZZIT"
- a cupboard or recess, esp. one used for hanging clothes.
- [Old French, diminutive of *clos* from Latin *clausum* enclosure & *clausus* past participle of *claudere* shut]

clostridial *adjective*
- "closs TRIDDY 'll"
- of, relating to, or caused by rod-shaped bacteria of the genus *Clostridium*, many of which cause disease (e.g. tetanus, botulism).
- [modern Latin *Clostridium* genus name from Greek *klōstēr* spindle]

closure *noun*
- "CLOE zhur"
- the act or process of closing.
- [Old French from Late Latin *clausura* from *claudere claus-* shut]

clotbur *noun*
- "CLOT bur"
- any of various plants with burr-like seeds, such as cocklebur, *Xanthium*, and burdock, *Arctium*.
- [dialect *clote* burdock + 'burr']

clothes *plural noun*
- "CLOZE" or "CLOATHZ"
- garments worn to cover the body.
- [Old English *clāthas* pl. of *clāth* cloth]

HOMOPHONES: *close*, *cloze*

clothier *noun*
- "CLOTHE ee ur"
- a maker or seller of clothes, esp. men's clothes.
- [Middle English *clother* from 'cloth']

cloture *noun*
- "CLOE chur" or "CLOE tyur"
- the closure of a debate.
- [French *clôture* from Old French *closure* CLOSURE]

Clovis *noun*
- "CLOE viss"
- a paleo-Indian culture of Central and North America, dated to about 11,500–11,000 years ago and earlier. The culture is distinguished by heavy leaf-shaped stone spearheads often found in conjunction with the bones of mammoths.
- [first found near *Clovis* in eastern New Mexico]

clozapine *noun*
- "CLOE zuh peen"
- a sedative of the benzodiazepine group used to treat schizophrenia.
- [as CHLORINE + BENZODIAZEPINE]

cloze *noun*
- "CLOZE"
- the exercise of supplying a word that has been omitted from a passage as a test of readability or comprehension.
- [representing a spoken abbreviation of CLOSURE]

HOMOPHONES: *close*, *clothes*

Cluniac *adjective*
- "CLOONY ack"
- of or relating to a monastic order founded at Cluny in E France in 910. The order was formed with the object of returning to the strict

Benedictine rule, and became centralized and influential in the 11th–12th c.

Clydesdale *noun*
- "CLIDES dale"
- a draft horse of a heavy powerful breed, usu. dark-coloured with thick white hair on the lower legs.
- [originally bred near the *Clyde* River in Scotland; 'dale' from Old English *dæl* valley]

clypeus *noun*
- "CLIPPY us"
- the hard protective area of an insect's head.
- [Latin, = round shield]

cnidarian *noun*
- "k'nye DERRY 'n"
- an aquatic invertebrate animal of a phylum that includes the coelenterates.
- [modern Latin from Greek *knidē* nettle]

coadjutor *noun*
- "co ADGE a tur"
- an assistant, esp. an assistant bishop.
- [Old French *coadjuteur* from Late Latin *coadjutor* (from *co-*, originally a form of *com-*, *cum* with + *adjutor*, from *adjuvare -jut-* help)]

coady *noun*
- "CO dee"
- *Cdn* (*Nfld*) a thick sweetened sauce, usu. made from boiled molasses.
- [20th c.: origin unknown]

coagulant *noun*
- "co AG yoo l'nt"
- a substance that produces coagulation.
- [as COAGULATE]

coagulate *verb*
- "co AG yuh late"
- change from a fluid to a solid or semi-solid state.
- [Latin *coagulare* from *coagulum* rennet]
- **coagulation** *noun*
- **coagulative** *adjective*
- **coagulator** *noun*

coalesce *verb*
- "co a LESS"
- come together and form one whole.
- [Latin *coalescere* (from *co-*, originally a form of *com-*, *cum* with + *alescere alit-* grow, from *alere* nourish)]
- **coalescence** *noun*
- **coalescent** *adjective*

coalition *noun*
- "co a LISH'n"
- a temporary alliance for combined action, esp. of distinct political parties forming a government.
- [medieval Latin *coalitio* (as COALESCE)]
- **coalitionist** *noun*

coaming *noun*
- "CO ming"
- a raised border around the hatches etc. of a ship to keep out water.
- [17th c.: origin unknown]

coarse *adjective*
- "CORSE"
- rough or loose in texture or grain; made of large particles.
- [Middle English: origin unknown]
- **coarsely** *adverb*
- **coarsen** *verb*
- **coarseness** *noun*

HOMOPHONES: *corse*, *course*

coati *noun*
- "co OTTY"
- any raccoon-like carnivorous mammal of the genera *Nasua* or *Nasuella*, with a long flexible snout and a long usu. ringed tail, found mainly in Central and South America.
- [Tupi from *cua* belt + *tim* nose]

coatimundi *noun*
- "co otta MUNDY"
- a coati.
- [as COATI + Tupi *mondi* solitary]

coax *verb*
- "COKES"
- persuade gradually by flattery or by continued patient trial.
- [16th c.: from 'make a *cokes* of' from obsolete *cokes* simpleton, of unknown origin]
- **coaxer** *noun*
- **coaxing** *noun*
- **coaxingly** *adverb*

coaxial *adjective*
- "co AX ee 'll"
- having a common axis.
- [Latin *co-*, originally a form of *com-*, *cum* with + AXIS]
- **coaxially** *adverb*

cobalt *noun*
- "CO bawlt"
- a silvery-white magnetic metallic element occurring naturally as a mineral in combination with sulphur and arsenic, and used in many alloys.
- [German *Kobalt*, prob. = KOBOLD in mines]
- **cobaltous** *adjective*

cobia *noun*
- "CO bee uh"
- a large slender predatory game fish, *Rachycentron canadum*, of the tropical Atlantic, Indian, and western Pacific Oceans.
- [19th c.: origin unknown]

Cobourger *noun*
- "CO burger"
- a resident of Cobourg, Ont.

cobra *noun*
- "CO bruh"
- any of a number of venomous Asian and

African snakes esp. of the genus *Naja*, which can dilate their necks to form a hood when excited.
• [Portuguese from Latin *colubra* snake]

coca *noun*
• "CO kuh"
• a S American shrub, *Erythroxylum coca*, of which the dried leaves are chewed as a stimulant.
• [Spanish from Quechua *cuca*]

cocaine *noun*
• "co CANE"
• a white crystalline alkaloid derived from coca leaves, used as a local anaesthetic or in various forms as a narcotic with euphoric effects.
• [as COCA]

coccidia *plural noun*
• "cock SIDDY uh"
• parasitic protozoa of a group that includes those that cause diseases such as coccidiosis and toxoplasmosis.
• [*coccidium* (modern Latin from Greek *kokkis* diminutive of *kokkos* berry)]
• **coccidian** *adjective*

coccidiosis *noun*
• "cock siddy OH sis"
• a disease of mammals and birds, esp. livestock, caused by any of various parasitic protozoa of the order Coccidia, affecting the intestine.
• [as COCCIDIA]

coccus *noun*
• "COCKUS"
• any spherical or roughly spherical bacterium.
• [modern Latin from Greek *kokkos* berry]
• **coccal** *adjective*
• **coccoid** *adjective*
HOMOPHONES: *caucus*

coccyx *noun*
• "COCK six"
• the small triangular bone at the base of the spinal column in humans and some apes; the tailbone.
• [Latin from Greek *kokkux -ugos* cuckoo (from being shaped like its bill)]
• **coccygeal** *adjective* "cock SIDGE ee 'll"

Cochin *noun*
• "CO chin"
• a fowl of an Asian breed with feathered legs.
• [*Cochin-China*, former name for what is now the southern part of Vietnam]

cochineal *noun*
• "CO chuh neel" or "co chuh NEEL"
• a scarlet dye used esp. for colouring food.
• [French *cochenille* or Spanish *cochinilla* from Latin *coccinus* scarlet, from Greek *kokkos* berry]

cochlea *noun*
• "COCKLY uh"
• the spiral cavity of the internal ear, in which the sensory reception of sound occurs.
• [Latin, = snail shell, from Greek *kokhlias*]
• **cochlear** *adjective*

Cochranite *noun*
• "COCK run ite"
• a resident of Cochrane, Alta.

cockade *noun*
• "cock ADE"
• a rosette etc. worn in a hat as a badge of office or party, or as part of a uniform.
• [French *cocarde* originally in *bonnet à la coquarde*, from feminine of obsolete *coquard* saucy, from *coq* cock]
• **cockaded** *adjective*

cockalorum *noun*
• "cocka LORUM"
• a self-important little man.
• [18th c.: arbitrary alteration of 'cock']

cockamamie *adjective*
ALSO SPELLED: **cockamamy**
• "COCKA may mee"
• ridiculous or incredible.
• [origin uncertain]

cockatiel *noun*
• "COCKA teel"
• a small delicately coloured crested Australian parrot, *Nymphicus hollandicus*.
• [Dutch *kaketielje*, prob. a diminutive of *kaketoe* cockatoo]

cockatrice *noun*
• "COCKA triss" or "COCKA treece"
• a mythical reptile with a lethal breath and look; a basilisk.
• [Old French *cocatris* from Latin *calcare* tread, track, rendering Greek *ikhneumōn* tracker: see ICHNEUMON]

cockchafer *noun*
• "COCK chafe ur"
• a large nocturnal beetle, *Melolontha melolontha*, which feeds on leaves and whose larva feeds on roots of crops etc.
• [perhaps from 'cock' as expressing size or vigour + CHAFER]

cockerel *noun*
• "COCK rull"
• a young rooster.
• [Middle English: diminutive of 'cock']

cocklebur *noun*
• "COCKLE bur"
• any of various plants with fruit covered in hooked bristles, esp. of the genus *Xanthium* of the daisy family.
• ['cockle', a type of plant, from Old English *coccul*, perhaps ultimately from Late Latin COCCUS + 'burr']

cockney *noun*
• "COCK nee"
• a native of the East End of London.
• [Middle English *cokeney* cock's egg, later derogatory for 'townsman']
• **cockneyism** *noun*

cockscomb *noun*
• "COX coam"
• the crest or comb of a rooster.
• ['cock' from Old English *cocc* and Old French *coq* prob. from medieval Latin *coccus* + 'comb' from Old English *camb*]
HOMOPHONES: *coxcomb*

coco *noun*
• "CO co"
• a tall tropical palm tree, *Cocos nucifera*, bearing coconuts.
• [Portuguese & Spanish *coco* grimace: the base of the shell resembles a face]
HOMOPHONES: *cocoa*

cocoa *noun*
• "CO co"
• a powder made from crushed cacao seeds, often with other ingredients.
• [alteration of CACAO]
HOMOPHONES: *coco*

coconut *noun*
• "CO kuh nut"
• a large ovate brown seed of the coco, with a hard shell and edible white fleshy lining enclosing a milky juice.
• [coco + 'nut']
• **coconutty** *adjective*

cocoon *noun*
• "kuh COON"
• a silky case spun by many insect larvae for protection as pupae.
• [French *cocon* from modern Provençal *coucoun* diminutive of *coca* shell]

cocooning *noun*
• "kuh COONING"
• the practice of spending one's leisure time in the home rather than by going out.
• [as COCOON]
• **cocooner** *noun*

cocotte *noun*
• "kuh COT"
• a small fireproof dish for cooking and serving an individual portion of food.
• [French, from a child's name for a hen]

coda *noun*
• "CO duh"
• the concluding passage of a musical composition, usu. forming an addition to the basic structure.
• [Italian from Latin *cauda* tail]

codec *noun*
• "CO deck"
• a device that converts an analog signal into an encoded digital form, and decodes digital signals into analog form, used in telephone systems and in video systems for computers.
• [blend of *coder-decoder*]

codeine *noun*
• "CO deen"
• an alkaloid derived from morphine and used to relieve pain.
• [Greek *kōdeia* poppy head]

codependent *adjective*
• "co duh PEN d'nt"
• emotionally or psychologically dependent on supporting or caring for another person, esp. a person with an addiction or illness.
• [Latin *co-*, originally a form of *com-*, *cum* with + DEPENDENT]
• **codependency** *noun*

codex *noun*
• "CO dex"
• an ancient manuscript text in book form.
• [Latin, = block of wood, tablet, book]

codicil *noun*
• "CO duh sill" or "CODDA sill"
• an addition explaining, modifying, or revoking a will or part of one.
• [Latin *codicillus*, diminutive of CODEX]

codify *verb*
• "CO duh fie" or "CODDA fie"
• arrange (laws etc.) systematically into a code.
• [French *codifier*, ultimately as CODEX]
• **codification** *noun*
• **codifier** *noun*

codomain *noun*
• "co duh MANE"
• a set that includes all the possible expressions of a given function.
• [Latin *co-*, originally a form of *com-*, *cum* with + DOMAIN]

codon *noun*
• "CO don"
• a sequence of three nucleotides, forming a unit of genetic code in a DNA or RNA molecule.
• ['code' (as CODEX)]

codswallop *noun*
• "CODS wollup"
• *Cdn, Brit., & Austral.* nonsense.
• [20th c.: origin unknown]

coefficient *noun*
• "co e FISH 'nt"
• a quantity placed before and multiplying an algebraic expression (e.g. 4 in $4x^y$).
• [Latin *co-*, originally a form of *com-*, *cum* with + EFFICIENT]

coelacanth *noun*
• "SEELA canth"
• a large bony marine fish, *Latimeria chalumnae*, formerly thought to be extinct, having a three-lobed tail fin and fleshy pectoral fins.
• [modern Latin *Coelacanthus* from Greek *koilos* hollow + *akantha* spine]

coelenterate *noun*
• "see LENTER ate"
• any marine animal of the phylum Coelenterata with a simple tube-shaped or cup-

shaped body, e.g. jellyfish, corals, and sea anemones.
• [modern Latin *Coelenterata* from Greek *koilos* hollow + *enteron* intestine]

coelom *noun*
ALSO SPELLED: **celom**
• "SEEL'm"
• the principal body cavity in animals, between the intestinal canal and the body wall.
• [Greek *koilōma* cavity]
• **coelomate** *adjective* (also **celomate**)
• **coelomic** *adjective* (also **celomic**)
"see LOMMIC" or "see LO mick"

coenzyme *noun*
• "CO en zime"
• a non-proteinaceous compound that assists in the action of an enzyme.
• [Latin *co-*, originally a form of *com-*, *cum* with + ENZYME]

coequal *adjective*
• "co EEK wul"
• equal to one another.
• [Latin *co-*, originally a form of *com-*, *cum* with + 'equal' from Latin *aequalis* from *aequus* even]
• **coequality** *noun*
• **coequally** *adverb*

coerce *verb*
• "co URSS"
• persuade or restrain (an unwilling person) by force.
• [Latin *coercēre* restrain (from *co-*, originally a form of *com-*, *cum* with + *arcēre* restrain)]
• **coercible** *adjective*
• **coercion** *noun* "co URSH 'n"
• **coercive** *adjective*
• **coercively** *adverb*
• **coerciveness** *noun*

coercivity *noun*
• "co ur SIVVA tee"
• the resistance of a magnetic material to changes in magnetization, esp. measured as the field intensity required to demagnetize it when fully magnetized.
• [as COERCE]

coeval *adjective*
• "co EE v'll"
• having the same age or date of origin.
• [Late Latin *coaevus* (from *co-*, originally a form of *com-*, *cum* with + Latin *aevum* age)]

coexist *verb*
• "co eg ZIST"
• exist together (in time or place).
• [Latin *co-*, originally a form of *com-*, *cum* with + back-formation of EXISTENCE]
• **coexistence** *noun*
• **coexistent** *adjective*

cofactor *noun*
• "CO fack tur"
• any substance (other than the substrate) whose presence is essential for the activity of an enzyme.
• [Latin *co-*, originally a form of *com-*, *cum* with + FACTOR]

coffer *noun*
• "COFFER"
• a box, esp. a large strongbox for valuables.
• [Old French *coffre* from Latin *cophinus* from Greek *kophinos* basket]
HOMOPHONES: *cougher*

cofferdam *noun*
• "COFFER dam"
• a watertight enclosure pumped dry to permit work below the waterline on building bridges etc., or for repairing a ship.
• [as COFFER + 'dam']

coffered *adjective*
• "COFFERD"
• (of a ceiling) having square sunken panels.
• [as COFFER]

coffle *noun*
• "COFF'll"
• a line of animals, slaves, etc., fastened together.
• [Arabic *ḳāfila* caravan]

cogeneration *noun*
• "co jenner AY sh'n"
• the utilization of otherwise wasted energy for useful heating or for generating electricity.
• [Latin *co-*, originally a form of *com-*, *cum* with + GENERATE]

cogent *adjective*
• "CO j'nt"
• (of arguments, reasons, etc.) convincing, compelling.
• [Latin *cogere* compel (from *co-*, originally a form of *com-*, *cum* with + *agere act-* drive)]
• **cogency** *noun*
• **cogently** *adverb*

cogitate *verb*
• "CODGE a tate"
• ponder, meditate.
• [Latin *cogitare* think (from *co-*, originally a form of *com-*, *cum* with + AGITATE)]
• **cogitation** *noun*
• **cogitator** *noun*

cogito *noun*
• "CODGE ee toe"
• the principle establishing the existence of a being from the fact of its thinking or awareness.
• [Latin, = I think, in the French philosopher Descartes's formula (1641) *cogito, ergo sum* 'I think, therefore I exist']

cognac *noun*
• "CON yack" or "CONE yack"
• a high-quality brandy, properly that distilled in Cognac in W France.

cognate *adjective*
• "COG nate"

• (of a word) having the same linguistic family or derivation (as another); representing the same original word or root (e.g. English *father*, German *Vater*, Latin *pater*).
• [Latin *cognatus* (from *co-*, originally a form of *com-*, *cum* with + *natus* born)]

cognition *noun*
• "cog NISH'n"
• the mental faculties of perception, thought, reason, and memory, as distinct from emotion and volition.
• [Latin *cognitio* (from *co-*, originally a form of *com-*, *cum* with + *gnoscere gnit-* apprehend)]
• **cognitive** *adjective* "COGNA tiv"
• **cognitively** *adverb*

cognizable *adjective*
ALSO SPELLED: esp. *Brit.* **-isable**
• "COG nizza bull" or "cog NIZE a bull"
• within the jurisdiction of a court.
• [as COGNIZANCE]
• **cognizably** *adverb* (also esp. *Brit.* **-isably**)

cognizance *noun*
• "COG nizz ince"
• knowledge or awareness; perception, notice.
• [Old French *conoisance*, ultimately from Latin *cognoscent-* from *cognitio*: see COGNITION]
• **cognizant** *adjective*

cognomen *noun*
• "cog NOME 'n"
• a name, esp. a nickname, epithet, or surname.
• [Latin, from *co-* together with + *gnomen*, *nomen* name]

cognoscenti *plural noun*
• "cog nuh SENTY" or "cog nuh SHENTY"
• people who are considered to be especially well informed about a subject.
• [Italian, lit. 'people who know', from Latin *cognoscent-* getting to know, from the verb *cognoscere* (as COGNITION)]

cohabit *verb*
• "co HABIT"
• live together amicably.
• [Latin *cohabitare* (from *co-*, originally a form of *com-*, *cum* with + *habitare* dwell)]
• **cohabitant** *noun*
• **cohabitation** *noun*
• **cohabitee** *noun*
• **cohabiter** *noun*

cohere *verb*
• "co HERE"
• (of parts or a whole) stick together, remain united.
• [Latin *cohaerēre cohaes-* (from *co-*, originally a form of *com-*, *cum* with + *haerēre* stick)]

coherent *adjective*
• "co HERE 'nt"
• (of a person) able to speak intelligibly and articulately.
• [Latin *cohaerēre cohaerent-* (as COHERE)]
• **coherence** *noun*
• **coherency** *noun*
• **coherently** *adverb*

cohesion *noun*
• "co HEE zh'n"
• the act or condition of sticking together.
• [Latin *cohaes-* (see COHERE) after *adhesion*]
• **cohesive** *adjective*
• **cohesively** *adverb*
• **cohesiveness** *noun*

coho *noun*
• "CO ho"
• a silver salmon, *Oncorhynchus kisutch*, of the N Pacific.
• [*cohose* (taken as pl.) from Halkomelem]

coif *noun*
• "KWOFF"
• a hairstyle.
• [abbreviation of COIFFURE]
HOMOPHONES: *quaff*

coiffeur *noun*
• "kwoff UR"
• a male hairdresser.
• [French]

coiffure *noun*
• "kwoff YOOR"
• a hairstyle.
• [French, from Old French *coife* headdress, from Late Latin *cofia* helmet]
• **coiffured** *adjective*

coincide *verb*
• "co in SIDE"
• occur at or during the same time.
• [medieval Latin *coincidere* (from *co-*, originally a form of *com-*, *cum* with + INCIDENT)]

coincidence *noun*
• "co INSA dince"
• a remarkable concurrence of events or circumstances without apparent causal connection.
• [medieval Latin *coincidentia* (as COINCIDE)]
• **coincidental** *adjective*
• **coincidentally** *adverb*

coincident *adjective*
• "co INSA d'nt"
• occurring together in space or time.
• [as COINCIDE]
• **coincidently** *adverb*

coir *noun*
• "COY ur"
• fibre from the outer husk of the coconut, used for ropes, matting, etc.
• [Malayalam *kāyar* cord, from *kāyaru* be twisted]

col *noun*
• "CAWL"
• a depression in a ridge or range of mountains, generally providing a pass from one slope to another.

• [French, = neck, from Latin *collum*]
HOMOPHONES: *caul, call*

colander *noun*
• "CAWL 'n dur" or "CULL 'n dur"
• a perforated metal or plastic container, used to strain off liquids.
• [Middle English, ultimately from Latin *colare* strain]

colby *noun*
• "COLE bee"
• a mild, soft-textured cheese resembling cheddar.
• [*Colby*, Wisconsin, where it was first made]

colcannon *noun*
• "cawl CAN 'n"
• an Irish and Scottish dish of cabbage and potatoes boiled and pounded.
• [Gaelic *cal ceannan*, lit. 'white-headed cabbage', from Latin *caulis* cabbage + Old Irish *ceann* head]

colchicine *noun*
• "COLLCHA seen" or "COLLKA seen"
• a yellow alkaloid obtained from colchicum, used in the treatment of gout.
• [as COLCHICUM]

colchicum *noun*
• "COLLCHA k'm" or "COLLKA k'm"
• any liliaceous plant of the genus *Colchicum*, esp. meadow saffron.
• [Latin from Greek *kolkhikon*, of *Colchis*, an ancient region south of the Caucasus mountains]

cole *noun*
• "COLE"
• any of various brassicas, esp. cabbage or rape.
• [Old Norse *kál* from Latin *caulis* stem, cabbage]
HOMOPHONES: *kohl, coal*

coleopteran *noun*
• "co lee OPTER 'n"
• any insect of the order Coleoptera, comprising the beetles and weevils, with front wings modified into sheaths to protect the hindwings, and biting mouthparts.
• [modern Latin *Coleoptera* from Greek *koleopteros* from *koleon* sheath + *pteron* wing]
• **coleopterist** *noun*
• **coleopterous** *adjective*

coleoptile *noun*
• "co lee OP tile"
• a hollow organ enclosing the first leaf of a germinating cereal grain.
• [Greek *koleon* sheath + *ptilon* feather]

coleslaw *noun*
• "COLE slaw"
• a salad of shredded raw cabbage with a dressing and often other vegetables, esp. carrots.
• [Dutch *koolsla*: as COLE + *sla*, shortened from *salade* salad, ultimately from Latin *sal* salt]

coleus *noun*
• "CO lee us"
• any plant of the genus *Coleus*, having variegated coloured leaves, frequently cultivated in gardens and as a houseplant.
• [modern Latin from Greek *koleon* sheath]

colic *noun*
• "COLLIC"
• severe spasmodic abdominal pain caused by gas or obstruction in the intestines.
• [French *colique* from Late Latin *colicus*]
• **colicky** *adjective*

coliform *adjective*
• "COLLA form"
• of or pertaining to a group of bacteria typified by *Escherichia coli*, which inhabit the large intestine of humans and animals and when present in water indicate fecal contamination.
• [modern Latin *coli* 'of the colon' + 'form']

coliseum *noun*
• "colla SEE um"
• a large amphitheatre, sports stadium, arena, etc.
• [medieval Latin *colosseum*, neuter of *colosseus* gigantic (as COLOSSUS)]

colitis *noun*
• "kuh LITE iss"
• inflammation of the lining of the colon.
• [COLON + Greek *-itis*, forming feminine of adjectives in *-itēs* (with *nosos* 'disease' implied)]

collaborate *verb*
• "kuh LABBER ate"
• work jointly, esp. in a literary or artistic production.
• [Latin *collaborare collaborat-* (from *com-* with + *laborare* work)]
• **collaboration** *noun*
• **collaborationist** *noun*
• **collaborative** *adjective*
• **collaboratively** *adverb*
• **collaborator** *noun*

collage *noun*
• "kuh LOZH"
• a form of art in which various materials (e.g. photographs, pieces of paper or cloth) are arranged and assembled or glued to a backing.
• [French, = gluing, from Greek *kolla* glue]
• **collagist** *noun*

collagen *noun*
• "COLLA j'n"
• a protein found in animal connective tissue which provides support and resiliency, used in injectable form in plastic surgery to eliminate wrinkles and scars, augment lip size, etc.
• [French *collagène* from Greek *kolla* glue + *-gène* = GENESIS]

collapse *noun*
• "kuh LAPS"

• the tumbling down or falling in of a structure or hollow body; caving in.
• [Latin *collapsus* past participle of *collabi* (from *com-* with + *labi* slip)]
• **collapsible** *adjective*

collar *noun*
• "COLLER"
• the part of a shirt, dress, coat, etc., that goes around the neck, either upright or folded over.
• [Anglo-French *coler* from Latin *collare* from *collum* neck]
• **collared** *adjective*
• **collarless** *adjective*
HOMOPHONES: *caller*, *choler*, *collard*

collarbone *noun*
• "COLLER bone"
• either of the two curved bones joining the breastbone and the shoulder blade.
• [as COLLAR + 'bone']

collard *noun*
• "COLLERD"
• a variety of cabbage without a distinct heart.
• [reduced form of *colewort*, from COLE + WORT]
HOMOPHONES: *collared*

collate *verb*
• "CO late" or "kuh LATE" or "CAWL ate"
• sort or arrange (pages) in the correct order.
• [Latin *collat-* past participle stem of *conferre* compare]
• **collator** *noun*

collateral *noun*
• "kuh LATTER'll"
• security pledged as a guarantee for repayment of a loan.
• [medieval Latin *collateralis* (from *com-* with + LATERAL)]
• **collateralize** *verb* (also esp. *Brit.* **-ise**)
• **collaterally** *adverb*

collation *noun*
• "co LAY sh'n" or "kuh LAY sh'n" or "cawl AY sh'n"
• a light informal meal; a snack.
• [as COLLATE]

colleague *noun*
• "CAW leeg"
• a person with whom one works, esp. in a profession or business.
• [French *collègue* from Latin *collega* (from *com-* with + *legare* depute)]

collect[1] *verb*
• "kuh LECT"
• bring or come together; assemble, accumulate.
• [French *collecter* or medieval Latin *collectare* from Latin *collectus* past participle of *colligere* (from *com-* with + *legere* pick)]
• **collection** *noun*
• **collector** *noun*

collect[2] *noun*
• "CAWL ect"
• a short prayer of the Anglican and Roman Catholic Churches, esp. one assigned to a particular day or season.
• [Old French *collecte* from Latin *collecta* feminine past participle of *colligere*: see COLLECT[1]]

collected *adjective*
• "kuh LECTED"
• calm and cool; not perturbed or distracted.
• [as COLLECT[1]]
• **collectedly** *adverb*

collectible *adjective*
ALSO SPELLED: esp. *Brit.* **collectable**
• "kuh LECTA bull"
• worth collecting.
• [as COLLECT[1]]
• **collectibility** *noun* (also esp. *Brit.* **collectability**)

collective *adjective*
• "kuh LECTIV"
• held in common.
• [as COLLECT[1]]
• **collectively** *adverb*
• **collectiveness** *noun*

collectivism *noun*
• "kuh LECTA vizm"
• the theory and practice of the collective ownership of land and the means of production.
• [as COLLECT[1]]
• **collectivist** *noun*
• **collectivistic** *adjective*
• **collectivization** *noun* (also esp. *Brit.* **-isation**)
• **collectivize** *verb* (also esp. *Brit.* **-ise**)

collectivity *noun*
• "cawl eck TIVVA tee"
• a group or community of people bound together by common beliefs or interests.
• [as COLLECT[1]]

colleen *noun*
• "caw LEEN"
• an Irish girl.
• [Irish *cailín*, diminutive of *caile* country woman]

college *noun*
• "CAW lidge"
• an establishment for further or higher education.
• [Old French *college* or Latin *collegium* from *collega* (as COLLEAGUE)]

collegial *adjective*
• "kuh LEE j'll" or "kuh LEEJY 'll"
• characterized by collaboration among colleagues.
• [as COLLEGE]
• **collegiality** *noun* "kuh leejy ALA tee"
• **collegially** *adverb*

collegian *noun*
- "kuh LEE j'n"
- a member of a college.
- [as COLLEGE]

collegiate *adjective*
- "kuh LEE jit"
- of or pertaining to colleges or universities.
- [Late Latin *collegiatus* (as COLLEGE)]

collenchyma *noun*
- "kuh LENKIM uh"
- a tissue strengthened by the thickening of cell walls, as in young shoots.
- [Greek *kolla* glue + *egkhuma* infusion]

collet *noun*
- "COLLIT"
- a slit sleeve with an external taper which is placed over a shaft and designed to tighten and grip it when pushed into an internally tapered socket.
- [French, diminutive of COL]

collide *verb*
- "kuh LIDE"
- strike together with an abrupt or violent impact.
- [Latin *collidere collis-* (from *com-* with + *laedere* strike, damage)]

collider *noun*
- "kuh LIDE ur"
- a particle accelerator emitting beams of particles which are made to collide.
- [as COLLIDE]

collie *noun*
- "COLLY" or "CO lee"
- a sheepdog of a breed originating in Scotland, with a long pointed nose and usu. dense long hair.
- [perhaps from *coll* coal (as being originally black)]

collier *noun*
- "COLLY ur"
- a coal miner.
- [Middle English, from Old English *col* coal]

colliery *noun*
- "CAWL yuh ree"
- a coal mine and its associated buildings.
- [as COLLIER]

collimate *verb*
- "COLLA mate"
- adjust the line of sight of (a telescope etc.).
- [Latin *collimare*, erroneous for *collineare* align (from *com-* with + *linea* line)]
- **collimation** *noun*

collimator *noun*
- "COLLA mater"
- a device for producing a parallel beam of rays or radiation.
- [as COLLIMATE]

collinear *adjective*
- "kuh LINNY ur" or "co LINNY ur"
- (of points) lying in the same straight line.
- [Latin *co-*, from *com-* with + LINEAR]
- **collinearity** *noun* "kuh linny ERRA tee"

collision *noun*
- "kuh LIZH'n"
- a violent impact of a moving body, esp. a vehicle, with another or with a fixed object.
- [Late Latin *collisio* (as COLLIDE)]
- **collisional** *adjective*

collocate *verb*
- "COLLA cate"
- (of a word) habitually associate with another.
- [Latin *collocare collocat-* (from *com-* with + *locare* to place)]
- **collocation** *noun*

collodion *noun*
- "kuh LOADY 'n"
- a syrupy solution of pyroxylin in a mixture of alcohol and ether, used in photography and surgery to form a thin flexible film.
- [Greek *kollōdēs* glue-like, from *kolla* glue]

colloid *noun*
- "CAWL oid"
- a substance consisting of ultramicroscopic particles.
- [Greek *kolla* glue]
- **colloidal** *adjective*

collop *noun*
- "COLLUP"
- a slice of meat.
- [Middle English, original sense 'bacon and eggs'; compare Old Swedish *kolhuppadher* roasted on coals, Swedish *kalops* stewed meat]

colloquial *adjective*
- "kuh LOKE wee 'll"
- belonging to or proper to ordinary or familiar conversation, not formal or literary.
- [Latin *colloquium* COLLOQUY]
- **colloquially** *adverb*

colloquialism *noun*
- "kuh LOKE wee 'll izm"
- a colloquial word or phrase.
- [as COLLOQUIAL]

colloquium *noun*
- "kuh LOKE wee um"
- an academic conference focused on a specific topic.
- [Latin: see COLLOQUY]

colloquy *noun*
- "COLLA kwee"
- the act of conversing.
- [Latin *colloquium* (from *com-* with + *loqui* speak)]

collotype *noun*
- "COLLA tipe"
- a thin sheet of gelatin exposed to light,

treated with reagents, and used to make high-quality prints by lithography.
• [Greek *kolla* glue + 'type', from French *type* or Latin *typus* from Greek *tupos* impression, figure, type, from *tuptō* strike]

collude *verb*
• "kuh LOOD"
• conspire together for a fraudulent or underhanded purpose; connive, plot.
• [Latin *colludere collus-* (from *com-* with + *ludere lus-* play)]
• **colluder** *noun*
• **collusion** *noun* "kuh LOO zh'n"
• **collusive** *adjective*

collywobbles *plural noun*
• "COLLY wobbles"
• a rumbling or pain in the stomach.
• [fanciful, from COLIC + 'wobble']

colobus *noun*
• "COLLA buss"
• any leaf-eating monkey of the genus *Colobus*, native to Africa, having shortened thumbs.
• [modern Latin from Greek *kolobos* docked]

colocynth *noun*
• "COLLA sinth"
• a plant of the gourd family, *Citrullus colocynthis*, bearing a pulpy fruit.
• [Latin *colocynthis* from Greek *kolokunthis*]

cologne *noun*
• "kuh LONE"
• a dilute solution of alcohol and a concentrate of perfume.
• [abbreviation of 'eau de cologne', French, lit. 'water of Cologne', the perfume originally being made in Cologne, Germany]

Colombian *noun*
• "kuh LUMBY 'n"
• a native or inhabitant of Colombia in South America.

colon *noun*
• "COLE 'n"
• the lower and greater part of the large intestine, from the cecum to the rectum.
• [Middle English, ultimately from Greek *kolon*]
• **colonic** *adjective*

colón *noun*
• "caw LON"
• the basic monetary unit of Costa Rica and El Salvador, equal to 100 centimos in Costa Rica and 100 centavos in El Salvador.
• [*Colón*, Spanish form of the name *Columbus*]

colonel *noun*
• "CUR n'll"
• (in Canada and the US) an officer in the armed forces ranking above a lieutenant colonel and below a brigadier general.
• [obsolete French *coronel* from Italian *colonnello* from *colonna* COLUMN]
• **colonelcy** *noun*
HOMOPHONES: *kernel*

colonnade *noun*
• "colla NADE"
• a row of columns, esp. supporting an entablature or roof.
• [French from *colonne* COLUMN]
• **colonnaded** *adjective*

colonoscope *noun*
• "kuh LONNA scope"
• an illuminated fibre optic tube introduced through the anus and used to examine the colon, remove polyps, or obtain tissue specimens.
• [as COLON + *skopos* target, from *skeptomai* look at]
• **colonoscopic** *adjective*
• **colonoscopy** *noun* "colla NOSCA pee" or "cola NOSCA pee"

colony *noun*
• "COLLA nee"
• a group of people who settle in a new territory (whether or not already inhabited) and form a community connected with a mother country.
• [Latin *colonia* from *colonus* farmer, from *colere* cultivate]
• **colonial** *adjective* "kuh LONEY 'll"
• **colonialism** *noun*
• **colonialist** *noun*
• **colonialization** *noun* (also esp. *Brit.* **-isation**)
• **colonialize** *verb* (also esp. *Brit.* **-ise**)
• **colonially** *adverb*
• **colonist** *noun*
• **colonization** *noun* (also esp. *Brit.* **-isation**)
• **colonize** *verb* (also esp. *Brit.* **-ise**)
• **colonizer** *noun* (also esp. *Brit.* **-iser**)

colophon *noun*
• "COLLA fon" or "COLLA f'n"
• a publisher's emblem or imprint, esp. on the title page of a book.
• [Late Latin from Greek *kolophōn* summit, finishing touch]

coloration *noun*
ALSO SPELLED: **colouration**
• "culler AY sh'n"
• colouring; a scheme or method of applying colour.
• [French *coloration* or Late Latin *coloratio* from *colorare* colour]

coloratura *noun*
• "culler a TURA" or "culler a TYURA" or "coller a TURA"
• elaborate ornamentation of a vocal melody with runs and trills.
• [Italian from Latin *colorare* colour]

colorectal *adjective*
• "co lo RECT'll"
• pertaining to or affecting the colon and the rectum.
• [COLON + RECTUM]

colorific *adjective*
• "culler IFFIC"
• producing colour.
• [French *colorifique* or modern Latin *colorificus* from *color* colour]

colorimeter *noun*
• "culler IMMA tur"
• an instrument for measuring the intensity of colour by comparison with a standard, used esp. to determine the concentration of a substance in solution.
• [Latin *color* colour + Greek *metron* measure]
• **colorimetric** *adjective* "culler a METRIC"
• **colorimetrically** *adverb*
• **colorimetry** *noun* "culler IMMA tree"

colossal *adjective*
• "kuh LOSS 'll"
• of immense size, scope, extent, or amount; huge, gigantic.
• [French from *colosse* COLOSSUS]
• **colossally** *adverb*

colossus *noun*
• "kuh LOSS us"
• a gigantic person, animal, building, etc.
• [Latin from Greek *kolossos*]

colostomy *noun*
• "kuh LOSSTA mee"
• an operation on the colon to make an opening in the abdominal wall to provide an artificial anus.
• [as COLON + Greek *stoma* mouth]

colostrum *noun*
• "kuh LOSSTRUM"
• the yellowish fluid secreted from the mammary glands in the first few days after giving birth, rich in protein and antibodies.
• [Latin]

colourant *noun*
ALSO SPELLED: **colorant**
• "CULLER 'nt"
• a colouring substance; pigment.
• [French *colorant*, present participle of *colorer* from Latin *colorare* to colour]

colposcopy *noun*
• "cawl POSCA pee"
• examination of the vagina and the neck of the uterus.
• [Greek *kolpos* womb + *skopos* target, from *skeptomai* look at]
• **colposcope** *noun*

colubrid *adjective*
• "CAWL yuh brid".
• of or relating to the large family Colubridae to which most non-venomous snakes belong.
• [Latin *coluber* snake]

colubrine *adjective*
• "CAWL yuh brine"
• snakelike.
• [Latin *colubrinus* from *coluber* snake]

columbarium *noun*
• "collum BERRY um"
• a room or building with niches and shelves for cinerary urns to be stored.
• [Latin, = pigeon house (from *columba* pigeon)]

columbine *noun*
• "COLLUM bine"
• any wild or cultivated plant of the genus *Aquilegia* with flowers said to resemble five clustered doves.
• [Old French *colombine* from medieval Latin *colombina herba* dovelike plant, from Latin *columba* dove]

columbite *noun*
• "kuh LUM bite"
• an ore of iron and niobium.
• [*Columbia*, a poetic name for America, + Greek *lithos* stone]

columbium *noun*
• "kuh LUMBY um"
• a rare grey-blue metallic transition element occurring naturally in several minerals and used in alloys for superconductors; niobium.
• [as COLUMBITE, in a specimen of which it was first discovered]

column *noun*
• "COLLUM"
• an upright cylindrical pillar often slightly tapering and usu. supporting an entablature or arch, or standing alone as a monument.
• [Latin *columna* pillar]
• **columnar** *adjective* "kuh LUM nur"
• **columned** *adjective*

columnist *noun*
• "COLLUM nist"
• a journalist contributing a regular column to a newspaper, magazine, etc.
• [as COLUMN]

colure *noun*
• "kuh LURE"
• either of two great circles intersecting at right angles at the celestial poles and passing through the ecliptic at either the equinoxes or the solstices.
• [Late Latin *colurus* from Greek *kolouros* truncated]

colza *noun*
• "CAWL zuh"
• a plant, *Brassica napus*, the seeds of which (rapeseeds) yield oil used in cooking, as a lubricant, and in soaps etc.
• [French *kolza(t)* from Low German *kōlsāt* (as COLE)]

coma *noun*
• "CO muh"
• a prolonged deep unconsciousness, caused esp. by severe injury or excessive use of drugs.
• [medieval Latin from Greek *kōma* deep sleep]

Comanche *noun*
• "kuh MANCHY"
• a member of an American Indian people of the southwestern US.
• [Spanish, from Comanche]

comatose *adjective*
• "CO muh tose" (rhymes with *GROSS*)
• in a coma.
• [as COMA]

combatant *noun*
• "k'm BAT'nt"
• a person engaged in fighting.
• [French *combattant* from *combattre* from Late Latin (from *com-* with + *batuere* fight)]

combative *adjective*
• "k'm BAT iv"
• ready or eager to fight; pugnacious.
• [as COMBATANT]
• **combatively** *adverb*
• **combativeness** *noun*

combinatorial *adjective*
• "com bin a TORY 'll"
• relating to combinations of items.
• [as COMBINE]

combine *verb*
• "k'm BINE"
• join together; unite for a common purpose.
• [Old French *combiner* or Late Latin *combinare* (from *com-* with + *bini* two)]
• **combinable** *adjective*
• **combination** *noun*
• **combinational** *adjective*
• **combinative** *adjective* "COM bin a tiv"
• **combinatory** *adjective*
• **combiner** *noun*

combustion *noun*
• "k'm BUS ch'n"
• burning; consumption by fire.
• [obsolete *combust* (adjective) from Latin *combustus* past participle of *comburere* burn up]
• **combustibility** *noun*
• **combustible** *adjective*
• **combustive** *adjective*

comedian *noun*
• "kuh MEEDY 'n"
• a humorous entertainer on stage, television, etc.
• [as COMEDY]

comedienne *noun*
• "kuh meedy EN"
• a female comedian.
• [French, as COMEDY]

comedist *noun*
• "COMMA dist"
• a writer of comedies.
• [as COMEDY]

comedo *noun*
• "COMMA doe"
• a blackhead.
• [Latin, = glutton, from *comedere* eat up]

comedy *noun*
• "COMMA dee"
• a play, film, etc., of an amusing or satirical character, usu. with a happy ending.
• [Old French *comedie* from Latin *comoedia* from Greek *kōmōidia* from *kōmōidos* comic poet, from *kōmos* revel]
• **comedic** *adjective* "kuh MEEDIC"

comely *adjective*
• "CUMLEE"
• (esp. of a person) pleasant to look at.
• [Middle English *cumelich*, *cumli* prob. from *becumelich* from 'become']
• **comeliness** *noun*

comestibles *plural noun*
• "kuh MESTA bulls"
• food.
• [French from medieval Latin *comestibilis* from Latin *comedere comest-* eat up]

comeuppance *noun*
• "kum UP ince"
• one's deserved fate or punishment.
• ['come' + 'up']

comfit *noun*
• "CUMFIT"
• a candy consisting of a nut, seed, etc., coated in sugar.
• [Old French *confit* from Latin *confectum* past participle of *conficere* prepare: see CONFECTION]

comfort *noun*
• "CUMFERT"
• consolation; relief in affliction.
• [Old French *confort(er)* from Late Latin *confortare* strengthen (from *com-* with + *fortis* strong)]
• **comforting** *adjective*
• **comfortingly** *adverb*
• **comfortless** *adjective*

comfortable *adjective*
• "CUMF tur bull" or "CUMFERT a bull"
• providing physical ease and relaxation.
• [as COMFORT]
• **comfortableness** *noun*
• **comfortably** *adverb*

comforter *noun*
• "CUMFERT ur"
• a warm quilt.
• [as COMFORT]

comfrey *noun*
• "CUMFREE"
• any of various herbs of the genus *Symphytum*, esp. *S. officinale* having large hairy leaves and clusters of usu. white or purple bell-shaped flowers.
• [Anglo-French *cumfrie*, ultimately from Latin *conferva* (from *com-* with + *fervēre* boil)]

comical *adjective*
• "COMMA k'll"
• funny; causing laughter.

• [Latin *comicus* from Greek *kōmikos* from *kōmos* revel]
• **comicality** *noun*
• **comically** *adverb*

Comice *noun*
• "COM iss"
• a large yellow dessert pear of a late-fruiting variety.
• [French, lit. = 'association, co-operative', referring to the *Comice Horticole* of Angers, France, where this variety was developed]

comity *noun*
• "COMMA tee"
• courtesy, civility; considerate behaviour towards others.
• [Latin *comitas* from *comis* courteous]

comma *noun*
• "COMMA"
• a punctuation mark (,) indicating a pause between parts of a sentence, or dividing items in a list, a string of figures, etc.
• [Latin from Greek *komma* clause]

commandant *noun*
• "COM'n dont" or "com'n DONT" or "com'n DANT"
• a commanding officer, esp. of a particular force, military academy, etc.
• [French *commandant*, or Italian or Spanish *commandante* from Late Latin *commandare* (as COMMEND)]

commandeer *verb*
• "com'n DEER"
• seize (men or goods) for military purposes.
• [South African Dutch *kommanderen* from French *commander* command]

commemorate *verb*
• "kuh MEMMER ate"
• preserve in memory by some celebration.
• [Latin *commemorare* (from *com-* with + *memorare* relate, from *memor* mindful)]
• **commemoration** *noun*
• **commemorative** *adjective*
• **commemorator** *noun*

commence *verb*
• "kuh MENCE"
• begin.
• [Old French *com(m)encier* from Romanic (from *com-* with + *initiare* INITIATE)]
• **commencement** *noun*

commend *verb*
• "kuh MEND"
• praise.
• [Latin *commendare* (from *com-* with + *mendare* = *mandare* entrust, from *manus* hand + *dare* give)]
• **commendable** *adjective*
• **commendably** *adverb*
• **commendation** *noun* "com'n DAY sh'n"

commendatory *adjective*
• "kuh MENDA tory"
• serving to present something as suitable for approval or acceptance.
• [Late Latin *commendatorius* (as COMMEND)]

commensalism *noun*
• "kuh MENSA lizm"
• an association between two organisms in which one benefits and the other derives no benefit or harm.
• [French *commensal* or medieval Latin *commensalis* 'eating at the same table' (from *com-* with + *mensa* table)]
• **commensal** *adjective*
• **commensality** *noun*

commensurable *adjective*
• "kuh MEN shur a bull" or "kuh MEN sur a bull" or "kuh MEN syur a bull"
• measurable by the same standard.
• [Late Latin *commensurabilis* (from *com-* with + *mensura* from *metiri mens-* measure)]
• **commensurability** *noun*
• **commensurably** *adverb*

commensurate *adjective*
• "kuh MEN shur it" or "kuh MEN sur it" or "kuh MEN syur it"
• having the same size, duration, etc.; co-extensive.
• [Late Latin *commensuratus* (from *com-* with + *mensura* from *metiri mens-* measure)]
• **commensurately** *adverb*

commentary *noun*
• "COM'n terry"
• a set of explanatory or critical notes on a text etc.
• [Latin *commentum* contrivance (in Late Latin also = interpretation), neuter past participle of *comminisci* devise]

commentate *verb*
• "COM'n tate"
• act as a commentator.
• [as COMMENTARY]
• **commentator** *noun*

commercial *adjective*
• "kuh MUR sh'll"
• of, engaged in, or concerned with, commerce.
• [French *commerce* or Latin *commercium* commerce (from *com-* with + *mercium* from *merx mercis* merchandise)]
• **commercialism** *noun*
• **commerciality** *noun* "kuh mershy ALA tee"
• **commercially** *adverb*

commercialize *verb*
ALSO SPELLED: esp. *Brit.* **-ise**
• "kuh MUR sh'll ize"
• exploit or spoil for the purpose of gaining profit.
• [as COMMERCIAL]
• **commercialization** *noun* (also esp. *Brit.* **-isation**)
• **commercialized** *adjective* (also esp. *Brit.* **-ised**)

commination *noun*
• "comma NAY sh'n"
• the threatening of divine vengeance.
• [Latin *comminatio* from *comminari* threaten]

comminatory *adjective*
• "COM'n a tory" or "kuh MINNA tory"
• threatening, punitive, or vengeful.
• [medieval Latin *comminatorius* (as COMMINATION)]

comminute *verb*
• "COM'n yute"
• reduce to small fragments.
• [Latin *comminuere comminut-* (from *com-* with + *minuere* lessen)]
• **comminution** *noun*

commis *noun*
• "COMMY"
• a junior chef.
• [originally = deputy, clerk, from French, past participle of *commettre* entrust (as COMMIT)]
HOMOPHONES: *commie*

commiserate *verb*
• "kuh MIZZER ate"
• express or feel sympathy or pity.
• [Latin *commiserari* (from *com-* with + *miserari* pity, from *miser* wretched)]
• **commiseration** *noun*
• **commiserative** *adjective*
• **commiserator** *noun*

commish *noun*
• "kuh MISH"
• a commissioner, esp. a commissioner of a professional sports league.
• [abbreviation]

commissar *noun*
• "COMMA sar"
• an official of the former Soviet Communist Party responsible for political education and organization.
• [Russian *komissar* from French *commissaire* (as COMMISSARY)]

commissariat *noun*
• "comma SERRY it"
• a department for the supply of food etc.
• [French *commissariat* & medieval Latin *commissariatus* (as COMMISSARY)]

commissary *noun*
• "COMMA serry"
• a deputy or delegate.
• [medieval Latin *commissarius* person in charge (as COMMIT)]

commission *noun*
• "kuh MISH'n"
• the authority to perform a task or certain duties.
• [Old French from Latin *commissio -onis* (as COMMIT)]

commissionaire *noun*
• "kuh misha NARE"
• a security guard or attendant.
• [French (as COMMISSION)]

commissioner *noun*
• "kuh MISH'n ur"
• a person appointed, esp. by a commission, to perform a specific task.
• [as COMMISSION]

commissure *noun*
• "COMMA syur"
• a junction, joint, or seam.
• [Latin *commissura* junction (as COMMIT)]
• **commissural** *adjective* "comma SYUR 'll"

commit *verb*
• "kuh MIT"
• entrust or consign for: safekeeping.
• [Latin *committere* join, entrust (from *com-* with + *mittere miss-* send)]
• **committable** *adjective*
• **committer** *noun*

commitment *noun*
• "kuh MIT m'nt"
• the process or an instance of committing oneself; a pledge or undertaking.
• [as COMMIT]

committal *noun*
• "kuh MIT'll"
• the act of committing a person to an institution, esp. prison or a mental hospital.
• [as COMMIT]

committed *adjective*
• "kuh MITTID"
• having a strong dedication to a cause or belief.
• [as COMMIT]

committee *noun*
• "kuh MITTY"
• a body of persons elected or appointed for a specific function by, and usu. out of, a larger body.
• [as COMMIT]

committeeman *noun*
• "kuh MITTY m'n"
• a person, esp. a man, who serves on a committee or committees, esp. frequently.
• [as COMMITTEE]

commode *noun*
• "kuh MODE"
• a chest of drawers.
• [French from Latin *commodus* convenient (from *com-* with + *modus* measure)]

commodification *noun*
• "kuh modda fuh CAY sh'n"
• the action of turning something into or treating something as a (mere) commodity.
• [as COMMODITY]
• **commodify** *verb*

commodious *adjective*
• "kuh MOADY us"
• roomy and comfortable.

• [French *commodieux* or from medieval Latin *commodiosus* from Latin *commodus* (as COMMODE)]
• **commodiously** *adverb*
• **commodiousness** *noun*

commodity *noun*
• "kuh MODDA tee"
• an article that can be bought and sold, esp. a product as opposed to a service.
• [Old French *commodité* or from Latin *commoditas* (as COMMODE)]
• **commoditization** *noun* (also esp. *Brit.* **-isation**)
• **commoditize** *verb* (also esp. *Brit.* **-ise**)

commodore *noun*
• "COMMA dore"
• (in Canada and the UK, and formerly also in the US) a naval officer ranking above captain and below rear admiral.
• [prob. from Dutch *komandeur* from French *commandeur* commander]

commonage *noun*
• "COM'n idge"
• a person's right to use another's property for pasturing animals or for fishing.
• [from 'common' from Old French *comun* from Latin *communis*]

commonality *noun*
• "com'n ALA tee"
• the sharing of an attribute.
• [as COMMONAGE]

commonalty *noun*
• "COM'n 'll tee"
• people without special rank or position, usu. viewed as an estate of the realm.
• [Old French *comunalté* from medieval Latin *communalitas -tatis* (as COMMONAGE)]

commonsensical *adjective*
• "com'n SENSA k'll"
• possessing or marked by common sense.
• ['common' + 'sense']

commonweal *noun*
• "COM'n weel"
• common well-being; the general good.
• [as COMMONAGE + WEAL]

commonwealth *noun*
• "COM'n welth"
• a community of people viewed as a political entity in which everyone has an interest.
• [as COMMONAGE + 'wealth']

commotion *noun*
• "kuh MOE sh'n"
• a confused and noisy disturbance or outburst.
• [Old French *commotion* or Latin *commotio* (from *com-* with + *motio -onis* motion)]

communal *adjective*
• "kuh MYOON 'll"
• relating or belonging to a community; for common use.
• [as COMMUNE]
• **communality** *noun*
• **communally** *adverb*

communalism *noun*
• "kuh MYOON'll izm"
• a principle of political organization based on federated communes.
• [as COMMUNE]
• **communalist** *noun*
• **communalistic** *adjective*

communard *noun*
• "COM yuh nard"
• a member of a commune.
• [French (as COMMUNE[1])]

commune[1] *noun*
• "COM yoon"
• a group of people, not necessarily related, sharing living accommodation and possessions, esp. as a political act.
• [French from medieval Latin *communia* neuter pl. of Latin *communis* common]

commune[2] *verb*
• "kuh MYOON"
• speak confidentially and intimately.
• [Old French *comuner* share, from *comun* from Latin *communis* common]

communicable *adjective*
• "kuh MYOONA kuh bull"
• (esp. of a disease) able to be passed on.
• [as COMMUNICATE]
• **communicability** *noun*

communicant *noun*
• "kuh MYOONA k'nt"
• a person who receives Holy Communion, esp. regularly.
• [Latin *communicare communicant-*]

communicate *verb*
• "kuh MYOONA cate"
• transmit or pass on (information) by speaking, writing, or other means.
• [Latin *communicare communicat-*]
• **communication** *noun*
• **communicational** *adjective*
• **communicative** *adjective*
"kuh MYOONA kuh tiv" or "kuh MYOONA kay tiv"
• **communicatively** *adverb*
• **communicator** *noun*
• **communicatory** *adjective*

communion *noun*
• "kuh MYOON y'n"
• an instance of sharing, esp. thoughts or feelings; fellowship.
• [as COMMUNE[2]]

communiqué *noun*
• "kuh MYOONA kay" or "kuh myoona CAY"
• an official communication, esp. a news report.
• [French, = communicated]

communism *noun*
• "COM yuh nizm"

• a system of society with property vested in the community and each member working for the common benefit according to his or her capacity and receiving according to his or her needs.
• [French *communisme* from *commun* common]
• **communist** *noun*
• **communistic** *adjective*

communitarian *noun*
• "kuh myoona TERRY 'n"
• a member of a community practising co-operation and some communism.
• [as COMMUNITY]
• **communitarianism** *noun*

community *noun*
• "kuh MYOONA tee"
• all the people living in a specific locality.
• [Old French *comuneté* from Latin *communitas -tatis* (as COMMONAGE)]

commutable *adjective*
• "kuh MUTE a bull"
• convertible into money; exchangeable.
• [Latin *commutabilis* (as COMMUTE)]
• **commutability** *noun*

commutate *verb*
• "COM yoo tate"
• regulate the direction of (an alternating current), esp. to make it a direct current.
• [as COMMUTE]

commutation *noun*
• "com yoo TAY sh'n"
• the act or process of changing (a judicial sentence etc.) to another less severe.
• [as COMMUTE]

commutative *adjective*
• "kuh MUTE a tiv"
• relating to or involving substitution.
• [as COMMUTE]

commutator *noun*
• "COM yoo tater"
• a device for reversing electric current.
• [as COMMUTE]

commute *verb*
• "kuh MUTE"
• travel to and from one's daily work, esp. from suburbs to the centre of a city by car or public transit.
• [Latin *commutare commutat-* (from *com-* with + *mutare* change)]
• **commuter** *noun*

commutershed *noun*
• "kuh MYOOTER shed"
• the region from within which it is possible to commute to work in a large, central city.
• [as COMMUTE + 'shed' as in 'watershed']

Comoran *noun*
• "COMMER 'n"
• a native or inhabitant of the Comoros in the Indian Ocean.

comose *adjective*
• "CO moce"
• (of seeds etc.) having hairs, downy.
• [Latin *comosus* from Greek *komē* hair of head]

Comox *noun*
• "CO mox"
• a member of an Aboriginal group, part of the Salishan linguistic group, living on Vancouver Island.
• [Comox, = 'land of plenty']

compadre *noun*
• "k'm PODRAY"
• friend, companion.
• [Spanish, = godfather]

companion *noun*
• "k'm PAN y'n"
• a person or animal with whom one spends a lot of time or with whom one travels.
• [Old French *compaignon*, lit. = 'one who breaks bread with another', ultimately from Latin *com* with + *panis* bread]

companionable *adjective*
• "k'm PAN y'n a bull"
• agreeable as a companion; sociable.
• [as COMPANION]
• **companionability** *noun*
• **companionableness** *noun*
• **companionably** *adverb*

companionship *noun*
• "k'm PAN y'n ship"
• good fellowship; friendship.
• [as COMPANION]

companionway *noun*
• "k'm PAN y'n way"
• a staircase to a cabin.
• [obsolete Dutch *kompanje* quarterdeck, from Old French *compagne* from Italian (*camera della*) *compagna* pantry, prob. ultimately related to COMPANION]

company *noun*
• "CUMPA nee"
• a number of people assembled; a crowd; an audience.
• [Anglo-French *compainie*, Old French *compai(g)nie* from Romanic (as COMPANION)]

comparable *adjective*
• "COMPER a bull" or "k'm PARE a bull"
• fit to be compared; worth comparing.
• [Old French *comparable* from *comparer* from Latin *comparare* (from *com-* with + *parare* from *par* equal)]
• **comparability** *noun*
• **comparably** *adverb*

comparative *adjective*
• "k'm PERRA tiv"
• measured or judged by estimating the similarity or dissimilarity between one thing and another; relative.
• [as COMPARABLE]
• **comparatively** *adverb*

comparator *noun*
- "k'm PERRA tur"
- a device for comparing a product, an output, etc., with a standard, esp. an electronic circuit comparing two signals.
- [as COMPARABLE]

comparison *noun*
- "k'm PERRA s'n"
- the act or an instance of comparing.
- [Old French *comparesoun* from Latin *comparatio -onis* (as COMPARABLE)]

compartment *noun*
- "k'm PART m'nt"
- a space within a larger space, separated from the rest by partitions, e.g. in a railway carriage, wallet, desk, etc.
- [French *compartiment* from Italian *compartimento* from Late Latin *compartiri* (from *com-* with + *partiri* share)]
- **compartmental** *adjective*
- **compartmentally** *adverb*
- **compartmentation** *noun*

compartmentalize *verb*
ALSO SPELLED: esp. *Brit.* **-ise**
- "k'm part MENT'll ize"
- divide into compartments or categories.
- [as COMPARTMENT]
- **compartmentalization** *noun* (also esp. *Brit.* **-isation**)

compass *noun*
- "CUMPUS"
- an instrument showing the direction of magnetic north and bearings from it.
- [Old French *compas*, ultimately from Latin *passus* pace]

compassion *noun*
- "k'm PASH'n"
- pity inclining one to help or be merciful.
- [Old French from Church Latin *compassio -onis* from *compati* (from *com-* with + *pati pass-* suffer)]
- **compassionate** *adjective*
- **compassionately** *adverb*

compatible *adjective*
- "k'm PATTA bull"
- able to coexist; well-suited; mutually tolerant.
- [French from medieval Latin *compatibilis* (as COMPASSION)]
- **compatibility** *noun*
- **compatibly** *adverb*

compatriot *noun*
- "k'm PAY tree it"
- a native or inhabitant of one's own country or region.
- [French *compatriote* from Late Latin *compatriota* (from *com-* with + *patriota* PATRIOT)]

compeer *noun*
- "COM peer" or "k'm PEER"
- an equal, a peer.
- [Old French *comper* (from *com-* with + *peer* from Latin *par* equal)]

compel *verb*
- "k'm PELL"
- force, oblige.
- [Latin *compellere compuls-* (from *com-* with + *pellere* drive)]

compellable *adjective*
- "k'm PELLA bull"
- (of a witness) able to be made to attend court or give evidence.
- [as COMPEL]

compelling *adjective*
- "k'm PELLING"
- arousing strong interest, attention, conviction, or admiration.
- [as COMPEL]
- **compellingly** *adverb*

compendious *adjective*
- "k'm PENDY us"
- (esp. of a book etc.) comprehensive but fairly brief.
- [as COMPENDIUM]
- **compendiously** *adverb*
- **compendiousness** *noun*

compendium *noun*
- "k'm PENDY um"
- a collection of detailed items of information, esp. in a book.
- [Latin, = what is weighed together, from *compendere* (from *com-* with + *pendere* weigh)]

compensate *verb*
- "COMP'n sate"
- recompense (a person).
- [Latin *compensare* (from *com-* with + *pensare* frequentative of *pendere pens-* weigh)]
- **compensation** *noun*
- **compensator** *noun*
- **compensatory** *adjective* "k'm PENSA tory" or "comp'n SAY tuh ree"

compère *noun*
- "COM pare"
- a master of ceremonies, esp. in a variety show etc.
- [French, = godfather, from Romanic (from *com-* with + *pater* father)]

compete *verb*
- "k'm PETE"
- strive for superiority or supremacy.
- [Latin *competere competit-*, in late sense 'strive after or contend for (something)' (from *com-* with + *petere* seek)]

competent *adjective*
- "COMPA t'nt"
- adequately qualified or capable.
- [Old French *competent* or Latin *competent-* (as COMPETE)]
- **competence** *noun*
- **competency** *noun*
- **competently** *adverb*

competition *noun*
- “compa TISH’n”
- the act or an instance of competing or contending with others (for supremacy, a position, a prize, etc.).
- [Late Latin *competitio* rivalry (as COMPETITIVE)]

competitive *adjective*
- “k’m PETTA tiv”
- involving, offered for, or by competition.
- [*competit-*, past participle stem of Latin *competere* COMPETE]
- **competitively** *adverb*
- **competitiveness** *noun*

competitor *noun*
- “k’m PETTA tur”
- a person who competes.
- [French *compétiteur* or Latin *competitor* (as COMPETE)]

compilation *noun*
- “compa LAY sh’n”
- the act of compiling.
- [Old French *compilation*, from *compiler* or its apparent source, Latin *compilare* plunder, plagiarize]

complacent *adjective*
- “k’m PLAY s’nt”
- smugly self-satisfied.
- [Latin *complacēre* (from *com-* with + *placēre* please)]
- **complacence** *noun*
- **complacency** *noun*
- **complacently** *adverb*

HOMOPHONES: *complaisant, complaisance*

complainant *noun*
- “k’m PLANE ’nt”
- a plaintiff in certain lawsuits.
- [Old French *complaignant* from *complaindre* from medieval Latin *complangere* bewail (as Latin *com-* with + *plangere planct-* lament)]

complaisant *adjective*
- “k’m PLAY z’nt” or “k’m PLAY s’nt”
- politely deferential.
- [French from *complaire* (stem *complais-*) acquiesce to please, from Latin *complacēre*: see COMPLACENT]
- **complaisance** *noun*

HOMOPHONES: *complacent, complacence*

compleat *adjective*
- “k’m PLEET”
- accomplished.
- [variant spelling of ‘complete’, esp. in 16th and 17th c., revived because of use in *The Compleat Angler* by I. Walton, English writer d.1683]

HOMOPHONES: *complete*

complected *adjective*
- “k’m PLECTED”
- having a (specified) complexion.
- [apparently from COMPLEXION]

complement *noun*
- “COMPLA m’nt”
- something that completes.
- [Latin *complementum* from *complēre* fill up]

HOMOPHONES: *compliment*

complementary *adjective*
- “compla MENTA ree”
- completing; forming a complement.
- [as COMPLEMENT]
- **complementarily** *adverb*

“compla men TERRA lee”
- **complementarity** *noun*

HOMOPHONES: *complimentary*

completist *noun*
- “k’m PLEET ist”
- an obsessive or indiscriminate collector.
- [from ‘complete’, from Old French *complet* or Latin *completus* past participle of *complēre* fill up]

complexion *noun*
- “k’m PLECK sh’n”
- the natural colour, texture, and appearance of the skin, esp. of the face.
- [Old French from Latin *complexio -onis* from *complexus* past participle of *complectere* embrace, assoc. with *complexus* braided: originally = combination of supposed qualities determining the nature of a body]
- **complexioned** *adjective*

complicate *verb*
- “COMPLA cate”
- make or become difficult, confused, or complex.
- [Latin *complicare complicat-* (from *com-* with + *plicare* fold)]
- **complicated** *adjective*
- **complicatedly** *adverb*
- **complicatedness** *noun*
- **complication** *noun*

complicity *noun*
- “k’m PLISSA tee”
- partnership in a crime or wrongdoing.
- [Middle English *complice* associate, from Old French, from Late Latin *complex, complic-* allied, from Latin *complicare* fold together (see COMPLICATE)]
- **complicit** *adjective*
- **complicitous** *adjective*

compliment *noun*
- “COMPLA m’nt”
- a spoken or written expression of praise.
- [French *complimenter* from Italian *complimento*, ultimately from Latin (as COMPLEMENT)]

HOMOPHONES: *complement*

complimentary *adjective*
- “compla MENTA ree”
- expressing a compliment; praising.
- [as COMPLIMENT]

HOMOPHONES: *complementary*

compline *noun*
- "COM plin" or "COM pline"
- the last of the canonical hours of prayer, said before retiring at night.
- [Old French *complie*, feminine past participle of obsolete *complir* complete, ultimately from Latin *complēre* fill up]

comply *verb*
- "k'm PLY"
- act in accordance (with a wish, command, regulation, etc.).
- [Italian *complire* from Catalan *complir*, Spanish *cumplir* from Latin *complēre* fill up]
- **compliance** *noun*
- **compliant** *adjective*
- **compliantly** *adverb*

component *noun*
- "k'm PONE 'nt"
- a part of a larger whole or system.
- [Latin *componere component-* (from *com-* with + *ponere* put)]
- **componential** *adjective*
- **componentry** *noun*

comport *reflexive verb*
- "k'm PORT"
- conduct oneself; behave.
- [Latin *comportare* (from *com-* with + *portare* carry)]
- **comportment** *noun*

compose *verb*
- "k'm POZE"
- construct or create (a work of art, esp. literature or music).
- [French *composer*, from Latin *componere* (from *com-* with + *ponere* put)]
- **composer** *noun*

composed *adjective*
- "k'm POZED"
- calm, unruffled.
- [as COMPOSE]

composite *adjective*
- "COMPA zit"
- made up of various parts; blended.
- [French from Latin *compositus* past participle of *componere* (from *com-* with + *ponere posit-* put)]
- **compositely** *adverb*
- **compositeness** *noun*

composition *noun*
- "compa ZISH'n"
- the act of putting together; formation or construction.
- [Old French, from Latin *compositio -onis* (as COMPOSITE)]
- **compositional** *adjective*
- **compositionally** *adverb*

compositor *noun*
- "k'm POZZA tur"
- a person who sets up type or text for printing.
- [Anglo-French *compositour* from Latin *compositor* (as COMPOSITE)]

composure *noun*
- "k'm POE zhur"
- a tranquil manner; calmness.
- [as COMPOSE]

compote *noun*
- "COM pote" or "COM pot"
- fruit preserved or cooked in syrup.
- [French from Old French *composte* (as COMPOSITE)]

comprador *noun*
ALSO SPELLED: **compradore**
- "compra DORE"
- an agent of a foreign power.
- [originally = a Chinese business agent of a foreign company, from Portuguese *comprador* buyer, from Late Latin *comparator* from Latin *comparare* purchase]

comprehend *verb*
- "com pree HEND"
- grasp mentally; understand (a person or a thing).
- [Old French *comprehender* or Latin *comprehendere comprehens-* (from *com-* with + *prehendere* grasp)]
- **comprehender** *noun*
- **comprehensibility** *noun*
- **comprehensible** *adjective*
- **comprehensibly** *adverb*
- **comprehension** *noun*

comprehensive *adjective*
- "com pree HENSIV"
- complete; including all or nearly all elements, aspects, etc.
- [French *compréhensif -ive* or Late Latin *comprehensivus* (as COMPREHEND)]
- **comprehensively** *adverb*
- **comprehensiveness** *noun*

compress *verb*
- "k'm PRESS"
- squeeze together.
- [Late Latin *compressare* frequentative of Latin *comprimere compress-* (from *com-* with + *premere* press)]
- **compressibility** *noun*
- **compressible** *adjective*
- **compression** *noun*
- **compressive** *adjective*
- **compressor** *noun*

comprise *verb*
- "k'm PRIZE"
- include; comprehend.
- [Old French, feminine past participle of *comprendre* COMPREHEND]

compromise *noun*
- "COMPRA mize"
- the settlement of a dispute by mutual concession.
- [Old French *compromis* from Late Latin *compromissum* neuter past participle of

compromittere (from *com-* with + *promittere* promise)]
• **compromiser** *noun*

compromised *adjective*
• "COMPRA mized"
• vulnerable, esp. unable to resist infection.
• [as COMPROMISE]

comptroller *noun*
• "k'n TROLE ur" or "comp TROLE ur"
• an official or executive in charge of financial affairs.
• [var. of 'controller', by erroneous assoc. with Latin *computare* count (see COMPUTE)]
HOMOPHONES: *controller*

compulsion *noun*
• "k'm PUL sh'n"
• the action of compelling; an obligation.
• [French from Late Latin *compulsio -onis* (as COMPEL)]

compulsive *adjective*
• "k'm PULSE iv"
• resulting or acting from, or as if from, compulsion.
• [medieval Latin *compulsivus* (as COMPEL)]
• **compulsively** *adverb*
• **compulsiveness** *noun*

compulsory *adjective*
• "k'm PULSER ee"
• required by law or a rule.
• [medieval Latin *compulsorius* (as COMPEL)]
• **compulsorily** *adverb*
• **compulsoriness** *noun*

compunction *noun*
• "k'm PUNK sh'n"
• an uneasy conscience; a feeling of remorse.
• [Old French *componction* from Church Latin *compunctio -onis* from Latin *compungere compunct-* (from *com-* with + *pungere* prick)]

compurgation *noun*
• "comper GAY sh'n"
• an acquittal from a charge or accusation obtained by the oaths of witnesses.
• [medieval Latin *compurgatio* from Latin *compurgare* (from *com-* with + *purgare* purify)]

compurgator *noun*
• "COMPER gay tur"
• (historically) a witness who swore to the innocence or good character of an accused person.
• [as COMPURGATION]

computational *adjective*
• "com pyoo TAY sh'n 'll"
• of or pertaining to computing.
• [as COMPUTE]

compute *verb*
• "k'm PYOOT"
• reckon or calculate (a number, an amount, etc.).
• [French *computer* or Latin *computare* (from *com-* with + *putare* reckon)]
• **computability** *noun*
• **computable** *adjective*
• **computation** *noun*
• **computing** *noun*

computer *noun*
• "k'm PYOO tur"
• an electronic device for storing and processing data (usu. in binary form), according to instructions given to it in a variable program.
• [as COMPUTE]
• **computerization** *noun* (also esp. *Brit.* **-isation**)
• **computerize** *verb* (also esp. *Brit.* **-ise**)
• **computerized** *adjective* (also esp. *Brit.* **-ised**)

computerese *noun*
• "k'm pyooter EEZ"
• the jargon associated with computers.
• [as COMPUTER]

computerphobia *noun*
• "k'm pyooter FOBEY uh"
• fear or mistrust of computer technology; an aversion to using computers.
• [as COMPUTER + PHOBIA]
• **computerphobe** *noun*
• **computerphobic** *adjective*

comrade *noun*
• "COMRAD"
• a workmate, friend, or companion.
• [earlier *cama- camerade*, via French *camerade*, *camarade* (originally feminine) and Spanish *camarada* roommate, from Latin *camera*]
• **comradely** *adjective*
• **comradeship** *noun*

concatenate *verb*
• "k'n CAT'n ate"
• link together (a chain of events, things, etc.).
• [Late Latin *concatenare* (from *com-* with + *catenare* from *catena* chain)]
• **concatenation** *noun*

concave *adjective*
• "CON cave"
• having an outline or surface curved like the interior of a circle or sphere.
• [Latin *concavus* (from *com-* with + *cavus* hollow)]
• **concavely** *adverb*
• **concavity** *noun* "k'n CAVVA tee"

conceal *verb*
• "k'n SEEL"
• keep secret.
• [Old French *conceler* from Latin *concelare* (from *com-* with + *celare* hide)]
• **concealment** *noun*

concealer *noun*
• "k'n SEELER"
• a cosmetic which covers blemishes and dark spots on the skin, esp. the circles under the eyes.
• [as CONCEAL]

concede *verb*
• "k'n SEED"
• admit to be true.
• [French *concéder* or Latin *concedere concess-* (from *com-* with + *cedere* yield)]
• **conceder** *noun*

conceit *noun*
• "k'n SEET"
• excessive pride in oneself or one's powers, abilities, etc.
• [Middle English from CONCEIVE after *deceit*, *deceive*, etc.]
• **conceited** *adjective*
• **conceitedly** *adverb*
• **conceitedness** *noun*

conceivable *adjective*
• "k'n SEEVA bull"
• capable of being grasped or imagined; understandable.
• [as CONCEIVE]
• **conceivability** *noun*
• **conceivably** *adverb*

conceive *verb*
• "k'n SEEVE"
• become pregnant.
• [Old French *conceiv-* stressed stem of *concevoir* from Latin *concipere concept-* (from *com-* with + *capere* take)]

concelebrate *verb*
• "k'n SELLA brate" or "con SELLA brate"
• (of two or more clergy) celebrate the Eucharist together.
• [Latin *concelebrare* (from *com-* with + *celebrare* CELEBRATE)]
• **concelebrant** *noun*
• **concelebration** *noun*

concentrate *verb*
• "CON s'n trate"
• focus all one's attention or mental ability.
• [French *concentrer* (from Latin *com-* with + CENTRE)]
• **concentration** *noun*
• **concentrative** *adjective*
• **concentrator** *noun*

concentrated *adjective*
• "CON s'n trated"
• (of an emotion etc.) intense, strong.
• [as CONCENTRATE]
• **concentratedly** *adverb*

concentric *adjective*
• "k'n SENTRIC"
• (esp. of circles) having a common centre.
• [medieval Latin *concentricus* (from *com-* with + *centricus* from *centrum* centre, from Greek *kentron* sharp point)]
• **concentrically** *adverb*
• **concentricity** *noun* "con sen TRISSA tee"

concept *noun*
• "CONSEPT"
• a general notion; an abstract idea.
• [Late Latin *conceptus* from *concept-*: see CONCEIVE]

conception *noun*
• "k'n SEP sh'n"
• the act or an instance of conceiving; the process of being conceived.
• [as CONCEPT]

conceptual *adjective*
• "k'n SEP choo 'll"
• of mental conceptions or concepts.
• [as CONCEPT]
• **conceptually** *adverb*

conceptualism *noun*
• "k'n SEP choo 'll izm"
• the theory that universals exist, but only as concepts in the mind.
• [as CONCEPT]
• **conceptualist** *noun*

conceptualize *verb*
ALSO SPELLED: esp. *Brit.* **-ise**
• "k'n SEP choo 'll ize"
• form a concept or idea of.
• [as CONCEPT]
• **conceptualization** *noun* (also esp. *Brit.* **-isation**)

concern *verb*
• "k'n SURN"
• be relevant or important to.
• [French *concerner* or Late Latin *concernere* (from *com-* with + *cernere* sift, discern)]
• **concerned** *adjective*
• **concernedly** *adverb*

concerning *preposition*
• "k'n SURNING"
• about, regarding.
• [as CONCERN]

concert *noun*
• "CON surt"
• a musical performance of usu. several separate compositions.
• [French *concert* (n.), *concerter* (v.) from Italian *concertare* harmonize]
• **concertgoer** *noun*

concerted *adjective*
• "k'n SURTED"
• combined together; jointly arranged or planned.
• [as CONCERT]

concertina *noun*
• "con sur TEENA"
• a musical instrument held in the hands and stretched and squeezed like bellows, having reeds and a set of buttons at each end to control the valves.
• [as CONCERT]

concertino *noun*
• "con sur TEENO"
• a simple or short concerto.
• [Italian, diminutive of CONCERTO]

concertize *verb*
ALSO SPELLED: esp. *Brit.* **-ise**
• "CONSURT ize"
• perform regularly in concerts.
• [as CONCERT]

concertmaster *noun*
• "CONSURT master"
• the principal first-violin player in an orchestra.
• [as CONCERT + 'master']

concerto *noun*
• "k'n CHAIR toe"
• a composition for a solo instrument or instruments accompanied by an orchestra.
• [Italian (see CONCERT)]

concession *noun*
• "k'n SESH'n"
• the act or an instance of conceding.
• [French *concession* from Latin *concessio* (as CONCEDE)]
• **concessional** *adjective*
• **concessionary** *adjective*

concessionaire *noun*
• "k'n sesh'n AIR"
• the operator or holder of a concession.
• [French *concessionnaire* (as CONCESSION)]

concessive *adjective*
• "k'n SESSIV"
• of or tending to concession.
• [Late Latin *concessivus* (as CONCEDE)]

conch *noun*
• "CONCH" or "CONK"
• a thick heavy spiral shell, occasionally bearing long projections, of various marine gastropod molluscs of the family Strombidae.
• [Latin *concha* shell, from Greek *kogkhē*]
HOMOPHONES: *conk*

concha *noun*
• "KONKA"
• any part resembling a shell, esp. the depression in the external ear leading to its central cavity.
• [Latin: see CONCH]

conchoidal *adjective*
• "con COID'll"
• (of a solid fracture etc.) resembling the surface of a bivalve shell.
• [as CONCH]

conchology *noun*
• "con COLLA jee"
• the scientific study of the shells of molluscs.
• [Latin *concha* shell, from Greek *kogkhē* + *logos* word]
• **conchological** *adjective*
• **conchologist** *noun*

concierge *noun*
• "concy AIRZH"
• an attendant at the entrance to an apartment or condominium building.
• [French, prob. ultimately from Latin *conservus* fellow slave]

conciliar *adjective*
• "k'n SILLY ur"
• of or concerning a council, esp. an ecclesiastical council.
• [medieval Latin *consiliarius* counsellor]

conciliate *verb*
• "k'n SILLY ate"
• attempt to settle an esp. labour dispute by hearing all disputants and recommending solutions.
• [Latin *conciliare* combine, gain (*concilium* COUNCIL)]
• **conciliation** *noun*
• **conciliator** *noun*
• **conciliatory** *adjective* "k'n SILLY a tory"

concise *adjective*
• "k'n SICE"
• (of speech, writing, style, or a person) brief but comprehensive in expression.
• [French *concis* or Latin *concisus* past participle of *concidere* (from *com-* with + *caedere* cut)]
• **concisely** *adverb*
• **conciseness** *noun*
• **concision** *noun* "k'n SIZH'n"

conclave *noun*
• "CON clave"
• a private meeting.
• [Old French from Latin *conclave* lockable room (from *com-* with + *clavis* key)]

conclude *verb*
• "k'n CLUDE"
• bring or come to an end.
• [Latin *concludere* (from *com-* with + *claudere* shut)]
• **conclusion** *noun*

conclusive *adjective*
• "k'n CLOO siv"
• decisive, convincing.
• [as CONCLUDE]
• **conclusively** *adverb*
• **conclusiveness** *noun*

concoct *verb*
• "k'n COCT"
• make by combining elements not usually mixed together, esp. from what is available.
• [Latin *concoquere concoct-* (from *com-* with + *coquere* cook)]
• **concocter** *noun*
• **concoction** *noun*

concomitant *adjective*
• "k'n COMMA t'nt"
• going together; associated.
• [Late Latin *concomitari* (from *com-* with + *comitari* from Latin *comes -mitis* companion)]
• **concomitantly** *adverb*

concord *noun*
• "CON cord"
• agreement or harmony between people or things.
• [Old French *concorde* from Latin *concordia* from *concors* of one mind (from *com-* with + *cors* from *cor cordis* heart)]
• **concordant** *adjective*
• **concordantly** *adverb*

concordance *noun*
• "k'n CORE dince"
• an alphabetized list of all the words in a text or group of texts, usu. with some accompanying text.
• [Old French from medieval Latin *concordantia* (as CONCORD)]
• **concordancer** *noun*
• **concordancing** *noun*

concordat *noun*
• "k'n CORE dat"
• an agreement, esp. between the Vatican and a secular government relating to matters of mutual interest.
• [French *concordat* or Latin *concordatum* neuter past participle of *concordare* (as CONCORD)]

concours *noun*
• "cong COOR"
• a competition.
• [French, as CONCUR]

concourse *noun*
• "CON corse"
• an open central area in a large public building, airport, etc.
• [Old French *concours* from Latin *concursus* (as CONCUR)]

concrescence *noun*
• "k'n CRESS ince"
• coalescence; growing together.
• [Latin *com-* with, after *excrescence* etc.]
• **concrescent** *adjective*

concrete *adjective*
• "CON creet"
• existing in a material form; real.
• [French *concret* or Latin *concretus* past participle of *concrescere* (from *com-* with + *crescere cret-* grow)]
• **concretely** *adverb*
• **concreteness** *noun*

concretion *noun*
• "k'n CREE sh'n"
• a hard solid concreted mass.
• [as CONCRETE]
• **concretionary** *adjective*

concretize *verb*
ALSO SPELLED: esp. *Brit.* **-ise**
• "CON creet ize"
• make concrete instead of abstract.
• [as CONCRETE]
• **concretization** *noun* (also esp. *Brit.* **-isation**)

concubinage *noun*
• "con CUBE 'n idge"
• the cohabitation of a man and woman not married to each other.
• [as CONCUBINE]

concubine *noun*
• "CON kyoo bine"
• a woman who lives with a man as his wife; a kept mistress.
• [Old French from Latin *concubina* (from *com-* with + *cubina* from *cubare* lie)]

concupiscence *noun*
• "k'n KYOOPA since"
• sexual desire.
• [Old French from Late Latin *concupiscentia* from Latin *concupiscere* begin to desire (from *com-* with + *cupere* desire)]
• **concupiscent** *adjective*

concur *verb*
• "k'n CUR"
• agree in opinion.
• [Latin *concurrere* (from *com-* with + *currere* run)]

concurrent *adjective*
• "k'n CUR 'nt"
• existing or in operation at the same time.
• [as CONCUR]
• **concurrence** *noun*
• **concurrently** *adverb*

concuss *verb*
• "k'n CUSS"
• subject to concussion.
• [Latin *concutere concuss-* (from *com-* with + *cutere* = *quatere* shake)]
• **concussive** *adjective*

concussion *noun*
• "k'n KUSH'n"
• a violent injury to the brain caused by shaking or jarring, usu. accompanied by loss of consciousness.
• [Latin *concussio* (as CONCUSS)]

condemn *verb*
• "k'n DEM"
• express utter disapproval of; censure.
• [Old French *condem(p)ner* from Latin *condemnare* (from *com-* with + *damnare* DAMN)]
• **condemnable** *adjective* "k'n DEMNA bull"
• **condemnation** *noun* "con dem NAY sh'n"
• **condemnatory** *adjective* "k'n DEMNA tory"
• **condemned** *adjective* "k'n DEMD"

condensate *noun*
• "k'n DEN sate" or "CON d'n sate"
• a substance produced by condensation.
• [as CONDENSE]

condense *verb*
• "k'n DENSE"
• reduce or be reduced from a gas or solid to a liquid.

• [French *condenser* or Latin *condensare* (from *com-* with + *densus* thick)]
• **condensation** *noun*

condenser *noun*
• "k'n DENSER"
• an apparatus or vessel for condensing vapour.
• [as CONDENSE]

condescend *verb*
• "conda SEND"
• be gracious enough (to do a thing) esp. while showing one's sense of dignity or superiority.
• [Old French *condescendre* from Church Latin *condescendere* (from *com-* with + DESCEND)]
• **condescending** *adjective*
• **condescendingly** *adverb*
• **condescension** *noun*

condign *adjective*
• "k'n DINE"
• (of a punishment etc.) severe and well-deserved.
• [Old French *condigne* from Latin *condignus* (from *com-* with + *dignus* worthy)]

condiment *noun*
• "CONDA m'nt"
• a spice or foodstuff used in small quantities to enhance the flavour of other foods, e.g. salt and pepper, vinegar, etc.
• [Latin *condimentum* from *condire* pickle]

condition *noun*
• "k'n DISH'n"
• a stipulation; something upon the fulfillment of which something else depends.
• [Latin *condicio -onis* from *condicere* (from *com-* with + *dicere* say)]
• **conditioned** *adjective*

conditional *adjective*
• "k'n DISH'n 'll"
• dependent; not absolute; containing a condition or stipulation.
• [as CONDITION]
• **conditionality** *noun*
• **conditionally** *adverb*

conditioner *noun*
• "k'n DISH'n ur"
• a substance or device that improves the condition of something, esp. a substance applied to the hair.
• [as CONDITION]

conditioning *noun*
• "k'n DISH'n ing"
• the act of bringing a person, animal, or thing into good condition.
• [as CONDITION]

condole *verb*
• "k'n DOLE"
• express sympathy with a person over a loss, grief, etc.
• [Late Latin *condolēre* (from *com-* with + *dolēre* suffer)]

condolence *noun*
• "k'n DOLE ince"
• an expression of sympathy.
• [as CONDOLE]

condominium *noun*
• "conda MINNY um"
• an apartment building, office building or townhouse complex containing units which are individually owned.
• [modern Latin (from *com-* with + *dominium* DOMINION)]

condone *verb*
• "k'n DONE" ("DONE" rhymes with *BONE*)
• forgive or overlook (an offence or wrongdoing).
• [Latin *condonare* (from *com-* with + *donare* give)]
• **condonation** *noun* "conda NAY sh'n"
• **condoner** *noun*

condor *noun*
• "CON dore"
• a large vulture, *Vultur gryphus*, of S America, having black plumage with a white neck ruff and a fleshy wattle on the forehead.
• [Spanish from Quechua *cuntur*]

condottiere *noun*
• "con dot YERRY"
• a leader or a member of a troop of mercenaries in Italy.
• [Italian from *condotto* troop under contract (*condotta*) from Latin *conductus* (from *com-* with + *ducere duct-* lead)]

conduce *verb*
• "k'n DOOCE" or "k'n DYOOCE"
• (usu. of an event or attribute) lead or contribute to (a result).
• [Latin *conducere conduct-* (from *com-* with + *ducere duct-* lead)]

conducive *adjective*
• "k'n DOO siv" or "k'n DYOO siv"
• contributing or helping (towards something).
• [as CONDUCE]

conduct *noun*
• "CON duct"
• behaviour; way of acting.
• [Latin *conductus* (from *com-* with + *ducere duct-* lead)]
• **conductible** *adjective*

conductance *noun*
• "k'n DUCK tince"
• the power of a specified material to conduct electricity.
• [as CONDUCT]

conduction *noun*
• "k'n DUCK sh'n"
• the transmission of heat through a substance from a region of higher temperature to a region of lower temperature.
• [as CONDUCT]

conductive *adjective*
- "k'n DUCTIV"
- having the property of conducting (esp. heat, electricity, etc.).
- [as CONDUCT]
- **conductively** *adverb*
- **conductivity** *noun*

conductor *noun*
- "k'n DUCT tur"
- a person who directs the performance of an orchestra or choir etc.
- [as CONDUCT]
- **conductorship** *noun*

conductress *noun*
- "k'n DUCK tress"
- a woman who collects fares in a bus etc.
- [as CONDUCT]

conduit *noun*
- "CON doo it" or "CON dyoo it"
- a channel or pipe for conveying liquids.
- [Old French *conduit* from medieval Latin *conductus* CONDUCT]

condyle *noun*
- "CON dill" or "CON dile"
- a rounded outgrowth at the end of a bone, forming an articulation with another bone.
- [French from Latin *condylus* from Greek *kondulos* knuckle]
- **condylar** *adjective*
- **condyloid** *adjective*

confabulate *verb*
- "k'n FAB yuh late"
- converse, chat.
- [Latin *confabulari* (from *com-* with + *fabulari* from *fabula* tale)]
- **confabulation** *noun*

confect *verb*
- "k'n FECT"
- make by putting together ingredients or materials.
- [Latin *conficere confect-* put together (from *com-* with + *facere* make)]

confection *noun*
- "k'n FECK sh'n"
- a sweet dessert or candy.
- [Old French from Latin *confectio -onis* (as CONFECT)]
- **confectioner** *noun*

confectionery *noun*
ALSO SPELLED: **confectionary**
- "k'n FECK sh'n airy"
- candy and other sweets.
- [as CONFECTION]

confederacy *noun*
- "k'n FEDDER a see"
- a league or alliance of persons, states, etc.
- [as CONFEDERATE]

confederate *adjective*
- "k'n FEDDER it"
- allied; joined by an agreement or treaty.
- [Late Latin *confoederatus* (from *com-* with + FEDERATE)]
- **confederated** *adjective* "k'n FEDDER ated"

confederation *noun*
- "k'n fedder AY sh'n"
- a union or alliance of peoples, countries, labour unions, etc.
- [French *confédération* (as CONFEDERATE)]
- **confederal** *adjective*
- **confederalism** *noun*

confederationist *noun*
- "k'n fedder AY sh'n ist"
- *Cdn* a supporter of Confederation.
- [as CONFEDERATE]

confer *verb*
- "k'n FUR"
- grant or bestow (a title, degree, favour, etc.).
- [Latin *conferre* (from *com-* with + *ferre* bring)]
- **conferee** *noun*
- **conferment** *noun*
- **conferral** *noun*

conference *noun*
- "CONFA rince"
- a meeting for discussion or presentation of information, esp. a regular one held by an association or organization.
- [French *conférence* or medieval Latin *conferentia* (as CONFER)]

confessor *noun*
- "k'n FESSER"
- a priest who hears confessions and gives spiritual counsel.
- [Old French *confesser* from Romanic from Latin *confessus* past participle of *confitēri* (from *com-* with + *fatēri* declare, avow)]

confetti *noun*
- "k'n FETTY"
- small bits of paper, usu. coloured, thrown on festive occasions, esp. at the bride and groom at weddings.
- [Italian, = sweetmeats, from Latin (as COMFIT)]

confidant *noun*
- "CONFA dawnt" or "confa DAWNT" or "CONFA dant" or "confa DANT"
- a person to whom secrets, problems or other private matters are confided.
- [18th-c. for earlier *confident*, prob. to represent the pronunciation of French *confidente* (as CONFIDE)]

HOMOPHONES: *confidante*

confidante *noun*
- "confa DAWNT" or "CONFA dawnt" or "CONFA dant" or "confa DANT"
- a woman to whom secrets, problems, or other private matters are confided.
- [as CONFIDANT]

HOMOPHONES: *confidant*

confide *verb*
• "k'n FIDE"
• tell (a secret etc.) in confidence.
• [Latin *confidere* (from *com-* with + *fidere* trust)]
• **confidingly** *adverb*

confidence *noun*
• "CONFA dince"
• belief in one's own abilities.
• [as CONFIDE]
• **confident** *adjective*
• **confidently** *adverb*

confidential *adjective*
• "confa DEN sh'll"
• secret.
• [as CONFIDE]
• **confidentiality** *noun* "confa denshy ALA tee"
• **confidentially** *adverb*

configure *verb*
• "k'n FIG yur" or "k'n FIGGER"
• arrange parts or elements in a particular form or figure.
• [Latin *configurare* (from *com-* with + *figurare* fashion)]
• **configurability** *noun*
• **configurable** *adjective*
• **configuration** *noun*
• **configurational** *adjective*

confirm *verb*
• "k'n FURM"
• provide support for the truth or correctness of; make definitely valid.
• [Old French *confermer* from Latin *confirmare* (from *com-* with + *firmus* firm)]
• **confirmatory** *adjective*

confirmand *noun*
• "CON fur mand"
• a person who is to be or has just been confirmed as a full member of the Christian Church.
• [as CONFIRM]

confirmation *noun*
• "con fur MAY sh'n"
• the act or an instance of confirming; the state of being confirmed.
• [as CONFIRM]
HOMOPHONES: *conformation*

confiscate *verb*
• "CONFA skate"
• take or seize by authority.
• [Latin *confiscare* (from *com-* with + *fiscare* from *fiscus* treasury)]
• **confiscable** *adjective* "k'n FISKA bull"
• **confiscation** *noun*
• **confiscator** *noun*
• **confiscatory** *adjective* "k'n FISKA tory"

confit *noun*
• "cõh FEE" (with a nasal *oh*)
• pork, duck, goose, turkey, etc., cooked slowly in its own fat, and preserved by storing in the fat.
• [French from Latin *confectum* something prepared]

Confiteor *noun*
• "k'n FEETY or"
• a Catholic prayer confessing sins, said esp. at the beginning of the Mass.
• [Latin *confiteor* I confess]

conflagration *noun*
• "confla GRAY sh'n"
• a great and destructive fire.
• [Latin *conflagratio* from *conflagrare* (from *com-* with + *flagrare* blaze)]

conflate *verb*
• "k'n FLATE"
• blend or fuse together.
• [Latin *conflare* (from *com-* with + *flare* blow)]
• **conflation** *noun*

conflict *noun*
• "CON flict"
• a state of opposition or hostilities.
• [Latin *confligere conflict-* (from *com-* with + *fligere* strike)]
• **conflictive** *adjective*
• **conflictual** *adjective*

confluence *noun*
• "CON floo ince"
• the place where two rivers etc. meet.
• [Latin *confluere* (from *com-* with + *fluere* flow)]

confluent *adjective*
• "CON floo 'nt"
• flowing together, uniting.
• [as CONFLUENCE]

conformance *noun*
• "k'n FOR mince"
• action or behaviour in accordance with established practice.
• [Old French *conformer* from Latin *conformare* (*com-* with + *forma* mould, form)]

conformation *noun*
• "con for MAY sh'n"
• the way in which a thing is formed; shape, structure.
• [as CONFORMANCE]
• **conformational** *adjective*
HOMOPHONES: *confirmation*

conformity *noun*
• "k'n FORMA tee"
• action or behaviour in accordance with established practice; compliance.
• [as CONFORMANCE]

confraternity *noun*
• "confra TURNA tee"
• a brotherhood devoted to religious or charitable work.
• [Old French *confraternité* from medieval Latin *confraternitas* (from *com-* with + FRATERNITY)]

confrere *noun*
• "CON frair"
• a fellow member of a profession, scientific body, etc.

• [Old French from medieval Latin *confrater* (from *com-* with + *frater* brother)]

Confucian *adjective*
• "k'n FYOO sh'n"
• of or relating to the Chinese philosopher Confucius (d.479 BC) or his philosophy.
• **Confucianism** *noun*
• **Confucianist** *noun*

confusable *adjective*
• "k'n FYOOZA bull"
• that is able or liable to be confused.
• [from 'confuse', 19th-c. back-formation from *confused* (14th c.) from Old French *confus* from Latin *confusus* from *confundere* mix up (from *com-* with + *fundere fus-* pour)]
• **confusability** *noun*

confusion *noun*
• "k'n FYOO zh'n"
• the act of confusing.
• [as CONFUSABLE]

confute *verb*
• "k'n FYOOT"
• prove (a person) to be in error.
• [Latin *confutare* restrain]
• **confutation** *noun* "con fyoo TAY sh'n"

conga *noun*
• "CONG guh"
• a Latin-American dance of African origin, usu. performed by people in a single line, one behind another, who take three steps forward and then kick.
• [Latin American Spanish from Spanish feminine form of *congo* of or pertaining to Congo]

congeal *verb*
• "k'n JEEL"
• make or become semi-solid by cooling.
• [Old French *congeler* from Latin *congelare* (from *com-* with + *gelare* from *gelu* frost)]
• **congealed** *adjective*

congee *noun*
• "CON jee"
• a thick Oriental soup made of rice.
• [Tamil *kañci*]

congelation *noun*
• "conja LAY sh'n"
• the process of congealing.
• [Old French *congelation* or Latin *congelatio* (as CONGEAL)]

congener *noun*
• "CONJA nur"
• a thing or person of the same kind or category as another, esp. animals or plants of a specified genus.
• [Latin]
• **congeneric** *adjective* "conja NARE ick"

congenial *adjective*
• "k'n JEENY 'll"
• (of a person, character, etc.) pleasant because akin to oneself in temperament or interests.
• [Latin *com-* with + GENIAL]
• **congeniality** *noun*
• **congenially** *adverb*

congenital *adjective*
• "k'n JENNIT'll"
• (esp. of a disease, defect, etc.) existing from birth.
• [Latin *congenitus* (from *com-* with + *genitus* past participle of *gigno* beget)]
• **congenitally** *adverb*

conger *noun*
• "CONG gur"
• any eel of the family Congridae, comprising scaleless sea eels usu. found in coastal waters, esp. *Conger conger*, a European conger reaching up to 3 metres in length and caught for food.
• [Greek *goggros*]

congeries *noun*
• "CONJA reez" or "con JEER eez"
• a disorderly collection; a mass or heap.
• [Latin, formed as CONGESTION]

congestion *noun*
• "k'n JESS ch'n"
• abnormal accumulation of blood or mucus in a part of the body.
• [Latin *congerere congest-* (from *com-* with + *gerere* bring)]
• **congested** *verb*
• **congestive** *adjective*

conglomerate *noun*
• "k'n GLOMMER it"
• a number of things or parts forming a heterogeneous mass.
• [Latin *conglomeratus* past participle of *conglomerare* (from *com-* with + *glomerare* from *glomus -eris* ball)]
• **conglomeration** *noun*

conglomerateur *noun*
• "k'n glommer a TURR"
• a person who forms or manages a corporate conglomerate.
• [CONGLOMERATE + common French suffix *-eur*; compare ENTREPRENEUR]

Congolese *adjective*
• "conga LEEZ"
• of or relating to Congo (formerly Zaire), the Republic of the Congo, or the region surrounding the Congo River.

congratulate *verb*
• "k'n GRATCH'll ate" or "k'n GRADGE'll ate"
• express pleasure at the happiness or good fortune or excellence of (a person).
• [Latin *congratulari* (from *com-* with + *gratulari* show joy, from *gratus* pleasing)]
• **congratulation** *noun*
• **congratulator** *noun*
• **congratulatory** *adjective*

congregant *noun*
- "CONGRA g'nt"
- a member of a congregation (esp. Jewish).
- [as CONGREGATE]

congregate *verb*
- "CONGRA gate"
- collect or gather into a crowd or mass.
- [Latin *congregare* (from *com-* with + *gregare* from *grex gregis* flock)]

congregation *noun*
- "congra GAY sh'n"
- a body assembled for religious worship.
- [as CONGREGATE]
- **congregational** *adjective*

Congregationalism *noun*
- "congra GAY sh'n 'll izm"
- a system of ecclesiastical organization whereby individual churches are largely self-governing.
- [as CONGREGATE]
- **Congregationalist** *noun*

congress *noun*
- "CONG gress"
- the national legislative body of the US, comprising the House of Representatives and the Senate.
- [Latin *congressus* from *congredi* (from *com-* with + *gradi* walk)]
- **congressional** *adjective*
- **congressman** *noun*
- **congressperson** *noun*
- **congresswoman** *noun*

congruent *adjective*
- "CONG groo 'nt" or "k'n GROO 'nt"
- suitable, agreeing.
- [Latin *congruere* agree]
- **congruence** *noun*
- **congruency** *noun*
- **congruently** *adverb*

congruous *adjective*
- "CONG groo us"
- suitable, agreeing; fitting.
- [Latin *congruus* (as CONGRUENT)]
- **congruity** *noun*
- **congruously** *adverb*

conic *adjective*
- "CONNIC"
- of, pertaining to, or resembling a cone.
- [modern Latin *conicus* from Greek *kōnikos* from *kōnos* cone]
- **conical** *adjective*
- **conically** *adverb*

conidium *noun*
- "kuh NIDDY um"
- a spore produced asexually by various fungi.
- [modern Latin diminutive from Greek *konis* dust]

conifer *noun*
- "CONNA fur"
- any evergreen tree of a group usu. bearing cones, including pines, yews, cedars, and redwoods.
- [Latin *conus* cone + *-fer* producing, from *ferre* bear]
- **coniferous** *adjective* "kuh NIFFER us"

coniine *noun*
- "CONEY een" or "CO neen"
- a poisonous alkaloid found in hemlock, that paralyzes the nerves.
- [Latin *conium* from Greek *kōneion* hemlock]

conjecture *noun*
- "k'n JECK chur"
- the formation of an opinion on incomplete information; guessing.
- [Old French *conjecture* or Latin *conjectura* from *conjicere* (from *com-* with + *jacere* throw)]
- **conjectural** *adjective*
- **conjecturally** *adverb*

conjugal *adjective*
- "CONJA g'll"
- of marriage or the relation between spouses.
- [Latin *conjugalis* from *conjux* consort (from *com-* with + *-jux -jugis* from root of *jungere* join)]

conjugate *verb*
- "CONJA gate"
- inflect (a verb) in its various forms of voice, mood, tense, number or person.
- [Latin *conjugare* yoke together (from *com-* with + *jugare* from *jugum* yoke)]
- **conjugative** *adjective*

conjugation *noun*
- "conja GAY sh'n"
- a system of verbal inflection.
- [as CONJUGATE]
- **conjugational** *adjective*

conjunct *adjective*
- "k'n JUNCT"
- joined together; combined; associated.
- [Latin *conjunctus* from *conjungere* (from *com-* with + *jungere junct-* join)]

conjunction *noun*
- "k'n JUNK sh'n"
- a word used to connect clauses or sentences or words in the same clause (e.g. *and, but, if*).
- [Old French *conjonction* from Latin *conjunctio -onis* (as CONJUNCT)]
- **conjunctional** *adjective*

conjunctiva *noun*
- "con junk TIVE uh" or "k'n JUNK tiv uh"
- the mucous membrane that covers the front of the eye and lines the inside of the eyelids.
- [medieval Latin (*membrana*) *conjunctiva* (as CONJUNCTIVE)]
- **conjunctival** *adjective*

conjunctive *adjective*
- "k'n JUNK tiv"
- serving to join; connective.
- [Late Latin *conjunctivus* (as CONJUNCT)]
- **conjunctively** *adverb*

conjunctivitis *noun*
• "k'n junk tiv ITE iss"
• inflammation of the conjunctiva.
• [CONJUNCTIVA + Greek *-itis*, forming feminine of adjectives in *-itēs* (with *nosos* 'disease' implied)]

conjuncture *noun*
• "k'n JUNK chur"
• a combination of events; a state of affairs.
• [obsolete French from Italian *congiuntura* (as CONJUNCT)]

conjure *verb*
• "CON jur"
• cause to appear or disappear as if by magic.
• [Old French *conjurer* plot, exorcise, from Latin *conjurare* band together by oath (from *com-* with + *jurare* swear)]
• **conjuration** *noun*

conjuring *noun*
• "CON jur ing"
• the performance of seemingly magical tricks, esp. by rapid movements of the hands.
• [as CONJURE]
• **conjuror** *noun* (also **conjurer**)

connate *adjective*
• "CON ate"
• existing in a person or thing from birth; innate.
• [Late Latin *connatus* past participle of *connasci* (from *com-* with + *nasci* be born)]

connectable *verb*
• "kuh NECT a bull"
• that can be joined to another thing.
• [Latin *connectere connex-* (from *com-* with + *nectere* bind)]
• **connector** *noun*

conniption *noun*
• "kuh NIP sh'n"
• a fit of anger, worry, etc.
• [19th c.: origin unknown]

connive *verb*
• "kuh NIVE"
• conspire.
• [French *conniver* or Latin *connivēre* shut the eyes (to)]
• **connivance** *noun*
• **conniver** *noun*
• **conniving** *adjective*

connoisseur *noun*
• "conna SUR" or "conna SOOR"
• an expert judge in matters of taste.
• [French, obsolete spelling of *connaisseur* from pres. stem of *connaître* know]
• **connoisseurial** *adjective*
• **connoisseurship** *noun*

connote *verb*
• "kuh NOTE"
• (of a word etc.) imply in addition to the literal or primary meaning.
• [medieval Latin *connotare* mark in addition (from *com-* with + *notare* from *nota* mark)]
• **connotation** *noun*
• **connotative** *adjective* "CONNA tate iv" or "kuh NOTE a tiv"

connubial *adjective*
• "kuh NEW bee 'll"
• of or relating to marriage or the relationship of spouses.
• [Latin *connubialis* from *connubium* (*nubium* from *nubere* marry)]

conodont *noun*
• "CO nuh dont" or "CONNA dont"
• any of various Paleozoic toothlike fossils of uncertain affinity.
• [Greek *kōnos* cone + *odont-*, *odous* tooth]

conoid *adjective*
• "CO noid"
• cone-shaped.
• [Greek *kōnos* cone]

conquer *verb*
• "CONKER"
• overcome and control (an enemy or territory) by military force.
• [Old French *conquerre* from Romanic from Latin *conquirere* (from *com-* with + *quaerere* seek, get)]
• **conquerable** *adjective*
• **conqueror** *noun*
HOMOPHONES: *conker*

conquest *noun*
• "CONG kwest"
• the act or an instance of conquering; the state of being conquered.
• [Old French *conquest(e)* from Romanic (as CONQUER)]

conquistador *noun*
• "con KWISTA dore" or "con KEESTA dore"
• a conqueror, esp. one of the Spanish conquerors of Mexico and Peru in the 16th c.
• [Spanish]

consanguinity *noun*
• "con sang GWINNA tee"
• relationship by descent from a common ancestor; blood relationship.
• [Latin *consanguinitas* (from *com-* with + *sanguis* blood)]
• **consanguineous** *adjective* "con sang GWINNY us"

conscience *noun*
• "CON shince"
• a moral sense of right and wrong esp. as felt by a person and affecting behaviour.
• [Old French from Latin *conscientia* from *conscire* be privy to (from *com-* with + *scire* know)]
• **conscienceless** *adjective*

conscientious *adjective*
• "conshy EN sh'ss"

• (of a person or conduct) diligent and scrupulous.
• [French *consciencieux* from medieval Latin *conscientiosus* (as CONSCIENCE)]
• **conscientiously** *adverb*
• **conscientiousness** *noun*

conscious *adjective*
• "CON sh'ss"
• awake and aware of one's surroundings and identity.
• [Latin *conscius* knowing with others or in oneself, from *conscire* (from *com-* with + *scire* know)]
• **consciously** *adverb*
• **consciousness** *noun*

conscript *verb*
• "k'n SCRIPT"
• enlist by conscription.
• [back-formation from CONSCRIPTION]

conscription *noun*
• "k'n SCRIP sh'n"
• compulsory enlistment for military service.
• [French from Late Latin *conscriptio* levying of troops, from Latin *conscribere conscript-* enrol (from *com-* with + *scribere* write)]

consecrate *verb*
• "CONSA crate"
• make or declare sacred; dedicate formally to a religious or divine purpose.
• [Latin *consecrare* (from *com-* with + *secrare* = *sacrare* dedicate, from *sacer* sacred)]
• **consecrated** *adjective*
• **consecration** *noun*
• **consecrator** *noun*
• **consecratory** *adjective*

consecutive *adjective*
• "k'n SECK yoo tiv"
• following continuously, in uninterrupted sequence.
• [French *consécutif -ive* from medieval Latin *consecutivus* from *consequi consecut-* overtake (from *com-* with + *sequi* pursue)]
• **consecutively** *adverb*
• **consecutiveness** *noun*

consensual *adjective*
• "k'n SEN shoo 'll"
• of or by consent or consensus.
• [as CONSENSUS]
• **consensually** *adverb*

consensus *noun*
• "k'n SEN suss"
• general agreement (of opinion, testimony, etc.).
• [Latin, = agreement, from *consentire* (from *com-* with + *sentire sens-* feel)]

consequence *noun*
• "CONSA kwince"
• the result or effect of an action or condition.
• [Old French from Latin *consequentia* (as CONSECUTIVE)]
• **consequent** *adjective*
• **consequential** *adjective* "consa KWEN sh'll"
• **consequentiality** *noun* "consa kwenshy ALA tee"
• **consequentially** *adverb*
• **consequently** *adverb*

consequentialism *noun*
• "consa KWEN sh'll izm"
• the doctrine that the morality of an action is to be judged solely by its consequences.
• [as CONSEQUENCE]
• **consequentialist** *adjective*

conservancy *noun*
• "k'n SURV 'n see"
• an organization concerned with the preservation of natural resources.
• [18th-c. alteration of obsolete *conservacy* from Anglo-French *conservacie* from Anglo-Latin *conservatia* from Latin *conservatio* from *conservare* (from *com-* + *servare* keep)]

conservation *noun*
• "con sur VAY sh'n"
• the action of conserving something, esp. preservation, protection, or restoration of the natural environment and of wildlife.
• [Latin *conservatio* from *conservare* (from *com-* + *servare* keep)]
• **conservational** *adjective*
• **conservationist** *noun*

conservatism *noun*
• "k'n SURV a tizm"
• any of several political philosophies, esp. one opposing radical reform, placing value in established institutions, and subjugating individual freedom to order, rank, security, and the good of the community, or one promoting individualism and non-intervention by the State.
• [as CONSERVATION]
• **conservative** *adjective*
• **conservatively** *adverb*

conservatoire *noun*
• "k'n SURV a twar" ("twar" rhymes with *FAR*)
• a (usu. European) school of music or other arts.
• [French from Italian *conservatorio* (as CONSERVATORY)]

conservator *noun*
• "k'n SURV a tur" or "CONSER vay tur"
• a person who preserves something, esp. in a museum etc.
• [as CONSERVATORY]

conservatory *noun*
• "k'n SURV a tory" or "k'n SURV a tree"
• a school of esp. classical music or other arts.
• [Late Latin *conservatorium* (as CONSERVATION)]

consider *verb*
• "k'n SIDDER"
• contemplate mentally, esp. in order to reach a conclusion.

• [Old French *considerer* from Latin *considerare* examine, perhaps from *com-* with + *sider-*, *sidus* constellation, star]
• **consideration** *noun*
• **considered** *adjective*

considerable *adjective*
• "k'n SIDDER a bull"
• enough in amount or extent to need consideration.
• [as CONSIDER]
• **considerably** *adverb*

considerate *adjective*
• "k'n SIDDER it"
• thoughtful towards other people; careful not to cause hurt or inconvenience.
• [as CONSIDER]
• **considerately** *adverb*

considering *preposition*
• "k'n SIDDER ing"
• in view of; taking into consideration.
• [as CONSIDER]

consigliere *noun*
• "consill YAIR ay"
• a top adviser to an organized crime boss.
• [Italian, = counsellor]

consign *verb*
• "k'n SINE"
• hand over; deliver to a person's possession or trust.
• [French *consigner* or Latin *consignare* mark with a seal (from *com-* with + SIGN)]
• **consignee** *noun*
• **consignment** *noun*
• **consignor** *noun*

consistency *noun*
• "k'n SIST 'n see"
• the degree of density, firmness, or viscosity, esp. of thick liquids.
• [French *consistence* or Late Latin *consistentia* from *consistere* exist (from *com-* with + *sistere* stop)]

consistent *adjective*
• "k'n SIS t'nt"
• compatible or in harmony; not contradictory.
• [Latin *consistere* (as CONSISTENCY)]
• **consistently** *adverb*

consistory *noun*
• "k'n SISTER ee"
• a council of cardinals presided over by the pope.
• [Anglo-French *consistorie* from Late Latin *consistorium* (as CONSISTENCY)]
• **consistorial** *adjective*

consociation *noun*
• "k'n so see AY sh'n"
• close association, esp. of Churches or religious communities.
• [Latin *consociatio*, *-onis* from *consociare* (from *com-* with + *socius* fellow)]
• **consociational** *adjective*

console[1] *verb*
• "k'n SOLE"
• comfort, esp. in grief or disappointment.
• [French *consoler* from Latin *consolari* (from *com-* with + *solari* soothe)]
• **consolable** *adjective*
• **consolation** *noun*
• **consolatory** *adjective* "k'n SOLLA tory"
• **consoler** *noun*
• **consolingly** *adverb*

console[2] *noun*
• "CON sole"
• a panel or unit accommodating a set of switches, controls, etc.
• [French, perhaps from *consolider* (as CONSOLIDATE)]

consolidate *verb*
• "k'n SOLLA date"
• combine (territories, companies, debts, etc.) into one whole.
• [Latin *consolidare* (from *com-* with + *solidare* from *solidus* solid)]
• **consolidated** *adjective*
• **consolidation** *noun*
• **consolidator** *noun*

consommé *noun*
• "CONSA may"
• a clear soup made with meat stock.
• [French, past participle of *consommer* from Latin *consummare* (as CONSUMMATE)]

consonance *noun*
• "CONSA nince"
• agreement, harmony.
• [Old French *consonance* (as CONSONANT)]

consonant *noun*
• "CONSA n'nt"
• a speech sound in which the breath is at least partly obstructed, and which to form a syllable must be combined with a vowel.
• [French from Latin *consonare* (from *com-* with + *sonare* sound, from *sonus* sound)]
• **consonantal** *adjective*

consortium *noun*
• "k'n SORTY um" or "k'n SORE sh'm"
• an association, esp. several large companies in a joint venture.
• [Latin, = partnership, from *consors* sharer, comrade (from *com-* with + *sors sortis* lot, destiny)]

conspecific *adjective*
• "con spuh SIFFIC"
• of the same species.
• [Latin *com-* with + SPECIFIC]

conspectus *noun*
• "k'n SPECK tuss"
• a general or comprehensive survey.
• [Latin from *conspicere conspect-* (from *com-* with + *spicere* look at)]

conspicuous *adjective*
• "k'n SPICK yoo us"
• clearly visible; striking to the eye; attracting notice.
• [Latin *conspicuus* (as CONSPECTUS)]
• **conspicuity** *noun* "con spick YOO a tee"
• **conspicuously** *adverb*
• **conspicuousness** *noun*

conspiracist *noun*
• "k'n SPEERA sist"
• a person who supports a conspiracy theory.
• [as CONSPIRACY]

conspiracy *noun*
• "k'n SPEERA see"
• a secret plan to commit a crime or do harm, often for political ends; a plot.
• [Anglo-French *conspiracie*, alteration of form of Old French *conspiration* from Latin *conspiratio -onis* (as CONSPIRE)]
• **conspirator** *noun*
• **conspiratorial** *adjective*
• **conspiratorially** *adverb*

conspire *verb*
• "k'n SPIRE"
• combine secretly to plan and prepare an unlawful or harmful act.
• [Old French *conspirer* from Latin *conspirare* agree, plot (from *com-* with + *spirare* breathe)]

constable *noun*
• "CONSTA bull"
• (in Canada, the UK, Australia, NZ, etc.) a police officer of the lowest rank.
• [Old French *conestable* from Late Latin *comes stabuli* count of the stable]

constabulary *noun*
• "k'n STAB yoo lerry"
• an organized body of police; a police force.
• [medieval Latin *constabularius* (as CONSTABLE)]

constancy *noun*
• "CON st'n see"
• the quality of being unchanging and dependable; faithfulness.
• [Latin *constantia* from *constare* (from *com-* with + *stare* stand)]

constantan *noun*
• "CON st'n tan"
• an alloy of copper and nickel used in electrical equipment.
• [from 'constant' (as CONSTANCY)]

constellate *verb*
• "CON stuh late"
• form into (or as if into) a constellation.
• [as CONSTELLATION]

constellation *noun*
• "con stuh LAY sh'n"
• a group of fixed stars whose outline is traditionally regarded as forming a particular figure.
• [Old French from Late Latin *constellatio -onis* (from *com-* with + *stella* star)]

consternate *verb*
• "CONSTER nate"
• dismay; fill with anxiety.
• [Latin *consternare* (from *com-* with + *sternere* throw down)]
• **consternation** *noun*

constipation *noun*
• "consta PAY sh'n"
• irregularity and difficulty in defecating.
• [Latin *constipare* (from *com-* with + *stipare* press)]
• **constipate** *verb*
• **constipated** *adjective*

constituency *noun*
• "k'n STITCH oo 'n see"
• a body of voters in a specified area who elect a representative member to a legislative body.
• [as CONSTITUTE]

constituent *adjective*
• "k'n STITCH oo 'nt"
• composing or helping to make up a whole.
• [Latin *constituent-* (as CONSTITUTE)]

constitute *verb*
• "CONSTA tute"
• be the components or essence of; make up, form.
• [Latin *constituere* (from *com-* with + *statuere* set up)]

constitution *noun*
• "consta TOO sh'n" or "consta TYOO sh'n"
• the body of fundamental principles or established precedents according to which a state or other organization is acknowledged to be governed.
• [as CONSTITUTE]
• **constitutional** *adjective*
• **constitutionalism** *noun*
• **constitutionalist** *noun*
• **constitutionality** *noun*
• **constitutionalize** *verb* (also esp. *Brit.* **-ise**)
• **constitutionally** *adverb*

constitutive *adjective*
• "k'n STITCH yoo tiv"
• having the power to establish or give organized existence to something.
• [as CONSTITUTE]
• **constitutively** *adverb*

constrictor *noun*
• "k'n STRICTER"
• any snake (esp. a boa) that kills by coiling around its prey and compressing it.
• [Latin *constringere constrict-* (from *com-* with + *stringere strict-* tie)]

construct *verb*
• "k'n STRUCT"
• make by fitting parts together; build, form (something physical or abstract).

• [Latin *construere construct-* (from *com-* with + *struere* pile, build)]
• **constructor** *noun*

constructivism *noun*
• "k'n STRUCK tiv izm"
• an orig. Russian artistic movement in which assorted (usu. mechanical or industrial) objects are combined into non-representational and mobile structural forms.
• [Russian *konstruktivizm* (as CONSTRUCT)]
• **constructivist** *noun*

construe *verb*
• "k'n STROO"
• interpret (words or actions).
• [Latin *construere* CONSTRUCT]
• **construable** *adjective*
• **construal** *noun*

consubstantial *adjective*
• "con sub STAN sh'll"
• of the same substance (esp. of the three persons of the Trinity).
• [Church Latin *consubstantialis* from *com-* with + SUBSTANTIAL]
• **consubstantiality** *noun*
"con sub stanshy ALA tee"

consubstantiation *noun*
• "con sub stanshy AY sh'n"
• the real substantial presence of the body and blood of Christ together with the bread and wine in the Eucharist.
• [modern Latin *consubstantiatio*, after *transubstantiatio* TRANSUBSTANTIATION, as CONSUBSTANTIAL]

consuetude *noun*
• "CON swuh tude"
• a custom, esp. one having legal force.
• [Old French *consuetude* or Latin *consuetudo -dinis* from *consuetus* accustomed]
• **consuetudinary** *adjective*

consul *noun*
• "CON s'll"
• an official appointed by a nation to live in a foreign city and protect the interests of the nation's citizens in the region and promote trade.
• [Latin, related to *consulere* take counsel]
• **consular** *adjective*
• **consulship** *noun*

consulate *noun*
• "CONSA lit"
• the building officially used by a consul.
• [as CONSUL]

consultant *noun*
• "k'n SUL t'nt"
• a person who gives professional advice or services in a specialized field, esp. on a freelance basis.
• [French *consulter* from Latin *consultare* frequentative of *consulere consult-* take counsel]
• **consultancy** *noun*

consultation *noun*
• "con s'll TAY sh'n"
• a meeting arranged to consult (esp. with a physician).
• [as CONSULTANT]

consumable *adjective*
• "k'n SUME a bull"
• that can be consumed; intended for consumption.
• [Latin *consumere* (from *com-* with + *sumere sumpt-* take up)]

consummate *adjective*
• "CONSA mit"
• complete, perfect, of the highest level.
• [Latin *consummare* (from *com-* with + *summare* complete, from *summus* utmost)]
• **consummately** *adverb*

consummation *noun*
• "consa MAY sh'n"
• the action of making (a marriage) legally complete by having sex.
• [as CONSUMMATE]

consumption *noun*
• "k'n SUMP sh'n"
• the using up of a resource.
• [Old French *consomption* from Latin *consumptio* (as CONSUMABLE)]

consumptive *adjective*
• "k'n SUMP tiv"
• of or tending to any disease causing wasting of tissues, esp. pulmonary tuberculosis (formerly called 'consumption').
• [medieval Latin *consumptivus* (as CONSUMPTION)]
• **consumptively** *adverb*

contagion *noun*
• "k'n TAY j'n"
• the communication of disease from one person to another by bodily contact.
• [Latin *contagio* (from *com-* with + *tangere* touch)]

contagious *adjective*
• "k'n TAY j'ss"
• (of a person) likely to transmit disease by direct or indirect contact.
• [as CONTAGION]
• **contagiously** *adverb*
• **contagiousness** *noun*

contaminate *verb*
• "k'n TAMMA nate"
• make impure by contact or mixture; pollute.
• [Latin *contaminare* (from *com-* with + *tamen-* related to *tangere* touch)]
• **contaminant** *noun*
• **contamination** *noun*

contango *noun*
• "k'n TANGO"
• the postponement of the transfer of stock from one account day to the next.
• [19th c.: prob. an arbitrary formation]

Conté *noun*
- "CON tay"
- a kind of hard, grease-free crayon used as a medium for artwork.
- [N. J. *Conté*, French inventor d.1805]

contemn *verb*
- "k'n TEM"
- despise; treat with contempt.
- [Old French *contemner* or Latin *contemnere* (from *com-* with + *temnere tempt-* despise)]
- **contemner** *noun* "k'n TEMMER" or "k'n TEMNER"

contemplate *verb*
- "CON t'm plate"
- look at or consider in a calm, reflective manner.
- [Latin *contemplari* (from *com-* with + *templum* place for observations)]
- **contemplation** *noun*
- **contemplator** *noun*

contemplative *adjective*
- "k'n TEMPLA tiv" or "CON t'm play tiv"
- of or given to (esp. religious) contemplation; meditative.
- [as CONTEMPLATE]
- **contemplatively** *adverb*

contemporaneous *adjective*
- "k'n temper AINY us"
- existing or occurring at the same time.
- [Latin *contemporaneus* (from *com-* with + *temporaneus* from *tempus -oris* time)]
- **contemporaneity** *noun* "k'n temper a NAY a tee"
- **contemporaneously** *adverb*
- **contemporaneousness** *noun*

contemporary *adjective*
- "k'n TEMPER airy"
- living or occurring at the same time.
- [medieval Latin *contemporarius* (as CONTEMPORANEOUS)]
- **contemporariness** *noun*

contemporize *verb*
- "k'n TEMPER ize"
- make up-to-date or fashionable.
- [as CONTEMPORARY]
- **contemporization** *noun* (also esp. *Brit.* **-isation**)

contempt *noun*
- "k'n TEMPT"
- a feeling that a person or a thing is beneath consideration or worthless, or deserving scorn or extreme reproach.
- [Latin *contemptus* (as CONTEMN)]
- **contemptible** *adjective*
- **contemptibly** *adverb*

contemptuous *adjective*
- "k'n TEMP choo us"
- showing contempt, scornful; insolent.
- [as CONTEMPT]
- **contemptuously** *adverb*

contention *noun*
- "k'n TEN sh'n"
- a point contended for in an argument.
- [French *contention* from Latin *contentio* from *contendere* contend (from *com-* with + *tendere tent-* stretch, strive)]

contentious *adjective*
- "k'n TEN sh'ss"
- argumentative, quarrelsome.
- [as CONTENTION]
- **contentiously** *adverb*
- **contentiousness** *noun*

conterminous *adjective*
- "con TURMIN us"
- having a common boundary.
- [Latin *conterminus* (from *com-* with + *terminus* boundary)]
- **conterminously** *adverb*

contessa *noun*
- "con TESSA"
- an Italian countess.
- [Italian from Late Latin *comitissa* from *comes comitis* companion]

contestant *noun*
- "k'n TESS t'nt"
- a person who takes part in a contest or competition.
- [French from Latin *contestari* (from *com-* with + *testis* witness)]

contestation *noun*
- "con tess TAY sh'n"
- an act or instance of disputation.
- [as CONTESTANT]
- **contestable** *adjective*
- **contestatory** *adjective*

context *noun*
- "CON text"
- the parts of something written or spoken that immediately precede and follow a word or passage and clarify its meaning.
- [Latin *contextus* (from *com-* with + *texere text-* weave)]
- **contextual** *adjective*
- **contextualization** *noun* (also esp. *Brit.* **-isation**)
- **contextualize** *verb* (also esp. *Brit.* **-ise**)
- **contextually** *adverb*

contextualism *noun*
- "k'n TEX choo 'll izm"
- any theory which emphasizes the importance of the context of inquiry in a particular question.
- [as CONTEXT]
- **contextualist** *adjective*

contiguous *adjective*
- "k'n TIG yoo us"
- touching, adjoining, in contact.
- [Latin *contiguus* (from *com-* with + *tangere* touch)]
- **contiguity** *noun* "conta GYOO a tee"
- **contiguously** *adverb*

continence *noun*
- "CON tin ince"
- the ability to control movements of the bowels and bladder.
- [Middle English from Latin from *continēre continent-* (from *com-* with + *tenēre* hold)]

contingency *noun*
- "k'n TINGE 'n see"
- a future event or circumstance which is possible but cannot be predicted with certainty.
- [as CONTINGENT]

contingent *noun*
- "k'n TINGE 'nt"
- a group with common origins, interests, etc. representing a larger body.
- [Latin *contingere* (from *com-* with + *tangere* touch)]
- **contingently** *adverb*

continual *adjective*
- "k'n TIN yoo 'll"
- constantly or frequently recurring.
- [as CONTINUE]
- **continually** *adverb*

continuance *noun*
- "k'n TIN yoo ince"
- a state of continuing in existence or operation.
- [as CONTINUE]

continuant *noun*
- "k'n TIN yoo 'nt"
- a speech sound in which the vocal tract is only partly closed, allowing the breath to pass through and the sound to be prolonged (as with *f*, *r*, *s*, *v*).
- [as CONTINUE]

continue *verb*
- "k'n TIN yoo"
- persist in, maintain, not stop (an action etc.).
- [Old French *continuer* from Latin *continuare* make or be CONTINUOUS]
- **continuation** *noun*

continuo *noun*
- "k'n TIN yoo oh"
- an accompaniment consisting of a bass line and harmonies which are indicated by figures, usu. played on a keyboard instrument.
- [*basso continuo* (Italian, = continuous bass)]

continuous *adjective*
- "k'n TIN yoo us"
- unbroken, uninterrupted.
- [Latin *continuus* uninterrupted, from *continēre* (from *com-* with + *tenēre* hold)]
- **continuity** *noun* "conta NEW a tee"
- **continuously** *adverb*
- **continuousness** *noun*

continuum *noun*
- "k'n TIN yoo um"
- anything seen as having a continuous structure without perceptibly distinct parts.
- [Latin, neuter of *continuus*: see CONTINUOUS]

contortion *noun*
- "k'n TOR sh'n"
- the act or process of twisting.
- [Latin *contortio* from *contorquēre contort-* (from *com-* with + *torquēre* twist)]

contortionist *noun*
- "k'n TOR sh'n ist"
- an entertainer who adopts contorted postures.
- [as CONTORTION]

contour *noun*
- "CON toor"
- an outline, esp. representing or bounding the shape of something with a curving form.
- [French from Italian *contorno* from *contornare* draw in outline (from Latin *com-* with + *tornare* turn)]

contoured *adjective*
- "CON toord"
- designed or shaped to fit a specific form.
- [as CONTOUR]

contra *noun*
- "CONTRA"
- a social form of American folk dance in which double lines of couples face one another as they dance, e.g. Virginia Reel.
- [French, *contredanses anglaises*, = 'English country dances']

contraband *noun*
- "CONTRA band"
- anything that has been smuggled, imported, or exported illegally.
- [Spanish *contrabanda* from Italian (Latin *contra* against + *bando* proclamation)]
- **contrabandist** *noun*

contrabass *noun*
- "CONTRA base"
- a double bass.
- [Italian *contra* against + *basso* BASS]
- **contrabassist** *noun*

contraception *noun*
- "contra SEP sh'n"
- the intentional prevention of pregnancy.
- [Latin *contra* against + CONCEPTION]
- **contraceptive** *adjective*

contractile *adjective*
- "k'n TRACK tile"
- capable of or producing contraction.
- [Latin *contractus* (from *com-* with + *trahere tract-* draw)]
- **contractility** *noun* "con track TILLA tee"

contractor *noun*
- "CON tracter"
- a person who undertakes a contract, esp. to provide materials, conduct building operations, etc.
- [as CONTRACTILE]

contractual *adjective*
- "k'n TRACK choo 'll"

• of, in the nature of, or secured by a contract.
• [as CONTRACTILE]
• **contractually** *adverb*

contracture *noun*
• "k'n TRACK chur"
• a shortening and hardening of fibrous tissues, esp. muscles and tendons, caused by spasms, scarring, etc.
• [as CONTRACTILE]

contradict *verb*
• "contra DICT"
• affirm the contrary of (a proposition, statement, etc.).
• [Latin *contradicere contradict-* (Latin *contra* against + *dicere* say)]
• **contradiction** *noun*
• **contradictorily** *adverb*
• **contradictoriness** *noun*
• **contradictory** *adjective*

contradistinguish *verb*
• "contra dis TING gwish"
• distinguish two things by contrasting them.
• [Latin *contra* against + DISTINGUISH]
• **contradistinction** *noun*

contraindicate *verb*
• "contra INDA cate"
• cause (a medication, course of treatment, etc.) to be inappropriate.
• [Latin *contra* against + INDICATE]
• **contraindication** *noun*

contralto *noun*
• "k'n TRAWL toe" or "k'n TRAL toe"
• the lowest female singing voice.
• [Italian (Latin *contra* against + ALTO)]

contraposition *noun*
• "contra puh ZISH'n"
• opposition, contrast.
• [Late Latin *contrapositio* (Latin *contra* against + *ponere posit-* place)]
• **contrapositive** *adjective*

contrapposto *noun*
• "contra POSSTO"
• (in sculpture) an asymmetrical arrangement of the human figure in which the line of the arms and shoulders contrast with, while balancing, those of the hips and legs.
• [Italian, past participle of *contrapporre*, counter, from Latin *contraponere*, place against (Latin *contra* against + *ponere posit-* place)]

contraption *noun*
• "k'n TRAP sh'n"
• a machine or device, esp. a strange, improvised, or particularly intricate one.
• [19th c.: perhaps from CONTRIVE, 'invention': assoc. with 'trap']

contrapuntal *adjective*
• "contra PUNT 'll"
• of, pertaining to, or of the nature of counterpoint, the art or technique of setting, writing, or playing a melody or melodies in conjunction with another, according to fixed rules.
• [Italian *contrappunto* counterpoint, from Latin *contrapunctum* (song) pricked or marked over against (the original melody), from *contra* against + *punctum*, from *pungere* prick]
• **contrapuntally** *adverb*
• **contrapuntist** *noun*

contrarian *noun*
• "con TRARE ee 'n"
• a person who opposes or rejects majority opinions, attitudes, etc., esp. in economic matters.
• [as CONTRARY]
• **contrarianism** *noun*

contrariety *noun*
• "contra RYE a tee"
• opposition in nature, quality, or action.
• [as CONTRARY]

contrariwise *adverb*
• "k'n TRERRY wise"
• on the other hand.
• [as CONTRARY]

contrary *adjective*
• "CON trerry"
• opposed in nature or tendency.
• [Anglo-French *contrarie*, Old French *contraire*, from Latin *contrarius* from *contra* against]
• **contrarily** *adverb*
• **contrariness** *noun*

contravene *verb*
• "contra VEEN"
• infringe, violate (a law, standards, guidelines, etc.).
• [Late Latin *contravenire* (Latin *contra* against + *venire vent-* come)]
• **contravener** *noun*
• **contravention** *noun*

contredanse *noun*
• "CONTRA dance"
• a quadrille-like variation of the English country dance.
• [French alteration of 'country dance' by association with Latin *contra* against]

contretemps *noun*
• "CONTRA tãh" (with a nasal *ah*)
• an awkward or unfortunate occurrence.
• [French, from Latin *contra* against + *tempus* time]

contribute *verb*
• "k'n TRIB yoot"
• give (money, an idea, help, etc.) towards a common purpose.
• [Latin *contribuere contribut-* (from *com-* with + *tribuere* bestow)]
• **contributing** *adjective*
• **contribution** *noun*
• **contributive** *adjective*
• **contributor** *noun*

contributory *adjective*
• "k'n TRIB yoo tory"
• contributing to a result; partly responsible for.
• [as CONTRIBUTE]

contrite *adjective*
• "CON trite" or "k'n TRITE"
• penitent; sincerely filled with guilt, regret, etc. and desirous of making amends.
• [Old French *contrit* from Latin *contritus* bruised (from *com-* with + *terere trit-* rub)]
• **contritely** *adverb*
• **contriteness** *noun*
• **contrition** *noun* "k'n TRISH'n"

contrivance *noun*
• "k'n TRIVE ince"
• a device or tool made for a particular purpose.
• [as CONTRIVE]

contrive *verb*
• "k'n TRIVE"
• devise.
• [Old French *controver* find, imagine, from medieval Latin *contropare* compare]

contrived *adjective*
• "k'n TRIVED" ("TRIVED" rhymes with *DIVED*)
• so obviously planned as to seem unnatural, artificial, or forced.
• [as CONTRIVE]

controversy *noun*
• "CONTRA vursy"
• a prolonged argument or dispute, esp. when conducted publicly and over a matter of opinion.
• [Latin *controversia* (as CONTROVERT)]
• **controversial** *adjective* "contra VUR sh'll"
• **controversialist** *noun*
• **controversially** *adverb*

controvert *verb*
• "contra VURT" or "CONTRA vurt"
• dispute, deny, oppose.
• [originally past participle; from French *controvers(e)* from Latin *controversus* (Latin *contra* against + *vertere vers-* turn)]
• **controverted** *adjective*
• **controvertible** *adjective*

contumacy *noun*
• "CONT yoo muh see"
• stubborn refusal to obey or comply.
• [Latin *contumacia* from *contumax*, perhaps related to *tumēre* swell]
• **contumacious** *adjective* "cont yoo MAY sh'ss"

contumely *noun*
• "CON tume lee"
• insulting or contemptuous language or treatment.
• [Old French *contumelie* from Latin *contumelia* (from *com-* with + *tumēre* swell)]
• **contumelious** *adjective* "con tume EELY us"

contusion *noun*
• "k'n TOO zh'n" or "k'n TYOO zh'n"
• a bruise or an injury which does not break the skin.
• [Late Latin *contusio* from Latin *contundere contus-* (from *com-* with + *tundere* thump)]

conundrum *noun*
• "kuh NUN drum"
• a riddle, esp. one with a pun in its answer.
• [16th c.: origin unknown]

conurbation *noun*
• "conner BAY sh'n"
• an extended urban area, esp. one consisting of several towns and merging suburbs.
• [Latin *com-, con-* with + *urbs urbis* city]

conure *noun*
• "con YUR"
• any of numerous Central and S American medium-sized parrots belonging to the genera *Aratinga*, *Pyrrhura*, and related genera, with mainly green plumage and a long gradated tail.
• [modern Latin *conurus* from Greek *kōnos* cone + *oura* tail]

convalesce *verb*
• "conva LESS"
• recover one's health after illness or medical treatment.
• [Latin *convalescere* (from *com-* with + *valēre* be well)]
• **convalescence** *noun*
• **convalescent** *adjective*

convection *noun*
• "k'n VECK sh'n"
• transference of heat in a gas or liquid by upward movement of the heated and less dense medium.
• [Late Latin *convectio* from Latin *convehere convect-* (from *com-* with + *vehere vect-* carry)]
• **convectional** *adjective*
• **convective** *adjective*

convector *noun*
• "k'n VECTER"
• a heating appliance that circulates warm air by convection.
• [as CONVECTION]

convene *verb*
• "k'n VEEN"
• call or arrange (a meeting etc.).
• [Latin *convenire convent-* assemble, agree, fit (from *com-* with + *venire* come)]
• **convenor** *noun* (also **convener**)

convenience *noun*
• "k'n VEEN yince"
• the quality of serving one's comfort, interests, or needs; suitability.
• [Middle English from Latin *convenientia* (as CONVENE)]
• **convenient** *adjective*
• **conveniently** *adverb*

conventicle *noun*
• "k'n VENTA k'll"
• a secret or unlawful religious meeting, esp. of dissenters.
• [Latin *conventiculum* (place of) assembly, diminutive of *conventus* (as CONVENE)]

convention *noun*
• "k'n VEN sh'n"
• general agreement, esp. on social behaviour etc. by implicit consent of the majority.
• [Old French from Latin *conventio -onis* (as CONVENE)]

conventional *adjective*
• "k'n VEN sh'n 'll"
• depending on or according with convention.
• [French *conventionnel* or Late Latin *conventionalis* (as CONVENTION)]
• **conventionality** *noun*
• **conventionalize** *verb* (also esp. *Brit.* **-ise**)
• **conventionally** *adverb*

conventioneer *noun*
• "k'n vensh'n EER"
• a person attending a convention.
• [as CONVENTION]

conventual *adjective*
• "k'n VEN choo 'll"
• of or belonging to a convent.
• [Old French *convent* from Latin *conventus* assembly (as CONVENE)]

converge *verb*
• "k'n VURJ"
• come together from several diverse points towards a common point.
• [Late Latin *convergere* (from *com-* with + *vergere* incline)]
• **convergence** *noun*
• **convergent** *adjective*

conversant *adjective*
• "k'n VURSE 'nt"
• well experienced or acquainted with a subject etc.
• [as CONVERSATION]

conversation *noun*
• "conver SAY sh'n"
• the informal exchange of ideas by spoken words.
• [Old French from Latin *conversatio -onis* from *conversari* keep company (with), frequentative of *convertere* convert, turn about (from *com-* with + *vertere* turn)]
• **conversational** *adjective*
• **conversationalist** *noun*
• **conversationally** *adverb*

conversazione *noun*
• "conver satsy OH nee"
• a social gathering usu. held by a learned or art society.
• [Italian from Latin (as CONVERSATION)]

convertible *adjective*
• "k'n VURTA bull"
• that may be converted.
• [Latin *convertere* convert, turn about (from *com-* with + *vertere* turn)]
• **convertibility** *noun*

convex *adjective*
• "CON vex"
• having an outline or surface curved like the exterior of a circle or sphere.
• [Latin *convexus* vaulted, arched]
• **convexity** *noun*
• **convexly** *adverb*

convey *verb*
• "k'n VAY"
• communicate (an idea, meaning, etc.).
• [Old French *conveier* from medieval Latin *conviare* (from Latin *com-* with + *via* way)]
• **conveyable** *adjective*
• **conveyor** *noun* (also **conveyer**)

conveyance *noun*
• "k'n VAY ince"
• the act or process of carrying.
• [as CONVEY]

conveyancer *noun*
• "k'n VAY ince ur"
• a person who transfers property from one owner to another.
• [as CONVEY]
• **conveyancing** *noun*

convivial *adjective*
• "kun VIVVY 'll"
• (of a person) friendly, fond of good company.
• [Latin *convivialis* from *convivium* feast (from *com-* with + *vivere* live)]
• **conviviality** *noun*
• **convivially** *adverb*

convocation *noun*
• "conva CAY sh'n"
• a formal assembly at a university or college for graduation ceremonies.
• [as CONVOKE]
• **convocational** *adjective*

convoke *verb*
• "k'n VOKE"
• call (people) together to a meeting etc.; summon to assemble.
• [Latin *convocare convocat-* (from *com-* with + *vocare* call)]

convoluted *adjective*
• "CONVA lute id"
• (of style, meaning, etc.) complicated, involved, difficult to comprehend.
• [past participle of *convolute* from Latin *convolutus* (from *com-* with + *volvere volut-* roll)]
• **convolutedly** *adverb*
• **convolution** *noun*
• **convolutional** *adjective*

convolve *verb*
- "k'n VOLVE"
- roll together; coil up.
- [Latin *convolvere* (as CONVOLUTED)]

convolvulus *noun*
- "k'n VOLVE yoo luss"
- any twining plant of the genus *Convolvulus*, with trumpet-shaped flowers, e.g. bindweed.
- [Latin, as CONVOLUTED]

convulsant *adjective*
- "k'n VULSE 'nt"
- producing convulsions.
- [as CONVULSE]

convulse *verb*
- "k'n VULSE"
- move violently or uncontrollably.
- [Latin *convellere convuls-* (from *com-* with + *vellere* pull)]

convulsion *noun*
- "k'n VULL sh'n"
- violent irregular motion of a limb or limbs or the body caused by involuntary contraction of muscles.
- [as CONVULSE]
- **convulsive** *adjective*
- **convulsively** *adverb*

coolabah *noun*
ALSO SPELLED: **coolibah**
- "COOLA bah"
- any of various gum trees, esp. *Eucalyptus microtheca*.
- [Kamilaroi (and related languages) *gulabaa*]

coolant *noun*
- "COOL'nt"
- a cooling agent, esp. fluid, to remove heat from an engine, nuclear reactor, etc.
- ['cool' + '-ant' after *lubricant*]

coolie *noun*
- "COOLY"
- an unskilled, low-paid labourer in or from India, China, or other Asian countries.
- [perhaps from *Kulī*, an aboriginal tribe of Gujarat, India]

HOMOPHONES: *coolly, coulis, coulee*

coolly *adverb*
- "COOLY"
- in a calm, unexcited manner.
- [Old English *cōl* cool, cold]

HOMOPHONES: *coolie, coulis, coulee*

coomb *noun*
ALSO SPELLED: **combe**
- "COOM"
- a valley or hollow on the side of a hill.
- [Old English *cumb*: compare CWM]

HOMOPHONES: *cwm, khoum*

coordinate *verb*
- "co ORD'n ate"
- bring (various parts, movements, activities, etc.) into a proper or required relation to ensure harmony or effective operation etc.
- [from *co-*, originally a form of Latin *com-*, *cum* with + Latin *ordinare ordinat-* from *ordo -inis* order]
- **coordinated** *adjective*
- **coordination** *noun*
- **coordinator** *noun*

copacetic *adjective*
- "co puh SETTIC"
- excellent; in good order.
- [20th c.: origin unknown]

copal *noun*
- "COPE'll"
- a resin from any of various tropical trees, used for varnish.
- [Spanish from Aztec *copalli* incense]

copepod *noun*
- "CO puh pod"
- any small aquatic crustacean of the class Copepoda, many of which form the minute components of plankton.
- [Greek *kōpē* oar handle + *pous podos* foot]

Copernican *adjective*
- "kuh PURNA k'n"
- of or relating to the Polish astronomer Nicolaus Copernicus (d.1543) or his work, esp. his theory that the planets (including the earth) revolve around the sun.

copiable *adjective*
- "COPPY a bull"
- that can or may be copied.
- [Old French *copie*, *copier* copy, ultimately from Latin *copia* abundance (in medieval Latin = transcript)]

copier *noun*
- "COPPY ur"
- a machine or person that copies (esp. documents).
- [as COPIABLE]

copious *adjective*
- "COPEY us"
- abundant, plentiful.
- [Old French *copieux* from Latin *copiosus* from *copia* plenty]
- **copiously** *adverb*
- **copiousness** *noun*

coplanar *adjective*
- "co PLANE ur"
- in the same plane.
- [from *co-*, originally a form of Latin *com-*, *cum* with + PLANAR]
- **coplanarity** *noun* "co pluh NERRA tee"

copolymer *noun*
- "CO polla mur"
- a polymer with units of more than one kind.
- [*co-*, originally a form of Latin *com-*, *cum* with + POLYMER]
- **copolymerize** *verb* (also esp. *Brit.* **-ise**)

copperas *noun*
• "COPPER us"
• green crystals of hydrated ferrous sulphate, esp. as an industrial product.
• [Middle English *coperose* from Old French *couperose* from medieval Latin *cup(e)rosa*: perhaps originally *aqua cuprosa* copper water]

coppice *noun*
• "COPPISS"
• an area of undergrowth and small trees, grown for periodic cutting.
• [Old French *copeïz*, ultimately from medieval Latin *colpus* blow, from *colaphus* from Greek *kolaphos* blow with the fist]
• **coppiced** *adjective*

copra *noun*
• "COPPRA"
• the dried kernels of the coconut.
• [Portuguese from Malayalam *koppara* coconut]

coprocessor *noun*
• "CO pross esser" or "CO pro sesser"
• a microprocessor providing additional functions to supplement a primary processor.
• [*co*-, originally a form of Latin *com*-, *cum* with + PROCESSOR]

coprolite *noun*
• "COPPRA lite"
• fossil dung or a piece of it.
• [Greek *kopros* dung + *lithos* stone]

coprophagy *noun*
• "cop ROFFA jee"
• the eating of dung.
• [Greek *kopros* dung + *phagein* eat]
• **coprophagous** *adjective* "cop ROFFA gus"

coprophilia *noun*
• "coppra FILLY uh" or "coppra FEELY uh"
• an abnormal interest in feces and defecation.
• [Greek *kopros* dung + *philos* dear, loving]

copse *noun*
• "COPS"
• a small wood or thicket.
• [shortened from COPPICE]
• **copsy** *adjective*

copula *noun*
• "COP yuh luh"
• a connecting word, esp. parts of the verbs *be*, *seem*, *look*, etc., connecting a subject and predicate.
• [Latin (from *co*-, originally a form of *com*-, *cum* with + *apere* fasten)]
• **copular** *adjective*

copulate *verb*
• "COP yuh late"
• have sexual intercourse.
• [Latin *copulare* fasten together (as COPULA)]
• **copulation** *noun*
• **copulatory** *adjective*

copulative *adjective*
• "COP yuh luh tiv"
• serving to connect.
• [as COPULA]

copyright *noun*
• "COPPY rite"
• the exclusive legal right granted for a specified period to an author, designer, etc., or another appointed person, to print, publish, perform, film, or record original literary, artistic, or musical material.
• [as COPIABLE + 'right']
• **copyrightable** *adjective*

copywriter *noun*
• "COPPY rite ur"
• a person who writes or prepares copy (esp. of advertising material) for publication.
• ['copy' + 'write']
• **copywriting** *noun*

coquetry *noun*
• "CO kuh tree"
• coquettish behaviour.
• [French *coquetterie* from *coqueter* (as COQUETTE)]

coquette *noun*
• "co KET"
• a woman who flirts.
• [French, feminine of *coquet* wanton, diminutive of *coq* cock]
• **coquettish** *adjective*
• **coquettishly** *adverb*
• **coquettishness** *noun*

coquina *noun*
• "co KEENA"
• a soft limestone of broken shells, used in road building.
• [Spanish, = cockle]

Coquitlamite *noun*
• "kuh KWIT lum ite"
• a resident of Coquitlam, BC.

coquito *noun*
• "co KEETO"
• a palm tree, *Jubaea chilensis*, native to Chile, yielding honey from its sap, and fibre.
• [Spanish, diminutive of *coco* coconut]

coracle *noun*
• "CORA k'll"
• a small boat of wickerwork covered with watertight material, used on Welsh and Irish lakes and rivers.
• [Welsh *corwgl* (*corwg* = Irish *currach* boat: compare CURRACH)]

coracoid *noun*
• "CORA coid"
• a short projection from the shoulder blade in vertebrates.
• [modern Latin *coracoides* from Greek *korakoeidēs* raven-like, from *korax -akos* raven]

coral *noun*
- "CORE 'll"
- a hard calcareous substance secreted by various marine polyps for support and habitation, and occurring in both single specimens and vast accumulations.
- [Old French from Latin *corallum* from Greek *korallion*, prob. of Semitic origin]

HOMOPHONES: *choral*

coralbells *noun*
- "CORE 'll bells"
- a herbaceous plant of the saxifrage family, *Heuchera sanguinea*, which has small pink bell-shaped flowers.
- [as CORAL + 'bell']

coralberry *noun*
- "CORE'll berry"
- a N American shrub, *Symphoricarpos orbiculata*, of the honeysuckle family, with deep red berries.
- [as CORAL + 'berry']

coralline *noun*
- "CORA line"
- any seaweed of the genus *Corallina* having a calcareous jointed stem.
- [French *corallin* & Italian *corallina* from Late Latin *corallinus* (as CORAL)]

corallite *noun*
- "CORA lite"
- the coral skeleton of a marine polyp.
- [Latin *corallum* CORAL + Greek *lithos* stone]

coralloid *adjective*
- "CORA loid"
- like or akin to coral.
- [as CORAL]

corbel *noun*
- "CORE bull"
- a projection of stone, timber, etc., jutting out from a wall to support a weight.
- [Old French, diminutive of *corp* crow, from Latin *corvus* raven (perhaps because of the shape of a corbel, resembling a crow's beak)]

corbie *noun*
- "CORBY"
- a raven.
- [Old French *corb*, *corp* from Latin *corvus* crow]

cord *noun*
- "CORD"
- long thin flexible material made from several twisted strands, esp. thicker than string and finer than rope.
- [Old French *corde* from Latin *chorda* from Greek *khordē* gut, string of musical instrument]
- **cording** *noun*

HOMOPHONES: *chord*

cordage *noun*
- "CORD idge"
- cords or ropes, esp. in the rigging of a ship.
- [as CORD]

cordate *adjective*
- "CORD ate"
- heart-shaped.
- [modern Latin *cordatus* from Latin *cor cordis* heart]

HOMOPHONES: *chordate*

corded *adjective*
- "CORD id"
- (of cloth) ribbed.
- [as CORD]

cordgrass *noun*
- "CORD grass"
- any grass of the genus *Spartina*, with rhizomatous roots and growing in wet or marshy ground.
- [as CORD + 'grass']

cordial *adjective*
- "CORE j'll" or "CORDY 'll"
- heartfelt, sincere.
- [medieval Latin *cordialis* from Latin *cor cordis* heart]
- **cordiality** *noun*
- **cordially** *adverb*

cordillera *noun*
- "core DILLER uh" or "cordil YAIR uh"
- a system or group of usu. parallel mountain ranges together with intervening plateaux etc., esp. as a major continental feature.
- [Spanish from *cordilla* diminutive of *cuerda* CORD]
- **cordilleran** *adjective*

cordite *noun*
- "CORD ite"
- a smokeless explosive made from nitrocellulose and nitroglycerine.
- [CORD (from its appearance) + Greek *lithos* stone]

cordless *adjective*
- "CORD less"
- (of an electrical appliance, telephone, etc.) working from an internal source of energy etc. (esp. a rechargeable battery).
- [as CORD]

cordon *noun*
- "CORD'n"
- a line or circle of police, soldiers, guards, etc., esp. preventing access to or from an area.
- [Italian *cordone* augmentative of *corda* CORD, & French *cordon* (as CORD)]

cordovan *noun*
- "CORDA v'n"
- a kind of soft leather made originally from goatskin and now from horsehide.
- [Spanish *cordovan* of Cordova (Cordoba) in S Spain, where it was originally made]

corduroy *noun*
- "CORDA roy"
- a thick cotton fabric with velvety ribs.

• [18th c.: prob. from CORD ribbed fabric + obsolete *duroy* coarse woollen fabric]

cordwood *noun*
• "CORD wood"
• wood that is or can easily be measured in cords (usu. 128 cu. ft., 3.6 cubic metres).
• [as CORD + 'wood']

corella *noun*
• "kuh RELLA"
• either of two small Australian cockatoos of the genus *Cacatua* with pink-tinged white plumage and blue skin around the eye.
• [Wiradhuri]

coreopsis *noun*
• "cory OP sis"
• any composite plant of the genus *Coreopsis*, having rayed usu. yellow flowers.
• [modern Latin from Greek *koris* bug + *opsis* appearance, with reference to the shape of the seed]

corgi *noun*
• "CORE gee" (with "G" as in *GEEK*)
• a short-legged breed of dog with a foxlike head.
• [Welsh from *cor* dwarf + *ci* dog]

coriaceous *adjective*
• "cory AY sh'ss"
• like leather; leathery.
• [Late Latin *coriaceus* from *corium* leather + adjective suffix *-aceus* of the nature of]

coriander *noun*
• "CORY ander"
• a plant, *Coriandrum sativum*, with leaves used for flavouring and small round aromatic fruits.
• [Old French *coriandre* from Latin *coriandrum* from Greek *koriannon*]

Corinthian *adjective*
• "kuh RINTH ee 'n"
• of ancient Corinth in S Greece.

Coriolis *adjective*
• "cory OH liss"
• designating an effect whereby a mass moving in a rotating system experiences a force acting perpendicular to the direction of motion and to the axis of rotation.
• [G. G. *Coriolis*, French scientist d.1843]

corium *noun*
• "CORY um"
• the dermis.
• [Latin, = skin]

corm *noun*
• "CORM"
• an underground swollen stem base of some plants, e.g. gladiolus.
• [modern Latin *cormus* from Greek *kormos* trunk with boughs lopped off]

cormorant *noun*
• "CORMER 'nt"
• any diving, fish-eating water bird of the family Phalacrocoracidae, having lustrous black plumage.
• [Old French *cormaran* from medieval Latin *corvus marinus* sea crow: for ending *-ant* compare *peasant*, *tyrant*]

corncrake *noun*
• "CORN crake"
• a slender European brown bird of the rail family, *Crex crex*, which has a harsh grating cry and lives in grassland.
• ['corn' + CRAKE]

cornea *noun*
• "CORNY uh"
• the transparent circular part of the front of the eyeball.
• [medieval Latin *cornea tela* horny tissue, from Latin *corneus* horny, from *cornu* horn]
• **corneal** *adjective*

cornel *noun*
• "CORN'll"
• any of various shrubs or small trees of the genus *Cornus*, including the flowering dogwoods, *C. florida* of eastern N America and *C. nuttallii* of western N America, and the low-growing bunchberry *C. canadensis*.
• [Middle English from Latin *cornus*]

cornet[1] *noun*
• "core NET"
• a brass instrument resembling a trumpet but shorter and wider.
• [Old French, ultimately from Latin *cornu* horn]
• **cornetist** *noun* (also **cornettist**)

cornet[2] *noun*
• "CORE nit"
• the fifth commissioned officer in a cavalry troop, who carried the colours.
• [earlier sense 'pennon, standard' from French *cornette* diminutive of *corne*, ultimately from Latin *cornua* horns]
• **cornetcy** *noun*

cornice *noun*
• "CORE niss"
• an ornamental moulding round the wall of a room just below the ceiling.
• [French *corniche* etc. from Italian *cornice*, perhaps from Latin *cornix -icis* crow]
• **corniced** *adjective*

corniche *noun*
• "CORE nish" or "core NEESH"
• a road cut into the edge of a cliff etc.
• [French: see CORNICE]
HOMOPHONES: *Cornish*

cornichon *noun*
• "corny SHÕH" (with a nasal *OH*)
• a tiny pickled cucumber.
• [French = pickled cucumber, diminutive of *corne* horn]

cornstalk *noun*
• "CORN stock"
• the stalk of a corn plant.
• ['corn' + STALK]

cornucopia *noun*
• "corn yuh COPEY uh"
• a symbol of plenty consisting of a goat's horn overflowing with flowers, fruit, and grain.
• [Late Latin from Latin *cornu copiae* horn of plenty]
• **cornucopian** *adjective*

corolla *noun*
• "kuh RAWL uh" or "kuh ROLE uh"
• a whorl or whorls of petals forming the inner envelope of a flower.
• [Latin, diminutive of *corona* crown]

corollary *noun*
• "kuh RAWL a ree"
• a proposition that follows from (and is often appended to) one already proved.
• [Latin *corollarium* money paid for a garland, gratuity: neuter adjective from COROLLA]

corona *noun*
• "kuh ROE nuh"
• a small circle of light round the sun or moon.
• [Latin, = crown]
• **coronal** *adjective* "kuh RONE'll" or "CORA nul"

coronagraph *noun*
• "kuh ROE nuh graff"
• an instrument for observing the sun's corona, esp. other than during a solar eclipse.
• [as CORONA + Greek *graphia* writing]

coronary *adjective*
• "CORA nerry"
• of or relating to the heart.
• [Latin *coronarius* from *corona* crown]

coronation *noun*
• "cora NAY sh'n"
• the act or ceremony of crowning a sovereign or a sovereign's consort.
• [Old French from medieval Latin *coronatio -onis* from *coronare* to crown, from CORONA]

coronavirus *noun*
• "kuh RONA vie russ"
• a virus having a roughly spherical shape with a crown-like appearance, causing respiratory ailments and gastroenteritis in humans.
• [as CORONA + VIRUS]

coroner *noun*
• "CORA nur"
• a public official responsible for investigating violent, suspicious, or accidental deaths, and certifying deaths occurring outside hospital.
• [Anglo-French *cor(o)uner* from *coro(u)ne* crown, reflecting the Latin title *custos placitorum coronae* 'guardian of the pleas of the crown']
• **coronership** *noun*

coronet *noun*
• "CORA net" or "cora NET"
• a small crown (esp. as worn, or used as a heraldic device, by a peer or peeress).
• [Old French *coronet(t)e* diminutive of *corone* crown]
• **coroneted** *adjective*

corozo *noun*
• "kuh ROE zoe"
• any of various tropical palm trees yielding palm oil.
• [Spanish, variant of dialect *carozo* fruit pit, core]

corporal *adjective*
• "CORPER 'll" or "CORE prull"
• of or relating to the human body.
• [Old French from Latin *corporalis* from *corpus -oris* body]
• **corporality** *noun*
• **corporally** *adverb*

corporation *noun*
• "corper AY sh'n"
• a group of people authorized to act as an individual and recognized in law as a single entity, esp. in business.
• [Late Latin *corporatio* from *corporare corporat-* form into a body (*corpus -oris*)]
• **corporate** *adjective* "CORPER it" or "CORE prit"
• **corporately** *adverb*
• **corporative** *adjective*
• **corporativism** *noun*

corporatism *noun*
• "CORE prit izm" or "CORPER it izm"
• a political ideology or system, esp. associated with fascist states, in which business, industry, labour, etc. are organized as corporate entities.
• [as CORPORATION]
• **corporatist** *adjective*

corporatize *verb*
ALSO SPELLED: esp. *Brit.* **-ise**
• "CORE pruh tize" or "CORPER a tize"
• to develop or convert (a small business operation) into a corporation.
• [as CORPORATION]
• **corporatization** *noun* (also esp. *Brit.* **-isation**)

corporeal *adjective*
• "core PORRY 'll"
• bodily, physical, material, esp. as distinct from spiritual.
• [Late Latin *corporealis* from Latin *corporeus* from *corpus -oris* body]
• **corporeality** *noun*
• **corporeally** *adverb*

corps *noun*
• "CORE"
• a body of troops with special duties.
• [French (as CORPSE)]
HOMOPHONES: *core*

corpse *noun*
• "CORPS"

- a dead (usu. human) body.
- [Middle English *corps* from Old French *cors* from Latin *corpus* body]

corpsman *noun*
- "CORE m'n"
- an enlisted medical auxiliary in the US army or navy.
- [as CORPS]

corpulent *adjective*
- "CORP yoo l'nt"
- portly; fat.
- [Latin *corpulentus* from *corpus* body]
- **corpulence** *noun*

corpus *noun*
- "CORE pus"
- a body or collection of writings, esp. by one author.
- [Latin, = body]

corpuscle *noun*
- "CORE pus'll"
- a minute body or cell in an organism, esp. the red or white cells in the blood of vertebrates.
- [Latin *corpusculum* (diminutive of CORPUS)]
- **corpuscular** *adjective* "core PUS kyuh lur"

corral *noun*
- "kuh RAL"
- a pen for cattle, horses, etc.
- [Spanish & Old Portuguese]

HOMOPHONES: *chorale*

correctitude *noun*
- "kuh RECTA tude"
- correctness, esp. conscious correctness of conduct.
- [19th c., from 'correct' (from Latin *corrigere correct-* from *com-* with + *regere* guide) + RECTITUDE]

corrector *noun*
- "kuh RECTER"
- something that provides a means of correction or prevents error.
- [Latin *corrigere correct-* (from *com-* with + *regere* guide)]

correlation *noun*
- "cora LAY sh'n"
- a mutual relation between two or more things.
- [medieval Latin *correlatio* (as CORRELATIVE)]
- **correlate** *verb*
- **correlational** *adjective*

correlative *adjective*
- "kuh RELLA tiv"
- having a mutual relation; corresponding.
- [medieval Latin *correlativus* (from *com-* with + RELATIVE)]
- **correlatively** *adverb*
- **correlativity** *noun*

correspond *verb*
- "cora SPOND"
- be analogous or similar.
- [French *correspondre* from medieval Latin *correspondere* (from *com-* with + *respondēre respons-* answer)]
- **correspondence** *noun*
- **corresponding** *adjective*
- **correspondingly** *adverb*

correspondent *noun*
- "cora SPOND 'nt"
- a person employed to contribute material for publication in a periodical or for broadcasting.
- [as CORRESPOND]

corretto *noun*
- "kuh RETTO"
- espresso laced with brandy or liqueur.
- [Italian, lit. = 'corrected']

corrida *noun*
- "core EEDA"
- a bullfight.
- [Spanish *corrida de toros* running of bulls]

corridor *noun*
- "CORA dore" or "CORA dur"
- a passage from which doors lead into rooms; hallway.
- [French from Italian *corridore* corridor, alteration (by association with *corridore* runner) of *corridoio* running place, from *correre* run, from Latin *currere*]

corrie *noun*
- "CORY"
- a circular hollow on a mountainside; a cirque.
- [Gaelic *coire* cauldron]

corrigendum *noun*
- "cora JEN dum"
- a thing to be corrected, esp. an error in a printed book.
- [Latin, neuter gerundive of *corrigere*: see CORRECTOR]

corroborate *verb*
- "kuh ROBBER ate"
- confirm or give support to (a statement or belief, or the person holding it), esp. in relation to witnesses in a law court.
- [Latin *corroborare* strengthen (from *com-* with + *roborare* from *robur -oris* strength)]
- **corroboration** *noun*
- **corroborative** *adjective*
- **corroborator** *noun*

corroboree *noun*
- "kuh ROBBER ee"
- a dance-drama ceremony of Australian Aboriginals, featuring song and rhythmical musical accompaniment.
- [Dharuk *garabari* a style of dancing]

corrode *verb*
- "kuh RODE"
- wear away, esp. by chemical action.
- [Latin *corrodere corros-* (from *com-* with + *rodere* gnaw)]

- **corroded** *adjective*
- **corrodible** *adjective*
- **corrosion** *noun*
- **corrosive** *adjective*
- **corrosively** *adverb*
- **corrosiveness** *noun*

corrugate *verb*
- "CORA gate"
- form into alternate ridges and grooves, esp. to strengthen.
- [Latin *corrugare* (from *com-* with + *rugare* from *ruga* wrinkle)]
- **corrugated** *adjective*
- **corrugation** *noun*

corrupt *adjective*
- "kuh RUPT"
- influenced by or using bribery or fraudulent activity.
- [Old French *corrupt* or Latin *corruptus* past participle of *corrumpere corrupt-* (from *com-* with + *rumpere* break)]
- **corrupter** *noun*
- **corruptibility** *noun*
- **corruptible** *adjective*
- **corruption** *noun*
- **corruptive** *adjective*
- **corruptly** *adverb*
- **corruptness** *noun*

corsage *noun*
- "core SOZH"
- an arrangement of flowers worn by a woman at the front of a dress below the shoulder, or at the waist or wrist, usu. on formal occasions.
- [Old French from *cors* body: see CORPSE]

corsair *noun*
- "core SARE"
- a pirate ship.
- [French *corsaire* from medieval Latin *cursarius* from *cursus* inroad, from *currere* run]

corse *noun*
- "CORSE" (rhymes with *HORSE*)
- a corpse.
- [var. of CORPSE]

HOMOPHONES: *coarse*, *course*

corselet *noun*
- "CORSE lit" or "CORSA let"
- a piece of armour covering the trunk but not the limbs.
- [Old French *corselet*, diminutive formed as CORSET]

corselette *noun*
- "corsa LET"
- a woman's foundation garment combining corset and brassiere.
- [as CORSELET]

corset *noun*
- "CORE set"
- a close-fitting undergarment worn by women to shape and support the torso.
- [Old French, diminutive of *cors* body: see CORPSE]
- **corseted** *adjective*
- **corsetry** *noun*

Corsican *adjective*
- "CORSA k'n"
- of or relating to the French island of Corsica north of Sardinia.

cortège *noun*
- "core TEZH"
- a procession, esp. for a funeral.
- [French, from Italian *corteggio*, from *corteggiare* attend court, from *corte* court, from Latin *cohors cohort-* yard, retinue]

Cortes *noun*
- "CORE tez"
- the legislative assembly of Spain and formerly of Portugal.
- [Spanish & Portuguese, pl. of *corte* from Latin *cohors, -hortis* yard, retinue]

cortex *noun*
- "CORE tex"
- the outer part of an organ, esp. of the brain or kidneys.
- [Latin *cortex, -icis* bark]
- **cortical** *adjective* "CORTA k'll"

corticate *adjective*
- "CORTA kit" or "CORTA cate"
- having bark or rind.
- [Latin *corticatus* (as CORTEX)]
- **cortication** *noun*

corticosteroid *noun*
- "corta co STARE oid"
- any of a group of steroid hormones produced in the adrenal cortex and concerned with regulation of salts and carbohydrates, inflammation, and sexual physiology.
- [as CORTEX + STEROID]

corticotrophin *noun*
- "corta co TRO fin"
- a hormone secreted by the pituitary gland and stimulating the adrenal glands.
- [as CORTEX + Greek *trophikos* from *trophē* nourishment, from *trephō* nourish]

cortisol *noun*
- "CORTA sawl"
- a steroid hormone produced by the adrenal cortex, used medicinally to treat inflammation and rheumatism.
- [as CORTISONE]

cortisone *noun*
- "CORTA zone"
- a steroid hormone produced by the adrenal cortex or synthetically, used medicinally esp. against inflammation and allergy.
- [abbreviation of 17-hydroxy-11-dehydro*corti*coster*one*]

Cortland *noun*
- "CORT l'nd"

- a red variety of apple.
- [*Cortland*, New York]

corundum *noun*
- "kuh RUN dum"
- extremely hard crystallized alumina, used esp. as an abrasive, and varieties of which, e.g. ruby and sapphire, are used for gemstones.
- [Tamil *kurundam* from Sanskrit *kuruvinda* ruby]

coruscate *verb*
- "CORA skate"
- give off flashing light; sparkle.
- [Latin *coruscare* glitter]
- **coruscant** *adjective*
- **coruscation** *noun*

corvée *noun*
- "CORE vay"
- a day's work of unpaid labour due to a feudal lord from a vassal.
- [Old French, ultimately from Latin *corrogare* ask for, collect (from *com-* with + *rogare* ask)]

corvette *noun*
- "core VET"
- a small naval escort vessel.
- [French from Middle Dutch *korf* kind of ship]

corvine *adjective*
- "CORE vine"
- of or akin to the raven or crow.
- [Latin *corvinus* from *corvus* raven]

corybantic *adjective*
- "cora BANTIC"
- wild, frenzied.
- [*Corybantes* priests of the mother goddess Cybele performing wild dances (Latin from Greek *Korubantes*)]

corydalis *noun*
- "kuh RIDDA liss"
- a plant of the genus *Corydalis* of the poppy family, with tubular flowers.
- [Greek *korudallis* crested lark (with reference to the flower, likened to the bird's spur)]

corymb *noun*
- "CORE imb" or "CORE im"
- a flat-topped cluster of flowers with the flower stalks proportionally longer lower down the stem.
- [French *corymbe* or Latin *corymbus* from Greek *korumbos* cluster]

coryphée *noun*
- "CORA fay"
- (in some ballet companies) a leading dancer in a corps de ballet.
- [French from Greek *koruphaios* leader of a chorus, from *koruphē* head]

coryza *noun*
- "kuh RIZE uh"
- a catarrhal inflammation of the mucous membrane in the nose; a cold in the head.
- [Latin from Greek *koruza* running at the nose]

cos *noun*
- "COSS"
- romaine lettuce.
- [Latin from Greek *Kōs*, island in the Aegean Sea, where it originated]

cosecant *noun*
- "co SEEK'nt"
- the ratio of the hypotenuse (in a right-angled triangle) to the side opposite an acute angle; the reciprocal of sine.
- [*co-*, originally a form of Latin *com-*, *cum* with + SECANT]

cosine *noun*
- "CO sine"
- the ratio of the side adjacent to an acute angle (in a right-angled triangle) to the hypotenuse.
- [*co-*, originally a form of Latin *com-*, *cum* with + SINE]

cosmetic *adjective*
- "cozz METTIC"
- intended to adorn or beautify the body, esp. the face.
- [French *cosmétique* from Greek *kosmētikos* from *kosmeō* adorn, from *kosmos* order, adornment]
- **cosmetically** *adverb*

cosmetician *noun*
- "cozma TISH'n"
- a person who sells or applies cosmetics for a living.
- [as COSMETIC]

cosmeticize *verb*

ALSO SPELLED: esp. *Brit.* **-ise**
- "cozz METTA size"
- treat with cosmetics.
- [as COSMETIC]

cosmetology *noun*
- "cozma TOLLA jee"
- the art or profession of applying cosmetics.
- [as COSMETIC + Greek *logos* word]
- **cosmetologist** *noun*

cosmogony *noun*
- "cozz MOGGA nee"
- a theory or account of the origin of the universe.
- [Greek *kosmogonia* from *kosmos* world + *-gonia* -begetting]
- **cosmogonic** *adjective* "cozma GONNIC"
- **cosmogonical** *adjective*
- **cosmogonist** *noun*

cosmography *noun*
- "cozz MOGGRA fee"
- a description or mapping of general features of the universe.
- [as COSMOS + *graphein* writing]
- **cosmographer** *noun*

cosmology *noun*
- "cozz MOLLA jee"
- the study of the origin and development of the universe.
- [French *cosmologie* or modern Latin *cosmologia* (as COSMOS + *logos* word)]
- **cosmological** *adjective*
- **cosmologically** *adverb*
- **cosmologist** *noun*

cosmonaut *noun*
- "COZMA not"
- an astronaut in the Russian or Soviet space program.
- [Russian *kosmonavt*, as COSMOS, after *astronaut*]

cosmopolis *noun*
- "cozz MOPPA liss"
- a cosmopolitan city.
- [Greek *kosmos* world + *polis* city]

cosmopolitan *adjective*
- "cozma POLLA t'n"
- of or from or knowing many parts of the world.
- [as COSMOPOLITE]
- **cosmopolitanism** *noun*
- **cosmopolitanize** *verb* (also esp. *Brit.* **-ise**)

cosmopolite *noun*
- "cozz MOPPLE ite"
- a cosmopolitan person.
- [French from Greek *kosmopolitēs* from *kosmos* world + *politēs* citizen]

cosmos *noun*
- "COZZ mose" ("MOSE" rhymes with *GROSS*)
- the universe, esp. as a well-ordered whole.
- [Greek *kosmos*]
- **cosmic** *adjective*
- **cosmical** *adjective*
- **cosmically** *adverb*

Cossack *noun*
- "COSS ack"
- a member of a people living on the northern shores of the Black and Caspian seas, originally famous for their military skill.
- [French *cosaque* from Russian *kazak* from Turki *quzzāq* nomad, adventurer]

cossack *noun*
- "COSS uck"
- *Cdn* (*Nfld*) a hooded pullover made of animal skin or heavy cotton.
- [alteration of CASSOCK]

cosset *verb*
- "COSS it"
- pamper.
- [dialect *cosset* = pet lamb, prob. from Anglo-French *coscet*, *cozet* from Old English *cotsǣta* cottager]

costal *adjective*
- "COST'll"
- of the ribs.
- [French from modern Latin *costalis* from Latin *costa* rib]

costard *noun*
- "COSS turd"
- a large ribbed variety of apple.
- [Anglo-French from *coste* rib, from Latin *costa*]

costermonger *noun*
- "COSTER mung gur" or "COSTER mong gur"
- a person who sells fruit, vegetables, etc., in the street from a cart.
- [COSTARD + MONGER]

costive *adjective*
- "COSTIV"
- constipated.
- [Old French *costivé* from Latin *constipatus*: see CONSTIPATION]
- **costively** *adverb*
- **costiveness** *noun*

costmary *noun*
- "COST merry"
- an aromatic composite plant, *Balsamita major*, formerly used in medicine and for flavouring ale.
- [Old English *cost* from Latin *costum* from Greek *kostos* from Arabic *kusṭ* an aromatic plant + (*St.*) *Mary* (with whom it was associated in medieval times)]

cotangent *noun*
- "CO tan j'nt"
- the ratio of the side adjacent to an acute angle (in a right-angled triangle) to the opposite side.
- [from *co-*, originally a form of Latin *com-*, *cum* with + TANGENT]

cote *noun*
- "COTE"
- a shelter, esp. for animals or birds; a shed or stall.
- [Old English from Germanic]

HOMOPHONES: *coat*

coteau *noun*
- "COE toe"
- (*West*) any of various kinds of elevated geographical features, such as a plateau, a divide between valleys, etc.
- [French *coteau* slope, hillside, from Latin *costa* side]

coterie *noun*
- "CO tur ee"
- a group of people who associate closely; a clique.
- [French, originally = association of tenants, ultimately from Middle Low German *kote* COTE]

coterminous *adjective*
- "co TURMIN us"
- having the same boundaries or extent (in space, time, or meaning).
- [*co-*, originally a form of Latin *com-*, *cum* with + TERMINUS]

cotillion *noun*
• "kuh TILL y'n" or "co TILL y'n"
• a formal ball, esp. one at which debutantes are presented.
• [French *cotillon* petticoat, diminutive of *cotte* from Old French *cote* coat]

cotinga *noun*
• "kuh TING guh"
• a tropical American bird of the passerine family Cotingidae, often with brilliant plumage.
• [French from Tupi *cutinga*]

cotoneaster *noun*
• "kuh tony ASTER"
• any rosaceous shrub of the genus *Cotoneaster*, bearing usu. bright red berries.
• [modern Latin from Latin *cotoneum* QUINCE + Latin *aster* denoting incomplete resemblance]

cotta *noun*
• "COTTA"
• a short surplice.
• [Italian, related to 'coat']

cottar *noun*
ALSO SPELLED: **cotter**
• "COTTER"
• a farm labourer or tenant occupying a cottage in return for labour as required.
• [Old English *cot* cottage, from Germanic, related to COTE + Scots agent suffix *-ar*]
HOMOPHONES: *cotter*

cottier *noun*
• "COTTY ur"
• an Irish peasant who rented a small portion of land at a price fixed by competition.
• [Old French *cotier* from medieval Latin *cotarius*: see COTERIE]

cotyledon *noun*
• "cot'll EED'n"
• an embryonic leaf in seed-bearing plants.
• [Latin, = pennywort, from Greek *kotulēdōn* cup-shaped cavity, from *kotulē* cup]
• **cotyledonary** *adjective*
• **cotyledonous** *adjective*

couchant *adjective*
• "COUCH 'nt"
• (of an animal) lying with the body resting on the legs and the head raised.
• [French, present participle of *coucher* lie down, from Latin *collocare* (from *com-* with + *locare* place)]

couchette *noun*
• "coo SHET"
• a railway car on European trains with seats convertible into sleeping berths.
• [French, = little bed, diminutive of *couche* (as COUCHANT)]

cougar *noun*
• "COO grr"
• a moderately large carnivorous mammal of the cat family, *Felis concolor*, with a tawny or greyish coat and long black-tipped tail, found in parts of N and S America.
• [French, representing Guarani *guaçu ara*]

coulee *noun*
• "COOLY"
• a deep ravine with steep sides, formed by heavy rain or melting snow.
• [French, feminine past participle of *couler* flow, from Latin *colare* strain, filter]
HOMOPHONES: *coulis, coolie, coolly*

coulis *noun*
• "COOLY"
• a purée of fruit, tomatoes, etc., thin enough to pour.
• [French from *couler*, as COULEE]
HOMOPHONES: *coulee, coolie, coolly*

coulisse *noun*
• "coo LEECE"
• a piece of side scenery or a space between two of these; the wings.
• [French from *coulis* sliding: see PORTCULLIS]

couloir *noun*
• "cool WARR" ("WARR" rhymes with *FAR*)
• a steep narrow gully on a mountainside.
• [French from *couler* glide: see COULEE]

coulomb *noun*
• "COO lom"
• the SI unit of electric charge, equal to the quantity of electricity conveyed in one second by a current of one ampere.
• [C. A. de *Coulomb*, French physicist d.1806]

coulter *noun*
ALSO SPELLED: **colter**
• "COLE tur"
• a vertical cutting wheel or blade fixed in front of a ploughshare.
• [Old English from Latin *culter*]

coumarin *noun*
• "COOMER in"
• an aromatic substance with the smell of new-mown hay, found in many plants and used in perfumery.
• [French *coumarine* from Tupi *cumarú* tonka bean]

council *noun*
• "COWN s'll"
• an advisory, deliberative, or administrative body of people formally constituted and meeting regularly.
• [Anglo-French *cuncile* from Latin *concilium* convocation, assembly, from *calare* summon: compare COUNSEL]
• **councilman** *noun*
• **councilwoman** *noun*
HOMOPHONES: *counsel*

councillor *noun*
• "COWN s'll ur"
• esp. *Cdn & Brit.* an elected member of a municipal council.

• [as COUNCIL]
• **councillorship** *noun*
HOMOPHONES: *counsellor*

counsel *noun*
• "COWN s'll"
• advice, esp. formally given.
• [Old French *c(o)unseil, conseiller* from Latin *consilium* consultation, advice]
• **counselling** *noun*
HOMOPHONES: *council*

counsellor *noun*
ALSO SPELLED: **counselor**
• "COWN s'll ur"
• a person who gives counsel; an adviser.
• [as COUNSEL]
HOMOPHONES: *councillor*

countenance *noun*
• "COUNTA nince"
• the face.
• [Anglo-French *c(o)untenance*, Old French *contenance* bearing, from *contenir* from Latin from *continēre continent-* (from *com-* with + *tenēre* hold)]

countercurrent *noun*
• "COUNTER cur 'nt"
• a current flowing in an opposite direction to another.
• [Old French *countre* from Latin *contra* against + CURRENT]

counterfactual *adjective*
• "counter FACK choo 'll"
• relating to or expressing what has not happened or is not the case.
• [Old French *countre* from Latin *contra* against + FACTUAL]

counterfeit *adjective*
• "COUNTER fit"
• (of money, documents, recordings, etc.) made in imitation; not genuine; forged.
• [Old French *countrefet, -fait*, past participle of *contrefaire* from Latin *contra* against + *facere* make]
• **counterfeiter** *noun*
• **counterfeiting** *noun*

counterfoil *noun*
• "COUNTER foil"
• the part of a cheque, receipt, etc., retained by the payer and containing details of the transaction.
• [Old French *countre* from Latin *contra* against + Old French *foil* from Latin *folium* leaf]

counterintuitive *adjective*
• "counter in TOO a tiv" or "counter in TYOO a tiv"
• contrary to intuition.
• [Old French *countre* from Latin *contra* against + INTUITION]

counterirritant *noun*
• "counter IRRA t'nt"
• something used to produce surface irritation of the skin, thereby counteracting more painful symptoms.
• [Old French *countre* from Latin *contra* against + IRRITATE]
• **counterirritation** *noun*

countermand *verb*
• "counter MAND"
• revoke (an order or command).
• [Old French *contremander* from medieval Latin *contramandare* (*contra* against + *mandare* order)]

countermeasure *noun*
• "COUNTER mezhur"
• an action taken to counteract a danger, threat, etc.
• [Old French *countre* from Latin *contra* against + MEASURE]

counteroffensive *noun*
• "counter a FENSIV"
• an attack made against an attacking force.
• [Old French *countre* from Latin *contra* against + OFFEND]

counterpane *noun*
• "COUNTER pane"
• a bedspread.
• [alteration (with assimilation to *pane* in obsolete sense 'cloth') from obsolete *counterpoint*, via Old French *contrepointe* (alteration of *cou(l)tepointe*) from medieval Latin *culcita puncta* 'quilted mattress']

counterpoise *noun*
• "COUNTER poyz"
• a force etc. equivalent to another on the opposite side.
• [Old French *contrepeis, -pois, contrepeser* (from Old French *countre* from Latin *contra* against + Old French *peis, pois* from Latin *pensum* weight)]

counterproductive *adjective*
• "counter pruh DUCTIV"
• having the opposite of the desired effect.
• [Old French *countre* from Latin *contra* against + Latin *productum*, neuter past participle of *producere* produce]

counterterrorism *noun*
• "counter TARE ur ism"
• measures to combat terrorism.
• [Old French *countre* from Latin *contra* against + TERRORISM]

countervail *verb*
• "counter VALE"
• counterbalance.
• [Anglo-French *contrevaloir* from Latin *contra valēre* be of worth against]
• **countervailable** *adjective*

counterweight *noun*
• "COUNTER wate"
• a counterbalancing weight.
• [Old French *countre* from Latin *contra* against + WEIGHT]

coup *noun*
• "COO"

• a notable or successful stroke or move.
• [French from medieval Latin *colpus* blow]
HOMOPHONES: *coo*

coupe *noun*
• "COOP"
• a two-door car with a hard roof, esp. one seating only two persons.
• [French *coupé*, past participle of *couper* cut (formed as COUP)]
HOMOPHONES: *coop*

couple *noun*
• "CUP'll"
• a set of two people or things.
• [Old French *cople*, *cuple*, *copler*, *cupler* from Latin *copulare*, Latin COPULA]
• **coupledom** *noun*

coupler *noun*
• "CUP lur"
• a person or thing that couples or links things together.
• [as COUPLE]

couplet *noun*
• "CUP lit"
• two successive lines of verse, usu. rhyming and of the same length.
• [French diminutive of *couple*, formed as COUPLE]

coupling *noun*
• "CUP ling"
• a link connecting railway cars etc.
• [as COUPLE]

coupon *noun*
• "COO pon" or "KYOO pon"
• a certificate entitling the bearer to a discount on a purchase etc.
• [French, = piece cut off, from *couper* cut: see COUPE]

courage *noun*
• "CUR idge"
• the ability to disregard fear; bravery.
• [Old French *corage*, from Latin *cor* heart]
• **courageous** *adjective* "cur AY juss"
• **courageously** *adverb*

courante *noun*
• "coo RANT"
• a running or gliding dance.
• [French, feminine present participle (as noun) of *courir* run, from Latin *currere*]

courgette *noun*
• "coor ZHET"
• a zucchini.
• [French, diminutive of *courge* gourd]

courier *noun*
• "CURRY ur"
• a person or company hired to convey documents, packages etc. from sender to recipient.
• [obsolete French, from Italian *corriere*, & from Old French *coreor*, both from Latin *currere* run]
HOMOPHONES: *currier*

course *noun*
• "CORSE"
• a continuous onward movement or progression.
• [Old French *cours* from Latin *cursus* from *currere curs-* run]
HOMOPHONES: *coarse*, *corse*

courser *noun*
• "CORSER"
• a swift horse.
• [Old French *corsier* (as COURSE)]
HOMOPHONES: *coarser*

courteous *adjective*
• "CURTY us"
• polite, kind, or considerate in manner; well-mannered.
• [Old French *corteis*, *curteis*, based on Latin *cohors* yard]
• **courteously** *adverb*
• **courteousness** *noun*

courtesan *noun*
• "CORTA zan"
• a prostitute, esp. one with wealthy or upper-class clients.
• [French *courtisane* from Italian *cortigiana*, feminine of *cortigiano* courtier, from *corte* court, from Latin *cohors* yard]

courtesy *noun*
• "CURTA see"
• courteous behaviour; good manners.
• [Old French *curtesie*, *co(u)rtesie* from *curteis* etc. COURTEOUS]

courtier *noun*
• "CORTY ur"
• a person who attends or frequents a sovereign's court.
• [Anglo-French *courte(i)our*, from Old French, from *cortoyer* be present at court, from *cort*, from Latin *cohors* yard or retinue]

couscous *noun*
• "COOSE coose" (rhymes with *GOOSE*)
• a type of North African pasta in granules made from crushed durum wheat.
• [French from Arabic *kuskus* from *kaskasa* to pound]

cousin *noun*
• "CUZZ'n"
• the child of one's uncle or aunt.
• [Old French *cosin*, *cusin*, from Latin *consobrinus* mother's sister's child]
• **cousinhood** *noun*
• **cousinly** *adjective*
• **cousinship** *noun*
HOMOPHONES: *cozen*

couth *adjective*
• "COOTH"
• cultured; well-mannered.
• [back-formation as antonym of UNCOUTH]

couture *noun*
- "coo CHOOR" or "coo TOOR" or "coo TYOOR"
- the design and manufacture of fashionable clothes.
- [French, = sewing, dressmaking, from *coudre* sew, from popular Latin *cosere*, from classical Latin *consuere*, from *suere* sew]

couturier *noun*
- "coo TOORY ay"
- a person who designs and oversees the making of high-fashion clothes.
- [French, as COUTURE]

couturière *noun*
- "coo toory AIR"
- a woman who designs and oversees the making of high-fashion clothes.
- [French, as COUTURE]

couvade *noun*
- "coo VOD"
- a custom in some cultures by which a father appears to undergo labour and childbirth when his child is being born.
- [French from *couver* hatch, from Latin *cubare* lie down]

couverture *noun*
- "coover TYOOR"
- chocolate for covering candies, cakes, etc.
- [French, = covering, from *couvrir* cover, from Latin *cooperire*, completely cover]

covalent *adjective*
- "co VALE 'nt"
- relating to, designating, or characterized by chemical bonds.
- [*co-*, originally a form of Latin *com-*, *cum* with + VALENCE]
- **covalence** *noun*
- **covalency** *noun*
- **covalently** *adverb*

coven *noun*
- "CUV'n"
- an assembly of witches.
- [var. of *covent*; see COVENANT]

covenant *noun*
- "CUVVA n'nt"
- an agreement; a contract.
- [Old French, present participle of *co(n)venir*, formed as CONVENE]
- **covenantal** *adjective*

covenanted *adjective*
- "CUVVA n'nt id"
- bound by a covenant.
- [as COVENANT]

coverlet *noun*
- "CUVVER lit"
- a bedspread.
- [Anglo-French *covrelet*, *-lit* from Old French *covrir* cover + *lit* bed]

covert *adjective*
- "CO vurt" or "co VURT" or "CUVVERT"
- secret or disguised.
- [Old French *covert* past participle of *covrir* cover, from Latin *cooperire* (*com-* with, *operire* cover)]
- **covertly** *adverb*

covet *verb*
- "CUVVIT"
- desire wrongfully or inordinately, esp. something belonging to another person.
- [Old French *coveitier* from Latin *cupiditas* (see CUPIDITY)]
- **covetable** *adjective*
- **coveted** *adjective*
- **covetous** *adjective*
- **covetously** *adverb*
- **covetousness** *noun*

covey *noun*
- "CUVVY"
- a brood of game birds, as partridges, ptarmigan, etc.
- [Old French *covee* from Romanic from Latin *cubare* lie]

cowabunga *interjection*
- "cow a BUNGA"
- expressing delight or satisfaction, or as a call to action.
- [prob. fanciful]

cowage *noun*
ALSO SPELLED: **cowhage**
- "COW idge"
- a climbing plant, *Mucuna pruritum*, having hairy pods which cause stinging and itching.
- [Hindi *kawāñch*]

cowardice *noun*
- "COW ur diss"
- lack of courage.
- [Old French *cuard*, *couard*, ultimately from Latin *cauda* tail]

Cowichan *noun*
- "COW itch 'n"
- a member of a Coast Salish Aboriginal people living on SE Vancouver Island.
- [*Kawutsun*, the name of a rock]

cowrie *noun*
ALSO SPELLED: **cowry**
- "COW ree"
- any gastropod mollusc of the family Cypraeidae, having a smooth glossy and usu. brightly coloured shell.
- [Urdu & Hindi *kauṛī*]

HOMOPHONES: *kauri*

coxa *noun*
- "COX uh"
- the hip bone or hip joint.
- [Latin]
- **coxal** *adjective*

coxcomb *noun*
- "COX coam"

• an ostentatiously conceited man; a dandy or fop.
• [= *cock's comb*, originally (a cap worn by) a jester]
• **coxcombry** *noun*
HOMOPHONES: *cockscomb*

Coxsackie *noun*
• "cock SACKY"
• any of a group of enteroviruses which cause various respiratory, neurological, and muscular diseases in humans.
• [named after *Coxsackie*, New York, where the first cases were diagnosed]

coxswain *noun*
• "COX'n" or "COX swane"
• a person who steers, esp. in a rowboat.
• [Middle English from *cock* small boat (from Old French *coque*, based on Latin *caudex, codex* block of wood) + SWAIN: compare BOATSWAIN]
• **coxswainship** *noun*

coyau *noun*
• "CAW yo"
• *Cdn* (*Que.*) a steep roof design having wing-like gables to channel runoff snow and ice; a bellcast roof.
• [French from Old French *coe* from Latin *cauda* tail]

coyote *noun*
• "kye OH tee" or "KYE ote" or "KYE oot"
• a wolflike wild dog, *Canis latrans*, native to N America, noted for its cunning.
• [Latin American Spanish from Aztec *coyotl*]

coypu *noun*
• "COY poo"
• an aquatic beaver-like rodent, *Myocastor coypus*, native to S America and kept in captivity for its fur.
• [Araucanian]

cozen *verb*
• "CUZZ'n"
• cheat, deceive, trick.
• [16th-c. cant, perhaps related to COUSIN]
• **cozenage** *noun*
HOMOPHONES: *cousin*

cracknel *noun*
• "CRACK n'll"
• a light crisp cracker.
• [Middle English from French *craquelin* from Middle Dutch *krākelinc* from *krāken* crack]

crake *noun*
• "CRAKE"
• any bird of the family Rallidae, often inhabiting marshes, esp. a corncrake.
• [Old Norse *kráka* (imitative)]

crampon *noun*
• "CRAM pon"
• a spiked iron plate fixed to a boot for walking on ice, climbing, etc.
• [French from Middle Dutch, Middle Low German *krampe*, Old High German *krampfo* from adjective meaning 'bent']

craniate *adjective*
• "CRAY nee ate"
• having a skull.
• [modern Latin *craniatus* from CRANIUM]

craniology *noun*
• "cray nee OLLA jee"
• the scientific study of the shape and size of the human skull.
• [as CRANIUM + Greek *logos* word]
• **craniological** *adjective*
• **craniologist** *noun*

craniometry *noun*
• "cray nee OMMA tree"
• the scientific measurement of skulls for study and comparison (e.g. in anthropology).
• [as CRANIUM + Greek *metron* measure]
• **craniometric** *adjective* "cray nee a METRIC"

craniosacral *adjective*
• "cray nee oh SAKE rull"
• designating a system of alternative medicine intended to relieve pain and tension by gentle manipulations of the skull regarded as harmonizing with a natural rhythm in the central nervous system.
• [as CRANIUM + SACRUM]

craniotomy *noun*
• "cray nee OTTA mee"
• surgical removal of a portion of the skull.
• [as CRANIUM + Greek *-tomia* cutting, from *temnō* cut]

cranium *noun*
• "CRAY nee um"
• the skull of a vertebrate.
• [medieval Latin from Greek *kranion* skull]
• **cranial** *adjective*

crankbait *noun*
• "CRANK bate"
• a plug type fishing lure which dives beneath the surface when retrieved.
• ['crank' + BAIT]

crannog *noun*
• "CRAN ug"
• an ancient lake-dwelling in Scotland or Ireland.
• [Irish from *crann* tree, beam]

crappie *noun*
• "CRAPPY"
• a N American freshwater sunfish of the genus *Pomoxis*.
• [Canadian French *crapet*]
HOMOPHONES: *crappy*

crapulous *adjective*
• "CRAP yoo luss"
• given to indulging in alcohol.
• [Late Latin *crapulentus* very drunk, from Latin *crapula* inebriation, from Greek *kraipalē* drunken headache]

- **crapulence** *noun*
- **crapulent** *adjective*

craquelure *noun*
- "CRACKA lure"
- a network of fine cracks in a painting caused by the shrinkage of its pigment or varnish over time.
- [French]

craton *noun*
- "CRAY tawn"
- a large stable block of the earth's crust.
- [alteration of *kratogen* from Greek *kratus* strength + GENESIS]
- **cratonic** *adjective*

cravat *noun*
- "cruh VAT"
- a scarf worn inside an open-necked shirt, esp. by men.
- [French *cravate* from German *Krawat*, *Kroat* from Serbo-Croatian *Hrvat* Croat]
- **cravatted** *adjective*

craven *adjective*
- "CRAY v'n"
- cowardly, obsequious.
- [Middle English *cravand* etc. perhaps from Old French *cravanté* defeated, past participle of *cravanter*, ultimately from Latin *crepare* burst]
- **cravenly** *adverb*
- **cravenness** *noun*

creatine *noun*
- "CREEA teen"
- a product of protein metabolism found in the muscles of vertebrates.
- [Greek *kreas* meat]

crèche *noun*
- "CRESH" or "CRAYSH"
- a nativity scene.
- [French, from Old French *creche* manger, crib, from Germanic]

credal *adjective*
ALSO SPELLED: **creedal**
- "CREED'll"
- pertaining to a creed or set of beliefs.
- [as CREDO]

credence *noun*
- "CREE dince"
- belief.
- [Old French from medieval Latin *credentia* from *credere* believe]

credential *noun*
- "cruh DEN sh'll"
- evidence of a person's achievements or trustworthiness, usu. in the form of certificates, references, etc.
- [medieval Latin *credentialis* (as CREDENCE)]
- **credentialed** *adjective*
- **credentialing** *noun*

credenza *noun*
- "cruh DENZA"
- a sideboard or buffet.
- [Italian from medieval Latin (as CREDENCE)]

credible *adjective*
- "CREDDA bull"
- (of a person or statement) believable or worthy of belief.
- [Latin *credibilis* from *credere* believe]
- **credibility** *noun*
- **credibly** *adverb*

creditable *adjective*
- "CREDDIT a bull"
- bringing credit or honour.
- [French *crédit* credit, from Italian *credito* or Latin *creditum* from *credere credit-* believe, trust]
- **creditability** *noun*
- **creditably** *adverb*

Créditiste *noun*
- "creddy TEEST"
- *Cdn* a member or supporter of the Quebec wing of the Social Credit Party.
- [French]

creditor *noun*
- "CREDDIT ur"
- a person to whom a debt is owing.
- [as CREDITABLE]

credo *noun*
- "CREE doe" or "CRAY doe"
- a set of principles held by a specified group, esp. as a philosophy.
- [Latin, = I believe]

credulous *adjective*
- "CRED yoo luss"
- too ready to believe; gullible.
- [Latin *credulus* from *credere* believe]
- **credulity** *noun* "cred YOOLA teedo"
- **credulously** *adverb*
- **credulousness** *noun*

creel *noun*
- "CREEL"
- a large wicker basket for fish.
- [Middle English, originally Scots: ultimate origin unknown]

cremate *verb*
- "CREE mate" or "cree MATE"
- burn (a corpse) to ashes, esp. after a funeral.
- [Latin *cremare* burn]
- **cremation** *noun*
- **cremator** *noun*

crematorium *noun*
- "creema TORY um"
- a building in which corpses are cremated.
- [modern Latin from *cremare* burn]

crematory *adjective*
- "CREEMA tory"
- of or relating to cremation.
- [as CREMATORIUM]

cremini *noun*
- "cruh MEENY"

• a brown variety of the common mushroom eaten before the cap has opened and fully matured.
• [Italian]

crenate *adjective*
• "CREE nate"
• having a notched edge or rounded teeth.
• [modern Latin *crenatus* from popular Latin *crena* notch]
• **crenation** *noun*

crenel *noun*
• "CREN'll"
• an indentation or gap in the parapet of a tower, castle, etc., originally for shooting through etc.
• [Old French *crenel*, ultimately from popular Latin *crena* notch]
• **crenellated** *adjective* (also **crenelated**)
• **crenellation** *noun* (also **crenelation**)

Creole *noun*
• "CREE ole"
• a descendant of European (esp. Spanish) settlers in the W Indies or Central or South America.
• [French *créole*, *criole* from Spanish *criollo*, prob. from Portuguese *crioulo* native, from *criar* breed, from Latin *creare* create]

creolize *verb*
ALSO SPELLED: esp. *Brit.* **-ise**
• "CREE ole ize"
• create a language from the contact of a European language (esp. English, French, or Portuguese) with another (esp. African) language.
• [as CREOLE]
• **creolization** *noun* (also esp. *Brit.* **-isation**)

creosote *noun*
• "CREEA sote"
• a dark brown oil distilled from coal tar, used as a wood preservative.
• [German *Kreosote* from Greek *kreas* flesh + *sōtēr* preserver, with reference to its antiseptic properties]
• **creosoted** *adjective*

crepe *noun*
• "CRAPE" or "CREP"
• a thin pancake, usu. with a savoury or sweet filling.
• [French from Old French *crespe* curled, from Latin *crispus*]
HOMOPHONES: *crape*

crêperie *noun*
• "CRAPE a ree"
• a restaurant serving crepes.
• [French]

crepey *noun*
• "CRAY pee"
• having a wrinkled surface.
• [as CREPE]
• **crepiness** *noun*

crepitate *verb*
• "CREPPA tate"
• make a crackling sound.
• [Latin *crepitare* frequentative of *crepare* creak]
• **crepitant** *adjective*
• **crepitation** *noun*

crepitus *noun*
• "CREPPIT us"
• a grating noise from the ends of a fractured bone rubbing together.
• [Latin from *crepare* rattle]

crepuscular *adjective*
• "cruh PUS kyuh lur"
• of twilight.
• [Latin *crepusculum* twilight]

crescendo *noun*
• "cresh ENDO"
• a passage gradually increasing in loudness.
• [Italian, participle of *crescere* grow (as CRESCENT)]

crescent *noun*
• "CRESS'nt"
• the curved sickle shape of the waxing or waning moon.
• [Old French *creissant*, from Latin *crescere* grow]
• **crescentic** *adjective* "cress ENTIC"

cresol *noun*
• "CREE sawl"
• any of three isomeric phenols present in creosote and used as disinfectants.
• [as CREOSOTE]

cresset *noun*
• "CRESSIT"
• a metal container for oil, coal, etc., lighted and usu. mounted on a pole for illumination.
• [Old French *cresset* from *craisse* = *graisse* grease, ultimately from Latin *crassus* fat]

cretaceous *adjective*
• "cruh TAY sh'ss"
• of the nature of chalk.
• [Latin *cretaceus* from *creta* chalk + adjective suffix *-aceus* of the nature of]

Cretan *noun*
• "CREET'n"
• a native or inhabitant of the Greek island of Crete.
HOMOPHONES: *cretin*

cretin *noun*
• "CRET'n" or "CREET'n"
• a person who is deformed and mentally retarded as the result of a thyroid deficiency.
• [French *crétin* from Swiss French *creitin*, *crestin* from Latin *Christianus* Christian]
• **cretinism** *noun*
• **cretinize** *verb* (also esp. *Brit.* **-ise**)
• **cretinous** *adjective*
HOMOPHONES: *Cretan*

cretonne *noun*
• "cruh TAWN"
• a heavy cotton fabric with a usu. floral

pattern printed on one or both sides, used for drapery.
• [French, from *Creton* in Normandy]

cretons *plural noun*
• "cruh TÕH" (with a nasal *OH*)
• *Cdn (Que.)* a spread of shredded pork cooked with onions in pork fat.
• [Canadian French, probably from Middle Dutch *kerte* cut]

crevasse *noun*
• "cruh VASS"
• a deep open crack, esp. in a glacier.
• [French from Old French *crevace*: see CREVICE]

crevice *noun*
• "CREV iss"
• a narrow opening or fissure, esp. in a rock or building etc.
• [Old French *crevace* from *crever* burst, from Latin *crepare*]

crewel *noun*
• "CROO 'll"
• a thin worsted yarn used for tapestry and embroidery.
• [Middle English *crule*, of unknown origin]
HOMOPHONES: *cruel*

cribbage *noun*
• "CRIB idge"
• a card game for two, three, or four players, in which the dealer may score from the cards in the crib , esp. using pegs in a board for keeping score.
• [17th c.: origin unknown]

cribriform *adjective*
• "CRIB ruh form"
• having numerous small holes.
• [Latin *cribrum* sieve + 'form']

cricoid *adjective*
• "CRY coid"
• ring-shaped.
• [modern Latin *cricoides* from Greek *krikoeidēs* from *krikos* ring]

Crimean *adjective*
• "cry MEE 'n"
• of or relating to the Crimea, a peninsula in S Ukraine, in the Black Sea.

criminal *noun*
• "CRIM 'n 'll"
• a person who has committed a crime or crimes.
• [Old French from Latin *crimen -minis* judgment, offence]
• **criminalistic** *adjective*
• **criminality** *noun*
• **criminally** *adverb*

criminalize *verb*
ALSO SPELLED: esp. *Brit.* **-ise**
• "CRIMMIN'll ize"
• turn (an activity) into a criminal offence by making it illegal.
• [as CRIMINAL]
• **criminalization** *noun* (also esp. *Brit.* **-isation**)

criminology *noun*
• "crim 'n OLLA jee"
• the scientific study of crime.
• [as CRIMINAL + Greek *logos* word]
• **criminological** *adjective*
• **criminologist** *noun*

crimson *adjective*
• "CRIM s'n"
• of a rich deep red inclining to purple.
• [Middle English *cremesin*, *crimesin*, ultimately from Arabic *ķirmizī* KERMES]

crinoid *noun*
• "CRIN oid"
• any echinoderm of the class Crinoidea, usu. sedentary with feathery arms, e.g. sea lilies and feather stars.
• [Greek *krinoeidēs* from *krinon* lily]
• **crinoidal** *adjective*

crinoline *noun*
• "CRINNA lin"
• a stiffened or hooped petticoat worn to make a skirt stand out.
• [French from Latin *crinis* hair + *linum* thread]
• **crinolined** *adjective*

crisis *noun*
• "CRICE iss"
• a time of danger or great difficulty.
• [Latin from Greek *krisis* decision, from *krinō* decide]

Crispin *noun*
• "CRISP'n"
• a large yellow or greenish-yellow cooking and eating apple.
• ['crisp' after the English personal name *Crispin*]

crista *noun*
• "CRISSTA"
• a ridge or crest.
• [Latin]
• **cristate** *adjective*

cristobalite *noun*
• "criss TOE buh lite"
• a principal form of silica, occurring as opal.
• [German *Cristobalit* from Cerro San *Cristóbal* in Mexico]

criterion *noun*
• "cry TEERY 'n"
• a principle or standard that a thing is judged by.
• [Greek *kritērion* means of judging]
• **criterial** *adjective*

critic *noun*
• "CRITTIC"
• a person who censures.
• [Latin *criticus* from Greek *kritikos* from *kritēs* judge, from *krinō* judge, decide]

critical *adjective*
• "CRITTA k'll"
• making or involving adverse or censorious comments or judgments.
• [Latin *criticus*: see CRITIC]
• **critically** *adverb*
• **criticalness** *noun*

criticality *adjective*
• "critta CALA tee"
• (of a nuclear reactor) the state of maintaining a self-sustaining chain reaction.
• [as CRITIC]

criticism *noun*
• "CRITTA sizm"
• finding fault; censure.
• [as CRITIC]
• **criticizable** *adjective* (also esp. *Brit.* **-isable**)
• **criticize** *verb* (also esp. *Brit.* **-ise**)
• **criticizer** *noun* (also esp. *Brit.* **-iser**)

critique *noun*
• "crit EEK"
• a critical essay or analysis; an instance or the process of formal criticism.
• [French from Greek *kritikē tekhnē* critical art, as CRITICISM]

Croatian *noun*
• "crow AY sh'n"
• a native or inhabitant of Croatia in the NW Balkan peninsula.

crochet *noun*
• "crow SHAY"
• a handicraft in which yarn is made up into a patterned fabric by means of a small slender hooked rod.
• [French, diminutive of *croc* hook]
• **crocheter** *noun* "crow SHAY ur"

crocidolite *noun*
• "crow SIDDA lite"
• a fibrous blue or green silicate of iron and sodium; blue asbestos.
• [Greek *krokis -idos* nap of cloth]

crocodile *noun*
• "CROCKA dile"
• any of a group of large tropical and subtropical amphibious reptiles with thick scaly skin, long tail, and long jaws (sometimes treated as a family, Crocodylidae) related to alligators.
• [Middle English from Old French *cocodrille* from medieval Latin *cocodrillus* from Latin *crocodilus* from Greek *krokodilos* from *krokē* pebble + *drilos* worm]

crocodilian *noun*
• "crocka DILL y'n"
• a reptile of the group including crocodiles and alligators, esp. one of the order Crocodylia, which also includes the caimans, the gharials, and numerous extinct animals, all large lizard-like semi-aquatic carnivores with a long powerful tail and jaws, short legs, and a covering of horny and bony plates.
• [as CROCODILE]

crocus *noun*
• "CROKE us"
• any dwarf plant of the genus *Crocus*, growing from a corm and having brilliant usu. yellow or purple flowers.
• [Middle English, = saffron, from Latin from Greek *krokos* crocus, of Semitic origin]

croissant *noun*
• "crwah SÃH" (with a nasal *AH*)
• a rich, flaky, crescent-shaped bread roll.
• [French, formed as CRESCENT]

crokinole *noun*
• "CROKE a nole"
• *Cdn* a game in which wooden discs are flicked across a round wooden board towards its centre.
• [French *croquignole* a flip, flick]

cromlech *noun*
• "CROM leck"
• a dolmen; a megalithic tomb.
• [Welsh from *crom* feminine of *crwm* bent + *llech* flat stone]

cronyism *noun*
• "CROW nee izm"
• the appointment of friends to political posts without due regard to their qualifications; patronage.
• [17th-c. *chrony*, (university slang) from Greek *khronios* long-standing, from *khronos* time]

croquet *noun*
• "crow CAY" or "CROW cay"
• a game played on a lawn, in which mallets are used to drive wooden balls through a series of hoops.
• [perhaps dialect form of French CROCHET hook]

croquette *noun*
• "crow KET"
• a fried, breaded roll or ball of mashed potato or minced meat etc.
• [French from *croquer* crunch]

crosse *noun*
• "CROSS"
• (in women's field lacrosse) the stick.
• [Canadian French from Old French *croce*, *croc* hook]
HOMOPHONES: *cross*

crostata *noun*
• "cross TATTA"
• an open-faced fruit tart with a lattice top.
• [Italian, = pie]

crostini *plural noun*
• "cross TEENY"
• small pieces of toasted bread topped with vegetables etc., served as an appetizer.
• [Italian, pl. of *crostino* little crust]

crotchet *noun*
• "CROTCH it"
• a quarter note.
• [Old French *crochet* diminutive of *croc* hook]

crotchety *adjective*
• "CROTCH a tee"
• peevish, irritable.
• [from a sense of CROTCHET 'an unfounded or perverse belief']
• **crotchetiness** *noun*

croton *noun*
• "CROTE 'n"
• any plant of the genus *Croton*, producing a capsule-like fruit.
• [modern Latin from Greek *krotōn* sheep tick, croton (from the shape of its seeds)]

croup *noun*
• "CROOP"
• an inflammation of the larynx and trachea in children, with a hard cough and difficulty in breathing.
• [*croup* to croak (imitative)]
• **croupy** *adjective*

croupier *noun*
• "CROOPY ur" or "CROOPY ay"
• the person in charge of a gaming table, raking in and paying out money etc.
• [French, originally = rider on the *croupe*, hindquarters of a horse]

crouton *noun*
• "CROO tawn"
• a small cube of fried or toasted bread used as a garnish for soups, salads, etc.
• [French from *croûte* crust, from Latin *crusta* rind, shell]

crozier *noun*
ALSO SPELLED: **crosier**
• "CROW zhur" or "CROZEY ur"
• a hooked staff carried by a bishop as a symbol of pastoral office.
• [originally = bearer of a crook, from Old French *crocier* & Old French *croisier* from *crois* cross]

cru *noun*
• "CROO"
• a French vineyard or wine-producing region.
• [French from *crû* grown]
HOMOPHONES: *crew*, *Kru*

crucial *adjective*
• "CROO sh'll"
• decisive, critical.
• [French from Latin *crux crucis* cross]
• **crucially** *adverb*

cruciate *adjective*
• "CROOSH ut"
• designating either of a pair of ligaments in the knee which cross each other and connect the femur and the tibia.
• [Latin *cruciatus* from *crux crucis* cross]

crucible *noun*
• "CROOSSA bull"
• a container in which metals or other materials are heated.
• [medieval Latin *crucibulum* night lamp, crucible (perhaps originally a lamp hanging in front of a crucifix), from Latin *crux crucis* cross]

crucifer *noun*
• "CROOSSA fur"
• a cruciferous plant.
• [as CRUCIFEROUS]

cruciferous *adjective*
• "croo SIFFER us"
• of the family Cruciferae, having flowers with four petals arranged in a cross, e.g. cabbage, mustard, etc.
• [modern Latin *Cruciferae* from Latin *crux, cruc-* cross + *-fer* bearing]

crucifix *noun*
• "CROOSSA fix"
• a model or image of a cross with a figure of Christ on it.
• [Old French from Church Latin *crucifixus* from Latin *cruci fixus* fixed to a cross]

cruciform *adjective*
• "CROOSSA form"
• cross-shaped (esp. of a church with transepts).
• [Latin *crux crucis* cross + 'form']

crucify *verb*
• "CROOSSA fie"
• put to death by fastening to a cross.
• [Old French *crucifier* from Late Latin *crucifigere* (as CRUCIFIX)]
• **crucifier** *noun*
• **crucifixion** *noun* "croossa FICK sh'n"

crudités *plural noun*
• "croody TAY"
• an hors d'oeuvre of mixed raw vegetables often served with a sauce into which they are dipped.
• [French pl. of *crudité* lit. rawness, from Latin *crudus* raw]

cruet *noun*
• "CROO it"
• a small container for salt, pepper, oil, or vinegar for use at table.
• [Old French *crue* pot, from Old Saxon *krūka*]

cruller *noun*
• "CRULLER" (rhymes with *DULLER*, *RULER*, or *FULLER*)
• a small, sweet cake made of a rich dough twisted or curled and deep-fried.
• [Dutch *kruller*, from *krullen* curl]
HOMOPHONES: *crueller*

crumhorn *noun*
• "CRUM horn"
• a medieval wind instrument with a double reed and a curved end.
• [German from *krumm* crooked + *Horn* horn]

crumpet *noun*
• "CRUM pit"
• a small, round, sponge-like yeast cake

resembling an English muffin, eaten toasted and buttered.
• [17th c.: origin uncertain]

crupper *noun*
• “CRUPPER”
• a strap buckled to the back of a saddle and looped under the horse’s tail to hold the harness back.
• [Old French *cropiere* (compare CROUPIER)]

crural *adjective*
• “CROOR’ll”
• of or pertaining to the leg.
• [French *crural* or Latin *cruralis* from *crus cruris* leg]

crusade *noun*
• “croo SADE”
• any of several medieval military expeditions made by Europeans to recover the Holy Land from the Muslims.
• [earlier *croisade* (French from *croix* cross) or *crusado* (Spanish from *cruz* cross)]
• **crusader** *noun*

crustacean *noun*
• “cruh STAY sh’n”
• any arthropod of the class Crustacea, having a hard shell and usu. aquatic, e.g. the crab, lobster, and shrimp.
• [modern Latin *crustaceus* from *crusta* rind, shell]
• **crustaceology** *noun* “cruh stay shee OLLA jee”
• **crustaceous** *adjective*

crustose *adjective*
• “cruss TOSE” (“TOSE” rhymes with *GROSS*)
• (esp. of a lichen) forming or resembling a crust.
• [Latin *crustosus* from *crusta* crust]

crux *noun*
• “CRUCKS”
• the decisive point at issue.
• [Latin, = cross]

cryobiology *noun*
• “cry oh by OLLA jee”
• the branch of biology dealing with the effects of very low temperatures on organisms, tissues, etc.
• [prefix *cryo-* extreme cold, from Greek *kruos* frost + BIOLOGY]
• **cryobiological** *adjective*
• **cryobiologist** *noun*

cryogen *noun*
• “CRY oh j’n”
• a substance used to produce very low temperatures.
• [prefix *cryo-* extreme cold, from Greek *kruos* frost + GENESIS]

cryogenics *noun*
• “cry oh JENNIX”
• the branch of physics dealing with the production and effects of very low temperatures.
• [prefix *cryo-* extreme cold, from Greek *kruos* frost + GENESIS]
• **cryogenic** *adjective*
• **cryogenically** *adverb*

cryolite *noun*
• “CRY oh lite”
• a lustrous mineral of sodium-aluminum fluoride, used in the manufacture of aluminum.
• [prefix *cryo-* extreme cold, from Greek *kruos* frost + Greek *lithos* stone]

cryonics *noun*
• “cry ONNIX”
• the practice or technique of deep-freezing human corpses in the hope of possible revival in the future.
• [contraction of CRYOGENICS]
• **cryonic** *adjective*
• **cryonicist** *noun* “cry ONNA sist”

cryopreservation *noun*
• “cry oh prezzer VAY sh’n”
• the freezing of living tissue, organs, sperm, etc. for storage and subsequent use.
• [prefix *cryo-* extreme cold, from Greek *kruos* frost + PRESERVATION]
• **cryopreserved** *adjective*

cryoprotectant *noun*
• “cry oh pro TECK t’nt”
• a substance that prevents the freezing of tissues, or prevents damage to cells etc. during freezing.
• [prefix *cryo-* extreme cold, from Greek *kruos* frost + PROTECTANT]

cryostat *noun*
• “CRY oh stat”
• an apparatus for maintaining chemical or organic samples at a very low steady temperature.
• [prefix *cryo-* extreme cold, from Greek *kruos* frost + Greek *statos* stationary]

cryosurgery *noun*
• “cry oh SUR jur ee”
• surgery using the local application of intense cold for anaesthesia or therapy.
• [prefix *cryo-* extreme cold, from Greek *kruos* frost + SURGERY]

crypt *noun*
• “CRIPT”
• an underground room or vault, esp. one beneath a church, used usu. as a burial place.
• [Latin *crypta* from Greek *kruptē* from *kruptos* hidden]

cryptanalysis *noun*
• “cripta NALA sis”
• the art or process of deciphering codes and ciphers by analysis.
• [CRYPT + ANALYSIS]
• **cryptanalyst** *noun* “cript ANNA list”

• **cryptanalytic** *adjective* "cript anna LITTIC"
• **cryptanalytical** *adjective*

cryptic *adjective*
• "CRIPTIC"
• obscure in meaning.
• [Late Latin *crypticus* from Greek *kruptikos* (as CRYPT)]
• **cryptically** *adverb*

cryptococcosis *noun*
• "cripto cock OH sis"
• infestation with a yeast-like fungus, *Cryptococcus neoformans*, usu. attacking the lungs and central nervous system.
• [modern Latin *cryptococcus*]
• **cryptococcal** *adjective*

cryptocrystalline *adjective*
• "cripto CRISSTA line" or "cripto CRISSTA leen"
• having symmetrically arranged constituent particles visible only when magnified.
• [as CRYPT + CRYSTALLINE]

cryptogam *noun*
• "CRIPTO gam"
• a plant that has no true flowers or seeds, e.g. ferns, mosses, algae, and fungi.
• [French *cryptogame* from modern Latin *cryptogamae* (*plantae*) formed as CRYPT + Greek *gamos* marriage]
• **cryptogamic** *adjective*
• **cryptogamous** *adjective* "crip TOGGA muss"

cryptogram *noun*
• "CRIPTO gram"
• a text written in code or cipher.
• [as CRYPT + Greek *gramma* thing written]
• **cryptogrammic** *adjective*

cryptography *noun*
• "crip TOGGRA fee"
• the art of writing or solving codes and ciphers.
• [as CRYPT + Greek *graphein* writing]
• **cryptographer** *noun*
• **cryptographic** *adjective*
• **cryptographically** *adverb*

cryptology *noun*
• "crip TOLLA jee"
• = CRYPTOGRAPHY.
• [as CRYPT + Greek *logos* word]
• **cryptological** *adjective*
• **cryptologist** *noun*

cryptomeria *noun*
• "cripto MEERY uh"
• a tall evergreen tree, *Cryptomeria japonica*, native to China and Japan, with long curved spirally arranged leaves and short cones.
• [as CRYPT + Greek *meros* part (because the seeds are enclosed by scales)]

cryptosporidiosis *noun*
• "cripto spory dee OH sis"
• an intestinal disease caused by infection with cryptosporidium, causing diarrhea and vomiting.
• [as CRYPTOSPORIDIUM]

cryptosporidium *noun*
• "cripto spore IDDY um"
• a parasitic coccidian protozoan found in the intestinal tract of many vertebrates, where it sometimes causes disease.
• [as CRYPT + modern Latin *sporidium* small spore]

cryptozoology *noun*
• "cripto zoo OLLA jee" or "cripto zo OLLA jee"
• the search for and study of animals whose existence or survival is disputed or unsubstantiated, such as the Loch Ness monster and the sasquatch.
• [as CRYPT + ZOOLOGY]
• **cryptozoological** *adjective*
• **cryptozoologist** *noun*

crystal *noun*
• "CRISS t'll"
• a piece of a homogeneous solid substance having a natural geometrically regular form with symmetrically arranged plane faces.
• [Old French *cristal* from Latin *crystallum* from Greek *krustallos* ice, crystal]
• **crystalline** *adjective* "CRISSTA line" or "CRISSTA leen"
• **crystallinity** *noun* "crissta LINNA tee"

crystallite *noun*
• "CRISSTA lite"
• a small crystal.
• [as CRYSTAL + Greek *lithos* stone]

crystallize *verb*
ALSO SPELLED: esp. *Brit.* **-ise**
• "CRISSTA lize"
• form or cause to form crystals.
• [as CRYSTAL]
• **crystallizable** *adjective* (also esp. *Brit.* **-isable**)
• **crystallization** *noun* (also esp. *Brit.* **-isation**)

crystallography *noun*
• "crisst'll OGGRA fee"
• the science of crystal form and structure.
• [as CRYSTAL + Greek *graphein* writing]
• **crystallographer** *noun*
• **crystallographic** *adjective*

crystalloid *adjective*
• "CRISST'll oid"
• crystal-like.
• [as CRYSTAL]

ctenoid *adjective*
• "TEE noid"
• (of fish scales) characterized by tiny toothlike processes.
• [Greek *kteis ktenos* comb]

ctenophore *noun*
• "TEENA for" or "TENNA for"
• any animal of the phylum Ctenophora,

comprising pelagic marine creatures resembling jellyfish and moving by means of stiff cilia borne on comb-like plates.
• [modern Latin *ctenophorus* (as CTENOID + Greek *-phoros -phoron* bearing, bearer, from *pherō* bear)]

cubeb *noun*
• "KYOO beb"
• a climbing plant, *Piper cubeba*, bearing pungent berries.
• [Old French *cubebe* ultimately from Arabic *kobāba, kubāba*]

cubical *adjective*
• "KYOOBA k'll"
• cube-shaped.
• [from 'cube' from French *cube* or Latin *cubus* from Greek *kubos*]
• **cubically** *adverb*
HOMOPHONES: *cubicle*

cubicle *noun*
• "KYOOBA k'll"
• a small partitioned space, esp. screened for privacy.
• [originally a sleeping compartment, from Latin *cubiculum* from *cubare* lie down]
HOMOPHONES: *cubical*

cubiform *adjective*
• "CUBE a form"
• cube-shaped.
• [as CUBICAL]

cubism *noun*
• "CUBE izm"
• a style and movement in art, esp. painting, in which objects are represented as an assemblage of geometrical forms.
• [as CUBICAL]
• **cubist** *noun*
• **cubistic** *adjective*

cubit *noun*
• "KYOOBIT"
• an ancient measure of length, approximately equal to the length of a forearm.
• [Latin *cubitum* elbow, cubit]

cubital *adjective*
• "KYOOBIT'll"
• of the forearm.
• [as CUBIT]

cuboid *adjective*
• "CUBE oid"
• cube-shaped; like a cube.
• [as CUBICAL]
• **cuboidal** *adjective*

cuckold *noun*
• "CUCK old"
• a man whose wife is unfaithful.
• [Middle English *cukeweld, cokewold*, from Old French *cucu* cuckoo, with reference to the cuckoo's habit of laying its eggs in other birds' nests]
• **cuckoldry** *noun*

cuckoo *noun*
• "COO coo" or "COOK oo"
• any of various birds of the family Cuculidae, e.g. the black-billed cuckoo *Coccyzus erythropthalmus* or yellow-billed cuckoo *C. americanus* of N America, with brown backs and white underparts, or the Eurasian grey or brown speckled bird, *Cuculus canorus*, which leaves its eggs in the nests of small birds and has a distinctive two-note call, the first hearing of which is regarded as a harbinger of spring.
• [Old French *cucu*, imitative]

cucurbit *noun*
• "kyoo CUR bit"
• any of various climbing or trailing plants of the family Cucurbitaceae bearing gourds, fleshy usu. large fruits with a hard skin.
• [Latin *cucurbita*]
• **cucurbitaceous** *adjective*

cudgel *noun*
• "CUDGE 'll"
• a short thick stick used as a weapon.
• [Old English *cycgel*, of unknown origin]

cuesta *noun*
• "KWESTA"
• a gentle slope, esp. one ending in a steep drop.
• [Spanish, = slope, from Latin *costa* side]

cuirass *noun*
• "kwuh RASS"
• a piece of armour consisting of breastplate and backplate fastened together.
• [Old French *cuirace*, ultimately from Late Latin *coriaceus* from *corium* leather]

cuirassier *noun*
• "kwih ruh SEER"
• a cavalry soldier wearing a cuirass.
• [French (as CUIRASS)]

cuisine *noun*
• "kwiz EEN"
• a style or method of cooking, esp. of a particular country or establishment.
• [French from Latin *coquina* from *coquere* to cook]

cuisse *noun*
• "KWISS"
• thigh armour.
• [Old French *cuisseaux* pl. of *cuissel* from Late Latin *coxale* from *coxa* hip]

culchie *noun*
ALSO SPELLED: **culshie**
• "CULCHEE"
• *derogatory* a country bumpkin.
• [perhaps alteration of *Kiltimagh*, a country town in County Mayo, Ireland]

Culdee *noun*
• "cull DEE"
• any of various Irish and Scottish monks in the 8th–12th c., who lived as hermits, usu. in

groups of thirteen on the analogy of Christ and his Apostles, until they and their Celtic Church were gradually brought under Roman Catholic rule.
• [from Irish *céile Dé* client of God]

culinary *adjective*
• "CULLA nerry" or "KYOOLA nerry"
• of or for cooking.
• [Latin *culinarius* from *culina* kitchen]
• **culinarily** *adverb*

cullet *noun*
• "CULLIT"
• recycled waste or broken glass used in glass-making.
• [var. of COLLET in sense 'portion of glass left on a blowing iron after removal of finished object']

culm *noun*
• "CULM"
• the stem of a plant, esp. of grasses.
• [Latin *culmus* stalk]

culminant *adjective*
• "CULMA n'nt"
• at or forming the top.
• [as CULMINATE]

culminate *verb*
• "CULMA nate"
• reach its highest or final point.
• [Late Latin *culminare culminat-* from *culmen* summit]
• **culmination** *noun*

culottes *plural noun*
• "coo LOTS" or "COO lots"
• a woman's garment that hangs like a skirt but has separate legs, like trousers; a divided skirt.
• [French, = knee breeches]

culpa *noun*
• "CULL puh" ("CULL" can rhyme either with *DULL* or with *PULL*)
• neglect resulting in damage; negligence.
• [Latin, = fault, blame]

culpable *adjective*
• "CULPA bull"
• deserving blame.
• [Latin *culpabilis* from *culpare* from *culpa* blame]
• **culpability** *noun*
• **culpably** *adverb*

culprit *noun*
• "CULL prit"
• a person accused of or guilty of an offence.
• [17th c.: originally in the formula *Culprit, how will you be tried?*, said by the Clerk of the Crown to a prisoner pleading Not Guilty: perhaps abbreviation of Anglo-French *Culpable: prest d'averrer* etc. (You are) guilty: (I am) ready to prove etc.]

cultigen *noun*
• "CULTA j'n"
• a plant species or variety known only in cultivation, esp. one with no known wild ancestor.
• [*culti*vated + GENESIS]

cultivar *noun*
• "CULTA var"
• a plant variety that has been produced in cultivation by selective breeding.
• [CULTIVATE + VARIETY]

cultivate *verb*
• "CULTA vate"
• prepare and use (soil etc.) for crops or gardening.
• [medieval Latin *cultivare* from *cultiva* (*terra*) arable (land) from *colere cult-* inhabit, till, worship]
• **cultivable** *adjective*
• **cultivated** *adjective*
• **cultivation** *noun*

cultivator *noun*
• "CULTA vater"
• a mechanical implement for breaking up the ground and uprooting weeds.
• [as CULTIVATE]

culture *noun*
• "CULL chur"
• the arts and other manifestations of human intellectual achievement regarded collectively.
• [French *culture* or Latin *cultura* (as CULTIVATE)]
• **cultural** *adjective*
• **culturally** *adverb*
• **cultured** *adjective*

cultus *noun*
• "CULT us"
• a system of religious worship; a cult.
• [Latin: see CULTIVATE]

culverin *noun*
• "CULVER in"
• a long cannon.
• [Old French *coulevrine* from *couleuvre* snake, ultimately from Latin *colubra*]

culvert *noun*
• "CULL vurt"
• an underground channel carrying water across a road etc.
• [18th c.: origin unknown]

cumber *verb*
• "CUMBER"
• hamper, hinder, inconvenience.
• [Middle English, prob. from ENCUMBER]

cumbersome *adjective*
• "CUMBER sum"
• inconvenient in size, weight, or shape; unwieldy.
• [as CUMBER]
• **cumbersomely** *adverb*
• **cumbersomeness** *noun*

cumbia *noun*
• "CUMBY uh"
• a form of dance music originating in Colombia.
• [Colombian Spanish, perhaps from Spanish *cumbé*, the name of a dance performed by blacks]

cumbrous *adjective*
• "CUMBRUSS"
• = CUMBERSOME.
• [as CUMBER]
• **cumbrously** *adverb*

cumin *noun*
• "CUMMIN" or "KYOO min"
• an umbelliferous plant, *Cuminum cyminum*, bearing aromatic seeds.
• [Old French from Latin *cuminum* from Greek *kuminon*, prob. of Semitic origin]

cummerbund *noun*
• "CUMMER bund"
• a wide, often horizontally pleated sash worn around the waist, esp. with a tuxedo.
• [Urdu & Persian *kamar-band* loin band]

cumulate *verb*
• "KYOO myoo late"
• accumulate, amass; combine.
• [Latin *cumulare* from *cumulus* heap]
• **cumulation** *noun*

cumulative *adjective*
• "KYOO myoo luh tiv"
• increasing or increased in amount, force, etc., by successive additions.
• [as CUMULATE]
• **cumulatively** *adverb*
• **cumulativeness** *noun*

cumulonimbus *noun*
• "kyoo myoo lo NIM buss"
• a cumulus cloud developed to a great height and producing rain or hail; a thundercloud.
• [as CUMULUS + NIMBUS]

cumulus *noun*
• "KYOO myoo luss"
• clouds formed in rounded masses heaped on each other above a flat base.
• [Latin, = heap]

cuneate *adjective*
• "KYOO nee ate"
• wedge-shaped.
• [Latin *cuneus* wedge]

cuneiform *adjective*
• "kyoo NAY a form" or "kyoo NEE a form"
• wedge-shaped.
• [French *cunéiforme* or modern Latin *cuneiformis* from Latin *cuneus* wedge]

cunit *noun*
• "KYOONIT"
• 100 cubic feet (2.832 cubic metres) of wood.
• [blend of 'cubic' and 'unit']

cupboard *noun*
• "CUBBERD"
• a recess or piece of furniture with a door and (usu.) shelves, in which things are stored.
• ['cup' + 'board']

cupel *noun*
• "KYOOP'll"
• a small flat porous vessel used in assaying gold or silver in the presence of lead.
• [French *coupelle* from Late Latin *cupella* diminutive of *cupa* tub]
• **cupellation** *noun*

cupidity *noun*
• "kyoo PIDDA tee"
• greed for gain; avarice.
• [Latin *cupiditas* from *cupidus* desirous]

cupola *noun*
• "KYOOPA luh"
• a rounded dome forming a roof or ceiling.
• [Italian from Late Latin *cupula* diminutive of *cupa* cask]
• **cupolaed** *adjective*

cuprammonium *noun*
• "kyoop ruh MOANY um" or "coop ruh MOANY um"
• a complex ion of divalent copper and ammonia, solutions of which dissolve cellulose.
• [Late Latin *cuprum* copper + AMMONIUM]

cupreous *adjective*
• "KYOOP ree us" or "COOP ree us"
• of or like copper.
• [Late Latin *cupreus* from *cuprum* copper]

cupric *adjective*
• "KYOOP rick" or "COOP rick"
• of copper, esp. divalent copper.
• [Late Latin *cuprum* copper]

cupriferous *adjective*
• "kyoo PRIFFER us"
• yielding copper.
• [Late Latin *cuprum* copper + *-fer* producing, from *ferre* bear]

cuprite *noun*
• "KYOOP rite" or "COOP rite"
• native cuprous oxide, a red mineral and major copper ore.
• [as CUPRIC]

cuprous *adjective*
• "KYOOP russ" or "COOP russ"
• of copper, esp. monovalent copper.
• [Late Latin *cuprum* copper]

cupule *noun*
• "KYOOP yool"
• a cup-shaped organ, receptacle, etc.
• [Late Latin *cupula* CUPOLA]

cur *noun*
• "CUR"
• a worthless or snappy dog.

• [Middle English, prob. originally in *cur-dog*, perhaps from Old Norse *kurr* grumbling]

curaçao *noun*
• "cure a SO"
• a liqueur of spirits flavoured with the peel of bitter oranges.
• [the island of *Curaçao* of the Netherlands Antilles, which produces these oranges]
HOMOPHONES: *curassow*

curacy *noun*
• "KYOORA a see"
• a curate's office or the tenure of it.
• [as CURATE]

curare *noun*
• "kyuh RAR ee" or "kuh RAR ee"
• a resinous bitter substance prepared from S American plants of the genera *Strychnos* and *Chondodendron*, paralyzing the motor nerves, formerly used to poison arrows and blowpipe darts by Aboriginals of S America, and as a muscle relaxant in surgery.
• [Carib]

curassow *noun*
• "cure a SO"
• any game bird of the family Cracidae, found in Central and S America.
• [anglicized from CURAÇAO]
HOMOPHONES: *curaçao*

curate *noun*
• "CURE it"
• a member of the clergy engaged as assistant to a parish priest.
• [medieval Latin *curatus* from Latin *cura* care]

curator *noun*
• "CURE ate ur"
• an employee of a museum, art gallery, etc., responsible for the collections.
• [late Middle English (denoting an ecclesiastical pastor) from Old French *curateur* or Latin *curator* (as CURATE)]
• **curatorial** *adjective*
• **curatorship** *noun*

curcuma *noun*
• "CUR kyoo muh"
• the spice turmeric.
• [medieval Latin or modern Latin from Arabic *kurkum* saffron, from Sanskrit *kuṅkuma*[m]]

curé *noun*
• "cure AY"
• a parish priest in Quebec, France, etc.
• [French from medieval Latin *curatus*: see CURATE]

curettage *noun*
• "cure ET idge" or "cure a TOZH"
• the use of or an operation involving the use of a curette.
• [French (as CURETTE)]

curette *noun*
• "cure ET"
• a surgeon's small scraping instrument.
• [French, from *curer* cleanse, from Latin *curare* take care of, from *cura* care]

curfew *noun*
• "CUR few"
• a regulation restricting or forbidding the public circulation of people, esp. requiring people to remain indoors between specified hours, usu. at night.
• [Middle English from Anglo-French *coeverfu*, Old French *cuevrefeu* from the stem of *couvrir* cover + *feu* fire]

Curia *noun*
• "CURE ee uh"
• the papal court; the government departments of the Vatican.
• [Latin: originally a division of an ancient Roman tribe, the senate house at Rome, a feudal court of justice]
• **Curial** *adjective*

curie *noun*
• "CURE ee"
• a unit of radioactivity, corresponding to 3.7×10^{10} disintegrations per second.
• [M. *Curie* (d.1934) & P. *Curie* (d.1906), French scientists]

curio *noun*
• "CURE ee oh"
• a rare or unusual object or person.
• [19th-c. abbreviation of CURIOSITY]

curiosa *plural noun*
• "cure ee OH suh"
• curiosities.
• [neuter pl. of Latin *curiosus*: see CURIOUS]

curiosity *noun*
• "cure ee OSSA tee"
• an eager desire to know; inquisitiveness.
• [as CURIOUS]

curious *adjective*
• "CURE ee us"
• eager to learn; inquisitive.
• [Old French *curios* from Latin *curiosus* careful, from *cura* care]
• **curiously** *adverb*
• **curiousness** *noun*

curium *noun*
• "CURE ee um"
• an artificially made transuranic radioactive metallic element, first produced by bombarding plutonium with helium ions.
• [M. *Curie* (d.1934) & P. *Curie* (d.1906), French scientists]

curlew *noun*
• "CUR loo"
• any wading bird of the genus *Numenius*, possessing a usu. long slender down-curved bill.
• [Old French *courlieu*, *courlis* originally imitative, but assimilated to *courliu* courier, from *courre* run + *lieu* place]

curlicue *noun*
- "CURLY kyoo"
- a decorative curl or twist.
- ['curly' + 'cue' (= pigtail)]

curmudgeon *noun*
- "cur MUDGE 'n"
- a bad-tempered person.
- [16th c.: origin unknown]
- **curmudgeonliness** *noun*
- **curmudgeonly** *adjective*

currach *noun*
ALSO SPELLED: **curragh**
- "CURRA"
- a coracle.
- [Irish: compare CORACLE]

currant *noun*
- "CUR 'nt"
- a dried fruit of a small seedless variety of grape grown in California and the Middle East and much used in cooking.
- [Middle English *raysons of coraunce* from Anglo-French, = grapes of Corinth (the original source)]

HOMOPHONES: *current*

currency *noun*
- "CUR 'n see"
- the money in general use in a country.
- [as CURRENT]

current *adjective*
- "CUR 'nt"
- belonging to the present time; happening now.
- [Old French *corant* from Latin *currere* run]
- **currently** *adverb*

HOMOPHONES: *currant*

curricle *noun*
- "CURRA k'll"
- a light open two-wheeled carriage drawn by two horses abreast.
- [Latin *curriculum*: see CURRICULUM]

curriculum *noun*
- "kuh RICK yuh lum"
- the subjects that are studied or prescribed for study in a school, school board, etc.
- [Latin, = course, race chariot, from *currere* run]
- **curricular** *adjective*

currier *noun*
- "CURRY ur"
- a person who dresses and colours tanned leather.
- [Old French *corier*, from Latin *coriarius* from *corium* leather]

HOMOPHONES: *courier*

curry *noun*
- "CURRY"
- a dish of meat, vegetables, etc., cooked in a highly spiced sauce, usu. served with rice.
- [Tamil]

cursillo *noun*
- "cur SEEYO"
- a short informal Christian spiritual retreat.
- [Spanish, = little course]

cursive *adjective*
- "CURSE iv"
- (of writing) done with joined characters.
- [medieval Latin (*scriptura*) *cursiva* from Latin *currere curs-* run]

cursor *noun*
- "CUR sur"
- a movable indicator on a computer screen identifying a particular position in the display, esp. the position that the program will operate on with the next keystroke.
- [Latin, = runner (as CURSIVE)]

HOMOPHONES: *curser*

cursorial *adjective*
- "cur SORRY 'll"
- having limbs adapted for running.
- [as CURSOR]

cursory *adjective*
- "CUR sur ee"
- hasty, hurried; superficial.
- [Latin *cursorius* of a runner (as CURSOR)]
- **cursorily** *adverb*
- **cursoriness** *noun*

curt *adjective*
- "CURT"
- noticeably or rudely brief.
- [Latin *curtus* cut short, abridged]
- **curtly** *adverb*
- **curtness** *noun*

curtail *verb*
- "cur TALE"
- cut short; reduce; terminate esp. prematurely.
- [obsolete *curtal* horse with docked tail, from French *courtault* from *court* short, from Latin *curtus*: assimilated to *tail*]
- **curtailment** *noun*

curtain *noun*
- "CURT'n"
- a piece of cloth etc. hung up as a screen, usu. movable sideways or upwards, esp. at a window or between the stage and auditorium of a theatre.
- [Old French *cortine* from Late Latin *cortina*, translation of Greek *aulaia* from *aulē* court]
- **curtained** *adjective*
- **curtainless** *adjective*

curtana *noun*
- "cur TONNA"
- an unpointed sword borne before English sovereigns at their coronation, as an emblem of mercy.
- [Anglo-Latin *curtana* (*spatha*) shortened (sword), from Old French *cortain*, from *cort* short, from Latin *curtus* cut short]

curtilage *noun*
• "CURTA lidge"
• a small court, yard, or piece of ground surrounding a house and forming one unit with it.
• [Old French *co(u)rtillage* from *co(u)rtil* small court, from *cort* court, ultimately from Latin *cohors -hortis* yard, retinue]

curtsy *noun*
ALSO SPELLED: **curtsey**
• "CURT see"
• a woman's or girl's formal greeting or salutation made by bending the knees with one foot in front of the other.
• [var. of COURTESY]

curule *adjective*
• "CURE ool"
• designating or relating to the authority exercised by the senior Roman magistrates, chiefly the consul and praetor, who were entitled to use the *sella curulis* ('curule seat' or seat of office).
• [Latin *curulis* from *currus* chariot (in which the chief magistrate was conveyed to the seat of office)]

curvaceous *adjective*
• "cur VAY sh'ss"
• (esp. of a woman) having a shapely figure with voluptuous breasts and hips.
• ['curve' + Latin adjective suffix *-aceus* of the nature of]

curvature *noun*
• "CURVA chur"
• the act or state of curving.
• [Old French from Latin *curvatura* from *curvus* bent]

curvifoliate *adjective*
• "curva FOLEY it"
• with the leaves bent back.
• [Latin *curvus* bent + FOLIATE]

curviform *adjective*
• "CURVA form"
• having a curved shape.
• [Latin *curvus* bent + 'form']

curvilinear *adjective*
• "curva LINNY ur"
• contained by or consisting of curved lines.
• [Latin *curvus* bent, after *rectilinear*]

cuscus *noun*
• "CUSS cuss"
• the aromatic fibrous root of an Indian grass, *Vetiveria zizanioides*, used for making fans etc.
• [Persian *kaškaš*]

cusec *noun*
• "KYOO seck"
• a unit of flow (esp. of water) equal to one cubic foot per second.
• [abbreviation]

cushion *noun*
• "COOSH'n" ("COOSH" rhymes with *BUSH*)
• a pad or bag of cloth etc. stuffed with a mass of soft material and used as a soft support for sitting etc.
• [Old French *co(i)ssin* from Gallo-Roman from Latin *culcita* mattress, cushion]
• **cushioned** *adjective*
• **cushioning** *noun*
• **cushiony** *adjective*

Cushitic *noun*
• "coosh ITTIC" ("COOSH" rhymes with *BUSH*)
• an Afro-Asiatic language family of NE Africa, including Somali, Galla, and other languages of Somalia and Ethiopia.
• [*Cush* an ancient country in the Nile valley]

cushy *adjective*
• "COOSHY" (rhymes with *BUSHY*)
• (of a job etc.) easy and pleasant.
• [Anglo-Indian from Urdu, Persian *khūsh* pleasant]
• **cushiness** *noun*

cuspidor *noun*
• "CUSSPA dore"
• a spittoon.
• [Portuguese, = spitter, from *cuspir* spit, from Latin *conspuere*]

cussed *adjective*
• "CUSS id"
• awkward and stubborn.
• [var. of 'cursed']
• **cussedly** *adverb*
• **cussedness** *noun*

custard *noun*
• "CUSS turd"
• a baked dish made with milk and eggs, usu. sweetened.
• [Middle English, earlier *crustarde* from Anglo-French from Old French *crouste* crust, from Latin *crusta* rind, shell]
• **custardy** *adjective*

custodian *noun*
• "cuss TOADY 'n"
• a person who has custody of and responsibility for another person, a thing, etc.
• [as CUSTODY, after *guardian*]
• **custodianship** *noun*

custody *noun*
• "CUSSTA dee"
• legal guardianship, esp. of a minor.
• [Latin *custodia* from *custos -odis* guardian]
• **custodial** *adjective* "cuss TOADY 'll"

custom *noun*
• "CUSS t'm"
• the usual way of behaving or acting.
• [Old French *custume*, ultimately from Latin *consuetudo -dinis*: see CONSUETUDE]
• **customarily** *adverb*
• **customary** *adjective*

customer *noun*
• "CUSSTA mur"
• a person who buys goods or services from a store or business.
• [as CUSTOM]

customize *verb*
ALSO SPELLED: esp. *Brit.* **-ise**
• "CUSSTA mize"
• make to order or modify according to individual requirements.
• [as CUSTOM]
• **customizability** *noun* (also esp. *Brit.* **-isability**)
• **customizable** *adjective* (also esp. *Brit.* **-isable**)
• **customization** *noun* (also esp. *Brit.* **-isation**)
• **customized** *adjective* (also esp. *Brit.* **-ised**)

cutaneous *adjective*
• "kyoo TAINY us"
• of the skin.
• [modern Latin *cutaneus* from Latin *cutis* skin]

cuticle *noun*
• "KYOOTA k'll"
• the dead skin at the base of a fingernail or toenail.
• [Latin *cuticula*, diminutive of *cutis* skin]
• **cuticular** *adjective* "kyoo TICK yuh lur"

cutis *noun*
• "KYOO tiss"
• the skin; the dermis.
• [Latin, = skin]

cutlass *noun*
• "CUT luss"
• a short sword with a slightly curved blade, esp. of the type formerly used by sailors.
• [French *coutelas*, ultimately from Latin *cultellus* small knife: see CUTLER]

cutler *noun*
• "CUT lur"
• a person who makes or deals in knives and similar utensils.
• [Old French *coutelier* from *coutel* from Latin *cultellus* diminutive of *culter* knife]

cutlery *noun*
• "CUTLER ee"
• knives, forks, and spoons for use at the table.
• [Old French *coutel(l)erie* (as CUTLER)]

cuvée *noun*
• "coo VAY"
• a blend or batch of wine.
• [French, = quantity filling a vat, from *cuve* cask, from Latin *cupa*]

cuvette *noun*
• "coo VET"
• a shallow vessel for liquid.
• [French, diminutive of *cuve* cask, from Latin *cupa*]

cwm *noun*
• "COOM"
• (in Wales) a valley or hollow on the side of a hill.
• [Welsh]
HOMOPHONES: *coomb, khoum*

cyan *adjective*
• "SYE ann"
• of a greenish-blue.
• [Greek *kuan(e)os* dark blue]

cyanamide *noun*
• "sye ANNA mide"
• a colourless crystalline amide of cyanogen.
• [CYANOGEN + AMIDE]

cyanic *adjective*
• "sye ANNIC"
• designating an unstable colourless pungent acid gas.
• [as CYANOGEN]

cyanide *noun*
• "SYE a nide"
• any of the highly poisonous salts or esters of hydrocyanic acid.
• [as CYANOGEN]

cyanoacrylate *noun*
• "sye a no a CRILL ate"
• any of a class of compounds which are cyanide derivatives of acrylates. They are easily polymerized and are used to make quick-setting adhesives.
• [CYANIDE + ACRYLATE]

cyanobacteria *plural noun*
• "sye a no back TEERY uh"
• any prokaryotic organisms of the division Cyanobacteria, found in many environments and capable of photosynthesizing.
• [Greek *kuan(e)os* dark blue + BACTERIA]
• **cyanobacterial** *adjective*

cyanocobalamin *noun*
• "sye a no kuh BALA min"
• a vitamin of the B complex, found in foods of animal origin such as liver, fish, and eggs, a deficiency of which can cause pernicious anemia.
• [CYANOGEN + *cobalamin* from COBALT + VITAMIN]

cyanogen *noun*
• "sye ANNA j'n"
• a colourless highly poisonous gas intermediate in the preparation of many fertilizers.
• [French *cyanogène* from Greek *kuanos* dark blue mineral, as being a constituent of Prussian blue]

cyanogenic *adjective*
• "sye anna JENNIC"
• capable of providing cyanide.
• [as CYANOGEN]

cyanosis *noun*
• "sye a NO sis"
• a bluish discoloration of the skin due to the presence of oxygen-deficient blood.
• [Greek *kuan(e)os* dark blue]
• **cyanotic** *adjective*

cybercafé *noun*
• "SYE bur caf ay"
• an Internet café.
• [CYBERNETICS + CAFÉ]

cybercrime *noun*
• "SYE bur crime"
• crime or a crime committed using computers or the Internet.
• [CYBERNETICS + 'crime' (see CRIMINAL)]
• **cybercriminal** *noun*

cyberculture *noun*
• "SYE bur cull chur"
• the social conditions brought about by computerization and the Internet; computers and the Internet viewed as a cultural phenomenon.
• [CYBERNETICS + CULTURE]

Cyberia *noun*
• "sye BEERY uh"
• the notional environment within which electronic communication occurs; the space of virtual reality, esp. viewed as a 'global village' or sphere of human interaction; cyberspace.
• [CYBERNETICS + *-ia* common ending for names of countries]
• **Cyberian** *noun*
HOMOPHONES: *Siberian*

cybernetics *noun*
• "sye bur NETTIX"
• the science of communications and automatic control systems in both machines and living things.
• [Greek *kubernētēs* steersman]
• **cybernetic** *adjective*
• **cybernetically** *adverb*
• **cybernetician** *noun*
• **cyberneticist** *noun* "sye bur NETTA sist"

cyberpunk *noun*
• "SYE bur punk"
• a style of science fiction featuring urban counterculture in a world of high technology and virtual reality.
• [CYBERNETICS + 'punk' of unknown origin]

cyberspace *noun*
• "SYE bur space"
• the forum in which the global electronic communications network operates.
• [CYBERNETICS + 'space']

cybersquatter *noun*
• "SYE bur skwotter"
• a person who registers well-known company or brand etc. names as Internet domain names, in the hope of later selling them back to the brand owner at a profit.
• [CYBERNETICS + 'squatter']
• **cybersquatting** *noun*

cyberstalking *noun*
• "SYE bur stocking"
• the repeated use of electronic communications to harass or frighten someone, e.g. by sending threatening emails.
• [CYBERNETICS + 'stalk']

cyberterrorism *noun*
• "SYE bur tare ur izm"
• terrorist acts consisting of hacking into a computer network, e.g. one belonging to the armed forces, a government, a utility, etc. to cause widespread havoc.
• [CYBERNETICS + TERRORISM]
• **cyberterrorist** *noun*

cyberwar *noun*
• "SYE bur wore"
• a conflict in which enemies attempt to hack into each other's computer networks to disrupt communications, shut down systems, steal information, etc.
• [CYBERNETICS + 'war']

cyborg *noun*
• "SYE borg"
• a person whose physical abilities are extended beyond normal human limitations by machine technology (as yet undeveloped).
• [CYBERNETICS + 'organism' (from French *organisme* from Latin *organum* instrument, from Greek *organon* tool)]

cycad *noun*
• "SYE cad"
• any of the palm-like plants of the order Cycadales (including fossil forms) inhabiting tropical and subtropical regions and often growing to a great height.
• [modern Latin *cycas, cycad-* from supposed Greek *kukas*, scribal error for *koikas*, pl. of *koix* Egyptian palm]

Cycladic *adjective*
• "sye CLADDIC"
• of the Cyclades islands in the S Aegean Sea, esp. of the Bronze Age civilization that flourished there.

cyclamate *noun*
• "SIKE la mate" or "SICK la mate"
• any of various compounds formerly used as artificial sweetening agents.
• [abbreviation of chemical name *cyclohexylsulphamate*]

cyclamen *noun*
• "SICK luh m'n"
• any plant of the genus *Cyclamen*, originating in Europe, having pink, red, or white flowers with reflexed petals, often grown as a houseplant.
• [medieval Latin from Greek *kuklaminos*, perhaps from *kuklos* circle, with reference to its bulbous roots]

cycle *noun*
• "SIKE 'll"
• a recurrent series or period (of events, phenomena, etc.).

• [Old French from Late Latin *cyclus* from Greek *kuklos* circle]

cyclic *adjective*
• "SIKE lick" or "SICK lick"
• recurring or revolving in cycles.
• [as CYCLE]
• **cyclical** *adjective*
• **cyclically** *adverb*

cycling *noun*
• "SIKE ling"
• travelling or touring on a bicycle etc.
• [as CYCLE]
• **cyclist** *noun*

cycloalkane *noun*
• "sike lo AL cane"
• a saturated cyclic hydrocarbon.
• [Greek *kuklos* circle + ALKANE]

cyclocross *noun*
• "SIKE lo cross"
• cross-country racing on bicycles.
• [CYCLING + 'cross-country']

cyclohexane *noun*
• "sike lo HEX ane"
• a colourless liquid cycloalkane used as a solvent and paint remover.
• [Greek *kuklos* circle + HEXANE]

cycloid *noun*
• "SIKE loid"
• the path traced out by a point on a circle when the circle is rolled along a straight line.
• [Greek *kuklos* circle]
• **cycloidal** *adjective*

cyclometer *noun*
• "sike LOMMA tur"
• an instrument for measuring circular arcs.
• [Greek *kuklos* circle + *metron* measure]

cyclone *noun*
• "SYE clone"
• a system of winds rotating inwards to an area of low barometric pressure; a depression.
• [prob. representing Greek *kuklōma* wheel, coil of a snake]
• **cyclonic** *adjective*

cycloparaffin *noun*
• "sike lo PERRA fin"
• = CYCLOALKANE.
• [Greek *kuklos* circle + PARAFFIN]

cyclopean *adjective*
ALSO SPELLED: **cyclopian**
• "sike lo PEE 'n" or "sike LOPEY 'n"
• (of ancient masonry) made with massive irregular blocks.
• [as CYCLOPS]

cyclopedia *noun*
ALSO SPELLED: **cyclopaedia**
• "sike luh PEEDY uh"
• an encyclopedia.
• [shortening of ENCYCLOPEDIA]
• **cyclopedic** *adjective* (also **cyclopaedic**)

cyclopropane *noun*
• "sike lo PRO pane"
• a colourless gaseous cycloalkane used as a general anaesthetic.
• [Greek *kuklos* circle + PROPANE]

Cyclops *noun*
• "SIKE lops"
• (in Greek mythology) a member of a race of one-eyed giants.
• [Latin from Greek *Kuklōps* from *kuklos* circle + *ōps* eye]

cyclorama *noun*
• "sike lo RAMMA"
• a circular panorama, curved wall, or cloth at the rear of a stage, esp. one used to represent the sky.
• [Greek *kuklos* circle + PANORAMA]
• **cycloramic** *adjective*

cyclosporin *noun*
ALSO SPELLED: **cyclosporine**
• "sike lo SPORE in"
• a peptide drug used to prevent the rejection of grafts and transplants.
• [Greek *kuklos* circle + *-sporum* part of the name of a fungus which produces it]

cyclostome *noun*
• "SIKE lo stome"
• a fish of the former taxon Cyclostomata, which includes primitive forms (the lampreys and hagfishes) having a round sucking mouth.
• [Greek *kuklos* circle + Greek *stoma* mouth]
• **cyclostomate** *adjective*

cyclotron *noun*
• "SIKE lo tron"
• an apparatus in which charged atomic and subatomic particles are accelerated by an alternating electric field while following an outward spiral or circular path in a magnetic field.
• [Greek *kuklos* circle + ELECTRON]

cygnet *noun*
• "SIG nit"
• a young swan.
• [Anglo-French *cignet* diminutive of Old French *cigne* swan, from medieval Latin *cycnus* from Greek *kuknos*]
HOMOPHONES: *signet*

cylinder *noun*
• "SILL'n dur"
• a uniform solid or hollow body with straight sides and a circular section.
• [Latin *cylindrus* from Greek *kulindros* from *kulindō* roll]
• **cylindrical** *adjective* "suh LINDRA k'll"
• **cylindrically** *adverb*

cyma *noun*
• "SYE muh"
• an ogee moulding of a cornice.
• [modern Latin from Greek *kuma* wave, wavy moulding]

cymbal *noun*
- "SIMBLE"
- a musical instrument consisting of a concave brass or bronze plate, struck with another or with a stick etc. to make a ringing sound.
- [Latin *cymbalum* from Greek *kumbalon* from *kumbē* cup]
- **cymbalist** *noun*

HOMOPHONES: *symbol, symbolist*

cymbidium *noun*
- "sim BIDDY um"
- any tropical orchid of the genus *Cymbidium*, with a hollow recess in the flower lip.
- [modern Latin from Greek *kumbē* cup]

cyme *noun*
- "SIME"
- an inflorescence in which the primary axis bears a single terminal flower that develops first, the system being continued by the axes of secondary and higher orders each with a flower.
- [French, var. of *cime* summit, ultimately from Greek *kuma* wave]
- **cymose** *adjective*

Cymric *adjective*
- "KIM rick"
- Welsh in language or culture.
- [Welsh *Cymru* Wales]

cynic *noun*
- "SINNIC"
- a person with little faith in human goodness who sarcastically doubts or despises sincerity and merit.
- [Latin *cynicus* from Greek *kunikos* from *kuōn kunos* dog, nickname for a school of ancient Greek philosophers founded by Antisthenes, marked by a belief in self-control as the essence of virtue and an ostentatious contempt for ease and pleasure]
- **cynical** *adjective*
- **cynically** *adverb*
- **cynicism** *noun* "SINNA sizm"

cynosure *noun*
- "SINNA shur" or "SINE a shur"
- a centre of attraction or admiration.
- [French *cynosure* or Latin *cynosura* from Greek *kunosoura* dog's tail (the Little Dipper), from *kuōn kunos* dog + *oura* tail]

cypress *noun*
- "SIPE riss"
- any coniferous tree of the genus *Cupressus* or *Chamaecyparis*, with hard wood and dark foliage.
- [Old French *cipres* from Late Latin *cypressus* from Greek *kuparissos*]

cyprinoid *adjective*
- "SIPRIN oid"
- of or like a carp.
- [Latin *cyprinus* from Greek *kuprinos* carp]

Cypriot *noun*
- "SIP ree it"
- a native or national of the island of Cyprus in the E Mediterranean.

cypripedium *noun*
- "sippra PEEDY um"
- any orchid of the genus *Cypripedium*, esp. the lady's slipper.
- [modern Latin from Greek *Kupris* Aphrodite + *pedilon* slipper]

cypsela *noun*
- "SIPSA luh"
- a dry single-seeded fruit formed from a double ovary of which only one develops into a seed, characteristic of the daisy family Compositae.
- [modern Latin from Greek *kupselē* hollow vessel]

Cyrenaic *adjective*
- "sye ruh NAY ick"
- of or denoting the hedonistic school of philosophy founded *c.*400 BC by Aristippus the Elder of Cyrene (in N Africa) which holds that pleasure is the highest good and that virtue is to be equated with the ability to enjoy.
- [from *Cyrene*]

Cyrillic *adjective*
- "suh RILLIC"
- denoting the alphabet derived from Greek, adapted by the Slavic peoples, and now used esp. for Russian and Bulgarian.
- [St. *Cyril*, Greek missionary d.869]

cyst *noun*
- "SIST"
- an abnormal sac containing fluid, pus, etc.
- [Late Latin *cystis* from Greek *kustis* bladder]
- **cystic** *adjective*

HOMOPHONES: *cist*

cysteine *noun*
- "SISTY een"
- a sulphur-containing amino acid, essential in the human diet and a constituent of many enzymes.
- [as CYSTINE]

cystine *noun*
- "SISTEEN" or "SISTIN"
- an organic base which is a naturally occurring dimer of cysteine.
- [Greek *kustis* bladder (because first found in urinary calculi)]

HOMOPHONES: *Sistine*

cystitis *noun*
- "sis TITE iss"
- an inflammation of the urinary bladder, often caused by infection, and usu. accompanied by frequent painful urination.
- [Greek *kustis* bladder + *-itis*, forming feminine of adjectives in *-itēs* (with *nosos* 'disease' implied)]

cystoscope *noun*
- "SISTA scope"

• an instrument inserted in the urethra for examining the urinary bladder.
• [Greek *kustis* bladder + *skopos* target, from *skeptomai* look at]
• **cystoscopic** *adjective*
• **cystoscopy** *noun* "sis TOSCA pee"

cytidine *noun*
• "SITE a deen"
• a nucleoside obtained from RNA by hydrolysis.
• [German *Cytidin* from Greek *kutos* vessel]

cytochrome *noun*
• "SITE oh crome"
• a compound consisting of a protein linked to a heme, which is involved in electron transfer reactions.
• [prefix *cyto-* cells, from Greek *kutos* vessel + CHROME]

cytogenetics *noun*
• "site oh juh NETTIX"
• the study of inheritance in relation to the structure and function of cells.
• [prefix *cyto-* cells, from Greek *kutos* vessel + GENETICS]
• **cytogenetic** *adjective* "site oh juh NETTIC"
• **cytogeneticist** *noun* "site oh juh NETTA sist"

cytokine *noun*
• "site oh KINE"
• any of various hormones secreted by certain cells of the immune system.
• [prefix *cyto-* cells, from Greek *kutos* vessel + Greek *kinein* move]

cytology *noun*
• "sye TOLLA jee"
• the microscopic study of cells, esp. to detect and identify disease.
• [prefix *cyto-* cells, from Greek *kutos* vessel + *logos* word]
• **cytological** *adjective*
• **cytologically** *adverb*
• **cytologist** *noun*

cytomegalovirus *noun*
• "site oh MEGGA lo vie russ"
• a kind of herpesvirus which usually produces very mild symptoms in an infected person but may cause severe neurological damage in the newborn and in people with weakened immune systems.
• [prefix *cyto-* cells, from Greek *kutos* vessel + Greek *megas megal-* great + VIRUS]

cytoplasm *noun*
• "SITE oh plazm"
• the protoplasmic content of a cell apart from its nucleus.
• [prefix *cyto-* cells, from Greek *kutos* vessel + PLASMA]
• **cytoplasmic** *adjective*

cytosine *noun*
• "SITE oh seen"
• one of the principal component bases of the nucleotides and the nucleic acids DNA and RNA, derived from pyrimidine.
• [prefix *cyto-* cells, from Greek *kutos* vessel]

cytoskeleton *noun*
• "SITE oh skella t'n"
• a network of protein filaments and tubules giving shape and coherence to a living cell.
• [prefix *cyto-* cells, from Greek *kutos* vessel + SKELETON]
• **cytoskeletal** *adjective*

cytosol *noun*
• "SITE oh sawl"
• the aqueous component of the cytoplasm of a cell, within which various organelles and particles are suspended.
• [prefix *cyto-* cells, from Greek *kutos* vessel + SOL(UBLE)]
• **cytosolic** *adjective*

cytotoxic *adjective*
• "site oh TOXIC"
• toxic to living cells.
• [prefix *cyto-* cells, from Greek *kutos* vessel + TOXIC]
• **cytotoxicity** *noun* "site oh tox ISSA tee"

czar *noun*
ALSO SPELLED: **tsar**
• "ZAR"
• the title of the former emperor of Russia.
• [Russian *czar'*, ultimately from Latin *Caesar*]
• **czardom** *noun* (also **tsardom**)
• **czarism** *noun* (also **tsarism**)
• **czarist** *adjective* (also **tsarist**)

czardas *noun*
• "CHAR das"
• a Hungarian dance with a slow start and a quick finish.
• [Hungarian *csárdás* from *csárda* inn]

czarevich *noun*
ALSO SPELLED: **tsarevich**
• "ZAR a vitch"
• the eldest son of an emperor of Russia.
• [Russian *czarevich* son of a czar]

czarina *noun*
ALSO SPELLED: **tsarina**
• "zar EENA"
• the title of the former empress of Russia.
• [Italian & Spanish *(c)zarina* from German *Czarin, Zarin*, feminine of *Czar, Zar*]

Czech *noun*
• "CHECK"
• a native or national of the Czech Republic or Czechoslovakia in central Europe.
• [Polish spelling of Bohemian *Čech*]
HOMOPHONES: *check, cheque*

Czechoslovakian *noun*
• "checka sluh VACKY 'n"
• a native or inhabitant of Czechoslovakia, a former country in central Europe.

Dd

dacha *noun*
• "DATCH uh"
• a country house or cottage in Russia.
• [Russian, lit. 'gift']

dachshund *noun*
• "DACKS h'nt" or "DOCKS h'nt"
• a breed of dog with short legs and a long body.
• [German, = badger dog]

dacite *noun*
• "DAY site"
• a volcanic rock similar to andesite but containing free quartz.
• [from *Dacia*, a Roman province in central Europe + Greek *lithos* stone]

dacoit *noun*
• "duh COIT"
• (in India or Burma) a member of a band of armed robbers.
• [Hindi *ḍakait* from *ḍākā* gang robbery]

dactyl *noun*
• "DACK t'll"
• a metrical foot consisting of one long or stressed syllable followed by two short or unstressed syllables.
• [Latin *dactylus* from Greek *daktulos* finger, the three bones corresponding to the three syllables]
• **dactylic** *adjective*

dado *noun*
• "DAY doe"
• the lower part of the wall of a room when visually distinct from the upper part.
• [Italian from Latin *datum* neuter past participle of *dare* give, play]

daemon *noun*
• "DEEM'n"
• in some operating systems, an unseen program that controls a peripheral device; a background task.
• [*d*isk + *a*nd *e*xecution *mon*itor]
HOMOPHONES: *demon*

daffodil *noun*
• "DAFFA dill"
• a bulbous plant, *Narcissus pseudonarcissus*, with a yellow trumpet-shaped crown.
• [earlier *affodill*, as ASPHODEL]

daguerreotype *noun*
• "duh GARE oh tipe"
• a photograph taken by an early photographic process employing an iodine-sensitized silvered plate and mercury vapour.
• [L. *Daguerre*, French inventor d.1851]

dahlia *noun*
• "DAILY uh" or "DOLLY uh"
• any composite garden plant of the genus *Dahlia*, of Mexican origin, cultivated for its many-coloured single or double flowers.
• [A. *Dahl*, Swedish botanist d.1789]

daikon *noun*
• "DIE con" or "DIE k'n"
• a long, thin, white oriental radish.
• [Japanese from Middle Chinese *dà* big + *gen* root]

Dáil *noun*
• "DOIL"
• the lower house of parliament in the Republic of Ireland.
• [Irish, = assembly (of Ireland)]

daimyo *noun*
ALSO SPELLED: **daimio**
• "DIME yo" or "DIMEY oh"
• in feudal Japan, any of the chief landowning nobles, vassals of the shogun.
• [Japanese from *dai* great + *myō* name]

daiquiri *noun*
• "DACKA ree"
• a cocktail of rum, sugar, and lime or lemon juice, etc.
• [*Daiquiri* in Cuba]

dais *noun*
• "DIE iss" or "DAY iss"
• a low platform, usu. at the upper end of a room and used to support a table, lectern, throne, etc.
• [Old French *deis* from Latin *discus* disc, dish, in medieval Latin = table]

daisy *noun*
• "DAY zee"
• a small composite plant, *Bellis perennis*, bearing flowers each with a yellow disc and white rays.

• [Old English *dæges ēage* day's eye, the flower opening in the morning]

Dakota *noun*
• "duh CO tuh"
• a member of a N American Aboriginal people inhabiting the upper Mississippi and Missouri river valleys.
• [Dakota *Dakhóta*, lit. 'allies']

dal *noun*
ALSO SPELLED: **dhal**
• "DOLL"
• a kind of lentil or split pea, a common foodstuff in India.
• [Hindi]
HOMOPHONES: *doll*

dalasi *noun*
• "doll OSSY"
• the chief monetary unit of Gambia.
• [name of an earlier local coin]

Daliesque *adjective*
• "dolly ESK"
• relating to or characteristic of the Spanish surrealist painter Salvador Dali (d.1989).

Dalit *noun*
• "DOLLIT"
• (in the traditional Indian caste system) a member of the lowest caste.
• [Hindi, from Sanskrit *dalita* oppressed]

dalliance *noun*
• "DALLY ince"
• a leisurely or frivolous passing of time.
• [Old French *dalier* chat]

Dalmatian *noun*
• "dal MAY sh'n"
• a breed of large dog having white, short hair with dark spots.
• [as DALMATIC, the dogs being originally from Dalmatia]

dalmatic *noun*
• "dal MATTIC"
• a wide-sleeved long loose vestment open at the sides, worn by deacons and bishops, and by English monarchs at their coronations.
• [Old French *dalmatique* or Late Latin *dalmatica* (*vestis* robe) of Dalmatia on the Adriatic coast of Croatia]

dalton *noun*
• "DOLL t'n"
• a unit of mass used to express atomic and molecular weights that is equal to one twelfth of the mass of an atom of carbon-12.
• [J. *Dalton*, English chemist d.1844]

daltonism *noun*
• "DOLL t'n izm"
• colour-blindness, esp. a congenital inability to distinguish between red and green.
• [French *daltonisme* from the name of J. *Dalton* (see DALTON) who gave the first detailed description of colour-blindness, based on his own inability to distinguish green from red]

Damara *noun*
• "duh MAR uh"
• a member of a people inhabiting mountainous parts of SW Africa and speaking the Nama language.
• [Nama]

damascene *verb*
• "DAMMA seen" or "damma SEEN"
• decorate (metal, esp. iron or steel) by etching or inlaying esp. with gold or silver, or with a watered pattern produced in welding.
• [*Damascene* of Damascus (in Syria), from Latin *Damascenus* from Greek *Damaskēnos*]

damask *noun*
• "DAM isk"
• a figured woven fabric (esp. silk or linen) with a pattern visible on both sides.
• [Middle English, ultimately from Latin *Damascus* (Damascus in Syria)]

dammar *noun*
• "DAMMER"
• any E Asian tree, esp. one of the genus *Agathis* or *Shorea*, yielding a resin used in varnish making.
• [Malay *damar*]

damn *verb*
• "DAM"
• curse (a person or thing).
• [Old French *damner* from Latin *damnare* inflict loss on, from *damnum* loss]
• **damning** *adjective* "DAMMING"
• **damningly** *adverb*
HOMOPHONES: *dam*

damnable *adjective*
• "DAM nuh bull"
• annoying.
• [as DAMN]
• **damnably** *adverb*

damnation *noun*
• "dam NAY sh'n"
• condemnation to eternal punishment, esp. in hell.
• [as DAMN]

damsel *noun*
• "DAM z'll"
• a young unmarried woman.
• [Old French *dam(e)isele*, ultimately from Latin *domina* mistress]

damselfish *noun*
• "DAM z'll fish"
• any of numerous brightly coloured tropical marine fishes of the family Pomacentridae.
• [as DAMSEL + 'fish']

damselfly *noun*
• "DAM z'll fly"
• any of various insects of the order Odonata,

like a dragonfly but with its wings folded over the body when resting.
• [as DAMSEL + 'fly']

damson *noun*
• "DAMZ'n"
• a small dark purple plum.
• [Middle English *damacene, -scene, -sene* from Latin *damascenum* (*prunum* plum) of *Damascus*: see DAMASCENE]

dandelion *noun*
• "DANDY lie 'n"
• a composite plant, *Taraxacum officinale*, with jagged leaves and a large bright yellow flower on a hollow stalk, followed by a globular head of seeds with downy tufts.
• [French *dent-de-lion* translation of medieval Latin *dens leonis* lion's tooth]

dandify *verb*
• "DANDA fie"
• cause to resemble a dandy, a man unduly devoted to style, smartness, and fashion in dress and appearance.
• [18th c.: perhaps an abbreviation of *Jack-a-dandy*: *dandy* may be a pet form of *Andrew*]
• **dandified** *adjective*

danseur *noun*
• "don SUR"
• a male ballet dancer.
• [French, = dancer]

danseuse *noun*
• "don SOOZ" (with "OO" as in *BOOK*)
• a female ballet dancer.
• [as DANSEUR]

Dantean *adjective*
• "DONTAY 'n" or "DANTAY 'n"
• relating to or characteristic of the Italian poet Dante Alighieri (d.1321) or his works, esp. *The Divine Comedy*, an allegorical journey through Hell, Purgatory, and Paradise.

daphne *noun*
• "DAFNY"
• any flowering shrub of the genus *Daphne*, e.g. the spurge laurel or mezereon.
• [Middle English, = laurel, from Greek *Daphnē*, a nymph who escaped Apollo's advances by being turned into a laurel bush]

daphnia *noun*
• "DAFNY uh"
• a minute semi-transparent freshwater crustacean with long antennae and prominent eyes, often used as food for aquarium fish.
• [modern Latin from *Daphne*: see DAPHNE]

Dari *noun*
• "DAR ee"
• the form of Persian spoken in Afghanistan.
• [Persian]

dariole *noun*
• "DERRY ole"
• a savoury or sweet dish cooked and served in a small mould usu. shaped like a flowerpot.
• [Old French]

Darjeeling *noun*
• "dar JEELING"
• the high-quality tea grown in the area around Darjeeling in NE India.

darnel *noun*
• "DARN 'll"
• any of several grasses of the genus *Lolium*, native to Europe and N Africa and naturalized in N America, planted as pasture grasses or to stabilize soil.
• [Middle English: apparently related to French *darnelle*]

darshan *noun*
• "DAR sh'n"
• an opportunity to see or an occasion of seeing a holy person or the image of a deity.
• [Hindi from Sanskrit *darśana* sight, seeing]

Darwinian *adjective*
• "dar WINNY 'n"
• of or relating to Charles Darwin's theory of the evolution of species by the action of natural selection.
• **Darwinism** *noun*
• **Darwinist** *noun*

dasheen *noun*
• "dash EEN"
• a cultivated variety of taro.
• [origin unknown]

dashiki *noun*
• "duh SHEEKY"
• a loose, usu. brightly coloured and patterned pullover shirt.
• [West African, prob. Yoruba from Hausa]

dastardly *adjective*
• "DASS t'rd lee"
• despicable.
• [*dastard* base coward, prob. from *dazed* past participle or obsolete *dasart* dullard, DOTARD]
• **dastardliness** *noun*

dasyure *noun*
• "DASSY ur"
• any of a number of carnivorous arboreal catlike marsupials of the genus *Dasyurus*, native to Australia and New Guinea.
• [French from modern Latin *dasyurus* from Greek *dasus* hairy + *oura* tail]

data *noun*
• "DATTA" or "DAY tuh"
• quantities or characters operated on by a computer.
• [pl. of DATUM]

database *noun*
• "DATTA base" or "DAY tuh base"
• an organized store of data, esp. one that may be accessed and manipulated by a computer.
• [as DATA + 'base']

datable *adjective*
- "DATE a bull"
- capable of being dated (to a particular time).
- [from 'date' (as DATUM)]

dative *noun*
- "DAY tiv"
- the case of nouns and pronouns (and words in grammatical agreement with them) indicating an indirect object or recipient.
- [Latin (*casus*) *dativus* from *dare dat-* give]

datum *noun*
- "DAT um" or "DATE um"
- a piece of information.
- [Latin, = thing given, neuter past participle of *dare* give]

datura *noun*
- "duh TYURA"
- any poisonous plant of the genus *Datura*, e.g. the thornapple.
- [modern Latin from Hindi *dhatura*]

daub *verb*
- "DOB"
- spread (paint, plaster, or some other thick substance) crudely or roughly on a surface.
- [Old French *dauber* from Latin *dealbare* whitewash, from *albus* white]
- **dauber** *noun*

daube *noun*
- "DOBE"
- a stew of braised meat (usu. beef) with wine etc.
- [French, from Italian *addobbo* seasoning, from *addobare* cook]

daughter *noun*
- "DOTTER"
- a girl or woman in relation to either or both of her parents.
- [Old English *dohtor* from Germanic]
- **daughterly** *adjective*

HOMOPHONES: *dodder*

daunt *verb*
- "DAWNT"
- discourage, intimidate.
- [Anglo-French *daunter* from Latin *domitare* frequentative of *domare* tame]
- **daunting** *adjective*
- **dauntingly** *adverb*

dauntless *adjective*
- "DAWNT less"
- intrepid, persevering.
- [as DAUNT]
- **dauntlessly** *adverb*
- **dauntlessness** *noun*

dauphin *noun*
- "DOFFIN" or "doe FÃ" (with a nasal *A*)
- the title borne by the eldest son of the king of France from 1349 to 1830.
- [French, from the family name of the lords of the Dauphiné in S central France, ultimately a nickname meaning 'dolphin']

Dauphinite *noun*
- "DOFFIN ite"
- a resident of Dauphin, Man.

daven *verb*
- "DOV'n"
- recite prayers.
- [Yiddish *davenen* pray]

davenport *noun*
- "DAV'n port"
- a large heavily upholstered sofa.
- [19th c.: from the name *Davenport*]

davit *noun*
- "DAV it" or "DAVE it"
- a small crane on board a ship, esp. one of a pair for suspending or lowering a lifeboat.
- [Old French *daviot* diminutive of *Davi* David]

Davy *noun*
- "DAY vee"
- a miner's safety lamp with the flame enclosed by wire gauze to prevent an explosion of gas.
- [Sir H. *Davy*, English chemist d.1829]

dawdle *verb*
- "DOD'll"
- walk or move slowly.
- [perhaps related to dialect *daddle*, *doddle* idle, dally]
- **dawdler** *noun*

HOMOPHONES: *doddle*, *dottle*

Dayak *noun*

ALSO SPELLED: **Dyak**
- "DIE ack"
- a member of a group of aboriginal peoples inhabiting parts of Borneo.
- [Malay, = upcountry]

deaccession *verb*
- "dee ack SESH'n"
- (of a museum, library, etc.) sell (a work).
- [from or after Latin *de* = off + ACCESSION]

deacon *noun*
- "DEEK'n"
- (in churches with a hierarchy) a minister of the third order, below bishop and priest.
- [Old English *diacon* from Church Latin *diaconus* from Greek *diakonos* servant]

deaconess *noun*
- "DEEK'n ess"
- a laywoman with functions similar to a deacon's.
- [as DEACON]

deactivate *verb*
- "dee ACTIV ate"
- make inactive or less reactive.
- [from or after Latin *de* = off + ACTIVATE]
- **deactivation** *noun*
- **deactivator** *noun*

dearth *noun*
- "DURTH"
- a scarcity or lack.
- [Middle English *derthe*, originally in the sense 'shortage and dearness of food']

debacle *noun*
- "duh BOCK 'll" or "duh BACK 'll"
- an utter failure or disaster.
- [French from *débâcler* unbar]

debatable *adjective*
- "de BAYTA bull"
- questionable; subject to dispute.
- [Old French *debatre*, *debat* from Romanic (Latin *de-*, *battuere* beat)]
- **debatably** *adverb*

debauch *verb*
- "duh BOTCH"
- corrupt morally.
- [French *débauche(r)*, of unknown origin]
- **debauched** *adjective*
- **debaucher** *noun*

debauchee *noun*
- "duh botch EE" or "duh bosh EE"
- a person addicted to excessive indulgence in sex, alcohol, drugs, etc.
- [as DEBAUCH]

debauchery *noun*
- "duh BOTCHA ree"
- excessive indulgence in pleasures of the flesh, esp. sex, alcohol, or drugs.
- [as DEBAUCH]

debenture *noun*
- "duh BEN chur"
- a sealed bond issued by a corporation or company in respect of a long-term (esp. fixed-interest) loan.
- [Latin *debentur* are owing, from *debēre* owe]

debilitate *verb*
- "de BILLA tate"
- enfeeble, enervate.
- [Latin *debilitare* (as DEBILITY)]
- **debilitating** *adjective*
- **debilitatingly** *adverb*
- **debilitation** *noun*
- **debilitative** *adjective*

debility *noun*
- "de BILLA tee"
- feebleness, esp. of health.
- [Old French *debilité* from Latin *debilitas -tatis* from *debilis* weak]

debit *noun*
- "DEBBIT"
- an entry in an account recording a sum owed or paid out.
- [French *débit* from Latin *debitum* DEBT]

debonair *adjective*
- "debba NARE"
- carefree, cheerful.
- [Old French *debonaire* = *de bon aire* of good disposition]
- **debonairly** *adverb*

debouch *verb*
- "duh BOUCH" (rhymes with *GROUCH*) or "duh BOOSH"
- emerge from a narrow or confined place into open ground.
- [French *déboucher* (Latin *de* = off + French *bouche* mouth)]
- **debouchment** *noun*

debridement *noun*
- "duh BREED m'nt"
- the removal of damaged tissue or foreign matter from a wound etc.
- [French, literally 'unbridling']

debrief *verb*
- "dee BREEF"
- discuss a completed mission, undertaking, or event with (a person).
- [from or after Latin *de* = off + BRIEF]
- **debriefing** *noun*

debris *noun*
- "duh BREE" or "deb REE"
- scattered fragments, esp. of something wrecked or destroyed.
- [French *débris* from obsolete *débriser* break down (Latin *de* = off + French *briser* break)]

debt *noun*
- "DET"
- a sum of money owed.
- [Old French *dette*, ultimately from Latin *debitum* past participle of *debēre* owe]
- **debtor** *noun*

debut *noun*
- "day BYOO" or "DAY byoo"
- the first public appearance of a person in a specified role, esp. a performer.
- [French from *débuter* lead off]

debutante *noun*
- "DEB yoo tont" or "DAY byoo tont"
- a (usu. wealthy) young woman making her social debut.
- [French, feminine participle of *débuter*: see DEBUT]

decade *noun*
- "DECK ade"
- a period of ten years.
- [French *décade* from Late Latin *decas -adis* from Greek *deka* ten]
- **decadal** *adjective* "DECKA d'll"

decadence *noun*
- "DECKA dince"
- moral or cultural deterioration, esp. after a peak or culmination of achievement.
- [French *décadence* from medieval Latin *decadentia* from *decadere* DECAY]
- **decadent** *adjective*
- **decadently** *adverb*

decaffeinate *verb*
• "dee CAFF'n ate"
• remove the caffeine from.
• [from or after Latin *de* = off + CAFFEINE]
• **decaffeinated** *adjective*
• **decaffeination** *noun*

decagon *noun*
• "DECKA gon"
• a plane figure with ten sides and angles.
• [Greek *deka* ten + *-gonos* -angled]
• **decagonal** *adjective* "deck AGGA n'll"

decahedron *noun*
• "decka HEED r'n"
• a solid figure with ten faces.
• [Greek *deka* ten + *hedra* base]

decal *noun*
• "DEE cal" or "DECK 'll"
• a picture or design transferred from specially prepared paper to the surface of glass, plastic, etc.
• [abbreviation of DECALCOMANIA]
HOMOPHONES: *deckle*

decalcify *verb*
• "dee CALSA fie"
• remove lime or calcareous matter from (a bone, tooth, etc.).
• [from or after Latin *de* = off + CALCIFY]
• **decalcification** *noun*
• **decalcifier** *noun*

decalcomania *noun*
• "dee calka MAINY uh"
• a process of transferring designs from specially prepared paper to the surface of glass, porcelain, etc.
• [French *décalcomanie* from *décalquer* transfer]

decalitre *noun*
ALSO SPELLED: esp. *US* **decaliter**
• "DECKA leeter"
• a metric unit of capacity, equal to 10 litres.
• [Greek *deka* ten + LITRE]

Decalogue *noun*
• "DECKA log"
• the Ten Commandments.
• [French *décalogue* or Church Latin *decalogus* from Greek *dekalogos* (after *hoi deka logoi* the Ten Commandments)]

decametre *noun*
ALSO SPELLED: esp. *US* **decameter**
• "DECKA meeter"
• a metric unit of length, equal to 10 metres.
• [Greek *deka* ten + METRE]

decanal *adjective*
• "dee CANE 'll" or "DECKA n'll"
• of a dean or deanery.
• [medieval Latin *decanalis* from Late Latin *decanus* dean, from *decem* ten; originally = chief of a group of ten]

decani *adjective*
• "dih CAINY" or "de CANNY"
• the side of a divided church choir on the right side when facing the altar.
• [Latin, genitive of *decanus* dean: see DECANAL]

decant *verb*
• "de CANT"
• gradually pour off (liquid, esp. wine or a solution) from one container to another, esp. without disturbing the sediment.
• [medieval Latin *decanthare* (from *de* from + CANTHUS, used for the lip of a beaker)]

decanter *noun*
• "de CANTER"
• a stoppered glass container into which wine or liquor is decanted.
• [AS DECANT]

decapitate *verb*
• "de CAPPA tate"
• remove the head or top of.
• [Late Latin *decapitare* (Latin *de* = off + *caput -itis* head)]
• **decapitation** *noun*

decapod *noun*
• "DECKA pod"
• any crustacean of the chiefly marine order Decapoda, characterized by five pairs of walking legs, e.g. shrimps, crabs, and lobsters.
• [French *décapode* from Greek *deka* ten + *pous podos* foot]

decarbonize *verb*
ALSO SPELLED: esp. *Brit.* **-ise**
• "dee CARB'n ize"
• remove carbon or carbonaceous deposits from (an internal combustion engine etc.).
• [from or after Latin *de* = off + *carbo- carbonis* charcoal]
• **decarbonization** *noun* (also esp. *Brit.* **-isation**)

decarboxylate *verb*
• "dee car BOX'll ate"
• remove a carboxyl group from (a molecule).
• [from or after Latin *de* = off + CARBOXYL]
• **decarboxylase** *noun*
• **decarboxylation** *noun*

decasyllable *noun*
• "DECKA silla bull"
• a metrical line of ten syllables.
• [Greek *deka* ten + SYLLABLE]
• **decasyllabic** *adjective*

decathlon *noun*
• "de CATH lon"
• an athletic contest in which each competitor takes part in ten events.
• [Greek *deka* ten + *athlon* contest]
• **decathlete** *noun*

decay *verb*
• "de CAY"
• rot, decompose.
• [Old French *decair* from Romanic (Latin *de* = off + *cadere* fall)]

decease *noun*
- "de SEECE"
- death.
- [Old French *deces* from Latin *decessus* from *decedere* (*de* = off + *cedere cess-* go)]
- **deceased** *adjective*

decedent *noun*
- "de SEED 'nt"
- a deceased person.
- [Latin *decedere* die: see DECEASE]

deceit *noun*
- "de SEET"
- the act or process of deceiving or misleading, esp. by concealing the truth.
- [Old French from past participle of *deceveir* from Latin *decipere* deceive (*de* = off + *capere* take)]
- **deceitful** *adjective*
- **deceitfully** *adverb*
- **deceitfulness** *noun*

deceive *verb*
- "de SEEVE"
- make (a person) believe what is false; mislead purposely.
- [Old French *deceivre* or *deceiv-* stressed, stem of *deceveir* (as DECEIT)]
- **deceivable** *adjective*
- **deceiver** *noun*

decelerate *verb*
- "dee SELLER ate"
- move more slowly, slow down.
- [Latin *de* = off + ACCELERATE]
- **deceleration** *noun*
- **decelerator** *noun*

decency *noun*
- "DEECE 'n see"
- correct and tasteful standards of behaviour as generally accepted.
- [Latin *decentia* from *decēre* be fitting]
- **decent** *adjective*

decennial *adjective*
- "de SENNY 'll"
- lasting ten years.
- [Latin *decennis* of ten years, from *decem* ten + *annus* year]
- **decennially** *adverb*

deception *noun*
- "de SEP sh'n"
- the act or an instance of deceiving; the process of being deceived.
- [Old French or Late Latin *deceptio* from *decipere* (as DECEIT)]

deceptive *adjective*
- "de SEPTIV"
- giving an appearance or impression different from the true one; misleading.
- [Old French *deceptif -ive* or Late Latin *deceptivus* (as DECEPTION)]
- **deceptively** *adverb*

decerebrate *adjective*
- "dee SERRA brit"
- having had the cerebrum removed.
- [from or after Latin *de* = off + CEREBRUM]

decertify *verb*
- "dee SERTA fie"
- revoke or renounce certification of (a person or thing, esp. a union).
- [from or after Latin *de* = off + CERTIFY]
- **decertification** *noun*

decibel *noun*
- "DESSA bull" or "DESSA bell"
- a unit (one-tenth of a bel) used in the comparison of two power levels relating to electrical signals or sound intensities, one of the pair usually being taken as a standard.
- [Latin *decimus* tenth + BEL]

decide *verb*
- "de SIDE"
- come to a resolution as a result of consideration.
- [French *décider* from Latin *decidere* (*de* = off + *cædere* cut)]
- **decidable** *adjective*

deciduous *adjective*
- "duh SIDGE oo us" or "duh SID yoo us"
- (of a tree) shedding its leaves annually.
- [Latin *deciduus* from *decidere* from *cadere* fall]

decigram *noun*
- "DESSA gram"
- a metric unit of mass, equal to 0.1 gram.
- [Latin *decem* ten + 'gram' from French *gramme* from Greek *gramma* small weight]

decile *noun*
- "DESS ile" or "DESS'll"
- any of the nine values of a random variable which divide a frequency distribution into ten groups, each containing one-tenth of the total population.
- [French *décile*, ultimately from Latin *decem* ten]

decilitre *noun*

ALSO SPELLED: esp. *US* **deciliter**
- "DESSA leeter"
- a metric unit of capacity, equal to 0.1 litre.
- [Latin *decimus* tenth + LITRE]

decimal *adjective*
- "DESSA m'll"
- (of a system of numbers, weights, measures, etc.) based on the number ten, in which the smaller units are related to the principal units as powers of ten (units, tens, hundreds, thousands, etc.).
- [modern Latin *decimalis* from Latin *decimus* tenth]
- **decimally** *adverb*

decimalize *verb*

ALSO SPELLED: esp. *Brit.* **-ise**
- "DESSA m'll ize"

• express as a decimal.
• [as DECIMAL]
• **decimalization** *noun* (also esp. *Brit.* **-isation**)

decimate *verb*
• "DESSA mate"
• destroy a large proportion of.
• [Latin *decimare* take the tenth man, from *decimus* tenth]
• **decimation** *noun*
• **decimator** *noun*

decimetre *noun*
ALSO SPELLED: esp. *US* **decimeter**
• "DESSA meeter"
• a metric unit of length, equal to 0.1 metre.
• [Latin *decimus* tenth + METRE]

decipher *verb*
• "dee SIFE ur"
• succeed in understanding (anything obscure or unclear).
• [from or after Latin *de* = off + CIPHER]
• **decipherable** *adjective*
• **decipherment** *noun*

decision *noun*
• "de SIZH'n"
• the act or process of deciding.
• [Old French *decision* or Latin *decisio* (as DECIDE)]

decisive *adjective*
• "de SICE iv"
• that decides an issue; conclusive.
• [French *décisif -ive* from medieval Latin *decisivus* (as DECIDE)]
• **decisively** *adverb*
• **decisiveness** *noun*

deckle *noun*
• "DECK'll"
• a device in a papermaking machine for limiting the size of the sheet.
• [German *Deckel* diminutive of *Decke* cover]
HOMOPHONES: *decal*

declamation *noun*
• "deckla MAY sh'n"
• the act or art of declaiming.
• [French *déclamation* or Latin *declamatio* from *declamare* from *de-* from, off + *clamare* cry out]
• **declamatory** *adjective* "de CLAMMA tory"

declarant *noun*
• "de CLARE 'nt"
• a person who makes a legal declaration.
• [as DECLARE]

declarative *adjective*
• "de CLARE a tiv"
• of the nature of, or making, a declaration.
• [as DECLARE]
• **declaratively** *adverb*

declare *verb*
• "de CLARE"
• announce openly or formally.
• [Latin *declarare* (*de* = off + *clarare* from *clarus* clear)]
• **declaration** *noun*
• **declaratory** *adjective*
• **declared** *adjective*
• **declaredly** *adverb* "de CLARE id lee"
• **declarer** *noun*

déclassé *adjective*
• "day class AY"
• that has fallen in social status.
• [French]

declassify *verb*
• "de CLASSA fie"
• declare (information etc.) to be no longer secret.
• [from or after Latin *de* = off + CLASSIFY]
• **declassification** *noun*

declension *noun*
• "duh CLEN sh'n"
• the variation of the form of a noun, pronoun, or adjective, by which its grammatical case, number, and gender are identified.
• [Old French *declinaison* from *decliner* DECLINE, after Latin *declinatio*]
• **declensional** *adjective*

declination *noun*
• "deckla NAY sh'n"
• the angular distance of a star etc. north or south of the celestial equator.
• [Latin *declinatio* (as DECLINE)]

decline *verb*
• "dee CLINE"
• deteriorate; lose strength or vigour.
• [Latin *declinare* (*de* = off + *clinare* bend)]
• **declinable** *adjective*
• **decliner** *noun*

declivity *noun*
• "de CLIVVA tee"
• a downward slope, esp. a piece of sloping ground.
• [Latin *declivitas* from *declivis* (*de* = off + *clivus* slope)]

Deco *noun*
• "DECKO"
• the predominant decorative art style of the period 1910–30, characterized by precise and boldly delineated geometric motifs, shapes, and strong colours.
• [French *décoratif* DECORATIVE]
HOMOPHONES: *dekko*

decoction *noun*
• "de COCK sh'n"
• a process of boiling down so as to extract some essence.
• [Late Latin *decoctio* (Latin *de* = off + *coquere coct-* boil)]

decode *verb*
• "dee CODE"
• convert (a coded message) into intelligible language.
• [from or after Latin *de* = off + 'code' (as CODEX)]
• **decodable** *adjective*

décolletage *noun*
• "day coll TOZH" or "day colla TOZH"
• a low neckline of a woman's dress etc.
• [French (Latin *de* = off + *collet* collar of a dress)]

décolleté *adjective*
• "day COLL tay"
• (of a dress etc.) having a low neckline.
• [French (as DÉCOLLETAGE)]

decolonize *verb*
ALSO SPELLED: esp. *Brit.* **-ise**
• "dee COLLA nize"
• (of a state) withdraw from (a colony), leaving it independent.
• [from or after Latin *de* = off + COLONIZE]
• **decolonization** *noun* (also esp. *Brit.* **-isation**)

decommission *verb*
• "dee kuh MISH'n"
• close down (a nuclear reactor etc.).
• [from or after Latin *de* = off + COMMISSION]

decompensation *noun*
• "dee comp'n SAY sh'n"
• failure of an organ to maintain functioning, esp. after a period of compensation for disease, deficiency, etc.
• [from or after Latin *de* = off + COMPENSATION]

decompose *verb*
• "dee k'm POZE"
• decay, rot.
• [from or after Latin *de* = off + COMPOSE]
• **decomposability** *noun*
• **decomposable** *adjective*
• **decomposition** *noun*

decompress *verb*
• "dee k'm PRESS"
• relieve or reduce pressure.
• [from or after Latin *de* = off + COMPRESS]
• **decompression** *noun*
• **decompressor** *noun*

decongestant *adjective*
• "dee k'n JESS t'nt"
• that relieves (esp. nasal) congestion.
• [from or after Latin *de* = off + CONGESTION]

deconsecrate *verb*
• "dee CONSA crate"
• transfer (esp. a building) from sacred to secular use.
• [from or after Latin *de* = off + CONSECRATE]
• **deconsecration** *noun*

decontaminate *verb*
• "dee k'n TAMMA nate"
• remove contamination or the risk of it from (an area, person, etc.) affected by radioactivity, infectious disease, harmful chemicals, etc.
• [from or after Latin *de* = off + CONTAMINATE]
• **decontamination** *noun*

decontextualize *verb*
ALSO SPELLED: esp. *Brit.* **-ise**
• "dee k'n TEX choo 'll ize"
• study or treat (a word, text, etc.) in isolation from its context.
• [from or after Latin *de* = off + CONTEXT]
• **decontextualization** *noun* (also esp. *Brit.* **-isation**)
• **decontextualized** *adjective* (also esp. *Brit.* **-ised**)

decor *noun*
• "day CORE" or "duh CORE" or "DAY core"
• the overall effect, style, etc. of the decorations and furnishings of a room, building, etc.
• [French from *décorer* (as DECORATE)]

decorate *verb*
• "DECKER ate"
• make (something) more attractive by adding colour, adornments, etc.
• [Latin *decorare decorat-* from *decus -oris* beauty]
• **decorated** *adjective*
• **decoration** *noun*
• **decorator** *noun*

decorative *adjective*
• "DECK ruh tiv" or "DECKER a tiv"
• serving to decorate.
• [as DECORATE]
• **decoratively** *adverb*
• **decorativeness** *noun*

decorous *adjective*
• "DECKER us"
• respecting good taste or propriety; dignified.
• [Latin *decorus* seemly]
• **decorously** *adverb*
• **decorousness** *noun*

decorticate *verb*
• "dee CORTA cate"
• remove the bark, rind, or husk from.
• [Latin *decorticare decorticat-* (*de* = off + *cortex -icis* bark)]
• **decortication** *noun*

decorum *noun*
• "de CORE um"
• seemliness, propriety.
• [Latin, neuter of *decorus* seemly]

decoupage *noun*
• "day coo POZH" or "day coo PAZH"
• the decoration of surfaces with paper cut-outs.
• [French, = the action of cutting out]

decouple *verb*
• "dee CUP'll"
• make separate or independent.
• [from or after Latin *de* = off + COUPLE]

- **decoupled** *adjective*
- **decoupling** *noun*

decrement *noun*
- "DECKRA m'nt"
- the act of decreasing.
- [Latin *decrementum* from *decrescere* (*de-* from, off + *crescere cret-* grow)]
- **decremental** *adjective*

decreolization *noun*
- "dee cree 'll ize AY sh'n"
- the modification of (a language) away from its creole characteristics.
- [from or after Latin *de* = off + CREOLIZE]

decrepit *adjective*
- "duh CREPPIT"
- weakened or worn out by age and infirmity.
- [Latin *decrepitus* (*de* = off + *crepitus* past participle of *crepare* creak)]
- **decrepitude** *noun*

decrescendo *noun*
- "dee cresh ENDO" or "day cresh ENDO"
- a gradual decrease in loudness.
- [Italian, participle of *decrescere* from Latin *decrescere* (*de-* from, off + *crescere cret-* grow)]

decretal *noun*
- "de CREET'll"
- a papal decree.
- [medieval Latin *decretale* from Late Latin (*epistola*) *decretalis* (letter) of decree, from Latin *decernere* decide (from *de-* off + *cernere* sift)]

decriminalize *verb*
ALSO SPELLED: esp. *Brit.* **-ise**
- "dee CRIMMIN'll ize"
- make or treat (an action etc.) as no longer criminal; legalize (esp. a drug, its possession, or use).
- [from or after Latin *de* = off + CRIMINAL]
- **decriminalization** *noun* (also esp. *Brit.* **-isation**)

decrypt *verb*
- "dee CRIPT"
- decipher or decode.
- [Latin *de-* off + CRYPTOGRAM]
- **decryption** *noun*

decumbent *adjective*
- "de CUM b'nt"
- (of a plant, shoot, etc.) lying or trailing on the ground with the extremity ascending.
- [Latin *decumbere decumbent-* lie down]

decussate *adjective*
- "dee CUSSATE"
- X-shaped.
- [Latin *decussatus* past participle of *decussare* divide in a cross shape, from *decussis* the numeral ten or the shape X, from *decem* ten]
- **decussation** *noun*

dedicate *verb*
- "DEDDA cate"
- devote (esp. oneself) to a noble task or purpose.
- [Latin *dedicare* (*de-* from, off + *dicare* declare, dedicate)]
- **dedicated** *adjective*
- **dedicatee** *noun*
- **dedication** *noun*
- **dedicatory** *adjective*

deduce *verb*
- "de DOOCE" or "de DYOOCE"
- infer; draw as a logical conclusion.
- [Latin *deducere* (*de* = off + *ducere duct-* lead)]
- **deducible** *adjective*

deductible *adjective*
- "de DUCTA bull"
- that may be deducted, esp. from tax to be paid or taxable income.
- [as DEDUCE]
- **deductibility** *noun*

deduction *noun*
- "de DUCK sh'n"
- the act or process of deducting.
- [Latin *deductio* (as DEDUCE)]

deductive *adjective*
- "de DUCTIV"
- of or reasoning by deduction.
- [medieval Latin *deductivus* (as DEDUCE)]
- **deductively** *adverb*

deerstalker *noun*
- "DEER stocker"
- a soft cloth cap with peaks in front and behind and earflaps usu. worn tied together at the crown.
- ['deer' + STALK]

deface *verb*
- "de FACE"
- spoil the appearance of; disfigure.
- [French *défacer*]
- **defaceable** *adjective*
- **defacement** *noun*
- **defacer** *noun*

defalcation *noun*
- "dee fal CAY sh'n"
- a misappropriation of money.
- [medieval Latin *defalcatio* (Latin *de* = off + Latin *falx -cis* sickle)]
- **defalcate** *verb* "DEE fal cate"

defamation *noun*
- "deffa MAY sh'n"
- the act of defaming or the fact of being defamed.
- [as DEFAME]
- **defamatory** *adjective* "de FAMMA tory"

defame *verb*
- "de FAME"
- attack the good reputation of; speak ill of.
- [Latin *diffamare* spread evil report (from *dis-* expressing negation + *fama* report)]
- **defamatory** *adjective* "de FAMMA tory"
- **defamer** *noun*

defamiliarize *verb*
ALSO SPELLED: esp. *Brit.* **-ise**
• "dee fuh MILL yuh rize"
• render (a word etc.) unfamiliar, esp. as a critical technique to revitalize the perception of words and their sounds by differentiation from ordinary language.
• [from or after Latin *de* = off + FAMILIARIZE]
• **defamiliarization** *noun* (also esp. *Brit.* **-isation**)

default *noun*
• "DEE fault" or "duh FAULT"
• failure to fulfill an obligation, esp. to appear, pay, or act in some way.
• [Old French *defaut(e)* from *defaillir* fail, from Romanic (Latin *de* = off + *fallere* deceive)]
• **defaulted** *adjective*
• **defaulter** *noun*

defeasance *noun*
• "de FEEZ ince"
• the act or process of rendering null and void.
• [Old French *defesance* from *de(s)faire* undo (Latin *de* = off + *faire* make, from Latin *facere*)]

defeasible *adjective*
• "de FEEZA bull"
• capable of annulment.
• [Anglo-French (as DEFEASANCE)]
• **defeasibility** *noun*
• **defeasibly** *adverb*

defeat *verb*
• "de FEET"
• overcome in a battle or other contest.
• [Old French *deffait*, *desfait* past participle of *desfaire* from medieval Latin *disfacere* (Latin *dis-* expressing negation + *facere* do)]

defeatism *noun*
• "de FEET izm"
• an excessive readiness to accept defeat.
• [as DEFEAT]
• **defeatist** *noun*

defecate *verb*
• "DEFFA cate"
• discharge feces from the body.
• [earlier as adjective, = purified, from Latin *defaecare* (*de* = off + *faex faecis* dregs)]
• **defecation** *noun*

defect *noun*
• "DEE fect"
• a shortcoming, failing, or imperfection.
• [Latin *defectus* from *deficere* desert, fail (*de* = off + *facere* do)]
• **defector** *noun*

defection *noun*
• "de FECK sh'n"
• the abandonment of one's country or cause.
• [as DEFECT]

defective *adjective*
• "de FECTIV"
• having a defect or defects; incomplete, imperfect, faulty.
• [as DEFECT]
• **defectively** *adverb*
• **defectiveness** *noun*

defendant *noun*
• "de FEND'nt"
• a person etc. sued or accused in a court of law.
• [Latin *defendere* (from *de-* off + *fendere* strike)]

defenestration *noun*
• "dee fenna STRAY sh'n"
• the action of throwing (esp. a person) out of a window.
• [modern Latin *defenestratio* (Latin *de* = off + *fenestra* window)]
• **defenestrate** *verb*

defensible *adjective*
• "de FENSA bull"
• justifiable; supportable by argument.
• [Late Latin *defensibilis* (as DEFENDANT)]
• **defensibility** *noun*
• **defensibly** *adverb*

defensive *adjective*
• "de FENSIV"
• done or intended for defence or to defend.
• [French *défensif -ive* from medieval Latin *defensivus* (as DEFENDANT)]
• **defensively** *adverb*
• **defensiveness** *noun*

defer *verb*
• "duh FUR"
• put off to a later time; postpone.
• [Middle English, originally the same as 'differ' from Latin *differre*, differ]
• **deferment** *noun*
• **deferral** *noun*

deference *noun*
• "DEFFER ince"
• courteous regard, respect.
• [French *déférence* from *déférer* from Latin *deferre* (from *de* off + *ferre* bring)]

deferential *adjective*
• "deffer EN sh'll"
• showing deference; respectful.
• [as DEFERENCE]
• **deferentially** *adverb*

defiance *noun*
• "duh FIE ince"
• open disobedience, bold resistance.
• [Old French *defiance* from *defier* (from Latin *dis-* expressing negation + *fidus* faithful)]
• **defiant** *adjective*
• **defiantly** *adverb*

defibrillation *noun*
• "dee fibbra LAY sh'n"
• the application of an electric shock to the heart to stop fibrillation and encourage the resumption of coordinated contractions.

• [from or after Latin *de* = off + FIBRILLATION]
• **defibrillator** *noun*

deficient *adjective*
• "de FISH 'nt"
• incomplete; not having enough of a specified quality or ingredient.
• [Latin *deficiens* participle of *deficere* (as DEFECT)]
• **deficiency** *noun*
• **deficiently** *adverb*

deficit *noun*
• "DEFFA sit"
• the amount by which a thing (esp. a sum of money) is too small.
• [French *déficit* from Latin *deficit* 3rd sing. pres. of *deficere* (as DEFECT)]

defilade *verb*
• "deffa LADE"
• shield (a position, troops, etc.) from observation or (enfilading) fire by utilizing natural obstacles or erecting fortifications.
• [French *défiler* (from Latin *de* = off + *filare* spin or *filum* thread)]

define *verb*
• "de FINE"
• give the exact meaning of (a word etc.).
• [ultimately from Latin *definire* (Latin *de* = off + *finire* finish, from *finis* end)]
• **definable** *adjective*
• **definer** *noun*
• **definition** *noun*

definite *adjective*
• "DEFF'n it"
• having exact and discernible limits.
• [Latin *definitus* past participle of *definire* (as DEFINE)]
• **definitely** *adverb*
• **definiteness** *noun*

definitive *adjective*
• "duh FINNA tiv"
• (of an answer, verdict, etc.) conclusive, decisive, final.
• [Old French *definitif -ive* from Latin *definitivus* (as DEFINE)]
• **definitively** *adverb*

deflagrate *verb*
• "DEFFLA grate" or "DEE fluh grate"
• burn away with sudden flame.
• [Latin *deflagrare* (Latin *de* = off + *flagrare* blaze)]
• **deflagration** *noun*

deflate *verb*
• "dee FLATE"
• let air or gas out of (a tire, balloon, etc.).
• [Latin *de-* off + INFLATE]
• **deflated** *adjective*
• **deflator** *noun*

deflation *noun*
• "dee FLAY sh'n"
• a general decrease in prices and rise in the purchasing value of money.
• [as DEFLATE]
• **deflationary** *adjective*
• **deflationist** *noun*

deflect *verb*
• "duh FLECT"
• bend or turn aside from a straight course or intended purpose.
• [Latin *deflectere* (Latin *de* = off + *flectere flex-* bend)]
• **deflection** *noun*
• **deflector** *noun*

defoliate *verb*
• "dee FOLEY ate"
• remove leaves from, esp. as a military tactic.
• [Late Latin *defoliare* from *de* = off + *folium* leaf]
• **defoliant** *noun*
• **defoliation** *noun*

deformation *noun*
• "de for MAY sh'n"
• the action or result of marring the appearance, excellence, etc.; disfigurement, defacement.
• [Old French *desformer* from Latin *deformare* from *de* = off + *forma* mould, form]
• **deformational** *adjective*

defraud *verb*
• "dee FROD"
• take or withhold rightful property, status, etc. from (a person) by fraud; cheat.
• [from or after Latin *de* = off + FRAUD]
• **defrauder** *noun*

defunct *adjective*
• "de FUNCT"
• no longer existing.
• [Latin *defunctus* dead, past participle of *defungi* (Latin *de* = off + *fungi* perform)]

degauss *verb*
• "dee GOUSE" (rhymes with *MOUSE*)
• neutralize the magnetism in (a thing) by encircling it with a current-carrying conductor.
• [Latin *de-* off + GAUSS]
• **degausser** *noun*

degenerate *verb*
• "duh JENNER ate"
• deteriorate physically, mentally, or morally.
• [Latin *degenerare* (Latin *de* = off + *genus -eris* race)]
• **degeneracy** *noun*
• **degenerately** *adverb*
• **degeneration** *noun*
• **degenerative** *adjective* "duh JENNER a tiv"

deglaciation *noun*
• "dee glay see AY sh'n"
• the disappearance of ice from a previously glaciated region.
• [from or after Latin *de* = off + 'glaciate' (as GLACIATED)]

degradation *noun*
- "deggra DAY sh'n"
- an action that humiliates or lowers a person in social position, status, etc.
- [as DEGRADE]

degrade *verb*
- "dee GRADE"
- lower in character or quality; debase.
- [Old French *degrader* from Church Latin *degradare* (Latin *de* = off + *gradus* step)]
- **degradability** *noun*
- **degradable** *adjective*

degressive *adjective*
- "dee GRESSIV"
- (of taxation) at successively lower rates on low amounts.
- [Latin *degredi* (Latin *de* = off + *gradi* walk)]

dehisce *verb*
- "dee HISS"
- gape or burst open (esp. of a pod or seed vessel or of a cut or wound).
- [Latin *dehiscere* (Latin *de* = off + *hiscere* (a form indicating the beginning of an action) from *hiare* gape)]
- **dehiscence** *noun*
- **dehiscent** *adjective*

dehumidify *verb*
- "dee hyoo MIDDA fie"
- reduce the degree of humidity of; remove moisture from (a gas, esp. air).
- [Latin *de* = off + *humidus* from *umēre* be moist]
- **dehumidification** *noun*
- **dehumidifier** *noun*

dehydrate *verb*
- "dee HY drate"
- remove water from (esp. foods for preservation and storage in bulk).
- [from or after Latin *de* = off + HYDRATE]
- **dehydrated** *adjective*
- **dehydration** *noun*
- **dehydrator** *noun*

dehydrogenase *noun*
- "dee hy DRAW j'n ace"
- an enzyme which helps the removal of hydrogen atoms from a particular molecule.
- [as DEHYDROGENATE]

dehydrogenate *verb*
- "dee hy DRAW j'n ate"
- remove a hydrogen atom or atoms from (a compound).
- [from or after Latin *de* = off + HYDROGENATE]
- **dehydrogenation** *noun*

deicide *noun*
- "DEE a side" or "DAY a side"
- the killing of a god.
- [Church Latin *deicida* from Latin *deus* god + *cidium* from *caedere* kill]

deictic *adjective*
- "DIKE tick"
- serving to relate that which is spoken of to the spatial and temporal context of the utterance, as the words *we*, *you*, *here*, *now*, *then*, and *that*.
- [Greek *deiktikos* from *deiktos* capable of proof, from *deiknumi* show]
- **deictically** *adverb*

deify *verb*
- "DEE a fie" or "DAY a fie"
- make a god of.
- [Old French *deifier* from Church Latin *deificare* from *deus* god]
- **deification** *noun*

deign *verb*
- "DANE"
- think fit; condescend.
- [Old French *degnier*, *deigner*, *daigner* from Latin *dignare*, *-ari* deem worthy, from *dignus* worthy]

HOMOPHONES: *Dane*

deindustrialize *verb*
ALSO SPELLED: esp. *Brit.* **-ise**
- "dee in DUSTRY'll ize"
- make (a region, nation, etc.) less or no longer industrial.
- [from or after Latin *de* = off + INDUSTRIALIZE]
- **deindustrialization** *noun* (also esp. *Brit.* **-isation**)
- **deindustrialized** *adjective* (also esp. *Brit.* **-ised**)

deinstitutionalize *verb*
ALSO SPELLED: esp. *Brit.* **-ise**
- "dee insta TOO sh'n 'll ize" or "dee insta TYOO sh'n 'll ize"
- remove from an institution or from the effects of institutional life.
- [from or after Latin *de* = off + INSTITUTION]
- **deinstitutionalization** *noun* (also esp. *Brit.* **-isation**)
- **deinstitutionalized** *adjective* (also esp. *Brit.* **-ised**)

deionize *verb*
ALSO SPELLED: esp. *Brit.* **-ise**
- "dee EYE a nize"
- remove the ions or ionic constituents from (water, air, etc.).
- [from or after Latin *de* = off + IONIZE]
- **deionization** *noun* (also esp. *Brit.* **-isation**)
- **deionized** *adjective* (also esp. *Brit.* **-ised**)
- **deionizer** *noun* (also esp. *Brit.* **-iser**)

deism *noun*
- "DEE izm"
- belief in the existence of a supreme being arising from reason rather than revelation.
- [Latin *deus* god]
- **deist** *noun*
- **deistic** *adjective*

deity *noun*
- "DEE a tee" or "DAY a tee"
- a god or goddess.

• [Old French *deité* from Church Latin *deitas -tatis* translation of Greek *theotēs* from *theos* god]

dejected *adjective*
• "dee JECTED"
• make sad or dispirited; depress.
• [Latin *dejicere* (*de-* from + *jacere* throw)]
• **dejectedly** *adverb*
• **dejection** *noun*

deke *noun*
• "DEEK"
• a fake shot or movement done to draw a defensive player out of position and thus create a better opportunity to score.
• [abbreviation of 'decoy' (perhaps from Dutch *de kooi* the decoy, from *de* the + *kooi* from Latin *cavea* cage)]

dekko *noun*
• "DECKO"
• a look or glance.
• [Hindi *dekho*, imperative of *dekhnā* look]
HOMOPHONES: *Deco*

delaminate *verb*
• "dee LAMMA nate"
• split into separate layers.
• [from or after Latin *de* = off + LAMINATE]
• **delamination** *noun*

delate *verb*
• "de LATE"
• inform against; impeach (a person).
• [Latin *delat-* (Latin *de* = off + *lat-* past participle stem of *ferre* carry)]
• **delation** *noun*
• **delator** *noun*

Delaware *noun*
• "DELLA ware"
• a member of an Aboriginal people formerly inhabiting the Delaware river basin in the northeastern US, some of whom moved north and now live near London, Ont.
• [the *Delaware* River]

dele *verb*
• "DEELY"
• delete or mark for deletion (a letter, word, etc.) from typeset material.
• [Latin, imperative of *delēre*: see DELETE]

delectable *adjective*
• "duh LECTA bull"
• (of food) delicious.
• [Latin *delectabilis* from *delectare* delight]
• **delectably** *adverb*

delectation *noun*
• "dee leck TAY sh'n"
• pleasure; enjoyment.
• [Old French (as DELECTABLE)]

delegacy *noun*
• "DELLA guh see"
• a system of delegating.
• [as DELEGATE]

delegate *noun*
• "DELLA git"
• a person chosen or elected to represent others at a conference, political convention, etc.
• [Latin *delegatus* (Latin *de* = off + *legare* depute)]

delegation *noun*
• "della GAY sh'n"
• a body of delegates; a number of people chosen to act as representatives.
• [Latin *delegatio* (as DELEGATE)]

delegitimize *verb*
ALSO SPELLED: esp. *Brit.* **-ise**
• "dee luh JITTA mize"
• withdraw legitimate status from (an organization, state, person, etc.).
• [from or after Latin *de* = off + LEGITIMIZE]
• **delegitimization** *noun* (also esp. *Brit.* **-isation**)

delete *verb*
• "duh LEET"
• remove or obliterate (written or printed matter).
• [Latin *delēre delet-* efface]
• **deletion** *noun*

deleterious *adjective*
• "della TEERY us"
• harmful (to the mind or body).
• [medieval Latin *deleterius* from Greek *dēlētērios* noxious]
• **deleteriously** *adverb*

Delft *noun*
• "DELFT"
• glazed, usu. blue and white, earthenware, made in Delft, the Netherlands.

deli *noun*
• "DELLY"
• a delicatessen.
• [abbreviation]

deliberate *adjective*
• "duh LIBBER it"
• intentional; done on purpose.
• [Latin *deliberatus* past participle of *deliberare* (Latin *de* = off + *librare* weigh, from *libra* balance)]
• **deliberately** *adverb*
• **deliberateness** *noun*

deliberation *noun*
• "duh libber AY sh'n"
• careful consideration.
• [as DELIBERATE]

deliberative *adjective*
• "duh LIBBER a tiv"
• of, characterized by, or appointed for the purpose of, deliberation or debate.
• [as DELIBERATE]

delicacy *noun*
• "DELLA kuh see"
• (esp. in craftsmanship or artistic or natural

beauty) fineness or intricacy of structure or texture; gracefulness.
• [as DELICATE]

delicate *adjective*
• "DELLA kit"
• fine in texture or structure; soft, slender, or slight.
• [Latin *delicatus*, of unknown origin]
• **delicately** *adverb*
• **delicateness** *noun*

delicatessen *noun*
• "della kuh TESS 'n"
• a place selling cooked meats, cheeses, and unusual or foreign prepared foods.
• [German *Delikatessen* or Dutch *delicatessen* from French *délicatesse* from *délicat* (as DELICATE)]

delicious *adjective*
• "duh LISH us"
• highly delightful and enjoyable to the taste or sense of smell.
• [Late Latin *deliciosus* from Latin *deliciae* delight]
• **deliciously** *adverb*
• **deliciousness** *noun*

delict *noun*
• "duh LICT" or "DEE lict"
• (in civil law jurisdictions) a civil wrong other than a breach of contract.
• [Latin *delictum* neuter past participle of *delinquere* offend (Latin *de* = off + *linquere* leave)]

delineate *verb*
• "duh LINNY ate"
• trace out by lines; trace or serve as the outline of.
• [Latin *delineare delineat-* (Latin *de* = off + *lineare* from *linea* line)]
• **delineation** *noun*
• **delineator** *noun*

delinquency *noun*
• "de LING kw'n see"
• minor crime such as vandalism, esp. when committed by young people.
• [Church Latin *delinquentia* from Latin *delinquens* participle of *delinquere* (as DELICT)]
• **delinquent** *noun*
• **delinquently** *adverb*

deliquesce *verb*
• "della KWESS"
• become liquid, melt.
• [Latin *deliquescere* (Latin *de* = off + *liquescere* inceptive of *liquēre* be liquid)]
• **deliquescence** *noun*
• **deliquescent** *adjective*

delirium *noun*
• "duh LEERY um"
• an acutely disordered state of mind involving incoherent speech, hallucinations, and frenzied excitement, occurring in metabolic disorders, intoxication, fever, etc.
• [Latin from *delirare* be deranged (Latin *de* = off + *lira* ridge between furrows)]
• **delirious** *adjective*
• **deliriously** *adverb*

deliver *verb*
• "duh LIVVER"
• distribute (letters, parcels, ordered goods, etc.) to the addressee or the purchaser.
• [Old French *delivrer* from Gallo-Roman (Latin *de* = off + LIBERATE)]
• **deliverability** *noun*
• **deliverable** *adjective*
• **deliverer** *noun*
• **delivery** *noun*

deliverance *noun*
• "duh LIVVER ince"
• the act or an instance of rescuing; the process of being rescued.
• [as DELIVER]

delocalized *adjective*
ALSO SPELLED: esp. *Brit.* **-ised**
• "dee LOKE'll ized"
• (of electrons) shared among more than two atoms in a molecule.
• [from or after Latin *de* = off + LOCALIZE]
• **delocalization** *noun* (also esp. *Brit.* **-isation**)

delouse *verb*
• "dee LOUSE"
• rid (a person or animal) of lice.
• [from or after Latin *de* = off + 'louse']

Delphic *adjective*
• "DELFIC"
• (of an utterance, prophecy, etc.) obscure, ambiguous, or enigmatic.
• [in allusion to the shrine of Apollo at *Delphi* in ancient Greece and the Delphic Oracle, whose often riddling responses to a wide range of religious, political, and moral questions were delivered in a state of ecstasy by the Pythia, the priestess of Apollo]

delphinium *noun*
• "del FINNY um"
• any garden plant of the genus *Delphinium*, of the buttercup family, with tall spikes of usu. blue flowers.
• [modern Latin from Greek *delphinion* larkspur, from *delphin* dolphin]

delphinoid *adjective*
• "DELF'n oid"
• of the family that includes dolphins, porpoises, grampuses, etc.
• [Greek *delphinoeidēs* from *delphin* dolphin]

delta *noun*
• "DELTA"
• a triangular tract of deposited earth, alluvium, etc., at the mouth of a river, formed by its diverging outlets.
• [from *delta* the fourth letter of the Greek alphabet (Δ, δ)]
• **deltaic** *adjective* "del TAY ick"

deltoid *noun*
• "DEL toid"
• a thick triangular muscle covering the shoulder joint and used for raising the arm away from the body.
• [French *deltoïde* or modern Latin *deltoides* from Greek *deltoeidēs* (as DELTA)]

delude *verb*
• "duh LOOD"
• deceive or mislead.
• [Latin *deludere* mock (Latin *de* = off + *ludere lus-* play)]
• **deluder** *noun*

deluge *noun*
• "DEL yoozh" or "DEL yoodge"
• a great flood.
• [French from Latin *diluvium*, related to *lavare* wash]

delusion *noun*
• "duh LOO zh'n"
• a false belief or impression.
• [Late Latin *delusio* (as DELUDE)]
• **delusional** *adjective*

delusive *adjective*
• "duh LOO siv"
• deceptive or unreal.
• [as DELUDE]

delusory *adjective*
• "duh LOOZERY"
• deceptive or unreal.
• [Late Latin *delusorius* (as DELUSION)]

deluxe *adjective*
• "de LUX"
• of a superior kind.
• [French *de luxe* of luxury, from Latin *luxus* abundance]

demagnetize *verb*
ALSO SPELLED: esp. *Brit.* **-ise**
• "dee MAGNA tize"
• remove the magnetic properties of.
• [from or after Latin *de* = off + MAGNETIZE]
• **demagnetization** *noun* (also esp. *Brit.* **-isation**)
• **demagnetizer** *noun* (also esp. *Brit.* **-iser**)

demagogue *noun*
ALSO SPELLED: *US* also **demagog**
• "DEMMA gog"
• a leader or orator who tries to win support by inflaming people's emotions and prejudices.
• [Greek *dēmagōgos* from *dēmos* the people + *agōgos* leading]
• **demagogic** *adjective* "demma GODGE ick" or "demma GOG ick"
• **demagoguery** *noun* "demma GOGGA ree"
• **demagogy** *noun* "DEMMA godge ee" or "DEMMA goggy"

demantoid *noun*
• "duh MAN toid"
• a lustrous green garnet.
• [German from *Demant* diamond]

demarcation *noun*
• "dee mar CAY sh'n"
• separation or distinction.
• [Spanish *demarcación* from *demarcar* mark the bounds of]
• **demarcate** *verb*
• **demarcator** *noun*

démarche *noun*
• "day MARSH"
• a political step or initiative.
• [French from *démarcher* take steps (Latin *de* = off + Late Latin *marcus* hammer)]

dematerialize *verb*
ALSO SPELLED: esp. *Brit.* **-ise**
• "dee muh TEERY 'll ize"
• make or become non-material or spiritual.
• [from or after Latin *de* = off + MATERIALIZE]
• **dematerialization** *noun* (also esp. *Brit.* **-isation**)

deme *noun*
• "DEEM"
• a political division of Attica in ancient Greece.
• [Greek *dēmos* the people]
HOMOPHONES: *deem*

demeanour *noun*
ALSO SPELLED: **demeanor**
• "duh MEENER"
• outward behaviour or bearing.
• [Old French *demener* from Romanic (Latin *de-* from + *minare* drive animals, from *minari* threaten), prob. influenced by obsolete *havour* behaviour]

dementia *noun*
• "duh MENSHA"
• a chronic or persistent disorder of the mental processes marked by memory disorders, personality changes, impaired reasoning, etc., due to brain disease or injury.
• [Latin from *demens* out of one's mind (*de-* from + *mens mentis* mind)]

demerara *noun*
• "demma RERRA"
• light brown raw sugar coming originally and chiefly from Demerara, a former Dutch colony (now part of Guyana) in S America.

demersal *adjective*
• "duh MUR s'll"
• (of a fish etc.) being or living near the sea bottom.
• [Latin *demersus* past participle of *demergere* (Latin *de* = off + *mergere* plunge)]

demesne *noun*
• "duh MEEN" or "duh MANE"
• landed property; an estate.
• [Old French *demeine* (later Anglo-French *demesne*) belonging to a lord, from Latin *dominicus*, from *dominus* lord]
HOMOPHONES: *demean*

demijohn *noun*
• "DEMMY jon"
• a bulbous narrow-necked bottle holding from 11 to 38 litres and usu. in a wicker cover.
• [prob. corruption of French *dame-jeanne* Lady Jane, assimilated to 'demi-' half (from French from medieval Latin *dimedius* half, for Latin *dimidius*) + the name *John*]

demilitarize *verb*
ALSO SPELLED: esp. *Brit.* **-ise**
• "dee MILLA tuh rize"
• remove a military organization or forces from (a frontier, a zone, etc.).
• [from or after Latin *de* = off + MILITARIZE]
• **demilitarization** *noun* (also esp. *Brit.* **-isation**)

demimondaine *noun*
• "DEMMY mon dane"
• a woman of a demimonde.
• [as DEMIMONDE]

demimonde *noun*
• "DEMMY mond"
• any group considered to be on the fringes of respectable society.
• [French, = half-world]

demineralize *verb*
ALSO SPELLED: esp. *Brit.* **-ise**
• "dee MINNER 'll ize"
• remove minerals from (water etc.).
• [from or after Latin *de* = off + MINERAL]
• **demineralization** *noun* (also esp. *Brit.* **-isation**)
• **demineralized** *adjective* (also esp. *Brit.* **-ised**)

demise *noun*
• "duh MIZE"
• death.
• [Anglo-French use of past participle of Old French *de(s)mettre* DISMISS]

demisemiquaver *noun*
• "demmy SEMMY kway vur"
• a thirty-second note.
• [French *demi-* half + *semi-* half + QUAVER (in Britain used to mean 'eighth note')]

demit *verb*
• "duh MIT"
• resign or abdicate (an office etc.).
• [French *démettre* from Latin *demittere* (Latin *de* = off + *mittere miss-* send)]

demitasse *noun*
• "DEMMY tass"
• a small cup used to serve strong black coffee.
• [French, = half-cup]

demiurge *noun*
• "DEMMY urge"
• (in Platonism) the creator of the universe.
• [Church Latin from Greek *dēmiourgos* craftsman, from *dēmios* public, from *dēmos* people + *-ergos* working]
• **demiurgic** *adjective*
• **demiurgical** *adjective*

democracy *noun*
• "duh MOCKRA see"
• a system of government by the whole population or all the eligible members of a state, typically through elected representatives.
• [French *démocratie* from Late Latin *democratia* from Greek *dēmokratia* from *dēmos* the people + *kratia* from *kratos* strength, power]
• **democrat** *noun*
• **democratic** *adjective*
• **democratically** *adverb*

democratize *verb*
ALSO SPELLED: esp. *Brit.* **-ise**
• "duh MOCKRA tize"
• make (a state, institution, etc.) democratic.
• [as DEMOCRACY]
• **democratization** *noun* (also esp. *Brit.* **-isation**)

démodé *adjective*
• "day mo DAY"
• out of fashion.
• [French, past participle of *démoder* (Latin *de* = off + French *mode* fashion from Latin *modus* way)]

demodulate *verb*
• "dee MODGE oo late" or "dee MOD yuh late"
• extract (a modulating signal) from the signal's carrier.
• [as MODULATE]
• **demodulation** *noun*
• **demodulator** *noun*

demography *noun*
• "dem OGGRA fee"
• the study of the structure of populations or population statistics, esp. those showing average age, income, marital status, etc.
• [Greek *dēmos* the people + *graphia* writing]
• **demographer** *noun*
• **demographic** *adjective*
• **demographically** *adverb*
• **demographics** *noun*

demoiselle *noun*
• "demwa ZELL"
• a small crane, *Anthropoides virgo*, native to Asia and North Africa.
• [French, = DAMSEL]

demolish *verb*
• "duh MAUL ish"
• pull down (a building).
• [French *démolir* from Latin *demoliri* (*de* = off, from + *moliri molit-* construct, from *moles* mass)]
• **demolisher** *noun*
• **demolition** *noun*
• **demolitionist** *noun*

demonetize *verb*
ALSO SPELLED: esp. *Brit.* **-ise**
• "dee MONNA tize"
• withdraw (a coin etc.) from use as money.
• [French *démonétiser* (Latin *de* = off, from + *moneta* money)]

• **demonetization** *noun* (also esp. *Brit.* **-isation**)

demoniac *adjective*
• "de MOANY ack"
• of or like demons.
• [medieval Latin *demon* from Latin *daemon* from Greek *daimōn* deity]
• **demoniacal** *adjective*

demonic *adjective*
• "de MONNIC"
• of or like demons.
• [as DEMONIAC]
• **demonically** *adverb*

demonstrable *adjective*
• "duh MONSTRA bull"
• capable of being shown or logically proved.
• [as DEMONSTRATE]
• **demonstrably** *adverb*

demonstrate *verb*
• "DEM 'n strate"
• describe and explain (a scientific theory, machine, etc.) with the help of examples, experiments, practical use, etc.
• [Latin *demonstrare* (*de* = off, from + *monstrare* show)]
• **demonstration** *noun*

demonstrative *adjective*
• "duh MONSTRA tiv"
• given to or marked by an open expression of feeling, esp. of affection.
• [as DEMONSTRATE]
• **demonstratively** *adverb*
• **demonstrativeness** *noun*

demonstrator *noun*
• "DEM'n stray tur"
• a person who takes part in a political protest.
• [as DEMONSTRATE]

demoralize *verb*
ALSO SPELLED: esp. *Brit.* **-ise**
• "de MORA lize"
• destroy (a person's) morale; make hopeless.
• [French *démoraliser* (*de-* off, from + MORALE)]
• **demoralization** *noun* (also esp. *Brit.* **-isation**)
• **demoralizing** *adjective* (also esp. *Brit.* **-ising**)
• **demoralizingly** *adverb* (also esp. *Brit.* **-isingly**)

demote *verb*
• "de MOTE"
• reduce to a lower rank or class.
• [*de-* off, from + 'promote' from Latin *promovēre promot-* (*pro-* in front of, *movēre* move)]
• **demotion** *noun*

demotic *noun*
• "de MOTTIC"
• the popular colloquial form of a language.
• [Greek *dēmotikos* from *dēmotēs* one of the people (*dēmos*)]

demulcent *adjective*
• "de MULL s'nt"
• soothing.
• [Latin *demulcēre* (*de-* off, from + *mulcēre* soothe)]

demur *verb*
• "duh MUR"
• raise scruples or objections.
• [Old French *demeurer* from Romanic (*de-* off, from + Latin *morari* delay)]
• **demurrer** *noun*

demure *adjective*
• "duh MYOOR" ("YOOR" rhymes with *TOUR*)
• composed; quiet and reserved.
• [Middle English, perhaps from Anglo-French *demuré* from Old French *demoré* past participle of *demorer* remain, stay (as DEMUR): influenced by Old French *meür* from Latin *maturus* ripe]
• **demurely** *adverb*
• **demureness** *noun*

demurrage *noun*
• "duh MUR idge"
• a rate or amount payable to a shipowner by a charterer for failure to load or discharge a ship within the time agreed.
• [Old French *demo(u)rage* from *demorer* (as DEMUR)]

demutualize *verb*
• "dee MYOO choo 'll ize"
• (of a mutual insurance company etc.) change from being owned by its members to a different type of ownership.
• [Latin *de* = off, from + MUTUAL]
• **demutualization** *noun* (also esp. *Brit.* **-isation**)

demystify *verb*
• "dee MISTA fie"
• clarify (obscure beliefs or subjects etc.); simplify; explain.
• [Latin *de* = off, from + MYSTIFY]
• **demystification** *noun*

demythologize *verb*
ALSO SPELLED: esp. *Brit.* **-ise**
• "dee mith OLLA jize"
• remove mythical elements from (a legend, famous person's life, etc.).
• [Latin *de* = off, from + MYTHOLOGY]

denar *noun*
• "DEE nar"
• the basic monetary unit of the former Yugoslav Republic of Macedonia.
• [Latin *denarius*]
HOMOPHONES: *dinar*

denarius *noun*
• "duh NERRY us"
• an ancient Roman silver coin.
• [Latin, = (coin) worth ten (of a smaller coin) (as DENARY)]

denary *adjective*
- "DEENER ee"
- of ten; decimal.
- [Latin *denarius* containing ten (*deni* by tens)]

HOMOPHONES: *deanery*

denationalize *verb*
ALSO SPELLED: esp. *Brit.* **-ise**
- "dee NASH'n 'll ize"
- transfer (a nationalized industry or institution etc.) from public to private ownership.
- [Latin *de* = off, from + *natio -onis* from *nasci nat-* be born]
- **denationalization** *noun* (also esp. *Brit.* **-isation**)

denaturalize *verb*
ALSO SPELLED: esp. *Brit.* **-ise**
- "dee NATCHER 'll ize"
- change the nature or properties of; make unnatural.
- [as DENATURE]
- **denaturalization** *noun* (also esp. *Brit.* **-isation**)

denature *verb*
- "de NAY chur"
- change the properties of (a protein etc.) by heat, acidity, etc.
- [Latin *de* = off, from + *natura* nature]
- **denaturant** *noun*
- **denaturation** *noun*
- **denatured** *adjective*

dendrimer *noun*
- "DEN druh mur"
- a synthetic polymer with a branching, treelike structure.
- [Greek *dendron* tree + POLYMER]

dendrite *noun*
- "DEN drite"
- a stone or mineral with natural treelike or mosslike markings.
- [French from Greek *dendritēs* (adjective) from *dendron* tree]
- **dendritic** *adjective* "den DRITTIC"

dendrobium *noun*
- "den DROE bee um"
- an orchid of the genus *Dendrobium*, frequently cultivated as an ornamental.
- [Greek *dendron* tree]

dendrochronology *noun*
- "dendro cruh NOLLA jee"
- a system of dating using the characteristic patterns of annual growth rings of trees to assign dates to timber.
- [Greek *dendron* tree + CHRONOLOGY]
- **dendrochronological** *adjective*
- **dendrochronologist** *noun*

dendroid *adjective*
- "DEN droid"
- tree-shaped.
- [Greek *dendrōdēs* treelike]

dendrology *noun*
- "den DRAWLA jee"
- the scientific study of trees.
- [Greek *dendron* tree + *logos* word]
- **dendrological** *adjective*
- **dendrologist** *noun*

Dene *noun*
- "DEN ay"
- a member of a group of Aboriginal peoples of the Athapaskan linguistic family, living esp. in the Canadian north.
- [Chipewyan *dene* person]

dene *noun*
- "DEEN"
- a narrow wooded valley.
- [Old English *denu*, related to 'den']

HOMOPHONES: *dean*

dengue *noun*
- "DENG gee" (with "G" as in *GEEK*)
- an infectious viral disease of the tropics causing a fever and acute pains in the joints.
- [West Indian Spanish, from Swahili *denga*, *dinga*, assimilated to Spanish *dengue* fastidiousness, with reference to the stiffness of the patient's neck and shoulders]

deniable *adjective*
- "de NIE a bull"
- that may be denied.
- [Old French *denier* from Latin *denegare* (*de-* off, from + *negare* say no)]
- **deniability** *noun*

denial *noun*
- "de NIE 'll"
- the act or an instance of denying.
- [as DENIABLE]

denier[1] *noun*
- "de NIE ur"
- a person who denies something.
- [as DENIABLE]

denier[2] *noun*
- "DEN yur"
- a unit of weight by which the fineness of silk, rayon, or nylon yarn is measured.
- [originally the name of a small coin: Middle English from Old French from Latin *denarius*]

denigrate *verb*
- "DENNA grate"
- defame or disparage the reputation of (a person).
- [Latin *denigrare* (*de-* off, from + *nigrare* from *niger* black)]
- **denigration** *noun*
- **denigrator** *noun*
- **denigratory** *adjective* "denna GRAY tur ee"

denitrify *verb*
- "dee NIE truh fie"
- remove the nitrates or nitrites from (soil etc.).
- [Latin *de* = off, from + NITRIFY]
- **denitrification** *noun*

denizen *noun*
- “DENNA z’n”
- an inhabitant or occupant.
- [Anglo-French *deinzein* from Old French *deinz* within, from Latin *de* from + *intus* within]
- **denizenship** *noun*

denominate *verb*
- “duh NOM’n ate”
- give a name to.
- [Latin *denominare* (*de-* off, from + NOMINATE)]
- **denominative** *adjective*

denomination *noun*
- “duh nom’n AY sh’n”
- a religious sect or body with a distinctive name and organization.
- [as DENOMINATE]
- **denominational** *adjective*
- **denominationalism** *noun*
- **denominationalist** *noun*

denominator *noun*
- “de NOM’n ater”
- the number below the line in a common fraction.
- [as DENOMINATE]

denotation *noun*
- “deeno TAY sh’n”
- the meaning or signification of a term, as distinct from its implications or connotations.
- [as DENOTE]

denote *verb*
- “dee NOTE”
- be a sign of; indicate.
- [French *dénoter* or from Latin *denotare* (*de-* off, from + *notare* mark, from *nota* note)]
- **denotative** *adjective*

denouement *noun*
- “day noo MÃH” (with a nasal *AH*)
- the final unravelling of a plot or complicated situation.
- [French *dénouement* from *dénouer* unknot (*de-* off, from + Latin *nodare* from *nodus* knot)]

densitometer *noun*
- “densa TOMMA tur”
- an instrument for measuring the photographic density of an image on a film or photographic print.
- [as DENSITY + Greek *metron* measure]

density *noun*
- “DENSA tee”
- the degree of compactness of a substance.
- [French *densité* from French *dense* or Latin *densus* dense]

dentalium *noun*
- “den TAILY um”
- any marine mollusc of the genus *Dentalium*, having a conical foot protruding from a tusk-like shell.
- [modern Latin from Late Latin *dentalis* from Latin *dens dentis* tooth]

dentalize *verb*
ALSO SPELLED: esp. *Brit.* **-ise**
- “DENT’ll ize”
- change into a dental sound.
- [Latin *dens dentis* tooth]

denticle *noun*
- “DENTA k’ll”
- a small tooth or toothlike projection, scale, etc.
- [Latin *denticulus* diminutive of *dens dentis* tooth]
- **denticulate** *adjective*

dentifrice *noun*
- “DENTA friss”
- a paste or powder for cleaning the teeth.
- [French from Latin *dentifricium* from *dens dentis* tooth + *fricare* rub]

dentil *noun*
- “DENTILL”
- each of a series of small rectangular blocks as a decoration under the moulding of a cornice in classical architecture.
- [obsolete French *dentille* diminutive of *dent* tooth, from Latin *dens dentis*]

HOMOPHONES: *dental*

dentine *noun*
- “DEN teen”
- a hard dense bony tissue forming the bulk of a tooth.
- [Latin *dens dentis* tooth]
- **dentinal** *adjective*

dentition *noun*
- “den TISH’n”
- the type, number, and arrangement of teeth in a species or individual.
- [Latin *dentitio* from *dentire* to teethe]

denture *noun*
- “DEN chur”
- an artificial replacement for one or more teeth carried on a removable plate or frame.
- [French from *dent* tooth]
- **denturism** *noun*
- **denturist** *noun*

denuclearize *verb*
ALSO SPELLED: esp. *Brit.* **-ise**
- “dee NEW clee ur ize”
- remove nuclear armaments from (a country etc.).
- [Latin *de* = off, from + NUCLEAR]
- **denuclearization** *noun* (also esp. *Brit.* **-isation**)

denude *verb*
- “duh NUDE”
- make naked or bare.
- [Latin *denudare* (*de-* off, from + *nudus* naked)]
- **denudation** *noun*

denunciation *noun*
- “duh nuncy AY sh’n”
- the act of denouncing (a person, policy, etc.); public condemnation.

• [Latin *denunciatio* from *denuntiare* (*de-* off, from, *nuntiare* make known, from *nuntius* messenger)]
• **denunciatory** *adjective* "duh NUNCY a tory"

deodar *noun*
• "DEEA dar"
• the Himalayan cedar *Cedrus deodara*, the tallest of the cedar family, with drooping branches bearing large barrel-shaped cones.
• [Hindi *dē' odār* from Sanskrit *deva-dāru* divine tree]

deodorant *noun*
• "dee OH dur 'nt"
• a substance sprayed or rubbed on to the body or sprayed into the air to remove or conceal unpleasant smells.
• [as DEODORIZE]

deodorize *verb*
ALSO SPELLED: esp. *Brit.* **-ise**
• "de OH dur ize"
• remove or destroy the (usu. unpleasant) smell of.
• [Latin *de* from + *odor* smell]
• **deodorization** *noun* (also esp. *Brit.* **-isation**)
• **deodorizer** *noun* (also esp. *Brit.* **-iser**)

deontic *adjective*
• "dee ONTIC"
• of or relating to duty and obligation as ethical concepts.
• [Greek *deont-* participle stem of *dei* it is right]

deontology *noun*
• "dee on TOLLA jee"
• the study of duty.
• [as DEONTIC]
• **deontological** *adjective*
• **deontologist** *noun*

deoxygenate *verb*
• "dee OXA j'n ate"
• remove oxygen, esp. free oxygen, from.
• [Latin *de* = off, from + OXYGENATE]
• **deoxygenated** *adjective*
• **deoxygenation** *noun*

deoxyribonucleic *adjective*
• "dee oxy rye bo new CLAY ick"
• designating the acid which is the self-replicating material present in nearly all living organisms, esp. as a constituent of chromosomes, and is the carrier of genetic information.
• [Latin *de* = off, from + OXYGEN + RIBONUCLEIC]

depanneur *noun*
• "deppa NUR"
• *Cdn* (*Que.*) a convenience store.
• [Canadian French]

departure *noun*
• "de PAR chur"
• the act or an instance of departing.
• [Old French *departeure*, ultimately from Latin *dispertire* divide]

dependable *adjective*
• "de PENDA bull"
• reliable.
• [Old French *dependre*, ultimately from Latin *dependēre* (*de* = off, from + *pendēre* hang)]
• **dependability** *noun*
• **dependably** *adverb*

dependant *noun*
ALSO SPELLED: **dependent**
• "de PEN d'nt"
• a person who relies on another esp. for financial support.
• [French *dépendant* present participle of *dépendre* (as DEPENDABLE)]

dependence *noun*
• "de PEND ince"
• the state of being dependent, esp. on financial or other support.
• [French *dépendance* (as DEPENDABLE)]

dependency *noun*
• "de PEN d'n see"
• a country or province controlled by another.
• [as DEPENDABLE]

dependent *adjective*
• "de PEN d'nt"
• depending, conditional.
• [as DEPENDANT]
• **dependently** *adverb*
HOMOPHONES: *dependant*

depersonalization *noun*
ALSO SPELLED: esp. *Brit.* **-isation**
• "dee purr s'n 'll ize AY sh'n"
• the loss of one's sense of identity.
• [as DEPERSONALIZE]

depersonalize *verb*
ALSO SPELLED: esp. *Brit.* **-ise**
• "dee PURR s'n 'll ize"
• make impersonal.
• [Latin *de* = off, from + PERSONALIZE]

depict *verb*
• "de PICT"
• represent in a drawing or painting etc.
• [Latin *depingere depict-* (*de-* off, from + *pingere* paint)]
• **depicter** *noun*
• **depiction** *noun*

depilate *verb*
• "DEP'll ate"
• remove the hair from.
• [Latin *depilare* (*de-* off, from + *pilare* from *pilus* hair)]
• **depilation** *noun*
• **depilatory** *adjective* "de PILLA tory"

deplete *verb*
• "de PLEET"
• reduce in numbers or quantity.
• [Latin *deplēre* (*de-* off, from + *plēre plet-* fill)]
• **depleter** *noun*
• **depletion** *noun*

deplorable *adjective*
• "de PLORA bull"
• exceedingly bad.
• [as DEPLORE]
• **deplorably** *adverb*

deplore *verb*
• "de PLORE"
• grieve over; regret.
• [ultimately from Latin *deplorare* (*de-* off, from + *plorare* bewail)]
• **deploringly** *adverb*

depolarize *verb*
ALSO SPELLED: esp. *Brit.* **-ise**
• "dee POE lur ize"
• reduce or remove the polarization of.
• [Latin *de* = off, from + POLARIZE]
• **depolarization** *noun* (also esp. *Brit.* **-isation**)

depoliticize *verb*
ALSO SPELLED: esp. *Brit.* **-ise**
• "dee puh LITTA size"
• make (a person, an organization, etc.) non-political.
• [Latin *de* = off, from + POLITICIZE]
• **depoliticization** *noun* (also esp. *Brit.* **-isation**)

depolymerize *verb*
ALSO SPELLED: esp. *Brit.* **-ise**
• "dee POLLA mur ize"
• break down into monomers or other smaller units.
• [Latin *de* = off, from + POLYMER]
• **depolymerization** *noun* (also esp. *Brit.* **-isation**)

deponent *adjective*
• "dee PONE 'nt"
• (of a verb, esp. in Latin or Greek) passive or middle in form but active in meaning.
• [Latin *deponere* (*de-* off, from + *ponere posit-* place): from the notion that the verb had laid aside the passive sense]

depopulate *verb*
• "dee POP yuh late"
• reduce the population of.
• [Latin *de* = off, from + POPULATE]
• **depopulation** *noun*

deportment *noun*
• "dee PORT m'nt"
• bearing, demeanour, or manners, esp. of a cultivated kind.
• [Old French *deportement* (Latin *de-* off, from + *portare* carry)]

deposit *noun*
• "de POZZIT"
• a sum of money placed or kept in an account in a bank.
• [Latin *depositum* (n.), medieval Latin *depositare* from Latin *deponere deposit-* (as DEPONENT)]

depositary *noun*
• "de POZZA terry"
• a person to whom something is entrusted; a trustee.
• [as DEPOSIT]

deposition *noun*
• "deppa ZISH'n" or "deepa ZISH'n"
• the act or an instance of depositing.
• [as DEPOSIT]

depositor *noun*
• "de POZZIT ur"
• a person who deposits money etc.
• [as DEPOSIT]

depository *noun*
• "dee POZZA tory"
• a place where something is deposited.
• [as DEPOSIT]

depot *noun*
• "DEEPO"
• a storehouse.
• [French *dépôt* from Latin (as DEPOSIT)]

deprave *verb*
• "de PRAVE"
• pervert or corrupt, esp. morally.
• [Latin *depravare* (*de-* off, from + *pravare* from *pravus* crooked)]
• **depravation** *noun* "deppra VAY sh'n"
• **depraved** *adjective*
• **depravity** *noun* "de PRAVVA tee"
HOMOPHONES: *deprivation*

deprecate *verb*
• "DEPPRA cate"
• express disapproval of or a wish against (a plan, proceeding, purpose, etc.); deplore; plead earnestly against.
• [Latin *deprecari* (*de-* off, from + *precari* pray)]
• **deprecatingly** *adverb*
• **deprecation** *noun*
• **deprecatory** *adjective* "DEPPRA kuh tory"

depreciate *verb*
• "duh PREESHY ate"
• diminish in value.
• [Late Latin *depretiare* (Latin *de-* off, from + *pretiare* from *pretium* price)]
• **depreciable** *adjective*
• **depreciatory** *adjective*

depreciation *noun*
• "duh preeshy AY sh'n"
• the amount of wear and tear (of a property etc.) for which a reduction may be made in a valuation, an estimate, or a balance sheet.
• [as DEPRECIATE]

depredation *noun*
• "deppra DAY sh'n"
• the act of despoiling, ravaging, or plundering.
• [French *déprédation* from Late Latin *depraedatio* (*de-* off, from + *praedatio -onis* from Latin *praedari* plunder)]

depress *verb*
• "de PRESS"
• make dispirited or dejected.

• [Old French *depresser* from Late Latin *depressare* (*de-* off, from + *pressare* frequentative of *premere* press)]
• **depressant** *adjective*
• **depressing** *adjective*
• **depressingly** *adverb*
• **depression** *noun*

depressible *adjective*
• “de PRESSA bull”
• that can be pushed or pulled down.
• [as DEPRESS]

depressor *noun*
• “de PRESSER”
• a muscle that causes the lowering of some part of the body.
• [as DEPRESS]

depressurize *verb*
ALSO SPELLED: esp. *Brit.* **-ise**
• “dee PRESHER ize”
• cause an appreciable drop in the pressure of the gas inside (a container), esp. to the ambient level.
• [Latin *de* = off, from + PRESSURIZE]
• **depressurization** *noun* (also esp. *Brit.* **-isation**)

deprivation *noun*
• “deppra VAY sh’n”
• the act or an instance of depriving.
• [Old French *depriver* from medieval Latin *deprivare* (*de-* from, Latin *privare* deprive)]
HOMOPHONES: *depravation*

depurate *verb*
• “DEPYER ate”
• make or become free from impurities.
• [medieval Latin *depurare* (*de-* off, from + *purus* pure)]
• **depuration** *noun*
• **depurative** *adjective* “duh PYUR a tiv”

deputation *noun*
• “dep yoo TAY sh’n”
• a group of people appointed to represent others, usu. for a specific purpose; a delegation.
• [as DEPUTE]

depute *verb*
• “de PYOOT”
• appoint as a deputy.
• [Old French *deputé* past participle of *deputer* from Latin *deputare* regard as, allot (*de-* off, from + *putare* think)]

deputy *noun*
• “DEP yuh tee”
• a person appointed or delegated to act for another or others.
• [Middle English var. of DEPUTE]
• **deputization** *noun* (also esp. *Brit.* **-isation**)
• **deputize** *verb* (also esp. *Brit.* **-ise**)
• **deputyship** *noun*

deracinate *verb*
• “dee RASS’n ate”
• tear up by the roots.
• [French *déraciner* (*de-* off, from + *racine* from Late Latin *radicina* diminutive of *radix* root)]
• **deracination** *noun*

derailleur *noun*
• “dee RAILER”
• a bicycle gear-shifting mechanism which switches the line of the chain while pedalling so that it jumps to a different sprocket.
• [French *dérailleur* (*de* from + ‘rail’ from Old French *reille* iron rod, from Latin *regula* rule, rail)]

deregulate *verb*
• “dee REG yuh late”
• remove regulations or restrictions from.
• [Latin *de* = off, from + REGULATE]
• **deregulation** *noun*
• **deregulator** *noun*
• **deregulatory** *adjective*

derelict *adjective*
• “DERRA lict”
• (esp. of property) ruined; dilapidated.
• [Latin *derelictus* past participle of *derelinquere* (*de-* off, from + *relinquere* leave)]

dereliction *noun*
• “derra LICK sh’n”
• neglect; failure to carry out one’s obligations.
• [as DERELICT]

deride *verb*
• “de RIDE”
• be scornful of; mock.
• [Latin *deridēre* (*de-* off, from + *ridēre ris-* laugh)]
• **deridingly** *adverb*

derision *noun*
• “de RIZH ’n”
• ridicule; mockery.
• [Old French from Late Latin *derisio -onis* (as DERIDE)]
• **derisible** *adjective*

derisive *adjective*
• “duh RICE iv”
• scoffing; ironical; scornful.
• [as DERIDE]
• **derisively** *adverb*
• **derisiveness** *noun*

derisory *adjective*
• “duh RICE a ree”
• scoffing; ironical; scornful.
• [Late Latin *derisorius* (as DERISION)]

derivative *adjective*
• “duh RIVVA tiv”
• derived from another source; not original.
• [as DERIVE]
• **derivatively** *adverb*

derive *verb*
• “duh RIVE”
• get, obtain, or form from a source.
• [Latin *derivare* (*de-* off, from + *rivus* stream)]
• **derivable** *adjective*

• **derivation** *noun* "derra VAY sh'n"
• **derivational** *adjective*

dermabrasion *noun*
• "durma BRAY zh'n"
• the surgical removal of superficial layers of skin with a rapidly revolving abrasive tool.
• [Greek *derma* skin + ABRADE]

dermatitis *noun*
• "durma TITE iss"
• inflammation of the skin.
• [Greek *derma -atos* skin + *-itis*, forming feminine of adjectives in *-itēs* (with *nosos* 'disease' implied)]

dermatoglyphics *noun*
• "durma toe GLIFFIX"
• the science or study of skin markings or patterns, esp. of the fingers, hands, and feet.
• [as DERMATITIS + Greek *gluphē* carving: see GLYPH]
• **dermatoglyphic** *adjective*

dermatology *noun*
• "durma TOLLA jee"
• the study of the diagnosis and treatment of skin disorders.
• [as DERMATITIS + Greek *logos* word]
• **dermatologic** *adjective*
• **dermatological** *adjective*
• **dermatologically** *adverb*
• **dermatologist** *noun*

dermis *noun*
• "DURMISS"
• (in general use) the skin.
• [modern Latin, after EPIDERMIS]
• **dermal** *adjective*
• **dermic** *adjective*

derogate *verb*
• "DERRA gate"
• take away a part from; detract from (a merit, a right, etc.).
• [Latin *derogare* (*de-* off, from + *rogare* ask)]
• **derogative** *adjective* "duh ROGGA tiv"

derogation *noun*
• "derra GAY sh'n"
• a lessening or impairment of (a law, authority, position, dignity, etc.).
• [as DEROGATE]

derogatory *adjective*
• "duh ROGGA tory"
• involving disparagement or discredit; insulting, depreciatory.
• [as DEROGATE]
• **derogatorily** *adverb*

derrick *noun*
• "DARE ick"
• a kind of crane for moving or lifting heavy weights, having a movable pivoted arm.
• [obsolete senses *hangman*, *gallows*, from the name of a London hangman *c.*1600]

Derridean *adjective*
• "duh RIDDY 'n"
• of or relating to the French deconstructionist philosopher Jacques Derrida (d.2004).

derrière *noun*
• "derry AIR"
• the buttocks.
• [French, = behind]

derringer *noun*
• "DARE in jur"
• a small large-bore pistol.
• [H. *Deringer*, US inventor d.1868]

derris *noun*
• "DARE iss"
• any woody tropical climbing leguminous plant of the genus *Derris*, bearing leathery pods.
• [modern Latin from Greek, = leather covering (with reference to its pod)]

dervish *noun*
• "DUR vish"
• a Muslim (specifically Sufi) religious man who has taken vows of poverty and austerity.
• [Turkish *derviş* from Persian *darvēsh* poor, a mendicant monk]

desalinate *verb*
• "dee SAL'n ate"
• remove salt from (esp. sea water).
• [Latin *de* = off, from + SALINE]
• **desalination** *noun*
• **desalinator** *noun*

desalinize *verb*
• "dee SAL'n ize"
• remove salt from (esp. sea water).
• [Latin *de* = off, from + SALINE]
• **desalinization** *noun*

desaparecido *noun*
• "dessa perray SEEDO"
• a person, esp. a perceived political activist, abducted by government or other forces in Central or S America, esp. in Argentina.
• [Spanish, lit. 'disappeared', past participle of *desaparacer* disappear]

descant *noun*
• "DESS cant"
• an independent soprano melody usu. sung or played above a basic melody, esp. of a hymn tune.
• [Old French *deschant* from medieval Latin *discantus* (*dis-* expressing negation + *cantus* song)]

descend *verb*
• "de SEND"
• go or come down (a hill, stairs, etc.).
• [Latin *descendere* (*de-* off, from + *scandere* climb)]
• **descent** *noun*
HOMOPHONES: *dissent*

descendant *noun*
• "de SEND'nt"
• a person or animal descended from another.
• [as DESCEND]

descender *noun*
- "de SENDER"
- a part of a letter that extends below the line.
- [as DESCEND]

describe *verb*
- "de SCRIBE"
- portray in words; give a detailed or graphic account of.
- [Latin *describere* (*de-* off, from + *scribere script-* write)]
- **describable** *adjective*
- **describer** *noun*
- **description** *noun*

descriptive *adjective*
- "de SCRIP tiv"
- serving or seeking to describe.
- [Late Latin *descriptivus* (as DESCRIBE)]
- **descriptively** *adverb*
- **descriptiveness** *noun*

descriptivism *noun*
- "de SCRIP tiv izm"
- the practice in dictionaries or linguistics of describing a language without comparing, endorsing, or condemning particular usage, vocabulary, etc.
- [as DESCRIBE]
- **descriptivist** *noun*

descriptor *noun*
- "de SCRIPTER"
- a word or expression etc. used to describe or identify.
- [Latin, = describer (as DESCRIBE)]

descry *verb*
- "duh SCRY"
- catch sight of; discern or detect.
- [Middle English (earlier senses 'proclaim') from Old French *descrier*: prob. confused with var. of obsolete *descrive* from Old French *descrivre* DESCRIBE]

desecrate *verb*
- "DESSA crate"
- violate (a venerated place or thing) with violence, profanity, etc.
- [*de* = off, from + CONSECRATE]
- **desecration** *noun*
- **desecrator** *noun*

desegregate *verb*
- "dee SEGGRA gate"
- abolish racial segregation in (schools etc.) or of (people etc.).
- [Latin *de* = off, from + SEGREGATE]
- **desegregation** *noun*

desensitize *verb*
ALSO SPELLED: esp. *Brit.* **-ise**
- "dee SENSA tize"
- reduce or destroy the sensitiveness of (photographic materials, an allergic person, etc.).
- [Latin *de* = off, from + SENSITIZE]
- **desensitization** *noun* (also esp. *Brit.* **-isation**)
- **desensitizer** *noun* (also esp. *Brit.* **-iser**)

desert[1] *verb*
- "duh ZURT"
- abandon, give up, leave without intention of returning.
- [French *déserter* from Late Latin *desertare* from Latin *desertus* (as DESERT[2])]
- **deserted** *adjective*
- **deserter** *noun*
- **desertion** *noun*

HOMOPHONES: *dessert*

desert[2] *noun*
- "DEZ urt"
- a dry, barren area of land, often sand-covered, characteristically desolate, with little fresh water and scanty vegetation.
- [Old French from Latin *desertus*, Church Latin *desertum* (n.), past participle of *deserere* leave, forsake]

desert[3] *noun*
- "duh ZURT"
- acts or qualities deserving reward or punishment.
- [Old French from *deservir* from Latin *deservire* (*de-* off, from = *servire* serve)]

HOMOPHONES: *dessert*

desertification *noun*
- "duh zurta fuh CAY sh'n"
- the transformation of fertile land into a desert or arid waste, esp. as a result of human activity.
- [as DESERT[2]]

deshabille *noun*
- "dezza BEEL"
- a state of being only partly or carelessly clothed.
- [French, = undressed]

desiccant *noun*
- "DESSIC 'nt"
- a drying or desiccating agent.
- [as DESICCATE]

desiccate *verb*
- "DESSA cate"
- remove the moisture from, dry (esp. food for preservation).
- [Latin *desiccare* (*de-* off, from + *siccus* dry)]
- **desiccated** *adjective*
- **desiccation** *noun*

desiccator *noun*
- "DESSA cater"
- an apparatus for desiccating fruit, milk, tanbark, etc.
- [as DESICCATE]

desiderative *adjective*
- "duh ZIDDER a tiv" or "duh SIDDER a tiv"
- (of a verb, conjugation, etc.) formed from

another verb etc. and denoting a desire to perform the action of that verb etc.
• [Late Latin *desiderativus* (as DESIDERATUM)]

desideratum *noun*
• "duh zidder AT um" or "duh sidder AT um"
• something lacking but needed and desired.
• [Latin neuter past participle of *desiderare* (*de-* off, from + *siderare* as in CONSIDER)]

design *noun*
• "de ZINE"
• a preliminary plan or sketch for the making or production of a building, machine, garment, etc.
• [ultimately from Latin *designare* DESIGNATE]

designate *verb*
• "DEZ ig nate"
• appoint to an office or function.
• [Latin *designare*, past participle *designatus* (*de-* off, from + *signare* from *signum* mark)]
• **designated** *adjective*
• **designation** *noun*
• **designator** *noun*

designed *adjective*
• "de ZINED" ("ZINED" rhymes with *FIND*)
• planned, purposed, intended.
• [as DESIGN]
• **designedly** *adverb*

designer *noun*
• "de ZINE ur"
• a person who makes artistic designs or plans for construction, e.g. for clothing, machines, theatre sets, etc.
• [as DESIGN]

designing *adjective*
• "de ZINE ing"
• crafty, artful, or scheming.
• [as DESIGN]

desire *noun*
• "de ZIRE"
• an unsatisfied longing or craving.
• [Old French *desir* from *desirer* from Latin *desiderare*, perhaps from *de-* down + *sidus sider-* star]
• **desirability** *noun*
• **desirable** *adjective*
• **desirably** *adverb*

desirous *predicative adjective*
• "duh ZYE russ"
• having desire, wishful, wanting.
• [as DESIRE]

desman *noun*
• "DESS m'n"
• any aquatic flesh-eating shrew-like mammal of two species, one originating in Russia (*Desmana moschata*) and one in the Pyrenees (*Galemys pyrenaicus*).
• [French & German from Swedish *desman-råtta* muskrat]

desmid *noun*
• "DESSMID"
• a microscopic unicellular freshwater alga of the family Desmidiaceae.
• [modern Latin genus name *Desmidium*, from Greek *desmos* band, chain]

desolate *adjective*
• "DESS'll it" or "DEZZ'll it"
• (of a person) forlorn, wretched, and usu. solitary.
• [Latin *desolatus* past participle of *desolare* (*de-* off, from + *solare* from *solus* alone)]
• **desolated** *adjective*
• **desolately** *adverb*
• **desolateness** *noun*
• **desolation** *noun*

desorb *verb*
• "dee SORB" or "dee ZORB"
• remove (a substance etc.) from a surface upon which it is adsorbed.
• [*de* = off, from + ADSORB]
• **desorption** *noun*

despair *noun*
• "dis PARE"
• the complete loss or absence of hope.
• [Old French *desespeir*, *desperer* from Latin *desperare* (*de-* off, from + *sperare* hope)]
• **despairing** *adjective*
• **despairingly** *adverb*

desperado *noun*
• "despa RODDO" or "despa RADDO"
• a desperate or reckless person, esp. a person ready for any deed of lawlessness or violence.
• [after DESPERATE]

desperate *adjective*
• "DESPER it"
• reckless from despair, esp. to the point of violence or lawlessness.
• [Latin *desperatus* past participle of *desperare* (*de-* off, from + *sperare* hope)]
• **desperately** *adverb*
• **desperation** *noun*

despicable *adjective*
• "duh SPICKA bull"
• vile, deserving to be despised, morally contemptible.
• [Late Latin *despicabilis* from *despicari* (*de-* off, from + *specere* look at)]
• **despicably** *adverb*

despise *verb*
• "de SPIZE"
• look down on (someone etc.) as inferior, worthless, or contemptible.
• [*despis-* pres. stem of Old French *despire* from Latin *despicere* (*de-* off, from + *specere* look at)]
• **despised** *adjective*
• **despiser** *noun*

despite *preposition*
• "de SPITE"
• notwithstanding; in spite of.

• [Old French *despit* from Latin *despectus* noun from *despicere* (as DESPISE)]

despoil *verb*
• "de SPOIL"
• spoil, destroy, make useless.
• [Old French *despoill(i)er* from Latin *despoliare* (*de-* off, from + *spoliare* spoil)]
• **despoiler** *noun*
• **despoliation** *noun* "duh spoley AY sh'n"

despondent *adjective*
• "de SPON d'nt"
• characterized by loss of courage or enthusiasm; dejected.
• [Latin *despondēre* give up, abandon (*de-* off, from + *spondēre* promise)]
• **despondence** *noun*
• **despondency** *noun*
• **despondently** *adverb*

despot *noun*
• "DESS pot"
• an absolute ruler.
• [French *despote* from medieval Latin *despota* from Greek *despotēs* master, lord]
• **despotic** *adjective*
• **despotically** *adverb*
• **despotism** *noun*

desquamate *verb*
• "DESKWA mate"
• (esp. of the skin in some diseases) come off in scales.
• [Latin *desquamare* (*de-* off, from + *squama* scale)]
• **desquamation** *noun*

dessert *noun*
• "duh ZURT"
• a sweet food, esp. as eaten at the end of a meal, e.g. cake, fruit, ice cream, etc.
• [French, past participle of *desservir* clear the table (French and Latin *dis-* expressing negation + *servir* serve, from Latin *servire*, from *servus* slave)]
HOMOPHONES: *desert*

destabilize *verb*
ALSO SPELLED: esp. *Brit.* **-ise**
• "dee STAY b'll ize"
• deprive of stability, render unstable.
• [Latin *de* = off, from + STABILIZE]
• **destabilization** *noun* (also esp. *Brit.* **-isation**)

destination *noun*
• "dest'n AY sh'n"
• a place to which a person or thing is going, the intended end of a journey.
• [Old French *destination* or Latin *destinatio* (as DESTINE)]

destine *verb*
• "DESS tin"
• set apart for or devote to a particular purpose, activity, etc.
• [French *destiner* from Latin *destinare* (*de-* off, from + *stanare* (unrecorded) settle, from *stare* stand)]

destined *adjective*
• "DESS tinned"
• having a future decided or planned beforehand, esp. by fate or as if by fate.
• [as DESTINE]

destiny *noun*
• "DESS tin ee"
• fate or the predetermined course of events.
• [Old French *destinée* from Romanic, past participle of *destinare*: see DESTINE]

destitute *adjective*
• "DESTA toot" or "DESTA tyoot"
• completely impoverished; without food, shelter, etc.
• [Latin *destitutus* past participle of *destituere* forsake (*de-* off, from + *statuere* place)]
• **destitution** *noun*

destrier *noun*
• "DESTREE ur"
• a warhorse.
• [Old French *destrier*, ultimately from Latin *dexter* right (as the knight's horse was led by the squire with the right hand)]

destroy *verb*
• "de STROY"
• demolish, pull or break down; shatter, smash to pieces.
• [Old French *destruire*, ultimately from Latin *destruere* (*de-* off, from + *struere struct-* build)]
• **destroyer** *noun*

destruct *verb*
• "de STRUCT"
• destroy (one's own rocket etc.) deliberately, esp. for safety reasons.
• [Latin *destruere* (as DESTROY) or as back-formation from DESTRUCTION]

destruction *noun*
• "de STRUCK sh'n"
• the act or an instance of destroying; the process of being destroyed.
• [Old French from Latin *destructio -onis* (as DESTROY)]
• **destructibility** *noun*
• **destructible** *adjective*
• **destructive** *adjective*
• **destructively** *adverb*
• **destructiveness** *noun*

desuetude *noun*
• "duh SOOA tude"
• the condition or state into which anything falls when one ceases to use or practise it; a state of disuse.
• [French *désuétude* or Latin *desuetudo* (*de-* off, from + *suescere suet-* be accustomed)]

desulphurize *verb*
ALSO SPELLED: esp. *Brit.* **-ise**, *US* **desulfurize**
• "dee SULFER ize"

• remove sulphur or sulphur compounds from.
• [Latin *de* = off, from + SULPHURIZE]
• **desulphurization** *noun* (also esp. *Brit.* **-isation**, *US* **desulfurization**)

desultory *adjective*
• "DESSLE tory"
• going constantly from one subject to another, esp. digressively and unmethodically.
• [Latin *desultorius* superficial, from *desultor* vaulter, from *desult-* (*de-* off, from + *salt-* past participle stem of *salire* leap)]
• **desultorily** *adverb*

detach *verb*
• "de TATCH"
• unfasten and remove; disconnect or disengage.
• [French *détacher* (*de-* off, from + ATTACH)]
• **detachability** *noun*
• **detachable** *adjective*

detached *adjective*
• "de TATCH't"
• impartial, unemotional.
• [as DETACH]
• **detachedly** "de TATCH id lee" *adverb*

detachment *noun*
• "de TATCH m'nt"
• a state of aloofness from or indifference to other people, public opinion, etc.
• [as DETACH]

detect *verb*
• "de TECT"
• discover or perceive the existence or presence of.
• [Latin *detegere detect-* (*de-* off, from + *tegere* cover)]
• **detectable** *adjective*
• **detectably** *adverb*
• **detection** *noun*

detective *noun*
• "de TECTIV"
• a person, esp. a member of a police force, employed to investigate crime.
• [as DETECT]

detector *noun*
• "de TECTER"
• a device which detects something liable to escape observation or indicates something out of the ordinary.
• [as DETECT]

detent *noun*
• "duh TENT"
• any stop or catch in a machine which, until released, prevents a motion.
• [French *détente* from Old French *destente* from *destendre* slacken (*de-* off, from + Latin *tendere*)]

détente *noun*
• "day TONT"
• an easing of strained relations esp. between nations.
• [French, = relaxation]

detention *noun*
• "duh TEN sh'n"
• an act or instance of detaining or being detained.
• [French *détention* or Late Latin *detentio* ultimately from Latin *detinēre detent-* (*de* = off, from + *tenēre* hold)]

deter *verb*
• "de TUR"
• discourage or prevent (a person) through fear or dislike of the consequences.
• [Latin *deterrēre* (*de-* off, from + *terrēre* frighten)]
• **determent** *noun*
• **deterrence** *noun*
• **deterrent** *noun*

detergent *noun*
• "de TUR j'nt"
• a water-soluble cleansing agent which combines with impurities and dirt to make them more soluble, and differs from soap in not forming a scum with the salts in hard water.
• [Latin *detergēre* (*de-* off, from + *tergēre ters-* wipe)]

deteriorate *verb*
• "de TEERY ur ate"
• make or become worse or lower in quality, character, etc.
• [Late Latin *deteriorare deteriorat-* from Latin *deterior* worse]
• **deterioration** *noun*

determinant *noun*
• "de TURMIN 'nt"
• a factor which decisively affects the nature or outcome of something.
• [as DETERMINE]

determinate *adjective*
• "de TURMIN it"
• limited in time, space, or character.
• [Latin *determinatus* past participle (as DETERMINE)]
• **determinacy** *noun*
• **determinately** *adverb*
• **determinateness** *noun*

determination *noun*
• "de turmin AY sh'n"
• firmness of purpose; resoluteness.
• [as DETERMINE]
• **determined** *adjective*
• **determinedly** *adverb* "de TUR m'nd lee"

determinative *adjective*
• "de TURMIN a tiv"
• serving to define, qualify, or direct.
• [as DETERMINE]
• **determinatively** *adverb*

determine *verb*
• "de TURMIN"
• find out or establish precisely.
• [Old French *determiner* from Latin *determinare* (*de-* off, from + *terminus* end)]
• **determinable** *adjective*
• **determiner** *noun*

determinism *noun*
• "de TURMIN izm"
• the doctrine that all events, including human action, are determined by causes regarded as external to the will.
• [as DETERMINE]
• **determinist** *noun*
• **deterministic** *adjective*
• **deterministically** *adverb*

detestable *adjective*
• "de TESTA bull"
• deserving to be detested; intensely hateful.
• [Latin *detestari* (*de* = off, from + *testari* call to witness, from *testis* witness)]
• **detestably** *adverb*

detestation *noun*
• "de test AY sh'n"
• intense dislike, hatred.
• [as DETESTABLE]

detonate *verb*
• "DET'n ate"
• set off (an explosive charge).
• [Latin *detonare detonat-* (*de-* off, from + *tonare* thunder)]
• **detonation** *noun*
• **detonative** *adjective*
• **detonator** *noun*

detoxify *verb*
• "dee TOXA fie"
• subject (an alcoholic or drug addict) to detoxification, the process of eliminating poison from the body.
• [Latin *de* = off, from + *toxicum* poison]
• **detoxification** *noun* "dee toxa fuh CAY sh'n"

detract *verb*
• "de TRACT"
• take something away from.
• [Latin *detrahere detract-* (*de-* off, from + *trahere* draw)]
• **detraction** *noun*
• **detractor** *noun*

detribalize *verb*
ALSO SPELLED: esp. *Brit.* **-ise**
• "dee TRIBE'll ize"
• make (a person) no longer a member of a tribe.
• [Latin *de* = off, from + Latin *tribus* tribe]
• **detribalization** *noun* (also esp. *Brit.* **-isation**)

detriment *noun*
• "DETTRA m'nt"
• harm, damage, disadvantage.
• [Latin *detrimentum* (*de-* off, from + *terere trit-* rub, wear)]
• **detrimental** *adjective* "dettra MENT'll"
• **detrimentally** *adverb*

detritivore *noun*
• "duh TRITTA vore"
• an animal that feeds on dead organic material, esp. plant detritus.
• [as DETRITUS + Latin *-vorus* from *vorare* devour]
• **detritivorous** *adjective*

detritus *noun*
• "duh TRITE us" or "DETTRA tuss"
• debris of any kind.
• [after French *détritus* matter produced by erosion, from Latin *detritus* (n.) = wearing down (as DETRIMENT)]
• **detrital** *adjective*

detumescence *noun*
• "dee too MESS ince" or "dee tyoo MESS ince"
• subsidence from a swollen state.
• [Latin *detumescere* (*de-* off, from + *tumescere* swell)]
• **detumescent** *adjective*

deuce *noun*
• "DOOCE" or "DYOOCE"
• the two in dice or playing cards.
• [Old French *deus* from Latin *duo* (accusative *duos*) two]
HOMOPHONES: *douce*

deuterate *verb*
• "DOOTER ate" or "DYOOTER ate"
• replace the usual isotope of hydrogen in (a substance) by deuterium.
• [as DEUTERIUM]
• **deuterated** *adjective*
• **deuteration** *noun*

deuterium *noun*
• "due TEERY um"
• a stable isotope of hydrogen with a mass about double that of the usual isotope.
• [modern Latin, from Greek *deuteros* second]

deuterocanonical *adjective*
• "dooter oh kuh NONNA k'll" or "dyooter oh kuh NONNA k'll"
• of or forming a secondary canon (of sacred writings), used esp. to designate those books of the Old Testament accepted as part of the canon by the Roman Catholic and Orthodox Churches but not by Protestants.
• [Greek *deuteros* second + CANON]

deuteron *noun*
• "DOOTER on" or "DYOOTER on"
• the nucleus of a deuterium atom, consisting of a proton and a neutron.
• [from DEUTERIUM]

Deutschmark *noun*
• "DOITCH mark"
• the former chief monetary unit of Germany, equal to 100 pfennigs.
• [German, = German mark]

deutzia *noun*
• "DYOOTSY uh" or "DOITSY uh"
• any ornamental shrub of the genus *Deutzia*, with usu. white flowers.
• [J. *Deutz* 18th-c. Dutch patron of botany]

deva *noun*
• "DAY vuh"
• a member of a class of divine beings in the Vedic period, which in Indian mythology are

benevolent (opposed to the asuras) and in Zoroastrianism are evil.
- [Sanskrit, = god]

devalue *verb*
- "dee VAL yoo"
- reduce the value of (a person, thing, etc.).
- [Old French, *de* from, + feminine past participle of *valoir* be worth, from Latin *valēre*]
- **devaluation** *noun*

Devanagari *noun*
- "dayva NAGGA ree"
- the alphabet used for Sanskrit, Hindi, and other Indian languages.
- [Sanskrit, = divine town script]

devastate *verb*
- "DEVVA state"
- lay waste; cause great destruction to.
- [Latin *devastare devastat-* (*de-* off, from + *vastare* lay waste)]
- **devastating** *adjective*
- **devastatingly** *adverb*
- **devastation** *noun*
- **devastator** *noun*

devein *verb*
- "dee VANE"
- remove the main central vein from (a shrimp).
- [Latin *de* = off, from + VEIN]

develop *verb*
- "duh VELLUP"
- make or become bigger or fuller.
- [French *développer* from Romanic]
- **developable** *adjective*
- **development** *noun*

developer *noun*
- "duh VELLUP ur"
- a person or company that develops land, esp. a speculative builder.
- [as DEVELOP]

developmental *adjective*
- "duh vellup MENT'll"
- pertaining to the process of achieving physical, mental, or social maturity.
- [as DEVELOP]
- **developmentally** *adverb*

deviant *adjective*
- "DEEVY 'nt"
- deviating or divergent, esp. from normal social standards.
- [as DEVIATE]
- **deviance** *noun*
- **deviancy** *noun*

deviate *verb*
- "DEEVY ate"
- turn aside or diverge (from a course of action, rule, truth, norm, etc.).
- [Late Latin *deviare deviat-* (*de-* off, from + *via* way)]
- **deviation** *noun*

devious *adjective*
- "DEEVY us"
- (of a person, plan etc.) not straightforward or sincere; underhand.
- [Latin *devius* (as DEVIATE)]
- **deviously** *adverb*
- **deviousness** *noun*

devise *verb*
- "de VIZE"
- plan or invent by careful thought.
- [Old French *deviser* ultimately from Latin *dividere divis-* DIVIDE]
- **devisable** *adjective*

devitalize *verb*
ALSO SPELLED: esp. *Brit.* **-ise**
- "dee VITE 'll ize"
- take away strength and vigour from.
- [Latin *de-* off, from + *vitalis* from *vita* life]
- **devitalization** *noun* (also esp. *Brit.* **-isation**)

devoid *adjective*
- "duh VOID"
- totally lacking or free from.
- [past participle of obsolete *devoid* cast out, from Old French *devoidier*]

devoir *noun*
- "duh VWAR" ("VWAR" rhymes with *FAR*)
- duty; one's best.
- [Old French *deveir* from Latin *debēre* owe]

devolution *noun*
- "devva LOO sh'n" or "deeva LOO sh'n"
- the delegation of power, esp. by central government to local or regional administration.
- [Late Latin *devolutio* (as DEVOLVE)]
- **devolutionary** *adjective*
- **devolutionism** *noun*
- **devolutionist** *noun*

devolve *verb*
- "de VOLVE"
- pass (work or duties) to (a deputy etc.).
- [Latin *devolvere devolut-* (*de-* off, from + *volvere* roll)]

Devonian *adjective*
- "duh VOE nee 'n"
- of or relating to the fourth period of the Paleozoic era, from about 408 to 360 million years BP, between the Silurian and Carboniferous periods. During this period, amphibians and forests first appeared.
- [medieval Latin *Devonia* Devonshire]

devotee *noun*
- "devvo TEE" or "devvo TAY"
- a zealous enthusiast or supporter.
- [Latin *devovēre devot-* (*de-* off, from + *vovēre* vow)]

devotion *noun*
- "de VOE sh'n"
- enthusiastic attachment or loyalty (to a person or cause); great love.
- [as DEVOTEE]

- **devotional** *adjective*
- **devotionalism** *noun*

dewan *noun*
ALSO SPELLED: **diwan**
- "duh WONN"
- a chief treasury official, finance minister, or prime minister of an Indian state.
- [Arabic & Persian *diwān* fiscal register]

dewar *noun*
- "DOOER" or "DYOOER"
- a double-walled vessel with a vacuum between the walls to reduce the transfer of heat, used for storing hot or cold liquids.
- [Sir J. *Dewar*, Scottish scientist d.1923]

HOMOPHONES: *doer*

dewlap *noun*
- "DEW lap"
- a loose fold of skin hanging from the throat of cattle, dogs, etc.
- ['dew' + 'lap' (lick)]

dexamethasone *noun*
- "decksa METHA zone"
- a synthetic corticosteroid used esp. as an anti-inflammatory agent.
- [from *dexa-* (blend of Greek *hex* six + Greek *deka* ten) + METHYL + CORTISONE]

dexterity *noun*
- "deck STARE a tee"
- manual or manipulative skill or adroitness; good physical coordination.
- [originally = 'right-handedness': French *dextérité* from Latin *dexteritas* from *dexter* on the right]

dexterous *adjective*
ALSO SPELLED: **dextrous**
- "DECKS truss"
- having or showing dexterity.
- [as DEXTERITY]
- **dexterously** *adverb* (also **dextrously**)

dextral *adjective*
- "DECKS trull"
- (of a person) right-handed.
- [medieval Latin *dextralis* from Latin *dextra* right hand]

dextran *noun*
- "DECK stran"
- an amorphous gum formed by the fermentation of sucrose etc.
- [German (as DEXTROSE + *-an* as in chemical names)]

dextroamphetamine *noun*
- "deck stro am FETTA meen"
- an amphetamine used as a central nervous system stimulant.
- [as DEXTROROTATORY + AMPHETAMINE]

dextromethorphan *noun*
- "deck stro muh THOR f'n"
- a cough suppressant acting by making the cough centre in the brain less sensitive to incoming stimuli.
- [DEXTROROTATORY + *methoxy* + *methylmorphinan*]

dextrorotatory *adjective*
- "deck stro roe TAY tuh ree"
- having the property of rotating the plane of a polarized light ray to the right.
- [Latin *dexter*, *dextra* on or to the right + ROTATE]
- **dextrorotation** *noun*

dextrose *noun*
- "DECK strose" (rhymes with *GROSS*)
- a dextrorotatory form of glucose.
- [formed as DEXTROROTATORY + GLUCOSE]

dhansak *noun*
ALSO SPELLED: **dansak**
- "DAN sack"
- a casserole of various meats and vegetables, a specialty of Parsi cuisine from western India.
- [Gujarati, from *dhan* wealth]

dharma *noun*
- "DARMA"
- (in Hinduism) the eternal law of the cosmos, inherent in the very nature of things, upheld (but neither created nor controlled) by the gods; in the context of individual action, it denotes the social rules codified in the law books.
- [Sanskrit, = decree, custom]

dharna *noun*
ALSO SPELLED: **dhurna**
- "DURNA" or "DARNA"
- (in India) a method of compelling payment or compliance by sitting at the debtor's or offender's door without eating until the demand is complied with.
- [Hindi *dharnā* placing, act of sitting in restraint]

Dharuk *noun*
- "DAR ook" ("OOK" rhymes with *BOOK*)
- an Aboriginal language of the area around Sydney, Australia, now extinct.
- [Dharuk]

dhobi *noun*
- "DOE bee"
- (in the Indian subcontinent) a washerman or washerwoman.
- [Hindi *dhobī* from *dhob* washing]

dholak *noun*
- "DOE lack"
- a medium-sized barrel-shaped or cylindrical drum, usu. with two heads, used in the Indian subcontinent.
- [Hindi *dholak*]

dhoti *noun*
- "DOE tee"
- the loincloth worn by male Hindus.
- [Hindi *dhotī*]

dhow *noun*
• "DOW" (rhymes with *HOW*)
• a lateen-rigged Arab ship used on the E African, Arabian, and Indian coasts.
• [19th c.: origin unknown]
HOMOPHONES: *Tao*

dhurrie *noun*
• "DURRY"
• a rug of heavy cotton cloth, originally used in the Indian subcontinent.
• [Hindi *darī*]

diabase *noun*
• "DIE a base"
• dolerite.
• [French, associated with Greek *diabasis* transition]

diabetes *noun*
• "die a BEET eez" or "die a BEET iss"
• any disorder of the metabolism characterized by excessive thirst and the production of large amounts of urine.
• [originally = siphon: Latin from Greek from *diabainō* go through]
• **diabetic** *adjective* "die a BETTIC"

diablerie *noun*
• "dee ABLA ree" or "die ABLA ree"
• sorcery; witchcraft.
• [French from *diable* from Latin *diabolus* devil (as DIABOLICAL)]

diabolical *adjective*
• "die a BOLLA k'll"
• of the Devil.
• [Latin *diabolus* devil, from Greek *diabolos* accuser, slanderer, from *dia* across + *ballō* to throw]
• **diabolically** *adverb*

diabolism *noun*
• "die AB'll izm"
• belief in or worship of the Devil.
• [as DIABOLICAL]
• **diabolist** *noun*

diabolize *verb*
ALSO SPELLED: esp. *Brit.* **-ise**
• "die AB'll ize"
• make into or represent as a devil.
• [as DIABOLICAL]

diabolo *noun*
• "dee ABBA lo" or "die ABBA lo"
• a game in which a two-headed top is thrown up and caught with a string stretched between two sticks.
• [Italian, = 'devil' (as DIABOLICAL): formerly called *devil on two sticks*]

diachronic *adjective*
• "die a CRONNIC"
• concerned with the historical development of a subject (esp. a language).
• [French *diachronique* (from Greek *dia* through + CHRONIC)]
• **diachronically** *adverb*
• **diachronous** *adjective* "die ACKRA nuss"
• **diachrony** *noun* "die ACKRA nee"

diaconal *adjective*
• "die ACKA n'll" or "dee ACKA n'll"
• of or pertaining to a deacon or deaconess.
• [Church Latin *diaconalis* from *diaconus* DEACON]

diaconate *noun*
• "die ACKA nit" or "dee ACKA nit"
• the office of deacon.
• [Church Latin *diaconatus* (as DIACONAL)]

diacritic *noun*
• "die a CRITTIC"
• a sign, e.g. an accent, diaeresis, cedilla, used to indicate different sounds or values of a letter.
• [Greek *diakritikos* (*dia* through + *kritikos* from *kritēs* judge, from *krinō* judge, decide)]
• **diacritical** *noun*

diadem *noun*
• "DIE a dem"
• a crown or headband worn as a sign of sovereignty.
• [Latin *diadema* from Greek *diadēma* (*dia* through + *deō* bind)]

diaeresis *noun*
ALSO SPELLED: *US* **dieresis**
• "die URRA sis"
• a mark (¨) over a vowel to indicate that it is sounded separately.
• [Latin from Greek, = separation]

diagenesis *noun*
• "die a JENNA sis"
• the transformation occurring during the conversion of sedimentation to sedimentary rock.
• [Greek *dia* through + GENESIS]
• **diagenetic** *adjective* "die a juh NETTIC"

diagnose *verb*
• "die ug NOCE" or "die ug NOZE"
• make a diagnosis of (a disease, a mechanical fault, etc.) from its symptoms.
• [as DIAGNOSIS]
• **diagnosable** *adjective*

diagnosis *noun*
• "die ug NO sis"
• the identification of an illness or disease by means of a patient's symptoms.
• [modern Latin from Greek (*dia* through + *gignōskō* recognize)]
• **diagnostic** *adjective* "die ug NOSS tick"
• **diagnostically** *adverb*
• **diagnostician** *noun* "die ug noss TISH'n"

diagnostics *noun*
• "die ug NOSS ticks"
• programs and other mechanisms used to detect and identify faults in hardware or software.
• [as DIAGNOSIS]

diagonal *adjective*
• "die AGGA n'll" or "die AG n'll"
• crossing a straight-sided figure from corner to corner.
• [Latin *diagonalis* from Greek *diagōnios* (*dia* through + *gōnia* angle)]
• **diagonally** *adverb*

diagram *noun*
• "DIE a gram"
• a drawing showing the general scheme or outline of an object and its parts.
• [Latin *diagramma* from Greek (*dia* through + *gramma* letter of the alphabet)]
• **diagrammatic** *adjective*
• **diagrammatically** *adverb*

diakinesis *noun*
• "die a kuh NEE sis"
• a stage during the prophase of meiosis when the separation of homologous chromosomes is complete and crossing over has occurred.
• [modern Latin (from Greek *dia* through + Greek *kinēsis* motion)]

dialect *noun*
• "DIE a lect"
• a form of speech peculiar to a particular region.
• [Latin *dialectus* from Greek *dialektos* discourse, from *dialegomai* converse]
• **dialectal** *adjective*
• **dialectological** *adjective*
• **dialectologist** *noun*
• **dialectology** *noun*

dialectic *noun*
• "die a LECK tick"
• the art of critically investigating the truth of opinions; the testing of truth by discussion.
• [Latin *dialectica* from Greek *dialektikē* (*tekhnē*) (art) of debate (as DIALECT)]
• **dialectical** *adjective*
• **dialectically** *adverb*
• **dialectician** *noun*
• **dialectics** *noun*

dialogic *adjective*
• "die a LODGE ick"
• of, pertaining to, or of the nature of dialogue.
• [as DIALOGUE]

dialogist *noun*
• "die ALA jist"
• a speaker in or writer of dialogue.
• [as DIALOGUE]

dialogue *noun*
ALSO SPELLED: *US* also **dialog**
• "DIE a log"
• conversation between two or more people.
• [Old French *dialoge* from Latin *dialogus* from Greek *dialogos* from *dialegomai* converse]

dialysis *noun*
• "die ALA sis"
• the separation of particles in a liquid by differences in their ability to pass through a membrane into another liquid.
• [Latin from Greek *dialusis* (*dia* through + *luō* set free)]
• **dialytic** *adjective* "die a LITTIC"

dialyze *verb*
ALSO SPELLED: esp. *Brit.* **-yse**
• "DIE a lize"
• subject to dialysis.
• [as DIALYSIS]
• **dialyzable** *adjective* (esp. *Brit.* **-ysable**)
• **dialyzer** *noun* (esp. *Brit.* **-yser**)

diamagnetic *adjective*
• "die a mag NETTIC"
• tending to become magnetized in a direction at right angles to the applied magnetic field.
• [Greek *dia* through + MAGNETIC]
• **diamagnetism** *noun*

diamanté *adjective*
• "dee a mon TAY" or "die a mon TAY"
• decorated with powdered crystal, sequins, or another sparkling substance.
• [French, past participle of *diamanter* set with diamonds, from *diamant* DIAMOND]

diamantine *adjective*
• "die a MAN tine"
• of or like diamonds.
• [French *diamantin* from *diamant* DIAMOND]

diameter *noun*
• "die AMMA tur"
• a straight line passing from side to side through the centre of a body or figure, esp. a circle or sphere.
• [Old French *diametre* from Latin *diametrus* from Greek *diametros* (*grammē*) (line) measuring across, from *dia* across, *metron* measure]
• **diametral** *adjective*
• **diametrical** *adjective*
• **diametrically** *adverb*

diamine *noun*
• "DIE a meen" or "die AM een"
• a compound whose molecule contains two amino groups, esp. when joined to radicals other than acid radicals.
• [Greek *dis* twice + AMINE]

diamond *noun*
• "DIE m'nd" or "DIE a m'nd"
• a usu. colourless or lightly tinted precious stone of great brilliance and hardness, used in jewellery and for cutting and abrading.
• [Old French *diamant* from medieval Latin *diamas diamant-* var. of Latin *adamas* ADAMANT, from Greek]

diamondback *noun*
• "DIE m'nd back"
• an edible freshwater terrapin, *Malaclemys terrapin*, native to N America, with diamond-shaped markings on its shell.
• [as DIAMOND + 'back']

diamondiferous *adjective*
• "die m'nd IFFER us" or "die a m'nd IFFER us"
• yielding diamonds.
• [DIAMOND + Latin *-fer* producing, from *ferre* bear]

dianthus *noun*
• "die ANTH us"
• any flowering plant of the genus *Dianthus*, e.g. a carnation or pink.
• [Greek *Dios* of Zeus + *anthos* flower]

diapason *noun*
• "die a PAY z'n" or "die a PAY s'n"
• a combination of notes or parts in a harmonious whole.
• [Middle English in sense 'octave' from Latin *diapason* from Greek *dia pasōn (khordōn)* through all (notes)]

diapause *noun*
• "DIE a pozz"
• a period of retarded or suspended development in some insects.
• [Greek *dia* through + *pausis*, from *pauō* stop]

diaper *noun*
• "DIPE ur" or "DIE a pur"
• a piece of folded cloth or disposable absorbent material wrapped around a baby's bottom to absorb and retain urine and feces.
• [Old French *diapre* from medieval Latin *diasprum* from medieval Greek *diaspros* (adjective) (Greek *dia* through + *aspros* white)]

diaphanous *adjective*
• "die AFFA nuss"
• (of fabric etc.) light and delicate, and almost transparent.
• [medieval Latin *diaphanus* from Greek *diaphanes* (Greek *dia* through + *phainō* show)]

diaphoresis *noun*
• "die a for EE sis"
• sweating, esp. artificially induced.
• [Late Latin from Greek from *diaphoreō* carry through]
• **diaphoretic** *adjective* "die a for ETTIC"

diaphragm *noun*
• "DIE a fram"
• (in mammals) a muscular, dome-shaped partition which separates the thorax from the abdomen, and whose contraction leads to expansion of the lungs in respiration.
• [Late Latin *diaphragma* from Greek (Greek *dia* through + *phragma -atos* from *phrassō* fence in)]
• **diaphragmatic** *adjective*

diapir *noun*
• "DIE a peer"
• an anticline in which the upper strata are pierced by a rock core from below.
• [Greek *diapeirainein* pierce through]
• **diapiric** *adjective*
• **diapirism** *noun*

diarchy *noun*
ALSO SPELLED: **dyarchy**
• "DIE arky"
• government by two independent authorities (esp. in India 1921–37).
• [Greek *dis* twice + Greek *-arkhia* rule, after *monarchy*]

diarrhea *noun*
ALSO SPELLED: esp. *Brit.* **diarrhoea**
• "die a REE uh"
• a condition of excessively frequent and loose bowel movements.
• [Late Latin from Greek *diarrhoia* (Greek *dia* through + *rheō* flow)]
• **diarrheal** *adjective* (also esp. *Brit.* **diarrhoeal**)

diary *noun*
• "DIE a ree"
• a daily written record of events, feelings, or thoughts.
• [Latin *diarium* from *dies* day]
• **diarist** *noun*
• **diaristic** *adjective*

Diaspora *noun*
• "die ASPER uh"
• the dispersion of the Jews among the Gentiles mainly in the 8th–6th c. BC.
• [Greek from *diaspeirō* (Greek *dia* through + *speirō* scatter)]
• **diasporic** *adjective* "die a SPORE ick"
• **diasporist** *noun*

diastase *noun*
• "DIE a stace"
• an amylase, esp. one that breaks down starch into maltose and is present in seeds and the pancreas.
• [French from Greek *diastasis* separation (Greek *dia* through + *stasis* placing)]
• **diastatic** *adjective*

diastole *noun*
• "die ASTA lee"
• the period between two contractions of the heart when the heart muscle relaxes and allows the chambers to fill with blood.
• [Late Latin from Greek *diastellō* (Greek *dia* through + *stellō* place)]
• **diastolic** *adjective* "die a STOLLIC"

diathermy *noun*
• "DIE a thurmy"
• the application of high-frequency electric currents to produce heat in the deeper tissues of the body, used during some surgical procedures and to treat arthritis, bursitis, fractures, etc.
• [German *Diathermie* from Greek *dia* through + *thermon* heat]

diathesis *noun*
• "die ATHA sis"
• a constitutional predisposition to a particular disease or condition.
• [modern Latin from Greek from *diatithēmi* arrange]

diatom *noun*
• "DIE a tum"
• a microscopic unicellular alga with a siliceous cell wall, found as plankton and forming fossil deposits.
• [modern Latin *Diatoma* (genus name) from Greek *diatomos* (Greek *dia* through + *temnō* cut)]

diatomaceous *adjective*
• "die a tuh MAY sh'ss"
• designating a soft, fine-grained deposit composed of fossil diatoms, used as a filter, filler, insulator, etc., in various manufacturing processes, and as an insecticide in gardening applications.
• [as DIATOM]

diatomic *adjective*
• "die a TOMMIC"
• consisting of two atoms.
• [Greek *dis* twice + ATOMICITY]

diatomite *noun*
• "die ATTA mite"
• a sedimentary rock composed of the siliceous skeletons of diatoms.
• [as DIATOM + Greek *lithos* stone]

diatonic *adjective*
• "die a TONNIC"
• (of a scale, interval, etc.) involving only notes proper to the prevailing key without chromatic alteration.
• [Late Latin *diatonicus* from Greek *diatonikos* at intervals of a tone (Greek *dia* through + *tonikos* from *tonos* tension)]

diatribe *noun*
• "DIE a tribe"
• a forceful verbal attack; a piece of bitter criticism.
• [French from Latin *diatriba* from Greek *diatribē* spending of time, discourse, from *diatribō* (Greek *dia* through + *tribō* rub)]

diazepam *noun*
• "die AZZA pam"
• a tranquilizing muscle-relaxant drug with anticonvulsant properties used to relieve anxiety, tension, etc.
• [benzo*diazepine* + *am*]

diazinon *noun*
• "die AZZA non"
• an organophosphorous insecticide derived from pyrimidine.
• [Greek *dis* twice + AZINE]

diazo *noun*
• "die AZZO"
• a copying or colouring process using a chemical compound containing two usu. multiply-bonded nitrogen atoms, often highly coloured.
• [Greek *dis* twice + French *azote* nitrogen, from Greek *azōos* without life]

dibasic *adjective*
• "die BASE ick"
• having two replaceable hydrogen atoms.
• [Greek *dis* twice + 'basic']

dichotomy *noun*
• "die COTTA mee"
• a division into two, esp. a sharply defined one.
• [modern Latin *dichotomia* from Greek *dikhotomia* from *dikho-* apart + Greek *-tomia* cutting, from *temnō* cut]
• **dichotomize** *verb* (also esp. *Brit.* **-ise**)
• **dichotomous** *adjective*

dichroic *adjective*
• "die CROW ick"
• (esp. of doubly refracting crystals) showing two colours.
• [Greek *dikhroos* (as Greek *dis* twice, *khrōs* colour)]
• **dichroism** *noun*

dichromatic *adjective*
• "die crow MATTIC"
• two-coloured.
• [Greek *dis* twice + Greek *khrōmatikos* from *khrōma -atos* colour]
• **dichromatism** *noun* "die CROW muh tizm"

Dickensian *adjective*
• "duh KENZY 'n"
• of or relating to the English novelist Charles Dickens (d.1870) or his work.

dicotyledon *noun*
• "die cot'll EED'n"
• any flowering plant having two cotyledons.
• [Greek *dis* twice + COTYLEDON]
• **dicotyledonous** *adjective*

dictate *verb*
• "DIC tate"
• say or read aloud (words to be written down or recorded).
• [Latin *dictare dictat-* frequentative of *dicere dict-* say]
• **dictation** *noun*

dictator *noun*
• "DIC tater"
• a ruler with unrestricted authority, esp. one who suppresses or succeeds a democratic government.
• [as DICTATE]
• **dictatorial** *adjective* "dicta TORY 'll"
• **dictatorially** *adverb*
• **dictatorship** *noun*

diction *noun*
• "DIC sh'n"
• the manner of enunciation in speaking or singing.
• [French *diction* or Latin *dictio* from *dicere dict-* say]

dictionary *noun*
• "DIC sh'n airy"

• a book that lists (usu. in alphabetical order) and explains the words of a language or gives equivalent words in another language.
• [medieval Latin *dictionarium* (*manuale* manual) & *dictionarius* (*liber* book) from Latin *dictio* (as DICTION)]

dictum *noun*
• "DIC tum"
• a formal utterance or pronouncement.
• [Latin, = neuter past participle of *dicere* say]

didactic *adjective*
• "die DACTIC"
• meant to instruct.
• [Greek *didaktikos* from *didaskō* teach]
• **didactically** *adverb*
• **didacticism** *noun* "die DACTA sizm"

didgeridoo *noun*
ALSO SPELLED: **didjeridoo**
• "didger ee DOO"
• a tubular wooden wind instrument of Australian Aboriginal origin, producing a low-pitched, resonant sound.
• [imitative]

dido *noun*
• "DIE doe"
• an antic, a caper, a prank.
• [19th c.: origin unknown]

didymium *noun*
• "dih DIMMY um"
• a mixture of praseodymium and neodymium, originally regarded as an element.
• [modern Latin from Greek *didumos* twin (from being closely associated with lanthanum)]

dieffenbachia *noun*
• "deef'n BACKY uh"
• any tropical American evergreen plant of the genus *Dieffenbachia*, of the arum family, often grown as a houseplant and having poisonous sap which can cause loss of the power of speech or death.
• [E. *Dieffenbach*, German naturalist d.1855]

dieldrin *noun*
• "dee ELDRIN"
• a crystalline insecticide produced by the oxidation of aldrin.
• [O. *Diels*, German chemist d.1954 + ALDRIN]

dielectric *adjective*
• "die uh LECK trick"
• insulating.
• [Greek *dia* through + ELECTRIC = through which electricity is transmitted (without conduction)]

diene *noun*
• "DIE een"
• any organic compound possessing two double bonds between carbon atoms.
• [Greek *dis* twice + '-ene' forming names of unsaturated hydrocarbons containing a double bond, from Greek *-ēnos*, adjective suffix denoting origin or source]

diesel *noun*
• "DEEZ'll"
• an internal combustion engine in which the heat produced by the compression of air in the cylinder ignites the fuel.
• [R. *Diesel*, German engineer d.1913]
• **dieselization** *noun* (also esp. *Brit.* **-isation**)
• **dieselize** *verb* (also esp. *Brit.* **-ise**)

dieselling *noun*
ALSO SPELLED: **dieseling**
• "DEEZ'll ing"
• the continued operation of an internal combustion engine after the ignition has been shut off.
• [as DIESEL]

dietary *adjective*
• "DIE a terry"
• of, relating to, or provided by diet.
• [medieval Latin *dietarium* from Latin *diaeta* from Greek *diaita* a way of life]

dietetics *noun*
• "die a TETTIX"
• the scientific study of diet and nutrition.
• [Latin *dieteticus* from Greek *diaitētikos* (as DIETARY)]
• **dietetic** *adjective*
• **dietetically** *adverb*

diethylstilbestrol *noun*
• "die eth'll still BESS trawl"
• a powerful synthetic estrogen formerly used to prevent miscarriage, withdrawn from use because of carcinogenic effects on offspring.
• [Greek *dis* twice + ETHYL + STILBESTROL]

dietitian *noun*
ALSO SPELLED: **dietician**
• "die a TISH'n"
• an expert in dietetics.
• [as DIETARY]

different *adjective*
• "DIFF r'nt"
• unlike, distinguishable in nature, form, or quality (from another).
• [Old French *different* from *differer* from Latin *differre*, differ, DEFER (from *dis-* expressing negation + *ferre* bear, tend)]
• **difference** *noun*
• **differently** *adverb*
• **differentness** *noun*

differentia *noun*
• "differ ENSHY uh"
• a distinguishing mark, esp. between species within a genus.
• [Latin: see DIFFERENT]

differential *adjective*
• "diffa REN sh'll"
• of, showing, or depending on a difference;

varying according to circumstances or relevant factors.
• [medieval & modern Latin *differentialis* (as DIFFERENT)]
• **differentially** *adverb*

differentiate *verb*
• "diffa REN shee ate"
• constitute a difference between or in.
• [medieval Latin *differentiare differentiat-* (as DIFFERENT)]
• **differentiable** *adjective*
• **differentiated** *adjective*
• **differentiation** *noun*
• **differentiator** *noun*

difficult *adjective*
• "DIFFA cult"
• needing much effort or skill.
• [back-formation from 'difficult', from Latin *difficultas* (*dis-* expressing negation + *facultas* FACULTY)]
• **difficultly** *adverb*
• **difficultness** *noun*
• **difficulty** *noun*

diffident *adjective*
• "DIFFA d'nt"
• shy, lacking self-confidence.
• [Latin *diffidere* (*dis-* expressing negation + *fidere* trust)]
• **diffidence** *noun*
• **diffidently** *adverb*

diffract *verb*
• "duh FRACT"
• (of the edge of an opaque body, a narrow slit, etc.) break up (a beam of light) into a series of dark or light bands or coloured spectra, or (a beam of radiation or particles) into a series of alternately high and low intensities.
• [Latin *diffringere diffract-*, from *frangere* break]
• **diffraction** *noun*
• **diffractive** *adjective*

diffractometer *noun*
• "duh frack TOMMA tur"
• an instrument for measuring diffraction, esp. in crystallographic work.
• [as DIFFRACT + Greek *metron* measure]

diffuse[1] *adjective*
• "dif FYOOSS"
• (of light, inflammation, etc.) spread out, diffused, not concentrated.
• [Latin *diffusus* extensive, from *fusus* past participle of *fundere* pour]
• **diffusely** *adverb*
• **diffuseness** *noun*
• **diffusive** *adjective*

diffuse[2] *adjective*
• "dif FYOOZ"
• disperse or be dispersed from a centre.
• [Latin *diffusus* extensive, from *fusus* past participle of *fundere* pour]
• **diffused** *adjective*
• **diffuser** *noun* (also **diffusor**)
• **diffusible** *adjective*
• **diffusion** *noun*
HOMOPHONES: *defuse*

diffusionism *noun*
• "dif FYOO zh'n izm"
• the theory that all or most cultural similarities are due to diffusion.
• [as DIFFUSE[2]]
• **diffusionist** *noun*

Digambara *noun*
• "dih GUMBA ruh"
• one of two principal sects of Jainism (the other is Svetambara), which was formed as a result of doctrinal schism in about AD 80 and continues today in parts of S India. Its adherents reject property ownership and usu. do not wear clothes.
• [Sanskrit, = sky-clad]

digamma *noun*
• "die GAMMA"
• the sixth letter (Ϝ, ϝ) of the early Greek alphabet, later disused.
• [Latin from Greek (as Greek *dis* twice, GAMMA)]

Digbyite *noun*
• "DIGBY ite"
• a resident of Digby, NS.

digerati *plural noun*
• "didger OTTY"
• people with expertise or professional involvement in information technology.
• [blend of DIGITAL + LITERATI]

digest *verb*
• "die JEST"
• assimilate (food) in the stomach and bowels.
• [Latin *digerere digest-* distribute, dissolve, digest, from *gerere* carry]
• **digestant** *noun*
• **digester** *noun*
• **digestibility** *noun*
• **digestible** *adjective*
• **digestion** *noun*

digestif *noun*
• "dee zhess TEEF"
• something which promotes good digestion, esp. a drink taken after a meal, e.g. a liqueur or brandy.
• [French: see DIGESTIVE]

digestive *adjective*
• "duh JESTIV" or "die JESTIV"
• of or relating to digestion.
• [Old French *digestif -ive* or Latin *digestivus* (as DIGEST)]
• **digestively** *adverb*

digicam *noun*
• "DIDGE a cam"
• a digital camera.
• [DIGITAL + CAMERA]

digit *noun*
- "DIDGE it"
- any numeral from 0 to 9, esp. when forming part of a number.
- [Latin *digitus* finger]

digital *adjective*
- "DIDGE it 'll"
- of or relating to a numerical digit or digits.
- [Latin *digitalis* (as DIGIT)]
- **digitalize** *verb* (also esp. *Brit.* **-ise**)
- **digitally** *adverb*

digitalin *noun*
- "didge it AL in"
- the pharmacologically active constituent(s) of the foxglove.
- [as DIGITALIS]

digitalis *noun*
- "didge it AL iss"
- a drug prepared from the dried leaves of foxgloves and containing substances that stimulate the heart muscle.
- [modern Latin, = pertaining to the finger, genus name of foxglove, influenced by German *Fingerhut* foxglove, thimble: see DIGITAL]

digitate *adjective*
- "DIDGE a tate"
- having separate fingers or toes.
- [Latin *digitatus* (as DIGIT)]

digitigrade *adjective*
- "DIDGE it a grade"
- (of an animal, e.g. dogs, cats, and rodents) walking on its toes and not touching the ground with its heels.
- [French from Latin *digitus* + *-gradus* -walking]

digitize *verb*
ALSO SPELLED: esp. *Brit.* **-ise**
- "DIDGE it ize"
- convert (pictures or sound etc.) into a digital form that can be processed by a computer.
- [as DIGIT]
- **digitization** *noun* (also esp. *Brit.* **-isation**)
- **digitizer** *noun* (also esp. *Brit.* **-iser**)

dignify *verb*
- "DIGNA fie"
- give dignity or distinction to.
- [Old French *dignefier* from Late Latin *dignificare* from *dignus* worthy]
- **dignified** *adjective*

dignitary *noun*
- "DIGNA terry"
- a person holding high rank or office.
- [as DIGNITY]

dignity *noun*
- "DIGNA tee"
- a composed and serious manner or style.
- [Old French *digneté*, *dignité* from Latin *dignitas -tatis* from *dignus* worthy]

digoxin *noun*
- "die JOXIN"
- a potentially poisonous steroid glycoside that is present in the foxglove etc. and is commonly used as a cardiac stimulant.
- [contraction of *digitoxin* (a similar, less widely used drug), blend of DIGITALIS + TOXIN]

digraph *noun*
- "DIE graff"
- a group of two letters representing one sound, as in *ph* and *ey*.
- [Greek *dis* twice + GRAPH]
- **digraphic** *adjective*

digress *verb*
- "die GRESS"
- depart from the main subject temporarily in speech or writing.
- [Latin *digredi digress-*, from *gradi* walk]
- **digression** *noun*
- **digressive** *adjective*
- **digressively** *adverb*
- **digressiveness** *noun*

dihedral *adjective*
- "die HEED rull"
- having or contained by two plane faces.
- [*dihedron* from Greek *dis* twice + *hedra* base]

dihydric *adjective*
- "die HY drick"
- containing two hydroxyl groups.
- [Greek *dis* twice + HYDROGEN]

diktat *noun*
- "DICK tat"
- a categorical statement or decree, esp. terms imposed after a war by a victor.
- [German, = DICTATE]

dilapidate *verb*
- "duh LAPPA date"
- fall or cause to fall into disrepair or ruin.
- [Latin *dilapidare* demolish, squander, from *lapis lapid-* stone]
- **dilapidated** *adjective*
- **dilapidation** *noun*

dilatation *noun*
- "die luh TAY sh'n"
- the widening or expansion of a hollow organ or cavity.
- [as DILATE]
- **dilatational** *adjective*

dilate *verb*
- "DIE late" or "die LATE"
- make or become wider or larger (esp. of an opening in the body).
- [Old French *dilater* from Latin *dilatare* spread out, from *latus* wide]
- **dilation** *noun*

dilator *noun*
- "DIE later"
- a muscle that dilates an organ.
- [as DILATE]

dilatory *adjective*
- "DILLA tory"
- given to or causing delay.

- [Late Latin *dilatorius* from *dilat-* past participle stem of *differre* DEFER]
- **dilatorily** *adverb*
- **dilatoriness** *noun*

dilemma *noun*
- "duh LEMMA"
- a situation in which a choice has to be made between two equally undesirable alternatives.
- [Latin from Greek (as Greek *dis* twice, *lēmma* premise)]

dilettante *noun*
- "DILLA tont"
- a person who studies a subject or area of knowledge superficially.
- [Italian from present participle of *dilettare* delight, from Latin *delectare*]
- **dilettantish** *adjective*
- **dilettantism** *noun*

diligent *adjective*
- "DILLA j'nt"
- careful and steady in application to one's work or duties.
- [Old French from Latin *diligens* assiduous, participle of *diligere* love, take delight in, from *legere* choose]
- **diligence** *noun*
- **diligently** *adverb*

diluent *adjective*
- "DILL yoo 'nt"
- that serves to dilute.
- [Latin *diluere diluent-* DILUTE]

dilute *verb*
- "die LOOT" or "duh LOOT"
- reduce the strength of (a fluid) by adding water or another solvent.
- [Latin *diluere dilut-* from *luere* wash]
- **diluted** *adjective*
- **diluter** *noun*
- **dilution** *noun*

diluvial *adjective*
- "die LOOVY 'll" or "duh LOOVY 'll"
- of or relating to a flood, esp. the Flood described in Genesis.
- [Late Latin *diluvialis* from *diluvium* DELUGE]

diluvium *noun*
- "die LOOVY um" or "duh LOOVY um"
- material deposited by the wind, a current of water, etc.
- [Latin: see DILUVIAL]

dimenhydrinate *noun*
- "die men HY druh nate"
- a medication used to counter nausea and vomiting and prevent motion sickness, the active ingredient in Gravol.
- [Greek *dis* twice + METHYL + HYDROGEN + AMINE]

dimension *noun*
- "duh MEN sh'n" or "die MEN sh'n"
- a measurable extent of any kind, as length, breadth, depth, area, and volume.
- [Latin *dimensio -onis* from *metiri mensus* measure]
- **dimensional** *adjective*
- **dimensionality** *noun*
- **dimensionally** *adverb*
- **dimensionless** *adjective*

dimer *noun*
- "DIE mur"
- a compound consisting of two identical molecules linked together.
- [Greek *dis* twice + *-mer* after POLYMER]
- **dimeric** *adjective* "die MARE ick"

dimerous *adjective*
- "DIE mur us"
- (of a plant) having two parts in a whorl etc.
- [modern Latin *dimerus* from Greek *dimerēs* bipartite]

dimeter *noun*
- "DIMMA tur"
- a line of verse consisting of two metrical feet.
- [Late Latin *dimetrus* from Greek *dimetros* (*dis* twice, *metron* measure)]

diminish *verb*
- "duh MIN ish"
- make or become smaller or less.
- [Middle English, blending of earlier *minish* from Old French *menusier* (from MINUTIA) and *diminue* from Old French *diminuer* from Latin *diminuere diminut-* break up small]
- **diminishable** *adjective*
- **diminished** *adjective*
- **diminishment** *noun*

diminuendo *noun*
- "dim in yoo ENDO"
- a gradual decrease in loudness.
- [Italian, participle of *diminuire* DIMINISH]

diminution *noun*
- "dim in YOO sh'n"
- the act or an instance of diminishing.
- [Old French from Latin *diminutio -onis* (as DIMINISH)]

diminutive *adjective*
- "duh MIN yoo tiv"
- remarkably small; tiny.
- [Old French *diminutif, -ive* from Late Latin *diminutivus* (as DIMINISH)]
- **diminutiveness** *noun*

dimity *noun*
- "DIMMA tee"
- a fairly sheer lightweight fabric of cotton or artificial fibres, often woven with fine stripes, checks, or printed patterns.
- [ultimately from Greek *dimitos* (*dis* twice, *mitos* warp thread)]

dimorphic *adjective*
- "die MORFIC"

• exhibiting, or occurring in, two distinct forms.
• [Greek *dimorphos* (*dis* twice, *morphē* form)]
• **dimorphism** *noun*

dinar *noun*
• "DEE nar"
• the chief monetary unit of certain countries esp. of the Middle East and North Africa.
• [Arabic & Persian *dīnār* from Greek *dēnarion* from Latin *denarius*: see DENIER[2]]
HOMOPHONES: *denar*

dinero *noun*
• "dee NERRO"
• money; cash.
• [Spanish]

dinette *noun*
• "die NET"
• a small room or part of a room used for eating meals.
• [as DINING]

dinghy *noun*
• "DING ee" or "DING gee" (with "G" as in *GEEK*)
• a small boat carried by a ship.
• [originally a rowboat used on Indian rivers, from Hindi *ḍiṅgī*]

dingo *noun*
• "DING go"
• a wild or half-domesticated Australian dog, *Canis dingo*.
• [Dharuk *din-gu* or *dayn-gu* 'domesticated dingo']

dingus *noun*
• "DING guss"
• a gadget or contraption.
• [Dutch *ding* thing]

dingy *adjective*
• "DINJY"
• dirty-looking.
• [perhaps ultimately from Old English *dynge* dung]
• **dingily** *adverb*
• **dinginess** *noun*

dining *noun*
• "DIE ning"
• the act of eating dinner.
• [Old French *diner*, *disner*, ultimately from Latin *dis-* expressing negation + Late Latin *jejunare* from *jejunus* fasting]

Dinka *noun*
• "DINKA"
• a member of a Sudanese people of the Nile basin.
• [Dinka *jieng* people]

dinkum *adjective*
• "DINK'm"
• genuine, right.
• [19th c.: origin unknown]

dinoflagellate *noun*
• "die no FLADGE a late"
• a unicellular aquatic organism with two flagella, of a group variously classed as algae and protozoa.
• [modern Latin *Dinoflagellata*, from Greek *dinos* whirling + Latin FLAGELLUM]

dinosaur *noun*
• "DIE nuh sore"
• an extinct reptile of the Mesozoic era, often of enormous size.
• [modern Latin *dinosaurus* from Greek *deinos* terrible + *sauros* lizard]
• **dinosaurian** *adjective*

dinothere *noun*
• "DIE no theer" (with "TH" as in *THIN*)
• any elephant-like animal of the extinct genus *Deinotherium*, having downward curving tusks.
• [modern Latin *dinotherium* from Greek *deinos* terrible + *thērion* wild beast]

diocese *noun*
• "DIE a seez" or "DIE a sis" or "DIE a seece"
• a district under the pastoral care of a bishop.
• [Old French *diocise* from Late Latin *diocesis* from Latin *dioecesis* from Greek *dioikēsis* administration (*dia* through + *oikeō* inhabit)]
• **diocesan** *adjective* "die OSSA s'n" or "die OSSA z'n"

diode *noun*
• "DIE ode"
• a semiconductor allowing the flow of current in one direction only and having two terminals.
• [Greek *dis* twice + ELECTRODE]

dioecious *adjective*
• "die EE sh'ss"
• having male and female organs on separate plants.
• [Greek *dis* twice + Greek *-oikos* -housed]

diol *noun*
• "DIE awl"
• any alcohol containing two hydroxyl groups in each molecule.
• [Greek *dis* twice + ALCOHOL]

Dionysiac *adjective*
• "die a NEECY ack"
• wildly sensual; unrestrained.
• [*Dionysus*, Greek god of fertility or wine]

dioptre *noun*
ALSO SPELLED: **diopter**
• "die OPTER"
• a unit of refractive power of a lens, equal to the reciprocal of its focal length in metres.
• [see DIOPTRIC]

dioptric *adjective*
• "die OPTRIC"
• serving as a medium for sight; assisting sight by refraction.
• [Greek *dioptrikos* from *dioptra* a kind of theodolite]

dioptrics *noun*
• "die OPTRIX"
• the part of optics dealing with refraction.
• [as DIOPTRIC]

diorama *noun*
• "die a RAMMA"
• a scenic painting in which changes in colour and direction of illumination simulate a sunrise etc.
• [Greek *dia* through + *horama -atos* from *horaō* see]
• **dioramic** *adjective*

diorite *noun*
• "DIE a rite"
• a coarse-grained plutonic igneous rock containing quartz.
• [French from Greek *diorizō* distinguish]

dioxan *noun*
• "die OX'n"
• a colourless toxic liquid used as a solvent.
• [Greek *dis* twice + OXYGEN]
HOMOPHONES: *dioxin*

dioxide *noun*
• "die OX ide"
• an oxide containing two atoms of oxygen which are not linked together.
• [Greek *dis* twice + OXYGEN]

dioxin *noun*
• "die OXIN"
• any of a class of cyclic compounds produced as chemical by-products, esp. the highly toxic tetrachlorodibenzoparadioxin (TCDD).
• [Greek *dis* twice + OXYGEN]
HOMOPHONES: *dioxan*

dipeptide *noun*
• "die PEP tide"
• a peptide formed by the combination of two amino acids.
• [Greek *dis* twice + PEPTIDE]

diphenhydramine *noun*
• "die fen HY druh meen"
• an antihistamine compound used for the symptomatic relief of allergies.
• [Greek *dis* twice + PHENYL + HYDROGEN + AMINE]

diphosphate *noun*
• "die FOSS fate"
• a compound with two phosphate groups in the molecule, or a salt with two phosphate anions per cation.
• [Greek *dis* twice + PHOSPHATE]

diphtheria *noun*
• "dif THEERY uh" or "dip THEERY uh"
• an acute infectious bacterial disease with inflammation of a mucous membrane esp. of the throat, resulting in the formation of a false membrane causing difficulty in breathing and swallowing.
• [French *diphthérie*, earlier *diphthérite* from Greek *diphthera* skin, hide]
• **diphtherial** *adjective*
• **diphtheritic** *adjective* "dif thur ITTIC" or "dip thur ITTIC"

diphthong *noun*
• "DIF thong" or "DIP thong"
• a speech sound in one syllable in which the articulation begins as for one vowel and moves as for another (as in *coin*, *loud*, and *side*).
• [French *diphtongue* from Late Latin *diphthongus* from Greek *diphthoggos* (as Greek *dis* twice, *phthoggos* voice)]
• **diphthongal** *adjective*
• **diphthongization** *noun* (also esp. *Brit.* **-isation**)
• **diphthongize** *verb* (also esp. *Brit.* **-ise**)

diplococcus *noun*
• "dipla COCKUS"
• any of various spherical bacteria that occur mainly in pairs.
• [Greek *diplous* double + COCCUS]

diplodocus *noun*
• "dip LODDA cuss" or "diplo DOE cuss"
• a huge plant-eating dinosaur of the genus *Diplodocus*, of the Jurassic period, with a long neck and long slender tail.
• [Greek *diplous* double + Greek *dokos* wooden beam]

diploid *adjective*
• "DIP loid"
• (of an organism or cell) having two complete sets of chromosomes per cell.
• [German (as Greek *diplous* double + *-oeidēs* from *eidos* form)]
• **diploidy** *noun*

diploma *noun*
• "dih PLOE muh"
• a certificate awarded for passing an examination, completing a course of study, etc.
• [Latin *diplōma*, letter of recommendation, from Greek *diplōma -atos* folded paper, from *diploō* to fold, from *diplous* double]

diplomacy *noun*
• "dih PLOE muh see"
• the management of international relations by negotiation.
• [French *diplomatie* from *diplomatique* from Latin DIPLOMA]
• **diplomatic** *adjective* "dipla MATTIC"
• **diplomatically** *adverb*
• **diplomatist** *noun*

diplomat *noun*
• "DIPLA mat"
• a person engaged by a government to conduct official negotiations with other countries; a member of a diplomatic service.
• [French *diplomate*, back-formation from *diplomatique*: see DIPLOMACY]

diplomate *noun*
• "DIPLA mate"
• a person who holds a diploma, esp. in medicine.
• [as DIPLOMA]

diplont *noun*
• "DIP lont"
• an animal or plant which has a diploid number of chromosomes in its cells (other than gametes).
• [Greek *diplous* double + Greek *ont-* stem of *ōn* being]

diplopia *noun*
• "dih PLOE pee uh"
• double vision.
• [Greek *diplous* double + *ōps* eye]

diplotene *noun*
• "DIPLO teen"
• a stage during the prophase of meiosis where paired chromosomes begin to separate.
• [Greek *diplous* double + Greek *tainia* band]

dipole *noun*
• "DIE pole"
• two equal and oppositely charged or magnetized poles separated by a distance.
• [Greek *dis* twice + 'pole']
• **dipolar** *adjective*

dipsomania *noun*
• "dipsa MAINY uh"
• an abnormal craving for alcohol.
• [Greek *dipso-* from *dipsa* thirst + MANIA]
• **dipsomaniac** *noun*

dipteran *noun*
• "DIPTER 'n"
• a dipterous insect.
• [modern Latin *diptera* from Greek *diptera* neuter pl. of *dipterous* two-winged (*dis* twice + *pteron* wing)]

dipterous *adjective*
• "DIPTER us"
• of or relating to the insect order Diptera, whose members (the 'true' flies) have two membranous wings, the hindwings being reduced to halteres or balancing organs, e.g. houseflies, mosquitoes, etc.
• [modern Latin *dipterus* from Greek *dipteros*: see DIPTERAN]

diptych *noun*
• "DIP tick"
• a pair of thematically linked paintings, photographs, sculptures, etc. on two panels.
• [Late Latin *diptycha* from Greek *diptukha* (as Greek *dis* twice, *ptukhē* fold)]

diram *noun*
• "DEER'm"
• a monetary unit of Tajikistan, equal to one-hundredth of a somoni.
• [Tajik]

Directoire *adjective*
• "dir eck TWAR" ("TWAR" rhymes with *FAR*)
• designating styles of clothing, furniture, etc. typical of the neoclassical style of the late 18th c. in France, characterized by simple lines and the use of antique ornamental motifs.
• [French (as DIRECTORY)]

directorate *noun*
• "dir ECTER it" or "die RECTER it"
• a government agency or subdivision of a ministry with a specific responsibility.
• [as DIRECTORY]

directory *noun*
• "dir ECTER ee" or "die RECTER ee"
• a book listing alphabetically or thematically a particular group of individuals (e.g. telephone subscribers) or organizations with various details.
• [Late Latin *directorium* from *directus* past participle of *dirigere direct-* from *regere* put straight]

directrix *noun*
• "dir ECTRIX" or "die RECTRIX"
• a fixed line used in describing a curve or surface.
• [medieval Latin from Late Latin *director*: see DIRECTORY]

dirge *noun*
• "DURJ"
• a lament for the dead, esp. forming part of a funeral service.
• [Latin *dirige* (imperative) direct, the first word in the Latin antiphon (from Psalm 5:8) in the Matins part of the Office for the Dead]

dirham *noun*
• "DUR um"
• the principal monetary unit of Morocco and the United Arab Emirates, equal to 100 francs in Morocco and 100 fils in the United Arab Emirates.
• [Arabic from Latin DRACHMA]
HOMOPHONES: *durum*

dirigible *noun*
• "DEER idge a bull"
• an airship.
• [Latin *dirigere* arrange, direct: see DIRECTORY]

dirigisme *noun*
• "dee ree ZHEEZ 'm"
• state control of economic and social matters.
• [French from *diriger* direct (see DIRECTORY)]
• ***dirigiste*** *adjective*

dirk *noun*
• "DURK"
• a long dagger, esp. as formerly worn by Scottish Highlanders.
• [17th-c. *durk*, of unknown origin]

dirndl *noun*
• "DURN d'll"
• a woman's dress styled in imitation of Alpine

peasant costume, with close-fitting bodice, tight waistband, and full skirt.
• [German dialect, diminutive of *Dirne* girl]

disabuse *verb*
• "dissa BYOOZ"
• free from a mistaken idea.
• [Latin *dis-* expressing negation + Latin *abusus* (*ab* off, away, from + *uti us-* use)]

disaccharide *noun*
• "die SACKA ride"
• a sugar whose molecule contains two linked monosaccharides.
• [Greek *dis* twice + SACCHARIDE]

disadvantage *noun*
• "diss'd VAN tidge"
• an unfavourable circumstance or condition.
• [Latin *dis-* expressing negation + ADVANTAGE]

disadvantaged *adjective*
• "diss'd VAN tijd"
• suffering from social or economic deprivation or discrimination.
• [as DISADVANTAGE]

disadvantageous *adjective*
• "dis ad v'n TAY juss"
• involving disadvantage or discredit.
• [as DISADVANTAGE]
• **disadvantageously** *adverb*

disaffected *adjective*
• "dissa FECTED"
• alienated and discontented, esp. with regard to authority.
• [past participle of *disaffect* (v.), originally = dislike, disorder (*dis-* expressing negation + AFFECT[1])]

disaffection *noun*
• "dissa FECK sh'n"
• discontentedness, esp. with political or social structures.
• [as DISAFFECTED]

disaffiliate *verb*
• "dissa FILLY ate"
• end the affiliation of.
• [Latin *dis-* expressing negation + AFFILIATE]
• **disaffiliation** *noun*

disaggregate *verb*
• "dis AGRA gate"
• separate into component parts; cease to treat as aggregated.
• [Latin *dis-* expressing negation + AGGREGATE]
• **disaggregation** *noun*

disagree *verb*
• "dissa GREE"
• hold a different opinion.
• [Latin *dis-* expressing negation + Old French *agreer*, ultimately from Latin *gratus* pleasing]
• **disagreement** *noun*

disagreeable *adjective*
• "dissa GREE a bull"
• unpleasant, not to one's liking.
• [as DISAGREE]
• **disagreeableness** *noun*
• **disagreeably** *adverb*

disallow *verb*
• "dissa LOW" ("LOW" rhymes with *COW*)
• refuse to allow or accept as valid; prohibit.
• [Latin *dis-* expressing negation + Old French *alouer* from Latin *allaudare* to praise, and medieval Latin *allocare* to place]
• **disallowance** *noun*

disambiguate *verb*
• "dissam BIG yoo ate"
• make unambiguous, esp. distinguish the various senses of (words in context).
• [Latin *dis-* expressing negation + AMBIGUOUS]
• **disambiguation** *noun*

disappear *verb*
• "dissa PEER"
• cease to be visible; pass from sight.
• [Latin *dis-* expressing negation + APPEAR]
• **disappearance** *noun*

disappoint *verb*
• "dissa POINT"
• fail to fulfill a desire or expectation of (a person).
• [French *désappointer* (*dis-* expressing negation + APPOINT)]
• **disappointed** *adjective*
• **disappointedly** *adverb*
• **disappointing** *adjective*
• **disappointingly** *adverb*
• **disappointment** *noun*

disapprobation *noun*
• "dis appro BAY sh'n"
• strong (esp. moral) disapproval.
• [Latin *dis-* expressing negation + APPROBATION]

disapprove *verb*
• "dissa PROOVE"
• have or express an unfavourable opinion.
• [Latin *dis-* expressing negation + APPROVE]
• **disapproval** *noun*
• **disapproving** *adjective*
• **disapprovingly** *adverb*

disarmament *noun*
• "dis ARMA m'nt"
• the reduction by a nation of its military forces and weapons.
• [Latin *dis-* expressing negation + ARMAMENT]

disarrange *verb*
• "dissa RANGE"
• bring into disorder.
• [Latin *dis-* expressing negation + ARRANGE]
• **disarrangement** *noun*

disarray *noun*
• "dissa RAY"
• disorder, confusion.
• [Latin *dis-* expressing negation + Anglo-French

araier, Old French *areer*, ultimately from a Germanic root, = prepare]

disarticulate *verb*
• "dis ar TICK yuh late"
• separate (a skeleton etc.) at the joints.
• [Latin *dis-* expressing negation + ARTICULATE]
• **disarticulation** *noun*

disassemble *verb*
• "dissa SEMBLE"
• take (a machine etc.) to pieces.
• [Latin *dis-* expressing negation + ASSEMBLE]
• **disassembly** *noun*

disassembler *noun*
• "dissa SEMBLER"
• a program for converting machine code into assembly language.
• [as DISASSEMBLE]

disassociate *verb*
• "dissa SO see ate" or "dissa SO shee ate"
• disconnect or become disconnected; separate.
• [Latin *dis-* expressing negation + ASSOCIATE]
• **disassociation** *noun*

disaster *noun*
• "diz ASTER"
• a great or sudden misfortune.
• [originally 'unfavourable aspect of a star', from French *désastre* or Italian *disastro* (*dis-* expressing negation + *astro* from Latin *astrum* star)]
• **disastrous** *adjective*
• **disastrously** *adverb*

disavow *verb*
• "dissa VOW"
• disclaim knowledge of, responsibility or support for, or belief in.
• [Latin *dis-* expressing negation + AVOWED]
• **disavowal** *noun*

disbelief *noun*
• "dis buh LEEF"
• lack of belief; failure to believe.
• [Latin *dis-* expressing negation + BELIEVE]
• **disbelieve** *verb*
• **disbeliever** *noun*
• **disbelievingly** *adverb*

disburden *verb*
• "dis BURD'n"
• relieve (a person, one's mind, etc.) of a burden.
• [Latin *dis-* expressing negation + 'burden']

disburse *verb*
• "dis BURSE"
• expend (money).
• [Old French *desbourser* (*dis-* expressing negation + BOURSE)]
• **disbursement** *noun*
• **disburser** *noun*
HOMOPHONES: *disperse*, *disperser*

discalced *adjective*
• "dis CALST"
• denoting or belonging to one of several strict orders of Catholic friars or nuns who go barefoot or wear only sandals.
• [var. of *discalceated* (after French *déchaux*) from Latin *discalceatus* (*dis-* expressing negation + *calceatus* from *calceus* shoe)]

discard *verb*
• "dis CARD"
• reject or get rid of as unwanted or superfluous.
• [Latin *dis-* expressing negation + 'card', from Old French *carte* from Latin *charta* from Greek *khartēs* papyrus leaf]
• **discardable** *adjective*

discarnate *adjective*
• "dis CAR nit"
• having no physical body; separated from the flesh.
• [Latin *dis-* expressing negation + *caro carnis* flesh]
• **discarnation** *noun*

discern *verb*
• "dis SURN"
• perceive through the senses, esp. by sight.
• [Old French *discerner* from Latin (*dis-* expressing negation + *cernere cret-* separate)]
• **discerner** *noun*
• **discernible** *adjective*
• **discernibly** *adverb*

discerning *adjective*
• "dis SURNING"
• having or showing good judgment, taste, or insight.
• [as DISCERN]
• **discerningly** *adverb*

discernment *noun*
• "dis SURN m'nt"
• good judgment or insight.
• [as DISCERN]

disciple *noun*
• "dis SIPE 'll"
• a follower or pupil of a leader, teacher, philosophy, etc.
• [Latin *discipulus* from *discere* learn]
• **discipleship** *noun*

discipline *noun*
• "DISSA plin"
• training, esp. of the mind and character, aimed at producing self-control, obedience, orderly conduct, etc.
• [Late Latin *disciplina* from *discipulus* DISCIPLE]
• **disciplinarian** *noun* "dissa plin AIRY 'n"
• **disciplinary** *adjective* "DISSA plin airy"

disclosure *noun*
• "dis CLOE zhur"
• the act or an instance of disclosing; the process of being disclosed.
• [Latin *dis-* expressing negation + CLOSURE]

discobolus *noun*
- "dis COBBA luss"
- a discus thrower in ancient Greece.
- [Latin from Greek *diskobolos* from *diskos* DISCUS + *-bolos* -throwing, from *ballō* to throw]

discography *noun*
- "dis COGGRA fee"
- a descriptive catalogue of sound recordings, esp. of a particular performer or composer.
- [as DISCUS + Greek *graphia* writing after *biography*]
- **discographer** *noun*
- **discographical** *adjective*

discoid *adjective*
- "DISC oid"
- disc-shaped.
- [Greek *diskoeidēs* (as DISCUS + *-oeidēs* from *eidos* form)]

discolour *verb*
ALSO SPELLED: **discolor**
- "dis CULLER"
- spoil or cause to spoil the colour of; stain; tarnish.
- [Latin *dis-* expressing negation + *color* colour]
- **discoloration** *noun* (also **discolouration**)

discombobulate *verb*
- "dis k'm BOB yuh late"
- disturb; disconcert.
- [prob. based on *discompose* or *discomfit*]
- **discombobulation** *noun*

discomfit *verb*
- "dis CUMFIT"
- disconcert, embarrass, or throw into confusion.
- [*disconfit* from Old French past participle of *desconfire* from Romanic (*dis-* expressing negation + Latin *conficere* put together: see CONFECTION)]
- **discomfiture** *noun*

discomfort *noun*
- "dis CUMFERT"
- a lack of ease; slight pain.
- [Latin *dis-* expressing negation + COMFORT]

discommode *verb*
- "disca MODE"
- inconvenience (a person etc.).
- [obsolete French *discommoder* var. of *incommoder* (*dis-* expressing negation + INCOMMODE)]

discompose *verb*
- "dis k'm POZE"
- disturb the composure of; agitate; disturb.
- [Latin *dis-* expressing negation + COMPOSE]
- **discomposure** *noun*

disconcert *verb*
- "disk'n SURT"
- disturb the composure of; agitate; fluster.
- [obsolete French *desconcerter* (*dis-* expressing negation + CONCERT)]
- **disconcertedly** *adverb*
- **disconcerting** *adjective*
- **disconcertingly** *adverb*

disconfirm *verb*
- "disk'n FURM"
- disprove or tend to disprove (a hypothesis etc.).
- [Latin *dis-* expressing negation + CONFIRM]
- **disconfirmation** *noun*

disconformity *noun*
- "disk'n FORMA tee"
- an unconformity in which strata of rock above and below are more or less parallel, the lower set having been eroded but not deformed.
- [Latin *dis-* expressing negation + CONFORMITY]

disconsolate *adjective*
- "dis CONSA lit"
- without consolation or comfort; unhappy.
- [medieval Latin *disconsolatus* (*dis-* expressing negation + *consolatus* past participle of Latin *consolari* console)]
- **disconsolately** *adverb*
- **disconsolation** *noun*

discontinue *verb*
- "disk'n TIN yoo"
- cease or cause to cease to exist or be made.
- [Latin *dis-* expressing negation + CONTINUE]
- **discontinuance** *noun*
- **discontinuation** *noun*

discontinuous *adjective*
- "disk'n TIN yoo us"
- lacking continuity in space or time; intermittent.
- [as DISCONTINUE]
- **discontinuity** *noun* "dis conta NEW a tee"
- **discontinuously** *adverb*

discord *noun*
- "DIS cord"
- disagreement; strife.
- [Old French *descord* (n.), *descorder* (v.) from Latin *discordare* from *discors* discordant (*dis-* expressing negation + *cor cord-* heart)]

discordant *adjective*
- "dis CORE d'nt"
- not in accord; incongruous.
- [as DISCORD]
- **discordance** *noun*
- **discordancy** *noun*
- **discordantly** *adverb*

discotheque *noun*
- "DISCO teck"
- a place or event at which recorded popular music is played for dancing, often with elaborate lighting and other special effects.
- [French, = record library]

discountenance *verb*
- "dis COUNTA nince"
- disconcert.

• [Latin *dis-* expressing negation + COUNTENANCE]

discourage *verb*
• "dis CUR idge"
• deprive of courage, confidence, or enthusiasm.
• [Old French *descouragier* (*dis-* expressing negation + COURAGE)]
• **discouragement** *noun*
• **discouraging** *adjective*
• **discouragingly** *adverb*

discourse *noun*
• "DIS corse"
• conversation; talk.
• [Latin *discursus* (*dis-* expressing negation + COURSE)]

discourteous *adjective*
• "dis CURTY us"
• impolite; rude.
• [Latin *dis-* expressing negation + COURTEOUS]
• **discourteously** *adverb*
• **discourteousness** *noun*

discourtesy *noun*
• "dis CURTA see"
• bad manners; rudeness.
• [as DISCOURTEOUS]

discredit *noun*
• "dis CREDDIT"
• harm to reputation.
• [Latin *dis-* expressing negation + CREDITABLE]
• **discreditable** *adjective*
• **discreditably** *adverb*
• **discredited** *adjective*

discreet *adjective*
• "dis CREET"
• circumspect in speech or action, esp. to avoid social disgrace or embarrassment.
• [Old French *discret -ete* from Latin *discretus* separate (*dis-* expressing negation + *cretus* past participle of *cernere* sift), with Late Latin sense from its derivative *discretio* discernment]
• **discreetly** *adverb*
• **discreetness** *noun*
HOMOPHONES: *discrete, discretely, discreteness*

discrepancy *noun*
• "dis CREP'n see"
• an illogical or surprising lack of compatibility or similarity between two or more facts.
• [Latin *discrepare* be discordant (*dis-* expressing negation + *crepare* creak)]
• **discrepant** *adjective*

discrete *adjective*
• "dis CREET"
• separate or individually distinct.
• [Latin *discretus*: see DISCREET]
• **discretely** *adverb*
• **discreteness** *noun*
HOMOPHONES: *discreet, discreetly, discreetness*

discretion *noun*
• "dis CRESH'n"
• the quality of being discreet; tact, circumspection.
• [Old French from Latin *discretio -onis* (as DISCREET)]

discretionary *adjective*
• "dis CRESH'n airy"
• used, adopted, etc. when considered necessary.
• [as DISCRETION]

discriminant *noun*
• "dis CRIM'n 'nt"
• a distinguishing feature or characteristic.
• [as DISCRIMINATE]

discriminate *verb*
• "dis CRIM'n ate"
• make or see a distinction; differentiate.
• [Latin *discriminare* from *discrimen -minis* distinction, from *discernere* DISCERN]
• **discriminative** *adjective*
• **discriminator** *noun*
• **discriminatory** *adjective* "dis CRIM'n a tory"

discriminating *adjective*
• "dis CRIM'n ate ing"
• able to discern, esp. distinctions.
• [as DISCRIMINATE]
• **discriminatingly** *adverb*

discrimination *noun*
• "dis crim'n AY sh'n"
• an act, instance, policy, etc. of unfavourable treatment based on prejudice, esp. regarding race, age, or sex.
• [as DISCRIMINATE]

discursive *adjective*
• "dis CURSE iv"
• rambling, digressive; passing indiscriminately from subject to subject.
• [medieval Latin *discursivus* from Latin *discurrere discurs-* (*dis-* expressing negation + *currere* run)]
• **discursively** *adverb*
• **discursiveness** *noun*

discus *noun*
• "DISK iss"
• a heavy thick-centred disc thrown in ancient Greek games.
• [Latin from Greek *diskos*]

discuss *verb*
• "dis CUSS"
• hold a conversation about.
• [Latin *discutere discuss-* disperse (*dis-* expressing negation + *quatere* shake)]
• **discussable** *adjective*
• **discussant** *noun*
• **discusser** *noun*
• **discussion** *noun*

disdain *noun*
• "dis DANE"
• a feeling or attitude of scorn or contempt.

• [Old French *desdeign(ier)*, ultimately from Latin *dedignari* (*de-* off, from + *dignari* from *dignus* worthy)]
• **disdainful** *adjective*
• **disdainfully** *adverb*

diseconomy *noun*
• "dissy CONNA mee"
• a lack or absence of economy.
• [Latin *dis-* expressing negation + ECONOMY]

disembark *verb*
• "dis'm BARK"
• leave or remove from a ship, aircraft, train, etc.
• [Latin *dis-* expressing negation + EMBARK]
• **disembarkation** *noun*

disembodied *adjective*
• "dis'm BOD eed"
• separated or free from the body or a concrete form.
• [Latin *dis-* expressing negation + EMBODY]
• **disembodiment** *noun*

disembogue *verb*
• "diss'm BO'g"
• (of a river etc.) pour forth (waters) at the mouth.
• [Spanish *desembocar* (*dis-* expressing negation + *en* in, *boca* mouth)]

disembowel *verb*
• "dis'm BOW'll" ("BOW" rhymes with *COW*)
• remove the bowels or entrails of.
• [Latin *dis-* expressing negation + 'bowel' from Old French *buel* from Latin *botellus* little sausage]
• **disembowelled** *adjective*
• **disembowelment** *noun*

disempower *verb*
• "dis'm POWER"
• remove the power to act from (a person, group, etc.).
• [Latin *dis-* expressing negation + EMPOWER]
• **disempowered** *adjective*
• **disempowerment** *noun*

disenchant *verb*
• "dis'n CHANT"
• disillusion; free from enchantment.
• [Latin *dis-* expressing negation + ENCHANT]
• **disenchanted** *adjective*

disencumber *verb*
• "dis'n CUMBER"
• free from encumbrance.
• [Latin *dis-* expressing negation + ENCUMBER]

disenfranchise *verb*
• "dis'n FRAN chize"
• deprive (a person) of the right to vote.
• [Latin *dis-* expressing negation + ENFRANCHISE]
• **disenfranchisement** *noun*

disenfranchised *adjective*
• "dis'n FRAN chized"
• deprived of (esp. social) rights and privileges deemed normative in a society.
• [as DISENFRANCHISE]

disengage *verb*
• "dis'n GAGE"
• detach, free, loosen, or separate (parts etc.).
• [Latin *dis-* expressing negation + ENGAGE]
• **disengaged** *adjective*
• **disengagement** *noun*

disentangle *verb*
• "dis'n TANGLE"
• extricate; free from complications, difficulties, etc.
• [Latin *dis-* expressing negation + ENTANGLE]
• **disentanglement** *noun*

disentitle *verb*
• "dis'n TITE'll"
• deprive of any rightful claim.
• [Latin *dis-* expressing negation + ENTITLE]

disequilibrium *noun*
• "dis eekwa LIBBRY um"
• a lack or loss of equilibrium, stability, or balance.
• [Latin *dis-* expressing negation + EQUILIBRIUM]

disestablish *verb*
• "dis es TAB lish"
• deprive (a Church) of a state connection and support; remove from a position as the national or state Church.
• [Latin *dis-* expressing negation + ESTABLISH]
• **disestablishment** *noun*

disesteem *noun*
• "dis es TEEM"
• low esteem or regard.
• [Latin *dis-* expressing negation + ESTEEM]

disfigure *verb*
• "dis FIG yur"
• spoil the appearance or beauty of; deface, deform.
• [Latin *dis-* expressing negation + FIGURE]
• **disfiguration** *noun*
• **disfigured** *adjective*
• **disfigurement** *noun*

disgorge *verb*
• "dis GORGE"
• vomit or eject (matter) from the throat or stomach.
• [Old French *desgorger* (*dis-* expressing negation + *gorge* throat, ultimately from Latin *gurges* whirlpool)]
• **disgorgement** *noun*

disgruntled *adjective*
• "dis GRUNT 'ld"
• discontented; irritated, annoyed.
• [Latin *dis-* expressing negation + *gruntle* obsolete frequentative of 'grunt']
• **disgruntlement** *noun*

disguise *verb*
• "dis GIZE" (with "G" as in *GIVE*)
• alter the appearance, dress, mannerisms, etc. of (a person) so as to conceal true identity.
• [Old French *desguis(i)er* (*dis-* expressing negation + GUISE)]
• **disguised** *adjective*

disharmony *noun*
• "dis HARMA nee"
• a lack of harmony or agreement; discord.
• [Latin *dis-* expressing negation + HARMONY]
• **disharmonious** *adjective* "dis har MOANY us"
• **disharmoniously** *adverb*

dishearten *verb*
• "dis HART'n"
• cause to lose courage, confidence, hope, etc.; make despondent.
• [Latin *dis-* expressing negation + 'heart']
• **disheartening** *adjective*
• **dishearteningly** *adverb*
• **disheartenment** *noun*

dishevelled *adjective*
ALSO SPELLED: esp. *US* **disheveled**
• "dish EV'ld"
• (of the hair, clothes, appearance, etc.) disordered, unkempt, untidy.
• [Middle English *dischevelee* from Old French *deschevelé* past participle (*dis-* expressing negation + *chevel* hair, from Latin *capillus*)]
• **dishevelment** *noun*

dishonest *adjective*
• "dis ONNIST"
• (of a person, act, or statement) fraudulent or insincere.
• [Latin *dis-* expressing negation + HONEST]
• **dishonestly** *adverb*
• **dishonesty** *noun*

dishonour *noun*
ALSO SPELLED: **dishonor**
• "dis ONNER"
• a state of shame, disgrace, or ignominy.
• [Latin *dis-* expressing negation + HONOUR]
• **dishonourable** *adjective* (also **dishonorable**)
• **dishonourableness** *noun* (also **dishonorableness**)
• **dishonourably** *adverb* (also **dishonorably**)

disillusion *noun*
• "dissa LOO zh'n"
• disenchantment, freedom from illusions.
• [Latin *dis-* expressing negation + ILLUSION]
• **disillusionment** *noun*

disincentive *noun*
• "dis'n SENTIV"
• something that tends to discourage a particular action etc.
• [Latin *dis-* expressing negation + INCENTIVE]

disinclination *noun*
• "dis incla NAY sh'n"
• unwillingness or reluctance.
• [Latin *dis-* expressing negation + INCLINATION]
• **disincline** *verb*
• **disinclined** *adjective*

disinfectant *noun*
• "dis'n FECK t'nt"
• a usu. commercially produced chemical liquid or spray that destroys germs etc.
• [Latin *dis-* expressing negation + *inficere infect-* taint (as *in-* in + *facere* make)]

disinflation *noun*
• "dis'n FLAY sh'n"
• a policy designed to counteract inflation without causing deflation, including such measures as restricting consumer spending by raising the interest rate and introducing price controls on commodities in short supply.
• [Latin *dis-* expressing negation + INFLATION]
• **disinflationary** *adjective*

disinformation *noun*
• "dis infur MAY sh'n"
• deliberately false information, esp. as supplied by governments, the military, etc.
• [Latin *dis-* expressing negation + *informare* give shape to, fashion, describe (*in-* in + *forma* form)]

disingenuous *adjective*
• "dis in JEN yoo us"
• insincere; lacking in frankness or honesty.
• [Latin *dis-* expressing negation + INGENUOUS]
• **disingenuously** *adverb*
• **disingenuousness** *noun*

disinherit *verb*
• "dis in HARE it"
• reject as one's heir; deprive of the right of inheritance.
• [Middle English from Latin *dis-* expressing negation + INHERIT in obsolete sense 'make heir']
• **disinheritance** *noun*

disintegrate *verb*
• "dis INTA grate"
• separate into component parts or fragments.
• [Latin *dis-* expressing negation + INTEGRATE]
• **disintegration** *noun*
• **disintegrator** *noun*

disinter *verb*
• "dis in TUR"
• exhume; remove or dig up from the ground.
• [Latin *dis-* expressing negation + INTER]
• **disinterment** *noun*

disinterest *noun*
• "dis IN trist" or "dis INTA rest"
• impartiality.
• [Latin *dis-* expressing negation + *interest*, 3rd sing. pres. of *interesse* matter, make a difference (*inter* between + *esse* be)]

disinterested *adjective*
• "dis IN triss tid" or "dis INTA rest id"

• unbiased, impartial; not influenced by one's own advantage.
• [as DISINTEREST]
• **disinterestedly** *adverb*
• **disinterestedness** *noun*

disjunct *adjective*
• "dis JUNCT"
• disconnected, separate, distinct.
• [as DISJUNCTURE]
• **disjunction** *noun*
• **disjunctive** *adjective*
• **disjunctively** *adverb*

disjuncture *noun*
• "dis JUNK chur"
• a disjointed state; a separation, a disconnection.
• [Latin *dis-* expressing negation + JUNCTURE]

dislocate *verb*
• "DIS luh cate" or "dis LO cate"
• disturb the normal connection of (esp. a joint in the body).
• [Latin *dis-* expressing negation + LOCATE]
• **dislocation** *noun*

dislodge *verb*
• "dis LODGE"
• remove from or leave an established or fixed position.
• [Old French *dis-* expressing negation + *loge* arbour, hut, from medieval Latin *laubia*, *lobia* lodge, from Germanic]
• **dislodgeable** *adjective*
• **dislodgement** *noun*

disloyal *adjective*
• "dis LOY'll"
• not loyal; unfaithful.
• [Old French *dis-* expressing negation + *loial* from Latin *legalis* legal]
• **disloyalist** *noun*
• **disloyally** *adverb*
• **disloyalty** *noun*

dismal *adjective*
• "DIZ m'll"
• causing or showing gloom; cheerless, miserable.
• [originally noun = unlucky days: Anglo-French *dis mal* from medieval Latin *dies mali* two days in each month held to be unpropitious]
• **dismally** *adverb*
• **dismalness** *noun*

dismiss *verb*
• "dis MISS"
• send away; cause (a person) to leave one's presence.
• [Middle English, originally as past participle after Old French *desmis* from medieval Latin *dismissus* (*dis-* expressing negation + Latin *mittere miss-* send)]
• **dismissal** *noun*
• **dismissible** *adjective*

dismissive *adjective*
• "dis MISSIV"
• disdainful; tending to dismiss from consideration.
• [as DISMISS]
• **dismissively** *adverb*
• **dismissiveness** *noun*

Disneyesque *adjective*
• "dizny ESK"
• of or like the work of the US animator Walt Disney (d.1966).

Disneyfication *noun*
• "dizny fuh CAY sh'n"
• the action or process of making something resemble cartoons, movies, or theme parks associated with the US animator Walt Disney (d.1966), esp. by idealizing, simplifying, or prettifying it.
• **Disneyfied** *adjective*

disobedient *adjective*
• "disso BEEDY 'nt"
• disobeying; rebellious, rule-breaking.
• [Latin *dis-* expressing negation + OBEDIENT]
• **disobedience** *noun*
• **disobediently** *adverb*

disobey *verb*
• "disso BAY"
• fail or refuse to obey (orders, rules, a person, etc.); disregard.
• [Latin *dis-* expressing negation + OBEY]

disoblige *verb*
• "disso BLIJE" (with "I" as in *RIDE*)
• refuse to consider the convenience or wishes of.
• [Latin *dis-* expressing negation + OBLIGE]
• **disobliging** *adjective*

disorganize *verb*
ALSO SPELLED: esp. *Brit.* **-ise**
• "dis ORGA nize"
• destroy the system, order, or organization of; throw into confusion.
• [Latin *dis-* expressing negation + medieval Latin *organizare* from Latin *organum* from Greek *organon* tool]
• **disorganization** *noun* (also esp. *Brit.* **-isation**)
• **disorganized** *adjective* (also esp. *Brit.* **-ised**)

disorient *verb*
• "dis ORRY 'nt"
• confuse (a person) as to his or her whereabouts or bearings.
• [Latin *dis-* expressing negation + Old French *orient*, *orienter* from Latin *oriens -entis* rising, sunrise, east, from *oriri* rise]
• **disorientation** *noun*

disorientate *verb*
• "dis ORRY 'n tate"
• = DISORIENT.
• [as DISORIENT]

disparage *verb*
• "dis PAIR idge"
• vilify or speak slightingly or critically of (a person, idea, etc.).
• [Old French *desparagier* marry unequally (*dis-* expressing negation + *parage* equality of rank, ultimately from Latin *par* equal)]
• **disparagement** *noun*
• **disparaging** *adjective*
• **disparagingly** *adverb*

disparate *adjective*
• "DISPA rit"
• essentially different in kind; without comparison or relation.
• [Latin *disparatus* separated (*dis-* expressing negation + *paratus* past participle of *parare* prepare), influenced in sense by Latin *dispar* unequal]
• **disparately** *adverb*
• **disparateness** *noun*

disparity *noun*
• "dis PERRA tee"
• a great difference or gap, esp. one regarded as unfair.
• [French *disparité* from Late Latin *disparitas -tatis* (*dis-* expressing negation + PARITY)]

dispassionate *adjective*
• "dis PASH'n it"
• calm, impartial; free from the influence or effect of strong emotion.
• [Latin *dis-* expressing negation + Late Latin *passio -onis* from Latin *pati pass-* suffer]
• **dispassion** *noun*
• **dispassionately** *adverb*
• **dispassionateness** *noun*

dispel *verb*
• "dis PELL"
• dissipate; disperse; scatter.
• [Latin *dispellere* (*dis-* expressing negation + *pellere* drive)]

dispensable *adjective*
• "dis PENSA bull"
• unnecessary or expendable.
• [as DISPENSE]
• **dispensability** *noun*

dispensary *noun*
• "dis PENSA ree"
• a place in a clinic, pharmacy, etc. where medicines are dispensed.
• [as DISPENSE]

dispense *verb*
• "dis PENSE"
• distribute or provide (a service or information) to a number of people.
• [Latin *dispensare* frequentative of *dispendere* weigh or pay out (*dis-* expressing negation + *pendere pens-* weigh)]
• **dispensation** *noun*
• **dispensational** *adjective*

dispenser *noun*
• "dis PENSER"
• an automatic machine that dispenses an item or a specific amount of something, e.g. money, soap, etc.
• [as DISPENSE]

dispersant *noun*
• "dis PURSE 'nt"
• a liquid or gas used to disperse small particles in a medium.
• [as DISPERSE]

disperse *verb*
• "dis PURSE"
• drive, throw, send, or scatter in different directions.
• [Latin *dispergere dispers-* (*dis-* expressing negation + *spargere* scatter)]
• **dispersal** *noun*
• **disperser** *noun*
• **dispersible** *adjective*
• **dispersion** *noun* "dis PURR zh'n"
• **dispersive** *adjective*
HOMOPHONES: *disburse*, *disburser*

dispirit *verb*
• "dis PEERIT"
• discourage; lower the morale of.
• [Latin *dis-* expressing negation + Anglo-French *(e)spirit*, Old French *esp(e)rit*, from Latin *spiritus* breath, spirit, from *spirare* breathe]
• **dispirited** *adjective*
• **dispiritedly** *adverb*
• **dispiritedness** *noun*
• **dispiriting** *adjective*
• **dispiritingly** *adverb*

displeasure *noun*
• "dis PLEZHUR"
• disapproval; dissatisfaction; anger.
• [Latin *dis-* expressing negation + PLEASURE]

disport *verb*
• "dis PORT"
• cavort, frolic, or enjoy oneself.
• [Old French *desporter* (*dis-* expressing negation + *porter* carry, from Latin *portare*)]

disposable *adjective*
• "dis POZE a bull"
• intended to be used once and then thrown away.
• [as DISPOSE]
• **disposability** *noun*

disposal *noun*
• "dis POZE'll"
• the act or an instance of getting rid of something.
• [as DISPOSE]

dispose *verb*
• "dis POZE"
• make willing; incline.
• [Old French *disposer* from Latin *disponere disposit-*]
• **disposed** *adjective*
• **disposer** *noun*

disposition *noun*
- "dispa ZISH'n"
- temperament or character, esp. as displayed in dealings with others.
- [Old French from Latin *dispositio* (*dis-* expressing negation + *ponere posit-* place)]
- **dispositional** *adjective*

dispossess *verb*
- "dispa ZESS"
- dislodge; oust (a person) from a dwelling etc.
- [Latin *dis-* expressing negation + POSSESS]
- **dispossessed** *adjective*
- **dispossession** *noun*
- **dispossessor** *noun*

dispraise *verb*
- "dis PRAZE"
- express disapproval or censure of.
- [Old French *despreisier*, ultimately from Late Latin *depretiare* DEPRECIATE]

disproportion *noun*
- "dispra POR sh'n"
- a lack of proportion.
- [Latin *dis-* expressing negation + PROPORTION]
- **disproportional** *adjective*
- **disproportionally** *adverb*
- **disproportionate** *adjective*
- **disproportionately** *adverb*

disprove *verb*
- "dis PROOVE"
- prove false; refute.
- [Latin *dis-* expressing negation + PROVE]
- **disprovable** *adjective*

disputable *adjective*
- "dis PYOOTA bull"
- open to question; contentious.
- [Old French *desputer* from Latin *disputare* estimate (*dis-* expressing negation + *putare* reckon)]
- **disputably** *adverb*

disputant *noun*
- "dis PYOOT'nt"
- a person who disputes or argues, esp. one who engages in public debate or disputation.
- [as DISPUTABLE]

disputation *noun*
- "dis pyoo TAY sh'n"
- the act or an instance of disputing or debating.
- [as DISPUTABLE]

disputatious *adjective*
- "dis pyoo TAY sh'ss"
- fond of or inclined to argument.
- [as DISPUTABLE]
- **disputatiously** *adverb*
- **disputatiousness** *noun*

disqualify *verb*
- "dis KWOLLA fie"
- debar from a competition or pronounce ineligible as a winner because of an infringement of the rules etc.
- [Latin *dis-* expressing negation + QUALIFY]
- **disqualification** *noun*

disquiet *verb*
- "dis KWY it"
- worry; trouble; deprive of peace.
- [Latin *dis-* expressing negation + QUIET]
- **disquieting** *adjective*
- **disquietingly** *adverb*
- **disquietude** *noun*

disquisition *noun*
- "dis kwiz ISH'n"
- a long or elaborate treatise or discourse on a subject.
- [French from Latin *disquisitio* (*dis-* expressing negation + *quaerere quaesit-* seek)]

disreputable *adjective*
- "dis REP yoo tuh bull"
- discreditable; of bad reputation.
- [as DISREPUTE]
- **disreputably** *adverb*

disrepute *noun*
- "dis re PYOOT"
- a lack of good reputation or respectability; discredit.
- [Latin *dis-* expressing negation + Old French *reputer* or Latin *reputare* (*re-* again + *putare* think)]

disrespect *noun*
- "dis re SPECT"
- a lack of respect or courtesy.
- [Latin *dis-* expressing negation + Old French *respect* from Latin *respectus* from *respicere* (*re-* again, *specere* look at) or from *respectare* frequentative of *respicere*]
- **disrespectful** *adjective*
- **disrespectfully** *adverb*

disrupt *verb*
- "dis RUPT"
- interrupt the flow or continuity of (a meeting, speech, etc.); bring disorder to.
- [Latin *disrumpere disrupt-* (*dis-* expressing negation + *rumpere* break)]
- **disrupter** *noun* (also **disruptor**)
- **disruption** *noun*
- **disruptive** *adjective*
- **disruptively** *adverb*
- **disruptiveness** *noun*

dissatisfy *verb*
- "dis SAT iss fie"
- make discontented; fail to satisfy.
- [Latin *dis-* expressing negation + SATISFY]
- **dissatisfaction** *noun*
- **dissatisfactory** *adjective*

dissaving *noun*
- "dis SAVING"
- the action of spending more than one has earned in a given period.
- [Latin *dis-* expressing negation + 'saving'

(from Old French *salver, sauver* from Late Latin *salvare* from Latin *salvus* safe)]

dissect *verb*
• "die SECT" or "dis SECT"
• cut into pieces.
• [Latin *dissecare dissect-* (*dis-* expressing negation + *secare* cut)]
• **dissection** *noun*
• **dissector** *noun*

dissemble *verb*
• "dis SEM bull"
• conceal one's motives; talk or act hypocritically.
• [Middle English, alteration (suggested by *semblance*) of obsolete *dissimule*, via Old French *dissimuler* from Latin *dissimulare* (*dis-* expressing negation + SIMULATE)]
• **dissemblance** *noun*
• **dissembler** *noun*

disseminate *verb*
• "dis SEMMA nate"
• scatter about, spread (esp. ideas) widely.
• [Latin *disseminare* (*dis-* expressing negation + *semen -inis* seed)]
• **disseminated** *adjective*
• **dissemination** *noun*
• **disseminator** *noun*

dissension *noun*
• "dis SEN sh'n"
• disagreement giving rise to discord.
• [Old French from Latin *dissensio* (*dis-* expressing negation + *sentire sens-* feel)]

dissent *verb*
• "dis SENT"
• think differently, disagree; express disagreement.
• [Latin *dissentire* (*dis-* expressing negation + *sentire* feel)]
• **dissenter** *noun*
• **dissenting** *adjective*
HOMOPHONES: *descent*

dissentient *adjective*
• "dis SEN sh'nt"
• disagreeing with a majority or official view.
• [as DISSENT]

dissertation *noun*
• "disser TAY sh'n"
• a detailed discourse on a subject, esp. one submitted in partial fulfillment of the requirements of a doctorate.
• [Latin *dissertatio* from *dissertare* discuss, frequentative of *disserere dissert-* examine (*dis-* expressing negation + *serere* join)]

disservice *noun*
• "dis SURVISS"
• an unhelpful or injurious act, esp. done when trying to help.
• [Latin *dis-* expressing negation + 'service' from Old French from Latin *servitium* from *servus* slave]

dissever *verb*
• "dis SEVVER"
• sever; divide into parts.
• [Anglo-French *dis(c)everer* from Late Latin *disseparare* (*dis-* expressing negation + SEPARATE)]

dissident *adjective*
• "DIS id 'nt"
• disagreeing, esp. with an established government, system, etc.
• [Latin *dissidēre* disagree (*dis-* expressing negation + *sedēre* sit)]
• **dissidence** *noun*

dissimilar *adjective*
• "dis SIM'll ur"
• unlike, not similar.
• [Latin *dis-* expressing negation + SIMILAR]
• **dissimilarity** *noun* "dis sim'll ERRA tee"
• **dissimilarly** *adverb*

dissimilate *verb*
• "dis SIM'll ate"
• change (a sound or sounds in a word) to another when the word originally had the same sound repeated, as in *purple*, originally *purpuran*.
• [Latin *dissimilis* (*dis-* expressing negation + *similis* like), after *assimilate*]
• **dissimilation** *noun*

dissimulate *verb*
• "dis SIM yuh late"
• dissemble.
• [Latin *dis-* expressing negation + SIMULATE]
• **dissimulation** *noun*

dissipate *verb*
• "DISSA pate"
• cause (a cloud, vapour, fear, darkness, etc.) to disappear or disperse.
• [Latin *dissipare dissipat-* (*dis-* expressing negation + *sipare* (unrecorded) throw)]
• **dissipative** *adjective*
• **dissipator** *noun*

dissipated *adjective*
• "DISSA pated"
• (of a person or way of life) overindulging in sensual pleasures.
• [as DISSIPATE]
• **dissipation** *noun*

dissociate *verb*
• "dis SO see ate" or "dis SO shee ate"
• disconnect or become disconnected; separate.
• [Latin *dissociare* (*dis-* expressing negation + *socius* companion)]
• **dissociation** *noun*
• **dissociative** *adjective*

dissoluble *adjective*
• "dis SAWL yoo bull"
• able to be disintegrated, loosened, or disconnected; soluble.
• [French *dissoluble* or Latin *dissolubilis* (*dis-* expressing negation + SOLUBLE)]
• **dissolubility** *noun*
• **dissolubly** *adverb*

dissolute *adjective*
• "DISSA loot"
• lax in morals; licentious.
• [Latin *dissolutus* past participle of *dissolvere* DISSOLVE]
• **dissolutely** *adverb*

dissolution *noun*
• "dissa LOO sh'n"
• disintegration; decomposition.
• [as DISSOLVE]

dissolve *verb*
• "diz OLVE"
• make or become liquid, esp. by immersion or dispersion in a liquid.
• [Latin *dissolvere dissolut-* (*dis-* expressing negation + *solvere* loosen)]
• **dissolvable** *adjective*

dissonant *adjective*
• "DISSA n'nt"
• discordant; not harmonious.
• [Old French *dissonant* or Latin *dissonare* (*dis-* expressing negation + *sonare* sound)]
• **dissonance** *noun*

dissuade *verb*
• "dis SWADE"
• discourage (a person); persuade against.
• [Latin *dissuadēre* (*dis-* expressing negation + *suadēre suas-* persuade)]
• **dissuasion** *noun*
• **dissuasive** *adjective*

dissymmetry *noun*
• "dis SIMMA tree"
• lack of symmetry.
• [Latin *dis-* expressing negation + SYMMETRY]
• **dissymmetric** *adjective* "diss'm METRIC"
• **dissymmetrical** *adjective*

distaff *noun*
• "DIS taff"
• a cleft stick holding wool or flax wound for spinning by hand.
• [Old English *distæf*, the first element being apparently related to Middle Low German *dise*, *disene* bunch of flax + 'staff' stick]

distal *adjective*
• "DIST'll"
• situated away from the centre of the body or point of attachment; terminal.
• [as DISTANCE]
• **distally** *adverb*

distance *noun*
• "DIS tince"
• the condition of being far off; remoteness.
• [Old French from Latin *distantia* from *distare* stand apart (as *dis-* expressing negation + *stare* stand)]
• **distant** *adjective*
• **distantly** *adverb*

distaste *noun*
• "dis TASTE"
• dislike; repugnance; aversion.
• [Latin *dis-* expressing negation + Old French *tast, taster* touch, try, taste, ultimately perhaps from Latin *tangere* touch + *gustare* taste]
• **distasteful** *adjective*
• **distastefully** *adverb*
• **distastefulness** *noun*

distelfink *noun*
• "DIST'll fink"
• a bird feeder, esp. for finches, consisting of a seed-filled tube suspended vertically, with perches and small feeding holes throughout.
• [German spelling of Pennsylvania Dutch *dischdelfink* goldfinch, from *dischdel* thistle + *fink* finch]

distemper *noun*
• "dis TEMPER"
• a disease of dogs, causing fever, coughing, and catarrh.
• [earlier as verb, = upset, derange: Middle English from Late Latin *distemperare* (*dis-* expressing negation + *temperare* mingle correctly)]

distempered *adjective*
• "dis TEMPERD"
• disordered, disturbed; uneasy.
• [as DISTEMPER]

distend *verb*
• "dis TEND"
• swell out by pressure from within.
• [Latin *distendere* (*dis-* expressing negation + *tendere tens-* stretch)]
• **distensibility** *noun*
• **distensible** *adjective*
• **distension** *noun*

distich *noun*
• "DISTICK"
• a pair of verse lines; a couplet.
• [Latin *distichon* from Greek *distikhon* (Greek *dis* twice + *stikhos* line)]

distichous *adjective*
• "DISTICK us"
• arranged in two opposite vertical rows.
• [as DISTICH]
• **distichously** *adverb*

distillate *noun*
• "DIST'll it" or "DIST'll ate"
• a product of distillation.
• [Latin *distillare* from *destillare* from *stilla* drop]

distillation *noun*
• "dist'll AY sh'n"
• the process of purifying (a liquid) by vaporizing it with heat, then condensing it with cold and collecting the result.
• [as DISTILLATE]

distillery *noun*
• "dis TILLER ee"
• a place where alcoholic liquor is distilled.
• [as DISTILLATE]
• **distiller** *noun*

distinct *adjective*
- "dis TINCT"
- not identical; separate; individual.
- [Latin *distinctus* past participle of *distinguere* DISTINGUISH]
- **distinctly** *adverb*
- **distinctness** *noun*

distinction *noun*
- "dis TINK sh'n"
- the act or an instance of discriminating or distinguishing.
- [as DISTINGUISH]

distinctive *adjective*
- "dis TINK tiv"
- distinguishing, characteristic.
- [as DISTINGUISH]
- **distinctively** *adverb*
- **distinctiveness** *noun*

distinguish *verb*
- "dis TING gwish"
- see or point out the difference of; draw distinctions.
- [Latin *distinguere* (*dis-* expressing negation + *stinguere stinct-* extinguish): compare EXTINGUISH]
- **distinguishable** *adjective*

distinguished *adjective*
- "dis TING gwisht"
- of high standing.
- [as DISTINGUISH]

distract *verb*
- "dis TRACT"
- draw away the attention of (a person, the mind, etc.).
- [Latin *distrahere distract-* (*dis-* expressing negation + *trahere* draw)]
- **distracted** *adjective*
- **distractedly** *adverb*
- **distractibility** *noun*
- **distractible** *adjective*
- **distraction** *noun*

distrain *verb*
- "dis TRAIN"
- impose distraint (on a person, goods, etc.).
- [Old French *destreindre* from Latin *distringere* (*dis-* expressing negation + *stringere strict-* draw tight)]

distraint *noun*
- "dis TRAINT"
- the seizure of chattels to make a person pay rent etc. or meet an obligation, or to obtain satisfaction by their sale.
- [as DISTRAIN]

distrait *adjective*
- "dis TRAY"
- not paying attention, absent-minded.
- [Old French *destrait* past participle of *destraire* (as DISTRACT)]

distraught *adjective*
- "dis TROT"
- extremely worried, upset, fearful, etc.
- [Middle English, alteration of obsolete *distract* (adjective) (as DISTRACT), after *straught*, obsolete past participle of 'stretch']

distress *noun*
- "dis TRESS"
- severe trouble, anxiety, sorrow, anguish, etc.
- [Old French *destresse* etc., from Gallo-Roman (as DISTRAIN)]
- **distressed** *adjective*
- **distressful** *adjective*
- **distressing** *adjective*
- **distressingly** *adverb*

distributary *noun*
- "dis TRIB yoo terry"
- a branch of a river or glacier that does not return to the main stream after leaving it (as in a delta).
- [as DISTRIBUTE]

distribute *verb*
- "dis TRIB yoot" or "DISTRA byoot"
- give shares of; deal out.
- [Latin *distribuere distribut-* (*dis-* expressing negation + *tribuere* assign)]
- **distributable** *adjective*
- **distribution** *noun*
- **distributional** *adjective*
- **distributive** *adjective*
- **distributively** *adverb*
- **distributor** *noun*
- **distributorship** *noun*

distributed *adjective*
- "dis TRIB yoo tid" or "DISTRA byooted"
- designating a computer system, process, etc. involving a number of independent interconnected computers.
- [as DISTRIBUTE]

distrust *noun*
- "dis TRUST"
- a lack of trust; doubt; suspicion.
- [Latin *dis-* expressing negation + Old Norse *traust* from *traustr* strong]
- **distrustful** *adjective*
- **distrustfully** *adverb*

disturb *verb*
- "dis TURB"
- break the rest, calm, order, or quiet of; interrupt.
- [Latin *disturbare* (*dis-* expressing negation + *turbare* from *turba* tumult)]
- **disturbance** *noun*
- **disturbed** *adjective*
- **disturber** *noun*
- **disturbing** *adjective*
- **disturbingly** *adverb*

disulfiram *noun*
- "die SULFER am"
- a synthetic compound used in the treatment

of alcoholics to make drinking alcohol produce unpleasant after-effects, such as nausea.
• [blend of DISULPHIDE and *thiuram* (from Greek *theion* sulphur + UREA + AMMONIUM)]

disulphide *noun*
ALSO SPELLED: **disulfide**
• "die SULL fide"
• a binary chemical containing two atoms of sulphur in each molecule.
• [Greek *dis* twice + SULPHIDE]

disyllable *noun*
• "die SILLA bull"
• a word or metrical foot of two syllables.
• [Greek *dis* twice + SYLLABLE]
• **disyllabic** *adjective* "die suh LABBIC"

dithyramb *noun*
• "DITHY ram" or "DITHY ramb" (with "TH" as in *THIN*)
• a wild choral hymn in ancient Greece, esp. to Dionysus.
• [Latin *dithyrambus* from Greek *dithurambos*, of unknown origin]
• **dithyrambic** *adjective* "dithy RAM bick"

Ditidaht *noun*
• "DITTY dat"
• a member of an Aboriginal people, part of the Nuu-chah-nulth, living on southern Vancouver Island.
• [Ditidaht, self-designation]

dittany *noun*
• "DIT 'n ee"
• any herb of the genus *Dictamnus*, formerly used medicinally.
• [Old French *dita(i)n* from medieval Latin *dictamus* from Latin *dictamnus* from Greek *diktamnon* perhaps from *Diktē*, a mountain in Crete]

ditto *noun*
• "DITTO"
• (in accounts, inventories, lists, etc.) the aforesaid, the same.
• [Italian dialect from Latin *dictus* past participle of *dicere* say]

dittography *noun*
• "dih TOGGRA fee"
• a copyist's mistaken repetition of a letter, word, or phrase.
• [Greek *dittos* double + *graphia* writing]
• **dittographic** *adjective*

ditzy *adjective*
ALSO SPELLED: **ditsy**
• "DITSY"
• (usu. of a woman) silly or foolish.
• [20th c.: origin unknown]
• **ditz** *noun*
• **ditziness** *noun* (also **ditsiness**)

diuresis *noun*
• "die ur EE sis"
• an increased excretion of urine.
• [modern Latin from Greek (*dia* through + *ourēsis* urination)]

diuretic *adjective*
• "die ur ETTIC"
• causing increased output of urine.
• [Late Latin *diureticus* from Greek *diourētikos* from *dioureō* urinate]

diurnal *adjective*
• "die UR n'll"
• of or during the day; not nocturnal.
• [Late Latin *diurnalis* from Latin *diurnus* from *dies* day]
• **diurnally** *adverb*

diva *noun*
• "DEEVA"
• a famous female opera singer.
• [Italian from Latin, = goddess]

divagate *verb*
• "DIE vuh gate"
• stray; digress.
• [Latin *divagari* (*dis-* expressing negation + *vagari* wander)]
• **divagation** *noun*

divalent *adjective*
• "die VALE 'nt"
• having a valence of two; bivalent.
• [Greek *dis* twice + *valent-* participial stem (as VALENCE)]
• **divalence** *noun*
• **divalency** *noun*

divan *noun*
• "dih VAN"
• a long, low, padded seat set against the wall of a room; a backless sofa.
• [French *divan* or Italian *divano* from Turkish *dīvān* from Arabic *dīwān* from Persian *dīvān* anthology, register, court, bench]

divaricate[1] *verb*
• "div ERRA cate"
• diverge, branch; separate widely.
• [Latin *divaricare* (Latin *dis-* expressing negation, *varicus* straddling)]
• **divarication** *noun*

divaricate[2] *adjective*
• "div ERRA kit"
• diverging, branching; separating widely.
• [as DIVARICATE[1]]

diverge *verb*
• "die VURJ"
• proceed in a different direction or in different directions from a point.
• [medieval Latin *divergere* (Latin *dis-* expressing negation, Latin *vergere* incline)]
• **divergence** *noun*
• **divergency** *noun*
• **divergent** *adjective*
• **divergently** *adverb*

diverse *adjective*
• "die VURSE" or "DIE vurse"
• unlike in nature or qualities; varied.

• [Old French from Latin *diversus* (*dis-* expressing negation + *versus* past participle of *vertere* turn)]
• **diversely** *adverb*
• **diversity** *noun*

diversify *verb*
• "die VURSA fie"
• make diverse; vary; modify.
• [Old French *diversifier* from medieval Latin *diversificare* (as DIVERSE)]
• **diversification** *noun*

diversion *noun*
• "die VUR zh'n" or "div UR zh'n"
• the act of diverting; deviation.
• [Late Latin *diversio* (as DIVERT)]
• **diversional** *adjective*
• **diversionary** *adjective*

divert *verb*
• "die VURT" or "div URT"
• turn aside from a direction or course; deflect.
• [French *divertir* from Latin *divertere* (Latin *dis-* expressing negation, *vertere* turn)]

diverticulitis *noun*
• "die vur tick yuh LITE iss"
• inflammation of a diverticulum.
• [as DIVERTICULUM + Greek *-itis*, forming feminine of adjectives in *-itēs* (with *nosos* 'disease' implied)]

diverticulosis *noun*
• "die vur tick yuh LO sis"
• the presence of abnormal diverticula, esp. in the intestine.
• [as DIVERTICULUM]

diverticulum *noun*
• "die vur TICK yuh lum"
• a blind tube or sac forming at weak points in the wall of a cavity or passage, esp. of the alimentary tract.
• [medieval Latin, var. of Latin *deverticulum* byway, from *devertere* from *vertere* turn]
• **diverticular** *adjective*

divertimento *noun*
• "div urta MENTO"
• a light and entertaining composition, often in the form of a suite for chamber orchestra.
• [Italian, = diversion]

divertissement *noun*
• "dee vare teece MÃH" (with a nasal *AH*)
• a diversion; an entertainment.
• [French, from *divertiss-* stem of *divertir* DIVERT]

divest *verb*
• "die VEST"
• sell off (a subsidiary company, investments, etc.).
• [earlier *devest* from Old French *desvestir* etc. (Latin *dis-* expressing negation, *vestire* from *vestis* garment)]
• **divestiture** *noun*
• **divestment** *noun*

divide *verb*
• "div IDE"
• separate or be separated into parts; break up; split.
• [Latin *dividere divis-* (Latin *dis-* expressing negation, *vid-* separate)]
• **divider** *noun*

dividend *noun*
• "DIVVA dend"
• a sum of money to be divided among a number of persons, esp. that paid by a company to shareholders.
• [Anglo-French *dividende* from Latin *dividendum* (as DIVIDE)]

divination *noun*
• "divva NAY sh'n"
• supposed insight into the future or the unknown gained by supernatural means.
• [Latin *divinatio* (as DIVINE)]
• **divinatory** *adjective*

divine *adjective*
• "div INE"
• of, from, or like God or a god.
• [Old French *devin -ine* from Latin *divinus* from *divus* godlike]
• **divinely** *adverb*
• **divineness** *noun*
• **diviner** *noun*

divinity *noun*
• "div INNA tee"
• the state or quality of being divine.
• [Old French *divinité* from Latin *divinitas -tatis* (as DIVINE)]

divinize *verb*
ALSO SPELLED: esp. *Brit.* **-ise**
• "DIV'n ize"
• make divine; deify.
• [as DIVINE]
• **divinization** *noun* (also esp. *Brit.* **-isation**)

divisible *adjective*
• "div IZZA bull"
• capable of being divided, physically or mentally.
• [Late Latin *divisibilis* (as DIVIDE)]
• **divisibility** *noun*

division *noun*
• "div IZH'n"
• the act or an instance of dividing; the process of being divided.
• [Old French *divisiun* from Latin *divisio -onis* (as DIVIDE)]
• **divisional** *adjective*
• **divisionally** *adverb*

divisionalize *verb*
ALSO SPELLED: esp. *Brit.* **-ise**
• "div IZH'n 'll ize"
• organize (a company etc.) into separate divisions.
• [as DIVISION]

• **divisionalization** *noun* (also esp. *Brit.* **-isation**)

divisive *adjective*

• "div ISS iv" or "div ICE iv" or "div IZZ iv"

• tending to divide, esp. in opinion; causing disagreement.

• [Late Latin *divisivus* (as DIVIDE)]

• **divisively** *adverb*

• **divisiveness** *noun*

divisor *noun*

• "div IZER"

• a number by which another is to be divided.

• [Latin *divisor* (as DIVIDE)]

HOMOPHONES: *devisor, deviser*

divot *noun*

• "DIVVIT"

• a piece of turf cut out by a golf club in making a stroke.

• [16th c.: origin unknown]

divulge *verb*

• "die VULGE" or "dih VULGE"

• disclose; reveal (a secret etc.).

• [Latin *divulgare* (Latin *dis-* expressing negation, *vulgare* publish, from *vulgus* common people)]

• **divulgence** *noun*

Diwali *noun*

ALSO SPELLED: **Divali**

• "dee WOLLY" or "dee VOLLY"

• a major Hindu festival held in October or November, honouring Lakshmi, the goddess of prosperity, during which gifts are exchanged and lamps lit.

• [Hindi *dīwalī* from Sanskrit *dīpāvalī* row of lights, from *dīpa* lamp]

dizzy *adjective*

• "DIZZY"

• giddy, unsteady.

• [Old English *dysig* from West Germanic]

• **dizzily** *adverb*

• **dizziness** *noun*

• **dizzying** *adjective*

• **dizzyingly** *adverb*

djellaba *noun*

ALSO SPELLED: **djellabah**, **jellaba**

• "JELLA buh"

• a loose, long-sleeved, hooded woollen cloak of a type originally worn by Arab men in North Africa.

• [Arabic *jallaba, jallābīya*]

djembe *noun*

• "JEMBA" or "JEMBAY"

• a kind of goblet-shaped hand drum originating in West Africa.

• [French *djembé*, from Mande (a West African language) *jembe*]

Djiboutian *noun*

• "jih BOOTY 'n"

• a native or inhabitant of Djibouti in NE Africa.

djinn *noun*

• "JIN"

• (in Muslim mythology) an intelligent being lower than the angels, able to appear in human and animal forms, and having power over people.

• [Arabic *jinnī*, pl. *jinn*]

HOMOPHONES: *gin*

dobra *noun*

• "DOBBRA"

• the basic monetary unit of São Tomé and Principe, equal to 100 centavos.

• [Portuguese *dóbra* doubloon]

dobro *noun*

• "DOBBRO"

• a type of acoustic guitar with steel resonating discs inside the body under the bridge, used in country and bluegrass music.

• [from the *Do(pěra) Bro(thers)*, its Czech-American inventors]

docent *noun*

• "DOE s'nt"

• a usu. voluntary guide in a museum, art gallery, zoo, etc.

• [German *Docent, Dozent*, from Latin *docent-* present participle stem of *docere* teach]

docile *adjective*

• "DOSS ile" or "DOE sile"

• submissive, easily managed.

• [Latin *docilis* from *docēre* teach]

• **docilely** *adverb*

• **docility** *noun*

doctor *noun*

• "DOCTER"

• a qualified practitioner of medicine; a physician or surgeon.

• [Old French *doctour* from Latin *doctor* from *docēre doct-* teach]

• **doctorial** *adjective* "dock TORY 'll"

• **doctorly** *adjective*

doctorate *noun*

• "DOCTER it"

• the highest university degree in any faculty.

• [as DOCTOR]

• **doctoral** *adjective*

doctrinaire *adjective*

• "dock trin AIR"

• seeking to apply a theory or doctrine in all circumstances without regard to practical considerations; theoretical and impractical.

• [French from *doctrine* DOCTRINE]

doctrine *noun*

• "DOCK trin"

• what is taught; a body of instruction.

• [Old French from Latin *doctrina* teaching (as DOCTOR)]

• **doctrinal** *adjective* "dock TRINE 'll" or "DOCK trin'll"

• **doctrinally** *adverb*

docudrama *noun*
• "DOCK yoo dramma" or "DOCK yoo dromma"
• a dramatized television film based on real events.
• [DOCUMENTARY + DRAMA]
• **docudramatist** *noun*

document *noun*
• "DOCK yoo m'nt"
• a piece of written or printed matter that provides a record or evidence of events, an agreement, ownership, identification, etc.
• [Old French from Latin *documentum* proof, from *docēre* teach]
• **documentable** *adjective*
• **documental** *adjective*
• **documenter** *noun*

documentary *noun*
• "dock yoo MENTA ree"
• a film or broadcast program based on real events, places, or circumstances and usu. intended primarily to record or inform.
• [as DOCUMENT]
• **documentarian** *noun*
• **documentarist** *noun*

documentation *noun*
• "dock yoo m'n TAY sh'n"
• the provision of documents.
• [as DOCUMENT]

dodder *verb*
• "DODDER"
• tremble or totter, esp. from age.
• [17th c.: var. of obsolete dial. *dadder*]
• **dodderer** *noun*
• **doddering** *adjective*
HOMOPHONES: *daughter*

dodecagon *noun*
• "doe DECKA gon"
• a plane figure with twelve sides.
• [Greek *dōdeka* twelve + *-gōnos* -angled]

dodecahedron *noun*
• "doe decka HEED r'n"
• a solid figure with twelve faces.
• [Greek *dōdeka* twelve + *hedra* base]
• **dodecahedral** *adjective*

dodecaphonic *adjective*
• "doe decka FONNIC"
• pertaining to or designating music using the twelve chromatic notes of the octave on an equal basis without dependence on a key system.
• [Greek *dōdeka* twelve]

dodgem *noun*
• "DODGE 'm"
• each of a number of small electrically driven cars in an enclosure at an amusement park etc., driven around and bumped into each other; a bumper car.
• ['dodge' + ''em']

dogbane *noun*
• "DOG bane"
• any of various herbaceous plants of the genus *Apocynum*, with small bell-shaped flowers.
• ['dog' + BANE]

doge *noun*
• "DOAJ" (with "OA" as in *BOAT*)
• the chief magistrate of Venice or Genoa.
• [French from Italian from Venetian *doze* from Latin *dux ducis* leader]

doggerel *noun*
• "DOGGER 'll"
• poor or trivial verse.
• [Middle English, apparently from 'dog' (of unknown origin)]

dogie *noun*
• "DOE gee" (with "G" as in *GEEK*)
• a motherless or neglected calf.
• [19th c.: origin unknown]

doily *noun*
• "DOY lee"
• a small ornamental mat of paper, lace, etc., e.g. on a table, or on a plate for cookies, sandwiches, etc.
• [originally the name of a fabric: from *Doiley*, the name of a draper]
• **doilied** *adjective*

dojo *noun*
• "DOE joe"
• a room or hall in which judo and other martial arts are practised.
• [Japanese, from *dō* way, pursuit + *jō* a place]

dolce *adverb*
• "DOLL chay"
• (as a musical direction) sweetly and softly.
• [Italian, = sweet]

doldrums *plural noun*
• "DOLE drums" or "DOLL drums"
• low spirits; a feeling of boredom or depression.
• [prob. from *dull* and *tantrum*]

dole *noun*
• "DOLE"
• benefits claimable by the unemployed from the government.
• [Old English *dāl* from Germanic]

dolerite *noun*
• "DOLLER ite"
• a coarse basaltic rock.
• [French *dolérite* from Greek *doleros* deceptive (because it is difficult to distinguish from diorite)]

dolichocephalic *adjective*
• "dolla co suh FALIC"
• having a long or narrow head.
• [Greek *dolikhos* long + CEPHALIC]

dollop *noun*
• "DOLL up"
• a shapeless lump of something soft, esp. food.
• [perhaps from Scandinavian]

dolma *noun*
• "DOLL muh"
• an E European delicacy of spiced rice or meat etc. wrapped in vine or cabbage leaves.
• [Turkish from *dolmak* fill, be filled]

dolman *noun*
• "DOLL m'n"
• a long Turkish robe open in front.
• [ultimately from Turkish *dolama*]
HOMOPHONES: *dolmen*

dolmen *noun*
• "DOLL m'n"
• a megalithic tomb with a large flat stone laid on upright ones.
• [French, perhaps from Cornish *tolmēn* hole of stone]
HOMOPHONES: *dolman*

dolomite *noun*
• "DOLLA mite" or "DOE luh mite"
• a mineral or rock of calcium magnesium carbonate.
• [French from D. de *Dolomieu*, French geologist d.1801]
• **dolomitic** *adjective* "dolla MITTIC" or "doe luh mittic"

dolorous *adjective*
• "DOLLER us"
• distressing, painful; doleful, dismal.
• [as DOLOUR]
• **dolorously** *adverb*

dolour *noun*
ALSO SPELLED: **dolor**
• "DOLLER"
• sorrow, distress.
• [Old French from Latin *dolor -oris* pain, grief]
HOMOPHONES: *dollar*

dolphin *noun*
• "DOLFIN"
• any of various porpoise-like sea mammals of the family Delphinidae having a slender beaklike snout.
• [Latin *delphinus* from Greek *delphis -inos*]

dolphinarium *noun*
• "dolfin AIRY um"
• an aquarium for dolphins, esp. one open to the public.
• [DOLPHIN + AQUARIUM]

domain *noun*
• "duh MAIN"
• an area under one rule; a realm.
• [French *domaine*, Old French *demeine* DEMESNE, assoc. with Latin *dominus* lord]
HOMOPHONES: *domaine*

domaine *noun*
• "duh MAIN"
• a vineyard.
• [French: see DOMAIN]
HOMOPHONES: *domain*

domestic *adjective*
• "duh MESTIC"
• of the home, household, or family affairs.
• [French *domestique* from Latin *domesticus* from *domus* home]
• **domestically** *adverb*
• **domesticity** *noun* "doe mess TISSA tee" or "domma STISSA tee"

domesticate *verb*
• "duh MESTA cate"
• tame (an animal) and keep it as a pet or for farm produce.
• [medieval Latin *domesticare* (as DOMESTIC)]
• **domesticable** *adjective*
• **domesticated** *adjective*
• **domestication** *noun*

domicile *noun*
• "DOMMA sile" or "DOMMA sill"
• a dwelling place; one's home.
• [Old French from Latin *domicilium* from *domus* home]

domiciliary *adjective*
• "domma SILLY airy"
• (esp. of medical care, etc.) of, relating to, or occurring at a person's home.
• [as DOMICILE]

dominant *adjective*
• "DOM'n 'nt"
• dominating, prevailing, most influential.
• [French from Latin *dominari* (as DOMINATE)]
• **dominance** *noun*
• **dominantly** *adverb*

dominate *verb*
• "DOM'n ate"
• have a commanding influence on; exercise control over.
• [Latin *dominari dominat-* from *dominus* lord]
• **dominating** *adjective*
• **domination** *noun*
• **dominator** *noun*

domineer *verb*
• "dom'n EER"
• behave in an arrogant and overbearing way.
• [Dutch *dominieren* from French *dominer*]
• **domineering** *adjective*
• **domineeringly** *adverb*

dominical *adjective*
• "duh MINNA k'll"
• of the Lord's Day; of Sunday.
• [Latin *dominicalis* from Latin *dominicus* from *dominus* lord]

Dominican *adjective*
• "duh MINNA k'n"
• of or relating to the mendicant Order of Friars Preaching, founded in 1215 by St.

Dominic and devoted to preaching and the study of theology.
• [medieval Latin *Dominicanus* from *Dominicus*, the Latin name of *Domingo* de Guzmán (St. *Dominic*), Spanish priest d.1221]

dominie *noun*
• "DOM'n ee"
• a schoolmaster.
• [later spelling of *domine* sir, vocative of Latin *dominus* lord]

dominion *noun*
• "duh MIN y'n"
• sovereign authority; control.
• [Old French from medieval Latin *dominio -onis* from Latin *dominium* from *dominus* lord]

domino *noun*
• "DOM'n oh"
• any of 28 small oblong tiles, marked with 0–6 dots on each half.
• [French, prob. from Latin *dominus* lord, but unexplained]

donair *noun*
• "doe NAIR"
• spiced lamb cooked on a spit, served in slices, and usu. rolled in pita bread.
• [Turkish *döner* rotating]

Donatist *noun*
• "DOE nuh tist"
• a member of a schismatic Christian group of the 4th–7th c., holding that only those living a blameless life belonged in the Church.
• [Late Latin *Donatista* follower of Donatus, 4th-c. Roman grammarian]
• **Donatism** *noun*

donga *noun*
• "DONG guh"
• a ravine or watercourse with steep sides caused by erosion.
• [Nguni]

dongle *noun*
• "DONG g'll"
• a software protection device which must be plugged into a computer to enable protected software to be used on it.
• [arbitrary formation]

donjon *noun*
• "DUN j'n" or "DON j'n"
• the great tower or innermost keep of a castle.
• [archaic spelling of DUNGEON]
HOMOPHONES: *dungeon*

donkey *noun*
• "DONKEE"
• a domestic ass.
• [earlier with pronunciation as *monkey*: perhaps from the man's name *Duncan*]

donkeyman *noun*
• "DONKEE m'n"
• a person in charge of a donkey engine.
• [as DONKEY]

donnée *noun*
• "don AY"
• the subject, theme, or primary motif of a literary work, opera, etc.
• [French, feminine past participle of *donner* give]

donnish *adjective*
• "DON ish"
• having a pedantic stiffness or gravity of manner like a university professor.
• [Italian and Spanish from Latin *dominus* lord]
• **donnishly** *adverb*
• **donnishness** *noun*

donnybrook *noun*
• "DONNY brook" (with "OO" as in *BOOK*)
• a scene of uproar and disorder; a brawl.
• [suburb of Dublin, Ireland, once famous for its annual fair]

donor *noun*
• "DOE nur"
• a person who gives or donates something, e.g. to a charity.
• [Anglo-French *donour* from Latin *donator -oris* from *donare* give]

doozy *noun*
ALSO SPELLED: **doozie**
• "DOOZY"
• something amazing, remarkable, or incredible.
• [20th c.: origin uncertain]

dopa *noun*
• "DOE puh"
• an amino acid derivative which is a precursor of dopamine.
• [German from **D**ioxy**p**henyl**a**lanine, former name of the compound]

dopamine *noun*
• "DOE puh meen"
• an amine present in the body as a neurotransmitter and a precursor of other substances including adrenalin.
• [DOPA + AMINE]
• **dopaminergic** *adjective* "doe puh min UR jick"

doppelgänger *noun*
• "DOP'll gang ur"
• a ghostly likeness or double of a living person.
• [German, = double-goer]

Doppler *noun*
• "DOP lur"
• a device, gauge, system, etc. operating on the principles of an increase (or decrease) in the frequency of sound, light, or other waves as the source and observer move towards (or away) from each other (the Doppler effect), esp. ultrasonic scanning machines.
• [C. *Doppler*, Austrian physicist d.1853]

dorado *noun*
• "duh RADDO"
• a blue and silver marine fish, *Coryphaena hippurus*, showing brilliant colours when dying out of water.
• [Spanish from Late Latin *deauratus* gilt, from *aurum* gold]

doré *noun*
• "dore AY"
• *Cdn* the walleye, *Stizostedion vitreum*.
• [French, = 'golden']

Dorian *noun*
• "DORRY 'n"
• a member of an ancient Hellenic people speaking the Doric dialect of Greek, inhabiting the Peloponnese and elsewhere.
• [Latin *Dorius* from Greek *Dōrios* from *Dōros*, the mythical ancestor]

Doric *adjective*
• "DORIC"
• relating to or denoting a classical order of architecture characterized by a plain, sturdy column and a thick square abacus resting on a rounded moulding.
• [Latin *Doricus* from Greek *Dōrikos* (as DORIAN)]

dormant *adjective*
• "DORE m'nt"
• lying inactive as in sleep; sleeping.
• [Old French, present participle of *dormir* from Latin *dormire* sleep]
• **dormancy** *noun*

dormer *noun*
• "DORE mur"
• a projecting upright window in a sloping roof.
• [Old French *dormëor* (as DORMANT)]

dormitory *noun*
• "DORMA tory"
• a university or college residence.
• [Latin *dormitorium* from *dormire dormit-* sleep]

dormouse *noun*
• "DORE mouse"
• any small mouselike hibernating rodent of the family Gliridae, having a long bushy tail.
• [Middle English: origin unknown]

doronicum *noun*
• "dore ONNA k'm"
• any plant of the genus *Doronicum*, with large yellow daisy-like flowers.
• [modern Latin, ultimately from Arabic *darānaj*]

dorsal *adjective*
• "DORE s'll"
• of, on, or near the back.
• [Late Latin *dorsalis* from Latin *dorsum* back]
• **dorsally** *adverb*

Dorset *noun*
• "DORE sit"
• a member of an Aboriginal people living in the eastern Arctic *c.*1000 BC–AD 1000, whose culture was displaced by that of the Inuit.
• [Cape *Dorset*, NU]

dorsum *noun*
• "DORE sum"
• the dorsal part of an organism or structure.
• [Latin, = back]

dory *noun*
• "DORY"
• any of various marine fish having a compressed body and flat head, esp. the John Dory, used as food.
• [French *dorée*, feminine past participle of *dorer* gild (as DORADO)]

dosa *noun*
• "DOE suh"
• (in southern Indian cooking) a pancake made from rice flour, typically served with a spiced vegetable filling.
• [Tamil *tōcai*]

dosage *noun*
• "DOE sidge"
• the size of a dose of medicine etc.
• [French from Late Latin *dosis* from Greek *dosis* gift, from *didōmi* give]

dosha *noun*
• "DOSH uh" or "DOE shuh"
• (in Ayurvedic medicine) each of the three humours circulating in the body and governing physiological activity, their differing proportions determining individual temperament, physical constitution, and (when imbalanced) giving rise to a disposition to particular physical and mental disorders.
• [Sanskrit *doṣa*, fault, disease, used by extension to refer to the three humours themselves]

dosimeter *noun*
• "doe SIMMA tur"
• a device used to measure an absorbed dose of ionizing radiation.
• [as DOSAGE + Greek *metron* measure]
• **dosimetric** *adjective* "dose a METRIC"
• **dosimetrist** *noun*
• **dosimetry** *noun*

dossal *noun*
• "DOSS'll"
• an ornamental cloth hanging behind an altar or around a chancel.
• [medieval Latin *dossale* from Late Latin *dorsalis* DORSAL]

dossier *noun*
• "DOSSY ay"
• a set of documents, esp. a collection of information about a person, event, or subject.
• [French, so called from the label on the back, from *dos* back, from Latin *dorsum*]

dotage *noun*
• "DOTE idge"

• the state of having the intellect impaired, esp. through old age; senility.
• [from obsolete sense of 'dote' 'be silly or feeble-minded']

dotal *adjective*
• "DOTE 'll"
• pertaining to a woman's dowry.
• [French from *dot* dowry, from Latin *dos dotis*]

dotard *noun*
• "DOTE 'rd"
• a senile person.
• [as DOTAGE]

dotterel *noun*
• "DOTTER'll"
• a small migrant plover, *Eudromias morinellus*.
• ['dote' named from the ease with which it is caught, taken to indicate stupidity]

dottle *noun*
• "DOT'll"
• a remnant of unburned tobacco in a pipe.
• [from 'dot' from Old English *dott* head of a boil]

doublet *noun*
• "DUB lit"
• a man's short close-fitting jacket, with or without sleeves.
• [Old French from *double* from Latin *duplus* double]

doubloon *noun*
• "duh BLOON"
• a Spanish gold coin.
• [French *doublon* or Spanish *doblón* from Latin *duplus* double]

doublure *noun*
• "doo BLOOR"
• an ornamental lining, usu. leather, inside a book cover.
• [French, = lining (*doubler* to line)]

doubt *noun*
• "DOUT"
• a feeling of uncertainty; an undecided state of mind.
• [Old French *doute* from Latin *dubitare* hesitate; modern spelling after Latin]
• **doubter** *noun*
• **doubtful** *adjective*
• **doubtfully** *adverb*
• **doubtfulness** *noun*
• **doubtingly** *adverb*
HOMOPHONES: *dout*

doubtless *adverb*
• "DOUT less"
• certainly, without doubt.
• [as DOUBT]
• **doubtlessly** *adverb*

douce *adjective*
• "DOOCE"
• sober, gentle, sedate.
• [Old French *dous douce* from Latin *dulcis* sweet]
HOMOPHONES: *deuce*

douche *noun*
• "DOOSH"
• a jet of liquid applied to part of the body for cleansing or medicinal purposes.
• [French from Italian *doccia* pipe, from *docciare* pour by drops, ultimately from Latin *ductus* leading, aqueduct, from *ducere duct-* lead]
• **douching** *noun*

dough *noun*
• "DOE"
• a thick mixture of flour, water, etc. for baking into bread, pastry, etc.
• [Old English *dāg* from Germanic]
• **doughiness** *noun*
• **doughy** *adjective*
HOMOPHONES: *doh, do, doe*

doughty *adjective*
• "DOUTY"
• fearless, valiant, stout-hearted.
• [Old English *dohtig* var. of *dyhtig* from Germanic]
• **doughtily** *adverb*
• **doughtiness** *noun*

Doukhobor *noun*
• "DOOKA bore"
• a member of a Russian Christian sect similar to the Society of Friends, many members of which migrated to Canada in 1899 after persecution for refusing military service.
• [Russian *Dukhobor*, from *dukh* spirit + *borets* wrestler]

doula *noun*
• "DOOLA"
• a person, esp. an experienced mother, who gives emotional support, practical help, and advice to a woman during pregnancy and childbirth and for the first few weeks after birth, esp. one who is hired to do so.
• [modern Greek from Greek *doulē* female slave]

doum *noun*
• "DOWM" (with "DOW" as in *DOWN*) or "DOOM"
• a palm tree, *Hyphaene thebaica*, with edible fruit.
• [Arabic *dawm*, *dūm*]
HOMOPHONES: *doom*

dour *adjective*
• "DOWER" or "DOOER"
• severe, stern, or sullenly obstinate in manner or appearance.
• [Middle English (originally Scots), prob. from Gaelic *dúr* dull, obstinate, perhaps from Latin *durus* hard]
• **dourly** *adverb*
• **dourness** *noun*
HOMOPHONES: *dower, dewar, doer*

dourocouli *noun*
• "dura COOLY"
• any nocturnal monkey of the genus *Aotus*, native to S America, having large staring eyes.
• [native name]

douse *verb*
ALSO SPELLED: **dowse**
• "DOUSE" (rhymes with *MOUSE*)
• drench or wet thoroughly with a liquid.
• [16th c.: perhaps related to Middle Dutch, Low German *dossen* strike]

dout *verb*
• "DOUT" (rhymes with *OUT*)
• *Cdn* (*Nfld*) *dialect* turn off or extinguish (a light, fire, cigarette, etc.).
• [coalesced form of *do out*]
HOMOPHONES: *doubt*

dovecote *noun*
• "DUV cote"
• a structure with nesting holes for domesticated pigeons.
• ['dove' + COTE]

dovekie *noun*
• "DUV kee"
• a small arctic auk, *Alle alle*.
• [Scots, diminutive of 'dove']

dowager *noun*
• "DOW a jur"
• a widow with a title or property derived from her late husband.
• [Old French *douag(i)ere* from *douage* (as DOWER)]

dowdy *adjective*
• "DOW dee"
• (of clothes) unfashionable; unattractively dull.
• [Middle English *dowd* slut, of unknown origin]
• **dowdily** *adverb*
• **dowdiness** *noun*

dowel *noun*
• "DOW'll" (rhymes with *TOWEL*)
• a headless peg of wood, metal, or plastic for holding together components of a structure without the peg itself showing.
• [Middle Low German *dovel*: compare THOLE]
• **dowelled** *adjective*

dowelling *noun*
ALSO SPELLED: **doweling**
• "DOW'll ing" (rhymes with *TOWELLING*)
• cylindrical rods for cutting into dowels.
• [as DOWEL]

dower *noun*
• "DOWER"
• a widow's share for life of her husband's estate.
• [Old French *douaire* from medieval Latin *dotarium* from Latin *dos dotis*]
• **dowerless** *adjective*
HOMOPHONES: *dour*

dowitcher *noun*
• "DOW itch ur"
• any N American wading bird of the genus *Limnodromus*, related to sandpipers and having a long, straight bill.
• [Iroquoian]

dowry *noun*
• "DOW ree"
• property or money brought by a bride to her husband at marriage.
• [Anglo-French *dowarie* DOWER]

dowse *verb*
• "DOWZ" (rhymes with *PLOWS*)
• search for underground water or minerals by holding a Y-shaped stick or rod which dips abruptly when over the right spot.
• [17th c.: origin unknown]
• **dowser** *noun*
• **dowsing** *noun*

doxology *noun*
• "dox OLLA jee"
• a liturgical formula of praise to God.
• [medieval Latin *doxologia* from Greek *doxologia* from *doxa* glory + *logos* word]

doxorubicin *noun*
• "docksa ROOBA sin"
• an antibiotic drug used to treat leukemia and other cancers.
• [d(e)ox(y) + Latin *rubus* red + '-cin' ending for antibiotics]

doxy *noun*
• "DOCKSY"
• a lover or mistress.
• [16th-c. cant: origin unknown]

doxycycline *noun*
• "docksy SIKE lin"
• a broad spectrum antibiotic of the tetracycline group used to treat some infections.
• [d(e)ox(y) + (TETRA)CYCLINE]

doyen *noun*
• "DOY 'n" or "doy EN" or "DWAH yã" (with a nasal *a*)
• the most senior or most prominent male member of a particular category or body of people.
• [French from Old French *deien*, from Late Latin *decanus* from *decem* ten; originally = chief of a group of ten]
HOMOPHONES: *doyenne*

doyenne *noun*
• "doy EN" or "dwah YEN"
• the most senior or most prominent female member of a particular category or body of people.
• [French, feminine of DOYEN]
HOMOPHONES: *doyen*

dozen *noun*
• "DUZZ'n"
• twelve, regarded collectively.

• [Old French *dozeine*, ultimately from Latin *duodecim* twelve]
• **dozenth** *adjective*

dracaena *noun*
• "druh SEENA"
• any of various shrubs and trees of the genera *Dracaena* and *Cordyline* (agave family) grown for their foliage.
• [modern Latin from Greek *drakaina*, feminine of *drakōn* dragon]

drachm *noun*
• "DRAM"
• a weight or measure formerly used by apothecaries, equivalent to 60 grains or one eighth of an ounce (3.89 grams), or 60 minims, one eighth of a fluid ounce.
• [Latin *drachma* from Greek *drakhmē* Attic weight and coin]
HOMOPHONES: *dram*

drachma *noun*
• "DRACKMA"
• the former chief monetary unit of Greece, now replaced by the euro.
• [Latin from Greek *drakhmē*]

draconian *adjective*
• "druh CONEY 'n"
• very harsh or severe (esp. of laws and their application).
• [*Draco*, 7th-c. BC Athenian legislator who prescribed death for nearly all offences]
• **draconianism** *noun*

draegerman *noun*
• "DRAY gur m'n"
• a member of a crew trained for underground rescue work.
• [A. B. *Dräger*, German scientist d.1928]

dragée *noun*
• "drazh AY"
• a sugar-coated almond, candy, etc.
• [French from Old French *dragie*, *dragee*, perhaps from Latin *tragemata* from Greek *tragēmata* spices]

dragoman *noun*
• "DRAGGA m'n"
• an interpreter or guide, esp. in countries speaking Arabic, Turkish, or Persian.
• [French from Italian *dragomano* from medieval Greek *dragomanos* from Arabic *tarjumān* from *tarjama* interpret, from Aramaic *targēm* from Assyrian *targumânu* interpreter]

dragonet *noun*
• "DRAG'n it"
• any marine spiny fish of the family Callionymidae, the males of which are brightly coloured.
• [French, diminutive of Old French *dragon*, from Latin *draco -onis* from Greek *drakōn* serpent]

dragoon *noun*
• "druh GOON"
• a mounted infantryman armed with a carbine.
• [originally = carbine (thought of as breathing fire), from French *dragon* dragon (as DRAGONET)]

drama *noun*
• "DRAMMA" or "DROMMA"
• a play for acting on stage or for broadcasting.
• [Late Latin from Greek *drama -atos* from *draō* do]

dramatic *adjective*
• "druh MATTIC"
• of drama or the study of drama.
• [as DRAMA]
• **dramatically** *adverb*

dramatics *noun*
• "druh MATTIX"
• the production and performance of plays.
• [as DRAMA]

dramatist *noun*
• "DRAMMA tist" or "DROMMA tist"
• a person who writes dramas; a playwright.
• [as DRAMA]

dramatize *verb*
ALSO SPELLED: esp. *Brit.* **-ise**
• "DRAMMA tize" or "DROMMA tize"
• adapt (a novel, incident, etc.) to form a dramatic work, esp. a play or film.
• [as DRAMA]
• **dramatization** *noun* (also esp. *Brit.* **-isation**)

dramaturge *noun*
• "DRAMMA turj" or "DROMMA turj"
• a consultant to a theatre company whose duties may involve the development of new works through script editing etc., historical research to assist in the mounting of older works, advising the artistic director on repertoire, etc.
• [French or German from Greek *dramatourgos* (as DRAMA, *-ergos* worker)]

dramaturgy *noun*
• "DRAMMA turjy" or "DROMMA turjy"
• the art of theatrical production; the theory of dramatics.
• [as DRAMATURGE]
• **dramaturgical** *adjective*
• **dramaturgically** *adverb*

dramedy *noun*
• "DRAMMA dee" or "DROMMA dee"
• a movie or television program which has both dramatic and comedic elements.
• [blend of DRAMA + COMEDY]

drastic *adjective*
• "DRASSTIC"
• having a strong or far-reaching effect; severe.
• [Greek *drastikos* from *draō* do]
• **drastically** *adverb*

Dravidian *noun*
• "druh VIDDY 'n"
• a member of a dark-skinned aboriginal

people of S India and Sri Lanka (including the Tamils and Kanarese).
• [Sanskrit *Dravida*, a province of S India]

dray *noun*
• "DRAY"
• a low cart without sides used esp. formerly by brewers for carrying heavy loads.
• [Old English *dræge* dragnet, *dragan* draw]

dreadful *adjective*
• "DREDFUL"
• terrible; causing great fear or suffering.
• [Old English *ādrǣdan*, *ondrǣdan* fear greatly]
• **dreadfully** *adverb*
• **dreadfulness** *noun*

dreadnought *noun*
• "DRED not"
• a type of battleship whose main armament was entirely big guns of the same calibre.
• [from the name of the first, launched in 1906]

drear *adjective*
• "DREER"
• dismal, dull, gloomy.
• [abbreviation of DREARY]

dreary *adjective*
• "DREERY"
• dismal, dull, gloomy.
• [Old English *drēorig* from *drēor* gore: related to *drēosan* to drop, from Germanic]
• **drearily** *adverb*
• **dreariness** *noun*

dreidel *noun*
ALSO SPELLED: **dreidl**
• "DRAY d'll"
• a four-sided spinning top with a Hebrew letter on each side.
• [Yiddish *dreydl* from Middle High German *drae(je)n* (German *drehen*) turn]

Dresden *noun*
• "DREZZ d'n"
• delicate and elaborate porcelain originally made at Dresden in E Germany, made at nearby Meissen since 1710.

dressage *noun*
• "druh SOZH"
• the training of a horse in obedience and deportment, esp. for competition.
• [French from *dresser* to train]

drivel *noun*
• "DRIV'll"
• silly nonsense; twaddle.
• [Old English *dreflian*]
• **driveller** *noun* (also *US* **driveler**)
• **drivelling** *adjective* (also esp. *US* **driveling**)

drizzle *noun*
• "DRIZZ'll"
• very fine rain.
• [prob. from Old English *drēosan* fall]
• **drizzly** *adjective*

drogue *noun*
• "DROE'g"
• a sea anchor.
• [18th c.: origin unknown]

droit *noun*
• "DROIT"
• a right or due.
• [Old French from Latin *directum* from *directus*: see DIRECTORY]

droke *noun*
• "DROKE"
• *Cdn* (*Nfld* & *Maritimes*) a grove of trees.
• [origin unknown]

droll *adjective*
• "DROLE"
• quaintly amusing.
• [French *drôle*, perhaps from Middle Dutch *drolle* little man]
• **drollery** *noun*
• **drollness** *noun*
• **drolly** *adverb*

dromedary *noun*
• "DROMMA derry"
• a domesticated camel with one hump, *Camelus dromedarius*, native to the deserts of N Africa and Arabia.
• [Late Latin *dromedarius*, ultimately from Greek *dromas -ados* runner]

drone *noun*
• "DRONE"
• a non-working male of the honeybee, whose sole function is to mate with fertile females.
• [Old English *drān*, *drǣn*, prob. from West Germanic]
• **droner** *noun*

drongo *noun*
• "DRONG go"
• any black bird of the family Dicruridae, native to India, Africa, and Australia, having a long forked tail.
• [Malagasy]

dropsy *noun*
• "DROPSEE"
• a condition characterized by an excess of watery fluid collecting in the cavities or tissues of the body.
• [Old French *idropesie*, ultimately from Latin *hydropisis* from Greek *hudrōps* dropsy (as HYDROUS)]
• **dropsical** *adjective*

dropwort *noun*
• "DROP wurt" or "DROP wort"
• a plant, *Filipendula vulgaris*, with tuberous root fibres.
• ['drop' + WORT]

droshky *noun*
• "DROSHKY"
• a Russian low four-wheeled open carriage.

• [Russian *drozhki*, diminutive of *drogi* wagon, from *droga* shaft]

drosophila *noun*
• "druh SOFFA luh"
• any fruit fly of the genus *Drosophila*, used extensively in genetic research.
• [modern Latin from Greek *drosos* dew, moisture + *philos* loving]

dross *noun*
• "DROSS" (rhymes with *CROSS*)
• material without value or worth.
• [Old English *drōs*]
• **drossy** *adjective*

drought *noun*
• "DROUT" (rhymes with *SHOUT*)
• the continuous absence of rain; dry weather.
• [Old English *drūgath* from *drȳge* dry]
• **droughty** *adjective*

drowsy *adjective*
• "DROWZY" ("DROW" rhymes with *COW*)
• half asleep; dozing.
• [prob. related to Old English *drūsian* be languid or slow, *drēosan* fall: compare DREARY]
• **drowse** *verb*
• **drowsily** *adverb*
• **drowsiness** *noun*

drugget *noun*
• "DRUG it"
• a coarse woven fabric used as a floor or table covering.
• [French *droguet*, of unknown origin]

druggist *noun*
• "DRUG ist"
• a pharmacist.
• [French *droguiste* from Old French *drogue*, of unknown origin]

Druid *noun*
• "DROO id"
• an ancient Celtic priest, magician, or soothsayer of Gaul, Britain, or Ireland.
• [French *druide* or Latin pl. *druidae*, *-des*, Greek *druidai* from Gaulish *druides*]
• **Druidic** *adjective* "droo ID ick"
• **Druidical** *adjective*
• **Druidism** *noun*

drumlin *noun*
• "DRUMLIN"
• a long oval mound of boulder clay moulded by glacial action.
• [Scottish Gaelic & Irish *druim* ridge]

drupe *noun*
• "DROOP"
• any fleshy or pulpy fruit enclosing a stone containing one or a few seeds, e.g. an olive, plum, or peach.
• [Latin *drupa* from Greek *druppa* olive]
HOMOPHONES: *droop*

drupelet *noun*
• "DROOP lit"
• a small drupe usu. in an aggregate fruit, e.g. a blackberry or raspberry.
• [as DRUPE]

druse *noun*
• "DROOZ"
• a crust of crystals lining a rock cavity.
• [French from German, = weathered ore]
HOMOPHONES: *Druze*

dryad *noun*
• "DRY ad" or "DRY ud"
• a nymph inhabiting a tree; a wood nymph.
• [Old French *dryade* from Latin from Greek *druas -ados* from *drus* tree]

dryas *noun*
• "DRY us"
• a rosaceous alpine plant of the genus *Dryas*, bearing white or yellow flowers.
• [Greek *druas* from *drus* tree]

dual *adjective*
• "DUE 'll"
• of two; twofold.
• [Latin *dualis* from *duo* two]
• **duality** *noun*
• **dualize** *verb* (also esp. *Brit.* **-ise**)
• **dually** *adverb*
HOMOPHONES: *duel*, *duellist*, *duly*

dualism *noun*
• "DUE 'll izm"
• the state of being twofold; duality.
• [as DUAL]
• **dualist** *noun*
• **dualistic** *adjective*
• **dualistically** *adverb*

duathlon *noun*
• "due ATH lon"
• a sporting event combining two disciplines, e.g. running and swimming, running and biking, etc.
• [DUAL, after PENTATHLON]
• **duathlete** *noun*

dubbin *noun*
• "DUBBIN"
• prepared grease for softening and waterproofing leather.
• [Old English from Old French *adober* 'equip with armour, repair', of unknown origin]

dubiety *noun*
• "due BY a tee"
• a feeling of doubt.
• [Late Latin *dubietas* from *dubium* doubt]

dubious *adjective*
• "DUE bee us"
• hesitating or doubting.
• [Latin *dubiosus* from *dubium* doubt]
• **dubiously** *adverb*
• **dubiousness** *noun*

dubnium *noun*
• "DUB nee um"

• a very unstable chemical element made by high-energy atomic collisions.
• [modern Latin, from *Dubna* in Russia, site of the Joint Nuclear Institute]

ducal *adjective*
• "DUKE'll"
• of, like, or pertaining to a duke or dukedom.
• [French from *duc* from Latin *dux ducis* leader]

ducat *noun*
• "DUCK it"
• any of various gold or silver coins, formerly current in most European countries.
• [medieval Latin *ducatus* DUCHY]

duchess *noun*
• "DUTCH iss"
• a duke's wife or widow.
• [Old French *duchesse* from medieval Latin *ducissa* (as DUCAL)]

duchesse *noun*
• "doo SHESS"
• mashed potatoes formed into croquettes or small cakes, or piped into fancy shapes, and then baked or fried to acquire a crisp surface.
• [French, = DUCHESS]

duchy *noun*
• "DUTCHY"
• a dukedom or the territory of a duke or duchess.
• [Old French *duché(e)* from medieval Latin *ducatus* from Latin *dux ducis* leader]
HOMOPHONES: *Dutchie*

ductile *adjective*
• "DUCK tile"
• (of a substance) flexible, pliant, malleable.
• [Latin *ductilis* from *ducere duct-* lead]
• **ductility** *noun* "duck TILLA tee"

dudgeon *noun*
• "DUDGE 'n"
• a feeling of anger, offence, or resentment.
• [16th c.: origin unknown]

due *adjective*
• "DUE"
• owing or payable as a debt or an obligation, whether immediately or at some future date.
• [Old French *deü*, ultimately from Latin *debitus* past participle of *debēre* owe]
HOMOPHONES: *dew, do*

duel *noun*
• "DUE 'll"
• a contest with deadly weapons arranged between two people in order to settle a point of honour.
• [Italian *duello* or Latin *duellum* (archaic form of *bellum* war), in medieval Latin = single combat]
• **dueller** *noun* (also *US* **dueler**)
• **duellist** *noun* (also *US* **duelist**)
HOMOPHONES: *dual, dualist*

duenna *noun*
• "due ENNA"
• an older woman acting as a governess, companion, or chaperone in charge of girls, esp. in a Spanish family.
• [Spanish *dueña* from Latin *domina* mistress]

duet *noun*
• "due ET"
• a performance by two voices, instrumentalists, etc.
• [German *Duett* or Italian *duetto* diminutive of *duo* duet, from Latin *duo* two]
• **duettist** *noun*

dugong *noun*
• "DOO gong"
• a marine mammal, *Dugong dugon*, of Asian seas and coasts.
• [ultimately from Malay *dūyong*]

duiker *noun*
ALSO SPELLED: **duyker**
• "DIKE ur"
• any of various small African antelopes of the genera *Cephalophus* and *Silvicapra*, esp. *S. grimmia*, usu. having a crest of long hair between its horns, widespread in southern African savannah and bush.
• [Dutch *duiker* diver, with reference to its habit of plunging through bushes when pursued]

dulcet *adjective*
• "DULL sit"
• (esp. of sound) sweet and soothing.
• [Middle English, earlier *doucet* from Old French diminutive of *doux* from Latin *dulcis* sweet]

dulcimer *noun*
• "DULLSA mur"
• a musical instrument with strings of graduated length stretched over a trapezoidal sounding board or box, played by being struck with hammers.
• [Old French *doulcemer*, said to represent Latin *dulce* sweet, *melos* song]

dullard *noun*
• "DULL'rd"
• a slow, dull, or stupid person.
• [Middle Low German, Middle Dutch *dul*, corresponding to Old English *dol* stupid]

dullsville *noun*
• "DULLZ vill"
• an extremely dull place or situation.
• [as DULLARD + French *ville* town]

dulse *noun*
• "DULSE" (rhymes with *PULSE*)
• an edible seaweed, *Rhodymenia palmata*, with red wedge-shaped fronds.
• [Irish & Gaelic *duileasg*]

duly *adverb*
• "DUE lee"
• in due manner, order, form, or time.

• [Old French *deü*, ultimately from Latin *debitus* past participle of *debēre* owe]
HOMOPHONES: *dually*

Duma *noun*
• "DOOMA"
• a legislative body in the ruling assembly of Russia and of some other republics of the former USSR.
• [Russian: originally an elective municipal council]

dumbbell *noun*
• "DUM bell"
• a short bar with a weight at each end, used for exercise, muscle building, etc.
• ['dumb' + 'bell']

dumdum *noun*
• "DUM dum"
• a kind of soft-nosed or hollow-nosed bullet that expands on impact to inflict extensive injuries.
• [*Dum-Dum* in India, where it was first produced]

dun *adjective*
• "DUN"
• dull greyish-brown.
• [Old English *dun, dunn*]
HOMOPHONES: *done*

dungaree *noun*
• "dun guh REE"
• a coarse, hard-wearing cotton fabric, often blue.
• [Hindi *dungrī*]

dungeon *noun*
• "DUN j'n"
• a strong underground cell for prisoners.
• [originally = *donjon*: Middle English from Old French *donjon*, ultimately from Latin *dominus* lord]
HOMOPHONES: *donjon*

dunlin *noun*
• "DUN lin"
• a long-billed Holarctic sandpiper, *Calidris alpina*, the male of which has a reddish back and a black patch on the front.
• [prob. from DUN]

dunnage *noun*
• "DUN idge"
• loose material, such as mats etc., stowed under or among cargo to prevent wetting or chafing.
• [Anglo-Latin *dennagium*, of unknown origin]

duodecimal *adjective*
• "due oh DESSA m'll"
• relating to or using a system of numerical notation that has 12 as a base.
• [Latin *duodecimus* twelfth, from *duodecim* twelve]
• **duodecimally** *adverb*

duodecimo *noun*
• "due oh DESSIM oh"
• a size of book or paper in which each leaf is one-twelfth of the size of a standard printing sheet.
• [Latin (*in*) *duodecimo* in a twelfth (as DUODECIMAL)]

duodenum *noun*
• "due oh DEE num" or "due ODDA num"
• the first part of the small intestine immediately below the stomach.
• [medieval Latin from *duodeni* from its length of about 12 fingers' breadth]
• **duodenal** *adjective*

duologue *noun*
• "DUE a log"
• a conversation between two people.
• [Latin *duo* or Greek *duo* two, after *monologue*]

duomo *noun*
• "DWOE moe"
• an Italian cathedral.
• [Italian from Latin *domus* house]

duopoly *noun*
• "due OPPA lee"
• a condition in which a particular market is controlled or dominated by only two suppliers, individuals, etc.
• [Greek *duo* two + *pōleō* sell, after *monopoly*]
• **duopolist** *noun*
• **duopolistic** *adjective*

duotone *noun*
• "DUE a tone"
• a halftone illustration in two colours from the same original with different screen angles.
• [Latin *duo* two + 'tone']

dupatta *noun*
• "duh PUTTA"
• a length of cloth worn as a scarf or head covering, typically with a shalwar, by women from the Indian subcontinent.
• [Hindi *dupaṭṭā*]

dupion *noun*
• "DUPEY 'n"
• a rough silk fabric woven from the threads of double cocoons.
• [French *doupion* from Italian *doppione* from *doppio* double]

duple *adjective*
• "DUPE 'll"
• double, twofold, or of two parts.
• [Latin *duplus* from *duo* two]

duplicate *adjective*
• "DUE pluh kit"
• copied or exactly like something already existing (in any number of copies).
• [Latin *duplicatus* past participle of *duplicare* from *duplex duplicis* from *duo* two + *plic-* fold]
• **duplicable** *adjective*
• **duplication** *noun*

- **duplicative** *adjective*
- **duplicator** *noun*

duplicity *noun*
- "due PLISSA tee"
- the quality or practice of being two-faced, deceitful in manner or conduct, or double-dealing.
- [Late Latin *duplicitas* (as DUPLICATE)]
- **duplicitous** *adjective*

durable *adjective*
- "DURE a bull"
- capable of lasting or able to withstand change, decay, or wear.
- [Old French from Latin *durabilis* from *durare* endure, from *durus* hard]
- **durability** *noun*
- **durably** *adverb*

duramen *noun*
- "due RAY men"
- the dense inner part of a tree trunk yielding the hardest timber.
- [Latin from *durare* harden]

duration *noun*
- "due RAY sh'n"
- the time during which something lasts or continues.
- [Old French from medieval Latin *duratio -onis* (as DURABLE)]
- **durational** *adjective*

durative *adjective*
- "DURE a tiv"
- denoting continuing action.
- [as DURATION]

durbar *noun*
- "DUR bar"
- the court of an Indian ruler.
- [Urdu from Persian *darbār* court]

durchkomponiert *adjective*
- "DURK compon eert"
- (of a composition) having a formal design which does not rely on repeated sections, esp. having different music for each verse.
- [German from *durch* through + *komponiert* composed]

duress *noun*
- "dur ESS" or "dyur ESS"
- compulsion, constraint, esp. imprisonment, threats, or violence.
- [Old French *duresse* from Latin *duritia* from *durus* hard]

durian *noun*
- "DURY 'n"
- a large tree, *Durio zibethinus*, native to SE Asia, bearing oval spiny fruits containing a creamy pulp with a fetid smell and an agreeable taste.
- [Malay *durīan* from *dūrī* thorn]

duricrust *noun*
- "DURA crust"
- a hard mineral crust formed near the surface of soil in semi-arid regions by evaporation of groundwater.
- [Latin *durus* hard + *crusta* rind, shell]

durmast *noun*
- "DUR mast"
- a Eurasian oak tree, *Quercus petraea*, having sessile flowers.
- [*dur-* (perhaps erroneous for DUN) + 'mast' the fruit of the beech, oak, chestnut, and other forest trees, esp. as food for pigs]

durra *noun*
ALSO SPELLED: **dhurra**
- "DURRA" (with "U" as in *DUCK*)
- a variety of sorghum, *Sorghum bicolor*, grown esp. in N Africa and the Indian subcontinent.
- [Arabic *ḏura*, *ḏurra*]

durum *noun*
- "DUR um" or "DYUR um"
- a kind of wheat, *Triticum durum*, having hard seeds and yielding a flour used in the manufacture of pasta.
- [Latin, neuter of *durus* hard]

HOMOPHONES: *dirham*

Dutchie *noun*
- "DUTCHY"
- *Cdn* a usu. square, raised, glazed doughnut containing raisins.
- [from 'Dutch' (of the Netherlands) from Middle Dutch *dutsch* etc. 'Netherlandish, German', Old High German *diutisc* national]

HOMOPHONES: *duchy*

duteous *adjective*
- "DUTY us"
- (of a person or conduct) dutiful, obedient.
- [as DUTY]
- **duteously** *adverb*
- **duteousness** *noun*

dutiable *adjective*
- "DUE tee a bull"
- liable to customs taxes or other duties.
- [as DUTY]

duty *noun*
- "DUE tee"
- a moral or legal obligation or responsibility.
- [Anglo-French *deweté*, *dueté* (as DUE)]
- **dutiful** *adjective*
- **dutifully** *adverb*
- **dutifulness** *noun*

duumvir *noun*
- "due UM vur" or "DUE 'm vur"
- one of two coequal magistrates or officials.
- [Latin from *duum virum* of the two men]

duumvirate *noun*
- "due UM vur it"
- a coalition of two people.
- [as DUUMVIR]

duvet *noun*
- "doo VAY" or "DOO vay"
- a quilt, filled with down or a synthetic fibre

with a high loft, used instead of an upper sheet and blankets.
• [French, lit. 'down']

duxelles *noun*
• "dook SELL"
• a seasoning or sauce of mushrooms, shallots, parsley, and onions.
• [French, possibly after the 17th-c. Marquis d'Uxelles, whose chef is said to have invented the recipe]

dwale *noun*
• "DWALE"
• a poisonous plant, *Atropa belladonna*, with purple flowers and purple-black berries.
• [prob. from Scandinavian]

dyad *noun*
• "DIE ad"
• two, a group of two, a pair, or a twofold entity.
• [Late Latin *dyas dyad-* from Greek *duas duados* from *duo* two]
• **dyadic** *adjective*

dybbuk *noun*
• "DIB ook"
• (in Jewish folklore) a wandering malevolent spirit that enters and possesses the body of a living person until exorcised.
• [Hebrew *dibbûḵ* from *dāḏaḵ* cling]

dye *noun*
• "DIE"
• a substance used to change the colour of hair, fabric, wood, etc.
• [Old English *deag, deagian*]
• **dyeable** *adjective*
• **dyer** *noun*
HOMOPHONES: *die, dire*

dynamic *adjective*
• "die NAMMIC"
• energetic; active.
• [French *dynamique* from Greek *dunamikos* from *dunamis* power]
• **dynamically** *adverb*

dynamics *noun*
• "die NAMMIX"
• the branch of mechanics concerned with the motion of bodies under the action of forces.
• [as DYNAMIC]
• **dynamicist** *noun* "die NAMMA sist"

dynamism *noun*
• "DIE nuh mizm"
• energizing or dynamic action or power.
• [Greek *dunamis* power]

dynamite *noun*
• "DIE nuh mite"
• a high explosive consisting of nitroglycerine mixed with an absorbent.
• [formed as DYNAMISM]
• **dynamiter** *noun*

dynamo *noun*
• "DIE nuh moe"
• a machine converting mechanical into electrical energy, esp. by rotating coils of copper wire in a magnetic field.
• [abbreviation of *dynamo-electric machine* from Greek *dunamis* power, force]

dynamometer *noun*
• "die nuh MOMMA tur"
• an instrument that measures the power output of an engine.
• [French *dynamomètre* from Greek *dunamis* power, force + *metron* measure]

dynast *noun*
• "DIE nast"
• a member of a powerful family, esp. a hereditary ruler.
• [Latin from Greek *dunastēs* from *dunamai* be able]

dynasty *noun*
• "DIE nuh stee"
• a line of hereditary rulers.
• [French *dynastie* or Late Latin *dynastia* from Greek *dunasteia* lordship (as DYNAST)]
• **dynastic** *adjective* "die NASTIC"
• **dynastically** *adverb*

dyne *noun*
• "DINE"
• a unit of force that, acting on a mass of one gram, increases its velocity by one centimetre per second every second along the direction that it acts.
• [French from Greek *dunamis* force, power]
HOMOPHONES: *dine*

dysentery *noun*
• "DISS'n terry" or "DISS'n tree"
• a disease with inflammation of the intestines, causing severe diarrhea with blood and mucus.
• [Latin *dysenteria* from Greek *dusenteria* (*dus-* bad, *enteria* from *entera* bowels)]
• **dysenteric** *adjective*

dysfunction *noun*
• "dis FUNK sh'n"
• an abnormality or impairment of function.
• [Greek *dus-* bad + 'function' from French *fonction* from Latin *functio -onis* from *fungi funct-* perform]
• **dysfunctional** *adjective*

dyskinesia *noun*
• "dis k'n EE zhuh"
• abnormality or impairment of voluntary movement.
• [Greek *dus-* bad + KINESIS]

dyslexia *noun*
• "dis LEXY uh"
• a general term for disorders that involve difficulty in learning to read or interpret words, letters, and other symbols, but that do not affect general intelligence.

• [German *Dyslexie* (Greek *dus-* bad, *lexis* speech)]
• **dyslexic** *adjective*

dysmenorrhea *noun*
ALSO SPELLED: **dysmenorrhoea**
• "dis menna REE uh"
• painful menstruation.
• [Greek *dus-* bad + post-classical Latin *menorrhoea* from Greek *meno-* month + *rheō* flow]

dyspepsia *noun*
• "dis PEPSY uh"
• indigestion.
• [Latin *dyspepsia* from Greek *duspepsia* (*dus-* bad, *peptos* cooked, digested)]
• **dyspeptic** *adjective* "dis PEPTIC"

dysphasia *noun*
• "dis FAY zhuh" or "dis FAZEY uh"
• lack of coordination in speech, owing to brain damage.
• [Greek *dusphatos* hard to utter (*dus-* bad, PHATIC)]

dysphoria *noun*
• "dis FORY uh"
• a state of unease or mental discomfort.
• [Greek *dusphoria* from *dusphoros* hard to bear (*dus-* bad, *pherō* bear)]
• **dysphoric** *adjective*

dysplasia *noun*
• "dis PLAY zhuh" or "dis PLAZEY uh"
• abnormal growth of tissues etc.
• [modern Latin, from Greek *dus-* bad + *plasis* formation]
• **dysplastic** *adjective*

dyspnea *noun*
ALSO SPELLED: esp. *Brit.* **dyspnoea**
• "disp NEE uh"
• difficult or laboured breathing.
• [Latin from Greek *duspnoia* (*dus-* bad, *pneō* breathe)]

dysprosium *noun*
• "dis PROZY um"
• a naturally occurring soft metallic element of the lanthanide series, used as a component in certain magnetic alloys.
• [modern Latin from Greek *dusprositos* hard to get at]

dystocia *noun*
• "dis TOE shuh"
• difficult or prolonged childbirth.
• [Greek *dus-* bad + *tokos* childbirth]

dystonia *noun*
• "dis TONY uh"
• a state of abnormal muscle tone, esp. a postural disorder marked by spasm of the trunk, neck, shoulders or limbs and due to disease of the basal ganglia of the brain.
• [Greek *dus-* bad + 'tone']
• **dystonic** *adjective*

dystopia *noun*
• "dis TOPEY uh"
• a nightmare vision of society, often as one dominated by a totalitarian state.
• [Greek *dus-* bad + UTOPIA]
• **dystopian** *adjective*

dystrophy *noun*
• "DISTRA fee"
• impaired nourishment of an organ or part of the body.
• [modern Latin *dystrophia* from Greek *dus-* bad + *-trophia* nourishment]
• **dystrophic** *adjective* "dis TROFFIC"

dysuria *noun*
• "dis YURY uh"
• painful or difficult urination.
• [Late Latin from Greek *dusouria* (*dus-* bad, *ouron* urine)]

Dzongkha *noun*
• "ZONKA"
• the official language of Bhutan, closely related to Tibetan.
• [Tibetan]

Ee

earache *noun*
- "EER ake"
- a (usu. prolonged) pain in the ear.
- [Old English *ēar* from Germanic + ACHE]

earnest *adjective*
- "URN ist"
- serious in intention; not trifling.
- [Old English *eornust*, *eornost*]
- **earnestly** *adverb*
- **earnestness** *noun*

earring *noun*
- "EERING"
- a piece of jewellery worn in or on (esp. the lobe of) the ear.
- ['ear' + 'ring']

earthenware *noun*
- "URTH'n ware"
- pottery, vessels, etc., made of clay fired to a porous state which can be made impervious to liquids by the use of a glaze.
- ['earth' + WARE]

easel *noun*
- "EEZ'll"
- a standing frame, usu. of wood, for supporting an artist's work, a blackboard, etc.
- [Dutch *ezel* = German *Esel* donkey]

eaves *plural noun*
- "EEVZ"
- the underside of a projecting roof.
- [originally sing., from Old English *efes*: prob. related to 'over']

eavesdrop *verb*
- "EEVZ drop"
- listen secretly to a private conversation.
- [from an earlier noun *eavesdrop* 'the ground onto which water drips from the eaves', prob. from Old Norse *upsardropi*; *eavesdropper* originally 'a person who listens by the wall (in the eavesdrop)': the modern verb by back-formation from 'eavesdropper']
- **eavesdropper** *noun*

eavestrough *noun*
- "EEVZ troff"
- (esp. *Cdn*) a shallow trough attached to the eaves of a building to collect runoff from the roof.
- [EAVES + TROUGH]

ebb *noun*
- "EB"
- the movement of the tide out to sea.
- [Old English *ebba*, *ebbian*]

Ebola *noun*
- "ib OLE uh"
- a tropical African virus that causes a severe, infectious, generally fatal hemorrhagic disease in humans.
- [the name of a river and district in Congo (formerly Zaire), where the disease was first observed in 1976]

Ebonics *noun*
- "ee BONNIX"
- American black English regarded as a language in its own right rather than as a dialect of standard English.
- [blend of EBONY + PHONICS]

ebonite *noun*
- "EBBA nite"
- a hard black vulcanized rubber.
- [EBONY + Greek *lithos* stone]

ebony *noun*
- "EBBA nee"
- a heavy hard dark wood used for furniture.
- [ultimately from Latin *ebenus*, Greek *ebenos* ebony tree, perhaps on the pattern of *ivory*]

ebullient *adjective*
- "e BULLY 'nt" ("BULLY" can rhyme either with *GULLY* or with *WOOLLY*)
- exuberant, high-spirited.
- [Latin *ebullire ebullient-* bubble out (Latin *ex* out of, *bullire* boil)]
- **ebullience** *noun*
- **ebulliently** *adverb*

écarté *noun*
- "ay CAR tay"
- a card game for two persons in which cards from a player's hand may be exchanged for others from the pack.
- [French, past participle of *écarter* discard]

eccentric *adjective*
- "eck SENTRIC"
- odd or capricious in behaviour or appearance; whimsical.

• [Late Latin *eccentricus* from Greek *ekkentros* from *ek* out of + *kentros* CENTRE]
• **eccentrically** *adverb*
• **eccentricity** *noun* "eck sen TRISSA tee"

ecclesial *adjective*
• "e CLEEZY 'll"
• of or relating to the Christian Church or the clergy.
• [Greek *ekklesia* assembly, church, from *ekklētos* summoned out from *ek* out + *kaleō* call]

ecclesiastic *noun*
• "e cleezy ASTIC"
• a member of the Christian clergy.
• [French *ecclésiastique* or Late Latin *ecclesiasticus* from Greek *ekklēsiastikos* from *ekklēsia* assembly, church: see ECCLESIAL]

ecclesiastical *adjective*
• "e cleezy ASTA k'll"
• of or relating to the Christian Church or the clergy.
• [as ECCLESIASTIC]
• **ecclesiastically** *adverb*

ecclesiology *noun*
• "e cleezy OLLA jee"
• the study of churches, esp. church building and decoration.
• [Greek *ekklēsia* assembly, church (see ECCLESIAL) + *logos* word]
• **ecclesiological** *adjective*
• **ecclesiologist** *noun*

eccrine *adjective*
• "ECK reen"
• designating or pertaining to those sweat glands which lose none of their cytoplasm during secretion.
• [Greek *ek* out of + *krinō* sift]

ecdysis *noun*
• "eck DIE sis"
• the action of casting off skin or shedding an exoskeleton etc.
• [modern Latin from Greek *ekdusis* from *ekduō* put off]

echelon *noun*
• "ESHA lon"
• a level or rank in an organization, in society, etc.; those occupying it.
• [French *échelon* from *échelle* ladder, from Latin *scala*]

echeveria *noun*
• "etch a VEERY uh"
• any succulent plant of the genus *Echeveria*, native to Central and S America, and grown in gardens and as a houseplant.
• [M. *Echeveri*, 19th-c. Mexican botanical illustrator]

echidna *noun*
• "e KIDNA"
• any of several egg-laying pouch-bearing mammals native to Australia and New Guinea, with a covering of spines, and having a long snout and long claws.
• [modern Latin from Greek *ekhidna* viper]

echinacea *noun*
• "ecka NAY shuh"
• a composite plant of the genus *Echinacea*, of eastern N America, esp. the purple coneflower, *E. purpurea*, cultivated as an ornamental.
• [as ECHINUS + Latin *-acea* 'of the nature of']

echinoderm *noun*
• "e KINE a durm" or "ECK'n a durm"
• any marine invertebrate of the phylum Echinodermata, usu. having a spiny skin, e.g. starfish and sea urchins.
• [ECHINUS + Greek *derma -atos* skin]

echinoid *noun*
• "e KINE oid"
• a sea urchin.
• [as ECHINUS]

echinus *noun*
• "e KINE us"
• any sea urchin of the genus *Echinus*.
• [Latin from Greek *ekhinos* hedgehog, sea urchin]

echo *noun*
• "ECKO"
• the repetition of a sound by the reflection of sound waves.
• [Latin from Greek *ēkhō*, related to *ēkhē* a sound]
• **echoer** *noun*
• **echoey** *adjective*
• **echoless** *adjective*

echocardiogram *noun*
• "ecko CARDY oh gram"
• a tracing or image obtained by echocardiography.
• [Latin *echo* from Greek *ēkhō*, related to *ēkhē* a sound + CARDIOGRAM]

echocardiography *noun*
• "ecko cardy OGGRA fee"
• the use of ultrasound waves to investigate the action of the heart.
• [Latin *echo* from Greek *ēkhō*, related to *ēkhē* a sound + CARDIOGRAPH]
• **echocardiograph** *noun*
• **echocardiographer** *noun*
• **echocardiographic** *adjective*

echoencephalogram *noun*
• "ecko en SEFFA luh gram"
• a tracing or image of the inside or contents of the skull obtained by by means of ultrasound.
• [Latin *echo* from Greek *ēkhō*, related to *ēkhē* a sound + ENCEPHALOGRAM]
• **echoencephalography** *noun*
"ecko en seffle OGGRA fee"

echogram *noun*
• "ECKO gram"
• a record produced by an echograph.

• [Latin *echo* from Greek *ēkhō*, related to *ēkhē* a sound + Greek *gramma* thing written]

echograph *noun*
• "ECKO graff"
• a device for measuring and recording ocean depths using sonic waves.
• [Latin *echo* from Greek *ēkhō*, related to *ēkhē* a sound + GRAPH]

echoic *adjective*
• "eck OH ick"
• (of a word) imitating the sound it represents; onomatopoeic.
• [as ECHO]
• **echoically** *adverb*

echolalia *noun*
• "ecko LAY lee uh"
• the meaningless repetition of another person's spoken words.
• [modern Latin from Greek *ēkhō* echo + *lalia* talk]

echolocation *noun*
• "ecko lo CAY sh'n"
• the location of objects by reflected sound.
• [Latin *echo* from Greek *ēkhō*, related to *ēkhē* a sound + LOCATION]
• **echolocate** *verb*

echovirus *noun*
• "ECKO vie russ"
• any of a group of enteroviruses sometimes causing mild meningitis, encephalitis, etc.
• [from *e*nteric *c*ytopathogenic *h*uman *o*rphan (because not originally assignable to any known disease) + VIRUS]

echt *adjective*
• "EKT"
• authentic, genuine, typical.
• [German]

eclair *noun*
• "ay CLAIR" or "e CLAIR"
• a small elongated cream puff filled with cream or custard and iced with chocolate or coffee icing.
• [French, lit. 'lightning flash']

eclampsia *noun*
• "e CLAMPSY uh"
• a condition involving convulsions leading to coma, occurring esp. in pregnant women.
• [modern Latin from French *eclampsie* from Greek *eklampsis* sudden development, from *eklampō* shine forth]
• **eclamptic** *adjective*

éclat *noun*
• "ay CLAW"
• brilliant display; dazzling effect.
• [French from *éclater* burst out]

eclectic *adjective*
• "e CLECTIC"
• deriving ideas, tastes, style, etc., from various sources.
• [Greek *eklektikos* from *eklegō* pick out]
• **eclectically** *adverb*
• **eclecticism** *noun* "e CLECTA sizm"

eclipse *noun*
• "e CLIPS"
• the obscuring of the reflected light from one celestial body by the passage of another between it and the eye or between it and its source of illumination.
• [Old French from Latin from Greek *ekleipsis* from *ekleipō* fail to appear, be eclipsed, from *leipō* leave]
• **eclipser** *noun*

ecliptic *noun*
• "e CLIPTIC"
• the sun's apparent path among the stars during the year.
• [Latin from Greek *ekleiptikos* (as ECLIPSE)]

eclogue *noun*
• "ECK log"
• a short poem, esp. a pastoral dialogue.
• [Latin *ecloga* from Greek *eklogē* selection, from *eklegō* pick out]

eclosion *noun*
• "e CLOE zh'n"
• the emergence of an insect from a pupa case or of a larva from an egg.
• [French *éclosion* from *éclore* hatch (Latin *ex* out of, *claudere* to close)]

ecocide *noun*
• "EEKO side"
• destruction of the natural environment.
• [as ECOLOGY + Latin *-cida, -cidium* from *caedere* kill]

ecology *noun*
• "e COLLA jee"
• the relations of organisms to one another and to their physical surroundings.
• [German *Ökologie* from Greek *oikos* house]
• **ecologic** *adjective*
• **ecological** *adjective*
• **ecologically** *adverb*
• **ecologist** *noun*

econometrics *noun*
• "e conna METRIX"
• the branch of economics that deals with the application of mathematics, esp. statistics, to economic data.
• [ECONOMY + METRIC]
• **econometric** *adjective*
• **econometrical** *adjective*
• **econometrician** *noun*
• **econometrist** *noun*

economical *adjective*
• "ecka NOMMA k'll" or "eeka NOMMA k'll"
• thrifty, careful in the use of resources, not wasteful.
• [as ECONOMY]
• **economically** *adverb*

economics *noun*
• "eeka NOMMIX" or "ecka NOMMIX"
• the social science of the production and distribution of wealth in theory and practice.
• [as ECONOMY]
• **economic** *adjective*

economist *noun*
• "e CONNA mist"
• an expert in or student of economics.
• [as ECONOMY]

economize *verb*
ALSO SPELLED: esp. *Brit.* **-ise**
• "e CONNA mize"
• practice economy, reduce expenses, or make savings in or on a commodity etc.
• [as ECONOMY]
• **economizer** *noun* (also esp. *Brit.* **-iser**)
• **economizing** *noun* (also esp. *Brit.* **-ising**)

economy *noun*
• "e CONNA mee"
• the wealth and resources of a community, esp. in terms of the production and consumption of goods and services.
• [French *économie* or Latin *oeconomia* from Greek *oikonomia* household management, from *oikos* house + *nemō* manage]

ecosphere *noun*
• "EEKO sfeer"
• the region of space around the sun or a star within which conditions compatible with the existence of life, esp. on planets, may theoretically occur.
• [ECOLOGY + SPHERE]

ecosystem *noun*
• "EEKO sist'm"
• a biological community of interacting organisms and their physical environment.
• [ECOLOGY + SYSTEM]

ecotage *noun*
• "EEKO tozh"
• acts of sabotage perpetrated in the name of environmental protection against individuals or companies perceived to be polluters, destroyers of natural resources, etc.
• [blend of ECOLOGICAL + SABOTAGE]

ecotone *noun*
• "EEKO tone"
• a region of transition between two ecological communities.
• [ECOLOGY + Greek *tonos*, lit. = 'tension']
• **ecotonal** *adjective*

ecotourism *noun*
• "eeko TOOR izm"
• tourism to exotic or wild, often threatened, natural environments, esp. intended to support conservation efforts.
• [ECOLOGY + 'tourism' from Old French *to(u)r* from Latin *tornus* from Greek *tornos* lathe]
• **ecotour** *noun*
• **ecotourist** *noun*

ecotoxicology *noun*
• "eeko toxa COLLA jee"
• the branch of science that deals with the nature, effects, and interactions of substances that are harmful to the environment.
• [ECOLOGY + TOXICOLOGY]

ecotype *noun*
• "EEKO tipe"
• a distinct form of a species occupying a particular habitat.
• [ECOLOGY + TYPE]
• **ecotypic** *adjective* "eeko TIPPIC"

ecru *noun*
• "AY croo"
• light brown or the colour of unbleached linen.
• [French *écru* unbleached, from *cru* raw]

ecstasy *noun*
• "EKSTA see"
• an overwhelming feeling of joy or rapture.
• [Old French *extasie* from Late Latin *extasis* from Greek *ekstasis* standing outside oneself, from *ek* out + *histēmi* to place]
• **ecstatic** *adjective* "ick STATTIC"
• **ecstatically** *adverb*

ectoblast *noun*
• "ECTO blast"
• the outermost layer of an embryo in early development, giving rise to epidermis and neural tissue.
• [Greek *ekto-* stem of *ektos* outside + *blastos* sprout]
• **ectoblastic** *adjective*

ectoderm *noun*
• "ECTO durm"
• the outermost layer of an embryo in early development, giving rise to epidermis and neural tissue.
• [Greek *ekto-* stem of *ektos* outside + DERMIS]
• **ectodermal** *adjective*
• **ectodermic** *adjective*

ectogenesis *noun*
• "ecto JENNA sis"
• reproduction occurring outside the body.
• [Greek *ekto-* stem of *ektos* outside + GENESIS]
• **ectogenetic** *adjective* "ecto juh NETTIC"
• **ectogenetically** *adverb*

ectomorph *noun*
• "ECTO morf"
• a person with a lean and delicate build of body and with a large skin surface in comparison with weight.
• [Greek *ekto-* stem of *ektos* outside + *morphē* form]
• **ectomorphic** *adjective*
• **ectomorphy** *noun*

ectoparasite *noun*
• "ecto PERRA site"
• a parasite that lives on the outside of its host.
• [Greek *ekto-* stem of *ektos* outside + PARASITE]
• **ectoparasitic** *adjective* "ecto perra SITTIC"

ectopic *adjective*
• "eck TOPPIC"
• occurring in an abnormal place or position.
• [modern Latin *ectopia* from Greek *ektopos* out of place]

ectoplasm *noun*
• "ECTO plazm"
• the dense, clear, outer layer of the cytoplasm in some cells.
• [Greek *ekto-* stem of *ektos* outside + PLASMA]
• **ectoplasmic** *adjective*

Ecuadorean *noun*
• "eckwa DORY 'n"
• a native or inhabitant of Ecuador in S America.

ecumene *noun*
• "ECK yoo meen"
• an inhabited area.
• [Greek *oikoumenē* the inhabited earth]

ecumenical *adjective*
• "eck yoo MENNA k'll" or "eek yoo MENNA k'll"
• of or representing the whole Christian world.
• [Late Latin *oecumenicus* from Greek *oikoumenikos* of the inhabited earth (*oikoumenē*)]
• **ecumenically** *adverb*

ecumenism *noun*
• "eck YOO m'n izm" or "ECK yoo m'n izm"
• the belief in or striving for the unity of Christians worldwide, transcending differences of doctrine.
• [as ECUMENICAL]

eczema *noun*
• "eck ZEE muh" or "ECKSA muh"
• non-infectious, superficial inflammation of the skin, usu. with itching and discharge from blisters.
• [modern Latin from Greek *ekzema -atos* from *ek* out + *zeō* boil]
• **eczematous** *adjective*

Edam *noun*
• "EE d'm" or "EE dam"
• a mild, round, pressed Dutch cheese, usu. pale yellow with a red rind.
• [*Edam*, a town in the NE Netherlands]

edamame *noun*
• "edda MAW may"
• a Japanese dish of salted green soybeans boiled in their pods, typically served as a snack or appetizer.
• [Japanese, literally 'beans on a branch']

edaphic *adjective*
• "e DAFFIC"
• of, pertaining to, produced, or influenced by the soil.
• [German *edaphisch* from Greek *edaphos* floor]

eddo *noun*
• "EDDO"
• a tropical aroid plant, *Colocasia esculenta*, with tuberous roots used as food; taro.
• [West African word]

edelweiss *noun*
• "AID'll vice"
• an alpine plant, *Leontopodium alpinum*, with woolly white bracts around the flower heads, growing in rocky places.
• [German from *edel* noble + *weiss* white]

edema *noun*
ALSO SPELLED: *Brit.* **oedema**
• "e DEEMA"
• a condition characterized by an excess of watery fluid collecting in the cavities or tissues of the body.
• [modern Latin, from Greek *oidēma*, from *oidein* to swell]
• **edematous** *adjective* (also esp. *Brit.* **oedematous**) "e DEMMA tuss"

Eden *noun*
• "EE d'n"
• a paradise or a delightful abode.
• [Late Latin from Greek *ēdēn* from Hebrew *'ēden*, originally = delight]
• **Edenic** *adjective* "e DEN ick"

edentate *adjective*
• "e DEN tate"
• having no or few teeth.
• [Latin *edentatus* (Latin *ex* out of, *dens dentis* tooth)]

edible *adjective*
• "EDDA bull"
• fit or suitable to be eaten.
• [Late Latin *edibilis* from *edere* eat]
• **edibility** *noun*

edict *noun*
• "EE dict"
• an order proclaimed by authority, esp. an ordinance or proclamation having the force of law.
• [Latin *edictum* from *edicere* proclaim]

edifice *noun*
• "EDDA fiss"
• a building, esp. a large, imposing, or stately one.
• [Old French from Latin *aedificium* from *aedis* dwelling + *-ficium* from *facere* make]

edify *verb*
• "EDDA fie"
• (of a circumstance, experience, etc.) instruct and improve morally or intellectually.
• [Old French *edifier* from Latin *aedificare* (as EDIFICE)]
• **edification** *noun*
• **edifying** *adjective*
• **edifyingly** *adverb*

editor *noun*
• "EDDA tur"
• a person who edits material for publication or broadcasting.
• [Late Latin, = producer (of games), publisher from *edere edit-* put out (*ex-* out, *dare* give)]
• **editorial** *adjective* "edda TORY 'll"

- **editorially** *adverb*
- **editorship** *noun*

editorialize *verb*
ALSO SPELLED: esp. *Brit.* **-ise**
- "edda TORY 'll ize"
- write editorials or comment editorially.
- [as EDITOR]
- **editorialist** *noun*

Edmontonian *noun*
- "ed m'n TONY 'n"
- a resident of Edmonton.

Edsonite *noun*
- "ED s'n ite"
- a resident of Edson, Alta.

educate *verb*
- "EDGE uh cate" or "ED yoo cate"
- give intellectual, moral, and social instruction to (a pupil, a child), esp. as a formal and prolonged process.
- [Latin *educare educat-*, related to *educere* EDUCE]
- **educability** *noun*
- **educable** *adjective*
- **educatable** *adjective*
- **educated** *adjective*
- **education** *noun*
- **educational** *adjective*
- **educationally** *adverb*
- **educationist** *noun*
- **educative** *adjective*
- **educator** *noun*

educe *verb*
- "e DYOOCE"
- evoke or bring out or develop from latent or potential existence.
- [Latin *educere educt-* lead out (Latin *ex* out of, *ducere* lead)]

edutainment *noun*
- "edge oo TANE m'nt" or "ed yoo TANE m'nt"
- entertainment with an educational aspect.
- [EDUCATE + 'entertainment' from French *entretenir*, ultimately from Latin *tenēre* hold]

Edwardian *adjective*
- "ed WAR dee 'n" ("WAR" can rhyme either with *FAR* or with *FOR*)
- of, characteristic of, or associated with the reign of Edward VII of England (1901–10).

eelpout *noun*
- "EEL pout"
- a freshwater fish, *Lota lota*, of the cod family, with a broad head and barbels.
- [Old English *ǣleputa*]

eerie *adjective*
- "EERY"
- gloomy, strange, or weird, esp. inspiring unease or fear.
- [originally Northern English and Scots *eri*, of obscure origin: compare Old English *earg* cowardly]
- **eerily** *adverb*
- **eeriness** *noun*

HOMOPHONES: *aerie*, *Erie*

efface *verb*
- "e FACE"
- rub or wipe out (a mark etc.).
- [French *effacer* (Latin *ex* out of, *facies* face)]
- **effacement** *noun*

effect *noun*
- "e FECT"
- the result or consequence of an action etc.
- [Old French *effect* or Latin *effectus* (Latin *ex* out of, *facere* make)]

HOMOPHONES: *affect*

effective *adjective*
- "e FECTIV"
- having a definite or desired effect.
- [as EFFECT]
- **effectively** *adverb*
- **effectiveness** *noun*
- **effectivity** *noun*

HOMOPHONES: *affective*, *affectivity*

effector *noun*
- "e FECTOR"
- an organ or cell acting in response to a stimulus.
- [as EFFECT]

effectual *adjective*
- "e FECK choo 'll"
- effective, efficacious, or capable of producing the intended result or effect.
- [as EFFECT]
- **effectuality** *noun*
- **effectually** *adverb*

effectuate *verb*
- "e FECK choo ate"
- cause to happen, put into effect, accomplish.
- [medieval Latin *effectuare* (as EFFECT)]

effeminate *adjective*
- "e FEMMA nit"
- (of a man) feminine in appearance or manner; unmasculine.
- [Latin *effeminatus* past participle of *effeminare* (*ex* out of, *femina* woman)]
- **effeminacy** *noun*
- **effeminately** *adverb*

effendi *noun*
- "ef FENDY"
- a man of education or standing in E Mediterranean or Arab countries.
- [Turkish *efendi* from modern Greek *afentēs* from Greek *authentēs* lord, master: see AUTHENTIC]

efferent *adjective*
- "EFFER 'nt"
- conducting outwards away from the central nervous system, an organ, etc.
- [Latin *efferre* (*ex* out of, *ferre* carry)]

effervesce *verb*
- "effer VESS"

• bubble or give off bubbles of gas, e.g. as a result of chemical reaction.
• [Latin *effervescere* (*ex* out of, *fervēre* be hot)]
• **effervescence** *noun*
• **effervescent** *adjective*

effete *adjective*
• "e FEET"
• decadent, degenerate, ineffectual, esp. as a result of overrefinement.
• [Latin *effetus* worn out by bearing young (*ex* out of, FETUS)]
• **effetely** *adverb*
• **effeteness** *noun*

efficacious *adjective*
• "effa CAY sh'ss"
• (of a thing) producing or sure to produce the desired effect; effective.
• [Latin *efficax* (as EFFICIENT)]
• **efficaciously** *adverb*
• **efficaciousness** *noun*
• **efficacy** *noun* "EFFA kuh see"

efficient *adjective*
• "e FISH 'nt"
• productive with minimum waste or effort.
• [Middle English from Latin *efficere* (*ex* out of, *facere* make, accomplish)]
• **efficiency** *noun*
• **efficiently** *adverb*

effigy *noun*
• "EFFA jee"
• a representation of a person in the form of a sculptured figure, dummy, etc.
• [Latin *effigies* from *effingere* to fashion]

effleurage *noun*
• "effla ROZH"
• a form of massage involving a circular inward stroking movement made with the flat or heel of the hand, used esp. during childbirth.
• [French from *effleurer* to skim, touch lightly]

effloresce *verb*
• "ef flor ESS"
• bloom or burst out into flower.
• [Latin *efflorescere* (*ex* out of, *florēre* to bloom, from *flos floris* flower)]
• **efflorescence** *noun*
• **efflorescent** *adjective*

effluence *noun*
• "EFF loo ince"
• a flowing out.
• [French *effluence* or medieval Latin *effluentia* from Latin *effluere efflux-* flow out (*ex* out of, *fluere* flow)]

effluent *noun*
• "EFF loo 'nt"
• sewage or industrial waste discharged into a body of water.
• [as EFFLUENCE]

effluvium *noun*
• "if LOOVY um"
• waste material or refuse, esp. when transported by water.
• [Latin, from *effluere* flow out]

efflux *noun*
• "EFF lucks"
• the action of flowing out or of emanating, e.g. of ions.
• [medieval Latin *effluxus* from *effluere* flow out]
• **effluxion** *noun*

effort *noun*
• "EFF'rt"
• strenuous physical or mental exertion.
• [French from Old French *esforcier*, ultimately from Latin *fortis* strong]
• **effortful** *adjective*
• **effortfully** *adverb*
• **effortless** *adjective*
• **effortlessly** *adverb*
• **effortlessness** *noun*

effrontery *noun*
• "e FRONTER ee"
• shameless insolence or impudent audacity.
• [French *effronterie* from *effronté*, ultimately from Late Latin *effrons -ontis* shameless (*ex* out of, *frons* forehead)]

effulgent *adjective*
• "e FUL j'nt" ("FUL" rhymes with *HULL*)
• radiant, resplendent, or shining out brilliantly.
• [Latin *effulgēre* shine forth (*ex* out of, *fulgēre* shine)]
• **effulgence** *noun*
• **effulgently** *adverb*

effusion *noun*
• "e FYOO zh'n"
• a copious outpouring.
• [Latin *effusio* from *effundere effus-* pour out (*ex* out of, *fundere* pour)]

effusive *adjective*
• "e FYOO siv"
• gushing, demonstrative, exuberant.
• [as EFFUSION]
• **effusively** *adverb*
• **effusiveness** *noun*

eft *noun*
• "EFT"
• a newt.
• [Old English *efeta*, of unknown origin]

egalitarian *adjective*
• "e gala TERRY 'n"
• of or relating to the principle of equal rights and opportunities for all.
• [French *égalitaire* from *égal* from Latin *aequalis* from *aequus* even]
• **egalitarianism** *noun*

eglantine *noun*
• "EGG l'n tine"
• a wild rose, *Rosa eglanteria*, with small fragrant leaves and flowers.

• [French *églantine* from Old French *aiglent*, ultimately from Latin *acus* needle]

ego *noun*
• "EEGO"
• oneself or the conscious, thinking subject.
• [Latin, = I]
• **egoless** *adjective*

egocentric *adjective*
• "eego SENTRIC"
• understanding the self as the centre of all experience with everything being considered only in relation to the self.
• [EGO + CENTRE]
• **egocentrically** *adverb*
• **egocentricity** *noun* "eego sen TRISSA tee"
• **egocentrism** *noun*

egoism *noun*
• "EEGO izm"
• an ethical theory that regards self-interest as the foundation of morality.
• [French *égoïsme*, ultimately from modern Latin *egoismus* (as EGO)]
• **egoist** *noun*
• **egoistic** *adjective*
• **egoistical** *adjective*
• **egoistically** *adverb*

egomania *noun*
• "eego MAINY uh"
• obsessive self-love or self-centredness.
• [as EGO + MANIA]
• **egomaniac** *noun*
• **egomaniacal** *adjective* "eego muh NIE a k'll"

egotism *noun*
• "EEGO tizm"
• the practice of continually talking about oneself.
• [as EGO]
• **egotist** *noun*
• **egotistic** *adjective*
• **egotistical** *adjective*
• **egotistically** *adverb*

egregious *adjective*
• "e GREEDGE iss"
• gross, flagrant, shocking, or outstandingly bad.
• [Latin *egregius* illustrious, lit. 'standing out from the flock' from *grex gregis* flock]
• **egregiously** *adverb*
• **egregiousness** *noun*

egress *noun*
• "EE gress"
• the action of going out or coming in.
• [Latin *egressus* from *egredi egress-* (*ex* out of, *gradi* to step)]

egret *noun*
• "EE grit"
• any of various herons of the genus *Egretta* or *Bulbulcus*, usu. having long white feathers in the breeding season.
• [Middle English, var. of AIGRETTE]

Egyptian *adjective*
• "e JIP sh'n"
• of or relating to ancient or modern Egypt, Egyptian, or Egyptians.

Egyptology *noun*
• "e jipt OLLA jee"
• the study of the language, history, and culture of ancient Egypt, esp. the branch of archaeology that deals with Egyptian antiquities.
• ['Egypt' + *logos* word]
• **Egyptological** *adjective*
• **Egyptologist** *noun*

eicosapentaenoic *adjective*
• "eye cossa penta ee NO ick"
• designating a polyunsaturated fatty acid found esp. in fish oils. In humans it is a metabolic precursor of prostaglandins.
• [Greek *eicosa-* twenty (the number of carbon atoms in the molecule) + *pente* five + '-ene' forming names of unsaturated hydrocarbons containing a double bond, from Greek *-ēnos*, adjective suffix denoting origin or source + *-oic* on the pattern of *methanoic*]

eider *noun*
• "IDER" (rhymes with *RIDER*)
• any large northern sea duck of the genera *Somateria* and *Polysticta*, esp. the common eider, *S. mollisima*, the male of which is largely black and white and the female dull brown, and which is the source of eiderdown, or the king eider.
• [Icelandic *aethr*]

eiderdown *noun*
• "IDER down" ("IDER" rhymes with *RIDER*)
• a quilt, sleeping bag, etc. stuffed with down (originally from the eider) or some other soft material, esp. as the upper layer of bedclothes.
• [as EIDER + 'down']

eidetic *adjective*
• "eye DETTIC"
• of, pertaining to, or designating a recollected mental image having unusual vividness and detail, as if actually visible.
• [German *eidetisch* from Greek *eidētikos* from *eidos* form]

eidolon *noun*
• "eye DOE lon"
• a spectre or phantom.
• [Greek *eidōlon*: see IDOL]

eigenfrequency *noun*
• "EYE g'n free kw'n see"
• any of the natural resonant frequencies of a system.
• [German *eigen* own + FREQUENT]

eigenfunction *noun*
• "EYE g'n funk sh'n"
• each of a set of independent functions which are solutions to a given differential equation.
• [German *eigen* own + 'function' from French

fonction from Latin *functio -onis* from *fungi funct-* perform]

eigenvalue *noun*
• "EYE g'n val yoo"
• each of a set of values of a parameter for which a differential equation has a non-zero solution, or eigenfunction, under given conditions.
• [German *eigen* own + 'value', from Old French *value*, feminine past participle of *valoir* be worth, from Latin *valēre*]

eighth *noun*
• "ATE 'th"
• the position in a sequence corresponding to the number 8 in the sequence 1–8.
• [Old English *ehta, eahta* eight]
• **eighthly** *adverb*

einkorn *noun*
• "INE corn"
• a kind of wheat (*Triticum monococcum*).
• [German from *ein* one + *Korn* seed]

Einsteinian *adjective*
• "ine STINEY 'n"
• of or relating to the German-American theoretical physicist Albert Einstein (d.1955) or his work.

einsteinium *noun*
• "ine STINEY um"
• a transuranic radioactive metallic element produced artificially from plutonium.
• [A. *Einstein*, German-American theoretical physicist d.1955]

eisteddfod *noun*
• "eye STETH vod" (with "TH" as in *BREATHE*) or "eye STED f'd"
• a congress of Welsh bards.
• [Welsh, lit. = 'session' from *eistedd* sit]
• **eisteddfodic** *adjective*

either *adjective*
• "EYE thur" or "EE thur" (with "TH" as in *THEN*)
• one or the other of two.
• [Old English *ǣgther* from Germanic]

eject *verb*
• "e JECT"
• send or drive out precipitately or by force.
• [Latin *ejicere eject-* (Latin *ex* out of, *jacere* throw)]
• **ejectable** *adjective*
• **ejection** *noun*
• **ejector** *noun*

ejecta *plural noun*
• "e JECTA"
• material that is thrown out, esp. from a volcano or a star.
• [Latin from *ejicere eject-* EJECT]

ejido *noun*
• "ay HEEDO"
• (in Mexico) a piece of land farmed communally under a system supported by the state.
• [Mexican Spanish, from Spanish, denoting common land on the road leading out of a village]

eke *verb*
• "EEK"
• contrive to make (a livelihood) or support (an existence).
• [Old English *ēacan*, related to Latin *augēre* increase]
HOMOPHONES: *eek*

ekka *noun*
• "ECKA"
• a small one-horse vehicle used in the Indian subcontinent.
• [Sanskrit, Hindi *ekkā* unit]

el *noun*
• "ELL"
• an elevated railway as part of a city's subway system.
• [abbreviation of 'elevated']
HOMOPHONES: *ell*

elaborate *adjective*
• "e LABBER it"
• carefully or minutely worked out.
• [Latin *elaboratus* past participle of *elaborare* (Latin *ex* out of, *labor* work)]
• **elaborately** *adverb*
• **elaborateness** *noun*
• **elaboration** *noun*

elaeagnus *noun*
• "elly AG nuss"
• any of various sometimes thorny trees of the genus *Elaeagnus*, esp. *E. angustifolia* bearing olive-shaped yellowish fruits.
• [modern Latin from Greek *elaiagnos* a kind of willow, from *elaia* olive tree + *agnos* chaste tree]

élan *noun*
• "ay LÃH" (with a nasal *AH*)
• style, vivacity, energy arising from enthusiasm.
• [French from *élancer* launch]

eland *noun*
• "EE l'nd"
• any antelope of the genus *Tragelaphus*, native to Africa, having spirally twisted horns, esp. the largest of living antelopes, *T. derbianus*.
• [Dutch, = moose]

elapse *verb*
• "e LAPS"
• (of time) pass by.
• [Latin *elabor elaps-* slip away]

elasmobranch *noun*
• "e LAZMA brank"
• any cartilaginous fish of the subclass Chondrichthyes, e.g. sharks, skates, rays.
• [modern Latin *elasmobranchii* from Greek *elasmos* beaten metal + *bragkhia* gills]

elasmosaur *noun*
• "e LAZMA sore"
• a large extinct marine reptile with paddle-like limbs and tough crocodile-like skin.
• [modern Latin from Greek *elasmos* beaten metal + *sauros* lizard]

elastane *noun*
• "e LASS tane"
• an elastic polyurethane fabric used in foundation garments, tights, bathing suits, and other tight-fitting stretchy garments.
• [as ELASTIC]

elastase *noun*
• "e LASS tace"
• a pancreatic enzyme which digests elastin.
• [as ELASTIN]

elastic *adjective*
• "e LASTIC"
• able to resume its normal bulk or shape spontaneously after contraction, dilatation, or distortion.
• [modern Latin *elasticus* from Greek *elastikos* propulsive, from *elaunō* drive]
• **elastically** *adverb*
• **elasticity** *noun* "e lass TISSA tee"

elasticated *adjective*
• "e LASTA cated"
• (of a fabric) made elastic by weaving with rubber thread.
• [as ELASTIC]

elasticized *adjective*
ALSO SPELLED: esp. *Brit.* **-ised**
• "e LASTA sized"
• (of a fabric) made elastic by weaving with rubber thread.
• [as ELASTIC]

elastin *noun*
• "e LASTIN"
• an elastic fibrous glycoprotein found in connective tissue.
• [as ELASTIC]

elastomer *noun*
• "e LASTA mur"
• a natural or synthetic rubber or rubber-like plastic.
• [as ELASTIC, after ISOMER]
• **elastomeric** *adjective* "e lasta MARE ick"

elate *verb*
• "e LATE"
• make very happy or proud; fill with joy.
• [Middle English from Latin *efferre elat-* raise]
• **elated** *adjective*
• **elatedly** *adverb*
• **elatedness** *noun*
• **elation** *noun*
HOMOPHONES: *illation*

elater *noun*
• "ELLA tur"
• a click beetle.
• [modern Latin from Greek *elatēr* driver, from *elaunō* drive]

eldritch *adjective*
• "ELD rich"
• weird; spooky.
• [16th c.: origin unknown]

elecampane *noun*
• "ella cam PANE"
• a sunflower-like plant, *Inula helenium*, with bitter aromatic leaves and roots, used in herbal medicine and cookery.
• [corruption of medieval Latin *enula* (for Latin *inula* from Greek *helenion) campana* (prob. = of the fields)]

elect *verb*
• "e LECT"
• choose (a person) by vote.
• [Latin *electus* past participle of *eligere elect-* (Latin *ex* out of, *legere* pick)]
• **electability** *noun*
• **electable** *adjective*
• **election** *noun*
• **elector** *noun*
• **electorship** *noun*

electioneer *verb*
• "e leck shuh NEER"
• take part in an election campaign.
• [as ELECT]
• **electioneering** *noun*

elective *adjective*
• "e LECTIV"
• (of an office or its holder) filled or appointed by election.
• [as ELECT]

electoral *adjective*
• "e LECTER 'll" or "e leck TORE 'll"
• relating to electors or elections.
• [as ELECT]
• **electorally** *adverb*

electorate *noun*
• "e LECTER it"
• the body of persons entitled to vote in a country or constituency.
• [as ELECT]

electret *noun*
• "e LECK trit"
• a permanently polarized piece of dielectric material, analogous to a permanent magnet.
• [ELECTRICITY + MAGNET]

electric *adjective*
• "e LECK trick"
• of, worked by, or charged with electricity.
• [modern Latin *electricus* from Latin *electrum* from Greek *ēlektron* amber, the rubbing of which causes electrostatic phenomena]
• **electrical** *adjective*
• **electrically** *adverb*

electrician *noun*
• "e leck TRISH'n"

• a person who installs or maintains electrical equipment, esp. professionally.
• [as ELECTRIC]

electricity *noun*
• "e leck TRISSA tee"
• a form of energy resulting from the existence of charged particles (electrons, protons, etc.), either statically as an accumulation of charge or dynamically as a current.
• [as ELECTRIC]

electrify *verb*
• "e LECTRA fie"
• charge with electricity; pass an electric current through.
• [as ELECTRIC]
• **electrification** *noun*
• **electrifier** *noun*

electro *noun*
• "e LECTRO"
• a copy made by the electrolytic deposition of copper on a mould, esp. for printing.
• [abbreviation]

electroacoustic *adjective*
• "e lectro a COO stick"
• involving the direct conversion of electrical into acoustic energy or vice versa.
• [ELECTRIC + ACOUSTIC]

electrocardiogram *noun*
• "e lectro CARDY oh gram"
• a chart or record produced by an electrocardiograph, used in the diagnosis of heart disease.
• [ELECTRIC + CARDIOGRAM]

electrocardiograph *noun*
• "e lectro CARDY oh graff"
• an instrument that records or displays the electric activity of the heart by means of electrodes attached to the skin.
• [ELECTRIC + CARDIOGRAPH]
• **electrocardiographic** *adjective*
• **electrocardiographically** *adverb*
• **electrocardiography** *noun*

electrochemistry *adjective*
• "e lectro KEMMA stree"
• the branch of science that deals with the relations between electrical and chemical phenomena.
• [ELECTRIC + CHEMISTRY]
• **electrochemical** *adjective*
• **electrochemically** *adverb*
• **electrochemist** *noun*

electrochromic *adjective*
• "e lectro CROME ick"
• changing colour when placed in an electric field.
• [ELECTRIC + CHROMIC]
• **electrochromism** *noun*

electroconvulsive *adjective*
• "e lectro k'n VULL siv"
• designating a method of treating certain mental illnesses in which an electric current is passed through the brain so as to produce a convulsion.
• [ELECTRIC + CONVULSIVE]

electrocute *verb*
• "e LECTRA cute"
• cause the death of (a person or animal) by means of an electric current.
• [ELECTRIC, after EXECUTE]
• **electrocution** *noun*

electrode *noun*
• "e LECTRODE"
• a conductor through which electricity enters or leaves an electrolyte, gas, vacuum, etc.
• [ELECTRIC + Greek *hodos* way]

electrodialysis *noun*
• "e lectro die ALA sis"
• dialysis in which the movement of ions is aided by electrodes placed on either side of a semi-permeable membrane.
• [ELECTRIC + DIALYSIS]

electrodynamics *noun*
• "e lectro die NAMMIX"
• the study of electric charges in motion, the forces created by electric and magnetic fields, and the relationship between them.
• [ELECTRIC + DYNAMIC]
• **electrodynamic** *adjective*

electroencephalogram *noun*
• "e lectro en SEFFA luh gram"
• a chart or record produced by an electroencephalograph.
• [ELECTRIC + ENCEPHALOGRAM]

electroencephalograph *noun*
• "e lectro en SEFFA luh graff"
• an instrument that records or displays the electrical activity of the brain, using electrodes attached to the scalp.
• [ELECTRIC + ENCEPHALOGRAPH]
• **electroencephalographic** *adjective*
• **electroencephalography** *noun*
"e lectro en seffle OGGRA fee"

electrologist *noun*
• "e leck TRAWLA jist"
• a person trained to remove excess body or facial hair using electrolysis.
• [ELECTRIC + *logos* word]

electroluminescence *noun*
• "e lectro loomin ESS ince"
• luminescence produced electrically, esp. by the application of a voltage.
• [ELECTRIC + LUMINESCENCE]
• **electroluminescent** *adjective*

electrolysis *noun*
• "e leck TRAWLA sis"
• chemical decomposition produced by passing an electric current through an electrolyte.
• [ELECTRIC + LYSIS]

- **electrolytic** *adjective* "e lectro LITTIC"
- **electrolytical** *adjective*
- **electrolytically** *adverb*

electrolyte *noun*
- "e LECTRA lite"
- a liquid, esp. that present in a battery, which contains ions and can be decomposed by electrolysis.
- [ELECTRIC + Greek *lutos* released from *luō* loosen]

electrolyze *verb*
ALSO SPELLED: esp. *Brit.* **-yse**
- "e LECTRA lize"
- subject to or treat by electrolysis.
- [ELECTROLYSIS after *analyze*]
- **electrolyzer** *noun* (esp. *Brit.* **-yser**)

electromagnet *noun*
- "e LECTRO magnet"
- a piece of soft iron that becomes magnetic when an electric current is passed through the coil surrounding it.
- [ELECTRIC + MAGNET]
- **electromagnetic** *adjective*
- **electromagnetically** *adverb*

electromagnetism *noun*
- "e lectro MAGNA tizm"
- the magnetic forces produced by electricity.
- [as ELECTROMAGNET]

electromechanical *adjective*
- "e lectro muh CANNA k'll"
- relating to the application of electricity to mechanical processes, devices, etc.
- [ELECTRIC + MECHANICAL]

electrometer *noun*
- "e leck TROMMA tur"
- an instrument for measuring small voltages without drawing any current from the circuit.
- [ELECTRIC + Greek *metron* measure]
- **electrometric** *adjective* "e lectro METRIC"
- **electrometry** *noun*

electromotive *adjective*
- "e lectro MOE tiv"
- producing or tending to produce an electric current.
- [ELECTRIC + Late Latin *motivus* from Latin *movēre mot-* move]

electromyogram *noun*
- "e lectro MY oh gram"
- a chart or record produced by an electromyograph.
- [ELECTRIC + Greek *mus muos* muscle, *gramma* thing written]

electromyograph *noun*
- "e lectro MY oh graff"
- an instrument that records or displays or converts into sound the electrical activity of muscle, using electrodes attached to the skin or inserted into the muscle.
- [ELECTRIC + Greek *mus muos* muscle, *graphia* writing]
- **electromyographic** *adjective*
- **electromyography** *noun*

electron *noun*
- "e LECTRON"
- a stable subatomic particle with a charge of negative electricity, found in all atoms and acting as the primary carrier of electricity in solids.
- [as ELECTRIC]

electronegative *adjective*
- "e lectro NEGGA tiv"
- (of an element) tending to acquire electrons in chemical reactions.
- [ELECTRIC + NEGATIVE]
- **electronegativity** *noun*

electronic *adjective*
- "e leck TRONNIC"
- produced by or involving the flow of electrons.
- [as ELECTRIC]
- **electronically** *adverb*

electronica *noun*
- "e leck TRONNA kuh"
- any of various kinds of electronically generated music.
- [as ELECTRONIC]

electronics *noun*
- "e leck TRONNIX"
- a branch of physics and technology concerned with the behaviour and movement of electrons in a vacuum, gas, semiconductor, etc.
- [as ELECTRONIC]

electrophilic *adjective*
- "e lectro FILLIC"
- having or involving an affinity for electrons.
- [ELECTRIC + Greek *philos* loving]
- **electrophile** *noun*

electrophoresis *noun*
- "e lectro for EE sis"
- the movement of charged particles in a fluid or gel under the influence of an electric field.
- [ELECTRIC + Greek *phorēsis* being carried]
- **electrophoretic** *adjective* "e lectro for ETTIC"
- **electrophoretically** *adverb*

electrophorus *noun*
- "e leck TROFFER us"
- a device for repeatedly generating static electricity by induction.
- [modern Latin from ELECTRIC + Greek *-phoros* bearing]

electrophysiology *noun*
- "e lectro fizzy OLLA jee"
- the branch of physiology that deals with the electrical phenomena associated with bodily processes.
- [ELECTRIC + PHYSIOLOGY]
- **electrophysiological** *adjective*
- **electrophysiologically** *adverb*

electroplate *verb*
• "e LECTRO plate"
• coat (a utensil etc.) by electrolytic deposition with chromium, silver, etc.
• [ELECTRIC + 'plate']
• **electroplater** *noun*

electroporation *noun*
• "e lectro por AY sh'n"
• the action or process of introducing DNA or chromosomes into the cells of bacteria etc. using a pulse of electricity to open the pores in the cell membranes briefly.
• [ELECTRIC + 'pore']

electropositive *adjective*
• "e lectro POZZA tiv"
• electrically positive.
• [ELECTRIC + POSITIVE]

electroscope *noun*
• "e LECTRO scope"
• an instrument for detecting and measuring electricity, esp. as an indication of the ionization of air by radioactivity.
• [ELECTRIC + Greek *skopos* target, from *skeptomai* look at]
• **electroscopic** *adjective*

electroshock *noun*
• "e LECTRO shock"
• a method of treating certain mental illnesses in which an electric current is passed through the brain so as to produce a convulsion.
• [ELECTRIC + 'shock' from French *choc* of unknown origin]

electrostatics *noun*
• "e lectro STATTIX"
• the study of stationary electric charges or fields as opposed to electric currents.
• [ELECTRIC + STATIC after *hydrostatic*]
• **electrostatic** *adjective*
• **electrostatically** *adverb*

electrotherapy *noun*
• "e lectro THERRA pee"
• the treatment of diseases by the use of electricity.
• [ELECTRIC + THERAPY]

electrothermal *adjective*
• "e lectro THURM'll"
• relating to heat electrically derived.
• [ELECTRIC + THERAPY]

electrotype *verb*
• "e LECTRO tipe"
• copy by the electrolytic deposition of copper on a mould, esp. for printing.
• [ELECTRIC + TYPE]
• **electrotyper** *noun*

electrovalent *adjective*
• "e lectro VALE 'nt"
• (of bonding) resulting from electrostatic attraction between ions.
• [ELECTRIC + *-valent* after *trivalent* etc.]
• **electrovalence** *noun*
• **electrovalency** *noun*

electroweak *adjective*
• "e lectro WEEK"
• relating to or denoting electromagnetic and weak interactions regarded as manifestations of the same interaction.
• [ELECTRIC + 'weak']

electrum *noun*
• "e LECK trum"
• an alloy of silver and gold used in ancient times.
• [Latin from Greek *ēlektron* amber, electrum]

electuary *noun*
• "e LECK choo airy"
• a medicinal substance mixed with honey or syrup.
• [Late Latin *electuarium*, prob. from Greek *ekleikton* from *ekleikhō* lick up]

eleemosynary *adjective*
• "ella MOSSA nerry"
• dependent on or supported by charity.
• [medieval Latin *eleemosynarius* from Late Latin *eleemosyna*: see ALMS]

elegant *adjective*
• "ELLA g'nt"
• tasteful, stylish, and refined in appearance.
• [French *élégant* or Latin *elegant-*, related to *eligere*: see ELECT]
• **elegance** *noun*
• **elegancy** *noun*
• **elegantly** *adverb*

elegiac *adjective*
• "ella JYE ick"
• (esp. of a work of art) having a pleasing quality of gentle and wistful mournfulness.
• [French *élégiaque*: see ELEGY]
• **elegiacally** *adverb*

elegy *noun*
• "ELLA jee"
• a song or poem of lamentation, esp. for the dead.
• [French *élégie* or Latin *elegia* from Greek *elegeia* from *elegos* mournful poem]
• **elegist** *noun*
• **elegize** *verb* (also esp. *Brit.* **-ise**)

element *noun*
• "ELLA m'nt"
• a component part or group; a contributing factor or thing.
• [Old French from Latin *elementum*]

elemental *adjective*
• "ella MENT'll"
• essential; basic.
• [as ELEMENT]

elementary *adjective*
• "ella MENTA ree"
• dealing with or arising from the simplest facts of a subject; rudimentary, introductory.

• [as ELEMENT]
• **elementarily** *adverb* "ella men TERRA lee"

elephant *noun*
• "ELLA f'nt"
• the largest living land animal, of which two species survive, the larger African (*Loxodonta africana*) and the smaller Indian (*Elephas maximus*), both with a trunk and long curved ivory tusks.
• [Old French *elefant*, ultimately from Latin *elephantus*, *elephans* from Greek *elephas -antos* ivory, elephant]
• **elephantine** *adjective*
• **elephantoid** *adjective*

elephantiasis *noun*
• "ella f'n TIE a sis"
• gross enlargement of the body, esp. the limbs, due to lymphatic obstruction by a nematode parasite transmitted by mosquitoes.
• [Latin from Greek (as ELEPHANT)]

Eleusinian *adjective*
• "el yoo SINNY 'n"
• of or relating to Eleusis near Athens, where annual celebrations were held in ancient times in honour of the goddess Demeter.
• [Latin *Eleusinius* from Greek *Eleusinios*]

elevate *verb*
• "ELLA vate"
• raise above the usual level or position.
• [Latin *elevare* raise (Latin *ex* out of, *levis* light)]
• **elevation** *noun*
• **elevational** *adjective*

elevator *noun*
• "ELLA vay tur"
• a platform or compartment housed in a shaft for raising and lowering persons or things to different floors of a building etc.
• [as ELEVATE]

elicit *verb*
• "e LISSIT"
• draw out or forth; evoke (an admission, response, etc.).
• [Latin *elicere elicit-* (Latin *ex* out of, *lacere* entice)]
• **elicitation** *noun*
• **elicitor** *noun*
HOMOPHONES: *illicit*

elide *verb*
• "e LIDE"
• omit (a vowel, consonant, or syllable) by elision.
• [Latin *elidere elis-* crush out (Latin *ex* out of, *laedere* knock)]

eligible *adjective*
• "ELLA juh bull"
• fit or entitled to be chosen for a position, award, etc.
• [French *éligible* from Late Latin *eligibilis* (as ELECT)]
• **eligibility** *noun*
• **eligibly** *adverb*

eliminate *verb*
• "e LIMMA nate"
• remove, get rid of.
• [Latin *eliminare* (Latin *ex* out of, *limen liminis* threshold)]
• **elimination** *noun*
• **eliminative** *adjective*
• **eliminator** *noun*

ELISA *noun*
• "e LIZE uh"
• a diagnostic technique for determining the amount of protein or other antigen in a blood sample by means of an enzyme-catalyzed colour change.
• [acronym from *e*nzyme-*l*inked *i*mmuno*s*orbent *a*ssay]

elision *noun*
• "e LIZH 'n"
• the omission of a vowel, consonant, or syllable in pronouncing (as in *I'm*, *let's*).
• [Late Latin *elisio* (as ELIDE)]

elite *noun*
• "e LEET" or "ay LEET"
• the best or choice part of a larger body or group.
• [French from past participle of *élire* from Romanic: related to ELECT]

elitism *noun*
• "e LEET izm" or "ay LEET izm"
• the advocacy or existence of an elite as a dominating element in a system or society.
• [as ELITE]
• **elitist** *noun*

elixir *noun*
• "e LIX ur"
• a preparation supposedly able to change metals into gold.
• [medieval Latin from Arabic *al-iksīr* from *al* the + *iksīr*, prob. from Greek *xērion* powder for drying wounds, from *xēros* dry]

Elizabethan *adjective*
• "e lizza BEETH 'n"
• of, belonging to, or characteristic of the period of Elizabeth I (d.1603).

ell *noun*
• "ELL"
• an extension of a building etc. which is at right angles to the main part.
• [representing the pronunciation of *L*, *l*, as the letter's name]
HOMOPHONES: *el*

ellagic *adjective*
• "el ADGE ick"
• designating an acid extracted from oak galls and various fruits and nuts. It has some ability to inhibit blood flow and retard the growth of cancer cells.
• [French *ellagique* (an anagram of *galle* gall nut + *-ique*), thus avoiding the form *gallique*, already in use]

ellipse *noun*
• "e LIPS"
• a regular oval, traced by a point moving in a plane so that the sum of its distances from two other points is constant, or resulting when a cone is cut by an oblique plane which does not intersect the base.
• [French from Latin *ellipsus* from Greek *elleipsis* from *elleipō* come short, from *en* in + *leipō* leave]

ellipsis *noun*
• "e LIP sis"
• the omission from a sentence of words not needed to complete the construction or sense.
• [as ELLIPSE]

ellipsoid *noun*
• "e LIP soid"
• a solid of which all the plane sections normal to one axis are circles and all the other plane sections are ellipses.
• [as ELLIPSE]
• **ellipsoidal** *adjective*

elliptic *adjective*
• "e LIP tick"
• of, relating to, or having the form of an ellipse or ellipsis.
• [Greek *elleiptikos* defective, from *elleipō* (as ELLIPSE)]
• **elliptically** *adverb*
• **ellipticity** *noun* "e lip TISSA tee"

elocution *noun*
• "ella KYOO sh'n"
• the art of clear and expressive speech, esp. of distinct pronunciation and articulation.
• [Latin *elocutio* from *eloqui elocut-* speak out (*ex* out of, *loqui* speak)]
• **elocutionary** *adjective*
• **elocutionist** *noun*

elongate *verb*
• "ee LONG gate" or "EE long gate"
• lengthen, prolong.
• [Late Latin *elongare* (Latin *ex* out of, *longus* long)]
• **elongated** *adjective*
• **elongation** *noun*

elope *verb*
• "e LOPE"
• run away secretly with a lover, esp. to get married.
• [Anglo-French *aloper* perhaps from a Middle English form *alope*, related to 'leap']
• **elopement** *noun*

eloquence *noun*
• "ELLA kwince"
• fluent and effective use of language or persuasive speaking or writing.
• [Old French from Latin *eloquentia* from *eloqui* speak out (*ex* out of, *loqui* speak)]
• **eloquent** *adjective*
• **eloquently** *adverb*

eluate *noun*
• "ELL yoo ate"
• a solution or gas stream obtained by elution.
• [as ELUTE]

elucidate *verb*
• "e LOO suh date"
• throw light on; explain, clarify.
• [Late Latin *elucidare* (Latin *ex* out of, LUCID)]
• **elucidation** *noun*
• **elucidative** *adjective*
• **elucidator** *noun*

elude *verb*
• "e LOOD"
• escape adroitly from (a danger, difficulty, pursuer, etc.); dodge.
• [Latin *eludere elus-* (*ex* out of, *ludere* play)]
HOMOPHONES: *allude*

elusive *adjective*
• "e LOO siv"
• difficult to find or catch; tending to elude.
• [as ELUDE]
• **elusively** *adverb*
• **elusiveness** *noun*
HOMOPHONES: *allusive, illusive, allusively, allusiveness*

elute *verb*
• "e LOOT"
• remove (an adsorbed substance) by washing with a solvent, esp. as a chromatographic technique.
• [Latin *eluere* wash out (*ex* out of, *luere lut-* wash)]
• **elution** *noun*

elutriate *verb*
• "e LOO tree ate"
• separate (lighter and heavier particles in a mixture) by suspension in an upward flow of liquid or gas.
• [Latin *elutriare elutriat-* (*ex* out of, *lutriare* wash)]
• **elutriation** *noun*

elver *noun*
• "ELVER"
• a young eel.
• [var. of *eel-fare* (see FARE) = a brood of young eels]

Elysian *noun*
• "e LEE zh'n" or "e LIZZY 'n"
• (in Greek mythology) designating the abode of the blessed after death.
• [Latin from Greek *Elusion* (*pedion* plain)]

elytron *noun*
• "ELLA tron"
• each of the two hard, often coloured wing-cases of a beetle or earwig.
• [Greek *elutron* sheath]

emaciated *adjective*
• "e MAY see ated"
• abnormally thin or feeble.

• [Latin *emaciare emaciat-* (*ex* out of, *macies* leanness)]
• **emaciation** *noun*

emanate *verb*
• "EMMA nate"
• issue, originate (from a source).
• [Latin *emanare* flow out]
• **emanation** *noun*
• **emanative** *adjective*

emancipate *verb*
• "e MANSA pate"
• free from restraint, esp. legal, social, or political.
• [Latin *emancipare* transfer property (*ex* out of, *manus* hand + *capere* take)]
• **emancipated** *adjective*
• **emancipation** *noun*
• **emancipator** *noun*
• **emancipatory** *adjective*

emasculate *verb*
• "e MASS kyoo late"
• deprive of force or vigour; make feeble or ineffective.
• [Latin *emasculatus* past participle of *emasculare* (*ex* out of, *masculus* diminutive of *mas* male)]
• **emasculation** *noun*
• **emasculator** *noun*
• **emasculatory** *adjective*

embalm *verb*
• "em BOM" or "em BAWLM"
• preserve (a corpse) from decay by means of arterial injection of a preservative, e.g. formaldehyde.
• [Old French *embaumer* (as BALM)]
• **embalmer** *noun*

embankment *noun*
• "em BANK m'nt"
• an earth or stone bank for keeping back water, or for carrying a road or railway.
• [from 'bank']

embargo *noun*
• "em BARGO"
• an order prohibiting ships from entering or leaving a country's ports, usu. issued in anticipation of war.
• [Spanish from *embargar* arrest]

embark *verb*
• "em BARK"
• put or go on board a ship or aircraft (to a destination).
• [French *embarquer* (Latin *in* in, *barca* ship's boat)]
• **embarkation** *noun*

embarrass *verb*
• "em BARE us"
• cause (a person) to feel awkward or self-conscious or ashamed.
• [French *embarrasser* (originally = hamper) from Spanish *embarazar* from Italian *imbarrare* bar in]
• **embarrassedly** *adverb*
• **embarrassingly** *adverb*
• **embarrassment** *noun*

embassy *noun*
• "EMBA see"
• the residence or offices of an ambassador.
• [earlier *ambassy* from Old French *ambassée* etc. from medieval Latin *ambasciata* from Romanic (as AMBASSADOR)]

embattled *adjective*
• "em BAT'ld"
• involved in a conflict or difficult undertaking.
• [Old French *embataillier* from *bataille*, ultimately from Late Latin *battualia* gladiatorial exercises, from Latin *battuere* beat]

embayment *noun*
• "em BAY m'nt"
• a portion of water or coast forming a bay.
• [Old French *baie* from Old Spanish *bahia*]

embellish *verb*
• "em BELL ish"
• beautify, adorn.
• [Old French *embellir* from *bel* handsome, from Latin *bellus*]
• **embellisher** *noun*
• **embellishment** *noun*

embezzle *verb*
• "em BEZZ'll"
• divert (money etc.) fraudulently to one's own use in violation of trust.
• [Anglo-French *embesiler* from Old French *besillier* maltreat, ravage, of unknown origin]
• **embezzlement** *noun*
• **embezzler** *noun*

embittered *adjective*
• "em BITTERD"
• intensely hostile, bitter, or discontented.
• [Old English *biter* having a disagreeable taste]
• **embitterment** *noun*

emblazon *verb*
• "em BLAY z'n"
• inscribe a conspicuous design, logo, slogan, etc. on (a surface).
• [as BLAZON]

emblem *noun*
• "EM blum"
• a symbol or representation typifying or identifying an institution, quality, etc.
• [Latin *emblema* from Greek *emblēma -matos* insertion, from *emballō* throw in, from *ballō* throw]
• **emblematic** *adjective*
• **emblematically** *adverb*

emblematize *verb*
ALSO SPELLED: esp. *Brit.* **-ise**
• "em BLEMMA tize"
• serve as an emblem of.
• [as EMBLEM]

embody *verb*
• "em BODY"
• give a concrete or discernible form to (an idea, concept, etc.).
• [from 'body' from Old English *bodig*, of unknown origin]
• **embodiment** *noun*

embolden *verb*
• "em BOLD'n"
• make bold; encourage.
• [Old English *bald* dangerous, from Germanic]

embolism *noun*
• "EMB'll izm"
• an obstruction of any artery by a clot of blood, air bubble, etc.
• [as EMBOLUS]

embolus *noun*
• "EMB'll us"
• an object causing an embolism.
• [Latin, = piston, from Greek *embolos* peg, stopper]
• **embolic** *adjective*

embonpoint *noun*
• "ãh bõh PWÃ" (with nasal *ah*, *oh*, and *A*)
• plumpness (of a person).
• [French *en bon point* in good condition]

emboss *verb*
• "em BOSS"
• carve or mould in relief.
• [Old French *boce* knob or stud in centre of shield]
• **embosser** *noun*
• **embossing** *noun*

embouchure *noun*
• "OMBA shoor"
• the mode of applying the mouth to the mouthpiece of a brass or woodwind instrument.
• [French from *emboucher* put in or to the mouth, from *bouche* mouth]

embourgeoisement *noun*
• "omm boor zhwozz MÃH" (with a nasal *AH*)
• conversion to a bourgeois outlook or way of life.
• [French, as BOURGEOIS]

embower *verb*
• "em BOWER" ("BOWER" rhymes with *FLOWER*)
• enclose as in a bower.
• [Old English *būr* garden, from Germanic]

embrace *verb*
• "em BRACE"
• hold (a person) closely in the arms, esp. as a sign of affection.
• [Old French *embracer*, ultimately from Latin *bracchium* arm]
• **embraceable** *adjective*
• **embracer** *noun*

embrasure *noun*
• "em BRAY zhur"
• the bevelling of a wall at the sides of a door or window; splaying.
• [French from *embraser* splay, of unknown origin]

embrittle *verb*
• "em BRIT'll"
• make or become brittle.
• [ultimately from a Germanic root related to Old English *brēotan* break up]
• **embrittlement** *noun*

embrocation *noun*
• "embro CAY sh'n"
• a liquid used for rubbing on the body to relieve muscular pain etc.
• [medieval Latin *embrocatio*, ultimately from Greek *embrokhē* lotion]

embroider *verb*
• "em BROY dur"
• decorate (cloth etc.) with needlework.
• [Anglo-French *enbrouder*]
• **embroiderer** *noun*
• **embroidery** *noun*

embroil *verb*
• "em BROIL"
• involve (a person, company, etc.) in conflict or difficulties.
• [Old French *embrouiller*]
• **embroilment** *noun*

embryo *noun*
• "EM bree oh"
• an unborn or unhatched offspring.
• [Late Latin *embryo -onis* from Greek *embruon* fetus, from *bruō* swell, grow]
• **embryoid** *adjective*
• **embryonal** *adjective* "em BRY 'n 'll"
• **embryonic** *adjective* "em bree ONNIC"
• **embryonically** *adverb*

embryogenesis *noun*
• "embree oh JENNA sis"
• the formation of an embryo.
• [as EMBRYO + GENESIS]

embryology *noun*
• "embree OLLA jee"
• the study of embryos.
• [as EMBRYO + *logos* word]
• **embryologic** *adjective*
• **embryological** *adjective*
• **embryologically** *adverb*
• **embryologist** *noun*

emend *verb*
• "e MEND"
• edit (a text etc.) to remove errors and corruptions.
• [Latin *emendare* (*ex* out of, *menda* fault)]
• **emendation** *noun*
HOMOPHONES: *amend*

emerald *noun*
• "EM ruld" or "EMMER uld"
• a bright green precious stone, a variety of beryl.

• [Old French *emeraude, esm-*, ultimately from Greek *smaragdos*]

emerg *noun*
• "e MURJ"
• *Cdn* the emergency department of a hospital.
• [abbreviation]
HOMOPHONES: *emerge*

emerge *verb*
• "e MURJ"
• come up or out into view, esp. when formerly concealed.
• [Latin *emergere emers-* (*ex* out of, *mergere* dip)]
• **emergence** *noun*
HOMOPHONES: *emerg*

emergency *noun*
• "e MURJ 'n see"
• a sudden state of danger, conflict, etc., requiring immediate action.
• [medieval Latin *emergentia* (as EMERGE)]

emergent *adjective*
• "e MURJ 'nt"
• becoming apparent; emerging.
• [as EMERGE]

emeritus *adjective*
• "e MERRIT us"
• retired and retaining one's title as an honour.
• [Latin, past participle of *emerēri* (*ex* out of, *merēri* earn)]

emerse *adjective*
• "e MURSE"
• (of part of an aquatic plant) reaching above the surface of the water.
• [as EMERGE]
• **emersed** *adjective*
HOMOPHONES: *immerse, immersed*

emersion *noun*
• "e MUR zh'n"
• the act or an instance of emerging.
• [Late Latin *emersio* (as EMERGE)]
HOMOPHONES: *immersion*

Emersonian *adjective*
• "emmer SO nee 'n"
• of or relating to the US poet and philosopher R. W. Emerson (d.1882) or his work.

emery *noun*
• "EMMER ee"
• a coarse rock of corundum and magnetite or hematite used for polishing metal or other hard materials.
• [French *émeri(l)* from Italian *smeriglio*, ultimately from Greek *smuris, smēris* polishing powder]

emesis *noun*
• "EMMA sis"
• vomiting.
• [Greek, from *emein* to vomit]

emetic *adjective*
• "e METTIC"
• that causes vomiting.
• [Greek *emetikos* from *emeō* vomit]

emic *adjective*
• "EEMIC"
• describing the structure of a particular language or culture in terms of its internal elements and their functioning, rather than in terms of any existing external scheme.
• [from PHONEMIC]

emigrate *verb*
• "EMMA grate"
• leave one's own country to settle in another.
• [Latin *emigrare emigrat-* (*ex* out of, *migrare* depart)]
• **emigrant** *noun*
• **emigration** *noun*

émigré *noun*
• "EMMA gray"
• an emigrant, esp. a political exile.
• [French, past participle of *émigrer* EMIGRATE]

eminent *adjective*
• "EMMA n'nt"
• distinguished, notable.
• [Latin *eminēre eminent-* jut]
• **eminence** *noun*
• **eminently** *adverb*

emir *noun*
• "em MEER"
• a title of various Muslim rulers, esp. in the Middle East.
• [French *émir* from Arabic *'amīr*]

emirate *noun*
• "EMMA rit" or "EMMA rate"
• the rank, domain, or reign of an emir.
• [as EMIR]

emissary *noun*
• "EMMA serry"
• a person sent as a diplomatic representative on a special mission.
• [Latin *emissarius* scout, spy (as EMIT)]

emission *noun*
• "e MISH'n"
• the process or an act of emitting.
• [Latin *emissio* (as EMIT)]

emissive *adjective*
• "e MISSIV"
• having the power to radiate light, heat, etc.
• [as EMIT]
• **emissivity** *noun*

emit *verb*
• "e MIT"
• send out (heat, light, exhaust, etc.).
• [Latin *emittere emiss-* (*ex* out of, *mittere* send)]
• **emitter** *noun*

Emmenthal *noun*
ALSO SPELLED: **Emmental**
• "EM 'n tawl"

• a kind of hard yellow Swiss cheese with many large holes in it, similar to Gruyère.
• [German *Emmentaler* from *Emmental* in Switzerland]

emmer *noun*
• "EMMER"
• a kind of wheat, *Triticum dicoccum*, grown mainly for fodder.
• [German dialect]

emmet *noun*
• "EMMIT"
• an ant.
• [Old English *ǣmete*]

emollient *adjective*
• "e MOLLY 'nt"
• that softens or soothes the skin.
• [Latin *emollire* (*ex* out of, *mollis* soft)]
• **emollience** *noun*

emolument *noun*
• "e MOLL yoo m'nt"
• a salary, fee, or profit from employment or office.
• [Old French *emolument* or Latin *emolumentum*, originally prob. 'payment for wheat grinding', from *emolere* (Latin *ex* out of, *molere* grind)]

emoticon *noun*
• "e MOTE a con"
• a (usu. sideways) representation of a facial expression constructed out of keyboard characters, added to an esp. email message to help establish the tone, e.g. ;-) representing a winking face or :-(representing a sad face.
• [blend of EMOTION + ICON]

emotion *noun*
• "e MOE sh'n"
• a strong mental or instinctive feeling such as love, sorrow, or fear.
• [earlier = agitation, disturbance of the mind, from French *émotion* from *émouvoir* excite]
• **emotional** *adjective*
• **emotionalism** *noun*
• **emotionalist** *noun*
• **emotionality** *noun*
• **emotionalize** *verb* (also esp. *Brit.* **-ise**)
• **emotionally** *adverb*
• **emotionless** *adjective*

emotive *adjective*
• "e MOE tiv"
• of or characterized by emotion.
• [Latin *emovēre emot-* (*ex* out of, *movēre* move)]
• **emotively** *adverb*
• **emotiveness** *noun*
• **emotivity** *noun* "eemo TIVVA tee"

empanada *noun*
• "empa NODDA"
• a baked or fried Spanish or Latin American turnover with a filling of meat, fish, cheese, fruit, or vegetables.
• [Spanish, feminine past participle of *empanar* bake or roll in pastry]

empathy *noun*
• "EMPA thee" (with "TH" as in *THIN*)
• the power of identifying oneself mentally with (and so fully comprehending) a person or object of contemplation.
• [translation of German *Einfühlung* from *ein* in + *Fühlung* feeling, after Greek *empatheia*: see SYMPATHY]
• **empathetic** *adjective*
• **empathetically** *adverb*
• **empathic** *adjective* "em PATHIC"
• **empathically** *adverb*
• **empathize** *verb* (also esp. *Brit.* **-ise**)

empennage *noun*
• "em PEN idge"
• the rear assembly of an aircraft, consisting of the stabilizer, elevators, fin, and rudder.
• [French from *empenner* to feather (an arrow)]

emperor *noun*
• "EMPER ur"
• the male sovereign of an empire.
• [Old French *emperere*, *empereor* from Latin *imperator -oris* from *imperare* command]
• **emperorship** *noun*

emphasis *noun*
• "EMFA sis"
• special importance or prominence attached to a thing, fact, idea, etc.
• [Latin from Greek from *emphainō* exhibit, from *phainō* show]
• **emphasize** *verb* (also esp. *Brit.* **-ise**)

emphatic *adjective*
• "em FATTIC"
• (of language, tone, or gesture) forcibly expressive.
• [Late Latin *emphaticus* from Greek *emphatikos* (as EMPHASIS)]
• **emphatically** *adverb*

emphysema *noun*
• "emfa ZEEMA" or "emfa SEEMA"
• enlargement of the air sacs of the lungs causing breathlessness.
• [Late Latin from Greek *emphusēma* from *emphusaō* puff up]
• **emphysematous** *adjective*

empirical *adjective*
• "em PEERA k'll"
• based or acting on observation or experiment, not on theory.
• [Latin *empiricus* from Greek *empeirikos* from *empeiria* experience, from *empeiros* skilled]
• **empiric** *adjective*
• **empirically** *adverb*

empiricism *noun*
• "em PEERA sizm"
• the theory that all knowledge is derived from sense-experience.
• [as EMPIRICAL]
• **empiricist** *noun*

emplace *verb*
- "em PLACE"
- put into a specified position; situate.
- [French *emplacement* from Old French *place* via Latin *platea* from Greek *plateia (hodos)* broad (way)]
- **emplacement** *noun*

emplane *verb*
- "em PLANE"
- go or put on board an airplane.
- [from 'plane', from Latin *planum* flat surface, neuter of *planus* plain (differentiated from 'plain' in 17th c.)]

employable *adjective*
- "em PLOYA bull"
- qualified for employment and available for work.
- [Old French *employer*, ultimately from Latin *implicari* be involved, from *implicare* enfold: see IMPLICATE]
- **employability** *noun*

emporium *noun*
- "em PORY um"
- a specialized retail store etc.
- [Latin from Greek *emporion* from *emporos* merchant]

empower *verb*
- "em POWER"
- authorize, license.
- [Anglo-French *poer* ultimately from Latin *posse* be able]
- **empowerment** *noun*

empress *noun*
- "EM press"
- the wife or widow of an emperor.
- [Old French *emperesse* feminine of *emperere* EMPEROR]

empty *adjective*
- "EM tee"
- containing nothing.
- [Old English *ǣmtig, ǣmetig* from *ǣmetta* leisure]
- **emptily** *adverb*
- **emptiness** *noun*

empurple *verb*
- "em PURP'll"
- make purple or red.
- [from 'purple' (Old English alteration of *purpure purpuran* from Latin *purpura* from Greek *porphura*)]

empyema *noun*
- "em pie EEMA" or "em pee EEMA"
- a collection of pus in a cavity, esp. in the pleura.
- [Late Latin from Greek *empuēma* from *empueō* suppurate, from *puon* pus]

empyrean *noun*
- "em PIRRY 'n"
- the highest heaven, as the sphere of fire in ancient cosmology or as the abode of God in early Christianity.
- [medieval Latin *empyreus* from Greek *empurios*, from *pur* fire]
- **empyreal** *adjective*

HOMOPHONES: *imperial*

emulate *verb*
- "EM yuh late"
- try to equal or excel.
- [Latin *aemulat-* rivalled, equalled, from *aemulari* from *aemulus* rival]
- **emulation** *noun*
- **emulative** *adjective*
- **emulator** *noun*

emulsifier *noun*
- "e MULL suh fie ur"
- any substance that stabilizes an emulsion, esp. a food additive used to stabilize processed foods.
- [as EMULSION]

emulsify *verb*
- "e MULL suh fie"
- convert into an emulsion.
- [as EMULSION]
- **emulsifiable** *adjective*
- **emulsification** *noun*

emulsion *noun*
- "e MULL sh'n"
- a fine dispersion of one liquid in another, esp. as paint, medicine, etc.
- [French *émulsion* or modern Latin *emulsio* from *emulgēre* (Latin *ex* out of, *mulgēre muls-* to milk)]

enable *verb*
- "in AY bull"
- give (a person etc.) the means or authority to do something.
- [from 'able', from Latin *habilis* handy, from *habēre* to hold]
- **enabler** *noun*

enabling *adjective*
- "in AY bling"
- (of legislation) empowering a person or body to take certain action.
- [as ENABLE]

enact *verb*
- "in ACT"
- establish (a law, legal penalty, etc.).
- [Middle English, ultimately from Latin *agere act-* do]
- **enaction** *noun*
- **enactive** *adjective*
- **enactment** *noun*

enamel *noun*
- "in AM'll"
- a glasslike opaque or semi-transparent coating on metallic or other hard surfaces for ornament or as a preservative lining.
- [Anglo-French *enameler, enamailler* from Old French *esmail* from Germanic]

- **enameller** *noun*
- **enamelwork** *noun*

enamour *verb*

ALSO SPELLED: **enamor**

- "in AMMER"
- inspire with love or liking.
- [Old French *enamourer* from *amourer* (as AMOUR)]

enantiodromia *noun*

- "en anty a DROMEY uh"
- the process by which something becomes its opposite, and the effects of this.
- [Greek, = running in contrary ways, from *enantio* opposite + *dromos* running]

enantiomer *noun*

- "en ANTY a mur"
- a molecule that is the mirror image of another.
- [Greek *enantios* opposite + *meros* part, share]
- **enantiomeric** *adjective* "en anty a MARE ick"
- **enantiomerically** *adverb*

enantiomorph *noun*

- "en ANTY a morf"
- a mirror image; a form (esp. of a crystal structure etc.) related to another as an object is to its mirror image.
- [German from Greek *enantios* opposite + *morphē* form]
- **enantiomorphic** *adjective*
- **enantiomorphism** *noun*
- **enantiomorphous** *adjective*

enarthrosis *noun*

- "en ar THROW sis"
- a ball-and-socket joint.
- [Greek from *enarthros* jointed, from *arthron* joint]

encaenia *noun*

- "en SEENY uh"
- *Cdn* (at the University of New Brunswick and the University of King's College in Halifax) graduation ceremonies.
- [Latin from Greek *egkainia*, from *kainos* new]

encamp *verb*

- "en CAMP"
- settle in a military camp.
- ['camp' from French *camp* from Italian *campo* from Latin *campus* level ground]
- **encampment** *noun*

encapsulate *verb*

- "en CAPS'll ate" or "en CAPS yuh late"
- enclose in or as in a capsule.
- [as CAPSULE]
- **encapsulation** *noun*
- **encapsulator** *noun*

encase *verb*

- "en CASE"
- put into a case.
- [from 'case' from Old French *casse*, *chasse*, from Latin *capsa* from *capere* hold]
- **encasement** *noun*

encaustic *adjective*

- "en COSS tick"
- (in painting, ceramics, etc.) using pigments mixed with hot wax, which are burned in as an inlay.
- [Latin *encausticus* from Greek *egkaustikos* (as CAUSTIC)]

enceinte *noun*

- "on SANT"
- an enclosure, esp. in fortification.
- [French, ultimately from Latin *cingere cinct-* gird: see CINCTURE]

encephalic *adjective*

- "ensa FALIC"
- of or relating to the brain.
- [Greek *egkephalos* brain, from *kephalē* head]

encephalitis *noun*

- "en seffa LITE iss"
- inflammation of the brain.
- [as ENCEPHALIC + Greek *-itis*, forming feminine of adjectives in *-itēs* (with *nosos* 'disease' implied)]
- **encephalitic** *adjective* "en seffa LITTIC"

encephalogram *noun*

- "en SEFFA luh gram"
- an X-ray photograph of the brain.
- [as ENCEPHALIC]

encephalograph *noun*

- "en SEFFA luh graff"
- an instrument that records or displays the electrical activity of the brain, using electrodes attached to the scalp.
- [as ENCEPHALIC]

encephalomyelitis *noun*

- "en seffa lo my a LITE iss"
- inflammation of the brain and spinal cord, esp. due to viral infection.
- [as ENCEPHALIC + MYELITIS]

encephalon *noun*

- "en SEFFA lon"
- the brain.
- [as ENCEPHALIC]

encephalopathy *noun*

- "en seffa LOPPA thee" (with "TH" as in *THIN*)
- disease of the brain.
- [as ENCEPHALIC + Greek *patheia* suffering]
- **encephalopathic** *adjective* "en seffa luh PATHIC"

enchant *verb*

- "en CHANT"
- charm, delight.
- [French *enchanter* from Latin *incantare* (Latin *in* in, *canere cant-* sing)]
- **enchantedly** *adverb*
- **enchanter** *noun*
- **enchanting** *adjective*
- **enchantingly** *adverb*
- **enchantment** *noun*
- **enchantress** *noun*

enchase *verb*
• "en CHASE"
• place (a jewel) in a setting.
• [French *enchâsser* (as ENCASE)]

enchilada *noun*
• "encha LODDA"
• a tortilla with chili sauce and usu. a filling, esp. meat.
• [Latin American Spanish, feminine past participle of *enchilar* season with chili]

encipher *verb*
• "en SIFE ur"
• write (a message etc.) in cipher.
• [as CIPHER]
• **encipherment** *noun*

encircle *verb*
• "en SURK'll"
• surround, encompass.
• [Old French *cercle* from Latin *circulus* diminutive of *circus* ring]
• **encirclement** *noun*

enclave *noun*
• "ON clave" or "EN clave"
• a portion of territory of one state surrounded by territory of another or others, as viewed by the surrounding territory.
• [French from *enclaver*, ultimately from Latin *clavis* key]

enclitic *adjective*
• "en CLITTIC"
• (of a word) pronounced with very little emphasis and usually shortened and forming part of the preceding word.
• [Late Latin *encliticus* from Greek *egklitikos*, from *klinō* lean]
• **enclitically** *adverb*

enclose *verb*
• "en CLOZE"
• surround with a wall, fence, etc.
• [Old French *enclos* past participle of *enclore*, ultimately from Latin *includere* (as INCLUDE)]
• **enclosure** *noun*

encode *verb*
• "en CODE"
• put (a message etc.) into code or cipher.
• [Old French *code* from Latin CODEX]
• **encoder** *noun*

encomium *noun*
• "en CO mee um"
• a formal or high-flown expression of praise.
• [Latin from Greek *egkōmion*, from *kōmos* revelry]
• **encomiastic** *adjective* "en co mee ASTIC"

encompass *verb*
• "en CUMPUS"
• surround or form a circle about.
• [as COMPASS]

encore *noun*
• "ON core"
• a call by an audience or spectators for the repetition of an item, or for a further item.
• [French, = once again]

encounter *verb*
• "en COUNT ur"
• meet, come across, esp. by chance or unexpectedly.
• [Old French *encontrer*, *encontre*, ultimately from Latin *contra* against]

encourage *verb*
• "en CUR idge"
• give courage, confidence, or hope to.
• [French *encourager* (as COURAGE)]
• **encouragement** *noun*
• **encourager** *noun*
• **encouraging** *adjective*
• **encouragingly** *adverb*

encroach *verb*
• "en CROACH"
• intrude, esp. on another's territory or rights.
• [Old French *encrochier* from *crochier* from *croc* hook, from Old Norse *krókr* hook]
• **encroacher** *noun*
• **encroachment** *noun*

encrust *verb*
• "en CRUST"
• cover with a crust.
• ['crust' from Old French *crouste* from Latin *crusta* rind, shell]

encrypt *verb*
• "en CRIPT"
• convert (data) into code, esp. to prevent unauthorized access.
• [as CRYPT]
• **encryption** *noun*

enculturation *noun*
• "in cull chur AY sh'n"
• the process by which the values and norms of a society are passed on to or acquired by its members.
• [as CULTURE]
• **enculturate** *verb*

encumber *verb*
• "en CUMBER"
• be a burden to.
• [Old French *encombrer* block up, from Romanic]
• **encumberment** *noun*
• **encumbrance** *noun*

encyclical *noun*
• "en SICK luh k'll"
• a papal letter addressed to bishops and all members of the Roman Catholic Church.
• [Late Latin *encyclicus* from Greek *egkuklios* from *kuklos* circle]

encyclopedia *noun*
ALSO SPELLED: **encyclopaedia**
• "en sike luh PEEDY uh"
• a book or set of books, usu. arranged

alphabetically, giving information on many subjects or on many aspects of one subject.
• [modern Latin from spurious Greek *egkuklopaideia* for *egkuklios paideia* all-round education: compare ENCYCLICAL]

encyclopedic *adjective*
ALSO SPELLED: **encyclopaedic**
• "en sike luh PEED ick"
• of, pertaining to, or resembling an encyclopedia, esp. in embracing all branches of learning.
• [as ENCYCLOPEDIA]

encyclopedist *noun*
ALSO SPELLED: **encyclopaedist**
• "en sike luh PEED ist"
• a person who writes, edits, compiles, or contributes to an encyclopedia.
• [as ENCYCLOPEDIA]

encyst *verb*
• "en SIST"
• enclose or become enclosed in a cyst.
• [as CYST]
• **encysted** *adjective*
• **encystment** *noun*
HOMOPHONES: *insist*

endanger *verb*
• "en DANE jur"
• place in danger.
• [from 'danger', earlier sense 'jurisdiction, power', from Old French *dangier*, ultimately from Latin *dominus* lord]
• **endangerment** *noun*

endear *verb*
• "en DEER"
• make dear to or beloved by.
• [Old English *dēore* from Germanic; compare Dutch *dier* beloved, German *teuer* expensive]
• **endearing** *adjective*
• **endearingly** *adverb*

endearment *noun*
• "en DEER m'nt"
• an expression of love, affection, or fondness such as a pet name, caress, etc.
• [as ENDEAR]

endeavour *verb*
ALSO SPELLED: **endeavor**
• "en DEVVER"
• try earnestly.
• [Middle English from *put oneself in devoir* 'do one's utmost': see DEVOIR]

endemic *adjective*
• "en DEMMIC"
• (of a disease, condition, etc.) of common occurrence or habitually present in a certain area as a result of permanent local factors.
• [modern Latin *endemicus* from Greek *endēmos* native, from *dēmos* the people]
• **endemically** *adverb*
• **endemicity** *noun* "en dem ISSA tee"
• **endemism** *noun* "END'm izm"

endocarditis *noun*
• "endo car DITE iss"
• inflammation of the endocardium.
• [ENDOCARDIUM + Greek *-itis*, forming feminine of adjectives in *-itēs* (with *nosos* 'disease' implied)]

endocardium *noun*
• "endo CARDY um"
• the smooth membrane lining the cavities and valves of the heart.
• [Greek *endon* within + *kardia* heart]

endocarp *noun*
• "ENDO carp"
• the innermost layer of the pericarp of a fruit, which lines the seed chamber.
• [Greek *endon* within + PERICARP]
• **endocarpal** *adjective*

endocrine *adjective*
• "ENDO crine" or "ENDO crin"
• (of a gland) secreting directly into the blood; ductless.
• [Greek *endon* within + *krinō* sift]

endocrinology *noun*
• "endo crin OLLA jee"
• the branch of medicine that deals with the structure and physiology of endocrine glands and hormones.
• [as ENDOCRINE + *logos* word]
• **endocrinological** *adjective*
• **endocrinologist** *noun*

endocytosis *noun*
• "endo sye TOE sis"
• the taking in of matter by a living cell by invagination of its membrane.
• [Greek *endon* within + *cyto-* cells, from Greek *kutos* vessel]

endoderm *noun*
• "ENDO durm"
• the innermost layer of an animal embryo in early development.
• [Greek *endon* within + *derma* skin]
• **endodermal** *adjective*

endodontics *noun*
• "endo DONTIX"
• the branch of dentistry that deals with the prevention, diagnosis, and treatment of diseases of tooth pulp and the surrounding tissues, e.g. root canals.
• [Greek *endon* within + *odous odont-* tooth]
• **endodontist** *noun*

endogamy *noun*
• "en DOGGA mee"
• the custom of marrying only within the same tribe, clan, community, etc.
• [Greek *endon* within + *gamos* marriage]
• **endogamic** *adjective* "endo GAMMIC"
• **endogamous** *adjective*

endogenous *adjective*
• "en DODGE a nuss"
• growing or originating from within.

• [Greek *endon* within + GENESIS]
• **endogenously** *adverb*

endolymph *noun*
• "ENDO limf"
• the fluid in the membranous labyrinth of the ear.
• [Greek *endon* within + LYMPH]
• **endolymphatic** *adjective*

endometriosis *noun*
• "endo meetree OH sis"
• a condition in which endometrial tissue grows in the pelvic cavity, resulting in pelvic pain and the formation of cysts.
• [as ENDOMETRIUM]

endometrium *noun*
• "endo MEETREE um"
• the mucous membrane lining the uterus.
• [Greek *endon* within + *mētra* womb]
• **endometrial** *adjective*
• **endometritis** *noun* "endo mee TRITE iss"

endomorph *noun*
• "ENDO morf"
• a person with a soft round build of body and a high proportion of fat tissue.
• [Greek *endon* within + *morphē* form]
• **endomorphic** *adjective*
• **endomorphy** *noun*

endomorphism *noun*
• "endo MORF izm"
• a change in cooling molten rock caused by reaction with the surrounding rock mass or assimilation of fragments of it.
• [as ENDOMORPH]

endoparasite *noun*
• "endo PERRA site"
• a parasite that lives on the inside of its host.
• [Greek *endon* within + PARASITE]
• **endoparasitic** *adjective* "endo perra SITTIC"

endophyte *noun*
• "ENDO fite"
• a plant growing inside a plant or animal.
• [Greek *endon* within + *phuton* plant, from *phuō* come into being]

endoplasm *noun*
• "ENDO plazm"
• the inner, usu. granular, fluid of the cytoplasm of some cells, e.g. amoebae.
• [Greek *endon* within + PLASMA]
• **endoplasmic** *adjective*

endorphin *noun*
• "en DORE fin"
• any of a group of peptide neurotransmitters occurring naturally in the brain and having pain-relieving properties.
• [French *endorphine* from *endogène* endogenous + MORPHINE]

endorse *verb*
• "en DORSE"
• declare one's approval of (a candidate etc.).
• [medieval Latin *indorsare* (Latin *in* in, *dorsum* back)]
• **endorsable** *adjective*
• **endorsation** *noun*
• **endorsee** *noun*
• **endorsement** *noun*
• **endorser** *noun*

endoscope *noun*
• "ENDO scope"
• a flexible instrument, consisting of illuminated optical tubes, designed for viewing the internal cavities or hollow organs of the body, such as the lungs, stomach, or bowel.
• [Greek *endon* within + *skopos* target, from *skeptomai* look at]
• **endoscopic** *adjective*
• **endoscopically** *adverb*
• **endoscopist** *noun* "en DOSCA pist"
• **endoscopy** *noun* "en DOSCA pee"

endoskeleton *noun*
• "ENDO skella t'n"
• an internal skeleton as found in vertebrates.
• [Greek *endon* within + SKELETON]
• **endoskeletal** *adjective*

endosperm *noun*
• "ENDO spurm"
• nutritive material surrounding the germ in some plant seeds.
• [Greek *endon* within + Latin *sperma* seed]

endospore *noun*
• "ENDO spore"
• a resistant, asexual spore that develops inside a vegetative bacterial cell.
• [Greek *endon* within + SPORE]

endothelium *noun*
• "endo THEELY um"
• a layer of cells lining the blood vessels, heart, and lymphatic vessels.
• [Greek *endon* within + *thēlē* teat]
• **endothelial** *adjective*

endothermic *adjective*
• "endo THURMIC"
• occurring or formed with the absorption of heat.
• [Greek *endon* within + *thermē* heat]
• **endothermy** *noun*

endotoxin *noun*
• "ENDO toxin"
• a toxin present inside a bacterial cell and released when the cell disintegrates.
• [Greek *endon* within + TOXIN]
• **endotoxic** *adjective*

endow *verb*
• "en DOW" ("DOW" rhymes with *COW*)
• bequeath or give a permanent income to (a person, institution, etc.).
• [Anglo-French *endouer* from Old French *douer* from Latin *dotare* from *dos dotis* DOWER]
• **endowed** *adjective*
• **endowment** *noun*

endue *verb*
• "en DYOO"
• invest or provide (a person) with qualities, powers, etc.
• [earlier = induct, put on clothes: Middle English from Old French *enduire* from Latin *inducere* lead in, assoc. in sense with Latin *induere* put on (clothes)]

endure *verb*
• "en DYUR" or "en DUR"
• (of a person) undergo (a difficulty, hardship, etc.), esp. without giving way.
• [Old French *endurer* from Latin *indurare* harden (Latin *in* in, *durus* hard)]
• **endurability** *noun*
• **endurable** *adjective*
• **endurance** *noun*
• **enduring** *adjective*
• **enduringly** *adverb*

enduro *noun*
• "en DYUR oh"
• a long-distance race for motor vehicles, designed to test endurance rather than speed.
• [as ENDURE]

enema *noun*
• "ENNA muh"
• the injection of liquid or gas into the rectum or colon, esp. to expel the contents.
• [Late Latin from Greek *enema* from *eniēmi* inject, from *hiēmi* send]

enemy *noun*
• "ENNA mee"
• a person or group actively nursing hatred for or seeking to harm another person, group, or cause.
• [Old French *enemi* from Latin *inimicus* (*in-* not, without, *amicus* friend)]

energetic *adjective*
• "enner JETTIC"
• having much energy or being strenuously active.
• [Greek *energētikos* from *energeō*, from *ergon* work]
• **energetically** *adverb*

energetics *noun*
• "enner JETTIX"
• the branch of science that deals with energy.
• [as ENERGETIC]

energize *verb*
ALSO SPELLED: esp. *Brit.* **-ise**
• "ENNER jize"
• infuse energy or vigour into (a person, work, movement, etc.).
• [as ENERGY]
• **energized** *adjective* (also esp. *Brit.* **-ised**)
• **energizer** *noun* (also esp. *Brit.* **-iser**)

energumen *noun*
• "enner GYOO m'n"
• an enthusiast or fanatic.
• [Late Latin *energumenus* from Greek *energoumenos* passive participle of *energeō*: see ENERGETIC]

energy *noun*
• "ENNER jee"
• a person's force, vigour, or capacity for and tendency to strenuous activity.
• [French *énergie* or Late Latin *energia* from Greek *energeia* from *ergon* work]

enervate *verb*
• "ENNER vate"
• deprive of vigour, vitality, or strength, mentally, morally, or physically.
• [Latin *enervatus* past participle of *enervare* (*ex* out of, *nervus* sinew)]
• **enervated** *adjective*
• **enervating** *adjective*
• **enervation** *noun*
HOMOPHONES: *innervate*

enfeeble *verb*
• "en FEEBLE"
• weaken, make feeble.
• [from 'feeble' from Old French *feble, fleible* from Latin *flebilis* lamentable, from *flēre* weep]
• **enfeebled** *adjective*
• **enfeeblement** *noun*

enfilade *noun*
• "en fill ADE"
• a suite of rooms with doorways in line with each other.
• [French from *enfiler*, from *fil* thread]

enfold *verb*
• "en FOLD"
• wrap up, envelop, or enclose.
• [Old English *falden, fealden* from Germanic]

enforce *verb*
• "en FORCE"
• compel performance or observance of (a law etc.).
• [Old French *enforcir*, *-ier*, ultimately from Latin *fortis* strong]
• **enforceability** *noun*
• **enforceable** *adjective*
• **enforcement** *noun*
• **enforcer** *noun*

enfranchise *verb*
• "en FRAN chize"
• grant (a person) the rights of a citizen, esp. the right to vote.
• [Old French *enfranchir*, from *franc franche* from medieval Latin *francus* free, from 'Frank' (since only Franks had full freedom in Frankish Gaul)]
• **enfranchisement** *noun*

engage *verb*
• "en GAGE"
• arrange to employ or hire (a person).
• [French *engager*]
• **engagement** *noun*
• **engager** *noun*

engagé *adjective*
• "on ga ZHAY"
• (of a writer, artist, etc.) showing social, moral, or political commitment.
• [French, past participle of *engager*: see ENGAGE]

engaged *adjective*
• "en GAGED"
• under a promise to marry.
• [as ENGAGE]

engaging *adjective*
• "en GAGE ing"
• pleasing, attractive, charming.
• [as ENGAGE]
• **engagingly** *adverb*

engender *verb*
• "en JEN dur"
• give rise to; bring about (a feeling etc.).
• [Old French *engendrer* from Latin *ingenerare* (Latin *in* in, *generare* GENERATE)]

engorge *verb*
• "en GORGE"
• cause to swell with blood, water, breast milk, or another fluid.
• [French *engorger* from Old French *gorge* throat, ultimately from Latin *gurges* whirlpool]
• **engorged** *adjective*
• **engorgement** *noun*

engram *noun*
• "EN gram"
• a supposed permanent and physical change in the brain accounting for the existence of memory.
• [German *Engramm* from Greek *en* in + *gramma* letter of the alphabet]
• **engrammatic** *adjective*

engrave *verb*
• "en GRAVE"
• inscribe, cut, or carve (a text or design) on a hard surface.
• [Old English *grafan* dig, engrave, from Germanic: related to 'groove']
• **engraved** *adjective*
• **engraver** *noun*
• **engraving** *noun*

engross *verb*
• "en GROSE" ("GROSE" rhymes with *DOSE*)
• (of an object of thought or feeling) fully occupy (the mind, affections, etc.).
• [Anglo-French *engrosser* from *en gros* wholesale]
• **engrossedly** *adverb*
• **engrossing** *adjective*
• **engrossment** *noun*

engulf *verb*
• "en GULF"
• flow over and swamp or swallow up as in a gulf, abyss, etc.
• [from 'gulf', from Old French *golfe* from Italian *golfo*, ultimately from Greek *kolpos* bosom, gulf]
• **engulfment** *noun*

enhance *verb*
• "en HANCE"
• heighten or intensify (qualities, powers, value, etc.).
• [Anglo-French *enhauncer*, prob. alteration from Old French *enhaucier*, ultimately from Latin *altus* high]
• **enhancement** *noun*
• **enhancer** *noun*

enharmonic *adjective*
• "en har MONNIC"
• of or having intervals smaller than a semitone (esp. such intervals as that between G sharp and A flat, these notes being made the same in a scale of equal temperament).
• [Late Latin *enharmonicus* from Greek *enarmonikos* from *harmonia* HARMONY]
• **enharmonically** *adverb*

enigma *noun*
• "in IG muh"
• a puzzling, perplexing, or unexplained thing.
• [Latin *aenigma* from Greek *ainigma -matos* from *ainissomai* speak allusively, from *ainos* fable]
• **enigmatic** *adjective* "en ig MATTIC"
• **enigmatical** *adjective*
• **enigmatically** *adverb*

enjambment *noun*
ALSO SPELLED: **enjambement**
• "en JAMB m'nt" or "en JAM m'nt"
• the continuation of a sentence without a pause beyond the end of a line, couplet, or stanza.
• [French *enjambement* from *enjamber*, from *jambe* leg]
• **enjamb** *verb*
• **enjambed** *adjective*

enjoin *verb*
• "en JOIN"
• command, order, or call upon (a person).
• [Old French *enjoindre* from Latin *injungere* (Latin *in* in, *jungere* join)]

enkephalin *noun*
• "en KEFFA lin"
• either of two morphine-like peptides occurring naturally in the brain and thought to control levels of pain.
• [Greek *egkephalos* brain]

enkindle *verb*
• "in KIN d'll"
• cause (flames) to flare up.
• [as KINDLE]

enlace *verb*
• "en LACE"
• encircle tightly.
• [Old French *enlacier*, ultimately from Latin *laqueus* noose]

enlarge *verb*
- "en LARGE"
- make or become larger or wider.
- [Old French *large* from feminine of Latin *largus* copious]
- **enlarged** *adjective*
- **enlargement** *noun*

enlarger *noun*
- "en LAR jur"
- an apparatus for producing photographic enlargements.
- [as ENLARGE]

enlighten *verb*
- "en LITE 'n"
- instruct or inform (about a subject).
- [from 'light', from Old English *lēoht, līht, līhtan* from Germanic]
- **enlightening** *adjective*
- **enlightenment** *noun*

enlightened *adjective*
- "en LITE 'nd"
- having or showing an understanding of people's needs, a situation, etc. that is not based on old-fashioned attitudes and prejudice.
- [as ENLIGHTEN]

enlist *verb*
- "en LIST"
- enrol in the armed forces.
- [from 'list', from Old English *liste* border, strip, from Germanic]
- **enlister** *noun*
- **enlistment** *noun*

enliven *verb*
- "en LIE v'n"
- animate, invigorate, give fuller life or spirit to.
- [from 'live', from Old English *libban, lifian,* from Germanic]
- **enlivener** *noun*
- **enlivening** *adjective*
- **enlivenment** *noun*

enmesh *verb*
- "en MESH"
- catch or entangle in or as in a net.
- [from 'mesh', from Middle Dutch *maesche* from Germanic]
- **enmeshment** *noun*

enmity *noun*
- "ENMA tee"
- the condition of being an enemy or a state of mutual hostility.
- [Old French *enemitié* from Romanic (as ENEMY)]

ennead *noun*
- "ENNY ad"
- a group of nine.
- [Greek *enneas enneados* from *ennea* nine]

ennoble *verb*
- "en NO bull"
- refine, dignify, or elevate in nature, character etc.
- [French *ennoblir* from Old French *noble* from Latin *(g)nobilis* noble]
- **ennoblement** *noun*
- **ennobling** *adjective*

ennui *noun*
- "on WEE"
- boredom or mental weariness from lack of occupation or interest.
- [French from Latin *in odio*: compare ODIUM]

enoki *noun*
- "ee NOCKY"
- a long-stemmed edible white Japanese mushroom with a tiny cap.
- [Japanese *enoki(-take)* Chinese nettle tree (mushroom)]

enormity *noun*
- "in ORMA tee"
- monstrous wickedness.
- [French *énormité* from Latin *enormitas -tatis* from *enormis* (as ENORMOUS)]

enormous *adjective*
- "in OR muss"
- huge, very great, excessive in size or intensity.
- [Latin *enormis* (*ex* out of, *norma* pattern, standard)]
- **enormously** *adverb*
- **enormousness** *noun*

enosis *noun*
- "en OH sis" or "ENNO sis"
- political union as an ideal or proposal, esp. that between Cyprus and Greece.
- [modern Greek *enōsis* from *ena* one]

enrage *verb*
- "en RAGE"
- make furious or very angry.
- [Old French *enrager*, from *rager*, ultimately from Latin RABIES]
- **enraged** *adjective*

enrapture *verb*
- "en RAP chur"
- give intense pleasure or joy to.
- [as RAPTURE]

enrich *verb*
- "en RICH"
- make wealthy or wealthier.
- [Old French *enrichir* from *riche* rich, powerful, of Germanic origin]
- **enriched** *adjective*
- **enriching** *adjective*
- **enrichment** *noun*

enrobe *verb*
- "en ROBE"
- cover with a coating.
- [Old French from Germanic (related to 'rob', original sense 'booty')]
- **enrober** *noun*

enrol *verb*
ALSO SPELLED: **enroll**
• "en ROLL"
• enter one's name on a list or register, esp. as a commitment to membership of a society, class, etc.
• [Old French *enroller* from *rolle* roll, from Latin *rotulus*, diminutive of *rota* wheel]
• **enrollee** *noun*
• **enrolment** *noun* (also **enrollment**)

ensconce *verb*
• "en SCONCE"
• establish or settle comfortably, safely, or secretly.
• [as SCONCE]

ensemble *noun*
• "on SOM bull"
• a thing viewed as the sum of its parts.
• [French, ultimately from Latin *insimul* (Latin *in* in, *simul* at the same time)]

enshrine *verb*
• "en SHRINE"
• enclose in or as in a shrine.
• [from 'shrine', Old English *scrīn* from Germanic from Latin *scrinium* case for books etc.]
• **enshrinement** *noun*

enshroud *verb*
• "en SHROUD" (rhymes with *LOUD*)
• cover with or as with a shroud.
• [Old English *scrūd* shroud]

ensign *noun*
• "EN sine" or "EN s'n"
• a military or naval standard, esp. a flag flown at the stern of a vessel to show its nationality.
• [Old French *enseigne* from Latin *insignia*: see INSIGNIA]

ensilage *noun*
• "EN sill idge" or "IN sill idge"
• the process of preserving green crops in a silo or pit without having previously dried them.
• [as SILO]

ensile *verb*
• "en SILE" or "in SILE"
• put (fodder) into a silo or closed pit for preservation.
• [French *ensiler* from Spanish *ensilar* (as SILO)]

enslave *verb*
• "en SLAVE"
• make (a person) completely subject to or dominated by habit, superstition, passion, etc.
• [from 'slave', from Old French *esclave* from medieval Latin *sclavus*, *sclava*, a captive]
• **enslavement** *noun*
• **enslaver** *noun*

ensnare *verb*
• "en SNARE"
• entrap, entangle in difficulties, or catch in or as in a snare.
• [as SNARE]

ensoul *verb*
• "en SOLE"
• endow with a soul.
• [from 'soul', from Old English *sāwol*, *sāwel*, *sāwl*, from Germanic]
• **ensoulment** *noun*

ensue *verb*
• "en SUE"
• be subsequent or happen afterwards.
• [Old French *ensuivre*, ultimately from Latin *sequi* follow]
• **ensuing** *adjective*

ensuite *noun*
• "on SWEET"
• a bathroom forming a single unit with another room, with one room leading into another.
• [French, = in sequence]

entablature *noun*
• "en TABLA chur"
• the upper part of a classical building supported by columns or a colonnade, comprising architrave, frieze, and cornice.
• [Italian *intavolatura* from *intavolare* board up (Latin *in* in, *tavola* table)]

entablement *noun*
• "en TABLE m'nt"
• a platform supporting a statue, above the dado and base.
• [French, from *entabler* from Old French *table* from Latin *tabula* plank, tablet, list]

entail *verb*
• "en TALE"
• necessitate as a consequence, have as an inevitable accompaniment, or involve unavoidably.
• [Middle English, from Anglo-French *taile* notch, cut, tax, from *taillier* cut, ultimately from Latin *talea* twig]
• **entailment** *noun*

entangle *verb*
• "en TANGLE"
• cause to get caught in something that is tangled or that impedes movement or extrication.
• [from 'tangle', prob. from Norwegian *taangel* from Old Norse *thöngull*]
• **entanglement** *noun*

entasis *noun*
• "ENTA sis"
• a slight convex curve in a column shaft to correct the visual illusion that straight sides give of curving inwards.
• [modern Latin from Greek from *enteinō* to stretch]

entelechy *noun*
• "en TELLA kee"
• (in Aristotle's use) the condition in which a potentiality has become an actuality, esp. the

soul, essential nature, or informing principle of a living thing.
• [Late Latin *entelechia* from Greek *entelekheia*, from *telos* end, perfection + *ekhein* be in a state]

entente *noun*
• "on TONT"
• a friendly understanding between nations.
• [French, = understanding (as INTENTION)]

enteric *adjective*
• "en TARE ick"
• of, pertaining to, or occurring in the intestines.
• [Greek *enterikos* from *enteron* intestine]

enteritis *noun*
• "enter ITE iss"
• inflammation of the small intestine, often causing diarrhea.
• [Greek *enteron* intestine + *-itis*, forming feminine of adjectives in *-itēs* (with *nosos* 'disease' implied)]

enterobacteria *noun*
• "enter oh back TEERY uh"
• a class of rod-like, Gram-negative bacteria that occur either normally or pathologically in the intestine, e.g. salmonella.
• [Greek *enteron* intestine + BACTERIA]

enterocolitis *noun*
• "enter oh kuh LITE iss"
• inflammation of the small intestine and the colon.
• [Greek *enteron* intestine + COLON + *-itis*, forming feminine of adjectives in *-itēs* (with *nosos* 'disease' implied)]

enterostomy *noun*
• "enter OSSTA mee"
• a surgical operation in which the small intestine is brought through the abdominal wall and opened, in order to bypass the stomach or the colon.
• [Greek *enteron* intestine + *stoma* mouth]

enterovirus *noun*
• "enter oh VIE russ"
• a genus of small RNA viruses which typically occur in the gastrointestinal tract, but include the poliovirus and the virus of hepatitis A.
• [Greek *enteron* intestine + VIRUS]

enterprise *noun*
• "ENTER prize"
• an undertaking, esp. a bold or difficult one.
• [Old French *entreprise* feminine past participle of *entreprendre* var. of *emprendre*, ultimately from Latin *prendere*, *prehendere* take]
• **enterpriser** *noun*

enterprising *adjective*
• "ENTER prize ing"
• ready to engage in enterprises.
• [as ENTERPRISE]
• **enterprisingly** *adverb*

enthalpy *noun*
• "ENTH'll pee" or "en THALPY"
• the total thermodynamic heat content of a system.
• [Greek *enthalpō* warm in, from *thalpō* to heat]

enthrall *verb*
ALSO SPELLED: **enthral**
• "en THRAWL" (rhymes with *DOLL*)
• captivate, please greatly.
• [as THRALL]
• **enthralling** *adjective*
• **enthrallment** *noun* (also **enthralment**)

enthrone *verb*
• "en THRONE"
• install (a king, bishop, etc.) on a throne, esp. ceremonially.
• [from 'throne', from Old French *trone* from Latin *thronus* from Greek *thronos* high seat]
• **enthronement** *noun*

enthusiasm *noun*
• "in THOOZY azm" or "in THYOOZY azm"
• strong interest or admiration.
• [French *enthousiasme* or Late Latin *enthusiasmus* from Greek *enthousiasmos* from *entheos* possessed by a god, inspired, from *theos* god]
• **enthuse** *verb*
• **enthusiast** *noun*
• **enthusiastic** *adjective*
• **enthusiastically** *adverb*

enthymeme *noun*
• "ENTH'm eem"
• a syllogism in which one premise is not explicitly stated.
• [Latin *enthymema* from Greek *enthumēma* from *enthumeomai* consider, from *thumos* mind]

entice *verb*
• "en TICE"
• lure or attract by the offer of pleasure or reward.
• [Old French *enticier* prob. from Romanic]
• **enticement** *noun*
• **enticer** *noun*
• **enticing** *adjective*
• **enticingly** *adverb*

entitle *verb*
• "en TITLE"
• give (a person etc.) a just claim.
• [from 'title' from Old French from Latin *titulus* placard, title]
• **entitlement** *noun*

entity *noun*
• "ENTA tee"
• a thing with distinct and independent existence.
• [French *entité* or medieval Latin *entitas* from Late Latin *ens* being]

entomb *verb*
• "in TOOM"
• place in or as in a tomb.

- [as TOMB]
- **entombment** *noun*

entomology *noun*
- "enta MOLLA jee"
- the study of the forms and behaviour of insects.
- [Greek *entomos* cut up (in neuter = 'insect') from *temnō* cut + *logos* word]
- **entomological** *adjective*
- **entomologist** *noun*

entomophagous *adjective*
- "enta MOFFA guss"
- insect-eating.
- [as ENTOMOLOGY + Greek *phagō* eat]

entomophilous *adjective*
- "enta MOFFA luss"
- pollinated by insects.
- [as ENTOMOLOGY + Greek *philos* dear, loving]

entourage *noun*
- "ONTA rozh"
- people attending an esp. important person.
- [French from *entourer* surround]

entrails *plural noun*
- "EN trails"
- the intestines of a person or animal.
- [Old French *entrailles* from medieval Latin *intralia* alteration of Latin *interaneus* internal, from *inter* among]

entrain *verb*
- "en TRAIN"
- (of a fluid) carry (particles etc.) along in its flow.
- [French *entraîner*, from *traîner* drag, ultimately from Latin *trahere* draw]
- **entrainment** *noun*

entrance[1] *noun*
- "EN trince"
- the act or an instance of coming or going in.
- [Old French from Latin *intrare* go in]

entrance[2] *verb*
- "en TRANCE"
- fill someone with wonder and delight, holding their entire attention.
- [Old French *transe* from *transir* depart, fall into a trance, from Latin *transire*: see TRANSIENT]
- **entrancement** *noun*
- **entrancing** *adjective*
- **entrancingly** *adverb*

entranceway *noun*
- "EN trince way"
- a passage or hallway at the entrance to a building etc.
- [as ENTRANCE[1]]

entrant *noun*
- "EN tr'nt"
- a person who enters a competition; a candidate in an examination etc.
- [French, present participle of *entrer*: see ENTRANCE[1]]

entrap *verb*
- "en TRAP"
- catch in or as in a trap.
- [from 'trap' from Old English *treppe*, *træppe*, related to Middle Dutch *trappe*, medieval Latin *trappa*, of uncertain origin]
- **entrapment** *noun*

entreat *verb*
- "en TREET"
- ask (a person) earnestly.
- [Old French *entraiter*, from *traiter* treat, from Latin *tractare* handle, frequentative of *trahere tract-* draw, pull]
- **entreatingly** *adverb*
- **entreaty** *noun*

entrechat *noun*
- "ontra SHAH"
- a jump in ballet, in which the dancer beats the legs in the air and criss-crosses them at least once.
- [French from Italian (*capriola*) *intrecciata* complicated (caper)]

entrecôte *noun*
- "ONTRA cote"
- a boned steak cut off the sirloin.
- [French from *entre* between + *côte* rib]

entree *noun*
- "ON tray"
- the main dish of a meal.
- [French, = 'entry']

entremets *noun*
- "ontra MAY"
- a sweet dish.
- [French from *entre* between + *mets* dish]

entrench *verb*
- "en TRENCH"
- establish firmly (in a defensible position, in office, etc.).
- [from 'trench' from Old French *trenche* (n.) *trenchier* (v.), ultimately from Latin *truncare* TRUNCATE]
- **entrenched** *adjective*
- **entrenchment** *noun*

entrepôt *noun*
- "ONTRA poe"
- a warehouse for temporary storage of goods in transit.
- [French from *entreposer* store, from *entre-* (from Latin *inter* between) + *poser* place]

entrepreneur *noun*
- "ontra pruh NUR"
- a person who starts or organizes a commercial enterprise, esp. one involving financial risk.
- [French from *entreprendre* undertake: see ENTERPRISE]
- **entrepreneurial** *adjective*
- **entrepreneurialism** *noun*
- **entrepreneurially** *adverb*
- **entrepreneurism** *noun*
- **entrepreneurship** *noun*

entresol *noun*
• "ONTRA sawl"
• a low storey between the ground floor and the floor above; a mezzanine floor.
• [French from *entre* between + *sol* ground]

entropy *noun*
• "ENTRA pee"
• a measure of the unavailability of a system's thermal energy for conversion into mechanical work.
• [German *Entropie*, from Greek *tropē* transformation]
• **entropic** *adjective* "en TROPPIC"
• **entropically** *adverb*

entrust *verb*
• "en TRUST"
• give responsibility for (a person or a thing) to a person in whom one has confidence.
• [from 'trust', from Old Norse *traust* from *traustr* strong]

entwine *verb*
• "en TWINE"
• twine together (a thing with or around another).
• [from 'twine', from Old English *twīn*, *twigin* linen, ultimately from the stem of *twi-* two]

enucleate *verb*
• "in NEW clee ate"
• extract (a tumour etc.).
• [Latin *enucleare* (*ex* out of, NUCLEUS)]
• **enucleation** *noun*

enumerate *verb*
• "in NYOOMER ate" or "in NOOMER ate"
• specify (items); mention one by one.
• [Latin *enumerare* (*ex* out of, *numerare* number)]
• **enumerable** *adjective*
• **enumeration** *noun*
• **enumerative** *adjective*
• **enumerator** *noun*
HOMOPHONES: *innumerable*

enunciate *verb*
• "in NUN see ate"
• pronounce (words) clearly.
• [Latin *enuntiare* (*ex* out of, *nuntiare* announce, from *nuntius* messenger)]
• **enunciation** *noun*

enuresis *noun*
• "en yur EE sis"
• involuntary urination.
• [modern Latin from Greek *enoureō* urinate in, from *ouron* urine]
• **enuretic** *adjective* "en yur ETTIC"

envelop *verb*
• "in VELLUP"
• wrap up or cover completely.
• [Old French *envoluper*]
• **envelopment** *noun*

envelope *noun*
• "ENVA lope" or "ONVA lope"
• a folded paper container, usu. with a sealable flap, for a letter etc.
• [as ENVELOP]

envenom *verb*
• "en VEN'm"
• put poison on or into; make poisonous.
• [as VENOM]

enviable *adjective*
• "ENVY a bull"
• (of a person or thing) exciting or likely to excite envy.
• [from 'envy', from Old French *envie* from Latin *invidia* from *invidēre* envy, from *vidēre* see]
• **enviably** *adverb*

envious *adjective*
• "ENVY us"
• feeling or showing envy.
• [as ENVIABLE]
• **enviously** *adverb*

environ *verb*
• "in VIE run"
• encircle, surround (esp. hostilely or protectively).
• [Old French *environer* from *environ* surroundings, from *en* in + *viron* circuit from *virer* turn, perhaps alteration of Latin *gyrare* GYRATE]

environment *noun*
• "en VIE run m'nt" or "en VIE urn m'nt"
• the physical surroundings, conditions, circumstances, etc., in which a person lives, works, etc.
• [as ENVIRON]
• **environmental** *adjective*
• **environmentalism** *noun*
• **environmentalist** *noun*
• **environmentally** *adverb*

environs *plural noun*
• "en VIRE enz"
• a surrounding district, esp. around an urban area.
• [as ENVIRON]

envisage *verb*
• "en VIZ idge"
• have a mental picture of (a thing or conditions not yet existing).
• [French *envisager* (as VISAGE)]
• **envisagement** *noun*

envision *verb*
• "en VIZH'n"
• envisage, visualize.
• [as VISION]

envoi *noun*
ALSO SPELLED: **envoy**
• "EN voy"
• a short stanza concluding a ballade etc.
• [Old French *envoi*, from *envoyer* (as ENVOY)]
HOMOPHONES: *envoy*

envoy *noun*
- "ON voy" or "EN voy"
- a messenger or representative, esp. on a diplomatic mission.
- [French *envoyé*, past participle of *envoyer* send, from *en voie* on the way, from Latin *via*]

HOMOPHONES: *envoi*

enzootic *adjective*
- "en zo OTTIC"
- (of a disease etc.) regularly affecting animals in a particular district.
- [Greek *en* in + *zōion* animal]

enzyme *noun*
- "EN zime"
- a protein produced by living cells and functioning as a catalyst in a specific biochemical reaction.
- [German *Enzym* from medieval Greek *enzumos* leavened, from Greek *en* in + *zumē* leaven]
- **enzymatic** *adjective*
- **enzymatically** *adverb*
- **enzymic** *adjective* "en ZIME ick"
- **enzymology** *noun*

Eocene *adjective*
- "EE oh seen"
- of, relating to, or denoting the second epoch of the Tertiary period, between the Paleocene and the Oligocene, lasting from about 54.9 to 38 million years BP and having evidence of an abundance of mammals.
- [Greek *ēōs* dawn + *kainos* new]

eolith *noun*
- "EE a lith"
- any of various roughly chipped flint objects found in Tertiary strata and originally thought to be early artifacts.
- [Greek *ēōs* dawn + *lithos* stone]

eon *noun*

ALSO SPELLED: **aeon**
- "EE on"
- a very long or indefinite period.
- [Church Latin from Greek *aiōn* age]

eosin *noun*
- "EE oh sin"
- a red fluorescent dye used esp. as a stain in optical microscopy.
- [Greek *ēōs* dawn]

eosinophil *noun*
- "ee oh SINNA fill"
- a white blood cell readily stained by eosin.
- [as EOSIN + Greek *philos* dear, loving]

eosinophilia *noun*
- "ee oh sinna FILLY uh" or "ee oh sinna FEELY uh"
- an increased number of eosinophils in the blood, as in some allergic disorders and parasitic infections.
- [as EOSINOPHIL]
- **eosinophilic** *adjective*

epact *noun*
- "EE pact"
- the number of days by which the solar year exceeds the lunar year.
- [French *épacte* from Late Latin *epactae* from Greek *epaktai (hēmerai)* intercalated (days), from *epagō* intercalate (*epi* upon, near to, in addition, *agō* bring)]

eparch *noun*
- "EPP ark"
- the chief bishop of an eparchy.
- [Greek *eparkhos* (*epi* upon, near to, in addition, *arkhos* ruler)]

eparchy *noun*
- "EPP arky"
- a diocese in an Eastern-rite church.
- [as EPARCH]

epaulette *noun*

ALSO SPELLED: **epaulet**
- "eppa LET" or "EPPA let"
- a decoration on the shoulder of a coat, jacket, etc., esp. on a uniform.
- [French *épaulette* diminutive of *épaule* shoulder, from Latin *spatula*: see SPATULA]

épée *noun*
- "ay PAY"
- a sharp-pointed duelling sword, often used with the end blunted.
- [French, = sword, from Old French *espee* from Latin *spatha*: see SPATHE]
- **épéeist** *noun*

epeirogeny *noun*
- "ep eye RODGE a nee"
- the regional uplift of extensive areas of the earth's crust.
- [Greek *ēpeiros* mainland + GENESIS]
- **epeirogenic** *adjective* "ep eye ruh JENNIC"

epenthesis *noun*
- "e PENTHA sis"
- the insertion of a letter or sound within a word, e.g. the sound inserted by some people in the pronunciation of *biathlon*.
- [Late Latin from Greek from *epentithēmi* insert (*epi* upon, near to, in addition + *tithēmi* place)]
- **epenthetic** *adjective*

epergne *noun*
- "e PURN"
- an ornament (esp. in branched form) for the centre of a dinner table, holding flowers or fruit.
- [18th c.: perhaps a corruption of French *épargne* saving, economy, in the phrase *taille* or *gravure d'épargne*, metal or etching in which parts are 'spared', i.e. left in relief]

ephah *noun*
- "EEFA"
- an ancient Hebrew unit of dry measure, approximately equal to a bushel or 33 litres.
- [Hebrew *'ēp̱āh*, prob. from Egyptian]

ephebe *noun*
• "EFF eeb"
• a young man of 18–20 undergoing military training in ancient Greece.
• [Latin *ephebus* from Greek *ephēbos* (*epi* upon, near to, in addition, *hēbē* early manhood)]
• **ephebic** *adjective*

ephedra *noun*
• "ef FEDDRA"
• any evergreen shrub of the genus *Ephedra*, with trailing stems and scale-like leaves. Some kinds are a source of ephedrine and are used medicinally.
• [modern Latin from Greek *ephedra* sitting upon]

ephedrine *noun*
• "ef FED rin"
• an alkaloid drug found in some ephedras, causing constriction of the blood vessels and widening of the bronchial passages, used to relieve asthma, hay fever, colds, etc.
• [as EPHEDRA]

ephemera *noun*
• "ef FEMMER uh" or "ef FEEMER uh"
• a winged insect of the genus *Ephemera* or the order Ephemeroptera, a mayfly.
• [modern Latin from Greek *ephēmeros* lasting only a day (*epi* upon, near to, in addition, *hēmera* day)]

ephemeral *adjective*
• "ef FEMMER 'll"
• lasting or of use for only a short time; transitory.
• [as EPHEMERA]
• **ephemerality** *noun* "ef femmer ALA tee"
• **ephemerally** *adverb*

ephemeris *noun*
• "if FEMMER iss" or "if FEEMER iss"
• a table of the predicted positions of a celestial body.
• [Latin from Greek *ephēmeris* diary (as EPHEMERAL)]

ephemeron *noun*
• "if FEMMER 'n" or "if FEEMER 'n"
• a thing (esp. a printed item) of short-lived interest or usefulness.
• [as EPHEMERA]

ephod *noun*
• "EE fod" or "EFF od"
• a vestment, resembling an embroidered apron, worn by priests in ancient Israel.
• [Hebrew *'ēpôḏ*]

ephor *noun*
• "EFFOR"
• any of five senior magistrates in ancient Sparta.
• [Greek *ephoros* overseer (*epi* upon, near to, in addition, *horaō* see)]
• **ephorate** *noun*

epiblast *noun*
• "EPPA blast"
• the outermost layer of a young embryo.
• [Greek *epi* upon, near to, in addition + *blastos* sprout]

epic *noun*
• "EPPIC"
• a long poem, typically one derived from ancient oral tradition, narrating the adventures or deeds of one or more heroic or legendary figures, e.g. the *Iliad*, *Paradise Lost*.
• [Latin *epicus* from Greek *epikos* from *epos* word, song]
• **epically** *adverb*

epicardium *noun*
• "eppa CARDY um"
• the visceral part of the serous pericardium, covering the heart.
• [Greek *epi* upon, near to, in addition + *-cardium*, after PERICARDIUM]
• **epicardial** *adjective*

epicene *adjective*
• "EPPA seen"
• denoting either sex without change of gender.
• [Late Latin *epicoenus* from Greek *epikoinos* (*epi* upon, near to, in addition, *koinos* common)]

epicentre *noun*
ALSO SPELLED: esp. *US* **epicenter**
• "EPPA senter"
• the point at which an earthquake reaches the earth's surface.
• [Greek *epikentros* (adjective) (*epi* upon, near to, in addition, CENTRE)]
• **epicentral** *adjective*

epicontinental *adjective*
• "eppa conta NENT'll"
• (of a sea) situated on a continental shelf.
• [Greek *epi* upon, near to, in addition + 'continent' from Latin *terra continens* (from *continēre content-* from *com-* with, *tenēre* hold) continuous land]

epicotyl *noun*
• "eppa COT'll"
• the region of an embryo or seedling stem above the cotyledon(s).
• [Greek *epi* upon, near to, in addition + COTYLEDON]

epicure *noun*
• "EPPA cure"
• a person who takes particular pleasure in fine food and drink.
• [medieval Latin *epicurus* one preferring sensual enjoyment, from *Epicurus*, Greek philosopher d.270 BC]
• **epicurean** *noun*
• **epicurism** *noun*

Epicureanism *noun*
• "eppa CURE ee 'n izm"
• an ancient school of philosophy, founded in

Athens by Epicurus, which advocated pleasure as the highest good, but of a restrained kind.
• [as EPICURE]

epicycle *noun*
• "EPPA sike'll"
• a small circle moving around the circumference of a larger one.
• [Greek *epi* upon, near to, in addition + CYCLE]
• **epicyclic** *adjective*

epicycloid *noun*
• "eppa SIKE loid"
• a curve traced by a point on the circumference of a circle rolling on the exterior of another circle.
• [Greek *epi* upon, near to, in addition + CYCLE]
• **epicycloidal** *adjective*

epidemic *noun*
• "eppa DEMMIC"
• a widespread occurrence of a disease in a community at a particular time.
• [ultimately from Greek *epidēmia* prevalence of disease, from *epidēmios* (adjective) (*epi* upon, near to, in addition, *dēmos* the people)]

epidemiology *noun*
• "eppa deemy OLLA jee"
• the study of the incidence and distribution of diseases, and of their control and prevention.
• [as EPIDEMIC + *logos* word]
• **epidemiologic** *adjective*
• **epidemiological** *adjective*
• **epidemiologically** *adverb*
• **epidemiologist** *noun*

epidermis *noun*
• "eppa DURMISS"
• the outer cellular layer of the skin.
• [Late Latin from Greek (*epi* upon, near to, in addition, *derma* skin)]
• **epidermal** *adjective*
• **epidermic** *adjective*
• **epidermoid** *adjective*

epididymis *noun*
• "eppa DIDDA miss"
• a convoluted duct behind the testis, along which sperm passes to the vas deferens.
• [Greek *epididumis* (*epi* upon, near to, in addition, *didumoi* testicles)]

epidote *noun*
• "EPPA dote"
• any of several rock-forming silicates of calcium, aluminum, and iron that occur as monoclinic usu. green crystals in many metamorphic rocks.
• [French *épidote* from Greek *epiddidonai* (*epi* upon, near to, in addition + *didonai* give, with reference to the great length of the crystals)]

epidural *adjective*
• "eppa DUR 'll" or "eppa DYUR 'll"
• on or around the dura mater, the tough outermost membrane enveloping the brain and spinal cord.
• [Greek *epi* upon, near to, in addition + 'dura (mater)', from medieval Latin = hard mother, translation of Arabic *al-'umm al-jāfiya* ('mother' in Arabic indicating the relationship of things)]

epigastrium *noun*
• "eppa GAS tree um"
• the part of the abdomen immediately over the stomach.
• [Late Latin from Greek *epigastrion* (neuter adjective) (*epi* upon, near to, in addition, *gastēr* belly)]
• **epigastric** *adjective*

epigeal *adjective*
• "eppa JEE 'll"
• having one or more cotyledons above the ground.
• [Greek *epigeios* (*epi* upon, near to, in addition, *gē* earth)]

epigene *adjective*
• "EPPA jeen"
• produced on the surface of the earth.
• [French *épigène* from Greek *epigenēs* (*epi* upon, near to, in addition, *genēs* born)]

epiglottis *noun*
• "eppa GLOTTISS"
• a flap of cartilage at the root of the tongue, which is depressed during swallowing to cover the windpipe.
• [Greek *epiglōttis* (*epi* upon, near to, in addition, *glōtta* tongue)]
• **epiglottal** *adjective*
• **epiglottic** *adjective*

epigone *noun*
• "EPPA gone" ("GONE" rhymes with *BONE*)
• a less distinguished follower or imitator of someone, esp. an artist of philosopher.
• [Greek *epigonoi* those born afterwards (*epi* upon, near to, in addition, root of *gignomai* be born)]
• **epigonic** *adjective*

epigram *noun*
• "EPPA gram"
• a pithy saying or remark expressing an idea in a clever and amusing way.
• [French *épigramme* or Latin *epigramma* from Greek *epigramma -atos* (*epi* upon, near to, in addition, *gramma* thing written)]
• **epigrammatic** *adjective*
• **epigrammatically** *adverb*
• **epigrammatist** *noun*

epigraph *noun*
• "EPPA graff"
• a quotation at the beginning of a chapter, book, etc.
• [Greek *epigraphē* from *epigraphō* (*epi* upon, near to, in addition, *graphō* write)]

epigraphy *noun*
• "ep PIGGRA fee"
• the study of (esp. ancient) inscriptions.
• [as EPIGRAPH]

- **epigrapher** *noun*
- **epigraphic** *adjective*
- **epigraphical** *adjective*
- **epigraphically** *adverb*
- **epigraphist** *noun*

epilation *noun*
- "eppa LAY sh'n"
- the removal of hair.
- [French *épiler* (compare DEPILATE)]
- **epilator** *noun*

epilepsy *noun*
- "EPPA lep see"
- a condition in which a person has intermittent attacks of disordered brain function, usu. causing loss of awareness or consciousness and sometimes convulsions.
- [Greek *epilēpsia* from *epilambanō* attack (*epi* upon, near to, in addition, *lambanō* take)]
- **epileptic** *adjective*

epilimnion *noun*
- "eppa LIMNY 'n"
- the upper layer of water in a stratified lake.
- [Greek *epi* upon, near to, in addition + *limnion* diminutive of *limnē* lake]

epilogue *noun*
- "EPPA log"
- the concluding part of a literary work.
- [Greek *epilogos* (*epi* upon, near to, in addition, *logos* speech)]

epimer *noun*
- "EPPA mur"
- either of two isomers with different configurations of atoms about one of several asymmetric carbon atoms present.
- [German (from Greek *epi* upon, near to, in addition, ISOMER)]
- **epimeric** *adjective* "eppa MARE ick"
- **epimerism** *noun*

epimerize *verb*
ALSO SPELLED: esp. *Brit.* **-ise**
- "ep PIMMER ize"
- convert (one epimer) into the other.
- [as EPIMER]

epinephrine *noun*
- "epp'n EFF rin"
- a hormone secreted by the adrenal glands, esp. in conditions of stress, increasing rates of blood circulation, breathing, and carbohydrate metabolism and preparing muscles for exertion; adrenalin.
- [Greek *epi* upon + *nephros* kidney]

epiphany *noun*
- "ep PIFFA nee"
- a Christian festival observed on 6 January or the following Sunday in the Western Church and on 19 January in Eastern-rite churches. In the Western Church it commemorates the manifestation of Jesus to the Magi; in Eastern Churches the baptism of Jesus.
- [Greek *epiphaneia* manifestation, from *epiphainō* reveal (*epi* upon, near to, in addition, *phainō* show)]
- **epiphanic** *adjective* "eppa FANNIC"
- **epiphanous** *adjective*

epiphenomenon *noun*
- "eppa fuh NOMMA n'n"
- a secondary symptom, which may occur simultaneously with a disease etc. but is not regarded as its cause or result.
- [Greek *epi* upon, near to, in addition + PHENOMENON]
- **epiphenomenal** *adjective*

epiphysis *noun*
- "e PIFFA sis"
- the end part of a long bone, initially growing separately from the shaft.
- [modern Latin from Greek *epiphusis* (*epi* upon, near to, in addition, *phusis* growth)]

epiphyte *noun*
- "EPPA fite"
- a plant growing but not parasitic on another, e.g. a moss.
- [Greek *epi* upon, near to, in addition + *phuton* plant]
- **epiphytic** *adjective* "eppa FITTIC"

episcopacy *noun*
- "e PISKA puh see"
- government of a Church by bishops.
- [as EPISCOPATE]

episcopal *adjective*
- "e PISKA p'll"
- of a bishop or bishops.
- [Church Latin *episcopalis* from *episcopus* BISHOP]
- **episcopalism** *noun*
- **episcopally** *adverb*

episcopalian *adjective*
- "e piska PAILY 'n"
- of or advocating government of a Church by bishops.
- [as EPISCOPAL]
- **episcopalianism** *noun*

episcopate *noun*
- "e PISKA pit"
- the office or tenure of a bishop.
- [Church Latin *episcopatus* from *episcopus* BISHOP]

episematic *adjective*
- "e pissa MATTIC"
- (of coloration, markings, etc.) serving to help recognition by animals of the same species.
- [Greek *epi* upon, near to, in addition + *sēma sēmatos* sign]

episiotomy *noun*
- "e peezy OTTA mee"
- a surgical cut made at the opening of the vagina during childbirth, to aid delivery.
- [Greek *epision* pubic region + *-tomia* cutting, from *temnō* cut]

episode *noun*
- "EPPA sode"
- one event or a group of events as part of a sequence.
- [Greek *epeisodion* (*epi* upon, near to, in addition + *eisodos* entry, from *eis* into + *hodos* way)]
- **episodic** *adjective* "eppa SODDIC"
- **episodically** *adverb*

epistaxis *noun*
- "eppa STACK sis"
- a nosebleed.
- [modern Latin from Greek (*epi* upon, near to, in addition, *stazō* drip)]

epistemic *adjective*
- "eppa STEEMIC" or "eppa STEMMIC"
- relating to knowledge or to the degree of its validation.
- [Greek *epistēmē* knowledge]
- **epistemically** *adverb*

epistemology *noun*
- "e pista MOLLA jee"
- the theory of knowledge, esp. with regard to its methods and validation.
- [as EPISTEMIC + *logos* word]
- **epistemological** *adjective*
- **epistemologically** *adverb*
- **epistemologist** *noun*

epistle *noun*
- "e PISS'll"
- or a letter, esp. a long one on a serious subject.
- [Old French from Latin *epistola* from Greek *epistolē* from *epistellō* send news (*epi* upon, near to, in addition, *stellō* send)]

epistolary *adjective*
- "e PISTA lerry"
- in the style or form of a letter or letters.
- [French *épistolaire* or Latin *epistolaris* (as EPISTLE)]

epistrophe *noun*
- "e PISTRA fee"
- the repetition of a word at the end of successive clauses.
- [Greek (*epi* upon, near to, in addition, *strophē* turning)]

epistyle *noun*
- "EPPA stile"
- (in classical architecture) a main beam resting across the tops of columns; an architrave.
- [French *épistyle* or Latin *epistylium* from Greek *epistulion* (*epi* upon, near to, in addition, *stulos* pillar)]

epitaph *noun*
- "EPPA taff"
- words written in memory of a person who has died, esp. as a tomb inscription.
- [Old French *epitaphe* from Latin *epitaphium* from Greek *epitaphion* funeral oration (*epi* upon, near to, in addition, *taphos* tomb)]

epitaxy *noun*
- "EPPA taxy"
- the growth of crystals on a crystalline substrate that determines their orientation.
- [French *épitaxie* (as Greek *epi* upon, near to, in addition, *taxis* arrangement)]
- **epitaxial** *adjective*

epithalamium *noun*
- "eppa thuh LAY mee um" (with "TH" as in *THIN*)
- a song or poem celebrating a marriage.
- [Latin from Greek *epithalamion* (*epi* upon, near to, in addition, *thalamos* bridal chamber)]

epithelium *noun*
- "eppa THEELY um"
- the tissue forming the outer layer of the body surface and lining many hollow structures.
- [modern Latin (from Greek *epi* upon, near to, in addition + *thēlē* teat)]
- **epithelial** *adjective*

epithet *noun*
- "EP ith et"
- an adjective or other descriptive word expressing a quality or attribute, esp. used with or as a name.
- [Greek *epitheton* from *epitithēmi* add (*epi* upon, near to, in addition, *tithēmi* place)]
- **epithetic** *adjective*

epitome *noun*
- "e PITTA mee"
- a typical example of a person or thing embodying a particular quality, class, etc.
- [Latin from Greek *epitomē* from *epitemnō* abridge (*epi* upon, near to, in addition, *temnō* cut)]

epitomize *verb*
ALSO SPELLED: esp. *Brit.* **-ise**
- "e PITTA mize"
- typify or be a perfect example of (a quality etc.).
- [as EPITOME]
- **epitomization** *noun* (also esp. *Brit.* **-isation**)

epizoon *noun*
- "eppa ZO on"
- an animal that lives on the surface of another, esp. a parasite.
- [modern Latin (from Greek *epi* upon, near to, in addition, *zōion* animal)]

epizootic *adjective*
- "eppa zo OTTIC"
- (of an animal disease) normally absent or infrequent in a population, but liable to become temporarily widespread.
- [French *épizootique* from *épizootie* (as EPIZOON)]

epoch *noun*
- "EE pock" or "EP ock" or "EP uck"
- a period of history or of a person's life marked by notable events.

• [modern Latin *epocha* from Greek *epokhē* stoppage]
• **epochal** *adjective*

epode *noun*
• "EP ode"
• a serious lyric poem composed of couplets in which a long line is followed by a shorter one.
• [French *épode* or Latin *epodos* from Greek *epōidos* (*epi* upon, near to, in addition, *ōidē* Attic form of *aoidē* song, from *aeidō* sing)]

eponym *noun*
• "EPPA nim"
• a person (real or imaginary) after whom a discovery, invention, place, institution, etc. is named or thought to be named.
• [Greek *epōnumos* (*epi* upon, near to, in addition, *-ōnumos* from *onoma* name)]

eponymous *adjective*
• "e PONNA muss"
• (of a person) giving their name to something.
• [as EPONYM]
• **eponymously** *adverb*

epoxide *noun*
• "e POX ide"
• a compound containing an oxygen atom bonded in a triangular arrangement to two carbon atoms.
• [Greek *epi* upon, near to, in addition + OXYGEN]

epoxy *adjective*
• "e POXY"
• relating to or derived from an epoxide, esp. designating epoxy resins and the substances made from them.
• [Greek *epi* upon, near to, in addition + OXYGEN]

epsilon *noun*
• "EPS'll on"
• the fifth letter of the Greek alphabet (Ε, ϵ).
• [Greek, = 'bare E' from *psilos* bare]

equable *adjective*
• "ECKWA bull"
• (of a person) not easily disturbed or angered.
• [Latin *aequabilis* (as EQUATE)]
• **equability** *noun*
• **equably** *adverb*

equal *adjective*
• "EE kwull"
• identical in amount, size, number, value, intensity, etc.
• [Latin *aequalis* from *aequus* even]
• **equally** *adverb*

equality *noun*
• "ee KWOLLA tee"
• the condition of being equal in quantity, magnitude, value, intensity, etc.
• [as EQUAL]

equalize *verb*
ALSO SPELLED: esp. *Brit.* **-ise**
• "EEKWA lize"
• make or become equal.
• [as EQUAL]
• **equalization** *noun* (also esp. *Brit.* **-isation**)
• **equalizer** *noun* (also esp. *Brit.* **-iser**)

equanimity *noun*
• "eckwa NIMMA tee"
• mental composure, evenness of temper, esp. in misfortune.
• [Latin *aequanimitas* from *aequanimis* from *aequus* even + *animus* mind]

equate *verb*
• "e KWATE"
• treat or regard as equal or equivalent.
• [Latin *aequare aequat-* from *aequus* equal]
• **equatable** *adjective*

equation *noun*
• "e KWAY zh'n"
• the action of making equal or equating.
• [as EQUATE]

equator *noun*
• "e KWAY tur"
• an imaginary line round the earth or other body, equidistant from the poles and marking the division between the northern and southern hemispheres.
• [as EQUATE]
• **equatorial** *adjective* "eckwa TORY 'll" or "eekwa TORY 'll"
• **equatorially** *adverb*
• **equatorward** *adverb*

equerry *noun*
• "ECKWA ree" or "e KWERRY"
• an officer of the British royal household attending members of the royal family.
• [earlier *esquiry* from Old French *esquierie* company of squires, prince's stables, from Old French *esquier* ESQUIRE: perhaps assoc. with Latin *equus* horse]

equestrian *adjective*
• "e KWESS tree 'n"
• of or relating to horses and horseback riding.
• [Latin *equestris* from *eques* horseman, knight, from *equus* horse]

equestrienne *noun*
• "e kwestry EN"
• a female skilled at horseback riding.
• [as EQUESTRIAN]

equiangular *adjective*
• "eekwee ANG gyuh lur" or "eckwee ANG gyuh lur"
• having all angles equal.
• [as EQUAL + ANGULAR]

equidistant *adjective*
• "eekwa DIS t'nt" or "eckwa DIS t'nt"
• separated by an equal distance or equal distances.
• [as EQUAL + Old French *distant* or Latin *distant-*

participle stem of *distare* stand apart, from *stare* stand]
- **equidistance** *noun*
- **equidistantly** *adverb*

equilateral *adjective*
- "eekwa LATTER'll"
- having all its sides equal in length.
- [as EQUAL + LATERAL]

equilibrate *verb*
- "e KWILLA brate"
- cause (two things) to balance or to come or stay in equilibrium.
- [Late Latin *aequilibrare aequilibrat-* (as EQUAL, *libra* balance)]
- **equilibration** *noun*
- **equilibrator** *noun*

equilibrist *noun*
- "e KWILLA brist"
- a person who performs feats of balancing, esp. on a tightrope.
- [as EQUILIBRIUM]

equilibrium *noun*
- "eekwa LIB ree um" or "eckwa LIB ree um"
- a condition of balance between opposing physical forces.
- [Latin (as EQUAL, *libra* balance)]

equine *adjective*
- "ECK wine" or "EEK wine"
- of, like, or affecting a horse or horses.
- [Latin *equinus* from *equus* horse]

equinoctial *adjective*
- "eckwa NOCK sh'll" or "eekwa NOCK sh'll"
- happening at or near the time of either equinox.
- [Old French *equinoctial* or Latin *aequinoctialis* (as EQUINOX)]

equinox *noun*
- "ECKWA nox" or "EEKWA nox"
- either of the two occasions in the year when the sun crosses the celestial equator and day and night are of equal length throughout the world.
- [Old French *equinoxe* or medieval Latin *equinoxium* for Latin *aequinoctium* (as EQUAL, *nox noctis* night)]

equipage *noun*
- "ECKWA pidge"
- personal items, equipment, tackle, etc. necessary for a particular undertaking.
- [French *équipage* from *équiper*, prob. from Old Norse *skipa* to man (a ship) from *skip* ship]

equipoise *noun*
- "ECKWA poyz" or "EEKWA poyz"
- a balanced state or equilibrium, esp. of intellectual, moral, or social forces or interests.
- [as EQUAL + Old French *pois* ultimately from Latin *pensum* weight, from *pendere pens-* weigh]

equipotential *adjective*
- "eckwa puh TEN sh'll"
- (of a surface or line) composed of points having the same or constant potential.
- [as EQUAL + POTENTIAL]

equitable *adjective*
- "ECKWA tuh bull"
- just or characterized by fairness or equity.
- [French *équitable* (as EQUITY)]
- **equitableness** *noun*
- **equitably** *adverb*

equitation *noun*
- "eckwa TAY sh'n"
- the art and practice of horsemanship and horseback riding.
- [French *équitation* or Latin *equitatio* from *equitare* ride a horse, from *eques equitis* horseman from *equus* horse]

equity *noun*
- "ECKWA tee"
- fairness, impartiality, even-handedness.
- [Old French *equité* from Latin *aequitas -tatis* from *aequus* fair]

equivalent *adjective*
- "e KWIVVA l'nt"
- equal in value, amount, importance, etc.
- [Old French from Late Latin *aequivalēre* (as EQUAL, *valēre* be worth)]
- **equivalence** *noun*
- **equivalency** *noun*
- **equivalently** *adverb*

equivocal *adjective*
- "e KWIVVA k'll"
- (of a word, expression, etc.) ambiguous or capable of more than one interpretation.
- [Late Latin *aequivocus* (as EQUAL, *vocare* call)]
- **equivocality** *noun*
- **equivocally** *adverb*
- **equivocalness** *noun*

equivocate *verb*
- "e KWIVVA kate"
- hedge, prevaricate, or use ambiguous words and expressions to mislead.
- [Late Latin *aequivocare* (as EQUIVOCAL)]
- **equivocation** *noun*
- **equivocator** *noun*

eradicate *verb*
- "e RADDA cate"
- get rid of, remove or destroy completely.
- [Latin *eradicare* tear up by the roots (*ex* out of, *radix -icis* root)]
- **eradicable** *adjective*
- **eradicant** *noun*
- **eradication** *noun*
- **eradicator** *noun*

erase *verb*
- "e RACE"
- rub out or obliterate (something written, typed, drawn, etc.).
- [Latin *eradere eras-* (*ex* out of, *radere* scrape)]
- **erasability** *noun*
- **erasable** *adjective*
- **eraser** *noun*

erasure *noun*
- “e RAY shur”
- an act or instance of erasing.
- [as ERASE]

erbium *noun*
- “URBY um”
- a soft, silvery metallic element of the lanthanide series.
- [modern Latin from *Ytterby* in Sweden, where it was first found]

erect *adjective*
- “e RECT”
- upright, vertical, not bending or stooping.
- [Latin *erigere erect-* set up (*ex* out of, *regere* direct)]
- **erectable** *adjective*
- **erection** *noun*
- **erectly** *adverb*
- **erectness** *noun*
- **erector** *noun*

erectile *adjective*
- “e RECK tile”
- that can be erected or become erect.
- [as ERECT]

eremite *noun*
- “ERRA mite”
- a hermit or recluse, esp. one under religious vows.
- [Old French, var. of *hermite, ermite* from Late Latin *eremita* from Greek *erēmitēs* from *erēmia* desert, from *erēmos* solitary]
- **eremitic** *adjective* “erra MITTIC”
- **eremitical** *adjective*
- **eremitism** *noun*

erg *noun*
- “URG”
- a unit of work or energy, equal to the amount of work done by a force of one dyne when its point of application moves one centimetre in the direction of action of the force.
- [Greek *ergon* work]

ergative *noun*
- “URGA tiv”
- a case of noun in some languages, such as Inuktitut or Basque, that identifies the doer of an action as the object rather than the subject of a verb.
- [Greek *ergatē* worker]
- **ergativity** *noun*

ergo *adverb*
- “AIR go” or “UR go”
- therefore.
- [Latin]

ergometer *noun*
- “air GOMMA tur”
- an instrument or machine which measures work or energy, esp. the work done during a period of exercise.
- [Greek *ergon* work + *metron* measure]

ergonomics *noun*
- “urga NOMMIX”
- the field of study that deals with the relationship between people and their working environment, esp. as it affects efficiency, safety, and ease of action.
- [Greek *ergon* work: compare ECONOMICS]
- **ergonomic** *adjective*
- **ergonomically** *adverb*
- **ergonomist** *noun* “ur GONNA mist”

ergosterol *noun*
- “ur GOSTER awl”
- a plant sterol, found in ergot and other fungi, that is converted to vitamin D_2 when irradiated with ultraviolet light.
- [ERGOT, after CHOLESTEROL]

ergot *noun*
- “UR gut”
- a disease of rye and other cereals caused by the fungus *Claviceps purpurea.*
- [French from Old French *argot* cock's spur, from the appearance produced]

ergotamine *noun*
- “ur GOTTA meen”
- the pharmacologically active isomer of an alkaloid present in some kinds of ergot, used chiefly to treat migraine.
- [as ERGOT]

ergotism *noun*
- “URGA tizm”
- poisoning produced by eating food affected by ergot.
- [as AMINE]

erica *noun*
- “ERRA kuh”
- any shrub or heath of the genus *Erica*, with small leathery leaves and bell-like flowers.
- [Latin from Greek *ereikē* heath]

ericaceous *adjective*
- “erra CAY sh'ss”
- of or relating to the plant family Ericaceae, which includes heathers, azaleas, and rhododendrons.
- [modern Latin *Ericaceae* from ERICA + adjective suffix *-aceus* of the nature of]

erigeron *noun*
- “e RIGGA ron”
- any composite herb of the genus *Erigeron*, with daisy-like flowers.
- [Greek *ērigerōn* from *ēri* early + *gerōn* old man, because some species bear grey down]

eristic *adjective*
- “air ISTIC”
- of, characterized by, or pertaining to disputation.
- [Greek *eristikos* from *erizō* wrangle from *eris* strife]

Eritrean *noun*
- “erra TREE 'n” or “erra TRAY 'n”
- a native or inhabitant of Eritrea in NE Africa.

ermine *noun*
- "UR min"
- a flesh-eating mammal, *Mustela erminea*, of the weasel family, having brown fur in the summer turning mainly white in the winter, with the tail remaining black-tipped.
- [Old French *(h)ermine* prob. from medieval Latin *(mus) Armenius* Armenian (mouse)]
- **ermined** *adjective*

Ermite *noun*
- "air MEET"
- a creamy, semi-soft, and salty blue veined cheese made in Quebec.
- [French *ermite* hermit]

erode *verb*
- "e RODE"
- wear away (esp. soil or rock), destroy or be destroyed gradually.
- [French *éroder* or Latin *erodere eros-* (Latin *ex* out of, *rodere ros-* gnaw)]
- **eroded** *adjective*
- **erodible** *adjective*

erogenous *adjective*
- "e RODGE a nuss"
- (esp. of a part of the body) sensitive to sexual stimulation.
- [as EROTIC + GENESIS]

eros *noun*
- "AIR oss" or "EER oss"
- earthly, romantic, or sexual love.
- [Greek]

erosion *noun*
- "e ROE zh'n"
- the wearing away of the earth's surface by wind, water, or glacial action.
- [French *érosion* from Latin *erosio* (as ERODE)]
- **erosional** *adjective*
- **erosive** *adjective*

erotic *adjective*
- "e ROTTIC"
- of or pertaining to sexual love.
- [French *érotique* from Greek *erōtikos* from *erōs erōtos* sexual love]
- **erotically** *adverb*
- **eroticism** *noun* "e ROTTA sizm"
- **eroticization** *noun* (also esp. *Brit.* **-isation**)
- **eroticize** *verb* (also esp. *Brit.* **-ise**)
- **eroticized** *adjective* (also esp. *Brit.* **-ised**)

erotica *noun*
- "e ROTTIC uh"
- intentionally erotic literature or art.
- [as EROTIC]

erotomania *noun*
- "e rotta MAINY uh"
- an obsessive erotic desire, esp. with fantasies, delusions, etc.
- [as EROTIC + MANIA]
- **erotomaniac** *noun*

err *verb*
- "AIR"
- be mistaken or incorrect.
- [Old French *errer* from Latin *errare* stray]

HOMOPHONES: *air, heir, are, ere*

errand *noun*
- "AIR 'nd"
- a short trip, often on another's behalf, to buy or deliver something, take a message, etc.
- [Old English *ǣrende* from Germanic]

errant *adjective*
- "AIR 'nt"
- erring, doing wrong, deviating from an accepted standard.
- [as ERR]
- **errancy** *noun*
- **errantry** *noun*

HOMOPHONES: *arrant*

erratic *adjective*
- "e RATTIC"
- inconsistently variable in conduct, opinions, etc.
- [Old French *erratique* from Latin *erraticus* (as ERR)]
- **erratically** *adverb*

erratum *noun*
- "e RATTUM"
- an error in a printed or written text, esp. one noted in a list appended to a book or published in a subsequent issue of a journal.
- [Latin, neuter past participle (as ERR)]

erroneous *adjective*
- "e RONEY us"
- incorrect, containing or arising from an error.
- [Latin *erroneus* from *erro -onis* vagabond (as ERR)]
- **erroneously** *adverb*
- **erroneousness** *noun*

error *noun*
- "AIR ur"
- a mistake.
- [Old French *errour* from Latin *error -oris* (as ERR)]
- **errorless** *adjective*

ersatz *adjective*
- "AIR zats" or "AIR sats"
- imitation (esp. of inferior quality).
- [German, = replacement]

Erse *adjective*
- "URSE" (rhymes with *PURSE*)
- Irish or Highland Gaelic.
- [early Scots form of 'Irish']

erstwhile *adjective*
- "URST wile"
- former, previous.
- [Old English *ǣrest* superlative of *ǣr* before]

erucic *adjective*
- "e ROO sick"

• designating a solid, unsaturated fatty acid present in mustard seeds and rape seeds.
• [Latin *eruca* rocket (the plant), caterpillar]

eructation *noun*
• "e ruck TAY sh'n"
• the act or an instance of belching.
• [Latin *eructatio* from *eructare* (Latin *ex* out of, *ructare* belch)]

erudite *adjective*
• "AIR oo dite" or "AIR yoo dite"
• (of a person) learned, scholarly.
• [Latin *eruditus* past participle of *erudire* instruct, train (Latin *ex* out of, *rudis* untrained)]
• **eruditely** *adverb*
• **erudition** *noun* "air oo DISH'n" or "air yoo DISH'n"

erupt *verb*
• "e RUPT"
• break out or burst forth suddenly or dramatically.
• [Latin *erumpere erupt-* (Latin *ex* out of, *rumpere* break)]
• **eruption** *noun*
• **eruptive** *adjective*
HOMOPHONES: *irrupt, irruption, irruptive*

erysipelas *noun*
• "erra SIPPA luss"
• an acute, sometimes recurrent, streptococcal infection characterized by large raised patches on the skin, esp. of the face and legs, with fever and severe general illness.
• [Latin from Greek *erusipelas*, perhaps related to *eruthros* red + a root *pel-* skin]

erythema *noun*
• "erra THEEMA" (with "TH" as in *THIN*)
• a superficial reddening of the skin, usu. in patches, as a result of injury or irritation.
• [modern Latin from Greek *eruthēma* from *eruthainō* be red, from *eruthros* red]
• **erythematous** *adjective*

erythroblast *noun*
• "e RITH roe blast"
• a nucleated cell which develops into an erythrocyte.
• [German, as ERYTHROCYTE + Greek *blastos* germ, sprout]

erythrocyte *noun*
• "e RITH roe site"
• one of the principal cells in the blood of vertebrates, containing the pigment hemoglobin and transporting oxygen and carbon dioxide to and from the tissues.
• [Greek *eruthros* red + Greek *kutos* vessel]
• **erythrocytic** *adjective* "e rith roe SITTIC"

erythroid *adjective*
• "ERRA throid"
• of or relating to erythrocytes.
• [as ERYTHROCYTE]

erythromycin *noun*
• "e rith roe MICE in"
• an antibiotic isolated from *Streptomyces erythreus*, similar in its effects to penicillin.
• [Greek *eruthros* red + *mukēs* fungus, mushroom]

erythropoiesis *noun*
• "e rith roe poy EE sis"
• the formation of red blood cells.
• [Greek *eruthros* red + *poiesis* creation]
• **erythropoietic** *adjective*

erythropoietin *noun*
• "e rith ro poy EETIN"
• a hormone, secreted by the kidneys, that increases the rate of formation of red blood cells, often used as a performance-enhancing drug.
• [as ERYTHROPOIESIS]

escalate *verb*
• "ESKA late"
• increase or develop (usu. rapidly) by stages.
• [back-formation from ESCALATOR]
• **escalating** *adjective*
• **escalation** *noun*

escalator *noun*
• "ESKA later"
• a moving staircase consisting of an endless chain of steps on a circulating belt driven by a motor.
• [from the stem of *escalade* climb a wall by ladder]

escallonia *noun*
• "eska LONEY uh"
• any evergreen shrub of the genus *Escallonia*, bearing pink, red, or white flowers.
• [*Escallon*, 18th-c. Spanish traveller]

escalope *noun*
• "ESKA lop"
• a thin, boneless slice of meat, esp. veal or turkey.
• [French (in Old French = shell)]

escapade *noun*
• "ESKA pade"
• a daring, reckless, or adventurous act.
• [French from Provençal or Spanish *escapada* (as ESCAPE)]

escape *verb*
• "iss CAPE"
• break free or free oneself by fleeing or struggling.
• [Old Northern French *escaper*, ultimately from medieval Latin (Latin *ex* out of, *cappa* cloak)]
• **escapable** *adjective*
• **escapee** *noun*
• **escaper** *noun*

escapement *noun*
• "iss CAPE m'nt"
• a mechanism in a clock or watch that alternately checks or releases the train by a

fixed amount and transmits a periodic impulse from the spring or weight to the balance wheel or pendulum.

• [French *échappement* from *échapper* ESCAPE]

escapism *noun*

• "iss CAPE izm"

• the tendency to seek distraction and relief from reality, esp. in the arts or through fantasy.

• [as ESCAPE]

• **escapist** *noun*

escapology *noun*

• "eska POLLA jee"

• the methods and techniques of escaping from confinement, esp. as a form of entertainment.

• [as ESCAPE + *logos* word]

• **escapologist** *noun*

escargot *noun*

• "es car GO"

• a snail as an item of food.

• [French from Provençal *escaragol* from Latin *conchylium* shellfish]

escarole *noun*

• "ESKA role"

• a variety of chicory with broad, crisp, undivided, and bitter-tasting leaves used in salads.

• [French, from Italian *scar(i)ola*, based on Latin *esca* food]

escarpment *noun*

• "es CARP m'nt"

• a long, steep-sided ridge, esp. one at the edge of a plateau or separating areas of land at different heights.

• [French *escarpement* from *escarpe* SCARP]

eschar *noun*

• "ESS car"

• a dry, dark scab, esp. one caused by burning.

• [Old French *eschare* or Late Latin *eschara* scar or scab, from Greek *eskhara* scab]

eschatology *noun*

• "eska TOLLA jee"

• the branch of theology concerned with last things, e.g. death, judgment, heaven, and hell.

• [Greek *eskhatos* last + *logos* word]

• **eschatological** *adjective*

• **eschatologist** *noun*

escheat *noun*

• "iss CHEET"

• the reversion of property to the state, or (in feudal law) to a lord, on the owner's dying without legal heirs.

• [Old French *eschete*, ultimately from Latin *excidere* (*ex* out of, *cadere* fall)]

eschew *verb*

• "es CHOO"

• carefully or deliberately avoid, abstain from, or shun.

• [Middle English from Old French *eschiver*, ultimately from Germanic: related to 'shy']

• **eschewal** *noun*

escort *noun*

• "ESS cort"

• one or more persons, vehicles, ships, etc. accompanying another, esp. for protection, security, or as a mark of rank or status.

• [French *escorte*, *escorter* from Italian *scorta* feminine past participle of *scorgere* conduct]

escritoire *noun*

• "es cree TWAR" ("TWAR" rhymes with *FAR*)

• a writing desk with drawers for papers, envelopes, etc. and usu. a hinged flap to conceal these.

• [French from Latin *scriptorium* writing room: see SCRIPTORIUM]

escrow *noun*

• "es CROW"

• money, property, or a written bond, kept in the custody of a third party until a specified condition has been fulfilled.

• [Anglo-French *escrowe*, Old French *escroe* scrap, scroll, from medieval Latin *scroda* from Germanic]

escudo *noun*

• "es COODO"

• the former principal monetary unit of Portugal (equal to 100 centavos) and, formerly, of some other countries that were or had been Portuguese or Spanish territories, e.g. Chile.

• [Spanish & Portuguese from Latin *scutum* shield]

escutcheon *noun*

• "es CUTCH 'n"

• a shield or emblem bearing a coat of arms.

• [Anglo-French & Old Northern French *escuchon*, ultimately from Latin *scutum* shield]

• **escutcheoned** *adjective*

esker *noun*

• "ESKER"

• a long, narrow ridge, usu. of sand and gravel, deposited in a river valley by a stream flowing under a former glacier or ice sheet.

• [Irish *eiscir*]

esophagus *noun*

ALSO SPELLED: esp. *Brit.* **oesophagus**

• "e SOFFA guss"

• the gullet or the part of the alimentary canal from the mouth to the stomach.

• [Greek *oisophagos*]

• **esophageal** *adjective* (also esp. *Brit.* **oesophageal**) "e soffa JEE 'll" or "e suh FADGE ee 'll"

esoteric *adjective*

• "esso TARE ick" or "ee so TARE ick"

• (of a doctrine, field of study, mode of speech, etc.) intended only for, or intelligible only to, the initiated or those with special knowledge.

• [Greek *esōterikos* from *esōterō* comparative of *esō* within]

• **esoterically** *adverb*

- **esotericism** *noun* "esso TERRA sizm" or "ee so TERRA sizm"
- **esotericist** *noun*

esoterica *noun*
- "essa TARE ick uh" or "ee suh TARE ick uh"
- esoteric details, items, or publications.
- [as ESOTERIC]

espadrille *noun*
- "espa DRILL"
- a light canvas shoe with a braided fibre sole.
- [French from Provençal *espardillo* from *espart* ESPARTO]

espalier *noun*
- "es PAL yur"
- a latticework or framework of stakes along which the branches of a tree or shrub are trained to grow flat against a wall etc.
- [French from Italian *spalliera* from *spalla* shoulder]
- **espaliered** *adjective*

Espanolian *noun*
- "espa NOLEY 'n"
- a resident of Espanola, Ont.

esparto *noun*
- "es PARTO"
- a coarse grass, *Stipa tenacissima*, native to Spain and N Africa, with tough narrow leaves, used to make ropes, wickerwork, and high-quality paper.
- [Spanish from Latin *spartum* from Greek *sparton* rope]

especial *adjective*
- "e SPESH 'll"
- notable, pre-eminent, or exceptional.
- [Old French from Latin *specialis* special]

especially *adverb*
- "e SPESH 'll ee"
- chiefly, pre-eminently.
- [as ESPECIAL]

Esperanto *noun*
- "esper ANTO"
- an artificial language invented in 1887 and based on roots common to the chief European languages with endings standardized.
- [the pen name (from Latin *sperare* hope) of its inventor, L. L. Zamenhof, Polish physician d.1917]
- **Esperantist** *noun*

espial *noun*
- "e SPY 'll"
- the act or an instance of catching sight of or of being seen.
- [Old French *espiaille* from *espier*: see ESPY]

espionage *noun*
- "ESS pee a nozh"
- the practice of spying or of using spies, esp. to obtain secret information.
- [French *espionnage* from *espionner* from *espion* spy]

esplanade *noun*
- "espla NADE" or "ESPLA nod"
- a level, open space along a waterfront, where people may walk or drive.
- [French from Spanish *esplanada* from *esplanar* make level, from Latin *explanare* (*ex* out of, *planus* level)]

espoir *noun*
- "ESP warr" ("WARR" rhymes with *FAR*)
- a category of competition for wrestlers between 17 and 20 years old.
- [French, lit. 'hope']

espouse *verb*
- "es POWZ"
- adopt or support (a cause, doctrine, etc.).
- [Old French *espouser* from Latin *sponsare* from *sponsus* past participle of *spondēre* betroth]
- **espousal** *noun*
- **espouser** *noun*

espresso *noun*
- "es PRESSO"
- strong, concentrated, black coffee made by forcing steam through ground coffee beans.
- [Italian, = pressed out]

esprit *noun*
- "es PREE"
- wit.
- [French from Latin *spiritus* spirit]

espy *verb*
- "es SPY"
- catch sight of or perceive, esp. at a distance.
- [Old French *espier*]

Esquimalt *noun*
- "esk WYE malt"
- a member of a Salishan Aboriginal group living near Esquimalt on Vancouver Island.

esquire *noun*
- "ESS kwire"
- a title appended to a man's surname when no other form of address is used, esp. as a formal form of address for letters.
- [Old French *esquier* from Latin *scutarius* shield bearer, from *scutum* shield]

Essene *noun*
- "ESS een"
- a member of an ancient Jewish ascetic sect who lived communally and are widely regarded as the authors of the Dead Sea Scrolls.
- [Latin pl. *Esseni* from Greek pl. *Essēnoi*]

essential *adjective*
- "e SEN sh'll"
- absolutely necessary; indispensable.
- [Late Latin *essentialis* from *esse* be]
- **essentiality** *noun* "e senshy ALA tee"
- **essentially** *adverb*

essentialism *noun*
- "e SEN sh'll izm"
- the belief that things have a set of characteristics which make them what they are,

and that the task of science and philosophy is their discovery and expression.
• [as ESSENTIAL]
• **essentialist** *noun*

essentialize *verb*
ALSO SPELLED: esp. *Brit.* **-ise**
• "e SEN sh'll ize"
• formulate in essential form; express the essential form of.
• [as ESSENTIAL]
• **essentialization** *noun* (also esp. *Brit.* **-isation**)

establish *verb*
• "es TAB lish"
• found or consolidate (a business, system, etc.) on a permanent basis.
• [Old French *establir* (stem *establiss-*) from Latin *stabilire* from *stabilis* stable, from *stare* stand]
• **established** *adjective*
• **establisher** *noun*
• **establishment** *noun*

establishmentarian *adjective*
• "es tab lish m'n TERRY 'n"
• adhering to or advocating the principle of an established church, a religious denomination recognized by a national government as its nation's official church.
• [as ESTABLISH]
• **establishmentarianism** *noun*

estaminet *noun*
• "es tammy NAY"
• a small French café or bistro selling alcoholic drinks.
• [French from Walloon *staminé* cowshed, from *stamo* a pole for tethering a cow, prob. from German *Stamm* stem]

estancia *noun*
• "es TANSY uh"
• a cattle ranch in Latin America or the southern US.
• [Spanish, lit. 'station', from medieval Latin *stancia* from Latin *stant-* present participle stem of *stare* to stand]

estate *noun*
• "es TATE"
• a property consisting of an extensive area of land usu. with a large house.
• [Old French *estat* (as STATUS)]

esteem *verb*
• "es TEEM"
• have a high regard for; greatly respect; think favourably of.
• [Old French *estimer* from Latin *aestimare* fix the price of]
• **esteemed** *adjective*

ester *noun*
• "ESTER"
• any of a class of organic compounds produced by replacing the hydrogen of an acid by an alkyl, aryl, etc. group, many of which occur naturally as oils and fats.
• [German, prob. from *Essig* vinegar + *Äther* ether]
• **esterification** *noun* "es terra fuh CAY sh'n"
• **esterify** *verb*

esterase *noun*
• "ESTER ace"
• an enzyme which hydrolyzes an ester into an acid and an alcohol, phenol, etc.
• [as ESTER]

Estevanite *noun*
• "ESTA van ite"
• a resident of Estevan, Sask.

estimable *adjective*
• "ESTA muh bull"
• worthy of esteem.
• [French from Latin *aestimabilis* (as ESTEEM)]
• **estimably** *adverb*

estimate *noun*
• "ESTA mit"
• a judgment or calculation of the approximate cost, value, size, etc. of something.
• [Latin *aestimare aestimat-* fix the price of]
• **estimated** *adjective*
• **estimation** *noun*
• **estimative** *adjective*
• **estimator** *noun*

Estonian *noun*
• "es TONY 'n"
• a native of Estonia on the Baltic Sea.

estop *verb*
• "es TOP"
• bar or preclude, esp. by estoppel.
• [Old French *estoper* from Late Latin *stuppare* stop up, from Latin *stuppa* tow]

estoppel *noun*
• "es TOP'll"
• the principle which precludes a person from asserting something contrary to what is implied by a previous action or statement of that person or by a previous pertinent judicial determination.
• [Old French *estouppail* bung, from *estoper* (as ESTOP)]

estradiol *noun*
ALSO SPELLED: *Brit.* also **oestradiol**
• "estra DIE awl"
• a major estrogen produced in the ovarian follicles of female mammals.
• [ESTRUS + Greek *dis* twice + ALCOHOL]

estrange *verb*
• "e STRANGE"
• cause (a person or group) to become unfriendly or distant; alienate.
• [Old French *estranger* from Latin *extraneare* treat as a stranger, from *extraneus* stranger]
• **estrangement** *noun*

estranged *adjective*
- "e STRANGED" ("STRANGED" rhymes with *CHANGED*)
- (of a spouse) no longer living with his or her spouse.
- [as ESTRANGE]

estreat *noun*
- "es TREET"
- a copy of a court record of a fine etc. for use in prosecution.
- [Anglo-French *estrete*, Old French *estraite* from *estraire* from Latin *extrahere* EXTRACT]

estrogen *noun*
ALSO SPELLED: *Brit.* **oestrogen**
- "ESTRA j'n"
- any of various steroid hormones developing and maintaining female characteristics of the body.
- [ESTRUS + GENESIS]
- **estrogenic** *adjective* (also esp. *Brit.* **oestrogenic**)
- **estrogenically** *adverb* (also esp. *Brit.* **oestrogenically**)

estrous *adjective*
ALSO SPELLED: *Brit.* **oestrous**
- "ESS truss"
- pertaining to estrus.
- [as ESTRUS]

HOMOPHONES: *estrus*

estrus *noun*
ALSO SPELLED: *Brit.* **oestrus**
- "ESS truss"
- a recurring period of sexual receptivity in many female mammals; heat.
- [Greek *oistros* gadfly, frenzy]

HOMOPHONES: *estrous*

estuary *noun*
- "ESS choo airy"
- the tidal mouth of a large river, where the tide meets the stream.
- [Latin *aestuarium* tidal channel, from *aestus* tide]
- **estuarial** *adjective*
- **estuarine** *adjective* "ESS choo a rine"

esurient *adjective*
- "e SURY 'nt"
- hungry.
- [Latin *esurire* be hungry, from *edere es-* eat]
- **esuriently** *adverb*

eta *noun*
- "AY tuh" or "EE tuh"
- the seventh letter of the Greek alphabet (Η, η).
- [Greek]

HOMOPHONES: *Ada*

étagère *noun*
- "ay ta ZHAIR"
- a piece of furniture with a number of open shelves on which to display ornaments etc.
- [French, from *étage* shelf, ultimately from Latin *stare* stand]

etalon *noun*
- "ETTA lon"
- a device consisting of two reflecting plates, for producing interfering light beams.
- [French *étalon* standard, from Old French *estel* post]

etchant *noun*
- "ETCH 'nt"
- a corrosive used in etching.
- [from 'etch', from Dutch *etsen* from German *ätzen* etch, from Old High German *azzen* cause to eat or to be eaten, from Germanic]

eternal *adjective*
- "e TURN'll"
- existing always; without an end or beginning in time.
- [Old French from Late Latin *aeternalis* from Latin *aeternus* from *aevum* age]
- **eternality** *noun* "e turn ALA tee"
- **eternalize** *verb* (also esp. *Brit.* **-ise**)
- **eternally** *adverb*
- **eternalness** *noun*
- **eternize** *verb* (also esp. *Brit.* **-ise**)

eternity *noun*
- "e TURNA tee"
- infinite or unending (esp. future) time.
- [Old French *eternité* from Latin *aeternitas -tatis* from *aeternus*: see ETERNAL]

Etesian *adjective*
- "e TEE zh'n"
- designating a dry NW wind blowing each summer in the eastern Mediterranean.
- [Latin *etesius* from Greek *etēsios* annual, from *etos* year]

ethanal *noun*
- "ETHA nawl"
- a colourless volatile liquid aldehyde, used in the synthesis of acetic acid and other chemical compounds; acetaldehyde.
- [ETHANE + ALDEHYDE]

HOMOPHONES: *ethanol*

ethane *noun*
- "ETH ane"
- a colourless odourless gaseous hydrocarbon of the alkane series, occurring in natural gas.
- [as ETHER]

ethanediol *noun*
- "ETH ane die awl"
- a colourless viscous hygroscopic liquid used as an antifreeze and in the manufacture of polyesters.
- [ETHANE + DIOL]

ethanol *noun*
- "ETHA nawl"
- a colourless volatile inflammable liquid forming the intoxicating element in wine, beer,

spirits, etc., and also used as a solvent, as fuel, etc.; alcohol.
• [ETHANE + ALCOHOL]
HOMOPHONES: *ethanal*

ethene *noun*
• "ETH een"
• a gaseous hydrocarbon of the alkene series, occurring in natural gas and crude oil, and used in the manufacture of polyethylene; ethylene.
• [ETHER + '-ene' forming names of unsaturated hydrocarbons containing a double bond, from Greek *-ēnos*, adjective suffix denoting origin or source]

ether *noun*
• "EE thur" (with "TH" as in *THIN*)
• a colourless volatile organic liquid used as an anaesthetic or solvent.
• [Old French *ether* or Latin *aether* from Greek *aithēr* from root of *aithō* burn, shine]
• **etheric** *adjective* "ee THARE ick" or "EE thare ick" (with "TH" as in *THIN*)

ethereal *adjective*
• "ith EERY 'll"
• light, airy.
• [Latin *aethereus, -ius* from Greek *aitherios* (as ETHER)]
• **ethereality** *noun*
• **ethereally** *adverb*

etherize *verb*
ALSO SPELLED: esp. *Brit.* **-ise**
• "EE thur ize"
• treat or anaesthetize with ether.
• [as ETHER]

ethic *noun*
• "ETHIC"
• a set of moral principles, esp. those of a specified religion, school of thought, etc.
• [Old French *éthique* or Latin *ethicus* from Greek *ēthikos* (as ETHOS)]
• **ethical** *adjective*
• **ethicality** *noun*
• **ethically** *adverb*

ethicist *noun*
• "ETHA sist"
• a person who studies ethics and makes recommendations about ethical dilemmas.
• [as ETHIC]

ethics *noun*
• "ETHIX"
• the science of morals in human conduct; moral philosophy.
• [as ETHIC]

Ethiopian *noun*
• "eethy OH pee 'n"
• a native or national of Ethiopia in E Africa.
• [*Ethiopia* from Latin *Aethiops* from Greek *Aithiops* from *aithō* burn + *ōps* face]

Ethiopic *noun*
• "eethy OPPIC" or "eethy OH pick"
• any of several Semitic languages related to Arabic and spoken in Ethiopia and neighbouring areas.
• [as ETHIOPIAN]

ethmoid *adjective*
• "ETH moid"
• of, pertaining to, or designating a square bone at the root of the nose forming part of the cranium, with perforations through which pass the olfactory nerves.
• [Greek *ēthmoeidēs* from *ēthmos* sieve]
• **ethmoidal** *adjective*

ethnic *adjective*
• "ETH nick"
• (of a population group) sharing a distinctive cultural and historical tradition, often associated with race, nationality, or religion.
• [Church Latin *ethnicus* from Greek *ethnikos* heathen, from *ethnos* nation]
• **ethnically** *adverb*
• **ethnicity** *noun* "eth NISSA tee"

ethnoarchaeology *noun*
• "ethno arky OLLA jee"
• the study of a society's institutions and organization based on examination of its material remains.
• [as ETHNIC + ARCHAEOLOGY]
• **ethnoarchaeological** *adjective*
• **ethnoarchaeologist** *noun*

ethnobotany *noun*
• "ethno BOT 'n ee"
• the traditional knowledge of a people concerning plants and their uses.
• [as ETHNIC + BOTANY]
• **ethnobotanical** *adjective*
• **ethnobotanist** *noun*

ethnocentric *adjective*
• "ethno SENTRIC"
• evaluating other races and cultures by criteria specific to one's own.
• [as ETHNIC + CENTRE]
• **ethnocentrically** *adverb*
• **ethnocentricity** *noun* "ethno sen TRISSA tee"
• **ethnocentrism** *noun*

ethnocide *noun*
• "ETHNO side"
• the deliberate and systematic destruction of the culture of an ethnic group, esp. within a larger community.
• [as ETHNIC + Latin *-cida, -cidium* from *caedere* kill]

ethnocultural *adjective*
• "ethno CULL chur 'll"
• pertaining to or having a particular ethnic group.
• [as ETHNIC + CULTURE]

ethnography *noun*
• "eth NOGGRA fee"

• the scientific description of human races and cultures.
• [as ETHNIC + Greek *graphein* writing]
• **ethnographer** *noun*
• **ethnographic** *adjective*
• **ethnographically** *adverb*

ethnohistory *noun*
• "ethno HISTER ee"
• the branch of knowledge that deals with the history of races and cultures, esp. non-Western ones.
• [as ETHNIC + Latin *historia* from Greek *historia* finding out, narrative, history, from *histōr* learned, wise man]
• **ethnohistorian** *noun*
• **ethnohistoric** *adjective*
• **ethnohistorical** *adjective*
• **ethnohistorically** *adverb*

ethnology *noun*
• "eth NOLLA jee"
• the branch of knowledge that deals with the characteristics of different peoples and the differences and relationships between them.
• [as ETHNIC + *logos* word]
• **ethnologic** *adjective*
• **ethnological** *adjective*
• **ethnologically** *adverb*
• **ethnologist** *noun*

ethnomethodology *noun*
• "ethno metha DOLLA jee"
• a method of sociological analysis that examines how individuals in everyday situations construct and maintain the social order of those situations.
• [as ETHNIC + French *méthode* or Latin *methodus* from Greek *methodos* pursuit of knowledge (*meta-* with, *hodos* way) + *logos* word]
• **ethnomethodological** *adjective*
• **ethnomethodologist** *noun*

ethnomusicology *noun*
• "ethno music OLLA jee"
• the study of the music of one or more (esp. non-European) cultures.
• [as ETHNIC + Old French *musique* from Latin *musica* from Greek *mousikē* (*tekhnē* art) of the Muses (*mousa* Muse) + *logos* word]
• **ethnomusicological** *adjective*
• **ethnomusicologist** *noun*

ethogram *noun*
• "EETHO gram"
• a list of the kinds of behaviour or activity observed in an animal.
• [Greek *ētho-* (see ETHOS) + *gramma* thing written]

ethology *noun*
• "ee THOLLA jee"
• the science of animal behaviour.
• [Latin *ethologia* from Greek *ēthologia* (as ETHOS + *logos* word)]
• **ethological** *adjective*
• **ethologically** *adverb*
• **ethologist** *noun*

ethos *noun*
• "EETH oss"
• the characteristic spirit or attitudes of a community, people, or system, or of a literary work etc.
• [modern Latin from Greek *ēthos* nature, disposition]

ethyl *noun*
• "ETH'll"
• the monovalent radical derived from ethane by removal of a hydrogen atom.
• [German (as ETHER)]

ethylene *noun*
• "ETH'll een"
• a gaseous hydrocarbon of the alkene series, occurring in natural gas and crude oil, and used in the manufacture of polyethylene.
• [as ETHYL]

ethyne *noun*
• "EETH ine" or "ETH ine"
• a colourless hydrocarbon gas, burning with a bright flame, used esp. in welding and formerly in lighting; acetylene.
• [as ETHYL]

etic *adjective*
• "ETTIC"
• designating a generalized non-structural approach to the description of a particular language or culture.
• [abbreviation of PHONETIC]

etiolated *adjective*
• "EETY a lated"
• (of a plant) pale from exclusion of light.
• [French *étioler* from Norman French *étieuler* grow into a stem, from *éteule*, ultimately from Latin *stipula* straw]
• **etiolation** *noun*

etiology *noun*
ALSO SPELLED: *Brit.* also **aetiology**
• "eety OLLA jee"
• the causation of diseases and disorders, esp. of a specific disease, as a subject of investigation.
• [Late Latin *aetiologia* from Greek *aitiologia* from *aitia* cause]
• **etiologic** *adjective* (also esp. *Brit.* **aetiologic**)
• **etiological** *adjective* (also esp. *Brit.* **aetiological**)
• **etiologically** *adverb* (also esp. *Brit.* **aetiologically**)

etiquette *noun*
• "ETTA kit" or "ETTA ket"
• the conventional rules of social or official behaviour.
• [French *étiquette* label, etiquette]

Etonian *noun*
- "ee TONY 'n"
- a past or present member of Eton College, an exclusive private school in S England.

étouffée *noun*
- "ay too FAY"
- a spicy Cajun stew made with vegetables and seafood.
- [French, lit. = 'smothered']

etrier *noun*
- "AY tree ay"
- a short rope ladder with a few rungs of wood or metal.
- [French, = stirrup]

Etruscan *adjective*
- "e TRUSS k'n"
- of ancient Etruria in central Italy, esp. its pre-Roman civilization and physical remains.
- [Latin *Etruscus*]

étude *noun*
- "ay TUDE"
- a short musical composition or exercise, usu. for one instrument, designed to improve the technique of the player.
- [French, = study, from Latin *studium* care, application, study]

etui *noun*
- "et TWEE"
- a small case for needles etc.
- [French *étui* from Old French *estui* prison]

etymology *noun*
- "etta MOLLA jee"
- the historically verifiable sources of the formation of a word and the development of its meaning.
- [Greek *etumologia* (as ETYMON + *logos* word)]
- **etymological** *adjective*
- **etymologically** *adverb*
- **etymologist** *noun*
- **etymologize** *verb* (also esp. *Brit.* **-ise**)

etymon *noun*
- "ETTA mon"
- the word that gives rise to a derivative or a borrowed or later form.
- [Latin from Greek *etumon* (neuter of *etumos* true), the literal sense or original form of a word]

eucalyptus *noun*
- "yooka LIP tuss"
- any tree of the genus *Eucalyptus*, native to Australasia, cultivated for its timber and for the oil from its leaves.
- [modern Latin from Greek *eu* well, easily + *kaluptos* covered, from *kaluptō* to cover, the unopened flower being protected by a cap]

eucharis *noun*
- "YOOKA riss"
- any bulbous plant of the genus *Eucharis*, native to S America, with white umbellate flowers.
- [Greek *eukharis* pleasing (*eu* well, easily, *kharis* grace)]

Eucharist *noun*
- "YOOKA rist"
- (in the Catholic, Anglican and Orthodox churches) the sacrament commemorating the Last Supper, in which bread and wine are consecrated and consumed.
- [ultimately from ecclesiastical Greek *eukharistia* thanksgiving, from Greek *eukharistos* grateful (*eu* well, easily, *kharizomai* offer willingly)]
- **Eucharistic** *adjective*
- **Eucharistically** *adverb*

euchre *noun*
- "YOO cur"
- a card game for two to four players in which the highest cards are the joker (if used), the jack of trumps, and the other jack of the same colour in a pack with the lower cards removed, the aim being to win at least three of the five tricks played.
- [19th c.: German dialect *Jucker(spiel)*]

Euclidean *adjective*
ALSO SPELLED: **Euclidian**
- "yoo CLIDDY 'n"
- of or relating to the Greek mathematician Euclid (*c.*300 BC), esp. the system of geometry based on his principles.

Eudist *noun*
- "YOO dist"
- a member of the Congregation of Jesus and Mary, an esp. teaching order of Roman Catholic priests.
- [St. John *Eudes*, d.1680]

eugenics *noun*
- "yoo JENNIX"
- the science of improving the (esp. human) population by controlled breeding for desirable inherited characteristics.
- [Greek *eu* well, easily + GENIC]
- **eugenic** *adjective*
- **eugenically** *adverb*
- **eugenicist** *noun* "yoo JENNA sist"
- **eugenist** *noun*

euglena *noun*
- "yoo GLEENA"
- a single-celled freshwater flagellate of the genus *Euglena*, which can form a green scum on stagnant water.
- [modern Latin genus name, from Greek *eu* well, easily + *glēnē* eyeball, socket of joint]

eukaryote *noun*
ALSO SPELLED: **eucaryote**
- "you CARRY oat"
- an organism consisting of a cell or cells in which the genetic material is DNA in the form

of chromosomes contained within a distinct nucleus.
• [Greek *eu* well, easily + *karyo-* denoting the nucleus of a cell, from *karuon* kernel + *-ote* as in ZYGOTE]
• **eukaryotic** *adjective* (also **eucaryotic**) "you carry OTTIC"

eulachon *noun*
• "YOOLA con"
• a small oily food fish, *Thaleichthys pacificus*, of the Pacific coast of N America, belonging to the smelt family.
• [Lower Chinook *úłxan*]

eulogy *noun*
• "YOOLA jee"
• speech or writing in praise of a person, esp. a person who has recently died.
• [medieval Latin *eulogium* from (apparently by confusion with Latin *elogium* epitaph) Late Latin *eulogia* praise, from Greek]
• **eulogist** *noun*
• **eulogistic** *adjective*
• **eulogize** *verb* (also esp. *Brit.* **-ise**)

eunuch *noun*
• "YOO nick"
• a castrated man, esp. one employed (historically) at an oriental harem or court.
• [Latin *eunuchus* from Greek *eunoukhos* lit. bedchamber attendant, from *eunē* bed + second element related to *ekhō* hold]

euonymus *noun*
• "yoo ONNA muss"
• any tree or shrub of the genus *Euonymus*, e.g. the spindle tree and burning bush.
• [Latin from Greek *euōnumos* of lucky name (*eu* well, easily, *onoma* name)]

eupeptic *adjective*
• "yoo PEPTIC"
• of or having good digestion.
• [Greek *eupeptos* (*eu* well, easily, *peptō* digest)]

euphemism *noun*
• "YOOFA mizm"
• a mild or vague expression substituted for one thought to be too harsh or direct, e.g. *pass away* for *die*.
• [Greek *euphēmismos* from *euphēmos* (*eu* well, easily, *phēmē* speaking)]
• **euphemistic** *adjective*
• **euphemistically** *adverb*
• **euphemize** *verb* (also esp. *Brit.* **-ise**)

euphonium *noun*
• "yoo FONEY um"
• a brass wind instrument of the tuba family, used esp. in brass and military bands.
• [modern Latin from Greek *euphōnos* (as EUPHONY)]

euphony *noun*
• "YOOFA nee"
• pleasantness of sound, esp. of a word or phrase; harmony.
• [French *euphonie* from Late Latin *euphonia* from Greek *euphōnia* (*eu* well, easily, *phōnē* sound)]
• **euphonic** *adjective* "yoo FONNIC"
• **euphonious** *adjective* "yoo FONEY us"
• **euphoniously** *adverb*

euphorbia *noun*
• "yoo FORBY uh"
• any plant of the genus *Euphorbia*, including spurges and poinsettia.
• [Latin *euphorbea* from *Euphorbus*, 1st-c. Greek physician]

euphoria *noun*
• "yoo FORY uh"
• a feeling or state of intense excitement and happiness.
• [Greek from *euphoros* well-bearing (*eu* well, easily, *pherō* bear)]
• **euphoric** *adjective*
• **euphorically** *adverb*

euphoriant *adjective*
• "yoo FOREY 'nt"
• inducing euphoria.
• [as EUPHORIA]

euphuism *noun*
• "YOO fyoo izm"
• an affected style of writing or speaking.
• [Greek *euphuēs* well endowed by nature: originally of writing imitating the elaborate style of *Euphues* by English writer J. Lyly (d.1606)]
• **euphuistic** *adjective*
• **euphuistically** *adverb*

Eurasian *adjective*
• "yur AY zh'n"
• of mixed European and Asian parentage.

eureka *interjection*
• "yur EEKA"
• I have found it! (announcing a discovery etc.).
• [Greek *heurēka* 1st person singular perfect of *heuriskō* find: attributed to the Greek mathematician Archimedes d.212 BC]

euro *noun*
• "YURO"
• the European currency unit adopted by the European Union, used in most of the EU countries.
• [as EUROPEAN]

Eurobond *noun*
• "YURO bond"
• an international bond issued outside the country in whose currency its value is stated.
• [as EUROPEAN + 'bond']

Eurocentric *adjective*
• "yuro SENTRIC"
• having or regarding Europe as its centre.
• [as EUROPEAN + CENTRE]
• **Eurocentricity** *noun* "yuro sen TRISSA tee"
• **Eurocentrism** *noun*

Eurocommunism *noun*
- "yuro COM yuh nizm"
- a form of Communism in Western European countries emphasizing acceptance of democratic institutions and independence of Soviet influence.
- [as EUROPEAN + COMMUNISM]
- **Eurocommunist** *adjective*

Eurocrat *noun*
- "YURO crat"
- a bureaucrat in the administration of the European Union.
- [as EUROPEAN + BUREAUCRAT]

Eurocurrency *noun*
- "YURO cur 'n see"
- currency, usu. American or Japanese, held in a European country and used for short and medium-term lending and borrowing.
- [as EUROPEAN + CURRENCY]

Eurodollar *noun*
- "YURO doller"
- a dollar deposited in a financial institution outside the US, originally in Europe but now in any country.
- [as EUROPEAN + 'dollar' from Low German *daler* from German *Taler*, short for *Joachimstaler*, a coin from the silver mine of *Joachimstal*, now *Jáchymov* in the Czech Republic]

Euromarket *noun*
- "YURO market"
- a market that emerged in the 1950s for financing international trade, backed by the commercial banks, large companies, and central banks of members of the European Union.
- [as EUROPEAN + 'market', ultimately from Latin *mercatus* from *mercari* buy]

European *adjective*
- "yura PEE 'n"
- of or in Europe.
- **Europeanism** *noun*
- **Europeanist** *noun*
- **Europeanization** *noun* (also esp. *Brit.* **-isation**)
- **Europeanize** *verb* (also esp. *Brit.* **-ise**)

Europhile *noun*
- "YURO file"
- a person who admires and likes Europe, its culture, etc.
- [as EUROPEAN + Greek *philos* dear, loving]
- **Europhilia** *noun* "yuro FILLY uh" or "yuro FEELY uh"
- **Europhiliac** *adjective*
- **Europhilic** *adjective*

Europhobe *noun*
- "YURO fobe"
- a person who opposes participation in the European Union.
- [as EUROPEAN + PHOBIA]
- **Europhobia** *noun*
- **Europhobic** *adjective*

europium *noun*
- "yur OPE ee um"
- a soft silvery metallic element of the lanthanide series, occurring naturally in small quantities.
- [modern Latin from *Europe*]

Eurotrash *noun*
- "YURO trash"
- rich European socialites, esp. those living or working in the US.
- [as EUROPEAN + 'trash', of unknown origin]

eurozone *noun*
- "YURO zone"
- the economic region formed by those member countries of the European Union that have adopted the euro.
- [as EUROPEAN + 'zone', from French *zone* or Latin *zona* girdle, from Greek *zōnē*]

eurythmic *adjective*
ALSO SPELLED: **eurhythmic**
- "yuh RITH mick" (with "TH" as in *THEM*)
- of or in harmonious proportion (esp. of architecture).
- [*eurhythmy* harmony of proportions, from Latin *eur(h)ythmia* from Greek *eurhuthmia* (*eu* well, easily, *rhuthmos* proportion, rhythm)]

eurythmics *noun*
ALSO SPELLED: **eurhythmics**
- "yuh RITH micks" (with "TH" as in *THEM*)
- harmony of bodily movement, esp. as developed with music and dance into a system of education.
- [as EURYTHMIC]

eurythmy *noun*
ALSO SPELLED: **eurhythmy**
- "yuh RITH mee" (with "TH" as in *THEM*)
- harmony of bodily movement, esp. as developed with music and dance into a system of education.
- [as EURYTHMIC]

Eustachian *adjective*
- "yoo STAY sh'n" or "yoo STAY shee 'n"
- designating the tube leading from the pharynx to the cavity of the middle ear and equalizing the pressure on each side of the eardrum.
- [Latin *Eustachius* = B. *Eustachio*, Italian anatomist d.1574]

eustasy *noun*
- "YOOSTA see"
- a change in sea level throughout the world caused by tectonic movements, melting of glaciers, etc.
- [back-formation from German *eustatisch* (adjective) (Greek *eu* well, easily, STATIC)]
- **eustatic** *adjective*

eutectic *adjective*
- "yoo TECK tick"
- (of a mixture, alloy, etc.) having the lowest

freezing point of any possible proportions of its constituents.
• [Greek *eutēktos* (Greek *eu* well, easily, *tēkō* melt)]

euthanasia *noun*
• "yootha NAY zhuh"
• an act of painlessly killing, esp. at the patient's request, a person or animal suffering from an incurable condition.
• [Greek (*eu* well, easily, *thanatos* death)]
• **euthanize** *verb* (also esp. *Brit.* **-ise**)

eutherian *noun*
• "yoo THEERY 'n"
• a mammal of the infraclass Eutheria, giving nourishment to its unborn young through a placenta (as in humans).
• [Greek *eu* well, easily + *thēr* wild beast]

eutrophic *adjective*
• "yoo TROFFIC"
• (of a lake etc.) rich in nutrients and therefore supporting a dense plant population, which kills animal life by depriving it of oxygen.
• [*eutrophy* from Greek *eutrophia* (*eu* well, easily, *trephō* nourish)]
• **eutrophicate** *verb*
• **eutrophication** *noun*
• **eutrophy** *noun* "YOOTRA fee"

evacuate *verb*
• "e VACK yoo ate"
• remove (people) from a place of danger to stay elsewhere for the duration of the danger.
• [Latin *evacuare* (*ex* out of, *vacuus* empty)]
• **evacuant** *noun*
• **evacuation** *noun*

evacuee *noun*
• "e vack yoo EE"
• a person evacuated from a place of danger.
• [as EVACUATE]

evade *verb*
• "e VADE"
• escape from, avoid (pursuers, arrest, etc.) esp. by guile or trickery.
• [French *évader* from Latin *evadere* (*ex* out of, *vadere vas-* go)]
• **evadable** *adjective*
• **evader** *noun*

evaginate *verb*
• "e VADGE 'n ate"
• turn (a tubular organ) inside out.
• [Latin *evaginare* (Latin *ex* out of, *vaginare* from *vagina* sheath, scabbard)]
• **evagination** *noun*

evaluate *verb*
• "e VAL yoo ate"
• assess, appraise.
• [back-formation from *evaluation* from French *évaluation* from *évaluer* (from Latin *ex* out of, *valēre* be worth)]
• **evaluable** *adjective*
• **evaluation** *noun*
• **evaluative** *adjective*
• **evaluator** *noun*

evanesce *verb*
• "evva NESS"
• fade from sight or existence; disappear.
• [Latin *evanescere* (*ex* out of, *vanus* empty)]
• **evanescence** *noun*
• **evanescent** *adjective*
• **evanescently** *adverb*

evangel *noun*
• "e VAN j'll"
• the Christian gospel.
• [Old French *evangile* from Church Latin *evangelium* from Greek *euaggelion* good news (*eu* well, easily, *aggelos* messenger)]

evangelical *adjective*
• "ee van JELLA k'll" or "evan JELLA k'll"
• of or according to the teaching of the gospel or the Christian religion.
• [Church Latin *evangelicus* from ecclesiastical Greek *euaggelikos* (as EVANGEL)]
• **evangelicalism** *noun*
• **evangelically** *adverb*

evangelize *verb*
ALSO SPELLED: esp. *Brit.* **-ise**
• "e VAN juh lize"
• preach the Christian gospel to.
• [Church Latin *evangelizare* from Greek *euaggelizomai* (as EVANGEL)]
• **evangelism** *noun*
• **evangelist** *noun*
• **evangelistic** *adjective*
• **evangelization** *noun* (also esp. *Brit.* **-isation**)
• **evangelizer** *noun* (also esp. *Brit.* **-iser**)

evaporate *verb*
• "e VAPPER ate"
• turn from solid or liquid into vapour.
• [Latin *evaporare* (*ex* out of, *vaporare* as VAPOUR)]
• **evaporable** *adjective*
• **evaporation** *noun*
• **evaporative** *adjective*
• **evaporator** *noun*

evaporite *noun*
• "e VAPPER ite"
• a natural salt or mineral deposit formed by evaporation of water.
• [EVAPORATE + Greek *lithos* stone]

evapotranspiration *noun*
• "e vappo transpa RAY sh'n"
• the process by which water is transferred from the land to the atmosphere by evaporation from the soil and other surfaces and by transpiration from plants.
• [EVAPORATE + 'transpiration' from French *transpirer* or medieval Latin *transpirare* (*trans-* across, *spirare* breathe)]

evasion *noun*
• "e VAY zh'n"
• the act or a means of evading a duty, question, etc.
• [Latin *evasio -onis* (as EVADE)]

evasive *adjective*
- "e VAY siv"
- seeking to evade something.
- [as EVADE]
- **evasively** *adverb*
- **evasiveness** *noun*

evection *noun*
- "e VECK sh'n"
- a perturbation of the moon's motion caused by the sun's attraction.
- [Latin *evectio* (*ex* out of, *vehere vect-* carry)]

eventful *adjective*
- "e VENT full"
- marked by many events or incidents, esp. noteworthy ones.
- ['event' from Latin *eventus* from *evenire event-* happen (*ex* out of, *venire* come)]
- **eventfully** *adverb*
- **eventfulness** *noun*

eventual *adjective*
- "e VEN choo 'll"
- occurring or existing in due course or at last; ultimate.
- [as EVENTFUL, after *actual*]
- **eventually** *adverb*

eventuality *noun*
- "e ven choo ALA tee"
- a possible event or outcome.
- [as EVENTUAL]

eventuate *verb*
- "e VEN choo ate"
- turn out in a specified way as the result.
- [as EVENTFUL, after *actuate*]
- **eventuation** *noun*

evert *verb*
- "e VURT"
- turn (an organ etc.) outwards or inside out.
- [Latin *evertere* (*ex* out of, *vertere vers-* turn)]
- **eversible** *adjective*
- **eversion** *noun*

HOMOPHONES: *avert*

every *adjective*
- "EV ree"
- each single.
- [Old English *ǣfre ǣlc* ever each]

evict *verb*
- "e VICT"
- expel (a tenant) from a property by legal process.
- [Latin *evincere evict-* (*ex* out of, *vincere* conquer)]
- **eviction** *noun*
- **evictor** *noun*

evidence *noun*
- "EVVA dince"
- the available facts, circumstances, etc. supporting or otherwise a belief, proposition, etc., or indicating whether or not a thing is true or valid.
- [Old French from Latin *evidentia* (as EVIDENT)]
- **evidential** *adjective* "evva DEN sh'll"
- **evidentially** *adverb*
- **evidentiary** *adjective* "evva DENSHA ree"

evident *adjective*
- "EVVA d'nt"
- plain or obvious (visually or intellectually).
- [Old French *evident* or Latin *evidēre evident-* (*ex* out of, *vidēre* see)]
- **evidently** *adverb*

evil *adjective*
- "EE v'll"
- morally bad; wicked.
- [Old English *yfel* from Germanic]
- **evilly** *adverb*
- **evilness** *noun*

evince *verb*
- "e VINCE"
- indicate or make evident.
- [Latin *evincere*: see EVICT]

eviscerate *verb*
- "e VISSER ate"
- disembowel.
- [Latin *eviscerare eviscerat-* (*ex* out of, VISCERA)]
- **evisceration** *noun*

evoke *verb*
- "e VOKE"
- inspire or draw forth (memories, an image, feelings, a response, etc.).
- [Latin *evocare* (*ex* out of, *vocare* call)]
- **evocation** *noun*
- **evocative** *adjective* "e VOCKA tiv"
- **evocatively** *adverb*
- **evocativeness** *noun*
- **evoker** *noun*

evolute *noun*
- "EVVA lute" or "EEVA lute"
- a curve which is the locus of the centres of curvature of another curve that is its involute.
- [Latin *evolutus* past participle (as EVOLVE)]

evolution *noun*
- "evva LOO sh'n" or "eeva LOO sh'n"
- gradual development, esp. from a simple to a more complex form.
- [Latin *evolutio* unrolling (as EVOLVE)]
- **evolutionarily** *adverb*
- **evolutionary** *adjective*
- **evolutionism** *noun*
- **evolutionist** *noun*
- **evolutionistic** *adjective*

evolve *verb*
- "e VOLVE"
- develop or come forth gradually.
- [Latin *evolvere evolut-* (*ex* out of, *volvere* roll)]
- **evolvability** *noun*
- **evolvable** *adjective*

evzone *noun*
- "EV zone"
- a member of a select Greek infantry regiment.

• [modern Greek *euzōnos* from Greek, = dressed for exercise (*eu* well, easily, *zōnē* belt)]

Ewe *adjective*
• "AY way"
• of or relating to a Kwa language of Ghana, Togo, and Benin in W Africa.
• [Ewe]

ewe *noun*
• "YOO"
• a female sheep.
• [Old English *ēowu* from Germanic]
HOMOPHONES: *yew, you*

ewer *noun*
• "YOO ur"
• a large pitcher or water jug with a wide mouth.
• [Old Northern French *eviere*, Old French *aiguiere*, ultimately from Latin *aquarius* of water, from *aqua* water]

exacerbate *verb*
• "ex ASSER bate" or "ig ZASSER bate"
• make (pain, a situation, etc.) worse.
• [Latin *exacerbare* (*ex* out of, *acerbus* bitter)]
• **exacerbation** *noun*

exactor *noun*
• "ig ZACTER"
• *Cdn* a bet on the first- and second-place finishers in a race, specifying their order of finish.
• [alteration of *exacta*, from Latin American Spanish *quiniela exacta* exact quinella]

exaggerate *verb*
• "eg ZADGE ur ate"
• give an impression of (a thing), esp. in speech or writing, that makes it seem larger or greater etc. than it really is.
• [Latin *exaggerare* (*ex* out of, *aggerare* heap up, from *agger* heap)]
• **exaggerated** *adjective*
• **exaggeratedly** *adverb*
• **exaggeration** *noun*
• **exaggerator** *noun*

exalt *verb*
• "eg ZAWLT" ("ZAWLT" rhymes with *SALT*)
• raise in rank or power etc.
• [Latin *exaltare* (*ex* out of, *altus* high)]
• **exaltation** *noun* "eg zawl TAY sh'n"
• **exaltedly** *adverb*
• **exaltedness** *noun*

example *noun*
• "eg ZAMPLE"
• a thing characteristic of its kind or illustrating a general rule.
• [Old French from Latin *exemplum* (as EXEMPT)]

exanthema *noun*
• "ex an THEEMA" (with "TH" as in *THIN*)
• a skin rash accompanying a disease such as scarlet fever or measles.
• [Late Latin from Greek *exanthēma* eruption, from *exantheō* (*ex* out of, *anthos* blossom)]

exarch *noun*
• "EX ark"
• (in Eastern-rite churches) a bishop lower in rank than a patriarch and having jurisdiction wider than the metropolitan of a diocese.
• [Church Latin from Greek *exarkhos* (*ex* out of, *arkhos* ruler)]
• **exarchate** *noun*

exasperate *verb*
• "eg ZASPER ate"
• irritate intensely.
• [Latin *exasperare exasperat-* (*ex* out of, *asper* rough)]
• **exasperatedly** *adverb*
• **exasperatingly** *adverb*
• **exasperation** *noun*

excavate *verb*
• "EX kuh vate"
• make (a hole or channel) by digging.
• [Latin *excavare* (*ex* out of, *cavus* hollow)]
• **excavation** *noun*
• **excavator** *noun*

exceed *verb*
• "eck SEED"
• be greater or more numerous than.
• [Old French *exceder* from Latin *excedere* (*ex* out of, *cedere cess-* go)]
HOMOPHONES: *accede*

exceedance *noun*
• "eck SEED ince"
• the exceeding of limits set by standards regulating pollution, etc.
• [as EXCEED]

exceeding *adjective*
• "eck SEEDING"
• surpassing in amount or degree.
• [as EXCEED]
• **exceedingly** *adverb*
HOMOPHONES: *acceding*

excel *verb*
• "eck SELL"
• be superior to.
• [Latin *excellere* (*ex* out of, *celsus* lofty)]

excellence *noun*
• "EX'll ince"
• the quality of being excellent; great merit.
• [Old French *excellence* or Latin *excellentia* (as EXCEL)]
• **excellent** *adjective*
• **excellently** *adverb*

Excellency *noun*
• "EX'll in see"
• a title used in addressing or referring to certain high officials, e.g. governors general, ambassadors, governors, and (in some countries) senior Church dignitaries.
• [Latin *excellentia* (as EXCEL)]

excelsior *noun*
• "eck SELL see or"
• soft wood shavings used for stuffing, packing, etc.
• [Latin, comparative of *excelsus* lofty]

except *verb*
• "eck SEPT"
• exclude from a general statement, condition, etc.
• [Latin *excipere except-* (*ex* out of, *capere* take)]
• **exception** *noun*
• **exceptionless** *adjective*
HOMOPHONES: *accept*

excepting *preposition*
• "eck SEPTING"
• not including; other than.
• [as EXCEPT]

exceptionable *adjective*
• "eck SEP sh'n a bull"
• open to objection.
• [as EXCEPT]
• **exceptionably** *adverb*

exceptional *adjective*
• "eck SEP sh'n 'll"
• forming an exception.
• [as EXCEPT]
• **exceptionality** *noun*
• **exceptionally** *adverb*

exceptionalism *noun*
• "eck SEP sh'n 'll izm"
• the belief that a certain thing is an exception in relation to others in its class.
• [as EXCEPT]

excerpt *noun*
• "ECK surpt" or "EG zurpt"
• a short extract from a book, film, piece of music, etc.
• [Latin *excerpere excerpt-* (*ex* out of, *carpere* pluck)]
• **excerptible** *adjective*
• **excerption** *noun*

excess *noun*
• "eck SESS"
• the state or an instance of exceeding.
• [Old French *exces* from Latin *excessus* (as EXCEED)]

excessive *adjective*
• "eck SESSIV"
• too much or too great.
• [as EXCESS]
• **excessively** *adverb*
• **excessiveness** *noun*

exchange *noun*
• "ex CHANGE"
• the act or an instance of giving one thing and receiving another in its place.
• [Old French *eschangier* from Romanic (*ex* out of, Late Latin *cambiare*, Latin *cambire* barter, prob. of Celtic origin)]
• **exchangeability** *noun*
• **exchangeable** *adjective*
• **exchanger** *noun*

exchequer *noun*
• "ex CHECKER"
• the former British government department in charge of national revenue.
• [Old French *eschequier* from medieval Latin *scaccarium* chessboard (its original sense, with reference to keeping accounts on a checkered cloth)]

excimer *noun*
• "ECKSA mur"
• a dimer existing only in an excited state, used in some lasers.
• [*excited* + DIMER]

excise[1] *noun*
• "ECK size"
• a duty or tax levied on goods and commodities produced or sold within the country of origin.
• [Middle Dutch *excijs*, *accijs*, perhaps from Romanic: related to CENSUS]
• **exciseman** *noun*

excise[2] *verb*
• "eck SIZE"
• remove (a passage of a book etc.).
• [Latin *excidere excis-* (*ex* out of, *caedere* cut)]
• **excision** *noun* "eck SIZH'n"

excite *verb*
• "eck SITE"
• rouse the feelings or emotions of (a person).
• [Old French *exciter* or Latin *excitare* frequentative of *exciēre* (*ex* out of, *ciēre* set in motion)]
• **excitability** *noun*
• **excitable** *adjective*
• **excitably** *adverb*
• **excitant** *adjective* "EX a t'nt" or "eck SITE 'nt"
• **excitation** *noun*
• **excitatory** *adjective* "EXA tuh tory"
• **excitedly** *adverb*
• **excitedness** *noun*
• **excitement** *noun*
• **exciter** *noun*
• **exciting** *adjective*
• **excitingly** *adverb*

exciton *noun*
• "eck SITE on" or "ECKSA tawn"
• a mobile concentration of energy in a crystal formed by an excited electron and an associated hole.
• [as EXCITE]

exclamation *noun*
• "ex cluh MAY sh'n"
• the act or an instance of exclaiming.
• [Old French *exclamation* or Latin *exclamatio* from *exclamare* exclaim, from *ex* out, *clamare* shout]

exclamatory *adjective*
• "ex CLAMMA tory"
• of or serving as an exclamation.
• [as EXCLAMATION]

exclave *noun*
• "EX clave"
• a portion of territory of one nation completely surrounded by territory of another or others, as viewed by the home territory.
• [Latin *ex-* out of + ENCLAVE]

exclosure *noun*
• "ex CLOE zhur"
• an area from which unwanted animals are excluded.
• [Latin *ex* out of + ENCLOSE]

exclude *verb*
• "ex CLUDE"
• shut or keep out (a person or thing) from a place, group, privilege, etc.
• [Latin *excludere exclus-* (*ex* out of, *claudere* shut)]
• **excludable** *adjective*
• **excluder** *noun*
• **exclusion** *noun*
• **exclusionary** *adjective*

exclusionist *adjective*
• "ex CLOO zh'n ist"
• favouring exclusion, esp. from rights or privileges.
• [as EXCLUDE]
• **exclusionism** *noun*

exclusive *adjective*
• "ex CLOO siv"
• excluding other things.
• [medieval Latin *exclusivus* (as EXCLUDE)]
• **exclusively** *adverb*
• **exclusiveness** *noun*
• **exclusivity** *noun*

exclusivism *noun*
• "ex CLOO siv izm"
• a policy or doctrine of (esp. national, racial, or religious) exclusiveness.
• [as EXCLUSIVE]
• **exclusivist** *adjective*

excogitate *verb*
• "ex CODGE a tate"
• think out; contrive.
• [Latin *excogitare excogitat-* (*ex* out of, *cogitare* COGITATE)]
• **excogitation** *noun*

excommunicate *verb*
• "ex kuh MYOONA cate"
• officially exclude (a person) from participation in the sacraments, or from formal communion with the Church.
• [Latin *excommunicare -atus* (*ex* out of, *communis* common)]
• **excommunication** *noun*

excoriate *verb*
• "ex COREY ate"
• censure severely.
• [Latin *excoriare excoriat-* (*ex* out of, *corium* hide)]
• **excoriation** *noun*

excrement *noun*
• "EX cruh m'nt"
• feces.
• [French *excrément* or Latin *excrementum* (as EXCRETE)]
• **excremental** *adjective*

excrescence *noun*
• "ex CRESS ince"
• an abnormal or morbid outgrowth on the body or a plant.
• [Latin *excrescentia* (*ex* out of, *crescere* grow)]
• **excrescent** *adjective*

excreta *plural noun*
• "ex CREETA"
• waste discharged from the body, esp. feces and urine.
• [Latin neuter pl.: see EXCRETE]

excrete *verb*
• "ex CREET"
• (of an animal or plant) separate and expel waste matter as a result of metabolism.
• [Latin *excernere excret-* (*ex* out of, *cernere* sift)]
• **excreter** *noun*
• **excretion** *noun*
• **excretory** *adjective* "EX cruh tory"

excruciating *adjective*
• "ex CROOSHY ate ing"
• (of physical or mental pain) intense, acute.
• [Latin *excruciare excruciat-* (*ex* out of, *cruciare* torment, from *crux crucis* cross)]
• **excruciatingly** *adverb*
• **excruciation** *noun*

exculpate *verb*
• "EX cull pate"
• free from blame.
• [medieval Latin *exculpare exculpat-* (*ex* out of, *culpa* blame)]
• **exculpation** *noun*
• **exculpatory** *adjective* "ex CULPA tory"

excursion *noun*
• "ex CUR zh'n"
• a short journey, esp. one made by a group of people together for pleasure.
• [Latin *excursio* from *excurrere excurs-* (*ex* out of, *currere* run)]
• **excursionist** *noun*

excursus *noun*
• "ex CUR suss"
• a detailed discussion of a special point in a book, usu. in an appendix.
• [Latin, verbal noun formed as EXCURSION]

excuse *verb*
• "ex KYOOZ"
• attempt to lessen the blame attaching to (a person, act, or fault).

• [Old French *escuser* from Latin *excusare* (*ex* out of, *causa* cause, accusation)]
• **excusable** *adjective*
• **excusably** *adverb*

execrable *adjective*
• "EX a cruh bull"
• abominable, detestable.
• [Old French from Latin *execrabilis* (as EXECRATE)]
• **execrably** *adverb*

execrate *verb*
• "EX a crate"
• express or feel abhorrence for.
• [Latin *exsecrare* (*ex* out of, *sacrare* devote, from *sacer* sacred, accursed)]
• **execration** *noun*

executant *noun*
• "eg ZECK yoo t'nt"
• a performer, esp. of music.
• [French *exécutant* present participle (as EXECUTE)]

execute *verb*
• "EX a cute"
• carry out a sentence of death on (a condemned person).
• [Old French *executer* from medieval Latin *executare* from Latin *exsequi exsecut-* (*ex* out of, *sequi* follow)]
• **executable** *adjective*
• **execution** *noun*
• **executionary** *adjective*
• **executioner** *noun*

executive *noun*
• "eg ZECK yoo tiv"
• a person or body with managerial or administrative responsibility in a business organization etc.; a senior business person.
• [medieval Latin *executivus* (as EXECUTE)]
• **executively** *adverb*

executor *noun*
• "eg ZECK yoo tur"
• a person appointed by a testator to carry out the terms of his or her will.
• [as EXECUTE]
• **executorship** *noun*
• **executory** *adjective*

executrix *noun*
• "eg ZECK yoo trix"
• a woman appointed by a testator to carry out the terms of his or her will.
• [as EXECUTE + Latin *-trix* feminine agent noun ending]

exegesis *noun*
• "ex a JEE sis"
• critical explanation of a text, esp. of Scripture.
• [Greek *exēgēsis* from *exēgeomai* interpret (*ex* out of, *hēgeomai* lead)]
• **exegetic** *adjective* "ex a JETTIC"
• **exegetical** *adjective*

exegete *noun*
• "EX a jeet"
• a person skilled at exegesis.
• [Greek *exēgētēs* (as EXEGESIS)]

exemplar *noun*
• "eg ZEM plur" or "eg ZEM plar"
• a model or pattern.
• [Old French *exemplaire* from Late Latin *exemplarium* (as EXAMPLE)]

exemplary *adjective*
• "eg ZEMPLA ree"
• fit to be imitated; outstandingly good.
• [Late Latin *exemplaris* (as EXAMPLE)]
• **exemplarily** *adverb* "eg zem PLERRA lee"
• **exemplariness** *noun*
• **exemplarity** *noun*

exemplify *verb*
• "eg ZEMPLA fie"
• illustrate by example.
• [medieval Latin *exemplificare* (as EXAMPLE)]
• **exemplification** *noun*

exemplum *noun*
• "eg ZEM plum"
• an example or model, esp. a moralizing or illustrative story.
• [Latin: see EXAMPLE]

exempt *adjective*
• "eg ZEMPT"
• free from an obligation or liability etc. imposed on others.
• [Latin *exemptus* past participle of *eximere exempt-* (*ex* out of, *emere* take)]
• **exemption** *noun*

exequies *plural noun*
• "EX a kweez"
• funeral rites.
• [Old French from Latin *exsequiae* (*ex* out of, *sequi* follow)]

exercise *noun*
• "EX ur size"
• activity requiring physical effort, done esp. as training or to sustain or improve health.
• [Old French *exercice* from Latin *exercitium* from *exercere exercit-* keep at work (*ex* out of, *arcēre* restrain)]
• **exercisable** *adjective*
• **exerciser** *noun*
HOMOPHONES: *exorcise*

exergue *noun*
• "eg ZURG" or "EX urg"
• a small space usu. on the reverse of a coin or medal, below the principal device.
• [French from medieval Latin *exergum* from Greek *ex-* (*ex* out of) + *ergon* work]

exert *verb*
• "eg ZURT"
• bring to bear (a quality, force, influence, etc.).
• [Latin *exserere exsert-* put forth (*ex* out of, *serere* bind)]
• **exertion** *noun*

exeunt *verb*
• "EX ee unt"
• (as a stage direction) (actors) leave the stage.
• [Latin, = they go out: 3rd pl. pres. of *exire* go out]

exfiltrate *verb*
• "ex FILL trate"
• withdraw (troops, spies, etc.) surreptitiously, esp. from danger.
• [Latin *ex* out of + INFILTRATE]
• **exfiltration** *noun*

exfoliant *noun*
• "ex FOLEY 'nt"
• a cosmetic product designed to remove dead cells from the surface of the skin.
• [as EXFOLIATE]

exfoliate *verb*
• "ex FOLEY ate"
• (of bone, the skin, a mineral, etc.) come off in scales or layers.
• [Late Latin *exfoliare exfoliat-* (*ex* out of, *folium* leaf)]
• **exfoliation** *noun*
• **exfoliative** *adjective*

exhale *verb*
• "ex HALE"
• breathe out (esp. air or smoke) from the lungs.
• [Old French *exhaler* from Latin *exhalare* (*ex* out of, *halare* breathe)]
• **exhalable** *adjective*
• **exhalation** *noun* "ex huh LAY sh'n"

exhaust *verb*
• "eg ZOST"
• consume or use up the whole of.
• [Latin *exhaurire exhaust-* (*ex* out of, *haurire* draw (water), drain)]
• **exhauster** *noun*
• **exhaustible** *adjective*
• **exhaustingly** *adverb*

exhaustion *noun*
• "eg ZOSS ch'n"
• a state of extreme physical or mental fatigue.
• [as EXHAUST]

exhaustive *adjective*
• "eg ZOSS tiv"
• thorough, comprehensive.
• [as EXHAUST]
• **exhaustively** *adverb*
• **exhaustiveness** *noun*
• **exhaustivity** *noun*

exhibit *verb*
• "eg ZIBBIT"
• show or reveal publicly (for amusement, in competition, etc.).
• [Latin *exhibēre exhibit-* (*ex* out of, *habēre* hold)]
• **exhibition** *noun* "ex a BISH'n"
• **exhibitor** *noun*

exhibitionism *noun*
• "ex a BISH'n izm"
• a tendency towards display or extravagant behaviour.
• [as EXHIBIT]
• **exhibitionist** *noun*
• **exhibitionistic** *adjective*
• **exhibitionistically** *adverb*

exhilarate *verb*
• "eg ZILLA rate"
• make (someone) feel very happy, elated, or excited.
• [Latin *exhilarare* (*ex* out of, *hilaris* cheerful)]
• **exhilarated** *adjective*
• **exhilarating** *adjective*
• **exhilaratingly** *adverb*
• **exhilaration** *noun*

exhort *verb*
• "eg ZORT"
• urge or advise strongly or earnestly.
• [Latin *exhortari* (*ex* out of, *hortari* exhort)]
• **exhortation** *noun*
• **exhortatory** *adjective*
• **exhorter** *noun*

exhume *verb*
• "ex OOM" or "eg ZOOM" or "ex YOOM"
• dig out, unearth (esp. a buried corpse).
• [medieval Latin *exhumare* (*ex* out of, *humus* ground)]
• **exhumation** *noun*

exigency *noun*
• "EX idge 'n see" or "eg ZIDGE 'n see"
• an urgent need or demand.
• [Late Latin *exigentia* (as EXIGENT)]

exigent *adjective*
• "EG zidge 'nt" or "EX idge 'nt"
• requiring much; exacting.
• [Latin *exigent-* completing, ascertaining, from the verb *exigere* (*ex* out of, *agere* drive)]

exiguous *adjective*
• "eg ZIG yoo us"
• scanty, small.
• [Latin *exiguus* scanty, from *exigere* weigh exactly: see EXIGENT]
• **exiguity** *noun*
• **exiguously** *adverb*
• **exiguousness** *noun*

exile *noun*
• "EG zile" or "EX ile"
• expulsion, or the state of being expelled, from one's native land or home, esp. for political reasons.
• [Old French *exil*, *exiler* from Latin *exilium* banishment]
• **exilic** *adjective* "eg ZILLIC" or "ex ILLIC"

existence *noun*
• "eg ZIS tince"
• the fact or condition of being or existing.
• [Old French *existence* or Late Latin *existentia* from Latin *exsistere* (*ex* out of, *stare* stand)]
• **existent** *adjective*

existential *adjective*
- "eg zis TEN sh'll" or "ex iss TEN sh'll"
- of or relating to existence.
- [as EXISTENCE]
- **existentially** *adverb*

existentialism *noun*
- "eg zis TEN sh'll izm" or "ex iss TEN sh'll izm"
- a philosophical theory emphasizing the existence of the individual person as a free and responsible agent isolated in an otherwise deterministic world.
- [as EXISTENCE]
- **existentialist** *noun*

exobiology *noun*
- "ex oh by OLLA jee"
- the branch of science that deals with the possibility of life on other planets or in space.
- [Greek *exo* outside + BIOLOGY]
- **exobiological** *adjective*
- **exobiologist** *noun*

exocrine *adjective*
- "EX oh crine"
- (of a gland) secreting through a duct.
- [Greek *exo* outside + *krinō* sift]

exocytosis *noun*
- "ex oh sye TOE sis"
- the release of matter by a living cell.
- [Greek *exo* outside + Greek *kutos* vessel]
- **exocytotic** *adjective*

exodus *noun*
- "EX a duss" or "EG zuh duss"
- a mass departure of people.
- [Church Latin from Greek *exodos* (*ex* out of, *hodos* way)]

exogamy *noun*
- "ex OGGA mee"
- marriage outside one's own community, clan, or tribe.
- [Greek *exo* outside + *-gamia* from *gamos* marriage]
- **exogamic** *adjective* "ex oh GAMMIC"
- **exogamous** *adjective*

exogenous *adjective*
- "ex ODGE a nuss"
- growing or originating from outside.
- [Greek *exo* outside + GENESIS]
- **exogenously** *adverb*

exon *noun*
- "EX on"
- a segment of a DNA or RNA molecule that contains coding information for a protein.
- [from 'express']

exonerate *verb*
- "eg ZONNER ate"
- free or declare free from guilt, blame, etc.
- [Latin *exonerare exonerat-* (*ex* out of, *onus, oneris* burden)]
- **exoneration** *noun*
- **exonerative** *adjective*

exophthalmos *noun*
- "ex off THAL muss"
- abnormal protrusion of the eyeball.
- [modern Latin from Greek *exophthalmos* having prominent eyes (*ex* out of, *ophthalmos* eye)]
- **exophthalmic** *adjective*

exorbitant *adjective*
- "eg ZORBA t'nt"
- (of a price, demand, etc.) grossly excessive.
- [Late Latin *exorbitare* (*ex* out of, *orbita* orbit)]
- **exorbitance** *noun*
- **exorbitantly** *adverb*

exorcise *verb*
ALSO SPELLED: **-ize**
- "EX ur size" or "EX or size"
- endeavour to expel (a supposed evil spirit) by religious ceremonies, prayers, etc.
- [French *exorciser* or Church Latin *exorcizare* from Greek *exorkizō* (*ex* out of, *horkos* oath)]
- **exorcism** *noun*
- **exorcist** *noun*

HOMOPHONES: *exercise*

exordium *noun*
- "ex ORDY um"
- the beginning or introductory part, esp. of a discourse or treatise.
- [Latin from *exordiri* (*ex* out of, *ordiri* begin)]
- **exordial** *adjective*

exoskeleton *noun*
- "ex oh SKELLA t'n"
- a rigid external covering for the body in certain animals, esp. arthropods, providing support and protection.
- [Greek *exo* outside + SKELETON]
- **exoskeletal** *adjective*

exosphere *noun*
- "EX oh sfeer"
- the outermost part of the atmosphere of a planet etc.
- [Greek *exo* outside + SPHERE]
- **exospheric** *adjective*

exoteric *adjective*
- "ex oh TARE ick"
- (of a doctrine, mode of speech, etc.) intended for, or intelligible to, those outside a select group.
- [Greek *exōterikos* from *exōterō*, comparative of *exō* outside: compare ESOTERIC]

exothermic *adjective*
- "ex oh THURMIC"
- (of a reaction) accompanied by, or (of a compound) formed with the liberation of heat.
- [Greek *exo* outside + *thermē* heat]
- **exothermally** *adverb*
- **exothermically** *adverb*

exotic *adjective*
- "eg ZOTTIC"
- introduced from or originating in or existing in a foreign or distant place.

• [Latin *exoticus* from Greek *exōtikos* from *exō* outside]
• **exotically** *adverb*
• **exoticism** *noun* "eg ZOTTA sizm"
• **exoticize** *verb* (also esp. *Brit.* **-ise**)
• **exoticness** *noun*

exotica *plural noun*
• "eg ZOTTIC uh"
• remarkably strange or rare things.
• [Latin, neuter pl. of *exoticus*: see EXOTIC]

exotoxin *noun*
• "EX oh toxin"
• a toxin released by a living bacterial cell into its surroundings.
• [Greek *exo* outside + TOXIN]

expand *verb*
• "ex PAND"
• increase in size, scope, or importance.
• [Latin *expandere expans-* spread out (*ex* out of, *pandere* spread)]
• **expandability** *noun*
• **expandable** *adjective*
• **expander** *noun*
• **expanding** *adjective*
• **expansibility** *noun*
• **expansible** *adjective*
• **expansion** *noun*
• **expansionary** *adjective*
• **expansive** *adjective*
• **expansively** *adverb*
• **expansiveness** *noun*

expansile *adjective*
• "ex PAN sile"
• of expansion.
• [as EXPAND]

expansionism *noun*
• "ex PAN sh'n"
• a policy or theory advocating esp. territorial or economic expansion.
• [as EXPAND]
• **expansionist** *noun*
• **expansionistic** *adjective*

expatiate *verb*
• "ex PAY shee ate"
• speak or write at length or in detail.
• [Latin *exspatiari* digress (*ex* out of, *spatium* space)]
• **expatiation** *noun*

expatriate *adjective*
• "ex PAY tree it"
• living abroad, esp. for a long period.
• [medieval Latin *expatriare* (*ex* out of, *patria* native country)]
• **expatriation** *noun*

expect *verb*
• "ex PECT"
• regard as likely; assume as a future event or occurrence.
• [Latin *exspectare* (*ex* out of, *spectare* look, frequentative of *specere* see)]
• **expectable** *adjective*
• **expectably** *adverb*
• **expectancy** *noun*
• **expectant** *adjective*
• **expectantly** *adverb*
• **expectation** *noun*

expectorate *verb*
• "ex PECTER ate"
• cough or spit out (phlegm etc.) from the chest or lungs.
• [Latin *expectorare expectorat-* (*ex* out of, *pectus -oris* breast)]
• **expectorant** *adjective*
• **expectoration** *noun*
• **expectorator** *noun*

expedient *adjective*
• "ex PEEDY 'nt"
• (of an action) convenient and practical although possibly improper or immoral.
• [Latin *expedire*: see EXPEDITE]
• **expedience** *noun*
• **expediency** *noun*
• **expediently** *adverb*

expedite *verb*
• "EXPA dite"
• assist the progress of; hasten (an action, process, etc.).
• [Latin *expedire expedit-* extricate, put in order (*ex* out of, *pes pedis* foot)]

expediter *noun*
ALSO SPELLED: **expeditor**
• "EXPA dite ur"
• an employee responsible for ensuring that work is done efficiently and on schedule.
• [as EXPEDITE]

expedition *noun*
• "expa DISH'n"
• a journey or voyage for a particular purpose, esp. tourism, exploration, or scientific research.
• [Old French from Latin *expeditio -onis* (as EXPEDITE)]
• **expeditionary** *adjective*
• **expeditioner** *noun*
• **expeditionist** *noun*

expeditious *adjective*
• "expa DISH us"
• acting or done with speed and efficiency.
• [as EXPEDITE]
• **expeditiously** *adverb*
• **expeditiousness** *noun*

expel *verb*
• "ex PELL"
• compel the departure of (a person) from a school, community, etc.
• [Latin *expellere expuls-* (*ex* out of, *pellere* drive)]
• **expellee** *noun*

expend *verb*
• "ex PEND"
• spend or use up (money, time, energy, etc.).

• [Latin *expendere expens-* (*ex* out of, *pendere* weigh)]
• **expenditure** *noun*

expendable *adjective*
• "ex PENDA bull"
• that may be sacrificed or dispensed with, esp. to achieve a purpose.
• [as EXPEND]
• **expendability** *noun*
• **expendably** *adverb*

expense *noun*
• "ex PENSE"
• cost incurred; payment of money.
• [Late Latin *expensa* (money) spent, past participle of Latin *expendere* EXPEND]

expensive *adjective*
• "ex PENSIV"
• costing much.
• [as EXPEND]
• **expensively** *adverb*
• **expensiveness** *noun*

experience *noun*
• "ex PEERY ince"
• actual observation of or practical acquaintance with facts or events.
• [Old French from Latin *experientia* from *experiri expert-* try]
• **experienceable** *adjective*
• **experienced** *adjective*
• **experiencer** *noun*

experiential *adjective*
• "ex peery EN sh'll"
• involving or based on experience.
• [as EXPERIENCE]
• **experientialism** *noun*
• **experientialist** *noun*
• **experientially** *adverb*

experiment *noun*
• "ex PERRA m'nt"
• a procedure undertaken to make a discovery, test a hypothesis etc., or demonstrate a known fact.
• [Old French *experiment* or Latin *experimentum* (as EXPERIENCE)]
• **experimental** *adjective*
• **experimentally** *adverb*
• **experimentation** *noun*
• **experimenter** *noun*

experimentalism *noun*
• "ex perra MENT'll izm"
• the empirical approach in philosophy or science.
• [as EXPERIMENT]
• **experimentalist** *noun*

expertise *noun*
• "ex purr TEEZ"
• expert skill, knowledge, or judgment.
• [French, from 'expert' from Old French from Latin *expertus* past participle of *experiri*: see EXPERIENCE]

expertize *verb*
ALSO SPELLED: esp. *Brit.* **-ise**
• "EX purr tize"
• give an expert opinion.
• [as EXPERTISE]

expiate *verb*
• "EX pee ate"
• atone for (guilt or sin).
• [Latin *expiare expiat-* (*ex* out of, *pius* devout)]
• **expiation** *noun*
• **expiator** *noun*
• **expiatory** *adjective* "EX pee a tory"

expiratory *adjective*
• "ex PIRE a tory"
• relating to the exhalation of air from the lungs.
• [as EXPIRE]

expire *verb*
• "ex PIRE"
• (of a period of time, validity, etc.) come to an end.
• [Old French *expirer* from Latin *exspirare* (*ex* out of, *spirare* breathe)]
• **expiration** *noun*
• **expiry** *noun*

explain *verb*
• "ex PLANE"
• make (something) clear or intelligible with detailed information etc.
• [Latin *explanare* (*ex* out of, *planus* flat, assimilated to 'plain')]
• **explainable** *adjective*
• **explainer** *noun*

explanation *noun*
• "expla NAY sh'n"
• the act or an instance of explaining.
• [Latin *explanatio* (as EXPLAIN)]

explanatory *adjective*
• "ex PLANNA tory"
• serving to explain.
• [Late Latin *explanatorius* (as EXPLAIN)]
• **explanatorily** *adverb*

expletive *noun*
• "EXPLA tiv" or "ex PLEE tiv"
• an oath, swear word, or other expression, used in an exclamation.
• [Late Latin *expletivus* (*ex* out of, *plēre plet-* fill)]

explicable *adjective*
• "ex PLICKA bull" or "EX plicka bull"
• that can be explained.
• [as EXPLICATE]

explicate *verb*
• "EXPLA cate"
• make clear, explain.
• [Latin *explicare explicat-* unfold (*ex* out of, *plicare plicat-* or *plicit-* fold)]
• **explication** *noun*
• **explicative** *adjective* "ex PLICKA tiv" or "EXPLA cay tiv"
• **explicator** *noun*

explicit *adjective*
• "ex PLISSIT"
• expressly stated or conveyed, leaving nothing merely implied; stated in detail.
• [French *explicite* or Latin *explicitus* (as EXPLICATE)]
• **explicitly** *adverb*
• **explicitness** *noun*

explode *verb*
• "ex PLODE"
• (of gas, gunpowder, a bomb, etc.) expand suddenly, burst, or fly into pieces with a loud noise owing to a release of internal energy.
• [earliest in sense 'show (a theory etc.) to be false or baseless', from Latin *explodere* hiss off the stage (*ex* out of, *plodere plos-* = *plaudere* clap)]
• **explodable** *adjective*
• **exploder** *noun*
• **explosion** *noun*
• **explosive** *adjective*
• **explosively** *adverb*
• **explosiveness** *noun*

exploit *noun*
• "ex PLOIT"
• utilize or take advantage of (esp. a person) for one's own ends.
• [Old French *esploit*, *exploiter*, ultimately from Latin *explicare*: see EXPLICATE]
• **exploitability** *noun*
• **exploitable** *adjective*
• **exploitation** *noun*
• **exploitative** *adjective*
• **exploiter** *noun*
• **exploitive** *adjective*

exploratory *adjective*
• "ex PLORA tory"
• (of discussion etc.) preliminary, serving to establish procedure etc.
• [as EXPLORE]

explore *verb*
• "ex PLORE"
• travel extensively (through a country etc.) in order to learn or discover about it.
• [French *explorer* from Latin *explorare* search out, from *ex-* out + *plorare* cry]
• **exploration** *noun*
• **explorational** *adjective*
• **explorative** *adjective*
• **explorer** *noun*

exponent *noun*
• "ex POE n'nt"
• a raised symbol or expression beside a numeral indicating how many times it is to be multiplied by itself, e.g. $2^3 = 2 \times 2 \times 2$.
• [Latin *exponere* (*ex* out of, *ponere posit-* put)]

exponential *adjective*
• "expa NEN shull"
• of or indicated by a mathematical exponent.
• [as EXPONENT]
• **exponentially** *adverb*

export *verb*
• "EX port" or "ex PORT"
• send out (goods, services, etc.) to another country, esp. for sale.
• [Latin *exportare* (*ex* out of, *portare* carry)]
• **exportability** *noun*
• **exportable** *adjective*
• **exportation** *noun*
• **exporter** *noun*

expose *verb*
• "ex POZE"
• remove the covering from or leave uncovered or unprotected.
• [Old French *exposer* after Latin *exponere*: see EXPONENT]
• **exposed** *adjective*
• **exposer** *noun*

exposé *noun*
• "expo ZAY"
• the act or an instance of revealing something discreditable.
• [French, past participle of *exposer* (as EXPOSE)]

exposition *noun*
• "expa ZISH'n"
• the action or process of stating or describing, in speech or writing; a detailed statement or description.
• [Old French *exposition*, or Latin *expositio* (as EXPONENT)]
• **expositional** *adjective*

expositor *noun*
• "ex POZZA tur"
• an expounder or interpreter.
• [as EXPOSE]

expository *adjective*
• "ex POZZA tory"
• intended to explain or describe something.
• [as EXPOSE]

expostulate *verb*
• "ex POSS chuh late" or "ex POSS tyuh late"
• make a protest; remonstrate earnestly.
• [Latin *expostulare expostulat-* (*ex* out of, *postulare* demand)]
• **expostulation** *noun*
• **expostulatory** *adjective*

exposure *noun*
• "ex POE zhur"
• the act or condition of exposing or being exposed (to cold, danger, radiation, an influence, etc.).
• [as EXPOSE]

expound *verb*
• "ex POUND"
• set out in detail (a doctrine, theory, etc.).
• [Old French *espondre* (as EXPONENT)]
• **expounder** *noun*

express *verb*
• "ex PRESS"
• represent or make known (thought, feelings, etc.) in words or by gestures, conduct, etc.

• [Old French *expresser* from Romanic (*ex* out of, Latin *pressare*, frequentative of *premere press-* press)]
• **expresser** *noun*
• **expressible** *adjective*
• **expression** *noun*
• **expressional** *adjective*
• **expressionless** *adjective*
• **expressionlessly** *adverb*
• **expressionlessness** *noun*

expressionism *noun*
• "ex PRESH'n izm"
• a style of painting, music, drama, etc., in which an artist or writer seeks to express emotional experience rather than impressions of the external world.
• [as EXPRESS]
• **expressionist** *noun*
• **expressionistic** *adjective*
• **expressionistically** *adverb*

expressive *adjective*
• "ex PRESSIV"
• full of expression.
• [as EXPRESS]
• **expressively** *adverb*
• **expressiveness** *noun*
• **expressivity** *noun*

expropriate *verb*
• "ex PRO pree ate"
• (esp. of the state) take away (property) from its owner.
• [medieval Latin *expropriare expropriat-* (*ex* out of, *proprium* property)]
• **expropriation** *noun*
• **expropriator** *noun*

expulsion *noun*
• "ex PUL sh'n"
• the act or an instance of expelling; the process of being expelled.
• [Latin *expulsio* (as EXPEL)]
• **expulsive** *adjective*

expunge *verb*
• "ex PUNGE"
• erase, remove (esp. a passage from a book or a name from a list).
• [Latin *expungere expunct-* (*ex* out of, *pungere* prick)]

expurgate *verb*
• "EX purr gate"
• remove matter thought to be objectionable from (a book etc.).
• [Latin *expurgare expurgat-* (*ex* out of, *purgare* cleanse)]
• **expurgation** *noun*
• **expurgator** *noun*

exquisite *adjective*
• "ex KWIZZIT" or "EX kwiz it"
• extremely beautiful or pleasing.
• [Latin *exquirere exquisit-* (*ex* out of, *quaerere* seek)]
• **exquisitely** *adverb*
• **exquisiteness** *noun*

exsanguinate *verb*
• "ex AN gwin ate"
• drain of blood.
• [Latin *exsanguinatus* (*ex* out of, *sanguis -inis* blood)]
• **exsanguination** *noun*

extant *adjective*
• "ex TANT" or "EX t'nt"
• (esp. of a document, species, etc.) still existing, surviving.
• [Latin *exstare exstant-* (*ex* out of, *stare* stand)]

extemporaneous *adjective*
• "ex temper AINY us"
• spoken or done without preparation; improvised.
• [as EXTEMPORE]
• **extemporaneously** *adverb*

extempore *adjective*
• "ex TEMPER ee"
• without preparation.
• [Latin *ex tempore* on the spur of the moment, lit. 'out of the time' from *tempus* time]

extemporize *verb*
ALSO SPELLED: esp. *Brit.* **-ise**
• "ex TEMPER ize"
• compose or produce (music, a speech, etc.) without preparation; improvise.
• [as EXTEMPORE]
• **extemporization** *noun* (also esp. *Brit.* **-isation**)

extend *verb*
• "ex TEND"
• lengthen or make larger in space or time.
• [Latin *extendere extens-* or *extent-* stretch out (*ex* out of, *tendere* stretch)]
• **extendability** *noun*
• **extendable** *adjective*
• **extender** *noun*
• **extendibility** *noun*
• **extendible** *adjective*
• **extensibility** *noun*
• **extensible** *adjective*
• **extension** *noun*
• **extensional** *adjective*
• **extensionally** *adverb*

extensive *adjective*
• "ex TENSIV"
• covering a large area in space or time.
• [French *extensif -ive* or Late Latin *extensivus* (as EXTEND)]
• **extensively** *adverb*
• **extensiveness** *noun*

extensometer *noun*
• "exten SOMMA tur"
• an instrument for measuring deformation of metal under stress.
• [Latin *extensus* (as EXTEND) + Greek *metron* measure]

extensor *noun*
• "ex TENSER"
• a muscle that extends or straightens out part of the body.
• [modern Latin (as EXTEND)]

extenuated *adjective*
• "ex TEN yoo ated"
• very thin.
• [Latin *extenuare extenuat-* make thin (*ex* out of, *tenuis* thin)]

extenuating *adjective*
• "ex TEN yoo ate ing"
• showing reasons why a wrong or illegal act, or a bad situation, should be judged less seriously or excused.
• [as EXTENUATED]
• **extenuation** *noun*

exterior *adjective*
• "ex TEERY ur"
• of or on the outer side.
• [Latin, comparative of *exterus* outside]
• **exteriority** *noun*
• **exteriorly** *adverb*

exteriorize *verb*
ALSO SPELLED: esp. *Brit.* **-ise**
• "ex TEERY ur ize"
• attribute an external existence to (states of consciousness).
• [as EXTERIOR]

exterminate *verb*
• "ex TURMIN ate"
• destroy utterly (esp. something living).
• [Latin *exterminare exterminat-* (*ex* out of, *terminus* boundary)]
• **extermination** *noun*
• **exterminator** *noun*
• **exterminatory** *adjective*

external *adjective*
• "ex TURN'll"
• of or situated on the outside or visible part.
• [medieval Latin from Latin *externus* from *exterus* outside]
• **externality** *noun*
• **externally** *adverb*

externalize *verb*
ALSO SPELLED: esp. *Brit.* **-ise**
• "ex TURN'll ize"
• treat (a fact, responsibility, etc.) as existing or occurring outside of oneself or in the external world.
• [as EXTERNAL]
• **externalization** *noun* (also esp. *Brit.* **-isation**)

exteroceptive *adjective*
• "exter oh SEPTIV"
• relating to stimuli produced outside an organism.
• [Latin *externus* exterior + RECEPTIVE]
• **exteroceptivity** *noun*
• **exteroceptor** *noun*

extinct *adjective*
• "ex TINCT"
• (of a species, language, etc.) no longer surviving in the world at large or in a specific locale.
• [Latin *exstinguere exstinct-* (*ex* out of, *stinguere* quench)]
• **extinction** *noun*

extinguish *verb*
• "ex TING gwish"
• quench, put out, or cause (a flame, light, etc.) to die out.
• [Latin *extinguere* (as EXTINCT): compare *distinguish*]
• **extinguishable** *adjective*
• **extinguisher** *noun*
• **extinguishment** *noun*

extirpate *verb*
• "EXTER pate"
• kill all the members of (a race, nation, etc.) or make (a species) extinct locally, but not globally.
• [Latin *exstirpare exstirpat-* (*ex* out of, *stirps* stem)]
• **extirpation** *noun*

extol *verb*
• "ex TOLE"
• praise enthusiastically.
• [Latin *extollere* (*ex* out of, *tollere* raise)]
• **extoller** *noun*

extort *verb*
• "ex TORT"
• obtain (esp. money) by force, threats, persistent demands, etc.
• [Latin *extorquēre extort-* (*ex* out of, *torquēre* twist)]
• **extorter** *noun*
• **extortion** *noun*
• **extortionist** *noun*
• **extortive** *adjective*

extortionate *adjective*
• "ex TORE sh'n it"
• (of a price etc.) exorbitant or grossly excessive.
• [as EXTORT]
• **extortionately** *adverb*

extracellular *adjective*
• "extra SELL yuh lur"
• situated or taking place outside a cell or cells.
• [Latin *extra* outside + CELLULAR]
• **extracellularly** *adverb*

extracorporeal *adjective*
• "extra core PORRY 'll"
• involving something situated or occurring outside the body.
• [Latin *extra* outside + CORPOREAL]
• **extracorporeally** *adverb*

extract *verb*
• "ex TRACT"
• remove or take out (a tooth etc.) from a containing body or cavity, usu. with some degree of effort, force, dexterity, etc.

• [Latin *extrahere extract-* (*ex* out of, *trahere* draw)]
• **extractability** *noun*
• **extractable** *adjective*
• **extraction** *noun*
• **extractor** *noun*

extractive *adjective*
• "ex TRACTIV"
• of, involving, or concerned with the extraction of natural resources or products, esp. non-renewable ones.
• [as EXTRACT]

extracurricular *adjective*
• "extra kuh RICK yuh lur"
• (of an activity or subject of study) not included in the normal curriculum.
• [Latin *extra* outside + CURRICULUM]
• **extracurricularly** *adverb*

extradition *noun*
• "extra DISH'n"
• the surrender or delivery of a person into the jurisdiction of another country in order that he or she may be tried by that country for crimes committed there.
• [French, from *ex-* out, from + *tradition* delivery, from *tradere* hand on, betray (*trans-* across, *dare* give)]
• **extraditable** *adjective* "extra DITE a bull"
• **extradite** *verb* "EXTRA dite"

extrados *noun*
• "ex TRAY doss"
• the upper or outer curve of an arch, esp. the upper curve of the voussoirs which form the arch.
• [Latin *extra* outside + *dos* back, from Latin *dorsum*]

extragalactic *adjective*
• "extra guh LACTIC"
• occurring or existing outside our galaxy, the Milky Way.
• [Latin *extra* outside + GALACTIC]

extrajudicial *adjective*
• "extra joo DISH'll"
• not legally authorized or outside the ordinary course of law or justice.
• [Latin *extra* outside + JUDICIAL]
• **extrajudicially** *adverb*

extralimital *adjective*
• "extra LIMMIT'll"
• situated, occurring, or derived from outside a particular area.
• [Latin *extra* outside + *limes limitis* boundary, frontier]

extralinguistic *adjective*
• "extra ling GWISTIC"
• outside the field of linguistics or the bounds of language.
• [Latin *extra* outside + LINGUISTIC]

extramarital *adjective*
• "extra MERRIT'll"
• involving or constituting a usu. sexual relationship between a married person and someone other than his or her spouse.
• [Latin *extra* outside + MARITAL]

extramundane *adjective*
• "extra MUN dane"
• outside or beyond the earth, material world, or physical universe.
• [Latin *extra* outside + MUNDANE]

extramural *adjective*
• "extra MYUR'll"
• (of courses etc.) taught or conducted off the premises of a university, college, or school.
• [Latin *extra muros* outside the walls]
• **extramurally** *adverb*

extraneous *adjective*
• "ex TRAINY us"
• of external origin or added from without.
• [Latin *extraneus* from *extra* outside]
• **extraneously** *adverb*
• **extraneousness** *noun*

extraordinaire *adjective*
• "ex trore din AIR" or "extra ore din AIR"
• remarkable, outstanding.
• [French, as EXTRAORDINARY]

extraordinary *adjective*
• "ex TRORE din airy" or "extra ORDIN airy"
• unusual, remarkable, or out of the regular course or order.
• [Latin *extraordinarius* from *extra ordinem* outside the usual order]
• **extraordinarily** *adverb*
• **extraordinariness** *noun*

extrapolate *verb*
• "ex TRAPPA late"
• infer more widely from a limited range of known facts.
• [Latin *extra* outside + INTERPOLATE]
• **extrapolation** *noun*
• **extrapolative** *adjective*
• **extrapolator** *noun*

extrapyramidal *adjective*
• "extra peer a MIDDLE"
• involving or designating nerves concerned with motor activity that descend from the cortex to the spine, e.g. the basal ganglia.
• [Latin *extra* outside + PYRAMID]

extrasensory *adjective*
• "extra SENSER ee"
• regarded as derived by means other than the known senses, e.g. by telepathy, clairvoyance, etc.
• [Latin *extra* outside + SENSORY]

extrasolar *adjective*
• "extra SO lur"
• outside the solar system.
• [Latin *extra* outside + SOLAR]

extraterrestrial *adjective*
• "extra tuh RESS tree 'll"
• existing or occurring beyond the earth or its atmosphere.
• [Latin *extra* outside + TERRESTRIAL]

extraterritorial *adjective*
• "extra terra TORY 'll"
• situated or (of laws etc.) valid outside a country's territory.
• [Latin *extra territorium* outside the territory]
• **extraterritoriality** *noun*

extravagant *adjective*
• "ex TRAVVA g'nt"
• immoderate, excessive, or wasteful in use of resources, esp. money.
• [medieval Latin *extravagari* (*extra* outside, *vagari* wander)]
• **extravagance** *noun*
• **extravagantly** *adverb*

extravaganza *noun*
• "ex travva GANZA"
• an event, festival, etc. featuring elaborate and colourful spectacle, massive participation, lavish expenditure, etc.
• [Italian *estravaganza* extravagance]

extravasate *verb*
• "ex TRAVVA sate"
• let or force out (a fluid, esp. blood) from its proper vessel.
• [Latin *extra* outside + *vas* vessel]
• **extravasation** *noun*

extravascular *adjective*
• "extra VASS kyuh lur"
• situated or occurring outside the vascular system.
• [Latin *extra* outside + VASCULAR]

extravehicular *adjective*
• "extra vee HICK yuh lur"
• occurring outside a spacecraft in space.
• [Latin *extra* outside + VEHICULAR]

extreme *adjective*
• "ex TREEM"
• reaching a high or the highest degree or being exceedingly great or intense.
• [Old French from Latin *extremus* superlative of *exterus* outward]
• **extremely** *adverb*
• **extremeness** *noun*

extremist *noun*
• "ex TREEMIST"
• a person who holds extreme opinions and advocates extreme measures.
• [as EXTREME]
• **extremism** *noun*

extremity *noun*
• "ex TREMMA tee"
• the very end or terminal portion of anything.
• [as EXTREME]

extremophile *noun*
• "ex TREMMA file"
• a micro-organism that lives in conditions of extreme temperature, acidity, alkalinity, or chemical concentration.
• [as EXTREME + Greek *philos* dear, loving]

extricate *verb*
• "EXTRA cate"
• free or disentangle (esp. a person) from a constraint or difficulty.
• [Latin *extricare extricat-* (*ex* out of, *tricae* perplexities)]
• **extrication** *noun*

extrinsic *adjective*
• "ex TRIN zick"
• not inherent, intrinsic, or essential.
• [Late Latin *extrinsicus* outward, from Latin *extrinsecus* (adverb) from *exter* outside + *secus* beside]
• **extrinsically** *adverb*

extropy *noun*
• "EXTRA pee"
• the pseudo-scientific principle that life will expand indefinitely and in an orderly, progressive way throughout the entire universe by the means of human intelligence and technology.
• [Latin *ex* out + ENTROPY]
• **extropian** *adjective* "ex TRO pee 'n"

extrovert *noun*
• "EXTRA vurt"
• a person whose thoughts and interests are predominantly concerned with things outside the self.
• [*extro-* (from Latin *extra* outside) + *vertere* turn]
• **extroversion** *noun*
• **extroverted** *adjective*

extrude *verb*
• "ex TRUDE"
• thrust, force out, or expel.
• [Latin *extrudere extrus-* (*ex* out of, *trudere* thrust)]
• **extruded** *adjective*
• **extruder** *noun*
• **extrusion** *noun*
• **extrusive** *adjective*

exuberant *adjective*
• "eg ZOOBER 'nt" or "eg ZYOOBER 'nt"
• (of people or their actions) lively, high-spirited, effusive in display of feelings.
• [French *exubérant* from Latin *exuberare* (*ex* out of, *uberare* be fruitful, from *uber* fertile)]
• **exuberance** *noun*
• **exuberantly** *adverb*

exudate *noun*
• "EGGZ yoo date"
• an exuded substance, esp. a mass of cells and fluid that has seeped out of blood vessels or an organ, e.g. in inflammation or malignancy.
• [as EXUDE]
• **exudative** *adjective* "ig ZYOO duh tiv"

exude *verb*
- "eg ZOOD" or "eg ZYOOD"
- (of a liquid, moisture, etc.) ooze out, escape or cause to escape gradually.
- [Latin *exsudare* (*ex* out of, *sudare* sweat)]
- **exudation** *noun*

exult *verb*
- "eg ZULT"
- have a feeling of triumph (over a person).
- [Latin *exsultare* (*ex* out of, *saltare* frequentative of *salire salt-* leap)]
- **exultancy** *noun*
- **exultant** *adjective*
- **exultantly** *adverb*
- **exultation** *noun*
- **exultingly** *adverb*

exurb *noun*
- "EX urb"
- a town or community beyond the suburbs of a large city.
- [Latin *ex* out of + *urbs* city]
- **exurban** *adjective*
- **exurbanite** *noun*
- **exurbia** *noun*

exuviae *plural noun*
- "eg ZOOVY ee"
- an animal's sloughed skin or covering.
- [Latin, = 'animal's skins', spoils of the enemy, from *exuere* divest oneself of]

eyas *noun*
- "EYE us"
- a young hawk, esp. one taken from the nest for training in falconry.
- [originally *nyas* from French *niais* ultimately from Latin *nidus* nest]

eyelet *noun*
- "EYE lit"
- a small hole in paper, leather, cloth, etc., for string or rope etc. to pass through.
- [Old French *oillet* diminutive of *oil* eye, from Latin *oculus*]

HOMOPHONES: *islet*

eyewear *noun*
- "EYE ware"
- glasses, contact lenses, goggles, etc. worn on the eyes.
- ['eye' + 'wear']

eyra *noun*
- "ERRA"
- a red form of jaguarundi.
- [Tupi *(e)irara*]

HOMOPHONES: *era*

eyrir *noun*
- "AY reer"
- a monetary unit of Iceland, equal to one-hundredth of a krona.
- [Icelandic, from Old Norse, literally 'ounce (of silver etc.) money', prob. from Latin *aureus* golden, a golden coin]

Fabian *noun*
• "FAY bee 'n"
• a member or supporter of the Fabian Society, a socialist organization founded in England in 1884 to promote cautious and gradual political change.
• [Latin *Fabianus* from *Fabius*, Roman general d.203 BC, who successfully wore down the Carthaginians by pursuing a strategy of caution and delay]
• **Fabianism** *noun*
• **Fabianist** *noun*

fabliau *noun*
• "FABBLY oh"
• a coarsely humorous short story in verse, popular in early French poetry.
• [French from Old French dialect *fabliaux*, *-ax* pl. of *fablel* diminutive of Old French *fabler* from Latin *fabulari* from *fabula* discourse, from *fari* speak]

fabricate *verb*
• "FABBRA cate"
• construct or manufacture, esp. from prepared components.
• [Latin *fabricare fabricat-* from *fabrica* fabric, from *faber* metalworker etc.]
• **fabrication** *noun*
• **fabricator** *noun*

fabrique *noun*
• "fab REEK"
• *Cdn* (*Que.*) a vestry or local parish body responsible for the maintenance, management, etc. of church property.
• [French, as FABRICATE]

fabulist *noun*
• "FAB yoo list"
• a person who relates or composes fables or legends.
• [French *fabuliste* from Latin *fabula* discourse, from *fari* speak]
• **fabulism** *noun*

fabulous *adjective*
• "FAB yoo luss"
• incredible, exaggerated, astonishing.
• [French *fabuleux* or Latin *fabulosus* from Latin *fabula* discourse, story, from *fari* speak]
• **fabulously** *adverb*
• **fabulousness** *noun*

facade *noun*
• "fuh SOD"
• the face of a building, esp. its principal front.
• [French, ultimately from Latin *facies*]

facet *noun*
• "FASS it"
• a particular aspect of a thing.
• [French *facette* diminutive of *face* face (as FACADE)]
• **faceted** *adjective*
• **faceting** *noun*

facetious *adjective*
• "fuh SEE sh'ss"
• not intended seriously or literally; ironic.
• [Latin *facetia* jest]
• **facetiously** *adverb*
• **facetiousness** *noun*

facial *adjective*
• "FAY sh'll"
• of or for the face.
• [French, as FACADE]
• **facially** *adverb*
HOMOPHONES: *fascial*

facies *noun*
• "FAY sheez"
• the appearance or facial expression of an individual, esp. when characteristic of a particular disease.
• [Latin, = 'face']

facile *adjective*
• "FASS ile" or "FASS eel"
• easily obtained or achieved and so not highly valued.
• [French *facile* easy or Latin *facilis* from *facere* do]
• **facilely** *adverb*
• **facileness** *noun*

facilitate *verb*
• "fuh SILLA tate"
• make (an action, result, etc.) easier, less difficult, or more easily achieved.
• [French *faciliter* from Italian *facilitare* from *facile* easy, from Latin *facilis*]
• **facilitation** *noun*

- **facilitative** *adjective*
- **facilitator** *noun*

facility *noun*
- "fuh SILLA tee"
- fluency, dexterity, or ease of speech, action, etc.
- [French *facilité* or Latin *facilitas* (as FACILE)]

facsimile *noun*
- "fack SIMMA lee"
- an exact copy, esp. of writing, printing, a picture, etc.
- [modern Latin from Latin *fac* imperative of *facere* make + *simile* neuter of *similis* like]

factious *adjective*
- "FACK sh'ss"
- relating or inclined to dissension.
- [French *factieux* from Latin *factio -onis* faction, from *facere fact-* do, make]
- **factiously** *adverb*
- **factiousness** *noun*

factitious *adjective*
- "fack TISH us"
- specially contrived, not genuine.
- [Latin *facticius* from *facere fact-* do, make]
- **factitiously** *adverb*
- **factitiousness** *noun*

factitive *adjective*
- "FACTA tiv"
- (of a verb) expressing the notion of making a thing to be of a certain character, e.g. *paint* the door green, and designating the object, complement, etc. of such a verb.
- [modern Latin *factitivus*, from Latin *factitare* frequentative of *facere fact-* do, make]

factor *noun*
- "FACTER"
- a circumstance, fact, or influence contributing to a result.
- [French *facteur* or Latin *factor* from *facere fact-* do, make]
- **factorable** *adjective*

factorage *noun*
- "FACTER idge"
- commission or charges payable to a factor (agent).
- [as FACTOR]

factorial *noun*
- "fack TORY 'll"
- the product of a number and all the whole numbers below it.
- [as FACTOR]
- **factorially** *adverb*

factorize *verb*
ALSO SPELLED: esp. *Brit.* **-ise**
- "FACTER ize"
- resolve into mathematical factors or express as a product of factors.
- [as FACTOR]
- **factorization** *noun* (also esp. *Brit.* **-isation**)

factory *noun*
- "FACTER ee"
- a building or buildings containing equipment for manufacturing or processing.
- [Portuguese *feitoria* and Late Latin *factorium*]

factotum *noun*
- "fack TOE tum"
- an employee who does all kinds of work, esp. as support staff.
- [medieval Latin from Latin *fac* imperative of *facere* do, make + *totum* neuter of *totus* whole]

factual *adjective*
- "FACK choo 'll"
- based on, concerned with, or of the nature of fact or facts.
- [as FACTUM, after 'actual']
- **factuality** *noun* "fack choo ALA tee"
- **factually** *adverb*

factum *noun*
- "FACT'm"
- *Cdn* a statement of the facts of a case and the legal arguments which will be made, filed by each party in an appeal.
- [French from Latin, = 'fact' from *facere* do]

facture *noun*
- "FACK chur"
- the quality of execution, esp. of the surface of a painting.
- [Old French from Latin *factura* from *facere fact-* do, make]

facula *noun*
- "FACK yoo luh"
- a bright spot or streak on the sun associated with sunspots and solar activity in general.
- [Latin, diminutive of *fax facis* torch]
- **facular** *adjective*

facultative *adjective*
- "FACK'll tuh tiv"
- (of actions, conditions, etc.) optional or permissive as opposed to compulsory.
- [French *facultatif -ive* (as FACULTY)]
- **facultatively** *adverb*

faculty *noun*
- "FACK'll tee"
- an aptitude or ability for a particular activity.
- [Old French *faculté* from Latin *facultas -tatis* from *facilis* easy]

fado *noun*
- "FODDO"
- a type of Portuguese folk song, usu. with guitar accompaniment, and often doleful or plaintive in tone.
- [Portuguese, lit. 'fate']

Faeroese *adjective*
ALSO SPELLED: **Faroese**
- "ferro EEZ"
- of or relating to the Faeroe Islands in the N Atlantic Ocean.

faggoting *noun*
• "FAGGUT ing"
• a type of embroidery in which some vertical threads are bound together so as to create a pattern of open rectangles alternating with cords of thread.
• [original sense 'bundle of sticks for fuel', from Old French *fagot*, from Italian *fagotto*, based on Greek *phakelos* bundle]

Fahrenheit *adjective*
• "FAIR 'n hite"
• of or measured on a scale of temperature on which water freezes at 32° and boils at 212° under standard conditions.
• [G. D. *Fahrenheit*, German physicist d.1736]

faience *noun*
• "FIE awnce"
• decorated and glazed earthenware and porcelain, e.g. Delft or majolica.
• [French *faïence* from Faenza in Italy, where first produced]

faille *noun*
• "FILE" or "FALE"
• a soft ribbed fabric of silk, rayon, etc.
• [French]
HOMOPHONES: *phial, file, fail*

fain *adjective*
• "FANE"
• willing under the circumstances.
• [Old English *fægen* from Germanic]
HOMOPHONES: *feign*

fainéant *noun*
• "FAY nay ãh" (with a nasal *ah*)
• an idle or ineffective person.
• [French from *fait* does + *néant* nothing]

fajita *noun*
• "fuh HEETA"
• a dish consisting of small strips of grilled spiced beef or chicken rolled in a tortilla and garnished with fried chopped vegetables and grated cheese and usu. guacamole, salsa, and sour cream.
• [Latin American Spanish, lit. 'little strip or belt']

fakir *noun*
• "FAY keer" or "fuh KEER"
• a Muslim or (rarely) Hindu religious mendicant or ascetic.
• [Arabic *faḳīr* needy man]

falafel *noun*
ALSO SPELLED: **felafel**
• "fuh LOFF'll"
• a spicy fried patty made of ground chickpeas or beans.
• [Arabic *falāfil*]

Falangist *noun*
• "fuh LAN jist"
• an adherent of the Falange movement, a Spanish fascist movement founded in the 1930s.

Falasha *noun*
• "fuh LASHA"
• an Ethiopian holding the Jewish faith.
• [Amharic, = exile, immigrant]

falcate *adjective*
• "FAL cate"
• curved like a sickle.
• [Latin *falcatus* from *falx falcis* sickle]

falchion *noun*
• "FAWL ch'n"
• a broad curved sword with a convex edge.
• [Old French *fauchon*, ultimately from Latin *falx falcis* sickle]

falciform *adjective*
• "FAL suh form"
• curved like a sickle.
• [Latin *falx falcis* sickle]

falcon *noun*
• "FAWL k'n" or "FAL k'n"
• any diurnal bird of prey of the family Falconidae, having long pointed wings, and sometimes trained to hunt small game for sport.
• [Old French *faucon* from Late Latin *falco -onis*, perhaps from Latin *falx* scythe, or from Germanic]

falconer *noun*
• "FAWL k'n ur" or "FAL k'n ur"
• a keeper and trainer of hawks.
• [as FALCON]

falconet *noun*
• "FAWL k'n it" or "FAL k'n it"
• a light cannon.
• [Italian *falconetto* diminutive of *falcone* FALCON]

falconry *noun*
• "FAWL k'n ree" or "FAL k'n ree"
• the breeding and training of hawks; the sport of hawking.
• [French *fauconnerie* (as FALCON)]

fallacy *noun*
• "FAL a see"
• a mistaken belief, esp. based on unsound argument.
• [Latin *fallacia* from *fallax -acis* deceiving, from *fallere* deceive]
• **fallacious** *adjective* "fuh LAY sh'ss"
• **fallaciously** *adverb*
• **fallaciousness** *noun*

fallible *adjective*
• "FAL a bull"
• capable of making mistakes.
• [medieval Latin *fallibilis* from Latin *fallere* deceive]
• **fallibility** *noun*
• **fallibly** *adverb*

Fallopian *adjective*
• "fuh LOPEY 'n"
• designating either of two tubes in female

mammals along which ova travel from the ovaries to the uterus.
- [*Fallopius*, Latinized name of G. *Fallopio*, Italian anatomist d.1562]

falsetto *noun*
- "fawl SETTO"
- a method of voice production used by male singers, esp. tenors, to sing notes higher than their normal range.
- [Italian, diminutive of *falso* from Latin *falsus* past participle of *fallere* deceive]

falsify *verb*
- "FALSE a fie"
- fraudulently alter or make false (a document, evidence, etc.).
- [Old English *fals* and Old French *fals, faus* from Latin *falsus* past participle of *fallere* deceive]
- **falsifiability** *noun*
- **falsifiable** *adjective*
- **falsification** *noun*
- **falsifier** *noun*

Falstaffian *adjective*
- "fawl STAFFY 'n"
- fat, jolly, or dissipated like Shakespeare's character Sir John Falstaff.

Fameuse *noun*
- "fuh MOOZ" (with "OO" as in *BOOK*)
- *Cdn* a variety of apple grown esp. in Quebec from the 17th to the 19th c.
- [Canadian French from French, lit. 'famous']

familiar *adjective*
- "fuh MILL yur"
- well known.
- [Old French *familier* from Latin *familiaris* (as FAMILY)]
- **familiarity** *noun* "fuh milly ERRA tee"
- **familiarly** *adverb*

familiarize *verb*
ALSO SPELLED: esp. *Brit.* **-ise**
- "fuh MILL yuh rize"
- make (a person) conversant or well acquainted.
- [as FAMILIAR]
- **familiarization** *noun* (also esp. *Brit.* **-isation**)

family *noun*
- "FAMMA lee" or "FAM lee"
- a group of people related by blood, legal or common-law marriage, or adoption.
- [Latin *familia* household, from *famulus* servant]
- **familial** *adjective* "fuh MILL y'll"

famine *noun*
- "FAMMIN"
- extreme scarcity of food.
- [Old French from *faim* from Latin *fames* hunger]

famish *verb*
- "FAM ish"
- reduce or be reduced to extreme hunger.
- [Middle English from obsolete *fame* from Old French *afamer*, ultimately from Latin *fames* hunger]
- **famished** *adjective*

fanatic *noun*
- "fuh NATTIC"
- a person filled with excessive and often misguided enthusiasm for something.
- [French *fanatique* or Latin *fanaticus* from *fanum* temple (originally in religious sense)]
- **fanatical** *adjective*
- **fanatically** *adverb*
- **fanaticism** *noun* "fuh NATTA sizm"

fancier *noun*
- "FANCY ur"
- a connoisseur or follower of some activity or thing.
- [as FANCY]

fanciful *adjective*
- "FANSA full"
- existing only in the imagination or fancy.
- [as FANCY]
- **fancifully** *adverb*
- **fancifulness** *noun*

fancy *adjective*
- "FANCY"
- elaborate; not plain.
- [contraction of FANTASY]
- **fancily** *adverb*
- **fanciness** *noun*

fandangle *noun*
- "fan DANGLE"
- a fantastic ornament.
- [perhaps from FANDANGO after *newfangle*]

fandango *noun*
- "fan DANGO"
- a lively Spanish dance for two in triple time, usu. accompanied by castanets and guitars.
- [Spanish: origin unknown]

fanfare *noun*
- "FAN fare"
- a short showy or ceremonious sounding of trumpets, bugles, etc.
- [French, imitative]

fanfaronade *noun*
- "fan ferra NADE"
- arrogant talk; bragging.
- [French *fanfaronnade* from *fanfaron* braggart (as FANFARE)]

fantasia *noun*
- "fan TAY zhuh" or "fan TAIZY uh"
- a musical or other composition free in form and often in improvisatory style, or which is based on several familiar tunes.
- [Italian, = FANTASY]

fantasist *noun*
- "FANTA sist"
- a writer of fantasies.
- [as FANTASY]

fantasize *verb*
ALSO SPELLED: esp. *Brit.* **-ise**
• "FANTA size"
• daydream about something one wishes to happen.
• [as FANTASY]
• **fantasizer** *noun* (also esp. *Brit.* **-iser**)

fantast *noun*
• "FAN tast"
• a visionary; a dreamer.
• [medieval Latin from Greek *phantastēs* boaster, from *phantazomai* make a show, from *phainō* show]

fantastic *adjective*
• "fan TASTIC"
• excellent, extraordinary.
• [orig. in sense 'existing only in the imagination, unreal', from Old French *fantastique* via medieval Latin from Greek *phantastikos* from *phatazein* make visible]
• **fantastically** *adverb*

fantasticate *verb*
• "fan TASTA cate"
• make something seem fanciful or fantastic.
• [as FANTASTIC]
• **fantastication** *noun*

fantasy *noun*
• "FANTA see"
• the faculty of inventing images, esp. extravagant or visionary ones.
• [Old French *fantasie* from Latin *phantasia* appearance, from Greek (as FANTAST)]

Fanti *noun*
ALSO SPELLED: **Fante**
• "FANTY"
• a member of a people inhabiting southern Ghana.
• [Fanti]

fanzine *noun*
• "FAN zeen"
• a magazine for fans, esp. those of science fiction, sport, or popular music.
• ['fan' + MAGAZINE]

farad *noun*
• "FAIR ud"
• the SI unit of capacitance, such that one coulomb of charge causes a potential difference of one volt.
• [shortening of FARADAY]

faraday *noun*
• "FERRA day"
• a unit of electric charge equal to Faraday's constant.
• [M. *Faraday*, English physicist and chemist d.1867]

faradic *adjective*
• "fuh RADDIC"
• inductive, induced.
• [as FARADAY]

farandole *noun*
• "fare 'n DOLL"
• a Provençal communal dance, usu. in 6/8 time.
• [French from modern Provençal *farandoulo*]

farceur *noun*
• "far SUR"
• an actor or writer of farces.
• [French from *farcer* act farces]

farcical *adjective*
• "FARSA k'll"
• extremely ludicrous or futile.
• [from 'farce', from French, originally = stuffing, from Old French *farsir* from Latin *farcire* to stuff, used metaphorically of interludes etc.]
• **farcicality** *noun*
• **farcically** *adverb*

farcy *noun*
• "FARCY"
• a bacterial disease of cattle, marked by swelling and inflammation of lymph nodes.
• [Old French *farcin* from Late Latin *farciminum* from *farcire* to stuff]
HOMOPHONES: *Farsi*

fare *noun*
• "FARE"
• the price a passenger has to pay to be conveyed by bus, airplane, etc.
• [Old English *fær*, *faru* journeying, *faran* (v.), from Germanic]
HOMOPHONES: *fair*

farfalle *plural noun*
• "far FOLLAY"
• bow-shaped pasta.
• [Italian, from *farfalla* butterfly]

farina *noun*
• "fuh REENA"
• the flour or meal of cereal, nuts, or starchy roots.
• [Latin from *far* corn]

farinaceous *noun*
• "ferra NAY sh'ss"
• consisting of or containing starch.
• [Latin from *far* corn]

farl *noun*
• "FARL"
• a thin cake, originally quadrant-shaped, of oatmeal or flour.
• [obsolete *fardel* quarter]

farmstead *noun*
• "FARM sted"
• a farm and its buildings regarded as a unit.
• ['farm' + HOMESTEAD]

faro *noun*
• "FERRO"
• a gambling card game in which bets are placed on the order of appearance of the cards.

• [French *pharaon* PHARAOH (said to have been the name of the king of hearts)]
HOMOPHONES: *farrow, pharaoh*

farouche *adjective*
• "fuh ROOSH"
• sullen, shy.
• [French from Old French *faroche, forache* from medieval Latin *forasticus* from Latin *foras* out of doors]
• **farouchely** *adverb*

farrago *noun*
• "fuh ROGGO"
• a medley or hodgepodge.
• [Latin *farrago farraginis* mixed, fodder, from *far* grain]
• **farraginous** *adjective* "fuh RADGE 'n us"

farrier *noun*
• "FERRY ur"
• a smith who shoes horses.
• [Old French *ferrier* from Latin *ferrarius* from *ferrum* iron, horseshoe]
• **farriery** *noun*

farrow *noun*
• "FERRO"
• a litter of pigs.
• [Old English *fearh, færh* pig]
• **farrowing** *noun*
HOMOPHONES: *faro, pharaoh*

Farsi *noun*
• "FARCY"
• the modern Persian language.
• [Persian: compare PARSI]
HOMOPHONES: *farcy*

farthingale *noun*
• "FARTHING gale" (with "TH" as in *THIS*)
• a framework of hoops or a hooped petticoat worn to expand a woman's skirt.
• [earlier *vardingale, verd-* from French *verdugale* from Spanish *verdugado* from *verdugo* rod]

fartlek *noun*
• "FART leck"
• a method of training for middle- and long-distance running, mixing fast with slow work.
• [Swedish from *fart* speed + *lek* play]

fasces *plural noun*
• "FASS eez"
• a bundle of elm or birch rods with a projecting axe blade, carried by a lictor as a symbol of a magistrate's power in ancient Rome.
• [Latin, pl. of *fascis* bundle]

fascia *noun*
• "FAY shuh" or "FASHA" or "FASHY uh"
• a flat horizontal band of wood, aluminum, etc. around the edge of a roof, to which eavestroughs are attached.
• [Latin, = band, door frame, etc.]
• **fascial** *adjective*
HOMOPHONES: *facial*

fasciated *adjective*
• "FASHY ated"
• (of contiguous parts) compressed or growing into one.
• [Latin *fasciatus* past participle of *fasciare* swathe (as FASCIA)]
• **fasciation** *noun*

fascicle *noun*
• "FASSA k'll"
• a separately published instalment of a book, usu. not complete in itself.
• [Latin *fasciculus* bundle, diminutive of *fascis*: see FASCES]
• **fasciculate** *adjective*
• **fasciculation** *noun*

fasciitis *noun*
• "fashy ITE iss"
• inflammation of the fascia of a muscle etc.
• [as FASCIA + Greek *-itis*, forming feminine of adjectives in *-itēs* (with *nosos* 'disease' implied)]

fascinate *verb*
• "FASSA nate"
• capture the interest of; attract irresistibly.
• [Latin *fascinare* from *fascinum* spell]
• **fascinated** *adjective*
• **fascinating** *adjective*
• **fascinatingly** *adverb*
• **fascination** *noun*
• **fascinator** *noun*

fascine *noun*
• "fass EEN"
• a bundle of rods, sticks, or plastic pipes bound together, used in construction or military operations for filling in marshy ground or other obstacles and for strengthening the sides of embankments, trenches, or ditches, etc.
• [French from Latin *fascina* from *fascis* bundle: see FASCES]

Fascism *noun*
• "FASH izm"
• extreme right-wing totalitarian nationalism in Italy or Germany in the mid-20th century.
• [Italian *fascismo* from *fascio* bundle, political group, from Latin *fascis* bundle: see FASCES]
• **Fascist** *noun*
• **Fascistic** *adjective*

fashion *noun*
• "FASH'n"
• the current popular custom or style, esp. in dress or social conduct.
• [Old French *façon*, from Latin *factio -onis* from *facere fact-* do, make]
• **fashionability** *noun*
• **fashionable** *adjective*
• **fashionableness** *noun*
• **fashionably** *adverb*
• **fashioner** *noun*
• **fashiony** *adjective*

fashionista *noun*
• "fash'n EESTA"

• a person employed in the creation or promotion of haute couture, as a designer, photographer, model, etc.
• [FASHION + *ista*, apparently after SANDINISTA etc.]

fastidious *adjective*
• "fass TIDDY us"
• scrupulous or over-scrupulous in matters of taste, cleanliness, propriety, etc.; fussy.
• [Latin *fastidiosus* from *fastidium* loathing]
• **fastidiously** *adverb*
• **fastidiousness** *noun*

fastigiate *adjective*
• "fass TIDGE ee ate"
• (of a tree etc.) having the branches more or less parallel to the main stem.
• [Latin *fastigium* gable top]

fatality *noun*
• "fay TALA tee" or "fuh TALA tee"
• an occurrence of death by accident or in war etc.
• [Old French *fatal* or Latin *fatalis* from Latin *fatum* that which is spoken, from *fari* speak]

fathom *noun*
• "FATH'm" (with "TH" as in *THEM*)
• a measure of six feet (1.8 m), esp. used in taking depth soundings.
• [Old English *fæthm* outstretched arms, from Germanic]
• **fathomable** *adjective*
• **fathomless** *adjective*
• **fathomlessly** *adverb*

fatigue *noun*
• "fuh TEEG"
• extreme tiredness after physical or mental exertion.
• [French *fatigue*, *fatiguer* from Latin *fatigare* tire out]

Fatiha *noun*
ALSO SPELLED: **Fatihah**
• "FAH tee huh"
• the short first sura of the Quran, used by Muslims as a prayer.
• [Arabic *fātiḥa* opening, from *fataḥa* to open]

fatuous *adjective*
• "FATCH oo us"
• vacantly silly; idiotic.
• [Latin *fatuus* foolish]
• **fatuity** *noun* "fa CHOO a tee"
• **fatuously** *adverb*
• **fatuousness** *noun*

fatwa *noun*
• "FAT wuh"
• (in Islamic countries) an authoritative ruling on a religious matter given by a mufti.
• [Arabic *fatwa*]

faubourg *noun*
• "FOE bur" or "FOE burg"
• a suburb, esp. of Paris.
• [French: compare medieval Latin *falsus burgus* not the city proper]

fauces *plural noun*
• "FOSS eez"
• the cavity at the back of the mouth from which the larynx and the pharynx open out.
• [Latin, = throat]
• **faucial** *adjective*

faucet *noun*
• "FOSSIT"
• a device by which a flow of water from a pipe can be controlled.
• [Old French *fausset* (denoting a tap for drawing liquor from a container) from Provençal *falset* from *falsar* to bore]
• **faucetry** *noun*

faun *noun*
• "FON"
• one of a class of Latin rural deities with a human face and torso and a goat's horns, legs, and tail, identified with the Greek satyrs.
• [Old French *faune* or Latin *Faunus*, god of wooded places]
HOMOPHONES: *fawn, Fon*

fauna *noun*
• "FONNA"
• the animal life of a particular region, geological period, or environment.
• [modern Latin from the name of a rural goddess, sister of Faunus, god of wooded places]
• **faunal** *adjective*

Faustian *adjective*
• "FOUSE tee 'n" ("FOUSE" rhymes with *HOUSE*)
• relating to or suggestive of Faust, a legendary German figure who sold his soul to the devil.

Fauve *noun*
• "FOVE"
• any of a group of French artists, active between 1905 and 1910, who painted in very bright colours mainly as a reaction against Impressionism.
• [French *fauve* wild beast]
• **Fauvism** *noun*
• **Fauvist** *noun*

faux *adjective*
• "FOE"
• false, imitation.
• [French, = false]
HOMOPHONES: *foe, pho*

favela *noun*
• "fuh VELLA"
• a Brazilian shack, slum, or shantytown.
• [Portuguese]

fawn *verb*
• "FON"
• (of a person) behave in an obsequious manner; affect a cringing pleasure or fondness.
• [Old English *fagnian*, *fægnian* (as FAIN)]
• **fawning** *adjective*

- **fawningly** *adverb*

HOMOPHONES: *faun, Fon*

fay *noun*
- "FAY"
- a fairy.
- [Old French *fae, faie* from Latin *fata* (pl.) the Fates]

HOMOPHONES: *fey*

faze *verb*
- "FAZE"
- disconcert, perturb, disorientate.
- [var. of *feeze* drive off, from Old English *fēsian*, of unknown origin]

HOMOPHONES: *phase*

fealty *noun*
- "FEEL tee"
- a feudal tenant's or vassal's fidelity to a lord.
- [Old French *feaulté* from Latin *fidelitas -tatis* from *fidelis* faithful, from *fides* faith]

feasible *adjective*
- "FEEZA bull"
- practicable; easily or conveniently done.
- [Old French *faisible* from *fais-* stem of *faire* from Latin *facere* do, make]
- **feasibility** *noun*
- **feasibly** *adverb*

feat *noun*
- "FEET"
- a noteworthy act or achievement.
- [Old French *fait, fet* (as FACTUM)]

HOMOPHONES: *feet*

feature *noun*
- "FEE chur"
- a distinctive or characteristic part of a thing.
- [Old French *faiture* form, from Latin *factura* formation: see FACTURE]
- **featured** *adjective*
- **featureless** *adjective*

featurette *noun*
- "fee chur ET"
- a short feature film.
- [as FEATURE]

febrifuge *noun*
- "FEB ruh fyoodge"
- a medicine or treatment that reduces fever.
- [French *fébrifuge* from Latin *febris* fever + modern Latin *-fugus* from Latin *fugare* put to flight]

febrile *adjective*
- "FEE brile" or "FEB rile"
- of or relating to fever; feverish.
- [French *fébrile* or medieval Latin *febrilis* from Latin *febris* fever]
- **febrility** *noun* "fuh BRILLA tee"

February *noun*
- "FEB roo airy" or "FEB yoo airy"
- the second month of the year, containing 28 days, except in a leap year when it has 29.
- [ultimately from Latin *februarius* from *februa* a purification feast held in this month]

feces *noun*

ALSO SPELLED: **faeces**
- "FEE seez"
- waste matter discharged from the bowels.
- [Latin *faeces*, pl. of *faex* dregs]
- **fecal** *adjective* (also **faecal**) "FEEK'll"

feckless *adjective*
- "FECK less"
- lacking in efficiency or vitality.
- [Scots *feck* from *effeck* var. of EFFECT]
- **fecklessly** *adverb*
- **fecklessness** *noun*

feculent *adjective*
- "FECK yoo l'nt"
- murky; filthy.
- [French *féculent* or Latin *faeculentus* (as FECES)]
- **feculence** *noun*

fecund *adjective*
- "FEEK'nd" or "FECK'nd"
- fertile; highly productive of offspring, fruit, etc.
- [French *fécond* or Latin *fecundus*]
- **fecundity** *noun*

fecundate *verb*
- "FEEK'n date" or "FECK'n date"
- make fruitful.
- [Latin *fecundare* from *fecundus* fruitful]
- **fecundation** *noun*

fedayee *noun*
- "fedda YEE"
- an Arab guerrilla operating esp. against Israel.
- [informal Arabic *fidā'iyīn* pl. from Arabic *fidā'ī* adventurer]

federal *adjective*
- "FEDDER'll"
- of a system of government in which power is divided between a central government and several regional ones.
- [Latin *foedus -eris* league, covenant]
- **federalism** *noun*
- **federalist** *noun*
- **federalization** *noun* (also esp. *Brit.* **-isation**)
- **federalize** *verb* (also esp. *Brit.* **-ise**)
- **federally** *adverb*

federate *verb*
- "FEDDER ate"
- organize or be organized on a federal basis.
- [as FEDERAL]
- **federated** *adjective*
- **federative** *adjective*

federation *noun*
- "fedder AY sh'n"
- a federal group of provinces, states, etc.
- [as FEDERAL]

fedora *noun*
- "fuh DORA"

• a low soft felt hat with a crown creased lengthwise.
• [*Fédora*, drama by V. Sardou (1882)]

feign *verb*
• "FANE"
• simulate or pretend to be affected by.
• [Middle English from *feign-* stem of Old French *feindre* from Latin *fingere* mould, contrive]
• **feigned** *adjective*
HOMOPHONES: *fain*

feint *noun*
• "FAINT"
• a sham move, attack, blow, etc. to divert attention or fool an opponent or enemy.
• [French *feinte*, feminine past participle of *feindre* FEIGN]
HOMOPHONES: *faint*

feisty *adjective*
• "FICE tee"
• spirited, energetic, forceful, or exuberant, esp. when faced with opposition.
• [late 19th c.: from earlier *feist*, *fist* small dog, from *fisting cur* or *hound*, a derogatory term for a lapdog, from Middle English *fist* break wind, of West Germanic origin]
• **feistily** *adverb*
• **feistiness** *noun*

Feldenkrais *noun*
• "FELD'n krice"
• a system designed to promote bodily and mental efficiency and well-being by conscious analysis of neuromuscular activity via exercises which improve flexibility and coordination and increase ease and range of motion.
• [M. *Feldenkrais*, Russian-born physicist and mechanical engineer d.1984]

feldspar *noun*
• "FELD spar"
• any of a group of aluminum silicates of potassium, sodium, or calcium, which are the most abundant minerals in the earth's crust.
• [German *Feldspat*, *-spath* from *Feld* field + *Spat*, *Spath* a crystalline, easily cleavable and non-lustrous mineral]
• **feldspathic** *adjective* "feld SPATHIC"

felicitate *verb*
• "fuh LISSA tate"
• congratulate (a person).
• [Late Latin *felicitare* make happy, from Latin *felix -icis* happy]
• **felicitation** *noun*

felicitous *adjective*
• "fuh LISSA tuss"
• (of a name, expression, etc.) strikingly apt.
• [as FELICITY]
• **felicitously** *adverb*
• **felicitousness** *noun*

felicity *noun*
• "fuh LISSA tee"
• happiness, bliss.
• [Old French *felicité* from Latin *felicitas -tatis* from *felix -icis* happy]

feline *adjective*
• "FEE line"
• of or relating to the cat family Felidae.
• [Latin *felinus* from *feles* cat]
• **felinity** *noun* "fuh LINNA tee"

fellah *noun*
• "FELLA"
• a peasant in an Arabic-speaking country, esp. Egypt.
• [Arabic *fallāḥ* husbandman, from *falaḥa* till the soil]
HOMOPHONES: *fella*

felon *noun*
• "FELL'n"
• a person who has been convicted of a usu. violent crime, (in the US) one classified as graver than a misdemeanour, usu. punishable by a prison term of more than one year.
• [Old French from medieval Latin *felo -onis*, of unknown origin]
• **felonious** *adjective* "fuh LONEY us"
• **feloniously** *adverb*
• **felony** *noun*

felquiste *noun*
• "fell KEEST"
• *Cdn* a member of the Front de Libération du Québec.
• [Canadian French]

felsic *adjective*
• "FELL sick"
• of, pertaining to, or designating a group of light coloured minerals including feldspar, quartz, and muscovite.
• [contraction of FELDSPAR + SILICA]

felucca *noun*
• "fuh LUCKA" or "fuh LOOKA" (with "OO" as in *FOOD*)
• a small boat propelled by lateen sails, oars, or both, formerly used along the Mediterranean coast and still in use on rivers, esp. the Nile.
• [Italian *felucca* from obsolete Spanish *faluca* from Arabic *fulk*, perhaps from Greek *epholkion* sloop]

feminine *adjective*
• "FEM'n in"
• of, pertaining to, or characteristic of women.
• [Old French *feminin -ine* or Latin *femininus* from *femina* woman]
• **femininely** *adverb*
• **feminineness** *noun*
• **femininity** *noun* "fem'n INNA tee"

feminism *noun*
• "FEM'n izm"
• the advocacy of equality of the sexes, esp. through the establishment of the political, social, and economic rights of women.
• [Latin *femina* woman]
• **feminist** *noun*

feminize *verb*
ALSO SPELLED: esp. *Brit.* **-ise**
• "FEM'n ize"
• make or become feminine or female.
• [as FEMINISM]
• **feminization** *noun* (also esp. *Brit.* **-isation**)
• **feminized** *adjective* (also esp. *Brit.* **-ised**)

femur *noun*
• "FEEMER"
• the thigh bone in vertebrates, the thick bone between the hip and the knee.
• [Latin *femur femoris* thigh]
• **femoral** *adjective* "FEMMER'll"

fencible *noun*
• "FENSA bull"
• (historically) a soldier liable only for defensive military service at home.
• [Middle English from DEFENSIBLE]

fenestra *noun*
• "fuh NESTRA"
• a small hole or opening in a bone etc., esp. one of two in the inner ear.
• [Latin, = window]

fenestrated *adjective*
• "FENNA strated" or "fuh NEST rated"
• having windows or openings.
• [as FENESTRA]

fenestration *noun*
• "fenna STRAY sh'n"
• the arrangement of windows in a building.
• [as FENESTRA]

Fenian *noun*
• "FEENY 'n"
• a member of a militant 19th-c. Irish-American nationalist organization aimed at overthrowing the British government in Ireland, responsible for a number of raids from the US into Canada.
• [Old Irish *féne* name of an ancient Irish people, confused with *fiann* guard of legendary kings]
• **Fenianism** *noun*

fennec *noun*
• "FENNIC"
• a small fox, *Vulpes zerda*, native to N Africa, having large pointed ears.
• [Arabic *fanak*]

fennel *noun*
• "FEN'll"
• a yellow-flowered fragrant umbelliferous plant, *Foeniculum vulgare*, with fragrant seeds and fine leaves used as flavouring.
• [Old English *finugl* etc. & Old French *fenoil* from Latin *feniculum* from *fenum* hay]
HOMOPHONES: *phenyl*

fenning *noun*
• "FENNING"
• a monetary unit of Bosnia and Herzegovina, equal to one-hundredth of a marka.
• [Bosnian]

fenugreek *noun*
• "FENYOO greek"
• a leguminous plant, *Trigonella foenum-graecum*, having aromatic seeds.
• [Old English *fenogrecum*, superseded in Middle English from Old French *fenugrec* from Latin *faenugraecum* (*fenum graecum* Greek hay), used by the Romans as fodder]

feoffment *noun*
• "FEFF m'nt"
• (historically) a mode of conveying a freehold estate by a formal transfer of possession.
• [Anglo-French *feoffement*, related to 'fee']
• **feoffee** *noun* "feff EE"
• **feoffor** *noun* "FEFFER"

feral *adjective*
• "FEER 'll" or "FARE 'll"
• (of animals) belonging to or forming a wild population ultimately descended from individuals which escaped from captivity or domestication.
• [Latin *ferus* wild]

Ferberize *verb*
• "FURBER ize"
• train (a baby) to fall asleep on its own by leaving it to cry for successively longer periods and returning only to speak comfortingly to it but not pick it up, feed it, or cuddle it.
• [R. *Ferber*, US pediatrician]

feria *noun*
• "FEERY uh" or "FERRY uh"
• (in the Christian church calendar) a weekday which is not a feast day.
• [Latin, = 'holiday']
• **ferial** *adjective*

fermata *noun*
• "fare MOTTA"
• a prolongation, of unspecified length, of a note or rest.
• [Italian, 'stop, pause']

fermi *noun*
• "FARE mee"
• a unit of length equal to 10^{-15} metre, formerly used in nuclear physics.
• [E. *Fermi*, Italian-American atomic physicist d.1954]

fermion *noun*
• "FURMY on"
• a subatomic particle, such as a nucleon, with half-integral spin.
• [as FERMI]

fermium *noun*
• "FURMY um"
• a transuranic radioactive metallic element produced artificially.
• [as FERMI]

Fernieite *noun*
• "FURNY ite"
• a resident of Fernie, BC.

ferocious *adjective*
• "fuh ROE sh'ss"
• fierce, savage, or wildly cruel or destructive.
• [Latin *ferox -ocis*]
• **ferociously** *adverb*
• **ferociousness** *noun*

ferocity *noun*
• "fuh ROSSA tee"
• the quality or state of being ferocious.
• [as FEROCIOUS]

ferrate *noun*
• "FARE ate"
• a salt formed from or as from ferric oxide and a base.
• [Latin *ferrum* iron]

ferret *noun*
• "FARE it"
• a small half-domesticated animal of the weasel family, *Mustela putorius furo*, kept as a pet or (in Europe) used to catch rabbits, rats, etc.
• [Old French *fu(i)ret* alteration of *fu(i)ron* from Late Latin *furo -onis* from Latin *fur* thief]
• **ferreter** *noun*
• **ferrety** *adjective*

ferric *adjective*
• "FARE ick"
• of or containing iron.
• [Latin *ferrum* iron]

ferrite *noun*
• "FARE ite"
• a compound, often with magnetic properties, formed from ferric oxide and a basic oxide or from ferric hydroxide and a base.
• [Latin *ferrum* iron]
• **ferritic** *adjective* "fuh RITTIC"

ferritin *noun*
• "FARE a tin"
• a water-soluble protein containing ferric iron, involved in storing iron in mammalian metabolism.
• [as FERRIC]

ferroconcrete *noun*
• "fair oh CON creet"
• concrete reinforced with steel.
• [as FERRIC + CONCRETE]

ferroelectric *adjective*
• "fair oh e LECK trick"
• exhibiting permanent electric polarization which varies in strength with the applied electric field.
• [as FERROUS + ELECTRIC]
• **ferroelectricity** *noun*
"fair oh e leck TRISSA tee"

ferromagnesian *adjective*
• "fair oh mag NEE zh'n"
• (of a rock or mineral) containing iron and magnesium as major components.
• [as FERROUS + MAGNESIUM]

ferromagnetism *noun*
• "fair oh MAGNA tizm"
• a phenomenon, evidenced by metallic iron, cobalt, and nickel, in which there is a high susceptibility to magnetization, the strength of which varies with the applied magnetizing field, and which may persist after removal of the applied field.
• [as FERROUS + MAGNET]
• **ferromagnetic** *adjective*

ferrous *adjective*
• "FAIR us"
• (of an alloy etc.) containing iron in significant quantities.
• [Latin *ferrum* iron]

ferruginous *adjective*
• "fuh ROODGE 'n us"
• (of rocks, minerals, etc.) of the nature of or containing iron or its compounds.
• [Latin *ferrugo -ginis* rust, from *ferrum* iron]

ferrule *noun*
• "FAIR ool"
• a usu. metal ring or cap strengthening the end of a stick or tube, used esp. to prevent splitting or wearing.
• [earlier *verrel* etc. from Old French *virelle, virol(e)*, from Latin *viriola* diminutive of *viriae* bracelet: assimilated to Latin *ferrum* iron]
HOMOPHONES: *ferule*

fertile *adjective*
• "FUR tile" or "FURTLE"
• (of soil) fruitful or rich in the materials needed to produce and support vegetation.
• [French from Latin *fertilis*]
• **fertility** *noun* "fur TILLA tee"

fertilize *verb*
ALSO SPELLED: esp. *Brit.* **-ise**
• "FURTA lize"
• make fertile or productive.
• [as FERTILE]
• **fertilizable** *adjective* (also esp. *Brit.* **-isable**)
• **fertilization** *noun* (also esp. *Brit.* **-isation**)

fertilizer *noun*
ALSO SPELLED: esp. *Brit.* **-iser**
• "FURTA lize ur"
• a chemical or natural substance added to soil to make it more fertile.
• [as FERTILE]

ferula *noun*
• "FAIR oo luh"
• any plant of the genus *Ferula*, esp. the giant fennel (*F. communis*), having a tall stick-like stem and thick roots.
• [Latin, = giant fennel, rod]

ferule *noun*
• "FAIR ool"
• a flat ruler with a widened end formerly used for beating children.
• [Middle English (as FERULA)]
HOMOPHONES: *ferrule*

fervent *adjective*
- "FUR v'nt"
- ardent, impassioned, intense.
- [Old French from Latin *fervēre* boil]
- **fervency** *noun*
- **fervently** *adverb*

fervid *adjective*
- "FUR vid"
- ardent, intense.
- [Latin *fervidus* (as FERVENT)]
- **fervidly** *adverb*

fervour *noun*
ALSO SPELLED: **fervor**
- "FUR vur"
- vehemence, passion, zeal.
- [Latin *fervor -oris* (as FERVENT)]

fescue *noun*
- "FESS kyoo"
- any grass of the genus *Festuca*, valuable for lawns, pasture, and fodder.
- [Old French *festu*, ultimately from Latin *festuca* stalk, straw]

festal *adjective*
- "FEST'll"
- of, like, or pertaining to a feast or festival.
- [Old French from Late Latin *festalis* from Latin *festus* joyous]

festivity *noun*
- "fess TIVVA tee"
- a celebration.
- [as FESTAL]

festoon *noun*
- "fess TOON"
- a garland of flowers, leaves, ribbons, etc. hung in a curve as a decoration.
- [French *feston* from Italian *festone* from *festa* from Latin *festus* joyous]

Festschrift *noun*
- "FEST shrift"
- a volume of writings collected and published in honour of a scholar, writer, etc., usu. presented to mark a specific occasion in his or her life.
- [German from *Fest* celebration + *Schrift* writing]

feta *noun*
- "FETTA"
- a very soft, white cheese made from ewe's milk or goat's milk, originally from Greece.
- [modern Greek *pheta*]

fetal *adjective*
ALSO SPELLED: esp. *Brit.* **foetal**
- "FEET'll"
- of or pertaining to a fetus.
- [as FETUS]

fete *noun*
- "FATE" or "FET"
- a festival, fair, or great entertainment.
- [French *fête* from Latin *festus* joyous]

HOMOPHONES: *fate*

fetid *adjective*
- "FET id" or "FEET id"
- stinking or foul smelling.
- [Latin *fetidus* from *fetēre* stink]
- **fetidly** *adverb*

fetish *noun*
- "FET ish"
- a form of sexual desire in which gratification is linked to an abnormal degree to a particular object, item of clothing, part of the body, etc.
- [French *fétiche* from Portuguese *feitiço* charm: originally adjective = made by art, from Latin *factitius* FACTITIOUS]
- **fetishism** *noun*
- **fetishist** *noun*
- **fetishistic** *adjective*
- **fetishization** *noun* (also esp. *Brit.* **-isation**)
- **fetishize** *verb* (also esp. *Brit.* **-ise**)

fetor *noun*
- "FEETER"
- an offensive smell.
- [Latin (as FETID)]

HOMOPHONES: *feeder*

fettuccine *noun*
ALSO SPELLED: **fettucini**
- "fet oo CHEENY"
- pasta made in ribbons.
- [Italian, pl. of diminutive of *fetta* slice, ribbon]

fetus *noun*
ALSO SPELLED: esp. *Brit.* **foetus**
- "FEET us"
- the unborn offspring of a mammal from the stage of development where the main features of an adult can be recognized, e.g. for a human, from eight weeks after conception.
- [Latin, = 'offspring']

feud *noun*
- "FYOOD"
- a prolonged mutual hostility, esp. between two families, tribes, etc., with murderous assaults in revenge for a previous injury.
- [Old French *fede* from Middle Dutch, Middle Low German *vēde* from Germanic, related to 'foe']

feudal *adjective*
- "FYOOD'll"
- of, according to, or resembling a medieval European politico-economic system of landholding which was based on a reciprocal arrangement between vassal (or peasant) and lord. The nobility held lands from the Crown in exchange for a specified amount of military service; the peasantry lived on their lord's land, and had to provide him with labour or a share of their produce in exchange for military protection.
- [medieval Latin *feudalis*, *feodalis* from *feudum*, *feodum* fee, perhaps from Germanic]
- **feudalism** *noun*

- **feudalist** *noun*
- **feudalistic** *adjective*

feuilleté *noun*
- "fuh yuh TAY"
- a filled puff pastry shell.
- [French, 'flaky']

feuilleton *noun*
- "fuh yuh TÕH" (with a nasal *OH*)
- a part of a European newspaper etc. devoted to fiction, criticism, light literature, etc.
- [French, 'leaflet']

fey *adjective*
- "FAY"
- having a strange, almost otherworldly, whimsical charm.
- [Old English *fæge* from Germanic]
- **feyness** *noun*

HOMOPHONES: *fay*

fez *noun*
- "FEZZ"
- a red felt cap with a flat top and tassel but no brim, worn by men in some Muslim countries and formerly the national headdress of Turkey.
- [Turkish, perhaps from the city of *Fez* in Morocco]

fiacre *noun*
- "fee ACK ur"
- a small, horse-drawn, four-wheeled carriage.
- [named after the Hôtel de St. *Fiacre*, Paris, where such vehicles were first hired out]

fiancé *noun*
- "fee ON say" or "fee on SAY"
- a man to whom one is engaged to be married.
- [French, past participle of *fiancer* betroth, from Old French *fiance* a promise, ultimately from Latin *fidere* to trust]

HOMOPHONES: *fiancée*

fiancée *noun*
- "fee ON say" or "fee on SAY"
- a woman to whom one is engaged to be married.
- [as FIANCÉ]

HOMOPHONES: *fiancé*

fianchetto *noun*
- "fee 'n CHETTO"
- the development of a bishop in chess by moving it one square to a long diagonal of the board.
- [Italian, diminutive of *fianco* flank]

fiasco *noun*
- "fee ASS co"
- a complete and ridiculous failure.
- [Italian, 'bottle' (with unexplained allusion) from Late Latin *flasco* flask]

fiat *noun*
- "FEE at" or "FIE at"
- a formal authorization.
- [Latin, 'let it be done']

fibril *noun*
- "FIE brill"
- a small or delicate fibre, esp. a constituent strand of an animal, vegetable, or synthetic fibre.
- [modern Latin *fibrilla* diminutive of Latin *fibra* fibre]
- **fibrillar** *adjective*

fibrillate *verb*
- "FIBBRA late"
- (of a muscle, esp. in the heart) undergo a quivering movement or contract irregularly fibril by fibril.
- [as FIBRIL]
- **fibrillation** *noun*

fibrin *noun*
- "FIE brin"
- an insoluble protein formed during blood clotting from fibrinogen.
- [Latin *fibra* fibre]
- **fibrinoid** *adjective*
- **fibrinous** *adjective*

fibrinogen *noun*
- "fie BRINNA j'n"
- a soluble blood plasma protein which produces fibrin when acted upon by the enzyme thrombin.
- [as FIBRIN + GENESIS]

fibroblast *noun*
- "FIE bro blast"
- a cell producing collagen fibres in connective tissue.
- [Latin *fibra* fibre + Greek *blastos* sprout]

fibroid *adjective*
- "FIE broid"
- of or characterized by fibrous tissue.
- [Latin *fibra* fibre]

fibroin *noun*
- "FIE bro in"
- a protein which is the chief constituent of silk and spider webs.
- [Latin *fibra* fibre]

fibroma *noun*
- "fie BRO muh"
- a fibrous tumour.
- [modern Latin from Latin *fibra* fibre + '-oma' forming nouns denoting tumours and other abnormal growths]

fibromyalgia *noun*
- "fie bro my AL juh"
- a rheumatic disorder of uncertain origin, characterized by chronic, diffuse muscular or musculoskeletal pain, with stiffness (esp. on waking) and localized tenderness at specific points on the body.
- [Latin *fibra* fibre + MYALGIA]

fibrosis *noun*
- "fie BRO sis"
- a thickening and scarring of connective tissue, usu. as a result of injury.

- [modern Latin from Latin *fibra* fibre]
- **fibrotic** *adjective* "fie BROTTIC"

fibrous *adjective*
- "FIE bruss"
- consisting of or like fibres.
- [Latin *fibra* fibre]

fibula *noun*
- "FIB yoo luh"
- the smaller and outer of the two bones between the knee and the ankle in terrestrial vertebrates.
- [Latin, = 'clasp' perhaps related to *figere* fix]
- **fibular** *adjective*

fiche *noun*
- "FEESH"
- a microfiche.
- [French, = slip of paper]

fichu *noun*
- "FEE shoo"
- a woman's small triangular shawl of lace etc. for the shoulders and neck.
- [French]

fictitious *adjective*
- "fick TISH us"
- imaginary, unreal.
- [Latin *ficticius* from *fingere* form, contrive]
- **fictitiously** *adverb*
- **fictitiousness** *noun*

fictive *adjective*
- "FICTIV"
- creating or created by imagination.
- [French *fictif -ive* or medieval Latin *fictivus* from *fingere* form, contrive]
- **fictiveness** *noun*

ficus *noun*
- "FEE kuss" or "FIKE us"
- a tree or shrub of the large genus *Ficus* (mulberry family), including the fig and the rubber plant.
- [Latin, = fig, fig tree]

fideism *noun*
- "FIE dee izm" or "FEE day izm"
- the doctrine that knowledge depends on faith or revelation rather than reason.
- [Latin *fides* faith]
- **fideist** *noun*
- **fideistic** *adjective*

Fidelista *noun*
- "fid ell EESTA"
- a follower of Cuban leader Fidel Castro (b.1927).

fidelity *noun*
- "fuh DELLA tee"
- faithfulness, loyalty.
- [French *fidélité* or Latin *fidelitas* (as FEALTY)]

fiducial *adjective*
- "fuh DOO sh'll" or "fuh DYOO sh'll"
- (of a line, point, etc.) assumed as a fixed basis of comparison.
- [Late Latin *fiducialis* from *fiducia* trust, from *fidere* to trust]

fiduciary *adjective*
- "fuh DOOSHY airy" or "fuh DYOOSHY airy"
- of or relating to a trust, trustee, or trusteeship.
- [Latin *fiduciarius* (as FIDUCIAL)]

fie *interjection*
- "FIE"
- expressing disgust, shame, or a pretense of outraged propriety.
- [Old French from Latin *fi*, an exclamation of disgust at a stench]

HOMOPHONES: *phi*

fief *noun*
- "FEEF"
- a piece of land held under the feudal system or in fee.
- [Old French *fieu*, etc. from medieval Latin *feodum*, *feudum*, perhaps from Frankish]

fiefdom *noun*
- "FEEF dum"
- a person's sphere of operation or control.
- [as FIEF]

fieldfare *noun*
- "FEELD fare"
- a thrush, *Turdus pilaris*, of northern Eurasia, having grey plumage with a speckled breast.
- [Middle English *feldefare*, perhaps as 'field' + FARE]

fiend *noun*
- "FEEND"
- an evil spirit, a demon.
- [Old English *fēond* from Germanic]
- **fiendish** *adjective*
- **fiendishly** *adverb*
- **fiendishness** *noun*
- **fiendlike** *adjective*

fierce *adjective*
- "FEERCE"
- vehemently aggressive or frightening in temper or action, violent.
- [Old French *fiers fier* proud, from Latin *ferus* savage]
- **fiercely** *adverb*
- **fierceness** *noun*

fiery *adjective*
- "FIRE ee"
- consisting of or flaming with fire.
- [Old English *fȳr* fire, from West Germanic]
- **fierily** *adverb*
- **fieriness** *noun*

fiesta *noun*
- "fee ESTA"
- a holiday or festivity.
- [Spanish, = feast]

figment *noun*
- "FIG m'nt"
- a thing invented or existing only in the imagination.
- [Latin *figmentum*, related to *fingere* fashion]

figural *adjective*
- "FIG yur 'll"
- figurative.
- [as FIGURE]

figuration *noun*
- "fig yur AY sh'n" or "figger AY sh'n"
- ornamentation by designs.
- [as FIGURE]

figurative *adjective*
- "FIG yur a tiv" or "FIGGER a tiv"
- metaphorical, not literal.
- [as FIGURE]
- **figuratively** *adverb*
- **figurativeness** *noun*

figure *noun*
- "FIG yur" or "FIGGER"
- the external form or shape of a thing.
- [Old French from Latin *figura*, *figurare*, related to *fingere* fashion]
- **figureless** *adjective*

figurine *noun*
- "fig yur EEN"
- a small moulded or carved figure; a statuette.
- [French from Italian *figurina* diminutive of *figura* FIGURE]

figwort *noun*
- "FIG wurt" or "FIG wort"
- any plant of the genus *Scrophularia* (family Scrophulariaceae), with dull purplish-brown flowers, once believed to be useful against scrofula.
- ['fig' from Old French *figue* from Provençal *fig(u)a*, ultimately from Latin *ficus* + WORT]

Fijian *adjective*
- "fee JEE 'n"
- of or relating to Fiji in the S Pacific, its people, or language.

fil *noun*
- "FILL"
- a monetary unit of Jordan and Iraq, equal to one-thousandth of a dinar.
- [Arabic]

HOMOPHONES: *fill*

filament *noun*
- "FILLA m'nt"
- a slender threadlike body or fibre (esp. in animal or vegetable structures).
- [French *filament* or modern Latin *filamentum* from Late Latin *filare* spin, from Latin *filum* thread]
- **filamentary** *adjective* "filla MENTA ree"
- **filamentous** *adjective*

filaria *noun*
- "fill AIRY uh"
- any threadlike parasitic nematode worm of the family Filariidae introduced into the blood by certain biting flies and mosquitoes.
- [modern Latin from Latin *filum* thread]
- **filarial** *adjective*

filariasis *noun*
- "filla RYE a sis" or "fil airy AY sis"
- a disease common in the tropics, caused by the presence of filarial worms in the lymph vessels.
- [as FILARIA]

filbert *noun*
- "FILL bert"
- any of various shrubs or small trees of the genus *Corylus*, esp. the cultivated hazel, *Corylus maxima*, bearing edible ovoid nuts.
- [Middle English *philliberd* etc. from Anglo-French *philbert*, dialect French *noix de filbert*, a nut ripe around St. Philibert's day (20 Aug.)]

filé *noun*
- "fee LAY" or "FEE lay"
- pounded or powdered sassafras leaves used to flavour and thicken soup, esp. gumbo.
- [French, past participle of *filer* twist]

filet *noun*
- "fuh LAY" or "FILL it"
- a fleshy boneless piece of meat or fish.
- [French, = thread]

HOMOPHONES: *fillet*

filial *adjective*
- "FILLY 'll"
- of or due from a son or daughter.
- [Old French *filial* or Late Latin *filialis* from *filius* son, *filia* daughter]

filiation *noun*
- "filly AY sh'n"
- the fact of being the child of one or two specified parents.
- [French from Late Latin *filiatio -onis* from Latin *filius* son]

filibeg *noun*
- "FILLA beg"
- a kilt.
- [Gaelic *feileadh-beag* little fold]

filibuster *noun*
- "FILLA buster"
- the obstruction of progress in a legislative assembly, esp. by prolonged speaking.
- [ultimately from Dutch *vrijbuiter* freebooter, a pirate or lawless adventurer, influenced by French *flibustier*, Spanish *filibustero*]
- **filibusterer** *noun*

filigree *noun*
- "FILLA gree"
- ornamental work of gold or silver or copper as fine wire formed into delicate tracery; fine metal openwork.
- [earlier *filigreen*, *filigrane* from French *filigrane*

from Italian *filigrana* from Latin *filum* thread + *granum* seed]
• **filigreed** *adjective*

Filipina *noun*
• "filla PEENA"
• a woman or girl who is a native or national of the Philippines.
• [Spanish, = Philippine]

Filipino *noun*
• "filla PEENO"
• a native or national of the Philippines in SE Asia.
• [Spanish, = Philippine]

filk *noun*
• "FILK"
• (among science fiction and fantasy fans) a type of popular music characterized by the use of familiar or traditional songs whose lyrics have been rewritten or parodied.
• [from a typographical error in the title of an essay 'The Influence of Science Fiction on Modern American Filk Music']

fillet *verb*
• "FILL it"
• remove bones from (fish or meat).
• [Old French *filet* from Romanic diminutive of Latin *filum* thread]
HOMOPHONES: *filet*

fillip *noun*
• "FILLIP"
• something that adds interest or excitement.
• [imitative]

filmography *noun*
• "film OGGRA fee"
• a list of films by one director etc. or on one subject.
• ['film' + Greek *graphia* writing, after *bibliography*]

filovirus *noun*
• "FEELO vie russ"
• a filamentous RNA virus of a genus which causes severe hemorrhagic fevers in humans and primates, and which includes the Ebola and Marburg viruses.
• [Latin *filum* thread + VIRUS]

fils[1] *noun*
• "FILCE"
• a monetary unit of Iraq, Bahrain, Jordan, Kuwait, and Yemen.
• [informal pronunciation of Arabic *fals*, a small copper coin]

***fils*[2]** *noun*
• "FEECE"
• (added to a surname to distinguish a son from a father) the son, junior.
• [French, = son]

fimbriate *adjective*
• "FIMBRY ate"
• fringed or bordered with hairs etc.
• [Latin *fimbriatus* from *fimbriae* fringe]

finagle *verb*
• "fuh NAY g'll"
• act or obtain dishonestly.
• [dialect *fainaigue* cheat]
• **finagler** *noun*

finale *noun*
• "fuh NALLY"
• the last movement of an instrumental composition.
• [Italian from Latin *finalis* final, from *finis* end]

finality *noun*
• "fuh NALA tee"
• the quality or fact of being final.
• [Latin *finalis* final, from *finis* end]

finance *noun*
• "FIE nance" or "fuh NANCE"
• the management of large amounts of money, esp. by governments or large companies.
• [Old French from *finer* settle a debt, from *fin* end]
• **financeable** *adjective*

financial *adjective*
• "fie NAN sh'll" or "fuh NAN sh'll"
• of or pertaining to revenue or money matters.
• [as FINANCE]
• **financially** *adverb*

financier *noun*
• "fie nan SEER" or "fuh nan SEER"
• a person who is concerned with or skilled in finance, esp. on a large scale.
• [French (as FINANCE)]

finca *noun*
• "FINKA"
• (in Spain and Spanish-speaking countries) a country estate; a ranch.
• [Spanish, from *fincar* cultivate, perhaps from Latin *figere* fix, fasten, plant]

finesse *noun*
• "fuh NESS"
• skill in dealing with people or situations cleverly or tactfully.
• [French, ultimately from Latin *finire* finish]

finial *noun*
• "FINNY 'll"
• an ornament finishing off the apex of a roof, pediment, gable, etc.
• [Old French *fin* from Latin *finis* end]

finicky *adjective*
• "FINNICK ee"
• over-particular, fastidious, or too fussy.
• [earlier *finical* (prob. originally university slang) from 'fine']

finis *noun*
• "fee NEE" or "FINNISS"
• (at the end of a book, film, etc.) the end.
• [Latin]

finish *verb*
• "FIN ish"

• complete, come or bring to an end.
• [Old French *fenir* from Latin *finire* from *finis* end]
• **finished** *adjective*
• **finisher** *noun*
HOMOPHONES: *Finnish*

finite *adjective*
• "FIE nite"
• having bounds, ends, or limits.
• [Latin *finitus* past participle of *finire* FINISH]
• **finitely** *adverb*
• **finiteness** *noun*
• **finitude** *noun* "FINNA tude"

finitism *noun*
• "FIE nite izm"
• belief in the finiteness of the world, God, etc.
• [as FINITE]

finito *adjective*
• "fin EETO"
• finished, ended.
• [Italian, as FINITE]

Finlandization *noun*
ALSO SPELLED: esp. *Brit.* **-isation**
• "fin l'nd ize AY sh'n"
• the process or result of becoming obliged to favour, or refrain from opposing, the interests of the former Soviet Union, as happened to Finland after 1944.
• **Finlandize** *verb* (also esp. *Brit.* **-ise**)

Finn *noun*
• "FIN"
• a native or national of Finland.
• [Old English *Finnas* pl.]
HOMOPHONES: *fin*

Finnic *adjective*
• "FINNICK"
• of or pertaining to the Finns, the group of people ethnically allied to the Finns, or the group of languages allied to Finnish.
• [as FINN]

Finnish *adjective*
• "FIN ish"
• of, pertaining to, or characteristic of Finland, the Finns, or their language.
• [as FINN]
HOMOPHONES: *finish*

fino *noun*
• "FEENO"
• a light-coloured dry sherry.
• [Spanish, = fine]

fioritura *noun*
• "fyora TURA"
• the usu. improvised decoration or elaboration of a melody by a performer.
• [Italian, = flowering, from *fiorire* to flower]

fipple *noun*
• "FIP'll"
• a complete or partial plug at the mouth end of a wind instrument, esp. a partial plug at the head of a recorder, whistle, etc. that leaves a narrow channel for air.
• [17th c.: origin unknown]

fir *noun*
• "FUR"
• any evergreen coniferous tree, esp. of the genus *Abies*, with needles borne singly on the stems.
• [Middle English, prob. from Old Norse *fyri-* from Germanic]
HOMOPHONES: *fur*

firkin *noun*
• "FUR kin"
• a small cask for liquids, butter, fish, etc.
• [Middle English *ferdekyn*, prob. from Middle Dutch *vierdekijn* (unrecorded) diminutive of *vierde* fourth]

firmament *noun*
• "FURMA m'nt"
• the arch or vault of the skies.
• [Old French from Latin *firmamentum* from *firmare* from *firmus* firm]

firman *noun*
• "fur MAN" or "FUR m'n"
• an edict or order issued by a Near Eastern ruler or official, esp. a grant, licence, passport, or permit.
• [Persian *fermān*, Sanskrit *pramāṇam* right measure]

firn *noun*
• "FEERN"
• crystalline or granular snow, esp. on the upper part of a glacier.
• [German from Old High German *firni* old]

firth *noun*
• "FURTH"
• an estuary or narrow inlet of the sea.
• [Middle English (originally Scots) from Old Norse *fjörthr* FJORD]

fisc *noun*
• "FISK"
• the public treasury.
• [French *fisc* or Latin *fiscus* rush basket, purse, treasury]

fiscal *adjective*
• "FISS k'll"
• of or related to public revenue, usu. taxes.
• [French *fiscal* or Latin *fiscalis* (as FISC)]
• **fiscally** *adverb*

fissile *adjective*
• "FISS ile" or "FISS'll"
• capable of undergoing nuclear fission.
• [Latin *fissilis* (as FISSURE)]

fission *noun*
• "FISH'n" or "FIZH'n"
• the spontaneous or impact-induced splitting of a heavy atomic nucleus, accompanied by a release of energy.
• [Latin *fissio* (as FISSURE)]
• **fissionable** *adjective*

fissiparous *adjective*
• "fiss IPPA russ"
• reproducing by fission.
• [Latin *fissus* past participle (as FISSURE) after VIVIPAROUS]
• **fissiparousness** *noun*

fissure *noun*
• "FISHER" or "FIZHER"
• an opening, usu. long and narrow, made by cracking, splitting, or separation of esp. rock or ice.
• [Old French or Latin *fissura* from *findere fiss-* cleave]
HOMOPHONES: *fisher*

fistful *noun*
• "FIST full"
• a quantity held in a fist.
• [as FISTIC]

fistic *adjective*
• "FISTICK"
• relating to boxing.
• [from 'fist', from Old English *fȳst* from West Germanic]

fisticuffs *noun*
• "FISTA cuffs"
• fighting with the fists.
• [prob. obsolete *fisty* adjective = FISTIC, + 'cuff' (strike, hit)]

fistula *noun*
• "FIST yoo luh"
• an abnormal or surgically made passage between a hollow organ and the body surface or between two hollow organs.
• [Latin, = pipe, flute]
• **fistulous** *adjective*

fitful *adjective*
• "FIT full"
• active or occurring spasmodically or intermittently.
• [Middle English *fit*, = position of danger, perhaps = Old English *fitt* conflict]
• **fitfully** *adverb*
• **fitfulness** *noun*

fixate *verb*
• "FIX ate"
• be or become obsessed with.
• [Latin *fixus* past participle of *figere* fix, fasten]
• **fixation** *noun*

fixative *noun*
• "FIXA tiv"
• a substance used to set or fix colours, hair, biological specimens, etc.
• [as FIXATE]

fixity *noun*
• "FIXA tee"
• a fixed state.
• [as FIXATE]

fjord *noun*
ALSO SPELLED: **fiord**
• "FYORD" or "FEE ord"
• a long, narrow, and deep inlet of sea between high cliffs.
• [Norwegian from Old Norse *fjörthr* from Germanic]

flabbergast *verb*
• "FLABBER gast"
• overwhelm with astonishment; dumbfound.
• [18th c.: perhaps from 'flabby' + AGHAST]
• **flabbergasted** *adjective*

flaccid *adjective*
• "FLASS id" or "FLACK sid"
• (of flesh etc.) lacking stiffness; hanging or lying loose; limp, flabby.
• [French *flaccide* or Latin *flaccidus* from *flaccus* flabby]
• **flaccidity** *noun*
• **flaccidly** *adverb*

flack *noun*
• "FLACK"
• a publicist.
• [20th c.: origin unknown]
• **flackery** *noun*
HOMOPHONES: *flak*

flagellant *noun*
• "FLADGE a l'nt" or "fluh JELL'nt"
• a person who scourges himself or herself or others as a religious discipline.
• [Latin *flagellare* to whip, from FLAGELLUM]

flagellate¹ *verb*
• "FLADGE a late"
• scourge, flog.
• [Latin *flagellat-* past participle stem of *flagellare*]
• **flagellation** *noun*
• **flagellator** *noun*
• **flagellatory** *adjective*

flagellate² *adjective*
• "FLADGE a lit" or "FLADGE a late"
• having flagella (see FLAGELLUM).
• [as FLAGELLUM]

flagellum *noun*
• "fluh JELLUM"
• a long lash-like appendage found esp. on microscopic organisms.
• [Latin, = whip, diminutive of *flagrum* scourge]
• **flagellar** *adjective*
• **flagelliform** *adjective*

flageolet¹ *noun*
• "fladge a LET" or "fladge a LAY" or "FLADGE a let"
• a small wind instrument resembling the recorder, having six principal holes, including two for the thumb, and sometimes keys.
• [French, diminutive of Old French *flag(e)ol* from Provençal *flajol*, of unknown origin]

flageolet² *noun*
• "fladge oh LAY" or "fladge oh LET"
• a kind of French kidney bean.
• [French, based on Latin *phaseolus* bean]

flagitious *adjective*
• "fluh JISH us"
• deeply criminal; utterly villainous.
• [Latin *flagitiosus* from *flagitium* shameful crime]
• **flagitiousness** *noun*

flagon *noun*
• "FLAG 'n"
• a large bottle in which wine etc., is sold.
• [Old French *flacon*, ultimately from Late Latin *flasco -onis* flask]

flagrant *adjective*
• "FLAY gr'nt"
• (of an offence or an offender) glaring; notorious; scandalous.
• [French *flagrant* or Latin *flagrant-* participle stem of *flagrare* blaze]
• **flagrancy** *noun*
• **flagrantly** *adverb*

flail *noun*
• "FLALE"
• a threshing tool consisting of a wooden staff with a short heavy stick swinging from it.
• [Old English prob. from Latin FLAGELLUM]

flair *noun*
• "FLARE"
• special talent, aptitude, or ability.
• [French *flairer* to smell, ultimately from Latin *fragrare* smell sweet]
HOMOPHONES: *flare*

flak *noun*
ALSO SPELLED: **flack**
• "FLACK"
• anti-aircraft fire.
• [German, abbreviation of *Flug(zeug)abwehrkanone*, anti-aircraft gun]
HOMOPHONES: *flack*

flambé *adjective*
• "flom BAY" or "flam BAY"
• (of food) covered with alcohol and set alight briefly.
• [French, past participle of *flamber* singe (as FLAMBEAU)]

flambeau *noun*
• "FLAMBO"
• a flaming torch, esp. composed of several thick waxed wicks.
• [French from *flambe* from Latin *flammula* diminutive of *flamma* flame]

flamboyant *adjective*
• "flam BOY 'nt"
• (of a person, behaviour, etc.) ostentatious; showy.
• [original sense designating architectural decoration marked by wavy flamelike lines, from French present participle of *flamboyer* from *flambe*: see FLAMBEAU]
• **flamboyance** *noun*
• **flamboyantly** *adverb*

flamen *noun*
• "FLAY m'n"
• a priest serving a particular deity in ancient Rome.
• [Latin]

flamenco *noun*
• "fluh MENCO"
• a style of music played (esp. on the guitar) and sung by Spanish gypsies.
• [Spanish, 'like a gypsy', lit. = 'a Flemish person', from Middle Dutch *Vlaminc*]

flamingo *noun*
• "fluh MINGO"
• any tall long-necked web-footed wading bird of the family Phoenicopteridae, with a crooked bill and pink, scarlet, and black plumage.
• [Portuguese *flamengo* from Provençal *flamenc* from *flama* flame]

flammable *adjective*
• "FLAMMA bull"
• easily set on fire; highly combustible.
• [Latin *flammare* from *flamma* flame]
• **flammability** *noun*

flammulated *adjective*
• "FLAM yuh lated"
• designating a small reddish-grey owl of North America, *Otus flammeolus*.
• [modern Latin *flammulatus* from Latin *flammula*, diminutive of *flamma* flame]

flâneur *noun*
• "fluh NUR"
• an idler; a lounger.
• [French from *flâner* lounge, loiter, from Norse *flana* wander about]

flange *noun*
• "FLANJ"
• a projecting flat rim, collar, or rib, used for strengthening or attachment, or (on a wheel) maintaining position on a rail.
• [17th c.: perhaps from *flange* widen out, from Old French *flangir*, from *flanche*, *flanc* flank, from Frankish]
• **flangeless** *noun*

flanger *noun*
• "FLAN jur"
• a vertical scraper for clearing snow from railway tracks to allow room for the wheel flanges.
• [as FLANGE]

flannel *noun*
• "FLAN'll"
• any of various loose-textured soft woollen or synthetic fabrics of plain or twilled weave and slightly napped on one side.
• [perhaps from Welsh *gwlanen* from *gwlān* wool]

flannelboard *noun*
• "FLAN'll bord"
• a piece of flannel as a base for paper or cloth cut-outs, used as a toy or a teaching aid.
• [as FLANNEL + BOARD]

flannelette *noun*
• "flan'll ET"
• a napped cotton fabric imitating the texture of flannel, used for sheets, pyjamas, etc.
• [as FLANNEL]

flannelgraph *noun*
• "FLAN'll graff"
• = FLANNELBOARD.
• [as FLANNEL + GRAPH]

flare *verb*
• "FLARE"
• burn or cause to burn suddenly with a bright unsteady flame.
• [16th c.: origin unknown]
HOMOPHONES: *flair*

flatulent *adjective*
• "FLATCH oo l'nt"
• causing formation of gas in the alimentary canal.
• [French from modern Latin *flatulentus* (as FLATUS)]
• **flatulence** *noun*
• **flatulently** *adverb*

flatus *noun*
• "FLATE us"
• gas in or from the stomach or bowels.
• [Latin, = blowing, from *flare* blow]

flaunt *verb*
• "FLONT"
• display ostentatiously (oneself or one's finery); show off; parade.
• [16th c.: origin unknown]

flautist *noun*
• "FLOT ist" or "FLOUT ist"
• a flute player.
• [Italian *flautista* from *flauto* flute, probably from Provençal *flaüt*, perhaps a blend of *flaujol* FLAGEOLET + *laüt* lute]

flavin *noun*
• "FLAY v'n"
• the chemical compound forming the nucleus of various natural yellow pigments.
• [Latin *flavus* yellow]

flavone *noun*
• "FLAY vone"
• any of a group of naturally occurring white or yellow pigments found in plants.
• [as FLAVIN + '-one' forming nouns denoting various compounds, from Greek *-ōnē* feminine patronymic]

flavonoid *noun*
• "FLAY vuh noid"
• any of a large class of plant pigments having a structure based on or similar to flavone, including anthocyanins, flavones, etc.
• [FLAVONE + Greek *-oeidēs* from *eidos* form]

flavoprotein *noun*
• "flay voe PRO teen"
• any of a group of conjugated proteins containing flavin that are involved in oxidation reactions in cells.
• [FLAVIN + PROTEIN]

flea *noun*
• "FLEE"
• a small wingless jumping insect of the order Siphonaptera, feeding on human and other blood.
• [Old English *flēa*, *flēah* from Germanic]
HOMOPHONES: *flee*

fleabag *noun*
• "FLEE bag"
• a cheap, rundown hotel.
• [as FLEA + 'bag']

fleabane *noun*
• "FLEE bane"
• any of various composite plants of the genus *Inula* or *Erigeron*, supposed to drive away fleas.
• [as FLEA + BANE]

fleapit *noun*
• "FLEE pit"
• a dingy dirty place, esp. a rundown cinema.
• [as FLEA + 'pit']

fleawort *noun*
• "FLEE wort"
• a plant of the genus *Senecio* of the daisy family, formerly thought to drive away fleas.
• [FLEA + WORT]

flèche *noun*
• "FLESH"
• a slender spire, often perforated with windows, esp. at the intersection of the nave and the transept of a church.
• [French, originally = arrow]
HOMOPHONES: *flesh*

flechette *noun*
• "flesh ET"
• a type of ammunition resembling a small dart, shot from a gun.
• [French *fléchette*, diminutive of *flèche* arrow]

fledgling *noun*
• "FLEDGE ling"
• a young bird.
• [obsolete *fledge* (adjective) fit to fly, from Old English *flycge*, from a Germanic root related to 'fly']

flee *verb*
• "FLEE"
• run or hurry away; escape (esp. from danger, threat, etc.).
• [Old English *flēon* from Germanic]
HOMOPHONES: *flea*

fleece *noun*
• "FLEECE"
• the woolly covering of a sheep or a similar animal.
• [Old English *flēos*, *flēs* from West Germanic]
• **fleeceable** *adjective*
• **fleeced** *adjective*

• ***fleecily*** *adverb*
• ***fleeciness*** *noun*
• ***fleecy*** *adjective*

fleer *verb*
• "FLEER"
• laugh impudently or mockingly; sneer; jeer.
• [Middle English, prob. from Scandinavian: compare Norwegian & Swedish dialect *flira* to grin]

fleet *noun*
• "FLEET"
• a number of warships under one commander-in-chief.
• [Old English *flēot* ship, shipping, from *flēotan* float]

fleeting *adjective*
• "FLEETING"
• transitory; brief.
• [Old English *flēotan* float, swim, from Germanic]
• ***fleetingly*** *adverb*

Fleming *noun*
• "FLEMMING"
• a native of medieval Flanders in what is now Belgium, France, and the Netherlands.
• [Old English from Old Norse *Flæmingi* & Middle Dutch *Vlāming* from root of *Vlaanderen* Flanders]

Flemish *adjective*
• "FLEM ish"
• of or relating to Flanders in Belgium, the Netherlands, and France.
• [Middle Dutch *Vlāmisch* (as FLEMING)]

flense *verb*
• "FLENCE"
• remove the blubber or skin from (a whale or seal).
• [Danish *flense*: compare Norwegian *flinsa*, *flunsa* flay]
• ***flenser*** *noun*

fleuron *noun*
• "flur ÕH" (with a nasal *OH*)
• a flower-shaped ornament on a building, a coin, a book, etc.
• [Old French *floron* from *flour* flower]

flews *plural noun*
• "FLOOZ"
• the hanging lips of a bloodhound etc.
• [16th c.: origin unknown]

flexible *adjective*
• "FLEX a bull"
• able to bend without breaking; pliable; pliant.
• [Latin *flectere flex-* bend]
• ***flexibility*** *noun*
• ***flexibly*** *adverb*

flexion *noun*
ALSO SPELLED: **flection**
• "FLECK sh'n"
• the act of bending or the condition of being bent, esp. of a limb or joint.
• [Latin *flexio* from *flectere flex-* bend]

flexography *noun*
• "flex OGGRA fee"
• a rotary letterpress technique using rubber or plastic plates and synthetic inks or dyes for printing on fabrics, plastics, etc., as well as on paper.
• [Latin *flectere flex-* bend + Greek *graphia* writing]
• ***flexographic*** *adjective*

flexor *noun*
• "FLEXER"
• a muscle that bends part of the body.
• [Latin *flectere flex-* bend]

flexuous *adjective*
• "FLECK shoo us"
• full of bends; winding.
• [Latin *flexuosus* from *flexus* bending from *flectere flex-* bend]

flexure *noun*
• "FLECK shur"
• the act of bending or the condition of being bent.
• [Latin *flectere flex-* bend]
• ***flexural*** *adjective*

flibbertigibbet *noun*
• "FLIBBER tee jibbit"
• a gossiping, frivolous, or restless person.
• [imitative of chatter]

flimsy *adjective*
• "FLIMZY"
• lightly or carelessly assembled; insubstantial, easily damaged.
• [17th c.: prob. from 'flim-flam' nonsense]
• ***flimsily*** *adverb*
• ***flimsiness*** *noun*

flippant *adjective*
• "FLIP'nt"
• lacking in seriousness; treating serious things lightly; disrespectful.
• [from 'flip']
• ***flippancy*** *noun*
• ***flippantly*** *adverb*

flirt *verb*
• "FLURT"
• show sexual interest in (a person) without any serious intent.
• [apparently symbolic, the elements *fl-* and *-irt* both suggesting sudden movement; compare with 'flick' and 'spurt'. The original verb senses were 'give someone a sharp blow' and 'sneer at'; the earliest noun senses were 'joke, gibe' and 'flighty girl' with a notion originally of cheeky behaviour, later of playfully amorous behaviour]
• ***flirtation*** *noun*
• ***flirtatious*** *adjective*
• ***flirtatiously*** *adverb*
• ***flirtatiousness*** *noun*
• ***flirty*** *adjective*

floc *noun*
- "FLOCK"
- a flocculent mass of fine particles.
- [abbreviation of FLOCCULUS]

HOMOPHONES: *flock*

flocculent *adjective*
- "FLOCK yoo l'nt"
- like tufts of wool.
- [as FLOCCULUS]
- **flocculate** *verb*
- **flocculation** *noun*
- **flocculence** *noun*

flocculus *noun*
- "FLOCK yoo luss"
- a small ovoid lobe in the undersurface of the cerebellum.
- [modern Latin, diminutive of *floccus* lock or tuft of wool]

floe *noun*
- "FLOW"
- a sheet of floating ice.
- [prob. from Norwegian *flo* from Old Norse *fló* layer]

HOMOPHONES: *flow*

floreat *verb*
- "FLORY at"
- may (he, she, or it) flourish.
- [Latin, 3rd sing. present subjunctive of *florēre* flourish]

Florentine *adjective*
- "FLOR 'n teen"
- of or relating to Florence in Italy.
- [French *Florentin -ine* or Latin *Florentinus* from *Florentia* Florence]

florescence *noun*
- "flor ESS ince"
- the process, state, or time of flowering.
- [modern Latin *florescentia* from Latin *florescere* from *florēre* bloom]

HOMOPHONES: *fluorescence*

floret *noun*
- "flor ET"
- each of the small flowers making up a composite flower head.
- [Latin *flos floris* flower]

floribunda *noun*
- "flora BUNDA"
- a plant, esp. a rose, bearing dense clusters of flowers.
- [modern Latin from *floribundus* freely flowering, from Latin *flos floris* flower, influenced by Latin *abundus* copious]

floriculture *noun*
- "FLORA cull chur"
- the cultivation of esp. ornamental flowers.
- [Latin *flos floris* flower + CULTURE, after *horticulture*]
- **floricultural** *adjective*
- **floriculturist** *noun*

florid *adjective*
- "FLOR id"
- (of a person's complexion) ruddy or flushed.
- [French *floride* or Latin *floridus* from *flos floris* flower]
- **floridity** *noun*
- **floridly** *adverb*
- **floridness** *noun*

Floridian *noun*
- "flor IDDY 'n"
- a native or inhabitant of Florida.

floriferous *adjective*
- "flor IFFER us"
- (of a seed or plant) producing many flowers.
- [Latin *florifer* from *flos floris* flower + *-fer* producing, from *ferre* bear]

florilegium *noun*
- "flora LEEJY um"
- an anthology of choice extracts from literature.
- [modern Latin from Latin *flos floris* flower + *legere* gather, translation of Greek *anthologion* ANTHOLOGY]

florin *noun*
- "FLOR in"
- a former British coin worth two shillings.
- [Old French from Italian *fiorino* diminutive of *fiore* flower, from Latin *flos floris*, the original coin having a figure of a lily on it]

florist *noun*
- "FLOR ist"
- a person who retails flowers and ornamental plants.
- [Latin *flos floris* flower]
- **floristry** *noun*

floristic *adjective*
- "flor ISTIC"
- relating to the study of the distribution of plants.
- [as FLORIST]
- **floristically** *adverb*
- **floristics** *noun*

floruit *verb*
- "FLOR oo it"
- (he or she) was alive and working; flourished (used of a person, esp. a painter, writer, etc., whose exact dates are unknown).
- [Latin, = he or she flourished]

flotilla *noun*
- "flo TILLA"
- a fleet of boats or small ships.
- [Spanish, diminutive of *flota* fleet, Old French *flote* multitude]

flotsam *noun*
- "FLOT sum"
- wreckage of a ship or its cargo found floating on the surface of the sea, a lake, etc.
- [Anglo-French *floteson* from *floter* float]

flour *noun*
• "FLOUR" (rhymes with *HOUR*)
• a fine powder obtained by grinding grain, esp. wheat, used for making bread, cakes, etc.
• [Middle English, different spelling of 'flower' in the sense 'finest part']
• **floured** *adjective*
• **flourless** *adjective*
• **floury** *adjective*
HOMOPHONES: *flower*

flourish *verb*
• "FLUR ish"
• (of a plant, tree, etc.) grow vigorously, thrive.
• [Middle English from Old French *florir*, ultimately from Latin *florēre* from *flos floris* flower]
• **flourishing** *adjective*

fluctuate *verb*
• "FLUCK choo ate"
• (of a price, number, rate, etc.) rise and fall or change irregularly.
• [Latin *fluctuare* from *fluctus* flow, wave, from *fluere fluct-* flow]
• **fluctuation** *noun*

flue *noun*
• "FLOO"
• a duct for the passage of smoke, waste gases, etc. in a chimney.
• [16th c.: origin unknown]
HOMOPHONES: *flu*, *flew*

fluent *adjective*
• "FLOO 'nt"
• (of speech or literary style) flowing naturally and readily.
• [Latin *fluere* flow]
• **fluency** *noun* "FLOO 'n see"
• **fluently** *adverb*

flugelhorn *noun*
• "FLOO g'll horn"
• a valved brass wind instrument with a cup-shaped mouthpiece and a wide conical bore, like a cornet but with a broader tone.
• [German *Flügelhorn* from *Flügel* wing + *Horn* horn]
• **flugelhornist** *noun*

fluid *noun*
• "FLOO id"
• a substance, esp. a gas or liquid, lacking definite shape and capable of flowing and yielding to the slightest pressure.
• [French *fluide* or Latin *fluidus* from *fluere* flow]
• **fluidity** *noun*
• **fluidly** *adverb*
• **fluidness** *noun*

fluidics *noun*
• "floo IDDIX"
• the study and technique of using small interacting flows and fluid jets for functions usu. performed by electronic devices.
• [as FLUID]
• **fluidic** *adjective*

fluidize *verb*
ALSO SPELLED: esp. *Brit.* **-ise**
• "FLOO id ize"
• cause (a finely divided solid) to acquire the characteristics of a fluid by the upward passage of a gas etc.
• [as FLUID]
• **fluidization** *noun* (also esp. *Brit.* **-isation**)
• **fluidized** *adjective* (also esp. *Brit.* **-ised**)

fluidram *noun*
• "FLOO a dram"
• a fluid drachm.
• [as FLUID + DRACHM]

flume *noun*
• "FLOOM"
• an artificial channel conveying water etc. for industrial use, esp. for the transport of logs or timber.
• [Old French *flum* from Latin *flumen* river, from *fluere* flow]

flummery *noun*
• "FLUMMER ee"
• empty compliments, nonsense, humbug.
• [Welsh *llymru*, of unknown origin]

flummox *verb*
• "FLUM ix"
• bewilder, confound, disconcert.
• [19th c.: prob. from dialect *flummock* make untidy, confuse]

fluorescein *noun*
• "FLUR a seen" or "FLUR a sin"
• an orange dye with a yellowish-green fluorescence, used in solution as an indicator in biochemistry and medicine.
• [as FLUORESCENCE]

fluorescence *noun*
• "flor ESS ince"
• the visible or invisible radiation produced from certain substances as a result of incident radiation of a shorter wavelength as X-rays, ultraviolet light, etc.
• [FLUORSPAR (which fluoresces) after OPALESCENCE]
• **fluoresce** *verb*
• **fluorescent** *adjective*
HOMOPHONES: *florescence*

fluoridate *verb*
• "FLORA date"
• add traces of fluoride to (drinking water etc.) to reduce or prevent tooth decay.
• [as FLUORIDE]
• **fluoridated** *adjective*
• **fluoridation** *noun*

fluoride *noun*
• "FLORIDE"
• a binary compound of fluorine, esp. as used to prevent tooth decay.
• [as FLUORINE]

fluorinate *verb*
• "FLOR 'n ate"
• introduce one or more fluorine atoms into (a compound or molecule), usu. in place of hydrogen.
• [as FLUORINE]
• **fluorinated** *adjective*
• **fluorination** *noun*

fluorine *noun*
• "FLOR een"
• a poisonous, pale yellow gaseous element of the halogen group occurring naturally in fluorite and cryolite, and the most reactive of all elements.
• [French (as FLUORSPAR)]

fluorite *noun*
• "FLOR ite"
• a mineral form of calcium fluoride.
• [Italian (as FLUORSPAR)]

fluorocarbon *noun*
• "FLORO carb'n"
• a synthetic, chemically stable compound formed by replacing one or more of the hydrogen atoms in a hydrocarbon with fluorine atoms.
• [as FLUORINE + 'carbon']

fluoroscope *noun*
• "FLORA scope"
• an instrument with a fluorescent screen on which X-ray images may be viewed without taking and developing X-ray photographs.
• [as FLUORESCENCE + Greek *skopos* target, from *skeptomai* look at]
• **fluoroscopic** *adjective*
• **fluoroscopically** *adverb*
• **fluoroscopy** *noun* "flor OSCA pee"

fluorosis *noun*
• "flor OH sis"
• poisoning by fluorine or its compounds characterized by mottling of dental enamel and by skeletal changes.
• [as FLUORINE]

fluorspar *noun*
• "FLOO or spar"
• = FLUORITE.
• [*fluor* 'a flow, a mineral used as a flux, fluorspar' from Latin *fluor* from *fluere* flow + FELDSPAR]

fluoxetine *noun*
• "floo OXA teen"
• an organic compound believed to inhibit the uptake of serotonin into the brain, used (orally, as the hydrochloride) as an antidepressant.
• [FLUORINE + OXYGEN + *etine* perhaps from *e* + a blend of TOLUENE + AMINE]

flutist *noun*
• "FLUTE ist"
• a flute player.
• [from 'flute' from Old French *fläute*, prob. from Provençal *fläut*, perhaps a blend of *flaujol* flageolet + *laüt* lute]

fluvial *adjective*
• "FLOOVY 'll"
• of or pertaining to a river or rivers.
• [Latin *fluvialis* from *fluvius* river, from *fluere* flow]

fluviatile *adjective*
• "FLOOVY a tile"
• of, found in, or produced by a river or rivers.
• [French from Latin *fluviatilis* from *fluviatus* moistened, from *fluvius* river]

fluvioglacial *adjective*
• "floovy oh GLAY sh'll"
• of or caused by streams from glacial ice, or the combined action of rivers and glaciers.
• [as FLUVIAL + GLACIAL]

fluxion *noun*
• "FLUCK sh'n"
• the rate at which a variable quantity changes; a derivative.
• [French *fluxion* or Latin *fluxio* from *fluere* flow]
• **fluxional** *adjective*

focaccia *noun*
• "fuh CATCH uh"
• a type of flat Italian bread usu. topped with herbs etc.
• [Italian from medieval Latin *focacius*, short for *panis focacius*, lit. 'bread cooked in the oven']

foible *noun*
• "FOY bull"
• a minor weakness or idiosyncrasy.
• [French, obsolete form of *faible* from Latin *flebilis* lamentable, from *flēre* weep]

folacin *noun*
• "FOL a sin" ("FOL" can rhyme either with *DOLL* or with *DOLE*)
• a vitamin of the B complex, found in leafy green vegetables, liver, and kidney, a deficiency of which causes pernicious anemia.
• [Latin *folium* leaf (because it is found esp. in green leaves) + *acid*]

folate *noun*
• "FOE late"
• a salt or ester of folic acid.
• [as FOLACIN]

folderol *noun*
• "FAWL dur awl"
• foolish chatter or ideas; nonsense.
• [originally as a nonsensical refrain in songs: perhaps from *falbala* trimming on a dress]

foley *noun*
• "FOLEY" (rhymes with *GOALIE*)
• designating sound effects in a motion picture etc. recorded separately from the shooting of the image and subsequently matched with it on the sound track.
• [J. *Foley*, US sound technician d.1967]

foliaceous *adjective*
• "foley AY sh'ss"
• of or like leaves.
• [Latin *foliaceus* leafy, from *folium* leaf + adjective suffix *-aceus* of the nature of]

foliage *noun*
• "FOLEY idge"
• leaves.
• [French *feuillage* from *feuille* leaf, from Old French *foille* from Latin *folium* leaf]
• **foliaged** *adjective*

foliar *adjective*
• "FOLEY ur"
• of or relating to leaves.
• [modern Latin *foliaris* from Latin *folium* leaf]

foliate *adjective*
• "FOLEY it"
• decorated with foils or depictions of leaves.
• [Latin *foliatus* leaved, from *folium* leaf]
• **foliation** *noun*

folio *noun*
• "FOLEY oh"
• a leaf of paper etc., esp. one numbered only on the front.
• [Latin, ablative of *folium* leaf, = *on leaf* (as specified)]

follicle *noun*
• "FOLLA k'll"
• a small secretory cavity, sac, or gland, esp. the gland or cavity at the root of a hair.
• [Latin *folliculus* diminutive of *follis* bellows]
• **follicular** *adjective* "fuh LICK yuh lur"

foment *verb*
• "foe MENT"
• instigate or stir up (trouble, sedition, etc.).
• [French *fomenter* from Late Latin *fomentare* from Latin *fomentum* poultice, lotion, from *fovēre* heat, cherish]
• **fomentation** *noun*
• **fomenter** *noun*

Fon *noun*
• "FON"
• a member of a W African people inhabiting the southern part of Benin.
• [Fon]
HOMOPHONES: *fawn, faun*

fondant *noun*
• "FOND'nt"
• a creamy, thick paste made of sugar and water, used as an icing or filling.
• [French, present participle of *fondre* melt, from Latin *fundere* pour]

fondue *noun*
• "fon DOO"
• a dish of flavoured melted cheese into which cubes of bread are dipped.
• [French, feminine past participle of *fondre* melt, from Latin *fundere* pour]

fontanelle *noun*
ALSO SPELLED: *US* **fontanel**
• "fonta NELL"
• a membranous space in an infant's skull at the angles of the parietal bones.
• [French *fontanelle* from modern Latin *fontanella* from Old French *fontenelle* diminutive of *fontaine* fountain]

fontina *noun*
• "fon TEENA"
• a mild, semi-soft to firm, pale yellow cow's-milk cheese.
• [Italian]

foofaraw *noun*
• "FOOFA raw"
• a fuss, commotion, or disturbance.
• [origin unknown]

foolscap *noun*
• "FULL scap" or "FOOLZ cap"
• a type of legal-sized writing paper, usu. lined.
• [named from the former watermark representing a fool's cap]

foosball *noun*
• "FOOS ball" or "FOOZ ball" ("FOOS" rhymes with *GOOSE*)
• a game played using a table resembling a miniature soccer field, with toy players which can be made to 'kick' the ball by rotating rods extending from the sides.
• [representing the pronunciation of German *Fussball* football]

forage *noun*
• "FOR idge"
• food for horses, cattle, etc., esp. hay or grass.
• [Old French *fourrage*]
• **forager** *noun*

foramen *noun*
• "for AY m'n"
• an opening, hole, or passage, esp. in a bone.
• [Latin *foramen -minis* from *forare* bore a hole]
• **foraminate** *adjective*

foraminifer *noun*
• "fora MINNA fur"
• any protozoan of the order Foraminifera, having a perforated shell through which amoeba-like pseudopodia emerge.
• [as FORAMEN + Latin *-fer* producing, from *ferre* bear]
• **foraminiferous** *adjective* "fora min IFFER us"

foray *noun*
• "FOR ay"
• a sudden attack; a raid or incursion.
• [Middle English, prob. earlier as verb: back-formation from *forayer* from Old French *forrier* forager]

forb *noun*
• "FORB"
• any herbaceous plant other than a grass.

• [Greek *phorbē* fodder, forage, from *ferbein* to feed]

forbear *verb*
• "for BARE"
• abstain or desist (from).
• [Old English *forberan*]
HOMOPHONES: *forebear*

forbearance *noun*
• "for BARE ince"
• patient self-control; tolerance.
• [as FORBEAR]

forceps *noun*
• "FOR seps"
• surgical pincers, used for grasping and holding.
• [Latin *forceps forcipis*]

forcible *adjective*
• "FORSA bull"
• done by or involving force.
• [Old French, from *force* ultimately from Latin *fortis* strong]
• **forcibly** *adverb*
HOMOPHONES: *forceable*

fore *adjective*
• "FOR"
• situated in front.
• [Old English from Germanic]
HOMOPHONES: *for, four*

forearm[1] *noun*
• "FOR arm"
• the part of the arm from the elbow to the wrist or the fingertips.
• [as FORE + 'arm' (body part)]

forearm[2] *verb*
• "for ARM"
• prepare or arm beforehand.
• [as FORE + 'arm' (provide with weapons)]

forebear *noun*
ALSO SPELLED: **forbear**
• "FOR bare"
• an ancestor.
• [FORE + obsolete *bear, beer* (related to 'be')]
HOMOPHONES: *forbear*

foreboding *noun*
• "for BODE ing"
• an expectation of trouble or evil; a presage or omen.
• [as FORE + BODE]
• **forebode** *verb*
• **forebodingly** *adverb*

forebrain *noun*
• "FOR brain"
• the anterior part of the brain, including the cerebrum, thalamus, and hypothalamus.
• [as FORE + 'brain']

forecast *verb*
• "FOR cast"
• predict; estimate or calculate beforehand.
• [as FORE + Old Norse *kasta*]
• **forecaster** *noun*
• **forecasting** *noun*

forecastle *noun*
• "FOKE s'll"
• the forward part of a ship where the crew has quarters.
• [as FORE + 'castle' from Old French *chastel* from Latin *castellum* diminutive of *castrum* fort]

forecheck *verb*
• "FOR check"
• (of a player or team) attempt to gain control of the puck by attacking aggressively in the opposing side's defensive zone before it can organize an attack.
• [FORE + 'check' from Old French *eschequier* play chess, give check to, and Old French *eschec*, ultimately from Persian *šāh* king]
• **forechecker** *noun*
• **forechecking** *noun*

foreclose *verb*
• "for CLOZE"
• stop (a mortgage) from being redeemable or (a mortgagor) from redeeming, esp. as a result of defaults in payment.
• [Old French *forclos* past participle of *forclore* from *for-* out, from Latin *foras* + Old French *clos-* stem of *clore* from Latin *claudere* shut]
• **foreclosure** *noun*

forecourt *noun*
• "FOR cort"
• an enclosed space in front of a building.
• [as FORE + 'court' from Old French *cort*, ultimately from Latin *cohors, -hortis* yard, retinue]

foredeck *noun*
• "FOR deck"
• the deck at the forward part of a ship.
• [as FORE + 'deck' from Middle English, = covering, from Middle Dutch *dec* roof, cloak]

foredoom *verb*
• "for DOOM"
• doom or condemn beforehand.
• [as FORE + 'doom' from Old English *dōm* statute, judgment, from Germanic: related to 'do']

forefather *noun*
• "FOR father"
• an ancestor.
• [as FORE + 'father' from Old English *fæder*]

forefinger *noun*
• "FOR finger"
• the finger next to the thumb.
• [as FORE + 'finger' from Old English]

forefoot *noun*
• "FOR foot"
• either of the front feet of a four-footed animal.
• [as FORE + 'foot' from Old English]

forefront *noun*
• "FOR frunt"
• the foremost part.
• [as FORE + 'front' from Old French *front* from Latin *frons frontis*]

forego *verb*
• "for GO"
• precede in place or time.
• [Old English *foregān*]
HOMOPHONES: *forgo*

foregoing *adjective*
• "for GO ing"
• preceding; previously mentioned.
• [as FOREGO]

foregone *verb*
• "for GON"
• (of a conclusion) that can be predicted with certainty.
• [as FOREGO]

foreground *noun*
• "FOR ground"
• the part of a view, esp. in a picture, that is nearest the observer.
• [as FORE + 'ground' from Old English *grund* from Germanic]

forehand *noun*
• "FOR hand"
• a stroke played with the palm of the hand facing the opponent.
• [as FORE + 'hand' from Old English]

forehead *noun*
• "FOR hed"
• the part of the face above the eyebrows.
• [as FORE + 'head' from Old English]

foreign *adjective*
• "FORRIN"
• of or from or situated in or characteristic of a country or a language other than one's own.
• [Old French *forein*, *forain*, ultimately from Latin *foras*, *-is* outside: for *-g-* compare *sovereign*]
• **foreigner** *noun*
• **foreignness** *noun*

forejudge *verb*
• "for JUDGE"
• judge or determine before knowing the evidence.
• [as FORE + 'judge' from Old French *juger* from Latin *judex judicis* from *jus* law + *-dicus* speaking]

foreknow *verb*
• "for NO"
• know beforehand; have prescience of.
• [as FORE + 'know' from Old English]
• **foreknowable** *adjective*
• **foreknowledge** *noun*

foreland *noun*
• "FOR land"
• a cape or promontory.
• [as FORE + 'land' from Old English]

foreleg *noun*
• "FOR leg"
• each of the front legs of a quadruped.
• [as FORE + 'leg' from Old English]

forelimb *noun*
• "FOR lim"
• any of the front limbs of an animal.
• [as FORE + 'limb' from Old English *lim* from Germanic]

forelock *noun*
• "FOR lock"
• a lock of hair growing just above the forehead.
• [as FORE + 'lock' (of hair) from Old English *locc*]

foreman *noun*
• "FOR m'n"
• a worker with supervisory responsibilities.
• [as FORE + 'man' from Old English]

foremast *noun*
• "FOR mast"
• the forward (lower) mast of a ship.
• [as FORE + 'mast' from Old English *mæst* from West Germanic]

foremost *adjective*
• "FOR most"
• the chief or most notable.
• [earlier *formost*, *formest*, superlative of Old English *forma* first, assimilated to FORE, 'most']

foremother *noun*
• "FOR mother"
• a female ancestor or predecessor.
• [as FORE + 'mother' from Old English]

forename *noun*
• "FOR name"
• a first name.
• [as FORE + 'name' from Old English *namen*]

forenoon *noun*
• "FOR noon"
• the part of the day before noon; the morning.
• [as FORE + 'noon' from Old English *nōn* from Latin *nona (hora)* ninth hour: originally = 3 p.m.]

forensic *adjective*
• "fuh REN zick"
• of or used in connection with courts of law, esp. in relation to crime detection.
• [Latin *forensis* from Latin *forum* public square or marketplace]
• **forensically** *adverb*

foreordain *verb*
• "for or DANE"
• predestinate; ordain beforehand.
• [as FORE + ORDAIN]
• **foreordination** *noun*

forepart *noun*
• "FOR part"
• the foremost part; the front.

• [as FORE + 'part' from Old French from Latin *pars partis*]

forepaw *noun*
• "FOR paw"
• either of the front paws of a quadruped.
• [as FORE + 'paw' from Old French *poue* etc., ultimately from Frankish]

forepeak *noun*
• "FOR peek"
• the front end of a hold or cabin in the angle of the bows of a ship.
• [as FORE + 'peak' prob. a back-formation from *peaked*, variant of dialect *picked* pointed]

foreperson *noun*
• "FOR person"
• a worker with supervisory responsibilities.
• [as FORE + 'person' from Latin *persona* actor's mask, character in a play, human being]

forequarters *plural noun*
• "FOR kwort urz"
• the front legs and adjoining parts of a quadruped.
• [as FORE + 'quarters' from Anglo-French *quarter*, Old French *quartier* from Latin *quartarius* fourth part (of a measure), from *quartus* fourth]

forerun *verb*
• "for RUN"
• go before.
• [as FORE + 'run' from Old English]

forerunner *noun*
• "FOR runner"
• a predecessor.
• [as FORERUN]

foresail *noun*
• "FOR sale" or "FOR s'll"
• the principal sail on a foremast (the lowest square sail, or the fore-and-aft bent on the mast, or the triangular before the mast).
• [as FORE + 'sail' from Old English *segel*]

foresee *verb*
• "for SEE"
• see or be aware of beforehand.
• [as FORE + 'see' from Old English]
• **foreseeability** *noun*
• **foreseeable** *adjective*
• **foreseeably** *adverb*
• **foreseer** *noun*

foreshadow *verb*
• "for SHADDO"
• be a warning or indication of (a future event).
• [as FORE + 'shadow', Old English *scead(u)we*, oblique case of *sceadu* shade]
• **foreshadowing** *noun*

foresheets *plural noun*
• "FOR sheets"
• the inner part of the bows of a boat with gratings for the bowman to stand on.
• [as FORE + 'sheet' (rope) from Old English *scēata*, Old Norse *skaut*]

foreshock *noun*
• "FOR shock"
• a lesser shock preceding the main shock of an earthquake.
• [as FORE + 'shock' from French *choc*, *choquer*, of unknown origin]

foreshore *noun*
• "FOR shore"
• the part of the shore between high- and low-water marks, or between the water and cultivated or developed land.
• [as FORE + 'shore' from Middle Dutch, Middle Low German *schōre*]

foreshorten *verb*
• "for SHORT'n"
• show or portray (an object) with the apparent shortening due to visual perspective.
• [as FORE + 'short' from Old English *sceort*]
• **foreshortening** *noun*

foreshow *verb*
• "for SHOW"
• foretell.
• [as FORE + 'show' from Old English *scēawian*]

foresight *noun*
• "FOR site"
• regard or provision for the future.
• [as FORE + 'sight' from Old English *(ge)sihth*]
• **foresighted** *adjective*
• **foresightedly** *adverb*
• **foresightedness** *noun*
• **foresightful** *adjective*

forestall *verb*
• "for STAWL"
• act in advance of in order to prevent.
• [Old English *foresteall* an ambush (as FORE, 'stall' from Old English, related to 'stand')]

forestay *noun*
• "FOR stay"
• a stay from the head of the foremast to the ship's deck to support the foremast.
• [as FORE + 'stay' from Old English *stæg* be firm, from Germanic]

foretaste *noun*
• "FOR taste"
• a small experience of something before it actually happens; a sample in anticipation.
• [as FORE + 'taste' from Old French *tast*, *taster* touch, try, taste, ultimately perhaps from Latin *tangere* touch + *gustare* taste]

foretell *verb*
• "for TELL"
• tell of or presage (an event etc.) before it takes place; predict, prophesy.
• [as FORE + 'tell' from Old English *tellan*]

forethought *noun*
• "FOR thot"
• care or provision for the future.
• [as FORE + 'thought' from Old English]

foretoken *noun*
• "FOR toke'n"
• a sign of something to come.
• [as FORE + 'token' from Old English *tāc(e)n*, related to 'teach']

foretop *noun*
• "FOR top"
• a platform at the top of a foremast.
• [as FORE + 'top' from Old English *topp*]

forewarn *verb*
• "for WORN"
• warn beforehand.
• [as FORE + 'warn' from Old English *war(e)nian*]

forewing *noun*
• "FOR wing"
• either of the two front wings of a four-winged insect.
• [as FORE + 'wing' from Old English]

forewoman *noun*
• "FOR woman"
• a female worker with supervisory responsibilities.
• [as FORE + 'woman' from Old English]

foreword *noun*
• "FOR wurd"
• introductory remarks at the beginning of a book, often by a person other than the author.
• [as FORE + 'word' from Old English]
HOMOPHONES: *forward*

foreyard *noun*
• "FOR yard"
• the lowest yard on a foremast.
• [as FORE + 'yard' from Old English *geard* enclosure, region, from Germanic: related to 'garden']

forfeit *noun*
• "FOR fit"
• a penalty for a breach of contract or neglect; a fine.
• [Middle English (= crime) from Old French *forfet*, *forfait* past participle of *forfaire* transgress (from Latin *foris* outside) + *faire* from Latin *facere* do]
• **forfeitable** *adjective*
• **forfeiter** *noun*
• **forfeiture** *noun*

forint *noun*
• "FOR int"
• the chief monetary unit of Hungary.
• [Hungarian from Italian *fiorino*: see FLORIN]

forlorn *adjective*
• "for LORN"
• sad and abandoned or lonely.
• [past participle of obsolete *forlese* from Old English *forlēosan*]
• **forlornly** *adverb*
• **forlornness** *noun*

formaldehyde *noun*
• "for MALDA hide"
• a colourless, pungent, toxic gas used as a disinfectant and preservative and in the manufacture of synthetic resins.
• ['formic (acid)' + ALDEHYDE]

formalin *noun*
• "FORMA lin"
• a colourless solution of formaldehyde in water used as a preservative for biological specimens etc.
• [as FORMALDEHYDE]

formerly *adverb*
• "FORMER lee"
• in the past; in former times.
• [Middle English from *forme* first, after FOREMOST]

formication *noun*
• "forma CAY sh'n"
• a sensation as of ants crawling over the skin.
• [Latin *formicatio* from *formica* ant]

formidable *adjective*
• "for MIDDA bull" or "FORMID a bull"
• inspiring fear or dread.
• [French *formidable* or Latin *formidabilis* from *formidare* fear]
• **formidableness** *noun*
• **formidably** *adverb*

formula *noun*
• "FOR mew luh"
• a set of chemical symbols showing the constituents of a substance and their relative proportions.
• [Latin, diminutive of *forma* form]
• **formulaic** *adjective* "for mew LAY ick"
• **formulaically** *adverb*

formulary *noun*
• "FOR mew lerry"
• a collection of formulas or set forms, esp. for religious use.
• [French *formulaire* or medieval Latin *formularius* (*liber* book) from Latin (as FORMULA)]

formulate *verb*
• "FOR mew late"
• express in a formula.
• [as FORMULA]
• **formulation** *noun*
• **formulator** *noun*

formulistic *adjective*
• "for mew LISTIC"
• adhering to or depending on conventional formulas.
• [as FORMULA]

forsake *verb*
• "for SAKE"
• give up; break off from; renounce.
• [Old English *forsacan* deny, renounce, refuse, from West Germanic; compare Old English *sacan* quarrel]
• **forsakenness** *noun*

forswear *verb*
- "for SWARE"
- abjure; renounce under oath.
- [Old English *forswerian*]

forsythia *noun*
- "for SITHY uh"
- any ornamental shrub of the genus *Forsythia* bearing bright yellow flowers in early spring.
- [modern Latin from W. *Forsyth*, English botanist d.1804]

forte *noun*
- "FORTAY"
- a person's strong point; a thing in which a person excels.
- [French *fort* strong, from Latin *fortis*]

fortepiano *noun*
- "fortay PIANO"
- a pianoforte (esp. with reference to an instrument of the 18th to early 19th c.).
- [as PIANOFORTE]

forth *adverb*
- "FORTH"
- forward.
- [Old English]

HOMOPHONES: *fourth*

fortissimo *adjective*
- "for TISSY moe"
- performed very loudly.
- [Italian, superlative of *forte* loud, from Latin *fortis* strong]

fortitude *noun*
- "FORTA tude"
- moral strength or courage, esp. in the endurance of pain or adversity.
- [French from Latin *fortitudo -dinis* from *fortis* strong]

fortnight *noun*
- "FORT nite"
- a period of two weeks.
- [Old English *fēowertīene niht* fourteen nights]
- **fortnightly** *adjective*

fortuitous *adjective*
- "for TOO it us" or "for TYOO it us"
- due to or characterized by chance, esp. lucky chance.
- [Latin *fortuitus* from *forte* by chance]
- **fortuitously** *adverb*
- **fortuitousness** *noun*
- **fortuity** *noun*

fortunate *adjective*
- "FOR chuh nit"
- favoured by fortune; lucky, prosperous.
- [Old French from Latin *fortuna* luck, chance]
- **fortunately** *adverb*

forty *noun*
- "FORTY"
- the product of four and ten.
- [Old English *fēowertig*]
- **fortieth** *adjective*
- **fortyfold** *adjective*
- **fortyish** *adjective*

forward *adjective*
- "FOR wurd"
- directed or moving towards a point in advance, onward, towards the front.
- [Old English *forweard*, var. of *forthweard*]
- **forwarder** *noun*
- **forwardly** *adverb*
- **forwardness** *noun*

HOMOPHONES: *foreword*

fossa *noun*
- "FOSSA"
- a shallow depression or cavity.
- [Latin, = ditch, feminine past participle of *fodere* dig]

fosse *noun*
- "FOSS"
- a long narrow trench or excavation, esp. in a fortification.
- [Old French from Latin *fossa*: see FOSSA]

fossick *verb*
- "FOSSICK"
- rummage, search.
- [19th c.: compare dialect *fossick* bustle about]
- **fossicker** *noun*

fossil *noun*
- "FOSS'll"
- the remains or impression of a prehistoric plant or animal, usu. petrified while embedded in rock, amber, etc..
- [French *fossile* from Latin *fossilis* from *fodere foss-* dig]
- **fossilization** *noun* (also esp. *Brit.* **-isation**)
- **fossilize** *verb* (also esp. *Brit.* **-ise**)

fossiliferous *adjective*
- "foss'll IFFER us"
- (of a rock or stratum) containing fossils or organic remains.
- [FOSSIL + Latin *-fer* producing, from *ferre* bear]

fossorial *adjective*
- "foss ORRY 'll"
- (of animals) burrowing.
- [medieval Latin *fossorius* from *fossor* digger (as FOSSIL)]

fouetté *noun*
- "FWET ay"
- a pirouette performed with a quick circular whipping movement of the raised leg.
- [French, past participle of *fouetter* whip]

foul *adjective*
- "FOWL"
- offensive to the senses; loathsome, stinking.
- [Old English *fūl* from Germanic]
- **foully** *adverb*
- **foulness** *noun*

HOMOPHONES: *fowl*

foulard *noun*
- "foo LARD"

• a thin soft material of silk or silk and cotton.
• [French]

fousty *adjective*
• "FOW stee" ("FOW" rhymes with *HOW*)
• *Cdn* (*Nfld*) mouldy, musty.
• [SW England dialect]

fovea *noun*
• "FOVEY uh"
• a small depression or pit, esp. the pit in the retina of the eye for focusing images.
• [Latin]
• **foveal** *adjective*
• **foveate** *adjective*

fowl *noun*
• "FOUL"
• any domestic cock or hen of various gallinaceous birds, kept for eggs and flesh.
• [Old English *fugol* from Germanic]
• **fowler** *noun*
• **fowling** *noun*
HOMOPHONES: *foul*

foyer *noun*
• "FOY ay"
• an entrance hall or other large area in a hotel, theatre, apartment building, etc.
• [French, = hearth, home, ultimately from Latin *focus* fire]

fracas *noun*
• "FRACK us"
• a noisy disturbance or quarrel.
• [French from *fracasser* from Italian *fracassare* make an uproar]

fractal *noun*
• "FRACK t'll"
• a curve or geometrical figure, each part of which has the same statistical character as the whole.
• ['fraction' (as FRACTIONATE)]

fractionate *verb*
• "FRACK sh'n ate"
• break up into parts.
• [Old French from Late Latin *fractio -onis* from Latin *frangere fract-* break]
• **fractionation** *noun*
• **fractionator** *noun*

fractious *adjective*
• "FRACK sh'ss"
• irritable, bad-tempered.
• ['fraction' (as FRACTIONATE) in obsolete sense 'brawling', prob. after 'factious' etc.]
• **fractiously** *adverb*
• **fractiousness** *noun*

fracture *noun*
• "FRACK chur"
• breakage or breaking, esp. of a bone or cartilage.
• [French *fracture* or from Latin *fractura* (as FRACTIONATE)]
• **fractured** *adjective*

fragrant *adjective*
• "FRAY gr'nt"
• pleasant smelling.
• [French *fragrant* or Latin *fragrare* smell sweet]
• **fragrance** *noun*
• **fragranced** *adjective*
• **fragrantly** *adverb*

frail *adjective*
• "FRALE"
• (of a person) physically weak or delicate.
• [Old French *fraile, frele* from Latin *fragilis* fragile, from *frangere* break]
• **frailly** *adverb*
• **frailness** *noun*
• **frailty** *noun*

Fraktur *noun*
• "FRACK tur"
• a German style of black-letter type, the normal type used for printing German from the 16th to the mid 20th c.
• [German]

franc *noun*
• "FRANK"
• the former chief monetary unit of France, Belgium, and Luxembourg.
• [Old French from *Francorum Rex* 'king of the Franks', the legend on the earliest gold coins so called (14th c.)]
HOMOPHONES: *frank*

franchise *noun*
• "FRAN chize"
• the right to vote in elections.
• [Old French from *franc, franche* free, from medieval Latin *francus* free, from 'Frank' (since only Franks had full freedom in Frankish Gaul)]
• **franchisee** *noun*
• **franchisor** *noun* (also **franchiser**)

Franciscan *noun*
• "fran SIS k'n"
• a monk or nun of an order founded in Italy in 1209 by St. Francis of Assisi (d.1226).
• [French *franciscain* from modern Latin *Franciscanus* from *Franciscus* Francis]

francium *noun*
• "FRANCY um"
• a radioactive metallic element occurring naturally in uranium and thorium ores.
• [modern Latin from *France* (the discoverer's country)]

francize *verb*
ALSO SPELLED: **-ise**
• "FRAN size"
• *Cdn* (*Que.*) cause (a person, business, etc.) to adopt French as an official or working language.
• [French *franciser*]
• **francization** *noun* (also **-isation**)

francolin *noun*
• "FRANCA lin"
• any medium-sized Eurasian or African partridge of the genus *Francolinus*.
• [French from Italian *francolino*]

francophile *noun*
• "FRANCA file"
• a person who admires French or francophone culture.
• ['franco-' French, from medieval Latin *Francus* Frank + Greek *philos* dear, loving]
• **francophilia** *noun* "franca FILLY uh" or "franca FEELY uh"

francophobe *noun*
• "FRANCA fobe"
• a person who dislikes francophones, or French or francophone culture.
• ['franco-' French, from medieval Latin *Francus* Frank + PHOBIA]
• **francophobia** *noun*

francophone *noun*
• "FRANCA fone"
• esp. *Cdn* a French-speaking person.
• ['franco-' French, from medieval Latin *Francus* Frank + Greek *phōnē* voice]

Francophonie *noun*
• "franca foe NEE"
• *Cdn* a loosely united group of nations in which French is a first, official, or culturally significant language.
• [French, as FRANCOPHONE]

frangible *adjective*
• "FRANJA bull"
• breakable, fragile.
• [Old French *frangible* or medieval Latin *frangibilis* from Latin *frangere* to break]
• **frangibility** *noun*

frangipane *noun*
• "FRANJA pane"
• a custard or cream flavoured with almonds and used as a filling.
• [French, earlier meaning a perfume resembling jasmine (as FRANGIPANI)]

frangipani *noun*
• "franja PANNY"
• any tree or shrub of the genus *Plumeria*, native to tropical America, esp. *P. rubra* with clusters of fragrant white, pink, or yellow flowers.
• [named after M. *Frangipani*, 16th-c. Italian marquis, inventor of a perfume for scenting gloves]

franglais *noun*
• "FRONG glay"
• those elements of the French language that have been recently borrowed from English.
• [French from *français* French + *anglais* English]

Frankenfood *noun*
• "FRANK 'n food"
• a genetically modified food.
• [blend of FRANKENSTEIN + 'food']

Frankenstein *noun*
• "FRANK 'n stine"
• a thing that becomes terrifying to its maker; a monster.
• [Baron *Frankenstein*, a character in and the title of a novel (1818) by English writer Mary Shelley (d.1851)]
• **Frankensteinian** *adjective*

frankincense *noun*
• "FRANK 'n sense"
• an aromatic gum resin obtained from trees of the genus *Boswellia*, used for burning as incense.
• [Old French *franc encens* pure incense]

frankum *noun*
• "FRANK um"
• *Cdn* (*Nfld*) the hardened resin of a spruce tree, often used as chewing gum.
• [shortening of *fran(c)kumsence*, 16th–17th c. var. of FRANKINCENSE, in sense 'spruce or fir resin']

Fransaskois *noun*
• "fron sas KWAH"
• *Cdn* a francophone resident of Saskatchewan.
• [Canadian French]

frantic *adjective*
• "FRANTIC"
• wildly excited; frenzied.
• [Middle English *frentik*, *frantik* from Old French *frenetique* from Latin *phreneticus*: see FRENETIC]
• **frantically** *adverb*
• **franticness** *noun*

frappé *adjective*
• "frap AY"
• (esp. of wine) iced, cooled.
• [French, past participle of *frapper* strike, ice (drinks)]

frascati *noun*
• "frass COTTY"
• a usu. white wine produced in the Frascati region of Italy.

frass *noun*
• "FRASS"
• a fine refuse left by insects boring.
• [German from *fressen* devour]

fraternal *adjective*
• "fruh TURN'll"
• of a brother or brothers.
• [medieval Latin *fraternalis* from Latin *fraternus* from *frater* brother]
• **fraternalism** *noun*
• **fraternally** *adverb*

fraternity *noun*
• "fruh TURNA tee"
• a male students' society in a university or college.
• [Old French *fraternité* from Latin *fraternitas -tatis* (as FRATERNAL)]

fraternize *verb*
ALSO SPELLED: esp. *Brit.* **-ise**
• "FRATTER nize"

• associate; make friends; behave as intimates.
• [French *fraterniser* & medieval Latin *fraternizare* from Latin *fraternus*: see FRATERNAL]
• **fraternization** *noun* (also esp. *Brit.* **-isation**)

fratricide *noun*
• "FRAT ruh side"
• the killing of one's brother or sister.
• [French *fratricide* or Late Latin *fratricidium*, Latin *fratricida*, from *frater fratris* brother + *-cida*, *-cidium* from *caedere* kill]
• **fratricidal** *adjective*

Frau *noun*
• "FROW" ("FROW" rhymes with *COW*)
• (often as a title) a married or widowed German woman.
• [German]

fraud *noun*
• "FROD"
• the action or an instance of deceiving someone in order to make money or obtain an advantage illegally.
• [Old French *fraude* from Latin *fraus fraudis* deceit, injury]
• **fraudster** *noun*
• **fraudulence** *noun*
• **fraudulent** *adjective* "FROD yoo l'nt"
• **fraudulently** *adverb*

fraught *adjective*
• "FROT"
• filled or attended with.
• [Middle English, past participle of obsolete *fraught* (v.) load with cargo, from Middle Dutch *vrachten* from *vracht* FREIGHT]

Fräulein *noun*
• "FROY line"
• (often as a title or form of address) an unmarried (esp. young) German woman.
• [German, diminutive of FRAU]

fraxinella *noun*
• "fraxa NELLA"
• an aromatic plant, *Dictamnus albus*, having foliage that emits an ethereal inflammable oil.
• [modern Latin, diminutive of Latin *fraxinus* ash tree]

frazil *noun*
• "FRAZZ'Il"
• slush consisting of small ice crystals formed in water too turbulent to freeze over.
• [Canadian French *frasil* snow floating in the water; compare French *fraisil* cinders]
HOMOPHONES: *frazzle*

frazzle *noun*
• "FRAZZ'Il"
• a worn or exhausted state.
• [19th c.: origin uncertain]
HOMOPHONES: *frazil*

Frederictonian *noun*
• "fred rick TONY 'n"
• a resident of Fredericton, NB.

freemartin *noun*
• "FREE mart'n"
• a female calf born as a twin to a male and sterile, probably as a result of exposure to male hormones in the uterus.
• [17th c.: origin unknown]

freesia *noun*
• "FREE zhuh" or "FREEZY uh"
• any bulbous plant of the genus *Freesia*, native to Africa, having fragrant coloured flowers.
• [modern Latin from F. H. T. *Freese*, German physician d.1876]

freight *noun*
• "FRATE"
• goods transported by water, air, or land.
• [Middle Dutch, Middle Low German *vrecht* var. of *vracht*: compare FRAUGHT]

freighter *noun*
• "FRATE ur"
• a ship or aircraft designed to carry freight.
• [as FREIGHT]

frenetic *adjective*
• "fruh NETTIC"
• frantic, frenzied.
• [Old French *frenetique* from Latin *phreneticus* from Greek *phrenitikos* from *phrenitis* delirium, from *phrēn phrenos* mind]
• **frenetically** *adverb*

frenulum *noun*
ALSO SPELLED: **fraenulum**
• "FREE nyuh lum"
• a small frenum.
• [modern Latin, diminutive of FRENUM]

frenum *noun*
ALSO SPELLED: **fraenum**
• "FREE num"
• a fold of mucous membrane or skin esp. under the tongue, checking the motion of an organ.
• [Latin, = bridle]

frenzy *noun*
• "FRENZY"
• mental derangement; wild excitement or agitation.
• [Old French *frenesie* from medieval Latin *phrenesia* from Latin *phrenesis* from Greek *phrēn* mind]
• **frenzied** *adjective*
• **frenziedly** *adverb*

frequent *adjective*
• "FREE kw'nt"
• occurring often or in close succession.
• [French *fréquent* or Latin *frequens -entis* crowded]
• **frequency** *noun*
• **frequently** *adverb*

frequentative *adjective*
• "free KWENTA tiv"
• expressing frequent repetition or intensity of action.
• [as FREQUENT]

frequenter *noun*
• "FREE kw'nt ur" or "free KWEN tur"
• a person who goes somewhere habitually.
• [as FREQUENT]

fresco *noun*
• "FRESCO"
• a painting done in watercolour on a wall or ceiling while the plaster is still wet.
• [Italian, = cool, fresh]
• **frescoed** *adjective*

freshet *noun*
• "FRESH it"
• a rush of fresh water flowing into the sea.
• [prob. from Old French *freschete* from *frais* fresh]

fresnel *noun*
• "fray NELL"
• a flat lens made of a number of concentric rings, to reduce spherical aberration.
• [A. J. *Fresnel*, French physicist d.1827]

Freudian *adjective*
• "FROY dee 'n"
• of or relating to the Austrian psychologist Sigmund Freud (d.1939), his theories, or his methods of psychoanalysis, esp. with reference to the importance of sexuality in human behaviour.
• **Freudianism** *noun*

friable *adjective*
• "FRY a bull"
• able to be easily crumbled or reduced to powder.
• [French *friable* or Latin *friabilis* from *friare* crumble]
• **friability** *noun*

friar *noun*
• "FRY ur"
• a member of any of certain religious orders of men, esp. the four mendicant orders (Augustinians, Carmelites, Dominicans, and Franciscans).
• [Old French *frere* from Latin *frater fratris* brother]
HOMOPHONES: *fryer*

friary *noun*
• "FRY ur ee"
• a house or building in which a community of friars live.
• [as FRIAR]

fricassee *noun*
• "FRICKA see"
• a dish of white meat such as chicken, veal, or rabbit, cut up, stewed in stock, and served in a thick white sauce.
• [French, feminine past participle of *fricasser* cut up and cook in a sauce]

fricative *adjective*
• "FRICKA tiv"
• (of a consonant sound) produced by the friction of the airstream through a narrow opening in the mouth.
• [modern Latin *fricativus* from Latin *fricare* rub]

fricot *noun*
• "free COE"
• *Cdn* (*Maritimes*) a hearty Acadian stew containing potatoes and meat, fish, or seafood.
• [French, 'stew']

friction *noun*
• "FRICK sh'n"
• the action of one surface or object rubbing against another.
• [French from Latin *frictio -onis* from *fricare* · *frict-* rub]
• **frictional** *adjective*
• **frictionless** *adjective*

frieze *noun*
• "FREEZE"
• any broad, horizontal band of sculpted, painted, or other decoration, esp. along a wall near the ceiling.
• [French *frise* from medieval Latin *frisium*, *frigium* from Latin *Phrygium* (*opus*) (work) of Phrygia (in Asia Minor)]
HOMOPHONES: *freeze*

frigate *noun*
• "FRIG it"
• *Cdn & Brit.* a naval escort vessel between a corvette and a destroyer in size.
• [French *frégate* from Italian *fregata*, of unknown origin]

frigid *adjective*
• "FRIDGE id"
• extremely cold.
• [Latin *frigidus* from *frigēre* be cold, from *frigus* (n.) cold]
• **frigidity** *noun*
• **frigidly** *adverb*
• **frigidness** *noun*

frijoles *plural noun*
• "free HOLE ace"
• (esp. in Mexican cooking) beans, esp. kidney beans.
• [Spanish, pl. of *frijol* bean, ultimately from Latin *phaseolus*]

frippery *noun*
• "FRIPPER ee"
• unnecessary items of ornament or decoration, e.g. in clothing.
• [French *friperie* from Old French *freperie* from *frepe* rag]

frisée *noun*
• "free ZAY"
• a curly-leaved plant, *Cichorium endivia*, used in salads.
• [French, from *chicorée frisée* 'curly endive']

Frisian *noun*
ALSO SPELLED: **Friesian**

• "FREE zh'n" or "FRIZZY 'n"
• a native or inhabitant of Friesland (an area comprising the N Netherlands and NW Germany).

frisson *noun*
• "FREE sawn" or "free SÕH" (with a nasal *OH*)
• an emotional thrill, esp. a shiver of excitement.
• [French, = shiver]

frites *plural noun*
• "FREET"
• french fries, esp. very thinly sliced ones.
• [French, short for *pommes frites* 'fried potatoes']

fritillary *noun*
• "fruh TILLER ee" or "FRITTLE airy"
• any liliaceous plant of the genus *Fritillaria*, having pendent bell-like flowers.
• [modern Latin *fritillaria* from Latin *fritillus* dice box]

frittata *noun*
• "fruh TATTA" or "fruh TOTTA"
• a type of omelette in which chopped vegetables, meat, etc. are incorporated into the beaten eggs before they are fried.
• [Italian]

friulano *noun*
• "free oo LANNO"
• *Cdn* a mild, pale yellow firm cow's-milk cheese of a kind made orig. in Friuli in NE Italy.
• [Italian, = 'Friulian']

Friulian *adjective*
• "free OOLY 'n"
• of or pertaining to Friuli in NE Italy, or the dialect spoken there.

frivolous *adjective*
• "FRIVVA luss"
• (of activities) silly or wasteful.
• [Latin *frivolus* silly, trifling]
• **frivolity** *noun*
• **frivolously** *adverb*
• **frivolousness** *noun*

frizzle *verb*
• "FRIZZ'll"
• form (hair) into tight curls.
• [16th c.: origin unknown]

froe *noun*
ALSO SPELLED: **frow**
• "FROE" (rhymes with *GO*)
• a wedge-shaped cleaving tool with a handle set at right angles to the blade.
• [abbreviation of *frower* from FROWARD 'turned away']
HOMOPHONES: *fro*

frogspawn *noun*
• "FROG spon"
• the soft, almost transparent jellylike mass of eggs of a frog.
• ['frog' + SPAWN]

froideur *noun*
• "frwah DUR"
• coolness or reserve (between people).
• [French, = 'coldness']

frolic *verb*
• "FROLLICK"
• play and move about cheerfully, excitedly, or energetically.
• [Dutch *vrolijk* from *vro* glad]
• **frolicker** *noun*
• **frolicsome** *adjective* "FROLLICK sum"
• **frolicsomely** *adverb*
• **frolicsomeness** *noun*

frontier *noun*
• "frun TEER" or "fron TEER"
• the border between two countries.
• [Anglo-French *frounter*, Old French *frontiere*, ultimately from Latin *frons frontis* front]
• **frontierless** *adjective*

frontiersman *noun*
• "frun TEERZ m'n" or "fron TEERZ m'n"
• a man living on a frontier, or on or beyond the borders of civilization.
• [as FRONTIER]

frontierswoman *noun*
• "frun TEERZ woman" or "fron TEERZ woman"
• a woman living on a frontier, or on or beyond the borders of civilization.
• [as FRONTIER]

frontispiece *noun*
• "FRUN tiss peece"
• an illustration facing the title page of a book or of one of its divisions.
• [French *frontispice* or Late Latin *frontispicium* facade, from Latin *frons frontis* front + *-spicium* from *specere* look: assimilated to 'piece']

frontlet *noun*
• "FRUNT lit"
• a piece of cloth hanging over the upper part of an altar frontal.
• [Old French *front* from Latin *frons, front-*, front, forehead]

fronton *noun*
• "FRUNT'n"
• a building in which pelota or jai alai is played.
• [French from Italian *frontone* from *fronte* forehead]

frottage *noun*
• "fruh TOZH"
• the technique or process of taking a rubbing from an uneven surface, such as grained wood, as a basis of a work of art.
• [French, = rubbing, from *frotter* rub]

froward *adjective*
• "FROE wurd"
• perverse, difficult to deal with, ungovernable.
• [late Old English *frāward* leading away from, away, based on Old Norse *frá* fro, from]

• **frowardly** *adverb*
• **frowardness** *noun*

frowst *noun*
• "FROUST" (rhymes with *JOUST*)
• stuffy warmth in a room.
• [back-formation from FROWSTY]

frowsty *adjective*
• "FROUSTY" ("FROUST" rhymes with *JOUST*)
• (of air in a room etc.) stale, stuffy, etc.
• [var. of FROWZY]

frowzy *adjective*
ALSO SPELLED: **frowsy**
• "FROWZY" (rhymes with *LOUSY*)
• musty, ill-smelling, close.
• [17th c.: origin unknown]
• **frowziness** *noun* (also **frowsiness**)

fructiferous *adjective*
• "fruck TIFFER us"
• bearing or producing fruit.
• [Latin *fructifer* from *fructus* fruit + *-fer* producing, from *ferre* bear]

fructify *verb*
• "FRUCTA fie"
• bear fruit or become fruitful.
• [Old French *fructifier* from Latin *fructificare* from *fructus* fruit]
• **fructification** *noun*

fructose *noun*
• "FROOK tose" or "FRUCK tose" ("FROOK" rhymes with *BOOK*; "TOSE" rhymes with *GROSS*)
• a simple sugar found in honey and fruits.
• [Latin *fructus* fruit]

frugal *adjective*
• "FROO g'll"
• sparing or economical; thrifty.
• [Latin *frugalis* from *frugi* economical]
• **frugality** *noun* "froo GALA tee"
• **frugally** *adverb*
• **frugalness** *noun*

frugivorous *adjective*
• "froo JIVVER us"
• (of an animal) feeding on fruit.
• [Latin *frux frugis* fruit + *-vorus* from *vorare* devour]

fruitarian *noun*
• "froo TERRY 'n"
• a person who eats only fruit.
• ['fruit', (from Old French from Latin *fructus* fruit, enjoyment, from *frui* enjoy) after *vegetarian*]
• **fruitarianism** *noun*

fruition *noun*
• "froo ISH'n"
• the bearing of fruit.
• [Old French from Late Latin *fruitio -onis* from *frui* enjoy, erroneously associated with 'fruit']

frumenty *noun*
• "FROO m'n tee"
• hulled wheat boiled in milk and seasoned with cinnamon, sugar, etc.
• [Old French *frumentee* from *frument* from Latin *frumentum* corn]

frustule *noun*
• "FRUST yool"
• the siliceous cell wall of a diatom.
• [French from Latin *frustulum* (as FRUSTUM)]

frustum *noun*
• "FRUST 'm"
• the remainder of a cone or pyramid whose upper part has been cut off by a plane parallel to its base.
• [Latin, = piece cut off]

fruticose *adjective*
• "FROOTA cose" (rhymes with *GROSS*)
• resembling a shrub.
• [Latin *fruticosus* from *frutex fruticis* bush]

fryer *noun*
• "FRY ur"
• a pot etc. for frying food, esp. in deep fat.
• [from 'fry' from Old French *frire* from Latin *frigere*]
HOMOPHONES: *friar*

fuchsia *noun*
• "FEW shuh"
• any shrub of the genus *Fuchsia*, with drooping red or purple or white flowers.
• [modern Latin from L. *Fuchs*, German botanist d.1566]

fuchsin *noun*
• "FOOK sin"
• a deep red aniline dye used in the pharmaceutical and textile processing industries.
• [FUCHSIA (from its resemblance to the colour of the flower)]

fucus *noun*
• "FYOOK us"
• any seaweed of the genus *Fucus*, with flat leathery fronds.
• [Latin, = rock lichen, from Greek *phukos*, of Semitic origin]
• **fucoid** *adjective*

fugacious *adjective*
• "few GAY sh'ss"
• fleeting, evanescent, hard to capture or keep.
• [Latin *fugax fugacis* from *fugere* flee]

fugitive *noun*
• "FEW juh tiv"
• a person who has escaped from a place or is in hiding, esp. to avoid arrest or persecution.
• [Old French *fugitif -ive* from Latin *fugitivus* from *fugere fugit-* flee]

fugleman *noun*
• "FEW g'll m'n"
• a soldier placed in front of a regiment etc. while drilling to show the motions and time.

• [German *Flügelmann* from *Flügel* wing + *Mann* man]

fugu *noun*
• "FOO goo"
• a pufferfish that is eaten as a Japanese delicacy after some highly poisonous parts have been removed.
• [Japanese]

fugue *noun*
• "FYOOG"
• a contrapuntal composition in which a short melody or phrase (the subject) is introduced by one part and successively taken up by others and developed by interweaving the parts.
• [French or Italian from Latin *fuga* flight]
• **fugal** *adjective*
• **fuguist** *noun*

führer *noun*
ALSO SPELLED: **fuehrer**
• "FYUR ur"
• a leader, esp. a tyrannical one.
• [German, = leader: part of the title assumed in 1934 by German dictator Adolf Hitler (d.1945)]
HOMOPHONES: *furor*

Fuji *noun*
• "FOO jee"
• a large firm-fleshed greenish apple with red highlights.
• [Mount *Fuji* in Japan]

Fulani *noun*
• "foo LANNY" or "FOO lan ee"
• a member of an African people of northern Nigeria and adjacent territories.
• [Hausa]

fulcrum *noun*
• "FULL crum" ("FULL" rhymes with *PULL* or *HULL*)
• the point against which a lever is placed to get a purchase or on which it turns or is supported.
• [Latin, = post of a couch, from *fulcire* to prop]

fulfill *verb*
ALSO SPELLED: **fulfil**
• "full FILL"
• bring to consummation, carry out (a prophecy or promise).
• [Old English *fullfyllan*]
• **fulfillment** *noun* (also **fulfilment**)

fulfilled *adjective*
• "full FILD"
• completely happy; satisfied.
• [as FULFILL]

fulfilling *adjective*
• "full FILLING"
• deeply satisfying.
• [as FULFILL]

fulgent *adjective*
• "FUL j'nt" ("FUL" rhymes with *HULL*)
• shining, brilliant.
• [Middle English from Latin *fulgēre* shine]

fulgurite *noun*
• "FUL gyoo rite" ("FUL" rhymes with *HULL*)
• a rocky substance of sand fused or vitrified by lightning.
• [Latin *fulgur* lightning]

fuliginous *adjective*
• "few LIDGE 'n us"
• sooty, dusky.
• [Late Latin *fuliginosus* from *fuligo -ginis* soot]

fullerene *noun*
• "FULLER een"
• any of several forms of carbon in which atoms are joined in a hollow structure.
• [as BUCKMINSTERFULLERENE]

fulmar *noun*
• "FULL mur"
• any medium-sized seabird of the genus *Fulmarus*, with a stout body, robust bill, and rounded tail.
• [originally Hebridean dialect: perhaps from Old Norse *fúll* FOUL (with reference to its smell) + *már* gull]

fulminant *adjective*
• "FULL m'n 'nt" ("FULL" rhymes either with *HULL* or with *PULL*)
• (of a disease or symptom) developing suddenly.
• [as FULMINATE]

fulminate *verb*
• "FULL m'n ate" ("FULL" rhymes either with *HULL* or with *PULL*)
• express censure loudly and forcefully.
• [Latin *fulminare fulminat-* from *fulmen -minis* lightning]
• **fulmination** *noun*

fulsome *adjective*
• "FULL sum"
• (of praise etc.) excessively complimentary or flattering; effusive, overdone.
• [Middle English from 'full']
• **fulsomely** *adverb*
• **fulsomeness** *noun*

fulvous *adjective*
• "FUL vuss" ("FUL" rhymes with *HULL*)
• brownish yellow, tawny.
• [Latin *fulvus*]

fumarole *noun*
• "FEW muh roll"
• an opening in or near a volcano, through which hot vapours emerge.
• [from obsolete Italian *fumaruolo*, from Late Latin *fumariolum* vent for smoke, a diminutive based on Latin *fumus* smoke]
• **fumarolic** *adjective* "fyooma ROLLIC"

fumet *noun*
• "few MET"
• a concentrated stock, usu. of game or fish, used as flavouring.

• [French from *fumer* fume, from Latin *fumus* smoke]

fumigate *verb*
• "FEW muh gate"
• disinfect (something contaminated or infested) with the fumes of certain chemicals.
• [Latin *fumigare fumigat-* from *fumus* smoke]
• **fumigant** *noun*
• **fumigation** *noun*
• **fumigator** *noun*

fumitory *noun*
• "FEW muh tory"
• an Old World plant of the genus *Fumaria*, with spikes of small tubular pink or white flowers.
• [Old French *fumeterre* from medieval Latin *fumus terrae* 'smoke from the earth' (because of its greyish leaves)]

funambulist *noun*
• "few NAM byoo list"
• a tightrope walker.
• [French *funambule* or Latin *funambulus* from *funis* rope + *ambulare* walk]

fundament *noun*
• "FUNDA m'nt"
• the buttocks or anus.
• [Old French *fondement* from Latin *fundamentum* from *fundare* from *fundus* bottom]

fundamental *adjective*
• "funda MENT'll"
• of, affecting, or serving as a base or foundation, essential, primary, original.
• [as FUNDAMENT]
• **fundamentality** *noun*
• **fundamentally** *adverb*

fundamentalism *noun*
• "funda MENT'll izm"
• strict maintenance of traditional Protestant beliefs such as the inerrancy of Scripture and literal acceptance of the creeds as fundamentals of Christianity.
• [as FUNDAMENTAL]
• **fundamentalist** *noun*

fundus *noun*
• "FUND us"
• the base of a hollow organ; the part furthest from the opening.
• [Latin, = bottom]

funeral *noun*
• "FYOONER 'll"
• a ceremony or service held shortly after a person's death, usu. including the person's burial or cremation.
• [Old French *funeraille* from medieval Latin *funeralia* neuter pl. of Late Latin *funeralis* from Latin *funus -eris* funeral]
• **funerary** *adjective* "FYOONER airy"
• **funereal** *adjective* "fyoo NEERY'll"
• **funereally** *adverb*

fungible *adjective*
• "FUNJA bull"
• precisely or acceptably replacing or replaceable by another item, mutually interchangeable, esp. of goods etc. contracted for, when a particular item is not specified.
• [medieval Latin *fungibilis* from *fungi (vice)* serve (in place of)]
• **fungibility** *noun*

fungicide *noun*
• "FUNGA side" or "FUNJA side"
• a fungus-destroying substance.
• [FUNGUS + Latin *-cida, -cidium* from *caedere* kill]
• **fungicidal** *adjective*

fungistatic *adjective*
• "funja STATTIC"
• inhibiting the growth of fungi.
• [as FUNGUS + STATIC]

fungo *noun*
• "FUN go"
• a fly ball hit in the air for practice.
• [origin unknown]

fungous *adjective*
• "FUNG guss"
• of, like, or caused by fungus.
• [as FUNGUS]
HOMOPHONES: *fungus*

fungus *noun*
• "FUNG guss"
• any of a group of unicellular, multicellular, or syncytial spore-producing organisms feeding on organic matter, including moulds, yeast, mushrooms, and toadstools.
• [Latin, perhaps from Greek *sp(h)oggos* SPONGE]
• **fungiform** *adjective* "FUNJA form"
• **fungivorous** *adjective* "fun JIVVER us"
• **fungoid** *adjective*
HOMOPHONES: *fungous*

funicular *adjective*
• "fuh NICK yuh lur"
• (of a railway, esp. on a mountainside) operating by cable with ascending and descending cars counterbalanced.
• [Latin *funiculus* from *funis* rope]

funkadelic *adjective*
• "funka DELLIC"
• designating a type of popular music which combines funk with elements derived from soul and psychedelic and rock (such as the use of highly amplified guitars and a heavy drum beat).
• [from *Funkadelic*, the name of a rock group formed 1968 by George Clinton (b.1940), after 'funk' + PSYCHEDELIC]

furan *noun*
• "FYUR 'n" or "fyur AN"
• a colourless liquid compound which has a planar five-membered ring in its molecule.
• [abbreviation of German *Furfuran*, from

furfurol, a volatile oil obtained by distilling bran, from Latin *furfur* bran]

furbelow *noun*
- "FURBA lo"
- a gathered strip or pleated border of a skirt or petticoat.
- [18th-c. var. of *falbala* flounce, trimming]
- **furbelowed** *adjective*

furbish *verb*
- "FUR bish"
- remove rust from, polish, burnish.
- [Old French *forbir* from Germanic]

furcula *noun*
- "FUR kyoo luh"
- a forked organ or structure, esp. the wishbone of a bird.
- [Latin, diminutive of *furca* fork]
- **furcular** *adjective*

furfuraceous *adjective*
- "fur fur AY sh'ss"
- (of skin) resembling bran or dandruff; scaly.
- [*furfur* scurf, from Latin *furfur* bran + adjective suffix *-aceus* of the nature of]

furl *verb*
- "FURL"
- roll up and secure (a sail, umbrella, flag, etc.).
- [French *ferler* from Old French *fer(m)* firm, from Latin *firmus* + Old French *lier* bind, from Latin *ligare*]
- **furlable** *adjective*

furlong *noun*
- "FUR long"
- an eighth of a mile, 220 yards (201.168 metres).
- [Old English *furlang* from *furh* furrow + *lang* long: originally = length of a furrow in a common field]

furlough *noun*
- "FUR lo"
- leave of absence, esp. granted to a soldier, missionary, or an inmate of a penitentiary.
- [Dutch *verlof* after German *Verlaub*]

furor *noun*
ALSO SPELLED: *Brit.* **furore**
- "FYUR or" or "FYUR ur"
- an outbreak of public anger or excitement.
- [Italian *furore* from Latin *furor -oris* from *furere* be mad]

HOMOPHONES: *führer*

furosemide *noun*
- "fuh ROE suh mide"
- a strong diuretic, used esp. in the treatment of edema.
- [ultimately from Latin *furfur* bran + *sem-* of unknown origin]

furtive *adjective*
- "FURTIV"
- done by stealth, clandestine, meant to escape notice.
- [French *furtif -ive* or Latin *furtivus* from *furtum* theft]
- **furtively** *adverb*
- **furtiveness** *noun*

furuncle *noun*
- "FYUR unk'll"
- an inflamed pus-filled swelling caused by infection of a hair follicle etc.; a boil.
- [Latin *furunculus*, lit. 'petty thief', also 'knob on a vine' (regarded as stealing the sap) from *fur* thief]

furunculosis *noun*
- "fyur unk yoo LO sis"
- a diseased condition in which boils appear.
- [modern Latin (as FURUNCLE)]

furze *noun*
- "FURZ"
- any spiny yellow-flowered shrub of the genus *Ulex*, esp. growing on European wastelands; gorse.
- [Old English *fyrs*, of unknown origin]
- **furzy** *adjective*

fusarium *noun*
- "few ZERRY um"
- a mould of a large genus which includes a number that cause plant diseases, esp. wilting.
- [modern Latin, from Latin *fusus* spindle]

fusee *noun*
ALSO SPELLED: **fuzee**
- "few ZEE"
- a conical pulley or wheel esp. in a watch or clock.
- [French *fusée* spindle, ultimately from Latin *fusus*]

fuselage *noun*
- "FEW suh lozh" or "FEW zuh lozh"
- the body of an airplane, to which the wings and tail are fitted.
- [French from *fuseler* cut into a spindle, from *fuseau* spindle, from Old French *fusel*, ultimately from Latin *fusus*]

fusible *adjective*
- "FYOOZ a bull"
- that can be easily fused or melted.
- [Old French, from Latin *fundere fus-* pour, melt]
- **fusibility** *noun*

fusiform *adjective*
- "FYOOZA form"
- shaped like a spindle or cigar, tapering at both ends.
- [Latin *fusus* spindle]

fusil *noun*
- "FYOOZ'll"
- a light musket.
- [French, ultimately from Latin *focus* hearth, fire]

fusilier *noun*
- "fyooza LEER"
- a member of any of several regiments formerly armed with fusils.
- [French (as FUSIL)]

fusillade *noun*
- "fyooza LADE" or "fyooza LOD" or "fyoossa LADE" or "fyoossa LOD"
- a continuous discharge of firearms.
- [French from *fusiller* shoot]

fusilli *plural noun*
- "foo SILLY" or "foo ZILLY" or "fyoo SILLY" or "fyoo ZILLY"
- pasta in the form of short spirals.
- [Italian, literally 'little spindles', diminutive of *fuso* spindle]

fustian *noun*
- "FUSTY 'n" or "FUSS ch'n"
- thick twilled cotton cloth with a short nap, usu. dyed in dark colours.
- [Old French *fustaigne* from medieval Latin *fustaneus* (adjective) relating to cloth from *Fostat* a suburb of Cairo, Egypt]

futhorc *noun*
- "FOO thork"
- the Scandinavian runic alphabet.
- [its first six letters *f, u, th, ö, r, k*]

futile *adjective*
- "FEW tile" or "FEW t'll"
- useless, ineffectual.
- [Latin *futilis* leaky, futile, related to *fundere* pour]
- **futilely** *adverb*
- **futility** *noun*

futon *noun*
- "FOO tawn"
- a mattress rolled out or unfolded for use as a bed.
- [Japanese]

futtock *noun*
- "FUT uck"
- each of the middle timbers of a ship's frame, between the floor and the top timbers.
- [Middle English *votekes* from Middle Low German from *fōt* foot + *-ken* diminutive ending]

futz *verb*
- "FUTS"
- spend time unproductively.
- [20th c.: origin uncertain, perhaps alteration of Yiddish *arumfartzen* fart around]

fylfot *noun*
- "FILL fut"
- a swastika.
- [perhaps from *fill-foot*, pattern to fill the foot of a painted window]

Gg

gabardine *noun*
ALSO SPELLED: **gaberdine**
• "GABBER deen" or "gabber DEEN"
• a smooth durable twill-woven cloth esp. of worsted or cotton.
• [var. of 'gaberdine', a long loose garment worn in the Middle Ages, from Old French *gauvardine* perhaps from Middle High German *wallevart* pilgrimage]

gabba *noun*
• "GABBA"
• a harsh, aggressive type of house music originating in Rotterdam, characterized by its extremely fast dance beat.
• [Dutch *gabber*]

Gabbeh *noun*
• "GAB ay"
• a hand-woven and knotted woollen rug with a very thick pile and geometric or symbolic designs, made by nomads in southern Iran.
• [Farsi, = 'raw, natural']

gabbro *noun*
• "GABRO"
• a dark granular plutonic rock of crystalline texture.
• [Italian from *Gabbro* in Tuscany]
• **gabbroic** *adjective*
• **gabbroid** *adverb*

gabion *noun*
• "GAY bee 'n"
• a rectangular or cylindrical metal basket for filling with earth or stones, used in engineering or (formerly) in fortification.
• [French from Italian *gabbione* from *gabbia* from Latin *cavea* cage]

Gabonese *noun*
• "gab 'n EEZ"
• a native or inhabitant of Gabon in W Africa.

gadoid *noun*
• "GAY doid"
• any marine fish of the cod family Gadidae, including haddock and whiting.
• [modern Latin *gadus* from Greek *gados* cod + Greek *-oeidēs* from *eidos* form]

gadolinite *noun*
• "GADDA lin ite"
• a dark crystalline mineral consisting of ferrous silicate of beryllium.
• [J. *Gadolin*, Finnish mineralogist d.1852]

gadolinium *noun*
• "gadda LINNY um"
• a soft silvery metallic element of the lanthanide series, occurring naturally in gadolinite.
• [modern Latin from GADOLINITE]

gadroon *noun*
• "guh DROON"
• a decoration on silverware etc., consisting of convex curves in a series forming an ornamental edge like inverted fluting.
• [French *godron*: prob. related to *goder* pucker]
• **gadrooned** *adjective*

gadwall *noun*
• "GAD wall"
• a brownish-grey freshwater duck, *Anas strepera*.
• [17th c.: origin unknown]

gadzooks *interjection*
• "gad ZOOKS"
• an expression of surprise, annoyance, asseveration, etc.
• [perhaps from *God's hooks*, i.e. God's nails]

Gael *noun*
• "GALE"
• a Gaelic Celt, formerly esp. a Scottish Celt.
• [Gaelic *Gaidheal*]
• **Gaeldom** *noun*
HOMOPHONES: *gale*

Gaelic *noun*
• "GALE ick"
• any of the Celtic languages spoken in Ireland and Scotland.
• [as GAEL]

Gaeltacht *noun*
• "GALE tuct"
• any or all of the regions in Ireland where the vernacular language is Irish.
• [Irish]

gaffe *noun*
• "GAFF"
• a blunder; an indiscreet act or remark.

• [French]
HOMOPHONES: *gaff*

Gaia
• "GUY uh" or "GAY uh"
• the earth viewed as a vast self-regulating organism.
• [Greek, = Earth]
• **Gaian** *adjective*

gaiety *noun*
• "GAY a tee"
• the state of being lighthearted or merry; mirth.
• [French *gaieté* from *gai*, of unknown origin]

gaijin *noun*
• "guy JIN"
• (in Japan) a foreigner; an alien.
• [Japanese, contraction of *gaikoku-jin* (*gaikaku* foreign country, *jin* person)]

gaillardia *noun*
• "gay LARDY uh"
• any composite plant of the genus *Gaillardia*, with showy flowers.
• [modern Latin from *Gaillard* de Marentoneau, 18th-c. French botanist]

gaily *adverb*
• "GAY lee"
• in a gay or lighthearted manner.
• [as GAIETY]

gait *noun*
• "GATE"
• a manner of walking; one's bearing as one walks.
• [var. of 'gate' street, way, from Old Norse *gata*, from Germanic]
• **gaited** *adjective*
HOMOPHONES: *gate, gated*

gaiter *noun*
• "GATER"
• a covering of cloth, leather, etc. for the ankle, or ankle and lower leg, and often extending to the instep, worn over the shoe.
• [French *guêtre*, prob. related to 'wrist']
• **gaitered** *adjective*
HOMOPHONES: *gator*

galactic *adjective*
• "guh LACTIC"
• of or relating to a galaxy or galaxies, esp. the Milky Way.
• [Greek *galaktias*, var. of *galaxias*: see GALAXY]

galactose *noun*
• "guh LACK tose" (rhymes with *GROSS*)
• a hexose sugar present in many polysaccharides, notably lactose.
• [Greek *gala galaktos* milk]

galago *noun*
• "guh LAY go"
• any small tree-climbing primate of the genus *Galago*, found in southern Africa, with large eyes and ears and a long tail.
• [modern Latin]

Galahad *noun*
• "GALA had"
• a person characterized by nobility, integrity, courtesy, etc.
• [Sir *Galahad* in Arthurian legend, a knight of immaculate purity]

galaktoboureko *noun*
• "guh lacto BURA co"
• a Greek dessert consisting of vanilla custard enclosed in phyllo pastry which is then soaked in flavoured syrup.
• [Greek *galakto* of milk + *boureko* pie]

galangal *noun*
• "guh LANG g'll"
• an aromatic rhizome of an E Asian plant of the genus *Alpinia* of the ginger family, used in cooking and medicine.
• [Old French *galingal* from Arabic *ḵalanjān*, said to be from Chinese *ge-liang-liang*, lit. = 'mild ginger from Ge']

galantine *noun*
• "GAL 'n teen"
• white meat or fish boned, cooked, pressed, and served cold in aspic etc.
• [Old French, alteration of *galatine* jellied meat, from medieval Latin *galatina*]

Galatian *noun*
• "guh LAY sh'n"
• a native or inhabitant of ancient Galatia in what is now central Turkey.

galaxy *noun*
• "GAL uck see"
• any of many independent systems of stars, gas, dust, etc., held together by gravitational attraction.
• [Old French *galaxie* from medieval Latin *galaxia*, Late Latin *galaxias* from Greek from *gala galaktos* milk, in reference to the Milky Way]

galbanum *noun*
• "GAL buh num"
• a bitter aromatic gum resin produced from kinds of ferula, used in perfumery.
• [Latin from Greek *khalbanē*, prob. of Semitic origin]

galea *noun*
• "GAY lee uh"
• a structure like a helmet in shape, form, or function.
• [Latin, = helmet]
• **galeate** *adjective*
• **galeated** *adjective*

galena *noun*
• "guh LEENA"
• lead sulphide, the principal ore of lead, found as grey, usu. cubic crystals with a metallic lustre.
• [Latin, = lead ore (in a partly purified state)]

Galenic *adjective*
• "gay LENNIC"

• of or relating to Galen, Greek physician d.199, or his methods.

galette *noun*
• "guh LET"
• a usu. savoury pancake, esp. one made of grated potatoes etc. or of a buckwheat batter.
• [French]

Galibi *noun*
• "guh LEEBY"
• a member of a S American Aboriginal people inhabiting French Guiana in northern S America.
• [Carib, = strong man]

Galician *noun*
• "guh LISH'n"
• a native or inhabitant of Galicia in SE Poland and W Ukraine.

Galilean[1] *noun*
• "gala LEE 'n"
• a native or inhabitant of ancient Galilee in N Palestine.

Galilean[2] *adjective*
• "gala LAY 'n" or "gala LEE 'n"
• of or relating to the Italian astronomer and physicist Galileo Galilei (d.1642), or his methods or discoveries.

galingale *noun*
• "GAL ing gale"
• an aromatic rhizome of an E Asian plant of the genus *Alpinia* of the ginger family, used in cooking and medicine.
• [Old English *gallengar*, Old French *galingal* from Arabic *kalanjān* from Chinese *ge-liang-jiang* mild ginger from Ge (in SE China)]

Galla *noun*
• "GALA"
• a member of a Hamitic people inhabiting mainly parts of Ethiopia and Kenya.
• [origin unknown]
HOMOPHONES: *gala*

gallant *adjective*
• "GAL'nt"
• brave, noble.
• [Old French *galant* participle of *galer* make merry]
• **gallantly** *adverb*
• **gallantry** *noun*

galleon *noun*
• "GAL ee 'n"
• a square-rigged ship with three or more decks and masts, having a high forecastle and poop, used chiefly by Spain from the 15th to the 18th c., originally as a warship and later as a trader.
• [Middle Dutch *galjoen* from French *galion* from *galie* galley, or from Spanish *galeón*]

galleria *noun*
• "gala REE uh"
• a collection of stores under one often high glass roof.
• [Italian]

gallery *noun*
• "GAL ur ee"
• a room or building for showing works of art.
• [French *galerie* from Italian *galleria* from medieval Latin *galeria*]
• **galleried** *adjective*

galley *noun*
• "GAL ee"
• a low flat single-decked vessel using sails and oars, and usu. rowed by slaves or criminals.
• [Old French *galie* from medieval Latin *galea*, medieval Greek *galaia*]

galliard *noun*
• "GAL ee ard"
• a lively dance usu. in triple time for two persons, popular in the 16th–17th c.
• [Old French *gaillard* valiant]

Gallic *adjective*
• "GAL ick"
• French or typically French.
• [Latin *Gallicus* from *Gallus* a Gaul]
• **Gallicize** *verb* (also esp. *Brit.* **-ise**) "GALA size"

Gallican *adjective*
• "GAL ick 'n"
• asserting the right of esp. the French Church to be in certain respects free from papal control.
• [Latin *Gallicanus*, from *Gallic-us* Gaulish, from *Gallus* Gaul]
• **Gallicanism** *noun*

Gallicism *noun*
• "GALA sizm"
• a French word or usage, esp. one adopted in another language.
• [as GALLIC]

galligaskins *plural noun*
• "gala GAS kins"
• breeches, trousers.
• [originally wide hose of the 16th–17th c., from obsolete French *garguesque* for *greguesque* from Italian *grechesca* feminine of *grechesco* Greek]

gallimaufry *noun*
• "gala MOFF ree"
• a heterogeneous mixture; a jumble or medley.
• [French *galimafrée*, of unknown origin]

gallinaceous *adjective*
• "gala NAY sh'ss"
• of or relating to the order Galliformes, which includes domestic poultry, pheasants, partridges, etc.
• [Latin *gallinaceus* from *gallina* hen, from *gallus* cock + adjective suffix *-aceus* of the nature of]

gallinule *noun*
• "GAL 'n yool"
• a moorhen.

• [modern Latin *gallinula*, diminutive of Latin *gallina* hen, from *gallus* cock]

gallipot *noun*
• "GALA pot"
• a small pot of earthenware, metal, etc., used for ointments etc.
• [prob. GALLEY + 'pot', because brought in galleys from the Mediterranean]

gallium *noun*
• "GAL ee um"
• a soft bluish-white metallic element which melts just above room temperature, used in high-temperature thermometers and semiconductors.
• [modern Latin from Latin *Gallia* France (so named patriotically by its discoverer Lecoq de Boisbaudran d.1912)]

gallivant *verb*
• "GALA vant"
• idly search for pleasure; gad about.
• [origin uncertain]

galliwasp *noun*
• "GALA wosp"
• any of various lizards of the Central American genus *Diploglossus*, esp. *D. monotropis* of the W Indies.
• [18th c.: origin unknown]

gallon *noun*
• "GAL 'n"
• (in Britain and other Commonwealth countries and formerly in Canada) a measure of capacity equal to eight pints and equivalent to 4.55 litres, used esp. for liquids.
• [Old Northern French *galon* from base of medieval Latin *gallēta*, *gallētum*, perhaps of Celtic origin]
• **gallonage** *noun*

galloon *noun*
• "guh LOON"
• a narrow close-woven braid of gold, silver, silk, cotton, nylon, etc., for binding dresses etc.
• [French *galon* from *galonner* trim with braid, of unknown origin]

gallop *noun*
• "GAL up"
• the fastest pace of a horse or other quadruped, with all the feet off the ground together in each stride.
• [Old French *galop*, *galoper*, from Frankish *wala hlaupan*, run well]
• **galloper** *noun*
HOMOPHONES: *galop*, *Gallup*

galloway *noun*
• "GALA way"
• a breed of hornless black beef cattle.
• [*Galloway* in SW Scotland]

galluses *plural noun*
• "GALA siz"
• suspenders.
• [pl. of *gallus* var. of 'gallows' from Old English *gealga*]

galoot *noun*
• "guh LOOT"
• a person, esp. a strange or clumsy one.
• [19th-c. Naut. slang: origin unknown]

galop *noun*
• "GAL up"
• a lively ballroom dance in duple time.
• [French: see GALLOP]
HOMOPHONES: *gallop*, *Gallup*

galore *adverb*
• "guh LORE"
• in abundance.
• [Irish *go leór* to sufficiency]

galosh *noun*
• "guh LOSH"
• a waterproof overshoe, usu. of rubber.
• [Old French *galoche* from Late Latin *gallicula* small Gallic shoe]

galumph *verb*
• "guh LUMF"
• move noisily or clumsily.
• [coined by Lewis Carroll, perhaps from GALLOP + TRIUMPH]

galvanic *adjective*
• "gal VANNIC"
• of or producing an electric current by chemical action.
• [as GALVANISM]
• **galvanically** *adverb*

galvanism *noun*
• "GAL v'n izm"
• electricity produced by chemical action.
• [French *galvanisme* from L. *Galvani*, Italian anatomist d.1798]

galvanize *verb*
ALSO SPELLED: esp. *Brit.* **-ise**
• "GALVA nize"
• rouse forcefully, esp. by shock or excitement.
• [French *galvaniser*: see GALVANISM]
• **galvanization** *noun* (also esp. *Brit.* **-isation**)
• **galvanizer** *noun* (also esp. *Brit.* **-iser**)

galvanometer *noun*
• "galva NOMMA tur"
• an instrument for detecting and measuring small electric currents.
• [as GALVANISM + Greek *metron* measure]
• **galvanometric** *adjective* "galva no METRIC"

Gamay *noun*
• "gam AY"
• a variety of black wine grape native to the Beaujolais district of France.
• [*Gamay*, a hamlet in Burgundy, France]

gambade *noun*
• "gam BOD"
• a horse's leap or bound.

• [French *gambade* & Spanish *gambado* from Italian & Spanish *gamba* leg]

Gambian *noun*
• "GAMBY 'n"
• a native or inhabitant of Gambia in W Africa.

gambier *noun*
• "GAMBY ur"
• an astringent extract of a tropical Asiatic plant used in tanning etc.
• [Malay *gambir* name of the plant]

gamboge *noun*
• "gam BOAJ" (with "OA" as in *BOAT*) or "gam BOOZH"
• a gum resin produced by various E Asian trees and used as a yellow pigment.
• [modern Latin *gambaugium* from *Cambodia* in SE Asia]

gambol *verb*
• "GAM bull"
• skip or frolic playfully.
• [as GAMBADE]
HOMOPHONES: *gamble*

gambrel *noun*
• "GAM brull"
• a roof with two sides, each of which has a shallower slope above a steeper one, as in many traditional barns.
• [Old Northern French *gamberel* from *gambier* forked stick, from *gambe* leg (from the resemblance to the shape of a horse's hind leg)]

gamelan *noun*
• "GAMMA lan"
• an Indonesian, esp. Javanese or Balinese, orchestra with a wide range of metal percussion instruments.
• [Javanese]

gametangium *noun*
• "gammy TANJY um"
• an organ in which gametes are formed.
• [as GAMETE + Greek *aggeion* vessel]

gamete *noun*
• "GAM eet"
• a mature haploid reproductive cell (male or female) which unites with another of the opposite sex in sexual reproduction to form a zygote.
• [modern Latin *gameta* from Greek *gametē* wife, from *gamos* marriage]
• **gametic** *adjective* "guh METTIC"

gametocyte *noun*
• "guh MEETO site"
• any cell that is in the process of developing into one or more gametes.
• [GAMETE + Greek *kutos* vessel]

gametogenesis *noun*
• "guh meeto JENNA sis"
• the process by which cells undergo meiosis to form gametes.
• [as GAMETE + GENESIS]

gametophyte *noun*
• "guh MEETO fite"
• the gamete-producing form of a plant that alternates with the asexual form in a plant that has alternation of generations.
• [GAMETE + Greek *phuton* plant, from *phuō* come into being]
• **gametophytic** *adjective* "guh meeto FITTIC"

gamin *noun*
• "GAMMIN"
• a street urchin.
• [French, = 'child']
HOMOPHONES: *gammon*

gamine *noun*
• "GAM een" or "guh MEEN"
• a girl with mischievous or boyish charm.
• [French, = 'young girl']

gamma *noun*
• "GAMMA"
• the third letter of the Greek alphabet (Γ, γ).
• [Greek]

gammon *noun*
• "GAM'n"
• the bottom piece of a flitch of bacon including a hind leg.
• [Old Northern French *gambon* from *gambe* leg: compare JAMB]
HOMOPHONES: *gamin*

gamut *noun*
• "GAM ut"
• the whole series or range or scope of anything.
• [medieval Latin *gamma ut* from GAMMA taken as the name for a note one tone lower than A of the classical scale + *ut* the first of six arbitrary names of notes forming the hexachord, being syllables (*ut*, *re*, *mi*, *fa*, *so*, *la*) in the Hymn for St. John Baptist's day: *Ut* queant laxis *re*sonare fibris *Mi*ra gestorum *fa*muli tuorum, *Sol*ve polluti *la*bii reatum, Sancte Iohannes]

ganache *noun*
• "guh NASH" or "guh NOSH"
• a whipped filling of chocolate and cream, used in cakes, truffles, etc.
• [French]

Gananoquean *noun*
• "ganna NOCK way 'n"
• a resident of Gananoque, Ont.

ganglion *noun*
• "GANGLY 'n"
• an enlargement or knot on a nerve etc. containing an assemblage of nerve cells.
• [Greek *gagglion*]
• **gangliar** *adjective*
• **ganglionated** *adjective*
• **ganglionic** *adjective*

gangrene *noun*
• "GANG green" or "gang GREEN"
• death and decomposition of a part of the

body tissue, usu. resulting from obstructed circulation or bacterial infection.
• [French *gangrène* from Latin *gangraena* from Greek *gaggraina*]
• **gangrenous** *adjective* "GANG grin us"

gangue *noun*
• "GANG"
• valueless earth etc. in which ore is found.
• [French from German *Gang* lode]
HOMOPHONES: *gang*

gannet *noun*
• "GANNIT"
• any seabird of the genus *Sula*, esp. the northern gannet, *Sula bassana*, catching fish by plunge-diving, and nesting in large colonies on ledges of coastal islands.
• [Old English *ganot* from Germanic, related to 'gander']

gannetry *noun*
• "GANNA tree"
• a place where gannets breed; a gannet colony.
• [as GANNET]

ganoid *adjective*
• "GAN oid"
• (of fish scales) enamelled; smooth and bright.
• [French *ganoïde* from Greek *ganos* brightness]

gantry *noun*
• "GAN tree"
• a bridge-like overhead structure whose span supports a suspended travelling crane, railway or road signals, etc.
• [prob. from *gawn*, dialect form of GALLON + 'tree']

garbanzo *noun*
• "gar BONZO"
• a leguminous plant, *Cicer arietinum*, with short swollen pods containing yellowish-brown pea-shaped seeds; a chickpea.
• [Spanish]

garboard *noun*
• "GAR bord"
• the first range of planks or plates laid on a ship's bottom next to the keel.
• [Dutch *gaarboord*, perhaps from *garen* gather + *boord* BOARD]

garburator *noun*
• "GARBA rater"
• *Cdn* a system installed in a kitchen sink, with blades in the drain to mulch refuse.
• [initial element from 'garbage', perhaps punningly after CARBURETOR or influenced by INCINERATOR]

garçon *noun*
• "gar SÕH" (with a nasal *OH*)
• a waiter in a French restaurant, hotel, etc.
• [French, = 'waiter', lit. 'boy']

Garda *noun*
• "GARDA"
• the state police force of the Irish Republic.
• [Irish *Garda Síochána* Civic Guard]

gardenia *noun*
• "gar DEENY uh"
• any tree or shrub of the genus *Gardenia*, with large white or yellow flowers and usu. a fragrant scent.
• [modern Latin from Dr. A. *Garden*, Scottish naturalist d.1791]

gargantuan *adjective*
• "gar GAN choo 'n"
• enormous, gigantic.
• [the name of a giant in the book *Gargantua* (1534) by French writer F. Rabelais (d.1553)]

garget *noun*
• "GAR git"
• inflammation of a cow's or ewe's udder.
• [perhaps from obsolete *garget* throat, from Old French *gargate*, *-guete*]

gargoyle *noun*
• "GAR goil"
• a grotesque carved human or animal face or figure projecting from the edge of a roof of (esp. a Gothic) building usu. as a spout to carry water clear of a wall.
• [Old French *gargouille* throat, gargoyle]
• **gargoyled** *adjective*
• **gargoylish** *adjective*

garibaldi *noun*
• "gare a BALL dee"
• a kind of loose blouse formerly worn by women or children, originally of bright red material imitating the shirts worn by the Italian patriot G. Garibaldi (d.1882) and his followers.

garish *adjective*
• "GARE ish"
• obtrusively bright; showy.
• [16th-c. *gaurish* apparently from obsolete *gaure* stare]
• **garishly** *adverb*
• **garishness** *noun*

garnet *noun*
• "GAR nit"
• a vitreous silicate mineral, esp. a transparent, deep red kind used as a gem.
• [Old French *grenat* from medieval Latin *granatum* POMEGRANATE, from its resemblance to the fruit's pulp]

garniture *noun*
• "GAR nitch ur"
• decoration or trimmings.
• [French from Old French *garnir* to equip or arm, from a Germanic verb, possibly related to 'warn']

garret *noun*
• "GARE it"
• a top-floor or attic room, esp. a dismal one.
• [Old French *garite* watchtower, from Germanic]

garrison *noun*
• "GARE iss 'n"

• the troops stationed in a fortress, town, etc., to defend it.
• [Old French *garison* from *garir* defend, furnish, from Germanic]

garrotte *noun*
ALSO SPELLED: **garotte**; *US* **garrote**
• "guh ROT"
• a wire or cord, esp. one with handles attached at each end, used for strangling a person.
• [French *garrotter* or Spanish *garrotear* from *garrote* a cudgel, of unknown origin]

garrulous *adjective*
• "GARE a luss"
• talkative, esp. on trivial matters.
• [Latin *garrulus* from *garrire* chatter]
• **garrulity** *noun* "guh ROOLA tee"
• **garrulously** *adverb*
• **garrulousness** *noun*

Gascon *noun*
• "GAS k'n"
• a native of Gascony in SW France.
• [French from Latin *Vasco -onis*]

gaseous *adjective*
• "GASSY us" or "GASH us"
• of or like gas.
• [from 'gas', invented by J. B. van Helmont, Belgian chemist d.1644, after Greek *khaos* chaos]

gasify *verb*
• "GASSA fie"
• convert or be converted into gas.
• [as GASEOUS]
• **gasification** *noun*
• **gasifier** *noun*

gasohol *noun*
• "GASSA hawl"
• a mixture of gasoline and ethyl alcohol used as fuel.
• [as GASEOUS + ALCOHOL]

gasoline *noun*
• "gass'll EEN"
• a volatile inflammable liquid obtained from petroleum and used as fuel in motor vehicles etc.
• [as GASEOUS + Latin *oleum* oil + '-ene' forming names of unsaturated hydrocarbons containing a double bond, from Greek *-ēnos*, adjective suffix denoting origin or source]

gasometer *noun*
• "gas OMMA tur"
• a large tank in which gas is stored for distribution by pipes to users.
• [French *gazomètre* from *gaz* gas + Greek *metron* measure]

gaspereau *noun*
• "GASPER oh"
• *Cdn* a fish of the herring family, *Alosa pseudoharengus*, found off the Atlantic coast of N America and in the Great Lakes; an alewife.
• [Canadian French *gaspareau*]

Gaspesian *noun*
• "gas PAY zh'n"
• *Cdn* a native or resident of the Gaspé Peninsula in E Quebec.

Gastarbeiter *noun*
• "GAST ar bite ur"
• a person with temporary permission to work in another country (esp. in W Europe).
• [German, from *Gast* guest + *Arbeiter* worker]

gasthaus *noun*
• "GAST house"
• a small inn or hotel in German-speaking countries.
• [German from *Gast* guest + *Haus* house]

gastrectomy *noun*
• "gas TRECTA mee"
• a surgical operation in which the whole or part of the stomach is removed.
• [GASTRIC + Greek *ektomē* excision, from *ek* out + *temnō* cut]

gastric *adjective*
• "GAS trick"
• of the stomach.
• [modern Latin *gastricus* from Greek *gastēr gast(e)ros* stomach]

gastrin *noun*
• "GAS trin"
• a polypeptide hormone, secreted by the stomach in response to the presence of food, which stimulates the secretion of gastric juice.
• [as GASTRIC]

gastritis *noun*
• "gas TRITE iss"
• inflammation of the lining of the stomach.
• [as GASTRIC + Greek *-itis*, forming feminine of adjectives in *-itēs* (with *nosos* 'disease' implied)]

gastroenteritis *noun*
• "gastro enter ITE iss"
• inflammation of the stomach and intestines.
• [as GASTRIC + Greek *enteron* intestine + *-itis*, forming feminine of adjectives in *-itēs* (with *nosos* 'disease' implied)]

gastroenterology *noun*
• "gastro enter OLLA jee"
• the branch of medicine which deals with disorders of the stomach and intestines.
• [as GASTROENTERITIS + *logos* word]
• **gastroenterological** *adjective*
• **gastroenterologist** *noun*

gastrointestinal *adjective*
• "gastro in TEST'n 'll"
• of or relating to the stomach and the intestines.
• [as GASTRIC + INTESTINAL]

gastrolith *noun*
• "GASTRO lith"
• a small stone swallowed by a bird, reptile, or fish, to aid digestion in the gizzard.
• [as GASTRIC + Greek *lithos* stone]

gastronome *noun*
- "GASTRA nome"
- a gourmet.
- [French from *gastronomie* GASTRONOMY]

gastronomy *noun*
- "gas TRONNA mee"
- the practice, study, or art of eating and drinking well.
- [French *gastronomie* from Greek *gastronomia* (as GASTRIC, *-nomia* from *nomos* law)]
- **gastronomic** *adjective* "gastra NOMMIC"
- **gastronomical** *adjective*
- **gastronomically** *adverb*

gastropod *noun*
- "GASTRA pod"
- any mollusc of the class Gastropoda that moves along by means of a large muscular foot, e.g. a snail, slug, etc.
- [French *gastéropode* from modern Latin *gasteropoda*,(as GASTRIC, Greek *pous podos* foot)]
- **gastropodous** *adjective* "gas TROPPA duss"

gastroscope *noun*
- "GASTRA scope"
- an optical instrument used for inspecting the interior of the stomach.
- [as GASTRIC + Greek *skopos* target, from *skeptomai* look at]
- **gastroscopic** *adjective*

gastrula *noun*
- "GAS troo luh"
- an embryonic stage developing from the blastula.
- [modern Latin from Greek *gastēr gast(e)ros* belly]

gastrulation *noun*
- "gas troo LAY sh'n"
- the process of formation of a gastrula from a blastula.
- [as GASTRULA]

gateau *noun*
- "ga TOE"
- any of various rich layer cakes, usu. containing cream or fruit.
- [French *gâteau* cake from Frankish *wastil* food]

gator *noun*
- "GATER"
- an alligator.
- [abbreviation]

HOMOPHONES: *gaiter*

Gatsbyesque *adjective*
- "gats bee ESK"
- resembling F. Scott Fitzgerald's novel *The Great Gatsby*, esp. in its depiction of the 1920s and of lavish wealth, glamour, and parties, or of its title character's ultimate discovery that his life is hollow.

gauche *adjective*
- "GOASH" (with "OA" as in *GOAT*)
- lacking ease or grace; socially awkward.
- [French, = left-handed, awkward]
- **gauchely** *adverb*
- **gaucheness** *noun*

gaucherie *noun*
- "go shur EE" or "GO shur ee"
- gauche manners.
- [French]

gaucho *noun*
- "GOW cho" ("GOW" rhymes with *HOW*)
- a cowboy from the S American pampas.
- [Spanish from Quechua]

gaud *noun*
- "GOD"
- a gaudy thing; a showy ornament.
- [perhaps through Anglo-French from Old French *gaudir* rejoice, from Latin *gaudēre*]

HOMOPHONES: *god*

gaudy *adjective*
- "GODDY"
- tastelessly or extravagantly bright or showy.
- [prob. from GAUD]
- **gaudily** *adverb*
- **gaudiness** *noun*

gauge *noun*
ALSO SPELLED: *US* **gage**
- "GAGE"
- a standard measure to which certain things must conform, esp. the measure of the inner diameter of an esp. shotgun barrel, representing the number of lead balls of that diameter required to make one pound.
- [Old Northern French *gauge*, *gauger*, of unknown origin]
- **gaugeable** *adjective* (also *US* **gageable**)

HOMOPHONES: *gage*

Gaul *noun*
- "GAWL"
- a native or inhabitant of ancient Gaul, corresponding to modern France, Belgium, the south Netherlands, SW Germany, and N Italy.
- **Gaulish** *adjective*

HOMOPHONES: *gall*

gauleiter *noun*
- "GOW lite ur" ("GOW" rhymes with *COW*)
- an official governing a district under Nazi rule.
- [German from *Gau* administrative district + *Leiter* leader]

Gaullism *noun*
- "GAWL izm"
- the principles and policies of the French general and statesman Charles de Gaulle (d.1970), characterized by their conservatism, nationalism, and advocacy of centralized government with strong executive authority vested in the Presidency.
- [French *Gaullisme*]
- **Gaullist** *noun*

gaunch *noun*
• "GONCH"
• *Cdn* (esp. *BC* & *Alta.*) underwear.
• [alteration of 'gotch', prob. of Eastern European origin: compare Hungarian *gatya*, Serbo-Croat *gaće*]

gaunt *adjective*
• "GONT"
• lean, haggard.
• [Middle English: origin unknown]
• **gauntly** *adverb*
• **gauntness** *noun*

gauntlet *noun*
• "GONT lit"
• a sturdy glove long enough to cover the wrist and part of the forearm.
• [Old French *gantelet* diminutive of *gant* glove, from Germanic]
• **gauntleted** *adjective*

gaur *noun*
• "GOUR" (rhymes with *HOUR*)
• a large wild ox, *Bos gaurus*, found in forests from India to Malaysia.
• [Sanskrit *gaura*]

gauss *noun*
• "GOUSE" (rhymes with *MOUSE*)
• a unit of magnetic induction, equal to one ten-thousandth of a tesla.
• [K. F. *Gauss*, German mathematician, astronomer, and physicist d.1855]

gauze *noun*
• "GOZZ"
• a thin transparent fabric of silk, cotton, etc.
• [French *gaze* from *Gaza* in Palestine]
• **gauzily** *adverb*
• **gauziness** *noun*
• **gauzy** *adjective*
HOMOPHONES: *Ghazi*

gavel *noun*
• "GAV 'll"
• a small hammer used by an auctioneer, or for calling a meeting to order.
• [19th c.: origin unknown]

gavotte *noun*
• "guh VOT"
• a medium-paced French dance popular in the 18th c.
• [French from Provençal *gavoto* from *Gavot* native of a region in the Alps]

gawk *verb*
• "GOCK"
• stare stupidly.
• [related to obsolete *gaw* gaze, from Old Norse *gá* heed]
• **gawker** *noun*
• **gawkish** *adjective*

gawky *adjective*
• "GOCKY"
• awkward or ungainly.
• [as GAWK]
• **gawkily** *adverb*
• **gawkiness** *noun*

gawmoge *noun*
• "ga MOE'g"
• *Cdn* (*Nfld*) a clownish, mischievous person.
• [Irish *gamóg* a clown or simpleton]

gawp *verb*
• "GOP"
• stare stupidly or obtrusively; gape.
• [earlier *gaup*, *galp* from Middle English *galpen* yawn]
• **gawper** *noun*

gayal *noun*
• "guh YAL"
• a semi-domesticated ox, *Bos frontalis*, of India and SE Asia, which is black or brown with white legs, and possibly a variety of the gaur.
• [Bengali]

Gazan *noun*
• "GAZ 'n" or "GOZ 'n"
• a resident of the Gaza Strip in Palestine.

gazania *noun*
• "guh ZANEY uh"
• any herbaceous plant of the genus *Gazania*, with showy yellow or orange daisy-shaped flowers.
• [18th c.: from Theodore of *Gaza*, Greek scholar d.1478]

gazebo *noun*
• "guh ZEE bo"
• a small structure in a garden, park, etc., usu. open or with screens on all sides to give a wide view.
• [perhaps jocular from 'gaze', in imitation of Latin future tenses ending in *-ēbo*: compare LAVABO]

gazelle *noun*
• "guh ZELL"
• any of various small graceful soft-eyed antelopes of Asia or Africa, esp. of the genus *Gazella*.
• [French prob. from Spanish *gacela* from Arabic *ġazāl*]

gazette *noun*
• "guh ZET"
• a newspaper (used esp. in names).
• [French from Italian *gazzetta*, originally Venetian *gazeta de la novita* 'a halfpennyworth of news' because sold for a *gazeta*, a Venetian small coin]

gazetteer *noun*
• "gazza TEER"
• a geographical index or dictionary.
• [earlier = journalist, for whom such an index was provided: from French *gazettier* from Italian *gazzettiere* (as GAZETTE)]

gazillion *noun*
• "guh ZILL y'n"
• an exaggeratedly large number.

- [alteration of 'billion']
- **gazillionaire** *noun*

gazpacho *noun*
- "guh SPATCH oh"
- a Spanish soup made from tomatoes, peppers, cucumbers, garlic, etc., and served cold.
- [Spanish]

gazump *verb*
- "guh ZUMP"
- (of a seller) raise the price of a property after having accepted an offer by (an intending buyer).
- [20th c.: origin uncertain]
- **gazumper** *noun*

gazunder *verb*
- "guh ZUNDER"
- (of a buyer) lower the amount of an offer made to (the seller) for a property, esp. just before exchange of contracts.
- [GAZUMP + 'under']

gean *noun*
- "GEEN" (with "G" as in *GEEK*)
- the wild sweet cherry, *Prunus avium*.
- [Old French *guine* (modern *guigne*)]

gecko *noun*
- "GECKO"
- any of various house lizards found in warm climates, with adhesive feet for climbing vertical surfaces.
- [Malay *chichak* etc., imitative of its cry]

Gehenna *noun*
- "guh HENNA"
- (in Judaism and the New Testament) a name for hell as a place of fiery torment for the wicked.
- [Church Latin from Greek from Hebrew *gê' hinnōm* hell, originally the valley of Hinnom near Jerusalem, where children were sacrificed]

geisha *noun*
- "GAY shuh"
- a Japanese hostess trained in entertaining men with dance and song.
- [Japanese]

gel *noun*
- "JELL"
- a semi-solid colloidal suspension or jelly, of a solid dispersed in a liquid.
- [abbreviation of GELATIN]

HOMOPHONES: *jell*

gelada *noun*
- "juh LODDA"
- a brownish gregarious baboon, *Theropithecus gelada*, with a bare red patch on its chest, native to Ethiopia.
- [Amharic *č'ällada*]

gelatin *noun*

ALSO SPELLED: **gelatine**
- "JELLA tin"
- a virtually colourless tasteless transparent water-soluble protein derived from collagen and obtained by prolonged boiling of animal skin, tendons, ligaments, etc., used in food preparation, photography, glue, etc.
- [French *gélatine* from Italian *gelatina* from *gelata* from Latin *gelare* freeze, from *gelu* frost]
- **gelatinization** *noun* (also esp. *Brit.* **-isation**)
- **gelatinize** *verb* (also esp. *Brit.* **-ise**)
- **gelatinous** *adjective* "juh LAT'n us"
- **gelatinously** *adverb*

gelation *noun*
- "juh LAY sh'n"
- solidification by freezing.
- [Latin *gelatio* from *gelare* freeze]

gelato *noun*
- "juh LOTTO"
- an Italian sherbet-like ice cream made with milk or cream and relatively low in butterfat.
- [Italian, = frozen from Latin *gelare* freeze, from *gelu* frost]

gelcap *noun*
- "JELL cap"
- a gelatin capsule containing a medication in liquid or gel form.
- [as GELATIN + 'cap']

gelcoat *noun*
- "JELL cote"
- a polyester resin coating applied to a mould on which fibreglass cloth is subsequently laid, setting to a hard surface over the fibreglass.
- [as GELATIN + 'coat']

gelid *adjective*
- "JELLID"
- icy, ice-cold.
- [Latin *gelidus* from *gelu* frost]

gelignite *noun*
- "JELLIG nite"
- a high explosive made from a gel of nitroglycerine and nitrocellulose in a base of wood pulp and sodium or potassium nitrate, much used in rock blasting.
- [GELATIN + Latin *ignis* fire + Greek *lithos* stone]

Gémeaux *noun*
- "zhay MOE"
- *Cdn* any of several awards presented by the Academy of Canadian Cinema and Television for excellence in Canadian French-language television.
- [French, = 'twins, Gemini']

Gemeinschaft *noun*
- "guh MINE shoft"
- a form of social integration based on personal ties; community.
- [German, from *gemein* common, general + *-schaft* -ship]

geminate *adjective*
- "JEM 'n ate"
- combined in pairs.

• [Latin *geminatus* past participle of *geminare* from *geminus* twin]
• **gemination** *noun*

Gemini *noun*
• "JEM 'n eye" or "JEM 'n ee"
• the third sign of the zodiac.
• [Latin, = twins]
• **Geminian** *noun* "jem 'n EYE 'n" or "jem 'n EE 'n"

gemma *noun*
• "JEMMA"
• a small cellular body in cryptogams that separates from the mother plant and starts a new one; an asexual spore.
• [Latin *gemma* bud, jewel]

gemmation *noun*
• "jem AY sh'n"
• reproduction by gemmae.
• [French from *gemmer* to bud, *gemme* bud, as GEMMA]

gemmule *noun*
• "JEM yool"
• a tough-coated dormant cluster of embryonic cells produced by a freshwater sponge, for development in more favourable conditions.
• [French *gemmule* or Latin *gemmula* little bud (as GEMMA)]

gemology *noun*
• "jem OLLA jee"
• the study of gems.
• [as GEMMA + *logos* word]
• **gemologist** *noun*

gemsbok *noun*
• "JEMS bock"
• a large antelope, *Oryx gazella*, of SW and E Africa, having long straight horns and black markings on the face and flanks.
• [Afrikaans from Dutch, = chamois]

gemütlich *adjective*
• "guh MOOT lick"
• pleasant and comfortable; cozy.
• [German]

gemütlichkeit *adjective*
• "guh MOOT lick kite"
• the quality of being *gemütlich*.
• [German]

gen *noun*
• "JEN"
• information.
• [perhaps from first syllable of *general information*]

gendarme *noun*
• "zhon DARM" or "ZHON darm"
• a soldier employed in specific public police duties, esp. in some French-speaking countries.
• [French from *gens d'armes* people of arms]

gendarmerie *noun*
• "zhon DARMER ee"
• a force of gendarmes.
• [as GENDARME]

gene *noun*
• "JEEN"
• a unit of heredity composed of DNA or RNA and forming part of a chromosome etc., that determines a particular characteristic of an individual.
• [German *Gen*: see GENESIS]
• **genic** *adjective*
HOMOPHONES: *jean*

genealogy *noun*
• "jeeny OLLA jee" or "jeeny ALA jee"
• a line of descent traced continuously from an ancestor.
• [Old French *genealogie* from Late Latin *genealogia* from Greek *genealogia* from *genea* race + *logos* word]
• **genealogical** *adjective*
• **genealogically** *adverb*
• **genealogist** *noun*

generalissimo *noun*
• "jenner a LEECY moe"
• the supreme commander of a combined military force consisting of army, navy, and air force units.
• [Italian, superlative of *generale* from Latin *generalis* (as GENUS)]

generate *verb*
• "JENNER ate"
• bring into existence; produce, evolve.
• [Latin *generare* beget (as GENUS)]
• **generable** *adjective*

generation *noun*
• "jenner AY sh'n"
• all the people born at a particular time, regarded collectively.
• [as GENERATE]
• **generational** *adjective*

generative *adjective*
• "JENNER a tiv"
• of or concerning procreation.
• [Latin *generare* beget (as GENUS)]

generator *noun*
• "JENNER ater"
• a machine for converting mechanical into electrical energy; a dynamo.
• [as GENERATE]

generic *adjective*
• "juh NARE ick"
• characteristic of or relating to an entire class; general, not specific or special.
• [French *générique* from Latin GENUS]
• **generically** *adverb*

generous *adjective*
• "JENNER us"
• (of a person or an institution) giving willingly more of something, esp. money, than is strictly necessary or expected.

• [Old French *genereus* from Latin *generosus* noble, magnanimous (as GENUS)]
• **generosity** *noun* "jenner OSSA tee"
• **generously** *adverb*
• **generousness** *noun*

genesis *noun*
• "JENNA sis"
• the origin, or mode of formation or generation, of a thing.
• [Latin from Greek from *gen-* be produced, root of *gignomai* become]

genet *noun*
• "JENNIT"
• any catlike mammal of the genus *Genetta*, native to Africa and S Europe, with spotted fur and a long ringed bushy tail.
• [Old French *genete* from Arabic *jarnaiṭ*]

genetics *noun*
• "juh NETTIX"
• the study of heredity and the variation of inherited characteristics.
• [as GENESIS]
• **genetic** *adjective*
• **genetically** *adverb*
• **geneticist** *noun* "juh NETTA sist"

geneva *noun*
• "juh NEEVA"
• gin made in Holland.
• [Dutch *genever* from Old French *genevre* from Latin *juniperus*, assimilated to *Geneva*, Switzerland]

genial *adjective*
• "JEENY 'll"
• jovial, sociable, kindly, cheerful.
• [Latin *genialis* (as GENIUS)]
• **geniality** *noun*
• **genially** *adverb*

genie *noun*
• "JEENY"
• (in Muslim mythology) an intelligent being lower than the angels, able to appear in human and animal forms, and having power over people.
• [French *génie* from Latin GENIUS: compare JINNI]

genista *noun*
• "juh NEESTA"
• any almost leafless shrub of the genus *Genista*, with a profusion of yellow pea-shaped flowers, e.g. dyer's broom.
• [Latin]

genistein *noun*
• "juh NIST ay in"
• a phytoestrogen found esp. in soybeans and flaxseed which may have cancer-fighting properties.
• [GENISTA, because originally isolated in dyer's broom]

genital *adjective*
• "JENNIT'll"
• of or relating to the reproductive organs.
• [Old French *génital* or Latin *genitalis* from *gignere genit-* beget]

genitalia *plural noun*
• "jenna TAILY uh"
• the genitals.
• [Latin, neuter pl. of *genitalis*: see GENITAL]

genitive *noun*
• "JENNA tiv"
• the case of nouns and pronouns (and words in grammatical agreement with them) corresponding to *of*, *from*, and other prepositions and indicating possession or close association.
• [Old French *genetif*, *-ive* or Latin *genitivus* from *gignere genit-* beget]

genitourinary *adjective*
• "jenna toe YURA nerry"
• of the genital and urinary organs.
• [as GENITAL + URINE]

genius *noun*
• "JEEN yuss"
• an exceptional intellectual or creative power or other natural ability or tendency.
• [Latin, from the root of *gignere* beget]

genlock *noun*
• "JEN lock"
• a device for maintaining synchronization between two different video signals, or between a video signal and a computer or audio signal, esp. enabling video images and computer graphics to be mixed.
• [GENERATOR + 'lock']
• **genlocking** *noun*

genoa *noun*
• "JENNO uh"
• a large jib or foresail used esp. on racing yachts.
• [*Genoa* in NW Italy]

genocide *noun*
• "JENNA side"
• the mass extermination of human beings, esp. of a particular race or nation.
• [Greek *genos* race + Latin *-cida*, *-cidium* from *caedere* kill]
• **genocidal** *adjective*

Genoese *adjective*
• "jenno EEZ"
• of or relating to Genoa in NW Italy.

genoise *noun*
• "ZHEN wozz"
• a sponge cake with melted butter incorporated into the batter.
• [French, = 'Genoese']

genome *noun*
• "JEE nome"

• the haploid set of chromosomes of an organism.
• [GENE + CHROMOSOME]
• **genomic** *adjective* "jee NOMMIC"

genomics *noun*
• "jee NOMMIX"
• the branch of molecular biology concerned with the structure, function, evolution, and mapping of genomes.
• [as GENOME]

genotoxic *adjective*
• "jeeno TOXIC"
• designating any substance, esp. a carcinogen, which has a direct and toxic effect upon the genetic material of an organism.
• [as GENE + TOXIC]
• **genotoxicity** *noun* "jeeno tox ISSA tee"

genotype *noun*
• "JEENO tipe" or "JENNO tipe"
• the genetic constitution of an individual.
• [German *Genotypus* (as GENE, TYPE)]
• **genotypic** *adjective* "jeeno TIPPIC" or "jenno TIPPIC"

genre *noun*
• "ZHON ruh"
• a kind or style, esp. of art or literature, e.g. novel, satire, science fiction.
• [French, = a kind from Old French *gendre*, ultimately from Latin GENUS]

gens *noun*
• "JENZ"
• a group of families sharing a name and claiming a common origin.
• [Latin, from the root of *gignere* beget]

gentamicin *noun*
• "jenta MICE in"
• a broad spectrum antibiotic used esp. for severe systemic infections.
• [from *genta-*, of unknown origin + alteration of '-mycin' suffix for antibiotics, from *mukēs* fungus, mushroom]

genteel *adjective*
• "jen TEEL"
• affectedly or ostentatiously refined, stylish, or polite.
• [earlier *gentile*, readoption of French *gentil* from Latin *gentilis*: see GENTILE]
• **genteelly** *adverb*
• **genteelness** *noun*

genteelism *noun*
• "jen TEEL izm"
• a word used because it is thought to be less vulgar than the commoner word, e.g. *perspire* for *sweat*.
• [as GENTEEL]

gentian *noun*
• "JEN sh'n" or "JEN shee 'n"
• any plant of the genus *Gentiana* or *Gentianella*, found esp. in mountainous regions, and usu. having violet or vivid blue trumpet-shaped flowers.
• [Old English from Latin *gentiana* from *Gentius* king of Illyria (on the E Adriatic coast)]

gentile *adjective*
• "JEN tile"
• not Jewish.
• [Latin *gentilis* from *gens gentis* family: see GENS]

gentility *noun*
• "jen TILLA tee"
• refined manners and habits, esp. as associated with wealthy and well-bred people.
• [Old French *gentilité* (as GENTILE)]

gentoo *noun*
• "JEN too"
• a penguin, *Pygoscelis papua*, esp. abundant in the Falkland Islands in the S Atlantic.
• [perhaps from Anglo-Indian *Gentoo* = Hindu, from Portuguese *gentio* GENTILE]

gentrify *verb*
• "JENTRA fie"
• convert (a working-class or inner-city neighbourhood etc.) into an area of middle-class residence.
• [as GENTRY]
• **gentrification** *noun*
• **gentrified** *adjective*
• **gentrifier** *noun*

gentry *plural noun*
• "JEN tree"
• people of high social standing.
• [prob. from obsolete *gentrice* from Old French *genterise* var. of *gentelise* nobility, from *gentil* gentle (as GENTILE)]

genuflect *verb*
• "JEN yoo flect"
• bend the knee to the ground, esp. in worship or as a sign of respect.
• [Church Latin *genuflectere genuflex-* from Latin *genu* the knee + *flectere* bend]
• **genuflection** *noun*

genuine *adjective*
• "JEN yoo 'n" or "JEN yoo ine"
• really coming from its stated, advertised, or reputed source.
• [Latin *genuinus* from *genu* knee, with reference to a father's acknowledging a newborn child by placing it on his knee: later associated with GENUS]
• **genuinely** *adverb*
• **genuineness** *noun*

genus *noun*
• "JEE nuss" or "JEN us"
• a taxonomic grouping of organisms having common characteristics distinct from those of other genera, usu. containing several or many species and being one of a series constituting a taxonomic family.
• [Latin *genus -eris* birth, race, stock]

geocentric *adjective*
• "jeeo SENTRIC"
• having or representing the earth as the centre; not heliocentric.
• [Greek *geō-* from *gē* earth + CENTRE]
• **geocentrically** *adverb*

geochemistry *noun*
• "jeeo KEMMA stree"
• the chemistry of the earth and its rocks, minerals, etc.
• [Greek *geō-* from *gē* earth + CHEMISTRY]
• **geochemical** *adjective*
• **geochemist** *noun*

geochronology *noun*
• "jeeo cruh NOLLA jee"
• the study and measurement of geological time by means of geological events.
• [Greek *geō-* from *gē* earth + CHRONOLOGY]
• **geochronological** *adjective*
• **geochronologist** *noun*

geode *noun*
• "JEE ode"
• a small cavity lined with crystals or other mineral matter.
• [Latin *geodes* from Greek *geōdēs* earthy, from *gē* earth]
• **geodic** *adjective* "jee ODDIC"

geodemographic *adjective*
• "jeeo demma GRAFFIC"
• of or pertaining to a combination of geographic and demographic information, obtained esp. by matching census data with neighbourhoods as defined by e.g. postal codes.
• [Greek *geō-* from *gē* earth + DEMOGRAPHY]
• **geodemographics** *noun*

geodesy *noun*
• "jee ODDA see"
• the branch of mathematics dealing with the figures and areas of the earth or large portions of it.
• [modern Latin from Greek *geōdaisia* (*geō-* from *gē* earth, *daiō* divide)]
• **geodesic** *adjective* "jeeo DEE sick" or "jeeo DESS ick"
• **geodesist** *noun*

geodetic *adjective*
• "jeeo DETTIC"
• of or relating to geodesy, esp. as applied to land surveying.
• [Greek *geōdaitēs* land surveyor, from *geōdaisia* GEODESY]

geoduck *noun*
• "GOOEY duck"
• a giant mud-burrowing bivalve mollusc, *Panopea generosa*, occurring on the west coast of N America, where it is collected for food.
• [Chinook Jargon from Salish *gwídeq*]

geography *noun*
• "jee OGGRA fee"
• the study of the earth's physical features, resources, and climate, and the physical aspects of its population.
• [Greek *geōgraphia* from *gē* earth + *-graphia* writing]
• **geographer** *noun*
• **geographical** *adjective*
• **geographically** *adverb*

geoid *noun*
• "JEE oid"
• the shape of the earth taken as mean sea level and its imagined extension under (or over) land areas.
• [Greek *geōeidēs* (*geō-* from *gē* earth, *-oeidēs* from *eidos* form)]

geology *noun*
• "jee OLLA jee"
• the science of the earth, including the composition, structure, and origin of its rocks.
• [Greek *geō-* from *gē* earth + *logos* word]
• **geological** *adjective*
• **geologically** *adverb*
• **geologist** *noun*

geomagnetism *noun*
• "jeeo MAGNA tizm"
• the study of the magnetic properties of the earth.
• [Greek *geō-* from *gē* earth + MAGNET]
• **geomagnetic** *adjective*
• **geomagnetically** *adverb*

geomancy *noun*
• "JEEO mancy"
• the art of siting buildings etc. auspiciously.
• [Greek *geō-* from *gē* earth + *manteia* divination]
• **geomancer** *noun*
• **geomantic** *adjective*

geomatics *noun*
• "jeeo MATTIX"
• computerization applied to geography.
• [GEOGRAPHY + 'informatics', translation of Russian *informatika* (from Latin *informare* give shape to, fashion, describe (*in* in, *forma* form))]

geometer *noun*
• "jee OMMA tur"
• a person skilled in geometry.
• [Greek *geō-* from *gē* earth]

geometry *noun*
• "jee OMMA tree"
• the branch of mathematics concerned with the properties and relations of points, lines, surfaces, and solids.
• [Old French *geometrie* from Latin *geometria* from Greek *geō-* from *gē* earth + *metron* measure]
• **geometric** *adjective* "jeeo METRIC"
• **geometrical** *adjective*
• **geometrically** *adverb*
• **geometrician** *noun* "jeeo muh TRISH'n"

geomorphology *noun*
• "jeeo mor FOLLA jee"
• the study of the physical features of the

surface of the earth and their relation to its underlying geological structures.
• [Greek *geō-* from *gē* earth + MORPHOLOGY]
• **geomorphic** *adjective*
• **geomorphological** *adjective*
• **geomorphologist** *noun*

geophysics *noun*
• "jeeo FIZZIX"
• the science concerned with all aspects of the physical properties and processes of the earth and planetary bodies, including seismology, gravity, magnetism, etc.
• [Greek *geō-* from *gē* earth + PHYSICS]
• **geophysical** *adjective*
• **geophysicist** *noun* "jeeo FIZZA sist"

geopolitics *noun*
• "jeeo POLLA ticks"
• the politics of a country as determined by its geographical features.
• [Greek *geō-* from *gē* earth + POLITIC]
• **geopolitical** *adjective*
• **geopolitically** *adverb*
• **geopolitician** *noun* "jeeo polla TISH'n"

Geordie *noun*
• "JORDY"
• a native of the area around Newcastle in NE England.
• [pet form of *George*]

georgette *noun*
• "jor JET"
• a thin silk or crepe dress material.
• [*Georgette* de la Plante, French dressmaker fl. *ca.* 1900]

georgic *adjective*
• "JOR jick"
• agricultural.
• [Latin *georgicus* from Greek *geōrgikos*, from *geōrgos* farmer]

Georginian *noun*
• "jor JEENY 'n"
• a resident of Georgina, Ont.

geosphere *noun*
• "JEEO sfeer"
• the solid surface of the earth.
• [Greek *geō-* from *gē* earth + SPHERE]

geostationary *adjective*
• "jeeo STAY sh'n airy"
• (of an artificial satellite of the earth) moving in such an orbit as to remain above the same point on the earth's surface.
• [Greek *geō-* from *gē* earth + STATIONARY]

geostrategic *adjective*
• "jeeo struh TEE jick"
• relating to the esp. military or economic global strategies of nations.
• [Greek *geō-* from *gē* earth + STRATEGY]

geostrophic *adjective*
• "jeeo STROFFIC"
• relating to or denoting the component of a wind or current that arises from a balance between pressure gradients and Coriolis forces.
• [Greek *geō-* from *gē* earth + *strophē* a turning, from *strephō* to turn]

geosynchronous *adjective*
• "jeeo SINK ruh nuss"
• (of an artificial satellite of the earth) moving in an orbit equal to the earth's period of rotation.
• [Greek *geō-* from *gē* earth + SYNCHRONOUS]

geotechnical *adjective*
• "jeeo TECKNA k'll"
• of or pertaining to practical applications of geological science in engineering, building, etc.
• [Greek *geō-* from *gē* earth + TECHNICAL]

geotropism *noun*
• "jee OTTRA pizm"
• plant growth in relation to gravity.
• [Greek *geō-* from *gē* earth + *tropikos* from *tropē* a turning, from *trepō* to turn]
• **geotropic** *adjective* "jeeo TROPPIC"

geranium *noun*
• "juh RAINY um"
• any herb or shrub of the genus *Geranium* bearing fruit shaped like the bill of a crane, e.g. cranesbill.
• [Latin from Greek *geranion* from *geranos* crane]

gerbera *noun*
• "JUR bur uh"
• any composite plant of the genus *Gerbera* of Africa or Asia.
• [T. *Gerber*, German naturalist d.1743]

gerbil *noun*
• "JUR bull"
• a mouselike desert rodent of the subfamily Gerbillinae, with long hind legs, esp. *Meriones unguiculatus* of Mongolia, commonly kept elsewhere as a pet.
• [French *gerbille* from modern Latin *gerbillus* diminutive of *gerbo* JERBOA]

gerenuk *noun*
• "JERRA nook" (rhymes with *BOOK*)
• an antelope, *Litocranius walleri*, native to E Africa, with a very long neck and small head.
• [Somali]

geriatric *adjective*
• "jerry ATTRIC"
• of or relating to old age or old people.
• [Greek *gēras* old age + *iatros* doctor]

geriatrics *noun*
• "jerry ATTRIX"
• a branch of medicine or social science dealing with the health and care of old people.
• [as GERIATRIC]
• **geriatrician** *noun*

germander *noun*
• "jur MANDER"
• any plant of the genus *Teucrium*, of the mint

family, of which some are cultivated as ornamentals and some are used in herbal medicine.
• [medieval Latin *germandra*, ultimately from Greek *khamaidrus* from *khamai* on the ground + *drus* oak]

germane *adjective*
• "jur MANE"
• relevant (to a subject under consideration).
• [Old French *germain* from Latin *germanus* genuine, of the same parent]
• **germanely** *adverb*
• **germaneness** *noun*

germanium *noun*
• "jur MAINY um"
• a lustrous brittle semi-metallic element occurring naturally in sulphide ores and used in semiconductors.
• [modern Latin from *Germanus* German]

germicide *noun*
• "JURMA side"
• a substance destroying germs, esp. those causing disease.
• [French *germe* from Latin *germen germinis* sprout + Latin *-cida, -cidium* from *caedere* kill]
• **germicidal** *adjective*

germinal *adjective*
• "JURMA n'll"
• relating to or of the nature of a germ or germs.
• [Latin *germen germin-* sprout]

germinate *verb*
• "JURMA nate"
• sprout, bud, or put forth shoots.
• [Latin *germinare germinat-* sprout]
• **germination** *noun*
• **germinative** *adjective*
• **germinator** *noun*

germplasm *noun*
• "JURM plazm"
• germ cells collectively; their genetic material.
• [French *germe* from Latin *germen germinis* sprout + PLASMA]

Geronimo *interjection*
• "juh RONNA moe"
• expressing exhilaration or exultation.
• [after *Geronimo*, Apache chief d.1909]

gerontocracy *noun*
• "jare on TOCKRA see"
• government by old people.
• [Greek *gerōn -ontos* old man + *kratia* from *kratos* strength, power]
• **gerontocrat** *noun* "jare ONTA crat"
• **gerontocratic** *adjective*

gerontology *noun*
• "jare 'n TOLLA jee"
• the scientific study of old age, the process of aging, and the special problems of old people.
• [Greek *gerōn -ontos* old man + *logos* word]
• **gerontological** *adjective*
• **gerontologist** *noun*

gerrymander *verb*
• "JERRY mander"
• manipulate the boundaries of (a constituency etc.) so as to give undue influence to some party or class.
• [the name of Governor *Gerry* of Massachusetts + (SALA)MANDER, from the shape of a district on a political map drawn when he was in office (1812)]
• **gerrymanderer** *noun*

gerund *noun*
• "JARE 'nd"
• a noun formed from a verb, in English ending in *-ing*, and designating an action or state, e.g. *smoking is bad for you*.
• [Late Latin *gerundium* from *gerundum* var. of *gerendum*, the gerund of Latin *gerere* do]

gerundive *noun*
• "juh RUN div"
• a form of a Latin verb and functioning as an adjective meaning 'that should or must be done' etc.
• [Late Latin *gerundivus* (*modus* mood) from *gerundium*: see GERUND]

Gesamtkunstwerk *noun*
• "guh ZAMT koonst vurk"
• a work of art in which drama, music, and other performing arts are integrated and each is subservient to the whole.
• [German, from *gesamt* total + *Kunstwerk* work of art]

Gesellschaft *noun*
• "guh ZELL shoft"
• a form of social integration based on impersonal ties, as duty to society or an organization.
• [German, from *Gesell(e)* companion + *-schaft* -ship]

gesso *noun*
• "JESSO"
• plaster of Paris or gypsum as used in painting as a ground or in sculpture.
• [Italian from Latin *gypsum*: see GYPSUM]
• **gessoed** *adjective*

gestalt *noun*
• "guh STAWLT" ("STAWLT" rhymes with *SALT*)
• an organized whole that is perceived as more than the sum of its parts.
• [German, = form, shape]
• **gestaltism** *noun*
• **gestaltist** *noun*

gestation *noun*
• "jess TAY sh'n"
• the process of carrying or being carried in the womb between conception and birth.
• [Latin *gestatio* from *gestare* frequentative of *gerere* carry]
• **gestate** *verb* "JESS tate"
• **gestational** *adjective*

gesticulate *verb*
- "jess TICK yuh late"
- use esp. lively gestures instead of or in addition to speech.
- [Latin *gesticulari* from *gesticulus* diminutive of *gestus* GESTURE]
- **gesticulation** *noun*
- **gesticulative** *adjective*
- **gesticulator** *noun*
- **gesticulatory** *adjective*

gesture *noun*
- "JESS chur"
- a movement of a limb or the body as an expression of thought or feeling.
- [medieval Latin *gestura* from Latin *gerere gest-* wield]
- **gestural** *adjective*
- **gesturally** *adverb*

gesundheit *interjection*
- "guh ZUN tite" or "guh ZOONT hite"
- expressing a wish of good health to a person who has just sneezed.
- [German, = health]

geum *noun*
- "JEE um"
- any rosaceous plant of the genus *Geum*, with rosettes of leaves and yellow, red, or white flowers.
- [modern Latin, var. of Latin *gaeum*]

gewgaw *noun*
- "GOO gaw"
- a gaudy ornament or trinket.
- [Middle English: origin unknown]

Gewürztraminer *noun*
- "guh VURTS truh meener"
- a variety of grape most associated with Alsace, France, but also grown in other cool climates.
- [German, from *Gewürz* spice, perfume + *Traminer* a grape and white wine originally from *Tramin*, now *Termeno*, in N Italy]

geyser *noun*
- "GUY zur"
- an intermittently gushing hot spring that throws up a tall column of water.
- [Icelandic *Geysir*, the name of a particular spring in Iceland, related to *geysa* to gush]

Ghanaian *noun*
- "guh NAY 'n"
- a native or inhabitant of Ghana in W Africa.

gharial *noun*
- "GARE ee 'll" or "GAR ee 'll"
- a large Indian crocodile, *Gavialis gangeticus*, having a long narrow snout widening at the nostrils.
- [Hindi]

ghastly *adjective*
- "GASTLY"
- horrible, frightful.
- [Middle English *gastlich* from obsolete *gast* terrify: *gh* after *ghost*]
- **ghastliness** *noun*

ghat *noun*
- "GOT"
- (in India) steps leading down to a river.
- [Hindi *ghāṭ*]

HOMOPHONES: *got*

ghazal *noun*
- "GOZZ awl"
- a usu. amatory Arabic, Turkish, Urdu, or esp. Persian lyric poem or song characterized by a limited number of stanzas and the recurrence of the same rhyme.
- [Persian from Arabic *ġazal*]

Ghazi *noun*
- "GOZZY"
- a Muslim fighter against non-Muslims.
- [Arabic *al-ġāzī* participle of *ġazā* raid]

HOMOPHONES: *gauzy*

ghee *noun*
- "GEE" (with "G" as in *GEESE*)
- clarified butter as used in Indian cuisine, esp. from the milk of a buffalo or cow.
- [Hindi *ghī* from Sanskrit *ghṛitá-* sprinkled]

HOMOPHONES: *gi*

gherao *noun*
- "gare OW"
- (in India and Pakistan) coercion of employers, by which their workers prevent them from leaving the premises until certain demands are met.
- [Hindi *gherna* besiege]

gherkin *noun*
- "GUR kin"
- a small variety of cucumber, or a young green cucumber, used for pickling.
- [Dutch *gurkkijn* (unrecorded), diminutive of *gurk*, from Slavic, ultimately from medieval Greek *aggourion*]

ghetto *noun*
- "GETTO" (with "G" as in *GET*)
- a part of a city, esp. a slum area, occupied by a minority group or groups.
- [perhaps from Italian *getto* foundry (applied to the site of the first ghetto in Venice in 1516)]

ghettoize *verb*
ALSO SPELLED: esp. *Brit.* **-ise**
- "GETTO ize" (with "G" as in *GET*)
- restrict to a certain category by prejudice.
- [as GHETTO]
- **ghettoization** *noun* (also esp. *Brit.* **-isation**)

ghoul *noun*
- "GOOL"
- an evil spirit or phantom.
- [Arabic *ġūla* desert demon believed to rob graves and devour corpses]
- **ghoulish** *adjective*
- **ghoulishly** *adverb*
- **ghoulishness** *noun*

gi *noun*
• "GEE" (with "G" as in *GEESE*)
• the loose white jacket worn in judo and karate.
• [Japanese]
HOMOPHONES: *ghee*

giaour *noun*
• "JOUR" (rhymes with *HOUR*)
• (historically) a non-Muslim, esp. a Christian.
• [Turkish *gâvur* from Persian *gaur* var. of *gabr*, prob. from Arabic *kāfir* infidel, from *kafara* not believe]

giardia *noun*
• "jee ARDY uh"
• a flagellate protozoan, *Giardia lamblia*, sometimes found in the mammalian intestines.
• [modern Latin genus name *Giardia* (from A. *Giard*, French biologist d.1908)]

giardiasis *noun*
• "jee ar DIE a sis"
• infection of the intestines with giardia, often from drinking untreated lake water, causing diarrhea etc.
• [as GIARDIA]

gib *noun*
• "JIB" or "GIB"
• a wood or metal bolt, wedge, or pin for holding a machine part etc. in place.
• [18th c.: origin unknown]
HOMOPHONES: *jib*

gibber *verb*
• "JIBBER"
• speak fast and inarticulately; chatter incoherently.
• [imitative]
• **gibbering** *noun*
HOMOPHONES: *jibber*

gibberellin *noun*
• "jibber ELL 'n"
• one of a group of plant hormones that stimulate the growth of leaves and shoots.
• [*Gibberella* a genus of fungi, diminutive of genus name *Gibbera* from Latin *gibber* hump]

gibberish *noun*
• "JIBBER ish"
• unintelligible or meaningless speech or writing; nonsense.
• [perhaps from GIBBER (but attested earlier) + '-ish' as used in *Spanish*, *Swedish*, etc.]

gibbet *noun*
• "JIBBIT"
• a gallows.
• [Old French *gibet* gallows, diminutive of *gibe* club, prob. from Germanic]

gibbous *adjective*
• "GIB us" (with "G" as in *GIVE*)
• (of a moon or planet) having the bright part greater than a semicircle and less than a circle.
• [Late Latin *gibbosus* from *gibbus* hump]

giblets *plural noun*
• "JIB lits"
• the liver, gizzard, heart, neck, etc., of a fowl, usu. removed and kept separate when the bird is prepared for cooking.
• [Old French *gibelet* game stew, perhaps from *gibier* game]

gigabyte *noun*
• "GIGGA bite" (with "G" as in *GIVE*)
• 1 073 741 824 (i.e. 2^{30}) bytes as a measure of data capacity, or loosely 1 000 000 000.
• [Greek *gigas* giant + BYTE]

gigahertz *noun*
• "GIGGA hurts" (with "G" as in *GIVE*)
• a measure of frequency equivalent to one million (10^9) cycles per second.
• [Greek *gigas* giant + HERTZ]

gigolo *noun*
• "JIGGA lo"
• a young man paid by an older woman to be her escort or lover.
• [French, formed as masculine of *gigole* dance hall woman]

gigot *noun*
• "zhee GO"
• a leg of mutton or lamb.
• [French, diminutive of dialect *gigue* leg]

gigue *noun*
• "ZHEEG"
• a lively piece of music in duple or triple time, often with dotted rhythms and forming the last movement of a suite.
• [French, from 'jig', of unknown origin]

gild *verb*
• "GILD" (with "G" as in *GIVE*)
• cover thinly with gold or a substance resembling gold.
• [Old English *gyldan* from Germanic]
• **gilder** *noun*
• **gilding** *noun*
HOMOPHONES: *guild, guilder*

gillie *noun*
ALSO SPELLED: **ghillie**
• "GILLY" (with "G" as in *GIVE*)
• a man or boy attending a person hunting or fishing.
• [Gaelic *gille* lad, servant]

gillyflower *noun*
• "JILLY flower"
• a clove-scented pink.
• [Old French *gilofre*, *girofle*, from medieval Latin from Greek *karuophullon* clove tree, from *karuon* nut + *phullon* leaf, assimilated to 'flower']

gilt *noun*
• "GILT" (with "G" as in *GIVE*)
• a young sow that has not been bred.
• [Old Norse *gyltr*]
HOMOPHONES: *guilt*

gimbal *noun*
• "JIMBLE" or "GIMBLE" (with "G" as in *GIVE*)
• a contrivance, usu. of rings and pivots, for keeping objects, esp. instruments such as a compass and chronometer, horizontal aboard a ship or aircraft, etc.
• [var. of earlier *gimmal* from Old French *gemel* double finger ring, from Latin *gemellus* diminutive of *geminus* twin]
• **gimballed** *adjective*

gimcrack *adjective*
• "JIM crack"
• showy but flimsy and worthless.
• [Middle English *gibecrake* a kind of ornament, of unknown origin]
• **gimcrackery** *noun*

gingham *noun*
• "GING um" (with "G" as in *GIVE*)
• a plain-woven cotton cloth of dyed yarn, esp. striped or checked.
• [Dutch *gingang* from Malay *ginggang* (originally adjective = striped)]

gingiva *noun*
• "JIN jiv uh" or "jin JIVE uh"
• the gums around the teeth.
• [Latin]
• **gingival** *adjective* "jin JIVE 'll"

gingivitis *noun*
• "jinja VITE iss"
• inflammation of the gums.
• [GINGIVA + Greek *-itis*, forming feminine of adjectives in *-itēs* (with *nosos* 'disease' implied)]

ginkgo *noun*
ALSO SPELLED: **gingko**
• "GINK go" or "GINKO" (with "G" as in *GIVE*)
• an originally Chinese and Japanese tree, *Ginkgo biloba*, with fan-shaped leaves and yellow flowers.
• [Japanese *ginkyo* from Chinese *yinxing* silver apricot]

ginormous *adjective*
• "jye NOR muss"
• *Cdn & Brit.* very large; enormous.
• ['giant' (Middle English *geant* (later influenced by Latin) from Old French, ultimately from Latin *gigas gigant-* from Greek) + ENORMOUS]

ginseng *noun*
• "JIN seng"
• any of several medicinal plants of the genus *Panax*, found in E Asia and N America.
• [Chinese *renshen* perhaps = man-image, with allusion to its forked root]

giraffe *noun*
• "juh RAFF"
• a ruminant mammal, *Giraffa camelopardalis* of Africa, the tallest living animal, with a long neck and forelegs and a skin of dark patches separated by lighter lines.
• [French *girafe*, Italian *giraffa*, ultimately from Arabic *zarāfa*]

girandole *noun*
• "JIR 'n dole"
• a revolving cluster of fireworks.
• [French from Italian *girandola* from *girare* GYRATE]

girasol *noun*
• "JIRRA sawl"
• a kind of opal reflecting a reddish glow.
• [originally = sunflower, from French *girasol* or Italian *girasole* from *girare* (as GIRANDOLE) + *sole* sun]

gird *verb*
• "GURD"
• encircle, attach, or secure with a belt or band.
• [Old English *gyrdan* from Germanic]

girder *noun*
• "GURDER"
• a large iron or steel beam or compound structure for bearing loads, esp. in bridge-building.
• [as GIRD]

girdle *noun*
• "GURD'll"
• a woman's corset extending from waist to thigh.
• [Old English *gyrdel*: see GIRD]

giro *noun*
• "JYE roe"
• a system of credit transfer between banks, post offices, etc.
• [German from Italian, = circulation (of money)]
HOMOPHONES: *gyro*

Girondin *noun*
• "zhee rõh DÃ" (with nasal *oh* and *A*)
• a member of the French moderate republican party in power during the Revolution 1791–93, so called because the party leaders were the deputies from the department of the Gironde in SW France.
• [French]

girt *adjective*
• "GURT"
• surrounded.
• [as GIRD]

girth *noun*
• "GURTH"
• the distance around a thing.
• [Old Norse *gjörth*, Gothic *gairda* from Germanic]

gist *noun*
• "JIST"
• the substance or essence of a matter.
• [Old French, 3rd sing. pres. of *gesir* lie, from Latin *jacēre*]

gîte *noun*
- "ZHEET"
- a furnished holiday house in a French-speaking area, usu. small and in a rural district.
- [originally = lodging: French from Old French *giste*, related to *gésir* lie]

Gitksan *noun*
- "git K'SAWN" (with "G" as in *GIVE*)
- an Aboriginal group living along the Skeena River in north central BC.
- [Gitksan *kitxsan*, lit. 'people of the Skeena River']

gittern *noun*
- "GITTERN" (with "G" as in *GIVE*)
- a medieval stringed instrument, a forerunner of the guitar.
- [Old French *guiterne*: compare CITTERN, GUITAR]

glabella *noun*
- "gluh BELLA"
- the smooth part of the forehead above and between the eyebrows.
- [modern Latin from Latin *glabellus* (adjective) diminutive of *glaber* smooth]
- **glabellar** *adjective*

glabrous *adjective*
- "GLAY bruss"
- free from hair or down; smooth skinned.
- [Latin *glaber glabri* hairless]

glacé *adjective*
- "GLASS ay" or "glass AY"
- (of fruit, esp. cherries) preserved in sugar, usu. resulting in a glossy surface.
- [French, past participle of *glacer* to ice, gloss from *glace* ice: see GLACIER]

glacial *adjective*
- "GLAY sh'll"
- of ice; icy.
- [French *glacial* or Latin *glacialis* icy, from *glacies* ice]
- **glacially** *adverb*

glaciated *adjective*
- "GLAY see ated"
- marked or polished by the action of ice.
- [past participle of *glaciate* from Latin *glaciare* freeze, from *glacies* ice]
- **glaciation** *noun*

glacier *noun*
- "GLAY shur" or "GLAY shee ur" or "GLAY see ur"
- a slowly-moving mass or river of ice formed by the accumulation and compaction of snow on mountains or in areas of prolonged cold climate.
- [French from *glace* ice, ultimately from Latin *glacies*]

glaciology *noun*
- "glay see OLLA jee" or "glay shee OLLA jee"
- the science of the internal dynamics and effects of glaciers.
- [Latin *glacies* ice + *logos* word]
- **glaciological** *adjective*
- **glaciologist** *noun*

glacis *noun*
- "GLASSY" or "GLASS iss" or "GLAY sis"
- a bank sloping down from a fort, on which attackers are exposed to the defenders' missiles etc.
- [French from Old French *glacier* to slip, from *glace* ice: see GLACIER]

HOMOPHONES: *glassy*

gladiator *noun*
- "GLADDY ater"
- a man trained to fight with a sword or other weapons at ancient Roman shows.
- [Latin from *gladius* sword]
- **gladiatorial** *adjective*

gladiolus *noun*
- "gladdy OH luss"
- any iridaceous plant of the genus *Gladiolus* with sword-shaped leaves and usu. brightly coloured flower spikes.
- [Latin, diminutive of *gladius* sword]

Glagolitic *adjective*
- "glagga LITTIC"
- of or relating to the alphabet ascribed to St. Cyril (d.869) and formerly used in writing some Slavic languages.
- [modern Latin *glagoliticus* from Serbo-Croatian *glagolica* Glagolitic alphabet, from Old Slavic *glagol* word]

glair *noun*
ALSO SPELLED: **glaire**
- "GLARE"
- an adhesive preparation made from egg whites, used in bookbinding etc.
- [Old French *glaire*, ultimately from Latin *clara* feminine of *clarus* clear]

HOMOPHONES: *glare*

glaive *noun*
- "GLAVE"
- a sword.
- [Old French, apparently from Latin *gladius* sword]

glamorize *verb*
ALSO SPELLED: **glamourize**, esp. *Brit.* **-ise**
- "GLAMMER ize"
- make glamorous or attractive.
- [as GLAMOUR]
- **glamorization** *noun* (also **glamourization**, esp. *Brit.* **-isation**)

glamour *noun*
ALSO SPELLED: **glamor**
- "GLAMMER"
- physical attractiveness, esp. when achieved by makeup, elegant clothing, etc.
- [18th c.: var. of GRAMMAR, with reference to

the occult practices associated with learning in the Middle Ages]
- **glamorous** *adjective*
- **glamorously** *adverb*
- **glamourless** *adjective* (also **glamorless**)

glamourpuss *noun*
ALSO SPELLED: **glamorpuss**
- "GLAMMER puss" (with "U" as in *PUT*)
- a glamorous person, esp. deliberately or affectedly so.
- [as GLAMOUR + 'puss']

glanders *plural noun*
- "GLANDERZ"
- a contagious disease of horses, caused by a bacterium and characterized by swellings below the jaw and mucous discharge from the nostrils.
- [Old French *glandre* from Latin *glandulae* throat glands]

glandular *adjective*
- "GLAND yuh lur"
- of or relating to a gland or glands.
- [French *glandulaire* (as GLANDERS)]

glasnost *noun*
- "GLAZ nost"
- (in the former Soviet Union) the policy or practice of more open consultative government and wider dissemination of information.
- [Russian *glasnost'*, lit. 'publicity', 'openness']

glassine *noun*
- "glass EEN"
- a glossy transparent paper.
- [from 'glass']

glassware *noun*
- "GLASS ware"
- articles made from glass, esp. drinking glasses, tableware, etc.
- ['glass' + WARE]

glasswort *noun*
- "GLASS wurt" or "GLASS wort"
- any plant of the genus *Salicornia* or *Salsola* formerly burned for use in glass-making.
- ['glass' + WORT]

Glaswegian *adjective*
- "glazz WEE j'n" or "glass WEE j'n"
- of or relating to Glasgow, Scotland.
- [*Glasgow* on the pattern of *Norwegian*]

glaucoma *noun*
- "glaw CO muh"
- a condition of the eye with increased pressure within the eyeball, causing gradual loss of sight.
- [Latin from Greek *glaukōma -atos*, ultimately from *glaukos*: see GLAUCOUS]

glaucous *adjective*
- "GLOCK us"
- of a dull greyish green or blue.
- [Latin *glaucus* from Greek *glaukos* bluish-green or bluish-grey]

glazier *noun*
- "GLAY zee ur" or "GLAY zhur"
- a person whose trade is glazing windows etc.
- [from 'glaze' from 'glass']
- **glaziery** *noun*

gleam *noun*
- "GLEEM"
- a reflected, brief, or faint light.
- [Old English *glǣm*]
- **gleamingly** *adverb*
- **gleamy** *adjective*

glean *verb*
- "GLEEN"
- collect or scrape together (news, facts, gossip, etc.) in small quantities.
- [Old French *glener* from Late Latin *glennare*, prob. of Celtic origin]
- **gleaner** *noun*
- **gleanings** *plural noun*

glebe *noun*
- "GLEEB"
- a piece of land serving as part of a clergyman's benefice and providing income.
- [Latin *gl(a)eba* clod, soil]

Gleichschaltung *noun*
- "GLIKE shall toong"
- the standardization of political, economic, and social institutions in authoritarian states.
- [German, from *gleich* same + *schalten* force or bring into line]

glengarry *noun*
- "glen GARE ee"
- a brimless Scottish hat with a cleft down the centre and usu. two ribbons hanging at the back, chiefly worn as part of Highland dress.
- [*Glengarry* in Scotland]

glenoid *adjective*
- "GLEE noid"
- designating a shallow depression on a bone, esp. the scapula and temporal bone, receiving the projection of another bone to form a joint.
- [French *glénoïde* from Greek *glēnoeidēs* from *glēnē* socket]

gley *noun*
- "GLAY"
- a tacky waterlogged soil grey to blue in colour.
- [Ukrainian, = sticky blue clay, related to 'clay']

glia *noun*
- "GLYE uh" or "GLEE uh"
- the connective tissue supporting the central nervous system.
- [Greek, = glue]
- **glial** *adjective*

glimpse *noun*
- "GLIMPS"
- a momentary or partial view.
- [Middle English *glimse* corresponding to

Middle High German *glimsen* from West Germanic]

glioma *noun*
• "glye OH muh"
• any malignant tumour of non-nervous cells in the nervous system.
• [from GLIA + '-oma' as in CARCINOMA]

gliosis *noun*
• "glye OH sis"
• reparative or pathological proliferation of glial cells.
• [from GLIA]

glissade *noun*
• "gliss ODD"
• an act of sliding down a steep slope of snow or ice, usu. on the feet with the support of an ice axe etc.
• [French from *glisser* slip, slide]

glissando *noun*
• "gliss ANDO"
• a continuous rapid slide of adjacent notes upwards or downwards.
• [Italian from French *glissant* sliding (as GLISSADE)]

glissé *noun*
• "GLEE say"
• a ballet step in which one foot is slid briskly outward from the body, extended slightly off the ground, and returned to a closed position.
• [French, past participle of *glisser*: see GLISSADE]

glisten *verb*
• "GLISS'n"
• shine, esp. like a wet object, snow, etc.; glitter.
• [Old English *glisnian* from *glisian* shine]
• **glisteningly** *adverb*

glister *verb*
• "GLISTER"
• sparkle; glitter.
• [Middle Low German *glistern*, Middle Dutch *glisteren*, related to GLISTEN]

glitterati *plural noun*
• "glitter OTTY"
• the fashionable, wealthy set of literary or show-business people.
• ['glitter' + LITERATI]

glitzy *adjective*
• "GLIT see"
• extravagant, ostentatious; tawdry, gaudy.
• ['glitter', after RITZY]
• **glitz** *noun*
• **glitzily** *adverb*
• **glitziness** *noun*

gloaming *noun*
• "GLOW ming"
• twilight; dusk.
• [Old English *glōmung* from *glōm* twilight, related to 'glow']

globalize *verb*
ALSO SPELLED: esp. *Brit.* **-ise**
• "GLOBE'll ize"
• develop or be developed so as to make possible international influence or operation.
• [Latin *globus* spherical object]
• **globalization** *noun* (also esp. *Brit.* **-isation**)

globigerina *noun*
• "glow bidger INE uh" or "glow bidger EENA"
• any planktonic protozoan of the genus *Globigerina*, living near the surface of the sea. The shells collect as a deposit over much of the ocean floor, called globigerina ooze.
• [modern Latin from Latin *globus* globe + *-ger* carrying]

globin *noun*
• "GLOW bin"
• any of various polypeptides forming the protein component of hemoglobin and related compound proteins.
• [abbreviation of HEMOGLOBIN]

globule *noun*
• "GLOB yool"
• a small globe or round particle; a drop.
• [French *globule* or Latin *globulus* from *globus* spherical object]
• **globular** *adjective*

globulin *noun*
• "GLOB yoo lin"
• any of a group of simple proteins characterized by solubility only in salt solutions and esp. forming a large fraction of blood serum protein.
• [archaic sense GLOBULE = blood corpuscle]

glockenspiel *noun*
• "GLOCK 'n speel" or "GLOCK 'n shpeel"
• a musical instrument consisting of a series of bells or metal bars or tubes suspended or mounted in a frame and struck by hammers.
• [German, = bell-play]

glomerulonephritis *noun*
• "gluh merra lo nuh FRITE iss"
• a disease of the kidneys, usu. allergic in origin, resulting in acute inflammation.
• [GLOMERULUS + Greek *-itis*, forming feminine of adjectives in *-itēs* (with *nosos* 'disease' implied)]

glomerulus *noun*
• "gluh MARE a luss" or "gluh MARE yuh luss"
• a cluster of small organisms, tissues, or blood vessels, esp. of the capillaries of the kidney.
• [modern Latin, diminutive of Latin *glomus -eris* ball]
• **glomerular** *adjective*

gloriosa *noun*
• "glory OH suh"
• a plant of the genus *Rudbeckia*, with daisy-like flowers.
• [Latin, = glorious]

glossary *noun*
• "GLOSSA ree"
• an alphabetical list of terms or words found in or relating to a specific subject or text, with explanations; a brief dictionary.
• [Latin *glossarium* from *glossa* explanation of a difficult word, from Greek *glōssa* tongue]
• **glossarial** *adjective* "gloss AIRY 'll"

glossolalia *noun*
• "glossa LAY lee uh"
• the power of speaking in unknown languages, regarded as one of the gifts of the Holy Spirit.
• [modern Latin from Greek *glōssa* tongue + *-lalia* speaking]

glossopharyngeal *adjective*
• "glosso fuh RINJY 'll"
• of or relating to the tongue and pharynx.
• [Greek *glōssa* tongue + *pharyngeal*: see PHARYNX]

glottis *noun*
• "GLOTTISS"
• the space at the upper end of the windpipe and between the vocal cords, affecting voice modulation through expansion or contraction.
• [modern Latin from Greek *glōttis* from *glōtta* var. of *glōssa* tongue]
• **glottal** *adjective*

glower *verb*
• "GLOWER" (rhymes with *FLOWER*)
• stare or scowl angrily.
• [origin uncertain: perhaps Scots var. of Middle English *glore* from Low German or Scandinavian, or from obsolete (Middle English) *glow* stare]
• **gloweringly** *adverb*

gloxinia *noun*
• "glock SINNY uh"
• a tropical plant, *Sinningia speciosa*, native to S America, with large bell-shaped flowers of various colours, cultivated as a houseplant.
• [modern Latin from B. P. *Gloxin*, 18th-c. German botanist]

glucagon *noun*
• "GLOOKA gon"
• a polypeptide hormone formed in the pancreas, which aids the breakdown of glycogen to glucose.
• [Greek *glukus* sweet + *agōn* leading]

glucocorticoid *noun*
• "glooko CORTA coid"
• any of a group of corticosteroids which are involved in the metabolism of carbohydrates, proteins, and fats.
• [as GLUCOSE + CORTICOSTEROID]

glucosamine *noun*
• "gloo KOSE a meen" ("KOSE" rhymes with *GROSS*)
• a crystalline amino sugar that is derived from glucose and is the principal constituent of chitin.
• [as GLUCOSE + AMINE]

glucose *noun*
• "GLOO kose" ("KOSE" rhymes with *GROSS*)
• a simple sugar containing six carbon atoms, found mainly in its dextrorotatory form, which is an important energy source in living organisms and obtainable from some carbohydrates by hydrolysis.
• [French from Greek *gleukos* sweet wine, related to *glukus* sweet]

glucoside *noun*
• "GLOO kuh side"
• a compound yielding glucose and other products upon hydrolysis.
• [as GLUCOSE]

glume *noun*
• "GLOOM"
• a membranous bract surrounding the spikelet of grasses or the florets of sedges.
• [Latin *gluma* husk]
HOMOPHONES: *gloom*

gluon *noun*
• "GLOO on"
• any of a group of elementary particles that are thought to bind quarks together.
• [from 'glue' from Old French *glu*, from Late Latin *glus glutis* from Latin *gluten*]

glutamate *noun*
• "GLOOTA mate"
• any salt or ester of glutamic acid, esp. a sodium salt used to enhance the flavour of food.
• [as GLUTAMIC]

glutamic *adjective*
• "gloo TAMMIC"
• designating a naturally occurring amino acid, a constituent of many proteins.
• [GLUTEN + AMINE]

glutamine *noun*
• "GLOOTA meen"
• a hydrophilic amino acid present in many proteins.
• [GLUTAMIC + AMINE]

glutathione *noun*
• "gloota THYE own" (with "TH" as in *THIN*)
• a compound present in the body and involved as a coenzyme in oxidation-reduction reactions in cells. It is derived from glutamic acid, cysteine, and glycine.
• [as GLUTAMIC]

glute *noun*
• "GLOOT"
• a gluteus muscle.
• [abbreviation]

gluten *noun*
• "GLOO t'n"
• a mixture of proteins present in cereal grains, responsible for the elastic cohesion of dough.
• [French from Latin *gluten glutinis* glue]

gluteus *noun*
- "GLOOTY us"
- any of the three muscles in each buttock.
- [modern Latin from Greek *gloutos* buttock]
- **gluteal** *adjective*

glutinous *adjective*
- "GLOOT 'n us"
- sticky; like glue.
- [French *glutineux* or Latin *glutinosus* (as GLUTEN)]
- **glutinously** *adverb*

glutton *noun*
- "GLUT 'n"
- an excessively greedy eater.
- [Old French *gluton, gloton* from Latin *glutto -onis* from *gluttire* swallow, *gluttus* greedy]
- **gluttonous** *adjective*
- **gluttonously** *adverb*
- **gluttony** *noun*

glycemic *adjective*
ALSO SPELLED: *Brit.* **glycaemic**
- "glye SEEMIC"
- designating an index describing the ability of a food to increase blood sugar, calculated as the increase in blood glucose over 2 hours after consuming 50 g of carbohydrate, expressed as a percentage of that after 50 g of glucose.
- ['glyco-' relating to or producing sugar, from Greek *glukus* sweet + *aimia* from Greek *haima* blood]

glyceride *noun*
- "GLISSER ide"
- any fatty-acid ester of glycerol.
- [as GLYCEROL]

glycerine *noun*
ALSO SPELLED: esp. *US* **glycerin**
- "GLISSER in"
- = GLYCEROL.
- [French *glycerin* from Greek *glukeros* sweet]

glycerol *noun*
- "GLISSER awl"
- a colourless sweet viscous liquid formed as a by-product in the manufacture of soap, used as an emollient and laxative, and for making explosives and antifreeze.
- [GLYCERINE + ALCOHOL]

glycine *noun*
- "GLYE sin"
- the simplest naturally occurring amino acid, a general constituent of proteins.
- [German *Glycin* from Greek *glukus* sweet]

glycogen *noun*
- "GLYE kuh j'n"
- a polysaccharide serving as a store of carbohydrates, esp. in animal tissues, and yielding glucose on hydrolysis.
- [Greek *glukus* sweet + GENESIS]
- **glycogenic** *adjective*

glycol *noun*
- "GLYE coll"
- a diol, esp. ethylene glycol.
- [GLYCERINE + ALCOHOL, originally as being intermediate between glycerine and alcohol]
- **glycolic** *adjective*

glycolipid *noun*
- "glye kuh LIPPID"
- any compound in which a sugar or other carbohydrate is combined with a lipid.
- [Greek *glukus* sweet + LIPID]

glycolysis *noun*
- "glye COLLA sis"
- the breakdown of glucose by enzymes in most living organisms to release energy and pyruvic acid or lactic acid.
- [Greek *glukus* sweet + *lusis* loosening]
- **glycolytic** *adjective*

glycoprotein *noun*
- "glye co PRO teen"
- any of a group of compounds consisting of a protein combined with a carbohydrate.
- [Greek *glukus* sweet + PROTEIN]

glycoside *noun*
- "GLYE kuh side"
- a compound formed from a simple sugar and another compound by replacement of a hydroxyl group in the sugar molecule. Many drugs and poisons derived from plants are glycosides.
- [Greek *glukus* sweet + GLUCOSIDE]
- **glycosidic** *adjective* "glye kuh SIDDIC"

glycosuria *noun*
- "glye kuh SYUR ee uh"
- a condition characterized by an excess of sugar in the urine, associated with diabetes, kidney disease, etc.
- [French *glycose* glucose + URINE]

glyph *noun*
- "GLIFF"
- a sculptured character or symbol.
- [French *glyphe* from Greek *gluphē* carving, from *gluphō* carve]
- **glyphic** *adjective*

glyphosate *noun*
- "GLIFE a sate"
- a non-selective systemic herbicide that is especially effective against perennial weeds.
- [GLYCINE + PHOSPHORUS]

glyptic *adjective*
- "GLIPTIC"
- of or concerning carving, esp. on precious stones.
- [French *glyptique* or Greek *gluptikos* from *gluptēs* carver, from *gluphō* carve]

glyptodont *noun*
- "GLIPTA dont"
- an extinct mammal of Cenozoic times whose few teeth were grooved, related to the

armadillos but much larger and with a bony shield round the body and tail.
• [modern Latin from Greek *gluptos* carved + *odous odontos* tooth]

gnarled *adjective*
• "NARLD"
• (of a tree, hands, etc.) knobbly, twisted, rugged.
• [var. of Middle English *knarled*, from *knarre*, related to Middle Low German, Middle Dutch, Middle High German *knorre* knobbed protuberance]

gnarly *adjective*
• "NARLY"
• = GNARLED.
• [as GNARLED]

gnash *verb*
• "NASH"
• grind (the teeth), esp. in anger or exasperation.
• [var. of obsolete *gnacche* or *gnast*, related to Old Norse *gnastan* a gnashing (imitative)]

gnat *noun*
• "NAT"
• any small two-winged biting fly, e.g. a midge or blackfly.
• [Old English *gnætt*]

gnatcatcher *noun*
• "NAT catcher"
• any of various tiny birds, related to the kinglets, of the genus *Polioptila*.
• [as GNAT + 'catch' from Anglo-French & Old Northern French *cachier*, Old French *chacier*, ultimately from Latin *captare* try to catch]

gnaw *verb*
• "NAW"
• bite persistently; wear away by biting.
• [Old English *gnagen*, ultimately imitative]
HOMOPHONES: *naw*

gnawing *adjective*
• "NAWING"
• persistent; worrying.
• [as GNAW]
• **gnawingly** *adverb*

gneiss *noun*
• "NICE"
• a usu. coarse-grained metamorphic rock foliated by mineral layers, principally of feldspar, quartz, and ferromagnesian minerals.
• [German]
• **gneissic** *adjective*
HOMOPHONES: *nice*

gnocchi *plural noun*
• "NYOCKY"
• an Italian dish of small dumplings usu. made from potato, semolina flour, etc.
• [Italian, pl. of *gnocco* from *nocchio* knot in wood]

gnome *noun*
• "NOME"
• a dwarfish legendary creature supposed to guard the earth's treasures underground; a goblin.
• [French from modern Latin *gnomus*, a word used by Swiss physician Paracelsus (d.1541) as a synonym of *Pygmaeus* denoting a mythical race of very small people said to inhabit parts of Ethiopia and India]
• **gnomish** *adjective*

gnomic *adjective*
• "NOME ick"
• expressed in or of the nature of short, pithy maxims or aphorisms.
• [Greek *gnōmikos* from *gnōmē* opinion from *gignōskō* know]

gnomon *noun*
• "NO mon"
• the rod or pin etc. on a sundial that shows the time by the position of its shadow.
• [French or Latin *gnomon* from Greek *gnōmōn* indicator etc. from *gignōskō* know]
• **gnomonic** *adjective* "no MONNIC"

gnosis *noun*
• "NO sis"
• esoteric knowledge of spiritual mysteries.
• [Greek *gnōsis* knowledge (as GNOMON)]

gnostic *adjective*
• "NOSS tick"
• relating to knowledge, esp. esoteric mystical knowledge.
• [Church Latin *gnosticus* from Greek *gnōstikos* (as GNOSIS)]

Gnosticism *noun*
• "NOSSTA sizm"
• a heretical movement prominent in the Christian Church in the 2nd c., emphasizing the power of gnosis, the supposed revealed knowledge of God, to redeem the spiritual element in humankind; they contrasted the supreme remote divine being with the demiurge or creator god, who controlled the world and was antagonistic to all that was purely spiritual.
• [as GNOSTIC]

gnu *noun*
• "NOO" or "NYOO"
• any antelope of the genus *Connochaetes*, native to S Africa, with a large erect head and brown stripes on the neck and shoulders.
• [Bushman *nqu*, prob. through Dutch *gnoe*]
HOMOPHONES: *nu*, *new*

Goan *noun*
• "GO 'n"
• a native or inhabitant of Goa on the west coast of India.
• **Goanese** *adjective*

goanna *noun*
• "go ANNA"
• any of various lizards, esp. large monitors of the genus *Varanus*.
• [corruption of IGUANA]

goatee *noun*
• "go TEE"
• a small beard on the point of the chin, like that of a goat.
• [from 'goat' from Old English *gāt* she-goat]
• **goateed** *adjective*

gobbet *noun*
• "GOBBIT"
• a piece or lump, esp. of raw meat, flesh, food, etc.
• [Old French *gobet* from *go(u)be* mouthful]

gobbledygook *noun*
ALSO SPELLED: **gobbledegook**
• "GOBBLE dee gook" ("GOOK" can rhyme either with *BOOK* or with *SPOOK*)
• unintelligible jargon.
• [prob. imitative of a male turkey]

Gobelin *noun*
• "GO buh lin" or "go BLÃ" (with a nasal *A*)
• a tapestry made at the Gobelins factory.
• [name of a state factory in Paris, called *Gobelins* after its original owners]

goblet *noun*
• "GOB lit"
• a drinking vessel with a foot and a stem, usu. of glass.
• [Old French *gobelet* diminutive of *gobel* cup, of unknown origin]

goblin *noun*
• "GOB lin"
• a mischievous ugly dwarf-like creature of folklore.
• [prob. from Anglo-French *gobelin*, medieval Latin *gobelinus*, prob. from name diminutive of *Gobel*, related to German *Kobold*: see COBALT]

goby *noun*
• "GO bee"
• any small marine fish of the family Gabiidae, having ventral fins joined to form a sucker or disc.
• [Latin *gobius*, *cobius* from Greek *kōbios* GUDGEON]

goddaughter *noun*
• "GOD dotter"
• a female godchild.
• ['God' + DAUGHTER]

Goderichite *noun*
• "GOD rich ite"
• a resident of Goderich, Ont.

godet *noun*
• "go DET" or "GO day"
• a triangular piece of material inserted in a dress, glove, etc.
• [French]

godetia *noun*
• "go DEESHA"
• a North American plant of the genus *Clarkia* with showy lilac to red flowers.
• [C. *Godet* Swiss botanist d.1879]

godforsaken *adjective*
• "GOD for sake 'n"
• (of a place) dismal; dreary; lacking in comfort.
• ['God' + FORSAKE]

godown *noun*
• "go DOWN"
• a warehouse in parts of E Asia, esp. in India.
• [Portuguese *gudão* from Malay *godong* perhaps from Telugu *gidangi* place where goods lie, from *kidu* lie]

godwit *noun*
• "GOD wit"
• any wading bird of the genus *Limosa*, with long legs and a long straight or slightly upcurved bill.
• [16th c.: of unknown origin]

Goethean *adjective*
ALSO SPELLED: **Goethian**
• "GOOTY 'n" (with "OO" as in *GOOD*)
• of, relating to, or characteristic of the German writer J. W. von Goethe (d.1832).

gofer *noun*
• "GO fur"
• a person who runs errands, esp. in an office.
• [representing a pronunciation of 'go for']
HOMOPHONES: *goffer*, *gopher*

goffer *verb*
• "GO fur" or "GOFF ur"
• make wavy, flute, or crimp (a lace edge, a trimming, etc.) with heated irons.
• [French *gaufrer* stamp with a patterned tool, from *gaufre* honeycomb, related to 'wafer', 'waffle']
HOMOPHONES: *gofer*, *gopher*

Goidel *noun*
• "GOID'l"
• a Celt who speaks Irish Gaelic, Scottish Gaelic, or Manx.
• [Old Irish *Góidel*]

Goidelic *noun*
• "goy DELLIC"
• the northern group of the Celtic languages, comprising Irish Gaelic, Scottish Gaelic, and Manx.
• [as GOIDEL]

goitre *noun*
ALSO SPELLED: esp. *US* **goiter**
• "GOY tur"
• a swelling of the neck resulting from enlargement of the thyroid gland.
• [French, back-formation from *goitreux* or from Provençal *goitron*, ultimately from Latin *guttur* throat]

- **goitred** *adjective* (also esp. *US* **goitered**)
- **goitrous** *adjective*

Golconda *noun*
- "gaul CONDA"
- a mine or source of wealth, advantages, etc.
- [city near Hyderabad, India]

golem *noun*
- "GO lum"
- (in Jewish legend) a clay figure supernaturally brought to life.
- [Yiddish *goylem* from Hebrew *gōlem* shapeless mass]

golliwog *noun*
- "GOLLY wog"
- a black-faced brightly dressed soft doll with fuzzy hair.
- [from *Golliwogg*, the name of a doll character in books by B. Upton, US writer d.1912; perhaps suggested by 'golly' + POLLYWOG]

gombeen *noun*
- "gom BEEN"
- usury.
- [Irish *gaimbín* perhaps from the same Old Celtic source as medieval Latin *cambire* change]
- **gombeenism** *noun*

gonadotropin *noun*
- "go nadda TRO pin"
- any of various hormones stimulating the activity of the gonads.
- [modern Latin *gonas gonad-* from Greek *gonē*, *gonos* generation, seed]
- **gonadotropic** *adjective*

gondola *noun*
- "GONDA luh"
- a light flat-bottomed boat used on Venetian canals, with a central cabin and a high point at each end, worked by one oar at the stern.
- [Venetian Italian, perhaps from Byzantine Greek *kondoura* small boat]

gondolier *noun*
- "gonda LEER"
- the oarsman on a gondola.
- [French from Italian *gondoliere* (as GONDOLA)]

gonfalon *noun*
- "GONFA lon"
- a banner, often with streamers, hung from a crossbar; a pennant.
- [Italian *gonfalone* from Germanic]
- **gonfalonier** *noun* "gonfa luh NEER"

goniff *noun*
ALSO SPELLED: **gonif**
- "GON if"
- a disreputable or dishonest person (often used as a general term of abuse).
- [Yiddish *ganev* from Hebrew *gannāb* thief]

goniometer *noun*
- "go nee OMMA tur"
- any of various instruments for measuring angles, as in crystallography, medicine (e.g. in the study of joints), etc.
- [French *goniomètre* from Greek *gōnia* angle + *metron* measure]
- **goniometric** *adjective* "go nee oh METRIC"
- **goniometry** *noun*

googol *noun*
- "GOOGLE"
- ten raised to the hundredth power (10^{100}).
- [arbitrary formation]

HOMOPHONES: *google*

googolplex *noun*
- "GOOGLE plex"
- ten raised to the power of a googol.
- [GOOGOL + *-plex* (from Latin *-plex -plicis* -fold)]

goombah *noun*
- "goom BAH"
- a member of a criminal gang; a Mafioso.
- [Italian dialect *compare* godfather, friend, accomplice]

goonda *noun*
- "GOONDA"
- (in the Indian subcontinent) a hired thug or bully.
- [Hindi *guṇḍā* rascal]

gopher *noun*
- "GO fur"
- a buff-coloured ground squirrel of the prairies of western N America; a Richardson's ground squirrel.
- [18th c.: origin uncertain]

HOMOPHONES: *gofer*, *goffer*

gopik *noun*
- "GO pick"
- a monetary unit of Azerbaijan, equal to one-hundredth of a manat.
- [Azerbaijani, = KOPECK]

goral *noun*
- "GOR'll"
- a goat-antelope, *Nemorhaedus goral*, native to mountainous regions from N India to Siberia, having short horns curving to the rear.
- [local (Himalayan) name]

gorgeous *adjective*
- "GOR juss"
- strikingly beautiful.
- [earlier *gorgayse*, *-yas* from Old French *gorgias* fine, elegant, of unknown origin]
- **gorgeously** *adverb*
- **gorgeousness** *noun*

gorget *noun*
- "GOR jit"
- a patch of colour on the throat of a bird, insect, etc.
- [Old French *gorgete* from *gorge* throat, ultimately from Latin *gurges* whirlpool]

gorgon *noun*
- "GOR g'n"
- a frightening or repulsive person, esp. a woman.

• [the *Gorgons*, three snake-haired sisters in Greek mythology with the power to turn anyone who looked at them to stone, from Greek *gorgos* terrible]

gorgonian *noun*
• "gor GO nee 'n"
• a usu. brightly coloured horny coral of the order Gorgonacea, having a treelike skeleton bearing polyps, e.g. a sea fan.
• [modern Latin (as GORGON), with reference to its petrifaction]

Gorgonzola *noun*
• "gor g'n ZOLE uh"
• a type of rich cheese with bluish-green veins.
• [*Gorgonzola*, a village in Northern Italy]

gorilla *noun*
• "guh RILLA"
• the largest anthropoid ape, *Gorilla gorilla*, native to Central Africa, having a large head, short neck, and prominent mouth.
• [adopted as the specific name in 1847 from Greek *Gorillai* an African tribe noted for hairiness]
HOMOPHONES: *guerrilla*

gorse *noun*
• "GORSE"
• any spiny yellow-flowered shrub of the genus *Ulex*, esp. growing on European wastelands.
• [Old English *gors(t)* related to Old High German *gersta*, Latin *hordeum*, barley]

Gorsedd *noun*
• "GOR seth" (with "TH" as in *BATHE*)
• a meeting of Welsh etc. bards and druids (esp. as a daily preliminary to the eisteddfod).
• [Welsh, lit. 'throne']

goshawk *noun*
• "GOSS hock"
• a large short-winged hawk, *Accipiter gentilis*.
• [Old English *gōs-hafoc* 'goose hawk']

gosling *noun*
• "GOZZ ling"
• a young goose.
• [Middle English, originally *gesling* from Old Norse *gæslingr*]

gospel *noun*
• "GOSS p'll"
• the teaching or revelation of Christ.
• [Old English *gōdspel* ('good', *spel* news), rendering Church Latin *bona annuntiatio*, *bonus nuntius* = *evangelium* EVANGEL: assoc. with 'God']

gospeller *noun*
ALSO SPELLED: *US* **gospeler**
• "GOS p'll ur"
• a person who preaches or promotes the Gospel or a gospel.
• [as GOSPEL]

gospelly *adjective*
• "GOS p'll ee"
• resembling gospel music.
• [as GOSPEL]

gossamer *noun*
• "GOSSA mur"
• a filmy substance of small spiders' webs.
• [Middle English *gos(e)somer(e)*, apparently from 'goose' + 'summer' (*goose summer* = St. Martin's summer, i.e. early November when geese were eaten, gossamer being common then)]

gossipmonger *noun*
• "GOSSIP mong gur" or "GOSSIP mung gur"
• a perpetrator of gossip.
• [earlier sense 'godparent': from Old English *godsibb* person related to one in God]

gossoon *noun*
• "goss OON"
• a lad.
• [earlier *garsoon* from French *garçon* boy]

Götterdämmerung *noun*
• "gotter DAMMER oong"
• the twilight (i.e. downfall) of the gods.
• [German, esp. as the title of an opera by Wagner]

gouache *noun*
• "goo OSH" or "GWOSH"
• a method of painting in opaque pigments ground in water and thickened with a glue-like substance.
• [French from Italian *guazzo*]

Gouda *noun*
• "GOO duh"
• a flat round usu. Dutch cheese with a yellow rind.
• [*Gouda*, in the Netherlands, where originally made]

gouge *noun*
• "GOWJ" ("GOW" rhymes with *COW*)
• a chisel with a concave blade, used in carpentry, sculpture, and surgery.
• [French from Late Latin *gubia*, perhaps of Celtic origin]
• **gouger** *noun*

goulash *noun*
• "GOO lash"
• a highly-seasoned Hungarian soup or stew of meat and vegetables, usu. flavoured with paprika.
• [Hungarian *gulyás-hús* from *gulyás* herdsman + *hús* meat]

gourami *noun*
• "GUR a mee" or "gur OMMY"
• a large freshwater fish, *Osphronemus goramy*, native to SE Asia, used as food.
• [Malay *gurāmi*]

gourd *noun*
• "GOORD"
• any of various fleshy usu. large fruits with a hard skin, often used as containers, ornaments, etc.

• [Old French *gourde*, ultimately from Latin *cucurbita*]
• **gourdful** *noun*
HOMOPHONES: *gourde*

gourde *noun*
• "GOORD"
• the basic monetary unit of Haiti, equal to 100 centimes.
• [French, feminine of *gourd*, heavy, dull]
HOMOPHONES: *gourd*

gourmand *noun*
• "goor MOND"
• a glutton.
• [Old French, of unknown origin]

gourmandise *noun*
• "goor mon DEEZ"
• the habits of a gourmand; gluttony.
• [French (as GOURMAND)]

gourmandize *verb*
ALSO SPELLED: esp. *Brit.* **-ise**
• "GOOR m'n dize"
• eat or devour voraciously.
• [as GOURMAND]

gourmet *noun*
• "gore MAY" or "GOOR may" or "GORE may"
• a connoisseur of good food, having a discerning palate.
• [French, = wine taster: sense influenced by GOURMAND]

govern *verb*
• "GUVVERN"
• rule or control (a state, subject, etc.) with authority; conduct the policy and affairs of (an organization etc.).
• [Old French *governer* from Latin *gubernare* steer, rule, from Greek *kubernaō*]
• **governability** *noun*
• **governable** *adjective*
• **governance** *noun*
• **government** *noun* "GUVVERN m'nt" or "GUVVER m'nt"
• **governmental** *adjective*
• **governmentally** *adverb*
• **governor** *noun*
• **governorate** *noun*
• **governorship** *noun*

governess *noun*
• "GUVVERN ess"
• a woman employed to teach children in a private household.
• [earlier *governeress* from Old French *governeresse* (as GOVERN)]
• **governessy** *adjective*

gowan *noun*
• "GOW 'n" ("GOW" rhymes with *COW*)
• a daisy.
• [prob. var. of dialect *gollan* ranunculus etc., and related to *gold* in *marigold*]

gowk *noun*
• "GOUK" (with "OU" as in *OUT*)
• an awkward or halfwitted person; a fool.
• [Old Norse *gaukr* from Germanic]

Graafian *adjective*
• "GROFFY 'n"
• designating a follicle in the mammalian ovary in which an ovum develops prior to ovulation.
• [R. de *Graaf*, Dutch anatomist d.1673]

graben *noun*
• "GROB 'n"
• a depression of the earth's surface between faults.
• [German, originally = ditch]

gracile *adjective*
• "GRASS ile" or "GRASSIL"
• slender; gracefully slender.
• [Latin *gracilis* slender]
• **gracility** *noun* "gruh SILLA tee"

gracious *adjective*
• "GRAY sh'ss"
• kindly, courteous.
• [Old French from Latin *gratia* from *gratus* pleasing: compare GRATEFUL]
• **graciously** *adverb*
• **graciousness** *noun*

gradation *noun*
• "gray DAY sh'n" or "gruh DAY sh'n"
• a stage of transition or advance.
• [Latin *gradatio* from *gradus* step]
• **gradate** *verb*
• **gradational** *adjective*
• **gradationally** *adverb*

gradient *noun*
• "GRAY dee 'nt"
• a stretch of road, railway, etc., that slopes from the horizontal.
• [prob. formed on 'grade' (from Latin *gradus* step) after *salient*]

gradual *adjective*
• "GRADGE oo 'll"
• taking place or progressing slowly or by degrees.
• [medieval Latin *gradualis*, *-ale* from Latin *gradus* step]
• **gradually** *adverb*
• **gradualness** *noun*

gradualism *noun*
• "GRADGE oo 'll izm"
• a policy of gradual reform rather than sudden change or revolution.
• [as GRADUAL]
• **gradualist** *noun*
• **gradualistic** *adjective*

graduand *noun*
• "GRADGE oo and"
• *Cdn & Brit.* a person about to receive a degree or other academic qualification.

• [medieval Latin *graduandus* gerundive of *graduare* GRADUATE]

graduate *noun*
• "GRADGE oo it"
• a person who has been awarded an academic degree.
• [medieval Latin *graduari* take a degree, from Latin *gradus* step]
• **graduation** *noun*

graduated *adjective*
• "GRADGE oo ated"
• arranged in grades or gradations; advancing or proceeding by degrees.
• [as GRADUATE]

Graecism *noun*
ALSO SPELLED: **Grecism**
• "GREE sizm"
• a Greek idiom, esp. as imitated in another language.
• [French *grécisme* or medieval Latin *Graecismus* from *Graecus* Greek]

Graecize *verb*
ALSO SPELLED: **Grecize**, esp. *Brit.* **Graecise**
• "GREE size"
• give a Greek character or form to.
• [Latin *Graecizare* (as GRAECISM)]

graffiti *plural noun*
• "gruh FEETY"
• inscriptions or drawings scribbled, scratched, or sprayed on a surface.
• [Italian, from *graffio* a scratch]
• **graffitist** *noun*

graham *adjective*
• "GRAY um" or "GRAM"
• designating unbolted whole wheat flour, or crackers etc. made from this.
• [Sylvester *Graham* (d.1851), US advocate of dietary reform]
HOMOPHONES: *gram*

grama *noun*
• "GRAMMA"
• any of various chiefly N American pasture and ornamental grasses of the genus *Bouteloua*.
• [Spanish, = 'grass']
HOMOPHONES: *gramma*

graminaceous *adjective*
• "gram'n AY sh'ss"
• of or like grass; grassy.
• [Latin *gramen -inis* grass + adjective suffix *-aceus* of the nature of]

gramma *noun*
• "GRAMMA" or "GRAMMAW"
• grandma.
• [corruption]
HOMOPHONES: *grama*

grammar *noun*
• "GRAMMER"
• the branch of language study or linguistics which deals with the means of showing the relationship between words in use, traditionally including morphology and syntax, and often phonology.
• [Old French *gramaire* from Latin *grammatica* from Greek *grammatikē* (*tekhnē*) (art) of letters, from *gramma -atos* letter of the alphabet]
• **grammarian** *noun* "gruh MERRY 'n"
• **grammarless** *adjective*
• **grammatical** *adjective* "gruh MATTA k'll"
• **grammaticality** *noun*
• **grammatically** *adverb*

gramophone *noun*
• "GRAMA fone"
• a record player.
• [formed by inversion of PHONOGRAM]

granary *noun*
• "GRAY nur ee" or "GRANNER ee"
• a storehouse for threshed grain.
• [Latin *granarium* from *granum* grain]

granddaughter *noun*
• "GRAN dotter"
• a female grandchild.
• ['grand' + DAUGHTER]

grandee *noun*
• "gran DEE"
• a Spanish or Portuguese nobleman of the highest rank.
• [Spanish & Portuguese *grande*]

grandeur *noun*
• "GRAND ur" or "GRAND yur" or "GRAN jur"
• majesty, splendour; dignity of appearance or bearing.
• [French from *grand* great, grand, from Latin *grandis* full-grown]

grandiflora *adjective*
• "grandy FLORA"
• bearing large flowers.
• [modern Latin (often used in specific names of large-flowered plants) from Latin *grandis* great + *flora* flower]

grandiloquent *adjective*
• "gran DILLA kw'nt"
• pompous or inflated in language.
• [Latin *grandiloquus* (*grandis* great, *-loquus* -speaking, from *loqui* speak)]
• **grandiloquence** *noun*
• **grandiloquently** *adverb*

grandiose *adjective*
• "grandy OSE" or "GRANDY ose" ("OSE" rhymes with *GROSS*)
• producing or meant to produce an imposing effect.
• [French from Italian *grandioso* from Latin *grandis* great]
• **grandiosely** *adverb*
• **grandiosity** *noun* "grandy OSSA tee"

granita *noun*
• "gruh NEETA"
• a coarse sherbet.
• [Italian (see GRANITE)]

granite *noun*
• "GRANNIT"
• a granular crystalline igneous rock of quartz, mica, feldspar, etc., used for building.
• [Italian *granito*, lit. 'grained' from *grano* from Latin *granum* grain]
• **granitic** *adjective* "gruh NITTIC"
• **granitoid** *adjective*

graniteware *noun*
• "GRANNIT ware"
• a speckled form of earthenware imitating the appearance of granite.
• [as GRANITE + WARE]

granivorous *adjective*
• "gruh NIVVER us"
• feeding on grain.
• [Latin *granum* grain + *-vorus* from *vorare* devour]
• **granivore** *noun*

granodiorite *noun*
• "granno DIE a rite"
• a coarse-grained plutonic rock containing quartz and plagioclase, between granite and diorite in composition.
• [GRANITE + DIORITE]

granola *noun*
• "gruh NO luh"
• a mixture of rolled oats, nuts, raisins, brown sugar, etc. eaten as a breakfast cereal or pressed into bars.
• [from *gran-* representing 'grain']

granulate *verb*
• "GRAN yuh late"
• form into grains.
• [as GRANULE]
• **granulation** *noun*
• **granulator** *noun*

granule *noun*
• "GRAN yool"
• a small grain.
• [Late Latin *granulum*, diminutive of Latin *granum* grain]

granulocyte *noun*
• "GRAN yoo luh site"
• any of various white blood cells having granules in their cytoplasm.
• [GRANULE + Greek *kutos* vessel]
• **granulocytic** *adjective* "gran yoo luh SITTIC"

granuloma *noun*
• "gran yoo LO muh"
• a mass of granulation tissue produced in any of various disease states, usu. in response to infection, inflammation, or the presence of a foreign substance.
• [as GRANULE]
• **granulomatous** *adjective*

graph *noun*
• "GRAFF"
• a visual symbol, esp. a letter or letters, representing a unit of sound or other feature of speech.
• [Greek *graphē* writing]

grapheme *noun*
• "GRAFF eem"
• a class of letters etc. representing a unit of sound.
• [Greek *graphē* writing + French *-ème* unit, from Greek *-ēma*]
• **graphemic** *adjective*
• **graphemically** *adverb*

graphic *adjective*
• "GRAFFIC"
• of or relating to the visual or descriptive arts, esp. writing and drawing.
• [Latin *graphicus* from Greek *graphikos* from *graphē* writing]
• **graphical** *adjective*
• **graphically** *adverb*
• **graphicness** *noun*

graphics *plural noun*
• "GRAFFIX"
• the products of the graphic arts, esp. commercial design or illustration.
• [as GRAPHIC]

graphite *noun*
• "GRAFF ite"
• a crystalline allotropic form of carbon used as a solid lubricant, in pencils, and as a moderator in nuclear reactors etc.
• [German *Graphit* from Greek *graphō* write]
• **graphitic** *adjective* "gruh FITTIC"
• **graphitize** *verb* (also esp. *Brit.* **-ise**)

graphology *noun*
• "gruh FOLLA jee"
• the study of handwriting esp. as a supposed guide to character.
• [Greek *graphē* writing + *logos* word]
• **graphological** *adjective*
• **graphologist** *noun*

graple *noun*
• "GRAPLE" (rhymes with *MAPLE*)
• *Cdn* (*Nfld*) a small anchor used to moor fishing equipment or small boats.
• [Old French *grapil* from Provençal, diminutive of *grapa* hook]

grapnel *noun*
• "GRAP n'll"
• a device with iron claws, attached to a rope and used for dragging or grasping.
• [Old French *grapon* from Germanic]

grappa *noun*
• "GRAPPA"
• a brandy distilled from the fermented residue of grapes after they have been pressed in winemaking.
• [Italian, lit. = 'grape stalk']

graptolite *noun*
- "GRAPTA lite"
- an extinct marine invertebrate animal found as a fossil in lower Paleozoic rocks.
- [Greek *graptos* marked with letters + *lithos* stone]

grasscycling *noun*
- "GRASS sike ling"
- the practice of leaving grass clippings on a lawn after mowing, so that they fall between the growing blades and act as fertilizer.
- [blend of 'grass' (Old English *græs* from Germanic, related to 'green', 'grow') + RECYCLE]
- **grasscycle** *verb*

grateful *adjective*
- "GRATE full"
- thankful; feeling or showing gratitude.
- [obsolete *grate* (adjective) from Latin *gratus* pleasing, thankful]
- **gratefully** *adverb*
- **gratefulness** *noun*

gratify *verb*
- "GRATTA fie"
- please, delight.
- [French *gratifier* or Latin *gratificari* do a favour to, make a present of, from *gratus* pleasing]
- **gratification** *noun*
- **gratifier** *noun*
- **gratifying** *adjective*
- **gratifyingly** *adverb*

gratin *noun*
- "gruh TĀ" (with a nasal *A*)
- a crisp brown crust usu. of bread crumbs or melted cheese.
- [French from *gratter* grate]

gratinée *adjective*
- "gra tee NAY"
- cooked with a crisp brown crust usu. of bread crumbs or melted cheese.
- [as GRATIN]
- **gratinéed** *adjective*

gratis *adjective*
- "GRAT iss"
- free; without charge.
- [Latin, contracted ablative pl. of *gratia* favour]

gratitude *noun*
- "GRATTA tude"
- the feeling of being grateful or the desire to express one's thanks.
- [French *gratitude* or medieval Latin *gratitudo* from *gratus* thankful]

gratuitous *adjective*
- "gruh TOO it us" or "gruh TYOO it us"
- uncalled for; unwarranted; lacking good reason.
- [Latin *gratuitus* spontaneous]
- **gratuitously** *adverb*
- **gratuitousness** *noun*

gratuity *noun*
- "gruh TOO it ee" or "gruh TYOO it ee"
- money given in recognition of services; a tip.
- [Old French *gratuité* or medieval Latin *gratuitas* gift, from Latin *gratus* grateful]

gravamen *noun*
- "gruh VAY m'n"
- the essential or most serious part of an accusation; the part that bears most heavily on the accused.
- [Late Latin, = inconvenience, from Latin *gravare* to load from *gravis* heavy]

grave[1] *adverb*
- "GRAW vay"
- (as a musical direction) with slow and solemn movement.
- [French or Italian from Latin *gravis* heavy, serious]

grave[2] *adjective*
- "GROV"
- designating a mark (`) placed over a vowel in some languages to denote pronunciation, length, etc., originally indicating low or falling pitch.
- [French, from Latin *gravis* heavy]

HOMOPHONES: *Graves*

gravel *noun*
- "GRAV'll"
- a mixture of coarse sand and small water-worn or pounded stones, used for paths and roads and as an aggregate.
- [Old French *gravel(e)* diminutive of *grave greve* shore]
- **gravelly** *adjective*

Gravenstein *noun*
- "GRAV 'n steen"
- a red, medium-sized cooking and eating apple streaked with yellow.
- [German name for *Graasten*, a village in Denmark (formerly in Germany)]

Graves *noun*
- "GROV"
- a light usu. white wine from Graves in SW France.

HOMOPHONES: *grave*

gravid *adjective*
- "GRAVVID"
- pregnant.
- [Latin *gravidus* from *gravis* heavy]

gravimeter *noun*
- "gruh VIMMA tur"
- an instrument for measuring the difference in the force of gravity from one place to another.
- [French *gravimètre* from Latin *gravis* heavy + Greek *metron* measure]

gravimetry *noun*
- "gruh VIMMA tree"
- the measurement of weight.

- [as GRAVIMETER]
- **gravimetric** *adjective* "gravva METRIC"

gravitas *noun*
- "GRAVVY tass" or "GROVVY toss"
- solemn demeanour; seriousness.
- [Latin from *gravis* serious]

gravitate *verb*
- "GRAVVA tate"
- move or be attracted to some source of influence.
- [modern Latin *gravitare* as GRAVITAS]
- **gravitation** *noun*
- **gravitational** *adjective*
- **gravitationally** *adverb*

graviton *noun*
- "GRAVVA tawn"
- a hypothetical quantum of gravitational energy.
- [as GRAVITY]

gravity *noun*
- "GRAVVA tee"
- the force that attracts a body towards the centre of the earth or towards any other physical body having mass.
- [French *gravité* or Latin *gravitas* from *gravis* heavy]

gravlax *noun*
- "GRAV lax"
- a Scandinavian dish of dry-cured salmon marinated in salt, sugar, and dill etc.
- [Swedish *gravlax*, from *grav* trench + *lax* salmon, from the former practice of marinating the salmon in a hole in the ground]

gravure *noun*
- "gruh VYUR"
- an image, plate, or print produced from a photographic negative transferred to a metal plate and etched in.
- [abbreviation of PHOTOGRAVURE]

gray *noun*
- "GRAY"
- the SI unit of the absorbed dose of ionizing radiation, corresponding to one joule per kilogram.
- [L. H. *Gray*, English radiobiologist d.1965]

HOMOPHONES: *grey*

grayling *noun*
- "GRAY ling"
- any silver-grey freshwater fish of the genus *Thymallus*, with a long high dorsal fin.
- [*gray* var. of 'grey' from Old English *græg*]

grazier *noun*
- "GRAY zhur"
- a person who feeds cattle for market.
- [Old English *grasian* from *græs* grass]

greave *noun*
- "GREEVE"
- a piece of armour for the shin.
- [Old French *greve* shin, greave, of unknown origin]

HOMOPHONES: *grieve*

grebe *noun*
- "GREEB"
- any diving bird of the family Podicipedidae, with a long neck, lobed toes, and almost no tail.
- [French *grèbe*, of unknown origin]

Grecian *adjective*
- "GREE sh'n"
- (of architecture or beauty) following Greek models or ideals.
- [Old French *grecien* or medieval Latin *graecianus* (unrecorded) from Latin *Graecia* Greece]

gregarious *adjective*
- "gruh GARRY us"
- fond of company.
- [Latin *gregarius* from *grex gregis* flock]
- **gregariously** *adverb*
- **gregariousness** *noun*

Gregorian *adjective*
- "gruh GORY 'n"
- designating the general calendar in use today, introduced in 1582 by Pope Gregory XIII as a correction of the Julian calendar, with 365 days in standard years and 366 days in all years exactly divisible by 4 except century years, which must be exactly divisible by 400 to have 366 days.

gremlin *noun*
- "GREMLIN"
- an imaginary mischievous sprite regarded as responsible for mechanical faults.
- [20th c.: origin unknown, but prob. after *goblin*]

gremolata *noun*
- "gremma LOTTA"
- a mixture of parsley, grated lemon rind, and garlic, used to add zest to a dish.
- [Italian]

Grenache *noun*
- "gruh NASH"
- a variety of esp. black grape that is widely planted in southern France, Spain, California, and elsewhere.
- [French]

grenade *noun*
- "gruh NADE"
- a small bomb, esp. one thrown by hand.
- [French from Old French *grenate* and Spanish *granada* POMEGRANATE]

Grenadian *noun*
- "gruh NAY dee 'n"
- a native or inhabitant of Grenada, in the W Indies.

grenadier *noun*
- "grenna DEER"
- a member of the first regiment of the British royal household infantry.
- [French (as GRENADE)]

grenadilla *noun*
- "grenna DILLA"
- a passion fruit.
- [Spanish *granadilla*, diminutive of *granada* POMEGRANATE]

grenadine *noun*
- "GRENNA deen"
- a sweet red syrup flavoured with pomegranates.
- [French from *grenade*: see GRENADE]

greyhound *noun*
- "GRAY hound"
- a breed of tall slender dog having keen sight and capable of high speed, used in racing.
- [Old English *grīghund* from *grīeg* female dog (unrecorded: compare Old Norse *grey*) + *hund* dog, related to 'hound']

greywacke *noun*
ALSO SPELLED: **graywacke**
- "GRAY wacka" or "GRAY wack"
- a dark and coarse-grained sandstone, usu. with an admixture of clay.
- [anglicized from German *Grauwacke* from *grau* grey: see WACKE]

grief *noun*
- "GREEF"
- deep or intense sorrow or mourning.
- [Anglo-French *gref*, Old French *grief* from *grever* GRIEVE]

grievance *noun*
- "GREE vince"
- a real or fancied cause for complaint.
- [Middle English, = injury, from Old French *grevance* (as GRIEF)]

grieve *verb*
- "GREEVE"
- suffer grief, esp. at another's death.
- [Old French *grever*, ultimately from Latin *gravare* from *gravis* heavy]
- **griever** *noun*

HOMOPHONES: *greave*

grievous *adjective*
- "GREEVE us"
- very severe or serious.
- [as GRIEVE]
- **grievously** *adverb*
- **grievousness** *noun*

griffin *noun*
ALSO SPELLED: **gryphon**
- "GRIFFIN"
- a mythical creature with an eagle's head and wings and a lion's body.
- [Old French *grifoun*, ultimately from Late Latin *gryphus* from Latin *gryps* from Greek *grups*]

HOMOPHONES: *griffon*

griffon *noun*
- "GRIFFIN"
- a small terrier-like breed of dog with coarse or smooth hair.
- [French, or var. of GRIFFIN]

HOMOPHONES: *griffin*

grig *noun*
- "GRIG"
- a small eel.
- [Middle English, originally = dwarf: origin unknown]

grille *noun*
ALSO SPELLED: **grill**
- "GRILL"
- a grating or latticed screen, used as a partition or to allow discreet vision.
- [French from Old French *graïlle* from medieval Latin *graticula*, *craticula*, diminutive of *cratis* hurdle]

HOMOPHONES: *grill*

grilse *noun*
- "GRILLS" (with "S" as in *PULSE*)
- a young salmon that has returned to fresh water from the sea for the first time.
- [Middle English: origin unknown]

grimace *noun*
- "GRIM iss"
- a distortion of the face made in disgust etc. or to amuse.
- [French from Spanish *grimazo* from *grima* fright]

grimalkin *noun*
- "grim AL kin" or "grim AWL kin"
- an old female cat.
- ['grey' + *Malkin* diminutive of the name *Matilda*]

griot *noun*
- "GREE oh" or "gree OH"
- (in W Africa) a member of a hereditary caste whose main function is to maintain an oral history of their tribe or village.
- [French]

grippe *noun*
- "GRIP"
- influenza.
- [French from *gripper* seize]

HOMOPHONES: *grip*

grisaille *noun*
- "gree ZYE"
- a method of painting in grey monochrome, often to imitate sculpture.
- [French from *gris* grey]

griseofulvin *noun*
- "grizzy oh FULL vin"
- an antibiotic used against fungal infections of the hair and skin.
- [modern Latin *griseofulvum* from medieval Latin *griseus* grey + Latin *fulvus* reddish yellow]

grisly *adjective*
• "GRIZZLY"
• causing horror, disgust, or fear.
• [Old English *grislic* terrifying]
• **grisliness** *noun*
HOMOPHONES: *grizzly*

gristle *noun*
• "GRISS'll"
• tough cartilaginous tissue, esp. as occurring in meat.
• [Old English *gristle*]
• **gristly** *adjective*

grizzly *noun*
• "GRIZZLY"
• a large brown bear with grey-tipped fur.
• [from 'grizzle', from Old French *grisel* from *gris* grey]
HOMOPHONES: *grisly*

groat *noun*
• "GROTE"
• an old English silver coin worth four old pence.
• [Middle Dutch *groot*, originally = great, i.e. thick (penny)]

groats *plural noun*
• "GROTES"
• hulled or crushed grain, esp. oats.
• [Old English *grotan* (pl.): compare *grot* fragment, *grēot* grit, *grytt* bran]

grocer *noun*
• "GROW sur" or "GROW shur"
• a person who owns or operates a grocery store.
• [Anglo-French *grosser*, originally one who sells in the gross, from Old French *grossier* from medieval Latin *grossarius* (as GROSS)]

grocery *noun*
• "GROW sur ee" or "GROW shur ee"
• food and other general household supplies.
• [as GROCER]

groceteria *noun*
• "grow suh TEERY uh"
• (used esp. in names) a usu. small grocery store.
• [GROCERY, after CAFETERIA]

grogram *noun*
• "GROG rum"
• a coarse fabric of silk, or of mohair and wool, or of a mixture of all these, often stiffened with gum.
• [French *gros grain* coarse grain (as GROSS, Latin *granum* grain)]

grommet *noun*
• "GROM it"
• a metal, plastic, or rubber eyelet, esp. placed in a hole to protect or insulate a rope or cable etc. passed through it.
• [obsolete French *grommette* from *gourmer* to curb, of unknown origin]

grosbeak *noun*
• "GROCE beak"
• any of various finch-like birds with heavy bills and usu. brightly coloured plumage.
• [French *grosbec* (as GROSS, *bec* beak)]

grosgrain *noun*
• "GROW grain"
• any of various heavily ribbed fabrics, esp. of silk or rayon.
• [French, = coarse grain (as GROSS, 'grain')]

gross *adjective*
• "GROCE"
• overfed, bloated; repulsively fat.
• [Old French *gros grosse* large, from Late Latin *grossus*]
• **grossly** *adverb*
• **grossness** *noun*

grosz *noun*
• "GROSH"
• a monetary unit of Poland, equal to one-hundredth of a zloty.
• [Polish]

grotesque *adjective*
• "grow TESK"
• comically or repulsively distorted; monstrous, unnatural.
• [Italian *grottesca* grotto-like (painting etc.) feminine of *grottesco* (as GROTTO)]
• **grotesquely** *adverb*
• **grotesqueness** *noun*
• **grotesquerie** *noun* (also **grotesquery**) "grow TESKER ee"

grotto *noun*
• "GROTTO"
• a small picturesque cave.
• [Italian *grotta*, ultimately from Latin *crypta* (as CRYPT)]

groundsel *noun*
• "GROUN s'll" ("GROUN" rhymes with *BROWN*)
• any composite plant of the genus *Senecio*, esp. *S vulgaris*, used as a food for caged birds.
• [Old English *grundeswylige*, *gundæswelgiæ* (perhaps = pus-absorber, from *gund* pus, with reference to use for poultices)]

groupware *noun*
• "GROOP ware"
• software designed to facilitate collective working by a number of different users.
• ['group' from French *groupe* from Italian *gruppo* + WARE]

grovel *verb*
• "GROV'll"
• behave obsequiously in seeking favour or forgiveness.
• [back-formation from obsolete *grovelling* (adverb) from *gruf* face down, from *on grufe* from Old Norse *á grúfu*, later taken as present participle]
• **groveller** *noun*
• **grovelling** *adjective*
• **grovellingly** *adverb*

groyne *noun*
ALSO SPELLED: esp. *US* **groin**
• "GROIN"
• a timber framework or low broad wall built out from a shore to check erosion of a beach.
• [dialect *groin* snout, from Old French *groign* from Late Latin *grunium* pig's snout]
HOMOPHONES: *groin*

grubstake *noun*
• "GRUB stake"
• material or provisions supplied to an enterprise in return for a share in the resulting profits (originally in prospecting for ore).
• ['grub' (food) + STAKE]
• **grubstaker** *noun*

gruesome *adjective*
• "GROO sum"
• horrible, grisly, disgusting.
• [Scots *grue* to shudder, from Scandinavian]
• **gruesomely** *adverb*
• **gruesomeness** *noun*

grunion *noun*
• "GRUN y'n"
• a slender Californian marine fish, *Leuresthes tenuis*, that comes ashore to spawn.
• [prob. from Spanish *gruñón* grunter]

Gruyère *noun*
• "groo YARE"
• a firm pale yellow cheese made from cow's milk.
• [*Gruyère*, a district in Switzerland where it was first made]

guacamole *noun*
• "gwocka MOLEY"
• a dip or spread made from mashed avocados mixed with chopped onion, tomatoes, chili peppers, and seasoning.
• [Latin American Spanish from Nahuatl *ahuacamolli* from *ahuacatl* avocado + *molli* sauce]

guaiacol *noun*
• "GWYE a coll"
• a liquid with a penetrating aromatic odour obtained by the fractional distillation of wood tar and the dry distillation of guaiacum resin.
• [GUAIACUM + ALCOHOL]

guaiacum *noun*
• "GWYE a k'm"
• any tree of the genus *Guaiacum*, native to tropical America.
• [modern Latin from Spanish *guayaco* of Haitian origin]

guaifenesin *noun*
• "gwye FENNA sin"
• a substance derived from guaiacol, having expectorant properties and commonly used in cough medicines.
• [GUAIACOL + respelling of PHENOL + arbitrary suffix *-esin*]

guan *noun*
• "GWON"
• any of various game birds of the family Cracidae, of tropical America.
• [from Latin American Spanish from Miskito *kwamu*]

guanaco *noun*
• "gwuh NOCKO"
• an Andean mammal, *Lama guanicoe*, related to the llama and camel, with a coat of soft pale brown hair used for wool.
• [Spanish, from Quechua *huanacu*]

guanine *noun*
• "GWON een"
• a purine found in all living organisms as a component base of DNA and RNA.
• [as GUANO]

guano *noun*
• "GWONNO"
• the excrement of seabirds, esp. that found in the islands off Peru and used as manure.
• [Spanish from Quechua *huanu* dung]

guar *noun*
• "GWARR" (rhymes with *FAR*)
• a drought-resistant leguminous plant, *Cyamopsis tetragonoloba*, grown esp. in the Indian subcontinent as a vegetable and fodder crop and as a source of guar gum.
• [Hindi *guār*]

guarana *noun*
• "gwuh RONNA"
• a Brazilian shrub, *Paullinia cupana*.
• [Tupi]

Guarani *noun*
• "gwar a NEE"
• a member of a S American Aboriginal people of Paraguay and adjacent regions.
• [Spanish]

guarantee *noun*
• "gare 'n TEE"
• a formal promise or assurance, esp. that an obligation will be fulfilled or that something is of a specified quality and durability.
• [earlier *garante*, perhaps from Spanish *garante* = French *garant* WARRANT: later influenced by French *garantie* guaranty]
HOMOPHONES: *guaranty*

guarantor *noun*
• "GARE 'n tor" or "GARE 'n tur"
• a person who gives a guarantee or guaranty.
• [as GUARANTY]

guaranty *noun*
• "GARE 'n tee"
• a written or other undertaking to answer for the payment of a debt or for the performance of an obligation by another person liable in the first instance.
• [Anglo-French *guarantie*, var. of *warantie* WARRANTY]
HOMOPHONES: *guarantee*

guard *verb*
• "GARD"
• watch over and defend or protect from harm.
• [Old French *garde, garder*, ultimately from West Germanic]

guarded *adjective*
• "GARD id"
• (of a remark etc.) cautious, avoiding commitment.
• [as GUARD]
• **guardedly** *adverb*
• **guardedness** *noun*

guardhouse *noun*
• "GARD house"
• a building used to accommodate a military guard or to detain prisoners.
• [as GUARD + 'house']

guardian *noun*
• "GARDY 'n"
• a defender, protector, or keeper.
• [Anglo-French *gardein*, Old French *garden* from Frankish, related to 'ward', 'warden']
• **guardianship** *noun*

guardrail *noun*
• "GARD rail"
• a rail fitted as a support or to prevent an accident, e.g. along the edge of a highway or balcony.
• [as GUARD + 'rail']

guardroom *noun*
• "GARD room"
• a room used to accommodate a military guard or to detain prisoners.
• [as GUARD + 'room']

guardsman *noun*
• "GARDZ m'n"
• a soldier belonging to a body of guards.
• [as GUARD + 'man']

Guatemalan *noun*
• "gwotta MOLL 'n"
• a native or inhabitant of Guatemala in Central America.

guava *noun*
• "GWOVVA"
• a small tropical American tree, *Psidium guajava*, bearing an edible pale yellow fruit with pink juicy flesh.
• [Spanish *guayaba* prob. from a S American name]

guayabera *noun*
• "gay a BERRA"
• a lightweight open-necked Cuban or Mexican shirt with two breast pockets and two pockets over the hips, typically having short sleeves and worn untucked.
• [Cuban Spanish: apparently orig. from the name of the *Yayabo* river, influenced by Spanish *guayaba* guava]

gubernatorial *adjective*
• "goober nuh TORY 'll"
• of or relating to a governor.
• [Latin *gubernator* governor]

gudgeon *noun*
• "GUDGE 'n"
• a small European freshwater fish, *Gobio gobio*, often used as bait.
• [Old French *goujon* from Latin *gobio -onis* GOBY]

Guelphite *noun*
• "GWELF ite"
• a resident of Guelph, Ont.

guenon *noun*
• "guh NON"
• any African monkey of the genus *Cercopithecus*, having a characteristic long tail, e.g. the vervet.
• [French: origin unknown]

guerdon *noun*
• "GURD'n"
• a reward or recompense.
• [Old French from medieval Latin *widerdonum* from West Germanic *widarlōn* (as 'with', 'loan'), assimilated to Latin *donum* gift]

Guernsey *noun*
• "GURN zee"
• a light brown and white dairy cow of a breed originally from the island of Guernsey in the English Channel.

guerrilla *noun*
ALSO SPELLED: **guerilla**
• "guh RILLA"
• a person taking part in an irregular war waged by small bands operating independently, often against a stronger, more organized force, with surprise attacks etc.
• [Spanish *guerrilla*, diminutive of *guerra* war]
HOMOPHONES: *gorilla*

guess *verb*
• "GESS" (with "G" as in *GET*)
• estimate or suppose without calculation or measurement, or on the basis of inadequate data.
• [Middle English *gesse*, of uncertain origin]
• **guessable** *adjective*
• **guesser** *noun*

guesstimate *noun*
ALSO SPELLED: **guestimate**
• "GESS tuh mit" (with "G" as in *GET*)
• an estimate based more on guesswork than calculation.
• [GUESS + ESTIMATE]

guesswork *noun*
• "GESS wurk" (with "G" as in *GET*)
• the process of or results obtained by guessing.
• [as GUESS + 'work']

guest *noun*
• "GEST" (with "G" as in *GET*)
• a person (usu. invited) visiting another's

house or invited to have a meal etc. at the expense of the inviter.
• [Old Norse *gestr* from Germanic]

guidance *noun*
• "GUY dince"
• advice or information aimed at resolving a problem, difficulty, etc.
• [Old French *guider* guide]

guide *noun*
• "GUY'd"
• a person who leads or shows the way, or directs the movements of a person or group.
• [Old French *guide*, earlier *guier*, ultimately from Germanic, related to 'wit']
• **guider** *noun*

guidebook *noun*
• "GUY'd book"
• a book of information about a place for visitors, tourists, etc.
• [as GUIDE + 'book']

guideline *noun*
• "GUY'd line"
• a principle or criterion guiding or directing action.
• [as GUIDE + 'line']

guidepost *noun*
• "GUY'd post"
• a post with a sign giving directions or information.
• [as GUIDE + 'post']

guideway *noun*
• "GUY'd way"
• a groove or track that guides movement, e.g. of a monorail.
• [as GUIDE + 'way']

Guiding *noun*
• "GUY ding"
• the Girl Guide movement.
• [as GUIDE]

guidon *noun*
• "GUY d'n"
• a pennant narrowing to a point or fork at the free end, esp. one used as the standard of a light cavalry regiment.
• [French from Italian *guidone* from *guida* (as GUIDANCE)]

guild *noun*
• "GILD" (with "G" as in *GIVE*)
• an association of people for mutual aid or the pursuit of a common goal.
• [prob. from Middle Low German, Middle Dutch *gilde* from Germanic: related to Old English *gild* payment, sacrifice]
• **guildsman** *noun*
• **guildswoman** *noun*
HOMOPHONES: *gild*

guilder *noun*
• "GILDER" (with "G" as in *GIVE*)
• the former chief monetary unit of the Netherlands, now replaced by the euro.
• [Middle English, alteration of Dutch *gulden*: see GULDEN]
HOMOPHONES: *gilder*

guildhall *noun*
• "GILD hall" (with "G" as in *GIVE*)
• the meeting place of a guild or corporation.
• [as GUILD + 'hall']

guile *noun*
• "GILE" (with "G" as in *GIVE*)
• clever and esp. deceitful behaviour.
• [Old French, prob. from Germanic]
• **guileful** *adjective*
• **guileless** *adjective*
• **guilelessly** *adverb*
• **guilelessness** *noun*

guillemot *noun*
• "GILLA mot" (with "G" as in *GIVE*)
• any of several diving seabirds of northern latitudes constituting the genera *Uria* and *Cepphus*, of the auk family, with black (or brown) and white plumage and pointed bills.
• [French from *Guillaume* William]

guilloche *noun*
• "gill OSH"
• an ornament imitating braided ribbons.
• [French *guillochis* (or *guilloche* the tool used)]

guillotine *noun*
• "GILLA teen" or "GEE a teen" (with "G" as in *GIVE*)
• a machine with a heavy knife blade sliding vertically in grooves, used for beheading.
• [French from J.-I. *Guillotin*, French physician d.1814, who recommended its use for executions in 1789]
• **guillotiner** *noun*

guilt *noun*
• "GILT"
• the fact of having committed a specified or implied offence.
• [Old English *gylt*, of unknown origin]
• **guiltily** *adverb*
• **guiltiness** *noun*
• **guiltless** *adjective*
• **guiltlessly** *adverb*
• **guiltlessness** *noun*
• **guilty** *adjective*
HOMOPHONES: *gilt*

guinea *noun*
• "GINNY" (with "G" as in *GIVE*)
• a former British gold coin worth 21 shillings, first minted in 1663 from gold imported from W Africa.
• [*Guinea* in W Africa]

Guinean *noun*
• "GINNY 'n" (with "G" as in *GIVE*)
• a native or inhabitant of Guinea in W Africa.

guiro *noun*
• "GEE roe" (with "G" as in *GIVE*) or "GWEE roe"

• a Latin American musical instrument consisting of a gourd with an artificially serrated surface which gives a rasping sound when scraped with a stick.
• [Spanish, = gourd]

guise *noun*
• "GIZE" (sounds like *GUYS*)
• an assumed appearance; a pretense.
• [Old French, ultimately from Germanic]

guitar *noun*
• "guh TAR"
• a usu. six-stringed musical instrument with a fretted fingerboard, played by plucking or strumming with the fingers or a plectrum.
• [Spanish *guitarra* (partly through French *guitare*) from Greek *kithara*: see CITTERN, GITTERN]
• **guitarist** *noun*

Gujarati *noun*
• "gooja ROTTY"
• the language of Gujarat in W India.

gulag *noun*
• "GOO lag"
• the system of forced-labour camps in the Soviet Union, esp. 1930–55.
• [Russian acronym, from *G*lavnoe *u*pravlenie ispravitel'no-trudovykh *lag*ereĭ, lit. 'Chief Administration for Corrective Labour Camps']

gulden *noun*
• "GOOL d'n" (with "OO" as in *GOOD*)
• the former chief monetary unit of the Netherlands.
• [Dutch & German, = 'golden']

gules *noun*
• "GYOOLZ"
• (in heraldry) red.
• [Old French *goules* red-dyed fur neck ornaments, from *gole* throat]

Gullah *noun*
• "GULLA"
• a member of a people living on the coast of S Carolina or the nearby sea islands.
• [perhaps a shortening of *Angola*, or from a tribal name *Golas*]

gullible *adjective*
• "GULLA bull"
• easily persuaded or deceived; credulous.
• [perhaps from obsolete *gull* yellow, from Old Norse *gulr*]
• **gullibility** *noun*

gumma *noun*
• "GUMMA"
• a small soft swelling occurring in the connective tissue of the liver, brain, testes, and heart, and characteristic of the late stages of syphilis.
• [modern Latin from Latin *gummi* gum]
• **gummatous** *adjective*

gummi *noun*
• "GUMMY"
• a rubbery, coloured and flavoured candy, often in the shape of animals, insects, etc.
• [German]
HOMOPHONES: *gummy*

gumption *noun*
• "GUMP sh'n"
• resourcefulness, initiative; enterprising spirit.
• [18th-c. Scots: origin unknown]

gunnel *noun*
• "GUN'll"
• any small eel-shaped marine fish of the family Pholidae.
• [17th c.: origin unknown]
HOMOPHONES: *gunwale*

gunnera *noun*
• "GUNNER uh"
• any plant of the genus *Gunnera* from S America and New Zealand, having large leaves and often grown for ornament.
• [J. E. *Gunnerus*, Norwegian botanist d.1773]

gunwale *noun*
ALSO SPELLED: **gunnel**
• "GUN 'll"
• the upper edge of the side of a boat or ship.
• ['gun' + WALE (because formerly used to support guns)]
HOMOPHONES: *gunnel*

guppy *noun*
• "GUPPY"
• a small freshwater fish, *Poecilia reticulata*, of the W Indies and S America, frequently kept in aquariums, and giving birth to live young.
• [R. J. L. *Guppy*, 19th-c. Trinidad clergyman who sent the first specimen to the British Museum]

gurdwara *noun*
• "gurd WARR uh" ("WARR" rhymes with *FAR*)
• a Sikh temple.
• [Punjabi *gurduārā* from Sanskrit *guru* teacher + *dvāra* door]

gurdy *noun*
• "GURDY"
• a winch on a fishing boat used to haul in a line, net, etc.
• [prob. from earlier 'hurdy-gurdy' a musical instrument with a droning sound, played by turning a handle, of imitative origin]

Gurkha *noun*
• "GURKA"
• a member of the principal Hindu race in Nepal.
• [name of locality from Sanskrit *goraksa* cowherd (from *go* cow + *rakṣ-* protect) as epithet of patron deity]

gurnard *noun*
• "GUR nurd"
• any marine fish of the family Triglidae,

having a large spiny head with mailed sides, and three finger-like pectoral rays used for walking on the seabed etc.
• [Old French *gornart* from *grondir* to grunt, from Latin *grunnire*]

gurney *noun*
• "GURNY"
• a wheeled stretcher used to transport patients in a hospital etc.
• [apparently named after J. T. *Gurney*, US designer of a two-wheeled horse-drawn cab in 1883]

gurry *noun*
• "GURRY"
• fish entrails or offal as refuse from cleaning fish.
• [origin unknown]

guru *noun*
• "GOO roo" or "GUR oo"
• a Hindu spiritual teacher or head of a religious sect.
• [Sanskrit *guru* elder, teacher]

gusset *noun*
• "GUSS it"
• a piece of material let into a garment etc. to strengthen or enlarge a part.
• [Old French *gousset* flexible piece filling up a joint in armour, from *gousse* pod, shell]
• **gusseted** *adjective*

gustatory *adjective*
• "GUSTA tory"
• concerned with tasting or the sense of taste.
• [Latin *gustat-* past participle stem of *gustare* to taste]

gusto *noun*
• "GUSS toe"
• zest; enthusiasm or vigour in doing something.
• [Italian from Latin *gustus* taste]

guttate *adjective*
• "GUT ate"
• having drop-like markings.
• [Latin *guttatus* speckled, from *gutta* drop]

guttural *adjective*
• "GUTTER'll"
• (of a sound) produced at the back of the throat.
• [French *guttural* or medieval Latin *gutturalis* from Latin *guttur* throat]
• **gutturally** *adverb*

Guyanese *noun*
• "guy a NEEZ"
• a native or inhabitant of Guyana in S America.

gybe *verb*
ALSO SPELLED: **jibe**
• "JIBE"
• (of a fore-and-aft sail or boom) swing across in wearing or running before the wind.
• [obsolete Dutch *gijben*]
HOMOPHONES: *jibe*

gymkhana *noun*
• "jim CONNA"
• an equestrian day event comprising races and other competitions on horseback, esp. for children.
• [Urdu, Persian, and Hindi *gendkhāna* ball house, racquet court, assimilated to GYMNASIUM]

gymnasium *noun*
• "jim NAY zee um"
• a room or building equipped for gymnastics, indoor sports, physical training, etc.
• [Latin from Greek *gumnasion* from *gumnazō* exercise, from *gumnos* naked]

gymnastics *plural noun*
• "jim NASTIX"
• exercises developing or displaying physical agility and coordination, usu. in competition.
• [French *gymnaste* or Greek *gumnastēs* athlete trainer, from *gumnazō*: see GYMNASIUM]
• **gymnast** *noun*
• **gymnastic** *adjective*
• **gymnastically** *adverb*

gymnatorium *noun*
• "jim nuh TORY um"
• a large room in a school, church hall, etc. that serves as both a gymnasium and an auditorium.
• [GYMNASIUM + AUDITORIUM]

gymnosophist *noun*
• "jim NOSSA fist"
• a member of an ancient contemplative Hindu sect wearing little clothing.
• [ultimately from Greek *gumnosophistai* from *gumnos* naked + SOPHIST]
• **gymnosophy** *noun*

gymnosperm *noun*
• "JIMNO spurm"
• any of various plants having seeds unprotected by an ovary, including conifers, cycads, and ginkgos.
• [Greek *gumnos* naked + *sperma* seed]
• **gymnospermous** *adjective*

gynecology *noun*
ALSO SPELLED: **gynaecology**
• "guy nuh COLLA jee"
• the science of the physiological functions and diseases of women and girls, esp. those affecting the reproductive system.
• [Greek *gunē* woman + *logos* word]
• **gynecological** *adjective* (also **gynaecological**)
• **gynecologically** *adverb* (also **gynaecologically**)
• **gynecologist** *noun* (also **gynaecologist**)

gynecomastia *noun*
ALSO SPELLED: **gynaecomastia**
• "guy nuh co MASTY uh"

• enlargement of a man's breasts, usu. due to hormone imbalance or hormone therapy.
• [Greek *gunē* woman + *mastos* breast]

gynocentric *adjective*
• "guy no SENTRIC"
• (of an attitude, viewpoint, society, etc.) based on women's perspectives.
• [Greek *gunē* woman + CENTRE]

gynoecium *noun*
ALSO SPELLED: **gynaeceum**
• "guy NEECY um" or "jye NEECY um"
• the carpels of a flower taken collectively.
• [modern Latin from Greek *gunaikeion* women's apartments (*gunē* woman, *oikos* house)]

gypsophila *noun*
• "jip SOFFA luh"
• any plant of the genus *Gypsophila*, with a profusion of small usu. white composite flowers, esp. baby's breath.
• [modern Latin from Greek *gupsos* chalk + *philos* loving]

gypsum *noun*
• "JIP sum"
• a hydrated form of calcium sulphate occurring naturally and used in the building industry and to make plaster of Paris.
• [Latin from Greek *gupsos* chalk]

gypsumboard *noun*
• "JIP sum bord"
• prefabricated sheets of plaster sandwiched between heavy paper, used for interior walls.
• [GYPSUM + BOARD]

gyrate *verb*
• "JYE rate" or "jye RATE"
• revolve around a fixed point or axis; go in a circle or spiral.
• [Latin *gyrare gyrat-* revolve, from *gyrus* ring, from Greek *guros*]
• **gyration** *noun*
• **gyratory** *adjective* "JIRE a tory"

gyre *verb*
• "JIRE" (rhymes with *FIRE*)
• whirl, gyrate.
• [Latin *gyrus* ring, from Greek *guros*]

gyrfalcon *noun*
• "JUR fawl k'n" or "JUR fal k'n"
• a large falcon, *Falco rusticolus*, of the northern hemisphere.
• [Old French *gerfaucon* from Frankish *gērfalco* from Old Norse *geirfálki*: see FALCON]

gyro[1] *noun*
• "JYE roe"
• a gyroscope.
• [abbreviation]
HOMOPHONES: *giro*

gyro[2] *noun*
• "YEE roe" or "JYE roe"
• a sandwich of pita bread filled with slices of spiced meat cooked on a spit, tomatoes, onions, etc.
• [modern Greek *guros* turning]
HOMOPHONES: *giro*

gyrocompass *noun*
• "JYE roe kum pus"
• a non-magnetic compass giving true north and bearings from it by means of a gyroscope.
• [as GYROSCOPE + COMPASS]

gyromagnetic *adjective*
• "jye roe mag NETTIC"
• of the magnetic and mechanical properties of a rotating charged particle.
• [as GYROSCOPE + MAGNET]

gyroscope *noun*
• "JYE ruh scope"
• a wheel or disc mounted so as to spin rapidly about an axis whose orientation is not fixed but is unperturbed by tilting of the mount, esp. used in stabilizers, gyrocompasses, navigation systems, etc.
• [French from Latin *gyrare gyrat-* revolve, from *gyrus* ring, from Greek *guros* + *skopos* target, from *skeptomai* look at]
• **gyroscopic** *adjective*
• **gyroscopically** *adverb*

gyrostabilizer *noun*
ALSO SPELLED: esp. *Brit.* **-iser**
• "JYE roe stay b'll ize ur"
• a gyroscopic device for maintaining the equilibrium of a ship, aircraft, platform, etc.
• [as GYROSCOPE + STABILIZE]

gyrus *noun*
• "JYE russ"
• a fold or convolution, esp. of the brain.
• [Latin from Greek *guros* ring]

haar *noun*
- "HAR"
- a cold sea fog on the east coast of England or Scotland.
- [perhaps from Old Norse *hárr* hoar, hoary]

habanera *noun*
- "habba NERRA" or "habba NYERRA"
- a Cuban dance in slow duple time.
- [Spanish, short for *danza habanera* 'dance of Havana']

habanero *noun*
- "habba NERRO"
- a small, green, fiery hot chili pepper.
- [Spanish *habanero* 'of Havana']

haberdasher *noun*
- "HABBER dasher"
- a dealer in men's clothing and accessories.
- [Middle English, prob. ultimately from Anglo-French *hapertas* perhaps the name of a fabric]
- **haberdashery** *noun*

habiliment *noun*
- "huh BILLA m'nt"
- clothes suited to a particular purpose.
- [Old French *habillement* from *habiller* fit out, from *habile* from Latin *habilis* handy, from *habēre* to hold]

habitant *noun*
- "abbey TÃH" (with a nasal *AH*)
- (in Canada) a French settler in rural Quebec up until the early 20th c., esp. a farmer.
- [French from Old French *habiter* from Latin *habitare* inhabit]

habituate *verb*
- "huh BIT choo ate"
- make or become accustomed or used to something, esp. to living in close contact with humans.
- [Late Latin *habituare* from Latin *habitus* from *habēre habit-* have, be constituted]
- **habituation** *noun*

habitué *noun*
- "huh BIT choo ay"
- a habitual visitor to a place.
- [French, past participle of *habituer* (as HABITUATE)]

háček *noun*
- "HATCH eck"
- a diacritical mark (ˇ) placed over letters to modify the sound in some Slavic and Baltic languages.
- [Czech, diminutive of *hák* hook]

hacienda *noun*
- "hassy ENDA"
- an estate or plantation in Spanish-speaking countries, esp. one used for farming or ranching.
- [Spanish from Latin *facienda* things to be done]

hackmatack *noun*
- "HACK muh tack"
- any of several N American larches, esp. *Larix laricina*, found in wet places across most of Canada; a tamarack.
- [perhaps from Western Abenaki]

hackney *noun*
- "HACK nee"
- a light harness horse with a compact body and a characteristic high-stepping trot.
- [Middle English, perhaps from *Hackney* in London, where horses were pastured]

hackneyed *adjective*
- "HACK need"
- (of a phrase etc.) made commonplace or trite by overuse.
- [as HACKNEY]

hacktivism *noun*
- "HACK tuh vizm"
- the commission of computer crimes, e.g. hacking into military or financial etc. computer systems, to further social or political ends.
- [blend of 'hack' + ACTIVISM]
- **hacktivist** *noun*

haddock *noun*
- "HAD uck"
- a marine fish, *Melanogrammus aeglefinus*, of the N Atlantic, related to the cod, but smaller, and popular as a food fish.
- [Middle English, prob. from Anglo-French *hadoc*, Old French *(h)adot*, of unknown origin]

hade *noun*
- "HADE"

- an incline from the vertical.
- [17th c., perhaps dialect form of *head*]

Hadith *noun*
- "HADDIT" or "ha DEET"
- a collection of traditions containing sayings of the Prophet Muhammad, which, with accounts of his daily practice, constitute the major source of guidance for Muslims after the Quran.
- [Arabic *ḥadīṯ* tradition]

hadron *noun*
- "HAD ron"
- any of a class of subatomic particles including baryons and mesons, which can take part in the strong interaction.
- [Greek *hadros* bulky]
- **hadronic** *adjective*

hadrosaur *noun*
- "HADRO sore"
- a large herbivorous usu. bipedal dinosaur of the family Hadrosauridae, of the late Cretaceous period, with jaws flattened like the bill of a duck.
- [modern Latin genus name *Hadrosaurus*, from Greek *hadros* thick, stout + *sauros* lizard]

hafiz *noun*
- "HAFF izz"
- a Muslim who knows the Quran by heart.
- [Persian from Arabic *ḥāfiz* guardian]

hafnium *noun*
- "HAFNY um"
- a silvery lustrous metallic element occurring naturally with zirconium, used in tungsten alloys for filaments and electrodes.
- [modern Latin from *Hafnia* Copenhagen]

Haggadah *noun*
- "ha GADDA" or "hagga DAH"
- the non-legal element of the Talmud, consisting esp. of illustrative legends or parables.
- [Hebrew, = tale, from *higgîd* tell]
- **Haggadic** *adjective*

haggard *adjective*
- "HAG'rd"
- looking exhausted and distraught, esp. from fatigue, worry, privation, etc.
- [French *hagard*, of uncertain origin: later influenced by 'hag']
- **haggardly** *adverb*
- **haggardness** *noun*

haggis *noun*
- "HAG iss"
- a Scottish dish consisting of a sheep's or calf's offal mixed with suet, oatmeal, etc., and boiled in a bag made from the animal's stomach or in an artificial bag.
- [Middle English: origin unknown]

hagiography *noun*
- "haggy OGGRA fee"
- the writing of the lives of saints.
- [Greek *hagios* holy + *graphia* writing]
- **hagiographer** *noun*
- **hagiographic** *adjective*
- **hagiographical** *adjective*

hagiology *noun*
- "haggy OLLA jee"
- literature dealing with the lives and legends of saints.
- [Greek *hagios* holy + *logos* word]
- **hagiological** *adjective*
- **hagiologist** *noun*

hahnium *noun*
- "HONNY um"
- the name formerly proposed by the American Chemical Society for the chemical element of atomic number 105 (now called DUBNIUM) and by IUPAC for element 108 (now called HASSIUM).
- [O. *Hahn*, German chemist d.1968]

Haida *noun*
- "HY duh"
- a member of an Aboriginal people living on the west coast of Canada.
- [Haida, = people]

haik *noun*
ALSO SPELLED: **haick**
- "HIKE" or "HAKE"
- a large outer wrap, usu. white, covering the head and body and worn by Arabs of both sexes.
- [Moroccan Arabic *ḥā'ik*]

HOMOPHONES: *hake, hike*

haiku *noun*
- "HY coo"
- a type of very short Japanese poem, having three parts, usu. 17 syllables, and often about a subject in nature.
- [Japanese]

hail *verb*
- "HALE"
- acclaim, commend, or endorse vigorously.
- [elliptical use of obsolete *hail* (adjective) from Old Norse *heill* healthy, whole]

HOMOPHONES: *hale*

Haileyburian *noun*
- "HALE ee burry 'n"
- a resident of Haileybury, Ont.

Haisla *noun*
- "HY sluh"
- a member of a major language group of northern Wakashan, living in the watershed of the Douglas Channel in NW BC.
- [Haisla, = those living at the river mouth and downriver]

Haitian *noun*
- "HAY sh'n"
- a native or inhabitant of Haiti in the Caribbean.

hajj *noun*
ALSO SPELLED: **hadj**
- "HADGE"

• the pilgrimage to Mecca undertaken in the twelfth month of the Muslim year, constituting one of the religious duties of Islam.
• [Arabic *ḥajj* pilgrimage]

hajji *noun*
ALSO SPELLED: **hadji**
• "HADGE ee"
• a Muslim who has been to Mecca as a pilgrim: also used as a title.
• [Persian *hājī* (partly through Turkish *hacı*) from Arabic *ḥajj*: see HAJJ]

hakim[1] *noun*
• "huh KEEM"
• (in India and Muslim countries) a physician.
• [Arabic *ḥakīm* wise man, physician]

hakim[2] *noun*
• "HOCK im"
• (in India and Muslim countries) a judge, ruler, or governor.
• [Arabic *ḥākim* governor]

Halacha *noun*
ALSO SPELLED: **Halakah**
• "huh LOCK huh"
• Jewish law and jurisprudence, based on the Talmud, esp. the Mishnah, and subsequent rabbinical rulings.
• [Aramaic *hᵃlāḵāh* law]
• **Halachic** *adjective* (also **Halakic**)

halal *adjective*
ALSO SPELLED: **hallal**
• "hal AL"
• designating food prepared as prescribed by Muslim law.
• [Arabic *ḥalāl* lawful]

halalah *noun*
• "huh LAL uh"
• a monetary unit of Saudi Arabia, equal to one-hundredth of a riyal.
• [Arabic]

halberd *noun*
• "HAL burd"
• a weapon consisting of a long handle ending in a combined spearhead and battle-axe, used esp. in the 15th and 16th c.
• [French *hallebarde* from Italian *alabarda* from Middle High German *helmbarde* from *helm* handle + *barde* hatchet]
• **halberdier** *noun* "hal bur DEER"

halcyon *adjective*
• "HAL see 'n"
• calm, peaceful.
• [Latin *(h)alcyon* from Greek *(h)alkuōn* kingfisher]

hale *adjective*
• "HALE"
• (esp. of an old person) strong and healthy.
• [Old English *hāl* whole]
HOMOPHONES: *hail*

haler *noun*
• "HAL ur"
• a monetary unit of the Czech Republic and Slovakia, equal to one-hundredth of a koruna.
• [Czech *haléř* from Middle High German *haller*]

halfpenny *noun*
• "HAY puh nee" or "HAPE nee"
• (in the UK) a former bronze coin worth half a penny, withdrawn in 1984.
• ['half' + 'penny']

halfpennyworth *noun*
• "HAY purth"
• as much as could be bought for a halfpenny.
• [as HALFPENNY + 'worth']

halibut *noun*
• "HALA bit"
• any of several very large flatfishes fished intensively for food.
• [Middle English from *haly* holy + obsolete sense of 'butt' flatfish, perhaps because eaten on holy days]

halide *noun*
• "HAL ide" or "HALE ide"
• a binary compound of a halogen with another group or element.
• [as HALOGEN]

Haligonian *noun*
• "hala GO nee 'n"
• a native or resident of Halifax, NS.
• [from medieval Latin *Haligonia* Halifax in N England]

haliotis *noun*
• "hally OH tiss"
• any edible gastropod mollusc of the genus *Haliotis* with an ear-shaped shell lined with mother-of-pearl.
• [Greek *hals hali-* sea + *ous ōt-* ear]

halite *noun*
• "HAL ite"
• rock salt.
• [modern Latin *halites* from Greek *hals* salt]

halitosis *noun*
• "hala TOE sis"
• bad breath.
• [modern Latin from Latin *halitus* breath]

Halkomelem *noun*
• "hawl kuh MAY lum"
• the Salishan language of the Halq'emeylem, an Aboriginal people living in southwestern BC.
• [Halkomelem]

Hallel *noun*
• "huh LALE" or "HA lell"
• a portion of the service for certain Jewish festivals, consisting of Psalms 113 to 118 inclusive.
• [Hebrew *hallēl* praise]

hallelujah *interjection*
• "hala LOO yuh" or "hollay LOO yuh"

• God be praised.
• [as ALLELUIA]

Hallstatt *adjective*
• "HAWL shtat"
• of or relating to the early Iron Age in Europe, as attested by archaeological finds at Hallstatt in Upper Austria.

hallucination *noun*
• "huh loo s'n AY sh'n"
• the apparent or alleged perception of an object not actually present.
• [Latin *hallucinatio (h)allucinari* wander in mind, from Greek *alussō* be uneasy]
• **hallucinate** *verb*
• **hallucinatory** *adjective* "huh LOO sin a tory"

hallucinogen *noun*
• "huh LOO sinna j'n"
• a drug causing hallucinations.
• [as HALLUCINATION + GENESIS]
• **hallucinogenic** *adjective*

hallux *noun*
• "HAL ux"
• the big toe.
• [modern Latin from Latin *allex*]

halo *noun*
• "HAY lo"
• a disc or circle of light shown surrounding the head of a sacred person.
• [medieval Latin from Latin from Greek *halōs* threshing floor, disc of the sun or moon]

halogen *noun*
• "HALA j'n"
• any of the group of non-metallic elements (fluorine, chlorine, bromine, iodine, and astatine) which form halides (e.g. sodium chloride) by simple union with a metal.
• [Greek *hals halos* salt + GENESIS]
• **halogenic** *adjective*

halogenation *noun*
• "hala juh NAY sh'n"
• the introduction of a halogen atom into a molecule.
• [as HALOGEN]
• **halogenated** *adjective* "huh LODGE a nated"

halon *noun*
• "HAY lon"
• any of a class of compounds in which the hydrogen atoms of a hydrocarbon (usually methane or ethane) are replaced by bromine and other halogens, many of which are gases noted for their lack of reactivity and useful in firefighting.
• [as HALOGEN]

haloperidol *noun*
• "hal oh PERRA doll" or "hay lo PERRA doll"
• a drug used to treat psychotic disorders, esp. mania.
• [HALOGEN + PIPERIDINE + ALCOHOL]

halophyte *noun*
• "HALA fite" or "HAY luh fite"
• a plant adapted to saline conditions.
• [Greek *hals halos* salt + *phuton* plant, from *phuō* come into being]
• **halophytic** *adjective* "hala FITTIC" or "hay luh FITTIC"

halothane *noun*
• "HALA thane"
• a volatile liquid used as a general anaesthetic, a halogenated derivative of ethane.
• [HALOGEN + ETHANE]

halteres *plural noun*
• "hal TEER eez"
• the balancing organs of dipterous insects.
• [Greek, = weights used to aid leaping, from *hallomai* to leap]

halvah *noun*
ALSO SPELLED: **halva**
• "HAL vuh"
• a sweet confection of sesame flour and honey.
• [Yiddish from Turkish *helva* from Arabic *ḥalwa* sweetmeat]

halwa *noun*
• "HAL wuh"
• a sweet Indian dish consisting of carrots or semolina boiled with milk, almonds, sugar, butter, and cardamom.
• [Arabic, lit. = 'sweetmeat']

halyard *noun*
• "HAL y'rd"
• a rope or tackle for raising or lowering a sail or yard etc.
• [Middle English *halier* from Old French *haler* from Old Norse *hala* drag, assoc. with 'yard' (unit of measure)]

hamadryad *noun*
• "hamma DRY ad"
• (in Greek and Roman mythology) a nymph who lives in a tree and dies when it dies.
• [Latin *hamadryas* from Greek *hamadruas* from *hama* with + *drus* tree]

hamadryas *noun*
• "hamma DRY us"
• a large Arabian baboon, *Papio hamadryas*, with a silvery-grey cape of hair over the shoulders, held sacred in ancient Egypt.
• [as HAMADRYAD]

hamamelis *noun*
• "hamma MEE liss"
• any shrub of the genus *Hamamelis*, e.g. witch hazel.
• [modern Latin from Greek *hamamēlis* medlar]

hamantaschen *noun*
• "HOM'n tosh'n"
• (in Jewish cuisine) a triangular pastry with a prune or poppyseed filling, served traditionally at Purim.
• [Yiddish, = 'Haman's hat' (Haman being a

Persian official who plotted to kill all Jews but was defeated by Esther)]

hamartia *noun*
• "huh MARTY uh"
• (in Greek tragedy) the fatal flaw leading to the destruction of the tragic hero or heroine.
• [Greek, = fault, failure]

hamatsa *noun*
• "huh MATSA"
• a dance among the Kwagiulth in which the main dancer is inspired by the spirit of a man-eating monster hungering for human flesh.
• [Kwagiulth]

hames *plural noun*
• "HAYMZ"
• two curved pieces of iron or wood forming the collar or part of the collar of a draft horse, to which the traces are attached.
• [Middle Dutch *hame*]

Hamiltonian *noun*
• "ham'll TONY 'n"
• a resident of Hamilton, Ont.

Hamite *noun*
• "HAM ite"
• a member of a group of North African peoples, including the ancient Egyptians and Berbers.
• [*Ham*, son of Noah, from whom they are supposedly descended]

Hamitic *noun*
• "huh MITTIC"
• a group of African languages including ancient Egyptian and Berber.
• [as HAMITE]

hamulus *noun*
• "HAM yoo luss"
• a hooklike projection.
• [Latin, diminutive of *hamus* hook]

Han *noun*
• "HON"
• a member of a small Aboriginal group living along the Yukon River.
• [Gwich'in *han-gwich'in* 'river dwellers']

Handelian *adjective*
• "han DEELY 'n"
• relating to or characteristic of the German baroque composer George Frederick Handel (d.1759) or his work.

handicap *noun*
• "HANDY cap"
• a disadvantage imposed on a superior competitor in order to make the chances more equal.
• [originally a game in which participants deposited forfeit money in a cap: the name prob. from the phrase *hand in cap*]
• **handicapper** *noun*

handicapped *adjective*
• "HANDY capt"
• suffering from a physical or mental disability.
• [as HANDICAP]

handicraft *noun*
• "HANDY craft"
• an art, skill, or trade that requires both manual and artistic ability.
• [Middle English, alteration of earlier 'handcraft' after HANDIWORK]

handiwork *noun*
• "HANDY wurk"
• work done or a thing made by hand, or by a particular person.
• [Old English *handgeweorc*, from 'hand' + *geweorc* something made, interpreted in the 16th c. as *handy* + *work*]

handkerchief *noun*
• "HANKER chiff" or "HANKER cheef"
• a square of cotton, linen, silk, etc., usu. carried in the pocket for wiping one's nose etc.
• ['hand' + KERCHIEF]

handsome *adjective*
• "HAN s'm"
• (of a person) good-looking.
• [Middle English, = easily handled, from 'hand']
• **handsomeness** *noun*
HOMOPHONES: *hansom*

handsomely *adverb*
• "HAN s'm lee"
• generously, liberally.
• [as HANDSOME]

hangar *noun*
• "HANG ur"
• a building with extensive floor area, for housing aircraft etc.
• [French, of unknown origin]
• **hangarage** *noun*
HOMOPHONES: *hanger*

Hanoverian *noun*
• "hanna VEERY 'n"
• a member of the British royal house from 1714 to the death of Queen Victoria in 1901, descended from George, elector of Hanover in N Germany.

Hansard *noun*
• "HAN surd"
• the official verbatim record of debates in parliaments in Canada, the UK, and many other parliaments throughout the Commonwealth.
• [T. C. *Hansard*, English printer d.1832, who first printed it]

Hanseatic *adjective*
• "hancy ATTIC"
• of or relating to a 13th–19th-c. commercial alliance of north German cities.
• [Middle High German *hanse*, Old High German, Gothic *hansa* company]

hansom *noun*
• "HAN s'm"
• a two-wheeled horse-drawn cab accommodating two inside, with the driver seated behind.
• [J. A. *Hansom*, English architect d.1882, who designed it]
HOMOPHONES: *handsome*

hantavirus *noun*
• "HANTA vie russ"
• any of various viruses of the family Bunyaviridae, spread mainly by rodents and causing acute respiratory disease, kidney failure, etc.
• [modern Latin from *Hantaan* River in Korea (where the virus was first isolated in 1976) + VIRUS]

Hanukkah *noun*
ALSO SPELLED: **Chanukah**
• "HONNA kuh"
• the eight-day Jewish festival of lights, usu. in December, commemorating the purification of the Temple in 165 BC.
• [Hebrew *ḥănukkāh* consecration]

hanuman *noun*
• "hanu MONN"
• a common grey monkey of India, *Presbytis entellus*, venerated by Hindus.
• [Hindi]

haphazard *adjective*
• "hap HAZZ'rd"
• done etc. by chance; random.
• [archaic 'hap' chance, luck, from Old Norse *happ* + HAZARD]
• **haphazardly** *adverb*
• **haphazardness** *noun*

haploid *adjective*
• "HAP loid"
• (of an organism or cell) with a single set of chromosomes.
• [German from Greek *haplous* single + *eidos* form]

haplology *noun*
• "hap LOLLA jee"
• the omission of a sound when this is repeated within a word (e.g. *mirror* pronounced MEER).
• [Greek *haplous* single + *logos* word]

haplotype *noun*
• "HAPLO tipe"
• a set of genetic determinants located on a single chromosome.
• [as HAPLOID + TYPE]

happenstance *noun*
• "HAP'n stance"
• a thing that happens by chance.
• ['happen' + CIRCUMSTANCE]

happi *noun*
• "HAPPY"
• a loose informal Japanese coat.
• [Japanese]
HOMOPHONES: *happy*

haptic *adjective*
• "HAPTIC"
• relating to the sense of touch.
• [Greek *haptikos* able to touch, from *haptō* fasten]

harangue *noun*
• "huh RANG"
• a lengthy and earnest speech.
• [Old French *arenge* from medieval Latin *harenga*, perhaps from Germanic]
• **haranguer** *noun*

harass *verb*
• "huh RASS" or "HARE us"
• trouble and annoy continually or repeatedly.
• [French *harasser* from Old French *harer* set a dog on]
• **harasser** *noun*
• **harassing** *noun*
• **harassingly** *adverb*
• **harassment** *noun*

harbinger *noun*
• "HAR b'n jur"
• a person or thing that announces or signals the approach of another.
• [earlier = 'one who provides lodging': Middle English *herbergere* from Old French from *herberge* lodging, from Germanic]

hardihood *noun*
• "HARDY hood" (with "OO" as in *GOOD*)
• boldness, daring.
• [Old French *hardi* past participle of *hardir* become bold, from Germanic, related to 'hard']

hardware *noun*
• "HARD ware"
• tools, building materials, and household articles.
• ['hard' + WARE]

hare *noun*
• "HAIR"
• any of various mammals of the family Leporidae, esp. of the genus *Lepus*, like a large rabbit, with tawny fur, long ears, short tail, and hind legs longer than forelegs, inhabiting fields, hills, etc.
• [Old English *hara* from Germanic]
HOMOPHONES: *hair*, *Herr*

harebell *noun*
• "HARE bell"
• a plant, *Campanula rotundifolia*, with slender stems and pale-blue bell-shaped flowers.
• [HARE + 'bell']

Haredi *noun*
• "ha REDDY"
• a member of any of various Orthodox Jewish sects characterized by strict adherence to the traditional form of Jewish law and rejection of modern secular culture, many of whom do not

recognize the modern state of Israel as a spiritual authority.
• [Hebrew, lit. 'one who trembles (in awe at the word of God)']

harelip *noun*
• "HARE lip"
• a congenital split in the upper lip, now more commonly called a 'cleft lip'.
• [HARE + 'lip']
• **harelipped** *adjective*

harem *noun*
• "HARE um"
• (historically, or in conservative Muslim communities) the women of a Muslim household, esp. the wives and concubines, living in a separate part of the house.
• [Arabic *ḥarām*, *ḥarīm*, originally = prohibited, prohibited place, from *ḥarama* prohibit]

harewood *noun*
• "HARE wood"
• stained sycamore wood used for making furniture.
• [German dialect *Ehre* from Latin *acer* maple + 'wood']

haricot *noun*
• "HERRY co"
• a variety of French bean with small white seeds.
• [French, perhaps from Aztec *ayacotl*]

Harijan *noun*
• "HAR ee j'n"
• a member of the class of untouchables in the Indian subcontinent.
• [Sanskrit, = a person dedicated to the god Vishnu, from *Hari* Vishnu, *jana* person]

harissa *noun*
• "HERRISS uh"
• a spicy, North African chili paste used as an accompaniment to couscous dishes.
• [Arabic *harīsa* a dish of meat and bulgur, from *harasa* crush, pound, tenderize by beating]

harlequin *noun*
• "HARLA kwin"
• a mute character in pantomime, usu. masked and dressed in a diamond-patterned costume.
• [French from earlier *Herlequin* leader of a legendary troupe of demon horsemen]

harlequinade *noun*
• "harla kwin ADE"
• the part of a pantomime featuring Harlequin.
• [French *arlequinade* (as HARLEQUIN)]

harlot *noun*
• "HAR lit"
• a prostitute or promiscuous woman.
• [Old French *harlot*, *herlot* lad, knave, vagabond]
• **harlotry** *noun*

harmattan *noun*
• "har MAT 'n"
• a parching dusty land-wind of the West African coast occurring from December to February.
• [Fanti or Twi *haramata*]

harmful *adjective*
• "HARM full"
• causing or likely to cause harm.
• [Old English *hearm* harm, from Germanic]
• **harmfully** *adverb*
• **harmfulness** *noun*

harmolodics *noun*
• "harma LODDIX"
• a form of free jazz in which musicians improvise simultaneously on a melodic line at various pitches.
• [coined by the American saxophonist Ornette Coleman (b.1930) and said to be a blend of *harmony*, *movement*, and *melodic*]
• **harmolodic** *adjective*

harmonic *adjective*
• "har MONNIC"
• of or characterized by harmony; harmonious.
• [as HARMONY]
• **harmonically** *adverb*

harmonica *noun*
• "har MONNA kuh"
• a small rectangular wind instrument with a row of metal reeds along its length, held against the lips and moved from side to side to produce different notes by blowing or sucking.
• [Latin, feminine sing. or neuter pl. of *harmonicus* harmonic (as HARMONY)]

harmonium *noun*
• "har MOANY um"
• a keyboard instrument in which the notes are produced by air driven through metal reeds by bellows operated by the feet.
• [French from Latin (as HARMONY)]

harmony *noun*
• "HARMA nee"
• a combination of simultaneously sounded musical notes to produce chords and chord progressions, esp. as having a pleasing effect.
• [Old French *harmonie* from Latin *harmonia* from Greek *harmonia* joining, concord, from *harmos* joint]
• **harmonious** *adjective* "har MOANY us"
• **harmoniously** *adverb*
• **harmoniousness** *noun*
• **harmonist** *noun*
• **harmonization** *noun* (also esp. *Brit.* **-isation**)
• **harmonize** *verb* (also esp. *Brit.* **-ise**)
• **harmonizer** *noun* (also esp. *Brit.* **-iser**)

harness *noun*
• "HAR nuss"
• the equipment of straps and fittings by which a horse or other draft animal is fastened to a cart etc. and controlled.
• [Old French *harneis* military equipment, from

Old Norse *hernest* (unrecorded) from *herr* army + *nest* provisions]
• **harnesser** *noun*

harpoon *noun*
• "har POON"
• a barbed spear-like missile with a rope attached, for hunting seals, whales, etc.
• [French *harpon* from *harpe* clamp, from Latin *harpa* from Greek *harpē* sickle]
• **harpooner** *noun*

harpsichord *noun*
• "HARPSA cord"
• a keyboard instrument with horizontal strings which are plucked mechanically.
• [obsolete French *harpechorde* from Late Latin *harpa* harp, + *chorda* string, the -*s*- being unexplained]
• **harpsichordist** *noun*

harpy *noun*
• "HARPY"
• (in Greek and Roman mythology) a monster with a woman's head and body and bird's wings and claws.
• [French *harpie* or Latin *harpyia* from Greek *harpuiai* snatchers (compare *harpazō* snatch)]

harquebus *noun*
• "HAR kwuh buss"
• an early type of portable gun supported on a tripod or on a forked rest.
• [French *(h)arquebuse*, ultimately from Middle Low German *hakebusse* or Middle High German *hakenbühse*, from *haken* hook + *busse* gun]

harridan *noun*
• "HARE a d'n"
• a bad-tempered woman.
• [17th-c. cant, perhaps from French *haridelle* old horse]

harrier *noun*
• "HERRY ur"
• any bird of prey of the genus *Circus*, with long wings for swooping over the ground.
• [originally *harrower* from *harrow* harry, rob, assimilated to 'harrier' a person who harries or lays waste]

harrow *noun*
• "HERRO"
• a heavy frame with iron teeth dragged over plowed land to break up clods, remove weeds, cover seed, etc.
• [Old Norse *hervi*]

harrowing *adjective*
• "HERRO ing"
• greatly distressing.
• [as HARROW]
• **harrowingly** *adverb*

harry *verb*
• "HERRY"
• ravage or despoil.
• [Old English *herian*, *hergian* from Germanic, related to Old English *here* army]
HOMOPHONES: *hairy*

hart *noun*
• "HART"
• the male of the European red deer, usu. over five years old.
• [Old English *heor(o)t* from Germanic]
HOMOPHONES: *heart*

hartal *noun*
• "HART'll"
• the closing of shops and offices in the Indian subcontinent as a mark of protest or sorrow.
• [Hindi *hartāl*, *haṭtāl* from Sanskrit *haṭṭa* shop + *tālaka* lock]

hartebeest *noun*
• "HARTA beest"
• any large African antelope of the genus *Alcelaphus*, with ringed horns bent back at the tips.
• [Afrikaans from Dutch *hert* HART + *beest* beast]

hartshorn *noun*
• "HARTS horn"
• an aqueous solution of ammonia used as smelling salts, formerly prepared from the horns of a deer.
• [as HART + 'horn']

haruspex *noun*
• "huh ROO specks"
• a Roman religious official who interpreted omens from the inspection of animals' entrails.
• [Latin]
• **haruspicy** *noun* "huh ROO spiss ee"

Hashemite *adjective*
• "HASHA mite"
• of, relating to, or denoting an Arab princely family claiming descent from Hashim, great-grandfather of Muhammad.

hashish *noun*
• "ha SHEESH" or "HASH eesh"
• a resinous product of the top leaves and tender parts of hemp, smoked or chewed for its narcotic effects.
• [Arabic *ḥašīš* dry herb; powdered hemp leaves]

Hasid *noun*
ALSO SPELLED: **Chassid**, **Hassid**
• "HASSID"
• a member of any of several mystical Jewish sects, esp. one founded in the 18th c.
• [Hebrew *ḥāsîḏ* pious]
• **Hasidic** *adjective* (also **Chassidic**, **Hassidic**) "huh SIDDIC"
• **Hasidism** *noun* (also **Chassidism**, **Hassidism**)

hassium *noun*
• "HASSY um"
• a very unstable chemical element made by high-energy atomic collisions.

• [modern Latin, from Latin *Hassias* Hesse (the German state); it was discovered in Darmstadt, Hesse in 1984]

hassock *noun*
• "HASS uck"
• a thick firm cushion used to rest the feet on or, esp. in church, to kneel on.
• [Old English *hassuc*]

hastate *adjective*
• "HASS tate"
• triangular like the head of a spear.
• [Latin *hastatus* from *hasta* spear]

hauberk *noun*
• "HOB urk"
• a coat of armour made of interlaced rings or chains, or overlapping plates, joined together flexibly.
• [Old French *hau(s)berc* from Frankish, = neck protection, from *hals* neck + *berg-* from *beorg* protection]

Haudenosaunee *noun*
• "hodda nuh SAW nee"
• = IROQUOIS.
• [Mohawk, lit. 'people of the longhouse']

haughty *adjective*
• "HOTTY"
• arrogantly self-admiring and disdainful.
• [extension of *haught* (adjective), earlier *haut* from Old French *haut* from Latin *altus* high]
• **haughtily** *adverb*
• **haughtiness** *noun*
HOMOPHONES: *hottie*

haul *verb*
• "HAWL"
• pull or drag forcibly.
• [Old French *haler* from Old Norse *hala*]
• **hauler** *noun*
HOMOPHONES: *hall*, *holler*

haulage *noun*
• "HAWL idge"
• the commercial transport of goods.
• [as HAUL]

haulback *noun*
• "HAWL back"
• a lighter line for drawing a cable back to its original position after it has been used to move a log away.
• [as HAUL + 'back']

haulm *noun*
ALSO SPELLED: **halm**
• "HOM"
• a stalk or stem.
• [Old English *h(e)alm* from Germanic]

haulout *noun*
• "HAWL out"
• the action of hauling a boat out of water.
• [as HAUL + 'out']

haunch *noun*
• "HONCH"
• the fleshy part of the buttock with the thigh.
• [Old French *hanche*, of Germanic origin: compare Low German *hanke* hind leg of a horse]

haunt *verb*
• "HONT"
• (of a ghost) visit (a place) regularly, usu. reputedly giving signs of its presence.
• [Old French *hanter* from Germanic]
• **haunted** *adjective*
• **haunter** *noun*

haunting *adjective*
• "HONT ing"
• (of a memory, melody, etc.) poignant, wistful, evocative.
• [as HAUNT]
• **hauntingly** *adverb*

Hausa *noun*
• "HOW suh" or "HOW zuh"
• a people of West Africa and the Sudan.
• [Hausa]

hausfrau *noun*
• "HOUSE frow" ("FROW" rhymes with *COW*)
• a housewife.
• [German from *Haus* house + *Frau* woman]

haute *adjective*
• "OAT" or "HOAT"
• upper-class, elegant, prestigious.
• [French, lit. = high]
HOMOPHONES: *oat*

hauteur *noun*
• "owe TUR"
• haughtiness of manner.
• [French from *haut* high]
HOMOPHONES: *auteur*

Havana *noun*
• "huh VANNA"
• a cigar made at Havana or elsewhere in Cuba.

havarti *noun*
• "huh VARTY"
• a mild, semi-soft Danish cheese with small irregular holes.
• [name of the farm of Hanne Nielsen, 19th c. Danish cheese maker]

haver *verb*
• "HAY vur"
• talk foolishly; babble.
• [18th c.: origin unknown]

haversack *noun*
• "HAVVER sack"
• a stout bag for provisions etc., carried on the back or over the shoulder.
• [French *havresac* from German *Habersack* from *Haber* oats + *Sack* sack]

haversine *noun*
• "HAVVER sine"
• half of a versed sine.
• [contraction]

havoc *noun*
• "HAVE ick"
• widespread destruction; great confusion or disorder.
• [Anglo-French *havok* from Old French *havo(t)*, of unknown origin]

Hawaiian *noun*
• "huh WYE 'n"
• a native of Hawaii in the N Pacific Ocean.

Hawkesburian *noun*
• "HOCKS burry 'n"
• a resident of Hawkesbury, Ont.

hawse *noun*
• "HOZZ"
• the part of a ship's bows through which the anchor cables pass.
• [prob. from Old Norse *háls* neck, ship's bow]

hawser *noun*
• "HOZZER"
• a thick rope or cable for mooring or towing a ship.
• [Old French *haucier* hoist, ultimately from Latin *altus* high]

haylage *noun*
• "HAY lidge"
• silage made from grass etc. which has been partially dried.
• [from 'hay', from Old English *hēg, hīeg, hīg* from Germanic + (SI)LAGE]

Hazara *noun*
• "ha ZAR uh"
• a member of a people of Mongolian descent inhabiting the mountainous region of central Afghanistan and parts of northern Iran and Pakistan.
• [Persian *hazār* thousand]

hazard *noun*
• "HAZZ'rd"
• a danger or risk.
• [Old French *hasard* from Spanish *azar* from Arabic *az-zahr* chance, luck]
• **hazardous** *adjective*
• **hazardously** *adverb*
• **hazardousness** *noun*

headdress *noun*
• "HED dress"
• an ornamental covering or band for the head.
• ['head' + 'dress']

hearken *verb*
ALSO SPELLED: **harken**
• "HARK'n"
• listen.
• [Old English *heorcnian*]

hearse *noun*
• "HURSE" (rhymes with *PURSE*)
• a vehicle for conveying the coffin at a funeral.
• [Old French *herse* harrow, from medieval Latin *herpica*, ultimately from Latin *hirpex -icis* large rake]

hearth *noun*
• "HARTH"
• the floor of a fireplace.
• [Old English *heorth* from West Germanic]

hearthstone *noun*
• "HARTH stone"
• a flat stone forming a hearth.
• [as HEARTH + 'stone']

heathen *noun*
• "HEE then"
• *derogatory* a person who does not belong to a widely held religion (esp. who is not Christian, Jewish, or Muslim) as regarded by those that do.
• [Old English *hǣthen* from Germanic]
• **heathendom** *noun*
• **heathenism** *noun*

heave *verb*
• "HEEVE"
• lift or haul (a heavy thing) with great effort.
• [Old English *hebban* from Germanic, related to Latin *capere* take]
• **heaver** *noun*

hebdomadal *adjective*
• "heb DOMMA d'll"
• weekly, esp. meeting weekly.
• [Late Latin *hebdomadalis* from Greek *hebdomas, -ados* from *hepta* seven]

hebetude *noun*
• "HEBBA tude"
• dullness, lethargy.
• [Late Latin *hebetudo* from *hebes, -etis* blunt]

Hebraic *adjective*
• "he BRAY ick"
• of Hebrew or the Hebrews.
• [Late Latin from Greek *Hebraikos* (as HEBRAISM)]

Hebraism *noun*
• "HEE bray izm"
• a Hebrew idiom or expression, esp. in the Greek of the Bible.
• [French *hébraïsme* or modern Latin *Hebraismus* from late Greek *Hebraïsmos* from Aramaic *'iḇray* from Hebrew *'iḇrî* one from the other side (of the river)]
• **Hebraize** *verb* (also esp. *Brit.* **-ise**)

Hebraist *noun*
• "HEE bray ist"
• a Hebrew scholar; an expert in Hebrew.
• [as HEBRAISM]

Hebridean *adjective*
• "hebra DEE 'n"
• of or relating to the Hebrides, a group of about 500 islands off the NW coast of Scotland.

hecatomb *noun*
• "HECKA toom"
• (in ancient Greece or Rome) a great public sacrifice, originally of 100 oxen.
• [Latin *hecatombe* from Greek *hekatombē* from *hekaton* hundred + *bous* ox]

hectare *noun*
• "HECK tare" or "HECK tar"
• a metric unit of land measure, equal to 100 ares (2.471 acres or 10,000 square metres).
• [French from Greek *hekaton* hundred, ARE]

hectic *adjective*
• "HECK tick"
• busy and confused; characterized by feverish excitement or haste.
• [Old French *etique* from Late Latin *hecticus* from Greek *hektikos* habitual, from *hexis* habit (originally applying to a habitual fever)]
• **hectically** *adverb*

hectogram *noun*
• "HECTO gram"
• a metric unit of mass, equal to one hundred grams.
• [French from Greek *hekaton* hundred + 'gram']

hectolitre *noun*
ALSO SPELLED: esp. *US* **hectoliter**
• "HECTO leeter"
• a metric unit of capacity, equal to one hundred litres.
• [French from Greek *hekaton* hundred, LITRE]

hectometre *noun*
ALSO SPELLED: esp. *US* **hectometer**
• "HECTO meeter"
• a metric unit of length, equal to one hundred metres.
• [French from Greek *hekaton* hundred, METRE]

hector *verb*
• "HECTER"
• bully, intimidate.
• [earlier 'swaggering fellow' from the legendary Trojan hero, *Hector*]
• **hectoring** *adjective*
• **hectoringly** *adverb*

heddle *noun*
• "HED'll"
• one of the sets of small cords or wires between which the warp is passed in a loom before going through the reed.
• [apparently from Old English *hefeld*]

hedonism *noun*
• "HEED'n izm" or "HED'n izm"
• belief in pleasure as the highest good and mankind's proper aim.
• [Greek *hēdonē* pleasure]
• **hedonic** *adjective* "hee DONNIC"
• **hedonist** *noun*
• **hedonistic** *adjective*

hedysarum *noun*
• "huh DISSA rum"
• a leguminous plant of the genus *Hedysarum* including both poisonous species and those with edible roots, e.g. licorice root.
• [Greek name for some plant, *hedysaron*, used by Swedish botanist C. Linnaeus (d.1778)]

Hegelian *adjective*
• "huh GAILY 'n"
• of or relating to the German philosopher G. W. F. Hegel (d.1831) or his philosophy of dialectical reasoning.

hegemon *noun*
• "HEDGE a monn"
• a paramount leader.
• [as HEGEMONY]

hegemony *noun*
• "huh JEMMA nee"
• leadership or dominance, esp. by one state or social group over others.
• [Greek *hēgemonia* from *hēgemōn* leader, from *hēgeomai* lead]
• **hegemonic** *adjective* "hedge a MONNIC"

hegira *noun*
ALSO SPELLED: **hejira**
• "huh JYE ruh" or "HEDGE a ruh"
• the Muslim era reckoned from the date (AD 622) of Muhammad's departure from Mecca to Medina.
• [medieval Latin *hegira* from Arabic *hijra* departure from one's country, from *hajara* separate]

heifer *noun*
• "HEFFER"
• a female domestic bovine animal that has not borne a calf, or has borne only one calf.
• [Old English *heahfore*]

height *noun*
• "HITE"
• the measurement from base to top or (of a standing person) from head to foot.
• [Old English *hēhthu* from Germanic]

heighten *verb*
• "HITE 'n"
• make or become higher or more intense.
• [as HEIGHT]
• **heightened** *adjective*

Heiltsuk *noun*
• "HILE tsook" (rhymes with *BOOK*)
• a member of an Aboriginal group living on the islands and waterways of Milbanke Sound in BC.
• [Heiltsuk, = 'people']

heinie *noun*
• "HY nee"
• the buttocks.
• [alteration of 'hinder' behind]

heinous *adjective*
• "HAY niss"
• (of a crime or criminal) utterly odious or wicked.
• [Old French *haïneus*, ultimately from *haïr* to hate, from Frankish]
• **heinously** *adverb*
• **heinousness** *noun*

heir *noun*
- "AIR"
- a person entitled to property or rank as the legal successor of its former owner.
- [Old French *eir* from Late Latin *herem* from Latin *heres -edis*]
- **heirless** *adjective*
- **heirship** *noun*

HOMOPHONES: *air, err, ere, are*

heiress *noun*
- "AIR iss"
- a woman entitled to property or rank as the legal successor of its former owner.
- [as HEIR]

heirloom *noun*
- "AIR loom"
- a piece of personal property that has been in a family for several generations.
- [HEIR + 'loom' in the sense 'tool']

heist *noun*
- "HICED" (rhymes with *PRICED*)
- a robbery.
- [representing a local pronunciation of 'hoist']

heldentenor *noun*
- "HELD'n tenner"
- a powerful tenor voice suitable for heroic roles in opera.
- [German from *Held* a hero + TENOR]

helenium *noun*
- "huh LEENY um"
- any composite plant of the genus *Helenium*, with daisy-like flowers having prominent central discs.
- [modern Latin from Greek *helenion*, possibly commemorating Helen of Troy]

heliacal *adjective*
- "huh LIE a k'll"
- relating to or near the sun.
- [Late Latin *heliacus* from Greek *hēliakos* from *hēlios* sun]

helianthemum *noun*
- "heely ANTHA mum"
- any evergreen shrub of the genus *Helianthemum*, with saucer-shaped flowers.
- [modern Latin from Greek *hēlios* sun + *anthemon* flower]

helianthus *noun*
- "heely ANTH us"
- any plant of the genus *Helianthus*, including the sunflower and Jerusalem artichoke.
- [modern Latin from Greek *hēlios* sun + *anthos* flower]

helical *adjective*
- "HELLA k'll" or "HEELA k'll"
- having the form of a helix.
- [as HELIX]
- **helically** *adverb*
- **helicoid** *adjective*

helichrysum *noun*
- "hella CRY z'm"
- any composite plant of the genus *Helichrysum*, with flowers retaining their appearance when dried.
- [Latin from Greek *helikhrusos*, from *helix* spiral + *khrusos* gold]

helicity *noun*
- "huh LISSA tee"
- helical character.
- [as HELICAL]

helicon *noun*
- "HELLA con"
- a large spiral bass tuba played encircling the player's head and resting on the shoulder.
- [Latin from Greek *Helikōn* Mount Helicon, legendary home of the Muses: later associated with HELIX]

helicopter *noun*
- "HELLA copter"
- a type of aircraft without wings, obtaining lift and propulsion from horizontally revolving overhead blades or rotors, and capable of moving vertically and horizontally.
- [French *hélicoptère* from Greek *helix* (see HELIX) + *pteron* wing]

heliocentric *adjective*
- "heely a SENTRIC"
- having, representing, or regarding the sun as centre.
- [Greek *hēlios* sun + CENTRE]
- **heliocentrism** *noun*

heliograph *noun*
- "HEELY a graff"
- a signalling apparatus reflecting sunlight in flashes from a movable mirror.
- [Greek *hēlios* sun + GRAPH]
- **heliographic** *adjective*

heliometer *noun*
- "heely OMMA tur"
- a refracting telescope with a split objective lens, used to measure angular distances between stars etc. (originally used for measuring the diameter of the sun).
- [Greek *hēlios* sun + *metron* measure]

heliotrope *noun*
- "HEELY a trope"
- any plant of the genus *Heliotropium*, with fragrant purple flowers.
- [Latin *heliotropium* from Greek *hēliotropion* plant turning its flowers to the sun, from *hēlios* sun + *-tropos* from *trepō* turn]

heliotropism *noun*
- "heely OTTRA pizm"
- the directional growth of a plant in response to sunlight.
- [as HELIOTROPE]
- **heliotropic** *adjective*

helipad *noun*
- "HELLA pad"
- a landing pad for helicopters.
- [as HELICOPTER + 'pad']

heliport *noun*
- "HELLA port"
- an airport or landing place for helicopters.
- [HELICOPTER + 'airport']

helitack *noun*
- "HELLA tack"
- the use of helicopters to fight forest fires, e.g. to deploy ground crews or to transport and release extinguishing substances.
- [blend of HELICOPTER + 'attack']

helium *noun*
- "HEELY um"
- a colourless, light, inert, gaseous element occurring in deposits of natural gas, used in airships and as a refrigerant.
- [Greek *hēlios* sun (having been first identified in the sun's atmosphere)]

helix *noun*
- "HEE lix"
- an object of coiled form, either a spiral curve round an axis like a corkscrew or a coiled curve in one plane like a watchspring.
- [Latin *helix -icis* from Greek *helix -ikos*]

hellacious *adjective*
- "hell AY sh'ss"
- hellish, extremely awful.
- ['hell' + *-acious*, perhaps suggested by BODACIOUS]
- **hellaciously** *adverb*

Helladic *adjective*
- "hell ADDIC"
- of or belonging to the Bronze Age culture of mainland Greece, lasting from *c.*2800-*c.*1200 BC.
- [Greek *Helladikos* from *Hellas -ados* Greece]

hellebore *noun*
- "HELLA bor"
- any evergreen plant of the genus *Helleborus*, having large white, green, or purplish flowers, e.g. the Christmas rose.
- [Old French *elebore* from Latin *elleborus* from Greek *(h)elleboros*]

helleborine *noun*
- "HELLA bor een"
- any orchid of the genus *Epipactis* or *Cephalanthera*.
- [French or Latin *helleborine* or Latin from Greek *helleborinē* plant like hellebore (as HELLEBORE)]

Hellene *noun*
- "HELL een"
- a native or citizen of modern Greece.
- [Greek *Hellēn* a Greek]
- **Hellenic** *adjective* "hell ENNIC"

Hellenism *noun*
- "HELLEN izm"
- Greek character or culture (esp. of ancient Greece).
- [as HELLENE]
- **Hellenization** *noun* (also esp. *Brit.* **-isation**)
- **Hellenize** *verb* (also esp. *Brit.* **-ise**)

Hellenist *noun*
- "HELLEN ist"
- an expert on Greek language or culture.
- [as HELLENE]

Hellenistic *adjective*
- "hellen ISTIC"
- of or relating to the period of Greek history, language, and culture from the death of Alexander the Great in 323 BC to the defeat of Cleopatra and Mark Antony by Octavian in 31 BC.
- [as HELLENE]

Hellerwork *noun*
- "HELLER wurk"
- a form of alternative therapy which combines massage, body movements, and exploration of emotional issues.
- [J. *Heller*, US engineer b.1940 who developed the method]

hellgrammite *noun*
- "HELLGRA mite"
- an aquatic larva of an insect, esp. the fly *Corydalus cornutus*, often used as fishing bait.
- [19th c.: origin unknown]

hellion *noun*
- "HELLY 'n"
- a rowdy, troublemaking, disreputable person.
- [perhaps from dialect *hallion* a worthless fellow, assimilated to 'hell']

helminth *noun*
- "HELL minth"
- any of various parasitic worms including flukes, tapeworms, and nematodes.
- [Greek *helmins -inthos* intestinal worm]
- **helminthic** *adjective*
- **helminthoid** *adjective*
- **helminthology** *noun*

helminthiasis *noun*
- "helmin THY a sis" (with "TH" as in *THICK*)
- a disease characterized by the presence of any of several parasitic worms in the body.
- [as HELMINTH]

helo *noun*
- "HEELO"
- a helicopter.
- [abbreviation]

helot *noun*
- "HELL it"
- a slave or serf.
- [Latin *helotes* pl. from Greek *heilōtes, -ōtai*, erroneously taken as = inhabitants of *Helos* near Sparta]
- **helotism** *noun*
- **helotry** *noun*

helve *noun*
- "HELVE"
- the handle or shaft of a weapon or a tool.
- [Old English *helfe* from West Germanic]

Helvetian *adjective*
- "hel VEE sh'n"
- Swiss.
- [Latin *Helvetia* Switzerland]

hemagglutinate *verb*
ALSO SPELLED: esp. *Brit.* **haemagglutinate**
- "heema GLOOT'n ate"
- cause (red blood cells) to coagulate.
- [Greek *haima* blood + AGGLUTINATE]
- **hemagglutination** *noun* (also esp. *Brit.* **haemagglutination**)

hemagglutinin *noun*
ALSO SPELLED: esp. *Brit.* **haemagglutinin**
- "heema GLOOT'n in"
- a substance, such as a viral protein, which causes hemagglutination.
- [as HEMAGGLUTINATE]

hemal *adjective*
ALSO SPELLED: esp. *Brit.* **haemal**
- "HEEM'll"
- of or concerning the blood or circulatory system.
- [Greek *haima* blood]

hematic *adjective*
ALSO SPELLED: esp. *Brit.* **haematic**
- "hee MATTIC"
- of or containing blood.
- [Greek *haimatikos* (as HEMATIN)]

hematin *noun*
ALSO SPELLED: esp. *Brit.* **haematin**
- "HEEMA tin"
- a bluish-black derivative of hemoglobin, formed by removal of the protein part and oxidation of the iron atom.
- [Greek *haima -matos* blood]

hematite *noun*
ALSO SPELLED: esp. *Brit.* **haematite**
- "HEEMA tite"
- ferric oxide occurring as a dark red mineral which constitutes an important ore of iron.
- [Latin *haematites* from Greek *haimatitēs* (*lithos*) blood-like (stone) (as HEMATIN)]

hematocele *noun*
ALSO SPELLED: esp. *Brit.* **haematocele**
- "HEEMA toe seel"
- a swelling caused by blood collecting in a body cavity.
- [Greek *haima -matos* blood = *kēlē* tumour]

hematocrit *noun*
ALSO SPELLED: esp. *Brit.* **haematocrit**
- "HEEMA toe crit"
- the ratio of the volume of red blood cells to the total volume of blood.
- [Greek *haima -matos* blood + *kritēs* judge]

hematology *noun*
ALSO SPELLED: esp. *Brit.* **haematology**
- "heema TOLLA jee"
- the branch of medicine that deals with the blood, esp. in disorders.
- [Greek *haima -matos* blood + *logos* word]
- **hematologic** *adjective* (also esp. *Brit.* **haematologic**)
- **hematological** *adjective* (also esp. *Brit.* **haematological**)
- **hematologist** *noun* (also esp. *Brit.* **haematologist**)

hematoma *noun*
ALSO SPELLED: esp. *Brit.* **haematoma**
- "heema TOE muh"
- a solid swelling of clotted blood within the tissues.
- [Greek *haima -matos* blood]

hematoxylin *noun*
ALSO SPELLED: esp. *Brit.* **haematoxylin**
- "heema TOXA lin"
- a colourless crystalline polycyclic phenol present in logwood that can be easily converted into red, blue, or purple dyes and used as a biological stain.
- [modern Latin *Haematoxylum* genus name for a Caribbean tree, from Greek *haima -matos* blood + *xulon* wood]

hematuria *noun*
ALSO SPELLED: esp. *Brit.* **haematuria**
- "heema TYUR ee uh"
- the presence of blood in urine.
- [Greek *haima -matos* blood + URINE]

heme *noun*
ALSO SPELLED: esp. *Brit.* **haem**
- "HEEM"
- a non-protein compound containing iron, and responsible for the red colour of hemoglobin.
- [Greek *haima* blood, or from HEMOGLOBIN]

hemerocallis *noun*
- "hemma roe CAL iss"
- any plant of the genus *Hemerocallis*, whose flowers last only a day; a day lily.
- [Latin *hemerocalles* from Greek *hēmerokalles*, a kind of lily, from *hēmera* day + *kallos* beauty]

hemicellulose *noun*
- "hemmy SELL yoo lose" (rhymes with *GROSS*)
- any of various polysaccharides forming the matrix of plant cell walls in which cellulose is embedded.
- [Greek *hēmi-* half + CELLULOSE]

hemichordate *noun*
- "hemmy CORD ate"
- a wormlike marine invertebrate of the phylum *Hemichordata*, comprising the acorn worms, possessing a notochord in the larval stage.
- [Greek *hēmi-* half + CHORDATE]

hemidemisemiquaver *noun*
- "HEMMY demmy SEMMY kway vur"
- a sixty-fourth note.
- [Greek *hēmi-* half + DEMISEMIQUAVER]

hemihedral *adjective*
- "hemmy HEED rull"
- (of a crystal) having half the number of planes required for symmetry of the holohedral form.
- [Greek *hēmi-* half + *hedra* base]

hemiola *noun*
- "heemy OH luh" or "hemmy OH luh"
- a rhythmic device consisting of superimposing two notes in the time of three, or three in the time of two, e.g. two dotted quarter notes in a 3/4 bar.
- [medieval Latin *hemiolia* from Greek *hēmiolia*, *-lios*, in the ratio of one and a half to one, from Greek *hēmi-* half + *holos* whole]

hemiplegia *noun*
- "hemmy PLEE juh"
- paralysis of one side of the body.
- [modern Latin from Greek *hēmiplēgia* paralysis (Greek *hēmi-* half, *plēgē* stroke)]
- **hemiplegic** *noun*

hemipterous *adjective*
- "hem IPTER us"
- of the insect order *Hemiptera* including aphids, bugs, and cicadas, with piercing or sucking mouthparts.
- [Greek *hēmi-* half + *pteron* wing]

hemisphere *noun*
- "HEM iss feer"
- a half of the earth, esp. as divided by the equator (into *northern* and *southern hemisphere*) or by an imaginary line passing through the poles (into *eastern* and *western hemisphere*).
- [Greek *hēmi-* half + SPHERE]
- **hemispheral** *adjective*
- **hemispheric** *adjective*
- **hemispherical** *adjective*
- **hemispherically** *adverb*

hemistich *noun*
- "HEMMISS tick"
- a half of a line of verse or a line of less than the usual length.
- [Late Latin *hemistichium* from Greek *hēmistikhion* (*hēmi-* half, *stikhion* from *stikhos* line)]

hemocoel *noun*
ALSO SPELLED: esp. *Brit.* **haemocoel**
- "HEEMA seel"
- the primary body cavity of most invertebrates, containing circulatory fluid.
- [Greek *haima* blood + *koilos* hollow, cavity]

hemocyanin *noun*
ALSO SPELLED: esp. *Brit.* **haemocyanin**
- "heema SYE a nin"
- an oxygen-carrying substance containing copper, present in the blood plasma of arthropods and molluscs, that is blue when oxygenated and colourless otherwise.
- [Greek *haima* blood + *cyanin* blue pigment (as CYAN)]

hemodialysis *noun*
ALSO SPELLED: esp. *Brit.* **haemodialysis**
- "heemo die ALA sis"
- the clinical purification of blood, e.g. of a person without adequately functioning kidneys, by dialysis.
- [Greek *haima* blood + DIALYSIS]

hemoglobin *noun*
ALSO SPELLED: esp. *Brit.* **haemoglobin**
- "HEEMA glow bin"
- a red, oxygen-carrying substance containing iron, present in the red blood cells of vertebrates.
- [shortened from *hematoglobin*, compound of HEMATIN + GLOBULIN]

hemolymph *noun*
ALSO SPELLED: esp. *Brit.* **haemolymph**
- "HEEMA limf"
- a fluid equivalent to blood in invertebrate animals.
- [Greek *haima* blood + LYMPH]

hemolysis *noun*
ALSO SPELLED: esp. *Brit.* **haemolysis**
- "hee MOLLA sis"
- the loss of hemoglobin from red blood cells.
- [Greek *haima* blood + LYSIS]
- **hemolytic** *adjective* (also esp. *Brit.* **haemolytic**)

hemophilia *noun*
ALSO SPELLED: esp. *Brit.* **haemophilia**
- "heema FILLY uh" or "heema FEELY uh"
- a usu. hereditary disorder with a tendency to bleed severely from even a slight injury, through the failure of the blood to clot normally.
- [Greek *haima* blood + *philos* dear, loving]
- **hemophiliac** *noun* (also esp. *Brit.* **haemophiliac**)
- **hemophilic** *adjective* (also esp. *Brit.* **haemophilic**)

hemorrhage *noun*
ALSO SPELLED: esp. *Brit.* **haemorrhage**
- "HEMMER idge"
- an escape of blood from a ruptured blood vessel, esp. when profuse.
- [ultimately from Greek *haimorrhagia* from *haima* blood + stem of *rhēgnumi* burst]
- **hemorrhagic** *adjective* (also esp. *Brit.* **haemorrhagic**) "hemmer ADGE ick"

hemorrhoid *noun*
ALSO SPELLED: esp. *Brit.* **haemorrhoid**
- "HEMMER oid"
- swollen veins at or near the anus.
- [Greek *haimorrhoides* (*phlebes*) bleeding (veins) from *haima* blood, *-rhoos* -flowing]

• **hemorrhoidal** *adjective* (also esp. *Brit.* **haemorrhoidal**)

hemostat *noun*
ALSO SPELLED: esp. *Brit.* **haemostat**
• "HEEMO stat"
• an instrument for stopping the flow of blood by compression of a blood vessel.
• [Greek *haima* blood + *statikos* from *sta-* stand]
• **hemostatic** *adjective* (also esp. *Brit.* **haemostatic**)

hendiadys *noun*
• "hen DIE a dis"
• the expression of an idea by two words connected with 'and', instead of one modifying the other, e.g. *nice and warm* for *nicely warm*.
• [medieval Latin from Greek *hen dia duoin* one thing by two]

henequen *noun*
• "HENNA ken"
• a Mexican agave, *Agave fourcroydes*.
• [Spanish *jeniquen*]

Henley *noun*
• "HENLEE"
• a long-sleeved pullover with a round neckline and a short buttoned placket.
• [possibly alluding to Henley in England, where prestigious rowing races are held]

henna *noun*
• "HENNA"
• a tropical shrub, *Lawsonia inermis*, having small pink, red, or white flowers.
• [Arabic *ḥinnā'*]
• **hennaed** *adjective*

heparin *noun*
• "HEPPA rin"
• a sulphur-containing polysaccharide with anticoagulant properties, present in the blood and various bodily organs and tissues.
• [Latin from Greek *hēpar* liver]
• **heparinization** *noun* (also esp. *Brit.* **-isation**)
• **heparinized** *adjective* (also esp. *Brit.* **-ised**)

hepatic *adjective*
• "hep ATTIC"
• of or relating to the liver.
• [Latin *hepaticus* from Greek *hēpatikos* from *hēpar -atos* liver]

hepatica *noun*
• "hep ATTIC uh"
• any plant of the genus *Hepatica*, with reddish-brown lobed leaves resembling the liver.
• [medieval Latin feminine of *hepaticus*: see HEPATIC]

hepatitis *noun*
• "heppa TITE iss"
• inflammation of the liver.
• [modern Latin: see HEPATIC + Greek *-itis*, forming feminine of adjectives in *-itēs* (with *nosos* 'disease' implied)]

Hepplewhite *noun*
• "HEP'll wite"
• a late 18th-c. style of furniture, originally as made by the English cabinetmaker George Hepplewhite (d.1786), characterized by lightness, delicacy, and graceful curves.

heptad *noun*
• "HEP tad"
• a group of seven.
• [Greek *heptas -ados* set of seven (*hepta*)]

heptagon *noun*
• "HEPTA gon"
• a plane figure with seven sides and angles.
• [Greek *hepta* seven + *-gonos* -angled]
• **heptagonal** *adjective* "hep TAGGA n'll"

heptahedron *noun*
• "hepta HEED r'n"
• a solid figure with seven faces.
• [Greek *hepta* seven + *hedra* base]
• **heptahedral** *adjective*

heptameter *noun*
• "hep TAMMA tur"
• a line or verse of seven metrical feet.
• [Latin *heptametrum* from Greek (*hepta* seven + *metron* measure)]

heptane *noun*
• "HEP tane"
• a liquid hydrocarbon of the alkane series, obtained from petroleum.
• [Greek *hepta* seven]

heptarchy *noun*
• "HEP tarky"
• government by seven rulers.
• [Greek *hepta* seven + *arkhō* rule]
• **heptarchic** *adjective*
• **heptarchical** *adjective*

Heptateuch *noun*
• "HEPTA tuke" or "HEPTA tyuke"
• the first seven books of the Bible.
• [Latin from Greek from *hepta* seven + *teukhos* book, volume]

heptathlon *noun*
• "hep TATH lon"
• an athletic contest, usu. for women, in which each competitor takes part in seven events.
• [Greek *hepta* seven, on the pattern of DECATHLON]
• **heptathlete** *noun*

heptavalent *adjective*
• "hepta VALE 'nt"
• having a valence of seven.
• [Greek *hepta* seven + VALENCE]

herb *noun*
• "HURB" or "URB"
• any plant with leaves, seeds, or flowers used for flavouring, food, medicine, scent, etc.
• [Old French *erbe* from Latin *herba* grass, green crops, herb]
• **herblike** *adjective*

herbaceous *adjective*
- "hur BAY sh'ss"
- (of a plant) not woody or not having a woody stem.
- [Latin *herbaceus* grassy, from *herba* grass, green crops, herb + adjective suffix *-aceus* of the nature of]
- **herbaceousness** *noun*

herbage *noun*
- "HURB idge" or "URB idge"
- herbs collectively.
- [Old French *erbage* from medieval Latin *herbaticum, herbagium* right of pasture, from Latin *herba* herb]

herbarium *noun*
- "hur BERRY um" or "ur BERRY um"
- a systematically arranged collection of dried plants.
- [as HERB + Latin *-arium*, neuter of adjectives in *-arius*]

herbicide *noun*
- "HURBA side" or "URBA side"
- a substance toxic to plants and used to destroy unwanted vegetation.
- [HERB + Latin *-cida, -cidium* from *caedere* kill]
- **herbicidal** *adjective*

herbivore *noun*
- "HURBA vore"
- an animal that feeds on plants.
- [Latin *herba* herb + *-vorus* from *vorare* devour]
- **herbivorous** *adjective* "hur BIVVER us"

herbology *noun*
- "hur BOLLA jee" or "ur BOLLA jee"
- the use of herbs to treat disease.
- [as HERB + *logos* word]
- **herbologist** *noun*

Hercules *noun*
- "HUR kyoo leez"
- a man of exceptional strength or size.
- [from the legendary hero *Hercules*, known for his great strength]
- **Herculean** *adjective* "hur kyoo LEE 'n" or "hur KYOO lee 'n"

Hercynian *adjective*
- "hur SINNY 'n"
- designating a time during which mountains were formed in the eastern hemisphere during the late Paleozoic era.
- [Latin *Hercynia silva* forested mountains of central Germany]

hereditable *adjective*
- "huh REDDA tuh bull"
- that can be inherited.
- [obsolete French *héréditable* or medieval Latin *hereditabilis* from Church Latin *hereditare* from Latin *heres -edis* heir]

hereditament *noun*
- "hare a DITTA m'nt" or "huh REDDA tuh m'nt"
- anything, esp. property, that can be inherited.
- [medieval Latin *hereditamentum* (as HEREDITABLE)]

hereditary *adjective*
- "huh REDDA terry"
- (of a characteristic, disease, etc.) able to be passed down from one generation to another.
- [Latin *hereditarius* (as HEREDITY)]
- **hereditarily** *adverb*

heredity *noun*
- "huh REDDA tee"
- the passing on of physical or mental characteristics genetically from one generation to another.
- [French *hérédité* or Latin *hereditas* heirship (as HEIR)]

Hereford *noun*
- "HUR furd" or "HARE a furd"
- an animal of a breed of red and white beef cattle.
- [*Hereford* in west central England, where it originated]

Herero *noun*
- "huh RERRO" or "huh REERO"
- a member of any of several peoples, speaking a Bantu language, of Namibia, Angola, and Botswana.
- [Herero]

heresiarch *noun*
- "huh REEZY ark"
- the leader or founder of a heresy.
- [Church Latin *haeresiarcha* from Greek *hairesiarkhēs* (as HERESY + *arkhēs* ruler)]

heresy *noun*
- "HARE a see"
- belief or practice contrary to the orthodox doctrine of a given religion.
- [Old French *(h)eresie*, from Church Latin *haeresis*, in Latin = school of thought, from Greek *hairesis* choice, sect, from *haireomai* choose]

heretic *noun*
- "HARE a tick"
- the holder of an unorthodox opinion in a subject, field, etc.
- [Old French *heretique* from Church Latin *haereticus* from Greek *hairetikos* able to choose (as HERESY)]
- **heretical** *adjective* "huh RETTA k'll"
- **heretically** *adverb*

heretofore *adverb*
- "heer too FOR"
- formerly, before this time.
- ['here' + 'to' + FORE]

heritable *adjective*
- "HARE a tuh bull"
- (of property) capable of being inherited by heirs-at-law.
- [Old French from *heriter* from Church Latin *hereditare*: see HEREDITABLE]
- **heritability** *noun*

heritage *noun*
• "HARE a tidge"
• things such as works of art, cultural achievements and folklore that have been passed on from earlier generations.
• [Old French (as HERITABLE)]

herm *noun*
• "HURM"
• a squared stone pillar with a head (esp. of Hermes) on top, used in ancient times as a boundary marker, signpost, etc.
• [Latin *Herma* from Greek *Hermes*, the messenger of the gods]

hermaphrodite *noun*
• "hur MAFFRA dite"
• an animal normally having both male and female sexual organs, e.g. many snails and earthworms.
• [*Hermaphroditus*, the son of Hermes and Aphrodite, who became joined with the nymph Salmacis in one body which retained characteristics of either sex]
• **hermaphroditic** *adjective* "hur maffra DITTIC"
• **hermaphroditism** *noun*

hermeneutics *noun*
• "hurma NOOTIX" or "hurma NYOOTIX"
• the branch of knowledge that deals with interpretation and the theories of interpretation, esp. of Scripture or literary texts.
• [Greek *hermēneutikos* from *hermēneuō* interpret]
• **hermeneutic** *adjective*
• **hermeneutical** *adjective*
• **hermeneutically** *adverb*

hermetic *adjective*
• "hur METTIC"
• completely airtight.
• [modern Latin *hermeticus* from *Hermes Trismegistus* 'thrice-greatest Hermes' (as the founder of alchemy)]
• **hermetical** *adjective*
• **hermetically** *adverb*
• **hermeticism** *noun* "hur METTA sizm"

hernia *noun*
• "HURNY uh"
• a rupture or the abnormal displacement and protrusion of part of an organ through the wall of the cavity containing it, esp. of the abdomen.
• [Latin]
• **herniated** *adjective* "HURNY ated"
• **herniation** *noun*

heroin *noun*
• "HARE oh in"
• a highly addictive white crystalline analgesic drug derived from morphine, often used as a narcotic.
• [German, from *heroisch* heroic (from Latin *heros* from Greek *hērōs* hero), from its effects on the user's self-esteem]
HOMOPHONES: *heroine*

heroine *noun*
• "HARE oh in"
• a woman noted or admired for nobility, courage, outstanding achievements, etc.
• [Greek *hērōinē*, feminine of *hērōs* hero]
HOMOPHONES: *heroin*

herpes *noun*
• "HUR peez"
• any of several infectious diseases caused by a herpesvirus and characterized by outbreaks of blisters on the skin etc.
• [Greek *herpēs -ētos* shingles, from *herpō* creep]
• **herpetic** *adjective* "hur PETTIC"

herpesvirus *noun*
• "HUR peez vie russ"
• any of a group of related viruses that includes those causing shingles and chicken pox, esp. *Herpesvirus hominis*, the cause of herpes simplex.
• [as HERPES + VIRUS]

herpetology *noun*
• "hurpa TOLLA jee"
• the branch of zoology concerned with the study of reptiles and amphibians.
• [Greek *herpeton* reptile, from *herpō* creep + *logos* word]
• **herpetological** *adjective*
• **herpetologist** *noun*

herring *noun*
• "HARE ing"
• any of various chiefly marine fishes of the family Clupeidae, which form shoals in coastal waters at spawning time, including several important food fishes esp. *Clupea harengus* of the N Atlantic or *C. pallasi* of the N Pacific.
• [Old English *hǣring, hēring* from West Germanic]

herringbone *noun*
• "HARE ing bone"
• any zigzag pattern or arrangement resembling the pattern of a herring's bones, as of stones, bricks, tiles, etc.
• [as HERRING + 'bone']

hertz *noun*
• "HURTS"
• the SI unit of frequency, equal to one cycle per second.
• [H. R. *Hertz*, German physicist d.1894]

Hertzian *adjective*
• "HURTS ee 'n"
• designating an electromagnetic wave of a length suitable for use in radio.
• [as HERTZ]

Herzegovinian *noun*
• "hurts a guh VEENY 'n"
• a native or inhabitant of Herzegovina, the southern part of Bosnia and Herzegovina in SE Europe.

hesitate *verb*
- "HEZZA tate"
- show or feel indecision or uncertainty; pause in doubt.
- [Latin *haesitare* frequentative of *haerēre haes-* stick fast]
- **hesitance** *noun*
- **hesitancy** *noun*
- **hesitant** *adjective*
- **hesitantly** *adverb*
- **hesitatingly** *adverb*
- **hesitation** *noun*

Hesperian *adjective*
- "hess PEERY 'n"
- western.
- [Latin *Hesperius* from Greek *Hesperios* as *hesperos* western, evening (star)]

Hesquiaht *noun*
- "HESS kwit"
- a member of a Nuu-chah-nulth Aboriginal group living on the west coast of Vancouver Island.
- [Hesquiaht, 'people who eat herring eggs off eel grass']

Hessian *noun*
- "HESH'n"
- coarse canvas esp. of jute used for sacking etc; burlap.
- [*Hesse*, a state of W Germany]

hetaera *noun*
- "huh TEERA"
- a courtesan or mistress, esp. in ancient Greece.
- [Greek *hetaira*, feminine of *hetairos* companion]

heteroclite *adjective*
- "HETTER a clite"
- abnormal.
- [Late Latin *heteroclitus* from Greek (*heteros* other, *klitos* from *klinō* bend, inflect)]
- **heteroclitic** *adjective* "hetter a CLITTIC"

heterocyclic *adjective*
- "hetter a SIKE lick" or "hetter a SICK lick"
- (of a compound) with a bonded ring of atoms of more than one kind.
- [Greek *heteros* other + CYCLE]

heterodox *adjective*
- "HETTER a dox"
- (of a person, opinion, etc.) not orthodox.
- [Late Latin *heterodoxus* from Greek (*heteros* other, *doxos* from *doxa* opinion)]
- **heterodoxy** *noun*

heterodyne *adjective*
- "HETTER a dine"
- relating to the production of a lower radio frequency from the combination of two almost equal high radio frequencies.
- [Greek *heteros* other + DYNE]

heterogeneous *adjective*
- "hetter a JEENY us"
- diverse in character.
- [medieval Latin *heterogeneus* from Greek *heterogenēs* (*heteros* other, *genos* kind)]
- **heterogeneity** *noun* "hetter a juh NAY a tee"
- **heterogeneously** *adverb*
- **heterogeneousness** *noun*

heterologous *adjective*
- "hetter OLLA guss"
- not homologous.
- [Greek *heteros* other + *logos* ratio, proportion]
- **heterology** *noun*

heteromorphism *noun*
- "hetter oh MORF izm"
- the quality or condition of existing in various forms.
- [Greek *heteros* other + *morphē* form]
- **heteromorphic** *adjective*
- **heteromorphous** *adjective*

heteronomous *adjective*
- "hetter ONNA muss"
- subject to an external law.
- [Greek *heteros* other + *nomos* law]
- **heteronomy** *noun*

heteropolar *adjective*
- "hetter oh POLE ur"
- having dissimilar poles, esp. with an armature passing north and south magnetic poles alternately.
- [Greek *heteros* other + POLAR]

heteropteran *noun*
- "hetter OPTER 'n"
- any insect of the suborder Heteroptera with non-uniform forewings having a thickened base and membranous tip.
- [Greek *heteros* other + *pteron* wing]
- **heteropterous** *adjective*

heterosexism *noun*
- "hetter oh SEX izm"
- discrimination or prejudice by heterosexuals against or towards homosexuals.
- [Greek *heteros* other + Old French *sexe* or Latin *sexus* sex]
- **heterosexist** *adjective*

heterosexual *adjective*
- "hetter oh SECK shoo 'll"
- feeling or involving sexual attraction to persons of the opposite sex.
- [as HETEROSEXISM]
- **heterosexuality** *noun*
- **heterosexually** *adverb*

heterotrophic *adjective*
- "hetter oh TROFFIC"
- deriving its nourishment and carbon requirements from organic substances; not autotrophic.
- [Greek *heteros* other + *trophos* feeder]

heterozygote *noun*
• "hetter oh ZYE gote"
• an individual having two different alleles of a particular gene or genes, and so giving rise to varying offspring.
• [Greek *heteros* other + ZYGOTE]
• **heterozygous** *adjective*

hetman *noun*
• "HET m'n"
• a Polish or Cossack military commander.
• [Polish, prob. from German *Hauptmann* captain]

heuchera *noun*
• "HYOO kur uh"
• any N American herbaceous plant of the genus *Heuchera*, with dark green round or heart-shaped leaves and tiny flowers.
• [modern Latin from J. H. von *Heucher*, German botanist d.1747]

heuristic *adjective*
• "hure ISTIC"
• allowing or assisting to discover.
• [Greek *heuriskō* find]
• **heuristically** *adverb*

hevea *noun*
• "HEEVY uh"
• any S American tree of the genus *Hevea*, yielding a milky sap used for making rubber.
• [modern Latin from Quechua *hyeve*]

hew *verb*
• "HYOO"
• chop or cut (a thing) with an axe, a sword, etc.
• [Old English *hēawan* from Germanic]
HOMOPHONES: *hue*

hexachord *noun*
• "HEXA cord"
• a diatonic series of six notes with a semitone between the third and fourth, used at three different pitches in medieval music.
• [Greek *hex* six + CHORD]

hexadecimal *adjective*
• "hexa DESSA m'll"
• relating to or using a system of numerical notation that has 16 rather than 10 as a base.
• [Greek *hex* six + DECIMAL]

hexagon *noun*
• "HEXA gon"
• a plane figure with six sides and angles.
• [Greek *hex* six + *-gonos* -angled]
• **hexagonal** *adjective* "hex AGGA n'll"
• **hexagonally** *adverb*

hexagram *noun*
• "HEXA gram"
• a figure formed by two intersecting equilateral triangles.
• [Greek *hex* six + *gramma* thing written]

hexahedron *noun*
• "hexa HEED r'n"
• a solid figure with six faces.
• [Greek *hex* six + *hedra* base]
• **hexahedral** *adjective*

hexameter *noun*
• "hex AMMA tur"
• a line or verse of six metrical feet.
• [Greek *hex* six + *metron* measure]
• **hexametric** *adjective* "hexa METRIC"

hexane *noun*
• "HEX ane"
• a liquid hydrocarbon of the alkane series.
• [Greek *hex* six + ALKANE]

hexapod *noun*
• "HEXA pod"
• any arthropod with six legs; an insect.
• [Greek *hexapous, hexapod-* (*hex* six, *pous pod-* foot)]

Hexateuch *noun*
• "HEXA tuke" or "HEXA tyuke"
• the first six books of the Old Testament.
• [Greek *hex* six + *teukhos* book]

hexavalent *adjective*
• "hexa VALE 'nt"
• having a valence of six.
• [Greek *hex* six + VALENCE]

hexose *noun*
• "HEX ose" (rhymes with *GROSS*)
• a monosaccharide with six carbon atoms in each molecule, e.g. glucose or fructose.
• [Greek *hex* six + ending of GLUCOSE]

heyday *noun*
• "HAY day"
• the flush or full bloom of youth, vigour, prosperity, etc.
• [archaic *heyday* expression of joy, surprise, etc.: compare Low German *heidi, heida*, exclamation denoting gaiety]

hiatus *noun*
• "hy AY tuss"
• a break or gap, esp. in a series, account, or chain of proof.
• [Latin, = gaping, from *hiare* gape]

hibachi *noun*
• "huh BOTCH ee" or "huh BATCH ee"
• a small, portable charcoal brazier with a grill.
• [Japanese, from *hi* fire + *hachi* bowl, pot]

hibernaculum *noun*
• "hy bur NACK yuh lum"
• a structure which protects a plant or animal during hibernation.
• [as HIBERNATE + Latin *-culus, -culum* forming diminutives]

hibernate *verb*
• "HY bur nate"
• (of some animals) spend the winter in a dormant state.
• [Latin *hibernare* from *hibernus* wintry]
• **hibernation** *noun*
• **hibernator** *noun*

Hibernian *adjective*
- "hy BURNY 'n"
- of or concerning Ireland.
- [Latin *Hibernia, Iverna* from Greek *Iernē* from Old Celtic]

hibiscus *noun*
- "hib ISS cuss" or "hy BISS cuss"
- any plant of the genus *Hibiscus*, often cultivated for its large bright-coloured flowers.
- [Latin from Greek *hibiskos* marsh mallow]

hiccup *noun*
- "HICKUP"
- an involuntary spasm of the diaphragm and respiratory organs, with sudden closure of the glottis and characteristic cough-like sound.
- [imitative]
- **hiccupy** *adjective*

hickory *noun*
- "HICKER ee"
- any N American tree of the genus *Carya*, yielding tough heavy wood, and bearing sometimes edible nuts.
- [earlier *pohickery*, from Virginia Algonquian *pocohiquara* milky drink prepared from hickory nuts]

hidalgo *noun*
- "hid ALGO"
- a Spanish gentleman.
- [Spanish from *hijo dalgo* 'son of something' (i.e. of an important person)]

hideous *adjective*
- "HIDDY us"
- frightful, repulsive, or revolting, to the senses or the mind.
- [Old French *hideus*, from Old French *hide* fear, of unknown origin]
- **hideosity** *noun* "hiddy OSSA tee"
- **hideously** *adverb*
- **hideousness** *noun*

hie *verb*
- "HY"
- go quickly.
- [Old English *hīgian* strive, pant, of unknown origin]

HOMOPHONES: *hi, high*

hierarch *noun*
- "HIRE ark"
- a chief priest.
- [medieval Latin from Greek *hierarkhēs* from *hieros* sacred + *-arkhēs* ruler]
- **hierarchal** *adjective*

hierarchy *noun*
- "HIRE arky"
- a system in which grades or classes of status or authority are ranked one above the other.
- [as HIERARCH]
- **hierarchic** *adjective* "hire ARKIC"
- **hierarchical** *adjective*
- **hierarchize** *verb* (also esp. *Brit.* **-ise**)

hieratic *adjective*
- "hire ATTIC"
- of or concerning priests.
- [Latin from Greek *hieratikos* from *hieraomai* be a priest, from *hiereus* priest]

hieroglyph *noun*
- "HY ruh gliff"
- a picture of an object representing a word, syllable, or sound, as used in ancient Egyptian and other writing.
- [back-formation from 'hieroglyphic', from Greek *hieroglyphikos* (*hieros* sacred, *gluphikos* from *gluphē* carving)]
- **hieroglyphic** *adjective* "hy ruh GLIFFIC"

hierophant *noun*
- "HIRE a fant"
- an initiating or presiding priest in ancient Greece; an official interpreter of sacred mysteries.
- [Late Latin *hierophantes* from Greek *hierophantēs* (*hieros* sacred, *phantēs* from *phainō* show)]
- **hierophantic** *adjective*

highfalutin *adjective*
- "hy fuh LOOT'n"
- absurdly pretentious.
- ['high' + *fluting* present participle of 'flute']

hijab *noun*
- "hidge OB" or "hidge AB"
- a veil worn by some Muslim women to cover the hair, forehead, etc.
- [Arabic]

hilarious *adjective*
- "huh LERRY us"
- exceedingly funny.
- [Latin *hilaris* from Greek *hilaros* cheerful]
- **hilariously** *adverb*
- **hilariousness** *noun*
- **hilarity** *noun*

hillock *noun*
- "HILL uck"
- a small hill or mound.
- [diminutive of 'hill']
- **hillocky** *adjective*

hilum *noun*
- "HY lum"
- the point of attachment of a seed to its seed vessel.
- [Latin, = little thing, trifle]

Himalayan *adjective*
- "himma LAY 'n"
- of or relating to the Himalayas, a vast mountain system in S Asia that includes Mount Everest.

himation *noun*
- "him ATTY 'n"
- the outer garment worn by the ancient Greeks over the left shoulder and under the right.
- [Greek]

Hinayana *noun*
- "heena YONNA"
- a name given by the followers of Mahayana Buddhism to the more orthodox and, as they thought, less central, schools of early Buddhism.
- [Sanskrit from *hīna* lesser + *yāna* vehicle]

Hindi *noun*
- "HIN dee"
- the most widely spoken language of N India.
- [Urdu *hindī* from *Hind* India]

hindrance *noun*
- "HIN drince"
- the act or an instance of hindering.
- [Old English *hindrian* from Germanic]

Hindu *noun*
- "HINDOO"
- a follower of Hinduism.
- [Urdu from Persian from *Hind* India]

Hinduism *noun*
- "HINDOO izm"
- the main religious and social system of India, including a belief in reincarnation, the worship of several gods, and an ordained caste system as the basis of society.
- [as HINDU]
- **Hinduize** *verb* (also esp. *Brit.* **-ise**)

Hindustani *noun*
- "hindoo STANNY"
- a group of mutually intelligible languages and dialects spoken in NW India, principally Hindi and Urdu.
- [Urdu from Persian *hindūstānī* (as HINDU + *-stān* country)]

hippeastrum *noun*
- "hippy ASTRUM"
- any S American bulbous plant of the genus *Hippeastrum* with showy white or red flowers.
- [modern Latin from Greek *hippeus* horseman (the leaves appearing to ride on one another) + *astron* star (from the shape of the flower)]

hippocampus *noun*
- "hippa CAMPUS"
- a sea horse.
- [Latin from Greek *hippokampos* from *hippos* horse + *kampos* sea monster]
- **hippocampal** *adjective*

hippocras *noun*
- "HIPPA crass"
- wine flavoured with spices.
- [Old French *ipocras* Hippocrates (see HIPPOCRATIC), prob. because strained through a filter called 'Hippocrates' sleeve']

Hippocratic *adjective*
- "hippa CRATTIC"
- designating an oath, taken by doctors prior to beginning medical practice, affirming their obligations and proper conduct.
- [medieval Latin *Hippocraticus* from *Hippocrates*, Greek physician d.377 BC, known as the father of modern medicine]

Hippocrene *noun*
- "HIPPA creen"
- poetic or literary inspiration.
- [name of a fountain sacred to the Muses: Latin from Greek *hippos* horse + *krēnē* fountain, as having been produced by a stroke of the winged horse Pegasus' hoof]

hippodrome *noun*
- "HIPPA drome"
- a dance hall.
- [French *hippodrome* or Latin *hippodromus* from Greek *hippodromos* from *hippos* horse + *dromos* race, course]

hippogriff *noun*
ALSO SPELLED: **hippogryph**
- "HIPPA griff"
- a mythical creature with the body and hindquarters of a horse and the wings and head of a griffon.
- [French *hippogriffe* from Italian *ippogrifo* from Greek *hippos* horse + Italian *grifo* GRIFFIN]

hippopotamus *noun*
- "hippa POTTA muss"
- a large thick-skinned four-legged mammal, *Hippopotamus amphibius*, native to Africa, inhabiting rivers, lakes, etc.
- [Latin from Greek *hippopotamos* from *hippos* horse + *potamos* river]

hiragana *noun*
- "heera GANNA"
- the cursive form of Japanese syllabic writing or kana.
- [Japanese, lit. 'plain kana']

hirsute *adjective*
- "hur SUTE"
- hairy, shaggy.
- [Latin *hirsutus*]
- **hirsuteness** *noun*
- **hirsutism** *noun*

Hispanic *adjective*
- "hiss PANNIC"
- of or relating to Spain or to Spanish-speaking countries.
- [Latin *Hispanicus* from *Hispania* Spain]
- **Hispanicize** *verb* (also esp. *Brit.* **-ise**)

Hispanist *noun*
- "HISS p'n ist"
- an expert in or student of the language, literature, and civilization of Spain or Spanish-speaking countries.
- [as HISPANIC]

hispid *adjective*
- "HISS pid"
- bristly; covered with short stiff hairs.
- [Latin *hispidus*]

histamine *noun*
- "HISTA min" or "HISTA meen"
- an amine causing contraction of smooth

muscle and dilation of capillaries, released by most cells in response to injury and in allergic and inflammatory reactions.
• [Greek *histos* web, tissue + AMINE]

histidine *noun*
• "HISTA deen"
• an amino acid present in proteins and from which histamine is derived.
• [Greek *histos* web, tissue]

histochemistry *noun*
• "histo KEMMA stree"
• the study of the identification and distribution of the chemical constituents of tissues by means of stains, indicators, and microscopy.
• [Greek *histos* web, tissue + CHEMISTRY]
• **histochemical** *adjective*

histocompatibility *noun*
• "histo k'm patta BILLA tee"
• compatibility between the tissue of different individuals, so that one accepts a graft from the other without giving an immune reaction.
• [Greek *histos* web, tissue + COMPATIBLE]

histogenesis *noun*
• "hista JENNA sis"
• the production and differentiation of organic tissues.
• [Greek *histos* web, tissue + GENESIS]
• **histogenetic** *adjective* "hista juh NETTIC"

histogram *noun*
• "HISTA gram"
• a chart consisting of rectangles (usu. drawn vertically from a base line) whose areas and positions are proportional to the value or range of a number of variables.
• [Greek *histos* mast + *gramma -atos* thing written]

histology *noun*
• "hiss TOLLA jee"
• the study of the microscopic structure of tissues.
• [Greek *histos* web, tissue + *logos* word]
• **histologic** *adjective*
• **histological** *adjective*
• **histologically** *adjective*
• **histologist** *noun*

histone *noun*
• "HISS tone"
• any of a group of proteins found in chromatin.
• [German *Histon* perhaps from Greek *histamai* arrest, or *histos* web, tissue]

histopathology *noun*
• "histo puh THOLLA jee"
• changes in tissues caused by disease.
• [Greek *histos* web, tissue + PATHOLOGY]
• **histopathologic** *adjective*
• **histopathological** *adjective*
• **histopathologist** *noun*

histoplasmosis *noun*
• "histo plazz MOE sis"
• infection with *Histoplasma capulatum*, a fungus found in the droppings of birds and bats in humid areas, which may be a transient benign infection of the lungs or a disseminated usu. fatal disease of the reticuloendothelial system.
• [Greek *histos* web, tissue + PLASMA]

historiated *adjective*
• "hiss TORY ated"
• decorated with historical, legendary, or emblematic designs.
• [Latin *historia* from Greek *historia* finding out, narrative, history, from *histōr* learned, wise man]

historicism *noun*
• "hiss TORRA sizm"
• the theory that social and cultural phenomena are determined by history.
• [as HISTORIATED]
• **historicist** *noun*

historicity *noun*
• "hista RISSA tee"
• the historical genuineness of an event etc.
• [as HISTORIATED]

historicize *verb*
• "hiss TORA size"
• make or represent as historical.
• [as HISTORIATED]
• **historicization** *noun* (also esp. *Brit.* **-isation**)
• **historicized** *adjective* (also esp. *Brit.* **-ised**)
• **historicizing** *noun* (also esp. *Brit.* **-ising**)

historiography *noun*
• "hiss tory OGGRA fee"
• the writing of history.
• [as HISTORIATED + Greek *graphia* writing]
• **historiographer** *noun*
• **historiographic** *adjective*
• **historiographical** *adjective*
• **historiographically** *adverb*

histrionic *adjective*
• "histry ONNIC"
• (of behaviour) theatrical; dramatically exaggerated.
• [Late Latin *histrionicus* from Latin *histrio -onis* actor]
• **histrionically** *adverb*

Hitchcockian *adjective*
• "hitch COCKY 'n"
• relating to or characteristic of the work of the English director of suspense films, Alfred Hitchcock (d.1980).

hitchhike *verb*
• "HITCH hike"
• travel by seeking free lifts in passing vehicles.
• ['hitch' + 'hike']
• **hitchhiker** *noun*
• **hitchhiking** *noun*

Hittite *noun*
- "HIT ite"
- a member of an ancient, non-Semitic people of Asia Minor and Syria.
- [Hebrew *Ḥittīm*]

Hmong *noun*
- "h'MONG"
- a member of a people living in isolated mountain villages throughout SE Asia.
- [Chinese, self-designation]

hoagie *noun*
ALSO SPELLED: **hoagy**
- "HOE gee" (with "G" as in *GEEK*)
- a sandwich made with a long roll or small loaf and filled with a variety of meats, cheeses, etc.; a sub.
- [origin unknown]

hoar *adjective*
- "HORE"
- grey-haired with age.
- [Old English *hār* from Germanic]

HOMOPHONES: *whore*

hoard *noun*
- "HORD"
- a stock or store (esp. of money) put away.
- [Old English *hord* from Germanic]
- **hoarder** *noun*

HOMOPHONES: *horde*

hoarding *noun*
- "HORDING"
- a temporary board fence erected around a construction site etc.
- [obsolete *hoard* from Anglo-French *h(o)urdis* from Old French *hourd*, *hort*, related to 'hurdle']

hoarfrost *noun*
- "HORE frost"
- frozen water vapour deposited in clear still weather on vegetation etc.
- [as HOAR + 'frost']

hoarse *adjective*
- "HORSE"
- (of the voice) rough and deep; husky; croaking.
- [Old Norse *hārs* (unrecorded) from Germanic]
- **hoarsely** *adverb*
- **hoarseness** *noun*

HOMOPHONES: *horse*

hoary *adjective*
- "HORY"
- (of hair) grey or white with age.
- [as HOAR]
- **hoarily** *adverb*
- **hoariness** *noun*

hoatzin *noun*
- "hoe AT sin"
- a tropical American bird, *Opisthocomus hoatzin*, whose young climb by means of hooked claws on their wings.
- [Latin American Spanish from Nahuatl *uatzin*, prob. imitative]

Hobbesian *adjective*
- "HOBZY 'n"
- of or relating to English philosopher Thomas Hobbes (d.1679).

hobbledehoy *noun*
- "HOBBLE dee hoy"
- a clumsy or awkward youth.
- [16th c.: origin unknown]

hobgoblin *noun*
- "HOB gob lin"
- a mischievous imp or sprite.
- [Middle English *hob*, familiar form of *Rob*, short for *Robin* or *Robert* + GOBLIN]

hocus *verb*
- "HOKE us"
- take in; hoax.
- [obsolete noun *hocus* = 'hocus-pocus' 17th-c. sham Latin for deception]

hodograph *noun*
- "HODDA graff"
- a curve in which the radius vector represents the velocity of a moving particle.
- [Greek *hodos* way + *graphia* writing]

Hogmanay *noun*
- "hog muh NAY"
- New Year's Eve.
- [17th c.: perhaps from Norman French *hoguinané* from Old French *aguillanneuf* (also = new year's gift)]

Hohokam *noun*
- "ho HO k'm"
- an extinct N American Aboriginal people.
- [Uto-Aztecan *hùhukam*, old one]

hoick *verb*
- "HOYK"
- lift or pull, esp. with a jerk.
- [perhaps var. of 'hike']

hoisin *noun*
- "HOY zin"
- a sweet, spicy, dark red sauce made from soybeans, vinegar, sugar, garlic, and various spices, widely used in southern Chinese cooking.
- [Cantonese *hoisin*, seafood, from *hoi* sea + *sin* fresh]

Hokan *noun*
- "HOE k'n"
- a group of languages spoken by certain Aboriginal peoples of California, the US southwest, and Mexico.
- [Hokan *hok* approximate form of 'two']

hokum *noun*
- "HOE k'm"
- sentimental, popular, sensational, or unreal situations, dialogue, etc., in a film or play etc.
- [20th c.: origin unknown]

Holarctic *adjective*
- "hoe LARK tick"
- of, relating to, or found throughout the Nearctic and Palearctic regions considered together as a single zoogeographical region.
- [Greek *holos* whole + ARCTIC]

Holi *noun*
- "HOE lee"
- the Hindu spring festival in honour of Krishna the amorous cowherd.
- [Hindi from Sanskrit *holī*]

HOMOPHONES: *holy, wholly, holey*

holily *adverb*
- "HOLE 'll ee"
- in a holy manner.
- [Old English *hālig* from Germanic, related to 'whole']

holism *noun*
ALSO SPELLED: **wholism**
- "HOLE izm"
- the treating of the whole person including mental and social factors rather than just the symptoms of a disease.
- [Greek *holos* whole]
- **holist** *noun* (also **wholist**)
- **holistic** *adjective* (also **wholistic**)
- **holistically** *adverb* (also **wholistically**)

hollandaise *noun*
- "HOLL'n daze"
- a creamy sauce of melted butter, egg yolks, lemon juice, etc., served esp. with fish or in eggs benedict.
- [French, feminine of *hollandais* Dutch, from *Hollande* Holland]

hollowware *noun*
- "HOLLOW ware"
- hollow articles of metal, china, etc., such as pots, kettles, jugs, etc.
- [Old English *holh* cave, related to 'hole' + WARE]

hollyhock *noun*
- "HOLLY hock"
- a tall plant, *Alcea rosea*, with large showy flowers of various colours.
- [Middle English (originally = marsh mallow) from 'holy' + obsolete *hock* mallow, Old English *hoc*, of unknown origin]

holm *noun*
- "HOME"
- an evergreen oak, *Quercus ilex*, with holly-like young leaves.
- [Middle English alteration of obsolete *holin* from Old English *hole(g)n* holly]

HOMOPHONES: *hom, home*

Holmesian *adjective*
- "HOME zee 'n"
- of, pertaining to, or characteristic of Sherlock Holmes, the brilliant amateur detective in the stories of the Scottish writer Arthur Conan Doyle (d.1930).

holmium *noun*
- "HOLE mee um"
- a soft silvery metallic element of the lanthanide series occurring naturally in apatite.
- [modern Latin from *Holmia* Stockholm, Sweden]

holocaust *noun*
- "HOLLA cost"
- a case of large-scale destruction, esp. by fire or nuclear war.
- [Old French *holocauste* from Late Latin *holocaustum* from Greek *holokauston* (*holos* whole, *kaustos* burned, from *kaiō* burn)]
- **holocaustal** *adjective*

Holocene *adjective*
- "HOLLA seen"
- of or relating to the second epoch of the Quaternary period, following the Pleistocene and lasting from about 10,000 years ago to the present, coinciding with the development of human agricultural settlement and civilization.
- [Greek *holos* whole + *kainos* new]

holoenzyme *noun*
- "hollow EN zime"
- the active complex of an enzyme with a coenzyme.
- [Greek *holos* whole + ENZYME]

hologram *noun*
- "HOLLA gram"
- a three-dimensional image formed by the interference of light beams from a coherent light source.
- [Greek *holos* whole + *gramma -atos* thing written]

holograph *adjective*
- "HOLLA graff"
- wholly written by hand by the person named as the author.
- [Greek *holos* whole + *graphia* writing]

holography *noun*
- "huh LOGGRA fee"
- the study or production of holograms.
- [as HOLOGRAPH]
- **holographic** *adjective*
- **holographically** *adverb*

holohedral *adjective*
- "holla HEED rull"
- having the full number of planes required by the symmetry of a crystal system.
- [Greek *holos* whole + *hedra* base]

holophyte *noun*
- "HOLLA fite"
- an organism that synthesizes complex organic compounds by photosynthesis.
- [Greek *holos* whole + *phuton* plant, from *phuō* come into being]
- **holophytic** *adjective* "holla FITTIC"

holothurian *noun*
- "holla THURRY 'n"

• any echinoderm of the class Holothurioidea, with a wormlike body, e.g. a sea cucumber.
• [modern Latin *Holothuria* (n.pl.) from Greek *holothourion*, a zoophyte]

holotype ***noun***
• "HOLLA tipe"
• the specimen used for naming and describing a species.
• [Greek *holos* whole + TYPE]

Holstein ***noun***
• "HOLE steen" or "HOLE stine"
• a large black and white breed of dairy cattle, noted for high milk production.
• [*Holstein* in NW Germany]

holster ***noun***
• "HOLE stur"
• a leather case for a pistol or revolver, worn on a belt or under an arm or fixed to a saddle.
• [17th c., synonymous with Dutch *holster*: origin unknown]

holubtsi ***plural noun***
• "HAUL up chee"
• *Cdn* (esp. *West*) cabbage rolls.
• [Ukrainian]

hom ***noun***
• "HOME"
• a plant yielding an intoxicating drink used in Vedic ritual.
• [Persian *hōm*, *hūm*, Avestan *haoma*]
HOMOPHONES: *holm*, *home*

homage ***noun***
• "HOM idge" or "OM idge"
• acknowledgement of superiority, dutiful reverence.
• [Old French *(h)omage* from medieval Latin *hominaticum* from Latin *homo -minis* man]

hombre ***noun***
• "OMM bray" or "HOM bray"
• a man.
• [Spanish]
HOMOPHONES: *ombré*

homburg ***noun***
• "HOM burg"
• a man's felt hat with a narrow curled brim and a lengthwise dent in the crown.
• [*Homburg* in Germany, where first worn]

homeopathy ***noun***
ALSO SPELLED: *Brit.* **homoeopathy**
• "homey OPPA thee" (with "TH" as in *THIN*)
• the treatment of disease by minute doses of drugs that in a healthy person would produce symptoms of the disease.
• [German *Homöopathie* from Greek *homoios* like + *patheia* suffering]
• **homeopath** ***noun*** (also *Brit.* **homoeopath**) "HOMEY oh path"
• **homeopathic** ***adjective*** (also *Brit.* **homoeopathic**) "homey oh PATHIC"
• **homeopathically** ***adverb*** (also *Brit.* **homoeopathically**)
• **homeopathist** ***noun*** (also *Brit.* **homoeopathist**) "homey OPPA thist"

homeostasis ***noun***
ALSO SPELLED: **homoeostasis**
• "homey oh STAY sis"
• the tendency towards a relatively stable equilibrium between interdependent elements, esp. as maintained by physiological processes.
• [modern Latin, from Greek *homoios* like + STASIS]
• **homeostatic** ***adjective*** (also **homoeostatic**)

homeotherm ***noun***
• "HOMEY oh thurm"
• an organism that maintains its body temperature at a constant level, usu. above that of the environment, by its metabolic activity; a warm-blooded organism.
• [modern Latin from Greek *homoios* like + *thermē* heat]
• **homeothermic** ***adjective***
• **homeothermy** ***noun***

Homeric ***adjective***
• "hoe MARE ick"
• of, or in the style of, the ancient Greek poet Homer or the epic poems ascribed to him (the *Iliad* and the *Odyssey*).

homestead ***noun***
• "HOME sted"
• (historically) an area of public land (usu. a quarter section) granted to a settler in exchange for a small fee, and on certain conditions, usu. that the settler establish a dwelling and cultivate a certain area of land within a specified time.
• [Old English *hāmstede* ('home', *stede* place)]
• **homesteader** ***noun***

homicide ***noun***
• "HOMMA side"
• the killing of a human being by another.
• [Old French from Latin *homicidium* (*Homo* man) + *-cida*, *-cidium* from *caedere* kill]
• **homicidal** ***adjective***

homily ***noun***
• "HOM'll ee"
• a sermon.
• [Greek *homilia* from *homilos* crowd]
• **homiletic** ***adjective*** "homma LETTIC"
• **homiletical** ***adjective***
• **homilist** ***noun***

hominid ***noun***
• "HOM 'n id"
• a primate of the family Hominidae, which includes human beings (*Homo sapiens*), and several fossil forms.
• [modern Latin *Hominidae* from Latin *homo hominis* man]

hominoid *adjective*
- "HOM 'n oid"
- like a human.
- [as HOMINID]

hominy *noun*
- "HOM 'n ee"
- coarsely ground kernels of corn esp. boiled with water or milk.
- [contraction of Virginia Algonquian *uskatahomen*]

homocentric *adjective*
- "homo SENTRIC" or "hommo SENTRIC"
- having the same centre.
- [Greek *homos* same + CENTRE]

homocysteine *noun*
- "homo SISTY een"
- an amino acid which occurs in the body as an intermediate in the metabolism of methionine and cysteine.
- [Greek *homos* same + CYSTEINE]

homogamy *noun*
- "huh MOGGA mee"
- a state in which the flowers of a plant are hermaphrodite or of the same sex.
- [Greek *homogamos* (*homos* same, *gamos* marriage)]
- **homogamous** *adjective*

homogenate *noun*
- "huh MAW j'n ate"
- a suspension produced by homogenizing.
- [as HOMOGENEOUS]

homogeneous *adjective*
- "homma JEENY us" or "home uh JEENY us"
- of the same kind.
- [medieval Latin *homogeneus* from Greek *homogenēs* (*homos* same, *genēs* from *genos* kind)]
- **homogeneity** *noun* "homma juh NAY a tee" or "home uh juh NAY a tee"
- **homogeneously** *adverb*
- **homogeneousness** *noun*

homogenetic *adjective*
- "homo juh NETTIC" or "hommo juh NETTIC"
- having a common descent or origin.
- [Greek *homos* same + GENESIS]

homogenize *verb*
ALSO SPELLED: esp. *Brit.* **-ise**
- "huh MODGE 'n ize"
- make or become homogeneous.
- [as HOMOGENEOUS]
- **homogenization** *noun* (also esp. *Brit.* **-isation**)
- **homogenized** *adjective* (also esp. *Brit.* **-ised**)
- **homogenizer** *noun* (also esp. *Brit.* **-iser**)

homogeny *noun*
- "huh MODGE a nee"
- similarity due to common descent.
- [as HOMOGENEOUS]
- **homogenous** *adjective*

homograft *noun*
- "HOMMA graft"
- a graft of living tissue from one to another of the same species but different genotype.
- [Greek *homos* same + 'graft' from Old French *grafe*, *grefe* from Latin *graphium* from Greek *graphion* stylus, from *graphō* write]

homograph *noun*
- "HOMMA graff"
- a word spelled like another but of different meaning or origin.
- [Greek *homos* same + *graphia* writing]
- **homographic** *adjective*

homologate *verb*
- "huh MOLLA gate"
- acknowledge, admit.
- [medieval Latin *homologare* agree, from Greek *homologeō* (*homos* same, *logos* word)]
- **homologation** *noun*

homologize *verb*
ALSO SPELLED: esp. *Brit.* **-ise**
- "huh MOLLA jize"
- be homologous; correspond.
- [as HOMOLOGOUS]

homologous *adjective*
- "huh MOLLA guss"
- having the same relation, relative position, etc.
- [medieval Latin *homologus* from Greek (*homos* same, *logos* ratio, proportion)]
- **homological** *adjective*
- **homology** *noun* "huh MOLLA jee"

homologue *noun*
ALSO SPELLED: **homolog**
- "HOMMA log"
- a homologous thing.
- [French from Greek *homologon* (neuter adjective) (as HOMOLOGOUS)]

homonym *noun*
- "HOMMA nim"
- a word of the same spelling or sound as another but of different meaning; a homograph or homophone.
- [Latin *homonymum* from Greek *homōnumon* (neuter adjective) (*homos* same, *onoma* name)]
- **homonymic** *adjective*
- **homonymous** *adjective*

homophobia *noun*
- "home uh FOBEY uh"
- a hatred or fear of or prejudice against homosexuals or homosexuality.
- [HOMOSEXUAL + PHOBIA]
- **homophobe** *noun*
- **homophobic** *adjective*

homophone *noun*
- "HOMMA fone"
- a word having the same sound as another but of different meaning or origin (e.g. *pair*, *pear*).
- [Greek *homos* same + *phōnē* voice]

homophonic *adjective*
• "homma FONNIC"
• in unison; characterized by movement of all parts to the same melody.
• [as HOMOPHONE]
• **homophonically** *adverb*
• **homophony** *noun* "hum MOFFA nee"

homopteran *noun*
• "huh MOPTER 'n"
• any insect of the suborder Homoptera, including aphids and cicadas, with wings of uniform texture.
• [Greek *homos* same + *pteron* wing]
• **homopterous** *adjective*

homosexual *adjective*
• "homo SECK shoo 'll"
• feeling or involving sexual attraction to persons of the same sex.
• [Greek *homos* same + Old French *sexe* or Latin *sexus* sex]
• **homosexuality** *noun*
• **homosexually** *adverb*

homosocial *adjective*
• "homo SO sh'll"
• of or relating to social interaction between members of the same sex, typically men.
• [Greek *homos* same + SOCIAL]

homozygote *noun*
• "homo ZYE gote"
• an individual having two identical alleles of a particular gene or genes and so breeding true for the corresponding characteristic.
• [Greek *homos* same + ZYGOTE]
• **homozygosity** *noun* "homo zye GOSSA tee"
• **homozygous** *adjective*

homunculus *noun*
• "huh MUNK yoo luss"
• a small person.
• [Latin *homunculus* from *homo -minis* man]

honest *adjective*
• "ONNIST"
• fair and just in character or behaviour, not cheating or stealing.
• [Old French *(h)oneste* from Latin *honestus* from *honos* HONOUR]
• **honestly** *adverb*
• **honesty** *noun*

honorand *noun*
• "ONNER and"
• a person to be honoured, esp. with an honorary degree.
• [Latin *honorandus* (as HONOUR)]

honorarium *noun*
• "onner AIRY um"
• a fee, esp. a voluntary payment for professional services rendered without the normal fee.
• [Latin, neuter of *honorarius*: see HONORARY]

honorary *adjective*
ALSO SPELLED: **honourary**
• "ONNER airy"
• conferred as an honour, without the usual requirements, functions, etc.
• [Latin *honorarius* (as HONOUR)]

honorific *adjective*
• "onna RIFFIC"
• conferring honour.
• [Latin *honorificus* (as HONOUR)]
• **honorifically** *adverb*

honour *noun*
ALSO SPELLED: **honor**
• "ONNER"
• high respect; glory; credit, reputation, good name.
• [Old French *(h)onor* (n.), *onorer* (v.) from Latin *honor, honorare*]
• **honourable** *adjective* (also **honorable**)
• **honourableness** *noun* (also **honorableness**)
• **honourably** *adverb* (also **honorably**)

hookah *noun*
• "HOOKA"
• an oriental tobacco pipe with a long tube passing through water for cooling the smoke as it is drawn through.
• [Urdu from Arabic *ḥuḳḳah* casket]

hooligan *noun*
• "HOOLA g'n"
• a noisy and violent person.
• [19th c.: perhaps from *Hooligan*, surname of a fictional rowdy Irish family]
• **hooliganism** *noun*

hoopoe *noun*
• "HOO poo"
• a salmon-pink Eurasian bird, *Upupa epops*, with black and white wings and tail, a large erectile crest, and a long downward-curving bill.
• [alteration of Middle English *hoop* from Old French *huppe* from Latin *upupa*, imitative of its cry]

hoosegow *noun*
• "HOOSE gow" ("HOOSE" rhymes with *MOOSE*; "gow" rhymes with *COW*)
• a prison.
• [Latin American Spanish *juzgao*, Spanish *juzgado* tribunal, from Latin *judicatum* neuter past participle of *judicare* judge]

Hoosier *noun*
• "HOO zhur"
• a native or inhabitant of the state of Indiana (used as a nickname).
• [origin unknown]

hootenanny *noun*
• "HOOT 'n annie"
• an informal gathering with folk music.
• [originally dialect, = 'gadget']

hopak *noun*
• "HOE pack"
• a lively Ukrainian dance in 2/4 time.
• [Ukrainian, from *hop*, interjection uttered during the dance]

Hopi *noun*
• "HOPEY"
• a member of a N American Aboriginal people living chiefly in NE Arizona.
• [Hopi]

hoplite *noun*
• "HOP lite"
• a heavily-armed foot soldier of ancient Greece.
• [Greek *hoplitēs* from *hoplon* weapon]

hora *noun*
• "HORA"
• a Jewish and Romanian traditional dance in which the dancers form a circle.
• [Hebrew *hōrāh*, Romanian *horă*]

horde *noun*
• "HORD"
• a large group, a gang.
• [Polish *horda* from Turkic *ordī*, *ordū* camp: compare URDU]
HOMOPHONES: *hoard*

horehound *noun*
• "HORE hound"
• a herbaceous plant, *Marrubium vulgare*, with a white cottony covering on its stem and leaves.
• [Old English *hāre hūne* from *hār* HOAR + *hūne* a plant]

horizon *noun*
• "huh RIZE 'n"
• the line at which the earth and sky appear to meet.
• [Old French *orizon(te)* from Late Latin *horizon -ontis* from Greek *horizōn* (*kuklos*) limiting (circle)]
• **horizonless** *adjective*

horizontal *adjective*
• "hora ZONT'll"
• parallel to the plane of the horizon, at right angles to the vertical.
• [French *horizontal* or modern Latin *horizontalis* (as HORIZON)]
• **horizontality** *noun*
• **horizontally** *adverb*

hormone *noun*
• "HORE mone"
• a regulatory substance produced in an organism and transported in tissue fluids such as blood or sap to stimulate cells or tissues into action.
• [Greek *hormōn* participle of *hormaō* impel]
• **hormonal** *adjective*
• **hormonally** *adverb*

hornblende *noun*
• "HORN blend"
• a dark brown, black, or green mineral occurring in many igneous and metamorphic rocks, and composed of calcium, magnesium, and iron silicates.
• [German (as 'horn', BLENDE)]

hornfels *noun*
• "HORN felz"
• a dark fine-grained metamorphic rock composed mainly of quartz, mica, and feldspars.
• [German, lit. = 'horned rock']

hornswoggle *verb*
• "HORN swog'll"
• cheat, hoax.
• [19th c.: origin unknown]
• **hornswoggler** *noun*

hornwort *noun*
• "HORN wurt" or "HORN wort"
• any aquatic rootless plant of the genus *Ceratophyllum*, with forked leaves.
• ['horn' + WORT]

horology *noun*
• "huh ROLLA jee"
• the art of measuring time or making clocks, watches, etc.; the study of this.
• [Greek *hōra* time + *logos* word]
• **horological** *adjective*
• **horologist** *noun*

horoscope *noun*
• "HORA scope"
• a forecast of a person's future based on a diagram showing the relative positions of the stars and planets at a particular time, e.g. the time of that person's birth.
• [French from Latin *horoscopus* from Greek *hōroskopos* from *hōra* time + *skopos* observer]
• **horoscopic** *adjective* "hora SCOPPIC"
• **horoscopy** *noun* "huh ROSCA pee"

horrendous *adjective*
• "huh REND us"
• horrifying; awful.
• [Latin *horrendus* gerundive of *horrēre*: see HORRID]
• **horrendously** *adverb*

horrible *adjective*
• "HORRA bull"
• causing or likely to cause horror; hideous, shocking.
• [Old French *(h)orrible* from Latin *horribilis* from *horrēre*: see HORRID]
• **horribleness** *noun*
• **horribly** *adverb*

horrid *adjective*
• "HORRID"
• horrible, revolting.
• [Latin *horridus* from *horrēre* bristle, shudder]
• **horridly** *adverb*
• **horridness** *noun*

horrific *adjective*
• "hor IFFIC"
• arousing horror; shocking, scandalizing.

• [French *horrifique* or Latin *horrificus* from *horrēre*: see HORRID]
• **horrifically** *adverb*
• **horrify** *verb*
• **horrifying** *adjective*
• **horrifyingly** *adverb*

horripilation *noun*
• "horra puh LAY sh'n"
• goosebumps.
• [Late Latin *horripilatio* from Latin *horrēre* to bristle + *pilus* hair]

horror *noun*
• "HORRER"
• an intense feeling of loathing and fear.
• [Old French *(h)orrour* from Latin *horror -oris* (as HORRID)]

horseleech *noun*
• "HORSE leech"
• a large freshwater leech of the genus *Haemopis*, feeding by swallowing not sucking.
• ['horse' + LEECH]

horst *noun*
• "HORST"
• a raised elongated block of land bounded by faults on both sides.
• [German, = heap]

hortative *adjective*
• "HORTA tiv"
• tending or serving to exhort.
• [Latin *hortativus* from *hortari* exhort]

hortatory *adjective*
• "HORTA tory"
• tending or serving to exhort.
• [Latin *hortari* exhort]

hortensia *noun*
• "hor TENSY uh"
• a kind of hydrangea, *Hydrangea macrophylla*, with large rounded infertile flower heads.
• [modern Latin from *Hortense* Lepaute, 18th-c. Frenchwoman]

horticulture *noun*
• "HORTA cull chur"
• the art or science of garden cultivation.
• [Latin *hortus* garden, after AGRICULTURE]
• **horticultural** *adjective*
• **horticulturalist** *noun*
• **horticulturally** *adverb*
• **horticulturist** *noun*

hosanna *noun*
• "hoe ZANNA"
• (in Biblical, Judaic, and Christian use) a shout of adoration.
• [Greek *hōsanna* from Hebrew *hôšaʿnā* for *hôšîʿa-nnâ* save now!]

hosiery *noun*
• "HOE zur ee" or "HOE zhur ee"
• stockings and socks collectively.
• [Old English *hosa* leggings, stockings]

hospice *noun*
• "HOSS piss"
• a home for people who are ill (esp. terminally).
• [French from Latin *hospitium* from *hospes -pitis* host, guest]

hospitable *adjective*
• "hoss PITTA bull" or "HOSPA tuh bull"
• giving or disposed to give welcome and entertainment to strangers or guests.
• [French from *hospiter* from medieval Latin *hospitare* entertain, from *hospes -pitis* host, guest]
• **hospitably** *adverb*

hosta *noun*
• "HOSS tuh"
• any perennial garden plant of the genus *Hosta* (formerly *Funkia*) with green or variegated ornamental leaves and loose clusters of tubular mauve or white flowers.
• [modern Latin, from N. T. *Host*, Austrian physician d.1834]

hostage *noun*
• "HOSS tidge"
• a person seized or held as security for the fulfillment of a condition.
• [Old French *(h)ostage* ultimately from Late Latin *obsidatus* 'the state of being a hostage' from Latin *obses obsidis* hostage]
• **hostageship** *noun*

hostel *noun*
• "HOSS t'll"
• a place providing temporary accommodation for the homeless etc.
• [Old French *(h)ostel* from medieval Latin *hospitale* neuter of Latin *hospitalis* (adjective) from *hospes -pitis* host, guest]
HOMOPHONES: *hostile*

hostelling *noun*
ALSO SPELLED: esp. *US* **hosteling**
• "HOSS t'll ing"
• the practice of staying in youth hostels, esp. while travelling.
• [as HOSTEL]
• **hosteller** *noun* (also esp. *US* **hosteler**)

hostelry *noun*
• "HOSS t'll ree"
• an inn.
• [as HOSTEL]

hostile *adjective*
• "HOSS tile" or "HOSS t'll"
• aggressively opposed; showing strong rejection or dislike.
• [French *hostile* or Latin *hostilis* from *hostis* stranger, enemy]
• **hostilely** *adverb*
• **hostility** *noun*
HOMOPHONES: *hostel*

hostler *noun*
• "HOSS lur" or "OSS lur"
• a stableman at an inn.

• [Middle English from *hosteler* from Anglo-French *hostiler*, Old French *(h)ostelier* (as HOSTEL)]

hotelier *noun*
• "hoe TELLY ur"
• a person who owns or manages a hotel.
• [French *hôtelier* from Old French *hostelier*: see HOSTEL]

Houdini *noun*
• "hoo DEENY"
• an ingenious escape.
• [H. *Houdini*, Hungarian-born US escape artist d.1926]

houngan *noun*
• "HOONG g'n"
• a voodoo priest.
• [Fon *hun* voodoo deity + *ga* chief]

houri *noun*
• "HOORY"
• a beautiful young woman, esp. in the Muslim Paradise.
• [French via Persian *ḥūrī* from Arabic *ḥūr* pl. of *ḥawra'* gazelle-like (of the eyes)]
HOMOPHONES: *hurry*

housecarl *noun*
ALSO SPELLED: **housecarle**
• "HOUSE carl"
• (historically) a member of the bodyguard of a Danish or English king or noble.
• [Old English *húscarl* from Old Norse *húskarl* from *hús* house + *karl* man]

houseleek *noun*
• "HOUSE leek"
• a plant, *Sempervivum tectorum*, with pink flowers and fleshy leaves, cultivated in gardens and as a houseplant.
• ['house' + LEEK]

housewifery *noun*
• "HOUSE wiffer ee"
• housekeeping.
• ['house' + 'wife']

hovel *noun*
• "HUV'll" or "HOV'll"
• a small miserable dwelling.
• [Middle English: origin unknown]

hover *verb*
• "HUVVER"
• (of a bird, insect, etc.) hang suspended in the air, esp. with a fluttering or wavering movement, by rapidly beating the wings.
• [Middle English from obsolete *hove* hover, linger]
• **hoverer** *noun*

hovercraft *noun*
• "HUVVER craft"
• a vehicle that travels over land or water supported on a cushion of air produced by jet engines.
• [as HOVER + 'craft']

hoverfly *noun*
• "HUVVER fly"
• any fly of the dipteran family Syrphidae, the members of which resemble wasps but are stingless and often hover in the air.
• [as HOVER + 'fly']

hoverport *noun*
• "HUVVER port"
• a terminal for hovercraft.
• [HOVERCRAFT + 'port']

howdah *noun*
• "HOW duh"
• a seat for two or more, usu. with a canopy, for riding on the back of an elephant.
• [Urdu *hawda* from Arabic *hawdaj* litter]

howitzer *noun*
• "HOW itz ur"
• a short, relatively light gun for high-angle firing of shells at low velocities.
• [Dutch *houwitser* from German *Haubitze* from Czech *houfnice* catapult]

hoya *noun*
• "HOY uh"
• any climbing shrub of the genus *Hoya*, with pink, white, or yellow waxy flowers.
• [modern Latin from T. *Hoy*, English gardener d.1821]

hoyden *noun*
• "HOY d'n"
• a boisterous girl; a tomboy.
• [originally = rude fellow, prob. from Middle Dutch *heiden* (= HEATHEN)]
• **hoydenish** *adjective*

hryvnya *noun*
ALSO SPELLED: **hryvnia**
• "HRIV nyuh"
• the monetary unit of Ukraine.
• [Ukrainian]

hubbub *noun*
• "HUB ub"
• a confused din, esp. from a crowd of people.
• [perhaps of Irish origin: compare Gaelic *ubub* interjection of contempt, Irish *abú*, used in battle cries]

hubris *noun*
• "HYOO briss"
• arrogant pride or presumption.
• [Greek]
• **hubristic** *adjective*
• **hubristically** *adverb*

hue *noun*
• "HYOO"
• a colour or tint.
• [Old English *hiew*, *hēw* form, beauty, from Germanic: compare Old Norse *hȳ* down on plants]
HOMOPHONES: *hew*

Huguenot *noun*
• "HYOO guh not" or "HYOO guh no"

• a French Protestant in the 16th or 17th c., esp. one persecuted for his or her beliefs or involved in civil war with the Catholic majority.
• [French, assimilation of *eiguenot* (from Dutch *eedgenot* from Swiss German *Eidgenoss* confederate) to the name of a Geneva burgomaster *Hugues*]

Huichol *noun*
• "wee CHOLE"
• a member of a Mexican Indian people.
• [Spanish, from Huichol]

hula *noun*
• "HOOLA"
• a Hawaiian dance with six basic steps and flowing arm movements symbolizing or imitating natural phenomena, historical events, etc.
• [Hawaiian]

hullabaloo *noun*
• "hulla buh LOO"
• an uproar or clamour.
• [18th c.: reduplication of *hallo, hullo*, etc.]

humane *adjective*
• "hyoo MANE" or "yoo MANE"
• benevolent, compassionate.
• [Old French *humain(e)* from Latin *humanus* from *homo* human being]
• **humanely** *adverb*
• **humaneness** *noun*

humanitarian *noun*
• "hyoo manna TERRY 'n" or "yoo manna TERRY 'n"
• a person who seeks to promote human welfare.
• [as HUMANE]
• **humanitarianism** *noun*

Humboldtonian *noun*
• "humbole TONY 'n"
• a resident of Humboldt, Sask.

humectant *adjective*
• "hyoo MECK t'nt"
• retaining or preserving moisture.
• [Latin *(h)umectant-* participle stem of *(h)umectare* moisten, from *umēre* be moist]

humerus *noun*
• "HYOOMER us"
• the bone of the upper arm in humans.
• [Latin, = shoulder]
• **humeral** *adjective*
HOMOPHONES: *humorous, humoral*

humic *adjective*
• "HYOO mick"
• of or consisting of humus.
• [as HUMUS]

humidify *verb*
• "hyoo MIDDA fie"
• make (air etc.) humid or damp.
• [French *humide* or Latin *humidus* from *umēre* be moist]
• **humidification** *noun*
• **humidifier** *noun*

humidistat *noun*
• "hyoo MIDDA stat"
• a machine or device which automatically regulates the humidity of the air in a room or building.
• [as HUMIDITY + Greek *statikos* from *sta-* stand]

humidity *noun*
• "hyoo MIDDA tee"
• the degree of moisture esp. in the atmosphere.
• [French *humide* or Latin *humidus* from *umēre* be moist]

humidor *noun*
• "HYOOMA dore"
• a room or container for keeping cigars or tobacco moist.
• [as HUMIDITY after *cuspidor*]

humiliate *verb*
• "hyoo MILLY ate"
• make humble; injure the dignity or self-respect of.
• [Late Latin *humiliare* from *humilis* lowly, from *humus* ground]
• **humiliating** *adjective*
• **humiliatingly** *adverb*
• **humiliation** *noun*
• **humiliator** *noun*

humility *noun*
• "hyoo MILLA tee"
• humbleness, meekness.
• [Old French *humilité* from Latin *humilitas -tatis* (as HUMILIATE)]

hummus *noun*
ALSO SPELLED: **hommos**
• "HUM us"
• a thick sauce or spread made from ground chickpeas and sesame oil flavoured with lemon and garlic.
• [Turkish *humus* mashed chickpeas]

humongous *adjective*
ALSO SPELLED: **humungous**
• "hyoo MUNG guss"
• huge, enormous.
• [20th c.: origin unknown]

humoral *adjective*
• "HYOOMER 'll"
• relating to body fluids, esp. as distinct from cells.
• [French *humoral* or medieval Latin *humoralis* from Latin *humor* moisture]
HOMOPHONES: *humeral*

humoresque *noun*
• "hyoomer ESK"
• a short lively piece of music.
• [German *Humoreske* from *Humor* humour]

humorist *noun*
- "HYOOMER ist"
- a person who is known for his or her humorous writing or talking.
- [Anglo-French *umour*, *humour*, Old French *umor*, *humor* from Latin *humor* moisture]
- **humoristic** *adjective*

humorous *adjective*
- "HYOOMER us"
- showing humour or a sense of humour.
- [as HUMORIST]
- **humorously** *adverb*
- **humorousness** *noun*

HOMOPHONES: *humerus*

humus *noun*
- "HYOO muss"
- the organic constituent of soil, usu. formed by the decomposition of plants and leaves by soil bacteria.
- [Latin, = soil]
- **humusy** *adjective*

Huntsvillian *noun*
- "hunts VILLY 'n"
- a resident of Huntsville, Ont.

hurdle *noun*
- "HURD'll"
- each of a series of light frames to be cleared by athletes in a race.
- [Old English *hyrdel* from Germanic]
- **hurdler** *noun*

HOMOPHONES: *hurtle*

hurley *noun*
- "HURLY"
- an Irish game somewhat resembling field hockey, played with broad sticks.
- [from 'hurl' Middle English, prob. imitative, but corresponding in form and partly in sense with Low German *hurreln*]

hurricane *noun*
- "HURRA cane"
- a tropical cyclone with winds greater than 65 knots (75 mph) accompanied by heavy rain, esp. one originating in the western North Atlantic.
- [Spanish *huracan* & Portuguese *furacão*, of Carib origin]

hurtle *verb*
- "HURT'll"
- move or hurl rapidly or with a clattering sound.
- ['hurt' from Old French *hurter*, *hurt*, ultimately perhaps from Germanic, in obsolete sense 'strike forcibly']

HOMOPHONES: *hurdle*

hussar *noun*
- "hoo ZARR" (with "HOO" as in *HOOK*)
- a soldier of a light cavalry regiment.
- [Hungarian *huszár* from Old Serbian *husar* from Italian *corsaro* CORSAIR]

Hussite *noun*
- "HUSS ite"
- a member of the movement begun by John Huss, Bohemian nationalist and religious reformer d.1415.
- **Hussitism** *noun*

hustings *noun*
- "HUSS tings"
- the political campaigning leading up to an election, e.g. canvassing votes and making speeches.
- [late Old English *husting* from Old Norse *hústhing* house of assembly]

Hutterite *noun*
- "HUTTER ite"
- a member of an Anabaptist sect living esp. in rural communal settlements and holding all property in common.
- [Jacob *Hutter*, Moravian Anabaptist d.1536]

Hutu *noun*
- "HOO too"
- a member of a Bantu-speaking people forming the majority population in Rwanda and Burundi.
- [Bantu]

HOMOPHONES: *hoodoo*

huzzah *noun*
- "huh ZAH"
- a shout or cheer; a hurrah.
- [earlier *huzza*, perhaps originally a sailor's cry when hauling: compare German *Hussa* a cry of pursuit and exaltation]

hwyl *noun*
- "HOO ill"
- an emotional quality inspiring impassioned eloquence.
- [Welsh]

hyacinth *noun*
- "HY a sinth"
- any bulbous plant of the genus *Hyacinthus* with racemes of usu. purplish-blue, pink, or white bell-shaped fragrant flowers.
- [French *hyacinthe* from Latin *hyacinthus* from Greek *huakinthos*, also the name of a youth from whose blood Apollo caused the flower to spring up]
- **hyacinthine** *adjective* "hy a SINTH een"

hyalin *noun*
- "HY a lin"
- a clear substance esp. produced as a result of the degeneration of certain body tissues.
- [Greek *hualos* glass]

HOMOPHONES: *hyaline*

hyaline *adjective*
- "HY a lin" or "HY a line" or "HY a leen"
- having a glassy or translucent appearance.
- [Latin *hyalinus* from Greek *hualinos* from *hualos* glass]

HOMOPHONES: *hyalin*

hyaloid *adjective*
• "HY a loid"
• designating a thin transparent membrane enveloping the vitreous humour of the eye.
• [French *hyaloïde* from Late Latin *hyaloides* from Greek *hualoeidēs* like glass, from *hualos* glass]

hyaluronic *adjective*
• "hy 'll yoo RONNIC"
• designating a viscous fluid carbohydrate found in synovial fluid, the vitreous humour of the eye, etc.
• [HYALOID + *-uronic* chemical suffix]

hybrid *noun*
• "HY brid"
• the offspring of two plants or animals of different species or varieties.
• [Latin *hybrida*, *(h)ibrida* offspring of a tame sow and wild boar, child of a freeman and slave, etc.]
• **hybridist** *noun*
• **hybridity** *noun*

hybridize *verb*
ALSO SPELLED: esp. *Brit.* **-ise**
• "HY brid ize"
• subject (a species etc.) to crossbreeding.
• [as HYBRID]
• **hybridizable** *adjective* (also esp. *Brit.* **-isable**)
• **hybridization** *noun* (also esp. *Brit.* **-isation**)
• **hybridizer** *noun* (also esp. *Brit.* **-iser**)

hybridoma *noun*
• "hy brid OH muh"
• a culture of cells produced by hybridization, esp. one in which myeloma cells are hybridized with antibody-producing lymphocytes, used to produce monoclonal antibodies.
• [as HYBRID + MYELOMA]

hydatid *noun*
• "HY duh tid"
• a cyst containing watery fluid (esp. one formed by, and containing, a tapeworm larva).
• [modern Latin *hydatis* from Greek *hudatis -idos* watery vesicle, from *hudōr hudatos* water]
• **hydatidiform** *adjective*

hydra *noun*
• "HY druh"
• a freshwater polyp of the genus *Hydra* with a tubular body and tentacles around the mouth.
• [Latin from Greek *hudra* water snake]

hydrangea *noun*
• "hy DRANE juh" or "hy DRANE jee uh"
• any shrub of the genus *Hydrangea* with large white, pink, or blue flowers.
• [modern Latin from Greek *hudōr* water + *aggos* vessel (from the cup shape of its seed capsule)]

hydrant *noun*
• "HY drint"
• a pipe, usu. on the side of the street, with a valve for drawing water from a main to which a firehose can be attached.
• [as HYDRATE]

hydrate *verb*
• "HY drate"
• cause to absorb water.
• [French from Greek *hudōr* water]
• **hydrated** *adjective*
• **hydration** *noun*
• **hydrator** *noun*

hydraulic *adjective*
• "hy DROLLIC"
• (of water, oil, etc.) conveyed through pipes or channels usu. by pressure.
• [Latin *hydraulicus* from Greek *hudraulikos* from *hudōr* water + *aulos* pipe]
• **hydraulically** *adverb*

hydraulics *noun*
• "hy DROLLIX"
• the science of the conveyance of liquids through pipes etc. esp. as motive power.
• [as HYDRAULIC]

hydrazine *noun*
• "HY druh zeen"
• a colourless alkaline liquid which is a powerful reducing agent and is used as a rocket propellant.
• [HYDROGEN + French *azote* nitrogen, from Greek *azōos* without life]

hydride *noun*
• "HY dride"
• a binary compound of hydrogen with an element, esp. with a metal.
• [as HYDROGEN]

hydro *noun*
• "HYDRO"
• *Cdn* electricity.
• [abbreviation of HYDROELECTRICITY]

hydrobromide *noun*
• "hydro BRO mide"
• a compound formed by the combination of hydrogen bromide and water with an organic radical.
• [HYDROGEN + BROMIDE]
• **hydrobromic** *adjective*

hydrocarbon *noun*
• "hydro CARB'n"
• a compound of hydrogen and carbon.
• [as HYDROGEN + 'carbon' from French *carbone* from Latin *carbo -onis* charcoal]

hydrocele *noun*
• "HYDRO seel"
• the accumulation of serous fluid in a body sac.
• [Greek *hudro-* from *hudōr* water + *kēlē* tumour]

hydrocephalus *noun*
• "hydro SEFFA luss"
• an accumulation of fluid in the brain, esp. in young children, which makes the head enlarge and can cause mental handicap.
• [Greek *hudro-* from *hudōr* water + *kephalē* head]
• **hydrocephalic** *adjective* "hydro suh FALIC"

hydrochloride *noun*
- "hydro CLOR ide"
- a compound of an organic base with hydrochloric acid.
- [HYDROGEN + CHLORIDE]
- **hydrochloric** *adjective*

hydrocortisone *noun*
- "hydro CORTA zone"
- a steroid hormone produced by the adrenal cortex, used medicinally to treat inflammation and rheumatism.
- [HYDROGEN + CORTISONE]

hydrocyanic *adjective*
- "hydro sye ANNIC"
- designating a highly poisonous volatile liquid with a characteristic odour of bitter almonds.
- [HYDROGEN + CYANIDE]

hydrodynamics *noun*
- "hydro die NAMMIX"
- the science of forces acting on or exerted by fluids (esp. liquids).
- [Greek *hudro-* from *hudōr* water + DYNAMIC]
- **hydrodynamic** *adjective*
- **hydrodynamicist** *noun*

"hydro die NAMMA sist"

hydroelectric *adjective*
- "hydro e LECK trick"
- generating electricity by utilization of water power.
- [Greek *hudro-* from *hudōr* water + ELECTRIC]
- **hydroelectricity** *noun*

"hydro e leck TRISSA tee"

hydrofluoric *adjective*
- "hydro FLORIC"
- designating a solution of the colourless liquid hydrogen fluoride in water.
- [Greek *hudro-* from *hudōr* water + FLUORIDE]

hydrofoil *noun*
- "HYDRO foil"
- a boat equipped with a device consisting of planes for lifting its hull out of the water to increase its speed.
- [Greek *hudro-* from *hudōr* water + 'airfoil' a structure with curved surfaces, e.g. a wing, fin, or tailplane, designed to give lift]

hydrogel *noun*
- "HYDRO jell"
- a gel in which the liquid component is water.
- [Greek *hudro-* from *hudōr* water + GEL]

hydrogen *noun*
- "HYDRA j'n"
- a colourless gaseous element, without taste or odour, the lightest of the elements and occurring in water and all organic compounds.
- [French *hydrogène* (as Greek *hudro-* from *hudōr* water + GENESIS)]
- **hydrogenous** *adjective* "hy DRAW j'n uss"

hydrogenase *noun*
- "hy DRAW j'n ace"
- any enzyme that catalyzes the reduction of a substrate by hydrogen, as in some micro-organisms.
- [as HYDROGEN]

hydrogenate *verb*
- "hy DRAW j'n ate"
- charge with or cause to combine with hydrogen.
- [as HYDROGEN]
- **hydrogenation** *noun*

hydrogeology *noun*
- "hydro jee OLLA jee"
- the branch of geology dealing with underground and surface water.
- [Greek *hudro-* from *hudōr* water + GEOLOGY]
- **hydrogeological** *adjective*
- **hydrogeologist** *noun*

hydrography *noun*
- "hy DRAW gruh fee"
- the science of surveying and charting seas, lakes, rivers, etc.
- [Greek *hudro-* from *hudōr* water + *graphia* writing]
- **hydrographer** *noun*
- **hydrographic** *adjective*
- **hydrographically** *adverb*

hydroid *noun*
- "HY droid"
- any usu. polypoid hydrozoan of the order Hydroida, including hydra.
- [as HYDRA]

hydrolase *noun*
- "HYDRO lace"
- any enzyme which catalyzes the hydrolysis of a substrate.
- [as HYDROLYSIS]

hydrology *noun*
- "hy DRAWLA jee"
- the science of the properties of the earth's water, esp. of its movement in relation to land.
- [Greek *hudro-* from *hudōr* water + *logos* word]
- **hydrologic** *adjective*
- **hydrological** *adjective*
- **hydrologist** *noun*

hydrolysis *noun*
- "hy DRAWLA sis"
- the chemical reaction of a substance with water, usu. resulting in decomposition.
- [Greek *hudro-* from *hudōr* water + LYSIS]
- **hydrolytic** *adjective* "hydro LITTIC"
- **hydrolyze** *verb* (also esp *Brit.* **-yse**)

"HYDRO lize"

hydrometer *noun*
- "hy DROMMA tur"
- an instrument for measuring the density of liquids.
- [Greek *hudro-* from *hudōr* water + *metron* measure]
- **hydrometric** *adjective* "hydro METRIC"
- **hydrometry** *noun*

hydropathy *noun*
• "hy DROPPA thee" (with "TH" as in *THIN*)
• the treatment of disorders by external and internal application of water.
• [Greek *hudro-* from *hudōr* water, after HOMEOPATHY]
• **hydropathic** *adjective*

hydrophilic *adjective*
• "hydro FILLIC"
• having an affinity for water.
• [Greek *hudro-* from *hudōr* water + *philos* loving]

hydrophobia *noun*
• "hydro FOBEY uh"
• a morbid aversion to water, esp. as a symptom of rabies in humans.
• [Greek *hudro-* from *hudōr* water + PHOBIA]
• **hydrophobic** *adjective*
• **hydrophobicity** *noun* "hydro foe BISSA tee"

hydrophone *noun*
• "HYDRO fone"
• an instrument for the detection of sound waves in water.
• [Greek *hudro-* from *hudōr* water + *phōneō* speak]

hydroplane *noun*
• "HYDRO plane"
• a light fast motorboat designed to skim over the surface of water.
• [Greek *hudro-* from *hudōr* water + 'plane']

hydroponics *noun*
• "hydro PONNIX"
• the process of growing plants in sand, gravel, or liquid, without soil and with added nutrients.
• [Greek *hudro-* from *hudōr* water + *ponos* labour]
• **hydroponic** *adjective*
• **hydroponically** *adverb*

hydroquinone *noun*
• "hydro KWIN own"
• a substance formed by the reduction of benzoquinone, used as a photographic developer and in skin-bleaching creams.
• [HYDROGEN + BENZOQUINONE]

hydrosphere *noun*
• "HYDRO sfeer"
• the waters of the earth's surface.
• [Greek *hudro-* from *hudōr* water + SPHERE]

hydrostatic *adjective*
• "hydro STATTIC"
• of the equilibrium of liquids and the pressure exerted by liquid at rest.
• [prob. from Greek *hudrostatēs* hydrostatic balance (*hudro-* from *hudōr* water + *sta-* stand)]
• **hydrostatically** *adverb*

hydrostatics *noun*
• "hydro STATTIX"
• the branch of mechanics concerned with the hydrostatic properties of liquids.
• [as HYDROSTATIC]

hydrotherapy *noun*
• "hydro THERRA pee"
• the use of water in the treatment of disorders, usu. exercises in swimming pools for arthritic or partially paralyzed patients.
• [Greek *hudro-* from *hudōr* water + THERAPY]
• **hydrotherapist** *noun*

hydrothermal *adjective*
• "hydro THURM'll"
• of or relating to the action of heated water in the earth's crust.
• [Greek *hudro-* from *hudōr* water + *thermē* heat]
• **hydrothermally** *adverb*

hydrous *adjective*
• "HY druss"
• containing water.
• [Greek *hudōr hudro-* water]

hydroxide *noun*
• "hy DROX ide"
• a metallic compound containing oxygen and hydrogen either in the form of the hydroxide ion (OH-) or the hydroxyl group (-OH).
• [HYDROGEN + OXYGEN]

hydroxyl *noun*
• "hy DROX'll"
• the monovalent group containing hydrogen and oxygen, as -OH.
• [HYDROGEN + OXYGEN]

hydrozoan *noun*
• "hydra ZO 'n"
• any aquatic coelenterate of the class Hydrozoa of mainly marine polyp or medusoid forms, including hydra and Portuguese man-of-war.
• [modern Latin *Hydrozoa* (as HYDRA, Greek *zōion* animal)]

hyena *noun*
• "hy EENA"
• any of several carnivorous scavenging animals somewhat resembling a dog, but with the hind limbs shorter than the forelimbs, belonging to the genera *Hyaena* and *Crocuta* (family Hyaenidae).
• [Old French *hyene* & Latin *hyaena* from Greek *huaina* feminine of *hus* pig]

hygiene *noun*
• "HY jeen"
• the branch of knowledge that deals with the maintenance of health, esp. the conditions and practices conducive to it.
• [French *hygiène* from modern Latin *hygieina* from Greek *hugieinē* (*tekhnē*) (art) of health, from *hugiēs* healthy]

hygienic *noun*
• "hy JEN ick" or "hy JEEN ick"
• conducive to health; clean and sanitary.
• [as HYGIENE]
• **hygienically** *adverb*

hygienist *noun*
• "hy JEN ist" or "hy JEEN ist"
• a person trained and licensed to act as a dentist's assistant, specializing in oral hygiene, cleaning and scaling teeth, etc.
• [as HYGIENE]

hygrometer *noun*
• "hy GROMMA tur"
• an instrument for measuring the humidity of the air or a gas.
• [Greek *hugro-* from *hugros* wet, moist + *metron* measure]
• **hygrometric** *adjective* "hy gruh METRIC"
• **hygrometry** *noun*

hygroscope *noun*
• "HY gruh scope"
• an instrument which indicates approximately the humidity of the air.
• [Greek *hugro-* from *hugros* wet, moist + *skopeō* look at]

hygroscopic *adjective*
• "hy gruh SCOPPIC"
• (of a substance) tending to absorb moisture from the air.
• [as HYGROSCOPE]
• **hygroscopicity** *noun*
"hy gruh scop ISSA tee"

hymeneal *adjective*
• "hy m'n EE 'll"
• of or concerning marriage.
• [*Hymen*, Greek god of marriage]

hymenium *noun*
• "hy MEENY um"
• the spore-bearing surface of certain fungi.
• [modern Latin from Greek *humenion* diminutive of *humēn* membrane]

hymenopteran *noun*
• "hy m'n OPTER 'n"
• any insect of the order Hymenoptera having four transparent wings, including bees, wasps, and ants.
• [modern Latin *hymenoptera* from Greek *humenopteros* membrane-winged (as HYMENIUM, *pteron* wing)]
• **hymenopterous** *adjective*

hymn *noun*
• "HIM"
• a song of praise, esp. to God in Christian worship, usu. a metrical composition sung in a religious service.
• [Old French *ymne* from Latin *hymnus* from Greek *humnos* song in praise of a god or hero]
• **hymnic** *adjective* "HIM nic"
HOMOPHONES: *him*

hymnal *noun*
• "HIM n'll"
• a hymn book.
• [as HYMN]

hymnary *noun*
• "HIMNA ree"
• a hymn book.
• [as HYMN]

hymnody *noun*
• "HIMNA dee"
• the singing or composition of hymns.
• [medieval Latin *hymnodia* from Greek *humnōidia* from *humnos* hymn: compare PSALMODY]

hymnology *noun*
• "him NOLLA jee"
• the composition or study of hymns.
• [as HYMN + *logos* word]
• **hymnologist** *noun*

hyoid *noun*
• "HY oid"
• a U-shaped bone in the neck which supports the tongue.
• [French *hyoïde* from modern Latin *hyoïdes* from Greek *huoeidēs* shaped like the letter upsilon (*hu*)]

hyoscine *noun*
• "HY a seen"
• a poisonous alkaloid found in plants of the nightshade family, esp. of the genus *Scopolia*, and used to prevent vomiting in motion sickness and as a preoperative medication for examination of the eye.
• [from HYOSCYAMINE]

hyoscyamine *noun*
• "hy a SYE a meen"
• a poisonous alkaloid obtained from henbane, having similar properties to scopolamine.
• [modern Latin *hyoscyamus* from Greek *huoskuamos* henbane, from *hus huos* pig + *kuamos* bean]

hype *noun*
• "HIPE"
• extravagant or intensive publicity or promotion.
• [20th c.: origin unknown]

hyper *adjective*
• "HIPE ur"
• hyperactive, highly strung; extraordinarily energetic.
• [abbreviation of HYPERACTIVE]

hyperactive *adjective*
• "hyper ACTIV"
• (of a person, esp. a child) abnormally active.
• [Greek *huper* over, beyond + Latin *activa* active]
• **hyperactively** *adverb*
• **hyperactivity** *noun*

hyperbaric *adjective*
• "hyper BARE ick"
• (of a gas) at a pressure greater than normal.
• [Greek *huper* over, beyond + *barus* heavy]

hyperbola *noun*
• "hy PURBA luh"
• the plane curve of two equal branches, produced when a cone is cut by a plane that makes a larger angle with the base than the side of the cone.
• [modern Latin from Greek *huperbolē* excess (*huper* over, beyond, *ballō* to throw)]
• **hyperbolic** *adjective* "hyper BOLLIC"
• **hyperbolically** *adverb*

hyperbole *noun*
• "hy PURBA lee"
• an exaggerated statement not meant to be taken literally.
• [Latin (as HYPERBOLA)]
• **hyperbolize** *verb* (also esp. *Brit.* **-ise**)

hyperboloid *noun*
• "hy PURBA loid"
• a solid or surface having plane sections that are hyperbolas, ellipses, or circles.
• [as HYPERBOLA]
• **hyperboloidal** *adjective*

hypercholesterolemia *noun*
ALSO SPELLED: esp. *Brit.* **hypercholesterolaemia**
• "hyper kuh lester aw LEEMY uh"
• an excess of cholesterol in the bloodstream.
• [Greek *huper* over, beyond + CHOLESTEROL + Greek *aimia* from *haima* blood]

hyperconscious *adjective*
• "hyper CON sh'ss"
• acutely or excessively aware.
• [Greek *huper* over, beyond + CONSCIOUS]

hypercritical *adjective*
• "hyper CRITTA k'll"
• excessively critical, esp. of small faults.
• [Greek *huper* over, beyond + CRITICAL]
• **hypercritically** *adverb*

hypercube *noun*
• "HYPER cube"
• a geometrical figure in four or more dimensions, analogous to a cube in three dimensions.
• [Greek *huper* over, beyond + French *cube* or Latin *cubus* from Greek *kubos* cube]

hyperdrive *noun*
• "HYPER drive"
• (in science fiction) a supposed propulsion system for travel in hyperspace.
• [Greek *huper* over, beyond + 'drive']

hyperemia *noun*
ALSO SPELLED: esp. *Brit.* **hyperaemia**
• "hyper EEMY uh"
• an excessive quantity of blood in the vessels supplying an organ or other part of the body.
• [modern Latin (from Greek *huper* over, beyond, *aimia* from *haima* blood)]
• **hyperemic** *adjective* (also esp. *Brit.* **hyperaemic**)

hyperextend *verb*
• "hyper ex TEND"
• bend (a limb, digit, etc.) so that it makes an abnormally great angle.
• [Greek *huper* over, beyond + EXTEND]
• **hyperextensibility** *noun*
• **hyperextensible** *adjective*
• **hyperextension** *noun*

hyperfocal *adjective*
• "hyper FOKE 'll"
• designating the distance on which a camera lens can be focused to bring the maximum range of object-distances into focus.
• [Greek *huper* over, beyond + Latin *focus* = hearth]

hyperglycemia *noun*
ALSO SPELLED: esp. *Brit.* **hyperglycaemia**
• "hyper glye SEEMY uh"
• an excess of glucose in the bloodstream, often associated with diabetes mellitus.
• [Greek *huper* over, beyond + GLUCOSE + *aimia* from *haima* blood]
• **hyperglycemic** *adjective* (also esp. *Brit.* **hyperglycaemic**)

hypericin *noun*
• "hy PERRA sin"
• a substance found in St John's Wort, credited with chemical and pharmacological properties similar to those of antidepressants.
• [from HYPERICUM]

hypericum *noun*
• "hy PERRA k'm"
• any shrub of the genus *Hypericum* with five-petalled yellow flowers.
• [Latin from Greek *hupereikon* (*huper* over, beyond, *ereikē* heath)]

hyperinflation *noun*
• "hyper in FLAY sh'n"
• monetary inflation at a very high rate.
• [Greek *huper* over, beyond + INFLATION]

hyperkinetic *adjective*
• "hyper kin ETTIC"
• characterized by excessive or spasmodic movement.
• [Greek *huper* over, beyond + KINETIC]

hyperlink *noun*
• "HYPER link"
• a link from a hypertext file or document to another location or file, typically activated by clicking on a highlighted word or image at a particular location on the screen.
• [Greek *huper* over, beyond + 'link']

hypermarket *noun*
• "HYPER market"
• (in Europe) a very large supermarket with extensive parking facilities.
• [Greek *huper* over, beyond + 'market']

hypermedia *noun*
• "hyper MEEDY uh"

• art, education, etc. using more than one medium of expression, communication, etc.
• [Greek *huper* over, beyond + MEDIATE]

hyperon *noun*
• "HYPER on"
• an unstable subatomic particle classified as a baryon, heavier than the neutron and proton.
• [Greek *huper* over, beyond]

hyperplasia *noun*
• "hyper PLAZEY uh" or "hyper PLAY zhuh"
• the enlargement of an organ or tissue from the increased production of cells.
• [Greek *huper* over, beyond + *plasis* formation]

hyperreal *adjective*
• "hyper REEL"
• (esp. of an artificial environment or an artistic creation) created or represented with such meticulous attention to detail as to appear more real than reality.
• [Greek *huper* over, beyond + 'real']
• **hyperrealism** *noun*
• **hyperrealist** *adjective*
• **hyperrealistic** *adjective*
• **hyperreality** *noun*

hypersensitive *adjective*
• "hyper SENSA tiv"
• abnormally or excessively sensitive.
• [Greek *huper* over, beyond + SENSITIVE]
• **hypersensitivity** *noun*

hypersonic *adjective*
• "hyper SONNIC"
• relating to speeds of more than five times the speed of sound (Mach 5).
• [Greek *huper* over, beyond + SONIC]
• **hypersonically** *adverb*

hyperspace *noun*
• "HYPER space"
• space of more than three dimensions, esp. (in science fiction) a notional space-time continuum in which motion and communication at speeds greater than that of light are supposedly possible.
• [Greek *huper* over, beyond + 'space']
• **hyperspatial** *adjective* "hyper SPAY sh'll"

hypertension *noun*
• "hyper TEN sh'n"
• abnormally high blood pressure.
• [Greek *huper* over, beyond + TENSION]
• **hypertensive** *adjective*

hypertext *noun*
• "HYPER text"
• a software system allowing extensive cross-referencing between related sections of text and associated graphic material.
• [Greek *huper* over, beyond + 'text']
• **hypertextual** *adjective*
• **hypertextually** *adverb*

hyperthermia *noun*
• "hyper THURMY uh"
• the condition of having a body temperature greatly above normal.
• [Greek *huper* over, beyond + *thermē* heat]
• **hyperthermic** *adjective*

hyperthyroidism *noun*
• "hyper THYE roid izm" (with "TH" as in *THIN*)
• overactivity of the thyroid gland, resulting in rapid heartbeat and an increased rate of metabolism.
• [Greek *huper* over, beyond + THYROID]
• **hyperthyroid** *noun*

hypertonic *adjective*
• "hyper TONNIC"
• (of muscles) having high tension.
• [Greek *huper* over, beyond + *tonos* tension, tone, from *teinō* stretch]

hypertrophy *noun*
• "hy PURTRA fee"
• the enlargement of an organ or tissue from the increase in size of its cells.
• [modern Latin *hypertrophia* (as Greek *huper* over, beyond, *-trophia* nourishment)]
• **hypertrophic** *adjective* "hyper TROFFIC"
• **hypertrophied** *adjective*

hyperventilation *noun*
• "hyper vent'll AY sh'n"
• breathing at an abnormally rapid rate, resulting in an increased loss of carbon dioxide, and often accompanied by dizziness.
• [Greek *huper* over, beyond + VENTILATE]
• **hyperventilate** *verb*

hypha *noun*
• "HY fuh"
• a filament in the mycelium of a fungus.
• [modern Latin from Greek *huphē* web]
• **hyphal** *adjective*

hyphen *noun*
• "HIFE 'n"
• the sign (-) used to join words semantically or syntactically (as in *pick-me-up*, *rock-forming*), to indicate the division of a word at the end of a line, or to indicate a missing or implied element (as in *man- and womankind*).
• [Late Latin from Greek *huphen* together, from *hupo* under + *hen* one]
• **hyphenate** *verb*
• **hyphenated** *adjective*
• **hyphenation** *noun*

hypnagogic *adjective*
• "hipna GODGE ick"
• of or pertaining to the state immediately before falling asleep.
• [French *hypnagogique* from Greek *hypnos* sleep, *agōgos* leading]

hypnosis *noun*
• "hip NO sis"
• a state like sleep in which the subject acts only on external suggestion.
• [modern Latin from Greek *hupnos* sleep]

hypnotherapy *noun*
- "hipno THERRA pee"
- psychotherapy involving the use of hypnotism.
- [as HYPNOSIS + THERAPY]
- **hypnotherapist** *noun*

hypnotic *adjective*
- "hip NOTTIC"
- of or producing hypnotism.
- [French *hypnotique* from Late Latin *hypnoticus* from Greek *hupnōtikos* from *hupnoō* put to sleep]
- **hypnotically** *adverb*

hypnotism *noun*
- "HIPNA tizm"
- the study or practice of hypnosis.
- [as HYPNOTIC]
- **hypnotist** *noun*

hypnotize *verb*
ALSO SPELLED: esp. *Brit.* **-ise**
- "HIPNA tize"
- produce hypnosis in.
- [as HYPNOTIC]
- **hypnotizable** *adjective* (also esp. *Brit.* **-isable**)

hypo *noun*
- "HYPO"
- a hypodermic needle, used to inject drugs etc. beneath the skin.
- [abbreviation]

hypoallergenic *adjective*
- "hypo al ur JENNIC"
- having little tendency, or a specially reduced tendency, to cause an allergic reaction.
- [Greek *hupo* under + ALLERGY + GENESIS]

hypoblast *noun*
- "HYPO blast"
- the innermost layer of an animal embryo in early development.
- [Greek *hupo* under + *blastos* sprout]

hypocaust *noun*
- "HYPO cost"
- a hollow space under the floor in ancient Roman houses, into which hot air was sent for heating a room or bath.
- [Latin *hypocaustum* from Greek *hupokauston* place heated from below (as *hupo* under, *kaiō*, *kau-* burn)]

hypochlorite *noun*
- "hypo CLOR ite"
- a salt of hypochlorous acid.
- [Greek *hupo* under + CHLORITE]

hypochlorous *adjective*
- "hypo CLOR us"
- designating an unstable acid existing only in dilute solution and used in bleaching and water treatment.
- [Greek *hupo* under + CHLORINE]

hypochondria *noun*
- "hypo CON dree uh"
- abnormal and unnecessary anxiety about one's health.
- [Late Latin from Greek *hupokhondria* soft parts of the body below the ribs, where melancholy was thought to arise (*hupo* under, *khondros* sternal cartilage)]
- **hypochondriac** *noun*

hypocotyl *noun*
- "hypo COT'll"
- the part of the stem of an embryo plant beneath the stalks of the seed leaves or cotyledons and directly above the root.
- [Greek *hupo* under + COTYLEDON]

hypocrisy *noun*
- "hip OCKRA see"
- the assumption or postulation of moral standards, principles, etc. to which one's own behaviour does not conform; dissimulation, pretense.
- [Old French *ypocrisie* from Church Latin *hypocrisis* from Greek *hupokrisis* acting of a part, pretense (*hupo* under, *krinō* decide, judge)]
- **hypocrite** *noun* "HIPPA crit"
- **hypocritical** *adjective*
- **hypocritically** *adverb*

hypocycloid *noun*
- "hypo SIKE loid"
- the curve traced by a point on the circumference of a circle rolling on the interior of another circle.
- [Greek *hupo* under + CYCLE]
- **hypocycloidal** *adjective*

hypodermic *adjective*
- "hypo DURMIC"
- of or relating to the area beneath the skin.
- [Greek *hupo* under, *derma* skin]
- **hypodermically** *adverb*

hypogastrium *noun*
- "hypa GAS tree um"
- the part of the central abdomen which is situated below the region of the stomach.
- [modern Latin from Greek *hupogastrion* (*hupo* under, *gastēr* belly)]
- **hypogastric** *adjective*

hypogeal *adjective*
- "hypa JEE 'll"
- (existing or growing) underground.
- [Late Latin *hypogeus* from Greek *hupogeios* (*hupo* under, *gē* earth)]

hypoglycemia *noun*
ALSO SPELLED: esp. *Brit.* **hypoglycaemia**
- "hypo glye SEEMY uh"
- a deficiency of glucose in the bloodstream.
- [Greek *hupo* under + GLUCOSE + *aimia* from *haima* blood]
- **hypoglycemic** *adjective* (also esp. *Brit.* **hypoglycaemic**)

hypoid *adjective*
- "HIPE oid"
- designating a gear with the pinion offset

from the centre-line of the wheel, to connect non-intersecting shafts.
• [perhaps from HYPERBOLOID]

hypomania *noun*
• "hypo MAINY uh"
• a minor form of mania.
• [modern Latin from German *Hypomanie* (*hupo* under, MANIA)]
• **hypomanic** *adjective* "hypo MANNIC"

hyponasty *noun*
• "HYPA nasty"
• the tendency in plant organs for growth to be more rapid on the underside.
• [Greek *hupo* under + *nastos* pressed]
• **hyponastic** *adjective*

hypophysis *noun*
• "hy POFFA sis"
• the pituitary gland.
• [modern Latin from Greek *hupophusis* offshoot (*hupo* under, *phusis* growth)]
• **hypophyseal** *adjective* (also **hypophysial**) "hypa FIZZY 'll"

hypostasis *noun*
• "hy POSSTA sis"
• an accumulation of fluid or blood in the lower parts of the body or organs under the influence of gravity, in cases of poor circulation.
• [Church Latin from Greek *hupostasis* (*hupo* under, STASIS standing, state)]

hypostatic *adjective*
• "hypa STATTIC"
• (in Christian theology) relating to the three persons of the Trinity.
• [Greek *hupo* under + STASIS standing, state]

hypostatize *verb*
• "hy POSSTA tize"
• make into or represent as a substance or concrete reality; embody, personify.
• [Greek *hupo* under + STASIS standing, state]
• **hypostatization** *noun* (also esp. *Brit.* **-isation**)

hypostyle *adjective*
• "HYPA stile"
• having a roof supported by pillars.
• [Greek *hupostulos* (*hupo* under, *stulos* column)]

hypotaxis *noun*
• "hypa TAX iss"
• the subordination of one clause to another.
• [Greek *hupotaxis* (*hupo* under, *taxis* arrangement)]
• **hypotactic** *adjective*

hypotension *noun*
• "hypo TEN sh'n"
• abnormally low blood pressure.
• [Greek *hupo* under + TENSION]
• **hypotensive** *adjective*

hypotenuse *noun*
• "hy POTTA noose" or "hy POTTA nooz" or "hy POTTA nyooz"
• the side opposite the right angle of a right-angled triangle.
• [Latin *hypotenusa* from Greek *hupoteinousa* (*grammē*) subtending (line) feminine participle of *hupoteinō* (*hupo* under, *teinō* stretch)]

hypothalamus *noun*
• "hypo THALLA muss"
• the region of the brain which controls body temperature, thirst, hunger, etc.
• [modern Latin formed from Greek *hupo* under, THALAMUS]
• **hypothalamic** *adjective*

hypothermia *noun*
• "hypo THURMY uh"
• the condition of having an abnormally low body temperature.
• [Greek *hupo* under + *thermē* heat]
• **hypothermic** *adjective*

hypothesis *noun*
• "hy POTHA sis"
• a proposition made as a basis for reasoning, without the assumption of its truth.
• [Late Latin from Greek *hupothesis* foundation (*hupo* under, THESIS)]
• **hypothesist** *noun*
• **hypothesize** *verb* (also esp. *Brit.* **-ise**)
• **hypothesizer** *noun* (also esp. *Brit.* **-iser**)
• **hypothetical** *adjective* "hypa THETTIC'll"
• **hypothetically** *adverb*

hypothyroidism *noun*
• "hypo THYE roid izm" (with "TH" as in *THIN*)
• subnormal activity of the thyroid gland, resulting in mental retardation in children, and mental and physical slowing in adults.
• [Greek *hupo* under + THYROID]
• **hypothyroid** *noun*

hypoventilation *noun*
• "hypo vent'll AY sh'n"
• breathing at an abnormally slow rate, resulting in an increased amount of carbon dioxide in the blood.
• [Greek *hupo* under + VENTILATION]

hypoxemia *noun*
ALSO SPELLED: esp. *Brit.* **hypoxaemia**
• "hy pock SEEMY uh"
• an abnormally low concentration of oxygen in the blood.
• [modern Latin (from Greek *hupo* under, OXYGEN, *aimia* from *haima* blood)]
• **hypoxemic** *adjective* (also esp. *Brit.* **hypoxaemic**)

hypoxia *noun*
• "hy POXY uh"
• a deficiency of oxygen reaching the tissues.
• [Greek *hupo* under + OXYGEN]
• **hypoxic** *adjective*

hyrax *noun*
• "HY rax"
• a mammal of the order Hyracoidea,

comprising small stumpy animals of Africa and the Middle East which resemble rodents but are actually related to ungulates and sirenians, having feet with nails like hoofs.
• [modern Latin from Greek *hurax* shrew mouse]

hyssop *noun*
• "HISSUP"
• any small bushy aromatic herb of the genus *Hyssopus*, esp. *H. officinalis*, formerly used medicinally.
• [Old English *(h)ysope* from Latin *hyssopus* from Greek *hyssōpos*, of Semitic origin]

hysterectomy *noun*
• "hista RECTA mee"
• the surgical removal of the uterus.
• [Greek *hustera* womb + *ektomē* excision, from *ek* out + *temnō* cut]
• **hysterectomize** *verb* (also esp. *Brit.* **-ise**)

hysteresis *noun*
• "hista REE sis"
• the lagging behind of an effect when its cause varies in amount etc., esp. of magnetic induction behind the magnetizing force.
• [Greek *husterēsis* from *hustereō* be behind, from *husteros* coming after]

hysteria *noun*
• "hiss TERRY uh" or "hiss TEERY uh"
• an emotional state, caused by grief or fear etc., accompanied by uncontrollable laughter, weeping, etc.
• [modern Latin from Greek *husterikos* of the womb (*hustera*), hysteria previously being thought to occur more frequently in women than in men and to be associated with the womb]
• **hysteric** *noun* "hiss TARE ick"
• **hysterical** *adjective*
• **hysterically** *adverb*

iamb *noun*
- "EYE amb"
- a metrical foot consisting of one short (or unstressed) followed by one long (or stressed) syllable.
- [anglicized from IAMBUS]
- **iambic** *adjective* "eye AM bick"

iambus *noun*
- "eye AM buss"
- a metrical foot consisting of one short (or unstressed) followed by one long (or stressed) syllable.
- [Latin from Greek *iambos* iambus, lampoon, from *iaptō* assail in words, from its use by Greek satirists]

iatrogenic *adjective*
- "eye atra JENNIC"
- (of a disease etc.) caused by medical examination or treatment.
- [Greek *iatros* physician + GENESIS]
- **iatrogenesis** *noun*

Iban *noun*
- "EE ban"
- a member of a group of non-Muslim indigenous peoples of Borneo.
- [Iban]

Iberian *adjective*
- "eye BEERY 'n"
- pertaining to the body of land including Spain and Portugal.
- [Latin from Greek *Ibēr* Spaniard]

ibex *noun*
- "EYE bex"
- a wild goat-antelope, *Capra ibex*, esp. of mountainous areas of Europe, N Africa, and Asia, with a chin beard and thick curved ridged horns.
- [Latin]

ibis *noun*
- "EYE biss"
- any wading bird of the family Threskiornithidae with a curved bill, long neck, and long legs, and nesting in colonies.
- [Latin from Greek]

Ibo *noun*
- "EE bo"
- a member of a people of SE Nigeria.
- [African name]

ibogaine *noun*
- "ib OH gane"
- a hallucinogenic compound derived from the roots of a West African shrub, sometimes used as a treatment for heroin or cocaine addiction.
- [from a blend of *iboga* (local name for the compound) and COCAINE]

ibuprofen *noun*
- "eye byoo PRO fin"
- an analgesic and anti-inflammatory drug used esp. as a stronger alternative to acetylsalicylic acid.
- [Greek *isos* equal + BUTYL + PROPIONIC + *-fen* representing PHENYL, elements of the chemical name]

iceberg *noun*
- "ICE burg"
- a large floating mass of ice detached from a glacier or ice sheet and carried out to sea.
- [prob. from Dutch *ijsberg* from *ijs* ice + *berg* hill]

icescape *noun*
- "ICE scape"
- a landscape covered with ice.
- ['ice' + 'landscape' from Middle Dutch *landscap*]

ichneumon *noun*
- "ick NEW m'n"
- any small hymenopterous insect of the family Ichneumonidae, depositing eggs in or on the larva of another insect as food for its own larva.
- [Latin from Greek *ikhneumōn* spider-hunting wasp, from *ikhneuō* trace, from *ikhnos* footstep]

ichor *noun*
- "IKE or"
- (in Greek mythology) fluid flowing like blood in the veins of the gods.
- [Greek *ikhōr*]
- **ichorous** *adjective*

ichthyology *noun*
- "ick thee OLLA jee" (with "TH" as in *THIN*)
- the study of fishes.
- [Greek *ikhthus* fish + *logos* word]

- **ichthyological** *adjective*
- **ichthyologist** *noun*

ichthyosaur *noun*
- "ICK thee a sore" (with "TH" as in *THIN*)
- any extinct marine reptile of the order Ichthyosauria, with long head, tapering body, four flippers, and usu. a large tail.
- [Greek *ikhthus* fish + *sauros* lizard]

icon *noun*
ALSO SPELLED: **ikon**
- "EYE con"
- a devotional painting or carving, usu. on wood, of Christ or another holy figure, esp. in the Eastern Church.
- [Latin from Greek *eikōn* image]

iconic *adjective*
- "eye CONNIC"
- of or having the nature of an image or portrait.
- [Latin *iconicus* from Greek *eikonikos* (as ICON)]
- **iconically** *adverb*
- **iconicity** *noun* "eye kuh NISSA tee"

iconoclasm *noun*
- "eye CONNA clazm"
- the breaking of images.
- [as ICONOCLAST after *enthusiasm* etc.]

iconoclast *noun*
- "eye CONNA clast"
- a person who attacks cherished beliefs or conventions.
- [medieval Latin *iconoclastes* from ecclesiastical Greek *eikonoklastēs* (as ICON, *klaō* break)]
- **iconoclastic** *adjective*
- **iconoclastically** *adverb*

iconography *noun*
- "ike 'n OGGRA fee"
- the visual images and symbols typical of an art form, an artistic movement, an artist, a culture, etc.
- [Greek *eikonographia* sketch (as ICON + *graphia* writing)]
- **iconographer** *noun*
- **iconographic** *adjective*
- **iconographical** *adjective*
- **iconographically** *adverb*

iconostasis *noun*
- "eye kuh NOSSTA sis" or "eye conna STASS iss"
- (in the Eastern Church) a screen bearing icons and separating the sanctuary from the nave.
- [modern Greek *eikonostasis* (from Greek *eikōn* likeness + STASIS)]

icosahedron *noun*
- "eye kuh suh HEED r'n"
- a solid figure with twenty faces.
- [Late Latin *icosahedrum* from Greek *eikosaedron* from *eikosi* twenty + *hedra* base]
- **icosahedral** *adjective*

icterus *noun*
- "ICKTER us"
- a condition with yellowing of the skin or whites of the eyes, often caused by obstruction of the bile duct or by liver disease; jaundice.
- [Latin from Greek *ikteros*]
- **icteric** *adjective* "ick TARE ick"

ictus *noun*
- "ICK tuss"
- rhythmical or metrical stress.
- [Latin, = blow, from *icere* strike]

ideate *verb*
- "EYE dee ate"
- imagine, conceive.
- [medieval Latin *ideare* form an idea, from Greek *idea* form, pattern from stem *id-* see]
- **ideation** *noun*
- **ideational** *adjective*
- **ideationally** *adverb*

ident *noun*
- "eye DENT"
- 'identification', esp. in informal or technical use.
- [abbreviation]

identical *adjective*
- "eye DENTA k'll"
- (of different things) exactly the same in every detail.
- [medieval Latin *identicus* (as IDENTITY)]
- **identically** *adverb*

identify *verb*
- "eye DENTA fie"
- establish the identity of; recognize.
- [medieval Latin *identificare* (as IDENTITY)]
- **identifiable** *adjective*
- **identifiably** *adverb*
- **identification** *noun*
- **identifier** *noun*

identity *noun*
- "eye DENTA tee"
- the quality or condition of being a specified person or thing.
- [Late Latin *identitas* from Latin *idem* same]

ideogram *noun*
- "IDDY a gram"
- a character symbolizing the idea of a thing without indicating the sequence of sounds in its name (e.g. a numeral, and many Chinese characters).
- [Greek *idea* form + *gramma* thing written]

ideograph *noun*
- "IDDY a graff"
- = IDEOGRAM.
- [Greek *idea* form + *graphia* writing]
- **ideographic** *adjective*

ideologue *noun*
- "EYE dee a log" or "eye DEE a log"
- an adherent of an ideology.
- [as IDEOLOGY]

ideology *noun*
• "eye dee OLLA jee" or "iddy OLLA jee"
• a system of ideas or way of thinking, usu. relating to politics or society, or to the conduct of a class or group, and regarded as justifying actions, esp. one that is held implicitly or adopted as a whole and maintained regardless of the course of events.
• [French *idéologie* (Greek *idea* form + *logos* word)]
• **ideological** *adjective*
• **ideologically** *adverb*
• **ideologist** *noun*

idiocy *noun*
• "IDDY a see"
• utter foolishness; idiotic behaviour or an idiotic action.
• [as IDIOT]

idiolect *noun*
• "IDDY a lect"
• the linguistic system of an individual person, differing in some details from that of all other speakers of the same dialect or language.
• [Greek *idios* own + *-lect* in DIALECT]
• **idiolectal** *adjective*

idiom *noun*
• "IDDY um"
• a group of words established by usage and having a meaning not deducible from those of the individual words, e.g. *down in the dumps*.
• [French *idiome* or Late Latin *idioma* from Greek *idiōma -matos* private property, from *idios* own, private]
• **idiomatic** *adjective*
• **idiomatically** *adverb*
• **idiomaticity** *noun* "iddy uh muh TISSA tee"

idiopathic *adjective*
• "iddy a PATHIC"
• (of a disease or condition) of unknown cause or arising spontaneously.
• [modern Latin *idiopathia* from Greek *idiopatheia* from *idios* own + *patheia* suffering]

idiosyncrasy *noun*
• "iddy oh SINKRA see"
• a person's particular way of thinking, behaving, etc. that is clearly different from that of others.
• [orig. in the sense 'physical constitution particular to an individual', from Greek *idiosugkrasia* from *idios* own + *sun* with + *krasis* mixture]
• **idiosyncratic** *adjective* "iddy oh sin KRATTIC"
• **idiosyncratically** *adverb*

idiot *noun*
• "IDDY it"
• a stupid person; an utter fool.
• [Old French from Latin *idiota* ignorant person, from Greek *idiōtēs* private person, layman, ignorant person, from *idios* own, private]
• **idiotic** *adjective*
• **idiotically** *adverb*

idle *adjective*
• "EYE d'll"
• (of a person) not working, doing nothing.
• [Old English *īdel* empty, useless]
• **idleness** *noun*
• **idly** *adverb*
HOMOPHONES: *idol*, *idyll*

idler *noun*
• "IDE lur"
• a person who idles or is idle.
• [as IDLE]

Ido *noun*
• "EE doe"
• an artificial universal language based on Esperanto.
• [Ido, = offspring]

idol *noun*
• "EYE d'll"
• an image of a deity etc. used as an object of worship.
• [Old French *idole* from Latin *idolum* from Greek *eidōlon* phantom, from *eidos* form]
HOMOPHONES: *idle*, *idyll*

idolatry *noun*
• "eye DOLLA tree"
• the worship of idols.
• [as IDOL + Greek *latreia* worship, from *latreuō* serve]
• **idolater** *noun*
• **idolatrous** *adjective*

idolize *verb*
ALSO SPELLED: esp. *Brit.* **-ise**
• "EYE d'll ize"
• admire, revere, or love greatly or excessively.
• [as IDOL]
• **idolization** *noun* (also esp. *Brit.* **-isation**)
• **idolizer** *noun* (also esp. *Brit.* **-iser**)

idyll *noun*
ALSO SPELLED: **idyl**
• "ID ill" or "EYE d'll"
• an extremely happy, peaceful, or picturesque episode or scene, typically an idealized or unsustainable one.
• [Latin *idyllium* from Greek *eidullion*, diminutive of *eidos* form]
• **idyllic** *adjective* "eye DILLIC" or "id ILLIC"
• **idyllically** *adverb*
HOMOPHONES: *idle*, *idol*

Iglulik *noun*
ALSO SPELLED: **Igloolik**
• "ig LOO lick"
• a member of an Inuit people inhabiting the eastern Arctic, esp. living on Baffin Island and the Melville Peninsula.
• [Inuktitut, = 'there is an igloo here']

igneous *adjective*
• "IG nee us"

• (of rock) having solidified from lava or magma.
• [Latin *igneus* from *ignis* fire]

ignite *verb*
• "ig NITE"
• set fire to; cause to burn.
• [Latin *ignire ignit-* from *ignis* fire]
• **ignitable** *adjective*
• **igniter** *noun*

ignition *noun*
• "ig NISH'n"
• the action of igniting the fuel in the cylinder of an internal combustion engine.
• [as IGNITE]

ignoble *adjective*
• "ig NO bull"
• dishonourable.
• [French *ignoble* or Latin *ignobilis* (Latin *in-* not, without, *nobilis* noble)]
• **ignobility** *noun*
• **ignobly** *adverb*

ignominy *noun*
• "ig NOMMA nee" or "IGNA min ee"
• dishonour, disgrace.
• [French *ignominie* or Latin *ignominia* (Latin *in-* not, without, *nomen* name)]
• **ignominious** *adjective* "igna MINNY us"
• **ignominiously** *adverb*
• **ignominiousness** *noun*

ignoramus *noun*
• "igna RAY muss" or "igna RAM us"
• an extremely ignorant person.
• [Latin, = we do not know: in legal use (formerly of a grand jury rejecting a bill) we take no notice of it; modern sense perhaps from a character in George Ruggle's *Ignoramus* (1615) exposing lawyers' ignorance]

ignorance *noun*
• "IGNA rince"
• lack of knowledge (about a thing).
• [French *ignorance* from Latin *ignorare* not know, ignore (*in* not, without, *gno-* know)]
• **ignorant** *adjective*
• **ignorantly** *adverb*

iguana *noun*
• "ig WONNA"
• any of various large lizards of the family Iguanidae native to America, the W Indies, and the Pacific islands, having a dorsal crest and throat appendages.
• [Spanish from Carib *iwana*]

iguanodon *noun*
• "ig WONNA don"
• a large extinct plant-eating dinosaur of the genus *Iguanodon*, of late Jurassic and early Cretaceous times, with forelimbs smaller than hind limbs.
• [IGUANA (from its resemblance to this), after *mastodon* etc.]

ikat *noun*
• "EE cat"
• a fabric made using an Indonesian technique of textile decoration in which warp or weft threads, or both, are tied at intervals and dyed before weaving.
• [Malay, = tie, fasten]

ikebana *noun*
• "icka BANNA"
• the art of Japanese flower arrangement, with formal display according to strict rules.
• [Japanese, = living flowers]

ileitis *noun*
• "illy ITE iss" or "eye lee ITE iss"
• inflammation of the ileum.
• [as ILEUM + Greek *-itis*, forming feminine of adjectives in *-itēs* (with *nosos* 'disease' implied)]

ileostomy *noun*
• "illy OSSTA mee" or "eye lee OSSTA mee"
• a surgical operation in which a damaged part is removed from the ileum and the cut end directed to an artificial opening in the abdominal wall.
• [ILEUM + Greek *stoma* mouth]

ileum *noun*
• "ILLY um" or "EYE lee um"
• the third and last portion of the small intestine.
• [var. of ILIUM]
• **ileac** *adjective*
• **ileal** *adjective*
HOMOPHONES: *ilium, iliac*

ileus *noun*
• "ILLY us" or "EYE lee us"
• any painful obstruction of the intestine, esp. of the ileum.
• [Latin from Greek *(e)ileos* colic]

ilex *noun*
• "EYE lex"
• any tree or shrub of the genus *Ilex*, esp. the common holly.
• [Latin]

iliac *adjective*
• "ILLY ack"
• of the lower body or ilium.
• [Late Latin *iliacus* (as ILIUM)]
HOMOPHONES: *ileac*

ilium *noun*
• "ILLY um"
• the bone forming the upper part of each half of the human pelvis.
• [Latin]
HOMOPHONES: *ileum*

illation *noun*
• "ill LAY sh'n"
• a deduction or conclusion.
• [Latin *illatio* from *illatus* past participle of *inferre* INFER]
HOMOPHONES: *elation*

illative *adjective*
• "ill LAY tiv" or "ILLA tiv"
• (of a word) stating or introducing an inference.
• [Latin *illativus* (as ILLATION)]
• **illatively** *adverb*

illegal *adjective*
• "ill LEE g'll"
• not legal.
• [Latin *in-* not, without + *legalis* from *lex legis* law]
• **illegality** *noun*
• **illegally** *adverb*

illegible *adjective*
• "ill LEDGE a bull"
• difficult or impossible to read; not legible.
• [Latin *in-* not, without + LEGIBLE]
• **illegibility** *noun*
• **illegibly** *adverb*

illegitimate *adjective*
• "illa JITTA mit"
• (of a child) born of parents not married to each other.
• [Latin *in-* not, without + LEGITIMATE]
• **illegitimacy** *noun*
• **illegitimately** *adverb*

illiberal *adjective*
• "ill LIBBER 'll"
• intolerant, narrow-minded.
• [Latin *in-* not, without + LIBERAL]
• **illiberality** *noun*
• **illiberally** *adverb*

illicit *adjective*
• "ill LISSIT"
• unlawful, forbidden.
• [Latin *in-* not, without + LICIT]
• **illicitly** *adverb*
• **illicitness** *noun*
HOMOPHONES: *elicit*

illimitable *adjective*
• "ill LIMMIT a bull"
• limitless, boundless.
• [Latin *in-* not, without, *limes limitis* boundary, frontier]
• **illimitably** *adverb*

illiquid *adjective*
• "ill LICK wid"
• (of assets) not easily converted into cash.
• [Latin *in-* not, without + LIQUID]
• **illiquidity** *noun*

illiterate *adjective*
• "ill LITTER it"
• unable to read or write.
• [Latin *in-* not, without + LITERATE]
• **illiteracy** *noun*
HOMOPHONES: *aliterate, aliteracy*

illogical *adjective*
• "ill LODGE a k'll"
• devoid of or contrary to logic.
• [Latin *in-* not, without + LOGIC]
• **illogic** *noun*
• **illogicality** *noun*
• **illogically** *adverb*

illume *verb*
• "ill LUME"
• light up; make bright.
• [shortening of ILLUMINE]

illuminance *noun*
• "ill LOOMIN ince"
• the amount of luminous flux per unit area.
• [as ILLUMINATE]

illuminate *verb*
• "ill LOOMIN ate"
• light up; make bright.
• [Latin *illuminare* (*in* in, *lumen luminis* light)]
• **illuminant** *noun*
• **illuminating** *adjective*
• **illuminatingly** *adverb*
• **illumination** *noun*
• **illuminator** *noun*

illuminati *plural noun*
• "ill loomin ATTY" or "ill loomin OTTY"
• persons claiming to possess special knowledge or enlightenment.
• [pl. of Latin *illuminatus* or Italian *illuminato* past participle (as ILLUMINATE)]
• **illuminism** *noun*
• **illuminist** *noun*

illumine *verb*
• "ill LOOMIN"
• light up; make bright.
• [Old French *illuminer* from Latin (as ILLUMINATE)]

illusion *noun*
• "ill LOO zh'n"
• deception, delusion.
• [French from Latin *illusio -onis* from *illudere* mock (*in* in, *ludere lus-* play)]
• **illusional** *adjective*
HOMOPHONES: *allusion*

illusionist *noun*
• "ill LOO zh'n ist"
• a person who produces illusions, esp. a conjuror.
• [as ILLUSION]
• **illusionism** *noun*
• **illusionistic** *adjective*

illusive *adjective*
• "ill LOO siv"
• = ILLUSORY.
• [medieval Latin *illusivus* (as ILLUSION)]
HOMOPHONES: *allusive, elusive*

illusory *adjective*
• "ill LOOZE a ree" or "ill LOOCE a ree"
• deceptive (esp. as regards value or content).
• [Church Latin *illusorius* (as ILLUSION)]

illustrate *verb*
• "ILL us trate"

• provide (a book, newspaper, etc.) with pictures.
• [Latin *illustrare* (*in* in, *lustrare* light up)]
• **illustration** *noun*
• **illustrational** *adjective*
• **illustrator** *noun*

illustrative *adjective*
• "ILL us tray tiv"
• serving as an explanation or example.
• [as ILLUSTRATE]

illustrious *adjective*
• "ill LUSS tree us"
• distinguished, renowned.
• [Latin *illustris* (as ILLUSTRATE)]
• **illustriously** *adverb*
• **illustriousness** *noun*

Illyrian *adjective*
• "ill LIRRY 'n"
• of or relating to ancient Illyria on the E Adriatic coast.

ilmenite *noun*
• "ILMA nite"
• a black ore of titanium.
• [*Ilmen* mountains in the Urals + Greek *lithos* stone]

imaginal *adjective*
• "im MADGE in 'll"
• of or an image or images.
• [Latin *imago imagin-* image]

imagine *verb*
• "im MADGE in"
• form a mental image or concept of.
• [Old French *imaginer* from Latin *imaginari* from *imago* image]
• **imaginable** *adjective*
• **imaginary** *adjective*
• **imagination** *noun*
• **imaginative** *adjective*
• **imaginatively** *adverb*
• **imaginer** *noun*

imagism *noun*
• "IM idge izm"
• a movement in early 20th-c. poetry which, in revolt against Romanticism, sought clarity of expression through the use of precise images and free verse.
• [Latin *imago* image]
• **imagist** *noun*
• **imagistic** *adjective*
• **imagistically** *adverb*

imago *noun*
• "im MAY go"
• the final and fully developed stage of an insect after all metamorphoses, e.g. a butterfly or beetle.
• [modern Latin sense of *imago* image]

imam *noun*
• "im AM" or "im OM"
• a leader of prayers in a mosque.
• [Arabic *'imām* leader, from *'amma* precede]
• **imamate** *noun*

Imari *noun*
• "im AR ee"
• designating a high-quality Japanese porcelain with rich decoration and delicate colouring.
• [a town in NW Kyushu, Japan]

imbecile *noun*
• "IMBA sill" or "IMBA sile"
• a stupid person.
• [French *imbécil(l)e* from Latin *imbecillus* (*in-* not, without, *baculum* stick) originally in sense 'without supporting staff']
• **imbecilic** *adjective* "imba SILLIC"
• **imbecility** *noun* "imba SILLA tee"

imbibe *verb*
• "im BIBE"
• drink (esp. alcoholic liquor).
• [Latin *imbibere* (*in* in, *bibere* drink)]
• **imbiber** *noun*
• **imbibition** *noun* "imba BISH'n"

imbricate *verb*
• "IMBRA cate"
• arrange (leaves, the scales of a fish, etc.), or be arranged, so as to overlap like roof tiles.
• [Latin *imbricare imbricat-* cover with roof tiles, from *imbrex -icis* roof tile, from *imber* shower of rain]
• **imbrication** *noun*

imbroglio *noun*
• "im BROLEY oh"
• a complicated, confused, or embarrassing situation, esp. a political or interpersonal one.
• [Italian *imbrogliare* confuse (as EMBROIL)]

imbue *verb*
• "im BYOO"
• inspire or permeate (with feelings, opinions, or qualities).
• [originally as past participle, from French *imbu* or Latin *imbutus* from *imbuere* moisten]

imide *noun*
• "IM ide"
• an organic compound containing the group (-CO.NH.CO.-) formed by replacing two of the hydrogen atoms in ammonia by carbonyl groups.
• [originally French: arbitrary alteration of AMIDE]

imine *noun*
• "IM een"
• a compound containing the group (-NH-) formed by replacing two of the hydrogen atoms in ammonia by other groups.
• [German *Imin* arbitrary alteration of *Amin* AMINE]

imipramine *noun*
• "im IPPRA meen"
• a tricyclic tertiary amine used to treat depression.
• [IMINE + PROPYL + AMINE]

imitate *verb*
• "IMMA tate"
• follow the example of; copy the action(s) of.
• [Latin *imitari imitat-*, related to *imago* image]
• **imitable** *adjective*
• **imitation** *noun*
• **imitative** *adjective*
• **imitatively** *adverb*
• **imitator** *noun*

immaculate *adjective*
• "im MACK yoo lit"
• pure, spotless; perfectly clean and tidy.
• [Latin *immaculatus* (*in-* not, without, *maculatus* from *macula* spot)]
• **immaculacy** *noun*
• **immaculately** *adverb*
• **immaculateness** *noun*

immanent *adjective*
• "IMMA n'nt"
• naturally present; indwelling, inherent.
• [Late Latin *immanēre* (Latin *in* in, *manēre* remain)]
• **immanence** *noun*
• **immanentism** *noun*
• **immanentist** *noun*
HOMOPHONES: *imminent, imminence*

immaterial *adjective*
• "imma TEERY 'll"
• of no essential consequence; unimportant, irrelevant.
• [Latin *in-* not, without + MATERIAL]
• **immateriality** *noun*

immaterialism *noun*
• "imma TEERY 'll izm"
• the doctrine that all things exist only as ideas or perceptions of a mind, that matter has no objective existence.
• [as IMMATERIAL]
• **immaterialist** *noun*

immature *adjective*
• "imma CHUR"
• (of cells, animals, etc.) not mature or fully developed.
• [Latin *in-* not, without + MATURE]
• **immaturely** *adverb*
• **immaturity** *noun*

immeasurable *adjective*
• "im MEZHUR a bull"
• not measurable; immense.
• [Latin *in-* not, without + MEASURE]
• **immeasurability** *noun*
• **immeasurably** *adverb*

immediate *adjective*
• "im MEEDY it"
• occurring or done at once or without delay.
• [French *immédiat* or Late Latin *immediatus* (Latin *in-* not, without, MEDIATE)]
• **immediacy** *noun*
• **immediately** *adverb*
• **immediateness** *noun*

immemorial *adjective*
• "im muh MORRY 'll"
• ancient beyond memory or record.
• [Latin *in-* not, without + MEMORIAL]
• **immemorially** *adverb*

immense *adjective*
• "im MENSE"
• immeasurably large or great; huge.
• [French from Latin *immensus* immeasurable (*in-* not, without, *mensus* past participle of *metiri* measure)]
• **immensity** *noun*

immensely *adverb*
• "im MENSE lee"
• very much.
• [as IMMENSE]

immerse *verb*
• "im MURSE"
• dip, plunge, or submerge in a liquid.
• [Latin *immergere* (*in* in, *mergere mers-* dip)]
HOMOPHONES: *emerse*

immersion *noun*
• "im MUR zh'n"
• a method of teaching a foreign language by the exclusive use of that language, usu. at a special school, in a special class, etc.
• [as IMMERSE]
HOMOPHONES: *emersion*

immigrate *verb*
• "IMMA grate"
• come as a permanent resident to a country other than one's native land.
• [Latin *immigrare* (*in* in, MIGRATE)]
• **immigrant** *noun*
• **immigration** *noun*

imminent *adjective*
• "IMMA n'nt"
• (of an event, esp. danger) impending; about to happen.
• [Latin *imminēre imminent-* overhang, project]
• **imminence** *noun*
• **imminently** *adverb*
HOMOPHONES: *immanent, immanence*

immiscible *adjective*
• "im MISSA bull"
• unable to be mixed.
• [Late Latin *immiscibilis* (Latin *in-* not, without, MISCIBLE)]
• **immiscibility** *noun*

immiseration *noun*
• "im mizzer AY sh'n"
• economic impoverishment.
• [translation of German *Verelendung*]

immobile *adjective*
• "im MOE bile" or "im MOE bull"
• not moving.
• [Latin *in-* not, without + *mobilis* from *movēre* move]
• **immobility** *noun*

immobilize *verb*
ALSO SPELLED: esp. *Brit.* **-ise**
• "im MOE b'll ize"
• make or keep immobile.
• [as IMMOBILE]
• **immobilization** *noun* (also esp. *Brit.* **-isation**)
• **immobilizer** *noun* (also esp. *Brit.* **-iser**)

immoderate *adjective*
• "im MODDER it"
• excessive; lacking moderation.
• [Latin *in-* not, without + MODERATE]
• **immoderately** *adverb*
• **immoderateness** *noun*
• **immoderation** *noun*

immodest *adjective*
• "im MOD ist"
• lacking modesty.
• [Latin *in-* not, without + *modestus* keeping due measure]
• **immodestly** *adverb*
• **immodesty** *noun*

immolate *verb*
• "IM'll ate"
• kill or offer as a sacrifice, esp. by burning.
• [Latin *immolare* sprinkle with sacrificial meal (*in* in, *mola* meal, ground grain)]
• **immolation** *noun*
• **immolator** *noun*

immoral *adjective*
• "im MOR'll"
• not conforming to accepted standards of morality.
• [Latin *in-* not, without + *moralis* from *mos moris* custom, pl. *mores* morals]
• **immoralist** *noun*
• **immorality** *noun*
• **immorally** *adverb*

immortal *adjective*
• "im MORT'll"
• living forever; not mortal.
• [Latin *in-* not, without + *mortalis* from *mors mortis* death]
• **immortality** *noun*
• **immortalization** *noun* (also esp. *Brit.* **-isation**)
• **immortalize** *verb* (also esp. *Brit.* **-ise**)
• **immortally** *adverb*

immortelle *noun*
• "im mor TELL"
• a flower of the daisy family with papery texture, retaining its shape and colour after being dried, esp. a helichrysum.
• [French, feminine of *immortel* IMMORTAL]

immovable *adjective*
• "im MOOVA bull"
• unable to be moved.
• [Latin *in-* not, without + *movere* move]
• **immovably** *adverb*

immune *adjective*
• "im MYOON"
• resistant to a particular infection, toxin, etc., owing to the presence of specific antibodies or sensitized white blood cells.
• [French from Latin *immunis* exempt from public service or charge (*in-* not, without, *munis* ready for service)]
• **immunity** *noun*

immunize *verb*
ALSO SPELLED: esp. *Brit.* **-ise**
• "IM yoo nize"
• make immune, esp. to infection, usu. by inoculation.
• [as IMMUNE]
• **immunization** *noun* (also esp. *Brit.* **-isation**)
• **immunizer** *noun* (also esp. *Brit.* **-iser**)

immunoassay *noun*
• "im myoono a SAY"
• the determination of the presence or quantity of a substance, esp. a protein, through its properties as an antigen or antibody.
• [as IMMUNE + ASSAY]

immunochemistry *noun*
• "im myoono KEMMA stree"
• the chemical study of immune systems.
• [as IMMUNE + CHEMISTRY]

immunocompromised *adjective*
• "im myoono COMPRA mized"
• having an impaired immune system.
• [as IMMUNE + COMPROMISE]

immunodeficiency *noun*
• "im myoono duh FISH'n see"
• a reduction in a person's normal immune defences.
• [as IMMUNE + DEFICIENT]
• **immunodeficient** *adjective*

immunofluorescence *noun*
• "im myoono fluh RESS ince"
• a technique for determining the location of an antigen or antibody in tissues by reaction with an antibody or antigen labelled with a fluorescent dye.
• [as IMMUNE + FLUORESCENCE]
• **immunofluorescent** *adjective*

immunogenic *adjective*
• "im myoono JENNIC"
• of, relating to, or possessing the ability to elicit an immune response.
• [as IMMUNE + GENESIS]
• **immunogenicity** *noun*
"im myoono juh NISSA tee"

immunoglobulin *noun*
• "im myoono GLOB yoo lin"
• any of a group of structurally related proteins which function as antibodies.
• [as IMMUNE + GLOBULIN]

immunology *noun*
• "im yoo NOLLA jee"
• the scientific study of resistance to infection in humans and animals.
• [as IMMUNE + Greek *logos* word]
• **immunologic** *adjective*
• **immunological** *adjective*
• **immunologically** *adverb*
• **immunologist** *noun*

immunosuppression *noun*
• "im myoono suh PRESH'n"
• the partial or complete suppression of the immune response of an individual, esp. to maintain the survival of an organ after a transplant operation.
• [as IMMUNE + SUPPRESS]
• **immunosuppressant** *noun*
• **immunosuppressed** *adjective*
• **immunosuppressive** *adjective*

immunotherapy *noun*
• "im myoono THERRA pee"
• the prevention or treatment of disease with substances that stimulate the immune response.
• [as IMMUNE + THERAPY]
• **immunotherapeutic** *adjective*
"im myoono therra PYOOTIC"

immure *verb*
• "im MYOOR"
• enclose within walls; imprison.
• [French *emmurer* or medieval Latin *immurare* (Latin *in* in, *murus* wall)]
• **immurement** *noun*

immutable *adjective*
• "im MUTE a bull"
• unchangeable.
• [Latin *in-* not, without + MUTABLE]
• **immutability** *noun*
• **immutably** *adverb*

impair *verb*
• "im PAIR"
• damage or weaken.
• [Old French *empeirier* (Latin *in* in, Late Latin *pejorare* from Latin *pejor* worse)]
• **impairment** *noun*

impaired *adjective*
• "im PAIRD"
• (of driving or the driver of a car, boat, snowmobile, etc.) adversely affected by alcohol or narcotics, specifically for legal purposes, having a blood alcohol level greater than .08.
• [as IMPAIR]

impala *noun*
• "im PALA"
• a medium-sized reddish-brown grazing antelope, *Aepyceros melampus*, of southern and eastern African savannah, the male of which has lyre-shaped horns.
• [Zulu]

impale *verb*
• "im PALE"
• transfix or pierce with a sharp instrument.
• [French *empaler* or medieval Latin *impalare* (Latin *in* in, *palus* stake)]
• **impalement** *noun*
• **impaler** *noun*

impalpable *adjective*
• "im PAL puh bull"
• not easily grasped by the mind; intangible.
• [Latin *in-* not, without + PALPABLE]
• **impalpability** *noun*
• **impalpably** *adverb*

impartial *adjective*
• "im PAR sh'll"
• treating all sides in a dispute etc. equally; unprejudiced, fair.
• [Latin *in-* not, without + *partialis* from *pars* part]
• **impartiality** *noun* "im parshy ALA tee"
• **impartially** *adverb*

impassable *adjective*
• "im PASSA bull"
• that cannot be traversed.
• [Latin *in-* not, without + 'passable' ultimately from Latin *passus* pace]
• **impassability** *noun*
• **impassably** *adverb*
HOMOPHONES: *impassible, impassibility*

impasse *noun*
• "IM pass"
• a position from which progress is impossible; deadlock.
• [French from Latin *in-* not, without, *passus* pace]

impassible *adjective*
• "im PASSA bull"
• (in Christian theology) not subject to suffering.
• [Latin *in-* not, without + PASSIBLE]
• **impassibility** *noun*
HOMOPHONES: *impassable, impassability*

impassioned *adjective*
• "im PASH'nd"
• deeply felt; ardent.
• [Latin *in* in + PASSION]

impassive *adjective*
• "im PASSIV"
• not feeling or showing emotion.
• [Latin *in-* not, without + PASSION]
• **impassively** *adverb*
• **impassivity** *noun* "im pass IVVA tee"

impasto *noun*
• "im PASS toe"
• the process of laying on paint thickly.
• [Italian *impastare* (Latin *in* in, *pastare* paste)]
• **impastoed** *adjective*

impatiens *noun*
• "im PAY shince"

• any plant of the genus *Impatiens*, including busy Lizzie and touch-me-not.
• [modern Latin from IMPATIENT]
HOMOPHONES: *impatience*

impatient *adjective*
• "im PAY sh'nt"
• lacking patience or tolerance.
• [Latin *in-* not, without + PATIENT]
• **impatience** *noun*
• **impatiently** *adverb*
HOMOPHONES: *impatiens*

impeccable *adjective*
• "im PECKA bull"
• (of behaviour, performance, etc.) faultless, exemplary.
• [Latin *impeccabilis* (*in-* not, without, *peccare* sin)]
• **impeccability** *noun*
• **impeccably** *adverb*

impecunious *adjective*
• "im puh KYOO nee us"
• having little or no money.
• [Latin *in-* not, without + obsolete *pecunious* having money, from Latin *pecuniosus* from *pecunia* money from *pecu* cattle]
• **impecuniosity** *noun*
"impa kyoo nee OSSA tee"
• **impecuniously** *adverb*
• **impecuniousness** *noun*

impedance *noun*
• "im PEE dince"
• the total effective resistance of an electric circuit etc. to alternating current, arising from ohmic resistance and reactance.
• [as IMPEDE]

impede *verb*
• "im PEED"
• retard by obstructing; hinder.
• [Latin *impedire* shackle the feet of (*in* in, *pes* foot)]

impediment *noun*
• "im PEDDA m'nt"
• a hindrance or obstruction.
• [Latin *impedimentum* (as IMPEDE)]
• **impedimental** *adjective*

impedimenta *plural noun*
• "im pedda MENTA"
• equipment for an expedition, esp. when considered as bulky or an encumbrance.
• [Latin, pl. of *impedimentum*: see IMPEDIMENT]

impel *verb*
• "im PELL"
• drive, force, or urge into action.
• [Latin *impellere* (*in* in, *pellere puls-* drive)]
• **impeller** *noun*

impenetrable *adjective*
• "im PENNA truh bull"
• that cannot be penetrated, pierced or entered.
• [Latin *in-* not, without + PENETRATE]
• **impenetrability** *noun*
• **impenetrably** *adverb*

impenitent *adjective*
• "im PENNA t'nt"
• not repentant or penitent.
• [Church Latin *impaenitens* (Latin *in-* not, without, PENITENT)]
• **impenitence** *noun*
• **impenitently** *adverb*

imperative *adjective*
• "im PERRA tiv"
• urgent.
• [Late Latin *imperativus* from *imperare* command (Latin *in* in, *parare* make ready)]
• **imperatively** *adverb*
• **imperativeness** *noun*

imperator *noun*
• "imper AT or" or "imper AY tur"
• (in ancient Rome) commander (a title conferred under the Republic on a victorious general and under the Empire on the emperor).
• [Latin (as IMPERATIVE)]
• **imperatorial** *adjective*

imperceptible *adjective*
• "imper SEPTA bull"
• that cannot be perceived.
• [Latin *in-* not, without + PERCEPTIBLE]
• **imperceptibility** *noun*
• **imperceptibly** *adverb*

impercipient *adjective*
• "imper SIPPY 'nt"
• lacking in perception.
• [Latin *in-* not, without + PERCIPIENT]
• **impercipience** *noun*

imperforate *adjective*
• "im PURR fur ate"
• not perforated.
• [Latin *in-* not, without + PERFORATE]

imperial *adjective*
• "im PEERY 'll"
• of or characteristic of an empire or comparable sovereign state.
• [Old French from Latin *imperialis* from *imperium* command, authority]
• **imperially** *adverb*
HOMOPHONES: *empyreal*

imperialism *noun*
• "im PEERY 'll izm"
• an imperial rule or system.
• [as IMPERIAL]
• **imperialist** *noun*
• **imperialistic** *adjective*
• **imperialistically** *adverb*
• **imperialize** *verb* (also esp. *Brit.* **-ise**)

imperil *verb*
• "im PARE 'll"
• bring or put into danger.
• [Latin *in* in + PERIL]

imperious *adjective*
• "im PEERY us"
• overbearing, domineering, expecting obedience.
• [Latin *imperiosus* from *imperium* command, authority]
• **imperiously** *adverb*
• **imperiousness** *noun*

imperium *noun*
• "im PEERY um"
• absolute power or authority.
• [Latin, = command, authority]

impermanent *adjective*
• "im PURMA n'nt"
• not permanent; transient.
• [Latin *in-* not, without + PERMANENT]
• **impermanence** *noun*
• **impermanently** *adverb*

impermeable *adjective*
• "im PURMY a bull"
• that cannot be penetrated.
• [French *imperméable* or Late Latin *impermeabilis* (Latin *in-* not, without, PERMEABLE)]
• **impermeability** *noun*

impermissible *adjective*
• "im purr MISSA bull"
• not allowable.
• [Latin *in-* not, without + PERMISSIBLE]
• **impermissibility** *noun*

impersonate *verb*
• "im PURSA nate"
• pretend to be (another person) in order to deceive others.
• [Latin *in* in + *persona* person]
• **impersonation** *noun*
• **impersonator** *noun*

impertinent *adjective*
• "im PURTA n'nt"
• rude or insolent; lacking proper respect.
• [Latin *in-* not, without + PERTINENT]
• **impertinence** *noun*
• **impertinently** *adverb*

imperturbable *adjective*
• "im purr TURBA bull"
• not excitable; calm.
• [Latin *in-* not, without + PERTURB]
• **imperturbability** *noun*
• **imperturbably** *adverb*

impervious *adjective*
• "im PURVY us"
• not responsive (to an argument, outside influence, etc.).
• [Latin *impervius* (*in-* not, without, PERVIOUS)]
• **imperviousness** *noun*

impetigo *noun*
• "impa TIE go"
• a contagious bacterial skin infection forming pustules and yellow crusty sores.
• [Latin *impetigo -ginis* from *impetere* assail]

impetuous *adjective*
• "im PETCH oo us"
• acting or done rashly or with sudden energy.
• [Old French *impetueux* from Late Latin *impetuosus* (as IMPETUS)]
• **impetuosity** *noun* "im petch oo OSSA tee"
• **impetuously** *adverb*
• **impetuousness** *noun*

impetus *noun*
• "IMPA tuss"
• the force or energy with which a body moves.
• [Latin, = assault, force, from *impetere* assail (*in* in, *petere* seek)]

impi *noun*
• "IMPY"
• a body of Zulu warriors or armed tribesmen.
• [Zulu, = regiment, armed band]

impinge *verb*
• "im PINGE"
• make an impact; have an effect.
• [Latin *impingere* drive (a thing) at (*in* in, *pangere* fix, drive)]
• **impingement** *noun*

impious *adjective*
• "IMPY us"
• not pious; lacking reverence for God or a god.
• [Latin *in-* not, without + PIOUS]
• **impiety** *noun* "im PIE a tee"
• **impiously** *adverb*
• **impiousness** *noun*

implacable *adjective*
• "im PLACKA bull"
• that cannot be appeased or placated.
• [Latin *in-* not, without + *placare* appease]
• **implacability** *noun*
• **implacably** *adverb*

implausible *adjective*
• "im PLOZZA bull"
• not plausible.
• [Latin *in-* not, without + PLAUSIBLE]
• **implausibility** *noun*
• **implausibly** *adverb*

implement *noun*
• "IMPLA m'nt"
• a tool, instrument, or utensil.
• [medieval Latin *implementa* (pl.) from *implēre* employ (Latin *in* in, *plēre plet-* fill)]
• **implementable** *adjective*
• **implementation** *noun*
• **implementer** *noun*

implicate *verb*
• "IMPLA cate"
• show (a person or thing) to be concerned or involved (in a charge, crime, etc.).
• [Latin *implicatus* past participle of *implicare* (*in* in, *plicare, plicat-* or *plicit-* fold)]

implication *noun*
• "impla CAY sh'n"

• what is involved in or implied by something else.
• [as IMPLICATE]

implicit *adjective*
• "im PLISSIT"
• implied though not plainly expressed.
• [French *implicite* or Latin *implicitus* (as IMPLICATE)]
• **implicitly** *adverb*
• **implicitness** *noun*

implode *verb*
• "im PLODE"
• burst or cause to burst inwards.
• [Latin *in* in + *-plodere*, after EXPLODE]
• **implosion** *noun*
• **implosive** *adjective*

implore *verb*
• "im PLORE"
• entreat (a person).
• [French *implorer* or Latin *implorare* invoke with tears (*in* in, *plorare* weep)]
• **imploringly** *adverb*

impolitic *adjective*
• "im POLLA tick"
• failing to possess or display prudence; unwise.
• [Latin *in-* not, without + POLITIC]

imponderable *adjective*
• "im PONDER a bull"
• that cannot be estimated or assessed in any definite way.
• [Latin *in-* not, without + French *pondérable* from Old French *ponderer* from Latin *ponderare* from *pondus -eris* weight]
• **imponderability** *noun*
• **imponderably** *adverb*

importunate *adjective*
• "im PORCH'n it"
• making persistent or pressing requests, demands for attention, etc.
• [Latin *importunus* inconvenient (*in-* not, without, *portunus* from *portus* harbour)]
• **importunately** *adverb*
• **importunity** *noun* "im pore TUNA tee"

importune *verb*
• "im pore TUNE"
• solicit (a person) pressingly; beg or demand insistently.
• [French *importuner* or medieval Latin *importunari* (as IMPORTUNATE)]

imposition *noun*
• "impa ZISH'n"
• the act or an instance of imposing; the process of being imposed.
• [Latin *impositiōn* from *imponere imposit-* inflict, deceive (*in* in, *ponere* put)]

impossible *adjective*
• "im POSSA bull"
• not possible; that cannot occur, exist, or be done.
• [Latin *in-* not, without + POSSIBLE]
• **impossibility** *noun*
• **impossibly** *adverb*

impost *noun*
• "IM post" ("POST" rhymes with *TOAST*)
• a tax, duty, or tribute.
• [French from medieval Latin *impost-* participle stem of Latin *imponere*: see IMPOSITION]

imposter *noun*
ALSO SPELLED: **impostor**
• "im POSS tur"
• a person who assumes a false character or pretends to be someone else.
• [French *imposteur* from Late Latin *impostor* (as IMPOST)]

imposture *noun*
• "im POSS chur"
• the act or an instance of fraudulent deception.
• [French from Late Latin *impostura* (as IMPOSTER)]

impotent *adjective*
• "IMPA t'nt"
• powerless; lacking all strength.
• [Latin *in-* not, without + POTENT]
• **impotence** *noun*
• **impotency** *noun*
• **impotently** *adverb*

impoverish *verb*
• "im POVVER ish"
• make poor.
• [Old French *empoverir* from *povre*, *poure* from Latin *pauper* poor]
• **impoverishment** *noun*

impracticable *adjective*
• "im PRACTIC a bull"
• impossible in practice.
• [Latin *in-* not, without + PRACTICABLE]
• **impracticability** *noun*
• **impracticably** *adverb*

impractical *adjective*
• "im PRACTIC 'll"
• not practical.
• [Latin *in-* not, without + PRACTICAL]
• **impracticality** *noun*
• **impractically** *adverb*

imprecation *noun*
• "impra CAY sh'n"
• a spoken curse; a malediction.
• [Latin *imprecatiōn* (*in* in, *precari* pray)]
• **imprecatory** *adjective* "IMPRA cayta ree" or "IMPRA kuh tory"

imprecise *adjective*
• "impra SICE"
• not precise.
• [Latin *in-* not, without + PRECISE]
• **imprecisely** *adverb*

- **impreciseness** *noun*
- **imprecision** *noun* "impra SIZH'n"

impregnable *adjective*
- "im PREGNA bull"
- (of a fortress etc.) that cannot be taken by force.
- [Old French *imprenable* (Latin *in-* not, without, *prendre* take)]
- **impregnability** *noun*
- **impregnably** *adverb*

impresario *noun*
- "impra SAR ee oh" or "impra SERRY oh"
- an organizer of public entertainments, esp. a manager or promoter of performing arts companies or productions.
- [Italian from *impresa* undertaking]

imprescriptible *adjective*
- "im pree SCRIPTA bull"
- (of rights) that cannot be taken away by prescription or lapse of time.
- [medieval Latin *imprescriptibilis* (Latin *in-* not, without, PRESCRIBE)]

imprest *noun*
- "IM prest"
- an advance; a loan.
- [originally *in prest* from Old French *prest* loan, advance pay, from *prester* from Latin *praestare* furnish (*prae-* before, *stare* stand)]

imprimatur *noun*
- "impra MATTER" or "impra MAYTER"
- an official licence to print (an ecclesiastical or religious book etc.).
- [Latin, = let it be printed]

improbable *adjective*
- "im PROBBA bull"
- not likely to be true or to happen.
- [Latin *in-* not, without + PROBABLE]
- **improbability** *noun*
- **improbably** *adverb*

impromptu *adjective*
- "im PROMP too"
- without preparation; on the spur of the moment; unrehearsed.
- [French from Latin *in promptu* in readiness: see PROMPT]

impropriety *noun*
- "impra PRY a tee"
- lack of propriety; indecency.
- [Latin *in-* not, without + PROPRIETY]

improvident *adjective*
- "im PROVVA d'nt"
- lacking foresight or care for the future.
- [Latin *in-* not, without + PROVIDENT]
- **improvidence** *noun*
- **improvidently** *adverb*

improvise *verb*
- "IMPRA vize"
- compose or perform (music, dialogue, etc.) on the spur of the moment, not working from a text or score, etc.
- [French *improviser* or Italian *improvvisare* from *improvviso* extempore, from Latin *improvisus* past participle (*in-* not, without, PROVIDE)]
- **improvisation** *noun* "impra vizz AY sh'n"
- **improvisational** *adjective*
- **improvisatory** *adjective*

"im PROVVA zuh tory"
- **improviser** *noun*

imprudent *adjective*
- "im PROO d'nt"
- rash, indiscreet.
- [Latin *in-* not, without + Old French *prudent* or Latin *prudens* = *providens* PROVIDENT]
- **imprudence** *noun*
- **imprudently** *adverb*

impudent *adjective*
- "IMP yoo d'nt"
- insolently disrespectful; impertinent.
- [Latin *impudens* (*in-* not, without, *pudēre* be ashamed)]
- **impudence** *noun*
- **impudently** *adverb*

impugn *verb*
- "im PYOON"
- challenge or call in question (a statement, action, someone's character, etc.).
- [Latin *impugnare* assail (*in* in, *pugnare* fight)]
- **impugnment** *noun*

impunity *noun*
- "im PYOONA tee"
- exemption from punishment or from the injurious consequences of an action.
- [Latin *impunitas* from *impunis* (*in-* not, without, *poena* penalty)]

impute *verb*
- "im PYOOT"
- regard (esp. something undesirable) as being done or caused or possessed by.
- [Old French *imputer* from Latin *imputare* enter in the account (*in* in, *putare* reckon)]
- **imputable** *adjective*
- **imputation** *noun*

inability *noun*
- "inna BILLA tee"
- the state of being unable.
- [Latin *in-* not, without + ABILITY]

inaccessible *adjective*
- "in ack SESSA bull"
- not accessible; that cannot be reached.
- [Latin *in-* not, without + ACCESSIBLE]
- **inaccessibility** *noun*
- **inaccessibly** *adverb*

inaccurate *adjective*
- "in ACK yur it"
- not accurate; inexact, imprecise, incorrect.
- [Latin *in-* not, without + ACCURATE]
- **inaccuracy** *noun*
- **inaccurately** *adverb*

inadequate *adjective*
- "in ADDA kwit"
- not adequate; insufficient.
- [Latin *in-* not, without + ADEQUATE]
- **inadequacy** *noun*
- **inadequately** *adverb*

inadmissible *adjective*
- "in ad MISSA bull"
- that cannot be admitted or allowed.
- [Latin *in-* not, without + ADMISSIBLE]
- **inadmissibility** *noun*

inadvertent *adjective*
- "in ad VUR t'nt"
- (of an action) unintentional.
- [Latin *in-* not, without + obsolete *advertent* attentive, from Latin *advertere* (as ADVERSE)]
- **inadvertence** *noun*
- **inadvertently** *adverb*

inadvisable *adjective*
- "in ad VIZE a bull"
- not advisable.
- [Latin *in-* not, without + ADVISABLE]
- **inadvisability** *noun*

inalienable *adjective*
- "in AYLEE 'n a bull"
- that cannot be transferred to another; not alienable.
- [Latin *in-* not, without + ALIENABLE]
- **inalienably** *adverb*

inalterable *adjective*
- "in ALTER a bull"
- not alterable; that cannot be changed.
- [Latin *in-* not, without + ALTER]
- **inalterably** *adverb*

inamorata *noun*
- "in ammer ATTA"
- a female lover.
- [feminine of INAMORATO]

inamorato *noun*
- "in ammer ATTO"
- a lover.
- [Italian, past participle of *inamorare* enamour (Latin *in* in, *amore* from *amor* love)]

inane *adjective*
- "in ANE"
- silly, senseless.
- [Latin *inanis* empty, vain]
- **inanely** *adverb*
- **inanity** *noun* "in ANNA tee"

inanimate *adjective*
- "in ANNA mit"
- not animate; not endowed with (esp. animal) life.
- [Latin *in-* not, without + ANIMATE]
- **inanimation** *noun*

inanition *noun*
- "inna NISH'n"
- exhaustion resulting from lack of nourishment.
- [Late Latin *inanitio* from Latin *inanire* make empty (as INANE)]

inapparent *adjective*
- "inna PARE 'nt"
- causing no noticeable signs or symptoms.
- [Latin *in-* not, without + APPARENT]

inapplicable *adjective*
- "inna PLICKA bull" or "in APP licka bull"
- not relevant or appropriate.
- [Latin *in-* not, without + APPLICABLE]
- **inapplicability** *noun*
- **inapplicably** *adverb*

inapposite *adjective*
- "in APPA zit"
- not apposite; unsuitable, not pertinent.
- [Latin *in-* not, without + APPOSITE]

inappropriate *adjective*
- "inna PRO pree it"
- not appropriate; unsuitable.
- [Latin *in-* not, without + APPROPRIATE[1]]
- **inappropriately** *adverb*
- **inappropriateness** *noun*

inarch *verb*
- "in ARCH"
- graft (a plant) by connecting a growing branch without separation from the parent stock.
- [Latin *in* in + 'arch' from Old French *arche*, ultimately from Latin *arcus* arc]

inarguable *adjective*
- "in ARG yoo a bull"
- that cannot be argued about or disputed.
- [Latin *in-* not, without + ARGUABLE]
- **inarguably** *adverb*

inarticulate *adjective*
- "in ar TICK yoo lit"
- unable to speak distinctly or express oneself clearly or fluently.
- [Latin *in-* not, without + ARTICULATE]
- **inarticulacy** *noun*
- **inarticulately** *adverb*
- **inarticulateness** *noun*

inasmuch *adverb*
- "in az MUCH"
- since, because, seeing or considering that.
- ['in' + 'as' + 'much']

inattentive *adjective*
- "inna TEN tiv"
- not paying due attention; heedless.
- [Latin *in-* not, without + ATTENTION]
- **inattention** *noun*
- **inattentively** *adverb*
- **inattentiveness** *noun*

inaudible *adjective*
- "in ODDA bull"
- not audible; not able to be heard.
- [Latin *in-* not, without + AUDIBLE]
- **inaudibility** *noun*
- **inaudibly** *adverb*

inaugurate *verb*
- "in OGG yur ate" or "in OGGER ate"
- admit (a person) formally to office.
- [Latin *inaugurare* (*in* in, *augurare* take omens: see AUGUR)]
- **inaugural** *adjective*
- **inauguration** *noun*
- **inaugurator** *noun*

inauspicious *adjective*
- "in oss PISH us"
- not conducive to success; unpromising.
- [Latin *in-* not, without + AUSPICIOUS]
- **inauspiciously** *adverb*
- **inauspiciousness** *noun*

inauthentic *adjective*
- "in aw THENTIC" (with "TH" as in *THIN*)
- not in fact what it is said to be.
- [Latin *in-* not, without + AUTHENTIC]
- **inauthenticity** *noun* "in oth en TISSA tee"

inbred *adjective*
- "IN bred"
- inborn, innate, inherent.
- [Latin *in-* not, without + 'breed']

Inca *noun*
- "INKA"
- a member of a S American Aboriginal people who established an empire in the central Andes before the Spanish conquest in the early 16th c.
- [Quechua, = lord, royal person]
- **Incaic** *adjective* "in CAY ick"
- **Incan** *adjective*

incalculable *adjective*
- "in CAL kyoo luh bull"
- too great for calculation.
- [Latin *in-* not, without + CALCULATE]
- **incalculability** *noun*
- **incalculably** *adverb*

incandescent *adjective*
- "in can DESS'nt"
- (of an electric or other light) produced by a glowing white-hot filament.
- [French from Latin *incandescere* (*in* in, *candescere* inceptive of *candēre* be white)]
- **incandesce** *verb*
- **incandescence** *noun*
- **incandescently** *adverb*

incantation *noun*
- "in can TAY sh'n"
- a magical formula chanted or spoken.
- [Old French from Late Latin *incantatio -onis* from *incantare* chant, bewitch (Latin *in* in, *cantare* sing)]
- **incant** *verb*
- **incantational** *adjective*
- **incantatory** *adjective* "in CANTA tory"

incapable *adjective*
- "in CAY puh bull"
- incompetent, not capable.
- [Latin *in-* not, without + CAPABLE]
- **incapability** *noun*
- **incapably** *adverb*

incapacitate *verb*
- "inca PASSA tate"
- render incapable or unfit.
- [as INCAPACITY]
- **incapacitant** *noun*
- **incapacitation** *noun*

incapacity *noun*
- "inca PASSA tee"
- inability; lack of the necessary power or resources.
- [Latin *in-* not, without + CAPACIOUS]

incarcerate *verb*
- "in CARSA rate"
- imprison or confine.
- [medieval Latin *incarcerare* (Latin *in* in, *carcer* prison)]
- **incarceration** *noun*
- **incarcerator** *noun*

incarnadine *adjective*
- "in CARNA dine"
- crimson or flesh-coloured.
- [French *incarnadin -ine* from Italian *incarnadino* (for *-tino*) from *incarnato* INCARNATE]

incarnate *adjective*
- "in CAR nit"
- (of a person, spirit, quality, etc.) embodied in flesh, esp. in human form.
- [Church Latin *incarnare incarnat-* make flesh (Latin *in* in, *caro carnis* flesh)]

incarnation *noun*
- "in car NAY sh'n"
- the form, appearance, or mode of presentation assumed by a person or thing at a particular time.
- [as INCARNATE]

incendiary *adjective*
- "in SENDY airy"
- (of a substance or device, esp. a bomb) designed to cause fires.
- [Latin *incendiarius* from *incendium* conflagration from *incendere incens-* set fire to]
- **incendiarism** *noun*

incense[1] *noun*
- "IN sense"
- a gum or spice producing a sweet smell when burned.
- [Old French *encens*, *encenser* from Church Latin *incensum* a thing burned, incense: see INCENDIARY]

incense[2] *verb*
- "in SENSE"
- enrage; make angry.
- [Old French *incenser* (as INCENDIARY)]

incentive *noun*
- "in SEN tiv"
- a motive or incitement, esp. to action.
- [Latin *incentivus* setting the tune, from *incinere incent-* sing to (*in* in, *canere* sing)]
- **incent** *verb*
- **incentivize** *verb* (also esp. *Brit.* **-ise**)

inception *noun*
- "in SEP sh'n"
- a beginning.
- [Old French *inception* or Latin *inceptio incipere incept-* begin (*in* in, *capere* take)]
- **inceptive** *adjective*

incertitude *noun*
- "in SURTA tude"
- uncertainty, doubt.
- [Latin *in-* not, without + CERTITUDE]

incessant *adjective*
- "in SESS'nt"
- unceasing, continual, repeated.
- [French *incessant* or Late Latin *incessans* (Latin *in-* not, without, *cessans* present participle of *cessare* CEASE)]
- **incessantly** *adverb*

inchoate *adjective*
- "in CO it" or "in CO ate"
- incipient, just begun.
- [Latin *inchoatus* past participle of *inchoare* (*in* in, *choare* begin)]
- **inchoately** *adverb*
- **inchoative** *adjective*

incidence *noun*
- "INSA dince"
- the fact, manner, or rate of occurrence or action of a phenomenon among a group of people.
- [as INCIDENT]

incident *noun*
- "INSA d'nt"
- an event or occurrence.
- [French *incident* or Latin *incidere* (*in* in, *cadere* fall)]

incidental *adjective*
- "insa DENT 'll"
- having a minor role in relation to a more important thing, event, etc.
- [as INCIDENT]

incidentally *adverb*
- "insa DENT 'll ee"
- by the way; as a further thought or unconnected remark.
- [as INCIDENT]

incinerate *verb*
- "in SINNER ate"
- destroy completely by burning; reduce to ashes.
- [medieval Latin *incinerare* (Latin *in* in, *cinis -eris* ashes)]
- **incineration** *noun*
- **incinerator** *noun*

incipient *adjective*
- "in SIPPY 'nt"
- beginning.
- [Latin *incipere incipient-* (as INCEPTION)]
- **incipience** *noun*

incise *verb*
- "in SIZE"
- cut into or make a cut in.
- [French *inciser* from Latin *incidere incis-* (*in* in, *caedere* cut)]
- **incised** *adjective*
- **incision** *noun* "in SIZH'n"

incisive *adjective*
- "in SICE iv"
- mentally sharp; acute.
- [as INCISE]
- **incisively** *adverb*
- **incisiveness** *noun*

incisor *noun*
- "in SIZE ur"
- a sharp cutting tooth, esp. in humans, any of the eight teeth at the front of the mouth.
- [as INCISE]

incite *verb*
- "in SITE"
- urge or stir up.
- [French *inciter* from Latin *incitare* (*in* in, *citare* rouse)]
- **incitement** *noun*
- **inciter** *noun*

incivility *noun*
- "in suh VILLA tee"
- rudeness, discourtesy.
- [Latin *in-* not, without + CIVILITY]

inclement *adjective*
- "in CLEM 'nt"
- (of the weather or climate) severe, esp. cold, rainy, or stormy.
- [Latin *in-* not, without + CLEMENT]
- **inclemency** *noun*

inclination *noun*
- "incla NAY sh'n"
- a disposition, tendency, or propensity.
- [Latin *inclinare* (*in* in, *clinare* bend)]

inclinometer *noun*
- "in clin OMMA tur"
- an instrument for measuring the angle between the direction of the earth's magnetic field and the horizontal.
- [as INCLINATION + Greek *metron* measure]

include *verb*
- "in CLUDE"
- involve, comprise, or reckon in as part of a whole.
- [Latin *includere inclus-* (*in* in, *claudere* shut)]
- **included** *adjective*
- **including** *preposition*
- **inclusion** *noun*

inclusive *adjective*
- "in CLOO siv"
- including, comprising.
- [medieval Latin *inclusivus* (as INCLUDE)]
- **inclusively** *adverb*
- **inclusiveness** *noun*
- **inclusivity** *noun*

incognito *adjective*
• "in cog NEETO"
• with one's name or identity kept secret.
• [Italian, = unknown, from Latin *incognitus* (*in-* not, without, *cognitus* past participle of *cognoscere* know)]

incognizant *adjective*
• "in COG niz 'nt"
• unaware; not knowing.
• [Latin *in-* not, without + COGNIZANCE]

incoherent *adjective*
• "in co HERE 'nt"
• (of a person) unable to speak intelligibly.
• [Latin *in-* not, without + COHERENT]
• **incoherence** *noun*
• **incoherency** *noun*
• **incoherently** *adverb*

incombustible *adjective*
• "in k'm BUSTA bull"
• that cannot be burned or consumed by fire.
• [Latin *in-* not, without + COMBUSTION]
• **incombustibility** *noun*

incommensurable *adjective*
• "inca MEN shur a bull" or "inca MEN sur a bull" or "inca MEN syur a bull"
• not worthy of being compared with; utterly disproportionate to.
• [Latin *in-* not, without + COMMENSURABLE]
• **incommensurability** *noun*

incommensurate *adjective*
• "inca MEN shur it" or "inca MEN sur it" or "inca MEN syur it"
• out of proportion; inadequate.
• [Latin *in-* not, without + COMMENSURATE]

incommode *verb*
• "inca MODE"
• hinder, inconvenience.
• [French *incommoder* or Latin *incommodare* (*in-* not, without, *commodus* convenient)]

incommunicable *adjective*
• "inca MYOONA kuh bull"
• that cannot be communicated or shared.
• [Latin *in-* not, without + COMMUNICABLE]

incommunicado *adjective*
• "in kuh myoona CODDO" or "in kuh myoona CADDO"
• without or deprived of the means of communication with others.
• [Spanish *incomunicado* past participle of *incomunicar* deprive of communication]

incomparable *adjective*
• "in COMPER a bull"
• without an equal; matchless.
• [Latin *in-* not, without + COMPARABLE]
• **incomparability** *noun*
• **incomparably** *adverb*

incompatible *adjective*
• "in k'm PATTA bull"
• opposed in character; discordant.
• [Latin *in-* not, without + COMPATIBLE]
• **incompatibility** *noun*

incompetent *adjective*
• "in COMPA t'nt"
• not qualified or able to perform a particular task or function.
• [Latin *in-* not, without + COMPETENT]
• **incompetence** *noun*
• **incompetency** *noun*
• **incompetently** *adverb*

incomprehensible *adjective*
• "in compra HENSA bull"
• that cannot be understood.
• [Latin *in-* not, without + COMPREHEND]
• **incomprehensibility** *noun*
• **incomprehensibly** *adverb*

incomprehension *noun*
• "in compra HEN sh'n"
• failure to understand.
• [as INCOMPREHENSIBLE]

incompressible *adjective*
• "in k'm PRESSA bull"
• that cannot be compressed into a smaller volume.
• [Latin *in-* not, without + COMPRESS]
• **incompressibility** *noun*

inconceivable *adjective*
• "in k'n SEEVA bull"
• unthinkable, unimaginable.
• [Latin *in-* not, without + CONCEIVABLE]
• **inconceivability** *noun*
• **inconceivably** *adverb*

inconclusive *adjective*
• "in k'n CLOO siv"
• (of an argument, evidence, or action) not leading to a definite decision, conclusion, or result.
• [Latin *in-* not, without + CONCLUSIVE]
• **inconclusively** *adverb*
• **inconclusiveness** *noun*

incongruous *adjective*
• "in CONG groo us"
• not appropriate; out of place.
• [Latin *in-* not, without + CONGRUOUS]
• **incongruity** *noun*
• **incongruously** *adverb*
• **incongruousness** *noun*

inconnu *noun*
• "IN kuh noo"
• a predatory freshwater salmonid game fish *Stenodus leucichthys*, of the Eurasian and N American Arctic.
• [French = 'unknown' (as INCOGNITO)]

inconsecutive *adjective*
• "in k'n SECK yoo tiv"
• not in order or following continuously.
• [Latin *in-* not, without + CONSECUTIVE]

inconsequent *adjective*
• "in CONSA kw'nt"
• irrelevant.

• [Latin *in-* not, without + CONSEQUENCE]
• **inconsequence** *noun*

inconsequential *adjective*
• "in consa KWEN sh'll"
• trivial, unimportant, of no consequence.
• [as INCONSEQUENT]
• **inconsequentiality** *noun*
"in consa kwenshy ALA tee"
• **inconsequentially** *adverb*

inconsiderable *adjective*
• "in k'n SIDDER a bull"
• of small size, value, etc.
• [Latin *in-* not, without + CONSIDERABLE]

inconsiderate *adjective*
• "in k'n SIDDER it"
• thoughtlessly causing hurt or inconvenience to others.
• [Latin *in-* not, without + CONSIDERATE]
• **inconsiderately** *adverb*
• **inconsiderateness** *noun*

inconsistent *adjective*
• "in k'n SIS t'nt"
• acting at variance with one's own principles or former conduct.
• [Latin *in-* not, without + CONSISTENT]
• **inconsistency** *noun*
• **inconsistently** *adverb*

inconsolable *adjective*
• "in k'n SOLE a bull"
• (of a person, grief, etc.) that cannot be consoled or comforted.
• [Latin *in-* not, without + CONSOLE[1]]
• **inconsolably** *adverb*

inconspicuous *adjective*
• "in k'n SPICK yoo us"
• not conspicuous; not easily noticed.
• [Latin *in-* not, without + CONSPICUOUS]
• **inconspicuously** *adverb*
• **inconspicuousness** *noun*

incontestable *adjective*
• "in k'n TESTA bull"
• unquestionable, indisputable, not open to argument.
• [Latin *in-* not, without + CONTESTATION]
• **incontestability** *noun*
• **incontestably** *adverb*

incontrovertible *adjective*
• "in contra VURTA bull"
• indisputable, indubitable.
• [Latin *in-* not, without + CONTROVERT]
• **incontrovertibility** *noun*
• **incontrovertibly** *adverb*

inconvenient *adjective*
• "in k'n VEEN y'nt"
• causing trouble, difficulty, or discomfort; not convenient.
• [Latin *in-* not, without + CONVENIENCE]
• **inconvenience** *noun*
• **inconveniently** *adverb*

inconvertible *adjective*
• "in k'n VURTA bull"
• (esp. of currency) not convertible into another form on demand.
• [Latin *in-* not, without + CONVERTIBLE]

incoordination *noun*
• "in co ord'n AY sh'n"
• lack of coordination, esp. of muscular action.
• [Latin *in-* not, without + COORDINATE]

incorporate *verb*
• "in CORPER ate"
• unite; form into one body or whole.
• [Late Latin *incorporare* (Latin *in* in, *corpus -oris* body)]
• **incorporation** *noun*
• **incorporator** *noun*

incorporated *adjective*
• "in CORPER ated"
• forming a legal corporation.
• [as INCORPORATE]

incorporeal *adjective*
• "in core PORRY 'll"
• without a body or material form.
• [Latin *incorporeus* (as INCORPORATE)]

incorrigible *adjective*
• "in CORE idge a bull"
• (of a person or habit) incurably bad or depraved.
• [Latin *in-* not, without + CORRECTOR]
• **incorrigibility** *noun*
• **incorrigibly** *adverb*

incorruptible *adjective*
• "in kuh RUPTA bull"
• unable to be corrupted, esp. unable to be bribed.
• [Latin *in-* not, without + CORRUPT]
• **incorruptibility** *noun*
• **incorruptibly** *adverb*

incredible *adjective*
• "in CREDDA bull"
• that cannot be believed.
• [Latin *in-* not, without + CREDIBLE]
• **incredibility** *noun*
• **incredibly** *adverb*

incredulous *adjective*
• "in CRED yoo luss"
• unwilling to believe, skeptical.
• [Latin *in-* not, without + CREDULOUS]
• **incredulity** *noun* "in cred YOOLA tee"
• **incredulously** *adverb*
• **incredulousness** *noun*

increment *noun*
• "INCRA m'nt"
• the action or process of increasing or becoming greater, esp. gradually.
• [Latin *incrementum* from *increscere* increase]
• **incremental** *adjective*
• **incrementalism** *noun*
• **incrementally** *adverb*

incriminate *verb*
- "in CRIM'n ate"
- tend to prove the guilt of.
- [Late Latin *incriminare* (Latin *in* in, *crimen* offence)]
- **incrimination** *noun*
- **incriminatory** *adjective* "in CRIM'n a tory"

incubate *verb*
- "INK yoo bate"
- sit on or artificially heat (eggs) in order to bring forth young birds etc.
- [Latin *incubare* (*in* in, *cubare cubit-* or *cubat-* lie)]
- **incubation** *noun*

incubator *noun*
- "INK yoo bate ur"
- an apparatus used to provide a suitable temperature and environment for a premature baby or one of low birth weight.
- [as INCUBATE]

incubus *noun*
- "INK yoo buss"
- a male demon believed to have sexual intercourse with sleeping women.
- [Late Latin, = Latin *incubo* nightmare (as INCUBATE)]

inculcate *verb*
- "IN cull cate"
- urge or impress (a fact, habit, idea, etc.) persistently.
- [Latin *inculcare* (*in* in, *calcare* tread, from *calx calcis* heel)]
- **inculcation** *noun*
- **inculcator** *noun*

inculpate *verb*
- "IN cull pate"
- involve in a charge; incriminate.
- [Late Latin *inculpare* (Latin *in* in, *culpare* blame, from *culpa* fault)]
- **inculpation** *noun*
- **inculpatory** *adjective* "in CULPA tory"

incumbent *adjective*
- "in KUM b'nt"
- currently holding office.
- [Anglo-Latin *incumbens* present participle of Latin *incumbere* lie upon (*in* in, *cubare* lie)]
- **incumbency** *noun*

incunabulum *noun*
- "in kyoo NAB yuh lum"
- a book printed at an early date, esp. before 1501.
- [Latin *incunabula* swaddling clothes, cradle (*in* in, *cunae* cradle)]

incur *verb*
- "in CUR"
- suffer, experience, or become subject to (something unpleasant) as a result of one's own behaviour etc.
- [Latin *incurrere incurs-* (*in* in, *currere* run)]
- **incurrable** *adjective*

incursion *noun*
- "in CUR zh'n"
- an invasion or attack, esp. when sudden or brief.
- [Middle English from Latin *incursio* (as INCUR)]

incus *noun*
- "INK us"
- the small anvil-shaped bone in the middle ear, in contact with the malleus and stapes.
- [Latin, = anvil]

incuse *noun*
- "in KYOOZ"
- an impression hammered or stamped on a coin.
- [Latin *incusus* past participle of *incudere* (*in* in, *cudere* forge)]

indecent *adjective*
- "in DEE s'nt"
- offending against recognized standards of decency.
- [Latin *in-* not, without + DECENCY]
- **indecency** *noun*
- **indecently** *adverb*

indecipherable *adjective*
- "in de SIFE ur a bull"
- that cannot be deciphered; incoherent or illegible.
- [Latin *in-* not, without + DECIPHER]

indecision *noun*
- "in de SIZH'n"
- lack of decision; hesitation.
- [Latin *in-* not, without + DECISION]

indecisive *adjective*
- "in de SICE iv"
- not decisive or conclusive.
- [Latin *in-* not, without + DECISIVE]
- **indecisively** *adverb*
- **indecisiveness** *noun*

indeclinable *adjective*
- "in de CLINE a bull"
- that cannot be declined.
- [Latin *in-* not, without + DECLINE]

indecorous *adjective*
- "in DECKER us"
- improper.
- [Latin *in-* not, without + DECOROUS]
- **indecorously** *adverb*
- **indecorousness** *noun*

indefatigable *adjective*
- "in duh FATTA guh bull"
- (of a person, quality, etc.) that cannot be tired out; unwearying, unremitting.
- [obsolete French *indéfatigable* or Latin *indefatigabilis* (*in-* not, without, *defatigare* wear out)]
- **indefatigability** *noun*
- **indefatigably** *adverb*

indefeasible *adjective*
- "in de FEEZA bull"

• (esp. of a claim, rights, etc.) that cannot be lost.
• [Latin *in-* not, without + DEFEASIBLE]
• **indefeasibility** *noun*
• **indefeasibly** *adverb*

indefectible *adjective*
• "in de FECTA bull"
• unfailing; not liable to defect or decay.
• [Latin *in-* not + Late Latin *defectibilis* (as DEFECT)]

indefensible *adjective*
• "in de FENSA bull"
• that cannot be defended, justified, or maintained in argument.
• [Latin *in-* not, without + DEFENSIBLE]
• **indefensibility** *noun*
• **indefensibly** *adverb*

indefinable *adjective*
• "in de FINE a bull"
• that cannot be defined or exactly described.
• [Latin *in-* not, without + DEFINE]
• **indefinably** *adverb*

indefinite *adjective*
• "in DEFF'n it"
• not clearly defined or stated; vague.
• [Latin *in-* not, without + DEFINITE]
• **indefiniteness** *noun*

indefinitely *adverb*
• "in DEFF'n it lee"
• for an unlimited time.
• [as INDEFINITE]

indehiscent *adjective*
• "in de HISS'nt"
• (of fruit) not splitting open when ripe.
• [Latin *in-* not, without + DEHISCE]
• **indehiscence** *noun*

indelible *adjective*
• "in DELLA bull"
• that cannot be rubbed out or (in abstract senses) removed; permanent.
• [French *indélébile* or Latin *indelebilis* (Latin *in-* not, without, *delebilis* from *delēre* efface)]
• **indelibility** *noun*
• **indelibly** *adverb*

indelicate *adjective*
• "in DELLA kit"
• coarse, unrefined.
• [Latin *in-* not, without, DELICATE]
• **indelicacy** *noun*
• **indelicately** *adverb*

indemnify *verb*
• "in DEMNA fie"
• protect or secure (a person) against harm, loss, etc.
• [Latin *indemnis* unhurt (*in-* not, without, *damnum* loss, damage)]
• **indemnification** *noun*

indemnity *noun*
• "in DEMNA tee"
• compensation for loss incurred.
• [French *indemnité* or Late Latin *indemnitas -tatis* (as INDEMNIFY)]

indene *noun*
• "IN deen"
• a colourless flammable liquid hydrocarbon obtained from coal tar and used in making synthetic resins.
• [INDOLE + '-ene' forming names of unsaturated hydrocarbons containing a double bond, from Greek *-ēnos*, adjective suffix denoting origin or source]

indenture *noun*
• "in DEN chur"
• a sealed agreement or contract, esp. a contract binding a person to service.
• [Anglo-French *endenture* from *endenter* from Anglo-Latin *indentare* (*in* in, *dens dentis* tooth)]
• **indentured** *adjective*
• **indentureship** *noun*

indépendantiste *noun*
• "an day pon don TEEST"
• *Cdn* a person who supports the idea of Quebec independence; a sovereignist.
• [French]

independent *adjective*
• "in de PEN d'nt"
• not depending on authority or control.
• [Latin *in-* not, without + DEPENDENT]
• **independence** *noun*
• **independently** *adverb*

indescribable *adjective*
• "in de SCRIBE a bull"
• too unusual or extreme to be described.
• [Latin *in-* not, without + DESCRIBE]
• **indescribably** *adverb*

indestructible *adjective*
• "in de STRUCTA bull"
• that cannot be destroyed.
• [Latin *in-* not, without + DESTROY]
• **indestructibility** *noun*
• **indestructibly** *adverb*

indeterminable *adjective*
• "in de TURMIN a bull"
• that cannot be ascertained.
• [Latin *in-* not, without + DETERMINE]

indeterminate *adjective*
• "in de TURMIN it"
• not fixed in extent, character, etc.
• [Latin *in-* not, without + DETERMINATE]
• **indeterminacy** *noun*
• **indeterminately** *adverb*

indeterminism *noun*
• "in de TURMIN izm"
• the belief that human action is not wholly determined by motives.
• [Latin *in-* not, without + DETERMINISM]
• **indeterministic** *adjective*

Indic *adjective*
• "INDIC"
• of or relating to a group of Indo-European languages comprising Sanskrit and the modern Indian languages which are its descendants.
• [Latin *Indicus* from Greek *Indikos* Indian]

indicate *verb*
• "INDA cate"
• point out; make known; show.
• [Latin *indicare* (*in* in, *dicare* make known)]
• **indication** *noun*
• **indicative** *adjective* "in DICKA tiv"
• **indicatively** *adverb*
• **indicator** *noun*

indicia *plural noun*
• "in DISHY uh"
• distinguishing or identifying marks.
• [pl. of Latin *indicium* from *index indicis* forefinger, informer, sign]

indict *verb*
• "in DITE"
• charge (a person) with a crime, esp. formally by legal process.
• [Anglo-French *enditer* from Old French *enditier* declare, from Romanic *indictare* (unrecorded: Latin *in* in, DICTATE)]
• **indictable** *adjective*
• **indictee** *noun*
• **indicter** *noun*
• **indictment** *noun*

indifference *noun*
• "in DIFF rince"
• lack of interest or attention.
• [Latin *in-* not, without + DIFFERENCE]

indifferent *adjective*
• "in DIFF r'nt"
• having no partiality for or against; having no interest in or sympathy for.
• [Latin *in-* not, without + DIFFERENT]
• **indifferently** *adverb*

indifferentism *noun*
• "in DIFF r'nt izm"
• an attitude of indifference, esp. in religious matters.
• [as INDIFFERENT]

indigene *noun*
• "INDA jeen"
• a native or aboriginal inhabitant of a region etc.
• [French *indigène* from Latin *indigena* (as INDIGENOUS)]

indigenize *verb*
ALSO SPELLED: esp. *Brit.* **-ise**
• "in DIDGE a nize"
• make indigenous; subject to native influence.
• [as INDIGENOUS]
• **indigenization** *noun* (also esp. *Brit.* **-isation**)

indigenous *adjective*
• "in DIDGE a nuss"
• (esp. of flora or fauna) originating naturally in a region.
• [Latin *indigena* from *indi-* = *in* in + *gen-* be born]
• **indigenously** *adverb*

indigent *adjective*
• "INDA j'nt"
• needy, poor.
• [Old French from Late Latin *indigēre* from *indi-* = *in* in + *egēre* need]
• **indigence** *noun*

indigestible *adjective*
• "inda JESTA bull"
• difficult or impossible to digest.
• [Latin *in-* not, without + DIGEST]
• **indigestibility** *noun*
• **indigestibly** *adverb*

indigestion *noun*
• "inda JESS ch'n"
• difficulty in digesting food.
• [Latin *in-* not, without + DIGEST]

indignant *adjective*
• "in DIG n'nt"
• feeling or showing scornful anger at supposed unjust or unfair conduct or treatment.
• [Latin *indignari indignant-* regard as unworthy (*in-* not, without, *dignus* worthy)]
• **indignantly** *adverb*
• **indignation** *noun* "in dig NAY sh'n"

indignity *noun*
• "in DIGNA tee"
• unworthy treatment.
• [Latin *in-* not, without + DIGNITY]

indigo *noun*
• "INDA go"
• a natural blue dye obtained from the indigo plant.
• [16th-c. *indico* (from Spanish), *indigo* (from Portuguese) from Latin *indicum* from Greek *indikon* Indian (dye)]

indiscernible *adjective*
• "in de SURNA bull"
• that cannot be discerned or distinguished from another.
• [Latin *in-* not, without + DISCERN]
• **indiscernibly** *adverb*

indiscipline *noun*
• "in DISSA plin"
• lack of discipline.
• [Latin *in-* not, without + DISCIPLINE]
• **indisciplined** *adjective*

indiscreet *adjective*
• "in dis CREET"
• not discreet; revealing secrets.
• [Latin *in-* not, without + DISCREET]
• **indiscreetly** *adverb*
HOMOPHONES: *indiscrete*

indiscrete *adjective*
- "in dis CREET"
- not divided into distinct parts.
- [Latin *in-* not, without + DISCRETE]

HOMOPHONES: *indiscreet*

indiscretion *noun*
- "in dis CRESH'n"
- lack of discretion; indiscreet conduct.
- [as INDISCREET]

indiscriminate *adjective*
- "in dis CRIM'n it"
- (of an action etc.) not distinguished by discernment or discrimination; haphazard, not selective.
- [Latin *in-* not, without + DISCRIMINATE]
- **indiscriminately** *adverb*
- **indiscriminateness** *noun*
- **indiscrimination** *noun*

indispensable *adjective*
- "in dis PENSA bull"
- that cannot be dispensed with; necessary.
- [Latin *in-* not, without + DISPENSABLE]
- **indispensability** *noun*
- **indispensably** *adverb*

indisputable *adjective*
- "in dis PYOOTA bull"
- that cannot be disputed.
- [Latin *in-* not, without + DISPUTABLE]
- **indisputability** *noun*
- **indisputably** *adverb*

indissoluble *adjective*
- "in dis SAWL yoo bull"
- that cannot be dissolved or decomposed.
- [Latin *in-* not, without + DISSOLUBLE]
- **indissolubility** *noun*
- **indissolubly** *adverb*

indistinct *adjective*
- "in dis TINCT"
- not distinct.
- [Latin *in-* not, without + DISTINCT]
- **indistinctly** *adverb*
- **indistinctness** *noun*

indistinguishable *adjective*
- "in dis TING gwish a bull"
- not distinguishable.
- [Latin *in-* not, without + DISTINGUISH]
- **indistinguishability** *noun*
- **indistinguishably** *adverb*

indium *noun*
- "INDY um"
- a soft silvery-white metallic element occurring naturally in zinc blende etc., used for electroplating and in semiconductors.
- [Latin *indicum* indigo, with reference to its characteristic spectral lines]

individual *adjective*
- "inda VIDGE oo 'll"
- single, separate.
- [Middle English, = indivisible, from medieval Latin *individualis* (*in-* not, without, *dividuus* from *dividere* DIVIDE)]
- **individually** *adverb*

individualism *noun*
- "inda VIDGE oo 'll izm"
- the habit or principle of being independent and self-reliant.
- [as INDIVIDUAL]
- **individualist** *noun*
- **individualistic** *adjective*
- **individualistically** *adverb*

individuality *noun*
- "inda vidge oo ALA tee"
- the sum of the attributes which distinguish one person or thing from others of the same kind; strongly marked individual character.
- [as INDIVIDUAL]

individualize *verb*

ALSO SPELLED: esp. *Brit.* **-ise**
- "inda VIDGE oo a lize"
- give an individual character to.
- [as INDIVIDUAL]
- **individualization** *noun* (also esp. *Brit.* **-isation**)

individuate *verb*
- "inda VIDGE oo ate"
- distinguish from others of the same kind; single out.
- [as INDIVIDUAL]
- **individuation** *noun*

indivisible *adjective*
- "inda VIZZA bull"
- not divisible.
- [Latin *in-* not, without + DIVISIBLE]
- **indivisibility** *noun*
- **indivisibly** *adverb*

indoctrinate *verb*
- "in DOC trin ate"
- teach (a person or group) systematically or for a long period to accept (esp. partisan or tendentious) ideas uncritically.
- [Latin *in-* not, without + DOCTRINE]
- **indoctrination** *noun*
- **indoctrinator** *noun*

indole *noun*
- "IN dole"
- an organic compound with a characteristic odour formed on the reduction of indigo.
- [INDIGO + Latin *oleum* oil]

indoleacetic *adjective*
- "indo luh SEETIC"
- any of the several isomeric acetic acid derivatives of indole, esp. one found as a natural growth hormone in plants.
- [INDOLE + ACETIC]

indolent *adjective*
- "INDA l'nt"
- lazy; wishing to avoid activity or exertion.

• [Late Latin *indolens* (Latin *in-* not, without, *dolēre* suffer pain)]
• **indolence** *noun*
• **indolently** *adverb*

Indology *noun*
• "in DOLLA jee"
• the study of the history, literature, etc. of India.
• ['India' + Greek *logos* word]
• **Indologist** *noun*

indomitable *adjective*
• "in DOMMIT a bull"
• impossible to subdue or defeat.
• [Late Latin *indomitabilis* (Latin *in-* not, without, *domitare* tame)]
• **indomitability** *noun*
• **indomitably** *adverb*

Indonesian *noun*
• "inda NEE zh'n"
• a native or national of Indonesia in SE Asia.

indri *noun*
• "IN dree"
• a large woolly black and white lemur of Madagascar, *Indri indri*, having long hind legs and a short tail and progressing by long leaps between trees.
• [Malagasy *indry* behold, mistaken for its name]

indubitable *adjective*
• "in DOO bit a bull" or "in DYOO bit a bull"
• that cannot be doubted.
• [French *indubitable* or Latin *indubitabilis* (Latin *in-* not, without, *dubitare* to doubt)]
• **indubitably** *adverb*

induce *verb*
• "in DUCE"
• prevail on; persuade.
• [Latin *inducere induct-* (*in* in, *ducere* lead)]
• **inducement** *noun*
• **inducer** *noun*
• **inducible** *adjective*

inductance *noun*
• "in DUCK tince"
• the property of an electric circuit that causes an electromotive force to be generated by a change in the current flowing.
• [as INDUCE]

inductor *noun*
• "in DUCTER"
• a component (in a circuit) which possesses inductance.
• [as INDUCE]

indulge *verb*
• "in DULGE"
• allow oneself to enjoy the pleasure of something.
• [Latin *indulgēre indult-* give free rein to]
• **indulgence** *noun*
• **indulgent** *adjective*
• **indulgently** *adverb*
• **indulger** *noun*

induna *noun*
• "in DOONA"
• a South African tribal councillor or headman.
• [Nguni *inDuna* captain, councillor]

indurate *verb*
• "IND yur ate"
• make or become hard.
• [Latin *indurare* (*in* in, *durus* hard)]

indusium *noun*
• "in DOOZY um" or "in DYOOZY um"
• a membranous shield covering the fruit cluster of a fern.
• [Latin, = tunic, from *induere* put on (a garment)]

industrialism *noun*
• "in DUSTRY 'll izm"
• a social or economic system in which manufacturing industries are prevalent.
• [as INDUSTRY]

industrialist *noun*
• "in DUSTRY 'll ist"
• a person engaged in the management of an industrial enterprise.
• [as INDUSTRY]

industrious *adjective*
• "in DUSTRY us"
• diligent, hard-working.
• [as INDUSTRY]
• **industriously** *adverb*
• **industriousness** *noun*

industry *noun*
• "INDUS tree"
• a branch of trade or manufacture.
• [French *industrie* or Latin *industria* diligence]
• **industrial** *adjective* "in DUSTRY 'll"
• **industrialization** *noun* (also esp. *Brit.* **-isation**)
• **industrialize** *verb* (also esp. *Brit.* **-ise**)
• **industrially** *adverb*

inebriate *verb*
• "in EEBRY ate"
• make drunk; intoxicate.
• [Latin *inebriatus* past participle of *inebriare* (*in* in, *ebrius* drunk)]
• **inebriated** *adjective*
• **inebriation** *noun*
• **inebriety** *noun* "in ee BRY a tee"

inedible *adjective*
• "in EDDA bull"
• not edible, esp. not suitable for eating.
• [Latin *in-* not, without + EDIBLE]
• **inedibility** *noun*

ineducable *adjective*
• "in EDGE oo kuh bull" or "in ED yoo kuh bull"
• incapable of being educated.
• [Latin *in-* not, without + EDUCATE]
• **ineducability** *noun*

ineffable *adjective*
- "in EFFA bull"
- unutterable; too great for description in words; indefinable.
- [Old French *ineffable* or Latin *ineffabilis* (Latin *in-* not, without, *effari* speak out, utter)]
- **ineffability** *noun*
- **ineffably** *adverb*

ineffaceable *adjective*
- "inna FACE a bull"
- that cannot be effaced.
- [Latin *in-* not, without + EFFACE]

ineffective *adjective*
- "inna FECTIV"
- not producing any effect or the desired effect.
- [Latin *in-* not, without + EFFECTIVE]
- **ineffectively** *adverb*
- **ineffectiveness** *noun*

ineffectual *adjective*
- "inna FECK choo 'll"
- without effect.
- [Latin *in-* not, without + EFFECTUAL]
- **ineffectuality** *noun*
- **ineffectually** *adverb*
- **ineffectualness** *noun*

inefficacious *adjective*
- "in effa CAY sh'ss"
- (of a remedy etc.) not producing the desired effect.
- [Latin *in-* not, without + EFFICACIOUS]
- **inefficaciously** *adverb*
- **inefficacy** *noun*

inefficient *adjective*
- "inna FISH 'nt"
- (of a machine, process, etc.) wasting time or resources.
- [Latin *in-* not, without + EFFICIENT]
- **inefficiency** *noun*
- **inefficiently** *adverb*

inegalitarian *adjective*
- "inny gala TERRY 'n"
- of or pertaining to inequality; favouring or marked by inequality.
- [Latin *in-* not, without + EGALITARIAN]
- **inegalitarianism** *noun*

inelastic *adjective*
- "inny LASTIC"
- not elastic.
- [Latin *in-* not, without + ELASTIC]
- **inelastically** *adverb*
- **inelasticity** *noun* "inny lass TISSA tee"

inelegant *adjective*
- "in ELLA g'nt"
- not elegant.
- [Latin *in-* not, without + ELEGANT]
- **inelegance** *noun*
- **inelegantly** *adverb*

ineligible *adjective*
- "in ELLA juh bull"
- not eligible; not having the appropriate or necessary qualifications (for an office, position, etc).
- [Latin *in-* not, without + ELIGIBLE]
- **ineligibility** *noun*

ineluctable *adjective*
- "inny LUCTA bull"
- unable to be resisted or avoided; inescapable.
- [Latin *ineluctabilis* (*in-* not, without, *eluctari* struggle out)]
- **ineluctability** *noun*
- **ineluctably** *adverb*

inequality *noun*
- "inny KWOLLA tee"
- lack of equality between persons or things; disparity in size, number, quality, etc.
- [Latin *in-* not, without + EQUALITY]

inequitable *adjective*
- "in ECKWA tuh bull"
- unfair, unjust.
- [Latin *in-* not, without + EQUITABLE]
- **inequitably** *adverb*

inequity *noun*
- "in ECKWA tee"
- unfairness, bias.
- [Latin *in-* not, without + EQUITY]

ineradicable *adjective*
- "inny RADDA kuh bull"
- unable to be eradicated or rooted out.
- [Latin *in-* not, without + ERADICATE]
- **ineradicably** *adverb*

inerrant *adjective*
- "in AIR 'nt"
- (esp. in reference to the Bible) incapable of being wrong.
- [Latin *inerrans* (*in-* not, without, ERR)]
- **inerrancy** *noun*
- **inerrantist** *noun*

inertia *noun*
- "in UR shuh"
- a property of matter by which it continues in its existing state of rest or uniform motion in a straight line, unless that state is changed by an external force.
- [Latin from *iners inert-* inert (*in-* not, without, *ars* art)]
- **inertial** *adjective*

inescapable *adjective*
- "in ess CAY puh bull"
- that cannot be escaped or avoided.
- [Latin *in-* not, without + ESCAPE]
- **inescapability** *noun*
- **inescapably** *adverb*

inessential *adjective*
- "inny SEN sh'll"
- not necessary; dispensable.
- [Latin *in-* not, without + ESSENTIAL]

inestimable *adjective*
- "in ESTA muh bull"
- too great, intense, precious, etc., to be estimated.

• [Latin *in-* not, without + ESTIMABLE]
• **inestimably** *adverb*

inevitable *adjective*
• "in EVVA tuh bull"
• unavoidable; sure to happen.
• [Latin *inevitabilis* (*in-* not, without, *evitare* avoid)]
• **inevitability** *noun*
• **inevitably** *adverb*

inexcusable *adjective*
• "in ex CYOOZ a bull"
• (of a person, action, etc.) that cannot be excused or justified.
• [Latin *in-* not, without + EXCUSE]
• **inexcusably** *adverb*

inexhaustible *adjective*
• "in eg ZOSSTA bull"
• that cannot be used up.
• [Latin *in-* not, without + EXHAUST]
• **inexhaustibility** *noun*
• **inexhaustibly** *adverb*

inexorable *adjective*
• "in EXER a bull"
• relentless.
• [French *inexorable* or Latin *inexorabilis* (Latin *in-* not, without, *exorare* entreat)]
• **inexorability** *noun*
• **inexorably** *adverb*

inexpedient *adjective*
• "in ex PEEDY 'nt"
• not expedient.
• [Latin *in-* not, without + EXPEDIENT]
• **inexpediency** *noun*

inexpensive *adjective*
• "in ex PENSIV"
• not expensive, cheap.
• [Latin *in-* not, without + EXPEDIENT]
• **inexpensively** *adverb*

inexperience *noun*
• "in ex PEERY ince"
• lack of experience, or of the resulting knowledge or skill.
• [Latin *in-* not, without + EXPERIENCE]
• **inexperienced** *adjective*

inexplicable *adjective*
• "in ex PLICKA bull"
• that cannot be explained or accounted for.
• [Latin *in-* not, without + EXPLICABLE]
• **inexplicability** *noun*
• **inexplicably** *adverb*

inexpressible *adjective*
• "in ex PRESSA bull"
• that cannot be expressed in words.
• [Latin *in-* not, without + EXPRESS]
• **inexpressibly** *adverb*

inextinguishable *adjective*
• "in ex TING gwish a bull"
• unquenchable; indestructible.
• [Latin *in-* not, without + EXTINGUISH]

inextricable *adjective*
• "in EX tricka bull" or "in ex TRICKA bull"
• (of a circumstance) that cannot be escaped from.
• [Latin *in-* not, without + EXTRICATE]
• **inextricably** *adverb*

infallible *adjective*
• "in FALA bull"
• incapable of error.
• [Latin *in-* not, without + FALLIBLE]
• **infallibility** *noun*
• **infallibly** *adverb*

infamous *adjective*
• "INFA muss"
• well-known for being bad, wicked, etc.; notorious.
• [Latin *in-* not, without + *fama* fame, renown]
• **infamously** *adverb*
• **infamy** *noun*

infanticide *noun*
• "in FANTA side"
• the killing of an infant soon after birth.
• [from 'infant', from Latin *infans* unable to speak (*in-* not, without, *fans fantis* present participle of *fari* speak) + *-cida, -cidium* from *caedere* kill]
• **infanticidal** *adjective*

infantile *adjective*
• "IN f'n tile"
• like or characteristic of a child.
• [Latin *infans* unable to speak (*in-* not, without, *fans fantis* present participle of *fari* speak)]
• **infantilism** *noun* "in FANT'll izm"
• **infantility** *noun* "in f'n TILLA tee"

infantilize *verb*
ALSO SPELLED: esp. *Brit.* **-ise**
• "in FANT'll ize"
• treat (a person) as a child or in a way that denies their maturity or experience.
• [as INFANTILE]
• **infantilization** *noun* (also esp. *Brit.* **-isation**)

infarct *noun*
• "IN farct"
• a small localized area of dead tissue caused by an inadequate blood supply.
• [modern Latin *infarctus* (Latin *in* in, *farcire farct-* stuff)]
• **infarcted** *adjective*
• **infarction** *noun*

infatuated *adjective*
• "in FATCH oo ated"
• affected by an intense fondness or admiration.
• [Latin *infatuare* (*in* in, *fatuus* foolish)]
• **infatuation** *noun*

infauna *noun*
• "IN fonna"
• any animals which live just below the surface of the seabed.
• [Danish *ifauna* (Latin *in* in, FAUNA)]
• **infaunal** *adjective*

infeasible *adjective*
• "in FEEZA bull"
• not feasible; that cannot easily be done.
• [Latin *in-* not, without + FEASIBLE]
• **infeasibility** *noun*

infelicity *noun*
• "in fuh LISSA tee"
• a thing that is inappropriate, esp. a remark or expression.
• [Latin *in-* not, without + FELICITY]
• **infelicitous** *adjective*
• **infelicitously** *adverb*

infer *verb*
• "in FUR"
• deduce or conclude from facts and reasoning.
• [Latin *inferre* (*in* in, *ferre* bring)]
• **inferable** *adjective* (also **inferrable**)
• **inference** *noun* "IN fur ince"
• **inferential** *adjective*
• **inferentially** *adverb*

inferior *adjective*
• "in FEERY ur"
• of lower rank, quality, etc.
• [Latin, comparative of *inferus* that is below]
• **inferiority** *noun* "in feery ORA tee"
• **inferiorly** *adverb*

infernal *adjective*
• "in FURN'll"
• of hell or the underworld.
• [Old French from Late Latin *infernalis* from Latin *infernus* situated below]
• **infernally** *adverb*

inferno *noun*
• "in FURNO"
• a raging fire.
• [Italian from Late Latin *infernus* (as INFERNAL)]

infertile *adjective*
• "in FUR tile" or "in FURTLE"
• not fertile.
• [Latin *in-* not, without + FERTILE]
• **infertility** *noun* "in fur TILLA tee"

infidel *noun*
• "INFA dell" or "INFA d'll"
• usu. *derogatory* a person who does not believe in religion or in a particular religion; an unbeliever.
• [French *infidèle* or Latin *infidelis* (*in-* not, without, *fidelis* faithful)]

infidelity *noun*
• "infa DELLA tee"
• disloyalty, or esp. unfaithfulness to a sexual partner.
• [as INFIDEL]

infiltrate *verb*
• "IN fill trate"
• gain entrance or access to surreptitiously and by degrees (as spies etc.).
• [Latin *in-* not, without + medieval Latin *filtrum* felt used as a filter]
• **infiltration** *noun*
• **infiltrator** *noun*

infinite *adjective*
• "INF 'n it"
• boundless, endless.
• [Latin *infinitus* (*in-* not, without, FINITE)]
• **infinitely** *adverb*
• **infiniteness** *noun*
• **infinity** *noun*

infinitesimal *adjective*
• "in finna TESS'm 'll"
• infinitely or very small.
• [modern Latin *infinitesimus* from INFINITE: compare CENTESIMAL]
• **infinitesimally** *adverb*

infinitive *noun*
• "in FINNA tiv"
• a form of a verb expressing the verbal notion without reference to a particular subject, tense, etc. (e.g. *see* in *we came to see*, or *let her see*).
• [Latin *infinitivus* (*in-* not, without, *finitivus* definite, from *finire finit-* define)]
• **infinitival** *adjective* "in finna TIVE 'll"
• **infinitivally** *adverb*

infinitude *noun*
• "in FINNA tude"
• the state of being infinite; boundlessness.
• [as INFINITE]

infirmary *noun*
• "in FURMA ree"
• a place for those who are ill in a boarding school, prison, camp, monastery, etc.
• [Latin *in-* not, without + *firmus* firm]

inflammable *adjective*
• "in FLAMMA bull"
• easily set on fire; flammable.
• [Old French *enflammer* from Latin *inflammare* (*in* in, *flamma* flame)]
• **inflammability** *noun*

inflammation *noun*
• "infla MAY sh'n"
• the act or an instance of inflaming.
• [Latin *inflammatio* from *inflammare* (*in* in, *flamma* flame)]

inflammatory *adjective*
• "in FLAMMA tory"
• (esp. of speeches, leaflets, etc.) tending to cause anger etc.
• [as INFLAMMATION]

inflate *verb*
• "in FLATE"
• distend (a balloon etc.) with air.
• [Latin *inflare inflat-* (*in* in, *flare* blow)]
• **inflatable** *adjective*
• **inflated** *adjective*
• **inflator** *noun*

inflation *noun*
• "in FLAY sh'n"
• a general increase in prices and fall in the purchasing value of money.

• [as INFLATE]
• **inflationary** *adjective*
• **inflationist** *noun*

inflexible *adjective*
• "in FLEXA bull"
• that cannot be changed or adapted to particular circumstances.
• [Latin *in-* not, without + FLEXIBLE]
• **inflexibility** *noun*
• **inflexibly** *adverb*

inflorescence *noun*
• "in flor ESS ince"
• the complete flower head of a plant including stems, stalks, bracts, and flowers.
• [modern Latin *inflorescentia* from Late Latin *inflorescere* (Latin *in* in, FLORESCENCE)]

influence *noun*
• "IN floo ince"
• the effect a person or thing has on another.
• [Old French *influence* or medieval Latin *influentia* inflow, from Latin *influere* flow in (*in* in, *fluere* flow)]
• **influenceable** *adjective*
• **influencer** *noun*

influent *adjective*
• "IN floo 'nt"
• flowing in.
• [Middle English from Latin (as INFLUENCE)]

influential *adjective*
• "in floo EN sh'll"
• having a great influence or power.
• [as INFLUENCE]
• **influentially** *adverb*

influenza *noun*
• "in floo ENZA"
• a highly contagious virus infection causing fever, severe aching, weakness, and coughing.
• [Italian from medieval Latin *influentia* INFLUENCE]
• **influenzal** *adjective*

influx *noun*
• "IN flux"
• a continual entry of people (esp. visitors or immigrants) into a place, esp. in large numbers.
• [French *influx* or Late Latin *influxus* (Latin *in* in, FLUXION)]

infomediary *noun*
• "info MEEDY airy"
• an Internet company that gathers and links information on particular subjects on behalf of commercial organizations and their potential customers.
• ['information' + INTERMEDIARY]

infomercial *noun*
• "INFO mur sh'll"
• a usu. lengthy television commercial which promotes a particular product using a documentary, testimonial, talk show, or demonstration format etc. to convey information.
• ['information' + COMMERCIAL]

infosphere *noun*
• "INFO sfeer"
• the sphere of human activity concerned with the collection and processing of information, esp. by computer.
• ['information' + SPHERE]

infotainment *noun*
• "info TANE m'nt"
• broadcast material intended both to entertain and to inform.
• ['information' + 'entertainment']

infrangible *adjective*
• "in FRANJA bull"
• unbreakable.
• [Latin *in-* not, without, FRANGIBLE]

infrasonic *adjective*
• "infra SONNIC"
• of or relating to sound waves with a frequency below the lower limit of human audibility.
• [Latin *infra* below, beneath + SONIC]
• **infrasonically** *adverb*

infrastructure *noun*
• "INFRA struck chur"
• the basic structural foundations of a society or enterprise; a substructure or foundation.
• [Latin *infra* below, beneath + Old French *structure* or Latin *structura* from *struere struct-* build]
• **infrastructural** *adjective*

infula *noun*
• "IN fyoola"
• either of the two ribbons on a bishop's mitre.
• [Latin, = woollen fillet worn by priest etc.]

infundibular *adjective*
• "in fun DIB yuh lur"
• funnel-shaped.
• [Latin *infundibulum* funnel, from *infundere* pour in (*in* in, *fundere* pour)]

infuriate *verb*
• "in FYURY ate"
• fill with fury; enrage.
• [Latin *in* in + *furia* from *furere* be mad]
• **infuriating** *adjective*
• **infuriatingly** *adverb*

infusible *adjective*
• "in FYOOZA bull"
• not able to be fused or melted.
• [Latin *infundere infus-* (*in* not, without, *fundere* pour)]
• **infusibility** *noun*

ingenious *adjective*
• "in JEENY us"
• clever at inventing, constructing, organizing, etc.; skilful; resourceful.
• [Middle English, = talented, from French

ingénieux or Latin *ingeniosus* from *ingenium* cleverness]
- **ingeniously** *adverb*
- **ingeniousness** *noun*

ingenue *noun*
- "on zhuh NOO"
- an innocent or unsophisticated young woman.
- [French, feminine of *ingénu* INGENUOUS]

ingenuity *noun*
- "in juh NEW a tee"
- skill in devising or contriving; ingeniousness.
- [Latin *ingenuitas* ingenuousness (as INGENUOUS): English meaning by confusion of INGENIOUS with INGENUOUS]

ingenuous *adjective*
- "in JEN yoo us"
- innocent; artless.
- [Latin *ingenuus* freeborn, frank (*in* in, root of *gignere* beget)]
- **ingenuously** *adverb*
- **ingenuousness** *noun*

ingest *verb*
- "in JEST"
- take in (food etc.); eat.
- [Latin *ingerere ingest-* (*in* in, *gerere* carry)]
- **ingestion** *noun*
- **ingestive** *adjective*

inglenook *noun*
- "INGLE nook"
- a space within the opening on either side of a large fireplace.
- [dialect (originally Scots) *ingle* fire burning on a hearth, perhaps from Gaelic *aingeal* fire, light, + Middle English *nok(e)* corner, of unknown origin]

ingot *noun*
- "ING git"
- a usu. oblong piece of cast metal, esp. of gold, silver, or steel.
- [Middle English: perhaps from 'in' + *goten* past participle of Old English *geotan* cast]

ingratiate *reflexive verb*
- "in GRAY shee ate"
- bring oneself into favour.
- [Latin *in gratiam* into favour]
- **ingratiating** *adjective*
- **ingratiatingly** *adverb*
- **ingratiation** *noun*

ingratitude *noun*
- "in GRATTA tude"
- a lack of due gratitude.
- [Latin *in-* not, without + GRATITUDE]

ingredient *noun*
- "in GREEDY 'nt"
- any of the foods that are combined to make a particular dish.
- [Latin *ingredi ingress-* enter (*in* in, *gradi* step)]

inguinal *adjective*
- "IN gwin 'll"
- of the groin.
- [Latin *inguinalis* from *inguen -inis* groin]

inhalant *noun*
- "in HAY l'nt"
- a medicinal preparation for inhaling.
- [as INHALE]

inhale *verb*
- "in HALE"
- breathe in.
- [Latin *inhalare* breathe in (*in* in, *halare* breathe)]
- **inhalation** *noun* "in huh LAY sh'n"

inhaler *noun*
- "in HALE ur"
- a portable device for administering a medicinal or anaesthetic gas or vapour, esp. to relieve nasal or bronchial congestion, e.g. in asthmatics.
- [as INHALE]

inharmonious *adjective*
- "in har MOANY us"
- not harmonious.
- [Latin *in-* not, without + HARMONY]

inhere *verb*
- "in HERE"
- exist essentially or permanently in.
- [Latin *inhaerēre inhaes-* (*in* in, *haerēre* to stick)]

inherent *adjective*
- "in HAIR 'nt" or "in HERE 'nt"
- existing in something, esp. as a permanent or characteristic attribute.
- [as INHERE]
- **inherently** *adverb*

inherit *verb*
- "in HAIR it"
- receive (property, rank, title, etc.) by legal descent or succession.
- [Old French *enheriter* from Late Latin *inhereditare* (Latin *in* in, *heres heredis* heir)]
- **inheritability** *noun*
- **inheritable** *adjective*
- **inheritance** *noun*
- **inheritor** *noun*

inheritrix *noun*
- "in HAIR a trix"
- an heiress; a woman who inherits.
- [as INHERIT]

inhibit *verb*
- "in HIBBIT"
- hinder, restrain, or prevent (an action or progress).
- [Latin *inhibēre* (*in* in, *habēre* hold)]
- **inhibitive** *adjective*
- **inhibitor** *noun*
- **inhibitory** *adjective*

inhibition *noun*
• "in huh BISH'n"
• a restraint on the direct expression of an instinct.
• [as INHIBIT]
• **inhibited** *adjective*

inhomogeneous *adjective*
• "in homma JEENY us" or "in home uh JEENY us"
• not homogeneous.
• [Latin *in-* not, without + HOMOGENEOUS]
• **inhomogeneity** *noun* "in homma juh NAY a tee" or "in home uh juh NAY a tee"

inhospitable *adjective*
• "in hoss PITTA bull"
• not hospitable.
• [Latin *in-* not, without + HOSPITABLE]
• **inhospitableness** *noun*
• **inhospitably** *adverb*
• **inhospitality** *noun*

inimical *adjective*
• "in IMMICK 'll"
• hostile.
• [Late Latin *inimicalis* from Latin *inimicus* (*in-* not, without, *amicus* friend)]
• **inimically** *adverb*

inimitable *adjective*
• "in IMMIT a bull"
• impossible to imitate.
• [Latin *in-* not, without + IMITATE]
• **inimitability** *noun*
• **inimitably** *adverb*

iniquity *noun*
• "in ICKWA tee"
• wickedness.
• [Old French *iniquité* from Latin *iniquitas -tatis* from *iniquus* (*in-* not, without, *aequus* just)]
• **iniquitous** *adjective*
• **iniquitously** *adverb*
• **iniquitousness** *noun*

initial *adjective*
• "in ISH'll"
• of, existing at, or occurring at the beginning; first.
• [Latin *initialis* from *initium* beginning, from *inire init-* go in]
• **initially** *adverb*

initialism *noun*
• "in ISH'll izm"
• a group of initial letters used as an abbreviation for a name or expression, each letter being pronounced separately, e.g. *CBC*.
• [as INITIAL]

initialize *verb*
ALSO SPELLED: esp. *Brit.* **-ise**
• "in ISH'll ize"
• set to the value or put in the condition appropriate to the start of an operation.
• [as INITIAL]
• **initialization** *noun* (also esp. *Brit.* **-isation**)

initiate *verb*
• "in ISHY ate"
• cause (a process or action) to begin.
• [Latin *initiare* from *initium*: see INITIAL]
• **initiation** *noun*
• **initiator** *noun*
• **initiatory** *adjective* "in ISHY a tory"

initiative *noun*
• "in ISHA tiv" or "in ISH yuh tiv"
• the ability to initiate things; enterprise, self-motivation.
• [French (as INITIATE)]

injera *noun*
• "in JEERA"
• a soft, white, spongy Ethiopian bread made from teff flour.
• [Amharic]

injudicious *adjective*
• "in joo DISH us"
• unwise, showing lack of judgment or discretion.
• [Latin *in-* not, without + JUDICIOUS]
• **injudiciously** *adverb*
• **injudiciousness** *noun*

injunction *noun*
• "in JUNK sh'n"
• an authoritative warning or order.
• [Late Latin *injunctio* from Latin *injungere* ENJOIN]
• **injunctive** *adjective*

injury *noun*
• "INJUR ee"
• physical harm or damage.
• [Anglo-French *injurie* from Latin *injuria* a wrong (*in-* not, without, *jus juris* right)]
• **injure** *verb*
• **injured** *adjective*
• **injurious** *adjective* "in JURY us"
• **injuriously** *adverb*

injustice *noun*
• "in JUSS tiss"
• a lack of fairness or justice.
• [Latin *in-* not, without + 'justice' from Old French *juste* from Latin *justus* from *jus* right]

inlier *noun*
• "IN lie ur"
• a structure or area of older rocks completely surrounded by newer rocks.
• ['in', after *outlier*]

innards *plural noun*
• "INNERDS"
• entrails.
• [dialect etc. pronunciation of *inwards*]

innate *adjective*
• "in ATE"
• inborn; natural.
• [Latin *innatus* (*in* in, *natus* past participle of *nasci* be born)]
• **innately** *adverb*
• **innateness** *noun*

innervate *verb*
• "INNER vate" or "in UR vate"
• supply (an organ etc.) with nerves or nervous stimulation.
• [Latin *in* in + *nervus* nerve]
• **innervation** *noun*
HOMOPHONES: *enervate*

innocent *adjective*
• "INNA s'nt"
• free from moral wrong; sinless.
• [Old French *innocent* or Latin *innocens innocent-* (Latin *in-* not, without, *nocēre* hurt)]
• **innocence** *noun*
• **innocently** *adverb*

innocuous *adjective*
• "in OCK yoo us"
• not injurious; harmless.
• [Latin *innocuus* (*in-* not, without, *nocuus* formed as INNOCENT)]
• **innocuously** *adverb*
• **innocuousness** *noun*

innominate *adjective*
• "in NOM'n it"
• not having a name; unnamed.
• [Late Latin *innominatus* (Latin *in-* not, without + NOMINATE)]

innovate *verb*
• "INNA vate"
• bring in new methods, ideas, etc.
• [Latin *innovare* make new, alter (*in* in, *novus* new)]
• **innovation** *noun*
• **innovative** *adjective*
• **innovatively** *adverb*
• **innovativeness** *noun*
• **innovator** *noun*
• **innovatory** *adjective*

Innu *noun*
• "IN oo"
• a member of an Aboriginal people living in Labrador and northern Quebec.
• [Innu *innu*, human being]

innuendo *noun*
• "in yoo ENDO"
• an allusive or oblique remark or hint, usu. disparaging.
• [Latin, = by nodding at, by pointing to: ablative gerund of *innuere* nod at (*in* in, *nuere* nod)]

innumerable *adjective*
• "in NOOMER a bull" or "in NYOOMER a bull"
• too many to be counted.
• [Latin *in-* not, without + NUMERABLE]
HOMOPHONES: *enumerable*

innumerate *adjective*
• "in NOOMER it" or "in NYOOMER it"
• without a basic knowledge of mathematics and arithmetic.
• [Latin *in-* not, without + NUMERATE]
• **innumeracy** *noun*

inoculate *verb*
• "in NOCK yuh late"
• treat (a person or animal) with a vaccine containing a dead or modified disease-causing agent, usu. by injection, to promote immunity against the disease.
• [originally in sense 'insert (a bud) into a plant': Latin *inoculare inoculat-* implant (*in* in, *oculus* eye, bud)]
• **inoculation** *noun*
• **inoculator** *noun*

inoculum *noun*
• "in OCK yoo I'm"
• any substance used for inoculation.
• [modern Latin (as INOCULATE)]

inoffensive *adjective*
• "inna FENSIV"
• not objectionable or offensive; not causing offence.
• [Latin *in-* not, without + OFFENSIVE]
• **inoffensively** *adverb*
• **inoffensiveness** *noun*

inoperable *adjective*
• "in OPPER a bull"
• that cannot be operated on successfully.
• [Latin *in-* not, without + *operari* to work, from *opus operis* work]

inoperative *adjective*
• "in OPPER a tiv"
• not working or taking effect.
• [as INOPERABLE]
• **inoperativeness** *noun*

inopportune *adjective*
• "in opper TUNE"
• not appropriate, esp. as regards time; inconvenient.
• [Latin *in-* not, without + OPPORTUNE]
• **inopportunely** *adverb*
• **inopportuneness** *noun*

inordinate *adjective*
• "in ORD'n it"
• unusually or disproportionately large; excessive.
• [Latin *inordinatus* (*in-* not, without, *ordinatus* past participle of *ordinare* ORDAIN)]
• **inordinately** *adverb*

inositol *noun*
• "in OH suh tawl"
• each of the nine stereoisomers in $C_6H_{12}0_6$, a substance acting as a growth factor in plants, animals, etc.
• [Greek *īno-* muscle + *lithos* stone + ALCOHOL]

inquisition *noun*
• "in kwuh ZISH'n"
• usu. *derogatory* an intensive search or investigation.
• [Old French from Latin *inquisitio -onis* examination from *inquirere* (*in* in, *quaerere quaesit-* seek)]

inquisitive *adjective*
• "in KWIZZA tiv"
• seeking knowledge; inquiring.
• [Old French *inquisitif -ive* from Late Latin *inquisitivus* (as INQUISITION)]
• **inquisitively** *adverb*
• **inquisitiveness** *noun*

inquisitor *noun*
• "in KWIZZA tur"
• an official investigator, esp. one who proceeds ruthlessly, unrelentingly, etc.
• [French *inquisiteur* from Latin *inquisitor -oris* (as INQUISITION)]
• **inquisitorial** *adjective* "in kwizza TORY 'll"
• **inquisitorially** *adverb*

insalubrious *adjective*
• "in suh LOO bree us"
• (of a place) seedy and rundown; unwholesome.
• [Latin *in-* not, without + SALUBRIOUS]

insanitary *adjective*
• "in SANNA terry"
• not sanitary; dirty or germ-carrying.
• [Latin *in-* not, without + SANITARY]

insatiable *adjective*
• "in SAY shuh bull"
• unable to be satisfied.
• [Old French *insaciable* or Latin *insatiabilis* (*in-* not, without, SATIATE)]
• **insatiability** *noun*
• **insatiably** *adverb*

insatiate *adjective*
• "in SAY shee it"
• never satisfied.
• [as INSATIABLE]

inscrutable *adjective*
• "in SCROOTA bull"
• wholly mysterious, impenetrable.
• [Church Latin *inscrutabilis* (Latin *in-* not, without, *scrutari* search: see SCRUTINY)]
• **inscrutability** *noun*
• **inscrutableness** *noun*
• **inscrutably** *adverb*

inseam *noun*
• "IN seem"
• the inner seam on the leg of a pair of pants, extending from crotch to cuff.
• ['in' + 'seam']

insecticide *noun*
• "in SECTA side"
• a substance used for killing insects.
• [Latin *insectum* (*animal*) notched (animal), from *insecare insect-* (*in* in, *secare* cut) + *-cida, -cidium* from *caedere* kill]
• **insecticidal** *adjective*

insectivore *noun*
• "in SECTA vore"
• any animal that feeds on insects, esp. a mammal of the order Insectivora, including shrews, hedgehogs, and moles.
• [Latin *insectum* (*animal*) notched (animal), from *insecare insect-* from *secare* cut + *-vorus* from *vorare* devour]
• **insectivorous** *adjective* "in sec TIVVER us"

inseminate *verb*
• "in SEMMA nate"
• introduce semen into (a female) by natural or artificial means.
• [Latin *inseminare* (*in* in, SEMEN)]
• **insemination** *noun*

insensate *adjective*
• "in SEN sate"
• without physical sensation or feeling; inanimate.
• [Church Latin *insensatus* (Latin *in-* not, without, *sensatus* from *sensus* faculty of feeling, thought, meaning, from *sentire sens-* feel)]
• **insensately** *adverb*

insensible *adjective*
• "in SENSA bull"
• without one's mental faculties; unconscious.
• [Latin *in-* not, without + SENSIBLE]
• **insensibility** *noun*
• **insensibly** *adverb*

insensitive *adjective*
• "in SENSA tiv"
• showing or feeling no sympathetic or emotional response; indifferent, callous.
• [Latin *in-* not, without + SENSITIVE]
• **insensitively** *adverb*
• **insensitivity** *noun*

insentient *adjective*
• "in SEN sh'nt"
• not sentient; inanimate.
• [Latin *in-* not, without + SENTIENT]
• **insentience** *noun*

inseparable *adjective*
• "in SEPPER a bull"
• unable or unwilling to be separated.
• [Latin *in-* not, without + SEPARATE]
• **inseparability** *noun*
• **inseparableness** *noun*
• **inseparably** *adverb*

inshallah *interjection*
• "in SHAL uh"
• if Allah wills it.
• [Arabic *in šā' Allah*]

insidious *adjective*
• "in SIDDY us"
• proceeding or progressing inconspicuously but harmfully.
• [Latin *insidiosus* cunning, from *insidiae* ambush (*in* in, *sedēre* sit)]
• **insidiously** *adverb*
• **insidiousness** *noun*

insight *noun*
• "IN site"

• the capacity of understanding hidden truths etc., esp. of character or situations.
• [Middle English, = 'discernment', prob. of Scandinavian & Low German origin]
• **insightful** *adjective*
• **insightfully** *adverb*

insignia *noun*
• "in SIG nee uh"
• a badge or distinguishing mark of military rank, office, or membership of an organization or other symbols of rank or authority.
• [Latin, pl. of *insigne* neuter of *insignis* distinguished (*in* in, *signis* from *signum* sign)]

insignificant *adjective*
• "in sig NIFFA k'nt"
• unimportant; trifling.
• [Latin *in-* not, without + SIGNIFICANT]
• **insignificance** *noun*
• **insignificantly** *adverb*

insincere *adjective*
• "in sin SEER"
• not sincere; not candid.
• [Latin *in-* not, without + SINCERE]
• **insincerely** *adverb*
• **insincerity** *noun*

insinuate *verb*
• "in SIN yoo ate"
• convey indirectly or obliquely; hint.
• [Latin *insinuare insinuat-* (*in* in, *sinuare* to curve)]
• **insinuating** *adjective*
• **insinuatingly** *adverb*
• **insinuation** *noun*

insipid *adjective*
• "in SIP id"
• lacking vigour or interest; dull, boring.
• [French *insipide* or Late Latin *insipidus* (Latin *in-* not, without, *sapidus* SAPID)]
• **insipidity** *noun*
• **insipidly** *adverb*
• **insipidness** *noun*

insistent *adjective*
• "in SIS t'nt"
• insisting; demanding positively or continually.
• [Latin *insistere* stand on, persist (*in* in, *sistere* stand)]
• **insistence** *noun*
• **insistently** *adverb*

insobriety *noun*
• "insa BRYE a tee"
• lack of sobriety; intemperance, esp. in drinking.
• [Latin *in-* not, without + SOBRIETY]

insolation *noun*
• "insa LAY sh'n"
• exposure to the sun's rays, esp. for drying or bleaching or as a medical treatment.
• [Latin *insolatio* from *insolare* (*in* in, *solare* from *sol* sun)]
HOMOPHONES: *insulation*

insolent *adjective*
• "IN suh l'nt"
• rude, disrespectful; offensively contemptuous or arrogant.
• [Middle English, = 'arrogant', from Latin *insolens* (*in-* not, without, *solens* present participle of *solēre* be accustomed)]
• **insolence** *noun*
• **insolently** *adverb*

insoluble *adjective*
• "in SAWL yoo bull"
• (of a difficulty, problem, etc.) incapable of being solved.
• [Latin *in-* not, without + SOLUBLE]

insolvent *adjective*
• "in SOLVE 'nt"
• unable to pay one's debts.
• [Latin *in-* not, without + SOLVENT]
• **insolvency** *noun*

insomnia *noun*
• "in SOMNY uh"
• habitual sleeplessness; inability to sleep.
• [Latin from *insomnis* sleepless (*in-* not, without, *somnus* sleep)]
• **insomniac** *noun*

insouciant *adjective*
• "in SOO see 'nt"
• carefree; unconcerned.
• [French (Latin *in-* not, without, *souciant* present participle of *soucier* care)]
• **insouciance** *noun*
• **insouciantly** *adverb*

inspector *noun*
• "in SPECTER"
• a person who inspects.
• [Latin *inspicere inspect-* (*in* in, *specere* look at), or its frequentative *inspectare*]
• **inspectorate** *noun*
• **inspectorial** *adjective*
• **inspectorship** *noun*

inspissated *adjective*
• "in SPISS ated"
• thickened; condensed.
• [Late Latin *inspissare inspissat-* (Latin *in* in, *spissus* thick)]

instance *noun*
• "IN stince"
• an example or illustration of.
• [Old French from Latin *instantia* (as INSTANTANEOUS)]

instantaneous *adjective*
• "in st'n TAINY us"
• occurring or done in an instant or instantly.
• [medieval Latin *instantaneus* from Latin *instans* from *instare instant-* be present, press upon (*in* in, *stare* stand) after Church Latin *momentaneus*]
• **instantaneity** *noun* "in stan tuh NAY a tee"
• **instantaneously** *adverb*
• **instantaneousness** *noun*

instantiate *verb*
- "in STAN shee ate"
- represent by an instance.
- [Latin *instantia*: see INSTANCE]
- **instantiation** *noun*

instauration *noun*
- "in stor AY sh'n"
- restoration; renewal.
- [Latin *instauratio* from *instaurare* renew]

instigate *verb*
- "INSTA gate"
- bring about by incitement or persuasion; provoke.
- [Latin *instigare instigat-* urge, incite (*in-* towards, *stigare* prick)]
- **instigation** *noun*
- **instigator** *noun*

instinct *noun*
- "IN stinct"
- an innate, usu. fixed, pattern of behaviour in most animals in response to certain stimuli.
- [Middle English, = 'impulse', from Latin *instinctus* from *instinguere* incite (Latin *in* in, *stinguere stinct-* prick)]
- **instinctive** *adjective*
- **instinctively** *adverb*
- **instinctual** *adjective*
- **instinctually** *adverb*

institute *noun*
- "INSTA tute"
- a society or organization for the promotion of science, education, etc.
- [Latin *institutum* design, precept, neuter past participle of *instituere* establish, arrange, teach (*in* in, *statuere* set up)]

institution *noun*
- "insta TOO sh'n" or "insta TYOO sh'n"
- the act or an instance of instituting.
- [as INSTITUTE]
- **institutional** *adjective*
- **institutionalism** *noun*
- **institutionally** *adverb*

institutionalize *verb*
ALSO SPELLED: esp. *Brit.* **-ise**
- "insta TOO sh'n 'll ize" or "insta TYOO sh'n 'll ize"
- establish in practice or custom.
- [as INSTITUTION]
- **institutionalization** *noun* (also esp. *Brit.* **-isation**)

institutionalized *adjective*
ALSO SPELLED: esp. *Brit.* **-ised**
- "insta TOO sh'n 'll ized" or "insta TYOO sh'n 'll ized"
- (of a prisoner, a long-term patient, etc.) made apathetic and dependent after a long period in an institution.
- [as INSTITUTIONALIZE]

instrument *noun*
- "INSTRA m'nt"
- a tool or implement, esp. for delicate or scientific work.
- [Old French *instrument* or Latin *instrumentum* from Latin *instruere* build, teach (*in* in, *struere* pile up)]
- **instrumented** *adjective*

instrumental *adjective*
- "instra MENT'll"
- serving as an instrument or means.
- [as INSTRUMENT]
- **instrumentality** *noun*
- **instrumentally** *adverb*

instrumentalism *noun*
- "instra MENT'll izm"
- a pragmatic philosophical approach which regards an activity (such as science, law, or education) chiefly as an instrument or tool for some practical purpose, rather than in more absolute or ideal terms.
- [as INSTRUMENT]

instrumentalist *noun*
- "instra MENT'll ist"
- a player of a musical instrument.
- [as INSTRUMENT]

instrumentation *noun*
- "instra m'n TAY sh'n"
- the arrangement or composition of music for a particular group of musical instruments.
- [as INSTRUMENT]

insubordinate *adjective*
- "in suh BORD'n it"
- refusing to obey instructions or show respect.
- [Latin *in-* not, without + SUBORDINATE]
- **insubordinately** *adverb*
- **insubordination** *noun*

insubstantial *adjective*
- "in sub STAN sh'll"
- lacking solidity or substance; weak, flimsy.
- [Latin *in-* not, without + SUBSTANTIAL]
- **insubstantiality** *noun*
"in sub stanshy ALA tee"
- **insubstantially** *adverb*

insufferable *adjective*
- "in SUFFER a bull"
- intolerable.
- [Latin *in-* not, without + *sufferre* suffer (*sub* under, *ferre* bear)]
- **insufferableness** *noun*
- **insufferably** *adverb*

insufficient *adjective*
- "in suh FISH 'nt"
- not sufficient; inadequate.
- [Latin *in-* not, without + SUFFICIENT]
- **insufficiency** *noun*
- **insufficiently** *adverb*

insufflate *verb*
- "INSA flate"
- blow or breathe (air, gas, powder, etc.) into a cavity of the body etc.

• [Late Latin *insufflare insufflat-* (Latin *in* in, *sufflare* blow upon)]
• **insufflation** *noun*

insular *adjective*
• "IN s'll ur" or "IN syuh lur"
• of or like an island.
• [Late Latin *insularis* (as INSULATE)]
• **insularity** *noun* "in sul ERRA tee" or "in syul ERRA tee"

insulate *verb*
• "IN s'll ate" or "IN syuh late"
• prevent the passage of electricity, heat, or sound from (a thing, room, etc.) by interposing non-conductors.
• [Latin *insula* island]
• **insulation** *noun*
• **insulative** *adjective*
• **insulator** *noun*
HOMOPHONES: *insolation*

insulin *noun*
• "IN s'll in" or "IN syuh lin"
• a polypeptide hormone produced in the pancreas by the islets of Langerhans, which regulates the amount of glucose in the blood, and the lack of which causes diabetes.
• [Latin *insula* island]

insuperable *adjective*
• "in SUPER a bull" or "in SUPE ruh bull"
• (of a barrier) impossible to surmount.
• [Latin *in-* not, without, + *superabilis* from *superare* overcome]
• **insuperably** *adverb*

insupportable *adjective*
• "in suh PORTA bull"
• unable to be endured; insufferable.
• [Latin *in-* not, without + *supportare* (*sub* under, *portare* carry)]
• **insupportably** *adverb*

insurgent *adjective*
• "in SUR j'nt"
• rising in active revolt; rebellious.
• [French from Latin *insurgere insurrect-* (*in* in, *surgere* rise)]
• **insurgence** *noun*
• **insurgency** *noun*

insurmountable *adjective*
• "in sur MOUNT a bull"
• unable to be surmounted or overcome.
• [Latin *in-* not, without + Old French *sur* (from Latin *super* above) + Old French *monter* (ultimately from Latin *mons montis* mountain)]
• **insurmountably** *adverb*

insurrection *noun*
• "in sur RECK sh'n"
• a rising in open resistance to established authority; a rebellion.
• [Old French from Late Latin *insurrectio -onis* (as INSURGENT)]
• **insurrectionary** *adjective*
• **insurrectionist** *noun*

intagliated *adjective*
• "in TALLY ated"
• decorated with surface carving.
• [Italian *intagliato* past participle of *intagliare* cut into]

intaglio *noun*
• "in TALLY oh"
• a gem with an incised design.
• [Italian (as INTAGLIATED)]

intangible *adjective*
• "in TANJA bull"
• unable to be touched; not solid.
• [Latin *in-* not, without + TANGIBLE]
• **intangibility** *noun*
• **intangibly** *adverb*

intarsia *noun*
• "in TARCY uh"
• the craft of using wood inlays, esp. as practised in 15th-c. Italy.
• [Italian *intarsio*]

integer *noun*
• "INTA jur"
• a whole number.
• [Latin (adjective) = untouched, whole]

integral *adjective*
• "INTA grull" or "in TEG rull"
• of a whole or necessary to the completeness of a whole.
• [Late Latin *integralis* (as INTEGER)]
• **integrality** *noun*
• **integrally** *adverb*

integrand *noun*
• "INTA grand"
• a function that is to be integrated.
• [Latin *integrandus* gerundive of *integrare*: see INTEGRATE]

integrate *verb*
• "INTA grate"
• combine (parts) into a whole.
• [Latin *integrare integrat-* make whole (as INTEGER)]
• **integrable** *adjective* "INTA gruh bull"
• **integrated** *adjective*
• **integration** *noun*
• **integrationist** *noun*
• **integrative** *adjective*

integrator *noun*
• "INTA grater"
• an instrument for indicating or registering the total amount or mean value of some physical quality, as area, temperature, etc.
• [as INTEGRATE]

integrin *noun*
• "INTA grin"
• any of a class of animal transmembrane proteins which are involved in the adhesion of cells to each other and to their substrate.
• [as INTEGER]

integrity *noun*
• "in TEGGRA tee"
• moral uprightness; honesty.
• [French *intégrité* or Latin *integritas* (as INTEGER)]

integument *noun*
• "in TEG yoo m'nt"
• a natural outer covering, as a skin, husk, rind, etc.
• [Latin *integumentum* from *integere* (*in* in, *tegere* cover)]
• **integumentary** *adjective*
"in teg yoo MENTA ree"

intellect *noun*
• "INTA lect"
• the faculty of reasoning, knowing, and thinking, as distinct from feeling.
• [Old French or Latin *intellectus* understanding (as INTELLIGENT)]

intellection *noun*
• "inta LECK sh'n"
• the action or process of understanding.
• [as INTELLECT]
• **intellective** *adjective*

intellectual *adjective*
• "inta LECK choo 'll"
• of or relating to the intellect.
• [as INTELLECT]
• **intellectualism** *noun*
• **intellectualist** *noun*
• **intellectuality** *noun*
• **intellectualization** *noun* (also esp. *Brit.* **-isation**)
• **intellectualize** *verb* (also esp. *Brit.* **-ise**)
• **intellectually** *adverb*

intelligent *adjective*
• "in TELLA j'nt"
• having the faculty of understanding; possessing or showing intelligence, esp. of a high level.
• [Latin *intelligere intellect-* understand (*inter* between, among, *legere* gather, pick out, read)]
• **intelligence** *noun*
• **intelligently** *adverb*

intelligentsia *noun*
• "in tella JENT see uh"
• the class of intellectuals regarded as possessing culture and political initiative.
• [Russian from Polish *inteligencja* from Latin *intelligentia* (as INTELLIGENT)]

intelligible *adjective*
• "in TELLA juh bull"
• able to be understood; comprehensible.
• [Latin *intelligibilis* (as INTELLIGENT)]
• **intelligibility** *noun*
• **intelligibly** *adverb*

intemperate *adjective*
• "in TEMPER it"
• (of a person, conduct, or speech) immoderate; unbridled; violent.
• [Latin *in-* not, without + *temperatus* past participle of *temperare* mingle]
• **intemperance** *noun*
• **intemperately** *adverb*

intendant *noun*
• "in TEN d'nt"
• a high-ranking administrative official in French, Portuguese, and Spanish provinces and colonies, responsible for economic development, settlement, and the administration of justice.
• [French from Latin *intendere* strain, direct, purpose (*in* in, *tendere* stretch, tend)]
• **intendancy** *noun*

intension *noun*
• "in TEN sh'n"
• the internal content of a concept.
• [Latin *intensio* (as INTENTION)]
• **intensional** *adjective*
• **intensionally** *adverb*
HOMOPHONES: *intention, intentional, intentionally*

intention *noun*
• "in TEN sh'n"
• a thing intended; an aim or purpose.
• [Old French from Latin *intentio* stretching, purpose, from *intendere intent-* or *intens-* strain, direct, purpose, from *tendere* stretch, tend]
• **intentional** *adjective*
• **intentionality** *noun*
• **intentionally** *adverb*
• **intentioned** *adjective*
HOMOPHONES: *intension, intensional, intensionally*

inter *verb*
• "in TUR"
• deposit (a corpse etc.) in the earth, a tomb, etc.; bury.
• [Old French *enterrer* from Romanic (Latin *in* in, *terra* earth)]
• **interment** *noun*

intercalary *adjective*
• "in TURKA lerry" or "inter CALA ree"
• (of a day or a month) inserted in the calendar to harmonize it with the solar year, e.g. 29 Feb. in leap years.
• [Latin *intercalari(u)s* (as INTERCALATE)]

intercalate *verb*
• "in TURKA late"
• insert (an intercalary day etc.).
• [Latin *intercalare intercalat-* (*inter* between, among, *calare* proclaim)]
• **intercalation** *noun*

intercalated *adjective*
• "in TURKA lated"
• (of strata etc.) interposed.
• [as INTERCALATE]

intercede *verb*
• "inter SEED"
• interpose or intervene on behalf of another; plead.

• [French *intercéder* or Latin *intercedere intercess-* intervene (*inter* between, among, *cedere* go)]

intercellular *adjective*
• "inter SELL yuh lur"
• located or occurring between cells.
• [Latin *inter* between, among + CELLULAR]

intercept *verb*
• "inter SEPT"
• seize, catch, or stop (a person, message, vehicle, ball, puck, etc.) going from one place to another.
• [Latin *intercipere intercept-* (*inter* between, among, *capere* take)]
• **interception** *noun*
• **interceptive** *adjective*

interceptor *noun*
• "inter SEPTER"
• an aircraft used to intercept enemy aircraft.
• [as INTERCEPT]

intercession *noun*
• "inter SESH'n"
• the act of interceding, esp. by prayer.
• [French *intercession* or Latin *intercessio* (as INTERCEDE)]
• **intercessor** *noun*
• **intercessory** *adjective*
HOMOPHONES: *intersession*

intercollegiate *adjective*
• "inter kuh LEE jit"
• existing or conducted between colleges or universities.
• [Latin *inter* between, among + COLLEGIATE]

intercolonial *adjective*
• "inter kuh LONEY 'll"
• existing or conducted between colonies.
• [Latin *inter* between, among + COLONY]

intercommunicate *verb*
• "inter kuh MYOONA cate"
• communicate reciprocally.
• [Latin *inter* between, among + COMMUNICATE]
• **intercommunication** *noun*

intercommunion *noun*
• "inter kuh MYOON y'n"
• mutual fellowship, esp. mutual sharing of the Eucharist by Christian denominations.
• [Latin *inter* between, among + COMMUNION]

intercommunity *noun*
• "inter kuh MYOONA tee"
• the quality of being common to various groups etc.
• [Latin *inter* between, among + COMMUNITY]

intercostal *adjective*
• "inter COST'll"
• between the ribs (of the body or a ship).
• [Latin *inter* between, among + COSTAL]

interdependent *adjective*
• "inter de PEND'nt"
• dependent on each other.
• [Latin *inter* between, among + DEPENDENT]
• **interdepend** *verb*
• **interdependence** *noun*
• **interdependency** *noun*
• **interdependently** *adverb*

interdict *noun*
• "INTER dict"
• an authoritative prohibition.
• [Latin *interdictum* past participle of *interdicere* interpose, forbid by decree (*inter* between, among, *dicere* say)]
• **interdiction** *noun*
• **interdictory** *adjective*

interdigitate *verb*
• "inter DIDGE a tate"
• interlock like clasped fingers.
• [Latin *inter* between, among + *digitus* finger]

interdisciplinary *adjective*
• "inter DISSA plin airy"
• of or between more than one branch of learning.
• [Latin *inter* between, among + DISCIPLINE]
• **interdisciplinarity** *noun*
"inter dissa plin ERRA tee"

interfere *verb*
• "inter FEER"
• (of a person) meddle; obstruct a process etc.
• [Old French *s'entreferir* strike each other (*inter* between, among, *ferir* from Latin *ferire* strike)]
• **interference** *noun*
• **interferential** *adjective* "inter fuh REN sh'll"
• **interferer** *noun*
• **interfering** *adjective*
• **interferingly** *adverb*

interferometer *noun*
• "inter fuh ROMMA tur"
• an instrument for measuring wavelengths etc. by means of interference phenomena.
• [as INTERFERE + Greek *metron* measure]
• **interferometric** *adjective*
"inter ferra METRIC"
• **interferometrically** *adverb*
• **interferometry** *noun*

interferon *noun*
• "inter FEER on"
• any of various proteins released by cells, usu. in response to a virus, and able to inhibit viral replication.
• [as INTERFERE]

intergalactic *adjective*
• "inter guh LACTIC"
• of or situated between two or more galaxies.
• [Latin *inter* between, among + GALACTIC]
• **intergalactically** *adverb*

intergenerational *adjective*
• "inter jenner AY sh'n 'll"
• existing or occurring between different generations of people.
• [Latin *inter* between, among + GENERATION]

interglacial *adjective*
• "inter GLAY sh'll"
• of or relating to a period of milder climate between glacial periods.
• [Latin *inter* between, among + GLACIAL]

intergovernmental *adjective*
• "inter guvern MENT'll" or "inter guvver MENT'll"
• concerning or conducted between two or more governments.
• [Latin *inter* between, among + GOVERN]
• **intergovernmentally** *adverb*

intergrade *verb*
• "INTER grade"
• merge gradually one into another by passing through a series of intermediate stages.
• [Latin *inter* between, among + *gradus* step]
• **intergradation** *noun*

interior *adjective*
• "in TEERY ur"
• inner.
• [Latin, comparative from *inter* among]
• **interiority** *noun*
• **interiorization** *noun* (also esp. *Brit.* **-isation**)
• **interiorize** *verb* (also esp. *Brit.* **-ise**)

interject *verb*
• "inter JECT"
• introduce abruptly, esp. into a conversation; remark parenthetically or as an interruption.
• [Latin *interjicere* (*inter* between, among, *jacere* throw)]
• **interjection** *noun*

interleukin *noun*
• "inter LOO kin"
• any of several glycoproteins produced by leukocytes for regulating immune responses.
• [Latin *inter* between, among + LEUKOCYTE]

interlinear *adjective*
• "inter LINNY ur"
• written or printed between the lines of a text.
• [Latin *inter* between, among + LINEAR]

interlocutor *noun*
• "inter LOCK yoo tur"
• a person who takes part in a dialogue or conversation.
• [modern Latin from Latin *interloqui interlocut-* interrupt in speaking (*inter* between, among, *loqui* speak)]
• **interlocution** *noun* "inter lo KYOO sh'n"
• **interlocutory** *adjective*

interloper *noun*
• "INTER lope ur"
• an intruder.
• [Latin *inter* between, among + *loper* as in *landloper* vagabond, from Middle Dutch *landlooper*]
• **interlope** *verb*

interlude *noun*
• "INTER lude"
• an intervening time, space, or event that contrasts with what goes before or after.
• [Middle English, = a light dramatic item between the acts of a morality play, from medieval Latin *interludium* (*inter* between, among, *ludus* play)]

intermediary *noun*
• "inter MEEDY airy"
• a person who acts as a link or helps to negotiate between two or more others; a mediator.
• [French *intermédiaire* from Italian *intermediario* from Latin *intermedius* (as INTERMEDIATE)]

intermediate *adjective*
• "inter MEEDY it"
• coming between two things in time, place, order, character, etc.
• [medieval Latin *intermediatus* (*inter* between, among, *medius* middle)]
• **intermediacy** *noun*
• **intermediately** *adverb*
• **intermediation** *noun*

intermetallic *adjective*
• "inter muh TALIC"
• designating compounds made from two or more metals.
• [Latin *inter* between, among + METAL]

intermezzo *noun*
• "inter METSO"
• a short connecting instrumental movement in an opera or other musical work.
• [Italian from Latin *intermedium* interval (as INTERMEDIATE)]

interminable *adjective*
• "in TURMIN a bull"
• endless; having no prospect of an end.
• [Latin *in-* not, without + TERMINUS]
• **interminably** *adverb*

intermittent *adjective*
• "inter MIT 'nt"
• occurring at intervals; not continuous or steady.
• [Latin *intermittere intermiss-* (*inter* between, among, *mittere* let go)]
• **intermittence** *noun*
• **intermittency** *noun*
• **intermittently** *adverb*

intermolecular *adjective*
• "inter muh LECK yuh lur"
• between molecules.
• [Latin *inter* between, among + MOLECULE]

intermontane *adjective*
• "inter MON tane"
• situated between mountains.
• [Latin *inter* between, among + MONTANE]

intern *noun*
• "IN turn"
• a recent medical graduate, resident and

working under supervision in a hospital as part of his or her training.
• [French *interne* from Latin *internus* internal]
• **internship** *noun*

internal *adjective*
• "in TURN'll"
• of or situated in the inside or invisible part.
• [modern Latin *internalis* (as INTERN)]
• **internality** *noun*
• **internally** *adverb*

internalize *verb*
ALSO SPELLED: esp. *Brit.* **-ise**
• "in TURN'll ize"
• make (attitudes, behaviour, etc.) part of one's nature by learning or unconscious assimilation.
• [as INTERNAL]
• **internalization** *noun* (also esp. *Brit.* **-isation**)

international *adjective*
• "inter NASH'n 'll"
• existing, involving, or carried on between two or more nations.
• [Latin *inter* between, among + *natio -onis* from *nasci nat-* be born]
• **internationalization** *noun* (also esp. *Brit.* **-isation**)
• **internationalize** *verb* (also esp. *Brit.* **-ise**)
• **internationally** *adverb*

internationalism *noun*
• "inter NASH'n 'll izm"
• the advocacy of a community of interests among nations.
• [as INTERNATIONAL]
• **internationalist** *noun*

internecine *adjective*
• "inter NESS een"
• mutually destructive.
• [originally = deadly, from Latin *internecinus* from *internecio* massacre, from *internecare* slaughter (*inter* between, among, *necare* kill)]

internist *noun*
• "IN turn ist"
• a specialist in internal medicine.
• [as INTERN]

internment *noun*
• "in TURN m'nt"
• the act of confining or obliging (a prisoner, alien, etc.) to reside within prescribed limits.
• [as INTERN]
• **internee** *noun*

internode *noun*
• "INTER node"
• a part of a stem between two of the knobs from which leaves arise.
• [Latin *inter* between, among + *nodus* knot]

internuclear *adjective*
• "inter NEW clee ur"
• between nuclei.
• [Latin *inter* between, among + NUCLEAR]

interoperable *adjective*
• "inter OPPER a bull"
• able to operate in conjunction.
• [Latin *inter* between, among + *operari* to work, from *opus operis* work]
• **interoperability** *noun*

interparliamentary *adjective*
• "inter parla MENTA ree"
• between parliaments.
• [Latin *inter* between, among + PARLIAMENT]

interpellate *verb*
• "in TURP'll ate"
• (in European parliaments) interrupt the order of the day by demanding an explanation from (the minister concerned).
• [Latin *interpellare interpellat-* (*inter* between, among, *pellere* drive)]
• **interpellation** *noun*
• **interpellator** *noun*
HOMOPHONES: *interpolate*, *interpolation*, *interpolator*

interpenetrate *verb*
• "inter PENNA trate"
• (of two things) penetrate each other.
• [Latin *inter* between, among + PENETRATE]
• **interpenetration** *noun*
• **interpenetrative** *adjective*

interpersonal *adjective*
• "inter PURR s'n 'll"
• (of relations) occurring between persons, esp. reciprocally.
• [Latin *inter* between, among + *persona* actor's mask, character in a play, human being]
• **interpersonally** *adverb*

interphase *noun*
• "INTER faze"
• the resting phase between successive divisions of a cell.
• [Latin *inter* between, among + PHASE]

interplanetary *adjective*
• "inter PLANNA terry"
• between planets.
• [Latin *inter* between, among + PLANET]

interpolate *verb*
• "in TURPA late"
• interject (a remark) in a conversation.
• [Latin *interpolare* furbish up (*inter* between, among, *polire* polish)]
• **interpolation** *noun*
• **interpolator** *noun*
HOMOPHONES: *interpellate*, *interpellation*, *interpellator*

interpose *verb*
• "inter POZE"
• place or insert (a thing) between others.
• [French *interposer* from Latin *interponere* put]
• **interposition** *noun*

interpret *verb*
• "in TURP rit"
• explain the meaning of.

• [Old French *interpreter* or Latin *interpretari* explain, translate, from *interpres -pretis* explainer]
• **interpretability** *noun*
• **interpretable** *adjective*
• **interpretation** *noun*
• **interpretational** *adjective*
• **interpretative** *adjective*
• **interpretive** *adjective*
• **interpretively** *adverb*

interpreter *noun*
• "in TURPRA tur"
• a person who translates from one language to another either orally or using sign language.
• [as INTERPRET]

interprovincial *adjective*
• "inter pruh VIN sh'll"
• situated or carried on between provinces.
• [Latin *inter* between, among + PROVINCIAL]
• **interprovincially** *adverb*

interracial *adjective*
• "inter RAY sh'll"
• existing between or affecting different races.
• [Latin *inter* between, among + French *racial* from Italian *razza*, of unknown origin]
• **interracially** *adverb*

interregnum *noun*
• "inter REG num"
• an interval when the normal government is suspended, esp. between successive reigns or regimes.
• [Latin (*inter* between, among, *regnum* reign)]

interrelate *verb*
• "inter re LATE"
• relate (two or more things) to each other.
• [Latin *inter* between, among + *referre relat-* bring back]
• **interrelatedness** *noun*
• **interrelation** *noun*
• **interrelationship** *noun*

interrogate *verb*
• "in TERRA gate"
• ask questions of (a person) esp. closely, thoroughly, or formally.
• [Latin *interrogare interrogat-* ask (*inter* between, among, *rogare* ask)]
• **interrogation** *noun*
• **interrogational** *adjective*
• **interrogator** *noun*

interrogative *adjective*
• "inter OGGA tiv"
• of or like a question; used in questions.
• [as INTERROGATE]
• **interrogatively** *adverb*

interrogatory *adjective*
• "inter OGGA tory"
• questioning; of or suggesting inquiry.
• [as INTERROGATE]

interrupt *verb*
• "inter UPT"
• act so as to break the continuous progress of (something) temporarily.
• [Latin *interrumpere interrupt-* (*inter* between, among, *rumpere* break)]
• **interrupter** *noun* (also **interruptor**)
• **interruptible** *adjective*
• **interruption** *noun*
• **interruptive** *adjective*

interscholastic *adjective*
• "inter skuh LASTIC"
• occurring between schools.
• [Latin *inter* between, among + SCHOLASTIC]

intersession *noun*
• "INTER sesh'n"
• *Cdn* a short university term, usu. in May and June, in which the course material usually covered in thirteen weeks is condensed into five or six weeks of intensive study.
• [Latin *inter* between, among + Old French *session* or Latin *sessio -onis* from *sedēre sess-* sit]
HOMOPHONES: *intercession*

interspecific *adjective*
• "inter spuh SIFFIC"
• relating to or occurring between one or more species.
• [Latin *inter* between, among + SPECIFIC]

intersperse *verb*
• "inter SPURSE"
• scatter; place here and there.
• [Latin *interspergere interspers-* (*inter* between, among, *spargere* scatter)]
• **interspersion** *noun*

intersquad *adjective*
• "INTER skwod"
• designating a competition between members of the same team.
• [Latin *inter* between, among + SQUAD]

interstadial *adjective*
• "inter STAIDY 'll"
• of or relating to a minor period of ice retreat during a glacial period.
• [Latin *inter* between, among + *stadium* stage]

interstellar *adjective*
• "INTER steller"
• occurring or situated between stars.
• [Latin *inter* between, among + STELLAR]

interstice *noun*
• "in TUR stiss"
• an intervening space.
• [Latin *interstitium* (*inter* between, among, *sistere stit-* stand)]
• **interstitial** *adjective* "inter STISH'll"
• **interstitially** *adverb*

intersubjective *adjective*
• "inter sub JECTIV"
• existing between or shared by more than one conscious mind.

• [Latin *inter* between, among + 'subjective' from Old French *suget* etc. from Latin *subjectus* past participle of *subjicere* (*sub* under, *jacere* throw)]
• **intersubjectively** *adverb*
• **intersubjectivity** *noun*

intertextuality *noun*
• "inter tex choo ALA tee"
• the relationship between esp. literary texts; the fact of relating or alluding to other texts.
• [Latin *inter* between, among + 'text' from Old Northern French *texte* from Latin *textus* tissue, literary style (in medieval Latin = Gospel) from Latin *texere text-* weave]
• **intertextual** *adjective*

interval *noun*
• "INTER v'll"
• an intervening time or space.
• [Middle English, ultimately from Latin *intervallum* space between ramparts, interval (*inter* between, among, *vallum* rampart)]
• **intervallic** *adjective* (also **intervalic**) "inter VALIC"

intervale *noun*
• "INTER vail"
• (*Maritimes, Nfld & New England*) a low, level tract of land, esp. along a river.
• [var. of INTERVAL, influenced by VALE through folk etymology]

intervene *verb*
• "inter VEEN"
• occur in time between events.
• [Latin *intervenire* (*inter* between, among, *venire* come)]
• **intervenor** *noun* (also **intervener**)
• **intervention** *noun*
• **interventional** *adjective*

interventionist *adjective*
• "inter VEN sh'n ist"
• favouring intervention, esp. by a government in its domestic economy or by one state in the affairs of another.
• [as INTERVENE]
• **interventionism** *noun*

intervertebral *adjective*
• "inter VURTA brull"
• between vertebrae.
• [Latin *inter* between, among + VERTEBRA]

intervocalic *adjective*
• "inter voe CALIC"
• occurring between vowels.
• [Latin *inter* between, among + VOCALIC]

intestate *adjective*
• "in TESS tate"
• not having made a will before death.
• [Latin *intestatus* (*in-* not, without, *testari testat-* make a will, from *testis* witness)]
• **intestacy** *noun*

intestine *noun*
• "in TESS tine" or "in TESS tin"
• the lower part of the alimentary canal from the end of the stomach to the anus.
• [Latin *intestinum* from *intestinus* internal]
• **intestinal** *adjective*

inti *noun*
• "INTY"
• a former monetary unit of Peru, equal to 100 centimos.
• [Spanish from Quechua *ynti*, sun, the Inca sun god]

intimate[1] *adjective*
• "INTA mit"
• closely acquainted; familiar, close.
• [Latin *intimus* inmost]
• **intimacy** *noun* "INTA muh see"
• **intimately** *adverb*

intimate[2] *verb*
• "INTA mate"
• state or make known.
• [Late Latin *intimare* announce, from Latin *intimus* inmost]
• **intimation** *noun*

intimidate *verb*
• "in TIMMA date"
• frighten or overawe, esp. to subdue or influence.
• [medieval Latin *intimidare* (Latin *in* in, *timidare* from *timidus* from *timēre* fear)]
• **intimidating** *adjective*
• **intimidatingly** *adverb*
• **intimidation** *noun*
• **intimidator** *noun*

intinction *noun*
• "in TINK sh'n"
• the dipping of the Eucharistic bread in the wine so that the communicant receives both together.
• [Late Latin *intinctio* from Latin *intingere intinct-* (*in* in, *tingere tinct-* dye, stain)]

intolerable *adjective*
• "in TOLLER a bull" ("TOLLER" rhymes with *COLLAR*)
• that cannot be endured.
• [Latin *in-* not, without + TOLERATE]
• **intolerably** *adverb*

intolerant *adjective*
• "in TOLLER 'nt" ("TOLLER" rhymes with *COLLAR*)
• not tolerant, esp. of views, beliefs, or behaviour differing from one's own.
• [Latin *in-* not, without + TOLERATE]
• **intolerance** *noun*
• **intolerantly** *adverb*

intonation *noun*
• "inta NAY sh'n"
• modulation of the voice; accent.
• [medieval Latin *intonare* (Latin *in* in, *tonus* tone)]
• **intonational** *adjective*

intoxicant *noun*
- "in TOXA k'nt"
- an intoxicating substance.
- [as INTOXICATE]

intoxicate *verb*
- "in TOXA cate"
- make drunk.
- [medieval Latin *intoxicare* (Latin *in* in, *toxicare* poison, from *toxicum*): see TOXIC]
- **intoxicating** *adjective*
- **intoxicatingly** *adverb*
- **intoxication** *noun*

intracellular *adjective*
- "intra SELL yuh lur"
- located or occurring within a cell or cells.
- [Latin *intra* inside + CELLULAR]
- **intracellularly** *adverb*

intracranial *adjective*
- "intra CRAINY 'll"
- within the skull.
- [Latin *intra* inside + CRANIUM]

intractable *adjective*
- "in TRACTA bull"
- hard to control or deal with.
- [Latin *in-* not, without + TRACTABLE]
- **intractability** *noun*
- **intractably** *adverb*

intrados *noun*
- "in TRAY doss"
- the lower or inner curve of an arch.
- [French from Latin *intra* inside, *dos* back, from Latin *dorsum*]

intramolecular *adjective*
- "intra muh LECK yuh lur"
- within a molecule.
- [Latin *intra* inside + MOLECULE]

intramural *adjective*
- "intra MYUR'll"
- taking place within a single (esp. educational) institution.
- [Latin *intra* inside + *muros* walls]
- **intramurally** *adverb*

intramuscular *adjective*
- "intra MUSS kyuh lur"
- in or into a muscle or muscles.
- [Latin *intra* inside + MUSCULAR]
- **intramuscularly** *adverb*

intransigent *adjective*
- "in TRANSA j'nt"
- uncompromising, stubborn.
- [French *intransigeant* from Spanish *los intransigentes*, a name adopted by the extreme republicans in the Cortes, ultimately formed from Latin *in-* not, without + *transigere transigent-* come to an understanding (*trans* across, *agere* act)]
- **intransigence** *noun*
- **intransigency** *noun*
- **intransigently** *adverb*

intransitive *adjective*
- "in TRANZA tiv"
- (of a verb or sense of a verb) that does not take or require a direct object (whether expressed or implied), e.g. *look* in *look at the sky*.
- [Latin *in-* not, without + TRANSITIVE]
- **intransitively** *adverb*
- **intransitivity** *noun*

intrapsychic *adjective*
- "intra SIKE ick"
- occurring or existing within the psyche or self.
- [Latin *intra* inside + PSYCHIC]

intraspecific *adjective*
- "intra spuh SIFFIC"
- produced, occurring, or existing within a single taxonomic species or between individuals of a single species.
- [Latin *intra* inside + SPECIFIC]

intrauterine *adjective*
- "intra YOOTER in" or "intra YOOTER ine"
- within the uterus.
- [Latin *intra* inside + UTERUS]

intravascular *adjective*
- "intra VASS kyuh lur"
- situated or occurring within a vessel of an animal or plant, esp. within a blood vessel.
- [Latin *intra* inside + VASCULAR]

intravenous *adjective*
- "intra VEE nuss"
- in or into a vein or veins.
- [Latin *intra* inside + VENOUS]
- **intravenously** *adverb*

intrepid *adjective*
- "in TREPPID"
- fearless; very brave.
- [French *intrépide* or Latin *intrepidus* (*in-* not, without, *trepidus* alarmed)]
- **intrepidity** *noun* "in truh PIDDA tee"
- **intrepidly** *adverb*

intricate *adjective*
- "INTRA kit"
- very complicated; perplexingly detailed.
- [Latin *intricare intricat-* (*in* in, *tricare* from *tricae* tricks)]
- **intricacy** *noun*
- **intricately** *adverb*

intrigue *verb*
- "in TREEG"
- provoke (a person's) interest or curiosity.
- [French *intriguer* from Italian *intrigare* from Latin (as INTRICATE)]
- **intriguer** *noun*
- **intriguing** *adjective* "in TREEG ing"
- **intriguingly** *adverb*

intrinsic *adjective*
- "in TRIN zick"
- inherent, essential; belonging naturally.
- [Middle English, = interior, from French

intrinsèque from Late Latin *intrinsecus* from Latin *intrinsecus* (adverb) inwardly]
- **intrinsically** *adverb*

introduce *verb*
- "intra DOOCE" or "intra DYOOCE"
- make (a person or oneself) known by name to another, esp. formally.
- [Latin *introducere introduct-* (*intro* within, *ducere* lead)]
- **introducer** *noun*
- **introduction** *noun*
- **introductory** *adjective*

introit *noun*
- "IN troit"
- a psalm or antiphon sung or said while the priest approaches the altar for the Eucharist.
- [Old French from Latin *introitus* from *introire introit-* enter (*intro* to the inside, *ire* go)]

introjection *noun*
- "intra JECK sh'n"
- the unconscious incorporation of external ideas into one's mind.
- [Latin *intro* to the inside + 'projection' from Latin *projectiōn* from *projicere* (*pro* in front (of), *jacĕre* throw)]
- **introject** *verb*

introspection *noun*
- "intra SPECK sh'n"
- the examination or observation of one's own mental and emotional processes etc.
- [Latin *introspicere introspect-* look inwards (*intro* to the inside, *specere* look)]
- **introspective** *adjective*
- **introspectively** *adverb*

introvert *noun*
- "INTRA vurt"
- a person predominantly concerned with his or her own thoughts and feelings rather than with external things.
- [Latin *intro* to the inside + *vert* as in INVERT]
- **introversion** *noun*
- **introverted** *adjective*

intubate *verb*
- "IN tube ate"
- insert a tube into the trachea for ventilation, usu. during anaesthesia.
- [Latin *in* in + *tuba* tube]
- **intubation** *noun*

intuit *verb*
- "in TOO it" or "in TYOO it"
- know by intuition.
- [Latin *intueri intuit-* consider (*in* in, *tueri* look)]

intuition *noun*
- "in too ISH'n" or "in tyoo ISH'n"
- the power of understanding situations or people's feelings immediately, without the need for conscious reasoning or study.
- [as INTUIT]
- **intuitive** *adjective* "in TOO a tiv" or "in TYOO a tiv"
- **intuitively** *adverb*
- **intuitiveness** *noun*

intuitionism *noun*
- "in too ISH'n izm" or "in tyoo ISH'n izm"
- the belief that primary truths and principles (esp. of ethics and metaphysics) are known directly by intuition.
- [as INTUIT]
- **intuitionist** *noun*

intussusception *noun*
- "inta suh SEP sh'n"
- the inversion of one portion of the intestine within another.
- [modern Latin *intussusceptio* from Latin *intus* within + *susceptio* from *suscipere* take up]

Inuinnaqtun *noun*
- "innoo ee NUCK toon"
- an Inuit language spoken in the Coronation Gulf area of the Central Arctic.
- [Inuktitut]

Inuit *noun*
- "IN yoo it" or "IN oo it" or "IN oo eet"
- any of several Aboriginal peoples inhabiting the Arctic coasts of Canada, Greenland, and Alaska.
- [Inuktitut *inuit* the people]

Inuk *noun*
- "in OOK" (with "OOK" as in *BOOK*)
- a member of any of the Inuit peoples.
- [Inuktitut *inuk* person]

inukshuk *noun*
- "in OOK shook" (with "OOK" as in *BOOK*)
- a figure of a human made of stones, originally used among the Inuit to scare caribou into an ambush, and as a marker to guide travellers, now also found as decorative sculptures in southern Canada.
- [Inuktitut]

Inuktitut *noun*
- "in OOK tuh toot" ("TOOT" rhymes with *FOOT*)
- the language of the Inuit.
- [Inuktitut]

inulin *noun*
- "IN yuh lin"
- a complex of sugar present in the root of various plants and used medically to test kidney function. It is a polysaccharide based on fructose.
- [Latin *inula* (identified by medieval herbalists with elecampane)]

inundate *verb*
- "IN un date"
- flood.
- [Latin *inundare* flow, from *unda* wave]
- **inundation** *noun*

Inupiaq *noun*
- "in OOPY ack"
- an Inuit language spoken in Canada, Alaska, and Greenland.
- [Inuktitut, from *inuk* person + *piaq* genuine]

Inupiat *noun*
- "in OOPY at"
- a member of an Inuit people inhabiting areas of northern Alaska.
- [INUPIAQ]

inure *verb*
- "in YUR"
- accustom (a person) to something esp. unpleasant.
- [Anglo-French *eneurer* from phrase *en eure* (both unrecorded) in use or practice, from *en* in + Old French *e(u)vre* work, from Latin *opera*]
- **inurement** *noun*

Inuvialuit *noun*
- "in oovy AL oo it"
- an Inuit people of the W Canadian Arctic, speaking Inuvialuktun.
- [Inuvialuktun]

Inuvialuk *noun*
- "in oovy AL ook" (with "OOK" as in *BOOK*)
- a member of the Inuvialuit people.
- [Inuvialuktun]

Inuvialuktun *noun*
- "in oovy a LOOK toon" (with "OOK" as in *BOOK*)
- an Inuit language of the western Arctic.
- [Inuvialuktun]

invaginate *verb*
- "in VADGE 'n ate"
- turn or double (a tubular anatomical structure) inside out or back within itself.
- [Latin *in* in + *vagina* sheath]
- **invagination** *noun*

invaluable *adjective*
- "in VAL yoo bull" or "in VAL yoo a bull"
- above valuation; inestimable.
- [Latin *in-* not, without + VALUABLE]
- **invaluably** *adverb*

invariable *adjective*
- "in VERRY a bull"
- unchangeable; always the same.
- [Latin *in-* not, without + VARY]
- **invariability** *noun*
- **invariably** *adverb*

invariant *adjective*
- "in VERRY 'nt"
- unvarying, invariable.
- [Latin *in-* not, without + VARY]
- **invariance** *noun*

invasion *noun*
- "in VAY zh'n"
- the act of invading or process of being invaded.
- [Latin *invadere invas-* (*in* in, *vadere* go)]

invasive *adjective*
- "in VAY siv"
- (of weeds, cancer cells, etc.) tending to spread.
- [as INVASION]
- **invasiveness** *noun*

invective *noun*
- "in VECTIV"
- insulting, abusive, or highly critical language.
- [Old French from Late Latin *invectivus* attacking (as INVEIGH)]

inveigh *verb*
- "in VAY"
- speak or write with strong hostility, esp. to denounce, reproach, or censure.
- [Latin *invehi* go into, assail (*in* in, *vehi* passive of *vehere vect-* carry)]

inveigle *verb*
- "in VAY g'll"
- entice; persuade by guile.
- [earlier *enve(u)gle* from Anglo-French *envegler*, Old French *aveugler* to blind, from *aveugle* blind, prob. from Romanic *ab oculis* (unrecorded) without eyes]
- **inveiglement** *noun*

inventor *noun*
- "in VENTER"
- a person who invents things, esp. as an occupation.
- [from 'invent', Middle English, = discover, from Latin *invenire invent-* find, contrive (*in* in, *venire vent-* come)]

inventory *noun*
- "IN v'n tory"
- a complete list of goods in stock, house contents, etc.
- [medieval Latin *inventorium* from Late Latin *inventarium* (as INVENTOR)]

invert *verb*
- "in VURT"
- turn upside down, inside out, or inwards.
- [Latin *invertere invers-* (*in* in, *vertere* turn)]
- **inverter** *noun*
- **invertibility** *noun*
- **invertible** *adjective*

invertase *noun*
- "in VURT ace"
- an enzyme from yeast which catalyzes the inversion of sucrose to produce invert sugar.
- [as INVERT]

invertebrate *adjective*
- "in VURTA brate" or "in VURTA brit"
- (of an animal) not having a backbone or spinal column.
- [modern Latin *invertebrata* (pl.) (Latin *in-* not, without, VERTEBRA)]

investigate *verb*
- "in VESTA gate"
- inquire into; examine; study carefully.
- [Latin *investigare investigat-* (*in* in, *vestigare* track)]
- **investigation** *noun*
- **investigational** *adjective*
- **investigator** *noun*
- **investigatory** *adjective*

investigative *adjective*
• "in VESTA gate iv" or "in VESTA guh tiv"
• (of journalism or broadcasting) investigating and seeking to expose malpractice, miscarriage of justice, etc.
• [as INVESTIGATE]

investiture *noun*
• "in VESTA chur"
• the formal investing of a person with honours or rank.
• [medieval Latin *investitura* from *investire investit-* (*in* in, *vestire* clothe, from *vestis* clothing)]

inveterate *adjective*
• "in VETTER it"
• (of a person) confirmed in an esp. undesirable habit etc.
• [Latin *inveterare inveterat-* make old (*in* in, *vetus veteris* old)]
• **inveteracy** *noun*
• **inveterately** *adverb*

invidious *adjective*
• "in VIDDY us"
• (of an action, conduct, attitude, etc.) likely to excite resentment or indignation against the person responsible, esp. by real or seeming injustice.
• [Latin *invidiosus* from *invidia* envy (*in-* not, without, *vidēre* see)]
• **invidiously** *adverb*
• **invidiousness** *noun*

invigilate *verb*
• "in VIDGE 'll ate"
• *Cdn & Brit.* supervise candidates at an examination.
• [originally = keep watch, from Latin *invigilare invigilat-* (*in* in, *vigilare* watch, from *vigil* watchful)]
• **invigilation** *noun*
• **invigilator** *noun*

invigorate *verb*
• "in VIGGER ate"
• give vigour or strength to.
• [Latin *in* in + medieval Latin *vigorare vigorat-* make strong]
• **invigorating** *adjective*
• **invigoratingly** *adverb*
• **invigoration** *noun*

invincible *adjective*
• "in VINSA bull"
• unconquerable; that cannot be defeated.
• [Latin *invincibilis* (*in-* not, without + *vincibilis* from *vincere* overcome)]
• **invincibility** *noun*
• **invincibleness** *noun*
• **invincibly** *adverb*

inviolable *adjective*
• "in VIE 'll a bull"
• not to be violated, dishonoured, or profaned.
• [French *inviolable* or Latin *inviolabilis* (Latin *in-* not, without, *violare, violat-* treat violently)]
• **inviolability** *noun*
• **inviolably** *adverb*

inviolate *adjective*
• "in VIE 'll it"
• not violated or profaned.
• [Latin *inviolatus* (*in-* not, without, *violare, violat-* treat violently)]

invisible *adjective*
• "in VIZZA bull"
• unable to be seen; that by its nature is not perceivable by the eye.
• [Latin *in-* not, without + VISIBLE]
• **invisibility** *noun*
• **invisibleness** *noun*
• **invisibly** *adverb*

invocation *noun*
• "in voe CAY sh'n"
• the act or an instance of invoking an authority, a precedent, etc.
• [Latin *invocare* (*in* in, *vocare* call)]
• **invocatory** *adjective* "in VOCKA tory"

involucre *noun*
• "INVA luker"
• a membranous envelope.
• [French *involucre* or Latin *involucrum* from *involvere involut-* (*in* in, *volvere* roll)]

involuntary *adjective*
• "in VOL 'n terry"
• not done willingly or by choice; unintentional.
• [Latin *in-* not, without + VOLUNTARY]
• **involuntarily** *adverb*

involute *adjective*
• "INVA lute"
• involved, intricate.
• [Latin *involutus* past participle of *involvere*: see INVOLUCRE]

involuted *adjective*
• "INVA luted"
• complicated, abstruse.
• [as INVOLUTE]

involution *noun*
• "inva LOO sh'n"
• the action of involving or the fact of being involved.
• [Latin *involutio* (as INVOLUTE)]
• **involutional** *adjective*

invulnerable *adjective*
• "in VULLNER a bull"
• that cannot be wounded or hurt, physically or mentally.
• [Latin *in-* not, without + VULNERABLE]
• **invulnerability** *noun*
• **invulnerably** *adverb*

iodide *noun*
• "EYE a dide"
• any compound of iodine with another element or group.
• [as IODINE]

iodinate *verb*
• "EYE a din ate" or "eye ODDA nate"
• treat or combine with iodine.
• [as IODINE]
• **iodination** *noun*

iodine *noun*
• "EYE a dine"
• a non-metallic element of the halogen group, forming black crystals and a violet vapour, used in medicine and photography, and important as an essential element for living organisms.
• [French *iode* from Greek *iōdēs* violet-like, from *ion* violet]
• **iodate** *noun*
• **iodic** *adjective* "eye ODDIC"

iodize *verb*
ALSO SPELLED: esp. *Brit.* **-ise**
• "EYE a dize"
• treat or impregnate with iodine.
• [as IODINE]
• **iodization** *noun* (also esp. *Brit.* **-isation**)

ion *noun*
• "EYE on" or "EYE 'n"
• an atom, molecule, or group that has lost one or more electrons (= CATION), or gained one or more electrons (= ANION).
• [Greek, neuter pres. participle of *eimi* go]
• **ionic** *adjective* "eye ONNIC"
• **ionically** *adverb*

Ionian *noun*
• "eye OH nee 'n"
• a native or inhabitant of ancient Ionia in western Asia Minor.

ionize *verb*
ALSO SPELLED: esp. *Brit.* **-ise**
• "EYE a nize"
• convert or be converted into an ion or ions.
• [as ION]
• **ionizable** *adjective* (also esp. *Brit.* **-isable**)
• **ionization** *noun* (also esp. *Brit.* **-isation**)

ionizer *noun*
• "EYE a nize ur"
• any thing which produces ionization, esp. a device used to improve the quality of the air in a room etc.
• [as ION]

ionophore *noun*
• "eye ONNA for"
• an agent which is able to transport ions across a lipid membrane in a cell.
• [ION + Greek *-phoros -phoron* bearing, bearer, from *pherō* bear]

ionosphere *noun*
• "eye ONNA sfeer"
• an ionized region of the atmosphere above the stratosphere, extending to about 1 000 km above the earth's surface and able to reflect radio waves for long-distance transmission around the earth.
• [as ION + SPHERE]
• **ionospheric** *adjective*

iota *noun*
• "eye OH tuh"
• the ninth letter of the Greek alphabet (Ι, ι).
• [Greek *iōta*]

ipecac *noun*
• "IPPA cack"
• ipecacuanha.
• [abbreviation]

ipecacuanha *noun*
• "ippa cack yoo ANNA"
• the root of a S American shrub, *Cephaelis ipecacuanha*, used as an emetic and expectorant.
• [Portuguese from Tupi-Guarani *ipekaaguéne* emetic creeper]

ipomoea *noun*
• "ippa MEE uh"
• any twining plant of the genus *Ipomoea*, having trumpet-shaped flowers, e.g. the sweet potato and morning glory.
• [modern Latin from Greek *ips ipos* worm + *homoios* like]

ipsilateral *adjective*
• "ipsa LATTER'll"
• belonging to or occurring on the same side of the body.
• [Latin *ipse* self + LATERAL]

Iqalungmiut *noun*
• "icka LOONG mee oot" ("OOT" rhymes with *FOOT*)
• a resident of Iqaluit, Nunavut.

Iranian *adjective*
• "ih RAINY 'n"
• of or relating to Iranians or Iran.

Iraqi *adjective*
• "ih RACKY" or "ih ROCKY"
• of or relating to Iraq or Iraqis.

irascible *adjective*
• "ih RASSA bull"
• irritable, hot-tempered, easily provoked to anger or resentment.
• [French from Late Latin *irascibilis* from Latin *irasci* grow angry, from *ira* anger]
• **irascibility** *noun*
• **irascibly** *adverb*

irenic *adjective*
ALSO SPELLED: **eirenic**
• "eye REENIC"
• aiming or aimed at peace.
• [Greek *eirēnikos* from *eirēnikos* peace]

iridaceous *adjective*
• "irra DAY sh'ss"
• of or relating to the family Iridaceae of plants growing from bulbs, corms, or rhizomes, e.g. iris, crocus, and gladiolus.
• [modern Latin *iridaceus* from Latin *iris iridis* from Greek *iris iridos* rainbow, iris + adjective suffix *-aceus* of the nature of]

iridescent *adjective*
• "irra DESS'nt"
• showing rainbow-like luminous or gleaming colours.
• [IRIDACEOUS + Latin *-escent-* used in verb forms to signify becoming]
• **iridescence** *noun*
• **iridescently** *adverb*

iridium *noun*
• "ir IDDY um"
• a hard white metallic element of the platinum group, used esp. in alloys.
• [modern Latin from Latin *iris iridis* rainbow]

iridology *noun*
• "irra DOLLA jee"
• (in alternative medicine) diagnosis by examination of the iris of the eye.
• [Greek *iris iridos* iris + *logos* word]
• **iridologist** *noun*

irk *verb*
• "URK"
• irritate, bore, annoy.
• [Middle English: origin unknown]
• **irksome** *adjective*
• **irksomely** *adverb*
• **irksomeness** *noun*

irony *noun*
• "EYE ruh nee" or "EYE ur nee"
• the expression of meaning using language that normally expresses the opposite.
• [Latin *ironia* from Greek *eirōneia* simulated ignorance, from *eirōn* dissembler]
• **ironic** *adjective* "eye RONNIC"
• **ironical** *adjective*
• **ironically** *adverb*
• **ironist** *noun*
• **ironize** *verb* (also esp. *Brit.* **-ise**)

Iroquoian *noun*
• "irra KWOY 'n"
• a major Aboriginal linguistic group, including Cayuga, Mohawk, Oneida, Onondaga, Seneca, and Tuscarora.
• [as IROQUOIS]

Iroquois *noun*
• "IRRA kwah"
• an Aboriginal confederacy of Iroquoian peoples (originally including the Cayuga, Mohawk, Oneida, Onondaga, and Seneca, and later also the Tuscarora) living in Ontario, Quebec, and New York.
• [French from Algonquin]

irradiance *noun*
• "ir RAIDY ince"
• the flux of radiant energy per unit area, normal to the direction of flow of radiant energy through a medium.
• [as IRRADIATE]

irradiate *verb*
• "ir RAIDY ate"
• subject to any form of radiation.
• [Latin *irradiare irradiat-* (*in* in, *radiare* from *radius* ray)]
• **irradiation** *noun*

irrational *adjective*
• "ir RASH'n 'll"
• illogical; unreasonable.
• [Latin *in-* not, without + *rationalis*, from *ratio* reckoning, reason]
• **irrationalism** *noun*
• **irrationalist** *noun*
• **irrationality** *noun*
• **irrationally** *adverb*

irreconcilable *adjective*
• "ir reck 'n SILE a bull"
• implacably hostile.
• [Latin *in-*, without + RECONCILE]
• **irreconcilability** *noun*
• **irreconcilably** *adverb*

irrecoverable *adjective*
• "ir re CUVVER a bull"
• that cannot be recovered or retrieved.
• [Latin *in-*, without + Old French *recovrer* from Latin *recuperare* RECUPERATE]
• **irrecoverably** *adverb*

irredeemable *adjective*
• "ir re DEEMA bull"
• that cannot be redeemed or bought back.
• [Latin *in-*, without + REDEEM]
• **irredeemably** *adverb*

irredentist *noun*
• "irra DENTIST"
• a person, originally in 19th-c. Italy, advocating the restoration to his or her country of any territory formerly belonging to it.
• [Italian *irredentista* from (*Italia*) *irredenta* unredeemed (Italy)]
• **irredentism** *noun*

irreducible *adjective*
• "irra DUCE a bull"
• that cannot be reduced or made smaller.
• [Latin *in-*, without + REDUCE]
• **irreducibility** *noun*
• **irreducibly** *adverb*

irrefragable *adjective*
• "ir REF ruh guh bull"
• (of a statement, argument, or person) unanswerable, indisputable.
• [Late Latin *irrefragabilis* (Latin *in-* not, without, *refragari* oppose)]

irrefutable *adjective*
• "ir re FUTE a bull"
• that cannot be refuted or disproved.
• [Latin *in-*, without + REFUTE]
• **irrefutably** *adverb*

irregular *adjective*
• "ir REG yuh lur"
• not regular; unsymmetrical, uneven; varying in form.
• [Latin *in-*, without + REGULAR]

- **irregularity** *noun* "ir reg yuh LERRA tee"
- **irregularly** *adverb*

irrelevant *adjective*
- "ir RELLA v'nt"
- not relevant; not applicable (to a matter in hand).
- [Latin *in-*, without + RELEVANT]
- **irrelevance** *noun*
- **irrelevancy** *noun*
- **irrelevantly** *adverb*

irreligion *noun*
- "ir re LIDGE 'n"
- disregard of or hostility to religion.
- [Latin *in-*, without + RELIGION]
- **irreligious** *adjective*

irremediable *adjective*
- "irry MEEDY a bull"
- that cannot be remedied.
- [Latin *irremediabilis* (*in-* not, without, REMEDY)]
- **irremediably** *adverb*

irremovable *adjective*
- "irry MOOVA bull"
- that cannot be removed, esp. from office.
- [Latin *in-*, without + Old French *removeir* from Latin *removēre remot-* (*re-* again, *movēre* move)]
- **irremovably** *adverb*

irreparable *adjective*
- "ir REP ruh bull"
- (of an injury, loss, etc.) that cannot be rectified or made good.
- [Latin *in-*, without + REPARABLE]
- **irreparably** *adverb*

irreplaceable *adjective*
- "irry PLACE a bull"
- that cannot be replaced if lost or damaged.
- [Latin *in-*, without + *re* again + Old French *place* via Latin *platea* from Greek *plateia (hodos)* broad (way)]
- **irreplaceability** *noun*
- **irreplaceably** *adverb*

irrepressible *adjective*
- "irry PRESSA bull"
- that cannot be repressed or restrained.
- [Latin *in-*, without + Middle English 'repress' from Latin *reprimere* (*re-* again, *premere* press)]
- **irrepressibility** *noun*
- **irrepressibly** *adverb*

irreproachable *adjective*
- "irry PROACH a bull"
- faultless, blameless.
- [Latin *in-*, without + Old French *reproche(r)* from Romanic (Latin *re-* again, *prope* near)]
- **irreproachability** *noun*
- **irreproachably** *adverb*

irresistible *adjective*
- "irry ZISTA bull"
- too strong or convincing to be resisted.
- [Latin *in-*, without + RESIST]
- **irresistibility** *noun*
- **irresistibly** *adverb*

irresolute *adjective*
- "ih REZZA loot"
- hesitant, undecided.
- [Latin *in-*, without + RESOLUTE]
- **irresolutely** *adverb*
- **irresoluteness** *noun*
- **irresolution** *noun*

irresolvable *adjective*
- "irry ZOLVA bull"
- that cannot be resolved into its components.
- [Latin *in-*, without + RESOLVABLE]
- **irresolvability** *noun*

irrespective *adjective*
- "irry SPECTIV"
- not taking into account; regardless of.
- [Latin *in-*, without + French *respectif -ive* from medieval Latin *respectivus* from Latin *respectus* from *respicere* (*re-* again, *specere* look at)]
- **irrespectively** *adverb*

irresponsible *adjective*
- "irry SPONSA bull"
- acting or done without due sense of responsibility.
- [Latin *in-*, without + RESPONSIBLE]
- **irresponsibility** *noun*
- **irresponsibly** *adverb*

irretrievable *adjective*
- "irry TREEVA bull"
- that cannot be retrieved or restored.
- [Latin *in-*, without + RETRIEVE]
- **irretrievably** *adverb*

irreverent *adjective*
- "ir REVVER 'nt" or "ir REV r'nt"
- lacking reverence; disrespectful.
- [Latin *in-*, without + REVERE]
- **irreverence** *noun*
- **irreverently** *adverb*

irreversible *adjective*
- "irry VURSA bull"
- not reversible or alterable, irrevocable.
- [Latin *in-*, without + REVERSE]
- **irreversibility** *noun*
- **irreversibly** *adverb*

irrevocable *adjective*
- "ir REVVA kuh bull" or "irry VOKE a bull"
- unalterable.
- [Latin *irrevocabilis* (*in-* not, without, REVOKE)]
- **irrevocability** *noun*
- **irrevocably** *adverb*

irrigate *verb*
- "IRRA gate"
- supply (land or a crop) with water, esp. by means of specially constructed channels or pipes.
- [Latin *irrigare* (*in* in, *rigare* moisten)]
- **irrigable** *adjective* "IRRA guh bull"
- **irrigation** *noun*
- **irrigator** *noun*

irritate *verb*
• "IRRA tate"
• excite to anger; annoy.
• [Latin *irritare irritat-*]
• **irritability** *noun*
• **irritable** *adjective*
• **irritably** *adverb*
• **irritancy** *noun*
• **irritant** *adjective*
• **irritatedly** *adverb*
• **irritating** *adjective*
• **irritatingly** *adverb*
• **irritation** *noun*
• **irritative** *adjective*

irrupt *verb*
• "ih RUPT"
• enter forcibly or violently.
• [Latin *irrumpere irrupt-* (*in* in, *rumpere* break)]
• **irruption** *noun*
• **irruptive** *adjective*
HOMOPHONES: *erupt, eruption, eruptive*

ischemia *noun*
ALSO SPELLED: esp. *Brit.* **ischaemia**
• "iss KEEMY uh"
• a reduction of the blood supply to part of the body.
• [modern Latin from Greek *iskhaimos* from *iskhō* keep back + *haima* blood]
• **ischemic** *adjective* (also esp. *Brit.* **ischaemic**)

ischium *noun*
• "ISS kee um"
• the curved bone forming the base of each half of the pelvis.
• [Latin from Greek *iskhion* hip joint: compare SCIATIC]
• **ischial** *adjective*

isentropic *adjective*
• "ice en TROPPIC"
• having constant or equal entropy.
• [Greek *isos* equal + ENTROPY]

isinglass *noun*
• "EYE zing glass"
• a kind of gelatin obtained from fish, esp. sturgeon, and used in making jellies, glue, etc.
• [corruption of obsolete Dutch *huisenblas* sturgeon's bladder, assimilated to 'glass']

isle *noun*
• "ILE"
• an island, esp. a small one (esp. in place names).
• [Middle English *ile* (later *isle*) via Old French *ile, isle* from Latin *insula*]
HOMOPHONES: *aisle*

islet *noun*
• "EYE lit"
• a small island.
• [Old French, diminutive of *isle* ISLE]
HOMOPHONES: *eyelet*

Ismaili *noun*
• "iz MAY lee"
• a member of a Shiite Muslim branch that seceded from the main group in the 8th c. over the question of succession to the position of imam.
• [*Ismail* a son of the patriarch Ibrāhim (= Abraham)]

isobar *noun*
• "ICE oh bar"
• a line on a map connecting positions having the same atmospheric pressure at a given time or on average over a given period.
• [Greek *isobarēs* of equal weight (*isos* equal, *baros* weight)]
• **isobaric** *adjective* "ice a BARE ick"

isochronous *adjective*
• "eye SOCKRA nuss"
• occurring at the same time.
• [Greek *isos* equal + *khronos* time]
• **isochronously** *adverb*

isoclinal *adjective*
• "ice oh CLINE 'll"
• (of a fold) in which the two limbs are parallel.
• [Greek *isos* equal + CLINE]

isocyanate *noun*
• "ice oh SYE a nate"
• the radical ·N=C=O, or any of the class of compounds containing this radical, some of which are used in making polyurethane.
• [Greek *isos* equal + *cyanate* (as CYANIC)]

isoelectric *adjective*
• "ice oh e LECK trick"
• having or involving no net electric charge or difference in electrical potential.
• [Greek *isos* equal + ELECTRIC]

isoenzyme *noun*
• "ice oh EN zime"
• one of two or more enzymes with identical function but different structure.
• [Greek *isos* equal + ENZYME]

isoflavone *noun*
• "ice oh FLAY vone"
• a phytoestrogen found in leguminous plants such as chickpeas and soybeans.
• [Greek *isos* equal + FLAVONE]
• **isoflavonoid** *noun*

isogloss *noun*
• "ICE oh gloss"
• a line on a map marking an area having a distinct linguistic feature.
• [Greek *isos* equal + *glōssa* tongue]

isohyet *noun*
• "ice oh HY it"
• a line on a map connecting places having the same amount of precipitation in a given period.
• [Greek *isos* equal + *huetos* rain]

isokinetic *adjective*
• "ice oh kin ETTIC"
• characterized by or producing a constant speed.
• [Greek *isos* equal + KINETIC]

isoleucine *noun*
• "ice oh LOO seen"
• an amino acid that is a constituent of proteins and an essential nutrient.
• [German *Isoleucin* (Greek *isos* equal, LEUCINE)]

isomer *noun*
• "ICE a mur"
• one of two or more compounds with the same molecular formula but a different arrangement of atoms and different properties.
• [German from Greek *isomerēs* sharing equally (*isos* equal, *meros* share)]
• **isomeric** *adjective* "ice a MARE ick"
• **isomerism** *noun*
• **isomerization** *noun* (also esp. *Brit.* **-isation**)
• **isomerize** *verb* (also esp. *Brit.* **-ise**)

isometric *adjective*
• "ice oh METRIC"
• of equal measure.
• [Greek *isometria* equality of measure (*isos* equal, *metron* measure)]
• **isometrically** *adverb*
• **isometry** *noun* "ice OMMA tree"

isometrics *noun*
• "ice oh METRIX"
• a system of physical exercises in which muscles are caused to act against each other or against a fixed object.
• [as ISOMETRIC]

isomorphic *adjective*
• "ice oh MORFIC"
• exactly corresponding in form and relations.
• [Greek *isos* equal + *morphē* form]
• **isomorph** *noun*
• **isomorphism** *noun*
• **isomorphous** *adjective*

isoniazid *noun*
• "ice oh NIE a zid"
• a soluble colourless crystalline compound used as a bacteriostatic drug, esp. in the treatment of tuberculosis.
• [Greek *isos* equal + NICOTINE + *hydrazide* (as HYDRAZINE)]

isopleth *noun*
• "ICE oh pleth"
• a line on a map connecting places having equal incidence of a geographical or meteorological feature.
• [Greek *isos* equal + *plēthos* fullness]

isopod *noun*
• "ICE oh pod"
• any crustacean of the order Isopoda, including sowbugs, often parasitic and having a flattened body with seven pairs of legs.
• [French *isopode* from modern Latin *Isopoda* (as Greek *isos* equal, *pous podos* foot)]

isopropyl *adjective*
• "ice oh PRO p'll"
• designating a colourless secondary alcohol used in antifreeze and as a solvent.
• [Greek *isos* equal + PROPYL]

isosceles *adjective*
• "eye SOSSA leez"
• (of a triangle) having two sides equal.
• [Late Latin from Greek *isoskelēs* (*isos* equal, *skelos* leg)]

isostasy *noun*
• "eye SOSTA see"
• the general state of equilibrium thought to exist within the earth's crust.
• [Greek *isos* equal + *stasis* station]
• **isostatic** *adjective*
• **isostatically** *adverb*

isotherm *noun*
• "ICE oh thurm"
• a line on a map connecting places having the same temperature at a given time or on average over a given period.
• [French *isotherme* (as Greek *isos* equal, *thermē* heat)]
• **isothermal** *adjective*
• **isothermally** *adverb*

isotonic *adjective*
• "ice oh TONNIC"
• designating or relating to a solution having the same osmotic pressure as some particular solution (esp. that in a cell, or a body fluid).
• [Greek *isotonos* (*isos* equal, 'tone')]
• **isotonically** *adverb*

isotope *noun*
• "ICE a tope"
• each of two or more forms of an element differing from each other in relative atomic mass, and in nuclear but not chemical properties.
• [Greek *isos* equal + *topos* place (i.e. in the periodic table of elements)]
• **isotopic** *adjective* "ice a TOPPIC"
• **isotopically** *adverb*

isotretinoin *noun*
• "ice oh truh TINNO in"
• an isomer of retinoic acid, given orally in the treatment of severe acne and other skin disorders.
• [Greek *isos* equal + TRETINOIN]

isotropic *adjective*
• "ice oh TROPPIC"
• having the same physical properties in all directions.
• [Greek *isos* equal + *tropos* turn]
• **isotropically** *adverb*
• **isotropy** *noun* "ice OTTRA pee"

Israeli *adjective*
• "iz RAY lee"
• of or relating to the modern state of Israel.

Israelite *noun*
• "IZ ree a lite" or "IZ ruh lite"
• a member of the ancient Hebrew nation or people, esp. an inhabitant of the northern kingdom of the Hebrews (*c.*930–721 BC).
• [Hebrew *yisrā'ēl* he that strives with God]

Issei *noun*
- "EE say"
- a member of the first generation of Japanese immigrants to N America, who immigrated in the late 19th and early 20th c.
- [Japanese, = generation]

issuant *adjective*
- "ISH oo 'nt"
- (esp. of a beast with only the upper part shown) rising from the bottom or top of a heraldic bearing.
- [as ISSUE]

issue *noun*
- "ISH oo"
- a giving out or circulation of shares, notes, stamps, etc.
- [Old French ultimately from Latin *exitus* past participle of *exire* go out (*ex* out of, *ire* go)]
- **issuable** *adjective*
- **issuance** *noun*
- **issueless** *adjective*
- **issuer** *noun*

isthmus *noun*
- "ISS muss" or "ISTH muss"
- a narrow piece of land connecting two larger bodies of land.
- [Latin from Greek *isthmos*]
- **isthmian** *adjective*

italic *adjective*
- "eye TALIC" or "ih TALIC"
- of the sloping kind of letters now used esp. for emphasis or distinction and in foreign words.
- [Latin *italicus* from Greek *italikos* Italian (because introduced by Aldo Manuzio of Venice)]
- **italicization** *noun* (also esp. *Brit.* **-isation**)
- **italicize** *verb* (also esp. *Brit.* **-ise**)

Italiot *noun*
- "ih TALLY it"
- an inhabitant of the Greek colonies in ancient Italy.
- [Greek *Italiōtēs* from *Italia* Italy]

iterate *verb*
- "ITTER ate"
- perform or utter repeatedly.
- [Latin *iterare iterat-* from *iterum* again]
- **iteration** *noun*

iterative *adjective*
- "ITTER a tiv" or "ITTER ay tiv"
- expressing frequent repetition or intensity of action.
- [as ITERATE]
- **iteratively** *adverb*

itinerant *adjective*
- "eye TINNER 'nt"
- travelling from place to place.
- [Late Latin *itinerari* travel, from Latin *iter itiner-* journey]
- **itinerancy** *noun*

itinerary *noun*
- "eye TINNER airy"
- a detailed route.
- [Late Latin *itinerarius* (as ITINERANT)]

ivermectin *noun*
- "eye vur MECK tin"
- a medication used for treating heartworm in dogs.
- [*i* + *avermectin*, an anthelmintic isolated from the bacterium *Streptomyces avermitilis*]

ivied *adjective*
- "EYE veed"
- overgrown with ivy.
- [Old English *īfig*]

Ivorian *noun*
- "eye VORY 'n"
- a person from Ivory Coast in W Africa.

ivory *noun*
- "EYE vur ee"
- a hard creamy-white substance composing the main part of the tusks of an elephant, hippopotamus, walrus, or narwhal.
- [Old French *yvoire* ultimately from Latin *ebur eboris*]

ixia *noun*
- "IXY uh"
- any iridaceous plant of the genus *Ixia* of S Africa, with large showy flowers.
- [Latin from Greek, a kind of thistle]

Iyengar *noun*
- "eye YEN gar"
- a type of hatha yoga focusing on the correct alignment of the body, making use of straps, wooden blocks, and other objects as aids to achieving the correct postures.
- [B. K. S. *Iyengar* Indian yoga teacher b.1918, who devised it]

Jj

jabiru *noun*
- "JABBY roo"
- a large stork, *Jabiru mycteria*, of Central and S America.
- [Tupi-Guarani *jabirú*]

jaborandi *noun*
- "jabba RANDY"
- any shrub of the genus *Pilocarpus*, of S America.
- [Tupi-Guarani *jaburandi*]

jabot *noun*
- "ZHABBO"
- an ornamental frill or ruffle of lace etc. on the front of a shirt or blouse.
- [French, originally = crop of a bird]

jacamar *noun*
- "JACKA mar"
- a small insect-eating bird with partly iridescent plumage, of the tropical S American family Galbulidae.
- [French, apparently from Tupi]

jacana *noun*
- "JACKA nuh" or "JASSA nuh"
- any of various small tropical wading birds of the family Jacanidae, with elongated toes and hind claws which enable them to walk on floating leaves etc.
- [Portuguese *jaçanã* from Tupi-Guarani *jasaná*]

jacaranda *noun*
- "jacka RANDA"
- any tropical American tree of the genus *Jacaranda*, with trumpet-shaped blue flowers.
- [Tupi-Guarani *jacarandá*]

jackal *noun*
- "JACK'll"
- any of various wild doglike mammals of the genus *Canis*, esp. *C. aureus*, found in Africa and S Asia, usu. hunting or scavenging for food in packs.
- [Turkish *çakal* from Persian *šagāl*]

jackanapes *noun*
- "JACKA napes"
- an impertinent person.
- [earliest as *Jack Napes* (1450): supposed to refer to the Duke of Suffolk, whose badge was an ape's clog and chain]

Jacobean *adjective*
- "jacka BEE 'n"
- of or relating to the reign of James I of England (d.1625).
- [modern Latin *Jacobaeus* from Church Latin *Jacobus* James, from Greek *Iakōbos* Jacob]

Jacobin *noun*
- "JACKA bin"
- a member of the most radical and ruthless of the political groups formed in the wake of the French Revolution; they instituted the Reign of Terror of 1793–4.
- [Old French from medieval Latin *Jacobinus* from Church Latin *Jacobus* James. The term was applied to the Dominican friars in Old French in reference to their church in Paris, St-Jacques, near which they built their first convent; the building eventually became the headquarters of the French revolutionary group]
- **Jacobinic** *adjective*
- **Jacobinical** *adjective*
- **Jacobinism** *noun*

Jacobite *noun*
- "JACKA bite"
- a supporter of the deposed James II and his descendants in their claim to the British throne after the Revolution of 1688.
- [as JACOBEAN]
- **Jacobitism** *noun*

jaconet *noun*
- "JACKA net"
- a lightweight cotton cloth with a smooth and slightly stiff finish.
- [Urdu *jagannāthi* from *Jagannath* (now Puri) in India, its place of origin: see JUGGERNAUT]

jacquard *noun*
- "JACK ard"
- an apparatus with perforated cards, fitted to a loom to facilitate the weaving of figured fabrics.
- [J. M. *Jacquard*, French inventor d.1834]

jactitation *noun*
- "jack tuh TAY sh'n"
- the restless tossing of the body in illness.
- [earlier *jactation*, from Latin *jactare* throw]

jadeite *noun*
- "JADE ite"
- a green, blue, or white sodium aluminum silicate form of jade.
- [French *le jade* for *l'ejade*, from Spanish *piedra de ijada* 'stone of the flank', i.e. stone for colic (which it was believed to cure) + Greek *lithos* stone]

jaeger *noun*
- "YAY gur"
- a seabird of the skua family, esp. one of the smaller kinds, of the genus *Stercorarius*.
- [German *Jäger* hunter, from *jagen* to hunt]

Jaffa *noun*
- "JAFFA"
- a large oval thick-skinned variety of orange.
- [*Jaffa*, Israel, near where it was first grown]

jagdwurst *noun*
- "YOG'd wurst"
- a cured German sausage with chunks of ham in a pâté base, often with whole mustard seeds, pistachios, and pimentos.
- [German, = 'hunter's sausage']

jaguar *noun*
- "JAG warr" ("WARR" rhymes with *FAR*) or "JAG yoo ar"
- a large carnivorous feline, *Panthera onca*, of Central and S America, mainly yellowish-brown with dark spots grouped in rosettes.
- [Tupi-Guarani *jaguara*]

jaguarundi *noun*
- "jag wuh RUNDY"
- a wild cat, *Felis yagouaroundi*, larger than the domestic cat, with a long body and tail and inhabiting forest and scrub from Arizona to Argentina.
- [Tupi-Guarani]

Jain *noun*
- "JINE"
- an adherent of a non-Brahmanical Indian religion characterized by its stress on non-violence and strict asceticism as means to liberation.
- [Hindi from Sanskrit *jainas* saint, victor, from *jīna* victorious]
- **Jainism** *noun*
- **Jainist** *noun*

jalapeno *noun*
- "hala PEE no" or "hala PEE nyo" or "hala PAY nyo"
- a very hot green chili pepper, used esp. in Mexican-style cooking.
- [Latin American Spanish *(chile) jalapeño*]

jalopy *noun*
- "juh LOPPY"
- a dilapidated old car, truck, etc.
- [20th c.: origin unknown]

jalousie *noun*
- "ZHALLA zee"
- a blind or shutter made of a row of angled slats to keep out rain etc. and control the influx of light.
- [French (as JEALOUS)]

Jamaican *noun*
- "juh MAKE 'n"
- a native or inhabitant of Jamaica.

jamb *noun*
- "JAM"
- a side post or surface of a doorway, window, or fireplace.
- [Old French *jambe* ultimately from Late Latin *gamba* hoof]

HOMOPHONES: *jam*

jambalaya *noun*
- "jam buh LIE uh"
- a Cajun dish of rice with shrimps, chicken, etc.
- [Louisiana French from modern Provençal *jambalaia*]

jamboree *noun*
- "jam buh REE"
- a celebration or merrymaking.
- [19th c.: origin unknown]

janissary *noun*
- "JANNA serry"
- a member of the Turkish infantry forming the Sultan's guard and the main fighting force of the Turkish army from the late 14th to early 19th c.
- [ultimately from Turkish *yeniçeri* from *yeni* new + *çeri* troops]

janitor *noun*
- "JANNA tur"
- a caretaker of a school, office building, etc., responsible for its cleaning, heating, etc.
- [Latin from *janua* door]
- **janitorial** *adjective*

Jansenism *noun*
- "JAN s'n izm"
- a Christian movement of the 17th and 18th c., characterized by asceticism and moral rigour.
- [C. O. *Jansen*, Flemish bishop and theologian d.1638]
- **Jansenist** *noun*

January *noun*
- "JAN yoo airy"
- the first month of the year.
- [Latin *Januarius* (*mensis*) (month) of Janus, the guardian god of gates and beginnings]

japonica *noun*
- "juh PONNA kuh"
- any flowering shrub of the genus *Chaenomeles*, esp. *C. speciosa*, with round white, green, or yellow edible fruits and bright red flowers.
- [modern Latin, feminine of *japonicus* Japanese]

jardinière *noun*
• "zhardy NYARE"
• an ornamental pot or stand for the display of growing plants.
• [French, lit. = 'female gardener']

jarl *noun*
• "YARL"
• a Norse or Danish chief.
• [Old Norse, originally = man of noble birth, related to 'earl']

jarrah *noun*
• "JA ruh"
• the Australian mahogany gum tree, *Eucalyptus marginata*.
• [Aboriginal *djarryl*]

jasmine *noun*
ALSO SPELLED: **jasmin**
• "JAZZ min"
• any of various ornamental shrubs of the genus *Jasminum* usu. with white or yellow flowers.
• [French *jasmin, jessemin* from Arabic *yās(a)mīn* from Persian *yāsamīn*]

jaundice *noun*
• "JON diss"
• a condition with yellowing of the skin or whites of the eyes, often caused by obstruction of the bile duct or by liver disease.
• [Old French *jaunice* yellowness, from *jaune* yellow]

jaunt *noun*
• "JONT"
• a short excursion for enjoyment.
• [16th c.: origin unknown]

jaunty *adjective*
• "JONTY"
• cheerful and self-confident; carefree.
• [earlier *jentee* from French *gentil* see GENTEEL]
• **jauntily** *adverb*
• **jauntiness** *noun*

javelin *noun*
• "JAVVA lin" or "JAV lin"
• a light spear thrown in a competitive sport or as a weapon.
• [French *javeline, javelot* from Gallo-Roman *gabalottus*]

javelina *noun*
• "havva LEENA"
• any of several dark-furred gregarious pig-like mammals of the family Tayassuidae, which inhabit forest and forest scrub in Central and S America; a peccary.
• [Spanish *jabalina*, from the feminine form of *jabalí* wild boar, from Arabic *jabali* mountaineer]

jealous *adjective*
• "JELLUS"
• envious or resentful (of a person or a person's advantages etc.).
• [Old French *gelos* from medieval Latin *zelosus* ZEALOUS]
• **jealously** *adverb*
• **jealousy** *noun*

jeepney *noun*
• "JEEP nee"
• (in the Philippines) a jitney bus converted from a Jeep.
• [blend of 'Jeep' + JITNEY]

Jeffersonian *adjective*
• "jeffer SO nee 'n"
• of or pertaining to US statesman Thomas Jefferson (d.1826) or his political principles, esp. minimal intervention by the state, individual rights, and democracy.
• **Jeffersonianism** *noun*

Jehovist *noun*
• "juh HOVE ist"
• the postulated author or authors of parts of the Hexateuch in which God is regularly named Jehovah.
• [medieval Latin *Iehoua(h)* from Hebrew *YHVH* (with the vowels of *adonai* 'my lord' included)]

jejune *adjective*
• "juh JUNE"
• intellectually unsatisfying; shallow.
• [originally = fasting, from Latin *jejunus*]
• **jejunely** *adverb*

jejunum *noun*
• "juh JUNE um"
• the part of the small intestine between the duodenum and ileum.
• [Latin, neuter of *jejunus* fasting]
• **jejunal** *adjective*

jeopardy *noun*
• "JEPPER dee"
• danger, esp. of severe harm or loss.
• [Middle English *iuparti* from Old French *ieu parti* divided (i.e. even) game, from Latin *jocus* game + *partitus* past participle of *partire* divide from *pars partis* part]
• **jeopardize** *verb* (also esp. *Brit.* **-ise**) "JEPPER dize"

jerboa *noun*
• "jur BOA"
• any small desert rodent of the family Dipodidae with long hind legs and the ability to make large jumps.
• [modern Latin from Arabic *yarbū'* flesh of loins, jerboa]

jeremiad *noun*
• "jerra MY ud" or "jerra MY ad"
• a doleful complaint or lamentation; a list of woes.
• [French *jérémiade* from *Jérémie* Jeremiah, with reference to the Lamentations of Jeremiah in the Old Testament]

jeroboam *noun*
• "jerra BO um"

• a wine bottle of 4 times the ordinary size.
• [*Jeroboam* King of Israel]

jersey ***noun***
• "JURZY"
• a soft, fine, usu. stretchy knitted fabric.
• [the island of *Jersey* in the English Channel]

Jerseyan ***noun***
• "JURZY'n"
• a native or inhabitant of New Jersey.

Jerusalemite ***noun***
• "jur OOSA l'm ite" or "jur OOZA l'm ite"
• a resident of Jerusalem.

Jesuit ***noun***
• "JEZH yoo it" or "JEZZ oo it" or "JEZH oo it"
• a member of the Society of Jesus, a Roman Catholic order founded by St. Ignatius Loyola and others in 1534.
• [French *jésuite* or modern Latin *Jesuita* from *Jesus*]
• **Jesuitical** ***adjective***
• **Jesuitically** ***adverb***

jeté ***noun***
• "zhet AY"
• a ballet jump or leap with one leg thrown forwards or outwards.
• [French, past participle of *jeter* throw, ultimately from Latin *jactare* frequentative of *jacere jact-* throw]

jetsam ***noun***
• "JET sum"
• discarded material washed ashore, esp. that thrown overboard to lighten a ship etc.
• [contraction of JETTISON]

jettison ***verb***
• "JETTA s'n" or "JETTA z'n"
• throw (esp. heavy material) overboard to lighten an aircraft, ship, hot-air balloon, etc.
• [Anglo-French *getteson*, Old French *getaison* from Latin *jactatio -onis* from *jactare* throw]

Jezebel ***noun***
• "JEZZA bell"
• a shameless or immoral woman.
• [*Jezebel*, denounced by Elijah for introducing the worship of Baal into ancient Israel]

jibba ***noun***
ALSO SPELLED: **jibbah, djibba, djibbah**
• "JIBBA"
• a long coat worn by Muslim men.
• [Egyptian var. of Arabic *jubba*]

jibe ***verb***
• "JIBE"
• agree; be in accord.
• [19th c.: origin unknown]
HOMOPHONES: *gybe*

jicama ***noun***
• "HEEKA muh"
• the crisp white-fleshed edible tuber of the yam bean, used esp. in Mexican cuisine.
• [Mexican Spanish *jícama* from Nahuatl *xicama*]

jihad ***noun***
• "jih HAD"
• a holy war undertaken by Muslims for the propagation or defence of Islam.
• [Arabic *jihād*]
• **jihadi** ***noun***

jinni ***noun***
ALSO SPELLED: **jinnee**
• "jin EE" or "JIN ee"
• (in Muslim mythology) an intelligent being lower than the angels, able to appear in human and animal forms, and having power over people.
• [Arabic *jinnī*, pl. *jinn*: compare GENIE]

jitney ***noun***
• "JIT nee"
• a bus or other vehicle carrying passengers for a low fare, originally five cents.
• [origin unknown]

jocose ***adjective***
• "juh KOSE" ("KOSE" rhymes with *GROSS*)
• playful or humorous.
• [Latin *jocosus* from *jocus* jest]
• **jocosely** ***adverb***
• **jocosity** ***noun*** "juh COSSA tee"

jocular ***adjective***
• "JOCK yuh lur"
• (of speech, action, etc.) of the nature of a joke; said, done, etc. jokingly.
• [Latin *jocularis* from *joculus* diminutive of *jocus* jest]
• **jocularity** ***noun*** "jock yoo LERRA tee"
• **jocularly** ***adverb***

jocund ***adjective***
• "JOCK 'nd"
• merry, cheerful.
• [Old French from Latin *jocundus*, *jucundus* from *juvare* delight]
• **jocundity** ***noun***

jodhpurs ***plural noun***
• "JOD purz"
• long breeches for riding etc., wide around the hips and thighs but close-fitting from the knee to the ankle.
• [*Jodhpur* in W India]

Johnsonian ***adjective***
• "jon SO nee 'n"
• of or relating to English lexicographer and writer Samuel Johnson (d.1784).

jojoba ***noun***
• "ho HO buh"
• a plant, *Simmondsia chinensis*, with seeds yielding an oily extract used in cosmetics etc.
• [Latin American Spanish]

Jonagold ***noun***
• "JOE nuh gold"
• an apple that is a cross of Jonathan and

Golden Delicious apples, with a yellowish-green skin with red stripes.

Jonah *noun*
- "JOE nuh"
- a person who seems to bring bad luck.
- [*Jonah* in the Bible, who was thrown overboard as a bringer of bad luck]

Jonamac *noun*
- "JOE nuh mack"
- an apple that is a cross of Jonathan and McIntosh.

Jonathan *noun*
- "JONNA th'n" (with "TH" as in *THIN*)
- a red-skinned cooking apple with a yellowish flesh.
- [*Jonathan* Hasbrouk, US lawyer d.1846]

jongleur *noun*
- "zhon GLUR"
- an itinerant minstrel in the Middle Ages.
- [French, var. of *jougleur* from Old French *jogler*, *jugler* from Latin *joculari* jest, from *joculus* diminutive of *jocus* jest]

jonquil *noun*
- "JON kwill"
- a bulbous plant, *Narcissus jonquilla*, with clusters of small fragrant yellow flowers.
- [modern Latin *jonquilla* or French *jonquille* from Spanish *junquillo* diminutive of *junco*: see JUNCO]

Jordanian *noun*
- "jor DAINY 'n"
- a native or inhabitant of Jordan in the Middle East.

jorum *noun*
- "JOR um"
- a large drinking bowl.
- [perhaps from the Biblical character *Joram* who 'brought with him vessels of silver, and vessels of gold' to King David]

jostle *verb*
- "JOSSLE"
- knock or come into rough collision with.
- [Middle English: earlier *justle* from 'joust' from Old French *juster* bring together, ultimately from Latin *juxta* near]
- **jostler** *noun*

joual *noun*
- "zhoo AWL"
- a variety of Canadian French considered to be uneducated, characterized by non-standard grammar and syntax and, esp. in cities, numerous English borrowings.
- [dialect Canadian French from French *cheval*, lit. 'horse']

jouissance *noun*
- "zhwee SONCE"
- pleasure or delight, esp. from the possession and use of something advantageous or pleasing.
- [French *jouir*, lit. 'enjoy' from Latin *gaudēre* be joyful]

joule *noun*
- "JOOL"
- the SI unit of work or energy equal to the work done by a force of one newton when its point of application moves one metre in the direction of action of the force, equivalent to a watt-second.
- [J. P. *Joule*, English physicist d.1889]

HOMOPHONES: *jewel*

journal *noun*
- "JUR n'll"
- a daily record of events; a diary.
- [Old French *jurnal* from Late Latin *diurnalis* DIURNAL]

journalese *noun*
- "jur n'll EEZ"
- a hackneyed style of language characteristic of some newspaper writing.
- [as JOURNAL]

journalism *noun*
- "JUR n'll izm"
- the work of collecting, writing, and reporting news items in the press or on television and radio.
- [as JOURNAL]
- **journalist** *noun*
- **journalistic** *adjective*
- **journalistically** *adverb*

journey *noun*
- "JUR nee"
- an act of going from one place to another, esp. at a long distance.
- [Old French *jornee* day, day's work or travel, ultimately from Latin *diurnus* daily]
- **journeyer** *noun*

journeyman *noun*
- "JUR nee m'n"
- a person who, having served an apprenticeship, is qualified to work in a craft or trade under the direction of another more qualified person.
- [JOURNEY in obsolete sense 'day's work' + 'man']

jovial *adjective*
- "JOE vee 'll"
- merry, convivial, hearty and good-humoured.
- [French from Late Latin *jovialis* of Jupiter, with reference to the supposed influence of the planet Jupiter on those born under it]
- **joviality** *noun* "joe vee ALA tee"
- **jovially** *adverb*

Jovian *adjective*
- "JOE vee 'n"
- (in Roman mythology) of or like the chief god, Jupiter.
- [Latin *Jovis* used as genitive of *Jupiter*]

jowar *noun*
• "jow AR" ("JOW" rhymes with *COW*)
• a variety of sorghum, *Sorghum bicolor*, grown esp. in N Africa and the Indian subcontinent.
• [Hindi *jawār*]

Joycean *adjective*
• "JOY see 'n"
• of or characteristic of the Irish writer James Joyce (d.1941) or his work.

jubilant *adjective*
• "JOOB'll 'nt"
• exultant, rejoicing, joyful.
• [Latin *jubilare jubilant-* shout for joy]
• **jubilance** *noun*
• **jubilantly** *adverb*

jubilate *verb*
• "JOOB'll ate"
• exult; be joyful.
• [Latin *jubilare* (as JUBILANT)]
• **jubilation** *noun*

jubilee *noun*
• "joob'll EE" or "JOOB'll ee"
• an anniversary, esp. the 25th, 50th, or 60th.
• [Old French *jubilé* from Late Latin *jubilaeus* (*annus*) (year) of jubilee, ultimately from Hebrew *yōḇēl*, originally = ram, ram's-horn trumpet]

Judaic *adjective*
• "joo DAY ick"
• of or characteristic of the Jews or Judaism.
• [Latin *Judaicus* from Greek *Ioudaïkos* from *Ioudaios* Jew]

Judaica *plural noun*
• "joo DAY ick uh"
• the literature, customs, ritual objects, artifacts, etc. which are of particular relevance to Jews or Judaism.
• [as JUDAIC]

Judaism *noun*
• "JOO day izm"
• the religion of the Jews, with a belief in one God and a basis in Mosaic and rabbinical teachings.
• [Late Latin *Judaismus* from Greek *Ioudaïsmos* (as JUDAIC)]

Judaize *verb*
ALSO SPELLED: esp. *Brit.* **-ise**
• "JOO day ize"
• follow Jewish customs or rites.
• [Late Latin *judaizare* from Greek *ioudaïzō* (as JUDAIC)]
• **Judaization** *noun* (also esp. *Brit.* **-isation**)
• **Judaized** *adjective* (also esp. *Brit.* **-ised**)
• **Judaizer** *noun* (also esp. *Brit.* **-iser**)

Judas *noun*
• "JOO duss"
• a person who betrays a friend.
• [*Judas* Iscariot, the apostle who betrayed Jesus for 30 pieces of silver]

Judean *adjective*
• "joo DEE 'n"
• of or relating to Judea in ancient Palestine.

judicare *noun*
• "JOODA care"
• *Cdn* a form of legal aid in which lawyers bill the province for services to poor clients rather than receiving a salary.
• [blend of JUDICIAL + 'care', after MEDICARE]

judicature *noun*
• "JOODA kuh chur"
• the administration of justice.
• [medieval Latin *judicatura* from Latin *judicare* to judge]

judicial *adjective*
• "joo DISH'll"
• of, done by, or proper to a court of law.
• [Latin *judicialis* from *judicium* judgment, from *judex* judge]
• **judicially** *adverb*

judiciary *noun*
• "joo DISHA ree" or "joo DISHY airy"
• the judges of a nation collectively.
• [Latin *judiciarius* (as JUDICIAL)]

judicious *adjective*
• "joo DISH us"
• sensible, prudent, proceeding from or showing sound judgment esp. in practical matters.
• [French *judicieux* from Latin *judicium* (as JUDICIAL)]
• **judiciously** *adverb*
• **judiciousness** *noun*

judo *noun*
• "JOO doe"
• a refined form of jiu-jitsu using principles of movement and balance, practised as a sport or form of physical exercise.
• [Japanese from *jū* gentle + *dō* way]
• **judoist** *noun*

judoka *noun*
• "JOO doe kuh"
• a person who practises or is an expert in judo.
• [Japanese, from JUDO + *-ka* person, profession]

juggernaut *noun*
• "JUGGER not"
• a huge or overwhelming force or object.
• [Hindi *Jagannath* from Sanskrit *Jagannātha* = lord of the world: name of an idol of Krishna in Hindu belief, carried in procession on a huge cart under which devotees are said to have formerly thrown themselves]

jugular *adjective*
• "JUG yuh lur"
• of the neck or throat.
• [Late Latin *jugularis* from Latin *jugulum* collarbone, throat, diminutive of *jugum* yoke]

juju *noun*
- "JOO joo"
- a charm or fetish of some W African peoples.
- [perhaps from French *joujou* toy]

jujube *noun*
- "JOO joob"
- any plant of the genus *Zizyphus* bearing edible acidic berry-like fruits.
- [French *jujube* or medieval Latin *jujuba*, ultimately from Greek *zizuphon*]

juku *noun*
- "JOO coo"
- (in Japan) a place of study, complementing one's normal schooling, where students cram, are tutored, etc. in preparation for university entrance examinations.
- [Japanese]

julep *noun*
- "JOO lep"
- a sweet iced alcoholic drink of bourbon flavoured with mint.
- [Old French from Arabic *julāb* from Persian *gulāb* from *gul* rose + *āb* water]

Julian *adjective*
- "JOO lee 'n"
- of or associated with Julius Caesar, Roman general and ruler d.44 BC.
- [Latin *Julianus* from *Julius*]

julienne *noun*
- "joo lee EN"
- food, esp. vegetables, cut into short thin strips.
- [French from the name *Jules* or *Julien*]
- **julienned** *adjective*

jumar *noun*
- "JOOMER"
- a clamp that is attached to a fixed rope and automatically tightens when weight is applied and relaxes when it is removed.
- [orig. in Swiss use; of unknown origin]

jumbie *noun*
- "JUMBY"
- a ghost; an evil spirit.
- [Kikongo *zumbi* fetish: compare ZOMBIE]

junco *noun*
- "JUNKO"
- any of several small birds of Central and N America of the genus *Junco*.
- [Spanish from Latin *juncus* rush plant]

junction *noun*
- "JUNK sh'n"
- a point at which two or more things are joined.
- [Latin *junctio* from *jungere junct-* join]
- **junctional** *adjective*

juncture *noun*
- "JUNK chur"
- a critical convergence of events; a critical point of time.
- [Latin *junctura* from *jungere junct-* join]

Jungian *adjective*
- "YOONG ee 'n" (with "OO" as in *BOOK*)
- of Swiss psychologist Carl Jung (d.1961) or his system of analytical psychology.

juniper *noun*
- "JOONA pur"
- any evergreen shrub or tree of the genus *Juniperus*, esp. *J. communis*, with prickly leaves and dark blue berry-like cones.
- [Latin *juniperus*]

Junker *noun*
- "YOON kur" (with "OO" as in *BOOK*)
- a member of an exclusive (Prussian) aristocratic party concerned with maintaining the exclusive privileges of their class.
- [German, earlier *Junkher* from Old High German *jung* young, *Herr* lord]
- **junkerdom** *noun*

Juno *noun*
- "JOO no"
- *Cdn* any of several awards presented by the Canadian Academy of Recording Arts and Sciences for excellence in Canadian music recording.
- [after the Roman goddess *Juno* and P. *Juneau* b.1922, chairman of the CRTC who introduced Canadian content rules for broadcasting]

Junoesque *adjective*
- "joo no ESK"
- (of a woman) imposingly tall and shapely.
- [the Roman goddess *Juno*]

junta *noun*
- "HOONTA" (with "OO" as in *BOOK*) or "HUNTA" or "JUNTA"
- a political or military clique or faction taking power after a revolution or coup.
- [Spanish & Portuguese from Latin *juncta*, feminine past participle (as JUNCTURE)]

Jurassic *adjective*
- "jur ASSIC"
- of or relating to the second period of the Mesozoic era, between 213 and 144 million years ago, between the Triassic and Cretaceous periods, with evidence of many large dinosaurs, the first birds (including Archaeopteryx), and mammals.
- [French *jurassique* from the *Jura* Mountains on the border of France and Switzerland + *-assic* from TRIASSIC]

jurat *noun*
- "JUR at"
- a statement of the circumstances in which an affidavit was made.
- [Latin *juratum* neuter past participle of *jurare* swear]

juridical *noun*
- "jur IDDA k'll"
- of judicial proceedings.
- [Latin *juridicus* from *jus juris* law + *-dicus* saying, from *dicere* say]
- **juridically** *adverb*

juried *adjective*
- "JUR eed"
- judged or selected by a jury or panel.
- [as JURY]

jurisconsult *noun*
- "jur iss k'n SULT"
- a person learned in law; a jurist.
- [Latin *jurisconsultus* from *jus juris* law + *consultus* skilled: see CONSULTANT]

jurisdiction *noun*
- "jur iss DICK sh'n"
- the administration of justice.
- [Latin *jurisdictio* from *jus juris* law + *dictio* DICTION]
- **jurisdictional** *adjective*

jurisprudence *noun*
- "jur iss PROO dince"
- the science or philosophy of law.
- [Late Latin *jurisprudentia* from Latin *jus juris* law + *prudentia* knowledge]
- **jurisprudential** *adjective* "jur iss proo DEN sh'll"

jurist *noun*
- "JUR ist"
- a person who is knowledgeable in legal matters, e.g. a judge, legal writer, etc.
- [French *juriste* or medieval Latin *jurista* from *jus juris* law]

juror *noun*
- "JUR ur"
- a member of a jury.
- [Old French *jureor* from Latin *jurator -oris* from *jurare jurat-* swear]

jury *noun*
- "JUREE"
- a body of usu. twelve persons sworn to render a verdict on the basis of evidence submitted to them in a court of justice.
- [Old French *juree* oath, inquiry, from *jurata* feminine past participle of Latin *jurare* swear]
- **juryman** *noun*
- **jurywoman** *noun*

HOMOPHONES: *Jewry*

jus *noun*
- "ZHOO"
- (esp. in French cuisine) an unthickened sauce.
- [French, = 'juice']

justiciable *adjective*
- "juss TISHA bull"
- liable to be tried in a court of justice; subject to jurisdiction.
- [Old French from *justicier* bring to trial, from medieval Latin *justitiare* from *justus* from *jus* right]

justify *verb*
- "JUSTA fie"
- show the justice or rightness of (a person, act, etc.).
- [French *justifier* from Late Latin *justificare* do justice to, from Latin *justus* just]
- **justifiability** *noun*
- **justifiable** *adjective*
- **justifiably** *adverb*
- **justification** *noun*
- **justificatory** *adjective* "juss TIFFA kuh tory"
- **justifier** *noun*

juvenal *noun*
- "JOOV'n 'll"
- a bird in its first full plumage, but not yet having adult plumage.
- [Latin *juvenalis*, = *juvenilis* (as JUVENILE)]

HOMOPHONES: *juvenile*

juvenile *adjective*
- "JOOV'n ile" or "JOOV'n 'll"
- young, youthful.
- [Latin *juvenilis* from *juvenis* young]
- **juvenility** *noun*

HOMOPHONES: *juvenal*

juvenilia *plural noun*
- "joova NILLY uh" or "joova NIE lee uh"
- works produced by an author or artist in youth.
- [as JUVENILE]

juxtapose *verb*
- "JUXTA poze" or "juxta POZE"
- place (things) side by side.
- [French *juxtaposer* from Latin *juxta* next, *ponere* place]
- **juxtaposition** *noun*
- **juxtapositional** *adjective*

ka *noun*
- "KAW"
- (in ancient Egypt) the spiritual part of an individual human being or god, which survived (with the soul) after death and could reside in a statue of the dead person.
- [Ancient Egyptian]

HOMOPHONES: *caw*

kabaddi *noun*
- "kuh BODDY"
- a game popular in northern India and Pakistan played between two teams of nine who rush and tackle one another.
- [Tamil]

Kabinett *noun*
- "kabba NET"
- a wine of exceptional quality, esp. one made in Germany from grapes that can ferment without added sugar.
- [German *Kabinettwein*, lit. 'cabinet or chamber wine', from its originally being kept in a special cellar]

kabloona *noun*
- "kuh BLOONA"
- a person who is not Inuit, esp. a white person.
- [Inuktitut *kabluna* bushy eyebrow]

kabocha *noun*
- "kuh BOTCHA"
- any of various Japanese pumpkins or squashes with a rough dark-green skin and a flattened turban shape.
- [Japanese]

kabuki *noun*
- "kuh BOO kee"
- a form of popular traditional Japanese drama with highly stylized song, acted by males only.
- [Japanese from *ka* song + *bu* dance + *ki* art]

kachina *noun*
- "kuh CHEENA"
- a Pueblo Indian ancestral spirit.
- [Hopi *kacina* supernatural]

Kaddish *noun*
- "CAD ish"
- a Jewish mourner's prayer.
- [Aramaic *ḳaddiš* holy]

HOMOPHONES: *caddish*, *cattish*

kaffeeklatsch *noun*
- "CAFFAY clatch"
- an informal gathering for conversation at which coffee is served, esp. one involving only women.
- [German *Kaffeeklatsch*, lit. 'coffee gossip']

Kaffir *noun*
- "CAFFER"
- a member of the Xhosa-speaking peoples of South Africa.
- [originally = a non-Muslim: Arabic *kāfir* infidel, from *kafara* not believe]

HOMOPHONES: *Kafir*

kaffiyeh *noun*

ALSO SPELLED: **keffiyeh**
- "kuh FEE yay"
- a headdress worn by Arab men, consisting of a square of material fastened by a cord around the crown of the head.
- [Arabic *keffiya*, *kūfiyya*, perhaps from Late Latin *cofea* headdress]

Kafir *noun*
- "CAFFER"
- a native of the Hindu Kush mountains of NE Afghanistan.
- [formed as KAFFIR]

HOMOPHONES: *Kaffir*

Kafkaesque *adjective*
- "kafka ESK"
- (of a situation, atmosphere, etc.) impenetrably oppressive, nightmarish, in a manner characteristic of the fictional world of the Czech novelist Franz Kafka (d.1924).

kahuna *noun*
- "kuh HOONA"
- an important person; a big shot.
- [Hawaiian *kahuna* priest, wise man]

Kaigani *noun*
- "kye GANNY"
- a member of a division of the Haida, who left the Queen Charlotte Islands in the early 18th c. and settled on the southern shores of Prince of Wales Island (Alaska).
- [Haida]

Kainai *plural noun*
- "KYE nye" (both syllables rhyme with *PIE*)

• a member of an Algonquian Aboriginal people of S Alberta.
• [Kainai, = 'many chiefs']

kaiser *noun*
• "KYE zur"
• an emperor, esp. the German Emperor, the Emperor of Austria, or the head of the Holy Roman Empire.
• [German *Kaiser* from Latin *Caesar*, family name of Julius Caesar and subsequently applied to other Roman emperors]

kaizen *noun*
• "kye ZEN"
• a Japanese business philosophy of continuous improvement of working practices, personal efficiency, etc.
• [Japanese, = improvement]

kaka *noun*
• "CAW caw"
• a large New Zealand parrot, *Nestor meridionalis*, with olive-brown plumage.
• [Maori]
HOMOPHONES: *caca*

kakapo *noun*
• "COCKA poe"
• an owl-like flightless New Zealand parrot, *Strigops habroptilus*.
• [Maori, = night kaka]

kakivak *noun*
• "KACKY vack"
• a three-pronged fish spear used by the Inuit.
• [Inuktitut]

kalamata *noun*
ALSO SPELLED: **calamata**
• "cala MATTA"
• a medium-sized, firm, flavourful, Greek variety of purplish-black olive.
• [*Kalamáta*, Greece, where they are grown]

kalanchoe *noun*
• "kal'n CO ee"
• a succulent plant of the mainly African genus *Kalanchoe*, which includes several houseplants, some producing miniature plants from the edges of the leaves.
• [modern Latin from French, ultimately from Chinese *gāláncài*]

Kalashnikov *noun*
• "kuh LASHNA coff"
• a type of rifle or submachine gun made in Russia.
• [M. T. *Kalashnikov* (b.1919), its Russian developer]

kale *noun*
• "KALE"
• a variety of cabbage which forms no compact head.
• [Middle English, northern form of COLE]

kaleidoscope *noun*
• "kuh LIE duh scope"
• a tube containing mirrors and pieces of coloured glass or paper, whose reflections produce changing patterns when the tube is rotated.
• [Greek *kalos* beautiful + *eidos* form + *skopos* target, from *skeptomai* look at]
• **kaleidoscopic** *adjective*
• **kaleidoscopically** *adverb*

kalimba *noun*
• "kuh LIM buh"
• a type of African thumb piano.
• [Bantu]

kalmia *noun*
• "KAL mee uh"
• a N American evergreen shrub of the genus *Kalmia*, esp. sheep laurel, *K. angustifolia*, with showy pink flowers.
• [modern Latin from P. *Kalm*, Swedish botanist d.1779]

Kalmuck *noun*
ALSO SPELLED: **Kalmyk**
• "KAL muck"
• a member of a Buddhist Mongolian people living in the west of the former USSR.
• [Russian *kalmyk*]

kalong *noun*
• "KAW long"
• any of several fruit bats of SE Asia and Indonesia, esp. the large common flying fox, *Pteropus vampyrus*.
• [Malay]

kalpa *noun*
• "KALPA"
• the period between the beginning and the end of the world considered as the day of Brahma (4,320 million human years).
• [Sanskrit]

kame *noun*
• "CAME"
• a short ridge of sand and gravel deposited from the water of a melted glacier.
• [Scots form of 'comb']

kameez *noun*
• "kuh MEEZ"
• a long tunic worn by many people from the Indian subcontinent, typically with a shalwar or churidars.
• [Arabic *ḳamīṣ*, perhaps from Late Latin *camisia* (see CHEMISE)]

kami *noun*
• "KOMMY"
• a divine being in the Shinto religion.
• [Japanese]

kamik *noun*
• "KOMMIC" or "KAMMIC"
• a traditional Inuit boot made from seal or caribou skin.
• [Inuktitut]
HOMOPHONES: *comic*

kamikaze *noun*
- "komma KOZZY" or "kamma KAZZY"
- (during the Second World War) a Japanese aircraft loaded with explosives and deliberately crashed by its pilot on its target.
- [Japanese from *kami* divinity + *kaze* wind]

Kamilaroi *noun*
- "kuh MILLER oy"
- an Aboriginal language formerly spoken in New South Wales and S Queensland, Australia.
- [Kamilaroi]

Kamloopsian *noun*
- "kam LOOPSY 'n"
- a resident of Kamloops, BC.

kampong *noun*
- "KAM pong"
- a Malayan enclosure or village.
- [Malay]

Kampuchean *noun*
- "kam poo CHEE 'n"
- a native or national of Cambodia in SE Asia.
- [variant name for 'Cambodia']

kana *noun*
- "KONNA"
- Japanese syllabic writing.
- [Japanese]

kanaka *noun*
- "kuh NACKA" or "kuh NOCKA"
- a South Sea Islander, esp. (formerly) one employed as a labourer in either Canada or Australia.
- [Hawaiian, = person, human being]

Kanarese *noun*
ALSO SPELLED: **Canarese**
- "kanna REEZ"
- a member of a Dravidian people living in western India.
- [*Kanara* in India]

kangaroo *noun*
- "kang guh ROO"
- a plant-eating marsupial of the genus *Macropus*, native to Australia and New Guinea, with a long tail and strongly developed hind quarters enabling it to travel by jumping.
- [*ganurru*, the name of a specific kind of kangaroo in Guugu Yimidhirr (an extinct Aboriginal language of N Queensland)]

Kanienkehaka *noun*
- "kan yen cay HOCKA"
- the Mohawk people.
- [Mohawk, = 'people of the flint']

kanji *noun*
- "KAN jee"
- Japanese writing using Chinese characters.
- [Japanese from *kan* Chinese + *ji* character]

Kannada *noun*
- "CANADA"
- the Kanarese language.
- [Kanarese]

Kantian *adjective*
- "KANTY 'n"
- of or relating to the German philosopher I. Kant (d.1804) or his work.

kaolin *noun*
- "KAY a lin"
- a fine soft white clay produced by the decomposition of other clays or feldspar, used esp. for making porcelain and in medicines.
- [French from Chinese *gaoling* the name of a mountain, from *gao* high + *ling* hill]
- **kaolinic** *adjective*

kaon *noun*
- "KAY on"
- a meson having a mass several times that of a pion.
- [*ka* representing the letter *K* (as symbol for the particle)]

kapellmeister *noun*
- "kuh PELL mice tur"
- the conductor of an orchestra, opera, choir, etc., attached to a German court.
- [German from *Kapelle* court orchestra, from Italian *cappella* chapel + *Meister* master]

kapok *noun*
- "KAY pock"
- a fine fibrous cotton-like substance found surrounding the seeds of a tropical tree, *Ceiba pentandra*, used for stuffing cushions, soft toys, etc.
- [ultimately from Malay *kāpoq*]

kappa *noun*
- "KAPPA"
- the tenth letter of the Greek alphabet (Κ, κ).
- [Greek]

kaput *predicative adjective*
- "kuh PUT" ("PUT" rhymes with *FOOT*)
- broken, ruined; done for.
- [German *kaputt*]

karahi *noun*
- "kuh RYE"
- a small, bowl-shaped frying pan with two handles used in Indian cooking, esp. for preparing balti dishes.
- [Hindi]

karakul *noun*
ALSO SPELLED: **caracul**
- "KA ruh k'll"
- a variety of Asian sheep with a dark curled fleece when young.
- [Russian]

karaoke *noun*
- "kerry OH kee"
- a form of entertainment in which people sing popular songs as soloists against a pre-recorded backing.
- [Japanese, = empty orchestra]

karat *noun*
ALSO SPELLED: **carat**

• "KARE it"
• a measure of purity of gold, pure gold being 24 karats.
• [as CARAT]
HOMOPHONES: *carat, caret, carrot*

karate *noun*
• "kuh ROTTY"
• a Japanese system of unarmed combat using the hands and feet as weapons.
• [Japanese from *kara* empty + *te* hand]

Karelian *adjective*
• "kuh REELY 'n"
• of or pertaining to Karelia, a region of N Europe straddling the Finnish–Russian border.

Karen *noun*
• "kuh REN"
• a member of a non-Burmese Mongoloid people, most of whom live in eastern Burma (Myanmar).
• [Burmese *ka-reng* 'wild unclean man']

karma *noun*
• "KARMA"
• the sum of a person's actions in previous states of existence, viewed as deciding his or her fate in future existences.
• [Sanskrit, = action, fate]
• **karmic** *adjective*
• **karmically** *adverb*

karoo *noun*
ALSO SPELLED: **karroo**
• "kuh ROO"
• semi-desert land in South Africa.
• [Khoikhoi, lit. = 'hard, dry']

karst *noun*
• "KARST"
• a limestone region with underground drainage and many cavities and passages caused by the dissolution of the rock.
• [the *Karst*, a limestone region in Slovenia]
• **karstic** *adjective*

karyokinesis *noun*
• "kerry oh kuh NEE sis"
• the division of a cell nucleus during mitosis.
• [Greek *karuon* kernel + *kinēsis* movement, from *kineō* move]

karyotype *noun*
• "KERRY a tipe"
• the number and structure of the chromosomes in the nucleus of a cell.
• [Greek *karuon* kernel + TYPE]
• **karyotypic** *adjective* "kerry a TIPPIC"
• **karyotyping** *noun*

kasha *noun*
• "CASH uh"
• a soft food made of boiled or baked grain, esp. buckwheat.
• [Russian]

Kashmiri *adjective*
• "cash MEERY"
• of or relating to Kashmir, a region on the border of India and NE Pakistan, or its people or language.

Kashruth *noun*
• "CASH rooth"
• the body of religious laws relating to the suitability of food, ritual objects, etc.
• [Hebrew, = 'legitimacy (in religion)': as KOSHER]

Kaska *noun*
• "CASS kuh"
• a member of a Dene Aboriginal group living in northwestern BC.
• [from the native name of a creek in the area]

kata *noun*
• "CAW taw"
• a system of basic exercises or postures used to teach and improve the execution of techniques in judo and other martial arts.
• [Japanese]

katabatic *adjective*
• "katta BATTIC"
• (of wind) caused by air flowing downwards.
• [Greek *katabatikos* from *katabainō* go down]

katakana *noun*
• "katta KONNA"
• an angular form of Japanese kana or writing.
• [Japanese, = side kana]

Kathak *noun*
• "kuh TUCK"
• a type of northern Indian classical dance alternating passages of mime with passages of dance.
• [Sanskrit *kathaka* professional storyteller, from *kathā* story]

Kathakali *noun*
• "kutta KAW lee"
• a form of dramatic dance of southern India, based on Hindu literature and characterized by masks, stylized costume and makeup, and frequent use of mime.
• [Malayalam, from Sanskrit *kathā* story + Malayalam *kali* play]

katsura *noun*
• "kat SURA"
• a tree native to eastern Asia, *Cercidiphyllum japonicum*, with leaves resembling redbud, grown as an ornamental.
• [Japanese]

katydid *noun*
• "KATEY did"
• any of various N American green grasshoppers of the family Tettigoniidae.
• [imitative of the sound it makes]

kauri *noun*
• "COW ree"
• a coniferous New Zealand tree, *Agathis*

australis, which produces valuable timber and a resin.
• [Maori]
HOMOPHONES: *cowrie*

kava *noun*
• "KOVVA"
• a Polynesian shrub, *Piper methysticum*.
• [Polynesian]

kayak *noun*
• "KYE ack"
• a one-man canoe consisting of a covered light wooden frame.
• [Inuktitut]
• **kayaker** *noun*
• **kayaking** *noun*
HOMOPHONES: *kiack*

kayo *verb*
• "KAY oh"
• knock out; stun by a blow.
• [representing pronunciation of 'KO' knock out]

Kazakh *noun*
• "kuh ZOCK"
• a member of a Turkic people of central Asia, esp. of Kazakhstan.

kea *noun*
• "KEE uh" or "KAY uh"
• a parrot, *Nestor notabilis*, of New Zealand, with brownish-green and red plumage.
• [Maori, imitative]

kebab *noun*
ALSO SPELLED: **kabob**
• "kuh BOB" or "kuh BAB"
• a dish of pieces of marinated meat and vegetables cooked and served on a skewer.
• [Urdu from Arabic *kabāb*]

kedgeree *noun*
• "KEDGE ur ee"
• an Indian dish of rice, split pulse, onions, eggs, etc.
• [Hindi *khichṛī*, Sanskrit *k'rsara* dish of rice and sesame]

keek *verb*
• "KEEK"
• peep; peek.
• [Middle English *kike*: compare Middle Dutch, Middle Low German *kīken*]

keeshond *noun*
• "KACE hond"
• a breed of dog with long thick grey hair; a variety of the spitz.
• [Dutch, from *Kees* pet form of male name Cornelius + *hond* dog]

kef *noun*
• "KEFF"
• a drowsy state induced by marijuana etc.
• [Arabic *kayf* enjoyment, well-being]

kefalotiri *noun*
ALSO SPELLED: **kefalotyri**
• "keffa lo TEERY"
• a hard, salty, yellow, Greek ewe's or goat's cheese similar to Parmesan.
• [Greek, = 'hat cheese', its shape being similar to that of a brimless hat]

keiretsu *noun*
• "kay RET soo"
• (in Japan) a conglomeration of businesses linked together by cross-shareholdings to form a robust corporate structure.
• [Japanese, from *kei* systems + *retsu* tier]

keister *noun*
ALSO SPELLED: **keester**
• "KEESTER"
• the buttocks.
• [origin unknown: original sense 'suitcase, satchel, handbag']

keloid *noun*
• "KEE loid"
• fibrous tissue formed at the site of a scar or injury.
• [Greek *khēlē* claw + Greek *-oeidēs* from *eidos* form]
• **keloidal** *adjective*

kelpie *noun*
• "KELPY"
• (in Scottish folklore) a water spirit, usu. in the form of a horse, reputed to delight in the drowning of travellers etc.
• [perhaps from Gaelic *cailpeach, colpach* bullock, colt]

kelt *noun*
• "KELT"
• a salmon or sea trout after spawning.
• [Middle English: origin unknown]
HOMOPHONES: *Celt*

kelvin *noun*
• "KELVIN"
• the SI unit of thermodynamic temperature, equal in magnitude to the degree Celsius.
• [William Thomson, 1st Baron *Kelvin*, Scottish physicist d.1907]

kempt *adjective*
• "KEMPT"
• combed; neatly kept.
• [past participle of (now dialect) *kemb* 'comb' from Old English *cemban* from Germanic]

kendo *noun*
• "KEN doe"
• a Japanese form of fencing with two-handed bamboo swords.
• [Japanese, = sword way]

kenning *noun*
• "KENNING"
• a compound expression in Old English and Old Norse poetry, e.g. *oar-steed* = ship.

• [Middle English, = 'teaching' etc. from Old English *cennan* know]

keno *noun*
• "KEENO"
• a game of chance resembling bingo, based on the drawing of numbers and covering of corresponding numbers on cards.
• [19th c.: origin unknown]

Kenoran *noun*
• "kuh NOR 'n"
• a resident of Kenora, Ont.

kenosis *noun*
• "kuh NO sis"
• the renunciation of the divine nature, at least in part, by Christ in the Incarnation.
• [Greek *kenōsis* from *kenoō* to empty, from *kenos* empty]
• **kenotic** *adjective* "kuh NOTTIC"

kenspeckle *adjective*
• "KEN speck'll"
• conspicuous.
• [*kenspeck* of Scandinavian origin]

kente *noun*
• "KEN tay"
• a brightly coloured banded woven fabric of Ghanaian origin.
• [Twi, = cloth]

kentledge *noun*
• "KENT ledge"
• pig iron etc. used as permanent ballast.
• [French *quintelage* ballast, assimilated to *kentle* obsolete var. of QUINTAL]

Kentvillite *noun*
• "KENT vill ite"
• a resident of Kentville, NS.

Kenyan *noun*
• "KEN y'n" or "KEEN y'n"
• a native or inhabitant of Kenya in E Africa.

kepi *noun*
• "KEPPY" or "KAY pee"
• a French military cap with a flat circular top and a horizontal peak.
• [French *képi* from Swiss German *käppi* diminutive of *kappe* cap]

keratectomy *noun*
• "kerra TECTA mee"
• a form of eye surgery which uses a laser to carve away part of the outer surface of the cornea.
• [KERATITIS + Greek *ektomē* excision, from *ek* out + *temnō* cut]

keratin *noun*
• "KERRA tin"
• a fibrous protein which occurs in hair, feathers, hooves, claws, horns, etc.
• [Greek *keras keratos* horn]
• **keratinization** *noun* (also esp. *Brit.* **-isation**)
• **keratinize** *verb* (also esp. *Brit.* **-ise**)

keratitis *noun*
• "kerra TITE iss"
• inflammation of the cornea of the eye.
• [*kerat-* denoting the cornea (from Greek *keras keratos* horn) + *-itis*, forming feminine of adjectives in *-itēs* (with *nosos* 'disease' implied)]

keratosis *noun*
• "kerra TOE sis"
• a skin condition marked by horny growths.
• [as KERATITIS]
• **keratotic** *adjective* "kerra TOTTIC"

keratotomy *noun*
• "kerra TOTTA mee"
• a surgical operation involving cutting into the cornea of the eye, esp. to correct myopia.
• [*kerat-* denoting the cornea (compare KERATITIS) + Greek *-tomia* cutting, from *temnō* cut]

kerchief *noun*
• "KUR chiff" or "KUR cheef"
• a cloth used to cover the head.
• [Anglo-French *courchef*, Old French *couvrechief* from *couvrir* cover + *chef* head, from Latin *caput*]
• **kerchiefed** *adjective*

kerf *noun*
• "KURF"
• a slit made by cutting, esp. with a saw.
• [Old English *cyrf* from Germanic]

kerfuffle *noun*
• "kur FUFF'll"
• *Cdn, Brit., & Austral.* a fuss or commotion.
• [Scots *curfuffle* from *fuffle* to disorder: imitative]

kermes *noun*
• "KUR meez"
• a small evergreen oak, *Quercus coccifera*, of the Mediterranean region.
• [French *kermès* from Arabic & Persian *ḳirmiz*: related to CRIMSON]

kermis *noun*
• "KUR miss"
• a periodical country fair, esp. in the Netherlands.
• [Dutch, originally = mass on the anniversary of the dedication of a church, when a yearly fair was held: from *kerk* church + *mis, misse* mass]

kermode *noun*
• "kur MOE dee"
• a subspecies of the black bear, *Ursus americanus kermodei*, which can have either black or white fur, found in the coastal mainland and some coastal islands of British Columbia.
• [F. *Kermode*, Canadian museum administrator d.1946]

kern *noun*
• "KURN"
• the part of a metal type projecting beyond its body or shank.

• [perhaps from French *carne* corner, from Old French *charne* from Latin *cardo cardinis* hinge]

• **kerned** *adjective*

kernel *noun*

• "KURN'll"

• a central, softer, usu. edible part within a hard shell of a nut, fruit stone, seed, etc.

• [Old English *cyrnel*, diminutive of 'corn']

HOMOPHONES: *colonel*

kerosene *noun*

• "KERRA seen"

• a petroleum distillate widely used as a fuel and solvent.

• [Greek *kēros* wax + '-ene' forming names of unsaturated hydrocarbons containing a double bond, from Greek *-ēnos*, adjective suffix denoting origin or source]

kersey *noun*

• "KURZY"

• a kind of coarse narrow cloth woven from short-stapled wool, usu. ribbed.

• [Middle English, prob. from *Kersey* in Suffolk]

kerseymere *noun*

• "KURZY meer"

• a twilled fine woollen cloth.

• [alteration of *cassimere*, var. of CASHMERE, assimilated to KERSEY]

kestrel *noun*

• "KESS trull"

• any of several falcons distinguished by the habit of hunting by sustained hovering, esp. the American kestrel *Falco sparverius* or the Eurasian kestrel *F. tinnunculus*, widely distributed in the Old World.

• [Middle English *castrell*, perhaps from French dialect *casserelle*, French *créc(er)elle*, perhaps imitative of its cry]

keta *noun*

• "KEETA"

• a salmon, *Oncorhynchus keta*, of the N American Pacific coast.

• [Russian]

kétaine *adjective*

• "kay TEN"

• *Cdn (Que.)* in poor taste; tacky or kitschy.

• [Canadian French]

ketamine *noun*

• "KEETA meen"

• an anaesthetic and painkilling drug, also used (illicitly) as a hallucinogen.

• [KETONE + AMINE]

ketone *noun*

• "KEE tone"

• any of a class of organic compounds in which two hydrocarbon groups are linked by a carbonyl group, e.g. propanone (acetone).

• [German *Keton* alteration of *Aketon* ACETONE]

• **ketonic** *adjective* "kuh TONNIC"

ketonuria *noun*

• "keeto NYURY uh"

• the excretion of abnormally large amounts of ketone bodies in the urine, characteristic of diabetes mellitus, starvation, etc.

• [as KETONE + URINE]

ketosis *noun*

• "kuh TOE sis"

• a condition characterized by raised levels of ketone bodies in the body, associated with fat metabolism and diabetes.

• [as KETONE]

• **ketotic** *adjective* "kuh TOTTIC"

kewpie *noun*

• "KYOOPY"

• a small chubby doll with a curl or topknot.

• ['Cupid' the Roman god of love]

Keynesian *adjective*

• "KANE zee 'n"

• of or relating to the theories of the English economist J. M. Keynes (d.1946), esp. regarding state control of the economy through money and taxation.

• **Keynesianism** *noun*

khadi *noun*

• "KODDY"

• Indian homespun cloth.

• [Punjabi, Hindi]

khaki *adjective*

• "CACKY" or "COCKY" or "CARKY"

• dust-coloured; dull brownish yellow.

• [Urdu *ḵākī* dust-coloured, from *ḵāk* dust]

HOMOPHONES: *cocky*

Khalsa *noun*

• "KAWL suh"

• the fraternity of warriors into which Sikh males are initiated at puberty.

• [Punjabi from Urdu from Persian *ḵāl(i)ṣa* from feminine of Arabic *ḵāl(i)ṣ* pure, free, belonging to]

khamsin *noun*

• "KAM sin"

• an oppressive hot south or southeast wind occurring in Egypt for about 50 days in March, April, and May.

• [Arabic *ḵamsīn* from *ḵamsūn* fifty]

khan *noun*

• "KON" or "KAN"

• (in the Middle East) an inn with a central court where caravans may rest.

• [Arabic *ḵān* inn]

HOMOPHONES: *can, con*

khat *noun*

• "KOT"

• a shrub, *Catha edulis*, grown in Arabia.

• [Arabic *ḳāt*]

HOMOPHONES: *cot, caught*

Khedive *noun*

• "kuh DEEV"

• the title of the viceroy of Egypt under Turkish rule 1867–1914.
• [French *khédive*, ultimately from Persian *kadīv* prince]
• **Khedival** *adjective*
• **Khedivial** *adjective*

Khmer *noun*
• "k'MAIR"
• a native of the ancient Khmer kingdom in SE Asia, or of modern Cambodia.
• [Khmer]

Khoikhoi *noun*
• "KOY koy"
• a member of a people of South Africa and Namibia; a Nama.
• [Nama, lit. 'men of men']

Khoisan *noun*
• "KOY sawn"
• a collective term for the Nama (Khoikhoi) and the San (Bushmen) of southern Africa.
• [KHOIKHOI + SAN]

khoum *noun*
• "KOOM"
• a monetary unit of Mauritania, equal to one-fifth of an ouguiya.
• [Arabic *kums* one-fifth]
HOMOPHONES: *coomb*, *cwm*

kiack *noun*
• "KYE ack"
• *Cdn* (*Nova Scotia*) a fish of the herring family, *Alosa pseudoharengus*, found off the Atlantic coast of N America and in the Great Lakes; an alewife or gaspereau.
• [prob. from Mi'kmaq]
HOMOPHONES: *kayak*

kiang *noun*
• "kye ANG"
• a wild Tibetan ass, *Equus hemionus kiang*, with a thick furry coat.
• [Tibetan *kyang*]

kibbeh *noun*
• "kib AY"
• an originally Middle Eastern dish of meatballs with bulgur wheat, onions, seasoning, etc.
• [Arabic]

kibbutz *noun*
• "ki BUTS" ("BUTS" rhymes with *PUTS*)
• a collective esp. farming settlement in Israel.
• [modern Hebrew *ḳibbūṣ* gathering]

kibbutznik *noun*
• "ki BUTS nick" ("BUTS" rhymes with *PUTS*)
• a member of a kibbutz.
• [Yiddish (as KIBBUTZ)]

kibe *noun*
• "KIBE"
• an ulcerated chilblain, esp. on the heel.
• [Middle English, prob. from Welsh *cibi*]

kibitka *noun*
• "kib IT kuh"
• a type of Russian hooded sled or wagon.
• [Russian from Tartar *kibitz*]

kibitz *verb*
• "KIBBITS"
• chat or joke lightheartedly.
• [Yiddish from German *kiebitzen* lapwing, busybody]
• **kibitzer** *noun*

kibosh *noun*
• "KYE bosh"
• nonsense.
• [19th c.: origin unknown]

kiddush *noun*
• "kid OOSH" or "KID ush"
• a ceremony of prayer and blessing over wine, performed by the head of a Jewish household at the meal ushering in the Sabbath or a holy day.
• [Hebrew *qiddūš* sanctification]

kielbasa *noun*
• "keel BOSSA"
• a type of highly seasoned sausage of Eastern European origin, usu. containing garlic.
• [Polish *kiełbasa* sausage]

kieselguhr *noun*
• "KEEZLE goor"
• a soft, fine-grained deposit composed of fossil diatoms, used as a filter, filler, insulator, etc., in various manufacturing processes, and as an insecticide in gardening applications; diatomaceous earth.
• [German from *Kiesel* gravel + dialect *Guhr* earthy deposit]

Kikongo *noun*
• "kih KONG go"
• the Bantu language of the Kongo people, used in the Republic of the Congo, Congo (formerly Zaire), and adjacent areas.
• [Kikongo, from *ki-* prefix + KONGO]

Kikuyu *noun*
• "kee KOO yoo"
• a member of a Bantu-speaking people constituting the largest ethno-linguistic group in Kenya.
• [Bantu]

kilderkin *noun*
• "KILL dur kin"
• a cask for liquids etc., usu. holding 18 imperial gallons (about 82 litres).
• [Middle English, alteration of *kinderkin* from Middle Dutch *kinderkin*, *kinneken*, diminutive of *kintal* QUINTAL]

kilim *noun*
• "kill EEM" or "KEE lim"
• a pileless woven carpet, rug, etc., made in Turkey and neighbouring areas to the east.
• [Turkish from Persian *gelīm*]

killick *noun*
- "KILLICK"
- a heavy stone used by small craft as an anchor.
- [17th c.: origin unknown]

killifish *noun*
- "KILLA fish"
- any of several small, often brightly coloured fish of the families Cyprinodontidae and Poeciliidae, esp. any of the genus *Fundulus*, found esp. in sheltered rivers and estuaries of eastern N America.
- [perhaps from *kill* stream, from Dutch *kil* + 'fish']

kilobyte *noun*
- "KILLA bite"
- 1,024 (i.e. 2^{10}) bytes as a measure of memory size.
- [French from Greek *khilioi* thousand + BYTE]

kilocalorie *noun*
- "KILLO cala ree"
- a calorie.
- [French from Greek *khilioi* thousand + CALORIE]

kilohertz *noun*
- "KILLA hurts"
- a measure of frequency equivalent to 1,000 cycles per second.
- [French from Greek *khilioi* thousand + HERTZ]

kilojoule *noun*
- "KILLA jool"
- 1,000 joules, esp. as a measure of the energy value of foods.
- [French from Greek *khilioi* thousand + JOULE]

kilolitre *noun*
ALSO SPELLED: **kiloliter**
- "KILLA leeter"
- 1,000 litres (equivalent to 220 imperial gallons).
- [French from Greek *khilioi* thousand + LITRE]

kilometrage *noun*
- "KILLA meeter idge"
- a number of kilometres travelled, used, etc., esp. by motor vehicle.
- [as KILOMETRE]

kilometre *noun*
ALSO SPELLED: **kilometer**
- "kuh LOMMA tur" or "KILLA meeter"
- a metric unit of measurement equal to 1 000 metres (approx. 0.62 miles).
- [French from Greek *khilioi* thousand + METRE]
- **kilometric** *adjective* "killa METRIC"

kilopascal *noun*
- "KILLO pask'll" or "killo pass CAL"
- a metric unit of pressure equal to 1 000 pascals.
- [French from Greek *khilioi* thousand + PASCAL]

kimberlite *noun*
- "KIMBER lite"
- a rare igneous blue-tinged rock sometimes containing diamonds, found in northern Canada, South Africa, and Siberia.
- [*Kimberley* in South Africa]

kimchee *noun*
ALSO SPELLED: **kimchi**
- "KIM chee"
- a dish of raw, highly spiced, pickled or fermented cabbage, the Korean national dish.
- [Korean]

kimono *noun*
- "kim OH no"
- a long loose Japanese robe worn with a sash.
- [Japanese]
- **kimonoed** *adjective*

kina *noun*
- "KEENA"
- the chief monetary unit of Papua New Guinea, equal to 100 toea.
- [Papuan]

kinase *noun*
- "KINE ace" or "KIN ace"
- any of various enzymes that catalyze the transfer of a phosphate group from ATP to another molecule.
- [from Greek *kinein* move]

Kincardinite *noun*
- "kin CAR d'n ite"
- a resident of Kincardine, Ont.

kindergarten *noun*
- "KIN dur gart'n"
- a class or school for young children, usu. five-year-olds, in preparation for grade one.
- [German, = children's garden]
- **kindergartner** *noun*

kindle *verb*
- "KIN d'll"
- light or set on fire (a flame, fire, substance, etc.), esp. gradually.
- [Old Norse *kynda*]

kindling *noun*
- "KIND ling" ("KIND" rhymes with *PINNED*)
- small sticks etc. for lighting fires.
- [as KINDLE]

kindred *noun*
- "KIN drid"
- one's relatives, referred to collectively.
- [Middle English from Old English *cynn* relatives, from Germanic + *-red* from Old English *ræden* condition]

kinematics *noun*
- "kinna MATTIX"
- the branch of mechanics concerned with the motion of objects without reference to the forces which cause the motion.
- [Greek *kinēma -matos* motion, from *kineō* move]
- **kinematic** *adjective*
- **kinematically** *adverb*

kinesics *noun*
- "kin EE sicks"
- the study of body movements and gestures which contribute to communication.
- [Greek *kinēsis* motion (as KINETIC)]

kinesiology *noun*
- "kuh neecy OLLA jee" or "kuh neezy OLLA jee"
- the study of the mechanics of esp. human body movements.
- [as KINESIS + *logos* word]
- **kinesiologist** *noun*

kinesis *noun*
- "kuh NEE sis"
- movement, motion.
- [Greek *kinēsis* movement]

kinesthesia *noun*
ALSO SPELLED: **kinaesthesia**
- "kin us THEEZY uh" or "kin us THEE zhuh" (with "TH" as in *THIN*)
- a sense of awareness of the position and movement of the voluntary muscles of the body.
- [Greek *kineō* move + *aisthēsis* sensation]
- **kinesthetic** *adjective* (also **kinaesthetic**) "kin us THETTIC"

kinetic *adjective*
- "kin ETTIC"
- of or due to motion.
- [Greek *kinētikos* from *kineō* move]
- **kinetically** *adverb*

kinin *noun*
- "KYE nin"
- any of a group of polypeptides of low molecular weight which are formed in tissue (from inactive precursors in the blood) in response to injury and have local effects that typically include pain and the dilatation of the blood vessels.
- [Greek *kinein* set in motion]

kinkajou *noun*
- "KINKA joo"
- a Central and S American nocturnal fruit-eating mammal, *Potos flavus*, related to the raccoon, with a prehensile tail and living in trees.
- [French *quincajou*, alteration of CARCAJOU influenced by Ojibwa *kwi:nkwa'a:ke:* wolverine]

kinnikinnick *noun*
- "kinny kin ICK"
- a mixture formerly used by some Aboriginal peoples of N America as a substitute for tobacco or for mixing with it, usu. consisting of dried bearberry or sumac leaves and the inner bark of dogwood or willow.
- [Delaware, = admixture]

kiosk *noun*
- "KEE osk"
- a light open-fronted booth or cubicle from which refreshments, newspapers, tickets, etc. are sold or information for tourists is provided.
- [French *kiosque* from Turkish *kiūshk* pavilion, from Persian *guš*]

Kiowa *noun*
- "KYE a wuh"
- a member of an Aboriginal people from the southern US plains.
- [Latin American Spanish *Caygua* from Kiowa *kóygú* (pl.)]

kir *noun*
- "KEER"
- a drink made from dry white wine and crème de cassis.
- [Canon Felix *Kir* d.1968, said to have invented the recipe]

kirpan *noun*
- "kir PAN" or "kir PON"
- the dagger or sword worn by Sikhs as a religious symbol.
- [Punjabi and Hindi *kirpān* from Sanskrit *kṛpāṇa* sword]

kirsch *noun*
- "KEERSH"
- a brandy distilled from the fermented juice of cherries.
- [German *Kirsche* cherry]

kismet *noun*
- "KIZZ met" or "KISS met"
- destiny, fate.
- [Turkish from Arabic *ḳisma(t)* from *ḳasama* divide]

Kiswahili *noun*
- "kiss wuh HEELY"
- a major language of the Bantu family, spoken widely in Kenya, Tanzania, and elsewhere in E Africa, where it serves as a lingua franca.
- [Swahili *ki-* prefix for an abstract or inanimate object + SWAHILI]

Kitimatian *noun*
- "kitty MAY sh'n"
- a resident of Kitimat, BC.

kitsch *noun*
- "KITCH"
- garish, tasteless, or sentimental art.
- [German]
- **kitschification** *noun*
- **kitschiness** *noun*
- **kitschy** *adjective*

Kitselas *noun*
- "KIT s'll us"
- a member of an Aboriginal people living along the Skeena River in northwestern BC.
- [Kitselas *git'selasu* = 'people of the canyon']

kittiwake *noun*
- "KITTY wake"
- either of two small gulls, *Rissa tridactyla* and *R. brevirostris*, nesting on sea cliffs.
- [imitative of its cry]

kiva *noun*
- "KEEVA"
- a chamber, built wholly or partly underground, used by male Pueblo Indians for religious rites etc.
- [Hopi]

kiwi *noun*
- "KEE wee"
- a flightless New Zealand bird of the genus *Apteryx* with hairlike feathers and a long bill.
- [Maori]

klaxon *noun*
- "KLAX'n"
- a horn, originally on a motor vehicle.
- [name of the manufacturing company]

kleptocracy *noun*
- "klep TOCKRA see"
- government by a group who enrich themselves on the country's resources.
- [Greek *klepto-* from *kleptēs* thief + *kratia* from *kratos* strength, power]
- **kleptocrat** *noun*

kleptomania *noun*
- "klepto MAINY uh"
- a recurrent urge to steal, usu. without regard for need or profit.
- [Greek *kleptēs* thief + MANIA]
- **kleptomaniac** *noun*

klezmer *noun*
- "KLEZZ mur"
- a member of a group of musicians playing traditional eastern European Jewish music.
- [Yiddish, contraction of Hebrew *kĕlēy zemer* musical instrument]

Klingon *noun*
- "KLING on"
- a member of a warlike humanoid alien species in the TV series *Star Trek* and its spinoffs.
- [invented name]

klipspringer *noun*
- "KLIP springer"
- a S African dwarf antelope, *Oreotragus oreotragus*, which can bound up and down rocky slopes.
- [Afrikaans from *klip* rock + *springer* jumper]

klister *noun*
- "KLISTER"
- a soft wax for applying to the running surface of skis to facilitate movement, used esp. when the temperature is above freezing.
- [Norwegian, = paste]

Klondiker *noun*
- "KLONDIKE ur"
- a prospector who took part in the Klondike gold rush of 1897–8 in the Yukon Territory.

kloof *noun*
- "KLOOF"
- a steep-sided ravine or valley.
- [Dutch, = cleft]

kludge *noun*
- "KLUDGE" (rhymes with *JUDGE*)
- an ill-assorted collection of poorly matching parts.
- [invented word, perhaps influenced by 'fudge']
- **kludgy** *adjective*

klutz *noun*
- "KLUTS"
- a clumsy, awkward person.
- [Yiddish, from German *Klotz* wooden block]
- **klutzy** *adjective*

klystron *noun*
- "KLICE tron"
- an electron tube that generates or amplifies microwaves by velocity modulation.
- [Greek *kluzō klus-* wash over + ELECTRON]

knack *noun*
- "NACK"
- an acquired or intuitive faculty of doing a thing adroitly.
- [Middle English, prob. identical with *knack* sharp blow or sound, from Low German, ultimately imitative]

knacker *noun*
- "NACKER"
- a buyer of useless horses for slaughter.
- [19th c.: origin unknown]

knackwurst *noun*
- "NOCK wurst"
- a type of short fat highly seasoned German sausage.
- [German from *knacken* make a cracking noise + *Wurst* sausage]

knap *verb*
- "NAP"
- break (esp. a stone) with a sharp blow from a hammer etc.
- [Middle English, imitative]
- **knapper** *noun*

HOMOPHONES: *nap*, *nappe*

knapsack *noun*
- "NAP sack"
- a bag of canvas, nylon, or other weatherproof material, carried strapped on the back by hikers, students, soldiers, etc.
- [Middle Low German, prob. from *knappen* bite + 'sack']

knapweed *noun*
- "NAP weed"
- any of various plants of the genus *Centaurea*, having thistle-like purple flowers.
- [Middle English, originally *knopweed* from *knop* knob + 'weed']

knar *noun*
- "NAR"
- a knot or protuberance in a tree trunk, root, etc.
- [Middle English *knarre*, related to Middle Low

German, Middle Dutch, Middle High German *knorre* knobbed protuberance]

knave *noun*
- "NAVE"
- a rogue, a scoundrel.
- [Old English *cnafa* boy, servant, from West Germanic]
- **knavery** *noun*
- **knavish** *adjective*

HOMOPHONES: *nave*

knawel *noun*
- "NAW 'll"
- any low-growing plant of the genus *Scleranthus*.
- [German *Knauel*]

knead *verb*
- "NEED"
- work (dough, clay, etc.) into a smooth mass by pressing and folding.
- [Old English *cnedan* from Germanic]
- **kneader** *noun*

HOMOPHONES: *need*

knell *noun*
- "NELL"
- the sound of a bell, esp. when rung solemnly for a death or funeral.
- [Old English *cnyll*, *cnyllan*: perhaps influenced by *bell*]

knickerbockers *plural noun*
- "NICKER bockerz"
- loose-fitting breeches gathered at the knee or calf.
- [Diedrich *Knickerbocker*, pretended author of *History of New York* (1809) by W. Irving, US writer d.1859]

knickers *plural noun*
- "NICKERZ"
- knickerbockers.
- [abbreviation of KNICKERBOCKERS]

knobkerrie *noun*
- "NOB kerry"
- a short stick with a knobbed head used as a weapon esp. in S Africa.
- [after Afrikaans *knopkierie*]

knoll *noun*
- "NOLE"
- a small hill or mound.
- [Old English *cnoll* hilltop, related to Middle Dutch, Middle High German *knolle* clod, Old Norse *knollr* hilltop]

knout *noun*
- "NOUT" (rhymes with *OUT*)
- a scourge used in imperial Russia, often causing death.
- [French from Russian *knut* from Icelandic *knútr*, related to 'knot']

HOMOPHONES: *nowt*

knowledge *noun*
- "NAW lidge"
- awareness or familiarity gained by experience (of a person, fact, or thing).
- [Middle English *knaulege*, with earlier *knawlechen* (v.) formed as 'know' + Old English *-lǣcan* from *lāc* the action of]
- **knowledgeability** *noun*
- **knowledgeable** *adjective*
- **knowledgeably** *adverb*

knur *noun*

ALSO SPELLED: **knurr**
- "NUR"
- a hard excrescence on the trunk of a tree.
- [Middle English *knorre*, var. of KNAR]

knurl *noun*
- "NURL"
- a small projecting knob, ridge, etc.
- [as KNUR]
- **knurled** *adjective*

koa *noun*
- "KOE uh"
- a Hawaiian tree, *Acacia koa*, which produces dark red wood.
- [Hawaiian]

koala *noun*
- "kuh WOLLA"
- an Australian bearlike marsupial, *Phascolarctos cinereus*, having thick grey fur and feeding on eucalyptus leaves.
- [Aboriginal *kūl(l)a*]

koan *noun*
- "KOE an"
- a paradoxical anecdote or riddle without a solution, used in Zen Buddhism to demonstrate the inadequacy of logical reasoning and provoke enlightenment.
- [Japanese, = public matter (for thought)]

kob *noun*
- "KOB"
- a grazing antelope, *Kobus kob*, native to African savannah.
- [Wolof *kooba*]

HOMOPHONES: *cob*

kobo *noun*
- "KOE boe"
- a monetary unit of Nigeria, equal to one-hundredth of a naira.
- [from 'copper']

kobold *noun*
- "KOE b'ld"
- (in Germanic mythology) a spirit who haunts houses or lives underground in mines or caves.
- [German]

Kodiak *noun*
- "KOE dee ack"
- a large variety of grizzly found in Alaska.
- [*Kodiak* Island, Alaska]

kofta *noun*
• "KOFF tuh"
• (in Indian cooking) a spiced meatball (or fish or vegetable ball).
• [Urdu and Persian *koftah* pounded meat]

kohl *noun*
• "KOLE"
• a black powder, usu. antimony sulphide or lead sulphide, used as eye makeup esp. in Eastern countries.
• [Arabic *kuḥl*]
HOMOPHONES: *coal, cole*

kohlrabi *noun*
• "kole RABBY" or "kole ROBBY"
• a variety of cabbage with an edible turnip-like swollen stem.
• [German from Italian *cavoli rape* (pl.) from medieval Latin *caulorapa* (as COLE, Latin *rapum, rapa* turnip)]

koi *noun*
• "KOY"
• a carp of a large ornamental variety bred in Japan.
• [Japanese]
HOMOPHONES: *coy*

koine *noun*
• "KOY nee"
• the common language of the Greeks from the close of the classical period to the Byzantine era.
• [Greek *koinē* (*dialektos*) common (language)]

kokanee *noun*
• "CO kuh nee"
• a non-migratory form of sockeye salmon found in lakes in western N America.
• [Shuswap]

kokum[1] *noun*
• "KOE k'm"
• (among Cree, Ojibwa, and some Metis peoples) a grandmother.
• [Algonquian]

kokum[2] *noun*
ALSO SPELLED: **kokam**
• "KOE k'm"
• an East Indian tree, *Garcinia indica*, related to the mangosteen, with round purple fruits used to impart an acidic flavour to foods, and the seeds of which yield an oil or butter used in soaps and skin preparations.
• [Hindi]

kolbassa *noun*
• "co buh SAW" or "COO buh saw" or "co BASSA"
• a type of highly seasoned sausage, usu. containing garlic.
• [Russian *kolbasa* or Ukrainian *kovbasa* sausage]
HOMOPHONES: *kubasa*

kolinsky *noun*
• "kuh LIN skee"
• the Siberian mink, *Mustela sibirica*, having a brown coat in winter.
• [Russian *kolinskiĭ* from *Kola* in NW Russia]

kolkhoz *noun*
• "KOLL kozz" or "kulk HOZZ"
• a collective farm in the former USSR.
• [Russian from *kollektivnoe khozyaĭstvo* collective farm]

komatik *noun*
ALSO SPELLED: **qamutik**
• "COMMA tick"
• an Inuit sled consisting of two parallel wooden runners connected by wooden slats, usu. pulled by a dog team or snowmobile.
• [Inuktitut *qamutiq*]

kombu *noun*
• "KOM boo"
• a brown seaweed of the genus *Laminaria*, used in Japanese cooking, esp. as a base for stock.
• [Japanese]

Kongo *noun*
• "KONG go"
• a member of a Bantu-speaking people inhabiting the region of the Congo River in west central Africa.
• [Kikongo]

kookaburra *noun*
• "KOOKA burra" (with "OO" as in *BOOK*)
• any Australian kingfisher of the genus *Dacelo*, esp. *D. novaeguineae*, which makes a strange laughing cry.
• [Wiradhuri *guguburra*]

kopeck *noun*
ALSO SPELLED: **kopek**
• "KOE peck"
• a monetary unit of Russia and some other countries of the former USSR, equal to one-hundredth of a ruble.
• [Russian *kopeĭka* diminutive of *kop'ë* lance (from the figure of Ivan IV bearing a lance instead of a sword in 1535)]

kopje *noun*
ALSO SPELLED: **koppie**
• "COPPY"
• a small hill.
• [Afrikaans *koppie*, Dutch *kopje*, diminutive of *kop* head]
HOMOPHONES: *copy*

kora *noun*
• "KORA"
• a stringed W African instrument resembling a harp.
• [from a W African language]

Korean *noun*
• "kuh REE 'n"
• a native or national of N Korea or S Korea in SE Asia.

korma *noun*
• "KORMA"

• a mildly-spiced Indian curry dish of meat or fish marinated in yogourt or curds.
• [Urdu *ḳormā* from Turkish *kavurma*]

koruna *noun*
• "KOR oo nuh" or "kuh ROONA"
• the chief monetary unit of the Czech Republic and Slovakia, equal to 100 haleru.
• [Czech, = crown]

kosher *adjective*
• "CO shur"
• (of food or premises in which food is sold, cooked, or eaten) fulfilling the requirements of Jewish law.
• [Hebrew *kāšēr* proper]

Kosovar *noun*
• "KOSSA var"
• an esp. Albanian-speaking native or inhabitant of Kosovo, an autonomous province of Serbia.

koto *noun*
• "KOE toe"
• a Japanese musical instrument with 13 long esp. silk strings.
• [Japanese]

koumiss *noun*
ALSO SPELLED: **kumiss**, **kumis**
• "KOO miss"
• a fermented liquor prepared from esp. mare's milk, used by Asian nomads and medicinally.
• [Tartar *kumiz*]

kouprey *noun*
• "KOOP ray"
• a rare grey ox, *Bos sauveli*, native to forests in SE Asia.
• [Cambodian]

kowtow *noun*
• "COW tow" ("TOW" rhymes with *COW*)
• the Chinese custom of kneeling and touching the ground with the forehead in worship or submission.
• [Chinese *ketou* from *ke* knock + *tou* head]

kraal *noun*
• "KRAL"
• a village of huts enclosed by a fence.
• [Afrikaans from Portuguese *corral*]

kraft *noun*
• "CRAFT"
• a kind of strong smooth brown wrapping paper.
• [German from Swedish, = strength]
HOMOPHONES: *craft*

krai *noun*
ALSO SPELLED: **kray**
• "CRY"
• an administrative territory of Russia.
• [Russian, = edge, border]
HOMOPHONES: *cry*

krait *noun*
• "KRITE"
• any venomous snake of the genus *Bungarus* of E Asia.
• [Hindi *karait*]

kremlin *noun*
• "KREM lin"
• a citadel within a Russian town.
• [French, from Russian *Kreml'*, of Tartar origin]

Kremlinology *noun*
• "krem lin OLLA jee"
• the study and analysis of Soviet or Russian policies.
• [as KREMLIN (the Kremlin in Moscow being the seat of Russian government) + *logos* word]
• **Kremlinologist** *noun*

kreplach *plural noun*
• "KREP lack"
• triangular dumplings of noodle dough filled with chopped meat or cheese and served with soup.
• [Yiddish *kreplech* pl. of *krepel* from dialect German *Kräppel* fritter]

kriegspiel *noun*
• "KREEG speel"
• a war game in which blocks representing armies etc. are moved about on maps.
• [German from *Krieg* war + *Spiel* game]

krill *noun*
• "KRILL"
• a small shrimp-like planktonic crustacean of the order Euphausiacea, important as food for fish, and for some whales and seals.
• [Norwegian *kril* tiny fish]

krimmer *noun*
• "KRIMMER"
• a grey or black fur obtained from the wool of young Crimean lambs.
• [German from *Krim* Crimea]

kris *noun*
• "KREECE"
• a Malay or Indonesian dagger with a wavy blade.
• [ultimately from Malay *k(i)rīs*]
HOMOPHONES: *crease*

Krishnaism *noun*
• "KRISHNA izm"
• (in Hinduism) the worship of Krishna as an incarnation of the god Vishnu.

krona *noun*
• "CROW nuh"
• the chief monetary unit of Sweden.
• [Swedish & Icelandic, = 'crown']
HOMOPHONES: *krone*

krone *noun*
• "CROW nuh"
• the chief monetary unit of Denmark and of Norway, equal to one hundred ore.
• [Danish & Norwegian, = 'crown']
HOMOPHONES: *krona*

kroon *noun*
• "KROON"
• the basic monetary unit of Estonia, equal to 100 sents.
• [Estonian, = 'crown']
HOMOPHONES: *croon*

Kru *noun*
ALSO SPELLED: **Kroo**
• "KROO"
• a member of a seafaring people on the coast of Liberia in W Africa.
• [W African]
HOMOPHONES: *crew, cru*

krugerrand *noun*
• "KROOGER rand" or "KROOGER ront"
• a South African gold coin.
• [S. J. P. *Kruger*, S African statesman d.1904, who is depicted on the coin + the gold-producing district of the *Rand* (also called the Witwatersrand)]

krummholz *noun*
• "KRUM holts"
• a region of dwarfed, crooked trees found in alpine regions, esp. just below the timberline.
• [German, 'crooked wood']

krypton *noun*
• "KRIP tawn"
• an inert gaseous element of the noble gas group, forming a small portion of the earth's atmosphere and used in fluorescent lamps etc.
• [Greek *krupton* hidden, neuter adjective from *kruptō* hide]

kryptonite *noun*
• "KRIPTA nite"
• a mythical mineral capable of defeating even the strongest man.
• [a substance in the *Superman* comic book series capable of incapacitating the otherwise invincible superhero]

Kshatriya *noun*
• "k'SHATTRY uh" or "k'SHOTTRY uh"
• a member of the second of the four great Hindu castes, the military caste.
• [Sanskrit from *kshatra* rule]

Ktunaxa *noun*
• "too NOKKA"
• a member of an Aboriginal people living in southeastern BC and northeastern Washington.
• [Ktunaxa, self-designation]

kubasa *noun*
• "coo baw SAW" or "KOO buh saw" or "ko BASSA"
• *Cdn* a garlic sausage of Ukrainian origin.
• [corruption of Ukrainian *kovbasa* sausage]
HOMOPHONES: *kolbassa*

kubie *noun*
• "COOBY"
• *Cdn* (*Alta.*) kubasa, esp. when eaten on a hot dog bun.
• [abbreviation of KUBASA]

kuchen *noun*
• "KOOK h'n"
• a cake topped with sliced fruit and sprinkled with sugar before baking.
• [German, 'cake']

kudlik *noun*
• "KOOD lick"
• an Inuit soapstone seal oil lamp, providing both light and heat.
• [Inuktitut *qulliq*]

kudos *noun*
• "KOO doze" or "KOO dose"
• expressions of praise.
• [Greek]

kudu *noun*
ALSO SPELLED: **koodoo**
• "KOO doo"
• either of two African antelopes, *Tragelaphus strepsiceros* or *T. imberbis*, with white stripes and corkscrew-shaped ridged horns.
• [Xhosa-Kaffir *iqudu*]

kudzu *noun*
• "KUD zoo"
• a quick-growing climbing plant, *Pueraria thunbergiana*, with reddish-purple flowers.
• [Japanese *kuzu*]

Kufic *noun*
ALSO SPELLED: **Cufic**
• "KOOFIC"
• an early angular form of the Arabic alphabet found chiefly in decorative inscriptions.
• [*Cufa*, a city south of Baghdad in Iraq]

kugel *noun*
• "KOO g'll"
• a baked sweet or savoury dish of potatoes or noodles mixed with eggs, cottage cheese, etc. and served as a separate course or as a side dish.
• [Yiddish 'ball' from Middle High German *kugel(e)* ball, globe]

kukri *noun*
• "COOK ree" ("COOK" rhymes with *BOOK*)
• a curved knife broadening towards the point, used by Gurkhas.
• [Nepalese *kukṛī*]
HOMOPHONES: *cookery*

kulak *noun*
• "KOO lack"
• a member of the landowning peasantry in Soviet Russia, persecuted after resisting forced collectivization in 1929.
• [Russian, = fist, tight-fisted person]

kulfi *noun*
• "KULL fee"
• an East Indian ice-cream-like dessert flavoured with nuts, esp. pistachios or almonds, and mangoes, etc.
• [Hindi/Urdu]

kummel *noun*
• "KOOM'll"

• a sweet liqueur flavoured with caraway and cumin seeds.
• [German (as CUMIN)]

kumquat *noun*
• "KUM kwot"
• an orange-like fruit with a sweet rind and acid pulp, used in preserves.
• [Cantonese var. of Mandarin *kin kü* golden orange]

kuna *noun*
• "KOONA"
• the basic monetary unit of Croatia, equal to 100 lipa.
• [Serbo-Croat, literally 'marten' (the fur of the marten was formerly a medium of exchange)]

kundalini *noun*
• "COONDA leeny"
• (in yoga) latent female energy believed to lie coiled at the base of the spine.
• [Sanskrit, *kuṇḍalinī*, lit. 'snake']

Kung *noun*
• "KOONG"
• a member of a San (Bushman) people of the Kalahari Desert in southern Africa, maintaining to some extent a nomadic way of life dependent on hunting and gathering.
• [Khoikhoi *!Kung*, lit. = 'people']

kurchatovium *noun*
• "kurcha TOE vee um"
• a name proposed in the former USSR for the artificial radioactive element of atomic number 104, now called RUTHERFORDIUM.
• [I. V. *Kurchatov*, Russian physicist d.1960]

Kurd *noun*
• "KURD"
• a member of a mainly pastoral Muslim people living chiefly in eastern Turkey, northern Iraq, western Iran, and eastern Syria.
• [Kurdish]
• **Kurdish** *adjective*
HOMOPHONES: *curd*

kurta *noun*
• "KURTA"
• a loose shirt or tunic worn by esp. Hindu men and women.
• [Urdu and Persian]

kurtosis *noun*
• "kur TOE sis"
• the sharpness of the peak of a frequency-distribution curve.
• [modern Latin from Greek *kurtōsis* bulging, from *kurtos* convex]

kurush *noun*
• "kuh ROOSH"
• a monetary unit of Turkey, equal to one-hundredth of a lira.
• [Turkish *kuruş*]

Kutenai *noun*
ALSO SPELLED: **Kootenay**, **Kootenai**
• "COOTA nay"
• a member of an Aboriginal people living in southeastern BC and northeastern Washington.
• [corruption of KTUNAXA]

Kuwaiti *noun*
• "coo WAY tee"
• a native or inhabitant of Kuwait on the NW coast of the Persian Gulf.

kvass *noun*
• "k'VASS"
• (esp. in Russia) a fermented beverage, low in alcohol, made from rye flour or bread with malt.
• [Russian *kvas*]

kvell *verb*
• "k'VELL"
• be extremely pleased or bursting with pride.
• [Yiddish *kveln* be delighted]

kvetch *verb*
• "k'VETCH"
• complain and whine, esp. continually.
• [Yiddish *kvetsh* from Yiddish verb *kvetshn* from German *quetschen* crush, press]
• **kvetching** *noun*
• **kvetchy** *adjective*

Kwa *noun*
• "KWAH"
• the group of related languages, spoken from Ivory Coast to Nigeria, which includes Ibo and Yoruba.
• [Kwa]
HOMOPHONES: *qua*

kwacha *noun*
• "KWOTCH uh"
• the chief monetary unit of Zambia and Malawi, equal to 100 ngwee in Zambia and 100 tambala in Malawi.
• [Bantu, = dawn]

Kwagiulth *noun*
• "kwah GEE oolt" (with "G" as in *GEEK*)
• a member of an Aboriginal people living in parts of coastal BC and northern Vancouver Island.
• [Kwagiulth *K'ʷágul*]

Kwakiutl *noun*
• "kwocky OOT'll"
• = KWAGIULTH.
• [corruption of KWAGIULTH]

Kwakwala *noun*
• "kwah KWOLLA"
• the Wakashan language of the Kwakwaka'wakw and Kwagiulth.
• [Kwakwala]

Kwanza *noun*
ALSO SPELLED: **Kwanzaa**
• "KWONZA"
• a festival observed from 26 Dec. to 1 Jan. in celebration of black cultural heritage.
• [Swahili *matunda ya kwanza* 'first fruits']

kwashiorkor *noun*
- "kwoshy OR core"
- a form of malnutrition caused by a severe dietary protein deficiency, esp. in young children in the tropics.
- [local name in Ghana]

kyanite *noun*
- "KYE a nite"
- a crystalline mineral of aluminum silicate, usu. blue, greenish, or colourless.
- [Greek *kuanos* dark blue + *lithos* stone]

kyat *noun*
- "kee AT"
- the chief monetary unit of Burma (Myanmar).
- [Burmese]

kylin *noun*
- "KEELIN"
- a mythical composite animal figured on Chinese and Japanese ceramics.
- [Chinese *qilin* from *qi* male + *lin* female]

kymograph *noun*
- "KIME a graff"
- an instrument for recording variations in pressure, e.g. in sound waves or in blood within blood vessels, by the trace of a stylus on a rotating cylinder.
- [Greek *kuma* wave + *graphia* writing]
- **kymographic** *adjective*

kyphosis *noun*
- "kye FOE sis"
- excessive outward curvature of the spine, causing hunching of the back.
- [modern Latin from Greek *kuphōsis* from *kuphos* bent]
- **kyphotic** *adjective* "kye FOTTIC"

Kyrgyz *noun*
ALSO SPELLED: **Kirghiz**
- "keer GIZZ" or "KUR gizz" (with "G" as in *GIVE*)
- a member of a traditionally nomadic Sunni Muslim Mongol people living chiefly in Kyrgyzstan but also in Tajikistan, Uzbekistan, and parts of China and Afghanistan.
- [Kyrgyz]

Kyrie *noun*
- "KEERY ay"
- a short repeated invocation (in Greek or translated) beginning with the words 'Lord, have mercy' used in many Christian liturgies, esp. at the beginning of the Eucharist or as a response in a litany.
- [Greek, 'Lord, have mercy']

laager *noun*
- "LOGGER"
- a camp or encampment, originally formed by a circle of wagons.
- [Afrikaans from Dutch *leger* camp, related to 'lair']

HOMOPHONES: *lager, logger*

laari *noun*
- "LAR ee"
- a monetary unit of the Maldives, equal to one-hundredth of a rufiyaa.
- [Persian]

Labanotation *noun*
- "LABBA no tay sh'n"
- a system of dance notation devised by the Hungarian-born dancer and choreographer Rudolf von Laban, born Rudolf Laban von Varlja (1879–1958).
- [*Laban* + 'notation' from Latin *nota* mark]

labarum *noun*
- "LABBA rum"
- a symbolic banner.
- [Late Latin: origin unknown]

labdanum *noun*
- "LABDA num"
- a gum resin from plants of the genus *Cistus*, used in perfumery etc.
- [Latin from Greek *ladanon* from *lēdon* mastic]

labellum *noun*
- "luh BELLUM"
- each of a pair of lobes at the tip of the proboscis in some insects.
- [Latin, diminutive of *labrum* lip]

labial *adjective*
- "LAY bee 'll"
- of the lips.
- [medieval Latin *labialis* from Latin *labia* lips]
- **labialize** *verb* (also esp. *Brit.* **-ise**)
- **labially** *adverb*

labiate *noun*
- "LAY bee ut"
- any plant of the family Labiatae, including mint and rosemary, having square stems and a corolla or calyx divided into two parts suggesting lips.
- [modern Latin *labiatus* (as LABIAL)]

labile *adjective*
- "LAY bile" or "LAY bill"
- (of a compound) liable to displacement or change esp. if an atom or group is easily replaced by other atoms or groups.
- [Late Latin *labilis* from *labi* to fall]
- **lability** *noun*

labiodental *adjective*
- "lay bee oh DEN t'll"
- (of a sound) made with the lips and teeth, e.g. *f* and *v*.
- [Latin *labia* lips + *dens dentis* tooth]

labiovelar *adjective*
- "lay bee oh VEELER"
- (of a sound) made with the lips and soft palate, e.g. *w*.
- [Latin *labia* lips + VELAR]

laboratory *noun*
- "LABBRA tory" or "luh BORA tory"
- a room or building fitted out for scientific experiments, research, teaching, or the manufacture of drugs and chemicals.
- [medieval Latin *laboratorium* from Latin *laborare* work]

laborious *adjective*
- "luh BORY us"
- needing hard work or toil.
- [Latin *laboriosus* from *labor* work]
- **laboriously** *adverb*
- **laboriousness** *noun*

Labrador *noun*
- "LAB ruh dore"
- a breed of retriever with a black or golden coat often used as a gun dog or as a guide for a blind person.
- [from *Labrador* in E Canada]

Labradorian *noun*
- "lab ruh DORY 'n"
- a native or inhabitant of Labrador.

labradorite *noun*
- "lab ruh DORE ite"
- a kind of plagioclase feldspar, often showing iridescence from internal reflective planes.
- [*Labrador* in E Canada + *lithos* stone]

labret *noun*
- "LAB rit"
- a piece of shell, bone, etc., inserted in the lip as an ornament.
- [as LABRUM]

labrum *noun*
- "LAY brum"
- the upper lip in the mouthparts of an insect.
- [Latin, = lip: related to LABIAL]

labrusca *noun*
- "luh BROOSKA" (with "OO" as in *BOOK*)
- a wild vine, *Vitis labrusca*, of eastern N America, from which many cultivated varieties have been derived.
- [Latin *labrusca*, a wild vine]

laburnum *noun*
- "luh BURN um"
- any small tree of the genus *Laburnum* with racemes of golden flowers yielding poisonous seeds.
- [Latin]

labyrinth *noun*
- "LABBER inth"
- a complicated irregular network of passages or paths etc.; a maze.
- [ultimately from Greek *laburinthos*]
- **labyrinthian** *adjective*
- **labyrinthine** *adjective* "labber INTH ine"

lac *noun*
- "LACK"
- a resinous substance secreted as a protective covering by an Asian scale insect, *Laccifer lacca*, living in trees, and used to make varnish and shellac.
- [ultimately from Hindi *lākh* from Prakrit *lakkha* from Sanskrit *lākṣā*]

HOMOPHONES: *lack*, *lakh*

Lacanian *adjective*
- "luh CANNY 'n"
- of or relating to the French psychoanalyst J. Lacan (d.1981).

laccolith *noun*
- "LACKA lith"
- a lens-shaped intrusion of igneous rock which thrusts the overlying strata into a dome.
- [Greek *lakkos* reservoir + *lithos* stone]

lacerate *verb*
- "LASSER ate"
- tear or cut (esp. flesh or tissue).
- [Latin *lacerare* from *lacer* torn]
- **lacerated** *adjective*
- **laceration** *noun*

lacertian *noun*
- "luh SURTY 'n"
- any reptile of the suborder Lacertilia, including lizards.
- [Latin *lacerta* lizard]

laches *noun*
- "LATCH iz" or "LAY chiz"
- unjustifiable, inexcusable, or unreasonable delay in performing a legal duty, asserting a right, claiming a privilege, etc.
- [Anglo-French *laches(se)*, Old French *laschesse* from *lasche*, ultimately from Latin *laxus* loose]

lachrymose *adjective*
- "LACKRA mose" ("MOSE" rhymes with *GROSS*)
- given to weeping; tearful.
- [Latin *lacrimosus* from *lacrima* tear]
- **lachrymosely** *adverb*
- **lachrymosity** *noun* "lackry MOSSA tee"

laciniate *adjective*
- "luh SINNY it"
- divided into deep narrow irregular segments; fringed.
- [Latin *lacinia* flap of a garment]
- **laciniation** *noun*

lackadaisical *adjective*
- "lacka DAZE a k'll"
- unenthusiastic, lacking vigour and determination.
- [archaic *lackaday*, *-daisy* (interj.), from 'alack' (prob. from 'ah' + 'lack')]
- **lackadaisically** *adverb*
- **lackadaisicalness** *noun*

lackey *noun*
- "LACKY"
- *derogatory* a servile political follower.
- [French *laquais*, obsolete *alaquais* from Catalan *alacay* = Spanish ALCALDE]

lacklustre *adjective*

ALSO SPELLED: esp. *US* **lackluster**
- "LACK luster"
- lacking in vitality, force, or conviction.
- ['lack' + LUSTRE]

Lacombian *noun*
- "la KOME bee 'n"
- a resident of Lacombe, Alta.

laconic *adjective*
- "luh CONNIC"
- (of a style of speech or writing) brief; concise; terse.
- [Latin from Greek *Lakōnikos* from *Lakōn* Spartan, the Spartans being known for their terse speech]
- **laconically** *adverb*
- **laconicism** *noun* "luh CONNA sizm"

lacquer *noun*
- "LACKER"
- a sometimes coloured varnish made of shellac dissolved in alcohol, or of synthetic substances, that dries to form a hard protective coating for wood, brass, etc.
- [obsolete French *lacre* sealing wax, from unexplained var. of Portuguese *laca* LAC]
- **lacquered** *adjective*

lacquerware *noun*
- "LACKER ware"
- decorative articles made of wood coated with

lacquer, often inlaid with ivory, mother-of-pearl, etc.
• [LACQUER + WARE]

lacrimal *adjective*
ALSO SPELLED: **lachrymal**
• "LACK ruh m'll"
• concerned in the secretion of tears.
• [medieval Latin *lachrymalis* from Latin *lacrima* tear]

lacrimation *noun*
• "lack ruh MAY sh'n"
• the flow of tears.
• [Latin *lacrimatio* from *lacrimare* weep (as LACRIMAL)]

lacrosse *noun*
• "luh CROSS"
• a game, originally played by N American Indians, in which a ball is thrown, carried and caught with a lacrosse stick.
• [French from *la* the + CROSSE]

lactase *noun*
• "LACK tace"
• any of a group of enzymes which catalyze the hydrolysis of lactose to glucose and galactose.
• [French from *lactose* LACTOSE]

lactate *verb*
• "LACK tate"
• (of mammals) secrete milk.
• [Latin *lactare* suckle, from *lac lactis* milk]
• **lactating** *adjective*
• **lactation** *noun* "lack TAY sh'n"

lacteal *adjective*
• "LACKTY 'll"
• of, pertaining to, consisting of, or resembling milk.
• [Latin *lacteus* from *lac lactis* milk]

lactic *adjective*
• "LACK tic"
• of, relating to, or obtained from milk.
• [Latin *lac lactis* milk]

lactiferous *adjective*
• "lack TIFFER us"
• yielding milk or milky fluid.
• [Late Latin *lactifer* (as LACTIC + *-fer* producing, from *ferre* bear)]

lactitol *noun*
• "LACK tuh tawl"
• an artificial sweetener derived from lactulose.
• [Latin *lac lactis* milk + ALCOHOL]

lactobacillus *noun*
• "lacto buh SILL us"
• any Gram-positive rod-shaped bacterium of the genus *Lactobacillus*, producing lactic acid from the fermentation of carbohydrates.
• [Latin *lac lactis* milk + BACILLUS]

lactometer *noun*
• "lack TOMMA tur"
• an instrument for testing the relative density of milk.
• [Latin *lac lactis* milk + Greek *metron* measure]

lactone *noun*
• "LACK tone"
• any of a class of cyclic esters formed by the elimination of water from a hydroxy-carboxylic acid.
• [German *Lacton*]

lactoprotein *noun*
• "lack toe PRO teen"
• a protein which occurs normally in milk.
• [Latin *lac lactis* milk + PROTEIN]

lactose *noun*
• "LACK tose" (rhymes with *GROSS*)
• a sugar that occurs in milk, and is less sweet than sucrose.
• [Latin *lac lactis* milk + GLUCOSE]

lactulose *noun*
• "LACK tyoo lose" (rhymes with *GROSS*)
• a disaccharide of galactose and fructose which is formed in heated milk by the isomerization of lactose.
• [Latin *lac lactis* milk + GLUCOSE]

lacuna *noun*
• "luh KYOO nuh"
• a hiatus, blank, or gap.
• [Latin, = pool, from *lacus* lake]
• **lacunar** *adjective*

lacustrine *adjective*
• "luh KUSS trine"
• of or relating to lakes.
• [Latin *lacus* lake, after *palustris* marshy]

lade *verb*
• "LADE"
• put cargo on board (a ship).
• [Old English *hladan*]
• **lading** *noun*
HOMOPHONES: *laid*

laden *adjective*
• "LAY d'n"
• having a high proportion of the specified quality, substance, etc.
• [as LADE]

Ladin *noun*
• "luh DEEN"
• the Rhaeto-Romance dialect of the Engadine area of SE Switzerland and the adjoining areas of N Italy.
• [Romansh, from Latin *latinus* Latin]

ladino *noun*
• "luh DEENO"
• a large variety of white clover (*Trifolium repens*) native to Italy and cultivated for fodder.
• [Italian]
HOMOPHONES: *Latino*

ladle *noun*
• "LAY d'll"
• a long-handled spoon with a cup-shaped bowl for serving or transferring liquids.

- [Old English *hlædel* from *hladan* LADE]
- **ladleful** *noun*

lagan *noun*
- "LAG'n"
- goods or wreckage lying on the bed of the sea, sometimes with a marking buoy etc. for later retrieval.
- [Old French, perhaps of Scandinavian origin]

lager *noun*
- "LOGGER"
- a kind of beer, effervescent and light in colour and body.
- [German *Lagerbier* beer brewed for keeping, from *Lager* store]

HOMOPHONES: *laager, logger*

laggard *noun*
- "LAG'rd"
- a dawdler; a person who lags behind.
- [from 'lag', originally = hindmost person, hang back: perhaps from a fanciful distortion of 'last' in a children's game (*fog, seg, lag,* = 1st, 2nd, last, in dialect)]
- **laggardly** *adjective*
- **laggardness** *noun*

lagniappe *noun*
- "lan YAP"
- something given as a bonus or gratuity.
- [Louisiana French, from Spanish *la ñapa*]

lagomorph *noun*
- "LAGGA morf"
- any mammal of the order Lagomorpha, including hares and rabbits.
- [Greek *lagōs* hare + *morphē* form]

Lagrangian *adjective*
- "luh GRONZHY 'n"
- designating each of five points in the plane of orbit of one body around another, e.g. the moon around the earth, at which a small third body can remain stationary with respect to both.
- [J. L. *Lagrange*, Italian-French mathematician d.1813]

lahal *noun*
- "LUH hawl" or "LUH hal"
- a game common amongst Pacific Northwest Aboriginal peoples in which teams attempt to win carved sticks by guessing in which hands of their opponents four bones are concealed. Singing, drumming, and often gambling accompany the game.
- [Pacific Northwest languages]

lahar *noun*
- "LAW har"
- a mudflow composed mainly of volcanic debris.
- [Javanese]

laic *adjective*
- "LAY ick"
- non-clerical.
- [Late Latin from Greek *laïkos* from *laos* people]
- **laicism** *noun* "LAY a sizm"

laicize *verb*

ALSO SPELLED: esp. *Brit.* **-ise**
- "LAY a size"
- make (an office etc.) tenable by lay people.
- [as LAIC]
- **laicization** *noun* (also esp. *Brit.* **-isation**)

laity *noun*
- "LAY a tee"
- lay people, as distinct from the clergy.
- [as LAIC]

lakh *noun*

ALSO SPELLED: **lac**
- "LACK" or "LOCK"
- a hundred thousand (rupees etc.).
- [Hindustani *lākh* from Sanskrit *lakṣa*]

HOMOPHONES: *lock, loch, lac, lack*

Lakota *noun*
- "luh CO tuh"
- a member of an Aboriginal people of western South Dakota.
- [Lakota *lakhóta* allies]

Lallans *noun*
- "LALL 'nz"
- a Lowland Scots dialect, esp. as a literary language.
- [var. of 'lowland']

lama *noun*
- "LOMMA" or "LAMMA"
- a Tibetan or Mongolian Buddhist monk.
- [Tibetan *blama* (with silent *b*)]

HOMOPHONES: *llama*

Lamaism *noun*
- "LOMMA izm" or "LAMMA izm"
- the system of doctrine and observances inculcated and maintained by lamas; Tibetan Buddhism.
- [as LAMA]
- **Lamaist** *noun*

Lamarckism *noun*
- "luh MARK izm"
- the theory of evolution devised by the French naturalist J. B. de Lamarck (d.1829), based on the inheritance of acquired characteristics.
- **Lamarckian** *noun*

lamasery *noun*
- "LOMMA serry" or "LAMMA serry"
- a monastery of lamas.
- [French *lamaserie* from *lama* LAMA]

Lamaze *noun*
- "luh MOZZ"
- designating a method of childbirth which emphasizes the use of psychological and physical preparation and breathing routines to control pain and minimize the need for drugs.
- [F. *Lamaze*, French physician d.1957, who advocated it]

lambada *noun*
- "lum BODDA"
- a fast erotic Brazilian dance which became internationally popular for a brief period in the late 1980s.
- [Portuguese, = a beating]

lambaste *verb*
- "lam BAYST"
- thrash; beat.
- ['lam' (beat) + BASTE]

lambda *noun*
- "LAM duh"
- the eleventh letter of the Greek alphabet (Λ, λ).
- [Greek *la(m)bda*]

lambent *adjective*
- "LAM b'nt"
- (of a flame or a light) playing on a surface with a soft radiance but without burning.
- [Latin *lambere lambent-* lick]
- **lambency** *noun*
- **lambently** *adverb*

lambert *noun*
- "LAM burt"
- a former unit of luminance, equal to the emission or reflection of one lumen per square centimetre.
- [J. H. *Lambert*, German physicist d.1777]

lambrequin *noun*
- "LAM bruh kin" or "LAM bur kin"
- a short piece of drapery hung over the top of a door or a window or draped on a mantelpiece.
- [French from Dutch (unrecorded) *lamperkin*, diminutive of *lamper* veil]

lamé *noun*
- "lam AY" or "LAM ay"
- a fabric with gold or silver threads interwoven.
- [French, ultimately from Latin *lamina* layer]

lamella *noun*
- "luh MELLA"
- a thin layer, membrane, scale, or plate-like tissue or part, esp. in bone tissue.
- [Latin, diminutive of *lamina*: see LAMINA]
- **lamellar** *adjective*
- **lamellate** *adjective* "LAMMA late"
- **lamellated** *adjective*

lamellibranch *noun*
- "luh MELLA brank"
- any of a group of aquatic molluscs of the class Bivalvia, with laterally compressed bodies enclosed within two hinged shells, e.g. oysters, mussels, etc.
- [LAMELLA + Greek *bragkhia* gills]

lamellicorn *noun*
- "luh MELLA corn"
- the former name for SCARABAEOID.
- [modern Latin *lamellicornis* from Latin *lamella* (see LAMELLA) + *cornu* horn]

lamina *noun*
- "LAMMA nuh"
- a thin plate or scale, e.g. of bone, stratified rock, or vegetable tissue.
- [Latin, = 'layer']
- **laminar** *adjective*
- **laminose** *adjective*

laminate *verb*
- "LAMMA nate"
- overlay with a thin plastic layer, metal plates, etc.
- [as LAMINA]
- **lamination** *noun*
- **laminator** *noun*

laminitis *noun*
- "lamma NITE iss"
- inflammation of the laminae of the hoof in horses and other animals.
- [as LAMINA + Greek *-itis*, forming feminine of adjectives in *-itēs* (with *nosos* 'disease' implied)]

Lammas *noun*
- "LAM us"
- the first day of August, formerly observed in England as harvest festival.
- [Old English *hlāfmæsse* (as 'loaf', 'mass')]

lammergeier *noun*
ALSO SPELLED: **lammergeyer**
- "LAMMER guy ur"
- a large Eurasian vulture, *Gypaetus barbatus*, with a very large wingspan (often of 3 m) and dark beard-like feathers on either side of its beak.
- [German *Lämmergeier*, from *Lämmer* lambs + *Geier* vulture]

lamppost *noun*
- "LAMP post"
- a tall post supporting a street light.
- ['lamp' + 'post']

lamprey *noun*
- "LAM pree"
- any eel-like aquatic vertebrate of the family Petromyzonidae, without scales, paired fins, or jaws, but having a sucker mouth with horny teeth and a rough tongue.
- [Old French *lampreie* from medieval Latin *lampreda*: compare Late Latin *lampetra* perhaps from Latin *lambere* lick + *petra* stone]

lanai *noun*
- "luh NYE"
- a porch or veranda, originally in Hawaii.
- [Hawaiian]

Lancastrian *noun*
- "lan CASS tree 'n"
- a follower of the House of Lancaster or of the Red Rose party supporting it in the Wars of the Roses in 15th-century England.

lancelet *noun*
- "LANCE lit"
- any small non-vertebrate fishlike chordate of

the family Branchiostomidae, that burrows in sand.
• [Old French *lancier* from Latin *lancea* + diminutive ending '-let', with reference to its thin form]

lanceolate *adjective*
• "LANCY a lit"
• shaped like the head of a lance, narrow and tapering at each end.
• [Late Latin *lanceolatus* from *lanceola* diminutive of *lancea* lance]

lancet *noun*
• "LANCE it"
• a small broad two-edged surgical knife with a sharp point.
• [Old French *lancette* (as LANCELET)]
• **lanceted** *adjective*

Land *noun*
• "LONT"
• a state of Germany or Austria.
• [German]

landau *noun*
• "LAN dow" ("DOW" rhymes with *HOW*)
• a four-wheeled horse-drawn carriage, with folding front and rear hoods enabling it to travel open, half-open, or closed.
• [*Landau* near Karlsruhe in Germany, where it was first made]

ländler *noun*
• "LEND lur"
• an Austrian dance in triple time, a precursor of the waltz.
• [German, from *Landl* Upper Austria]

langlauf *noun*
• "LANG louf" (with "OU" as in *LOUD*)
• cross-country skiing; a cross-country skiing race.
• [German, = long run]

langouste *noun*
• "long GOOST"
• a spiny lobster.
• [French, from Provençal *langosta* from Latin *locusta* grasshopper]

langoustine *noun*
• "long goo STEEN"
• a small European lobster, *Nephrops norvegicus*.
• [French, as LANGOUSTE]

language *noun*
• "LANG gwidge"
• the method of human communication, either spoken or written, consisting of the use of words in an agreed way.
• [Old French *langage*, ultimately from Latin *lingua* tongue]

languid *adjective*
• "LANG gwid"
• moving slowly and involving little physical effort or emotion.
• [French *languide* or Latin *languidus* (as LANGUISH)]
• **languidly** *adverb*
• **languidness** *noun*

languish *verb*
• "LANG gwish"
• be or grow feeble; lose or lack vitality.
• [Old French *languir*, ultimately from Latin *languēre*]

languor *noun*
• "LANG gur"
• the state or feeling, often pleasant, of being lazy and lacking energy.
• [Old French from Latin *languor -oris* (as LANGUISH)]
• **languorous** *adjective*
• **languorously** *adverb*

langur *noun*
• "lung GOOR"
• any of various Asian long-tailed monkeys esp. of the genus *Presbytis*.
• [Hindi]

lanolin *noun*
• "LANNA lin"
• a fat found naturally on sheep's wool and used purified for cosmetics etc.
• [German from Latin *lana* wool + *oleum* oil]

lansquenet *noun*
• "LANCE kuh nit"
• a card game of German origin.
• [French from German *Landsknecht* (*Land* land, *Knecht* soldier, from Old High German *kneht* boy, youth, hero)]

lantana *noun*
• "lan TAY nuh" or "lan TANNA" or "lan TONNA"
• any evergreen shrub of the genus *Lantana*, with usu. yellow or orange flowers.
• [modern Latin]

lanthanide *noun*
• "LANTHA nide"
• any of a series of 15 metallic elements from lanthanum (at. no.: 57) to lutetium (at. no.: 71), inclusive, in the periodic table, having similar chemical properties.
• [German *Lanthanid* (as LANTHANUM)]

lanthanum *noun*
• "LANTHA num"
• a silvery metallic element which is used in the manufacture of alloys and catalysts.
• [Greek *lanthanō* escape notice, from having remained undetected in cerium oxide]

lanugo *noun*
• "luh NEW go"
• fine soft hair, esp. that which covers the body and limbs of a human fetus.
• [Latin, = 'down', from *lana* wool]

lanyard *noun*
• "LAN yurd" or "LAN yard"
• a cord hanging around the neck or looped

around the shoulder, to which a knife, a whistle, etc., may be attached.
• [Old French *laniere*, *lasniere*: assimilated to 'yard']

Laodicean *adjective*
• "lay oh duh SEE 'n"
• lukewarm or half-hearted, esp. in religion or politics.
• [Latin *Laodicea* in Asia Minor (with reference to the early Christians there)]

Laotian *noun*
• "LOW sh'n" ("LOW" rhymes with *HOW*) or "luh OH sh'n"
• a native or national of Laos in SE Asia.

laparoscope *noun*
• "LAPPA ruh scope"
• a fibre optic instrument inserted through the abdominal wall to give a view of the organs in the abdomen.
• [Greek *lapara* flank + *skopos* target, from *skeptomai* look at]
• **laparoscopic** *adjective*
• **laparoscopy** *noun* "lappa ROSCA pee"

laparotomy *noun*
• "lappa ROTTA mee"
• a surgical incision into the abdominal cavity for exploration or diagnosis.
• [Greek *lapara* flank + *-tomia* cutting, from *temnō* cut]

lapel *noun*
• "luh PELL"
• the part of the front of a coat, jacket, etc., which is folded over towards either shoulder.
• [Old English *læppa* fold, flap]
• **lapelled** *adjective*

lapidary *adjective*
• "LAPPA derry"
• concerned with stone or stones.
• [Latin *lapidarius* from *lapis -idis* stone]

lapilli *plural noun*
• "luh PILL eye"
• stone fragments ejected from volcanoes.
• [Italian from Latin, pl. diminutive of *lapis* stone]

Lapp *noun*
• "LAP"
• a member of the indigenous population of the extreme north of Scandinavia.
• [Swedish *Lapp*, perhaps originally a term of contempt: compare Middle High German *lappe* simpleton]
• **Lappish** *adjective*
HOMOPHONES: *lap*

lappet *noun*
• "LAP it"
• a small flap or fold of a garment etc.
• [Old English *læppa* fold, flap]
• **lappeted** *adjective*

lapstrake *noun*
• "LAP strake"
• a boat having external planks overlapping downwards and secured with clinched copper nails.
• ['lap' + STRAKE]

larboard *noun*
• "LAR burd"
• the left-hand side (looking forward) of a ship, boat, or aircraft.
• [Middle English *lade-*, *ladde-*, *lathe-* (perhaps = LADE + BOARD): later assimilated to *starboard*]

larceny *noun*
• "LARCE 'n ee"
• the theft of personal property.
• [Old French *larcin* from Latin *latrocinium* from *latro* robber, mercenary, from Greek *latreus*]
• **larcenist** *noun*
• **larcenous** *adjective*
• **larcenously** *adverb*

lardon *noun*
• "LAR d'n"
• a strip of fat bacon used to lard meat.
• [French *lardon* from Old French *lard* bacon, from Latin *lardum*, *laridum*, related to Greek *larinos* fat]

lares *plural noun*
• "LARE eez"
• gods worshipped, together with the penates, by households in ancient Rome.
• [Latin]

largesse *noun*
ALSO SPELLED: **largess**
• "lar JESS" or "lar ZHESS"
• generosity in bestowing money or gifts upon others.
• [Old French *largesse*, ultimately from Latin *largus* copious]

larghetto *adverb*
• "lar GETTO" (with "G" as in *GET*)
• in a fairly slow tempo.
• [Italian, diminutive of *largo* broad]

lari *noun*
• "LAR ee"
• a monetary unit of Georgia, equal to one hundred tetri.
• [Georgian]

lariat *noun*
• "LERRY it"
• a lasso.
• [Spanish *la reata* from *reatar* tie again (*re-* again, Latin *aptare* adjust from *aptus* apt, fit)]

larigan *noun*
ALSO SPELLED: **larrigan**
• "LAR a g'n" or "LARE a g'n"
• a tanned leather moccasin boot almost reaching the knee.
• [origin unknown]

larrikin *noun*
- "LAR a kin"
- a hooligan.
- [also English dialect: perhaps from the name *Larry* (pet form of *Lawrence*)]

larrup *verb*
- "LARE up"
- thrash.
- [dialect: perhaps from 'lather']

larvicide *noun*
- "LARVA side"
- a preparation adapted to kill larvae.
- ['larva' (Latin, = ghost, mask) + *-cida, -cidium* from *caedere* kill]
- **larvicidal** *adjective*

laryngectomy *noun*
- "lare in JECTA mee"
- surgical removal of the larynx.
- [LARYNX + Greek *ektomē* excision, from *ek* out + *temnō* cut]

laryngitis *noun*
- "lare in JITE us"
- inflammation of the larynx.
- [as LARYNX + Greek *-itis*, forming feminine of adjectives in *-itēs* (with *nosos* 'disease' implied)]

laryngology *noun*
- "lare ing GOLLA jee"
- the branch of medicine that deals with the larynx.
- [as LARYNX + *logos* word]
- **laryngologist** *noun*

laryngoscope *noun*
- "luh RING guh scope"
- an instrument for examining the larynx, or for inserting a tube through it.
- [as LARYNX + Greek *skopos* target, from *skeptomai* look at]

laryngotomy *noun*
- "lare ing GOTTA mee"
- a surgical incision of the larynx, esp. to provide an air passage when breathing is obstructed.
- [as LARYNX + Greek *-tomia* cutting, from *temnō* cut]

larynx *noun*
- "LARE inx"
- the hollow muscular organ forming an air passage to the lungs and holding the vocal cords in humans and other mammals; the voice box.
- [modern Latin from Greek *larugx -ggos*]
- **laryngeal** *adjective* "luh RINJY 'll"

lasagna *noun*
ALSO SPELLED: **lasagne**
- "luh ZON yuh"
- pasta in the form of wide ribbons, usu. with ruffled edges.
- [Italian, from Latin *lasanum* cooking pot]

lascar *noun*
- "LASKER"
- a sailor from India or SE Asia.
- [ultimately from Urdu & Persian *laškar* army]

lascivious *adjective*
- "luh SIVVY us"
- lustful.
- [Late Latin *lasciviosus* from Latin *lascivia* lustfulness, from *lascivus* sportive, wanton]
- **lasciviously** *adverb*
- **lasciviousness** *noun*

lase *verb*
- "LAZE"
- function as or in a laser.
- [back-formation from LASER]

HOMOPHONES: *laze*

laser *noun*
- "LAY zur"
- a device that generates an intense beam of coherent monochromatic light (or other electromagnetic radiation) by stimulated emission from excited atoms or molecules. Lasers are used in drilling and cutting, alignment and guidance, surgery, recording and playing compact discs, etc.
- [*l*ight *a*mplification by *s*timulated *e*mission of *r*adiation]

lassi *noun*
- "LASSY"
- a drink, originally from the Indian subcontinent, made from a buttermilk or yogourt base with water.
- [Hindi]

HOMOPHONES: *lassie*

lassitude *noun*
- "LASSA tude"
- languor, weariness.
- [French *lassitude* or Latin *lassitudo* from *lassus* tired]

lasso *noun*
- "la SOO" or "LASS oh"
- a rope with a noose at one end, used esp. in N America for catching cattle etc.
- [Spanish *lazo* lace]
- **lassoer** *noun*

latent *adjective*
- "LAY t'nt"
- concealed, dormant.
- [Latin *latēre latent-* be hidden]
- **latency** *noun*
- **latently** *adverb*

lateral *adjective*
- "LATTER'll"
- of, at, towards, or from the side or sides.
- [Latin *lateralis* from *latus lateris* side]
- **laterally** *adverb*

laterite *noun*
- "LATTER ite"
- a red or yellow ferruginous clay, friable and hardening in air, used for making roads in the tropics.

• [Latin *later* brick + Greek *lithos* stone]
• **lateritic** *adjective* "latter ITTIC"

latex *noun*
• "LAY tex"
• a milky fluid of mixed composition found in various plants and trees, esp. the rubber tree, and used for commercial purposes.
• [Latin, = liquid]

lathe *noun*
• "LATHE" (rhymes with *BATHE*)
• a machine for shaping wood, metal, etc., by means of a rotating drive which turns the piece being worked on against changeable cutting tools.
• [prob. related to Old Danish *lad* structure, frame, from Old Norse *hlath*, related to *hlatha* LADE]

lathi *noun*
• "LATTY"
• (in India) a long heavy iron-bound bamboo stick used as a weapon, esp. by police.
• [Hindi *lāṭhī*]
HOMOPHONES: *laddie*

latitude *noun*
• "LATTA tude"
• the angular distance on its meridian of any place on the earth's surface from the equator, expressed in degrees and minutes north or south of the equator.
• [Middle English, = breadth, from Latin *latitudo -dinis* from *latus* broad]
• **latitudinal** *adjective* "latta TUDE 'n 'll"
• **latitudinally** *adverb*

latitudinarian *adjective*
• "latta tude 'n AIRY 'n"
• allowing latitude esp. in religion; showing no preference among varying creeds and forms of worship.
• [as LATITUDE]
• **latitudinarianism** *noun*

latke *noun*
• "LAT kuh"
• (in Jewish cooking) a pancake made with grated potato.
• [Yiddish from Russian *latka* earthenware cooking vessel, (dialect) dish cooked in such a vessel]

latrine *noun*
• "luh TREEN"
• a communal lavatory, esp. in a camp, barracks, etc.
• [French from Latin *latrina*, shortening of *lavatrina* from *lavare* wash]

latte *noun*
• "LAT ay" or "LOT ay"
• a drink made by adding a shot of espresso coffee to a cup of frothy hot milk.
• [Italian, abbreviation of *caffe latte*, lit. = 'coffee milk']

latten *noun*
• "LAT'n"
• an alloy of copper and zinc, often rolled into sheets, and formerly used for monumental brasses and church articles.
• [Old French *laton*, *leiton* brass]
HOMOPHONES: *Latin*

lattice *noun*
• "LAT iss"
• a structure of crossed laths or bars with spaces between, used as a screen, fence, etc.
• [Old French *lattis* from *latte* lath, from West Germanic]
• **latticed** *adjective*

latticework *noun*
• "LAT iss wurk"
• laths arranged in lattice formation.
• [as LATTICE + 'work']

laud *verb*
• "LOD"
• praise or extol.
• [Latin *laudare*, from Latin *laus laudis* praise]
• **laudability** *noun*
• **laudable** *adjective* "LOD a bull"
• **laudably** *adverb*
• **laudatory** *adjective*

laudanum *noun*
• "LODDA num"
• a solution containing morphine and prepared from opium, formerly used as a narcotic painkiller.
• [modern Latin, the name given by Swiss physician Paracelsus (d.1541) to a costly medicament, later applied to preparations containing opium: perhaps var. of LABDANUM]

launcher *noun*
• "LON chur"
• a structure or device to hold a rocket, missile, etc. during launching.
• [Anglo-French *launcher* from Latin *lancea* lance]

launder *verb*
• "LON dur"
• wash and dry (clothes, bed or table linen, etc.).
• [Middle English *launder* (n.) washer of linen, contraction of *lavander* from Old French *lavandier*, ultimately from Latin *lavanda* things to be washed, neuter pl. gerundive of *lavare* wash]
• **launderer** *noun*
• **laundress** *noun*

launderette *noun*
ALSO SPELLED: **laundrette**
• "lon DRET"
• a laundromat.
• [as LAUNDER]

laundromat *noun*
• "LONDRA mat"
• an establishment with coin-operated washing machines and dryers for public use.

• [from LAUNDRY + *-mat*, suffix designating establishments using automatic machines]

laundry *noun*
• "LON dree"
• clothes or linen for laundering or newly laundered.
• [contraction of *lavendry* (from Old French *lavanderie*), influenced by LAUNDER]
• **laundryman** *noun*
• **laundrywoman** *noun*

laureate *noun*
• "LORRY it"
• a person who is honoured for outstanding creative or intellectual achievement.
• [Latin *laureatus* from *laurea* laurel wreath, from *laurus* laurel]
• **laureateship** *noun*

laurel *noun*
• "LORE 'll"
• a Mediterranean tree, *Laurus nobilis*, having deep green leaves and purple berries.
• [Old French *lorier* from Provençal *laurier* from Latin *laurus*]

Laurentian *adjective*
• "luh REN sh'n"
• designating or pertaining to a geological region in eastern Canada of Precambrian age or the period in which it was formed, esp. designating a group of granites found northwest of the St. Lawrence River.
• [Latin *Laurentius* Laurence, from the *St. Lawrence River*]

laurustinus *noun*
• "lora STYE nuss"
• an evergreen winter-flowering shrub, *Viburnum tinus*, with dense glossy green leaves and white or pink flowers.
• [modern Latin from Latin *laurus* laurel + *tinus* wild laurel]

lavabo *noun*
• "luh VAY bo" or "luh VABBO"
• the ritual washing of the celebrant's hands at the offertory of the Mass.
• [Latin, = I will wash, first word of Psalm 26:6]

lavage *noun*
• "luh VOZH" or "LAV idge"
• the washing out of a body cavity, such as the colon or stomach, with water or a medicated solution.
• [French from *laver* wash: see LAVE]

lavaliere *noun*
ALSO SPELLED: **lavalier**, **lavalliere**
• "lavva LEER"
• a small microphone worn hanging around the neck.
• [Louise de *la Vallière*, French courtesan d.1710]

lavatera *noun*
• "lavva TERRA"
• a plant of the genus *Lavatera*, of the mallow family, bearing pink, white, or purple flowers.
• [modern Latin, after the brothers *Lavater*, 17th- and 18th-c. Swiss naturalists]

lavatory *noun*
• "LAVVA tory"
• a toilet.
• [Middle English, = washing vessel, from Late Latin *lavatorium* from Latin *lavare lavat-* wash]
• **lavatorial** *adjective*

lave *verb*
• "LAVE" (rhymes with *SAVE*)
• wash, bathe.
• [Old French *laver* from Latin *lavare* wash, perhaps coalescing with Old English *lafian*]

lavender *noun*
• "LAV 'n dur"
• any small evergreen shrub of the genus *Lavandula*, with narrow leaves and blue, purple, or pink aromatic flowers.
• [Anglo-French *lavendre*, ultimately from medieval Latin *lavandula*]

laver *noun*
• "LAY vur" or "LAVVER"
• any of various edible seaweeds, esp. *Porphyra umbilicalis*, having sheet-like fronds.
• [Latin]

lavish *adjective*
• "LAV ish"
• giving or producing in large quantities; profuse.
• [Middle English from obsolete *lavish*, *lavas* (n.) profusion, from Old French *lavasse* deluge of rain, from *laver* wash]
• **lavishly** *adverb*
• **lavishness** *noun*

lawrencium *noun*
• "luh RENCY um"
• an artificially made transuranic radioactive metallic element.
• [E. O. *Lawrence*, US physicist d.1958]

lawyer *noun*
• "LOYER"
• a member of the legal profession.
• [Middle English *law(i)er* from 'law']
• **lawyerly** *adjective*

laxative *adjective*
• "LAXA tiv"
• tending to stimulate or facilitate evacuation of the bowels.
• [Old French *laxatif -ive* or Late Latin *laxativus* from Latin *laxare* loosen]

lazaret *noun*
ALSO SPELLED: **lazarette**
• "lazza RET"
• a hospital for diseased people, esp. lepers.
• [(French *lazaret*) from Italian *lazzaretto* from *lazzaro* from medieval Latin *lazarus* with biblical allusion to *Lazarus*, a beggar covered with sores]

Lazarist *noun*
• "LAZZA rist"
• a member of a religious body, the Congregation of the Mission, established at the priory of St. Lazare in Paris in 1625 by St. Vincent de Paul.

lea *noun*
• "LEE"
• a piece of meadowland, or pasture land, or arable land.
• [Old English *lēa(h)* from Germanic]
HOMOPHONES: *lee*

leach *verb*
• "LEECH"
• make (a liquid) percolate through some material.
• [prob. representing Old English *leccan* to water, from West Germanic]
• **leachability** *noun*
• **leachable** *adjective*
HOMOPHONES: *leech*

leachate *noun*
• "LEECH ate"
• a quantity of liquid that has percolated through a solid and leached out some of the constituents.
• [as LEACH]

league *noun*
• "LEEG"
• a collection of people, countries, groups, etc., combining for a particular purpose, esp. mutual protection or co-operation.
• [French *ligue* or Italian *liga*, var. of *lega* from *legare* bind, from Latin *ligare*]

leaguer *noun*
• "LEEGER"
• a member of a league.
• [as LEAGUE]

leak *noun*
• "LEEK"
• a hole in a pipe, container, etc. caused by wear or damage, through which matter, esp. liquid or gas, passes accidentally in or out.
• [Middle English prob. from Low German]
• **leakage** *noun*
• **leaker** *noun*
• **leakiness** *noun*
• **leaky** *adjective*
HOMOPHONES: *leek*

Leamingtonian *noun*
• "leeming TONY 'n"
• a resident of Leamington, Ont.

lease *noun*
• "LEECE"
• an agreement by which the owner of a building, apartment, vehicle, piece of land, etc. allows another to use it for a specified time in return for payment.
• [Old French *lais*, *leis* from *lesser*, *laissier* leave, from Latin *laxare* make loose (*laxus*)]
• **leasable** *adjective*
• **leaser** *noun*

leaseback *noun*
• "LEECE back"
• the leasing of a property back to the vendor.
• [as LEASE + 'back']

leasehold *noun*
• "LEECE hold"
• the holding of property by lease.
• [as LEASE + 'hold']
• **leaseholder** *noun*

leaven *noun*
• "LEV 'n"
• a substance added to dough to make it ferment and rise, esp. yeast, or fermenting dough reserved for the purpose.
• [Old French *levain* from Gallo-Roman spec. use of Latin *levamen* relief, from *levare* lift]
• **leavener** *noun*

leavening *noun*
• "LEV 'n ing"
• a substance, e.g. yeast or baking powder, that causes dough or batter to rise.
• [as LEAVEN]

Lebanese *noun*
• "lebba NEEZ"
• a native or inhabitant of Lebanon on the E coast of the Mediterranean.

Lebensraum *noun*
• "LAY b'nz roum" (with "ROU" as in *ROUND*)
• the territory which a nation etc. believes is needed for its natural development.
• [German, = living space (originally with reference to Germany, esp. in the 1930s)]

lechery *noun*
• "LETCHER ee"
• unrestrained indulgence of sexual desire.
• [Old French *lecheor* etc. from *lechier* live in debauchery or gluttony, from Frankish, related to 'lick']
• **lecher** *noun*
• **lecherous** *adjective*
• **lecherously** *adverb*
• **lecherousness** *noun*

lecithin *noun*
• "LESS a thin"
• any of a group of phospholipids found naturally in animals, egg yolk, and some higher plants.
• [Greek *lekithos* egg yolk]

lectern *noun*
• "LECK turn"
• a stand for holding a book in a church, esp. for a bible from which readings are made.
• [Old French *let(t)run*, medieval Latin *lectrum* from *legere lect-* read]

lectin *noun*
• "LECK tin"
• any of a class of proteins, usu. of plant origin,

causing the agglutination of particular cell types.
• [Latin *legere*, *lect-* choose, select]

lection *noun*
• "LECK sh'n"
• a reading of a text found in a particular copy or edition.
• [Latin *lectio* reading (as LECTERN)]

lectionary *noun*
• "LECK sh'n airy"
• a list of portions of Scripture for reading at a religious service.
• [as LECTION]

lector *noun*
• "LECTER"
• a person designated to read aloud certain readings, prayers, psalms, etc. at Mass.
• [Latin from *legere lect-* read]

lecture *noun*
• "LECK chur"
• a discourse giving information about a subject to a class or other audience.
• [Old French *lecture* or medieval Latin *lectura* from Latin (as LECTOR)]
• **lecturer** *noun*
• **lectureship** *noun*

lederhosen *plural noun*
• "LAY dur hoze 'n"
• leather shorts with braces worn by men in Bavarian traditional dress.
• [German, = leather trousers]

Leducian *noun*
• "luh DOOSHY 'n"
• a resident of Leduc, Alta.

lee *noun*
• "LEE"
• shelter given by a neighbouring object.
• [Old English *hlēo* from Germanic]
HOMOPHONES: *lea*

leech *noun*
• "LEECH"
• any freshwater or terrestrial annelid worm of the class Hirudinea with suckers at both ends, esp. *Hirudo medicinalis*, a bloodsucking parasite of vertebrates formerly much used medically.
• [Old English *lǣce*]
HOMOPHONES: *leach*

leek *noun*
• "LEEK"
• an alliaceous plant, *Allium porrum*, with flat overlapping leaves forming an elongated cylindrical bulb, used as food and as a Welsh national emblem.
• [Old English *lēac* from Germanic]
HOMOPHONES: *leak*

leer *verb*
• "LEER"
• look slyly or lasciviously or maliciously.
• [perhaps from obsolete *leer* cheek, from Old English *hlēor*, as though 'to glance over one's cheek']
• **leeringly** *adverb*
HOMOPHONES: *lehr*

leery *adjective*
• "LEERY"
• wary.
• [perhaps from obsolete *leer* looking askance, from LEER]
• **leeriness** *noun*

lees *plural noun*
• "LEEZ"
• the sediment of wine etc.
• [pl. of Middle English *lie* from Old French *lie* from medieval Latin *lia* from Gaulish]

leeward *adjective*
• "LEE wurd" or "LOO urd"
• on or towards the side sheltered from the wind.
• [as LEE + 'toward']

leeway *noun*
• "LEE way"
• allowable deviation or freedom of action.
• [as LEE + 'way']

legacy *noun*
• "LEGGA see"
• a gift left in a will.
• [Old French *legacie* legateship, from medieval Latin *legatia* from Latin *legare* bequeath]

legate *noun*
• "LEG it"
• a member of the clergy representing the Pope.
• [Old English from Old French *legat* from Latin *legatus* past participle of *legare* depute, delegate]
• **legateship** *noun*

legatee *noun*
• "legga TEE"
• the recipient of a legacy.
• [as LEGATOR]

legation *noun*
• "luh GAY sh'n"
• a body of deputies.
• [as LEGATE]

legato *adverb*
• "luh GOTTO"
• in a smooth flowing manner, without breaks between notes.
• [Italian, = bound, past participle of *legare* from Latin *ligare* bind]

legator *noun*
• "luh GAY tur"
• the giver of a legacy.
• [archaic *legate* bequeath, from Latin *legare* (as LEGACY)]

legend *noun*
• "LEDGE 'nd"
• a traditional story sometimes popularly

regarded as historical but unauthenticated; a myth.
• [Old French *legende* from medieval Latin *legenda* what is to be read, neuter pl. gerundive of Latin *legere* read]
• **legendarily** *adverb*
• **legendary** *adjective*

legerdemain *noun*
• "ledge ur duh MAIN"
• sleight of hand; conjuring or juggling.
• [French *léger de main* light of hand, dexterous]

legible *adjective*
• "LEDGE a bull"
• (of handwriting, print, etc.) clear enough to read; readable.
• [Late Latin *legibilis* from *legere* read]
• **legibility** *noun*
• **legibly** *adverb*

legion *noun*
• "LEE j'n"
• a vast host, multitude, or number.
• [Old French from Latin *legio -onis* from *legere* choose]

legionary *noun*
• "LEE j'n airy"
• an ancient Roman soldier.
• [Old French from Latin *legio -onis* from *legere* choose]

legionella *noun*
• "leeja NELLA"
• the bacterium *Legionella pneumophila*, which causes legionnaires' disease.
• [as LEGION]

legionnaire *noun*
• "leeja NAIR"
• a member of a foreign legion.
• [French *légionnaire* (as LEGION)]

legislation *noun*
• "ledge iss LAY sh'n"
• the process of making laws.
• [Late Latin *legis latio* from *lex legis* law + *latio* proposing, from *lat-* past participle stem of *ferre* bring]
• **legislate** *verb*
• **legislative** *adjective*
• **legislatively** *adverb*

legislator *noun*
• "LEDGE iss later"
• a member of a legislative body.
• [as LEGISLATION]

legislature *noun*
• "LEDGE iss lay chur"
• the legislative body of a nation, province, etc.
• [as LEGISLATION]

legit *adjective*
• "luh JIT"
• legitimate.
• [abbreviation]

legitimate *adjective*
• "luh JITTA mit"
• (of a child) born of parents lawfully married to each other, entitled in law to full filial rights.
• [medieval Latin *legitimare* from Latin *legitimus* lawful, from *lex legis* law]
• **legitimacy** *noun*
• **legitimately** *adverb*
• **legitimating** *adjective*
• **legitimation** *noun*
• **legitimization** *noun* (also esp. *Brit.* **-isation**)
• **legitimize** *verb* (also esp. *Brit.* **-ise**)
• **legitimizing** *noun* (also esp. *Brit.* **-ising**)

legitimism *noun*
• "luh JITTA mizm"
• adherence to a sovereign or pretender whose claim is based on direct descent (esp. in French and Spanish history).
• [as LEGITIMATE]
• **legitimist** *noun*

legume *noun*
• "LEG yume"
• any seed, pod, or other edible part of a plant of the family Leguminosae used as food.
• [French *légume* from Latin *legumen -minis* from *legere* pick, because they can be picked by hand]
• **leguminous** *adjective* "leg YUME in us"

lehr *noun*
• "LEER"
• a slow-cooling, tunnel-like furnace used for the annealing of glass.
• [17th c.: origin unknown]
HOMOPHONES: *leer*

lei *noun*
• "LAY" or "LAY ee"
• a garland of flowers, feathers, shells, etc. often given as a symbol of affection.
• [Hawaiian]
HOMOPHONES: *lay*, *ley*

Leicester *noun*
• "LESTER"
• a kind of mild firm cheese, usu. orange-coloured and originally made in Leicestershire, England.

leishmaniasis *noun*
• "leesh muh NIE a sis"
• any of several diseases caused by parasitic protozoans of the genus *Leishmania* transmitted by the bite of sandflies.
• [W. B. *Leishman*, British physician d.1926]

leister *noun*
• "LEESTER"
• a pronged spear for catching salmon.
• [Old Norse *ljóstr* from *ljósta* to strike]

leisure *noun*
• "LEE zhur" or "LEZH ur"
• free time; time at one's own disposal.
• [Anglo-French *leisour*, Old French *leisir*, ultimately from Latin *licēre* be allowed]
• **leisured** *adjective*

leisurely *adjective*
- "LEE zhur lee" or "LEZH ur lee"
- relaxed, having leisure, able to proceed without haste.
- [as LEISURE]
- **leisureliness** *noun*

leitmotif *noun*
ALSO SPELLED: **leitmotiv**
- "LITE moe teef"
- a recurrent theme associated throughout a musical, literary, etc. composition with a particular person, idea, or situation.
- [German *Leitmotiv* (as 'lead', 'motive')]

lek *noun*
- "LECK"
- a patch of ground used by groups of certain birds during the breeding season as a setting for the males' display and their meeting with the females.
- [perhaps from Swedish *leka* to play]

Lekwiltok *noun*
- "LECK will tock"
- a member of large group of the Kwakwaka'wakw living between Knight and Bute Inlets, on the west coast of BC.
- [Lekwiltok]

lemma *noun*
- "LEMMA"
- an assumed or demonstrated proposition used in an argument or proof.
- [Latin from Greek *lēmma -matos* thing assumed, from the root of *lambanō* take]

lemonade *noun*
- "LEM'n ade"
- a drink made of lemon juice and water, usu. sweetened with sugar.
- [French *limonade* from Old French *limon* lemon]

lempira *noun*
- "lem PEERA"
- the chief monetary unit of Honduras, equal to 100 centavos.
- [named after *Lempira*, 16th-c. chieftain who opposed the Spanish conquest of Honduras]

lemur *noun*
- "LEEMER"
- any arboreal primate of the family Lemuridae native to Madagascar, with a pointed snout and long tail.
- [modern Latin from Latin *lemures* (pl.) spirits of the dead, from its spectre-like face]

length *noun*
- "LENGTH" or "LENKTH" or "LENTH"
- the linear extent of a thing from end to end.
- [Old English *lengthu* from Germanic]
- **lengthily** *adverb*
- **lengthiness** *noun*
- **lengthy** *adjective*

lenient *adjective*
- "LEENY 'nt"
- merciful, tolerant, not disposed to severity.
- [Latin *lenire lenit-* soothe, from *lenis* gentle]
- **leniency** *noun*
- **leniently** *adverb*

Leninism *noun*
- "LENNIN izm"
- Marxism as interpreted and applied by the Russian revolutionary and statesman V. I. Lenin (d.1924).
- **Leninist** *noun*

lenition *noun*
- "lee NISH'n"
- the process or result of a consonant being weakly articulated or lost.
- [Latin *lenis* soft, after German *Lenierung*]

lenticel *noun*
- "LENTA sell"
- any of the raised pores in the stems of woody plants that allow gas exchange between the atmosphere and the internal tissues.
- [modern Latin *lenticella* diminutive of Latin *lens lentis* lentil]

lenticular *adjective*
- "len TICK yuh lur"
- having a flattened shape with a dense centre and thin edges, like a lentil or biconvex lens.
- [Latin *lenticularis* (as LENTIL)]

lentil *noun*
- "LENT'll"
- a leguminous plant, *Lens culinaris*, yielding edible biconvex seeds.
- [Old French *lentille* from Latin *lenticula* from *lens lentis* lentil]

leone *noun*
- "lee OWN" or "lee OH nee"
- the basic monetary unit of Sierra Leone, equal to 100 cents.
- [from the name of Sierra Leone]

leonine *adjective*
- "LEE a nine"
- like a lion.
- [Old French *leonin -ine* or Latin *leoninus* from *leo leonis* lion]

leopard *noun*
- "LEPPERD"
- any large African or Asian flesh-eating cat, *Panthera pardus*, with either a black-spotted yellowish-fawn or all black coat.
- [Old French from Late Latin from late Greek *leopardos* from *leōn leontos* lion, *pardos* leopard]

leopardess *noun*
- "LEPPERD ess"
- a female leopard.
- [as LEOPARD]

leotard *noun*
- "LEE a tard"

• a close-fitting one-piece garment worn by dancers, gymnasts, etc.
• [J. *Léotard*, French trapeze artist d.1870]

leper *noun*
• "LEPPER"
• a person suffering from leprosy.
• [Old French *lepre* from Latin *lepra* from Greek, feminine of *lepros* scaly, from *lepos* scale]

lepidopterist *noun*
• "leppa DOPTER ist"
• a person who studies or collects butterflies.
• [as LEPIDOPTEROUS]

lepidopterous *adjective*
• "leppa DOPTER us"
• of the order Lepidoptera of insects, with four scale-covered wings often brightly coloured, including butterflies and moths.
• [Greek *lepis -idos* scale + *pteron* wing]
• **lepidopteran** *adjective*

leprechaun *noun*
• "LEPRA con"
• a small, usu. mischievous being of human form in Irish folklore, often associated with shoemaking or buried treasure.
• [Old Irish *luchorpán* from *lu* small + *corp* body]

leprosarium *noun*
• "lepra SERRY um"
• a hospital for people with leprosy.
• [as LEPROSY]

leprosy *noun*
• "LEPRA see"
• a contagious bacterial disease that affects the skin, mucous membranes, and nerves, causing disfigurement.
• [Old French from Late Latin *leprosus* from *lepra*: see LEPER]
• **leprous** *adjective* "LEP russ"

lepton *noun*
• "LEPT'n"
• a former Greek monetary unit worth one-hundredth of a drachma.
• [Greek *lepton* (*nomisma* coin) neuter of *leptos* small]

leptospirosis *noun*
• "lepta spuh ROE sis"
• an infectious disease caused by bacteria of the genus *Leptospira*, that occurs in rodents, dogs, and other mammals, and can be transmitted to humans.
• [Greek *leptos* fine, small, thin, delicate + *speira* coil]

leptotene *noun*
• "LEPTA teen"
• the first stage of the prophase of meiosis in which each chromosome is apparent as two fine chromatids.
• [Greek *leptos* fine, small, thin, delicate + *tainia* band]

lesion *noun*
• "LEE zh'n"
• a pathological change in the functioning or structure of an organ, organism, etc.
• [Old French from Latin *laesio -onis* from *laedere laes-* injure]
• **lesioned** *adjective*

lessor *noun*
• "less OR"
• a person who lets a property by lease.
• [Anglo-French from *lesser*: see LEASE]

lethal *adjective*
• "LEETH'll"
• causing or sufficient to cause death.
• [Latin *let(h)alis* from *letum* death]
• **lethality** *noun* "lee THALA tee"
• **lethally** *adverb*

lethargy *noun*
• "LETH ur jee"
• lack of energy or vitality; a torpid, inert, or apathetic state.
• [Old French *litargie* from Late Latin *lethargia* from Greek *lēthargia* from *lēthargos* forgetful, from *lēth-*, *lanthanomai* forget]
• **lethargic** *adjective* "luth AR jick"
• **lethargically** *adverb*

lettuce *noun*
• "LET iss"
• a composite plant, *Lactuca sativa*, with crisp edible leaves used in salads.
• [Middle English *letus(e)*, related to Old French *laituë* from Latin *lactuca* from *lac lactis* milk, with reference to its milky juice]

leu *noun*
• "LAY oo"
• the basic monetary unit of Romania and Moldova, equal to 100 bani.
• [Romanian, = lion]

leucine *noun*
• "LOO seen"
• an amino acid which is a constituent of most proteins and is essential in the diet of vertebrates.
• [French from Greek *leukos* white]

leucotomy *noun*
• "loo COTTA mee"
• the surgical cutting of white nerve fibres of the frontal lobes of the brain, formerly used to treat intractable psychiatric disorders.
• [Greek *leukos* white + *-tomia* cutting, from *temnō* cut]

leukemia *noun*
ALSO SPELLED: esp. *Brit.* **leukaemia**
• "loo KEEMY uh"
• any of a group of malignant diseases in which the bone marrow and other blood-forming organs produce increased numbers of leukocytes.
• [modern Latin from German *Leukämie* from Greek *leukos* white + *haima* blood]
• **leukemic** *adjective* (also esp. *Brit.* **leukaemic**)

leukocyte *noun*
ALSO SPELLED: **leucocyte**
• "LOO kuh site"
• a white blood cell.
• [Greek *leukos* white + *kutos* vessel]
• **leukocytic** *adjective* (also **leucocytic**) "loo kuh SITTIC"

leukocytosis *noun*
ALSO SPELLED: **leucocytosis**
• "loo co sye TOE sis"
• an increase in the number of leukocytes in the blood.
• [as LEUKOCYTE]

leukoma *noun*
ALSO SPELLED: **leucoma**
• "loo CO muh"
• a white opacity in the cornea of the eye.
• [Greek *leukos* white]

leukopenia *noun*
ALSO SPELLED: **leucopenia**
• "loo kuh PEENY uh"
• a reduction in the number of white cells in the blood.
• [Greek *leukos* white + *penia* poverty]

leukosis *noun*
ALSO SPELLED: **leucosis**
• "loo CO sis"
• a leukemic disease of animals, esp. any of a group of malignant viral diseases of poultry (*avian* or *fowl leukosis*) or of cattle (*bovine leukosis*).
• [Greek *leukos* white]

leukotriene *noun*
• "loo kuh TRY een"
• any of a group of biologically active metabolites related to prostaglandins, originally isolated from leukocytes, and contributing to asthma, other bronchial reactions, etc.
• [Greek *leukos* white + *tri* three]

levator *noun*
• "luh VAY tur"
• a muscle whose contraction causes the raising of a part of the body.
• [Latin, = one who lifts, from *levare* raise]

levee[1] *noun*
• "LEVVY"
• *Cdn* a New Year's Day reception held by the Governor General or by a Lieutenant-Governor, or by a mayor, bishop, etc.
• [French *levé* var. of *lever* rising, from *lever* to rise: see LEVY]
HOMOPHONES: *levy*

levee[2] *noun*
• "LEVVY" or "luh VEE"
• an embankment against river floods.
• [French *levée* feminine past participle of *lever* raise: see LEVY]
HOMOPHONES: *levy*

leveret *noun*
• "LEVVER et"
• a young hare, esp. one in its first year.
• [Anglo-French, diminutive of *levre*, Old French *lievre* from Latin *lepus leporis* hare]

leviathan *noun*
• "luh VIE a th'n" (with "TH" as in *THIN*)
• a sea monster.
• [Late Latin from Hebrew *liwyāṯān*]

levirate *noun*
• "LEEVA rit" or "LEVVA rit"
• a custom of the ancient Jews and some other peoples by which a man is obliged to marry his brother's widow.
• [Latin *levir* brother-in-law]

levitate *verb*
• "LEVVA tate"
• rise and float in the air (esp. with reference to spiritualism).
• [Latin *levis* light, after GRAVITATE]
• **levitation** *noun*
• **levitator** *noun*

Levite *noun*
• "LEE vite"
• a member of the tribe of Levi, esp. of that part of it which provided assistants to the priests in the worship in the Jewish temple.
• [Late Latin *levita* from Greek *leuitēs* from *Leui* from Hebrew *lēwî* Levi]
• **Levitical** *adjective* "luh VITTA k'll"

levity *noun*
• "LEVVA tee"
• the treatment of a serious matter with humour or in a manner lacking due respect.
• [Latin *levitas* from *levis* light]

levodopa *noun*
• "leeva DOE puh"
• the levorotatory form of dopa, used to treat Parkinson's disease.
• [as LEVOROTATORY + DOPA]

levonorgestrel *noun*
• "leevo nor JESS trull"
• a synthetic steroid hormone which has a similar effect to progesterone and is used in some contraceptive pills.
• [LEVOROTATORY + *norgestrel* a synthetic steroid hormone]

levorotatory *adjective*
ALSO SPELLED: esp. *Brit.* **laevorotatory**
• "leevo ROE tuh tory"
• having the property of rotating the plane of a polarized light ray to the left (counter-clockwise facing the oncoming radiation).
• [Latin *laevus* left + ROTATE]

levulose *noun*
ALSO SPELLED: esp. *Brit.* **laevulose**
• "LEEVE yoo lose" (rhymes with *GROSS*)
• a simple sugar found in honey and fruits; fructose.
• [LEVOROTATORY + GLUCOSE]

levy *verb*
• "LEVVY"
• raise (contributions, taxes) or impose (a rate, toll, fee, etc.) as a levy.
• [Old French *levee* feminine past participle of *lever* from Latin *levare* raise, from *levis* light]
• **leviable** *adjective*
HOMOPHONES: *levee*

lewd *adjective*
• "LUDE"
• lustful, lecherous, wanton.
• [Old English *lǣwede* lay (non-clerical), of unknown origin]
• **lewdly** *adverb*
• **lewdness** *noun*

lewis *noun*
• "LOO iss"
• an iron contrivance for gripping heavy blocks of stone or concrete for lifting.
• [18th c.: origin unknown]

lewisite *noun*
• "LOO iss ite"
• a dark oily liquid or gas that causes respiratory irritation and produces blisters, developed for use in chemical warfare.
• [W. L. *Lewis*, US chemist d.1943]

lexeme *noun*
• "LEX eem"
• a basic lexical unit of a language comprising one or several words, the elements of which do not separately convey the meaning of the whole.
• [LEXICON + French *-ème* unit, from Greek *-ēma*]

lexical *adjective*
• "LEXA k'll"
• of the words of a language.
• [as LEXICON]
• **lexically** *adverb*

lexicography *noun*
• "lexa COGGRA fee"
• the compiling, writing, or editing of dictionaries.
• [as LEXICON + Greek *graphia* writing]
• **lexicographer** *noun*
• **lexicographic** *adjective*
• **lexicographical** *adjective*
• **lexicographically** *adverb*

lexicology *noun*
• "lexa COLLA jee"
• the study of the form, history, and meaning of words.
• [as LEXICON + Greek *logos* word]
• **lexicological** *adjective*
• **lexicologically** *adverb*
• **lexicologist** *noun*

lexicon *noun*
• "LEXA con"
• a dictionary, esp. of Greek, Hebrew, Syriac, or Arabic.
• [modern Latin from Greek *lexikon* (*biblion* book), neuter of *lexikos* from *lexis* word, from *legō* speak]

lexis *noun*
• "LEX iss"
• words, vocabulary.
• [Greek: see LEXICON]

ley *noun*
• "LAY"
• a field temporarily under grass.
• [Middle English (originally adjective), perhaps from Old English, related to 'lay', 'lie']
HOMOPHONES: *lay, lei*

Lhasa *noun*
• "LASSA"
• a breed of small long-coated dog, often gold or grey and white.
• [*Lhasa*, the capital of Tibet; second term from Tibetan]

liable *adjective*
• "LIE a bull" or "LIE bull"
• legally bound.
• [Middle English perhaps from Anglo-French from Old French *lier* from Latin *ligare* bind]
• **liability** *noun* "lie a BILLA tee"
HOMOPHONES: *libel*

liaison *noun*
• "lee AY zon"
• communication or co-operation, esp. between groups within an organization.
• [French from *lier* bind, from Latin *ligare*]
• **liaise** *verb* "lee AZE"

liana *noun*
• "lee ANNA"
• any of several climbing and twining plants of tropical forests.
• [French *liane, lierne* clematis, of uncertain origin]

lias *noun*
• "LIE us"
• the lower strata of the Jurassic system of rocks, consisting of shales and limestones rich in fossils.
• [Old French *liois* hard limestone, prob. from Germanic]
• **Liassic** *adjective* "lie ASSIC"

liatris *noun*
• "lie AT riss"
• any of various N American plants of the genus *Liatris*, of the composite family, cultivated for their long spikes of purple or white flower heads.
• [19th c.: origin unknown]

libation *noun*
• "lie BAY sh'n"
• the pouring out of a drink offering to a god.
• [Latin *libatio* from *libare* pour as offering]

libel *noun*
• "LIE bull"
• a published false statement damaging to a person's reputation.

• [Old French from Latin *libellus* diminutive of *liber* book]
• **libeller** *noun* (also **libeler**)
• **libellous** *adjective* (also **libelous**)
• **libellously** *adverb* (also **libelously**)
HOMOPHONES: *liable*

liberal *adjective*
• "LIBBER 'll"
• given freely.
• [Middle English, originally = befitting a free man, from Old French from Latin *liberalis* from *liber* free (man)]
• **liberally** *adverb*
• **liberalness** *noun*

liberalism *noun*
• "LIBBER 'll izm"
• a political and social philosophy emphasizing the freedom of the individual, democratic government characterized by progress and reform, and the protection of civil liberties.
• [as LIBERAL]

liberality *noun*
• "libber ALA tee"
• generosity.
• [as LIBERAL]

liberalize *verb*
ALSO SPELLED: esp. *Brit.* **-ise**
• "LIBBER 'll ize"
• make or become more liberal or less strict.
• [as LIBERAL]
• **liberalization** *noun* (also esp. *Brit.* **-isation**)
• **liberalizer** *noun* (also esp. *Brit.* **-iser**)

liberate *verb*
• "LIBBER ate"
• set at liberty, set free.
• [Latin *liberare liberat-* from *liber* free]
• **liberation** *noun*
• **liberationist** *noun*
• **liberator** *noun*
• **liberatory** *adjective* "LIBBER a tory"

Liberian *noun*
• "lie BEERY 'n"
• a native or inhabitant of Liberia in W Africa.

libertarian *noun*
• "libber TERRY 'n"
• an advocate of liberty, esp. of an almost absolute freedom of expression and action.
• [as LIBERTY]
• **libertarianism** *noun*

libertine *noun*
• "LIBBER teen" or "LIBBER tine"
• a man who behaves without moral principles or a sense of responsibility, esp. in sexual matters.
• [Latin *libertinus* freedman, from *libertus* made free, from *liber* free]
• **libertinage** *noun* "LIBBER teen idge"
• **libertinism** *noun*

liberty *noun*
• "LIBBER tee"
• freedom from captivity, imprisonment, slavery, or despotic control.
• [Old French *liberté* from Latin *libertas -tatis*, from *liber* free]

libido *noun*
• "luh BEE doe"
• the sexual drive or instinct.
• [Latin *libidinosus* from *libido -dinis* lust]
• **libidinal** *adjective* "luh BID'n 'll"
• **libidinally** *adverb*
• **libidinous** *adjective* "luh BID'n us"
• **libidinously** *adverb*
• **libidinousness** *noun*

Libra *noun*
• "LEE bruh"
• the seventh sign of the zodiac.
• [Latin, originally = pound weight]
• **Libran** *noun*

librarian *noun*
• "lie BRERRY 'n"
• a person professionally trained in library science.
• [as LIBRARY]
• **librarianship** *noun*

library *noun*
• "LIE brerry"
• a collection of books, periodicals, recordings, electronic reference materials, etc. for use by the public or by members of a group.
• [Old French *librairie* from Latin *libraria* (*taberna* shop), feminine of *librarius* bookseller's, of books, from *liber libri* book]

libration *noun*
• "lie BRAY sh'n"
• an apparent oscillation of a heavenly body, esp. the moon, by which the parts near the edge of the disc are alternately in view and out of view.
• [Latin *libratio* from *librare* from *libra* balance]

libretto *noun*
• "lib RETTO"
• the text of an opera or other long musical vocal work.
• [Italian, diminutive of *libro* book, from Latin *liber libri*]
• **librettist** *noun*

Libyan *adjective*
• "LIBBY 'n"
• of or relating to Libya in N Africa.

licensure *noun*
• "LICE 'n shur"
• the granting of a licence, esp. to carry on a profession.
• [Old French *licence* from Latin *licentia* from *licēre* be lawful]

licentiate *noun*
• "lie SEN shee ut" or "lie SEN shut"

• a holder of a certificate of competence to practise a certain profession.
• [as LICENSURE]

licentious *adjective*
• "lie SEN sh'ss"
• sexually promiscuous or unrestrained.
• [Latin *licentiosus* from *licentia*: see LICENSURE]
• **licentiously** *adverb*
• **licentiousness** *noun*

lichen *noun*
• "LIKE 'n"
• any plant organism of the group Lichenes, composed of a fungus and an alga in symbiotic association, usu. of green, grey, or yellow tint and growing on and colouring rocks, tree trunks, roofs, walls, etc.
• [Latin from Greek *leikhēn*]
• **lichened** *adjective*
• **lichenology** *noun*
• **lichenous** *adjective*
HOMOPHONES: *liken*

licit *adjective*
• "LISSIT"
• not forbidden; lawful.
• [Latin *licitus* past participle of *licēre* be lawful]
• **licitly** *adverb*

licorice *noun*
ALSO SPELLED: **liquorice**
• "LICKER ish" or "LICK rish"
• a black, rubbery candy flavoured with a substance extracted from the root of the leguminous plant *Glycyrrhiza glabra*.
• [Anglo-French *lycorys*, Old French *licoresse* from Late Latin *liquiritia* from Greek *glukurrhiza* from *glukus* sweet + *rhiza* root]
HOMOPHONES: *lickerish, liquorish*

lictor *noun*
• "LICTER"
• an officer attending the consul or other magistrate in ancient Rome, bearing the fasces, and executing sentence on offenders.
• [Latin, perhaps related to *ligare* bind]

lidar *noun*
• "LIE dar"
• a detection system which works on the principle of radar, but uses light from a laser.
• [blend of 'light' + 'radar']

lido *noun*
• "LEEDO" or "LIE doe"
• a public open-air swimming pool or beach.
• [Italian from *Lido*, a beach near Venice]

lidocaine *noun*
• "LIE doe cane"
• a local anaesthetic for the gums, mucous membranes, or skin, usu. given by injection.
• [from ACETANILIDE + COCAINE]

Liebfraumilch *noun*
• "LEEB frow milk" ("FROW" rhymes with *COW*)
• a light white wine from the Rhine region.
• [German from *Liebfrau* the Virgin Mary, the patroness of the convent where it was first made + *Milch* milk]

Liechtensteiner *noun*
• "LEEK t'n stine ur"
• a native or inhabitant of the Alpine principality of Liechtenstein.

lied *noun*
• "LEED" or "LEET"
• a type of German song, esp. of the Romantic period, usu. for solo voice with piano accompaniment.
• [German]
HOMOPHONES: *lead*

liege *adjective*
• "LEEJ" or "LEEZH"
• usu. (of a superior) entitled to receive or (of a vassal) bound to give feudal service or allegiance.
• [Old French *lige, liege* from medieval Latin *laeticus*, prob. from Germanic]

lien *noun*
• "LEEN"
• a right over another's property to protect a debt charged on that property.
• [French from Old French *loien* from Latin *ligamen* bond, from *ligare* bind]
HOMOPHONES: *lean*

lieu *noun*
• "LOO" or "LYOO"
• (in Canada) designating time taken off work in compensation for overtime worked.
• [French from Latin *locus* place]
HOMOPHONES: *loo*

lieutenant *noun*
• "lef TEN'nt" or "loo TEN'nt"
• a deputy or substitute acting for a superior.
• [Old French (as LIEU, TENANT)]
• **lieutenancy** *noun*

lifebuoy *noun*
• "LIFE boy"
• a buoyant support (usu. a ring) for keeping a person afloat in water, esp. in an emergency.
• ['life' + BUOY]

ligament *noun*
• "LIGGA m'nt"
• a short band of tough flexible fibrous connective tissue linking bones together.
• [Latin *ligamentum* bond, from *ligare* bind]
• **ligamentary** *adjective* "ligga MENTA ree"
• **ligamentous** *adjective*

ligand *noun*
• "LIG'nd"
• an ion or molecule attached to a metal atom by covalent bonding in which both electrons are supplied by one atom.
• [Latin *ligandus*, gerundive of *ligare* bind]

ligase *noun*
• "LIG ace"
• an enzyme which catalyzes the linking

together of two molecules, esp. with a simultaneous conversion of ATP to ADP.
• [Latin *ligare* bind]

ligate *verb*
• "lie GATE"
• tie up (a bleeding artery etc.).
• [Latin *ligare ligat-* bind]
• **ligation** *noun*

ligature *noun*
• "LIGGA chur"
• a tie or bandage, esp. in surgery for a bleeding artery etc.
• [Late Latin *ligatura* from Latin *ligare ligat-* tie, bind]

lightning *noun*
• "LITE ning"
• a flash of bright light produced by an electric discharge between clouds or between clouds and the ground.
• [Middle English, differentiated from *lightening*, verbal noun from 'lighten']
HOMOPHONES: *lightening*

lightweight *adjective*
• "LITE wate"
• (of a person, animal, garment, etc.) of below average weight.
• ['light' + WEIGHT]

ligneous *adjective*
• "LIG nee us"
• (of a plant) woody.
• [Latin *ligneus* from *lignum* wood]

lignify *verb*
• "LIG nuh fie"
• make or become woody by the deposition of lignin.
• [Latin *lignum* wood]
• **lignification** *noun*

lignin *noun*
• "LIG nin"
• a complex organic polymer deposited in the cell walls of many plants making them rigid and woody.
• [Latin *lignum* wood]

lignite *noun*
• "LIG nite"
• a soft brown coal showing traces of plant structure, intermediate between bituminous coal and peat.
• [Latin *lignum* wood]

ligulate *adjective*
• "LIG yuh late"
• having strap-shaped florets.
• [as LIGULE]

ligule *noun*
• "LIG yool"
• a narrow projection from the top of the sheath which encloses a leaf of a grass.
• [Latin *ligula* strap, spoon, from *lingere* lick]

Ligurian *adjective*
• "lih GYOORY 'n"
• of or relating to Liguria in NW Italy, its people, or their language or dialect.

ligustrum *noun*
• "lih GUS trum"
• any evergreen shrub of the genus *Ligustrum*, esp. *L. vulgare* bearing small white flowers and black berries, and used for hedges.
• [Latin]

likuta *noun*
• "lih COOTA"
• a monetary unit of Congo (formerly Zaire), equal to one-hundredth of a zaire.
• [Kikongo]

lilac *noun*
• "LIE l'k" or "LIE lock" or "LIE lack"
• any shrub or small tree of the genus *Syringa*, esp. *S. vulgaris* with fragrant purple, mauve, pink, or white blossoms.
• [obsolete French from Spanish from Arabic *līlāk* from Persian *līlak*, var. of *nīlak* bluish, from *nīl* blue]

lilangeni *noun*
• "lee lan GAY nee"
• the basic monetary unit of Swaziland, equal to 100 cents.
• [Bantu, from *li-*, singular prefix (*ema-*, plural prefix) + *-langeni* member of royal family]

liliaceous *adjective*
• "lilly AY sh'ss"
• of or relating to the family Liliaceae of plants with elongated leaves growing from a corm, bulb, or rhizome, e.g. tulip, lily, or onion.
• [Latin *lilium* lily + adjective suffix *-aceus* of the nature of]

Lilliputian *noun*
• "lilla PYOO sh'n"
• a diminutive person or thing.
• [the imaginary country of *Lilliput* in *Gulliver's Travels* by Irish satirist J. Swift (d.1745), inhabited by people 15 cm (6 inches) high]

Lillooet *noun*
• "LILL oo et"
• a member of a Salishan Aboriginal people living in southwestern BC, northeast of Vancouver, also called the Stl'atl'imx.
• [the native name for Mount Currie]

limbic *adjective*
• "LIM bick"
• of or relating to a part of the brain concerned with basic emotions and instinctive actions.
• [French *limbique*, from Latin *limbus* edge]

limerick *noun*
• "LIMMER ick"
• a humorous or comic form of five-line poem with a rhyme scheme *aabba*.
• [said to be from the chorus 'will you come up

to Limerick?' sung between improvised verses at a gathering: from *Limerick* in Ireland]

liminal *adjective*
- "LIMMA n'll"
- of or relating to a transitional or initial stage.
- [Latin *limin-*, *limen* threshold]
- **liminality** *noun* "lim 'n ALA tee"

limn *verb*
- "LIM"
- paint or draw (a picture or portrait); portray (a subject).
- [obsolete *lumine* illuminate, from Old French *luminer* from Latin *luminare*: see LUMEN]
- **limner** *noun* "LIM nur"

HOMOPHONES: *limb*

limnology *noun*
- "lim NOLLA jee"
- the study of the physical phenomena of lakes and other fresh waters.
- [Greek *limnē* lake + *logos* word]
- **limnological** *adjective*
- **limnologist** *noun*

Limoges *noun*
- "lim OAZH" (with "OA" as in *BOAT*)
- porcelain and painted enamels produced in Limoges in west central France.

limonene *noun*
- "LIM'n een"
- a colourless liquid hydrocarbon with a lemon-like scent, present in the oils of citrus fruits and other essential oils.
- [modern Latin *limonum* lemon + '-ene' forming names of unsaturated hydrocarbons containing a double bond, from Greek *-ēnos*, adjective suffix denoting origin or source]

limonite *noun*
- "LIE m'n ite"
- an amorphous secondary material now recognized as a mixture of hydrous ferric oxides and important as an iron ore.
- [German *Limonit*, prob. from Greek *leimōn* meadow, after the earlier German name *Wiesenerz* lit. 'meadow ore']

limonium *noun*
- "lim OANY um"
- any maritime plant of the genus *Limonium*, with small brightly coloured funnel-shaped flowers, used in dried flower arrangements.
- [Greek *leimōnion* from *leimōn* meadow]

Limousin *noun*
- "lee moo ZÃ" (with a nasal *A*)
- a breed of white beef cattle originating in the province of Limousin in central France.

limousine *noun*
- "limma ZEEN" or "LIMMA zeen"
- a large luxurious automobile, often with a partition behind the driver.
- [French, originally a caped cloak worn in the province of *Limousin* in central France]

linage *noun*
- "LINE idge"
- the number of lines in printed or written matter.
- [from Middle English *line*, *ligne* from Old French *ligne*, ultimately from Latin *linea* from *linum* flax, & from Old English *līne* rope, series]

Lincolnite *noun*
- "LINK'n ite"
- a resident of Lincoln, Ont.

linctus *noun*
- "LINK tuss"
- a syrupy medicine, esp. a soothing cough mixture.
- [Latin from *lingere* lick]

lindane *noun*
- "LIN dane"
- a synthetic organochlorine insecticide, now generally restricted in use owing to its toxicity and persistence in the environment.
- [T. van der *Linden*, Dutch chemist b.1884]

lineage *noun*
- "LINNY idge"
- lineal descent; ancestry, pedigree.
- [as LINAGE]

lineal *adjective*
- "LINNY 'll"
- in the direct line of descent or ancestry.
- [as LINAGE]
- **lineally** *adverb*

lineament *noun*
- "LINNY a m'nt"
- a distinctive feature or characteristic, esp. of the face.
- [Latin *lineamentum* from *lineare* make straight, from *linea* line]

linear *adjective*
- "LINNY ur"
- of or in lines; in lines rather than masses.
- [Latin *linearis* from *linea* line]
- **linearity** *noun* "linny ERRA tee"
- **linearize** *verb* (also esp. *Brit.* **-ise**)
- **linearly** *adverb*

lineation *noun*
- "linny AY sh'n"
- a marking with or drawing of lines.
- [Latin *lineatio* from *lineare* make straight]

Lingala *noun*
- "ling GOLLA"
- a Bantu language used by over 8 million people as a lingua franca in northern parts of the Republic of the Congo and the Democratic Republic of the Congo (formerly Zaire).
- [a local name]

lingerie *noun*
- "LAWN zhuh ray" or "lawn zhuh RAY"
- women's underwear and nightclothes.
- [French from *linge* linen]

lingonberry *noun*
• "LING g'n berry"
• the cowberry, *Vaccinium vitis-idaea*, of northern regions, esp. typically in Scandinavia, where the berries are used in cooking.
• [from Swedish *lingon* cowberry + 'berry']

lingual *adjective*
• "LING gwul"
• of or formed by the tongue.
• [medieval Latin *lingualis* from Latin *lingua* tongue, language]
• **lingually** *adverb*

linguiform *adjective*
• "LING gwuh form"
• tongue-shaped.
• [Latin *lingua* tongue + 'form' from Old French *forme* from Latin *forma* mould, form]

linguine *plural noun*
ALSO SPELLED: **linguini**
• "ling GWEENY"
• pasta in the form of narrow ribbons.
• [Italian, pl. of *linguina*, diminutive of *lingua* tongue]

linguist *noun*
• "LING gwist"
• a person skilled in languages or linguistics.
• [Latin *lingua* language]

linguistic *adjective*
• "ling GWISTIC"
• of or relating to language or the study of languages.
• [as LINGUIST]
• **linguistically** *adverb*
• **linguistics** *noun*

liniment *noun*
• "LINNA m'nt"
• a medicated lotion, usu. made with oil, for rubbing onto the body to relieve pain.
• [Late Latin *linimentum* from Latin *linire* smear]

Linnaean *adjective*
• "lin EE 'n" or "lin AY 'n"
• of or relating to Swedish botanist C. Linnaeus (d.1778) or his system of binary nomenclature in the classification of plants and animals.

linnet *noun*
• "LINNIT"
• a small common Eurasian songbird related to the finches, *Carduelis cannabina*, with brown and grey plumage, formerly kept as a cage bird.
• [Old French *linette* from *lin* flax (the bird feeding on flax seeds)]

linoleic *adjective*
• "linno LEE ick" or "linno LAY ick"
• designating a polyunsaturated fatty acid occurring as a glyceride in linseed and other oils and essential in the human diet.
• [Latin *linum* flax + OLEIC]

linolenic *adjective*
• "linno LENNIC" or "linno LEENIC"
• designating a polyunsaturated fatty acid (with one more double bond than linoleic acid) occurring as a glyceride in linseed and other oils and essential in the human diet.
• [German *Linolensaüre* linolenic acid, from *Linolsaüre* LINOLEIC (acid) with *-ene-* inserted + *Saüre* acid]

linoleum *noun*
• "lin OH lee um"
• a floor covering, originally consisting of thickened linseed oil and powdered wood etc. applied to a backing, now more commonly made of vinyl.
• [Latin *linum* flax + *oleum* oil]
• **linoleumed** *adjective* "lin OH lee umd"

lintel *noun*
• "LINT'll"
• a horizontal supporting piece of timber, stone, concrete, etc., across the top of a door or window.
• [Old French *lintel* threshold, from Romanic *limitale* (unrecorded), influenced by Late Latin *liminare* from Latin *limen* threshold]

lipa *noun*
• "LEEPA"
• a monetary unit of Croatia, equal to one-hundredth of a kuna.
• [Serbo-Croat, literally 'lime tree']

lipase *noun*
• "LIE pace" or "LIP ace"
• any enzyme that catalyzes the breakdown of fats.
• [Greek *lipos* fat]

lipid *noun*
• "LIPPID"
• any of a group of organic compounds that are insoluble in water but soluble in organic solvents, including fatty acids, oils, waxes, and steroids.
• [French *lipide* (as LIPASE)]

lipidosis *noun*
• "lippid OH sis"
• any disorder of lipid metabolism in the body tissues.
• [as LIPID]

Lipizzaner *noun*
ALSO SPELLED: **Lippizaner**
• "lippit SANNER"
• a horse of a fine white breed used esp. in displays of dressage.
• [German from *Lippiza* in Slovenia]

lipoid *adjective*
• "LIP oid"
• resembling fat.
• [as LIPID]

lipophilic *adjective*
• "lippo FILLIC" or "lie po FILLIC"
• tending to combine with or dissolve in lipids or fats.

• [Greek *lipos* fat + *philos* dear, loving]
• **lipophilicity** *noun* "lippo fuh LISSA tee" or "lie po fuh LISSA tee"

lipoprotein *noun*
• "lippo PRO teen" or "lie po PRO teen"
• any of a group of soluble proteins that combine with and transport fat or other lipids in the blood plasma.
• [Greek *lipos* fat + PROTEIN]

liposculpture *noun*
• "LIPPO sculp chur" or "LIE po sculp chur"
• a type of liposuction in which saline solution combined with local anaesthetic and adrenaline is introduced into the tissues before fat is removed, and which allows for greater sculpting of the tissue.
• [Greek *lipos* fat + SCULPTURE]

liposome *noun*
• "LIPPA soam" or "LIE po soam"
• a minute artificial spherical sac usu. of a phospholipid membrane enclosing an aqueous core, esp. used to carry drugs to specific tissues.
• [Greek *lipos* fat + *sōma* body]

liposuction *noun*
• "LIPPO suck sh'n" or "LIE po suck sh'n"
• a technique in cosmetic surgery for removing excess fat from under the skin by suction.
• [Greek *lipos* fat + SUCTION]

liquefy *verb*
ALSO SPELLED: **liquify**
• "LICKWA fie"
• make or become liquid.
• [French *liquéfier* from Latin *liquefacere* from *liquēre* be liquid]
• **liquefaction** *noun*
• **liquefactive** *adjective*
• **liquefier** *noun*

liquescent *adjective*
• "lih KWESS'nt"
• becoming or apt to become liquid.
• [Latin *liquescere* (as LIQUEFY)]

liqueur *noun*
• "lih CURE"
• any of several strong sweet alcoholic spirits, variously flavoured, usu. drunk after a meal.
• [French, = LIQUOR]

liquid *adjective*
• "LICK wid"
• (of a material substance) having a consistency like that of water or oil, flowing freely but of constant volume.
• [Latin *liquidus* from *liquēre* be liquid]
• **liquidity** *noun*
• **liquidly** *adverb*
• **liquidness** *noun*
• **liquidy** *adjective*

liquidambar *noun*
• "lick wid AMBER"
• any tree of the genus *Liquidambar* yielding a resinous gum.
• [modern Latin apparently from Latin *liquidus* (see LIQUID) + medieval Latin *ambar* amber]

liquidate *verb*
• "LICK wid ate"
• wind up the affairs of (a company or firm) by ascertaining liabilities and apportioning assets.
• [medieval Latin *liquidare* make clear (as LIQUID)]
• **liquidation** *noun*
• **liquidator** *noun*

liquidize *verb*
ALSO SPELLED: esp. *Brit.* **-ise**
• "LICK wid ize"
• reduce (esp. food) to a liquid or puréed state, esp. using an electric blender.
• [as LIQUID]
• **liquidizer** *noun* (also esp. *Brit.* **-iser**)

liquor *noun*
• "LICKER"
• an alcoholic drink, esp. produced by distillation.
• [Old French *lic(o)ur* from Latin *liquor -oris* (as LIQUID)]
HOMOPHONES: *licker*

lira *noun*
• "LEERA"
• the former chief monetary unit of Italy, used also in San Marino and the Vatican City, now replaced by the euro.
• [Italian from Provençal *liura* from Latin *libra* pound (weight etc.)]

lisianthus *noun*
• "lissy ANTH us"
• a plant, *Eustoma grandiflorum*, with delicate roselike white, purple, or pink flowers.
• [modern Latin from Greek *lysis* breaking up, dissolving + *anthos* flower, the original tropical American plant so called being used as a cathartic]

lisle *noun*
• "LYLE"
• a fine smooth cotton thread for stockings etc.
• [*Lisle*, former spelling of *Lille* in N France, where originally made]

lissome *adjective*
ALSO SPELLED: **lissom**
• "LISSUM"
• lithe, supple, agile.
• [ultimately from LITHE]
• **lissomely** *adverb*
• **lissomeness** *noun*

listeria *noun*
• "liss TEERY uh"
• any motile rod-like bacterium of the genus *Listeria*, esp. *L. monocytogenes* infecting humans and animals eating contaminated food.
• [modern Latin from J. *Lister*, English surgeon d.1912]

listeriosis *noun*
- "liss teery OH sis"
- infection with, or a disease caused by, listerias, contracted esp. by the ingestion of contaminated food or silage.
- [as LISTERIA]

listserv *noun*
- "LIST surv"
- an email system which automatically sends messages to all subscribers on specific mailing lists, in special interest groups, etc.
- ['list' + 'serve']

litany *noun*
- "LITTA nee"
- a series of petitions for use in church services or processions, usu. recited by the clergy and responded to in a recurring formula by the people.
- [Old French *letanie* from Church Latin *litania* from Greek *litaneia* prayer, from *litē* supplication]

litas *noun*
- "LEE tass"
- the basic monetary unit of Lithuania, equal to 100 cents.
- [Lithuanian]

literal *adjective*
- "LITTER'll"
- taking words in their usual or primary sense without metaphor or allegory.
- [Old French *literal* or Late Latin *litteralis* from Latin *littera* letter of alphabet, (in pl.) epistle, literature]
- **literality** *noun*
- **literalize** *verb* (also esp. *Brit.* **-ise**)
- **literally** *adverb*
- **literalness** *noun*

HOMOPHONES: *littoral*

literalism *noun*
- "LITTER'll izm"
- insistence on a literal interpretation; adherence to the letter.
- [as LITERAL]
- **literalist** *noun*
- **literalistic** *adjective*

literary *adjective*
- "LITTER airy"
- of, constituting, or occupied with books or literature or written composition, esp. of the kind valued for quality of form.
- [Latin *litterarius* from *littera* letter of alphabet, (in pl.) epistle, literature]
- **literarily** *adverb*
- **literariness** *noun*

literate *adjective*
- "LITTER it"
- able to read and write.
- [Latin *litteratus* from *littera* letter of alphabet, (in pl.) epistle, literature]
- **literacy** *noun*
- **literately** *adverb*

literati *plural noun*
- "litter OTTY"
- educated and intelligent people who produce or are well-versed in literature.
- [Latin, pl. of *literatus* from Latin *litera*, *littera* letter of alphabet, (in pl.) epistle, literature]

literature *noun*
- "LITTER a chur" or "LIT ruh chur"
- written works, esp. those whose value lies in beauty of language or in emotional effect.
- [Middle English, = literary culture, from Latin *litteratura* (as LITERATE)]

lithe *adjective*
- "LITHE" (with "LI" as in *LIE* and "THE" as in *BATHE*)
- moving or bending easily and gracefully; supple.
- [Old English *līthe* from Germanic]
- **lithely** *adverb*
- **litheness** *noun*

lithic *adjective*
- "LITHIC"
- of, like, or made of stone.
- [Greek *lithikos* (as LITHIUM)]

lithified *adjective*
- "LITHA fide"
- formed into stone.
- [Greek *lithos* stone]
- **lithification** *noun*

lithium *noun*
- "LITH ee um"
- a soft silver-white metallic element, the lightest metal, used in alloys and in batteries.
- [modern Latin *lithia* lithium oxide, alteration of earlier *lithion* from Greek neuter of *litheios* from *lithos* stone]

litho *noun*
- "LITH oh"
- = LITHOGRAPHY.
- [abbreviation]

lithography *noun*
- "lith OGGRA fee"
- a process of obtaining prints from a stone or metal surface so treated that what is to be printed can be inked but the remaining area rejects ink.
- [German *Lithographie* (Greek *lithos* stone, *graphia* writing)]
- **lithograph** *noun*
- **lithographer** *noun*
- **lithographic** *adjective*
- **lithographically** *adverb*

lithology *noun*
- "lith OLLA jee"
- the general physical characteristics of a rock, esp. as discernible without a microscope.
- [Greek *lithos* stone + *logos* word]
- **lithologic** *adjective*
- **lithological** *adjective*
- **lithologically** *adverb*

lithophyte *noun*
- "LITHA fite"
- a plant that grows on stone.
- [Greek *lithos* stone + *phuton* plant, from *phuō* come into being]

lithosphere *noun*
- "LITH us feer"
- the rigid outer portion of the earth including the crust and the outermost mantle, above the asthenosphere.
- [Greek *lithos* stone + SPHERE]
- **lithospheric** *adjective*

lithotomy *noun*
- "lith OTTA mee"
- the surgical removal of a stone from the urinary tract, esp. the bladder.
- [Late Latin from Greek *lithotomia* (*lithos* stone, *-tomia* cutting, from *temnō* cut)]

lithotripsy *noun*
- "LITHA trip see"
- a treatment using ultrasound to shatter a stone in the bladder into small particles that can be passed through the urethra.
- [Greek *lithos* stone + *tripsis* rubbing, from *tribo* rub]

lithotripter *noun*
- "LITHA tripter"
- a machine which generates and focuses ultrasonic waves to shatter stones in the bladder or kidney.
- [as LITHOTRIPSY]

Lithuanian *noun*
- "lith oo AY nee 'n" or "lith yoo AY nee 'n"
- a native or inhabitant of Lithuania on the Baltic Sea.

litigant *noun*
- "LITTA g'nt"
- a party to a lawsuit.
- [French (as LITIGATE)]

litigate *verb*
- "LITTA gate"
- take a claim or dispute to a law court; be a party to a lawsuit.
- [Latin *litigare litigat-* from *lis litis* lawsuit]
- **litigable** *adjective* "LITTA guh bull"
- **litigation** *noun*
- **litigator** *noun*

litigious *adjective*
- "luh TIDGE us"
- fond of or given to litigation or carrying on lawsuits, esp. unreasonably so.
- [Old French *litigieux* or Latin *litigiosus* from *litigium* litigation: see LITIGATE]
- **litigiously** *adverb*
- **litigiousness** *noun*

litotes *noun*
- "lie TOE teez"
- ironic understatement, esp. the expressing of an affirmative by the negative of its contrary, e.g. *no mean feat* for some great accomplishment.
- [Late Latin from Greek *litotēs* from *litos* plain, meagre]

litre *noun*

ALSO SPELLED: esp. *US* **liter**
- "LEETER"
- a metric unit of capacity, formerly defined as the volume of one kilogram of water under standard conditions, now equal to 1 cubic decimetre (about 35 oz.).
- [French from *litron*, an obsolete measure of capacity, from medieval Latin from Greek *litra* a Sicilian monetary unit]

HOMOPHONES: *leader*

littérateur *noun*
- "litter a TUR"
- a writer of literary or critical works; a literary person.
- [French, as LITERATURE]

littoral *adjective*
- "LITTER'll"
- of or on the shore of the sea, a lake, etc.
- [Latin *littoralis* from *litus litoris* shore]

HOMOPHONES: *literal*

liturgics *noun*
- "lih TUR jicks"
- the branch of knowledge that deals with liturgies, their form, origin, etc.
- [as LITURGY]

liturgy *noun*
- "LITTER jee"
- public worship, esp. in accordance with a prescribed form.
- [French *liturgie* or Late Latin *liturgia* from Greek *leitourgia* public worship, from *leitourgos* minister, from *leit-* public + *ergon* work]
- **liturgical** *adjective*
- **liturgically** *adverb*
- **liturgist** *noun*

livelihood *noun*
- "LIVE lee hood" ("LIVE" rhymes with *DIVE*, and with "OO" as in *GOOD*)
- a way of earning a living; an occupation.
- [Old English *līflād* from *līf* life + *lād* course: assimilated to obsolete *livelihood* liveliness]

Liverpudlian *noun*
- "livver PUD lee 'n"
- a native of Liverpool, England.
- [jocular from *Liverpool* + 'puddle']

liverwort *noun*
- "LIVVER wurt" or "LIVVER wort"
- any small leafy or thalloid bryophyte of the class Hepaticae, of which some have liver-shaped parts.
- ['liver' + WORT]

liverwurst *noun*
• "LIVVER wurst"
• a cooked sausage having a high proportion of esp. pork liver.
• ['liver' + German *Wurst* sausage]

livery *noun*
• "LIVVER ee"
• a distinctive uniform worn by servants in a particular household.
• [Old French *livrée*, feminine past participle of *livrer* deliver]
• **liveried** *adjective*

livid *adjective*
• "LIVVID"
• furiously angry.
• [French *livide* or Latin *lividus* from *livēre* be bluish]
• **lividity** *noun*
• **lividly** *adverb*
• **lividness** *noun*

Livonian *noun*
• "liv OH nee 'n"
• a person from the region of Livonia, comprising most of Latvia and Estonia.

livre *noun*
• "LEEV ruh"
• an old French monetary unit, worth one pound of silver.
• [French from Latin *libra* pound]

lixiviate *verb*
• "lick SIVVY ate"
• separate (a substance) into soluble and insoluble constituents by the percolation of liquid.
• [Latin *lixivius* made into lye, from *lix* lye]
• **lixiviation** *noun*

lizard *noun*
• "LIZZ'rd"
• any reptile of the suborder Lacertilia, having usu. a long body and tail, four legs, movable eyelids, and a rough or scaly hide.
• [Old French *lesard(e)* from Latin *lacertus*]

llama *noun*
• "LAMMA" or "LOMMA"
• a S American ruminant, *Lama glama*, kept as a beast of burden and for its soft woolly fleece.
• [Spanish, prob. from Quechua]
HOMOPHONES: *lama*

llano *noun*
• "LANNO" or "L'YANNO"
• a treeless grassy plain or steppe, esp. in S America.
• [Spanish from Latin *planum* plain]

loath *adjective*
• "LOATH" (rhymes with *BOTH*)
• disinclined, reluctant, unwilling.
• [Old English *lāth* from Germanic]

loathe *verb*
• "LOTHE" (with "TH" as in *BATHE*)
• regard with disgust; abominate, detest.
• [Old English *lāthian* from Germanic, related to LOATH]
• **loather** *noun*
• **loathing** *noun*

loathsome *adjective*
• "LOTHE sum" (with "THE" either as in *BATH* or as in *BATHE*)
• arousing hatred or disgust; offensive, repulsive.
• [Middle English from *loath* disgust, from LOATHE]
• **loathsomely** *adverb*
• **loathsomeness** *noun*

lobar *adjective*
• "LOE bur"
• of the lungs.
• [Late Latin from Greek *lobos* lobe, pod]

lobate *adjective*
• "LOE bate"
• having a lobe or lobes; lobed.
• [as LOBAR]
• **lobation** *noun*

lobectomy *noun*
• "luh BECTA mee"
• the excision of a lobe of an organ such as the thyroid gland, lung, etc.
• [LOBAR + Greek *ektomē* excision, from *ek* out + *temnō* cut]

lobelia *noun*
• "luh BEELY uh"
• any plant of the genus *Lobelia*, with blue, scarlet, white, or purple flowers having a deeply cleft corolla.
• [M. de *Lobel*, Flemish botanist in England d.1616]

lobotomy *noun*
• "luh BOTTA mee"
• surgical incision into a lobe, esp. the prefrontal lobe of the brain, formerly used to treat intractable psychiatric disorders.
• [Greek *lobos* lobe, pod + *-tomia* cutting, from *temnō* cut]
• **lobotomize** *verb* (also esp. *Brit.* **-ise**)

lobscouse *noun*
• "LOB scouse" (rhymes with *HOUSE*)
• a sailor's dish of meat stewed with vegetables and ship's biscuit.
• [18th c.: origin unknown: compare Dutch *lapskous*, Danish, Norwegian, German *Lapskaus*]

lobule *noun*
• "LOB yool"
• a small lobe or a subdivision of a lobe.
• [Greek *lobos* lobe]
• **lobular** *adjective*
• **lobulate** *adjective*

local *adjective*
• "LO k'll"
• belonging to, existing in, or pertaining to a

particular locality as opposed to the country as a whole.
• [Old French from Late Latin *localis* from Latin *locus* place]
• **locally** *adverb*
• **localness** *noun*

locale *noun*
• "lo CAL"
• a scene or locality, esp. with reference to an event or occurrence taking place there.
• [French *local* (n.) (as LOCAL), respelt to indicate stress: compare MORALE]

localism *noun*
• "LO k'll izm"
• preference for what is local.
• [as LOCAL]

locality *noun*
• "lo CALA tee"
• an area or district considered as the site occupied by certain people or things or as the scene of certain activities; a neighbourhood.
• [French *localité* or Late Latin *localitas* (as LOCAL)]

localize *verb*
ALSO SPELLED: esp. *Brit.* **-ise**
• "LO k'll ize"
• restrict or assign to a particular place.
• [as LOCAL]
• **localizable** *adjective* (also esp. *Brit.* **-isable**)
• **localization** *noun* (also esp. *Brit.* **-isation**)
• **localized** *adjective* (also esp. *Brit.* **-ised**)
• **localizer** *noun* (also esp. *Brit.* **-iser**)

locate *verb*
• "lo CATE" or "LO cate"
• discover the exact place or position of.
• [Latin *locare locat-* from *locus* place]
• **locatable** *adjective*
• **locator** *noun*

location *noun*
• "lo CAY sh'n"
• a particular place; the place or position in which a person or thing is.
• [as LOCATE]
• **locational** *adjective*

locative *noun*
• "LOCKA tiv"
• (in some languages) the case of nouns, pronouns, and adjectives, expressing location.
• [formed as LOCATE, after *vocative*]

loch *noun*
• "LOCK"
• a lake in Scotland.
• [Middle English from Gaelic]
HOMOPHONES: *lakh*, *lock*

loche *noun*
• "LOSH"
• *Cdn* (*North*) a freshwater fish, *Lota lota*, of the cod family, with a broad head and barbels.
• [French *loche* from Gaulish *leuka* whiteness, with reference to the colour of its flesh]

lochia *noun*
• "LOCKY uh" or "LO kee uh"
• a discharge from the uterus after childbirth.
• [modern Latin from Greek *lokhia* neuter pl. of *lokhios* of childbirth]
• **lochial** *adjective*

locomotion *noun*
• "lo kuh MOE sh'n"
• motion or the power of motion from one place to another.
• [Latin *loco* ablative of *locus* place + *motio* motion]

locomotive *noun*
• "lo kuh MOE tiv"
• an engine, powered by diesel fuel or electricity, used for pulling trains.
• [as LOCOMOTION]

locomotor *adjective*
• "lo kuh MOTER"
• of or relating to locomotion.
• [LOCOMOTION + 'motor' (Latin, = mover)]

loculus *noun*
• "LOCK yoo luss"
• each of a number of small separate cavities.
• [Latin, diminutive of *locus*: see LOCUS]
• **locular** *adjective*

locum *noun*
• "LOE k'm"
• a temporary substitute, esp. for a doctor, lawyer, minister, etc.
• [medieval Latin *locum tenens*, one holding a place: see LOCUS, TENANT]

locus *noun*
• "LO cuss"
• a position or point, esp. in a text, treatise, etc.
• [Latin, = place]

locust *noun*
• "LO kust"
• any of various grasshoppers of the family Acrididae, migrating in swarms and destroying vegetation.
• [Old French *locuste* from Latin *locusta* lobster, locust]

locution *noun*
• "lo KYOO sh'n"
• a word or phrase, esp. considered in regard to style or idiom.
• [Old French *locution* or Latin *locutio* from *loqui locut-* speak]
• **locutionary** *adjective*

lode *noun*
• "LODE"
• a vein of metal ore.
• [var. of 'load']
HOMOPHONES: *load*

loden *noun*
- "LODE 'n"
- a thick waterproof woollen cloth.
- [German, originally woven by peasants living in *Loderers*, Austria]

lodicule *noun*
- "LODDA kyool"
- a small green or white scale below the ovary of a grass flower.
- [Latin *lodicula* diminutive of *lodix* coverlet]

loess *noun*
- "LO ess"
- a deposit of fine light-coloured windblown dust found esp. in the basins of large rivers and very fertile when irrigated.
- [German *Löss* from Swiss German *lösch* loose, from *lösen* loosen]

logan *noun*
- "LO g'n"
- *Cdn* (*Nfld*) a leather boot with a rubber foot, reaching to below the knee, worn in winter or when working in the bush.
- [origin unknown]

loganberry *noun*
- "LO g'n berry"
- a hybrid, *Rubus loganobaccus*, between a blackberry and a raspberry, with dark red acid fruits.
- [J. H. *Logan*, US horticulturalist d.1928 + 'berry']

logarithm *noun*
- "LOGGA rith'm"
- a figure representing the power to which a fixed number or base must be raised to produce a given number, used to simplify calculations as the addition and subtraction of logarithms is equivalent to multiplication and division.
- [modern Latin *logarithmus* from Greek *logos* reckoning, ratio + *arithmos* number]
- **logarithmic** *adjective*
- **logarithmically** *adverb*

loge *noun*
- "LOAZH" (with "OA" as in *LOAD*)
- a seating area in a theatre, usu. elevated above the orchestra level and on the side.
- [French, from Old French *loge* arbour, hut, from medieval Latin *laubia*, *lobia* lodge, from Germanic]

loggia *noun*
- "LO juh" or "LODGE uh"
- an open-sided gallery or arcade.
- [Italian, = 'lodge', as LOGE]

logic *noun*
- "LODGE ick"
- the science of reasoning, proof, thinking, or inference.
- [Old French *logique* from Late Latin *logica* from Greek *logikē* (*tekhnē*) (art) of reason, from *logos* word]
- **logical** *adjective*
- **logicality** *noun*
- **logically** *adverb*
- **logician** *noun* "lodge ISH'n"

logistics *noun*
- "luh JIST icks"
- the organization of moving, lodging, and supplying troops and equipment.
- [French *logistique* from *loger* lodge (as LOGE)]
- **logistic** *adjective*
- **logistical** *adjective*
- **logistically** *adverb*

logocentric *noun*
- "lo go SENTRIC"
- centred on reason.
- [Greek *logos* word + CENTRE]
- **logocentrism** *noun*

logogram *noun*
- "LOGGA gram"
- a sign or character representing a word, e.g. the symbol & representing the word *and*.
- [Greek *logos* word + *gramma* thing written]

logorrhea *noun*
ALSO SPELLED: esp. *Brit.* **logorrhoea**
- "logga REE uh"
- an excessive flow of words esp. in mental illness.
- [Greek *logos* word + *rhoia* flow]

logotype *noun*
- "LOGGA tipe"
- a single piece of type that prints a word or group of separate letters.
- [Greek *logos* word + TYPE]

logy *adjective*
- "LO gee" (with "G" as in *GEEK*)
- dull and heavy in motion or thought.
- [origin uncertain: compare Dutch *log* heavy, dull]

loiter *verb*
- "LOY tur"
- hang about; linger idly.
- [Middle Dutch *loteren* wag about]
- **loiterer** *noun*

lollapalooza *noun*
ALSO SPELLED: **lalapalooza**
- "lolla puh LOOZA"
- an excellent or attractive person or thing.
- [fanciful formation]

Lollard *noun*
- "LOLL'rd"
- any of a group of radical Christians in the Middle Ages who followed or held opinions similar to those of the 14th-c. religious reformer John Wycliffe (d.1384).
- [Middle Dutch *lollaerd* from *lollen* mumble]
- **Lollardism** *noun*

lollipop *noun*
- "LOLLY pop"
- a large flat or round candy on a small stick, held in the hand and sucked.
- [perhaps from dialect *lolly* tongue]

lollop *verb*
- "LOLLUP"
- move forward in bounds, esp. in a loose-limbed way.
- [prob. from 'loll', of imitative origin]

Lombard *noun*
- "LOM bard"
- a native of Lombardy in N Italy.
- **Lombardic** *adjective*

lomentum *noun*
- "lo MEN tum"
- the pod of some leguminous plants, breaking up when mature into one-seeded joints.
- [Latin *lomentum* bean-meal (originally a cosmetic) from *lavare* wash]
- **lomentaceous** *adjective* "lo m'n TAY sh'ss"

longan *noun*
- "LONG g'n"
- an edible juicy fruit from a plant (*Dimocarpus longan*) related to the lychee, cultivated in SE Asia.
- [Chinese *lóngyǎn*, lit. = 'dragon's eye']

longeron *noun*
- "LONJER 'n"
- a longitudinal member of a plane's fuselage.
- [French, = girder]

longevity *noun*
- "lon JEVVA tee"
- long life.
- [Late Latin *longaevitas* from Latin *longus* long + *aevum* age]

longicorn *noun*
- "LONJA corn"
- a longhorn beetle.
- [modern Latin *longicornis* from Latin *longus* long + *cornu* horn]

longitude *noun*
- "LON juh tude" or "LONG guh tude"
- the angular distance east or west from a standard meridian such as Greenwich to the meridian of any place.
- [Latin *longitudo -dinis* from *longus* long]

longitudinal *adjective*
- "lon juh TUDE'n 'll" or "long guh TUDE'n 'll"
- of or in length.
- [as LONGITUDE]
- **longitudinally** *adverb*

longueur *noun*
- "lon GUR"
- a tedious passage in a book etc.
- [French, = length]

lonicera *noun*
- "luh NISSER uh"
- any shrub of the genus *Lonicera* with fragrant yellow, orange, white or pink flowers; a honeysuckle.
- [A. *Lonicerus*, German botanist d.1586]

loofah *noun*
ALSO SPELLED: **loofa**
- "LOOFA"
- a climbing gourd-like plant, *Luffa cylindrica*, native to Asia, producing edible marrow-like fruits.
- [Egyptian Arabic *lūfa*, the plant]

loosestrife *noun*
- "LOOSE strife"
- any plant of the genus *Lysimachia*, e.g. the European garden loosestrife, *L. vulgaris*, naturalized in N America.
- ['loose' + 'strife', taking the Greek name *lusimakhion* (from *Lusimakhos*, its discoverer) as if directly from *luō* undo + *makhē* battle]

lophophore *noun*
- "LO fuh for" or "LOFFA for"
- a horseshoe-shaped structure bearing ciliated tentacles around the mouth of bryozoans, brachiopods, etc.
- [Greek *lophos* crest + *-phoros -phoron* bearing, bearer, from *pherō* bear]
- **lophophorate** *adjective* "luh FOFFER ate" or "lo fuh FOR ate"

loppet *noun*
- "LOPPIT"
- a long-distance cross-country ski race in which all competitors start together.
- [Norwegian *løpet*, definite sing. of *løp* race, run, running (cognate with English *lope*)]

loquacious *adjective*
- "lo KWAY sh'ss"
- talkative.
- [Latin *loquax -acis* from *loqui* talk]
- **loquaciously** *adverb*
- **loquaciousness** *noun*
- **loquacity** *noun* "lo KWASSA tee"

loquat *noun*
- "LO kwot"
- a rosaceous tree, *Eriobotrya japonica*, bearing small yellow egg-shaped fruits.
- [Chinese dialect *luh kwat* rush orange]

lordosis *noun*
- "lor DOE sis"
- inward curvature of the spine.
- [modern Latin from Greek *lordōsis* from *lordos* bent backwards]
- **lordotic** *adjective* "lor DOTTIC"

Lorelei *noun*
- "LORA lie"
- a dangerously fascinating woman; a temptress.
- [name of a siren said to lure Rhine boatmen to destruction]

lorgnette *noun*
- "lor NYET"
- a pair of eyeglasses or opera glasses held by a long handle.
- [French from *lorgner* to squint]

lorikeet *noun*
• "LORA keet"
• any of various small brightly coloured parrots of the subfamily Loriinae, including the rainbow lorikeet.
• [diminutive of LORY, after *parakeet*]

loris *noun*
• "LOR iss"
• either of two small tailless nocturnal primates of the subfamily Lorisinae, with small ears, very short tails, and opposable thumbs.
• [French perhaps from obsolete Dutch *loeris* clown]

lorry *noun*
• "LORY"
• a truck.
• [19th c.: origin uncertain]
HOMOPHONES: *lory*

lory *noun*
• "LORY"
• any of various brightly coloured Australasian parrots of the subfamily Loriinae.
• [Malay *lūri*]
HOMOPHONES: *lorry*

lose *verb*
• "LOOZ"
• be deprived of or cease to have, esp. by negligence or misadventure.
• [Old English *losian* perish, destroy, from *los* loss]
• **loser** *noun*
• **losing** *noun*

Lothario *noun*
• "luh THARE ee oh" or "luh THAR ee oh" (with "TH" as in *THIN*)
• a man known for many sexual conquests.
• [a character in Rowe's *Fair Penitent* (1703)]

loti *noun*
• "LO tee" or "LOO tee"
• the basic monetary unit of Lesotho, equal to 100 lisente.
• [Sesotho]

lotus *noun*
• "LO tuss"
• (in Greek mythology) a legendary plant inducing luxurious languor when eaten.
• [Latin from Greek *lōtos*, of Semitic origin]

louche *adjective*
• "LOOSH"
• disreputable, shifty.
• [French, lit. 'squinting']

Loucheux *noun*
• "LOO shoo"
• a member of an Athapaskan Aboriginal people living in Alaska, the Yukon, and the NWT, also called the Gwich'in.
• [French, 'squinting', translation of Gwich'in *Tukkuth*, lit. 'people of the slanting eyes', one of the Gwich'in bands]

louis *noun*
• "LOOEY"
• a former French gold coin worth about 20 francs.
• [*Louis*, the name of kings of France]

loungey *adjective*
• "LOWN jee" ("LOWN" rhymes with *BROWN*)
• (of a place) conducive to lounging; comfortable.
• [perhaps from obsolete *lungis* lout]

loupe *noun*
• "LOOP"
• a small magnifying glass used by jewellers etc.
• [French]
HOMOPHONES: *loop*

lousewort *noun*
• "LOUSE wurt" or "LOUSE wort" ("LOUSE" rhymes with *HOUSE*)
• any plant of the genus *Pedicularis* with purple-pink flowers found in marshes and wet places.
• ['louse' + WORT]

louvre *noun*
ALSO SPELLED: **louver**
• "LOOVER"
• each of a set of overlapping slats, esp. in a door, designed to admit air and some light.
• [Old French *lover*, *lovier* skylight, prob. from Germanic]
• **louvred** *adjective*

lovage *noun*
• "LUV idge"
• a S European herb, *Levisticum officinale*, used for flavouring etc.
• [Middle English *loveache* alteration of Old French *levesche* from Late Latin *levisticum* from Latin *ligusticum* neuter of *ligusticus* Ligurian]

lovat *noun*
• "LUV it"
• a muted green colour found esp. in tweed and woollen garments.
• [*Lovat*, a place in Highland Scotland]

lovey *noun*
• "LUVVY"
• love, sweetheart (esp. as a form of address).
• [from 'love']

lozenge *noun*
• "LOZ inj"
• a rhombus or diamond figure.
• [Old French *losenge*, probably derived from the base of Spanish *losa*, Portuguese *lousa* slab, Late Latin *lausiae (lapides)* (stone) slabs]

luau *noun*
• "LOO ow"
• a Hawaiian party or feast usu. accompanied by some form of entertainment.
• [Hawaiian *lū'au*]

Lubavitcher *noun*
• "LOOBA vitch ur" or "loo BAH vuh chur"

• a member of a group of Hasidic Jews founded in the 18th c., stressing piety and missionary work.

• [from *Lubavich*, a town in Russia near Smolensk, an important centre for the group in the 19th c.]

lubricant *noun*
• "LOOBRA k'nt"
• a substance used to reduce friction.
• [as LUBRICATE]

lubricate *verb*
• "LOOBRA cate"
• reduce friction in (machinery etc.) by applying oil or grease etc.
• [Latin *lubricare lubricat-* from *lubricus* slippery]
• **lubrication** *noun*
• **lubricator** *noun*

lubricious *adjective*
• "loo BRISH us"
• lewd, prurient.
• [Latin *lubricus* slippery]
• **lubricity** *noun* "loo BRISSA tee"

lucent *adjective*
• "LOO s'nt"
• shining, luminous.
• [Latin *lucēre* shine, from *lux* light]
• **lucency** *noun*

lucerne *noun*
ALSO SPELLED: **lucern**
• "loo SURN"
• a leguminous plant, *Medicago sativa*, with clover-like leaves and flowers used for fodder; alfalfa.
• [French *luzerne* from modern Provençal *luzerno* glow-worm, with reference to its shiny seeds]

lucid *adjective*
• "LOO sid"
• expressing or expressed clearly; easy to understand.
• [Latin *lucidus* (perhaps through French *lucide* or Italian *lucido*) from *lucēre* shine, from *lux* light]
• **lucidity** *noun*
• **lucidly** *adverb*
• **lucidness** *noun*

luciferase *noun*
• "loo SIFFER ace"
• an enzyme which catalyzes a reaction by which a luciferin produces light.
• [as LUCIFERIN]

luciferin *noun*
• "loo SIFFER in"
• a substance in an organism such as the firefly which can produce light when oxidized in the presence of a specific enzyme.
• [Old English *lucifer* from Latin, = light-bringing, morning star (*lux* light, *-fer* from *ferre* bring)]

lucrative *adjective*
• "LOO cruh tiv"
• profitable, yielding financial gain.
• [Latin *lucrativus* from *lucrari* to gain]
• **lucratively** *adverb*
• **lucrativeness** *noun*

lucre *noun*
• "LOO cur"
• financial profit or gain.
• [French *lucre* or Latin *lucrum*]

lucubration *noun*
• "loo kyoo BRAY sh'n"
• literary writings, esp. of a pedantic or elaborate character.
• [Latin *lucubratio* from *lucubrare* work by lamplight, from *lux* light]

Lucullan *adjective*
• "loo CULL'n"
• (esp. of food) profusely luxurious.
• [Licinius *Lucullus*, Roman general d. *c.*56 BC, known for his luxurious tastes]

Luddite *noun*
• "LUD ite"
• a member of any of the bands of English artisans who rioted against mechanization and destroyed machinery (1811–16).
• [perhaps from Ned *Lud*, who destroyed machinery *c.*1779]
• **Luddism** *noun*

ludic *adjective*
• "LOODIC"
• spontaneously playful.
• [French *ludique*, from Latin *ludere* to play, from *ludus* sport]
• **ludically** *adverb*

ludicrous *adjective*
• "LOODA cruss"
• absurd or ridiculous; laughable.
• [Latin *ludicrus* prob. from *ludicrum* stage play]
• **ludicrously** *adverb*
• **ludicrousness** *noun*

ludo *noun*
• "LOODO"
• a simple board game in which counters are moved around according to the throw of dice.
• [Latin, = I play]

Luftwaffe *noun*
• "LOOFT voffa"
• the German air force up to the end of the Second World War.
• [German from *Luft* air + *Waffe* weapon]

luge *noun*
• "LOOZH"
• a light sled with runners for one or two people, ridden in a sitting or supine position.
• [Swiss French]
• **luger** *noun*

lugubrious *adjective*
• "loo GOO bree us"
• doleful, mournful, dismal.

• [Latin *lugubris* from *lugēre* mourn]
• **lugubriously** *adverb*
• **lugubriousness** *noun*

lulu *noun*
• "LOO loo"
• a remarkable, incredible, or memorable person or thing, esp. for its unpleasantness.
• [19th c., perhaps from *Lulu*, pet form of *Louise*]

luma *noun*
• "LOOMA"
• a monetary unit of Armenia, equal to one-hundredth of a dram.
• [Armenian]

lumbago *noun*
• "lum BAY go"
• rheumatic pain in the muscles of the lower back.
• [Latin from *lumbus* loin]

lumbar *adjective*
• "LUMBER" or "LUM bar"
• relating to the loin, esp. the lower back area.
• [medieval Latin *lumbaris* from Latin *lumbus* loin]
HOMOPHONES: *lumber*

lumen *noun*
• "LOOMIN"
• the SI unit of luminous flux, equal to the amount of light emitted per second in a unit solid angle of one steradian from a uniform source of one candela.
• [Latin *lumen luminis* a light, an opening]

luminaire *noun*
• "LOOMIN air"
• a unit consisting of an electric light and its fittings.
• [French, as LUMINARY]

luminance *noun*
• "LOOMIN ince"
• the state or quality of reflecting light.
• [Latin *luminare* illuminate (as LUMEN)]

luminary *noun*
• "LOOMIN airy"
• a prominent member of a group or gathering.
• [Old French *luminarie* or Late Latin *luminarium* from Latin LUMEN]

luminescence *noun*
• "loomin ESS ince"
• the emission of light by a substance that has not been heated, as in fluorescence and phosphorescence.
• [as LUMEN + Latin *-escent-* used in verb forms to signify becoming]
• **luminescent** *adjective*

luminous *adjective*
• "LOOMIN us"
• full of or shedding light; radiant, bright, shining.
• [Old French *lumineux* or Latin *luminosus*, as LUMEN]
• **luminosity** *noun* "loomin OSSA tee"
• **luminously** *adverb*
• **luminousness** *noun*

lummox *noun*
• "LUM ix"
• a clumsy or stupid person.
• [19th c. in US & dialect: origin unknown]

lumpectomy *noun*
• "lump ECTA mee"
• the surgical removal of a usu. cancerous lump from the breast.
• ['lump' + Greek *ektomē* excision, from *ek* out + *temnō* cut]

lumpen *adjective*
• "LUMP 'n"
• *derogatory* ignorantly contented, boorish, stupid; uninterested in revolutionary advancement.
• [back-formation from LUMPENPROLETARIAT]

lumpenproletariat *noun*
• "lump'n pro luh TERRY ut"
• (esp. in Marxist terminology) the unorganized and unpolitical lower orders of society, not interested in revolutionary advancement.
• [German from *Lumpen* rag, rogue: see PROLETARIAT]

lumpia *noun*
• "LUMPY uh"
• an Indonesian spring roll served with a sauce for dipping.
• [Dutch *loempia* from Indonesian *lumpia*]

lunar *adjective*
• "LOONER"
• of, relating to, resembling, or determined by the moon.
• [Latin *lunaris* from *luna* moon]

lunate *adjective*
• "LOON ate"
• crescent-shaped.
• [Latin *lunatus* from *luna* moon]

lunatic *noun*
• "LOONA tick"
• an insane person.
• [Old French *lunatique* from Late Latin *lunaticus* from Latin *luna* moon]
• **lunacy** *noun*

lunation *noun*
• "loo NAY sh'n"
• the interval between new moons, about 29½ days.
• [medieval Latin *lunatio* (as LUNATIC)]

luncheon *noun*
• "LUNCH'n"
• a lunch, esp. a formal one.
• [17th c.: origin unknown]

luncheonette *noun*
• "lunch'n ET"
• a small restaurant or snack bar serving light lunches.
• [as LUNCHEON]

Lunenburger *noun*
• "LOON'n burger"
• a resident of Lunenburg, NS.

lunette *noun*
• "loo NET"
• an arched aperture in a domed ceiling to admit light.
• [French, diminutive of *lune* moon, from Latin *luna*]

lungi *noun*
• "LOON gee" (with "OO" as in *LOOK* and with "G" as in *GEEK*)
• a length of cotton cloth, usu. worn as a loincloth in India, or as a skirt in Burma (Myanmar) where it is the national dress for both sexes.
• [Urdu]

lungwort *noun*
• "LUNG wurt" or "LUNG wort"
• any herbaceous plant of the genus *Pulmonaria*, esp. *P. officinalis* with white-spotted leaves likened to a diseased lung.
• ['lung' + WORT]

lunisolar *adjective*
• "loona SO lur"
• of or concerning the sun and moon.
• [Latin *luna* moon + *sol* sun]

lunula *noun*
• "LOON yoo luh"
• a crescent-shaped mark, esp. the white area at the base of the fingernail.
• [Latin, diminutive of *luna* moon]

Lupercalia *noun*
• "looper CAY lee uh"
• an ancient Roman festival of purification and fertility, held on 15 February at a cave called the Lupercal.

lupine[1] *noun*
ALSO SPELLED: **lupin**
• "LOO pin"
• any plant of the genus *Lupinus*, with long tapering spikes of blue, purple, pink, white, or yellow flowers.
• [Latin *lupinus* '(grass) of the wolf']

lupine[2] *adjective*
• "LOO pine"
• of or like a wolf or wolves.
• [Latin *lupinus* from *lupus* wolf]

lupini *noun*
• "loo PEENY"
• the seed of a large-seeded bitter variety of lupine, eaten as food.
• [Italian, pl. of *lupino* LUPINE[1]]

lupous *adjective*
• "LOO pus"
• pertaining to lupus.
• [Latin, = wolf]
HOMOPHONES: *lupus*

lupus *noun*
• "LOO pus"
• any of various ulcerous or erosive skin diseases, esp. lupus erythematosus.
• [Latin, = wolf]
• **lupoid** *adjective*
HOMOPHONES: *lupous*

luscious *adjective*
• "LUSH us"
• richly sweet in taste or smell.
• [Middle English perhaps alteration of obsolete *licious* from DELICIOUS]
• **lusciously** *adverb*
• **lusciousness** *noun*

Lusitanian *adjective*
• "loo suh TAY nee 'n"
• of or relating to Lusitania, the ancient Roman province comprising modern Spain and Portugal.

lustration *noun*
• "luss TRAY sh'n"
• purification by expiatory sacrifice, ceremonial washing, or other such rite.
• [Latin *lustrare* (as LUSTRUM)]

lustre *noun*
ALSO SPELLED: esp. *US* **luster**
• "LUSTER"
• gloss, brilliance, or sheen.
• [French from Italian *lustro* from *lustrare* from Latin *lustrare* illuminate]
• **lustreless** *adjective* (also esp. *US* **lusterless**)
• **lustrous** *adjective*
• **lustrously** *adverb*
• **lustrousness** *noun*

lustreware *noun*
ALSO SPELLED: esp. *US* **lusterware**
• "LUSTER ware"
• ceramics with an iridescent glaze.
• [LUSTRE + WARE]

lustrum *noun*
• "LUS trum"
• a period of five years.
• [Latin, an originally purificatory sacrifice after a quinquennial census]

lusus *noun*
• "LOO suss"
• a freak of nature.
• [Latin]

lute *noun*
• "LOOT"
• a guitar-like instrument with a long neck and a pear-shaped body, much used in the 14th–17th c.

• [French *lut*, *leüt*, prob. from Provençal *laüt* from Arabic *al-'ūd*]
HOMOPHONES: *loot*

luteal *adjective*
• "LOOTY 'll"
• of or pertaining to the corpus luteum, a hormone-secreting mass of tissue that develops in the ovary after discharge of an ovum, remaining in existence only if pregnancy has begun.
• [as LUTEIN]

lutein *noun*
• "LOOTY in"
• a pigment of a deep yellow colour found in egg yolk etc.
• [Latin *luteum* yolk of egg, neuter of *luteus* yellow]

luteinizing *adjective*
ALSO SPELLED: esp. *Brit.* **-ising**
• "LOOTIN ize ing"
• designating a hormone secreted by the anterior pituitary gland that in females stimulates ovulation and in males stimulates the synthesis of androgen.
• [as LUTEIN]

lutenist *noun*
• "LOO t'n ist"
• a lute player.
• [medieval Latin *lutanista* from *lutana* LUTE]

lutetium *noun*
• "loo TEESHY um"
• a silvery metallic element of the lanthanide series.
• [French *lutécium* from Latin *Lutetia* the ancient name of Paris, France, the home of its discoverer]

Lutheran *noun*
• "LOOTH ur in"
• a member of the Church which accepts the Augsburg Confession of 1530, with justification by faith alone as a cardinal doctrine.
• [Martin *Luther* German religious reformer d.1546]
• **Lutheranism** *noun*

luthier *noun*
• "LOOTY ur"
• a maker of stringed instruments, esp. those of the violin family and guitars.
• [French from *luth* LUTE]

Lutz *noun*
• "LUTS"
• a jump in which the skater takes off from the back outside edge of one skate, using the toe of the free foot to assist the takeoff, and lands, after at least one complete rotation in the air, on the back outside edge of the other skate.
• [prob. from the name of Gustave *Lussi* b.1898, who invented it]

luxe *noun*
• "LUCKS" or "LOOKS"
• luxury.
• [French from Latin *luxus*]
HOMOPHONES: *lux*

Luxembourger *noun*
• "LUCKS 'm burger"
• a native or national of the Grand Duchy of Luxembourg in NW Europe.

Luxemburgish *noun*
• "LUCKS 'm burg ish"
• a form of German spoken in the Grand Duchy of Luxembourg.

luxuriant *adjective*
• "lug ZHURRY 'nt" or "luck SHURRY 'nt"
• (of vegetation, hair, etc.) lush, profuse in growth.
• [Latin *luxuriare* grow rank, from *luxuria* LUXURY]
• **luxuriance** *noun*
• **luxuriantly** *adverb*

luxuriate *verb*
• "lug ZHURRY ate" or "luck SHURRY ate"
• take self-indulgent delight in, enjoy in a luxurious manner.
• [as LUXURY]

luxurious *adjective*
• "lug ZHURRY us" or "luck SHURRY us"
• characterized by luxury; sumptuous, rich.
• [as LUXURY]
• **luxuriously** *adverb*
• **luxuriousness** *noun*

luxury *noun*
• "LUCK shur ee" or "LUG zhur ee"
• choice or costly surroundings, possessions, food, etc.; luxuriousness.
• [Old French *luxurie*, *luxure* from Latin *luxuria* from *luxus* abundance]

lwei *noun*
• "luh WAY"
• a monetary unit of Angola, equal to one-hundredth of a kwanza.
• [Angolan name]

lycanthropy *noun*
• "lie CAN thruh pee"
• the mythical transformation of a person into a wolf.
• [modern Latin *lycanthropia* from Greek *lukanthrōpia* from *lukos* wolf + *anthrōpos* man]
• **lycanthrope** *noun* "LIKE 'n thrope"
• **lycanthropic** *adjective* "like 'n THROPPIC"

lycée *noun*
• "lee SAY"
• a public secondary school in France.
• [French from Latin (as LYCEUM)]

Lyceum *noun*
• "lie SEE um"
• (esp. in the names of buildings) a concert hall or theatre.

• [Latin from Greek *Lukeion* the garden at Athens in which Aristotle taught philosophy, neuter of *Lukeios* epithet of Apollo (from whose neighbouring temple the Lyceum was named)]

lychee ***noun***
ALSO SPELLED: **litchi**, **lichee**
• "LEE chee"
• a sweet fleshy fruit with a thin spiny skin.
• [Chinese *lizhi*]

lycopene ***noun***
• "LIKE a peen"
• a red carotenoid pigment and antioxidant present in tomatoes and some fruits.
• [from the variant *lycopin* (from modern Latin *Lycopersicon*, a genus name including the tomato) + '-ene' forming names of unsaturated hydrocarbons containing a double bond, from Greek *-ēnos*, adjective suffix denoting origin or source]

lycopod ***noun***
• "LIKE a pod"
• any of various clubmosses, esp. of the genus *Lycopodium*.
• [anglicized form of LYCOPODIUM]

lycopodium ***noun***
• "like a POE dee um"
• = LYCOPOD.
• [modern Latin from Greek *lukos* wolf + *pous podos* foot]

Lydian ***noun***
• "LIDDY 'n"
• a native or inhabitant of ancient Lydia in W Asia Minor.

lye ***noun***
• "LIE"
• any strong alkaline solution, esp. of potassium hydroxide used for washing or cleansing.
• [Old English *lēag* from Germanic]
HOMOPHONES: *lie*

lymph ***noun***
• "LIMF"
• a colourless fluid containing white blood cells, drained from the tissues and conveyed through the body in the lymphatic system.
• [French *lymphe* or Latin *lympha*, *limpa* water]
• **lymphoid** ***adjective***

lymphadenopathy ***noun***
• "limf ad'n OPPA thee" (with "TH" as in *THIN*)
• chronic swelling of the lymph nodes.
• [as LYMPH + Greek *adēn* gland + *patheia* suffering]

lymphatic ***adjective***
• "lim FATTIC"
• of or secreting or conveying lymph.
• [as LYMPH]

lymphoblast ***noun***
• "LIMFA blast"
• an abnormal cell resembling a large lymphocyte, produced in large numbers in a form of leukemia.
• [as LYMPH + Greek *blastos* sprout]
• **lymphoblastic** ***adjective***

lymphocyte ***noun***
• "LIMFA site"
• a form of leukocyte occurring in the blood, in lymph, etc.
• [LYMPH + Greek *kutos* vessel]
• **lymphocytic** ***adjective*** "limfa SITTIC"

lymphokine ***noun***
• "LIMFA kine"
• any of various soluble substances released by lymphocytes which are thought to be involved in cell-mediated immunity but to lack the antigen-specificity of antibodies.
• [LYMPH + Greek *kinein* move]

lymphoma ***noun***
• "lim FOE muh"
• any malignant tumour of the lymph nodes, excluding leukemia.
• [as LYMPH + *-oma* from CARCINOMA]

lynch ***verb***
• "LINCH"
• (of a body of people) put (a person) to death, esp. by hanging, for an alleged offence without a legal trial.
• [*Lynch's law*, after Capt. W. *Lynch* of Virginia *c.*1780]
• **lyncher** ***noun***
• **lynching** ***noun***

lynx ***noun***
• "LINKS"
• any of various small to medium-sized members of the cat family typically having a short tail, tufted ears, and mottled or spotted fur, esp. *Lynx canadensis* of northern N America or the smaller *Lynx lynx*, which inhabits forest in NW Europe and northern Asia.
• [Latin from Greek *lugx*]
HOMOPHONES: *links*

lyophilic ***adjective***
• "lie a FILLIC"
• (of a colloid) readily dispersed by a solvent.
• [Greek *luō* loosen, dissolve + *philos* loving]

lyophilize ***verb***
ALSO SPELLED: esp. *Brit.* **-ise**
• "lie OFF'll ize"
• freeze-dry.
• [as LYOPHILIC]
• **lyophilization** ***noun*** (also esp. *Brit.* **-isation**)

lyophobic ***adjective***
• "lie a FOE bick"
• (of a colloid) not lyophilic.
• [Greek *luō* loosen, dissolve + PHOBIC (see PHOBIA)]

lyrate ***adjective***
• "LIRE ate"
• lyre-shaped.
• [as LYRE]

lyre *noun*
- "LIRE"
- an ancient stringed instrument like a small U-shaped harp, played usu. with a plectrum and accompanying the voice.
- [Old French *lire* from Latin *lyra* from Greek *lura*]
- **lyrist** *noun*

HOMOPHONES: *liar*

lyrebird *noun*
- "LIRE bird"
- any Australian bird of the family Menuridae, the male of which has a lyre-shaped tail display.
- [as LYRE + 'bird']

lyric *adjective*
- "LEER ick"
- (of poetry) expressing the writer's emotions, usu. briefly and in stanzas or recognized forms.
- [as LYRE]
- **lyrical** *adjective*
- **lyrically** *adverb*
- **lyricism** *noun* "LEERA sizm"

lyricist *noun*
- "LEERA sist"
- a person who writes the words to a song.
- [as LYRIC]

lyse *verb*
- "LIZE" or "LICE"
- bring about or undergo lysis.
- [back-formation from LYSIS]

HOMOPHONES: *lice*

lysergic *adjective*
- "lie SUR jick"
- designating a crystalline acid extracted from ergot or prepared synthetically.
- [hydro*lysis* + *ergot*]

lysin *noun*
- "LICE in"
- a protein in the blood able to cause lysis.
- [as LYSIS]

lysine *noun*
- "LICE een"
- a basic amino acid which is a constituent of most proteins and essential in the diet of vertebrates.
- [as LYSIS]

lysis *noun*
- "LICE iss"
- the disintegration of a cell.
- [Latin from Greek *lusis* loosening, from *luō* loosen]

lysosome *noun*
- "LICE a soam"
- a cytoplasmic organelle in eukaryotic cells containing degradative enzymes enclosed in a membrane.
- [as LYSIS + Greek *sōma* body]
- **lysosomal** *adjective*

lysozyme *noun*
- "LICE a zime"
- an enzyme found in tears and egg white which catalyzes the destruction of cell walls of certain bacteria.
- [LYSIS + ENZYME]

lythrum *noun*
- "LITH rum"
- a genus of plants including among others the purple loosestrife.
- [modern Latin from Greek *lythron* gore, from the colour of the flowers]

lytic *adjective*
- "LITTIC"
- of, relating to, or causing lysis.
- [as LYSIS]

Mm

macabre *adjective*
• "muh COBBRA" or "muh COB" or "muh CABBRA"
• grim, gruesome.
• [Old French *macabré* perhaps from *Macabé* a Maccabee, with reference to a miracle play showing the slaughter of the Maccabees (see MACCABEAN)]

macadam *noun*
• "muh CAD 'm"
• material for road building with successive layers of compacted broken stone.
• [J. L. *McAdam*, British surveyor d.1836, who advocated using this material]
• **macadamize** *verb* (also esp. *Brit.* **-ise**)

macadamia *noun*
• "macka DAY mee uh"
• any evergreen tree of the genus *Macadamia*, esp. *M. ternifolia*, bearing edible nutlike seeds.
• [J. *Macadam*, Australian chemist d.1865]

macaque *noun*
• "muh CACK"
• any monkey of the genus *Macaca*, including the rhesus monkey and Barbary ape, having prominent cheek pouches and usu. a long tail.
• [French from Portuguese *macaco* from Bantu *makaku* some monkeys, from *kaku* monkey]

Macarena *noun*
• "macka RAY nuh"
• a dance performed with hand and body language, including exaggerated hip motion, to 16 beats of music.
• [from a Spanish female given name, or from the name of a barrio of Seville]

macaroni *noun*
• "macka ROE nee"
• a tubular variety of pasta, usu. cut into short pieces.
• [Italian *maccaroni* from late Greek *makaria* 'food made from barley', from ancient Greek *makaarios* blessed (because originally a funeral or charitable meal)]

macaronic *noun*
• "macka RONNIC"
• verse in which vernacular words are introduced in the context of another language, esp. Latin.
• [modern Latin *macaronicus* from obsolete Italian *macaronico*, jocularly formed as MACARONI]

macaroon *noun*
• "macka ROON"
• a small light cookie made with egg whites, sugar, and ground almonds or coconut.
• [French *macaron* from Italian (as MACARONI)]

Macassar *noun*
• "muh CASSER"
• a kind of oil formerly used by men to make their hair shine and lie flat.
• [*Macassar*, a former name for Ujung Pandang in Indonesia, from where its ingredients were said to come]

macaw *noun*
• "muh CAW"
• any long-tailed brightly coloured parrot of the genus *Ara* or *Anodorhynchus*, native to S and Central America.
• [Portuguese *macao*, of unknown origin]

Maccabean *adjective*
• "macka BEE 'n"
• of, pertaining to, or reminiscent of Judas Maccabaeus or the Maccabees, who led a Jewish revolt in Judea from around 167 BC.

macchiato *noun*
• "macky OTTO"
• coffee served with a very small amount of hot milk or milk froth.
• [Italian *(caffè) macchiato*, from *caffè* coffee + *macchiato* stained]

macédoine *noun*
• "MASSA dwon"
• mixed vegetables or fruit, esp. cut up small or in jelly.
• [French, = Macedonia, with reference to the mixture of peoples there]

Macedonian *adjective*
• "massa DOE nee 'n"
• of or relating to the ancient region of Macedonia, the modern Greek region of Macedonia, or the Former Yugoslav Republic of Macedonia.

macerate *verb*
- "MASSER ate"
- make or become soft by soaking.
- [Latin *macerare macerat-*]
- **maceration** *noun*
- **macerator** *noun*

Mach *noun*
- "MOCK" or "MACK"
- the ratio of the speed of a body to the speed of sound in the surrounding medium.
- [E. *Mach*, Austrian physicist d.1916]

HOMOPHONES: *mock, mack, mac, Mac*

machaca *noun*
- "muh CHOCKA"
- a Mexican dish consisting of strips of dried meat (esp. beef) shredded, pounded to a pulp, and fried with onions, egg, tomatoes, peppers, etc.
- [Mexican Spanish from Spanish *machacar* to pound, to crush]

mâche *noun*
- "MOSH"
- a plant, *Valerianella locusta*, used in salad.
- [French]

HOMOPHONES: *mosh*

macher *noun*
- "MACK hur"
- usu. *derogatory* an important or overbearing person.
- [Yiddish *makher*, from Middle High German *Macher* doer, active person]

machete *noun*
- "muh SHETTY"
- a broad heavy knife, originally used in Central America and the W Indies as an implement and weapon.
- [Spanish from *macho* hammer, from Late Latin *marcus*]

Machiavellian *adjective*
- "macky a VELLY 'n"
- elaborately cunning; scheming, unscrupulous.
- [Niccolò dei *Machiavelli*, Italian political philosopher d.1527, who advocated resort to morally questionable methods in the interests of the state]
- **Machiavellianism** *noun*

machicolate *verb*
- "muh CHICKA late"
- furnish (a parapet etc.) with openings between supporting corbels for dropping stones etc. on attackers.
- [Old French *machicoler*, ultimately from Provençal *machacol* from *macar* crush + *col* neck]
- **machicolated** *adjective*
- **machicolation** *noun*

machination *noun*
- "masha NAY sh'n" or "macka NAY sh'n"
- a cunning plot or scheme.
- [Latin *machinari* contrive from *machina* from Greek *makhana* from *mēkhos* contrivance]

machismo *noun*
- "muh CHIZ moe" or "muh KIZ moe"
- exaggerated or aggressive pride in being male.
- [Spanish from *macho* male, from Latin *masculus*]

Machmeter *noun*
- "MOCK meeter" or "MACK meeter"
- an instrument indicating airspeed in the form of a Mach number.
- [as MACH + Greek *metron* measure]

macho *adjective*
- "MOTCH oh" or "MATCH oh"
- aggressively or ostentatiously masculine.
- [as MACHISMO]

mackerel *noun*
- "MACK rull"
- any of various swift-swimming pelagic fishes of the family Scombridae, of which several are commercially important as food fishes, esp. *Scomber scombrus*, of the N Atlantic and Mediterranean, which approaches the shore in shoals in summer for spawning.
- [Old French *maquerel*]

mackinaw *noun*
- "MACK 'n aw"
- a heavy, napped and felted woollen cloth, now usu. with a plaid design.
- [*Mackinaw* City, Michigan, an important trading post]

mackintosh *noun*

ALSO SPELLED: **macintosh**
- "MACK 'n tosh"
- a waterproof coat or cloak.
- [C. *Macintosh*, Scottish inventor d.1843, who originally patented the cloth]

HOMOPHONES: *McIntosh*

macle *noun*
- "MACK'll"
- a diamond or other crystal that is twinned.
- [French from Latin *macula* blemish: see MACULA]

macramé *noun*
- "MACRA may"
- the art of knotting cord or string in patterns to make decorative articles.
- [Turkish *makrama* bedspread, from Arabic *mikrama*]

macro *noun*
- "MACRO"
- a series of abbreviated instructions expanded automatically when required.
- [independent use of the prefix *macro-* from Greek *makro-* from *makros* long, large]

macrobiotic *adjective*
- "macro by OTTIC"
- relating to or following an originally Zen

Buddhist dietary system intended to prolong life, usu. comprised of pure vegetable foods, brown rice, etc.
• [Greek *makro-* from *makros* long, large + *biōtikos* fit for life, from *bios* life]

macrocarpa *noun*
• "macro CARPA"
• an evergreen tree, *Cupressus macrocarpa*, often cultivated for hedges or windbreaks.
• [modern Latin from Greek *makro-* from *makros* long, large + *karpos* fruit]

macrocephalic *adjective*
• "macro suh FALIC"
• having a long or large head.
• [Greek *makro-* from *makros* long, large + *kephalē* head]
• **macrocephaly** *noun* "macro SEFFA lee"

macrocosm *noun*
• "MACRO cozm"
• the universe; the whole of all nature.
• [Greek *makro-* from *makros* long, large + COSMOS]
• **macrocosmic** *adjective*

macroeconomics *noun*
• "macro eeka NOMMIX" or "macro ecka NOMMIX"
• the study of large-scale or general economic factors, e.g. national productivity.
• [Greek *makro-* from *makros* long, large + ECONOMICS]
• **macroeconomic** *adjective*
• **macroeconomist** *noun* "macro e CONNA mist"

macroevolution *noun*
• "macro evva LOO sh'n"
• major evolutionary change, esp. over a long period.
• [Greek *makro-* from *makros* long, large + EVOLUTION]
• **macroevolutionary** *adjective*

macromolecule *noun*
• "macro MOLLA kyool"
• a molecule containing a very large number of atoms and having a very high molecular weight, e.g. a molecule of a polymer, protein, or nucleic acid.
• [Greek *makro-* from *makros* long, large + MOLECULE]
• **macromolecular** *adjective* "macro muh LECK yuh lur"

macron *noun*
• "MACK ron"
• a written or printed mark (¯) over a long or stressed vowel.
• [Greek *makron* neuter of *makros* large]

macronutrient *noun*
• "macro NEW tree 'nt"
• a chemical required in relatively large amounts for the growth and development of living organisms.
• [Greek *makro-* from *makros* long, large + NUTRIENT]

macrophage *noun*
• "MACRO fage" ("FAGE" rhymes with *CAGE*)
• a large phagocytic white blood cell usu. occurring at points of infection.
• [Greek *makro-* from *makros* long, large + *-phagos* from *phagein* eat]
• **macrophagous** *adjective* "mack ROFFA guss"

macrophyte *noun*
• "MACRO fite"
• any plant, esp. an aquatic plant, large enough to be discerned by the naked eye.
• [Greek *makro-* from *makros* long, large + *phuton* plant, from *phuō* come into being]

macropod *noun*
• "MACRO pod"
• any plant-eating mammal of the family Macropodidae native to Australia and New Guinea, including kangaroos and wallabies.
• [Greek *makro-* from *makros* long, large + *pous podos* foot]

macroscopic *adjective*
• "macro SCOPPIC"
• visible to the naked eye.
• [Greek *makro-* from *makros* long, large + *skopos* target, from *skeptomai* look at]
• **macroscopically** *adverb*

macula *noun*
• "MACK yoo luh"
• a dark spot, esp. a permanent one, in the skin, e.g. a freckle.
• [Latin, = spot, mesh]
• **macular** *adjective*
• **maculation** *noun*

Madagascan *noun*
• "madda GAS k'n"
• a native or inhabitant of Madagascar off the east coast of Africa.

Madawaskan *noun*
• "madda WOSS k'n"
• a resident of the Madawaska region of NW New Brunswick.

Madeira *noun*
• "muh DEERA"
• a fortified white wine from the Portuguese island of Madeira.

Madeiran *noun*
• "muh DEER'n"
• a native or inhabitant of the Portuguese island of Madeira, off the NW coast of Africa.

madeleine *noun*
• "MADDA len"
• a small, shell-shaped sponge cake.
• [French]

Madelinot *noun*
• "madda lee NO"
• a resident or native of the Îles de la

Madeleine (Magdalen Islands) in the Gulf of St. Lawrence.
• [French]

Mademoiselle *noun*
• "mad mwuh ZELL"
• a title or form of address used of or to an unmarried French-speaking woman, corresponding to Miss or madam.
• [French from *ma* my + *demoiselle* DAMSEL]

maderization *noun*
• "madder ize AY sh'n"
• a form of oxidation which gives white wine a brownish colour and caramelized flavour like that of Madeira.
• [French *madérisation*, from *madériser*, from *Madère* Madeira]
• **maderized** *adjective* (also esp. *Brit.* **-ised**)

madras *noun*
• "muh DRASS"
• a strong cotton fabric with brightly coloured or white stripes, checks, etc.
• [*Madras*, the former name for Chennai, India]

madrepore *noun*
• "MADRA pore"
• any perforated coral of the genus *Madrepora*.
• [Italian *madrepora* from *madre* mother + *poro* pore]

madrigal *noun*
• "MADRA g'll"
• a usu. 16th-c. or 17th-c. part-song for several voices, usu. arranged in elaborate counterpoint and without instrumental accompaniment.
• [Italian *madrigale* from medieval Latin *matricalis* mother (church)]
• **madrigalist** *noun*

madroño *noun*
• "muh DRO nyo"
• an evergreen tree, *Arbutus menziesii*, of western N America, with white flowers, red berries, and glossy leaves.
• [Spanish]

Maecenas *noun*
• "my SEEN us"
• a generous patron of literature or art.
• [Gaius (Cilnius) Maecenas, Roman statesman d.8 BC, patron of poets]

maelstrom *noun*
• "MAIL strum"
• a great whirlpool.
• [early modern Dutch from *malen* grind, whirl + *stroom* stream]

maenad *noun*
• "MEEN ad"
• a female worshipper or follower of Bacchus, the Roman god of wine.
• [Latin *Maenas Maenad-* from Greek *Mainas -ados* from *mainomai* rave]
• **maenadism** *noun*

maestoso *adjective*
• "my STO zo"
• to be performed majestically.
• [Italian]

maestro *noun*
• "MY stro"
• a distinguished musician, esp. a conductor or performer.
• [Italian, = master]

mafic *adjective*
• "MAFFIC"
• of, pertaining to, or designating a group of dark coloured, mainly ferromagnesian minerals.
• [contraction of MAGNESIUM + FERRIC]

magalogue *noun*
• "MAGGA log"
• a promotional catalogue or sales brochure designed to resemble a high-quality magazine.
• [blend of MAGAZINE + CATALOGUE]

magazine *noun*
• "magga ZEEN"
• a periodical publication containing articles, stories, etc. by various writers, usu. with photographs, illustrations, etc.
• [French *magasin* from Italian *magazzino* from Arabic *makẕin* pl. of *makẕan* storehouse, from *kazana* store up]

magdalen *noun*
• "MAGDA l'n"
• a reformed prostitute.
• [Mary *Magdalene* of Magdala (Luke 8:2), identified (prob. wrongly) with the sinner of Luke 7:37]

Magdalenian *adjective*
• "magda LEENY 'n"
• of the culture of the latest paleolithic period in Europe, characterized by fine horn and bone tools and a strong artistic tradition.
• [French *Magdalénien* of La *Madeleine*, Dordogne, France, where remains were found]

magenta *noun*
• "muh JENTA"
• a brilliant mauvish-crimson shade.
• [*Magenta* in N Italy, site of a battle (1859) fought shortly before the dye was discovered]

magic *noun*
• "MADGE ick"
• the supposed art of influencing events by the occult control of nature or spirits.
• [Old French *magique* from Late Latin *magica* n., from Greek *magikos* (as MAGUS)]
• **magical** *adjective*
• **magically** *adverb*

magician *noun*
• "madge ISH'n"
• a person skilled in or practising magic or sorcery.
• [as MAGIC]

magisterial *adjective*
• "madge iss TEERY 'll"
• imperious, dictatorial.
• [medieval Latin *magisterialis* from Late Latin *magisterius* from Latin *magister* master]
• **magisterially** *adverb*

magisteriate *noun*
• "madge iss TEERY it"
• *Cdn* an alternative name for a master's degree.
• [as MAGISTERIAL]

magisterium *noun*
• "madge iss TEERY um"
• the teaching function and authority of the Church.
• [Latin, = the office of a master (as MAGISTERIAL)]

magistrate *noun*
• "MADGE iss trate"
• an official conducting a court for minor cases and preliminary hearings.
• [Latin *magistratus* from *magister* master]
• **magistracy** *noun*
• **magistrateship** *noun*
• **magistrature** *noun*

Maglemosian *noun*
• "mag'll MOZEY 'n"
• a N European mesolithic culture, characterized by bone and stone implements.
• [*Maglemose* in Denmark, where articles from it were found]

magnanimous *adjective*
• "mag NANNA muss"
• nobly generous; not petty in feelings or conduct.
• [Latin *magnanimus* from *magnus* great + *animus* soul]
• **magnanimity** *noun* "magna NIMMA tee"
• **magnanimously** *adverb*

magnate *noun*
• "MAG nate" or "MAG nit"
• a wealthy and influential person, esp. in business.
• [Late Latin *magnas -atis* from Latin *magnus* great]
HOMOPHONES: *magnet*

magnesia *noun*
• "mag NEE zhuh" or "mag NEESHA" or "mag NEEZ yuh"
• magnesium oxide, a white refractory solid used in ceramics etc.
• [medieval Latin from Greek *Magnēsia* (*lithos*) (stone) of Magnesia in Asia Minor, originally referring to loadstone]
• **magnesian** *adjective*

magnesite *noun*
• "MAGNA site"
• a white or grey mineral form of magnesium carbonate.
• [as MAGNESIA]

magnesium *noun*
• "mag NEEZY um"
• a silvery metallic element occurring naturally in magnesite and dolomite, used for making light alloys and important as an essential element in living organisms.
• [as MAGNESIA]

magnet *noun*
• "MAG nit"
• a piece of iron, steel, alloy, ore, etc., usu. in the form of a bar or horseshoe, having properties of attracting or repelling iron.
• [Latin *magnes magnetis* from Greek *magnēs* = *Magnēs -ētos* (*lithos*) (stone) of Magnesia: compare MAGNESIA]
• **magnetic** *adjective*
• **magnetically** *adverb*
• **magnetism** *noun*
• **magnetization** *noun* (also esp. *Brit.* **-isation**)
• **magnetize** *verb* (also esp. *Brit.* **-ise**)
HOMOPHONES: *magnate*

magnetite *noun*
• "MAGNA tite"
• magnetic iron oxide, an important ore of iron.
• [as MAGNET + Greek *lithos* stone]

magneto *noun*
• "mag NEETO"
• an electric generator using permanent magnets and producing high voltage, esp. for the ignition of an internal combustion engine.
• [abbreviation of 'magneto-electric' of, pertaining to, or involving electric currents induced in a conducting material by its motion in a magnetic field]

magnetograph *noun*
• "mag NEETA graff"
• an instrument for recording measurements of magnetic quantities.
• [as MAGNET + Greek *graphia* writing]

magnetohydrodynamic *adjective*
• "mag neeto hydro die NAMMIC"
• of, pertaining to, or involving an electrically conducting fluid, as a plasma or molten metal, acted on by a magnetic field.
• [as MAGNET + Greek *hudro-* from *hudōr* water + DYNAMIC]
• **magnetohydrodynamics** *noun*

magnetometer *noun*
• "magna TOMMA tur"
• an instrument measuring magnetic forces, esp. the earth's magnetism.
• [as MAGNET + Greek *metron* measure]
• **magnetometric** *adjective*
"mag neeto METRIC"
• **magnetometry** *noun*

magneton *noun*
• "MAGNA tawn"
• a unit of magnetic moment in atomic and nuclear physics.
• [as MAGNET]

magnetosphere *noun*
• "mag NEETA sfeer"
• the not necessarily spherical region surrounding a planet, star, etc. in which its magnetic field is effective and prevails over other magnetic fields.
• [as MAGNET + SPHERE]
• **magnetospheric** *adjective*

magnetron *noun*
• "MAGNA tron"
• an electron tube for amplifying or generating microwaves, with the flow of electrons controlled by an external magnetic field.
• [MAGNET + ELECTRON]

magnificent *adjective*
• "mag NIFFA s'nt"
• splendid; remarkable; impressive.
• [ultimately from Latin *magnus* great]
• **magnificence** *noun*
• **magnificently** *adverb*

magnifico *noun*
• "mag NIFFIC oh"
• a magnate or grandee, esp. a Venetian one.
• [Italian, = MAGNIFICENT]

magnify *verb*
• "MAGNA fie"
• make (a thing) appear larger than it is, as with a lens.
• [Old French *magnifier* or Latin *magnificare* (as MAGNIFICENT)]
• **magnifiable** *adjective*
• **magnification** *noun*
• **magnifier** *noun*

magniloquent *adjective*
• "mag NILLA kw'nt"
• grand or grandiose in speech.
• [Latin *magniloquus* from *magnus* great + *-loquus* -speaking]
• **magniloquence** *noun*
• **magniloquently** *adverb*

magnitude *noun*
• "MAGNA tude"
• great size or extent.
• [Latin *magnitudo* from *magnus* great]

magnolia *noun*
• "mag NO lee uh"
• any tree or shrub of the genus *Magnolia*, cultivated for its dark green foliage and large waxlike flowers in spring.
• [modern Latin from P. *Magnol*, French botanist d.1715]

maguey *noun*
• "MAG way"
• an agave plant, esp. one yielding pulque.
• [Spanish from Haitian]

magus *noun*
• "MAY guss"
• a member of a priestly caste of ancient Persia.
• [Latin from Greek *magos* from Old Persian *magus*]

maharaja *noun*
ALSO SPELLED: **maharajah**
• "maw huh RODGE uh"
• a title of some Indian princes of high rank.
• [Hindi *mahārājā* from *mahā* great + RAJA]

maharanee *noun*
ALSO SPELLED: **maharani**
• "maw huh RONNY"
• the title of a maharaja's wife or widow.
• [Hindi *mahārānī* from *mahā* great + RANI]

maharishi *noun*
• "maw huh REESHY"
• a great Hindu sage or spiritual leader.
• [Hindi from Sanskrit *mahā* great + RISHI]

mahatma *noun*
• "muh HATMA" or "muh HOTMA"
• (in India etc.) a person regarded with reverence, love, and respect.
• [Sanskrit *mahātman* from *mahā* great + *ātman* soul]

Mahayana *noun*
• "maw huh YONNA"
• a school of Buddhism with syncretistic features, practised in China, Japan, and Tibet.
• [Sanskrit from *mahā* great + *yāna* vehicle]

Mahdi *noun*
• "MODDY"
• a spiritual and temporal messiah expected by Muslims.
• [Arabic *mahdīy* he who is guided right, past participle of *hadā* guide]
• **Mahdism** *noun*
• **Mahdist** *noun*

Mahican *noun*
• "muh HEE k'n"
• a member of an American Indian people formerly inhabiting the Upper Hudson Valley in New York State.
• [Mahican, said to mean 'wolf']

mahogany *noun*
• "muh HOGGA nee"
• a rich, reddish-brown wood used for furniture.
• [17th c.: origin unknown]

mahonia *noun*
• "muh HOE nee uh"
• any evergreen shrub of the genus *Mahonia*, with yellow bell-shaped or globular flowers.
• [scientific Latin from Bernard *McMahon*, US naturalist d.1816]

mahout *noun*
• "muh HOUT" ("HOUT" rhymes with *OUT*)
• (in India etc.) an elephant driver or keeper.
• [Hindi *mahāut* from Sanskrit *mahāmātra* high official, lit. 'great in measure']

maidan *noun*
• "my DON"
• an open space in or near a town in India.
• [Urdu from Arabic *maydān*]

maieutic *adjective*
• "may OOTIC"
• (of the Socratic mode of inquiry) serving to bring a person's latent ideas into clear consciousness.
• [Greek *maieutikos* from *maieuomai* act as a midwife, from *maia* midwife]

maillot *noun*
• "my YO"
• a woman's one-piece bathing suit.
• [French, from *maille* stitch, from Latin *macula* stitch, stain]

maintenance *noun*
• "MAINTA nince" or "MAINT nince"
• the action or process of maintaining or being maintained.
• [Old French from *maintenir*, ultimately from Latin *manu tenēre* hold in the hand]

maisonette *noun*
ALSO SPELLED: **maisonnette**
• "maze a NET"
• a part of a house, apartment building, etc., forming separate living accommodation, usu. on two floors and having a separate entrance.
• [French *maisonnette*, diminutive of *maison* house, from Latin *mansio*: see MANSE]

maize *noun*
• "MAZE"
• a cereal plant, *Zea mays*, native to N America, yielding large, edible, usu. yellow grains set in rows on a cob; corn.
• [French *maïs* or Spanish *maiz*, of Carib origin]
HOMOPHONES: *maze*

majesty *noun*
• "MADGE a stee"
• impressive dignity or beauty.
• [Old French *majesté* from Latin *majestas* from *major*, comparative of *magnus* great]
• **majestic** *adjective*
• **majestically** *adverb*

majolica *noun*
ALSO SPELLED: **maiolica**
• "muh JAW lick uh" or "muh YAW lick uh"
• a type of earthenware with coloured decoration on an opaque white glaze.
• [Italian from former name of the Spanish Mediterranean island of Majorca]

majoritarian *adjective*
• "muh jorra TERRY 'n"
• governed by or believing in majority rule.
• [as MAJORITY]
• **majoritarianism** *noun*

majority *noun*
• "muh JORRA tee"
• the greater number or part.
• [medieval Latin *majoritas* from *major*, comparative of *magnus* great]

majuscule *noun*
• "MADGE a skyool"
• a large letter, whether capital or uncial.
• [French from Latin *majuscula* (*littera* letter), diminutive of *major* (see MAJORITY)]

maki *noun*
• "MACKY"
• a dish consisting of sushi and raw vegetables wrapped in a sheet of seaweed.
• [Japanese, from *maku* to roll (up) + SUSHI]

mako *noun*
• "MAY co"
• a large blue mackerel shark of the genus *Isurus*, of tropical and temperate oceans worldwide.
• [Maori]

malabsorption *noun*
• "mal ub ZORP sh'n"
• imperfect absorption of food material by the small intestine.
• [French *mal* badly, from Latin *male* + ABSORB]

malacca *noun*
• "muh LACKA"
• a cane from the stem of the palm tree *Calamus scipionum*, having a rich brown colour and used for walking sticks etc.
• [*Malacca* (var. of *Melaka*) in Malaysia]

malachite *noun*
• "MALA kite"
• a bright green mineral of hydrous copper carbonate, taking a high polish and used ornamentally.
• [Greek *molokhitis* from *molokhē* = *malakhē* mallow]

malacology *noun*
• "mala COLLA jee"
• the study of molluscs.
• [Greek *malakos* soft + *logos* word]
• **malacological** *adjective*
• **malacologist** *noun*

malacostracan *noun*
• "mala COSTRA k'n"
• any crustacean of the class Malacostraca, including crabs, shrimps, lobsters, and krill.
• [Greek *malakos* soft + *ostrakon* shell]

maladaptive *adjective*
• "mala DAP tiv"
• (of an individual, species, etc.) failing to adjust adequately to the environment, and undergoing emotional, behavioural, physical, or mental repercussions.
• [French *mal* badly, from Latin *male* + *adaptare* (*ad-* to, *aptare* from *aptus* fit)]
• **maladaptation** *noun*
• **maladapted** *adjective*

maladjusted *adjective*
• "mala JUSTED"
• not correctly adjusted.

• [French *mal* badly, from Latin *male* + ADJUST]
• **maladjustment** *noun*

maladroit *adjective*
• "mala DROIT"
• clumsy; bungling.
• [French (*mal* badly, from Latin *male* + ADROIT)]
• **maladroitly** *adverb*
• **maladroitness** *noun*

malady *noun*
• "MALA dee"
• an ailment; a disease.
• [Old French *maladie* from *malade* sick, ultimately from Latin *male* ill + *habitus* past participle of *habēre* have]

Malaga *noun*
• "MALA guh"
• a sweet fortified wine from Malaga in S Spain.

Malagasy *adjective*
• "mala GASSY"
• of or relating to Madagascar.
• [originally *Malegass*, *Madegass* from *Madagascar*]

malaise *noun*
• "muh LAZE"
• a non-specific bodily discomfort not associated with the development of a disease.
• [Old French *mal* bad + *aise* ease, ultimately from Latin *adjacens* ADJACENT]

malamute *noun*
ALSO SPELLED: **malemute**
• "MALA mute"
• a dog of a breed developed in Alaska, with a thick grey or black and white coat, pointed ears, and a plumed tail curling over the back.
• [Inupiaq *malimiut*, a people of the Kolzebue Sound, Alaska, who developed the breed]

malapropism *noun*
• "MALA prop izm"
• the use of a word in mistake for one sounding similar, to comic effect, e.g. *consummated* for *consommé*.
• [Mrs. *Malaprop* (from MALAPROPOS) in R. B. Sheridan's *The Rivals* (1775)]

malapropos *adjective*
• "mala pruh POE"
• inopportune; inappropriate.
• [French *mal à propos* from *mal* ill: see APROPOS]

malar *adjective*
• "MALE ur"
• of the cheek.
• [modern Latin *malaris* from Latin *mala* jaw]
HOMOPHONES: *mailer*

malaria *noun*
• "muh LERRY uh"
• an intermittent and remittent fever caused by a protozoan parasite of the genus *Plasmodium*, introduced by the bite of a mosquito.
• [Italian *mal'aria* bad air, because the disease was formerly believed to be caused by the unwholesome condition of the atmosphere in marshy districts of Italy and other hot countries]
• **malarial** *adjective*

malarkey *noun*
• "muh LARKY"
• humbug; nonsense.
• [20th c.: origin unknown]

malathion *noun*
• "mala THYE 'n" (with "TH" as in *THIN*)
• an insecticide containing phosphorus, with low toxicity to other animals.
• [diethyl *maleate* + *thio-* acid]

Malawian *noun*
• "muh LAW wee 'n"
• a native or inhabitant of Malawi in south central Africa.

Malayalam *noun*
• "mala YOLL'm"
• the Dravidian language of the state of Kerala in S India.
• [Malayalam, from *mala* mountain + *āḷ* man]

Malbec *noun*
• "MAL beck"
• a variety of black grape, native to areas of SW France, but now also widely cultivated elsewhere, esp. in Latin America.
• [19th c.: origin unknown]

Maldivian *noun*
• "mawl DIVVY 'n"
• a native or inhabitant of the Maldives in the Indian Ocean.

malediction *noun*
• "mala DICK sh'n"
• a curse.
• [Latin *maledictio* from *maledicere* speak evil of, from *male* ill + *dicere dict-* speak]

malefactor *noun*
• "MALA facter"
• a criminal; an evildoer.
• [Latin *malefacere malefact-* from *male* ill + *facere* do]
• **malefaction** *noun*

malefic *adjective*
• "muh LEFFIC"
• (of magical arts etc.) harmful; baleful.
• [Latin *maleficus* from *male* ill]

maleficent *adjective*
• "muh LEFFA s'nt"
• hurtful; malicious.
• [*maleficence* formed as MALEFIC after *malevolence*]
• **maleficence** *noun*

maleic *adjective*
• "muh LAY ick"
• designating a colourless crystalline organic acid used in making synthetic resins.
• [French *maléique* (as MALIC)]

malevolent *adjective*
• "muh LEVVA l'nt"
• wishing evil to others.
• [Latin *malevolens* from *male* ill + *volens* willing, participle of *velle*]
• **malevolence** *noun*
• **malevolently** *adverb*

malfeasance *noun*
• "mal FEEZ ince"
• evildoing; illegal action.
• [Anglo-French *malfaisance* from Old French *malfaisant* (*mal* badly, from Latin *male*, *faisant* participle of *faire* do, from Latin *facere*): compare MISFEASANCE]
• **malfeasant** *noun*

Malian *noun*
• "MOLLY 'n"
• a native or inhabitant of Mali in W Africa.

malic *adjective*
• "MAL ick"
• designating an organic acid found in apples and other fruits.
• [French *malique* from Latin *malum* apple]

malice *noun*
• "MAL iss"
• the intention to do evil or to injure another person.
• [Latin *malitia* from *malus* bad]
• **malicious** *adjective* "muh LISH us"
• **maliciously** *adverb*
• **maliciousness** *noun*

malign *adjective*
• "muh LINE"
• (of a thing) injurious.
• [Latin *malignus* from *malus* bad: compare BENIGN]
• **maligner** *noun*
• **malignity** *noun* "muh LIG nuh tee"
• **malignly** *adverb*
HOMOPHONES: *moline*

malignant *adjective*
• "muh LIG n'nt"
• (of a disease) very virulent or infectious.
• [as MALIGN]
• **malignancy** *noun*
• **malignantly** *adverb*

malinger *verb*
• "muh LING gur"
• exaggerate or feign illness in order to escape duty, work, etc.
• [back-formation from *malingerer* apparently from French *malingre*, perhaps from *mal* badly, from Latin *male* + *haingre* weak]
• **malingerer** *noun*

Maliseet *noun*
• "MALA seet"
• a member of an Aboriginal people now occupying northwestern New Brunswick and eastern Quebec.
• [French *Malecite*, from Mi'kmaq *mali·sit*, lit. 'a person who speaks poorly or incomprehensibly']

mallard *noun*
• "MAL 'rd" or "MAL ard"
• a common wild duck or drake, *Anas platyrhynchos*, of the northern hemisphere, the male of which has a green head, narrow white collar, chestnut breast, and a blue patch on the wings.
• [Old French prob. from *maslart* (unrecorded)]

malleable *adjective*
• "MAL ee a bull"
• (of metal etc.) able to be hammered or pressed permanently out of shape without breaking or cracking.
• [medieval Latin *malleabilis* from Latin *malleare* to hammer, from *malleus* hammer]
• **malleability** *noun*

mallee *noun*
• "MAL ee"
• any of several types of eucalyptus, esp. *Eucalyptus dumosa*, that flourish in arid areas.
• [prob. from Wemba-wemba *mali*]

malleolus *noun*
• "muh LEE a luss"
• a bony protuberance of the tibia or fibula on either side of the ankle.
• [Latin, diminutive of *malleus* hammer]

malleus *noun*
• "MAL ee us"
• a small bone in the middle ear transmitting the vibrations of the tympanum to the incus.
• [Latin, = hammer]

malmsey *noun*
• "MAWM zee"
• a strong sweet wine originally from Greece, now chiefly from the Portuguese island of Madeira.
• [Middle Dutch *malemeseye* via Old French from *Monemvasia* in S Greece]

malnourished *adjective*
• "mal NUR isht"
• suffering from malnutrition.
• [French *mal* badly, from Latin *male* + NOURISH]
• **malnourishment** *noun*

malnutrition *noun*
• "mal new TRISH'n"
• a dietary condition resulting from the absence of some foods or essential elements necessary for health; insufficient nutrition.
• [French *mal* badly, from Latin *male* + NUTRITION]

malocclusion *noun*
• "mala CLOO zh'n"
• imperfect positioning of the teeth when the jaws are closed.
• [French *mal* badly, from Latin *male* + OCCLUSION]

malodorous *adjective*
- "mal OH dur us"
- foul smelling.
- [French *mal* badly, from Latin *male* + ODOROUS]

malolactic *adjective*
- "mal oh LACTIC"
- designating bacterial fermentation which converts malic acid (in wine) to lactic acid.
- [MALIC + LACTIC]

Malpighian *adjective*
- "mal PIGGY 'n"
- designating a layer of proliferating cells in the epidermis.
- [M. *Malpighi*, Italian microscopist d.1694]

Maltese *noun*
- "maul TEEZ"
- a native or national of the Mediterranean island of Malta.

Malthusian *adjective*
- "mal THOOZY 'n"
- of or relating to the theories of English economist T. R. Malthus (d.1834), esp. his assertion that population increases faster than the means of subsistence, and must therefore be controlled to avert catastrophe.
- **Malthusianism** *noun*

maltose *noun*
- "MAUL tose" (rhymes with *GROSS*)
- a sugar produced by the hydrolysis of starch under the action of the enzymes in malt, saliva, etc.
- [Old English *m(e)alt* malt (from Germanic, related to 'melt') + *-ose* as in GLUCOSE]

Malvasia *noun*
- "mal vuh SEE uh"
- a variety of grape used to make white and red wines, esp. in Italy.
- [Italian form of *Monemvasia*: see MALMSEY]

malversation *noun*
- "mal vur SAY sh'n"
- corrupt behaviour in a position of trust.
- [French from *malverser* from Latin *male* badly + *versari* behave]

mamateek *noun*
- "MAM a teek"
- a type of wigwam used by the Beothuk.
- [Beothuk]

mamilla *noun*
- "muh MILLA"
- the nipple of a woman's breast.
- [Latin, diminutive of MAMMA]
- **mamillary** *adjective*

mamma *noun*
- "MAM uh"
- a milk-secreting organ of female mammals.
- [Old English from Latin]
- **mammiform** *adjective*

mammal *noun*
- "MAM'll"
- any warm-blooded animal of the vertebrate class Mammalia, members of which are characterized by the possession of mammary glands in the female and a four-chambered heart, including human beings, carnivores, ungulates, rodents, whales, etc.
- [modern Latin *mammalia* neuter pl. of Latin *mammalis* (as MAMMA)]
- **mammalian** *adjective* "muh MAILY 'n"
- **mammalogist** *noun* "muh MALA jist"
- **mammalogy** *noun*

mammary *adjective*
- "MAMMER ee"
- of the human female breasts or milk-secreting organs of other mammals.
- [as MAMMA]

mammee *noun*
- "ma MEE"
- a tropical American tree, *Mammea americana*, with large red-rinded yellow-pulped fruit.
- [Spanish *mamei* from Haitian]

mammogram *noun*
- "MAM a gram"
- an image obtained by mammography.
- [as MAMMA + Greek *gramma* thing written]

mammography *noun*
- "muh MOGGRA fee"
- an X-ray technique of diagnosing and locating abnormalities (esp. tumours) of the breasts.
- [MAMMA + *graphia* writing]

Mammon *noun*
- "MAM'n"
- wealth regarded as an idol or as an evil influence.
- [Aramaic *māmōn* riches]

mammoth *noun*
- "MAM uth"
- any large extinct elephant of the genus *Mammuthus*, with a hairy coat and curved tusks.
- [Russian *mamo(n)t*]

mana *noun*
- "MONNA"
- (esp. in Polynesian, Melanesian, and Maori belief) an impersonal supernatural power which can be associated with people or objects and which can be transmitted or inherited.
- [Maori]

manacle *noun*
- "MANNA k'll"
- a fetter or shackle for the hand; a handcuff.
- [Old French *manicle* handcuff, from Latin *manicula* diminutive of *manus* hand]

manage *verb*
- "MAN idge"
- organize; regulate; be in charge of (a business, household, team, a person's career, etc.).

• [orig. in sense 'put (a horse) through the paces of the manège', from Italian *maneggiare*, *maneggio* ultimately from Latin *manus* hand]
• **manageability** *noun*
• **manageable** *adjective*
• **manageableness** *noun*
• **manageably** *adverb*
• **management** *noun*
• **manager** *noun*
• **manageress** *noun*
• **managerial** *adjective* "manna JEERY 'll"
• **managerially** *adverb*
• **managing** *adjective*

manakin *noun*
• "MANNA kin"
• any small bird of the family Pipridae of Central and S America, the males of which are often brightly coloured.
• [var. of MANIKIN]
HOMOPHONES: *mannequin*, *manikin*

mañana *adverb*
• "mun YONNA"
• in the indefinite future (esp. to indicate procrastination).
• [Spanish, = tomorrow]

manat *noun*
• "MAN at"
• the basic monetary unit of Azerbaijan and Turkmenistan, equal to 100 gopik in Azerbaijan and 100 tenesi in Turkmenistan.
• [Azerbaijani and Turkmen]

manatee *noun*
• "MANNA tee"
• any large aquatic plant-eating mammal of the genus *Trichechus*, with paddle-like forelimbs, no hind limbs, and a powerful tail.
• [Spanish *manati* from Carib *manattouï*]

manchineel *noun*
• "mancha NEEL"
• a Caribbean tree, *Hippomane mancinella*, with a poisonous and caustic milky sap and acrid apple-like fruit.
• [French *mancenille* from Spanish *manzanilla* diminutive of *manzana* apple]

Manchu *noun*
• "man CHOO"
• a member of a people in China, descended from a Tartar people, who formed the last imperial dynasty (1644–1912).
• [Manchu, = pure]

Manchurian *adjective*
• "man CHURRY 'n"
• of or relating to Manchuria in NE China.

manciple *noun*
• "MANSA pull"
• an officer or steward who buys provisions for a college, monastery, etc.
• [Latin *mancipium* purchase, from *manceps* buyer, from *manus* hand + *capere* take]

Mancunian *noun*
• "man KYOONY 'n"
• a native of Manchester, England.
• [Latin *Mancunium* Manchester]

Mandaean *noun*
• "man DEE 'n"
• a member of a Gnostic sect surviving in Iraq and claiming descent from John the Baptist.
• [Aramaic *mandaiia* Gnostics, from *manda* knowledge]

mandala *noun*
• "MANDA luh"
• a symbolic circular figure representing the universe in Hinduism and Buddhism.
• [Sanskrit *máṇḍala* disc]

mandamus *noun*
• "man DAY muss"
• a judicial writ issued as a command to an inferior court, or ordering a person to perform a public or statutory duty.
• [Latin, = we command]

mandarin *noun*
• "MANDER in"
• a small flattish deep-coloured orange with a loose skin.
• [French *mandarine*, perhaps from 'mandarin', a Chinese official (from Portuguese *mandarim* from Malay from Hindi *mantrī* from Sanskrit *mantrin* counsellor), with reference to the official's yellow robes]

mandarinate *noun*
• "MANDER in it"
• a body of bureaucrats, known derogatorily as 'mandarins'.
• [as MANDARIN]

mandatory *adjective*
• "MANDA tory"
• compulsory.
• [Latin *mandatum*, neuter past participle of *mandare* command, from *manus* hand + *dare* give]
• **mandatorily** *adverb*

mandible *noun*
• "MANDA bull"
• the jaw, esp. the lower jaw in mammals and fishes.
• [Old French *mandible* or Late Latin *mandibula* from *mandere* chew]
• **mandibular** *adjective* "man DIB yuh lur"
• **mandibulate** *adjective*

mandolin *noun*
• "manda LIN"
• a musical instrument resembling a lute, having paired metal strings plucked with a plectrum.
• [French *mandoline* from Italian *mandolino* diminutive of *mandola*, an early form of mandolin]
• **mandolinist** *noun*

mandorla *noun*
- "man DORE luh"
- a pointed oval used as an aureole in medieval sculpture and painting.
- [Italian, = almond]

mandrel *noun*
- "MAN drull"
- a shaft inserted into a workpiece to secure it to a lathe.
- [16th c.: origin unknown]

mandrill *noun*
- "MAN drill"
- a large W African baboon, *Mandrillus sphinx*, with a brightly coloured red and blue face, the male having a blue rump.
- [prob. from 'man' + 'drill', a West African baboon, *Papio leucophaeus*, related to the mandrill]

manducate *verb*
- "MAND yoo cate"
- chew; eat.
- [Latin *manducare* chew, from *manduco* guzzler, from *mandere* chew]

manège *noun*
- "ma NEZH"
- a riding school.
- [French *manège* from Italian (as MANAGE)]

manes *plural noun*
- "MON aze" or "MAY neez"
- the deified souls of dead ancestors in ancient Roman belief.
- [Latin]

mangabey *noun*
- "MANGA bay"
- any small long-tailed W African monkey of the genus *Cercocebus*.
- [*Mangabey*, a region of Madagascar]

manganese *noun*
- "MANGA neez"
- a grey brittle metallic transition element used with steel to make alloys.
- [Italian *manganese*, alteration of MAGNESIA]

mangel *noun*
- "MANG g'll"
- a large kind of beet, *Beta vulgaris*, used as cattle food.
- [German *Mangoldwurzel* from *Mangold* beet + *Wurzel* root]

HOMOPHONES: *mangle*

mangonel *noun*
- "MANGA n'll"
- a military engine for throwing stones etc.
- [Old French *mangonel(le)*, from medieval Latin *manganellus* diminutive of Late Latin *manganum* from Greek *manganon*, axis of a pulley]

mangosteen *noun*
- "MANGA steen"
- a white juicy-pulped fruit with a thick reddish-brown rind.
- [Malay *manggustan*]

manhattan *noun*
- "man HAT'n"
- a cocktail made of vermouth, whisky, etc.
- [*Manhattan* in New York City]

Manhattanite *noun*
- "man HAT'n ite"
- a resident of Manhattan in New York City.

mania *noun*
- "MAY nee uh"
- mental illness marked by periods of great excitement and violence.
- [Late Latin from Greek, = madness, from *mainomai* be mad]

maniac *noun*
- "MAY nee ack"
- a person exhibiting extreme symptoms of wild behaviour etc.; an insane person.
- [Late Latin *maniacus* from late Greek *maniakos* (as MANIA)]
- **maniacal** *adjective* "muh NIE a k'll"
- **maniacally** *adverb*

manic *adjective*
- "MANNIC"
- of or affected by mania.
- [as MANIA]
- **manically** *adverb*

Manichaean *noun*
ALSO SPELLED: **Manichean**
- "manna KEE 'n"
- an adherent of a religious system of the 3rd–5th c., representing Satan in a state of everlasting conflict with God.
- [*Manichaeus*, Persian prophet d. *c.*274]
- **Manichaeism** *noun* (also **Manicheism**)

manicotti *noun*
- "manna COTTY"
- large tubular pasta, usu. served stuffed with ricotta cheese and covered with tomato sauce.
- [Italian, pl. of *manicotto* sleeve, muff]

manicure *noun*
- "MANNA cure"
- a usu. professional cosmetic treatment of the hands and fingernails.
- [French from Latin *manus* hand + *cura* care]
- **manicured** *adjective*
- **manicurist** *noun*

manifest *adjective*
- "MANNA fest"
- clear or obvious to the eye or mind.
- [Latin *manifestus*, *manifestare* from *manus* hand + *festus* (unrecorded) struck]
- **manifestation** *noun*
- **manifestly** *adverb*

manifesto *noun*
- "manna FESS toe"
- a public declaration of principles, intentions, purposes, etc.
- [Italian from *manifestare* from Latin (as MANIFEST)]

manifold *adjective*
• "MANNA fold"
• many and various.
• [Old English *manigfeald* (as 'many' + the suffix '-fold', original sense 'folded in so many layers')]

manikin *noun*
ALSO SPELLED: **mannikin**
• "MANNA kin"
• a little person; a dwarf.
• [Dutch *manneken*, diminutive of *man* man]
HOMOPHONES: *manakin*, *mannequin*

manila *noun*
ALSO SPELLED: **manilla**
• "muh NILLA"
• the strong fibre of a Philippine tree, *Musa textilis*, used for rope etc.
• [*Manila*, capital of the Philippines]

manioc *noun*
• "MANNY ock"
• the starchy tuberous root of a tropical tree, used as food in tropical countries; cassava.
• [Tupi *mandioca*]

maniple *noun*
• "MANNA pull"
• a subdivision of a Roman legion, containing 120 or 60 men.
• [Latin *manipulus* handful, troop, from *manus* hand]

manipulate *verb*
• "muh NIP yuh late"
• handle, treat, or use, esp. skilfully (a tool, question, material, etc.).
• [modern Latin *manipulatio* (as MANIPLE)]
• **manipulability** *noun*
• **manipulable** *adjective*
• **manipulation** *noun*
• **manipulator** *noun*

manipulative *adjective*
• "muh NIP yoo luh tiv"
• characterized by unscrupulous exploitation of a situation, person, etc., for one's own ends.
• [as MANIPULATE]
• **manipulativeness** *noun*

Manitoban *noun*
• "manna TOE b'n"
• a person from Manitoba.

manitou *noun*
• "MANNA too"
• a good or evil spirit as an object of reverence, esp. among the Cree and Ojibwa.
• [Algonquian *manito*, *-tu* 'he has surpassed']

manna *noun*
• "MANNA"
• the substance miraculously supplied as food to the Israelites in the wilderness (Exod. 16).
• [Aramaic *mannā* from Hebrew *mān*, explained as = *mān hū?* what is it?, but prob. = Arabic *mann* exudation of common tamarisk (*Tamarix gallica*)]

mannequin *noun*
• "MANNA kin"
• a three-dimensional model of a human body, used when making clothes or esp. for displaying them in stores.
• [French, = MANIKIN]
HOMOPHONES: *manakin*, *manikin*

manoeuvre *noun*
ALSO SPELLED: **maneuver**
• "muh NOOVER"
• a planned and controlled movement or series of moves.
• [French *manœuvre* from medieval Latin *manuoperare* from Latin *manus* hand + *operari* to work]
• **manoeuvrability** *noun* (also **maneuverability**)
• **manoeuvrable** *adjective* (also **maneuverable**)
• **manoeuvrer** *noun* (also **maneuverer**)

manometer *noun*
• "muh NOMMA tur"
• a pressure gauge for gases and liquids.
• [French *manomètre* from Greek *manos* thin + *metron* measure]
• **manometric** *adjective* "manna METRIC"
• **manometry** *noun*

manor *noun*
• "MANNER"
• a large house with lands.
• [Old French *maneir*, from Latin *manēre* remain]
• **manorial** *adjective* "muh NORRY 'll"
HOMOPHONES: *manner*

manqué *adjective*
• "mong CAY"
• that might have been but is not; unfulfilled.
• [French, past participle of *manquer* miss]

mansard *noun*
• "MAN sard"
• a roof which has four sloping sides, each of which becomes steeper halfway down.
• [French *mansarde* from F. *Mansart*, French architect d.1666]
• **mansarded** *adjective*

manse *noun*
• "MANCE"
• the house, owned by a congregation, of an esp. Presbyterian or United Church minister.
• [medieval Latin *mansus* house, from *manēre* remain]

mansion *noun*
• "MAN sh'n"
• a large house.
• [Latin *mansio* 'a staying' (as MANSE)]

manslaughter *noun*
• "MAN slotter"
• the killing of a human being.
• ['man' + SLAUGHTER]

mansuetude *noun*
• "MAN swuh tude"
• meekness, docility, gentleness.
• [Latin *mansuetudo* from *mansuetus* gentle, tame, from *manus* hand + *suetus* accustomed]

mantel *noun*
• "MANT'II"
• a structure of wood, marble, etc. above and around a fireplace.
• [var. of MANTLE]
HOMOPHONES: *mantle*

mantelet *noun*
• "MANTA lit"
• a woman's short loose sleeveless mantle.
• [Old French, diminutive of *mantel* MANTLE]

mantic *adjective*
• "MANTIC"
• of or concerning divination or prophecy.
• [Greek *mantikos* from *mantis* prophet]

manticore *noun*
• "MANTA core"
• a fabulous monster having the body of a lion, the head of a man, porcupine's quills, and the tail or sting of a scorpion.
• [Latin *manticora* representing Greek *mantikhōras*, corrupt reading in Aristotle for *martikhoras* from an Old Persian word for 'man-eater']

mantid *noun*
• "MANTID"
• any insect of the family Mantidae, feeding on other insects etc.
• [as MANTIS]

mantilla *noun*
• "man TILLA"
• a lace scarf worn by Spanish women over the hair and shoulders.
• [Spanish, diminutive of *manta* MANTLE]

mantis *noun*
• "MAN tiss"
• any insect of the family Mantidae, feeding on other insects etc.
• [Greek, = prophet]

mantissa *noun*
• "man TISSA"
• the part of a logarithm after the decimal point.
• [Latin, = makeweight]

mantle *noun*
• "MANT'II"
• a loose sleeveless cloak.
• [Latin *mantellum* cloak]
HOMOPHONES: *mantel*

mantra *noun*
• "MANTRA"
• a word or sound repeated to aid concentration in meditation.
• [Sanskrit, = instrument of thought, from *man* think]

mantua *noun*
• "MAN tyoo uh"
• a woman's loose gown of the 17th–18th c.
• [corruption of *manteau* (French, as MANTLE) after *Mantua* in Italy]

manual *adjective*
• "MAN yoo 'II"
• of or relating to the hand or hands.
• [Latin *manualis* from *manus* hand]
• **manually** *adverb*

manufacture *noun*
• "man yoo FAC chur"
• the making of articles esp. in a factory etc.
• [French from Italian *manifattura* & Latin *manufactum* made by hand]
• **manufacturability** *noun*
• **manufacturable** *adjective*
• **manufacturer** *noun*

manuka *noun*
• "MON oo kuh" or "ma NOO kuh"
• a small tree, *Leptospermum scoparium*, native to New Zealand and Tasmania, yielding aromatic leaves which are sometimes used for tea and nectar which produces a honey which has antibiotic properties.
• [Maori]

manumatic *adjective*
• "man yoo MATTIC"
• (of a motor vehicle or its transmission) using gears that are changed manually by the driver but without the need of a clutch pedal.
• [blend of MANUAL + AUTOMATIC]

manumit *verb*
• "man yoo MIT"
• set (a slave) free.
• [Latin *manumittere* from *manus* hand + *emittere* send forth]
• **manumission** *noun*

manuscript *noun*
• "MAN yoo script"
• a book, document, etc. written by hand.
• [medieval Latin *manuscriptus* from *manu* by hand + *scriptus* past participle of *scribere* write]

manzanilla *noun*
• "manza NILLA"
• a pale very dry Spanish sherry.
• [Spanish, lit. 'camomile']

manzanita *noun*
• "manza NEETA"
• any of several evergreen shrubs of the genus *Arctostaphylos*, of the southwestern US.
• [Spanish, diminutive of *manzana* apple]

Maoism *noun*
• "MOW izm" ("MOW" rhymes with *COW*)
• the Communist doctrines of Mao Zedong (d.1976) as formerly practised in China, having as a central idea permanent revolution and stressing the importance of the peasantry, of

small-scale industry, and of agricultural collectivization.

• **Maoist** *noun*

Maori *noun*

• "MOW ree" ("MOW" rhymes with *COW*)

• a member of the Polynesian aboriginal people of New Zealand.

• [Maori]

maquette *noun*

• "muh KET"

• a sculptor's or architect's small preliminary model.

• [French from Italian *machietta* diminutive of *macchia* spot, from Latin *macula* stain]

maquiladora *noun*

• "macky la DORA"

• a Mexican factory taking advantage of cheap labour, run by a foreign company and exporting its products to the country of that company.

• [Latin American Spanish from *maquilar* assemble]

maquillage *noun*

• "macky YOZH"

• makeup; cosmetics.

• [French from *maquiller* make up, from Old French *maquier* to do, from Middle Dutch *maken* make]

Maquis *noun*

• "ma KEE"

• the French resistance movement during the German occupation (1940–45).

• [French, = brushwood, from Corsican Italian *macchia* thicket]

marabou *noun*

ALSO SPELLED: **marabout**

• "MA ruh boo"

• a large W African stork, *Leptoptilos crumeniferus*.

• [French from Arabic *murābiṭ* holy man (see MARABOUT), the stork being regarded as holy]

marabout *noun*

• "MA ruh boot"

• a Muslim hermit or monk, esp. in N Africa.

• [French from Portuguese *marabuto* from Arabic *murābiṭ* holy man, from *ribāṭ* frontier station, where he acquired merit by combat against the infidel]

maraca *noun*

• "muh ROCKA" or "muh RACKA"

• a hollow gourd or gourd-shaped container filled with beans, pebbles, etc. and usu. shaken in pairs as a percussion instrument.

• [Portuguese *maracá*, prob. from Tupi]

maraschino *noun*

• "merra SHEE no" or "merra SKEE no"

• a strong sweet liqueur made from a small black Dalmatian cherry.

• [Italian from *marasca* small black cherry, from *amaro* bitter, from Latin *amarus*]

marasmus *noun*

• "muh RAZ muss"

• severe loss of weight in a person, esp. an undernourished child.

• [modern Latin from Greek *marasmos* from *marainō* wither]

• **marasmic** *adjective*

Maratha *noun*

ALSO SPELLED: **Mahratta**

• "muh ROTTA" or "muh RATTA"

• a member of a Hindu people native to the Indian state of Maharashtra.

• [Hindi *Marhaṭṭa* from Sanskrit *Māhārāshṭra* great kingdom]

Marathi *noun*

ALSO SPELLED: **Mahratti**

• "muh ROTTY" or "muh RATTY"

• the Indic language of the Marathas.

• [MARATHA]

marathon *noun*

• "MERRA thon"

• a long-distance running race, usu. of 26 miles 385 yards (42.195 km).

• [*Marathon* in Greece, scene of a victory over the Persians in 490 BC: a messenger was said to have run to Athens with the news, but the account has no authority]

• **marathoner** *noun*

maraud *verb*

• "muh ROD"

• go about in search of things to steal, people to attack, etc.

• [French *marauder* from *maraud* rogue]

• **marauder** *noun*

marbleize *verb*

ALSO SPELLED: esp. *Brit.* **-ise**

• "MAR b'll ize"

• stain or colour to look like variegated marble.

• [Old French *marbre*, *marble*, from Latin *marmor* from Greek *marmaros* shining stone]

Marburg *noun*

• "MAR burg"

• designating the virus of an acute, often fatal, hemorrhagic febrile disease originally transmitted to humans from the green monkey.

• [*Marburg*, Germany, where the first major outbreak occurred (1967)]

marc *noun*

• "MARK"

• the residue of pressed grapes etc.

• [French from *marcher* tread, from Late Latin *marcus* hammer]

HOMOPHONES: *mark*, *marque*

marcasite *noun*

• "MARKA site"

• a yellowish crystalline iron sulphide mineral.

• [medieval Latin *marcasita*, from Arabic *markašīṯā* from Persian]

marcato *adjective*
• "mar COTTO"
• (of music) played with emphasis.
• [Italian, = marked]

marcel *noun*
• "mar SELL"
• a deep wave in the hair created with a hot curling iron, popular as a hairstyle esp. in the twenties and thirties.
• [*Marcel* Grateau, Paris hairdresser d.1936, who invented the method]

marchioness *noun*
• "marsha NESS"
• the wife or widow of a marquess.
• [medieval Latin *marchionissa* from *marchio* captain of the marches (borderlands)]

marconi *noun*
• "mar CO nee"
• *Cdn* (*Nfld*) a radio, esp. one used for two-way communications.
• [G. *Marconi*, Italian radio pioneer d.1937]

mare *noun*
• "MAR ay" or "MAR ee"
• the sea under the jurisdiction of a particular country.
• [Latin, = sea]

margarine *noun*
• "MAR juh rin"
• a butter substitute made from vegetable oils or animal fats with milk etc.
• [French, misapplication of a chemical term, from *margarique*, from Greek *margaron* pearl]

margarita *noun*
• "marga REETA"
• a cocktail made with tequila, lime juice, and orange liqueur, typically served in a glass with a salt-coated rim.
• [Spanish equivalent of female first name Margaret]
HOMOPHONES: *margherita*

margay *noun*
• "MAR gay"
• a small wild S American cat, *Felis wiedii*.
• [French from Tupi *mbaracaïa*]

margherita *adjective*
• "marga REETA"
• designating a pizza topped with cheese, tomatoes, and traditionally also basil.
• [Italian *margherita* from the name of *Margherita* Teresa Giovanna of Savoy (d.1926), Queen of Italy 1878–1900, the colours of mozzarella, tomatoes, and basil being white, red, and green like the Italian flag]
HOMOPHONES: *margarita*

margin *noun*
• "MARJIN"
• the edge or border of a surface.
• [Latin *margo -ginis* edge]
• **marginal** *adjective*
• **marginality** *noun*
• **marginally** *adverb*

marginalia *plural noun*
• "marjin AILY uh"
• marginal notes.
• [medieval Latin, neuter pl. of *marginalis*, as MARGIN]

marginalize *verb*
ALSO SPELLED: esp. *Brit.* **-ise**
• "MARJIN a lize"
• make or treat as insignificant.
• [as MARGIN]
• **marginalization** *noun* (also esp. *Brit.* **-isation**)

margrave *noun*
• "MAR grave"
• the hereditary title of some princes of the Holy Roman Empire (originally of a military governor of a border province).
• [Middle Dutch *markgrave* border count ('mark' + *grave* count, from Old Low German *grēve*)]

margravine *noun*
• "MARGRA veen"
• the wife of a margrave.
• [Dutch *markgravin* (as MARGRAVE)]

marguerite *noun*
• "marga REET"
• a daisy, esp. the ox-eye daisy, *Chrysanthemum leucanthemum*.
• [French from Latin *margarita* from Greek *margaritēs* from *margaron* pearl]

mariachi *noun*
• "merry ATCH ee" or "merry OTCH ee"
• an itinerant Mexican folk band.
• [Mexican Spanish *mariache*, *mariachi* street singer]

Marian *adjective*
• "MERRY 'n"
• of or relating to the Virgin Mary.
• [Latin *Maria* Mary]

mariculture *noun*
• "MERRA cull chur"
• the cultivation of the living resources of the sea (such as algae, shellfish, or esp. fish).
• [Latin *mare* sea + CULTURE]

marigold *noun*
• "MERRA gold"
• any plant of the genus *Calendula* or *Tagetes*, with golden or bright yellow flowers.
• [Middle English from *Mary* (prob. the Virgin) + dialect *gold*, Old English *golde*, prob. related to 'gold']

marijuana *noun*
• "merra WONNA"
• the dried leaves, flowering tops, and stems of the hemp, used as an intoxicating drug usu. smoked in cigarettes; cannabis.
• [Latin American Spanish]

marimba *noun*
• "muh RIM buh"
• a kind of deep-toned xylophone, originating in Africa and consisting of wooden keys on a frame with a tuned resonator beneath each key.
• [Congolese]

marina *noun*
• "muh REENA"
• a specially designed harbour with moorings for pleasure boats etc.
• [Italian & Spanish feminine adjective from *marino* from Latin (as MARINE)]

marinade *noun*
• "MERRA nade" or "merra NADE"
• a mixture of wine, vinegar, oil, spices, etc., in which meat, fish, etc., is soaked before cooking.
• [French from Spanish *marinada*, via *marinar* pickle in brine, from *marino* (as MARINE)]

marinara *adjective*
• "merra NARE uh" or "mar a NAR uh"
• designating a sauce made from tomatoes, onions, herbs, etc., usu. served with pasta.
• [Italian *alla marinara* sailor-fashion]

marinate *verb*
• "MERRA nate"
• soak (meat, fish, etc.) in a marinade.
• [Italian *marinare* or French *mariner* (as MARINE)]
• **marination** *noun*

marine *adjective*
• "muh REEN"
• of, found in, or produced by the sea.
• [Latin *marinus*, from *mare* sea]

mariner *noun*
• "MARE 'n ur"
• a sailor.
• [as MARINE]

Mariolatry *noun*
• "merry OLLA tree"
• idolatrous worship of the Virgin Mary.
• [Latin *Maria* Mary + '-latry', after IDOLATRY]

Mariology *noun*
• "merry OLLA jee"
• the study of the Virgin Mary in Christian belief.
• [Latin *Maria* Mary + *logos* word]

marionberry *noun*
• "MERRY 'n berry"
• a large black berry produced by crossing loganberry and blackberry cultivars.
• [*Marion* County, Oregon, where the variety was tested]

marionette *noun*
• "merry a NET"
• a puppet worked from above by strings.
• [French *marionnette* from *Marion* diminutive of *Marie* Mary]

mariposa *noun*
• "merra POZE uh"
• any of various lilies of western N America of the genus *Calochortus* with showy flowers of three petals.
• [Spanish, = 'butterfly']

Marist *noun*
• "MARE ist"
• a member of a Roman Catholic religious order of priests, the Society of Mary.
• [French *Mariste* from *Marie* Mary]

marital *adjective*
• "MERRIT'll"
• of marriage or the relations between spouses.
• [Latin *maritalis* from *maritus* husband]
• **maritally** *adverb*

maritime *adjective*
• "MERRA time"
• connected with the sea or seafaring.
• [Latin *maritimus* from *mare* sea]

Maritimer *noun*
• "MERRA timer"
• *Cdn* a resident of the Maritime Provinces of New Brunswick, Nova Scotia, or Prince Edward Island.

marjoram *noun*
• "MAR juh rum"
• either of two aromatic herbaceous plants, *Origanum vulgare*, or *Origanum marjorana*.
• [Old French *majorane* from medieval Latin *majorana*, of unknown origin]

marka *noun*
• "MARKA"
• the basic monetary unit of Bosnia and Herzegovina, equal to one hundred fenning.
• [Bosnian]
HOMOPHONES: *markka*

markhor *noun*
• "MAR cor"
• a large spiral-horned wild goat, *Capra falconeri*, of N India.
• [Persian *mār-kwār* from *mār* serpent + *k̲wār* -eating]

markka *noun*
• "MARKA"
• the former chief monetary unit of Finland, now replaced by the euro.
• [Finnish]
HOMOPHONES: *marka*

marlin *noun*
• "MAR lin"
• any of several large marine game fishes and food fishes of the swordfish family (genera *Makaira* and *Tetrapterus*) with the upper jaw elongated to form a pointed snout.
• [MARLINSPIKE, with reference to its pointed snout]
HOMOPHONES: *marline*

marline *noun*
- "MAR lin"
- a thin line of two strands.
- [Dutch *marlijn* from *marren* bind + *lijn* line]

HOMOPHONES: *marlin*

marlinspike *noun*
ALSO SPELLED: **marlinespike**
- "MAR lin spike"
- a pointed iron tool used to separate strands of rope or wire.
- [originally apparently *marling spike* from *marl* fasten with marline (from Dutch *marlen* frequentative of Middle Dutch *marren* bind) + 'spike']

marmalade *noun*
- "MARMA lade"
- a preserve of citrus fruit, usu. bitter oranges, made like jam.
- [French *marmelade* from Portuguese *marmelada* quince jam, from *marmelo* quince, from Latin *melimelum* from Greek *melimēlon* from *meli* honey + *mēlon* apple]

marmoreal *adjective*
- "mar MORRY 'll"
- of or like marble.
- [Latin *marmoreus* from *marmor* marble, from Greek *marmaros* shining stone]
- **marmoreally** *adverb*

marmoset *noun*
- "MARMA zet"
- any of several small tropical American monkeys of the family Callitricidae, having a long bushy tail.
- [Old French *marmouset* grotesque image, of unknown origin]

marmot *noun*
- "MAR mit"
- any burrowing rodent of the genus *Marmota*, with a heavy-set body and short bushy tail.
- [French *marmotte* prob. from Romansh *murmont* from Latin *murem montis* mountain mouse]

Maronite *noun*
- "MERRA nite"
- a member of a Christian church of Syrian origin, living chiefly in Lebanon and in communion with the Roman Catholic Church.
- [medieval Latin *Maronita* from *Maro*, the name of the 5th-c. Syrian founder]

marque *noun*
- "MARK"
- a make or brand, esp. of motor vehicle.
- [French, = 'mark']

HOMOPHONES: *mark, marc*

marquee *noun*
- "mar KEE"
- a canopy over the entrance to a large building.
- [MARQUISE, taken as pl. & assimilated to '-ee' ending]

HOMOPHONES: *marquis*

marquess *noun*
- "MAR kwiss"
- a British nobleman ranking between a duke and an earl.
- [var. of MARQUIS]

marquetry *noun*
ALSO SPELLED: **marqueterie**
- "MARKA tree"
- inlaid work in wood, ivory, etc., esp. as used for the decoration of furniture.
- [French *marqueterie* from *marqueter* variegate, from MARQUE]

marquis *noun*
- "mar KEE"
- a European nobleman ranking between a duke and a count.
- [Old French *marchis* from Romanic]

HOMOPHONES: *marquee*

marquise *noun*
- "mar KEEZ"
- the wife or widow of a marquis.
- [French, feminine of MARQUIS]

marram *noun*
- "MARE um"
- a coarse shore grass, *Ammophila brevigulata* or *A. arenaria*, that binds sand with its tough rhizomes.
- [Old Norse *marálmr* from *marr* sea + *hálmr* HAULM]

marriage *noun*
- "MARE idge"
- the legal or religious union of two people.
- [Old French *mariage* from *marier* marry, from Latin *maritare* from *maritus* husband]

marriageable *adjective*
- "MARE idge a bull"
- (of a person) fit for marriage, esp. of an appropriate age.
- [as MARRIAGE]
- **marriageability** *noun*

Marsala *noun*
- "mar SALA" or "mar SOLLA"
- a dark sweet fortified dessert wine.
- [*Marsala* in Sicily, where originally made]

Marseillaise *noun*
- "mar say YEZZ"
- the national anthem of France.
- [French, feminine adjective from *Marseille* Marseilles, the anthem having first been sung by patriots from there]

marshal *noun*
- "MAR sh'll"
- (in titles of ranks) a high-ranking officer in the armed forces of some countries.
- [Middle English via Old French *mareschal* and Late Latin *mariscalcus* from Germanic, literally 'horse servant']
- **marshaller** *noun*
- **marshalship** *noun*

HOMOPHONES: *martial*

marshmallow *noun*
• "MARSH mell oh" or "MARSH mal oh"
• a very soft, fluffy, usu. white candy made of sugar, egg white, gelatin, etc.
• [originally a type of plant, from 'marsh' from Old English *mer(i)sc* + 'mallow' from Old English *meal(u)we*]

marsupial *noun*
• "mar SOOPY 'll"
• any mammal of the order Marsupialia, characterized by being born incompletely developed and usu. carried and suckled in a pouch on the mother's belly.
• [modern Latin *marsupialis* from Latin *marsupium* from Greek *marsupion* pouch, diminutive of *marsipos* purse]

martagon *noun*
• "MARTA g'n"
• a lily, *Lilium martagon*, with small purple turban-like flowers.
• [French from Turkish *martagān* a form of turban]

marten *noun*
• "MAR t'n"
• any weasel-like carnivore of the genus *Martes* found in forests of Eurasia and N America, esp. the pine marten.
• [Middle Dutch *martren* from Old French (*peau*) *martrine* marten (fur), from *martre* from West Germanic]
HOMOPHONES: *martin*

martensite *noun*
• "MAR t'n zite"
• a hard, very brittle solid solution of carbon in iron, the chief constituent of hardened steel, formed when steel is quenched very rapidly.
• [A. *Martens*, German metallurgist d.1914 + Greek *lithos* stone]
• **martensitic** *adjective* "mar t'n ZITTIC"

martial *adjective*
• "MAR sh'll"
• of or appropriate to warfare or the military.
• [Latin *martialis* of Mars, the Roman god of war]
• **martially** *adverb*
HOMOPHONES: *marshal*

Martian *adjective*
• "MAR sh'n"
• of the planet Mars.
• [Latin *Martianus* from *Mars*]

martin *noun*
• "MART'n"
• any of several birds belonging to the swallow family Hirundinidae, e.g. the purple martin.
• [prob. from St. *Martin*]
HOMOPHONES: *marten*

martinet *noun*
• "mar t'n ET"
• a strict (originally military or naval) disciplinarian.
• [J. *Martinet*, 17th-c. French drill master]

martingale *noun*
• "MAR t'n gale"
• a strap, or set of straps, fastened at one end to the noseband of a horse and at the other end to the girth, to prevent rearing etc.
• [French, of uncertain origin]

martini *noun*
• "mar TEENY"
• a cocktail made of dry vermouth and usu. gin.
• [*Martini* & Rossi, Italian firm selling vermouth]

Martiniquan *noun*
• "marta NEEK'n"
• a person from the French island of Martinique in the W Indies.

Martinmas *noun*
• "MAR t'n muss"
• St. Martin's day, 11 Nov.
• [Middle English from St. *Martin* + 'mass']

martlet *noun*
• "MART lit"
• an imaginary footless bird in heraldic arms.
• [French *martelet* alteration of *martinet* diminutive from MARTIN]

martyr *noun*
• "MARTER"
• a person who is put to death for refusing to renounce a faith or belief.
• [Church Latin *martyr* from Greek *martur*, *martus -uros* witness]
• **martyrdom** *noun*
• **martyrish** *adjective*

martyrology *noun*
• "marter OLLA jee"
• a list or register of martyrs.
• [as MARTYR + *logos* word]
• **martyrological** *adjective*
• **martyrologist** *noun*

marvel *noun*
• "MARV'll"
• a wonderful thing.
• [Old French *merveille*, *merveiller* from Late Latin *mirabilia* neuter pl. of Latin *mirabilis* from *mirari* wonder at: see MIRACLE]
• **marveller** *noun* (also esp. *US* **marveler**)
• **marvellous** *adjective* (also esp. *US* **marvelous**)
• **marvellously** *adverb* (also esp. *US* **marvelously**)
• **marvellousness** *noun* (also esp. *US* **marvelousness**)

marzipan *noun*
• "MARZA pan"
• a paste of ground almonds, sugar, etc., moulded into decorative shapes or used to coat large cakes.
• [German from Italian *marzapane*]

mas *noun*
• "MASS"
• (in Trinidad, and subsequently elsewhere) a masquerade, esp. one held as part of an annual carnival parade.
• [abbreviation of MASQUE]
HOMOPHONES: *mass*

masa *noun*
• "MASSA"
• a type of dough made from cornmeal and used to make tortillas etc.
• [Spanish]

Masai *noun*
• "MASS eye"
• a pastoral people living in Kenya and Tanzania.
• [Bantu]

masala *noun*
• "muh SALA"
• any of various spice mixtures ground into a paste or powder for use in Indian cooking.
• [Urdu *maṣālaḥ*, ultimately from Arabic *maṣāliḥ* ingredients, materials]

mascara *noun*
• "mass KERRA"
• a cosmetic applied to the eyelashes to make them look darker and thicker.
• [Italian *mascara*, *maschera* mask]
• **mascaraed** *adjective*

mascarpone *noun*
• "mass car PONY"
• a soft mild Italian cream cheese.
• [Italian]

mascon *noun*
• "MASS con"
• a concentration of dense matter below parts of the moon's surface, producing a gravitational pull.
• [*mass concentration*]

mascot *noun*
• "MASS cot"
• a person, animal, or thing that is supposed to bring good luck to or represent a team, school, etc.
• [French *mascotte* from modern Provençal *mascotto* feminine diminutive of *masco* witch]

masculine *adjective*
• "MASS kyoo lin"
• of or characteristic of men.
• [Old French *masculin -ine* from Latin *masculinus* from *mas* a male]
• **masculinity** *noun*
• **masculinize** *verb* (also esp. *Brit.* **-ise**)

masculinist *noun*
• "MASS kyoo lin ist"
• an advocate of the rights of men.
• [as MASCULINE]

maser *noun*
• "MAY zur"
• a device using the stimulated emission of radiation by excited atoms to amplify or generate coherent monochromatic electromagnetic radiation in the microwave range.
• [*m*icrowave *a*mplification by the *s*timulated *e*mission of *r*adiation]
HOMOPHONES: *mazer*

mashie *noun*
• "MASHY"
• a golf club formerly used for lofting or for medium distances.
• [perhaps from French *massue* club]

masjid *noun*
• "MASS jid"
• a mosque.
• [Arabic, lit. 'place of prostration']

maskinonge *noun*
• "MASK 'n onj" or "MASK 'n onjy"
• a large N American pike, *Esox masquinongy*, esp. of the Great Lakes.
• [ultimately from Ojibwa, = great fish]

masochism *noun*
• "MASSA kizm"
• the condition or state of deriving gratification from one's own pain or humiliation.
• [L. von Sacher-*Masoch*, Austrian novelist d.1895, who described cases of it]
• **masochist** *noun*
• **masochistic** *adjective*
• **masochistically** *adverb*

mason *noun*
• "MAY s'n"
• a person who builds with stone or brick.
• [Old French *masson*, *maçonner*, Old Northern French *machun*, prob. ultimately from Germanic]
• **masonry** *noun*

Masonic *adjective*
• "muh SONNIC"
• of or relating to Freemasons, an international fraternity for mutual help and fellowship (the *Free and Accepted Masons*), with elaborate secret rituals.
• [as MASON]

Masorah *noun*
ALSO SPELLED: **Massorah**
• "muh SORE uh" or "massa RAH"
• a body of traditional information and comment on the correct text of the Hebrew Bible.
• [Hebrew *māsōreṯ*, perhaps = bond]

Masorete *noun*
ALSO SPELLED: **Massorete**
• "MASSA reet"
• any of the Jewish scholars who contributed to the formation of the Masorah.
• [French *Massoret* & modern Latin *Massoreta*,

originally a misuse of Hebrew (see MASORAH), assimilated to words ending in '-ete']
• **Masoretic** *adjective* (also **Massoretic**) "massa RETTIC"

masque *noun*
• "MASK"
• a dramatic and musical entertainment esp. of the 16th and 17th c., originally of pantomime, later with metrical dialogue.
• [French *masque* mask, from Italian *maschera* from Arabic *maskara* buffoon, from *sakira* to ridicule]
• **masquer** *noun*
HOMOPHONES: *mask, masker*

masquerade *noun*
• "maska RAID"
• a false show or pretense.
• [French *mascarade* from Spanish *mascarada* from *máscara* mask]
• **masquerader** *noun*

massacre *noun*
• "MASSA cur"
• a general slaughter (of persons, occasionally of animals).
• [Old French, of unknown origin]

massage *noun*
• "muh SOZH"
• the rubbing, kneading, etc., of muscles and joints of the body esp. with the hands, for relaxation, to stimulate circulation, increase suppleness, etc.
• [French, from *masser* treat with massage, perhaps via Portuguese *amassar* knead, from *massa* dough]
• **massager** *noun*

massasauga *noun*
• "massa SOGGA"
• a small spotted venomous N American rattlesnake, *Sistrurus catenatus*.
• [Ojibwa, = 'great river mouth']

masseter *noun*
• "muh SEETER"
• either of two chewing muscles which run from the temporal bone to the lower jaw.
• [Greek *masētēr* from *masaomai* chew]

masseur *noun*
• "ma SUR"
• a person who provides massage professionally.
• [French from *masser*: see MASSAGE]

masseuse *noun*
• "ma SOOCE" or "ma SUHZ"
• a woman who provides massage professionally.
• [French from *masser*: see MASSAGE]

massicot *noun*
• "MASSA cot"
• yellow lead monoxide, used as a pigment.
• [French, perhaps related to Italian *marzacotto* unguent, prob. from Arabic *mashakūnyā*]

massif *noun*
• "ma SEEF" or "MASS if"
• a large mountain mass; a compact group of mountain heights.
• [French *massif* used as noun, from Old French *massiz*, ultimately from Latin *massa* mass]

mastectomy *noun*
• "mass TECTA mee"
• the surgical removal of all or part of a breast.
• [Greek *mastos* breast + *ektomē* excision, from *ek* out + *temnō* cut]

mastic *noun*
• "MASS tick"
• a gum or resin exuded from the bark of the mastic tree, used in making varnish.
• [Old French from Late Latin *mastichum* from Latin *mastiche* from Greek *mastikhē*, perhaps from *mastikhaō* (see MASTICATE) with reference to its use as chewing gum]

masticate *verb*
• "MASTA cate"
• grind or chew (food) with one's teeth.
• [Late Latin *masticare masticat-* from Greek *mastikhaō* gnash the teeth]
• **mastication** *noun*
• **masticator** *noun*
• **masticatory** *adjective*

mastitis *noun*
• "mass TITE iss"
• an inflammation of the mammary gland (the breast or udder).
• [Greek *mastos* breast + *-itis*, forming feminine of adjectives in *-itēs* (with *nosos* 'disease' implied)]

mastodon *noun*
• "MASTA don"
• a large extinct mammal of the genus *Mammut*, resembling the elephant but having nipple-shaped tubercles on the crowns of its molar teeth.
• [modern Latin from Greek *mastos* breast + *odous odontos* tooth]

mastoid *adjective*
• "MASS toid"
• shaped like a woman's breast.
• [French *mastoïde* or modern Latin *mastoides* from Greek *mastoeidēs* from *mastos* breast]

mastoiditis *noun*
• "mass toid ITE iss"
• inflammation of the mastoid process, a conical prominence on the temporal bone behind the ear, to which muscles are attached.
• [as MASTOID + Greek *-itis*, forming feminine of adjectives in *-itēs* (with *nosos* 'disease' implied)]

matador *noun*
• "MATTA dore"
• a bullfighter whose task is to kill the bull.

• [Spanish from *matar* kill, from Persian *māt* dead]

maté *noun*
• "MAT ay"
• an infusion of the leaves of a S American shrub, *Ilex paraguariensis.*
• [Spanish *mate* from Quechua *mati*]

matelot *noun*
• "MAT lo"
• *Cdn & Brit.* a sailor.
• [French. from Middle Dutch *mattenoot*, lit. = bedmate]

matelote *noun*
• "MATTA lote"
• a dish of fish etc. with a sauce of wine and onions.
• [French (as MATELOT)]

materfamilias *noun*
• "may tur fuh MILLY us"
• the female head of a family or household.
• [Latin from *mater* mother + *familia* family]

material *noun*
• "muh TEERY 'll"
• the matter from which a thing is made.
• [Old French *materiel*, *-al*, from Late Latin *materialis* from Latin *materia* timber, substance, subject of discourse]
• **materiality** *noun*

materialism *noun*
• "muh TERRY 'll izm"
• a tendency to prefer material possessions and physical comfort to spiritual values.
• [as MATERIAL]
• **materialist** *noun*
• **materialistic** *adjective*
• **materialistically** *adverb*

materialize *verb*
ALSO SPELLED: esp. *Brit.* **-ise**
• "muh TEERY 'll ize"
• become actual fact.
• [as MATERIAL]
• **materialization** *noun* (also esp. *Brit.* **-isation**)

materially *adverb*
• "muh TEERY 'll ee"
• substantially, considerably.
• [as MATERIAL]

matériel *noun*
• "muh terry EL"
• available means or resources, esp. materials and equipment used in warfare.
• [French (as MATERIAL)]

maternal *adjective*
• "muh TURN'll"
• of or like a mother.
• [Old French *maternel* or Latin *maternus* from *mater* mother]
• **maternally** *adverb*

maternity *noun*
• "muh TURNA tee"
• for women during and just after childbirth.
• [medieval Latin *maternitas -tatis* from Latin *maternus* from *mater* mother]

mathematics *noun*
• "math a MATTIX"
• the abstract, deductive science of number, quantity, space, and arrangement.
• [ultimately from Greek *mathēma -matos* science, from *manthanō* learn]
• **mathematical** *adjective*
• **mathematically** *adverb*
• **mathematician** *noun*

matinee *noun*
• "mat 'n AY"
• an afternoon performance at a theatre, concert hall, etc.
• [French, = 'what occupies a morning' (extended in fashionable French society to the dinner hour, 6 or 7 p.m.), from *matin* morning (as MATINS)]

matins *noun*
ALSO SPELLED: **mattins**
• "MAT inz"
• a service of morning prayer in the Anglican Church.
• [Old French *matines* from Church Latin *matutinas*, accusative feminine pl. adjective from Latin *matutinus* of the morning, from *Matuta* dawn goddess]

matriarch *noun*
• "MAY tree ark"
• a woman who is the head of a family or tribe.
• [Latin *mater* mother, after PATRIARCH]
• **matriarchal** *adjective*

matriarchy *noun*
• "MAY tree arky"
• a form of social organization in which the mother is the head of the family and descent is reckoned through the female line.
• [as MATRIARCH]

matric *noun*
• "muh TRICK"
• matriculation.
• [abbreviation]

matricide *noun*
• "MATRA side"
• the killing of one's mother.
• [Latin *matricida*, *matricidium* from *mater matris* mother + *-cida*, *-cidium* from *caedere* kill]
• **matricidal** *adjective*

matriculate *verb*
• "muh TRICK yuh late"
• be enrolled at a college or university.
• [medieval Latin *matriculare matriculat-* enrol, from Late Latin *matricula* register, diminutive of Latin MATRIX]
• **matriculation** *noun*

matrilineal *adjective*
• "matra LINNY 'll"
• of or based on kinship with the mother or the female line.
• [Latin *mater matris* mother + LINEAL]
• **matrilineage** *noun* "matra LINNY idge"
• **matrilineally** *adverb*

matrilocal *adjective*
• "matra LO k'll"
• of or denoting a custom in marriage where the married couple goes to live with the wife's community.
• [Latin *mater matris* mother + LOCAL]
• **matrilocality** *noun*

matrimony *noun*
• "MATRA moany"
• the rite or institution of marriage.
• [Anglo-French *matrimonie* from Latin *matrimonium* from *mater matris* mother]
• **matrimonial** *adjective*
• **matrimonially** *adverb*

matrix *noun*
• "MAY trix"
• an environment or substance in which a thing is developed.
• [Latin, = breeding female, womb, from *mater matris* mother]

matron *noun*
• "MAY trun"
• a middle-aged or elderly married woman, esp. a dignified, staid, or portly one of high social standing.
• [Latin *matrona* from *mater matris* mother]
• **matronly** *adjective*

matryoshka *noun*
ALSO SPELLED: **matrioshka**
• "ma TREE osh kuh"
• a set of hollow and usu. decorated wooden doll figures of differing sizes, each one made so as to nest inside the next largest.
• [Russian *matrëshka*]

Matsqui *noun*
• "MAT skwee"
• a member of a Salishan Aboriginal people, a subgroup of the Halq'emeylem, living in the Lower Fraser valley of BC.
• [Halkomelem, = 'easy portage, easy travelling', in reference to the ease of ascending creeks from the Fraser and portaging over a nearby height of land]

matsutake *noun*
• "matsoo TOCK ay"
• an edible mushroom of the genus *Tricholoma*, found in pine forests and much prized as a delicacy.
• [Japanese *matsu* pine + *take* mushroom]

matte *adjective*
• "MAT"
• (of a colour, surface, etc.) dull, without lustre.
• [French *mat*]
HOMOPHONES: *mat*

mattock *noun*
• "MAT uck"
• an agricultural tool shaped like a pickaxe, with an adze and a chisel edge as the ends of the head.
• [Old English *mattuc*, of unknown origin]

mattress *noun*
• "MA triss"
• a large fabric case stuffed with soft, firm, or springy material, or a similar case filled with air or water, used on or as a bed.
• [Old French *materas* from Italian *materasso* from Arabic *almaṭraḥ* the place, the cushion, from *ṭaraḥa* throw]

mature *adjective*
• "muh CHUR"
• with fully developed powers of body and mind; adult.
• [Latin *maturus* timely, early]
• **maturation** *noun* "matcher AY sh'n"
• **maturational** *adjective*
• **maturely** *adverb*
• **maturity** *noun*

matutinal *adjective*
• "mat yoo TINE 'll" or "muh TYOO t'n 'll"
• of or occurring in the morning.
• [Late Latin *matutinalis* from Latin *matutinus*: see MATINS]

matzo *noun*
ALSO SPELLED: **matzoh**, **matzah**
• "MOTT so" or "MOTT suh"
• a flat, crisp, unleavened bread for Passover.
• [Yiddish from Hebrew *maṣṣāh*]

maudlin *adjective*
• "MOD lin"
• foolishly sentimental or self-pitying.
• [Old French *Madeleine* from Church Latin *Magdalena* MAGDALEN, with reference to pictures of Mary Magdalen weeping]

maul *verb*
• "MAUL" (sounds like *MALL*)
• (of an animal) tear and mutilate (a person, prey etc.).
• [Old French *mail* from Latin *malleus* hammer]
• **mauler** *noun*
• **mauling** *noun*
HOMOPHONES: *mall, moll*

maunder *verb*
• "MAWN dur"
• talk in a dreamy or rambling manner.
• [perhaps from obsolete *maunder* beggar, to beg]

Mauritanian *noun*
• "mora TAY nee 'n"
• a native or inhabitant of the W African country of Mauritania.

Mauritian *noun*
• "muh RISH'n"
• a native or inhabitant of Mauritius in the Indian Ocean.

mausoleum *noun*
- "mozza LEE um"
- a large and grand tomb.
- [Latin from Greek *Mausōleion* from *Mausōlos* Mausolus king of Caria in SW Asia Minor (4th c. BC), to whose tomb the name was originally applied]

mauve *adjective*
- "MOAVE" (rhymes with *STOVE*)
- pale purple.
- [French, lit. 'mallow', from Latin *malva*]

mauzy *adjective*
ALSO SPELLED: **mausy**
- "MOZZY"
- *Cdn* (*Nfld*) (of weather) foggy, damp, or misty, esp. producing condensation on objects.
- [English dialect *mosey* muggy, foggy]

maven *noun*
- "MAY v'n"
- an expert or connoisseur.
- [Hebrew *mēḇīn*]

maverick *noun*
- "MAV rick"
- an unorthodox or independent-minded person.
- [S. A. *Maverick*, Texas engineer and rancher d.1870, who did not brand his cattle]

mawkish *adjective*
- "MOCK ish"
- sentimental in a feeble or sickly way.
- [obsolete *mawk* maggot, from Old Norse *mathkr* from Germanic]
- **mawkishly** *adverb*
- **mawkishness** *noun*

maxilla *noun*
- "mack SILLA"
- the jaw or jawbone, esp. the upper jaw in most vertebrates.
- [Latin, = jaw]
- **maxillary** *adjective* "mack SILLER ee" or "MAXA lerry"

mayonnaise *noun*
- "MAY a naze"
- a thick creamy dressing made of egg yolks, oil, vinegar, etc.
- [French, perhaps from *mahonnais -aise* of Port *Mahon* on the Spanish Mediterranean island of Minorca]

mayor *noun*
- "MAY ur" or "MARE"
- the head of a municipal corporation, esp. of a city or town.
- [Old French *maire* from Latin *major*, comparative of *magnus* great]
- **mayoral** *adjective*
- **mayorship** *noun*

HOMOPHONES: *mare*

mayoralty *noun*
- "MAY ur 'll tee" or "MARE 'll tee"
- the office of mayor.
- [as MAYOR]

mayoress *noun*
- "MAY ur ess"
- a woman holding the office of mayor.
- [as MAYOR]

mazard *noun*
ALSO SPELLED: **mazzard**
- "MAZZ 'rd"
- the wild sweet cherry, *Prunus avium*, of Europe.
- [alteration of MAZER]

Mazdaism *noun*
- "MAZDA izm"
- Zoroastrianism, a dualistic religious system, based on the concept of a conflict between a spirit of light and good and a spirit of darkness and evil.
- [Avestan *mazda*, the supreme god of ancient Persian religion]

mazer *noun*
- "MAY zur"
- a hardwood drinking bowl, usu. silver-mounted.
- [Old French *masere* from Germanic]

HOMOPHONES: *maser*

mazuma *noun*
- "muh ZOOMA"
- money, cash.
- [Yiddish from Hebrew *mĕzummān*, from *zimmēn* prepare]

mazurka *noun*
- "muh ZURKA"
- a usu. lively Polish dance in triple time, usu. with a slide and hop.
- [French *mazurka* or German *Masurka*, from Polish *mazurka* denoting a woman from the province of Mazovia]

mbaqanga *noun*
- "baw KONG guh" or "m'baw KONG guh"
- an upbeat form of South African popular music blending the influences of Zulu rhythms, blues, rock, and jazz.
- [Zulu *umbaqanga* steamed corn bread]

McCarthyism *noun*
- "muh CARTHY izm"
- (esp. in the US) the policy of hunting out suspected Communists and removing them from government departments or other positions, esp. as pursued by Joseph McCarthy (d.1957).
- **McCarthyite** *adjective*

McGuffin *noun*
ALSO SPELLED: **MacGuffin**
- "muh GUFF'n"
- (in a film, novel, or other form of narrative fiction) a particular event, object, factor, etc., initially presented as being of great significance

to the story, but often having little actual importance for the plot as it develops.
• [prob. from the surname *McGuffin*, allegedly borrowed by Alfred Hitchcock from a humorous story involving a diversion of this kind]

McIntosh *noun*
• "MACK 'n tosh"
• a medium-sized, deep red, cooking and eating apple with green blotches.
• [J. McIntosh (1777–1845), Canadian farmer and apple breeder, who first discovered it]
HOMOPHONES: *mackintosh*

McLuhanesque *adjective*
• "muh cloo 'n ESK"
• characteristic or suggestive of the work of the Canadian communications theorist Marshall McLuhan (d.1980).

mead *noun*
• "MEED"
• an alcoholic drink of fermented honey and water.
• [Old English *me(o)du* from Germanic]
HOMOPHONES: *meed, Mede*

meadow *noun*
• "MEDDO"
• a piece of grassland, esp. one used for hay or for grazing animals.
• [Old English *mǣdwe*, oblique case of *mǣd*]
• **meadowy** *adjective*

meadowland *noun*
• "MEDDO land"
• land used for the cultivation of grass, esp. for hay.
• [as MEADOW]

meadowlark *noun*
• "MEDDO lark"
• any of several N American songbirds of the genus *Sturnella* related to the blackbirds but speckled brown with yellow underparts, esp. the eastern meadowlark, *S. magna*, or western meadowlark, *S. neglecta*, which has a characteristic bubbling song.
• [as MEADOW + 'lark']

meadowsweet *noun*
• "MEDDO sweet"
• a rosaceous plant, *Filipendula ulmaria*, common in meadows and damp places, with creamy-white fragrant flowers.
• [as MEADOW + 'sweet']

Meafordite *noun*
• "MEEFURD ite"
• a resident of Meaford, Ont.

meagre *adjective*
ALSO SPELLED: **meager**
• "MEE gur"
• lacking in amount or quality.
• [Anglo-French *megre* from Latin *macer*]
• **meagrely** *adverb* (also **meagerly**)
• **meagreness** *noun* (also **meagerness**)

meander *verb*
• "mee ANDER"
• wander randomly.
• [Latin *maeander* from Greek *Maiandros*, the name of a winding river in Phrygia in Asia Minor]
• **meandering** *adjective*

measles *plural noun*
• "MEEZ 'lz"
• an acute infectious viral disease marked by red spots on the skin.
• [Middle English *masele(s)* prob. from Middle Low German *masele*, Middle Dutch *masel* pustule (compare Dutch *mazelen* measles), Old High German *masala*: change of form prob. due to assimilation to Middle English *meser* leper]

measly *adjective*
• "MEEZLY"
• ridiculously small in size, amount, or value.
• [as MEASLES]

measure *noun*
• "MEZHUR"
• a size or quantity found by measuring.
• [Old French *mesure* from Latin *mensura* from *metiri mens-* measure]
• **measurability** *noun*
• **measurable** *adjective*
• **measurably** *adverb*
• **measured** *adjective*
• **measurement** *noun*
• **measurer** *noun*

measureless *adjective*
• "MEZHUR less"
• not measurable; infinite.
• [as MEASURE]
• **measurelessly** *adverb*

meatus *noun*
• "mee AY tuss"
• a tubular channel or passage in the body, esp. that leading into the ear.
• [Latin, = passage from *meare* flow, run]

mecca *noun*
• "MECKA"
• a place which attracts people of a particular group.
• [*Mecca* in Saudi Arabia, birthplace of the Prophet Muhammad and chief place of Muslim pilgrimage]

mechanic *noun*
• "muh CANNIC"
• a skilled worker who makes or uses or repairs machinery, esp. engines.
• [Old French *mecanique* or Latin *mechanicus* from Greek *mēkhanikos* from *mēkhos* contrivance]

mechanical *adjective*
• "muh CANNA k'll"
• of or relating to machines or mechanisms.
• [Latin *mechanicus* (as MECHANIC)]
• **mechanically** *adverb*

mechanician *noun*
- "mecka NISH'n"
- a person skilled in constructing machinery.
- [as MECHANIC]

mechanics *noun*
- "muh CANNIX"
- the branch of applied mathematics dealing with motion and tendencies to motion.
- [as MECHANIC]

mechanism *noun*
- "MECKA nizm"
- the structure or adaptation of parts of a machine.
- [modern Latin *mechanismus* from Greek (as MECHANIC)]

mechanist *noun*
- "MECKA mist"
- a mechanician.
- [as MECHANIC]
- **mechanistic** *adjective*
- **mechanistically** *adverb*

mechanize *verb*
ALSO SPELLED: esp. *Brit.* **-ise**
- "MECKA nize"
- make mechanical; give a mechanical character to.
- [as MECHANIC]
- **mechanization** *noun* (also esp. *Brit.* **-isation**)
- **mechanizer** *noun* (also esp. *Brit.* **-iser**)

mechanoreceptor *noun*
- "mecka no re SEPTER"
- a sensory receptor that responds to mechanical stimuli such as touch or sound.
- [MECHANIC + RECEPTOR]
- **mechanoreception** *noun*
- **mechanoreceptive** *adjective*

mechatronics *noun*
- "mecka TRONNIX"
- technology combining electronics and mechanical engineering, esp. in developing new manufacturing techniques.
- [blend of MECHANIC + ELECTRONICS]

Mechlin *noun*
- "MECKLIN"
- lace made at Mechlin (now Mechelen or Malines) in Belgium.

mechoui *noun*
- "MAY shwee"
- *Cdn (Que.)* a meal of meat, esp. lamb or mutton, roasted on a spit over a fire.
- [French from North African Arabic *mashwi* grilled foods]

meconium *noun*
- "muh CONEY um"
- a dark substance forming the first feces of a newborn infant.
- [Latin, lit. 'poppy juice', from Greek *mēkōnion* from *mēkōn* poppy]

medal *noun*
- "MED'll"
- a piece of metal, usu. in the form of a disc, struck or cast with an inscription or device to commemorate an event etc., or awarded as a distinction to a soldier, scholar, athlete, etc., for services rendered, for proficiency, etc.
- [French *médaille* from Italian *medaglia*, ultimately from Latin *metallum* METAL]
- **medalled** *adjective* (also esp. *US* **medaled**)

HOMOPHONES: *meddle, metal, mettle*

medallion *noun*
- "muh DAL y'n"
- a large medal.
- [French *médaillon* from Italian *medaglione* augmentative of *medaglia* (as MEDAL)]

medallist *noun*
ALSO SPELLED: esp. *US* **medalist**
- "MED'll ist"
- a recipient of a (specified) medal.
- [as MEDAL]

meddle *verb*
- "MED'll"
- interfere in or busy oneself unduly with others' concerns.
- [Old French *medler*, var. of *mesler*, ultimately from Latin *miscēre* mix]
- **meddler** *noun*
- **meddlesome** *adjective*
- **meddlesomely** *adverb*
- **meddlesomeness** *noun*

HOMOPHONES: *medal, mettle, metal, medlar, mettlesome*

Mede *noun*
- "MEED"
- a member of an Indo-European people which established an empire in Media in Persia (modern Iran) in the 7th c. BC.
- [Latin *Medi* (pl.) from Greek *Mēdoi*]

HOMOPHONES: *mead, meed*

medevac *noun*
ALSO SPELLED: **medivac**
- "MEDDA vac"
- the transportation of sick or wounded patients by air to hospital, esp. from a remote location, a battlefield, etc.
- [from MED(ICAL) + EVAC(UATE)]

medial *adjective*
- "MEEDY 'll"
- situated in the middle.
- [Late Latin *medialis* from Latin *medius* middle]
- **medially** *adverb*

median *adjective*
- "MEEDY 'n"
- situated in the middle.
- [French *médiane* or Latin *medianus* (as MEDIAL)]

mediant *noun*
- "MEEDY 'nt"
- the third note of a diatonic scale of any key.
- [French *médiante* from Italian *mediante*

participle of obsolete *mediare* come between, from Latin (as MEDIATE)]

mediastinum *noun*
- "meedy a STYE num"
- a membranous middle septum, esp. between the lungs.
- [modern Latin from medieval Latin *mediastinus* medial, after Latin *mediastinus* drudge, from *medius* middle]
- **mediastinal** *adjective*

mediate *verb*
- "MEEDY ate"
- intervene (between parties in a dispute) to produce agreement or reconciliation.
- [Late Latin *mediare mediat-* from Latin *medius* middle]
- **mediation** *noun*
- **mediator** *noun*
- **mediatory** *adjective*

medic *noun*
- "MEDDIC"
- a doctor or medical student.
- [Latin *medicus* physician, from *medēri* heal]

HOMOPHONES: *medick*

medicable *adjective*
- "MEDDA kuh bull"
- able to be treated or cured medically.
- [Latin *medicabilis* (as MEDICATE)]

medical *adjective*
- "MEDDA k'll"
- of or relating to the science or practice of medicine in general.
- [as MEDIC]
- **medically** *adverb*

medicalize *verb*
ALSO SPELLED: esp. *Brit.* **-ise**
- "MEDDA k'll ize"
- involve medicine in; view in medical terms, esp. unnecessarily.
- [as MEDIC]
- **medicalization** *noun* (also esp. *Brit.* **-isation**)

medicament *noun*
- "muh DICKA m'nt" or "MEDDA kuh m'nt"
- a substance used for medical treatment.
- [French *médicament* or Latin *medicamentum* (as MEDICATE)]

medicare *noun*
- "MEDDA care"
- (in Canada) a national health care program financed by taxation and administered by the provinces and territories.
- [MEDICAL + 'care']

medicate *verb*
- "MEDDA cate"
- treat medically; administer medication to.
- [Latin *medicari medicat-* administer remedies to, from *medicus*: see MEDIC]

medication *noun*
- "medda CAY sh'n"
- a substance used for medical treatment.
- [as MEDICATE]

medicinal *adjective*
- "muh DISS'n 'll"
- (of a substance) having healing properties.
- [Old French from Latin *medicinalis* (as MEDICINE)]
- **medicinally** *adverb*

medicine *noun*
- "MEDDA sin"
- the science or practice of the diagnosis, treatment, and prevention of disease, esp. as distinct from surgical methods.
- [Old French *medecine* from Latin *medicina* from *medicus*: see MEDIC]

medick *noun*
ALSO SPELLED: **medic**
- "MEDDIC"
- any leguminous plant of the genus *Medicago*, esp. alfalfa.
- [Latin *medica* from Greek *Mēdikē poa* Median grass]

HOMOPHONES: *medic*

medico *noun*
- "MEDDIC oh"
- a doctor or medical student.
- [Italian from Latin (as MEDIC)]

medieval *adjective*
ALSO SPELLED: esp. *Brit.* **mediaeval**
- "mid EE v'll" or "meddy EE v'll"
- of, or in the style of, the Middle Ages.
- [modern Latin *medium aevum* from Latin *medius* middle + *aevum* age]
- **medievalism** *noun* (also esp. *Brit.* **mediaevalism**)
- **medievalist** *noun* (also esp. *Brit.* **mediaevalist**)
- **medievalize** *verb* (also esp. *Brit.* **mediaevalise**)
- **medievally** *adverb* (also esp. *Brit.* **mediaevally**)

medina *noun*
- "muh DEENA"
- the old Arab or non-European quarter of a N African town.
- [Arabic, literally 'town']

mediocre *adjective*
- "meedy OKER" ("OKER" rhymes with *JOKER*)
- of middling quality, neither good nor bad.
- [French *médiocre* or from Latin *mediocris* of middle height or degree, from *medius* middle + *ocris* rugged mountain]
- **mediocrity** *noun* "meedy OCKRA tee"

meditate *verb*
- "MEDDA tate"
- exercise the mind in (esp. religious) contemplation.
- [Latin *meditari* contemplate]

- **meditation** *noun*
- **meditational** *adjective*
- **meditative** *adjective*
- **meditatively** *adverb*
- **meditator** *noun*

Mediterranean *adjective*
• "medda tuh RAINY 'n"
• of or characteristic of the Mediterranean Sea between Europe and Africa, countries bordering it, or their inhabitants.
• [Latin *mediterraneus* inland, from *medius* middle + *terra* land]

medlar *noun*
• "MED lur"
• a rosaceous tree, *Mespilus germanica*, bearing small brown apple-like fruits.
• [Old French *medler* from Latin *mespila* from Greek *mespilē*, *-on*]
HOMOPHONES: *meddler*

medley *noun*
• "MEDLY"
• a varied mixture; a miscellany.
• [Old French *medlee* var. of *meslee* from Romanic (as MEDDLE)]

Medoc *noun*
• "may DOCK" or "MED ock"
• a fine red wine from the Médoc region of SW France.

medulla *noun*
• "muh DULLA"
• the inner region of certain organs or tissues usu. when it is distinguishable from the outer region or cortex, as in hair or a kidney.
• [Latin, = pith, marrow, prob. related to *medius* middle]
• **medullary** *adjective*

medusa *noun*
• "muh DOO suh" or "muh DYOO suh"
• a jellyfish.
• [*Medusa*, one of the Gorgons (see GORGON)]
• **medusan** *adjective*
• **medusoid** *noun*

meed *noun*
• "MEED"
• a reward.
• [Old English *mēd* from West Germanic, related to Gothic *mizdō*, Greek *misthos* reward]
HOMOPHONES: *mead*, *Mede*

meerkat *noun*
• "MEER cat"
• a South African burrowing mongoose, *Suricata suricatta*, with grey and black stripes.
• [Dutch, = sea cat]

meerschaum *noun*
• "MEER shum" or "MEER shom"
• a soft white form of hydrated magnesium silicate, chiefly found in Turkey, which resembles clay.
• [German, = seafoam, from *Meer* sea + *Schaum* foam, translation of Persian *kef-i-daryā*, with reference to its frothiness]

megabyte *noun*
• "MEGGA bite"
• 1,048,576 (i.e. 2^{20}) bytes as a measure of data capacity, or loosely 1,000,000 bytes.
• [Greek *mega* from *megas* great + BYTE]

megahertz *noun*
• "MEGGA hurts"
• one million hertz, esp. as a measure of frequency of radio transmissions.
• [Greek *mega* from *megas* great + HERTZ]

megalith *noun*
• "MEGGA lith"
• a large stone, esp. one placed upright as a monument or part of one.
• [Greek *mega* from *megas* great + *lithos* stone]
• **megalithic** *adjective*

megalomania *noun*
• "megga luh MAINY uh"
• a mental disorder producing delusions of grandeur.
• [Greek *mega* from *megas* great + MANIA]
• **megalomaniac** *adjective*
• **megalomaniacal** *adjective*
"megga lo muh NIE a k'll"

megalopolis *noun*
• "megga LOPPA liss"
• a very large city.
• [Greek *mega* from *megas* great + *polis* city]
• **megalopolitan** *adjective*
"megga luh POLLA t'n"

megalosaur *noun*
• "MEGGA luh sore"
• a large flesh-eating dinosaur of the genus *Megalosaurus*, with stout hind legs and small forelimbs.
• [Greek *mega* from *megas* great + *sauros* lizard]

megapixel *noun*
• "MEGGA pix'll"
• 1,048,576 or 2^{20} pixels, esp. as a unit of graphic resolution.
• [Greek *mega* from *megas* great + PIXEL]

megapode *noun*
• "MEGGA pode"
• any bird of the family Megapodidae, native to Australasia, that builds a mound of debris for the incubation of its eggs, e.g. a mallee fowl.
• [modern Latin *Megapodius* (genus name) formed as Greek *mega* from *megas* great + *pous podos* foot]

megawatt *noun*
• "MEGGA wot"
• one million watts, esp. as a measure of electrical power as generated by power stations.
• [Greek *mega* from *megas* great + WATT]

megohm *noun*
• "MEG ome"
• one million ohms.
• [Greek *mega* from *megas* great + OHM]

meiosis *noun*
• "my OH sis"
• a type of cell division that results in daughter cells with half the chromosome number of the parent cell.
• [modern Latin from Greek *meiōsis* from *meioō* lessen, from *meiōn* less]
• **meiotic** *adjective* "my OTTIC"
• **meiotically** *adverb*
HOMOPHONES: *miosis, miotic*

Meissen *noun*
• "MICE 'n"
• Dresden china.
• [*Meissen*, Germany, where it has been made since 1710]

Meistersinger *noun*
• "MICE tur singer"
• a member of one of the 14th–16th-c. German guilds for lyric poets and musicians.
• [German from *Meister* master + *Singer* singer]

meitnerium *noun*
• "mite NEERY um"
• a very unstable chemical element made by high-energy atomic collisions.
• [modern Latin, from Lise *Meitner*, Austrian-born Swedish physicist d.1968]

melamine *noun*
• "MELLA meen"
• a white crystalline compound that can be copolymerized with formaldehyde to give thermosetting resins.
• [*melam* (arbitrary) + AMINE]

melancholia *noun*
• "mell'n CO lee uh"
• a mental illness marked by depression and ill-founded fears.
• [Late Latin: see MELANCHOLY]
• **melancholic** *adjective* "mell'n COLLIC"
• **melancholically** *adverb*

melancholy *noun*
• "MELL'n colly"
• a pensive sadness.
• [Old French *melancolie* and Late Latin *melancholia* from Greek *melagkholia*, from *melas melanos* black + *kholē* bile]

Melanesian *noun*
• "mella NEE zh'n"
• a native or inhabitant of Melanesia in the W Pacific.

mélange *noun*
• "may LAWNZH"
• a mixture, a medley.
• [French from *mêler* mix (as MEDDLE)]

melanin *noun*
• "MELLA nin"
• a dark brown to black pigment occurring in the hair, skin, and iris of the eye, that is responsible for tanning of the skin when exposed to sunlight.
• [Greek *melas melanos* black]

melanism *noun*
• "MELLA nizm"
• the unusual darkening of body tissues caused by excessive production of melanin, esp. as a form of colour variation in animals.
• [as MELANIN]
• **melanic** *adjective* "muh LANNIC"

melanoma *noun*
• "mella NOMA"
• a usu. malignant tumour of melanin-forming cells, usu. in the skin.
• [MELANIN + CARCINOMA]

melanosis *noun*
• "mella NO sis"
• = MELANISM.
• [modern Latin from Greek (as MELANIN)]
• **melanotic** *adjective* "mella NOTTIC"

melatonin *noun*
• "mella TOE nin"
• an indole derivative formed in the pineal gland of various mammals, which inhibits melanin formation and is thought to be concerned with regulating the reproductive cycle.
• [MELANIN + SEROTONIN]

Melchite *noun*
• "MELL kite"
• a Christian of the eastern Orthodox or Catholic Churches originating in Syria and Egypt, following the Byzantine rite, which historically accepted the Orthodox faith of the ecumenical Councils of Ephesus and Chalcedon, as did the Emperor.
• [Church Latin *Melchitae* from Byzantine Greek *Melkhitai* representing Syriac *malkāyā* royalists, from *malkā* king]

melee *noun*
• "MAY lay" or "MELL ay" or "mell AY"
• a confused fight, skirmish, or scuffle.
• [French (as MEDLEY)]

melilot *noun*
• "MELLA lot"
• a leguminous plant of the genus *Melilotus*, with trifoliate leaves, long spikes of small flowers, and a scent of hay when dried.
• [(Old) French *mélilot* via Latin *melilotus* from Greek *melilōtos* 'honey lotus']

meliorate *verb*
• "MEELY a rate"
• improve.
• [Late Latin *meliorare* from Latin *melior* better]
• **melioration** *noun*
• **meliorative** *adjective*

meliorism *noun*
• "MEELY a rizm"
• a doctrine that the world may be made better by properly directed human effort.
• [Latin *melior* better]
• **meliorist** *noun*
• **melioristic** *adjective*

melisma *noun*
- "muh LIZMA"
- the prolongation of one syllable of text over a number of notes.
- [Greek, lit. 'song']
- **melismatic** *adjective* "mel iz MATTIC"

melliferous *adjective*
- "mel IFFER us"
- yielding or producing honey.
- [Latin *mellifer* from *mel* honey + *-fer* producing, from *ferre* bear]

mellifluous *adjective*
- "mel IFF loo us"
- (of a voice, words, etc.) pleasing, musical, flowing.
- [Late Latin *mellifluus* from *mel* honey + *fluere* flow]
- **mellifluent** *adjective*
- **mellifluously** *adverb*
- **mellifluousness** *noun*

melodeon *noun*
- "muh LOADY 'n"
- a small organ popular in the 19th c., similar to the harmonium.
- [MELODY + HARMONIUM with Graecized ending]

melodrama *noun*
- "MELLO dramma" or "MELLO dromma"
- a sensational dramatic piece with crude appeals to the emotions and usu. a happy ending.
- [French *mélodrame* from Greek *melos* music + French *drame* DRAMA]
- **melodramatic** *adjective*
- **melodramatically** *adverb*
- **melodramatize** *verb* (also esp. *Brit.* **-ise**)

melodramatics *noun*
- "mello druh MATTIX"
- melodramatic behaviour, action, or writing.
- [as MELODRAMA]

melody *noun*
- "MELLA dee"
- an arrangement of single notes in a musically expressive succession.
- [Old French *melodie* from Late Latin *melodia* from Greek *melōidia* from *melos* song]
- **melodic** *adjective* "muh LODDIC"
- **melodically** *adverb*
- **melodious** *adjective* "muh LOADY us"
- **melodiously** *adverb*
- **melodiousness** *noun*
- **melodist** *noun*
- **melodize** *verb* (also esp. *Brit.* **-ise**)

melton *noun*
- "MELT'n"
- cloth with a close-cut nap, used for jackets, overcoats, etc.
- [*Melton Mowbray* in central England]

Melvillite *noun*
- "MELL vill ite"
- a resident of Melville, Sask.

membrane *noun*
- "MEM brane"
- any pliable sheet-like structure acting as a boundary, lining, or partition in an organism.
- [Latin *membrana* skin of body, parchment, from *membrum* limb]
- **membranous** *adjective* "MEM brun us"

meme *noun*
- "MEEM"
- an element of a culture or system of behaviour that is passed from one individual to another by non-genetic means, esp. imitation.
- [Greek *mimēma* 'that which is imitated', after GENE]

memento *noun*
- "muh MENTO"
- an object kept as a reminder or a souvenir of a person or an event.
- [Latin, imperative of *meminisse* remember]

memoir *noun*
- "MEM warr" ("WARR" rhymes with *FAR*)
- an autobiography or a written account of one's memory of certain events or people.
- [French *mémoire* (masculine), special use of *mémoire* (feminine) MEMORY]
- **memoirist** *noun*

memorabilia *plural noun*
- "memmer a BEEL yuh"
- souvenirs of memorable events, people, periods, etc.
- [Latin, neuter pl. (as MEMORABLE)]

memorable *adjective*
- "MEMMER a bull"
- worth remembering, not to be forgotten.
- [French *mémorable* or Latin *memorabilis* from *memorare* bring to mind, from *memor* mindful]
- **memorability** *noun*
- **memorableness** *noun*
- **memorably** *adverb*

memorandum *noun*
- "memma RAN dum"
- a written note or communication esp. in business between people working for the same organization.
- [Latin neuter sing. gerundive of *memorare*: see MEMORABLE]

memorial *noun*
- "muh MORRY 'll"
- an object, institution, or custom established in memory of a person or event.
- [Old French *memorial* or Latin *memorialis* (as MEMORY)]
- **memorialist** *noun*

memorialize *verb*

ALSO SPELLED: esp. *Brit.* **-ise**
- "muh MORRY 'll ize"
- commemorate.
- [as MEMORIAL]
- **memorialization** *noun* (also esp. *Brit.* **-isation**)
- **memorializer** *noun* (also esp. *Brit.* **-iser**)

memorize *verb*
ALSO SPELLED: esp. *Brit.* **-ise**
• "MEMMER ize"
• commit to memory, learn by heart.
• [as MEMORY]
• **memorization** *noun* (also esp. *Brit.* **-isation**)
• **memorizer** *noun* (also esp. *Brit.* **-iser**)
• **memorizing** *noun* (also esp. *Brit.* **-ising**)

memory *noun*
• "MEMMER ee"
• the faculty by which things are recalled to or kept in the mind.
• [Old French *memorie* from Latin *memoria* from *memor* mindful, remembering]

memsahib *noun*
• "MEM suh hib" or "MEM saw ib"
• a European married woman in India, as spoken of or to by Indians.
• ['ma'am' + SAHIB]

menace *noun*
• "MEN iss"
• a dangerous thing or person.
• [ultimately from Latin *minax -acis* threatening, from *minari* threaten]
• **menacing** *adjective*
• **menacingly** *adverb*

ménage *noun*
• "may NAZH" or "may NOZH"
• a domestic establishment, a household.
• [Old French *manaige*, ultimately from Latin (as MANSION)]

menagerie *noun*
• "muh NAZH ur ee" or "muh NADGE ur ee" or "muh NOZH ur ee"
• a collection of wild animals in captivity for exhibition etc.
• [French *ménagerie* (as MÉNAGE)]

menaquinone *noun*
• "menna KWIN own"
• one of the K vitamins, produced by bacteria found in the large intestine, essential for the blood clotting process.
• [chemical derivative of *me*thyl-*na*phtho*quinone*]

menarche *noun*
• "men ARKY"
• the onset of first menstruation.
• [modern Latin formed as Greek *mēn mēnos* month + *arkhē* beginning]

mendacious *adjective*
• "men DAY sh'ss"
• lying, untruthful; false.
• [Latin *mendax -dacis* lying, perhaps from *mendum* fault]
• **mendaciously** *adverb*
• **mendacity** *noun* "men DASSA tee"

mendelevium *noun*
• "menda LEEVY um"
• an artificially made transuranic radioactive metallic element.
• [D. I. *Mendeleev*, Russian chemist d.1907]

Mendelism *noun*
• "MEND'll izm"
• the theory of heredity based on the recurrence of certain inherited characteristics transmitted by genes.
• [G. *Mendel*, Czech monk and pioneer geneticist d.1884]
• **Mendelian** *adjective* "men DEELY 'n"

mendicant *adjective*
• "MENDA k'nt"
• begging.
• [Latin *mendicare* beg, from *mendicus* beggar, from *mendum* fault]
• **mendicancy** *noun*

menhaden *noun*
• "men HAY d'n"
• any large herring-like fish of the genus *Brevoortia*, of the E coast of N America, yielding valuable oil and used for fertilizer.
• [Algonquian: compare Narragansett *munnawhatteaûg*]

menhir *noun*
• "MEN heer"
• a single, tall, upright usu. prehistoric monumental stone.
• [Breton *men* stone + *hir* long]

menial *adjective*
• "MEENY 'll"
• (esp. of unskilled work) of the nature of drudgery; servile, degrading.
• [Old French *meinee* household]
• **menially** *adverb*

meninges *plural noun*
• "men IN jeez"
• the three membranes that line the skull and vertebral canal and enclose the brain and spinal cord (dura mater, arachnoid, pia mater).
• [modern Latin from Greek *mēnigx -iggos* membrane]
• **meningeal** *adjective* "muh NINJY 'll"

meningitis *noun*
• "men in JITE iss"
• an inflammation of the meninges of the brain or spinal cord due to infection by viruses or bacteria.
• [as MENINGES + Greek *-itis*, forming feminine of adjectives in *-itēs* (with *nosos* 'disease' implied)]

meningococcus *noun*
• "men inga COCKUS" or "men inja COCKUS"
• a bacterium, *Neisseria meningitidis*, involved in some forms of meningitis and cerebrospinal infection.
• [as MENINGES + COCCUS]
• **meningococcal** *adjective*

meniscus *noun*
• "muh NISK us"
• the curved upper surface of a liquid in a tube etc., caused by surface tension or capillarity.
• [modern Latin from Greek *mēniskos* crescent, diminutive of *mēnē* moon]
• **meniscoid** *adjective*

Mennonite *noun*
• "MEN 'n ite"
• a member of a Protestant denomination originating in the 16th c., emphasizing adult baptism and rejecting the taking of oaths, military service, and the holding of public office.
• [*Menno* Simons, its founder, d.1561]
• **Mennonitism** *noun*

meno *adverb*
• "MAY no"
• (in music) less.
• [Italian]

menology *noun*
• "min OLLA jee"
• a calendar, esp. that of the Greek Church, with biographies of the saints.
• [modern Latin *menologium* from ecclesiastical Greek *mēnologion* from *mēn* month + *logos* account]

menopause *noun*
• "MENNA pozz"
• the final cessation of menstruation.
• [modern Latin *menopausis* (*meno*- menstruation, from Greek *mēn mēnos* month, 'pause' from Latin *pausa* from Greek *pausis*, from *pauō* stop)]
• **menopausal** *adjective*

menorah *noun*
• "men ORE uh"
• a candelabrum with usu. seven branches, used at home and in the synagogue on Sabbaths and holidays.
• [Hebrew, = candlestick]

menorrhagia *noun*
• "menna RAY jee uh"
• abnormally heavy bleeding at menstruation.
• [Greek *mēn mēnos* month + *rhēgnumi* burst]

menorrhea *noun*
ALSO SPELLED: **menorrhoea**
• "menna REE uh"
• ordinary flow of blood at menstruation.
• [Greek *mēn mēnos* month + *rhoia* from *rheō* flow]

mensch *noun*
• "MENSH"
• an admirable or honourable person.
• [Yiddish from German 'person']

menses *plural noun*
• "MEN seez"
• blood and mucosal tissue etc. discharged from the uterus at menstruation.
• [Latin, pl. of *mensis* month]

Menshevik *noun*
• "MEN shuh vick"
• a member of a minority faction of the Russian Socialist Party who opposed the radical Bolshevik policies following the overthrow of the czar in 1917.
• [Russian *Men'shevik* a member of the minority (*men'she* less)]

menstruant *noun*
• "MEN stroo 'nt"
• a woman who is menstruating.
• [as MENSTRUATE]

menstruate *verb*
• "MEN strate"
• (of sexually mature, non-pregnant women) discharge blood and mucosal tissue etc. from the uterus through the vagina, normally at intervals of about one lunar month.
• [Late Latin *menstruare menstruat-* from *mensis* month]
• **menstrual** *adjective* "MEN strull" or "MEN stroo 'll"
• **menstruating** *adjective*
• **menstruation** *noun*

menstruum *noun*
• "MEN strum"
• a solvent.
• [Latin, neuter of *menstruus* monthly, from *mensis* month, from the alchemical parallel between transmutation into gold and the supposed action of menses on the ovum]

mensuration *noun*
• "men sur AY sh'n"
• the act or action of measuring.
• [Late Latin *mensuratio* (as MEASURE)]

mentality *noun*
• "men TALA tee"
• mental character or disposition.
• [Old French *mental* or Late Latin *mentalis* from Latin *mens mentis* mind]

mentation *noun*
• "men TAY sh'n"
• mental activity.
• [Latin *mens -ntis* mind]

menthol *noun*
• "MEN tholl" (rhymes with *DOLL*)
• a mint-tasting organic alcohol found in oil of peppermint etc., used as a flavouring and to relieve local pain.
• [German from Latin *mentha* mint]

mentholated *adjective*
• "MENTHA lated"
• treated with or containing menthol.
• [as MENTHOL]

mentor *noun*
• "MEN tor"
• an experienced and trusted adviser or guide.
• [Greek *Mentōr*, adviser of the young Telemachus in Homer's *Odyssey*]

• **mentoring** *noun*
• **mentorship** *noun*

meperidine *noun*
• "muh PERRA deen"
• a narcotic analgesic used for moderate to severe pain, the generic name for Demerol.
• [METHYL + PIPERIDINE]

Mephistopheles *noun*
• "meffa STOFFA leez"
• a fiendish person.
• [name of an evil spirit to whom Faust, in a 16th-c. German legend, sold his soul]
• **Mephistophelean** *adjective* "meffa stoffa LEE 'n"
• **Mephistophelian** *adjective* "meffa stuh FEELY 'n"

mephitis *noun*
• "muh FITE iss"
• a noxious emanation, esp. from the earth.
• [Latin]
• **mephitic** *adjective* "muh FITTIC"

merbromin *noun*
• "mare BRO min"
• a fluorescein derivative containing bromine and mercury, obtained as greenish iridescent scales which dissolve in water to give a red solution used as an antiseptic.
• [from MERCURY + BROMINE]

mercantile *adjective*
• "MURK'n tile"
• of or pertaining to trade, traders, or trading.
• [French from Italian from *mercante* ultimately from Latin *mercari* trade, from *merx mercis* merchandise]

mercantilism *noun*
• "MURK'n till izm" or "mur CANTA lizm"
• the economic theory that trade generates wealth and is stimulated by the accumulation of bullion, which a government should encourage by promoting exports and restricting imports.
• [as MERCANTILE]
• **mercantilist** *noun*
• **mercantilistic** *adjective*

mercaptan *noun*
• "mur CAP t'n"
• any organic compound containing an alcohol-like group but with sulphur in place of oxygen.
• [modern Latin *mercurium captans* capturing mercury]

mercenary *adjective*
• "MURSE a nerry"
• primarily concerned with money or other material reward.
• [Latin *mercenarius* from *merces -edis* reward]
• **mercenariness** *noun*

mercerized *adjective*
ALSO SPELLED: esp. *Brit.* **-ised**
• "MUR sur ized"
• (of cotton fabric or thread) treated under tension with caustic alkali to give greater strength and impart lustre.
• [J. *Mercer*, alleged inventor of the process d.1866]

merchandise *noun*
• "MUR ch'n dice" or "MUR ch'n dize"
• the commodities of commerce, goods to be bought and sold.
• [Old French *marchandise* from *marchand*, ultimately from Latin *mercari* trade, from *merx mercis* merchandise]
• **merchandiser** *noun*
• **merchandising** *noun*

Mercian *noun*
• "MURSHY 'n" or "MURCY 'n"
• a native or inhabitant of the former Anglo-Saxon kingdom of Mercia in central England.

merciful *adjective*
• "MURCY full"
• having, showing, or feeling mercy.
• [Old French *merci* mercy, from Latin *merces -edis* reward, in Late Latin pity, thanks]
• **mercifully** *adverb*
• **mercifulness** *noun*

merciless *adjective*
• "MURCY less"
• pitiless, unrelenting.
• [as MERCIFUL]
• **mercilessly** *adverb*
• **mercilessness** *noun*

mercurial *adjective*
• "mur KYURY 'll"
• (of a person) lively, quick to react and often changing.
• [as MERCURY]
• **mercurially** *adverb*

Mercurian *adjective*
• "mur KYUR ee 'n"
• of or relating to the planet Mercury.

mercury *noun*
• "MUR kyur ee"
• a toxic silvery-white heavy liquid metallic element used in barometers, thermometers, and amalgams.
• [*Mercury*, Roman messenger god]
• **mercuric** *adjective* "mur KYUR ick"
• **mercurous** *adjective* "MUR kyur us"

mere *adjective*
• "MEER"
• having no greater extent, range, value, power, or importance than the designation implies.
• [Anglo-French *meer* from Latin *merus* unmixed]
• **merely** *adverb*

merengue *noun*
• "muh RENG gay"
• a dance of Dominican and Haitian origin, with alternating long and stiff-legged steps.
• [probably American Spanish; compare

perhaps with the sense 'upheaval, disorder', attested in Argentina, Paraguay, and Uruguay]

meretricious *adjective*
- "merra TRISH us"
- (of decorations, literary style, etc.) showily attractive but valueless.
- [Latin *meretricius* from *meretrix -tricis* prostitute, from *merēri* be hired]
- **meretriciously** *adverb*
- **meretriciousness** *noun*

merganser *noun*
- "mur GAN sur"
- any of various diving fish-eating northern ducks of the genus *Mergus*, with a long narrow serrated hooked bill, esp. the common merganser, *M. merganser*, the male of which has a glossy green head and black and white body, and the female of which has a conspicuous crest, and the red-breasted merganser, *M. serrator*.
- [modern Latin from Latin *mergus* diver, from *mergere* dive + *anser* goose]

merge *verb*
- "MURJ"
- combine or be combined.
- [Latin *mergere mers-* dip, plunge, partly via legal Anglo-French *merger*]
- **merged** *adjective*
- **merging** *noun*

merger *noun*
- "MUR jur"
- the combining of two commercial companies etc. into one.
- [as MERGE]

merguez *noun*
- "mur GEZZ" (with "G" as in *GET*)
- a spicy sausage made of beef and lamb, and coloured with red peppers, originally made in parts of North Africa.
- [French *merguez* from Arabic *mirkās, mirqās*]

meridian *noun*
- "mur IDDY 'n"
- a great circle passing through the celestial poles and zenith of a given place on the earth's surface.
- [Old French *meridien* or Latin *meridianus* (adjective) from *meridies* midday, from *medius* middle + *dies* day]

meridional *adjective*
- "mur IDDY 'n 'll"
- of or in the south (esp. of Europe).
- [Old French from Late Latin *meridionalis* from Latin *meridies*: see MERIDIAN]

meringue *noun*
- "mur ANG"
- a mixture of stiffly beaten egg white and sugar.
- [French, of unknown origin]

merino *noun*
- "mur EENO"
- a variety of sheep with long fine wool.
- [Spanish *merino*, probably from Arabic *Marīnī* member of the Banū Marīn, a Berber people and former dynasty of Morocco, from whose territory sheep were imported to Spain]

meristem *noun*
- "MERRA stem"
- a plant tissue consisting of actively dividing cells forming new tissue.
- [Greek *meristos* divisible, from *merizō* divide, from *meros* part, after *xylem*]
- **meristematic** *adjective* "merra stuh MATTIC"

merit *noun*
- "MERRIT"
- the quality of being entitled to reward or gratitude.
- [Latin *meritum* price, value, = past participle of *merēri* earn, deserve]

meritocracy *noun*
- "merra TOCKRA see"
- government or the holding of power by persons selected competitively according to merit.
- [as MERIT + Greek *kratia* from *kratos* strength, power]
- **meritocratic** *adjective*

meritorious *adjective*
- "merra TORY us"
- (of a person or act) having merit; deserving reward, praise, or gratitude.
- [as MERIT]

merle *noun*
- "MURL"
- a dog, esp. a collie, having a light-coloured coat with dark markings, esp. blue-grey fur speckled or streaked with black.
- [from *merled*, *mirled* variants of *marled*, perhaps from Old French *merelé* from *merelle*, counter]

merlin *noun*
- "MURLIN"
- a small European or N American falcon, *Falco columbarius*, that hunts small birds.
- [Anglo-French *merilun* from Old French *esmerillon* augmentative of *esmeril* from Frankish]

merlon *noun*
- "MUR lon"
- the solid part of an embattled parapet between two embrasures.
- [French from Italian *merlone* from *merlo* battlement]

Merlot *noun*
- "mur LO" or "mare LO"
- a variety of black grape used in winemaking.
- [French from *merle* blackbird, with allusion to the colour of the grapes]

mermaid *noun*
• "MUR made"
• an imaginary half-human sea creature, with the head and trunk of a woman and the tail of a fish.
• [Middle English from *mere* sea + 'maid']

merman *noun*
• "MUR man"
• an imaginary half-human sea creature, with the head and trunk of a man and the tail of a fish.
• [as MERMAID + 'man']

Merovingian *adjective*
• "merro VINJY 'n"
• of or relating to the Frankish dynasty reigning in Gaul and Germany *c.*500–750.
• [French *mérovingien* from medieval Latin *Merovingi* from Latin *Meroveus* name of the reputed founder]

merriment *noun*
• "MERRY m'nt"
• exuberant enjoyment; being merry.
• [Old English *myrige* merry, from Germanic]

mesa *noun*
• "MAY suh"
• an isolated flat-topped hill with steep sides, found in landscapes with horizontal strata.
• [Spanish, lit. 'table', from Latin *mensa*]

mésalliance *noun*
• "may zally AWNCE"
• a marriage with a person thought to be of a lower social position.
• [French, from Old French *mes-* badly, ultimately from Latin *minus* less + ALLIANCE]

mescal *noun*
• "MESS cal"
• any of several plants of the genus *Agave* found in Mexico and the southwestern US, used as sources of fermented liquor, food, or fibre, esp. the American aloe, *Agave americana*.
• [Spanish *mezcal* from Nahuatl *mexcalli*]

mescaline *noun*
ALSO SPELLED: **mescalin**
• "MESKA lin"
• a hallucinogenic alkaloid present in mescal buttons.
• [as MESCAL]

mesclun *noun*
• "MESK lun"
• a kind of green salad made from a selection of lettuces, typically with other edible leaves and flowers.
• [Provençal, = 'mixture', from *mesclar* mix, from Old French *mes(c)ler*, from medieval Latin *misculāre* mix thoroughly, from Latin *miscēre*]

mesembryanthemum *noun*
• "mez embry ANTHA mum"
• any of various succulent plants esp. of the genus *Mesembryanthemum* of S Africa, having daisy-like flowers in a wide range of bright colours that fully open in sunlight.
• [modern Latin from Greek *mesembria* noon + *anthemon* flower]

mesencephalon *noun*
• "mez en SEFFA lon"
• the part of the brain developing from the middle of the primitive or embryonic brain.
• [Greek *mesos* middle + *encephalon* brain: see ENCEPHALIC]

mesentery *noun*
• "MESS'n terry"
• a double layer of peritoneum attaching the stomach, small intestine, pancreas, spleen, and other abdominal organs to the posterior wall of the abdomen.
• [medieval Latin *mesenterium* from Greek *mesenterion* (as Greek *mesos* middle, *enteron* intestine)]
• **mesenteric** *adjective* "mess'n TERRIC"
• **mesenteritis** *noun* "mess enter ITE iss"

meshuga *adjective*
ALSO SPELLED: ***meshugga***, ***meshuggah***
• "muh SHUGGA"
• mad, crazy; stupid.
• [Yiddish *meshuge* from Hebrew *měshuggā'*]

mesial *adjective*
• "MEEZY 'Il"
• of, in, or directed towards the middle line of a body.
• [Greek *mesos* middle]
• **mesially** *adverb*

mesic *adjective*
• "MEZZIC" or "MEEZIC"
• (of a habitat) containing a moderate amount of moisture.
• [Greek *mesos* middle]

mesmerism *noun*
• "MEZMUR izm"
• the process or practice of inducing a hypnotic state by the influence of an operator over the will and nervous system of the patient.
• [F. A. *Mesmer*, Austrian physician d.1815]
• **mesmeric** *adjective* "mez MARE ick"
• **mesmerically** *adverb*
• **mesmerist** *noun*

mesmerize *verb*
ALSO SPELLED: esp. *Brit.* **-ise**
• "MEZMUR ize"
• fascinate, hold spellbound.
• [as MESMERISM]

mesne *adjective*
• "MEEN"
• intermediate.
• [var. of Anglo-French *meen* from Old French *meien*, *moien* from Latin *medianus* MEDIAN]
HOMOPHONES: *mean*, *mien*

mesoblast *noun*
• “MEZZO blast”
• = MESODERM.
• [Greek *mesos* middle + *blastos* sprout]

mesoderm *noun*
• “MEZZO durm”
• the middle germ layer of an embryo.
• [Greek *mesos* middle + *derma* skin]
• **mesodermal** *adjective*

mesolithic *adjective*
• “mezzo LITHIC”
• of or concerning the part of the Stone Age between the paleolithic and neolithic periods.
• [Greek *mesos* middle + *lithos* stone]

mesomorph *noun*
• “MEZZO morf”
• a person with a compact and muscular build of body.
• [Greek *mesos* middle + *morphē* form]
• **mesomorphic** *adjective*

meson *noun*
• “MEZZ on” or “MEEZ on”
• any of a class of elementary particles believed to participate in the forces that hold nucleons together in the atomic nucleus.
• [earlier *mesotron*: compare Greek *mesos* middle]
• **mesonic** *adjective* “muh ZONNIC”

mesopause *noun*
• “MEZZO pozz” or “MEEZO pozz”
• the boundary in the atmosphere between the mesosphere and the thermosphere, at which the temperature stops decreasing with increasing height and begins to increase.
• [Greek *mesos* middle + Latin *pausa* from Greek *pausis*, from *pauō* stop]

mesophyll *noun*
• “MEZZO fill”
• the inner tissue of a leaf.
• [Greek *mesos* middle + *phullon* leaf]

mesophyte *noun*
• “MEZZO fite”
• a plant needing only a moderate amount of water.
• [Greek *mesos* middle + *phuton* plant, from *phuō* come into being]

Mesopotamian *adjective*
• “messa puh TAY mee ’n”
• of or relating to ancient Mesopotamia in what is now Iraq.

mesosphere *noun*
• “MEZZO sfeer”
• the region of the atmosphere extending from the top of the stratosphere to an altitude of about 50 miles.
• [Greek *mesos* middle + SPHERE]
• **mesospheric** *adjective*

mesothelioma *noun*
• “messo theely OH muh”
• a tumour of the lungs, or of the lining of the pleural or abdominal cavities, associated esp. with exposure to asbestos.
• [Greek *mesos* middle + (EPI)THELIUM + CARCINOMA]

Mesozoic *adjective*
• “mezzo ZO ick” or “messo ZO ick”
• of or relating to the geological era between the Paleozoic and Cenozoic, comprising the Triassic, Jurassic, and Cretaceous periods. The Mesozoic lasted from about 248 to 65 million years BP, and was a time of abundant vegetation.
• [Greek *mesos* middle + *zōē* life]

mesquite *noun*
• “mess KEET”
• any N American leguminous tree of the genus *Prosopis*, esp. *P. juliflora*.
• [Latin American Spanish *mezquite* from Nahuatl *mizquitl*]

messenger *noun*
• “MESS ’n jur”
• a person who carries a message.
• [Old French *messager*, ultimately from Latin *mittere miss-* send: *-n-* as in *harbinger*, *passenger*, etc.]

Messiah *noun*
• “muh SYE uh”
• the promised deliverer of the Jews, as prophesied in the Hebrew Bible.
• [ultimately from Hebrew *māšîaḥ* anointed]
• **Messiahship** *noun*

messianic *adjective*
• “messy ANNIC”
• of, pertaining to, or characteristic of the Messiah or a messiah.
• [French *messianique* (as MESSIAH) after *rabbinique* rabbinical]
• **messianism** *noun* “muh SYE a nizm”

messuage *noun*
• “MESS widge”
• a dwelling with outbuildings and land assigned to its use.
• [Anglo-French: perhaps an alternative form of *mesnage* dwelling]

mestiza *noun*
• “mess TEEZA”
• a woman who is a mestizo.
• [as MESTIZO]

mestizo *noun*
• “mess TEEZO”
• (in Latin America) a person of mixed European and Aboriginal descent.
• [Spanish, ultimately from Latin *mixtus*, past participle of *miscēre* mix]

metabolism *noun*
• “muh TABBA lizm”
• all the chemical processes that occur within a

living organism, resulting in energy production and growth.
• [Greek *metabolē* change (*meta* with, after, *bolē* from *ballō* throw)]
• **metabolic** *adjective* "metta BOLLIC"
• **metabolically** *adverb*
• **metabolizable** *adjective* (also esp. *Brit.* **-isable**)
• **metabolize** *verb* (also esp. *Brit.* **-ise**)

metabolite *noun*
• "muh TABBA lite"
• a substance formed in or necessary for metabolism.
• [as METABOLISM]

metacarpus *noun*
• "metta CARP us"
• the set of five bones of the hand that connects the wrist to the fingers.
• [Greek *meta* with, after, CARPUS]
• **metacarpal** *adjective*

metacentre *noun*
ALSO SPELLED: esp. *US* **metacenter**
• "METTA senter"
• the point of intersection between a line (vertical in equilibrium) through the centre of gravity of a floating body and a vertical line through the centre of pressure after a slight angular displacement, which must be above the centre of gravity to ensure stability.
• [Greek *meta* with, after + CENTRE]
• **metacentric** *adjective*

metadata *noun*
• "METTA datta" or "METTA day tuh"
• a set of data that describes and gives information about other data.
• [Greek *meta* with, after + DATA]

metafiction *noun*
• "METTA fick sh'n"
• a work of fiction in which the author self-consciously alludes to the artificiality or literariness of a work by parodying or departing from novelistic conventions (esp. naturalism) and traditional narrative techniques.
• [Greek *meta* with, after + 'fiction' from Old French from Latin *fictio -onis* from *fingere* form, contrive]
• **metafictional** *adjective*
• **metafictionist** *noun*

metagenesis *noun*
• "metta JENNA sis"
• the alternation of generations between sexual and asexual reproduction.
• [Greek *meta* with, after + GENESIS]
• **metagenetic** *adjective* "metta juh NETTIC"

metal *noun*
• "MET'll"
• any of a class of substances (including many chemical elements) which are in general lustrous, malleable, fusible, ductile solids and good conductors of heat and electricity, e.g. gold, silver, iron, brass, steel.
• [Old French *metal* or Latin *metallum* from Greek *metallon* mine]
• **metallic** *adjective* "muh TALIC"
• **metallically** *adverb*
• **metallicity** *noun* "met'll ISSA tee"
HOMOPHONES: *mettle, medal, meddle*

metalanguage *noun*
• "METTA lang gwidge"
• a language used for the description or analysis of another language.
• [Greek *meta* with, after + LANGUAGE]

metaldehyde *noun*
• "muh TALDA hide"
• a solid that is a low polymer of acetaldehyde and is used to kill slugs and snails and as a fuel for cooking and heating.
• [Greek *meta* with, after + ALDEHYDE]

metalhead *noun*
• "MET'll hed"
• a fan of heavy metal music.
• [as METAL + 'head']

metalinguistics *noun*
• "metta ling GWISTIX"
• the branch of linguistics that deals with metalanguages.
• [Greek *meta* with, after + LINGUISTIC]
• **metalinguistic** *adjective*

metallize *verb*
ALSO SPELLED: esp. *Brit.* **metallise**; *US* **metalize**
• "MET'll ize"
• render metallic.
• [as METAL]
• **metallization** *noun* (also esp. *Brit.* **metallisation**; *US* **metalization**)

metallography *noun*
• "metta LOGGRA fee"
• the descriptive science of the structure and properties of metals.
• [as METAL + Greek *graphia* writing]
• **metallographic** *adjective*
• **metallographically** *adverb*

metalloid *adjective*
• "METTA loid"
• having the form or appearance of a metal.
• [as METAL]

metallurgy *noun*
• "METTA lur jee"
• the science concerned with the production, purification, and properties of metals and their application.
• [Greek *metallon* metal + *-ourgia* working]
• **metallurgic** *adjective* "metta LUR jick"
• **metallurgical** *adjective*
• **metallurgically** *adverb*
• **metallurgist** *noun*

metalware *noun*
- "MET'll ware"
- utensils or other articles made of metal.
- [as METAL + WARE]

metamere *noun*
- "METTA meer"
- each of several similar body segments containing the same internal structures e.g. in an earthworm.
- [Greek *meta* with, after + *meros* part]
- **metamerism** *noun* "muh TAMMER izm"

metameric *adjective*
- "metta MARE ick"
- having the same proportional composition and molecular weight, but different functional groups and chemical properties.
- [as METAMERE]
- **metamer** *noun* "METTA mur"

metamorphic *adjective*
- "metta MORFIC"
- of or marked by metamorphosis.
- [as METAMORPHOSIS]
- **metamorphism** *noun*

metamorphosis *noun*
- "metta MORFA sis" or "metta more FOE sis"
- a change of form (by natural or supernatural means).
- [Latin from Greek *metamorphōsis* from *metamorphoō* transform (*meta* with, after, *morphoō* from *morphē* form)]
- **metamorphose** *verb* "metta MORE foze"

metaphase *noun*
- "METTA faze"
- the stage of meiotic or mitotic cell division when the chromosomes become attached to the spindle fibres.
- [Greek *meta* with, after + PHASE]

metaphor *noun*
- "METTA for"
- the application of a name or descriptive term or phrase to an object or action to which it is imaginatively but not literally applicable, e.g. *a glaring error.*
- [Greek *metaphora*, from *metapherō* transfer]
- **metaphoric** *adjective*
- **metaphorical** *adjective*
- **metaphorically** *adverb*

metaphrase *noun*
- "METTA fraze"
- literal translation.
- [Greek *metaphrasis* from *metaphrazō* 'word differently']
- **metaphrastic** *adjective* "metta FRASTIC"

metaphysic *noun*
- "metta FIZZIC"
- a system of metaphysics.
- [as METAPHYSICS]

metaphysics *noun*
- "metta FIZZIX"
- the branch of philosophy that deals with the first principles of things, including such concepts as being, knowing, substance, essence, cause, identity, time, and space.
- [medieval Latin *metaphysica*, ultimately from Greek *ta meta ta phusika* the things after the Physics, from the sequence of Aristotle's works]
- **metaphysical** *adjective*
- **metaphysically** *adverb*
- **metaphysician** *noun*

metaplasia *noun*
- "metta PLAY zhuh" or "metta PLAZEY uh"
- an abnormal change in the nature of a tissue.
- [modern Latin from German *Metaplase* from Greek *metaplasis* (*meta* with, after, *plasis* from *plassō* to mould)]
- **metaplastic** *adjective*

metapsychology *noun*
- "metta sye COLLA jee"
- the study of the nature and functions of the mind beyond what can be studied experimentally.
- [Greek *meta* with, after + PSYCHOLOGY]
- **metapsychological** *adjective*

metastable *adjective*
- "metta STAY bull"
- (of a state of equilibrium) stable only under small disturbances.
- [Greek *meta* with, after + Old French *estable* from Latin *stabilis* from *stare* stand]
- **metastability** *noun*

metastasis *noun*
- "muh TASTA sis"
- the transfer of a disease, etc. from one part of the body to another; esp. the development of secondary tumours at a distance from a primary site of cancer.
- [Late Latin from Greek from *methistēmi* change]
- **metastasize** *verb* (also esp. *Brit.* **-ise**)
- **metastatic** *adjective* "metta STATTIC"

metatarsus *noun*
- "metta TAR suss"
- the part of the human foot between the ankle and the toes.
- [Greek *meta* with, after + TARSUS]
- **metatarsal** *adjective*

metathesis *noun*
- "muh TATHA sis"
- the transposition of sounds or letters in a word.
- [Late Latin from Greek *metatithēmi* transpose]
- **metathetic** *adjective* "metta THETTIC"
- **metathetical** *adjective*

metazoan *noun*
- "metta ZO 'n"
- any animal of the subkingdom Metazoa, having multicellular and differentiated tissues and comprising all animals except protozoa and sponges.

• [*Metazoa* from Greek *meta* with, after + *zōia* pl. of *zōion* animal]

mete *verb*
• "MEET"
• apportion or allot (a punishment or reward).
• [Old English *metan* from Germanic]
HOMOPHONES: *meat, meet*

metempsychosis *noun*
• "met'm sye CO sis"
• the supposed transmigration of the soul of a human being or animal at death into a new body of the same or a different species.
• [Greek *metempsukhōsis* (*meta* with, after, *psukhē* soul)]

meteor *noun*
• "MEETY ur" or "MEETY or"
• a small body of matter from outer space that becomes incandescent as a result of friction with the earth's atmosphere and is visible as a streak of light.
• [modern Latin *meteorum* from Greek *meteōron* neuter of *meteōros* lofty (*meta* with, after, *aeirō* raise)]
• **meteoric** *adjective* "meety ORIC"
• **meteorically** *adverb*

meteorite *noun*
• "MEETY ur ite"
• a rock or metal fragment formed from a meteor of sufficient size to reach the earth's surface without burning up completely in the atmosphere.
• [as METEOR]
• **meteoritic** *adjective* "meety ur ITTIC"

meteorograph *noun*
• "MEETY ur a graff" or "meety ORRA graff"
• an apparatus that records several meteorological phenomena at the same time.
• [as METEOROLOGY + Greek *graphia* writing]

meteoroid *noun*
• "MEETY ur oid"
• any small body moving in the solar system that becomes visible as it passes through the earth's atmosphere as a meteor.
• [as METEOR]
• **meteoroidal** *adjective*

meteorology *noun*
• "meety ur OLLA jee"
• the study of the processes and phenomena of the atmosphere, esp. as a means of forecasting the weather.
• [Greek *meteōrologia* (as METEOR)]
• **meteorological** *adjective*
• **meteorologically** *adverb*
• **meteorologist** *noun*

meter *noun*
• "MEETER"
• a thing that measures, esp. an instrument for recording a quantity of gas, electricity, etc. supplied, present, or needed, or a device in a taxi measuring the time and distance travelled and the fare payable.
• [Middle English from METE]
HOMOPHONES: *metre*

methadone *noun*
• "METHA done" ("DONE" rhymes with *BONE*)
• a potent narcotic analgesic drug used to relieve severe pain, and as a substitute for morphine or heroin.
• [6-di*meth*ylamino-4,4-*d*iphenyl-3-heptan*one*]

methamphetamine *noun*
• "meth am FETTA meen"
• an amphetamine derivative with quicker and longer action, used as a stimulant.
• [METHYL + AMPHETAMINE]

methane *noun*
• "METH ane"
• a colourless odourless inflammable gaseous hydrocarbon, the simplest in the alkane series, and the main constituent of natural gas.
• [as METHYL]

methanoic *adjective*
• "metha NO ick"
• designating a colourless irritant volatile acid used in textile finishing etc.
• [as METHANE]

methanol *noun*
• "METHA nawl"
• a colourless volatile inflammable liquid, used as a solvent.
• [METHANE + ALCOHOL]

methaqualone *noun*
• "meth ACKWA lone"
• a hypnotic and sedative drug derived from quinazoline.
• [METHYL + *-a-* + QUININE + French *azote* nitrogen, from Greek *azōos* without life + '-one' forming nouns denoting various compounds, from Greek *-ōnē* feminine patronymic]

methionine *noun*
• "meth EYE a neen"
• an amino acid which contains sulphur and is an important constituent of proteins.
• [METHYL + Greek *theion* sulphur]

methotrexate *noun*
• "metho TREX ate"
• a cytotoxic orange-brown powder which is a folic acid antagonist used to treat certain cancers.
• [from *meth-* + elements of unknown origin]

Methuselah *noun*
• "muh THOOZA luh"
• a very old person or thing.
• [*Methuselah*, grandfather of Noah, said to have lived 969 years (Gen. 5:27)]

methyl *noun*
• "METH'll"
• the monovalent hydrocarbon radical $-CH_3$, present in many organic compounds.

• [see METHYLENE]
• **methylic** *adjective* "muh THILLIC"

methylate *verb*
• "METH'll ate"
• mix or impregnate with methanol.
• [as METHYL]
• **methylation** *noun*

methylene *noun*
• "METH'll een"
• the highly reactive divalent group of atoms CH_2.
• [French *méthylène* from Greek *methu* wine + *hulē* wood + '-ene' forming names of unsaturated hydrocarbons containing a double bond, from Greek *-ēnos*, adjective suffix denoting origin or source]

methylphenidate *noun*
• "meth'll FENNA date"
• a synthetic drug that stimulates the sympathetic and central nervous systems and is used to improve mental activity in attention deficit disorder and other conditions.
• [METHYL + PHENYL + PIPERIDINE + ACETATE]

metical *noun*
• "metta CAWL"
• the basic monetary unit of Mozambique, equal to 100 centavos.
• [Portuguese *matical*, from Arabic *mitḵāl* Arabian unit of weight, from *taḳala* weigh]

meticulous *adjective*
• "muh TICK yoo luss"
• giving great or excessive attention to details.
• [Latin *meticulosus* from *metus* fear]
• **meticulously** *adverb*
• **meticulousness** *noun*

métier *noun*
• "mate YAY" or "MATE yay"
• one's trade, profession, or department of activity.
• [French, ultimately from Latin *ministerium* service]

Metis *noun*
• "may TEE"
• (esp. in Canada) a person of mixed Aboriginal and European descent.
• [French *métis*, Old French *mestis*, from Romanic: related to MESTIZO]

metonym *noun*
• "METTA nim"
• a word used in metonymy.
• [back-formation from METONYMY, after *synonym*]

metonymy *noun*
• "muh TAWNA mee"
• the substitution of the name of an attribute or adjunct for that of the thing meant, e.g. *Crown* for *monarch*, *pigskin* for *football*.
• [Greek *metōnumia* (*meta* with, after, *onoma*, *onuma* name)]
• **metonymic** *adjective* "metta NIM ick"
• **metonymical** *adjective*
• **metonymically** *adverb*

metope *noun*
• "METTA pee" or "MET ope"
• a square space between triglyphs in a Doric frieze.
• [Greek *metopē* (*meta* with, after, *opē* hole for a beam end)]

metre *noun*
ALSO SPELLED: **meter**
• "MEETER"
• a metric unit and the base SI unit of linear measure, equal to about 39.4 inches, and reckoned as the length of the path travelled by light in a vacuum during $^{1}/_{299,792,458}$ of a second.
• [French *mètre* from Greek *metron* measure]
HOMOPHONES: *meter*

metric *adjective*
• "MET rick"
• of or pertaining to the metre or metric system.
• [French *métrique* (as METRE)]

metricate *verb*
• "METRA cate"
• change or adapt to a metric system of measurement.
• [as METRIC]
• **metrication** *noun*

metritis *noun*
• "muh TRITE iss"
• inflammation of the womb.
• [Greek *mētra* womb + *-itis*, forming feminine of adjectives in *-itēs* (with *nosos* 'disease' implied)]

metrology *noun*
• "muh TRAWLA jee"
• the scientific study of measurement.
• [Greek *metron* measure + *logos* word]
• **metrological** *adjective*

metronome *noun*
• "METRA nome"
• an instrument marking time at a selected rate by giving a regular tick.
• [Greek *metron* measure + *nomos* law]
• **metronomic** *adjective* "metra NOMMIC"
• **metronomically** *adverb*

metronymic *adjective*
• "metra NIMMIC"
• (of a name) derived from the name of a mother or female ancestor.
• [Greek *mētēr mētros* mother, after PATRONYMIC]

metropolis *noun*
• "muh TROPPA liss"
• a large, busy city, esp. the main city of a country or region.
• [Greek *mētropolis* parent state, from *mētēr mētros* mother + *polis* city]

- **metropolitan** *adjective* "metra POLLA t'n"
- **metropolitanism** *noun*

metrorrhagia *noun*
- "meetra RAY jee uh"
- abnormal bleeding from the uterus.
- [modern Latin from Greek *mētra* uterus + *-rrhage* as HEMORRHAGE]

mettle *noun*
- "MET'll"
- the quality of a person's disposition or temperament.
- [var. of METAL]
- **mettlesome** *adjective*

HOMOPHONES: *metal, meddle, medal, meddlesome*

meunière *adjective*
- "mun YAIR"
- (esp. of fish) cooked or served in lightly browned butter with lemon juice and parsley.
- [French (*à la*) *meunière* (in the manner of) a miller's wife]

Meursault *noun*
- "mur SO"
- a (usu. white) burgundy wine produced near Beaune, France.
- [*Meursault*, in the Côte d'Or]

mews *noun*
- "MYOOZ"
- a set of stables around an open yard or along a lane.
- [pl. (now used as sing.) of 'mew', a cage for hawks, esp. while moulting (from Old French *mue* from *muer* moult, from Latin *mutare* change), originally referring to the royal stables on the site of hawks' mews at Charing Cross, London]

HOMOPHONES: *muse*

meze *noun*
- "MAY zay"
- (in Turkish, Greek, and Middle Eastern cooking) a selection of hot and cold dishes, typically served as an hors d'oeuvre.
- [Turkish, lit. 'appetizer', from Persian *maza* to relish]

mezereon *noun*
- "muh ZEERY 'n"
- a small European and Asian shrub, *Daphne mezereum*, with fragrant purplish-red flowers and red berries.
- [medieval Latin from Arabic *māzaryūn*]

mezuzah *noun*
- "muh ZOO zuh"
- a parchment inscribed with religious texts and attached in a case to the doorpost of a Jewish house as a sign of faith.
- [Hebrew *mᵉzûzāh* doorpost]

mezzanine *noun*
- "MEZZA neen"
- a low storey between two others (usu. between the ground floor and the second floor).
- [French from Italian *mezzanino*, diminutive of *mezzano* middle, from Latin *medianus* MEDIAN]

mezzo *adverb*
- "METSO"
- (in music) half, moderately.
- [Italian, from Latin *medius* middle]

mezzotint *noun*
- "METSO tint" or "MEZZO tint"
- a method of printing or engraving in which the surface of a plate is roughened by scraping so that it produces tones and halftones.
- [Italian *mezzotinto* from *mezzo* half + *tinto* tint]

mho *noun*
- "MOE"
- the reciprocal of an ohm, a former unit of conductance.
- [OHM reversed]

HOMOPHONES: *mow, mot, mo*

miasma *noun*
- "my AZMA" or "mee AZMA"
- an infectious or noxious vapour, esp. from putrescent organic matter, which pollutes the atmosphere.
- [Greek, = defilement, from *miainō* pollute]
- **miasmal** *adjective*
- **miasmatic** *adjective*
- **miasmic** *adjective*

mica *noun*
- "MIKE uh"
- any of a group of silicate minerals with a layered structure, esp. muscovite.
- [Latin, = crumb]
- **micaceous** *adjective* "my CAY sh'ss"

micelle *noun*
- "miss ELL" or "my SELL"
- an aggregate of molecules in a colloidal solution, as formed e.g. by detergents.
- [modern Latin *micella* diminutive of Latin *mica* crumb]

Michaelmas *noun*
- "MICK'll muss"
- the feast of St. Michael, 29 September.
- [Old English *sancte Micheles mæsse* Saint Michael's mass]

Michigander *noun*
- "misha GANDER"
- a resident of Michigan.

mickey *noun*
- "MICKY"
- *Cdn* a half bottle of liquor, usu. 375 ml.
- [20th c.: origin uncertain]

microanalysis *noun*
- "micro a NALA sis"
- the quantitative analysis of chemical compounds using a sample of a few milligrams.
- [Greek *mikro-* from *mikros* small + ANALYSIS]
- **microanalytic** *adjective* "micro anna LITTIC"

microarray *noun*
• "micro a RAY"
• a set of DNA sequences representing the entire set of genes of an organism, arranged in a grid pattern for use in genetic testing.
• [Greek *mikro-* from *mikros* small + ARRAY]

microbe *noun*
• "MIKE robe"
• a minute living being; a micro-organism (esp. a bacterium causing disease or fermentation).
• [French from Greek *mikros* small + *bios* life]
• **microbial** *adjective* "my CROW bee 'll"
• **microbic** *adjective*

microbiology *noun*
• "micro by OLLA jee"
• the scientific study of micro-organisms, e.g. bacteria, viruses, and fungi.
• [Greek *mikro-* from *mikros* small + BIOLOGY]
• **microbiological** *adjective*
• **microbiologically** *adverb*
• **microbiologist** *noun*

microbrewery *noun*
• "MICRO broory" or "MICRO broo ur ee"
• a brewery which produces beer on a small scale, and which usu. specializes in high-quality brands made with natural ingredients.
• [Greek *mikro-* from *mikros* small + 'brewery']
• **microbrew** *noun*
• **microbrewer** *noun*

microbrowser *noun*
• "MICRO brow zur"
• an Internet browser for use with cellphones and other hand-held devices with small screens.
• [Greek *mikro-* from *mikros* small + BROWSE]

microburst *noun*
• "MICRO burst"
• a particularly violent wind shear, esp. during a thunderstorm.
• [Greek *mikro-* from *mikros* small + 'burst']

microcassette *noun*
• "MICRO kuh set"
• a small audio cassette for use in a tape recorder, answering machine, etc.
• [Greek *mikro-* from *mikros* small + CASSETTE]

microcephaly *noun*
• "micro SEFFA lee"
• an abnormal smallness of the head in relation to the rest of the body.
• [Greek *mikro-* from *mikros* small + *kephalē* head]
• **microcephalic** *adjective*

microchip *noun*
• "MICRO chip"
• a tiny wafer of semiconducting material used to make an integrated circuit.
• [Greek *mikro-* from *mikros* small + 'chip']

microcircuit *noun*
• "MICRO sur kit"
• a minute electric circuit, esp. an integrated circuit.
• [Greek *mikro-* from *mikros* small + CIRCUIT]
• **microcircuitry** *noun*

microclimate *noun*
• "MICRO clime it"
• the climate of a small local area or enclosed space, esp. as differing from the surroundings.
• [Greek *mikro-* from *mikros* small + CLIMATE]
• **microclimatic** *adjective* "micro cly MATTIC"
• **microclimatically** *adverb*

microcode *noun*
• "MICRO code"
• a machine-code instruction that effects a basic operation in a computer system.
• [Greek *mikro-* from *mikros* small + 'code']

microcomputer *noun*
• "MICRO k'm pyoo tur"
• a small computer that contains a microprocessor as its central processing unit.
• [Greek *mikro-* from *mikros* small + COMPUTER]

microcontroller *noun*
• "MICRO k'n trole ur"
• a control device which incorporates a microprocessor.
• [Greek *mikro-* from *mikros* small + 'controller' (from Anglo-French *contreroller* keep a copy of a roll of accounts, from medieval Latin *contrarotulare* (*contra-* against, *rotulus* roll))]

microcosm *noun*
• "MICRO cozm"
• a miniature representation.
• [French *microcosme* or medieval Latin *microcosmus* from Greek *mikros kosmos* little world]
• **microcosmic** *adjective*
• **microcosmically** *adverb*

microdot *noun*
• "MICRO dot"
• a microphotograph of a document etc. reduced to the size of a dot.
• [Greek *mikro-* from *mikros* small + 'dot' from Old English *dott* head of a boil, perhaps influenced by Dutch *dot* knot]

microeconomics *noun*
• "micro eeka NOMMIX" or "micro ecka NOMMIX"
• the branch of economics that deals with small-scale economic factors such as individual commodities, producers, consumers, etc.
• [Greek *mikro-* from *mikros* small + ECONOMICS]
• **microeconomic** *adjective*

microelectronics *noun*
• "micro e leck TRONNIX"
• the design, manufacture, and use of microchips and microcircuits.
• [Greek *mikro-* from *mikros* small + ELECTRONICS]
• **microelectronic** *adjective*

microenvironment *noun*
• "MICRO en vie run m'nt" or "MICRO en vie urn m'nt"
• the immediate small-scale environment of a thing, esp. as a distinct part of a larger environment.
• [Greek *mikro-* from *mikros* small + ENVIRONMENT]
• **microenvironmental** *adjective*

microevolution *noun*
• "micro evva LOO sh'n"
• evolutionary change within a species or small group of organisms, esp. over a short period.
• [Greek *mikro-* from *mikros* small + EVOLUTION]
• **microevolutionary** *adjective*

microfibre *noun*
ALSO SPELLED: esp. *US* **microfiber**
• "MICRO fie bur"
• a lightweight, water-resistant polyester used esp. for outerwear, swimsuits, etc.
• [Greek *mikro-* from *mikros* small + 'fibre' from French from Latin *fibra*]

microfiche *noun*
• "MICRO feesh"
• a flat rectangular piece of film bearing microphotographs of the pages of a printed text or document.
• [Greek *mikro-* from *mikros* small + FICHE]

microfilm *noun*
• "MICRO film"
• a length of film bearing microphotographs of documents etc.
• [Greek *mikro-* from *mikros* small + 'film']

microfine *adjective*
• "MICRO fine"
• (of a powder etc.) ground to a very fine consistency.
• [Greek *mikro-* from *mikros* small + 'fine']

microform *noun*
• "MICRO form"
• microphotographic reproduction on film or paper of a manuscript etc.
• [Greek *mikro-* from *mikros* small + 'form']

microgram *noun*
• "MICRO gram"
• one-millionth of a gram.
• [Greek *mikro-* from *mikros* small + 'gram']

micrograph *noun*
• "MICRO graff"
• a photograph taken by means of a microscope.
• [MICROSCOPE + PHOTOGRAPH]

microgravity *noun*
• "MICRO gravva tee"
• very weak gravity, as in an orbiting spacecraft.
• [Greek *mikro-* from *mikros* small + GRAVITY]

microgroove *noun*
• "MICRO groove"
• a very narrow groove on a long-playing record.
• [Greek *mikro-* from *mikros* small + 'groove' from Middle English, = mine shaft, from obsolete Dutch *groeve* furrow, from Germanic]

microhabitat *noun*
• "MICRO habba tat"
• a habitat which is of small or limited extent and which differs in character from some surrounding more extensive habitat.
• [Greek *mikro-* from *mikros* small + 'habitat' (Latin, = it dwells, as HABITANT)]

microinstruction *noun*
• "micro in STRUCK sh'n"
• a machine-code instruction that effects a basic operation in a computer system.
• [Greek *mikro-* from *mikros* small + 'instruction' from Latin *instruere instruct-* build, teach (*in* in, *struere* pile up)]

microlepidoptera *plural noun*
• "micro leppa DOPTER uh"
• the numerous small moths that are of interest only to specialists.
• [Greek *mikro-* from *mikros* small + modern Latin *Lepidoptera*: see LEPIDOPTEROUS]

microlight *noun*
• "MICRO lite"
• a very small, light, low-speed, one- or two-seater aircraft with an open frame.
• [Greek *mikro-* from *mikros* small + 'light']

microlith *noun*
• "MICRO lith"
• a minute worked flint usu. as part of a composite tool.
• [Greek *mikro-* from *mikros* small + *lithos* stone]
• **microlithic** *adjective*

micromanage *verb*
• "MICRO man idge"
• supervise or control with excessive attention to small details.
• [Greek *mikro-* from *mikros* small + MANAGE]
• **micromanagement** *noun*
• **micromanager** *noun*

micrometer *noun*
• "my CROMMA tur"
• a gauge for accurately measuring small distances, thicknesses, etc.
• [Greek *mikro-* from *mikros* small + *metron* measure]
• **micrometry** *noun*

micrometre *noun*
• "MICRO meeter"
• one-millionth of a metre.
• [Greek *mikro-* from *mikros* small + METRE]

microminiaturization *noun*
ALSO SPELLED: esp. *Brit.* **-isation**
• "micro minna chur ize AY sh'n"
• the manufacture of very small electronic devices by using integrated circuits.
• [Greek *mikro-* from *mikros* small + MINIATURE]

micron *noun*
- "MY cron"
- one-millionth of a metre.
- [Greek *mikron* neuter of *mikros* small]

Micronesian *adjective*
- "micro NEE zh'n"
- of or relating to Micronesia in the W Pacific, or to its people or their languages.

micronutrient *noun*
- "micro NEW tree 'nt"
- a chemical element or substance required in trace amounts for the growth and development of living organisms.
- [Greek *mikro-* from *mikros* small + NUTRIENT]

microphone *noun*
- "MICRA fone"
- an instrument for converting sound waves into electrical energy variations which may be reconverted into sound after transmission by wire or radio or after recording.
- [Greek *mikro-* from *mikros* small + *phōnē* voice, sound]
- **microphonic** *adjective* "micro FONNIC"

microphotograph *noun*
- "micro FOE tuh graff"
- a photograph reduced to a very small size.
- [Greek *mikro-* from *mikros* small + PHOTOGRAPH]
- **microphotographic** *adjective*
- **microphotography** *noun* "micro fuh TOGGRA fee"

microprocessor *noun*
- "micro PROSS esser" or "micro PRO sesser"
- an integrated circuit that contains all the functions of a central processing unit of a computer.
- [Greek *mikro-* from *mikros* small + PROCESSOR]

microprogram *noun*
- "MICRO pro gram"
- a microinstruction program that controls the functions of a central processing unit of a computer.
- [Greek *mikro-* from *mikros* small + 'program' from Greek *programma -atos*, from *prographō* write publicly (*pro* before, *graphō* write)]

microproof *adjective*
- "MICRO proof"
- (of a dish, container, etc.) able to be used in a microwave oven.
- [as MICROWAVE + 'proof' from Old French *proeve* and Late Latin *proba* from Latin *probare* (see PROVE)]

micropyle *noun*
- "MICRO pile"
- a small opening in the surface of an ovule, through which pollen passes.
- [Greek *mikro-* from *mikros* small + *pulē* gate]

microsatellite *noun*
- "MICRO satta lite"
- a set of short repeated DNA sequences at a particular locus on a chromosome, which vary in number in different individuals and so can be used for genetic fingerprinting.
- [Greek *mikro-* from *mikros* small + SATELLITE]

microscooter *noun*
- "MICRO scooter"
- a small two-wheeled foldable aluminum scooter for both children and adults.
- [Greek *mikro-* from *mikros* small + 'scooter' (origin unknown)]

microscope *noun*
- "MICRA scope"
- an instrument magnifying small objects by means of a lens or lenses so as to reveal details invisible to the naked eye.
- [modern Latin *microscopium* (Greek *mikro-* from *mikros* small, *skopos* target, from *skeptomai* look at)]
- **microscopist** *noun* "my CROSCA pist"
- **microscopy** *noun* "my CROSCA pee"

microscopic *adjective*
- "micra SCOPPIC"
- so small as to be visible only with a microscope.
- [as MICROSCOPE]
- **microscopically** *adverb*

microscopical *adjective*
- "micra SCOPPIC'll"
- of or pertaining to a microscope.
- [as MICROSCOPE]

microsome *noun*
- "MICRO soam"
- a small particle of organelle fragments obtained by centrifugation of homogenized cells.
- [Greek *mikro-* from *mikros* small + *sōma* body]
- **microsomal** *adjective*

microsphere *noun*
- "MICRO sfeer"
- a minute sphere, esp. one obtained by cooling a solution of a proteinoid.
- [Greek *mikro-* from *mikros* small + SPHERE]

microspore *noun*
- "MICRO spore"
- the smaller of the two kinds of spore produced by some ferns.
- [Greek *mikro-* from *mikros* small + SPORE]

microstructure *noun*
- "MICRO struck chur"
- (in a metal or other material) the arrangement of crystals etc. which can be made visible and examined with a microscope.
- [Greek *mikro-* from *mikros* small + 'structure' from Old French *structure* or Latin *structura* from *struere struct-* build]
- **microstructural** *adjective*

microsurgery *noun*
- "MICRO sur jur ee"

• intricate surgery performed using microscopes, enabling the tissue to be operated on with miniaturized precision instruments.
• [Greek *mikro-* from *mikros* small + SURGERY]
• **microsurgeon** *noun*
• **microsurgical** *adjective*

microswitch *noun*
• "MICRO switch"
• a switch that can be operated rapidly by a small movement.
• [Greek *mikro-* from *mikros* small + 'switch', probably from Low German]

microtome *noun*
• "MICRO tome"
• an instrument for cutting extremely thin sections of material for examination under a microscope.
• [Greek *mikro-* from *mikros* small + *tomia* cutting]

microtone *noun*
• "MICRO tone"
• an interval smaller than a semitone.
• [Greek *mikro-* from *mikros* small + 'tone' from Old French *ton* or Latin *tonus* from Greek *tonos* tension, tone, from *teinō* stretch]
• **microtonal** *adjective*
• **microtonality** *noun*
• **microtonally** *adverb*

microtubule *noun*
• "MICRO toob yool"
• a minute protein filament occurring in cytoplasm and involved in forming the spindles during cell division etc.
• [Greek *mikro-* from *mikros* small + TUBULE]

microvillous *adjective*
• "micro VILL us"
• of or pertaining to microvilli.
• [as MICROVILLUS]
HOMOPHONES: *microvillus*

microvillus *noun*
• "micro VILL us"
• any of a number of minute projections from the surface of some cells.
• [Greek *mikro-* from *mikros* small + VILLUS]
• **microvillar** *adjective*
HOMOPHONES: *microvillous*

microwave *noun*
• "MICRO wave"
• an electromagnetic wave with a wavelength in the range 0.001–0.3 m.
• [Greek *mikro-* from *mikros* small + 'wave' from Old English]
• **microwaveable** *adjective* (also **microwavable**)

microwinery *noun*
• "MICRO wine ur ee"
• a winery which produces wine on a small scale, and which usu. specializes in high-quality or natural wines.
• [Greek *mikro-* from *mikros* small + 'winery']

micturition *noun*
• "mick chur ISH'n"
• urination.
• [Latin *micturire micturit-*, desiderative from *mingere mict-* urinate]
• **micturate** *verb*

middling *adjective*
• "MID ling"
• moderately good.
• [Middle English, of Scots origin]

middy *noun*
• "MIDDY"
• a midshipman.
• [abbreviation]
HOMOPHONES: *midi*

Midewiwin *noun*
• "mih DAY wuh win"
• a shamanic society among the Ojibwa and Algonquin, devoted to the understanding of herbal remedies and spiritual knowledge.
• [Ojibwa]

midi *noun*
• "MIDDY"
• a garment of medium length, usu. reaching to mid-calf.
• ['mid' after 'mini']
HOMOPHONES: *middy*

Midrash *noun*
• "MID rash"
• an ancient commentary on part of the Hebrew scriptures.
• [Biblical Hebrew *mid̲rāš* commentary]
• **Midrashic** *adjective*

midwifery *noun*
• "mid WIFFER ee"
• the work or profession of a person (usu. a woman) trained to assist women in pregnancy and childbirth.
• [Middle English, prob. from obsolete prep. *mid* with + *wife* woman, in the sense of 'a person who is with the mother']

mien *noun*
• "MEEN"
• a person's look or bearing, as showing character or mood.
• [prob. from obsolete *demean* behave, from Old French *demener* from Romanic (Latin *de-* off, from, *minare* drive animals, from *minari* threaten), assimilated to French *mine* expression]
HOMOPHONES: *mean*, *mesne*

might *noun*
• "MITE"
• great bodily or mental strength.
• [Old English *miht*, *mieht* from Germanic]
• **mightily** *adverb*
• **mightiness** *noun*
• **mighty** *adjective*
HOMOPHONES: *mite*

mignonette *noun*
• "minya NET"
• any of various plants of the genus *Reseda*, esp. *R. odorata*, with fragrant grey-green flowers.
• [French *mignonnette*, diminutive of *mignon* small]

migraine *noun*
• "MY grain"
• a recurrent throbbing headache that usually affects one side of the head, often accompanied by nausea and disturbance of vision.
• [French from Late Latin *hemicrania* from Greek *hēmikrania* (*hēmi-* half + CRANIUM): originally of a headache confined to one side of the head]

migrate *verb*
• "MY grate"
• (of people) move from one place of residence to another, esp. in a different country.
• [Latin *migrare migrat-*]
• **migrant** *adjective*
• **migration** *noun*
• **migrational** *adjective*
• **migrator** *noun*
• **migratory** *adjective* "MY gruh tory"

mihrab *noun*
• "MEE rab"
• a niche or slab in a mosque, used to show the direction of Mecca.
• [Arabic *miḥrāb* praying place]

mikado *noun*
• "muh CODDO"
• the emperor of Japan.
• [Japanese from *mi* august + *kado* door]

mikveh *noun*
ALSO SPELLED: **mikvah, mikva**
• "MICK vuh"
• a bath in which certain Jewish ritual purifications are performed.
• [Yiddish *mikve* from Hebrew *miqweh*, lit. 'collection, mass, esp. of water']

mil *noun*
• "MILL"
• one thousandth of an inch (0.0254 mm), as a unit of measure for the diameter of wire, thickness of a film, etc.
• [Latin *millesimum* thousandth, from *mille* thousand]
HOMOPHONES: *mill*

Milanese *adjective*
• "milla NEEZ"
• of or relating to Milan, Italy.

mileage *noun*
• "MY lidge"
• distance travelled in miles.
• [Old English *mil*, ultimately from Latin *mil(l)ia*, pl. of *mille* thousand]

milfoil *noun*
• "MILL foil"
• the common yarrow, *Achillea millefolium*, with small white flowers and finely divided leaves.
• [Middle English via Old French from Latin *millefolium* from *mille* thousand + *folium* leaf, suggested by Greek *muriophullon*]

miliary *adjective*
• "MILLY airy" or "MILL yuh ree"
• like a millet seed in size or form.
• [Latin *miliarius* from *milium* millet]

milieu *noun*
• "mil YOO" (with "OO" as in *HOOD*)
• one's environment or social surroundings.
• [French from *mi* mid + *lieu* place]

militant *adjective*
• "MILLA t'nt"
• combative; aggressively active esp. in support of a (usu. political) cause.
• [Old French from Latin (as MILITATE)]
• **militancy** *noun*
• **militantism** *noun*
• **militantly** *adverb*

militaria *plural noun*
• "milla TERRY uh"
• military articles of historical interest.
• [as MILITARY]

militarism *noun*
• "MILLA tuh rizm"
• the policy of maintaining a strong military capability.
• [as MILITARY]
• **militarist** *noun*
• **militaristic** *adjective*
• **militaristically** *adverb*

militarize *verb*
ALSO SPELLED: esp. *Brit.* **-ise**
• "MILLA tuh rize"
• equip with military resources.
• [as MILITARY]
• **militarization** *noun* (also esp. *Brit.* **-isation**)

military *adjective*
• "MILLA terry"
• of, relating to, or characteristic of soldiers or armed forces.
• [French *militaire* or Latin *militaris* from *miles militis* soldier]
• **militarily** *adverb*

militate *verb*
• "MILLA tate"
• (of facts or evidence) have force or effect.
• [Latin *militare militat-* from *miles militis* soldier]

militia *noun*
• "muh LISHA"
• a military force raised from the civilian population and supplementing a regular army in an emergency.
• [Latin, = military service, from *miles militis* soldier]
• **militiaman** *noun*

milkwort *noun*
• "MILK wurt" or "MILK wort"
• any plant of the genus *Polygala*, formerly supposed to increase women's milk.
• ['milk' + WORT]

millenarian *adjective*
• "milla NERRY 'n"
• of or related to the period of 1,000 years during which (according to one interpretation of Rev. 20:1–5) Christ will reign in person on earth.
• [as MILLENARY]
• **millenarianism** *noun*

millenary *noun*
• "MILLA nerry" or "mill ENNER ee"
• a period of 1,000 years.
• [Late Latin *millenarius* consisting of a thousand, from *milleni* distributive of *mille* thousand]
HOMOPHONES: *millinery*

millennialism *noun*
• "mill ENNY 'll izm"
• the belief in the imminence of the period of 1,000 years during which (according to one interpretation of Rev. 20:1–5) Christ will reign in person on earth.
• [as MILLENNIUM]
• **millennialist** *noun*

millennium *noun*
• "mill ENNY um"
• a period of 1,000 years.
• [modern Latin from Latin *mille* thousand, on the pattern of BIENNIUM]
• **millennial** *adjective*

millet *noun*
• "MILLIT"
• any of various cereal plants, esp. *Panicum miliaceum*, bearing a large crop of small nutritious seeds.
• [French, diminutive of *mil* from Latin *milium*]

milliammeter *noun*
• "milly AMMA tur"
• an instrument for measuring electrical current in milliamperes.
• [MILLIAMPERE + Greek *metron* measure]

milliampere *noun*
• "milly AM pair"
• one thousandth of an ampere, a measure for small electrical currents.
• [Latin *mille* thousand + AMPERE]

millibar *noun*
• "MILLA bar"
• one thousandth of a bar, the cgs unit of atmospheric pressure equivalent to 100 pascals.
• [Latin *mille* thousand + Greek *baros* weight]

milligram *noun*
• "MILLA gram"
• one thousandth of a gram.
• [Latin *mille* thousand + French *gramme* from Greek *gramma* small weight]

millilitre *noun*
ALSO SPELLED: esp. *US* **milliliter**
• "MILLA leeter"
• one thousandth of a litre (0.002 pint).
• [Latin *mille* thousand + LITRE]

millimetre *noun*
ALSO SPELLED: esp. *US* **millimeter**
• "MILLA meeter"
• one thousandth of a metre (0.039 in.).
• [Latin *mille* thousand + Greek *metron* measure]

milliner *noun*
• "MILLA nur"
• a person who makes or sells women's hats.
• [originally = vendor of goods from *Milan*, Italy]
• **millinery** *noun* "MILLA nerry"
HOMOPHONES: *millenary*

millionaire *noun*
• "MILL y'n air" or "mill y'n AIR"
• a person whose assets are worth at least one million dollars, pounds, etc.
• [French, from Old French *million*, prob. from Italian *millione* from *mille* thousand + *-one* augmentative suffix]
• **millionairess** *noun*

millipede *noun*
• "MILLA peed"
• any arthropod of the class Diplopoda, having a long segmented body with two pairs of legs on each segment.
• [Latin *millepeda* wood louse, from *mille* thousand + *pes pedis* foot]

millisecond *noun*
• "MILLA seck'nd"
• one thousandth of a second.
• [Latin *mille* thousand + 'second' from Old French from Latin *secundus* from *sequi* follow]

millivolt *noun*
• "MILLA volt"
• one thousandth of a volt.
• [Latin *mille* thousand + 'volt' from the name of A. *Volta*, Italian physicist d.1824]

millwright *noun*
• "MILL rite"
• a person who maintains or repairs mill machinery.
• ['mill' + WRIGHT]

milo *noun*
• "MY lo"
• a drought-resistant variety of sorghum grown esp. in the central US.
• [Sesotho *maili*]

milpa *noun*
• "MILPA"
• (in Central America and Mexico) a small cultivated field, usu. of corn.
• [Latin American Spanish]

milquetoast *noun*
- "MILK toast"
- a timid, submissive person.
- [Caspar *Milquetoast*, a cartoon character created by H. T. Webster, US cartoonist, in 1924]

Miltonian *noun*
- "mill TONY 'n"
- a resident of Milton, Ont.

mimeograph *noun*
- "MIMMY a graff"
- a duplicating machine which produces copies from a stencil.
- [Greek *mimeomai* imitate + *graphia* writing]

mimesis *noun*
- "muh MEE sis" or "my MEE sis"
- a close external resemblance of an animal (or part of one) to another animal or to a plant or inanimate object; a similar resemblance in a plant.
- [Greek *mimēsis* from *mimeisthai* to imitate]
- **mimetic** *adjective* "muh METTIC"
- **mimetically** *adverb*

mimic *verb*
- "MIMMIC"
- imitate (a person, gesture, manner of speech, etc.) esp. to entertain or ridicule.
- [Latin *mimicus* from Greek *mimikos* from *mimos* mime]
- **mimicker** *noun*
- **mimicry** *noun* "MIMMIC ree"

mimosa *noun*
- "mim OH zuh" or "mim OH suh"
- any leguminous shrub of the genus *Mimosa*, esp. the sensitive plant, *M. pudica*, having globular flowers and sensitive leaves which droop when touched.
- [modern Latin, apparently from Latin *mimus* from Greek *mimos* mime (from being as sensitive as animals) + *-osa* feminine suffix]

mimulus *noun*
- "MIM yoo luss"
- any flowering plant of the genus *Mimulus*, including the N American plants musk and the monkey flower.
- [modern Latin, apparently diminutive of Latin *mimus* from Greek *mimos* mime, perhaps with reference to its mask-like flowers]

minaret *noun*
- "minna RET" or "MINNA ret"
- a slender turret connected with a mosque and having a balcony from which the muezzin calls at hours of prayer.
- [French *minaret* or Spanish *minarete* from Turkish *minare* from Arabic *manār(a)* lighthouse, minaret, from *nār* fire, light]
- **minareted** *adjective*

minatory *adjective*
- "MINNA tory"
- threatening, menacing.
- [Late Latin *minatorius* from *minari minat-* threaten]

mincha *noun*
- "MINK huh"
- the Jewish daily afternoon worship.
- [Hebrew *minḥāh*, lit. 'gift, offering']

mindful *adjective*
- "MIND full"
- taking heed or care; being conscious.
- [from 'mind', from Old English]
- **mindfully** *adverb*
- **mindfulness** *noun*

mineral *noun*
- "MINNER 'll"
- a substance that occurs naturally in the earth and is not formed from animal or vegetable matter.
- [medieval Latin *minerale*, neuter of *mineralis* from *minera* ore]
- **mineralization** *noun* (also esp. *Brit.* **-isation**)
- **mineralize** *verb* (also esp. *Brit.* **-ise**)
- **mineralogical** *adjective*
- **mineralogically** *adverb*
- **mineralogist** *noun* "minna RAWLA jist" or "minna RALA jist"
- **mineralogy** *noun*

minestrone *noun*
- "minna STRONE ee"
- a soup containing vegetables and pasta, beans, or rice.
- [Italian, from *minestra* soup, from *minestrare* serve at table, from Latin *ministrare* minister]

mingy *adjective*
- "MINJY"
- mean, stingy.
- [perhaps from 'mean' and STINGY]
- **mingily** *adverb*

miniature *adjective*
- "MINNA chur" or "MINNY a chur"
- much smaller than normal.
- [Italian *miniatura* from medieval Latin *miniatura* from Latin *miniare* from *minium* red lead, vermilion]
- **miniaturization** *noun* (also esp. *Brit.* **-isation**)
- **miniaturize** *verb* (also esp. *Brit.* **-ise**)

miniaturist *noun*
- "MINNA chur ist" or "MINNY a chur ist"
- a painter of very small portraits.
- [as MINIATURE]

minim *noun*
- "MINNIM"
- a half note.
- [Latin *minimus* smallest]

minimalist *adjective*
- "MINNIM a list"
- (esp. of an aesthetic style) constituting or characterized by the minimum required; not elaborate.

- [as MINIMUM]
- **minimalism** *noun*
- **minimalistic** *adjective*

minimax *noun*
- "MINNY max"
- the lowest of a set of maximum values.
- [MINIMUM + 'maximum' neuter of Latin *maximus*, superlative of *magnus* great]

minimum *noun*
- "MINNA mum"
- the least possible or attainable amount.
- [Latin, neuter of *minimus* least]
- **minimal** *adjective*
- **minimally** *adverb*
- **minimization** *noun* (also esp. *Brit.* **-isation**)
- **minimize** *verb* (also esp. *Brit.* **-ise**)
- **minimizer** *noun* (also esp. *Brit.* **-iser**)

minion *noun*
- "MIN y'n"
- a follower or underling of a powerful person, esp. a servile or unimportant one.
- [French *mignon*, Old French *mignot*, of Gaulish origin]

HOMOPHONES: *minyan*

minister *noun*
- "MIN iss tur"
- (in Canada, the UK, and other Commonwealth countries) a head of a government department.
- [Old French *ministre* from Latin *minister* servant, from *minus* less]
- **ministerial** *adjective* "min iss TEERY 'll"
- **ministerially** *adverb*

ministrant *noun*
- "MIN iss tr'nt"
- a person who ministers to another's needs.
- [as MINISTER]

ministration *noun*
- "min iss TRAY sh'n"
- aid or service.
- [Old French *ministration* or Latin *ministratio* (as MINISTER)]

ministry *noun*
- "MIN iss tree"
- a government department headed by a minister.
- [Latin *ministerium* (as MINISTER)]

miniver *noun*
- "MINNA vur"
- plain white fur used in ceremonial robes of state.
- [Anglo-French *menuver*, Old French *menu vair* from *menu* small, *vair* fur obtained from a variety of Russian red squirrel with grey back and white belly, used widely in the 13th and 14th c. for linings and trimmings]

minke *noun*
- "MINKA"
- a small baleen whale, *Balaenoptera acutorostrata*, with a pointed snout.
- [prob. from *Meincke*, the name of a Norwegian whaler]

minneola *noun*
- "minny OH luh"
- a thin-skinned, deep-reddish variety of tangelo.
- [*Minneola*, a town in Florida]

minnesinger *noun*
- "MINNA singer"
- a German lyric poet and singer of the 12th–14th c.
- [German, = love singer]

Minnesotan *noun*
- "minna SO t'n"
- a resident of Minnesota.

Minoan *adjective*
- "min OH 'n"
- of or relating to the Bronze Age civilization centred on Crete (*c.*3000–1100 BC).
- [*Minos*, legendary king of Crete]

minor *adjective*
- "MY nur"
- lesser or comparatively small in size or importance.
- [Latin, = smaller, less, related to *minuere* lessen]

HOMOPHONES: *miner*

Minorcan *noun*
- "min ORK'n"
- a native or inhabitant of the Spanish Mediterranean island of Minorca.

Minorite *noun*
- "MINER ite"
- a Franciscan friar or Friar Minor, so called because the Franciscans regarded themselves as of humbler rank than members of other orders.
- [as MINOR]

minority *noun*
- "my NORRA tee" or "min ORRA tee"
- a smaller number or part, esp. within a political party or structure.
- [French *minorité* or medieval Latin *minoritas* from Latin *minor*: see MINOR]

minoxidil *noun*
- "min OXA dill"
- a pyrimidine derivative used to treat hypertension, which can also promote hair growth when applied topically.
- [AMINO + OXYGEN + *-il*, of unknown origin]

minster *noun*
- "MIN stur"
- a large or important church, esp. a cathedral.
- [Old English *mynster* from Church Latin *monasterium* from Greek *monastērion* MONASTERY]

minstrel *noun*
- "MIN strull"
- a medieval singer or musician, esp. singing or reciting poetry.

• [Old French *menestral* entertainer, servant, from Provençal *menest(ai)ral* officer, employee, musician, from Late Latin *ministerialis* official, officer]

minstrelsy *noun*
• "MIN strul see"
• the minstrel's art.
• [as MINSTREL]

minuend *noun*
• "MIN yoo end"
• a quantity or number from which another is to be subtracted.
• [Latin *minuendus* gerundive of *minuere* diminish]

minuet *noun*
• "min yoo ET"
• a slow stately dance for two in triple time, popular esp. in the 17th and 18th c.
• [French *menuet*, originally adjective = fine, delicate, diminutive of *menu* small]

minuscule *adjective*
• "MINNA skyool"
• extremely small or unimportant.
• [French from Latin *minuscula* (*littera* letter) diminutive of *minor*: see MINOR]
• **minuscular** *adjective* "min USS kyuh lur"

minutia *noun*
• "min OO shuh" or "min OOSHY uh" or "min YOO shuh" or "min YOOSHY uh"
• a precise, trivial, or minor detail.
• [Latin, = smallness, in pl. trifles, from *minutus* small]

minyan *noun*
• "MIN y'n" or "min YAWN"
• the quorum of ten males over thirteen years of age required for traditional Jewish public worship.
• [Hebrew *minyān* count, reckoning]
HOMOPHONES: *minion*

Miocene *adjective*
• "MY a seen"
• of or relating to the fourth epoch of the Tertiary period, between the Oligocene and the Pliocene, lasting from about 24.6 to 5.1 million years ago, a period of great earth movements during which the Alps and Himalayas were being formed.
• [Greek *meiōn* less + *kainos* new]

miosis *noun*
ALSO SPELLED: **myosis**
• "my OH sis"
• excessive constriction of the pupil of the eye.
• [Greek *muō* shut the eyes]
• **miotic** *adjective* (also **myotic**) "my OTTIC"
HOMOPHONES: *meiosis, meiotic*

mirabelle *noun*
• "MIRRA bell"
• a European variety of plum tree, bearing small round yellow fruit.
• [French, as MYROBALAN]

miracle *noun*
• "MIRRA k'll"
• an extraordinary event attributed to some supernatural power.
• [Old French from Latin *miraculum* object of wonder, from *mirari* wonder, from *mirus* wonderful]
• **miraculous** *adjective* "muh RACK yoo lus"
• **miraculously** *adverb*
• **miraculousness** *noun*

mirador *noun*
• "mirra DOR"
• a turret or tower etc. attached to a building, and commanding an excellent view.
• [Spanish from *mirar* to look]

mirage *noun*
• "mur OZH"
• an optical illusion caused by atmospheric conditions, esp. the appearance of a sheet of water in a desert or on a hot road from the reflection of light.
• [French from *se mirer* be reflected, from Latin *mirare* look at]

Miramichier *noun*
• "meera muh SHEE ur"
• a resident of Miramichi, NB.

Miranda *adjective*
• "muh RANDA"
• designating or pertaining to the duty of the police in the US to inform a person taken into custody of his or her right to legal counsel and the right to remain silent under questioning.
• [*Miranda* versus Arizona, the case that led to the US Supreme Court ruling on the matter]

Mirandize *verb*
ALSO SPELLED: esp. *Brit.* **-ise**
• "muh RAN dize"
• inform a person of their Miranda rights.
• [as MIRANDA]

mirepoix *noun*
• "meera PWAH"
• sautéed chopped vegetables, usu. including carrots and onions, used in sauces etc.
• [French, from Duc de *Mirepoix*, French general d.1757]

mirex *noun*
• "MY rex"
• an organochlorine insecticide used esp. against ants.
• [origin unknown]

mirid *noun*
• "MIR id" or "MY rid"
• a heteropteran bug of the family Miridae (formerly Capsidae), which includes numerous plant pests.
• [modern Latin *Miris* genus name, from *mirus* wonderful]

mirin *noun*
• "MEE rin"

• a sweet, golden coloured Japanese rice wine, used esp. in cooking.
• [Japanese, from *mi-* taste + *-rin* to remove astringency, both from Middle Chinese]

mirliton *noun*
• "MURLA t'n"
• a vine, *Sechium edule*, native to tropical America and cultivated elsewhere for its fruit.
• [French, = 'reed pipe', of unknown origin]

mirth *noun*
• "MURTH"
• merriment, laughter.
• [Old English *myrgth* (related to 'merry')]
• **mirthful** *adjective*
• **mirthfulness** *noun*
• **mirthless** *adjective*
• **mirthlessly** *adverb*
• **mirthlessness** *noun*

misadventure *noun*
• "miss ad VEN chur"
• a misfortune.
• [Old French *mesaventure* from *mesavenir* turn out badly (*mes-* badly, ultimately from Latin *minus* neuter of *minor* less + *advenire* from *ad* to + *venire* come)]

misalign *verb*
• "missa LINE"
• give the wrong alignment to.
• [prefix *mis-* badly, from Old English *mis-* badly + ALIGN]
• **misaligned** *adjective*
• **misalignment** *noun*

misalliance *noun*
• "missa LIE ince"
• an unsuitable alliance, esp. an unsuitable marriage.
• [prefix *mis-* badly, from Old English *mis-* badly + ALLIANCE]
• **misally** *verb* "missa LIE"

misallocation *noun*
• "miss ala CAY sh'n"
• inappropriate or wrongful allocation, esp. of money.
• [prefix *mis-* badly, from Old English *mis-* + ALLOCATE]

misandry *noun*
• "miss ANDRY"
• the hatred of men.
• [Greek *misos* hatred + *andr- aner* man, on the pattern of MISOGYNY]

misanthrope *noun*
• "MISS 'n thrope" or "MIZZ 'n thrope"
• a person who hates humans.
• [French from Greek *misanthrōpos* from *misos* hatred + *anthrōpos* man]
• **misanthropic** *adjective* "miss 'n THROPPIC" or "mizz 'n THROPPIC"
• **misanthropy** *noun* "miss ANTHRA pee" or "mizz ANTHRA pee"

misapply *verb*
• "missa PLY"
• apply (a theory, a term, funds, etc.) wrongly.
• [prefix *mis-* badly, from Old English *mis-* badly + APPLY]
• **misapplication** *noun*

misapprehend *verb*
• "miss ap ree HEND"
• misunderstand (words, a person).
• [prefix *mis-* badly, from Old English *mis-* badly + APPREHEND]
• **misapprehension** *noun*

misappropriate *verb*
• "missa PRO pree ate"
• apply (usu. another's money) to one's own use, or to a wrong use.
• [prefix *mis-* badly, from Old English *mis-* badly + APPROPRIATE[2]]
• **misappropriation** *noun*

misbegotten *adjective*
• "miss be GOT'n"
• badly conceived, designed, or planned.
• [prefix *mis-* badly, from Old English *mis-* badly + 'begotten' past participle of 'beget' be the father of, from Old English *begietan*]

misbehave *verb*
• "miss bee HAVE" ("HAVE" rhymes with *SAVE*)
• (of a person, machine, etc.) behave badly.
• [prefix *mis-* badly, from Old English *mis-* badly + 'behave' (as BEHAVIOUR)]
• **misbehaviour** *noun*

miscalculate *verb*
• "miss CAL kyoo late"
• calculate (amounts, results, etc.) wrongly.
• [prefix *mis-* badly, from Old English *mis-* badly + CALCULATE]
• **miscalculation** *noun*

miscall *verb*
• "miss CALL"
• = MISNAME.
• [prefix *mis-* badly, from Old English *mis-* badly + 'call']

miscarriage *noun*
• "MISS care idge"
• the expulsion of a fetus from the womb before it can survive independently, esp. before the 28th week of pregnancy; a spontaneous abortion.
• [prefix *mis-* badly, from Old English *mis-* badly + CARRIAGE]
• **miscarry** *verb*

miscast *verb*
• "miss CAST"
• assign an unsuitable role to (a performer).
• [prefix *mis-* badly, from Old English *mis-* badly + 'cast' from Old Norse *kasta* throw]

miscegenation *noun*
- "muh sedge 'n AY sh'n" or "missa j'n AY sh'n"
- the interbreeding of races, esp. of whites and non-whites.
- [Latin *miscēre* mix + *genus* race]

miscellanea *plural noun*
- "missa LAY nee uh"
- a collection of miscellaneous items.
- [Latin neuter pl. (as MISCELLANEOUS)]

miscellaneous *adjective*
- "missa LAY nee us"
- of mixed composition or character.
- [Latin *miscellaneus* from *miscellus* mixed, from *miscēre* mix]

miscellany *noun*
- "MISSA lay nee"
- a mixture, a medley.
- [French *miscellanées* (feminine pl.) or Latin MISCELLANEA]

mischance *noun*
- "miss CHANCE"
- bad luck.
- [Old French *meschance* from *mes-* (ultimately from Latin *minus* neuter of *minor* less) + *chëance chëoir* fall, ultimately from Latin *cadere*]

mischief *noun*
- "MISS chiff"
- conduct which is troublesome, but not malicious, esp. in children.
- [Old French *meschief* from *meschever* from *mes-* (ultimately from Latin *minus* neuter of *minor* less), *chever* come to an end (from *chef* head: see CHIEF)]

mischievous *adjective*
- "MISS chiv us"
- (of a person) disposed to mischief.
- [Anglo-French *meschevous* from Old French *meschever*: see MISCHIEF]
- **mischievously** *adverb*
- **mischievousness** *noun*

miscible *adjective*
- "MISSA bull"
- capable of being mixed.
- [medieval Latin *miscibilis* from Latin *miscēre* mix]
- **miscibility** *noun*

miscommunication *noun*
- "miss kuh myoona CAY sh'n"
- failure to communicate adequately.
- [prefix *mis-* badly, from Old English *mis-* badly + COMMUNICATE]

misconceive *verb*
- "miss k'n SEEVE"
- have a wrong idea or conception.
- [prefix *mis-* badly, from Old English *mis-* badly + CONCEIVE]
- **misconceived** *adjective*
- **misconceiver** *noun*
- **misconception** *noun*

misconduct *noun*
- "miss CON duct"
- improper or unprofessional behaviour.
- [prefix *mis-* badly, from Old English *mis-* badly + CONDUCT]

misconstrue *verb*
- "miss k'n STROO"
- interpret (a word, action, etc.) wrongly.
- [prefix *mis-* badly, from Old English *mis-* badly + CONSTRUE]
- **misconstruction** *noun*

miscount *verb*
- "miss COUNT"
- count wrongly.
- [Anglo-Norman *mesconter* from *mes-* (ultimately from Latin *minus* neuter of *minor* less) + *conter* (as COMPUTE)]

miscreant *noun*
- "MISS cree 'nt"
- an immoral or criminal person.
- [Old French *mescreant* (*mes-* (ultimately from Latin *minus* neuter of *minor* less), *creant* participle of *croire* from Latin *credere* believe)]

miscue *noun*
- "MISS kyoo"
- an error or blunder.
- [prefix *mis-* badly, from Old English *mis-* badly + 'cue' (of unknown origin)]

misdeal *verb*
- "miss DEEL"
- make a mistake in dealing (cards).
- [prefix *mis-* badly, from Old English *mis-* badly + 'deal' from Old English *dǣl*, *dǣlan*]

misdeed *noun*
- "miss DEED"
- an evil deed, a wrongdoing; a crime.
- [Old English *misdǣd*]

misdemeanour *noun*
ALSO SPELLED: **misdemeanor**
- "miss duh MEENER"
- a minor wrongdoing.
- [prefix *mis-* badly, from Old English *mis-* badly + DEMEANOUR]

misdescribe *verb*
- "miss de SCRIBE"
- describe inaccurately.
- [prefix *mis-* badly, from Old English *mis-* badly + DESCRIBE]
- **misdescription** *noun*

misdiagnose *verb*
- "miss die ug NOCE" or "miss die ug NOZE"
- diagnose incorrectly.
- [prefix *mis-* badly, from Old English *mis-* badly + DIAGNOSIS]
- **misdiagnosis** *noun*

misdial *verb*
- "miss DILE"
- dial (a telephone number etc.) incorrectly.
- [prefix *mis-* badly, from Old English *mis-* badly

+ 'dial' from Middle English, = sundial, from medieval Latin *diale* clock dial, ultimately from Latin *dies* day]

misdirect *verb*
• "miss die RECT" or "miss dir ECT"
• direct (a person, letter, blow, etc.) wrongly.
• [prefix *mis-* badly, from Old English *mis-* badly + 'direct': see DIRECTORY]
• **misdirected** *adjective*
• **misdirection** *noun*

misdoing *noun*
• "miss DOOING"
• a misdeed.
• [prefix *mis-* badly, from Old English *mis-* badly + 'do']

misdoubt *verb*
• "miss DOUT"
• have doubts or misgivings about the truth or existence of.
• [prefix *mis-* badly, from Old English *mis-* badly + DOUBT]

misemploy *verb*
• "miss em PLOY"
• employ or use wrongly or improperly.
• [prefix *mis-* badly, from Old English *mis-* or Old French *mes-* (ultimately from Latin *minus* neuter of *minor* less) + 'employ': see EMPLOYABLE]

miser *noun*
• "MY zur"
• a person who hoards wealth and lives miserably.
• [Latin, = wretched]
• **miserliness** *noun*
• **miserly** *adjective*

miserable *adjective*
• "MIZZ ruh bull" or "MIZZER a bull"
• wretchedly unhappy or uncomfortable.
• [French *misérable* from Latin *miserabilis* pitiable, from *miserari* to pity, from *miser* wretched]
• **miserableness** *noun*
• **miserably** *adverb*

misericord *noun*
• "mizz AIRY cord"
• a shelving projection on the underside of a hinged seat in a choir stall serving (when the seat is turned up) to help support a person standing.
• [Old French *misericorde* from Latin *misericordia* from *misericors* compassionate, from stem of *miserēri* pity + *cor cordis* heart]

misery *noun*
• "MIZZER ee"
• great discomfort of mind or body.
• [Old French *misere* or Latin *miseria* (as MISER)]

misfeasance *noun*
• "miss FEEZ ince"
• a transgression, esp. the wrongful exercise of lawful authority.
• [Old French *mesfaisance* from *mesfaire* misdo (*mes-* badly (ultimately from Latin *minus* neuter of *minor* less), *faire* do, from Latin *facere*): compare MALFEASANCE]

misfire *verb*
• "miss FIRE"
• (of a gun, motor engine, etc.) fail to go off or start or function regularly.
• [prefix *mis-* badly, from Old English *mis-* badly + 'fire' from Old English *fȳr*]

misfit *noun*
• "MISS fit"
• a person unsuited to a particular kind of environment, occupation, etc.
• [prefix *mis-* badly, from Old English *mis-* badly + 'fit', of unknown origin]

misfortune *noun*
• "miss FOR ch'n"
• bad luck.
• [prefix *mis-* badly, from Old English *mis-* badly + 'fortune', from Old French *fortune* from Latin *fortuna* luck, chance]

misgiving *noun*
• "miss GIVING"
• a feeling of mistrust or apprehension.
• [prefix *mis-* badly, from Old English *mis-* badly + 'give' from Old English *g(i)efan*]

misgovern *verb*
• "miss GUVVERN"
• govern (a country etc.) badly.
• [prefix *mis-* badly, from Old English *mis-* badly + GOVERN]
• **misgovernment** *noun*

misguided *adjective*
• "miss GUY did"
• mistaken in thought or action.
• [prefix *mis-* badly, from Old English *mis-* badly + GUIDE]
• **misguidance** *noun*
• **misguide** *verb*
• **misguidedly** *adverb*
• **misguidedness** *noun*

mishandle *verb*
• "miss HAND'll"
• deal with incorrectly or ineffectively.
• [prefix *mis-* badly, from Old English *mis-* badly + 'handle', from 'hand' from Old English]

mishap *noun*
• "MISS hap"
• an unlucky accident.
• [prefix *mis-* badly, from Old English *mis-* badly + 'hap' from Old Norse *happ* chance, luck]

mishear *verb*
• "miss HEER"
• hear incorrectly or imperfectly.
• [prefix *mis-* badly, from Old English *mis-* badly + 'hear' from Old English]

Mishnah *noun*
• "MISHNA"
• an authoritative collection of exegetical

material embodying the oral tradition of Jewish law, which forms the first part of the Talmud.
• [Hebrew *mišnāh* (teaching by) repetition]
• **Mishnaic** *adjective* "mish NAY ick"

misidentify *verb*
• "miss eye DENTA fie"
• identify erroneously.
• [prefix *mis-* badly, from Old English *mis-* badly + IDENTIFY]
• **misidentification** *noun*

misinformed *adjective*
• "miss in FORMD"
• (of a person) incorrectly informed; having an incorrect or imperfect knowledge of or acquaintance with the facts.
• [prefix *mis-* badly, from Old English *mis-* badly + 'inform' from Old French *enfo(u)rmer* from Latin *informare* give shape to, fashion, describe (*in* in, *forma* form)]
• **misinform** *verb*
• **misinformation** *noun*

misinterpret *verb*
• "miss in TUR prit"
• interpret wrongly; draw a wrong inference from.
• [prefix *mis-* badly, from Old English *mis-* badly + INTERPRET]
• **misinterpretation** *noun*
• **misinterpreter** *noun*

misjudge *verb*
• "miss JUDGE"
• judge wrongly.
• [prefix *mis-* badly, from Old English *mis-* badly + 'judge' from Old French *juger* from Latin *judex judicis* from *jus* law + *-dicus* speaking]
• **misjudgment** *noun* (also **misjudgement**)

Miskito *noun*
• "miss KEETO"
• a member of an Aboriginal people of the Atlantic coast of Nicaragua and Honduras.
• [the name in Miskito]
HOMOPHONES: *mosquito*

mislabel *verb*
• "miss LAY bull"
• attach an incorrect label to.
• [prefix *mis-* badly, from Old English *mis-* badly + 'label' from Old French, = ribbon, prob. from Germanic]

mislay *verb*
• "miss LAY"
• unintentionally put (a thing) where it cannot readily be found.
• [prefix *mis-* badly, from Old English *mis-* badly + 'lay' from Old English]

mislead *verb*
• "miss LEED"
• cause (a person) to have a wrong idea or impression about something.
• [prefix *mis-* badly, from Old English *mis-* badly + 'lead' from Old English]
• **misleader** *noun*
• **misleading** *adjective*
• **misleadingly** *adverb*
• **misleadingness** *noun*

mismanage *verb*
• "miss MAN idge"
• manage badly or dishonestly.
• [prefix *mis-* badly, from Old English *mis-* badly + MANAGE]
• **mismanagement** *noun*

mismatch *verb*
• "miss MATCH"
• match unsuitably or incorrectly.
• [prefix *mis-* badly, from Old English *mis-* badly + 'match' from Old English *gemæcca* mate, companion, from Germanic]

mismeasure *verb*
• "miss MEZHUR"
• measure or estimate incorrectly.
• [prefix *mis-* badly, from Old English *mis-* badly + MEASURE]
• **mismeasurement** *noun*

misname *verb*
• "miss NAME"
• call by a wrong or inappropriate name.
• [prefix *mis-* badly, from Old English *mis-* badly + 'name' from Old English *nama*]

misnomer *noun*
• "miss NOME ur"
• a name or term used wrongly.
• [Anglo-French from Old French *mesnom(m)er* (*mes-* ultimately from Latin *minus* neuter of *minor* less, *nommer* name, from Latin *nominare*, formed as NOMINAL)]

miso *noun*
• "MEE so"
• a paste made from fermented soybeans and barley or rice malt, used in Japanese cooking.
• [Japanese]

misogyny *noun*
• "miss AW juh nee"
• the hatred of women.
• [Greek *misos* hatred + *gunē* woman]
• **misogynist** *noun*
• **misogynistic** *adjective*
• **misogynous** *adjective*

misperception *noun*
• "miss purr SEP sh'n"
• a wrong or incorrect perception.
• [prefix *mis-* badly, from Old English *mis-* badly + PERCEPTION]
• **misperceive** *verb* "miss purr SEEVE"

misplace *verb*
• "miss PLACE"
• put in the wrong place.
• [prefix *mis-* badly, from Old English *mis-* badly + 'place' from Old French *place* via Latin *platea* from Greek *plateia* (*hodos*) broad (way)]
• **misplacement** *noun*

misplay *verb*
• "miss PLAY"
• play (a ball, card, etc.) in a wrong or ineffective manner.
• [prefix *mis-* badly, from Old English *mis-* badly + 'play' from Old English *pleg(i)an*, originally = to exercise]

misprint *noun*
• "MISS print"
• a mistake in printing.
• [prefix *mis-* badly, from Old English *mis-* badly + 'print' from Old French *priente, preinte*, feminine past participle of *preindre* press, from Latin *premere*]

misprision *noun*
• "miss PRIZH'n"
• the deliberate concealment of one's knowledge of a crime, treason, etc.
• [Anglo-French *mesprisioun* from Old French *mesprison* error, from *mesprendre* to mistake (Old French *mes-* (ultimately from Latin *minus* neuter of *minor* less), *prendre* take)]

misprize *verb*
• "miss PRIZE"
• despise, scorn; fail to appreciate.
• [Old French *mesprisier* (*mes-* (ultimately from Latin *minus* neuter of *minor* less), *pris-* (stem of *preisier* praise, from Late Latin *pretiare* from Latin *pretium* price))]

mispronounce *verb*
• "miss pruh NOUNCE"
• pronounce (a word etc.) wrongly.
• [prefix *mis-* badly, from Old English *mis-* badly + 'pronounce' from Old French *pronuncier* from Latin *pronuntiare* (*pro* in front (of), for, *nuntiare* announce, from *nuntius* messenger)]
• **mispronunciation** *noun* "miss pruh nuncy AY sh'n"

misquote *verb*
• "miss KWOTE"
• quote wrongly.
• [prefix *mis-* badly, from Old English *mis-* badly + QUOTE]
• **misquotation** *noun*

misread *verb*
• "miss REED"
• read or interpret (text, a situation, etc.) wrongly.
• [prefix *mis-* badly, from Old English *mis-* badly + 'read' from Old English]
• **misreading** *noun*

misremember *verb*
• "miss re MEMBER"
• remember imperfectly or incorrectly.
• [prefix *mis-* badly, from Old English *mis-* badly + 'remember' from Old French *remembrer* from Late Latin *rememorari* (Latin *re-* again, *memor* mindful)]

misreport *verb*
• "miss re PORT"
• give a false or incorrect report of.
• [prefix *mis-* badly, from Old English *mis-* badly + 'report' from Old French *reporter* from Latin *reportare* (*re-* again, *portare* bring)]

misrepresent *verb*
• "miss rep re ZENT"
• represent wrongly; give a false or misleading account or idea of.
• [prefix *mis-* badly, from Old English *mis-* badly + REPRESENTATION]
• **misrepresentation** *noun*
• **misrepresentative** *adjective*

misrule *noun*
• "miss RULE"
• bad government.
• [prefix *mis-* badly, from Old English *mis-* badly + 'rule' from Old French *reule*, *reuler* from Late Latin *regulare* from Latin *regula* straight stick]

missal *noun*
• "MISS'l"
• a book containing the texts used in the service of the Mass throughout the year.
• [medieval Latin *missale* neuter of Church Latin *missalis* of the Mass, from *missa* Mass]
HOMOPHONES: *missile*

missalette *noun*
• "missa LET"
• a small booklet containing the liturgy, prayers, readings, hymns, etc. for Masses for a week or a month.
• [as MISSAL]

misshapen *adjective*
• "miss SHAPE 'n"
• ill-shaped, deformed, distorted.
• [prefix *mis-* badly, from Old English *mis-* badly + 'shape' from Old English *gesceap* creation]
• **misshape** *verb*
• **misshapenly** *adverb*
• **misshapenness** *noun*

missile *noun*
• "MISS'l" or "MISS ile"
• a destructive, self-propelling projectile, esp. a nuclear weapon, that is directed automatically or by remote control.
• [Latin *missilis* from *mittere miss-* send]
• **missileer** *noun*
• **missilery** *noun* "MISS 'll ree"
HOMOPHONES: *missal*

Mississauga *noun*
• "missa SOGGA"
• a member of an Ojibwa Aboriginal people living in S Ontario.
• [Ojibwa *misizaagii* 'inhabitant of the large river outlet' (referring to the *Mississagi* river draining into Lake Huron, where the group was first encountered by the French)]

Mississaugan *noun*
• "missa SOG'n"
• a resident of Mississauga, Ont.

Mississippian *noun*
- "missa SIPPY 'n"
- a native or resident of Mississippi.

missive *noun*
- "MISSIV"
- an esp. official letter.
- [medieval Latin *missivus* from Latin *mittere miss-* send]

misspeak *verb*
- "miss SPEEK"
- speak wrongly or improperly.
- [prefix *mis-* badly, from Old English *mis-* badly + 'speak' from Old English *sprecan*, later *specan*]

misspell *verb*
- "miss SPELL"
- spell wrongly.
- [prefix *mis-* badly, from Old English *mis-* badly + 'spell' from Old French *espel(l)er*, from Frankish]
- **misspelled** *adjective*
- **misspelling** *noun*

misspent *adjective*
- "miss SPENT"
- wastefully or irresponsibly spent, passed, etc.
- [prefix *mis-* badly, from Old English *mis-* badly + 'spend' from Old English *spendan* from Latin *expendere* (see EXPEND)]
- **misspend** *verb*

misstate *verb*
- "miss STATE"
- state wrongly or inaccurately.
- [prefix *mis-* badly, from Old English *mis-* badly + 'state' partly from ESTATE, partly from Latin STATUS]
- **misstatement** *noun*

misstep *noun*
- "MISS step"
- an inappropriate or clumsy action.
- [prefix *mis-* badly, from Old English *mis-* badly + 'step' from Old English *stæpe*]

mistake *noun*
- "miss TAKE"
- a misconception about the meaning of something; an incorrect idea or opinion.
- [Old Norse *mistaka* take badly]
- **mistakable** *adjective*

mistaken *adjective*
- "miss TAKE'n"
- wrong in opinion or judgment.
- [as MISTAKE]
- **mistakenly** *adverb*

mistime *verb*
- "miss TIME"
- say or do at the wrong time.
- [prefix *mis-* badly, from Old English *mis-* badly + 'time' from Old English *tīma*]
- **mistiming** *noun*

mistitle *verb*
- "miss TITE 'll"
- give the wrong title or name to.
- [prefix *mis-* badly, from Old English *mis-* badly + 'title' from Old French *title* from Latin *titulus* placard, title]

mistletoe *noun*
- "MISS'll toe"
- a parasitic plant, *Viscum album*, growing on apple and other trees and bearing white glutinous berries in winter.
- [Old English *misteltān*]

mistral *noun*
- "MISS trull" or "miss TRALL"
- a cold north wind that blows down the Rhone valley and southern France into the Mediterranean.
- [French & Provençal]

mistranslate *verb*
- "miss TRANZ late"
- translate incorrectly.
- [prefix *mis-* badly, from Old English *mis-* badly + TRANSLATE]
- **mistranslation** *noun*

mistreat *verb*
- "miss TREET"
- treat wrongly, badly, or abusively.
- [prefix *mis-* badly, from Old English *mis-* badly + 'treat' from Old French *traitier* from Latin *tractare* handle, frequentative of *trahere tract-* draw, pull]
- **mistreatment** *noun*

mistrial *noun*
- "MISS try'll"
- a trial rendered invalid through some error in the proceedings.
- [prefix *mis-* badly, from Old English *mis-* badly + TRIAL]

mistrust *verb*
- "miss TRUST"
- be suspicious of; doubt the truth, validity, or genuineness of.
- [prefix *mis-* badly, from Old English *mis-* badly + 'trust' from Old Norse *treysta*, assimilated to the noun *traust* from *traustr* strong]
- **mistrustful** *adjective*
- **mistrustfully** *adverb*

mistype *verb*
- "miss TIPE"
- type wrongly.
- [prefix *mis-* badly, from Old English *mis-* badly + TYPE]

misunderstand *verb*
- "miss under STAND"
- fail to understand correctly.
- [prefix *mis-* badly, from Old English *mis-* badly + 'understand' from Old English *understandan*]
- **misunderstanding** *noun*
- **misunderstood** *adjective*

"miss under STOOD" (rhymes with *WOOD*)

misuse *verb*
• "miss YOOZ"
• use wrongly or improperly; apply to the wrong purpose.
• [prefix *mis-* badly, from Old English *mis-* badly + 'use' from Old French *us*, *user*, ultimately from Latin *uti us-* use]
• **misusage** *noun* "miss YOO sidge"
• **misuser** *noun*

Mithraism *noun*
• "MITH ray izm"
• the cult of the ancient Persian god Mithras.
• **Mithraic** *adjective* "mith RAY ick"
• **Mithraist** *noun*

mitigate *verb*
• "MITTA gate"
• make milder or less intense or severe; moderate or give relief from.
• [Latin *mitigare mitigat-* from *mitis* mild]
• **mitigable** *adjective* "MITTA guh bull"
• **mitigation** *noun*
• **mitigator** *noun*
• **mitigatory** *adjective* "MITTA guh tory"

mitochondrion *noun*
• "mite a CON dree 'n"
• an organelle found in most eukaryotic cells, containing enzymes for respiration and energy production.
• [modern Latin from Greek *mitos* thread + *khondrion* diminutive of *khondros* granule]
• **mitochondrial** *adjective*

mitogen *noun*
• "MITE a j'n"
• a substance or agent that induces or stimulates mitosis.
• [as MITOSIS + GENESIS]
• **mitogenic** *adjective*

mitosis *noun*
• "my TOE sis"
• a type of cell division that results in two daughter cells each having the same number and kind of chromosomes as the parent nucleus.
• [modern Latin from Greek *mitos* thread]
• **mitotic** *adjective* "my TOTTIC"
• **mitotically** *adverb*

mitral *adjective*
• "MY trull"
• designating or pertaining to the mitral valve, a two-cusped valve between the left atrium and the left ventricle of the heart.
• [modern Latin *mitralis* from Latin *mitra* girdle]

mitre *noun*
ALSO SPELLED: esp. *US* **miter**
• "MITE ur"
• a tall, deeply-cleft headdress worn by bishops and abbots, forming in outline the shape of a pointed arch.
• [Old French from Latin *mitra* from Greek *mitra* girdle, turban]
• **mitred** *adjective* (also esp. *US* **mitered**)

mitrewort *noun*
• "MITE ur wurt" or "MITE ur wort"
• a woodland plant of the genus *Mitella*, found east of the Rockies, with small white fringed flowers.
• [MITRE + WORT]

Mitteleuropean *adjective*
• "mit'll yura PEE 'n"
• from or pertaining to central Europe.
• [German]

mitzvah *noun*
• "MITS vuh"
• a precept or commandment in Judaism.
• [Hebrew *miṣwāh* commandment]

Mixtec *noun*
• "MEE steck"
• a member of an Aboriginal people of Central America.
• [Spanish from Nahuatl *mixtecah* 'person from a cloudy place']

mizzen *noun*
ALSO SPELLED: **mizen**
• "MIZZ'n"
• the lowest fore-and-aft sail of a fully rigged ship's mizzen-mast.
• [French *misaine* from Italian *mezzana* mizzen-sail, feminine of *mezzano* middle: see MEZZANINE]

mnemonic *adjective*
• "nuh MONNIC"
• of or designed to aid the memory.
• [medieval Latin *mnemonicus* from Greek *mnēmonikos* from *mnēmōn* mindful]
• **mnemonically** *adverb*

mnemonics *noun*
• "nuh MONNIX"
• the art of improving memory, esp. by artificial aids.
• [as MNEMONIC]

Moabite *adjective*
• "MOE a bite"
• of Moab, an ancient region by the Dead Sea, or its people.

moat *noun*
• "MOTE"
• a deep defensive ditch round a castle, town, etc., usu. filled with water.
• [Old French *mote*, *motte* mound]
HOMOPHONES: *mote*

mobocracy *noun*
• "mob OCKRA see"
• rule or government by a mob.
• ['mob' (abbreviation of *mobile*, short for Latin *mobile vulgus* excitable crowd, from *mobilis* from *movēre* move) + Greek *kratia* from *kratos* strength, power]

moccasin *noun*
• "MOCKA sin"
• a type of soft leather slipper or shoe with combined sole and heel, as originally worn by some N American Aboriginal peoples.
• [Virginia Algonquian and other N American Aboriginal languages *mockasin, makisin*]
• **moccasined** *adjective*

mocha *noun*
• "MOE kuh"
• a coffee of fine quality.
• [*Mocha*, a port on the Red Sea, from where the coffee first came]

mochaccino *noun*
• "moe kuh CHEENO"
• a cappuccino flavoured with chocolate syrup.
• [blend of MOCHA + CAPPUCCINO]

mockumentary *noun*
• "mock yoo MENTA ree"
• a film, radio drama, etc. written and presented as a straightforward documentary, which is actually a spoof or parody of the profiled subject.
• [blend of 'mock' (from Old French *mo(c)quer* deride) + DOCUMENTARY]

modacrylic *noun*
• "modda CRILLIC"
• a synthetic, acrylic-based fibre.
• [from 'modified acrylic']

moderate *adjective*
• "MODDER it"
• avoiding extremes in conduct, opinions, or expression.
• [Latin *moderatus* past participle of *moderare* reduce, control]
• **moderately** *adverb*
• **moderateness** *noun*
• **moderatism** *noun*

moderation *noun*
• "modder AY sh'n"
• the process or an instance of moderating.
• [as MODERATE]

moderato *adjective*
• "modder OTTO"
• performed at a moderate pace.
• [Italian (as MODERATE)]

moderator *noun*
• "MODDER ate ur"
• a chairperson of a discussion on television or radio.
• [as MODERATE]

moderne *noun*
• "moe DAIRN"
• a style of architecture and interior design originating in the US in the late 1920s as an adaptation of European Art Deco, and similarly characterized by austere geometrical shapes, strong colours, and frequent use of chrome, enamel, bronze, and polished stone.
• [French, = 'modern', ultimately from Latin *modo* just now]

modicum *noun*
• "MODDA k'm"
• a small quantity.
• [Latin, = short distance or time, neuter of *modicus* moderate, from *modus* measure]

modify *verb*
• "MODDA fie"
• make partial or minor changes in; alter without radical transformation.
• [Old French *modifier* from Latin *modificare* from *modus* measure]
• **modifiable** *adjective*
• **modification** *noun*
• **modifier** *noun*

modillion *noun*
• "muh DILL y'n"
• a projecting bracket placed in series under the corona of a cornice in the Corinthian and other orders.
• [French *modillon* from Italian *modiglione*, ultimately from Latin *mutulus* mutule]

modular *adjective*
• "MOD yuh lur" or "MODGE oo lur"
• of or pertaining to modules or moduli.
• [modern Latin *modularis* from Latin *modulus*: see MODULUS]
• **modularity** *noun* "mod yuh LERRA tee" or "modge oo LERRA tee"
• **modularization** *noun* (also esp. *Brit.* **-isation**)

modulate *verb*
• "MOD yuh late" or "MODGE uh late"
• regulate or adjust.
• [Latin *modulari modulat-* to measure, from *modus* measure]
• **modulation** *noun*
• **modulator** *noun*
• **modulatory** *adjective*

module *noun*
• "MOD yool" or "MODGE ool"
• a standardized part or independent unit used in construction or assembly, esp. of furniture, a building, or an electronic system.
• [French *module* or Latin *modulus*: see MODULUS]

modulo *preposition*
• "MOD yoo lo"
• using, or with respect to, a modulus.
• [Latin, ablative of MODULUS]

modulus *noun*
• "MOD yoo luss"
• the magnitude of a real number without regard to its sign.
• [Latin, = measure, diminutive of *modus*]

mogul *noun*
• "MOE g'll"
• an important or influential person.
• [Persian *mugūl*: see MUGHAL]

Mohegan *noun*
• "moe HEE g'n"
• a member of an Algonquian people formerly inhabiting part of Connecticut.
• [Mohegan]

mohel *noun*
• "MOIL"
• a person trained to perform ritual circumcisions according to Jewish law.
• [Hebrew *mōhēl*]

moho *noun*
• "MOE hoe"
• a boundary of discontinuity separating the earth's crust and mantle.
• [A. *Mohorovičić*, Yugoslav seismologist d.1936]

moi *pronoun*
• "MWAH"
• as a tongue-in-cheek rejoinder to being accused of something of which one knows one is guilty; what, me?
• [French, = 'me']

moidore *noun*
• "MOY dore"
• a Portuguese gold coin, current in England in the 18th c.
• [Portuguese *moeda d'ouro* money of gold]

moiety *noun*
• "MOY a tee"
• a half, either of two equal parts.
• [Old French *moité, moitié* from Latin *medietas -tatis* middle, from *medius* (adjective) middle]

moiré *noun*
• "more AY" or "mwor AY"
• a fabric, often silk, having a pattern of glossy wavy bars.
• [French, past participle of *moirer* (earlier *mouaire*) from 'mohair', ultimately from Arabic *mukayyar*, lit. 'choice, select']

mojito *noun*
• "moe HEETO" or "moe JEETO"
• a cocktail originating in Cuba and consisting of white rum, lime or lemon juice, sugar, fresh mint, ice, and carbonated or soda water.
• [Cuban Spanish from stem of Spanish *mojado* wet + diminutive *-ito*]

mojo *noun*
• "MOE joe"
• magic, voodoo.
• [prob. of African origin]

moksha *noun*
• "MOCK shuh"
• (in Hinduism) the final release of the soul from the cycle of reincarnations.
• [Sanskrit *mokṣa*]

molal *adjective*
• "MOLE 'll"
• (of a solution) containing one mole, or a specified number of moles, of solute per kilogram of solvent.
• [German *Mol* from *Molekül* MOLECULE]
• **molality** *noun* "muh LALLA tee"

molar *adjective*
• "MOE lur"
• (of a tooth) serving to grind, esp. designating any of the back teeth of mammals.
• [Latin *molaris* from *mola* millstone]

molasses *noun*
• "muh LASS iss" or "muh LASS izz"
• a thick, dark, uncrystallized syrup drained from raw sugar during refining, often used in animal feed etc.
• [Portuguese *melaço* from Late Latin *mellaceum* grape juice before or during fermentation, from *mel* honey]

Moldovan *noun*
• "MAUL duh v'n"
• a native or inhabitant of Moldova in SE Europe.

mole *noun*
• "MOE lay"
• a highly spiced Mexican sauce made chiefly from chili peppers and chocolate, served with meat.
• [Mexican Spanish from Nahuatl *molli* sauce, stew]

molecule *noun*
• "MOLLA cule"
• the smallest fundamental unit (usu. a group of atoms) of a chemical compound that can take part in a chemical reaction.
• [French *molécule* from modern Latin *molecula* diminutive of Latin *moles* mass]
• **molecular** *adjective* "muh LECK yuh lur"
• **molecularity** *noun* "muh leck yuh LERRA tee"
• **molecularly** *adverb*

moline *adjective*
• "muh LINE"
• (of a cross) having each extremity broadened and curved back.
• [prob. from Anglo-French *moliné* from *molin* mill, because of the resemblance to the iron support of a millstone]
HOMOPHONES: *malign*

mollify *verb*
• "MOLLA fie"
• appease, pacify.
• [French *mollifier* or Latin *mollificare* from *mollis* soft]
• **mollification** *noun*
• **mollifier** *noun*

mollusc *noun*
ALSO SPELLED: esp. *US* **mollusk**
• "MOLL usk"
• any invertebrate of the phylum Mollusca, with a soft body and usu. a hard shell, including limpets, snails, cuttlefish, oysters, mussels, etc.
• [modern Latin *mollusca* neuter pl. of Latin *molluscus* from *mollis* soft]

• **molluscan** *adjective* (also esp. *US* **molluskan**) "muh LUSK 'n"

molten *adjective*
• "MOLE t'n"
• melted, esp. made liquid by heat.
• [archaic past participle of 'melt']

molto *adverb*
• "MOLL toe"
• (as a musical direction) very.
• [Italian from Latin *multus* much]

moly *noun*
• "MOLE ee"
• an alliaceous plant, *Allium moly*, with small yellow flowers.
• [Latin from Greek *mōlu*]

molybdenite *noun*
• "muh LIBDA nite"
• molybdenum disulphide as an ore.
• [as MOLYBDENUM]

molybdenum *noun*
• "muh LIBDA num"
• a silver-white brittle metallic transition element occurring naturally in molybdenite and used in steel to give strength and resistance to corrosion.
• [modern Latin, earlier *molybdena*, originally = molybdenite, lead ore: Latin *molybdena* from Greek *molubdaina* plummet, from *molubdos* lead]

momentous *adjective*
• "moe MEN tuss"
• having great importance.
• [as MOMENTUM]
• **momentously** *adverb*
• **momentousness** *noun*

momentum *noun*
• "moe MEN tum"
• the quantity of motion of a moving body, measured as a product of its mass and velocity.
• [Latin from *movimentum* from *movēre* move]

monad *noun*
• "MON ad" or "MOE nad"
• the number one; a unit.
• [French *monade* or Late Latin *monas monad-* from Greek *monas -ados* unit, from *monos* alone]
• **monadic** *adjective*

monadnock *noun*
• "muh NAD nock"
• a steep-sided isolated hill resistant to erosion and rising above a plain.
• [Mount *Monadnock* in New Hampshire, US]

monandry *noun*
• "muh NAN dree"
• the custom of having only one husband at a time.
• [Greek from *monos* alone, after *polyandry*]
• **monandrous** *adjective*

monarch *noun*
• "MON ark"
• a sovereign with the title of king, queen, emperor, empress, or the equivalent.
• [Greek *monarkhēs, -os*, from *monos* alone + *arkhō* to rule]
• **monarchal** *adjective*
• **monarchic** *adjective* "muh NARKIC"
• **monarchical** *adjective*
• **monarchism** *noun*
• **monarchist** *noun*
• **monarchy** *noun*

monastery *noun*
• "MONNA sterry"
• the residence of a religious community, esp. of monks living in seclusion.
• [Church Latin *monasterium* from ecclesiastical Greek *monastērion* from *monazō* live alone, from *monos* alone]

monastic *adjective*
• "muh NASTIC"
• of or relating to monasteries or the religious communities living in them.
• [as MONASTERY]
• **monastically** *adverb*
• **monasticism** *noun* "muh NASTA sizm"

monaural *adjective*
• "mon OR'll"
• (of sound reproduction) using only one channel of transmission.
• [Greek *monos* single + AURAL]

monazite *noun*
• "MONNA zite"
• a phosphate mineral containing rare-earth elements and thorium.
• [German *Monazit* from Greek *monazō* live alone (because of its rarity)]

Monctonian *noun*
• "munk TONY 'n"
• a resident of Moncton, NB.

mondaine *adjective*
• "mon DEN"
• of the fashionable world.
• [French, feminine of *mondain*: see MUNDANE]

Monegasque *noun*
• "monna GASK"
• a native or inhabitant of the principality of Monaco on the NW Mediterranean coast.
• [French]

monetarism *noun*
• "MONNA tuh rizm"
• the theory or practice of controlling the supply of money as the chief method of stabilizing the economy.
• [as MONETARY]
• **monetarist** *noun*

monetary *adjective*
• "MONNA terry"
• of or pertaining to coinage or currency.
• [French *monétaire* or Late Latin *monetarius* from Latin *moneta* mint, money, originally a title

of the goddess Juno, in whose temple at Rome money was minted]
• **monetarily** *adverb*

monetize *verb*
ALSO SPELLED: esp. *Brit.* **-ise**
• "MONNA tize"
• give a fixed value as currency.
• [French *monétiser* from Latin (as MONETARY)]
• **monetization** *noun* (also esp. *Brit.* **-isation**)

moneywort *noun*
• "MUNNY wurt" or "MUNNY wort"
• a trailing evergreen plant, *Lysimachia nummularia*, with round glossy leaves and yellow flowers.
• ['money' + WORT]

monger *noun*
• "MONG gur" or "MUNG gur"
• a dealer or trader.
• [Old English *mangere* from *mangian* to traffic, from Germanic, ultimately from Latin *mango* dealer]

mongo *noun*
• "MONG go"
• a monetary unit of Mongolia, equal to one-hundredth of a tugrik.
• [Mongolian *möngö* silver]

Mongol *adjective*
• "MONG g'll"
• of or relating to the Asian people now inhabiting Mongolia or their language.
• [Mongolian, said to be from *mong* brave]

Mongolian *noun*
• "mong GOALIE 'n"
• a native or inhabitant of Mongolia in E Asia.

Mongoloid *adjective*
• "MONG guh loid"
• of or relating to the division of humankind including the indigenous peoples of E Asia, SE Asia, and the Arctic region of N America, characteristically having dark eyes, straight hair, pale ivory to dark skin, and little facial or body hair.
• [as MONGOL]

mongrel *noun*
• "MONG grull"
• a dog of no definable type or breed.
• [earlier *meng-*, *mang-* from Germanic: prob. related to 'mingle']
• **mongrelism** *noun*
• **mongrelization** *noun* (also esp. *Brit.* **-isation**)
• **mongrelize** *verb* (also esp. *Brit.* **-ise**)

moniker *noun*
ALSO SPELLED: **monicker**
• "MONNICK ur"
• a name.
• [19th c.: origin unknown]

monism *noun*
• "MON izm" or "MOAN izm"
• any theory denying the duality of matter and mind.
• [modern Latin *monismus* from Greek *monos* single]
• **monist** *noun*
• **monistic** *adjective*

monition *noun*
• "muh NISH'n"
• a warning (of danger).
• [Old French from Latin *monitio -onis* (as MONITOR)]

monitor *noun*
• "MONNO tur"
• any of various persons or devices for observing, checking, or warning about a situation, operation, etc.
• [Latin from *monēre monit-* warn]
• **monitorial** *adjective*
• **monitoring** *noun*

monitory *adjective*
• "MONNA tory"
• serving as a warning (of danger).
• [as MONITOR]

monoamine *noun*
• "monno a MEEN" or "monno AM een"
• any compound having a single amine group in its molecule.
• [Greek *monos* single, alone + AMINE]

monobloc *adjective*
• "MONNO block"
• made as, contained in, or involving a single casting.
• [French (Greek *monos* single, alone + French *bloc* block from Middle Dutch *blok*)]

monocarpic *adjective*
• "monno CARPIC"
• bearing fruit only once.
• [Greek *monos* single, alone + *karpos* fruit]

monocausal *adjective*
• "monno COZZ'll"
• in terms of a sole cause.
• [Greek *monos* single, alone + 'cause']

monochromatic *adjective*
• "monno crow MATTIC"
• (of light or other radiation) of a single wavelength or frequency.
• [Greek *monos* single, alone + CHROMATIC]
• **monochromatically** *adverb*

monochromatism *noun*
• "monno CROW muh tizm"
• complete colour-blindness in which all colours appear as shades of one colour.
• [as MONOCHROMATIC]

monochrome *noun*
• "MONNO crome"
• a photograph or picture done in one colour or different tones of this, or in black and white only.

• [ultimately from Greek *monokhrōmatos* (*monos* single, alone, *khrōmatos* from *khrōma* colour)]
• **monochromic** *adjective*

monocle *noun*
• "MONNA k'll"
• a single eyeglass, kept in position by the muscles around the eye.
• [French, originally adjective from Late Latin *monoculus* one-eyed (Greek *monos* single, alone, *oculus* eye)]
• **monocled** *adjective*

monocline *noun*
• "MONNO cline"
• a bend in rock strata that are otherwise uniformly dipping or horizontal.
• [Greek from *monos* single, alone + *klinō* lean, dip]
• **monoclinal** *adjective*

monoclinic *adjective*
• "monno CLINNIC"
• (of a crystal) having one axial intersection oblique.
• [Greek from *monos* single, alone + *klinō* lean, slope]

monoclonal *adjective*
• "monno CLONE 'll"
• forming a single clone; derived from a single individual or cell.
• [Greek *monos* single, alone + CLONE]

monocoque *noun*
• "MONNO cock"
• an aircraft or vehicle structure in which the chassis is integral with the body.
• [French (Greek *monos* single, alone + French *coque* shell)]

monocot *noun*
• "MONNO cot"
• = MONOCOTYLEDON.
• [abbreviation]

monocotyledon *noun*
• "monno cot'll EED'n"
• any flowering plant with a single cotyledon.
• [Greek *monos* single, alone + COTYLEDON]
• **monocotyledonous** *adjective*

monocracy *noun*
• "muh NOCKRA see"
• government by one person only.
• [Greek *monos* single, alone + *kratia* from *kratos* strength, power]
• **monocratic** *adjective*

monocropping *noun*
• "MONNO cropping"
• the practice of planting the same crop in the same field year after year.
• [Greek *monos* single, alone + 'crop']
• **monocrop** *noun*

monocular *adjective*
• "muh NOCK yuh lur"
• of or pertaining to one eye only.
• [Late Latin *monoculus* having one eye]

monoculture *noun*
• "MONNO cull chur"
• the cultivation of a single crop to the exclusion of others.
• [Greek *monos* single, alone + CULTURE]
• **monocultural** *adjective*

monocycle *noun*
• "MONNO sike'll"
• a single-wheeled cycle, esp. as used by acrobats.
• [Greek *monos* single, alone + CYCLE]

monocyte *noun*
• "MONNO site"
• a large leukocyte with a simple nucleus, developing into a macrophage.
• [Greek *monos* single, alone + *kutos* vessel]
• **monocytic** *adjective* "monno SITTIC"

monodrama *noun*
• "MONNO dramma" or "MONNO dromma"
• a dramatic piece for one performer.
• [Greek *monos* single, alone + DRAMA]

monody *noun*
• "MONNA dee"
• an ode sung by a single actor in a Greek tragedy.
• [Late Latin *monodia* from Greek *monōidia* from *monōidos* singing alone]
• **monodic** *adjective* "muh NODDIC"
• **monodist** *noun*

monoecious *adjective*
• "muh NEE sh'ss"
• with unisexual male and female organs on the same plant.
• [modern Latin *Monoecia* the class of such plants, from Greek *monos* single + *oikos* house]

monofilament *noun*
• "MONNO filla m'nt"
• a single strand of synthetic fibre.
• [Greek *monos* single, alone + FILAMENT]

monogamy *noun*
• "muh NOGGA mee"
• the practice or state of being married to one person at a time.
• [French *monogamie* from Church Latin from Greek *monogamia* (*monos* single, alone, *gamos* marriage)]
• **monogamist** *noun*
• **monogamous** *adjective*
• **monogamously** *adverb*

monogenesis *noun*
• "monno JENNA sis"
• the theory of the development of all beings from a single cell.
• [Greek *monos* single, alone + GENESIS]
• **monogenetic** *adjective* "monno juh NETTIC"

monoglot *adjective*
• "MONNA glot"
• speaking, writing, or understanding only one language.

• [Greek *monoglōttos* (*monos* single, alone, *glōtta* tongue)]

monogram *noun*
• "MONNA gram"
• two or more letters, esp. a person's initials, combined in one design and marked on items of clothing etc.
• [Greek *monos* single, alone + *gramma* thing written]
• **monogrammed** *adjective*

monograph *noun*
• "MONNA graff"
• a separate treatise on a single subject or an aspect of it.
• [Greek *monos* single, alone, *graphia* writing]
• **monographer** *noun*
• **monographic** *adjective*

monohull *noun*
• "MONNO hull"
• a boat with a single hull.
• [Greek *monos* single, alone + 'hull']

monohybrid *noun*
• "monno HY brid"
• a hybrid that is heterozygous for alleles of one gene.
• [Greek *monos* single, alone + HYBRID]

monokini *noun*
• "monno KEENY"
• a woman's one-piece bathing suit equivalent to the lower half of a bikini.
• [Greek from *monos* single, alone + BIKINI, by false or humorous association with 'bi-' twice]

monolayer *noun*
• "MONNO lay ur"
• a layer only one molecule in thickness.
• [Greek *monos* single, alone + 'layer']

monolingual *adjective*
• "monna LING gwul" or "monna LING gyoo 'll"
• knowing or using only one language.
• [Greek *monos* single, alone + LINGUAL]
• **monolingualism** *noun*

monolith *noun*
• "MONNA lith"
• a single block of stone, esp. shaped into a pillar or monument.
• [French *monolithe* from Greek *monolithos* (*monos* single, alone, *lithos* stone)]
• **monolithic** *adjective*
• **monolithically** *adverb*

monologue *noun*
• "MONNA log"
• a long speech in a play, film, etc. spoken by one actor, esp. when alone.
• [French from Greek *monologos* speaking alone (*monos* single, alone, *logos* word)]
• **monologic** *adjective* "monna LODGE ick"
• **monological** *adjective*
• **monologist** *noun* (also **-loguist**)
"MONNA log ist"
• **monologize** *verb* (also esp. *Brit.* **-ise**)
"muh NOLLA jize"

monomania *noun*
• "monno MAINY uh"
• obsession of the mind by one idea or interest.
• [Greek *monos* single, alone + MANIA]
• **monomaniac** *noun*
• **monomaniacal** *adjective*
"monno muh NIE a k'll"

monomer *noun*
• "MONNO mur"
• a unit in a dimer, trimer, or polymer.
• [Greek *monos* single, alone + POLYMER]
• **monomeric** *adjective* "monno MARE ick"

monomial *adjective*
• "muh NO mee 'll"
• (of an algebraic expression) consisting of one term.
• [Greek from *monos* single, alone, after *binomial*]

monomolecular *adjective*
• "monno muh LECK yuh lur"
• (of a layer) only one molecule in thickness.
• [Greek *monos* single, alone + MOLECULE]

monomorphic *adjective*
• "monno MORFIC"
• not changing form during development.
• [Greek *monos* single, alone + *morphē* form]
• **monomorphism** *noun*

mononuclear *adjective*
• "monno NEW clee ur"
• having one nucleus.
• [Greek *monos* single, alone + NUCLEAR]

mononucleosis *noun*
• "monno new clee OH sis"
• an abnormally high proportion of monocytes in the blood, esp. an infectious viral disease characterized by swelling of the lymph glands and prolonged lassitude.
• [Greek from *monos* single, alone + NUCLEUS]

monophonic *adjective*
• "monna FONNIC"
• (of sound reproduction) using only one channel of transmission.
• [Greek from *monos* alone, single + *phōnē* sound]
• **monophonically** *adverb*

monophthong *noun*
• "MON uf thong"
• a single vowel sound.
• [Greek *monophthoggos* (*monos* single, alone, *phthoggos* sound)]
• **monophthongal** *adjective*

monophyletic *adjective*
• "monno fie LETTIC"
• (of a group of organisms) descended from a common evolutionary ancestor or ancestral group, esp. one not shared with any other group.
• [Greek *monos* single, alone + PHYLETIC]

Monophysite *noun*
- "muh NOFFA site"
- a person who holds that there is only one nature (partly divine, partly and subordinately human) in the person of Christ.
- [Church Latin *monophysita* from ecclesiastical Greek *monophusitēs* (Greek *monos* single, alone, *phusis* nature)]

monoplane *noun*
- "MONNO plane"
- an airplane with one set of wings.
- [Greek *monos* single, alone + 'plane']

monopole *noun*
- "MONNO pole"
- a single electric charge or magnetic pole, esp. a hypothetical isolated magnetic pole.
- [Greek *monos* single, alone + 'pole']

monopolize *verb*
ALSO SPELLED: esp. *Brit.* **-ise**
- "muh NOPPA lize"
- obtain exclusive possession or control of (a trade or commodity etc.).
- [as MONOPOLY]
- **monopolization** *noun* (also esp. *Brit.* **-isation**)
- **monopolizer** *noun* (also esp. *Brit.* **-iser**)

monopoly *noun*
- "muh NOPPA lee"
- the exclusive possession or control of the trade in a commodity or service.
- [Latin *monopolium* from Greek *monopōlion* (*monos* single, alone, *pōleō* sell)]
- **monopolist** *noun*
- **monopolistic** *adjective*
- **monopolistically** *adverb*

monoprint *noun*
- "MONNO print"
- an impression on paper made from an inked design painted on glass or metal.
- [Greek *monos* single, alone + 'print']

monorail *noun*
- "MONNA rail"
- a railway in which the track consists of a single rail, usu. elevated with the train units suspended from it.
- [Greek *monos* single, alone + 'rail']

monosaccharide *noun*
- "monno SACKA ride"
- a sugar that cannot be hydrolyzed to give a simpler sugar, e.g. glucose.
- [Greek *monos* single, alone + SACCHARIDE]

monospermous *adjective*
- "monno SPUR muss"
- having one seed.
- [Greek from *monos* single, alone + Greek *sperma* seed]

monosyllable *noun*
- "monno SILLA bull"
- a word of one syllable.
- [Greek *monos* single, alone + SYLLABLE]
- **monosyllabic** *adjective* "monno suh LABBIC"
- **monosyllabically** *adverb*

monotheism *noun*
- "monno THEE izm" (with "TH" as in *THICK*)
- the doctrine or belief that there is only one God.
- [Greek *monos* single, alone + *theos* god]
- **monotheist** *noun*
- **monotheistic** *adjective*
- **monotheistically** *adverb*

monotint *noun*
- "MONNO tint"
- a photograph or picture done in one colour or different tones of this, or in black and white only.
- [Greek *monos* single, alone + 'tint']

monotone *noun*
- "MONNA tone"
- a sound or utterance continuing or repeated on one note without change of pitch.
- [Greek *monos* single, alone + 'tone']
- **monotonic** *adjective* "monna TONNIC"
- **monotonically** *adverb*

monotony *noun*
- "muh NOTTA nee"
- lack of interesting variety; dull or tedious routine.
- [as MONOTONE]
- **monotonous** *adjective*
- **monotonously** *adverb*

monotreme *noun*
- "MONNO treem"
- any mammal of the order Monotremata, native to Australia and New Guinea, including the duckbill and echidna, laying large yolky eggs through a common opening for urine, feces, etc.
- [Greek *monos* single, alone + *trēma -matos* hole]

monotypic *adjective*
- "monno TIPPIC"
- having only one type or representative.
- [Greek *monos* single, alone + TYPE]

monounsaturated *adjective*
- "monno un SATCHER ated"
- (of a compound, esp. a fat or oil molecule) containing one double bond.
- [Greek *monos* single, alone + SATURATE]

monovalent *adjective*
- "monno VALE 'nt"
- having a valence of one; univalent.
- [Greek *monos* single, alone + VALENCE]

monoxide *noun*
- "muh NOX ide"
- an oxide containing one oxygen atom.
- [Greek from *monos* single, alone + OXYGEN]

monozygotic *adjective*
- "monno zye GOTTIC"
- (of twins, triplets, etc.) derived from a single ovum; identical.
- [Greek *monos* single, alone + ZYGOTE]

Monseigneur *noun*
• "mon sen YUR"
• a title given to an eminent French person, esp. a prince, cardinal, archbishop, or bishop.
• [French from *mon* my + *seigneur* lord, ultimately from Latin *senior* older, comparative of *senex* old man]

Monsieur *noun*
• "muh SYUH"
• the title or form of address used of or to a French-speaking man, corresponding to Mr. or sir.
• [French from *mon* my + *sieur* lord, ultimately from Latin *senior* older, comparative of *senex* old man]

Monsignor *noun*
• "m'n SEEN yur" or "mon SEEN yur"
• a title in the Roman Catholic Church bestowed by the Pope on priests, either in conjunction with an office or as an honorary title for distinguished service.
• [Italian, after MONSEIGNEUR: see SIGNOR]

monstera *noun*
• "mon STEERA"
• any climbing plant of the genus *Monstera*, including Swiss cheese plant.
• [modern Latin, perhaps from Latin *monstrum* monster (from the odd appearance of its leaves)]

monstrance *noun*
• "MON strince"
• a receptacle, usu. of gold or silver, with an open or transparent compartment in which the consecrated Host is exposed for veneration.
• [Middle English, = demonstration, from medieval Latin *monstrantia* from Latin *monstrare* show]

monstrosity *noun*
• "mon STROSSA tee"
• a huge, hideous, or outrageous thing, esp. an unsightly building.
• [Late Latin *monstrositas* (as MONSTROUS)]

monstrous *adjective*
• "MON struss"
• of or like a monster in appearance, fearsomeness, etc.
• [Old French *monstreux* or Latin *monstrosus* from *monstrum* portent, monster, from *monēre* warn]
• **monstrously** *adverb*
• **monstrousness** *noun*

montage *noun*
• "mon TOZH"
• a combination of images in quick succession to compress background information or provide atmosphere.
• [French from *monter* from Latin *mons montis* mountain]

Montagnais *noun*
• "MON tan yay"
• a member of an Innu people living in the barrens between Hudson Bay and the Labrador coast.
• [French, = mountaineer]

Montanan *noun*
• "mon TAN'n"
• a resident of Montana.

montane *adjective*
• "MON tane"
• of or inhabiting mountainous country.
• [Latin *montanus* from *mons montis* mountain]

montbretia *noun*
• "mon BREESHA"
• a hybrid plant of the genus *Crocosmia*, with bright orange-yellow trumpet-shaped flowers.
• [modern Latin from A. F. E. Coquebert de *Montbret*, French botanist d.1801]

monte *noun*
• "MONTY"
• a Spanish game of chance, played with 40 cards.
• [Spanish, = mountain, heap of cards]
HOMOPHONES: *monty*

Montenegrin *noun*
• "monta NAY grin"
• a native or inhabitant of Montenegro in the Balkans.

Montessori *noun*
• "monta SORRY"
• the system of education (esp. of young children) propounded by Italian educator Maria Montessori (d.1952) that seeks to develop natural interests and activities rather than use formal teaching methods.

montmorillonite *noun*
• "mont muh RILLA nite"
• any of a group of clay minerals which undergo reversible expansion on absorbing water, including the main constituents of fuller's earth and bentonite.
• [*Montmorillon*, a town in France]

Montrachet *noun*
• "mont ra SHAY"
• a white burgundy made from Chardonnay grapes from a single vineyard called Le Montrachet, in the Côte de Beaune district of Burgundy.

monument *noun*
• "MON yoo m'nt"
• anything enduring that serves to commemorate or make celebrated, esp. a structure or building.
• [French from Latin *monumentum*, from *monēre* remind]

monumental *adjective*
• "mon yoo MENT'll"
• extremely great; stupendous.
• [as MONUMENT]
• **monumentality** *noun*
• **monumentally** *adverb*

monumentalize *verb*
ALSO SPELLED: esp. *Brit.* **-ise**
• "mon yoo MENT'll ize"
• record or commemorate by or as by a monument.
• [as MONUMENT]

mor *noun*
• "MORE"
• humus formed under acid conditions.
• [Danish]
HOMOPHONES: *moor, more, Moor*

moraine *noun*
• "muh RAIN"
• a ridge or mound of rock debris etc. carried and deposited by a glacier.
• [French from Italian dialect *morena* from French dialect *mor(re)*, from Romanic]
• **morainal** *adjective*
• **morainic** *adjective*

morale *noun*
• "muh RAL"
• the amount of confidence, enthusiasm, determination, etc. that a person or group has at a particular time.
• [French *moral* from Latin *moralis* from *mos moris* custom, pl. *mores* morals, respelled to preserve the pronunciation]

morass *noun*
• "muh RASS"
• an entanglement; a disordered situation, esp. one impeding progress.
• [Dutch *moeras* (assimilated to *moer* moor, heath) from Middle Dutch *marasch* from Old French *marais* marsh, from medieval Latin *mariscus*]

moratorium *noun*
• "mora TORY um"
• a temporary prohibition or suspension (of an activity).
• [modern Latin, neuter of Late Latin *moratorius* delaying, from Latin *morari morat-* to delay, from *mora* delay]

Moravian *noun*
• "muh RAY vee 'n"
• a native of Moravia in the Czech Republic.

moray *noun*
• "MORE ay"
• any tropical eel-like fish of the family Muraenidae.
• [Portuguese *moreia* from Latin from Greek *muraina*]

mordant *adjective*
• "MORE d'nt"
• (of sarcasm etc.) caustic, biting.
• [French, participle of *mordre* bite, from Latin *mordēre*]
• **mordancy** *noun*
• **mordantly** *adverb*
HOMOPHONES: *mordent*

mordent *noun*
• "MORE d'nt"
• a musical ornament consisting of one rapid alternation of a written note with the note immediately below or above it.
• [German from Italian *mordente* participle of *mordēre* bite]
HOMOPHONES: *mordant*

morel *noun*
• "muh RELL"
• an edible fungus, *Morchella esculenta*, with a honeycombed cap.
• [French *morille* from Dutch *morilje*]

morello *noun*
• "muh RELLO"
• a sour kind of dark cherry.
• [Italian *morello* blackish, from medieval Latin *morellus*, diminutive of Latin *Maurus* Moor]

mores *plural noun*
• "MORE aze" or "MORE eez"
• customs or conventions regarded as essential to or characteristic of a community.
• [Latin, pl. of *mos* custom]

Moresque *adjective*
• "more ESK"
• (of art or architecture) Moorish in style or design.
• [French from Italian *moresco* from *Moro* Moor]

morganatic *adjective*
• "more g'n ATTIC"
• of or relating to a marriage between a person of high rank and another of lower rank, the spouse and children having no claim to the possessions or title of the person of higher rank.
• [French *morganatique* or German *morganatisch* from medieval Latin *matrimonium ad morganaticam* 'marriage with a morning gift', the husband's gift to the wife after consummation being his only obligation in such a marriage]
• **morganatically** *adverb*

morgue *noun*
• "MORG"
• a mortuary.
• [French, originally the name of a Paris mortuary]

moribund *adjective*
• "MORE a bund"
• at the point of death.
• [Latin *moribundus* from *mori* die]

Mormon *noun*
• "MORE m'n"
• a member of the Church of Jesus Christ of Latter-day Saints, a millenary religion founded in 1830 by Joseph Smith on the basis of revelations in the Book of Mormon.
• **Mormonism** *noun*

mornay *noun*
• "MORE nay"

• a cheese-flavoured white sauce.
• [named after *Mornay*, the French cook and eldest son of Joseph Voiron, 19th c. inventor of the sauce]

Moro *noun*
• "MORO"
• a member of a group of Muslim peoples of the Philippines.
• [Spanish, = 'Moor']

Moroccan *noun*
• "muh ROCKIN"
• a native or inhabitant of Morocco in NW Africa.

morocco *noun*
• "muh ROCKO"
• a fine flexible leather made (originally in Morocco) from goatskins tanned with sumac, used esp. in bookbinding and shoemaking.

morose *adjective*
• "muh ROSE" ("ROSE" rhymes with *GROSS*)
• sullen and ill-tempered.
• [Latin *morosus* peevish etc., from *mos moris* manner]
• **morosely** *adverb*
• **moroseness** *noun*

morph *verb*
• "MORF"
• alter or transform (an image) by computer.
• [extracted from METAMORPHOSIS]

morpheme *noun*
• "MORE feem"
• a morphological element considered with respect to its functional relations in a linguistic system.
• [French *morphème* from Greek *morphē* form, after PHONEME]
• **morphemic** *adjective*
• **morphemically** *adverb*

morphine *noun*
• "MORE feen"
• an analgesic and narcotic drug obtained from opium and used medicinally to relieve pain.
• [German *Morphin* & modern Latin *morphia* from *Morpheus* god of sleep]

morphogenesis *noun*
• "morfa JENNA sis"
• the development of form in organisms.
• [modern Latin from Greek *morphē* form + GENESIS]
• **morphogenetic** *adjective* "morfa juh NETTIC"
• **morphogenic** *adjective*

morphology *noun*
• "more FOLLA jee"
• the study of the forms of organisms.
• [Greek *morphē* form + *logos* word]
• **morphologic** *adjective*
• **morphological** *adjective*
• **morphologically** *adverb*
• **morphologist** *noun*

mortadella *noun*
• "morta DELLA"
• a large spiced sausage usu. made of pork and pork fat and eaten cold.
• [Italian diminutive, from Latin *murtatum* seasoned with myrtle berries]

mortar *noun*
• "MORTER"
• a mixture of lime with cement, sand, and water, used in building to bond bricks or stones.
• [Old French *mortier*, originally a vessel made of hard material, in which ingredients are pounded with a pestle, with transference from the vessel to the substance made in it, from Latin *mortarium*: partly from Low German]

mortarboard *noun*
• "MORTER bord"
• an academic cap with a stiff flat square top.
• [because of its resemblance to a board for carrying mortar]

mortgage *noun*
• "MORE gidge" (with "G" as in *GIVE*)
• an agreement by which money is lent by a bank, trust company, etc. for buying a house or other property, the property itself being the security.
• [Old French, = dead pledge, from *mort* from Latin *mortuus* dead + *gage* from Germanic (related to 'wage')]
• **mortgageable** *adjective*

mortgagee *noun*
• "more gidge EE" (with "G" as in *GIVE*)
• the creditor in a mortgage, e.g. a bank, trust company, etc.
• [as MORTGAGE]

mortgagor *noun*
• "MORE gidge or" (with "G" as in *GIVE*)
• the debtor in a mortgage.
• [as MORTGAGE]

mortician *noun*
• "more TISH'n"
• an undertaker.
• [Latin *mors mortis* death]

mortify *verb*
• "MORTA fie"
• cause (a person) to feel shamed or humiliated.
• [Old French *mortifier* from Church Latin *mortificare* kill, subdue, from *mors mortis* death]
• **mortification** *noun*
• **mortifying** *adjective*
• **mortifyingly** *adverb*

mortise *noun*
ALSO SPELLED: **mortice**
• "MORE tiss"
• a hole in a piece of wood etc. designed to receive the end of another part, esp. a tenon.
• [Old French *mortoise* from Arabic *murtazz* fixed in]
• **mortiser** *noun*

mortmain *noun*
- "MORT mane"
- the status of lands or tenements held inalienably by an ecclesiastical or other corporation.
- [Old French *mortemain* from medieval Latin *mortua manus* dead hand, prob. in allusion to impersonal ownership]

mortuary *noun*
- "MORE choo airy"
- a room or building in which dead bodies may be kept until burial or cremation.
- [Anglo-French *mortuarie* from medieval Latin *mortuarium* from Latin *mortuarius* from *mortuus* dead]

morula *noun*
- "MORE oo luh"
- a fully segmented ovum from which a blastula is formed.
- [modern Latin, diminutive of Latin *morum* mulberry]

mosaic *noun*
- "moe ZAY ick"
- a picture or pattern produced by an arrangement of small variously coloured pieces of glass or stone etc.
- [French *mosaïque* from Italian *mosaico* from medieval Latin *mosaicus, musaicus* from Greek *mous(e)ion* mosaic work, from *mousa* muse]
- **mosaicist** *noun* "moe ZAY a sist"

mosasaur *noun*
- "MOE suh sore"
- any large extinct marine reptile of the genus *Mosasaurus*, with a long slender body and flipper-like limbs.
- [modern Latin from *Mosa*, Meuse River (near which it was first discovered) + Greek *sauros* lizard]

moselle *noun*
- "moe ZELL"
- a light medium-dry white wine produced in the valley of the Mosel River in Germany.

mosey *verb*
- "MOE zee"
- walk in a leisurely or aimless manner.
- [19th c.: origin unknown]

moshav *noun*
- "moe SHOV"
- a co-operative association of Israeli smallholders.
- [Hebrew *mošāḇ*, lit. 'dwelling']

mosque *noun*
- "MOSK"
- a Muslim place of worship.
- [French *mosquée* from Italian *moschea* from Arabic *masjid*]

mosquito *noun*
- "muh SKEETO"
- any of various slender biting insects, esp. of the genus *Culex, Anopheles*, or *Aedes*, the female of which punctures the skin of humans and other animals with a long proboscis to suck their blood and transmits diseases such as malaria and encephalitis.
- [Spanish & Portuguese, diminutive of *mosca* from Latin *musca* fly]

HOMOPHONES: *Miskito*

mot *noun*
- "MOE"
- a witty saying.
- [French, = word, ultimately from Latin *muttum* uttered sound, from *muttire* murmur]

HOMOPHONES: *mow, mo, mho*

mote *noun*
- "MOTE"
- a speck of dust.
- [Old English *mot*, corresponding to Dutch *mot* dust, sawdust, of unknown origin]

HOMOPHONES: *moat*

motet *noun*
- "moe TET"
- a short sacred choral composition.
- [Old French, diminutive of *mot*: see MOT]

motherlode *noun*
- "MUTHER lode" (with "TH" as in *THIS*)
- the main vein of a system.
- ['mother' + LODE]

motif *noun*
- "moe TEEF"
- a distinctive feature or dominant idea in artistic or literary composition.
- [French from Old French *motif* from Late Latin *motivus* from *movere* move]

motile *adjective*
- "MOE tile"
- capable of motion.
- [Latin *motus* motion]
- **motility** *noun* "moe TILLA tee"

motivic *adjective*
- "MOE tiv ick"
- of or relating to a motif or motifs.
- [as MOTIF]

motley *adjective*
- "MOT lee"
- of varied character.
- [Middle English *mottelay*, perhaps ultimately related to MOTE]

motmot *noun*
- "MOT mot"
- a bird of the tropical American family Momotidae, some members of which have two long tail feathers like racquets.
- [Latin American Spanish, imitative]

motorsailer *noun*
- "MOE tur sailer"
- a boat equipped with both sails and an engine.
- ['motor' + SAILER]

motte *noun*
- "MOT"
- a mound forming the site of a castle, camp, etc.
- [Old French *mote* (as MOAT)]

moue *noun*
- "MOO"
- an expression of displeasure or sulking; a pout.
- [French]

HOMOPHONES: *moo*

mouflon *noun*
ALSO SPELLED: **moufflon**
- "MOOF lon"
- a wild mountain sheep with chestnut-brown wool, *Ovis orientalis*, found in mountainous regions from Iran to Asia Minor, and thought to be the closest relation of the domestic sheep.
- [French *mouflon* from Italian *muflone* from Romanic]

mouillé *adjective*
- "moo YAY"
- (of a consonant, esp. *ll* in Spanish or French, *gl* and *gn* in Italian, etc.) palatalized, pronounced with a sound.
- [French, = wetted, from popular Latin *molliare* soften (bread) by soaking, from Latin *mollis* soft]

mountebank *noun*
- "MOUNTA bank"
- a swindler; a charlatan.
- [Italian *montambanco* = *monta in banco* climb on bench]

mourn *verb*
- "MORN"
- feel or show deep sorrow or regret for (a dead person, a lost thing, a past event, etc.).
- [Old English *murnan*]
- **mourner** *noun*

HOMOPHONES: *morn*

mournful *adjective*
- "MORN full"
- doleful, sad, sorrowing.
- [as MOURN]
- **mournfully** *adverb*
- **mournfulness** *noun*

mourning *noun*
- "MORNING"
- the expression of deep sorrow, esp. for a loss, death, etc.
- [as MOURN]

HOMOPHONES: *morning*

mourvèdre *noun*
- "moor VEDRA"
- a variety of vine of the species *Vitis vinifera*, yielding black grapes used in winemaking, widely grown in Spain, Southern France, California, and elsewhere.
- [French, perhaps from *Murviedro*, the name of a town in Valencia, Spain, where the grape is grown]

moussaka *noun*
- "moo SOCKA"
- a Greek and eastern Mediterranean baked dish of ground meat, eggplant, etc. with white sauce.
- [modern Greek or Turkish]

mousse *noun*
- "MOOSE"
- a dessert of whipped cream, eggs, etc., usu. flavoured with fruit or chocolate.
- [French, = moss, froth]

HOMOPHONES: *moose*

mousseline *noun*
- "MOOSE leen" or "moose LEEN"
- a muslin-like fabric of silk etc.
- [French: see MUSLIN]

moustache *noun*
ALSO SPELLED: **mustache**
- "MUSS tash" or "muh STASH"
- the hair on the upper lip, esp. as left to grow by men.
- [French from Italian *mostaccio* from Greek *mustax -akos*]
- **moustached** *adjective* (also **mustached**)

Mousterian *adjective*
- "moo STEERY 'n"
- of or relating to the main culture of the middle paleolithic period, associated with Neanderthal peoples and dated to *c.*80,000–35,000 BC.
- [French *moustiérien* from *Le Moustier* a cave in SW France, where remains were found]

moxa *noun*
- "MOX uh"
- a downy substance from the dried leaves of *Artemisia moxa* etc., burned on the skin in oriental medicine as a counterirritant.
- [Japanese *mogusa* from *moe kusa* burning herb]

moxibustion *noun*
- "mox a BUSS ch'n"
- the burning of moxa on or near the skin.
- [MOXA + COMBUSTION]

moxie *noun*
- "MOXY"
- force of character, energy, ingenuity.
- [proprietary name of a soft drink]

Mozambican *noun*
- "moe zam BEEK 'n"
- a native or inhabitant of Mozambique on the east coast of southern Africa.

Mozartian *adjective*
- "mote SARTY 'n"
- relating to or characteristic of the Austrian composer W. A. Mozart (d.1791).

mozzarella *noun*
- "motsa RELLA" or "mutsa RELLA"
- a white Italian cheese originally made of buffalo milk.

• [Italian, diminutive of *mozza*, a kind of cheese, from *mozzare*, cut off]

mu *noun*
• "MYOO"
• the twelfth Greek letter (M, μ).
• [Greek]
HOMOPHONES: *mew*

mucho *adjective*
• "MOOCH oh"
• much.
• [Spanish]

mucilage *noun*
• "MYOOSA lidge"
• a solution of gum or glue in water, used as an adhesive.
• [French from Late Latin *mucilago -ginis* musty juice (MUCUS)]
• **mucilaginous** *adjective*
"myoosa LADGE 'n us"

mucopolysaccharide *noun*
• "myoo co polly SACKA ride"
• any of a group of polysaccharides whose molecules contain sugar residues and are often found as components of connective tissue.
• [as MUCUS + POLYSACCHARIDE]

mucosa *noun*
• "myoo CO suh"
• a mucous membrane.
• [modern Latin, feminine of *mucosus*: see MUCOUS]
• **mucosal** *adjective*

mucous *adjective*
• "MYOO cuss"
• of, resembling, secreting, or covered with mucus.
• [Latin *mucosus* (as MUCUS)]
• **mucosity** *noun* "myoo COSSA tee"
HOMOPHONES: *mucus*

mucro *noun*
• "MYOO crow"
• a sharp-pointed part or organ.
• [Latin *mucro -onis* sharp point]

mucus *noun*
• "MYOO cuss"
• a slimy substance, usu. not miscible with water, secreted by a mucous membrane or gland.
• [Latin]
HOMOPHONES: *mucous*

Muenster *noun*
• "MOON stur" (with "OO" as in *TOOK*)
• a fairly strong soft-ripened cheese, having a washed rind cured in a solution of brine or seasoned wine or beer.
• [*Munster* in Alsace, France]

muesli *noun*
• "MYOOZ lee"
• a breakfast food of crushed cereals (usu. oats), dried fruits, nuts, etc., eaten with milk.
• [Swiss German]

muezzin *noun*
• "moo EZZIN"
• a Muslim crier who proclaims the hours of prayer usu. from a minaret.
• [Arabic *mu'aḏḏin* participle of *'aḏḏana* proclaim]

mufti *noun*
• "MUFF tee"
• a Muslim legal expert empowered to give rulings on religious matters.
• [Arabic *muftī*, participle of *'aftā* decide a point of law]

Mughal *noun*
• "MOOG'll"
• a Mongolian.
• [Persian *muğūl* MONGOL]

mugho *noun*
ALSO SPELLED: **mugo**
• "MYOOGO" or "MOOGO"
• a dwarf pine, *Pinus mugo*, of the mountains of central and southern Europe, much used in landscaping.
• [French *mugho* from Italian *mugo*]

mugwort *noun*
• "MUG wurt" or "MUG wort"
• any of various plants of the genus *Artemisia*, esp. *A. vulgaris*, with silver-grey aromatic foliage.
• [Old English *mucgwyrt*, lit. = 'midge plant']

mujahedeen *plural noun*
ALSO SPELLED: **mujahideen**, **mujahedin**, **mujahidin**
• "mooja huh DEEN"
• guerrilla fighters in Islamic countries, esp. supporting Muslim fundamentalism.
• [Persian & Arabic *mujāhidīn* pl. of *mujāhid* one who fights a jihad]

mukluk *noun*
• "MUCK luck"
• a winter boot with a heavy rubber sole and a high fabric upper, usu. with laces.
• [Yupik *maklak* bearded seal]

muktuk *noun*
• "MUCK tuck"
• a traditional Inuit food consisting of the skin and surface blubber of a whale, esp. a beluga or narwhal, either dried, cooked, or eaten raw.
• [Inuit]

mulatto *noun*
• "moo LATTO" or "moo LOTTO"
• (historically) a person of mixed white and black parentage.
• [Spanish *mulato* young mule or mulatto, from *mulo* mule]

mulberry *noun*
• "MULL berry" or "MULLBER ee"
• any deciduous tree of the genus *Morus* (family Moraceae), esp. *M. alba*, the white mulberry, grown originally for feeding silkworms, and *M.*

rubra of eastern N America, the red mulberry, with juicy edible fruit.
• [Middle English *mol-*, *mool-*, *mulberry*, with dissimilation from *murberie* from Old English *mōrberie*, from Latin *morum*]

mulct *verb*
• "MULKT"
• extract money from by fine or taxation.
• [French *mulcter* from Latin *mulctare* from *mulcta* a fine]

muleteer *noun*
• "myoola TEER"
• a mule driver.
• [French *muletier* from *mulet* diminutive of Old French *mul* mule]

mullah *noun*
• "MULLA" or "MOOLA" (with "OO" as in *WOOL*)
• a Muslim learned in Islamic theology and sacred law.
• [Persian, Turkish, Urdu *mullā* from Arabic *mawlā*]

mullein *noun*
• "MULL'n"
• any herbaceous plant of the genus *Verbascum*, with woolly leaves and yellow flowers.
• [Old French *moleine* from Gaulish]

mullet *noun*
• "MULL it"
• any fish of the family Mullidae (the red mullet) or Mugilidae (the grey mullet), usu. with a thick body and a large blunt-nosed head, commonly used as food.
• [Old French *mulet* diminutive of Latin *mullus* red mullet, from Greek *mollos*]

mulligan *noun*
• "MULLA g'n"
• a stew made from odds and ends of food.
• [apparently from the surname *Mulligan*]

mulligatawny *noun*
• "mulla guh TAWNY"
• a highly seasoned soup originally from India.
• [Tamil *milagutannir*, lit. 'pepper water']

mullion *noun*
• "MULL y'n"
• a vertical bar dividing the panes of glass in a window.
• [prob. an altered form of Middle English *monial*, from Old French *moinel* middle, from *moien* (as MEDIAN)]
• **mullioned** *adjective*

multiaxial *adjective*
• "multy AXY 'll"
• of or involving several axes.
• [Latin *multus* much, many + AXIS]

multicellular *adjective*
• "multy SELL yuh lur"
• having or involving many cells.
• [Latin *multus* much, many + CELLULAR]
• **multicellularity** *noun*
"multy sell yuh LERRA tee"

multidisciplinary *adjective*
• "multy DISSA plin airy"
• combining or involving many separate disciplines or fields of endeavour.
• [Latin *multus* much, many + DISCIPLINE]

multifactorial *adjective*
• "multy fack TORY 'll"
• involving or dependent on a number of factors, esp. genes or causes.
• [Latin *multus* much, many + FACTORIAL]

multifarious *adjective*
• "multy FERRY us"
• many and various.
• [Latin *multifarius*]
• **multifariously** *adverb*
• **multifariousness** *noun*

multilateral *adjective*
• "multy LATTER'll"
• (of an agreement, treaty, conference, etc.) in which three or more parties participate.
• [Latin *multus* much, many + LATERAL]
• **multilateralism** *noun*
• **multilateralist** *noun*
• **multilaterally** *adverb*

multilingual *adjective*
• "multy LING gwul" or "multy LING gyoo 'll"
• in or using several languages.
• [Latin *multus* much, many + LINGUAL]
• **multilingualism** *noun*

multinomial *noun*
• "multy NO mee 'll"
• = POLYNOMIAL.
• [Latin *multus* much, many, after *binomial*]

multiparous *adjective*
• "mull TIPPER us"
• bringing forth many young at a birth.
• [Latin *multus* much, many + *-parus* -bearing, from *parere* bring forth]

multipartite *adjective*
• "multy PAR tite"
• divided into many parts.
• [Latin *multus* much, many + 'part']

multiple *adjective*
• "MULTA p'll"
• having many parts, elements, or individual components.
• [French from Late Latin *multiplus* from Latin *multiplex* from (*multus* much, many, *-plex -plicis* -fold)]
• **multiply** *adverb* "MULTA plee"

multiplicand *noun*
• "multa pluh CAND"
• a quantity to be multiplied by a multiplier.
• [medieval Latin *multiplicandus* gerundive of Latin *multiplicare* (as MULTIPLE)]

multiplicity *noun*
• "multa PLISSA tee"
• manifold variety.
• [Late Latin *multiplicitas* (as MULTIPLE)]

multiply
• "MULTA ply"
• obtain from (a number) another that is a specified number of times its value.
• [Old French *multiplier* from Latin *multiplicare* from *multi* many, *plicare* fold]
• **multiplication** *noun*
• **multiplicative** *adjective* "multa PLICKA tiv" or "multa pluh CAY tiv"
• **multiplier** *noun*

multiprocessor *noun*
• "multy PRO sesser"
• a computer capable of performing multiprocessing.
• [Latin *multus* much, many + PROCESSOR]

multiprogramming *noun*
• "multy PRO gramming"
• the execution of two or more independent programs concurrently.
• [Latin *multus* much, many + 'program']

multitudinous *adjective*
• "multa TUDE in us"
• very numerous.
• [Old French from Latin *multitudo -dinis* from *multus* many]

multivalent *adjective*
• "multy VALE 'nt"
• having or susceptible of many applications, interpretations, meanings, or values.
• [Latin *multus* much, many + VALENCE]
• **multivalence** *noun*
• **multivalency** *noun*

multivariate *adjective*
• "multy VERRY it"
• involving or having two or more variable quantities.
• [Latin *multus* much, many + VARIATE]

mummery *noun*
• "MUMMER ee"
• ridiculous ceremonial, esp. religious ritual regarded as silly or hypocritical.
• [Old French *momerie*]

mummichog *noun*
• "MUMMY chog"
• a black and silver killifish, *Fundulus heteroclitus*, common in marshy coastal waters of N America.
• [Narragansett *moammitteaug*]

mummify *verb*
• "MUMMA fie"
• embalm and preserve (a body) in the form of a mummy.
• [French *momie* from medieval Latin *mumia* from Arabic *mūmiyā* from Persian *mūm* wax]
• **mummification** *noun*
• **mummified** *adjective*

mundane *adjective*
• "mun DANE" or "MUN dane"
• dull, routine; of or pertaining to everyday life.
• [Old French *mondain* from Late Latin *mundanus* from Latin *mundus* world]
• **mundanely** *adverb*
• **mundaneness** *noun*
• **mundanity** *noun* "mun DANNA tee"

municipal *adjective*
• "myoo NISSA p'll" or "myoona SIPPLE"
• of, concerning, or operated by a municipality or its government.
• [Latin *municipalis* from *municipium* free city, from *municeps -cipis* citizen with privileges, from *munia* civic offices + *capere* take]
• **municipally** *adverb*

municipality *noun*
• "myoo nissa PALA tee"
• a city, town, or district having local government.
• [as MUNICIPAL]

munificent *adjective*
• "myoo NIFFA s'nt"
• (of a giver or a gift) splendidly generous, bountiful.
• [Latin *munificent-*, var. stem of *munificus* from *munus* gift]
• **munificence** *noun*
• **munificently** *adverb*

muniment *noun*
• "MYOONA m'nt"
• a document kept as evidence of rights or privileges etc.
• [Old French from Latin *munimentum* defence, in medieval Latin 'title deed', from *munire munit-* fortify]

munition *noun*
• "myoo NISH'n"
• military weapons, ammunition, equipment, and stores.
• [French from Latin *munitio -onis* fortification (as MUNIMENT)]

Munsee *noun*
• "MUNCY"
• a member of either of two groups of Aboriginal people living esp. in New Jersey and New York, but with a small population near St. Thomas, Ont.
• [Munsee *mán'si:w* person of Minisink Island]

muntjac *noun*
ALSO SPELLED: **muntjak**
• "MUNT jack"
• any small deer of the genus *Muntiacus* native to SE Asia, the male having tusks and small antlers.
• [local name in W Java]

muon *noun*
• "MYOO on"
• an unstable elementary particle like an electron, but with a much greater mass.
• [μ (MU), as the symbol for it]
• **muonic** *adjective*

murage *noun*
• "MYUR idge"

• a tax levied for building or repairing the walls of a town.
• [Old French *mur* from Latin *murus* wall]

muriatic *adjective*
• "myoory ATTIC"
• designating an acid formed by a solution of the colourless gas hydrogen chloride in water.
• [Latin *muriaticus* from *muria* brine]
• **muriate** *noun* "MYOORY it" or "MYOORY ate"

murine *adjective*
• "MYOOR ine"
• of or like a mouse or mice.
• [Latin *murinus* from *mus muris* mouse]

murmur *noun*
• "MUR mur"
• a softly spoken or nearly inarticulate utterance.
• [Old French *murmurer* from Latin *murmurare*: compare Greek *mormurō* (of water) roar, Sanskrit *marmaras* noisy]
• **murmurer** *noun*
• **murmuring** *adjective*
• **murmurous** *adjective*

murrain *noun*
• "MUR in"
• an infectious disease of cattle, carried by parasites.
• [Anglo-French *moryn*, Old French *morine* from *morir* from Latin *mori* die]

murre *noun*
• "MUR"
• an auk or guillemot.
• [16th c.: origin unknown]
HOMOPHONES: *myrrh*

murrelet *noun*
• "MUR lit"
• any of several small auks of the N Pacific, of the genera *Brachyramphus* and *Synthliboramphus*.
• [as MURRE]

Muscadet *noun*
• "MUSKA day"
• a white wine from the Loire region of France.
• [French from *muscade* nutmeg, from *musc* musk]

muscadine *noun*
• "MUSKA din" or "MUSKA dine"
• any of a group of species and varieties of wine grape native to Mexico and the southeastern US, typically having thick skins and a musky flavour.
• [prob. alteration of MUSCATEL]

muscarine *noun*
• "MUSKER in"
• a poisonous alkaloid from the fungus *Amanita muscaria*.
• [Latin *muscarius* from *musca* fly]
• **muscarinic** *adjective*

muscat *noun*
• "MUSS cat"
• a variety of white, red, or black grape with a musky scent, grown in warm climates for wine or raisins or as table grapes.
• [French from Provençal *muscat muscade* (adjective) from *musc* musk]

muscatel *noun*
• "muska TELL"
• = MUSCAT.
• [Old French from Provençal diminutive of *muscat*: see MUSCAT]

muscle *noun*
• "MUSS'll"
• a fibrous tissue with the ability to contract, producing movement in or maintaining the position of an animal body.
• [French from Latin *musculus* diminutive of *mus* mouse, from the fancied mouselike form of some muscles]
• **muscled** *adjective*
• **muscleless** *adjective*
• **muscly** *adjective*
HOMOPHONES: *mussel*

muscleman *noun*
• "MUSS'll man"
• a man with highly developed muscles.
• [as MUSCLE]
HOMOPHONES: *Mussulman*

musclewood *noun*
• "MUSS'll wood"
• a tree of eastern N America, *Carpinus caroliniana*, with strong wood and smoothly ridged bark.
• [as MUSCLE + 'wood']

muscovado *noun*
• "muska VODDO"
• an unrefined sugar made from the juice of sugar cane by evaporation and draining off the molasses.
• [Spanish *mascabado* (sugar) of the lowest quality]

Muscovite *noun*
• "MUSKA vite"
• a native or citizen of Moscow, Russia.
• [modern Latin *Muscovita* from *Muscovia* from Russian *Moskva* Moscow]

muscular *adjective*
• "MUSS kyuh lur"
• having well-developed muscles.
• [earlier *musculous* (as MUSCLE)]
• **muscularity** *noun* "muss kyuh LERRA tee"
• **muscularly** *adverb*

musculature *noun*
• "MUSS kyoo luh chur"
• the muscular system of a body or organ.
• [French from Latin (as MUSCLE)]

musculoskeletal *adjective*
• "muss kyoo lo SKELLA t'll"
• of or relating to the musculature and skeleton together.
• [as MUSCLE + SKELETAL]

museology *noun*
• "muze ee OLLA jee"
• the science or practice of organizing and managing museums.
• [Latin *museum* from Greek *mouseion* seat of the Muses + *logos* word]
• **museological** *adjective*
• **museologist** *noun*

musette *noun*
• "myoo ZET"
• a kind of small bagpipe with bellows, common in the French court in the 17th–18th c.
• [Old French, diminutive of *muse* bagpipe]

musicale *noun*
• "myoozy CAL"
• a concert or musical social evening.
• [French feminine adjective from Old French *musique* from Latin *musica* from Greek *mousikē* (*tekhnē* art) of the Muses]

muskeg *noun*
• "MUSS keg"
• a swamp or bog in northern N America, consisting of a mixture of water and partly dead vegetation, often covered by a layer of sphagnum or other mosses.
• [Cree *maske:k*]

muskellunge *noun*
• "MUSKA lunge"
• a large N American pike, *Esox masquinongy*, esp. of the Great Lakes.
• [Algonquian]

muskie *noun*
• "MUSKY"
• a muskellunge.
• [abbreviation]
HOMOPHONES: *musky*

Muskogean *noun*
• "muska JEE 'n" or "muss KO jee 'n"
• a language family of southeastern N America, including Creek, Seminole, Choctaw, and Chickasaw.
• [as MUSKOGEE]

Muskogee *noun*
• "muss KO jee"
• a member of a N American Aboriginal people forming part of the Creek Confederacy.
• [Creek *ma:skó:ki*]

muslin *noun*
• "MUZZ lin"
• a cotton or cotton blend fabric of a plain weave.
• [French *mousseline* from Italian *mussolina* from *Mussolo* Mosul in Iraq, where it was made]

mussel *noun*
• "MUSS'll"
• any bivalve mollusc of the genus *Mytilus*, living in sea water and often used for food.
• [Old English *mus(c)le* & Middle Low German *mussel*, ultimately related to Latin *musculus* (as MUSCLE)]
HOMOPHONES: *muscle*

mustachio *noun*
• "muh STASHY oh"
• a moustache, esp. a large one.
• [Spanish *mostacho* & Italian *mostaccio* (as MOUSTACHE)]
• **mustachioed** *adjective*

mustelid *noun*
• "MUSTA lid" or "muss TELLID"
• a mammal of the family *Mustelidae*, including weasels, otters, badgers, skunks, martens, etc.
• [modern Latin *Mustelidae* from Latin *mustela* weasel]

mutable *adjective*
• "MUTE a bull"
• liable or subject to change or alteration.
• [Latin *mutabilis* from *mutare* change]
• **mutability** *noun*

mutagen *noun*
• "MUTE a j'n"
• an agent causing or promoting mutation, e.g. radiation.
• [as MUTABLE + GENESIS]
• **mutagenesis** *noun*
• **mutagenic** *adjective*
• **mutagenicity** *noun* "mute a juh NISSA tee"
• **mutagenized** *adjective* (also esp. *Brit.* **-ised**)

mutant *adjective*
• "MYOO t'nt"
• resulting from mutation.
• [Latin *mutant-* participle from *mutare* change]

mutilate *verb*
• "MUTE 'll ate"
• injure or damage (a person or animal or a part of the body) very severely, e.g. by removal of a limb or organ.
• [Latin *mutilare* from *mutilus* maimed]
• **mutilation** *noun*
• **mutilator** *noun*

mutiny *noun*
• "MUTE 'n ee"
• an open revolt against constituted authority, esp. by soldiers or sailors against their officers.
• [obsolete *mutine* from French *mutin* rebellious, from *muete* movement, ultimately from Latin *movēre* move]
• **mutineer** *noun* "mute 'n EER"
• **mutinous** *adjective*
• **mutinously** *adverb*

Mutsu *noun*
• "MUT soo"
• a large yellow or greenish-yellow cooking and eating apple.
• [Japanese]

mutual *adjective*
• "MYOO choo 'll"
• (of feelings, actions, etc.) experienced or done

by each of two or more parties with reference to the other or others; reciprocal.
• [Old French *mutuel* from Latin *mutuus* mutual, borrowed, related to *mutare* change]
• **mutuality** *noun*
• **mutually** *adverb*
HOMOPHONES: *mutuel, mutule*

mutualism *noun*
• "MYOO choo 'll izm"
• the doctrine that mutual dependence is necessary to social well-being.
• [as MUTUAL]
• **mutualist** *noun*
• **mutualistic** *adjective*

mutuel *noun*
• "MYOO choo 'll"
• a form of betting in which those backing the first three places divide the losers' stakes (less the operator's commission).
• [abbreviation of PARIMUTUEL]
HOMOPHONES: *mutule, mutual*

mutule *noun*
• "MYOO chool"
• a block derived from the ends of wooden beams projecting under a Doric cornice.
• [French from Latin *mutulus*]
HOMOPHONES: *mutuel, mutual*

muumuu *noun*
• "MOO moo"
• a woman's usu. brightly coloured and patterned loose-fitting dress.
• [Hawaiian]

muzhik *noun*
ALSO SPELLED: **moujik**
• "MOO zhick"
• a Russian peasant.
• [Russian *muzhik*]

myalgia *noun*
• "my AL juh"
• a pain in a muscle or group of muscles.
• [modern Latin from Greek *mus* muscle + Greek *algia* from *algos* pain]
• **myalgic** *adjective*

myasthenia *noun*
• "my us THEENY uh"
• a condition causing abnormal weakness of certain muscles.
• [modern Latin from Greek *mus* muscle: compare ASTHENIA]
• **myasthenic** *adjective* "my us THENNIC"

mycelium *noun*
• "my SEELY um"
• the vegetative part of a fungus, consisting of microscopic threadlike hyphae.
• [modern Latin from Greek *mukēs* mushroom, after EPITHELIUM]
• **mycelial** *adjective*

Mycenaean *adjective*
• "my suh NEE 'n"
• of or relating to the late Bronze Age civilization in Greece depicted in the Homeric poems and represented by finds at Mycenae and elsewhere.

mycobacterium *noun*
• "mike oh back TEERY um"
• any of various Gram-positive, aerobic, filament-forming bacteria of the genus *Mycobacterium* or the family Mycobacteriaceae, including the causative agents of tuberculosis and leprosy.
• [Greek *mukēs* fungus, mushroom + BACTERIA]
• **mycobacterial** *adjective*

mycology *noun*
• "my COLLA jee"
• the study of fungi.
• [Greek *mukēs* fungus, mushroom + *logos* word]
• **mycological** *adjective*
• **mycologically** *adverb*
• **mycologist** *noun*

mycoplasma *noun*
• "mike oh PLAZMA"
• any of a group of mainly parasitic micro-organisms smaller than bacteria and without a cell wall.
• [Greek *mukēs* fungus, mushroom + PLASMA]

mycorrhiza *noun*
• "mike a RIZE uh"
• a symbiotic association of a fungus and the roots of a plant.
• [Greek *mukēs* fungus, mushroom + *rhiza* root]
• **mycorrhizal** *adjective*

mycosis *noun*
• "my CO sis"
• any disease caused by a fungus, e.g. ringworm.
• [Greek *mukēs* fungus, mushroom]
• **mycotic** *adjective* "my COTTIC"

mycotoxin *noun*
• "mike a TOXIN"
• any toxic substance produced by a fungus.
• [Greek *mukēs* fungus, mushroom + TOXIN]

mydriasis *noun*
• "muh DRY a sis"
• excessive dilation of the pupil of the eye.
• [Latin from Greek *mudriasis*]

myelin *noun*
• "MY a lin"
• a white substance which forms a sheath around certain nerve fibres.
• [Greek *muelos* marrow]
• **myelinated** *adjective*
• **myelination** *noun*

myelitis *noun*
• "my a LITE iss"
• inflammation of the spinal cord.
• [modern Latin from Greek *muelos* marrow + Greek *-itis*, forming feminine of adjectives in *-itēs* (with *nosos* 'disease' implied)]

myeloid *adjective*
• "MY a loid"
• of or relating to bone marrow or the spinal cord.
• [Greek *muelos* marrow]

myeloma *noun*
• "my a LO muh"
• a malignant tumour of the bone marrow.
• [modern Latin, as MYELITIS + *-oma* as CARCINOMA]

mylodon *noun*
• "MY luh d'n"
• an extinct gigantic ground sloth of the genus *Mylodon*, with cylindrical teeth, remains of which are found in deposits formed during the ice age of the Pleistocene epoch in S America.
• [modern Latin from Greek *mulē* mill, molar + *odous odontos* tooth]

mynah *noun*
ALSO SPELLED: **myna**
• "MY nuh"
• any of various SE Asian starlings, esp. *Gracula religiosa*, able to mimic the human voice.
• [Hindi *mainā*]

myocardium *noun*
• "my oh CARDY um"
• the muscular tissue of the heart.
• [Greek *mus muos* muscle + *kardia* heart]
• **myocardial** *adjective*
• **myocarditis** *noun* "my oh car DITE iss"

myofibril *noun*
• "my oh FIE brill"
• any of the elongated contractile threads found in striated muscle cells.
• [Greek *mus muos* muscle + FIBRIL]

myogenic *adjective*
• "my a JENNIC"
• originating in muscle tissue.
• [Greek *mus muos* muscle + GENESIS]

myoglobin *noun*
• "my oh GLOW bin"
• an oxygen-carrying protein containing iron and found in muscle cells.
• [Greek *mus muos* muscle + GLOBIN]

myology *noun*
• "my OLLA jee"
• the study of the structure and function of muscles.
• [Greek *mus muos* muscle + *logos* word]

myopia *noun*
• "my OH pee uh"
• short-sightedness.
• [modern Latin from French from Late Latin *myops* from Greek *muōps* from *muō* shut + *ōps* eye]
• **myopic** *adjective* "my OPPIC"
• **myopically** *adverb*

myosin *noun*
• "MY oh sin"
• a protein which with actin forms the contractile filaments of muscle.
• [Greek *mus muos* muscle]

myotonia *noun*
• "my a TONY uh"
• an inability to relax or delay in relaxing a voluntary muscle.
• [Greek *mus muos* muscle + *tonos* tone]
• **myotonic** *adjective*

myriad *noun*
• "MEERY ad"
• an indefinitely great number.
• [Late Latin *mirias miriad-* from Greek *murias -ados* from *murioi* 10,000]

myriapod *noun*
• "MEERY a pod"
• any land-living arthropod of the group Myriapoda, with numerous leg-bearing segments, e.g. centipedes and millipedes.
• [modern Latin *Myriapoda* (as MYRIAD, Greek *pous podos* foot)]

myrmidon *noun*
• "MURMA don"
• an unquestioning follower or servant etc.
• [Latin *Myrmidones* (pl.) from Greek *Murmidones*, a warlike people who went with Achilles to Troy]

myrobalan *noun*
• "my ROBBA l'n"
• a tree, *Prunus cerasifera*, native to SW Asia, with solitary white flowers and red fruits.
• [French *myrobolan* or Latin *myrobalanum* from Greek *murobalanos* from *muron* unguent + *balanos* acorn]

myrrh *noun*
• "MUR"
• a gum resin from several trees of the genus *Commiphora* used, esp. in the Near East, in perfumery, medicine, incense, etc.
• [Old English *myrra, myrre* from Latin *myrr(h)a* from Greek *murra*, of Semitic origin]
• **myrrhic** *adjective*
• **myrrhy** *adjective*
HOMOPHONES: *murre*

myrtle *noun*
• "MURTLE"
• an evergreen shrub of the genus *Myrtus* with aromatic foliage and white flowers, esp. *M. communis*, bearing purple-black ovoid berries.
• [medieval Latin *myrtilla, -us* diminutive of Latin *myrta, myrtus* from Greek *murtos*]

mystery *noun*
• "MISTER ee"
• a secret, hidden, or inexplicable matter.
• [Old French *mistere* or Latin *mysterium* from Greek *mustērion*, related to MYSTIC]
• **mysterious** *adjective* "miss TEERY us"
• **mysteriously** *adverb*
• **mysteriousness** *noun*

mystic *noun*
• "MISTIC"
• a person who seeks by contemplation and self-surrender to obtain unity or identity with or absorption into the Deity or the ultimate reality, or who believes in the spiritual apprehension of truths that are beyond the understanding.
• [Old French *mystique* or Latin *mysticus* from Greek *mustikos* from *mustēs* initiated person, from *muō* close the eyes or lips, initiate]
• **mystical** *adjective*
• **mystically** *adverb*
• **mysticism** *noun* "MISTA sizm"

mystify *verb*
• "MISTA fie"
• bewilder, confuse.
• [French *mystifier* (as MYSTIC or MYSTERY)]
• **mystification** *noun*
• **mystifying** *adjective*
• **mystifyingly** *adverb*

mystique *noun*
• "miss TEEK"
• an atmosphere of mystery and importance evoking admiration, surrounding some activity or person; charisma.
• [French (as MYSTIC)]

myth *noun*
• "MITH"
• a traditional narrative usu. involving supernatural or imaginary persons and embodying popular ideas on natural or social phenomena etc.
• [modern Latin *mythus* from Late Latin *mythos* from Greek *muthos*]
• **mythic** *adjective*
• **mythical** *adjective*
• **mythically** *adverb*

mythicize *verb*
ALSO SPELLED: esp. *Brit.* **-ise**
• "MITHA size"
• treat (a story etc.) as a myth; interpret mythically.
• [as MYTH]
• **mythicization** *noun* (also esp. *Brit.* **-isation**)

mythmaker *noun*
• "MITH maker"
• a creator of myths or folklore.
• [as MYTH + 'maker']
• **mythmaking** *noun*

mythography *noun*
• "mith OGGRA fee"
• a collection of myths.
• [as MYTH + Greek *graphia* thing written]
• **mythographer** *noun*

mythology *noun*
• "mith OLLA jee"
• a body of myths.
• [as MYTH + Greek *logos* word]
• **mythologic** *adjective*
• **mythological** *adjective*
• **mythologically** *adverb*
• **mythologist** *noun*
• **mythologization** *noun* (also esp. *Brit.* **-isation**)
• **mythologize** *verb* (also esp. *Brit.* **-ise**)
• **mythologizer** *noun* (also esp. *Brit.* **-iser**)

mythomania *noun*
• "mith oh MAINY uh"
• an abnormal tendency to exaggerate or tell lies.
• [as MYTH + MANIA]
• **mythomaniac** *noun*

mythopoeia *noun*
• "mith oh PEE uh"
• the making of myths.
• [Greek *muthos* myth + *poieō* make]
• **mythopoeic** *adjective*
• **mythopoetic** *adjective* "mith oh poe ETTIC"

mythos *noun*
• "MITH oss" or "MY thoss"
• a myth; a body of myths.
• [Late Latin: see MYTH]

myxedema *noun*
ALSO SPELLED: esp. *Brit.* **myxoedema**
• "mix a DEEMA"
• a syndrome caused by hypothyroidism, resulting in thickening of the skin, weight gain, mental dullness, loss of energy, and sensitivity to cold.
• [Greek *muxa* mucus + EDEMA]

myxoma *noun*
• "mix OH muh"
• a benign tumour of mucous or gelatinous tissue.
• [modern Latin (Greek *muxa* mucus + *-oma* as CARCINOMA)]
• **myxomatous** *adjective*

myxomatosis *noun*
• "mix oh muh TOE sis"
• an infectious usu. fatal viral disease in rabbits, causing swelling of the mucous membranes.
• [as MYXOMA]

myxomycete *noun*
• "mix oh MY seet"
• a slime-like aggregate of small simple organisms that reproduce by means of spores, found esp. in damp habitats on land.
• [Greek *muxa* mucus + *-mycetes* from *mukēs -ētos* mushroom]

myxovirus *noun*
• "MIX oh vie russ"
• any of a group of viruses including the influenza virus.
• [Greek *muxa* mucus + VIRUS]

Nn

nabob *noun*
• "NAY bob"
• a very rich or influential person.
• [Portuguese *nababo* or Spanish *nabab*, from Urdu (as NAWAB)]

Nabokovian *adjective*
• "nabba CO vee 'n"
• of or relating to the Russian-American novelist V. Nabokov (d.1977).

nacelle *noun*
• "nuh SELL"
• a streamlined housing or tank for something on the outside of an aircraft or motor vehicle.
• [French, from Late Latin *navicella* diminutive of Latin *navis* ship]

naches *noun*
• "NUCK huss"
• pride or gratification, esp. at the achievements of one's children.
• [Yiddish *nakhes*, from Hebrew *naḥaṯ* contentment]

nacho *noun*
• "NOTCH oh"
• a tortilla chip topped with cheese, salsa, peppers, etc. and broiled.
• [20th c.: origin uncertain, possibly from Mexican Spanish *Nacho*, pet form of the male forename Ignacio (with reference to the supposed creator of the dish)]

nacre *noun*
• "NAY kur"
• a smooth iridescent substance forming the inner layer of the shell of some molluscs.
• [French]
• **nacreous** *adjective* "NAY cree us"

nada *noun*
• "NODDA"
• nothing.
• [Spanish]

nadir *noun*
• "NAY deer"
• the part of the celestial sphere directly below an observer.
• [Old French from Arabic *naẓīr* (*as-samt*) opposite (to the zenith)]

naga *noun*
• "NOGGA"
• (in Hinduism) a member of a race of semi-divine creatures, half-snake half-human.
• [Sanskrit, = serpent]

Nahuatl *noun*
• "naw WOT'll" or "NAW wot'll"
• a member of a group of Aboriginal peoples of S Mexico and Central America, including the Aztecs.
• [Spanish from Nahuatl]
• **Nahuatlan** *adjective*

naiad *noun*
• "NIE ad"
• a water nymph.
• [Latin *Naïas Naïad-* from Greek *Naias -ados* from *naō* flow]

nainsook *noun*
• "NANE sook" (with "OO" as in *HOOK*)
• a fine soft cotton fabric, used esp. for baby clothes.
• [Hindi *nainsukh* from *nain* eye + *sukh* pleasure]

naira *noun*
• "NIE ruh"
• the chief monetary unit of Nigeria, equal to 100 kobo.
• [contraction of *Nigeria*]

naive *adjective*
• "nie EEV"
• artless; innocent; unaffected.
• [French, feminine of *naïf* from Latin *nativus* native]
• **naively** *adverb*
• **naiveness** *noun*

naïveté *noun*
ALSO SPELLED: **naivety**
• "nie eeva TAY" or "nie EEVA tee"
• the state or quality of being naive.
• [French (as NAIVE)]

nakfa *noun*
• "NACK fuh"
• the basic monetary unit of Eritrea, equal to one hundred cents.
• [*Nakfa*, the name of the town where the country's armed struggle against the Ethiopian regime was launched]

Nakota *noun*
• "nuh CO tuh"
• a member of an Aboriginal people living in S Saskatchewan and NE Montana; an Assiniboine.
• [Sioux, = 'allies']

naloxone *noun*
• "nuh LOX own"
• a synthetic drug, similar to morphine, which blocks opiate receptors in the nervous system.
• [contraction of *N-allylnoroxymorphone*]

naltrexone *noun*
• "nal TRECK sown"
• a synthetic drug, similar to morphine, which blocks opiate receptors in the nervous system and is used chiefly in the treatment of heroin addiction.
• [contraction of *N-allylnoroxymorphone*, with the insertion of the arbitrary element *-trex-*]

Nama *noun*
• "NOMMA"
• a member of a people of South Africa and Namibia.
• [Nama]

Namibian *noun*
• "nuh MIBBY 'n"
• a native or inhabitant of Namibia in southern Africa.

Nanaimoite *noun*
• "nuh NIE mo ite"
• a resident of Nanaimo, BC.

nanometre *noun*
ALSO SPELLED: **nanometer**
• "NANNO meeter"
• one billionth of a metre.
• [Latin *nano* from Greek *nanos* dwarf + METRE]

nanosecond *noun*
• "NANNO seck'nd"
• one billionth of a second.
• [Latin *nano* from Greek *nanos* dwarf + 'second']

nanotechnology *noun*
• "nanno teck NOLLA jee"
• the branch of technology that deals with dimensions and tolerances of less than 100 nanometres, esp. the manipulation of individual atoms and molecules.
• [Latin *nano* from Greek *nanos* dwarf + TECHNOLOGY]
• **nanotechnological** *adjective*
• **nanotechnologist** *noun*

napalm *noun*
• "NAY pom"
• a jellied gasoline produced from naphthenic acid, other fatty acids, and aluminum, used in incendiary bombs.
• [NAPHTHENE + PALMITIC]

napery *noun*
• "NAY purr ee"
• household linen, esp. table linen.
• [Old French *naperie* from *nape* from Latin *mappa* napkin]

naphtha *noun*
• "NAP thuh" or "NAF thuh"
• a colourless, flammable petroleum distillate used as a fuel and solvent.
• [Latin from Greek, = 'flammable volatile liquid issuing from the earth']

naphthalene *noun*
• "NAF thuh leen" or "NAP thuh leen"
• a white crystalline aromatic substance produced by the distillation of coal tar and used in mothballs and the manufacture of dyes etc.
• [NAPHTHA + '-ene' forming names of unsaturated hydrocarbons containing a double bond, from Greek *-ēnos*, adjective suffix denoting origin or source]
• **naphthalic** *adjective* "naf THALIC" or "nap THALIC"

naphthene *noun*
• "NAF theen" or "NAP theen"
• any of a group of cycloalkanes obtained from petroleum.
• [NAPHTHA + '-ene' forming names of unsaturated hydrocarbons containing a double bond, from Greek *-ēnos*, adjective suffix denoting origin or source]
• **naphthenic** *adjective*

napoleon *noun*
• "nuh POLEY 'n"
• a dessert comprised of thin layers of puff pastry and a filling of cream, custard, etc.
• [French *napoléon* from *Napoléon*, name of 19th-c. French emperors]

Napoleonic *adjective*
• "nuh poley ONNIC"
• of, relating to, or characteristic of the French Emperor Napoleon I (d.1821) or his time.

nappe *noun*
• "NAP"
• a sheet of rock that has moved sideways over neighbouring strata, usu. as a result of overthrust.
• [French *nappe* tablecloth]
HOMOPHONES: *nap*, *knap*

naproxen *noun*
• "nuh PROX 'n"
• an anti-inflammatory analgesic substance given orally as a painkiller and in the treatment of some forms of arthritis.
• [NAPHTHALENE + PROPIONIC + OXYGEN]

narcissism *noun*
• "NARSA sizm"
• excessive or erotic interest in oneself, one's physical features, etc.
• [*Narcissus*, mythological youth who fell in love with his own reflection]
• **narcissist** *noun*
• **narcissistic** *adjective*

narcissus *noun*
- "nar SISS us"
- any bulbous plant of the genus *Narcissus*, esp. *N. poeticus* bearing a heavily scented single flower with an undivided corona edged with crimson and yellow.
- [Latin from Greek *narkissos*, perhaps from *narkē* numbness, with reference to its narcotic effects]

narcolepsy *noun*
- "NARKA lepsy"
- a disease with fits of sleepiness and drowsiness.
- [Greek *narkē* numbness, after EPILEPSY]
- **narcoleptic** *adjective*

narcosis *noun*
- "nar CO sis"
- a state of drowsiness or unconsciousness induced by a narcotic drug.
- [Greek *narkōsis* from *narkoun* make numb]

narcoterrorism *noun*
- "narco TARE ur izm"
- terrorism associated with illicit drugs, esp. directed against law enforcement.
- [NARCOTIC + TERRORISM]
- **narcoterrorist** *noun*

narcotic *adjective*
- "nar COTTIC"
- (of a substance) inducing drowsiness, sleep, stupor, or insensibility.
- [Old French *narcotique* or medieval Latin from Greek *narkōtikos* (as NARCOSIS)]
- **narcotically** *adverb*
- **narcotize** *verb* (also esp. *Brit.* **-ise**)
"NARKA tize"

nardoo *noun*
- "nar DOO"
- a clover-like plant, *Marsilea drummondii*, native to Australia.
- [various Aboriginal languages *ngardu*, *nhaadu*]

nares *plural noun*
- "NARE eez"
- the nostrils.
- [pl. of Latin *naris*]

narghile *noun*
ALSO SPELLED: **nargileh**
- "NAR g'll ee"
- an oriental tobacco pipe with the smoke drawn through water; a hookah.
- [Persian *nārgileh* (*nārgil* coconut)]

Narragansett *noun*
- "narra GAN set"
- an Algonquian language of Rhode Island, now virtually extinct.
- [Algonquian, = people of the small point (of land)]

narrate *verb*
- "NARE ate" or "nuh RATE"
- give a continuous story or account of.
- [Latin *narrare narrat-*]
- **narratable** *adjective*
- **narration** *noun*
- **narrator** *noun*
- **narratorial** *adjective*

narrative *noun*
- "NERRA tiv"
- a spoken or written account of connected events in order of happening.
- [as NARRATE]
- **narratively** *adverb*

narratology *noun*
- "nerra TOLLA jee"
- the branch of knowledge that deals with the structure and function of narrative.
- [as NARRATE + Greek *logos* word]
- **narratological** *adjective*
- **narratologist** *noun*

narthex *noun*
- "NAR thex"
- a lobby inside the main entrance to a church building.
- [Latin from Greek *narthēx*]

narwhal *noun*
- "NAR w'll"
- a white Arctic whale, *Monodon monoceros*, the male of which has a long straight spirally fluted tusk developed from one of its teeth.
- [Dutch *narwal* from Danish *narhval* from *hval* whale: compare Old Norse *náhvalr* (perhaps from *nár* corpse, with reference to its skin colour)]

nary *adjective*
- "NERRY"
- not a; no.
- [from *ne'er (never) a*]

nasal *adjective*
- "NAZE'll"
- of, for, or relating to the nose.
- [French *nasal* or medieval Latin *nasalis* from Latin *nasus* nose]
- **nasality** *noun*
- **nasalization** *noun* (also esp. *Brit.* **-isation**)
- **nasalize** *verb* (also esp. *Brit.* **-ise**)
- **nasally** *adverb*

nascent *adjective*
- "NAY s'nt" or "NASS'nt"
- just beginning to be; not yet mature.
- [Latin *nasci nascent-* be born]
- **nascency** *noun*

naseberry *noun*
- "NAZE berry"
- a large tropical American evergreen tree, *Manilkara zapota*, with edible fruit and durable wood, and sap from which chicle is obtained; a sapodilla.
- [Spanish & Portuguese *néspera* medlar, from Latin (see MEDLAR): assimilated to 'berry']

Naskapi *noun*
- "nuh SKAPPY"

• a member of an Innu people living along the north shores of the Gulf of St. Lawrence and the St. Lawrence River.
• [Naskapi]

nasogastric *adjective*
• "nay zo GAS trick"
• supplying the stomach via the nose.
• [NASAL + GASTRIC]

nasturtium *noun*
• "nuh STUR sh'm"
• a trailing plant, *Tropaeolum majus*, with rounded edible leaves and bright orange, yellow, or red flowers.
• [Latin, apparently from *naris* nose + *torquere* to twist]

natal *adjective*
• "NATE 'll"
• of or pertaining to one's birth.
• [Latin *natalis* from *nasci nat-* be born]

nates *plural noun*
• "NAY teez"
• the buttocks.
• [Latin]

nativity *noun*
• "nuh TIVVA tee"
• the birth of Christ.
• [Late Latin *nativitas* from Latin *nasci nat-* be born]

natron *noun*
• "NAY tron" or "NAY trun"
• a mineral form of hydrated sodium salts found in dried lake beds.
• [French from Spanish *natrón* from Arabic *naṭrūn* from Greek *nitron* NITRE]

naturopathy *noun*
• "natch ur OPPA thee" or "nay chur OPPA thee" (with "TH" as in *THIN*)
• the treatment of disease etc. without drugs, usu. involving diet, exercise, massage, etc.
• ['nature' from Latin *natura*, from *nasci nat-* be born + Greek *patheia* suffering]
• **naturopath** *noun* "NATCH ur a path"
• **naturopathic** *adjective*

naughty *adjective*
• "NOTTY"
• (esp. of children) disobedient; badly behaved.
• [Middle English from *naught* nothing]
• **naughtily** *adverb*
• **naughtiness** *noun*
HOMOPHONES: *knotty, knottiness, noddy*

nauplius *noun*
• "NOPPLEE us"
• the first larval stage of some crustaceans.
• [Latin, = a kind of shellfish, or from Greek *Nauplios* son of Poseidon, god of the sea]

Nauruan *noun*
• "NOW roo 'n"
• a native or inhabitant of Nauru in the SW Pacific Ocean.

nausea *noun*
• "NOZZY uh" or "NOZH uh"
• a feeling of sickness with an inclination to vomit.
• [Latin from Greek *nausia* seasickness, from *naus* ship]
• **nauseate** *verb* "NOZZY ate"
• **nauseated** *adjective*
• **nauseating** *adjective*
• **nauseatingly** *adverb*

nauseous *adjective*
• "NOSH us" or "NOZH us" or "NOZZY us"
• affected with nausea, sick.
• [as NAUSEA]

nautch *noun*
• "NOTCH"
• a performance of professional Indian dancing girls.
• [Urdu (Hindi) *nāch* from Prakrit *nachcha* from Sanskrit *nṛitja* dancing]
HOMOPHONES: *notch*

nautical *adjective*
• "NOTTA k'll"
• of or concerning sailors or ships; naval; maritime.
• [French *nautique* or from Latin *nauticus* from Greek *nautikos* from *nautēs* sailor from *naus* ship]
• **nautically** *adverb*

nautilus *noun*
• "NOT'll us"
• any cephalopod of the genus *Nautilus* with a light brittle spiral shell.
• [Latin from Greek *nautilos*, lit. sailor (as NAUTICAL)]

Navajo *noun*
ALSO SPELLED: **Navaho**
• "NAVVA hoe"
• a member of an Athapaskan people of Arizona, Utah, and New Mexico.
• [Spanish, = pueblo]

naval *adjective*
• "NAY v'll"
• of, in, for, etc. the navy or a navy.
• [Latin *navalis* from *navis* ship]
HOMOPHONES: *navel*

navarin *noun*
• "nav a RÃ" (with a nasal *A*)
• a casserole of mutton or lamb with vegetables.
• [French, possibly after the battle of *Navarino* (1827)]

navel *noun*
• "NAY v'll"
• a rounded depression in the centre of the belly caused by the detachment of the umbilical cord; the umbilicus.
• [Old English *nafela* from Germanic]
HOMOPHONES: *naval*

navicular *adjective*
• "nuh VICK yuh lur"
• boat-shaped.
• [Latin *navicula* diminutive of *navis* ship]

navigable *adjective*
• "NAVVA guh bull"
• (of a river, the sea, etc.) affording a passage for ships.
• [as NAVIGATE]
• **navigability** *noun*

navigate *verb*
• "NAVVA gate"
• manage or direct the course of (a ship, aircraft, etc.).
• [Latin *navigare*, from *navis* ship + *agere* drive]
• **navigation** *noun*
• **navigational** *adjective*
• **navigator** *noun*

nawab *noun*
• "nuh WAB" or "nuh WOB"
• the title of a governor or nobleman in India.
• [Urdu *nawwāb* pl. from Arabic *nā'ib* deputy: compare NABOB]

Naxalite *noun*
• "NAX'll ite"
• (in the Indian subcontinent) a member of an armed revolutionary group advocating Maoist communism.
• [from *Naxal(bari)* the name of an area of West Bengal, India]

Nazarene *noun*
• "NAZZA reen" or "nazza REEN"
• a native or inhabitant of Nazareth.
• [Greek *Nazarēnos*, from *Nazaret* Nazareth, Galilean childhood home of Jesus]

Nazirite *noun*
ALSO SPELLED: **Nazarite**
• "NAZZA rite"
• a Hebrew who had taken certain vows of abstinence; an ascetic.
• [Late Latin *Nazaraeus* from Hebrew *nāzīr* from *nāzar* to separate or consecrate oneself]

Ndebele *noun*
• "unda BEELY" or "unda BAY lee"
• a member of a Nguni people.
• [the name in the Nguni languages]

Neanderthal *adjective*
• "nee ANDER tholl" or "nee ANDER toll" (with "OLL" as in *DOLL*)
• of or belonging to the type of human widely distributed in paleolithic Europe, with a retreating forehead and massive brow ridges.
• [*Neanderthal*, a region in Germany where remains were found]

neap *noun*
• "NEEP"
• a tide just after the first and third quarters of the moon when there is least difference between high and low water.
• [Old English *nēpflōd*, of unknown origin]
HOMOPHONES: *neep*

Neapolitan *noun*
• "nee a POLLA t'n"
• a native or citizen of Naples in Italy.
• [Latin *Neapolitanus* from Latin *Neapolis* Naples, from Greek from *neos* new + *polis* city]

Nearctic *adjective*
• "nee ARK tick" or "nee AR tick"
• of or relating to the Arctic and the temperate parts of N America as a zoogeographical region.
• [Greek *neos* new + ARCTIC]

Nebbiolo *noun*
• "nebby OH lo"
• a black wine grape grown in Piedmont in northern Italy.
• [Italian]

nebuchadnezzar *noun*
• "neb oo k'd NEZZER" or "neb yoo k'd NEZZER"
• a wine bottle of about 20 times the standard size.
• [*Nebuchadnezzar*, Babylonian king d.562 BC]

nebula *noun*
• "NEB yoo luh"
• a cloud of gas and dust in space, sometimes glowing and sometimes appearing as a dark silhouette against other glowing matter.
• [Latin, = mist]
• **nebular** *adjective*

nebulizer *noun*
ALSO SPELLED: esp. *Brit.* **-iser**
• "NEB yoo lize ur"
• a device for producing a fine spray of liquid.
• [as NEBULA]
• **nebulize** *verb* (also esp. *Brit.* **-ise**)

nebulous *adjective*
• "NEB yoo luss"
• hazy, indistinct, vague.
• [Latin *nebulosus* (as NEBULA)]
• **nebulosity** *noun* "neb yoo LOSSA tee"
• **nebulously** *adverb*
• **nebulousness** *noun*

necessary *adjective*
• "NESSA serry"
• requiring to be done, achieved, etc.; requisite, essential.
• [Latin *necessarius* from *necesse* needful]
• **necessarily** *adverb*

necessitarian *noun*
• "nuh sessa TERRY 'n"
• a person who holds that all action is predetermined and free will is impossible.
• [as NECESSITY]
• **necessitarianism** *noun*

necessitate *verb*
• "nuh SESSA tate"
• make necessary (esp. as a result).
• [as NECESSITY]

necessitous *adjective*
• "nuh SESSA tuss"
• poor; needy.
• [as NECESSITY]

necessity *noun*
• "nuh SESSA tee"
• an indispensable thing.
• [Latin *necessitas -tatis* from *necesse* needful]

neckerchief *noun*
• "NECKER chiff" or "NECKER cheef"
• a square of cloth worn around the neck.
• ['neck' + KERCHIEF]

necklace *noun*
• "NECK luss"
• a chain or string of beads, precious stones, links, etc., worn as an ornament around the neck.
• ['neck' + 'lace']

necrobiosis *noun*
• "neck roe by OH sis"
• decay in the tissues of the body, esp. swelling of the collagen bundles in the dermis.
• [Greek *nekro-* from *nekros* corpse + *biōsis* mode of life, from *bios* life]
• **necrobiotic** *adjective*

necrology *noun*
• "nuh CRAWLA jee"
• a list of recently dead people.
• [Greek *nekro-* from *nekros* corpse + *logos* word]
• **necrological** *adjective*
• **necrologist** *noun*

necromancy *noun*
• "NECKRA mancy"
• the prediction of the future by the supposed communication with the dead.
• [Old French *nigromancie* from medieval Latin *nigromantia* changed (by assoc. with Latin *niger nigri* black) from Late Latin *necromantia* from Greek *nekromanteia* from *nekros* corpse + *manteia* divination]
• **necromancer** *noun*
• **necromantic** *adjective*

necrophobia *noun*
• "neckra FOBEY uh"
• an abnormal fear of death or dead bodies.
• [Greek *nekro-* from *nekros* corpse + PHOBIA]

necropolis *noun*
• "nuh CROPPA liss"
• an ancient cemetery or burial place.
• [Greek *nekro-* from *nekros* corpse + *polis* city]

necropsy *noun*
• "NECK rop see"
• a post-mortem examination conducted to determine the cause of death; an autopsy.
• [Greek *nekro-* from *nekros* corpse, after AUTOPSY]

necrosis *noun*
• "nuh CROW sis"
• the death or decay of part or all of an organ or tissue due to disease, injury, or deficiency of nutrients, esp. as one of the symptoms of gangrene or pulmonary tuberculosis.
• [modern Latin from Greek *nekrōsis* from *nekros* corpse]
• **necrotic** *adjective* "nuh CROTTIC"
• **necrotize** *verb* (also esp. *Brit.* **-ise**) "NECKRA tize"

nectar *noun*
• "NECTER"
• a sugary substance produced by plants to attract pollinating insects and made into honey by bees.
• [Latin from Greek *nektar*]

nectarine *noun*
• "necta REEN"
• a variety of peach with a thin brightly coloured smooth skin and firm flesh.
• [originally as adjective, = nectar-like, from NECTAR]

nectary *noun*
• "NECTA ree"
• the nectar-secreting organ of a flower or plant.
• [as NECTAR]

née *adjective*
• "NAY"
• (used in adding a married woman's maiden name after her surname) born.
• [French, feminine past participle of *naître* be born]
HOMOPHONES: *nay, neigh*

neem *noun*
• "NEEM"
• a tree, *Azadirachta indica* (mahogany family), whose leaves and bark are used medicinally in the Indian subcontinent.
• [Hindi *nīm*]

neep *noun*
• "NEEP"
• a turnip.
• [Old English *nǣp* from Latin *napus*]
HOMOPHONES: *neap*

Neepawan *noun*
• "NEEPA w'n"
• a resident of Neepawa, Man.

nefarious *adjective*
• "nuh FERRY us"
• wicked; iniquitous.
• [Latin *nefarius* from *nefas* wrong, from *ne-* not + *fas* divine law]
• **nefariously** *adverb*
• **nefariousness** *noun*

negate *verb*
• "nuh GATE"
• nullify, make ineffective, invalidate.
• [Latin *negare negat-* deny]
• **negation** *noun*
• **negator** *noun*

negative *adjective*
• "NEGGA tiv"
• expressing or implying denial, prohibition, or refusal.
• [Late Latin *negativus* (as NEGATE)]
• **negatively** *adverb*
• **negativeness** *noun*
• **negativity** *noun*

negativism *noun*
• "NEGGA tiv izm"
• the tendency to be negative in attitude, action, or position.
• [as NEGATIVE]
• **negativist** *noun*
• **negativistic** *adjective*

negligee *noun*
• "NEG luh zhay"
• a woman's light nightgown or dressing gown made of delicate, semi-transparent fabric and trimmed with lace etc.
• [French, past participle of *négliger* from Latin *neglegere neglect-* from *neg-* not + *legere* choose, pick up]

negligence *noun*
• "NEG luh jince"
• a lack of reasonable or proper care and attention; carelessness.
• [Latin *negligentia* from *negligere* = *neglegere*: see NEGLIGEE]
• **negligent** *adjective*
• **negligently** *adverb*

negligible *adjective*
• "NEG lidge a bull"
• not worth considering or noticing; insignificant.
• [obsolete French from *négliger* neglect (as NEGLIGEE)]
• **negligibly** *adverb*

negotiate *verb*
• "nuh GO shee ate"
• confer with others in order to reach a compromise or agreement.
• [Latin *negotiari* from *negotium* business, from *neg-* not + *otium* leisure]
• **negotiable** *adjective* "nuh GO shuh bull"
• **negotiated** *adjective*
• **negotiating** *noun*
• **negotiation** *noun*
• **negotiator** *noun*

Negroid *adjective*
• "NEE groid"
• denoting, concerning, or belonging to one of the group of human populations having dark skin, tightly curled hair, and a broad flattish nose, indigenous to sub-Saharan Africa and parts of Melanesia in the W Pacific.
• [Spanish & Portuguese *Negro* black, from Latin *niger nigri* black]

negus *noun*
• "NEE guss"
• a hot drink of port or sherry mixed with water, sugar, lemon, and spice.
• [Col. F. *Negus* d.1732, its inventor]

neigh *noun*
• "NAY"
• the high whinnying sound of a horse.
• [Old English *hnægan*, of imitative origin]
HOMOPHONES: *nay*, *née*

neighbour *noun*
ALSO SPELLED: **neighbor**
• "NAY bur"
• a person, institution, etc., resident or established next door to or near or nearest another.
• [Old English *nēahgebūr* (as NIGH: *gebūr*, compare BOOR)]
• **neighbouring** *adjective* (also **neighboring**)

neighbourhood *noun*
ALSO SPELLED: **neighborhood**
• "NAY bur hood" (with "OO" as in *GOOD*)
• a district, esp. considered in reference to the character or circumstances of its inhabitants.
• [as NEIGHBOUR]

neighbourly *adjective*
ALSO SPELLED: **neighborly**
• "NAY bur lee"
• characteristic of a good neighbour; friendly; kind.
• [as NEIGHBOUR]
• **neighbourliness** *noun* (also **neighborliness**)

neither *adjective*
• "NIE thur" or "NEE thur" (with "TH" as in *THEN*)
• not the one nor the other (of two things); not either.
• [Middle English *naither*, *neither* from Old English *nowther* contraction of *nōhwæther*: assimilated to EITHER]

nekton *noun*
• "NECK t'n"
• free-swimming aquatic animals collectively.
• [German from Greek *nēkton* neuter of *nēktos* swimming, from *nēkhō* swim]
• **nektonic** *adjective* "neck TONNIC"

nelumbo *noun*
• "nuh LUMBO"
• either of two water lilies of the genus *Nelumbo*, the sacred lotus of the East, *N. nucifera*, bearing red flowers, and the yellow-flowered American lotus, *N. lutea*.
• [modern Latin from Sinhalese *nelum(bu)*]

nematic *adjective*
• "nuh MATTIC"
• designating or involving a state of a liquid crystal in which the molecules are oriented in parallel but not arranged in well-defined planes.
• [Greek *nēma nēmat-* thread]

nematocyst *noun*
• "nuh MATTA sist" or "NEMMA tuh sist"

• a specialized cell in a jellyfish etc. containing a coiled thread that can be projected as a sting.
• [as NEMATODE + CYST]

nematode *noun*
• "NEMMA tode"
• any parasitic or free-living worm of the phylum Nematoda, with a slender unsegmented cylindrical shape.
• [Greek *nēma -matos* thread]

nemertean *noun*
• "nuh MURTY 'n"
• any marine ribbon worm of the phylum Nemertea, often very long and brightly coloured, found in tangled knots in coastal waters of Europe and the Mediterranean.
• [modern Latin *Nemertes* from Greek *Nēmertēs* name of a sea nymph]

nemesia *noun*
• "nuh MEE zhuh"
• any chiefly S African plant of the genus *Nemesia*, cultivated for its variously coloured and irregular flowers.
• [modern Latin from Greek *nemesion*, the name of a similar plant]

nemesis *noun*
• "NEMMA sis"
• a long-standing or persistent rival, enemy, or tormentor.
• [Greek, = righteous indignation, from *nemō* give what is due]

neoclassical *adjective*
• "neeo CLASSA k'll"
• of or relating to a revival or development of a classical style or treatment in art, literature, music, etc.
• [Greek *neos* new + CLASSICISM]
• **neoclassicism** *noun* "neeo CLASSA sizm"
• **neoclassicist** *noun*

neocortex *noun*
• "neeo CORE tex"
• the most recently evolved part of the cerebral cortex, involved in sight and hearing in advanced reptiles and in mammals.
• [Greek *neos* new + CORTEX]
• **neocortical** *adjective*

neodymium *noun*
• "neeo DIMMY um"
• a silver-grey naturally occurring metallic element of the lanthanide series used in colouring glass etc.
• [Greek *neos* new + DIDYMIUM]

neolithic *adjective*
• "neeo LITHIC"
• of or relating to the later Stone Age, when ground or polished stone weapons and implements prevailed.
• [Greek *neos* new + *lithos* stone]

neologism *noun*
• "nee OLLA jizm"
• a new word or expression.
• [French *néologisme* (Greek *neos* new + *logos* word)]
• **neologist** *noun*
• **neologistic** *adjective*
• **neologize** *verb* (also esp. *Brit.* **-ise**)

neomycin *noun*
• "neeo MICE in"
• an antibiotic, related to streptomycin, used to treat a wide variety of bacterial infections.
• [Greek *neos* new + *mukēs* fungus, mushroom]

neonate *noun*
• "NEEO nate"
• a newborn child, esp. an infant less than four weeks old.
• [modern Latin *neonatus* (Greek *neos* new, Latin *nasci nat-* be born)]
• **neonatal** *adjective*
• **neonatologist** *noun*
• **neonatology** *noun*

neophobia *noun*
• "neeo FOBEY uh"
• a fear or dislike of what is new.
• [Greek *neos* new + PHOBIA]
• **neophobic** *adjective*

neophyte *noun*
• "NEEO fite"
• a beginner; a novice.
• [Church Latin *neophytus* from New Testament Greek *neophutos* newly planted (Greek *neos* new, *phuton* plant)]

neoplasm *noun*
• "NEEO plazm"
• a new and abnormal growth of tissue in some part of the body, esp. a tumour.
• [Greek *neos* new + *plasma* formation]
• **neoplastic** *adjective*

Neoplatonism *noun*
• "neeo PLATE'n izm"
• a philosophical and religious system based on Platonic ideas and developed by the followers of Plotinus (d. *c.*270).
• [Greek *neos* new + PLATONISM]
• **Neoplatonic** *adjective* "neeo pluh TONNIC"
• **Neoplatonist** *noun*

neoprene *noun*
• "NEEO preen"
• any of various strong synthetic rubbers which are resistant to oil, heat, and weathering.
• [Greek *neos* new + *chloroprene* etc. (perhaps from PROPYL + '-ene' forming names of unsaturated hydrocarbons containing a double bond, from Greek *-ēnos*, adjective suffix denoting origin or source)]

neoteny *noun*
• "nee OTTA nee"
• the retention of juvenile features in the adult form of some animals, e.g. an axolotl.
• [German *Neotenie* (Greek *neos* new + *teinō* extend)]

- **neotenic** *adjective* "neeo TENNIC"
- **neotenous** *adjective*

neotropical *adjective*
- "neeo TROPPA k'll"
- of or relating to tropical and S America as a biogeographical region.
- [Greek *neos* new + 'tropical' from Latin *tropicus* from Greek *tropikos* from *tropē* turning, from *trepō* turn]

Nepalese *adjective*
- "neppa LEEZ"
- of or from Nepal.

Nepali *noun*
- "nuh POLLY"
- a native or national of Nepal in S Asia.

nephrectomy *noun*
- "nuh FRECTA mee"
- the surgical removal of a kidney.
- [Greek *nephros* kidney + *ektomē* excision, from *ek* out + *temnō* cut]

nephrite *noun*
- "NEFF rite"
- a green, yellow, or white calcium magnesium silicate form of jade.
- [German *Nephrit* from Greek *nephros* kidney, with reference to its supposed efficacy in treating kidney disease]

nephritis *noun*
- "neff RITE iss"
- inflammation of the kidneys.
- [Late Latin from Greek *nephros* kidney + Greek *-itis*, forming feminine of adjectives in *-itēs* (with *nosos* 'disease' implied)]

nephron *noun*
- "NEFF ron"
- each of the functional units in the kidney, through which filtrate passes before emerging as urine.
- [Greek *nephros* kidney]
- **nephritic** *adjective* "neff RITTIC"

nepotism *noun*
- "NEPPA tizm"
- favouritism shown to relatives in bestowing employment or conferring privileges.
- [French *népotisme* from Italian *nepotismo* from *nepote* nephew: originally with reference to popes with illegitimate sons called nephews]
- **nepotist** *noun*
- **nepotistic** *adjective*

neptunium *noun*
- "nep TUNE ee um"
- a radioactive transuranic metallic element produced when uranium atoms absorb bombarding neutrons.
- [*Neptune*, as the next planet beyond Uranus]

nereid *noun*
- "NEERY id"
- a sea nymph.
- [Latin *Nereïs Nereïd-* from Greek *Nērēis -idos* daughter of the sea god Nereus]

neroli *noun*
- "NEERA lee"
- an essential oil from the flowers of the Seville orange, used in perfumery.
- [Italian *neroli*, from the name of Anna-Maria de la Tremoille, the wife of the Prince of *Nerola* in Italy, who is said to have discovered the oil *ca.* 1670]

nervous *adjective*
- "NUR vuss"
- worried, anxious.
- [Middle French *nerveux* sinewy, strong, from Latin *nervus*, related to Greek *neuron*]
- **nervously** *adverb*
- **nervousness** *noun*

nervure *noun*
- "NUR vyoor"
- each of the hollow tubes that form the framework of an insect's wing; a venule.
- [French, from *nerf* nerve]

Nestorian *adjective*
- "ness TORY 'n"
- of or relating to an early Christian doctrine that there were distinct divine and human persons in Christ, maintained by some ancient Churches of the Middle East.
- [*Nestorius*, Patriarch of Constantinople d. *c.*451]
- **Nestorianism** *noun*

netiquette *noun*
- "NETTA kit"
- the informal code of conduct governing effective and polite use of the Internet.
- [blend of 'Net' + ETIQUETTE]

Netsilingmiut *plural noun*
- "net sill ING mee oot"
- an Inuit people inhabiting an area of Nunavut around the Boothia Peninsula and Pelly Bay.
- [Inuit, = 'people of the seal']

netsuke *noun*
- "NET sooky" ("OOT" rhymes with *FOOT*)
- (in Japan) a carved button-like ornament, esp. of ivory or wood, formerly worn to suspend articles from a belt.
- [Japanese]

neume *noun*
- "NOOM" or "NYOOM"
- a sign in plainsong indicating a note or group of notes to be sung to a syllable.
- [Old French *neume* from medieval Latin *neu(p)ma* from Greek *pneuma* breath]

neural *adjective*
- "NYUR 'll" or "NUR 'll"
- of or relating to a nerve or the central nervous system.
- [Greek *neuron* nerve]
- **neurally** *adverb*

neuralgia *noun*
• "nyur AL juh" or "nur AL juh"
• an intense intermittent pain along the course of a nerve, esp. in the head or face.
• [as NEURAL + Greek *algia* from *algos* pain]
• **neuralgic** *adjective*

neurasthenia *noun*
• "nyur us THEENY uh" or "nur us THEENY us"
• an ill-defined medical condition characterized by lassitude, fatigue, headache, and irritability, associated chiefly with emotional disturbance.
• [Greek *neuron* nerve + ASTHENIA]
• **neurasthenic** *adjective*

neuritis *noun*
• "nyur ITE iss" or "nur ITE iss"
• inflammation of a nerve or nerves, usu. with pain and loss of function.
• [formed as NEURAL + Greek *-itis*, forming feminine of adjectives in *-itēs* (with *nosos* 'disease' implied)]
• **neuritic** *adjective* "nyur ITTIC" or "nur ITTIC"

neuroanatomy *noun*
• "nyuro a NATTA mee" or "nuro a NATTA mee"
• the anatomy of the nervous system.
• [Greek *neuron* nerve + ANATOMY]
• **neuroanatomical** *adjective* "nyuro anna TOMMA k'll" or "nuro anna TOMMA k'll"
• **neuroanatomist** *noun*

neurobiology *noun*
• "nyuro by OLLA jee" or "nuro by OLLA jee"
• the biology of the nervous system.
• [Greek *neuron* nerve + BIOLOGY]
• **neurobiological** *adjective*
• **neurobiologist** *noun*

neuroblastoma *noun*
• "nyuro blass TOE muh" or "nuro blass TOE muh"
• a tumour composed of embryonic cells from which nerve fibres originate, esp. a malignant tumour originating in the adrenal gland.
• [Greek *neuron* nerve + *blastos* sprout + *-oma* as CARCINOMA]

neurochemical *adjective*
• "nyuro KEMMA k'll" or "nuro KEMMA k'll"
• of or pertaining to the chemistry of the nervous system.
• [Greek *neuron* nerve + CHEMICAL]
• **neurochemist** *noun*
• **neurochemistry** *noun*

neurodegenerative *adjective*
• "nyuro de JENNER a tiv" or "nuro de JENNER a tiv"
• (of a disease) causing degeneration of the nervous system.
• [Greek *neuron* nerve + DEGENERATE]
• **neurodegeneration** *noun*

neurogenic *adjective*
• "nyuro JENNIC" or "nuro JENNIC"
• caused by or arising in nervous tissue.
• [Greek *neuron* nerve + GENESIS]

neurohormone *noun*
• "nyuro HORE mone" or "nuro HORE mone"
• a hormone produced by nerve cells and secreted into the circulation.
• [Greek *neuron* nerve + HORMONE]
• **neurohormonal** *adjective*

neuroleptic *adjective*
• "nyuro LEPTIC" or "nuro LEPTIC"
• tending or able to reduce nervous tension by depressing nerve function.
• [Greek *neuron* nerve + *lēptikos* disposed to take, from *lambanō* take]

neurolinguistics *noun*
• "nyuro ling GWISTIX" or "nuro ling GWISTIX"
• the branch of linguistics dealing with the relationship between language and the structure and functioning of the brain.
• [Greek *neuron* nerve + LINGUISTICS]
• **neurolinguistic** *adjective*

neurology *noun*
• "nyur OLLA jee" or "nur OLLA jee"
• the branch of biology or esp. medicine that deals with the anatomy, functions, and organic disorders of nerves and the nervous system.
• [modern Latin *neurologia* from Greek *neuron* nerve + *logos* word]
• **neurologic** *adjective*
• **neurological** *adjective*
• **neurologically** *adverb*
• **neurologist** *noun*

neuroma *noun*
• "nyur OH muh" or "nur OH muh"
• a tumour on a nerve or in nerve tissue.
• [Greek *neuron* nerve + *-oma* as CARCINOMA]

neuromuscular *adjective*
• "nyuro MUSS kyuh lur" or "nuro MUSS kyuh lur"
• pertaining to, consisting of, or resembling both nerves and muscle tissue.
• [Greek *neuron* nerve + MUSCULAR]

neuron *noun*
• "NYUR on" or "NUR on"
• a specialized cell transmitting nerve impulses; a nerve cell.
• [Greek *neuron* nerve]
• **neuronal** *adjective* "nyur OH n'll" or "nur OH n'll"

neuropathology *noun*
• "nyuro puh THOLLA jee" or "nuro puh THOLLA jee"
• the branch of pathology that deals with diseases and disorders of the nervous system.
• [Greek *neuron* nerve + PATHOLOGY]
• **neuropathological** *adjective*
• **neuropathologist** *noun*

neuropathy *noun*
• "nyur OPPA thee" or "nur OPPA thee" (with "TH" as in *THIN*)
• a disease or dysfunction of one or more peripheral nerves, typically causing numbness or weakness.
• [Greek *neuron* nerve + *patheia* suffering]

neuropeptide *noun*
• "nyuro PEP tide" or "nuro PEP tide"
• any short-chain protein in the nervous system which is capable of acting as a neurotransmitter.
• [Greek *neuron* nerve + PEPTIDE]

neurophysiology *noun*
• "nyuro fizzy OLLA jee" or "nuro fizzy OLLA jee"
• the physiology of the nervous system.
• [Greek *neuron* nerve + PHYSIOLOGY]
• **neurophysiological** *adjective*
• **neurophysiologist** *noun*

neuropsychology *noun*
• "nyuro sye COLLA jee" or "nuro sye COLLA jee"
• the study of the relationship between the nervous system (esp. the brain) and behaviour.
• [Greek *neuron* nerve + PSYCHOLOGY]
• **neuropsychological** *adjective*
• **neuropsychologist** *noun*

neuropteran *noun*
• "nyur OPTER 'n" or "nur OPTER 'n"
• any insect of the order Neuroptera, including lacewings, having four finely-veined membranous leaflike wings.
• [Greek *neuron* nerve + *pteron* wing]
• **neuropterous** *adjective*

neuroscience *noun*
• "NYURO sye ince" or "NURO sye ince"
• any or all of the sciences dealing with the structure and function of the nervous system and brain.
• [Greek *neuron* nerve + SCIENCE]
• **neuroscientist** *noun*

neurosis *noun*
• "nyur OH sis" or "nur OH sis"
• a mild mental illness, not attributable to organic cause, characterized by symptoms of stress such as anxiety, depression, obsessive behaviour, hypochondria, etc., without loss of contact with reality.
• [modern Latin from Greek *neuron* nerve]
• **neurotic** *adjective* "nur OTTIC" or "nyur OTTIC"
• **neurotically** *adverb*
• **neuroticism** *noun* "nyur OTTA sizm" or "nur OTTA sizm"

neurosurgery *noun*
• "nyuro SUR jur ee" or "nuro SUR jur ee"
• surgery performed on the nervous system, esp. the brain and spinal cord.
• [Greek *neuron* nerve + SURGERY]
• **neurosurgeon** *noun*
• **neurosurgical** *adjective*

neurotoxin *noun*
• "nyuro TOXIN" or "nuro TOXIN"
• any poison which acts on the nervous system.
• [Greek *neuron* nerve + TOXIN]
• **neurotoxic** *adjective*
• **neurotoxicity** *noun* "nyuro tox ISSA tee" or "nuro tox ISSA tee"

neurotransmitter *noun*
• "nyuro TRANZ mitter" or "nuro TRANZ mitter"
• a chemical substance released from a nerve fibre that effects the transfer of an impulse to another nerve or muscle.
• [Greek *neuron* nerve + TRANSMITTER]
• **neurotransmission** *noun*

neuter *verb*
• "NOOTER" or "NYOOTER"
• castrate or spay (an animal).
• [Latin *neuter* neither, from *ne-* not + *uter* either]
• **neutered** *adjective*
• **neutering** *noun*

neutral *adjective*
• "NEW trull"
• not helping or supporting either of two opposing sides, esp. countries at war or in dispute; impartial.
• [Latin *neutralis* of neuter gender (as NEUTER)]
• **neutralism** *noun*
• **neutralist** *noun*
• **neutrality** *noun* "new TRALA tee"
• **neutrally** *adverb*

neutralize *verb*
ALSO SPELLED: esp. *Brit.* **-ise**
• "NOOTRA lize" or "NYOOTRA lize"
• counterbalance; render ineffective by an opposite force or effect.
• [French *neutraliser* from medieval Latin *neutralizare* (as NEUTRAL)]
• **neutralization** *noun* (also esp. *Brit.* **-isation**)
• **neutralizer** *noun* (also esp. *Brit.* **-iser**)

neutrino *noun*
• "new TREE no"
• any of a group of stable elementary particles with zero electric charge and probably zero mass, which travel at the speed of light.
• [Italian, diminutive of *neutro* neutral (as NEUTER)]

neutron *noun*
• "NEW tron"
• an elementary particle of about the same mass as a proton but without an electric charge, present in all atomic nuclei except those of ordinary hydrogen.
• [as NEUTRAL]

neutrophil *adjective*
• "NOOTRO fill" or "NYOOTRO fill"
• (esp. of a cell or tissue) that can be stained with natural dyes, but usu. not readily with either acidic or basic dyes.
• [as NEUTRAL + Greek *philos* dear, loving]
• **neutrophilic** *adjective*

névé *noun*
• "NAY vay"
• an expanse of crystalline or granular snow on the upper part of a glacier, not yet compressed into ice.
• [Swiss French, = glacier, ultimately from Latin *nix nivis* snow]

nevus *noun*
ALSO SPELLED: **naevus**
• "NEE vuss"
• a birthmark in the form of a raised red patch on the skin.
• [Latin]

newbie *noun*
• "NEW bee"
• a novice at some activity.
• [arbitrary formation from 'new']

newel *noun*
• "NEW 'll"
• the supporting central post of winding stairs.
• [Old French *nouel* knob, from medieval Latin *nodellus* diminutive of Latin *nodus* knot]

newsstand *noun*
• "NEWS stand"
• a stall for the sale of newspapers.
• ['news' + 'stand']

nexus *noun*
• "NEX us"
• a connected group, series, or network.
• [Latin from *nectere nex-* bind]

Ngbandi *noun*
• "'ng BANDY"
• a Niger-Congo language of N Congo (formerly Zaire).
• [Ngbandi]

ngultrum *noun*
• "'ng GUL trum"
• the basic monetary unit of Bhutan, equal to 100 chetrum.
• [Dzongkha]

Nguni *noun*
• "'ng GOONY"
• a member of a group of Bantu-speaking peoples living mainly in southern Africa.
• [Zulu]

ngwee *noun*
• "'ng GWEE"
• a monetary unit of Zambia, equal to one-hundredth of a kwacha.
• [a local word]

niacin *noun*
• "NIE a sin"
• a vitamin of the B complex, found in milk, liver, and yeast, a deficiency of which causes pellagra; vitamin B_3.
• [*nic*otinic *acid*]

niacinamide *noun*
• "nie a SINNA mide"
• the amide of niacin, which is interconvertible with niacin in living organisms, providing a source of vitamin B_3.
• [as NIACIN + AMIDE]

Niagara *noun*
• "nie AGRA"
• an outpouring, a deluge.
• [Niagara Falls on the Ontario/New York border]

Niagaran *noun*
• "nie AG run"
• a resident of the Niagara Peninsula in Ontario.

niblick *noun*
• "NIB lick"
• an iron with a large round heavy head, used esp. for playing out of bunkers.
• [19th c.: origin unknown, perhaps an alteration of Scottish *neb laigh* a broken nose, with reference to the short club face]

nicad *noun*
• "NIE cad"
• a battery, often rechargeable, with a nickel anode and a cadmium cathode.
• [NICKEL + CADMIUM]

Nicaraguan *noun*
• "nicka ROG w'n" or "nicka RAG w'n"
• a native or inhabitant of Nicaragua in Central America.

Nicene *adjective*
• "NIE seen" or "nie SEEN"
• designating a creed which is a formal statement of Christian belief based on that adopted at the first Council of Nicaea in 325.
• [Late Latin *Nicenus* of Nicaea (in Asia Minor)]

niche *noun*
• "NEESH" or "NITCH"
• a shallow recess, esp. in a wall to contain a statue etc.
• [French from *nicher* make a nest, ultimately from Latin *nidus* nest]

Nichiren *noun*
• "NISHER 'n"
• a Japanese Buddhist sect founded by the religious teacher Nichiren (1222–82).

nickel *noun*
• "NICK'll"
• a malleable ductile silver-white metallic transition element, occurring naturally in various minerals and used in special steels, in magnetic alloys, and as a catalyst.
• [abbreviation of German *Kupfernickel* copper-coloured ore from which nickel was first obtained, from *Kupfer* copper + *Nickel* demon, with reference to the ore's failure to yield copper]

nickelodeon *noun*
• "nick'll OH dee 'n"
• a jukebox.
• [NICKEL + MELODEON]

nicker *verb*
• "NICKER"
• neigh.
• [imitative]

niçoise *adjective*
• "nee SWOZZ"
• designating food (esp. a salad) garnished with tomatoes, capers, anchovies, etc.
• [French, = of Nice (on the Mediterranean coast)]

nicotiana *noun*
• "nicko tee ANNA" or "nicko shee ANNA"
• any of several plants of the genus *Nicotiana* of the nightshade family, esp. *N. tabacum* and its cultivars grown for their narcotic leaves which are used for smoking, and other cultivated varieties grown for their fragrant flowers, or for the production of insecticides; tobacco.
• [modern Latin *nicotiana (herba)* tobacco (plant), named after J. *Nicot*, 16th-c. French diplomat who introduced tobacco to France]

nicotinamide *noun*
• "nicka TEENA mide" or "nicka TINNA mide"
• the amide of niacin, having a similar role in the diet.
• [as NICOTINE + AMIDE]

nicotine *noun*
• "NICKA teen" or "nicka TEEN"
• a colourless poisonous alkaloid present in tobacco.
• [French from NICOTIANA]
• **nicotinic** *adjective*

nictitating *adjective*
• "NICKTA tate ing"
• designating a clear membrane forming a third eyelid in amphibians, birds, and some other animals, that can be drawn across the eye to give protection without loss of vision.
• [medieval Latin *nictitare* frequentative of Latin *nictare* blink]

nidus *noun*
• "NIE duss"
• a place in which an insect etc. deposits its eggs, or in which spores or seeds develop.
• [Latin, = nest]

niece *noun*
• "NEECE"
• a daughter of one's brother or sister, or of one's brother-in-law or sister-in-law.
• [Old French, ultimately from Latin *neptis* granddaughter]

niello *noun*
• "nee ELLO"
• a black composition of sulphur with silver, lead, or copper, for filling engraved lines in silver or other metal.
• [Italian from Latin *nigellus* diminutive of *niger* black]
• **nielloed** *adjective*

Nietzschean *adjective*
• "NEETCHY 'n"
• of or characteristic of the thought of German philosopher F. Nietzsche (d.1900), known for repudiating compassion for the weak and exalting the 'will to power'.

Nigerian *noun*
• "nie JEERY 'n"
• a native or inhabitant of Nigeria in W Africa.

niggardly *adjective*
• "NIG 'rd lee"
• stingy, parsimonious.
• [Middle English, alteration of earlier (obsolete) *nigon*, prob. of Scandinavian origin]
• **niggardliness** *noun*

nigh *adjective*
• "NIE"
• often (esp. of a momentous event) near; approaching.
• [Old English *nēh*, *nēah*]

nightingale *noun*
• "NITE ing gale"
• any small reddish-brown bird of the genus *Luscinia*, esp. *L. megarhynchos*, of which the male sings melodiously, esp. at night.
• [Old English *nihtegala* (whence obsolete *nightgale*) from Germanic]

nihilism *noun*
• "NIE 'll izm"
• the rejection of all moral and religious principles.
• [Latin *nihil* nothing]
• **nihilist** *noun*
• **nihilistic** *adjective*

Nikkei *noun*
• "NEE cay"
• a figure indicating the relative price of representative shares on the Tokyo Stock Exchange.
• [*Nikkei* from Japanese abbreviation of the name of a financial newspaper]

nil *noun*
• "NILL"
• nothing; no number or amount (often as a score in games).
• [Latin, = *nihil* nothing]

nilgai *noun*
• "NEEL guy"
• a large short-horned Indian antelope, *Boselaphus tragocamelus*.
• [Hindi *nīlgāī* from *nīl* blue + *gāī* cow]

Nilotic *adjective*
• "nile OTTIC"
• of or relating to the Nile or the Nile region of Africa.
• [Latin *Niloticus* from Greek *Neilōtikos* from *Neilos* Nile]

nimbostratus *noun*
• "nimbo STRAT us"

• cloud forming a low diffuse dark grey layer, often with falling rain or snow.
• [modern Latin, from NIMBUS + STRATUS]

nimbus *noun*
• "NIM buss"
• a bright cloud or halo investing a deity or person or thing.
• [Latin, = cloud, aureole]
• **nimbused** *adjective* "NIM bust"

nincompoop *noun*
• "NIN k'm poop"
• a simpleton; a fool.
• [17th c.: origin unknown]

ninety *noun*
• "NINE tee"
• the product of nine and ten.
• [Old English *nigontig*]
• **ninetieth** *adjective*
• **ninetyfold** *adjective*

ninja *noun*
• "NINJA"
• a person skilled in an originally Japanese martial art characterized by stealthy movement and camouflage.
• [Japanese]

ninny *noun*
• "NINNY"
• a foolish or simple-minded person.
• [perhaps from *innocent*]

ninth *noun*
• "NINE'th"
• the position in a sequence corresponding to the number 9 in the sequence 1–9.
• [from 'nine' from Old English *nigon*]
• **ninthly** *adverb*

niobium *noun*
• "nie OH bee um"
• a rare grey-blue metallic transition element occurring naturally in several minerals and used in alloys for superconductors.
• [*Niobe* daughter of Tantalus: so called because first found in TANTALITE]

nipa *noun*
• "NEEPA"
• an E Indian palm tree, *Nypa fruticans*, with a creeping trunk and large feathery leaves.
• [Spanish & Portuguese from Malay *nīpah*]

Nipponese *noun*
• "NIPP 'n eez"
• a Japanese person.
• [Japanese *Nippon* Japan, lit. 'land of the rising sun']

nirvana *noun*
• "nur VANNA" or "nur VONNA"
• (in Buddhism) perfect bliss and release from karma, attained by the extinction of individuality.
• [Sanskrit *nirvāṇa* from *nirvā* be extinguished, from *nis* out + *vā-* to blow]
• **nirvanic** *adjective*

Nisei *noun*
• "nee SAY"
• a Canadian or American whose parents were immigrants from Japan.
• [Japanese, lit. 'second generation']

nisi *adjective*
• "NICE ee"
• that takes effect only on certain conditions.
• [Latin, = 'unless']

nitrate *noun*
• "NIE trate"
• any salt or ester of nitric acid.
• [French (as NITRE)]
• **nitration** *noun*

nitre *noun*
ALSO SPELLED: esp. *US* **niter**
• "NITE ur"
• saltpetre, potassium nitrate.
• [Old French from Latin *nitrum* from Greek *nitron*, of Semitic origin]

nitric *adjective*
• "NIE trick"
• of or containing nitrogen, esp. in the quinquevalent state.
• [as NITROGEN]

nitride *noun*
• "NIE tride"
• a binary compound of nitrogen with a more electropositive element.
• [as NITROGEN]

nitrify *verb*
• "NIE truh fie"
• impregnate with nitrogen.
• [as NITROGEN]
• **nitrification** *noun*

nitrile *noun*
• "NIE trile"
• an organic compound consisting of an alkyl radical bound to a cyanide radical.
• [as NITROGEN]

nitrite *noun*
• "NIE trite"
• any salt or ester of nitrous acid.
• [as NITROGEN]

nitro *noun*
• "NIE tro"
• nitroglycerine.
• [abbreviation]

nitrobenzene *noun*
• "nie tro BEN zeen"
• a yellow oily liquid made by the nitration of benzene and used to make aniline etc.
• [as NITROGEN + BENZENE]

nitrocellulose *noun*
• "nie tro SELL yoo lose" (rhymes with *GROSS*)
• a highly flammable material made by treating cellulose with concentrated nitric acid,

used in the manufacture of explosives and celluloid.
• [as NITROGEN + CELLULOSE]

nitrogen *noun*
• "NIE tro j'n"
• a colourless odourless unreactive gaseous element that forms four-fifths of the earth's atmosphere and is an essential constituent of proteins, nucleic acids, and other biological molecules.
• [French *nitrogène* (as NITRE, GENESIS)]
• **nitrogenous** *adjective* "nie TRODGE a nuss"

nitroglycerine *noun*
ALSO SPELLED: **nitroglycerin**
• "nie tro GLISSER in"
• an explosive yellow liquid made by reacting glycerol with a mixture of concentrated sulphuric and nitric acids, used as an explosive and medically as a vasodilator.
• [as NITROGEN + GLYCEROL]

nitrosamine *noun*
• "nie TRO suh meen" or "nie tro SAM een"
• any of a group of carcinogenic substances containing the chemical group :N-N:O.
• [as NITRE + AMINE]

nitrous *adjective*
• "NIE truss"
• of, like, or impregnated with nitrogen, esp. in the trivalent state.
• [as NITRE]

Nobel *noun*
• "no BELL"
• any of six international prizes awarded annually for physics, chemistry, physiology or medicine, literature, economics, and the promotion of peace.
• [A. *Nobel*, Swedish chemist d.1896, whose large fortune from inventing dynamite enabled him to endow the prizes]
• **Nobelist** *noun*

nobelium *noun*
• "no BEELY um"
• an artificially produced radioactive transuranic metallic element.
• [A. *Nobel*, Swedish chemist d.1896]

nobiliary *adjective*
• "nuh BILL yuh ree"
• of the nobility.
• [French *nobiliaire* from Latin *(g)nobilis*]

nobility *noun*
• "no BILLA tee"
• nobleness of character, mind, birth, or rank.
• [Old French *nobilité* or Latin *nobilitas* from *(g)nobilis*]

nock *noun*
• "NOCK"
• a notch at either end of a bow for holding the string.
• [Middle English, perhaps = *nock* forward upper corner of some sails, from Middle Dutch *nocke*]
HOMOPHONES: *knock*

noctambulist *noun*
• "nock TAM byoo list"
• a sleepwalker.
• [Latin *nox noct-* night + *ambulare* walk]
• **noctambulism** *noun*

noctilucent *adjective*
• "nockta LOO s'nt"
• designating a high-altitude cloud that is luminous at night, esp. in summer in high latitudes.
• [from Latin *nox, noct-* night + *lucere* shine]

noctule *noun*
• "NOCK tule"
• a large bat, *Nyctalus noctula*, of temperate and subtropical Eurasia and N Africa.
• [French from Italian *nottola* bat]

nocturn *noun*
• "NOCK turn"
• a part of matins originally said at night.
• [see NOCTURNAL]
HOMOPHONES: *nocturne*

nocturnal *adjective*
• "nock TURN'll"
• of or relating to the night.
• [Late Latin *nocturnalis* from Latin *nocturnus* of the night, from *nox noctis* night]
• **nocturnally** *adverb*

nocturne *noun*
• "NOCK turn"
• a short composition of a romantic nature, usu. for piano.
• [French (as NOCTURN)]
HOMOPHONES: *nocturn*

nodal *adjective*
• "NODE 'll"
• of or pertaining to a node or nodes.
• [Latin *nodus* knot]

nodule *noun*
• "NOD yool" or "NODGE 'll"
• a small rounded lump of anything.
• [Latin *nodulus* diminutive of *nodus* knot]
• **nodular** *adjective*
• **nodulated** *adjective*
• **nodulation** *noun*

Noel *noun*
• "no ELL"
• Christmas.
• [French from Latin *natalis (dies)* (day) of birth]

noetic *adjective*
• "no ETTIC" or "no EETIC"
• of the intellect.
• [Greek *noētikos* from *noētos* intellectual, from *noeō* apprehend]

nogoodnik *noun*
• "no GOOD nick"

• a no-good person.
• ['no' + 'good' + suffix *-nik* from Russian and Yiddish, forming nouns denoting a person associated with a specified thing or quality]

noir *adjective*
• "NWARR" (rhymes with *FAR*)
• having the characteristics of film noir, a film genre, popular esp. in the 1940s, characterized by urban gangster settings and contrasty photography.
• [French, = 'black']
• **noirish** *adjective*

noisette *noun*
• "nwah ZET"
• a small round piece of meat etc.
• [French, diminutive of *noix* nut]

noisome *adjective*
• "NOY s'm"
• harmful, noxious.
• [Middle English from obsolete *noy* from 'annoy' from Old French *anuier*, ultimately from Latin *in odio* hateful]
• **noisomeness** *noun*

nomen *noun*
• "NO men"
• an ancient Roman's second name, indicating the gens, as in Marcus *Tullius* Cicero.
• [Latin, = name]

nomenclature *noun*
• "NO m'n clay chur" or "NOM'n clay chur"
• a set or system of names, esp. as used in a particular science etc.
• [Latin *nomenclatura* from *nomen* name + *calare* call]
• **nomenclatural** *adjective*

nomenklatura *noun*
• "no m'n cluh TURA"
• (in the former Soviet Union) a select list or group of people from whom upper-level government positions were filled.
• [Russian from Latin *nomenclatura*: see NOMENCLATURE]

nominal *adjective*
• "NOM'n 'll"
• existing in name only; not real or actual.
• [Latin *nominalis* from *nomen -inis* name]
• **nominally** *adverb*

nominalism *noun*
• "NOM'n 'll izm"
• the doctrine that universals or abstract concepts are mere names without any corresponding reality.
• [as NOMINAL]
• **nominalist** *noun*
• **nominalistic** *adjective*

nominalize *verb*
ALSO SPELLED: esp. *Brit.* **-ise**
• "NOM'n 'll ize"
• form a noun from (a verb, adjective, etc.), e.g. *output*, *truth*, from *put out*, *true*.
• [as NOMINAL]
• **nominalization** *noun* (also esp. *Brit.* **-isation**)

nominate *verb*
• "NOM'n ate"
• propose (a candidate) for election.
• [Latin *nominare nominat-* (as NOMINAL)]
• **nomination** *noun*
• **nominator** *noun*
• **nominee** *noun* "nom'n EE"

nominative *noun*
• "NOM'n a tiv"
• the case of nouns, pronouns, and adjectives, expressing the subject of a verb.
• [Latin *nominativus* (as NOMINATE)]

nomogram *noun*
• "NOMMA gram" or "NO muh gram"
• a graphical presentation of relations between quantities whereby the value of one may be found by simple geometrical construction (e.g. drawing a straight line) from those of others.
• [Greek *nomo-* from *nomos* law + *gramma* thing written]
• **nomographic** *adjective*
• **nomographically** *adverb*
• **nomography** *noun*

nomothetic *adjective*
• "nomma THETTIC" or "no muh THETTIC"
• of or relating to the study or discovery of general scientific laws.
• [obsolete *nomothete* legislator, from Greek *nomothetēs*]

nonage *noun*
• "NO nidge" or "NON idge"
• the state of being under full legal age, minority.
• [Old French *nonage* from Latin *non* not, *aetas -atis* age]

nonagenarian *noun*
• "no nuh juh NERRY 'n" or "nonna juh NERRY 'n"
• a person from 90 to 99 years old.
• [Latin *nonagenarius* from *nonageni* distributive of *nonaginta* ninety]

nonagon *noun*
• "NONNA gon"
• a plane figure with nine sides and angles.
• [Latin *nonus* ninth, after HEXAGON]

nonary *adjective*
• "NO nur ee"
• (of a scale of notation) having nine as its base.
• [Latin *nonus* ninth]

nonbelligerency *noun*
• "non buh LIDGER 'n see"
• a lack of belligerency.
• [Latin *non* not + BELLIGERENT]
• **nonbelligerent** *adjective*

nonce *noun*
• "NONSE" (rhymes with *RESPONSE*)
• designating a word or phrase etc. coined for one specific occasion.
• [Middle English *than anes* = for the one, altered by wrong division]

nonchalant *adjective*
• "non shuh LONT" or "NON shuh lont"
• calm and casual, unmoved, unexcited, indifferent.
• [French, participle of *nonchaloir* from *non* not, *chaloir* be concerned]
• **nonchalance** *noun*
• **nonchalantly** *adverb*

noncommittal *adjective*
• "non kuh MIT'll"
• avoiding commitment to a definite opinion or course of action.
• [Latin *non* not + COMMIT]
• **noncommittally** *adverb*

nonconformist *noun*
• "non k'n FORMIST"
• a person who does not conform to a prevailing principle.
• [Latin *non* not + CONFORMANCE]
• **nonconformism** *noun*
• **nonconformity** *noun*

nondescript *adjective*
• "non duh SCRIPT"
• lacking distinctive characteristics; uninteresting, dull.
• [Latin *non* not + *descript* described, from *descriptus* (as DESCRIBE)]
• **nondescriptly** *adverb*
• **nondescriptness** *noun*

none *noun*
• "NONE" (rhymes with *TONE*)
• the office of the fifth of the canonical hours of prayer, originally said at the ninth hour (3 p.m.).
• [Latin *nona* feminine sing. of *nonus* ninth]
HOMOPHONES: *known*

nonentity *noun*
• "non ENTA tee"
• a person or thing of no importance.
• [medieval Latin *nonentitas* non-existence]

nones *plural noun*
• "NONES" (rhymes with *BONES*)
• in the ancient Roman calendar, the ninth day before the ides by inclusive reckoning, i.e. the 7th day of March, May, July, October, the 5th of other months.
• [Old French *nones* from Latin *nonae* feminine pl. of *nonus* ninth]

nonet *noun*
• "no NET"
• a composition for nine voices or instruments.
• [Italian *nonetto* from *nono* ninth, from Latin *nonus*]

nonfeasance *noun*
• "non FEEZ ince"
• failure to perform an act required by law.
• [Latin *non* not + MISFEASANCE]

nonpareil *adjective*
• "non puh RAY" or "non puh RYE"
• unrivalled or unique.
• [French from *non* not + *pareil* equal, from popular Latin *pariculus* diminutive of Latin *par*]

nonplussed *adjective*
ALSO SPELLED: *US* **nonplused**
• "non PLUST"
• perplexed.
• [Latin *non plus* not more]

nonresistance *noun*
• "non re ZIST ince"
• failure to resist; a lack of resistance.
• [Latin *non* not + RESIST]
• **nonresistant** *adjective*

nonsense *noun*
• "NON sense"
• spoken or written words that have no meaning, or make no sense.
• [Latin *non* not + *sensus* faculty of feeling, thought, meaning, from *sentire sens-* feel]
• **nonsensical** *adjective*
• **nonsensicality** *noun*
• **nonsensically** *adverb*

nonsuch *noun*
ALSO SPELLED: **nonesuch**
• "NUN such"
• a person or thing that is unrivalled, a paragon.
• ['none' + 'such']

noogie *noun*
• "NOOG ee" (with "OO" as in *NOOK*)
• the act or an instance of rubbing esp. a person's head with one's knuckles, either as a prank or to express affection.
• [origin unknown, perhaps diminutive of 'knuckle']

nootropic *adjective*
• "no a TROPPIC"
• (of a drug) used to enhance memory or other cognitive functions.
• [French *nootrope* from Greek *noos* mind + *tropē* turning]

nopal *noun*
• "NOPE 'll"
• any American cactus of the genus *Nopalea*, esp. *N. cochinellifera* grown in plantations for breeding cochineal.
• [French & Spanish from Nahuatl *nopalli* cactus]

noradrenalin *noun*
ALSO SPELLED: **noradrenaline**
• "nora DREN'll in"
• a hormone released by the adrenal medulla

and by sympathetic nerve endings as a neurotransmitter.
• ['normal' + ADRENALIN]

Nordic *adjective*
• "NORDIC"
• of or relating to a physical type of northern Germanic peoples characterized by tall stature and fair colouring.
• [French *nordique* from *nord* north]

nordicity *noun*
• "nor DISSA tee"
• *Cdn* a measure of the degree of northernness of a high-latitude place, calculated by assigning values to ten criteria, including latitude, summer heat, and annual cold.
• [as NORDIC]

norepinephrine *noun*
• "nor epp'n EFF rin"
• = NORADRENALIN.
• ['normal' + EPINEPHRINE]

norethindrone *noun*
• "nor ETH'n drone"
• a progestin used in oral contraceptives, often in combination with an estrogen.
• [alteration and rearrangement of chemical name]

nori *noun*
• "NORY"
• edible seaweed of the genus *Porphyra*, eaten either fresh or dried in sheets.
• [Japanese]

normative *adjective*
• "NORMA tiv"
• of or establishing a norm.
• [French *normatif -ive* from Latin *norma* carpenter's square]
• ***normatively*** *adverb*
• ***normativity*** *noun*

normotensive *adjective*
• "normo TENSIV"
• having or designating a normal blood pressure.
• ['normal' + TENSION]

norsteroid *noun*
• "nor STARE oid"
• a steroid lacking a methyl side chain or having one of its rings contracted by one methylene group.
• ['normal' + STEROID]

northernness *noun*
• "NOR thurn ness" (with "TH" as in *THEN*)
• the quality of being of or in the north.
• [Old English *northerne*]

Northumbrian *adjective*
• "nor THUMBRY 'n"
• of or relating to ancient Northumbria or modern Northumberland in NE England.

Norwegian *noun*
• "nor WEE j'n"
• a native or national of Norway in N Europe.
• [medieval Latin *Norvegia* from Old Norse *Norvegr*, assimilated to *Norway*]

nosography *noun*
• "nuh SOGGRA fee"
• the systematic description of diseases.
• [Greek *nosos* disease + *graphia* writing]

nosology *noun*
• "nuh SOLLA jee"
• the branch of medical science dealing with the classification of diseases.
• [Greek *nosos* disease + *logos* word]
• ***nosological*** *adjective* "nossa LODGE a k'll"
• ***nosologically*** *adverb*
• ***nosologist*** *noun*

nostalgia *noun*
• "noss TAL juh" or "nuh STAL juh"
• sentimental yearning for a period of the past; regretful or wistful memory of an earlier time.
• [modern Latin, from Greek *nostos* return home + *algia* from *algos* pain]
• ***nostalgic*** *adjective*
• ***nostalgically*** *adverb*
• ***nostalgist*** *noun*

nostoc *noun*
• "NOSS tock"
• any gelatinous blue-green alga of the genus *Nostoc*, that can fix nitrogen from the atmosphere.
• [name invented by Swiss physician Paracelsus (d.1541)]

nostril *noun*
• "NOSS trull"
• either of two external openings of the nasal cavity in vertebrates that admit air to the lungs and smells to the olfactory nerves.
• [Old English *nosthyrl*, *nosterl* from *nosu* nose + *thȳr(e)l* hole]

nostrum *noun*
• "NOSS trum"
• a quack remedy, a patent medicine, esp. one prepared by the person recommending it.
• [Latin, neuter of *noster* our, used in sense 'of our own make']

notable *adjective*
• "NOTE a bull"
• worthy of note; striking, remarkable, eminent.
• [Latin *nota* mark]
• ***notability*** *noun*
• ***notably*** *adverb*

notary *noun*
• "NOTE a ree"
• a person authorized to perform certain legal formalities, esp. to draw up or certify contracts, deeds, etc.
• [Latin *notarius* secretary, from *nota* mark]
• ***notarial*** *adjective* "no TERRY 'll"

- **notarially** *adverb*
- **notarize** *verb* (also esp. *Brit.* **-ise**)

noticeable *adjective*
- "NO tiss a bull"
- easily seen or noticed; perceptible.
- [from 'notice' from Old French from Latin *notitia* being known, from *notus* past participle of *noscere* know]
- **noticeably** *adverb*

notifiable *adjective*
- "no tuh FIE a bull"
- (of a disease, crop, pest, etc.) requiring that the appropriate authorities be notified.
- [as NOTIFY]

notify *verb*
- "NO tuh fie"
- inform or give notice to (a person).
- [Old French *notifier* from Latin *notificare* from *notus* known]
- **notification** *noun*

notochord *noun*
- "NO tuh cord"
- a cartilaginous skeletal rod supporting the body in all embryo and some adult chordate animals.
- [Greek *nōton* back + CHORDATE]

notorious *adjective*
- "no TORY us" or "nuh TORY us"
- well known, esp. unfavourably.
- [medieval Latin *notorius* from Latin *notus* known]
- **notoriety** *noun* "no tuh RYE a tee"
- **notoriously** *adverb*

nougat *noun*
- "NOO git"
- a candy made from sugar or honey, nuts, and egg white.
- [French from Provençal *nogat* from *noga* nut]

nourish *verb*
- "NUR ish"
- sustain with food.
- [Old French *norir* from Latin *nutrire*]
- **nourisher** *noun*

nourishment *noun*
- "NUR ish m'nt"
- something that nourishes; sustenance, food.
- [as NOURISH]
- **nourishing** *adjective*
- **nourishingly** *adverb*

nous *noun*
- "NOUSE" (rhymes with *MOUSE*)
- common sense; gumption.
- [Greek, = intellect]

nouveau *adjective*
- "NOO voe" or "noo VOE"
- (of a person) having recently become the thing specified.
- [French, = new]

nouvelle *adjective*
- "noo VELL"
- of, pertaining to, or characteristic of nouvelle cuisine, a modern style of (esp. French) cooking that avoids traditional rich sauces and emphasizes the freshness of the ingredients and attractive presentation.
- [French, = new]

novel *noun*
- "NOV'll"
- a fictitious prose story of considerable length and complexity, esp. one representing character and action with some degree of realism.
- [Italian *novella* (*storia* story) feminine of *novello* new, from Latin *novellus* from *novus* new]
- **novelist** *noun*
- **novelistic** *adjective*

novelette *noun*
- "nov'll ET"
- a short novel.
- [as NOVEL]
- **novelettish** *adjective*

novelize *verb*
ALSO SPELLED: esp. *Brit.* **-ise**
- "NOV'll ize"
- make into a novel.
- [as NOVEL]
- **novelization** *noun* (also esp. *Brit.* **-isation**)

novella *noun*
- "nuh VELLA"
- a short novel or narrative story.
- [Italian: see NOVEL]

novelty *noun*
- "NOV'll tee"
- newness; new character.
- [Old French *novelté* from *novel* from Latin *novellus* from *novus* new]

novena *noun*
- "no VEENA"
- a devotion consisting of special prayers or services on nine successive days.
- [medieval Latin from Latin *novem* nine]

novice *noun*
- "NOV iss"
- a beginner; an inexperienced person.
- [Latin *novicius* from *novus* new]

novitiate *noun*
- "no VISHY it" or "nuh VISH it"
- the period of being a novice.
- [French *noviciat* or medieval Latin *noviciatus* (as NOVICE)]

novocaine *noun*
- "NO vuh cane"
- a local anaesthetic derived from benzoic acid.
- [Latin *novus* new + COCAINE]

noxious *adjective*
- "NOCK sh'ss"
- harmful, injurious.
- [from Latin *noxius* from *noxa* harm]

• **noxiously** *adverb*
• **noxiousness** *noun*

nu *noun*
• "NYOO"
• the thirteenth letter of the Greek alphabet (N, ν).
• [Greek]
HOMOPHONES: *gnu, new*

nuance *noun*
• "NEW awnce"
• a subtle difference in or shade of meaning, feeling, colour, etc.
• [French from *nuer* to shade, ultimately from Latin *nubes* cloud]
• **nuanced** *adjective*

Nubian *adjective*
• "NOOBY 'n" or "NYOOBY 'n"
• of or relating to Nubia, an ancient region of S Egypt and N Sudan.

nubile *adjective*
• "NEW bile"
• (of a woman) sexually attractive.
• [Latin *nubilis* suitable for marriage, from *nubere* become the wife of]
• **nubility** *noun*

nubuck *noun*
• "NOO buck"
• a type of cow, pig, or lamb skin which is brushed to give it the feel and look of suede.
• [respelling of 'new' + 'buck' (buckskin)]

nuchal *adjective*
• "NEW k'll"
• of or relating to the nape of the neck.
• [*nucha* nape, from medieval Latin *nucha* medulla oblongata, from Arabic *nuka*' spinal marrow]

nuclear *adjective*
• "NEW clee ur"
• of, relating to, or constituting a nucleus.
• [as NUCLEUS]

nuclease *noun*
• "NEW clee ace"
• any enzyme that catalyzes the breakdown of nucleic acids.
• [as NUCLEUS]

nucleate *adjective*
• "NEW clee it"
• having a nucleus.
• [Late Latin *nucleare nucleat-* form a kernel (as NUCLEUS)]
• **nucleation** *noun*

nucleic *adjective*
• "new CLAY ick"
• designating either of two complex organic substances (DNA and RNA) present in living cells, whose molecules consist of many nucleotides linked in a long chain.
• [as NUCLEUS]

nucleolus *noun*
• "new clee OH luss"
• a small dense spherical structure in the nucleus of a cell during interphase.
• [Late Latin, diminutive of Latin *nucleus*: see NUCLEUS]
• **nucleolar** *adjective*

nucleon *noun*
• "NEW clee on"
• a proton or neutron.
• [as NUCLEUS]

nucleonics *noun*
• "new clee ONNIX"
• the branch of science and technology concerned with atomic nuclei and nucleons, esp. the exploitation of nuclear power.
• [NUCLEAR, after *electronics*]
• **nucleonic** *adjective*

nucleoprotein *noun*
• "new clee oh PRO teen"
• a complex of nucleic acid and protein.
• [as NUCLEUS + PROTEIN]

nucleoside *noun*
• "NEW clee oh side"
• an organic compound consisting of a purine or pyrimidine base linked to a sugar, e.g. adenosine.
• [as NUCLEUS]

nucleosynthesis *noun*
• "new clee oh SINTHA sis"
• the cosmic formation of atoms more complex than the hydrogen atom.
• [as NUCLEUS + SYNTHESIS]
• **nucleosynthetic** *adjective*

nucleotide *noun*
• "NEW clee a tide"
• an organic compound consisting of a nucleoside linked to a phosphate group.
• [as NUCLEUS]

nucleus *noun*
• "NEW clee us"
• the central part or thing around which others are collected.
• [Latin, = kernel, inner part, diminutive of *nux nucis* nut]

nuclide *noun*
• "NEW clide"
• a distinct kind of atom or nucleus characterized by a specific number of protons and neutrons.
• [NUCLEUS + Greek *eidos* form]

nudibranch *noun*
• "NOODY brank" or "NYOODY brank"
• a marine gastropod of the order Nudibranchia, with exposed gills and a vestigial shell; a sea slug.
• [modern Latin *Nudibranchia*, from Latin *nudus* nude + BRANCHIA]

• **nudibranchiate** *noun* "noody BRANKY it" or "nyoody BRANKY it"

nudnik *noun*
• "NOOD nick"
• a pestering, nagging, or irritating person.
• [Yiddish from Russian *nudnyĭ* tedious, boring]

Nuer *noun*
• "NOOER"
• a member of an African people of southeastern Sudan and Ethiopia, traditionally rearers of cattle.
• [the name in Dinka]

nugatory *adjective*
• "NOOGA tory" or "NYOOGA tory"
• futile, trifling, worthless.
• [Latin *nugatorius* from *nugari* to trifle, from *nugae* jests]

nuisance *noun*
• "NOOSE ince" or "NYOOSE ince"
• a person, thing, or circumstance causing trouble, annoyance, or inconvenience.
• [Old French, = hurt, from *nuire nuis-* from Latin *nocēre* to hurt]

nullah *noun*
• "NULLA"
• a dry riverbed or ravine, esp. in the Indian subcontinent.
• [Hindi *nālā*]

nullify *verb*
• "NULLA fie"
• make legally null and void; annul, invalidate.
• [post-classical Latin *nullificare* to hold in contempt, despise, from Latin *nullus* none]
• **nullification** *noun*

nullipara *noun*
• "null IPPER uh"
• a female who has never borne a child.
• [modern Latin from Latin *nullus* none + *-para* feminine of *-parus* from *parere* bear children]
• **nulliparous** *adjective*

nullipore *noun*
• "NULLA pore"
• any of various seaweeds able to secrete lime.
• [Latin *nullus* none + *porus* from Greek *poros* passage, pore]

nullity *noun*
• "NULLA tee"
• the fact of being null and void; invalidity, esp. of marriage.
• [French *nullité* from Latin *nullus* none]

numdah *noun*
• "NUMDA"
• an embroidered felt rug from India etc.
• [Urdu *namdā* from Persian *namad* carpet]

numen *noun*
• "NEW men"
• a local or presiding deity or spirit.
• [Latin *numen -minis*]

numerable *adjective*
• "NOOMER a bull" or "NYOOMER a bull"
• that can be counted.
• [Latin *numerabilis* from *numerare* to number]

numeral *noun*
• "NOOMER 'll" or "NYOOMER 'll"
• a word, figure, or group of figures denoting a number.
• [Late Latin *numeralis* from Latin *numerus* number]

numerate *adjective*
• "NOOMER it" or "NYOOMER it"
• acquainted with the basic principles of mathematics, esp. arithmetic.
• [Latin *numerus* number, after *literate*]
• **numeracy** *noun*

numeration *noun*
• "noomer AY sh'n" or "nyoomer AY sh'n"
• a method or process of numbering or computing.
• [as NUMERABLE]

numerator *noun*
• "NOOMER ate ur" or "NYOOMER ate ur"
• the number above the line in a common fraction showing how many of the parts indicated by the denominator are taken (e.g. 2 in $^2/_3$).
• [as NUMERABLE]

numerical *adjective*
• "new MERRA k'll"
• of, pertaining to, or characteristic of a number or numbers.
• [medieval Latin *numericus* from Latin *numerus* number]
• **numerically** *adverb*

numerology *noun*
• "noomer OLLA jee" or "nyoomer OLLA jee"
• the study of the supposed occult or esoteric significance of numbers.
• [Latin *numerus* number + Greek *logos* word]
• **numerological** *adjective*
• **numerologist** *noun*

numerous *adjective*
• "NOOMER us" or "NYOOMER us"
• great in number.
• [Latin *numerosus* from *numerus* number]
• **numerously** *adverb*
• **numerousness** *noun*

numinous *adjective*
• "NEW min us"
• spiritual.
• [Latin *numen*: see NUMEN]
• **numinosity** *noun* "new min OSSA tee"

numismatic *adjective*
• "new miz MATTIC"
• of or relating to coins or medals.
• [French *numismatique* from Latin *numisma* from Greek *nomisma -atos* current coin, from *nomizō* use currently]

- **numismatically** *adverb*
- **numismatics** *noun*
- **numismatist** *noun* "new MIZZ muh tist"

numnah *noun*
- "NUMNA"
- a saddle cloth or pad placed under a saddle.
- [Urdu *namdā*: see NUMDAH]

nunatak *noun*
- "NUN attack"
- an isolated peak of rock projecting above a surface of inland ice or snow.
- [Greenlandic]

Nunavummiut *plural noun*
- "noona VOOMY it"
- the people inhabiting the territory of Nunavut.
- [Inuktitut]

nunchaku *noun*
- "nun CHACK oo"
- a Japanese martial arts weapon consisting of two usu. hardwood sticks joined together with a strap, chain, etc.
- [Japanese]

nunciature *noun*
- "NUNCY a chur"
- the office or tenure of a nuncio.
- [Italian *nunziatura* (as NUNCIO)]

nuncio *noun*
- "NUNCY oh" or "NOONCY oh"
- a papal ambassador to a foreign court or government.
- [Italian from Latin *nuntius* messenger]

nunnery *noun*
- "NUNNER ee"
- a convent.
- [Old English *nunne* and Old French *nonne* nun, from Church Latin *nonna* feminine of *nonnus* monk, originally a title given to an elderly person]

nuptial *adjective*
- "NUP sh'll"
- of or relating to marriage or weddings.
- [Latin *nuptialis* from *nuptiae* wedding, from *nubere nupt-* wed]

nursling *noun*
- "NURSE ling"
- an infant or baby animal that is being suckled.
- [Old French *norice*, *nurice* nurse, from Late Latin *nutricia* feminine of Latin *nutricius* from *nutrix -icis* from *nutrire* NOURISH]

nurturance *noun*
- "NUR chur ince"
- emotional and physical nourishment and care given to someone.
- [as NURTURE]
- **nurturant** *adjective*

nurture *noun*
- "NUR chur"
- the process of bringing up or training (esp. children).
- [Old French *nour(e)ture* (as NOURISH)]
- **nurturer** *noun*

nutant *adjective*
- "NEW t'nt"
- nodding, drooping.
- [Latin *nutare* nod]

nutation *noun*
- "new TAY sh'n"
- a periodic oscillation of the earth's poles.
- [Latin *nutatio* (as NUTANT)]

nutgall *noun*
- "NUT gaul"
- a growth found on dyer's oak, used as a dyestuff.
- ['nut' + 'gall' from Old French *galle* fungal growth, from Latin *galla*]

nutraceutical *noun*
- "nootra SOOTA k'll"
- a food containing health-giving additives and having medicinal benefit.
- [blend of NUTRITION + PHARMACEUTICAL]

nutria *noun*
- "NEW tree uh"
- the skin or fur of a coypu.
- [Spanish, = otter]

nutrient *noun*
- "NEW tree 'nt"
- any substance that provides essential nourishment for the maintenance of life.
- [Latin *nutrire* nourish]

nutriment *noun*
- "NOOTRA m'nt" or "NYOOTRA m'nt"
- a nourishing substance.
- [Latin *nutrimentum* (as NUTRIENT)]

nutrition *noun*
- "new TRISH'n"
- the process by which humans or animals utilize food for the proper functioning of the organism.
- [French *nutrition* or Late Latin *nutritio* (as NUTRIENT)]
- **nutritional** *adjective*
- **nutritionally** *adverb*
- **nutritionist** *noun*

nutritious *adjective*
- "new TRISH us"
- rich in nutrients.
- [as NUTRITION]
- **nutritiously** *adverb*
- **nutritiousness** *noun*

nutritive *adjective*
- "NOOTRA tiv" or "NYOOTRA tiv"
- of, pertaining to, or concerned in nutrition.
- [medieval Latin *nutritivus* (as NUTRIENT)]

Nuxalk *noun*
- "nook HAWLK"
- a member of a Salishan Aboriginal people of the central BC coast.
- [Nuxalk *nuxalk*, the name for the Bella Coola Valley]

nyala *noun*
- "NYALA"
- a large antelope, *Tragelaphus angasi*, native to southern Africa, with curved horns having a single complete turn.
- [Zulu]

nyctalopia *noun*
- "nicta LOPEY uh"
- the inability to see in dim light or at night.
- [Late Latin from Greek *nuktalōps* from *nux nuktos* night + *alaos* blind + *ōps* eye]

nyctitropic *adjective*
- "nicta TROPPIC"
- (of plant movements) occurring at night and caused by changes in light and temperature.
- [Greek *nukti-* combining form of *nux nuktos* night + *tropos* turn]

nylon *noun*
- "NIE lon"
- any of various synthetic polyamide fibres having a protein-like structure, with tough, lightweight, elastic properties, used for textiles, cord, etc.
- [invented word, after *cotton*, *rayon*]

nymph *noun*
- "NIMF"
- any of various mythological semi-divine spirits regarded as maidens and associated with aspects of nature, esp. rivers and woods.
- [Latin *nympha* from Greek *numphē*]
- **nymphal** *adjective*
- **nymphean** *adjective* "nim FEE 'n"

nymphalid *adjective*
- "nim FAL id"
- of or relating to the large family Nymphalidae of butterflies with degenerate forelegs.
- [modern Latin genus name *Nymphalis*, from Latin *nympha* NYMPH]

nymphet *noun*
- "nim FETT" or "NIMF it"
- a sexually attractive girl or young woman.
- [as NYMPH]

nympholepsy *noun*
- "NIMFA lepsy"
- ecstasy or frenzy caused by desire of the unattainable.
- [from Greek *numpholēptos* caught by nymphs (as NYMPH, *lambanō* take) after *epilepsy*]
- **nympholept** *noun*
- **nympholeptic** *adjective*

nystagmus *noun*
- "niss TAG muss"
- a rapid, involuntary, and usu. lateral movement of the eyeball.
- [Greek *nustagmos* nodding]
- **nystagmic** *adjective*

nystatin *noun*
- "NICE tuh tin" or "NISS tuh tin"
- an antibiotic used esp. to treat fungal infections.
- [*New York State* (where developed)]

Nyungar *noun*
- "NYOONG ur"
- an Aboriginal language of SW Australia, now extinct.
- [Nyungar]

oakum *noun*
• "OAK 'm"
• a loose fibre obtained by picking old rope to pieces and used esp. in caulking.
• [Old English *ǣcumbe*, *ācumbe*, lit. 'off-combings']

Oakvillian *noun*
• "oak VILLY 'n"
• a resident of Oakville, Ont.

oasis *noun*
• "oh AY sis"
• a fertile spot in a desert, where water is found.
• [Late Latin from Greek, apparently of Egyptian origin]

oast *noun*
• "OAST" (rhymes with *TOAST*)
• a kiln for drying hops.
• [Old English *āst* from Germanic]

oasthouse *noun*
• "OAST house"
• a building containing a kiln for drying hops.
• [OAST + 'house']

obbligato *noun*
ALSO SPELLED: **obligato**
• "obbly GOTTO"
• an accompaniment, usu. special and unusual in effect, forming an integral part of a composition.
• [Italian, = obligatory, from Latin *obligatus* past participle (as OBLIGE)]

obconical *adjective*
• "ob CONNA k'll"
• in the form of an inverted cone.
• [Latin *ob* towards, against, in the way of + CONIC]

obcordate *adjective*
• "ob CORD ate"
• in the shape of a heart and attached at the pointed end.
• [Latin *ob* towards, against, in the way of + CORDATE]

obdurate *adjective*
• "OB dyur it" or "OB dur it"
• stubborn, unyielding.
• [Latin *obduratus* past participle of *obdurare* (*ob* towards, against, in the way of, *durare* harden, from *durus* hard)]
• **obduracy** *noun*
• **obdurately** *adverb*
• **obdurateness** *noun*

obeah *noun*
• "OH bee uh"
• a kind of sorcery or witchcraft practised esp. in the W Indies.
• [Twi *ɔ-bayifo* sorcerer, from *bayi* sorcery]

obedience *noun*
• "oh BEEDY ince"
• the act or practice of obeying.
• [Latin *obedientia* (as OBEY)]
• **obedient** *adjective*
• **obediently** *adverb*

obeisance *noun*
• "oh BAY since" or "oh BEE since"
• homage, submission, deference.
• [Old French *obeissance* (as OBEY)]
• **obeisant** *adjective*

obelisk *noun*
• "OBBA lisk"
• a tapering usu. four-sided stone pillar set up as a monument or landmark etc.
• [Greek *obeliskos* diminutive of *obelos* spit for roasting meat etc.]

obelus *noun*
• "OBBA luss"
• a symbol (†) used as a reference mark in printed matter or to indicate that a person is deceased.
• [Latin from Greek *obelos* (as OBELISK)]

obese *adjective*
• "oh BEECE"
• very fat; corpulent.
• [Latin *obesus* (as *ob* towards, against, in the way of, *edere* eat)]
• **obesity** *noun*

obey *verb*
• "oh BAY"
• carry out the command of.
• [Old French *obeir* from Latin *obedire* (*ob* towards, against, in the way of, *audire* hear)]
• **obeyer** *noun*

obfuscate *verb*
- "OB fuss cate"
- obscure or confuse (a mind, topic, etc.).
- [Late Latin *obfuscare* (*ob* towards, against, in the way of, *fuscus* dark)]
- **obfuscation** *noun*
- **obfuscatory** *adjective* "ob FUSS kuh tory"

obi *noun*
- "OH bee"
- a sash worn with a Japanese kimono.
- [Japanese]

obituary *noun*
- "oh BIT choo airy"
- a notice of a death, esp. in a newspaper, usu. comprising a brief biographical sketch of the deceased.
- [medieval Latin *obituarius* from Latin *obitus* death, from *obire obit-* die (*ob* towards, against, in the way of, *ire* go)]
- **obituarist** *noun*

objectionable *adjective*
- "ub JECK sh'n a bull"
- unpleasant, offensive, undesirable, disapproved of.
- [from 'object' from medieval Latin *objectum* thing presented to the mind, past participle of Latin *objicere* (*ob* towards, against, in the way of, *jacere ject-* throw)]
- **objectionably** *adverb*

objet *noun*
- "ob ZHAY"
- an object displayed as an ornament.
- [French, lit. 'object']

oblanceolate *adjective*
- "ob LANCY a lit"
- (esp. of leaves) lanceolate with the more pointed end at the base.
- [Latin *ob* towards, against, in the way of + LANCEOLATE]

oblast *noun*
- "OB last"
- an administrative division or region in Russia and the former Soviet Union, and in some constituent republics of the former Soviet Union.
- [Russian]

oblate *noun*
- "OB late"
- a person dedicated to a monastic or religious life or work.
- [French from medieval Latin *oblatus* from *offere oblat-* offer (*ob* towards, against, in the way of, *ferre* bring)]

oblation *noun*
- "oh BLAY sh'n"
- a thing offered to a divine being.
- [Late Latin *oblatio* (as OBLATE)]

obligate *verb*
- "OBLA gate"
- bind (a person) legally or morally.
- [Latin *obligare obligat-* (as OBLIGE)]
- **obligation** *noun*
- **obligational** *adjective*
- **obligatorily** *adverb* "uh bligga TORA lee"
- **obligatory** *adjective* "uh BLIGGA tory"

oblige *verb*
- "uh BLIJE" (with "I" as in *RIDE*)
- constrain, compel.
- [Old French *obliger* from Latin *obligare* (*ob* towards, against, in the way of, *ligare* bind)]
- **obliger** *noun*

obligee *noun*
- "ob lidge EE"
- a person to whom another is bound by contract or other legal procedure.
- [as OBLIGE]

obliging *adjective*
- "uh BLY jing"
- courteous, accommodating; ready to do a service or kindness.
- [as OBLIGE]
- **obligingly** *adverb*
- **obligingness** *noun*

obligor *noun*
- "obla GOR"
- a person who is bound to another by contract or other legal procedure.
- [as OBLIGE]

oblique *adjective*
- "oh BLEEK" or "uh BLEEK"
- slanting; declining from the vertical or horizontal.
- [French from Latin *obliquus*]
- **obliquely** *adverb*
- **obliqueness** *noun*
- **obliquity** *noun* "uh BLICK wuh tee"

obliterate *verb*
- "oh BLITTER ate"
- blot out; efface, erase, destroy.
- [Latin *obliterare* (*ob* towards, against, in the way of, *litera* letter)]
- **obliteration** *noun*
- **obliterative** *adjective*
- **obliterator** *noun*

oblivion *noun*
- "uh BLIVVY 'n"
- a state in which one is no longer aware or conscious of what is happening.
- [Old French from Latin *oblivio -onis* from *oblivisci* forget]

oblivious *adjective*
- "uh BLIVVY us"
- unaware or unconscious of.
- [as OBLIVION]
- **obliviously** *adverb*
- **obliviousness** *noun*

obloquy *noun*
- "OBLA kwee"

• the state of being generally ill spoken of.
• [Late Latin *obloquium* contradiction, from Latin *obloqui* deny (*ob* towards, against, in the way of, *loqui* speak)]

obnoxious *adjective*
• "ob NOCK sh'ss"
• annoying, irritating, disliked, offensive.
• [originally = vulnerable (to harm), from Latin *obnoxiosus* or *obnoxius* (*ob* towards, against, in the way of, *noxa* harm: assoc. with NOXIOUS)]
• **obnoxiously** *adverb*
• **obnoxiousness** *noun*

oboe *noun*
• "OH bo"
• a woodwind double-reed instrument of treble pitch and a plaintive tone.
• [Italian *oboe* or French *hautbois* from *haut* high + *bois* wood]
• **oboist** *noun*

obol *noun*
• "OB'll"
• an ancient Greek coin, equal to one-sixth of a drachma.
• [Greek *obolos*, var. of *obelos* OBELUS]

obovate *adjective*
• "ob OH vate"
• (of a leaf) ovate with the narrower end at the base.
• [Latin *ob* towards, against, in the way of + OVATE]

obscene *adjective*
• "ub SEEN"
• offensively or repulsively indecent, esp. by offending accepted sexual morality.
• [French *obscène* or Latin *obsc(a)enus* ill-omened, abominable]
• **obscenely** *adverb*

obscenity *noun*
• "ub SENNA tee"
• an obscene word, action, etc.
• [as OBSCENE]

obscurantism *noun*
• "ub SKYOOR 'nt izm"
• opposition to knowledge and enlightenment.
• [*obscurant* from German from Latin *obscurans* from *obscurare*: see OBSCURE]
• **obscurant** *noun*
• **obscurantist** *noun*

obscure *adjective*
• "ub SKYOOR"
• not clearly expressed or easily understood.
• [Old French *obscur* from Latin *obscurus* dark]
• **obscuration** *noun*
• **obscurely** *adverb*
• **obscurity** *noun*

obsequies *plural noun*
• "OBSA kweez"
• funeral rites.
• [Anglo-French *obsequie* from medieval Latin *obsequiae* from Latin *exsequiae* funeral rites (see EXEQUIES): assoc. with *obsequium* (see OBSEQUIOUS)]

obsequious *adjective*
• "ub SEE kwee us"
• servilely obedient or attentive.
• [Latin *obsequiosus* from *obsequium* compliance (*ob* towards, against, in the way of, *sequi* follow)]
• **obsequiously** *adverb*
• **obsequiousness** *noun*

observance *noun*
• "ub ZUR vince"
• the act or process of keeping or performing a law, duty, custom, ritual, etc.
• [as OBSERVE]

observatory *noun*
• "ub ZURVA tory"
• a room or building equipped for the observation of natural, esp. astronomical or meteorological, phenomena.
• [as OBSERVE]

observe *verb*
• "ub ZURV"
• perceive, note; take notice of; become conscious of.
• [Latin *observare* watch (*ob* towards, against, in the way of, *servare* keep)]
• **observable** *adjective*
• **observably** *adverb*
• **observant** *adjective*
• **observantly** *adverb*
• **observation** *noun*
• **observational** *adjective*
• **observationally** *adverb*
• **observer** *noun*

obsidian *noun*
• "ub SIDDY 'n"
• a dark glassy volcanic rock formed from hardened lava.
• [Latin *obsidianus*, error for *obsianus* from *Obsius*, the name of the discoverer of a similar stone]

obsolescent *adjective*
• "obsa LESS'nt"
• becoming obsolete; going out of use or date.
• [Latin *obsolescere obsolescent-* (*ob* towards, against, in the way of, *solēre* be accustomed)]
• **obsolescence** *noun*

obsolete *adjective*
• "obsa LEET"
• disused, discarded, antiquated, outmoded, out of date.
• [Latin *obsoletus* past participle (as OBSOLESCENT)]
• **obsoletely** *adverb*
• **obsoleteness** *noun*

obstacle *noun*
• "OBSTA k'll"
• a person or thing that obstructs progress.
• [Old French from Latin *obstaculum* from

obstare impede (*ob* towards, against, in the way of, *stare* stand)]

obstetric *adjective*
• "ub STET rick"
• of or relating to childbirth and associated processes.
• [modern Latin *obstetricus* for Latin *obstetricius* from *obstetrix* midwife, from *obstare* be present (*ob* towards, against, in the way of, *stare* stand)]
• **obstetrically** *adverb*
• **obstetrician** *noun* "obsta TRISH'n"
• **obstetrics** *noun*

obstinate *adjective*
• "OB stin it"
• stubborn, intractable.
• [Latin *obstinatus* past participle of *obstinare* persist (*ob* towards, against, in the way of, *stare* stand)]
• **obstinacy** *noun*
• **obstinately** *adverb*

obstreperous *adjective*
• "ub STREPPER us"
• unruly; resisting control.
• [Latin *obstreperus* from *obstrepere* (*ob* towards, against, in the way of, *strepere* make a noise)]
• **obstreperously** *adverb*
• **obstreperousness** *noun*

obtrude *verb*
• "ub TRUDE"
• be or become obtrusive.
• [Latin *obtrudere obtrus-* (*ob* towards, against, in the way of, *trudere* push)]
• **obtruder** *noun*
• **obtrusion** *noun*

obtrusive *adjective*
• "ub TRUE siv"
• unpleasantly or unduly noticeable.
• [as OBTRUDE]
• **obtrusively** *adverb*
• **obtrusiveness** *noun*

obtuse *adjective*
• "ub TUCE"
• dull-witted; slow to understand.
• [late Middle English (in the sense 'blunt') from Latin *obtusus* past participle of *obtundere* beat against]
• **obtusely** *adverb*
• **obtuseness** *noun*

obverse *noun*
• "OB vurse" or "ob VURSE"
• the side of a coin or medal etc. bearing the head or principal design.
• [Latin *obversus* past participle (as OBVERT)]
• **obversely** *adverb*

obvert *verb*
• "ub VURT"
• alter (a proposition) so as to infer another proposition with a contradictory predicate, e.g. *no men are immortal* to *all men are mortal*.
• [Latin *obvertere obvers-* (*ob* towards, against, in the way of, *vertere* turn)]
• **obversion** *noun*

obviate *verb*
• "OB vee ate"
• get around or do away with (a need, inconvenience, etc.).
• [Late Latin *obviare* oppose (*ob* towards, against, in the way of, *via* way)]
• **obviation** *noun*

ocarina *noun*
• "ocka REENA"
• a small egg-shaped wind instrument with finger holes.
• [Italian from *oca* goose (from its shape)]

occasion *noun*
• "uh CAY zh'n"
• a special or noteworthy event or happening.
• [Old French *occasion* or Latin *occasio* juncture, reason, from *occidere occas-* go down (*ob* towards, against, in the way of, *cadere* fall)]

occasional *adjective*
• "uh CAY zh'n 'll"
• happening, done, consumed, etc. infrequently; not regular.
• [as OCCASION]
• **occasionally** *adverb*

Occident *noun*
• "OCKSA d'nt"
• the West.
• [Latin *occidens -entis* setting, sunset, west (as OCCASION)]
HOMOPHONES: *oxidant*

occidental *adjective*
• "ocksa DENT'll"
• of the Occident, as distinct from oriental.
• [as OCCIDENT]

occipital *adjective*
• "ock SIPPA t'll"
• belonging to or situated in or on the occiput.
• [as OCCIPUT]

occiput *noun*
• "OXA putt"
• the back of the head.
• [Latin *occiput* (*ob* towards, against, in the way of, *caput* head)]

Occitan *noun*
• "OXA tan"
• the group of Romance dialects spoken south of the Loire.
• [French, from *oc* (from Latin *hoc*) the form for *yes* (as opposed to *oui* north of the Loire)]
• **Occitanian** *noun* "oxa TAINY 'n"

occlude *verb*
• "uh CLUDE"
• stop up or close (pores, an orifice, a passage, etc.).
• [Latin *occludere occlus-* (*ob* towards, against, in the way of, *claudere* shut)]

- **occlusion** *noun*
- **occlusive** *adjective*

occult *adjective*
- "uh CULT"
- involving the supernatural; mystical, magical.
- [Latin *occulere occult-* (*ob* towards, against, in the way of, *celare* hide)]
- **occultation** *noun*
- **occultism** *noun*
- **occultist** *noun*
- **occultly** *adverb*

occupancy *noun*
- "OCK yuh p'n see"
- the act, condition, or fact of occupying something or of being occupied.
- [as OCCUPY]

occupant *noun*
- "OCK yuh p'nt"
- a person who occupies, resides in, or is in a place etc.
- [as OCCUPY]

occupation *noun*
- "ock yuh PAY sh'n"
- what occupies one; a means of passing one's time.
- [as OCCUPY]
- **occupational** *adjective*

occupy *verb*
- "OCK yuh pie"
- reside in; be the tenant of.
- [Latin *occupare* seize (*ob* towards, against, in the way of, *capere* take)]
- **occupier** *noun*

occur *verb*
- "uh CUR" or "oh CUR"
- come into being as an event or process at or during some time; happen.
- [Latin *occurrere* go to meet, present itself (*ob* towards, against, in the way of, *currere* run)]
- **occurrence** *noun*

ocean *noun*
- "OH sh'n"
- a large expanse of sea, esp. each of the main areas called the Atlantic, Pacific, Indian, Arctic, and Antarctic Oceans.
- [Latin *oceanus* from Greek *ōkeanos* stream encircling the earth's disc]
- **oceanic** *adjective* "oh shee ANNIC" or "oh see ANNIC"
- **oceanward** *adverb*

oceanarium *noun*
- "oh sh'n AIRY um"
- a large sea water aquarium for keeping sea animals.
- [OCEAN + '-arium', after *aquarium*]

oceanfront *adjective*
- "OH sh'n frunt"
- on the shore of an ocean.
- [OCEAN + 'front']

Oceanian *adjective*
- "oh shee ANNY 'n" or "oh see ANNY 'n"
- of or relating to Oceania, which consists of the islands of the Pacific and adjacent seas, sometimes including Australasia and the Malay archipelago.

Oceanid *noun*
- "oh SEE 'n id"
- an ocean nymph.
- [Greek *ōkeanis -idos* daughter of Oceanus, the personification of the river encircling the whole world]

oceanography *noun*
- "oh sh'n OGGRA fee"
- the study of the oceans.
- [as OCEAN + Greek *graphia* writing]
- **oceanographer** *noun*
- **oceanographic** *adjective*

oceanside *adjective*
- "OH sh'n side"
- near, by, on or along the shore of an ocean.
- [OCEAN + 'side' from Old English *sīde*]

oceanview *adjective*
- "OH sh'n vyoo"
- designating a room etc. with a view of an ocean.
- [OCEAN + 'view' from Anglo-French *v(i)ewe*, Old French *vēue* feminine past participle from *vēoir* see, from Latin *vidēre*]

ocellus *noun*
- "aw SELL us"
- each of the simple, as opposed to compound, eyes of insects etc.
- [Latin, diminutive of *oculus* eye]
- **ocellar** *adjective*
- **ocellated** *adjective* "OSSA lated"

ocelot *noun*
- "AW suh lot" or "OH suh lot"
- a medium-sized cat, *Felis pardalis*, native to S and Central America, having a deep yellow or orange coat with black striped and spotted markings.
- [French from Nahuatl *ocelotl* jaguar]

oche *noun*
- "OCKY"
- the line behind which the players stand when throwing darts.
- [20th c.: origin uncertain (perhaps connected with Old French *ochen* cut a deep notch in)]

ochlocracy *noun*
- "ock LOCKRA see"
- mob rule.
- [French *ochlocratie* from Greek *okhlokratia* from *okhlos* mob + *kratia* power]
- **ochlocrat** *noun*
- **ochlocratic** *adjective*

ochre *noun*
ALSO SPELLED: *US* also **ocher**
- "OH cur"

• a mineral of clay and ferric oxide, used as a pigment varying from light yellow to brown or red.
• [Greek ōkhra yellow ochre]

ocker *noun*
• "OCKER"
• a boorish or aggressive Australian (esp. as a stereotype).
• [20th c.: origin uncertain]

ocotillo *noun*
• "oh kuh TEELYO"
• a spiny scarlet-flowered desert shrub, *Fouquieria splendens*, of Mexico and the southwestern US.
• [Latin American Spanish, diminutive from Nahuatl *ocotl* torch]

octad *noun*
• "OCTAD"
• a group of eight.
• [Late Latin *octas octad-* from Greek *oktas -ados* from *oktō* eight]

octagon *noun*
• "OCTA gon"
• a plane figure with eight sides and angles.
• [Latin *octagonos* from Greek *octagōnos* (*oktō* eight, *-gonos* -angled)]
• **octagonal** *adjective* "ock TAGGA n'll"
• **octagonally** *adverb*

octahedron *noun*
• "octa HEED r'n"
• a solid figure contained by eight (esp. triangular) plane faces.
• [Greek *oktaedron* (*oktō* eight, *hedra* base)]
• **octahedral** *adjective*

octal *adjective*
• "OCT'll"
• pertaining to or designating a system of numerical notation in which the base is 8, using digits 0 through 7.
• [Greek *oktō* eight]

octamerous *adjective*
• "ock TAMMER us"
• (of a plant etc.) having eight parts.
• [Greek *oktō* eight, *-meros* having (a specified number of) parts, sharing]

octane *noun*
• "OCK tane"
• a colourless inflammable hydrocarbon of the alkane series.
• [Greek *oktō* eight]

octant *noun*
• "OCK t'nt"
• an arc of a circle equal to one eighth of the circumference.
• [Latin *octans octant-* half-quadrant from *octo* eight]

octavalent *adjective*
• "octa VALE 'nt"
• having a valence of eight.
• [Greek *oktō* eight + VALENCE]

octave *noun*
• "OCTIV"
• a series of eight notes occupying the interval between (and including) two notes, one having twice or half the frequency of vibration of the other.
• [Old French from Latin *octava* eighth (reckoned inclusively)]

octavo *noun*
• "ock TOV oh" or "ock TAY vo"
• a size of book or page given by folding a standard sheet three times to form a quire of eight leaves.
• [Latin *in octavo* in an eighth, from *octavus* eighth]

octennial *adjective*
• "ock TENNY 'll"
• lasting eight years.
• [Late Latin *octennium* period of eight years]

octet *noun*
• "OCK tet"
• a composition for eight voices or instruments.
• [Italian *ottetto* or German *Oktett* from Latin *octo* eight]

octodecimo *noun*
• "octo DESSIM oh"
• a size of book or page given by folding a standard sheet into eighteen leaves.
• [*in octodecimo* from Latin *octodecimus* eighteenth]

octogenarian *noun*
• "octa juh NERRY 'n"
• a person from 80 to 89 years old.
• [Latin *octogenarius* from *octogeni* distributive of *octoginta* eighty]

octopod *noun*
• "OCTA pod"
• any cephalopod of the order Octopoda, with eight arms usu. having suckers, and a round sacklike body, including octopuses.
• [Greek *oktōpous -podos* from *oktō* eight + *pous* foot]

octopus *noun*
• "OCTA puss"
• any cephalopod mollusc of the genus *Octopus* having eight suckered arms, a soft sacklike body, and strong beaklike jaws.
• [Greek *oktōpous*: see OCTOPOD]

octosyllable *noun*
• "octa SILLA bull"
• a verse or word with eight syllables.
• [Late Latin *octosyllabus* (Latin *octo* eight + SYLLABLE)]
• **octosyllabic** *adjective* "octa suh LABBIC"

octroi *noun*
• "OCK trwah"
• a duty levied in some countries on goods entering a town.

• [French from *octroyer* grant, from medieval Latin *auctorizare*: see AUTHORIZE]

octuple *adjective*
• "ock TUPPLE"
• eightfold.
• [French *octuple* or Latin *octuplus* (adjective) from *octo* eight]

ocular *adjective*
• "OCK yuh lur"
• of or connected with the eyes or sight; visual.
• [Late Latin *ocularis* from Latin *oculus* eye]
• **ocularly** *adverb*

oculist *noun*
• "OCK yuh list"
• a person who specializes in the medical treatment of eye disorders or defects.
• [French *oculiste* from Latin *oculus* eye]

odalisque *noun*
• "OH duh lisk"
• an Eastern female slave or concubine, esp. in the Turkish Sultan's seraglio.
• [French from Turkish *odalik* from *oda* chamber + *lik* function]

Odawa *noun*
• "oh DAH wah"
• a member of an Aboriginal people formerly living along the Ottawa River, and now living esp. on Manitoulin Island in Lake Huron.
• [Ojibwa, self-designation]

odeum *noun*
• "OH dee um" or "oh DEE um"
• a building for musical performances, esp. among the ancient Greeks and Romans.
• [French *odéum* or Latin *odeum* from Greek *ōideion* from *aeidō* sing]
HOMOPHONES: *odium*

odious *adjective*
• "OH dee us"
• hateful, repulsive.
• [Latin *odiosus* (as ODIUM)]
• **odiously** *adverb*
• **odiousness** *noun*

odium *noun*
• "OH dee um"
• a general or widespread dislike or reprobation incurred by a person or associated with an action.
• [Latin, = hatred, from *odi* to hate]
HOMOPHONES: *odeum*

odometer *noun*
• "oh DOMMA tur"
• an instrument for measuring the distance travelled by a vehicle.
• [French *odomètre* from Greek *hodos* way, *metron* measure]
• **odometry** *noun*

odontoid *adjective*
• "oh DON toid"
• toothlike.
• [Greek *odontoeidēs* (*odous odont-* tooth, *eidos* form)]

odontology *noun*
• "oh don TOLLA jee"
• the scientific study of the structure and diseases of teeth.
• [Greek *odous odont-* tooth, *logos* word]
• **odontological** *adjective*
• **odontologist** *noun*

odorant *noun*
• "OH dur 'nt"
• a substance giving off a smell, esp. one used to give a particular scent or odor to a product.
• [Latin *odor -oris* smell, scent]

odoriferous *adjective*
• "oh dur IFFER us"
• diffusing an intense odour, esp. an unpleasant one.
• [as ODORANT + *-fer* producing, from *ferre* bear]
• **odoriferously** *adverb*

odorous *adjective*
• "OH dur us"
• having a scent or odour.
• [as ODORANT]
• **odorously** *adverb*

odyssey *noun*
• "ODDA see"
• a series of wanderings; a long adventurous journey.
• [The *Odyssey*, title of an epic poem attributed to Homer describing the adventures of *Odysseus* (Ulysses) on his journey home from Troy]
• **Odyssean** *adjective* "oh DISSY 'n"

oenology *noun*
• "ee NOLLA jee"
• the study of wines.
• [Greek *oinos* wine + *logos* word]
• **oenological** *adjective*
• **oenologist** *noun*

oenophile *noun*
• "EENA file"
• a connoisseur of wines.
• [as OENOLOGY + Greek *philos* dear, loving]
• **oenophilic** *adjective*
• **oenophilist** *noun* "ee NOFF'll ist"

oersted *noun*
• "UR sted"
• a unit of magnetic field strength equivalent to 79.58 amperes per metre.
• [H. C. *Oersted*, Danish physicist d.1851]

oeuvre *noun*
• "OOV ruh" (with "OO" as in *HOOD*)
• the works of an author, painter, composer, filmmaker, etc., esp. regarded collectively.
• [French, = work, from Latin *opera*]

offal *noun*
• "OFF'll"
• the less valuable edible parts of a carcass, esp. the entrails and internal organs.

• [Middle Dutch *afval* from *af* off + *vallen* fall]
HOMOPHONES: *awful*

offence *noun*
ALSO SPELLED: **offense**
• "uh FENCE"
• an illegal act; a transgression or misdemeanour.
• [originally = stumbling, stumbling block: Middle English & Old French *offens* from Latin *offensus* annoyance, and Middle English & French *offense* from Latin *offensa* a striking against, hurt, displeasure, both from *offendere* (as *ob* towards, against, in the way of, *fendere fens-* strike)]

offend *verb*
• "uh FEND"
• cause offence to or resentment in; wound the feelings of.
• [Old French *offendre* from Latin (as OFFENCE)]
• **offender** *noun*
• **offending** *adjective*

offensive *adjective*
• "uh FENSIV"
• giving or meant or likely to give offence; insulting.
• [as OFFENCE]
• **offensively** *adverb*
• **offensiveness** *noun*

official *adjective*
• "uh FISH'll"
• of or relating to an office or its tenure or duties.
• [Middle English from Old French from Latin *officialis* from *officium* performance of a task (in medieval Latin also office, divine service) (from *opus* work + *facere fic-* do)]
• **officialdom** *noun*
• **officialism** *noun*
• **officially** *adverb*

officialese *noun*
• "uh fish'll EEZ"
• turgid or pedantic language supposedly characteristic of official documents and correspondence.
• [as OFFICIAL]

officiate *verb*
• "uh FISHY ate"
• act in an official capacity, esp. on a particular occasion.
• [medieval Latin *officiare* perform a divine service (*officium*): see OFFICIAL]
• **officiant** *noun*
• **officiation** *noun*
• **officiator** *noun*

officious *adjective*
• "uh FISH us"
• asserting one's authority aggressively; domineering.
• [Latin *officiosus* obliging, from *officium*: see OFFICIAL]
• **officiously** *adverb*
• **officiousness** *noun*

ogee *adjective*
• "OH jee" or "oh JEE"
• showing in section a double continuous S-shaped curve.
• [apparently from OGIVE, as being the usual moulding in groin ribs]

ogham *noun*
ALSO SPELLED: **ogam**
• "OG um"
• an ancient British and Irish alphabet of twenty characters formed by parallel strokes on either side of or across a continuous line.
• [Old Irish *ogam*, referred to *Ogma*, its supposed inventor]

ogive *noun*
• "OH jive" or "oh JIVE"
• a pointed or Gothic arch.
• [French, of unknown origin]
• **ogival** *adjective*

ogle *verb*
• "OH g'll"
• eye amorously, lecherously, or covetously.
• [prob. Low German or Dutch: compare Low German *oegeln*, frequentative of *oegen* look at]
• **ogler** *noun*

Ohioan *noun*
• "oh HY oh 'n"
• a resident of Ohio.

ohm *noun*
• "OME"
• the SI unit of resistance, transmitting a current of one ampere when subjected to a potential difference of one volt.
• [G. S. *Ohm*, German physicist d.1854]
• **ohmic** *adjective*
HOMOPHONES: *om*

ohmmeter *noun*
• "OME meeter"
• an instrument for measuring electrical resistance.
• [OHM + Greek *metron* measure]

oidium *noun*
• "oh IDDY um"
• any of several kinds of fungal spore, formed by the breaking up of fungal hyphae into cells.
• [modern Latin from Greek *ōion* egg + *-idion* diminutive suffix]

Ojibwa *noun*
ALSO SPELLED: **Ojibway, Ojibwe**
• "oh JIB way"
• a member of an Algonquian people living esp. around Lake Superior and certain adjacent areas.
• [Ojibwa, from a root meaning 'puckered', with reference to their moccasins]

Oka *noun*
• "OH kuh"

• *Cdn* a variety of semi-soft cured cheese originally made by Trappist monks.
• [from *Oka*, Quebec, where this cheese is made]

Okanagan *noun*
• "oh kuh NOG'n"
• a member of an Aboriginal people living in southern BC.
• [*Okanagan* Lake, in BC]

okapi *noun*
• "oh KAPPY"
• a ruminant mammal, *Okapia johnstoni*, native to central Africa, with a head resembling that of a giraffe and a body resembling that of a zebra, having a dark chestnut coat and transverse stripes on the hindquarters and upper legs only.
• [local word]

okra *noun*
• "OAK ruh"
• a plant, *Abelmoschus esculentus*, yielding long ridged seed pods.
• [apparently West African: compare Ibo *okuro* okra, Twi *nkrakra* broth]

Oktoberfest *noun*
• "ock TOE bur fest"
• an annual beer festival celebrated in Munich, Germany and other areas of German settlement in late September and early October.
• [German, *Oktober* October + *Fest* festivity, celebration]

oleaginous *adjective*
• "oh lee ADGE 'n us"
• having the properties of or producing oil.
• [French *oléagineux* from Latin *oleaginus* from *oleum* oil]

oleander *noun*
• "oh lee ANDER"
• an evergreen poisonous shrub, *Nerium oleander*, native to the Mediterranean and bearing clusters of white, pink, or red flowers.
• [medieval Latin]

oleaster *noun*
• "oh lee ASTER"
• any of various sometimes thorny trees of the genus *Elaeagnus*, esp. *E. angustifolia* bearing olive-shaped yellowish fruits.
• [Latin from *olea* olive tree + suffix '-aster' denoting incomplete resemblance]

oleate *noun*
• "OH lee ate"
• a salt or ester of oleic acid.
• [as OLEIC]

olecranon *noun*
• "oh LECKRA non" or "oh lee CRAY non"
• a bony prominence on the upper end of the ulna at the elbow.
• [Greek *ōle(no)kranon* from *ōlenē* elbow + *kranion* head]

olefin *noun*
ALSO SPELLED: **olefine**
• "OH luh fin"
• any of a series of unsaturated aliphatic hydrocarbons containing a double bond and having the general formula C_nH_{2n}, including ethylene and propylene; an alkene.
• [French *oléfiant* oil-forming (with reference to oily ethylene dichloride)]

oleic *adjective*
• "oh LEE ick"
• designating an unsaturated fatty acid present in many fats and soaps.
• [Latin *oleum* oil]

oleo *adjective*
• "OH lee oh"
• designating a system containing a telescopic strut, used esp. in aircraft undercarriages, which absorbs shocks by causing oil to be forced through a small valve into a hollow piston where the strut is compressed.
• [Latin *oleum* oil]
HOMOPHONES: *olio*

oleograph *noun*
• "OH lee oh graff"
• a print made to resemble an oil painting.
• [Latin *oleum* oil + Greek *graphia* writing]
• **oleographic** *adjective*
• **oleography** *noun*

oleomargarine *noun*
• "oh lee oh MAR juh rin"
• = MARGARINE.
• [Latin *oleum* oil + MARGARINE]

oleoresin *noun*
• "oh lee oh REZZIN"
• a natural or artificial mixture of essential oils and a resin, e.g. balsam.
• [Latin *oleum* oil + RESIN]

oleum *noun*
• "OH lee um"
• concentrated sulphuric acid containing excess sulphur trioxide in solution forming a dense corrosive liquid.
• [Latin, = oil]

olfaction *noun*
• "ol FACK sh'n"
• the act or capacity of smelling; the sense of smell.
• [Latin *olfactus* a smell, from *olēre* to smell + *facere fact-* make]
• **olfactory** *adjective*

olibanum *noun*
• "oh LIBBA num"
• an aromatic gum resin from any tree of the genus *Boswellia*, used as incense.
• [Late Latin *libanus* from Greek *libanos* frankincense, of Semitic origin]

oligarch *noun*
• "OLLA gark"
• a member of an oligarchy.

- [Greek *oligarkhēs* from *oligoi* few + *arkhō* to rule]

oligarchy *noun*
- "OLLA garky"
- government by a small group of people.
- [as OLIGARCH]
- **oligarchic** *adjective*
- **oligarchical** *adjective*
- **oligarchically** *adverb*

Oligocene *adjective*
- "AWL igga seen"
- of or relating to the third epoch of the Tertiary period, between the Eocene and the Miocene, from about 38 to 24.6 million years ago, a time of falling temperatures.
- [Greek *oligos* small, *oligoi* few, *kainos* new]

oligochaete *noun*
- "OLLA go keet"
- an annelid worm of the division Oligochaeta, which includes the earthworms.
- [Greek *oligos* small, *oligoi* few, *khaitē* long hair (taken as 'bristle'), so called as having fewer bristles than polychaetes]

oligonucleotide *noun*
- "olla go NEW clee a tide"
- a polynucleotide whose molecules contain a relatively small number of nucleotides.
- [Greek *oligos* small, *oligoi* few + NUCLEOTIDE]

oligopoly *noun*
- "olla GOPPA lee"
- a state of limited competition between a small number of producers or sellers.
- [Greek *oligos* small, *oligoi* few + MONOPOLY]
- **oligopolist** *noun*
- **oligopolistic** *adjective*

oligosaccharide *noun*
- "olla go SACKA ride"
- any carbohydrate whose molecules are composed of a relatively small number of monosaccharide units.
- [Greek *oligos* small, *oligoi* few + SACCHARIDE]

oligotrophic *adjective*
- "olla go TROFFIC"
- (of a lake etc.) relatively poor in plant nutrients.
- [Greek *oligos* small, *oligoi* few, *trophē* food]
- **oligotrophy** *noun* "olla GOTTRA fee"

olivaceous *adjective*
- "olla VAY sh'ss"
- olive green; of a dusky yellowish green.
- [Latin *oliva* from Greek *elaia*, from *elaion* oil + Latin adjective suffix *-aceus* of the nature of]

olivine *noun*
- "OLLA veen"
- a naturally occurring form of magnesium-iron silicate, usu. olive green and found in igneous rocks.
- [Latin *oliva* olive]

ollie *noun*
- "OLLY"
- (in skateboarding and snowboarding) a jump performed without the aid of a takeoff ramp, executed by pushing the back foot down on the tail of the board, bringing the board off the ground.
- [20th c.: origin unknown]

Olmec *noun*
- "AWL meck"
- a member of a prehistoric people inhabiting the coast of Veracruz and western Tabasco on the Gulf of Mexico (*c.*1200–400 BC) who established what was probably the first Meso-American civilization.
- [Nahuatl *Olmecatl*, literally 'inhabitants of the rubber country']

oloroso *noun*
- "olla ROE so"
- a heavy dark medium-sweet sherry.
- [Spanish, lit. 'fragrant']

Olympiad *noun*
- "a LIMPY ad"
- a period of four years between Olympic Games, used by the ancient Greeks in dating events.
- [Latin *Olympias Olympiad-* from Greek *Olumpias Olumpiad-* from *Olumpios*: see OLYMPIC]

Olympian *adjective*
- "a LIMPY 'n"
- of or associated with Mount Olympus in Greece, traditionally the home of the Greek gods.
- [as OLYMPIC]

Olympic *adjective*
- "a LIMPIC"
- of or pertaining to the modern Olympic Games.
- [Latin *Olympicus* from Greek *Olumpikos* of *Olympus* (home of the gods) or *Olympia* (in S Greece)]

om *noun*
- "OME"
- a mystic syllable used as a mantra and at the beginning and end of prayers etc.
- [Sanskrit *om*, *om*, sometimes regarded as composed of three sounds, *a-u-m*, symbolizing the three major Hindu deities]

HOMOPHONES: *ohm*

omadhaun *noun*
- "OMMA don"
- a foolish person.
- [Irish *amadán*]

Omani *noun*
- "oh MANNY" or "oh MONNY"
- a native or inhabitant of Oman on the Arabian peninsula.

omasum *noun*
- "oh MAY sum"

- the third stomach of a ruminant.
- [Latin, = steer's tripe]

ombré *adjective*
- "OMM bray"
- (of a fabric etc.) having gradual shading of colour from light to dark.
- [French, past participle of *ombrer* to shadow (as UMBER)]

HOMOPHONES: *hombre*

ombudsman *noun*
- "OMM budz m'n"
- an official appointed by a government to investigate individuals' complaints against public authorities etc.
- [Swedish, = legal representative]

omega *noun*
- "oh MAY guh" or "oh MEGGA"
- the last (24th) letter of the Greek alphabet (Ω, ω).
- [Greek, *ō mega* = great O]

omelette *noun*

ALSO SPELLED: **omelet**
- "OMM lit"
- a dish of beaten eggs cooked in a frying pan and served plain or filled with cheese, meat, vegetables, etc.
- [French *omelette*, obsolete *amelette* by metathesis from *alumette* var. of *alumelle* from *lemele* knife blade, from Latin *lamella*: see LAMELLA]

omen *noun*
- "OH m'n"
- an occurrence or object regarded as portending good or evil.
- [Latin *omen ominis*]

omentum *noun*
- "oh MEN tum"
- a fold of peritoneum connecting the stomach with other abdominal organs.
- [Latin]
- **omental** *adjective*

omertà *noun*
- "oh MARE tuh"
- a code of silence, esp. as practised by the Mafia.
- [Italian, = conspiracy of silence]

omicron *noun*
- "OMMA cron" or "OME a cron"
- the fifteenth letter of the Greek alphabet (O, o).
- [Greek, *o mikron* = small o]

ominous *adjective*
- "OMM 'n us"
- threatening; indicating disaster or difficulty.
- [Latin *ominosus* (as OMEN)]
- **ominously** *adverb*
- **ominousness** *noun*

omit *verb*
- "oh MIT"
- leave out; not insert or include.
- [Latin *omittere omiss-* (as *ob* towards, against, in the way of, *mittere* send)]
- **omissible** *adjective*
- **omission** *noun* "oh MISH'n"

ommatidium *noun*
- "omma TIDDY um"
- a structural element in the compound eye of an insect.
- [modern Latin from Greek *ommatidion* diminutive of *omma ommat-* eye]

omnibus *noun*
- "OMNA buss"
- a volume containing several novels etc. previously published separately.
- [French from Latin (dative pl. of *omnis*), = for all]

omnicompetent *adjective*
- "omna COMPA t'nt"
- able to deal with all matters.
- [Latin *omnis* all + COMPETENT]
- **omnicompetence** *noun*

omnidirectional *adjective*
- "omna duh RECK sh'n 'll"
- of equal sensitivity or power in all (esp. horizontal) directions.
- [Latin *omnis* all + 'directional' from Latin *directio* (as DIRECTORY)]

omnifarious *adjective*
- "omna FERRY us"
- of all sorts or varieties.
- [Late Latin *omnifarius*]

omnipotent *adjective*
- "omm NIPPA t'nt"
- having great or absolute power.
- [Latin *omnipotens* (as *omnis* all + POTENT)]
- **omnipotence** *noun*
- **omnipotently** *adverb*

omnipresent *adjective*
- "omna PREZZ 'nt"
- present everywhere at the same time.
- [medieval Latin *omnipraesens* (*omnis* all, *praesens -entis* participle of *praeesse* be at hand (*prae-* before, *esse* be))]
- **omnipresence** *noun*

omniscient *adjective*
- "omm NISSY 'nt" or "omm NISH 'nt"
- having infinite or very extensive knowledge.
- [medieval Latin *omnisciens -entis* (*omnis* all, *scire* know)]
- **omniscience** *noun*
- **omnisciently** *adverb*

omnivorous *adjective*
- "omm NIVVER us"
- feeding on many kinds of food, esp. on both plants and flesh.
- [Latin *omnivorus* from *omnis* all + *-vorus* from *vorare* devour]
- **omnivore** *noun*
- **omnivorously** *adverb*
- **omnivorousness** *noun*

omphalos *noun*
• "OMFA loss"
• a conical stone (esp. that at Delphi) representing the navel of the earth.
• [Greek, = navel, hub]

onager *noun*
• "ONNA gur"
• a wild ass, esp. *Equus hemionus* of Central Asia.
• [ultimately from Greek *onagros* from *onos* ass + *agrios* wild]

oncogene *noun*
• "ONKA jeen"
• a gene which can transform a cell into a tumour cell.
• [Greek *ogkos* mass + GENE]

oncogenic *adjective*
• "onko JENNIC"
• causing development of a tumour or tumours.
• [Greek *ogkos* mass + GENESIS]
• **oncogenicity** *noun* "onko juh NISSA tee"

oncology *noun*
• "on COLLA jee"
• the branch of medicine dealing with the diagnosis and treatment of cancerous tumours.
• [Greek *ogkos* mass + *logos* word]
• **oncologist** *noun*

Oneida *noun*
• "oh NIDE uh"
• a member of an Iroquois people formerly living in New York State, and now living esp. along the Thames River near London, Ont.
• [Oneida, lit. 'people of the stone']

oneiric *adjective*
• "uh NIRE ick"
• of or relating to dreams or dreaming.
• [Greek *oneiros* dream]

oneiromancy *noun*
• "uh NIRE a mancy"
• the interpretation of dreams.
• [Greek *oneiros* dream + *manteia* divination]

onerous *adjective*
• "OWN ur us" or "ONNER us"
• burdensome; causing or requiring trouble.
• [Old French *onereus* from Latin *onerosus* from *onus oneris* burden]
• **onerously** *adverb*
• **onerousness** *noun*

onomastic *adjective*
• "onna MASTIC"
• relating to the origin and formation of (esp. personal) proper names.
• [Greek *onomastikos* from *onoma* name]
• **onomastics** *noun*

onomatopoeia *noun*
• "onna matta PEE uh"
• the formation of a word from a sound associated with what is named (e.g. *cuckoo*, *sizzle*).
• [Late Latin from Greek *onomatopoiia* word-making, from *onoma -matos* name + *poieō* make]
• **onomatopoeic** *adjective*
• **onomatopoeically** *adverb*

Onondaga *noun*
• "on on DOGGA"
• a member of an Iroquois people now living esp. on the Six Nations reserve near Brantford, Ont.
• [Onondaga *onó:tà'ke*, the name of the main Onondaga village, lit. 'on the hill']

onslaught *noun*
• "ON slot"
• a fierce attack.
• [earlier *anslaight* from Middle Dutch *aenslag* from *aen* on + *slag* blow, assimilated to obsolete *slaught* slaughter]

Ontarian *noun*
• "on TERRY 'n"
• a native or inhabitant of Ontario.

ontogenesis *noun*
• "onta JENNA sis"
• the origin and development of an individual.
• [Greek *ōn ont-* being, present participle of *eimi* be + GENESIS]
• **ontogenetic** *adjective* "onta juh NETTIC"
• **ontogenetically** *adverb*

ontology *noun*
• "on TOLLA jee"
• the branch of metaphysics dealing with the nature of being.
• [modern Latin *ontologia* from Greek *ōn ont-* being + *logos* word]
• **ontological** *adjective*
• **ontologically** *adverb*
• **ontologist** *noun*

onus *noun*
• "OH nuss"
• a burden, duty, or responsibility.
• [Latin]

onyx *noun*
• "ONNIX"
• a semi-precious variety of agate with different colours in layers.
• [Old French *onix* from Latin from Greek *onux* fingernail, onyx]

oocyte *noun*
• "OH a site"
• an immature ovum in an ovary.
• [Greek *ōion* egg, *kutos* vessel]

oogamous *adjective*
• "oh OGGA muss"
• reproducing by the union of mobile male and immobile female cells.
• [Greek *ōion* egg, *gamos* marriage]
• **oogamy** *noun*

oogenesis *noun*
• "oh a JENNA sis"
• the production or development of an ovum.
• [Greek *ōion* egg + GENESIS]

Ookpik *noun*
- "OOK pick"
- *Cdn* a doll resembling an owl, originally handcrafted of sealskin by Inuit artisans, now mass-produced and sold as a souvenir.
- [Inuktitut *ukpik* snowy owl]

oolite *noun*
- "OH a lite"
- a sedimentary rock, usu. limestone, consisting of rounded grains made up of concentric layers.
- [French *oölithe* from Greek *ōion* egg, *lithos* stone]
- **oolitic** *adjective* "oh a LITTIC"

oology *noun*
- "oh OLLA jee"
- the study or collecting of birds' eggs.
- [Greek *ōion* egg + *logos* word]
- **oological** *adjective*
- **oologist** *noun*

oolong *noun*
- "OO long"
- a dark kind of tea, grown esp. in China, that is partially fermented before it is dried.
- [Chinese *wulong* black dragon]

oompah *noun*
- "OOM pah"
- a representation of the repetitive rhythmical playing of lower brass instruments, esp. in German and E European dance music.
- [imitative]

oophorectomy *noun*
- "oh a fuh RECTA mee"
- the surgical removal of one or both ovaries.
- [modern Latin *oophoron* ovary (from Greek *ōophoros* egg-bearing) + Greek *ektomē* excision, from *ek* out + *temnō* cut]

opa *noun*
- "OH puh"
- (among people of German descent) grandfather; grandpa.
- [German]

HOMOPHONES: *opah*

opacify *verb*
- "oh PASSA fie"
- make or become opaque.
- [as OPAQUE]
- **opacification** *noun*
- **opacifier** *noun*

opacity *noun*
- "oh PASSA tee"
- the state of being opaque.
- [French *opacité* from Latin *opacitas -tatis* (as OPAQUE)]

opah *noun*
- "OH puh"
- a large rare deep-sea fish, *Lampris guttatus*, usu. having a silver-blue back with white spots and crimson fins.
- [West African name]

HOMOPHONES: *opa*

opal *noun*
- "OH pull"
- a quartz-like form of hydrated silica, usu. white or colourless and sometimes showing changing colours, often used as a gemstone.
- [French *opale* or Latin *opalus* prob. ultimately from Sanskrit *upalas* precious stone]

opalescent *adjective*
- "oh puh LESS'nt"
- showing changing colours like an opal.
- [as OPAL]
- **opalesce** *verb*
- **opalescence** *noun*

opaline *adjective*
- "OH puh line"
- opal-like, opalescent, iridescent.
- [as OPAL]

opaque *adjective*
- "oh PAKE"
- not transmitting light.
- [Middle English *opak* from Latin *opacus*: spelling now assimilated to French]
- **opaquely** *adverb*
- **opaqueness** *noun*

operator *noun*
- "OPPER ater"
- a person operating a machine etc., esp. one who operates a telephone switchboard.
- [Latin, from *operari* to work, from *opus operis* work]

operculum *noun*
- "uh PURK yuh lum"
- a flap-like structure covering the gills in a fish.
- [Latin from *operire* cover]
- **opercular** *adjective*
- **operculate** *adjective*

operetta *noun*
- "opper ETTA"
- a theatrical production, usu. of a comic nature, combining songs with spoken dialogue.
- [Italian, diminutive of *opera*, from Latin, = labour, work]

operon *noun*
- "OPPER on"
- a unit made up of linked genes thought to regulate other genes responsible for protein synthesis.
- [from French *opérer* work]

ophicleide *noun*
- "OFFA clide"
- an obsolete usu. bass brass wind instrument developed from the serpent.
- [French *ophicléide* from Greek *ophis* serpent + *kleis kleidos* key]

ophidian *noun*
• "oh FIDDY 'n"
• any reptile of the suborder Serpentes (formerly Ophidia), including snakes.
• [modern Latin *Ophidia* from Greek *ophis* snake]

ophthalmia *noun*
• "off THALMY uh" or "opp THALMY uh"
• an inflammation of the eye, esp. conjunctivitis.
• [Late Latin from Greek *ophthalmos* eye]

ophthalmic *adjective*
• "off THAL mick" or "opp THAL mick"
• of or relating to the eye and its diseases.
• [Latin *ophthalmicus* from Greek *ophthalmikos* (as OPHTHALMIA)]

ophthalmology *noun*
• "off th'll MOLLA jee" or "opp th'll MOLLA jee"
• the scientific study of the eye.
• [Greek *ophthalmos* eye + *logos* word]
• **ophthalmological** *adjective*
• **ophthalmologist** *noun*

ophthalmoscope *noun*
• "off THALMA scope" or "opp THALMA scope"
• an instrument for inspecting the retina and other parts of the eye.
• [as OPHTHALMIA + Greek *skopos* target, from *skeptomai* look at]
• **ophthalmoscopic** *adjective*
• **ophthalmoscopy** *noun* "off th'll MOSCA pee" or "opp th'll MOSCA pee"

opiate *noun*
• "OH pee it"
• a drug containing or derived from opium, usu. to ease pain or induce sleep.
• [medieval Latin *opiatus*, *-um*, *opiare* from Latin *opium*: see OPIUM]

opinion *noun*
• "uh PIN y'n"
• a belief or assessment based on grounds short of proof.
• [Latin *opinio -onis* from *opinari* think, believe]

opinionated *adjective*
• "uh PIN y'n ated"
• conceitedly assertive or dogmatic in one's opinions.
• [obsolete *opinionate* in the same sense, from OPINION]

opioid *noun*
• "OH pee oid"
• any compound resembling cocaine and morphine in its addictive properties or physiological effects.
• [OPIUM + Greek *-oeidēs* from *eidos* form]

opium *noun*
• "OH pee um"
• a reddish-brown heavy-scented addictive drug prepared from the juice of the opium poppy, used in medicine as an analgesic and narcotic; it is the source of both morphine and heroin.
• [Greek *opion* poppy juice, from *opos* juice]

opopanax *noun*
• "oh POPPA nax"
• an umbelliferous plant, *Opopanax chironium*, with yellow flowers.
• [Greek from *opos* juice + *panax* formed as PANACEA]

opossum *noun*
• "a POSSUM"
• any mainly tree-living marsupial of the family Didelphidae, having a prehensile tail and hind feet with an opposable thumb, esp. the common N. American species, *Didelphis virginiana*, which is the size of a cat.
• [Virginia Algonquian *āpassūm*]

opponent *noun*
• "uh POE n'nt"
• a person who opposes or belongs to an opposing side.
• [Latin *opponere opponent-* (*ob* towards, against, in the way of, *ponere* place)]
• **opponency** *noun*

opportune *adjective*
• "opper TUNE"
• (of a time) well-chosen or especially favourable or appropriate.
• [Latin *opportunus* (*ob* towards, against, in the way of, *portus* harbour), originally of the wind driving towards the harbour]
• **opportunely** *adverb*
• **opportuneness** *noun*

opportunism *noun*
• "opper TUNE izm"
• the adaptation of policy or judgment to circumstances or opportunity, esp. regardless of principle.
• [as OPPORTUNE]
• **opportunist** *noun*
• **opportunistic** *adjective*
• **opportunistically** *adverb*

opportunity *noun*
• "opper TUNA tee"
• a good chance; a favourable occasion.
• [as OPPORTUNE]

opposable *adjective*
• "a POZE a bull"
• (of the thumb in primates) capable of facing and touching the other digits on the same hand.
• [as OPPOSE]

oppose *verb*
• "a POZE"
• resist; set oneself against; argue against.
• [Old French *opposer* from Latin *opponere*: see OPPONENT]
• **opposer** *noun*
• **opposing** *adjective*
• **opposition** *noun* "oppa ZISH'n"
• **oppositional** *adjective*
• **oppositionist** *noun*

opposite *adjective*
• "OPPA zit"
• having a position on the other or further side, facing or back to back.
• [Latin *oppositus* past participle of *opponere*: see OPPONENT]
• **oppositely** *adverb*
• **oppositeness** *noun*

oppress *verb*
• "a PRESS"
• keep in subservience by coercion.
• [medieval Latin *oppressare*]
• **oppressed** *adjective*
• **oppression** *noun*
• **oppressive** *adjective*
• **oppressively** *adverb*
• **oppressiveness** *noun*
• **oppressor** *noun*

opprobrious *adjective*
• "a PRO bree us"
• (of language) severely scornful; abusive.
• [as OPPROBRIUM]
• **opprobriously** *adverb*

opprobrium *noun*
• "a PRO bree um"
• disgrace or bad reputation attaching to some act or conduct.
• [Latin from *opprobrum* (*ob* towards, against, in the way of, *probrum* disgraceful act)]

opsimath *noun*
• "OPSA math"
• a person who learns only late in life.
• [Greek *opsimathēs* from *opse* late + *math-* learn]

opsonin *noun*
• "OPP s'n in"
• a substance (often an antibody) in blood plasma which combines with foreign cells and makes them more susceptible to phagocytosis.
• [Greek *opsōnion* victuals]
• **opsonic** *adjective* "opp SONNIC"

opsonize *verb*
ALSO SPELLED: esp. *Brit.* **-ise**
• "OPP s'n ize"
• make more susceptible to phagocytosis.
• [as OPSONIN]
• **opsonization** *noun* (also esp. *Brit.* **-isation**)

optic *adjective*
• "OPTIC"
• of or relating to the eye, vision, or light.
• [French *optique* or medieval Latin *opticus* from Greek *optikos* from *optos* seen]
• **optical** *adjective*
• **optically** *adverb*

optician *noun*
• "opp TISH'n"
• a maker or seller of optical instruments, esp. eyeglasses and contact lenses.
• [French *opticien* from medieval Latin *optica* (as OPTIC)]

optics *noun*
• "OPTIX"
• the scientific study of sight and the behaviour of light, or of other radiation or particles.
• [as OPTIC]

optimal *adjective*
• "OPTA m'll"
• best or most favourable, esp. under a particular set of circumstances.
• [Latin *optimus* best]
• **optimality** *noun*
• **optimally** *adverb*

optimism *noun*
• "OPT'm izm"
• an inclination to hopefulness and confidence; a tendency to take a favourable view of circumstances or prospects.
• [French *optimisme* from Latin OPTIMUM]
• **optimist** *noun*
• **optimistic** *adjective*
• **optimistically** *adverb*

optimize *verb*
ALSO SPELLED: esp. *Brit.* **-ise**
• "OPT'm ize"
• make the best or most effective use of (a situation, an opportunity, etc.).
• [Latin *optimus* best]
• **optimization** *noun* (also esp. *Brit.* **-isation**)
• **optimizer** *noun* (also esp. *Brit.* **-iser**)

optimum *noun*
• "OPTA mum"
• the most favourable conditions (for growth, reproduction, etc.).
• [Latin, neuter (as n.) of *optimus* best]

optoelectronics *noun*
• "opto e leck TRONNIX"
• the branch of technology concerned with the combined use of electronics and light.
• [as OPTIC + ELECTRONIC]
• **optoelectronic** *adjective*

optometry *noun*
• "opp TOMMA tree"
• the science or profession of measuring eyesight, detecting eye disease, and prescribing corrective lenses (but not drugs or medicines).
• [Greek *optos* seen, visible + *metron* measure]
• **optometric** *adjective* "opta METRIC"
• **optometrist** *noun*

opulent *adjective*
• "OPP yoo l'nt"
• ostentatiously rich; wealthy.
• [Latin *opulens*, *opulent-* from *opes* wealth]
• **opulence** *noun*
• **opulently** *adverb*

opuntia *noun*
• "oh PUNSHY uh"
• any cactus of the genus *Opuntia*, with jointed cylindrical or elliptical stems and barbed bristles.

• [Latin plant name from *Opus -untis* in Locris in ancient Greece]

opus *noun*
• "OH pus"
• a separate musical composition or set of compositions of any kind.
• [Latin, = work]

opuscule *noun*
• "uh PUS kyool"
• a minor (esp. musical or literary) work.
• [French from Latin *opusculum* diminutive of OPUS]

orache *noun*
ALSO SPELLED: **orach**
• "OR itch"
• any of various plants of the genus *Atriplex* of the goosefoot family, with red, yellow, or green leaves, esp. garden orache, *A. hortensis*, cultivated for its edible leaves.
• [Anglo-French *arasche* from Latin *atriplex* from Greek *atraphaxus*]

oracle *noun*
• "ORA k'll"
• a place at which advice or prophecy was sought from the gods in classical antiquity.
• [Latin *oraculum* from *orare* speak]
• **oracular** *adjective* "or ACK yuh lur"
• **oracularly** *adverb*
HOMOPHONES: *auricle*

oracy *noun*
• "ORA see"
• the ability to express oneself fluently in speech and to understand a spoken language.
• [Latin *os oris* mouth, after *literacy*]

oral *adjective*
• "OR'll"
• by word of mouth; spoken; not written.
• [Late Latin *oralis* from Latin *os oris* mouth]
• **orally** *adverb*
HOMOPHONES: *aural, aurally*

oralism *noun*
• "OR'll izm"
• the principle that profoundly deaf people should learn to communicate by speech and lip-reading without the use of sign language.
• [as ORAL]
• **oralist** *adjective*

orality *noun*
• "or ALA tee"
• the quality of being spoken or verbally communicated.
• [as ORAL]

orangeade *noun*
• "OR inj ade"
• a non-alcoholic drink flavoured with orange.
• ['orange' (Old French *orenge*, ultimately from Arabic *nāranj* from Persian *nārang*) + LEMONADE]

orangutan *noun*
• "a RANG a tan"
• a large red long-haired tree-living ape, *Pongo pygmaeus*, native to Borneo and Sumatra, with characteristic long arms and hooked hands and feet.
• [Malay *ōrang ūtan* wild man]

oration *noun*
• "or AY sh'n"
• a formal speech, discourse, etc., esp. when ceremonial.
• [Latin *oratio* discourse, prayer, from *orare* speak, pray]
• **orator** *noun* "ORA tur"

Oratorian *noun*
• "ora TORY 'n"
• a member of the Institute of the Oratory of St. Philip Neri, a Roman Catholic society of priests.
• [as ORATORIO]

oratorio *noun*
• "ora TORY oh"
• a semi-dramatic work for orchestra and voices esp. on a sacred theme, performed without costume, scenery, or action.
• [Italian from Church Latin *oratorium* ORATORY, originally of musical services at the church of the Oratory of St. Philip Neri in Rome]

oratory *noun*
• "ORA tory"
• the art or practice of formal speaking, esp. in public.
• [Latin *ars oratoria* art of speaking from *oratorius* from *orare* pray, speak]
• **oratorical** *adjective*

orature *noun*
• "ORA chur"
• a body of poetry, tales, etc. preserved through oral transmission as part of a particular culture, esp. a pre-literate one.
• [blend of ORAL + LITERATURE]

orbicular *adjective*
• "or BICK yuh lur"
• circular and flat; disc-shaped; ring-shaped.
• [Late Latin *orbicularis* from Latin *orbiculus* diminutive of *orbis* ring]

orca *noun*
• "ORKA"
• the killer whale.
• [French *orque* or Latin *orca* a kind of whale]

Orcadian *adjective*
• "or CAY dee 'n"
• of or relating to the Orkney Islands off the north coast of Scotland.
• [Latin *Orcades* Orkney Islands]

orchard *noun*
• "OR churd"
• a piece of enclosed land with fruit trees.
• [Old English *ortgeard* from Latin *hortus* garden + 'yard']
• **orcharding** *noun*
• **orchardist** *noun*

orchestra *noun*
• "OR kiss truh"
• a usu. large group of instrumentalists, esp. combining strings, woodwinds, brass, and percussion.
• [Latin from Greek *orkhēstra* from *orkheomai* to dance (originally the part of the theatre in which the chorus danced)]
• **orchestral** *adjective* "or KESS trull"
• **orchestrally** *adverb*

orchestrate *verb*
• "OR kiss trate"
• arrange, score, or compose (music) for orchestral performance.
• [as ORCHESTRA]
• **orchestration** *noun*
• **orchestrator** *noun*

orchid *noun*
• "OR kid"
• any epiphytic or terrestrial plant of the family Orchidaceae, bearing flowers in fantastic shapes and brilliant colours, usu. having one petal larger than the others and variously spurred, lobed, pouched, etc.
• [modern Latin *Orchid(ac)eae* from Latin *orchis*: see ORCHIS]
• **orchidaceous** *adjective* "or kid AY sh'ss"
• **orchidist** *noun*

orchil *noun*
• "OR chill"
• a red or violet dye from lichen, esp. from *Roccella tinctoria*, often used in litmus.
• [Old French *orcheil* etc., perhaps ultimately from Latin *herba urceolaris* a plant for polishing glass pitchers]

orchis *noun*
• "OR kiss"
• any orchid of the genus *Orchis*, with a tuberous root and an erect fleshy stem having a spike of usu. purple or red flowers.
• [Latin from Greek *orkhis*, originally = testicle (with reference to the shape of its tuber)]

orchitis *noun*
• "or KITE iss"
• inflammation of the testicles.
• [modern Latin from Greek *orkhis* testicle + Greek *-itis*, forming feminine of adjectives in *-itēs* (with *nosos* 'disease' implied)]

orcin *noun*
• "OR sin"
• a crystalline substance, becoming red in air, extracted from any of several lichens and used to make dyes.
• [modern Latin *orcina* from Italian *orcello* orchil]

ordain *verb*
• "or DANE"
• bestow the office of minister, priest, or deacon on (a person).
• [Anglo-French *ordeiner*, Old French *ordein-* stressed stem of *ordener* from Latin *ordinare* from *ordo -inis* order]
• **ordainer** *noun*

ordinal *noun*
• "ORD'n 'll"
• a number defining a thing's position in a series, e.g. 'first', 'second', 'third', etc.
• [Late Latin *ordinalis* from Latin *ordo -inis* order]

ordinance *noun*
• "ORD'n ince"
• an authoritative order; a decree.
• [medieval Latin *ordinantia* from Latin *ordinare*: see ORDAIN]
HOMOPHONES: *ordnance*

ordinand *noun*
• "ORD'n and"
• a candidate for ordination.
• [Latin *ordinandus*, gerundive of *ordinare* ORDAIN]

ordinary *adjective*
• "ORD'n airy"
• regular, normal, customary, usual.
• [Latin *ordinarius* orderly, from *ordo -inis* order]
• **ordinarily** *adverb*
• **ordinariness** *noun*

ordinate *noun*
• "ORD'n it"
• a straight line from any point drawn parallel to one coordinate axis and meeting the other, usually a coordinate measured parallel to the vertical.
• [Latin *linea ordinata applicata* line applied parallel, from *ordinare*: see ORDAIN]

ordination *noun*
• "ord'n AY sh'n"
• the act of ordaining or conferring holy orders on a priest, minister, etc.
• [Latin *ordinatio* (as ORDAIN)]

ordnance *noun*
• "ORD nince"
• mounted guns; cannon.
• [Middle English var. of ORDINANCE]
HOMOPHONES: *ordinance*

Ordovician *adjective*
• "orda VISSY 'n" or "ordo VISHY 'n"
• of or relating to the second period of the Paleozoic era, lasting from about 505 to 438 million years ago, between the Cambrian and Silurian periods, characterized by the diversification of many invertebrate groups and the appearance of the first vertebrates.
• [Latin *Ordovices* ancient British tribe in N Wales]

ordure *noun*
• "OR dyoor"
• excrement; dung.
• [Old French from *ord* foul, from Latin *horridus*: see HORRID]

ore *noun*
• "URRA"
• a Scandinavian monetary unit equal to one-hundredth of a krona or krone.
• [Danish, Norwegian *øre*, Swedish *öre*]

oread *noun*
• "ORRY ad"
• (in Greek and Roman mythology) a mountain nymph.
• [Latin *oreas -ados* from Greek *oreias* from *oros* mountain]

orecchiette *plural noun*
• "ora KYETTY"
• a pasta dish of small ear-shaped noodles.
• [Italian, lit. 'little ears']

oregano *noun*
• "a REGGA no"
• the dried leaves of wild marjoram used as a culinary herb.
• [Spanish, = ORIGANUM]

Oregonian *noun*
• "ora GO nee 'n"
• a resident of Oregon.

organdy *noun*
ALSO SPELLED: esp. *Brit.* **organdie**
• "ORG'n dee"
• a fine translucent cotton muslin, usu. stiffened.
• [French *organdi*, of unknown origin]

organelle *noun*
• "orga NELL"
• any of various organized or specialized structures which form part of a cell.
• [modern Latin *organella* diminutive of *organum*, from Greek *organon* tool]

organochlorine *noun*
• "org'n oh CLORE een"
• any of a large group of pesticides and other synthetic organic compounds with chlorinated aromatic molecules.
• ['organic' (from Latin *organum* organ, from Greek *organon* tool) + CHLORINE]

organogenesis *noun*
• "org'n oh JENNA sis"
• the production or development of the organs of an animal or plant.
• ['organ' (from Latin *organum* organ, from Greek *organon* tool) + GENESIS]

organoleptic *adjective*
• "org'n oh LEPTIC"
• affecting the organs of sense.
• ['organ' (from Latin *organum* organ, from Greek *organon* tool) + Greek *lēptikos* disposed to take, from *lambanō* take]

organometallic *adjective*
• "org'n oh muh TALIC"
• (of a compound) organic and containing a metal.
• ['organic' (from Latin *organum* organ, from Greek *organon* tool) + METAL]

organon *noun*
• "ORG'n on"
• an instrument of thought, esp. a means of reasoning or a system of logic.
• [Greek *organon* & Latin *organum* organ, from Greek *organon* tool]

organophosphorus *noun*
• "org'n oh FOSS fur us"
• an organic compound that contains phosphorus.
• ['organic' (from Latin *organum* organ, from Greek *organon* tool) + PHOSPHORUS]
• **organophosphate** *noun*
• **organophosphorous** *adjective*

organum *noun*
• "ORG'n um"
• (in medieval music) a part sung as an accompaniment below or above a melody, usu. at an interval of a fourth or fifth.
• [Latin, = organ]

organza *noun*
• "ore GANZA"
• a thin stiff transparent silk or synthetic dress fabric.
• [prob. from French *organsin* strong silk thread, from Italian *organzino*, from *Organzi*, the European name of *Urgench*, a town in Uzbekistan, known in the Middle Ages for its silk trade]

orgeat *noun*
• "OR jee ut" or "OR jat"
• a cooling drink made from barley or almonds and orange flower water.
• [French from Provençal *orjat* from *ordi* barley, from Latin *hordeum*]

orgulous *adjective*
• "ORG yoo luss"
• haughty, proud.
• [Old French *orguillus* from *orguill* pride, from Frankish]

orgy *noun*
• "OR jee"
• a wild festivity esp. with much drinking and indiscriminate sexual activity.
• [originally pl., from French *orgies* from Latin *orgia* from Greek *orgia* secret rites]
• **orgiastic** *adjective*
• **orgiastically** *adverb*

oribi *noun*
• "ORA bee"
• a small S African grazing antelope, *Ourebia ourebi*, having a reddish-fawn back and white underparts.
• [prob. Khoisan]

oriel *noun*
• "ORRY 'll"

• a window built out from the wall of a building, usu. supported by corbels.
• [Old French *oriol* gallery, of unknown origin]
HOMOPHONES: *oriole*

orifice *noun*
• "ORA fiss"
• a usu. small opening or aperture, esp. the mouth of a bodily organ or other cavity.
• [French from Late Latin *orificium* from *os oris* mouth + *facere* make]

oriflamme *noun*
• "ORA flam"
• the sacred scarlet silk banner of St. Denis given to early French kings by the abbot of St. Denis on setting out for war.
• [Old French from Latin *aurum* gold + *flamma* flame]

origami *noun*
• "ora GAMMY"
• the Japanese art of folding paper into decorative shapes and figures.
• [Japanese from *ori* fold + *kami* paper]

origanum *noun*
• "or IGGA num"
• any plant of the genus *Origanum*, esp. wild marjoram.
• [Latin *origanum* from Greek *origanon*]

Orillian *noun*
• "uh RILL y'n"
• a resident of Orillia, Ont.

oriole *noun*
• "ORRY 'll" or "ORRY ole"
• any New World bird of the genus *Icterus*, esp. the northern oriole.
• [Old French *oriol* from Latin *aureolus* diminutive of *aureus* golden, from *aurum* gold]
HOMOPHONES: *oriel, aureole*

Orisha *noun*
• "ORA shaw"
• (in southern Nigeria) any of several minor gods or spirits. The term is also used in various religious cults of South America and the Caribbean.
• [Yoruba]

orison *noun*
• "ORA z'n"
• a prayer.
• [Old French *oreison* from Latin (as ORATION)]

Oriya *noun*
• "or EE yuh"
• a native of the State of Orissa in India.
• [Hindi]

Orkneyman *noun*
• "ORK nee m'n"
• *Cdn* (historically) a native or inhabitant of the Orkney Islands working in the N American fur trade, esp. with the Hudson's Bay Company.

orlop *noun*
• "OR lop"
• the lowest deck of a ship with three or more decks.
• [Middle Dutch *overloop* covering, from *overloopen* run over]

ormolu *noun*
• "ORMA loo"
• gilded bronze; a gold-coloured alloy of copper, zinc, and tin used to decorate furniture, make ornaments, etc.
• [French *or moulu* powdered gold (for use in gilding)]

ornament *noun*
• "ORNA m'nt"
• a thing used or serving to adorn, esp. a small trinket, vase, figure, etc.
• [Latin *ornamentum* equipment, from *ornare* adorn]
• **ornamentation** *noun*

ornamental *adjective*
• "orna MENT'll"
• serving as an ornament; decorative.
• [as ORNAMENT]
• **ornamentalism** *noun*
• **ornamentally** *adverb*

ornery *adjective*
• "ORNER ee"
• grumpily stubborn.
• [var. of ORDINARY]
• **orneriness** *noun*

ornithic *adjective*
• "or NITHIC"
• of or relating to birds.
• [Greek *ornithikos* birdlike, from *ornis ornithos* bird]

ornithischian *adjective*
• "orna THISKY 'n" or "orna THISHY 'n" (with "TH" as in *THIN*)
• of or relating to the order Ornithischia, including dinosaurs with a pelvic structure like that of birds.
• [modern Latin, from Greek *ornis ornithos* bird + *iskhion* hip joint]

ornithology *noun*
• "orna THOLLA jee"
• the branch of zoology that deals with the study of birds.
• [modern Latin *ornithologia* from Greek *ornithologos* treating of birds (*ornis ornithos* bird + *logos* word)]
• **ornithological** *adjective*
• **ornithologist** *noun*

ornithopod *noun*
• "OR nitha pod"
• a bipedal herbivorous ornithischian dinosaur of the suborder Ornithopoda.
• [modern Latin, from Greek *ornis ornith-* bird + *pous pod-* foot]

ornithopter *noun*
• "OR nith opter"
• a machine designed to achieve flight by means of flapping wings.
• [French (Greek *ornis ornithos* bird + *ptero* wing)]

orogeny *noun*
• "or ODGE a nee"
• the process of the formation of mountains.
• [Greek *oros* mountain + GENESIS]
• **orogenic** *adjective* "ora JENNIC"

orography *noun*
• "or OGGRA fee"
• the branch of physical geography dealing with the formation and features of mountains.
• [Greek *oros* mountain, *graphia* writing]
• **orographic** *adjective*

Oromoctonian *noun*
• "ora mock TONY 'n"
• a resident of Oromocto, NB.

orotund *adjective*
• "ORA tund"
• (of the voice or phrasing) full, resonant; imposing.
• [Latin *ore rotundo* with rounded mouth]
• **orotundity** *noun*
• **orotundly** *adverb*

orphan *noun*
• "OR f'n"
• a child or young animal deprived by death of one or usu. both parents.
• [Late Latin *orphanus* from Greek *orphanos* bereaved]
• **orphaned** *adjective*
• **orphanhood** *noun*

orphanage *noun*
• "OR f'n idge"
• a usu. residential institution for the care and education of orphans.
• [as ORPHAN]

Orphic *adjective*
• "OR fick"
• of or concerning the legendary Greek musician Orpheus or the mysteries, doctrines, etc. associated with him.
• [Latin *Orphicus* from Greek *Orphikos* from *Orpheus*]

orphrey *noun*
• "OR free"
• an ornamental stripe or border or separate piece of ornamental needlework, esp. on ecclesiastical vestments.
• [Middle English *orfreis* (taken as pl.) (gold) embroidery, from Old French from medieval Latin *aurifrisium* etc. from Latin *aurum* gold + *Phrygius* Phrygian, also 'embroidered']

orpiment *noun*
• "ORPA m'nt"
• a mineral form of arsenic trisulphide, formerly used as a dye and artist's pigment.
• [Old French from Latin *auripigmentum* from *aurum* gold + *pigmentum* pigment]

orpine *noun*
ALSO SPELLED: **orpin**
• "ORPIN"
• a succulent herbaceous purple-flowered plant, *Sedum telephium*.
• [Old French *orpine*, prob. alteration of ORPIMENT, originally of a yellow-flowered species of the same genus]

orrery *noun*
• "ORRER ee"
• a mechanical, usu. clockwork, model of the solar system.
• [the fourth Earl of *Orrery* d.1731, for whom one was made]

orris *noun*
• "OR iss"
• any plant of the genus *Iris*, esp. *I. florentina*.
• [16th c.: apparently an unexplained alteration of 'iris']

orrisroot *noun*
• "OR iss root"
• the fragrant rootstock of the orris, used as a flavouring and in perfumery.
• [as ORRIS + 'root']

ortanique *noun*
• "ort'n EEK"
• a citrus fruit produced by crossing an orange and a tangerine.
• [*or*ange + *tan*gerine + un*ique*]

orthochromatic *adjective*
• "ortho crow MATTIC"
• giving fairly correct relative intensity to colours in photography by being sensitive to all except red.
• [Greek *orthos* straight + CHROMATIC]

orthoclase *noun*
• "ORTHO clace"
• a common alkali feldspar usu. occurring as variously coloured crystals, used in ceramics and glass-making.
• [Greek *orthos* straight, *klasis* breaking]

orthodontics *noun*
• "ortha DONTIX"
• the branch of dentistry that deals with treatment of irregular alignment of the teeth and jaws.
• [Greek *orthos* straight, *odous odont-* tooth]
• **orthodontic** *adjective*
• **orthodontist** *noun*

orthodox *adjective*
• "ORTHA docks"
• holding correct or currently accepted opinions, esp. on religious doctrine, morals, etc.
• [Greek *orthodoxos* (*orthos* straight, *doxa* opinion)]
• **orthodoxly** *adverb*

orthodoxy *noun*
• "ORTHA docksy"
• the quality or character of being orthodox.
• [as ORTHODOX]

orthoepy *noun*
• "ORTHO eppy" or "or THOE a pee" (with "TH" as in *THIN*)
• the scientific study of the correct pronunciation of words.
• [Greek *orthoepeia* correct speech (*orthos* straight, *epos* word)]
• **orthoepic** *adjective*
• **orthoepist** *noun*

orthogenesis *noun*
• "ortho JENNA sis"
• evolutionary change in a defined direction, esp. as supposedly caused by internal tendency rather than external influence.
• [Greek *orthos* straight + GENESIS]
• **orthogenetic** *adjective* "ortho juh NETTIC"

orthogonal *adjective*
• "orth OGGA n'll"
• of, involving, or at right angles; rectangular.
• [French from *orthogone* (Greek *orthos* straight, *-gonos* -angled)]
• **orthogonality** *noun*

orthography *noun*
• "or THOGGRA fee"
• correct or conventional spelling.
• [Greek *orthographia* (*orthos* straight, *graphia* writing)]
• **orthographer** *noun*
• **orthographic** *adjective*
• **orthographical** *adjective*
• **orthographically** *adverb*

orthopaedics *noun*
ALSO SPELLED: **orthopedics**
• "ortha PEEDIX"
• the branch of medicine dealing with the correction of deformities of bones or muscles or the treatment of impairments of the skeletal system.
• [French *orthopédie* (Greek *orthos* straight, *paideia* rearing of children, the treatment being originally for children)]
• **orthopaedic** *adjective* (also **orthopedic**)
• **orthopaedist** *noun* (also **orthopedist**)

orthopteran *noun*
• "or THOPTER 'n"
• any insect of the order Orthoptera, with straight narrow forewings, and hind legs modified for jumping etc., including grasshoppers and crickets.
• [Greek *orthos* straight, *pteros* wing]
• **orthopterous** *adjective*

orthoptic *adjective*
• "or THOPTIC"
• relating to the correct or normal use of the eyes.
• [Greek *orthos* straight, *optikos* of sight: see OPTIC]
• **orthoptist** *noun*

orthoptics *noun*
• "or THOPTIX"
• the branch of medicine that deals with the treatment of defective binocular vision by means of eye exercises.
• [as ORTHOPTIC]

orthorhombic *adjective*
• "ortho ROMBIC"
• (of a crystal) characterized by three mutually perpendicular axes which are unequal in length, as in topaz and talc.
• [Greek *orthos* straight + RHOMBUS]

orthotic *noun*
• "or THOTTIC"
• a moulded insert for a shoe etc. designed to improve posture and gait.
• [Greek *orthos* straight]
• **orthotist** *noun* "ORTHA tist"

ortolan *noun*
• "ORTA l'n"
• a small European bird, *Emberiza hortulana*, eaten as a delicacy.
• [French from Provençal, lit. 'gardener', from Latin *hortulanus* from *hortulus* diminutive of *hortus* garden]

Orvieto *noun*
• "orv YETTO" or "orvy ETTO"
• a usu. dry white wine made near Orvieto in central Italy.

Orwellian *adjective*
• "or WELLY 'n"
• of or characteristic of the work of the English writer George Orwell (d.1950), esp. with reference to the totalitarian development of the state as depicted in *Nineteen Eighty-Four* and *Animal Farm*.

oryx *noun*
• "ORRIX"
• any large straight-horned antelope of the genus *Oryx*, native to Africa and Arabia.
• [Greek *orux* stonemason's pickaxe, from its pointed horns]

orzo *noun*
• "ORZO"
• a variety of pasta shaped like grains of rice or barley.
• [Italian, = 'barley']

Osage *noun*
• "oh SAGE" or "OH sage"
• a member of a N American Indian people formerly inhabiting the Osage river valley, Missouri.
• [Osage *Wazhazhe*, one of the three bands composing this people]

Oscan *noun*
• "OSS k'n"
• the ancient language of Campania in south

central Italy, related to Latin and surviving only in inscriptions.
• [Latin *Oscus*, the Osci, an ancient people of Campania]

oscillate *verb*
• "OSS'll ate"
• swing to and fro like a pendulum.
• [Latin *oscillare oscillat-* swing]
• **oscillating** *adjective*
• **oscillation** *noun*
• **oscillator** *noun*
• **oscillatory** *adjective* "uh SILLA tory" or "OSS'll a tory"

oscillogram *noun*
• "uh SILLA gram"
• a record obtained from an oscillograph.
• [as OSCILLATE + Greek *gramma* thing written]

oscillograph *noun*
• "uh SILLA graff"
• a device for displaying or recording oscillations as a continuous curve.
• [as OSCILLATE + Greek *graphia* writing]
• **oscillographic** *adjective*
• **oscillography** *noun*

oscilloscope *noun*
• "uh SILLA scope"
• a device for viewing oscillations by a display on the screen of a cathode ray tube.
• [as OSCILLATE + Greek *skopos* target, from *skeptomai* look at]
• **oscilloscopic** *adjective*

oscine *adjective*
• "OSSIN"
• of or relating to the suborder Oscines of passerine birds including many of the songbirds.
• [Latin *oscen -cinis* songbird (*ob* towards, against, in the way of, *canere* sing)]

oscular *adjective*
• "OSS kyuh lur"
• of or relating to the mouth.
• [Latin *osculum* mouth, kiss, diminutive of *os* mouth]

osculate *verb*
• "OSS kyuh late"
• (of a curve or surface) touch (another curve or surface) without crossing, so as to have a common tangent.
• [Latin *osculari* kiss (as OSCULAR)]
• **osculation** *noun*
• **osculatory** *adjective* "OSS kyuh luh tory"

osculum *noun*
• "OSS kyuh lum"
• a mouth-like aperture, esp. of a sponge.
• [Latin: see OSCULAR]

osier *noun*
• "OH zee ur"
• any of various willows, esp. *Salix viminalis*, with long flexible shoots used in basketwork.
• [Old French: compare medieval Latin *auseria* osier bed]

Osmanli *adjective*
• "ozz MANLY" or "oss MANLY"
• of or relating to the Turkish dynasty founded by Osman (Othman) I (d.1326), or the empire it ruled.
• [Turkish from *Osman* from Arabic *'uṯmān* (see OTTOMAN) + *-li* adjective suffix]

osmium *noun*
• "OZZ mee um"
• a hard bluish-white transition element, the heaviest known metal, occurring naturally in association with platinum and used in certain alloys.
• [Greek *osmē* smell (from the pungent smell of its tetroxide)]
• **osmic** *adjective*

osmoregulation *noun*
• "ozzmo reg yuh LAY sh'n"
• the maintenance of constant osmotic pressure in the fluids of an organism by control of water and salt levels etc.
• [as OSMOSIS + REGULATE]

osmosis *noun*
• "ozz MOE sis"
• the passage of a solvent through a semi-permeable partition into a more concentrated solution, so as to make the concentration on the two sides more nearly equal.
• [originally *osmose*, after French from Greek *ōsmos* push]
• **osmotic** *adjective* "ozz MOTTIC"
• **osmotically** *adverb*

osmunda *noun*
• "ozz MUNDA"
• any fern of the genus *Osmunda*, esp. the royal fern, having large divided fronds.
• [of uncertain origin]

osprey *noun*
• "OSS pray" or "OSS pree"
• a large bird of prey, *Pandion haliaetus*, with a brown back and white markings, feeding on fish, which it catches in its claws after making a spectacular dive from the air.
• [Old French *ospres*, apparently ultimately from Latin *ossifraga* osprey, from *os* bone + *frangere* break]

ossein *noun*
• "OSSY in"
• the collagen of bones.
• [Latin *osseus* (as OSSEOUS)]

osseous *adjective*
• "OSSY us"
• of, pertaining to, consisting of, or resembling bone.
• [Latin *osseus* from *os ossis* bone]

Ossetian *noun*
• "aw SEE sh'n"

• a native or inhabitant of Ossetia in SE Europe, divided between Russia and Georgia.

ossicle *noun*
• "OSSA k'll"
• any small bone, esp. of the middle ear.
• [Latin *ossiculum* diminutive of *os ossis* bone]

ossify *verb*
• "OSSA fie"
• turn into bone or bony tissue; harden.
• [French *ossifier* from Latin *os ossis* bone]
• **ossification** *noun*

ossuary *noun*
• "OSS yoo airy"
• a receptacle for the bones of the dead; a charnel house.
• [Late Latin *ossuarium* from *os ossis* bone]

osteitis *noun*
• "osty ITE iss"
• inflammation of the substance of a bone.
• [Greek *osteon* bone + *-itis*, forming feminine of adjectives in *-itēs* (with *nosos* 'disease' implied)]

ostensible *adjective*
• "oss TENSA bull"
• apparent, but not necessarily real.
• [French from medieval Latin *ostensibilis* from Latin *ostendere ostens-* stretch out to view (*ob* towards, against, in the way of, *tendere* stretch)]
• **ostensibly** *adverb*

ostentation *noun*
• "oss ten TAY sh'n"
• a pretentious and vulgar display esp. of wealth and luxury.
• [Latin *ostentatio -onis* from *ostentare* frequentative of *ostendere*: see OSTENSIBLE]
• **ostentatious** *adjective*
• **ostentatiously** *adverb*

osteoarthritis *noun*
• "ostee oh ar THRITE iss"
• a degenerative disease of joint cartilage causing pain and stiffness esp. in those middle aged and older.
• [Greek *osteon* bone + ARTHRITIS]

osteoblast *noun*
• "OSTEE oh blast"
• a mesodermal cell which secretes the substance of bone.
• [Greek *osteon* bone, *blastos* sprout]
• **osteoblastic** *adjective*

osteoclast *noun*
• "OSTEE oh clast"
• a large cell which absorbs bone tissue during growth and healing.
• [Greek *osteon* bone, *klastēs* sprout]
• **osteoclastic** *adjective*

osteogenesis *noun*
• "osty oh JENNA sis"
• the formation of bone.
• [Greek *osteon* bone + GENESIS]
• **osteogenetic** *adjective* "osty oh juh NETTIC"

osteology *noun*
• "ostee OLLA jee"
• the study of the structure and function of the skeleton and bony structures.
• [Greek *osteon* bone, *logos* word]
• **osteological** *adjective*
• **osteologically** *adverb*
• **osteologist** *noun*

osteomalacia *noun*
• "ostee oh muh LAY shuh"
• softening of the bones, often through a deficiency of vitamin D and calcium.
• [modern Latin (Greek *osteon* bone, *malakos* soft)]
• **osteomalacic** *adjective* "ostee oh muh LASSIC"

osteomyelitis *noun*
• "ostee oh my a LITE iss"
• inflammation of the bone or bone marrow, usu. due to infection.
• [Greek *osteon* bone + MYELITIS]

osteopathy *noun*
• "ostee OPPA thee" (with "TH" as in *THIN*)
• a system of healing based on the theory that some disorders can be alleviated by treatment of the skeleton and musculature using manipulation and massage.
• [Greek *osteon* bone, *patheia* suffering]
• **osteopath** *noun*
• **osteopathic** *adjective*

osteoporosis *noun*
• "ostee oh puh ROE sis"
• a condition of fragile, porous bones caused by loss of the protein and mineral content of bone tissue, esp. as a result of hormonal changes, or deficiency of calcium or vitamin D.
• [Greek *osteon* bone, *poros* passage, pore]
• **osteoporotic** *adjective* "ostee oh puh ROTTIC"

osteosarcoma *noun*
• "ostee oh sar CO muh"
• a malignant tumour of bone, esp. one involving proliferation of osteoblasts.
• [Greek *osteon* bone + SARCOMA]

osteotomy *noun*
• "ostee OTTA mee"
• the surgical cutting of a bone, esp. to allow realignment.
• [Greek *osteon* bone, *-tomia* cutting, from *temnō* cut]

ostinato *noun*
• "ossta NOTTO"
• a persistent phrase or rhythm repeated through all or part of a piece.
• [Italian, = OBSTINATE]

ostium *noun*
• "OSTEE um"
• an opening into a vessel or body cavity.
• [Latin, = door, opening]

ostomy *noun*
• "OSTA mee"
• an operation that involves making a permanent artificial opening in the body.
• [extracted from *colostomy*, *ileostomy*, etc.]

Ostpolitik *noun*
• "OST polla teek"
• the foreign policy, esp. of détente, of many western European countries with reference to the Communist bloc.
• [German from *Ost* east + *Politik* politics]

ostracize *verb*
ALSO SPELLED: esp. *Brit.* **-ise**
• "OSTRA size"
• exclude (a person) from a society, favour, privileges, etc. by common consent; refuse to associate with.
• [Greek *ostrakizō* from *ostrakon* shell, potsherd (used to write a name on in voting)]
• **ostracism** *noun*

ostrich *noun*
• "OST rich"
• a large African swift-running flightless bird, *Struthio camelus*, with long legs and two toes on each foot.
• [Old French *ostric(h)e* from Latin *avis* bird + Late Latin *struthio* from Greek *strouthiōn* ostrich, from *strouthos* sparrow, ostrich]
• **ostrichlike** *adjective*

Ostrogoth *noun*
• "OSTRA goth"
• a member of the Eastern branch of the Goths, who conquered Italy in the 5th–6th c.
• [Late Latin *Ostrogothi* (pl.) from Germanic *austro-* (unrecorded) east + Late Latin *Gothi* Goths]
• **Ostrogothic** *adjective*

otic *adjective*
• "OTTIC" or "OH tick"
• of or relating to the ear.
• [Greek *ōtikos* from *ous ōtos* ear]

otiose *adjective*
• "OH tee ose" (rhymes with *GROSS*)
• serving no practical purpose; not required; functionless.
• [Latin *otiosus* from *otium* leisure]
• **otioseness** *noun*

otitis *noun*
• "oh TITE iss"
• inflammation of the ear.
• [modern Latin from Greek *ous ōtos* ear, *-itis*, forming feminine of adjectives in *-itēs* (with *nosos* 'disease' implied)]

otolaryngology *noun*
• "oh tuh lare in GOLLA jee"
• the study of diseases of the ear and throat.
• [Greek *ous ōtos* ear + LARYNGOLOGY]
• **otolaryngological** *adjective*
• **otolaryngologist** *noun*

otolith *noun*
• "OH tuh lith"
• any of the small particles of calcium carbonate found in the inner ear of vertebrates, important as sensors of gravity and acceleration.
• [Greek *ous ōtos* ear, *lithos* stone]
• **otolithic** *adjective*

otology *noun*
• "oh TOLLA jee"
• the study of the anatomy, functions, and diseases of the ear.
• [Greek *ous ōtos* ear, *logos* word]
• **otological** *adjective*
• **otologist** *noun*

otorhinolaryngology *noun*
• "oh tuh rine oh lare 'n GOLLA jee"
• the study of diseases of the ear, nose, and throat.
• [Greek *ous ōtos* ear, *rhis rhinos* nostril, nose + LARYNGOLOGY]
• **otorhinolaryngologist** *noun*

otoscope *noun*
• "OH tuh scope"
• an apparatus for examining the eardrum and the passage leading to it from the ear.
• [Greek *ous ōtos* ear, *skopos* target, from *skeptomai* look at]
• **otoscopic** *adjective*

ottoman *noun*
• "OTTA m'n"
• a footstool or low upholstered seat, usu. square and without a back or arms, sometimes serving as a box.
• [French *ottomane* from Arabic *'uṯmānī* 'of Othman' (designating the Turkish dynasty founded by Osman (Othman) I (d.1326), or the empire it ruled)]

ouananiche *noun*
• "WANNA nish"
• *Cdn* a landlocked lake variety of Atlantic salmon, found in Newfoundland and Labrador, Quebec, and Ontario.
• [Canadian French from Montagnais *wananish* 'little salmon']

oubliette *noun*
• "oobly ET"
• a secret dungeon with access only through a trap door.
• [French from *oublier* forget, as OBLIVION]

ouguiya *noun*
ALSO SPELLED: **ougiya**
• "oo GEEYA" (with "G" as in *GEEK*)
• the basic monetary unit of Mauritania, equal to five khoums.
• [French from Mauritanian Arabic *ūgiyya*, ultimately from Latin *uncia* ounce]

outmanoeuvre *verb*
ALSO SPELLED: **outmaneuver**
• "out muh NOOVER"

• use skill and cunning to secure an advantage over (a person).
• ['out' + MANOEUVRE]

outpoll *verb*
• "out POLE"
• receive more votes than (an opponent) in an election, opinion poll, etc.
• ['out' + POLL]

outrageous *adjective*
• "out RAY juss"
• deeply shocking and unacceptable.
• [Old French *outrageus* from *outrage* from *outrer* exceed, from *outre* from Latin *ultra* beyond]
• **outrageously** *adverb*
• **outrageousness** *noun*

outré *adjective*
• "oo TRAY"
• outside the bounds of what is usual or proper.
• [French, past participle of *outrer*: see OUTRAGEOUS]

outro *noun*
• "OUT tro"
• a concluding section, esp. of a broadcast program or a piece of music.
• ['out', on the pattern of 'intro', from abbreviation of INTRODUCTION]

outtake *noun*
• "OUT take"
• a length of film or tape rejected in editing.
• ['out' + 'take']

ouzel *noun*
ALSO SPELLED: **ousel**
• "OOZ'll"
• any of several stocky short-tailed songbirds constituting the genus *Cinclus* and family Cinclidae, which habitually bob up and down, frequent fast-flowing streams, and swim and walk under water to feed, esp. *C. mexicanus* of western N America, or *C. cinclus* of Eurasia.
• [Old English *ōsle* blackbird, of unknown origin]

ouzo *noun*
• "OOZ oh"
• a Greek aniseed-flavoured liquor.
• [modern Greek]

oval *adjective*
• "OH v'll"
• egg-shaped, ellipsoidal.
• [medieval Latin *ovalis* (as OVUM)]

Ovambo *noun*
• "oh VAMBO"
• a member of a Bantu-speaking people inhabiting N Namibia.
• [a local name, from *ova-* (prefix denoting a plural) + *ambo* man of leisure]

ovary *noun*
• "OVER ee"
• each of the female reproductive organs in which ova are produced.
• [modern Latin *ovarium* (as OVUM)]
• **ovarian** *adjective* "oh VERRY 'n"
• **ovariectomy** *noun* "oh verry ECTA mee"

ovate *adjective*
• "OH vate"
• egg-shaped as a solid or in outline; oval.
• [Latin *ovatus* (as OVUM)]

ovation *noun*
• "oh VAY sh'n"
• an enthusiastic reception, esp. spontaneous and sustained applause.
• [Latin *ovatio* from *ovare* exult]
• **ovational** *adjective*

overabundant *adjective*
• "over a BUN d'nt"
• in excessive quantity.
• ['over' + ABUNDANT]
• **overabundance** *noun*
• **overabundantly** *adverb*

overachieve *verb*
• "over a CHEEVE"
• do more than might be expected (esp. scholastically).
• ['over' + ACHIEVE]
• **overachievement** *noun*
• **overachiever** *noun*

overcapacity *noun*
• "over kuh PASSA tee"
• the resources to produce more goods, handle more business, etc. than is needed at a particular time.
• ['over' + CAPACITY]

overcapitalize *verb*
ALSO SPELLED: esp. *Brit.* **-ise**
• "over CAPPA t'll ize"
• fix or estimate the capital of (a company etc.) too high.
• ['over' + CAPITALIZE]

overcautious *adjective*
• "over COSH us"
• excessively cautious.
• ['over' + CAUTION]
• **overcaution** *noun*
• **overcautiously** *adverb*
• **overcautiousness** *noun*

overcommit *verb*
• "over kuh MIT"
• commit (esp. oneself) to an excessive degree.
• ['over' + COMMIT]
• **overcommitment** *noun*

overcompensate *verb*
• "over COM p'n sate"
• compensate excessively for (something).
• ['over' + COMPENSATE]
• **overcompensation** *noun*

overconfident *adjective*
• "over CONFA d'nt"
• excessively confident.

• ['over' + CONFIDENT]
• **overconfidence** *noun*
• **overconfidently** *adverb*

overemphasis *noun*
• "over EMFA sis"
• excessive emphasis.
• ['over' + EMPHASIS]
• **overemphasize** *verb* (also esp. *Brit.* **-ise**)

overenthusiasm *noun*
• "over en THOOZY azm" or "over en THYOOZY azm"
• excessive enthusiasm.
• ['over' + ENTHUSIASM]
• **overenthusiastic** *adjective*
• **overenthusiastically** *adverb*

overexert *verb*
• "over eg ZURT"
• exert too much.
• ['over' + EXERT]
• **overexertion** *noun*

overfamiliar *adjective*
• "over fuh MILL yur"
• excessively familiar.
• ['over' + FAMILIAR]
• **overfamiliarity** *noun* "over fuh milly ERRA tee"

overfulfill *verb*
ALSO SPELLED: **overfulfil**
• "over full FILL"
• fulfill (a plan, quota, etc.) beyond expectation or before the appointed time.
• ['over' + FULFILL]
• **overfulfillment** *noun* (also **-fulfilment**)

overgenerous *adjective*
• "over JENNER us"
• excessively generous.
• ['over' + GENEROUS]
• **overgenerously** *adverb*

overhaul *verb*
• "OVER hawl"
• take to pieces in order to examine.
• [originally Naut., = release (rope tackle) by slackening, from 'over' + HAUL]

overhype *verb*
• "over HIPE"
• promote with excessive hype.
• ['over' + HYPE]
• **overhyped** *adjective*

overindulge *verb*
• "over in DULGE"
• indulge to excess.
• ['over' + INDULGE]
• **overindulgence** *noun*
• **overindulgent** *adjective*

overladen *adjective*
• "over LAY d'n"
• bearing or carrying too large a load.
• ['over' + LADE]

overmantel *noun*
• "OVER mant'll"
• ornamental shelves etc. over a mantelpiece.
• ['over' + MANTEL]

overmedicate *verb*
• "over MEDDA cate"
• prescribe too many drugs for.
• ['over' + MEDICATE]
• **overmedicated** *adjective*

overpopulated *adjective*
• "over POP yuh lated"
• having too large a population.
• ['over' + POPULATE]
• **overpopulation** *noun*

overrate *verb*
• "over RATE"
• rate or esteem too highly.
• ['over' + 'rate' (Old French and medieval Latin *rata* (from Latin *pro rata parte* or *portione* 'according to the proportional share') from *ratus*, past participle of *rēri* reckon)]
• **overrated** *adjective*

overreach *verb*
• "over REECH"
• exceed (the limits of a person's authority etc.).
• ['over' + 'reach' from Old English *rǣcan*]
• **overreacher** *noun*
• **overreaching** *noun*

overreact *verb*
• "over ree ACT"
• respond more forcibly etc. than is justified.
• ['over' + 'react' (from medieval Latin *reagere react-* (*re-* again, *agere* do, act))]
• **overreaction** *noun*

overrefine *verb*
• "over ree FINE"
• refine too much.
• ['over' + 'refine' (Latin *re-* again, *finire* finish)]
• **overrefinement** *noun*

overreliance *noun*
• "over ree LIE ince"
• excessive reliance.
• ['over' + RELIANCE]

overrepresent *verb*
• "over rep ree ZENT"
• cause to be present in numbers higher than would be expected statistically.
• ['over' + REPRESENTATION]

override *verb*
• "over RIDE"
• have or claim precedence or superiority over.
• ['over' + 'ride' from Old English *rīdan*]

overriding *adjective*
• "over RIDE ing"
• foremost; taking precedence.
• [as OVERRIDE]

overripe *adjective*
• "over RIPE"

• (esp. of fruit etc.) past its best; excessively ripe.
• ['over' + 'ripe' from Old English *rīpe*]
• **overripeness** *noun*

overruff *verb*
• "over RUFF"
• play a higher trump than another player.
• ['over' + 'ruff' trump at cards, originally the name of a card game: from Old French *roffle*, *rouffle*, = Italian *ronfa* (perhaps alteration of *trionfo* trump)]

overrule *verb*
• "over RULE"
• set aside (a decision, argument, proposal, etc.) by exercising a superior authority.
• ['over' + 'rule' from Old French *reule*, *reuler* from Late Latin *regulare* from Latin *regula* straight stick]

overrun *verb*
• "over RUN"
• (esp. of something undesirable) swarm or spread over.
• ['over' + 'run' from Old English *rinnan*]

overschedule *verb*
• "over SKED joo 'll" or "over SKED jool" or "over SHED jool" or "over SHED yool"
• schedule too many activities for (a person).
• ['over' + SCHEDULE]

overstimulate *verb*
• "over STIM yuh late"
• stimulate or excite excessively.
• ['over' + STIMULUS]
• **overstimulation** *noun*

oversubtle *adjective*
• "over SUTTLE"
• excessively subtle; not plain or clear.
• ['over' + SUBTLE]

overt *adjective*
• "oh VURT" or "OH vurt"
• unconcealed; done openly.
• [Old French past participle of *ovrir* open, from Latin *aperire*]
• **overtly** *adverb*
• **overtness** *noun*

overture *noun*
• "OVER chur"
• an orchestral piece opening an opera, musical, ballet, etc.
• [Old French from Latin *apertura* APERTURE]

overweening *adjective*
• "over WEENING"
• arrogant, presumptuous, conceited.
• ['over' + archaic *ween* be of the opinion; think, suppose, from Old English *wēnan*]

overweight *adjective*
• "over WATE"
• in excess of a weight considered normal or desirable.
• ['over' + WEIGHT]

overwhelm *verb*
• "over WELM"
• overpower.
• ['over' + 'whelm' = overturn, from Old English]
• **overwhelming** *adjective*
• **overwhelmingly** *adverb*
• **overwhelmingness** *noun*

overwrite *verb*
• "over RITE"
• write on top of (other writing).
• ['over' + WRITE]

overwrought *adjective*
• "over ROT"
• overexcited, nervous, distraught.
• ['over' + 'wrought' archaic past participle of 'work']

overzealous *adjective*
• "over ZELLIS"
• too zealous in one's attitude, behaviour, etc.; excessively enthusiastic.
• ['over' + ZEALOUS]

Ovidian *adjective*
• "oh VIDDY 'n"
• of or relating to the Roman poet Ovid (d. *c.*17).

oviduct *noun*
• "OH vuh duct"
• the tube through which an ovum passes from the ovary.
• [Latin *ovum* egg + 'duct' (as DUCTILE)]
• **oviductal** *adjective*

oviform *adjective*
• "OH vuh form"
• egg-shaped.
• [Latin *ovum* egg + 'form' (from Latin *forma* form)]

ovine *adjective*
• "OH vine"
• of or like sheep.
• [Late Latin *ovinus* from Latin *ovis* sheep]

oviparous *adjective*
• "oh VIPPER us"
• producing young by means of eggs expelled from the body before they are hatched.
• [Latin *ovum* egg + *-parus* -bearing, from *parere* bring forth]
• **oviparity** *noun* "oh vuh PERRA tee"
• **oviparously** *adverb*

ovipositor *noun*
• "oh vuh POZZIT ur"
• a pointed tubular organ with which a female insect deposits her eggs.
• [modern Latin from Latin *ovum* egg + *positor* from *ponere posit-* to place]
• **oviposit** *verb*
• **oviposition** *noun*

ovolo *noun*
• "OH vuh loh"
• a convex moulding with an outline of a quarter circle.

• [Italian diminutive of *ovo* egg from Latin OVUM]

ovotestis *noun*
• "oh vuh TEST iss"
• an organ producing both ova and spermatozoa.
• [OVUM + TESTIS]

ovoviviparous *adjective*
• "oh voe viv IPPER us"
• producing young by means of eggs hatched within the body.
• [OVUM + VIVIPAROUS]
• **ovoviviparity** *noun* "oh voe vivva PERRA tee"

ovulate *verb*
• "OV yuh late"
• produce ova or ovules, or discharge them from the ovary.
• [modern Latin *ovulum* (as OVULE)]
• **ovulation** *noun*
• **ovulatory** *adjective* "OV yuh luh tory"

ovule *noun*
• "OH vyool" or "OV yool"
• the part of the ovary of seed plants that contains the germ cell; an unfertilized seed.
• [French from medieval Latin *ovulum*, diminutive of OVUM]
• **ovular** *adjective*

ovum *noun*
• "OH vum"
• a mature reproductive cell of female animals, produced by the ovary.
• [Latin, = egg]

oxalic *adjective*
• "ock SALIC"
• designating a very poisonous and sour acid found in sorrel and rhubarb leaves.
• [Greek *oxalis* wood sorrel]
• **oxalate** *noun* "OXA late"

oxalis *noun*
• "OXA liss"
• any plant of the genus *Oxalis*, with trifoliate leaves.
• [Latin from Greek from *oxus* sour]

oxidant *noun*
• "OXA d'nt"
• an oxidizing agent.
• [French *oxidant* from *oxygène* OXYGEN + *-ide* after *acide* acid, from Latin *acidus* from *acēre* be sour]
HOMOPHONES: *Occident*

oxidase *noun*
• "OXA dace"
• any of a class of enzymes that react with molecular oxygen to form water or hydrogen peroxide.
• [French *oxydase*, from *oxyde* (as OXIDANT)]

oxidize *verb*
ALSO SPELLED: esp. *Brit.* **-ise**
• "OXA dize"
• combine or cause to combine with oxygen.
• [from 'oxide' (as OXIDANT)]
• **oxidation** *noun*
• **oxidational** *adjective*
• **oxidative** *adjective*
• **oxidizable** *adjective* (also esp. *Brit.* **-isable**)
• **oxidized** *adjective* (also esp. *Brit.* **-ised**)
• **oxidizer** *noun* (also esp. *Brit.* **-iser**)

oxidizing *adjective*
• "OXA dize ing"
• designating a substance that brings about oxidation by being reduced and gaining electrons.
• [as OXIDIZE]

Oxonian *adjective*
• "ox OH nee 'n"
• of or relating to Oxford (England) or Oxford University.
• [*Oxonia* Latinized name of *Ox(en)ford*]

oxyacetylene *adjective*
• "oxy a SETTA leen"
• of or using a mixture of oxygen and acetylene, esp. in cutting or welding metals.
• [as OXYGEN + ACETYLENE]

oxyacid *noun*
• "OXY assid"
• an acid containing oxygen.
• [OXYGEN + 'acid' from Latin *acidus* from *acēre* be sour]

oxygen *noun*
• "OXA j'n"
• a colourless tasteless odourless gaseous element, occurring naturally in air, water, and most minerals and organic substances, and essential to plant and animal life.
• [French *oxygène* acidifying principle (Greek *oxu-* from *oxus* sharp + GENESIS: it was at first held to be the essential principle in the formation of acids)]
• **oxygenic** *adjective*
• **oxygenous** *adjective* "ock SIDGE a nuss"

oxygenate *verb*
• "OXA j'n ate"
• supply, treat, or mix with oxygen; oxidize.
• [French *oxygéner* (as OXYGEN)]
• **oxygenation** *noun*
• **oxygenator** *noun*

oxyhemoglobin *noun*
ALSO SPELLED: esp. *Brit.* **oxyhaemoglobin**
• "oxy HEEMA glow bin"
• a bright red complex formed when hemoglobin combines with oxygen.
• [as OXYGEN + HEMOGLOBIN]

oxymoron *noun*
• "oxy MORE on"
• a figure of speech in which apparently contradictory terms appear in conjunction, e.g. *faith unfaithful kept him falsely true.*
• [Greek *oxumōron* neuter of *oxumōros* pointedly foolish, from *oxus* sharp + *mōros* foolish]

- **oxymoronic** *adjective*
- **oxymoronically** *adverb*

oxytetracycline *noun*
- "oxy tetra SIKE lin"
- an antibiotic related to tetracycline.
- [as OXYGEN + TETRACYCLINE]

oxytocin *noun*
- "oxy TOE sin"
- a hormone released by the pituitary gland that causes increased contraction of the uterus during labour and stimulates the ejection of milk into the ducts of the breasts.
- [*oxytocic* accelerating parturition, from Greek *oxutokia* sudden delivery (*oxus* sharp, *tokos* childbirth)]

oxytone *adjective*
- "OXY tone"
- (esp. in ancient Greek) having an acute accent on the last syllable.
- [Greek *oxutonos* (*oxus* sharp, *tonos* tone)]

oxytrope *noun*
- "OXY trope"
- any of various leguminous plants of the genus *Oxytropis*, with pinnate leaves and racemes of flowers, some cultivated, some poisonous to livestock.
- [Greek *oxy* sharp + *tropis* keel]

oyamel *noun*
- "OY a mell"
- a large fir tree, *Abies religiosa*, of mountainous regions in Mexico, forests of which provide the wintering grounds of the monarch butterfly.
- [Mexican Spanish from Aztec *oyametl*]

oyez *interjection*
ALSO SPELLED: **oyes**
- "oh YES" or "oh YEZ"
- uttered, usu. three times, by a public crier or a court officer to command silence and attention.
- [Old French *oiez*, *oyez*, imperative pl. of *oïr* hear, from Latin *audire*]

Pp

paan *noun*
• "PAN"
• the leaf of the betel palm wrapped around a preparation of betel nuts and lime and chewed.
• [Hindi *pān* betel leaf, from Sanskrit *parṇà*, feather, leaf]
HOMOPHONES: *pan, panne*

pabulum *noun*
• "PAB yuh lum"
• food, esp. for the mind.
• [Latin 'food', from *pascere* feed]

paca *noun*
• "PACKA"
• either of two rodents of Mexico and northern S America related to the agoutis and cavies and constituting the genus *Agouti*, esp. *A. paca*, hunted locally for food.
• [Spanish & Portuguese, from Tupi]

pace *preposition*
• "PAW chay"
• (in stating a contrary opinion) with due deference to (the person named).
• [Latin, ablative of *pax* peace]

pachinko *noun*
• "puh CHINKO"
• a Japanese form of pinball.
• [Japanese]

pachisi *noun*
• "puh CHEEZY"
• a four-handed Indian board game with six cowries used like dice.
• [Hindi, = of 25 (the highest throw)]

pachyderm *noun*
• "PACKY durm"
• any thick-skinned mammal, esp. an elephant or rhinoceros.
• [French *pachyderme* from Greek *pakhudermos* from *pakhus* thick + *derma -matos* skin]
• **pachydermatous** *adjective*
"packy DURMA tuss"

pachysandra *noun*
• "packy SANDRA"
• any of various N American and eastern Asian evergreen shrubs of the genus *Pachysandra*, of the box family, esp. the Japanese *P. terminalis*, grown as ground cover.
• [Greek *pakhus* thick + *andr-* man (with reference to the thick stamens)]

pachytene *noun*
• "PACKY teen"
• a stage during the prophase of meiosis when the chromosomes thicken and may exchange genes by crossing over.
• [Greek *pakhus* thick + *tainia* band]

pacific *adjective*
• "puh SIFFIC"
• characterized by or tending to peace; tranquil.
• [French *pacifique* or Latin *pacificus* from *pax pacis* peace]
• **pacifically** *adverb*

pacifism *noun*
• "PASSA fizm"
• the belief that war and violence are morally unjustified and that all disputes should be settled by peaceful means.
• [French *pacifisme* from *pacifier* PACIFY]
• **pacifist** *noun*
• **pacifistic** *adjective*

pacify *verb*
• "PASSA fie"
• appease (a person, anger, etc.).
• [Old French *pacifier* or Latin *pacificare* (as PACIFIC)]
• **pacification** *noun*
• **pacifier** *noun*

Packham *noun*
• "PACK 'm"
• a large, bumpy green pear with smooth white sweet and juicy flesh, grown esp. in the southern hemisphere.
• [C. H. *Packham*, Australian fruit grower d.1909]

paczki *noun*
• "PUNCH kee"
• a round doughnut with a filling of jam, prunes, lemon, custard, etc., traditionally eaten by Poles on Shrove Tuesday.
• [Polish]

pademelon *noun*
• "PADDA mell'n"

• any small wallaby of the genus *Thylogale*, inhabiting the coastal scrub of Australia.
• [earlier *paddymelon*, prob. alteration of Dharuk *badimaliyan*]

padouk *noun*
• "puh DOOK" (rhymes with *SPOOK*)
• any hardwood tree of the genus *Pterocarpus*.
• [Burmese]

padre *noun*
• "POD ray" or "PAD ray"
• a Christian clergyman, esp. a Roman Catholic priest.
• [Italian, Spanish, & Portuguese, = father, priest, from Latin *pater patris* father]

padrone *noun*
• "puh DRONE ee" or "puh DRONE ay"
• a boss, a manager.
• [Italian]

paean *noun*
• "PEE 'n"
• a song of praise or triumph.
• [Latin from Doric Greek *paian* 'hymn of thanksgiving to Apollo' (invoked by the name *Paian*, originally the Homeric name for the physician of the gods)]
HOMOPHONES: *paeon*, *peon*

paella *noun*
• "pie AY uh" or "pie ELLA"
• a Spanish dish of rice, saffron, chicken, seafood, etc.
• [Catalan from Old French *paele* from Latin *patella* pan]

paeon *noun*
• "PEE 'n"
• a metrical foot of one long syllable and three short syllables in any order.
• [Latin from Greek *paiōn*, the Attic form of *paian* PAEAN]
HOMOPHONES: *paean*, *peon*

pagan *noun*
• "PAY g'n"
• a person holding religious beliefs other than those of any of the main religions of the world, esp. formerly regarded by Christians as unenlightened or heathen.
• [Latin *paganus* villager, rustic, from *pagus* country district: in Christian Latin = civilian, heathen]
• **paganism** *noun*

pageant *noun*
• "PADGE 'nt"
• a brilliant spectacle, esp. an elaborate parade.
• [Middle English *pagyn*, of unknown origin]

pageantry *noun*
• "PADGE 'n tree"
• elaborate or sumptuous show or display.
• [as PAGEANT]

paginate *verb*
• "PADGE 'n ate"
• assign numbers to the pages of a book etc.
• [French *paginer* from Latin *pagina* page]
• **pagination** *noun*

pagoda *noun*
• "puh GO duh"
• a Hindu or Buddhist temple or sacred building, esp. a many-tiered tower, in India and the Far East.
• [Portuguese *pagode*, prob. ultimately from Persian *butkada* idol temple]

Pahlavi *noun*
• "PAH luh vee"
• an Aramaic-based writing system used in Persia from the 2nd c. BC to the advent of Islam in the 7th c. AD.
• [Persian *pahlawī*, via *pahlav* from *parthava* Parthia]

pahoehoe *noun*
• "puh HOEY hoey"
• lava forming smooth undulating or ropy masses.
• [Hawaiian]

paillette *noun*
• "pal YET" or "pie YET"
• a spangle.
• [French, diminutive of *paille* from Latin *palea* straw, chaff]

paisa *noun*
• "PAY suh"
• a coin and monetary unit of India, Pakistan, and Nepal, equal to one-hundredth of a rupee.
• [Hindi]

paisley *noun*
• "PAZE lee"
• a distinctive detailed pattern of curved feather-shaped figures.
• [*Paisley*, in Scotland]

pakeha *noun*
• "PACK a huh"
• a white person as opposed to a Maori.
• [Maori]

Pakistani *noun*
• "packa STANNY"
• a native or inhabitant of Pakistan in S Asia.

pakora *noun*
• "puh KORA"
• a piece of cauliflower, carrot, or other vegetable, coated in seasoned batter and deep-fried.
• [Hindi]

palacsinta *noun*
• "pal a CHINTA"
• (in Hungarian cuisine) a thin pancake eaten as a dessert, filled esp. with jam, cottage cheese, nuts, or chocolate.
• [Hungarian *palacsinta* pancake]

paladin *noun*
• "PAL a din"
• any of the twelve peers of Charlemagne's

court, of whom the Count Palatine was the chief.
• [French *paladin* from Italian *paladino* from Latin *palatinus*: see PALATINE]

palais *noun*
• "PAL ay"
• a public hall for dancing.
• [French *palais* (*de danse*) (dancing) hall, from Old French *palais* from Latin *Palatium* Palatine (hill) in Rome where the house of the emperor was situated]

palanquin *noun*
ALSO SPELLED: **palankeen**
• "pal 'n KEEN"
• (in India and the East) a covered litter for one passenger.
• [Portuguese *palanquim*: compare Hindi *pālkī* from Sanskrit *palyanka* bed, couch]

palatable *adjective*
• "PAL a tuh bull"
• pleasant to taste.
• [as PALATE]
• **palatability** *noun*
• **palatableness** *noun*
• **palatably** *adverb*

palatal *noun*
• "PAL a t'll"
• (of a sound) made by placing the surface of the tongue against the hard palate, e.g. *y* in *yes*.
• [Latin *palatum*]
• **palatalization** *noun* (also esp. *Brit.* **-isation**)
• **palatalize** *verb* (also esp. *Brit.* **-ise**)

palate *noun*
• "PAL it"
• a structure closing the upper part of the mouth cavity in vertebrates.
• [Latin *palatum*]
HOMOPHONES: *palette, pallet*

palatial *adjective*
• "puh LAY sh'll"
• (of a building) like a palace, esp. spacious and splendid.
• [Latin (as PALAIS)]
• **palatially** *adverb*

palatinate *noun*
• "puh LAT'n it"
• territory under the jurisdiction of a Count Palatine, any of several counts in the German Empire, each having supreme jurisdiction within his own territory.
• [as PALATINE]

palatine *adjective*
• "PAL a tine" or "PAL a tin"
• (of an official or feudal lord) having local authority that elsewhere belongs only to a sovereign.
• [French *palatin -ine* from Latin *palatinus* from *Palatium* Palatine (hill) in Rome where the house of the emperor was situated]

palaver *noun*
• "puh LAV ur"
• fuss and bother, esp. prolonged.
• [Portuguese *palavra* word, from Latin (as PARABLE)]

palazzo *noun*
• "puh LAT so" or "puh LOT so"
• a palatial mansion; a large imposing building.
• [Italian from Latin *palatium*, palace (as PALATINE)]

palea *noun*
• "PAY lee uh"
• the upper bract of the floret of a grass.
• [Latin, = chaff]

Palearctic *adjective*
ALSO SPELLED: esp. *Brit.* **Palaearctic**
• "paily ARK tick" or "pally ARK tick"
• of the Arctic and temperate parts of the Old World.
• [Greek *palaios* ancient + ARCTIC]

paleoanthropology *noun*
ALSO SPELLED: esp. *Brit.* **palaeoanthropology**
• "paily oh anthra POLLA jee" or "pally oh anthra POLLA jee"
• the branch of anthropology concerned with fossil hominids.
• [Greek *palaios* ancient + ANTHROPOLOGY]
• **paleoanthropological** *adjective* (also esp. *Brit.* **palaeoanthropological**)
• **paleoanthropologist** *noun* (also esp. *Brit.* **palaeoanthropologist**)

paleobotany *noun*
ALSO SPELLED: esp. *Brit.* **palaeobotany**
• "paily oh BOT 'n ee" or "pally oh BOT 'n ee"
• the study of fossil plants.
• [Greek *palaios* ancient + BOTANY]
• **paleobotanical** *adjective* (also esp. *Brit.* **palaeobotanical**)
• **paleobotanist** *noun* (also esp. *Brit.* **palaeobotanist**)

Paleocene *adjective*
ALSO SPELLED: esp. *Brit.* **Palaeocene**
• "PAILY oh seen" or "PALLY oh seen"
• of or relating to the earliest epoch of the Tertiary period, between the Cretaceous period and the Eocene epoch, lasting from about 65 to 55 million years BP, characterized by a sudden diversification of mammals.
• [Greek *palaios* ancient + *kainos* new]

paleoclimatology *noun*
ALSO SPELLED: esp. *Brit.* **palaeoclimatology**
• "paily oh clime a TOLLA jee" or "pally oh clime a TOLLA jee"
• the study of the climate in geologically past times.
• [Greek *palaios* ancient + CLIMATOLOGY]
• **paleoclimatologist** *noun* (also esp. *Brit.* **palaeoclimatologist**)

paleoecology *noun*
ALSO SPELLED: esp. *Brit.* **palaeoecology**
• "paily oh ee COLLA jee" or "pally oh ee COLLA jee"
• the ecology of extinct and prehistoric organisms.
• [Greek *palaios* ancient + ECOLOGY]
• **paleoecological** *adjective* (also esp. *Brit.* **palaeoecological**)
• **paleoecologist** *noun* (also esp. *Brit.* **palaeoecologist**)

paleogeography *noun*
ALSO SPELLED: esp. *Brit.* **palaeogeography**
• "paily oh jee OGGRA fee" or "pally oh jee OGGRA fee"
• the study of the geographical features at periods in the geological past.
• [Greek *palaios* ancient + GEOGRAPHY]
• **paleogeographer** *noun* (also esp. *Brit.* **palaeogeographer**)

paleography *noun*
ALSO SPELLED: esp. *Brit.* **palaeography**
• "paily OGGRA fee" or "pally OGGRA fee"
• the study of writing and documents from the past.
• [Greek *palaios* ancient + *graphia* writing]
• **paleographer** *noun* (also esp. *Brit.* **palaeographer**)
• **paleographic** *adjective* (also esp. *Brit.* **palaeographic**)
• **paleographical** *adjective* (also esp. *Brit.* **palaeographical**)
• **paleographically** *adverb* (also esp. *Brit.* **palaeographically**)

paleolithic *adjective*
ALSO SPELLED: esp. *Brit.* **palaeolithic**
• "paily oh LITHIC" or "pally oh LITHIC"
• of or relating to the early phase of the Stone Age, lasting for about 2.5 million years until the end of the last ice age.
• [Greek *palaios* ancient + *lithos* stone]

paleomagnetism *noun*
ALSO SPELLED: esp. *Brit.* **palaeomagnetism**
• "paily oh MAGNA tizm" or "pally oh MAGNA tizm"
• the study of the magnetism remaining in rocks.
• [Greek *palaios* ancient + MAGNET]
• **paleomagnetic** *adjective* (also esp. *Brit.* **palaeomagnetic**)

paleontology *noun*
ALSO SPELLED: esp. *Brit.* **palaeontology**
• "paily 'n TOLLA jee" or "pally 'n TOLLA jee"
• the branch of science that deals with extinct and fossil animals and plants.
• [Greek *palaios* ancient + *onta* neuter pl. of *ōn* being, participle of *eimi* be + *logos* word]
• **paleontological** *adjective* (also esp. *Brit.* **palaeontological**)
• **paleontologist** *noun* (also esp. *Brit.* **palaeontologist**)

Paleozoic *adjective*
ALSO SPELLED: esp. *Brit.* **Palaeozoic**
• "paily oh ZO ick" or "pally oh ZO ick"
• of or relating to the geological era between the Precambrian and the Mesozoic, comprising the Cambrian, Ordovician, Silurian, Devonian, Carboniferous, and Permian periods, and lasting from about 590 to 248 million years ago. The earliest hard-shelled fossils are from this era.
• [Greek *palaios* ancient + *zōē* life, *zōos* living]

Palestinian *adjective*
• "pala STINNY 'n"
• of or relating to Palestine in the Middle East.

palestra *noun*
• "puh LESTRA"
• a wrestling school or gymnasium.
• [Latin *palaestra* from Greek *palaistra* from *palaiō* wrestle]

palette *noun*
• "PAL it"
• a thin board or slab or other surface, usu. with a hole for the thumb, on which an artist lays and mixes colours.
• [French, diminutive of *pale* shovel, from Latin *pala* spade]
HOMOPHONES: *palate, pallet*

palfrey *noun*
• "PAUL free"
• a horse for ordinary riding, esp. for women.
• [Old French *palefrei* from medieval Latin *palefredus*, Late Latin *paraveredus* from Greek *para* beside, extra, + Latin *veredus* light horse, of Gaulish origin]

Pali *noun*
• "PALLY"
• an Indic language used in the canonical books of Buddhists.
• [Pali *pāli-bhāsā*, from *pāli* line, canon + *bhāsā* language]
HOMOPHONES: *pally*

palimony *noun*
• "PALA moany"
• an allowance made by one member of an unmarried couple to the other after separation.
• [blend of 'pal' (as PALLY) + ALIMONY]

palimpsest *noun*
• "PAL imp sest"
• a piece of writing material or manuscript on which the original writing has been effaced to make room for other writing.
• [Latin *palimpsestus* from Greek *palimpsēstos* from *palin* again + *psēstos* rubbed smooth]
• **palimpsestic** *adjective*

palindrome *noun*
• "PAL in drome"
• a word or phrase that reads the same backwards as forwards, e.g. *rotator*, or *nurses run*.
• [Greek *palindromos* running back again, from *palin* again + *drom-* run]
• **palindromic** *adjective* "pal in DROMMIC"
• **palindromist** *noun*

palingenesis *noun*
- "pal 'n JENNA sis"
- regeneration, rebirth.
- [Greek *palin* again + *genesis* birth]
- **palingenetic** *adjective* "pal 'n juh NETTIC"

palisade *noun*
- "pala SADE"
- a fence of pales or iron railings.
- [French *palissade* from Provençal *palissada* from *palissa* paling, ultimately from Latin *palus* stake]

pall *noun*
- "PAUL"
- a cloth spread over a coffin, hearse, or tomb.
- [Old English *pæll*, from Latin *pallium* cloak]

HOMOPHONES: *pawl*, *pol*

Palladian *adjective*
- "puh LAY dee 'n"
- in the neoclassical style of Italian architect A. Palladio (d.1580).
- **Palladianism** *noun*

palladium *noun*
- "puh LAY dee um"
- a white ductile metallic element occurring naturally in various ores and used in chemistry as a catalyst and for making jewellery.
- [modern Latin from *Pallas*, an asteroid discovered just before the element]

pallbearer *noun*
- "PAUL bare ur"
- a person helping to carry or officially escorting a coffin at a funeral.
- [as PALL + 'bear']

pallet *noun*
- "PAL it"
- a portable platform for transporting and storing loads.
- [French *palette*: see PALETTE]
- **palletize** *verb* (also esp. *Brit.* **-ise**)

HOMOPHONES: *palate*, *palette*

palliasse *noun*

ALSO SPELLED: **paillasse**
- "PALLY ass"
- a straw mattress.
- [French *paillasse* from Italian *pagliaccio*, ultimately from Latin *palea* straw]

palliate *verb*
- "PALLY ate"
- alleviate (disease or its symptoms) without curing it.
- [Late Latin *palliare* to cloak, from *pallium* cloak]
- **palliation** *noun*
- **palliative** *noun* "PALLY a tiv"
- **palliatively** *adverb*

pallid *adjective*
- "PAL id"
- pale.
- [Latin *pallidus* pale]
- **pallidly** *adverb*
- **pallidness** *noun*

pallium *noun*
- "PALLY um"
- a narrow circular shoulder band with pendants, esp. that sent by the Pope to an archbishop as a symbol of authority.
- [Latin]

pallor *noun*
- "PAL ur"
- pallidness, paleness.
- [Latin from *pallēre* be pale]

pally *adjective*
- "PAL ee"
- like a pal; friendly.
- [Romany = brother, mate, ultimately from Sanskrit *bhrātr* brother]

HOMOPHONES: *Pali*

palm *noun*
- "POM" or "PAULM"
- the inner surface of the hand between the wrist and fingers.
- [Old French *paume* from Latin *palma*: later assimilated to Latin]
- **palmar** *adjective* "PAL mur" or "PAUL mur" or "POMMER"
- **palmful** *noun*

HOMOPHONES: *pom*, *palmer*

palmaceous *adjective*
- "pal MAY sh'ss"
- of or pertaining to the Palmae or palm family.
- [Latin *palma* palm of the hand, the palm leaf being likened to a spread hand, + adjective suffix *-aceus* of the nature of]

palmer *noun*
- "POMMER" or "PAUL mur"
- a pilgrim returning from the Holy Land with a palm branch or leaf.
- [Anglo-French *palmer* from medieval Latin *palmarius* pilgrim]

HOMOPHONES: *palmar*

palmette *noun*
- "pal MET"
- an ornament of radiating petals like a palm leaf.
- [French, diminutive of *palme* palm tree, (ultimately as PALM, the palm tree's leaf being likened to a spread hand)]

palmetto *noun*
- "pal METTO" or "paul METTO"
- a small palm tree, e.g. any of various fan palms of the genus *Sabal* or *Chamaerops*.
- [Spanish *palmito*, diminutive of *palma* palm tree, assimilated to Italian words in *-etto*]

palmier *noun*
- "PAL mee ay"
- a sweet crisp pastry shaped like a palm leaf.
- [French, = palm tree]

palmitate *noun*
- "PAL muh tate" or "PAUL muh tate"
- a salt or ester of palmitic acid.
- [as PALMITIC]

palmitic *adjective*
- "pal MITTIC" or "paul MITTIC"
- designating a saturated fatty acid, solid at room temperature, found in palm oil and other vegetable and animal fats.
- [French *palmitique*, from *palme* palm tree]

palmyra *noun*
- "pal MY ruh"
- an Asian palm, *Borassus flabellifer*, with fan-shaped leaves used for matting etc.
- [Portuguese *palmeira* palm tree, assimilated to *Palmyra*, an ancient Syrian city]

palomino *noun*
- "pala MEENO"
- a golden or tan-coloured horse with a light-coloured mane and tail, originally bred in the southwestern US.
- [Latin American Spanish from Spanish *palomino* young pigeon, from *paloma* dove, from Latin *palumba*]

palooka *noun*
- "puh LOO kuh"
- an oaf or lout.
- [origin unknown]

paloverde *noun*
- "pal oh VURDY"
- any yellow-flowered thorny tree of the genus *Cercidium*.
- [Latin American Spanish, = green tree]

palpable *adjective*
- "PAL puh bull"
- that can be touched or felt.
- [Late Latin *palpabilis* (as PALPATE)]
- **palpability** *noun*
- **palpably** *adverb*

palpate *verb*
- "PAL pate"
- examine (esp. medically) by touch.
- [Latin *palpare palpat-* touch gently]
- **palpation** *noun*

palpebral *adjective*
- "pal PEE brull"
- of or relating to the eyelids.
- [Late Latin *palpebralis* from Latin *palpebra* eyelid]

palpitate *verb*
- "PALPA tate"
- pulsate, throb.
- [Latin *palpitare* frequentative of *palpare* touch gently]
- **palpitant** *adjective*
- **palpitation** *noun*

palsa *noun*
- "PAL suh"
- a landform of subarctic regions, consisting of a mound or ridge of peat covered with vegetation and containing a core of frozen peat or mineral soil.
- [Swedish *palse* (pl. *palsar*) from Finnish and Lappish *palsa*]

palsgrave *noun*
- "PAUL's grave"
- a German Count Palatine.
- [Dutch *paltsgrave* from *palts* palatinate + *grave* count]

palsy *noun*
- "PAUL zee"
- paralysis, esp. with involuntary tremors.
- [Middle English *parlesi* from Old French *paralisie*, ultimately from Latin *paralysis*: see PARALYSIS]
- **palsied** *adjective*

paltry *adjective*
- "PAUL tree"
- trifling, meagre.
- [16th c.: from *paltry* trash, apparently from *palt*, *pelt* rubbish: compare Low German *paltrig* ragged]
- **paltriness** *noun*

palynology *noun*
- "pala NOLLA jee"
- the study of pollen, spores, etc., esp. from archaeological or geological deposits, e.g. for carbon dating and the investigation of past environments.
- [Greek *palunō* sprinkle + *logos* word]
- **palynological** *adjective*
- **palynologist** *noun*

pampas *plural noun*
- "PAM pus"
- large treeless plains in S America.
- [Spanish from Quechua *pampa* plain]

pamphlet *noun*
- "PAM flit"
- a small, usu. unbound booklet or leaflet containing information.
- [Middle English from *Pamphilet*, the familiar name of the 12th-c. Latin love poem *Pamphilus seu de Amore*]

pamphleteer *noun*
- "pam fluh TEER"
- a writer or issuer of (esp. political) pamphlets.
- [as PAMPHLET]
- **pamphleteering** *noun*

panacea *noun*
- "panna SEE uh"
- a universal remedy; a cure for all ills.
- [Latin from Greek *panakeia* from *panakēs* all-healing (as *pan* neuter of *pas* all, *akos* remedy)]
- **panacean** *adjective*

panache *noun*
- "puh NASH"
- assertiveness or flamboyance of style or manner.

• [French from Italian *pennacchio* from Late Latin *pinnaculum* diminutive of *pinna* feather]

panama *noun*
• "PANNA muh"
• a hat of straw-like material made from the leaves of a palm-like plant.
• [*Panama* in Central America]

Panamanian *noun*
• "panna MAINY 'n"
• a native or inhabitant of Panama in Central America.

panatela *noun*
ALSO SPELLED: **panatella**
• "panna TELLA"
• a long thin cigar.
• [Latin American Spanish *panatela*, = long thin biscuit, from Italian *panatella* diminutive of *panata*, ultimately from Latin *panis* bread]

pancetta *noun*
• "pan CHETTA"
• cured belly of pork, usu. in a long casing.
• [Italian, dim. of *pancia* belly]

panchayat *noun*
• "p'n CHY ut" ("CHY" rhymes with *BY*)
• a village council in India.
• [Hindi from Sanskrit *pancha* five]

panchromatic *adjective*
• "pan crow MATTIC"
• (of a photographic film etc.) sensitive to all visible colours of the spectrum.
• [Greek *pan* neuter of *pas* all + CHROMATIC]

pancreas *noun*
• "PAN cree us"
• a gland near the stomach supplying the duodenum with digestive fluid and secreting insulin into the blood.
• [modern Latin from Greek *pagkreas* (as *pan* neuter of *pas* all, *kreas -atos* flesh)]
• **pancreatic** *adjective* "pan cree ATTIC"
• **pancreatitis** *noun* "pan cree a TITE iss"

pancreatin *noun*
• "PAN cree a tin"
• a digestive extract containing pancreatic enzymes, prepared from animal pancreases.
• [as PANCREAS]

pandanus *noun*
• "pan DAY nuss" or "pan DAN us"
• a tropical tree or shrub of the genus *Pandanus*, with a twisted stem, aerial roots, and spiral tufts of long narrow leaves at the top.
• [modern Latin from Malay *pandan*]

pandect *noun*
• "PAN dect"
• a complete body of laws.
• [French *pandecte* or Latin *pandecta pandectes* from Greek *pandektēs* all-receiver (*pan* neuter of *pas* all, *dektēs* from *dekhomai* receive)]

pandemic *adjective*
• "pan DEMMIC"
• (of a disease) prevalent over a whole country or the world.
• [Greek *pandēmos* (*pan* neuter of *pas* all, *dēmos* people)]

pandemonium *noun*
• "panda MOANY um"
• uproar; utter confusion.
• [modern Latin (place of all demons in Milton's *Paradise Lost*) from Greek *pan* neuter of *pas* all + *daimōn* demon, deity]

pandowdy *noun*
• "pan DOW dee"
• a baked pudding of sliced apples topped with a tea-biscuit crust.
• [origin unknown]

paneer *noun*
• "pan EER"
• a mild milk curd cheese similar to cottage cheese, originally from N India, Iran, and Afghanistan.
• [from Hindi or Persian *panīr*, cheese]

panegyric *noun*
• "panna JEE rick" or "panna JYE rick"
• a laudatory or praising discourse, speech, etc.
• [French *panégyrique* from Latin *panegyricus* from Greek *panēgurikos* of public assembly (*pan* neuter of *pas* all, *ēguris* = *agora* assembly)]
• **panegyrical** *adjective*
• **panegyrist** *noun*
• **panegyrize** *verb* (also esp. *Brit.* **-ise**) "PANNA juh rize"

panettone *noun*
• "panna TONY"
• a usu. tall bread-like cake made with eggs and raisins, candied fruit, etc.
• [Italian, from *panetto*, diminutive of *pane* bread, from Latin *panis*]

panforte *noun*
• "pan FORTAY"
• a hard, spicy, Sienese cake containing nuts, candied peel, and honey.
• [Italian, from *pane* bread, and *forte* strong]

panga *noun*
• "PANG guh"
• a bladed African tool like a machete.
• [Swahili]

Panglossian *adjective*
• "pan GLOSSY 'n"
• unrealistically optimistic.
• [from *Pangloss*, the philosopher and tutor in Voltaire's *Candide* (1759)]

pangolin *noun*
• "pang GO lin"
• any scaly anteater of the genus *Manis*, native to Asia and Africa, having a small head with elongated snout and tongue, and a tapering tail.

• [Malay *peng-gōling* roller (from its habit of rolling itself up)]

panicle *noun*

• "PANNA k'll"

• a loose branching cluster of flowers, as in oats.

• [Latin *paniculum* diminutive of *panus* thread]

• **panicled** *adjective*

panino *noun*

• "puh NEENO"

• a crusty, originally Italian, white, elongated bread roll.

• [Italian, diminutive of *pane* bread]

panjandrum *noun*

• "pan JAN drum"

• a mock title for an important person.

• [apparently invented in nonsense verse by S. Foote 1755]

panleukopenia *noun*

ALSO SPELLED: **panleucopenia**

• "pan loo kuh PEENY uh"

• feline distemper.

• [Greek *pan* neuter of *pas* all + LEUKOPENIA]

pannacotta *noun*

• "panna COTTA"

• an Italian dessert made with flavoured sweetened cream set with gelatin, usu. in a mould.

• [Italian, lit. 'cooked cream']

panne *noun*

• "PAN"

• a velvet-like fabric of silk or rayon with a flattened pile.

• [French, from Latin *penna* feather]

HOMOPHONES: *paan, pan*

pannier *noun*

• "PAN yur" or "PAN yay"

• a basket, esp. one of a pair carried by a beast of burden.

• [Old French *panier* from Latin *panarium* breadbasket, from *panis* bread]

panoply *noun*

• "PANNA plee"

• a complete or splendid array.

• [French *panoplie* or modern Latin *panoplia* full armour, from Greek (*pan* neuter of *pas* all, *oplia* from *hopla* arms)]

• **panoplied** *adjective*

panopticon *noun*

• "pan OPTA con"

• a circular prison with cells arranged around a central well, from which prisoners could at all times be observed.

• [Greek *panoptos* seen by all, *panoptēs* all-seeing]

panorama *noun*

• "panna RAMMA"

• an unbroken view of a surrounding region.

• [Greek *pan* neuter of *pas* all + *horama* view, from *horaō* see]

• **panoramic** *adjective*

• **panoramically** *adverb*

pantalets *plural noun*

ALSO SPELLED: **pantalettes**

• "panta LETS"

• long underpants worn by women and girls in the 19th c., with a frill at the bottom of each leg.

• [diminutive of PANTALOON]

pantaloon *noun*

• "panta LOON"

• men's close-fitting breeches fastened below the calf or at the foot.

• [French *pantalon* from Italian *Pantalone* character in *commedia dell'arte* wearing these]

pantechnicon *noun*

• "pan TECKNA con"

• a large van for transporting furniture.

• [Greek *pan* neuter of *pas* all + *technic* (as TECHNICS) originally as the name of a bazaar and then a furniture warehouse]

pantheism *noun*

• "PANTH ee izm"

• the belief or philosophical theory that God and the universe are identical (implying a denial of the personality and transcendence of God); the identification of God with the forces of nature and with natural substances.

• [Greek *pan* neuter of *pas* all + *theos* god]

• **pantheist** *noun*

• **pantheistic** *adjective*

• **pantheistical** *adjective*

• **pantheistically** *adverb*

pantheon *noun*

• "PANTH ee on"

• a building in which illustrious dead are buried or have memorials.

• [Greek *pantheion* (*pan* neuter of *pas* all, *theion* holy from *theos* god)]

pantograph *noun*

• "PANTA graff"

• an instrument for copying a plan or drawing etc. on a different scale by a system of jointed rods.

• [Greek *pas pantos* all, *-graphos* writing]

• **pantographic** *adjective*

pantomime *noun*

• "PANTA mime"

• the use of gestures and facial expression to convey meaning, esp. in drama and dance.

• [French *pantomime* or Latin *pantomimus* from Greek *pantomimos* (*pas pantos* all, *mimos* mime)]

• **pantomimic** *adjective* "panta MIMMIC"

pantothenic *adjective*

• "panta THENNIC"

• designating an acid which is a vitamin of the B complex, found in rice, bran, and many other foods, and essential for the oxidation of fats and carbohydrates.

• [Greek *pantothen* from every side]

pantywaist *noun*
• "PANTY waste"
• a childish, effeminate, or cowardly man or boy.
• [originally a child's outfit consisting of pants and a top joined with buttons at the waist]

panzerotto *noun*
• "panza ROTTO"
• *Cdn* a baked pizza-like turnover, consisting of dough folded into a sealed pocket, filled with tomato sauce, cheese, etc.
• [Italian *panzarotto* from *panza*, obsolete form of *pancia* belly, from its shape]

papacy *noun*
• "PAPE a see"
• a pope's office or tenure.
• [medieval Latin *papatia* from *papa* pope]

Papago *noun*
• "PAPPA go" or "POPPA go"
• a member of an American Indian people of the southwestern US and northern Mexico.
• [Spanish from American Indian name]

papain *noun*
• "puh PAY in"
• a protein-digesting enzyme obtained from unripe papayas, used to tenderize meat and as a food supplement to aid digestion.
• [as PAPAYA]

papal *adjective*
• "PAPE 'll"
• of or relating to a pope or to the papacy.
• [medieval Latin *papalis* from Church Latin *papa* bishop, pope, from ecclesiastical Greek *papas* = Greek *pappas* father]
• **papally** *adverb*

paparazzi *plural noun*
• "pappa RAT see" or "poppa ROT see"
• freelance photographers who pursue celebrities to get photographs of them.
• [Italian, from the name of a character in the film *La Dolce Vita* (1960) by Italian director F. Fellini (d.1993)]

papaya *noun*
• "puh PIE uh"
• an elongated melon-shaped fruit with edible orange flesh and small black seeds.
• [from Spanish & Portuguese, of Carib origin]

papilionaceous *adjective*
• "puh pill y'n AY sh'ss"
• (of a plant) with a corolla like a butterfly.
• [modern Latin *papilionaceus* from Latin *papilio -onis* butterfly + adjective suffix *-aceus* of the nature of]

papilla *noun*
• "puh PILLA"
• a small nipple-like protuberance in a part or organ of the body.
• [Latin, = nipple, diminutive of *papula*: see PAPULE]
• **papillary** *adjective* "PAP'll airy" or "puh PILLER ee"
• **papillate** *adjective* "PAP'll ate"
• **papillose** *adjective* "PAP'll ose" ("OSE" rhymes with *GROSS*)

papilloma *noun*
• "pap'll OH muh"
• a wart-like usu. benign tumour.
• [as PAPILLA + '-oma' as CARCINOMA]

papillon *noun*
• "puh PILL y'n"
• a breed of toy spaniel with ears suggesting the form of a butterfly.
• [French, = butterfly, from Latin *papilio -onis*]

papoose *noun*
• "puh POOSE" ("POOSE" rhymes with *GOOSE*)
• a young N American Indian child.
• [Algonquian *papoos*]

pappadum *noun*
ALSO SPELLED: **pappadam, papadum, poppadum**
• "POPPA dum"
• a thin, crisp, spiced roasted or fried chip made from lentil flour and eaten with Indian food.
• [Tamil *pappaḍam*]

pappardelle *plural noun*
• "pap ar DELL ay"
• pasta in the form of broad flat ribbons, usu. served with a meat sauce.
• [Italian from *pappare* eat greedily]

pappus *noun*
• "PAP us"
• a group of hairs on the fruit of thistles, dandelions, etc.
• [Latin from Greek *pappos*]
• **pappose** *adjective*

paprika *noun*
• "PAP rick uh" or "puh PREE kuh"
• a condiment made from the dried ground fruits of certain (esp. red) varieties of the sweet pepper, *Capsicum annuum*.
• [Hungarian]

paprikash *noun*
ALSO SPELLED: **paprikas**
• "PAP rick ash"
• a Hungarian stew of usu. chicken or veal with tomato, green pepper, and paprika, thickened with sour cream.
• [Hungarian]

Papuan *noun*
• "PAP oo 'n" or "POP oo 'n"
• a native or inhabitant of Papua, the SE half of the island of New Guinea.

papule *noun*
• "PAP yool"
• a pimple.
• [Latin *papula*]
• **papular** *adjective*

papyrus *noun*
• "puh PIE russ"
• a writing material prepared in ancient Egypt from the pithy stem of an aquatic plant, *Cyperus papyrus*.
• [Latin *papyrus* from Greek *papuros*]
• **papyrological** *adjective*
• **papyrologist** *noun*
• **papyrology** *noun* "papper OLLA jee"

parabiosis *noun*
• "perra by OH sis"
• the anatomical union of a pair of organisms, either naturally (as in conjoined twins) or surgically.
• [modern Latin, from Greek *para* beside, past, beyond + Greek *biōsis* mode of life, from *bios* life]
• **parabiotic** *adjective*

parable *noun*
• "PERRA bull" or "PA ruh bull"
• a narrative of imagined events used to illustrate a moral or spiritual lesson.
• [Old French *parabole* from Late Latin sense 'allegory, discourse' of Latin *parabola* comparison]

parabola *noun*
• "puh RABBA luh"
• an open plane curve formed by the intersection of a cone with a plane parallel to its side, resembling the path of a projectile under the action of gravity.
• [modern Latin from Greek *parabolē* placing side by side, comparison (*para* beside, past, beyond, *bolē* a throw, from *ballō*)]
• **parabolic** *adjective* "perra BOLLIC" or "pa ruh BOLLIC"
• **parabolically** *adverb*

paraboloid *noun*
• "puh RABBA loid"
• a solid generated by the rotation of a parabola about its axis of symmetry.
• [as PARABOLA]
• **paraboloidal** *adjective*

paracetamol *noun*
• "pa ruh SEETA maul"
• = ACETAMINOPHEN.
• [*para-acetylaminophenol*]

parachute *noun*
• "PERRA shoot"
• a device allowing a person or object to fall (esp. from an airplane) at a safe rate, or retarding other motion, by increasing air resistance, consisting of a fabric sheet along whose perimeter are attached ropes secured to the person or object.
• [French (*para-* from Italian from Latin *parare* defend + CHUTE)]
• **parachutist** *noun*

Paraclete *noun*
• "PERRA cleet"
• the Holy Spirit as advocate or counsellor.
• [Old French *paraclet* from Late Latin *paracletus* from Greek *paraklētos* called in aid (*para* beside, past, beyond, *klētos* from *kaleō* call)]

paradichlorobenzene *noun*
• "perra die cloro BEN zeen"
• a crystalline compound, $C_6H_4Cl_2$, used as a mothproofing agent.
• [Greek *para* beside, past, beyond + *dis* twice + CHLORINE + BENZENE]

paradiddle *noun*
• "PERRA did'll"
• a basic drum roll produced by alternate beating of sticks.
• [imitative]

paradigm *noun*
• "PERRA dime"
• an example or pattern followed; a typical instance.
• [Late Latin *paradigma* from Greek *paradeigma* from *paradeiknumi* show side by side (*para* beside, past, beyond, *deiknumi* show)]
• **paradigmatic** *adjective* "perra dig MATTIC"

paradise *noun*
• "PERRA dice"
• (in some religions) heaven as the ultimate abode of the just.
• [Old French *paradis* from Late Latin *paradisus* from Greek *paradeisos* from Avestan *pairidaēza* park]
• **paradisaical** *adjective* "perra duh SAY a k'll"
• **paradisal** *adjective*
• **paradisiacal** *adjective* "perra duh SYE a k'll"
• **paradisical** *adjective* "perra DISSA k'll"

paradox *noun*
• "PERRA dox"
• a seemingly absurd or self-contradictory statement which, when investigated or explained, may prove to be well-founded or true.
• [originally = a statement contrary to accepted opinion, from Late Latin *paradoxum* from Greek *paradoxon* neuter adjective (*para* beside, past, beyond, *doxa* opinion)]
• **paradoxical** *adjective*
• **paradoxically** *adverb*

paraffin *noun*
• "PERRA fin"
• a translucent, inflammable, waxy or oily substance obtained by distillation from petroleum and shale and used esp. in candles, cosmetics, and polishes, and for coating and sealing.
• [German (1830) from Latin *parum* little + *affinis* related, from the small affinity it has for other substances]

paragoge *noun*
• "perra GODGE ee"
• the addition of a letter or syllable to a word in some contexts or as a language develops, e.g. *t* in *peasant*.
• [Late Latin from Greek *paragōgē* derivation

(Greek *para* beside, past, beyond, *agōgē* from *agō* lead)]
- **paragogic** *adjective*

paragon *noun*
- "PERRA gon"
- a model of excellence.
- [obsolete French from Italian *paragone* touchstone, from medieval Greek *parakonē* whetstone]

Paraguayan *noun*
- "pa ruh GWAY 'n" or "pa ruh GWYE 'n"
- a native or inhabitant of Paraguay in central S America.

parakeet *noun*
- "PERRA keet"
- any of various small usu. long-tailed parrots.
- [Old French *paroquet*, Italian *parrocchetto*, Spanish *periquito*, perhaps ultimately from diminutive of *Pierre* etc. Peter]

paralanguage *noun*
- "PERRA lang gwidge"
- elements or factors in communication that are ancillary to language proper, e.g. intonation and gesture.
- [from or after Greek *para* beside, past, beyond + 'language']

paraldehyde *noun*
- "puh RALDA hide"
- a colourless liquid cyclic polymer of acetaldehyde, used formerly as a narcotic and sedative.
- [Greek *para* beside, past, beyond + ALDEHYDE]

paralegal *noun*
- "perra LEE g'll"
- a person trained in subsidiary legal matters, but not fully qualified as a lawyer; a legal aide.
- [Greek *para* beside, past, beyond + 'legal']

paralipomena *plural noun*
- "perra luh POMMA nuh"
- the books of Chronicles in the Hebrew Bible, containing particulars omitted from Kings.
- [Church Latin from Greek *paraleipomena* from *paraleipō* omit (*para* beside, past, beyond, *leipō* leave)]

paralipsis *noun*
- "perra LIP sis"
- the device of giving emphasis by professing to say little or nothing of a subject, as in *not to mention their unpaid debts of several millions.*
- [Late Latin from Greek *paraleipsis* passing over (*para* beside, past, beyond, *leipsis* from *leipō* leave)]

parallax *noun*
- "PERRA lax"
- the apparent difference in the position or direction of an object caused when the observer's position is changed.
- [Greek *parallaxis* change, from *parallassō* to alternate (*para* beside, past, beyond, *allassō* exchange, from *allos* other)]
- **parallactic** *adjective*

parallel *adjective*
- "PERRA lell"
- (of lines or planes) side by side and having the same distance continuously between them.
- [Greek *parallēlos* (*para* beside, past, beyond, *allēlos* one another)]
- **parallelism** *noun*

parallelepiped *noun*
- "perra lell EPPA ped" or "perra lella PIPE id"
- a solid figure bounded by six parallelograms, of which opposite pairs are parallel.
- [Greek *parallēlepipedon* (as PARALLEL, *epipedon* plane surface)]

parallelogram *noun*
- "perra LELLA gram"
- a four-sided plane rectilinear figure with opposite sides parallel.
- [Greek *parallēlogrammon* (as PARALLEL, *grammē* line)]

paralysis *noun*
- "puh RALLA sis"
- loss of the ability to move a part of the body, usu. as a result of disease or injury to the nervous system.
- [Latin from Greek *paralusis* from *paraluō* disable (*para* beside, past, beyond, *luō* loosen)]
- **paralytic** *adjective* "perra LITTIC"
- **paralytically** *adverb*
- **paralyze** *verb* (also **-yse**)
- **paralyzed** *adjective* (also **-ysed**)
- **paralyzingly** *adverb* (also **-ysingly**)

paramagnetic *adjective*
- "perra mag NETTIC"
- (of a body or substance) tending to become weakly magnetized so as to lie parallel to a magnetic field force.
- [Greek *para* beside, past, beyond + MAGNET]
- **paramagnetism** *noun*

paramecium *noun*
ALSO SPELLED: esp. *Brit.* **paramoecium**
- "perra MEECY um"
- any freshwater protozoan of the genus *Paramecium*, of a characteristic slipper-like shape covered with cilia.
- [modern Latin from Greek *paramēkēs* oval (*para* beside, past, beyond, *mēkos* length)]

paramedic *noun*
- "perra MEDDIC"
- a paramedical worker, esp. one who works in ambulances and is trained in first aid, emergency care, etc.
- [Greek *para* beside, past, beyond + MEDICAL]

paramedical *adjective*
- "perra MEDDA k'll"
- (of services etc.) supplementing and supporting medical work.
- [as PARAMEDIC]

parameter ***noun***
• "puh RAMMA tur"
• a distinguishing or defining characteristic or feature, esp. one that may be measured or quantified.
• [modern Latin from Greek *para* beside + *metron* measure]
• **parametric** ***adjective*** "perra METRIC"
HOMOPHONES: *perimetric*

parameterize ***verb***
ALSO SPELLED: esp. *Brit.* **-ise**
• "puh RAMMA tur ize"
• describe or represent in terms of a parameter or parameters.
• [as PARAMETER]
• **parameterization** ***noun*** (also esp. *Brit.* **-isation**)

paramilitary ***adjective***
• "perra MILLA terry"
• (of an organization, unit, etc.) not a professional military force, but having an ancillary or analogous function, organization, or status.
• [Greek *para* beside, past, beyond + MILITARY]

paramo ***noun***
• "PERRA moe"
• a high treeless plateau in tropical S America.
• [Spanish & Portuguese from Latin *paramus*]

paramount ***adjective***
• "PERRA mount"
• pre-eminent, requiring first consideration; superior to others in importance, influence, etc.
• [Anglo-French *paramont* from Old French *par* by + *amont* above]
• **paramountcy** ***noun***
• **paramountly** ***adverb***

paramour ***noun***
• "PERRA moor"
• an illicit lover of a married person.
• [Old French *par amour* by love]

parang ***noun***
• "PARE ang"
• a large heavy Malayan knife used for clearing vegetation etc.
• [Malay]

paranoia ***noun***
• "perra NOYA"
• a mental illness characterized by delusions of persecution, unwarranted jealousy, or exaggerated self-importance.
• [modern Latin from Greek from *paranoos* distracted (Greek *para* beside, past, beyond, *noos* mind)]
• **paranoiac** ***adjective***
• **paranoiacally** ***adverb***
• **paranoic** ***adjective***
• **paranoid** ***adjective***

paranormal ***adjective***
• "perra NORM'll"
• designating, pertaining to, or involving phenomena or powers such as telekinesis, clairvoyance, etc., whose operation is outside the scope of known laws of nature or normal objective investigation.
• [Greek *para* beside, past, beyond + 'normal' from Latin *norma* carpenter's square]

parapente ***noun***
• "PERRA pont"
• the activity (sometimes practised as an organized sport) of gliding by means of an airfoil parachute launched from high ground.
• [French *parapente* (as PARACHUTE + *pente* slope, incline, gradient, sloping flight path)]

parapet ***noun***
• "PERRA pet"
• a low wall at the edge of a roof, balcony, etc., or along the sides of a bridge, pier, etc.
• [French *parapet* or Italian *parapetto* breast-high wall (*para-* from Latin *parare* defend, *petto* breast, from Latin *pectus*)]

paraph ***noun***
• "PARE uf"
• a flourish after a signature, originally as a precaution against forgery.
• [French *paraphe* from medieval Latin *paraphus* for *paragraphus* from Greek *paragraphos* short stroke marking a break in sense (*para* beside, *graphō* write)]

paraphernalia ***plural noun***
• "perra fuh NAILY uh"
• miscellaneous belongings, items of equipment, accessories, etc.
• [originally = property owned by a married woman, from medieval Latin *paraphernalia* from Late Latin *parapherna* from Greek *parapherna* property apart from a dowry (Greek *para* beside, past, beyond, *pherna* from *phernē* dower)]

paraphrase ***noun***
• "PERRA fraze"
• a free rendering or rewording of a passage.
• [Greek *paraphrasis* from *paraphrazō* (*para* beside, past, beyond *phrazō* tell)]
• **paraphrasable** ***adjective***
• **paraphrastic** ***adjective*** "perra FRASTIC"

paraplegia ***noun***
• "perra PLEE juh"
• paralysis of the legs and part or the whole of the trunk.
• [modern Latin from Greek *paraplēgia* from *paraplēssō* (*para* beside, past, beyond, *plēssō* strike)]
• **paraplegic** ***adjective***

paraprofessional ***noun***
• "perra pruh FESH'n 'll"
• a person without professional training to whom a particular aspect of a professional task is designated.
• [Greek *para* beside + PROFESSIONAL]

parapsychology ***noun***
• "perra sye COLLA jee"
• the study of mental phenomena outside the

sphere of the ordinary, e.g. hypnosis, telepathy, etc.
• [Greek *para* beside + PSYCHOLOGY]
• **parapsychological** *adjective*
• **parapsychologist** *noun*

paraquat *noun*
• "PERRA kwot"
• a quick-acting, highly toxic herbicide that is rendered inactive on contact with the soil.
• [Greek *para* beside, past, beyond + QUATERNARY (from the position of the bond between the two parts of the molecule relative to quaternary nitrogen atom)]

paraselene *noun*
• "perra suh LEENY"
• a bright spot, esp. an image of the moon, on a lunar halo.
• [modern Latin (Greek *para* beside, past, beyond, *selēnē* moon)]

parasite *noun*
• "PERRA site"
• an organism living in or on another and benefiting at the expense of the other.
• [Greek *parasitos* one who eats at another's table (*para* beside, past, beyond, *sitos* food)]
• **parasitic** *adjective* "perra SITTIC"
• **parasitical** *adjective*
• **parasitically** *adverb*
• **parasiticide** *noun* "perra SITTA side"
• **parasitism** *noun*
• **parasitization** *noun* (also esp. *Brit.* **-isation**)
• **parasitize** *verb* (also esp. *Brit.* **-ise**)
• **parasitological** *adjective*
• **parasitologist** *noun*
• **parasitology** *noun*

parasitoid *noun*
• "PERRA sit oid"
• an insect whose larvae live as parasites which eventually kill their hosts, e.g. an ichneumon wasp.
• [as PARASITE]

parasol *noun*
• "PERRA sawl"
• a light umbrella used to give shade from the sun.
• [French from Italian *parasole* (from Latin *parare* defend, *sol* sun)]

parastatal *adjective*
• "perra STATE 'll"
• (of an industrial organization etc.) having some political authority and serving the nation indirectly, esp. in some African countries.
• [Greek *para* beside + 'state' from Latin STATUS]

parasympathetic *adjective*
• "perra simpa THETTIC"
• relating to one of the major divisions of the autonomic nervous system, whose nerves leave the spinal cord in the cranial or sacral region, and which is associated more with calmness and rest than with alertness.
• [Greek *para* beside, past, beyond + SYMPATHETIC, because some of these nerves run alongside sympathetic nerves]

parasynthesis *noun*
• "perra SINTHA sis"
• a derivation from a compound, e.g. *black-eyed* from *black eye(s)* + *-ed*.
• [Greek *parasunthesis* (*para* beside, past, beyond, SYNTHESIS)]
• **parasynthetic** *adjective* "perra sin THETTIC"

parataxis *noun*
• "perra TAX iss"
• the placing of clauses etc. one after another, without words to indicate coordination or subordination, e.g. *Tell me, how are you?*
• [Greek *parataxis* (*para* beside, past, beyond, *taxis* arrangement, from *tassō* arrange)]
• **paratactic** *adjective* "perra TACTIC"
• **paratactically** *adverb*

paratha *noun*
• "puh ROTHA"
• (in esp. Indian cookery) a piece of flat unleavened bread fried in butter, ghee, etc. on a griddle.
• [Hindi *parāṭhā*]

parathion *noun*
• "perra THYE 'n" (with "TH" as in *THIN*)
• a sulphur-containing organophosphorous agricultural insecticide which is also highly toxic to mammals.
• [Greek *para* beside, past, beyond + *theion* sulphur]

parathyroid *noun*
• "perra THYE roid" (with "TH" as in *THIN*)
• a gland next to the thyroid, secreting a hormone that regulates calcium and phosphate levels in the body.
• [Greek *para* beside + THYROID]

paratyphoid *noun*
• "perra TIFE oid"
• a fever resembling typhoid but less severe and caused by different, though related, bacteria.
• [Greek *para* beside + TYPHOID]

paravane *noun*
• "PERRA vane"
• a device attached by wire to a ship, esp. one used to cut the moorings of submerged mines, having vanes or planes to keep it at a desired depth.
• [Greek *para* beside + VANE]

pare *verb*
• "PAIR"
• trim by cutting away the surface or edge.
• [Old French *parer* adorn, peel (fruit), from Latin *parare* prepare]
• **parer** *noun*

HOMOPHONES: *pair*, *pear*, *père*

paregoric *noun*
• "perra GORIC"
• a camphorated tincture of opium used to reduce pain.
• [Late Latin *paregoricus* from Greek *parēgorikos* soothing (*para* beside, past, beyond, *-agoros* speaking, from *agora* assembly)]

parenchyma *noun*
• "puh RENK im uh"
• the functional part of a gland or organ as distinguished from the connective and supporting tissue.
• [Greek *paregkhuma* something poured in besides (*para* beside, past, beyond, *egkhuma* infusion, from *egkheō* pour in)]
• **parenchymal** *adjective*
• **parenchymatous** *adjective*
"puh ren KIMMA tuss"

parenteral *adjective*
• "puh RENTER 'll"
• involving or designating the introduction of a substance into the body other than by the mouth or intestine, esp. by injection.
• [Greek *para* beside, past, beyond + Greek *enteron* intestine]
• **parenterally** *adverb*

parenthesis *noun*
• "puh RENTHA sis"
• a word, clause, or sentence inserted as an explanation or afterthought into a passage which is grammatically complete without it, usu. marked off by brackets, dashes, or commas.
• [Greek *parenthesis* from *parentithēmi* put in beside]
• **parenthesize** *verb* (also esp. *Brit.* **-ise**)
• **parenthetic** *adjective* "pair 'n THETTIC"
• **parenthetical** *adjective*
• **parenthetically** *adverb*

paresis *noun*
• "puh REE sis" or "PERRA sis"
• partial paralysis.
• [modern Latin from Greek from *pariēmi* let go (*para* beside, past, beyond, *hiēmi* let go)]
• **paretic** *adjective* "puh RETTIC"

paresthesia *noun*
ALSO SPELLED: esp. *Brit.* **paraesthesia**
• "pare us THEEZY uh" or "pare us THEE zhuh" (with "TH" as in *THIN*)
• abnormal sensations caused esp. by pressure on or damage to peripheral nerves.
• [Greek *para* beside, past, beyond + Greek *aisthēsis* sensation]

pareve *adjective*
ALSO SPELLED: **parve**
• "PAR a vuh" or "PARVA"
• (of food) being or containing neither meat nor dairy and so kosher for use with either according to Jewish dietary laws (includes fruit, vegetables, fish, many synthetic products, etc.).
• [Yiddish *parev(e)*, lit. 'neutral']

parfait *noun*
• "par FAY"
• a layered dessert consisting of ice cream, sauces, crushed fruit, etc. served in a tall glass.
• [French *parfait*, perfect]

parfleche *noun*
• "PAR flesh"
• an esp. buffalo hide from which the hair has been removed and which has been dried on a frame.
• [Canadian French *parflèche* from French *parer* from Italian *parare* ward off + French *flèche* arrow]

parging *noun*
• "PAR jing"
• a thin layer of mortar, roughcast, etc. covering a wall, brickwork, etc. for protection or to create a smooth surface.
• [Old French *pargeter*, *parjeter* from *par* all over + *jeter* throw]

parhelion *noun*
• "par HEELY 'n"
• a bright spot on a solar halo, frequently occurring in pairs on either side of the sun and prismatically coloured, caused by reflection of light by atmospheric ice crystals.
• [Latin *parelion* from Greek (*para* beside, past, beyond, *hēlios* sun)]
• **parhelic** *adjective*

pariah *noun*
• "puh RYE uh"
• a social outcast.
• [Tamil *paṛaiyar* pl. of *paṛaiyan* hereditary drummer, from *paṛai* drum]

parietal *adjective*
• "puh RYE a t'll"
• of the wall of the body or the lining of any of its cavities.
• [French *pariétal* from Latin *paries -etis* wall]

parimutuel *noun*
• "perra MYOO choo 'll"
• a form of betting in which those backing the first three places divide the losers' stakes (less the operator's commission).
• [French, = mutual stake]

paring *noun*
• "PARE ing"
• a thin portion cut or peeled from the surface of a thing; a shaving.
• [as PARE]
HOMOPHONES: *pairing*

parish *noun*
• "PARE ish"
• an area of ecclesiastical jurisdiction having a church and clergy.
• [Old French *paroche*, *paroisse* from Church Latin *parochia*, *paroechia* from Greek *paroikia* sojourning, from *paroikos* (*para* beside, past, beyond, *-oikos* -dwelling, from *oikeō* dwell)]
HOMOPHONES: *perish*

parishioner *noun*
- "puh RISH'n ur"
- a member of or someone who attends a particular church.
- [obsolete *parishen* from Middle English from Old French *parossien*, formed as PARISH]

Parisian *adjective*
- "puh REE zh'n" or "puh REEZY 'n"
- of, relating to, or typical of Paris or the people of Paris.
- [French *parisien*]

Parisienne *noun*
- "puh reezy EN"
- a Parisian girl or woman.
- [French feminine of *Parisien* Parisian]

parity *noun*
- "PERRA tee"
- equality or equal status.
- [French *parité* or Late Latin *paritas* from Latin *par* = equal, equality]

parkade *noun*
- "par CADE"
- *Cdn* a parking garage.
- ['park' + ARCADE]

parkette *noun*
- "par KET"
- *Cdn* (*S Ont.*) a small park in a city, usu. less than a block and containing a grassy area, small gardens, benches, etc.
- [diminutive of 'park']

parlance *noun*
- "PAR lince"
- a particular way of speaking, esp. as regards choice of words, idiom, etc.
- [Old French from *parler* speak, ultimately from Latin *parabola* (see PARABLE): in Late Latin = 'speech']

parlay *verb*
- "par LAY" or "PAR lay" or "PARLY"
- exploit (a circumstance), transform (an advantage etc.) into something greater.
- [French *paroli* from Italian from *paro* like, from Latin *par* equal]

HOMOPHONES: *parley*

parley *noun*
- "PARLY"
- an informal conference, under truce, with an enemy, for discussing the mutual arrangement of matters such as terms for armistice, exchange of prisoners, etc.
- [perhaps from Old French *parlee*, feminine past participle of *parler* speak: see PARLANCE]

HOMOPHONES: *parlay*

parliament *noun*
- "PARLA m'nt"
- the highest legislative body in certain countries, including Canada. In Canada the federal parliament consists of the Sovereign, the House of Commons, and the Senate.
- [Old French *parlement* speaking (as PARLANCE)]
- **parliamentary** *adjective* "parla MENTA ree"

parliamentarian *noun*
- "parla m'n TERRY 'n"
- a member of a parliament, esp. one well-versed in its procedures.
- [as PARLIAMENT]

parlous *adjective*
- "PAR luss"
- dangerous or difficult.
- [Middle English, = PERILOUS]
- **parlously** *adverb*
- **parlousness** *noun*

Parmesan *noun*
- "PARMA zhon" or "PARMA zan"
- a kind of hard dry cheese made originally at Parma in N Italy and used esp. in grated form.
- [French from Italian *parmigiano* of Parma]

parmigiana *adjective*
- "parma JONNA" or "parma ZHANNA"
- made or served with Parmesan cheese.
- [Italian, feminine of *parmigiano*]

Parnassian *adjective*
- "par NASSY 'n"
- of Parnassus in Greece, in antiquity sacred to the Muses.

parochial *adjective*
- "puh ROKEY 'll"
- (of affairs, views, etc.) merely local, narrow or restricted in scope.
- [Church Latin *parochialis* (as PARISH)]
- **parochialism** *noun*
- **parochiality** *noun*
- **parochially** *adverb*

parody *noun*
- "PERRA dee"
- humorous exaggerated imitation of an author, literary work, style, etc., esp. for purposes of ridicule.
- [Late Latin *parodia* or Greek *parōidia* burlesque poem (*para* beside, past, beyond, *ōidē* ode)]
- **parodic** *adjective* "puh RODDIC"
- **parodically** *adverb*
- **parodist** *noun*
- **parodistic** *adjective*

parol *adjective*
- "puh ROLE"
- expressed or given orally; verbal, not in writing.
- [Old French *parole* (as PAROLE)]

HOMOPHONES: *parole*

parole *noun*
- "puh ROLE"
- the release of a prisoner, temporarily for a special purpose or completely, before the expiry of a sentence, on the promise of good behaviour.
- [French, = word: see PARLANCE]
- **parolee** *noun*

HOMOPHONES: *parol*

paronomasia *noun*
- "perra nuh MAZEY uh"
- a play on words; a pun.
- [Latin from Greek *paronomasia* (*para* beside, past, beyond, *onomasia* naming, from *onoma* a name)]

paronym *noun*
- "PERRA nim"
- a word cognate with another.
- [Greek *parōnumon*, neuter of *parōnumos* (*para* beside, past, beyond, *onuma* name)]
- **paronymous** *adjective* "puh RONNA muss"

parotid *adjective*
- "puh ROTTID"
- situated near the ear.
- [French *parotide* or Latin *parotis parotid-* from Greek *parōtis -idos* (*para* beside, past, beyond, *ous ōtos* ear)]

parotitis *noun*
- "perra TITE iss"
- inflammation of the parotid gland, a salivary gland in front of the ear.
- [PAROTID + Greek *-itis*, forming feminine of adjectives in *-itēs* (with *nosos* 'disease' implied)]

Parousia *noun*
- "puh ROOZY uh"
- the prophesied return of Christ to earth on Judgment Day.
- [Greek, 'presence, coming']

paroxysm *noun*
- "PARE uck sizm" or "puh ROCK sizm"
- a sudden attack or outburst (of rage, laughter, etc.).
- [medieval Latin *paroxysmus* from Greek *paroxusmos* from *paroxunō* exasperate (*para* beside, past, beyond, *oxunō* sharpen, from *oxus* sharp)]
- **paroxysmal** *adjective*

paroxytone *adjective*
- "puh ROXY tone"
- (esp. in ancient Greek) having an acute accent on the last syllable but one.
- [*para* beside, past, beyond, OXYTONE]

parquet *noun*
- "par CAY" or "PAR cay"
- a flooring of short strips or blocks of wood arranged in an esp. geometric pattern, usu. sold in square, interlocking tiles.
- [French, = small compartment, floor, diminutive of *parc* park]

parquetry *noun*
- "PARKA tree"
- inlaid work of blocks of various woods arranged in a geometric pattern, esp. for furniture or flooring.
- [as PARQUET]

parr *noun*
- "PAR"
- a young salmon between the stages of fry and smolt, distinguished by dark rounded patches evenly spaced along its sides.
- [18th c.: origin unknown]

HOMOPHONES: *par*

parricide *noun*
- "PERRA side" or "PAR a side"
- the killing of a near relative, esp. of a parent.
- [French *parricide* or Latin *parricidium*, of uncertain origin, associated in Latin with *pater* father and *parens* parent + *-cida, -cidium* from *caedere* kill]
- **parricidal** *adjective*

parry *verb*
- "PERRY"
- avert or ward off (a weapon or attack), esp. with a countermove.
- [prob. representing French *parez* imperative of *parer* from Italian *parare* ward off]

HOMOPHONES: *perry*

parsec *noun*
- "PAR seck"
- a unit of stellar distance, equal to about 3.25 light years (3.08×10^{16} metres), the distance at which the mean radius of the earth's orbit subtends an angle of one second of arc.
- [PARALLAX + 'second']

Parsi *noun*

ALSO SPELLED: **Parsee**
- "par SEE" or "PAR see"
- an adherent of Zoroastrianism, esp. a descendant of the Zoroastrian Persians who fled to India in the 7th–8th c. to escape Muslim persecution.
- [Persian *pārsī* Persian, from *pārs* Persia]

parsimony *noun*
- "PARSA moany"
- extreme or excessive carefulness in the use of money or other resources; miserliness, stinginess.
- [Latin *parsimonia, parcimonia* from *parcere pars-* spare]
- **parsimonious** *adjective*
- **parsimoniously** *adverb*
- **parsimoniousness** *noun*

parsley *noun*
- "PAR slee"
- a biennial herb, *Petroselinum crispum*, with white flowers and flavourful leaves, used for seasoning and garnishing food.
- [Old French *peresil*, and Old English *petersilie*, ultimately from Latin *petroselinum* from Greek *petroselinon*]
- **parsleyed** *adjective* "PAR sleed"

parson *noun*
- "PAR s'n"
- any (esp. Protestant) member of the clergy.
- [Old French *persone* from Latin *persona* person (in medieval Latin 'rector')]
- **parsonical** *adjective* "par SONNA k'll"

parsonage *noun*
• "PAR s'n idge"
• a church house provided for a parson; a rectory.
• [as PARSON]

parterre *noun*
• "par TARE"
• a level space in a garden occupied by flower beds arranged formally.
• [French, = *par terre* on the ground]

parthenogenesis *noun*
• "partha no JENNA sis"
• reproduction from an ovum without fertilization, esp. as a normal process in invertebrates and lower plants.
• [modern Latin from Greek *parthenos* virgin + GENESIS]
• **parthenogenetic** *adjective*
"partha no juh NETTIC"
• **parthenogenetically** *adverb*

Parthian *adjective*
• "PARTHY 'n"
• of or relating to ancient Parthia in what is now Iran.

participate *verb*
• "par TISSA pate"
• share or take part (in).
• [Latin *participare* from *particeps -cipis* taking part]
• **participant** *noun*
• **participation** *noun*
• **participative** *adjective*
• **participator** *noun*
• **participatory** *adjective* "par TISSA puh tory"

participle *noun*
• "PARTA sipple"
• a word formed from a verb, e.g. *going, gone, being, been*, and used in compound verb forms, e.g. *is going, has been*, or as an adjective, e.g. *working woman, burnt toast*.
• [Old French, by-form of *participe* from Latin *participium* (as PARTICIPATE)]
• **participial** *adjective* "parta SIPPY 'll"
• **participially** *adverb*

particle *noun*
• "PARTA k'll"
• a very small bit or piece of something.
• [Latin *particula* from *pars partis* part]

particleboard *noun*
• "PARTA k'll bord"
• a rigid sheet or panel made from compressed wood chips, splinters, sawdust, and resin.
• [PARTICLE + BOARD]

particular *adjective*
• "par TICK yuh lur"
• relating to or considered as one thing or person as distinct from others; individual.
• [Latin *particularis* (as PARTICLE)]
• **particularity** *noun* "par tick yuh LERRA tee"

particularism *noun*
• "par TICK yuh lur izm"
• exclusive devotion to one party, sect, etc.
• [as PARTICULAR]
• **particularist** *noun*
• **particularistic** *adjective*

particularize *verb*
ALSO SPELLED: esp. *Brit.* **-ise**
• "par TICK yuh lur ize"
• mention or describe particularly; name specially or one by one.
• [as PARTICULAR]
• **particularization** *noun* (also esp. *Brit.* **-isation**)

particularly *adverb*
• "par TICK yuh lare lee"
• especially, very.
• [as PARTICULAR]

particulate *adjective*
• "par TICK yuh lit" or "par TICK yuh late"
• in the form of separate particles.
• [Latin *particula* PARTICLE]

partisan *noun*
• "PARTA zan" or "PARTA z'n"
• an adherent or supporter of a party, person, or cause, esp. a zealous supporter.
• [French from Italian dialect *partigiano* etc. from *parte* from Latin *pars partis* part]
• **partisanship** *noun*

partita *noun*
• "par TEETA"
• a set of instrumental compositions, originally in dance style, to be played in succession.
• [Italian, feminine past participle of *partire* divide, from Latin *pars partis* part]

partition *noun*
• "par TISH'n"
• division into parts, esp. of a country with separate areas of government.
• [Latin *partitio -onis* from *partiri* to part]
• **partitioned** *adjective*
• **partitionist** *noun*

partitive *adjective*
• "PARTA tiv"
• (of a word, form, etc.) denoting part of a collective group or quantity.
• [French *partitif -ive* or medieval Latin *partitivus* (as PARTITION)]
• **partitively** *adverb*

parturient *adjective*
• "par TURY 'nt" or "par CHURY 'nt"
• about to give birth.
• [Latin *parturire* be in labour, inceptive of *parere part-* bring forth]

parturition *noun*
• "par tur ISH'n" or "par chur ISH'n"
• the act of bringing forth young; childbirth.
• [Late Latin *parturitio* (as PARTURIENT)]

parure *noun*
• "puh RUR"
• a set of jewels or other ornaments intended to be worn together.
• [Old French from *parer* (see PARE)]

parvenu *noun*
• "PARVA noo"
• a person of obscure origin who has gained wealth or position.
• [French, past participle of *parvenir* arrive, from Latin *pervenire* (from *venire* come)]

parvis *noun*
ALSO SPELLED: **parvise**
• "PAR viss"
• an enclosed area in front of a cathedral, church, etc.
• [Old French, ultimately from Late Latin *paradisus* PARADISE, a court in front of St. Peter's, Rome]

parvovirus *noun*
• "PARVO vie russ"
• any of a class of small viruses affecting vertebrate animals, esp. one which causes contagious disease in dogs.
• [Latin *parvus* small + VIRUS]

pas *noun*
• "PAH"
• a step in dancing, esp. in ballet.
• [French, = step]
HOMOPHONES: *pa*, *pah*, *paw*

pascal *noun*
• "PASK'll"
• the SI unit of pressure, equal to one newton per square metre.
• [B. *Pascal*, French mathematician and physicist d.1662]
HOMOPHONES: *paschal*

paschal *adjective*
• "PASK 'll"
• of or relating to Easter.
• [Church Latin *paschalis* from *pascha* from Greek *paskha* from Aramaic *pasḥa*, related to Hebrew *pesaḥ* Passover]
HOMOPHONES: *pascal*

pashm *noun*
• "PASH 'm"
• the under-fur of some Tibetan animals, esp. that of goats as used for cashmere shawls.
• [Persian *pašm* wool]

pashmina *noun*
• "pash MEENA"
• fine quality material made from goat's wool; a fine cashmere.
• [Persian *pashmīn* woollen]

Pashto *noun*
• "PASH toe"
• the Indo-Iranian language of the Pashtuns, an official language of Afghanistan, and spoken also in NW Pakistan.
• [Pashto]

Pashtun *noun*
• "pash TOON"
• a member of a Pashto-speaking people inhabiting NW Pakistan and SE Afghanistan.
• [name in Pashto]

paska *noun*
• "PASS kuh" or "POSS kuh"
• *Cdn* a rich, usu. decorated, egg bread, often containing dried fruits, traditional at Easter among people of Ukrainian origin.
• [Ukrainian and Russian, = Easter]

pasquinade *noun*
• "pass kwuh NADE"
• a lampoon or satire, originally one displayed in a public place.
• [Italian *pasquinata* from *Pasquino*, a statue in Rome on which abusive Latin verses were annually posted]

passable *adjective*
• "PASSA bull"
• barely satisfactory; just adequate.
• [Old French from *passer*, ultimately from Latin *passus* pace]
• **passably** *adverb*
HOMOPHONES: *passible*

passacaglia *noun*
• "passa CALLY uh"
• an instrumental piece usu. with a short theme in the bass constantly repeated with the upper parts of the music varied.
• [Italian from Spanish *pasacalle* from *pasar* pass + *calle* street: originally often played in the streets]

Passamaquoddy *noun*
• "passa muh KWODDY"
• a member of a N American Aboriginal people inhabiting parts of SE Maine and (formerly) SW New Brunswick.
• [Passamaquoddy or Mi'kmaq *peskutumaquadik* place where there are pollock]

passant *adjective*
• "PASS'nt"
• (of a heraldic animal) walking and looking to the dexter side, with three paws on the ground and the right forepaw raised.
• [Old French, participle of *passer* pass, ultimately from Latin *passus* pace]

passé *adjective*
• "pass AY"
• no longer fashionable or topical; out of date.
• [French, past participle of *passer* (as PASSABLE)]

passel *noun*
• "PASS'll"
• an indeterminate number or quantity; a group.
• [representing a pronunciation of 'parcel' from Old French *parcelle*, ultimately from Latin *particula* (as PARTICULAR)]

passementerie *noun*
• "pass MENTRY"
• a trimming of gold or silver lace, braid, beads, etc.
• [French from *passement* gold lace etc. from *passer* (as PASSABLE)]

passenger *noun*
• "PASS'n jur"
• a traveller in or on a public or private conveyance (other than the driver, pilot, crew, etc.).
• [Old French *passager* (adjective) passing (as PASSABLE): *-n-* as in *messenger* etc.]

passerine *noun*
• "PASSER een"
• any perching bird of the order Passeriformes, having feet with three toes pointing forward and one pointing backwards, including sparrows and most land birds.
• [Latin *passer* sparrow]

passible *adjective*
• "PASSA bull"
• capable of feeling or suffering.
• [Old French *passible* or Late Latin *passibilis* from Latin *pati pass-* suffer]
• **passibility** *noun*
HOMOPHONES: *passable*

passim *adverb*
• "PASS im"
• (of allusions or references in a published work) to be found at various places throughout the text.
• [Latin from *passus* scattered, from *pandere* spread]

passion *noun*
• "PASH'n"
• strong barely controllable emotion.
• [Late Latin *passio -onis* from Latin *pati pass-* suffer]
• **passional** *adjective*
• **passionate** *adjective* "PASH'n it"
• **passionately** *adverb*
• **passionateness** *noun*
• **passionless** *adjective*

Passiontide *noun*
• "PASH'n tide"
• the last two weeks of Lent.
• [as PASSION + 'tide' (Old English, = 'time')]

passivate *verb*
• "PASSA vate"
• make (esp. metal) passive.
• [Latin *passivus* (as PASSION)]
• **passivation** *noun*

pastel *noun*
• "pass TELL"
• a crayon consisting of powdered pigments bound with a gum solution.
• [French *pastel* or Italian *pastello*, diminutive of *pasta* from Late Latin *pasta* small, square medicinal lozenge, from Greek *pastē*, from *pastos* sprinkled]
• **pastelist** *noun* (also **pastellist**)

pastern *noun*
• "PASS turn"
• the part of a horse's foot between the fetlock and the hoof.
• [Middle English *pastron* from Old French *pasturon* from *pasture* hobble, ultimately from Latin *pastorius* of a shepherd: see PASTOR]

pasteurize *verb*
ALSO SPELLED: esp. *Brit.* **-ise**
• "PASS chur ize" or "PASS tur ize"
• subject (milk etc.) to the process of partial sterilization by heating.
• [L. *Pasteur*, French bacteriologist d.1895]
• **pasteurization** *noun* (also esp. *Brit.* **-isation**)
• **pasteurizer** *noun* (also esp. *Brit.* **-iser**)

pasticcio *noun*
• "pass TEECH oh"
• a musical pastiche.
• [Italian: see PASTICHE]

pastiche *noun*
• "pass TEESH"
• a medley, esp. a picture or a musical composition, made up from or imitating various sources.
• [French from Italian *pasticcio*, ultimately from Late Latin *pasta* (as PASTEL)]
• **pasticheur** *noun* "pass tee SHUR"

pastille *noun*
• "pass TEEL"
• a small candy, lozenge, or chocolate.
• [French from Latin *pastillus* little loaf, lozenge, from *panis* loaf]

pastime *noun*
• "PASS time"
• a pleasant recreation or hobby.
• ['pass' + 'time']

pastis *noun*
• "pass TEECE"
• an aniseed-flavoured aperitif.
• [French]

pastitsio *noun*
• "pass TEETSY oh"
• a Greek dish consisting of a layer of ground meat in a tomato sauce between two layers of macaroni in a cheese cream sauce.
• [Greek]

pastor *noun*
• "PASS tur"
• (often as a title or form of address) a minister or priest in charge of a church or a congregation.
• [Old French *pastour* from Latin *pastor -oris* shepherd, from *pascere past-* feed, graze]
• **pastorship** *noun*

pastoral *adjective*
• "PASS tur 'll"

• of, relating to, or associated with shepherds or flocks and herds.
• [Middle English from Latin *pastoralis* (as PASTOR)]
• **pastoralism** *noun*
• **pastorally** *adverb*

pastorale *noun*
• "pass tur AL" or "pass tur AL ee"
• a slow instrumental composition, usu. with drone notes in the bass suggestive of a shepherd's bagpipes.
• [Italian (as PASTORAL)]

pastoralist *noun*
• "PASS tur 'll ist"
• a farmer of sheep or cattle.
• [as PASTORAL]

pastorate *noun*
• "PASS tur it"
• the office or tenure of a pastor.
• [as PASTOR]

pastrami *noun*
• "puh STROMMY"
• seasoned smoked beef brisket, usu. cut in thin slices for sandwiches.
• [Yiddish from Romanian *pastramă* cured meat, prob. of Turkish origin]

pasty[1] *noun*
• "PAST ee"
• a piece of pastry folded around a usu. savoury filling, baked without a dish to shape it.
• [Old French *pasté*, ultimately from Late Latin *pasta* (as PASTEL)]

pasty[2] *adjective*
• "PASTE ee"
• unhealthily pale (esp. in complexion).
• [from 'paste', ultimately from Late Latin *pasta* (as PASTEL)]
• **pastily** *adverb*
• **pastiness** *noun*

pataca *noun*
• "puh TAY kuh"
• the basic monetary unit of Macao, equal to 100 avos.
• [Spanish and Portuguese]

patagium *noun*
• "puh TAY jee um"
• the wing membrane of a bat or similar animal.
• [medieval Latin use of Latin *patagium* from Greek *patageion* gold edging]

Patagonian *adjective*
• "patta GO nee 'n"
• of or relating to Patagonia in S Argentina.

pataphysics *noun*
• "PATTA fizzix"
• the branch of philosophy that deals with an imaginary realm additional to metaphysics.
• [from Greek *ta epi ta metaphusika*, literally 'the works imposed on the Metaphysics'. The concept was introduced by Alfred Jarry, French writer of the Absurd]
• **pataphysical** *adjective*

patchouli *noun*
• "puh CHOOLY"
• a strongly scented E Indian plant, *Pogostemon cablin*.
• [Tamil *pacculi*]

pâte *noun*
• "PAT"
• the paste of which porcelain is made.
• [French, = paste (as PASTEL)]
HOMOPHONES: *pat*

pâté *noun*
• "pat AY" or "PAT ay"
• a rich paste or spread of ground or puréed and seasoned meat or fish etc., usu. served as an appetizer.
• [French from Old French *pasté* (as PASTY[1])]

patella *noun*
• "puh TELLA"
• the kneecap.
• [Latin, diminutive of *patina*: see PATEN]
• **patellar** *adjective*
• **patellate** *adjective* "puh TELL ut"

paten *noun*
• "PAT'n"
• a shallow dish used for the bread at the Eucharist.
• [Old French *patene* or Latin *patena*, *patina* shallow dish, from Greek *patanē* a plate]
HOMOPHONES: *patten*

patency *noun*
• "PAT 'n see" or "PAY t'n see"
• obviousness.
• [Old French *patent* and Latin *patēre* lie open]

patent *noun*
• "PAT 'nt" or "PAY t'nt"
• a government authority to an individual or organization conferring a right or title, esp. the sole right to make or use or sell some invention.
• [Old French *patent* and Latin *patēre* lie open]
• **patentability** *noun*
• **patentable** *adjective*

patentee *noun*
• "pat 'n TEE" or "pay t'n TEE"
• a person, company, etc. that takes out or holds a patent.
• [as PATENT]

patently *adverb*
• "PAT 'nt lee" or "PAY t'nt lee"
• obviously, plainly.
• [Old French *patent* and Latin *patēre* lie open]

patentor *noun*
• "PAT 'n tur" or "PAY t'n tur"
• a person or body that grants a patent.
• [as PATENT]

paterfamilias *noun*
- "patter fuh MILLY us" or "pay tur fuh MILLY us"
- the male head of a family or household.
- [Latin, = father of the family]

paternal *adjective*
- "puh TURN'll"
- of or like or appropriate to a father.
- [Late Latin *paternalis* from Latin *paternus* from *pater* father]
- **paternally** *adverb*

paternalism *noun*
- "puh TURN'll izm"
- the policy of governing in a paternal way, or behaving paternally to one's associates or subordinates.
- [as PATERNAL]
- **paternalist** *adjective*
- **paternalistic** *adjective*
- **paternalistically** *adverb*

paternity *noun*
- "puh TURNA tee"
- fatherhood.
- [Late Latin *paternitas*]

paternoster *noun*
- "patter NOSS tur"
- the Lord's Prayer, esp. in Latin.
- [Old English from Latin *pater noster* our father]

pathetic *adjective*
- "puh THETTIC"
- arousing pity or sadness or contempt.
- [Late Latin *patheticus* from Greek *pathētikos* (as PATHOS)]
- **pathetically** *adverb*

pathogen *noun*
- "PATHA j'n"
- an agent causing disease.
- [as PATHOS + GENESIS]
- **pathogenic** *adjective*
- **pathogenicity** *noun* "patha juh NISSA tee"

pathogenesis *noun*
- "patha JENNA sis"
- the manner of development of a disease.
- [as PATHOS + GENESIS]
- **pathogenetic** *adjective* "patha juh NETTIC"

pathologize *verb*
ALSO SPELLED: esp. *Brit.* **-ise**
- "puh THOLLA jize"
- cause (someone or something) to be considered abnormal or ill.
- [as PATHOLOGY]

pathology *noun*
- "puh THOLLA jee"
- the science of bodily diseases.
- [as PATHOS + Greek *logos* word]
- **pathologic** *adjective*
- **pathological** *adjective*
- **pathologically** *adverb*
- **pathologist** *noun*

pathophysiology *noun*
- "patho fizzy OLLA jee"
- the disordered physical processes associated with disease or injury.
- [as PATHOS + PHYSIOLOGY]
- **pathophysiological** *adjective*

pathos *noun*
- "PAY thoss"
- a quality in speech, writing, events, etc. that excites pity or sadness.
- [Greek *pathos* suffering, related to *paskhō* suffer, *penthos* grief]

patient *adjective*
- "PAY sh'nt"
- having or showing calm endurance of hardship, provocation, pain, delay, etc.
- [Old French from Latin *patiens -entis* pres. part. of *pati* suffer]
- **patience** *noun*
- **patiently** *adverb*

patina *noun*
- "puh TEENA" or "PAT in uh"
- a film, usu. green, formed on the surface of old bronze.
- [Italian from Latin *patina* dish]
- **patinated** *adjective* "PAT 'n ated"
- **patination** *noun*

patisserie *noun*
- "puh TEECE a ree"
- a bakeshop where fancy, esp. French, pastries are made, sold, and usu. served.
- [French *pâtisserie* from medieval Latin *pasticium* pastry, from *pasta* paste]

patois *noun*
- "pat WAH" or "PAT wah"
- a non-standard local dialect.
- [French, = rough speech, perhaps from Old French *patoier* treat roughly, from *patte* paw]

patootie *noun*
- "puh TOOTY"
- the buttocks.
- [perhaps alteration of POTATO]

patriarch *noun*
- "PAY tree ark"
- the male head of a family or tribe.
- [Old French *patriarche* from Church Latin *patriarcha* from Greek *patriarkhēs* from *patria* family, from *patēr* father + *-arkhēs* -ruler]

patriarchal *adjective*
- "pay tree ARK 'll"
- of or pertaining to a patriarch or to patriarchy.
- [as PATRIARCH]
- **patriarchalist** *noun*
- **patriarchally** *adverb*

patriarchate *noun*
- "PAY tree ark it"
- the office, see, or residence of an ecclesiastical patriarch.
- [as PATRIARCH]

patriarchy *noun*
- "PAY tree arky"
- a system of society, government, etc., ruled by a man and with descent through the male line.
- [as PATRIARCH]
- **patriarchism** *noun*

patriate *verb*
- "PAY tree ate"
- *Cdn* bring (legislation, esp. a constitution) under the authority of the autonomous country to which it applies, used with reference to laws passed on behalf of that country by its former mother country.
- [from REPATRIATE]
- **patriation** *noun*

patrician *noun*
- "puh TRISH'n"
- a member of the ancient Roman nobility.
- [Old French *patricien* from Latin *patricius* having a noble father, from *pater patris* father]

patriciate *noun*
- "puh TRISH it"
- a patrician order; an aristocracy.
- [Latin *patriciatus* (as PATRICIAN)]

patricide *noun*
- "PATRA side"
- the killing of one's father.
- [Late Latin *patricida, patricidium*, alteration of Latin *parricida, parricidium* (see PARRICIDE) by association with *pater* father]
- **patricidal** *adjective*

patrilineal *adjective*
- "patra LINNY 'll"
- of or relating to, or based on kinship with, the father or descent through the male line.
- [Latin *pater patris* father + LINEAL]
- **patrilineally** *adverb*

patrilocal *adjective*
- "patra LO k'll"
- designating or pertaining to a pattern of marriage in which the couple settles in the husband's home or community.
- [Latin *pater patris* father + LOCAL]
- **patrilocality** *noun*

patrimony *noun*
- "PATRA moany"
- a heritage.
- [Old French *patrimoine* from Latin *patrimonium* from *pater patris* father]
- **patrimonial** *adjective*

patriot *noun*
- "PAY tree it"
- a person who is ardently devoted to the well-being or interests of his or her country.
- [French *patriote* from Late Latin *patriota* from Greek *patriōtēs* from *patrios* of one's fathers, from *patēr patros* father]
- **patriotic** *adjective*
- **patriotically** *adverb*
- **patriotism** *noun*

Patriote *noun*
- "pat ree OT"
- *Cdn* a supporter of reformer L. J. Papineau (d.1871) in the Rebellion of Lower Canada (1837).
- [French = PATRIOT]

patristics *noun*
- "puh TRISS ticks"
- the branch of Christian theology that deals with the early Christian theologians or their writings.
- [from Latin *pater patris* father]
- **patristic** *adjective*

patron *noun*
- "PAY trin"
- a person who gives financial or other support to a person, cause, arts organization, work of art, etc.
- [Old French from Latin *patronus* protector of clients, defender, from *pater patris* father]
- **patroness** *noun*

patronage *noun*
- "PAY truh nidge" or "PATTRA nidge"
- the support, promotion, or encouragement given by a patron.
- [as PATRON]

patronal *adjective*
- "puh TRO n'll"
- of or relating to a patron saint.
- [as PATRON]

patronize *verb*
ALSO SPELLED: esp. *Brit.* **-ise**
- "PAY truh nize" or "PATTRA nize"
- treat condescendingly.
- [as PATRON]
- **patronizer** *noun* (also esp. *Brit.* **-iser**)
- **patronizing** *adjective* (also esp. *Brit.* **-ising**)
- **patronizingly** *adverb* (also esp. *Brit.* **-isingly**)

patronymic *noun*
- "patra NIMMIC"
- a name derived from the name of a father or ancestor, e.g. *Johnson, O'Brien, Ivanovich, Fitzgerald*.
- [Late Latin *patronymicus* from Greek *patrōnumikos* from *patrōnumos* from *patēr patros* father + *onuma, onoma* name]

patroon *noun*
- "puh TROON"
- a landowner with manorial privileges under the Dutch governments of New York and New Jersey.
- [Dutch, = PATRON]

patten *noun*
- "PAT'n"
- a shoe or clog with a raised sole or set on an iron ring, for walking in mud etc.
- [Old French *patin* from *patte* paw]

HOMOPHONES: *paten*

patulous *adjective*
- "PAT yoo luss"
- (of branches etc.) spreading.
- [Latin *patulus* from *patēre* be open]

paua *noun*
- "POW uh" ("POW" rhymes with *HOW*)
- a large edible New Zealand shellfish of the genus *Haliotis*.
- [Maori]

paucity *noun*
- "POSSA tee"
- smallness of number or quantity.
- [Latin *paucitas* from *paucus* few]

paulownia *noun*
- "puh LO nee uh"
- any Chinese tree of the genus *Paulownia*, with fragrant purple flowers.
- [Anna *Paulovna*, Russian princess d.1865]

paunch *noun*
- "PONCH"
- the belly or stomach, esp. when protruding.
- [Anglo-French *pa(u)nche*, ultimately from Latin *pantex panticis* bowels]
- **paunchiness** *noun*
- **paunchy** *adjective*

pauper *noun*
- "POPPER"
- a very poor person.
- [Latin, = poor]
- **pauperdom** *noun*
- **pauperism** *noun*
- **pauperization** *noun* (also esp. *Brit.* **-isation**)
- **pauperize** *verb* (also esp. *Brit.* **-ise**)

HOMOPHONES: *popper*

paupiette *noun*
- "poe PYET"
- a long thin slice of fish, meat, etc., esp. rolled and stuffed with a filling.
- [French, prob. from Italian *polpetta*, from Latin *pulpa* pulp]

pavane *noun*
- "puh VAN" or "puh VON"
- a stately dance in elaborate clothing.
- [French *pavane* from Spanish *pavana*, perhaps from *pavon* peacock]

pavé *noun*
- "PAV ay"
- a setting of jewels placed closely together so that no metal is visible.
- [French, past participle of *paver* from Latin *pavimentum* from *pavire* beat, ram]

pavilion *noun*
- "puh VILL y'n"
- a summer house or other decorative building in a garden or park.
- [Old French *pavillon* from Latin *papilio -onis* butterfly, tent]
- **pavilioned** *adjective*

pavlova *noun*
- "pav LO vuh"
- a large round meringue shell filled with whipped cream and fruit.
- [A. *Pavlova*, Russian ballet dancer d.1931]

Pavlovian *adjective*
- "pav LO vee 'n"
- of or relating to Russian physiologist I. P. Pavlov (d.1936) or his work, esp. on conditioned reflexes.

pavonine *adjective*
- "PAVVA nine"
- of or like a peacock.
- [Latin *pavoninus* from *pavo -onis* peacock]

pawky *adjective*
- "POCKY"
- drily humorous.
- [Scots & Northern English dialect *pawk* trick, of unknown origin]
- **pawkily** *adverb*
- **pawkiness** *noun*

pawl *noun*
- "PAUL"
- a pivoted, usu. curved, bar or lever whose free end engages with the teeth of a cogwheel or ratchet so that it can only turn or move one way.
- [perhaps from Low German & Dutch *pal*, related to *pal* fixed]

HOMOPHONES: *pall, pol*

peaceable *adjective*
- "PEECE a bull"
- disposed to peace; unwarlike.
- [Old French *peisible* from Latin *pax* peace]
- **peaceableness** *noun*
- **peaceably** *adverb*

peafowl *noun*
- "PEE foul"
- a pheasant of the genus *Pavo*, a peacock or peahen.
- [Old English *pēa* from Latin *pavo* peacock + FOWL]

peal *noun*
- "PEEL"
- the loud ringing of a bell or bells, esp. a series of changes.
- [Middle English *pele* from *apele* APPEAL]

HOMOPHONES: *peel*

pearlescent *adjective*
- "purl ESS'nt"
- having or producing the appearance of mother-of-pearl.
- [Old French *perle*, prob. from Latin *perna* leg (applied to leg-of-mutton-shaped bivalve) + Latin *-escent* used in verb forms to signify becoming]
- **pearlescence** *noun*

pearlized *adjective*

ALSO SPELLED: esp. *Brit.* **-ised**
- "PURL ized"
- treated so as to resemble mother-of-pearl; iridescent.
- [Old French *perle*, prob. from Latin *perna* leg (applied to leg-of-mutton-shaped bivalve)]

peasant *noun*
- "PEZZ'nt"

- a usu. poor farmer of low social status who owns or rents a small piece of land for cultivation (chiefly in historical use or with reference to subsistence farming in poorer countries).
- [Anglo-French *paisant*, Old French *païsent*, from *païs* country, ultimately from Latin *pagus* canton]
- **peasanty** *adjective*

peasantry *noun*
- "PEZZ'n tree"
- peasants collectively.
- [as PEASANT]

peavey *noun*
ALSO SPELLED: **peavy**
- "PEEVY"
- a logging implement consisting of a long pole ending in a metal spike and hinged hook.
- [J. *Peavey*, its US inventor]

pec *noun*
- "PECK"
- a pectoral muscle.
- [abbreviation]

HOMOPHONES: *peck*

peccadillo *noun*
- "pecka DILLO"
- a trifling offence; a minor sin.
- [Spanish *pecadillo*, diminutive of *pecado* sin, from Latin (as PECCANT)]

peccant *adjective*
- "PECK'nt"
- sinning; guilty of an offence.
- [French *peccant* or Latin *peccare* sin]
- **peccancy** *noun*

peccary *noun*
- "PECKA ree"
- any of several dark-furred gregarious pig-like mammals of the family Tayassuidae, which inhabit forest and forest scrub in Central and S America.
- [Carib *pakira*]

pecorino *noun*
- "pecka REENO"
- an Italian cheese made from ewes' milk.
- [Italian from *pecorino* (adjective) of ewes, from *pecora* sheep]

pecten *noun*
- "PECK t'n"
- a comb-like structure of various kinds in animal bodies.
- [Latin *pecten pectinis* comb]
- **pectinate** *adjective*

HOMOPHONES: *pectin*

pectin *noun*
- "PECK tin"
- any of various soluble gelatinous polysaccharides found in ripe fruits etc. and used as a setting agent in jams and jellies.
- [Greek *pēktos* congealed, from *pēgnumi* make solid]
- **pectic** *adjective*

HOMOPHONES: *pecten*

pectoral *adjective*
- "PECTER 'll"
- of or relating to the breast or chest; thoracic.
- [Latin *pectorale pectus pectoris* breast, chest]

peculate *verb*
- "PECK yuh late"
- embezzle (money).
- [Latin *peculari* related to *peculium*: see PECULIAR]
- **peculation** *noun*
- **peculator** *noun*

peculiar *adjective*
- "puh KYOOL yur"
- strange; odd; unusual.
- [Latin *peculiaris* of private property, from *peculium* from *pecu* cattle]
- **peculiarity** *noun* "puh kyooly ERRA tee"
- **peculiarly** *adverb*

pecuniary *adjective*
- "puh KYOONY airy"
- of, concerning, or consisting of, money.
- [Latin *pecuniarius* from *pecunia* money, from *pecu* cattle]
- **pecuniarily** *adverb*

pedagogue *noun*
- "PEDDA gog"
- a teacher.
- [Latin *paedagogus* from Greek *paidagōgos* from *pais paidos* boy + *agōgos* guide]

pedagogy *noun*
- "PEDDA godge ee"
- the art or science of teaching; teaching.
- [French *pédagogie* from Greek *paidagōgia* (as PEDAGOGUE)]
- **pedagogic** *adjective*
- **pedagogical** *adjective*
- **pedagogically** *adverb*
- **pedagogics** *noun*

pedal *noun*
- "PED'll"
- any of several types of foot-operated levers or controls for mechanisms, esp.: either of a pair of levers for transmitting power to a bicycle or tricycle wheel etc.
- [French *pédale* via Italian *pedale* from Latin *pedalis* from *pes pedis* foot]
- **pedaller** *noun* (also **pedaler**)

HOMOPHONES: *peddle, peddler, petal*

pedalo *noun*
- "PEDDA lo"
- a small recreational pontoon boat usu. with paddlewheels, propelled by means of pedals.
- [as PEDAL]

pedant *noun*
- "PED'nt"
- a person excessively concerned with trifling

details or who insists on strict adherence to formal rules or literal meaning at the expense of a wider view.
• [French *pédant* from Italian *pedante*: apparently formed as PEDAGOGUE]
• **pedantic** *adjective* "puh DANTIC"
• **pedantically** *adverb*
• **pedantry** *noun*

pedate *adjective*
• "PED ate"
• having feet.
• [Latin *pedatus* from *pes pedis* foot]

peddle *verb*
• "PED'll"
• sell (goods), esp. in small quantities, as a peddler.
• [back-formation from PEDDLER]
HOMOPHONES: *pedal, petal*

peddler *noun*
ALSO SPELLED: **pedlar**
• "PED lur"
• a travelling seller of small items esp. carried in a pack etc.
• [Middle English *pedlere* alteration of *pedder* from *ped* pannier, of unknown origin]
HOMOPHONES: *pedaller*

pedestal *noun*
• "PEDDA st'll"
• a base supporting a column or pillar.
• [French *piédestal* via Italian *piedestallo*, from *piè* foot (from Latin *pes pedis*) + *di* of + *stallo* stall]

pedestrian *noun*
• "puh DESS tree 'n"
• a person on foot rather than in a vehicle.
• [French *pédestre* or Latin *pedester -tris*]

pedestrianize *verb*
ALSO SPELLED: esp. *Brit.* **-ise**
• "puh DESTRY 'n ize"
• close (part of an urban area) to vehicular traffic and make accessible only to pedestrians.
• [as PEDESTRIAN]
• **pedestrianization** *noun* (also esp. *Brit.* **-isation**)

pediatrics *noun*
ALSO SPELLED: esp. *Brit.* **paediatrics**
• "peedy ATTRIX"
• the branch of medicine dealing with children and their diseases.
• [Greek *pais paid-* child, *iatros* physician]
• **pediatric** *adjective* (also esp. *Brit.* **paediatric**)
• **pediatrician** *noun* (also esp. *Brit.* **paediatrician**) "peedy a TRISH'n"

pedicab *noun*
• "PEDDY cab"
• a small pedal-operated vehicle, usu. a rickshaw-like tricycle, serving as a taxi.
• [as PEDAL + 'cab' abbreviation of CABRIOLET]

pedicel *noun*
• "PEDDA s'll"
• a small (esp. subordinate) stalklike structure in a plant or animal, esp. each stalk bearing an individual flower in a branched inflorescence.
• [modern Latin *pedicellus* & Latin *pediculus* diminutive of *pes pedis* foot]
• **pedicellate** *adjective* "PEDDA s'll ate"

pedicle *noun*
• "PEDDA k'll"
• a small stalklike structure, esp. one supporting a seed, gland, tumour, etc.
• [Latin *pediculus*, diminutive of *ped pedis* foot]
• **pediculated** *adjective* "puh DIC yuh lated"

pediculicide *noun*
• "pedda KYOOL a side"
• a substance that kills lice.
• [from Latin *pediculus* louse + *-cida, -cidium* from *caedere* kill]

pediculosis *noun*
• "puh dick yuh LO sis"
• an infestation with lice.
• [from Latin *pediculus* louse]

pedicure *noun*
• "PEDDA cure"
• treatment of the feet, either remedial, as in the removal of corns and bunions, or cosmetic, as in the trimming, painting, etc. of the toenails.
• [French *pédicure* from Latin *pes pedis* foot + *curare* take care of, from *cura* care]
• **pedicurist** *noun*

pedigree *noun*
• "PEDDA gree"
• a recorded line of descent of a person or esp. a purebred domestic or pet animal.
• [Middle English *pedegru* etc. from Anglo-French from Old French *pie de grue* (unrecorded) crane's foot, a mark denoting succession in pedigrees]
• **pedigreed** *adjective*

pediment *noun*
• "PEDDA m'nt"
• the triangular part crowning the front of a building in the classical style.
• [earlier *pedament, periment*, perhaps corruption of PYRAMID]
• **pedimental** *adjective*
• **pedimented** *adjective*

pedology *noun*
• "puh DOLLA jee"
• the scientific study of soil, esp. its formation, nature, and classification.
• [Russian *pedologiya* from Greek *pedon* ground]
• **pedological** *adjective*
• **pedologist** *noun*

pedometer *noun*
• "puh DOMMA tur"
• an instrument for estimating the distance travelled on foot by recording the number of steps taken.

• [French *pédomètre* from Latin *pes pedis* foot + Greek *metron* measure]

peduncle *noun*
• "puh DUNK'll"
• the stalk of a flower, fruit, or cluster, esp. a main stalk bearing a solitary flower or subordinate stalks.
• [modern Latin *pedunculus* from Latin *pes pedis* foot]
• **peduncular** *adjective*
• **pedunculate** *adjective* "puh DUNK yuh lit"
• **pedunculated** *adjective*

peen *noun*
• "PEEN"
• the wedge-shaped or thin or curved end of a hammer-head.
• [17th c.: also *pane*, apparently from French *panne* from Dutch *pen* from Latin *pinna* point]

peepul *noun*
ALSO SPELLED: **pipal**
• "PEEP'll"
• an Indian fig tree, *Ficus religiosa*, regarded as sacred by Buddhists.
• [Hindi *pīpal* from Sanskrit *pippala*]
HOMOPHONES: *people*

pegmatite *noun*
• "PEGMA tite"
• a coarsely crystalline type of granite commonly occurring in igneous intrusions.
• [Greek *pēgma -atos* thing joined together, from *pēgnumi* fasten]
• **pegmatitic** *adjective* "pegma TITTIC"

Peigan *noun*
ALSO SPELLED: **Piegan**
• "pee GAN"
• a member of an Aboriginal people, a part of the Blackfoot Confederacy, living in S Alberta and NW Montana.
• [Blackfoot *piikániwa* Peigan]

peignoir *noun*
• "pay NWAR"
• a woman's loose dressing gown or bathrobe.
• [French from *peigner* to comb]

pejorative *adjective*
• "puh JORRA tiv"
• (of a word, an expression, etc.) expressing contempt and criticism or disapproval.
• [French *péjoratif -ive* from Late Latin *pejorare* make worse (*pejor*)]
• **pejoration** *noun*
• **pejoratively** *adverb*

pekan *noun*
• "PECK'n"
• a large N American arboreal carnivore of the weasel family, *Martes pennanti*, valued for its fur.
• [Canadian French from Abenaki *pékané*]

Peke *noun*
• "PEEK"
• a Pekingese dog.
• [abbreviation]
HOMOPHONES: *peak, peek, pique*

Pekingese *noun*
• "pee king EEZ" or "pee kin EES"
• a lapdog of a short-legged breed with long hair and a snub nose.
• [as *Peking* former name of *Beijing*, China]

pekoe *noun*
• "PEE co"
• a high-quality black tea, made from leaves picked when very young.
• [Chinese dialect *pek-ho* from *pek* white + *ho* down, the leaves being so young as to have down on them]
HOMOPHONES: *picot*

pelage *noun*
• "PELL idge"
• the fur, hair, wool, etc. of a mammal.
• [French from *poil* hair]

Pelagian *adjective*
• "puh LAY jee 'n"
• of or concerning the monk Pelagius (4th–5th c.) or his theory denying the doctrine of original sin.
• **Pelagianism** *noun*

pelagic *adjective*
• "puh LADGE ick"
• of or performed on the open sea.
• [Latin *pelagicus* from Greek *pelagikos* of the sea (*pelagos*)]

pelargonium *noun*
• "peller GO nee um"
• any plant of the genus *Pelargonium*, with red, pink, or white flowers and fragrant leaves.
• [modern Latin from Greek *pelargos* stork: compare GERANIUM]

Pelham *noun*
• "PELL'm"
• a horse's bit combining a curb and a snaffle.
• [the surname *Pelham*]

Pelhamite *noun*
• "PELL'm ite"
• a resident of Pelham, Ont.

pelican *noun*
• "PELLA k'n"
• any large gregarious waterfowl of the family Pelecanidae with a large bill and a pouch in the throat for storing fish.
• [Old English *pellican* & Old French *pelican* from Late Latin *pelicanus* from Greek *pelekan* prob. from *pelekus* axe, with reference to its bill]

pelisse *noun*
• "puh LEECE"
• a woman's cloak with armholes or sleeves, reaching to the ankles.
• [French from medieval Latin *pellicia* (*vestis*) (garment) of fur, from *pellis* skin]
HOMOPHONES: *police*

pelite *noun*
• "PEEL ite"
• a sediment or sedimentary rock composed of very fine clay or mud particles.
• [Greek *pēlos* clay, mud]
• **pelitic** *adjective* "puh LITTIC"

pellagra *noun*
• "puh LAGGRA" or "puh LAY gruh" or "puh LOGGRA"
• a disease caused by niacin deficiency, characterized by dermatitis, diarrhea, and mental disturbance.
• [Italian from *pelle* skin, after PODAGRA]
• **pellagrous** *adjective*

pellet *noun*
• "PELL it"
• a small, hard, compressed mass of something.
• [Middle English from Old French *pelote* from Latin *pila* ball]
• **pelletization** *noun* (also esp. *Brit.* **-isation**)
• **pelletize** *verb* (also esp. *Brit.* **-ise**)
• **pelletizer** *noun* (also esp. *Brit.* **-iser**)
• **pelletizing** *noun* (also esp. *Brit.* **-ising**)

pellicle *noun*
• "PELLA k'll"
• a thin skin, membrane, or film covering a surface, enclosing a cavity, etc.
• [French *pellicule* from Latin *pellicula*, diminutive of *pellis* skin]
• **pellicular** *adjective* "puh LICK yuh lur"

pellitory *noun*
• "PELLA tory"
• a composite plant, *Anacyclus pyrethrum*, with a pungent-flavoured root, used as a local irritant etc.
• [alteration of Middle English from Old French *peletre*, *peretre* from Latin *pyrethrum* from Greek *purethron* feverfew]

pellucid *adjective*
• "puh LOO sid"
• (of water, light, etc.) transparent, clear.
• [Latin *pellucidus* from *perlucēre* (from *lucēre* shine)]
• **pellucidity** *noun*
• **pellucidly** *adverb*

pelorus *noun*
• "puh LOR us"
• a sighting device like a ship's compass for taking bearings of a distant object.
• [perhaps from *Pelorus*, reputed name of Hannibal's pilot]

pelota *noun*
• "puh LOTTA" or "puh LO tuh"
• a Basque or Spanish game played in a walled court with a ball and basket-like racquets attached to the hand.
• [Spanish, = ball, augmentative of *pella*, from Latin *pila*]

peloton *noun*
• "PELLA tawn"
• the main field or group of cyclists in a race.
• [French, lit. 'small ball' (because of the concentrated grouping of the pack)]

Pembrokian *noun*
• "pem BROOKY 'n" (with "OO" as in *BOOK*)
• a resident of Pembroke, Ont.

pemmican *noun*
• "PEM ick 'n"
• pounded, dried meat (usu. buffalo) mixed to a paste with melted fat, berries, etc. originally made by N American Indians and adapted by fur traders etc.
• [Cree *pimecan* from *pime* fat]

pemphigus *noun*
• "PEMFA guss"
• any of several skin diseases characterized by the formation of watery blisters or eruptions on the skin.
• [modern Latin from Greek *pemphix -igos* bubble]
• **pemphigoid** *adjective*

penal *adjective*
• "PEEN'll"
• of or concerning punishment or its infliction.
• [Old French *penal* or Latin *poenalis* from *poena* pain]
• **penally** *adverb*

penalize *verb*
ALSO SPELLED: esp. *Brit.* **-ise**
• "PEEN'll ize" or "PEN'll ize"
• subject (a person) to a penalty for breaking a rule etc.
• [as PENAL]
• **penalization** *noun* (also esp. *Brit.* **-isation**)

penalty *noun*
• "PEN'll tee"
• a punishment, esp. a fine, for a breach of law, contract, etc.
• [French *pénalité* from medieval Latin *penalitas* (as PENAL)]

penance *noun*
• "PEN ince"
• an act of self-punishment as reparation for guilt.
• [Old French from Latin *paenitentia* (as PENITENT)]

penates *plural noun*
• "puh NAT eez" or "puh NAT aze"
• (in Roman mythology) the household gods, esp. the protectors of the storeroom.
• [Latin from *penus* provision of food]

penchant *noun*
• "PEN ch'nt"
• an inclination; a strong or habitual liking.
• [French, present participle of *pencher* incline]

pendant *noun*
• "PEN d'nt"
• a hanging jewel etc., esp. one attached to a necklace, bracelet, etc.

• [Old French from *pendre* hang, from Latin *pendere*]
HOMOPHONES: *pendent*

pendent *adjective*
• "PEN d'nt"
• hanging.
• [Middle English (as PENDANT)]
• **pendency** *noun*
HOMOPHONES: *pendant*

pendentive *noun*
• "pen DEN tiv"
• a curved triangle of vaulting formed by the intersection of a dome with its supporting arches.
• [French *pendentif -ive* (adjective) (as PENDANT)]

pendulous *adjective*
• "PEND yuh luss"
• (of a part of the body) tending to droop heavily, lacking firmness.
• [Latin *pendulus* from *pendēre* hang]
• **pendulously** *adverb*

pendulum *noun*
• "PEND yuh lum"
• a weight suspended so as to swing freely, esp. a rod with a weighted end regulating the movement of a clock's works.
• [Latin neuter adjective (as PENDULOUS)]

peneplain *noun*
ALSO SPELLED: **peneplane**
• "PEENA plane"
• a low, nearly featureless tract of land produced esp. by erosion.
• [Latin *paene* almost + 'plain' from Old French *plain* from Latin *planus* flat]

penetralia *plural noun*
• "penna TRAILY uh"
• innermost shrines or recesses.
• [Latin, neuter pl. of *penetralis* interior (as PENETRATE)]

penetrate *verb*
• "PENNA trate"
• find access into or through, esp. forcibly.
• [Latin *penetrare* place or enter within, from *penitus* interior]
• **penetrability** *noun*
• **penetrable** *adjective*
• **penetrant** *adjective*
• **penetrating** *adjective*
• **penetratingly** *adverb*
• **penetration** *noun*
• **penetrative** *adjective*
• **penetrator** *noun*

penicillate *adjective*
• "PENNA sillit" or "penna SILLIT"
• having or forming a small tuft or tufts.
• [Latin *penicillum* paintbrush, diminutive of *peniculus* brush, diminutive of *penis* tail]

penicillin *noun*
• "penna SILL in"
• any of various antibiotics produced naturally by moulds of the genus *Penicillium*, or synthetically, and able to prevent the growth of certain disease-causing bacteria.
• [modern Latin *Penicillium* genus name from Latin *penicillum* (as PENICILLATE)]

peninsula *noun*
• "puh NIN suh luh" or "puh NIN syuh luh"
• a piece of land almost surrounded by water or projecting far into a sea or lake etc.
• [Latin *paeninsula* from *paene* almost + *insula* island]
• **peninsular** *adjective*

penitent *adjective*
• "PENNA t'nt"
• regretting and wishing to atone for sins etc.; repentant.
• [Old French from Latin *paenitens* from *paenitēre* repent]
• **penitence** *noun*
• **penitential** *adjective* "penna TEN sh'll"
• **penitentially** *adverb*
• **penitently** *adverb*

penitentiary *noun*
• "penna TENSHER ee"
• a prison.
• [medieval Latin *paenitentiarius* (as PENITENT)]

pennant *noun*
• "PEN'nt"
• a tapering flag, esp. that flown at the masthead of a vessel in commission.
• [blend of PENDANT and PENNON]

penne *noun*
• "PEN ay"
• pasta in the form of short tubes with the ends cut diagonally.
• [Italian, pl. of *penna* quill]

penniless *adjective*
• "PENNY less"
• having no money; poor, destitute.
• [Old English *penig* penny]
• **pennilessly** *adverb*
• **pennilessness** *noun*

pennon *noun*
• "PENN'n"
• a long narrow flag, triangular or swallow-tailed, esp. as the military ensign of lancer regiments.
• [Old French from Latin *penna* feather]

Pennsylvanian *noun*
• "pen s'll VAINY 'n"
• a native or inhabitant of Pennsylvania.

pennywort *noun*
• "PENNY wurt" or "PENNY wort"
• any of several wild plants with rounded leaves.
• [from 'penny' + WORT]

Penobscot *noun*
• "puh NOB scot"

• a member of an Algonquian people of the Penobscot River valley in Maine.
• [Abenaki]

penology *noun*
• "pee NOLLA jee"
• the study of the prevention and punishment of crime and of the penal system.
• [Latin *poena* penalty + *logos* word]
• **penological** *adjective*
• **penologist** *noun*

pensée *noun*
• "pon SAY"
• a thought or reflection put into literary form; an aphorism.
• [French, = thought, from Late Latin *pensāre* think, from Latin *pensāre* weigh, judge]

pensile *adjective*
• "PEN sile"
• hanging down, suspended; pendulous.
• [Latin *pensilis* from *pendēre pens-* hang]

pension[1] *noun*
• "PEN sh'n"
• a regular payment made by a government to people above a specified age, to the disabled, or to such a person's surviving dependants.
• [Old French from Latin *pensio -onis* payment, from *pendere pens-* pay]
• **pensionability** *noun*
• **pensionable** *adjective*
• **pensioner** *noun*

pension[2] *noun*
• "pon SYŌH" (with a nasal *OH*)
• a European, esp. French, boarding house providing full or half board at a fixed rate.
• [French: see PENSION[1]]

penstemon *noun*
• "pen STEE m'n" or "PENSTA m'n"
• any N American herbaceous plant of the genus *Penstemon*, with showy flowers and five stamens, one of which is sterile.
• [modern Latin, from Greek *pente* five + *stēmōn* warp, used for 'stamen']

pentachlorophenol *noun*
• "penta cloro FEE nawl"
• a colourless crystalline acidic solid, C_6Cl_5OH, used in insecticides, fungicides, weed killers, wood preservatives, etc.
• [Greek *pente* five + CHLOROPHENOL]

pentacle *noun*
• "PENTA k'll"
• a figure used as a symbol, esp. in magic, e.g. a pentagram.
• [medieval Latin *pentaculum* from Greek *pente* five]

pentadactyl *adjective*
• "penta DACK t'll"
• having five toes or fingers.
• [Greek *pente* five + DACTYL]

pentagon *noun*
• "PENTA gon"
• a plane figure with five sides and angles.
• [Greek *pente* five + *-gonos* -angled]
• **pentagonal** *adjective* "pen TAGGA n'll"

pentagram *noun*
• "PENTA gram"
• a five-pointed star formed by extending the sides of a pentagon both ways until they intersect, formerly used as a mystic symbol.
• [Greek *pentagrammon* (*pente* five, *gramma* thing written)]

pentahedron *noun*
• "penta HEED r'n"
• a solid figure with five faces.
• [Greek *pente* five + *hedra* base]
• **pentahedral** *adjective*

pentamerous *adjective*
• "pen TAMMER us"
• having five parts in a flower whorl.
• [Greek *pente* five, *-meros* having (a specified number of) parts, sharing]

pentameter *noun*
• "pen TAMMA tur"
• a verse of five feet, e.g. English iambic verse of ten syllables.
• [Greek *pente* five + *metron* measure]

pentamidine *noun*
• "pen TAMMA deen"
• a drug used to treat protozoal infections, esp. in AIDS patients.
• [PENTANE + *amidine* (as AMIDE)]

pentane *noun*
• "PEN tane"
• a hydrocarbon of the alkane series.
• [Greek *pente* five + ALKANE]

pentangle *noun*
• "PEN tangle"
• = PENTAGRAM.
• [Middle English perhaps from medieval Latin *pentaculum* PENTACLE, assimilated to Latin *angulus* angle]

Pentateuch *noun*
• "PENTA tuke" or "PENTA tyuke"
• the first five books of the Bible (Genesis, Exodus, Leviticus, Numbers, and Deuteronomy), called the Torah by Jews, and traditionally ascribed to Moses.
• [Church Latin *pentateuchus* from ecclesiastical Greek *pentateukhos* (*pente* five, *teukhos* implement, book)]
• **Pentateuchal** *adjective*

pentathlon *noun*
• "pen TATH lon"
• an athletic competition in which participants engage in five different events usu. in a single day or over two days, including fencing, shooting, swimming, riding, and cross-country running.

- [Greek from *pente* five + *athlon* contest]
- **pentathlete** *noun* "pen TATH leet"

pentatonic *adjective*
- "penta TONNIC"
- (of a scale) consisting of five notes, usu. without semitones, equivalent to an ordinary major scale with the fourth and seventh omitted.
- [Greek *pente* five + *tonos* tension, tone, from *teinō* stretch]

pentavalent *adjective*
- "penta VALE 'nt"
- having a valence of five; quinquevalent.
- [Greek *pente* five + VALENCE]

Pentecost *noun*
- "PENTA cost"
- a Christian festival observed on the seventh Sunday after Easter, commemorating the descent of the Holy Spirit on the disciples.
- [Church Latin *pentecoste* from Greek *pentēkostē (hēmera)* fiftieth (day)]

Pentecostal *adjective*
- "penta COST'll"
- of or designating Christian denominations and individuals who emphasize charismatic forms of worship, e.g. speaking in tongues, healing, and uninhibited expressions of praise, and are often fundamentalist in outlook.
- [as PENTECOST]
- **Pentecostalism** *noun*
- **Pentecostalist** *adjective*

pentimento *noun*
- "penta MENTO"
- a visible trace of an earlier composition or alteration, seen through later layers of paint on a canvas.
- [Italian, = repentance, correction]

pentobarbital *noun*
- "penta BARBA tawl"
- a narcotic and sedative barbiturate drug formerly used to relieve insomnia.
- [Greek *pente* five + BARBITAL]

pentose *noun*
- "PEN tose" (rhymes with *GROSS*)
- any monosaccharide containing five carbon atoms, including ribose.
- [Greek *pente* five + '-ose' as in GLUCOSE]

pentyl *noun*
- "PEN till"
- an alkyl radical derived from pentane.
- [as PENTANE]

penultimate *adjective*
- "pen ULTA mit"
- last but one; second-last.
- [Latin *paenultimus* from *paene* almost + *ultimus* last, after *ultimate*]

penumbra *noun*
- "pen UM bruh"
- the partly shaded region around the shadow of an opaque body, esp. that around the total shadow of the moon or earth in an eclipse.
- [modern Latin from Latin *paene* almost + *umbra* shadow]
- **penumbral** *adjective*

penury *noun*
- "PEN yur ee"
- destitution; poverty.
- [Latin *penuria*, perhaps related to *paene* almost]
- **penurious** *adjective* "pen YURY us"
- **penuriously** *adverb*
- **penuriousness** *noun*

peon *noun*
- "PEE on"
- a menial or drudge.
- [Portuguese *peão* & Spanish *peon* from medieval Latin *pedo -onis* walker, from Latin *pes pedis* foot]
- **peonage** *noun*

HOMOPHONES: *paean, paeon*

peony *noun*
- "PEE a nee"
- any herbaceous plant of the genus *Paeonia*, with large globular red, pink, or white flowers, often double in cultivated varieties.
- [Old English *peonie* from Latin *peonia* from Greek *paiōnia* from *Paiōn*, physician of the gods]

peplum *noun*
- "PEP lum"
- a short flounce etc. at waist level, esp. of a blouse or jacket over a skirt.
- [Latin from Greek *peplos* woman's outer garment]

pepo *noun*
- "PEEPO"
- any fleshy fruit of the melon or cucumber type, with numerous seeds and surrounded by a hard skin.
- [Latin, = pumpkin, from Greek *pepōn* abbreviation of *pepōn sikuos* ripe gourd]

pepperoni *noun*
- "peppa ROE nee"
- a hard, highly-seasoned sausage made with beef and pork.
- [Italian *peperone* chili]

pepsin *noun*
- "PEP sin"
- an enzyme contained in the gastric juice, which hydrolyzes proteins.
- [German from Greek *pepsis* digestion]

peptic *adjective*
- "PEP tick"
- concerning or promoting digestion.
- [Greek *peptikos* able to digest (as PEPTONE)]

peptide *noun*
- "PEP tide"
- any of a group of organic compounds

consisting of two or more amino acids bonded in sequence.
• [German *Peptid*, back-formation (as POLYPEPTIDE)]

peptone *noun*
• "PEP tone"
• a protein fragment formed by hydrolysis in the process of digestion.
• [German *Pepton* from Greek *peptos*, neuter *pepton* cooked]

Péquiste *noun*
• "pay KEEST"
• *Cdn* a supporter or member of the Parti Québécois.
• [Canadian French, from the initial letters of Parti Québécois]

peradventure *adverb*
• "purr ad VEN chur"
• perhaps.
• [Old French *per* or *par auenture* by chance]

perambulate *verb*
• "purr AM byoo late"
• walk through, over, or about (streets, the country, etc.).
• [Latin *perambulare perambulat-* (*per* through, *ambulare* walk)]
• **perambulation** *noun*
• **perambulatory** *adjective*
"purr AMB yuh luh tory"

perambulator *noun*
• "purr AM byoo later"
• a baby carriage.
• [as PERAMBULATE]

percale *noun*
• "purr CALE"
• a closely woven cotton fabric used esp. for bedsheets.
• [French, of uncertain origin]

perceive *verb*
• "purr SEEVE"
• become aware or conscious of (something); come to realize or understand.
• [Old French *perçoivre*, from Latin *percipere* (*per* through, *capere* take)]
• **perceivable** *adjective*
• **perceived** *adjective*
• **perceiver** *noun*

percentage *noun*
• "purr SENT idge"
• a rate or proportion per cent.
• [from *per cent*, perhaps an abbreviation of pseudo-Latin *per centum* for every hundred]

percentile *noun*
• "purr SEN tile"
• one of 99 values of a variable dividing a population into 100 equal groups as regards the value of that variable.
• [as PERCENTAGE]

percept *noun*
• "PURR sept"
• an object of perception.
• [Latin *perceptum* perceived (thing), neuter past participle of *percipere* PERCEIVE, after *concept*]

perceptible *adjective*
• "purr SEPTA bull"
• capable of being perceived by the senses or intellect.
• [Old French *perceptible* or Late Latin *perceptibilis* from Latin (as PERCEIVE)]
• **perceptibility** *noun*
• **perceptibly** *adverb*

perception *noun*
• "purr SEP sh'n"
• the faculty of perceiving.
• [Latin *perceptio* (as PERCEIVE)]
• **perceptional** *adjective*
• **perceptual** *adjective*
• **perceptually** *adverb*

perceptive *adjective*
• "purr SEPTIV"
• capable of perceiving.
• [medieval Latin *perceptivus* (as PERCEIVE)]
• **perceptively** *adverb*
• **perceptiveness** *noun*
• **perceptivity** *noun*

perchance *adverb*
• "purr CHANCE"
• by chance.
• [Anglo-French *par chance* from *par* by, *ch(e)aunce*, Old French *chëance chëoir* fall, ultimately from Latin *cadere*]

Percheron *noun*
• "PURCH a ron" or "PURSH a ron"
• a breed of heavy draft horse combining strength with agility and speed.
• [French, originally bred in le *Perche*, a district of N France]

perchlorate *noun*
• "purr CLOR ate"
• a salt or ester of perchloric acid.
• [as PERCHLORIC]

perchloric *adjective*
• "purr CLORIC"
• designating a colourless toxic liquid acid that contains chlorine in its highest oxidation state and is a powerful oxidizing agent.
• [chemical prefix *per-* having the maximum of some element in combination, from Latin *per* through + CHLORINE]

perchloroethylene *noun*
• "purr cloro ETH'll een"
• an inert colourless liquid used as a dry-cleaning fluid.
• [as PERCHLORIC + ETHYLENE]

percipient *adjective*
• "purr SIPPY 'nt"
• able to perceive; conscious.

• [Latin (as PERCEIVE)]
• **percipience** *noun*
• **percipiently** *adverb*

percolate *verb*
• "PURK'll ate"
• (of liquid etc.) filter or ooze gradually (esp. through a porous surface).
• [Latin *percolare* (*per* through, *colare* strain, from *colum* strainer)]
• **percolation** *noun*

percolator *noun*
• "PURK a later"
• a machine for making coffee by circulating boiling water through ground beans.
• [as PERCOLATE]

percuss *verb*
• "purr KUSS"
• tap (a part of the body) gently with a finger or an instrument as part of a diagnosis.
• [Latin *percutere percuss-* strike (*per* through, *cutere* = *quatere* shake)]

percussion *noun*
• "purr CUSH'n" ("CUSH" rhymes with *MUSH*)
• the playing of music by striking instruments with sticks etc.
• [as PERCUSS]
• **percussionist** *noun*
• **percussive** *adjective*
• **percussively** *adverb*
• **percussiveness** *noun*

percutaneous *adjective*
• "purr kyoo TAINY us"
• made or done through the skin.
• [Latin *per cutem* through the skin]

perdition *noun*
• "purr DISH'n"
• eternal death; damnation.
• [Church Latin *perditio* from Latin *perdere* destroy (*per* through, *dere dit-* = *dare* give)]

perdurable *adjective*
• "purr DURE a bull"
• permanent; eternal; durable.
• [Old French from Late Latin *perdurabilis* (*per* through, DURABLE)]
• **perdurability** *noun*
• **perdurably** *adverb*

père *noun*
• "PARE"
• (added to a surname to distinguish a father from a son) the father, senior.
• [French, = father]
HOMOPHONES: *pair, pare, pear*

peregrinate *verb*
• "PERRA grin ate"
• travel; journey, esp. extensively or at leisure.
• [Latin *peregrinari* (as PEREGRINE)]
• **peregrination** *noun*
• **peregrinator** *noun*

peregrine *noun*
• "PERRA grin"
• a falcon, *Falco peregrinus*, much prized for hawking on account of its fast and accurate flight.
• [Latin *peregrinus* from *peregre* abroad, from *per* through + *ager* field]

peremptory *adjective*
• "purr EMP tur ee"
• (of a statement or command) admitting no denial or refusal.
• [Anglo-French *peremptorie*, Old French *peremptoire* from Latin *peremptorius* deadly, decisive, from *perimere perempt-* destroy, cut off (*per* through, *emere* take, buy)]
• **peremptorily** *adverb*
• **peremptoriness** *noun*

perennial *adjective*
• "puh RENNY 'll"
• (of a plant) lasting several years.
• [Latin *perennis* (*per* through, *annus* year)]
• **perennially** *adverb*

perestroika *noun*
• "perra STROY kuh"
• (in the former Soviet Union) the policy or practice of restructuring or reforming the economic and political system, esp. during the period 1985–91.
• [Russian *perestroĭka* = restructuring]

perfervid *adjective*
• "purr FUR vid"
• impassioned; very intense.
• [modern Latin *perfervidus* (*per* through, FERVID)]
• **perfervidly** *adverb*
• **perfervidness** *noun*

perfidy *noun*
• "PURR fid ee"
• breach of faith; treachery.
• [Latin *perfidia* from *perfidus* treacherous (*per* through, *fidus* from *fides* faith)]
• **perfidious** *adjective* "purr FIDDY us"
• **perfidiously** *adverb*

perfoliate *adjective*
• "purr FOLEY it"
• (of a plant) having the stalk apparently passing through the leaf.
• [modern Latin *perfoliatus* (*per* through, FOLIATE)]

perforate *verb*
• "PURR fur ate"
• make a hole or holes through; pierce.
• [Latin *perforare* (*per* through, *forare* pierce)]
• **perforated** *adjective*
• **perforation** *noun*
• **perforator** *noun*

performance *noun*
• "purr FOR mince"
• the act or process of performing or carrying out.

• [Anglo-French *parfourmer* from Old French *parfournir* (assimilated to *forme* 'form') from *par* through + *fournir* furnish]

performative *adjective*
• "purr FORMA tiv"
• denoting an utterance that effects an action by being spoken or written (e.g. *I bet, I apologize*).
• [as PERFORMANCE]

perfunctory *adjective*
• "purr FUNK tur ee"
• done merely for the sake of getting through a duty; superficial; mechanical.
• [Late Latin *perfunctorius* careless, from Latin *perfungi perfunct-* (*per* through, *fungi* perform)]
• **perfunctorily** *adverb*
• **perfunctoriness** *noun*

perfuse *verb*
• "purr FYOOZ"
• cause a fluid to pass through (an organ etc.).
• [Latin *perfundere perfus-* (*per* through, *fundere* pour)]
• **perfusion** *noun*

pergola *noun*
• "PURR guh luh"
• an arbour or covered walk, formed of growing plants trained over trellises.
• [Italian from Latin *pergula* projecting roof, from *pergere* proceed]

peri *noun*
• "PEERY"
• any of a group of fairy-like beings in Persian mythology.
• [Persian *pārī*]

perianth *noun*
• "PERRY anth"
• the outer part of a flower.
• [French *périanthe* from modern Latin *perianthium* (as Greek *peri* around, about, *anthos* flower)]

pericardium *noun*
• "perra CARDY um"
• the membranous sac enclosing the heart.
• [modern Latin from Greek *perikardion* (as Greek *peri* around, about + *kardia* heart)]
• **pericardial** *adjective*
• **pericarditis** *noun* "perra car DITE iss"

pericarp *noun*
• "PERRA carp"
• the part of a fruit formed from the wall of the ripened ovary.
• [French *péricarpe* from Greek *perikarpion* pod, shell (*peri* around, about, *karpos* fruit)]

perichondrium *noun*
• "perra CON dree um"
• the membrane enveloping cartilage tissue (except at the joints).
• [Greek *peri* around, about + *khondros* cartilage]

pericope *noun*
• "puh RICKA pee"
• a short passage or paragraph, esp. a portion of Scripture read in public worship.
• [Late Latin from Greek *perikopē* (*peri* around, about, *kopē* cutting, from *koptō* cut)]

peridot *noun*
• "PERRA dot"
• a green variety of olivine, used esp. as a semi-precious stone.
• [Old French *peritot*, of unknown origin]

peridotite *noun*
• "perra DOE tite"
• any of a group of plutonic rocks containing little or no feldspar but much olivine.
• [as PERIDOT]
• **peridotitic** *adjective* "perra doe TITTIC"

perigee *noun*
• "PERRA jee"
• the point in the orbit of a celestial body or satellite where it is nearest the earth.
• [French *périgée* from modern Latin from Greek *perigeion* round the earth (*peri* around, about, *gē* earth)]
• **perigean** *adjective* "perra JEE 'n"

periglacial *adjective*
• "perra GLAY sh'll"
• of or relating to a region adjoining a glacier.
• [Greek *peri* around, about + GLACIAL]

perigynous *adjective*
• "puh RIDGE in us"
• (of stamens) situated around the pistil or ovary.
• [modern Latin *perigynus* (Greek *peri* around, about, *gunē* woman)]

perihelion *noun*
• "perra HEELY 'n"
• the point of a planet's or comet's orbit nearest to the sun's centre.
• [Graecized from modern Latin *perihelium* (as Greek *peri* around, about, *hēlios* sun)]

peril *noun*
• "PARE 'll"
• serious and immediate danger.
• [Old French from Latin *peric(u)lum*, experiment, risk, danger, from base of *experiri* try + *-culum* diminutive ending]

perilla *noun*
• "puh RILLA"
• any of several plants of the genus *Perilla*, comprising annual herbs native to eastern Asia, esp. *P. frutescens*, grown in Asia as an oilseed, medicinal, and culinary plant, and sometimes elsewhere as an ornamental plant on account of its coloured (often purple) leaves.
• [18th c.: origin unknown]

perilous *adjective*
• "PERRA luss"
• full of risk; dangerous; hazardous.

• [as PERIL]
• **perilously** *adverb*
• **perilousness** *noun*

perilune *noun*
• "PERRA lune"
• the point in a body's lunar orbit where it is closest to the moon's centre.
• [Greek *peri* around, about + Latin *luna* moon, after *perigee*]

perilymph *noun*
• "PERRA limf"
• the fluid in the labyrinth of the ear.
• [Greek *peri* around, about + LYMPH]

perimenopause *noun*
• "perra MENNA pozz"
• the time of life occurring in the years just before menopause.
• [Greek *peri* around, about + MENOPAUSE]
• **perimenopausal** *adjective*

perimeter *noun*
• "puh RIMMA tur"
• the circumference or outline of a closed figure.
• [Greek *perimetros* (*peri* around, about, *metros* from *metron* measure)]
• **perimetric** *adjective* "perra METRIC"
HOMOPHONES: *parametric*

perinatal *adjective*
• "perra NATE 'll"
• of or relating to the time immediately before and after birth.
• [Greek *peri* around, about + NATAL]
• **perinatally** *adverb*

periodate *noun*
• "puh RYE a date"
• a salt or ester of an acid containing iodine.
• [chemical prefix *per-* having the maximum of some element in combination, from Latin *per* through + IODINE]

periodic *adjective*
• "peery ODDIC"
• appearing or occurring at regular intervals.
• [Old French *periode* from Latin *periodus* from Greek *periodos* (*peri* around, about, *odos* = *hodos* way)]
• **periodically** *adverb*
• **periodicity** *noun* "peery a DISSA tee"

periodical *noun*
• "peery ODDA k'll"
• a magazine etc. that is published at regular intervals, e.g. monthly or weekly.
• [as PERIODIC]

periodization *noun*
ALSO SPELLED: esp. *Brit.* **-isation**
• "peery id ize AY sh'n"
• the division of history into periods.
• [as PERIODIC]

periodontics *noun*
• "perry a DON tix"
• the branch of dentistry concerned with the gums and other structures surrounding and supporting the teeth.
• [Greek *peri* around, about, *odous odont-* tooth]
• **periodontal** *adjective*
• **periodontist** *noun*

periodontology *noun*
• "perry a don TOLLA jee"
• = PERIODONTICS.
• [as PERIODONTICS + Greek *logos* word]

periosteum *noun*
• "perry OSSTY um"
• a membrane enveloping the bones where no cartilage is present.
• [modern Latin from Greek *periosteon* (*peri* around, about, *osteon* bone)]
• **periosteal** *adjective*
• **periostitis** *noun* "perry oss TITE iss"

peripatetic *adjective*
• "perra puh TETTIC"
• going from place to place; itinerant.
• [Greek *peripatētikos* from *peripateō* (*peri* around, about, *pateō* walk)]
• **peripatetically** *adverb*
• **peripateticism** *noun* "perra puh TETTA sizm"

peripeteia *noun*
• "perra puh TIE uh" or "perra puh TEE uh"
• (esp. in a literary work) a sudden change of fortune.
• [Greek (*peri* around, about, *pet-* from *piptō* fall)]

peripheral *adjective*
• "puh RIFFER 'll"
• of minor importance; marginal.
• [as PERIPHERY]
• **peripherally** *adverb*

periphery *noun*
• "puh RIFFER ee"
• the boundary of an area or surface.
• [Late Latin *peripheria* from Greek *periphereia* circumference (*peri* around, about, *phereia* from *phero* bear)]

periphrasis *noun*
• "puh RIFF ruh sis"
• a roundabout way of speaking; circumlocution.
• [Latin from Greek from *periphrazō* (*peri* around, about, *phrazō* declare)]
• **periphrastic** *adjective* "perra FRASS tick"
• **periphrastically** *adverb*

peripteral *adjective*
• "puh RIPTER 'll"
• (of a classical temple) surrounded by a single row of columns.
• [Greek *peripteron* (*peri* around, about, Greek *pteron* wing)]

periscope *noun*
• "PERRA scope"
• an apparatus with mirrors or prisms

arranged in a tube so that the user can view the area above, e.g. the surface of the sea from a submerged submarine.
• [Greek *peri* around, about, *skopos* target, from *skeptomai* look at]
• **periscopic** *adjective*
• **periscopically** *adverb*

perish *verb*
• "PARE ish"
• be destroyed; suffer death or ruin.
• [Old French *perir* from Latin *perire* pass away (*per* though, *ire* go)]
• **perishability** *noun*
• **perishable** *adjective*
• **perishableness** *noun*
HOMOPHONES: *parish*

perisher *noun*
• "PARE ish ur"
• an annoying person.
• [as PERISH]

perishing *adjective*
• "PARE ish ing"
• freezing cold, extremely chilly.
• [as PERISH]
• **perishingly** *adverb*

perisperm *noun*
• "PERRA spurm"
• a mass of nutritive material outside the embryo sac in some seeds.
• [Greek *peri* around, about + *sperma* seed]

perissodactyl *adjective*
• "puh risso DACK t'll"
• of or relating to the order Perissodactyla of ungulate mammals with one main central toe, or a single toe, on each foot, including horses, rhinoceroses, and tapirs.
• [modern Latin *Perissodactyla*, from Greek *perissos* uneven + *daktulos* finger, toe]

peristalsis *noun*
• "perra STAL sis"
• the involuntary muscular wavelike movements by which the contents of the alimentary canal etc. are propelled along.
• [modern Latin from Greek *peristellō* wrap around (*peri* around, about, *stellō* place)]
• **peristaltic** *adjective*
• **peristaltically** *adverb*

peristome *noun*
• "PERRA stome"
• a fringe of small teeth around the mouth of a capsule in mosses and certain fungi.
• [modern Latin *peristoma* from Greek *peri* around, about + *stoma* mouth]

peristyle *noun*
• "perra STILE"
• a row of columns surrounding a temple, court, cloister, etc.; a space surrounded by columns.
• [Latin *peristylum* from Greek *peristulon* (*peri* around, about, *stulos* pillar)]

peritoneum *noun*
• "perra tuh NEE um"
• the serous membrane lining the cavity of the abdomen.
• [Late Latin from Greek *peritonaion* (*peri* around, about, *tonaion* from *-tonos* stretched)]
• **peritoneal** *adjective*

peritonitis *noun*
• "perra tuh NITE iss"
• an inflammatory disease of the peritoneum.
• [as PERITONEUM + Greek *-itis*, forming feminine of adjectives in *-itēs* (with *nosos* 'disease' implied)]

perivascular *adjective*
• "perra VASS kyuh lur"
• situated or occurring around a blood vessel.
• [Greek *peri* around, about + VASCULAR]

periwig *noun*
• "PERRA wig"
• a wig.
• [alteration of PERUKE, with *-wi-* for French *-u-* sound]

periwinkle *noun*
• "PERRA winkle"
• any plant of the genus *Vinca*, esp. an evergreen trailing plant with blue or white flowers.
• [Anglo-French *pervenke*, Old French *pervenche* from Late Latin *pervinca*]

perjury *noun*
• "PURR jur ee"
• a breach of an oath, esp. the act of wilfully telling an untruth when on oath.
• [Latin *perjurium* false oath, from the verb *perjurare* (*per* through, *jurare* swear)]
• **perjure** *reflexive verb*
• **perjured** *adjective*
• **perjurer** *noun*
• **perjurious** *adjective*
HOMOPHONES: *purger*

perlite *noun*
• "PURL ite"
• a glassy type of vermiculite, expandable to a solid form by heating, used for insulation, as a plant growth medium, etc.
• [French from *perle* pearl]

permaculture *noun*
• "PURMA cull chur"
• the development of agricultural ecosystems intended to be complete and self-sustaining.
• [PERMANENT + AGRICULTURE]
• **permacultural** *adjective*
• **permaculturist** *noun*

permanent *adjective*
• "PURMA n'nt"
• lasting, or intended to last or function, indefinitely without change.
• [Old French *permanent* or Latin *permanēre* (*per* through, *manēre* remain)]
• **permanence** *noun*

- **permanency** *noun*
- **permanently** *adverb*

permanganate *noun*
- "purr MANG guh nate" or "purr MANG guh nit"
- any salt of permanganic acid, esp. potassium permanganate.
- [as PERMANGANIC]

permanganic *adjective*
- "purr mang GANNIC"
- designating an acid containing heptavalent manganese.
- [chemical prefix *per-* having the maximum of some element in combination, from Latin *per* through + *manganic* (as MANGANESE)]

permeable *adjective*
- "PURMY a bull"
- capable of being permeated.
- [Latin *permeabilis* (as PERMEATE)]
- **permeability** *noun*

permeate *verb*
- "PURMY ate"
- penetrate throughout; pervade; saturate.
- [Latin *permeare permeat-* (*per* through, *meare* pass, go)]
- **permeation** *noun*

permethrin *noun*
- "purr MEETH rin"
- a synthetic pyrethroid used as an insecticide, esp. against disease-carrying insects.
- [chemical prefix *per-* having the maximum of some element in combination, from Latin *per* through + *-m-* + PYRETHRIN]

Permian *adjective*
- "PURMY 'n"
- of or relating to the final period of the Paleozoic era, lasting from about 286 to 248 million years ago, between the Carboniferous and Triassic periods.
- [*Perm*, Russia]

permissible *adjective*
- "purr MISSA bull"
- allowable.
- [French or from medieval Latin *permissibilis* (as PERMISSION)]
- **permissibility** *noun*
- **permissibly** *adverb*

permission *noun*
- "purr MISH'n"
- consent; authorization.
- [Latin *permissio* from *permittere* (*per* through, *mittere miss-* let go)]

permissive *adjective*
- "purr MISSIV"
- allowing or characterized by great or excessive freedom of behaviour.
- [medieval Latin *permissivus* (as PERMISSION)]
- **permissively** *adverb*
- **permissiveness** *noun*

permittivity *noun*
- "purma TIVVA tee"
- a quantity measuring the ability of a substance to store electrical energy in an electric field.
- [as PERMISSION]

permute *verb*
- "purr MUTE"
- alter the sequence or arrangement of.
- [Latin *permutare* (*per* through, *mutare* change)]
- **permutate** *verb*
- **permutation** *noun*
- **permutational** *adjective*

pernicious *adjective*
- "purr NISH us"
- having a harmful effect, esp. in a gradual or subtle way.
- [Latin *perniciosus* from *pernicies* ruin, *per* through, *nex necis* death]
- **perniciously** *adverb*
- **perniciousness** *noun*

pernickety *adjective*
- "purr NICKA tee"
- = PERSNICKETY.
- [19th-c. Scots: origin unknown]

perogy *noun*
ALSO SPELLED: **perogie**, **perogi**, **pierogi**, **pirogi**, **pyrogy**
- "purr OH gee" (with "gee" as in *GEEK*)
- a dough dumpling stuffed with potato, cheese, etc., boiled and then optionally fried, and usu. served with onions, sour cream, etc.
- [Polish *pierogi* (singular *piaróg*) or Ukrainian *pyrohy*]

peroneal *adjective*
- "perra NEE'll"
- relating to or near the fibula.
- [modern Latin *peronaeus* peroneal muscle, from *perone* fibula, from Greek *peronē* pin, fibula]

perorate *verb*
- "PERRA rate"
- sum up and conclude a speech.
- [Latin *perorare perorat-* (*per* through *orare* speak)]
- **peroration** *noun*

peroxidase *noun*
- "puh ROXA dace"
- any of a class of enzymes found esp. in plants, which catalyze the oxidation of a substrate by hydrogen peroxide.
- [as PEROXIDE]

peroxide *noun*
- "purr OX ide"
- a colourless viscous unstable liquid with strong oxidizing properties.
- [chemical prefix *per-* having the maximum of some element in combination, from Latin *per* through + 'oxide' (see OXIDANT)]

perpendicular *adjective*
• "purr p'n DICK yuh lur"
• at right angles to the plane of the horizon.
• [Latin *perpendicularis* from *perpendiculum* plumb line, *per* through, *pendēre* hang]
• **perpendicularity** *noun* "purr p'n dick yuh LERRA tee"
• **perpendicularly** *adverb*

perpetrate *verb*
• "PURR puh trate"
• commit or perform (a crime, blunder, or anything outrageous).
• [Latin *perpetrare perpetrat-* (*per* through, *patrare* effect)]
• **perpetration** *noun*
• **perpetrator** *noun*

perpetual *adjective*
• "purr PETCH oo 'll"
• eternal; lasting forever or indefinitely.
• [Latin *perpetualis* from *perpetuus* from *perpes -etis* continuous]
• **perpetually** *adverb*
• **perpetuate** *verb*
• **perpetuation** *noun*
• **perpetuator** *noun*
• **perpetuity** *noun* "purpa CHOO a tee" or "purpa TYOO a tee" or "purpa TOO a tee"

perplexity *noun*
• "purr PLEXA tee"
• bewilderment; the state of being perplexed.
• [obsolete adjective *perplex*, from Old French *perplexe* or Latin *perplexus* (*per* through, *plexus*, past participle of *plectere* plait, braid)]

perquisite *noun*
• "PURR kwuh zit"
• an incidental benefit attached to employment etc., e.g. the use of a company car.
• [medieval Latin *perquisitum* from Latin *perquirere* search diligently for (*per* through, *quaerere* seek)]

perron *noun*
• "PARE 'n"
• an exterior staircase leading up to a main entrance to a church or other (usu. large) building.
• [Old French, ultimately from Latin *petra* stone]

perry *noun*
• "PERRY"
• a drink like cider, made from the fermented juice of pears.
• [Old French *peré*, ultimately from Latin *pirum* pear]
HOMOPHONES: *parry*

persecute *verb*
• "PURSA kyoot"
• subject (a person etc.) to hostility or ill-treatment, esp. on the grounds of race or political or religious belief.
• [ultimately from Late Latin *persecutor* from Latin *persequi* (*per* through, *sequi secut-* follow, pursue)]
• **persecution** *noun*
• **persecutor** *noun*
• **persecutory** *adjective*

perseverate *verb*
• "purr SEVVER ate"
• tend to prolong or repeat an action, thought, or utterance after the original stimulus has ceased.
• [as PERSEVERE]
• **perseveration** *noun*

persevere *verb*
• "pursa VEER"
• continue steadfastly or determinedly; persist.
• [Latin *perseverare* persist, from *perseverus* very strict (*per* through, *severus* severe)]
• **perseverance** *noun*

Persian *noun*
• "PURR zh'n"
• a native or inhabitant of ancient or modern Persia (now Iran).

persiflage *noun*
• "PURSA flozh"
• light raillery, banter.
• [French *persifler* banter, from *siffler* whistle]

persimmon *noun*
• "purr SIM'n"
• any evergreen tree of the genus *Diospyros* bearing edible orange pulpy fruits.
• [corruption of Algonquian *pessemmins*]

persistent *adjective*
• "purr SIS t'nt"
• continuing in spite of obstacles, attempts at control, etc.; persisting.
• [Latin *persistere* (*per* through, *sistere* stand)]
• **persistence** *noun*
• **persistency** *noun*
• **persistently** *adverb*

persnickety *adjective*
• "purr SNICKA tee"
• fussy; fastidious.
• [alteration of PERNICKETY]

personage *noun*
• "PURR s'n idge"
• a person, esp. of rank or importance.
• [as PERSONATE]

personal *adjective*
• "PURR s'n 'll"
• one's own; individual; private.
• [as PERSONATE]

personalism *noun*
• "PURR s'n 'll izm"
• any of various systems of thought which maintain the primacy of the (human or divine) person on the basis that reality has meaning only through the conscious minds of people.
• [as PERSONATE]
• **personalist** *adjective*

personality *noun*
• "purr s'n ALA tee"
• the assemblage of qualities or characteristics which makes a person a distinctive individual.
• [Late Latin *personalitas -tatis* (as PERSONATE)]

personalize *verb*
ALSO SPELLED: esp. *Brit.* **-ise**
• "PURR s'n 'll ize"
• make personal; adapt to individual persons' needs etc.
• [as PERSONATE]
• **personalization** *noun* (also esp. *Brit.* **-isation**)

personally *adverb*
• "PURR s'n a lee"
• in person.
• [as PERSONATE]

personalty *noun*
• "purr s'n 'll tee"
• one's personal property or estate.
• [as PERSONATE]

personate *verb*
• "PURR s'n ate"
• play the part of (a character in a drama etc.; another type of person).
• [Late Latin *personare personat-* from *persona* actor's mask, character in a play, human being]
• **personation** *noun*
• **personator** *noun*

personify *verb*
• "purr SONNA fie"
• attribute a human nature or characteristics to (an abstraction or thing).
• [French *personnifier* (as PERSONATE)]
• **personification** *noun*
• **personifier** *noun*

personnel *noun*
• "purr s'n ELL"
• a body of employees, persons involved in a public undertaking, armed forces, etc.
• [French, originally *adjective* = personal]

perspective *noun*
• "purr SPECTIV"
• the art of drawing solid objects on a two-dimensional surface so as to give the right impression of relative positions, size, etc.
• [medieval Latin *perspectiva* (*ars* art) from *perspicere perspect-* (*per* through, *specere spect-* look)]
• **perspectival** *adjective* "purr speck TIVE 'll" ("TIVE" rhymes with *DIVE*)

perspicacious *adjective*
• "purr spick AY sh'ss"
• having or showing discernment or insight; perceptive.
• [Latin *perspicax -acis* from *perspicere* look through (*per* through, *specere* look)]
• **perspicaciously** *adverb*
• **perspicaciousness** *noun*
• **perspicacity** *noun* "purr spuh CASSA tee"

perspicuous *adjective*
• "purr SPICK yoo us"
• easily understood; clearly expressed.
• [Middle English, = transparent, from Latin *perspicuus* (as PERSPECTIVE)]
• **perspicuity** *noun* "purr spick YOO a tee"
• **perspicuously** *adverb*
• **perspicuousness** *noun*

perspire *verb*
• "purr SPIRE"
• sweat.
• [Latin *perspirare* (*per* through, *spirare* breathe)]
• **perspiration** *noun* "purspa RAY sh'n"

persuade *verb*
• "purr SWADE"
• cause (another person or oneself) to believe; convince.
• [Latin *persuadēre* (*per* through, *suadēre suas-* advise)]
• **persuadable** *adjective*
• **persuader** *noun*
• **persuasible** *adjective*
• **persuasion** *noun* "purr SWAY zh'n"
• **persuasive** *adjective*
• **persuasively** *adverb*
• **persuasiveness** *noun*

pertain *verb*
• "purr TANE"
• relate or have reference to.
• [Old French *partenir* from Latin *pertinēre* (*per* through, *tenēre* hold)]

pertinacious *adjective*
• "purr t'n AY sh'ss"
• stubborn; persistent; obstinate (in a course of action etc.).
• [Latin *pertinax* (*per* through, *tenax* tenacious)]
• **pertinaciously** *adverb*
• **pertinaciousness** *noun*
• **pertinacity** *noun* "purr t'n ASSA tee"

pertinent *adjective*
• "PURR t'n 'nt"
• relevant to the matter in hand; apposite.
• [Old French *pertinent* or Latin *pertinēre* (as PERTAIN)]
• **pertinence** *noun*
• **pertinently** *adverb*

perturb *verb*
• "purr TURB"
• disturb mentally; agitate.
• [Old French *pertourber* from Latin (*per* through, *turbare* disturb)]
• **perturbable** *adjective*
• **perturbation** *noun*
• **perturbingly** *adverb*

pertussis *noun*
• "purr TUSS iss"
• whooping cough.
• [modern Latin *per* through, *tussis* cough]

peruke *noun*
• "purr OOK"
• a wig.

• [French *perruque* from Italian *perrucca parrucca*, of unknown origin]

peruse *verb*
• "purr OOZE"
• read or study thoroughly or carefully.
• [Middle English, originally = use up, prob. from Anglo-Latin from Romanic (from 'use')]
• **perusal** *noun*
• **peruser** *noun*

Peruvian *noun*
• "purr OOVY 'n"
• a native or inhabitant of Peru in S America.

pervade *verb*
• "purr VADE"
• spread throughout, permeate.
• [Latin *pervadere* (*per* through, *vadere vas-* go)]
• **pervasion** *noun* "purr VAY zh'n"

pervasive *adjective*
• "purr VAY siv"
• pervading.
• [as PERVADE]
• **pervasively** *adverb*
• **pervasiveness** *noun*

perverse *adjective*
• "purr VURSE"
• (of a person or action) deliberately or stubbornly departing from what is reasonable or required.
• [Latin *perversus* (as PERVERT)]
• **perversely** *adverb*
• **perverseness** *noun*
• **perversion** *noun*
• **perversity** *noun*

pervert *verb*
• "purr VURT"
• turn (a person or thing) aside from its proper use or nature.
• [Latin *pervertere* (*per* through, *vertere vers-* turn)]
• **perverter** *noun*

pervious *adjective*
• "PURVY us"
• permeable.
• [Latin *pervius* (*per* through, *vius* from *via* way)]
• **perviousness** *noun*

Pesach *noun*
• "PAY sack"
• the Passover festival.
• [Hebrew *Pesaḥ*]

peseta *noun*
• "puh SAY tuh"
• the former basic monetary unit of Spain, now replaced by the euro.
• [Spanish, diminutive of *pesa* weight, from Latin *pensa* pl. of *pensum* weight]

pesewa *noun*
• "puh SAY wuh"
• a monetary unit of Ghana, equal to one-hundredth of a cedi.
• [Fanti, = 'penny']

Peshitta *noun*
• "puh SHEETA"
• the ancient Syriac version of the Bible, used in Syriac-speaking Christian countries from the early 5th c. and still the official Bible of the Syrian Christian Churches.
• [Syriac, = simple, plain]

peshmerga *noun*
• "pesh MURGA"
• a member of a Kurdish nationalist revolutionary army established in the early 1960s.
• [Kurdish *pêşmerge* from *pêş* in front of + *merg* death]

peso *noun*
• "PAY so"
• the basic monetary unit of several Latin American countries and of the Philippines, equal to 100 centésimos in Uruguay and 100 centavos elsewhere.
• [Spanish, = weight, from Latin *pensum* weight]

pessary *noun*
• "PESSA ree"
• a device worn in the vagina to support the uterus or as a contraceptive.
• [Late Latin *pessarium*, *pessulum* from *pessum*, *pessus* from Greek *pessos* oval stone]

pessimism *noun*
• "PESSA mizm"
• a tendency to take a gloomy view of circumstances or expect the worst outcome.
• [Latin *pessimus* worst]
• **pessimist** *noun*
• **pessimistic** *adjective*
• **pessimistically** *adverb*

pesticide *noun*
• "PESTA side"
• a chemical preparation for destroying insects or other organisms harmful to cultivated plants or to animals.
• ['pest' from French *peste* or Latin *pestis* plague + Latin *-cida*, *-cidium* from *caedere* kill]
• **pesticidal** *adjective*

pestiferous *adjective*
• "pes TIFFER us"
• irritating, annoying.
• [Latin *pestifer*, *-ferus* from *pestis* plague, + *-fer* producing, from *ferre* bear]

pestilence *noun*
• "PESTA lince"
• a fatal epidemic disease, esp. bubonic plague.
• [Old French from Latin *pestilentia* from *pestis* plague]
• **pestilent** *adjective*
• **pestilential** *adjective* "pesta LEN sh'll"
• **pestilentially** *adverb*
• **pestilently** *adverb*

pestle *noun*
• "PESS'll"

• a club-shaped instrument for pounding substances in a mortar.
• [Old French *pestel* from Latin *pistillum* from *pinsare pist-* to pound]

pesto *noun*
• "PESTO"
• an Italian sauce of crushed basil leaves, pine nuts, garlic, Parmesan cheese, and olive oil, usu. served with pasta.
• [Italian, from *pestare* pound, crush]

petabyte *noun*
• "PETTA bite"
• 1,125,899,906,842,624 (i.e. 2^{50}) bytes (a million gigabytes).
• [prefix *peta-* denoting a factor of 10^{15}, perhaps from *penta* from Greek *pente* five]

petal *noun*
• "PET'll"
• each of the parts of the corolla of a flower.
• [modern Latin *petalum*, in Late Latin metal plate, from Greek *petalon* leaf, from *petalos* outspread]
• **petalled** *adjective*
• **petaloid** *adjective*
HOMOPHONES: *pedal, peddle*

pétanque *noun*
• "pay TONK"
• a French game similar to boule.
• [French]

petard *noun*
• "puh TARD"
• a small bomb used to blast down a door etc.
• [French *pétard* from *péter* break wind]

petasus *noun*
• "PETTA suss"
• an ancient Greek hat with a low crown and broad brim, esp. (in Greek mythology) as worn by Hermes.
• [Latin from Greek *petasos*]

petechia *noun*
• "puh TEEKY uh"
• a small red or purple spot as a result of bleeding into the skin.
• [modern Latin from Italian *petecchia* a freckle or spot on one's face]
• **petechial** *adjective*

petersham *noun*
• "PEETER sh'm"
• thick corded silk ribbon used for stiffening in dressmaking etc.
• [Lord *Petersham*, English army officer d.1851]

pethidine *noun*
• "PETHA deen"
• a synthetic soluble analgesic used esp. in childbirth.
• [perhaps from PIPERIDINE (from which the drug is derived) + ETHYL]

petiole *noun*
• "PETTY ole"
• the slender stalk joining a leaf to a stem.
• [French *pétiole* from Latin *petiolus* little foot, stalk]
• **petiolar** *adjective*
• **petiolate** *adjective* "PETTY 'll it"

petite *adjective*
• "puh TEET"
• (of a woman) of small and dainty build.
• [French, feminine of *petit* = small, from Romanic, perhaps imitative of child's speech]

petition *noun*
• "puh TISH'n"
• a supplication or request.
• [Latin *petitio -onis*, from *petit-*, past participle stem of *petere*, aim at, lay claim to, ask, seek]
• **petitioner** *noun*

Petrarchan *adjective*
• "puh TRARK 'n"
• of, pertaining to, or characteristic of Italian poet Petrarch (d.1374), esp. denoting a sonnet of the kind used by him, with an octave rhyming *abbaabba*, and a sestet usu. rhyming *cdcdcd* or *cdecde*.

petrel *noun*
• "PET rull"
• any of various seabirds of the family Procellariidae or Hydrobatidae, with mainly black (or brown) and white plumage and usu. a hooked bill, usu. flying far from land.
• [17th c. (also *pitteral*), of uncertain origin: later assoc. with St. Peter, from the bird's habit of flying low with the legs dangling, giving the appearance of walking on water (Matt. 14:30)]
HOMOPHONES: *petrol*

petrifaction *noun*
• "petra FACK sh'n"
• the process of fossilization whereby organic matter is turned into a stony substance.
• [as PETRIFY]

petrify *verb*
• "PETRA fie"
• paralyze with fear, astonishment, etc.
• [French *pétrifier* from medieval Latin *petrificare* from Latin *petra* rock, from Greek]

Petrine *adjective*
• "PEE trine"
• of or relating to St. Peter or his teachings or writings.
• [Latin *Petrus* Peter]

petrochemical *noun*
• "petro KEMMA k'll"
• a substance industrially obtained from petroleum or natural gas.
• [PETROLEUM + CHEMICAL]

petrochemistry *noun*
• "petro KEMMA stree"
• the branch of chemistry dealing with petroleum and natural gas.
• [PETROLEUM + CHEMICAL]

petrodollar *noun*
• "PETRO doller"
• a unit of currency earned by a country etc. from petroleum exports.
• [PETROLEUM + 'dollar' from Low German *daler* from German *Taler*, short for *Joachimstaler*, a coin from the silver mine of *Joachimstal*, now *Jáchymov* in the Czech Republic]

petroglyph *noun*
• "PETRO gliff"
• a rock carving, esp. a prehistoric one.
• [Greek *petros* stone or *petra* rock, *glyphē* carving]

petrography *noun*
• "puh TROG ruh fee"
• the scientific description of the composition and formation of rocks.
• [Greek *petros* stone or *petra* rock, *graphia* writing]
• **petrographer** *noun*
• **petrographic** *adjective*
• **petrographically** *adverb*

petrol *noun*
• "PET rull"
• gasoline.
• [French *pétrole* from medieval Latin *petroleum*: see PETROLEUM]
HOMOPHONES: *petrel*

petrolatum *noun*
• "petra LOT'm"
• petroleum jelly.
• [modern Latin from PETROL]

petroleum *noun*
• "puh TROLE ee um"
• a dark viscous hydrocarbon oil found in the upper strata of the earth, refined for use as a fuel for heating and in internal combustion engines, for lighting, as a solvent, etc.
• [medieval Latin from Latin *petra* rock, from Greek + Latin *oleum* oil]

Petrolian *noun*
• "puh TROLE ee 'n"
• a resident of Petrolia, Ont.

petrology *noun*
• "puh TRAWLA jee"
• the study of the origin, structure, composition, etc., of rocks.
• [Greek *petros* stone or *petra* rock + *logos* word]
• **petrologic** *adjective*
• **petrological** *adjective*
• **petrologist** *noun*

petrous *adjective*
• "PET russ"
• denoting the hard part of the temporal bone protecting the inner ear.
• [Latin *petrosus* from Latin *petra* rock, from Greek]

petticoat *noun*
• "PETTY cote"
• a woman's or girl's undergarment in the form of a skirt or a skirt and bodice.
• [Middle English from *petty coat*]
• **petticoated** *adjective*

pettifog *verb*
• "PETTY fog"
• quibble or wrangle about petty points.
• [back-formation from *pettifogger*, from Middle English *pety* (see PETITE) + *fogger* underhand dealer, prob. from *Fugger* family of merchants in Augsburg, Germany, in the 15th–16th c.]
• **pettifogger** *noun*
• **pettifoggery** *noun*
• **pettifogging** *adjective*
• **pettifoggingly** *adverb*

pettish *adjective*
• "PETTISH"
• peevish, petulant; easily put out.
• [origin unknown]
• **pettishly** *adverb*
• **pettishness** *noun*

petulant *adjective*
• "PET yoo l'nt" or "PETCH oo l'nt"
• peevishly impatient or irritable.
• [French *pétulant* from Latin *petulans -antis* from *petere* seek]
• **petulance** *noun*
• **petulantly** *adverb*

Petun *noun*
• "puh TOON"
• a member of an Aboriginal people living in SW Ontario; defeated by the Iroquois in the mid 17th c., they were absorbed into neighbouring Aboriginal groups.
• [French from Tupi-Guarani *petȳ* tobacco]

petunia *noun*
• "puh TUNE yuh"
• any plant of the genus *Petunia* with white, purple, red, etc., funnel-shaped flowers.
• [modern Latin from French *petun* from Tupi-Guarani *petȳ* tobacco]

pewee *noun*
• "PEE wee"
• a N American tyrant flycatcher of the genus *Contopus*.
• [imitative of the bird's call]
HOMOPHONES: *peewee*

peyote *noun*
• "pay OH tee"
• any Mexican cactus of the genus *Lophophora*, esp. *L. williamsii* having no spines and button-like tops when dried.
• [Latin American Spanish from Nahuatl *peyotl*]

peyotism *noun*
• "pay OH tizm"
• the sacramental taking of a hallucinogenic drug containing mescaline prepared from peyote, observed as a religion by some American Indians.
• [as PEYOTE]

pfennig *noun*
• "p'FEN ig" or "FEN ig"
• a former German monetary unit, equal to one-hundredth of a mark.
• [German, related to 'penny']

phaeton *noun*
• "FAY t'n" or "FAY a t'n"
• a light open four-wheeled carriage, usu. drawn by a pair of horses.
• [French *phaéton* from *Phaethon*, son of the Greek sun god, who was allowed to drive the chariot of the sun for a day, with disastrous results]

phage *noun*
• "FAGE"
• a bacteriophage.
• [abbreviation]

phagocyte *noun*
• "FAGGA site"
• a type of cell capable of engulfing and absorbing foreign matter, esp. a leukocyte ingesting bacteria in the body.
• [Greek *phag-* eat + *kutos* vessel]
• **phagocytic** *adjective* "fagga SITTIC"

phagocytosis *noun*
• "fagga sye TOE sis"
• the ingestion of bacteria etc. by phagocytes.
• [as PHAGOCYTE]
• **phagocytize** *verb* (also esp. *Brit.* **-ise**) "FAGGA site ize"
• **phagocytose** *verb*

phalange *noun*
• "FAL anj" or "fuh LANJ"
• a bone of the finger or toe.
• [French from Latin *phalanx*: see PHALANX]
• **phalangeal** *adjective* "fuh LAN jee 'll"

phalanger *noun*
• "fuh LAN jur"
• any of various marsupials of the family Phalangeridae.
• [French from Greek *phalaggion* spider's web, from the webbed toes of its hind feet]

phalanx *noun*
• "FAL anx" or "FAIL anx"
• a line of battle, esp. a body of ancient Macedonian infantry drawn up in close order.
• [Latin from Greek *phalagx -ggos*]

phalarope *noun*
• "FALA rope"
• any small wading or swimming bird of the subfamily Phalaropodinae, with a straight bill and lobed feet.
• [French from modern Latin *Phalaropus*, from Greek *phalaris* coot + *pous podos* foot]

phanerogam *noun*
• "FANNER a gam"
• a plant that has stamens and pistils, a flowering plant.
• [French *phanérogame* from Greek *phaneros* visible + *gamos* marriage]
• **phanerogamic** *adjective*
• **phanerogamous** *adjective* "fanna ROGGA muss"

Phanerozoic *adjective*
• "fanner a ZO ick"
• designating or pertaining to the whole of geological time since the beginning of the Cambrian, as contrasted with the Precambrian.
• [Greek *phaneros* visible + *zōē* life]

phantasm *noun*
• "FAN tazm"
• an illusion, a phantom.
• [Greek *phantasma* from *phantazō* make visible, from *phainō* show]
• **phantasmal** *adjective* "fan TAZ m'll"
• **phantasmic** *adjective*

phantasmagoria *noun*
• "fan tazzma GORY uh"
• a shifting series of real or imaginary figures as seen in a dream or as created as an effect in a film etc.
• [prob. from French *fantasmagorie* (as PHANTASM + fanciful ending)]
• **phantasmagoric** *adjective*
• **phantasmagorical** *adjective*

phantom *noun*
• "FANT'm"
• a ghost; an apparition; a spectre.
• [Old French *fantosme*, ultimately from Greek *phantasma* (as PHANTASM)]

pharaoh *noun*
• "FARE oh"
• the ruler of ancient Egypt.
• [Old English from Church Latin *Pharao* from Greek *Pharaō* from Hebrew *par'ōh* from Egyptian *pr-'o* great house]
• **pharaonic** *adjective* "fare ay ONNIC"
HOMOPHONES: *faro, farrow*

Pharisee *noun*
• "FERRA see"
• a member of an ancient Jewish sect, distinguished by strict observance of the traditional and written law, and commonly held to have pretensions to superior sanctity.
• [Church Latin *pharisaeus* from Greek *Pharisaios* from Aramaic *p'rīšayyâ* pl. from Hebrew *pārûš* separated]
• **Pharisaic** *adjective* "ferra SAY ick"
• **Pharisaical** *adjective*
• **Pharisaism** *noun* "FERRA say izm"
• **Phariseeism** *noun*

pharma *noun*
• "FARMA"
• a pharmaceutical company.
• [abbreviation of PHARMACEUTICAL]

pharmacare *noun*
• "FARMA care"
• *Cdn* (in some provinces) a system of

subsidization of drug costs, esp. by the government.
• [PHARMACY + 'care']

pharmaceutical *adjective*
• "farma SOOTA k'll"
• of or engaged in pharmacy.
• [Late Latin *pharmaceuticus* from Greek *pharmakeutikos* from *pharmakeutēs* druggist, from *pharmakon* drug]
• **pharmaceutically** *adverb*

pharmacist *noun*
• "FARMA sist"
• a person qualified to prepare and dispense drugs and to give expert advice on their use and effects.
• [as PHARMACY]

pharmacognosy *noun*
• "farma COGNA see"
• the science of drugs, esp. relating to medicinal products in their natural or unprepared state.
• [Greek *pharmakon* drug + *gnōsis* knowledge]

pharmacokinetics *noun*
• "farma co kuh NETTIX"
• the branch of pharmacology that deals with the movement of drugs within the body.
• [as PHARMACY + KINETIC]
• **pharmacokinetic** *adjective*
• **pharmacokinetically** *adverb*

pharmacology *noun*
• "farma COLLA jee"
• the branch of medicine that deals with the uses, effects, and modes of action of drugs.
• [as PHARMACY + Greek *logos* word]
• **pharmacologic** *adjective*
• **pharmacological** *adjective*
• **pharmacologically** *adverb*
• **pharmacologist** *noun*

pharmacopoeia *noun*
• "farma kuh PEE uh"
• a book, esp. one officially published, containing a list of pharmaceutical drugs with directions for use.
• [modern Latin from Greek *pharmakopoiia* from *pharmakopoios* drug maker (*pharmakon* drug + *-poios* making)]

pharmacy *noun*
• "FARMA see"
• the preparation and the dispensing of (esp. medicinal) drugs.
• [medieval Latin *pharmacia* from Greek *pharmakeia* practice of the druggist, from *pharmakeus* from *pharmakon* drug]

pharos *noun*
• "FARE oss"
• a lighthouse or a beacon to guide sailors.
• [Latin from Greek *Pharos* island off Alexandria where a famous lighthouse stood]

pharynx *noun*
• "FARE inx"
• a cavity, with enclosing muscles and mucous membrane, behind the nose and mouth, connecting them to the esophagus.
• [modern Latin from Greek *pharugx -ggos*]
• **pharyngeal** *adjective* "fuh RINJY 'll"
• **pharyngitis** *noun* "fare in JITE iss"

phase *noun*
• "FAZE"
• a distinct period or stage in a process of change or development.
• [ultimately from Greek *phasis* appearance, from *phainō phan-* show]
• **phasic** *adjective*
HOMOPHONES: *faze*

phaser *noun*
• "FAY zur"
• (esp. in science fiction) a usu. hand-held weapon incorporating a laser beam whose 'phase' can supposedly be altered to create different effects (such as stunning, annihilation, etc.) on the target.
• [as PHASE]

phat *adjective*
• "FAT"
• excellent; cool.
• [20th c.: origin unknown]
HOMOPHONES: *fat*

phatic *adjective*
• "FATTIC"
• (of speech etc.) used to convey general sociability rather than to communicate a specific meaning, e.g. 'nice morning, eh?'.
• [Greek *phatos* spoken]

pheasant *noun*
• "FEZZ'nt"
• any of several long-tailed game birds of the family Phasianidae, originally from Asia.
• [Anglo-French *fesaunt* from Old French *faisan* from Latin *phasianus* from Greek *phasianos* (bird) of the river *Phasis* in Asia Minor]

pheasantry *noun*
• "FEZZ'n tree"
• a place where pheasants are reared or kept.
• [as PHEASANT]

phencyclidine *noun*
• "fen SIKE luh deen"
• a piperidine derivative used as a veterinary anaesthetic and a hallucinogenic drug.
• [PHENYL + CYCLE + PIPERIDINE]

phenobarbital *noun*
• "feeno BARBA tawl"
• a narcotic and sedative barbiturate drug used esp. to treat epilepsy.
• [prefix *pheno-* derived from benzene, from Greek *phainō* shine (with reference to substances used for illumination), show + BARBITAL]

phenocryst *noun*
• "FEENA crist" or "FENNA crist"
• a large or conspicuous crystal in porphyritic rock.
• [French *phénocryste* from prefix *pheno-* derived from benzene, from Greek *phainō* shine (with reference to substances used for illumination), show + CRYSTAL]

phenol *noun*
• "FEE nawl"
• a white hygroscopic mildly acidic crystalline solid, used in dilute form as an antiseptic and disinfectant.
• [French *phénole* from *phène* benzene (from Greek *phainō* shine) + ALCOHOL]

phenolic *adjective*
• "fuh NAWL ick"
• of the nature of, derived from, or containing a phenol, esp. containing or designating a hydroxyl group bonded directly to a benzene ring.
• [as PHENOL]

phenolphthalein *noun*
• "fee nawl THAY leen"
• a white crystalline solid used in solution as an acid-base indicator and medicinally as a laxative.
• [PHENOL + *phthal* from NAPHTHALENE]

phenom *noun*
• "FEE nom"
• an unusually gifted person, a prodigy.
• [abbreviation of PHENOMENON]

phenomenal *adjective*
• "fuh NOMMA n'll"
• extraordinary, remarkable, prodigious.
• [as PHENOMENON]
• **phenomenalize** *verb* (also esp. *Brit.* **-ise**)
• **phenomenally** *adverb*

phenomenalism *noun*
• "fuh NOMMA n'll izm"
• the doctrine that human knowledge is confined to the appearances presented to the senses.
• [as PHENOMENON]
• **phenomenalist** *noun*
• **phenomenalistic** *adjective*

phenomenology *noun*
• "fuh nomma NOLLA jee"
• the science of phenomena as distinct from that of being (ontology).
• [as PHENOMENON + Greek *logos* word]
• **phenomenological** *adjective*
• **phenomenologically** *adverb*
• **phenomenologist** *noun*

phenomenon *noun*
• "fuh NOMMA non" or "fuh NOMMA nun"
• a fact, circumstance, or occurrence that appears or is perceived, esp. one of which the cause is in question.
• [Late Latin from Greek *phainomenon* neuter present participle of *phainomai* appear, from *phainō* show]

phenothiazine *noun*
• "feeno THYE a zeen" (with "TH" as in *THIN*)
• a heterocyclic compound which is used to treat parasitic infestations of animals.
• [prefix *pheno-* derived from benzene, from Greek *phainō* shine (with reference to substances used for illumination), show + *theion* sulphur + AZINE]

phenotype *noun*
• "FEENO tipe"
• a set of observable characteristics of an individual or group as determined by its genotype and environment.
• [German *Phaenotypus* (Greek *phainō* shine, show + TYPE)]
• **phenotypic** *adjective* "feeno TIPPIC"
• **phenotypically** *adverb*

phenyl *noun*
• "FEN'll" or "FEEN'll"
• the monovalent radical formed from benzene by the removal of a hydrogen atom.
• [prefix *pheno-* derived from benzene, from Greek *phainō* shine (with reference to substances used for illumination), show]
HOMOPHONES: *fennel*

phenylalanine *noun*
• "fen'll ALA neen" or "feen'll ALA neen"
• an amino acid widely distributed in plant proteins and essential in the human diet.
• [PHENYL + ALANINE]

phenylbutazone *noun*
• "fen'll BYOOTA zone"
• a white or cream-coloured crystalline solid which was formerly used as an analgesic, esp. for the relief of rheumatic pain and inflammation, and as an antipyretic, but now largely restricted to veterinary use.
• [PHENYL + BUTYL + French *azote* nitrogen, from Greek *azōos* without life + '-one' forming nouns denoting various compounds, from Greek *-ōnē* feminine patronymic]

phenylephrine *noun*
• "fen'll EFF rin"
• a compound related to adrenalin which is used (usu. in the form of its crystalline hydrochloride) as a vasoconstrictor and as a nasal decongestant.
• [PHENYL + EPINEPHRINE]

phenylketonuria *noun*
• "fen'll keeta NYURY uh"
• an inherited inability to metabolize phenylalanine, ultimately leading to mental deficiency if untreated.
• [PHENYL + KETONE + URINE]

phenytoin *noun*
• "fenna TOE in"
• an anticonvulsant used to treat epilepsy.

• [PHENYL + *hydantoin*, a cyclic derivative of urea]

pheromone *noun*
• "FERRA mone"
• a chemical substance secreted and released by an animal for detection and response by another usu. of the same species.
• [Greek *pherō* convey + HORMONE]
• **pheromonal** *adjective*

phi *noun*
• "FIE" (rhymes with *PIE*)
• the twenty-first letter of the Greek alphabet (Φ, φ).
• [Greek]
HOMOPHONES: *fie*

phial *noun*
• "FILE"
• a small glass bottle, esp. for liquid medicine.
• [Latin *phiola phiala* from Greek *phialē*, a broad flat vessel: compare VIAL]
HOMOPHONES: *faille, file*

Philadelphian *noun*
• "filla DELFY 'n"
• a resident of Philadelphia, Pennsylvania.

philadelphus *noun*
• "filla DELL fuss"
• any highly-scented deciduous flowering shrub of the genus *Philadelphus*, esp. the mock orange.
• [modern Latin from Greek *philadelphos* loving one's brother]

philander *verb*
• "fill ANDER"
• have casual affairs with many women; womanize.
• [*philander* (n.) used in Greek literature as the proper name of a lover, from Greek *philandros* fond of men, from *philos* dear, loving, *anēr* male person]
• **philanderer** *noun*

philanthrope *noun*
• "FILL 'n thrope"
• a person who gives to charity on a large scale.
• [as PHILANTHROPIC]

philanthropic *adjective*
• "fill 'n THROPPIC"
• benevolent towards others, esp. in giving charity on a large scale.
• [French *philanthropique* from Greek *philanthrōpos* (*philos* dear, loving, *anthrōpos* human being)]
• **philanthropically** *adverb*
• **philanthropist** *noun* "fill ANTHRA pist"
• **philanthropy** *noun*

philately *noun*
• "fill ATTA lee"
• the collection and study of postage stamps.
• [French *philatélie* from Greek *philos* dear, loving, *ateleia* exemption from payment, from *a-* not + *telos* toll, tax]
• **philatelic** *adjective* "filla TELLIC"
• **philatelically** *adverb*
• **philatelist** *noun*

philharmonic *adjective*
• "fill har MONNIC" or "filler MONNIC"
• fond of music.
• [Greek *philos* dear, loving, HARMONIC]

philippic *noun*
• "fill IPPIC"
• a bitter verbal attack or denunciation.
• [Latin *philippicus* from Greek *philippikos* the name of Demosthenes' speeches against *Philip* II of Macedon (d.336 BC), and later of Cicero's against Mark Antony]

Philippine *adjective*
• "FILLA peen"
• of or relating to the Philippines or their people; Filipino.

philistine *noun*
• "FILLA steen" or "FILLA stine"
• a person who is hostile or indifferent to culture, the arts, etc., or one whose interests or tastes are commonplace or material.
• [French *Philistin* or Late Latin *Philistinus* from Greek *Philistinos* = *Palaistinos* from Hebrew *p^e lištî* member of a people opposing the Israelites in ancient Palestine]
• **philistinism** *noun* "FILLA stin izm"

philodendron *noun*
• "filla DEN drun"
• any tropical American climbing plant of the genus *Philodendron*, with bright foliage, often grown as a houseplant.
• [Greek *philos* dear, loving, *dendron* tree]

philology *noun*
• "fill OLLA jee"
• the branch of language that deals with the structure, historical development, and relationships of a language or languages.
• [French *philologie* from Latin *philologia* love of learning, from Greek (*philos* dear, loving + *logos* word)]
• **philological** *adjective*
• **philologist** *noun*

philosophe *noun*
• "FILLA soff"
• a philosopher, esp. any of the humanistic French philosophers of the 18th c.
• [French, = 'philosopher' (as PHILOSOPHY)]

philosophy *noun*
• "fill OSSA fee"
• the use of reason and argument in seeking truth and knowledge of reality, esp. of the causes and nature of things and of the principles governing existence, the material universe, perception of physical phenomena, and human behaviour.

• [Latin *philosophia* wisdom, from Greek (*philos* dear, loving, *sophos* wise)]
• **philosopher** *noun*
• **philosophic** *adjective* "filla SOFFIC"
• **philosophical** *adjective*
• **philosophically** *adverb*
• **philosophize** *verb* (also esp. *Brit.* **-ise**)
• **philosophizer** *noun* (also esp. *Brit.* **-iser**)

philtre *noun*
ALSO SPELLED: esp. *US* **philter**
• "FILTER"
• a drink supposed to excite sexual love in the drinker; a love potion.
• [French *philtre* from Latin *philtrum* from Greek *philtron* from *phileō* to love]
HOMOPHONES: *filter*

phiz *noun*
ALSO SPELLED: **phizz**
• "FIZZ"
• the face.
• [abbreviation of *phiznomy* = PHYSIOGNOMY]
HOMOPHONES: *fizz*

phlebitis *noun*
• "fluh BITE iss"
• inflammation of the walls of a vein.
• [modern Latin from Greek *phleps phlebos* vein + *-itis*, forming feminine of adjectives in *-itēs* (with *nosos* 'disease' implied)]
• **phlebitic** *adjective* "fluh BITTIC"

phlebotomy *noun*
• "fluh BOTTA mee"
• the surgical opening or puncture of a vein.
• [Greek *phleps phlebos* vein + *-tomia* cutting, from *temnō* cut]
• **phlebotomist** *noun*
• **phlebotomize** *verb* (also esp. *Brit.* **-ise**)

phlegm *noun*
• "FLEM"
• the thick viscous substance secreted by the mucous membranes of the respiratory passages, discharged by coughing.
• [Old French *fleume* from Late Latin *phlegma* from Greek *phlegma -atos* inflammation, from *phlegō* burn]
• **phlegmy** *adjective* "FLEMMY"

phlegmatic *adjective*
• "fleg MATTIC"
• stolidly calm; unexcitable, unemotional.
• [as PHLEGM]
• **phlegmatically** *adverb*

phloem *noun*
• "FLOE em"
• the tissue conducting food material in plants.
• [Greek *phloos* bark]

phlogiston *noun*
• "floe JIST'n" or "floe JIST on"
• a substance formerly supposed to exist in all combustible bodies, and to be released in combustion.
• [modern Latin from Greek *phlogizō* set on fire, from *phlox phlogos* flame]

phlox *noun*
• "FLOX"
• any cultivated plant of the genus *Phlox*, with scented clusters of esp. white, blue, and red flowers.
• [Latin from Greek *phlox*, the name of a plant (lit., 'flame')]

pho *noun*
• "FOE"
• a Vietnamese soup of rice noodles and vegetables in usu. beef broth.
• [Vietnamese]
HOMOPHONES: *foe, faux*

phobia *noun*
• "FOBEY uh"
• an abnormal or morbid fear or aversion.
• [Latin from Greek, = fear]
• **phobic** *adjective*

phoebe *noun*
• "FEEBY"
• any small N American tyrant flycatcher of the genus *Sayornis*.
• [imitative: influenced by the woman's name *Phoebe*]

Phoenician *noun*
• "fuh NEESH 'n"
• a member of a people of ancient Phoenicia in Lebanon and the Syrian coast, or of its colonies.

phoenix *noun*
• "FEE nix"
• a mythical bird, the only one of its kind, that after living for five or six centuries in the Arabian desert, burned itself on a funeral pyre and rose from the ashes with renewed youth to live through another cycle.
• [Latin *phoenix* from Greek *phoinix* Phoenician, purple, phoenix]

phonate *verb*
• "FOE nate"
• utter a vocal sound.
• [Greek *phōnē* voice]
• **phonation** *noun*
• **phonatory** *adjective* "FOE nuh tory"

phoneme *noun*
• "FOE neem"
• any of the units of sound in a specified language that distinguish one word from another, e.g. *p*, *b*, *d*, *t* as in *pad, pat, bad, bat* in English.
• [French *phonème* from Greek *phōnēma* sound, speech, from *phōneō* speak]
• **phonemic** *adjective* "fuh NEE mick"
• **phonemics** *noun*

phonetic *adjective*
• "fuh NETTIC"
• representing vocal sounds.

• [modern Latin *phoneticus* from Greek *phōnētikos* from *phōneō* speak]
• **phonetically** *adverb*
• **phonetician** *noun* "foe nuh TISH'n"
• **phonetics** *noun*

phonics *noun*
• "FONNIX"
• a method of teaching reading by associating letters or groups of letters with particular sounds.
• [as PHONETIC]

phonogram *noun*
• "FOE nuh gram"
• a symbol representing a spoken sound.
• [Greek *phōnē* sound, *gramma* thing written]

phonograph *noun*
• "FOE nuh graff"
• a record player.
• [Greek *phōnē* sound, *graphia* writing]

phonology *noun*
• "fuh NOLLA jee"
• the study of sounds in a language.
• [Greek *phōnē* sound, *logos* word]
• **phonological** *adjective*
• **phonologically** *adverb*
• **phonologist** *noun*

phonon *noun*
• "FOE non"
• a quantum of sound or elastic vibrations.
• [Greek *phōnē* sound, after PHOTON]

phony *adjective*
ALSO SPELLED: **phoney**
• "FOE nee"
• sham; counterfeit; fake.
• [20th c.: origin unknown]
• **phonily** *adverb*
• **phoniness** *noun* (also **phoneyness**)

phooey *interjection*
• "FOO ee"
• an expression of disgust or contempt.
• [imitative]

phoresy *noun*
• "FORA see"
• an association in which one organism is carried by another, without being a parasite.
• [French *phorésie* from Greek *phorēsis* being carried]
• **phoretic** *adjective* "for ETTIC"

phosgene *noun*
• "FOZZ jeen"
• a colourless poisonous gas (carbonyl chloride), formerly used in warfare.
• [Greek *phōs* light + GENESIS, with reference to its original production by the action of sunlight on chlorine and carbon monoxide]

phosphatase *noun*
• "FOSS fuh tace" or "FOSS fuh taze"
• any enzyme that catalyzes the synthesis or hydrolysis of an organic phosphate.
• [as PHOSPHATE]

phosphate *noun*
• "FOSS fate"
• any salt or ester of phosphoric acid.
• [French from *phosphore* PHOSPHORUS]
• **phosphatic** *adjective* "foss FATTIC"

phosphene *noun*
• "FOSS feen"
• the sensation of light patterns produced by irritation of the retina, as by pressure on the eyeball.
• [Greek *phōs* light + *phainō* show]
HOMOPHONES: *phosphine*

phosphide *noun*
• "FOSS fide"
• a binary compound of phosphorus with another element or group.
• [as PHOSPHORUS]

phosphine *noun*
• "FOSS feen"
• a colourless foul-smelling poisonous gaseous compound of phosphorus and hydrogen.
• [as PHOSPHORUS]
• **phosphinic** *adjective*
HOMOPHONES: *phosphene*

phospholipid *noun*
• "foss fuh LIPPID"
• any lipid consisting of a phosphate group and one or more fatty acids, including those forming cell membranes.
• [as PHOSPHORUS + LIPID]

phosphoprotein *noun*
• "foss foe PRO teen"
• any protein that contains phosphorus other than in a nucleic acid or a phospholipid.
• [as PHOSPHORUS + PROTEIN]

phosphor *noun*
• "FOSS fur"
• a synthetic fluorescent or phosphorescent substance esp. used in cathode ray tubes.
• [German from Latin *phosphorus* PHOSPHORUS]

phosphorescence *noun*
• "foss fuh RESS ince"
• radiation similar to fluorescence but detectable after excitation ceases.
• [as PHOSPHORUS]
• **phosphoresce** *verb*
• **phosphorescent** *adjective*
• **phosphorescently** *adverb*

phosphoric *adjective*
• "foss FORIC"
• containing phosphorus, esp. in its higher valence of five.
• [as PHOSPHORUS]

phosphorite *noun*
• "FOSS fur ite"
• a non-crystalline form of apatite.
• [as PHOSPHORUS]

phosphorous *adjective*
• "FOSS fur us"

• containing phosphorus, esp. in its lower valence of three.
• [as PHOSPHORUS]
HOMOPHONES: *phosphorus*

phosphorus *noun*
• "FOSS fur us"
• a non-metallic element occurring naturally in various phosphate rocks and existing in allotropic forms, esp. as a poisonous whitish waxy substance burning slowly at ordinary temperatures and so appearing luminous in the dark, and a reddish form used in matches, fertilizers, etc.
• [Latin, = morning star, from Greek *phōsphoros* from *phōs* light + *-phoros* -bringing]
HOMOPHONES: *phosphorous*

phosphorylate *verb*
• "foss FOR'll ate"
• introduce a phosphate group into (an organic molecule etc.).
• [as PHOSPHORUS]
• **phosphorylation** *noun*

phot *noun*
• "FOT" or "FOTE"
• a unit of illumination equal to one lumen per square centimetre.
• [Greek *phōs phōtos* light]

photic *adjective*
• "FOE tick"
• of or relating to light.
• [Greek *phōs phōtos* light]

photobiology *noun*
• "foto by OLLA jee"
• the study of the effects of light on living organisms.
• [Greek *phōs phōtos* light + BIOLOGY]

photochemistry *noun*
• "foto KEMMA stree"
• the study of the chemical effects of light.
• [Greek *phōs phōtos* light + CHEMISTRY]
• **photochemical** *adjective*
• **photochemically** *adverb*

photochromic *adjective*
• "foto CROME ick"
• changing colour or shade reversibly in light of a particular frequency or intensity.
• [Greek *phōs phōtos* light + *khrōma* colour]

photocollage *noun*
• "foto kuh LOZH"
• a technique of collage using photographs, parts of photographs, or photographic negatives.
• [Greek *phōs phōtos* light + COLLAGE]

photocomposition *noun*
• "foto compa ZISH'n"
• typesetting using characters on photographic film or directly from a photographic image.
• [PHOTOGRAPH + COMPOSITION]

photodegradable *adjective*
• "foto de GRADE a bull"
• capable of being decomposed by the action of light, esp. sunlight.
• [Greek *phōs phōtos* light + DEGRADE]

photodiode *noun*
• "foto DIE ode"
• a semiconductor diode the resistance of which depends on the degree of illumination.
• [Greek *phōs phōtos* light + DIODE]

photodynamic *adjective*
• "foto die NAMMIC"
• involving or causing a toxic response to light, esp. ultraviolet light.
• [Greek *phōs phōtos* light + DYNAMIC]

photoelectric *adjective*
• "foto e LECK trick"
• marked by or using emissions of electrons from substances exposed to light.
• [Greek *phōs phōtos* light + ELECTRIC]
• **photoelectricity** *noun*
"foto e leck TRISSA tee"

photoelectron *noun*
• "foto e LECTRON"
• an electron released from an atom by the action of a photon, esp. one emitted from a solid surface by the action of light.
• [Greek *phōs phōtos* light + ELECTRON]

photoemission *noun*
• "foto e MISH'n"
• the emission of electrons from a surface by the action of light incident on it.
• [Greek *phōs phōtos* light + EMISSION]

photogenic *adjective*
• "foto JENNIC"
• (esp. of a person) having an appearance that looks pleasing in photographs.
• [as PHOTOGRAPH + GENESIS]
• **photogenically** *adverb*

photogrammetry *noun*
• "foto GRAMA tree"
• the use of photography for surveying and mapping.
• [PHOTOGRAPH + Greek *gramma* thing written + *metron* measure]
• **photogrammetric** *adjective*
"foto gruh METRIC"
• **photogrammetrist** *noun*

photograph *noun*
• "FOTO graff"
• a picture formed by means of the chemical action of light or other radiation on sensitive film.
• [Greek *phōs phōtos* light + GRAPH]
• **photographable** *adjective*
• **photographer** *noun* "fuh TOGGRA fur"
• **photographic** *adjective*
• **photographically** *adverb*
• **photography** *noun*

photogravure *noun*
• "foto gruh VYUR"
• an image, plate, or print produced from a photographic negative transferred to a metal plate and etched in.
• [French (Greek *phōs phōtos* light + French *gravure* engraving (as ENGRAVE))]

photojournalism *noun*
• "foto JURN'll izm"
• the art or practice of relating news through the use of photographs, with or without an accompanying text, esp. in magazines etc.
• [PHOTOGRAPH + JOURNALISM]
• **photojournalist** *noun*
• **photojournalistic** *adjective*

photolithography *noun*
• "foto lith OGGRA fee"
• lithography in which the image is photographically transferred to the printing surface.
• [PHOTOGRAPH + LITHOGRAPHY]
• **photolithographer** *noun*
• **photolithographic** *adjective*

photolysis *noun*
• "foe TOLLA sis"
• decomposition or dissociation of molecules by the action of light.
• [Greek *phōs phōtos* light + LYSIS]
• **photolytic** *adjective* "foe tuh LITTIC"

photomechanical *adjective*
• "foto muh CANNA k'll"
• relating to or denoting processes in which photography is involved in the making of a printing plate.
• [PHOTOGRAPH + MECHANICAL]

photometer *noun*
• "foe TOMMA tur"
• an instrument for measuring light or for comparing the intensities of light from different sources.
• [Greek *phōs phōtos* light + *metron* measure]
• **photometric** *adjective* "foto METRIC"
• **photometry** *noun*

photomicrograph *noun*
• "foto MICRO graff"
• a photograph of an image produced by a microscope.
• [PHOTOGRAPH + MICROGRAPH]
• **photomicrography** *noun*

photomontage *noun*
• "foto mon TOZH"
• the technique of constructing a montage from photographic images.
• [PHOTOGRAPH + MONTAGE]

photomultiplier *noun*
• "foto MULTA ply ur"
• an instrument containing a photocell and a series of electrodes, used to detect and amplify the light from very faint sources.
• [Greek *phōs phōtos* light + MULTIPLY]

photon *noun*
• "FOE tawn"
• a quantum of light or other electromagnetic radiation, the energy of which is proportional to the frequency of radiation.
• [Greek *phōs phōtos* light, after *electron*]
• **photonic** *adjective*

photonics *noun*
• "foe TONNIX"
• the branch of technology concerned with the properties and transmission of photons, e.g. in fibre optics.
• [as PHOTON]

photoperiod *noun*
• "FOTO peery id"
• the period of daily illumination which an organism receives.
• [Greek *phōs phōtos* light + PERIODIC]
• **photoperiodic** *adjective*

photoperiodism *noun*
• "foto PEERY id izm"
• the phenomenon whereby many plants and animals are stimulated or inhibited in reproduction and other functions by the lengths of the daily periods of light and darkness to which they are subjected.
• [as PHOTOPERIOD]

photophobia *noun*
• "foto FOBEY uh"
• an abnormal sensitivity of the eyes to light.
• [Greek *phōs phōtos* light + PHOBIA]
• **photophobic** *adjective*

photophore *noun*
• "FOTO for"
• a light-producing organ in certain fishes and other animals.
• [Greek *phōtophoros* light-bearing, from *phōs phōtos* light + *-phoros -phoron* bearing, bearer, from *pherō* bear]

photorealism *noun*
• "foto REEL izm"
• detailed and unidealized representation in art, esp. of banal, mundane, or sordid aspects of life.
• [PHOTOGRAPH + 'realism' from Anglo-French *real* = Old French *reel* from Late Latin *realis* from Latin *res* thing]
• **photorealist** *noun*
• **photorealistic** *adjective*

photoreceptor *noun*
• "foto ree SEPTER"
• any living structure that responds to incident light, esp. a cell in which light is converted to a nervous or other signal.
• [Greek *phōs phōtos* light + RECEPTOR]

photorefractive *adjective*
• "foto ruh FRACTIV"
• designating a form of eye surgery which uses a laser to carve away part of the outer surface of the cornea.

• [Greek *phōs phōtos* light + Latin *refringere refract-* (*re-* again, *frangere* break)]

photosensitive *adjective*
• "foto SENSA tiv"
• reacting chemically, electrically, etc., to light.
• [Greek *phōs phōtos* light + SENSITIVE]
• **photosensitivity** *noun*

photosphere *noun*
• "FOTO sfeer"
• the luminous surface layer of the sun or other star, below the chromosphere, from which its light and heat radiate.
• [Greek *phōs phōtos* light + SPHERE]
• **photospheric** *adjective*

photostat *noun*
• "FOTO stat"
• a photocopier.
• [originally a trademark]
• **photostatic** *adjective*

photosynthesis *noun*
• "foto SINTHA siss"
• the process in which the energy of sunlight is used by organisms, esp. green plants, to synthesize carbohydrates from carbon dioxide and water.
• [Greek *phōs phōtos* light + SYNTHESIS]
• **photosynthesize** *verb* (also esp. *Brit.* **-ise**)
• **photosynthetic** *adjective* "foto sin THETTIC"
• **photosynthetically** *adverb*

photosystem *noun*
• "FOTO sist'm"
• either of the two biochemical mechanisms in plants by which light is converted into useful energy.
• [Greek *phōs phōtos* light + SYSTEM]

phototransistor *noun*
• "foto tran ZISTER"
• a transistor that responds to incident light by generating and amplifying an electric current.
• [Greek *phōs phōtos* light + TRANSISTOR]

phototropism *noun*
• "foto TROPE izm" or "fuh TOTTRA pizm"
• the tendency of a plant etc. to bend or turn towards or away from a source of light.
• [Greek *phōs phōtos* light, *tropos*, from *trepō* to turn]
• **phototrophic** *adjective*
• **phototropic** *adjective*

photovoltaics *noun*
• "foto voll TAY icks"
• the branch of science and technology that deals with the production of electric current at the junction of two substances exposed to light.
• [Greek *phōs phōtos* light + VOLTAIC]
• **photovoltaic** *adjective*

phrase *noun*
• "FRAZE"
• a small group of words forming a conceptual unit, but not a sentence, esp. such a group without a predicate or finite verb.
• [earlier *phrasis* from Latin from Greek *phrazō* declare, tell]
• **phrasal** *adjective* "FRAZE 'll"
• **phrasally** *adverb*
• **phrasing** *noun*

phraseology *noun*
• "fray zee OLLA jee"
• a choice or arrangement of words.
• [modern Latin *phraseologia* from Greek *phraseōn* genitive pl. of *phrasis* PHRASE + *logos* word]
• **phraseological** *adjective*

phreak *noun*
• "FREEK"
• a person who makes fraudulent use of a telephone system by electronic means, esp. for computer hacking etc.
• [alteration of 'freak' with *ph-* from *phone*]
• **phreaking** *noun*
HOMOPHONES: *freak*

phreatic *adjective*
• "free ATTIC"
• (of water) situated underground in the zone of saturation.
• [Greek *phrear phreatos* well]

phrenic *adjective*
• "FRENNIC"
• of or relating to the diaphragm.
• [French *phrénique* from Greek *phrēn phrenos* diaphragm]

phrenology *noun*
• "fruh NOLLA jee"
• the study of the shape and size of the cranium as a supposed indication of character and mental faculties.
• [Greek *phrēn phrenos* diaphragm, mind (once thought to be located in the diaphragm) + *logos* word]
• **phrenological** *adjective*
• **phrenologist** *noun*

Phrygian *adjective*
• "FRIDGE ee 'n"
• of or relating to Phrygia in ancient Asia Minor.

phthalic *adjective*
• "f'THALIC" or "THALIC"
• designating a crystalline acid derived from benzene, with two carboxylic acid groups attached to the benzene ring.
• [abbreviation of NAPHTHALIC: see NAPHTHALENE]
• **phthalate** *noun* "f'THAL ate" or "THAL ate"

phthisis *noun*
• "f'THICE iss" or "THICE iss"
• any progressive wasting disease, esp. pulmonary tuberculosis.
• [Latin from Greek from *phthinō* to decay]
• **phthisic** *adjective*
• **phthisical** *adjective*

phycology *noun*
- "fie COLLA jee"
- the study of algae.
- [Greek *phukos* seaweed + *logos* word]
- **phycological** *adjective*
- **phycologist** *noun*

phycomycete *noun*
- "fike oh MY seet"
- any of various fungi which typically form a non-septate mycelium.
- [Greek *phukos* seaweed + pl. of Greek *mukēs* mushroom]

phylactery *noun*
- "fill ACTER ee"
- either of two small leather boxes containing Biblical texts in Hebrew, worn by Jewish men during morning prayer on all days except the Sabbath as a reminder to keep the law.
- [Old French from Late Latin *phylacterium* from Greek *phulaktērion* amulet, from *phulassō* guard]

phyletic *adjective*
- "fie LETTIC"
- of or relating to the development of a species or other group.
- [Greek *phuletikos* from *phuletēs* tribesman, from *phulē* tribe]
- **phyletically** *adverb*

phyllo *noun*
ALSO SPELLED: **filo**
- "FIE lo" or "FEE lo"
- a kind of dough capable of being stretched into very thin leaves which may then be layered together to make sweet and savoury pastries, e.g. baklava.
- [Greek *phullo-* from *phullon* leaf]

phyllode *noun*
- "FILL ode"
- a flattened leaf stalk resembling and functioning as a leaf.
- [modern Latin *phyllodium* from Greek *phullōdēs* leaflike, from *phullon* leaf]

phylloquinone *noun*
- "fie lo KWIN own"
- one of the K vitamins, found in cabbage, spinach, and other leafy green vegetables, and essential for the blood clotting process.
- [Greek *phullo-* from *phullon* leaf + QUINONE]

phyllotaxis *noun*
- "fillo TAX iss"
- the arrangement of leaves on an axis or stem.
- [Greek *phullo-* from *phullon* leaf, *taxis* order]
- **phyllotactic** *adjective*

phylloxera *noun*
- "fill ox EERA" or "fill OX ur uh"
- any plant louse of the genus *Phylloxera*, esp. of a species attacking vines.
- [modern Latin from Greek *phullon* leaf + *xēros* dry]

phylogeny *noun*
- "fie LODGE a nee"
- the evolutionary development and diversification of groups of organisms, or particular features of organisms.
- [Greek *phullo-* from *phullon* leaf]
- **phylogenetic** *adjective* "fie lo juh NETTIC"
- **phylogenetically** *adverb*

phylum *noun*
- "FIE lum"
- a taxonomic rank below kingdom comprising a class or classes and subordinate taxa.
- [modern Latin from Greek *phulon* race]

physiatrist *noun*
- "fuh ZYE a trist"
- a person who uses physical agents such as light, heat, etc. to diagnose or treat deformity, disease, or injury.
- [as PHYSICAL + Greek *iatreia* healing]

physic *noun*
- "FIZZIC"
- a medicine.
- [Old French *fisique* medicine, from Latin *physica* from Greek *phusikē* (*epistēmē*) (knowledge) of nature]

physical *adjective*
- "FIZZIC 'll"
- of or concerning the body.
- [medieval Latin *physicalis* from Latin *physica* (as PHYSIC)]
- **physicality** *noun*
- **physically** *adverb*
- **physicalness** *noun*

physicalism *noun*
- "FIZZIC 'll izm"
- the theory that all reality must eventually be expressible in the language of physics.
- [as PHYSIC]
- **physicalist** *noun*
- **physicalistic** *adjective*

physician *noun*
- "fuh ZISH'n"
- a person legally qualified to practise medicine, esp. a specialist in non-surgical medical diagnosis and treatment.
- [Old French *fisicien* (as PHYSIC)]

physicochemical *adjective*
- "fizzic oh KEMMA k'll"
- of or relating to physics and chemistry or to physical chemistry.
- [as PHYSICAL + CHEMICAL]

physics *noun*
- "FIZZIX"
- the science dealing with the properties and interactions of matter and energy.
- [pl. of *physic* physical (thing), after Latin *physica*, Greek *phusika* natural things, from *phusis* nature]
- **physicist** *noun* "FIZZA sist"

physio *noun*
- "FIZZY oh"
- *Cdn & Brit.* a physiotherapist.
- [abbreviation]

physiocracy *noun*
- "fizzy OCKRA see"
- government according to a supposed natural order, esp. as advocated by the French physiocrats.
- [French *physiocratie* (Greek *phusis* nature + *kratia* from *kratos* strength, power)]

physiocrat *noun*
- "FIZZY oh crat"
- a member of an 18th-c. group of French economists who held that agriculture, rather than manufacturing or trade, was the source of all wealth and that agricultural products should be highly priced. They stressed the necessity of free trade and coined the term *laissez-faire*.
- [as PHYSIOCRACY]
- **physiocratic** *adjective*

physiognomy *noun*
- "fizzy ONNA mee"
- a person's face or expression, esp. viewed as indicative of the mind or character.
- [Old French *phisonomie* from medieval Latin *phisonomia* from Greek *phusiognōmonia* judging of a person's nature (by the features) (Greek *phusis* nature, *gnōmōn* judge)]
- **physiognomic** *adjective* "fizzy a NOMMIC"
- **physiognomical** *adjective*
- **physiognomist** *noun*

physiography *noun*
- "fizzy OGGRA fee"
- physical geography; geomorphology.
- [French *physiographie* (Greek *phusis* nature, *graphia* writing)]
- **physiographer** *noun*
- **physiographic** *adjective*
- **physiographical** *adjective*

physiology *noun*
- "fizzy OLLA jee"
- the science that deals with the normal functioning of living organisms and their parts.
- [Greek *phusis* nature + *logos* word]
- **physiologic** *adjective*
- **physiological** *adjective*
- **physiologically** *adverb*
- **physiologist** *noun*

physiotherapy *noun*
- "fizzy oh THERRA pee"
- esp. *Cdn & Brit.* the treatment of disease, injury, deformity, etc., by physical methods including manipulation, massage, infrared heat treatment, remedial exercise, etc., rather than by drugs.
- [PHYSICAL + THERAPY]
- **physiotherapist** *noun*

physique *noun*
- "fizz EEK"
- the form, size, and development of a person's body.
- [French, originally adjective (as PHYSIC)]

phytochemistry *noun*
- "fite oh KEMMA stree"
- the chemistry of plants and plant products.
- [Greek *phuton* plant, from *phuō* come into being + CHEMISTRY]
- **phytochemical** *adjective*
- **phytochemist** *noun*

phytochrome *noun*
- "FITE oh crome"
- a blue-green pigment found in many plants, and regulating various developmental processes according to the nature and timing of the light it absorbs.
- [Greek *phuton* plant, from *phuō* come into being + *khrōma* colour]

phytoestrogen *noun*
- "fite oh ESTRA j'n"
- an estrogen found in plants.
- [Greek *phuton* plant, from *phuō* come into being + ESTROGEN]

phytogenesis *noun*
- "fite oh JENNA sis"
- the science of the origin or evolution of plants.
- [Greek *phuton* plant, from *phuō* come into being + GENESIS]

phytogeography *noun*
- "fite oh jee OGGRA fee"
- the geographical distribution of plants.
- [Greek *phuton* plant, from *phuō* come into being + GEOGRAPHY]
- **phytogeographer** *noun*
- **phytogeographic** *adjective*

phytonutrient *noun*
- "fite oh NEW tree 'nt"
- a substance found in certain plants which is believed to be beneficial to human health and help prevent various diseases.
- [Greek *phuton* plant, from *phuō* come into being + NUTRIENT]

phytopathology *noun*
- "fite oh puh THOLLA jee"
- the study of plant diseases.
- [Greek *phuton* plant, from *phuō* come into being + PATHOLOGY]
- **phytopathological** *adjective*
- **phytopathologist** *noun*

phytophagous *adjective*
- "fie TOFFA guss"
- (esp. of an insect or other invertebrate) feeding on plants.
- [Greek *phuton* plant, from *phuō* come into being + *phagō* eat]

phytoplankton *noun*
- "fite oh PLANK t'n"
- plankton consisting of microscopic plants.

• [Greek *phuton* plant, from *phuō* come into being + PLANKTON]

phytotoxin *noun*
• "fite oh TOXIN"
• a substance poisonous or injurious to plants, esp. one produced by a parasite.
• [Greek *phuton* plant, from *phuō* come into being + TOXIN]
• **phytotoxic** *adjective*
• **phytotoxicity** *noun* "fite oh tox ISSA tee"

pi *noun*
• "PIE"
• the sixteenth letter of the Greek alphabet (Π, π).
• [Greek]
HOMOPHONES: *pie*

piaffe *verb*
• "pee AFF"
• (of a horse) move esp. on the spot with a high, slow, trotting step.
• [French *piaffer* to strut]

pianism *noun*
• "PEE a nizm"
• the art or technique of piano playing.
• [from 'piano', abbreviation of PIANOFORTE]
• **pianistic** *adjective*
• **pianistically** *adverb*

pianissimo *adjective*
• "pee a NISSY moe"
• performed very softly.
• [Italian, superlative of *piano* soft]

pianoforte *noun*
• "pee anno FORTAY"
• a piano.
• [Italian, earlier *piano e forte* soft and loud, expressing its gradation of tone]

pianola *noun*
• "pee a NO luh"
• a kind of automatic piano; a player piano.
• [apparently diminutive of 'piano']

piassava *noun*
• "pee a SOVVA"
• a stout fibre obtained from the leaf stalks of various American and African palm trees.
• [Portuguese from Tupi *piaçába*]

piastre *noun*
ALSO SPELLED: esp. *US* **piaster**
• "pee ASTER"
• a small coin and monetary unit of Egypt, Lebanon, and Syria, equal to one-hundredth of a pound.
• [French *piastre* from Italian *piastra* (*d'argento*) plate (of silver), from Latin *emplastrum* plaster]

piazza *noun*
• "pee AT suh" or "pee OT suh"
• a public square or marketplace esp. in an Italian town.
• [Italian, from Latin *platea* place, from Greek *plateia* (*hodos*) broad (way)]

pibroch *noun*
• "PEE brock"
• a series of esp. martial or funerary variations on a theme for the bagpipes.
• [Gaelic *piobaireachd* art of piping, from *piobair* piper, from *piob* from English 'pipe']

pica *noun*
• "PIKE uh"
• a tendency or craving to eat substances other than normal food, occurring during childhood or pregnancy, or as a symptom of disease.
• [modern Latin or medieval Latin, = magpie]
HOMOPHONES: *pika*

picador *noun*
• "PICK a dore"
• a mounted person with a lance who goads the bull in a bullfight.
• [Spanish from *picar* prick]

picante *adjective*
• "puh CON tay"
• (of food) hot, spicy, sharply seasoned.
• [Spanish, present participle of *picar* prick, bite]

picaresque *adjective*
• "picka RESK"
• (of a style of fiction) dealing with the episodic adventures of rogues etc.
• [French from Spanish *picaresco* from *pícaro* rogue]

picaroon *noun*
• "picka ROON"
• a long pole fitted with a spike or hook, used in logging and fishing.
• [perhaps from French *piqueron* little pike, dart, goad, from *pique* pike]

picayune *adjective*
• "picka YUNE"
• contemptible; petty.
• [French *picaillon* a Piedmontese coin, cash, from Provençal *picaioun*, of unknown origin]

piccalilli *noun*
• "picka LILLY"
• a condiment of pickled, chopped vegetables, mustard, and hot spices.
• [18th c.: perhaps from 'pickle' + CHILI]

piccata *noun*
• "pick ATTA"
• a dish of sautéed esp. veal cutlets with a sauce of lemon juice and parsley, sometimes with white wine and capers.
• [Italian]

piccolo *noun*
• "PICKA lo"
• a small flute sounding an octave higher than the ordinary flute.
• [Italian, = small (flute)]

pickerel *noun*
• "PICKER'll"
• a walleye.

• [Middle English, diminutive of 'pike' from Old English *pīc* point, prick (because of the fish's pointed jaw)]

pickerelweed *noun*
• "PICKER'll weed"
• an aquatic plant of eastern N America, *Pontederia cordata*, with a spike of blue flowers and large arrowhead-shaped leaves.
• [as PICKEREL + 'weed' from Old English *wēod*]

Pickwickian *adjective*
• "pick WICKY 'n"
• of or like Mr. Pickwick in Dickens's *Pickwick Papers*, esp. in being jovial, plump, etc.

picnic *noun*
• "PICK nick"
• an outing or excursion including a packed meal eaten out of doors.
• [French *pique-nique*, of unknown origin]
• **picnicker** *noun*
• **picnicky** *adjective*

picot *noun*
• "PEE co"
• any of a series of small loops worked in lace or embroidery forming an ornamental edging etc.
• [French, diminutive of *pic* peak, point]
HOMOPHONES: *pekoe*

picric *adjective*
• "PICK rick"
• designating a yellow crystalline acid obtained by nitrating phenol, used in dyeing and in the manufacture of explosives.
• [Greek *pikros* bitter]

Pict *noun*
• "PICT"
• a member of an ancient people of N Britain who fought against the Roman invaders and eventually amalgamated with the Scots before the Middle Ages.
• [Late Latin *Picti* perhaps from *pingere pict-* paint, tattoo]
• **Pictish** *adjective*

pictograph *noun*
• "PICTA graff"
• a pictorial symbol or sign.
• [Latin *pingere pict-* paint + Greek *graphia* writing]
• **pictographic** *adjective*

Pictonian *noun*
• "pick TONY 'n"
• a resident of Pictou, NS.

pictorial *adjective*
• "pick TORY 'll"
• of or expressed in a picture or pictures.
• [Late Latin *pictorius* from Latin *pictor* painter from *pingere pict-* paint]
• **pictorially** *adverb*

picturesque *adjective*
• "pick chur ESK"
• (of landscape, buildings, etc.) beautiful or striking, esp. in a quaint way.
• [French *pittoresque* from Italian *pittoresco* from *pittore* painter, from Latin (as PICTORIAL): assimilated to 'picture']
• **picturesquely** *adverb*
• **picturesqueness** *noun*

piddock *noun*
• "PID uck"
• any rock-boring bivalve mollusc of the family Pholadidae, used for bait.
• [18th c.: origin unknown]

pidgin *noun*
• "PIDGE 'n"
• a form of a language simplified or altered by non-native speakers and containing vocabulary from two or more languages, used for communication between people not having a common language.
• [corruption of *business*]
• **pidginization** *noun* (also esp. *Brit.* **-isation**)
• **pidginize** *verb* (also esp. *Brit.* **-ise**)
HOMOPHONES: *pigeon*

piebald *adjective*
• "PIE bald" ("BALD" rhymes with *CALLED*)
• (usu. of an animal, esp. a horse) having irregular patches of two colours, esp. black and white.
• [from 'pie' magpie (because of the magpie's black-and-white plumage) + 'bald' in the obsolete sense 'streaked with white']

piece *noun*
• "PEECE"
• one of the distinct portions forming part of or broken off from a larger object; a bit; a part.
• [Old French *piece* from Romanic, prob. of Gaulish origin]
HOMOPHONES: *peace*

piecemeal *adverb*
• "PEECE meel"
• piece by piece; gradually; separately.
• [Middle English from PIECE + *-meal* from Old English *mǣlum* in the sense 'measure, quantity taken at one time']

piecework *noun*
• "PEECE wurk"
• work paid for by the amount produced.
• [as PIECE + 'work']
• **pieceworker** *noun*

pied *adjective*
• "PIDE"
• partly of one colour, partly of another or others.
• [Middle English: see PIEBALD]

piedmont *noun*
• "PEED mont"
• a gentle slope leading from the foot of mountains to a region of flat land.
• [Italian *piemonte* mountain foot, the name of a region at the foot of the Alps]

Piedmontese *adjective*
- "peed mon TEEZ"
- of or relating to Piedmont in NW Italy.

pier *noun*
- "PEER"
- a structure of iron, wood, concrete, etc., raised on piles and leading out into the sea, a lake, etc., used as a landing stage and promenade.
- [Middle English *per* from Anglo-Latin *pera*, of unknown origin]

HOMOPHONES: *peer*

pierce *verb*
- "PEERCE"
- (of a sharp instrument etc.) penetrate the surface of.
- [Old French *percer* from Latin *pertundere* bore through (*per* through, *tundere tus-* thrust)]
- **pierced** *adjective*
- **piercer** *noun*

piercing *adjective*
- "PEER sing"
- (of voices, sounds, etc.) very high and loud; shrill.
- [as PIERCE]
- **piercingly** *adverb*

Pierrot *noun*
- "PYARE oh"
- a male figure in French pantomime, typically white-faced with a sad expression and dressed in a loose white clown's costume.
- [French, diminutive of *Pierre* Peter]

Pietà *noun*
- "pee et AW"
- a picture or sculpture of the Virgin Mary holding the dead body of Christ on her lap or in her arms.
- [Italian from Latin (as PIETY)]

pietism *noun*
- "PIE a tizm"
- pious sentiment.
- [German *Pietismus* (as PIETY)]
- **pietist** *noun*
- **pietistic** *adjective*
- **pietistical** *adjective*

piety *noun*
- "PIE a tee"
- the quality of being pious.
- [Old French *pieté* from Latin *pietas -tatis* dutifulness (as PIOUS)]

piezo *adjective*
- "pie EEZO"
- piezoelectric.
- [abbreviation]

piezoelectricity *noun*
- "pie eezo e leck TRISSA tee"
- electric polarization in a substance resulting from the application of mechanical stress, esp. in certain crystals.
- [Greek *piezō* press + ELECTRIC]
- **piezoelectric** *adjective*
- **piezoelectrically** *adverb*

piezometer *noun*
- "pie a ZOMMA tur"
- an instrument for measuring the magnitude or direction of pressure.
- [Greek *piezō* press + *metron* measure]

pigeon *noun*
- "PIDGE 'n"
- any of several large usu. grey and white birds of the family Columbidae, esp. *Columba livia*, often domesticated and bred and trained to carry messages etc.
- [Middle English from Old French *pijon* from Late Latin *pipio -onis* (imitative)]
- **pigeonry** *noun* "PIDGE 'n ree"

HOMOPHONES: *pidgin*

pigeonhole *noun*
- "PIDGE 'n hole"
- each of a set of compartments in a cabinet or on a wall for papers, letters, etc.
- [as PIGEON + 'hole']

pigment *noun*
- "PIG m'nt"
- colouring matter used as paint or dye, usu. as an insoluble suspension.
- [Latin *pigmentum* from *pingere* paint]
- **pigmentary** *adjective* "PIG m'n terry"

pigmentation *noun*
- "pig m'n TAY sh'n"
- the natural colouring of plants, animals, etc.
- [as PIGMENT]

pignoli *plural noun*
- "peen YO lee"
- pine nuts.
- [Italian]

pika *noun*
- "PIKE uh"
- any small rabbit-like mammal of the genus *Ochotona*, with small ears and no tail, found in the mountains and deserts of western N America.
- [Tungus *piika*]

HOMOPHONES: *pica*

pilaf *noun*
- "PEE laff"
- a Middle Eastern or Indian dish of spiced rice or wheat with meat, fish, vegetables, etc.
- [Turkish *pilâv*]

pilaster *noun*
- "pill ASTER"
- a rectangular column, esp. one projecting from a wall.
- [French *pilastre* from Italian *pilastro* from medieval Latin *pilastrum* from Latin *pila* pillar]
- **pilastered** *adjective*

Pilates *noun*
- "puh LOT eez"

• a system of exercises using specialized apparatus, designed to improve physical strength, flexibility, and posture, and enhance mental awareness and control of body movement.
• [named after the German physical fitness specialist Joseph *Pilates* d.1967]

pilchard *noun*
• "PILL churd"
• a small marine fish, *Sardinia pilchardus* of the herring family which is an important food fish of European waters, the young often marketed as sardines.
• [16th-c. *pilcher* etc.: origin unknown]

pileated *adjective*
• "PILLY ated"
• (of a bird) having a conspicuous cap or crest.
• [Latin *pileatus* capped, from *pileus* felt cap]

pileus *noun*
• "PIE lee us"
• the spore-bearing circular structure surmounting the stipe in a mushroom or toadstool, which has an undersurface composed of radiating plates or gills.
• [Latin, = felt cap]
• **pileate** *adjective*

pilfer *verb*
• "PILL fur"
• steal (objects) esp. in small quantities.
• [Old French *pelfrer* pillage, of unknown origin]
• **pilferage** *noun* "PILFER idge"
• **pilferer** *noun*

pilgrim *noun*
• "PILL grim"
• a person who journeys to a sacred place for religious reasons.
• [Middle English *pilegrim* from Provençal *pelegrin* from Latin *peregrinus* stranger: see PEREGRINE]

pilgrimage *noun*
• "PILL grim idge"
• a pilgrim's journey.
• [as PILGRIM]

Pilipino *noun*
• "pilla PEENO"
• the national language of the Philippines.
• [Tagalog from Spanish *Filipino*]

pillage *verb*
• "PILL idge"
• plunder; sack (a place or a person).
• [Old French from *piller* plunder]
• **pillager** *noun*

pillar *noun*
• "PILLER"
• a tall, upright column of stone, wood, metal, etc., used as a support for a building or as an ornament or monument etc.
• [Anglo-French *piler*, Old French *pilier*, ultimately from Latin *pila* pillar]
• **pillared** *adjective*
• **pillarless** *adjective*

pillion *noun*
• "PILL y'n"
• seating for a passenger behind a motorcyclist.
• [Gaelic *pillean*, *pillin* diminutive of *pell* cushion, from Latin *pellis* skin]

pillory *noun*
• "PILLER ee"
• a wooden framework with holes for the head and hands, enabling the public to assault or ridicule a person so imprisoned.
• [Old French *pilori* etc.: prob. from Provençal *espilori* of uncertain origin]

pilose *adjective*
• "PIE lose" (rhymes with *GROSS*)
• covered with hair.
• [Latin *pilosus* from *pilus* hair]
• **pilosity** *noun* "pie LOSSA tee"

Pilsner *noun*
ALSO SPELLED: **Pilsener**
• "PILL znur" or "PILL snur"
• a pale lager beer with a strong flavour of hops.
• [*Pilsen*, in the Czech Republic, where first brewed]

pimento *noun*
• "pim ENTO"
• a pepper with a relatively mild taste.
• [Spanish *pimiento* from Latin *pigmentum* PIGMENT, in medieval Latin = spice]

pimpernel *noun*
• "PIMPER nell"
• any plant of the genus *Anagallis*, esp. one with small esp. scarlet flowers closing in rainy or cloudy weather.
• [Old French *pimpernelle* ultimately from Latin *piper* pepper]

pinafore *noun*
• "PINNA for"
• a decorative apron-like garment, usu. with buttons or ties at the back, worn over a dress, esp. by small girls.
• ['pin' + 'afore' before, (because originally pinned on the front of a dress)]

pinata *noun*
• "pin YOTTA" or "peen YOTTA"
• an originally Mexican brightly decorated crock or papier mâché figure filled with candies or small toys etc. and suspended overhead to be broken by a blindfolded person waving a stick.
• [Spanish, = jug, pot]

pincers *plural noun*
• "PINCE urz"
• a gripping tool resembling scissors but with blunt usu. concave jaws to hold a nail etc. for extraction.

• [Middle English *pinsers*, *pinsours* from Anglo-French from Old French *pincier* pinch]

pineal *adjective*
• "PINNY 'll" or "PINE ee 'll"
• shaped like a pine cone.
• [French *pinéal* from Latin *pinea* pine cone]

pineapple *noun*
• "PINE apple"
• a tropical plant, *Ananas comosus*, with a spiral of sword-shaped leaves and a thick stem bearing a large fruit developed from many flowers.
• ['pine' + 'apple', from the fruit's resemblance to a pine cone]

pinetum *noun*
• "pie NEET um"
• a plantation of pine trees or other conifers for scientific or ornamental purposes.
• [Latin from *pinus* pine]

pingo *noun*
• "PING go"
• a dome-shaped mound found in permafrost areas, consisting of a layer of soil over a large core of ice.
• [Inuit *pinguq* nunatak]

pinguid *adjective*
• "PING gwid"
• fat, oily, or greasy.
• [Latin *pinguis* fat]

pinion *verb*
• "PIN y'n"
• bind the arms of (a person).
• [Old French *pignon* the outer part of a bird's wing, usu. including the flight feathers, ultimately from Latin *pinna* feather]
HOMOPHONES: *Pinyin*

pinna *noun*
• "PINNA"
• the auricle; the external part of the ear.
• [Latin, = *penna* feather, wing, fin]

pinnace *noun*
• "PINN us"
• any of various kinds of small boats used by a larger ship.
• [French *pinnace*, *pinasse*, ultimately from Latin *pinus* pine]

pinnacle *noun*
• "PINNA k'll"
• the culmination or climax (of endeavour, success, etc.).
• [Old French *pin(n)acle* from Late Latin *pinnaculum* from *pinna* wing, point]

pinnate *adjective*
• "PIN ate"
• (of a compound leaf) having leaflets arranged on either side of the stem, usu. in pairs opposite each other.
• [Latin *pinnatus* feathered (as PINNA)]

pinniped *adjective*
• "PINNA ped"
• denoting any aquatic mammal with limbs ending in fins.
• [Latin *pinna* fin + *pes ped-* foot]

pinnule *noun*
• "PIN yool"
• the secondary division of a pinnate leaf.
• [Latin *pinnula* diminutive of *pinna* fin, wing]
• **pinnular** *adjective*

pinochle *noun*
• "PEE nuck'll"
• a card game with a double pack of 48 cards (nine to ace only).
• [German *Binokel*, the name of a card game, from French *binocle*, lit. = 'two-eyed']

pinole *noun*
• "puh NO lee"
• flour made from parched cornflour, esp. mixed with sweet flour made of mesquite beans, sugar, etc.
• [Latin American Spanish from Aztec *pinolli*]

piñon *noun*
ALSO SPELLED: **pinyon**
• "pee NYON"
• a pine, *Pinus cembra*, bearing edible seeds.
• [Spanish from Latin *pinea* pine cone]

Pinot *noun*
• "pee NO"
• any of several varieties of black or white or greyish-blue grape used in winemaking.
• [French, var. of earlier *Pineau*, from *pin* pine + *-eau* diminutive suffix (from the shape of the grape cluster)]

Pinteresque *adjective*
• "pin tur ESK"
• typical of the plays of English playwright Harold Pinter (b.1930), esp. having disjointed dialogue.

pintle *noun*
• "PIN t'll"
• a pin or bolt, esp. one on which some other part turns.
• [Old English *pintel* penis, of unknown origin: compare Old Frisian etc. *pint*]

pinto *adjective*
• "PIN toe"
• piebald.
• [Spanish, = mottled, ultimately from Latin *pictus* past participle of *pingere* paint]

pinwale *adjective*
• "PIN wale"
• (of a fabric, esp. corduroy) having very thin wales.
• ['pin' + WALE]

Pinyin *noun*
• "PIN yin"
• a system of romanized spelling for transliterating Chinese.

• [Chinese *pīn-yīn*, lit. 'spell sound']
HOMOPHONES: *pinion*

pion *noun*
• "PIE on"
• a meson having a mass approximately 270 times that of an electron.
• [PI (the letter used as a symbol for the particle)]
• **pionic** *adjective* "pie ONNIC"

pioneer *noun*
• "pie a NEER"
• an initiator of a new enterprise, an inventor, etc.
• [French *pionnier* foot soldier, pioneer, Old French *paonier*, *peon(n)ier* (as PEON)]
• **pioneering** *adjective*

pious *adjective*
• "PIE us"
• devout; religious.
• [Latin *pius* dutiful, pious]
• **piously** *adverb*
• **piousness** *noun*

piperidine *noun*
• "pih PERRA deen" or "pih PERRA din"
• a peppery-smelling liquid formed by the reduction of pyridine.
• [Latin *piper* pepper]

pipette *noun*
• "pipe ET" or "pip ET"
• a slender tube for transferring or measuring small quantities of liquids esp. in chemistry.
• [French, diminutive of *pipe* pipe, ultimately from Latin *pipare* peep, chirp]

pipistrelle *noun*
• "pippa STRELL"
• any bat of the genus *Pipistrellus*, native to temperate regions and feeding on insects.
• [French from Italian *pipistrello*, *vip-*, from Latin *vespertilio* bat, from *vesper* evening]

pipit *noun*
• "PIPPIT"
• any of various birds of the family Motacillidae, esp. of the genus *Anthus*, found worldwide and having brown plumage often heavily streaked with a lighter colour.
• [prob. imitative]

pippin *noun*
• "PIPPIN"
• an apple grown from seed.
• [Old French *pepin*, of unknown origin]

pipsissewa *noun*
• "pip SISSA wah"
• an evergreen plant of the wintergreen family, *Chimaphila umbellata*, with whorls of shiny leaves and a cluster of waxy white or pink flowers.
• [Abenaki *kpi-pskwāhsawe* 'flower of the woods']

pipsqueak *noun*
• "PIP skweek"
• a contemptibly small, weak, or insignificant person or thing.
• [imitative]

piquant *adjective*
• "pee CONT" or "pee CANT" or "PEE cant"
• agreeably pungent, sharp, or appetizing.
• [French, present participle of *piquer* (as PIQUE)]
• **piquancy** *noun* "PEEK 'n see"
• **piquantly** *adverb*

pique *verb*
• "PEEK"
• wound the pride of, irritate.
• [French *piquer* prick, irritate, from Romanic]
HOMOPHONES: *peak*, *peek*, *Peke*

piqué *noun*
• "pee CAY"
• a stiff ribbed cotton or other fabric.
• [French, past participle of *piquer*: see PIQUE]

piquet *noun*
• "pick ET"
• a game for two players with a pack of 32 cards (seven to ace only).
• [French, of unknown origin]

piranha *noun*
• "puh RONNA" or "puh RANNA"
• any of various freshwater predatory fish of the genera *Pygocentrus*, *Rooseveltiella*, or *Serrasalmus*, native to S America and having sharp cutting teeth.
• [Portuguese from Tupi, var. of *piraya* scissors]

pirate *noun*
• "PIE rit"
• a person who robs ships at sea.
• [Latin *pirata* from Greek *peiratēs* from *peiraō* attempt, assault]
• **piracy** *noun*
• **piratic** *adjective* "pie RATTIC"
• **piratical** *adjective*

pirogue *noun*
• "pih ROE'g"
• a long narrow canoe made from a single tree trunk.
• [French, prob. from Galibi]

piroshki *noun*
• "pih ROSHKY"
• a small turnover of pastry filled with meat, fish, rice, etc.
• [Russian *pirozhki*, pl. of *pirozhok*, diminutive of *pirog*, a large pie]

pirouette *noun*
• "peer oo ET"
• a rapid turn or spin made esp. by a dancer while balanced on the point of the toe or the ball of the foot.
• [French, = spinning top]

piscatorial *adjective*
• "piska TORY 'll"
• of or concerning fish, fishermen, or fishing.

• [Latin *piscātōrius* from *piscātor* from *piscāt-*, past participial stem of *piscārī* to fish]
• **piscatorially** *adverb*

Pisces *noun*
• "PICE eez"
• the twelfth sign of the zodiac.
• [Latin, pl. of *piscis* fish]
• **Piscean** *noun* "PICE ee 'n"

pisciculture *noun*
• "PISSA cull chur"
• the breeding and rearing of fish by artificial means.
• [Latin *piscis* fish, after *agriculture* etc.]
• **piscicultural** *adjective*
• **pisciculturist** *noun*

piscina *noun*
• "piss EENA" or "piss INE uh"
• a stone basin for draining water used in the Mass, found chiefly in Roman Catholic and pre-Reformation churches.
• [Latin from *piscis* fish]

piscine *adjective*
• "PISS ine"
• of or concerning fish.
• [Latin *piscis* fish]

piscivorous *adjective*
• "piss IVVER us"
• fish-eating.
• [Latin *piscis* fish + *-vorus* from *vorare* devour]

pisiform *adjective*
• "PISSA form"
• pea-shaped.
• [modern Latin *pisiformis* from *pisum* pea]

pismire *noun*
• "PISS mire"
• an ant.
• [Middle English from 'piss' (from smell of anthill) + obsolete *mire* ant]

pissaladière *noun*
• "PISS alad yare"
• a Provençal open tart resembling pizza, typically made with tomato sauce topped with onions, anchovies, and olives.
• [French from Occitan (Nice) *pissaladiera* from *pissalat* anchovy (from Occitan *peis* fish (from Latin *piscis* fish)) + *salat*, past participle of *salar* to salt, from Latin *sal* salt]

pissoir *noun*
• "pee SWARR" ("SWARR" rhymes with *FAR*)
• a public urinal.
• [French]

pistachio *noun*
• "piss TASHY oh"
• an evergreen tree, *Pistacia vera*, bearing small brownish-green flowers and ovoid reddish fruit.
• [Italian *pistaccio* and Spanish *pistacho*, via Latin *pistacium* and Greek *pistakion*, from Persian *pistah*]

piste *noun*
• "PEEST"
• a ski run of compacted snow.
• [French from Italian *pista* from popular Latin *pistāre* crush]

pistil *noun*
• "PIST'll"
• the female organs of a flower, comprising the stigma, style, and ovary.
• [French *pistile* or Latin *pistillum* PESTLE]
• **pistillate** *adjective*
HOMOPHONES: *pistol*

pistol *noun*
• "PIST'll"
• a small firearm designed to be held in one hand.
• [obsolete French from German *Pistole* from Czech *pišt'al*, of which the original meaning was 'whistle', hence 'a firearm' by the resemblance in shape]
HOMOPHONES: *pistil*

pistole *noun*
• "piss TOLE"
• a gold coin of Spain or other European countries.
• [French *pistole* abbreviation of *pistolet*, of uncertain origin]

piston *noun*
• "PISS t'n"
• a disc or short cylinder fitting closely within a tube in which it moves up and down against a liquid or gas, used in an internal combustion engine to impart motion, or in a pump to receive motion.
• [French from Italian *pistone* var. of *pestone* augmentative of *pestello* PESTLE]

pistou *noun*
• "PEE stoo"
• a sauce or paste made from crushed basil, garlic, cheese, etc., used esp. in Provençal dishes.
• [Provençal, = Italian PESTO]

pita *noun*
• "PEETA"
• a flat hollow unleavened, usu. round bread which can be split and filled with salad etc.
• [modern Greek, = a cake]

pitchblende *noun*
• "PITCH blend"
• a mineral form of uranium oxide occurring in pitch-like masses and yielding radium.
• [German *Pechblende* (*Pech* 'pitch' sticky resinous substance obtained by distilling tar or turpentine, from Latin *pix picis* + BLENDE)]

piteous *adjective*
• "PITTY us"
• deserving or causing pity; wretched.
• [Anglo-French *pitous*, Old French *pitos* from Romanic (as PIETY)]
• **piteously** *adverb*
• **piteousness** *noun*

Pithecanthropus *noun*
- "pithy CANTHRA pus"
- a genus name formerly applied to some fossil hominids of the species *Homo erectus*, named from remains found in Java in 1891.
- [Greek *pithēkos* ape + *anthrōpos* man]

pithos *noun*
- "PITH oss"
- a large storage jar.
- [Greek]

pitiable *adjective*
- "PITTY a bull"
- deserving or causing pity.
- [Old French *pité* from Latin *pietas* (as PIETY)]
- **pitiably** *adverb*

pitiful *adjective*
- "PITTA full"
- deserving of or arousing pity.
- [as PITIABLE]
- **pitifully** *adverb*
- **pitifulness** *noun*

pitiless *adjective*
- "PITTY less"
- showing no pity; cruel.
- [as PITIABLE]
- **pitilessly** *adverb*
- **pitilessness** *noun*

piton *noun*
- "PEE tawn"
- a peg or spike driven into a rock or crack to support a climber or a rope.
- [French, = eyebolt]

pitot *noun*
- "PEETO"
- a device consisting of an open-ended right-angled tube used to measure the speed or flow of a fluid.
- [H. *Pitot*, French physicist d.1771]

pitta *noun*
- "PIT uh"
- a brightly coloured passerine bird with a strong bill and short tail, of the Old World genus *Pitta* and family Pittidae.
- [Telegu *piṭṭa* '(young) bird']

pittance *noun*
- "PIT ince"
- a scanty or meagre allowance, remuneration, etc.
- [Old French *pitance* from medieval Latin *pi(e)tantia* from Latin *pietas* 'pity']

pituitary *noun*
- "pih TOO a terry" or "pih TYOO a terry"
- a small ductless gland at the base of the brain secreting various hormones essential for growth and other bodily functions.
- [Latin *pituitarius* secreting phlegm, from *pituita* phlegm]

più *adverb*
- "PYOO"
- (as a musical direction) more.
- [Italian]

HOMOPHONES: *pew*

pivot *noun*
- "PIVVIT"
- a short shaft or pin on which something turns or oscillates.
- [French, of uncertain origin]
- **pivotal** *adjective*

pixel *noun*
- "PIX'll"
- any of the minute areas of uniform illumination of which an image on a television or computer screen is composed.
- [abbreviation of *picture element*]

pixelate *verb*

ALSO SPELLED: **pixellate**
- "PIX'll ate"
- display as or divide into pixels.
- [as PIXEL]
- **pixelated** *noun* (also **pixellated**)
- **pixelation** *noun* (also **pixellation**)

HOMOPHONES: *pixilated*, *pixillation*

pixie *noun*

ALSO SPELLED: **pixy**
- "PIXY"
- a small fairy, often portrayed with pointed ears and a pointed hat.
- [17th c.: origin unknown]
- **pixieish** *adjective* (also **pixyish**)

pixilated *adjective*

ALSO SPELLED: **pixillated**
- "PIX'll ated"
- bewildered; crazy.
- [var. of *pixie-led* (as PIXIE)]

HOMOPHONES: *pixelated*

pixillation *noun*

ALSO SPELLED: **pixilation**
- "pix'll AY sh'n"
- a theatrical and cinematographic technique whereby human characters move or appear to move as if artificially animated.
- [from PIXILATED]

HOMOPHONES: *pixelation*

pizza *noun*
- "PEETSA"
- a food consisting of a flat round base of dough baked with a topping of tomato sauce and cheese and other garnishes, e.g. meat, vegetables, etc.
- [Italian, = pie]

pizzazz *noun*

ALSO SPELLED: **pizazz**
- "puh ZAZZ"
- verve, energy, liveliness, sparkle.
- [perhaps invented by D. Vreeland, fashion editor in the 1930s of *Harper's Bazaar*]

pizzelle *noun*
- "peet SELL ay"
- a thin, slightly sweet, waffle-like Italian wafer biscuit.

• [Italian, as PIZZA + *elle* plural diminutive ending]

pizzeria *noun*
• "peetsa REE uh"
• a place where pizzas are made, sold, or eaten.
• [Italian (as PIZZA)]

pizzicato *adverb*
• "pitsa COTTO"
• plucking the strings of a violin etc. with the finger.
• [Italian, past participle of *pizzicare* twitch, from *pizzare* from *pizza* edge]

placard *noun*
• "PLACK ard" or "PLACK'rd"
• a printed or handwritten poster used esp. as an advertisement, in protest demonstrations, picket lines, etc.
• [Old French *placquart* from *plaquier* to plaster, from Middle Dutch *placken*]

placate *verb*
• "pluh CATE" or "PLACK ate" or "PLAY cate"
• pacify; conciliate.
• [Latin *placare placat-* please, appease]
• **placatingly** *adverb*
• **placatory** *adjective* "PLACKA tory"

placebo *noun*
• "pluh SEE bo"
• a pill, medicine, etc. prescribed for psychological reasons but having no physiological effect.
• [Latin, = I shall be acceptable or pleasing (first word of Ps. 116:9 in the Vulgate) from *placēre* 'please']

placenta *noun*
• "pluh SENTA"
• a flattened circular organ in the uterus of pregnant eutherian mammals, nourishing and maintaining the fetus through the umbilical cord and expelled after birth.
• [Latin from Greek *plakous -ountos* flat cake, from the root of *plax plakos* flat plate]
• **placental** *adjective*

placer *noun*
• "PLASSER"
• a deposit of sand, gravel, etc., in the bed of a stream etc., containing valuable minerals, e.g. gold, in particles.
• [Latin American Spanish, related to *placel* sandbank, from *plaza* 'place']

placid *adjective*
• "PLASSID"
• (of a person) not easily aroused or disturbed; peaceful.
• [French *placide* or Latin *placidus* from *placēre* please]
• **placidity** *noun*
• **placidly** *adverb*
• **placidness** *noun*

placoid *adjective*
• "PLACK oid"
• (of a fish scale) consisting of a hard base embedded in the skin and a spiny backward projection.
• [Greek *plax plakos* flat plate]

plagal *adjective*
• "PLAY g'll"
• (of a church mode) containing sounds between the dominant and its octave.
• [medieval Latin *plagalis* from *plaga* plagal mode, via Latin *plagius* from medieval Greek *plagios* (in classical Greek = oblique) from Greek *plagos* side]

plage *noun*
• "PLAZH"
• an unusually bright region on the sun.
• [French, = beach, from Italian *piaggio* hillside, from Greek *plagios* oblique]

plagiarize *verb*
ALSO SPELLED: esp. *Brit.* **-ise**
• "PLAY juh rize"
• take and use (the thoughts, writings, inventions, etc. of another person) as one's own.
• [Latin *plagiarius* kidnapper, from *plagium* a kidnapping, from Greek *plagion*]
• **plagiarism** *noun*
• **plagiarist** *noun*
• **plagiaristic** *adjective*
• **plagiarizer** *noun* (also esp. *Brit.* **-iser**)

plagioclase *noun*
• "PLAY jee a clace"
• a series of feldspar minerals forming glassy crystals.
• [Greek *plagios* oblique, from *plagos* side + *klasis* cleavage]

plague *noun*
• "PLAIG"
• a contagious bacterial disease characterized by fever and delirium, with the formation of buboes and sometimes infection of the lungs.
• [Latin *plaga* 'stroke, wound', prob. from Greek *plaga*, *plēgē*]

plaice *noun*
• "PLACE"
• either of two flatfishes having a brown back and a white underside, much used for food, the N Atlantic fish *Hippoglossoides platessoides* or the European *Pleuronectes platessa*.
• [Old French *plaïz* from Late Latin *platessa* apparently from Greek *platus* broad]
HOMOPHONES: *place*

plaid *noun*
• "PLAD"
• checkered or tartan, esp. woollen, twilled cloth.
• [Gaelic *plaide*, of unknown origin]

plaintiff *noun*
• "PLANE tiff"

• a person who brings a case against another into court.
• [Old French *plaintif* (adjective) (as PLAINTIVE)]

plaintive *adjective*
• "PLANE tiv"
• expressing sorrow; mournful, sad.
• [Old French (*-if*, *-ive*) from *plainte* from *plaindre* from Latin *plangere planct-* lament]
• **plaintively** *adverb*
• **plaintiveness** *noun*

plait *noun*
• "PLATE"
• a length of hair, straw, etc., in three or more interlaced strands; a braid.
• [Old French *pleit* 'a fold', ultimately from Latin *plicare* 'to fold']
HOMOPHONES: *plate*

planar *adjective*
• "PLANE ur"
• of, relating to, or in the form of a plane surface.
• [Latin *planum* flat surface]
HOMOPHONES: *planer*, *plainer*

planarian *noun*
• "pluh NERRY 'n"
• any flatworm of the class Turbellaria, usu. living in fresh water.
• [modern Latin *Planaria*, the genus name, feminine of Latin *planarius* lying flat]

planchet *noun*
• "PLAN shet"
• a plain metal disc from which a coin is made.
• [diminutive of *planch* slab of metal, from Old French *planche* from Late Latin *planca* board, from *plancus* flat-footed]

planchette *noun*
• "plan SHET"
• a small usu. heart-shaped board on casters with a pencil that is supposedly caused to write spirit messages when a person's fingers rest lightly on it.
• [French, diminutive of *planche*: see PLANCHET]

planer *noun*
• "PLANE ur"
• a tool consisting of a wooden or metal block with a projecting steel blade, used to smooth a wooden surface by paring shavings from it.
• [Old French *plane* var. of *plaine* from Late Latin *plana* from Latin *planus* plain, flat]
HOMOPHONES: *planar*, *plainer*

planet *noun*
• "PLANNIT"
• a celestial body moving in an elliptical orbit around a star, esp.: any of the nine large rocky or gaseous bodies orbiting the sun: Mercury, Venus, Earth, Mars, Jupiter, Saturn, Uranus, Neptune, and Pluto.
• [Late Latin *planeta*, *planetes* from Greek *planētēs* wanderer, planet, from *planaomai* wander]
• **planetary** *adjective*
• **planetology** *noun*
• **planetwide** *adjective*

planetarium *noun*
• "planna TERRY um"
• a domed building in which images of stars, planets, constellations, etc. are projected for public entertainment or education.
• [as PLANET]

planetesimal *noun*
• "planna TESS'm 'll"
• any of a vast number of minute planets or planetary bodies.
• [PLANET, after *infinitesimal*]

planetoid *noun*
• "PLANNA toid"
• an asteroid.
• [as PLANET]

plangent *adjective*
• "PLAN j'nt"
• (of a sound) loud and reverberating.
• [Latin *plangere plangent-* lament]
• **plangency** *noun*
• **plangently** *adverb*

planimeter *noun*
• "pluh NIMMA tur"
• an instrument for mechanically measuring the area of a plane figure.
• [French *planimètre* from Latin *planus* level + Greek *metron* measure]
• **planimetric** *adjective* "planna METRIC"
• **planimetrical** *adjective*
• **planimetrically** *adverb*
• **planimetry** *noun*

planish *verb*
• "PLANNISH"
• flatten (metal) with a smooth-faced hammer or between rollers.
• [Old French *planir* smooth from *plain* plane]
• **planisher** *noun*

planisphere *noun*
• "PLANNA sfeer"
• a map formed by the projection of a sphere or part of a sphere on a plane, esp. to show the appearance of the heavens at a specific time or place.
• [medieval Latin *planisphaerium* (from Latin *planus* plain, flat, SPHERE): influenced by French *planisphère*]
• **planispheric** *adjective* "planna SFARE ick"

planktivorous *adjective*
• "plank TIVVER us"
• eating plankton.
• [as PLANKTON + Latin *-vorus* from *vorare* devour]

plankton *noun*
• "PLANK t'n"
• the chiefly microscopic organisms drifting or floating in the sea or fresh water.

• [German from Greek *plagktos* wandering, from *plazomai* wander]
• **planktonic** *adjective* "plank TONNIC"

planoconcave *adjective*
• "plane oh CON cave" or "plane oh k'n CAVE"
• (of a lens etc.) with one surface plane and the other concave.
• [Latin *planus* flat + CONCAVE]

planoconvex *adjective*
• "plane oh CON vex" or "plane oh k'n VEX"
• (of a lens etc.) with one surface plane and the other convex.
• [Latin *planus* flat + CONVEX]

Plantagenet *adjective*
• "plan TADGE a nit"
• of or relating to the English royal house which held the throne from the accession of Henry II (1154) to the deposition of Richard II (1399).
• [Latin *planta genista* sprig of gorse, said to be worn as a crest by and given as a nickname to Geoffrey, count of Anjou, the father of Henry II]

plantain *noun*
• "plan TANE" or "PLAN tane"
• any plant of the genus *Plantago*, with a rosette of leaves and seeds used as food for birds and as a mild laxative.
• [Old French from Latin *plantago -ginis* from *planta* sole of the foot (from its broad prostrate leaves)]

plantar *adjective*
• "PLANTER"
• of or relating to the sole of the foot.
• [Latin *plantaris* from *planta* sole]
HOMOPHONES: *planter*

plantigrade *adjective*
• "PLANTA grade"
• (of an animal) walking on the soles of its feet.
• [French from modern Latin *plantigradus* from Latin *planta* sole + *-gradus* -walking]

plaque *noun*
• "PLACK"
• an ornamental usu. metal tablet, esp. affixed to a building in commemoration.
• [French from Dutch *plak* tablet, from *plakken* stick]

plasma *noun*
• "PLAZMA"
• the colourless fluid part of blood, lymph, or milk, in which corpuscles or fat globules are suspended.
• [Late Latin, = mould, from Greek *plasma -atos* from *plassō* 'to shape']
• **plasmatic** *adjective* "plazz MATTIC"
• **plasmic** *adjective*

plasmid *noun*
• "PLAZZ mid"
• a genetic structure in a cell that can replicate independently of the chromosomes, esp. a circular DNA strand in a bacterium or protozoan.
• [as PLASMA]

plasmin *noun*
• "PLAZMIN"
• a proteolytic enzyme which destroys blood clots by attacking fibrin.
• [as PLASMA]

plasminogen *noun*
• "plazz MINNA j'n"
• the inactive precursor, present in blood, of the enzyme plasmin.
• [as PLASMIN + GENESIS]

plasmodesma *noun*
• "plazma DEZMA"
• a narrow thread of cytoplasm that passes through cell walls and allows communication between plant cells.
• [PLASMA + Greek *desma* bond, fetter]

plasmodium *noun*
• "plazz MOE dee um"
• any parasitic protozoan of the genus *Plasmodium*, including those causing malaria in humans.
• [modern Latin from PLASMA]
• **plasmodial** *adjective*

plasmolysis *noun*
• "plazz MOLLA sis"
• contraction of the protoplast of a plant cell as a result of loss of water from the cell.
• [modern Latin (as PLASMA, LYSIS)]

plasticize *verb*
ALSO SPELLED: esp. *Brit.* **-ise**
• "PLASTA size"
• make plastic or mouldable, esp. by the addition of a plasticizer.
• [as PLASTIQUE]
• **plasticized** *adjective* (also esp. *Brit.* **-ised**)

plasticizer *noun*
• "PLASTA sizer"
• a substance (typically a solvent) added to a synthetic resin to produce or promote plasticity and flexibility and reduce brittleness.
• [as PLASTIQUE]

plastid *noun*
• "PLASS tid"
• any small organelle in the cytoplasm of a plant cell, containing pigment or food.
• [German from Greek *plastos* shaped]

plastique *noun*
• "plass TEEK"
• plastic explosive.
• [French, literally 'plastic' from Latin *plasticus* from Greek *plastikos*, from *plassō* 'mould']

plastron *noun*
• "PLASS tr'n"
• a fencer's leather-covered breastplate.
• [French from Italian *piastrone* augmentative

of *piastra* breastplate, from Latin *emplastrum* 'plaster']
• **plastral** *adjective*

plateau *noun*
• "pla TOE"
• an area of fairly level high ground.
• [French from Old French *platel* diminutive of *plat* flat surface]

platen *noun*
• "PLAT'n"
• a plate in a printing press which presses the paper against the type.
• [Old French *platine* a flat piece, from *plat* flat]

platinoid *noun*
• "PLAT'n oid"
• an alloy of copper, zinc, nickel, and tungsten.
• [as PLATINUM]

platinum *noun*
• "PLAT'n um"
• a ductile malleable silvery-white metallic element occurring naturally in nickel and copper ores, unaffected by simple acids and fusible only at a very high temperature, used in making jewellery and laboratory apparatus.
• [modern Latin from earlier *platina* from Spanish, diminutive of *plata* silver]

platitude *noun*
• "PLATTA tude"
• a trite or commonplace remark, esp. one solemnly delivered.
• [French from *plat* flat, after *certitude*, *multitudinous*, etc.]
• **platitudinize** *verb* (also esp. *Brit.* **-ise**) "platta TUDE 'n ize"
• **platitudinous** *adjective*

Platonic *adjective*
• "pluh TONNIC"
• of or associated with the Greek philosopher Plato (d. *c.*347 BC) or his ideas.
• [Latin *Platonicus* from Greek *Platōnikos* from *Platōn* Plato]
• **Platonically** *adverb*

Platonism *noun*
• "PLATE'n izm"
• the philosophy of Plato (d. *c.*347 BC) or his followers.
• **Platonist** *noun*

platoon *noun*
• "pluh TOON"
• a subdivision of a company, a tactical unit commanded by a lieutenant and usu. divided into three sections of ten to twelve soldiers.
• [French *peloton* small ball, diminutive of *pelote*: see PELLET]

Plattdeutsch *noun*
• "PLAT doitch"
• modern Low German, the group of dialects of Germany spoken in the lowland areas of the north, most closely related to Dutch and Frisian.
• [German from Dutch *Platduitsch*, from *plat* low, flat + *Duitsch* German]

platyhelminth *noun*
• "platty HELL minth"
• any invertebrate of the phylum Platyhelminthes, including flatworms, flukes, and tapeworms.
• [Greek *platu-* from *platus* broad, flat + HELMINTH]

platypus *noun*
• "PLATTA puss"
• an Australian aquatic egg-laying mammal, *Ornithorhynchus anatinus*, having a pliable duck-like bill, webbed feet, and sleek grey fur.
• [modern Latin from Greek *platu-* from *platus* broad, flat, *pous podos* foot]

platyrrhine *adjective*
• "PLATTA rine"
• (of primates) having nostrils far apart and directed forwards or sideways.
• [Greek *platu-* from *platus* broad, flat, *rhis rhin-* nose]

plaudit *noun*
• "PLODDIT"
• an emphatic expression of approval.
• [shortened from Latin *plaudite* applaud, imperative pl. of *plaudere plaus-* applaud, said by Roman actors at the end of a play]

plausible *adjective*
• "PLOZZA bull"
• (of an argument, statement, etc.) seeming reasonable, believable, or probable.
• [Latin *plausibilis* (as PLAUDIT)]
• **plausibility** *noun*
• **plausibly** *adverb*

playa *noun*
• "PLY uh"
• a flat area of silt or sand at the bottom of a desert basin, dry except after rain.
• [Spanish, = beach, from Late Latin *plagia*]

playwright *noun*
• "PLAY rite"
• a person who writes plays; a dramatist.
• ['play' + WRIGHT]

playwriting *noun*
• "PLAY rite ing"
• the activity or process of writing plays.
• ['play' + WRITE]

pleach *verb*
• "PLEECH"
• entwine or interlace (esp. branches to form a hedge).
• [Middle English *pleche* from Old French *pla(i)ssier*, ultimately from Latin *plectere* braid]

pleasance *noun*
• "PLEZZ ince"
• a secluded enclosure or part of a garden, esp. one attached to a large house.
• [Old French *plaisance* (as PLEASANT)]

pleasant *adjective*
• "PLEZZ'nt"
• pleasing to the mind, feelings, or senses.
• [Old French *plaisant* from *plaisir* from Latin *placēre* please]
• **pleasantly** *adverb*
• **pleasantness** *noun*

pleasantry *noun*
• "PLEZZ'n tree"
• a pleasant or amusing remark, esp. made in casual conversation.
• [as PLEASANT]

pleasurable *adjective*
• "PLEZHUR a bull"
• causing pleasure; agreeable.
• [as PLEASURE]
• **pleasurableness** *noun*
• **pleasurably** *adverb*

pleasure *noun*
• "PLEZHUR"
• a feeling of satisfaction or joy.
• [Middle English & Old French *plesir, plaisir* (as PLEASANT), used as a noun]

plebeian *noun*
• "pluh BEE 'n"
• a commoner, esp. in ancient Rome.
• [Latin *plebeius* from *plebs plebis* the common people]
• **plebeianism** *noun*

plebiscite *noun*
• "PLEBBA site"
• the direct vote of all electors on an important public question, e.g. a change in the constitution.
• [French *plébiscite* from Latin *plebiscitum* from *plebs plebis* the common people + *scitum* decree, from *sciscere* vote for]
• **plebiscitary** *adjective* "pluh BISSA terry"

plectrum *noun*
• "PLECK trum"
• a thin flat piece of plastic or horn etc. held in the hand and used to pluck a string, esp. of a guitar.
• [Latin from Greek *plēktron* from *plēssō* strike]

pleiotropy *noun*
• "ply OTTRA pee"
• the production by a single gene of two or more apparently unrelated effects.
• [Greek *pleiōn* more + *tropē* turning]
• **pleiotropic** *adjective* "ply a TROPPIC"
• **pleiotropism** *noun*

Pleistocene *adjective*
• "PLICE tuh seen"
• of or relating to the first epoch of the Quaternary period, between the Pliocene and the Holocene, lasting from about 2,000,000 to 10,000 years BP, and notable for a succession of ice ages and the evolution of modern humankind.
• [Greek *pleistos* most + *kainos* new]

plenary *adjective*
• "PLENNER ee"
• entire, unqualified, absolute.
• [Late Latin *plenarius* from *plenus* full]

plenipotentiary *noun*
• "plenna puh TENSHER ee"
• a person (esp. a diplomat) invested with the full power of independent action.
• [medieval Latin *plenipotentiarius* from *plenus* full + *potentia* power]

plenitude *noun*
• "PLENNA tude"
• fullness, completeness.
• [Late Latin *plenitudo* from *plenus* full]

plenteous *adjective*
• "PLENTY us"
• plentiful.
• [Old French *plentivous* from *plentif -ive* from *plenté* plenty, from Latin *plenitas -tatis* from *plenus* full]
• **plenteously** *adverb*
• **plenteousness** *noun*

plentiful *adjective*
• "PLENTA full"
• abundant, copious.
• [as PLENTEOUS]
• **plentifully** *adverb*
• **plentifulness** *noun*

plenum *noun*
• "PLEE num"
• a full assembly of people or a committee etc.
• [Latin, neuter of *plenus* full]

pleochroic *adjective*
• "plee a CROW ick"
• showing different colours when viewed in different directions.
• [Greek *pleiōn* more + *-khroos* from *khrōs* colour]
• **pleochroism** *noun*

pleomorphism *noun*
• "plee a MORF izm"
• crystallization in two or more fundamentally different forms.
• [Greek *pleiōn* more + *morphē* form]
• **pleomorphic** *adjective*

pleonasm *noun*
• "PLEE a nazm"
• the use of more words than are needed to give the sense, e.g. *see with one's eyes.*
• [Late Latin *pleonasmus* from Greek *pleonasmos* from *pleonazō* be superfluous]
• **pleonastic** *adjective*
• **pleonastically** *adverb*

plesiosaur *noun*
• "PLEECY a sore"
• any of a group of extinct marine reptiles with a broad flat body, short tail, long flexible neck, and large paddle-like limbs.
• [modern Latin from Greek *plēsios* near + *sauros* lizard]

plethora *noun*
• "PLETH ur uh"
• an abundance.
• [Late Latin from Greek *plēthōrē* from *plēthō* be full]
• **plethoric** *adjective* "PLETH ur ick" or "pluh THORIC"

pleura *noun*
• "PLURA"
• each of a pair of serous membranes lining the thorax and enveloping the lungs in mammals.
• [medieval Latin from Greek, = side of the body, rib]
• **pleural** *adjective*
HOMOPHONES: *plural*

pleurisy *noun*
• "PLURA see"
• inflammation of the pleura, marked by pain in the chest or side, fever, etc.
• [Old French *pleurisie* from Late Latin *pleurisis* alteration of Latin *pleuritis* from Greek (as PLEURA)]
• **pleuritic** *adjective* "plur ITTIC"

pleuropneumonia *noun*
• "pluro new MOANY uh"
• pneumonia complicated with pleurisy.
• [as PLEURA + PNEUMONIA]

plew *noun*
• "PLOO"
• (historically) a beaver pelt.
• [Canadian French *pêlu* = French *poilu* hairy, from *poil* hair]

plexor *noun*
• "PLEX ur"
• a small hammer used to test reflexes and in percussing.
• [Greek *plēxis* percussion]

plexus *noun*
• "PLEX us"
• a network of nerves or blood vessels in an animal body.
• [Latin from *plectere plex-* braid]
• **plexiform** *adjective*

pliable *adjective*
• "PLY a bull"
• bending easily; supple.
• [French from *plier* bend, from Latin *plicare* fold]
• **pliability** *noun*
• **pliableness** *noun*
• **pliably** *adverb*

pliant *adjective*
• "PLY 'nt"
• bending, lithe, flexible; able to be bent or folded.
• [Old French (as PLIABLE)]
• **pliancy** *noun*

plicate *adjective*
• "PLY cate"
• folded, crumpled, corrugated.
• [Latin *plicatus* past participle of *plicare* fold]
• **plicated** *adjective*

plication *noun*
• "pluh CAY sh'n"
• the act of folding.
• [medieval Latin *plicatio* or Latin *plicare* fold, after *complication*]

plié *noun*
• "PLEE ay"
• a ballet movement in which the knees are bent outwards in line with the turned out feet.
• [French, past participle of *plier* bend: see PLIABLE]

pliers *plural noun*
• "PLY urz"
• pincers with gripping jaws usu. having parallel serrated surfaces, used for holding small objects, bending wire, etc.
• [(dialect) *ply* bend (as PLIABLE)]

plimsoll *noun*
• "PLIM s'll"
• a rubber-soled canvas leisure or sports shoe.
• [prob. from the resemblance of the side of the sole, usu. white with a coloured line through the middle, to a Plimsoll line, a marking on a ship's side showing the limit of legal submersion under various sea conditions, named for S. *Plimsoll*, English politician d.1898, promoter of the Merchant Shipping Act of 1876]

Pliocene *adjective*
• "PLY a seen"
• of or relating to the last epoch of the Tertiary period, between the Miocene and the Pleistocene, lasting from about 5.1 to 2 million years ago, during which many mammals that had flourished earlier in the Tertiary become extinct.
• [Greek *pleiōn* more + *kainos* new]

plissé *adjective*
• "PLEE say"
• (of cloth etc.) chemically treated so as to give a wrinkled or puckered effect.
• [French, past participle of *plisser* pleat]

ploidy *noun*
• "PLOY dee"
• the number of sets of chromosomes in a cell.
• [after DIPLOIDY, POLYPLOIDY , etc.]

plosion *noun*
• "PLOE zh'n"
• the sudden release of breath in the pronunciation of a stop consonant.
• [shortening of EXPLOSION]

plosive *adjective*
• "PLOE siv"
• pronounced with a sudden release of breath.
• [shortening of EXPLOSIVE]

plover *noun*
• "PLUVVER"
• any plump-breasted shorebird of the family Charadriidae, usu. having a pigeon-like bill.

• [Old French *plo(u)vier*, ultimately from Latin *pluvia* rain]

ploye *noun*
• "PLOY"
• *Cdn* a buckwheat pancake in Acadian cuisine.
• [Acadian French, alteration of *plogue*, from English 'plug', because of the heavy nature of the dish]
HOMOPHONES: *ploy*

plumage *noun*
• "PLOO midge"
• a bird's feathers.
• [Old French, from *plume* feather, from Latin *plūma* down]
• **plumaged** *adjective*

plumb *noun*
• "PLUM"
• a ball of lead or other heavy material, esp. one attached to the end of a line for finding the depth of water or determining the vertical on an upright surface.
• [prob. ultimately from Latin *plumbum* lead, assimilated to Old French *plomb* lead]
HOMOPHONES: *plum*

plumbago *noun*
• "plum BAY go"
• any plant of the genus *Plumbago*, with grey or blue flowers.
• [Latin from *plumbum* lead]

plumbeous *adjective*
• "PLUM bee us"
• of the dull grey colour of lead.
• [Latin *plumbeus* from *plumbum* 'lead']

plumber *noun*
• "PLUMMER"
• a person who fits and repairs the water pipes, water tanks, etc. in a building.
• [Old French *plommier* from Latin *plumbarius* from *plumbum* 'lead']
• **plumbing** *noun*

plumbic *adjective*
• "PLUM bick"
• containing lead esp. in its tetravalent form.
• [Latin *plumbum* lead]

plumbism *noun*
• "PLUM bizm"
• acute or chronic poisoning by absorption of lead into the body.
• [Latin *plumbum* lead]

plumbous *adjective*
• "PLUM buss"
• containing lead in its divalent form.
• [Latin *plumbum* lead]

plume *noun*
• "PLUME"
• a feather, esp. a large one used for ornament.
• [Old French from Latin *pluma* down]
• **plumed** *adjective*
• **plumeless** *adjective*
• **plumelike** *adjective*
• **plumy** *adjective*

plumeria *noun*
• "ploo MERRY uh"
• a fragrant flowering tropical tree of a genus that includes frangipani.
• [modern Latin, named after Charles *Plumier*, French botanist d.1704]

plummet *verb*
• "PLUM it"
• drop, fall, or plunge rapidly.
• [Old French *plommet* diminutive (as PLUMB)]

plumose *adjective*
• "PLUME ose" ("OSE" rhymes with *GROSS*)
• feathered.
• [Latin *plumosus* (as PLUME)]

plumule *noun*
• "PLUME yool"
• the rudimentary shoot or stem of an embryo plant.
• [French *plumule* or Latin *plumula*, diminutive (as PLUME)]

pluot *noun*
• "PLOO ott"
• a hybrid fruit that is 75% plum and 25% apricot.
• [blend of 'plum' (from Old English *plūme* via medieval Latin *pruna* from Latin *prunum*) + APRICOT]

pluperfect *adjective*
• "ploo PURR fict"
• (of a tense) denoting an action completed prior to some past point of time specified or implied, formed in English by *had* and the past participle, as: *he had gone by then.*
• [modern Latin *plusperfectum* from Latin *plus quam perfectum* more than perfect]

Plutino *noun*
• "ploo TEENO"
• any of a number of small planet-like bodies orbiting the sun beyond Neptune.
• [the planet *Pluto* (because they have a similar orbit) + Italian diminutive suffix *-ino*]

plutocracy *noun*
• "ploo TOCKRA see"
• government by the wealthy.
• [Greek *ploutokratia* from *ploutos* wealth + *kratia* from *kratos* strength, power]
• **plutocrat** *noun* "PLOOTO crat"
• **plutocratic** *adjective*
• **plutocratically** *adverb*

pluton *noun*
• "PLOO tawn"
• an intrusive body of plutonic rock, esp. a large one.
• [back-formation from PLUTONIC]

Plutonian *adjective*
• "ploo TONY 'n"
• of or pertaining to the planet Pluto.
• [Latin *Plutonius* from Greek *Ploutōnios*]

plutonic *adjective*
• "ploo TONNIC"
• pertaining to or designating igneous rock formed by intense heat at great depths below the earth's surface.
• [formed as PLUTONIAN]

plutonium *noun*
• "ploo TONY um"
• a dense silvery radioactive metallic transuranic element of the actinide series, used in some nuclear reactors and weapons.
• [*Pluto* (as the next planet beyond Neptune)]

pluvial *adjective*
• "PLOOVY 'll"
• designating a period of relatively high average rainfall in low and intermediate latitudes during the geological past.
• [Latin *pluvialis* from *pluvia* rain]

plyometrics *noun*
• "ply oh METRIX"
• a form of exercise that involves rapid and repeated stretching and contracting of the muscles, designed to increase strength.
• [Greek *plio* more + METRIC]
• **plyometric** *adjective*

pneumatic *adjective*
• "new MATTIC"
• of or relating to air, wind, or gases.
• [Greek *pneumatikos* from *pneuma* wind, from *pneō* breathe]
• **pneumatically** *adverb*
• **pneumatics** *noun*

pneumatophore *noun*
• "new MATTA for"
• the gaseous cavity of various hydrozoans, such as the Portuguese man-of-war.
• [Greek (as PNEUMATIC + *-phoros -phoron* bearing, bearer, from *pherō* bear)]

pneumococcus *noun*
• "new muh COCKUS"
• a paired bacterium, *Streptococcus pneumoniae*, associated with pneumonia and sometimes meningitis.
• [as PNEUMONIA + COCCUS]
• **pneumococcal** *adjective*

pneumoconiosis *noun*
• "new muh conny OH sis"
• a lung disease caused by inhalation of dust or small particles.
• [PNEUMONIA + Greek *konis* dust]

pneumonia *noun*
• "new MOANY uh"
• a bacterial or other infection causing inflammation of one or both lungs causing the air sacs to fill with pus and become solid.
• [Latin from Greek from *pneumōn* lung]
• **pneumonic** *adjective* "new MONNIC"

pneumonitis *noun*
• "new muh NITE iss"
• inflammation of the lungs, esp. caused by a viral or unknown agent.
• [as PNEUMONIA + Greek *-itis*, forming feminine of adjectives in *-itēs* (with *nosos* 'disease' implied)]

pneumothorax *noun*
• "new mo THOR ax"
• the presence of air or gas in the pleural cavity of the thorax, caused by the perforation of the chest wall or the lungs.
• [as PNEUMONIA + THORAX]

poblano *noun*
• "poe BLANNO"
• a large dark green chili pepper of a mild-flavoured variety.
• [Spanish]

poco *adverb*
• "POE coe"
• (in musical directions) a little; rather.
• [Italian]

podagra *noun*
• "puh DAG ruh"
• gout of the foot, esp. the big toe.
• [Latin from Greek *pous podos* foot + *agra* seizure]

podiatry *noun*
• "puh DIE a tree"
• a medical specialty involving the care of the feet and treatment of foot disorders by surgery, manipulation of soft tissue, medication, etc.
• [Greek *pous podos* foot + *iatros* physician]
• **podiatric** *adjective* "poe dee ATTRIC"
• **podiatrist** *noun*

podium *noun*
• "POE dee um"
• a raised platform or dais at the front of a hall or stage.
• [Latin from Greek *podion* diminutive of *pous pod-* foot]

podzol *noun*
• "POD zoll" ("ZOLL" rhymes with *DOLL*)
• an acidic, generally infertile soil with minerals leached from its surface layers into a lower stratum.
• [Russian from *pod* under, *zola* ashes]
• **podzolic** *adjective*
• **podzolize** *verb* (also esp. *Brit.* **-ise**)

poesy *noun*
• "POE a zee"
• poetry.
• [ultimately from Greek *poēsis* = *poiēsis* making, poetry]

poetaster *noun*
• "POE it aster"
• a paltry or inferior poet.
• [modern Latin, from Greek *poētēs* = *poiētēs* maker, poet + suffix '-aster' forming nouns denoting poor quality]

poeticize *verb*
ALSO SPELLED: esp. *Brit.* **-ise**
• "poe ETTA size"
• give a poetic character to.
• [ultimately from Greek *poētēs* = *poiētēs* maker, poet]

pogonia *noun*
• "puh GO nee uh"
• any of various small orchids, esp. rose pogonia, *Pogonia ophioglossoides*, of eastern N America, with a pink flower with a crested lip.
• [modern Latin from Greek *pogonion* beard]

pogrom *noun*
• "poe GROM"
• an organized massacre, originally and especially of Jews in Russia.
• [Russian, = devastation, from *gromit'* destroy]

poi *noun*
• "POY"
• a Hawaiian dish made from the fermented root of the taro, *Colocasia esculenta*.
• [Polynesian]

poignant *adjective*
• "POIN y'nt"
• deeply moving, touching.
• [Old French, present participle of *poindre* prick, from Latin *pungere*]
• **poignance** *noun*
• **poignancy** *noun*
• **poignantly** *adverb*

poikilotherm *noun*
• "POY killa thurm"
• an organism that regulates its body temperature by behavioural means, such as basking or burrowing; a cold-blooded organism.
• [Greek *poikilos* multicoloured, changeable + *thermē* heat]
• **poikilothermal** *adjective*
• **poikilothermic** *adjective*

poilu *noun*
• "pwah LOO"
• a nickname for a French private soldier, esp. one who served in the First World War.
• [French, lit. = 'hairy' from *poil* hair]

poinciana *noun*
• "poin see ANNA"
• any tropical tree of the genus *Poinciana*, with bright showy red flowers.
• [modern Latin from M. de *Poinci*, 17th-c. governor in the W Indies + *-ana* feminine suffix]

poinsettia *noun*
• "poin SETTA" or "poin SETTY uh"
• a shrub, *Euphorbia pulcherrima*, with large showy scarlet or pink bracts surrounding small yellow flowers, often grown as a houseplant.
• [modern Latin from J. R. *Poinsett*, US diplomat d.1851]

pointe *noun*
• "POINT"
• the tip of the toe or toes in ballet, or the toe of a pointe shoe.
• [French, 'tiptoe' from Latin *punctum* from *pungere punct-* prick]
HOMOPHONES: *point*

pointelle *noun*
• "poin TELL"
• knitwear incorporating eyelet holes giving a lacy effect.
• [as POINTE + suffix '-elle']

pointillism *noun*
• "POINT'll izm"
• a technique of Impressionist painting in which luminous effects are produced by tiny dots of pure colours, which seem to blend when viewed.
• [French *pointillisme* from *pointiller* mark with dots]
• **pointillist** *noun*
• **pointillistic** *adjective*

poisha *noun*
• "POY shuh"
• a monetary unit of Bangladesh, equal to one-hundredth of a taka.
• [Bengali, alteration of PAISA]

polar *adjective*
• "POE lur"
• of or near a pole of the earth or a celestial body, or of the celestial sphere.
• [French *polaire* or modern Latin *polaris* from *polus* (north or south) pole, from Greek *polos* pivot, axis, sky]

polarimeter *noun*
• "poe luh RIMMA tur"
• an instrument used to measure the polarization of light or the effect of a substance on the rotation of the plane of polarized light.
• [as POLAR + Greek *metron* measure]
• **polarimetric** *adjective* "poe luh ruh METRIC"
• **polarimetry** *noun*

polariscope *noun*
• "poe LERRA scope"
• an instrument for showing the polarization of light.
• [as POLAR + *skopos* target, from *skeptomai* look at]
• **polariscopic** *adjective*

polarity *noun*
• "puh LERRA tee"
• the tendency of a lodestone, magnetized bar, etc., to point with its extremities to the magnetic poles of the earth.
• [as POLAR]

polarize *verb*
ALSO SPELLED: esp. *Brit.* **-ise**
• "POE lur ize"
• restrict the vibrations of (a transverse wave, esp. light) to one direction.
• [as POLAR]
• **polarizable** *adjective* (also esp. *Brit.* **-isable**)

• **polarization** *noun* (also esp. *Brit.* **-isation**)
• **polarizer** *noun* (also esp. *Brit.* **-iser**)

polarography *noun*
• "poe luh ROGGRA fee"
• the analysis by measurement of current-voltage relationships in electrolysis between mercury electrodes.
• [as POLAR + Greek *graphia* writing]
• **polarographic** *adjective*

polder *noun*
• "POLE dur"
• a piece of low-lying land reclaimed from the sea or a river, esp. in the Netherlands.
• [Dutch]

polemic *noun*
• "puh LEMMIC"
• a controversial discussion.
• [medieval Latin *polemicus* from Greek *polemikos* from *polemos* war]
• **polemically** *adverb*
• **polemicist** *noun* "puh LEMMA sist"
• **polemicize** *verb* (also esp. *Brit.* **-ise**)

polenta *noun*
• "puh LENTA"
• cornmeal boiled in water and often baked or fried.
• [Italian from Latin, = pearl barley]

poliomyelitis *noun*
• "poley oh my a LITE iss"
• an infectious viral disease that affects the central nervous system and which can cause temporary or permanent paralysis.
• [modern Latin from Greek *polios* grey + *muelos* marrow + *-itis*, forming feminine of adjectives in *-itēs* (with *nosos* 'disease' implied)]

poliovirus *noun*
• "POLEY oh vie russ"
• any of a group of enteroviruses, including those that cause poliomyelitis.
• [abbreviation of POLIOMYELITIS + VIRUS]

polis *noun*
• "POE liss"
• a city state, esp. in ancient Greece.
• [Greek, = city]

politburo *noun*
• "PAUL it byoor oh"
• the principal policy-making committee of a Communist party, esp. in the former USSR.
• [Russian *politbyuro* from *politícheskoe byuró* political bureau]

politesse *noun*
• "polly TESS"
• formal politeness.
• [French]

politic *adjective*
• "POLLA tick"
• (of an action) judicious, expedient.
• [ultimately from Greek *politikos* from *politēs* citizen, from *polis* city]
• **politicly** *adverb*

political *adjective*
• "puh LITTA k'll"
• of or concerning the state or its government, or public affairs generally.
• [as POLITIC]
• **politically** *adverb*

politician *noun*
• "polla TISH'n"
• a person engaged in or concerned with politics, esp. as a practitioner.
• [as POLITIC]

politicize *verb*
ALSO SPELLED: esp. *Brit.* **-ise**
• "puh LITTA size"
• give a political character to.
• [as POLITIC]
• **politicization** *noun* (also esp. *Brit.* **-isation**)

politico *noun*
• "puh LITTA co"
• a politician or political enthusiast.
• [Spanish or Italian (as POLITIC)]

politics *noun*
• "POLLA ticks"
• the art and science of government.
• [as POLITIC]

polity *noun*
• "POLLA tee"
• a form or process of civil government or constitution.
• [Latin *politia* from Greek *politeia* from *politēs* citizen, from *polis* city]

polka *noun*
• "POLE kuh" or "POE kuh"
• a lively dance of Bohemian origin for couples in duple time.
• [French and German from Czech *půlka* half-step, from *půl* half]

poll *noun*
• "POLE"
• the process of voting at an election.
• [Middle English, originally = head, perhaps from Middle Dutch *pol* top, summit]
HOMOPHONES: *pole, Pole*

pollard *noun*
• "PAWL'rd"
• an animal that has lost or cast its horns; an ox, sheep, or goat of a hornless breed.
• [as POLL]

pollen *noun*
• "PAWL 'n"
• the fine dust-like grains discharged from the male part of a flower containing the gamete that fertilizes the female ovule.
• [Latin *pollen pollinis* fine flour, dust]

pollex *noun*
• "PAWL ex"
• the innermost digit of a forelimb, usu. the thumb in primates.
• [Latin, = thumb or big toe]

pollinate *verb*
• "PAWL 'n ate"
• fertilize (a plant) with pollen.
• [as POLLEN]
• **pollination** *noun*
• **pollinator** *noun*

polling *noun*
• "POLE ing"
• the registering or casting of votes.
• [as POLL]

polliniferous *adjective*
• "pawl 'n IFFER us"
• bearing or producing pollen.
• [as POLLEN + *-fer* producing, from Latin *ferre* bear]

pollock *noun*
ALSO SPELLED: **pollack**
• "PAWL uck"
• a greenish food fish of the cod family, *Pollachius virens*, inhabiting the N Atlantic, having a characteristic protruding jaw; an important food fish.
• [earlier (Scots) *podlock*: origin unknown]

pollster *noun*
• "POLE stur"
• a person who conducts or analyzes opinion polls.
• [as POLL]

pollute *verb*
• "puh LOOT"
• contaminate or defile (the environment).
• [Middle English from Latin *polluere pollut-*]
• **pollutant** *adjective*
• **polluted** *adjective*
• **polluter** *noun*
• **pollution** *noun*

Pollyanna *noun*
• "polly ANNA"
• a cheerful optimist; an excessively cheerful person.
• [unfailingly optimistic character in a novel (1913) by E. Porter]
• **Pollyannaish** *adjective*
• **Pollyannaism** *noun*

pollywog *noun*
ALSO SPELLED: **polliwog**
• "POLLY wog"
• a tadpole.
• [earlier *polwigge*, *polwygle* from POLL + wiggle]

polonaise *noun*
• "pawla NAZE"
• a dance of Polish origin, consisting chiefly of an intricate march or procession in triple time.
• [French, feminine of *polonais* Polish, from medieval Latin *Polonia* Poland]

polonium *noun*
• "puh LONEY um"
• a rare radioactive metallic element, occurring naturally in uranium ores.
• [French & modern Latin from medieval Latin *Polonia* Poland (the native country of Marie Curie, its discoverer d.1934)]

poltergeist *noun*
• "POLE tur geist" ("GEIST" rhymes with *PRICED*)
• a noisy mischievous ghost, esp. one manifesting itself by physical damage.
• [German from *poltern* create a disturbance + *Geist* ghost]

poltroon *noun*
• "pawl TROON"
• a spiritless coward.
• [French *poltron* from Italian *poltrone* perhaps from *poltro* sluggard]
• **poltroonery** *noun*

poly *noun*
• "POLLY"
• polyester.
• [abbreviation]

polyacrylamide *noun*
• "polly a CRILLA mide"
• a synthetic resin made by polymerizing acrylamide, esp. a water-soluble polymer used to form or stabilize gels and as a thickening or clarifying agent.
• [POLYMER + ACRYLAMIDE]

polyamide *noun*
• "polly AM ide"
• any of a class of condensation polymers produced from the interaction of an amino group of one molecule and a carboxylic acid group of another, and which includes many synthetic fibres such as nylon.
• [as POLYMER + AMIDE]

polyandry *noun*
• "POLLY andry"
• polygamy in which a woman has more than one husband.
• [Greek *polu-* from *polus* much, *polloi* many + *andry* from Greek *anēr andros* man]
• **polyandrous** *adjective*

polyanthus *noun*
• "polly ANTH us"
• a plant cultivated from hybridized primulas.
• [modern Latin, from Greek *polu-* from *polus* much, *polloi* many + Greek *anthos* flower]

polybag *noun*
• "POLLY bag"
• a bag made of polyethylene, used esp. for packaging etc.
• [POLYETHYLENE + 'bag']
• **polybagged** *adjective*
• **polybagging** *noun*

polycarbonate *noun*
• "polly CARB'n ate"
• any of a class of polymers in which the units are linked through a carbonate group, mainly used as moulding materials.
• [POLYMER + CARBONATE]

polychaete *noun*
- "POLLY keet"
- any aquatic annelid worm of the class Polychaeta, including lugworms and ragworms, having numerous bristles on the fleshy lobes of each body segment.
- [Greek *polu-* from *polus* much, *polloi* many + *khaitē* mane (taken to mean 'bristle')]
- **polychaetan** *adjective*
- **polychaetous** *adjective*

polychlorinated *adjective*
- "polly CLOR 'n ated"
- designating any of several toxic aromatic compounds containing two benzene molecules in which hydrogens have been replaced by chlorine atoms, formed as waste in industrial processes.
- [POLYMER + CHLORINATE]

polychrome *adjective*
- "POLLY crome"
- painted, printed, or decorated in many colours.
- [French from Greek *polukhrōmos* (*polus* much, *polloi* many, *khrōma* colour)]
- **polychromatic** *adjective*
- **polychromatism** *noun*
"polly CROW muh tizm"
- **polychromed** *adjective*
- **polychromic** *adjective*
- **polychromous** *adjective*

polychromy *noun*
- "POLLY crome ee"
- the art of painting in several colours, esp. as applied to ancient pottery, architecture, etc.
- [as POLYCHROME]

polycotton *noun*
- "POLLY cot'n"
- fabric made from a mixture of cotton and polyester fibre.
- [POLYESTER + 'cotton' from Old French *coton* from Arabic *ḳuṭn*]

polycrystalline *adjective*
- "polly CRISSTA line" or "polly CRISSTA leen"
- (of a solid substance) consisting of many crystalline parts at various orientations, e.g. a metal casting.
- [Greek *polu-* from *polus* much, *polloi* many + CRYSTAL]

polycyclic *adjective*
- "polly SIKE lick"
- having more than one ring of atoms in the molecule.
- [Greek *polu-* from *polus* much, *polloi* many + CYCLE]

polycystic *adjective*
- "polly SIS tick"
- designating a disease in which an organ exhibits diffuse cystic change.
- [Greek *polu-* from *polus* much, *polloi* many + CYST]

polydactyl *adjective*
- "polly DACT'll"
- (of a person or animal) having more than five fingers or toes on one (or on each) hand or foot.
- [Greek *polu-* from *polus* much, *polloi* many + DACTYL]

polydrug *adjective*
- "POLLY drug"
- of, relating to, or designating, (the abuse of) several drugs together.
- [Greek *polu-* from *polus* much, *polloi* many + 'drug' from Old French *drogue*, of unknown origin]

polyester *noun*
- "polly ESTER"
- any of a group of condensation polymers used to form synthetic fibres or to make resins.
- [as POLYMER + ESTER]

polyethylene *noun*
- "polly ETH'll een"
- a tough light thermoplastic polymer of ethylene, usu. translucent and flexible or opaque and rigid, used for packaging and insulating materials.
- [as POLYMER + ETHYLENE]

polygamous *adjective*
- "puh LIGGA muss"
- having more than one wife or husband at the same time.
- [Greek *polugamos* (*polus* much, *polloi* many, *-gamos* marrying)]
- **polygamist** *noun*
- **polygamously** *adverb*
- **polygamy** *noun*

polygene *noun*
- "POLLY jeen"
- each of a group of independent genes that collectively affect a characteristic.
- [Greek *polu-* from *polus* much, *polloi* many + GENE]
- **polygenic** *adjective* "polly JENNIC"

polygenesis *noun*
- "polly JENNA sis"
- the (usu. postulated) origination of a race or species from several independent stocks.
- [Greek *polu-* from *polus* much, *polloi* many + GENESIS]
- **polygenetic** *adjective* "polly juh NETTIC"

polyglot *adjective*
- "POLLY glot"
- of many languages.
- [French *polyglotte* from Greek *poluglōttos* (*polus* much, *polloi* many, *glōtta* tongue)]
- **polyglotism** *noun* (also **polyglottism**)

polygon *noun*
- "POLLY gon"
- a plane figure with usu. four or more sides and angles.
- [Late Latin *polygonum* from Greek *polugōnon* (*polus* much, *polloi* many + *-gōnos* angled)]
- **polygonal** *adjective* "puh LIGGA n'll"

polygonum *noun*
- "puh LIG 'n um"
- any plant of the genus *Polygonum*, with small bell-shaped flowers.
- [modern Latin from Greek *polugonon*]

polygraph *noun*
- "POLLY graff"
- a machine designed to detect and record changes in several different physiological characteristics (e.g. rates of pulse and breathing), used esp. as a lie detector.
- [Greek *polu-* from *polus* much, *polloi* many + *graphia* writing]
- **polygrapher** *noun*

polygyny *noun*
- "puh LIDGE a nee"
- polygamy in which a man has more than one wife.
- [Greek *polu-* from *polus* much, *polloi* many + *gyny* from Greek *gunē* woman]
- **polygynous** *adjective* "puh LIDGE a nuss"

polyhedron *noun*
- "polly HEED r'n"
- a solid figure with many (usu. more than six) faces.
- [Greek *poluedron* neuter of *poluedros* (*polus* much, *polloi* many, *hedra* base)]
- **polyhedral** *adjective*

polyhistor *noun*
- "polly HISTER"
- a person of much or varied learning; a great scholar.
- [Latin]

polymath *noun*
- "POLLY math"
- a person of much or varied learning; a great scholar.
- [Greek *polumathēs* (*polus* much, *polloi* many, *math-* stem *manthanō* learn)]
- **polymathic** *adjective*
- **polymathy** *noun* "puh LIMMA thee" (with "TH" as in *THIN*)

polymer *noun*
- "POLLA mur"
- a compound composed of one or more large molecules that are formed from repeated units of smaller molecules.
- [German from Greek *polumeros* having many parts (*polus* much, *polloi* many, *meros* share)]
- **polymeric** *adjective* "polla MARE ick"
- **polymerism** *noun*
- **polymerization** *noun* (also esp. *Brit.* **-isation**)
- **polymerize** *verb* (also esp. *Brit.* **-ise**)

polymerase *noun*
- "POLLA mur ace"
- any enzyme which catalyzes the formation of a polymer, esp. of DNA or RNA.
- [as POLYMER]

polymerous *adjective*
- "puh LIMMER us"
- having many parts.
- [as POLYMER]

polymorphism *noun*
- "polly MORF izm"
- the existence of various different forms in the successive stages of the development of an organism.
- [Greek *polu-* from *polus* much, *polloi* many + METAMORPHOSIS]
- **polymorphic** *adjective*
- **polymorphous** *adjective*

Polynesian *adjective*
- "polla NEE zh'n"
- of or relating to Polynesia in the central Pacific.

polynomial *noun*
- "polly NO mee 'll"
- an expression of more than two algebraic terms, esp. the sum of several terms that contain different powers of the same variable(s).
- [Greek *polu-* from *polus* much, *polloi* many, after *multinomial*]

polynucleotide *noun*
- "polly NEW clee a tide"
- a polymeric compound that is composed of many nucleotides.
- [Greek *polu-* from *polus* much, *polloi* many + NUCLEOTIDE]

polynya *noun*
- "puh LIN yuh"
- a stretch of open water surrounded by ice, esp. in the Arctic seas.
- [Russian from *pole* field]

polyolefin *noun*
- "polly OH luh fin"
- a synthetic resin that is a polymer of an olefin.
- [as POLYMER + OLEFIN]

polyp *noun*
- "POLLIP"
- a small usu. benign growth protruding from a mucous membrane.
- [French *polype* from Latin *polypus* from Greek *pōlupos*, *polupous* cuttlefish (*polus* much, *polloi* many, *pous podos* foot)]

polypary *noun*
- "POLLIP airy"
- the common stem or support of a colony of polyps, marine animals such as jellyfish, corals, and sea anemones.
- [modern Latin *polyparium* (as POLYP)]

polypeptide *noun*
- "polly PEP tide"
- a peptide formed by the combination of about ten or more amino acids.
- [German *Polypeptid* (as Greek *polu-* from *polus* much, *polloi* many, PEPTONE)]

polyphase *adjective*
- "POLLY faze"
- (of a device or circuit) designed to supply or use simultaneously several alternating currents of the same voltage but with different phases.
- [Greek *polu-* from *polus* much, *polloi* many + PHASE]
- **polyphasic** *adjective* "polly FAY zick"

polyphenol *noun*
- "polly FEE nawl"
- a compound containing more than one phenolic hydroxyl group.
- [Greek *polu-* from *polus* much, *polloi* many + PHENOL]

polyphony *noun*
- "puh LIFFA nee"
- the style of simultaneously combining a number of parts, each forming an individual melody and harmonizing with the others.
- [Greek *poluphōnia* (*polus* much, *polloi* many, *phōnē* voice, sound)]
- **polyphonal** *adjective*
- **polyphonic** *adjective* "polly FONNIC"
- **polyphonically** *adverb*
- **polyphonous** *adjective*

polyphosphate *noun*
- "polly FOSS fate"
- any of various complex phosphates, used esp. in detergents or as food additives.
- [Greek *polu-* from *polus* much, *polloi* many + PHOSPHATE]

polyphyletic *adjective*
- "polly fie LETTIC"
- (of a group of organisms) derived from more than one common evolutionary ancestor or ancestral group.
- [Greek *polu-* from *polus* much, *polloi* many + PHYLETIC]

polyploid *noun*
- "POLLY ploid"
- a nucleus or organism that contains more than two sets of chromosomes.
- [German (Greek *polu-* from *polus* much, *polloi* many + HAPLOID)]
- **polyploidy** *noun* "POLLY ploidy"

polypod *adjective*
- "POLLY pod"
- having many feet.
- [French *polypode* from Greek (as POLYP)]

polypody *noun*
- "POLLY poe dee"
- any fern of the genus *Polypodium*, usu. found in woods growing on trees, walls, and stones.
- [Latin *polypodium* from Greek *polupodion* (as POLYP)]

polypoid *adjective*
- "POLLIP oid"
- of or like a polyp.
- [as POLYP]

polypropylene *noun*
- "polly PRO puh leen"
- any of various polymers of propylene including thermoplastic materials used for films, fibres, or moulding materials.
- [POLYMER + PROPYLENE]

polyrhythm *noun*
- "POLLY rith'm" (with "TH" as in *THEM*)
- the use of two or more different rhythms simultaneously.
- [Greek *polu-* from *polus* much, *polloi* many + RHYTHM]
- **polyrhythmic** *adjective*

polysaccharide *noun*
- "polly SACKA ride"
- any of a group of carbohydrates, including starch, cellulose, and glycogen, whose molecules consist of a number of sugar molecules bonded together.
- [Greek *polu-* from *polus* much, *polloi* many + SACCHARIDE]

polysemy *noun*
- "puh LISSA mee" or "polly SEEMY"
- the existence of many meanings (of a word etc.).
- [Greek *polu-* from *polus* much, *polloi* many + Greek *sēma* sign]
- **polysemic** *adjective* "polly SEE mick"
- **polysemous** *adjective* "puh LISSA muss" or "polly SEEM us"

polystyrene *noun*
- "polly STYE reen"
- a thermoplastic polymer of styrene, usu. hard and colourless or expanded with a gas to produce a lightweight rigid white substance, used for insulation and in packaging.
- [POLYMER + STYRENE]

polysyllabic *adjective*
- "polly suh LABBIC"
- (of a word) having many syllables.
- [as POLYSYLLABLE]
- **polysyllabically** *adverb*

polysyllable *noun*
- "POLLY silla bull"
- a polysyllabic word.
- [Greek *polu-* from *polus* much, *polloi* many + SYLLABLE]

polytechnic *noun*
- "polly TECK nick"
- an institution of higher education offering courses in many (esp. vocational) subjects at degree level or below.
- [French *polytechnique* from Greek *polutekhnos* (*polus* much, *polloi* many, *tekhnē* art)]

polytetrafluoroethylene *noun*
- "polly tetra floro ETH'll een"
- a tough translucent polymer resistant to chemicals and used to coat cooking utensils etc.
- [POLYMER + Greek *tetra* four + FLUORINE + ETHYLENE]

polytheism *noun*
- "polly THEE izm" (with "TH" as in *THICK*)
- the belief in or worship of more than one god.
- [French *polythéisme* from Greek *polutheos* of many gods (*polus* much, *polloi* many, *theos* god)]
- **polytheist** *noun*
- **polytheistic** *adjective* "polly thee ISTIC"

polythene *noun*
- "POLLY theen"
- polyethylene.
- [as POLYETHYLENE]

polytonality *noun*
- "polly toe NALA tee"
- the simultaneous use of two or more keys in a composition.
- [Greek *polus* much, *polloi* many + 'tonal' from Old French *ton* or Latin *tonus* from Greek *tonos* tension, tone, from *teinō* stretch]
- **polytonal** *adjective* "polly TONE'll"

polyunsaturate *noun*
- "polly un SATCHER ate"
- a polyunsaturated fat or fatty acid.
- [as POLYUNSATURATED]

polyunsaturated *adjective*
- "polly un SATCHER ated"
- (of a compound, esp. a fat or oil molecule) containing several double or triple bonds and thus not encouraging the formation of cholesterol in the blood.
- [Greek *polus* much, *polloi* many + UNSATURATED]

polyurethane *noun*
- "polly YURA thane"
- a polymer used in adhesives, paints, plastics, rubbers, foams, etc.
- [POLYMER + URETHANE]

polyvalent *adjective*
- "polly VALE 'nt"
- having a valence of more than two, or several valencies.
- [Greek *polus* much, *polloi* many + VALENCE]
- **polyvalence** *noun*

polyvinyl *noun*
- "polly VINE'll"
- a soft plastic polymer used in paints and adhesives.
- [POLYMER + VINYL]

polyzoan *noun*
- "polly ZO 'n"
- any aquatic invertebrate animal of the group Bryozoa (now regarded as comprising the phyla Ectoprocta and Entoprocta), which form colonies often suggesting mossy growths on rocks, seaweeds, etc.
- [Greek *polu-* from *polus* much, *polloi* many + *zōia* animals]

pomace *noun*
- "PUM iss"
- (esp. in cider making) the pulpy residue remaining after fruit has been crushed to extract its juice.
- [medieval Latin *pomacium* cider, from Latin *pomum* apple]

HOMOPHONES: *pumice*

pomade *noun*
- "puh MADE" or "puh MOD"
- scented ointment for the hair and the skin of the head.
- [French *pommade* from Italian *pomata* from medieval Latin from Latin *pomum* apple (from which it was originally made)]

pomander *noun*
- "puh MANDER"
- a ball of mixed aromatic substances placed in a cupboard etc. or carried in a box, bag, etc. as a protection against infection.
- [earlier *pom(e)amber* from Anglo-French from Old French *pome d'embre* from medieval Latin *pomum de ambra* apple of ambergris]

pomarine *adjective*
- "POMMER ine"
- designating a large, Arctic-breeding jaeger, *Stercocarius pomarinus*, having dark brown plumage, sometimes with pale underparts.
- [French *pomarin* from Greek *pōma* lid + *rhin-* nose, all jaegers having the nostrils somewhat covered by a horny plate forming the ridge of the bill]

pome *noun*
- "POME"
- a firm-fleshed fruit in which the carpels from the central core enclose the seeds, e.g. the apple, pear, and quince.
- [Old French, ultimately from *poma* pl. of Latin *pomum* fruit, apple]

HOMOPHONES: *poem*

pomegranate *noun*
- "POMMA grannit"
- an orange-sized fruit with a tough golden-orange outer skin containing many seeds in a red pulp.
- [Old French *pome grenate* (as POME, Latin *granatum* having many seeds, from *granum* seed)]

pomelo *noun*
- "PUMMA lo"
- the largest citrus fruit, with a thick yellow skin and bitter pulp.
- [19th c.: origin unknown]

Pomeranian *noun*
- "pommer AY nee 'n"
- a breed of small dog with long silky hair, a pointed muzzle, a tail curling over the back, and pricked ears.
- [*Pomerania* in N Europe, now divided between Germany and Poland]

pomfret *noun*
- "POM frut"

• a deep-bodied fish of open seas, of the family Bramidae, typically having scales on the dorsal and anal fins.
• [apparently from Portuguese *pampo*]

pommel *noun*
• "PUM'll"
• a knob, esp. at the end of a sword hilt.
• [Old French *pomel* from Romanic *pomellum* (unrecorded), diminutive of Latin *pomum* fruit, apple]
HOMOPHONES: *pummel*

pomology *noun*
• "puh MOLLA jee"
• the science of fruit growing.
• [Latin *pomum* fruit + Greek *logos* word]
• **pomological** *adjective*
• **pomologist** *noun*

pompadour *noun*
• "POMPA dore"
• a woman's hairstyle with the hair in a high turned-back roll around the face.
• [the Marquise de *Pompadour*, mistress of Louis XV of France, d.1764]
• **pompadoured** *adjective*

pompano *noun*
• "POMPA no"
• any of various tropical fishes having a deep, laterally compressed, angular body, many of which are caught for sport.
• [Spanish *pámpano*]

pompous *adjective*
• "POM pus"
• self-important, affectedly grand or solemn.
• [Old French *pompeux* from Late Latin *pomposus* from Latin *pompa* from Greek *pompē* procession, pomp, from *pempō* send]
• **pomposity** *noun* "pom POSSA tee"
• **pompously** *adverb*
• **pompousness** *noun*

ponderosa *noun*
• "ponder OH suh"
• a pine tree of western N America, *Pinus ponderosa*.
• [modern Latin, feminine of Latin *ponderosus*: see PONDEROUS]

ponderous *adjective*
• "PONDER us"
• heavy; unwieldy.
• [Latin *ponderosus* from *pondus -eris* weight]
• **ponderously** *adverb*
• **ponderousness** *noun*

pongal *noun*
• "PONG 'll"
• the Tamil New Year festival at which new rice is cooked.
• [Tamil *poṅkal* boiling]

pongee *noun*
• "pon JEE"
• a soft usu. unbleached type of Chinese silk fabric.
• [perhaps from Chinese dialect *pun-chī* own loom, i.e. homemade]

pongid *noun*
• "PON jid"
• any ape of the family Pongidae, including gorillas, chimpanzees, and orangutans.
• [modern Latin *Pongidae* from *Pongo* the genus name from Congolese *mpongo*]

poniard *noun*
• "PON yurd"
• a small slim dagger.
• [French *poignard* from Old French *poignal* from medieval Latin *pugnale* from Latin *pugnus* fist]

pönnukökur *noun*
• "PONNA kook ur" ("KOOK" rhymes with *BOOK*)
• an originally Icelandic crepe made with eggs, sugar, and milk, often served sprinkled with both white and brown sugar and rolled.
• [Icelandic]

pons *noun*
• "PONZ"
• the part of the brain stem that links the medulla oblongata and the thalamus.
• [Latin, = bridge]

pontifex *noun*
• "PONTA fex"
• a member of the principal college of priests in ancient Rome.
• [Latin *pontifex -ficis* from *pons pontis* bridge + *-fex* from *facere* make]

pontiff *noun*
• "PON tiff"
• the Pope.
• [French *pontife* (as PONTIFEX)]
• **pontifical** *adjective* "pon TIFFA k'll"
• **pontifically** *adverb*

pontificate *verb*
• "pon TIFFA cate"
• be pompously dogmatic.
• [Latin *pontificatus* (as PONTIFEX)]
• **pontification** *noun*

Ponzi *adjective*
• "PONZY"
• designating a form of fraud in which belief in the success of a non-existent enterprise is fostered by payment of quick returns to the first investors from money invested by others.
• [C. *Ponzi*, perpetrator of such a fraud in 1919–20, d.1949]

popinjay *noun*
• "POPPIN jay"
• a fop, a conceited person.
• [Old French *papingay* etc. from Spanish *papagayo* from Arabic *babaġā*: assimilated to 'jay']

poplar *noun*
- "POP lur"
- any tree of the genus *Populus*, with a usu. rapidly growing trunk and tremulous leaves.
- [Anglo-French *popler* from Latin *populus*]

poplin *noun*
- "POP lin"
- a plain-woven fabric usu. of cotton, with a corded surface.
- [obsolete French *papeline* perhaps from Italian *papalina* (feminine) PAPAL, from the papal town Avignon where it was made]

popliteal *adjective*
- "pop LITTY 'll" or "popla TEE 'll"
- of the hollow at the back of the knee.
- [modern Latin *popliteus* from Latin *poples -itis* this hollow]

poppet *noun*
- "POPPIT"
- a small or endearing person.
- [Middle English *popet(te)*, ultimately from Latin *pup(p)a*: compare PUPPET]

populace *noun*
- "POP yuh liss"
- the people living in a given area.
- [French from Italian *popolaccio* from *popolo* people + *-accio* pejorative suffix]

HOMOPHONES: *populous*

popular *adjective*
- "POP yuh lur"
- liked or admired by many people or by a specified group.
- [Latin *popularis* from *populus* people]
- **popularism** *noun*
- **popularity** *noun* "pop yuh LERRA tee"
- **popularization** *noun* (also esp. *Brit.* **-isation**)
- **popularize** *verb* (also esp. *Brit.* **-ise**)
- **popularizer** *noun* (also esp. *Brit.* **-iser**)
- **popularly** *adverb*

populate *verb*
- "POP yuh late"
- inhabit; form the population of (a town, country, etc.).
- [medieval Latin *populare populat-* (as POPULAR)]

population *noun*
- "pop yuh LAY sh'n"
- the inhabitants of a place, country, etc. referred to collectively.
- [Late Latin *populatio* from *populus* people]

populist *noun*
- "POP yuh list"
- a member or adherent of a political party seeking support mainly from the ordinary people.
- [Latin *populus* people]
- **populism** *noun*

populous *adjective*
- "POP yoo luss"
- having many inhabitants; densely populated.
- [Late Latin *populosus* (as POPULIST)]
- **populously** *adverb*
- **populousness** *noun*

HOMOPHONES: *populace*

porbeagle *noun*
- "POR bee g'll"
- a large shark of the N Atlantic and Mediterranean, *Lamna nasus*, having a pointed snout.
- [18th-c. Cornish dialect, of unknown origin]

porcelain *noun*
- "PORSA lin"
- a hard vitrified translucent ceramic.
- [French *porcelaine* cowrie, porcelain, from Italian *porcellana* from *porcella* diminutive of *porca* sow, from Latin *porca* feminine of *porcus* pig]
- **porcelainize** *verb* (also esp. *Brit.* **-ise**)

porcine *adjective*
- "POR sine"
- of or like pigs.
- [French *porcin* or from Latin *porcinus* from *porcus* pig]

porcini *noun*
- "por CHEENY"
- a mushroom with a glossy brown cap and a fat stem.
- [Italian, lit. 'little pigs']

porcupine *noun*
- "PORK yoo pine"
- any rodent of the family Erethizontidae native to the Americas, esp. the common porcupine *Erethizon dorsatum*, or of the family Hystricidae native to Africa, Asia, and SE Europe, having defensive spines or quills.
- [Middle English (originally applied to a European animal) from Old French *porc espin* from Provençal *porc espi(n)*, ultimately from Latin *porcus* pig + *spina* thorn]

pore *verb*
- "PORE"
- be absorbed in studying (a book etc.).
- [perhaps from Old English *puriān* (unrecorded)]

HOMOPHONES: *poor, pour*

porgy *noun*
- "PORG ee"
- any of numerous fishes found esp. in N American Atlantic coastal waters, esp. a fish of the family Sparidae, which includes several food fishes.
- [18th c.: origin uncertain: compare Spanish & Portuguese *pargo*]

pornography *noun*
- "por NOGGRA fee"
- the explicit description or exhibition of sexual activity in literature, films, etc., intended to stimulate erotic rather than aesthetic or emotional feelings.

• [Greek *pornographos* writing about prostitutes, from *pornē* prostitute + *graphō* write]
• **pornographer** *noun*
• **pornographic** *adjective*
• **pornographically** *adverb*

porous *adjective*
• "POR us"
• full of pores.
• [Old French *poreux* from Latin *porus* from Greek *poros* passage, pore]
• **porosity** *noun* "por OSSA tee"
• **porously** *adverb*
• **porousness** *noun*

porphyria *noun*
• "por FEERY uh"
• any of a group of genetic disorders associated with abnormal metabolism of various pigments.
• [modern Latin from PORPHYRIN]

porphyrin *noun*
• "POR fur in"
• any of a class of pigments whose molecules contain a flat ring of four linked heterocyclic rings, occurring widely in nature esp. as derivatives containing metal atoms, e.g. heme and chlorophyll.
• [Greek *porphura* purple]

porphyry *noun*
• "POR fur ee"
• a hard rock quarried in ancient Egypt, composed of crystals of white or red feldspar in a red matrix.
• [medieval Latin *porphyreum* from Greek *porphuritēs* from *porphura* purple]
• **porphyritic** *adjective* "por fur ITTIC"

porpoise *noun*
• "POR pus"
• any of various small toothed whales of the family Phocaenidae, esp. of the genus *Phocaena*, with a low triangular dorsal fin and a blunt rounded snout.
• [Old French *po(u)rpois* etc., ultimately from Latin *porcus* pig + *piscis* fish]

porridge *noun*
• "POR idge"
• a dish consisting of oats or another cereal boiled in water or milk.
• [16th c.: alteration of POTTAGE]
• **porridgy** *adjective*

porringer *noun*
• "POR in jur"
• a small bowl, often with a handle, for soup, stew, etc.
• [earlier *pottinger* from Old French *potager* from *potage* (see POTTAGE): -n- as in *messenger* etc.]

portage *noun*
• "por TOZH"
• the carrying of boats or goods between two navigable waters or around an unnavigable section of a river etc.
• [Old French from *porter* from Latin *portare* carry]

portal *noun*
• "PORT 'll"
• a doorway or gate etc., esp. a large and elaborate one.
• [medieval Latin *portale* (neuter adjective) from *porta* gate]

portamento *noun*
• "porta MENTO"
• the act or an instance of gliding from one note to another in singing, playing the violin, etc.
• [Italian, = carrying]

portcullis *noun*
• "port KULL iss"
• a strong heavy grating sliding up and down in vertical grooves, lowered to block a gateway in a fortress etc.
• [Old French *porte coleïce* sliding door, from *porte* door, from Latin *porta* + *col(e)ïce* feminine of *couleïs* sliding, ultimately from Latin *colare* filter]
• **portcullised** *adjective*

Porte *noun*
• "PORT"
• the Ottoman court at Constantinople.
• [French (*la Sublime Porte* = the exalted gate), translation of Turkish title of the central office of the Ottoman government]
HOMOPHONES: *port*

portend *verb*
• "por TEND"
• foreshadow as an omen.
• [Latin *portendere portent-* from *por-* alteration of *pro* in front (of) + *tendere* stretch]

portent *noun*
• "POR tent" or "POR t'nt"
• an omen, a significant sign of something to come.
• [as PORTEND]

portentous *adjective*
• "por TEN tuss"
• like or serving as a portent.
• [as PORTENT]
• **portentously** *adverb*
• **portentousness** *noun*

portfolio *noun*
• "port FOLEY oh"
• a case for keeping loose sheets of paper, drawings, etc.
• [Italian *portafogli* from *portare* carry + *foglio* leaf, from Latin *folium*]

portico *noun*
• "PORTA co"
• a colonnade; a roof supported by columns at regular intervals usu. attached as a porch to a building.
• [Italian from Latin *porticus* porch, from *porta* passage]
• **porticoed** *adjective*

portière *noun*
• "port YARE"
• a curtain hung over a door or doorway.
• [French from *porte* door, from Latin *porta*]

portmanteau *noun*
• "port man TOE" or "port MAN toe"
• a travelling bag for clothes etc., esp. of leather and opening into two equal parts.
• [French *portmanteau* from *porter* carry, from Latin *portare* + *manteau* coat (as MANTLE)]

portobello *noun*
• "porta BELLO"
• a brown variety of the common mushroom, *Agaricus bisporus*, harvested and eaten when mature.
• [origin uncertain]

portolan *noun*
• "PORTO lan"
• a book of sailing directions with charts, descriptions of harbours, etc.
• [Italian *portolano* from *porto* from Latin *portus* port]

portrait *noun*
• "POR trit" or "POR trate"
• a representation of a person or animal, esp. of the face, made by drawing, painting, photography, etc.
• [French, past participle of Old French *portraire* from *por-* alteration of *pro* in front (of) + *traire* draw, from Latin *trahere* portray]
• **portraitist** *noun*

portraiture *noun*
• "PORTRA chur"
• the art of painting or taking portraits.
• [as PORTRAIT]

Portuguese *noun*
• "por chuh GEEZ" (with "GEE" as in *GEEK*)
• a native or national of Portugal.
• [Portuguese *portuguez* from medieval Latin *portugalensis*]

portulaca *noun*
• "porch a LACKA"
• any of various succulent, bright-flowered plants, native to the tropics, of the genus *Portulaca*.
• [Latin, = PURSLANE]

poseur *noun*
• "poe ZUR"
• a person who poses for effect or behaves affectedly.
• [French from *poser* from Late Latin *pausare* pause]

posit *verb*
• "POZZIT"
• state or assume as a fact; postulate.
• [Latin *ponere posit-* place]

position *noun*
• "puh ZISH'n"
• a place occupied by a person or thing.
• [Latin *positio -onis* (as POSIT)]
• **positional** *adjective*
• **positionally** *adverb*
• **positioner** *noun*

positive *adjective*
• "POZZA tiv"
• (of a person) convinced, confident, or overconfident in his or her opinion.
• [Latin *positivus* (as POSIT)]
• **positively** *adverb*
• **positiveness** *noun*
• **positivity** *noun*

positivism *noun*
• "POZZA tiv izm"
• the philosophical system of French philosopher Auguste Comte (d.1857), recognizing only non-metaphysical facts and observable phenomena, and rejecting metaphysics and theism.
• [as POSITIVE]
• **positivist** *noun*
• **positivistic** *adjective*

positron *noun*
• "POZZA tron"
• a subatomic particle with a positive charge equal to the negative charge of an electron and having the same mass as an electron.
• [POSITIVE + ELECTRON]

posse *noun*
• "POSSY"
• a body of men summoned by a sheriff etc. to find a criminal, maintain order, etc.
• [medieval Latin, = power, from Latin *posse* be able]

possess *verb*
• "puh ZESS"
• hold as property; own.
• [Old French *possesser* from Latin *possidēre possess-* from *potis* able + *sedēre* sit]
• **possession** *noun*
• **possessor** *noun*
• **possessory** *adjective* "puh ZESSER ee"

possessive *adjective*
• "puh ZESSIV"
• showing a desire to possess or retain what one already owns.
• [as POSSESS]
• **possessively** *adverb*
• **possessiveness** *noun*

posset *noun*
• "POSSIT"
• a drink made of hot milk curdled with ale, wine, etc., often flavoured with spices, formerly much used as a remedy for colds etc.
• [Middle English *poshote*: origin unknown]

possibility *noun*
• "possa BILLA tee"
• the state or fact of being possible, or an occurrence of this.
• [as POSSIBLE]

possible *adjective*
- "POSSA bull"
- capable of existing or happening; that may be managed, achieved, etc.
- [Latin *possibilis* from *posse* be able]
- **possibly** *adverb*

possum *noun*
- "POSS um"
- any of various small or moderate-sized marsupials of Australasia, chiefly arboreal and typically having a short snout, large eyes, and a prehensile tail.
- [abbreviation of OPOSSUM]

posterior *adjective*
- "poss TEERY ur"
- situated behind or at the back.
- [Latin, comparative of *posterus* following, from *post* after]
- **posteriority** *noun*
- **posteriorly** *adverb*

posterity *noun*
- "poss TERRA tee"
- all succeeding generations.
- [Latin *posteritas -tatis* from *posterus*: see POSTERIOR]

postern *noun*
- "POSS turn"
- a back door.
- [Old French *posterne*, *posterle*, from Late Latin *posterula* diminutive of *posterus*: see POSTERIOR]

postglacial *adjective*
- "post GLAY sh'll"
- formed or occurring after a glacial period.
- [Latin *post* after + GLACIAL]

postgraduate *adjective*
- "POST gradge oo it"
- (of a course of study) carried on after completing a bachelor's degree.
- [Latin *post* after + GRADUATE]

posthumous *adjective*
- "POSS tyuh muss" or "POSS chuh muss"
- occurring after death.
- [Latin *postumus* last (superlative from *post* after): in Late Latin *posth-* by assoc. with *humus* ground]
- **posthumously** *adverb*

postilion *noun*
ALSO SPELLED: **postillion**
- "poss TILL y'n"
- a person who rides the leading left-hand horse of a team or pair drawing a coach etc. when there is no coachman.
- [French *postillon* from Italian *postiglione* post boy, from *posta* post, mail, ultimately from Latin *ponere posit-* place]

postlude *noun*
- "POST lood"
- a piece of esp. organ music played at the conclusion of a church service.
- [Latin *post* after + PRELUDE]

postnatal *adjective*
- "post NATE 'll"
- characteristic of or relating to the period after childbirth.
- [Latin *post* after + NATAL]
- **postnatally** *adverb*

postpaid *adjective*
- "POST pade"
- on which postage has been paid.
- [as 'postage' + 'paid']

postpartum *adjective*
- "post PART um"
- following childbirth.
- [Latin *post partum* after childbirth]

postpone *verb*
- "post PONE"
- put off to a future time; arrange (an event etc.) to take place at a later time; defer.
- [Latin *postponere* (*post* after, *ponere posit-* place)]
- **postponable** *adjective*
- **postponement** *noun*

postposition *noun*
- "POST puh zish'n"
- a word or particle, esp. an enclitic, placed after the word it modifies, e.g. *-ward* in *homeward* and *at* in *the books we looked at*.
- [Late Latin *postpositio* (as POSTPONE)]
- **postpositional** *adjective*

postscript *noun*
- "POST script"
- an additional paragraph or remark, usu. at the end of a letter after the signature and introduced by 'PS'.
- [Latin *postscriptum* neuter past participle of *postscribere* (*post* after, *scribere* write)]

postulant *noun*
- "POSS tyoo l'nt" or "POSS choo l'nt"
- a candidate, esp. for admission into a religious order.
- [French *postulant* or Latin *postulans -antis* (as POSTULATE)]
- **postulancy** *noun*

postulate *verb*
- "POSS tyuh late" or "POSS chuh late"
- assume as a necessary condition, esp. as a basis for reasoning; take for granted.
- [Latin *postulare postulat-* demand]
- **postulation** *noun*

postulator *noun*
- "POSS tyuh later" or "POSS chuh later"
- a person, usu. a priest, who presents a case for the canonization or beatification of a candidate.
- [as POSTULATE]

posture *noun*
- "POSS chur"
- a position of a person's body when sitting or standing.

• [French from Italian *postura* from Latin *positura* from *ponere posit-* place]
• **postural** *adjective*

posturer *noun*
• "POSS chur ur"
• a person who behaves in a way that is intended to impress or mislead others.
• [as POSTURE]

potable *adjective*
• "POE tuh bull"
• drinkable.
• [French *potable* or Late Latin *potabilis* from Latin *potare* drink]
• **potability** *noun*

potage *noun*
• "paw TOZH"
• thick soup.
• [French (as POTTAGE)]

potassium *noun*
• "puh TASSY um"
• a soft silver-white metallic element occurring naturally in sea water and various minerals, an essential element for living organisms, and forming many useful compounds used industrially.
• [from 'potash' (17th-c. *pot-ashes* from Dutch *pot-asschen*: originally obtained by leaching vegetable ashes and evaporating the solution in iron pots)]
• **potassic** *adjective*

potation *noun*
• "poe TAY sh'n"
• a drink.
• [Old French *potation* or Latin *potatio* from *potare* drink]

potato *noun*
• "puh TAY toe"
• a starchy plant tuber that is cooked and used for food.
• [Spanish *patata* var. of Taino *batata*]

Potawatomi *noun*
• "potta WOTTA mee"
• a member of an Aboriginal people living originally around Lake Michigan, now found in southwestern Ontario, Kansas, and Oklahoma.
• [Ojibwa *potewatami*]

poteen *noun*
• "paw TEEN"
• alcohol made illicitly, usu. from potatoes.
• [Irish *poitín* diminutive of *pota* pot]

Potemkin *adjective*
• "puh TEM kin"
• designating things which are sham, insubstantial, or consist of little or nothing behind an impressive facade.
• [after 'Potemkin village', one of the sham villages said to have been built in the Crimea by Russian officer G. *Potemkin*, favourite of Catherine the Great, in advance of a 1787 visit by the empress]

potent *adjective*
• "POE t'nt"
• powerful; strong.
• [Latin *potens -entis* present participle of *posse* be able]
• **potency** *noun*
• **potently** *adverb*

potentate *noun*
• "POE t'n tate"
• a person who possesses great power, esp. a monarch or ruler.
• [Old French *potentat* or Latin *potentatus* dominion (as POTENT)]

potential *adjective*
• "puh TEN sh'll"
• capable of coming into being or action; latent.
• [Late Latin *potentialis* from *potentia* (as POTENT)]
• **potentiality** *noun* "puh tenshy ALA tee"
• **potentially** *adverb*

potentiate *verb*
• "puh TEN shee ate"
• make more powerful, esp. increase the effectiveness of (a drug).
• [POTENT, on the pattern of SUBSTANTIATE]
• **potentiation** *noun*

potentilla *noun*
• "poe t'n TILLA"
• any herbaceous plant or shrub of the genus *Potentilla*; a cinquefoil.
• [medieval Latin, diminutive of Latin *potens* POTENT]

potentiometer *noun*
• "puh tenshy OMMA tur"
• an instrument for measuring or adjusting small electrical potentials.
• [POTENTIAL + Greek *metron* measure]
• **potentiometric** *adjective* "puh tenshy a METRIC"

potion *noun*
• "POE sh'n"
• a liquid medicine, poison, magic charm, etc.
• [Old French from Latin *potio -onis* from *potus* having drunk]

potpourri *noun*
• "poe puh REE"
• a mixture of dried petals and spices used to perfume a room, cupboard, etc.
• [French, = rotten pot]

potsherd *noun*
• "POT shurd"
• a broken piece of ceramic material, esp. one found on an archaeological site.
• ['pot' + SHERD]

pottage *noun*
• "POT idge"

• soup, stew.
• [Old French *potage* from *pot* from popular Latin *potus* drinking cup]

potto *noun*
• “POTTO”
• a West African lemur-like mammal, *Perodicticus potto*.
• [perhaps from Guinea dialect]

pouf *noun*
• “POOF”
• a soft projecting mass of material on a dress, headdress, etc.
• [French, ultimately imitative]
• **poufed** *adjective*
HOMOPHONES: *pouffe, poof*

pouffe *noun*
ALSO SPELLED: **pouf**
• “POOF”
• a large firm cushion used as a low seat or footstool.
• [French *pouf*; ultimately imitative]
HOMOPHONES: *pouf, poof*

poulard *noun*
• “poo LARD”
• a domestic hen that has been spayed and fattened for eating.
• [French *poularde* from *poule* hen]

poult *noun*
• “POLT”
• a young domestic fowl, turkey, pheasant, etc.
• [Middle English, contraction from PULLET]

poulterer *noun*
• “POLT ur ur”
• a dealer in poultry and usu. game.
• [Old French *pouletier* (as PULLET)]

poultice *noun*
• “POLE tiss”
• a soft medicated and usu. heated mass applied to the body and kept in place with muslin etc., for relieving soreness and inflammation.
• [originally *pultes* (pl.) from Latin *puls pultis* pottage, pap, etc.]

poultry *noun*
• “POLE tree”
• domestic fowls (chickens, turkeys, ducks, geese, etc.), esp. as a source of food.
• [Old French *pouletrie* (as POULTERER)]

poundal *noun*
• “POUND’ll”
• a unit of force equal to the force required to give a mass of one pound an acceleration of one foot per second per second.
• [‘pound’ (ultimately from Latin *pondo* Roman pound weight of 12 ounces) + *-al* perhaps after *quintal*]

poutine *noun*
• “poo TEEN”
• *Cdn* a dish of french fries topped with cheese curds and a sauce, usu. gravy.
• [Canadian French]

poverty *noun*
• “POVVER tee”
• the state of being poor; want of the necessities of life.
• [Old French *poverte, poverté* from Latin *paupertas -tatis* from *pauper* poor]

Powhatan *noun*
• “POWA tan” (with “OW” as in *HOW*)
• a member of an Algonquian Indian people of eastern Virginia.
• [Virginia Algonquian]

powwow *noun*
• “POW wow”
• a cultural gathering among some N American Aboriginal peoples, with dancing, music, eating, etc.
• [Algonquian *powah, powwaw* magician (lit. ‘he dreams’)]

practicable *adjective*
• “PRACK ticka bull”
• that can be done or used.
• [French *praticable* from *pratiquer* put into practice (as PRACTICAL)]
• **practicability** *noun*
• **practicableness** *noun*
• **practicably** *adverb*

practical *adjective*
• “PRACTA k’ll”
• of or concerned with practice or use rather than theory.
• [Late Latin *practicus* from Greek *praktikos* from *prassō* do, act]
• **practicality** *noun* “practa CALA tee”
• **practicalness** *noun*

practically *adverb*
• “PRACTIC lee”
• virtually, almost.
• [as PRACTICAL]

practician *noun*
• “prack TISH’n”
• a worker; a practitioner.
• [obsolete French *practicien* from *practique* from medieval Latin *practica* from Greek *praktikē* feminine of *praktikos*: see PRACTICAL]

practicum *noun*
• “PRACTIC um”
• a course of practical training through experience working in a particular field.
• [Late Latin, neuter of *practicus*, from Greek *praktikos*, from *prattein* do]

practitioner *noun*
• “prack TISH’n ur”
• a person practising a profession, esp. medicine.
• [obsolete *practitian* = PRACTICIAN]

praecipe *noun*
- "PREE sip ee"
- a writ demanding action or an explanation of non-action.
- [Latin (the first word of the writ), imperative of *praecipere* enjoin: see PRECEPT]

praenomen *noun*
- "pree NOME 'n"
- an ancient Roman's first or personal name (e.g. *Marcus* Tullius Cicero).
- [Latin from *prae* before + *nomen* name]

praetor *noun*
- "PREETER" or "PREE tor"
- (in ancient Rome) each of two magistrates ranking below consul.
- [French *préteur* or Latin *praetor* (perhaps as Latin *prae-* before, *ire it-* go)]
- **praetorial** *adjective*
- **praetorian** *adjective*
- **praetorship** *noun*

pragmatic *adjective*
- "prag MATTIC"
- dealing with matters with regard to their practical requirements or consequences.
- [Late Latin *pragmaticus* from Greek *pragmatikos* from *pragma -matos* deed]
- **pragmatically** *adverb*
- **pragmatism** *noun* "PRAG muh tizm"
- **pragmatist** *noun*

pragmatics *noun*
- "prag MATTIX"
- the branch of linguistics dealing with language in use.
- [as PRAGMATIC]

prahu *noun*
ALSO SPELLED: **prau**
- "PRAH oo"
- a Malay boat, esp. with a large triangular sail and a canoe-like outrigger.
- [Malay *prāū, prāhū*]

prairie *noun*
- "PRERRY"
- a large area of usu. treeless and flat grassland, esp. in western Canada.
- [French from Old French *praerie*, ultimately from Latin *pratum* meadow]

Prakrit *noun*
- "PROCK rit"
- any of the (esp. ancient or medieval) vernacular dialects of North and Central India existing alongside or derived from Sanskrit.
- [Sanskrit *prākṛta* unrefined: compare SANSKRIT]

praline *noun*
- "PRAY leen" or "PRAW leen"
- a confection made by browning nuts in boiling sugar, often crushed and used as a topping or in ice cream etc.
- [French from Marshal de Plessis-*Praslin*, French soldier d.1675, whose cook invented it]

prana *noun*
- "PRANNA"
- (in Hinduism) breath as a life-giving force.
- [Sanskrit]

prandial *adjective*
- "PRANDY 'll"
- of dinner or lunch.
- [Latin *prandium* meal]

praseodymium *noun*
- "pray zee a DIMMY um"
- a soft silvery metallic element of the lanthanide series, occurring naturally in various minerals and used in catalyst mixtures.
- [German *Praseodym* from Greek *prasios* (adjective) leek-green, from *prason* leek (from its green salts), + German *Didym* DIDYMIUM]

pratie *noun*
- "PRATE ee"
- *Cdn* (*Nfld*) & *Irish* a potato.
- [corruption]

pratincole *noun*
- "PRAT in cole"
- any of various birds of the subfamily Glareolinae, inhabiting sandy and stony areas and feeding on insects.
- [modern Latin *pratincola* from Latin *pratum* meadow + *incola* inhabitant]

prawn *noun*
- "PRON"
- any of various marine crustaceans, resembling a shrimp but usu. larger.
- [Middle English *pra(y)ne*, of unknown origin]

praxis *noun*
- "PRAX iss"
- accepted practice or custom.
- [medieval Latin from Greek, = doing, from *prassō* do]

preadolescent *adjective*
- "pree add'll ESS'nt"
- (of a child) having nearly reached adolescence.
- [Latin *prae* before + ADOLESCENT]
- **preadolescence** *noun*

preamble *noun*
- "PREE amble"
- a preliminary statement or introduction.
- [Late Latin *praeambulus* (adjective) going before (Latin *prae* before, *ambulare* walk)]

preamplifier *noun*
- "pree AMPLA fie ur"
- an electronic device that amplifies a very weak signal (e.g. from a microphone or pickup) and transmits it to a main amplifier.
- [Latin *prae* before + AMPLIFY]
- **preamplified** *adjective*

prebend *noun*
- "PREB'nd"
- an honorary canon.
- [Old French *prebende* from Late Latin

praebenda pension, neuter pl. gerundive of Latin *praebēre* grant, from *prae* forth + *habēre* hold]

prebendal *adjective*
- "preb END'Il"
- of or relating to a prebend or a prebendary.
- [as PREBEND]

prebendary *noun*
- "PREB'nd airy"
- an honorary canon.
- [medieval Latin *praebendarius* (as PREBEND)]
- **prebendaryship** *noun*

prebiotic *adjective*
- "pree by OTTIC"
- existing or occurring before the emergence of life.
- [Latin *prae* before + BIOTIC]

Precambrian *adjective*
- "pree CAME bree 'n" or "pree CAM bree 'n"
- of or relating to the earliest geological era including the whole of the earth's history from its origin about 4,600 million years ago to the beginning of the Cambrian period about 590 million years ago.
- [Latin *prae* before + CAMBRIAN]

precancerous *adjective*
- "pree CAN sur us"
- tending to develop into cancer.
- [Latin *prae* before + 'cancer' from Latin, = crab, cancer, after Greek *karkinos*]

precarious *adjective*
- "pruh KERRY us"
- uncertain; dependent on chance.
- [Latin *precarius* obtained by entreaty, from *prex precis* prayer]
- **precariously** *adverb*
- **precariousness** *noun*

precede *verb*
- "pree SEED"
- come or go before in time, order, importance, etc.
- [Latin *praecedere* (*prae-* before, *cedere cess-* go)]
- **precedence** *noun* "PRESSA dince"

precedent *noun*
- "PRESSA d'nt"
- a previous case or legal decision etc. taken as a guide for subsequent cases or as a justification.
- [as PRECEDE]

precentor *noun*
- "pre SENTER"
- a person who leads the singing or (in a synagogue) the prayers of a congregation.
- [Latin *praecentor* from *praecinere* (*prae-* before, *canere* sing)]
- **precentorship** *noun*

precept *noun*
- "PREE sept"
- a command; a rule of conduct.
- [Latin *praeceptum* neuter past participle of *praecipere praecept-* warn, instruct (as Latin *prae-* before, *capere* take)]

preceptor *noun*
- "pre SEPTER"
- a teacher or instructor.
- [as PRECEPT]
- **preceptorship** *noun*

precession *noun*
- "pre SESH'n"
- the slow movement of the axis of a spinning body around another axis.
- [Late Latin *praecessio* (as PRECEDE)]
- **precess** *verb*
- **precessional** *adjective*

HOMOPHONES: *procession, processional*

precinct *noun*
- "PREE sinct"
- an enclosed or clearly defined area, e.g. around a cathedral, college, etc.
- [medieval Latin *praecinctum* neuter past participle of *praecingere* encircle (as Latin *prae-* before, *cingere* gird)]

preciosity *noun*
- "preshy OSSA tee"
- overrefinement in art or language, esp. in the choice of words.
- [as PRECIOUS]

precious *adjective*
- "PRESH us"
- of great value or worth.
- [Old French *precios* from Latin *pretiosus* from *pretium* price]
- **preciously** *adverb*
- **preciousness** *noun*

precip *noun*
- "pree SIP"
- precipitation.
- [abbreviation]

precipice *noun*
- "PRESSA piss"
- a vertical or steep face of a rock, cliff, mountain, etc.
- [French *précipice* or Latin *praecipitium* falling headlong, precipice (as PRECIPITOUS)]

precipitant *adjective*
- "pre SIPPA t'nt"
- headlong; violently hurried.
- [obsolete French *précipitant* present participle of *précipiter* (as PRECIPITATE)]

precipitate *verb*
- "pre SIPPA tate"
- hasten the occurrence of; cause to occur prematurely.
- [Latin *praecipitare praecipitat-* from *praeceps praecipitis* headlong (*prae-* before, *caput* head)]
- **precipitately** *adverb* "pre SIPPA tut lee"
- **precipitateness** *noun*
- **precipitator** *noun*

precipitation *noun*
- "pre sippa TAY sh'n"
- rain or snow etc. falling to the ground.
- [French *précipitation* or Latin *praecipitatio* (as PRECIPITATE)]

precipitous *adjective*
- "pruh SIPPA tuss"
- of or like a precipice.
- [obsolete French *précipiteux* from Latin *praeceps* (as PRECIPITATE)]
- **precipitously** *adverb*
- **precipitousness** *noun*

précis *noun*
- "PRAY see"
- a summary or abstract, esp. of a text or speech.
- [French, = PRECISE (as n.)]

precise *adjective*
- "pre SICE"
- accurately expressed.
- [French *précis -ise* from Latin *praecidere praecis-* cut short (*prae-* before, *caedere* cut)]
- **precisely** *adverb*
- **preciseness** *noun*
- **precision** *noun* "pre SIZH'n"

preclude *verb*
- "pree CLUDE"
- prevent, exclude.
- [Latin *praecludere praeclus-* (*prae-* before, *claudere* shut)]
- **preclusion** *noun*

precocial *adjective*
- "pre CO sh'll"
- (of a bird) having young that can feed themselves as soon as they are hatched.
- [Latin *praecox -cocis* (as PRECOCIOUS)]

precocious *adjective*
- "pre CO sh'ss"
- (of a person, esp. a child) prematurely developed in some faculty or characteristic.
- [Latin *praecox -cocis* from *praecoquere* ripen fully (*prae-* before, *coquere* cook)]
- **precociously** *adverb*
- **precociousness** *noun*
- **precocity** *noun* "pruh COSSA tee"

precognition *noun*
- "pree cog NISH'n"
- (supposed) foreknowledge, esp. of a supernatural kind.
- [Late Latin *praecognitio* (*prae* before, COGNITION)]
- **precognitive** *adjective* "pree COGNA tiv"

preconceive *verb*
- "pree k'n SEEVE"
- form (an idea or opinion etc.) beforehand.
- [Latin *prae* before + CONCEIVE]

preconception *noun*
- "pree k'n SEP sh'n"
- a preconceived idea.
- [as PRECONCEIVE]

precondition *noun*
- "pree k'n DISH'n"
- a prior condition, that must be fulfilled before other things can be done.
- [Latin *prae* before + CONDITION]

preconize *verb*
ALSO SPELLED: esp. *Brit.* **-ise**
- "PREE kuh nize"
- proclaim or commend publicly.
- [medieval Latin *praeconizare* from Latin *praeco -onis* herald]
- **preconization** *noun* (also esp. *Brit.* **-isation**)

preconscious *adjective*
- "pree CON sh'ss"
- preceding consciousness.
- [Latin *prae* before + CONSCIOUS]
- **preconsciousness** *noun*

precordial *adjective*
- "pree CORDY 'll"
- in front of or about the heart.
- [Latin *prae* before + CORDIAL]

precursor *noun*
- "pree CUR sur"
- a forerunner.
- [Latin *praecursor* from *praecurrere praecurs-* (*prae-* before, *currere* run)]
- **precursory** *adjective*

predacious *adjective*
ALSO SPELLED: **predaceous**
- "pre DAY sh'ss"
- (of an animal) predatory.
- [Latin *praeda* booty: compare *audacious*]

predation *noun*
- "pre DAY sh'n"
- the act of despoiling, ravaging, or plundering.
- [Latin *praedatio -onis* taking of booty, from Latin *praeda* booty]

predator *noun*
- "PREDDA tur"
- an animal naturally preying on others.
- [Latin *praedator* plunderer, from *praedari* seize as plunder, from *praeda* booty]
- **predatorily** *adverb*
- **predatoriness** *noun*
- **predatory** *adjective* "PREDDA tory"

predecease *verb*
- "pree duh SEECE"
- die earlier than (another person).
- [Latin *prae* before + DECEASE]

predecessor *noun*
- "PREDDA sesser" or "PREEDA sesser"
- a former holder of an office or position with respect to a later holder.
- [Old French *predecesseur* from Late Latin *praedecessor* (Latin *prae-* before, *decessor* retiring officer, as DECEASE)]

predella *noun*
- "pre DELLA"

• an altar step, or raised shelf at the back of an altar.
• [Italian, = stool]

predestinarian *noun*
• "pree dest'n AIRY 'n"
• a person who believes in predestination.
• [as PREDESTINATE]

predestinate *verb*
• "pree DEST'n ate"
• determine beforehand.
• [Church Latin *praedestinare praedestinat-* (Latin *prae-* before, *destinare* establish)]
• **predestine** *verb* "pree DESS tin"

predestination *noun*
• "pree dest'n AY sh'n"
• (as a belief or doctrine) the divine foreordaining of all that will happen, esp. with regard to the salvation of some and not others.
• [as PREDESTINATE]

predetermine *verb*
• "pree de TURMIN"
• determine or decree beforehand.
• [Latin *prae* before + DETERMINE]
• **predetermination** *noun*

predicament *noun*
• "pree DICKA m'nt"
• a difficult, unpleasant, or embarrassing situation.
• [Late Latin *praedicamentum* thing predicated: see PREDICATE]

predicant *adjective*
• "PREDDA k'nt"
• (of a religious order, esp. the Dominicans) engaged in preaching.
• [Latin *praedicans* participle of *praedicare* (as PREDICATE)]

predicate *verb*
• "PREDDA cate"
• assert or affirm as true or existent.
• [Latin *praedicare praedicat-* proclaim (*prae-* before, *dicare* declare)]
• **predication** *noun*

predicative *adjective*
• "pruh DICKA tiv"
• (of an adjective or noun) forming or contained in the predicate, as *old* in *the dog is old* (but not in *the old dog*) and *house* in *there is a large house.*
• [Latin *praedicativus* (as PREDICATE)]
• **predicatively** *adverb*

predilection *noun*
• "predda LECK sh'n" or "preeda LECK sh'n"
• a preference or special liking.
• [French *prédilection*, ultimately from Latin *praediligere praedilect-* prefer (*prae-* before, *diligere* select): see DILIGENT]

prednisone *noun*
• "PREDNA zone"
• a synthetic drug similar to cortisone, used to relieve rheumatic and allergic conditions and to treat leukemia.
• [perhaps from *pre*(gnane) (a synthetic hydrocarbon) + *diene* + cort*isone*]

predominantly *adverb*
• "pre DOM'n 'nt lee"
• mainly; for the most part.
• [as PREDOMINATE]

predominate *verb*
• "pre DOM'n ate"
• have or exert control.
• [medieval Latin *praedominari* (Latin *prae-* before, DOMINATE)]
• **predominance** *noun*
• **predominant** *adjective*

predynastic *adjective*
• "pree die NASTIC"
• of or relating to a period before the normally recognized dynasties (esp. of ancient Egypt).
• [Latin *prae* before + DYNASTY]

prefabricate *verb*
• "pree FABBRA cate"
• manufacture sections of (a building or piece of furniture) to enable quick or easy assembly on site.
• [Latin *prae* before + FABRICATE]
• **prefabricated** *adjective*
• **prefabrication** *noun*

preface *noun*
• "PREFF iss"
• an introduction to a book stating its subject, scope, etc.
• [Old French from medieval Latin *praefatia* for Latin *praefatio* from *praefari* (*prae-* before, *fari* speak)]
• **prefatory** *adjective* "PREFFA tory"

prefect *noun*
• "PREE fect"
• a chief officer, magistrate, governor, etc.
• [Latin *praefectus* past participle of *praeficere* set in authority over (*prae-* before, *facere* make)]

prefecture *noun*
• "PREE feck chur"
• a district under the government of a prefect.
• [as PREFECT]
• **prefectural** *adjective*

prefer *verb*
• "pruh FUR"
• choose instead; like better.
• [Old French *preferer* from Latin *praeferre* (*prae-* before, *ferre* bear, carry)]
• **preference** *noun* "PREFFER ince"

preferable *adjective*
• "PREFFER a bull" or "pruh FURRA bull"
• to be preferred.
• [as PREFER]
• **preferability** *noun*
• **preferably** *adverb*

preferential *adjective*
- "preffer EN sh'll"
- of or involving preference.
- [as PREFER]
- **preferentially** *adverb*

preferment *noun*
- "pruh FUR m'nt"
- promotion to office.
- [as PREFER]

prefigure *verb*
- "pre FIG yur"
- represent beforehand by a figure or type.
- [Church Latin *praefigurare* (*prae-* before, FIGURE)]
- **prefiguration** *noun*
- **prefigurative** *adjective*
- **prefigurement** *noun*

pregnant *adjective*
- "PREG n'nt"
- (of a woman or female animal) having a child or young developing in the uterus.
- [French *prégnant* or Latin *praegnans -antis*, earlier *praegnas* (prob. as Latin *prae-* before, *(g)nasci* be born)]
- **pregnancy** *noun*

prehensile *adjective*
- "pree HEN sile"
- (of a tail or limb) capable of grasping.
- [French *préhensile* from Latin *prehendere prehens-* (*prae* before, *hendere* grasp)]

prehension *noun*
- "pre HEN sh'n"
- the action of grasping or seizing.
- [Latin *prehensio* (as PREHENSILE)]

prehistoric *adjective*
- "pree hiss TORIC"
- of or relating to the period before written records.
- [Latin *prae* before + 'historic' (as HISTORIATED)]
- **prehistorian** *noun*
- **prehistorically** *adverb*
- **prehistory** *noun*

prejudice *noun*
- "PREDGE a diss"
- a preconceived opinion.
- [Old French *prejudice* from Latin *praejudicium* (*prae-* before, *judicium* judgment)]
- **prejudicial** *adjective* "predge a DISH'll"
- **prejudicially** *adverb*

prejudiced *adjective*
- "PREDGE a dist"
- not impartial; bigoted.
- [as PREJUDICE]

prelate *noun*
- "PRELLIT"
- a high ecclesiastical dignitary, e.g. a bishop.
- [Old French *prelat* from medieval Latin *praelatus* civil dignitary, past participle (used as a noun) of Latin *praeferre* carry before, place before in esteem]

preliminary *adjective*
- "pruh LIMMA nerry"
- introductory, preparatory; initial.
- [modern Latin *praeliminaris* or French *préliminaire* (Latin *prae* before, *limen liminis* threshold)]
- **preliminarily** *adverb*

prelinguistic *adjective*
- "pree ling GWISTIC"
- existing or occurring before the development of language or the acquisition of speech.
- [Latin *prae* before + LINGUISTIC]

preliterate *adjective*
- "pre LITTER it"
- of or relating to a society or culture that has not developed the use of writing.
- [Latin *prae* before + LITERATE]

prelude *noun*
- "PRAY lood" or "PRELL yood"
- an action, event, or situation serving as an introduction.
- [French *prélude* or medieval Latin *praeludium* from Latin *praeludere praelus-* (*prae-* before, *ludere* play)]
- **preludial** *adjective* "prell YOODY 'll"

premarital *adjective*
- "pree MERRIT'll"
- existing or (esp. of sexual relations) occurring before marriage.
- [Latin *prae* before + MARITAL]

premature *adjective*
- "preema CHUR" or "premma CHUR"
- occurring or done before the usual or proper time; too early.
- [Latin *praematurus* very early (*prae-* before, MATURE)]
- **prematurely** *adverb*
- **prematurity** *noun*

premaxillary *adjective*
- "pree mack SILLER ee"
- in front of the upper jaw.
- [Latin *prae* before + MAXILLA]

premedication *noun*
- "pree medda CAY sh'n"
- medication to prepare for an operation or other treatment.
- [Latin *prae* before + MEDICATION]

premeditate *verb*
- "pree MEDDA tate"
- think out or plan (an action) beforehand.
- [Latin *prae* before + MEDITATE]
- **premeditated** *adjective*
- **premeditation** *noun*

premenopausal *adjective*
- "pree menna POZZ'll"
- preceding menopause.
- [Latin *prae* before + MENOPAUSE]

premenstrual *adjective*
• "pree MEN strull" or "pree MEN stroo 'll"
• of, occurring, or experienced before menstruation.
• [Latin *prae* before + MENSTRUAL]

premier *noun*
• "PREEM yeer" or "PREEM yur" or "PREE meer"
• *Cdn* the first minister of a province or territory.
• [Old French = first, from Latin (as PRIMARY)]
• **premiership** *noun*

premiere *noun*
• "preem YEER" or "prem YARE"
• the first performance or showing of a play, film, etc.
• [French, feminine of *premier* (adjective) (as PREMIER)]

premillennialism *noun*
• "pree mill ENNY 'll izm"
• the doctrine or belief that the Second Coming of Christ will precede the millennium.
• [Latin *prae* before + MILLENNIUM]
• **premillennial** *adjective*
• **premillennialist** *noun*

premise *noun*
ALSO SPELLED: **premiss**
• "PREM iss"
• a previous statement or proposition from which another is inferred or follows as a conclusion.
• [Old French *premisse* and medieval Latin *praemissa* (*propositio*) (proposition) set in front, from Latin *praemittere praemiss-* (*prae-* before, *mittere* send)]

premium *noun*
• "PREEMY um"
• an amount to be paid for a contract of insurance.
• [Latin *praemium* booty, reward (*prae-* before, *emere* buy, take)]

premolar *adjective*
• "pree MOLE ur"
• in front of a molar tooth.
• [Latin *prae* before + MOLAR]

premonition *noun*
• "premma NISH'n"
• a forewarning; a presentiment.
• [Late Latin *praemonitio* from Latin *praemonēre praemonit-* (*prae-* before, *monēre* warn)]
• **premonitorily** *adverb*
• **premonitory** *adjective* "pree MONNA tory"

prenatal *adjective*
• "pree NATE 'll"
• of or concerning the period before childbirth.
• [Latin *prae* before + NATAL]
• **prenatally** *adverb*

preoccupy *verb*
• "pre OCK yuh pie"
• (of a thought etc.) dominate or engross the mind of (a person) to the exclusion of other thoughts.
• [Latin *praeoccupare* seize beforehand]
• **preoccupation** *noun*
• **preoccupied** *adjective*

preoperative *adjective*
• "pre OPPER a tiv"
• of or related to the period or a condition before an operation.
• [Latin *prae* before + OPERATOR]
• **preoperatively** *adverb*

preparation *noun*
• "prepper AY sh'n"
• the act or an instance of preparing; the process of being prepared.
• [French *préparation* from *préparer* or Latin *praeparare* (*prae* before, *parare* make ready)]

preparative *adjective*
• "pruh PERRA tiv"
• preparatory.
• [as PREPARATION]
• **preparatively** *adverb*

preparatory *adjective*
• "PREPPER a tory" or "pruh PERRA tory"
• serving to prepare; introductory.
• [as PREPARATION]

prepense *adjective*
• "pre PENCE"
• deliberate, intentional.
• [alteration of earlier *purpense* from Anglo-French & Old French *purpenser* from *por-* beforehand and *penser* think]

preponderant *adjective*
• "pre PONDER 'nt"
• surpassing in influence, power, number, or importance; predominant, preponderating.
• [Latin *praeponderant-* weighing more]
• **preponderance** *noun*
• **preponderantly** *adverb*

preponderate *verb*
• "pre PONDER ate"
• be greater in number, quantity, or importance.
• [Latin *praeponderare* from *prae-* before and *pondere* consider]

preposition *noun*
• "preppa ZISH'n"
• a word governing (and usu. preceding) a noun or pronoun and expressing a relation to another word or element, as in: 'the man *on* the platform', 'came *after* dinner', 'what did you do it *for*?'.
• [Latin *praepositio* from *praeponere praeposit-* (*prae-* before, *ponere* place)]
• **prepositional** *adjective*
• **prepositionally** *adverb*

prepositive *adjective*
• "pre POZZA tiv"
• (of a word, particle, etc.) that should be placed before.
• [Late Latin *praepositivus* (as PREPOSITION)]

prepossessing *adjective*
• "pree puh ZESSING"
• attractive, appealing.
• [Latin *prae* before + POSSESS]

preposterous *adjective*
• "pre POSS tur us"
• utterly absurd; outrageous; contrary to nature, reason, or common sense.
• [Latin *praeposterus* reversed, absurd (*prae-* before, *posterus* coming after)]
• **preposterously** *adverb*
• **preposterousness** *noun*

prepotent *adjective*
• "pre POE t'nt"
• greater than others in power, influence, etc.
• [Latin *praepotent-* having greater power, from Latin *prae-* before + *posse* be able]
• **prepotence** *noun*
• **prepotency** *noun*

preprandial *adjective*
• "pree PRANDY 'll"
• before dinner or lunch.
• [Latin *prae* before + *prandium* a meal]

preprocessor *noun*
• "pree PROSS esser" or "pree PRO sesser"
• a computer program that modifies data to conform with the input requirements of another program.
• [Latin *prae* before + PROCESSOR]

prepubescent *adjective*
• "pree pyoo BESS'nt"
• occurring prior to puberty.
• [Latin *prae* before + PUBESCENT]

prequel *noun*
• "PREE kwull"
• a story, film, etc., whose events or concerns precede those of an existing work.
• [Latin *prae* before + SEQUEL]

prerequisite *adjective*
• "pree RECKWA zit"
• required as a precondition.
• [Latin *prae* before + REQUISITE]

prerogative *noun*
• "pruh ROGGA tiv"
• a right or privilege exclusive to an individual or class.
• [Latin *praerogativa* privilege (originally to vote first) from *praerogativus* asked first (*prae-* before, *rogare* ask)]

presage *noun*
• "PRESS idge"
• an omen or portent.
• [French *présage*, *présager* from Latin *praesagium* from *praesagire* forebode (*prae-* before, *sagire* perceive keenly)]

presbyopia *noun*
• "prezz bee OH pee uh"
• far-sightedness caused by loss of elasticity of the eye lens, occurring esp. in middle and old age.
• [modern Latin from Greek *presbus* old man + *ōps ōpos* eye]
• **presbyopic** *adjective* "prezz bee OPPIC"

presbyter *noun*
• "PRESS buh tur" or "PREZZ buh tur"
• an elder in the early Christian Church.
• [Church Latin from Greek *presbuteros* elder, comparative of *presbus* old]

presbyterial *noun*
• "press buh TEERY 'll" or "prezz buh TEERY 'll"
• *Cdn* a women's group belonging to a presbytery in the Presbyterian or United Churches.
• [as PRESBYTER]

Presbyterian *noun*
• "press buh TEERY 'n" or "prezz buh TEERY 'n"
• a member of any of various branches of a more or less Calvinistic Protestant denomination based on the principle of ecclesiastical government by presbyteries.
• [Church Latin *presbyterium* (as PRESBYTER)]
• **Presbyterianism** *noun*

presbytery *noun*
• "PRESS buh tree" or "PREZZ buh tree"
• (in the Presbyterian and United Churches) an ecclesiastical body made up of all of the ministers from a specific district together with an equal number of elders.
• [as PRESBYTER]

prescient *adjective*
• "PRESSY 'nt" or "PRESH 'nt"
• having foresight or foreknowledge.
• [Latin *praescire praescient-* know beforehand (*prae-* before, *scire* know)]
• **prescience** *noun*
• **presciently** *adverb*

prescind *verb*
• "pree SIND"
• leave out of consideration.
• [Latin *praescindere* (*prae-* before, *scindere* cut)]

prescribe *verb*
• "pre SCRIBE"
• advise the use of (a medicine etc.), esp. by an authorized prescription.
• [Latin *praescribere praescript-* direct in writing (*prae-* before, *scribere* write)]
• **prescriber** *noun*
HOMOPHONES: *proscribe*

prescript *noun*
• "PREE script"
• an ordinance, law, or command.

• [Latin *praescriptum* neuter past participle: see PRESCRIBE]

prescription *noun*
• "pre SCRIP sh'n"
• a doctor's (usu. written) instruction for the composition and use of a medicine.
• [Latin *praescriptio -onis* (as PRESCRIBE)]
HOMOPHONES: *proscription*

prescriptive *adjective*
• "pre SCRIP tiv"
• of or relating to the imposition or enforcement of a rule or method.
• [Late Latin *praescriptivus* (as PRESCRIBE)]
• **prescriptively** *adverb*
• **prescriptiveness** *noun*
• **prescriptivism** *noun*
• **prescriptivist** *noun*
HOMOPHONES: *proscriptive*

presentable *adjective*
• "pre ZENTA bull"
• of good appearance; fit to be presented to other people.
• [Old French from Latin *praesens -entis* participle of *praeesse* be at hand (*prae* before, *esse* be)]
• **presentability** *noun*
• **presentableness** *noun*
• **presentably** *adverb*

presentation *noun*
• "prez'n TAY sh'n"
• the act or an instance of presenting; the process of being presented.
• [as PRESENTABLE]
• **presentational** *adjective*
• **presentationally** *adverb*

presentiment *noun*
• "pre ZENTA m'nt" or "pre SENTA m'nt"
• a vague expectation; a foreboding (esp. of misfortune).
• [obsolete French *présentiment* (Latin *prae* before, SENTIMENT)]

presentism *noun*
• "PREZZ 'nt izm"
• the viewing of all cultural and social phenomena in the context of present-day attitudes, without regard for historical context.
• [as PRESENTABLE]
• **presentist** *noun*

presentment *noun*
• "pre ZENT m'nt"
• the act or an instance of presenting or being presented, esp. the presentation of a statement on oath by a jury, or of a bill, note, etc., as payment.
• [as PRESENTABLE]

preservationist *noun*
• "prezzer VAY sh'n ist"
• a supporter or advocate of preservation, esp. of antiquities, historic buildings, natural areas, etc.
• [as PRESERVE]

preservative *noun*
• "pre ZURVA tiv"
• a substance for preserving perishable foodstuffs, wood, etc.
• [as PRESERVE]

preserve *verb*
• "pre ZURV"
• keep safe or free from harm, decay, etc.
• [Old French *preserver* from Late Latin *praeservare* (*prae-* before, *servare* keep)]
• **preservation** *noun*
• **preserver** *noun*

preside *verb*
• "pre ZIDE"
• be in a position of authority, esp. as the chairperson or president of a meeting.
• [French *présider* from Latin *praesidēre* (*prae-* before, *sedēre* sit)]

president *noun*
• "PREZZA d'nt"
• the elected head of a republican state.
• [Old French from Latin (as PRESIDE)]
• **presidency** *noun*
• **presidential** *adjective* "prezza DEN sh'll"
• **presidentially** *adverb*

presidium *noun*
ALSO SPELLED: **praesidium**
• "pruh SIDDY um" or "pruh ZIDDY um"
• a standing executive committee in a Communist country, esp. in the former USSR.
• [Russian *prezidium* from Latin *praesidium* protection etc. (as PRESIDE)]

presocratic *adjective*
• "pree suh CRATTIC"
• (of Greek philosophy) of the time before Socrates (d.399 BC).
• [Latin *prae* before + SOCRATIC]

pressure *noun*
• "PRESH ur"
• the exertion of continuous force on or against a body by another in contact with it.
• [Middle English from Latin *pressura*, from *pressare*, frequentative of *premere press-* press]

pressurize *verb*
ALSO SPELLED: esp. *Brit.* **-ise**
• "PRESH ur ize"
• maintain normal atmospheric pressure in (an aircraft cabin etc.) at a high altitude.
• [as PRESSURE]
• **pressurization** *noun* (also esp. *Brit.* **-isation**)

prestidigitation *noun*
• "presta didge a TAY sh'n"
• the practice of conjuring or juggling; sleight of hand.
• [French *prestidigitateur* from *preste* nimble (as PRESTO) + Latin *digitus* finger]
• **prestidigitator** *noun*
"presta DIDGE a tay tur"

prestige *noun*
• "press TEEZH" or "press TEEJ"
• respect, reputation, or influence derived from achievements, power, wealth, etc.
• [French, = illusion, glamour, from Late Latin *praestigium* from *praestigiae* juggler's tricks]
• **prestigeful** *adjective*
• **prestigious** *adjective* "press TEEDGE us" or "press TIDGE us"
• **prestigiously** *adverb*
• **prestigiousness** *noun*

prestissimo *adverb*
• "press TISSY moe"
• (as a musical direction) in a very quick tempo.
• [Italian, superlative of PRESTO]

presto *adverb*
• "PRESS toe"
• (as a musical direction) in quick tempo.
• [Italian from Late Latin *praestus* from Latin *praesto* ready]

presumably *adverb*
• "pre ZOOMA blee" or "pre ZYOOMA blee"
• as may reasonably be presumed.
• [as PRESUME]

presume *verb*
• "pre ZOOM" or "pre ZYOOM"
• suppose to be true; take for granted.
• [Old French *presumer* from Latin *praesumere* anticipate, venture (*prae-* before, *sumere* take)]
• **presumable** *adjective*

presumptive *adjective*
• "pre ZUMP tiv"
• giving grounds for presumption.
• [French *présomptif -ive* from Late Latin *praesumptivus* (as PRESUME)]
• **presumptively** *adverb*

presumptuous *adjective*
• "pre ZUMP choo us"
• unduly or overbearingly confident.
• [Old French *presumptueux* from Late Latin *praesumptuosus* (as PRESUME)]
• **presumption** *noun*
• **presumptuously** *adverb*
• **presumptuousness** *noun*

presynaptic *adjective*
• "pree sin APTIC"
• existing or occurring prior to meiotic synapsis.
• [Latin *prae* before + SYNAPTIC]

pretension *noun*
• "pre TEN sh'n"
• an assertion of a claim.
• [medieval Latin *praetensio, -tio* (*prae* before, *tendere tent-*, later *tens-* stretch)]

pretentious *adjective*
• "pre TEN sh'ss"
• making an excessive claim to great merit, importance, fashionableness, etc. esp. without good cause.
• [French *prétentieux* (as PRETENSION)]
• **pretentiously** *adverb*
• **pretentiousness** *noun*

preterite *adjective*
ALSO SPELLED: **preterit**
• "PRETTER it"
• expressing a past action or state.
• [Old French *preterite* or Latin *praeteritus* past participle of *praeterire* pass (*praeter* past, beyond, *ire it-* go)]

preternatural *adjective*
• "pree tur NATCH ur 'll"
• outside the ordinary course of nature; supernatural.
• [Latin *praeter* past, beyond, *natura*, from *nasci nat-* be born]
• **preternaturalism** *noun*
• **preternaturally** *adverb*

pretzel *noun*
• "PRETS'll"
• a crisp salted biscuit made in the shape of a knot or a stick.
• [German]
• **pretzelled** *adjective*

prevail *verb*
• "pre VALE"
• be victorious or gain mastery.
• [Latin *praevalēre* (*prae* before, *valēre* have power), influenced by AVAIL]

prevailing *adjective*
• "pre VALE ing"
• most usual or widespread.
• [as PREVAIL]
• **prevailingly** *adverb*

prevalent *adjective*
• "PREVVA l'nt"
• generally existing or occurring.
• [as PREVAIL]
• **prevalence** *noun*
• **prevalently** *adverb*

prevaricate *verb*
• "pre VERRA cate"
• speak or act evasively or misleadingly.
• [Latin *praevaricari* walk crookedly, practise collusion, in Church Latin 'transgress' (as Latin *prae-* before, *varicari* straddle, from *varus* bent, knock-kneed)]
• **prevarication** *noun*
• **prevaricator** *noun*

prey *noun*
• "PRAY"
• an animal that is hunted or killed by another for food.
• [Old French *preie* from Latin *praeda* booty]
HOMOPHONES: *pray*

priest *noun*
• "PREEST"
• an ordained minister of the Roman Catholic or Orthodox Church, or of the Anglican Church

(above a deacon and below a bishop), authorized to perform certain rites and administer certain sacraments.
• [Old English *prēost*, ultimately from Church Latin *presbyter*: see PRESBYTER]
• **priestlike** *adjective*
• **priestliness** *noun*
• **priestly** *adjective*

priestess *noun*
• "PREEST ess"
• a female priest of a non-Christian religion.
• [as PRIEST]

priesthood *noun*
• "PREEST hood" (with "OO" as in *GOOD*)
• the office or position of priest.
• [as PRIEST]

primacy *noun*
• "PRIME a see"
• the state or position of being first in order, importance, or authority; pre-eminence.
• [Old French *primatie* or medieval Latin *primatia* (as PRIMATE)]

primal *adjective*
• "PRIME 'll"
• primitive, primeval.
• [medieval Latin *primalis* from Latin *primus* first]

primary *adjective*
• "PRY merry" or "PRY muh ree"
• of the first importance; chief.
• [Latin *primarius*, from *primus* first]
• **primarily** *adverb* "pry MERRA lee"

primate *noun*
• "PRIME ate"
• any animal of the order Primates, the highest order of mammals, including tarsiers, lemurs, apes, monkeys, and humans.
• [Old French *primat* from Latin *primas -atis* (adjective) of the first rank, from *primus* first]
• **primatological** *adjective*
• **primatologist** *noun*
• **primatology** *noun* "prime a TOLLA jee"

primavera *noun*
• "preema VERRA"
• a Central American tree, *Cybistax donnell-smithii*, bearing yellow blooms.
• [Spanish & Italian, = spring (the season), from Latin *primus* first + *ver* spring]

primeval *adjective*
ALSO SPELLED: **primaeval**
• "pry MEE v'll"
• of or relating to the first age of the world.
• [Latin *primaevus* from *primus* first + *aevum* age]
• **primevally** *adverb* (also **primaevally**)

primigravida *noun*
• "preema GRAVVID uh" or "prime a GRAVVID uh"
• a woman who is pregnant for the first time.
• [modern Latin feminine from Latin *primus* first + *gravidus* pregnant: see GRAVID]

primipara *noun*
• "pry MIPPA ruh"
• a woman who is giving birth for the first time.
• [modern Latin feminine from *primus* first + *-parus* from *parere* bring forth]
• **primiparity** *noun* "pry muh PERRA tee"
• **primiparous** *adjective*

primitive *adjective*
• "PRIMMA tiv"
• early, ancient; at an early stage of civilization.
• [Latin *primitivus* first of its kind, from *primitus* in the first place, from *primus* first]
• **primitively** *adverb*
• **primitiveness** *noun*
• **primitivity** *noun*

primitivism *noun*
• "PRIMMA tiv izm"
• primitive behaviour.
• [as PRIMITIVE]
• **primitivist** *noun*

primo *noun*
• "PREEMO"
• the leading or upper part in a duet etc.
• [Italian, = 'first']

primogenitor *noun*
• "prime oh JENNA tur"
• the earliest ancestor of a people etc.
• [var. of *progenitor*, after PRIMOGENITURE]

primogeniture *noun*
• "prime oh JENNA chur" or "preemo JENNA chur"
• the fact or condition of being the first-born child.
• [medieval Latin *primogenitura* from Latin *primo* first + *genitura* from *gignere genit-* beget]

primordial *adjective*
• "pry MORDY 'll"
• existing at or from the beginning, primeval.
• [Late Latin *primordialis* (as PRIMORDIUM)]
• **primordially** *adverb*

primordium *noun*
• "pry MORDY um"
• an organ or tissue in the early stages of development.
• [Latin, neuter of *primordius* original, from *primus* first + *ordiri* begin]

primula *noun*
• "PRIM yoo luh"
• any plant of the genus *Primula*, bearing flowers in a wide variety of colours during the spring, including primroses, cowslips, and polyanthuses.
• [medieval Latin, feminine of *primulus* diminutive of *primus* first]

principal *adjective*
• "PRINCE a pull"
• first in rank or importance; chief.

• [Old French from Latin *principalis* first, original, from *princeps principis* first, chief, sovereign, from *primus* first + *capere* take]
• **principally** *adverb* "PRINCE a plee"
• **principalship** *noun*
HOMOPHONES: *principle*

principality *noun*
• "prince a PALA tee"
• a state ruled by a prince.
• [Old French *principalité* from Late Latin *principalitas -tatis* (as PRINCIPAL)]

principate *noun*
• "PRINCE a pate"
• the rule of the early Roman emperors during which some republican forms were retained.
• [Old French *principat* or Latin *principatus* first place (as PRINCIPAL)]

principle *noun*
• "PRINCE a pull"
• a fundamental truth or law as the basis of reasoning or action.
• [Old French *principe* from Latin *principium* source, (in pl.) foundations (as PRINCIPAL)]
HOMOPHONES: *principal*

principled *adjective*
• "PRINCE a puld"
• based on or having (esp. praiseworthy) principles of behaviour.
• [as PRINCIPLE]

prion[1] *noun*
• "PRY 'n"
• a small saw-billed petrel of the genus *Pachyptila*, of southern seas.
• [modern Latin (former genus name) from Greek *priōn* a saw]

prion[2] *noun*
• "PRY on"
• a protein particle associated with and believed to be the cause of encephalopathies such as scrapie, BSE, and Creutzfeldt-Jakob disease.
• [by rearrangement from '*pro*teinaceous *in*fectious particle']

prior *adjective*
• "PRIRE"
• earlier.
• [Latin, = former, elder, comparative of Old Latin *pri* = Latin *prae* before]
• **priorship** *noun*

prioress *noun*
• "PRIRE ess"
• a female superior of a house of any of various orders of nuns.
• [as PRIOR]

priority *noun*
• "pry ORRA tee"
• something that is given prior or special attention or considered more important.
• [as PRIOR]
• **prioritization** *noun* (also esp. *Brit.* **-isation**)
• **prioritize** *verb* (also esp. *Brit.* **-ise**)

priory *noun*
• "PRIRE ee"
• a monastery governed by a prior or a convent governed by a prioress.
• [as PRIOR]

prism *noun*
• "PRIZM"
• a solid geometric figure whose two ends are similar, equal, and parallel rectilinear figures, and whose sides are parallelograms.
• [Late Latin *prisma* from Greek *prisma prismatos* thing sawn, from *prizō* to saw]
• **prismatic** *adjective* "prizz MATTIC"
• **prismatically** *adverb*

prismoid *noun*
• "PRIZ moid"
• a body like a prism, with similar but unequal parallel polygonal ends.
• [as PRISM]
• **prismoidal** *adjective*

pristine *adjective*
• "priss TEEN"
• in its original condition.
• [Latin *pristinus* former]

privacy *noun*
• "PRY vuh see" or "PRIVVA see"
• the state of being private and undisturbed.
• [from 'private' from Latin *privatus*, originally past participle of *privare* deprive]

privateer *noun*
• "pry vuh TEER"
• an armed vessel owned and officered by private individuals holding a government commission and authorized for war service.
• [as PRIVACY, after *volunteer*]
• **privateering** *noun*

privation *noun*
• "pry VAY sh'n"
• lack of the comforts or necessities of life.
• [Latin *privatio* (as PRIVACY)]

privative *adjective*
• "PRIVVA tiv"
• consisting in or marked by the loss or removal or absence of some quality or attribute.
• [French *privatif -ive* or Latin *privativus* (as PRIVATION)]

privet *noun*
• "PRIVVIT"
• any evergreen shrub of the genus *Ligustrum*, esp. *L. vulgare* bearing small white flowers and black berries, and used for hedges.
• [16th c.: origin unknown]

privilege *noun*
• "PRIV a lidge" or "PRIV lidge"
• a special right or advantage available only to a particular person or a group of people.
• [Old French *privilege* from Latin *privilegium*

bill or law affecting an individual, from *privus* private + *lex legis* law]
• **privileged** *adjective*

privity *noun*
• "PRIVVA tee"
• a relation between two parties that is recognized by law, e.g. that of blood, lease, or service.
• [Old French *privetè* from medieval Latin *privitas -tatis* from Latin *privus* private]

privy *adjective*
• "PRIVVY"
• sharing in the secret of (a person's plans etc.).
• [Old French *privé* from Latin *privatus* private]
• **privily** *adverb*

probable *adjective*
• "PROBBA bull"
• that may be expected to happen or prove true; likely.
• [Old French from Latin *probabilis* from *probare* prove]
• **probabilistic** *adjective* "probba bull ISTIC"
• **probability** *noun*
• **probably** *adverb*

probate *noun*
• "PRO bate"
• the official proving of a will.
• [Latin *probatum* neuter past participle of *probare* PROVE]

probation *noun*
• "pro BAY sh'n"
• a system of suspending the sentence on an offender subject to a period of good behaviour under supervision.
• [Old French *probation* or Latin *probatio* (as PROVE)]
• **probationary** *adjective*

probationer *noun*
• "pro BAY sh'n ur"
• a person who is serving a trial period in a job to which they are newly appointed.
• [as PROBATION]

probative *adjective*
• "PROBE a tiv"
• affording proof; evidential.
• [Latin *probativus* (as PROVE)]

probity *noun*
• "PRO bit ee" or "PROB it ee"
• uprightness, honesty.
• [Latin *probitas* from *probus* good]

proboscidean *adjective*
ALSO SPELLED: **proboscidian**
• "probba SIDDY 'n"
• of the mammalian order Proboscidea, including elephants and their extinct relatives.
• [modern Latin *Proboscidea* (as PROBOSCIS)]

proboscis *noun*
• "pro BOSS kiss" or "pro BOSS iss"
• the long flexible trunk or snout of some mammals, e.g. an elephant or tapir.
• [Latin *proboscis -cidis* from Greek *proboskis* from *proboskō* (*pro* before, *boskō* feed)]

procaine *noun*
• "PRO cane"
• a synthetic compound used as a local anaesthetic.
• [Latin *pro* in front of, instead of + COCAINE]

procedure *noun*
• "pro SEE jur"
• a way of proceeding, esp. a mode of conducting business or a legal action.
• [French *procédure* (as PROCEED)]
• **procedural** *adjective*
• **procedurally** *adverb*

proceed *verb*
• "pro SEED"
• go forward or on further; make one's way.
• [Old French *proceder* from Latin *procedere process-* (Latin *pro* in front of, *cedere* go)]

proceeding *noun*
• "pro SEEDING"
• an action or piece of conduct.
• [as PROCEED]

proceeds *plural noun*
• "PRO seeds"
• money produced by a transaction or other undertaking.
• [pl. of obsolete *proceed* (n.) from PROCEED]

process[1] *noun*
• "PRO sess" or "PRAW sess"
• a course of action or proceeding, esp. a series of stages in manufacture or some other operation.
• [Old French *proces* from Latin *processus* (as PROCEED)]
• **processable** *adjective*

process[2] *verb*
• "pro SESS"
• walk in procession.
• [back-formation from PROCESSION]

procession *noun*
• "pruh SESH'n"
• a number of people or vehicles etc. moving forward in orderly succession, esp. at a ceremony, demonstration, or festivity.
• [Old French from Latin *processio -onis* (as PROCEED)]
HOMOPHONES: *precession*

processional *adjective*
• "pruh SESH'n 'll"
• of processions.
• [medieval Latin *processionalis* (adjective), *-ale* (n.) (as PROCESSION)]
HOMOPHONES: *precessional*

processor *noun*
• "PRO sesser" or "PRAW sesser"
• a person or company etc. that processes something, esp. food.
• [as PROCESS[1]]

proclitic *adjective*
• "pro CLITTIC"
• (of a monosyllable) closely attached in pronunciation to a following word and having itself no accent.
• [modern Latin *procliticus* from Greek *proklinō* lean forward, after Late Latin *encliticus*: see ENCLITIC]

proclivity *noun*
• "pro CLIVVA tee"
• a tendency or inclination.
• [Latin *proclivitas* from *proclivis* inclined (*pro* in front of, *clivus* slope)]

proconsul *noun*
• "pro CON s'll"
• (in ancient Rome) a governor of a province, in the later republic usu. an ex-consul.
• [Latin, earlier *pro consule* (one acting) for the consul]
• **proconsular** *adjective* "pro CON syuh lur"

procrastinate *verb*
• "pro CRASS t'n ate"
• delay or postpone action.
• [Latin *procrastinare procrastinat-* (Latin *pro* in front of, *crastinus* of tomorrow, from *cras* tomorrow)]
• **procrastination** *noun*
• **procrastinator** *noun*

procreate *verb*
• "PRO cree ate"
• bring (offspring) into existence by the natural process of reproduction.
• [Latin *procreare procreat-* (*pro* in front of, *creare* create)]
• **procreation** *noun*
• **procreative** *adjective*
• **procreator** *noun*

Procrustean *adjective*
• "pro CRUSTY 'n"
• seeking to enforce uniformity by forceful or ruthless methods.
• [*Procrustes*, legendary Greek robber who forced travellers to lie on a bed and made them fit it by stretching their limbs or cutting off the appropriate length of leg]

proctology *noun*
• "prock TOLLA jee"
• the branch of medicine concerned with the anus and rectum.
• [Greek *prōktos* anus + *logos* word]
• **proctological** *adjective*
• **proctologist** *noun*

proctor *noun*
• "PROCK tur"
• a person who supervises students in an examination etc.
• [Middle English, syncopation of PROCURATOR]

proctoscope *noun*
• "PROCTA scope"
• a medical instrument for inspecting the rectum.
• [Greek *prōktos* anus + *skopos* target, from *skeptomai* look at]
• **proctoscopic** *adjective*
• **proctoscopy** *noun* "prock TOSCA pee"

procumbent *adjective*
• "pruh KUM b'nt"
• lying on the face; prostrate.
• [Latin *procumbere* fall forwards (*pro* in front of, *cumbere* lay oneself)]

procuration *noun*
• "prock yur AY sh'n"
• the action of procuring, obtaining, or bringing about.
• [as PROCURATOR]

procurator *noun*
• "PROCK yur ay tur"
• an agent or proxy, esp. one who has power of attorney.
• [Latin *procurator* administrator, finance-agent, from *procurare* take care of, manage (*pro* in front of, *curare* see to)]
• **procuratorial** *adjective* "prock yur a TORY 'll"
• **procuratorship** *noun*

prodigal *adjective*
• "PRODDA g'll"
• recklessly wasteful.
• [medieval Latin *prodigalis* from Latin *prodigus* lavish]
• **prodigality** *noun* "prodda GALA tee"
• **prodigally** *adverb*

prodigious *adjective*
• "pruh DIDGE us"
• marvellous or amazing.
• [Latin *prodigiosus* (as PRODIGY)]
• **prodigiously** *adverb*
• **prodigiousness** *noun*

prodigy *noun*
• "PRODDA jee"
• a person endowed with exceptional qualities or abilities, esp. a precocious child.
• [Latin *prodigium* portent]

prodrome *noun*
• "PRO drome" or "PROD rome"
• a premonitory symptom.
• [French from modern Latin from Greek *prodromos* precursor (*pro* before, *dromos* running)]
• **prodromal** *adjective* "pruh DROME 'll"
• **prodromic** *adjective* "pruh DROMMIC"

producible *adjective*
• "pro DOOSSA bull" or "pro DYOOSSA bull"
• that can be produced.
• [Latin *producere* (*pro-* in front of, *ducere duct-* lead)]
• **producibility** *noun*

productivity *noun*
• "prod uck TIVVA tee"

• the capacity to produce.
• [as PRODUCIBLE]

proem *noun*
• "PRO em"
• a preface or preamble to a book or speech.
• [Old French *proeme* or Latin *prooemium* from Greek *prooimion* prelude (*pro* before, *oimē* song)]

profane *adjective*
• "pro FANE"
• not belonging to what is sacred or Biblical; secular.
• [Latin *profanus* before (i.e. outside) the temple, not sacred (*pro* in front of, *fanum* temple)]
• **profanation** *noun* "proffa NAY sh'n"
• **profanely** *adverb*
• **profaner** *noun*

profanity *noun*
• "pro FANNA tee"
• a swear word.
• [Late Latin *profanitas* (as PROFANE)]

profess *verb*
• "pruh FESS"
• claim openly to have (a quality or feeling).
• [Latin *profitēri profess-* declare publicly (*pro* before, *fatēri* confess)]

professed *adjective*
• "pruh FEST"
• self-acknowledged.
• [as PROFESS]
• **professedly** *adverb* "pruh FESSID lee"

profession *noun*
• "pruh FESH'n"
• a vocation or calling, esp. one that involves some branch of advanced learning or science.
• [as PROFESS]
• **professional** *adjective*
• **professionalization** *noun*
• **professionalize** *verb*
• **professionally** *adverb*

professionalism *noun*
• "pruh FESH'n 'll izm"
• the skill or qualities required or expected of members of a profession.
• [as PROFESS]

professor *noun*
• "pruh FESSER"
• a university teacher.
• [Latin *profitēri profess-* declare publicly (*pro* in front of, *fatēri* confess)]
• **professorate** *noun* "pruh FESSER it"
• **professorial** *adjective* "proffa SORRY 'll"
• **professorially** *adverb*
• **professoriate** *noun* "proffa SORRY it"
• **professorship** *noun*

proficient *adjective*
• "pruh FISH 'nt"
• competent or skilled at doing or using something.
• [Latin *proficiens proficient-* from *proficere profect-* advance (*pro* in front of, *facere* do)]
• **proficiency** *noun*
• **proficiently** *adverb*

profit *noun*
• "PROFFIT"
• financial gain; excess of returns over outlay.
• [Old French from Latin *profectus* progress, profit, from *proficere profect-* advance (*pro-* for, *facere* do)]
• **profitability** *noun*
• **profitable** *adjective*
• **profitableness** *noun*
• **profitably** *adverb*
• **profitless** *adjective*
HOMOPHONES: *prophet*

profiteer *verb*
• "PROFFIT eer"
• make or seek to make excessive profits, esp. illegally or in black market conditions.
• [as PROFIT]

profiterole *noun*
• "pruh FITTER ole"
• a small cream puff usu. filled with whipped cream or ice cream and covered with chocolate sauce.
• [French, diminutive of *profit* profit (originally used to mean 'a small treat')]

profligate *adjective*
• "PROFF lig it"
• shamelessly immoral.
• [Latin *profligatus* dissolute, past participle of *profligare* overthrow, ruin (*pro* in front of, *fligere* strike down)]
• **profligacy** *noun*
• **profligately** *adverb*

progenitive *adjective*
• "pro JENNA tiv"
• capable of or connected with the production of offspring.
• [as PROGENITOR]

progenitor *noun*
• "pro JENNA tur"
• the ancestor of a person, animal, or plant.
• [Latin *progenitor* from *progignere progenit-* (*pro* in front of, *gignere* beget)]
• **progenitorial** *adjective* "pro jenna TORY 'll"

progeny *noun*
• "PRODGE a nee"
• the offspring of a person or other organism.
• [Old French *progenie* from Latin *progenies* from *progignere* (as PROGENITOR)]

progesterone *noun*
• "pro JESTER own"
• a steroid hormone released by the corpus luteum which stimulates the preparation of the uterus for pregnancy.
• [PROGESTIN + STEROL]

progestin *noun*
• "pro JESS tin"
• any of a group of steroid hormones (including progesterone) that maintain pregnancy and prevent further ovulation during it.
• [Greek *pro* before + GESTATION]

proglottid *noun*
• "pro GLOTTID"
• each segment in the strobila of a tapeworm that contains a complete reproductive system.
• [modern Latin from Greek *proglōssis* (*pro* before, *glōssis* from *glōssa, glōtta* tongue), from its shape]

prognathous *adjective*
• "prog NAY thuss" or "PROG nuh thuss" (with "TH" as in *THIN*)
• having a projecting jaw.
• [Greek *pro* before + *gnathos* jaw]
• **prognathic** *adjective* "prog NATHIC"

prognosis *noun*
• "prog NO sis"
• a forecast.
• [Greek *prognōsis* (*pro* before, *gignōskō* know)]
• **prognostic** *adjective* "prog NOSS tick"
• **prognosticate** *verb*
• **prognostication** *noun*
• **prognosticator** *noun*

programmatic *adjective*
• "pro gruh MATTIC"
• of the nature of or according to a program, schedule, or method.
• [Greek *programma -atos*, from *prographō* write publicly (*pro* before, *graphō* write)]
• **programmatically** *adverb*

prohibit *verb*
• "pro HIBBIT"
• formally forbid, esp. by authority.
• [Latin *prohibēre* (*pro* in front of, *habēre* hold)]
• **prohibitive** *adjective* "pro HIBBA tiv"
• **prohibitively** *adverb*
• **prohibitiveness** *noun*
• **prohibitory** *adjective* "pro HIBBA tory"

prohibition *noun*
• "pro hib ISH'n" or "pro a BISH'n"
• the act or an instance of forbidding; a state of being forbidden, esp. the forbidding of the sale and consumption of alcohol.
• [as PROHIBIT]
• **prohibitionary** *adjective*
• **prohibitionism** *noun*
• **prohibitionist** *noun*

projector *noun*
• "pruh JECTER"
• an apparatus containing a source of light and a system of lenses for projecting slides or film on to a screen.
• [Latin *projectum* neuter past participle of *projicere* (*pro* in front (of), *jacĕre* throw)]

prokaryote *noun*
ALSO SPELLED: **procaryote**
• "pro KERRY ote"
• a single-celled organism which has neither a distinct nucleus with a membrane nor other specialized organelles, e.g. a bacterium, a blue-green alga.
• [Greek *pro* before + *karuon* kernel + *-ote* as in ZYGOTE]
• **prokaryotic** *adjective* (also **procaryotic**) "pro kerry OTTIC"

prolactin *noun*
• "pro LACK tin"
• a hormone released from the anterior pituitary gland that stimulates milk production after childbirth.
• [Latin *pro* in front (of) + LACTATE]

prolapse *noun*
• "PRO laps"
• the forward or downward displacement of a part or organ.
• [Latin *prolabi prolaps-* (*pro* in front (of), *labi* slip)]

prolate *adjective*
• "PRO late"
• (of a spheroid) lengthened in the direction of a polar diameter.
• [Latin *prolatus* past participle of *proferre* prolong (*pro* in front (of), *ferre* carry)]

prole *noun*
• "PROLE"
• a proletarian.
• [abbreviation]

prolegomenon *noun*
• "pro luh GOMMA non"
• an introduction or preface to a book etc., esp. when critical or discursive.
• [Latin from Greek, neuter passive present participle of *prolegō* (*pro* before, *legō* say)]

prolepsis *noun*
• "pro LEP sis"
• the anticipation and answering of possible objections in rhetorical speech.
• [Greek *prolēpsis* from *prolambanō* anticipate (*pro* before, *lambanō* take)]
• **proleptic** *adjective*

proletariat *noun*
• "pro luh TERRY it"
• wage earners collectively, esp. those without capital and dependent on selling their labour.
• [French *prolétariat* from Latin *proletarius* from *proles* offspring, denoting a person having no wealth in property, who only served the state by producing offspring]
• **proletarian** *adjective*
• **proletarianism** *noun*
• **proletarianization** *noun* (also esp. *Brit.* **-isation**)
• **proletarianize** *verb* (also esp. *Brit.* **-ise**)

proliferate *verb*
- "pruh LIFFER ate"
- reproduce.
- [as PROLIFEROUS]
- **proliferation** *noun*
- **proliferative** *adjective* "pruh LIFFER a tiv"
- **proliferator** *noun*

proliferous *adjective*
- "pruh LIFFER us"
- (of a plant) producing many leaf or flower buds; growing luxuriantly.
- [Latin *proles* offspring + *-fer* producing, from *ferre* bear]

prolific *adjective*
- "pruh LIFFIC"
- producing many offspring or much output.
- [medieval Latin *prolificus* (as PROLIFEROUS)]
- **prolificacy** *noun*
- **prolifically** *adverb*

proline *noun*
- "PRO leen" or "PRO lin"
- an amino acid with a cyclic molecule, present in many proteins, esp. collagen.
- [contraction of chemical name *pyrrolidine*-2-carboxylic acid]

prolix *adjective*
- "PRO lix" or "pro LIX"
- (of speech, writing, etc.) lengthy; tedious.
- [Latin *prolixus* poured forth, extended (*pro* in front (of), *liquēre* be liquid)]
- **prolixity** *noun* "pro LICKS a tee"

prolocutor *noun*
- "pro LOCK yuh tur"
- a chairperson of a synod or committee in the Anglican Church.
- [Latin from *proloqui prolocut-* (*pro* in front (of), *loqui* speak)]

prologue *noun*
- "PRO log"
- a preface or introduction to a literary or musical work, esp. an introductory speech or short poem addressed to the audience by one of the actors in a play.
- [Old French *prologue* from Latin *prologus* from Greek *prologos* (*pro* before, *logos* speech)]

promenade *noun*
- "promma NAD" or "promma NOD" or "promma NADE"
- a walk, or sometimes a ride or drive, taken esp. for display, leisure, etc.
- [French from *se promener* walk, reflexive of *promener* take for a walk]
- **promenader** *noun*

promethazine *noun*
- "pro METH a zeen"
- an antihistamine drug used to treat allergies, motion sickness, etc.
- [PROPYL + di*meth*ylamine + phenothi*azine*]

Promethean *adjective*
- "pro MEETHY 'n"
- daring or inventive like Prometheus, a demigod in Greek myth who was punished for stealing fire from the gods and giving it to humans along with other skills.

promethium *noun*
- "pro MEETHY um"
- a radioactive metallic element of the lanthanide series occurring in nuclear waste material.
- [from *Prometheus*: see PROMETHEAN]

prominent *adjective*
- "PROMMA n'nt"
- jutting out; projecting.
- [Latin *prominēre* jut out: compare EMINENT]
- **prominence** *noun*
- **prominently** *adverb*

promiscuous *adjective*
- "pruh MISS kyoo us"
- (of a person) having frequent and diverse sexual relationships, esp. transient ones.
- [Latin *promiscuus* (*pro* in front (of), *miscēre* mix)]
- **promiscuity** *noun* "promma SKYOO a tee"
- **promiscuously** *adverb*
- **promiscuousness** *noun*

promissory *adjective*
- "PROMMA sorry"
- conveying or implying a promise.
- [medieval Latin *promissorius* from Latin *promissor promittere* put forth, promise (*pro* in front (of), *mittere* send)]

promontory *noun*
- "PROM'n tory"
- a point of high land jutting out into the sea etc.; a headland.
- [medieval Latin *promontorium* alteration (influenced by *mons montis* mountain) from Latin *promunturium* (perhaps from Latin *pro* in front (of), *mons*)]

prompt *adjective*
- "PROMPT"
- (of a person) acting without delay.
- [Latin *promptus* past participle of *promere prompt-* produce (*pro* for, *emere* take)]
- **prompting** *noun*
- **promptly** *adverb*
- **promptness** *noun*

prompter *noun*
- "PROMPT ur"
- a person seated out of sight of the audience who provides lines to the actors in case they forget.
- [as PROMPT]

promulgate *verb*
- "PROM'll gate"
- make known to the public; disseminate; promote (a cause etc.).

• [Latin *promulgare* (*pro* in front (of), *mulgēre* milk, cause to come forth)]
• **promulgation** *noun*
• **promulgator** *noun*

pronate *verb*
• "PRO nate"
• put (the hand, forearm, etc.) into a prone position (with the palm etc. downwards).
• [back-formation from *pronation* from Latin *pronus* from *pro* forwards]
• **pronation** *noun*
• **pronator** *noun*

pronominal *adjective*
• "pro NOM 'n 'll"
• of, concerning, or being, a pronoun.
• [Late Latin *pronominalis* from Latin *pronomen* (*pro* in front (of), *nomen, nominis* noun)]

pronunciamento *noun*
• "pro nuncy a MENTO"
• a pronouncement, proclamation, or manifesto, esp. a political one.
• [Spanish]

pronunciation *noun*
• "pruh nuncy AY sh'n"
• the way in which a word, language, etc. is pronounced, esp. with reference to a standard.
• [Old French *prononciation* or Latin *pronuntiatio* (*pro* in front (of), *nuntiare* announce, from *nuntius* messenger)]

propaganda *noun*
• "proppa GANDA"
• an organized program of publicity, selected information, etc., used to propagate a doctrine, practice, etc.
• [Italian from modern Latin *congregatio de propaganda fide* congregation for propagation of the faith]
• **propagandist** *noun*
• **propagandistic** *adjective*
• **propagandistically** *adverb*
• **propagandize** *verb* (also esp. *Brit.* **-ise**)

propagate *verb*
• "PROPPA gate"
• breed specimens of (a plant, animal, etc.) by natural processes from the parent stock.
• [Latin *propagare propagat-* multiply plants from layers, from *propago* (*pro* in front (of), *pangere* fix, layer)]
• **propagation** *noun*
• **propagative** *adjective*
• **propagator** *noun*

propane *noun*
• "pro PANE"
• a gaseous hydrocarbon of the alkane series used as bottled fuel.
• [as PROPIONIC]

propanone *noun*
• "PRO puh none" (rhymes with *TONE*)
• a colourless volatile liquid ketone valuable as a solvent for paints, varnishes, nail polish, etc.; acetone.
• [PROPANE + '-one' forming nouns denoting various compounds, from Greek *-ōnē* feminine patronymic]

propel *verb*
• "pruh PELL"
• drive or push forward.
• [Latin *propellere* (*pro* in front (of), *pellere puls-* drive)]

propellant *noun*
• "pruh PELL'nt"
• a thing that propels.
• [as PROPEL]
HOMOPHONES: *propellent*

propellent *adjective*
• "pruh PELL'nt"
• propelling; capable of driving or pushing forward.
• [as PROPEL]
HOMOPHONES: *propellant*

propene *noun*
• "PRO peen"
• a gaseous hydrocarbon of the alkene series used in the manufacture of chemicals; propylene.
• [PROPANE + ALKENE]

propensity *noun*
• "pruh PENSA tee"
• an inclination or tendency.
• [Latin *propensus* inclined, past participle of *propendēre* (*pro* in front (of), *pendēre* hang)]

prophase *noun*
• "PRO faze"
• the phase in cell division in which chromosomes contract and each becomes visible as two chromatids.
• [Greek *pro* before + PHASE]

prophecy *noun*
• "PROFFA see"
• a divinely inspired utterance.
• [Old French *profecie* from Late Latin *prophetia* from Greek *prophēteia* (as PROPHET)]

prophesy *verb*
• "PROFFA sye"
• foretell (an event etc.).
• [Old French *profecier* (as PROPHECY)]
• **prophesier** *noun*

prophet *noun*
• "PROFFIT"
• a teacher or interpreter of the supposed will of God.
• [Greek *prophētēs* spokesman (*pro* before, *phētēs* speaker, from *phēmi* speak)]
• **prophetess** *noun*
• **prophethood** *noun*
HOMOPHONES: *profit*

prophetic *adjective*
• "pruh FETTIC"

• containing a prediction.
• [as PROPHET]
• **prophetical** *adjective*
• **prophetically** *adverb*

prophylactic *adjective*
• "proffa LACTIC"
• tending to prevent disease.
• [French *prophylactique* from Greek *prophulaktikos* from *prophulassō* (*pro* before, *phulassō* guard)]
• **prophylactically** *adverb*

prophylaxis *noun*
• "proffa LAX iss"
• preventive treatment against disease.
• [modern Latin, from Greek *pro* before + Greek *phulaxis* act of guarding]

propinquity *noun*
• "pruh PINK wuh tee"
• nearness in space; proximity.
• [Latin *propinquitas* from *propinquus* near, from *prope* near to]

propionic *adjective*
• "pro pee ONNIC"
• designating a colourless sharp-smelling liquid carboxylic acid used for inhibiting the growth of mould in bread.
• [French *propionique* (Greek *pro* before, *piōn* fat), as being the first member of the fatty acid series to form fats]
• **propionate** *noun* "PRO pee 'n ate"

propitiate *verb*
• "pruh PISHY ate"
• appease (an offended person etc.).
• [Latin *propitiare* (as PROPITIOUS)]
• **propitiation** *noun*
• **propitiator** *noun*
• **propitiatory** *adjective* "pruh PISHY a tory"

propitious *adjective*
• "pruh PISH us"
• (of an omen etc.) favourable.
• [Latin *propitius* favourable]
• **propitiously** *adverb*
• **propitiousness** *noun*

propolis *noun*
• "PROPPA liss"
• a red resinous substance collected from buds by bees, for use in constructing hives.
• [Latin from Greek *propolis* suburb, bee glue, from Greek *pro* before + *polis* city]

proponent *noun*
• "pruh PONE 'nt"
• a person advocating a motion, theory, or proposal.
• [Latin *proponere* (*pro* in front (of), *ponere posit-* place)]

proportion *noun*
• "pruh POR sh'n"
• a comparative part or share.
• [Old French *proportion* or Latin *proportio* (*pro* in front (of), *portio -onis* portion)]
• **proportioned** *adjective*

proportional *adjective*
• "pruh POR sh'n 'll"
• in due proportion; comparable.
• [as PROPORTION]
• **proportionality** *noun*
• **proportionally** *adverb*

proportionate *adjective*
• "pruh POR sh'n it"
• = PROPORTIONAL.
• [as PROPORTION]
• **proportionately** *adverb*

proposition *noun*
• "proppa ZISH'n"
• a plan proposed; a proposal.
• [Old French *proposition* or Latin *propositio* (as PROPONENT)]
• **propositional** *adjective*

propranolol *noun*
• "pro PRANNA loll"
• a beta blocker, used mainly in the treatment of cardiac arrhythmia.
• [PROPYL + *propanol* (PROPANE + ALCOHOL) with reduplication of *-ol*]

proprietary *adjective*
• "pruh PRY a terry" or "pruh PRY a tree"
• (of a name) owned and used for a particular product only by a particular company.
• [Late Latin *proprietarius* from *proprietas -tatis* property, from *proprius* one's own, special]

proprietor *noun*
• "pruh PRY a tur"
• the owner of a business.
• [as PROPRIETARY]
• **proprietorial** *adjective* "pruh pry a TORY 'll"
• **proprietorially** *adverb*
• **proprietorship** *noun*

proprietress *noun*
• "pruh PRY a tress"
• a woman who owns a business.
• [as PROPRIETARY]

propriety *noun*
• "pruh PRY a tee"
• suitableness; rightness.
• [Middle English, = ownership, peculiarity, from Old French *propriete* property (as PROPRIETARY)]

proprioceptive *adjective*
• "pro pree a SEPTIV"
• relating to stimuli produced and perceived within an organism, esp. relating to the position and movement of the body.
• [Latin *proprius* own + RECEPTIVE]
• **proprioception** *noun*
• **proprioceptor** *noun*

propulsion *noun*
• "pruh PUL sh'n" ("PUL" rhymes with *GULL*)
• the act or an instance of driving or pushing forward.
• [medieval Latin *propulsio* from Latin *propellere* (as PROPEL)]
• **propulsive** *adjective*

propyl *noun*
• "PRO p'll"
• either of two isomeric radicals derived from propane.
• [as PROPIONIC]

propylaeum *noun*
• "prop'll EE um"
• a monumental gate or entranceway to a temple, esp. the entrance to the Acropolis at Athens.
• [Latin from Greek *propulaion* (*pro* before, *pulē* gate)]

propylene *noun*
• "PRO puh leen"
• a gaseous hydrocarbon of the alkene series used in the manufacture of chemicals.
• [as PROPYL]

propyne *noun*
• "PRO pine"
• a gaseous alkyne, methyl acetylene.
• [as PROPYL]

prorogue *verb*
• "pro ROE'g"
• discontinue the meetings of (a parliament etc.) without dissolving it.
• [Old French *proroger*, *-guer* from Latin *prorogare* prolong (*pro* in front (of), *rogare* ask)]
• **prorogation** *noun* "pro ruh GAY sh'n"

prosaic *adjective*
• "pro ZAY ick"
• like prose, lacking poetic beauty.
• [Old French from Latin *prosa* (*oratio*) straightforward (discourse), feminine of *prosus*, earlier *prorsus* direct]
• **prosaically** *adverb*

proscenium *noun*
• "pro SEENY um"
• an arch that forms a frame at the front of a stage.
• [Latin from Greek *proskēnion* (*pro* before, *skēnē* stage)]

prosciutto *noun*
• "pruh SHOO toe"
• Italian cured ham, usu. served raw and thinly sliced as an hors d'oeuvre.
• [Italian = ham]

proscribe *verb*
• "pro SCRIBE"
• reject or denounce (a practice etc.) as dangerous etc.
• [Latin *proscribere* (*pro* in front (of), *scribere script-* write)]
• **proscription** *noun* "pro SCRIP sh'n"
• **proscriptive** *adjective*
HOMOPHONES: *prescribe*, *prescriptive*, *prescription*

Prosecco *noun*
• "pro SECKO"
• a fizzy white wine from northeastern Italy.
• [Italian]

prosecute *verb*
• "PROSSA kyoot"
• institute legal proceedings against (a person).
• [Latin *prosequi prosecut-* (*pro* in front (of), *sequi* follow)]
• **prosecutable** *adjective*
• **prosecution** *noun*
• **prosecutor** *noun* "PROSSA kyooter"
• **prosecutorial** *adjective* "prossa kyoo TORY 'll"

proselyte *noun*
• "PROSS'll ite"
• a person converted, esp. recently, from one opinion, creed, party, etc., to another.
• [Late Latin *proselytus* from Greek *prosēluthos* stranger, convert (*pros* towards, stem *ēluth-* of *erkhomai* come)]
• **proselytism** *noun* "PROSS'll a tizm"

proselytize *verb*
ALSO SPELLED: esp. *Brit.* **-ise**
• "PROSS'll a tize"
• attempt to persuade others to adopt one's own belief, esp. in religion.
• [as PROSELYTE]
• **proselytization** *noun* (also esp. *Brit.* **-isation**)
• **proselytizer** *noun* (also esp. *Brit.* **-iser**)

prosenchyma *noun*
• "pross EN kim uh"
• a plant tissue of elongated cells with interpenetrating tapering ends, occurring esp. in vascular tissue.
• [Greek *pros* toward + *egkhuma* infusion, after *parenchyma*]
• **prosenchymal** *adjective*
• **prosenchymatous** *adjective* "pross en KIMMA tuss"

prosify *verb*
• "PROZE a fie"
• turn into prose.
• [as PROSAIC]

prosimian *noun*
• "pro SIMMY 'n"
• a primitive primate of the suborder *Prosimii*, which includes lemurs, lorises, galagos, and tarsiers.
• [Greek *pro* before + SIMIAN]

prosit *interjection*
• "PRO zit"
• an expression used in drinking a person's health etc.
• [German from Latin, = may it benefit]

prosody *noun*
• "PROZZA dee" or "PROSSA dee"
• the systematic study of versification, covering the principles of metre, rhythm, rhyme, and stanza forms.
• [Latin *prosodia* accent, from Greek *prosōidia* (*pros* towards, *ōidē* Attic form of *aoidē* song, from *aeidō* sing)]
• **prosodic** *adjective* "pruh SODDIC"
• **prosodically** *adverb*
• **prosodist** *noun*

prosopography *noun*
• "prossa POGGRA fee"
• a description of a person's appearance, personality, social and family connections, career, etc.
• [modern Latin *prosopographia* from Greek *prosōpon* face, person, *graphia* writing]
• **prosopographer** *noun*
• **prosopographic** *adjective*
• **prosopographical** *adjective*

prosopopoeia *noun*
ALSO SPELLED: **prosopopeia**
• "prossa puh PEE uh"
• a figure of speech in which an imaginary or absent person is represented as speaking or acting; the introduction of a pretended speaker.
• [Latin from Greek *prosōpopoiia* from *prosōpon* person + *poieō* make]

prospect *verb*
• "PROSS pect"
• explore a region for minerals.
• [Latin *prospectus*: see PROSPECTUS]
• **prospecting** *noun*
• **prospector** *noun*

prospective *adjective*
• "pruh SPECTIV"
• expected; potential.
• [obsolete French *prospectif -ive* or Late Latin *prospectivus* (as PROSPECTUS)]
• **prospectively** *adverb*

prospectus *noun*
• "pruh SPECTUS"
• a printed document advertising or describing a commercial enterprise etc., esp. to attract investors.
• [Latin, = prospect, from *prospicere* (*pro* in front (of), *specere* look)]

prostacyclin *noun*
• "prossta SIKE lin"
• a compound of the prostaglandin type that is produced in arterial walls and that functions as an anticoagulant and vasodilator.
• [from PROSTAGLANDIN + CYCLIC]

prostaglandin *noun*
• "prossta GLAND 'n"
• any of a group of hormone-like substances that cause muscle contraction and which may be used to induce labour.
• [German (from PROSTATE + Latin *glandulae* throat glands)]

prostate *noun*
• "PROSS tate"
• a gland surrounding the neck of the bladder in male mammals and releasing a fluid forming part of the semen.
• [French from modern Latin *prostata* from Greek *prostatēs* one that stands before (*pro* before, *statos* standing)]
• **prostatic** *adjective* "pross TATTIC"

prostatectomy *noun*
• "prossta TECTA mee"
• surgical removal of all or part of the prostate.
• [as PROSTATE + Greek *ektomē* excision, from *ek* out + *temnō* cut]

prosthesis *noun*
• "pross THEE sis" (with "TH" as in *THIN*)
• an artificial part supplied to remedy a deficiency, e.g. a false breast, leg, tooth, etc.
• [Late Latin from Greek *prosthesis* from *prostithēmi* (*pros* towards, *tithēmi* place)]
• **prosthetic** *adjective* "pross THETTIC"
• **prosthetics** *noun*

prosthodontics *noun*
• "pross thuh DONTIX" (with "TH" as in *THIN*)
• the branch of dentistry concerned with the design, manufacture, and fitting of artificial replacements for teeth and other parts of the mouth.
• [from PROSTHESIS, on the pattern of ORTHODONTICS]
• **prosthodontist** *noun*

prostrate *adjective*
• "PROSS trate"
• lying face downwards.
• [Latin *prostratus* past participle of *prosternere* (*pro* in front (of), *sternere strat-* lay flat)]
• **prostration** *noun*

protactinium *noun*
• "pro tack TINNY um"
• a radioactive metallic element whose chief isotope yields actinium by decay.
• [German from Greek *prōto-* from *prōtos* first, ACTINIUM]

protagonist *noun*
• "pro TAGGA nist"
• the principal character in a work of fiction, film, drama, etc.
• [Greek *prōtagōnistēs* (*prōto-* from *prōtos* first, *agōnistēs* actor)]

protamine *noun*
• "PRO tuh meen"
• any of a class of simple proteins found combined with nucleic acids (esp. in fish sperm) that may be combined with insulin to slow its absorption.
• [Greek *prōto-* from *prōtos* first + AMINE]

protasis *noun*
• "PROTTA sis"
• the clause expressing the condition in a conditional sentence, e.g. *If you asked my opinion* in *If you asked my opinion, I would agree.*
• [Latin, from Greek *protasis* proposition (*pro* before, *teinō* stretch)]
• **protatic** *adjective* "pruh TATTIC"

protea *noun*
• "PRO tee uh"
• any shrub of the genus *Protea* native to southern Africa, with cone-like flower heads.
• [modern Latin from *Proteus* (see PROTEAN), with reference to the many species]

protean *adjective*
• "PRO tee 'n" or "pro TEE 'n"
• variable, taking many forms.
• [after *Proteus*, minor Greek sea god who could assume different shapes]

protease *noun*
• "PRO tee ace"
• an enzyme that breaks down proteins and peptides.
• [as PROTEIN]

protectant *noun*
• "pruh TECK t'nt"
• a substance that provides protection, e.g. against ultraviolet radiation, rust, frost, etc.
• [Latin *protegere protect-* (*pro* in front (of), *tegere* cover)]

protector *noun*
• "pruh TECK tur"
• a person who protects.
• [as PROTECTANT]
• **protectress** *noun*

protectorate *noun*
• "pruh TECK tur it"
• a territory that is controlled and protected by a larger state.
• [as PROTECTANT]

protege *noun*
• "PRO tuh zhay" or "PROTTA zhay"
• a person whose welfare and career are looked after by an influential person, esp. over a long period.
• [French *protégé*, past participle of *protéger* from Latin *protegere* (see PROTECTANT)]

protein *noun*
• "PRO teen"
• any of a group of organic compounds composed of one or more chains of amino acids and forming an essential part of all living organisms.
• [French *protéine*, German *Protein* from Greek *prōteios* primary]

proteinaceous *adjective*
• "pro tuh NAY sh'ss"
• of the nature of or consisting of protein.
• [PROTEIN + Latin adjective suffix *-aceus* of the nature of]

proteinoid *noun*
• "PRO t'n oid"
• a polypeptide or mixture of polypeptides obtained by heating a mixture of amino acids.
• [as PROTEIN]

proteolysis *noun*
• "pro tee OLLA sis"
• the splitting of proteins or peptides by the action of enzymes esp. during the process of digestion.
• [modern Latin from PROTEIN + LYSIS]
• **proteolytic** *adjective* "pro tee a LITTIC"

proteomics *noun*
• "pro tee OMMIX"
• the branch of molecular biology concerned with the behaviour and interaction of proteins within cells.
• [as PROTEIN, after GENOMICS]

Proterozoic *adjective*
• "pro tur oh ZO ick"
• of or relating to the later part of the Precambrian era, from about 2.5 billion to 570 million years ago, characterized by the appearance of life.
• [Greek *proteros* former + *zōē* life, *zōos* living]

Protestant *noun*
• "PROTTA st'nt"
• a member or follower of any of the western Christian Churches that are separate from the Roman Catholic Church in accordance with the principles of the Reformation.
• [modern Latin *protestans*, participle of Latin *protestari* (*pro* in front (of), *testari* assert, from *testis* witness)]
• **Protestantism** *noun*

proteus *noun*
• "PRO tee us" or "PRO tyooce"
• any bacterium of the genus *Proteus*, usu. found in the intestines and feces.
• [as PROTEAN]

prothalamium *noun*
• "pro thuh LAY mee um" (with "TH" as in *THIN*)
• a song or poem to celebrate a forthcoming wedding.
• [title of a poem by E. Spenser (d.1599), after EPITHALAMIUM]

prothallus *noun*
• "pro THAL us"
• the gametophyte of certain plants, esp. a fern.
• [modern Latin from Greek *pro* before + Greek *thallos* green shoot]

prothonotary *noun*
• "pro thoe NOTE a ree" or "pruh THONNA terry" (with "TH" as in *THIN*)
• a chief clerk in some law courts.
• [medieval Latin *protonotarius* from late Greek *protonotarios* (*prōto-* from *prōtos* first, NOTARY)]

protist *noun*
• "PRO tist"
• any usu. unicellular organism of the kingdom Protista regarded as intermediate between or distinct from animals and plants, including bacteria, fungi, algae, and protozoa.
• [modern Latin *Protista* from Greek *prōtista* neuter pl. superlative from *prōtos* first]
• **protistology** *noun*

protium *noun*
• "PRO tee um"
• the ordinary isotope of hydrogen.
• [modern Latin from Greek *prōto-* from *prōtos* first]

protocol *noun*
• "PRO tuh coll"
• official, esp. diplomatic, formality and etiquette observed on state occasions etc.
• [medieval Latin *protocollum* from Greek *protokollon* fly-leaf (Greek *prōto-* from *prōtos* first, *kolla* glue)]

protolanguage *noun*
• "PRO toe lang gwidge"
• a hypothetical parent language from which actual languages or dialects are derived.
• [Greek *prōto-* from *prōtos* first + LANGUAGE]

protoplanet *noun*
• "PRO toe plannit"
• a large diffuse body of matter in the process of accretion in a solar or stellar orbit, postulated as a preliminary stage in the evolution of a planet.
• [Greek *prōto-* from *prōtos* first + PLANET]
• **protoplanetary** *adjective*
"pro toe PLANNA terry"

protoplasm *noun*
• "PRO tuh plazm"
• the material comprising the living part of a cell, consisting of a nucleus embedded in membrane-enclosed cytoplasm.
• [Greek *protoplasma* (*prōto-* from *prōtos* first, PLASMA)]
• **protoplasmic** *adjective*

protoplast *noun*
• "PRO tuh plast"
• the protoplasm of one cell.
• [Greek *protoplastos* (Greek *prōto-* from *prōtos* first, *plassō* mould)]
• **protoplastic** *adjective*

prototherian *noun*
• "pro toe THEERY 'n"
• any mammal of the subclass Prototheria, including monotremes.
• [Greek *prōto-* from *prōtos* first + *thēr* wild beast]

prototype *noun*
• "PRO tuh tipe"
• an original thing or person of which or whom copies, imitations, improved forms, representations, etc. are made.
• [Greek *prōto-* from *prōtos* first + TYPE]
• **prototypal** *adjective*

prototypical *adjective*
• "pro tuh TIPPA k'll"
• constituting the essential type of; ideal.
• [as PROTOTYPE]
• **prototypically** *adverb*

protozoan *noun*
• "pro tuh ZO 'n"
• any usu. unicellular and microscopic organism of the subkingdom Protozoa, including amoebae and ciliates.
• [modern Latin (Greek *prōto-* from *prōtos* first, *zōion* animal)]
• **protozoal** *adjective*

protractor *noun*
• "pruh TRACTER" or "PRO tracter"
• an instrument for measuring angles, usu. in the form of a semicircle graduated by degrees.
• [Latin *protrahere protract-* (*pro* in front (of), *trahere* draw)]

protrude *verb*
• "pro TRUDE"
• extend beyond or above a surface; project.
• [Latin *protrudere* (*pro* in front (of), *trudere trus-* thrust)]
• **protrusion** *noun* "pro TRUE zh'n"
• **protrusive** *adjective* "pro TRUE siv"

protrusible *adjective*
• "pruh TRUE suh bull"
• (of a limb etc.) adapted or able to be protruded.
• [as PROTRUDE]

protuberant *adjective*
• "pruh TUBE ur 'nt"
• bulging out; prominent.
• [Late Latin *protuberare* (*pro* in front (of), *tuber* bump)]
• **protuberance** *noun*

Proustian *adjective*
• "PROOSTY 'n"
• of or relating to the work of the French writer M. Proust (d.1922), esp. referring to the recovery of the lost past through the stimulation of unconscious memory.

prove *verb*
• "PROOVE"
• demonstrate the truth of by evidence or argument.
• [Old French *prover* from Latin *probare* test, approve, demonstrate, from *probus* good]
• **provable** *adjective*
• **provably** *adverb*

proven *adjective*
• "PROOV'n"
• shown to be such through trial and experience.
• [as PROVE]

provenance *noun*
• "PROVVA nince"
• the place of origin or history, esp. of a work of art, etc.
• [French from *provenir* from Latin *provenire* (*pro* in front (of), *venire* come)]

Provençal *adjective*
• "prov on SAL"
• of or concerning the language, inhabitants, landscape, etc. of Provence in SE France.

provender *noun*
• "PROV'n dur"
• animal fodder.
• [Old French *provendre*, ultimately from Latin *praebenda* (see PREBEND)]

provenience *noun*
• "pruh VEENY ince"
• = PROVENANCE.
• [Latin *provenire* from *venire* come]

provide *verb*
• "pruh VIDE"
• supply, furnish.
• [Latin *providēre* (*pro* in front (of), *vidēre vis-* see)]

provided *conjunction*
• "pruh VIDE id"
• on the condition or understanding (that).
• [as PROVIDE]

providence *noun*
• "PROVVA dince"
• the protective care of God or nature.
• [Old French *providence* or Latin *providentia* from *providēre* (*pro* in front (of), *vidēre vis-* see)]

provident *adjective*
• "PROVVA d'nt"
• having or showing foresight.
• [Middle English from Latin (as PROVIDENCE)]
• **providently** *adverb*

providential *adjective*
• "provva DEN sh'll"
• of or by divine foresight or intervention.
• [as PROVIDENCE]
• **providentially** *adverb*

provincial *adjective*
• "pruh VIN sh'll"
• of, pertaining to, or under the jurisdiction of a province or provinces.
• [Old French from Latin *provincia* charge, province]
• **provinciality** *noun* "pruh vinshy ALA tee"
• **provincially** *adverb*

provincialism *noun*
• "pruh VINSH'll izm"
• an attitude or manners reflecting a limited or restricted view of life and current events; narrow-mindedness.
• [as PROVINCIAL]
• **provincialist** *noun*

provincialization *noun*
ALSO SPELLED: esp. *Brit.* **-isation**
• "pruh vinsh'll ize AY sh'n"
• *Cdn* the transfer (of responsibilities, etc.) to the provincial level.
• [as PROVINCIAL]
• **provincialize** *verb* (also esp. *Brit.* **-ise**)

provision *noun*
• "pruh VIZH'n"
• the act or an instance of providing.
• [Old French from Latin *provisio -onis* (as PROVIDE)]
• **provisioner** *noun*
• **provisioning** *noun*

provisional *adjective*
• "pruh VIZH'n 'll"
• providing for immediate needs only; temporary.
• [as PROVISION]
• **provisionality** *noun*
• **provisionally** *adverb*

proviso *noun*
• "pruh VIZE oh"
• a stipulation.
• [Latin, neuter ablative past participle of *providēre* PROVIDE, in medieval Latin phrase *proviso quod* it being provided that]

provisory *adjective*
• "pruh VIZE ur ee"
• temporary, provisional.
• [French *provisoire* or medieval Latin *provisorius* (as PROVIDE)]
• **provisorily** *adverb*

provocateur *noun*
• "pruh vocka TUR"
• a person who provokes a disturbance; an agitator.
• [French, = 'instigator, provoker']

provocative *adjective*
• "pruh VOCKA tiv"
• intentionally causing anger, annoyance, controversy, etc.
• [obsolete French *provocatif -ive* from Late Latin *provocativus* (as PROVOKE)]
• **provocatively** *adverb*
• **provocativeness** *noun*

provoke *verb*
• "pruh VOKE"
• annoy, disturb, or harass.
• [Old French *provoquer* from Latin *provocare* (*pro* in front (of), *vocare* call)]
• **provocation** *noun*

provolone *noun*
• "pro voe LO nay" or "provva LO nee" or "PROVVA lone"
• a type of mellow cow's-milk cheese originally made in southern Italy, often smoked after drying and moulded into the shape of a pear.
• [Italian *provola* from Latin *probula* buffalo's-milk cheese]

provost *noun*
- "PROV ust"
- a high administrative officer in a university.
- [Old English *profost* & Anglo-French *provost*, *prevost* from medieval Latin *propositus* for *praepositus* past participle of *praeponere* set over (*prae-* before, *ponere posit-* place)]
- **provostship** *noun*

proximal *adjective*
- "PROCK sim 'll"
- situated towards the centre of the body or point of attachment.
- [Latin *proximus* nearest]
- **proximally** *adverb*

proximate *adjective*
- "PROXA mit"
- nearest or next before or after (in place, order, time, causation, thought process, etc.).
- [Latin *proximatus* past participle of *proximare* draw near (as PROXIMAL)]
- **proximately** *adverb*
- **proximity** *noun* "prock SIMMA tee"

proximo *adjective*
- "PROCK sim oh"
- of next month.
- [Latin *proximo mense* in the next month]

pruinose *adjective*
- "PROO in ose" ("OSE" rhymes with *GROSS*)
- covered with white powdery granules; frosted in appearance.
- [Latin *pruinosus* from *pruina* hoarfrost]

prunella *noun*
- "proo NELLA"
- any plant of the genus *Prunella*, esp. *P. vulgaris*, bearing pink, purple, or white flower spikes, and formerly thought to cure quinsy.
- [modern Latin, = quinsy: earlier *brunella* diminutive of medieval Latin *brunus* brown]

prurient *adjective*
- "PRURY 'nt"
- having or showing an excessive interest in sexual matters.
- [Latin *prurire* itch, be wanton]
- **prurience** *noun*
- **pruriently** *adverb*

pruritus *noun*
- "prur ITE us"
- severe itching of the skin.
- [Latin, = itching]
- **pruritic** *adjective* "prur ITTIC"

Prussian *noun*
- "PRUSH'n"
- a native or inhabitant of the former German kingdom or state of Prussia.

psalm *noun*
- "SOM" or "SAWLM"
- any of the sacred songs contained in the biblical Book of Psalms.
- [Greek *psalmos* song sung to a harp, from *psallō* pluck]
- **psalmic** *adjective*
- **psalmist** *noun*

psalmody *noun*
- "SOMMA dee" or "SAL muh dee"
- the practice or art of singing psalms, hymns, etc., esp. in public worship.
- [Late Latin *psalmodia* from Greek *psalmōidia* singing to a harp (as PSALM, *ōidē* song)]

psalter *noun*
- "SALTER" (rhymes with *ALTER*)
- the Book of Psalms.
- [Late Latin *psalterium* from Greek *psaltērion* stringed instrument (*psallō* pluck)]

HOMOPHONES: *salter*

psalterium *noun*
- "saul TEERY um"
- the third stomach of a ruminant; the omasum.
- [Latin (see PSALTER): named from its book-like form]

psaltery *noun*
- "SALTER ee" ("SALTER" rhymes with *ALTER*)
- an ancient and medieval instrument like a dulcimer but played by plucking the strings with the fingers or a plectrum.
- [as PSALTER]

HOMOPHONES: *saltery*

psephology *noun*
- "suh FOLLA jee" or "p'suh FOLLA jee"
- the statistical study of elections, voting, etc.
- [Greek *psēphos* pebble, vote + *logos* word]
- **psephologist** *noun*

pseud *adjective*
- "SOOD" or "SYOOD"
- intellectually or socially pretentious; not genuine.
- [abbreviation of PSEUDO]

pseudepigrapha *plural noun*
- "sooda PIGGRA fuh" or "syooda PIGGRA fuh"
- Jewish writings ascribed to various Old Testament prophets etc. but written during or just before the early Christian period.
- [neuter pl. of Greek *pseudepigraphos* with false title (*pseudēs* false, *pseudos* falsehood, EPIGRAPH)]
- **pseudepigraphic** *adjective*

pseudo *adjective*
- "SOO doe" or "SYOO doe"
- sham; spurious.
- [Greek *pseudēs* false, *pseudos* falsehood]

pseudocarp *noun*
- "SOODO carp" or "SYOODO carp"
- a fruit formed from parts other than the ovary, e.g. the strawberry or fig.
- [Greek *pseudēs* false, *pseudos* falsehood + *karpos* fruit]

pseudoephedrine *noun*
• "soodo a FED rin" or "syoodo a FED rin"
• a dextrorotatory compound commonly used as a nasal decongestant.
• [Greek *pseudēs* false, *pseudos* falsehood + EPHEDRINE]

pseudomorph *noun*
• "SOODA morf" or "SYOODA morf"
• a crystal etc. consisting of one mineral with the form proper to another.
• [Greek *pseudēs* false, *pseudos* falsehood + *morphē* form]
• **pseudomorphic** *adjective*

pseudonym *noun*
• "SOODA nim" or "SYOODA nim"
• a fictitious name, esp. one assumed by an author.
• [Greek *pseudōnymos* (*pseudēs* false, *pseudos* falsehood, *-ōnumos* from *onoma* name)]
• **pseudonymity** *noun* "sooda NIMMA tee" or "syooda NIMMA tee"
• **pseudonymous** *adjective* "soo DONNA muss" or "syoo DONNA muss"
• **pseudonymously** *adverb*

pseudopod *noun*
• "SOODO pod" or "SYOODO pod"
• = PSEUDOPODIUM.
• [modern Latin (as PSEUDOPODIUM)]

pseudopodium *noun*
• "soodo POE dee um" or "syoodo POE dee um"
• (in amoeboid cells) a temporary protrusion of protoplasm for movement, feeding, etc.
• [modern Latin (from Greek *pseudēs* false, *pseudos* falsehood + PODIUM)]

psi *noun*
• "SYE" or "p'SYE"
• the twenty-third letter of the Greek alphabet (Ψ, ψ).
• [Greek]
HOMOPHONES: *sigh, xi*

psilocybin *noun*
• "silla SYE bin"
• a hallucinogenic alkaloid found in Mexican mushrooms of the genus *Psilocybe*.
• [*Psilocybe* from Greek *psilos* bald + *kubē* head]

psittacine *adjective*
• "SITTA sine"
• of or relating to parrots; parrot-like.
• [Latin *psittacinus* from *psittacus* from Greek *psittakos* parrot]

psittacosis *noun*
• "sitta CO sis"
• a contagious viral disease of birds transmissible (esp. from parrots) to human beings as a form of pneumonia.
• [modern Latin from Latin *psittacus* (as PSITTACINE)]

psoas *noun*
• "SO us" or "SO ass"
• either of two muscles used in flexing the hip joint.
• [Greek, accusative pl. of *psoa*, taken as sing.]

psoriasis *noun*
• "suh RYE a sis"
• a skin disease marked by red scaly patches.
• [Greek *psōriasis* from *psōriaō* have an itch, from *psōra* itch]
• **psoriatic** *adjective* "sorry ATTIC"

psych *verb*
• "SIKE"
• prepare (oneself or another person) mentally for an ordeal etc.
• [abbreviation of PSYCHOLOGY]

psyche *noun*
• "SIKE ee"
• the soul; the spirit.
• [Latin from Greek *psukhē* breath, life, soul]

psychedelia *plural noun*
• "sike a DELLY uh" or "sike a DEELY uh"
• psychedelic articles, esp. posters, paintings, music, etc.
• [as PSYCHEDELIC]

psychedelic *adjective*
• "sike a DELLIC"
• expanding the mind's awareness etc., esp. through the use of hallucinogenic drugs.
• [irregular from Greek (as PSYCHE, *dēlos* clear, manifest)]
• **psychedelically** *adverb*

psychiatry *noun*
• "sye KYE a tree"
• the study and treatment of mental disease.
• [as PSYCHE + *iatreia* healing, from *iatros* healer]
• **psychiatric** *adjective* "sike ee ATTRIC"
• **psychiatrically** *adverb*
• **psychiatrist** *noun*

psychic *adjective*
• "SIKE ick"
• (of a person) considered to have occult powers, such as telepathy, clairvoyance, etc.
• [Greek *psukhikos* (as PSYCHE)]
• **psychical** *adjective*
• **psychically** *adverb*

psycho *noun*
• "SIKE oh"
• a psychopath.
• [abbreviation]

psychoacoustics *noun*
• "sike oh a COO sticks"
• the branch of psychology concerned with the perception of sound and its physiological effects.
• [Greek *psukho* breath, life, soul + ACOUSTIC]
• **psychoacoustic** *adjective*
• **psychoacoustically** *adverb*

psychoactive *adjective*
• "sike oh ACTIV"

• (esp. of a drug) affecting the mind.
• [Greek *psukho* breath, life, soul + 'active']

psychoanalysis *noun*
• "sike oh a NALA sis"
• a therapeutic method of treating mental disorders by investigating the interaction of conscious and unconscious elements in the mind and bringing repressed fears and conflicts into the conscious mind.
• [Greek *psukho* breath, life, soul + ANALYSIS]
• **psychoanalyst** *noun*
• **psychoanalytic** *adjective*
"sike oh anna LITTIC"
• **psychoanalytical** *adjective*
• **psychoanalytically** *adverb*
• **psychoanalyze** *verb* (also esp. *Brit.* **-yse**)
"sike oh ANNA lize"

psychobabble *noun*
• "SIKE oh babble"
• writing or talk filled with psychiatric jargon, esp. concerning personality and relationships, esp. when used by lay people with little regard for accuracy.
• [Greek *psukho* breath, life, soul + 'babble' (imitative)]

psychobiography *noun*
• "sike oh by OGGRA fee"
• biography dealing esp. with the psychology of the subject.
• [Greek *psukho* breath, life, soul + BIOGRAPHY]
• **psychobiographer** *noun*
• **psychobiographical** *adjective*

psychobiology *noun*
• "sike oh by OLLA jee"
• the branch of science that deals with the biological basis of behaviour and mental phenomena.
• [Greek *psukho* breath, life, soul + BIOLOGY]
• **psychobiological** *adjective*
• **psychobiologist** *noun*

psychodrama *noun*
• "SIKE oh dramma" or "SIKE oh dromma"
• a form of psychotherapy in which patients act out events from their past.
• [Greek *psukho* breath, life, soul + DRAMA]

psychodynamics *noun*
• "sike oh die NAMMIX"
• the study of the activity of and the interrelation between the various parts of an individual's personality or psyche.
• [Greek *psukho* breath, life, soul + DYNAMIC]
• **psychodynamic** *adjective*
• **psychodynamically** *adverb*

psychogenesis *noun*
• "sike oh JENNA sis"
• the study of the origin of the mind's development.
• [Greek *psukho* breath, life, soul + GENESIS]

psychogenic *adjective*
• "sike oh JENNIC"
• having a psychological origin or cause rather than a physical one.
• [as PSYCHOGENESIS]

psychographics *noun*
• "sike oh GRAFFIX"
• the study and classification of people according to their attitudes, aspirations, etc., esp. in market research.
• [Greek *psukho* breath, life, soul + *graphia* writing]
• **psychographic** *adjective*

psychohistory *noun*
• "sike oh HISTER ee"
• the interpretation of historical events with the aid of psychological theory.
• [Greek *psukho* breath, life, soul + 'history' (see HISTORIATED)]
• **psychohistorian** *noun*
• **psychohistorical** *adjective*

psychokinesis *noun*
• "sike oh kuh NEE sis"
• the movement of objects supposedly by mental effort without the action of natural forces.
• [Greek *psukho* breath, life, soul + KINESIS]
• **psychokinetic** *adjective* "sike oh kin ETTIC"

psycholinguistics *noun*
• "sike oh ling GWISTIX"
• the study of the psychological aspects of language and language-learning.
• [Greek *psukho* breath, life, soul + LINGUISTICS]
• **psycholinguist** *noun*
• **psycholinguistic** *adjective*

psychology *noun*
• "sye COLLA jee"
• the scientific study of the human mind and its functions, esp. those affecting behaviour in a given context.
• [Greek *psukho* breath, life, soul + *logos* word]
• **psychological** *adjective*
• **psychologically** *adverb*
• **psychologist** *noun*
• **psychologize** *verb* (also esp. *Brit.* **-ise**)

psychometrics *noun*
• "sike oh METRIX"
• the science of measuring mental capacities and processes.
• [Greek *psukho* breath, life, soul + *metron* measure]
• **psychometrician** *noun*
"sike oh muh TRISH'n"

psychometry *noun*
• "sye COMMA tree"
• the supposed divination of facts about events, people, etc., from inanimate objects associated with them.
• [Greek *psukho* breath, life, soul + *metron* measure]
• **psychometric** *adjective* "sike oh METRIC"
• **psychometrically** *adverb*
• **psychometrist** *noun*

psychomotor *adjective*
- "SIKE oh moter"
- concerning the study of movement resulting from mental activity.
- [Greek *psukho* breath, life, soul + 'motor']

psychoneuroimmunology *noun*
- "sike oh nyur oh im yoo NOLLA jee" or "sike oh nur oh im yoo NOLLA jee"
- the study of the effect of the mind on health and resistance to disease.
- [Greek *psukho* breath, life, soul + Greek *neuron* nerve + IMMUNOLOGY]

psychoneurosis *noun*
- "sike oh nyur OH sis" or "sike oh nur OH sis"
- a mild mental illness, not attributable to organic cause, characterized by symptoms of stress such as anxiety, depression, obsessive behaviour, hypochondria, etc., without loss of contact with reality.
- [Greek *psukho* breath, life, soul + NEUROSIS]
- **psychoneurotic** *adjective*

psychopath *noun*
- "SIKE oh path"
- a person suffering from chronic mental disorder esp. with abnormal or violent social behaviour.
- [Greek *psukho* breath, life, soul + *patheia* suffering]
- **psychopathic** *adjective*
- **psychopathically** *adverb*

psychopathology *noun*
- "sike oh puh THOLLA jee"
- the scientific study of mental disorders.
- [Greek *psukho* breath, life, soul + PATHOLOGY]
- **psychopathological** *adjective*
- **psychopathologist** *noun*

psychopathy *noun*
- "sye COPPA thee" (with "TH" as in *THIN*)
- psychopathic or psychologically abnormal behaviour.
- [as PSYCHOPATH]

psychopharmacology *noun*
- "sike oh farma COLLA jee"
- the branch of science that deals with the effects of drugs on the mind and behaviour.
- [Greek *psukho* breath, life, soul + PHARMACOLOGY]
- **psychopharmacological** *adjective* "sike oh farma kuh LODGE a k'll"
- **psychopharmacologist** *noun*

psychophysics *noun*
- "sike oh FIZZIX"
- the branch of science that deals with the relations between mental states and physical events and processes.
- [Greek *psukho* breath, life, soul + PHYSICS]
- **psychophysical** *adjective*
- **psychophysicist** *noun* "sike oh FIZZA sist"

psychophysiology *noun*
- "sike oh fizzy OLLA jee"
- the branch of physiology dealing with mental phenomena.
- [Greek *psukho* breath, life, soul + PHYSIOLOGY]
- **psychophysiological** *adjective*

psychopomp *noun*
- "SIKE oh pomp"
- a mythical conductor of souls to the place of the dead.
- [Greek *psukhopompos*, from *psukhē* PSYCHE + *pompos* conductor]

psychosexual *adjective*
- "sike oh SECK shoo 'll"
- of or involving the psychological aspects of the sexual impulse.
- [Greek *psukho* breath, life, soul + 'sexual']
- **psychosexually** *adverb*

psychosis *noun*
- "sye CO sis"
- a severe mental derangement, esp. when resulting in delusions and loss of contact with external reality.
- [Greek *psukhōsis* from *psukhoō* give life to (as PSYCHE)]

psychosocial *adjective*
- "sike oh SO sh'll"
- of or involving the influence of social factors or human interactive behaviour.
- [Greek *psukho* breath, life, soul + SOCIAL]
- **psychosocially** *adverb*

psychosomatic *adjective*
- "sike oh suh MATTIC"
- (of an illness etc.) caused or aggravated by mental conflict, stress, etc.
- [Greek *psukho* breath, life, soul + SOMATIC]
- **psychosomatically** *adverb*

psychosurgery *noun*
- "sike oh SUR jur ee"
- brain surgery as a means of treating mental disorder.
- [Greek *psukho* breath, life, soul + SURGERY]
- **psychosurgical** *adjective*

psychotherapy *noun*
- "sike oh THERRA pee"
- the treatment of mental disorder by psychological means.
- [Greek *psukho* breath, life, soul + THERAPY]
- **psychotherapeutic** *adjective* "sike oh therra PYOOTIC"
- **psychotherapist** *noun*

psychotic *adjective*
- "sye COTTIC"
- of or characterized by a psychosis.
- [as PSYCHOSIS]
- **psychotically** *adverb*

psychotropic *noun*
- "sike oh TROPPIC"
- (of a drug) acting on the mind.
- [Greek *psukho* breath, life, soul *tropē* turning]

psychrometer *noun*
• "sike ROMMA tur"
• a thermometer consisting of a dry bulb and a wet bulb for measuring atmospheric humidity.
• [Greek *psukhros* cold + Greek *metron* measure]
• **psychrometric** *adjective* "sike roe METRIC"

psyllium *noun*
• "SILLY um"
• a leafy-stemmed Mediterranean plantain, *Plantago afra*.
• [Latin from Greek *psullion*, from *psulla* flea, because of the seeds' appearance]
HOMOPHONES: *cilium*

ptarmigan *noun*
• "TARMA g'n"
• any of various game birds of Arctic regions of the genus *Lagopus*, resembling a grouse but with feathered toes and predominantly white plumage in winter.
• [Gaelic *tàrmachan*: *p-* after Greek words in *pt-*]

pteridology *noun*
• "terry DOLLA jee"
• the study of ferns.
• [Greek *pteris -idos* fern + *logos* word]
• **pteridological** *adjective*
• **pteridologist** *noun*

pteridophyte *noun*
• "TERRID a fite"
• any vascular non-flowering plant of the division Pteridophyta, including ferns, clubmosses, and horsetails.
• [Greek *pteris -idos* fern + *phuton* plant]

pterodactyl *noun*
• "terra a DACK t'll"
• a large extinct flying birdlike reptile with a long slender head and neck.
• [Greek *pteron* wing + *daktulos* finger]

pteropod *noun*
• "TERRA pod"
• a marine gastropod with the middle part of its foot expanded into a pair of wing-like lobes.
• [Greek *pteron* wing + *pous podos* foot]

pterosaur *noun*
• "TERRA sore"
• any of a group of extinct flying reptiles with large bat-like wings, including pterodactyls.
• [Greek *pteron* wing + *saura* lizard]

Ptolemaic *adjective*
• "tolla MAY ick"
• of or relating to the Greek astronomer Ptolemy (2nd c.) or his theories, esp. his geocentric and epicyclic theory of planetary motion.

ptomaine *noun*
• "TOE mane"
• any of various amine compounds, some toxic, in putrefying animal and vegetable matter.
• [French *ptomaïne* from Italian *ptomaina* from Greek *ptōma* corpse]

ptyalin *noun*
• "TIE a lin"
• an enzyme which hydrolyzes certain carbohydrates and is found in the saliva of humans and some other animals.
• [Greek *ptualon* spittle]

puberty *noun*
• "PYOOBER tee"
• the period during which adolescents reach sexual maturity and become capable of reproduction.
• [Latin *pubertas* from *puber* adult]
• **pubertal** *adjective*

pubes *noun*
• "PYOO beez"
• the lower part of the abdomen at the front of the pelvis, covered with hair from puberty.
• [Latin]

pubescence *noun*
• "pyoo BESS ince"
• the time when puberty begins.
• [French *pubescence* or medieval Latin *pubescentia* from Latin *pubescere* reach puberty]
• **pubescent** *adjective*

pubic *adjective*
• "PYOO bick"
• of or relating to the pubes or pubis.
• [as PUBES]

pubis *noun*
• "PYOO biss"
• either of a pair of bones forming the two sides of the pelvis.
• [Latin *os pubis* bone of the PUBES]

publican *noun*
• "PUBLIC'n"
• a tax collector, esp. one who held a contract for the collection of taxes in a specific area.
• [Latin *publicanus* from *publicum* public revenue]

publicity *noun*
• "pub LISSA tee"
• the action or fact of publicizing someone or something or of being publicized.
• [French *publicité* from Old French *public* or Latin *publicus* from *pubes* adult]
• **publicist** *noun*

publicize *verb*
ALSO SPELLED: esp. *Brit.* **-ise**
• "PUBBLA size"
• make publicly known; advertise, promote.
• [as PUBLICITY]

puce *noun*
• "PYUCE" (rhymes with *MOOSE*)
• a dark reddish purple.
• [French, = flea(-colour), from Latin *pulex -icis*]

pueblo *noun*
• "PWEB lo"
• a town or village in Latin America, esp. an Indian settlement.
• [Spanish, = people, from Latin *populus*]

puerile *adjective*
- "PURE ile"
- trivial, childish, immature.
- [French *puéril* or Latin *puerilis* from *puer* boy]
- **puerilely** *adverb*
- **puerility** *noun* "pure ILLA tee"

puerperal *adjective*
- "pyoo UR purr 'll"
- of or caused by childbirth.
- [Latin *puerperus* from *puer* child + *-parus* bearing]

puggree *noun*
ALSO SPELLED: **pugree**
- "PUG ree"
- an Indian turban.
- [Hindi *pagṛī* turban]

pugilist *noun*
- "PYOO j'll ist"
- a boxer, esp. a professional.
- [Latin *pugil* boxer]
- **pugilism** *noun*
- **pugilistic** *adjective*

pugnacious *adjective*
- "pug NAY sh'ss"
- quarrelsome; disposed to fight.
- [Latin *pugnax -acis* from *pugnare* fight, from *pugnus* fist]
- **pugnaciously** *adverb*
- **pugnaciousness** *noun*
- **pugnacity** *noun* "pug NASSA tee"

puisne *adjective*
- "PYOONY"
- *Cdn & Brit.* denoting a judge of a superior court inferior in rank to chief justices.
- [Old French from *puis* from Latin *postea* afterwards + *né* born, from Latin *natus*]

HOMOPHONES: *puny*

puissance *noun*
- "PYOO iss ince" or "PWISS ince" or "pwee SONCE"
- a test of a horse's ability to jump large obstacles in show jumping.
- [Old French (as PUISSANT)]

puissant *adjective*
- "PYOO iss 'nt" or "PWEECE 'nt" or "PWISS'nt"
- having great power or influence; mighty.
- [Old French from Latin *posse* be able: compare POTENT]
- **puissantly** *adverb*

puja *noun*
ALSO SPELLED: **pooja**
- "POO juh"
- a Hindu rite of worship; a prayer.
- [Sanskrit]

pukka *adjective*
ALSO SPELLED: **pukkah**, **pucka**
- "PUCKA"
- genuine.
- [Hindi *pakkā* cooked, ripe, substantial]

pul *noun*
- "POOL"
- a monetary unit of Afghanistan, equal to one-hundredth of an afghani.
- [Pashto from Persian *pūl* copper coin]

HOMOPHONES: *pool*

pula *noun*
- "PULL uh"
- the basic monetary unit of Botswana, equal to 100 thebe.
- [Setswana, = rain]

pulchritude *noun*
- "PUL cruh tude"
- beauty.
- [Latin *pulchritudo -dinis* from *pulcher -chri* beautiful]
- **pulchritudinous** *adjective* "pul cruh TUDE in us"

pule *verb*
- "PYOOL"
- cry querulously or weakly; whine, whimper.
- [16th c.: prob. imitative: compare French *piauler*]

pullet *noun*
- "PULL it"
- a young hen, esp. one less than one year old.
- [Old French *poulet* diminutive of *poule*, ultimately feminine of Latin *pullus* chicken]

pulley *noun*
- "PULL ee"
- a grooved wheel or set of wheels for a cord etc. to pass over, set in a block and used for changing the direction of a force.
- [Old French *polie* prob. ultimately from medieval Greek *polidion* (unrecorded) pivot, diminutive of *polos* (north or south) pole]

pullulate *verb*
- "PUL yuh late"
- (of a seed, shoot, etc.) bud, sprout, germinate.
- [Latin *pullulare* sprout, from *pullulus* diminutive of *pullus* young of an animal]
- **pullulation** *noun*

pulmonary *adjective*
- "PUL m'n airy"
- of or relating to the lungs.
- [Latin *pulmonarius* from *pulmo -onis* lung]

pulpit *noun*
- "PUL pit" ("PUL" rhymes with *HULL* or *FULL*)
- a lectern or raised usu. enclosed platform in a church etc. from which the preacher delivers a sermon.
- [Latin *pulpitum* scaffold, platform]

pulque *noun*
- "PULK"
- an originally Mexican fermented drink made from the sap of the maguey.
- [17th c.: Latin American Spanish, from Nahuatl *puliúhki* decomposed]

pulsar *noun*
- "PUL sarr"
- a celestial object, thought to be a rapidly rotating neutron star, emitting regular pulses of radio waves and other electromagnetic radiation.
- [*puls*ating *st*ar, after *quasar*]

pulsate *verb*
- "PUL sate"
- expand and contract rhythmically; throb.
- [Latin *pulsare* frequentative of *pellere puls-* drive, beat]
- **pulsation** *noun*
- **pulsator** *noun*

pulsatile *adjective*
- "PULSA tile"
- of or having the property of pulsation.
- [as PULSATE]

pulsatilla *noun*
- "pulsa TILLA"
- any plant of the genus *Pulsatilla*, esp. the pasque flower.
- [modern Latin diminutive of *pulsata* feminine past participle (as PULSATE), because it quivers in the wind]

pulverize *verb*
ALSO SPELLED: esp. *Brit.* **-ise**
- "PUL vur ize"
- reduce to fine particles.
- [Late Latin *pulverizare* from *pulvis pulveris* dust]
- **pulverization** *noun* (also esp. *Brit.* **-isation**)
- **pulverizer** *noun* (also esp. *Brit.* **-iser**)

pumice *noun*
- "PUM iss"
- a light porous volcanic rock often used as an abrasive in cleaning or polishing substances.
- [Old French *pomis* from Latin *pumex pumicis* (dialect *pom-*)]

HOMOPHONES: *pomace*

pummel *verb*
- "PUM'll"
- pound or thump repeatedly.
- [alteration of POMMEL]

HOMOPHONES: *pommel*

pumpernickel *noun*
- "PUMPER nick'll"
- a dense, dark, slightly sour rye bread.
- [German, earlier = lout, bumpkin, of uncertain origin]

puncheon *noun*
- "PUNCH'n"
- a large cask for liquids etc. holding from 150 to 545 litres.
- [Old French *poinson, po(i)nchon*, of unknown origin]

Punchinello *noun*
- "punch'n ELLO"
- the chief character in a traditional Italian puppet show.
- [Neapolitan dialect *Polecenella*, Italian *Pulcinella*, perhaps diminutive of *pollecena*, young turkeycock with a hooked beak, from *pulcino* chicken, ultimately from Latin *pullus*]

punctate *adjective*
- "PUNK tate"
- marked or studded with points, dots, spots, etc.
- [Latin *punctum* point]
- **punctation** *noun*

punctilio *noun*
- "punk TILLY oh"
- a fine or petty point of conduct or procedure.
- [Italian *puntiglio* & Spanish *puntillo* diminutive of *punto* from Latin *punctum* point]

punctilious *adjective*
- "punk TILLY us"
- attentive to formality or etiquette.
- [French *pointilleux* from *pointille* from Italian (as PUNCTILIO)]
- **punctiliously** *adverb*
- **punctiliousness** *noun*

punctual *adjective*
- "PUNK choo 'll"
- neither early nor late; precisely on time.
- [medieval Latin *punctualis* from Latin *punctum* point]
- **punctuality** *noun*
- **punctually** *adverb*

punctuate *verb*
- "PUNK choo ate"
- insert punctuation marks in.
- [medieval Latin *punctuare punctuat-* (as PUNCTUAL)]

punctuation *noun*
- "punk choo AY sh'n"
- the system or arrangement of marks used in writing to separate sentences and phrases etc. and to clarify meaning.
- [as PUNCTUATE]

puncture *noun*
- "PUNK chur"
- a small hole in a tire resulting in an escape of air.
- [Latin *punctura* from *pungere punct-* prick]

punditocracy *noun*
- "pundit OCKRA see"
- elite members of the news media, typically seen as having political power in their own right.
- [Sanskrit *paṇḍita* learned + Greek *kratia* from *kratos* strength, power]

pungent *adjective*
- "PUN j'nt"
- having a sharp or strong taste or smell.
- [Latin *pungent-* present participle of *pungere* prick]
- **pungency** *noun*
- **pungently** *adverb*

Punic *adjective*
• "PYOONIC"
• of or relating to ancient Carthage in North Africa.
• [Latin *Punicus*, *Poenicus* from *Poenus* from Greek *Phoinix* Phoenician]

punitive *adjective*
• "PYOONA tiv"
• inflicting or intended to inflict punishment.
• [medieval Latin *punitivus* from *punit-* punished, from the verb *punire*]
• **punitively** *adverb*

Punjabi *noun*
• "poon JABBY" or "pun JABBY"
• a native or inhabitant of Punjab, now divided between India and Pakistan.

punkah *noun*
• "PUNKA"
• (in India) a fan usu. made from the leaf of the palmyra.
• [Hindi *pankhā* fan, from Sanskrit *pakṣaka* from *pakṣa* wing]

punnet *noun*
• "PUN it"
• a small light basket or container for fruit or vegetables.
• [19th c.: perhaps diminutive of dialect *pun* pound]

pupa *noun*
• "PYOO puh"
• an inactive immature form of an insect, being the resting stage between larva and adult, e.g. a chrysalis.
• [modern Latin from Latin *pupa* girl, doll]
• **pupal** *adjective*
HOMOPHONES: *pupil*

pupate *verb*
• "PYOO pate"
• become a pupa.
• [as PUPA]
• **pupation** *noun*

pupil *noun*
• "PYOO p'll"
• a person who is taught by another, esp. a schoolchild or student in relation to a teacher.
• [Middle English, originally = orphan, ward, from Old French *pupille* or Latin *pupillus*, *-illa*, diminutive of *pupus* boy, *pupa* girl]
• **pupillage** *noun* (also **pupilage**) "PYOO p'll idge"
• **pupillary** *adjective* "PYOO p'll airy"
HOMOPHONES: *pupal*

puppet *noun*
• "PUPPIT"
• a small figure representing a human being or animal and moved by various means as entertainment, e.g. by pulling strings attached to its limbs or by putting one's hand inside it.
• [later form of POPPET]
• **puppeteer** *noun*
• **puppeteering** *noun*
• **puppetry** *noun*

Purana *noun*
• "poo RONNA"
• any of a class of Sanskrit sacred writings on Hindu mythology, folklore, etc.
• [Sanskrit *purāṇa* ancient legend, ancient, from *purā* formerly]
• **Puranic** *adjective*

purblind *adjective*
• "PURR blind"
• partly blind; having impaired or defective vision.
• [Middle English *pur(e) blind* from 'pure', originally in sense 'utterly']
• **purblindness** *noun*

purchase *verb*
• "PURR chiss"
• acquire by payment; buy.
• [Anglo-French *purchacer* seek to obtain (Old French *pur-* from Latin *por-* variant of *pro* for, Old French *chace chacier*, ultimately from Latin *capere* take)]
• **purchasable** *adjective*
• **purchaser** *noun*

purdah *noun*
• "PURDA"
• a system in certain Muslim and Hindu societies of screening women from strangers by means of a veil or curtain.
• [Urdu & Persian *pardah* veil, curtain]

purée *noun*
• "pure AY" or "PURE ay"
• a pulp of vegetables or fruit etc. reduced to a smooth thick liquid.
• [French]

purfle *noun*
• "PURF'll"
• an ornamental border, esp. on a violin etc.
• [Old French *porfil*, *porfiler*, ultimately from Latin *filum* thread]
• **purfling** *noun*

purgation *noun*
• "purr GAY sh'n"
• purification.
• [Old French *purgation* or Latin *purgatio* from *purgare* purify, from *purus* pure]

purgative *adjective*
• "PURGA tiv"
• serving to purify.
• [Old French *purgatif -ive* or Late Latin *purgativus* (as PURGATION)]

purgatory *noun*
• "PURGA tory"
• the condition or supposed place of spiritual cleansing, esp. of those dying in the grace of God but having to expiate venial sins etc.
• [Anglo-French *purgatorie* from medieval Latin

purgatorium from *purgare* purify, from *purus* pure]
• **purgatorial** *adjective*

puri *noun*
• "POO ree"
• (in Indian cooking) a small round cake of unleavened wheat flour deep-fried in ghee or oil.
• [Hindi]

purify *verb*
• "PYURA fie"
• cleanse or make pure.
• [Old French, from *pur* from Latin *purus* pure]
• **purification** *noun*
• **purificatory** *adjective* "pure IFFA kuh tory"
• **purifier** *noun*

Purim *noun*
• "POO rim"
• a Jewish spring festival commemorating the defeat of Haman's plot to massacre the Jews (Esther 9).
• [Hebrew, pl. of *pūr*, perhaps = 'lot' (from the casting of lots by Haman)]

purine *noun*
• "PYOOR een"
• an organic nitrogenous base forming uric acid on oxidation.
• [German *Purin* (from Latin *purus* pure + *uricum* uric acid)]

purist *noun*
• "PYUR ist"
• a stickler for or advocate of scrupulous correctness or authenticity, e.g. in language or art.
• [as PURIFY]
• **purism** *noun*
• **puristic** *adjective*

puritan *noun*
• "PURE a t'n"
• a member of a group of English Protestants who regarded the Reformation of the Church under Elizabeth I (d.1603) as incomplete and sought to simplify and regulate forms of worship.
• [Latin *purus* pure]
• **puritanism** *noun*

puritanical *adjective*
• "pure a TANNA k'll"
• practising, affecting, or advocating strict religious or moral behaviour, esp. one opposed to pleasure.
• [as PURITAN]
• **puritanically** *adverb*

purity *noun*
• "PURE it ee"
• pureness, cleanness; freedom from physical or moral pollution.
• [Latin *purus* pure]

purl *noun*
• "PURL"
• a knitting stitch made by putting the needle through the front of the previous stitch and passing the yarn around the back of the needle.
• [origin unknown]
HOMOPHONES: *pearl*

purlieu *noun*
• "PURL yoo"
• the outskirts; an outlying region.
• [Middle English *purlew*, prob. alteration (suggested by French *lieu* place) from Anglo-French *purale(e)*, Old French *pourallee* 'a going round to settle the boundaries' from *po(u)raler* traverse]

purlin *noun*
• "PURL in"
• a horizontal beam along the length of a roof, resting on principals and supporting the common rafters or boards.
• [Middle English: origin uncertain]

purloin *verb*
• "purr LOIN"
• steal, pilfer.
• [Anglo-French *purloigner* put away, do away with (Old French *pur-* from Latin *por-* variant of *pro* for, *loign* far, from Latin *longe*)]
• **purloiner** *noun*

purport *verb*
• "purr PORT"
• profess; be intended to seem.
• [Old French *purport* from *purporter* from medieval Latin *proportare* (*pro* for, *portare* carry)]
• **purportedly** *adverb*

purpose *noun*
• "PURR piss"
• something to be attained; a thing intended.
• [Old French *porpos*, *purpos* from Latin *proponere* (as PROPONENT)]
• **purposeless** *adjective*
• **purposelessly** *adverb*
• **purposelessness** *noun*

purposeful *adjective*
• "PURR piss full"
• having or indicating purpose.
• [as PURPOSE]
• **purposefully** *adverb*
• **purposefulness** *noun*

purposely *adverb*
• "PURR piss lee"
• on purpose; intentionally.
• [as PURPOSE]

purposive *adjective*
• "PURR puss iv"
• having or serving a purpose.
• [as PURPOSE]
• **purposively** *adverb*
• **purposiveness** *noun*

purpura *noun*
• "PURR pyoor uh"
• a rash of purple spots on the skin caused by internal bleeding from small blood vessels.
• [Latin from Greek *porphura* purple]

purslane *noun*
• "PURSE lane"
• any of various plants of the genus *Portulaca*, esp. *P. oleracea*, with green or golden leaves, used as a herb and salad vegetable.
• [Old French *porcelaine* (compare PORCELAIN) alteration of Latin *porcil(l)aca, portulaca*]

pursuance *noun*
• "purr SUE ince"
• the carrying out or observance (of a plan, idea, etc.).
• [as PURSUE]

pursuant *adverb*
• "purr SUE 'nt"
• conforming to or in accordance with.
• [Middle English, = prosecuting, from Old French *po(u)rsuiant* participle of *po(u)rsu(iv)ir* (as PURSUE): assimilated to Anglo-French *pursuer* and PURSUE]

pursue *verb*
• "purr SUE"
• follow with intent to overtake or capture or do harm to.
• [Anglo-French *pursuer* = Old French *porsivre* etc., ultimately from Latin *prosequi* follow after]
• **pursuer** *noun*

pursuit *noun*
• "purr SUTE"
• the act or an instance of pursuing.
• [Old French *poursuite* (as PURSUE)]

purulent *adjective*
• "PYUR oo l'nt" or "PYUR yoo l'nt"
• consisting of or containing pus.
• [French *purulent* or Latin *purulentus* from *pus puris* pus]
• **purulence** *noun*
• **purulently** *adverb*

purvey *verb*
• "purr VAY"
• provide or supply (food, provisions, or esp. shady or dishonest information, services, etc.) esp. as one's business.
• [Anglo-French *purveier*, Old French *porveiir* from Latin *providēre* PROVIDE]
• **purveyor** *noun*

purview *noun*
• "PURR vyoo"
• the scope or range of a document, scheme, etc.
• [Anglo-French *purveü*, Old French *porveü* past participle of *porveiir* (as PURVEY)]

Pushtu *noun*
• "PUSH too" ("PUSH" rhymes with *HUSH*)
• = PASHTO.
• [Persian *puštū*]

Pushtun *noun*
• "PUSH toon" ("PUSH" rhymes with *HUSH*)
• = PASHTUN.
• [Persian *puštūn*]

pusillanimous *adjective*
• "pyoo suh LANNA muss"
• lacking courage; timid.
• [Church Latin *pusillanimis* from *pusillus* very small + *animus* mind]
• **pusillanimity** *noun*
"pyoo suh luh NIMMA tee"
• **pusillanimously** *adverb*

pustule *noun*
• "PUS chool" or "PUST yool"
• a pimple containing pus.
• [Old French *pustule* or Latin *pustula*]
• **pustular** *adjective*
• **pustulate** *verb*
• **pustulation** *noun*
• **pustulous** *adjective*

putative *adjective*
• "PYOO tuh tiv"
• reputed, supposed.
• [Old French *putatif -ive* or Late Latin *putativus* from Latin *putare* think]
• **putatively** *adverb*

putrefy *verb*
• "PYOO truh fie"
• become or make putrid; go bad.
• [Latin *putrefacere* from *puter putris* rotten]
• **putrefaction** *noun*
• **putrefactive** *adjective*

putrescent *adjective*
• "pyoo TRESS'nt"
• in the process of rotting.
• [Latin *putrescere* inceptive of *putrēre* (as PUTRID)]
• **putrescence** *noun*

putrid *adjective*
• "PYOO trid"
• decomposed, rotten.
• [Latin *putridus* from *putrēre* to rot, from *puter putris* rotten]
• **putridity** *noun*
• **putridly** *adverb*
• **putridness** *noun*

putsch *noun*
• "PUTCH" (rhymes with *BUTCH*)
• an attempt at political revolution; a violent uprising.
• [Swiss German, = thrust, blow]
• **putschist** *noun*

puttanesca *adjective*
• "poota NESKA"
• denoting a pasta sauce of tomatoes, garlic, olives, anchovies, etc.
• [Italian, from *puttana* prostitute (the sauce is said to have been devised by prostitutes as one which could be cooked quickly between clients' visits)]

puttee *noun*
• "PUTT ee"
• a long strip of cloth wound spirally round the leg from ankle to knee for protection and support.
• [Hindi *paṭṭī* band, bandage]
HOMOPHONES: *putty*

putto *noun*
• "PUT oh"
• a representation of a naked child (esp. a cherub or a cupid) in (esp. Renaissance) art.
• [Italian, = boy, from Latin *putus*]

putz *noun*
• "PUTTS" (rhymes with *NUTS*)
• a fool; a stupid person.
• [Yiddish]

pya *noun*
• "p'YUH"
• a monetary unit of Burma (Myanmar), equal to one-hundredth of a kyat.
• [Burmese]

pyelonephritis *noun*
• "pie a lo nuh FRITE iss"
• inflammation of the kidney and its pelvis, caused by a bacterial infection.
• [Greek *puelos* pelvis (lit. = trough, basin) + NEPHRITIS]

pygmy *noun*
ALSO SPELLED: **pigmy**
• "PIG mee"
• a member of any of several small-statured peoples of equatorial Africa and parts of SE Asia.
• [Latin *pygmaeus* from Greek *pugmaios* dwarf, from *pugmē* the length from elbow to knuckles, fist]

pyjamas *plural noun*
ALSO SPELLED: **pajamas**
• "puh JOM uz" or "puh JAM uz"
• a suit of loose trousers, shorts, or underpants and a top for sleeping in.
• [Urdu *pā(ē)jāma* from Persian *pae, pay* leg + *jāma* clothing]

pylon *noun*
• "PIE lon"
• a plastic, usu. orange cone used to mark areas of roads etc.
• [Greek *pulōn* from *pulē* gate]

pylorus *noun*
• "pie LOR us"
• the opening from the stomach into the duodenum.
• [Late Latin from Greek *pulōros, pulouros* gatekeeper, from *pulē* gate + *ouros* warder]
• **pyloric** *adjective*

pyorrhea *noun*
ALSO SPELLED: *Brit.* **pyorrhoea**
• "pie a REE uh"
• a disease of periodontal tissue causing shrinkage of the gums and loosening of the teeth.
• [Greek *puo-* from *puon* pus + *rhoia* flux, from *rheō* flow]

pyracantha *noun*
• "pie ruh CANTH uh"
• any evergreen thorny shrub of the genus *Pyracantha*, having white flowers and bright red or yellow berries.
• [Latin from Greek *purakantha*]

pyramid *noun*
• "PEERA mid"
• a monumental structure, usu. of stone, with a square base and sloping sides meeting centrally at an apex, esp. an ancient Egyptian royal tomb.
• [Latin *pyramis* from Greek *puramis -idos*]
• **pyramidal** *adjective* "peer AMMA d'll" or "peera MIDDLE"
• **pyramidic** *adjective*

pyre *noun*
• "PIRE"
• a heap of combustible material esp. on which a corpse is burned.
• [Latin *pyra* from Greek *pura* from *pur* fire]

Pyrenean *adjective*
• "peera NEE 'n"
• of or relating to the Pyrenees mountain range on the border between France and Spain.

pyrethrin *noun*
• "pie REETH rin"
• any of a class of compounds found in pyrethrum flowers and used in the manufacture of insecticides.
• [as PYRETHRUM]

pyrethroid *noun*
• "pie REETH roid"
• any of a group of substances similar to pyrethrins in structure and properties.
• [as PYRETHRUM]

pyrethrum *noun*
• "pie REETH rum"
• any of several aromatic chrysanthemums of the genus *Tanacetum*, esp. *T. coccineum*.
• [Latin from Greek *purethron* feverfew]

pyretic *adjective*
• "pie RETTIC"
• of, for, or producing fever.
• [modern Latin *pyreticus* from Greek *puretos* fever]

pyrexia *noun*
• "pie REXY uh"
• fever.
• [modern Latin from Greek *purexis* from *puressō* be feverish, from *pur* fire]

pyridine *noun*
• "PEERA deen"
• a colourless volatile odorous liquid, formerly

obtained from coal tar, used as a solvent and in chemical manufacture.
• [Greek *pur* fire]

pyridoxine *noun*
• "peera DOX in"
• a vitamin of the B complex found in yeast, and important in the body's use of unsaturated fatty acids.
• [PYRIDINE + OXYGEN]

pyrimidine *noun*
• "peer IMMA deen"
• a cyclic organic nitrogenous base.
• [German *Pyrimidin* from *Pyridin* (as PYRIDINE, IMIDE)]

pyrite *noun*
• "PIE rite"
• a yellow lustrous form of iron disulphide.
• [Latin from Greek *puritēs* of fire (*pur*)]
• **pyritic** *adjective* "pie RITTIC"
• **pyritize** *verb* (also esp. *Brit.* **-ise**) "PIE rite ize"

pyroclastic *adjective*
• "pie roe CLASTIC"
• of or formed from fragments of rock from a volcanic eruption.
• [Greek *puro-* from *pur* fire + CLASTIC]

pyroelectric *adjective*
• "pie roe e LECK trick"
• having the property of becoming electrically charged when heated.
• [Greek *puro-* from *pur* fire + ELECTRIC]

pyrogenic *adjective*
• "pie roe JENNIC"
• producing heat, esp. in the body.
• [Greek *puro-* from *pur* fire + GENESIS]

pyrography *noun*
• "pire OGGRA fee"
• the technique of burning designs on white wood etc. with a heated metal rod.
• [Greek *puro-* from *pur* fire + *graphia* writing]
• **pyrographer** *noun*

pyrola *noun*
• "pie ROLE uh"
• a wintergreen of the genus *Pyrola*.
• [medieval and modern Latin, diminutive of Latin *pyrus* pear]

pyrolysis *noun*
• "pie RAWLA sis"
• chemical decomposition brought about by heat.
• [Greek *puro-* from *pur* fire + LYSIS]
• **pyrolytic** *adjective* "pie ruh LITTIC"
• **pyrolyze** *verb* (also **-yse**)

pyromania *noun*
• "pie roe MAINY uh"
• an obsessive desire to set things on fire.
• [Greek *puro-* from *pur* fire + MANIA]
• **pyromaniac** *noun*
• **pyromaniacal** *adjective*
"pie roe muh NIE a k'll"

pyrometer *noun*
• "pie ROMMA tur"
• an instrument for measuring high temperatures, esp. in furnaces and kilns.
• [Greek *puro-* from *pur* fire + *metron* measure]
• **pyrometric** *adjective* "pie roe METRIC"
• **pyrometrically** *adverb*
• **pyrometry** *noun*

pyrope *noun*
• "PIE rope"
• a deep red variety of garnet.
• [Old French *pirope* from Latin *pyropus* from Greek *purōpos* gold-bronze, lit. fiery-eyed, from *pur* fire + *ōps* eye]

pyrophoric *adjective*
• "pie roe FORIC"
• (of a substance) liable to ignite spontaneously on exposure to air.
• [modern Latin *pyrophorus* from Greek *purophoros* fire-bearing, from *pur* fire + *pherō* bear]

pyrosis *noun*
• "pie ROE sis"
• heartburn.
• [modern Latin from Greek *purōsis* from *puroō* set on fire, from *pur* fire]

pyrotechnic *adjective*
• "pie roe TECK nick"
• of or relating to fireworks.
• [Greek *puro-* from *pur* fire + *tekhnē* art]
• **pyrotechnical** *adjective*
• **pyrotechnician** *noun*
• **pyrotechnics** *noun*

pyroxene *noun*
• "pie ROX een"
• any of a group of minerals commonly found as components of igneous rocks, composed of silicates of calcium, magnesium, and iron.
• [Greek *puro-* from *pur* fire + *xenos* stranger (because supposed to be alien to igneous rocks)]

pyroxylin *noun*
• "pie ROX'll in"
• a form of nitrocellulose, soluble in ether and alcohol, used as a basis for lacquers, artificial leather, etc.
• [French *pyroxyline* (Greek *puro-* from *pur* fire, *xulon* wood)]

pyrrhic *adjective*
• "PEER ick"
• (of a victory) won at too great a cost to be of use to the victor.
• [*Pyrrhus* of Epirus, who defeated the Romans at Asculum in 279 BC but sustained heavy losses]

Pyrrhonism *noun*
• "PEER'n izm"
• the philosophy of Pyrrho of Elis (d. *c.*270 BC), maintaining that certainty of knowledge is unattainable.
• [Greek *Purrhōn* Pyrrho]
• **Pyrrhonist** *noun*

pyruvate *noun*
- "pie ROO vate"
- any salt or ester of pyruvic acid.
- [as PYRUVIC]

pyruvic *adjective*
- "pie ROO vic"
- designating an organic acid occurring as an intermediate in many metabolic pathways.
- [Greek *puro-* from *pur* fire + Latin *uva* grape]

pysanka *noun*
- "PISS'n kuh"
- *Cdn* a hand-painted Ukrainian Easter egg, usu. having elaborate and intricate designs.
- [Ukrainian]

Pythagorean *adjective*
- "pie thagga REE 'n"
- of or relating to the Greek philosopher Pythagoras (d. *c.*480 BC) or his philosophy, esp. designating the theorem attributed to Pythagoras that the square on the hypotenuse of a right-angled triangle is equal to the sum of the squares on the other two sides.

Pythian *adjective*
- "PITHY 'n"
- of or relating to Delphi (in central Greece) or its ancient oracle of Apollo.
- [Latin *Pythius* from Greek *Puthios* from *Puthō*, an older name of Delphi]

python *noun*
- "PIE thon"
- any constricting snake of the family Pythonidae, esp. of the genus *Python*, found throughout the tropics in the Old World.
- [Latin from Greek *Puthōn*, a huge serpent slain by Apollo]
- **pythonic** *adjective*

pythoness *noun*
- "PIE thuh ness"
- the Pythian priestess.
- [Late Latin *pythonissa* feminine of *pytho* from Greek *puthōn* soothsaying demon: compare PYTHON]

pyx *noun*
ALSO SPELLED: **pix**
- "PIX"
- the vessel in which the consecrated bread of the Eucharist is kept.
- [Latin (as PYXIS)]

HOMOPHONES: *pix*

pyxidium *noun*
- "pick SIDDY um"
- a seed capsule with a top that comes off like the lid of a box.
- [modern Latin from Greek *puxidion*, diminutive of *puxis*: see PYXIS]

pyxis *noun*
- "PIX iss"
- a small box or casket.
- [Latin from Greek *puxis* from *puxos* box]

qadi *noun*
ALSO SPELLED: **cadi, kadi**
• "KADDY" or "KAY dee"
• a civil judge in a Muslim community.
• [Arabic *ḳāḍī* from *ḳaḍā* to judge]
HOMOPHONES: *caddy, catty*

Qallunaaq *noun*
• "ka LOO nack"
• *Cdn (North)* a person who is not Inuit, esp. a white person.
• [Inuktitut]

Qatari *noun*
• "ka TAR ee"
• a native or inhabitant of the sheikdom of Qatar on the Persian Gulf.

qawwali *noun*
• "kuh WOLLY"
• a style of Muslim devotional music now associated particularly with Sufis in Pakistan.
• [Arabic *qawwāli*, from *qawwāl* loquacious, also 'singer']

qi *noun*
• "CHEE"
• the physical life force postulated by certain Chinese philosophers to flow through the body.
• [Chinese *qì* air, breath]

qibla *noun*
• "KIBLA"
• the direction of the Kaaba (the sacred building at Mecca), to which Muslims turn at prayer.
• [Arabic *ḳibla* that which is opposite]

qigong *noun*
• "chee GOONG" (with "OO" as in *BOOK*)
• a system of techniques to focus and strengthen qi, including breathing exercises, meditation, and hand and arm movements, used in alternative medicine and in martial-arts training.
• [QI + Chinese *kung* work]

qiviut *noun*
• "KIVVY oot"
• *Cdn (North) & Alaska* fine, soft wool from the underbelly of a muskox.
• [Inuktitut]

qua *conjunction*
• "KWAY" or "KWUH"
• in the capacity of; as being.
• [Latin, ablative feminine sing. of *qui* who]
HOMOPHONES: *Kwa*

quad *noun*
• "KWOD"
• a quadrangle.
• [abbreviation]

quadragenarian *noun*
• "kwodra juh NERRY 'n"
• a person from 40 to 49 years old.
• [Late Latin *quadragenarius* from *quadrageni* distributive of *quadraginta* forty]

Quadragesima *noun*
• "kwodra JESSIM uh"
• the first Sunday in Lent.
• [Late Latin, feminine of Latin *quadragesimus* fortieth, from *quadraginta* forty, Lent having 40 days]

quadrangle *noun*
• "KWOD rangle"
• a four-sided plane figure, esp. a square or rectangle.
• [Old French from Late Latin *quadrangulum* square, neuter of *quadrangulus* (*quadri-* from *quattuor* four, *angulus* angle)]
• **quadrangular** *adjective*

quadrant *noun*
• "KWOD r'nt"
• a quarter of a circle's circumference.
• [Latin *quadrans -antis* quarter, from *quattuor* four]

quadraphonic *adjective*
ALSO SPELLED: **quadrophonic**
• "kwodra FONNIC"
• (of sound reproduction) using four transmission channels.
• [Latin *quadri-* from *quattuor* four + STEREOPHONIC]
• **quadraphonically** *adverb* (also **quadrophonically**)
• **quadraphonics** *noun* (also **quadrophonics**)
• **quadraphony** *noun* (also **quadrophony**) "kwod ROFFA nee"

quadrat *noun*
• "KWOD rit"
• a small area marked out for study.
• [var. of QUADRATE]
HOMOPHONES: *quadrate*

quadrate *adjective*
• "KWOD rit"
• square or rectangular.
• [Latin *quadrare quadrat-* make square, from *quattuor* four]
HOMOPHONES: *quadrat*

quadratic *adjective*
• "kwod RATTIC"
• involving the second and no higher power of an unknown quantity or variable.
• [French *quadratique* or modern Latin *quadraticus* (as QUADRATE)]

quadrature *noun*
• "KWODRA chur"
• the process of constructing a square with an area equal to that of a figure bounded by a curve, e.g. a circle.
• [French *quadrature* or Latin *quadratura* (as QUADRATE)]

quadrennial *adjective*
• "kwod RENNY 'll"
• lasting four years.
• [as QUADRENNIUM]
• **quadrennially** *adverb*

quadrennium *noun*
• "kwod RENNY um"
• a period of four years.
• [Latin *quadriennium* (*quadri-* from *quattuor* four, *annus* year)]

quadric *adjective*
• "KWOD rick"
• (of a surface) described by an equation of the second degree.
• [Latin *quadra* square]

quadriceps *noun*
• "KWODRA seps"
• a large four-headed muscle at the front of the thigh, the chief extensor of the knee.
• [modern Latin (Latin *quadri-* from *quattuor* four, BICEPS)]

quadrifid *adjective*
• "KWODRA fid"
• having four divisions or lobes.
• [Latin *quadrifidus* (*quadri-* from *quattuor* four, *findere fid-* cleave)]

quadrilateral *adjective*
• "kwodra LATTER'll"
• having four sides.
• [Latin *quadri-* from *quattuor* four + LATERAL]

quadrille *noun*
• "kwod RILL"
• a square dance usu. performed by four couples and containing five figures, each of which is a complete dance in itself.
• [French from Spanish *cuadrilla* troop, company, from *cuadra* square or Italian *quadriglia* from *quadra* square]

quadrillion *noun*
• "kwod RILL y'n"
• a thousand raised to the fifth power (10^{15}).
• [originally one million raised to the fourth power (10^{24}), from French (Latin *quadri-* from *quattuor* four, after *million*, from Old French, prob. from Italian *millione* from *mille* thousand + *-one* augmentative suffix)]
• **quadrillionth** *noun*

quadripartite *adjective*
• "kwodra PAR tite"
• consisting of four parts.
• [Latin *quadripartitus* (*quadri-* from *quattuor* four + *partire* part)]

quadriplegia *noun*
• "kwodra PLEE juh"
• paralysis of all four limbs.
• [modern Latin (Latin *quadri-* from *quattuor* four, Greek *plēgē* blow, strike)]
• **quadriplegic** *adjective*

quadrivalent *adjective*
• "kwodra VALE 'nt"
• having a valence of four.
• [Latin *quadri-* from *quattuor* four + VALENCE]

quadrivium *noun*
• "kwod RIVVY um"
• a medieval university course of arithmetic, geometry, astronomy, and music.
• [Latin, = the place where four roads meet (*quadri-* from *quattuor* four, *via* road)]

quadroon *noun*
• "kwod ROON"
• the offspring of a white person and a mulatto; a person of one quarter black ancestry.
• [Spanish *cuarterón* from *cuarto* fourth, assimilated to Latin *quadri-* from *quattuor* four]

quadrumanous *adjective*
• "kwod ROOMA nuss"
• (of primates other than humans) four-handed, i.e. with opposable digits on all four limbs.
• [modern Latin *quadrumana* neuter pl. of *quadrumanus* (Latin *quadri-* from *quattuor* four, Latin *manus* hand)]

quadruped *noun*
• "KWODRA ped"
• a four-footed animal, esp. a four-footed mammal.
• [Latin *quadrupes -pedis* from *quadru-* var. of *quadri-* from *quattuor* four + *pes ped-* foot]
• **quadrupedal** *adjective* "kwod ROOPA d'll" or "kwodra PEED'll"

quadruple *adjective*
• "kwod RUPE'll"
• fourfold.

• [French from Latin *quadruplus* (Latin *quadri-* from *quattuor* four, *-plus* as in *duplus* DUPLE)]
• **quadruply** *adverb*

quadruplet *noun*
• "kwod RUPE lit"
• each of four children born at one birth.
• [QUADRUPLE, after *triplet*]

quadruplex *noun*
• "KWODRA plex"
• *Cdn* a building divided into four self-contained residences.
• [as QUADRUPLE, after *duplex*]

quadruplicate *adjective*
• "kwod ROOPLA kit"
• fourfold.
• [Latin *quadruplicare* from *quadruplex -plicis* fourfold]
• **quadruplication** *noun*

quaestor *noun*
• "KWEESTER"
• either of two ancient Roman magistrates with mainly financial responsibilities.
• [Latin from *quaerere quaesit-* seek]

quaff *verb*
• "KWOFF"
• drink deeply or in long drafts.
• [16th c.: perhaps imitative]
• **quaffable** *adjective*
• **quaffer** *noun*
HOMOPHONES: *coif*

quag *noun*
• "KWAG"
• a marshy or boggy place.
• [related to dialect *quag* (v.) = shake: prob. imitative]
• **quaggy** *adjective*

quagga *noun*
• "KWAGGA"
• an extinct zebra formerly native to southern Africa, with yellowish-brown stripes on the head, neck, and foreparts.
• [Xhosa-Kaffir *iqwara*]

quagmire *noun*
• "KWAG mire" or "KWOG mire"
• a soft boggy or marshy area that gives way underfoot.
• [QUAG + 'mire' from Old Norse *mýrr* boggy ground]

quahog *noun*
ALSO SPELLED: **quahaug**
• "KWAH hog" (with "KWAH" either as in *QUALITY* or as in *QUACK*)
• the edible round clam *Venus mercenaria*, of the Atlantic coast of N America.
• [Narragansett *poquaûhock*]

quaich *noun*
• "KWAKE"
• a kind of drinking cup, usu. of wood and with two handles.
• [Gaelic *cuach* cup, prob. from Latin *caucus*]
HOMOPHONES: *quake*

quail *noun*
• "KWALE"
• any small short-tailed bird of the genus *Coturnix*, related to the partridge, esp. the migratory *C. coturnix*, raised for its flesh and eggs.
• [Old French *quaille* from medieval Latin *coacula* (prob. imitative)]

quale *noun*
• "KWOLLY"
• a quality or property as perceived or experienced by a person.
• [Latin, neuter of *qualis* of what kind]

qualify *verb*
• "KWOLLA fie"
• make competent or fit for a position or purpose.
• [French *qualifier* from medieval Latin *qualificare* from Latin *qualis* such as]
• **qualifiable** *adjective*
• **qualification** *noun*
• **qualificatory** *adjective* "KWOL if icka tory"
• **qualifier** *noun*

qualifying *adjective*
• "KWOLLA fie ing"
• serving to determine those that qualify.
• [as QUALIFY]

qualitative *adjective*
• "KWOLLA tay tiv"
• concerned with or depending on quality or qualities.
• [as QUALITY]
• **qualitatively** *adverb*

quality *noun*
• "KWOLLA tee"
• the standard of something when compared to other things like it.
• [Old French *qualité* from Latin *qualitas -tatis* from *qualis* of what kind]

qualm *noun*
• "KWOM" or "KWOLM" (with "OL" as in *DOLL*)
• a misgiving; an uneasy doubt.
• [16th c.: origin uncertain]
• **qualmish** *adjective*

quandary *noun*
• "KWON dree" or "KWON dur ee"
• a state of perplexity concerning what to do in a difficult situation.
• [16th c.: origin uncertain]

quango *noun*
• "KWANG go"
• a semi-public administrative body outside the civil service but with financial support from and senior members appointed by the government.
• [abbreviation of *quasi* (or *quasi-autonomous*) non-government(al) organization]

- **quangocracy** *noun* "kwang GOCKRA see"
- **quangocrat** *noun*

quantal *adjective*
- "KWONT'Il"
- of or relating to a quantum or quantum theory.
- [Latin *quantus* how much]
- **quantally** *adverb*

quantify *verb*
- "KWONTA fie"
- determine the quantity of.
- [medieval Latin *quantificare* (as QUANTAL)]
- **quantifiable** *adjective*
- **quantification** *noun*
- **quantifier** *noun*

quantitate *verb*
- "KWONTA tate"
- ascertain the quantity or extent of, measure.
- [as QUANTITY]
- **quantitation** *noun*

quantitative *adjective*
- "KWONTA tate iv"
- concerned with quantity.
- [as QUANTITY]
- **quantitatively** *adverb*

quantitive *adjective*
- "KWONTA tiv"
- = QUANTITATIVE.
- [as QUANTITY]
- **quantitively** *adverb*

quantity *noun*
- "KWONTA tee"
- an indefinite number or amount.
- [Old French *quantité* from Latin *quantitas -tatis* from *quantus* how much]

quantize *verb*
ALSO SPELLED: esp. *Brit.* **-ise**
- "KWON tize"
- form into quanta; restrict the number of possible values of a quantity so that certain variables can assume only certain discrete magnitudes.
- [as QUANTUM]
- **quantization** *noun* (also esp. *Brit.* **-isation**)

quantum *noun*
- "KWON tum"
- a discrete quantity of energy proportional in magnitude to the frequency of radiation it represents.
- [Latin, neuter of *quantus* how much]

quarantine *noun*
- "KWORE 'n teen" or "kwore 'n TEEN"
- isolation imposed on persons or animals that have arrived from elsewhere or been exposed to, and might spread, infectious or contagious disease.
- [Italian *quarantina* forty days, from *quaranta* forty]

quark *noun*
- "KWARK" or "KWORK"
- any of a class of unobserved subatomic particles with a fractional electric charge, of which protons, neutrons, and other hadrons are thought to be composed.
- [invented word, assoc. with 'Three quarks for Muster Mark' in James Joyce's *Finnegans Wake* (1939)]

quarry *noun*
- "KWORRY"
- an open-air excavation from which stone for building etc. is or has been obtained by cutting, blasting, etc.
- [medieval Latin *quareria* from Old French *quarriere* from Latin *quadrum* square]
- **quarrier** *noun*
- **quarryman** *noun*

quartan *adjective*
- "KWORT'n"
- (of a fever etc.) recurring every seventy-two hours.
- [Old French *quartaine* from Latin (*febris* fever) *quartana* from *quartus* fourth]

quartet *noun*
- "kwor TET"
- a composition for four voices or instruments.
- [French *quartette* from Italian *quartetto* from *quarto* fourth, from Latin *quartus*]

quartic *adjective*
- "KWORTIC"
- involving the fourth and no higher power of an unknown quantity or variable.
- [Latin *quartus* fourth]

quartier *noun*
- "cart YAY"
- in French-speaking regions, a district or area, esp. of a city.
- [French from Latin *quartarius* fourth part (of a measure), from *quartus* fourth]

quartile *noun*
- "KWOR tile"
- one of three values of a variable dividing a population into four equal groups as regards the value of that variable.
- [medieval Latin *quartilis* from Latin *quartus* fourth]

quarto *noun*
- "KWORTO"
- the size given by folding a (usu. specified) sheet of paper twice, yielding 4 leaves or 8 pages.
- [Latin (*in*) *quarto* (in) the fourth (of a sheet), ablative of *quartus* fourth]

quartz *noun*
- "KWORTS"
- a mineral consisting of silica, crystallizing in colourless or white hexagonal prisms, often coloured by impurities (as amethyst, citrine,

cairngorm), and found widely in igneous and metamorphic rocks.
• [German *Quarz* from West Slavic *kwardy*, corresponding to Czech *tvrdý* hard]

quartzite *noun*
• "KWORTS ite"
• a hard, metamorphic rock consisting mainly of granular quartz.
• [as QUARTZ]

quasar *noun*
• "KWAY zar" or "KWAY sar"
• any of a class of starlike celestial objects, apparently of great size and remoteness, often associated with a spectrum with a large red shift and intense radio emission.
• [*quasi*-stellar]

quash *verb*
• "KWOSH"
• suppress; crush (speculation, a plan, an uprising etc.).
• [Old French *quasser*, *casser* annul, from Late Latin *cassare* from *cassus* null, void, or from Latin *cassare* frequentative of *quatere* shake]

quasi *adjective*
• "KWOZZY" or "KWOZZ eye"
• resembling, similar to.
• [Latin, = as if, almost]

quassia *noun*
• "KWOSHA"
• an evergreen tree, *Quassia amara*, native to S America.
• [G. *Quassi*, 18th-c. Surinamese slave, who discovered its medicinal properties]

quatercentenary *noun*
• "kwotter sen TENNER ee" or "kwotter sen TEENER ee"
• a four-hundredth anniversary.
• [Latin *quater* four times + CENTENARY]

quaternary *adjective*
• "KWOTTER nerry" or "kwuh TURNER ee"
• having four parts.
• [Latin *quaternarius* from *quaterni* (distributive of *quattuor* four)]

quaternion *noun*
• "kwuh TURNY 'n"
• a group of four.
• [Late Latin *quaternio -onis* (as QUATERNARY)]

quatrain *noun*
• "KWOT rain"
• a stanza of four lines, usu. with alternate rhymes.
• [French from *quatre* four, from Latin *quattuor*]

quatrefoil *noun*
• "CATRA foil"
• a four-pointed or four-leafed figure, esp. as an ornament in architectural tracery, resembling a flower or clover leaf.
• [Anglo-French from *quatre* four + *foil* leaf, from Latin *folium* leaf]

quattrocento *noun*
• "kwot roe CHENTO"
• the fifteenth century in Italy.
• [Italian, = 400 used with reference to the years 1400–99]

quaver *verb*
• "KWAY vur"
• (esp. of a voice or musical sound) vibrate, shake, tremble.
• [Middle English from *quave*, perhaps from Old English *cwafian* (unrecorded: compare *cwacian* quake)]
• **quaveringly** *adverb*
• **quavery** *adjective*

quay *noun*
• "KEE"
• a solid stationary artificial landing place lying alongside or projecting into water for loading and unloading boats, ships, etc.
• [Old French *kay* from Gaulish *caio* from Old Celtic]
HOMOPHONES: *key*

quayside *noun*
• "KEE side"
• the land forming or near a quay.
• [as QUAY]

queasy *adjective*
• "KWEEZY"
• feeling or tending to feel sick or nauseous.
• [Middle English *queysy*, *coisy* perhaps related to Old French *coisir* hurt]
• **queasily** *adverb*
• **queasiness** *noun*

Québécois *noun*
• "kay beck WAH"
• *Cdn* a francophone native or inhabitant of Quebec.

Québécoise *noun*
• "kay beck WAHZ"
• *Cdn* a francophone woman who is a native or inhabitant of Quebec.

Quechua *noun*
• "KETCH wuh"
• a member of a S American Indian people of Peru and neighbouring countries.
• [Spanish from Quechua]
• **Quechuan** *adjective*

quell *verb*
• "KWELL"
• put an end to (something), esp. by force; suppress.
• [Old English *cwellan* kill, from Germanic]

quench *verb*
• "KWENCH"
• satisfy (thirst) by drinking.
• [Old English *-cwencan* extinguish]
• **quencher** *noun*

quenelle *noun*
• "kuh NELL"

• a small dumpling-like ball of minced or chopped seasoned fish or meat usu. cooked by poaching.
• [French from German *knödel* dumpling]

quercetin *noun*
• "KWUR set in"
• a yellow crystalline pigment present in plants, used as a food supplement to reduce allergic responses or boost immunity.
• [probably from Latin *quercetum* oak grove (from *quercus* oak)]

quern *noun*
• "KWURN"
• a hand mill for grinding grain.
• [Old English *cweorn(e)* from Germanic]

querulous *adjective*
• "KWARE a luss"
• of a whining, complaining, or peevish nature or disposition.
• [Late Latin *querulosus* or Latin *querulus* from *queri* complain]
• **querulously** *adjective*
• **querulousness** *noun*

query *noun*
• "KWEER ee"
• a question or inquiry.
• [anglicized form of *quaere* from Latin *quaerere* ask]

quesadilla *noun*
• "kay suh DEE yuh"
• a dish of vegetables and grated cheese etc., stuffed between two tortillas, usu. baked or fried and served with salsa, sour cream, etc.
• [Spanish *quesada* cheese (ultimately from Latin *caseus*) + *illa* diminutive suffix]

questionnaire *noun*
• "kwess ch'n AIR"
• a formulated series of questions, esp. for statistical study or market research.
• [French from *questionner* from Latin *quaestio -onis* from *quaerere quaest-* seek]

quetzal *noun*
• "KWET z'll" or "KWET s'll"
• any of various brilliantly coloured birds of the family Trogonidae, esp. the Central and S American *Pharomachrus mocinno*, the male of which has long green tail coverts.
• [Spanish from Aztec from *quetzalli* the bird's tail feather]

queue *noun*
• "CUE"
• a line or sequence of persons, vehicles, etc., awaiting their turn to be attended to or to proceed.
• [French from Latin *cauda* tail]
HOMOPHONES: *cue*

quiche *noun*
• "KEESH"
• a pastry shell containing a mixture of eggs, milk, cream, cheese, etc., with vegetables, meat, fish, etc.
• [French from Alsatian dialect *Küchen* (German *Kuchen*) cake]

quid *noun*
• "KWID"
• one pound sterling.
• [prob. from *quid* the nature of a thing, from Latin *quid* what, something]

quiddity *noun*
• "KWIDDA tee"
• the essence of a person or thing; what makes a thing what it is.
• [medieval Latin *quidditas* from Latin *quid* what]

quiescent *adjective*
• "kwee ESS'nt"
• motionless, inert.
• [Latin *quiescere* from *quies* QUIET]
• **quiescence** *noun*

quiet *adjective*
• "KWY it"
• making little or no sound.
• [Old French *quiet(e)* from Latin *quietus* past participle of *quiescere* be quiet]
• **quietly** *adverb*
• **quietness** *noun*

quieten *verb*
• "KWY it 'n"
• make quiet.
• [as QUIET]

quietism *noun*
• "KWY it izm"
• religious mysticism based on the rejection of outward forms of devotion in favour of passive contemplation and extinction of the will.
• [Italian *quietismo* (as QUIET)]
• **quietist** *noun*
• **quietistic** *adjective*

quietude *noun*
• "KWY a tude"
• a state of quiet.
• [as QUIET]

quietus *noun*
• "kwy EET us"
• something which puts an end to or represses something.
• [medieval Latin *quietus est* he is quit, used as a form of receipt]

quillwort *noun*
• "KWILL wurt" or "KWILL wort"
• any grasslike plant of the genus *Isoetes*.
• ['quill' + WORT]

quinacrine *noun*
• "KWINNA crin" or "KWINNA creen"
• an anti-malarial drug derived from acridine.
• [*quinine* + *acridine*]

quinary *adjective*
- "KWINE a ree"
- of the number five.
- [Latin *quinarius* from *quini* distributive of *quinque* five]

quinazoline *noun*
- "kwuh NAZZ'll een"
- a yellow basic crystalline solid which has a bicyclic structure of fused benzene and pyrimidine rings.
- [Spanish from Quechua *kina* bark + ALCOHOL with inserted *-az-* from French *azote* nitrogen, from Greek *azōos* without life]

quince *noun*
- "KWINCE"
- a hard acid pear-shaped fruit used as a preserve or flavouring.
- [Middle English, originally collect. pl. of obsolete *quoyn*, *coyn*, from Old French *cooin* from Latin *cotoneum* var. of *cydoneum* (apple) of *Cydonia* in Crete]

quincentenary *noun*
- "kwin sen TENNER ee" or "kwin sen TEENER ee"
- a five-hundredth anniversary.
- [Latin *quinque* five + CENTENARY]
- **quincentennial** *adjective*

quincunx *noun*
- "KWIN kunks"
- five objects set so that four are at the corners of a square or rectangle and the fifth is at its centre, e.g. the five on dice or cards.
- [Latin, = five-twelfths from *quinque* five, *uncia* twelfth]
- **quincuncial** *adjective* "kwin KUN sh'll"

quinella *noun*
- "kwin ELLA"
- a form of betting in which the better must select the first-place and second-place winners in a race, not necessarily in the correct order.
- [Latin American Spanish *quiniela*]

quinine *noun*
- "KWIN ine" or "KWINE ine" or "KWIN een"
- an alkaloid found esp. in cinchona bark.
- [*quina* cinchona bark, from Spanish *quina* from Quechua *kina* bark]

quinoa *noun*
- "KEEN wuh"
- any of several annual goosefoots grown by the Indians of the Andes for their edible starchy seeds.
- [Spanish spelling of Quechua *kinua*, *kinoa*]

quinoline *noun*
- "KWINNA leen"
- an oily amine obtained from the distillation of coal tar or by synthesis and used in the preparation of drugs etc.
- [Spanish *quina* (as QUININE) + ALCOHOL]

quinolone *noun*
- "KWINNA lone"
- any of several related antibiotics that inhibit the reproduction of micro-organisms, and are used to treat infections that have become resistant to other antibiotics.
- [QUINOLINE + '-one' forming nouns denoting various compounds, from Greek *-ōnē* feminine patronymic]

quinone *noun*
- "KWIN own" or "kwin OWN"
- a yellow crystalline derivative of benzene with the hydrogen atoms on opposite carbon atoms replaced by two of oxygen.
- [Spanish *quina* (as QUININE) + '-one' forming nouns denoting various compounds, from Greek *-ōnē* feminine patronymic]

quinquagenarian *noun*
- "kwin kwuh juh NERRY 'n"
- a person from 50 to 59 years old.
- [Latin *quinquagenarius* from *quinquageni* distributive of *quinquaginta* fifty]

Quinquagesima *noun*
- "kwin kwuh JESSIM uh"
- the Sunday before the beginning of Lent.
- [medieval Latin, feminine of Latin *quinquagesimus* fiftieth, from *quinquaginta* fifty, after QUADRAGESIMA]

quinquennium *noun*
- "kwin KWENNY um"
- a period of five years.
- [Latin from *quinque* five + *annus* year]
- **quinquennial** *adjective*
- **quinquennially** *adverb*

quinquereme *noun*
- "KWIN kwuh reem"
- an ancient Roman galley with five files of oarsmen on each side.
- [Latin *quinqueremis* (*quinque* five, *remus* oar)]

quinquevalent *adjective*
- "KWIN kwuh vale 'nt"
- having a valence of five.
- [Latin *quinque* five + VALENCE]

quinsy *noun*
- "KWINZY"
- an inflammation of the throat, esp. an abscess in the region around the tonsils.
- [Old French *quinencie* from medieval Latin *quinancia* from Greek *kunagkhē* from *kun-* dog + *agkhō* throttle]

HOMOPHONES: *quinzhee*

quinta *noun*
- "KINTA" or "KWINTA"
- (in Spain, Portugal, and Latin America) a large house or villa in the country or on the outskirts of a town.
- [Spanish & Portuguese, from *quinta parte* fifth part (originally the part of a farm's produce paid as rent)]

quintal *noun*
- “KWINT'll”
- a hundredweight (112 lb.), used e.g. as a measure for dried salt cod.
- [Old French *quintal*, medieval Latin *quintale* from Arabic *ḳinṭār*, based on Latin *centenarius* containing a hundred]

quintessence *noun*
- “kwint ESS ince”
- the most essential part of any substance; a refined extract.
- [originally (in ancient philosophy) a fifth substance (beside the four elements) forming heavenly bodies and pervading all things, from French from medieval Latin *quinta essentia* fifth essence]
- **quintessential** *adjective* “kwinta SEN sh'll”
- **quintessentially** *adverb*

quintet *noun*
- “kwin TET”
- a composition for five voices or instruments.
- [French *quintette* from Italian *quintetto* from *quinto* fifth, from Latin *quintus*]

quintillion *noun*
- “kwin TILL y'n”
- a thousand raised to the sixth power (10^{18}).
- [originally one million raised to the fifth power (10^{30}), from Latin *quintus* fifth, after *million*, from Old French, prob. from Italian *millione* (*mille* thousand + *-one* augmentative suffix)]
- **quintillionth** *adjective*

quintuple *adjective*
- “kwin TUPPLE”
- fivefold; consisting of five parts.
- [French *quintuple* from Latin *quintus* fifth, after QUADRUPLE]

quintuplet *noun*
- “kwin TUP lit”
- each of five children born at one birth.
- [as QUINTUPLE]

quintuplicate *adjective*
- “kwin TUP luh kit”
- fivefold.
- [as QUINTUPLE]

quinzhee *noun*
ALSO SPELLED: **quinzie**
- “KWINZY”
- a shelter created by piling up snow, letting it settle, and then hollowing out the interior.
- [Athapaskan, = ‘bowl-shaped depression in snow; shelter’]

HOMOPHONES: *quinsy*

quipu *noun*
- “KEE poo” or “KWIP oo”
- the ancient Peruvians’ substitute for writing by variously knotting threads of various colours.
- [Quechua, = knot]

quire *noun*
- “KWIRE”
- four sheets of paper etc. folded to form eight leaves, as often in medieval manuscripts.
- [Old French *qua(i)er*, ultimately from Latin *quaterni* set of four (as QUATERNARY)]

HOMOPHONES: *choir*

quirt *noun*
- “KWURT”
- a short-handled riding whip with a braided leather lash.
- [Spanish *cuerda* CORD]

quisling *noun*
- “KWIZ ling”
- a person co-operating with an occupying enemy; a collaborator or fifth columnist.
- [V. *Quisling*, Norwegian army officer and diplomat d.1945, who collaborated with the German occupying force in Norway (1940–45)]

Quispammer *noun*
- “kwiss PAMMER”
- a resident of Quispamsis, NB.

quitch *noun*
- “KWITCH”
- any of several grasses of the genus *Agropyron*, esp. *A. repens*, having long creeping roots; couch grass.
- [Old English *cwice*, perhaps related to ‘quick’]

quite *adverb*
- “KWITE”
- completely; entirely; wholly; to the utmost extent; in the fullest sense.
- [Middle English from obsolete *quite* (adjective) = ‘quit’]

quittance *noun*
- “KWIT ince”
- a release.
- [Old French *quitance* from *quiter* from medieval Latin *quittus* from Latin *quietus* QUIET]

quiver *verb*
- “KWIVVER”
- tremble or vibrate slightly.
- [Middle English from obsolete *quiver* nimble: compare QUAVER]
- **quiveringly** *adverb*
- **quivery** *adjective*

quixotic *adjective*
- “kwick SOTTIC”
- extravagantly and romantically chivalrous; paying no heed to material interests in comparison with honour or devotion.
- [Don *Quixote*, hero of a romance by Spanish writer M. de Cervantes (d.1616), from Spanish *quixote* thigh armour]
- **quixotically** *adverb*
- **quixotism** *noun* “KWICK suh tizm”

quizzical *adjective*
• "KWIZZA k'll"
• expressing or done with mild or amused perplexity.
• [origin unknown]
• **quizzicality** *noun*
• **quizzically** *adverb*

quodlibet *noun*
• "KWOD luh bet"
• a topic or point for philosophical or theological discussion.
• [Latin from *quod* what + *libet* it pleases one]

quoin *noun*
• "COIN"
• an external angle of a building.
• [var. of 'coin' from Old French, = corner, stamping die, from Latin *cuneus* wedge]
• **quoining** *noun*
HOMOPHONES: *coin*

quoit *noun*
• "KOIT"
• a game consisting of aiming and throwing flat rings of rope or metal to encircle or land as near as possible to a peg.
• [Middle English: origin unknown]

quondam *adjective*
• "KWON dam"
• that once was; sometime; former.
• [Latin (adverb), = formerly]

quorum *noun*
• "KWORE um"
• the fixed minimum number of members that must be present to make the proceedings of an assembly, society, or meeting valid.
• [Latin, = of whom (we wish that you be two, three, etc.), in the wording of commissions]

quota *noun*
• "KWOTE uh"
• the share that an individual person or company is obliged to contribute to or entitled to take from a total.
• [medieval Latin *quota* (*pars*) how great (a part), feminine of *quotus* from *quot* how many]

quote *verb*
• "KWOTE"
• cite or appeal to (an author, book, etc.) in confirmation of some view.
• [Middle English, earlier 'mark with numbers', from medieval Latin *quotare* from *quot* how many, or as QUOTA]
• **quotability** *noun*
• **quotable** *adjective*
• **quotation** *noun*

quoth *verb*
• "KWOATH"
• said.
• [Old English *cwæth* past of *cwethan* say, from Germanic]

quotidian *adjective*
• "kwo TIDDY 'n"
• daily, of every day.
• [Old French *cotidien* & Latin *cotidianus* from *cotidie* daily]

quotient *noun*
• "KWO sh'nt"
• a result obtained by dividing one quantity by another.
• [Latin *quotiens* how many times, from *quot* how many]

Quran *noun*
ALSO SPELLED: **Koran**
• "kuh RAN"
• the Islamic sacred book, believed to be the word of God as dictated to Muhammad and written down in Arabic.
• [Arabic *qur'ān* recitation, from *qara'a* read]
• **Quranic** *adjective* (also **Koranic**)

QWERTY *adjective*
• "KWUR tee"
• denoting the standard keyboard on English-language word processors, typewriters, etc.
• [acronym from *q*, *w*, *e*, *r*, *t*, and *y* as the first keys on the top row of letters]

rabaska *noun*
• "ra BASKA"
• *Cdn (Que.)* a large birchbark or cedar canoe, about 8 m long with a high, usu. decorated, bow and stern, which can hold 10 to 12 people.
• [Canadian French, alteration of *Athabaska*, the canoes being originally used for the fur trade into the Athabasca region of Alberta]

rabbet *noun*
• "RABBIT"
• a step-shaped channel etc. cut along the edge or face or projecting angle of a length of wood etc., usu. to receive the edge or tongue of another piece.
• [Old French *rab(b)at* abatement, recess, from *rabattre* REBATE]
HOMOPHONES: *rabbit*

rabbi *noun*
• "RAB eye"
• a Jewish scholar or teacher, esp. of the law.
• [Hebrew *rabbî* my master, from *rab̲* master + pronominal suffix]
• **rabbinical** *adjective* "ruh BINNA k'll"

rabbinate *noun*
• "RAB 'n it"
• the position or office of a rabbi.
• [as RABBI]

Rabelaisian *adjective*
• "rab'll AY zee 'n"
• of or like the French writer F. Rabelais (d.1553) or his writings, esp. displaying earthy humour.

rabid *adjective*
• "RABBID"
• (of a person, feelings, opinions, etc.) unreasoning; fanatical.
• [Latin *rabidus* from *rabere* rave]
• **rabidly** *adverb*

rabies *noun*
• "RAY beez"
• a contagious and fatal viral disease of dogs, cats, raccoons, and other animals, transmissible through the saliva to humans and causing madness and convulsions.
• [Latin from *rabere* rave]

raceme *noun*
• "ruh SEEM"
• a flower cluster with the separate flowers attached by short equal stalks at equal distances along a central stem.
• [Latin *racemus* cluster of grapes]

racemic *adjective*
• "ruh SEEMIC" or "ruh SEMMIC"
• composed of equal numbers of dextrorotatory and levorotatory molecules of a compound.
• [as RACEME, originally of tartaric acid in grape juice]
• **racemization** *noun* (also esp. *Brit.* **-isation**)

racemose *adjective*
• "RASSA mose" ("MOSE" rhymes with *GROSS*)
• in the form of a raceme.
• [as RACEME]

rachis *noun*
• "RAY kiss"
• a stem of grass etc. bearing flower stalks at short intervals.
• [modern Latin from Greek *rhakhis* spine]

rachitis *noun*
• "ruh KITE iss"
• rickets.
• [modern Latin from Greek *rhakhitis* (as RACHIS + Greek *-itis*, forming feminine of adjectives in *-itēs* (with *nosos* 'disease' implied))]
• **rachitic** *adjective* "ruh KITTIC"

raclette *noun*
• "ra CLET"
• a Swiss dish of melted cheese, usu. eaten with potatoes.
• [French, = small scraper, from the practice of holding the cheese over the heat and scraping it on to a plate as it melts]

raconteur *noun*
• "rack on TUR"
• a teller of anecdotes.
• [French from *raconter* relate, from Old French *co(u)nter, co(u)nte* from Late Latin *computus, computare* compute]

radar *noun*
• "RAY dar"
• a method for detecting the position and

speed of aircraft, ships, or other objects, by sending out pulses of high-frequency electromagnetic waves.
• [*ra*dio *d*etection *a*nd *r*anging]

radial *adjective*
• "RAY dee 'll"
• of, concerning, or in rays.
• [as RADIUS]
• **radially** *adverb*

radian *noun*
• "RAY dee 'n"
• a unit of angle, equal to an angle at the centre of a circle the arc of which is equal in length to the radius; 1 radian is the same as 57.296°.
• [as RADIUS]

radiant *adjective*
• "RAY dee 'nt"
• emitting rays of light.
• [Latin *radiare* (as RADIUS)]
• **radiance** *noun*
• **radiantly** *adverb*

radiate *verb*
• "RAY dee ate"
• emit rays of light, heat, or other electromagnetic waves.
• [Latin *radiare radiat-* (as RADIUS)]
• **radiative** *adjective* "RAY dee a tiv"

radiation *noun*
• "ray dee AY sh'n"
• the act or an instance of radiating; the process of being radiated.
• [as RADIATE]

radiator *noun*
• "RAIDY ate ur" or "RADDY ate ur"
• a thing that radiates or emits light, heat, or sound.
• [as RADIATE]

radical *adjective*
• "RADDA k'll"
• of the root or roots; fundamental.
• [Late Latin *radicalis* from Latin *radix radicis* root]
• **radicalism** *noun*
• **radicalization** *noun* (also esp. *Brit.* **-isation**)
• **radicalize** *verb* (also esp. *Brit.* **-ise**)
• **radically** *adverb*
HOMOPHONES: *radicle*

radicchio *noun*
• "ruh DEEKY oh"
• a variety of chicory with dark red leaves, used esp. in salads.
• [Italian, = chicory]

radicle *noun*
• "RADDA k'll"
• the part of a plant embryo that develops into the primary root; a rootlet.
• [Latin *radicula* (as RADIX)]
• **radicular** *adjective* "ruh DICK yuh lur"
HOMOPHONES: *radical*

radioactivity *noun*
• "radio ack TIVVA tee"
• the spontaneous disintegration of atomic nuclei, with the emission of usu. penetrating radiation or particles.
• [RADIATION + ACTIVITY]
• **radioactive** *adjective*
• **radioactively** *adverb*

radiobiology *noun*
• "radio by OLLA jee"
• the biology concerned with the effects of radiation on organisms and the application in biology of radiological techniques.
• [RADIATION + BIOLOGY]
• **radiobiological** *adjective*
• **radiobiologist** *noun*

radiocarbon *noun*
• "radio CARB'n"
• a radioactive isotope of carbon.
• [RADIOACTIVE + 'carbon' (see CARBONACEOUS)]

radiochemistry *noun*
• "radio KEMMA stree"
• the chemistry of radioactive materials.
• [RADIOACTIVE + CHEMISTRY]
• **radiochemical** *adjective*
• **radiochemist** *noun*

radioelement *noun*
• "radio ELLA m'nt"
• a natural or artificial radioactive element or isotope.
• [RADIOACTIVE + ELEMENT]

radiogenic *adjective*
• "radio JENNIC"
• produced by radioactivity.
• [RADIOACTIVE + GENESIS]

radiogram *noun*
• "RADIO gram"
• a picture obtained by X-rays, gamma rays, etc.
• [RADIOACTIVE + Greek *gramma* thing written]

radiograph *noun*
• "RADIO graff"
• = RADIOGRAM.
• [RADIOACTIVE + Greek *graphia* writing]
• **radiographer** *noun*
• **radiographic** *adjective*
• **radiographically** *adverb*
• **radiography** *noun*

radioisotope *noun*
• "radio ICE a tope"
• a radioactive isotope.
• [RADIOACTIVE + ISOTOPE]
• **radioisotopic** *adjective* "radio ice a TOPPIC"

radiolarian *noun*
• "radio LERRY 'n"
• any marine protozoan of the order Radiolaria, having a siliceous skeleton and radiating pseudopodia.
• [modern Latin *radiolaria* from Latin *radiolus* diminutive of RADIUS]

radiology *noun*
- "raidy OLLA jee"
- the scientific study of X-rays and other high-energy radiation, esp. as used in medicine.
- [RADIATION + Greek *logos* word]
- **radiologic** *adjective*
- **radiological** *adjective*
- **radiologist** *noun*

radiometer *noun*
- "raidy OMMA tur"
- an instrument for measuring the intensity or force of radioactivity.
- [RADIOACTIVE + Greek *metron* measure]
- **radiometric** *adjective* "radio METRIC"
- **radiometry** *noun*

radionuclide *noun*
- "radio NEW clide"
- a radioactive nuclide.
- [RADIOACTIVE + NUCLIDE]

radiopaque *adjective*
- "raidy oh PAKE"
- opaque to X-rays or similar radiation.
- [RADIATION + OPAQUE]
- **radiopacity** *noun* "radio PASSA tee"

radiophonic *adjective*
- "radio FONNIC"
- of or relating to synthetic sound, esp. music, produced electronically.
- [RADIATION + Greek *phōnē* sound]

radioscopy *noun*
- "raidy OSCA pee"
- the examination by X-rays etc. of objects opaque to light.
- [RADIATION + Greek *skopos* target, from *skeptomai* look at]
- **radioscopic** *adjective*

radiosonde *noun*
- "RADIO sond"
- a miniature radio transmitter broadcasting information about pressure, temperature, etc., from various levels of the atmosphere, carried esp. by balloon.
- ['radio' (from RADIUS) + SONDE]

radiotherapy *noun*
- "radio THERRA pee"
- the treatment of cancer and other diseases by X-rays or other forms of radiation.
- [RADIATION + THERAPY]
- **radiotherapeutic** *adjective* "radio therra PYOOTIC"
- **radiotherapist** *noun*

radium *noun*
- "RAIDY um"
- a radioactive metallic element originally obtained from pitchblende etc., used esp. in luminous materials and in radiotherapy.
- [Latin *radius* ray]

radius *noun*
- "RAIDY us"
- a straight line from the centre to the circumference of a circle or sphere.
- [Latin, = staff, spoke, ray]

radix *noun*
- "RAY dix"
- a number or symbol used as the basis of a numeration scale, e.g. ten in the decimal system.
- [Latin, = root]

radome *noun*
- "RAY dome"
- a dome or other structure, transparent to radio waves, protecting radar equipment, esp. on the outer surface of an aircraft.
- [blend of RADAR + 'dome' from French *dôme* from Italian *duomo* cathedral, dome, from Latin *domus* house]

radon *noun*
- "RAY don"
- a naturally occurring gaseous radioactive inert element arising from the disintegration of radium, and used in radiotherapy.
- [RADIUM, on the pattern of *argon* etc.]

radula *noun*
- "RAD yoo luh"
- a file-like structure in molluscs for scraping off food particles and drawing them into the mouth.
- [Latin, = scraper, from *radere* scrape]
- **radular** *adjective*

raffia *noun*
- "RAFFY uh"
- a palm tree, *Raphia ruffia*, native to Madagascar, having very long leaves.
- [Malagasy]

raga *noun*
- "RAGGA"
- a pattern of notes used as a basis for improvisation in Indian music.
- [Sanskrit, = colour, musical tone]

HOMOPHONES: *ragga*

ragamuffin *noun*
- "RAGGA muffin"
- a person in ragged dirty clothes, esp. a child.
- [prob. based on 'rag', probably from Old Norse *roggvathr* tufted: compare 14th-c. *ragamoffyn*, the name of a demon]

HOMOPHONES: *raggamuffin*

ragg *noun*
- "RAG"
- a strong wool fibre treated so as to retain its natural oils.
- [Norwegian, = fur, goat hair; compare Norwegian *raggesokk*, thick skiing socks made from goat hair or coarse wool]

HOMOPHONES: *rag*

ragga *noun*
- "RAGGA"
- a style of popular music combining elements of reggae and hip hop.

• [RAGGAMUFFIN, from the style of clothing worn by its followers]
HOMOPHONES: *raga*

raggamuffin *noun*
ALSO SPELLED: **ragamuffin**
• "RAGGA muffin"
• an exponent or follower of ragga, typically dressing in ragged clothes.
• [see RAGAMUFFIN]
HOMOPHONES: *ragamuffin*

raglan *noun*
• "RAG l'n"
• an overcoat without shoulder seams, the sleeves running in a sloping line from the neck to under the arms.
• [Lord *Raglan*, Brit. commander d.1855]

ragout *noun*
• "rag OO"
• a stew.
• [French *ragoût* from *ragoûter* revive the taste of, from Latin *gustare* taste]

ragwort *noun*
• "RAG wurt" or "RAG wort"
• any yellow-flowered ragged-leaved plant of the genus *Senecio*.
• ['rag' probably from Old Norse *roggvathr* tufted + WORT]

rai *noun*
• "RYE"
• a style of popular music which fuses Arabic and Algerian folk elements with western styles.
• [perhaps from Arabic *ha er-ray* 'that's the thinking, here is the view', a phrase frequently found in the songs]
HOMOPHONES: *rye, wry*

raillery *noun*
• "RAILER ee"
• good-humoured ridicule; rallying.
• [French *raillerie* from *railler* from Provençal *ralhar* jest, ultimately from Latin *rugire* bellow]

raiment *noun*
• "RAY m'nt"
• clothing.
• [Middle English from obsolete *arrayment* (as ARRAY)]

raisin *noun*
• "RAY z'n"
• a partially dried grape.
• [Old French, ultimately from Latin *racemus* cluster of grapes]
• **raisiny** *adjective*

raita *noun*
• "RYE tuh"
• an Indian side dish of chopped cucumber (or other vegetables) and spices in yogourt.
• [Hindi *rāytā*]

Raj *noun*
• "ROZH" or "RODGE"
• the period of British rule in the Indian subcontinent before 1947.
• [Hindi *rāj* reign]

raja *noun*
ALSO SPELLED: **rajah**
• "ROZH uh" or "RODGE uh"
• an Indian king or prince.
• [Hindi *rājā* from Sanskrit *rājan* king]

Rajasthani *adjective*
• "rodge a STANNY" or "radge a STANNY"
• of or relating to Rajasthan in W India.

Rajput *noun*
• "RODGE poot" ("POOT" can rhyme either with *FOOT* or with *BOOT*)
• a member of a Hindu soldier caste claiming Kshatriya descent.
• [Hindi *rājpūt* from Sanskrit *rājan* king + *putrá* son]

raki *noun*
• "ruh KEE" or "RACKY"
• any of various alcoholic liquors made in E Europe and the Middle East.
• [Turkish *raqi*]

raku *noun*
• "RACK oo"
• a kind of Japanese lead-glazed earthenware, primarily for use in the tea ceremony.
• [Japanese, lit. 'enjoyment']

rale *noun*
• "RAL" (rhymes with *PAL*)
• an abnormal rattling sound heard in the auscultation of unhealthy lungs.
• [French from *râler* to rattle, from *racler* to scrape, from Provençal *rasclar*, ultimately from Latin *rasus* shaved]

rallentando *adverb*
• "ral 'n TANDO"
• (as a musical direction) with a gradual decrease of speed.
• [Italian]

raloxifene *noun*
• "ruh LOXA feen"
• an anti-estrogen drug given orally as the hydrochloride for the prevention of osteoporosis in post-menopausal women.
• [invented name]

Ramadan *noun*
• "RAMMA dan" or "ROMMA don"
• the ninth month of the Muslim year, during which strict fasting is observed from sunrise to sunset.
• [Arabic *ramaḍān* from *ramaḍa* be hot; reason for name uncertain]

rambunctious *adjective*
• "ram BUNK sh'ss"
• active; full of energy.
• [19th c.: origin unknown]
• **rambunctiously** *adverb*
• **rambunctiousness** *noun*

rambutan *noun*
• "ram BOOT 'n"
• a red plum-sized prickly fruit.
• [Malay *rambūtan* from *rambut* hair, in allusion to its spines]

ramekin *noun*
• "RAMMA kin"
• a small, usu. round dish for baking and serving an individual portion of food.
• [French *ramequin*, of Low German or Dutch origin]

ramen *plural noun*
• "ROM 'n"
• quick-cooking noodles, usu. served in a broth with meat and vegetables.
• [Japanese from Chinese *la* pull + *mian* noodle]

ramie *noun*
• "RAMMY"
• a tall E Asian plant of the genus *Boehmeria nivea*, of the nettle family.
• [Malay *rāmī*]

ramify *verb*
• "RAMMA fie"
• form branches or subdivisions or offshoots, branch out.
• [French *ramifier* from medieval Latin *ramificare* from Latin *ramus* branch]
• **ramification** *noun*

ramin *noun*
• "ra MEEN"
• any Malaysian tree of the genus *Gonystylus*, esp. *G. bancanus*.
• [Malay]

ramose *adjective*
• "RAY mose" ("MOSE" rhymes with *GROSS*)
• branched; branching.
• [Latin *ramosus* from *ramus* branch]

rampant *adjective*
• "RAMP 'nt"
• unchecked, flourishing excessively.
• [Old French, participle of *ramper* creep, crawl, from Frankish]
• **rampantly** *adverb*

ramsons *plural noun*
• "RAM s'nz"
• a broad-leaved garlic, *Allium ursinum*, with elongate pungent-smelling bulbous roots.
• [Old English *hramsan* pl. of *hramsa* wild garlic, later taken as sing.]

ranchera *noun*
• "ran CHAIR uh"
• a genre of Mexican popular music characterized by songs about the land, usu. accompanied by accordion, guitar, and bass.
• [Mexican Spanish from Spanish *rancho* group of persons eating together, the genre having arisen in Mexican cattle-ranching country]

ranchero *noun*
• "ran CHAIR oh"
• a rancher, esp. in Mexico and the southwestern US.
• [Spanish (as RANCHERA)]

ranchette *noun*
• "ran CHET"
• a small cattle ranch or piece of ranchland.
• [diminutive of 'ranch': see RANCHERA]

rancid *adjective*
• "RAN sid"
• (of fats, oils, or fatty meats such as bacon) smelling or tasting rank and stale as a result of oxidation.
• [Latin *rancidus* stinking]
• **rancidity** *noun*

rancour *noun*
ALSO SPELLED: esp. *US* **rancor**
• "RANKER"
• inveterate bitterness, malignant hate, spitefulness.
• [Old French from Late Latin *rancor -oris* (as RANCID)]
• **rancorous** *adjective*
• **rancorously** *adverb*
HOMOPHONES: *ranker*

rang *noun*
• "RÃH" (with a nasal *AH*)
• *Cdn* (*Que.*) a row of long lots, usu. along a road.
• [French, = row, range]

rangatira *noun*
• "rang guh TEERA"
• a Maori chief or noble.
• [Maori]

rangy *adjective*
• "RAIN jee"
• (of a person) tall and slim.
• [from 'range' from Old French *range* row, rank, via *ranger* from *rang* rank, from Germanic]

rani *noun*
ALSO SPELLED: **ranee**
• "RAN ee"
• a raja's wife or widow; a Hindu queen.
• [Hindi *rānī* = Sanskrit *rājnī* feminine of *rājan* king]

ranunculaceous *adjective*
• "ruh nunk yoo LAY sh'ss"
• of or relating to the family Ranunculaceae of flowering plants, including clematis and delphiniums.
• [Latin RANUNCULUS + adjective suffix *-aceus* of the nature of]

ranunculus *noun*
• "ruh NUNK yoo luss"
• any plant of the genus *Ranunculus*, usu. having bowl-shaped flowers with many stamens and carpels, including buttercups and crowfoots.
• [Latin, originally diminutive of *rana* frog]

rapacious *adjective*
• "ruh PAY sh'ss"
• greedy, grasping, extortionate.

• [Latin *rapax -acis* from *rapere* snatch]
• **rapaciously** *adverb*
• **rapaciousness** *noun*
• **rapacity** *noun* "ruh PASSA tee"

rapier *noun*
• "RAY pee ur"
• a light slender sword used for thrusting.
• [prob. from Dutch *rapier* or Low German *rappir*, from French *rapière*, of unknown origin]

rapine *noun*
• "RAP ine" or "RAP in"
• plundering, robbery.
• [Old French or from Latin *rapina* from *rapere* seize]

rapini *plural noun*
• "ruh PEENY"
• the edible leaves of an immature white turnip.
• [Italian]

rappel *verb*
• "ruh PELL"
• descend a steep rock face by using a doubled rope coiled round the body and fixed at a higher point.
• [French, = recall, from *rappeler* (*re-* again, APPEAL)]
HOMOPHONES: *repel*

rapport *noun*
• "ruh PORE"
• a relationship or communication, esp. when useful and harmonious.
• [French from *rapporter* (*re-* again, *porter* from Latin *portare* carry)]

rapporteur *noun*
• "rap ore TUR"
• a person who prepares an account of the proceedings of a committee etc. for a higher body.
• [French (as RAPPORT)]

rapprochement *noun*
• "ra prosh MÃH" (with a nasal *AH*)
• the establishment or resumption of harmonious relations, esp. between nations.
• [French from *rapprocher* (*re-* again, APPROACH)]

rapscallion *noun*
• "rap SKAL y'n"
• a rascal, scamp, or rogue.
• [earlier *rascallion*, perhaps from RASCAL]

rapt *adjective*
• "RAPT"
• fully absorbed or intent, enraptured.
• [Latin *raptus* past participle of *rapere* seize]
• **raptly** *adverb*
• **raptness** *noun*
HOMOPHONES: *wrapped*

raptor *noun*
• "RAPTER"
• any bird of prey, e.g. an owl, falcon, etc.
• [Latin, = ravisher, plunderer, from *rapere rapt-* seize]
• **raptorial** *adjective*

rapture *noun*
• "RAP chur"
• ecstatic delight, mental transport.
• [obsolete French *rapture* or medieval Latin *raptura* (as RAPT)]
• **rapturous** *adjective*
• **rapturously** *adverb*

rarefy *verb*
ALSO SPELLED: **rarify**
• "RERRA fie"
• make or become less dense or solid.
• [Old French *rarefier* from Latin *rarefacere*, from *rarus* rare + *facere* make]
• **rarefaction** *noun*
• **rarefied** *adjective* (also **rarified**)

raring *adjective*
• "RARE ing"
• enthusiastic, eager.
• [participle of *rare*, dialect var. of 'roar' (of imitative origin) or 'rear' (from Germanic)]

rarity *noun*
• "RARE it ee"
• rareness.
• [Latin *raritas* from *rarus* rare]

Rarotongan *noun*
• "rare a TONG g'n"
• a native or inhabitant of the S Pacific island of Rarotonga.

rascal *noun*
• "RASS k'll"
• a dishonest or mischievous person, esp. a child.
• [Old French *rascaille* rabble, prob. ultimately from Latin *radere ras-* scrape]
• **rascality** *noun*
• **rascally** *adjective*

raspberry *noun*
• "RAZZ berry"
• a bramble of the genus *Rubus*, esp. *R. idaeus*, having usu. red berries consisting of numerous drupelets on a conical receptacle.
• [16th-c. *rasp* (now dialect) from obsolete *raspis*, of unknown origin, + 'berry' from Germanic]

Rastafarian *noun*
• "rasta FERRY 'n"
• a member of a sect of Jamaican origin regarding blacks as a chosen people and the former Emperor Haile Selassie of Ethiopia (d.1975, entitled *Ras Tafari*) as God.
• **Rastafarianism** *noun*

raster *noun*
• "RASTER"
• a pattern of horizontal lines of pixels composing an image on a cathode ray tube display or for printing etc.

• [German, = screen, from Latin *rastrum* rake, from *radere ras-* scrape]

rasterize *verb*
ALSO SPELLED: esp. *Brit.* **-ise**
• "RASTER ize"
• convert (a digitized image) into a form that can be displayed on a cathode ray tube or printed.
• [as RASTER]
• **rasterization** *noun* (also esp. *Brit.* **-isation**)
• **rasterizer** *noun* (also esp. *Brit.* **-iser**)

ratafia *noun*
• "ratta FEE uh"
• a liqueur flavoured with almonds or kernels of peach, apricot, or cherry.
• [French, perhaps related to TAFIA]

rataplan *noun*
• "ratta PLAN"
• a drumming sound.
• [French: imitative]

ratatouille *noun*
• "ratta TOO ee"
• a vegetable dish made of stewed onions, zucchini, tomatoes, eggplants, and peppers.
• [French dialect, from French *touiller*, stir, from Latin *tudiculare* crush, stir]

rathskeller *noun*
• "ROTS keller" or "RATS keller"
• a bar or restaurant in a basement.
• [German, = (restaurant in) town-hall cellar]

ratio *noun*
• "RAY shee oh" or "RAY sho"
• the quantitative relation between two similar magnitudes determined by the number of times one contains the other integrally or fractionally.
• [Latin from *ratus*, past participle of *rēri* reckon]

ratiocinate *verb*
• "ratty OSSA nate" or "rashy OSSA nate"
• go through logical processes, reason, esp. using syllogisms.
• [Latin *ratiocinari* (as RATIO)]
• **ratiocination** *noun*
• **ratiocinative** *adjective*

ration *noun*
• "RASH'n"
• a fixed official allowance of food, clothing, etc., in a time of shortage.
• [French from Italian *razione* or Spanish *ración* from Latin *ratio -onis* reckoning, RATIO]

rational *adjective*
• "RASH'n 'll"
• of or based on reasoning or reason.
• [orig. = 'having the ability to reason', from Latin *rationalis*, from *ratio* reckoning, reason]
• **rationality** *noun*
• **rationally** *adverb*

rationale *noun*
• "rasha NAL"
• the fundamental reason or logical basis of anything.
• [modern Latin, neuter of Latin *rationalis*: see RATIONAL]

rationalism *noun*
• "RASH'n 'll ism"
• the theory that reason is the foundation of certainty in knowledge.
• [as RATIONAL]
• **rationalist** *noun*
• **rationalistic** *adjective*
• **rationalistically** *adverb*

rationalize *verb*
ALSO SPELLED: esp. *Brit.* **-ise**
• "RASH'n 'll ize"
• offer or subconsciously adopt a rational but specious explanation of (one's behaviour or attitude).
• [as RATIONAL]
• **rationalization** *noun* (also esp. *Brit.* **-isation**)
• **rationalizer** *noun* (also esp. *Brit.* **-iser**)

ratite *adjective*
• "RAT ite"
• (of a bird) having a keelless breastbone, and unable to fly.
• [Latin *ratis* raft]

ratoon *noun*
• "ruh TOON"
• a new shoot springing from a root of sugar cane etc. after cropping.
• [Spanish *retoño* sprout]

rattan *noun*
• "ruh TAN"
• any East Indian climbing palm of the genus *Calamus* etc. with long thin jointed pliable stems often used to make wickerwork, furniture, etc.
• [earlier *rot(t)ang* from Malay *rōtan* prob. from *raut* pare]

raucous *adjective*
• "ROCK us"
• harsh-sounding, loud and hoarse.
• [Latin *raucus*]
• **raucously** *adverb*
• **raucousness** *noun*

raunchy *adjective*
• "RON chee"
• coarse, earthy; sexually provocative.
• [20th c.: origin unknown]
• **raunch** *noun*
• **raunchily** *adverb*
• **raunchiness** *noun*

ravage *verb*
• "RAV idge"
• devastate, plunder; damage.
• [French *ravage(r)* alteration of *ravine* rush of water]

ravel *verb*
• "RAV 'll"
• entangle or become entangled or knotted.
• [prob. from Dutch *ravelen* tangle, fray out]

ravelin *noun*
• "RAV lin"
• an outwork of fortifications, with two faces forming a salient angle.
• [French from obsolete Italian *ravellino*, of unknown origin]

raven *verb*
• "RAV 'n"
• plunder, rob.
• [Old French *raviner* ravage, ultimately from Latin *rapina* RAPINE]
HOMOPHONES: *ravin*

ravenous *adjective*
• "RAV 'n us"
• very hungry, famished.
• [Old French *ravineus* from *raviner* ravage, ultimately from Latin *rapina* RAPINE]
• **ravenously** *adverb*

ravin *noun*
• "RAV in"
• robbery, plundering.
• [Old French *ravine* from Latin *rapina* RAPINE]
HOMOPHONES: *raven*

ravine *noun*
• "ruh VEEN"
• a narrow, steep-sided valley, esp. one formed by erosion by running water.
• [French (as RAVIN)]
• **ravined** *adjective*

ravioli *noun*
• "ravvy OH lee"
• small squares of pasta stuffed with minced meat, cheese, spinach, etc.
• [Italian]

raze *verb*
• "RAZE"
• completely destroy; tear down.
• [Middle English *rase* = wound slightly, from Old French *raser* shave close, ultimately from Latin *radere ras-* scrape]
HOMOPHONES: *raise*

razor *noun*
• "RAY zur"
• an instrument with a sharp blade or blades used in cutting hair or bristles esp. from the skin.
• [as RAZE]
HOMOPHONES: *raiser*

razorback *noun*
• "RAY zur back"
• an animal with a sharp ridged back, esp. a semi-wild hog of the southern US.
• [as RAZOR + 'back']

razorbill *noun*
• "RAY zur bill"
• an auk, *Alca torda*, with a sharp-edged bill, breeding along the coasts of the N Atlantic.
• [as RAZOR + 'bill']

razzmatazz *noun*
• "RAZZ muh tazz"
• glitter, showiness, pageantry; a flamboyant often insincere display, as of publicity.
• [prob. alteration of 'razzle-dazzle']

reacquaint *verb*
• "ree a KWAINT"
• make (a person or oneself) acquainted again.
• [Latin *re-* again, etc. + ACQUAINT]
• **reacquaintance** *noun*

reacquire *verb*
• "ree a KWIRE"
• acquire anew.
• [Latin *re-* again, etc. + ACQUIRE]
• **reacquisition** *noun* "ree ackwa ZISH'n"

reactance *noun*
• "ree ACT ince"
• a component of impedance in an AC circuit, due to capacitance or inductance or both.
• [Latin *re-* again, back, etc. + 'act']

reactant *noun*
• "ree ACT 'nt"
• a substance that takes part in and undergoes change during a reaction.
• [as REACTANCE]

reactionary *adjective*
• "ree ACK sh'n airy"
• tending to oppose (esp. political) change and advocate return to a former system.
• [Latin *re-* again, back + Latin *actio -onis* from *agere act-* do]

reactivate *verb*
• "ree ACTIV ate"
• restore to a state of activity; bring into action again.
• [Latin *re-* again + ACTIVATE]
• **reactivation** *noun*

reactive *adjective*
• "ree ACTIV"
• showing reaction.
• [as REACTIVATE]
• **reactivity** *noun*

reactor *noun*
• "ree ACK tur"
• a person or thing that reacts.
• [Latin *re-* again + *actor* from *agere act-* do]

readjust *verb*
• "ree a JUST"
• adjust again.
• [Latin *re-* again + ADJUST]
• **readjustment** *noun*

reaffirm *verb*
• "ree a FURM"
• affirm again.
• [Latin *re-* again + AFFIRM]
• **reaffirmation** *noun*

Reaganite *noun*
• "RAY g'n ite"

• (in the US) an advocate or supporter of the policies and principles of Ronald Reagan, US president 1981–89.
• **Reaganesque** *adjective* "ray g'n ESK"
• **Reaganism** *noun*

Reaganomics *noun*
• "ray g'n OMMIX"
• (in the US) the economic policies advocated by Ronald Reagan, US president 1981–89.
• ['Reagan' + ECONOMICS]

reagent *noun*
• "ree AY j'nt"
• a substance used to test for the presence of another substance by means of the reaction which it produces.
• [Latin *re-* again + AGENT]

real *noun*
• "ray AL"
• the basic monetary unit in Brazil, introduced in 1994, equal to 100 centavos.
• [Spanish & Portuguese, noun use of *real* (adjective) royal, from Latin *regalis* regal from *rex* king]

realgar *noun*
• "ree AL gur"
• an orange-red monoclinic sulphide of arsenic that is an important source of that element, used as a pigment and in fireworks.
• [medieval Latin from Arabic *rahj al-ḡār* dust of the cave]

realign *verb*
• "ree a LINE"
• adjust or alter the direction of.
• [Latin *re-* again + ALIGN]
• **realignment** *noun*

reallocate *verb*
• "ree ALA cate"
• allocate again or differently.
• [Latin *re-* again + ALLOCATE]
• **reallocation** *noun*

realm *noun*
• "RELM"
• a kingdom.
• [Old French *realme*, *reaume*, from Latin *regimen -minis* (see REGIMEN): influenced by Old French *reiel* royal]

realpolitik *noun*
• "ray al polla TEEK"
• politics based on realities and material needs, rather than on morals or ideals.
• [German]
• ***realpolitiker*** *noun*

realtor *noun*
• "REEL tur"
• a real estate agent.
• [from 'realty' from Old French *reel*, Late Latin *realis* from Latin *res* thing]

ream *noun*
• "REEM"
• twenty quires or 500 (formerly 480) sheets of paper (or a larger number, to allow for waste).
• [Old French *raime* etc., ultimately from Arabic *rīzma* bundle]

reamer *noun*
• "REEMER"
• a tool for enlarging or finishing drilled holes.
• [origin uncertain]

reanalyze *verb*
ALSO SPELLED: esp. *Brit.* **-yse**
• "ree ANNA lize"
• analyze again; subject to further analysis.
• [Latin *re-* again + ANALYZE]
• **reanalysis** *noun* "ree a NALA sis"

reanimate *verb*
• "ree ANNA mate"
• resuscitate; restore to life.
• [Latin *re-* again + ANIMATE]
• **reanimation** *noun*

reap *verb*
• "REEP"
• cut (a crop, esp. grain) as a harvest.
• [Old English *ripan*, *reopan*, of unknown origin]
• **reaper** *noun*

reappear *verb*
• "ree a PEER"
• appear again or as previously.
• [Latin *re-* again + APPEAR]
• **reappearance** *noun*

reapply *verb*
• "ree a PLY"
• apply again, esp. submit a further application (for a position etc.).
• [Latin *re-* again + APPLY]
• **reapplication** *noun*

reappoint *verb*
• "ree a POINT"
• appoint again to a position previously held.
• [Latin *re-* again + APPOINT]
• **reappointment** *noun*

reapportion *verb*
• "ree a POR sh'n"
• apportion again or differently.
• [Latin *re-* again + APPORTION]
• **reapportionment** *noun*

reappraise *verb*
• "ree a PRAZE"
• appraise or assess again.
• [Latin *re-* again + APPRAISE]
• **reappraisal** *noun*

rearrange *verb*
• "ree a RANGE"
• arrange again in a different way.
• [Latin *re-* again + ARRANGE]
• **rearrangement** *noun*
• **rearranging** *noun*

rearrest *verb*
- "ree a REST"
- arrest again.
- [Latin *re-* again + ARREST]

reassemble *verb*
- "ree a SEMBLE"
- assemble again or into a former state.
- [Latin *re-* again + ASSEMBLE]
- **reassembly** *noun*

reassert *verb*
- "ree a SURT"
- assert again.
- [Latin *re-* again + ASSERT]
- **reassertion** *noun*

reassess *verb*
- "ree a SESS"
- assess again, esp. differently.
- [Latin *re-* again + ASSESS]
- **reassessment** *noun*

reassign *verb*
- "ree a SINE"
- assign again or differently.
- [Latin *re-* again + ASSIGN]
- **reassignment** *noun*

reassure *verb*
- "ree a SHUR"
- restore confidence to; dispel the apprehensions of.
- [Latin *re-* again + ASSURE]
- **reassurance** *noun*
- **reassuring** *adjective*
- **reassuringly** *adverb*

reattach *verb*
- "ree a TATCH"
- attach again or in a former position.
- [Latin *re-* again + ATTACH]
- **reattachment** *noun*

reattain *verb*
- "ree a TANE"
- attain again.
- [Latin *re-* again + ATTAIN]
- **reattainment** *noun*

Réaumur *adjective*
- "RAY oh myoor"
- expressed in or related to the Réaumur scale of temperature at which water freezes at 0° and boils at 80°.
- [R. de *Réaumur*, French physicist d.1757]

reave *verb*
- "REEVE"
- forcibly deprive of.
- [Old English *rēafian* from Germanic]

HOMOPHONES: *reeve*, *reive*

rebarbative *adjective*
- "ree BARBA tiv"
- irritating, unattractive, objectionable.
- [French *rébarbatif -ive* from *barbe* beard]

rebate *noun*
- "REE bate"
- a partial refund of money paid.
- [earlier = diminish: Middle English from Old French *rabattre* (*re-* again, ABATE)]
- **rebatable** *adjective*

rebbe *noun*
- "REBBA"
- a Jewish religious leader or rabbi.
- [Yiddish from Hebrew *rabbi* rabbi]

rebbetzin *noun*
- "REBBIT s'n"
- the wife of a rabbi.
- [Yiddish from Hebrew, feminine form of *rabbi* rabbi]

rebec *noun*

ALSO SPELLED: **rebeck**
- "REE beck"
- a medieval usu. three-stringed instrument played with a bow.
- [French *rebec* var. of Old French *rebebe rubebe* from Arabic *rabāb*]

rebel *noun*
- "REB'll"
- a person who fights against, resists, or refuses allegiance to the established government.
- [Old French *rebelle*, *rebeller* from Latin *rebellis* (*re-* again, *bellum* war)]

rebellion *noun*
- "ruh BELL y'n"
- open resistance to authority, esp. organized armed resistance to an established government.
- [as REBEL]

rebozo *noun*
- "ruh BOE so"
- a long scarf covering the head and shoulders, traditionally worn by Spanish and Mexican women.
- [Spanish]

rebus *noun*
- "REE buss"
- a type of puzzle or visual pun in which a word is represented by pictures etc. suggesting its parts; for example, the letters CR followed by a picture of an eye would constitute a rebus for the word *cry*.
- [French *rébus* from Latin *rebus*, ablative pl. of *res* thing]

rebut *verb*
- "re BUT"
- refute or disprove (evidence or a charge).
- [Anglo-French *rebuter*, Old French *rebo(u)ter* (*re-* again, *boter* butt (charge with the head))]
- **rebuttable** *adjective*
- **rebuttal** *noun*

rebutter *noun*
- "re BUTTER"
- a refutation.
- [as REBUT]

recalcitrant *adjective*
- "re CALSA tr'nt"
- resisting discipline or authority; obstinately disobedient.
- [Latin *recalcitrare* (*re-* again, *calcitrare* kick out with the heels, from *calx calcis* heel)]
- **recalcitrance** *noun*
- **recalcitrantly** *adverb*

recalculate *verb*
- "ree CAL kyoo late"
- calculate again.
- [Latin *re-* again + CALCULATE]
- **recalculation** *noun*

recalesce *verb*
- "ree kuh LESS"
- grow hot again (esp. of iron allowed to cool from white heat, whose temperature rises at a certain point for a short time).
- [Latin *recalescere* (*re-* again, *calescere* grow hot)]
- **recalescent** *adjective*

recapitalize *verb*
ALSO SPELLED: esp. *Brit.* **-ise**
- "ree CAPPA t'll ize"
- capitalize (shares etc.) again.
- [Latin *re-* again + CAPITALIZE]
- **recapitalization** *noun* (also esp. *Brit.* **-isation**)

recapitulate *verb*
- "ree kuh PITCH'll ate"
- go briefly through (the main points of a speech, argument, etc.) again; summarize.
- [Latin *recapitulare* (*re-* again, *capitulum* chapter)]
- **recapitulation** *noun*

recce *noun*
- "RECKY"
- a reconnaissance.
- [abbreviation]

recede *verb*
- "re SEED"
- withdraw or move backwards from a previous position or away from an observer, or appear to do so.
- [Latin *recedere* (*re-* again, *cedere cess-* go)]

HOMOPHONES: *reseed*

receipt *noun*
- "re SEET"
- the act or an instance of receiving or being received into one's possession.
- [Anglo-French & Old Northern French *receite* from medieval Latin *recepta* feminine past participle of Latin *recipere* RECEIVE: *-p-* inserted after Latin]
- **receipted** *adjective*

HOMOPHONES: *reseat*

receive *verb*
- "re SEEVE"
- acquire or accept (something offered or given).
- [Old French *receivre, reçoivre* from Latin *recipere recept-* (*re-* again, *capere* take)]
- **receivable** *adjective*
- **receiver** *noun*

received *adjective*
- "re SEEVD"
- generally accepted as authoritative or true.
- [as RECEIVE]

receivership *noun*
- "re SEEVER ship"
- the state of being dealt with by a person appointed by a court to manage the property of a bankrupt or insane person, or property under litigation.
- [as RECEIVE]

recension *noun*
- "re SEN sh'n"
- the revision of a text.
- [Latin *recensio* from *recensēre* revise (*re-* again, *censēre* review)]

receptacle *noun*
- "re SEPTA k'll"
- a container or vessel in which something is stored or deposited.
- [Old French *receptacle* from Latin *receptaculum* (as RECEPTION)]

reception *noun*
- "re SEP sh'n"
- the act or an instance of receiving or the process of being received, esp. of a person into a place or group.
- [Old French *reception* or Latin *receptio* (as RECEIVE)]

receptionist *noun*
- "re SEP sh'n ist"
- a person employed in an organization to welcome and direct visitors, answer the telephone, etc.
- [as RECEPTION]

receptive *adjective*
- "re SEPTIV"
- quick or able to receive impressions or ideas.
- [French *réceptif -ive* or medieval Latin *receptivus* (as RECEIVE)]
- **receptiveness** *noun*
- **receptivity** *noun*

receptor *noun*
- "re SEP tur"
- a cell or group of cells, found in the eyes, ears, nose, etc., specialized to detect a particular stimulus, such as light, heat, or a drug, and to initiate the transmission of impulses via the sensory nerves.
- [Old French *receptour* or Latin *receptor* (as RECEIVE)]

recess *noun*
- "REE sess"
- a short break between classes, esp. in elementary school.
- [Latin *recessus* (as RECEDE)]

recessed *adjective*
- "REE sest"
- placed in such a way as to be flush or set back from the surface in which it is set.
- [as RECESS]

recession *noun*
- "re SESH'n"
- a temporary decline in economic activity or prosperity associated with lower levels of production and employment.
- [as RECESS]
- **recessional** *adjective*
- **recessionary** *adjective*

recessive *adjective*
- "re SESSIV"
- (of an inherited characteristic) appearing in offspring only when not masked by a dominant characteristic inherited from one parent.
- [as RECESS]
- **recessiveness** *noun*

réchauffé *noun*
- "RAY show fay"
- a warmed-up dish.
- [French past participle of *réchauffer* (*re-* again, CHAFE)]

recherché *adjective*
- "re SHARE shay"
- carefully sought out; rare or exotic.
- [French, past participle of *rechercher* (*re-* again, *chercher* seek, from Late Latin *cīrcāre* go about, from Latin *circa* around)]

rechristen *verb*
- "ree CRISS'n"
- give a new name to.
- [Latin *re-* again + CHRISTEN]

recidivist *noun*
- "re SID iv ist"
- a person who relapses into crime.
- [French *récidiviste* from *récidiver* from medieval Latin *recidivare* from Latin *recidivus* from *recidere* (*re-* again, *cadere* fall)]
- **recidivism** *noun*

recipe *noun*
- "RESSA pee"
- a statement of the ingredients and procedure required for preparing a dish.
- [2nd sing. imperative (as used in prescriptions) of Latin *recipere* take, RECEIVE]

recipient *noun*
- "re SIPPY 'nt"
- a person who receives something.
- [French *récipient* from Italian *recipiente* or Latin *recipiens* from *recipere* RECEIVE]

reciprocal *adjective*
- "re SIPPRA k'll"
- in return.
- [Latin *reciprocus*, ultimately from *re-* back + *pro* forward]
- **reciprocality** *noun*
- **reciprocally** *adverb*
- **reciprocity** *noun* "ressa PROSSA tee"

reciprocate *verb*
- "re SIPPRA cate"
- return or requite (affection etc.).
- [Latin *reciprocare reciprocat-* (as RECIPROCAL)]
- **reciprocation** *noun*
- **reciprocator** *noun*

recirculate *verb*
- "ree SUR kyoo late"
- circulate again, esp. make available for reuse.
- [Latin *re-* again + CIRCULATE]
- **recirculation** *noun*

recitalist *noun*
- "re SITE'll ist"
- a person who performs often in musical recitals.
- [as RECITE]

recitative *noun*
- "ressa tuh TEEVE"
- declamatory speech-like singing used esp. in opera or oratorio for advancing the plot.
- [Italian *recitativo* (as RECITE)]

recite *verb*
- "re SITE"
- repeat aloud or declaim (a poem or passage) from memory, esp. before an audience.
- [Old French *reciter* or Latin *recitare* (*re-* again, CITE)]
- **recital** *noun*
- **recitation** *noun* "ressa TAY sh'n"
- **reciter** *noun*

reclamation *noun*
- "reckla MAY sh'n"
- the act of reclaiming something.
- [Latin *reclamation* from *reclamare* cry out against (*re-* again, *clamare* shout)]

reclassify *verb*
- "ree CLASSA fie"
- classify again or differently.
- [Latin *re-* again + CLASSIFY]
- **reclassification** *noun*

recline *verb*
- "re CLINE"
- lie or cause to lie backwards in a horizontal or leaning position, esp. in resting.
- [Old English *recliner* or Latin *reclinare* bend back, recline (*re-* back, *clinare* bend)]
- **reclining** *adjective*

recliner *noun*
- "re CLINE ur"
- a comfortable chair for reclining in, usu. with adjustable back and footrest.
- [as RECLINE]

reclothe *verb*
- "ree CLOTHE" (with "TH" as in *THIS*)
- clothe again or differently.
- [Latin *re-* again + 'clothe' of unknown origin]

recluse *noun*
• "RECK luce" or "ruh KLUCE"
• a person preferring or living in seclusion or isolation.
• [Old French *reclus recluse* past participle of *reclure* from Latin *recludere reclus-* (*re-* again, *claudere* shut)]
• **reclusion** *noun*
• **reclusive** *adjective*

recognizance *noun*
• "ruh COG niz ince"
• a bond by which a person undertakes before a court or magistrate to observe some condition, e.g. to appear when summoned.
• [Old French *recon(n)issance* (*re-* again, COGNIZANCE)]

recognize *verb*
ALSO SPELLED: esp. *Brit.* **-ise**
• "RECK ug nize"
• identify (a person or thing) as already known; know again.
• [Old French *recon(n)iss-* stem of *reconnaistre* from Latin *recognoscere recognit-* (*re-* again, *cognoscere* learn)]
• **recognition** *noun*
• **recognizability** *noun* (also esp. *Brit.* **-isability**)
• **recognizable** *adjective* (also esp. *Brit.* **-isable**)
• **recognizably** *adverb* (also esp. *Brit.* **-isably**)
• **recognizer** *noun* (also esp. *Brit.* **-iser**)

recoilless *adjective*
• "re COIL less"
• (of a gun) having a reduced or eliminated tendency to move backwards upon firing.
• [Old French *reculer* (*re-* again, Latin *culus* buttocks)]

recollect *verb*
• "recka LECT"
• remember.
• [Latin *recolligere recollect-* (*re-* again, COLLECT[1])]
• **recollection** *noun*
• **recollective** *adjective*

Récollet *noun*
• "RECKA lay"
• a member of the reformed branch of the Franciscan Observants, founded in France in the late 16th c., and active in New France.
• [French *récollet*, from medieval Latin *recollectus*, past participle of *recolligere*, gather again]

recolonize *verb*
ALSO SPELLED: esp. *Brit.* **-ise**
• "ree COLLA nize"
• colonize again.
• [Latin *re-* again + COLONY]
• **recolonization** *noun* (also esp. *Brit.* **-isation**)

recombination *noun*
• "ree comba NAY sh'n"
• the rearrangement, esp. by crossing over in chromosomes, of genes to form a combination different from that of its parents.
• [Latin *re-* again + COMBINE]
• **recombinant** *adjective* "ree COMBA n'nt"

recommence *verb*
• "recka MENCE"
• begin again.
• [Latin *re-* again + COMMENCE]

recommend *verb*
• "recka MEND"
• suggest as fit for some purpose or use.
• [Middle English from medieval Latin *recommendare* (*re-* again, COMMEND)]
• **recommendable** *adjective*
• **recommendation** *noun*
• **recommender** *noun*

recommission *verb*
• "ree kuh MISH'n"
• commission again.
• [Latin *re-* again + COMMISSION]

recommit *verb*
• "ree kuh MIT"
• commit again.
• [Latin *re-* again + COMMIT]
• **recommitment** *noun*
• **recommittal** *noun*

recompense *verb*
• "RECKUM pence"
• make amends to (a person) or for (a loss etc.); compensate.
• [Old French *recompense(r)* from Late Latin *recompensare* (*re-* again, COMPENSATE)]

recompile *verb*
• "ree kum PILE"
• compile (a computer program) again or differently.
• [Latin *re-* again + *compilare* plunder, plagiarize]
• **recompilation** *noun*

reconceptualize *verb*
ALSO SPELLED: esp. *Brit.* **-ise**
• "ree k'n SEP choo 'll ize"
• conceptualize again or differently.
• [Latin *re-* again + CONCEPTUALIZE]
• **reconceptualization** *noun* (also esp. *Brit.* **-isation**)

reconcile *verb*
• "RECK'n sile"
• make friendly again after an estrangement.
• [Old French *reconcilier* or Latin *reconciliare* (*re-* again, *conciliare* CONCILIATE)]
• **reconcilable** *adjective*
• **reconciler** *noun*
• **reconciliation** *noun* "reck'n silly AY sh'n"
• **reconciliatory** *adjective*

recondite *adjective*
• "RECK'n dite" or "re CON dite"
• (of a subject or knowledge) abstruse; out of the way; little known.

• [Latin *reconditus* (*re-* again, *conditus* past participle of *condere* hide)]

recondition *verb*
• "ree k'n DISH'n"
• overhaul, refit, renovate.
• [Latin *re-* again + CONDITION]

reconfigure *verb*
• "ree k'n FIG yur"
• configure again or differently, esp. adapt (a computer system) to a new task by altering its configuration.
• [Latin *re-* again + CONFIGURE]
• **reconfiguration** *noun*

reconnaissance *noun*
• "re CONNA since"
• a survey of a region, esp. a military examination to locate an enemy or ascertain strategic features.
• [French (earlier *-oissance*) from stem of *reconnaître* (as RECONNOITRE)]

reconnect *verb*
• "ree kuh NECT"
• connect again.
• [Latin *re-* again + *connectere connex-* (*com-* with, *nectere* bind)]
• **reconnection** *noun*

reconnoitre *verb*
ALSO SPELLED: **reconnoiter**
• "recka NOY tur"
• make a reconnaissance of (an area, enemy position, etc.).
• [obsolete French *reconnoître* from Latin *recognoscere* RECOGNIZE]

reconquer *verb*
• "ree CONG kur"
• conquer again.
• [Latin *re-* again + CONQUER]
• **reconquest** *noun*

reconsecrate *verb*
• "ree CONSA crate"
• consecrate (a church etc.) again.
• [Latin *re-* again + CONSECRATE]
• **reconsecration** *noun*

recontextualize *verb*
ALSO SPELLED: esp. *Brit.* **-ise**
• "ree k'n TEX choo'll ize"
• contextualize again or differently.
• [Latin *re-* again + CONTEXT]
• **recontextualization** *noun* (also esp. *Brit.* **-isation**)

reconvene *verb*
• "ree k'n VEEN"
• convene again, esp. (of a meeting etc.) after a pause in proceedings.
• [Latin *re-* again + CONVENE]

recoup *verb*
• "re COOP"
• recover or regain (a loss).
• [French *recouper* (*re-* again, *couper* cut)]
• **recoupable** *adjective*
• **recoupment** *noun*

recreation *noun*
• "reck ree AY sh'n"
• the process or means of entertaining oneself.
• [Old French from Latin *recreatio -onis* from *recreare* create again, renew]
• **recreational** *adjective*
• **recreationally** *adverb*
• **recreationist** *noun*

recriminalize *verb*
ALSO SPELLED: esp. *Brit.* **-ise**
• "ree CRIMMIN'll ize"
• make (an activity which once had been a criminal offence) into a criminal offence again.
• [Latin *re-* again + CRIMINALIZE]
• **recriminalization** *noun* (also esp. *Brit.* **-isation**)

recriminate *verb*
• "re CRIM'n ate"
• make mutual or counter accusations.
• [medieval Latin *recriminare* (*re-* again, *criminare* accuse, from *crimen* crime)]
• **recrimination** *noun*
• **recriminatory** *adjective*

recrudesce *verb*
• "ree crew DESS"
• (of a disease or difficulty etc.) break out again, esp. after a dormant period.
• [back-formation from *recrudescent* from Latin *recrudescere* (*re-* again, *crudus* raw)]
• **recrudescence** *noun*
• **recrudescent** *adjective*

recruit *noun*
• "re CROOT"
• a serviceman or servicewoman newly enlisted and not yet fully trained.
• [earlier = reinforcement, from obsolete French dialect *recrute*, ultimately from French *recroître* increase again, from Latin *recrescere*]
• **recruiter** *noun*
• **recruitment** *noun*

recrystallize *verb*
ALSO SPELLED: esp. *Brit.* **-ise**
• "ree CRISSTA lize"
• crystallize again.
• [Latin *re-* again + CRYSTALLIZE]
• **recrystallization** *noun* (also esp. *Brit.* **-isation**)

rectal *adjective*
• "RECK t'll"
• of or relating to the rectum.
• [as RECTUM]
• **rectally** *adverb*

rectangle *noun*
• "RECK tangle"
• a plane figure with four straight sides and four right angles, esp. one with the adjacent sides unequal.
• [French *rectangle* or medieval Latin

rectangulum from Late Latin *rectiangulum* from Latin *rectus* straight + *angulus* angle]
• **rectangular** *adjective*
• **rectangularity** *noun*
"reck tang gyuh LERRA tee"
• **rectangularly** *adverb*

rectify *verb*
• "RECTA fie"
• adjust or make right; correct, amend.
• [Old French *rectifier* from medieval Latin *rectificare* from Latin *rectus* right]
• **rectifiable** *adjective*
• **rectification** *noun*
• **rectifier** *noun*

rectilinear *adjective*
• "recta LINNY ur"
• bounded or characterized by straight lines.
• [Late Latin *rectilineus* from Latin *rectus* straight + *linea* line]
• **rectilinearity** *noun* "recta linny ERRA tee"
• **rectilinearly** *adverb*

rectitude *noun*
• "RECTA tude"
• moral uprightness.
• [Old French *rectitude* or Late Latin *rectitudo* from Latin *rectus* right]

recto *noun*
• "RECK toe"
• the right-hand page of an open book.
• [Latin *recto* (*folio*) on the right (leaf)]

rector *noun*
• "RECTER"
• (in the Church of England) the incumbent of a parish where all tithes formerly passed to the incumbent.
• [Old French *rectour* or Latin *rector* ruler, from *regere rect-* rule]
• **rectorate** *noun*
• **rectorial** *adjective*
• **rectorship** *noun*

rectory *noun*
• "RECTER ee"
• a rector's house.
• [as RECTOR]

rectrix *noun*
• "RECK trix"
• a bird's strong tail feather directing flight.
• [Latin, feminine of *rector* ruler: see RECTOR]

rectum *noun*
• "RECK tum"
• the final section of the large intestine, terminating at the anus.
• [Latin *rectum* (*intestinum*) straight (intestine)]

rectus *noun*
• "RECK tuss"
• a straight muscle.
• [Latin, = straight]

recumbent *adjective*
• "re KUM b'nt"
• lying down; reclining.
• [Latin *recumbere* recline (*re-* back, *cumbere* lie)]
• **recumbency** *noun*

recuperate *verb*
• "re COOPER ate"
• recover from illness, exhaustion, financial loss, etc.
• [Latin *recuperare recuperat-* recover]
• **recuperation** *noun*
• **recuperative** *adjective* "re COOPER a tiv"

recur *verb*
• "re CUR"
• occur again; be repeated.
• [Latin *recurrere recurs-* (*re-* again, *currere* run)]
• **recurrence** *noun*
• **recurrent** *adjective*
• **recurrently** *adverb*
• **recursion** *noun*
• **recursive** *adjective*
• **recursively** *adverb*

recusant *noun*
• "RECK yoo z'nt" or "ruh KYOOZ 'nt"
• a person who refuses submission to an authority or compliance with a regulation, esp. one who refused to attend services of the Church of England.
• [as RECUSE]
• **recusancy** *noun*

recuse *verb*
• "re KYOOZ"
• (of a judge etc.) withdraw from hearing a case because of a possible conflict of interest or lack of impartiality.
• [Latin *recusare* refuse]
• **recusal** *noun*

recycle *verb*
• "re SIKE 'll"
• return (material) to a previous stage of a cyclic process, esp. convert (waste) to reusable material.
• [Latin *re-* again + CYCLE]
• **recyclability** *noun*
• **recyclable** *adjective*
• **recycler** *noun*
• **recycling** *noun*

redact *verb*
• "re DACT"
• put into literary form; edit for publication.
• [Latin *redigere redact-* (*red-* again, *agere* bring)]
• **redaction** *noun*
• **redactional** *adjective*
• **redactor** *noun*

redan *noun*
• "rid ANN"
• a fieldwork with two faces forming a salient angle.
• [French from *redent* notching (*re-* again, *dent* tooth)]

redcurrant *noun*
• "RED cur 'nt"
• a widely cultivated shrub, *Ribes rubrum*.
• ['red' + CURRANT]

redd *noun*
- "RED"
- a hollow in a riverbed made by a trout or salmon to spawn in.
- [17th c.: origin unknown]

HOMOPHONES: *red, read*

reddle *noun*
- "RED'll"
- red ochre; ruddle.
- [var. of RUDDLE]

redecorate *verb*
- "ree DECKER ate"
- decorate again or differently.
- [Latin *re-* again + DECORATE]
- **redecoration** *noun*

rededicate *verb*
- "ree DEDDA cate"
- dedicate anew.
- [Latin *re-* again + DEDICATE]
- **rededication** *noun*

redeem *verb*
- "re DEEM"
- buy back; recover by expenditure of effort or by a stipulated payment.
- [Old French *redimer* or Latin *redimere redempt-* (*red-* again, *emere* buy)]
- **redeemable** *adjective*
- **redeemer** *noun*
- **redemption** *noun*
- **redemptive** *adjective*

Redemptorist *noun*
- "re DEMP tur ist"
- a member of the Congregation of the Most Holy Redeemer, a Roman Catholic order of priests and lay brothers founded in 1732 by St. Alphonsus Liguori, devoted chiefly to preaching, esp. through parish missions and retreats.
- [Latin *redemptor* redeemer (as REDEEM)]

redetermine *verb*
- "ree de TURMIN"
- determine again or differently.
- [Latin *re-* again + DETERMINE]
- **redetermination** *noun*

redingote *noun*
- "REDDING goat"
- a woman's long coat with a cutaway front or a contrasting piece on the front.
- [French from English *riding-coat*]

redissolve *verb*
- "ree diz OLVE"
- dissolve again.
- [Latin *re-* again + DISSOLVE]
- **redissolution** *noun*

redistribute *verb*
- "ree dis TRIB yoot"
- distribute again or differently.
- [Latin *re-* again + DISTRIBUTE]
- **redistribution** *noun*
- **redistributionist** *noun*
- **redistributive** *adjective*

redivide *verb*
- "ree div IDE"
- divide again or differently.
- [Latin *re-* again + DIVIDE]
- **redivision** *noun*

redivivus *adjective*
- "redda VEE vuss"
- come back to life.
- [Latin (*re-* again, *vivus* living)]

redolent *adjective*
- "REDDA l'nt"
- strongly reminiscent or suggestive or mentally associated.
- [Old French *redolent* or Latin *redolēre* (*red-* again, *olēre* smell)]
- **redolence** *noun*
- **redolently** *adverb*

redoubt *noun*
- "re DOUT"
- an outwork or fieldwork usu. square or polygonal and without flanking defences.
- [French *redoute* from obsolete Italian *ridotta* from medieval Latin *reductus* refuge, from past participle of Latin *reducere* withdraw (see REDUCE): *-b-* after DOUBT (compare REDOUBTABLE)]

redoubtable *adjective*
- "re DOUT a bull"
- formidable, esp. as an opponent.
- [Old French *redoutable* from *redouter* fear (*re-* again, DOUBT)]
- **redoubtably** *adverb*

redound *verb*
- "re DOUND"
- (of an action etc.) make a great contribution to (one's credit or advantage etc.).
- [Middle English, originally = overflow, from Old French *redonder* from Latin *redundare* surge (*red-* again, *unda* wave)]

redpoll *noun*
- "RED pole"
- any of various Holarctic finches, with red crests.
- ['red' + POLL]

reduce *verb*
- "re DOOCE" or "re DYOOCE"
- make or become smaller or less.
- [Middle English in sense 'restore to original or proper position', from Latin *reducere reduct-* (*re-* again, *ducere* bring)]
- **reducer** *noun*
- **reducibility** *noun*
- **reducible** *adjective*
- **reduction** *noun*

reductase *noun*
- "re DUCK tace"
- an enzyme which promotes chemical reduction.
- [as REDUCE]

reductionism *noun*
• "re DUCK sh'n izm"
• the tendency to or principle of analyzing complex things into simple constituents.
• [as REDUCE]
• **reductionist** *noun*
• **reductionistic** *adjective*

reductive *adjective*
• "re DUCTIV"
• tending to present a subject or problem in a simplified form, esp. one viewed as crude.
• [as REDUCE]
• **reductively** *adverb*
• **reductiveness** *noun*

redundant *adjective*
• "re DUN d'nt"
• superfluous; not needed.
• [Latin *redundare redundant-* (as REDOUND)]
• **redundancy** *noun*
• **redundantly** *adverb*

reduplicate *verb*
• "ree DUPE luh cate"
• make double.
• [Latin *re-* again + DUPLICATE]
• **reduplication** *noun*
• **reduplicative** *adjective*

redux *adjective*
• "re DUCKS"
• brought back, revived, restored.
• [Latin, from *reducere* bring back]

reebok *noun*
• "REE bock"
• a small southern African antelope, *Pelea capreolus*, with sharp horns.
• [Dutch, = roebuck]

reedbuck *noun*
• "REED buck"
• any of various African antelopes of the genus *Redunca*, characterized by their whistling calls and high bouncing jumps.
• ['reed' + 'buck']

reek *verb*
• "REEK"
• smell strongly and unpleasantly.
• [Old English *rēocan* from Germanic]
• **reeky** *adjective*
HOMOPHONES: *wreak*

reel *noun*
• "REEL"
• a cylindrical device on which film, tape, etc., or thread, yarn, wire, etc., are wound.
• [Old English *hrēol*, of unknown origin]
• **reeler** *noun*
HOMOPHONES: *real, riel*

reeve *noun*
• "REEVE"
• *Cdn* (in Ontario and the Western provinces) the elected leader of the council of a town or other rural municipality.
• [Old English *(ge)rēfa, girœfa*]
• **reeveship** *noun*
HOMOPHONES: *reave, reive*

refashion *verb*
• "ree FASH'n"
• change the composition or appearance of (something); fashion again or differently.
• [Latin *re-* again + FASHION]

refectory *noun*
• "re FECTER ee"
• a room used for communal meals, esp. in a monastery or college.
• [Late Latin *refectorium* from Latin *reficere* refresh (*re-* again, *facere* make)]

refer *verb*
• "re FUR"
• allude (to) or describe.
• [Old French *referer* from Latin *referre* carry back (*re-* again, *ferre* bring)]
• **referable** *adjective*

referee *noun*
• "reffer EE"
• an official who supervises a hockey, basketball, etc. game or boxing match to ensure that the competitors obey the rules.
• [as REFER]
• **refereed** *adjective*
• **refereeing** *noun*

reference *noun*
• "REFFER ince"
• an allusion.
• [as REFER]
• **referential** *adjective*
• **referentiality** *noun* "reffer enshy ALA tee"

referendum *noun*
• "reffa REN dum"
• the process of referring a political question to the electorate for a direct decision by general vote.
• [Latin, gerund or neuter gerundive of *referre*: see REFER]

referent *noun*
• "REFFER 'nt"
• the idea or thing that a word etc. symbolizes.
• [as REFER]

referral *noun*
• "re FUR 'll"
• the referring of an individual to an expert or specialist for advice, esp. the directing of a patient by a general practitioner to a medical specialist.
• [as REFER]

refinish *verb*
• "ree FIN ish"
• apply a new finish to (a surface).
• [Latin *re-* again + FINISH]

reflectance *noun*
• "re FLECT ince"
• a measure of the proportion of light or other

radiation that a surface (of a particular substance) reflects or scatters.
• [Old French *reflecter* or Latin *reflectere* (*re-* again, *flectere flex-* bend)]

reflectivity *noun*
• "re fleck TIVVA tee"
• the property of reflecting light or radiation, esp. reflectance as measured independently of the thickness of a material.
• [as REFLECTANCE]

reflector *noun*
• "re FLECTER"
• a piece of glass or metal etc. for reflecting light in a required direction, e.g. a red one on the back of a bicycle.
• [as REFLECTANCE]

reflexive *adjective*
• "re FLEX iv"
• triggered by, or as if by, reflex.
• [as REFLECTANCE]
• **reflexively** *adverb*
• **reflexiveness** *noun*
• **reflexivity** *noun* "re flex IVVA tee"

reflexology *noun*
• "ree flex OLLA jee"
• a technique for treating tension, alleviating symptoms by massaging points on the feet, hands, and head.
• [Latin *reflexus* (as REFLECTANCE) + Greek *logos* word]
• **reflexologist** *noun*

reflux *noun*
• "REE flux"
• a backward flow.
• [Latin *re-* again, back + *fluxus* flow, from *fluere* to flow]

refocus *verb*
• "ree FOKE us"
• (of a camera lens) adjust the focus of.
• [Latin *re-* again + *focus* hearth]

reformation *noun*
• "reffer MAY sh'n"
• the act of reforming or process of being reformed, esp. a radical change for the better in political or religious or social affairs.
• [Latin *re-* again + *forma* mould, form]
• **reformational** *adjective*

reformatory *noun*
• "re FORMA tory"
• an institution to which young offenders are sent to be reformed.
• [as REFORMATION]

refract *verb*
• "re FRACT"
• (of water, air, glass, etc.) deflect (a ray of light, sound, etc.) at a certain angle when it enters obliquely from another medium.
• [Latin *refringere refract-* (*re-* again, *frangere* break)]
• **refracted** *adjective*
• **refraction** *noun*
• **refractive** *adjective*
• **refractivity** *noun*

refractometer *noun*
• "re frack TOMMA tur"
• an instrument for measuring a refractive index.
• [as REFRACT + Greek *metron* measure]

refractor *noun*
• "re FRACTER"
• a refracting medium or lens.
• [as REFRACT]

refractory *adjective*
• "re FRACTER ee"
• stubborn, unmanageable, rebellious.
• [alteration of obsolete *refractary* from Latin *refractarius* (as REFRACT)]
• **refractoriness** *noun*

refrigerate *verb*
• "re FRIDGE ur ate"
• make or become cool or cold.
• [Latin *refrigerare* (*re-* again, *frigus frigoris* cold)]
• **refrigerant** *noun*
• **refrigerated** *adjective*
• **refrigeration** *noun*
• **refrigerator** *noun*

refuge *noun*
• "REF yoodge"
• a shelter from pursuit, danger, or trouble.
• [Old French from Latin *refugium* (*re-* again, *fugere* flee)]

refugee *noun*
• "ref yoo JEE"
• a person taking refuge, esp. in a foreign country, from war, persecution, or natural disaster.
• [French *réfugié* past participle of (*se*) *réfugier* (as REFUGE)]

refugium *noun*
• "re FYOO jee um"
• an area in which a population of organisms can survive through a period of unfavourable conditions, esp. glaciation.
• [Latin, = place of refuge]

refulgent *adjective*
• "re FUL j'nt" ("FUL" rhymes with *HULL*)
• shining, radiant; gloriously bright.
• [Latin *refulgēre* (*re-* again, *fulgēre* shine)]

refurbish *verb*
• "ree FUR bish"
• brighten up, redecorate.
• [Latin *re-* again + FURBISH]
• **refurbished** *adjective*
• **refurbishing** *noun*
• **refurbishment** *noun*

refusenik *noun*
• "re FUZE nick"

• a Jew in the former Soviet Union who was refused permission to emigrate to Israel.
• ['refuse' (Old French *refuser*, prob. ultimately from Latin *recusare* (see RECUSE) after *refutare* REFUTE) + *-nik* from Russian]

refute *verb*
• "re FYOOT"
• prove the falsity or error of (a statement etc. or the person proposing it).
• [Latin *refutare* (*re-* again: compare CONFUTE)]
• **refutability** *noun*
• **refutable** *adjective*
• **refutation** *noun* "reff yoo TAY sh'n"

regal *adjective*
• "REE g'll"
• of, like, or fit for a monarch.
• [Old French *regal* or Latin *regalis* from *rex regis* king]
• **regality** *noun*
• **regally** *adverb*

regale *verb*
• "re GALE"
• entertain or divert with (talk etc.).
• [French *régaler* from Old French *gale* pleasure]

regalia *plural noun*
• "re GALE yuh"
• any distinctive or elaborate clothes or accoutrements.
• [medieval Latin, = royal privileges, from Latin neuter pl. of *regalis* REGAL]

regatta *noun*
• "re GATTA"
• a marine sporting event consisting of a series of races of boats, yachts, etc.
• [Italian (Venetian) *regata*, lit. = 'contest']

regenerate *verb*
• "ree JENNER ate"
• reconstitute in a new and improved form; revive.
• [Latin *re-* again + GENERATE]
• **regeneration** *noun*
• **regenerative** *adjective*
• **regenerator** *noun*

regent *noun*
• "REE j'nt"
• a person appointed to administer a country or state because the monarch is a minor, absent, or incapacitated.
• [Old French *regent* or Latin *regere* rule]
• **regency** *noun*

reggae *noun*
• "REG ay"
• a W Indian style of popular music indigenous to the black culture of Jamaica, developed from an eclectic mix of African religious music, Christian black revival songs, New Orleans rhythm and blues, and Rastafarian liturgical music.
• [Caribbean English, possibly related to Yoruba *ręgę-ręgę* in a rough manner or Hausa *rega* shake]

regicide *noun*
• "REDGE a side"
• the act of killing a king.
• [Latin *rex regis* king + *-cida, -cidium* from *caedere* kill]
• **regicidal** *adjective*

regie *noun*
• "ray ZHEE"
• *Cdn* (*Que.*) any of several Quebec government bodies regulating insurance, housing, language, etc.
• [French, = 'government agency' from Latin *regere* direct]

regild *verb*
• "ree GILD" (with "G" as in *GIVE*)
• gild again, esp. to renew faded or worn gilding.
• [Latin *re-* again + GILD]

regime *noun*
• "ray ZHEEM"
• a method of government or dominance of a country or state, esp. one that is or is considered to be oppressive.
• [French *régime* (as REGIMEN)]

regimen *noun*
• "REDGE a m'n"
• a prescribed course of exercise, way of life, or diet.
• [Latin from *regere* rule]

regiment *noun*
• "REDGE a m'nt"
• a permanent unit of an army usu. commanded by a colonel and divided into several companies, troops, or batteries and often into two battalions.
• [Old French from Late Latin *regimentum* (as REGIMEN)]
• **regimental** *adjective*

regimentation *noun*
• "redge a m'n TAY sh'n"
• the action of imposing order; the process by which (people etc.) are integrated in a system, institution, etc.
• [as REGIMENT]
• **regimented** *adjective*

Reginan *noun*
• "re JYE n'n"
• a resident of Regina, Sask.

region *noun*
• "REE j'n"
• a (usu. specified) area of land or division of the earth's surface without fixed limits but having definable features such as climate, fauna, flora, etc.
• [Old French from Latin *regio -onis* direction, district, from *regere* direct]
• **regional** *adjective*

- **regionalism** *noun*
- **regionalist** *noun*
- **regionalization** *noun* (also esp. *Brit.* **-isation**)
- **regionalize** *verb* (also esp. *Brit.* **-ise**)
- **regionally** *adverb*

regisseur *noun*
- "ray zhee SUR"
- a person who stages a theatrical production, esp. a ballet.
- [French *régisseur* stage manager, from *régir* direct, govern, from Latin *regere* direct]

register *noun*
- "REDGE iss tur"
- an official list or record of births, deaths, marriages, guests, students in attendance at school, etc.
- [Old French *registre* or medieval Latin *regestrum, registrum*, alteration of *regestum* from Late Latin *regesta* things recorded (*re-* again, Latin *gerere gest-* carry)]
- **registration** *noun*
- **registrational** *adjective*

registered *adjective*
- "REDGE iss turd"
- recorded; officially set down, esp. in a register.
- [as REGISTER]

registrant *noun*
- "REDGE iss tr'nt"
- a person who registers or has registered for something, such as a conference, course, etc.
- [as REGISTER]

registrar *noun*
- "REDGE iss trar"
- an official responsible for keeping a register or official records.
- [medieval Latin *registrarius* from *registrum* REGISTER]
- **registrarship** *noun*

registry *noun*
- "REDGE iss tree"
- a place or office where registers or records are kept.
- [as REGISTER]

regnal *adjective*
- "REG n'll" ("REG" rhymes with *LEG*)
- of or pertaining to a reign or monarch.
- [Anglo-Latin *regnalis* (as REIGN)]

regnant *adjective*
- "REG n'nt"
- (of things, qualities, etc.) predominant, prevalent.
- [Latin *regnare* REIGN]

regolith *noun*
- "REGGA lith"
- unconsolidated solid material covering the bedrock of a planet.
- [erroneously from Greek *rhēgos* rug, blanket + *lithos* stone]

regrettable *adjective*
- "re GRETTA bull"
- (of events or conduct) unfortunate, unwelcome; deserving censure.
- [French from Old French *regreter* bewail]
- **regrettably** *adverb*

regular *adjective*
- "REG yuh lur"
- usual, standard, customary.
- [Old French *reguler* from Latin *regularis* from *regula* rule]
- **regularity** *noun* "reg yuh LERRA tee"
- **regularization** *noun* (also esp. *Brit.* **-isation**)
- **regularize** *verb* (also esp. *Brit.* **-ise**)
- **regularly** *adverb*

regulate *verb*
- "REG yuh late"
- govern or control by law; subject to esp. legal restrictions.
- [Late Latin *regulare regulat-* from Latin *regula* rule]
- **regulation** *noun*
- **regulative** *adjective*
- **regulator** *noun*
- **regulatory** *adjective* "REG yuh luh tory"

regurgitate *verb*
- "re GURGE a tate"
- bring (swallowed food) up again to the mouth.
- [medieval Latin *regurgitare* (*re-* again, Latin *gurges gurgitis* whirlpool)]
- **regurgitation** *noun*

rehabilitate *verb*
- "ree huh BILLA tate"
- restore (a person) to effectiveness or normal life by training etc., esp. after imprisonment, injury, addiction, or illness.
- [originally in the sense 'restore to former privileges' from medieval Latin *rehabilitare*, *re-* again + *habilitare* make able]
- **rehabilitation** *noun*
- **rehabilitative** *adjective*

rehearse *verb*
- "re HURSE"
- practise (a play, recital, ceremony, etc.) for later public performance.
- [Anglo-French *rehearser*, Old French *reherc(i)er*, perhaps formed *re-* again + *hercer* to harrow, from *herse* harrow: see HEARSE]
- **rehearsal** *noun*

rehoboam *noun*
- "ree huh BO um"
- a wine bottle of about six times the standard size.
- [*Rehoboam* King of Israel]

rehydrate *verb*
- "ree HY drate"
- absorb water again after dehydration.

• [Latin *re-* again + HYDRATE]
• **rehydratable** *adjective*
• **rehydration** *noun*

Reich *noun*
• "RIKE"
• the former German nation or Commonwealth, esp. the the Nazi regime, 1933–45.
• [German, = empire]

reify *verb*
• "REE a fie" or "RAY a fie"
• convert (a concept, abstraction, etc.) into a thing; materialize.
• [Latin *res* thing]
• **reification** *noun*

reign *verb*
• "RAIN"
• hold royal office; be king or queen.
• [Old French *reigne* kingdom, from Latin *regnare* from *rex regis* king]
• **reigning** *adjective*
HOMOPHONES: *rein, rain*

reignite *verb*
• "ree ig NITE"
• ignite again.
• [Latin *re-* again + IGNITE]
• **reignition** *noun* "ree ig NISH'n"

reiki *noun*
• "RAY kee"
• a healing technique based on the principle that a therapist can channel energy into a patient by means of touch, to activate the natural healing processes of the patient's body and restore physical and emotional well-being.
• [Japanese, lit. 'universal life energy']

reimagine *verb*
• "ree im ADGE in"
• imagine again, esp. reinterpret (an event, a work of art, etc.) imaginatively; rethink.
• [Latin *re-* again + IMAGINE]

reimburse *verb*
• "ree im BURSE"
• repay (a person who has expended money).
• [Latin *re* again, back + obsolete *imburse* put in a purse, from medieval Latin *imbursare* (*in* in, *bursa* purse, from Greek *bursa* hide, leather)]
• **reimbursable** *adjective*
• **reimbursement** *noun*

reimpose *verb*
• "ree im POZE"
• impose again, esp. after a lapse.
• [Latin *re-* again + French *imposer* from Latin *imponere imposit-* inflict, deceive (*in* in, *ponere* put)]
• **reimposition** *noun*

rein *noun*
• "RAIN"
• a long narrow strap with each end attached to the bit, used to guide or check a horse etc. in riding or driving.
• [Old French *rene, reigne*, earlier *resne*, ultimately from Latin *retinēre* retain]
HOMOPHONES: *reign, rain*

reincarnation *noun*
• "ree in car NAY sh'n"
• the rebirth of a soul in a new body.
• [Latin *re-* again + INCARNATION]
• **reincarnate** *verb* "ree in CAR nate"
• **reincarnate** *adjective* "ree in CAR nit"

reincorporate *verb*
• "ree in CORPER ate"
• incorporate afresh.
• [Latin *re-* again + INCORPORATE]
• **reincorporation** *noun*

reindeer *noun*
• "RAIN deer"
• a subarctic deer, *Rangifer tarandus*, of which both sexes have large antlers, domesticated in northern Eurasia for drawing sleds and as a source of milk, flesh, and hide.
• [Old Norse *hreindýri* from *hreinn* reindeer, caribou + *dýr* animal, deer]

reinjure *verb*
• "ree INJUR"
• injure again.
• [Latin *re-* again + INJURE]
• **reinjury** *noun*

reinsert *verb*
• "ree in SURT"
• insert again.
• [Latin *re-* again + *inserere* (*in* in, *serere sert-* join)]
• **reinsertion** *noun*

reinstall *verb*
• "ree in STAWL"
• install again.
• [Latin *re-* again + medieval Latin *installare* (*in* in, *stallare* from *stallum* stall)]
• **reinstallation** *noun*

reinstitute *verb*
• "ree INSTA tute"
• institute or establish again.
• [Latin *re-* again + INSTITUTE]

reinsure *verb*
• "ree in SHUR"
• insure again (esp. of an insurance company securing itself by transferring some or all of the risk to another insurer).
• [Latin *re-* again + Anglo-French *enseürer* from Old French *aseürer* ASSURE]
• **reinsurance** *noun*
• **reinsurer** *noun*

reintegrate *verb*
• "ree INTA grate"
• restore wholeness or unity to.
• [Latin *re-* again + INTEGRATE]
• **reintegration** *noun*

reinter *verb*
- "ree in TUR"
- inter (a corpse) again.
- [Latin *re-* again + INTER]
- **reinterment** *noun*

reinterpret *verb*
- "ree in TUR prit"
- interpret again or differently.
- [Latin *re-* again + INTERPRET]
- **reinterpretation** *noun*

reintroduce *verb*
- "ree intra DYOOCE" or "ree intra DOOCE"
- introduce again.
- [Latin *re-* again + *introducere introduct-* (*intro* to the inside, *ducere* lead)]
- **reintroduction** *noun*

reinvent *verb*
- "ree in VENT"
- invent again.
- [Latin *re-* again + INVENTOR]
- **reinvention** *noun*

reinvest *verb*
- "ree in VEST"
- invest again (esp. money made from one investment in other investments etc.).
- [Latin *re-* again + Italian *investire* from Latin *investire investit-* (*in* in, *vestire* clothe, from *vestis* clothing)]
- **reinvestment** *noun*

reinvigorate *verb*
- "ree in VIGGER ate"
- impart fresh vigour to.
- [Latin *re-* again + INVIGORATE]
- **reinvigoration** *noun*

reishi *noun*
- "RAY ee shee"
- a mushroom, *Ganoderma lucidum*, with a shiny cap which typically grows on dead or dying timber, found in Asia and North America.
- [Japanese]

reiterate *verb*
- "ree ITTER ate"
- say or do again or repeatedly.
- [Latin *re-* again + ITERATE]
- **reiteration** *noun*
- **reiterative** *adjective*

reive *verb*
- "REEVE"
- make raids; plunder.
- [var. of REAVE]
- **reiver** *noun*

HOMOPHONES: *reeve, reave*

rejuvenate *verb*
- "re JOOVA nate"
- make young or as if young again.
- [Latin *re-* again + *juvenis* young]
- **rejuvenation** *noun*
- **rejuvenator** *noun*

rekindle *verb*
- "re KIN d'll"
- kindle again.
- [Latin *re-* again + KINDLE]

relapse *verb*
- "re LAPS"
- experience a return of an illness after partial or apparently complete recovery.
- [Latin *relabi relaps-* (*re-* again, *labi* slip)]
- **relapser** *noun*

relative *adjective*
- "RELLA tiv"
- considered or having significance in relation to something else; not absolute.
- [Old French *relatif -ive* or Late Latin *relativus* having reference or relation, from *referre relat-* bring back]
- **relatively** *adverb*
- **relativization** *noun* (also esp. *Brit.* **-isation**)
- **relativize** *verb* (also esp. *Brit.* **-ise**)

relativism *noun*
- "RELLA tiv izm"
- the doctrine or belief that knowledge, truth, morality, etc., are relative and not absolute.
- [as RELATIVE]
- **relativist** *noun*
- **relativistic** *adjective*
- **relativistically** *adverb*

relativity *noun*
- "rella TIVVA tee"
- the fact or state of being relative.
- [as RELATIVE]

relaxant *noun*
- "re LAX 'nt"
- a drug etc. that reduces tension and produces relaxation, esp. of muscles.
- [Latin *relaxare* (*re-* again, *laxus* loose)]

relegate *verb*
- "RELLA gate"
- consign or dismiss to an inferior or less important position, category, etc.
- [Latin *relegare relegat-* (*re-* again, *legare* send)]
- **relegation** *noun*

relevant *adjective*
- "RELLA v'nt"
- bearing on or having reference to the matter in hand.
- [medieval Latin *relevans*, participle of Latin *relevare* RELIEVE]
- **relevance** *noun*
- **relevancy** *noun*
- **relevantly** *adverb*

relic *noun*
- "RELLIC"
- an object interesting because of its age or association with the past.
- [Old French *relique* from Latin *reliquiae* from *reliquus* remaining (*re-* again + *linquere liq-* leave)]

relict *noun*
• "RELL ict"
• a species, structure, etc., surviving from a previous age or in changed circumstances after the disappearance of related species, structures, etc.
• [Latin *relinquere relict-* leave behind (*re-* again, *linquere* leave)]

relief *noun*
• "re LEEF"
• the alleviation of or deliverance from pain, distress, anxiety, etc.
• [Old French *relief*, from *relever*: see RELIEVE]

relieve *verb*
• "re LEEVE"
• bring or provide aid or assistance to.
• [Old French *relever* from Latin *relevare* (*re-* again, *levis* light)]
• **relievable** *adjective*
• **reliever** *noun*

relieved *predicative adjective*
• "re LEEVD"
• freed from anxiety or distress.
• [as RELIEVE]
• **relievedly** *adverb* "re LEEV id lee"

relievo *noun*
• "re LEEV oh"
• a method of moulding or carving or stamping in which the design stands out from the surface, with projections proportioned to and more or less closely approximating those of the objects depicted.
• [Italian *rilievo* (as RELIEF)]

religion *noun*
• "re LIDGE 'n"
• the belief in a superhuman controlling power, esp. in a personal God or gods entitled to obedience and worship.
• [Old French from Latin *religio -onis* obligation, bond, reverence]
• **religionist** *noun*
• **religionless** *adjective*
• **religious** *adjective*
• **religiously** *adverb*
• **religiousness** *noun*

religiose *adjective*
• "re LIDGY ose" ("OSE" rhymes with *GROSS*)
• excessively religious.
• [Latin *religiosus* (as RELIGION)]
• **religiosity** *noun* "re lidgy OSSA tee"

relinquish *verb*
• "re LINK wish"
• surrender or resign (a right or possession).
• [Old French *relinquir* from Latin *relinquere* (*re-* again, *linquere* leave)]
• **relinquishment** *noun*

reliquary *noun*
• "RELLA kwerry"
• a receptacle for religious relics.
• [French *reliquaire* (as RELIC)]

relleno *noun*
• "ray YAY no"
• a battered, deep-fried, stuffed green pepper.
• [Latin American Spanish, = 'stuffed']

reluctant *adjective*
• "re LUCK t'nt"
• unwilling or disinclined.
• [Latin *reluctari* (*re-* again, *luctari* struggle)]
• **reluctance** *noun*
• **reluctantly** *adverb*

rely *verb*
• "re LIE"
• depend on with confidence or assurance.
• [Middle English (earlier senses 'rally, be a vassal of') from Old French *relier* bind together, from Latin *religare* (*re-* again, *ligare* bind)]
• **reliability** *noun*
• **reliable** *adjective*
• **reliably** *adverb*
• **reliance** *noun*
• **reliant** *adjective*

remanent *adjective*
• "REMMA n'nt"
• remaining, residual.
• [Latin *remanēre* (*re-* again, *manēre* stay)]
• **remanence** *noun*

remanufacture *verb*
• "ree man yoo FACK chur"
• manufacture again.
• [Latin *re-* again + MANUFACTURE]

remediation *noun*
• "ruh meedy AY sh'n"
• the action of remedying something, esp. the reversing or stopping of environmental damage.
• [Latin *remediatio(n-)* from *remediare* heal, cure (as REMEDY)]
• **remediate** *verb*

remedy *noun*
• "REMMA dee"
• a medicine or treatment (for a disease etc.).
• [Anglo-French *remedie* or Latin *remedium* (*re-* again, *medēri* heal)]
• **remediable** *adjective* "re MEEDY a bull"
• **remedial** *adjective*

remembrance *noun*
• "re MEM brince"
• the act of remembering or process of being remembered.
• [Old French from *remembrer* from Late Latin *rememorari* (*re-* again, Latin *memor* mindful)]

remineralize *verb*
ALSO SPELLED: esp. *Brit.* **-ise**
• "ree MINNER 'll ize"
• restore the depleted mineral content of (a part of the body, esp. the bones or teeth).
• [Latin *re-* again + MINERAL]
• **remineralization** *noun* (also esp. *Brit.* **-isation**)

reminiscence *noun*
• "remma NISS ince"
• the recalling of one's past experiences or events, esp. with enjoyment.
• [Late Latin *reminiscentia* from Latin *reminisci* remember]
• **reminisce** *verb*
• **reminiscent** *adjective*
• **reminiscently** *adverb*

remise *verb*
• "re MIZE"
• surrender or make over (a right or property).
• [French from *remis*, *remise* past participle of *remettre* put back: compare REMIT]

remit *verb*
• "re MIT"
• cancel or refrain from exacting or inflicting (a debt or punishment etc.).
• [Latin *remittere remiss-* (*re-* again, *mittere* send)]
• **remissible** *adjective*
• **remittable** *adjective*
• **remittal** *noun*

remittance *noun*
• "re MIT ince"
• money sent, esp. by mail, for goods or services or as an allowance.
• [as REMIT]

remittent *adjective*
• "re MIT 'nt"
• (esp. of a fever) that abates at intervals.
• [as REMIT]

remnant *noun*
• "REM n'nt"
• a small remaining quantity.
• [Old French *remenant* from *remenoir* remain, ultimately from Latin *remanēre* (*re-* again, *manēre* stay)]

remonstrate *verb*
• "REM 'n strate"
• make a protest; argue forcibly.
• [medieval Latin *remonstrare* (*re-* again, *monstrare* show)]
• **remonstrance** *noun* "re MON strince"
• **remonstration** *noun*

remora *noun*
• "REMMER uh"
• any of various marine fish of the family Echeneidae, which attach themselves by modified sucker-like fins to other fish and to ships.
• [Latin, = hindrance (*re-* again, *mora* delay, from the former belief that the fish slowed ships down)]

remortgage *verb*
• "ree MORE gidge"
• mortgage again; revise the terms of an existing mortgage on (a property).
• [Latin *re-* again, back, etc. + MORTGAGE]

remoulade *noun*
• "ray muh LAWD" or "ray moo LAWD"
• a cold mayonnaise-based sauce, usu. with capers, mustard, herbs, chopped pickles and hard-boiled egg yolks.
• [French, perhaps ultimately from Latin *armoracea* horseradish]

remunerate *verb*
• "re MYOONER ate"
• reward; pay for services rendered.
• [Latin *remunerari* (*re-* again, *munus muneris* gift)]
• **remuneration** *noun*
• **remunerative** *adjective* "re MYOONER a tiv"

Renaissance *noun*
• "RENNA sonce" or "re NAY sonce"
• the period in Western European history in the 14th–16th c. of intensified classical scholarship and humanism, marked by advances in art and literature under the influence of classical models, and generally held to be the transition between the Middle Ages and the modern world.
• [French *renaissance* (*re-* again, French *naissance* birth, from Latin *nascentia* or French *naître naiss-* be born, from Romanic: compare NASCENT)]

renal *adjective*
• "REEN'll"
• of or concerning the kidneys.
• [French *rénal* from Late Latin *renalis* from Latin *renes* kidneys]

renascent *adjective*
• "re NAY s'nt"
• springing up anew; being reborn.
• [Latin *renasci* (*re-* again, *nasci* be born)]
• **renascence** *noun*

rendezvous *noun*
• "RON day voo"
• an agreed or regular meeting place.
• [French *rendez-vous* present yourselves, from *rendre*, ultimately from Latin *reddere reddit-* (*re-* again, *dare* give)]

renegade *noun*
• "RENNA gade"
• a person who deserts a party or principles.
• [Spanish *renegado* from medieval Latin *renegatus* (*re-* again, Latin *negare* deny)]

renege *verb*
• "re NEG" or "re NAIG"
• go back on one's word; change one's mind; recant.
• [medieval Latin *renegare* (*re-* again, Latin *negare* deny)]

renegotiate *verb*
• "ree nuh GO shee ate"
• negotiate again or on different terms.
• [Latin *re-* again, back, etc. + NEGOTIATE]
• **renegotiable** *adjective* "re nuh GO shuh bull"
• **renegotiation** *noun*

reniform *adjective*
• "REENA form"
• kidney-shaped.
• [Latin *ren* kidney]

renin *noun*
• "REEN in"
• a proteolytic enzyme secreted by the kidneys, which helps regulate blood pressure.
• [Latin *ren* kidney]

renminbi *noun*
• "REN min bee"
• the national currency of the People's Republic of China, introduced in 1948.
• [Chinese, from *rénmín* people + *bì* currency]

rennet *noun*
• "REN it"
• curdled milk found in the stomach of an unweaned calf, used in curdling milk for cheese, junket, etc.
• [Middle English, prob. from an Old English form *rynet* (unrecorded), related to 'run']

rennin *noun*
• "REN in"
• an enzyme secreted into the stomach of unweaned mammals causing the clotting of milk.
• [as RENNET]

renominate *verb*
• "ree NOMMA nate"
• nominate for a further term of office.
• [Latin *re-* again, back, etc. + NOMINATE]
• **renomination** *noun*

renounce *verb*
• "re NOUNCE" (rhymes with *BOUNCE*)
• consent formally to abandon; surrender; give up (a claim, right, possession, etc.).
• [Old French *renoncer* from Latin *renuntiare* (*re-* again, *nuntiare* announce)]
• **renouncement** *noun*
• **renouncer** *noun*

renovate *verb*
• "RENNA vate"
• remodel or install new fixtures etc. in (a building or part of it).
• [Latin *renovare* (*re-* again, *novus* new)]
• **renovation** *noun*
• **renovator** *noun*

renown *noun*
• "re NOWN" ("NOWN" rhymes with *CROWN*)
• fame; high distinction.
• [Anglo-French *ren(o)un*, Old French *renon*, *renom* from *renomer* make famous (*re-* again, Latin *nominare* NOMINATE)]
• **renowned** *adjective*

rente *noun*
• "RONT"
• *Cdn* an annual payment made (in cash or produce) by a tenant to a landowner under the seigneurial system.
• [French from *rendre* present, ultimately from Latin *reddere reddit-* (*re-* again, *dare* give)]

rentier *noun*
• "ronty AY"
• a person living on dividends from property, investments, etc.
• [French from *rente* dividend: see RENTE]

renunciation *noun*
• "re nuncy AY sh'n"
• the act or an instance of renouncing or giving up.
• [Old French *renonciation* or Late Latin *renuntiatio* (as RENOUNCE)]
• **renunciant** *noun*

reoccupy *verb*
• "ree OCK yuh pie"
• occupy again.
• [Latin *re-* again, back, etc. + OCCUPY]
• **reoccupation** *noun*

reoccur *verb*
• "ree a CUR"
• occur again or habitually.
• [Latin *re-* again, back, etc. + OCCUR]
• **reoccurrence** *noun*

reoffend *verb*
• "ree a FEND"
• offend again; commit a further (esp. criminal) offence.
• [Latin *re-* again, back, etc. + OFFEND]
• **reoffender** *noun*

reorient *verb*
• "ree ORRY 'nt"
• give a new direction to (ideas etc.); redirect (a thing).
• [Latin *re-* again, back, etc. + Old French *orient*, *orienter* from Latin *oriens -entis* rising, sunrise, east, from *oriri* rise]

reorientate *verb*
• "ree ORRY 'n tate"
• = REORIENT.
• [as REORIENT]
• **reorientation** *noun*

repand *adjective*
• "re PAND"
• with an undulating margin; wavy.
• [Latin *repandus* (*re-* again, *pandus* bent)]

reparable *adjective*
• "REP ruh bull" or "REPPER a bull" or "re PAIR a bull"
• (of a loss etc.) that can be made good.
• [French from Latin *reparabilis* from *reparare* (*re-* again, *parare* make ready)]

reparation *noun*
• "reppa RAY sh'n"
• the act or an instance of making amends.
• [as REPARABLE]
• **reparative** *adjective* "REPPER a tiv" or "re PERRA tiv"

repartee *noun*
• "rep ar TAY" or "rep ar TEE"
• the practice or faculty of making witty retorts; sharpness or wit in quick reply.
• [French *repartie* feminine past participle of *repartir* start again, reply promptly (*re-* again, *partir* part)]

repartition *verb*
• "ree par TISH'n"
• partition again.
• [Latin *re-* again, back, etc. + PARTITION]

repast *noun*
• "re PAST"
• a meal, esp. of a specified kind.
• [Old French *repaistre* from Late Latin *repascere repast-* feed]

repatriate *verb*
• "re PAY tree ate"
• restore (a person) to his or her native land.
• [Late Latin *repatriare* (*re-* again, *patria* native land)]
• **repatriation** *noun*

repeal *verb*
• "re PEEL"
• revoke, rescind, or annul (a law, act of parliament, etc.).
• [Anglo-French *repeler*, Old French *rapeler* (*re-* again, APPEAL)]
• **repealable** *adjective*

repeat *verb*
• "re PEET"
• say or do over again.
• [Old French *repeter* from Latin *repetere* (*re-* again, *petere* seek)]
• **repeatability** *noun*
• **repeatable** *adjective*
• **repeated** *adjective*
• **repeatedly** *adverb*
• **repeater** *noun*

repechage *noun*
• "reppa SHOZH"
• (in rowing etc.) an extra contest in which the runners-up in the eliminating heats compete for a place in the final.
• [French *repêcher* fish out, rescue, from *pêcher* to fish, from Latin *piscāri* from *piscis* fish]

repel *verb*
• "re PELL"
• drive back; ward off; repulse.
• [Latin *repellere* (*re-* again, *pellere puls-* drive)]
• **repellency** *noun*
• **repellent** *adjective*
• **repellently** *adverb*
• **repeller** *noun*
HOMOPHONES: *rappel*

repent[1] *verb*
• "re PENT"
• wish one had not done, regret (one's wrongdoing, omission, etc.); resolve not to continue (a wrongdoing etc.).
• [Old French *repentir* (*re-* again, *pentir*, ultimately from Latin *paenitēre* be penitent)]
• **repentance** *noun*
• **repentant** *adjective*
• **repenter** *noun*

repent[2] *adjective*
• "REEP 'nt"
• creeping, esp. growing along the ground or just under the surface.
• [Latin *repere* creep]

repercussion *noun*
• "ree purr KUSH'n" or "rep ur KUSH'n" ("KUSH" rhymes with *MUSH*)
• an indirect effect or reaction following an event or action.
• [Old French *repercussion* or Latin *repercussio* (*re-* again, PERCUSSION)]

repertoire *noun*
• "REPPER twar" or "REPPA twar" ("TWAR" rhymes with *FAR*)
• a stock of pieces etc. that a company or a performer knows or is prepared to perform.
• [French *répertoire* from Late Latin (as REPERTORY)]

repertory *noun*
• "REPPER tory" or "REPPA tory"
• = REPERTOIRE.
• [Late Latin *repertorium* from Latin *reperire repert-* find]

répétiteur *noun*
• "re petta TUR"
• a tutor or coach of musicians, esp. opera singers.
• [French, as REPETITION]

repetition *noun*
• "reppa TISH'n"
• the act or an instance of repeating or being repeated.
• [French *répétition* or Latin *repetitio* (as REPEAT)]
• **repetitious** *adjective*
• **repetitiously** *adverb*
• **repetitiousness** *noun*
• **repetitive** *adjective* "re PETTA tiv"
• **repetitively** *adverb*
• **repetitiveness** *noun*

rephrase *verb*
• "re FRAZE"
• express in an alternative way.
• [Latin *re-* again + PHRASE]

repine *verb*
• "re PINE"
• fret or complain; be discontented.
• [Latin *re-* again, back, etc. + Old English *pīnian*, related to obsolete English *pine* punishment, from Germanic from medieval Latin *pena*, Latin *poena*]

replenish *verb*
• "re PLEN ish"
• fill up again.

• [Old French *replenir* (*re-* again, *plenir* from *plein* full, from Latin *plenus*)]
• **replenisher** *noun*
• **replenishment** *noun*

replete *adjective*
• "re PLEET"
• filled or well-supplied with.
• [Old French *replet replete* or Latin *repletus* past participle of *replēre* (*re-* again, *plēre plet-* fill)]
• **repletion** *noun*

replevin *noun*
• "re PLEVVIN"
• the provisional restoration or recovery of distrained goods pending the outcome of trial and judgment.
• [Old French *replevir* (as REPLEVY)]

replevy *verb*
• "re PLEVVY"
• recover by replevin.
• [Old French *replevir* recover, from Germanic]

replica *noun*
• "REP lick uh"
• a facsimile, an exact copy.
• [Italian, as REPLICATE]

replicant *noun*
• "REP lick'nt"
• (in science fiction) a genetically engineered replica of a human being.
• [as REPLICATE]

replicate *verb*
• "REP luh cate"
• repeat (an experiment etc.).
• [Latin *replicare* (*re-* again, *plicare* fold)]
• **replicability** *noun*
• **replicable** *adjective*
• **replication** *noun*
• **replicative** *adjective*
• **replicator** *noun*

repopulate *verb*
• "ree POP yuh late"
• populate again or increase the population of.
• [Latin *re-* again, back, etc. + POPULATE]
• **repopulation** *noun*

reportage *noun*
• "rep or TOZH"
• the describing of events, esp. the reporting of news etc. for the press and for broadcasting.
• [French, from Old French *reporter* from Latin *reportare* (*re-* again, *portare* bring)]

reportorial *adjective*
• "re pore TORY 'll"
• of or typical of journalists.
• [as REPORTAGE, after *editorial*]
• **reportorially** *adverb*

repository *noun*
• "re POZZA tory"
• a place where things are stored or may be found, esp. a warehouse or museum.
• [obsolete French *repositoire* or Latin *repositorium* from Latin *reponere reposit-* (*re-* again, *ponere* place)]

repossess *verb*
• "ree puh ZESS"
• regain possession of (esp. property or goods on which repayment of a debt is in arrears).
• [Latin *re-* again, back, etc. + POSSESS]
• **repossession** *noun*
• **repossessor** *noun*

repoussé *adjective*
• "re POO say"
• hammered into relief from the reverse side.
• [French, past participle of *repousser* (*re-* again, *pousser* push)]

reprehend *verb*
• "rep re HEND"
• rebuke; blame; find fault with.
• [Latin *reprehendere* (*re-* again, *prehendere* seize)]
• **reprehensible** *adjective* "rep re HENSA bull"
• **reprehension** *noun*

representation *noun*
• "rep re zen TAY sh'n"
• the act or an instance of representing or being represented.
• [Latin *re-* again, back, etc. + *praesentare* from *praesens -entis* participle of *praeesse* be at hand (*prae-* before, *esse* be)]

representational *adjective*
• "rep re zen TAY sh'n 'll"
• (of a painting etc.) depicting an object as it actually appears to the eye.
• [as REPRESENTATION]
• **representationalism** *noun*
• **representationalist** *adjective*

representative *adjective*
• "rep re ZENTA tiv"
• typical of a class or category.
• [as REPRESENTATION]
• **representatively** *adverb*
• **representativeness** *noun*

repressor *noun*
• "re PRESSER"
• a substance which acts on an operon to inhibit enzyme synthesis.
• [Latin, from *reprimere* (*re-* again, *premere* press)]

reprieve *verb*
• "re PREEVE"
• relieve or rescue from impending punishment.
• [Middle English as past participle *repryed* from Old French *repris* past participle of *reprendre* (*re-* again, *prendre* from Latin *prehendere* take): 16th-c. *-v-* unexplained]

reprimand *noun*
• "REP ruh mand"
• an official or sharp rebuke (for a fault etc.).
• [French *réprimande(r)* from Spanish *reprimenda*

from Latin *reprimenda* neuter pl. gerundive of *reprimere* repress (*re-* again, *premere* press)]

reprisal *noun*
- "re PRIZE 'll"
- retaliation against an enemy involving the infliction of equal or greater injuries.
- [Anglo-French *reprisaille* from medieval Latin *reprisalia* from *repraehensalia* (as REPREHEND)]

reprise *noun*
- "re PRIZE" or "re PREEZ"
- a repeated passage in music.
- [French, feminine past participle of *reprendre* (see REPRIEVE)]

reprobate *noun*
- "REP ruh bate"
- an unprincipled person; a person of highly immoral character.
- [Latin *reprobare reprobat-* disapprove (*re-* again, *probare* approve)]
- **reprobation** *noun*

reproduce *verb*
- "ree pro DOOCE" or "ree pro DYOOCE"
- produce a copy or representation of.
- [Latin *re-* again, back, etc. + *prōdūcere* (*pro-* in front of, *ducere duct-* lead)]
- **reproducer** *noun*
- **reproducibility** *noun*
- **reproducible** *adjective*
- **reproducibly** *adverb*

reprography *noun*
- "re PROGGRA fee"
- the science and practice of copying documents by photography, xerography, etc.
- [REPRODUCE + Greek *graphia* writing]
- **reprographic** *adjective*

reprove *verb*
- "re PROOVE"
- rebuke (a person, a person's conduct etc.).
- [Old French *reprover* from Late Latin *reprobare* disapprove: see REPROBATE]
- **reprover** *noun*
- **reproving** *adjective*
- **reprovingly** *adverb*

reptile *noun*
- "REP tile"
- any cold-blooded scaly animal of the class Reptilia, including snakes, lizards, crocodiles, turtles, tortoises, etc.
- [Late Latin *reptilis* from Latin *repere rept-* crawl]
- **reptilian** *adjective* "rep TILLY 'n"

repudiate *verb*
- "re PYOODY ate"
- disown; disavow; reject.
- [Latin *repudiare* from *repudium* divorce]
- **repudiation** *noun*
- **repudiator** *noun*

repugnance *noun*
- "re PUG nince"
- antipathy; aversion.
- [Latin *repugnantia* from *repugnare* oppose (*re-* again, *pugnare* fight)]
- **repugnant** *adjective*

reputable *adjective*
- "REP yoo tuh bull"
- having a good reputation; respectable.
- [Latin *reputare* (*re-* again, *putare* think)]
- **reputably** *adverb*

reputation *noun*
- "rep yoo TAY sh'n"
- what is generally said or believed about a person's or thing's character or standing.
- [as REPUTABLE]
- **reputational** *adjective*

requiem *noun*
- "RECK wee em"
- a Mass for the repose of the souls of the dead.
- [the accusative of Latin *requies* rest, the initial word of the Mass]

require *verb*
- "re KWIRE"
- need; depend on for success or fulfillment.
- [Old French *requere*, ultimately from Latin *requirere* (*re-* again, *quaerere* seek)]
- **requirement** *noun*

requisite *adjective*
- "RECK wuh zit"
- required by circumstances; necessary to success etc.
- [Latin *requisitus* past participle (as REQUIRE)]

requisition *noun*
- "reck wuh ZISH'n"
- an official order for the use of property or materials, esp. by an army during a war.
- [French *réquisition* or Latin *requisitio* (as REQUIRE)]
- **requisitionist** *noun*

requite *verb*
- "re KWITE"
- make return for (a service).
- [Latin *re-* again + *quite* var. of 'quit': see QUIETUS]
- **requital** *noun*

reredos *noun*
- "REER doss" or "REE re doss"
- an ornamental screen covering the wall at the back of an altar.
- [Anglo-French from Old French *areredos* from *arere* behind + *dos* back: compare ARREARS]

reroute *verb*
- "ree ROOT" or "ree ROUT"
- send or carry by a different route.
- [Latin *re-* again, back, etc. + ROUTE]

reschedule *verb*
- "ree SKED joo 'll" or "ree SKED jool" or "ree SHED yool" or "ree SHED zhool"
- alter the schedule of; replan.
- [Latin *re-* again, back, etc. + SCHEDULE]

rescind *verb*
• "re SIND"
• abrogate, revoke, cancel.
• [Latin *rescindere rescissⁿ-* (*re-* again, *scindere* cut)]
• **rescission** *noun* "re SIZH'n"

resculpt *verb*
• "ree SCULPT"
• change the shape of.
• [Latin *re-* again, back, etc. + SCULPTURE]

resect *verb*
• "re SECT"
• cut out part of (a lung etc.).
• [Latin *resecare resect-* (*re-* again, *secare* cut)]
• **resection** *noun*

reseda *noun*
• "re SEEDA"
• any plant of the genus *Reseda*, with sweet-scented flowers, e.g. a mignonette.
• [Latin, perhaps from imperative of *resedare* assuage, with reference to its supposed curative powers]

resemble *verb*
• "re ZEM bull"
• be like; have a similarity to, or features in common with, or the same appearance as.
• [Old French *resembler* (*re-* again, *sembler* from Latin *similare* from *similis* like)]
• **resemblance** *noun*

resent *verb*
• "re ZENT"
• show or feel indignation at; be aggrieved by (a circumstance, action, or person).
• [obsolete French *resentir* (*re-* again, Latin *sentire* feel)]
• **resentful** *adjective*
• **resentfully** *adverb*
• **resentment** *noun*

reserpine *noun*
• "REZZER peen"
• an alkaloid obtained from plants of the genus *Rauwolfia*, used as a tranquilizer and in the treatment of hypertension.
• [German *Reserpin* from modern Latin species name *Rauwolfia serpentina* (named after L. *Rauwolf*, German botanist d.1596)]

reserve *verb*
• "re ZURV"
• postpone, put aside, keep back for a later occasion or special use.
• [Old French *reserver* from Latin *reservare* (*re-* again, *servare* keep)]
• **reservation** *noun*
• **reserver** *noun*

reserved *adjective*
• "re ZURVD"
• reticent; slow to reveal emotion or opinions; uncommunicative.
• [as RESERVE]
• **reservedly** *adverb* "re ZUR vid lee"
• **reservedness** *noun*

reservist *noun*
• "re ZURV ist"
• a member of a country's reserve forces.
• [as RESERVE]

reservoir *noun*
• "REZZER vwar" or "REZZA vwar" ("VWAR" rhymes with *FAR*)
• a large natural or artificial lake or pool used for collecting and storing water for public and industrial use, irrigation, etc.
• [French *réservoir* from *réserver* RESERVE]

reside *verb*
• "re ZIDE"
• (of a person) have one's home, dwell permanently.
• [French *résider* or Latin *residēre* (*re-* again, *sedēre* sit)]
• **residence** *noun*
• **residency** *noun*
• **resident** *noun*
• **residential** *adjective*
• **residentially** *adverb*

residuary *adjective*
• "re ZIDGE oo airy"
• of the residue of an estate.
• [as RESIDUE]

residue *noun*
• "REZZA due"
• what is left over or remains; a remainder; the rest.
• [Old French *residu* from Latin *residuum*: see RESIDUUM]
• **residual** *adjective* "re ZIDGE oo 'll"
• **residually** *adverb*

residuum *noun*
• "re ZIDGE oo um"
• a substance left after combustion, evaporation, etc.; a deposit, a sediment.
• [Latin, neuter of *residuus* remaining, from *residēre*: see RESIDE]

resign *verb*
• "re ZINE"
• give up office, one's employment, etc.
• [Old French *resigner* from Latin *resignare* unseal, cancel (*re-* again, *signare* sign, seal)]
• **resignation** *noun* "rezzig NAY sh'n"
• **resigner** *noun*

resigned *adjective*
• "re ZINED" ("ZINED" rhymes with *FIND*)
• having resigned oneself; submissive, acquiescent.
• [as RESIGN]
• **resignedly** *adverb* "re ZINE id lee"

resile *verb*
• "re ZILE"
• (of something stretched or compressed) recoil to resume a former size and shape; spring back.
• [obsolete French *resilir* or Latin *resilire* (*re-* again, *salire* jump)]

resilient *adjective*
- "re ZILL y'nt"
- (of a substance etc.) recoiling; springing back; resuming its original shape after bending, stretching, compression, etc.
- [Latin *resiliens resilient-* (as RESILE)]
- **resilience** *noun*
- **resiliency** *noun*
- **resiliently** *adverb*

resin *noun*
- "REZZIN"
- an adhesive inflammable substance insoluble in water, secreted by some plants, and often extracted by incision, esp. from fir and pine.
- [Latin *resina* & medieval Latin *rosina, rosinum*]
- **resinoid** *adjective*
- **resinous** *adjective*
- **resiny** *adjective*

resist *verb*
- "re ZIST"
- withstand the action or effect of; repel.
- [Old French *resister* or Latin *resistere* (*re-* again, *sistere* stop, reduplication of *stare* stand)]
- **resistance** *noun*
- **resistant** *adjective*
- **resister** *noun*
- **resistible** *adjective*
- **resistive** *adjective*
- **resistivity** *noun*

HOMOPHONES: *resistor*

resistless *adjective*
- "re ZIST less"
- irresistible; relentless.
- [as RESIST]

resistor *noun*
- "re ZIST ur"
- a device having resistance to the passage of an electrical current.
- [as RESIST]

HOMOPHONES: *resister*

resoluble *adjective*
- "re ZOL yuh bull"
- that can be resolved.
- [French *résoluble* or Latin *resolubilis* (as RESOLVE, after *soluble*)]

resolute *adjective*
- "REZZA loot"
- (of a person or a person's mind or action) determined; decided; firm of purpose; not vacillating.
- [Latin *resolutus* past participle of *resolvere* (see RESOLVE)]
- **resolutely** *adverb*
- **resoluteness** *noun*

resolution *noun*
- "rezza LOO sh'n"
- a formal expression of opinion or intention by a legislative body or meeting.
- [Latin *resolutio* (as RESOLVE)]

resolvable *adjective*
- "re ZOLVE a bull"
- that can be settled or solved.
- [as RESOLVE]
- **resolvability** *noun*
- **resolver** *noun*

resolve *verb*
- "re ZOLVE"
- make up one's mind; decide firmly.
- [Latin *resolvere resolut-* (*re-* again, *solvere solut-* unfasten, release)]
- **resolved** *adjective*
- **resolvedly** *adverb* "re ZOL vid lee"
- **resolvedness** *noun*

resonant *adjective*
- "REZZA n'nt"
- (of sound) echoing, resounding; continuing to sound; reinforced or prolonged by reflection or synchronous vibration.
- [French *résonnant* or Latin *resonare resonant-* (*re-* again, *sonare* sound)]
- **resonance** *noun*
- **resonantly** *adverb*
- **resonate** *verb*

resonator *noun*
- "REZZA nate ur"
- a device responding to a specific vibration frequency, and used for detecting it when it occurs in combination with other sounds.
- [as RESONANT]

resorb *verb*
- "re SORB" or "re ZORB"
- absorb again.
- [Latin *resorbēre resorpt-* (*re-* again, *sorbēre* absorb)]
- **resorption** *noun*
- **resorptive** *adjective*

resorcinol *noun*
- "re ZORSA nawl"
- a crystalline organic compound usu. made by synthesis and used in the production of dyes, drugs, resins, glues, etc.
- [RESIN + ORCIN]

resort *noun*
- "re ZORT"
- a place frequented esp. for holidays or for a specified purpose or quality.
- [Old French *resortir* (*re-* again, *sortir* come or go out)]

resound *verb*
- "re ZOUND"
- (of a place) ring or echo.
- [Latin *re-* again, back, etc. + Old French *soner* sound, from Latin *sonāre* from *sonus* sound]
- **resounding** *adjective*
- **resoundingly** *adverb*

resource *noun*
- "REE zorce" or "re ZORCE" or "REE sorce" or "re SORCE"

• the means available to achieve an end, fulfill a function, etc.
• [French *ressource*, *ressourse*, feminine past participle of Old French dialect *resourdre* (*re-* again, Latin *surgere* rise)]
• **resourceful** *adjective*
• **resourcefully** *adverb*
• **resourcefulness** *noun*
• **resourceless** *adjective*
• **resourcelessness** *noun*
• **resourcing** *noun*

respirator *noun*
• "RESPER ate ur"
• an apparatus for maintaining artificial respiration.
• [as RESPIRE]

respire *verb*
• "re SPIRE"
• inhale and exhale air; breathe.
• [Old French *respirer* or from Latin *respirare* (*re-* again, *spirare* breathe)]
• **respirable** *adjective*
• **respiration** *noun*
• **respiratory** *adjective* "RESPER a tory" or "RESPRA tory"

respite *noun*
• "RESS pite" or "RESS pit"
• an interval of rest or relief.
• [Old French *respit* from Latin *respectus* respect, from *respicere* (*re* again, *specere* look at)]

resplendent *adjective*
• "re SPLEN d'nt"
• brilliant, dazzlingly or gloriously bright.
• [Latin *resplendēre* (*re-* again, *splendēre* glitter)]
• **resplendence** *noun*
• **resplendently** *adverb*

respondent *noun*
• "re SPAWN d'nt"
• a person who replies to something, esp. one supplying information for a survey or questionnaire or responding to an advertisement.
• [Old French *respondre* answer, ultimately from Latin *respondēre respons-* answer (*re-* again, *spondēre* pledge)]

responsible *adjective*
• "re SPONSA bull"
• liable to be called to account (to a person or for a thing).
• [obsolete French from Latin *respondēre*: see RESPONDENT]
• **responsibility** *noun*
• **responsibly** *adverb*

responsorial *adjective*
• "re spawn SORRY 'll"
• relating to or involving (liturgical) responses.
• [as RESPONDENT]

responsory *noun*
• "re SPONSA ree"
• a church anthem said or sung by a soloist and choir after a reading.
• [as RESPONDENT]

restaurant *noun*
• "RESTA ront"
• a commercial establishment where meals are prepared, served, and eaten.
• [French from *restaurer* from Latin *restaurare* restore]

restaurateur *noun*
• "ress tur a TUR"
• a person who owns or manages a restaurant.
• [French (as RESTAURANT)]

restenosis *noun*
• "ree stuh NO sis"
• the recurrence of abnormal narrowing of an artery or valve after corrective surgery.
• [Latin *re-* again, back, etc. + STENOSIS]

restitution *noun*
• "resta TOO sh'n" or "resta TYOO sh'n"
• the act or an instance of restoring something lost or stolen to its proper owner.
• [Old French *restitution* or Latin *restitutio* from *restituere restitut-* restore (*re-* again, *statuere* establish)]
• **restitutive** *adjective* "RESTA too tiv" or "RESTA tyoo tiv"

restoration *noun*
• "ress tur AY sh'n"
• the return of something to a former or original state.
• [French from Latin *restaurer* (as RESTAURANT)]
• **restorationist** *noun*

restorationism *noun*
• "ress tur AY sh'n izm"
• the doctrine that all people will ultimately be restored to a state of happiness in the future life.
• [as RESTORATION]

restorative *adjective*
• "re STORA tiv"
• tending or able to restore health or strength.
• [as RESTORATION]

resultant *adjective*
• "re ZUL t'nt" ("ZUL" rhymes with *HULL*)
• occurring as a result; consequent.
• [medieval Latin *resultare* from Latin (*re-* again, *saltare* frequentative of *salire* jump)]

resume *verb*
• "re ZOOM" or "re ZYOOM"
• begin again or continue after an interruption.
• [Old French *resumer* or Latin *resumere resumpt-* (*re-* again, *sumere* take)]
• **resumption** *noun*
• **resumptive** *adjective*

resumé *noun*
• "REZZA may" or "REZZ yoo may"
• a brief account of one's education,

experience, previous employment, and interests, usu. submitted with a job application.

• [French past participle of *résumer* (as RESUME)]

resurgence *noun*

• "re SURGE ince"

• a renewed prominence or popularity.

• [Latin *resurgere resurrect-* (*re-* again, *surgere* rise)]

• **resurgent** *adjective*

resurrect *verb*

• "rezza RECT"

• bring back from obscurity or disrepair; revive.

• [back-formation from RESURRECTION]

resurrection *noun*

• "rezza RECK sh'n"

• the act or an instance of rising from the dead.

• [Old French from Late Latin *resurrectio -onis* (as RESURGENCE)]

resuscitate *verb*

• "re SUSSA tate"

• revive from unconsciousness or apparent death.

• [Latin *resuscitare* (*re-* again, *suscitare* raise)]

• **resuscitation** *noun*

• **resuscitator** *noun*

resveratrol *noun*

• "rez VEERA trawl"

• an antioxidant naturally occurring in certain nuts and fruits, esp. grapes, present in grape products such as red wine, and supposed to reduce cholesterol levels and inhibit cancer growth.

• [blend of RESORCINOL + modern Latin *veratrum* hellebore]

retable *noun*

• "re TAY bull"

• a frame enclosing painted or decorated panels above the back of an altar.

• [French *rétable, retable* from Spanish *retablo* (as RETABLO)]

retablo *noun*

• "re TAB lo"

• a retable, esp. in Latin America.

• [Spanish from medieval Latin *retrotabulum* rear table (*retro* backwards, *tabula* plank, tablet, list)]

retaliate *verb*

• "re TALLY ate"

• respond to an injury, insult, assault, etc. in like manner; attack in return.

• [Latin *retaliare* (*re-* again, *talis* such)]

• **retaliation** *noun*

• **retaliatory** *adjective* "re TALLY a tory"

retardant *adjective*

• "re TAR d'nt"

• tending to slow or resist; capable of remaining unaffected by.

• [French *retarder* from Latin *retardare* (*re-* again, *tardus* slow)]

• **retardance** *noun*

• **retardancy** *noun*

retch *verb*

• "RETCH"

• make an attempt to vomit, esp. involuntarily and without effect.

• [var. of (now dialect) *reach* from Old English *hræcan* spit, Old Norse *hrækja* from Germanic, of imitative origin]

• **retching** *noun*

HOMOPHONES: *wretch*

rete *noun*

• "REETY"

• an elaborate network or plexus of blood vessels and nerve cells.

• [Latin *rete* net]

HOMOPHONES: *reedy*

retention *noun*

• "re TEN sh'n"

• the act or an instance of retaining; the state of being retained.

• [Old French *retention* or Latin *retentio* from *retinēre retent-* retain (*re-* again, *tenēre* hold)]

• **retentive** *adjective*

• **retentiveness** *noun*

reticence *noun*

• "RETTA since"

• the avoidance of saying all one knows or feels, or of saying more than is necessary.

• [Latin *reticentia* from *reticēre* (*re-* again, *tacēre* be silent)]

• **reticent** *adjective*

reticle *noun*

• "RETTA k'll"

• a network of fine threads or lines in the focal plane or eyepiece of an optical instrument to help accurate observation and measurement.

• [Latin *reticulum*: see RETICULUM]

reticulate *verb*

• "re TICK yuh late"

• divide or be divided in fact or appearance into a network.

• [Latin *reticulatus* reticulated (as RETICULUM)]

• **reticulation** *noun*

reticule *noun*

• "RETTIC yool"

• a woman's small handbag, usu. with a drawstring closure, made of netting or other fabric.

• [French *réticule* from Latin (as RETICULUM)]

reticulocyte *noun*

• "re TICK yoo lo site"

• an immature red blood cell having a granular or reticulated appearance when suitably stained.

• [from RETICUL(ATED) + Greek *kutos* vessel]

reticuloendothelial *adjective*

• "re tick yuh lo endo THEELY 'll" (with "TH" as in *THIEF*)

• of, pertaining to, or designating a diverse system of fixed and circulating phagocytic cells involved in the immune response, common esp. in the liver, spleen, and lymphatic system.
• [RETICUL(UM) + ENDOTHELIAL]

reticulum *noun*
• "re TICK yuh lum"
• a netlike structure.
• [Latin, diminutive of *rete* net]
• **reticular** *adjective*

retina *noun*
• "RETTIN uh"
• a light-sensitive layer at the back of the eyeball that triggers nerve impulses through the optic nerve to the brain where the visual image is formed.
• [medieval Latin from Latin *rete* net]
• **retinal** *adjective*

retinitis *noun*
• "rettin ITE iss"
• inflammation of the retina.
• [RETINA + Greek *-itis*, forming feminine of adjectives in *-itēs* (with *nosos* 'disease' implied)]

retinoblastoma *noun*
• "rettin oh blass TOE muh"
• a rare, malignant, familial tumour of the retina in young children.
• [RETINA + *blasto* combining form of Greek *blastos* sprout + CARCINOMA]

retinoic *adjective*
• "rettin OH ick"
• designating an acid chemically related to vitamin A, used esp. as a topical ointment esp. in the treatment of wrinkles and other skin disorders.
• [as RETINA]

retinol *noun*
• "RETTA nawl"
• a vitamin found in green and yellow vegetables, egg yolk, and fish-liver oil, essential for growth and vision in dim light; vitamin A.
• [RETINA + ALCOHOL]

retinopathy *noun*
• "rettin OPPA thee" (with "TH" as in *THIN*)
• any (esp. non-inflammatory) disease of the retina.
• [as RETINA + Greek *patheia* suffering]

retinue *noun*
• "RETTA new"
• a body of attendants accompanying an important person.
• [Old French *retenue* feminine past participle of *retenir*: see RETENTION]

retort *noun*
• "re TORT"
• an incisive, witty, or angry reply.
• [Latin *retorquēre retort-* (*re-* again, *torquēre* twist)]

retract *verb*
• "re TRACT"
• withdraw or revoke (a statement, accusation, proposal, etc.).
• [Latin *retractare* (*re-* again, *trahere tract-* draw)]
• **retractable** *adjective*
• **retraction** *noun*
• **retractive** *adjective*

retractile *adjective*
• "re TRACK tile"
• capable of being retracted.
• [as RETRACT]

retractor *noun*
• "re TRACK tur"
• a muscle used for retracting.
• [as RETRACT]

retransmit *verb*
• "ree tranz MIT"
• transmit (esp. radio signals or broadcast programs) back again or to a further distance.
• [Latin *re-* again, back, etc. + *trans-* across, *mittere miss-* send]
• **retransmission** *noun*

retreatant *noun*
• "re TREET 'nt"
• a person participating in a religious or corporate etc. retreat.
• [Old French *retraiter* (v.) from Latin *retrahere*: see RETRACT]

retribution *noun*
• "rettra BYOO sh'n"
• punishment for a crime, injury, etc.; vengeance.
• [Late Latin *retributio* (*re-* again, *tribuere tribut-* assign)]
• **retributive** *adjective* "re TRIB yoo tiv"

retrieve *verb*
• "re TREEVE"
• regain possession of; recover and bring back.
• [Old French *retroeve-* stressed stem of *retrover* (*re-* again, *trover* find)]
• **retrievable** *adjective*
• **retrieval** *noun*

retriever *noun*
• "re TREEVER"
• a breed of dog used for retrieving game.
• [as RETRIEVE]

retro *noun*
• "RETRO"
• style or fashion imitating the past, esp. in dress, music, etc.
• [French *rétro*, abbreviation of *rétrograde* RETROGRADE]

retroactive *adjective*
• "retro ACTIV"
• (esp. of legislation) applying to the past as well as to the present or future; retrospective.
• [Latin *retro* backwards + 'active' from Latin *agere act-* do]

- **retroactively** *adverb*
- **retroactivity** *noun*

retrofit *verb*
- "RETRO fit"
- modify (machinery, vehicles, etc.) to incorporate changes and developments introduced after manufacture.
- [RETRO(ACTIVE) + '(re)fit']

retroflex *adjective*
- "RETRO flex"
- pronounced with the tip of the tongue curled up towards the hard palate.
- [Latin *retroflectere retroflex-* (*retro* backwards, *flectere* bend)]
- **retroflexion** *noun*

retrograde *adjective*
- "RETRO grade"
- directed backwards; retreating.
- [Latin *retrogradus* (*retro* backwards, *gradus* step, *gradi* walk)]

retrogress *verb*
- "retro GRESS"
- go back; move backwards.
- [Latin *retro-* backwards, after 'progress' from Latin *progressus* from *progredi* (*pro-* in front of, *gradi* walk)]
- **retrogression** *noun*
- **retrogressive** *adjective*

retrorocket *noun*
- "RETRO rock it"
- an auxiliary rocket for slowing down a spacecraft etc., e.g. when re-entering the earth's atmosphere.
- [Latin *retro-* backwards + 'rocket' from French *roquette* from Italian *rochetto* diminutive of *rocca* distaff, with reference to its cylindrical shape]

retrorse *adjective*
- "re TRORSE" (rhymes with *HORSE*)
- turned back or down.
- [Latin *retrorsus* = *retroversus* (*retro* backwards, *versus* past participle of *vertere* turn)]

retrospect *noun*
- "RETRA spect"
- a survey of past time or events.
- [Latin *retro* backwards, after PROSPECT]
- **retrospection** *noun*
- **retrospective** *adjective*
- **retrospectively** *adverb*

retroverted *adjective*
- "RETRO vurted"
- (of the womb) having a backward inclination.
- [as RETRORSE]
- **retroversion** *noun*

retrovirus *noun*
- "RETRO vie russ"
- any of a group of RNA viruses which insert a DNA copy of their genome into the host cell in order to replicate, e.g. HIV.
- [modern Latin from initial letters of *reverse transcriptase* + VIRUS]
- **retroviral** *adjective*
- **retrovirologist** *noun*
- **retrovirology** *noun*

retsina *noun*
- "ret SEENA"
- a Greek white wine flavoured with resin.
- [modern Greek *retsini* from *retine* pine resin]

retuse *adjective*
- "re TYUCE"
- having a broad end with a central depression.
- [Latin *retundere retus-* (*re-* again, *tundere* beat)]

Reuben *noun*
- "ROO b'n"
- a sandwich containing corned beef, sauerkraut, and usu. Swiss cheese, made with rye bread and served hot.
- [20th c.: origin unknown]

reunify *verb*
- "ree YOONA fie"
- restore (esp. separated territories) to a political unity.
- [Latin *re-* again, back, etc. + French *unifier* or Late Latin *unificare* from *unus* one]
- **reunification** *noun*

reunite *verb*
- "ree yoo NITE"
- bring or come back together.
- [Latin *re-* again, back, etc. + *unire unit-* from *unus* one]
- **reunion** *noun*

reupholster *verb*
- "re up HOLE stur"
- repair or replace the stuffing, springs, covering, etc. of (a piece of furniture).
- [Latin *re-* again, back, etc. + UPHOLSTER]
- **reupholstery** *noun*

reuse *verb*
- "ree YOOZ"
- use again or more than once.
- [Latin *re-* again, back, etc. + 'use']
- **reusability** *noun*
- **reusable** *adjective*
- **reused** *adjective*

revaccinate *verb*
- "re VACK sin ate"
- vaccinate again.
- [Latin *re-* again, back, etc. + VACCINATE]
- **revaccination** *noun*

revalue *verb*
- "re VAL yoo"
- assess the value of something again.
- [Latin *re-* again, back, etc. + Old French *value*, feminine past participle of *valoir* be worth, from Latin *valēre*]
- **revaluation** *noun*

revanchism *noun*
- "re VANCH izm"

• a policy of seeking to retaliate, esp. to recover lost territory.
• [French *revanche* from Late Latin *revindicare* (*re-* again, *vindicare* lay claim to)]
• **revanchist** *noun*

revegetate *verb*
• "ree VEDGE a tate"
• produce a new growth of vegetation on (disturbed or barren ground).
• [Latin *re-* again, back, etc. + VEGETATE]
• **revegetation** *noun*

reveille *noun*
• "REVVA lee"
• a signal given in the morning, usu. on a drum or bugle, to waken soldiers and indicate that it is time to rise.
• [French *réveillez* imperative pl. of *réveiller* awaken (*re-* again, *veiller* from Latin *vigilare* keep watch)]

réveillon *noun*
• "rev ay ÕH" (with a nasal *OH*)
• (among francophones) a festive meal on Christmas morning after midnight Mass or on New Year's Eve.
• [French, as REVEILLE]

revel *verb*
• "REV'll"
• take great delight in.
• [Old French *reveler* riot, from Latin *rebellare* REBEL]
• **reveller** *noun* (also *US* **reveler**)

revelation *noun*
• "revva LAY sh'n"
• the act or an instance of making something known.
• [Latin, from *revēlāre* reveal]

revelatory *adjective*
• "REVVA luh tory"
• serving to reveal, esp. something significant.
• [as REVELATION]

revelry *noun*
• "REV'll ree"
• the action of revelling or merrymaking; boisterous gaiety or mirth.
• [as REVEL]

Revelstokian *noun*
• "rev'll STOE kee in"
• a resident of Revelstoke, BC.

revenant *noun*
• "REVVA n'nt"
• a person who has returned, esp. supposedly from the dead.
• [French, present participle of *revenir*: see REVENUE]

revenue *noun*
• "REVVA new"
• income, esp. of a large amount, from any source.
• [Old French *revenu(e)* past participle of *revenir* from Latin *revenire* return (*re-* again, *venire* come)]

revenuer *noun*
• "REVVA newer"
• a person who collects taxes or customs duties etc.
• [as REVENUE]

reverberate *verb*
• "re VURBA rate"
• (of sound, light, or heat) be returned or echoed or reflected repeatedly.
• [Latin *reverberare* (*re-* again, *verberare* lash, from *verbera* (pl.) scourge)]
• **reverberant** *adjective*
• **reverberation** *noun*
• **reverberative** *adjective*
• **reverberator** *noun*

revere *verb*
• "re VEER"
• hold in deep and usu. affectionate or religious respect; venerate.
• [French *révérer* or Latin *reverēri* (*re-* again, *verēri* fear)]
• **reverence** *noun* "REVVER ince"
• **reverent** *adjective*
• **reverential** *adjective*
• **reverentially** *adverb*
• **reverently** *adverb*
HOMOPHONES: *revers*

reverend *noun*
• "REV r'nd" or "REVVER 'nd"
• a clergyman.
• [Old French *reverend* or Latin *reverendus* gerundive of *reverēri*: see REVERE]

reverie *noun*
• "REVVER ee"
• a state of absent-minded meditation or musing; a daydream.
• [Old French *reverie* rejoicing, revelry, from *rever* be delirious, of unknown origin]

revers *noun*
• "re VEER"
• the turned-back edge of a garment revealing the undersurface.
• [French, = REVERSE]
HOMOPHONES: *revere*

reverse *verb*
• "re VURSE"
• turn the other way around or up or inside out.
• [Old French *revers* (n.), *reverser* (v.), from Latin *revertere revers-* (*re-* again, *vertere* turn)]
• **reversal** *noun*
• **reversely** *adverb*
• **reverser** *noun*
• **reversibility** *noun*
• **reversible** *adjective*
• **reversibly** *adverb*

revert *verb*
• "re VURT"
• return to a former state or condition.

• [Old French *revertir* or Latin *revertere* (as REVERSE)]
• **reversion** *noun*
• **reversionary** *adjective*

revertible *adjective*
• "re VURT a bull"
• (of property) subject to reversion.
• [as REVERT]

revet *verb*
• "re VET"
• face (a rampart, wall, etc.) with masonry, esp. in fortification.
• [French *revêtir* from Late Latin *revestire* (*re-* again, *vestire* clothe, from *vestis*)]

revetment *noun*
• "re VET m'nt"
• a retaining wall or facing, esp. supporting an embankment etc.
• [as REVET]

revise *verb*
• "re VIZE"
• examine or re-examine and improve or amend (esp. written or printed matter).
• [French *réviser* look at, or Latin *revisere* (*re-* again, *visere* intensive of *vidēre vis-* see)]
• **revisable** *adjective*
• **reviser** *noun*
• **revision** *noun* "re VIZH'n"
• **revisionary** *adjective*

revisionism *noun*
• "re VIZH'n izm"
• a policy of revision or modification, esp. of Marxism on evolutionary socialist (rather than revolutionary) or pluralist principles.
• [as REVISE]
• **revisionist** *noun*

revitalize *verb*
ALSO SPELLED: esp. *Brit.* **-ise**
• "re VITE 'll ize"
• imbue with new life and vitality.
• [Latin *re-* again, back, etc. + *vitalis* from *vita* life]
• **revitalization** *noun* (also esp. *Brit.* **-isation**)

revival *noun*
• "re VIE v'll"
• an improvement in the condition or strength of something; a recovery.
• [as REVIVE]

revivalism *noun*
• "re VIE v'll izm"
• belief in or the promotion of a revival, esp. of religious fervour.
• [as REVIVE]
• **revivalist** *noun*
• **revivalistic** *adjective*

revive *verb*
• "re VIVE" (rhymes with *DIVE*)
• come or bring back to consciousness or life or strength.
• [Late Latin *revivere* (*re-* again, Latin *vivere* live)]
• **revivable** *adjective*

revivify *verb*
• "re VIVVA fie"
• restore to animation, activity, vigour, or life.
• [as REVIVE]
• **revivification** *noun*

revoke *verb*
• "re VOKE"
• rescind, withdraw, or cancel (a licence, decision, promise, etc.).
• [Latin *revocare* (*re-* again, *vocare* call)]
• **revocable** *adjective* "REVVA kuh bull" or "re VOKE a bull"
• **revocation** *noun* "revva CAY sh'n"

revolute *adjective*
• "REVVA loot"
• having a rolled-back edge.
• [Latin *revolutus* past participle of *revolvere*: see REVOLVE]

revolution *noun*
• "revva LOO sh'n"
• the forcible overthrow of a government or social order, in favour of a new system.
• [as REVOLUTE]
• **revolutionist** *noun*

revolutionary *adjective*
• "revva LOO sh'n airy"
• involving a complete or dramatic change.
• [as REVOLUTION]
• **revolutionize** *verb* (also esp. *Brit.* **-ise**)

revolve *verb*
• "re VOLVE"
• turn or cause to turn around, esp. on an axis; rotate.
• [Latin *revolvere* (*re-* again, *volvere* roll)]

revolver *noun*
• "re VOLVE ur"
• a pistol with revolving chambers enabling several shots to be fired without reloading.
• [as REVOLVE]

revue *noun*
• "re VYOO"
• a theatrical entertainment of a series of short usu. satirical sketches and songs.
• [French, = 'review', from *revoir* (*re-* again, *voir* see, from Latin *vidēre*)]
HOMOPHONES: *review*

revulsion *noun*
• "re VULL sh'n"
• abhorrence; a sense of loathing.
• [French *revulsion* or Latin *revulsio* (*re-* again, *vellere vuls-* pull)]

reweigh *verb*
• "ree WAY"
• weigh again.
• [Latin *re-* again, back, etc. + WEIGH]

rewrap *verb*
• "ree RAP"
• wrap again or differently.
• [Latin *re-* again, back, etc. + 'wrap' of unknown origin]

rewritable *adjective*
• "ree RITE a bull"
• (of a data storage device or medium) capable of being overwritten with new data, esp. designating a type of optical storage medium on which data can be written, and subsequently erased and rewritten, by the user.
• [as REWRITE]

rewrite *verb*
• "ree RITE"
• write again or differently.
• [Latin *re-* again, back, etc. + WRITE]

rhapsode *noun*
• "RAP sode"
• a reciter of epic poems, esp. of Homer in ancient Greece.
• [Greek *rhapsōidos* from *rhaptō* stitch + *ōidē* song]

rhapsodize *verb*
ALSO SPELLED: esp. *Brit.* **-ise**
• "RAPSA dize"
• talk or write about a person or thing with great enthusiasm.
• [as RHAPSODY]
• **rhapsodist** *noun*

rhapsody *noun*
• "RAPSA dee"
• an exaggeratedly enthusiastic or ecstatic expression of feeling.
• [Latin *rhapsodia* from Greek *rhapsōidia* (as RHAPSODE)]
• **rhapsodic** *adjective* "rap SODDIC"
• **rhapsodical** *adjective*
• **rhapsodically** *adverb*

rhatany *noun*
• "RATTA nee"
• either of two American shrubs, *Krameria trianda* and *K. argentea*, having an astringent root when dried.
• [modern Latin *rhatania* from Portuguese *ratanha*, Spanish *ratania*, from Quechua *rataña*]

rhea *noun*
• "REE uh"
• any of several S American flightless birds of the family Rheidae, like but smaller than an ostrich.
• [modern Latin genus name from Latin from Greek *Rhea*, the mother of Zeus]

Rhenish *adjective*
• "REEN ish" or "REN ish"
• of the Rhine and the Swiss, German, French, or Dutch regions adjoining it.
• [Anglo-French *reneis* from Latin *Rhenanus* from *Rhenus* Rhine]

rhenium *noun*
• "REENY um"
• a rare metallic element of the manganese group, occurring naturally in molybdenum ores and used in the manufacture of superconducting alloys.
• [modern Latin from Latin *Rhenus* see RHENISH]

rheology *noun*
• "ree OLLA jee"
• the science dealing with the flow and deformation of matter.
• [Greek *rheos* stream + *logos* word]
• **rheological** *adjective*
• **rheologist** *noun*

rheostat *noun*
• "REE a stat"
• an instrument used to control a current by varying the resistance.
• [Greek *rheos* stream + *statos* stationary]
• **rheostatic** *adjective*

rhesus *noun*
• "REECE us"
• a small catarrhine monkey, *Macaca mulatta*, common in N India.
• [modern Latin, arbitrary use of Latin *Rhesus* from Greek *Rhēsos*, mythical Thracian king]

rhetor *noun*
• "REE tur"
• an ancient Greek or Roman teacher or professor of rhetoric.
• [Greek *rhētōr*]
HOMOPHONES: *reader*

rhetoric *noun*
• "RETTER ick"
• the art of effective or persuasive speaking or writing.
• [Greek *rhētorikē* (*tekhnē*) (art) of rhetoric (as RHETOR)]
• **rhetorical** *adjective* "ruh TORRA k'll"
• **rhetorically** *adverb*
• **rhetorician** *noun* "retter ISH'n"

rheum *noun*
• "ROOM"
• a watery discharge from a mucous membrane, esp. of the eyes or nose.
• [Old French *reume* ultimately from Greek *rheuma -atos* stream, from *rheō* flow]
• **rheumy** *adjective*
HOMOPHONES: *room, roomy, roomie*

rheumatism *noun*
• "ROOMA tizm"
• any disease marked by inflammation and pain in the joints, muscles, or fibrous tissue, esp. rheumatoid arthritis.
• [ultimately from Greek *rheumatismos* from *rheumatizō* from *rheuma* stream; the disease was originally supposed to be caused by the internal flow of 'watery' humours]
• **rheumatic** *adjective* "roo MATTIC"
• **rheumaticky** *adjective*

rheumatoid *adjective*
- "ROOMA toid"
- having the character of rheumatism.
- [as RHEUMATISM]

rheumatology *noun*
- "rooma TOLLA jee"
- the study of rheumatic diseases.
- [as RHEUMATISM + Greek *logos* word]
- **rheumatological** *adjective*
- **rheumatologist** *noun*

rhinal *adjective*
- "RINE'll"
- of a nostril or the nose.
- [Greek *rhis rhinos* nose]

rhinestone *noun*
- "RINE stone"
- an imitation diamond.
- [translation of French *caillou du Rhin*, lit. 'pebble of the Rhine']

rhinitis *noun*
- "rye NITE iss"
- inflammation of the mucous membrane of the nose.
- [Greek *rhis rhinos* nose + *-itis*, forming feminine of adjectives in *-itēs* (with *nosos* 'disease' implied)]

rhino *noun*
- "RYE no"
- a rhinoceros.
- [abbreviation]

rhinoceros *noun*
- "rye NOSSER us"
- any of various large thick-skinned plant-eating ungulates of the family Rhinocerotidae of Africa and S Asia, with one horn or in some cases two horns on the nose and plated or folded skin.
- [Latin from Greek *rhinokerōs* (*rhis rhinos* nose, *keras* horn)]

rhinoplasty *noun*
- "RYE no plasty"
- plastic surgery of the nose.
- [Greek *rhis rhinos* nose + *plastos* formed, moulded]
- **rhinoplastic** *adjective*

rhinovirus *noun*
- "RYE no vie russ"
- any of a group of very small RNA viruses including those which cause some forms of the common cold.
- [Greek *rhis rhinos* nose + VIRUS]

rhizobium *noun*
- "rye ZO bee um"
- a nitrogen-fixing soil bacterium of the genus *Rhizobium*, found esp. in the root nodules of leguminous plants.
- [modern Latin genus name, from Greek *rhiza* root + Greek *bios* life]

rhizoid *adjective*
- "RYE zoid"
- rootlike.
- [Greek *rhiza* root]
- **rhizoidal** *adjective*

rhizome *noun*
- "RYE zome"
- an underground rootlike stem bearing both roots and shoots.
- [Greek *rhizōma* from *rhizoō* take root from *rhiza* root]
- **rhizomatous** *adjective*

rhizopod *noun*
- "RYE zo pod"
- any protozoan of the superclass Rhizopoda, forming rootlike pseudopodia, e.g. an amoeba.
- [Greek *rhiza* root + *pous podos* foot]

rho *noun*
- "ROE"
- the seventeenth letter of the Greek alphabet (Ρ, ρ).
- [Greek]

HOMOPHONES: *roe*, *row*

rhodamine *noun*
- "ROAD a min"
- any of various red synthetic dyes used to colour textiles.
- [Greek *rhodon* rose + AMINE]

Rhodesian *noun*
- "roe DEE zh'n"
- a native or inhabitant of Rhodesia, a former country (now Zimbabwe) in southern Africa.

rhodium *noun*
- "ROADY um"
- a hard white metallic element of the platinum group, occurring naturally in platinum ores and used in making alloys and plating jewellery.
- [Greek *rhodon* rose (from the colour of the solution of its salts)]

rhodochrosite *noun*
- "roe doe CROW site"
- a mineral form of manganese carbonate occurring in pink, brown, or grey crystals.
- [Greek *rhodokhrous* rose-coloured]

rhododendron *noun*
- "rode a DEN drun"
- any evergreen shrub or small tree of the genus *Rhododendron*, with usu. large clusters of trumpet-shaped flowers.
- [Latin, = oleander, from Greek (*rhodon* rose, *dendron* tree)]

rhodopsin *noun*
- "roe DOP sin"
- a light-sensitive pigment in the retina.
- [Greek *rhodon* rose + *opsis* sight]

rhodora *noun*
- "re DORA"

- a N American pink-flowered shrub, *Rhodora canadense*.
- [modern Latin from Latin plant name from Greek *rhodon* rose]

rhomb *noun*
- "ROM"
- = RHOMBUS.
- [French *rhombe* or Latin *rhombus*]
- **rhombic** *adjective* "ROM bick"

HOMOPHONES: *Rom*

rhombohedron *noun*
- "romba HEED r'n"
- a solid bounded by six equal rhombuses.
- [RHOMBUS, *hedra* base]
- **rhombohedral** *adjective*

rhomboideus *noun*
- "rom BOY dee us"
- a muscle connecting the shoulder blade to the vertebrae.
- [modern Latin *rhomboideus* RHOMBOID]

rhombus *noun*
- "ROM buss"
- a parallelogram with oblique angles and equal sides.
- [Latin from Greek *rhombos*]
- **rhomboid** *adjective*

rhotic *adjective*
- "ROE tick"
- of or relating to a dialect or variety of English in which *r* is pronounced before a consonant (as in *hard*) and at the ends of words (as in *far*).
- [Greek *rhot-*, stem of RHO]

rhubarb *noun*
- "ROO barb"
- any of various plants of the genus *Rheum*, esp. *R. rhaponticum*, producing long fleshy dark red leaf stalks used cooked as food.
- [Old French *r(e)ubarbe*, shortening of medieval Latin *r(h)eubarbarum*, alteration (by assoc. with Greek *rhēon* rhubarb) of *rhabarbarum* foreign 'rha', ultimately from Greek *rha* + *barbaros* foreign]

rhumb *noun*
- "RUM"
- any of the 32 points of the compass.
- [French *rumb* prob. from Dutch *ruim* room, assoc. with Latin *rhombus*: see RHOMBUS]

HOMOPHONES: *rum*

rhyme *noun*
- "RIME"
- the quality shared by words or syllables that have or end with the same sound as each other, esp. when such words etc. are used at the ends of lines of poetry.
- [Old French *rime* from medieval Latin *rithmus*, *rythmus* from Latin from Greek *rhuthmos* RHYTHM]
- **rhymer** *noun*

HOMOPHONES: *rime*

rhymester *noun*
- "RIME stur"
- a writer of (esp. simple) rhymes.
- [as RHYME]

rhyolite *noun*
- "RYE a lite"
- a fine-grained volcanic rock of granitic composition.
- [German *Rhyolit* from Greek *rhuax* lava stream + *lithos* stone]
- **rhyolitic** *adjective* "rye a LITTIC"

rhythm *noun*
- "RITH'm" (with "TH" as in *THEM*)
- a measured flow of words and phrases in verse or prose determined by various relations of long and short or accented and unaccented syllables.
- [French *rhythme* or Latin *rhythmus* from Greek *rhuthmos*, related to *rhēo* flow]
- **rhythmic** *adjective* "RITH mick" (with "TH" as in *THEM*)
- **rhythmical** *adjective*
- **rhythmically** *adverb*
- **rhythmicity** *noun* "rith MISSA tee" (with "TH" as in *THEM*)
- **rhythmless** *adjective*

rial *noun*
- "REE all" or "RYE'll"
- the chief monetary unit of Iran and Oman, equal to 1,000 baizas in Oman.
- [Persian from Arabic *riyal* from Spanish *real* royal]

HOMOPHONES: *riyal, rile*

ribald *adjective*
- "RYE b'ld" or "RIB'ld"
- (of language or its user) referring to sexual matters in a rude but humorous way.
- [Old French *ribau(l)d* from *riber* pursue licentious pleasures, from Germanic]
- **ribaldry** *noun* "RYE b'll dree" or "RIBBLE dree"

riband *noun*
- "RIB'nd"
- a ribbon.
- [Old French *riban*]

ribavirin *noun*
- "rye buh VIE rin"
- a drug which interferes with the synthesis of viral nucleic acids and is used to treat some viral infections.
- [RIBOSE + VIRUS]

Ribier *noun*
- "RIB yur"
- a variety of large, round, purple-black grape, orig. French but much grown in the US as a table grape.
- [French]

riboflavin *noun*
- "rye bo FLAY v'n"
- a vitamin of the B complex, found in

liver, milk, and eggs, essential for energy production.
• [RIBOSE + Latin *flavus* yellow]

ribonucleic *adjective*
• "rye bo noo CLAY ick"
• designating a nucleic acid yielding ribose on hydrolysis, present in living cells, esp. in ribosomes where it is involved in protein synthesis.
• [RIBOSE + NUCLEIC]

ribose *noun*
• "RYE bose" (rhymes with *GROSS*)
• a sugar found in many nucleosides and in several vitamins and enzymes.
• [German, alteration of *Arabinose*, a related sugar]

ribosome *noun*
• "RYE buh soam"
• each of the minute particles consisting of RNA and associated proteins found in the cytoplasm of living cells, concerned with the synthesis of proteins.
• [RIBONUCLEIC + Greek *soma* body]
• **ribosomal** *adjective*

ricercar *noun*
• "ree chair CAR"
• an elaborate contrapuntal instrumental composition in fugal or canonic style, esp. of the 16th–18th c.
• [Italian, = seek out]

ricin *noun*
• "RICE in"
• a toxic substance obtained from castor oil beans and causing gastroenteritis, jaundice, and heart failure.
• [modern Latin *ricinus communis* castor oil]

rickettsia *noun*
• "rih KETSY uh"
• a parasitic micro-organism of the genus *Rickettsia* causing typhus and other febrile diseases.
• [modern Latin from H. T. *Ricketts*, US pathologist d.1910]
• **rickettsial** *adjective*

rickey *noun*
• "RICKY"
• a drink of lime juice, soda water, and usu. gin.
• [20th c.: prob. from the surname *Rickey*]

ricochet *noun*
• "RICK a shay"
• the action of a projectile, esp. a shell or bullet, in rebounding off a surface.
• [French, of unknown origin]

ricotta *noun*
• "rih COTTA"
• a soft Italian cheese with a texture resembling that of fine cottage cheese, used esp. in pasta dishes and desserts.
• [Italian, = re-cooked, from Latin *recoquere* (*re-* again, *coquere* cook)]

rictus *noun*
• "RICK tuss"
• the expanse or gape of a mouth or beak.
• [Latin, = open mouth, from *ringi rict-* to gape]
• **rictal** *adjective*

riddance *noun*
• "RID ince"
• the act of getting rid of something.
• [Middle English *rid* free of something unwanted, earlier = 'clear (land etc.)' from Old Norse *rythja*]

ridicule *noun*
• "RIDDICK yool"
• derision or mockery.
• [French from Latin *ridiculus* laughable, from *ridēre* laugh]

ridiculous *adjective*
• "rih DICK yoo luss"
• unreasonable, absurd.
• [as RIDICULE]
• **ridiculously** *adverb*
• **ridiculousness** *noun*

riel *noun*
• "REE'll"
• the basic monetary unit of Cambodia, equal to one hundred sen.
• [Khmer]
HOMOPHONES: *real, reel*

Riesling *noun*
• "REEZ ling" or "REECE ling"
• a kind of dry white wine produced in Germany, Austria, and elsewhere.
• [German]

rifampin *noun*
• "riff AM pin"
• a reddish-brown crystalline antibiotic given orally to treat a range of diseases, esp. tuberculosis.
• [prob. ultimately from Italian *riformare* reform]

rigatoni *noun*
• "rigga TONY"
• pasta in the form of short broad hollow fluted tubes.
• [Italian, from *rigato* past participle of *rigare* draw a line, make fluting, from *riga* a line]

righteous *adjective*
• "RYE ch'ss"
• (of a person or conduct) morally right; virtuous.
• [Old English *rihtwīs*]
• **righteously** *adverb*
• **righteousness** *noun*

rigid *adjective*
• "RIDGE id"
• not flexible; that cannot be bent.

• [French *rigide* or Latin *rigidus* from *rigēre* be stiff]
• **rigidify** *verb*
• **rigidity** *noun*
• **rigidly** *adverb*

rigmarole *noun*
• "RIG muh role"
• a lengthy and complicated procedure.
• [originally *ragman roll* = a catalogue, of unknown origin]

rigor *noun*
• "RIGGER"
• stiffening of the body after death.
• [Latin from *rigēre* be stiff]
HOMOPHONES: *rigger, rigour*

rigour *noun*
ALSO SPELLED: **rigor**
• "RIGGER"
• severity, strictness, harshness.
• [Old French *rigour* from Latin *rigor* (as RIGOR)]
• **rigorous** *adjective*
• **rigorously** *adverb*
HOMOPHONES: *rigor, rigger*

rijsttafel *noun*
• "RICE toff'll"
• an originally SE Asian meal consisting of a selection of different foods (such as eggs, meat, fish, fruit, curry, etc.) mixed with rice and served in separate dishes.
• [Dutch, from *rijst* rice + *tafel* table]

rille *noun*
ALSO SPELLED: **rill**
• "RILL"
• a cleft or narrow valley on the moon's surface.
• [German]
HOMOPHONES: *rill*

rillettes *plural noun*
• "ree YET"
• a soft pâté of small pieces of shredded pork, poultry, etc., cooked for a long time in fat.
• [French, from Old French *rille* piece of pork, from *reille* plank, from Latin *regula* straight stick]

rime *noun*
• "RIME"
• frost, esp. formed from cloud or fog.
• [Old English *hrīm*]
• **rimy** *adjective*
HOMOPHONES: *rhyme*

rinderpest *noun*
• "RIN dur pest"
• a virulent infectious disease of ruminants (esp. cattle).
• [German from *Rinder* cattle + *Pest* pest, plague]

ringette *noun*
• "ring ET"
• *Cdn* a game resembling hockey, played (esp. by women and girls) on ice with a straight stick and a rubber ring.
• [diminutive of 'ring' from Old English *hring* from Germanic]

ringgit *noun*
• "RING git"
• the basic monetary unit of Malaysia, equivalent to 100 cents.
• [Malay *ringgit* jagged or toothed (with allusion to the serrated edge of a milled coin as opposed to the unserrated edge of the rial, an unmilled coin)]

rinse *verb*
• "RINCE"
• wash with clean water, esp. to remove soap or detergent.
• [Old French *rincer, raincier*, of unknown origin]
• **rinsable** *adjective*
• **rinser** *noun*

Rioja *noun*
• "ree OH huh"
• wine produced in Rioja, a district in N Spain.

riparian *adjective*
• "rih PERRY 'n"
• of or on a riverbank.
• [Latin *riparius* from *ripa* bank]

riposte *noun*
• "rih PAWST"
• a quick sharp reply or retort.
• [French *ri(s)poste, ri(s)poster* from Italian *risposta* response]

rishi *noun*
• "RISHY"
• a Hindu sage or saint.
• [Sanskrit *ṛiṣi*]

risible *adjective*
• "RIZZA bull"
• laughable, ludicrous.
• [Late Latin *risibilis* from Latin *ridēre ris-* laugh]
• **risibility** *noun*
• **risibly** *adverb*

risotto *noun*
• "rizz OTTO"
• an Italian dish of esp. arborio rice cooked in broth with various other ingredients, as meat, onions, etc.
• [Italian, from *riso* rice]

risqué *adjective*
• "riss CAY"
• slightly indecent or liable to shock slightly.
• [French, past participle of *risquer* from Italian *risco* danger, *riscare* run into danger]

rissole *noun*
• "RISS ole"
• a compressed mixture of meat and spices, coated in bread crumbs and fried.
• [French from Old French *ruissole, roussole,*

ultimately from Late Latin *russeolus* reddish, from Latin *russus* red]

ritard *noun*
• "rih TARD"
• a ritardando passage in a musical composition.
• [abbreviation]
HOMOPHONES: *retard*

ritardando *adverb*
• "rit ar DANDO"
• (as a musical direction) with a gradual decrease of speed.
• [Italian]

rite *noun*
• "RITE"
• a religious or solemn observance or act.
• [Old French *rit*, *rite* or Latin *ritus* (esp. religious) usage]
HOMOPHONES: *right*, *write*, *wright*

ritornello *noun*
• "rit or NELLO"
• a short instrumental refrain, interlude, etc., in a vocal work.
• [Italian, diminutive of *ritorno* return]

ritual *noun*
• "RICH oo 'll"
• a prescribed order of performing rites.
• [Latin *ritualis* (as RITE)]
• **ritualism** *noun*
• **ritualist** *noun*
• **ritualistic** *adjective*
• **ritualistically** *adverb*
• **ritualization** *noun* (also esp. *Brit.* **-isation**)
• **ritualize** *verb* (also esp. *Brit.* **-ise**)
• **ritually** *adverb*

ritzy *adjective*
• "RITZY"
• high-class, luxurious.
• [*Ritz*, the name of luxury hotels, from C. *Ritz*, Swiss hotel owner d.1918]
• **ritz** *noun*
• **ritziness** *noun*

riverine *adjective*
• "RIVER ine"
• of or on a river or riverbank; riparian.
• [Anglo-French *river* river or riverbank, ultimately from Latin *riparius* from *ripa* bank]

riverside *noun*
• "RIVER side"
• the ground along a riverbank.
• [as RIVERINE]

rivet *noun*
• "RIVVIT"
• a nail or bolt for holding together metal plates etc., its headless end being beaten out or pressed down when in place.
• [Old French from *river* clench, of unknown origin]
• **riveter** *noun*

riviera *noun*
• "rivvy ERRA"
• a coastal region with a subtropical climate, vegetation, etc., esp. that of SE France and NW Italy.
• [Italian, = seashore]

rivulet *noun*
• "RIV yuh lit"
• a small stream or brook.
• [obsolete *riveret* from French, diminutive of *rivière* river, perhaps after Italian *rivoletto* diminutive of *rivolo* diminutive of *rivo* from Latin *rivus* stream]

riyal *noun*
• "REE all" or "RYE'll"
• the chief monetary unit of Saudi Arabia, Qatar, and Yemen, equal to 100 halalah in Saudi Arabia, 100 dirhams in Qatar, and 100 fils in Yemen.
• [Persian from Arabic *riyal* from Spanish *real* royal]
HOMOPHONES: *rial*

roadstead *noun*
• "ROAD sted"
• a partly sheltered piece of water near the shore in which ships can ride at anchor.
• ['road' from Old English *rād* from *rīdan* ride + *stead* in obsolete sense 'place']

roan *adjective*
• "RONE"
• (of an animal, esp. a horse or cow) having a coat of which the prevailing colour is thickly interspersed with hairs of another colour, esp. bay or sorrel or chestnut mixed with white or grey.
• [Old French, of unknown origin]

robata *noun*
• "roe BATTA"
• a type of charcoal grill used in Japanese cooking.
• [Japanese, lit. = 'open fireplace']

robinia *noun*
• "ruh BINNY uh"
• any N American tree or shrub of the genus *Robinia*, e.g. a locust tree or false acacia.
• [modern Latin, from J. *Robin*, 17th-c. French gardener]

roc *noun*
• "ROCK"
• a gigantic bird of Eastern legend.
• [Spanish *rocho*, ultimately from Arabic *ruk*]
HOMOPHONES: *rock*

rocaille *noun*
• "roe KYE"
• an 18th-c. style of ornamentation characterized by ornate rock and shell motifs.
• [French from *roc*, of unknown origin]

rocambole *noun*
• "ROCK'm bole"

• an alliaceous plant with a garlic-like bulb that is sometimes used for seasoning.
• [French from German *Rockenbolle*]

rochet *noun*
• "ROTCH it"
• a vestment resembling a surplice, used chiefly by bishops and abbots.
• [Old French, diminutive of a Germanic word related to Old High German *roch* coat]

rockumentary *noun*
• "rock yoo MENTA ree"
• a documentary about rock music and musicians.
• ['rock' + DOCUMENTARY]

Rockwellian *adjective*
• "rock WELLY'n"
• like or pertaining to the work of US painter Norman Rockwell (d.1978), characterized by sentimentality and nostalgia.

rococo *adjective*
• "ruh CO co" or "ROE kuh co"
• of a late baroque style of decoration prevalent in 18th-c. continental Europe, with asymmetrical patterns involving scroll-work, shell motifs, etc.
• [French, jocular alteration of ROCAILLE]

rode *noun*
• "ROAD"
• a rope securing an anchor or net.
• [origin unknown]
HOMOPHONES: *road*

rodent *noun*
• "ROAD 'nt"
• any mammal of the order Rodentia with strong incisors and no canine teeth, e.g. rat, mouse, squirrel, beaver, porcupine.
• [Latin *rodere ros-* gnaw]
• **rodential** *adjective* "roe DEN sh'll"

rodenticide *noun*
• "roe DENTA side"
• a poison used to kill rodents.
• [as RODENT + Latin *-cida, -cidium* from *caedere* kill]

rodeo *noun*
• "ROADY oh"
• a display or competition exhibiting the skills of riding broncos, roping cattle, wrestling steers, etc.
• [Spanish from *rodear* go round, ultimately from Latin *rotare* ROTATE]
HOMOPHONES: *roadeo*

rodney *noun*
• "ROD nee"
• *Cdn* (*Nfld*) a small fishing boat or punt.
• [origin unknown]

rodomontade *noun*
• "rodda m'n TADE" or "rodda m'n TAD"
• boastful or bragging talk or behaviour.
• [French from obsolete Italian *rodomontada* from French *rodomont* & Italian *rodomonte* from the name of a boastful character in the *Orlando* epics]

roe *noun*
• "ROE"
• the mass of eggs in a female fish's ovary.
• [Middle English *row(e), rough*, from Middle Low German, Middle Dutch *roge(n)*, Old High German *rogo, rogan*, Old Norse *hrogn*]
HOMOPHONES: *row, rho*

roebuck *noun*
• "ROE buck"
• the male of a small European and Asian deer, *Capreolus capreolus*.
• [Old English *rā(ha)* + 'buck']

roentgen *noun*
ALSO SPELLED: **röntgen**
• "RONT gun" or "RUNT gun"
• a unit of ionizing radiation, the amount producing one electrostatic unit of positive or negative ionic charge in one cubic centimetre of air under standard conditions.
• [W. K. *Roentgen*, German physicist d.1923]

roentgenography *noun*
• "runt gun OGGRA fee"
• photography using X-rays.
• [as ROENTGEN + PHOTOGRAPHY]
• **roentgenographic** *adjective*

rogation *noun*
• "roe GAY sh'n"
• a solemn supplication consisting of the litany of the saints chanted on the three days before Ascension Day.
• [Latin *rogatio* from *rogare* ask]

rogue *noun*
• "ROE'g"
• a dishonest or unprincipled person.
• [16th-c. cant word: origin unknown]
• **roguery** *noun* "ROE gur ee"

roguish *adjective*
• "ROE gish"
• playfully mischievous.
• [as ROGUE]
• **roguishly** *adverb*
• **roguishness** *noun*

role *noun*
• "ROLE"
• an actor's part in a play, film, etc.
• [French *rôle* and obsolete French *roule, rolle*, = 'roll', from Latin *rotulus*, diminutive of *rota* wheel]
HOMOPHONES: *roll*

rollicking *adjective*
• "RAWLA king"
• exuberantly lively and amusing.
• [19th-c., prob. dialect: perhaps from 'romp' + 'frolic']

rollmop *noun*
• "ROLE mop"
• a rolled uncooked pickled herring fillet.
• [German *Rollmops*]

romaine *noun*
• “roe MAIN”
• a variety of lettuce with crisp narrow leaves forming a long upright head.
• [French, feminine of *romain* Roman]

romaji *noun*
• “ROME a jee”
• a system of Romanized spelling used to transliterate Japanese.
• [Japanese]

romance *noun*
• “ROE mance” or “roe MANCE”
• a love affair.
• [Old French *romanz*, *-ans*, *-ance*, ultimately from Latin *Romanicus* ROMANIC]

romancer *noun*
• “roe MANCER”
• a writer of romances, esp. in the medieval period.
• [as ROMANCE]

Romanesque *noun*
• “roe m’n ESK”
• a style of architecture prevalent in Europe *c.*900–1200, with massive vaulting and round arches.
• [French from *roman* ROMANCE]

Romanian *noun*
• “roe MAINY ’n”
• a native or inhabitant of Romania in SE Europe.

Romanic *noun*
• “roe MANNIC”
• the languages descended from Latin regarded collectively.
• [Latin *Romanicus* Roman]

Romano *noun*
• “roe MANNO”
• a strong-tasting hard cheese, originally made in Italy.
• [Italian, = ‘Roman’]

Romansh *noun*
• “roe MANSH”
• the Rhaeto-Romance language spoken in the Swiss canton of Grisons; it is an official language of Switzerland.
• [Romansh *Ruman(t)sch*, *Roman(t)sch* from medieval Latin *romanice* (adverb) (as ROMANCE)]

romanticism *noun*
• “roe MANTA sizm”
• adherence to a romantic style in art, music, etc.
• [as ROMANCE]
• **romanticist** *noun*

romanticize *verb*
ALSO SPELLED: esp. *Brit.* **-ise**
• “roe MANTA size”
• make or render romantic or unreal.
• [as ROMANCE]
• **romanticization** *noun* (also esp. *Brit.* **-isation**)

Romany *noun*
• “ROMMA nee”
• a gypsy.
• [Romany *Romani*, feminine and pl. of *Romano* (*adjective*), from *Rom* man]

Romeo *noun*
• “ROAMY oh”
• a passionate male lover or seducer.
• [the hero of Shakespeare’s play *Romeo and Juliet*]

rondeau *noun*
• “RON doe”
• a poem of ten or thirteen lines with only two rhymes throughout and with the opening words used twice as a refrain.
• [French, earlier *rondel* from Old French *rond* ‘round’ from Latin *rotundus* ROTUND]
HOMOPHONES: *rondo*

rondel *noun*
• “ROND’ll”
• a rondeau, esp. one of special form.
• [as RONDEAU]

rondo *noun*
• “RON doe”
• a form of composition with a recurring theme, often found in the final movement of a sonata or concerto etc.
• [Italian from French *rondeau*: see RONDEAU]
HOMOPHONES: *rondeau*

Ronga *noun*
• “RONG guh”
• a member of a Bantu-speaking people of southern Mozambique.
• [Ronga]

ronin *noun*
• “ROE nin”
• (in feudal Japan) a lordless wandering samurai; an outlaw.
• [Japanese]

rooibos *noun*
• “ROY boss”
• an evergreen South African shrub of the genus *Aspalathus* belonging to the family Leguminosae, and cultivated for its leaves which are used to make a kind of tea.
• [Afrikaans, from *rooi* red + *bos* bush]

roomette *noun*
• “room ET”
• a private single compartment in the sleeping car of a train.
• [diminutive of ‘room’]

roommate *noun*
• “ROOM mate”
• a person who lives in the same apartment, room, etc. as another.
• [‘room’ + ‘mate’]

roquefort *noun*
- "ROKE furt" or "ROKE fort" or "ROCK for"
- a soft blue cheese made from ewes' milk.
- [*Roquefort* in S. France]

roquet *verb*
- "ROE cay" or "ROE key"
- cause one's ball to strike (another ball).
- [apparently arbitrary alteration of CROQUET, originally used in the same sense]

rorqual *noun*
- "ROAR kwull"
- any of various baleen whales of the family Balaenopteridae characterized by a pleated throat and small dorsal fin, esp. the finback or the minke whale.
- [French from Norwegian *røyrkval* from Old Icelandic *reythr* the specific name + *hvalr* whale]

Rorschach *adjective*
- "ROAR shack" or "ROAR shock"
- designating or pertaining to a type of personality test in which a standard set of ink blots is presented one by one to the subject, who is asked to describe what they suggest or resemble.
- [H. *Rorschach*, Swiss psychiatrist d.1922]

rosacea *noun*
- "roe ZAY shuh"
- a condition in which certain blood vessels enlarge, giving the cheeks and nose a flushed appearance.
- [Latin, feminine of *rosaceus* in the sense 'rose-coloured']

rosaceous *adjective*
- "roe ZAY sh'ss"
- relating or belonging to the large plant family Rosaceae, which includes the rose.
- [Latin *rosaceus* from *rosa* rose + adjective suffix *-aceus* of the nature of]

rosary *noun*
- "ROZA ree"
- a form of Catholic devotion accompanying the contemplation of fifteen mysteries (now usu. in groups of five) in which fifteen decades (sets of ten) of Hail Marys are repeated, each decade preceded by an Our Father and followed by a Glory Be.
- [Latin *rosarium* rose garden, neuter of *rosarius*, from *rosa* rose]

rosé *noun*
- "roe ZAY"
- any pale red or pink wine, coloured by only brief contact with the skins of red grapes.
- [French, lit. 'pink']

roseate *adjective*
- "ROZE ee it"
- having a partly pink plumage.
- [Latin *roseus* rosy, from *rosa* rose]

rosemaling *noun*
- "ROZE mal ing"
- the art of painting wooden furniture etc. with flower motifs.
- [Norwegian, = rose painting]

roseola *noun*
- "roe ZEE a luh" or "rozy OLA"
- a rosy rash in measles and similar diseases.
- [modern var. of RUBEOLA from Latin *roseus* rose-coloured]

rosette *noun*
- "rose ET"
- an ornament or other object carved, moulded, shaped, or arranged to resemble or represent a rose.
- [French diminutive of *rose* rose]

roshi *noun*
- "ROE shee"
- the spiritual leader of a community of Zen Buddhist monks.
- [Japanese]

Rosicrucian *noun*
- "roze a CROO sh'n"
- a member of a 17th–18th-c. society, said to have been founded by Christian Rosenkreuz in 1484, devoted to metaphysical and mystical lore, such as that concerning the prolongation of life and power over the elements and elemental spirits.
- [modern Latin *rosa crucis* (or *crux*), as Latinization of German *Rosenkreuz*]
- **Rosicrucianism** *noun*

rosin *noun*
- "ROZZIN"
- the solid amber residue obtained after the distillation of crude turpentine oleoresin, or of naphtha extract from pine stumps, used in adhesives, varnishes, inks, etc. It is also used, esp. powdered, to prevent slipping when applied to the bows of stringed instruments, the hands of baseball players etc., and dancers' shoes.
- [Middle English, alteration of RESIN]
- **rosiny** *adjective*

rösti *plural noun*
- "ROOSTY" (with "OO" as in *BOOK*)
- a dish of grated potatoes, sometimes flavoured with onion or bacon, compacted into a large cake and fried.
- [Swiss German from German *rösten* roast, grill]

rostral *adjective*
- "ROSS trull"
- near the region of the nose and mouth.
- [as ROSTRUM]
- **rostrally** *adverb*

rostrum *noun*
- "ROSS trum"
- a platform or pulpit for public speaking.
- [Latin, = beak, from *rodere ros-* gnaw: originally *rostra* in the Roman forum adorned with beaks of captured galleys]

rota *noun*
• "ROE tuh"
• a rotational order of people, duties to be done, etc.
• [Latin, = wheel]

Rotarian *noun*
• "roe TERRY 'n"
• a member of a Rotary Club, a charitable society for businesspeople and professionals.

rotary *adjective*
• "ROE tuh ree"
• acting by rotation.
• [medieval Latin *rotarius* (as ROTA)]

rotate *verb*
• "ROE tate"
• move around an axis or centre; spin, revolve.
• [Latin *rotare* from *rota* wheel]
• **rotatable** *adjective*
• **rotation** *noun*
• **rotational** *adjective*
• **rotationally** *adverb*
• **rotatory** *adjective* "ROE tuh tory"

rotator *noun*
• "roe TAY tur"
• a muscle that rotates a limb etc.
• [as ROTATE]

rotavirus *noun*
• "ROE tuh vie russ"
• any of a class of wheel-shaped double-stranded RNA viruses, some of which cause acute enteritis in humans.
• [modern Latin, from Latin *rota* wheel + VIRUS]
• **rotaviral** *adjective*

rote *noun*
• "ROTE"
• a mechanical practice, routine, performance, etc.
• [Middle English: origin unknown]

rotenone *noun*
• "ROE t'n own"
• a toxic crystalline substance, $C_{23}H_{22}O_6$, obtained from the roots of derris and other plants, used as an insecticide.
• [Japanese *rotenon* from *roten* derris]

roti *noun*
• "ROE tee"
• a dish of Indian origin, common in the Caribbean, consisting of a flat pancake or unleavened bread folded over usu. a spicy meat filling with chickpeas.
• [Hindi *roti* bread]
HOMOPHONES: *roadie*

rotifer *noun*
• "ROE tuh fur"
• any minute aquatic animal of the phylum Rotifera, with rotatory organs used in swimming and feeding.
• [modern Latin *rotiferus* from Latin *rota* wheel + *-fer* bearing]

rotini *noun*
• "roe TEENY"
• a variety of pasta in small spirals.
• [Italian, = 'little wheels']

rotisserie *noun*
• "roe TISSER ee"
• a usu. motor-driven rotating spit for roasting meat esp. over a barbecue or in an oven.
• [French *rôtisserie* from Old French *rostir* roast, from Germanic]

rotogravure *noun*
• "roe tuh gruh VYUR"
• a printing system using a rotary press with intaglio cylinders, usu. running at high speed for long print runs of magazines, stamps, etc.
• [German *Rotogravur* (name of a company) assimilated to PHOTOGRAVURE]

rotor *noun*
• "ROE tur"
• a rotary part of a machine, esp. in the distributor of an internal combustion engine.
• [as ROTATOR]

rotoscope *noun*
• "ROE tuh scope"
• a device which projects and enlarges individual frames of filmed live action to permit them to be used to create cartoon animation and composite film sequences.
• [origin obscure: perhaps the same word as 19th-c. *rotascope*, denoting a kind of gyroscope]

Rottweiler *noun*
• "ROT wile ur"
• a breed of large, stocky, powerful dog having short coarse hair with black and tan markings, a broad head with pendent ears, and usu. a docked tail.
• [German from *Rottweil* in SW Germany]

rotund *adjective*
• "roe TUND"
• round, circular, spherical.
• [Latin *rotundus* from *rotare* ROTATE]
• **rotundity** *noun*

rotunda *noun*
• "roe TUNDA"
• a circular hall or room.
• [earlier *rotonda* from Italian *rotonda* (*camera*) round (chamber), feminine of *rotondo* round (as ROTUND)]

roué *noun*
• "ROO ay"
• a debauched man, esp. an elderly one.
• [French, past participle of *rouer* break (a person) on the wheel (the punishment said to be deserved by such a womanizer), from *roue* wheel, from Latin *rota*]

rouge *noun*
• "ROOZH"
• a red powder or cream used for colouring the cheeks.
• [French, = red, from Latin *rubeus*]

rough *adjective*
- "RUFF"
- having an uneven or irregular surface, not smooth or level or polished.
- [Old English *rūh* from West Germanic]
- **roughen** *verb*
- **roughness** *noun*

HOMOPHONES: *ruff*

roughage *noun*
- "RUFF idge"
- the part of a foodstuff that cannot be digested or absorbed; dietary fibre.
- [as ROUGH]

roughcast *noun*
- "RUFF cast"
- plaster of lime and gravel, used on outside walls.
- [ROUGH + 'cast']

roughhouse *noun*
- "RUFF house"
- boisterous or rambunctious play or wrestling, esp. indoors.
- [ROUGH + 'house']
- **roughhousing** *noun*

roughing *noun*
- "RUFFING"
- an unnecessary or excessive use of force for which a player is given a penalty.
- [as ROUGH]

roughly *adverb*
- "RUFF lee"
- approximately.
- [as ROUGH]

HOMOPHONES: *ruffly*

roughneck *noun*
- "RUFF neck"
- a rough or rowdy person.
- [ROUGH + 'neck']

roughout *adjective*
- "RUFF out"
- designating informal outdoor clothing, or materials used for making outdoor clothing, accessories, etc.
- [ROUGH + 'out']

roughrider *noun*
- "RUFF rider"
- a person who breaks in or can ride unbroken horses.
- [ROUGH + 'rider']

roughshod *adjective*
- "RUFF shod"
- (of a horse) having shoes with nailheads projecting to prevent slipping.
- [ROUGH + 'shod']

roughy *noun*
- "RUFFY"
- any of several rough-skinned fish of the family Trachichthyidae, esp. the orange roughy.
- [perhaps from ROUGH]

rouille *noun*
- "ROO ee"
- a Provençal sauce made from pounded red peppers, garlic, olive oil, and bread crumbs or potatoes, blended with stock and served with bouillabaisse or other fish dishes.
- [French, lit. 'rust', the colour of this sauce]

roulade *noun*
- "roo LOD"
- any of various dishes cooked or served in the shape of a roll, esp. a slice of meat or a piece of sponge cake spread with a filling and rolled up.
- [French from *rouler* to roll]

roulette *noun*
- "roo LET"
- a gambling game in which a ball is dropped onto a revolving wheel with numbered compartments in the centre of a table, players betting on the number at which the ball will come to rest.
- [French, diminutive of *rouelle* from Late Latin *rotella* diminutive of Latin *rota* wheel]

rouletted *adjective*
- "roo LET id"
- (of a sheet of postage stamps) perforated.
- [as ROULETTE]

roundel *noun*
- "ROUND'll"
- a small circular object, esp. a decorative medallion.
- [Old French *rondel(le)* from Old French *rond* round, from Latin *rotundus* ROTUND]

roundelay *noun*
- "ROUND a lay"
- a short simple song with a refrain.
- [French *rondelet*, assimilated to *virelay*, a medieval song or lyric poem]

roup *noun*
- "ROOP"
- an infectious respiratory disease of poultry.
- [16th c.: origin unknown]
- **roupy** *adjective*

rouse *verb*
- "ROUZE" (rhymes with *COWS*)
- bring out of sleep; wake.
- [originally as a hawking and hunting term, so prob. from Anglo-French: origin unknown]
- **rousable** *adjective*
- **rouser** *noun*

rousing *adjective*
- "ROUZE ing" ("ROUZE" rhymes with *COWS*)
- exciting, stirring.
- [as ROUSE]
- **rousingly** *adverb*

route *noun*
- "ROOT" or "ROUT"
- a way or course taken (esp. regularly) in getting from a starting point to a destination.

• [Old French *r(o)ute* road, ultimately from Latin *ruptus* broken]
HOMOPHONES: *root, rout*

routine *noun*
• "roo TEEN"
• a regular course or procedure, an unvarying performance of certain acts.
• [French (as ROUTE)]
• **routinely** *adverb*
• **routinization** *noun* (also esp. *Brit.* **-isation**)
• **routinize** *verb* (also esp. *Brit.* **-ise**)

roux *noun*
• "ROO"
• a mixture of fat (esp. butter) and flour used to thicken sauces etc.
• [French, = browned (butter), red, from Provençal *ros*, Italian *rosso* from Latin *russus* red]
HOMOPHONES: *rue, roo*

rowan *noun*
• "ROW 'n" ("ROW" rhymes with *CROW* or *COW*)
• any of various small trees of the genus *Sorbus*, with delicate pinnate leaves and scarlet berries; a mountain ash.
• [Scandinavian, corresponding to Norwegian *rogn, raun*, Icelandic *reynir*]

rowel *noun*
• "ROW 'll" ("ROW" rhymes with *COW*)
• a spiked revolving disc at the end of a spur.
• [Old French *roel(e)* from Late Latin *rotella* diminutive of Latin *rota* wheel]

rubato *noun*
• "roo BOTTO"
• the temporary disregarding of strict tempo in music.
• [Italian, = robbed]

rube *noun*
• "ROOB"
• a country bumpkin.
• [abbreviation of the name *Reuben*]

rubel *noun*
• "ROO bull"
• a monetary unit of Belarus.
• [Belarusian, as RUBLE]
HOMOPHONES: *ruble*

rubella *noun*
• "roo BELLA"
• an acute infectious viral disease with a red rash; German measles.
• [modern Latin, neuter pl. of Latin *rubellus* reddish]

rubellite *noun*
• "ROOBA lite"
• a red variety of tourmaline.
• [Latin *rubellus* reddish]

Rubenesque *adjective*
• "roob'n ESK"
• (esp. of a woman's body) plump and voluptuous.
• [with reference to P. P. *Rubens*, Flemish painter d.1640, whose paintings depicted such women]

rubeola *noun*
• "roo BEE a luh" or "ruby OH luh"
• measles.
• [medieval Latin from Latin *rubeus* red]

Rubicon *noun*
• "ROOBA con"
• a boundary which, once crossed, signifies irrevocable commitment; a point of no return.
• [a stream in NE Italy which marked the ancient boundary of Julius Caesar's province; by taking his army across it into Italy in 49 BC, he committed himself to war against the Senate]

rubicund *adjective*
• "ROOBA kund"
• (of a face, complexion, or person in these respects) ruddy, high-coloured.
• [French *rubicond* or Latin *rubicundus* from *rubēre* be red]
• **rubicundity** *noun*

rubidium *noun*
• "roo BIDDY um"
• a soft silvery element occurring naturally in various minerals and as the radioactive isotope rubidium-87.
• [Latin *rubidus* red (with reference to its spectral lines)]

ruble *noun*
ALSO SPELLED: *Brit.* **rouble**
• "ROO bull"
• the chief monetary unit of Russia and some other former republics of the USSR, equal to 100 kopecks.
• [French from Russian *rubl'*]
HOMOPHONES: *rubel*

rubric *noun*
• "ROO brick"
• a heading or passage in red or special lettering.
• [Old French *rubrique, rubrice* or Latin *rubrica* (*terra*) red (earth or ochre) as writing material, related to *rubeus* red]

rubricate *verb*
• "ROOBRA cate"
• mark with red; print or write in red.
• [Latin *rubricare* from *rubrica*: see RUBRIC]
• **rubrication** *noun*
• **rubricator** *noun*

ruche *noun*
• "ROOSH"
• a frill or gathering of lace etc. as a trimming.
• [French from medieval Latin *rusca* tree bark, of Celtic origin]
• **ruched** *adjective*
• **ruching** *noun*

ruckus *noun*
• "RUCK us"

• a noisy disturbance; an uproar or commotion.
• [compare RUCTION, 'rumpus']

ruction *noun*
• "RUCK sh'n"
• a disturbance or tumult.
• [19th c.: origin unknown]

rudbeckia *noun*
• "rud BECKY uh"
• any of various tall plants constituting the genus *Rudbeckia* of the composite family, native to N America, bearing yellow or orange flowers with a prominent conical dark-coloured disc, and including black-eyed Susan and various coneflowers.
• [modern Latin from O. *Rudbeck*, Swedish botanist d.1740]

rudd *noun*
• "RUD"
• a European freshwater fish of the carp family, *Scardinius erythrophthalmus*, with red fins.
• [apparently related to *rud* red colour, from Old English *rudu*]

ruddle *noun*
• "RUD'll"
• a red ochre, esp. of a kind used for marking sheep.
• [related to obsolete *rud*: see RUDD]

ruderal *adjective*
• "ROODER'll"
• (of a plant) growing on or in rubbish or rubble.
• [modern Latin *ruderalis* from Latin *rudera* pl. of *rudus* rubble]

rudiment *noun*
• "ROODA m'nt"
• the elements or first principles of a subject.
• [French *rudiment* or Latin *rudimentum* (*rudis* unwrought, after *elementum* element)]
• **rudimentarily** *adverb* "rooda men TERRA lee"
• **rudimentariness** *noun* "rooda MENTA ree nuss"
• **rudimentary** *adjective*

rue *verb*
• "ROO"
• repent of; bitterly feel the consequences of; wish to be undone or non-existent.
• [Old English *hrēow*, *hrēowan*]
HOMOPHONES: *roo*, *roux*

rueful *adjective*
• "ROO full"
• expressing sorrow or regret in a genuine or humorous way.
• [Middle English, from RUE]
• **ruefully** *adverb*
• **ruefulness** *noun*

ruff *noun*
• "RUFF"
• a projecting starched frill worn round the neck esp. in the 16th c.
• [perhaps a variant of ROUGH]
HOMOPHONES: *rough*

ruffian *noun*
• "RUFFY 'n"
• a violent lawless person.
• [French *ruf(f)ian* from Italian *ruffiano*, perhaps from dialect *rofia* scurf]
• **ruffianism** *noun*
• **ruffianly** *adverb*

rufiyaa *noun*
• "ROO fee yuh"
• the basic monetary unit of the Maldives, equal to 100 laari.
• [Maldivian]

rufous *adjective*
• "ROO fuss"
• (esp. of animals) reddish brown.
• [Latin *rufus* red, reddish]

rugelach *noun*
• "ROOGA lock"
• (in Jewish cuisine) a type of small cookie consisting of pastry rolled up to form a crescent shape over a filling of cinnamon sugar, nuts, etc.
• [Yiddish]

rugosa *noun*
• "roo GO suh"
• a Japanese rose, *Rosa rugosa*, which has dark green wrinkled leaves and deep pink flowers.
• [Latin, feminine of *rugosus* (see RUGOSE) used as specific epithet]

rugose *adjective*
• "ROO gose" or "roo GOSE" (rhymes with *GROSS*)
• wrinkled, corrugated.
• [Latin *rugosus* from *ruga* wrinkle]
• **rugosity** *noun* "roo GOSSA tee"

rumbustious *adjective*
• "rum BUSS ch'ss"
• boisterous, noisy, uproarious.
• [prob. var. of *robustious* boisterous, from French *robuste* or Latin *robustus* firm and hard, from *robus*, *robur* oak, strength]

rumen *noun*
• "ROO m'n"
• the first stomach of a ruminant, in which food, esp. cellulose, is partly digested by bacteria.
• [Latin *rumen ruminis* throat]

ruminant *noun*
• "ROOMA n'nt"
• an animal that chews the cud regurgitated from its rumen.
• [Latin *ruminari ruminant-* (as RUMEN)]

ruminate *verb*
• "ROOMIN ate"
• meditate, ponder.
• [as RUMINANT]

- **rumination** *noun*
- **ruminative** *adjective* "ROOMIN a tiv"
- **ruminatively** *adverb*

rummage *verb*
- "RUM idge"
- search, esp. untidily and unsystematically.
- [earlier as noun in obsolete sense 'arranging of casks etc. in a hold': Old French *arrumage* from *arrumer* stow (*ad-* to + *run* ship's hold, from Middle Dutch *ruim* room)]
- **rummager** *noun*

runcible *adjective*
- "RUNCE a bull"
- designating a fork curved like a spoon, with three broad prongs, one edged.
- [nonsense word used by English humorist E. Lear (d.1888), perhaps after *rouncival* large pea]

runcinate *adjective*
- "RUNCE a nit"
- (of a leaf) sawtoothed, with lobes pointing towards the base.
- [modern Latin *runcinatus* from Latin *runcina* plane (tool for smoothing, formerly taken to mean 'saw')]

rune *noun*
- "ROON"
- any of the letters of the earliest Germanic alphabet used by Scandinavians and Anglo-Saxons from about the 3rd c. and formed by modifying Roman or Greek characters to suit carving.
- [Old Norse *rún* (only in pl. *rúnar*) magic sign, related to Old English *rūn*]
- **runic** *adjective*

runnel *noun*
- "RUN'll"
- a brook or small stream.
- [later form (assimilated to 'run') of *rinel* from Old English *rynel*]

rupee *noun*
- "roo PEE"
- the basic monetary unit of India, Pakistan, Sri Lanka, Nepal, Mauritius, and the Seychelles, equal to 100 paisa in India, Pakistan, and Nepal, and 100 cents in Sri Lanka, Mauritius, and the Seychelles.
- [Hindi *rūpiyah* from Sanskrit *rūpya* wrought silver]

Rupertite *noun*
- "ROOPERT ite"
- a native or resident of Prince Rupert, BC.

rupiah *noun*
- "roo PEE uh"
- the basic monetary unit of Indonesia.
- [as RUPEE]

Ruritanian *adjective*
- "rur a TAINY 'n"
- relating to or characteristic of courtly intrigue and romantic adventure or its setting.
- [*Ruritania*, an imaginary setting in SE Europe of *The Prisoner of Zenda* and other novels by A. Hope, English writer d.1933]

Russophile *noun*
- "RUSSO file"
- a person who is fond of Russia or the Russians.
- ['Russia' + Greek *philos* dear, loving]

Russophobe *noun*
- "RUSSO fobe"
- a person who fears or hates Russia or the Russians.
- ['Russia' + PHOBIA]
- **Russophobia** *noun*

rustic *adjective*
- "RUSS tick"
- having a simplicity and charm that is typical of the countryside.
- [Latin *rusticus* from *rus* the country]
- **rustically** *adverb*
- **rusticity** *noun* "russ TISSA tee"

rusticate *verb*
- "RUSS tick ate"
- retire to or live in the country.
- [as RUSTIC]
- **rustication** *noun*

rustle *verb*
- "RUSS'll"
- make or cause to make a gentle sound as of dry leaves blown in a breeze.
- [Middle English *rustel* etc. (imitative): compare obsolete Flemish *ruysselen*, Dutch *ritselen*]

rutabaga *noun*
- "ROOTA bay guh" or "ROOTA bag uh"
- a cruciferous plant, *Brassica napus*, with a large yellow-fleshed root, originally from Sweden.
- [Swedish dialect *rotabagge*]

Ruthenian *noun*
- "roo THEENY 'n"
- a native or inhabitant of the region of Ruthenia, now in W Ukraine.

ruthenium *noun*
- "roo THEENY um"
- a rare hard white metallic transition element, occurring naturally in platinum ores, and used as a chemical catalyst and in certain alloys.
- [medieval Latin *Ruthenia* Russia (from its discovery in ores from the Urals)]

rutherfordium *noun*
- "ruther FORDY um" ("RUTHER" rhymes with *MOTHER*)
- a very unstable chemical element made by high-energy atomic collisions.
- [E. *Rutherford*, New Zealand-born physicist d.1937]

rutile *noun*
- "ROO tile"
- a mineral form of titanium dioxide.
- [French *rutile* or German *Rutil* from Latin *rutilus* reddish]

Rwandan *noun*
- "roo ON d'n"
- a native or inhabitant of Rwanda in central Africa.

rye *noun*
- "RYE"
- a cereal plant, *Secale cereale*, with spikes bearing florets which yield wheat-like grains.
- [Old English *ryge* from Germanic]

HOMOPHONES: *rai*, *wry*

ryegrass *noun*
- "RYE grass"
- any forage or lawn grass of the genus *Lolium*, esp. *L. perenne*.
- [obsolete *ray-grass*, of unknown origin]

ryokan *noun*
- "ree OAK'n"
- a traditional Japanese inn.
- [Japanese]

ryot *noun*
- "RYE it"
- an Indian peasant.
- [Urdu *ra'īyat* from Arabic *ra'īya* flock, subjects, from *ra'ā* to pasture]

HOMOPHONES: *riot*

Ss

Saanich *noun*
• "SAN itch"
• a member of a division of Straits people living on the Saanich Peninsula.
• [Straits, lit. 'elevated', with reference to the likeness of nearby Mount Newton's profile to a raised rump]

sabadilla *noun*
• "sabba DILLA"
• a Mexican plant, *Schoenocaulon officinale.*
• [Spanish *cebadilla* diminutive of *cebada* barley]

sabayon *noun*
• "SAB eye yon"
• a dessert consisting of egg yolks, sugar, and (esp. Marsala) wine, whipped to a frothy texture over gentle heat and served warm or cold.
• [French from Italian *sabaione*, var. of ZABAGLIONE]

Sabbatarian *noun*
• "sabba TERRY 'n"
• a Christian who favours observing Sunday strictly as the Sabbath.
• [Late Latin *sabbatarius* from Latin *sabbatum*: see SABBATH]
• **Sabbatarianism** *noun*

Sabbath *noun*
• "SAB uth"
• a day of rest and religious observance for Jews and Christians.
• [ultimately from Hebrew *šabbāṯ* from *šāḇaṯ* to rest]

sabbatical *adjective*
• "suh BATTA k'll"
• (of leave) granted at intervals to a professor or teacher for study or travel, originally every seventh year.
• [Late Latin *sabbaticus* from Greek *sabbatikos* of the Sabbath]

sabicu *noun*
• "SABBA coo"
• a Caribbean tree, *Lysiloma latisiliqua*, grown for timber.
• [Cuban Spanish *sabicú*]

Sabine *adjective*
• "SAB ine" ("INE" rhymes with *DINE*)
• of or relating to a people of the central Apennines in ancient Italy.
• [Latin *Sabinus*]

sabot *noun*
• "sa BOE" or "SABBO"
• a kind of simple shoe hollowed out from a block of wood.
• [French, blend of *savate* shoe + *botte* boot]
• **saboted** *adjective* "SAB ode"

sabotage *noun*
• "SABBA tozh" or "SABBA tazh"
• deliberate damage to or destruction of property, esp. in order to disrupt the production of goods or as a political or military act.
• [French from *saboter* make a noise with sabots, bungle, wilfully destroy: see SABOT]

saboteur *noun*
• "sabba TUR"
• a person who commits sabotage.
• [French]

sabra *noun*
• "SABBRA"
• a Jew born in Israel.
• [modern Hebrew *sābrāh* opuntia fruit]

sabre *noun*
ALSO SPELLED: esp. *US* **saber**
• "SAY bur"
• a cavalry sword with a curved blade.
• [French, earlier *sable* from German *Sabel*, *Säbel*, *Schabel* from Polish *szabla* or Hungarian *szablya*]

sac *noun*
• "SACK"
• a bag-like cavity, enclosed by a membrane, in an animal or plant.
• [French *sac* or Latin *saccus* sack]
HOMOPHONES: *sack*

saccade *noun*
• "sa COD"
• a brief rapid movement of the eye between fixation points.
• [French, = violent pull, from Old French *saquer*, *sachier* pull]
• **saccadic** *adjective*

saccharide *noun*
• "SACKA ride"

• any of a group of soluble usu. sweet-tasting crystalline carbohydrates found esp. in plants, e.g. glucose, and also in milk and blood.
• [modern Latin *saccharum* sugar]

saccharin *noun*
• "SACK a rin" or "SACK rin"
• a very sweet substance used as a substitute for sugar.
• [German (as SACCHARIDE)]
HOMOPHONES: *saccharine*

saccharine *adjective*
• "SACK a rin" or "SACK rin"
• sweet; sugary.
• [as SACCHARIN]
HOMOPHONES: *saccharin*

saccharose *noun*
• "SACK a rose" (rhymes with *GROSS*)
• sucrose.
• [modern Latin *saccharum* sugar + GLUCOSE]

saccule *noun*
• "SACK yool"
• a small sac or cyst.
• [Latin *sacculus* (as SAC)]
• **saccular** *adjective*

sacerdotal *adjective*
• "sasser DOTE'll" or "sacker DOTE'll"
• of priests or the priestly office; priestly.
• [Latin *sacerdotalis* from *sacerdos -dotis* priest]

sachem *noun*
• "SAY chum"
• the supreme chief of some N American Aboriginal peoples.
• [Narragansett, = SAGAMORE]

Sachertorte *noun*
• "SACKER tort"
• a Viennese chocolate cake with apricot jam filling and chocolate icing.
• [German, from Franz *Sacher* Austrian pastry chef, its inventor + *Torte* cake]

sachet *noun*
• "sash AY"
• a small perfumed bag.
• [French, diminutive of *sac* from Latin *saccus*]
HOMOPHONES: *sashay*

sackbut *noun*
• "SACK butt"
• an early form of trombone, of the Renaissance period.
• [French *saquebute*, earlier *saqueboute* hook for pulling a man off a horse, from *saquer* pull, *boute* butt]

Sackvillian *noun*
• "sack VILLY in"
• a resident of Sackville, NB.

sacral *adjective*
• "SAKE rull"
• of or relating to the sacrum.
• [as SACRUM]

sacralize *verb*
ALSO SPELLED: esp. *Brit.* **-ise**
• "SAKE ruh lize"
• endow with sacred significance.
• [French *sacraliser* from Latin *sacrum* sacred thing, from *sacer* sacred]
• **sacralization** *noun* (also esp. *Brit.* **-isation**)

sacrament *noun*
• "SACKRA m'nt"
• a religious ceremony or act of the Christian Churches regarded as an outward and visible sign of inward and spiritual grace: applied by the Eastern, pre-Reformation Western, and Roman Catholic Churches to the seven rites of baptism, confirmation, the Eucharist, penance, anointing of the sick, ordination, and matrimony, but restricted by most Protestants to baptism and the Eucharist.
• [Old French *sacrement* from Latin *sacramentum* solemn oath etc., from *sacrare* hallow, from *sacer* sacred, used in Christian Latin as translation of Greek *mustērion* mystery]
• **sacramental** *adjective*
• **sacramentalism** *noun*
• **sacramentalist** *noun*
• **sacramentalize** *verb* (also esp. *Brit.* **-ise**)
• **sacramentally** *adverb*

sacrarium *noun*
• "suh CRERRY um"
• the sanctuary of a church.
• [Latin from *sacer sacri* holy]

sacrifice *noun*
• "SACKRA fice"
• the act of giving up something valued for the sake of something else more important or worthy.
• [Old French from Latin *sacrificium* from *sacrificus* from *sacer sacri* holy]
• **sacrificial** *adjective* "sackra FISH'll"
• **sacrificially** *adverb*

sacrilege *noun*
• "SACKRA lidge"
• the violation or misuse of what is regarded as sacred.
• [Old French from Latin *sacrilegium* from *sacrilegus* stealer of sacred things, from *sacer sacri* sacred + *legere* take possession of]
• **sacrilegious** *adjective* "sackra LIDGE us"
• **sacrilegiously** *adverb*

sacristan *noun*
• "SACK riss t'n"
• a person in charge of a sacristy and its contents.
• [as SACRISTY]

sacristy *noun*
• "SACK riss tee"
• a room in a church or chapel, where the vestments, sacred vessels, etc., are kept and the celebrant can prepare for a service.
• [medieval Latin *sacristia* from *sacer sacri* holy]

sacroiliac *adjective*
- "sack roe ILLY ack" or "sake roe ILLY ack"
- relating to the sacrum and the ilium, esp. designating the rigid joint between them at the back of the pelvis.
- [SACRUM + ILIUM]

sacrosanct *adjective*
- "SACK roe sanct"
- (of a person, place, law, etc.) most sacred; inviolable; exempt from charge or criticism etc.
- [Latin *sacrosanctus* from *sacro* ablative of *sacrum* sacred rite + *sanctus* holy]
- **sacrosanctity** *noun*

sacrum *noun*
- "SACK rum" or "SAKE rum"
- a triangular bone formed from fused vertebrae and situated between the two hip bones of the pelvis.
- [Latin *os sacrum* translation of Greek *hieron osteon* sacred bone (from its sacrificial use)]

Sadducee *noun*
- "SAD yoo see"
- a member of a Jewish sect or party of the time of Christ that denied the resurrection of the dead, the existence of spirits, and the obligation of the traditional oral law.
- [Old English *sadducēas* from Late Latin *Sadducaeus* from Greek *Saddoukaios* from Hebrew *ṣᵉdûḳî*, prob. = descendant of Zadok (2 Sam. 8:17)]
- **Sadducean** *adjective* "sad yoo SEE 'n"

sadhu *noun*
ALSO SPELLED: **saddhu**
- "SAW doo"
- (in India) a holy man, sage, or ascetic.
- [Sanskrit, = holy man]

Sadlermiut *noun*
- "sad LUR mee oot" ("OOT" rhymes with *FOOT*)
- a member of an extinct Aboriginal people formerly living on Southampton Island, Hudson Bay.
- [variant of Inuktitut *Sallirmiut* from *Salliq* 'large flat island' (designating Southampton Island in Hudson Bay) + *-miut* the people of]

safari *noun*
- "suh FAR ee"
- a hunting or scientific expedition, esp. in East Africa.
- [Swahili from Arabic *safara* to travel]

safflower *noun*
- "SAF flower"
- an orange-flowered thistle-like plant, *Carthamus tinctorius*, whose seeds yield an edible oil.
- [Dutch *saffloer* or German *Safflor* via Old French *saffleur* from obsolete Italian *saffiore* from Arabic *aṣfar*]

saffron *noun*
- "SAFF run"
- an orange-yellow flavouring and food colouring made from the dried stigmas of the crocus, *Crocus sativus*.
- [Old French *safran* from Arabic *za'farān*]
- **saffroned** *adjective*
- **saffrony** *adjective*

safranine *noun*
- "SAFFRA neen"
- any of a large group of mainly red dyes used in biological staining etc.
- [French *safranine* (as SAFFRON): originally of dye from saffron]

sagacious *adjective*
- "suh GAY sh'ss"
- mentally penetrating; gifted with discernment; having practical wisdom.
- [Latin *sagax sagacis*]
- **sagaciously** *adverb*
- **sagacity** *noun* "suh GASSA tee"

sagamore *noun*
- "SAG a more"
- the supreme chief of some N American Aboriginal peoples.
- [Penobscot *sagamo*]

saggar *noun*
ALSO SPELLED: **sagger**
- "SAGGER"
- a protective fireclay box enclosing ceramic ware while it is being fired.
- [prob. contraction of 'safeguard']

sagittal *adjective*
- "SADGE a t'll"
- of or relating to the suture between the parietal bones of the skull.
- [French from medieval Latin *sagittalis* from *sagitta* arrow]

Sagittarius *noun*
- "sadge a TERRY us"
- the ninth sign of the zodiac.
- [Latin, = archer, from *sagitta* arrow]
- **Sagittarian** *adjective*

sagittate *adjective*
- "SADGE a tate"
- shaped like an arrowhead.
- [Latin *sagitta* arrow]

sago *noun*
- "SAY go"
- a kind of starch, made from the powdered pith of the sago palm and used in puddings etc.
- [Malay *sāgū* (originally through Portuguese)]

saguaro *noun*
- "suh GWARR oh"
- a giant cactus, *Carnegiea gigantea*, of the SW United States and Mexico.
- [Latin American Spanish]

Saharan *adjective*
- "suh HAIR 'n" or "suh HAR 'n"
- of or relating to the Sahara Desert in N Africa.

Sahelian *adjective*
• "suh HEELY 'n"
• of or relating to the Sahel, a vast semi-arid region south of the Sahara Desert.

sahib *noun*
• "SAW hib" or "SAW ib"
• (in India) a polite form of address, often placed after a person's name or title.
• [Urdu from Arabic *ṣāḥib* friend, lord]

saiga *noun*
• "SYE guh" or "SAY guh"
• a gazelle, *Saiga tatarica*, of the Asian steppes, distinguished by an inflated snout.
• [Russian]

sailer *noun*
• "SAILER"
• a sailing vessel, esp. one that sails in a specified way.
• [Old English *segel* sail]
HOMOPHONES: *sailor*

sailor *noun*
• "SAILER"
• a member of a ship's crew, esp. one below the rank of officer.
• [as SAILER]
• **sailorly** *adjective*
HOMOPHONES: *sailer*

sainfoin *noun*
• "SANE foin" or "SAN foin"
• a leguminous plant, *Onobrychis viciifolia*, grown for fodder and having pink flowers.
• [obsolete French *saintfoin* from modern Latin *sanum foenum* wholesome hay (because of its medicinal properties)]

saintpaulia *noun*
• "s'nt POLLY uh"
• any plant of the genus *Saintpaulia*, esp. the African violet.
• [Baron W. von *Saint Paul*, German soldier d.1910, its discoverer]

sake *noun*
ALSO SPELLED: **saki**
• "SACKY" or "SOCKY"
• a Japanese alcoholic drink made from fermented rice.
• [Japanese]
HOMOPHONES: *saki*

saker *noun*
• "SAY kur"
• a large falcon, *Falco cherrug*, used in hawking, esp. the larger female bird.
• [Old French *sacre* from Arabic *ṣaḳr*]

saki *noun*
• "SOCKY"
• any monkey of the genus *Pithecia* or *Chiropotes*, native to S America, having coarse fur and a long non-prehensile tail.
• [French from Tupi *çahy*]
HOMOPHONES: *sake*

Sakta *noun*
• "SHOCK tuh"
• a member of a Hindu sect worshipping the Sakti.
• [Sanskrit *śākta* relating to power or to the SAKTI]

Sakti *noun*
ALSO SPELLED: **Shakti**
• "SHACK tee"
• (in Hinduism) the female principle, esp. when personified as the wife of a god.
• [Sanskrit *śakti* power, divine energy]
• **Saktism** *noun* (also **Shaktism**)

salaam *noun*
• "suh LOM"
• (in Muslim countries and India) the salutation 'Peace'.
• [Arabic *salām*]

salacious *adjective*
• "suh LAY sh'ss"
• lustful; lecherous.
• [Latin *salax salacis* from *salire* leap]
• **salaciously** *adverb*
• **salaciousness** *noun*

salal *noun*
• "suh LAL"
• a shrub of western N America, *Gaultheria shallon*, with racemes of pink or white flowers and edible purple-black berries.
• [Chinook Jargon *sallal*]

salamander *noun*
• "SAL a mander"
• any tailed scaleless newt-like amphibian of the order Caudata.
• [ultimately from Greek *salamandra*]
• **salamandrine** *adjective* "sal a MAN drin"

salami *noun*
• "suh LOMMY"
• a highly-seasoned dried sausage often flavoured with garlic.
• [Italian, pl. of *salame*, from Late Latin *salare* (unrecorded) to salt]

salary *noun*
• "SAL a ree"
• a fixed regular payment made by an employer to an employee, esp. payment made for professional or non-manual work, usu. expressed as an annual sum.
• [Anglo-French *salarie*, Old French *salaire* from Latin *salarium* originally soldier's salt-money, from *sal* salt]

salaryman *noun*
• "SAL a ree m'n"
• (in Japan) a white-collar worker.
• [Japanese, from SALARY]

salbutamol *noun*
• "sal BYOOTA maul"
• a drug used esp. as a bronchodilator to treat asthma.
• [from SALICYLIC + BUTYL + AMINE + ALCOHOL]

Salchow *noun*
- "SOW cow" ("SOW" rhymes with *COW*)
- a figure-skating jump from the backward inside edge of one skate to the backward outside edge of the other, with a full turn in the air.
- [U. *Salchow*, Swedish skater d.1949]

salep *noun*
- "SAL up"
- a starchy preparation of the dried tubers of various orchids, used in cookery and formerly medicinally.
- [French from Turkish *sālep* from Arabic (*kuṣa-'l-*) *ta'lab* fox, fox's testicles]

Salesian *noun*
- "suh LEE zh'n"
- a member of an educational religious society within the Roman Catholic Church, founded in Italy by St. John Bosco in 1859.
- [St. François de *Sales*, French bishop d.1622]

Salian *adjective*
- "SAILY 'n"
- of or relating to the Salii, a 4th-c. Frankish people living near the Ijssel River in what is now the Netherlands, from which the Merovingians were descended.
- [Late Latin *Salii*]

Salic *adjective*
- "SAL ick" or "SAY lick"
- = SALIAN.
- [French *Salique* or medieval Latin *Salicus* from *Salii* (as SALIAN)]

salicin *noun*
- "SAL a sin"
- a bitter crystalline glucoside with analgesic properties, found in willow bark.
- [French *salicine* from Latin *salix -icis* willow]

salicional *noun*
- "suh LISHA n'll"
- an organ stop with a soft reedy tone like that of a willow pipe.
- [German from Latin *salix* willow]

salicylate *noun*
- "suh LISS'll ate"
- a salt or ester of salicylic acid.
- [as SALICYLIC]

salicylic *adjective*
- "salla SILLIC"
- designating a bitter chemical used as a fungicide and in the production of acetylsalicylic acid and dyestuffs.
- [*salicyl* its radical, from French *salicyle* (as SALICIN)]

salient *adjective*
- "SAY lee 'nt"
- most important or notable.
- [Latin *salire* leap]
- **salience** *noun*
- **saliency** *noun*
- **saliently** *adverb*

saliferous *adjective*
- "suh LIFFER us"
- (of rock etc.) containing much salt.
- [Latin *sal* salt + *-fer* producing, from *ferre* bear]

salina *noun*
- "suh LIE nuh"
- a salt lake.
- [Spanish from medieval Latin, = salt pit (as SALINE)]

saline *adjective*
- "SAY leen"
- (of natural waters, springs, etc.) impregnated with or containing salt or salts.
- [Middle English from Latin *sal* salt]
- **salinity** *noun* "suh LINNA tee"
- **salinization** *noun* (also esp. *Brit.* **-isation**)
- **salinometer** *noun* "sal a NOMMA tur"

Salish *noun*
- "SAL ish" or "SAY lish"
- a member of an Aboriginal people inhabiting lower Vancouver Island and the mainland north of Vancouver and around the Fraser River delta.
- [Sne Nay Muxw *sé'liš* Flatheads]

Salishan *noun*
- "SAL ish 'n" or "SAY lish 'n"
- an Aboriginal language group of the west coast of N America, including Comox, Halkomelem, Lillooet, Nuxalk, Okanagan, Sechelt, Shuswap, Squamish Straits and Nlaka'pamux.
- [as SALISH]

saliva *noun*
- "suh LIE vuh"
- liquid secreted into the mouth by glands to provide moisture and facilitate chewing and swallowing; spittle.
- [Middle English from Latin]
- **salivary** *adjective* "SAL a verry"

salivate *verb*
- "SAL a vate"
- secrete or discharge saliva esp. in excess or in greedy anticipation.
- [as SALIVA]
- **salivation** *noun*

sallet *noun*
- "SAL it"
- a light helmet with an outward-curving rear part, worn as part of medieval armour.
- [French *salade*, ultimately from Latin *caelare* engrave, from *caelum* chisel]

salmagundi *noun*
- "sal muh GUNDY"
- a dish of chopped meat, anchovies, eggs, onions, etc., and seasoning.
- [French *salmigondis* game stew, from *sel* salt + *condir* seasoning]

salmanazar *noun*
- "sal muh NAY zur"

• a wine bottle of about 12 times the standard size.
• [*Shalmaneser* king of Assyria (2 Kings 17–18)]

salmi *noun*
• "SAWL mee"
• a ragout or casserole made esp. of partly roasted game birds stewed in a rich sauce made with wine and the cooking juices.
• [French, abbreviation formed as SALMAGUNDI]

salmon *noun*
• "SAM'n"
• a migratory fish of the family Salmonidae, esp. of the genus *Salmo*, much prized for its pink flesh.
• [Old French *saumon* from Latin *salmo -onis*]

salmonberry *noun*
• "SAM'n berry"
• any of several pink- or orange-fruited N American brambles, esp. the pink-flowered *Rubus spectabilis* of the west coast.
• [as SALMON + 'berry']

salmonella *noun*
• "salma NELLA"
• a bacterium of the genus *Salmonella* comprising pathogenic rod-shaped forms, some of which cause food poisoning, typhoid, and paratyphoid in people and various diseases in animals.
• [modern Latin from D. E. *Salmon*, US veterinary surgeon d.1914]

salmonellosis *noun*
• "salma nell OH sis"
• infection with, or a disease caused by, salmonellae.
• [as SALMONELLA]

salmonid *adjective*
• "SALMA nid"
• of or relating to the family Salmonidae, which includes salmon and trout.
• [as SALMON]

salmonoid *noun*
• "SAMMA noid"
• a fish of the family Salmonidae or the superfamily Salmonoidea.
• [as SALMON]

salopettes *plural noun*
• "sal a PETS"
• weather-resistant pants with a high waist and shoulder straps, worn esp. for skiing.
• [French *salopette*, = 'bib overalls' + *-s* by analogy with *trousers* etc.]

Salopian *noun*
• "suh LO pee 'n"
• a native or inhabitant of Shropshire, England.
• [Anglo-French *Salopesberia* from Middle English from Old English *Scrobbesbyrig* Shrewsbury, in Shropshire]

salpicon *noun*
• "SAL pick on"
• a mixture of finely chopped meat, fish, vegetables, or eggs bound together in a thick sauce and used for fillings and stuffings.
• [French, from Spanish *salpicar* sprinkle (with salt)]

salpiglossis *noun*
• "sal puh GLOSS iss"
• any solanaceous plant of the genus *Salpiglossis*, cultivated for its funnel-shaped flowers.
• [modern Latin, from Greek *salpigx* trumpet + *glōssa* tongue]

salpingectomy *noun*
• "sal p'n JECT a mee"
• the surgical removal of the Fallopian tube or tubes, esp. to remove a cyst or tumour or to sterilize.
• [Latin *salpinx* Fallopian tubes, from Greek *salpigx salpiggos*, lit. 'trumpet' + Greek *ektomē* excision, from *ek* out + *temnō* cut]

salpingitis *noun*
• "sal p'n JITE iss"
• inflammation of the Fallopian tube or tubes caused by bacterial infection.
• [Latin *salpinx* Fallopian tubes, from Greek *salpigx salpiggos*, lit. 'trumpet' + Greek *-itis*, forming feminine of adjectives in *-itēs* (with *nosos* 'disease' implied)]

salsa *noun*
• "SAWL suh" or "SAL suh"
• a Latin American spicy sauce made with tomatoes or fruit and chilies etc. and used usu. as a dip or garnish.
• [Spanish from Latin *salsus* from *salere sals-* to salt, from *sal* salt]

salsify *noun*
• "SAL suh fee"
• a plant of the genus *Tragopogon*, esp. *T. porrifolius*, with long, thin, white-fleshed cylindrical roots.
• [French *salsifis* from obsolete Italian *salsefica*, of unknown origin]

saltcellar *noun*
• "SALT seller"
• a small container for holding salt.
• ['salt' from Old English *s(e)alt s(e)altan* + obsolete *saler* from Anglo-French from Old French *salier* salt box, from Latin (as SALARY), assimilated to CELLAR]

saltie *noun*
• "SAWL tee"
• an ocean-going ship.
• [from 'salt' from Old English *s(e)alt s(e)altan*]
HOMOPHONES: *salty*

saltigrade *adjective*
• "SAL tuh grade"
• (of arthropods) moving by leaping or jumping.
• [modern Latin *Saltigradae* from Latin *saltus* leap, from *salire salt-* + *-gradus* walking]

saltimbocca *noun*
• "sal tim BOCKA"
• an Italian dish consisting of thin pieces of veal, each individually wrapped around a slice of prosciutto and a sage leaf and braised in wine.
• [Italian, from *saltare* to leap + *in* into + *bocca* mouth]

saltine *noun*
• "sawl TEEN"
• a salted cracker.
• [from 'salt' from Old English *s(e)alt s(e)altan*]

saltire *noun*
• "SAWL tire"
• an X-shaped cross.
• [Old French *sau(l)toir* etc. stirrup cord, stile, saltire, from medieval Latin *saltatorium* from *saltare* frequentative of *salire salt-* leap]

saltwort *noun*
• "SALT wurt" or "SALT wort"
• any of various plants which tolerate saline conditions, esp. of the genus *Salsola*.
• ['salt' + WORT]

salubrious *adjective*
• "suh LOO bree us"
• conducive or favourable to good health; healthy.
• [Latin *salubris* from *salus* health]
• **salubriously** *adverb*
• **salubriousness** *noun*
• **salubrity** *noun*

Saluki *noun*
• "suh LOO kee"
• a breed of tall swift slender dog having a fringed tail and feet, large ears, and a silky coat.
• [Arabic *salūḳī*, from *Salūk* a town in Arabia]

salutary *adjective*
• "SAL yoo terry"
• producing good effects; beneficial.
• [French *salutaire* or Latin *salutaris* from *salus -utis* health]

salutation *noun*
• "sal yoo TAY sh'n"
• a sign or expression of greeting or recognition of another's arrival or departure.
• [Old French *salutacion* from Latin *salutationem* from *salutare* salute, from *salus -utis* health]
• **salutatory** *adjective* "suh LOO tuh tory"

Salvadoran *adjective*
• "salva DORE 'n"
• of or relating to El Salvador in Central America.

salvage *verb*
• "SAL vidge"
• save or recover (materials) from a shipwreck, fire, etc.
• [French from medieval Latin *salvagium* from Latin *salvare* save]
• **salvageable** *adjective*
• **salvager** *noun*

salvation *noun*
• "sal VAY sh'n"
• the act of saving or being saved.
• [Old French *sauvacion, salvacion*, from Church Latin *salvatio -onis* from *salvare* save]

salvationism *noun*
• "sal VAY sh'n izm"
• the principles or methods of the Salvation Army, an international evangelical organization with a military structure founded by William Booth in 1865 for the revival of Christianity and assistance to the poor and homeless.
• [as SALVATION]
• **salvationist** *noun*

salver *noun*
• "SAL vur"
• a tray usu. of silver or other metal, on which drinks, letters, etc. are presented.
• [French *salve* tray for presenting food to the king, from Spanish *salva* testing of food, from *salvar* save: assoc. with *platter*]
HOMOPHONES: *salvor*

salvia *noun*
• "SAL vee uh"
• any plant of the genus *Salvia* of the mint family, esp. *S. splendens* with red or blue flowers.
• [Latin, = 'sage' (the herb)]

salvific *adjective*
• "sal VIFFIC"
• causing or able to cause salvation.
• [Latin *salvificus* saving]

salvo *noun*
• "SAL vo"
• the simultaneous or concentrated discharge of artillery or other weapons in battle or as a salute.
• [earlier *salve* from French from Italian *salva* SALUTATION]

salvor *noun*
• "SAL vur"
• a person engaged in, assisting in, or attempting salvage.
• [as SALVAGE]
HOMOPHONES: *salver*

samadhi *noun*
• "suh MADDY"
• a state of concentration induced by meditation.
• [Sanskrit *samādhi* contemplation]

samara *noun*
• "SAMMER uh" or "suh MAR uh"
• a dry fruit in which the pericarp is extended to form a wing, as in the elm, ash, maple, sycamore, etc.
• [modern Latin from Latin, = elm seed]

Samaritan *noun*
• "suh MARE a t'n"
• a charitable or helpful person.
• [Late Latin *Samaritanus* from Greek *Samareitēs*

from *Samareia* Samaria (with reference to Luke 10:33 etc.)]
• **Samaritanism** *noun*

samarium *noun*
• "suh MERRY um"
• a soft silvery metallic element of the lanthanide series, occurring naturally in monazite etc. and used in making ferromagnetic alloys.
• [*samarskite* the mineral in which its spectrum was first observed, from *Samarski* name of a 19th-c. Russian official]

sambal *noun*
• "SAM bull"
• (in Malayan and Indonesian cooking) a hot mixture of chilies, onions, and spices, used as a relish with other foods.
• [Malay]

sambuca *noun*
• "sam BOO kuh"
• an Italian aniseed-flavoured liqueur traditionally served aflame with a coffee bean floating on top.
• [Latin *sambucus* elder tree]

samfu *noun*
• "SAM foo"
• a casual outfit consisting of a jacket and pants, worn by Chinese women and sometimes men.
• [Cantonese]

Samhain *noun*
• "SOW in" or "SOWN" ("SOW" rhymes with *HOW*)
• (in Britain) a Celtic festival marking the beginning of winter, celebrated on 1 Nov.
• [Irish *Samhain*]

Sami *plural noun*
• "SOMMY"
• the Lapps collectively.
• [Lappish (earlier *Sabme, Samek*), ultimate origin unknown]

Samian *noun*
• "SAY mee 'n"
• a native or inhabitant of the Greek island of Samos.

Samiel *noun*
• "SAMMY 'll"
• a hot dry dust-laden wind blowing at intervals esp. in the Arabian desert; a simoom.
• [Turkish *samyeli* hot wind, from Arabic *samm* poison + Turkish *yel* wind]

samite *noun*
• "SAM ite" or "SAME ite"
• a rich medieval dress fabric of silk occasionally interwoven with gold.
• [Old French *samit* from medieval Latin *examitum* from medieval Greek *hexamiton* from Greek *hexa-* six + *mitos* thread]

samizdat *noun*
• "SAM iz dat"
• a system of clandestine publication of banned literature in the USSR.
• [Russian, = self-publishing house]

Samnite *noun*
• "SAM nite"
• a member of a people of ancient Italy often at war with republican Rome.
• [Latin *Samnites* (pl.), related to *Sabinus* SABINE]

Samoan *noun*
• "suh MOE 'n"
• a native or inhabitant of Samoa in Polynesia.

samosa *noun*
• "suh MOE suh"
• an Indian snack consisting of a triangular pastry stuffed with a spicy mixture of diced vegetables or meat, fried in ghee or oil.
• [Persian and Urdu]

samovar *noun*
• "SAMMA var"
• a metal, usu. ornate, Russian urn for making tea, with an internal heating tube to keep water at boiling point.
• [Russian, from *samo-* self + *varit* boil]

Samoyed *noun*
• "SAMMA yed"
• a breed of white dog, once used for working in the Arctic, having a thick shaggy coat, stocky build, pricked ears, and a tail curling over the back.
• [Russian *samoed*]
• **Samoyedic** *adjective*

samphire *noun*
• "SAM fire"
• an umbelliferous maritime rock plant, *Crithmum maritimum*, with aromatic fleshy leaves used as a salad vegetable.
• [earlier *samp(i)ere* from French (*herbe de*) *Saint Pierre* St. Peter('s herb)]

sampladelic *adjective*
• "sam pluh DELLIC"
• denoting a type of dance music that is psychedelic or disorienting in nature and created using samples or other digital technology.
• ['sample' from Anglo-French *assample*, Old French *essample* EXAMPLE + PSYCHEDELIC]

samsara *noun*
• "sum SARR uh"
• the endless cycle of death and rebirth to which life in the material world is bound.
• [Sanskrit *saṃsāra* a wandering through]

samskara *noun*
• "sum SCAR uh"
• a purificatory ceremony or rite marking an event in one's life.
• [Sanskrit *saṃskāra* a making perfect, preparation]

samurai *noun*
- "SAM a rye"
- in feudal Japan, a member of a military caste, esp. a member of the class of military retainers of the daimyos.
- [Japanese]

San *noun*
- "SAWN"
- a member of the aboriginal Bushmen of southern Africa.
- [Nama]

sanatorium *noun*
- "sanna TORY um"
- an establishment for the medical treatment and recuperation of convalescents and those suffering chronic mental or physical disorders, tuberculosis, etc.
- [modern Latin from Latin *sanare* cure]

Sancerre *noun*
- "son SAIR"
- a light white (occasionally red) wine, produced in the area around Sancerre, in central France.

sanctify *verb*
- "SANKTA fie"
- consecrate; make holy.
- [Old French *saintifier* from Church Latin *sanctificare* from Latin *sanctus* holy]
- **sanctification** *noun*

sanctimonious *adjective*
- "sankta MOANY us"
- affecting or pretending piety, sanctity, or holiness.
- [Latin *sanctimonia* sanctity, from *sanctus* holy]
- **sanctimoniously** *adverb*
- **sanctimoniousness** *noun*
- **sanctimony** *noun* "SANKTA moany"

sanction *noun*
- "SANK sh'n"
- approval, permission, or encouragement granted for a particular action.
- [French from Latin *sanctio -onis* from *sancire sanct-* make sacred]

sanctity *noun*
- "SANKTA tee"
- holiness of life; saintliness.
- [Old French *sain(c)tité* or Latin *sanctitas*, from *sanctus* holy]

sanctuary *noun*
- "SANK choo airy"
- a holy place such as a church or temple etc.
- [Anglo-French *sanctuarie* from Latin *sanctuarium*, from *sanctus* holy]

sanctum *noun*
- "SANK tum"
- a holy place.
- [Latin, neuter of *sanctus* holy, past participle of *sancire* consecrate]

Sanctus *noun*
- "SANK tuss" or "SONK tuss"
- the prayer beginning 'Holy, holy, holy' said or sung at the end of the Eucharistic preface in some Christian liturgies.
- [Latin, = holy]

sandal *noun*
- "SAND'll"
- a light open shoe consisting of a sole attaching to the foot with light straps, worn esp. in warm weather.
- [Latin *sandalium* from Greek *sandalion* diminutive of *sandalon* wooden shoe, prob. of Asiatic origin]
- **sandalled** *adjective* (also esp. *US* **sandaled**)

sandalfoot *noun*
- "SAND'll foot"
- designating pantyhose etc. that do not have visibly reinforced toes or heels and which are suitable for wearing with sandals and open-toed shoes.
- [SANDAL + 'foot']

sandalwood *noun*
- "SAND'll wood"
- the scented wood of any of several trees of the genus *Santalum*, esp. the white sandalwood, *Santalum album*, of India, used esp. in carving and incense.
- [SANDAL + 'wood']

sandarac *noun*
ALSO SPELLED: **sandarach**
- "SAND a rack"
- the gummy resin of a North African conifer, *Tetraclinis articulata*, used in making varnish.
- [Latin *sandaraca* from Greek *sandarakē*, of Asiatic origin]

sandhi *noun*
- "SANDY"
- the process whereby the form or sound of a word changes as a result of its position in a phrase, e.g. the change from *a* to *an* before a vowel.
- [Sanskrit *saṃdhi* putting together]

HOMOPHONES: *sandy*

Sandinista *noun*
- "sanda NEECE tuh" or "sanda NISS tuh"
- a member of a revolutionary Nicaraguan guerrilla organization founded by Sandíno.
- [Augusto César *Sandíno*, Nicaraguan revolutionary leader d.1934]

sandwich *noun*
- "SAND witch" or "SAN witch" or "SAM witch"
- two or more slices of usu. buttered bread with a filling of meat, cheese, etc. between them.
- [4th Earl of *Sandwich*, English nobleman d.1792, said to have eaten food in this form so as not to leave the gaming table]

sandwort *noun*
- "SAND wurt" or "SAND wort"

• any low-growing plant of the genus *Arenaria*, usu. bearing small white flowers.
• ['sand' + WORT]

sangar *noun*
• "SANG gur"
• a stone breastwork or parapet around a hollow; a fortified lookout.
• [Persian & Pashto, prob. from Persian *sang* stone]

sangha *noun*
• "SONG uh"
• the Buddhist monastic order, including monks, nuns, and novices.
• [Hindi *saṅgha* from Sanskrit *saṃgha* community, from *sam* together + *han* come in contact]

sangiovese *noun*
• "san joe VAY zay"
• a vine yielding a black grape used in making Chianti and other Italian red wines.
• [Italian]

Sango *noun*
• "SANG go"
• a dialect of Ngbandi.
• [Ngbandi]

sangria *noun*
• "sang GREE uh"
• a drink of red wine with water, sugar, fruit juice, sliced citrus fruit, and usu. soda water.
• [Spanish, = bleeding, from Latin *sanguis -inis* blood]

sanguinary *adjective*
• "SANG gwin airy"
• characterized or accompanied by bloodshed; bloody.
• [Latin *sanguinarius* from *sanguis -inis* blood]

sanguine *adjective*
• "SANG gwin"
• optimistic; confident.
• [Old French *sanguin -ine* blood-red, from Latin *sanguineus* (as SANGUINARY)]
• **sanguinely** *adverb*

Sanhedrin *noun*
• "san HED rin"
• the highest court of justice and the supreme council in ancient Jerusalem with 71 members.
• [late Hebrew *sanhedrîn* from Greek *sunedrion* (*sun* with, *hedra* base)]

sanitarian *noun*
• "sanna TERRY 'n"
• a person who studies sanitation or is in favour of sanitary reform.
• [as SANITARY]

sanitarium *noun*
• "sanna TERRY um"
• = SANATORIUM.
• [pseudo-Latin from Latin *sanitas* health]

sanitary *adjective*
• "SANNA terry"
• of or pertaining to the conditions affecting health, the promotion of good health, or protection against infection.
• [French *sanitaire* from Latin *sanitas* health]
• **sanitarily** *adverb*

sanitation *noun*
• "sanna TAY sh'n"
• systems designed to protect or promote health.
• [as SANITARY]

sanitize *verb*
ALSO SPELLED: esp. *Brit.* **-ise**
• "SANNA tize"
• make (something) hygienic or thoroughly free from germs; sterilize, disinfect.
• [as SANITARY]
• **sanitization** *noun* (also esp. *Brit.* **-isation**)
• **sanitizer** *noun* (also esp. *Brit.* **-iser**)

sanity *noun*
• "SANNA tee"
• the state of being sane.
• [Latin *sanitas* from *sanus* healthy]

sannyasi *noun*
ALSO SPELLED: **sanyasi**
• "sun YASSY"
• a wandering Hindu fakir; a religious mendicant.
• [Hindi & Urdu *sannyāsī* from Sanskrit *saṃnyāsin* laying aside, from *saṃ* together, *ni* down, *as* throw]

sans *preposition*
• "SONZ" or "SÃH" (with a nasal *AH*)
• without.
• [Old French *san(z)*, *sen(s)*, ultimately from Latin *sine*, influenced by *absentia* in the absence of]

Sansei *noun*
• "SAN say"
• a N American whose grandparents were immigrants from Japan.
• [Japanese, from *san* three + *sei* generation]

sanseveria *noun*
ALSO SPELLED: **sansevieria**
• "san suh VEERY uh"
• any of various tropical African and Asian plants constituting the genus *Sansevieria*, of the agave family, having stiff erect leaves yielding a tough fibre and which include the houseplant mother-in-law's tongue, *S. trifasciata*.
• [modern Latin, from Raimondo di Sangro, Prince of *Sanseviero* in Italy d.1771]

Sanskrit *noun*
• "SAN scrit"
• the ancient Indo-Aryan language of the Indian subcontinent, the principal language of religious writings and scholarship, the source of some of the modern languages of the area (such

as Hindi, Bengali, etc.), and now also one of the languages recognized for official use in India.
• [Sanskrit *saṃskṛta* composed, elaborated, from *saṃ* together, *kṛ* make, *-ta* past participle ending]
• **Sanskritic** *adjective* "san SCRITTIC"
• **Sanskritist** *noun*

Santee *noun*
• "san TEE"
• a member of a Dakota group originally inhabiting Minnesota, now also living in Manitoba and Saskatchewan.
• [Dakota *Is(y)ati*, said to refer to a former residence at Knife Lake, Minnesota]

Santeria *noun*
• "santa REE uh"
• an Afro-Cuban religion that combines elements of Catholicism with the worship of Yoruba deities.
• [Spanish, lit. 'holiness, sanctity']

santero *noun*
• "san TARE oh"
• a priest of Santeria.
• [Spanish]

santim *noun*
• "SAN teem"
• a monetary unit of Latvia, equal to one-hundredth of a lat.
• [Latvian *santims*, from French *centime* + Latvian masculine ending *-s*]

santolina *noun*
• "santa LEE nuh"
• any aromatic shrub of the genus *Santolina*, with finely divided leaves and small usu. yellow flowers.
• [modern Latin, var. of SANTONICA]

santonica *noun*
• "san TAWNA kuh"
• a shrubby wormwood plant, *Artemisia cina*, yielding santonin.
• [Latin from *Santones* a tribe living in SW Gaul]

santonin *noun*
• "SANTA nin"
• a toxic drug extracted from santonica and other plants of the genus *Artemisia*, used as an anti-parasitic agent.
• [as SANTONICA]

sapele *noun*
• "suh PEE lee"
• any of several large West African hardwood trees of the genus *Entandrophragma*.
• [West African name]

sapid *adjective*
• "SAPPID"
• having (esp. an agreeable) flavour; savoury; palatable; not insipid.
• [Latin *sapidus* from *sapere* taste]

sapient *adjective*
• "SAY pee 'nt"
• wise, or attempting to appear wise.
• [Old French *sapient* or Latin participle stem of *sapere* be wise]
• **sapience** *noun*

sapodilla *noun*
• "sappa DILLA"
• a large tropical American evergreen tree, *Manilkara zapota*, with edible fruit and durable wood, and sap from which chicle is obtained.
• [Spanish *zapotillo* diminutive of *zapote* from Aztec *tzápotl*]

saponify *verb*
• "suh PONNA fie"
• turn (fat or oil) into soap by reaction with an alkali.
• [French *saponifier* from Latin *sapo -onis* soap]
• **saponification** *noun*

saponin *noun*
• "SAPPA nin"
• any of a group of plant glycosides, esp. those derived from the bark of the tree *Quillaja saponaria*, that foam when shaken with water and are used in detergents and fire extinguishers.
• [French *saponine* from Latin *sapo -onis* soap]

sappanwood *noun*
• "SAP'n wood"
• the heartwood of an E Indian tree, *Caesalpinia sappan*, formerly used as a source of red dye.
• [Dutch *sapan* from Malay *sapang*, of S Indian origin]

Sapphic *adjective*
• "SAFFIC"
• of or relating to the Greek poet Sappho (7th c. BC) or her lyric poetry.

sapphire *noun*
• "SAFF ire"
• a transparent blue precious stone consisting of corundum.
• [Old French *safir* from Latin *sapphirus* from Greek *sappheiros* prob. = lapis lazuli]
• **sapphirine** *adjective* "SAFFA rine"

saprogenic *adjective*
• "sapra JENNIC"
• causing or produced by putrefaction.
• [Greek *sapros* putrid + GENESIS]

saprophagous *adjective*
• "suh PROFFA guss"
• feeding on decaying matter.
• [Greek *sapros* putrid + *phagō* eat]

saprophyte *noun*
• "SAPRA fite"
• any plant or micro-organism living on dead or decayed organic matter.
• [Greek *sapros* putrid + *phuton* plant, from *phuō* come into being]
• **saprophytic** *adjective* "sapra FITTIC"

saraband *noun*
ALSO SPELLED: **sarabande**
• "SERRA band"
• a stately Spanish dance of the 17th and 18th c.
• [French *sarabande* from Spanish & Italian *zarabanda*]

Saracen *noun*
• "SERRA s'n"
• an Arab or Muslim at the time of the Crusades.
• [Old French *sarrazin, sarracin* from Late Latin *Saracenus* from late Greek *Sarakēnos* perhaps from Arabic *šarķī* eastern]
• **Saracenic** *adjective* "serra SENNIC"

sarangi *noun*
• "suh RANG gee" (with "G" as in *GIVE*)
• an Indian stringed instrument played with a bow.
• [Hindi *sāraṅgī*]

sarcasm *noun*
• "SAR cazm"
• the use of bitter or wounding, esp. ironic, remarks; language consisting of such remarks.
• [French *sarcasme* or Late Latin *sarcasmus* from late Greek *sarkasmos*, from Greek *sarkazō* tear flesh, in late Greek 'gnash the teeth, speak bitterly', from *sarx sarkos* flesh]
• **sarcastic** *adjective* "sar CASS tick"
• **sarcastically** *adverb*

Sarcee *noun*
• "SAR see" or "sar SEE"
• a member of a small Aboriginal group living on the Bow River near Calgary, the only Athapaskan people living within the Plains area.
• [Blackfoot *saaxsiiwa*]

sarcoma *noun*
• "sar CO muh"
• a malignant tumour of connective or other non-epithelial tissue.
• [modern Latin from Greek *sarkōma* from *sarkoō* become fleshy, from *sarx sarkos* flesh]
• **sarcomatosis** *noun*
• **sarcomatous** *adjective*

sarcophagus *noun*
• "sar COFFA guss"
• a stone coffin, esp. one adorned with a sculpture or inscription.
• [Latin from Greek *sarkophagos* flesh-consuming (as SARCOMA, *-phagos* -eating)]

sarcoplasm *noun*
• "SARKA plazm"
• the cytoplasm in which muscle fibrils are embedded.
• [Greek *sarx sarkos* flesh + PLASMA]

sardine *noun*
• "sar DEEN"
• any of various fish of the herring family.
• [Old French *sardine* = Italian *sardina* from Latin from *sarda* from Greek, perhaps from *Sardō* Sardinia]

Sardinian *noun*
• "sar DINNY 'n"
• a native or inhabitant of the Italian island of Sardinia.

sardonic *adjective*
• "sar DONNIC"
• (of laughter, a person's character, etc.) bitterly mocking or cynical.
• [French *sardonique* from Latin *sardonius* from Greek *sardonios* of Sardinia, alteration of *sardanios* Homeric epithet of bitter or scornful laughter]
• **sardonically** *adverb*
• **sardonicism** *noun* "sar DONNA sizm"

sardonyx *noun*
• "SAR don ix"
• onyx in which white layers alternate with sard.
• [Latin from Greek *sardonux* (prob. from Greek *sardios* a yellow or orange-red carnelian, prob. from *Sardō* Sardinia + ONYX)]

sargasso *noun*
• "sar GASSO"
• any seaweed of the genus *Sargassum*, with berry-like air vessels, found floating in island-like masses, esp. in the Sargasso Sea.
• [Portuguese *sargaço*, of unknown origin]

sari *noun*
ALSO SPELLED: **saree**
• "SAR ee"
• a length of cotton or silk draped around the body, traditionally worn as a main garment by Indian women.
• [Hindi *sāṛ(h)ī*]

sarin *noun*
• "SAR in"
• an organic phosphorus compound used as a nerve gas.
• [German]

Sarmatian *adjective*
• "sar MAY sh'n"
• of or relating to ancient Sarmatia in E Europe.

sarmentose *adjective*
• "SAR m'n tose" (rhymes with *GROSS*)
• having long thin trailing shoots.
• [Latin *sarmentosus* from *sarmenta* (pl.) twigs, brushwood, from *sarpere* to prune]

Sarnian *noun*
• "SARNY 'n"
• a resident of Sarnia, Ont.

sarnie *noun*
• "SARNY"
• a sandwich.
• [prob. representing a slang or dialect pronunciation of the first element of SANDWICH]

sarod *noun*
• "suh ROAD"
• a stringed musical instrument of India, played with a bow.
• [Urdu, from Persian *surod* song, melody]

sarong *noun*
• "suh RONG"
• a Malay and Javanese garment, worn by both sexes, consisting of a long strip of (often striped) cloth worn tucked around the waist or under the armpits.
• [Malay, lit. 'sheath']

saros *noun*
• "SAR oss"
• a period of about 18 years between repetitions of eclipses.
• [Greek from Babylonian *šār(u)* 3,600 (years)]

sarsaparilla *noun*
• "saspa RILLA"
• a preparation of the dried roots of various plants of the genus *Smilax*, used to flavour some drinks and medicines and formerly as a tonic.
• [Spanish *zarzaparilla* from *zarza* bramble, prob. + diminutive of *parra* vine]

sarsen *noun*
• "SAR s'n"
• a sandstone boulder carried by ice during a glacial period.
• [prob. var. of SARACEN]

sartorial *adjective*
• "sar TORY 'll"
• of or relating to clothes or clothing.
• [Latin *sartor* tailor, from *sarcire sart-* patch]
• **sartorially** *adverb*

sartorius *noun*
• "sar TORY us"
• the long narrow muscle running across the front of each thigh.
• [modern Latin from Latin *sartor* tailor (the muscle being used in adopting a tailor's cross-legged posture)]

sashimi *noun*
• "sa SHEE mee"
• a Japanese dish of garnished raw fish in thin slices.
• [Japanese, from *sashi* pierce + *mi* flesh]

Saskatchewanian *noun*
• "suh scatch a WONNY 'n"
• a resident of Saskatchewan.

Saskatonian *noun*
• "saska TONY in"
• a resident of Saskatoon.

saskatoon *noun*
• "saska TOON"
• *Cdn* (*Prairies*) a shrub, *Amelanchier alnifolia*, of western N America, bearing berries.
• [Cree *misa:skwato:min*, from *misa:skwat* saskatoon + *min* berry]

sasquatch *noun*
• "SASK watch"
• a supposed yeti-like animal of northwestern N America.
• [Halkomelem]

sassaby *noun*
• "SASSA bee"
• a southern African antelope, *Damaliscus lunatus*, similar to the hartebeest.
• [Setswana *tsessébe*, *-ábi*]

sassafras *noun*
• "SASSA frass"
• a small tree, *Sassafras albidum*, native to N America, with aromatic leaves and bark.
• [Spanish *sasafrás* or Portuguese *sassafraz*, of unknown origin]

Sassenach *noun*
• "SASSA nack"
• usu. *derogatory* an English person.
• [Gaelic *Sasunnoch*, Irish *Sasanach* from Latin *Saxones* Saxons]

sastrugi *plural noun*
• "sa STROO gee" (with "G" as in *GIVE*)
• wavelike irregularities on the surface of hard polar snow, caused by winds.
• [Russian *zastrugi* small ridges]

satang *noun*
• "sa TANG"
• a monetary unit of Thailand, equal to one-hundredth of a baht.
• [Thai from Pali *sata* hundred]

satanic *adjective*
• "suh TANNIC" or "say TANNIC"
• of, like, or befitting Satan or Satanism.
• [from 'Satan', Hebrew *śāṭān* lit. 'adversary' from *śāṭan* oppose, plot against]
• **satanically** *adverb*

Satanism *noun*
• "SAY tun izm"
• the worship of Satan.
• [as SATANIC]
• **Satanist** *noun*

satay *noun*
ALSO SPELLED: **saté**
• "sa TAY" or "SAT ay"
• an Indonesian and Malaysian dish consisting of small pieces of meat grilled on a skewer and usu. served with spicy peanut sauce.
• [Malayan *satai sate*, Indonesian *sate*]

satchel *noun*
• "SATCH'll"
• a small bag usu. of leather and hung from the shoulder with a strap, for carrying books etc. esp. to and from school.
• [Old French *sachel* from Latin *saccellus* small sack]

sateen *noun*
• "sa TEEN"

• cotton fabric woven like satin with a glossy surface.
• [*satin* after *velveteen*]

satellite *noun*
• "SATTA lite"
• a celestial body orbiting the earth or another planet.
• [French *satellite* or Latin *satelles satellitis* attendant]

satiate *verb*
• "SAY shee ate"
• gratify (desire, or a desirous person) to the full.
• [Latin *satiatus* past participle of *satiare* from *satis* enough]
• **satiation** *noun*

satiety *noun*
• "suh TIE a tee"
• the state of being or feeling satiated.
• [obsolete French *sacieté* from Latin *satietas -tatis* from *satis* enough]

satin *noun*
• "SAT in"
• a fabric of silk or various synthetic fibres, with a glossy surface on one side produced by a twill weave with the weft threads almost hidden.
• [Old French from Arabic *zaytūnī* of *Tsinkiang* in China]
• **satiny** *adjective*

satinwood *noun*
• "SAT in wood"
• a tree, *Chloroxylon swietenia*, native to central and southern India and Ceylon (Sri Lanka).
• [SATIN + 'wood']

satire *noun*
• "SAT ire"
• the use of ridicule, irony, sarcasm, etc., to expose folly or vice or to lampoon an individual.
• [French *satire* or Latin *satira* later form of *satura* medley]
• **satiric** *adjective* "suh TEER ick"
• **satirical** *adjective*
• **satirically** *adverb*
• **satirist** *noun* "SAT ur ist"
• **satirization** *noun* (also esp. *Brit.* **-isation**)
• **satirize** *verb* (also esp. *Brit.* **-ise**)

satisfy *verb*
• "SAT iss fie"
• meet the expectations or desires of; comply with (a demand).
• [Old French *satisfier* from Latin *satisfacere satisfact-* from *satis* enough]
• **satisfaction** *noun*
• **satisfactorily** *adverb*
• **satisfactoriness** *noun*
• **satisfactory** *adjective*
• **satisfiable** *adjective*
• **satisfying** *adjective*
• **satisfyingly** *adverb*

satori *noun*
• "suh TORY"
• sudden enlightenment.
• [Japanese]

satrap *noun*
• "SAT rap"
• a provincial governor in the ancient Persian Empire.
• [Old French *satrape* or Latin *satrapa* from Greek *satrapēs* from Old Persian *xšathra-pāvan* country protector]

satrapy *noun*
• "SATRA pee"
• a province ruled over by a satrap.
• [as SATRAP]

satsang *noun*
• "SAT sang" or "SUT sung"
• a spiritual discourse or sacred gathering.
• [Sanskrit *satsaṅga* association with good men]

satsuma *noun*
• "SAT sum uh" or "sat SOO muh"
• a variety of tangerine originally grown in Japan.
• [*Satsuma*, a former province of Japan]

saturate *verb*
• "SATCHER ate"
• fill with moisture; soak thoroughly.
• [Latin *saturare* from *satur* full]
• **saturable** *adjective*
• **saturated** *adjective*
• **saturation** *noun*

saturnalia *noun*
• "satter NAILY uh"
• the festival of the Roman agriculture god Saturn, characterized by unrestrained merrymaking for all.
• [Latin]

Saturnian *adjective*
• "suh TURNY in"
• of or relating to the planet Saturn.

saturniid *noun*
• "sa TURNY id"
• any large moth of the family Saturniidae of silk moths.
• [modern Latin]

saturnine *adjective*
• "SATTER nine"
• having a sluggish gloomy temperament.
• [Old French *saturnin* from medieval Latin *Saturninus* of Saturn (identified with lead by the alchemists and associated with slowness and gloom by the astrologers)]

satyagraha *noun*
• "sut YOGGRA huh"
• a policy of passive resistance to British rule advocated by Indian nationalist Mahatma Gandhi (d.1948).
• [Sanskrit from *satya* truth + *āgraha* obstinacy]

satyr *noun*
• "SAT ur" or "SATE ur"
• (in Greek mythology) one of a class of Greek woodland gods with a horse's ears and tail, or (in Roman representations) with a goat's ears, tail, legs, and budding horns.
• [Old French *satyre* or Latin *satyrus* from Greek *saturos*]
• **satyric** *adjective*
HOMOPHONES: *Seder*

satyrid *noun*
• "suh TEER id"
• any butterfly of the family Satyridae, with distinctive eyelike markings on the wings.
• [as SATYR]

saucier *noun*
• "SO see ay"
• a chef who prepares sauces.
• [French]

Saudi *noun*
• "SOWDY" or "SODDY" ("SOWDY" rhymes with *HOWDY*)
• a native or national of Saudi Arabia.

sauerbraten *noun*
• "SOUR brot'n"
• a roast of beef marinated in vinegar with peppercorns, onions, and other seasonings before cooking.
• [German, from *sauer* sour + *Braten* roast meat]

sauerkraut *noun*
• "SOUR crout"
• finely chopped pickled cabbage.
• [German from *sauer* sour + *Kraut* vegetable]

sauger *noun*
• "SOGGER"
• a N American fish of the perch family, *Stizoostedion canadense*, with a large mouth.
• [19th c.: origin unknown]

Sauk *noun*
• "SOCK"
• a member of an Algonquian people inhabiting parts of the central US, formerly in Wisconsin, Illinois, and Iowa, now in Oklahoma and Kansas.
• [Canadian French *Saki* from Ojibwa *osākī* (compare Sauk *asākīwa* person of the outlet)]
HOMOPHONES: *sock*

Saulteaux *noun*
ALSO SPELLED: **Salteaux**
• "SO toe"
• a member of an Aboriginal people formerly living on the shore of Lake Superior north of Sault Ste. Marie, and now living esp. in Manitoba.
• [French, = 'people of the rapids' from *sault* rapids]

Saultite *noun*
• "SOO ite"
• a resident of Sault Ste. Marie, Ont.

sauna *noun*
• "SAWNA"
• a special room heated to a high temperature to clean and refresh the body.
• [Finnish]

saunter *verb*
• "SAWN tur"
• walk or go slowly; amble, stroll.
• [Middle English, = muse: origin unknown]
• **saunterer** *noun*

saurian *adjective*
• "SORRY in"
• of or like a lizard.
• [modern Latin *Sauria* from Greek *saura* lizard]

saurischian *adjective*
• "sore ISS kee 'n" or "sore ISHY 'n"
• of or relating to the order Saurischia of dinosaurs with a pelvic structure like that of lizards.
• [modern Latin *Saurischia*, from Greek *sauros* lizard + *iskhion* hip joint]

sauropod *noun*
• "SORRO pod"
• any of a group of plant-eating dinosaurs with a long neck and tail, and four thick limbs.
• [Greek *saura* lizard + *pous pod-* foot]

saury *noun*
• "SORRY"
• any of various elongated marine fishes of the family Scomberescocidae, having narrow beaklike jaws, esp. *Scomberesox saurus* of the N Atlantic and southern hemisphere or *Cololabis saira* of the N Pacific.
• [perhaps from Late Latin from Greek *sauros* horse mackerel]
HOMOPHONES: *sorry*

sausage *noun*
• "SAW sidge"
• minced pork, beef, or other meat seasoned and often mixed with other ingredients, usu. encased in cylindrical form in a skin.
• [Old Northern French *saussiche* from medieval Latin *salsicia* from Latin *salsus* from *salere sals-* to salt, from *sal* salt]

sauté *verb*
• "SAW tay" or "saw TAY" or "so TAY"
• fry (food) quickly in a little hot fat.
• [French, past participle of *sauter* jump]

Sauternes *noun*
• "so TURN"
• a sweet white wine from Sauternes in the Bordeaux region of SW France.

Sauvignon *noun*
• "so veen YÕH" (with a nasal *OH*)
• a variety of white grape used in winemaking.
• [French]

savannah *noun*
ALSO SPELLED: **savanna**
• "suh VANNA"

• a grassy plain in tropical and subtropical regions, with few or no trees.
• [Spanish *zavana* perhaps of Carib origin]

savant *noun*
• "sa VONT" or "sa VÃH" (with a nasal *AH*)
• a learned person, esp. a distinguished scientist etc.
• [French, participle of *savoir* know (as SAPIENT)]

savate *noun*
• "suh VAT"
• a form of boxing in which feet and fists are used.
• [French, originally a kind of shoe: compare SABOT]

saveloy *noun*
• "SAVVA loy"
• a seasoned red pork sausage, dried and smoked, and sold ready to eat.
• [corruption of French *cervelas*, *-at*, from Italian *cervellata* (*cervello* brain)]

savin *noun*
ALSO SPELLED: **savine**
• "SAV in"
• a bushy juniper, *Juniperus sabina*, usu. spreading horizontally, and yielding oil formerly used in the treatment of amenorrhea.
• [Old English from Old French *savine* from Latin *sabina* (*herba*) Sabine (herb)]

savory *noun*
• "SAVER ee"
• any herb of the genus *Satureja*, esp. summer savory, *S. hortensis*, and winter savory, *S. montana*, used esp. in cookery.
• [Middle English *saverey*, perhaps from Old English *sætherie* from Latin *satureia*]
HOMOPHONES: *savoury*

savoury *adjective*
ALSO SPELLED: **savory**
• "SAVER ee"
• having an appetizing taste or smell.
• [Old French *savouré* tasty, fragrant, past participle of *savourer* taste, from Latin *sapor -oris* from *sapere* to taste]
• **savourily** *adverb* (also **savorily**)
• **savouriness** *noun* (also **savorily**)
HOMOPHONES: *savory*

Savoy *noun*
• "SA voy" or "suh VOY"
• a hardy variety of cabbage with wrinkled leaves.
• [*Savoy* in SE France]

Savoyard *noun*
• "suh VOY ard" or "sa voy ARD"
• a native of Savoy in SE France.
• [French from *Savoie* Savoy]

sawyer *noun*
• "SOY ur" or "SAW yur"
• a person who saws timber professionally.
• [Middle English, earlier *sawer*, from 'saw', Old English *saga*]

saxatile *adjective*
• "SAXA tile" or "SAXA till"
• living or growing on or among rocks.
• [French *saxatile* or Latin *saxatilis* from *saxum* rock]

saxifrage *noun*
• "SAXA fraydge" or "SAXA fradge"
• any plant of the genus *Saxifraga*, growing on rocky or stony ground and usu. bearing small white, yellow, or red flowers.
• [Old French *saxifrage* or Late Latin *saxifraga* (*herba*) from Latin *saxum* rock + *frangere* break]

saxophone *noun*
• "SAXA fone"
• a metal woodwind reed instrument in several sizes and registers, the most recognizable form of which has an upturned bell, used esp. in jazz and popular music.
• [*Sax*, name of its Belgian inventors, + Greek *phōnē* sound]
• **saxophonist** *noun*

sayonara *interjection*
• "sye a NAR uh"
• goodbye.
• [Japanese, lit. 'if it be so']

sayyid *noun*
• "SAY id"
• a Muslim claiming descent from Muhammad through Husain, the prophet's elder grandson.
• [Arabic, lit. 'lord, prince']

scabbard *noun*
• "SCAB'rd"
• a sheath for a sword, bayonet, etc.
• [Middle English *sca(u)berc* etc. from Anglo-French prob. from Frankish]

scabies *noun*
• "SKAY beez"
• a contagious skin disease causing severe itching.
• [Latin from *scabere* scratch]

scabious *noun*
• "SKAY bee us"
• any of various plants with pink, white or esp. blue pincushion-shaped flowers, esp. of the genus *Scabiosa* or *Knautia*.
• [medieval Latin *scabiosa* (*herba*) formerly regarded as a cure for skin disease: see SCABIES]

scabrous *adjective*
• "SKAB russ"
• having a rough surface; bearing short stiff hairs, scales, etc.
• [French *scabreux* or Late Latin *scabrosus* from Latin *scaber* rough]
• **scabrously** *adverb*
• **scabrousness** *noun*

scad *noun*
• "SKAD"
• any of numerous fish of the family

Carangidae, usu. having an elongated body and very large spiky scales.
• [17th c.: origin unknown]

scads *plural noun*
• "SKADZ"
• large quantities.
• [19th c.: origin unknown]

scaffold *noun*
• "SKAFF old" or "SKAFF 'ld"
• a raised wooden platform used for the execution of criminals.
• [Anglo-French from Old French *(e)schaffaut*, earlier *escadafaut*]
• **scaffolder** *noun*

scaffolding *noun*
• "SKAFF old ing" or "SKAFFLE ding"
• a temporary structure formed of poles, planks, etc., erected by workers and used by them while building or repairing a house etc.
• [as SCAFFOLD]

scagliola *noun*
• "skal YO luh"
• imitation stone or plaster mixed with glue.
• [Italian *scagliuola* diminutive of *scaglia* scale, from Germanic]

scalable *adjective*
• "SCALE a bull"
• capable of being scaled or climbed.
• [Old French *escaler* or medieval Latin *scalare* from Latin *scala* from *scandere* climb]
• **scalability** *noun*

scalar *adjective*
• "SKAY lur"
• (of a quantity) having only magnitude, not direction.
• [Latin *scalaris* from *scala* ladder; see SCALABLE]
HOMOPHONES: *scaler*

scald *verb*
• "SKAWLD"
• burn (the skin etc.) with hot liquid or steam.
• [Old Northern French *escalder* from Late Latin *excaldare* (Latin *ex* out of, *calidus* hot)]
HOMOPHONES: *skald*

scalding *adjective*
• "SKAWL ding"
• extremely hot.
• [as SCALD]

scalene *adjective*
• "SKAY leen" or "skay LEEN"
• (of a triangle) having three unequal sides.
• [Late Latin *scalenus* from Greek *skalēnos* unequal, related to *skolios* bent]

scaler *noun*
• "SCAY lur"
• a person who scales (measures the volume of) timber or logs.
• [Old Norse *skál* bowl, from Germanic]
HOMOPHONES: *scalar*

scallion *noun*
• "SKAL y'n"
• a shallot or green onion; any long-necked onion with a small bulb.
• [Anglo-French *scal(o)un* = Old French *escalo(i)gne*, ultimately from Latin *Ascalonia (caepa)* (onion) of *Ascalon* in ancient Palestine]

scallop *noun*
• "SKAL up" or "SKAWL up"
• any of various bivalve molluscs of the family Pectinidae, used as food.
• [Old French *escalope*, prob. from Germanic]

scalloper *noun*
• "SKAL up ur" or "SKAWL up ur"
• a boat for fishing for scallops.
• [as SCALLOP]

scalloping *noun*
• "SKAL up ing" or "SKAWL up ing"
• an ornamental edging cut in material in imitation of the edge of a scallop shell.
• [as SCALLOP]

scaloppine *noun*
ALSO SPELLED: **scallopini**
• "skal a PEENY" or "skawl a PEENY"
• thin, boneless slices of meat, esp. veal, sautéed or fried.
• [Italian, plural of *scaloppina*, diminutive of *scaloppa* escalope]

scalpel *noun*
• "SKAL pull"
• a surgeon's small sharp knife shaped for holding like a pen.
• [French *scalpel* or Latin *scalpellum* diminutive of *scalprum* chisel, from *scalpere* scratch]

scaly *adjective*
• "SKAY lee"
• covered in or having many scales or flakes.
• [Old French *escale* from Germanic, related to SCALER]
• **scaliness** *noun*

scamp *noun*
• "SKAMP"
• a rascal; a rogue.
• [*scamp* rob on highway, prob. from Middle Dutch *schampen* decamp, from Old French *esc(h)amper* (Latin or Greek *ex* out of, Latin *campus* field)]
• **scampish** *adjective*

scamper *verb*
• "SKAM pur"
• run and skip impulsively or playfully.
• [prob. formed as SCAMP]

scampi *plural noun*
• "SKAMPY"
• large prawns.
• [Italian]

scan *verb*
• "SKAN"
• look at intently or quickly.

• [Latin *scandere* climb: in Late Latin = scan verses (from the raising of one's foot in marking rhythm)]

scandal *noun*
• "SKAND'll"
• a person, thing, event, or circumstance causing general public outrage or indignation.
• [Old French *scandale* from Church Latin *scandalum* from Greek *skandalon* snare, stumbling block]
• **scandalize** *verb* (also esp. *Brit.* **-ise**)
• **scandalous** *adjective*
• **scandalously** *adverb*
• **scandalousness** *noun*

scandalmonger *noun*
• "SKAND'll mong gur" or "SKAND'll mung gur"
• a person who spreads malicious scandal.
• [as SCANDAL + MONGER]

Scandinavian *noun*
• "skanda NAVY 'n"
• a native or inhabitant of Scandinavia in N Europe.

scandium *noun*
• "SKANDY um"
• a rare soft silver-white metallic element occurring naturally in lanthanide ores.
• [modern Latin from *Scandia* Scandinavia (source of the minerals containing it)]

scannable *adjective*
• "SKANNA bull"
• that can be scanned.
• [as SCAN]

scanner *noun*
• "SKANNER"
• a device for scanning, systematically examining, reading, or monitoring something.
• [as SCAN]

scansion *noun*
• "SKAN sh'n"
• the metrical scanning of verse.
• [Latin *scansio* (Late Latin of metre) from *scandere scans-* climb]

scant *adjective*
• "SKANT"
• barely sufficient; deficient.
• [Old Norse *skamt* neuter of *skammr* short]
• **scantily** *adverb*
• **scantiness** *noun*
• **scantly** *adverb*
• **scanty** *adjective*

scantling *noun*
• "SKANT ling"
• a timber beam of small cross-section.
• [alteration from obsolete *scantlon*, from Old French *escantillon* sample]

scaphoid *noun*
• "SKAFF oid"
• a boat-shaped bone in the foot or hand.
• [modern Latin *scaphoides* from Greek *skaphoeidēs* from *skaphos* boat]

scapula *noun*
• "SKAP yoo luh"
• the shoulder blade.
• [Late Latin, sing. of Latin *scapulae*]
• **scapular** *adjective* "SKAP yuh lur"

scarab *noun*
• "SCARE ub"
• the sacred dung beetle of ancient Egypt.
• [Latin *scarabaeus* from Greek *skarabeios*]

scarabaeid *noun*
• "scare a BEE id"
• any beetle of the family Scarabaeidae, typically having strong spiky forelegs for burrowing.
• [as SCARAB]

scarabaeoid *noun*
• "scare a BEE oid"
• a beetle of a large group, superfamily Scarabaeoidea, having plate-like terminal segments in the antennae, including the largest-known beetles, such as the stag beetle, cockchafer, dung beetle, etc.
• [as SCARAB]

scarce *adjective*
• "SKAIRCE"
• (esp. of food, money, etc.) insufficient for the demand; scanty.
• [Old French *eschars* from Latin *excerpere*: see EXCERPT]
• **scarcity** *noun* "SCARE suh tee"

scarcely *adverb*
• "SCARE slee"
• hardly; barely; only just.
• [as SCARCE]

scaremonger *noun*
• "SCARE mong gur" or "SCARE mung gur"
• a person who spreads frightening reports or rumours.
• ['scare' from Middle English *skerre* from Old Norse *skirra* frighten, from *skjarr* timid + MONGER]
• **scaremongering** *noun*

scarifier *noun*
• "SCARE a fie ur"
• a machine for loosening soil, esp. in reforestation.
• [as SCARIFY]

scarify *verb*
• "SCARE a fie"
• make superficial incisions in.
• [French *scarifier* from Late Latin *scarificare* from Latin *scarifare* from Greek *skariphaomai* from *skariphos* stylus]
• **scarification** *noun*

scarlatina *noun*
• "scar luh TEENA"
• an infectious bacterial fever, affecting esp. children, with a scarlet rash; scarlet fever.

• [modern Latin from Italian *scarlattina* (*febbre* fever) diminutive of *scarlatto* SCARLET]

scarlet *noun*
• "SCAR lit"
• a brilliant red colour tinged with orange.
• [Old French *escarlate*: ultimate origin unknown]

scarp *noun*
• "SKARP"
• the inner wall or slope of a ditch in a fortification.
• [Italian *scarpa*]

scarper *verb*
• "SCAR pur"
• run away; escape.
• [prob. from Italian *scappare* escape, influenced by rhyming slang *Scapa Flow* = go]

scat *noun*
• "SKAT"
• excrement; the droppings of an animal, esp. a carnivore.
• [Greek *skōr skatos* dung]
HOMOPHONES: *skat*

scathe *verb*
• "SCATHE" (rhymes with *BATHE*)
• injure esp. by blasting, scorching, or withering.
• [Old Norse *skatha* = Old English *sceathian*]

scathing *adjective*
• "SCATHE ing" ("SCATHE" rhymes with *BATHE*)
• witheringly scornful; showing contempt; severe, harsh.
• [as SCATHE]
• **scathingly** *adverb*

scatology *noun*
• "skuh TOLLA jee"
• a morbid interest in excrement.
• [Greek *skōr skatos* dung + *logos* word]
• **scatological** *adjective* "skatta LODGE a k'll"

scatty *adjective*
• "SKATTY"
• scatterbrained; disorganized.
• [abbreviation]
• **scattily** *adverb*
• **scattiness** *noun*

scaup *noun*
• "SCOP"
• either of two diving ducks of the genus *Aythya*, the males having a dark head and breast and a white-sided body, the greater scaup, *A. marila* of Canada and Eurasia, or the lesser scaup, *A. affinis* of N America.
• [*scaup* Scots var. of *scalp* mussel bed, which it frequents]

scavenge *verb*
• "SKAV inj"
• search for and collect (useful items) from among usu. discarded material.
• [back-formation from *scavenger*, Middle English *scavager* from Anglo-French *scawager* from *scawage* from Old Northern French *escauwer* inspect, from Flemish *scauwen*, related to 'show': for *-n-* compare MESSENGER]
• **scavenger** *noun*

scena *noun*
• "SHANE uh"
• a scene or part of an opera.
• [Italian from Latin: see SCENE]

scenario *noun*
• "sen AIRY oh" or "sen ARRY oh"
• an outline of the plot of a play, film, opera, etc., with details of the scenes, situations, etc.
• [Italian (as SCENA)]

scenarist *noun*
• "suh NAIR ist"
• a writer of film or television scenarios.
• [as SCENARIO]

scend *noun*
• "SEND"
• the impulse given by a wave or waves.
• [alteration of 'send' or DESCEND]
HOMOPHONES: *send*

scene *noun*
• "SEEN"
• a place in which events in real life, drama, or fiction occur; the locality of an event etc.
• [Latin *scena* from Greek *skēnē* tent, stage]

scenery *noun*
• "SEENA ree"
• the general appearance of the natural features of a landscape, esp. when picturesque.
• [earlier *scenary* from Italian SCENARIO]
HOMOPHONES: *senary*

scenester *noun*
• "SEEN stur"
• a person associated with or immersed in a specific cultural scene.
• [as SCENE]

scenic *adjective*
• "SEE nick"
• (esp. of natural scenery) picturesque; impressive or beautiful.
• [as SCENE]
• **scenically** *adverb*

scenography *noun*
• "see NOGGRA fee"
• the painting or design of theatrical scenery.
• [as SCENE + Greek *graphia* writing]
• **scenographer** *noun*
• **scenographic** *adjective* "seena GRAFFIC"

scent *noun*
• "SENT"
• a distinctive, esp. pleasant, smell.
• [Middle English *sent* via Old French *sentir* perceive, smell, from Latin *sentire*: the *-c-* (added in 17th c.) is unexplained]
• **scented** *adjective*
• **scentless** *adjective*
HOMOPHONES: *sent, cent*

sceptre *noun*
ALSO SPELLED: *US* **scepter**
• "SEP tur"
• a staff borne esp. at a coronation as a symbol of sovereignty.
• [Old French *(s)ceptre* from Latin *sceptrum* from Greek *skēptron* from *skēptō* lean on]
• **sceptred** *adjective* (also esp. *US* **sceptered**)

schadenfreude *noun*
• "SHADDEN froy duh"
• the malicious enjoyment of another's misfortunes.
• [German from *Schaden* harm + *Freude* joy]

schedule *noun*
• "SKED joo 'll" or "SKED jool" or "SHED jool" or "SHED yool"
• a list or plan of intended events, times, etc.; a timetable.
• [Old French *cedule* from Late Latin *schedula* slip of paper, diminutive of *scheda* from Greek *skhedē* papyrus leaf]
• **scheduler** *noun*
• **scheduling** *noun*

scheelite *noun*
• "SHEE lite"
• calcium tungstate in its mineral crystalline form, an important ore of tungsten.
• [C. W. *Scheele*, Swedish chemist d.1786]

schefflera *noun*
• "SHEFFLER uh"
• any of various tropical and subtropical plants of the genus *Schefflera*, esp. the umbrella tree, *S. actinophylla*, with glossy leaves, often grown as a houseplant.
• [modern Latin, from J. C. *Scheffler*, 18th-c. botanist of Danzig]

schema *noun*
• "SKEEMA"
• a synopsis, outline, or diagram.
• [Greek *skhēma -atos* form, figure]

schematism *noun*
• "SKEEMA tizm"
• a schematic arrangement or presentation.
• [as SCHEME]

scheme *noun*
• "SKEEM"
• a systematic plan or arrangement for work, action, etc.
• [Latin *schema* from Greek (as SCHEMA)]
• **schematic** *adjective* "skeem ATTIC" or "skim ATTIC"
• **schematically** *adverb*
• **schematization** *noun* (also esp. *Brit.* **-isation**)
• **schematize** *verb* (also esp. *Brit.* **-ise**)
• **schemer** *noun*

scheming *adjective*
• "SKEEM ing"
• artful, cunning, or deceitful.
• [as SCHEME]

scherzando *adverb*
• "skairt SANDO"
• (as a musical direction) in a playful manner.
• [Italian, gerund of *scherzare* to jest (as SCHERZO)]

scherzo *noun*
• "SKAIRT so"
• a vigorous, light, or playful composition, usu. as a movement in a symphony, sonata, etc.
• [Italian, lit. 'jest']

schilling *noun*
• "SHILLING"
• the former chief monetary unit of Austria, now replaced by the euro.
• [German]
HOMOPHONES: *shilling*

schipperke *noun*
• "SKIPPER kee" or "SKIPPER kuh" or "SHIPPER kee" or "SHIPPER kuh"
• a breed of small black tailless dog with a ruff of fur around its neck.
• [Dutch dialect, = little boatman, from its use as a watchdog on barges]

schism *noun*
• "SKIZM"
• the division of a group into opposing sections or parties.
• [Church Latin *schisma* from Greek *skhisma -atos* cleft, from *skhizō* to split]
• **schismatic** *adjective*
• **schismatically** *adverb*

schist *noun*
• "SHIST"
• a foliated metamorphic rock composed of layers of different minerals and splitting into thin irregular plates.
• [French *schiste* from Latin *schistos* from Greek *skhistos* split (as SCHISM)]
• **schistose** *adjective*
• **schistosity** *noun* "shis TOSSA tee"

schistosome *noun*
• "SHISTO soam"
• a tropical flatworm of the genus *Schistosoma* which is parasitic in blood vessels in the human pelvic region.
• [Greek *skhistos* divided (as SCHISM) + *sōma* body]

schistosomiasis *noun*
• "shista so MY a sis"
• a chronic tropical disease produced by schistosomes.
• [as SCHISTOSOME]

schizanthus *noun*
• "skit SANTH us"
• any plant of the genus *Schizanthus*, with showy flowers in various colours, and finely-divided leaves.
• [modern Latin from Greek *skhizō* to split + *anthos* flower]

schizocarp *noun*
• "SKIT suh carp"
• any of a group of dry fruits that split into single-seeded parts when ripe.
• [Greek *skhizō* to split + *karpos* fruit]

schizoid *adjective*
• "SKITS oid"
• (of a person or personality etc.) tending to or resembling schizophrenia or a schizophrenic, but usu. without delusions.
• [as SCHIZOPHRENIA]

schizophrenia *noun*
• "skitsa FREENY uh" or "skitsa FRENNY uh"
• a mental disease marked by a breakdown in the relation between thoughts, feelings, and actions, frequently accompanied by delusions and retreat from social life.
• [modern Latin, from Greek *skhizō* to split + *phrēn* mind]
• **schizophrenic** *adjective* "skitsa FRENNIC"

schizotype *noun*
• "SKITSA tipe"
• a personality type in which mild symptoms of schizophrenia are present.
• [as SCHIZOPHRENIA + TYPE]
• **schizotypal** *adjective*

schlemiel *noun*
ALSO SPELLED: **shlemiel**
• "shluh MEEL"
• an awkward or unlucky person.
• [Yiddish *shlumiel*]

schlep *verb*
ALSO SPELLED: **schlepp**, **shlep**
• "SHLEP"
• carry (esp. something burdensome); drag.
• [Yiddish *shlepn* from German *schleppen* drag]
• **schlepper** *noun* (also **shlepper**)
• **schleppy** *adjective* (also **shleppy**)

schlieren *noun*
• "SHLEER 'n"
• a visually discernible area or stratum of different density in a transparent medium.
• [German, pl. of *Schliere* streak]

schlock *noun*
ALSO SPELLED: **shlock**
• "SHLOCK"
• cheap, shoddy or defective goods.
• [Yiddish *shlak* an apoplectic stroke, *schlog* wretch, untidy person, apoplectic stroke]
• **schlocky** *adjective* (also **shlocky**)
HOMOPHONES: *schlockey*

schlockey *noun*
• "SHLOCK ee"
• *Cdn* a children's game played on a four-foot by eight-foot framed plywood sheet stationed between two players, in which each player, using a cut-off hockey stick, attempts to score by shooting a puck past a centre barrier and through a hole in the framing board at the opposing end.
• [punningly after 'hockey' + SCHLOCKY]
HOMOPHONES: *schlocky*

schlockmeister *noun*
ALSO SPELLED: **shlockmeister**
• "SHLOCK mice tur"
• a person who produces trashy films, music, etc.
• [as SCHLOCK + German *Meister* master]

schlub *noun*
ALSO SPELLED: **shlub**
• "SHLUB"
• a clumsy, stupid, or untidy person.
• [Yiddish, perhaps from Polish *żłób*, blockhead]

schlump *noun*
ALSO SPELLED: **shlump**
• "SHLUMP"
• a slow or slovenly person; a slob, a fool.
• [apparently related to Yiddish *shlumperdik* dowdy and German *Schlumpe* slattern]

schmaltz *noun*
ALSO SPELLED: **shmaltz**
• "SHMAWLTS"
• sentimentality, esp. in music, drama, etc.
• [Yiddish from German *Schmalz* dripping, lard]
• **schmaltzy** *adjective* (also **shmaltzy**)

schmear *noun*
ALSO SPELLED: **schmeer**
• "SHMEER" or "shuh MEER"
• everything (possible or available); every aspect of the situation.
• [Yiddish *schmirn*, flatter, grease; compare German *shmieren*, smear]

schmo *noun*
ALSO SPELLED: **shmoe**
• "SHMOE"
• an ordinary, unremarkable person.
• [alteration of SCHMUCK]

schmooze *verb*
ALSO SPELLED: **shmooze**
• "SHMOOZ"
• talk, chat, esp. at a social function; network.
• [Yiddish *schmuesn* talk, converse, chat, *schmues* (noun) from Hebrew *shĕmūʻah* rumour]
• **schmoozefest** *noun* (also **shmoozefest**)
• **schmoozer** *noun* (also **shmoozer**)
• **schmoozy** *adjective* (also **shmoozy**)

schmuck *noun*
ALSO SPELLED: **shmuck**
• "SHMUCK"
• an objectionable or contemptible person; idiot.
• [Yiddish *shmok* penis]
• **schmucky** *adjective* (also **shmucky**)

schnapps *noun*
• "SHNAPS" or "SHNOPPS"
• any of various strong usu. colourless spirits made from grain, with added flavourings such as peppermint, peach, etc.

• [German, = dram of liquor, from Low German & Dutch *snaps* mouthful]

schnauzer *noun*
• "SHNOW zur" or "SHNOUT zur" ("SHNOW" rhymes with *NOW*)
• a German breed of dog with a close wiry coat and heavy whiskers round the muzzle.
• [German from *Schnauze* muzzle, snout]

schnitzel *noun*
• "SHNITS'll"
• a thin cutlet, esp. of veal or pork, breaded and fried.
• [German, = slice]

schnook *noun*
• "SHNOOK"
• a foolish or contemptible person.
• [perhaps from German *Schnucke* small sheep, or from Yiddish *shnuk* snout]

schnorrer *noun*
ALSO SPELLED: **shnorrer**
• "SHNORE ur"
• a beggar or scrounger; a layabout.
• [Yiddish from German *Schnurrer*]

schnozz *noun*
ALSO SPELLED: **schnoz**
• "SHNOZZ"
• the nose.
• [Yiddish *shnoytz* from German *Schnauze* snout]

scholar *noun*
• "SKAWLER"
• a learned person, esp. in language, literature, etc.; an academic.
• [Old English *scol(i)ere* & Old French *escol(i)er* from Late Latin *scholaris* from Latin *schola* school]
• **scholarly** *adjective*

scholarship *noun*
• "SKAWLER ship"
• academic achievement; learning of a high level.
• [as SCHOLAR]

scholastic *adjective*
• "skuh LASTIC"
• of or concerning universities, schools, education, teachers, etc.
• [Latin *scholasticus* from Greek *skholastikos* studious, via *skholazō* be at leisure, devote one's leisure to study, from *skholē* leisure]
• **scholastically** *adverb*

scholasticism *noun*
• "skuh LASTA sizm"
• the educational tradition of medieval universities, characterized esp. by a method of philosophical and theological speculation which aimed at a better understanding of Christianity by defining, systematizing, and reasoning.
• [as SCHOLASTIC]

scholiast *noun*
• "SKOE lee ast"
• an ancient or medieval scholar, esp. a grammarian, who annotated ancient literary texts.
• [medieval Greek *skholiastēs* from *skholiazō* write scholia: see SCHOLIUM]
• **scholiastic** *adjective*

scholium *noun*
• "SKOE lee um"
• a marginal note or explanatory comment, esp. by an ancient grammarian on a classical text.
• [modern Latin from Greek *skholion* from *skholē* disputation, leisure, school]

schooner *noun*
• "SKOONER"
• a fore-and-aft rigged ship with two or more masts, the foremast being smaller than the other masts.
• [18th c.: origin uncertain]

schottische *noun*
• "shaw TEESH"
• a kind of slow polka.
• [German *der schottische Tanz* the Scottish dance]

schtum *adjective*
ALSO SPELLED: **shtum**
• "SHTUM"
• silent, non-communicative.
• [Yiddish, from German *stumm* quiet]

schuss *noun*
• "SHUSS" (with "U" as in *PUT*)
• a straight downhill run on skis.
• [German, lit. 'shot']

schwa *noun*
• "SHWAH"
• the indistinct unstressed vowel sound as in *a* moment *ago*.
• [German from Hebrew *šᵉwā*, apparently from *šaw'* emptiness]

sciatic *adjective*
• "sye ATTIC"
• of the hip.
• [French *sciatique* from Late Latin *sciaticus* from Latin *ischiadicus* from Greek *iskhiadikos* subject to sciatica, from *iskhion* hip joint]

sciatica *noun*
• "sye ATTIC uh"
• neuralgia of the hip and thigh; a pain in the sciatic nerve.
• [as SCIATIC]

science *noun*
• "SYE ince"
• the intellectual and practical activity encompassing the systematic study of the structure and behaviour of the physical and natural world through observation and experiment.

• [Old French from Latin *scientia* from *scire* know]

scientific *adjective*
• "sye 'n TIFFIC"
• (of an investigation etc.) according to rules laid down in exact science for performing observations and testing the soundness of conclusions.
• [as SCIENCE]
• **scientifically** *adverb*

scientism *noun*
• "SYE 'n tizm"
• a method or doctrine regarded as characteristic of scientists.
• [as SCIENCE]
• **scientistic** *adjective*

scientist *noun*
• "SYE 'n tist"
• a person with expert knowledge of a (usu. physical or natural) science.
• [as SCIENCE]

scilicet *adverb*
• "SILLA set"
• that is to say; namely (introducing a word to be supplied or an explanation of an ambiguity).
• [Middle English from Latin, = *scire licet* one is permitted to know]

scilla *noun*
• "SILLA"
• any liliaceous plant of the genus *Scilla*, related to the bluebell, usu. bearing small blue star-shaped or bell-shaped flowers and having long glossy strap-like leaves.
• [Latin from Greek *skilla*]

Scillonian *noun*
• "sill OANY 'n"
• a resident of the Scilly Isles off SW England.

scimitar *noun*
• "SIM it ur"
• an oriental curved sword usu. broadening towards the point.
• [French *cimeterre*, Italian *scimitarra*, etc., of unknown origin]

scintigraphy *noun*
• "sin TIGGRA fee"
• the use of a radioisotope and a device for detecting and recording flashes produced in a material by an ionizing particle to get an image or record of a bodily organ etc.
• [SCINTILLATE + Greek *graphia* writing]

scintilla *noun*
• "sin TILLA"
• a trace, a tiny amount.
• [Latin]

scintillate *verb*
• "SINT'll ate"
• talk cleverly or wittily; be brilliant.
• [Latin *scintillare* (as SCINTILLA)]
• **scintillant** *adjective*
• **scintillating** *adjective*
• **scintillatingly** *adverb*
• **scintillation** *noun*

scion *noun*
• "SYE 'n"
• a shoot of a plant etc., esp. one cut for grafting or planting.
• [Old French *cion*, *sion* shoot, twig, of unknown origin]

scirrhus *noun*
• "SEER us" or "SKEER us"
• a carcinoma which is hard to the touch.
• [modern Latin from Greek *skirros* from *skiros* hard]
• **scirrhous** *adjective*
HOMOPHONES: *cirrus*

scissile *adjective*
• "SIS ile"
• able to be cut or divided.
• [Latin *scissilis* from *scindere sciss-* cut]

scission *noun*
• "SISH'n"
• the act or an instance of cutting; the state of being cut.
• [Old French *scission* or Late Latin *scissio* (as SCISSILE)]

scissors *plural noun*
• "SIZZ urz"
• an instrument for cutting fabric, paper, hair, etc., having two pivoted blades with finger and thumb holes in the handles, operating by closing on the material to be cut.
• [Middle English *sisoures* from Old French *cisoires* from Late Latin *cisoria* pl. of *cisorium* cutting instrument (as CHISEL): assoc. with Latin *scindere sciss-* cut]
• **scissor** *verb*

sclera *noun*
• "SKLEERA"
• the white of the eye; a white membrane coating the eyeball.
• [modern Latin from feminine of Greek *sklēros* hard]
• **scleral** *adjective*

sclerenchyma *noun*
• "skluh RENK im uh"
• the woody tissue found in a plant, formed from lignified cells and usu. providing support.
• [modern Latin from Greek *sklēros* hard + *egkhuma* infusion, after *parenchyma*]

sclerite *noun*
• "SKLEER ite" or "SKLAIR ite"
• a component section of an exoskeleton, esp. each of the plates forming the skeleton of an arthropod.
• [Greek *sklēros* hard]

scleroderma *noun*
• "SKLEERA durma" or "SKLERRA durma"

• a chronic hardening of the skin and connective tissue.
• [Greek *sklēros* hard + *derma* skin]

sclerophyll *noun*
• "SKLEERA fill" or "SKLERRA fill"
• any woody plant with leathery leaves retaining water.
• [Greek *sklēros* hard + *phullon* leaf]
• **sclerophyllous** *adjective*

scleroprotein *noun*
• "skleer oh PRO teen" or "sklair oh PRO teen"
• any insoluble structural protein.
• [Greek *sklēros* hard + PROTEIN]

sclerosed *adjective*
• "SKLUH roast" or "SKLUH rozed"
• affected by sclerosis.
• [as SCLEROSIS]

sclerosis *noun*
• "skluh ROE sis"
• an abnormal hardening of body tissue.
• [Greek *sklērōsis* from *sklēroō* harden]
• **sclerosing** *adjective*
• **sclerotic** *adjective* "skluh ROTTIC"

sclerotherapy *noun*
• "skleer a THERRA pee" or "sklerra THERRA pee"
• the treatment of varicose veins etc. by the injection of a hardening agent.
• [Greek *sklēros* hard + THERAPY]

sclerous *adjective*
• "SKLEER us" or "SKLAIR us"
• hardened; bony.
• [Greek *sklēros* hard]

scoff *verb*
• "SKOFF"
• speak derisively, esp. of serious subjects; mock; be scornful.
• [perhaps from Scandinavian: compare early modern Danish *skuf*, *skof* jest, mockery]
• **scoffer** *noun*

scofflaw *noun*
• "SCOFF law"
• a person who flouts the law, esp. a person not complying with various laws which are difficult to enforce effectively.
• [from SCOFF + 'law']

scold *verb*
• "SKOLD"
• rebuke or chide (esp. a child).
• [prob. from Old Norse *skáld* SKALD]
• **scolding** *noun*
• **scoldingly** *adverb*

scolex *noun*
• "SKOE lex"
• the head of a larval or adult tapeworm.
• [modern Latin from Greek *skōlēx* worm]

scoliosis *noun*
• "skoe lee OH sis"
• an abnormal lateral curvature of the spine.
• [modern Latin from Greek *skolios* bent]
• **scoliotic** *adjective*

scombroid *noun*
• "SKOM broid"
• any marine fish of the family Scombridae, including mackerels, tunas, and bonitos, or of the superfamily Scombroidea.
• [Latin from Greek *skombros* tuna or mackerel]
• **scombrid** *noun*

sconce *noun*
• "SKONCE"
• a semicircular or triangular lighting fixture attached to a wall.
• [Old French *esconse* lantern, or medieval Latin *sconsa* from Latin *absconsa* feminine past participle of *abscondere* hide: see ABSCOND]

scone *noun*
• "SKON" or "SKONE"
• a small quick bread often containing raisins or currants, usu. served with butter and jam.
• [originally Scots, perhaps from Middle Dutch *schoon(broot)*, Middle Low German *schon(brot)* fine (bread)]

scooch *verb*
• "SKOOCH"
• move quickly.
• [orig. unknown]

scopolamine *noun*
• "skuh POLE a meen"
• a poisonous alkaloid found in plants of the nightshade family, esp. of the genus *Scopolia*, and used to prevent vomiting in motion sickness and as a preoperative medication for examination of the eye.
• [*Scopolia* genus name of the plants yielding it, from G. A. *Scopoli*, Italian naturalist d.1788 + AMINE]

scopula *noun*
• "SKOP yoo luh"
• any of various small brushlike structures, esp. on the legs of spiders.
• [Late Latin, diminutive of Latin *scopa*, twig, broom]

scorbutic *adjective*
• "score BYOO tick"
• relating to, resembling, or affected with scurvy.
• [modern Latin *scorbuticus* from medieval Latin *scorbutus* scurvy, perhaps from Middle Low German *schorbūk* from *schoren* break + *būk* belly]

scoria *noun*
• "SKORRY uh"
• cellular lava, or fragments of it.
• [Latin from Greek *skōria* refuse, from *skōr* dung]
• **scoriaceous** *adjective* "skorry AY sh'ss"

Scorpio *noun*
• "SCORPY oh"
• the eighth sign of the zodiac.

• [Latin (as SCORPION)]
• **Scorpian** *adjective*
HOMOPHONES: *scorpion*

scorpioid *adjective*
• "SCORPY oid"
• of, relating to, or resembling a scorpion; of the scorpion order.
• [as SCORPION]

scorpion *noun*
• "SCORPY 'n"
• an arachnid of the order Scorpionida, with lobster-like pincers and a jointed tail that can be bent over to inflict a poisoned sting on prey held in its pincers.
• [Old French from Latin *scorpio -onis* from *scorpius* from Greek *skorpios*]
HOMOPHONES: *Scorpian*

scorzonera *noun*
• "skorza NEERA"
• a composite plant, *Scorzonera hispanica*, with long tapering purple-brown roots.
• [Italian from *scorzone* venomous snake, ultimately from medieval Latin *curtio*]

scoter *noun*
• "SCOTE ur"
• each of three northern diving ducks of the genus *Melanitta*, which breed in the Arctic and Subarctic and overwinter off coasts further south, esp. the surf scoter or the white-winged scoter.
• [17th c.: origin unknown]

scotia *noun*
• "SKOE shuh"
• a concave moulding, esp. at the base of a column.
• [Latin from Greek *skotia* from *skotos* darkness, with reference to the shadow produced]

scotoma *noun*
• "skaw TOE muh"
• a partial loss of vision or blind spot in an otherwise normal visual field.
• [Late Latin from Greek *skotōma* from *skotoō* darken, from *skotos* darkness]

Scotticism *noun*
• "SCOTTA sizm"
• a Scottish phrase, word, or idiom.
• [from *Scotland*]

Scottie *noun*
• "SCOTTY"
• a Scottish terrier.
• [from *Scotland*]

scoundrel *noun*
• "SKOUN drull"
• a person who shows no moral principles or conscience.
• [16th c.: origin unknown]
• **scoundrelism** *noun*
• **scoundrelly** *adjective*

scour *verb*
• "SKOUR"
• cleanse or brighten (esp. metal) by rubbing, esp. with soap, chemicals, or an abrasive substance.
• [Middle Dutch, Middle Low German *schūren* from Old French *escurer* from Late Latin *excurare* clean (off), from *ex-* away + *curare* to clean]
• **scourer** *noun*

scourge *noun*
• "SKURJ"
• a whip used for punishment, esp. of people.
• [Old French *escorge* (n.), *escorgier* (v.) (ultimately Latin *ex* out of, *corrigia* thong, whip)]

Scouse *noun*
• "SKOUSE" (rhymes with *HOUSE*)
• the dialect of Liverpool, England.
• [abbreviation of LOBSCOUSE]

scow *noun*
• "SKOW" (rhymes with *COW*)
• a flat-bottomed boat used as a barge etc.
• [Dutch *schouw* ferry boat]

scowl *noun*
• "SKOWL"
• a severe frown producing a sullen, bad-tempered, or threatening look on a person's face.
• [Middle English, prob. from Scandinavian: compare Danish *skule* look down or sidelong]
• **scowler** *noun*

scrag *noun*
• "SKRAG"
• the inferior, lean end of a neck of mutton or lamb.
• [perhaps alteration of dialect *crag* neck, related to Middle Dutch *crāghe*, Middle Low German *krage*]

scraggly *adjective*
• "SKRAG lee"
• sparse and irregular; ragged.
• [as SCRAG]

scraggy *adjective*
• "SKRAG ee"
• thin and bony.
• [as SCRAG]
• **scraggily** *adverb*
• **scragginess** *noun*

scran *noun*
• "SKRAN"
• food, eatables.
• [18th c.: origin unknown]

scrapie *noun*
• "SCRAPE ee"
• a disease of sheep involving the central nervous system and characterized by lack of coordination and itching causing affected animals to rub against trees etc., and thought to be caused by a virus-like agent such as a prion.

• [from 'scrape' from Old Norse *skrapa* or Middle Dutch *schrapen*]

scrapple *noun*
• "SKRAPPLE"
• scraps of pork etc. stewed with cornmeal and shaped into large cakes.
• [from 'scrap' from Old Norse *skrap*, related to *skrapa* scrape]

scravel *verb*
• "SKRAV'll"
• *Cdn* (*Nfld*) move quickly, scramble.
• [perhaps alteration of 'scrabble' from Middle Dutch *schrabbelen* frequentative of *schrabben* scrape]

scrawl *verb*
• "SKRAWL"
• write in a hurried untidy way.
• [perhaps from obsolete *scrawl* sprawl, alteration of 'crawl']
• **scrawly** *adjective*

scrawny *adjective*
• "SKRAWNY"
• lean, scraggy.
• [var. of dialect *scranny*: compare archaic *scrannel* (of sound) weak, feeble]
• **scrawniness** *noun*

scree *noun*
• "SKREE"
• small loose stones.
• [prob. back-formation from *screes* (pl.), ultimately from Old Norse *skritha* landslide, related to *skrítha* glide]

screech *noun*
• "SKREECH"
• a harsh high-pitched scream etc.
• [16th-c. var. of Middle English *scritch* (imitative)]
• **screecher** *noun*
• **screechy** *adjective*

screed *noun*
• "SKREED"
• a long usu. tiresome piece of writing or speech.
• [Middle English, prob. var. of 'shred' from Old English *scrēad* (unrecorded) piece cut off, *scrēadian* from West Germanic]

scrim *noun*
• "SKRIM"
• a theatrical drop made of an open-weave fabric that looks opaque when lit from in front but becomes transparent when lit from behind.
• [18th c.: origin unknown]

scrimmage *noun*
• "SKRIM idge"
• a rough or confused struggle; a brawl.
• [var. of SKIRMISH]
• **scrimmager** *noun*

scrimp *verb*
• "SKRIMP"
• be sparing or parsimonious.
• [18th c., originally Scots: perhaps related to 'shrimp', prob. related to Middle Low German *schrempen* wrinkle, Middle High German *schrimpfen* contract]
• **scrimper** *noun*

scrimshander *noun*
• "SKRIM shander"
• a person who scrimshaws.
• [as SCRIMSHAW]

scrimshaw *verb*
• "SKRIM shaw"
• adorn (whalebone, ivory, shells, etc.) with carved or coloured designs.
• [19th c.: perhaps from a surname]

scrip *noun*
• "SKRIP"
• a provisional certificate of money subscribed to a bank or company etc. entitling the holder to a formal certificate and dividends.
• [abbreviation of *subscription receipt*]

scriptorium *noun*
• "skrip TORY um"
• a room set apart for writing, esp. in a monastery.
• [medieval Latin from Latin *scriptum*, neuter past participle of *scribere* write]
• **scriptorial** *adjective*

scripture *noun*
• "SKRIP chur"
• writings sacred to a religion or group, esp. the Bible.
• [Latin *scriptura* (as SCRIPTORIUM)]
• **scriptural** *adjective*
• **scripturally** *adverb*

scritch *noun*
• "SKRITCH"
• a quiet scraping or scratching sound.
• [imitative]
• **scritching** *noun*

scrivener *noun*
• "SKRIVVEN ur"
• a copyist or drafter of documents.
• [Middle English from obsolete *scrivein* from Old French *escrivein*, ultimately from Latin *scriba* from *scribere* write]

scrob *verb*
ALSO SPELLED: **scrawb**
• "SKRAWB"
• *Cdn* (*Nfld*) & *Irish* scratch or scrape with or as with claws; claw.
• [origin uncertain; compare Irish *scrábaim*, *scrabhaim* scrape]

scrod *noun*
• "SKRAWD"
• a young cod or haddock, esp. as food.
• [19th c.: perhaps related to 'shred']

scrofula *noun*
• "SKROFF yoo luh"
• a disease with glandular swellings, prob. a form of tuberculosis.

• [Late Latin *scrofulae* (pl.) scrofulous swelling, diminutive of Latin *scrofa* a sow]
• **scrofulous** *adjective*

scrum *noun*
• "SKRUM"
• *Cdn* a situation where a crowd of reporters surround and interrogate a politician in an impromptu, informal, or disorderly manner.
• [abbreviation of SCRUMMAGE]

scrummage *noun*
• "SKRUM idge"
• an arrangement of the forwards of each team in rugby in two opposing groups, each with arms interlocked and heads down, with the ball thrown in between them to restart play.
• [as SCRIMMAGE]
• **scrummager** *noun*

scrummy *adjective*
• "SKRUMMY"
• (esp. of food) excellent; delicious.
• [as SCRUMPTIOUS]

scrumptious *adjective*
• "SKRUMP sh'ss"
• delicious.
• [19th c.: origin unknown]
• **scrumptiously** *adverb*
• **scrumptiousness** *noun*

scrumpy *noun*
• "SKRUMPY"
• rough cider, esp. as made in the West Country of England.
• [dialect *scrump* small apple]

scruncheon *noun*
ALSO SPELLED: **scrunchion**, **scrunchin**
• "SKRUN sh'n"
• *Cdn* (*Nfld*) small pieces of pork fat or fatback fried to a crisp and usu. eaten with fish and brewis.
• [origin uncertain; perhaps related to English dialect *scrunchings* table scraps]

scruple *noun*
• "SCREW pull"
• regard to the morality or propriety of an action.
• [French *scrupule* or Latin *scrupulus* from *scrupus* rough pebble, anxiety]

scrupulous *adjective*
• "SCREW pyoo luss"
• conscientious or thorough even in small matters.
• [French *scrupuleux* or Latin *scrupulosus* (as SCRUPLE)]
• **scrupulosity** *noun* "screw pyoo LOSSA tee"
• **scrupulously** *adverb*
• **scrupulousness** *noun*

scrutineer *noun*
• "screw tin EER"
• *Cdn & Brit.* a person who scrutinizes or examines something, esp. the conduct and result of a ballot.
• [as SCRUTINY]

scrutiny *noun*
• "SCREW tuh nee"
• a close examination or investigation.
• [Latin *scrutinium* from *scrutari* search, from *scruta* rubbish: originally of rag collectors]
• **scrutinize** *verb* (also esp. *Brit.* **-ise**)
• **scrutinizer** *noun* (also esp. *Brit.* **-iser**)

scry *verb*
• "SKRY" (rhymes with *CRY*)
• divine, esp. by crystal gazing or looking in a mirror or water.
• [shortening from DESCRY]
• **scryer** *noun*

scuba *noun*
• "SKOOBA"
• a portable breathing apparatus for divers, consisting of cylinders of compressed air strapped on the back, feeding air automatically through a mask or mouthpiece.
• [acronym from *s*elf-*c*ontained *u*nderwater *b*reathing *a*pparatus]

scud *verb*
• "SKUD"
• fly or run straight, fast, and lightly; skim along.
• [perhaps alteration of SCUT, as if to race like a hare]

scuff *verb*
• "SKUFF"
• graze or brush against.
• [imitative]
• **scuffed** *adjective*

scuffle *noun*
• "SKUFF'll"
• a confused struggle or disorderly fight at close quarters; a tussle.
• [prob. from Scandinavian: compare Swedish *skuffa* to push, related to 'shove']

scull *noun*
• "SKULL"
• either of a pair of small oars used by a single rower.
• [Middle English: origin unknown]
• **sculler** *noun*
HOMOPHONES: *skull*

scullery *noun*
• "SKULL a ree"
• a small kitchen or room at the back of a house for washing dishes etc.
• [Anglo-French *squillerie*, Old French *escuelerie* from *escuele* dish, from Latin *scutella* salver, diminutive of *scutra* wooden platter]

scullion *noun*
• "SKULL y'n"
• a servant employed to wash dishes and perform other menial kitchen tasks.
• [Middle English: origin unknown]

sculpin *noun*
• "SKULL pin"
• any of numerous fish of the family Cottidae, native to non-tropical regions, having large spiny heads.
• [perhaps from obsolete *scorpene* from Latin *scorpaena* from Greek *skorpaina* a fish]

sculpture *noun*
• "SKULP chur"
• the art of making forms, often representational, in the round or in relief by chiselling stone, carving wood, modelling clay, casting metal, etc.
• [Latin *sculptura* from *sculpere sculpt-* carve]
• **sculpt** *verb*
• **sculpting** *noun*
• **sculptor** *noun*
• **sculptress** *noun*
• **sculptural** *adjective*
• **sculpturally** *adverb*

scumble *verb*
• "SCUM bull"
• modify (a painting) by applying a thin opaque coat of paint to give a softer or duller effect.
• [perhaps frequentative of 'scum' skim, from Middle Low German, Middle Dutch *schūm*, Old High German *scūm* from Germanic]

scuncheon *noun*
• "SKUN sh'n"
• the inside face of a door jamb, window frame, etc.
• [Old French *escoinson* (Latin *ex* out of, *cuneus* wedge)]

scunner *noun*
• "SKUNNER"
• *Cdn* (*Nfld*) a lookout in a crow's nest who directs a ship, esp. through ice floes.
• [from *scun*, perhaps alteration of 'con' direct the steering of (a ship), apparently weakened form of obsolete *cond*, *condie*, from French *conduire* from Latin *conducere* CONDUCT]

scup *noun*
• "SKUP"
• a kind of porgy, *Stenostomus chrysops*, of the Atlantic coast of N America.
• [Narragansett *mishcup* thick-scaled, from *mishe* large + *cuppi* scale]

scupper *noun*
• "SKUPPER"
• a hole in a ship's side to carry off water from the deck.
• [Old French *escopir* from Romanic *skuppire* (unrecorded) to spit: originally imitative]

scuppernong *noun*
• "SKUPPER nong"
• a variety of the muscadine grape native to the basin of the Scuppernong River in N Carolina.

scurf *noun*
• "SKURF"
• flakes on the surface of the skin, cast off as fresh skin develops below, esp. those of the head; dandruff.
• [Old English, prob. from Old Norse & earlier Old English *sceorf*, related to *sceorfan* gnaw, *sceorfian* cut to shreds]
• **scurfy** *adjective*

scurrilous *adjective*
• "SKUR a luss"
• (of a person or language) grossly or indecently abusive.
• [French *scurrile* or Latin *scurrilus* from *scurra* buffoon]
• **scurrility** *noun*
• **scurrilously** *adverb*
• **scurrilousness** *noun*

scurry *verb*
• "SKURRY"
• run or move hurriedly, esp. with short quick steps; scamper.
• [abbreviation of *hurry-scurry*; reduplication of 'hurry' (imitative)]

scurvy *noun*
• "SKURVY"
• a disease caused by a deficiency of vitamin C, characterized by swollen bleeding gums and the opening of previously healed wounds.
• [as SCURF by assoc. with French *scorbut* (compare SCORBUTIC)]
• **scurvily** *adverb*

scut *noun*
• "SKUT"
• a short tail, esp. of a hare, rabbit, or deer.
• [Middle English: origin unknown: compare obsolete *scut* short, shorten]

scutage *noun*
• "SKYOOT idge"
• money paid to a feudal lord by a landowner or vassal instead of military service.
• [medieval Latin *scutagium* from Latin *scutum* shield]

scutch *verb*
• "SKUTCH"
• dress (fibrous material, esp. retted flax) by beating.
• [Old French *escouche*, *escoucher* (dialect), *escousser*, ultimately from Latin *excutere excuss-* (*ex* out of, *quatere* shake)]

scutcheon *noun*
• "SKUTCH'n"
• a shield or emblem bearing a coat of arms.
• [Middle English from ESCUTCHEON]

scute *noun*
• "SKYOOT"
• each of the shield-like plates or scales forming the bony covering of a crocodile, sturgeon, turtle, armadillo, etc.
• [Latin (as SCUTUM)]

scutellum *noun*
• "skyoo TELLUM"
• a scale, plate, or any shield-like formation on

a plant, insect, bird, etc., esp. one of the horny scales on a bird's foot.
• [modern Latin diminutive of Latin *scutum* shield]

scutter *verb*
• "SKUTTER"
• scurry.
• [perhaps alteration of 'scuttle' hurry, compare dial. *scuddle* frequentative of SCUD]

scuttle *noun*
• "SKUT'll"
• a bucket, usu. with a sloping lip for pouring, carrying, and holding a small supply of coal.
• [Old Norse *skutill*, Old High German *scuzzila* from Latin *scutella* dish]

scuttlebutt *noun*
• "SKUTTLE but"
• rumour, gossip.
• [originally denoting a water butt on the deck of a ship, providing drinking water: from *scuttled butt*]

scutum *noun*
• "SKYOO t'm"
• each of the shield-like plates or scales forming the bony covering of a crocodile, sturgeon, turtle, armadillo, etc.
• [Latin, = oblong shield]

scutwork *noun*
• "SKUT wurk"
• tedious menial work.
• [origin unknown]

scuzzball *noun*
• "SKUZZ ball"
• a filthy, sleazy, or shady person.
• [as SCUZZY + 'ball']

scuzzy *adjective*
• "SKUZZY"
• squalid, sleazy, abhorrent, or disgusting.
• [prob. an abbreviation of 'disgusting' from Old French *degoust*, *desgouster*, or Italian *disgusto*, *disgustare* (Latin *dis-* expressing negation, GUSTO)]
• **scuzz** *noun*
• **scuzziness** *noun*

scyphozoan *noun*
• "sife a ZO 'n"
• any marine jellyfish of the class Scyphozoa, with tentacles bearing stinging cells.
• [modern Latin *scyphus* from Greek *skuphos* a drinking cup with two handles below the level of the rim + *zōion* animal]

scythe *noun*
• "SYTHE" (with "TH" as in *SOOTHE*)
• an agricultural tool consisting of a pole with two short handles projecting from it and a long thin curving blade at the bottom, which is swung over the ground to cut grass, grain, etc.
• [Old English *sīthe* from Germanic]

Scythian *adjective*
• "SITHY 'n" (with "TH" as in *THEE*)
• of or relating to ancient Scythia north and east of the Black Sea.

seaborgium *noun*
• "see BORG ee um"
• a very unstable chemical element made by high-energy atomic collisions.
• [G. T. *Seaborg*, US chemist d.1999]

seaborne *adjective*
• "SEE born"
• carried over or supported by the sea.
• ['sea' + 'borne' past participle of 'bear' carry, from Old English *beran*]

seafaring *adjective*
• "SEE fare ing"
• travelling by sea.
• ['sea' + FARE]
• **seafarer** *noun*

seagirt *adjective*
• "SEE gurt"
• surrounded by sea.
• ['sea' + GIRT]

seakale *noun*
• "SEE cale"
• a cruciferous maritime plant, *Crambe maritima*, with white flowers and wavy coarsely-toothed leaves, the shoots of which are cultivated and eaten as a vegetable.
• ['sea' + KALE]

sealant *noun*
• "SEEL'nt"
• any of various substances used to prevent air or water from passing through cracks, seams, joints, etc.
• ['seal' from Anglo-French *seal*, Old French *seel* from Latin *sigillum* diminutive of *signum* sign]

Sealyham *noun*
• "SEELY ham"
• a breed of small stocky wire-haired terrier, having a medium-length usu. white coat, drooping ears, a small erect tail, and a square bearded muzzle.
• [*Sealyham* in S Wales]

seamstress *noun*
• "SEEM striss" or "SEM striss"
• a woman who makes and mends clothing, esp. professionally.
• [Old English *sēamestre* feminine from *sēamere* tailor]

Seanad *noun*
• "SHAN id"
• the upper House of Parliament in the Republic of Ireland.
• [Irish, = senate]

seance *noun*
• "SAY awnce"
• a meeting at which spiritualists attempt to make contact with the dead.
• [French *séance* from Old French *seoir* from Latin *sedēre* sit]

sear *verb*
- "SEER"
- burn or scorch the surface of.
- [Old English *sēarian* from Germanic]

HOMOPHONES: *cere, seer, sere*

sebaceous *adjective*
- "suh BAY sh'ss"
- fatty; of or relating to tallow or fat.
- [Latin *sebaceus* from *sebum* tallow + adjective suffix *-aceus* of the nature of]

seborrhea *noun*
ALSO SPELLED: *Brit.* **seborrhoea**
- "sebba REE uh"
- excessive discharge of sebum from the sebaceous glands.
- [SEBUM + Greek *rheō* flow]
- **seborrheic** *adjective* (also *Brit.* **seborrhoeic**)

sebum *noun*
- "SEEB um"
- the oily secretion of the sebaceous glands which lubricates and protects the hair and skin.
- [modern Latin from Latin *sebum* grease]

sec *adjective*
- "SECK"
- (of wine) dry.
- [French from Latin *siccus*]

secant *noun*
- "SEEK'nt"
- a line cutting a curve at one or more points.
- [French *sécant(e)* from Latin *secare secant-* cut]

secateurs *plural noun*
- "sekka TURZ"
- a pair of pruning shears that can be used with one hand to clip usu. thin branches and flowers etc.
- [French *sécateur* cutter, from Latin *secare* cut]

secco *noun*
- "SECKO"
- the process or technique of painting on dry plaster with colours mixed in water.
- [Italian, = dry, from Latin *siccus*]

secede *verb*
- "suh SEED"
- withdraw formally from an alliance, an association, a federal union, or a political or religious organization.
- [Latin *secedere secess-* (*se* apart, without, *cedere* go)]
- **seceder** *noun*
- **secession** *noun* "suh SESH'n"
- **secessional** *adjective*

secessionism *noun*
- "suh SESH'n izm"
- the principles of those in favour of secession.
- [as SECEDE]
- **secessionist** *noun*

Sechelt *noun*
- "SEE shelt"
- a member of an Aboriginal people living on the coast of BC, north of Vancouver.
- [Sechelt, = 'land between two waters']

seclude *verb*
- "suh CLUDE"
- keep (a person) sequestered or shut up in order to prevent access or influence from outside.
- [Latin *secludere seclus-* (*se* apart, without, *claudere* shut)]
- **secluded** *adjective*
- **seclusion** *noun*

secobarbital *noun*
- "secko BARBA tawl"
- a sedative and hypnotic derivative of barbituric acid, used esp. for preoperative sedation.
- [SECO(NDARY) + BARBITAL]

second *verb*
- "suh COND"
- remove (an officer) temporarily from a regiment or corps for employment on the staff or in some other extra-regimental appointment.
- [French *en second* in the second rank (of officers)]
- **secondee** *noun*
- **secondment** *noun*

secondary *adjective*
- "SECK'n derry"
- second in rank, sequence, importance, etc. to what is primary.
- [Latin *secundarius* of the second class or quality, from *secundus* second, from *sequi* follow]
- **secondarily** *adverb*
- **secondariness** *noun*

secondo *noun*
- "suh CONDO"
- the second or lower part in a duet etc.
- [Italian from Latin *secundus* second, from *sequi* follow]

secrecy *noun*
- "SEE cruh see"
- the ability or tendency to withhold information or keep things secret.
- [Old French *secret* secret, from Latin *secretus* separate, set apart, from *secernere secret-* (*se* apart, without, *cernere* sift)]

secretagogue *noun*
- "suh CREETA gog"
- a substance which promotes secretion.
- [from SECRETION + Greek *agōgos* leading, eliciting]

secretaire *noun*
- "seckra TARE"
- a writing desk with drawers and pigeonholes, and usu. a bookcase above.
- [French (as SECRETARY)]

secretariat *noun*
- "seckra TERRY it"
- a permanent administrative and executive

department of a government or similar organization.
• [French *secrétariat* from medieval Latin *secretariatus* (as SECRETARY)]

secretary *noun*
• "SECKRA terry"
• a person employed by an individual or a company to manage or assist with files, records, and correspondence, make appointments, etc.
• [Late Latin *secretarius* from *secretus* separate, set apart, from *secernere secret-* (*se* apart, without, *cernere* sift)]
• **secretarial** *adjective*
• **secretaryship** *noun*

secretin *noun*
• "suh CREE t'n"
• a hormone released into the bloodstream by the duodenum, esp. in response to acidity, to stimulate secretion by the liver and pancreas.
• [as SECRETION]

secretion *noun*
• "suh CREE sh'n"
• the production and release of a specific substance by a cell, gland, or organ into a cavity or vessel or into the surrounding medium either for a function in the organism or for excretion.
• [French *sécrétion* or Latin *secretio* separation from *secernere secret-* (*se* apart, without, *cernere* sift)]
• **secrete** *verb* "suh CREET"
• **secretory** *adjective*

sectarian *adjective*
• "sec TERRY 'n"
• of or concerning a body of people subscribing to religious doctrines usu. different from those of an established church from which they have separated.
• [Old French *secte* or Latin *secta* sect, from the stem of *sequi secut-* follow]
• **sectarianism** *noun*

sectary *noun*
• "SECTER ee"
• a member of a religious or political sect.
• [as SECTARIAN]

sector *noun*
• "SECTER"
• a distinct part or branch of an economy.
• [Late Latin, techn. use of Latin *sector* cutter from *secare sect-* cut]
• **sectoral** *adjective*
• **sectorial** *adjective*

secular *adjective*
• "SECK yuh lur"
• concerned with or belonging to the material world and the affairs of this world as opposed to the eternal or spiritual world.
• [Latin *saecularis* from *saeculum* generation, age]
• **secularism** *noun*
• **secularist** *noun*
• **secularity** *noun* "seck yuh LERRA tee"
• **secularly** *adverb*

secularize *verb*
ALSO SPELLED: esp. *Brit.* **-ise**
• "SECK yuh lur ize"
• dissociate from religious or spiritual concerns; convert to material and temporal purposes.
• [as SECULAR]
• **secularization** *noun* (also esp. *Brit.* **-isation**)

secund *adjective*
• "suh KUND"
• (of leaves) arranged on one side only.
• [Latin *secundus* (as SECONDARY)]
• **secundly** *adverb*

Secwepemc *noun*
• "suck WEP muck"
• a member of an Aboriginal people living in the Thompson River area of BC (also called SHUSWAP).
• [Secwepemc, self-designation]

sedan *noun*
• "suh DAN"
• a luxury car for four or more people.
• [perhaps alteration of Italian dialect, ultimately from Latin *sella* saddle, from *sedēre* sit]

sedation *noun*
• "suh DAY sh'n"
• the action of sedating a person or thing.
• [French *sédation* or Latin *sedatio* from *sedatus* past participle of *sedare* settle, from *sedēre* sit]

sedative *noun*
• "SEDDA tiv"
• a drug, influence, etc., that tends to calm or soothe.
• [as SEDATION]

sedentary *adjective*
• "SED'n terry"
• (of work etc.) characterized by much sitting and little physical exercise.
• [French *sédentaire* or Latin *sedentarius* from *sedēre* sit]
• **sedentariness** *noun*

Seder *noun*
• "SAY dur"
• a Jewish ritual service and ceremonial dinner for the first night or first two nights of the Passover.
• [Hebrew *sēḏer* order]
HOMOPHONES: *satyr*

sederunt *noun*
• "suh DARE 'nt"
• (in some Presbyterian Churches) a single sitting of a church court.
• [Latin, = (the following persons) sat, from *sedēre* sit]

sedile *noun*
• "suh DIE lee"
• each of usu. three stone seats for priests in the south wall of a chancel, often canopied and decorated.
• [Latin, = seat, from *sedēre* sit]

sediment *noun*
• "SEDDA m'nt"
• matter that settles to the bottom of a liquid; dregs.
• [French *sédiment* or Latin *sedimentum* (as SEDILE)]
• **sedimentary** *adjective* "sedda MENTA ree"
• **sedimentation** *noun*

sedimentology *noun*
• "sedda m'n TOLLA jee"
• the branch of geology that deals with the nature and properties of sediments and sedimentary rocks.
• [as SEDIMENT + Greek *logos* word]
• **sedimentological** *adjective*
• **sedimentologist** *noun*

sedition *noun*
• "suh DISH'n"
• conduct or speech inciting to rebellion or a breach of public order.
• [Old French *sedition* or Latin *seditio* from *sed-* = *se* apart, without + *ire it-* go]
• **seditious** *adjective*
• **seditiously** *adverb*

sedulous *adjective*
• "SED yoo luss"
• persevering, diligent, assiduous.
• [Latin *sedulus* zealous]
• **sedulously** *adverb*

sedum *noun*
• "SEED um" or "SED um"
• any plant of the genus *Sedum*, with fleshy leaves and star-shaped yellow, pink, or white flowers, e.g. stonecrop.
• [Latin, = houseleek]

see *noun*
• "SEE"
• the area under the authority of a bishop or archbishop; a diocese.
• [Anglo-French *se(d)* ultimately from Latin *sedes* seat, from *sedēre* sit]
HOMOPHONES: *sea*, *si*

seep *verb*
• "SEEP"
• ooze, filter, or percolate slowly.
• [perhaps dialect form of Old English *sipian* to soak]
• **seepage** *noun*

seer *noun*
• "SEER"
• a person who sees.
• [Old English *sēon* see, from Germanic]
HOMOPHONES: *sere*, *sear*, *cere*

seersucker *noun*
• "SEER sucker"
• material of linen, cotton, etc., with a puckered surface.
• [Persian *šir o šakar*, lit. 'milk and sugar']

seethe *verb*
• "SEETHE"
• boil, bubble over.
• [Old English *sēothan* from Germanic]
• **seethingly** *adverb*

segment *noun*
• "SEG m'nt"
• each of several parts into which a thing is or can be divided or marked off.
• [Latin *segmentum* from *secare* cut]
• **segmental** *adjective*
• **segmentally** *adverb*
• **segmentary** *adjective* "SEG m'n terry"
• **segmentation** *noun*

segregate *verb*
• "SEGGRA gate"
• put apart from the rest; isolate.
• [Latin *segregare* (*se* apart, without, *grex gregis* flock)]
• **segregation** *noun*
• **segregational** *adjective*
• **segregationist** *noun*
• **segregative** *adjective*

segue *verb*
• "SEG way"
• go on without a pause into the next section.
• [Italian, = follows]

sei *noun*
• "SAY"
• a small rorqual, *Balaenoptera borealis*.
• [Norwegian *sejhval* sei whale]
HOMOPHONES: *say*

seicento *noun*
• "say CHENTO"
• the style of Italian art and literature of the 17th c.
• [Italian, = 600, used with reference to the years 1600–99]

seiche *noun*
• "SAYSH"
• a fluctuation in the water level of a lake etc., usu. caused by changes in barometric pressure.
• [Swiss French, perhaps from German *Seiche* sinking (of water)]

seigneur *noun*
• "seen YUR"
• *Cdn* a holder of land under the seigneurial system, a system of land tenure established in New France, based on the feudal system, under which land was owned by seigneurs who rented it to tenant farmers and provided mills, a court system, and other services.
• [French from Latin *senior*, older, older man, comparative of *senex senis* old man, old]
• **seigneurial** *adjective*

seigneury *noun*
- "SEEN yur ee"
- *Cdn* a tract of land held by a seigneur under the seigneurial system.
- [as SEIGNEUR]

seigniorage *noun*
ALSO SPELLED: **seignorage**
- "SEEN yur idge"
- a profit made by issuing currency, esp. by issuing coins rated above their intrinsic value.
- [Old French *seignorage, seigneurage* (as SEIGNEUR)]

seine *noun*
- "SANE"
- a fishing net for encircling fish, with floats at the top and weights at the bottom edge, and usu. hauled ashore.
- [Old French *saïne*, & Old English *segne* from West Germanic from Latin *sagena* from Greek *sagēnē* net]
- **seiner** *noun*
- **seining** *noun*

HOMOPHONES: *sane, saner*

seisin *noun*
ALSO SPELLED: **seizin**
- "SEE zin"
- possession of land by freehold.
- [Old French *seisine* (as SEIZE)]

HOMOPHONES: *season*

seismic *adjective*
- "SIZE mick"
- of or relating to an earthquake or earthquakes or other vibrations of the earth and its crust.
- [Greek *seismos* earthquake, from *seiō* shake]
- **seismically** *adverb*

seismicity *noun*
- "size MISSA tee"
- seismic activity; esp. the frequency of earthquakes per unit area in a region.
- [as SEISMIC]

seismogram *noun*
- "SIZE muh gram"
- a record given by a seismograph.
- [as SEISMIC + Greek *gramma* thing written]

seismograph *noun*
- "SIZE muh graff"
- an instrument that records the force, direction, etc. of earthquakes.
- [as SEISMIC + Greek *graphia* writing]
- **seismographic** *adjective*

seismology *noun*
- "size MOLLA jee"
- the scientific study and recording of earthquakes and related phenomena.
- [as SEISMIC + Greek *logos* word]
- **seismological** *adjective*
- **seismologically** *adverb*
- **seismologist** *noun*

seize *verb*
- "SEEZ"
- take hold of forcibly or suddenly.
- [Old French *seizir, saisir* give seisin, from Frankish from Latin *sacire* from Germanic]
- **seizer** *noun*
- **seizure** *noun* "SEE zhur"

HOMOPHONES: *Caesar*

seizing *noun*
- "SEE zing"
- a cord or cords used for taking hold.
- [as SEIZE]

sejant *adjective*
- "SEE j'nt"
- (of an animal) sitting upright on its haunches.
- [properly *seiant* from Old French var. of *seant* sitting, from *seoir* from Latin *sedēre* sit]

Sejm *noun*
ALSO SPELLED: **Seim**
- "SAME"
- the lower house of parliament in Poland.
- [Polish]

HOMOPHONES: *same*

Sekani *noun*
- "suh CANNY"
- a member of an Aboriginal group living on the western slope of the Rocky Mountains in north central BC.
- [Sekani, = 'people of the rocks, people of the mountains']

sekt *noun*
- "ZEKT"
- a German sparkling white wine.
- [German]

selachian *noun*
- "sill AKEY in"
- any fish of the subclass Selachii, including sharks and dogfish.
- [modern Latin *Selachii* from Greek *selakhos* shark]

selah *interjection*
- "SEELA"
- often used at the end of a verse in Psalms and Habakkuk, presumed to be a musical direction.
- [Hebrew *selāh*]

selenite *noun*
- "SELLA nite"
- a form of gypsum occurring as transparent crystals or thin plates.
- [Latin *selenites* from Greek *selēnitēs lithos* moonstone, from *selēnē* moon]

selenium *noun*
- "suh LEENY um"
- a non-metallic element occurring naturally in various metallic sulphide ores and characterized by the variation of its electrical resistivity with intensity of illumination.
- [modern Latin from Greek *selēnē* moon]

selenography *noun*
• "seela NOGGRA fee"
• the study or mapping of the moon.
• [Greek *selēnē* moon + *graphia* writing]
• **selenographer** *noun*
• **selenographic** *adjective*

selenology *noun*
• "seela NOLLA jee"
• the scientific study of the moon.
• [Greek *selēnē* moon + *logos* word]
• **selenologist** *noun*

Selkirkian *noun*
• "sell KURKY in"
• a resident of Selkirk, Man.

seltzer *noun*
• "SELT sur"
• natural effervescent mineral water.
• [German *Selterser* (adjective) from *(Nieder)selters* in Germany, site of a mineral spring]

selvage *noun*
ALSO SPELLED: **selvedge**
• "SELL vidge"
• an edging that prevents cloth from unravelling (either an edge along the warp or a specially woven edging).
• [Middle English from 'self' + 'edge', after Dutch *selfegghe*]

semantic *adjective*
• "suh MANTIC"
• relating to meaning in language; relating to the denotations and connotations of words.
• [French *sémantique* from Greek *sēmantikos* significant, from *sēmainō* signify, from *sēma* sign]
• **semantically** *adverb*
• **semanticist** *noun* "suh MANTA sist"
• **semantics** *noun*

semaphore *noun*
• "SEMMA for"
• a system of sending messages by holding the arms or two flags in certain positions according to an alphabetic code.
• [French *sémaphore*, from Greek *sēma* sign + *-phoros -phoron* bearing, bearer, from *pherō* bear]
• **semaphoric** *adjective*
• **semaphorically** *adverb*

semblance *noun*
• "SEM blince"
• the outward or superficial appearance of something.
• [Old French from *sembler* from Latin *similare*, *simulare* SIMULATE]

semé *adjective*
ALSO SPELLED: **semée**
• "SEMMY" or "SEM ay"
• (in heraldry) covered with small bearings of indefinite number (e.g. stars, fleurs-de-lys).
• [French, past participle of *semer* to sow, from Latin *semen seminis* seed]
HOMOPHONES: *semi*

sememe *noun*
• "SEM eem" or "SEE meem"
• the unit of meaning carried by a morpheme.
• [as SEMANTIC + MORPHEME]

semen *noun*
• "SEE m'n"
• the reproductive fluid of male animals, containing spermatozoa in suspension.
• [Latin *semen seminis* seed, from *serere* to sow]
HOMOPHONES: *seaman*

semester *noun*
• "suh MESTER"
• an academic session occupying half of the academic year, lasting usu. for 15 to 18 weeks.
• [German from Latin *semestris* six-monthly, from *sex* six + *mensis* month]

semestering *noun*
• "suh MESTER ing"
• *Cdn* an educational system in which the school year is divided into two terms having school days with a reduced number of longer periods, with the whole year's course material in any given subject concentrated into one or the other term.
• [as SEMESTER]
• **semestered** *adjective*

semibreve *noun*
• "SEMMY breev"
• a whole note.
• [French, Italian, etc. or Latin *semi-* half + BREVE]

semiconductor *noun*
• "semmy k'n DUCK tur" or "sem eye k'n DUCK tur"
• a solid substance that is a non-conductor when pure or at a low temperature but has a conductivity between that of insulators and that of most metals when containing a suitable impurity or at a higher temperature and is used in integrated circuits, transistors, diodes, etc.
• [French, Italian, etc. or Latin *semi-* half + CONDUCT]
• **semiconducting** *adjective*

semicylinder *noun*
• "semmy SILL'n dur" or "sem eye SILL'n dur"
• half of a cylinder cut longitudinally.
• [French, Italian, etc. or Latin *semi-* half + CYLINDER]
• **semicylindrical** *adjective*

semidiameter *noun*
• "semmy die AMMA tur" or "sem eye die AMMA tur"
• half of a diameter.
• [French, Italian, etc. or Latin *semi-* half + DIAMETER]

semifreddo *noun*
• "semmy FRAY doe"
• an Italian ice-cream-like dessert, often with cookies, nuts, cake, chocolate, etc. incorporated, served chilled or slightly frozen.
• [Italian, from *semi* half and *freddo* cold]

Sémillon *noun*
- "semmy YÕH" (with a nasal *OH*)
- a white grape grown esp. in France.
- [French dialect, ultimately from Latin *semen* seed]

seminal *adjective*
- "SEMMA n'll"
- of or relating to semen.
- [Old French *seminal* or Latin *seminalis* (as SEMEN)]
- **seminally** *adverb*

seminar *noun*
- "SEMMA nar"
- a small group of students, esp. at a university, meeting to discuss or study a particular topic with a teacher.
- [German (as SEMINARY)]

seminary *noun*
- "SEMMA nerry"
- a training college for priests, rabbis, etc.
- [Latin *seminarium* seedbed, neuter of *seminarius* (adjective) (as SEMEN)]
- **seminarian** *noun*
- **seminarist** *noun*

seminiferous *adjective*
- "semma NIFFER us"
- bearing seed.
- [Latin *semin-* from SEMEN + *-fer* producing, from *ferre* bear]

Seminole *noun*
- "SEM in ole"
- a member of any of several groupings of N American Aboriginal peoples comprising Creek Confederacy emigrants to Florida or their descendants in Florida and Oklahoma.
- [Creek *simanó:ni* from Latin American Spanish *cimarrón* wild, untamed; runaway slave]

semiology *noun*
- "semmy OLLA jee" or "seemy OLLA jee"
- = SEMIOTICS.
- [Greek *sēmeion* sign, from *sēma* mark + *logos* word]
- **semiological** *adjective*
- **semiologist** *noun*

semiotics *noun*
- "semmy OTTIX" or "seemy OTTIX"
- the study of signs and symbols in various fields, esp. language.
- [Greek *sēmeiōtikos* of signs (as SEMIOLOGY)]
- **semiotic** *adjective*
- **semiotically** *adverb*
- **semiotician** *noun* "semmy a TISH'n"

semiquaver *noun*
- "SEMMY kway vur"
- a sixteenth note.
- [French, Italian, etc. or Latin *semi-* half + QUAVER]

Semite *noun*
- "SEM ite" or "SEEM ite"
- a member of any of the peoples supposed to be descended from Shem, son of Noah, including esp. the Jews, Arabs, Assyrians, and Phoenicians.
- [modern Latin *Semita* from Late Latin from Greek *Sēm* Shem]

Semitic *adjective*
- "suh MITTIC"
- of or relating to the Semites, esp. the Jews.
- [as SEMITE]

semolina *noun*
- "semma LEENA"
- the hard grains left after the milling of flour, used esp. in making pasta.
- [Italian *semolino* diminutive of *semola* bran, from Latin *simila* flour]

sempervivum *noun*
- "semper VIE vum"
- a succulent plant of the genus *Sempervivum*, esp. the houseleek.
- [modern Latin genus name, from Latin *semper* always + *vivus* living]

sempiternal *adjective*
- "sempa TURN'll"
- eternal, everlasting.
- [Old French *sempiternel* from Late Latin *sempiternalis* from Latin *sempiternus* from *semper* always + *aeternus* eternal]

semplice *adverb*
- "SEM plitch ay" or "SEM plitch ee"
- (as a musical direction) in a simple style of performance.
- [Italian, from Latin *simplus* simple]

sempre *adverb*
- "SEM pray" or "SEM pree"
- (as a musical direction) throughout, always.
- [Italian, from Latin *semper* always]

senary *adjective*
- "SEENER ee" or "SENNER ee"
- of six, by sixes.
- [Latin *senarius* from *seni* distributive of *sex* six]

HOMOPHONES: *scenery*

senate *noun*
- "SENNIT"
- (in Canada) the upper chamber of Parliament, consisting of senators appointed to represent the regions of Canada.
- [Old French *senat* from Latin *senatus* from *senex* old man]
- **senator** *noun*
- **senatorial** *adjective*
- **senatorship** *noun*

HOMOPHONES: *sennet*

sendal *noun*
- "SEND'll"
- a thin rich silk material.
- [Old French *cendal*, ultimately from Greek *sindōn*]

sene *noun*
• "SENNY"
• a monetary unit of Samoa, equal to one-hundredth of a tala.
• [Samoan]

Seneca *noun*
• "SENNA kuh"
• a member of one of the founding members of the Iroquois Five Nations confederacy, now living in Ontario and New York.
• [Dutch *Sennec(a)s* the upper Iroquois people collectively, ultimately from Algonquian]

Senegalese *noun*
• "senna guh LEEZ"
• a native or inhabitant of Senegal in W Africa.

Senegambian *adjective*
• "senna GAMBY 'n"
• of or relating to the W African region between the Senegal and Gambia rivers.

senesce *verb*
• "suh NESS"
• grow old.
• [Latin *senescere* from *senex* old]
• **senescence** *noun*
• **senescent** *adjective*

seneschal *noun*
• "SENNA sh'll"
• the steward or major-domo of a medieval great house.
• [Old French from medieval Latin *seniscalus* from Germanic, = old servant]

seniti *noun*
• "SEN itty"
• a monetary unit of Tonga, equal to one-hundredth of a pa'anga.
• [Tongan, from 'cent']

senna *noun*
• "SENNA"
• a cassia tree, or a laxative prepared from the dried pods of this.
• [medieval Latin *sena* from Arabic *sanā*]

sennet *noun*
• "SENNIT"
• a signal call on a trumpet or cornet (in the stage directions of Elizabethan plays).
• [perhaps var. of SIGNET]
HOMOPHONES: *senate*

señor *noun*
• "sen YORE"
• a title used of or to a Spanish-speaking man.
• [Spanish from Latin *senior* old man, from *senex* old]
HOMOPHONES: *signor*

señora *noun*
• "sen YORE uh"
• a title used of or to a Spanish-speaking married woman.
• [Spanish, feminine of SEÑOR]
HOMOPHONES: *signora*

señorita *noun*
• "sen yuh REETA"
• a title used of or to a Spanish-speaking unmarried woman.
• [Spanish, diminutive of SEÑORA]

sensei *noun*
• "sen SAY"
• (in martial arts) a teacher.
• [Japanese, from *sen* previous + *sei* birth]

sensibility *noun*
• "sensa BILLA tee"
• openness to emotional impressions, susceptibility, sensitiveness.
• [as SENSIBLE]

sensible *adjective*
• "SENSA bull"
• having or showing wisdom or common sense; reasonable, judicious.
• [Latin *sensibilis* from *sensus* faculty of feeling, thought, meaning, from *sentire sens-* feel]
• **sensibleness** *noun*
• **sensibly** *adverb*

sensitive *adjective*
• "SENSA tiv"
• very open to or acutely affected by external stimuli or mental impressions.
• [Old French *sensitif, -ive* or Latin *sensitivus* from *sensus* faculty of feeling, thought, meaning, from *sentire sens-* feel]
• **sensitively** *adverb*
• **sensitiveness** *noun*
• **sensitivity** *noun*

sensitize *verb*
ALSO SPELLED: esp. *Brit.* **-ise**
• "SENSA tize"
• make sensitive.
• [as SENSITIVE]
• **sensitization** *noun* (also esp. *Brit.* **-isation**)
• **sensitizer** *noun* (also esp. *Brit.* **-iser**)

sensitometer *noun*
• "sensa TOMMA tur"
• a device for measuring sensitivity to light.
• [SENSITIVE + Greek *metron* measure]

sensor *noun*
• "SENSER"
• a device giving a signal for the detection or measurement of a physical property to which it responds.
• [SENSORY, after 'motor']
HOMOPHONES: *censor, censer*

sensorium *noun*
• "sen SORRY um"
• the seat of sensation, the brain, brain and spinal cord, or grey matter of these.
• [Late Latin from Latin *sentire sens-* feel]
• **sensorial** *adjective*
• **sensorially** *adverb*

sensory *adjective*
• "SENSA ree"
• of sensation or the senses.

• [as SENSORIUM]
• **sensorily** *adverb*

sensual *adjective*
• "SEN shoo 'll"
• of or depending on the senses only and not on the intellect or spirit; carnal, fleshly.
• [Late Latin *sensualis* from Latin *sensus* faculty of feeling, thought, meaning, from *sentire* sens- feel]
• **sensualism** *noun*
• **sensualist** *noun*
• **sensuality** *noun* "sen shoo ALA tee"
• **sensualize** *verb* (also esp. *Brit.* **-ise**)
• **sensually** *adverb*

sensuous *adjective*
• "SEN shoo us"
• of or derived from or affecting the senses, esp. aesthetically rather than sensually.
• [as SENSUAL]
• **sensuously** *adverb*
• **sensuousness** *noun*

sent *noun*
• "SENT"
• a monetary unit of Estonia, equal to one-hundredth of a kroon.
• [Estonian, = cent]
HOMOPHONES: *scent, cent*

sente *noun*
• "SENTY"
• a monetary unit of Lesotho, equal to one-hundredth of a loti.
• [Sesotho]

sentential *adjective*
• "sen TEN sh'll"
• of a sentence.
• [Latin *sententia* opinion, from *sentire* be of opinion]

sententious *adjective*
• "sen TEN sh'ss"
• (of a person) fond of pompous moralizing.
• [as SENTENTIAL]
• **sententiously** *adverb*
• **sententiousness** *noun*

sentient *adjective*
• "SEN sh'nt"
• having the power of perception by the senses.
• [Latin *sentire* feel]
• **sentience** *noun*
• **sentiency** *noun*
• **sentiently** *adverb*

sentiment *noun*
• "SENTA m'nt"
• a view of or attitude towards a situation or event; an opinion or point of view.
• [medieval Latin *sentimentum* from Latin *sentire* feel]

sentimental *adjective*
• "senta MENT'll"
• of or prompted by feelings of tenderness, sadness, or nostalgia.
• [as SENTIMENT]
• **sentimentalism** *noun*
• **sentimentalist** *noun*
• **sentimentality** *noun*
• **sentimentalization** *noun* (also esp. *Brit.* **-isation**)
• **sentimentalize** *verb* (also esp. *Brit.* **-ise**)
• **sentimentally** *adverb*

sentinel *noun*
• "SEN tin 'll"
• a sentry or lookout; a guard.
• [French *sentinelle* from Italian *sentinella*, of unknown origin]

sepal *noun*
• "SEEP'll" or "SEP'll"
• each of the divisions or leaves of the calyx.
• [French *sépale*, modern Latin *sepalum*, perhaps formed as SEPARATE + PETAL]

separate *adjective*
• "SEPPER it" or "SEP rit"
• forming a unit that is or may be regarded as apart or by itself; physically disconnected, distinct, or individual.
• [Latin *separare separat-* (*se-* apart, without, *parare* make ready)]
• **separability** *noun*
• **separable** *adjective*
• **separably** *adverb*
• **separately** *adverb*
• **separateness** *noun*
• **separation** *noun*

separatist *noun*
• "SEPPRA tist"
• a person who favours separation, esp. for political or ecclesiastical independence; (in Canada) a person who favours the secession of Quebec or the Western provinces from Canada.
• [as SEPARATE]
• **separatism** *noun*

separator *noun*
• "SEPPA ray tur"
• a machine or device for separating, e.g. cream from milk or egg yolk from egg white.
• [as SEPARATE]

Sephardi *noun*
• "suh FARDY"
• a Jew of Spanish or Portuguese descent.
• [Late Hebrew, from *sᵉpāraḏ*, a country mentioned in Obad. 20 and taken to be Spain]
• **Sephardic** *adjective*

sepia *noun*
• "SEEPY uh"
• a dark reddish-brown colour associated particularly with monochrome photographs of the 19th and early 20th centuries.
• [Latin from Greek *sēpia* cuttlefish]

sepoy *noun*
• "SEE poy"
• (in India) a native soldier serving under British or other European orders.

• [Urdu & Persian *sipāhī* soldier, from *sipāh* army]

seppuku *noun*
• "suh POO coo"
• ritual suicide by disembowelment with a sword, formerly practised by Samurai to avoid dishonour.
• [Japanese]

sepsis *noun*
• "SEP sis"
• the state of being septic.
• [modern Latin from Greek *sēpsis* from *sēpō* make rotten]

sept *noun*
• "SEPT"
• a clan, esp. in Ireland.
• [prob. alteration of 'sect' (see SECTARIAN)]

septate *adjective*
• "SEP tate"
• having a septum or septa; partitioned.
• [as SEPTUM]
• **septation** *noun*

septenarius *noun*
• "septa NERRY us"
• a verse of seven feet, esp. a trochaic or iambic tetrameter lacking a syllable in the last foot.
• [Latin from *septeni* distributive of *septem* seven]

septenary *adjective*
• "SEPTA nerry" or "sep TEENA ree"
• of seven, by sevens, on the basis of seven.
• [Latin *septenarius* (as SEPTENARIUS)]

septennial *adjective*
• "sep TENNY 'll"
• lasting for seven years.
• [Late Latin *septennis* from Latin *septem* seven + *annus* year]

septet *noun*
• "sep TET"
• a composition for seven performers.
• [Latin *septem* seven]

septicemia *noun*
ALSO SPELLED: *Brit.* **septicaemia**
• "septa SEEMY uh"
• blood poisoning.
• [modern Latin from Greek *sēptikos* from *sēpō* make rotten + *haima* blood]
• **septicemic** *adjective* (also esp. *Brit.* **septicaemic**)

septillion *noun*
• "sep TILL y'n"
• a thousand raised to the eighth power (10^{24} and 10^{42} respectively).
• [French from *sept* seven, after *billion* etc.]

septoria *noun*
• "sep TORY uh"
• any of numerous parasitic fungi constituting the genus *Septoria*.
• [modern Latin *Septoria* from Latin SEPTUM]

septuagenarian *noun*
• "sept wuh juh NERRY 'n" or "sep chwa juh NERRY 'n" or "septa juh NERRY 'n"
• a person from 70 to 79 years old.
• [Latin *septuagenarius* from *septuageni* distributive of *septuaginta* seventy]

Septuagesima *noun*
• "sep tyoo a JESSIM uh"
• the Sunday before Sexagesima.
• [Latin, = seventieth (day), formed as SEPTUAGINT, perhaps after QUINQUAGESIMA or with reference to the period of 70 days from Septuagesima to the Saturday after Easter]

Septuagint *noun*
• "SEPT wuh j'nt" or "sep TOO a j'nt" or "SEP choo a j'nt"
• a Greek version of the Hebrew Scriptures including the Apocrypha, said to have been made about 270 BC by about 70 translators.
• [Latin *septuaginta* seventy]

septum *noun*
• "SEP t'm"
• a partition, such as that between the nostrils or the chambers of a shell.
• [Latin *s(a)eptum* from *saepire saept-* enclose, from *saepes* hedge]
• **septal** *adjective*

sepulchre *noun*
ALSO SPELLED: *US* **sepulcher**
• "SEPPLE cur"
• a tomb esp. cut in rock or built of stone or brick, a burial vault or cave.
• [Old French from Latin *sepulc(h)rum* from *sepelire sepult-* bury]
• **sepulchral** *adjective* "se PUL crull" ("PUL" rhymes with *HULL*)
• **sepulchrally** *adverb*

sequel *noun*
• "SEE kwull"
• what follows after or as a result of an earlier event.
• [Old French *sequelle* or Latin *sequel(l)a* from *sequi* follow]

sequela *noun*
• "suh KWEE luh"
• a condition or symptom following a disease.
• [Latin from *sequi* follow]

sequence *noun*
• "SEE kwince"
• succession, coming after or next.
• [Late Latin *sequentia* from Latin *sequens* present participle of *sequi* follow]

sequencer *noun*
• "SEE kwin sur"
• a programmable electronic device for storing sequences of musical notes, chords, rhythms, etc. and transmitting them when required to an electronic musical instrument.
• [as SEQUENCE]

sequential *adjective*
• "suh KWEN sh'll"
• forming a sequence, consequence, or sequela.
• [as SEQUENCE]
• **sequentiality** *noun* "suh kwenshy ALA tee"
• **sequentially** *adverb*

sequester *verb*
• "suh KWESS tur"
• seclude, isolate, set apart.
• [Old French *sequestrer* or Late Latin *sequestrare* commit for safekeeping, from Latin *sequester* trustee]

sequestrate *verb*
• "suh KWESS trate"
• confiscate, appropriate.
• [as SEQUESTER]
• **sequestration** *noun* "see kwiss TRAY sh'n"
• **sequestrator** *noun* "SEE kwiss traiter"

sequestrum *noun*
• "suh KWEST rum"
• a piece of dead bone or other tissue detached from the surrounding parts.
• [modern Latin, neuter of Latin *sequester* standing apart]

sequin *noun*
• "SEEK win"
• a circular spangle for attaching to clothing as an ornament.
• [French from Italian *zecchino* from *zecca* a mint, from Arabic *sikka* a die]
• **sequined** *adjective* (also **sequinned**)

sequoia *noun*
• "suh KWOY uh"
• a Californian evergreen coniferous tree, *Sequoia sempervirens*, of very great height and breadth.
• [modern Latin genus name, from *Sequoiah*, the name of a Cherokee]

serac *noun*
• "se RACK"
• a pinnacle or ridge of ice on the surface of a glacier where crevasses intersect.
• [Swiss French *sérac*, originally the name of a compact white cheese]

seraglio *noun*
• "suh RALLY oh"
• a harem.
• [Italian *serraglio* from Turkish from Persian *sarāy* palace: compare SERAI]

serai *noun*
• "suh RYE"
• (in the Middle East) an inn with a central court where caravans may rest; a caravanserai.
• [Turkish from Persian (as SERAGLIO)]

serape *noun*
ALSO SPELLED: **sarape**
• "suh RAPPY"
• a shawl or blanket worn as a cloak esp. in Mexico.
• [Latin American Spanish]

seraph *noun*
• "SARE uff"
• a supernatural being with three pairs of wings (Isaiah 6:2).
• [back-formation from *seraphim* (compare CHERUB) (pl.) from Late Latin from Greek *seraphim* from Hebrew *śᵉrāpīm*]
• **seraphic** *adjective* "suh RAFFIC"
• **seraphically** *adverb*
HOMOPHONES: *serif*

sere *adjective*
• "SEER"
• (esp. of a plant, landscape, etc.) withered, dried.
• [var. of SEAR]
HOMOPHONES: *cere, seer, sear*

serenade *noun*
• "serra NADE"
• a piece of music sung or played in the open air, esp. by a lover at night under the window of his beloved.
• [French *sérénade* from Italian *serenata* from *sereno* SERENE]
• **serenader** *noun*

serenata *noun*
• "serra NATTA"
• a cantata with a pastoral subject.
• [Italian (as SERENADE)]

serendipity *noun*
• "sare 'n DIPPA tee"
• the faculty of making happy and unexpected discoveries by accident.
• [coined by English writer and politician Horace Walpole (d.1797) after *The Three Princes of Serendip* (now Sri Lanka), a fairy tale]
• **serendipitous** *adjective*
• **serendipitously** *adverb*

serene *adjective*
• "suh REEN"
• placid, tranquil, unperturbed.
• [Latin *serenus*]
• **serenely** *adverb*
• **serenity** *noun* "suh RENNA tee"

serf *noun*
• "SURF"
• (under the feudal system) a labourer who was not free to move from the land on which he worked.
• [Old French from Latin *servus* slave]
• **serfdom** *noun*
HOMOPHONES: *surf*

serge *noun*
• "SURJ"
• a durable twilled woollen or worsted fabric used mainly for clothing.
• [Old French, ultimately from Latin *serica* (*lana*) from *sericum* silk, neuter of *sericus* from *seres* from Greek *Sēres* an oriental people]
HOMOPHONES: *surge*

sergeant *noun*
- "SAR j'nt"
- (in the Canadian Army and Air Force and other armies) a non-commissioned officer ranking above master corporal and below warrant officer.
- [Old French *sergent* from Latin *serviens -entis* servant, from *servire* serve]

serger *noun*
- "SUR jur"
- a machine used for close-stitching or overcasting to prevent material from fraying at the edge.
- [as SERGE]

serial *noun*
- "SEERY 'll"
- a story, play, or film which is published, broadcast, or shown in regular instalments.
- [as SERIES]
- **seriality** *noun*
- **serialization** *noun* (also esp. *Brit.* **-isation**)
- **serialize** *verb* (also esp. *Brit.* **-ise**)
- **serially** *adverb*

HOMOPHONES: *cereal*

serialism *noun*
- "SEERY 'll izm"
- a compositional technique in which a fixed series of notes, esp. the twelve notes of the chromatic scale, are used to generate the harmonic and melodic basis of a piece and are subject to change only in specific ways.
- [as SERIAL]
- **serialist** *noun*

seriate *adjective*
- "SEERY it"
- in the form of a series; in orderly sequence.
- [as SERIAL]
- **seriation** *noun*

sericulture *noun*
- "SERRA cull chur"
- silkworm breeding.
- [French *sériciculture* from Late Latin *sericum* silk: see SERGE, CULTURE]

seriema *noun*
- "serry EE muh"
- any S American bird of the family Cariamidae, having a long neck and legs and a crest above the bill.
- [modern Latin from Tupi *siriema* etc. crested]

series *noun*
- "SEER eez"
- a number of things of which each is similar to the preceding or in which each successive pair are similarly related; a sequence, succession, order, row, or set.
- [Latin, = row, chain, from *serere* join, connect]

serif *noun*
- "SARE if"
- a slight projection finishing off a stroke of a letter as in T contrasted with T.
- [perhaps from Dutch *schreef* dash, line, from Germanic]
- **serifed** *adjective*

HOMOPHONES: *seraph*

serigraph *noun*
- "SERRA graff"
- a print made by silkscreen printing.
- [formed irregularly from Latin *sericum* silk: see SERGE]

serine *noun*
- "SARE een" or "SEER een" or "SARE in" or "SEER in"
- a hydrophilic amino acid present in proteins.
- [Latin *sericum* silk]

seriocomic *adjective*
- "seery oh COMMIC"
- combining the serious and the comic; jocular in intention but simulating seriousness or vice versa.
- [as SERIOUS + COMEDY]
- **seriocomedy** *noun*

serious *adjective*
- "SEERY us"
- thoughtful, earnest, sober, sedate, responsible, not reckless or given to trifling.
- [Old French *serieux* or Late Latin *seriosus* from Latin *serius*]
- **seriously** *adverb*
- **seriousness** *noun*

sermon *noun*
- "SUR m'n"
- a spoken or written discourse on a religious or moral subject, esp. a discourse based on a text or passage of Scripture and delivered in a service by way of religious instruction or exhortation.
- [Old French from Latin *sermo -onis* discourse, talk]
- **sermonic** *adjective* "sur MONNIC"
- **sermonize** *verb* (also esp. *Brit.* **-ise**)
- **sermonizer** *noun* (also esp. *Brit.* **-iser**)

sermonette *noun*
- "surma NET"
- a short sermon.
- [as SERMON]

seroconversion *noun*
- "seero k'n VUR zh'n"
- a change from a seronegative to a seropositive state.
- [SERUM + Latin *convertere* convert, turn about (from *com-* with + *vertere* turn)]
- **seroconvert** *verb*

serology *noun*
- "suh RAWLA jee"
- the scientific study of blood sera and their effects.
- [SERUM + Greek *logos* word]
- **serologic** *adjective*
- **serological** *adjective*
- **serologically** *adverb*
- **serologist** *noun*

seronegative *adjective*
• "seero NEGGA tiv"
• giving a negative result in a test of blood serum, e.g. for presence of a virus.
• [SERUM + NEGATIVE]
• **seronegativity** *noun*

seropositive *adjective*
• "seero POZZA tiv"
• giving a positive result in a test of blood serum, e.g. for presence of a virus.
• [SERUM + POSITIVE]
• **seropositivity** *noun*

serosa *noun*
• "suh ROE suh"
• a serous membrane.
• [modern Latin, feminine of medieval Latin *serosus* SEROUS]
• **serosal** *adjective*

serotinous *adjective*
• "sur OTT in us"
• (of a pine etc. cone) remaining long unopened, slow to release seed.
• [Latin *serotinus* late]

serotonin *noun*
• "serra TOE nin"
• a compound present in blood platelets and serum, which constricts the blood vessels and acts as a neurotransmitter.
• [SERUM + 'tonic' from Greek *tonos* tension, tone, from *teinō* stretch]

serotype *noun*
• "SEERO tipe"
• a serologically distinguishable strain of a micro-organism.
• [SERUM + TYPE]

serous *adjective*
• "SEER us"
• of or like or producing serum; watery.
• [as SERUM]

serpent *noun*
• "SUR p'nt"
• a snake, esp. of a large kind.
• [Old French from Latin *serpens -entis* participle of *serpere* creep]
• **serpentine** *adjective* "SURP'n tine" or "SURP'n teen"

serranid *noun*
• "suh RAN id" or "SERRA nid"
• any marine fish of the family Serranidae, comprising heavy predatory fishes such as sea basses and groupers.
• [modern Latin *Serranus* (genus name) from Latin *serra* saw]

serrano *noun*
• "suh RONNO"
• a hot chili pepper with green, red, or yellow skin, used in salsas etc.
• [Spanish, = from the mountain]

serrated *adjective*
• "suh RATED"
• having a sawlike edge.
• [Late Latin *serrare serrat-* from Latin *serra* saw]
• **serration** *noun*

serried *adjective*
• "SARE eed"
• (of ranks of soldiers, rows of trees, etc.) pressed together; without gaps; close.
• [prob. from French *serré* past participle of *serrer* close, ultimately from Latin *sera* lock]

serrulate *adjective*
• "SERRA late" or "SERRA let"
• finely serrated; with a series of small notches.
• [modern Latin *serrulatus* from Latin *serrula* diminutive of *serra* saw]
• **serrulation** *noun*

serum *noun*
• "SEER um"
• the amber-coloured protein-rich liquid in which blood cells are suspended and which separates out when blood coagulates.
• [Latin, = whey]

serval *noun*
• "SURV'll"
• a tawny black-spotted long-legged African cat, *Felis serval*.
• [French from Portuguese *cerval* deer-like, from *cervo* deer, from Latin *cervus*]

servant *noun*
• "SURV'nt"
• a person hired to carry out the orders of an individual or corporate employer, esp. a person employed in a house on domestic duties or as a personal attendant.
• [Old French *servant* from *servir* from Latin *servire*, from *servus* slave]
• **servanthood** *noun*
• **servantless** *adjective*

servery *noun*
• "SURVER ee"
• a counter or room from which meals are served in a cafeteria etc.
• [as SERVANT]

serveware *noun*
• "SURVE ware"
• items on or from which food etc. is served, e.g. bowls, butter dishes, shakers, creamers, etc.
• [as SERVANT + WARE]

service *noun*
• "SUR viss"
• a southern European tree of the rose family, *Sorbus domestica*, with cream-coloured flowers, and small round or pear-shaped fruit eaten when overripe.
• [earlier *serves*, pl. of obsolete *serve*, via Old English *syrfe* from Germanic, ultimately from Latin *sorbus*]

serviceable *adjective*
• "SURVISS a bull"
• useful or usable.
• [as SERVANT]
• **serviceability** *noun*
• **serviceably** *adverb*

serviceberry *noun*
• "SURVISS berry"
• any N American shrub or small tree of the genus *Amelanchier*.
• [as SERVICE + 'berry']

serviette *noun*
• "survy ET"
• *Cdn & Brit.* a napkin for use at table, esp. a paper one.
• [Old French from *servir* serve, from Latin *servire*, from *servus* slave]

servile *adjective*
• "SUR vile"
• slavish, fawning; completely dependent.
• [Latin *servilis* from *servus* slave]
• **servilely** *adverb*
• **servility** *noun* "sur VILLA tee"

servitor *noun*
• "SURVA tur"
• a servant.
• [Latin, from *servire* serve, from *servus* slave]

servitude *noun*
• "SURVA tude"
• slavery.
• [Old French from Latin *servitudo -inis* from *servus* slave]

servomechanism *noun*
• "SUR vo mecka nizm"
• a powered mechanism producing motion or forces at a higher level of energy than the input level, e.g. in the brakes and steering of large motor vehicles, esp. where feedback is employed to make the control automatic.
• [Latin *servus* slave + MECHANISM]

sesame *noun*
• "SESSA mee"
• an E Indian herbaceous plant, *Sesamum indicum*, with seeds used as food and yielding an edible oil.
• [Latin *sesamum* from Greek *sēsamon, sēsamē*]

sesamoid *adjective*
• "SESSA moid"
• shaped like a sesame seed; nodular (esp. of small independent bones developed in tendons passing over an angular structure such as the kneecap and the navicular bone).
• [as SESAME]

Sesotho *noun*
• "se SOO too"
• the South Eastern Bantu language of the Sotho.
• [Sesotho, from *se-* prefix + SOTHO]

sesquicentenary *noun*
• "sess kwee sen TENNER ee" or "sess kwee sen TEENER ee"
• a one-hundred-and-fiftieth anniversary.
• [Latin *sesqui-* one and a half (*semi-* half, *-que* and) + CENTENARY]

sesquicentennial *noun*
• "sess kwee sen TENNY 'll"
• a one-hundred-and-fiftieth anniversary.
• [Latin *sesqui-* one and a half (*semi-* half, *-que* and) + CENTENNIAL]

sesquipedalian *adjective*
• "sess kwee puh DAILY 'n"
• (of a word) long, polysyllabic.
• [from Latin *sesquipedalis* a foot and a half long]

sessile *adjective*
• "SESS ile"
• (of a flower, leaf, eye, etc.) attached directly by its base without a stalk or peduncle.
• [Latin *sessilis* from *sedēre sess-* sit]

sesterce *noun*
• "SESS turce"
• an ancient Roman coin and monetary unit equal to one quarter of a denarius.
• [Latin *sestertius* (*nummus* coin) = 2½ from *semis* half + *tertius* third]

sestet *noun*
• "sess TET"
• the last six lines of a sonnet.
• [Italian *sestetto* from *sesto* from Latin *sextus* a sixth]

sestina *noun*
• "sess TEENA"
• a form of rhymed or unrhymed poem with six stanzas of six lines and a final triplet, all stanzas having the same six words at the line endings in six different sequences.
• [Italian (as SESTET)]

seta *noun*
• "SEETA"
• stiff hair; bristle.
• [Latin, = bristle]
• **setaceous** *adjective* "see TAY sh'ss"

setose *adjective*
• "SEE tose" (rhymes with *GROSS*)
• bristly.
• [Latin *seta* bristle]

Setswana *noun*
• "set SWONNA"
• the Bantu language of the Tswana.
• [Setswana *se-* language prefix + TSWANA]

settee *noun*
• "set EE"
• a seat (usu. upholstered), with a back and usu. arms, for more than one person.
• [18th c.: perhaps a fanciful var. of 'settle' bench, from Old English *setl* place to sit, from Germanic]

Seussian *adjective*
• "SOO see 'n"
• of or characteristic of 'Dr. Seuss' (Theodore Seuss Geisel), US writer and illustrator of children's books d.1991.

sever *verb*
• "SEV ur"
• divide, break, or make separate, esp. by cutting.
• [Old French *sevrer* ultimately from Latin *separare* SEPARATE]
• **severable** *adjective*

several *adjective*
• "SEV rull"
• more than two but not many.
• [Anglo-French from Anglo-Latin *separalis* from Latin *separ* SEPARATE]

severally *adverb*
• "SEV r'll ee"
• separately; individually.
• [as SEVERAL]

severalty *noun*
• "SEV r'll tee"
• separateness.
• [as SEVERAL]

severance *noun*
• "SEV ur ince"
• the act or an instance of severing.
• [as SEVER]

Sèvres *noun*
• "SEVRA"
• fine porcelain, often with elaborate decoration, made at Sèvres in the suburbs of Paris.

sevruga *noun*
• "sev ROOGA"
• a migratory sturgeon, *Acipenser stellatus*, of the Caspian and Black Sea basins.
• [Russian *sevryuga*]

sexagenarian *noun*
• "sexa juh NERRY 'n"
• a person from 60 to 69 years old.
• [Latin *sexagenarius* from *sexageni* distributive of *sexaginta* sixty]

Sexagesima *noun*
• "sexa JESSIM uh"
• the second Sunday before Lent.
• [Church Latin, = sixtieth (day), prob. named loosely as preceding QUINQUAGESIMA]

sexagesimal *adjective*
• "sexa JESSIM 'll"
• of sixtieths.
• [Latin *sexagesimus* (as SEXAGESIMA)]

sexcentenary *noun*
• "sek sen TENNER ee" or "sek sen TEENER ee"
• a six-hundredth anniversary.
• [Latin *sex* six + CENTENARY]

sexennial *adjective*
• "sek SENNY 'll"
• lasting six years.
• [Latin *sex* six + *annus* year]

sexpartite *adjective*
• "sex PAR tite"
• divided into six parts.
• [Latin *sex* six + *partire* part]

sext *noun*
• "SEXT"
• the office of the fourth canonical hour of prayer, originally said at the sixth hour of the day (i.e. noon).
• [Latin *sexta hora* sixth hour]
HOMOPHONES: *sexed*

sextant *noun*
• "SEX t'nt"
• an instrument with a graduated arc of 60° used in navigation and surveying for measuring the angular distance of objects by means of mirrors.
• [Latin *sextans -ntis* sixth part]

sextet *noun*
• "sex TET"
• a musical composition for six voices or instruments.
• [alteration of SESTET after Latin *sex* six]

sextillion *noun*
• "sex TILL y'n"
• a thousand raised to the seventh power (10^{21} and 10^{36} respectively).
• [French from Latin *sex* six, after *septillion* etc.]

sexton *noun*
• "SEX t'n"
• a person who looks after a church and churchyard, often acting as bell-ringer and gravedigger.
• [Anglo-French, Old French *segerstein, secrestein* from medieval Latin *sacristanus* SACRISTAN]

sextuple *adjective*
• "sex TUPPLE"
• sixfold.
• [medieval Latin *sextuplus*, from Latin *sex* six]

sextuplet *noun*
• "sex TUP lit"
• each of six children born at one birth.
• [as SEXTUPLE]

Seychellois *noun*
• "say shell WAH"
• a native or inhabitant of the Seychelles in the Indian Ocean.

sforzando *adjective*
• "sfort SANDO"
• (as a musical direction) with sudden emphasis.
• [Italian, verbal noun and past participle of *sforzare* use force]

sfumato *adjective*
- "sfoo MOTTO"
- with indistinct outlines.
- [Italian, past participle of *sfumare* shade off, from *fumare* smoke]

sgraffito *noun*
- "sgraw FEETO"
- a form of decoration made by scratching through wet plaster on a wall or through slip on ceramic ware, showing a different-coloured undersurface.
- [Italian, past participle of *sgraffire* scratch, from *graffio* scratch]

Shabbat *noun*
- "shaw BOT"
- the Jewish Sabbath.
- [Hebrew *šabbāt* Sabbath]

Shabbos *noun*
ALSO SPELLED: **Shabbes**
- "SHOB us"
- the Jewish Sabbath.
- [Yiddish from Hebrew *šabbāt* Sabbath]

shaddock *noun*
- "SHAD uck"
- the largest citrus fruit, with a thick yellow skin and bitter pulp; a pomelo.
- [Capt. *Shaddock*, who introduced it to the W Indies in the 17th c.]

shadoof *noun*
- "shuh DOOF"
- a pole with a bucket and counterweight used esp. in Egypt for raising water.
- [Egyptian Arabic *šādūf*]

shaganappi *noun*
- "shagga NAPPY"
- *Cdn (West)* thread, cord, or thong made of rawhide.
- [Swampy Cree *pi-ša-kana-piy* (compare Cree *pi-ša-kan* leather, *-a-piy* string)]

shaggymane *noun*
- "SHAGGY mane"
- a mushroom of the genus *Coprinus*, with a cap that peels in shaggy strips.
- ['shaggy' from Old English *sceacga*, related to Old Norse *skegg* beard, Old English *sceaga* coppice + 'mane' (Old English *manu* from Germanic)]

shagreen *noun*
- "sha GREEN"
- a kind of untanned leather with a rough granulated surface.
- [var. of CHAGRIN in the sense 'rough skin']

shah *noun*
- "SHAW"
- a title of the former monarch of Iran.
- [Persian *šāh* from Old Persian *kšāytiya* king]
- **shahdom** *noun*

HOMOPHONES: *pshaw*

shahid *noun*
ALSO SPELLED: **shaheed**
- "shuh HEED"
- a Muslim martyr.
- [Arabic *šhīd* witness, martyr]

shahtoosh *noun*
ALSO SPELLED: **shatoosh**
- "shuh TOOSH"
- high-quality fabric made from the wool of the chiru.
- [via Punjabi from Persian *šāh* king + Kashmiri *tośa* fine shawl material]

Shakespearean *adjective*
ALSO SPELLED: **Shakespearian**
- "shake SPEERY 'n"
- of or relating to the English poet and dramatist William Shakespeare (d.1616).
- **Shakespeareanism** *noun* (also **Shakespearianism**)

shako *noun*
- "SHAKE oh"
- a cylindrical peaked military hat with a plume.
- [French *schako* from Hungarian *csákó (süveg)* peaked (cap), from *csák* peak, from German *Zacken* spike]

shakuhachi *noun*
- "shackoo HATCH ee"
- a Japanese bamboo flute.
- [Japanese from *shaku* a measure of length + *hachi* eight (tenths)]

shale *noun*
- "SHALE"
- soft finely stratified rock that splits easily, consisting of consolidated mud or clay.
- [prob. from German *Schale* from Old English *sc(e)alu* related to Old Norse *skál* scale]

shallop *noun*
- "SHALLUP"
- a boat for use in shallow waters.
- [French *chaloupe* from Dutch *sloep* sloop]

shallot *noun*
- "shuh LOT" or "SHALL it"
- a variety of onion which forms clumps of small bulbs.
- [French *eschalotte* alteration of Old French *eschaloigne*: see SCALLION]

shalom *interjection*
- "shuh LOME"
- a Jewish salutation at meeting or parting.
- [Hebrew *šālôm* peace]

shalwar *noun*
- "shul WARR"
- a pair of light, loose, pleated trousers tapering to a tight fit around the ankles, worn by women from the Indian subcontinent, typically with a matching kameez.
- [Persian and Urdu *šalwār*]

shamal *noun*
• "shuh MAWL"
• a hot, dry northwesterly wind blowing across the Persian Gulf in summer, typically causing sandstorms.
• [Arabic *šamāl* north (wind)]

shaman *noun*
• "SHAY m'n"
• a person regarded as having access to the world of good and evil spirits, esp. among some peoples of northern Asia and N America.
• [German *Schamane* & Russian *shaman* from Tungus *samán*]
• **shamanic** *adjective* "shuh MANNIC"
• **shamanically** *adverb*
• **shamanism** *noun*
• **shamanistic** *adjective*
• **shamanistically** *adverb*

shamateur *noun*
• "SHAMMA chur" or "SHAMMA tur"
• a sports player who makes money from sporting activities though classed as an amateur.
• ['sham' + AMATEUR]
• **shamateurism** *noun*

shamba *noun*
• "SHAM buh"
• (in East Africa) a cultivated plot of ground; a farm or plantation.
• [Kiswahili]

shambolic *adjective*
• "sham BOLLIC"
• chaotic, unorganized.
• ['shambles', prob. after SYMBOLIC]

shamiana *noun*
• "SHOMMY onna"
• (in India) a large tent.
• [Persian *shāmiyāna*]

shamisen *noun*
• "SHAMMA s'n"
• a Japanese guitar with a long neck, no frets, and three strings of waxed silk, played with a plectrum.
• [Japanese from Chinese *san-hsien* from *san* three + *hsien* string]

shamus *noun*
• "SHAY muss"
• a detective.
• [20th c.: origin uncertain]

Shan *noun*
• "SHAWN" or "SHAN"
• a member of a group of Thai peoples inhabiting parts of SE Asia.
• [Burmese]

shanghai *verb*
• "SHANG hy" or "shang HY"
• trick or force (a person) into doing something or going somewhere.
• [*Shanghai*, China]

Shanghainese *adjective*
• "shang hy NEEZ"
• of or relating to Shanghai, China.

Shango *noun*
• "SHANG go"
• a religious cult originating in W Nigeria and now chiefly practised in parts of the Caribbean.
• [Yoruba]

shantung *noun*
• "shan TUNG"
• a fabric of silk or artificial fibres, with slubs in the yarn producing a slightly rough surface.
• [*Shantung* (also *Shandong*) in China]

Shaolin *noun*
• "shau LIN" ("SHAU" rhymes with *HOW*)
• a martial art which developed in NE central China.
• [the Buddhist monastery of *Shaolin* (founded AD 495), where it originated]

shapely *adjective*
• "SHAPE lee"
• well formed or proportioned.
• [Old English *gesceap* creation, shape, from Germanic]
• **shapeliness** *noun*

sharia *noun*
ALSO SPELLED: **shariah**
• "shuh REE uh"
• Islamic canonical law based on the teachings of the Quran and the traditions of the Prophet.
• [Arabic *šarīʻa*]

sharif *noun*
ALSO SPELLED: **sherif**
• "shuh REEF"
• a descendant of Muhammad through his daughter Fatima, entitled to wear a green turban or veil.
• [Arabic *šarīf* noble, from *šarafa* be exalted]

shashlik *noun*
• "SHASH lick"
• (in Asia and E Europe) a kebab of mutton and garnishes.
• [Russian *shashlyk*, ultimately from Turkish *şiş* spit, skewer]

Shastra *noun*
• "SHOSS truh"
• Hindu sacred writings.
• [Hindi *śāstr*, Sanskrit *śāstra*]

Shavian *adjective*
• "SHAY vee 'n"
• of or in the manner of the Irish writer G. B. Shaw (d.1950) or his ideas.
• [*Shavius*, Latinized form of *Shaw*]

Shavuot *noun*
ALSO SPELLED: **Shavuoth**
• "shuh VOO ut" or "shaw voo OTT"
• the Jewish harvest festival, on the fiftieth day after the second day of Passover.

• [Hebrew *šāḇûʻôṯ*, = weeks, with reference to the weeks between Passover and Shavuot]

shawarma *noun*
• "shuh WARR muh" ("WARR" rhymes with *FAR*)
• (in the cuisine of certain Arabic countries) meat cooked on a spit and served in thin slices, often rolled in pita bread.
• [Syrian Arabic *shāwirma* from Turkish *çevirme* piece of meat roasted on a spit, from *çevirme* turn, rotate]

shawm *noun*
• "SHOM"
• a medieval double-reed wind instrument with a sharp penetrating tone.
• [Old French *chalemie*, ultimately from Latin *calamus* from Greek *kalamos* reed]

Shawnee *noun*
• "shaw NEE"
• a member of an Algonquian people formerly resident in the eastern US and now chiefly in Oklahoma.
• [Delaware *ša:wano:w*]

shea *noun*
• "SHEE" or "SHEE uh"
• a W African tree, *Vitellaria paradoxa*, bearing nuts containing a large amount of fat.
• [from a W African name]
HOMOPHONES: *Shia*, *she*

sheaf *noun*
• "SHEEF"
• a pile or bundle of things, esp. paper.
• [Old English *scēaf* from Germanic]

shear *verb*
• "SHEER"
• clip the wool off (a sheep etc.).
• [Old English *sceran* from Germanic]
• **shearer** *noun*
HOMOPHONES: *sheer*

shearling *noun*
• "SHEER ling"
• a sheep that has been shorn once.
• [as SHEAR]

shearwater *noun*
• "SHEER water"
• any of a number of seabirds of the family Procellariidae, related to petrels, which habitually skim low over the open sea with wings outstretched.
• [as SHEAR + 'water']

sheath *noun*
• "SHEETH"
• a close-fitting cover, esp. for the blade of a knife or sword.
• [Old English *scæth*, *scēath*]
• **sheathless** *adjective*

sheathe *verb*
• "SHEETHE" (with "TH" as in *BATHE*)
• put into a sheath.
• [as SHEATH]

sheathing *noun*
• "SHEETHE ing" (with "TH" as in *BATHE*)
• a protective casing or covering.
• [as SHEATH]

sheave *verb*
• "SHEEVE"
• make (grain) into sheaves.
• [as SHEAF]

shebeen *noun*
• "shuh BEEN"
• (esp. in Ireland, Scotland, Newfoundland, and South Africa) an unlicensed house selling alcoholic liquor.
• [Anglo-Irish *síbín* from *séibe* mugful]

sheer *adjective*
• "SHEER"
• complete; nothing more than.
• [Middle English *schere* prob. from dialect *shire* pure, clear, from Old English *scīr* from Germanic]
• **sheerly** *adverb*
• **sheerness** *noun*
HOMOPHONES: *shear*

shehnai *noun*
ALSO SPELLED: **shenai**
• "shen EYE"
• a double-reed wind instrument of northern India, similar to the oboe.
• [Hindi and Urdu *śahnāī*, from Persian *šāhnāy*]

sheik *noun*
ALSO SPELLED: **sheikh**
• "SHEEK" or "SHAKE"
• a chief or head of an Arab tribe, family, or village.
• [ultimately from Arabic *šayḵ* old man, sheikh, from *šāḵa* be or grow old]
• **sheikdom** *noun* (also **sheikhdom**)
HOMOPHONES: *chic*, *shake*

sheila *noun*
• "SHEELA"
• a girl or young woman.
• [originally *shaler* (of unknown origin): assimilated to the name *Sheila*]

shekel *noun*
• "SHECK'll"
• the chief monetary unit of modern Israel.
• [Hebrew *šeḳel* from *šāḳal* weigh]

Shekinah *noun*
ALSO SPELLED: **Shekhinah**
• "shuh KINE uh" ("KINE" rhymes with *FINE*)
• (in Judaism) the glory of the divine presence, conventionally represented as light or interpreted (in kabbalism) as a divine feminine aspect.
• [late Hebrew *šākan* dwell, rest]

shelduck *noun*
• "SHELL duck"
• any bright-plumaged large goose-like wild duck of the genus *Tadorna*, esp. *T. tadorna* of

shores and brackish inland waters in Eurasia and N Africa.
- [Middle English prob. from dialect *sheld* pied, related to Middle Dutch *schillede* variegated, + 'duck']

shellac *noun*
- "shuh LACK"
- lac resin melted into thin flakes and used for making varnish.
- ['shell' + LAC, translation of French *laque en écailles* lac in thin plates]

shellacking *noun*
- "shuh LACKING"
- a severe defeat or beating.
- [as SHELLAC]

Shelta *noun*
- "SHELL tuh"
- an ancient hybrid secret language used by Irish tinkers, gypsies, etc.
- [19th c.: origin unknown]

shelter *noun*
- "SHELL tur"
- a structure built to give protection, esp. from the weather or from attack.
- [16th c.: perhaps from obsolete *sheltron* phalanx, from Old English *scieldtruma* (as SHIELD, *truma* troop)]
- **sheltered** *adjective*
- **shelterer** *noun*
- **shelterless** *adjective*

shelterbelt *noun*
- "SHELL tur belt"
- a line of trees etc. serving to break the force of the wind.
- [as SHELTER + 'belt']

shelterwood *noun*
- "SHELL tur wood"
- mature trees left standing to provide shelter in which saplings can grow.
- [as SHELTER + 'wood']

sheltie *noun*
ALSO SPELLED: **shelty**
- "SHELL tee"
- a Shetland pony or sheepdog.
- [prob. representing Old Norse *Hjalti* Shetlander (as pronounced in Orkney)]

shemozzle *noun*
ALSO SPELLED: **schemozzle**
- "shuh MOZZ'll"
- a brawl or commotion.
- [Yiddish after Late Hebrew *šel-lō'-mazzāl* of no luck]

shen *noun*
- "SHEN"
- (in Chinese thought) the spiritual element of a person's psyche.
- [Chinese *shén*]

shenanigan *noun*
- "shuh NANNA g'n"
- high-spirited behaviour; nonsense.
- [19th c.: origin unknown]

shepherd *noun*
- "SHEP'rd"
- a person employed to tend sheep, esp. at pasture.
- [Old English *scēaphierde* sheep herd]

shepherdess *noun*
- "SHEP'rd ess"
- a woman who tends and rears sheep.
- [as SHEPHERD]

Sheraton *noun*
- "SHARE a t'n"
- the style of furniture introduced in England *c.*1790 by Thomas Sheraton (d.1806), known for its delicate and graceful forms.

sherbet *noun*
- "SHUR bit"
- a frozen dessert, similar to ice cream, made from water, milk, and sugar, and usu. fruit-flavoured.
- [Turkish *şerbet*, Persian *šerbet* from Arabic *šarba* drink, from *šariba* to drink: compare SYRUP]

Sherbrooker *noun*
- "SHUR brooker"
- a resident of Sherbrooke, Que.

sherd *noun*
- "SHURD"
- a broken piece of ceramic material, esp. one found on an archaeological site.
- [Old English *sceard*]

sheriff *noun*
- "SHARE if"
- *Cdn* an appointed official responsible for court administration and trial preparation, the selection of jury panels, the serving of legal documents, and the seizure and sale of property to settle damage claims.
- [Old English *scīr-gerēfa* (shire county, REEVE)]
- **sheriffdom** *noun*

Sherpa *noun*
- "SHUR puh"
- a member of a Himalayan people living on the border of Nepal and Tibet renowned for their skill in mountaineering.
- [Tibetan *sharpa* inhabitant of an eastern country]

sherry *noun*
- "SHERRY"
- a fortified wine originally from S Spain.
- [earlier *sherris* from Spanish (*vino de*) *Xeres* (now Jerez de la Frontera) in S Spain]
- **sherried** *adjective*

sherwani *noun*
- "shur WONNY"
- a knee-length coat buttoning to the neck, worn by men from the Indian subcontinent.

• [Urdu and Persian *širwānī* 'from Shirvan' (referring to a town in NE Persia)]

shewbread *noun*
• "SHOW bred"
• (historically) twelve loaves that were displayed in the Jewish Temple and renewed each Sabbath.
• ['shew' old variant of 'show' + 'bread']

Shia *noun*
ALSO SPELLED: **Shiah**
• "SHEE uh"
• one of the two main branches of Islam, esp. in Iran, that rejects the first three Sunni caliphs and regards Ali, the fourth caliph, as Muhammad's first successor.
• [Arabic *šī'a* party (of Ali, Muhammad's cousin and son-in-law d.661)]
HOMOPHONES: *shea*

shiatsu *noun*
• "shee AT soo"
• a kind of therapy of Japanese origin, in which pressure is applied with the fingers or palms to certain points of the body.
• [Japanese, = finger pressure]

shibboleth *noun*
• "SHIBBA leth"
• a long-standing formula, doctrine, or phrase, etc., held to be true (esp. unreflectingly) by a party or group.
• [Hebrew *šibbōleṯ* ear of wheat, used as a test of nationality for its difficult pronunciation (Judg. 12:6)]

shield *noun*
• "SHEELD"
• a piece of metal, wooden, acrylic, etc. armour, carried on the arm or in the hand to deflect blows from the head or body.
• [Old English *sc(i)eld* from Germanic: prob. originally = board]

shieling *noun*
• "SHEE ling"
• a roughly constructed hut originally esp. for use by shepherds.
• [Scots *shiel* hut: Middle English, of unknown origin]

shigella *noun*
• "shig ELLA"
• any airborne bacterium of the genus *Shigella*, some of which cause dysentery.
• [modern Latin from K. *Shiga*, Japanese bacteriologist d.1957 + diminutive suffix]

shigellosis *noun*
• "shigga LO sis"
• infection with, or a disease caused by, shigella bacteria.
• [as SHIGELLA]

shiitake *noun*
• "shih TOCKY" or "shih TOCK ay" or "shih TACKY" or "shih TACK ay"
• an edible mushroom, *Lentinus edodes*, cultivated on oak logs etc.
• [Japanese, from *shii* a kind of oak + *take* mushroom]

Shiite *noun*
• "SHEE ite"
• an adherent of the Shia branch of Islam.
• **Shiism** *noun*

shillelagh *noun*
• "shill AY lee" or "shill AY luh"
• a thick stick or club of blackthorn or oak used in Ireland esp. as a weapon.
• [*Shillelagh* in Co. Wicklow, Ireland]

shinkansen *noun*
• "sheen CON sen"
• (in Japan) a high-speed passenger train; a bullet train.
• [Japanese, from *shin* new + *kansen* main line]

Shinto *noun*
• "SHIN toe"
• a religious system incorporating the worship of ancestors, nature spirits and other divinities, and prior to 1945 the state religion of Japan, founded on a belief in the divinity of the Japanese emperor.
• [Japanese from Chinese *shen dao* way of the gods]
• **Shintoism** *noun*
• **Shintoist** *noun*

shipwreck *noun*
• "SHIP reck"
• the destruction of a ship by a storm, sinking, etc.
• ['ship' + WRECK]

shipwright *noun*
• "SHIP rite"
• a carpenter employed in the manufacture or repair of ships.
• ['ship' + WRIGHT]

shiraz *noun*
• "shuh RAZZ"
• the variety of Syrah produced in Australia and South Africa.
• [alteration of French *syrah* influenced by the city of *Shiraz* in Iran, based on the belief that the vine was brought from Iran by the Crusaders]

shirk *verb*
• "SHURK"
• shrink from; avoid, evade, or attempt to get out of (duty, work, responsibility, fighting, etc.).
• [obsolete *shirk* (n.) sponger, perhaps from German *Schurke* scoundrel]
• **shirker** *noun*

shiro *noun*
• "SHEER oh"
• a medium-sized yellow plum.
• [origin unknown: perhaps from Japanese *shiro* white]

shirred *adjective*
• "SHEERD" or "SHURD"
• (of material, curtains, a dress etc.) gathered with several parallel rows of stitches in order to provide decoration and (of an article of clothing) a better or more comfortable fit.
• [19th c.: origin unknown]
HOMOPHONES: *sherd*

shirring *noun*
• "SHEER ing" or "SHUR ing"
• multiple rows of stitching in the material of a garment etc. forming a decorative gathering or smocking.
• [19th c.: origin unknown]
HOMOPHONES: *shearing*

shirttail *noun*
• "SHURT tale"
• the lower curved part of a shirt below the waist.
• ['shirt' + 'tail']

shiur *noun*
• "SHEE oor"
• a Talmudic study session, usu. led by a rabbi.
• [Hebrew *šî'ūr* measure, portion]

shiva *noun*
ALSO SPELLED: **shivah**
• "SHIVVA"
• a period of seven days' mourning for the dead beginning immediately after the funeral.
• [Hebrew *šib̲'āh* seven]

shivaree *noun*
• "SHIVVA ree"
• a noisy celebration or gathering.
• [corruption of CHARIVARI]
HOMOPHONES: *shivery*

shmatte *noun*
ALSO SPELLED: **schmatte**
• "SHMATTA"
• clothing.
• [Yiddish *schmatte*, from Polish *szmata* rag]

Shoah *noun*
• "SHOW uh"
• the mass murder esp. of Jews under the Nazi regime; the Holocaust.
• [modern Hebrew, lit. = 'catastrophe']

shoal *noun*
• "SHOLE"
• a school of fish, porpoises, etc.
• [prob. readoption of Middle Dutch *schōle* school (of fish)]

shochet *noun*
• "SHOW cut"
• a person officially certified as competent to kill cattle and poultry in the manner prescribed by Jewish law.
• [Hebrew *šōḥēṭ* slaughtering]

shofar *noun*
• "SHOW fur"
• a trumpet made of a ram's horn used by Jews in religious ceremonies and, in Biblical times, as a war trumpet.
• [Hebrew *šôp̄ār*]
HOMOPHONES: *chauffeur*

shogun *noun*
• "SHOW gun"
• any of a succession of hereditary commanders-in-chief in feudal Japan who were generally the real rulers of the country until 1867.
• [Japanese, = general, from Chinese *jiang jun*]

shogunate *noun*
• "SHOW gun it"
• the title or position of shogun.
• [as SHOGUN]

shoji *noun*
• "SHOW jee"
• (in Japan) a sliding outer or inner door made of a latticed screen covered usu. with white translucent paper.
• [Japanese]

Shona *noun*
• "SHOW nuh"
• a member of any of several related Bantu-speaking peoples inhabiting Mashonaland in N Zimbabwe and parts of Zambia and Mozambique.
• [a local name]

shortening *noun*
• "SHORT'n ing" or "SHORT ning"
• a soft fat that produces a crisp flaky effect in baked products, such as pastry, esp. a solid white fat made from hydrogenated vegetable oils, sometimes combined with lard.
• [as 'short' from Old English *sceort*]

Shoshone *noun*
ALSO SPELLED: **Shoshoni**
• "shuh SHOW nee"
• a member of a N American Aboriginal people of Wyoming, Idaho, Nevada, and neighbouring states.
• [19th c.: origin unknown]

shotcrete *noun*
• "SHOT creet"
• a mixture of cement, sand, and water applied through a hose.
• ['shot' (past participle of 'shoot') + (CON)CRETE]

Shotokan *noun*
• "show TOE can"
• one of the five main styles of karate.
• [Japanese, from *shō* right, true + *to* way + *kan* mansion]

showpiece *noun*
• "SHOW peece"
• an item of work presented for exhibition or display.
• ['show' from Old English *scēawian* + PIECE]

shoyu *noun*
- "SHOW yoo"
- a type of Japanese soy sauce.
- [Japanese, = 'soy']

shrapnel *noun*
- "SHRAP n'll"
- fragments of a bomb etc. thrown out by an explosion.
- [Gen. H. *Shrapnel*, British soldier d.1842, inventor of the shell]

shrewd *adjective*
- "SHROOD"
- showing astute powers of judgment; clever and judicious.
- [Middle English, = malignant, from 'shrew' in sense 'evil person or thing', or past participle of obsolete *shrew* to curse, from 'shrew' (mouse)]
- **shrewdly** *adverb*
- **shrewdness** *noun*

shriek *verb*
- "SHREEK"
- utter a shrill screeching sound or words esp. in pain or terror.
- [imitative]
- **shrieker** *noun*

shrivel *verb*
- "SHRIV'll"
- contract or wither into a wrinkled, folded, rolled-up, contorted, or dried-up state.
- [perhaps from Old Norse: compare Swedish dialect *skryvla* to wrinkle]

shtetl *noun*
- "SHTET'll" or "SHTATE 'll"
- a small Jewish town or village in E Europe.
- [Yiddish, = little town]

shtick *noun*
ALSO SPELLED: **schtick**
- "SHTICK"
- a theatrical routine, gimmick, etc.
- [Yiddish from German *Stück* piece]

shtreimel *noun*
- "SHTRAY m'll"
- a round, broad-brimmed hat edged with fur worn by some Hasidic Jews.
- [Yiddish, from Middle High German *streimel* stripe, strip]

shul *noun*
- "SHOOL"
- a synagogue.
- [Yiddish from German *Schule* school]

Shuswap *noun*
- "SHOO swop"
- a member of an Aboriginal people living in the Thompson River area of BC.
- [corruption of Shuswap *Secwepemc*, self-designation]

shvitz *verb*
ALSO SPELLED: **schvitz**
- "SHVITS"
- sweat.
- [Yiddish, = 'sweat']

shyster *noun*
- "SHICE tur"
- a person, esp. a lawyer, who uses unscrupulous methods.
- [19th c.: origin uncertain]

si *noun*
- "SEE"
- the seventh note of a major scale.
- [French from Italian, perhaps from the initials of *Sancte Iohannes*: see GAMUT]

HOMOPHONES: *see, sea*

siamang *noun*
- "SYE a mang" or "SEE a mang"
- a large black gibbon, *Hylobates syndactylus*, native to Sumatra and the Malay peninsula.
- [Malay]

Siamese *noun*
- "sye a MEEZ" or "sye MEEZ"
- a native of Siam (now Thailand) in SE Asia.

Siberian *adjective*
- "sye BEERY 'n"
- of or relating to Siberia in N Asia.

HOMOPHONES: *Cyberian*

sibilant *adjective*
- "SIBBLE 'nt"
- (of a letter or set of letters, as *s, sh*) articulated with a hissing sound.
- [Latin *sibilare sibilant-* hiss]
- **sibilance** *noun*
- **sibilancy** *noun*

sibyl *noun*
- "SIBBLE"
- any of the women in ancient times supposed to utter the oracles and prophecies of a god.
- [Latin *Sibylla* from Greek *Sibulla*]

sibylline *adjective*
- "SIBBA line"
- of or from a sibyl.
- [as SIBYL]

sic *adverb*
- "SICK"
- used, spelled, etc., as written (confirming, or calling attention to, the form of quoted or copied words).
- [Latin, = so, thus]

HOMOPHONES: *sick*

Sicilian *noun*
- "sis ILL y'n"
- a native or inhabitant of the Italian island of Sicily.

sidereal *adjective*
- "sye DEERY 'll"
- of or concerning the constellations or fixed stars.
- [Latin *sidereus* from *sidus sideris* star]

siderite *noun*
• "SIDDER ite"
• a mineral form of ferrous carbonate that is a source of iron and occurs in sedimentary rocks and ore veins as translucent usu. brown or yellow crystals.
• [Greek *sidēros* iron]
• **sideritic** *adjective* "sidder ITTIC"

siderophore *noun*
• "SIDDER oh for"
• an agent which binds and transports iron in micro-organisms.
• [Greek *sidēros* iron + *-phoros -phoron* bearing, bearer, from *pherō* bear]

sidewhisker *noun*
• "SIDE wisker"
• hair growing on the side of a man's face and cheeks; sideburns.
• ['side' from Old English *sīde* + WHISKER]

sidle *verb*
• "SIDE 'll"
• move in a sly, guileful, or devious manner.
• [back-formation from *sideling* sidelong]

siege *noun*
• "SEEDGE" or "SEEZH"
• a military operation in which an attacking army attempts to force the surrender of a fortified place by surrounding it and cutting off supplies and communication etc.
• [Old French *sege* seat, from *assegier* BESIEGE]

siemens *noun*
• "SEE minz"
• the SI unit of conductance, equal to one reciprocal ohm.
• [W. von *Siemens*, German electrical engineer d.1892]

Sienese *adjective*
• "see a NEEZ"
• of or pertaining to Siena, Italy.

sienna *noun*
• "see ENNA"
• a kind of iron-rich earth used as a pigment in oil and watercolour painting.
• [Italian (*terra di*) *Sienna* (earth of) Siena (in Tuscany)]

sierra *noun*
• "see ERRA"
• a long jagged mountain chain, esp. in Spain, the US, or Latin America.
• [Spanish from Latin *serra* saw]

siesta *noun*
• "see ESTA"
• an afternoon nap or rest, esp. one taken during the hottest hours of the day in a country with an especially warm climate.
• [Spanish from Latin *sexta* (*hora*) sixth hour]

sieur *noun*
• "SYUR"
• a title for a member of the minor nobility, e.g. a seigneur, in France or New France.
• [Old French, = lord (as SEIGNEUR)]

sieve *noun*
• "SIV"
• a device consisting of a meshed or perforated surface enclosed in a frame, used to separate coarse particles from finer ones or from a liquid.
• [Old English *sife* from W Germanic]

sievert *noun*
• "SEE vurt"
• an SI unit of dosage of ionizing radiation, defined as that which delivers a joule of energy per kilogram of recipient mass.
• [R. M. *Sievert*, Swedish radiologist b.1896]

sigh *verb*
• "SYE"
• emit a long deep audible breath as an expression of sadness, weariness, longing, relief, etc.
• [Middle English *sihen*]
HOMOPHONES: *psi*, *xi*

sigil *noun*
• "SIDGE 'll"
• a mark or seal; a signet.
• [from Latin *sigillum* seal, diminutive of *signum*, sign]

siglum *noun*
• "SIG lum"
• a letter (esp. an initial) or other symbol used to denote a word in a book, esp. to refer to a particular text.
• [Late Latin *sigla* (pl.), perhaps from *singula* neuter pl. of *singulus* single]

sigma *noun*
• "SIG muh"
• the eighteenth letter of the Greek alphabet (Σ, σ, or, when final, ς), represented in English by *S*, *s*, its uncial form having the shape of English *C*.
• [Latin from Greek]

sigmoid *adjective*
• "SIG moid"
• curved like the uncial sigma (C); crescent-shaped.
• [Greek *sigmoeidēs* (see SIGMA)]

sigmoidoscopy *noun*
• "sig moy DOSCA pee"
• an examination of the lower intestine (sigmoid colon) by means of a flexible tube inserted through the anus.
• [as SIGMOID + Greek *skopos* target, from *skeptomai* look at]
• **sigmoidoscope** *noun*

sign *noun*
• "SINE"
• an indication or suggestion of a quality or state.

• [Old French *signe*, *signer* from Latin *signum*, *signare*]
HOMOPHONES: *sine*, *syne*

signage *noun*
• "SINE idge"
• signs collectively, esp. those used commercially for identifying or advertising a store or business etc.
• [as SIGN]

signatory *noun*
• "SIG nuh tory"
• a person, party, or country that has signed a particular document, such as a treaty.
• [Latin *signatorius* of sealing, from *signare signat-* mark]

signature *noun*
• "SIG nuh chur"
• a person's name, initials, or distinctive mark used in signing a letter, document, etc.
• [medieval Latin *signatura* (Late Latin = marking of sheep), as SIGNATORY]

signboard *noun*
• "SINE bord"
• a board displaying the name or logo of a store, hotel, or other business.
• [SIGN + BOARD]

signee *noun*
• "sye NEE"
• a person who has signed a contract, register, etc.
• [as SIGN]

signet *noun*
• "SIG nit"
• a small seal, usu. set in a ring, used with or instead of a signature to authenticate a document.
• [Old French *signet* or medieval Latin *signetum* (as SIGN)]
HOMOPHONES: *cygnet*

significant *adjective*
• "sig NIFFA k'nt"
• of great importance or consequence.
• [Latin *significare*: see SIGNIFY]
• **significance** *noun*
• **significantly** *adverb*

signified *noun*
• "SIG nuh fide"
• the idea or meaning conventionally indicated by the signifier, as distinct from the external object to which it refers.
• [as SIGNIFY]

signifier *noun*
• "SIG nuh fie ur"
• a physical medium (such as a sound, symbol, image, etc.) expressing meaning, as distinct from the meaning expressed.
• [as SIGNIFY]

signify *verb*
• "SIG nuh fie"
• be a sign or symbol of; represent, denote.
• [Old French *signifier* from Latin *significare* (as SIGN)]
• **signification** *noun* "sig nuh fuh CAY sh'n"

signor *noun*
• "see NYOR"
• used as a title (preceding the surname or other designation) of, or as a respectful form of address to, an Italian or Italian-speaking man, corresponding to English Mr. or sir.
• [Italian from Latin *senior* old man]
HOMOPHONES: *señor*

signora *noun*
• "see NYORRA"
• used as a title (preceding the surname or other designation) of, or as a respectful form of address to, an Italian or Italian-speaking married woman, corresponding to English Mrs. or madam.
• [Italian, feminine of SIGNOR]
HOMOPHONES: *señora*

signorina *noun*
• "seen yuh REENA"
• used as a title (preceding the surname or other designation) of, or as a respectful form of address to, an Italian or Italian-speaking unmarried woman.
• [Italian, diminutive of SIGNORA]

sika *noun*
• "SEEKA"
• a small forest-dwelling deer, *Cervus nippon*, native to Japan and widely naturalized elsewhere.
• [Japanese *shika*]

Sikh *noun*
• "SEEK" or "SICK"
• a member of a monotheistic religion founded in Punjab by Guru Nanak (d.1539), combining Hindu and Islamic elements.
• [Punjabi, Hindi, from Sanskrit *śisya* disciple]
HOMOPHONES: *seek*, *sick*

Sikhism *noun*
• "SEEK izm" or "SICK izm"
• the beliefs and principles of the Sikhs.
• [as SIKH]

siksik *noun*
• "SEEK seek"
• *Cdn (North)* a large squirrel, *Spermophilus parryii*, with a dappled greyish-brown coat, of N Canada and Asia; the Arctic ground squirrel.
• [Inuktitut, imitative of its call]

Siksika *noun*
• "sick SICKA"
• a member of an Aboriginal people, part of the Blackfoot, living in central Alberta.
• [Blackfoot, from *siksi-* black + *-ka* foot]

silage *noun*
• "SYE lidge"
• green crops preserved by pressure esp. in a silo or occasionally in a stack.
• [alteration of ENSILAGE after *silo*]

silenus *noun*
• "sye LEE nuss"
• (in Greek and Roman mythology) a bearded old man like a satyr, sometimes with the tail and legs of a horse.
• [Latin from Greek *seilēnos*]

Silesian *adjective*
• "sye LEEZY in"
• of or relating to the central European region of Silesia, now largely in SW Poland.

silhouette *noun*
• "silla WET"
• a portrait or representation of a thing showing the outline only, usu. done in solid black and placed on a white or contrasting background.
• [Étienne de *Silhouette*, French author and politician d.1767]

silica *noun*
• "SILLA kuh"
• a hard mineral substance, silicon dioxide, occurring in many rocks, soils, and sands as flint, opal, or crystals of quartz, etc., used esp. in the manufacture of glass and ceramics.
• [Latin *silex -icis* flint, on the pattern of *alumina* etc.]
• **siliceous** *adjective* (also **silicious**) "suh LISH us"

silicate *noun*
• "SILLA kit"
• any of the many insoluble compounds of a metal combined with silicon and oxygen, which include many rock-forming minerals such as mica, feldspar, garnet, tourmaline, etc.
• [as SILICA]

silicic *adjective*
• "suh LISSIC"
• pertaining to, consisting of, or formed from silicon or silica.
• [as SILICA]

silicify *verb*
• "sill ISSA fie"
• convert into or impregnate with silica.
• [as SILICA]
• **silicification** *noun*

silicon *noun*
• "SILLA con"
• a non-metallic element occurring abundantly in the earth's crust in oxides and silicates, used in electronic components for its semiconducting properties, as well as in the manufacture of glass.
• [Latin *silex -icis* flint (after *carbon, boron*), alteration of earlier *silicium*]

silicone *noun*
• "SILLA cone"
• any of the many polymeric organic compounds of silicon and oxygen used as electrical insulators, waterproofing agents, adhesives, and rubbers.
• [as SILICON]

silicosis *noun*
• "silla CO sis"
• lung fibrosis caused by the inhalation of dust containing silica.
• [as SILICA]
• **silicotic** *adjective* "silla COTTIC"

siliqua *noun*
• "SILLICK wuh"
• the long narrow seed pod of a cruciferous plant.
• [Latin, = pod]
• **siliquose** *adjective*
• **siliquous** *adjective*

sillimanite *noun*
• "SILLA muh nite"
• an aluminum silicate occurring in orthorhombic crystals or fibrous masses.
• [B. *Silliman*, US chemist d.1864]

silo *noun*
• "SYE lo"
• a tall cylinder or pit in which green corn or hay etc. is pressed and kept for fodder, undergoing fermentation.
• [Spanish from Latin *sirus* from Greek *siros* grain pit]

Silurian *adjective*
• "suh LOORY 'n"
• of or relating to the third period of the Paleozoic era, lasting from about 438 to 408 million years BP, between the Ordovician and Devonian periods. The first land plants and the first true fish appeared during this period.
• [Latin *Silures*, a people of ancient SE Wales]

silviculture *noun*
• "SILVA cull chur"
• the branch of forestry concerned with the growing and cultivation of trees.
• [French from Latin *silva* a wood + French *culture* CULTURE]
• **silvicultural** *adjective*
• **silviculturist** *noun*

simcha *noun*
• "SIM chuh" or "SIM kuh"
• a Jewish private party or celebration.
• [Hebrew *śimḥāh* rejoicing]

Simconian *noun*
• "sim CONEY 'n"
• a resident of Simcoe, Ont.

simethicone *noun*
• "suh METHA cone"
• the active ingredient in many preparations to relieve intestinal gas, which causes mucus-trapped gas bubbles to form larger bubbles which are more easily eliminated.
• [SILICA + METHYL + SILICONE]

simian *adjective*
• "SIMMY 'n"
• of or concerning the anthropoid apes.

• [Latin *simia* ape, perhaps from Latin *simus* from Greek *simos* flat-nosed]

similar *adjective*
• "SIM'll ur"
• of the same nature or kind; alike.
• [French *similaire* or medieval Latin *similaris* from Latin *similis* like]
• **similarity** *noun* "sim'll ERRA tee"
• **similarly** *adverb*

simile *noun*
• "SIMMA lee"
• a figure of speech involving the explicit comparison of two different things, often using the words 'like' or 'as', e.g. *as brave as a lion.*
• [Middle English from Latin, neuter of *similis* like]

similitude *noun*
• "suh MILLA tude"
• the quality or state of being similar; similarity.
• [Old French *similitude* or Latin *similitudo* (as SIMILE)]

Simmental *noun*
• "SIMM'n tawl"
• a breed of large red and white cattle farmed for both milk and meat.
• [a valley in central Switzerland]

simoleon *noun*
• "sim OLEY 'n"
• a dollar.
• [perhaps after 'napoleon', a gold twenty-franc piece minted in the reign of Napoleon I]

simony *noun*
• "SIMON ee" or "SIMMON ee"
• the buying or selling of ecclesiastical privileges, e.g. pardons or benefices.
• [Old French *simonie* from Late Latin *simonia* from *Simon* Magus (Acts 8:18)]
• **simoniac** *adjective* "suh MOANY ack"

simoom *noun*
• "suh MOOM"
• a hot dry dust-laden wind blowing at intervals esp. in the Arabian desert.
• [Arabic *samūm* from *samma* to poison]

simpatico *adjective*
ALSO SPELLED: **sympatico**
• "sim PATTA co"
• congenial, likeable.
• [Italian & Spanish (as SYMPATHY)]

simpleton *noun*
• "SIMP'll t'n"
• a foolish, gullible, or halfwitted person.
• ['simple', after surnames derived from place names in *-ton*]

simplicity *noun*
• "sim PLISSA tee"
• the fact or condition of being simple.
• [Old French *simplicité* or Latin *simplicitas* from *simplus* simple]

simplify *verb*
• "SIMPLA fie"
• make simple; make easy or easier to do or understand.
• [Latin *simplus* simple]
• **simplification** *noun*

simplistic *adjective*
• "sim PLISS tick"
• excessively or affectedly simple.
• [Latin *simplus* simple]
• **simplistically** *adverb*

simply *adverb*
• "SIMP lee"
• in a simple manner.
• [Latin *simplus* simple]

simulacrum *noun*
• "sim yoo LAKE rum"
• an image of something.
• [Latin (as SIMULATE)]

simulate *verb*
• "SIM yuh late"
• pretend to have or feel (an attribute or feeling).
• [Latin *simulare* from *similis* like]
• **simulation** *noun*
• **simulator** *noun*

simulated *adjective*
• "SIM yuh lated"
• made to resemble the real thing but not genuinely such.
• [as SIMULATE]

simulcast *noun*
• "SYE mul cast" or "SIMMLE cast"
• a simultaneous transmission of the same program on radio and television, or on two or more channels, in two or more languages, etc.
• [SIMULTANEOUS + 'broadcast']
• **simulcasting** *noun*

simultaneous *adjective*
• "sye mul TAINY us" or "simmle TAINY us"
• occurring or operating at the same time.
• [medieval Latin *simultaneus* from Latin *simul* at the same time, prob. after *instantaneous* etc.]
• **simultaneity** *noun* "simmle tuh NAY a tee" or "sye mul tuh NAY a tee"
• **simultaneously** *adverb*

Sinaitic *adjective*
• "sye nay ITTIC"
• of or relating to Mount Sinai or of the Sinai peninsula in NE Egypt.
• [var. of *Sinaic* from *Sinai* from Hebrew *sīnay*, with *t* added for euphony]

sincere *adjective*
• "sin SEER"
• free from pretense or deceit; the same in reality as in appearance.
• [Latin *sincerus* clean, pure]
• **sincerely** *adverb*
• **sincerity** *noun* "sin SERRA tee"

sinciput *noun*
• "SINSA put"
• the front of the skull from the forehead to the crown.
• [Latin from *semi-* half + *caput* head]

sine *noun*
• "SINE"
• the trigonometric function that is equal to the ratio of the side opposite a given angle (in a right-angled triangle) to the hypotenuse.
• [Latin *sinus* curve, fold of a toga, used in medieval Latin as translation of Arabic *jayb* bosom, sine]
HOMOPHONES: *sign, syne*

sinecure *noun*
• "SINNA cure"
• a position that requires little or no work but usu. yields profit or honour.
• [Latin *sine cura* without care]
• **sinecurist** *noun*

sinew *noun*
• "SIN you"
• tough fibrous tissue uniting muscle to bone; a tendon.
• [Old English *sin(e)we* from Germanic]
• **sinewy** *adjective*

sinfonia *noun*
• "sinfa NEE uh" or "sin FONEY uh"
• a symphony.
• [Italian, = SYMPHONY]

sinfonietta *noun*
• "sinfa NYETTA"
• a short or simple symphony.
• [Italian, diminutive of *sinfonia*: see SINFONIA]

sinful *adjective*
• "SIN full"
• (of a person) committing sin, esp. habitually.
• [Old English *syn(n)* sin]
• **sinfully** *adverb*
• **sinfulness** *noun*

Singaporean *noun*
• "sing a PORRY 'n"
• a native or inhabitant of Singapore in SE Asia.

singe *verb*
• "SINGE" (rhymes with *HINGE*)
• burn superficially or lightly.
• [Old English *sencgan* from West Germanic]

singular *adjective*
• "SING gyuh lur"
• unique; much beyond the average; extraordinary.
• [Old French *singuler* from Latin *singularis* from *singulus*, related to *simplus* simple]
• **singularity** *noun* "sing gyuh LERRA tee"
• **singularization** *noun* (also esp. *Brit.* **-isation**)
• **singularize** *verb* (also esp. *Brit.* **-ise**)
• **singularly** *adverb*

Sinhalese *noun*
• "sin huh LEEZ" or "sinna LEEZ"
• a member of a people originally from N India and now forming the majority of the population of Sri Lanka.
• [Sanskrit *sinhalam* Sri Lanka]

sinister *adjective*
• "SIN iss tur"
• suggestive of evil; looking malignant or villainous.
• [Old French *sinistre* or Latin *sinister* left]
• **sinisterly** *adverb*
• **sinisterness** *noun*

sinistral *adjective*
• "SINN iss trull"
• left-handed.
• [as SINISTER]
• **sinistrality** *noun*

sinologue *noun*
• "SINE a log" or "SINNA log"
• an expert in sinology.
• [French, from Greek *Sinai* the Chinese + *-logos* speaking]

sinology *noun*
• "sye NOLLA jee" or "sin OLLA jee"
• the study of Chinese language, history, customs, etc.
• [as SINOLOGUE]
• **sinological** *adjective*
• **sinologist** *noun*

sinsemilla *noun*
• "sinsa MILLA"
• a seedless form of the cannabis plant, having a particularly high narcotic content.
• [Latin American Spanish, lit. 'without seed']
• **sinsemillan** *adjective*

sinuate *adjective*
• "SIN yoo ate"
• wavy-edged; with distinct inward and outward bends along the edge.
• [Latin *sinuatus* past participle of *sinuare* bend]

sinuous *adjective*
• "SIN yoo us"
• with many curves.
• [French *sinueux* or Latin *sinuosus* (as SINUS)]
• **sinuosity** *noun* "sin you OSSA tee"
• **sinuously** *adverb*

sinus *noun*
• "SYE nuss"
• a cavity of bone or tissue, esp. in the skull connecting with the nostrils.
• [Latin, = bosom, recess]

sinusitis *noun*
• "sye nuh SITE iss"
• inflammation of a nasal sinus.
• [SINUS + Greek *-itis*, forming feminine of adjectives in *-itēs* (with *nosos* 'disease' implied)]

sinusoid *noun*
• "SINE a soid"

• a curve having the form of a sine wave.
• [French *sinusoïde* from Latin *sinus*: see SINUS]
• **sinusoidal** *adjective*
• **sinusoidally** *adverb*

Siouan *noun*
• "SOO 'n"
• an Aboriginal language family including Dakota and Assiniboine (the only Siouan languages spoken in Canada), Lakota, Sioux, and Omaha.
• [as SIOUX]

Sioux *noun*
• "SOO"
• a member of a group of N American Aboriginal peoples chiefly inhabiting the upper Mississippi and Missouri river basins.
• [N American French from *Nadouessioux* from Ojibwa (Odawa dialect) *nātowēssiwak*: French pl. ending *-x* replaced Ojibwa pl. ending *-ak*]
HOMOPHONES: *sue, sou, xu*

siphon *noun*
ALSO SPELLED: esp. *Brit.* **syphon**
• "SIFE 'n"
• a pipe or tube used for conveying liquid from one level to a lower level, using the liquid pressure differential to force a column of the liquid up to a higher level before it falls to the outlet.
• [ultimately from Greek *siphōn* pipe]
• **siphonage** *noun* (also esp. *Brit.* **syphonage**)
• **siphonal** *adjective* (also esp. *Brit.* **syphonal**)
• **siphonic** *adjective* (also esp. *Brit.* **syphonic**) "sye FONNIC"

siphonophore *noun*
• "sye FONNA for"
• any usu. translucent marine hydrozoan of the order Siphonophora, e.g. the Portuguese man-of-war.
• [as SIPHON + Greek *-phoros -phoron* bearing, bearer, from *pherō* bear]

sirdar *noun*
• "SUR dar"
• (esp. in the Indian subcontinent) a person of high political or military rank.
• [Urdu *sardār* from Persian *sar* head + *dār* possessor]

sirenian *adjective*
• "sye REENY in"
• of the order Sirenia of large aquatic plant-eating mammals, with stocky streamlined bodies, forelimbs modified as flippers, and no hind limbs, e.g. the manatee and dugong.
• [modern Latin *Sirenia* from Late Latin *Sirena* fem. from Latin from Greek *Seirēn* woman whose singing lured unwary sailors on to rocks]

sirloin *noun*
• "SUR loin"
• the choicer part of a loin of beef, from in front of the rump.
• [Old French *surloigne* (*sur* above, from Latin *super* above, beyond, *loigne* ultimately from Latin *lumbus* loin)]

sirocco *noun*
ALSO SPELLED: **scirocco**
• "sih ROE co"
• a hot, oppressive, often dusty or rainy wind blowing from N Africa across the Mediterranean to southern Europe.
• [French from Italian *scirocco*, ultimately from Arabic *Šarūķ* east wind]

sisal *noun*
• "SICE 'll"
• a Mexican plant, *Agave sisalana*, with large fleshy leaves.
• [*Sisal*, the port of Yucatan, Mexico]

siskin *noun*
• "SIS kin"
• any of various small streaked yellowish-green finches of the genus *Carduelis*, esp. the N American pine siskin, *C. pinus*, or the Eurasian common siskin, *C. spinus*, allied to the goldfinch.
• [Middle Dutch *siseken* diminutive, related to Middle Low German *sisek*, Middle High German *zīse, zīsec*, of Slavic origin]

Sistine *adjective*
• "SIS teen"
• of any of the Popes called Sixtus, esp. Sixtus IV.
• [Italian *Sistino* from *Sisto* Sixtus]
HOMOPHONES: *cystine, cysteine*

sistrum *noun*
• "SIS trum"
• a jingling metal instrument used by the ancient Egyptians esp. in the worship of the nature goddess Isis.
• [Latin from Greek *seistron* from *seiō* shake]

Sisyphean *adjective*
• "sissa FEE in"
• (of toil) endless and fruitless like that of Sisyphus in Greek mythology, whose punishment in Hades was to roll a heavy stone to the top of a hill, from which it always rolled down again.

sitar *noun*
• "sih TAR" or "SIT ar"
• a long-necked Indian lute with movable frets.
• [Urdu, Persian *sitār*]
• **sitarist** *noun*

site *noun*
• "SITE"
• the ground chosen or used for a town or building.
• [Anglo-French *site* or Latin *situs* local position]
HOMOPHONES: *sight, cite*

situate *verb*
• "SITCH oo ate"
• put in a certain position or circumstances.
• [medieval Latin *situare situat-* from Latin *situs* site]

- **situation** *noun*
- **situational** *adjective*
- **situationally** *adverb*

situationism *noun*
- "sitch oo AY sh'n izm"
- the theory that human behaviour is determined by surrounding circumstances rather than by personal qualities.
- [as SITUATE]
- **situationist** *noun*

Siwash *noun*
- "SYE wash"
- *Cdn (West)* a thick woollen sweater decorated with symbols or animals from Aboriginal mythology.
- [Chinook Jargon, from Canadian French *sauvage* wild, native]

sizar *noun*
- "SYE zur"
- an undergraduate at Cambridge University or at Trinity College, Dublin, receiving financial help from the college and formerly having certain menial duties.
- ['size' = ration]
- **sizarship** *noun*

HOMOPHONES: *sizer*

sjambok *noun*
- "SHAM bock"
- (in South Africa) a long stiff whip, originally made of rhinoceros hide.
- [Afrikaans from Malay *samboq*, *chambok* from Urdu *chābuk*]

skald *noun*
ALSO SPELLED: **scald**
- "SKAWLD" or "SKALD"
- (in ancient Scandinavia) a composer and reciter of poems honouring heroes and their deeds.
- [Old Norse *skáld*, of unknown origin]
- **skaldic** *adjective* (also **scaldic**)

HOMOPHONES: *scald*

skat *noun*
- "SKAT"
- a three-handed card game with bidding.
- [German from Italian *scarto* a discard, from *scartare* discard]

HOMOPHONES: *scat*

skean *noun*
- "SKEEN" or "SKEE in"
- a Gaelic dagger formerly used in Ireland and Scotland.
- [Gaelic *sgian* knife]

skeet *noun*
- "SKEET"
- a shooting sport in which a clay target is thrown from a trap to simulate the flight of a bird.
- [Old Norse *skjóta* shoot]

skeg *noun*
- "SKEG"
- the after part of a vessel's keel or a projection from it.
- [Old Norse *skeg* beard, perhaps via Dutch *scheg(ge)*]

skein *noun*
- "SKANE"
- a loosely coiled bundle of yarn or thread.
- [Old French *escaigne*, of unknown origin]

skeleton *noun*
- "SKELLA t'n"
- a hard internal or external framework of bones, cartilage, shell, woody fibre, etc., supporting or containing the body of an animal or plant.
- [modern Latin from Greek, neuter of *skeletos* dried-up, from *skellō* dry up]
- **skeletal** *adjective*
- **skeletally** *adverb*
- **skeletonic** *adjective* "skella TONNIC"
- **skeletonize** *verb* (also esp. *Brit.* **-ise**)

skeptic *noun*
ALSO SPELLED: **sceptic**
- "SKEP tick"
- a person who doubts the validity of accepted beliefs in a particular subject.
- [via French and Latin from Greek *skeptikos*, from *scepsis* inquiry, doubt]
- **skeptical** *adjective* (also **sceptical**)
- **skeptically** *adverb* (also **sceptically**)
- **skepticism** *noun* (also **scepticism**) "SKEPTA sizm"

skerry *noun*
- "SKERRY"
- *Cdn (Nfld)* a reef or rocky island.
- [Orkney dialect from Old Norse *sker*]

HOMOPHONES: *scary*

skew *adjective*
- "SKYOO"
- oblique, slanting, set askew.
- [Old Northern French *eskiu(w)er* (v.) = Old French *eschuer*: see ESCHEW]
- **skewness** *noun*

HOMOPHONES: *SKU*

skewback *noun*
- "SKYOO back"
- the sloping face of the abutment on which an extremity of an arch rests.
- [as SKEW + 'back']

skewbald *adjective*
- "SKYOO bawld"
- (of an animal) with irregular patches of white and another colour (properly not black).
- [Middle English *skued* (origin uncertain), after PIEBALD]

skewer *noun*
- "SKYOO ur"
- a long metal or wooden pin for holding meat,

vegetables, etc. compactly together while cooking.
• [Middle English: origin unknown]

skijoring *noun*
• "SKEE jore ing" or "shee JUR ing"
• a winter sport in which a skier is towed by a horse or vehicle.
• [Norwegian *skikjøring* (*ski* from Old Norse *skíth* billet, snowshoe, *kjøre* drive)]
• **skijorer** *noun*

skilful *adjective*
ALSO SPELLED: **skillful**
• "SKILL full"
• having or showing skill; practised, expert, adroit, ingenious.
• [Old Norse *skil* distinction]
• **skilfully** *adverb* (also **skillfully**)
• **skilfulness** *noun* (also **skillfulness**)

skillet *noun*
• "SKILLIT"
• a frying pan.
• [Middle English, perhaps from Old French *escuelete* diminutive of *escuele* platter, from Late Latin *scutella*]

skimmia *noun*
• "SKIMMY uh"
• any evergreen shrub of the genus *Skimmia*, native to E Asia, with red berries.
• [modern Latin from Japanese]

skirl *noun*
• "SKURL"
• the shrill sound characteristic of bagpipes.
• [prob. Scandinavian: ultimately imitative]

skirmish *noun*
• "SKUR mish"
• a piece of irregular or unpremeditated fighting esp. between small or outlying parts of armies or fleets; a slight engagement.
• [Old French *eskirmir*, *escremir* from Frankish]
• **skirmisher** *noun*

skirr *verb*
• "SKUR"
• move rapidly esp. with a whirring sound.
• [perhaps related to 'scour']

skive *verb*
• "SKIVE" (rhymes with *HIVE*)
• split or pare (hides, leather, etc.).
• [Old Norse *skífa*, related to Middle English *schīve* slice]
• **skiver** *noun*

skivvy *noun*
• "SKIVVY"
• *derogatory* a female domestic servant.
• [20th c.: origin unknown]

skol *noun*
• "SKAWLL" or "SKOLE"
• used as a toast in drinking.
• [Danish *skaal*, Swedish *skål*, from Old Norse *skál* bowl]

skookum *adjective*
• "SKOOK um" (with "OO" as in *COOK*)
• esp. *Cdn* (*West*) excellent, impressive, good.
• [Chinook Jargon]

skordalia *noun*
• "score DALLY uh"
• a Greek dip of cold whipped potatoes and garlic served with pita bread.
• [modern Greek, = garlic sauce, from Greek *skordo* garlic]

skua *noun*
• "SKYOO uh"
• any of various large predatory seabirds of the family Stercorariinae, typically having brown or brown and white plumage and a strongly hooked bill, breeding in polar or cold regions, and with a habit of robbing other seabirds of food by forcing them to disgorge the fish they have caught.
• [modern Latin from Faroese *skúgvur*, Old Norse *skúfr*]

skulduggery *noun*
ALSO SPELLED: **skullduggery**
• "skull DUGGER ee"
• trickery; unscrupulous behaviour.
• [earlier *sculduddery*, originally Scots = unchastity (18th c.: origin unknown)]

skulk *verb*
• "SKULK"
• move stealthily, lurk, or keep oneself concealed, esp. in a cowardly or sinister way.
• [Middle English from Scandinavian: compare Norwegian *skulka* lurk, Danish *skulke*, Swedish *skolka* shirk]
• **skulker** *noun*

skull *noun*
• "SKULL"
• the bony case of the brain of a vertebrate.
• [Middle English *scolle*: origin unknown]
• **skulled** *adjective*
HOMOPHONES: *scull*

skullcap *noun*
• "SKULL cap"
• a small close-fitting peakless cap.
• [as SKULL + 'cap' from Late Latin *cappa*, perhaps from Latin *caput* head]

slainte *interjection*
• "SLANCHA"
• a Gaelic toast: good health!
• [Gaelic *sláinte*, lit. 'health']

slalom *noun*
• "SLAW lum"
• a downhill ski race on a zigzag course marked by artificial obstacles, usu. flags, and descended singly by each competitor in turn.
• [Norwegian, lit. 'sloping track']
• **slalomer** *noun*

slattern *noun*
• "SLAT urn"
• a promiscuous woman; a slut.

• [17th c.: related to *slattering* slovenly, from dialect *slatter* to spill, slop, waste, frequentative of *slat* strike]
• **slatternliness** *noun*
• **slatternly** *adjective*

slaty *adjective*
• "SLAITY"
• resembling slate in colour, texture, or appearance.
• [Old French *esclate* slate, fem. form of *esclat* slat, splinter, from *esclater* split]

slaughter *noun*
• "SLOTTER"
• the killing of an animal or animals for food.
• [Middle English *slahter*, ultimately from Old Norse *slátr* butcher's meat, related to 'slay']
• **slaughterer** *noun*
• **slaughterous** *adjective*

slaughterhouse *noun*
• "SLOTTER house"
• a place where animals are butchered for food.
• [as SLAUGHTER + 'house']

Slavey *noun*
• "SLAY vee"
• a member of a number of Dene Aboriginal groups living in the Mackenzie River basin in western NWT.
• [translation of Cree *awahkān* captive, slave]

Slavonic *adjective*
• "sluh VONNIC"
• of, pertaining to, or designating the branch of Indo-European languages including Russian, Polish, Ukrainian, and Czech, spoken throughout most of Central and Eastern Europe.
• [medieval Latin *S(c)lavonicus* from *S(c)lavonia* country of Slavs, from *Sclavus*, identical to *sclavus* slave, the Slavic peoples having been reduced to a servile state by conquest during the 9th c.]

Slavophile *noun*
• "SLAVVA file"
• an admirer or champion of Slavic languages, culture, history, etc.
• [as SLAVONIC + Greek *philos* dear, loving]

sleazebag *noun*
• "SLEEZ bag"
• a sordid, despicable, or shady person.
• [as SLEAZY]

sleazoid *noun*
• "SLEE zoid"
• a corrupt or vulgar person; a sleaze.
• [as SLEAZY]

sleazy *adjective*
• "SLEEZY"
• disreputable or corrupt.
• [17th c.: origin unknown]
• **sleaze** *noun*
• **sleazily** *adverb*
• **sleaziness** *noun*

sleeveen *noun*
• "sluh VEEN" or "slee VEEN"
• *Cdn (Nfld)* & *Irish* an untrustworthy or mischievous person; a rascal.
• [Irish *slighbhín, slíbhín* a sly person]

sleigh *noun*
• "SLAY"
• a sled, esp. a large one drawn by horses and used to convey passengers over snow and ice.
• [Dutch *slee*]
• **sleighing** *noun*
HOMOPHONES: *slay*

sleight *noun*
• "SLITE"
• a deceptive trick or movement.
• [Middle English *sleghth* from Old Norse *slœgth* from *slœgr* sly]
HOMOPHONES: *slight*

sleuth *noun*
• "SLOOTH"
• a detective or investigator.
• [originally in *sleuth-hound* bloodhound: Old Norse *slóth* track, trail]

slew *verb*
ALSO SPELLED: **slue**
• "SLOO"
• turn or swing around, esp. without moving from a position.
• [18th-c. Naut.: origin unknown]
HOMOPHONES: *slough*

Sliammon *noun*
• "sly OMMON"
• a dialect of mainland Comox spoken in the area surrounding Powell River, BC.
• [Sliammon]

slipperwort *noun*
• "SLIPPER wurt" or "SLIPPER wort"
• = CALCEOLARIA.
• ['slipper' + WORT]

slivovitz *noun*
• "SLIVVA vits"
• a dry slightly bitter colourless plum brandy made esp. in Romania and Serbia.
• [Serbo-Croat *šljivovica* from *šljiva* plum]

sloe *noun*
• "SLOW"
• the fruit of the blackthorn, a small blue-black drupe with a sharp sour taste.
• [Old English *slā(h)* from Germanic]
HOMOPHONES: *slow*

slogan *noun*
• "SLOE g'n"
• a word or phrase that is easy to remember, used by a political party or in advertising etc. to attract people's attention or suggest an idea quickly.
• [Gaelic *sluagh-ghairm* from *sluagh* army + *gairm* shout]
• **sloganed** *adjective*
• **sloganize** *verb* (also esp. *Brit.* **-ise**)

sloganeer *verb*
- "sloe g'n EER"
- devise or use slogans.
- [as SLOGAN]
- **sloganeering** *noun*

slouch *verb*
- "SLOUCH"
- stand or sit with the back, shoulders, and neck bent or drooping forwards.
- [16th c.: origin unknown]
- **slouchy** *adjective*

slough[1] *noun*
ALSO SPELLED: **slew**
- "SLOO" or "SLOU" (rhymes with *HOW*)
- an area of soft miry ground; a swamp or quagmire.
- [Old English *slōh, slō(g)*]

HOMOPHONES: *slew*

slough[2] *noun*
ALSO SPELLED: **sluff**
- "SLUFF"
- a part that an animal sheds, esp. a snake's skin.
- [Middle English, perhaps related to Low German *slu(we)* husk]
- **sloughy** *adjective* (also **sluffy**)

Slovak *noun*
- "SLOE vack"
- a native or inhabitant of Slovakia in central Europe.
- [Slovak etc. *Slovák*, related to SLOVENIAN]

sloven *noun*
- "SLOV 'n" or "SLUV 'n"
- a person who is habitually untidy or careless.
- [Middle English perhaps from Flemish *sloef* dirty or Dutch *slof* careless]
- **slovenliness** *noun*
- **slovenly** *adjective*

Slovenian *noun*
- "sluh VEENY 'n"
- an inhabitant of Slovenia in south-central Europe.
- [German *Slowene* from Slovenian etc. *Slovenec* from Old Slavic *Slov-*, perhaps related to *slovo* word]

sluggard *noun*
- "SLUG'rd"
- a lazy sluggish person.
- [Middle English from *slug* (v.) be slothful]
- **sluggardliness** *noun*
- **sluggardly** *adverb*

sluice *noun*
- "SLOOCE"
- a sliding gate or other contrivance for controlling the volume or flow of water.
- [Middle English from Old French *escluse*, ultimately from Latin *excludere* EXCLUDE]

slumgullion *noun*
- "slum GULLY 'n"
- sludge, esp. watery stew.
- [origin unknown]

slurry *noun*
- "SLURRY"
- a semi-liquid mixture of fine particles and water; thin mud.
- [Middle English, related to dialect *slur* thin mud]

slype *noun*
- "SLIPE"
- a covered way or passage, esp. between a cathedral etc. transept and the chapter house or deanery.
- [perhaps = *slipe* a long narrow piece of ground]

smalt *noun*
- "SMAWLT"
- glass coloured blue with cobalt.
- [French from Italian *smalto* from Germanic]

smear *verb*
- "SMEER"
- daub or mark with a greasy or sticky substance or with something that stains.
- [Old English *smierwan* from Germanic]
- **smeary** *adjective*

smectic *adjective*
- "SMECK tic"
- designating or involving a state of a liquid crystal in which the molecules are oriented in parallel and arranged in well-defined planes (compare NEMATIC).
- [Latin *smecticus*, Greek *smēktikos* cleansing (from the soap-like consistency)]

smew *noun*
- "SMYOO"
- a small merganser, *Mergus albellus*.
- [17th c., related to *smeath, smee* = smew, widgeon, etc.]

smilax *noun*
- "SMY lax"
- any climbing shrub of the genus *Smilax*, the roots of some species of which yield sarsaparilla.
- [Latin from Greek, = bindweed]

smirch *verb*
- "SMURCH"
- mark, soil, or smear (a thing, a person's reputation, etc.).
- [Middle English: origin unknown]

smirk *noun*
- "SMURK"
- a conceited, smug, scornful, or silly smile.
- [Old English *sme(a)rcian*]
- **smirker** *noun*
- **smirkingly** *adverb*
- **smirky** *adjective*

smithereens *plural noun*
- "smither EENZ" ("SMITHER" rhymes with *WITHER*)
- small fragments.
- [probably from Irish *smidirin*]

smolt *noun*
- (Rhymes with *BOLT*)
- a young salmon migrating to the sea for the first time.
- [Middle English (originally Scots & Northern English): origin unknown]

smooth *adjective*
- "SMOOTH" (with "TH" as in *BATHE*)
- having a relatively even and regular surface; free from perceptible projections, lumps, indentations, and roughness.
- [Old English *smōth*]
- **smoothable** *adjective*
- **smoother** *noun*
- **smoothish** *adjective*
- **smoothly** *adverb*
- **smoothness** *noun*

smoothbore *noun*
- "SMOOTH bore" (with "TH" as in *BATHE*)
- a gun with an unrifled barrel.
- [as SMOOTH + 'bore' the hollow of a firearm barrel, from Old English *borian*]

smorgasbord *noun*
- "SMORE gus bord"
- a buffet offering a wide variety of dishes.
- [Swedish, from *smörgas* '(slice of) bread and butter' (from *smör* butter + *gås* goose, lump of butter) + *bord* table]

smoulder *verb*
ALSO SPELLED: **smolder**
- "SMOLE dur"
- burn slowly with smoke but without a flame; slowly burn internally or invisibly.
- [Middle English, related to Low German *smöln*, Middle Dutch *smölen*]
- **smouldering** *adjective* (also **smoldering**)

sneezewort *noun*
- "SNEEZE wurt" or "SNEEZE wort"
- a kind of yarrow, *Achillea ptarmica*, whose dried leaves are used to induce sneezing.
- ['sneeze' Middle English *snese*, apparently alteration of obsolete *fnese* from Old English *-fnēsan*, Old Norse *fnýsa* & replacing earlier and less expressive *nese* + WORT]

snippet *noun*
- "SNIP it"
- a small fragment or bit.
- [Low German & Dutch *snippen* imitative]
- **snippety** *adjective*

snivel *verb*
- "SNIV'll"
- cry and sniff in a miserable way.
- [Old English *snyflan* (unrecorded) from *snofl* mucus]
- **sniveller** *noun*
- **snivelling** *adjective*
- **snivellingly** *adverb*
- **snivelly** *adjective*

snorkel *noun*
- "SNORK 'll"
- a breathing tube for an underwater swimmer.
- [German *Schnorchel*]
- **snorkeller** *noun*

snye *noun*
- "SNY" (rhymes with *TRY*)
- *Cdn* (*E Ont.*) a side channel, esp. one that bypasses a falls or rapids and rejoins the main river downstream, creating an island.
- [Canadian French *chenail*, French *chenal* channel]

soapwort *noun*
- "SOPE wurt" or "SOPE wort"
- a European plant, *Saponaria officinalis*, naturalized in N America, with pink or white flowers and leaves yielding a soapy substance.
- ['soap' + WORT]

soar *verb*
- "SORE"
- fly or rise high.
- [Old French *essorer* ultimately from Latin (*ex* out of, *aura* breeze)]
- **soarer** *noun*
- **soaring** *adjective*
- **soaringly** *adverb*

HOMOPHONES: *sore*

Soave *noun*
- "SWAH vay"
- a dry white wine produced in the region around Soave.
- [*Soave*, a town in N Italy]

sobriety *noun*
- "suh BRYE a tee"
- the state of being sober.
- [Old French *sobrieté* from *sobre* from Latin *sobrius*]

sobriquet *noun*
ALSO SPELLED: **soubriquet**
- "SO brick ay"
- a nickname.
- [French, originally = 'tap under the chin']

soca *noun*
- "SO kuh"
- a kind of calypso music with elements of soul, originally from Trinidad.
- ['soul' + CALYPSO]

socage *noun*
ALSO SPELLED: **soccage**
- "SOCK idge"
- a feudal tenure of land involving payment of rent or other non-military service to a superior.
- [Anglo-French *socage* from *soc* from Old English *sōcn* SOKE]

sociable *adjective*
- "SO shuh bull"
- fitted for or liking the society of other people; ready and willing to talk and act with others.
- [French *sociable* or Latin *sociabilis* from *sociare* to unite, from *socius* companion]
- **sociability** *noun*

• **sociableness** *noun*
• **sociably** *adverb*

social *adjective*
• "SO sh'll"
• of or relating to society or its organization.
• [French *social* or Latin *socialis* allied, from *socius* friend]
• **sociality** *noun* "so shee ALA tee"
• **socially** *adverb*

socialism *noun*
• "SO shuh lizm"
• a political and economic theory of social organization which advocates that the community as a whole should own and control the means of production, distribution, and exchange.
• [French *socialisme* (as SOCIAL)]
• **socialist** *noun*
• **socialistic** *adjective*
• **socialistically** *adverb*

socialite *noun*
• "SO shuh lite"
• a person who is well-known in fashionable society and goes to a lot of fashionable parties.
• [as SOCIAL]

socialize *verb*
ALSO SPELLED: esp. *Brit.* **-ise**
• "SO shuh lize"
• act in a sociable manner.
• [as SOCIAL]
• **socialization** *noun* (also esp. *Brit.* **-isation**)

society *noun*
• "suh SYE a tee"
• the sum of human conditions and activity regarded as a whole functioning interdependently.
• [French *société* from Latin *societas -tatis* from *socius* companion]
• **societal** *adjective*
• **societally** *adverb*

sociobiology *noun*
• "so see oh by OLLA jee" or "so shee oh by OLLA jee"
• the scientific study of the biological aspects of social behaviour.
• [as SOCIETY + BIOLOGY]
• **sociobiological** *adjective*
• **sociobiologically** *adverb*
• **sociobiologist** *noun*

sociolinguistic *adjective*
• "so see oh ling GWISTIC" or "so shee oh ling GWISTIC"
• relating to or concerned with language in its social aspects.
• [as SOCIETY + LINGUISTIC]
• **sociolinguist** *noun*
• **sociolinguistically** *adverb*
• **sociolinguistics** *noun*

sociology *noun*
• "so see OLLA jee" or "so shee OLLA jee"
• the study of the development, structure, and functioning of human society.
• [as SOCIETY + Greek *logos* word]
• **sociological** *adjective*
• **sociologically** *adverb*
• **sociologist** *noun*

sociometry *noun*
• "so see OMMA tree" or "so shee OMMA tree"
• the study of relationships within a group of people.
• [as SOCIETY + Greek *metron* measure]
• **sociometric** *adjective* "so see a METRIC" or "soo shee a METRIC"

sociopath *noun*
• "SO see a path" or "SO shee a path"
• a person with a personality disorder manifesting itself in extreme anti-social attitudes and behaviour, particularly a lack of moral responsibility or social conscience.
• [as SOCIETY, after PSYCHOPATH]
• **sociopathic** *adjective*
• **sociopathy** *noun* "so see OPPA thee" or "so shee OPPA thee" (with "TH" as in *THIN*)

socle *noun*
• "SOKE'll"
• a plain low block or plinth serving as a support for a column, urn, statue, etc., or as the foundation of a wall.
• [French from Italian *zoccolo* originally 'wooden shoe' from Latin *socculus* from *soccus* sock]

Socratic *adjective*
• "suh CRATTIC"
• of or relating to the Greek philosopher Socrates (d.399 BC) or his work, esp. the method associated with him of seeking the truth by a series of questions and answers.
• **Socratically** *adverb*

sodality *noun*
• "so DALA tee"
• a confraternity or association, esp. a Catholic religious guild or brotherhood.
• [French *sodalité* or Latin *sodalitas* from *sodalis* comrade]

sodium *noun*
• "SO dee um"
• a soft silver-white reactive metallic element, occurring naturally in soda, salt, etc., that is important in industry and is an essential element in living organisms.
• [late Middle English *soda*, from medieval Latin, from Arabic *suwwad* saltwort]
• **sodic** *adjective*

Sodom *noun*
• "SOD um"
• a depraved or corrupt place.
• [*Sodom* in ancient Palestine, destroyed for its wickedness (Gen. 18–19)]

soffit *noun*
• "SOFF it"
• the undersurface of an arch, a balcony, overhanging eaves, etc.

• [French *soffite* or Italian *soffitta*, *-itto*, ultimately from Latin *suffixus* (as SUFFIX)]

soigné *adjective*
• "SWON yay"
• carefully finished or arranged; well-groomed.
• [past participle of French *soigner* take care, from *soin* care]

sojourn *noun*
• "SO jurn"
• a temporary stay.
• [Old French *sojorn* etc. from Latin *sub* under, close to, towards + *diurnum* day]
• **sojourner** *noun*

soke *noun*
• "SOKE"
• a right of local jurisdiction.
• [Anglo-Latin *sōca* from Old English *sōcn* prosecution, from Germanic]
HOMOPHONES: *soak*

sol *noun*
• "SOLL" (rhymes with *DOLL*)
• a liquid suspension of a colloid.
• [abbreviation of SOLUTION]

solace *noun*
• "SOLL us"
• comfort in distress, disappointment, or tedium.
• [Old French *solas* from Latin *solatium* from *solari* CONSOLE[1]]

solanaceous *adjective*
• "solla NAY sh'ss"
• of or relating to the plant family Solanaceae, including potatoes, nightshades, and tobacco.
• [modern Latin *solanaceae* from Latin *sōlānum* nightshade + adjective suffix *-aceus* of the nature of]

solanine *noun*
• "SOLLA neen"
• a poisonous compound present in green potatoes and in related plants.
• [Latin *sōlānum* nightshade]

solar *adjective*
• "SO lur"
• of, relating to, or reckoned by the sun.
• [Latin *solaris* from *sol* sun]

solarium *noun*
• "suh LERRY um"
• a room, balcony, etc. fitted with extensive areas of glass to provide exposure to the sun.
• [Latin, = sundial, sunning place (as SOLAR)]

solarize *verb*
ALSO SPELLED: esp. *Brit.* **-ise**
• "SO luh rize"
• undergo or cause to undergo change in the relative darkness of parts of an image by long exposure.
• [as SOLAR]
• **solarization** *noun* (also esp. *Brit.* **-isation**)

solder *noun*
• "SODDER"
• a fusible alloy used to join less fusible metals or wires etc.
• [Old French *soudure* from *souder* from Latin *solidare* fasten, from *solidus* solid]
• **solderable** *adjective*
• **solderer** *noun*
• **solderless** *adjective*

soldier *noun*
• "SOLE jur"
• a person serving in or having served in an army.
• [via Old French *soldier* from *soulde* (soldier's) pay, from Latin *solidus*: see SOLIDUS]
• **soldierly** *adjective*

soldiery *noun*
• "SOLE jur ee"
• soldiers, esp. of a specified character.
• [as SOLDIER]

sole *noun*
• "SOLE"
• any of various flatfish of the family Pleuronectidae or Soleidae, used as food.
• [Old French from Provençal *sola*, ultimately from Latin *solea* (the sole of a shoe, named from its shape)]
HOMOPHONES: *soul*

solecism *noun*
• "SOLLA sizm"
• a mistake of grammar or idiom; a blunder in the manner of speaking or writing.
• [French *solécisme* or Latin *soloecismus* from Greek *soloikismos* from *soloikos* speaking incorrectly]

solemn *adjective*
• "SOLLUM"
• serious and dignified.
• [Old French *solemne* from Latin *sol(l)emnis* customary, celebrated at a fixed date, from *sollus* entire]
• **solemness** *noun*
• **solemnity** *noun* "suh LEM nuh tee"
• **solemnly** *adverb*

solemnize *verb*
ALSO SPELLED: esp. *Brit.* **-ise**
• "SOLLUM nize"
• duly perform (a ceremony esp. of marriage).
• [as SOLEMN]
• **solemnization** *noun* (also esp. *Brit.* **-isation**)

solenoid *noun*
• "SOLE a noid" or "SOLLA noid"
• a cylindrical coil of wire acting as a magnet when carrying electric current.
• [French *solénoïde* from Greek *sōlēn* channel, pipe + Greek *-oeidēs* from *eidos* form]
• **solenoidal** *adjective*

solicit *verb*
• "suh LISSIT"

• ask repeatedly or earnestly for or seek or invite (business etc.).
• [Old French *solliciter* from Latin *sollicitare* agitate, from *sollicitus* anxious, from *sollus* entire + *citus* past participle, = set in motion]
• **solicitation** *noun*

solicitor *noun*
• "suh LISSA tur"
• *Cdn* a lawyer.
• [as SOLICIT]

solicitous *adjective*
• "suh LISSA tuss"
• showing interest or concern.
• [Latin *sollicitus* (as SOLICIT)]
• **solicitously** *adverb*
• **solicitousness** *noun*

solicitude *noun*
• "suh LISSA tude"
• the state of being solicitous; solicitous behaviour.
• [as SOLICIT]

solidarity *noun*
• "solla DARE a tee"
• unity or agreement of feeling or action, esp. among individuals with a common interest.
• [French *solidarité* from *solidaire* from *solide* solid (as SOLIDUS)]

solidify *verb*
• "suh LIDDA fie"
• make or become solid.
• [as SOLIDUS]
• **solidification** *noun*
• **solidifier** *noun*

solidity *noun*
• "suh LIDDA tee"
• the state of being solid; firmness.
• [as SOLIDUS]

solidus *noun*
• "SOLLID us"
• an oblique stroke (/) used in writing fractions (¾), to separate other figures and letters, or to denote alternatives (*and/or*) and ratios (*miles/day*).
• [Middle English, originally a gold coin of the later Roman Empire, from Latin *solidus* solid, related to *salvus* safe, *sollus* entire]

solifluction *noun*
• "so luh FLUCK sh'n"
• the gradual movement of wet soil etc. down a slope.
• [Latin *solum* soil + *fluctio* flowing, from *fluere fluct-* flow]

soliloquy *noun*
• "suh LIL a kwee"
• the act of talking when alone or regardless of any hearers, esp. in drama.
• [Late Latin *soliloquium* from Latin *solus* alone + *loqui* speak]
• **soliloquist** *noun*
• **soliloquize** *verb* (also esp. *Brit.* **-ise**)

solipsism *noun*
• "SOLLIP sizm"
• the view that the self is all that exists, or is all that can be known.
• [Latin *solus* alone + *ipse* self]
• **solipsist** *noun*
• **solipsistic** *adjective*
• **solipsistically** *adverb*

solitaire *noun*
• "SOLLA tare"
• a game for one player in which cards taken in random order have to be arranged in certain groups or sequences.
• [French from Latin *solitarius* (as SOLITARY)]

solitary *adjective*
• "SOLLA terry"
• living alone; not gregarious; without companions; lonely.
• [Latin *solitarius* from *solus* alone]
• **solitarily** *adverb*
• **solitariness** *noun*

solitude *noun*
• "SOLLA tude"
• the state of being or living alone; solitariness.
• [Old French *solitude* or Latin *solitudo* from *solus* alone]

solmization *noun*
ALSO SPELLED: esp. *Brit.* **-isation**
• "sawl muh ZAY sh'n"
• a system of associating each note of a scale with a particular syllable, now usu. *do re mi fa so la ti*, with do as C in the fixed-do system and as the keynote in the movable-do or tonic sol-fa system.
• [French *solmisation* (*sol* from Latin *solve*, *mi* from Latin *mira*: see GAMUT)]

Solomon *noun*
• "SOLLA m'n"
• a very wise person.
• [*Solomon*, King of Israel in the 10th c. BC, famed for his wisdom]
• **Solomonic** *adjective* "solla MONNIC"

Solon *noun*
• "SO lawn"
• a wise lawmaker.
• [*Solon*, Athenian statesman d. *c.*560 BC]

solstice *noun*
• "SOLE stiss" or "SAWL stiss"
• either of the two times in the year when the sun reaches its highest or lowest point in the sky at noon, marked by the longest and shortest days.
• [Old French from Latin *solstitium* from *sol* sun + *sistere stit-* make stand]
• **solstitial** *adjective*

solubilize *verb*
ALSO SPELLED: esp. *Brit.* **-ise**
• "SAWL yoo bull ize"
• make soluble or more soluble.
• [as SOLUBLE]
• **solubilization** *noun* (also esp. *Brit.* **-isation**)

soluble *adjective*
- "SAWL yoo bull"
- that can be dissolved, esp. in water.
- [Old French from Late Latin *solubilis* from *solvere solut-* unfasten, release]
- **solubility** *noun*

solus *adjective*
- "SOLE us"
- (esp. in a stage direction) alone, unaccompanied.
- [Latin]

HOMOPHONES: *soulless*

solute *noun*
- "SAWL yoot"
- a dissolved substance.
- [Latin *solutum*, neuter of *solutus*: see SOLUBLE]

solution *noun*
- "suh LOO sh'n"
- the act or a means of solving a problem or difficulty.
- [Old French from Latin *solutio -onis* (as SOLUBLE)]

Solutrean *adjective*
- "suh LOO tree 'n"
- of or relating to an upper paleolithic culture in W Europe, following the Aurignacian and dated to c.21,000–18,000 years ago.
- [*Solutré* in E France, where remains of it were found]

solvate *verb*
- "SOLVE ate"
- enter or cause to enter combination with a solvent.
- [as SOLUBLE]
- **solvation** *noun*

solvency *noun*
- "SOLVE 'n see"
- the state of having enough money to meet one's liabilities.
- [as SOLVENT]

solvent *noun*
- "SOLVE 'nt"
- a liquid that dissolves.
- [as SOLUBLE]

som *noun*
- "SOAM"
- a monetary unit of Kyrgyzstan and Uzbekistan, equal to 100 tiyin.
- [Kyrgyz and Uzbek, 'rouble']

soma *noun*
- "SO muh"
- the body as distinct from the soul.
- [Greek *sōma -atos* body]

Somali *noun*
- "suh MOLLY" or "suh MALLY"
- a member of a Hamitic Muslim people of Somalia in E Africa.
- [African name]
- **Somalian** *adjective*

somatic *adjective*
- "suh MATTIC"
- of or relating to the body, esp. as distinct from the mind.
- [Greek *sōmatikos* (as SOMA)]
- **somatically** *adverb*

somatization *noun*
- "so muh tuh ZAY sh'n"
- the production of recurrent and multiple medical symptoms with no discernible organic cause.
- [as SOMATIC]

somatosensory *adjective*
- "suh matto SENSER ee"
- relating to or denoting a sensation (such as pressure, pain, or warmth) which can occur anywhere in the body, in contrast to one localized at a sense organ (e.g. sight, hearing, or taste).
- [as SOMATIC + SENSORY]

somatostatin *noun*
- "suh matto STAT'n"
- a hormone secreted in the pancreas and pituitary gland which inhibits gastric secretion and somatotropin release.
- [as SOMATOTROPIN + STATIC]

somatotropin *noun*
- "suh matto TRO pin"
- a growth hormone secreted by the pituitary gland.
- [as SOMATIC, Greek *tropikos* from *tropē* turning, from *trepō* turn]

somatotype *noun*
- "suh MATTO tipe"
- physique expressed in relation to various extreme types.
- [as SOMATIC + TYPE]

sombre *adjective*

ALSO SPELLED: esp. *US* **somber**
- "SOM bur"
- gloomy, shadowy.
- [French *sombre* from Old French *sombre* (n.), ultimately from Latin *sub* under, close to, towards + *umbra* shade]
- **sombrely** *adverb* (also esp. *US* **somberly**)
- **sombreness** *noun* (also esp. *US* **somberness**)

sombrero *noun*
- "som BRARE oh"
- a broad-brimmed felt or straw hat worn esp. in Mexico.
- [Spanish from *sombra* shade (as SOMBRE)]

somersault *noun*
- "SUMMER salt"
- an acrobatic movement in which a person turns head over heels in the air or on the ground, making a complete revolution.
- [Old French *sombresault* alteration of *sobresault*, ultimately from Latin *supra* above + *saltus* leap, from *salire* to leap]

somite *noun*
- "SO mite"
- each of several similar body segments containing the same internal structures e.g. in an earthworm.
- [Greek *sōma* body]
- **somitic** *adjective* "so MITTIC"

sommelier *noun*
- "som'll YAY"
- a wine waiter.
- [French, = butler, from *somme* pack (as SUMPTER)]

somnambulism *noun*
- "som NAM byoo lizm"
- sleepwalking.
- [Latin *somnus* sleep + *ambulare* walk]
- **somnambulant** *adjective*
- **somnambulantly** *adverb*
- **somnambulate** *verb*
- **somnambulist** *noun*
- **somnambulistic** *adjective*

somnolent *adjective*
- "SOMNA l'nt"
- sleepy, drowsy.
- [Old French *sompnolent* or Latin *somnolentus* from *somnus* sleep]
- **somnolence** *noun*

somoni *noun*
- "saw MOANY"
- the basic monetary unit of Tajikistan, equal to one hundred dirams.
- [Tajik, from the name of Ismail *Samani*, the 9th-c. founder of the Tajik nation]

sonant *adjective*
- "SONE 'nt"
- (of a sound) voiced and syllabic.
- [Latin *sonare sonant-* sound]

sonata *noun*
- "suh NOTTA" or "suh NATTA"
- a composition for one instrument or two (one usu. being a piano accompaniment), usu. in several movements with one (esp. the first) or more in sonata form.
- [Italian, = sounded (originally as distinct from sung): feminine past participle of *sonare* sound]

sonatina *noun*
- "sonna TEENA"
- a simple or short sonata.
- [Italian, diminutive of SONATA]

sonde *noun*
- "SOND"
- a device sent up to obtain information about atmospheric conditions, esp. = RADIOSONDE.
- [French, = line for sounding]

sone *noun*
- "SONE"
- a unit of subjective loudness.
- [Latin *sonus* sound]

songwriter *noun*
- "SONG rite ur"
- a writer of songs or the music for them.
- ['song' from Old English *sang* + WRITE]
- **songwriting** *noun*

sonic *adjective*
- "SONNIC"
- of or relating to or using sound or sound waves.
- [Latin *sonus* sound]
- **sonically** *adverb*

sonnet *noun*
- "SONNIT"
- a poem of fourteen lines using any of a number of formal rhyme schemes, in English typically in iambic pentameter.
- [French *sonnet* or Italian *sonetto* diminutive of *suono* from Latin *sonus* sound]
- **sonneteer** *noun*
- **sonneteering** *noun*

sonny *noun*
- "SUNNY"
- a familiar form of address to a young boy or man who is one's junior.
- [Old English *sunu* son, from Germanic]

HOMOPHONES: *sunny*, *Sunni*

sonobuoy *noun*
- "SONNA boy"
- a buoy for detecting underwater sounds and transmitting them by radio.
- [Latin *sonus* sound + BUOY]

sonogram *noun*
- "SONNA gram"
- the visual image produced by reflected sound waves in a diagnostic ultrasound examination.
- [Latin *sonus* sound + Greek *gramma* thing written]

sonograph *noun*
- "SONNA graff"
- an instrument which analyzes sound into its component frequencies and produces a graphical record of the results.
- [Latin *sonus* sound + Greek *graphia* writing]
- **sonographer** *noun*
- **sonographic** *adjective*
- **sonographically** *adverb*
- **sonography** *noun*

sonorous *adjective*
- "SONN ur us" or "SONE ur us"
- having a loud, full, or deep sound; resonant.
- [Latin *sonorus* from *sonor* sound]
- **sonority** *noun*
- **sonorously** *adverb*
- **sonorousness** *noun*

soopollalie *noun*
- "SOAP a lally"
- *Cdn* (*BC*) a shrub of the N American genus *Shepherdia* of the oleaster family.
- [from *soop*, var. of 'soap' (because the fruits yield saponin) + Chinook Jargon *olallie* berry]

soothe *verb*
• "SOOTH" (with "TH" as in *BATHE*)
• bring or restore (a person or feelings etc.) to a peaceful or tranquil state; calm.
• [Old English *sōthian* verify, from *sōth* true]
• **soothing** *adjective*
• **soothingly** *adverb*

soothsayer *noun*
• "SOOTH sayer" ("SOOTH" rhymes with *TOOTH*)
• a person who predicts future events; a prophet.
• [Middle English, = one who says the truth: see SOOTHE]
• **soothsaying** *noun*

sophism *noun*
• "SOFF izm"
• a plausible but false argument, esp. one intended to deceive or display ingenuity in reasoning.
• [Old French *sophime* from Latin from Greek *sophisma* clever device, from *sophos* wise]

sophist *noun*
• "SOFF ist"
• a person who reasons with clever but fallacious arguments.
• [as SOPHISM]
• **sophistic** *adjective*
• **sophistical** *adjective*
• **sophistically** *adverb*

sophisticate *verb*
• "suh FISTA cate"
• deprive (a person) of natural simplicity or innocence, esp. through education or experience.
• [medieval Latin *sophisticare* tamper with, from *sophisticus* (as SOPHISM)]
• **sophistication** *noun*

sophisticated *adjective*
• "suh FISTA cated"
• (of a person) worldly, cultured, and refined; discriminating in taste and judgment.
• [as SOPHISTICATE]
• **sophisticatedly** *adverb*

sophistry *noun*
• "SOFF iss tree"
• the use of intentionally deceptive or specious arguments or reasoning, esp. as a dialectic exercise.
• [as SOPHISM]

sophomore *noun*
• "SOFFA more"
• (esp. in the US) a student in his or her second year of high school, college, or university.
• [earlier *sophumer* from *sophum*, obsolete var. of SOPHISM]
• **sophomoric** *adjective* "soffa MORIC"

soporific *adjective*
• "soppa RIFFIC"
• tending to induce or produce sleep.
• [Latin *sopor* sleep]
• **soporifically** *adverb*

soppressata *noun*
• "soppra SOTTA"
• a kind of dense unsmoked Italian salami.
• [Italian, lit. = 'compressed']

sopranino *noun*
• "soppra NEENO"
• an instrument of a pitch higher than that of a soprano, esp. a recorder or saxophone.
• [Italian, diminutive of SOPRANO]

soprano *noun*
• "suh PRANNO"
• the highest singing voice.
• [Italian from *sopra* above, from Latin *supra*]

sora *noun*
• "SORA"
• a small N American marsh bird, *Porzana carolina*.
• [origin uncertain]

sorbet *noun*
• "sore BAY"
• a soft water ice made with fruit juice or fruit purée served esp. between main courses to cleanse the palate and reinvigorate the appetite, or as a dessert.
• [French from Italian *sorbetto* from Turkish *şerbet* from Arabic *šarba* to drink: compare SHERBET]

sorbitol *noun*
• "SORE bit awl"
• a sweet crystalline alcohol found in some fruit, used commercially as a substitute for sugar.
• [*sorb* (from French *sorbe* or Latin *sorbus* service tree, *sorbum* serviceberry) + ALCOHOL]

sorcerer *noun*
• "SORE sur ur"
• a person who claims to use magic powers; a wizard or magician.
• [obsolete *sorcer* from Old French *sorcier*, ultimately from Latin *sors sortis* lot]
• **sorcerous** *adjective*
• **sorcery** *noun*

sorceress *noun*
• "SORE sur ess"
• a woman who claims to use magic powers.
• [as SORCERER]

sordid *adjective*
• "SORE did"
• immoral, base, degenerate.
• [French *sordide* or Latin *sordidus* from *sordēre* be dirty]
• **sordidly** *adverb*
• **sordidness** *noun*

sordino *noun*
• "sore DEENO"
• a mute for a bowed or wind instrument.
• [Italian from *sordo* mute, from Latin *surdus*]

sorghum *noun*
• "SORE gum"

• any tropical cereal grass of the genus *Sorghum*, e.g. durra.
• [modern Latin from Italian *sorgo*, perhaps from unrecorded Romanic *syricum* (*gramen*) Syrian (grass)]

Soroptimist *noun*
• "suh ROPTA mist"
• a member of an international association of clubs for professional and business women.
• [Latin *soror* sister + OPTIMIST]

sororal *adjective*
• "suh ROAR 'll"
• of, pertaining to, or characteristic of a sister or sisterhood.
• [Latin *soror* sister]

sorority *noun*
• "suh ROAR a tee"
• a society for female students in a university or college.
• [Latin *soror* sister, after *fraternity*]

sorosis *noun*
• "suh ROE sis"
• a fleshy compound fruit, e.g. a pineapple or mulberry, derived from the ovaries of several flowers.
• [modern Latin from Greek *sōros* heap]
HOMOPHONES: *cirrhosis*

sorption *noun*
• "SORP sh'n"
• absorption or adsorption occurring jointly or separately.
• [back-formation from *absorption*, *adsorption*]

sorrel *noun*
• "SORE 'll"
• any of several plants of the genus *Rumex* having acid leaves, esp. *R. acetosa*, a plant of meadows with hastate leaves sometimes used in salads and for flavouring.
• [Old French *surele*, *sorele* from Germanic]

sorrowful *adjective*
• "SORRA full"
• feeling sorrow or grief; unhappy, sad.
• [Old English *sorh*, *sorg* sorrow]
• **sorrowfully** *adverb*
• **sorrowfulness** *noun*

sortie *noun*
• "SORE tee"
• a sudden emergence, dash, or attack made by troops from a besieged garrison.
• [French, feminine past participle of *sortir* go out]

sorus *noun*
• "SORE us"
• a heap or cluster, esp. of spore cases on the underside of a fern leaf, or in a fungus or lichen.
• [modern Latin from Greek *sōros* heap]

sostenuto *adverb*
• "soss ten OO toe"
• (as a musical direction) in a sustained or prolonged manner.
• [Italian, past participle of *sostenere* SUSTAIN]

soteriology *noun*
• "so teery OLLA jee"
• the doctrine of salvation.
• [Greek *sōtēria* salvation + *logos* word]
• **soteriological** *adjective*

Sothic *adjective*
• "SO thick"
• of or relating to Sirius, the Dog Star, esp. with reference to the ancient Egyptian year fixed by its heliacal rising.
• [Greek *Sōthis*, an Egyptian name for Sirius, the Dog Star]

Sotho *noun*
• "SOO too"
• a member of a Bantu-speaking people chiefly inhabiting Lesotho, Botswana, and the Transvaal.
• [Bantu]

sou *noun*
• "SOO"
• a former French coin of low value.
• [French, originally pl. *sous* from Old French *sout* from Latin SOLIDUS]
HOMOPHONES: *sue*, *xu*, *Sioux*

soubrette *noun*
• "soo BRET"
• a pert maidservant or similar female character in a play, ballet, or musical comedy.
• [French from Provençal *soubreto* feminine of *soubret* coy, from *sobrar* from Latin *superare* be above]

souchong *noun*
• "SOO shong"
• a fine black kind of China tea.
• [Chinese *xiao* small + *zhong* sort]

souffle *noun*
• "SOOF'll"
• a low murmur audible in a stethoscope, caused chiefly by the flow of blood through an organ.
• [French from *souffler* blow, from Latin *sufflare*]

soufflé *noun*
• "soo FLAY"
• a light spongy dish usu. made by adding egg yolks and a sweet or savoury filling to stiffly beaten egg whites then baked until puffy.
• [French past participle (as SOUFFLE)]
• **souffléd** *adjective*

sough *verb*
• "SOW" (rhymes with *COW*)
• make a moaning, whistling, or rushing sound as of the wind in trees etc.
• [Old English *swōgan* resound]
HOMOPHONES: *sow*

souk *noun*
ALSO SPELLED: **suk, sukh, suq**
• "SOOK" (rhymes with *LUKE*)
• an open marketplace or bazaar in Muslim countries.
• [Arabic *sūḳ*]

soukous *noun*
• "SOO koose"
• a style of African popular music characterized by syncopated rhythms and intricate contrasting guitar melodies, originating in Congo (formerly Zaire).
• [Congolese alteration of French *secouer* to shake]

soulless *adjective*
• "SOLE less"
• lacking sensitivity; cruel, ruthless.
• [Old English *sāwol* soul]
• **soullessly** *adverb*
• **soullessness** *noun*
HOMOPHONES: *solus*

soupçon *noun*
• "SOUP sawn"
• a very small amount; a dash, or hint.
• [French from Old French *sou(s)peçon* from medieval Latin *suspectio -onis*: see SUSPICION]

sourdough *noun*
• "SOUR doe"
• a leaven for making bread etc. consisting of fermenting dough, originally the dough left over from a previous baking.
• [Old English *sūr* sour + DOUGH]

sousaphone *noun*
• "SOOZA fone" or "SOOSA fone"
• a large brass wind instrument, similar to a tuba, which encircles the player's body with the bell above the player's head.
• [J. P. *Sousa*, US composer and bandmaster d.1932, after *saxophone*]

souse *verb*
• "SOUSE"
• soak, immerse, or drench (a thing) in liquid.
• [Old French *sous*, of Germanic origin]

soutache *noun*
• "soo TASH"
• a narrow flat ornamental braid used to trim clothing.
• [French from Hungarian *sujtás*]

soutane *noun*
• "soo TAN"
• a cassock worn by a priest.
• [French from Italian *sottana* from *sotto* under, from Latin *subtus*]

souvenir *noun*
• "soova NEER"
• a usu. inexpensive article given or purchased as a reminder of a place visited or an event witnessed etc.; a memento or keepsake.
• [French from *souvenir* remember, from Latin *subvenire* occur to the mind (*sub* under, close to, towards, *venire* come)]

souvlaki *noun*
• "soov LACKY" or "soov LOCKY"
• a Greek dish of pieces of marinated meat, esp. lamb or pork, grilled on a skewer.
• [modern Greek *soublaki* from *soubla* skewer]

sovereign *noun*
• "SOV r'n"
• the recognized supreme ruler of a people or country under monarchical government; a monarch.
• [Old French *so(u)verain* from Latin: -g- by assoc. with *reign*]
• **sovereignly** *adverb*

sovereignist *noun*
• "SOV r'n ist"
• *Cdn* a supporter of Quebec's right to self-government; an adherent to the principle of sovereignty-association or full independence.
• [as SOVEREIGN]

sovereignty *noun*
• "SOV r'n tee"
• the absolute and independent authority of a community, nation, etc.; the right to autonomy or self-government.
• [as SOVEREIGN]

Soviet *noun*
• "SO vee it"
• a citizen of the former Soviet Union.
• [Russian *sovet* council]
• **Sovietism** *noun*
• **Sovietization** *noun* (also esp. *Brit.* **-isation**)
• **Sovietize** *verb* (also esp. *Brit.* **-ise**)

Sovietologist *noun*
• "so vee a TOLLA jist"
• a person who studies the former Soviet Union.
• [as SOVIET + Greek *logos* word]

sozzled *adjective*
• "SOZZ 'ld"
• very drunk.
• [past participle of dialect *sozzle* mix sloppily (prob. imitative)]

spacefaring *noun*
• "SPACE fare ing"
• the action or activity of travelling in space.
• ['space' (as SPACIOUS) + FARE]
• **spacefarer** *noun*

spacious *adjective*
• "SPAY sh'ss"
• having ample space; roomy.
• [Middle French *spacieux* from Old French *espace* from Latin *spatium* space]
• **spaciously** *adverb*
• **spaciousness** *noun*

spadix *noun*
• "SPAY dix"

• a spike of flowers closely arranged around a fleshy axis and usu. enclosed in a spathe.
• [Latin from Greek, = palm branch]

spaetzle *plural noun*
• "SHPETS luh" or "SHPETS 'll"
• very small egg noodles made by forcing dough through a colander directly into boiling water.
• [German dialect, lit. 'little sparrows']

spaghetti *noun*
• "spuh GETTY"
• pasta made in solid thin strings, thicker than vermicelli.
• [Italian, pl. of diminutive of *spago* string]
• **spaghettilike** *adjective*

spaghettini *plural noun*
• "spagga TEENY"
• very thin spaghetti.
• [Italian, diminutive of SPAGHETTI]

spall *noun*
• "SPAWL"
• a splinter or chip, esp. of rock.
• [Middle English (also *spale*): origin unknown]
• **spalling** *noun*

Spallumcheenite *noun*
• "SPAL um cheen ite" ("SPAL" rhymes with *PAL*)
• a resident of Spallumcheen, BC.

spanakopita *noun*
• "spanna ko PEETA"
• an originally Greek phyllo pastry stuffed with spinach, feta cheese, etc.
• [modern Greek, from *spanaki* spinach + *pita* cake, pie]

spandrel *noun*
• "SPAN drull"
• the almost triangular space between one side of the outer curve of an arch, a wall, and the ceiling or framework.
• [perhaps from Anglo-French *spaund(e)re*, or from *espaundre* EXPAND]

Spaniard *noun*
• "SPAN yurd"
• a native or national of Spain.
• [Old French *Espaignart* from *Espaigne* Spain]

spaniel *noun*
• "SPAN y'll"
• a dog of any of various breeds with a long silky coat and drooping ears.
• [Old French *espaigneul* Spanish (dog), from Romanic *Hispaniolus* (unrecorded) from *Hispania* Spain]

Spartan *adjective*
• "SPART 'n"
• of or relating to Sparta in ancient Greece.

spartina *noun*
• "spar TEENA"
• any grass of the genus *Spartina*, with rhizomatous roots and growing in wet or marshy ground.
• [Greek *spartinē* rope]

spasm *noun*
• "SPAZM"
• a sudden involuntary muscular contraction.
• [Old French *spasme* or Latin *spasmus* from Greek *spasmos*, *spasma* from *spaō* pull]

spasmodic *adjective*
• "spazz MODDIC"
• of, caused by, or subject to, a spasm or spasms.
• [modern Latin *spasmodicus* from Greek *spasmōdēs* (as SPASM)]
• **spasmodically** *adverb*

spastic *adjective*
• "SPASS tick"
• affected by or pertaining to a spasm or sudden involuntary movements.
• [Latin *spasticus* from Greek *spastikos* pulling, from *spaō* pull]
• **spastically** *adverb*
• **spasticity** *noun* "spass TISSA tee"

spathe *noun*
• "SPATHE" (rhymes with *BATHE*)
• a large bract or pair of bracts enveloping a spadix or flower cluster.
• [Latin from Greek *spathē* broad blade etc.]

spatial *adjective*
ALSO SPELLED: **spacial**
• "SPAY sh'll"
• of or concerning space.
• [Latin *spatium* space]
• **spatiality** *noun* (also **spaciality**) "spay shee ALA tee"
• **spatialize** *verb* (also **spacialize**, esp. *Brit.* **-ise**)
• **spatially** *adverb* (also **spacially**)

spatiotemporal *adjective*
• "spay shee oh TEMPER 'll"
• belonging to both space and time or to space-time.
• [Latin *spatium* space + TEMPORAL]
• **spatiotemporally** *adverb*

Spätlese *noun*
• "SHPET lay zuh"
• a white, esp. German, wine made from grapes harvested late in the season.
• [German, from *spät* late + *Lese* picking, vintage]

spatula *noun*
• "SPATCH oo luh"
• any of various cooking utensils, esp.: an implement with a broad flexible rubber blade, used to scrape the sides of a bowl etc.
• [Latin, var. of *spathula*, diminutive of *spatha* SPATHE]

spatulate *adjective*
• "SPATCH oo lit"
• having a broad rounded end.
• [as SPATULA]

spavin *noun*
• "SPAV in"
• enlargement of a horse's hock, often leading to lameness.
• [Old French *espavin*, var. of *esparvain* from Germanic]

spavined *adjective*
• "SPAV ind"
• (of a horse) affected with spavin.
• [as SPAVIN]

spawn *verb*
• "SPON"
• (of a fish, frog, mollusc, or crustacean) produce or fertilize (eggs).
• [Anglo-French *espaundre* shed roe, Old French *espandre* EXPAND]
• **spawner** *noun*

spearwort *noun*
• "SPEER wurt" or "SPEER wort"
• an aquatic plant, *Ranunculus lingua*, with thick hollow stems, long narrow spear-shaped leaves, and yellow flowers.
• ['spear' (Old English *spere*) + WORT]

spec *noun*
• "SPECK"
• a detailed working description; a specification or specifications.
• [abbreviation of SPECIFICATION]
HOMOPHONES: *speck*

special *adjective*
• "SPESH'll"
• particularly good; exceptional; out of the ordinary.
• [Old French *especial* ESPECIAL or Latin *specialis* (as SPECIES)]
• **specially** *adverb*
• **specialness** *noun*

specialist *noun*
• "SPESH'll ist"
• a person who is trained in a particular branch of a profession, esp. medicine.
• [as SPECIAL]
• **specialism** *noun*

specialize *verb*
ALSO SPELLED: esp. *Brit.* **-ise**
• "SPESH 'll ize"
• be or become a specialist.
• [as SPECIAL]
• **specialization** *noun* (also esp. *Brit.* **-isation**)

specialty *noun*
• "SPESH'll tee"
• a special pursuit, product, operation, etc., to which a company or a person gives special attention.
• [as SPECIAL]

speciation *noun*
• "spee shee AY sh'n" or "spee see AY sh'n"
• the formation of new species in the course of evolution.
• [as SPECIES]
• **speciate** *verb*

specie *noun*
• "SPEE shee" or "SPEE see"
• coin money as opposed to paper money.
• [Latin, ablative of SPECIES in phrase *in specie*]

species *noun*
• "SPEE seez" or "SPEE sheez"
• a class of things having some common characteristics.
• [Latin, = appearance, kind, beauty, from *specere* look]

speciesism *noun*
• "SPEE seez izm" or "SPEE sheez izm"
• an assumption of human superiority leading to the exploitation of animals.
• [as SPECIES]
• **speciesist** *adjective*

specific *adjective*
• "spuh SIFFIC"
• clearly defined; definite, precise.
• [Late Latin *specificus* (as SPECIES)]
• **specifically** *adverb*
• **specificity** *noun* "spessa FISSA tee"

specify *verb*
• "SPESSA fie"
• name or mention expressly.
• [Old French *specifier* or Late Latin *specificare* (as SPECIFIC)]
• **specifiable** *adjective*
• **specification** *noun*
• **specifier** *noun*

specimen *noun*
• "SPESSA m'n"
• an individual or part taken as an example of a class or whole, esp. when used for investigation or scientific examination.
• [Latin from *specere* look]

specious *adjective*
• "SPEE sh'ss"
• superficially plausible or genuine but actually wrong or false.
• [Middle English, = beautiful, from Latin *speciosus* (as SPECIES)]
• **speciously** *adverb*
• **speciousness** *noun*

spectacle *noun*
• "SPECTA k'll"
• a public show, ceremony, etc.
• [Old French from Latin *spectaculum* from *spectare* frequentative of *specere* look]

spectacled *adjective*
• "SPECTA k'ld"
• wearing eyeglasses.
• [as SPECTACLE]

spectacles *plural noun*
- "SPECTA k'lz"
- a pair of eyeglasses.
- [as SPECTACLE]

spectacular *adjective*
- "speck TACK yuh lur"
- beautiful in a dramatic and eye-catching way.
- [SPECTACLE, after *oracular* etc.]
- **spectacularly** *adverb*

spectator *noun*
- "SPECK tay tur"
- a person who looks on at a show, game, incident, etc.
- [French *spectateur* or Latin *spectator* from *spectare*: see SPECTACLE]
- **spectate** *verb*
- **spectatorial** *adjective* "specta TORY 'll"
- **spectatorship** *noun*

spectre *noun*
ALSO SPELLED: *US* **specter**
- "SPECK tur"
- a ghost.
- [French *spectre* or Latin *spectrum*: see SPECTRUM]
- **spectral** *adjective*
- **spectrally** *adverb*

spectrogram *noun*
- "SPECTRO gram"
- a record obtained with a spectrograph.
- [SPECTRUM + Greek *gramma* thing written]

spectrograph *noun*
- "SPECTRO graff"
- an apparatus for photographing or otherwise recording spectra.
- [SPECTRUM + Greek *graphia* writing]
- **spectrographic** *adjective*
- **spectrographically** *adverb*
- **spectrography** *noun* "speck TROGGRA fee"

spectroheliograph *noun*
- "spectro HEELY a graff"
- an instrument for taking photographs of the sun in the light of one wavelength only.
- [SPECTRUM + HELIOGRAPH]

spectrometer *noun*
- "speck TROMMA tur"
- an instrument used for the measurement of observed spectra.
- [SPECTRUM + Greek *metron* measure]
- **spectrometric** *adjective* "spectra METRIC"
- **spectrometry** *noun*

spectrophotometer *noun*
- "spectro foe TOMMA tur"
- an instrument for measuring the intensity of light in various parts of the spectrum, esp. as transmitted or emitted by a substance or solution at a particular wavelength.
- [SPECTRUM + PHOTOMETER]
- **spectrophotometric** *adjective* "spectro foe tuh METRIC"
- **spectrophotometry** *noun*

spectroscope *noun*
- "SPECTRO scope"
- an instrument for producing and recording spectra for examination.
- [as SPECTRUM + Greek *skopos* target, from *skeptomai* look at]
- **spectroscopic** *adjective*
- **spectroscopist** *noun*
- **spectroscopy** *noun* "speck TROSCA pee"

spectrum *noun*
- "SPECK trum"
- a band of colours, as seen in a rainbow etc., produced by separation of the components of light by their different degrees of refraction according to wavelength.
- [Latin, = image, apparition, from *specere* to look]

specular *adjective*
- "SPECK yuh lur"
- of or having the properties of a mirror.
- [Latin *specularis* (as SPECULUM)]

speculate *verb*
- "SPECK yuh late"
- form a theory or conjecture, esp. without a firm factual basis; meditate.
- [Latin *speculari* spy out, observe, from *specula* watchtower, from *specere* look]
- **speculation** *noun*
- **speculator** *noun*

speculative *adjective*
- "SPECK yuh luh tiv"
- of, based on, engaged in, or inclined to speculation.
- [as SPECULATE]
- **speculatively** *adverb*
- **speculativeness** *noun*

speculum *noun*
- "SPECK yuh lum"
- an instrument to hold open or dilate a part of the body, esp. the vagina, for examination.
- [Latin, = mirror, from *specere* look]

speiss *noun*
- "SPICE"
- a compound of arsenic, iron, etc., formed in smelting certain lead ores.
- [German *Speise* food, amalgam]

HOMOPHONES: *spice*

speleology *noun*
- "speely OLLA jee"
- the scientific study of caves.
- [French *spéléologie* from Latin *spelaeum* from Greek *spēlaion* cave + *logos* word]
- **speleological** *adjective*
- **speleologist** *noun*

spelt *noun*
- "SPELT"
- a species of wheat, *Triticum aestivum*.
- [Old English from Old Saxon *spelta* (Old High German *spelza*), Middle English from Middle Low German, Middle Dutch *spelte*]

spelunker *noun*
- “spil LUNK ur”
- a person who explores caves, esp. as a hobby.
- [obsolete *spelunk* cave, from Latin *spelunca*]
- **spelunking** *noun*

spencer *noun*
- “SPEN sur”
- a short close-fitting jacket.
- [prob. from the 2nd Earl *Spencer*, English politician d.1834]

spermaceti *noun*
- “spurma SETTY”
- a white waxy substance produced by the sperm whale to aid buoyancy, and used in the manufacture of candles, ointments, etc.
- [medieval Latin from Late Latin *sperma* sperm + *ceti* genitive of *cetus* from Greek *kētos* whale, from the belief that it was whale spawn]

spermary *noun*
- “SPURMER ee”
- an organ in which human or animal sperms are generated.
- [Late Latin *sperma* sperm, from Greek *sperma -atos* seed, from *speirō* sow]

spermatic *adjective*
- “spur MATTIC”
- of or relating to a sperm or spermary.
- [Late Latin *sperma* sperm, from Greek *sperma -atos* seed, from *speirō* sow]

spermatid *noun*
- “SPURMA tid”
- an immature male sex cell formed from a spermatocyte, which may develop into a spermatozoon.
- [as SPERMATIC]

spermatocyte *noun*
- “spur MATTA site”
- a cell produced from a spermatogonium and which may divide by meiosis into spermatids.
- [Late Latin *sperma* sperm, from Greek *sperma -atos* seed, from *speirō* sow + Greek *kutos* vessel]

spermatogenesis *noun*
- “spur matta JENNA sis”
- the production or development of mature spermatozoa.
- [Late Latin *sperma* from Greek *sperma -atos* seed, from *speirō* sow + GENESIS]

spermatogonium *noun*
- “spur matta GO nee um”
- a cell produced at an early stage in the formation of spermatozoa, from which spermatocytes develop.
- [Late Latin *sperma* from Greek *sperma -atos* seed, from *speirō* sow + modern Latin *gonium* from Greek *gonos* offspring, seed]
- **spermatogonical** *adjective*

spermatophore *noun*
- “spur MATTA for”
- an albuminous capsule containing spermatozoa found in various invertebrates.
- [Late Latin *sperma* sperm + Greek *-phoros -phoron* bearing, bearer, from *pherō* bear]

spermatophyte *noun*
- “spur MATTA fite”
- any seed-bearing plant.
- [Greek *sperma -atos* seed, from *speirō* sow + *phuton* plant, from *phuō* come into being]

spermatozoid *noun*
- “spur matta ZO id”
- the mature motile male sex cell of some plants.
- [as SPERMATOZOON]

spermatozoon *noun*
- “spur matta ZO on”
- the mature motile male sex cell of an animal, by which the ovum is fertilized.
- [Late Latin *sperma* from Greek *sperma -atos* seed, from *speirō* sow + *zōion* animal]
- **spermatozoal** *adjective*
- **spermatozoan** *adjective*

spermicide *noun*
- “SPURMA side”
- a substance able to kill spermatozoa.
- [SPERMATOZOON + Latin *-cida, -cidium* from *caedere* kill]
- **spermicidal** *adjective*
- **spermicidally** *adverb*

sphagnum *noun*
- “SFAG num” or “SPAG num”
- any moss of the genus *Sphagnum*, growing in bogs, with spongy, absorbent leaves and stems, and used as packing esp. for plants, as a soil conditioner or fertilizer, etc.
- [modern Latin from Greek *sphagnos* a moss]

sphalerite *noun*
- “SFAL ur ite”
- any naturally occurring metal sulphide.
- [Greek *sphaleros* deceptive]

sphenoid *adjective*
- “SFEE noid”
- wedge-shaped.
- [modern Latin *sphenoides* from Greek *sphēnoeidēs* from *sphēn* wedge]
- **sphenoidal** *adjective*

sphere *noun*
- “SFEER”
- a solid figure, or its surface, with every point on its surface equidistant from its centre.
- [Old French *espere* from Late Latin *sphera*, Latin from Greek *sphaira* ball]
- **spheric** *adjective*
- **spherical** *adjective* “SFEERA k'll” or “SFERRA k'll”
- **spherically** *adverb*
- **sphericity** *noun* “sfeer ISSA tee”

spheroid *noun*
- “SFEER oid”

• a body resembling or approximating to a sphere in shape, esp. one formed by the revolution of an ellipse about one of its axes.
• [as SPHERE]
• **spheroidal** *adjective*

spherule *noun*
• "SFEER ool"
• a small sphere.
• [as SPHERE]

spherulite *noun*
• "SFEERA lite"
• a vitreous globule as a constituent of volcanic rocks.
• [as SPHERULE + Greek *lithos* stone]
• **spherulitic** *adjective* "sfeera LITTIC"

sphincter *noun*
• "SFINK tur"
• a ring of muscle surrounding and serving to guard or close an opening or tube, esp. the anus.
• [Latin from Greek *sphigktēr* from *sphiggō* bind tight]

sphingid *noun*
• "SFIN gid" (with "G" as in *GIVE*)
• any hawk moth of the family Sphingidae.
• [as SPHINX]

sphinx *noun*
• "SFINKS"
• (in Greek mythology) the winged monster of Thebes NW of Athens, having a woman's head and a lion's body, whose riddle Oedipus guessed and who consequently killed herself.
• [Latin from Greek *Sphigx*, apparently from *sphiggō* draw tight]

sphygmomanometer *noun*
• "sfig mo muh NOMMA tur"
• an instrument for measuring blood pressure.
• [Greek *sphugmo-* from *sphugmos* pulse, from *sphuzō* to throb + MANOMETER]
• **sphygmomanometric** *adjective* "sfig mo manna METRIC"

spica *noun*
• "SPIKE uh"
• a spiral bandage shaped like a figure eight, often applied to parts such as the thumb.
• [Latin, = spike, ear of corn, related to *spina* spine]

spiccato *noun*
• "spick OTTO"
• a style of staccato playing on stringed instruments involving bouncing the bow on the strings.
• [Italian, = detailed, distinct]

spicule *noun*
• "SPICK yool"
• any small sharp-pointed body.
• [modern Latin *spicula*, *spiculum*, diminutives of SPICA]
• **spicular** *adjective*
• **spiculate** *adjective* "SPICK yoo lit"

spiderwort *noun*
• "SPIDER wurt" or "SPIDER wort"
• any plant of the genus *Tradescantia*, esp. *T. virginiana*, having flowers with long hairy stamens.
• ['spider' + WORT]

spiel *noun*
• "SHPEEL" or "SPEEL"
• a long or prepared speech or story, esp. a sales pitch.
• [German, = play, game]
• **spieler** *noun*

Spielbergian *adjective*
• "speel BURG ee 'n"
• relating to or characteristic of the work of US film director and producer Steven Spielberg (b.1947).

spigot *noun*
• "SPIG it"
• a small peg or plug, esp. for insertion into the vent of a cask.
• [Middle English, perhaps from Provençal *espigou(n)* from Latin *spiculum* diminutive of *spicum* = SPICA]

spikenard *noun*
• "SPIKE nard"
• a Himalayan plant of the valerian family, *Nardostachys grandiflora*.
• [Middle English, ultimately from medieval Latin *spica nardi* (as SPICA + Greek *nardostakhus* from Greek *nardos* a plant)]

spillikin *noun*
• "SPILL ick in"
• a thin strip of wood etc., esp. as used in the game of jackstraws, in which a heap of them is to be removed one at a time without moving the others.
• ['spill' a thin strip of wood, folded or twisted paper, etc., used for lighting a fire, from Middle Dutch, Middle Low German *spile*, = wooden peg + diminutive suffix *-kin*]

spinach *noun*
• "SPIN itch"
• a green garden vegetable, *Spinacia oleracea*, with succulent leaves.
• [prob. Middle Dutch *spinaetse*, *spinag(i)e*, from Old French *espinage*, *espinache* from medieval Latin *spinac(h)ia* etc. from Arabic *'isfānāḵ* from Persian *ispānāḵ*: perhaps assimilated to Latin *spina* spine, with reference to its prickly seeds]
• **spinachy** *adjective*

spinarama *noun*
• "spinna RAMA"
• *Cdn* an evasive move, esp. in hockey, consisting of an abrupt 360-degree turn.
• ['spin' from Old English *spinnan* + PANORAMA]

spinel *noun*
• "spin EL"
• any of a group of hard crystalline minerals of

various colours, consisting chiefly of oxides of magnesium and aluminum.
• [French *spinelle* from Italian *spinella*, diminutive of *spina* spine]

spinet *noun*
• "SPIN it" or "spin ET"
• a small harpsichord with oblique strings.
• [obsolete French *espinette* from Italian *spinetta* virginal, spinet, diminutive of *spina* thorn, with reference to the plucked strings]

spinifex *noun*
• "SPIN if ex"
• any Australian grass of the genus *Spinifex*, with coarse, spiny leaves.
• [modern Latin from Latin *spina* spine + *-fex* maker, from *facere* make]

spinnaker *noun*
• "SPINNA cur"
• a large triangular sail carried opposite the mainsail of a racing yacht running before the wind.
• [fanciful from *Sphinx*, name of yacht first using it, perhaps after *spanker*]

spinneret *noun*
• "SPINNER et"
• any of various organs through which the silk, gossamer, or thread of spiders, silkworms, and certain other insects is produced.
• ['spin' (see SPINARAMA)]

spinney *noun*
• "SPINNY"
• a small wood; a thicket.
• [Old French *espinei* from Latin *spinetum* thicket, from *spina* thorn]
HOMOPHONES: *spinny*

spinose *adjective*
• "SPINE ose"
• having spines, spiny.
• [Latin *spina* spine, thorn]

spinster *noun*
• "SPIN stur"
• a woman, esp. an older one, thought unlikely to marry.
• [Middle English, originally = woman who spins]
• **spinsterhood** *noun*
• **spinsterish** *adjective*

spinto *noun*
• "SPIN toe"
• a lyric soprano or tenor voice of powerful dramatic quality.
• [Italian, past participle of *springere* push]

spinule *noun*
• "SPIN yool"
• a small spine.
• [Latin *spinula* diminutive of *spina* spine]

spiracle *noun*
• "SPY ruh k'll"
• an external respiratory opening in insects, whales, and some fish.
• [Latin *spiraculum* from *spirare* breathe]
• **spiracular** *adjective* "spy RACK yuh lur"

spirant *adjective*
• "SPY runt"
• (of a consonant sound) produced by the friction of the airstream through a narrow opening in the mouth.
• [Latin *spirare spirant-* breathe]

spirea *noun*
ALSO SPELLED: **spiraea**
• "spy REE uh"
• any rosaceous shrub of the genus *Spiraea*, with clusters of small white or pink flowers.
• [Latin from Greek *speiraia* from *speira* coil]

spirillum *noun*
• "spy RILLUM"
• any bacterium of the genus *Spirillum*, characterized by a rigid spiral structure.
• [modern Latin, diminutive of Latin *spira* spiral, from Greek *speira* coil]

spiritual *adjective*
• "SPEER itch oo 'll"
• of or relating to the human spirit or soul; not of physical things.
• [Old French *spirituel* from Latin *spiritus* breath, spirit, from *spirare* breathe]
• **spirituality** *noun*
• **spiritually** *adverb*

spiritualism *noun*
• "SPEER itch oo 'll izm"
• the belief that the spirits of the dead can communicate with the living, esp. through mediums.
• [as SPIRITUAL]
• **spiritualist** *noun*
• **spiritualistic** *adjective*

spiritualize *verb*
ALSO SPELLED: esp. *Brit.* **-ise**
• "SPEER itch oo 'll ize"
• make (a person or a person's character, thoughts, etc.) spiritual; elevate.
• [as SPIRITUAL]
• **spiritualization** *noun* (also esp. *Brit.* **-isation**)

spirituous *adjective*
• "SPEER itch oo us"
• containing much alcohol.
• [as SPIRITUAL]

spirochete *noun*
ALSO SPELLED: esp. *Brit.* **spirochaete**
• "SPY ro keet"
• any of various flexible spirally twisted bacteria of the order Spirochaetales, esp. one that causes syphilis.
• [Latin *spira*, Greek *speira* coil + Greek *khaitē* long hair]

spirogyra *noun*
• "spy ro JYE ruh"
• any freshwater alga of the genus *Spirogyra*, with cells containing spiral bands of chlorophyll.
• [modern Latin from Latin *spira*, Greek *speira* coil + Greek *guros gura* round]

spirometer *noun*
• "spy ROMMA tur"
• an instrument for measuring the air capacity of the lungs.
• [as SPIRANT + Greek *metron* measure]
• **spirometry** *noun*

spirulina *noun*
• "spy ruh LEENA"
• any alga of the genus *Spirulina*, found growing in dense tangled masses in warm alkaline lakes in Africa and Central and S America.
• [from modern Latin genus name *Spirulina*]

spittoon *noun*
• "spit TOON"
• a metal or earthenware pot with esp. a funnel-shaped top, used for spitting into.
• ['spit' from Old English *spittan*, of imitative origin]

spitz *noun*
• "SPITS"
• a small breed of dog with a pointed muzzle, esp. a Pomeranian.
• [German *Spitz(hund)* from *spitz* pointed + *Hund* dog]

spiv *noun*
• "SPIV"
• a man, often characterized by flashy dress, who makes a living by illicit or unscrupulous dealings.
• [20th c.: origin unknown]
• **spivvish** *adjective*
• **spivvy** *adjective*

splanchnic *adjective*
• "SPLANK nick"
• of or relating to the viscera; intestinal.
• [modern Latin *splanchnicus* from Greek *splagkhnikos* from *splagkhna* entrails]

spleenwort *noun*
• "SPLEEN wurt" or "SPLEEN wort"
• any fern of the genus *Asplenium*, formerly used as a remedy for disorders of the spleen.
• ['spleen' from Old French *esplen* from Latin *splen* from Greek *splēn* + WORT]

splendiferous *adjective*
• "splen DIFFER us"
• splendid.
• ['splendour' (from Anglo-French *splendeur* or Latin *splendor* from *splendēre* to shine) + *-fer* producing, from *ferre* bear]
• **splendiferously** *adverb*
• **splendiferousness** *noun*

splenectomy *noun*
• "splin ECTA mee"
• the surgical excision of the spleen.
• [Greek *splēn* spleen + *ektomē* excision, from *ek* out + *temnō* cut]

splenetic *adjective*
• "splin ETTIC"
• ill-tempered; peevish.
• [Late Latin *spleneticus* (as SPLEENWORT), from the earlier belief that the spleen was the seat of such feelings]
• **splenetically** *adverb*

splenic *adjective*
• "SPLEE nick" or "SPLEN ick"
• of or in the spleen.
• [French *splénique* or Latin *splenicus* from Greek *splēnikos* (as SPLENECTOMY)]

splenius *noun*
• "SPLEENY us"
• either section of muscle on each side of the neck and back serving to draw back the head.
• [modern Latin from Greek *splēnion* bandage]
• **splenial** *adjective*

splenomegaly *noun*
• "spleeno MEGGA lee"
• a pathological enlargement of the spleen.
• [Greek *splēn* spleen + *mega* from *megas* great]

spoliation *noun*
• "spo lee AY sh'n"
• plunder or pillage, esp. of neutral vessels in war.
• [Latin *spoliatio* from *spoliare* from *spolium* spoil, plunder]
• **spoliator** *noun*

spondee *noun*
• "SPON dee"
• a foot consisting of two long (or stressed) syllables.
• [ultimately from Greek *spondeios* (*pous* foot) from *spondē* libation, as being characteristic of music accompanying libations]
• **spondaic** *adjective* "spon DAY ick"

spondylitis *noun*
• "spon dil ITE iss"
• inflammation of the vertebrae.
• [Latin *spondylus* vertebra, from Greek *spondulos* + *-itis*, forming feminine of adjectives in *-itēs* (with *nosos* 'disease' implied)]
• **spondylitic** *adjective* "spon dil ITTIC"

sponge *noun*
• "SPUNJ"
• any sessile aquatic animal of the phylum Porifera, with a porous bag-like body structure and a rigid or elastic internal skeleton.
• [Old English via Latin *spongia* from Greek *spoggia, spoggos*]
• **spongeable** *adjective*
• **spongelike** *adjective*
• **spongily** *adverb*
• **sponginess** *noun*
• **spongy** *adjective*

sponger *noun*
• "SPUN jur"
• a person who contrives to live at another's expense.
• [as SPONGE]

spongiform *adjective*
• "SPUNJA form"
• spongelike; spongy.
• [as SPONGE + Latin *forma* form]

sponson *noun*
• "SPON s'n"
• a projection from the side of a warship or tank to enable a gun to be trained forward and aft.
• [19th c.: origin unknown]

sponsor *noun*
• "SPON sur"
• a person who supports an activity done for charity by pledging money in advance.
• [Latin *spondēre spons-* promise solemnly]
• **sponsorial** *adjective* "spon SORRY 'il"
• **sponsorship** *noun*

spontaneous *adjective*
• "spon TAINY us"
• acting or done or occurring because of a sudden impulse from within; not planned or caused or suggested by external forces.
• [Late Latin *spontaneus* from *sponte* of one's own accord]
• **spontaneity** *noun* "sponta NAY a tee"
• **spontaneously** *adverb*

spoor *noun*
• "SPOOR" (rhymes with *TOUR*)
• the track or scent of a person or animal, esp. the footprints of a wild animal hunted as game.
• [Afrikaans from Middle Dutch *spo(o)r* from Germanic]

sporadic *adjective*
• "spuh RADDIC"
• occurring only here and there or occasionally, separate, scattered.
• [medieval Latin *sporadicus* from Greek *sporadikos* from *sporas -ados* scattered: compare *speirō* to sow]
• **sporadically** *adverb*

sporangium *noun*
• "spuh RAN jee um"
• a receptacle in which spores are found.
• [modern Latin from Greek *spora* spore + *aggeion* vessel]
• **sporangial** *adjective*

spore *noun*
• "SPORE"
• a specialized reproductive cell of many plants and micro-organisms.
• [modern Latin *spora* from Greek *spora* sowing, seed, from *speirō* sow]
HOMOPHONES: *spoor*

sporocyst *noun*
• "SPORA sist"
• an intermediate stage in the life cycle of various parasites.
• [as SPORE + CYST]

sporogenesis *noun*
• "spora JENNA sis"
• the process of spore formation.
• [as SPORE + GENESIS]

sporophore *noun*
• "SPORA for"
• a spore-bearing structure esp. in a fungus.
• [as SPORE + Greek *-phoros -phoron* bearing, bearer, from *pherō* bear]

sporophyte *noun*
• "SPORA fite"
• the asexual form of a plant that has alternation of generations between this and the gamete-producing form (gametophyte).
• [as SPORE + Greek *phuton* plant, from *phuō* come into being]
• **sporophytic** *adjective* "spora FITTIC"

sporozoite *noun*
• "spora ZO ite"
• a small motile stage in the life cycle of some protozoans, e.g. the malaria parasite, usually produced inside a host.
• [as SPORE + Greek *zoion* animal]

sporran *noun*
• "SPORE 'n"
• a pouch, usu. of leather or sealskin covered with fur etc., worn in front of the kilt as part of Highland costume.
• [Gaelic *sporan* from medieval Latin *bursa* purse]

sporulate *verb*
• "SPORE yuh late"
• form spores or sporules.
• [as SPORE]
• **sporulation** *noun*

sporule *noun*
• "SPORE yool"
• a small spore or a single spore.
• [French *sporule* or modern Latin *sporula* (as SPORE)]

Sprechgesang *noun*
• "SHPRECK guh zong"
• a style of dramatic vocalization between speech and song.
• [German, lit. 'speech song']

sprightly *adjective*
• "SPRITE lee"
• characterized by animation or cheerful vitality; brisk, lively, spirited.
• [*spright* var. of 'sprite' from *sprit* var. of 'spirit' (see SPIRITUAL)]
• **sprightliness** *noun*

springbok *noun*
• "SPRING bock"

• a southern African gazelle, *Antidorcas marsupialis*, with the ability to run with high springing jumps.
• [Afrikaans from Dutch *springen* spring, leap + *bok* antelope]

spritz *verb*
• "SPRITS"
• sprinkle, squirt, or spray (something) with a liquid.
• [German *spritzen* to squirt]
• **spritzy** *adjective*

spritzer *noun*
• "SPRITS ur"
• a mixture of wine and soda water.
• [German *Spritzer* a splash, as SPRITZ]

sprue *noun*
• "SPROO"
• a channel through which molten metal or plastic is poured into a mould.
• [19th c.: origin unknown]

spry *adjective*
• "SPRY" (rhymes with *TRY*)
• nimble, active, lively.
• [18th c.: origin unknown]
• **spryly** *adverb*

spudgel *noun*
• "SPUDGE 'll"
• *Cdn* (*Nfld*) a metal or wooden bucket attached to a long pole used esp. to bail water from a boat or to draw water from a well.
• [18th c.: origin unknown]

spumante *noun*
• "spoo MANTY" or "spoo MONTAY"
• any of a number of Italian sparkling white wines, the most important of which is Asti.
• [Italian, = 'sparkling']

spume *noun*
• "SPYOOM"
• foam or froth on or from a liquid.
• [Old French (*e*)*spume* or Latin *spuma*]
• **spumy** *adjective*

spumoni *noun*
• "spuh MOANY"
• a kind of rich layered ice cream with candied fruit and nuts.
• [Italian *spumone* from *spuma* SPUME]

spurge *noun*
• "SPURJ"
• any plant of the genus *Euphorbia*, exuding an acrid milky juice once used medicinally as a purgative.
• [Old French *espurge* from *espurgier* from Latin *expurgare* (*ex* out of, *purgare* purify, from *purus* pure)]

spurious *adjective*
• "SPUR ee us" or "SPYOOR ee us"
• not proceeding from the reputed origin, source, or author; not genuine or authentic.
• [Latin *spurius* false]
• **spuriously** *adverb*
• **spuriousness** *noun*

spurn *verb*
• "SPURN"
• reject or refuse (a person or thing) in a way that indicates contempt.
• [Old English *spurnan, spornan*]

sputum *noun*
• "SPYOO t'm"
• saliva, spittle.
• [Latin, neuter past participle of *spuere* spit]

squab *noun*
• "SKWOB"
• a newly hatched or very young bird, esp. an unfledged pigeon.
• [17th c.: origin unknown: compare obsolete *quab* shapeless thing, Swedish dialect *sqvabba* fat woman]

squabble *noun*
• "SKWOBBLE"
• a petty or noisy quarrel; a dispute.
• [prob. imitative: compare Swedish dialect *sqvabbel* a dispute]
• **squabbler** *noun*

squad *noun*
• "SKWOD"
• a small group of people sharing a task etc.
• [French *escouade* var. of *escadre* from Italian *squadra* square, from Latin *quadra* square]

squadron *noun*
• "SKWOD r'n"
• a principal division of an armoured or cavalry regiment consisting of two or more troops.
• [Italian *squadrone* (as SQUAD)]

squalene *noun*
• "SKWAY leen"
• an oily liquid hydrocarbon which occurs in shark liver oil and human sebum, and is a metabolic precursor of sterols.
• [Latin *squalus* a kind of marine fish]

squalid *adjective*
• "SKWOLL id"
• rundown, degenerate, unsanitary, esp. through neglect or poverty.
• [Latin *squalidus* from *squalēre* be rough or dirty]

squall *noun*
• "SKWOLL"
• a sudden and short-lived violent storm or gust of wind, esp. with rain, snow, or sleet.
• [prob. from 'squeal' (imitative)]
• **squally** *adjective*

squalor *noun*
• "SKWOLL ur"
• the state of being filthy or squalid.
• [Latin, as SQUALID]

squama *noun*
• "SKWAY muh"
• a scale on an animal or plant.
• [Latin *squama*]
• **squamate** *adjective*

Squamish *noun*
• "SKWOM ish"
• a member of an Aboriginal people living in southwestern BC.
• [alteration of Squamish name for themselves]

squamous *adjective*
• "SKWAY muss"
• (of a substance) covered with or composed of scales.
• [Latin *squama* scale]

squander *verb*
• "SKWON dur" ("SKWON" rhymes with *LAWN*)
• spend (time, money, etc.) recklessly or lavishly; use or consume in a wasteful manner.
• [16th c.: origin unknown]
• **squanderer** *noun*

squawk *noun*
• "SKWAWK" (rhymes with *HAWK*)
• a loud harsh cry esp. of a bird.
• [imitative]
• **squawker** *noun*

squeamish *adjective*
• "SKWEE mish"
• easily turned sick, disgusted, or faint.
• [Middle English var. of *squeamous* (now dialect), from Anglo-French *escoymos*, of unknown origin]
• **squeamishly** *adverb*
• **squeamishness** *noun*

squeegee *noun*
• "SKWEE jee"
• an implement with a handle attached to a wide rubber blade used to remove the excess liquid from glass when cleaning windows.
• [*squeege*, strengthened form of 'squeeze']

squelch *verb*
• "SKWELCH"
• walk or tread heavily in mud, on wet ground, or with water in the shoes, so as to make a sucking sound.
• [imitative]
• **squelchy** *adjective*

squib *noun*
• "SKWIB"
• a small firework burning with a hissing sound and usu. a final slight explosion.
• [16th c.: origin unknown: perhaps imitative]

squidgy *adjective*
• "SKWIDGE ee"
• soft, squashy, soggy, or moist.
• [imitative]

squiffed *adjective*
• "SKWIFT"
• slightly drunk.
• [19th c.: origin unknown]

squiffy *adjective*
• "SKWIF ee"
• = SQUIFFED.
• [19th c.: origin unknown]

squiggle *noun*
• "SKWIG 'll"
• a short curly or wavy line, esp. in handwriting or doodling.
• [imitative]
• **squiggly** *adjective*

squill *noun*
• "SKWILL"
• a scilla, typically with star-shaped blue flowers.
• [Middle English via Latin *squilla*, *scilla* from Greek *skilla*]

squillion *noun*
• "SKWILL y'n"
• an indefinite very large number.
• [fanciful, after *million*]

squinch *noun*
• "SKWINCH"
• a straight or arched structure across an interior angle of a square tower to carry a superstructure, e.g. a dome.
• [var. of obsolete *scunch*, abbreviation of SCUNCHEON]

squire *noun*
• "SKWIRE"
• (in Britain) a country gentleman, esp. the chief landowner in a country district.
• [Old French *esquier* ESQUIRE]
• **squirely** *adjective*

squirearch *noun*
ALSO SPELLED: **squirarch**
• "SKWIRE ark"
• (in Britain) a member of the class of landowners, esp. having political or social influence.
• [as SQUIRE, after MONARCH etc.]
• **squirearchical** *adjective* (also **squirarchical**)
• **squirearchy** *noun* (also **squirarchy**)

squirm *verb*
• "SKWURM"
• wriggle, writhe.
• [imitative, prob. assoc. with 'worm']
• **squirmy** *adjective*

squirrel *noun*
• "SKWUR 'll"
• any of various slender agile arboreal rodents having a long bushy tail, a furry coat, and pointy ears, esp. of the genus *Sciurus* and related genera, noted for hoarding nuts for food in winter.
• [Old French *esquireul*, ultimately from Latin *sciurus* from Greek *skiouros* from *skia* shade + *oura* tail]

squirrelly *adjective*
• "SKWUR 'll ee"
• restless, fidgety, anxious.
• [as SQUIRREL]

squirt *verb*
• "SKWURT"
• eject or propel (a liquid or semi-liquid substance) in a jet-like stream, esp. from a small opening.
• [Middle English, imitative]
• **squirter** *noun*

Sri *noun*
ALSO SPELLED: **Shri**
• "SHREE" or "SREE"
• (in the Indian subcontinent) a title of respect preceding the name of a deity or distinguished person, or the title of a sacred book.
• [Sanskrit, = 'beauty']

stability *noun*
• "stuh BILLA tee"
• the quality or state of being stable.
• [Old French *estableté* from Latin *stabilis* from *stare* stand]

stabilize *verb*
ALSO SPELLED: *Brit.* **-ise**
• "STAY b'll ize"
• make or become stable.
• [as STABILITY]
• **stabilization** *noun* (also esp. *Brit.* **-isation**)
• **stabilizer** *noun* (also esp. *Brit.* **-iser**)

staccato *adverb*
• "stuh CATTO" or "stuh COTTO"
• (as a musical direction) with each note sharply detached or separated from the others.
• [Italian, past participle of *staccare* = *distaccare* DETACH]

stacte *noun*
• "STACK tee"
• a sweet spice used by the ancient Jews in making incense.
• [Latin from Greek *staktē* from *stazō* drip]

stadium *noun*
• "STAY dee um"
• an athletic or sports ground with tiers of seats for spectators.
• [Latin from Greek *stadion*]

stadtholder *noun*
ALSO SPELLED: **stadholder**
• "STOD hole dur" or "STOT hole dur" or "STAT hole dur"
• the chief magistrate of the United Provinces of the Netherlands.
• [Dutch *stadhouder* deputy, from *stad* place + *houder* holder]

stagette *noun*
• "stag ET"
• an all-female celebration in honour of a woman about to marry.
• ['stag' adult male deer + feminine diminutive *-ette*]

stagflation *noun*
• "stag FLAY sh'n"
• a state of inflation without a corresponding increase of demand and employment.
• [as STAGNANT + INFLATION]

stagnant *adjective*
• "STAG n'nt"
• (of liquid) motionless, having no current.
• [Latin *stagnare stagnant-* from *stagnum* pool]
• **stagnancy** *noun*
• **stagnantly** *adverb*

staid *adjective*
• "STADE"
• serious and dull; sedate.
• [= *stayed*, past participle of 'stay' from Old French *ester* from Latin *stare* stand]
• **staidly** *adverb*
• **staidness** *noun*

staithe *noun*
• "STAYTHE" (rhymes with *BATHE*)
• a wharf, esp. a waterside coal depot equipped for loading vessels.
• [Old Norse *stöth* landing stage]

stake *noun*
• "STAKE"
• a stout stick or post sharpened at one end and driven into the ground as a support, boundary mark, etc.
• [Old English *staca* from West Germanic, related to 'stick']
HOMOPHONES: *steak*

stakeholder *noun*
• "STAKE hole dur"
• an independent party with whom each of those who make a wager deposits the money etc. wagered.
• [as STAKE + 'holder']

stakeout *noun*
• "STAKE out"
• a continuous secret watch by the police.
• [as STAKE + 'out']

Stakhanovite *noun*
• "stuh CONNA vite"
• a worker (esp. in the former USSR) who increases his output to an exceptional extent, and so gains special awards.
• [A. G. *Stakhanov*, Russian coal miner d.1977]
• **Stakhanovism** *noun*

stalactite *noun*
• "stuh LACK tite" or "STAL uck tite"
• a tapering deposit of calcite hanging down like an icicle from the roof of a cave, cliff overhang, etc., formed by dripping water.
• [modern Latin *stalactites* from Greek *stalaktos* dripping, from *stalassō* drip]

stalagmite *noun*
• "stuh LAG mite" or "STAL ug mite"
• a mound or tapering column of calcite rising

from the floor of a cave etc., deposited by dripping water and often uniting with a stalactite.
• [modern Latin *stalagmites* from Greek *stalagma* a drop, from *stalassō* (as STALACTITE)]

Stalinism *noun*
• "STAL in ism" or "STOL in ism"
• the policies followed by the Soviet leader J. Stalin (d.1953), esp. centralization, totalitarianism, and the pursuit of Communism.
• **Stalinist** *noun*

stalk *noun*
• "STOCK"
• the main stem of a herbaceous plant.
• [Middle English *stalke*, prob. diminutive of (now dialect) *stale* rung of a ladder, long handle, from Old English *stalu*]
• **stalked** *adjective*
• **stalkless** *adjective*
• **stalklike** *adjective*
• **stalky** *adjective*
HOMOPHONES: *stock*, *stocky*

stalker *noun*
• "STOCKER"
• a person who stalks, hounds, or follows a particular person, esp. stealthily or obsessively.
• [Old English *stalk* pursue or approach stealthily: related to 'steal']
HOMOPHONES: *stocker*

stalwart *adjective*
• "STAWL wurt"
• strongly built, sturdy.
• [Scots var. of obsolete *stalworth* from Old English *stǣlwierthe* from *stǣl* place, *worth* worth]
• **stalwartly** *adverb*

stamen *noun*
• "STAY m'n"
• the male fertilizing organ of a flowering plant, including the anther containing pollen.
• [Latin *stamen* warp in an upright loom, thread]

stamina *noun*
• "STAMMA nuh"
• the ability to endure prolonged physical or mental strain; staying power, power of endurance.
• [Latin, pl. of STAMEN in sense 'warp, threads spun by the Fates']

staminate *adjective*
• "STAM in it" or "STAM in ate"
• (of a plant) having stamens, esp. stamens but not pistils.
• [as STAMINA]

stampede *noun*
• "stam PEED"
• a sudden flight and scattering of a number of horses, cattle, etc.
• [Spanish *estampida* crash, uproar, ultimately from Germanic, related to 'stamp']
• **stampeder** *noun*

stance *noun*
• "STANCE" (rhymes with *DANCE*)
• an attitude or position of the body, esp. in sports.
• [French from Italian *stanza* standing place, chamber, stanza, ultimately from Latin *stare* stand]

stanchion *noun*
• "STAN ch'n"
• a post or pillar, an upright support, a vertical strut.
• [Anglo-French *stanchon*, prob. ultimately from Latin *stare* stand]

standard *noun*
• "STAN durd"
• an object or quality or measure serving as a basis or example or principle to which others conform or should conform or by which the accuracy or quality of others is judged.
• [Anglo-French *estaundart*, Old French *estendart* from *estendre*, as EXTEND]
• **standardization** *noun* (also esp. *Brit.* **-isation**)
• **standardize** *verb* (also esp. *Brit.* **-ise**)

standardbred *noun*
• "STAN durd bred"
• a horse of a breed able to attain a specified speed, developed esp. for harness racing.
• [as STANDARD + 'bred' past tense of 'breed']

stannous *adjective*
• "STAN us"
• of or relating to bivalent tin.
• [Late Latin *stannum* tin]

stapelia *noun*
• "stuh PEELY uh"
• any southern African plant of the genus *Stapelia*, with flowers having an unpleasant smell.
• [modern Latin from J. B. von *Stapel*, Dutch botanist d.1636]

stapes *noun*
• "STAY peez"
• a small stirrup-shaped bone in the ears of mammals.
• [modern Latin from medieval Latin *stapes* stirrup]

staphylococcus *noun*
• "staffa luh COCKUS"
• any bacterium of the genus *Staphylococcus*, occurring in grape-like clusters, and sometimes causing pus formation usu. in the skin and mucous membranes of animals.
• [Greek *staphulē* bunch of grapes + COCCUS]
• **staphylococcal** *adjective*

starwort *noun*
• "STAR wurt" or "STAR wort"
• a plant of the genus *Stellaria* with starlike flowers.
• ['star' + WORT]

Stasi *noun*
• "SHTAZZY"
• the internal security force of the former German Democratic Republic, abolished in 1989.
• [German, from *Sta*ats*si*cherheit(sdienst) 'state security (service)']

stasis *noun*
• "STAY sis" or "STASS iss"
• a state of inactivity or equilibrium.
• [modern Latin from Greek from *sta-* stand]

stater *noun*
• "STAY tur"
• an ancient Greek gold or silver coin.
• [Late Latin from Greek *statēr*]
HOMOPHONES: *stator*

static *adjective*
• "STATTIC"
• stationary; not acting or changing; passive.
• [modern Latin *staticus* from Greek *statikos* from *sta-* stand]
• **statically** *adverb*

statice *noun*
• "STAT us"
• any maritime plant of the genus *Limonium*, with small brightly coloured funnel-shaped flowers, used in dried flower arrangements.
• [Latin from Greek, feminine of *statikos* STATIC (with reference to staunching of blood)]
HOMOPHONES: *status*

staticky *adjective*
• "STATTA kee"
• (of reception of telecommunications and broadcasts) affected by electrical disturbances producing interference.
• [as STATIC]

statics *noun*
• "STATTIX"
• the science of bodies at rest or of forces in equilibrium.
• [as STATIC]

stationary *adjective*
• "STAY sh'n airy"
• remaining in one place, not moving.
• [Latin *stationarius* from *stare* stand]
HOMOPHONES: *stationery*

stationery *noun*
• "STAY sh'n airy"
• writing paper.
• [as STATIONARY; stationers originally so called because their shops were in a fixed location]
HOMOPHONES: *stationary*

statism *noun*
• "STATE izm"
• centralized state administration and control of social and economic affairs.
• ['state' from Latin STATUS]
• **statist** *noun*

statistics *noun*
• "stuh TISTIX"
• the science of collecting and analyzing numerical data, esp. in or for large quantities, and usu. inferring proportions in a whole from proportions in a representative sample.
• [German *Statistik* of the State]
• **statistic** *noun*
• **statistical** *adjective*
• **statistically** *adverb*
• **statistician** *noun* "statta STISH'n"

stator *noun*
• "STAY tur"
• the stationary part of a machine, esp. of an electric motor or generator.
• [STATIONARY, after ROTOR]
HOMOPHONES: *stater*

statuary *adjective*
• "STATCH oo airy"
• of or for statues.
• [as STATUE]

statue *noun*
• "STATCH oo"
• a sculptured, cast, carved, or moulded figure of a person or animal, esp. life-size or larger.
• [Old French from Latin *statua* from *stare* stand]
• **statued** *adjective*

statuesque *adjective*
• "statch oo ESK"
• like a statue in size, dignity, or lack of movement.
• [as STATUE]
• **statuesquely** *adverb*
• **statuesqueness** *noun*

statuette *noun*
• "statch oo ET"
• a small statue; a statue less than life-size.
• [as STATUE]

stature *noun*
• "STATCH ur"
• a person's natural height.
• [Old French from Latin *statura* from *stare stat-* stand]
• **statured** *adjective*

status *noun*
• "STAT us" or "STATE us"
• the social or professional position of a person or thing in relation to others; relative importance.
• [Latin, = standing, from *stare* stand]
HOMOPHONES: *statice*

statute *noun*
• "STATCH oot"
• a decree or enactment passed by a legislative body, and expressed in a formal document.
• [Old French *statut* from Late Latin *statutum* neuter past participle of Latin *statuere* set up, from *status*: see STATUS]

statutory *adjective*
- "STATCH a tory" or "STATCH oo tory"
- required, permitted, or enacted by statute.
- [as STATUTE]
- **statutorily** *adverb*

staunch *adjective*
- "STONCH"
- trustworthy, loyal.
- [Old French *estanche* feminine of *estanc* from Romanic]
- **staunchly** *adverb*
- **staunchness** *noun*

stave *noun*
- "STAVE"
- each of the curved pieces of wood forming the sides of a cask, pail, etc.
- [Middle English, back-formation from *staves*, pl. of 'staff' from Old English *stæf* stick]

steadfast *adjective*
- "STED fast"
- constant, firm, unwavering.
- [Old English *stedefæst*]
- **steadfastly** *adverb*
- **steadfastness** *noun*

steading *noun*
- "STED ing"
- a farmstead.
- [Old English *stede* place, from Germanic]

steady *adjective*
- "STEDDY"
- firmly fixed or supported or standing or balanced; not tottering, rocking, or wavering.
- [Old English *stede* place]
- **steadily** *adverb*
- **steadiness** *noun*

steak *noun*
- "STAKE"
- a thick slice of meat (esp. beef) or fish, often cut for broiling, frying, barbecuing, etc.
- [Old Norse *steik* related to *steikja* roast on spit, *stikna* be roasted]

HOMOPHONES: *stake*

steakette *noun*
- "stake ET"
- *Cdn* a thin patty of ground beef, meant to be cooked quickly.
- [as STEAK]

stearic *adjective*
- "STEER ick" or "STEE a rick"
- derived from stearin.
- [French *stéarique* from Greek *stear steatos* tallow]
- **stearate** *noun*

HOMOPHONES: *steric*

stearin *noun*
- "STEER in"
- a white crystalline substance which is the main constituent of tallow and suet.
- [French *stéarine*, as STEARIC]

steatite *noun*
- "STEE a tite"
- a soapstone or other impure form of talc.
- [Latin *steatitis* from Greek *steatītēs* from *stear steatos* tallow]

steatopygous *adjective*
- "stee utto PIE guss" or "stee a TOP ig us"
- having an excess of fat on the buttocks.
- [modern Latin (as STEATITE + Greek *pugē* rump)]
- **steatopygia** *noun* "stee utto PIDGY uh"
- **steatopygic** *adjective*

steenbok *noun*
- "STEEN bock"
- an African dwarf antelope, *Raphicerus campestris*.
- [Dutch from *steen* stone + *bok* buck]

stegosaurus *noun*
- "stegga SORE us"
- a small-headed plant-eating dinosaur of the suborder Stegosauria, with a double row of large bony plates (or spines) along the back.
- [modern Latin from Greek *stegē* covering + *sauros* lizard]

stein *noun*
- "STINE"
- a large (usu. earthenware) mug, esp. for beer.
- [German, lit. 'stone']

Steinbacher *noun*
- "STINE backer"
- a resident of Steinbach, Man.

steinbock *noun*
- "STINE bock"
- an ibex native to the Alps.
- [German from *Stein* stone + *Bock* buck]

stela *noun*
- "STEE luh"
- an upright slab or pillar usu. with an inscription and sculpture, used in ancient times esp. as a tombstone.
- [Latin from Greek (as STELE)]

stele *noun*
- "STEEL" or "STEELY"
- the axial cylinder of vascular tissue in the stem and roots of most plants.
- [Greek *stēlē* standing block]
- **stelar** *adjective*

HOMOPHONES: *steel, steal, steely, steelie, stealer*

stellar *adjective*
- "STELLER"
- of or relating to a star or stars.
- [Late Latin *stellaris* from Latin *stella* star]

stellate *adjective*
- "STELL ate"
- arranged like a star; radiating.
- [Latin *stellatus* from *stella* star]

stemma *noun*
- "STEMMA"

• a family tree; a pedigree.
• [Latin from Greek *stemma* wreath, from *stephō* wreathe]

stencil *noun*
• "STEN s'll"
• a thin sheet of plastic, metal, cardboard, etc., in which a pattern or lettering is cut, used to produce a corresponding pattern on the surface beneath it by applying ink, paint, etc. to the cut-out areas.
• [Old French *estanceler* sparkle, cover with stars, from *estencele* spark, ultimately from Latin *scintilla*]

stenography *noun*
• "stuh NOGGRA fee"
• shorthand or the art of writing shorthand.
• [Greek *stenos* narrow + *graphia* writing]
• **stenographer** *noun*
• **stenographic** *adjective*

stenosis *noun*
• "stuh NO sis"
• the abnormal narrowing of a passage in the body.
• [modern Latin from Greek *stenōsis* narrowing, from *stenoō* make narrow, from *stenos* narrow]
• **stenotic** *adjective* "stuh NOTTIC"

stenotype *noun*
• "STENNO tipe"
• a machine like a typewriter for recording speech in phonetic shorthand.
• [STENOGRAPHY + TYPE]

stentorian *adjective*
• "sten TORY 'n"
• (of a voice, sound, etc.) very loud and powerful.
• [Greek *Stentōr*, herald in the Trojan War]

stephanotis *noun*
• "steffa NO tiss"
• any climbing tropical plant of the genus *Stephanotis*, cultivated for its fragrant waxy usu. white flowers.
• [modern Latin from Greek, = fit for a wreath, from *stephanos* wreath]

steppe *noun*
• "STEP"
• a level grassy unforested plain, esp. in SE Europe and Siberia.
• [Russian *step'*]
HOMOPHONES: *step*

steradian *noun*
• "stuh RAY dee 'n"
• the SI unit of solid angle, equal to the angle at the centre of a sphere subtended by a part of the surface equal in area to the square of the radius.
• [Greek *stereos* solid + RADIAN]

stere *noun*
• "STEER"
• a unit of volume equal to one cubic metre.
• [French *stère* from Greek *stereos* solid]
HOMOPHONES: *steer*

stereochemistry *noun*
• "sterry oh KEMMA stree"
• the branch of chemistry dealing with the three-dimensional arrangement of atoms in molecules.
• [Greek *stereos* solid, having three dimensions + CHEMISTRY]
• **stereochemical** *adjective*

stereoisomer *noun*
• "sterry oh ICE a mur"
• any of two or more compounds differing only in their spatial arrangement of atoms.
• [Greek *stereos* solid, having three dimensions + ISOMER]

stereolithography *noun*
• "sterry oh lith OGGRA fee"
• a technique or process for creating three-dimensional objects, in which a computer-controlled moving laser beam is used to build up the required structure, layer by layer, from a liquid polymer that hardens on contact with laser light.
• [Greek *stereos* solid, having three dimensions + LITHOGRAPHY]

stereophonic *adjective*
• "sterry oh FONNIC"
• (of sound reproduction) using two or more channels so that the sound has the effect of being distributed and of coming from more than one source.
• [Greek *stereos* solid, having three dimensions + *phōne* sound]
• **stereophonically** *adverb*
• **stereophony** *noun* "sterry AW fun ee"

stereopsis *noun*
• "sterry OP sis"
• the perception of depth produced by combining the visual images from both eyes; binocular vision.
• [Greek *stereos* solid, having three dimensions + *opsis* sight]
• **stereoptic** *adjective*

stereopticon *noun*
• "sterry OPTA k'n" or "sterry OPTA con"
• a projector which combines two images to give a three-dimensional effect, or makes one image dissolve into another.
• [Greek *stereos* solid, having three dimensions + *optikon*, neuter of *optikos* OPTIC]

stereoscope *noun*
• "STERRY uh scope"
• a device by which two photographs of the same object taken at slightly different angles are viewed together, giving an impression of depth and solidity as in ordinary human vision.
• [Greek *stereos* solid, having three dimensions + *skopos* target, from *skeptomai* look at]
• **stereoscopic** *adjective*

- **stereoscopically** *adverb*
- **stereoscopy** *noun*

stereospecific *adjective*
- "sterry oh spuh SIFFIC"
- of or relating to a particular stereoisomer of a substance.
- [STEREOISOMER + SPECIFIC]
- **stereospecifically** *adverb*
- **stereospecificity** *noun*

"sterry oh spess if ISSA tee"

stereotaxis *noun*
- "sterry oh TAX iss"
- surgery involving the accurate positioning of probes etc. inside the brain.
- [Greek *stereos* solid + *taxis* orientation]
- **stereotactic** *adjective*
- **stereotaxic** *adjective*

stereotype *noun*
- "STERRY oh tipe"
- a preconceived, standardized, and oversimplified impression of the characteristics which typify a person, situation, etc.
- [French *stéréotype* from Greek *stereos* solid, having three dimensions + TYPE, originally a solid plate used in printing]
- **stereotypic** *adjective* "sterry oh TIPPIC"
- **stereotypical** *adjective*
- **stereotypically** *adverb*
- **stereotypy** *noun*

steric *adjective*
- "STEER ick"
- relating to the spatial arrangement of atoms in a molecule.
- [Greek *stereos* solid]
- **sterically** *adverb*

HOMOPHONES: *stearic*

sterile *adjective*
- "STARE ile" or "STARE ill"
- (of humans or animals) not able to produce children or young; infertile.
- [French *stérile* or Latin *sterilis*]
- **sterilely** *adverb*
- **sterility** *noun* "stuh RILLA tee"

sterilize *verb*

ALSO SPELLED: esp. *Brit.* **-ise**
- "STARE a lize"
- make sterile.
- [as STERILE]
- **sterilizable** *adjective* (also esp. *Brit.* **-isable**)
- **sterilization** *noun* (also esp. *Brit.* **-isation**)
- **sterilizer** *noun* (also esp. *Brit.* **-iser**)

sterlet *noun*
- "STUR lit"
- a small sturgeon, *Acipenser ruthenus*, found in the Caspian Sea area and yielding fine caviar.
- [Russian *sterlyad'*]

sterling *adjective*
- "STUR ling"
- of or in British money.
- [prob. from late Old English *steorling* (unrecorded) from *steorra* star (because some early Norman pennies bore a small star)]

sternum *noun*
- "STUR num"
- the breastbone.
- [modern Latin from Greek *sternon* chest]
- **sternal** *adjective*

steroid *noun*
- "STARE oid"
- any of a group of organic compounds with a characteristic structure of four rings of carbon atoms, including many hormones, alkaloids, and vitamins, used to treat various diseases and to increase muscle size.
- [STEROL + Greek *-oeidēs* from *eidos* form]
- **steroidal** *adjective*

sterol *noun*
- "STARE awl"
- any of a group of naturally occurring steroid alcohols.
- [CHOLESTEROL, ERGOSTEROL, etc.]

stertorous *adjective*
- "STUR tur us"
- (of breathing etc.) laboured and noisy; sounding like snoring.
- [*stertor*, modern Latin from Latin *stertere* snore]
- **stertorously** *adverb*

stethoscope *noun*
- "STETHA scope" (with "TH" as in *THIN*)
- an instrument used in listening to the action of the heart, lungs, etc., usu. consisting of a circular piece placed against the chest or back, with flexible tubes leading to earpieces.
- [French *stéthoscope* from Greek *stēthos* breast + *skopos* target, from *skeptomai* look at]
- **stethoscopic** *adjective* "stetha SCOPPIC"
- **stethoscopy** *noun* "steth OSCA pee"

stetson *noun*
- "STET s'n"
- a slouch hat with a very wide brim and a high crown, associated with cowboys of the western US and Canada.
- [J. B. *Stetson*, US hat maker d.1906]

Stettlerite *noun*
- "STET lur ite"
- a resident of Stettler, Alta.

stevedore *noun*
- "STEVE a dore"
- a person employed in loading and unloading ships.
- [Spanish *estivador* from *estivar* stow a cargo, from Latin *stipare* pack tight]
- **stevedoring** *noun*

steward *noun*
- "STOO urd" or "STYOO urd"
- a passengers' attendant on an aircraft, ship, or train.

• [Old English *stīweard* from *stig* prob. = house, hall + *weard* ward]
• **stewardship** *noun*

stewardess *noun*
• "STOO urd ess" or "STYOO urd ess"
• a female flight attendant.
• [as STEWARD]

stichomythia *noun*
• "stick oh MITHY uh"
• dialogue in alternate lines of verse, used in disputation in Greek drama, and characterized by antithesis and repetition.
• [modern Latin from Greek *stikhomuthia*, from *stikhos* row, line of verse + *muthos* speech]

stifle *verb*
• "STIFE 'll"
• prevent or constrain (an activity or idea).
• [perhaps alteration of Middle English *stuffe*, *stuffle* from Old French *estouffer*]
• **stifler** *noun*

stifling *adjective*
• "STIFE ling"
• unbearably hot.
• [as STIFLE]
• **stiflingly** *adverb*

stigma *noun*
• "STIG muh"
• a mark or sign of disgrace or discredit.
• [Latin from Greek *stigma -atos* a mark made by a pointed instrument, a brand, a dot]
• **stigmatic** *adjective*
• **stigmatist** *noun*

stigmatize *verb*
ALSO SPELLED: esp. *Brit.* **-ise**
• "STIGMA tize"
• describe as discreditable or undesirable.
• [as STIGMA]
• **stigmatization** *noun* (also esp. *Brit.* **-isation**)

stilbene *noun*
• "STILL been"
• an aromatic hydrocarbon forming phosphorescent crystals.
• [French from Greek *stilbō* glitter + '-ene' forming names of unsaturated hydrocarbons containing a double bond, from Greek *-ēnos*, adjective suffix denoting origin or source]

stilbestrol *noun*
ALSO SPELLED: *Brit.* **stilboestrol**
• "still BESS trawl"
• a powerful synthetic estrogen derived from stilbene.
• [STILBENE + ESTRUS]

stile *noun*
• "STILE"
• an arrangement of steps allowing people but not cattle to climb over a fence or wall.
• [Old English *stigel* from a Germanic root *stig-* (unrecorded) climb]
HOMOPHONES: *style*

stiletto *noun*
• "still ETTO"
• a short dagger with a thick blade.
• [Italian, diminutive of *stilo* dagger (as STYLUS)]

stillage *noun*
• "STILL idge"
• a bench, frame, etc., for keeping articles off the floor while draining, drying, waiting to be packed, etc.
• [apparently from Dutch *stellagie* scaffold, from *stellen* to place]

stillson *noun*
• "STILL s'n"
• a large wrench with jaws that tighten as pressure is increased.
• [D. C. *Stillson*, its inventor d.1899]

stimulant *noun*
• "STIM yuh l'nt"
• an agent that stimulates, esp. a drug or alcoholic drink.
• [Latin *stimulare stimulant-* urge, goad]

stimulate *verb*
• "STIM yuh late"
• apply or act as a stimulus to.
• [as STIMULANT]
• **stimulating** *adjective*
• **stimulatingly** *adverb*
• **stimulation** *noun*
• **stimulative** *adjective*
• **stimulator** *noun*
• **stimulatory** *adjective* "STIMYA luh tory"

stimulus *noun*
• "STIM yuh luss"
• a thing that rouses to activity or energy.
• [Latin, = goad, spur, incentive]

stingy *adjective*
• "STIN jee"
• (of a person) having or displaying an unwillingness to give, spend, or use anything up.
• [perhaps from dial. *stinge* sting]
• **stingily** *adverb*
• **stinginess** *noun*

stipend *noun*
• "STIPE end"
• a salary or fixed regular sum paid for the services of a teacher, public official, or clergyman.
• [Old French *stipend(i)e* or Latin *stipendium* from *stips* wages + *pendere* to pay]

stipendiary *adjective*
• "stip EN jur ee" or "stip EN dee airy" or "stye PEN jur ee" or "stye PEN dee airy"
• receiving a stipend; working for pay, not voluntarily.
• [as STIPEND]

stipes *noun*
• "STIPE eez"
• a stalk or stem, such as that which supports the pileus or cap of a mushroom or toadstool.
• [Latin, = log, tree trunk]
• **stipitate** *adjective* "STIPPA tate"

stipple *verb*
• "STIP'll"
• draw, paint, or engrave (a surface, illustration, etc.) with dots, small spots, or flecks instead of lines.
• [Dutch *stippelen* frequentative of *stippen* to prick, from *stip* point]
• **stippler** *noun*

stipulate *verb*
• "STIP yuh late"
• demand or specify as an essential part or condition of an agreement or contract etc.
• [Latin *stipulari*]
• **stipulated** *adjective*
• **stipulation** *noun*

stipule *noun*
• "STIP yool"
• a small leaflike appendage of a leaf, usu. occurring in pairs at the base of a petiole where the leaf joins the stem.
• [French *stipule* or Latin *stipula* straw]

stirrup *noun*
• "STUR up"
• either of a pair of supports for the foot of a person riding a horse, consisting of a metal loop with a flat base and a leather strap which attaches this loop to each side of a saddle.
• [Old English *stigrāp* from *stigan* climb (as STILE) + 'rope']

stitchwort *noun*
• "STITCH wurt" or "STITCH wort"
• any plant of the genus *Stellaria*, esp. *S. media*, naturalized in N America, with an erect stem and white starry flowers, once thought to cure a stitch in the side.
• ['stitch' (Old English *stice*) + WORT]

stoa *noun*
• "STOE uh"
• a portico or roofed colonnade in ancient Greek architecture.
• [Greek: compare STOIC]

stochastic *adjective*
• "stuh CASTIC"
• determined by a random distribution or pattern of probabilities, so that its behaviour may be analyzed statistically but not predicted precisely.
• [Greek *stokhastikos* from *stokhazomai* aim at, guess, from *stokhos* aim]
• **stochastically** *adverb*

stockinette *noun*
ALSO SPELLED: **stockinet**
• "stock 'n ET"
• an elastic knitted material used esp. to make clothes, such as underwear.
• [prob. from *stocking-net*]

stogie *noun*
• "STOE gee" (with "G" as in *GEEK*)
• a cigar.
• [originally *stoga*, short for *Conestoga* in Pennsylvania]

Stoic *noun*
• "STOE ick"
• a member of the ancient Greek school of philosophy founded at Athens by Zeno *c.*308 BC, which taught control of one's feelings and passions and advocated indifference to the vicissitudes of fortune and pleasure and pain.
• [Latin *stoicus* from Greek *stōikos* from STOA (with reference to Zeno's teaching in the *Stoa Poikilē* or Painted Porch at Athens)]
• **Stoicism** *noun* "STOE a sizm"

stoically *adverb*
• "STOE ick lee"
• with indifference, fortitude, and the ability to endure pain without complaining.
• [as STOIC]

stolid *adjective*
• "STOLLID" (rhymes with *SOLID*)
• failing or unlikely to feel or express emotion.
• [obsolete French *stolide* or Latin *stolidus*]
• **stolidity** *noun*
• **stolidly** *adverb*
• **stolidness** *noun*

stollen *noun*
• "STAWL 'n"
• a rich bread with dried fruit and nuts, eaten esp. at Christmas.
• [German]

stolon *noun*
• "STOE lawn"
• a horizontal stem or branch that takes root at points along its length, forming new plants.
• [Latin *stolo -onis*]
• **stoloniferous** *adjective* "stoe lawn IFFER us"

stoma *noun*
• "STOE muh"
• any of the minute pores in the epidermis of a leaf or stem of a plant which allow movement of gases in and out of the plant.
• [modern Latin from Greek *stoma -atos* mouth]
• **stomal** *adjective*
• **stomatal** *adjective* "stoe MAT 'll" or "STOE mut'll"

stomatitis *noun*
• "stoe muh TITE us"
• inflammation of the mucous membrane of the mouth.
• [as STOMA + Greek *-itis*, forming feminine of adjectives in *-itēs* (with *nosos* 'disease' implied)]

stomatology *noun*
• "stoe muh TOLLA jee"

• the scientific study of the mouth or its diseases.
• [as STOMA + Greek *logos* word]
• **stomatological** *adjective*
• **stomatologist** *noun*

stonewort *noun*
• "STONE wurt" or "STONE wort"
• any of several chiefly freshwater algae of the family Characeae, with whorls of short branches, often partly encrusted with calcium carbonate.
• ['stone' + WORT]

Stoney *noun*
• "STOE nee"
• a member of an Aboriginal people now living in southern Alberta, and formerly living in southern Manitoba and southern Saskatchewan.
• [so called because of their traditional use of hot stones for boiling water]
HOMOPHONES: *stony*

stooge *noun*
• "STOOJ"
• an unquestioningly loyal or obsequious assistant.
• [20th c.: origin unknown]

stook *noun*
• "STOOK" (rhymes either with *LOOK* or with *LUKE*)
• *Cdn & Brit.* a small stack of bales of hay or straw, or sheaves of grain, collected in a field, esp. to hasten drying.
• [Middle English *stouk*, from or related to Middle Low German *stūke*]
• **stooker** *noun*
• **stooking** *noun*

storax *noun*
• "STORE ax"
• a fragrant resin, obtained from the tree *Styrax officinalis* and formerly used in perfume.
• [Latin from Greek, var. of STYRAX]

storey *noun*
ALSO SPELLED: **story**
• "STORE ee"
• a single level of a house or building including rooms or offices located on it; a floor.
• [Anglo-Latin *historia* history: see STORIED (perhaps originally meaning a tier of painted windows or sculpture)]
HOMOPHONES: *story*

storied *adjective*
• "STORE eed"
• celebrated in or associated with stories or legend; legendary.
• [from 'story' from Latin *historia* from Greek *historia* finding out, narrative, history, from *histōr* learned, wise man]

stotin *noun*
• "staw TEEN"
• a monetary unit of Slovenia, equal to one-hundredth of a tolar.
• [Slovene]

stotinka *noun*
• "staw TINKA"
• a monetary unit of Bulgaria, equal to one-hundredth of a lev.
• [Bulgarian, = hundredth]

stoup *noun*
• "STOOP"
• a basin for holy water, as at the entrance of a church etc.
• [Old Norse *staup* (= Old English *stēap*) from Germanic]
HOMOPHONES: *stoop, stupe*

strabismus *noun*
• "struh BIZ muss"
• the abnormal condition of one or both eyes not correctly aligned in direction; a squint.
• [modern Latin from Greek *strabismos* from *strabizō* squint, from *strabos* squinting]
• **strabismic** *adjective*

stracciatella *noun*
• "stratcha TELLA"
• an Italian soup made by adding beaten eggs and Parmesan cheese to broth.
• [Italian, from *stracciare* tear up]

Stradivarius *noun*
• "stradda VERRY us"
• a violin or other stringed instrument made by the Italian luthier Antonio Stradivari (d.1737) or his family.

strafe *verb*
• "STRAFE"
• attack repeatedly with bullets or bombs from aircraft flying low over their target.
• [jocular adaptation of German catchword (1914) *Gott strafe England* may God punish England]

straight *adjective*
• "STRATE"
• extending uniformly in the same direction; without a curve or bend etc.
• [Middle English, past participle of STRETCH]
• **straighten** *verb*
• **straightener** *noun*
• **straightish** *adjective*
• **straightly** *adverb*
• **straightness** *noun*
HOMOPHONES: *strait, straiten, straitly, straitness*

straightforward *adjective*
• "strate FOR wurd"
• honest or frank.
• [as STRAIGHT + FORWARD]
• **straightforwardly** *adverb*
• **straightforwardness** *noun*

strait *noun*
• "STRATE"
• a narrow passage of water connecting two seas or large bodies of water.
• [Old French *estreit* tight, narrow, from Latin *strictus* strict, past participle of *stringere* tighten]
• **straitly** *adverb*

• **straitness** *noun*
HOMOPHONES: *straight, straightly, straightness*

straiten *verb*
• "STRATE 'n"
• restrict in range or scope.
• [as STRAIT]
HOMOPHONES: *straighten*

straitened *adjective*
• "STRATE 'nd"
• of or marked by poverty.
• [as STRAIT]
HOMOPHONES: *straightened*

straitjacket *noun*
ALSO SPELLED: **straightjacket**
• "STRATE jack it"
• a strong garment with long sleeves which are tied in the back to prevent the person wearing it from acting violently.
• [as STRAIT + 'jacket']

straitlaced *adjective*
ALSO SPELLED: **straightlaced**
• "STRATE layst"
• severely virtuous; morally scrupulous; puritanical.
• [as STRAIT + 'lace']

Straits *noun*
• "STRATES"
• a N American Aboriginal language of British Columbia, part of the Salishan language group, spoken along the straits off the southern tip of Vancouver Island.

strake *noun*
• "STRAKE"
• a continuous line of planking or plates from the stem to the stern of a ship.
• [Middle English: prob. related to Old English *streccan* stretch]

stramonium *noun*
• "struh MOANY um"
• any poisonous plant of the genus *Datura*, e.g. the thornapple; datura.
• [modern Latin, perhaps from Tartar *turman* horse medicine]

strangulate *verb*
• "STRANG gyoo late"
• constrict or compress (an organ, duct, hernia, etc.) so as to prevent circulation or the passage of a fluid.
• [Latin *strangulare strangulat-* from Greek *straggalaō* from *straggalē* halter: compare *straggos* twisted]
• **strangulation** *noun*

strappado *noun*
• "struh PODDO"
• a form of torture in which the victim is secured to a rope and made to fall from a height almost to the ground then stopped with a jerk.
• [French *(e)strapade* from Italian *strappata* from *strappare* snatch]

stratagem *noun*
• "STRATTA jem"
• a cunning plan or scheme, esp. for deceiving an enemy.
• [ultimately from Greek *stratēgēma* from *stratēgeō* be a general (*stratēgos*) from *stratos* army + *agō* lead]

strategy *noun*
• "STRATTA jee"
• an esp. long-range policy designed for a particular purpose.
• [French *stratégie* from Greek *stratēgia* generalship, from *stratēgos*: see STRATAGEM]
• **strategic** *adjective* "struh TEE jick"
• **strategically** *adverb*
• **strategist** *noun*
• **strategize** *verb* (also esp. *Brit.* **-ise**)

strath *noun*
• "STRATH"
• a broad mountain valley.
• [Gaelic *srath*]

strathspey *noun*
• "strath SPAY"
• a slow Scottish dance with gliding steps in quadruple metre.
• [*Strathspey*, valley of the Spey River]

stratify *verb*
• "STRATTA fie"
• arrange in strata.
• [French *stratifier* (as STRATUM)]
• **stratification** *noun*
• **stratified** *adjective*

stratigraphy *noun*
• "struh TIGGRA fee"
• the order and relative position of strata.
• [STRATUM + Greek *graphia* writing]
• **stratigrapher** *noun*
• **stratigraphic** *adjective* "stratta GRAFF ick"
• **stratigraphical** *adjective*
• **stratigraphically** *adverb*

stratocumulus *noun*
• "stratto KYOO myoo luss"
• cloud formed as a low layer of clumped or broken grey masses.
• [as STRATUS + CUMULUS]

stratosphere *noun*
• "STRATTA sfeer"
• a layer of atmospheric air above the troposphere extending to about 50 km above the earth's surface, in which the lower part changes little in temperature and the upper part increases in temperature with height.
• [STRATUM + SPHERE after *atmosphere*]
• **stratospheric** *adjective* "stratta SFEER ick" or "stratta SFARE ick"
• **stratospherically** *adverb*

stratovolcano *noun*
• "stratto voll CAY no"
• a volcano built up of alternate layers of lava and ash.
• [as STRATUM + VOLCANO]

stratum *noun*
- "STRAT um"
- a layer or set of successive layers of any deposited substance.
- [Latin, = something spread or laid down, neuter past participle of *sternere* strew]

stratus *noun*
- "STRAT us"
- cloud forming a continuous horizontal sheet.
- [Latin, past participle of *sternere*: see STRATUM]

strength *noun*
- "STRENGTH" or "STRENTH" (with "TH" as in *THIN*)
- the state of being strong; the degree to which or respect in which a person or thing is strong.
- [Old English *strengthu* from Germanic]
- **strengthen** *verb*
- **strengthener** *noun*
- **strengthless** *adjective*

strenuous *adjective*
- "STREN yoo us"
- requiring or using great effort.
- [Latin *strenuus* brisk]
- **strenuously** *adverb*
- **strenuousness** *noun*

streptocarpus *noun*
- "strep toe CARP us"
- a southern African plant of the genus *Streptocarpus*, with funnel-shaped flowers, often violet or pink, and spirally twisted fruits.
- [Greek *streptos* twisted + *karpos* fruit]

streptococcus *noun*
- "strep toe COCKUS"
- any bacterium of the genus *Streptococcus*, usu. occurring in chains, some of which cause infectious diseases.
- [Greek *streptos* twisted, from *strephō* turn + COCCUS]
- **streptococcal** *adjective*

streptokinase *noun*
- "strep toe KYE nace"
- an enzyme produced by some streptococci and used to treat inflammation and blood clots.
- [STREPTOCOCCUS + Greek *kinein* move]

streptomycin *noun*
- "strep toe MICE in"
- an antibiotic produced by the bacterium *Streptomyces griseus*, effective against many disease-producing bacteria.
- [Greek *streptos* (as STREPTOCOCCUS) + *mukēs* fungus]

stressor *noun*
- "STRESSER" or "STRESS or"
- a situation, experience, event, or other stimulus that causes stress.
- [Middle English *stress* from DISTRESS, or partly from Old French *estresse* narrowness, oppression, ultimately from Latin *strictus* strict: see STRAIT]

streusel *noun*
- "STROOZ'll" or "STROOSS'll"
- a crumbly mixture of flour, butter, sugar, and usu. cinnamon, used as a topping or filling for cakes etc.
- [German, from *streuen* to sprinkle]

strew *verb*
- "STROO"
- scatter or spread or be scattered or spread over a surface.
- [Old English *stre(o)wian*]
- **strewer** *noun*

stria *noun*
- "STRY uh"
- a linear mark on a surface.
- [Latin]

striate *adjective*
- "STRY it"
- marked with striae.
- [as STRIA]
- **striated** *adjective* "stry ATE id"
- **striation** *noun*

strident *adjective*
- "STRY d'nt"
- loud and harsh.
- [Latin *stridere strident-* creak]
- **stridency** *noun*
- **stridently** *adverb*

stridulate *verb*
- "STRID yuh late"
- (of insects, esp. the cicada and grasshopper) make a shrill sound by rubbing esp. the legs or wing-cases together.
- [French *striduler* from Latin *stridulus* creaking (as STRIDENT)]
- **stridulation** *noun*

strigil *noun*
- "STRIDGE ill"
- an instrument with a curved blade, used in ancient Rome and Greece to scrape sweat and dirt from the skin after exercise.
- [Latin *strigilis* from *stringere* graze]

stringendo *adjective*
- "strin JENDO"
- (as a musical direction) with increasing speed.
- [Italian from *stringere* press: see STRINGENT]

stringent *adjective*
- "STRIN j'nt"
- (of rules etc.) strict, precise; requiring exact performance; leaving no loophole or discretion.
- [Latin *stringere* draw tight]
- **stringency** *noun*
- **stringently** *adverb*

stringhalt *noun*
- "STRING halt" ("HALT" rhymes with *FAULT*)
- spasmodic movement of a horse's hind leg.
- ['string' + 'halt']

strobila *noun*
• "stroe BYE luh"
• a chain of proglottids in a tapeworm.
• [modern Latin from Greek *strobilē* twisted lint plug, from *strephō* twist]

strobile *noun*
• "STROE bile"
• the cone of a pine etc.
• [French *strobile* or Late Latin *strobilus* from Greek *strobilos* from *strephō* twist]

stroboscope *noun*
• "STROBE a scope"
• an instrument for determining speeds of rotation etc. by shining a bright light at intervals so that a rotating object appears stationary.
• [Greek *strobos* whirling + *skopos* target, from *skeptomai* look at]
• **stroboscopic** *adjective*
• **stroboscopically** *adverb*

stroganoff *noun*
• "STROE guh noff"
• a dish of strips of beef cooked in a sauce containing mushrooms and sour cream.
• [P. *Stroganoff*, Russian diplomat, d.1817]

stroma *noun*
• "STROE muh"
• the framework of an organ or cell.
• [modern Latin from Late Latin from Greek *strōma* coverlet]
• **stromatic** *adjective*

stromatolite *noun*
• "stroe MATTA lite"
• a mound built up of layers of blue-green algae and trapped sediment, found in lagoons in Australasia and fossilized in Precambrian rocks elsewhere.
• [STROMA + Greek *lithos* stone]
• **stromatolitic** *adjective* "stroe matta LITTIC"

strontia *noun*
• "STRON shuh"
• strontium oxide.
• [*strontian* native strontium carbonate, from Strontian in Scotland, where it was discovered]

strontium *noun*
• "STRONSHY um" or "STRON shum" or "STRONTY um"
• a soft silver-white metallic element occurring naturally in various minerals.
• [as STRONTIA]

strophe *noun*
• "STROE fee"
• a turn in dancing made by an ancient Greek chorus.
• [Greek *strophē*, lit. + turning, from *strephō* turn]
• **strophic** *adjective*

strudel *noun*
• "STROO d'll"
• a dessert of thin pastry rolled up around a usu. fruit filling and baked.
• [German *Strudel*, lit. = 'whirlpool']

struma *noun*
• "STROOMA"
• a disease with glandular swellings; scrofula.
• [Latin, = scrofulous tumour]
• **strumous** *adjective*

strychnine *noun*
• "STRICK nine" or "STRICK neen" or "STRICK nin"
• a bitter and highly poisonous vegetable alkaloid obtained from plants of the genus *Strychnos* (esp. nux vomica).
• [French from Latin *strychnos* from Greek *strukhnos* a kind of nightshade]

stubborn *adjective*
• "STUB urn"
• unreasonably obstinate.
• [Middle English *stiborn*, *stoburn*, etc., of unknown origin]
• **stubbornly** *adverb*
• **stubbornness** *noun*

stucco *noun*
• "STUCKO"
• plaster or cement used for coating wall surfaces or moulding into architectural decorations.
• [Italian, of Germanic origin]
• **stuccoed** *adjective*

stultify *verb*
• "STUL tuh fie"
• make ineffective, useless, or futile, esp. as a result of tedious routine.
• [Late Latin *stultificare* from Latin *stultus* foolish]
• **stultification** *noun*
• **stultifier** *noun*

stultifying *adjective*
• "STUL tuh fie ing"
• extremely tedious or boring.
• [as STULTIFY]
• **stultifyingly** *adverb*

stunsail *noun*
• "STUN s'll"
• a sail set on a small extra yard and boom beyond the leech of a square sail in light winds.
• [contraction, representing the ordinary pronunciation, of 'studding sail', of unknown origin]

stupa *noun*
• "STOOPA"
• a round usu. domed building erected as a Buddhist shrine.
• [Sanskrit *stūpa*]

stupefacient *noun*
• "stoopa FAY sh'nt" or "styoopa FAY sh'nt"
• a drug causing semi-consciousness.
• [as STUPEFY]

stupefy ***verb***
- "STOOPA fie" or "STYOOPA fie"
- make stupid or insensible.
- [French *stupéfier* from Latin *stupefacere*, from *stupēre* be amazed]
- **stupefaction** ***noun***
- **stupefier** ***noun***
- **stupefying** ***adjective***
- **stupefyingly** ***adverb***

stupendous ***adjective***
- "stoo PEN duss" or "styoo PEN duss"
- amazing or prodigious, esp. in terms of size or degree.
- [Latin *stupendus* gerundive of *stupēre* be amazed at]
- **stupendously** ***adverb***

stupor ***noun***
- "STOOPER" or "STYOOPER"
- a condition of near-unconsciousness characterized by great reduction in mental activity and responsiveness, caused by disease, narcotics, alcohol, etc.
- [Middle English from Latin (as STUPENDOUS)]
- **stuporous** ***adjective***

sturgeon ***noun***
- "STUR j'n"
- any large mailed shark-like fish of the family Acipenseridae etc. swimming upriver to spawn, used as food and a source of caviar and isinglass.
- [Old French *esturgeon*, ultimately from Germanic]

Stygian ***adjective***
- "STIDGE ee 'n"
- (in Greek mythology) of or relating to the Styx, a river in Hades.
- [Latin *stugius* from Greek *stugios* from *Stux -ugos* Styx, from *stugnos* hateful, gloomy]

style ***noun***
- "STILE"
- a kind or sort, esp. in regard to appearance and form.
- [Old French *stile*, *style* from Latin *stilus*: spelling *style* due to association with Greek *stulos* column]
- **styleless** ***adjective***
- **stylelessness** ***noun***
- **styler** ***noun***

HOMOPHONES: *stile*, *stylus*

stylet ***noun***
- "STILE it"
- a slender pointed instrument; a stiletto.
- [French *stilet* from Italian STILETTO]

stylish ***adjective***
- "STILE ish"
- fashionable; elegant, chic.
- [as STYLE]
- **stylishly** ***adverb***
- **stylishness** ***noun***

stylist ***noun***
- "STILE ist"
- a person employed by a firm to create, coordinate, or promote new styles or designs, esp. of clothes or cars.
- [as STYLE]

stylistic ***adjective***
- "stile ISTIC"
- of or concerning esp. literary or artistic style.
- [as STYLE]
- **stylistically** ***adverb***

stylistics ***noun***
- "stile ISTIX"
- the study of literary or linguistic style.
- [as STYLE]

stylite ***noun***
- "STILE ite"
- an ancient or medieval ascetic living on top of a pillar.
- [ecclesiastical Greek *stulitēs* from *stulos* pillar]

stylized ***adjective***

ALSO SPELLED: esp. *Brit.* **-ised**
- "STILE ized"
- painted, drawn, etc. in a fixed, conventional, or artificial style.
- [as STYLE]
- **stylization** ***noun*** (also esp. *Brit.* **-isation**)

styloid ***adjective***
- "STILE oid"
- resembling a stylus or pen.
- [modern Latin *styloides* from Greek *stuloeidēs* from *stulos* pillar]

stylus ***noun***
- "STILE us"
- an ancient implement for writing on wax etc., having a pointed end for inscribing characters and a flat broad end for erasing and smoothing the writing surface.
- [erroneous spelling of Latin *stilus*: compare STYLE]

HOMOPHONES: *styleless*

stymie ***verb***
- "STYE mee"
- obstruct, thwart (a person, project, etc.).
- [19th c.: origin unknown]

styptic ***adjective***
- "STIP tic"
- (of a drug etc.) that checks bleeding.
- [Latin *stypticus* from Greek *stuptikos* from *stuphō* contract]

styrax ***noun***
- "STYE rax"
- storax resin.
- [Latin from Greek *sturax*: compare STORAX]

styrene ***noun***
- "STYE reen"
- a liquid hydrocarbon, easily polymerized and used in making plastics etc.
- [STYRAX + '-ene' forming names of unsaturated hydrocarbons containing a double

bond, from Greek *-ēnos*, adjective suffix denoting origin or source]

suable *adjective*
- "SOO a bull"
- liable to be sued; legally subject to legal process.
- [Anglo-French *suer* from Old French *siu-* etc. stem of *sivre* from Latin *sequi* follow]

suasion *noun*
- "SWAY zh'n"
- persuasion as opposed to force.
- [Old French *suasion* or Latin *suasio* from *suadēre suas-* urge]
- **suasive** *adjective*

suave *adjective*
- "SWOV"
- (of a person, manners, etc.) charming, smooth; polite; sophisticated.
- [French *suave* or Latin *suavis* agreeable]
- **suavely** *adverb*
- **suaveness** *noun*
- **suavity** *noun*

subaltern *noun*
- "sub ALL turn" or "SUB 'll turn"
- a person of inferior rank or status.
- [Late Latin *subalternus* from *alternus* (see ALTERNATE[1])]

subantarctic *adjective*
- "sub ant ARK tick" or "sub ant AR tick"
- of, pertaining to, or situated in regions immediately north of the Antarctic Circle.
- [Latin *sub-* under + ANTARCTIC]

subaquatic *adjective*
- "subba KWOTTIC" or "subba KWATTIC"
- partly aquatic.
- [Latin *sub-* under + AQUATIC]

subaqueous *adjective*
- "sub AKE wee us" or "sub ACK wee us"
- existing, formed, or taking place under water.
- [Latin *sub-* under + AQUEOUS]
- **subaqueously** *adverb*

subarctic *noun*
- "sub ARK tick" or "sub AR tick"
- the region immediately south of the Arctic Circle.
- [Latin *sub-* under + ARCTIC]

subcategory *noun*
- "sub CATTA gory"
- a secondary or subordinate category.
- [Latin *sub-* under + CATEGORY]
- **subcategorization** *noun* (also esp. *Brit.* **-isation**)
- **subcategorize** *verb* (also esp. *Brit.* **-ise**)

subcellular *adjective*
- "sub SELL yuh lur"
- situated or occurring within a cell or cells.
- [Latin *sub-* under + CELLULAR]

subclause *noun*
- "SUB clozz"
- a subsidiary section of a clause.
- [Latin *sub-* under + CLAUSE]

subclavian *adjective*
- "sub CLAY vee 'n"
- lying or extending under the collarbone.
- [modern Latin *subclavius* (*sub* under, close to, towards, *clavis* key): compare CLAVICLE]

subcommittee *noun*
- "SUB kuh mitty"
- a body of people appointed by a committee, usu. composed of a selection of its own members, esp. to study or deal with a specific issue or an aspect of a larger matter.
- [Latin *sub-* under + COMMITTEE]

subconscious *noun*
- "sub CON sh'ss"
- the part of the mind which influences actions etc. without one's full awareness.
- [Latin *sub-* under + CONSCIOUS]
- **subconsciously** *adverb*
- **subconsciousness** *noun*

subcontinent *noun*
- "sub CON tin 'nt"
- a large section of a continent having a certain geographical or political identity or independence.
- [Latin *sub-* under + 'continent' (from Latin *terra continens* (from *continēre content-* from *com-* with, *tenēre* hold) continuous land)]
- **subcontinental** *adjective*

subcontractor *noun*
- "SUB k'n track tur" or "sub CON track tur"
- an individual or company that carries out work for a company as part of a larger contract.
- [Latin *sub-* under + CONTRACTOR]

subcortical *adjective*
- "sub CORTA k'll"
- pertaining to or situated in the region underlying a cortex, esp. that of the brain.
- [Latin *sub-* under + CORTICAL (see CORTEX)]

subcritical *adjective*
- "sub CRITTA k'll"
- below a critical level, value, threshold, etc.
- [Latin *sub-* under + CRITICAL]

subcutaneous *adjective*
- "sub kyoo TAY nee us"
- situated or introduced just under the skin.
- [Latin *sub-* under + CUTANEOUS]
- **subcutaneously** *adverb*

subdeacon *noun*
- "SUB deek'n"
- (in some Christian churches) a minister of the order next below a deacon.
- [Latin *sub-* under + DEACON]

subdirectory *noun*
- "SUB dir eck tur ee" or "SUB die reck tur ee"

- a directory that is itself contained in another directory.
- [Latin *sub-* under + DIRECTORY]

subdiscipline *noun*
- "sub DISSA plin"
- a subordinate branch of a discipline.
- [Latin *sub-* under + DISCIPLINE]

subdivide *verb*
- "sub div IDE"
- divide (a thing) into smaller parts or portions.
- [Latin *sub-* under + DIVIDE]

subdivision *noun*
- "SUB dih vizh'n"
- an area of land divided into plots for sale or development.
- [Latin *sub-* under + DIVISION]

subdominant *noun*
- "sub DOM'n 'nt"
- the fourth note of the diatonic scale of any key.
- [Latin *sub-* under + DOMINANT]

subduction *noun*
- "sub DUCK sh'n"
- the sideways and downward movement of the edge of a plate of the earth's crust into the mantle beneath a neighbouring lithospheric plate.
- [Latin *sub-* under + *ducere duct-* lead]
- **subduct** *verb*

subdue *verb*
- "sub DOO" or "sub DYOO"
- overcome or overpower (a person or animal etc.) by physical force or violence.
- [Middle English *sodewe* from Old French *so(u)duire* from Latin *subducere* (*sub* under, close to, towards, *ducere* lead, bring) used with the sense of *subdere* conquer (*sub* under, close to, towards, *-dere* put)]

subdued *adjective*
- "sub DOOD" or "sub DYOOD"
- (of a colour, light, or sound, etc.) reduced in or lacking intensity or force.
- [as SUBDUE]

subdural *adjective*
- "sub DYUR 'll" or "sub DUR 'll"
- situated or occurring between the dura mater and the arachnoid membrane of the brain and spinal cord.
- [Latin *sub-* under + *dura mater* the tough outermost membrane enveloping the brain and spinal cord, from Latin *dura* hard]

subfusc *adjective*
- "SUB fusk"
- dull; gloomy; drab.
- [Latin *subfuscus* from *fuscus* dark brown]

subgenus *noun*
- "sub JEE nuss"
- a taxonomic category below a genus.
- [Latin *sub-* under + GENUS]

subglacial *adjective*
- "sub GLAY sh'll"
- existing or occurring under or at the bottom of a glacier.
- [Latin *sub-* under + GLACIAL]

subjacent *adjective*
- "sub JAY s'nt"
- situated below; underlying.
- [Latin *subjacēre* (*sub* under, close to, towards, *jacēre* lie)]
- **subjacency** *noun*

subjugate *verb*
- "SUB juh gate"
- bring (a country, people, etc.) into subjection; conquer, vanquish.
- [Late Latin *subjugare* bring under the yoke (*sub* under, close to, towards, *jugum* yoke)]
- **subjugation** *noun*
- **subjugator** *noun*

subjunctive *noun*
- "sub JUNK tiv"
- a mood of verbs used to express a condition, wish, fear, possibility, command, suggestion, uncertainty, or hypothetical situation, e.g. *if I were rich* or *I wish I were beautiful.*
- [French *subjonctif -ive* or Late Latin *subjunctivus* from Latin *subjungere*, from *sub-* in addition + *jungere* to join, translation of Greek *hupotaktikos*]

sublessee *noun*
- "sub less EE"
- a person who holds a sublease.
- [Latin *sub-* under + LEASE]

sublessor *noun*
- "sub less OR"
- a person who grants a sublease.
- [Latin *sub-* under + LESSOR]

sublethal *adjective*
- "sub LEETH'll"
- having an effect that is nearly lethal or fatal.
- [Latin *sub-* under + LETHAL]

sublimate *verb*
- "SUB luh mate"
- divert or channel the energy of (a primitive esp. sexual impulse) into a more highly valued or acceptable activity.
- [Latin *sublimare sublimat-* as SUBLIME]
- **sublimation** *noun*

sublime *adjective*
- "sub LIME"
- of the most exalted, grand, or noble kind; of a high intellectual, moral, or spiritual level.
- [Latin *sublimis* (*sub* under, second element perhaps related to *limen* threshold, *limus* oblique)]
- **sublimely** *adverb*
- **sublimity** *noun* "sub LIMMA tee"

subliminal *adjective*
- "sub LIMMA n'll"
- (of a stimulus, message, advertisement, etc.)

operating below the threshold of sensation or consciousness; having an influence upon the mind without one being aware of it.
• [Latin *sub* under, close to, towards, *limen -inis* threshold]
• **subliminally** *adverb*

sublittoral *adjective*
• "sub LITTER'll"
• of or concerning the region from the line of the sea at low tide to the edge of the continental shelf.
• [Latin *sub-* under + LITTORAL]

sublunary *adjective*
• "sub LOONER ee"
• situated or existing beneath the moon.
• [Late Latin *sublunaris* (*sub* under, close to, towards, LUNAR)]

subluxation *noun*
• "sub luck SAY sh'n"
• partial dislocation.
• [Latin *sub* under, close to, towards + Latin *luxat-*, past participle stem of *luxare*, from *luxus* dislocated]

submarine *noun*
• "sub muh REEN" or "SUB muh reen"
• a vessel capable of operating under water.
• [Latin *sub-* under + MARINE]

submariner *noun*
• "sub MERRA ner"
• a person who travels in or operates a submarine.
• [as SUBMARINE]

submaxillary *adjective*
• "sub mack SILLER ee"
• (esp. of a pair of salivary glands) beneath the upper jaw.
• [Latin *sub-* under + MAXILLA]

submediant *noun*
• "sub MEEDY 'nt"
• the sixth note of the diatonic scale of any key.
• [Latin *sub-* under + MEDIANT]

submerge *verb*
• "sub MURJ"
• immerse, dip, or place in a liquid.
• [Latin *submergere* (*sub* under, close to, towards, *mergere mers-* dip)]
• **submerged** *adjective*
• **submergence** *noun*
• **submersion** *noun* "sub MUR sh'n" or "sub MUR zh'n"

submersed *adjective*
• "sub MURST"
• submerged.
• [Latin *submers-* past participle stem of *submergere* SUBMERGE]

submersible *noun*
• "sub MURSA bull"
• a submarine operating under water for short periods, used esp. for exploration.
• [as SUBMERGE]

submicroscopic *adjective*
• "sub micra SCOPPIC"
• too small to be seen by an ordinary microscope.
• [Latin *sub-* under + MICROSCOPIC]

subminiature *adjective*
• "sub MINNA chur" or "sub MINNY a chur"
• (esp. of electronic components, photographic equipment, etc.) of greatly reduced size.
• [Latin *sub-* under + MINIATURE]

submissive *adjective*
• "sub MISSIV"
• obedient, subservient, meek.
• [Latin *submittere* (*sub* under, *mittere miss-* send)]
• **submissively** *adverb*
• **submissiveness** *noun*

subnuclear *adjective*
• "sub NEW clee ur"
• occurring in or smaller than an atomic nucleus.
• [Latin *sub-* under + NUCLEAR]

suboceanic *adjective*
• "sub oh shee ANNIC" or "sub oh see ANNIC"
• occurring or existing below the ocean or beneath the ocean floor.
• [Latin *sub-* under + OCEAN]

suboptimal *adjective*
• "sub OPTA m'll"
• less than optimal; not of the highest level, standard, or quality, etc.
• [Latin *sub-* under + OPTIMAL]

suborbital *adjective*
• "sub ORBIT'll"
• designating or having a trajectory that does not make a complete orbit of a planet.
• [Latin *sub-* under + *orbita* course, track (in medieval Latin eye cavity): fem. of *orbitus* circular, from *orbis* ring]

subordinate *adjective*
• "suh BORD'n it"
• (of a person, position, etc.) of inferior rank; dependent upon the authority or power of another.
• [medieval Latin *subordinare*, *subordinat-* (Latin *sub* under, close to, towards, *ordinare* ordain)]
• **subordinately** *adverb*
• **subordination** *noun*

subphylum *noun*
• "sub FIE lum"
• a taxonomic category below a phylum.
• [Latin *sub-* under + PHYLUM]

subpoena *noun*
• "suh PEENA"
• a writ issued by a court or other authorized body requiring the attendance of a person at a stated time and place, usu. to testify or present evidence, subject to penalty for non-compliance.
• [Latin *sub poena* under penalty (the first words of the writ)]

subrogation *noun*
• "sub ruh GAY sh'n"
• the principle that a person paying a debt on behalf of another may succeed to the rights of that person in order to obtain restitution for that payment of debt.
• [Late Latin *subrogatio* from *subrogare* choose as substitute (*sub* under, close to, towards, *rogare* ask)]
• **subrogate** *verb*

subsequence *noun*
• "sub SEE kwince"
• a sequence derived from another by the omission of a number of terms.
• [Latin *sub-* under + SEQUENCE]

subsequent *adjective*
• "SUB suh kw'nt"
• following a specified event etc. in time, esp. as a consequence.
• [Old French *subsequent* or Latin *subsequi* (*sub* under, close to, towards, *sequi* follow)]
• **subsequently** *adverb*

subservient *adjective*
• "sub SURVEE 'nt"
• slavishly submissive, servile, obsequious.
• [Latin *subserviens subservient-* (*sub* under, close to, towards, *servus* slave)]
• **subservience** *noun*
• **subserviency** *noun*

subsidiary *adjective*
• "sub SIDDY airy" or "sub SIDGE ur ee"
• serving to assist or supplement; auxiliary.
• [Latin *subsidiarius* (as SUBSIDY)]

subsidy *noun*
• "SUB sid ee"
• money granted by a government to producers of certain goods to enable them to sell the goods to the public at a low price, to compete with foreign competition, or to avoid laying off employees.
• [Anglo-French *subsidie* from Latin *subsidium* assistance]
• **subsidization** *noun* (also esp. *Brit.* **-isation**)
• **subsidize** *verb* (also esp. *Brit.* **-ise**)
• **subsidized** *adjective* (also esp. *Brit.* **-ised**)

subsistence *noun*
• "sub SIST ince"
• the means of supporting life; a livelihood.
• [Latin *subsistere* stand firm (*sub-* under, *sistere* set, stand)]

subspecialty *noun*
• "sub SPESH'll tee"
• a secondary specialty within a branch of esp. science or medicine.
• [Latin *sub-* under + SPECIALTY]
• **subspecialist** *noun*
• **subspecialize** *verb* (also esp. *Brit.* **-ise**)

subspecies *noun*
• "SUB spee seez" or "SUB spee sheez"
• a morphologically distinct subdivision of a species, esp. one geographically or ecologically isolated from other such subdivisions.
• [Latin *sub-* under + SPECIES]
• **subspecific** *adjective* "sub spuh SIFFIC"

substance *noun*
• "SUB stince"
• the essential esp. solid matter of which a physical thing consists or is made.
• [Old French from Latin *substantia* (*sub* under, close to, towards, *stare* stand)]

substantial *adjective*
• "sub STAN sh'll"
• of real importance or value.
• [as SUBSTANCE]
• **substantiality** *noun* "sub stanshy ALA tee"
• **substantially** *adverb*

substantiate *verb*
• "sub STAN shee ate"
• prove the truth of (a charge, statement, claim, etc.); demonstrate or verify by evidence.
• [medieval Latin *substantiare* give substance to (as SUBSTANCE)]
• **substantiation** *noun*

substituent *adjective*
• "sub STITCH oo 'nt"
• (of a group of atoms) replacing another atom or group in a compound, esp. replacing hydrogen in an organic compound.
• [Latin *substituere substituent-* (*sub* under, *statuere* set up)]

substrate *noun*
• "SUB strate"
• a layer of soil, earth, clay, or rock beneath the surface.
• [anglicized from SUBSTRATUM]

substratum *noun*
• "SUB strat um"
• a foundation or basis.
• [modern Latin, past participle of Latin *substernere* (*sub* under, close to, towards, *sternere* strew): compare STRATUM]

subsume *verb*
• "sub SOOM" or "sub SYOOM"
• include (a thing) in a larger group, class, or category; incorporate, absorb.
• [medieval Latin *subsumere* (*sub* under, close to, towards, *sumere sumpt-* take)]
• **subsumption** *noun*

subterfuge *noun*
• "SUB tur fyoodge"
• a deceitful statement or action resorted to in an attempt to avoid blame, justify an argument, conceal something, etc.
• [French *subterfuge* or Late Latin *subterfugium* from Latin *subterfugere* escape secretly, from *subter* beneath + *fugere* flee]

subterranean *adjective*
• "sub tuh RAINY 'n"
• existing, occurring, or done under the earth's surface.
• [Latin *subterraneus* (*sub* under, close to, towards, *terra* earth)]
• **subterraneously** *adverb*

subtle *adjective*
• "SUTTLE"
• difficult to perceive or detect; not easily grasped or understood.
• [Old French *sotil* from Latin *subtilis*]
• **subtlety** *noun* "SUTTLE tee"
• **subtly** *adverb* "SUTTLE ee"

subtrahend *noun*
• "SUB truh hend"
• a quantity or number to be subtracted.
• [Latin *subtrahendus* gerundive of *subtrahere* subtract (*sub* under, *trahere* draw)]

subulate *adjective*
• "SUB yuh lit" or "SUB yuh late"
• slender and tapering to a point.
• [Latin *subula* awl]

suburb *noun*
• "SUB urb"
• a residential district lying just beyond or just within the boundaries of a city.
• [Old French *suburbe* or Latin *suburbium* (*sub* under, close to, towards, *urbs urbis* city)]
• **suburban** *adjective*
• **suburbanite** *noun*
• **suburbanization** *noun* (also esp. *Brit.* **-isation**)
• **suburbanize** *verb* (also esp. *Brit.* **-ise**)

suburbia *noun*
• "suh BURBY uh"
• the suburbs collectively.
• [as SUBURB]

subwoofer *noun*
• "SUB woof ur" (with "OO" as in *GOOD*)
• a loudspeaker component designed to reproduce very low bass frequencies.
• [Latin *sub-* under + 'woofer' (from imitative 'woof')]

succeed *verb*
• "suck SEED"
• accomplish one's purpose; have success; prosper.
• [Old French *succeder* or Latin *succedere* (*sub* under, close to, towards, *cedere cess-* go)]
• **succeeder** *noun*

success *noun*
• "suck SESS"
• the accomplishment of an aim; a favourable outcome.
• [Latin *successus* (as SUCCEED)]
• **successful** *adjective*
• **successfully** *adverb*
• **successfulness** *noun*

succession *noun*
• "suck SESH'n"
• the process of following in order; succeeding.
• [as SUCCEED]
• **successional** *adjective*

successive *adjective*
• "suck SESSIV"
• following one after another.
• [as SUCCEED]
• **successively** *adverb*

successor *noun*
• "suck SESSER"
• a person who or thing which succeeds another in an office, function, or position.
• [as SUCCEED]

succinct *adjective*
• "suh SINCT" or "suck SINCT"
• briefly expressed; terse, concise.
• [Latin *succinctus* past participle of *succingere* tuck up (*sub* under, close to, towards, *cingere* gird)]
• **succinctly** *adverb*
• **succinctness** *noun*

succinic *adjective*
• "suck SINNIC"
• designating a crystalline dibasic acid derived from amber etc.
• [French *succinique* from Latin *succinum* amber]
• **succinate** *noun*

succotash *noun*
• "SUCKA tash"
• a dish of corn and lima beans boiled together.
• [Narragansett *msiquatash*]

succour *noun*
ALSO SPELLED: *US* **succor**
• "SUCKER"
• aid; assistance, esp. in time of need.
• [Old French *socours* from medieval Latin *succursus* from Latin *succurrere* (*sub* under, close to, towards, *currere curs-* run)]
HOMOPHONES: *sucker*

succubus *noun*
• "SUCK yuh buss"
• a female demon believed to have sexual intercourse with sleeping men.
• [Late Latin *succuba* prostitute, medieval Latin *succubus* from *succubare* (*sub* under, close to, towards, *cubare* lie)]

succulent *adjective*
• "SUCK yoo l'nt"
• juicy; palatable.
• [Latin *succulentus* from *succus* juice]
• **succulence** *noun*
• **succulently** *adverb*

succumb *verb*
• "suh KUM"
• be forced to give way; be overcome.
• [Old French *succomber* or Latin *succumbere* (*sub* under, close to, towards, *cumbere* lie)]

succussion *noun*
• "suh KUSH'n"
• vigorous shaking, esp. in the preparation of a homeopathic remedy.
• [Latin *succutere succuss-* (*sub* under, close to, towards, *cutare* = *quatere* shake)]
• **succuss** *verb* "suh KUSS"

sucralose *noun*
• "SUKE ruh lose" ("LOSE" rhymes with *GROSS*)
• an artificial sweetener, synthetic chlorinated sucrose.
• [alteration of SUCROSE]

sucrose *noun*
• "SOO krose" ("KROSE" rhymes with *GROSS*)
• common sugar, a disaccharide obtained from sugar cane, sugar beet, etc.
• [French *sucre* sugar, from Old French *sukere* from Italian *zucchero* prob. from medieval Latin *succarum* from Arabic *sūkkar*]

suction *noun*
• "SUCK sh'n"
• the act or an instance of sucking.
• [Late Latin *suctio* from Latin *sugere suct-* suck]

suctorial *adjective*
• "suck TORY 'll"
• adapted for or capable of sucking.
• [modern Latin *suctorius* (as SUCTION)]

Sudanese *noun*
• "sooda NEEZ"
• a native or inhabitant of Sudan in NE Africa.

sudarium *noun*
• "soo DERRY um"
• a cloth for wiping the face.
• [Latin, = napkin, from *sudor* sweat]

sudatorium *noun*
• "sooda TORY um"
• a hot-air or steam bath.
• [Latin, neuter of *sudatorius*, from *sudare* sweat]

Sudburian *noun*
• "sud BERRY 'n" or "sud BURRY 'n"
• a resident of Sudbury, Ont.

sudorific *adjective*
• "sooda RIFFIC"
• (of a drug) causing sweating.
• [modern Latin *sudorificus* from Latin *sudor* sweat]

Sudra *noun*
• "SOO druh"
• a member of the worker caste, lowest of the four Hindu castes.
• [Sanskrit *śūdra*]

suede *noun*
• "SWADE"
• leather, orig. kidskin, with the flesh side rubbed to make a velvety nap.
• [French (*gants de*) *Suède* (gloves of) Sweden]
HOMOPHONES: *swayed*

suet *noun*
• "SOO it"
• the hard white fat on the kidneys or loins of oxen, sheep, etc., used to make dough etc.
• [Anglo-French from Old French *seu* from Latin *sebum* tallow]
• **suety** *adjective*

suete *noun*
• "SWET"
• *Cdn* (*Cape Breton*) a very strong southeasterly wind in the west coastal areas of the Cape Breton Highlands.
• [Acadian French, corruption of French *sud-est* southeast]
HOMOPHONES: *sweat*

suffice *verb*
• "suh FICE"
• be enough or adequate.
• [Old French *suffire* (*suffis-*) from Latin *sufficere* (*sub* under, *facere* make)]

sufficient *adjective*
• "suh FISH 'nt"
• sufficing, adequate, enough.
• [as SUFFICE]
• **sufficiency** *noun* "suh FISH'n see"
• **sufficiently** *adverb*

suffix *noun*
• "SUFFIX"
• a verbal element added at the end of a word to form a derivative, e.g. *-ation*, *-fy*, *-ing*, *-itis*.
• [*suffixum*, *suffixus* past participle of Latin *suffigere* (*sub* under, close to, towards, *figere fix-* fasten)]
• **suffixation** *noun*

suffocate *verb*
• "SUFFA cate"
• choke or kill by stopping breathing, esp. by pressure, fumes, etc.
• [Latin *suffocare* (*sub* under, close to, towards, *fauces* throat)]
• **suffocating** *adjective*
• **suffocatingly** *adverb*
• **suffocation** *noun*

Suffolk *noun*
• "SUFF ick"
• a breed of black-faced sheep.
• [*Suffolk* in E England]

suffragan *adjective*
• "SUFFRA g'n"
• designating a bishop in relation to his or her archbishop or metropolitan.
• [Anglo-French & Old French, representing medieval Latin *suffraganeus* assistant (bishop), from Latin *suffragium* (see SUFFRAGE): originally of a bishop summoned to vote in synod]

suffrage *noun*
• "SUFF ridge"
• the right of voting in political elections.
• [Latin *suffragium*, partly through French *suffrage*]

suffragette *noun*
- "suffra JET"
- a woman engaged in esp. militant activity in favour of women's suffrage, esp. in the early 20th c.
- [as SUFFRAGE + feminine ending *-ette*]

suffragist *noun*
- "SUFFRA jist"
- a person who advocates the extension of the suffrage, esp. to women.
- [as SUFFRAGE]
- **suffragism** *noun*

suffuse *verb*
- "suh FYOOZ"
- (of colour, moisture, etc.) spread from within to colour or moisten.
- [Latin *suffundere suffus-* (*sub* under, close to, towards, *fundere* pour)]
- **suffusion** *noun*

Sufi *noun*
- "SOOFY"
- a member of any of various spiritual orders within Islam characterized by asceticism and mysticism.
- [Arabic *ṣūfī*, perhaps from *ṣūf* wool (from the wool garment worn)]
- **Sufic** *adjective*
- **Sufism** *noun*

suggest *verb*
- "suh JEST" or "sug JEST"
- propose (a theory, plan, or hypothesis).
- [Latin *suggerere suggest-* (*sub* under, close to, towards, *gerere* bring)]
- **suggestion** *noun*

suggestible *adjective*
- "suh JESTA bull" or "sug JESTA bull"
- open to suggestion; easily swayed.
- [as SUGGEST]
- **suggestibility** *noun*

suggestive *adjective*
- "suh JESTIV" or "sug JESTIV"
- conveying a suggestion; evocative.
- [as SUGGEST]
- **suggestively** *adverb*
- **suggestiveness** *noun*

suicide *noun*
- "SOO a side"
- the intentional killing of oneself.
- [modern Latin *suicida*, *suicidium* from Latin *sui* of oneself + *-cida, -cidium* from *caedere* kill]
- **suicidal** *adjective*
- **suicidally** *adverb*

suint *noun*
- "SWINT"
- the dried sweat of sheep deposited in the wool.
- [French from *suer* sweat]

suite *noun*
- "SWEET"
- a set of things belonging together, esp. a set of rooms in a hotel etc. for use by one person or group of people.
- [French from Old French *si(e)ute* from fem. past participle of a Romanic alteration of Latin *sequi* follow]

HOMOPHONES: *sweet*

suitor *noun*
- "SOOTER"
- a man seeking to marry a specified woman; a wooer.
- [Anglo-French *suitour* from Latin *secutor -oris*, from *sequi secut-* follow]

sukiyaki *noun*
- "soo kee OCKY"
- a Japanese dish of sliced meat simmered with vegetables and sauce.
- [Japanese]

Sukkot *noun*
- "suh COTE"
- the Jewish autumn harvest and thanksgiving festival commemorating the sheltering of the Israelites in the wilderness.
- [Hebrew *sukkôṯ* pl. of *sukkāh* thicket, hut]

sulcate *adjective*
- "SULL cate"
- grooved, fluted, channelled.
- [Latin *sulcatus*, past participle of *sulcare* furrow (as SULCUS)]

sulcus *noun*
- "SULL kuss"
- a groove or furrow, esp. on the surface of the brain.
- [Latin]

sully *verb*
- "SULL ee"
- disgrace or tarnish (a person's reputation or character, a victory, etc.).
- [perhaps from French *souiller* ultimately from Latin *sucula* diminutive of *sus* pig]

sulpha *noun*

ALSO SPELLED: **sulfa**
- "SULFA"
- any drug derived from sulphanilamide.
- [abbreviation]

sulphamethoxazole *noun*

ALSO SPELLED: **sulfamethoxazole**
- "sulfa meth OXA zole"
- a sulphonamide used to treat respiratory and urinary tract infections.
- [SULPHA + METHYL + OXYGEN + French *azote* nitrogen, from Greek *azōos* without life]

sulphanilamide *noun*

ALSO SPELLED: **sulfanilamide**
- "sulfa NILLA mide"
- a colourless sulphonamide drug with antibacterial properties.
- [*sulphanilic* (SULPHUR, ANILINE) + AMIDE]

sulphate *noun*
ALSO SPELLED: **sulfate**
• "SULL fate"
• a salt or ester of sulphuric acid.
• [French *sulfate* from Latin *sulphur*]
• **sulphation** *noun* (also **sulfation**)

sulphide *noun*
ALSO SPELLED: **sulfide**
• "SULL fide"
• a binary compound of sulphur.
• [as SULPHUR]

sulphite *noun*
ALSO SPELLED: **sulfite**
• "SULL fite"
• a salt or ester of sulphurous acid.
• [French *sulfite* alteration of *sulfate* SULPHATE]

sulphonamide *noun*
ALSO SPELLED: **sulfonamide**
• "sull FONNA mide"
• a substance derived from an amide of a sulphonic acid, able to prevent the multiplication of some pathogenic bacteria.
• [SULPHONE + AMIDE]

sulphonate *noun*
ALSO SPELLED: **sulfonate**
• "SULL fuh nate"
• a salt or ester of sulphonic acid.
• [as SULPHONE]

sulphone *noun*
ALSO SPELLED: **sulfone**
• "SULL fone"
• an organic compound containing the SO_2 group united directly to two carbon atoms.
• [German *Sulfon* (as SULPHUR)]
• **sulphonic** *adjective* (also **sulfonic**) "sull FONNIC"

sulphonylurea *noun*
ALSO SPELLED: **sulfonylurea**
• "sull fuh nill yuh REE uh"
• any of a group of compounds containing the group $SO_2NHCONH$, some of which are hypoglycemic drugs used to treat diabetes.
• [SULPHONE + UREA]

sulphoxide *noun*
ALSO SPELLED: **sulfoxide**
• "sull FOX ide"
• any organic compound containing the group SO joined to two carbon atoms.
• [SULPHUR + OXYGEN]

sulphur *noun*
ALSO SPELLED: **sulfur**
• "SULL fur"
• a pale yellow non-metallic element having crystalline and amorphous forms, burning with a blue flame and a suffocating smell, and used in making gunpowder, matches, and sulphuric acid, in the vulcanizing of rubber, and as an antiseptic and fungicide.
• [Anglo-French *sulf(e)re*, Old French *soufre* from Latin *sulfur*, *sulp(h)ur*]
• **sulphurous** *adjective* (also **sulfurous**)
• **sulphury** *adjective* (also **sulfury**)

sulphureous *adjective*
ALSO SPELLED: **sulfureous**
• "sull FYURY us"
• sulphur-coloured; yellow.
• [as SULPHUR]

sulphuric *adjective*
ALSO SPELLED: **sulfuric**
• "sull FYURE ick"
• containing hexavalent sulphur.
• [as SULPHUR]

sulphurize *verb*
ALSO SPELLED: **sulfurize**; esp. *Brit.* **sulphurise**
• "SULFER ize"
• impregnate, fumigate, or treat with sulphur, esp. in bleaching.
• [as SULPHUR]
• **sulphurization** *noun* (also **sulfurization**; esp. *Brit.* **sulphurisation**)

Sulpician *noun*
• "sull PISH'n"
• a member of a Roman Catholic society of diocesan priests founded in Paris in 1641 and established in New France in 1657, concerned esp. with the training of priests.
• [from the church of Saint-*Sulpice* in Paris, the congregation's first seminary]

sultan *noun*
• "SULL t'n"
• a Muslim sovereign.
• [French *sultan* or medieval Latin *sultanus* from Arabic *sulṭān* power, ruler, from *saluṭa* rule]
• **sultanate** *noun*

sultana *noun*
• "sull TANNA"
• a seedless raisin used in puddings, cakes, etc.
• [Italian, feminine of *sultano* = SULTAN]

sultry *adjective*
• "SULL tree"
• (of the atmosphere or the weather) hot or oppressive; close.
• [obsolete *sulter* swelter (see SWELTER)]
• **sultrily** *adverb*
• **sultriness** *noun*

sumac *noun*
ALSO SPELLED: **sumach**
• "SOO mack"
• any of various shrubs or trees of the genus *Rhus*, having cone-shaped clusters of reddish fruits.
• [Old French *sumac* or medieval Latin *sumac(h)* from Arabic *summāk*]

Sumatran *adjective*
• "soo MAW tr'n"
• of or relating to the Indonesian island of Sumatra.

sumatriptan *noun*
• "sooma TRIP tan"
• a generic drug used to relieve migraine

headaches by constricting dilated blood vessels in the brain.
• [invented name]

Sumerian *adjective*
• "soo MERRY 'n"
• of or relating to the early and non-Semitic element in the civilization of ancient Babylonia.
• [*Sumer*, an ancient region of SW Asia in present-day Iraq]

summa *noun*
• "SOOMA"
• a summary of what is known of a subject.
• [Middle English from Latin *summa* main part, fem. of *summus* highest]

summarily *adverb*
• "suh MERRA lee"
• without the customary legal formalities.
• [as SUMMARY]

summary *noun*
• "SUMMER ee"
• a brief account; an abridgement.
• [Latin *summarium* from Latin *summa* (as SUMMA)]
• **summarist** *noun*
• **summarize** *verb* (also esp. *Brit.* **-ise**)
• **summarizer** *noun* (also esp. *Brit.* **-iser**)
HOMOPHONES: *summery*

summation *noun*
• "suh MAY sh'n"
• the finding of a total or sum; an addition.
• [as SUMMA]
• **summational** *adjective*
• **summative** *adjective*

summerfallow *noun*
• "SUMMER fal oh" ("FAL" rhymes with *PAL*) or "SUMMER follow"
• esp. *Cdn* agricultural land left fallow in the summer to allow moisture and nutrient levels to recover.
• ['summer' + 'fallow' from Old English *fealh*]

sumo *noun*
• "SOO moe"
• a Japanese form of heavyweight wrestling in which a wrestler wins a bout by forcing his opponent outside a circle or making him touch the ground with any part of the body except the soles of the feet.
• [Japanese]

sumpter *noun*
• "SUMP tur"
• a pack horse or other beast of burden.
• [Old French *som(m)etier* from Late Latin from Greek *sagma -atos* packsaddle]

sumptuary *adjective*
• "SUMP choo airy"
• relating to or denoting laws that limit private expenditure on food, clothing, and personal items.
• [Latin *sumptuarius* from *sumptus* cost, from *sumere sumpt-* take]

sumptuous *adjective*
• "SUMP choo us"
• rich, lavish, magnificent.
• [Old French *somptueux* from Latin *sumptuosus* (as SUMPTUARY)]
• **sumptuosity** *noun* "sump choo OSSA tee"
• **sumptuously** *adverb*
• **sumptuousness** *noun*

sundae *noun*
• "SUN day" or "SUN dee"
• a dish of ice cream topped with chocolate or butterscotch sauce, fruit, whipped cream, nuts, etc.
• [perhaps from 'Sunday']
HOMOPHONES: *Sunday*

sundew *noun*
• "SUN doo" or "SUN dyoo"
• any small insect-consuming bog plant of the family Droseraceae, esp. of the genus *Drosera* with hairs secreting drops of moisture.
• ['sun' + 'dew']

sundry *adjective*
• "SUN dree"
• various; several.
• [Old English *syndrig* separate]

Sunna *noun*
• "SOONA"
• a traditional portion of Muslim law based on Muhammad's words or acts, accepted (together with the Quran) as authoritative by Muslims.
• [Arabic, = form, way, course, rule]

Sunni *noun*
• "SOONY"
• one of the two main branches of Islam, commonly described as orthodox, and differing from the Shia in its understanding of the Sunna and in its rejection of Ali (d.661) as Muhammad's first successor.
• [as SUNNA]

superabundant *adjective*
• "sooper a BUN d'nt"
• abounding beyond what is normal or right.
• [Latin *super* above, beyond + ABUNDANT]
• **superabundance** *noun*
• **superabundantly** *adverb*

superannuated *adjective*
• "sooper AN yoo ated"
• retired because of age or disability.
• [from medieval Latin *superannuatus* from Latin *super* above, beyond + *annus* year]
• **superannuable** *adjective*
• **superannuate** *verb*

superannuation *noun*
• "sooper anyoo AY sh'n"
• a pension paid to a retired person.
• [as SUPERANNUATED]

superb *adjective*
• "soo PURB"
• excellent; fine.
• [French *superbe* or Latin *superbus* proud]
• **superbly** *adverb*
• **superbness** *noun*

supercalender *verb*
• "sooper CAL'n dur"
• give a highly glazed finish to (paper) by extra calendering.
• [Latin *super* above, beyond + CALENDER]

superciliary *adjective*
• "sooper SILLY a ree"
• of or concerning the eyebrow; over the eye.
• [Latin *supercilium* eyebrow (as Latin *super* above, beyond, *cilium* eyelid)]

supercilious *adjective*
• "sooper SILLY us"
• assuming an air of contemptuous indifference or superiority.
• [Latin *superciliosus* (as SUPERCILIARY)]
• **superciliously** *adverb*
• **superciliousness** *noun*

superconductivity *noun*
• "sooper con duck TIVVA tee"
• the property of zero electrical resistance in some substances at very low absolute temperatures.
• [Latin *super* above, beyond + CONDUCTIVE]
• **superconducting** *adjective*
• **superconductive** *adjective*
• **superconductor** *noun*

supercontinent *noun*
• "SOOPER con tin 'nt"
• each of several large land masses thought to have divided to form the present continents in the geological past.
• [Latin *super* above, beyond + 'continent' (from Latin *terra continens* (from *continēre content-* from *com-* with, *tenēre* hold) continuous land)]

supererogation *noun*
• "sooper erra GAY sh'n"
• the performance of more than duty requires.
• [Late Latin *supererogatio* from *supererogare* pay in addition (Latin *super* above, beyond, *erogare* pay out)]
• **supererogatory** *adjective*
"sooper a ROGGA tory"

superfetation *noun*
• "sooper fee TAY sh'n"
• a second conception during pregnancy giving rise to embryos of different ages in the uterus.
• [ultimately from Latin *superfetare* (*super* above, beyond, FETUS)]

superficial *adjective*
• "sooper FISH'll"
• of or on the surface; lacking depth.
• [Late Latin *superficialis* from Latin (as SUPERFICIES)]
• **superficiality** *noun* "sooper fishy ALA tee"
• **superficially** *adverb*

superficies *noun*
• "sooper FISHY eez"
• a surface.
• [Latin (*super* above, beyond, *facies* face)]

superfluidity *noun*
• "sooper floo IDDA tee"
• the property of flowing without friction or viscosity, as in liquid helium below about 2.18 kelvins.
• [Latin *super* above, beyond + FLUID]
• **superfluid** *noun*

superfluous *adjective*
• "soo PURR floo us"
• more than enough, redundant, needless.
• [Latin *superfluus* (*super* above, beyond, *fluere* to flow)]
• **superfluity** *noun* "sooper FLOO a tee"
• **superfluously** *adverb*

superheterodyne *adjective*
• "sooper HETTER a dine"
• denoting or characteristic of a system of radio reception in which a local variable oscillator is tuned to beat at a constant ultrasonic frequency with carrier wave frequencies, making it unnecessary to vary the amplifier tuning and securing greater selectivity.
• [SUPERSONIC + HETERODYNE]

superinduce *verb*
• "sooper in DUCE"
• introduce or induce in addition.
• [Latin *super* above, beyond + INDUCE]
• **superinduction** *noun*

superintend *verb*
• "sooper in TEND"
• be responsible for the management or arrangement of (an activity etc.).
• [Church Latin *superintendere* (*super* above, beyond, INTENDANT), translation of Greek *episkopō*]
• **superintendence** *noun*
• **superintendency** *noun*
• **superintendent** *noun*

superior *adjective*
• "soo PEERY ur" or "suh PEERY ur"
• in a higher position; of higher rank.
• [Old French *superiour* from Latin *superior -oris*, comparative of *superus* that is above, from *super* above]
• **superiority** *noun*
• **superiorly** *adverb*

superlative *adjective*
• "soo PURLA tiv"
• of the highest quality or degree.
• [Old French *superlatif -ive* from Latin *superlatus* (*super* above, beyond, *latus* past participle of *ferre* take)]
• **superlatively** *adverb*
• **superlativeness** *noun*

superluminal *adjective*
- "sooper LOOM in 'll"
- of or having a speed greater than that of light.
- [Latin *super* above, beyond, *lumen luminis* light]

superlunary *adjective*
- "sooper LOONER ee"
- situated beyond the moon.
- [medieval Latin *superlunaris* (*super* above, beyond, LUNAR)]

supernal *adjective*
- "soo PURR n'll"
- heavenly; divine.
- [Old French *supernal* from Latin *supernus* from *super* above]
- **supernally** *adverb*

supernatant *adjective*
- "sooper NAY t'nt"
- floating on the surface of a liquid.
- [Latin *super* above, beyond + *natant* swimming, from Latin *natare* swim]

supernumerary *adjective*
- "sooper NOOMER airy" or "sooper NYOOMER airy"
- in excess of the normal number; extra.
- [Late Latin *supernumerarius* (soldier) added to a legion already complete, from Latin *super numerum* beyond the number]

superordinate *adjective*
- "sooper ORD'n it"
- of superior importance or rank.
- [Latin *super* above, beyond, after *subordinate*]

supersaturate *verb*
- "sooper SATCHER ate"
- add to (esp. a solution) beyond saturation point.
- [Latin *super* above, beyond + SATURATE]
- **supersaturation** *noun*

supersede *verb*
- "sooper SEED"
- adopt or appoint another person or thing in place of.
- [Old French *superseder* from Latin *supersedēre* be superior to (*super* above, beyond, *sedēre sess-* sit)]
- **supersession** *noun*

supersonic *adjective*
- "sooper SONNIC"
- designating or having a speed greater than that of sound.
- [Latin *super* above, beyond + SONIC]
- **supersonically** *adverb*

superstition *noun*
- "sooper STISH'n"
- irrational belief, esp. as based on fear of or reverence for the supernatural.
- [Old French *superstition* or Latin *superstitio* (Latin *super* above, beyond, *stare stat-* stand)]
- **superstitious** *adjective*
- **superstitiously** *adverb*
- **superstitiousness** *noun*

superstratum *noun*
- "SOOPER strat um"
- an overlying stratum.
- [Latin *super* above, beyond + STRATUM]

superterrestrial *adjective*
- "sooper tuh RESS tree 'll"
- in or belonging to a region above the earth.
- [Latin *super* above, beyond + TERRESTRIAL]

supervene *verb*
- "sooper VEEN"
- occur as an interruption in or a change from some state.
- [Latin *supervenire supervent-* (*super* above, beyond, *venire* come)]
- **supervenient** *adjective*
- **supervention** *noun*

supervise *verb*
- "SOOPER vize"
- superintend, oversee the execution of (a task etc.).
- [medieval Latin *supervidēre supervis-* (*super* above, beyond, *vidēre* see)]
- **supervision** *noun*
- **supervisor** *noun*
- **supervisory** *adjective*

supinate *verb*
- "SOO pin ate"
- put (a hand or foreleg etc.) into a supine position (with the palm etc. upwards).
- [as SUPINE]
- **supination** *noun*

supinator *noun*
- "SOO pin ate ur"
- a muscle in the forearm effecting supination.
- [as SUPINE]

supine *adjective*
- "SOO pine"
- lying face upwards.
- [Latin *supinus*, related to *super*]
- **supinely** *adverb*
- **supineness** *noun*

supplant *verb*
- "suh PLANT"
- dispossess and take the place of, esp. by underhand means.
- [Old French *supplanter* or Latin *supplantare* trip up (*sub* under, close to, towards, *planta* sole)]
- **supplanter** *noun*

supple *adjective*
- "SUP'll"
- bending and moving easily and gracefully; flexible.
- [Old French *souple* ultimately from Latin *supplex supplicis* submissive]
- **suppleness** *noun*

supplejack *noun*
- "SUP'll jack"
- any of various strong twining tropical shrubs, esp. *Berchemia scandens.*
- [as SUPPLE]

supplement *noun*
- "SUPPLA m'nt"
- a thing or part added to remedy deficiencies.
- [Latin *supplementum* (*sub* under, close to, towards, *plēre* fill)]
- **supplemental** *adjective*
- **supplementally** *adverb*
- **supplementarily** *adverb* "suppla men TERRA lee"
- **supplementary** *adjective* "suppla MENTA ree"
- **supplementation** *noun*

suppletion *noun*
- "suh PLEE sh'n"
- the act or an instance of supplementing, esp. the occurrence of unrelated forms to supply gaps in conjugation (e.g. *went* as the past of *go*).
- [Old French from medieval Latin *suppletio -onis* from Latin *supplēre* (*sub* under, *plēre* fill)]

suppliant *adjective*
- "SUP lee 'nt"
- supplicating.
- [French *supplier* beseech, from Latin (as SUPPLICATE)]
- **suppliantly** *adverb*

supplicate *verb*
- "SUP luh cate"
- petition humbly to (a person) or for (a thing).
- [Latin *supplicare* (*sub* under, close to, towards, *plicare* bend)]
- **supplicant** *adjective*
- **supplication** *noun*
- **supplicatory** *adjective* "SUP luh kuh tory"

support *verb*
- "suh PORT"
- carry all or part of the weight of.
- [Old French *supporter* from Latin *supportare* (*sub* under, *portare* carry)]
- **supportable** *adjective*
- **supportably** *adverb*
- **supporter** *noun*
- **supporting** *adjective*
- **supportless** *adjective*

supportive *adjective*
- "suh PORT iv"
- providing support or encouragement.
- [as SUPPORT]
- **supportively** *adverb*
- **supportiveness** *noun*

suppose *verb*
- "suh POSE"
- assume, esp. in default of knowledge; be inclined to think.
- [Old French *supposer*]
- **supposable** *adjective*

supposed *adjective*
- "suh POZED"
- generally accepted as being so; believed.
- [as SUPPOSE]
- **supposedly** *adverb* "suh POZE id lee"

supposition *noun*
- "suppa ZISH'n"
- a fact or idea etc. supposed.
- [Old French, from *supposer* (as SUPPOSE)]
- **suppositional** *adjective*

suppository *noun*
- "suh POZZA tory"
- a medical preparation in the form of a cone, cylinder, etc., to be inserted into the rectum or vagina to melt.
- [medieval Latin *suppositorium*, neuter of Late Latin *suppositorius* placed underneath]

suppress *verb*
- "suh PRESS"
- end the activity or existence of, esp. forcibly.
- [Latin *supprimere suppress-* (*sub* under, close to, towards, *premere* press)]
- **suppressible** *adjective*
- **suppression** *noun*
- **suppressive** *adjective*
- **suppressor** *noun*

suppressant *noun*
- "suh PRESS'nt"
- a suppressing or restraining agent.
- [as SUPPRESS]

suppurate *verb*
- "SUP yuh rate"
- form pus; fester.
- [Latin *suppurare* (*sub* under, close to, towards, *purare* form pus, from *pus puris* pus)]
- **suppuration** *noun*
- **suppurative** *adjective*

supra *adverb*
- "SOOPRA"
- above or earlier on (in a text).
- [Latin, = above]

supranational *adjective*
- "soop ruh NATIONAL"
- transcending national limits.
- [Latin *supra* above + 'national' from Latin *natio -onis* nation, from *nasci nat-* be born]
- **supranationalism** *noun*
- **supranationality** *noun*

supraorbital *adjective*
- "soopra ORBIT'll"
- situated above the orbit of the eye.
- [Latin *supra* above + 'orbit' from Latin *orbita* course, track (in medieval Latin eye cavity): fem. of *orbitus* circular, from *orbis* ring]

suprarenal *adjective*
- "soopra REEN 'll"
- situated above the kidneys.
- [Latin *supra* above + RENAL]

supremacist *noun*
• "suh PREMMA sist" or "soo PREMMA sist"
• a person who believes in or advocates the supremacy of a particular group.
• [as SUPREME]
• **supremacism** *noun*

supremacy *noun*
• "suh PREMMA see" or "soo PREMMA see"
• the state of being supreme in authority, rank, or power.
• [as SUPREME]

supreme *adjective*
• "soo PREEM" or "suh PREEM"
• highest in authority, rank, or power.
• [Latin *supremus*, superlative of *superus* that is above, from *super* above]
• **supremely** *adverb*

supremo *noun*
• "suh PREEMO" or "soo PREEMO"
• a person who has supreme authority; a ruler or leader.
• [Spanish, = SUPREME]

sura *noun*
• "SOORA" (with "OO" as in *BOOK*)
• a chapter or section of the Quran.
• [Arabic *sūra*, prob. from Syriac *ṣūrṭā* scripture]

sural *adjective*
• "SYUR'll"
• of or relating to the calf of the leg.
• [modern Latin *suralis* from Latin *sura* calf]

surcease *noun*
• "sur SEECE"
• relief.
• [Old French *sursis*, past participle of Old French *surseoir* refrain, delay, from Latin (as SUPERSEDE), assimilated to CEASE]

surcingle *noun*
• "SUR sing g'll"
• a strap or belt passed around the body of a horse to keep a blanket, pack, saddle, etc. in place.
• [Old French *surcengle* (Old French *sur* from Latin *super* above, beyond, *cengle* girth, from Latin *cingula* from *cingere* gird)]

surd *adjective*
• "SURD"
• (of a number) irrational.
• [Latin *surdus* deaf, mute, by mistranslating into Latin of Greek *alogos* irrational, speechless, through Arabic *jaḏr aṣamm* deaf root]

Sûreté *noun*
• "soora TAY"
• *Cdn* the provincial police force of Quebec.
• [French, = 'police force', lit. 'safety']

surety *noun*
• "SHOORA tee" (with "OO" as in *BOOK*)
• a person who assumes responsibility for the obligation of another, such as the payment of a debt or an appearance in court.
• [Old French *surete* from *sur* safe, sure, from Latin *securus* secure]

surf *noun*
• "SURF"
• the swell of the sea breaking on the esp. shallow shore of a beach or a reef.
• [apparently from obsolete *suff*, of unknown origin, perhaps assimilated to *surge*]
• **surflike** *adjective*
• **surfy** *adjective*
HOMOPHONES: *serf*

surfactant *noun*
• "sur FACK t'nt"
• a substance which reduces surface tension of a liquid.
• [*surface-active*]

surfeit *noun*
• "SUR fit"
• a large or excessive amount.
• [Old French *sorfe(i)t*, *surfe(i)t* (Latin *super* above, beyond, *facere fact-* do)]
• **surfeited** *adjective*

surficial *adjective*
• "sur FISH'll"
• of or relating to the earth's surface.
• ['surface' (from French *surface* from Latin *superficies*), after *superficial*]

surge *noun*
• "SURJ"
• a sudden or violent rush, onset, or burst.
• [Old French *sourdre sourge-*, or *sorgir* from Catalan, from Latin *surgere* rise]
HOMOPHONES: *serge*

surgeon *noun*
• "SUR j'n"
• a medical practitioner qualified to practise surgery.
• [Old French *serurgien* (as SURGERY)]

surgery *noun*
• "SUR jur ee"
• the branch of medicine concerned with treatment of injuries or disorders of the body by incision, manipulation, or alteration of organs etc.
• [Old French *surgerie* from Latin *chirurgia* from Greek *kheirourgia* handiwork, surgery, from *kheir* hand + *erg-* work]
• **surgical** *adjective*
• **surgically** *adverb*

suricate *noun*
• "SOOR uh cate" (with "OO" as in *BOOK*)
• a South African burrowing mongoose, *Suricata suricatta*, with grey and black stripes; a meerkat.
• [French, of African origin]

surimi *noun*
• "soo REEMY"
• a white relatively tasteless and odourless

paste made from minced fish, used esp. to produce imitation crabmeat and lobster meat.
• [Japanese, lit. 'minced flesh']

Surinamese *noun*
• "soora nuh MEEZ" (with "OO" as in *BOOK*)
• a native or inhabitant of Suriname in northern S America.

surly *adjective*
• "SUR lee"
• rude, ill-natured, unfriendly; gruff.
• [alteration of spelling of obsolete *sirly* haughty, from 'sir']
• **surlily** *adverb*
• **surliness** *noun*

surmise *verb*
• "sur MIZE"
• form an opinion that something may be true without sufficient evidence to be certain; infer, conjecture, suspect.
• [Old French feminine past participle of *surmettre* accuse, from Late Latin *supermittere supermiss-* (Latin *super* above, beyond, *mittere* send)]

surmount *verb*
• "sur MOUNT"
• overcome (an obstacle, difficulty, impediment, etc.).
• [Old French *surmunter, so(u)rmonter* from medieval Latin *supermontare* (Latin *super* above, beyond, *montare* climb)]
• **surmountable** *adjective*

surmullet *noun*
• "sur MULL it"
• a fish of tropical and subtropical oceans, related to the perch, and having two long barbels under the chin.
• [French *surmulet* from Old French *sor* red + *mulet* MULLET]

surname *noun*
• "SUR name"
• a hereditary name common to all members of a family, as distinct from a given name; a family name.
• [Old French *surnum* from Latin *super* above, beyond + Latin *nomen* name]

surpass *verb*
• "sur PASS"
• be greater, better than, or superior to; excel.
• [French *surpasser* (Old French *sur* from Latin *super* above, beyond, *passus* pace)]
• **surpassable** *adjective*

surpassing *adjective*
• "sur PASSING"
• that surpasses what is ordinary; exceptional, matchless.
• [as SURPASS]
• **surpassingly** *adverb*

surplice *noun*
• "SUR pliss" or "SUR plus"
• a loose white vestment with wide sleeves, reaching the knees or feet and worn usu. over a cassock by clergy, choir members, altar servers, etc.
• [Old French *sourpelis*, from medieval Latin *superpellicium* (Latin *super* above, beyond, *pellicia* PELISSE)]
• **surpliced** *adjective*
HOMOPHONES: *surplus*

surplus *noun*
• "SUR plus"
• an amount left over when requirements have been met; what remains of what is needed or already used.
• [Old French *s(o)urplus* from medieval Latin *superplus* (Latin *super* above, beyond, + *plus* more)]
• **surplusage** *noun*
HOMOPHONES: *surplice*

surprise *noun*
• "sur PRIZE"
• an unexpected or astonishing event, circumstance, or thing.
• [Old French, feminine past participle of *surprendre* (Old French *sur* from Latin *super* above, beyond, *prendre* from Latin *praehendere* seize)]
• **surprised** *adjective*
• **surprising** *adjective*
• **surprisingly** *adverb*

surrealism *noun*
• "suh REEL izm"
• a 20th-c. movement in art and literature aiming to explore and express the subconscious mind and to move beyond the accepted conventions of reality by representing the irrational imagery of dreams using such techniques as automatism, the irrational juxtaposition of images, and the creation of mysterious symbols.
• [*sur-* from Latin *super* above, beyond + 'real' from Late Latin *realis* from Latin *res* thing]
• **surreal** *adjective*
• **surrealist** *noun*
• **surrealistic** *adjective*
• **surrealistically** *adverb*
• **surreality** *noun* "surry ALA tee"
• **surreally** *adverb*

surrebutter *noun*
• "surra BUTTER"
• the plaintiff's reply to the defendant's rebutter.
• [Old French *sur* from Latin *super* above, beyond + REBUTTER, after SURREJOINDER]
• **surrebuttal** *noun*

surrejoinder *noun*
• "surra JOIN dur"
• the plaintiff's reply to the defendant's rejoinder.
• [Old French *sur* from Latin *super* above, beyond + 'rejoinder' from Old French *rejoindre*

rejoign- (*re* again, *joindre* (stem *joign-*) from Latin *jungere junct-* join)]

surrender *verb*
- "suh RENDER"
- give up possession or control of (something) to another, esp. on compulsion or demand; relinquish, yield.
- [Old French *surrendre* (Old French *sur* from Latin *super* above, beyond, *rendre*, ultimately from Latin *reddere reddit-* (*re* again, *dare* give))]

surreptitious *adjective*
- "sur up TISH us"
- obtained, done, etc. in secret or by stealth or illicit means; clandestine.
- [Latin *surrepticius -itius* from *surripere surrept-* (*super* above, beyond, *rapere* seize)]
- **surreptitiously** *adverb*
- **surreptitiousness** *noun*

surrey *noun*
- "SURRY"
- a light four-wheeled carriage with two seats facing forwards.
- [originally of an adaptation of the *Surrey cart*, originally made in Surrey, England]

Surreyite *noun*
- "SURRY ite"
- a resident of Surrey, BC.

surrogacy *noun*
- "SURRA guh see"
- the practice of surrogate motherhood.
- [as SURROGATE]

surrogate *noun*
- "SURRA git" (with "G" as in *GET*)
- a person or thing taking the place of another; a substitute.
- [Latin *surrogatus* past participle of *surrogare* elect as a substitute (*super* above, beyond, *rogare* ask)]

surround *verb*
- "suh ROUND"
- stand or be situated around; extend around, encircle.
- [Middle English = overflow, from Old French *s(o)uronder* from Late Latin *superundare* (Latin *super* above, beyond, *undare* flow, from *unda* wave)]

surrounding *adjective*
- "suh ROUND ing"
- located or situated around.
- [as SURROUND]

surtax *noun*
- "SUR tax"
- a higher rate of tax levied on personal incomes above a certain level.
- [*sur-* from Latin *super* above, beyond + 'tax' from Latin *taxare* censure, charge, compute, perhaps from Greek *tassō* fix]

surtout *noun*
- "sur TOO"
- a man's overcoat or frock coat.
- [French from *sur* over + *tout* everything]

surveillance *noun*
- "sur VALE ince"
- close observation or supervision, esp. of an enemy or suspected person.
- [French from *surveiller* (Old French *sur* from Latin *super* above, beyond, *veiller* from Latin *vigilare* keep watch)]

survey *noun*
- "SUR vay"
- a general and comprehensive discussion, description, view, consideration, or treatment of something.
- [Old French *so(u)rveeir* (pres. stem *survey-*) from medieval Latin *supervidēre* (Latin *super* above, beyond, *vidēre* see)]

surveying *noun*
- "sur VAY ing" or "SUR vay ing"
- the scientific measurement of land for making maps, preparing for development, etc.; the business or occupation of a surveyor.
- [as SURVEY]
- **surveyor** *noun*

survivalism *noun*
- "sur VIVE'll izm"
- a policy of trying to ensure the survival of oneself, one's business, or one's social or national group, esp. in the face of competition or event of a natural disaster, catastrophic event, or foreign invasion.
- [as SURVIVE]
- **survivalist** *noun*

survive *verb*
- "sur VIVE"
- continue to live or exist, esp. after some event; remain alive or existent.
- [Old French *sourvivre* from Latin *supervivere* (*super* above, beyond, *vivere* live)]
- **survivability** *noun*
- **survivable** *adjective*
- **survival** *noun*
- **survivor** *noun*
- **survivorship** *noun*

susceptible *adjective*
- "suh SEPTA bull"
- likely to be affected by; prone or vulnerable to.
- [Late Latin *susceptibilis* from Latin *suscipere suscept-* (*sub* under, close to, towards, *capere* take)]
- **susceptibility** *noun*
- **susceptibly** *adverb*

sushi *noun*
- "SOOSHY"
- a Japanese snack of balls or squares of cold boiled rice flavoured with vinegar, salt, and sugar, and garnished with a variety of toppings, e.g. raw fish, egg, seaweed, or vegetables.
- [Japanese]

suspensory *adjective*
• "suh SPENCER ee"
• (of a ligament, muscle, bandage, etc.) holding an organ or limb etc. suspended.
• [French *suspensoir* from Old French *suspendre* from Latin *suspendere suspens-* (*sub* under, *pendere* hang)]

suspicion *noun*
• "suh SPISH'n"
• the feeling or state of mind of a person who suspects.
• [Anglo-French *suspeciun* from medieval Latin *suspectio -onis* from Latin *suspicere* (*sub* under, *specere* look): assimilated to French *suspicion* & Latin *suspicio*]
• **suspicious** *adjective*
• **suspiciously** *adverb*
• **suspiciousness** *noun*

sustain *verb*
• "suh STANE"
• provide with the basic necessities required to support or preserve life, livelihood, or existence; provide for the needs of.
• [Old French *so(u)stein-*, stressed stem of *so(u)stenir*, from Latin *sustinēre sustent-* (*sub-* from *sub* under, close to, towards, *tenēre* hold)]
• **sustained** *adjective*
• **sustainer** *noun*
• **sustaining** *adjective*
• **sustainment** *noun*

sustainable *adjective*
• "suh STANE a bull"
• (esp. of development) that conserves an ecological balance by avoiding depletion of natural resources.
• [as SUSTAIN]
• **sustainability** *noun*
• **sustainably** *adverb*

sustenance *noun*
• "SUSTA nince"
• a means of sustaining life; nourishment.
• [Anglo-French *sustenaunce* (as SUSTAIN)]

susurration *noun*
• "soossa RAY sh'n" or "syoossa RAY sh'n"
• a sound of whispering or rustling.
• [as SUSURRUS]
• **susurrant** *adjective*
• **susurrating** *adjective*

susurrus *noun*
• "soo SUH russ" or "syoo SUH russ"
• a low soft whispering or rustling sound; a susurration.
• [Latin, of imitative origin]

sutler *noun*
• "SUT lur"
• a person following an army and selling provisions etc. to the soldiers.
• [obsolete Dutch *soeteler* from *soetelen* befoul, perform menial duties, from Germanic]

Sutra *noun*
• "SOOTRA"
• an aphorism or set of aphorisms in Hindu literature.
• [Sanskrit *sūtra* thread, rule, from *siv* sew]

suttee *noun*
ALSO SPELLED: **sati**
• "suh TEE" or "SUT ee"
• the Hindu practice of a widow immolating herself on her husband's funeral pyre.
• [Hindi & Urdu from Sanskrit *satī* faithful wife, from *sat* good]

suture *noun*
• "SOO chur"
• the joining of the edges of a wound or incision by stitching.
• [French *suture* or Latin *sutura* from *suere sut-* sew]
• **sutural** *adjective*
• **sutured** *adjective*
• **sutureless** *adjective*

suzerain *noun*
• "SOOZER 'n"
• a feudal overlord.
• [French, apparently from *sus* above, from Latin *sursum* upward, after *souverain* SOVEREIGN]
• **suzerainty** *noun*

Suzuki *adjective*
• "suh ZOOKY"
• designating, pertaining to, or using a method of teaching the violin (esp. to young children), characterized by exercises involving large groups and parental participation.
• [Shin'ichi *Suzuki*, Japanese violin teacher d.1998]

svelte *adjective*
• "SVELT"
• slender, graceful, elegant.
• [French from Italian *svelto*]

Svengali *noun*
• "sven GAL ee" or "sven GAWL ee"
• a person who exercises a controlling or mesmeric influence on another, esp. for a sinister purpose.
• [a character in the novel *Trilby* by French-born English writer G. Du Maurier (d.1896)]

Svetambara *noun*
• "svet UMBER uh"
• a member of one of the two principal sects of Jainism (the other is that of the Digambaras), which was formed AD *c.*80 and survives today in parts of India. The sect is characterized by asceticism and the wearing of white clothing.
• [Sanskrit, = white-clad]

Swabian *adjective*
• "SWAY bee 'n"
• of or relating to the region of Swabia, now divided between SW Germany, Switzerland, and France.

swage *noun*
- "SWAYJ" (rhymes with *stage*)
- a tool, die, or stamp for bending and shaping wrought iron etc. by hammering or pressure.
- [French *s(o)uage* decorative groove, of unknown origin]

Swahili *noun*
- "swuh HEELY" or "swaw HEELY"
- a member of a Bantu-speaking people of the central E African coast and the adjacent island of Zanzibar.
- [Arabic *sawāḥil*, pl. of *sāḥil* coast]

swain *noun*
- "SWANE"
- a young lover or suitor.
- [Old Norse *sveinn* lad = Old English *swān* swineherd, from Germanic]

swale *noun*
- "SWALE"
- a low or hollow place, esp. a marshy depression or hollow between ridges.
- [16th c.: origin unknown]

swami *noun*
- "SWOMMY"
- a Hindu male religious teacher.
- [Hindi *swāmī* master, prince, from Sanskrit *svāmin*]

swannery *noun*
- "SWONNER ee"
- a place where swans are bred.
- [from 'swan']

swaraj *noun*
- "swuh RADGE"
- self-government or independence for India.
- [Sanskrit, = self-ruling: compare RAJ]
- ***swarajist*** *noun*

sward *noun*
- "SWORE'd"
- the upper layer of soil usu. covered with grass or weeds; turf.
- [Old English *sweard* skin]

swarf *noun*
- "SWORF"
- waste debris produced by a machining operation esp. in the form of wet or greasy grit abraded from a grindstone or axle during use, metal filings or ribbons, stone chips, etc.
- [Old Norse *svarf* dust, from filing]

swarthy *adjective*
- "SWOR thee" (with "TH" as in *THIS*)
- of a dark colour or complexion.
- [var. of obsolete *swarty* from Old English *sweart* dark]
- **swarthiness** *noun*

swastika *noun*
- "swuh STEEKA" or "SWOSS ticka"
- an ancient symbol in the form of a cross with each of its four arms of equal length bent at right angles at the end, all in the same direction and usu. clockwise.
- [Sanskrit *svastika* from *svastí* well-being, from *sú* good + *astí* being]

swath *noun*
- "SWOTH" (with "TH" as in *THIN*)
- a strip in a field or lawn that has been left clear after the passage of a mower, scythe, etc.
- [Old English *swæth, swathu*]

HOMOPHONES: *swathe*

swathe *verb*
- "SWATHE" (rhymes either with *CLOTH* or with *BATHE*)
- wrap (a person etc.) in bandages or clothes.
- [Old English *swathian*]

HOMOPHONES: *swath*

swather *noun*
- "SWOTHER" (with "TH" either as in *THIN* or as in *THIS*)
- a machine used to cut grain and deposit it in a row to dry and be collected.
- [as SWATH]

Swazi *noun*
- "SWOZZY"
- a member of a people inhabiting Swaziland and parts of Mpumalanga in South Africa.
- [*Mswati*, name of a former king of the Swazi]

Swedenborgian *adjective*
- "sweed'n BORG ee 'n"
- of or relating to the Swedish scientific and religious writer E. Swedenborg (d.1772) or his followers.

sweepstakes *noun*
- "SWEEP stakes"
- a form of gambling in which all the money bet on the result of a contest is paid to the winner or winners.
- ['sweep' + STAKE]

swelter *verb*
- "SWELL tur"
- be uncomfortably hot.
- [base of (now dialect) *swelt* from Old English *sweltan* perish, from Germanic]
- **sweltering** *adjective*
- **swelteringly** *adverb*

swimmeret *noun*
- "SWIMMA ret"
- (in crustaceans) an abdominal limb adapted for swimming.
- ['swim']

swingletree *noun*
- "SWING g'll tree"
- a crossbar pivoted in the middle, to which the traces are attached in a cart, plow, etc.
- [Middle English from Middle Dutch *swinghel* + 'tree']

swirl *verb*
- "SWURL"

• move or flow or carry along with or as with a whirling motion.
• [Middle English (originally as noun): originally Scots, perhaps of Low German or Dutch origin]
• **swirly** *adjective*

switchel *noun*
• "SWITCH'll"
• *Cdn* (*Nfld*) weak tea without milk and sweetened with molasses, drunk esp. by fishermen and sealers at sea.
• [origin unknown]

switcheroo *noun*
• "switcha ROO"
• a change, reversal, or exchange, esp. a surprising or deceptive one.
• ['switch', probably from Low German]

swivel *noun*
• "SWIV'll"
• a fastening or coupling device between two parts enabling one to revolve without turning the other.
• [Middle English from Old English *swīfan* sweep]

sword *noun*
• "SORD"
• a weapon usu. of metal with a long blade and hilt with a hand guard, used esp. for thrusting or striking, and often worn as part of ceremonial dress.
• [Old English *sw(e)ord* from Germanic]

swordbearer *noun*
• "SORD bare ur"
• an official carrying the sovereign's etc. sword on a formal occasion.
• [as SWORD + 'bear' from Old English *beran*]

swordfern *noun*
• "SORD furn"
• any of several ferns with long narrow fronds, esp. the N American *Polystichum munitum* and the tropical *Nephrolepis exaltata*.
• [SWORD + 'fern' from Old English *fearn*]

swordfish *noun*
• "SORD fish"
• a large marine fish, *Xiphias gladius*, with an extended sword-like upper jaw.
• [SWORD + 'fish' from Old English *fisc*]

swordplay *noun*
• "SORD play"
• fencing.
• [SWORD + 'play' from Old English *pleg(i)an* (*v.*), originally = (to) exercise]

swordsman *noun*
• "SORDZ m'n"
• a person of (usu. specified) skill with a sword.
• [SWORD + 'man' from Old English]
• **swordsmanship** *noun*

swordtail *noun*
• "SORD tale"
• a tropical fish, *Xiphophorus helleri*, with a long tail.
• [SWORD + 'tail' from Old English *tægl*]

sybarite *noun*
• "SIBBA rite"
• a person who is self-indulgent or devoted to sensuous luxury.
• [originally an inhabitant of Sybaris in S Italy, noted for luxury, from Latin *sybarita* from Greek *subaritēs*]
• **sybaritic** *adjective* "sibba RITTIC"
• **sybaritical** *adjective*
• **sybaritically** *adverb*
• **sybaritism** *noun*

sycamine *noun*
• "SICKA min" or "SICKA mine"
• (in the Bible) the black mulberry tree, *Morus nigra*.
• [Latin *sycaminus* from Greek *sukaminos* mulberry tree, from Hebrew *šiḳmāh* sycamore, assimilated to Greek *sukon* fig]

sycamore *noun*
• "SICKA more"
• an eastern N American plane tree, *Platanus occidentalis*, having greyish-brown peeling bark.
• [Old French *sic(h)amor* from Latin *sycomorus* from Greek *sukomoros* from *sukon* fig + *moron* mulberry]

syce *noun*
ALSO SPELLED: **sice**
• "SICE" (rhymes with *ICE*)
• (esp. in India) a groom; a servant who looks after horses.
• [Persian, Urdu from Arabic *sā'is*, *sāyis*]

syconium *noun*
• "sye CONEY um"
• a fleshy hollow receptacle developing into a multiple fruit as in the fig.
• [modern Latin from Greek *sukon* fig]

sycophant *noun*
• "SICKA fant" or "SIKE a fant" or "SICKA f'nt" or "SIKE a f'nt"
• a person who acts obsequiously towards someone in order to gain advantage; a servile flatterer.
• [ultimately from Greek *sukophantēs* informer, from *sukon* fig + *phainō* show: the reason for the name is uncertain, and association with informing against the illegal exportation of figs from ancient Athens cannot be substantiated]
• **sycophancy** *noun*
• **sycophantic** *adjective*
• **sycophantically** *adverb*

Sydneyite *noun*
• "SID nee ite"
• a resident of Sydney, NS.

Sydneysider *noun*
• "SID nee sider"
• a resident of Sydney, Australia.

syenite *noun*
• "SYE 'n ite"
• a grey crystalline rock of feldspar and hornblende with or without quartz.
• [French *syénite* from Latin *Syenites* (*lapis*) (stone) of *Syene* in Egypt]
• **syenitic** *adjective* "sye 'n ITTIC"

syllabary *noun*
• "SILLA berry"
• a list of characters representing syllables and (in some languages or stages of writing) serving the purpose of an alphabet.
• [as SYLLABLE]

syllabication *noun*
• "sil abba CAY sh'n"
• division into or articulation by syllables.
• [as SYLLABLE]
• **syllabify** *verb*

syllabize *verb*
ALSO SPELLED: esp. *Brit.* **-ise**
• "SILLA bize"
• divide into or articulate by syllables.
• [as SYLLABLE]

syllable *noun*
• "SILLA bull"
• a unit of pronunciation uttered without interruption, forming the whole or a part of a word and usu. having one vowel sound often with a consonant or consonants before or after: there are two syllables in *water* and three in *inferno*.
• [Anglo-French *sillable* from Old French *sillabe* from Latin *syllaba* from Greek *sullabē* (as Greek *sun-* from *sun* with, *lambanō* take)]
• **syllabic** *adjective* "suh LABBIC"
• **syllabically** *adverb*
• **syllabicity** *noun* "silla BISSA tee"
• **syllabled** *adjective*

syllabub *noun*
• "SILLA bub"
• a drink made of milk mixed with wine, cider, rum, etc. and often sweetened, spiced, and served warm.
• [16th c.: origin unknown]

syllabus *noun*
• "SILLA buss"
• the program or outline of a course of study, teaching, etc.
• [modern Latin, originally a misreading of Latin *sittybas* accusative pl. of *sittyba* from Greek *sittuba* title slip or label]

syllepsis *noun*
• "sil EP sis"
• a figure of speech in which a word is applied to two others in different senses, e.g. *caught the train and a bad cold*, or to two others of which it grammatically suits one only, e.g. *neither they nor it is working*.
• [Late Latin from Greek *sullēpsis* taking together, from *sullambanō*: see SYLLABLE]
• **sylleptic** *adjective*

syllogism *noun*
• "SILLA jizm"
• a form of reasoning in which a conclusion is drawn from two given or assumed propositions (premises): a common or middle term is present in the two premises but not in the conclusion, which may be invalid, e.g. *all trains are long; some buses are long; therefore some buses are trains*: the common term is *long*.
• [Greek *sullogismos* from *sullogizomai* (as Greek *sun-* from *sun* with, *logizomai* to reason, from *logos* reason)]
• **syllogistic** *adjective*
• **syllogistically** *adverb*
• **syllogize** *verb* (also esp. *Brit.* **-ise**)

sylph *noun*
• "SILF"
• an elemental spirit of the air.
• [modern Latin *sylphes*, German *Sylphen* (pl.), perhaps based on Latin *sylvestris* of the woods + *nympha* nymph]
• **sylphlike** *adjective*

sylva *noun*
ALSO SPELLED: **silva**
• "SILVA"
• the trees of a region, epoch, or environment.
• [Latin *silva* a wood]

sylvan *adjective*
ALSO SPELLED: **silvan**
• "SILV'n"
• of the woods.
• [as SYLVA]

symbiont *noun*
• "SIM bee ont" or "SIM by ont"
• an organism living in symbiosis.
• [Greek *sumbiōn -ountos* participle of *sumbioō* live together (as SYMBIOSIS)]

symbiosis *noun*
• "sim bye OH sis" or "sim bee OH sis"
• an interaction between two different organisms living in close physical association, usu. to the advantage of both.
• [modern Latin from Greek *sumbiōsis* a living together, from *sumbioō* live together, *sumbios* companion (*sun* with, *bios* life)]
• **symbiotic** *adjective*
• **symbiotically** *adverb*

symbol *noun*
• "SIM bull"
• a thing conventionally regarded as typifying, representing, or recalling something, esp. an idea or quality.
• [Latin *symbolum* from Greek *sumbolon* mark, token (*sun* with, *ballō* throw)]
• **symbolic** *adjective*
• **symbolical** *adjective*
• **symbolically** *adverb*
• **symbolism** *noun*
• **symbolist** *noun*
• **symbolistic** *adjective*

• **symbolization** *noun* (also esp. *Brit.* **-isation**)
• **symbolize** *verb* (also esp. *Brit.* **-ise**)
HOMOPHONES: *cymbal*, *cymbalist*

symbology *noun*
• "sim BOLLA jee"
• the branch of knowledge that deals with the use of symbols.
• [as SYMBOL + Greek *logos* word]
• **symbological** *adjective*

symmetry *noun*
• "SIMMA tree"
• correct proportion of the parts of a thing; balance, harmony.
• [obsolete French *symmétrie* or Latin *summetria* from Greek (*sun* with, *metron* measure)]
• **symmetric** *adjective* "suh METRIC"
• **symmetrical** *adjective*
• **symmetrically** *adverb*
• **symmetrize** *verb* (also esp. *Brit.* **-ise**)

sympathectomy *noun*
• "simpa THECTA mee" (with "TH" as in *THIN*)
• the surgical removal of a sympathetic ganglion etc.
• [as SYMPATHY + Greek *ektomē* excision, from *ek* out + *temnō* cut]

sympathize *verb*
ALSO SPELLED: esp. *Brit.* **-ise**
• "SIMPA thize" (with "TH" as in *THIN*)
• feel or express sympathy; share a feeling or opinion.
• [as SYMPATHY]
• **sympathizer** *noun* (also esp. *Brit.* **-iser**)

sympathomimetic *adjective*
• "simpa tho muh METTIC"
• (of a drug) producing physiological effects characteristic of the sympathetic nervous system by promoting the stimulation of sympathetic nerves.
• [as SYMPATHY + MIMESIS]

sympathy *noun*
• "SIMPA thee" (with "TH" as in *THIN*)
• the act of sharing or tendency to share in an emotion or sensation or condition of another person or thing.
• [Latin *sympathia* from Greek *sumpatheia* (*sun* with, *pathēs* from *pathos* feeling)]
• **sympathetic** *adjective*
• **sympathetically** *adverb*

sympatric *adjective*
• "sim PATRICK"
• occurring within the same geographical area (compare ALLOPATRIC).
• [Greek *sun* with, *patra* fatherland]

sympetalous *adjective*
• "sim PETTA luss"
• having the petals united.
• [Greek *sun* with + PETAL]

symphonist *noun*
• "SIMF'n ist"
• a composer of symphonies.
• [as SYMPHONY]

symphony *noun*
• "SIM fuh nee"
• an elaborate composition usu. for full orchestra, and in several movements with one or more in sonata form.
• [Middle English, = harmony of sound, from Old French *symphonie* from Latin *symphonia* from Greek *sumphōnia* (*sun* with, *-phōnos* from *phōnē* sound)]
• **symphonic** *adjective*
• **symphonically** *adverb*

symphysis *noun*
• "SIM fuh sis"
• the process of growing together.
• [modern Latin from Greek *sumphusis* (*sun* with, *phusis* growth)]
• **symphyseal** *adjective* "sim FIZZY 'll"

sympodium *noun*
• "sim POE dee um"
• the apparent main axis or stem of a vine etc., made up of successive secondary axes.
• [modern Latin (from Greek *sun* with, Greek *pous podos* foot)]
• **sympodial** *adjective*

symposium *noun*
• "sim POZEY um"
• a conference or meeting to discuss a particular subject.
• [Latin from Greek *sumposion* (*sun* with, *-potēs* drinker)]

symptom *noun*
• "SIMP t'm"
• a change in the physical or mental condition of a person, regarded as evidence of a disorder.
• [Greek *sumptōma -atos* chance, symptom, from *sumpiptō* happen (*sun* with, *piptō* fall)]
• **symptomatic** *adjective*
• **symptomatically** *adverb*
• **symptomless** *adjective*

symptomatology *noun*
• "simpta muh TOLLA jee"
• the branch of medicine concerned with the study and interpretation of symptoms.
• [as SYMPTOM + Greek *logos* word]

synagogue *noun*
• "SINNA gog"
• the building where a Jewish assembly or congregation meets for religious observance and instruction.
• [Old French *sinagoge* from Late Latin *synagoga* from Greek *sunagōgē* meeting (*sun* with, *agō* bring)]
• **synagogal** *adjective*

synapomorphy *noun*
• "sin APPO morfy"
• the possession by two organisms of a characteristic (not necessarily the same in each)

that is derived from one characteristic in an organism from which they both evolved.
• [Greek *sun* with + *apo* from, away + *morphē* form]
• **synapomorphic** *adjective*

synapse *noun*
• "SIN aps" or "suh NAPS" or "SYE naps" or "sye NAPS"
• a junction of two nerve cells, consisting of a minute gap across which impulses pass by diffusion of a neurotransmitter.
• [Greek *synapsis* (*sun* with, *hapsis* from *haptō* join)]
• **synaptic** *adjective*
• **synaptically** *adverb*

sync *noun*
ALSO SPELLED: **synch**
• "SINK"
• synchronization.
• [abbreviation]
HOMOPHONES: *sink*

syncarpous *adjective*
• "sin CARP us"
• (of a flower or fruit) having the carpels united.
• [Greek *sun* with + *karpos* fruit]

synchro *noun*
• "SINK roe"
• a synchronizing device.
• [abbreviation]

synchrocyclotron *noun*
• "sink roe SIKE luh tron"
• a cyclotron able to achieve higher energies by decreasing the frequency of the accelerating electric field as the particles increase in energy and mass.
• [as SYNCHRONIZE + CYCLOTRON]

synchromesh *noun*
• "SINK roe mesh"
• a system of gear changing, esp. in motor vehicles, in which the driving and driven gearwheels are made to revolve at the same speed during engagement by means of a set of friction clutches, thereby easing the change.
• [abbreviation of *synchronized mesh*]

synchronic *adjective*
• "sing CRONNIC"
• describing a subject (esp. a language) as it exists at one point in time.
• [Late Latin *synchronus*: see SYNCHRONOUS]
• **synchronically** *adverb*

synchronicity *noun*
• "sink ruh NISSA tee"
• the simultaneous occurrence of events which appear significantly related but have no discernible connection.
• [as SYNCHRONIC]

synchronism *noun*
• "SINK ruh nizm"
• = SYNCHRONY.
• [Greek *sugkhronismos* (as SYNCHRONOUS)]
• **synchronistic** *adjective*
• **synchronistically** *adverb*

synchronize *verb*
ALSO SPELLED: esp. *Brit.* **-ise**
• "SINK ruh nize"
• cause to occur at the same time.
• [as SYNCHRONOUS]
• **synchronization** *noun* (also esp. *Brit.* **-isation**)
• **synchronizer** *noun* (also esp. *Brit.* **-iser**)

synchronous *adjective*
• "SINK ruh nuss"
• existing or occurring at the same time.
• [Late Latin *synchronus* from Greek *sugkhronos* (*sun* with, *khronos* time)]
• **synchronously** *adverb*

synchrony *noun*
• "SINK ruh nee"
• the state of being synchronic or synchronous.
• [as SYNCHRONOUS]

synchrotron *noun*
• "SINK ruh tron"
• a cyclotron in which the magnetic field strength increases with the energy of the particles to keep their orbital radius constant.
• [as SYNCHRONOUS + CYCLOTRON]

syncline *noun*
• "SINK line"
• a fold in rock from whose axis the strata incline upwards on either side.
• [Greek *sun* with, *klinō* lean]
• **synclinal** *adjective*
• **synclinally** *adverb*

syncopated *adjective*
• "SINKA pated"
• displace the beats or accents in (a passage) so that strong beats become weak and vice versa.
• [Late Latin *syncopare* swoon (as SYNCOPE)]
• **syncopation** *noun*
• **syncopator** *noun*

syncope *noun*
• "SINKA pee"
• the omission of interior sounds or letters in a word.
• [Late Latin *syncopē* from Greek *sugkopē* (*sun* with, *koptō* strike, cut off)]
• **syncopal** *adjective*

syncretism *noun*
• "SINK ruh tizm"
• the process or an instance of attempting to unify or reconcile differing schools of thought, religions, etc.
• [modern Latin *syncretismus* from Greek *sugkrētismos*, from *sugkrētizō* (of two parties) 'combine against a third' (*sun* with, *krēs* Cretan, originally of ancient Cretan communities)]
• **syncretic** *adjective* "sin CRETTIC"
• **syncretist** *noun*

- **syncretistic** *adjective*
- **syncretize** *verb* (also esp. *Brit.* **-ise**)

syncytium *noun*
- "sin SITTY um"
- a mass of cytoplasm with several nuclei, not divided into separate cells.
- [Greek *sun* with, *kutos* vessel]
- **syncytial** *adjective*

syndactyly *noun*
- "sin DACK til ee"
- the condition of having some or all of the fingers or toes wholly or partly united as in webbed feet etc.
- [Greek *sun* with + *daktulos* finger]

syndic *noun*
- "SIN dick"
- a government official in various countries.
- [French from Late Latin *syndicus* from Greek *sundikos* (*sun* with, *-dikos* from *dikē* justice)]
- **syndical** *adjective*

syndicalism *noun*
- "SIN dick'll izm"
- a movement for transferring the ownership and control of the means of production and distribution to workers' unions.
- [French *syndicalisme* from *syndical* (as SYNDIC)]
- **syndicalist** *noun*

syndicate *noun*
- "SIN duh kit"
- a combination of individuals or commercial firms to promote some common interest.
- [French *syndicat* from medieval Latin *syndicatus* from Late Latin *syndicus*: see SYNDIC]

syndication *noun*
- "sin duh CAY sh'n"
- the practice of making television or radio programs available to independent broadcasters.
- [as SYNDICATE]

syndrome *noun*
- "SIN drome" or "SIN drum"
- a group of symptoms or pathological signs which consistently occur together.
- [modern Latin from Greek *sundromē* (*sun* with, *dromē* from *dramein* to run)]
- **syndromic** *adjective* "sin DROMMIC"

synecdoche *noun*
- "suh NECK duh key"
- a figure of speech in which a part is made to represent the whole or vice versa, e.g. *new faces at the meeting; Italy won by two goals.*
- [Latin from Greek *sunekdokhē* (*sun* with, *ekdokhē* from *ekdekhomai* take up)]
- **synecdochic** *adjective* "sin eck DOCKIC"
- **synecdochical** *adjective*
- **synecdochically** *adverb*

syneresis *noun*
ALSO SPELLED: **synaeresis**
- "suh NEERA sis"
- the contraction of two vowels into a diphthong or single vowel.
- [Late Latin from Greek *sunairesis* (*sun* with, *hairesis* from *haireō* take)]

synergist *noun*
- "SINNER jist"
- a substance, organ, or other agent that participates in an effect of synergy.
- [as SYNERGY]

synergy *noun*
- "SINNER jee"
- the interaction or co-operation of two or more drugs, agents, organizations, etc., to produce an effect that exceeds or enhances the sum of their individual effects.
- [Greek *sunergos* working together (*sun* with, *ergon* work)]
- **synergetic** *adjective*
- **synergistic** *adjective*
- **synergistically** *adverb*
- **synergize** *verb* (also esp. *Brit.* **-ise**)

synesthesia *noun*
ALSO SPELLED: **synaesthesia**
- "sin us THEE zhuh" or "sin us THEEZY uh" (with "TH" as in *THIN*)
- the production of a mental sense impression relating to one sense by the stimulation of another sense, as in the association of certain sounds with colours.
- [modern Latin from Greek *sun* with, after *anaesthesia*]
- **synesthetic** *adjective* (also **synaesthetic**)

syngamy *noun*
- "SING guh mee"
- the fusion of gametes or nuclei in reproduction.
- [Greek *sun*, *gamos* marriage]

synod *noun*
- "SIN id"
- a church council attended by delegated clergy and sometimes laity.
- [Late Latin *synodus* from Greek *sunodos* meeting (*sun* with, *hodos* way)]
- **synodal** *adjective*
- **synodical** *adjective* "sin ODDA k'll"

synodic *adjective*
- "sin ODDIC"
- relating to or involving the conjunction of stars, planets, etc.
- [as SYNOD]

synonym *noun*
- "SINNA nim"
- a word or phrase that means exactly or nearly the same as another in the same language, e.g. *shut* and *close.*
- [Latin *synonymum* from Greek *sunōnumon* neuter of *sunōnumos* (*sun* with, *onoma* name): compare ANONYMOUS]
- **synonymic** *adjective*
- **synonymity** *noun*

- **synonymous** *adjective* "sin ONNA muss"
- **synonymously** *adverb*
- **synonymy** *noun* "sin ONNA mee"

synopsis *noun*
- "sin OP sis"
- a summary or outline.
- [Late Latin from Greek (*sun* with, *opsis* seeing)]
- **synopsize** *verb* (also esp. *Brit.* **-ise**)
- **synoptic** *adjective*
- **synoptical** *adjective*
- **synoptically** *adverb*

synovial *adjective*
- "sye NO vee 'll"
- denoting or relating to a viscous fluid lubricating joints and tendon sheaths.
- [modern Latin *synovia*, formed probably arbitrarily by Paracelsus (d.1541)]

synovitis *noun*
- "sye no VITE iss" or "sinno VITE iss"
- inflammation of the synovial membrane.
- [as SYNOVIAL + Greek *-itis*, forming feminine of adjectives in *-itēs* (with *nosos* 'disease' implied)]

syntagma *noun*
- "sin TAG muh"
- a word or phrase forming a syntactic unit.
- [Late Latin from Greek *suntagma* (as SYNTAX)]
- **syntagmatic** *adjective*
- **syntagmatically** *adverb*

syntax *noun*
- "SIN tax"
- the order of words in which they convey meaning collectively by their connection and relation.
- [French *syntaxe* or Late Latin *syntaxis* from Greek *suntaxis* (*sun* with, *taxis* from *tassō* arrange)]
- **syntactic** *adjective* "sin TACTIC"
- **syntactical** *adjective*
- **syntactically** *adverb*

synthase *noun*
- "SIN thace" (with "TH" as in *THIN*)
- an enzyme which catalyzes the linking together of two molecules, esp. without the direct involvement of ATP.
- [as SYNTHESIS]

synthesis *noun*
- "SINTHA sis"
- the process or result of building up separate elements, esp. ideas, into a connected whole, esp. into a theory or system.
- [Latin from Greek *sunthesis* (*sun* with, THESIS)]
- **synthesist** *noun*

synthesize *verb*
ALSO SPELLED: esp. *Brit.* **-ise**
- "SINTHA size"
- make (something) by synthesis, esp. chemically.
- [as SYNTHESIS]

synthesizer *noun*
ALSO SPELLED: esp. *Brit.* **-iser**
- "SINTHA sizer"
- an electronic musical instrument, esp. operated by a music keyboard, producing a wide variety of sounds by generating and combining signals of different frequencies.
- [as SYNTHESIS]
- **synthesist** *noun*

synthespian *noun*
- "sin THESS pee 'n"
- a computer-generated character who may appear to interact with human actors in a film, or as part of an animated film using only such characters.
- [blend of SYNTHETIC + THESPIAN]

synthetase *noun*
- "SINTHA tace"
- an enzyme which catalyzes a particular synthesis, esp. a ligase or a synthase.
- [as SYNTHETIC]

synthetic *adjective*
- "sin THETTIC"
- made by chemical synthesis, esp. to imitate a natural product.
- [Greek *sunthetikos* from *sunthetos* from *suntithēmi* (*sun* with, *tithēmi* put)]
- **synthetical** *adjective*
- **synthetically** *adverb*

Syrah *noun*
- "SEERA"
- a variety of black grape used in winemaking, grown originally in the Rhone valley of France, now also esp. in Australia and South Africa.
- [French, earlier *sirrah*: see SHIRAZ, where the early form *scyras* may have influenced the spelling]

Syriac *noun*
- "SEERY ack"
- the language of ancient Syria, western Aramaic, now only in liturgical use in the Maronite and Syrian Catholic Churches, the Syrian Jacobite Church, and the Nestorian Church.

Syrian *noun*
- "SEERY 'n"
- a native or inhabitant of Syria in the Middle East.

syringa *noun*
ALSO SPELLED: **seringa**
- "suh RING guh"
- any of various white-flowered, heavy-scented shrubs, esp. *Philadelphus coronarius*; mock orange.
- [modern Latin, formed as SYRINX (with reference to the use of its stems as pipestems)]

syringe *noun*
- "suh RINJ"
- a tube with a nozzle and piston or bulb for sucking in and ejecting liquid in a fine stream.
- [medieval Latin *syringa* (as SYRINX)]

syrinx *noun*
- "SUR inks"
- a set of pan pipes.
- [Latin *syrinx -ngis* from Greek *surigx suriggos* pipe, channel]
- **syringeal** *adjective* "suh RINJY 'll"

syrphid *adjective*
- "SUR fid"
- of or relating to the dipteran family Syrphidae, which includes the hoverflies.
- [modern Latin *Syrphidae* from the genus name *Syrphis*, from Greek *surphos* gnat]

syrup *noun*
ALSO SPELLED: *US* also **sirup**
- "SUR up"
- any of various very sweet liquids used e.g. as a topping, to flavour a drink, to preserve canned fruit, as a form of medicine, etc.
- [Old French *sirop* or medieval Latin *siropus* from Arabic *šarāb* beverage]
- **syrupy** *adjective* (also *US* **sirupy**)

system *noun*
- "SIST'm"
- a complex whole; a set of connected things, parts, institutions, etc.; an organized body of material or immaterial things.
- [Greek *sustēma -atos* (*sun* with, *histēmi* set up)]
- **systemless** *adjective*

systematic *adjective*
- "sista MATTIC"
- methodical; done or conceived according to a plan or system.
- [as SYSTEM]
- **systematically** *adverb*

systematics *noun*
- "sista MATTIX"
- the study or a system of classification; taxonomy.
- [as SYSTEM]

systematist *noun*
- "SISTA muh tist" or "sis TEMMA tist"
- a person who constructs or follows an esp. biological classification.
- [as SYSTEM]
- **systematism** *noun*

systematize *verb*
ALSO SPELLED: esp. *Brit.* **-ise**
- "SIST'm a tize"
- make systematic.
- [as SYSTEM]
- **systematization** *noun* (also esp. *Brit.* **-isation**)
- **systematizer** *noun* (also esp. *Brit.* **-iser**)

systemic *adjective*
- "sis TEMMIC"
- of or concerning the whole body, not confined to a particular part.
- [as SYSTEM]
- **systemically** *adverb*

systemize *verb*
ALSO SPELLED: esp. *Brit.* **-ise**
- "SIST'm ize"
- make systematic.
- [as SYSTEM]
- **systemization** *noun* (also esp. *Brit.* **-isation**)
- **systemizer** *noun* (also esp. *Brit.* **-iser**)

systole *noun*
- "SISTA lee"
- the contraction of the heart, when blood is pumped into the arteries.
- [Late Latin from Greek *sustolē* from *sustellō* contract]
- **systolic** *adjective* "sis TAW lick"

syzygy *noun*
- "SIZZA jee"
- conjunction or opposition, esp. of the moon with the sun.
- [Late Latin *syzygia* from Greek *suzugia* from *suzugos* yoked, paired (*sun* with, *zugon* yoke)]

Szechuan *noun*
ALSO SPELLED: **Szechwan**
- "SETCH wahn" or "SESH wahn" or "setch WAHN" or "sesh WAHN"
- designating food cooked in the distinctively spicy style of cuisine originating in Szechuan (also called *Sichuan*) in central China.

Tt

tabard *noun*
- "TAB'rd"
- a herald's official coat emblazoned with the arms of the sovereign.
- [Old French *tabart*, of unknown origin]

tabbouleh *noun*
- "tuh BOO lee"
- a Syrian and Lebanese salad made with bulgur, parsley, onion, mint, lemon juice, oil, and spices.
- [Arabic *tabbūla*]

Taberite *noun*
- "TAY bur ite"
- a resident of Taber, Alta.

tabernacle *noun*
- "TABBER nack'll"
- a tent used as a sanctuary for the Ark of the Covenant by the Israelites during the Exodus.
- [Old French from Latin *tabernaculum* tent, diminutive of *taberna* hut]

tabla *noun*
- "TAB luh" or "TOB luh"
- (in Indian music) a pair of small drums played with the hands.
- [Persian and Urdu *tablah*, Hindi *tablā*, from Arabic *ṭabl* drum]

tablature *noun*
- "TABLA chur"
- a form of notation, esp. for the guitar or the lute, in which lines, figures, and letters are used, e.g. with parallel lines representing the strings and numbers indicating the frets to be fingered.
- [French from Italian *tavolatura*, from *tavolare* set to music]

tableau *noun*
- "TAB lo" or "tab LO"
- a picturesque presentation.
- [French, = picture, diminutive of *table* from Latin *tabula* plank, tablet, list]

taboo *noun*
ALSO SPELLED: **tabu**
- "tuh BOO" or "tab OO"
- a system or the act of setting a person or thing apart as sacred or accursed.
- [Tongan *tabu*]

tabor *noun*
- "TAY bur"
- a small drum, esp. one used to accompany a pipe.
- [Old French *tabour*, *tabur*: compare TABLA, Persian *tabīra* drum]

tabular *adjective*
- "TAB yuh lur"
- of or arranged in tables or lists.
- [Latin *tabularis* (as TABLEAU)]
- **tabularly** *adverb*

tabulate *verb*
- "TAB yuh late"
- arrange (figures or facts) in tabular form.
- [Late Latin *tabulare tabulat-* from *tabula* table]
- **tabulation** *noun*
- **tabulator** *noun*

tabun *noun*
- "TAW boon" (with "OO" as in *BOOK*)
- an organic phosphorus compound used as a nerve gas.
- [German]

tacamahac *noun*
- "TACKA muh hack"
- a resinous gum obtained from certain tropical trees esp. of the genus *Calophyllum*.
- [obsolete Spanish *tacamahaca* from Aztec *tecomahiyac*]

tacet *verb*
- "TASS it" or "TAY sit"
- an instruction for a particular voice or instrument to be silent.
- [Latin, = is silent]

HOMOPHONES: *tacit*

tachism *noun*
- "TASH izm"
- a form of action painting with dabs of colour arranged randomly to evoke a subconscious feeling.
- [French *tachisme* from *tache* stain]
- **tachist** *noun*

tachograph *noun*
- "TACKA graff"
- a device used esp. in transport trucks and buses etc. for automatically recording speed and travel time.
- [Greek *takhos* speed + Greek *graphia* writing]

tachometer *noun*
• "tuh COMMA tur"
• an instrument for measuring the rate of rotation of a shaft and hence the speed or velocity of a vehicle.
• [Greek *takhos* speed + *metron* measure]

tachycardia *noun*
• "tacky CARDY uh"
• an abnormally rapid heart rate.
• [Greek *takhus* swift, *kardia* heart]

tachygraphy *noun*
• "tuh KIGGRA fee"
• stenography, esp. that of the ancient Greeks and Romans.
• [Greek *takhus* swift, *graphia* writing]

tachyon *noun*
• "TACKY on"
• a hypothetical particle that travels faster than light.
• [Greek *takhus* swift]

tacit *adjective*
• "TASS it"
• understood or implied without being stated.
• [Latin *tacitus* silent, from *tacēre* be silent]
• **tacitly** *adverb*
HOMOPHONES: *tacet*

taciturn *adjective*
• "TASSA turn"
• reserved in speech; saying little; uncommunicative.
• [French *taciturne* or Latin *taciturnus* (as TACIT)]
• **taciturnity** *noun*
• **taciturnly** *adverb*

taco *noun*
• "TOCKO" or "TACKO"
• a fried corn tortilla folded over and filled with ground meat, tomatoes, lettuce, shredded cheese, guacamole, etc.
• [Latin American Spanish]

taconite *noun*
• "TACKA nite"
• a type of chert used as an iron ore in parts of N America.
• [*Taconic* Range of mountains in eastern New York State + Greek *lithos* stone]

tacrine *noun*
• "TACK reen"
• a synthetic drug used in Alzheimer's disease to inhibit the breakdown of acetylcholine by cholinesterase and thereby enhance neurological function.
• [from Greek *tetra* four + ACRIDINE]

taffeta *noun*
• "TAFFA tuh"
• a fine lustrous silk or silk-like fabric.
• [Old French *taffetas* or medieval Latin *taffata*, ultimately from Persian *tāfta* past participle of *tāftan* twist]

taffrail *noun*
• "TAFF rale"
• the upper part of the flat portion of a ship's stern above the transom.
• [earlier *tafferel* from Dutch *taffereel* panel, diminutive of *tafel* table: assimilated to 'rail']

tafia *noun*
• "TAFFY uh"
• rum distilled from molasses etc.
• [18th c.: origin uncertain]

Tagalog *noun*
• "tuh GAL og"
• the language of the Philippine Islands.
• [Tagalog from *taga* native + *ilog* river]

tagetes *noun*
• "tuh JEE teez"
• any plant of the genus *Tagetes*, esp. any of various marigolds with bright orange or yellow flowers.
• [modern Latin from Latin *Tages* an Etruscan god]

Tagish *noun*
• "TAG ish"
• a member of an Aboriginal people living esp. in the southern Yukon Territory.
• [Tagish, = 'fish trap']

tagliatelle *noun*
• "tal yuh TELLY"
• a type of pasta made in narrow ribbons.
• [Italian, from *tagliare* to cut]

tahini *noun*
• "tuh HEENY"
• a paste or sauce made from ground sesame seeds.
• [modern Greek *takhini*, from Arab *ṭaḥīnā*, from *ṭaḥana* grind, crush]

Tahitian *noun*
• "tuh HEE sh'n" or "tuh HEETY 'n"
• a native or inhabitant of the island of Tahiti in the S Pacific.

Tahltan *noun*
• "TAWL tan"
• a member of an Aboriginal people living in the area of the Stikine River, BC.
• [origin uncertain]

tahr *noun*
• "TAR"
• any goatlike mammal of the genus *Hemitragus*, esp. *H. jemlahicus* of the Himalayas.
• [Local (Himalayan) name]
HOMOPHONES: *tar*

tahsil *noun*
• "ta SEEL"
• (in the Indian subcontinent) an administrative division comprising several villages, formerly esp. for revenue administration.
• [Urdu *taḥṣīl* from Arabic, = collection]

taiga *noun*
• "TIE guh"
• any of the swampy coniferous forests of subarctic N America, Europe, and Asia, usu. lying between Arctic tundra to the north and aspen parkland or steppe to the south; the boreal forest.
• [Russian]

taiko *noun*
• "TIKE oh"
• any of a variety of Japanese two-headed drums made of a hollow wooden shell the opening of which is covered with cowhide.
• [Japanese *tai* big + *ko* drum]

tailor *noun*
• "TAY lur"
• a person who alters clothing and makes suits and jackets etc. to measure.
• [Old French *tailleur* cutter, from *taillier* cut, ultimately from Latin *talea* twig]
• **tailored** *adjective*
• **tailoring** *noun*

Taino *adjective*
• "TIE no"
• designating or pertaining to an extinct Arawak people formerly inhabiting the Greater Antilles and the Bahamas in the West Indies.
• [Taino *taino* noble, lord]

taipan *noun*
• "TIE pan"
• the head of a foreign business in China.
• [Chinese]

Taiwanese *noun*
• "tie wonn EEZ"
• a native or inhabitant of Taiwan.

Taizé *noun*
• "TAY zay"
• a style of Christian worship characterized by the repetitive singing of simple harmonized tunes interspersed with reading, prayers, and periods of silence.
• [the name of a village in Burgundy, France, the site of an ecumenical Christian community founded in 1948]

Tajik *noun*
ALSO SPELLED: **Tadzhik**
• "taw JEEK"
• a native or inhabitant of the republic of Tajikistan in central Asia.
• [Persian, = 'someone who is neither an Arab nor a Turk']

tajine *noun*
ALSO SPELLED: **tagine**
• "ta ZHEEN"
• a traditional shallow earthenware Moroccan cooking pot with a conical lid.
• [French from Arabic *ṭagīn*, perhaps ultimately from Greek]

taka *noun*
• "TACKA"
• the basic monetary unit of Bangladesh, equal to 100 poisha.
• [Bengali]

takin *noun*
• "TACK in"
• a large shaggy horned ruminant, *Budorcas taxicolor*, of Tibet, Bhutan, and northern Burma (Myanmar), related to the muskox.
• [local Tibeto-Burman name]

tala *noun*
• "TAL uh"
• any of the traditional rhythmic patterns of Indian music.
• [Sanskrit *tāla* hand clapping]

talaria *plural noun*
• "tuh LERRY uh"
• winged sandals or small wings attached to the ankles of some gods and goddesses, such as Mercury and Iris.
• [Latin, neuter pl. of *talaris* from *talus* ankle]

talc *noun*
• "TALC" (with "AL" as in *PAL*)
• a monoclinic hydrated silicate of magnesium occurring as white, grey, or pale green masses or translucent laminae that are very soft and have a greasy feel, used esp. as a lubricant.
• [French *talc* or medieval Latin *talcum*, from Arabic *ṭalḳ* from Persian *ṭalk*]
• **talcy** *adjective* "TAL kee"

talcum *noun*
• "TAL k'm"
• a preparation of powdered talc, usu. scented or medicated for general cosmetic use.
• [medieval Latin: see TALC]

Taleggio *noun*
• "tuh LEDGY oh"
• a type of soft Italian cheese made from cow's milk.
• [Italian, from the name of the *Taleggio* valley in Lombardy]

tales *noun*
• "TAY leez"
• a writ for summoning jurors to supply a deficiency.
• [Latin *tales* (*de circumstantibus*) such (of the bystanders), the first words of the writ]

talesman *noun*
• "TAY luss m'n" or "TAILZ m'n"
• a person summoned by a *tales*.
• [as TALES]

talipes *noun*
• "TALA peez"
• a congenitally deformed foot, usu. turned downward and inward so that the person walks on the outer edge of the foot; a club foot.
• [modern Latin from Latin *talus* ankle + *pes* foot]

talipot *noun*
• "TALA pot"
• a tall S Indian palm, *Corypha umbraculifera*, with very large fan-shaped leaves that are used as sunshades etc.
• [Malayalam *tālipat*, Hindi *tālpāt* from Sanskrit *tālapattra* from *tāla* palm + *pattra* leaf]

talisman *noun*
• "TAL iz m'n" or "TAL iss m'n"
• an object, esp. an inscribed ring or stone, supposed to be endowed with magic powers esp. of averting evil from or bringing good luck to its holder.
• [French & Spanish, = Italian *talismano*, from medieval Greek *telesmon*, Greek *telesma* completion, religious rite, from *teleō* complete, from *telos* end]
• **talismanic** *adjective*
• **talismanically** *adverb*

tallis *noun*
• "TAL iss"
• a shawl worn by Jewish men, esp. at prayer.
• [Rabbinical Hebrew *ṭallīt* from *ṭillel* to cover]

Talmud *noun*
• "TALL mood" or "TAL mood" ("MOOD" rhymes with *GOOD*)
• the body of Jewish civil and ceremonial law and legend comprising the Mishnah and the Gemara.
• [late Hebrew *talmûḏ* instruction, from Hebrew *lāmaḏ* learn]
• **Talmudic** *adjective*
• **Talmudical** *adjective*
• **Talmudist** *noun*

talon *noun*
• "TAL 'n"
• a claw of an animal, esp. of a bird or beast of prey.
• [Old French, = heel, ultimately from Latin *talus*: see TALUS]
• **taloned** *adjective*

talus *noun*
• "TAY luss"
• a small bone in the foot, articulating with the tibia to form the ankle joint.
• [Latin, = ankle, heel]

tamale *noun*
• "tuh MOLLY" or "tuh MALLY"
• a Mexican food of seasoned ground meat wrapped in cornmeal dough and steamed or baked in corn husks.
• [Latin American Spanish *tamal*, pl. *tamales*]

tamandua *noun*
• "tuh MAND yoo uh"
• any small Central and South American arboreal anteater of the genus *Tamandua*, with a prehensile tail used in climbing.
• [Portuguese from Tupi *tamanduà*]

tamarack *noun*
• "TAMMA rack"
• any of several N American larches, esp. *Larix laricina*, found in wet places across most of Canada.
• [Canadian French *tamarac*, prob. from Algonquian]

tamari *noun*
• "tuh MAR ee"
• a Japanese variety of rich wheat-free soy sauce.
• [Japanese]

tamarin *noun*
• "TAMMER in"
• any of numerous small neotropical monkeys with fine silky coats and long bushy tails which belong to the genera *Saguinus* and *Leontopithecus*, and together with marmosets constitute the family Callithricidae.
• [French from Carib]

tamarind *noun*
• "TAMMER ind"
• the fruit of the tree *Tamarindus indica*, a brown pod containing one to twelve seeds embedded in a soft brown sticky acid pulp, valued for its laxative qualities and also used to make esp. chutney and cold drinks.
• [medieval Latin *tamarindus* from Arabic *tamr-hindī* Indian date]

tamarisk *noun*
• "TAMMER isk"
• any shrub of the genus *Tamarix*, usu. with long slender branches and small pink or white flowers, that thrives by the sea.
• [Late Latin *tamariscus*, Latin *tamarix*]

tambala *noun*
• "tam BOLLA" ("BOLL" rhymes with *DOLL*)
• a monetary unit of Malawi, equal to one-hundredth of a kwacha.
• [Nyanja, lit. = 'cockerel']

tambour *noun*
• "TAM bur"
• a flexible sliding shutter or door on a desk, cabinet, etc., made of strips of wood attached to a canvas backing.
• [French from *tabour* TABOR]
• **tamboured** *adjective*
HOMOPHONES: *timbre*

tamboura *noun*
ALSO SPELLED: **tambura**
• "tam BOORA" (with "OO" as in *BOOK*)
• a long-necked fretless type of lute with a round body and usu. four wire strings, used to provide a drone accompaniment in Indian music.
• [Arabic *ṭanbūra*]

tambourine *noun*
• "tam buh REEN"
• a musical instrument consisting of a hoop with a skin stretched over one side and pairs of small jingling discs in slots around the

circumference, played by shaking, striking, or drawing the fingers across the skin.
• [French, diminutive of TAMBOUR]

Tamil *noun*
• "TAM'il"
• a member of a Dravidian people inhabiting the southern Indian subcontinent and parts of Sri Lanka.
• [Tamil]
• **Tamilian** *noun*

tamoxifen *noun*
• "tuh MOX if en"
• a drug which acts as an estrogen antagonist, used to treat breast cancer and infertility in women.
• [arbitrary formation based on *trans*, *amine*, *oxy-*, *phenol*, parts of the drug's chemical name]

tampion *noun*
• "TAMPY 'n"
• a wooden stopper for the muzzle of a gun.
• [Old French *tampon*, nasalized var. of *tapon*]

tamponade *noun*
• "tampa NADE"
• compression of the heart by an accumulation of fluid in the pericardial sac.
• [as TAMPION]

tanager *noun*
• "TANNA jur"
• any small New World bird of the subfamily Thraupinae, the male usu. having brightly coloured plumage.
• [modern Latin *tanagra* from Tupi *tangara*]

tandoor *noun*
• "TAN door" (with "OO" as in *BOOK*)
• a clay oven of a kind used originally in N India and Pakistan.
• [Urdu]

tandoori *noun*
• "tan DOORY" (with "OO" as in *BOOK*)
• a style of Indian cooking based on the use of a tandoor.
• [Urdu, Persian, Arabic]

tangelo *noun*
• "TANJA lo"
• a hybrid citrus fruit, a cross between a tangerine and a grapefruit or pomelo.
• [TANGERINE + POMELO]

tangent *noun*
• "TAN j'nt"
• a straight line touching a curve or curved surface so that it meets it at a point but does not intersect it at that point.
• [Latin *tangere tangent-* touch]
• **tangency** *noun*
• **tangential** *adjective* "tan JEN sh'll"
• **tangentially** *adverb*

tangerine *noun*
• "tan juh REEN"
• a mandarin orange, esp. one with a sweeter or tangier flavour and darker colour of peel.
• [originally *tangerine orange* from *Tanger* (former name of *Tangier*, Morocco)]

tangible *adjective*
• "TAN juh bull"
• perceptible by touch; having material form.
• [French *tangible* or Late Latin *tangibilis*, from *tangere* touch]
• **tangibility** *noun*
• **tangibly** *adverb*

tanist *noun*
• "TANNIST"
• the heir apparent to a Celtic chief, usu. his most vigorous adult relation, chosen by election.
• [Irish & Gaelic *tánaiste* heir]
• **tanistry** *noun*

tankard *noun*
• "TANK'rd"
• a tall mug with a handle and sometimes a hinged lid, esp. of silver or pewter for beer.
• [Middle English: origin unknown: compare Middle Dutch *tanckaert*]

tannin *noun*
• "TAN in"
• any of a group of complex organic compounds found in tea, certain tree barks, and oak galls, used in leather production and as a mordant and astringent.
• [French *tanin* prob. from medieval Latin *tanare*, *tannare* tan]
• **tannate** *noun*
• **tannic** *adjective*

tansy *noun*
• "TANZY"
• any plant of the genus *Tanacetum*, esp. *T. vulgare* with yellow button-like flowers and aromatic leaves, formerly used in medicines and cookery.
• [Old French *tanesie* from medieval Latin *athanasia* immortality, from Greek]

tantalite *noun*
• "TANTA lite"
• a rare dense black mineral, the principal source of the element tantalum.
• [as TANTALUM + Greek *lithos* stone]

tantalum *noun*
• "TANTA lum"
• a rare hard white metallic element occurring naturally in tantalite, resistant to heat and the action of acids, and used in surgery and for electronic components.
• [formed as TANTALUS with reference to its non-absorbent quality]

tantalus *noun*
• "TANTA luss"
• a stand in which decanters may be locked up but visible.
• [*Tantalus*, who in Greek mythology was

punished in the underworld by being provided with fruit and water which receded when he reached for them]

tantamount *adjective*
• "TANTA mount"
• equivalent to.
• [from obsolete verb *tantamount* from Italian *tanto montare* 'amount to so much']

Tanzanian *noun*
• "tanza NEE 'n"
• a native or inhabitant of Tanzania in E Africa.

Tao *noun*
• "TOW" or "DOW" (rhymes with *COW*)
• (in Taoism) the absolute being or principle underlying the universe; ultimate reality.
• [Chinese *dào* way, path, right way (of life), reason]
HOMOPHONES: *tau, dhow*

Taoiseach *noun*
• "TEE shuck"
• the prime minister of the Irish Republic.
• [Irish, = chief, leader]

Taoism *noun*
• "TOW izm" or "DOW izm" ("TOW" and "DOW" rhyme with *COW*)
• a Chinese philosophy based on the writings of Lao-tzu (fl. 6th c. BC), advocating humility and religious piety.
• [Chinese *dao* (right) way]
• **Taoist** *noun*
• **Taoistic** *adjective*

tapa *noun*
• "TAPPA"
• the bark of a paper mulberry tree.
• [Polynesian]

tapas *plural noun*
• "TAP us"
• small savoury Spanish appetizers, esp. served with wine or beer.
• [Spanish]

tapenade *noun*
• "tappa NOD"
• a Provençal dish, usu. served as an hors d'oeuvre, made mainly from puréed black olives, capers, and anchovies.
• [French, from Provençal *tapeno* caper]

tapestry *noun*
• "TAP us tree"
• a thick textile fabric in which coloured weft threads are woven to form pictures or designs.
• [Old French *tapisserie* from *tapis* from Late Latin *tapetium* from Greek *tapētion* diminutive of *tapēs tapētos* tapestry]
• **tapestried** *adjective*

tapetum *noun*
• "tuh PEET um"
• a light-reflecting part of the choroid membrane in the eyes of certain mammals, e.g. cats.
• [Late Latin from Latin *tapete* carpet]

taphonomy *noun*
• "ta FONNA mee"
• the science concerned with the process of fossilization.
• [Greek *taphos* grave + Greek *-nomia* denoting an area of knowledge or the laws governing it, related to *nomos* law]
• **taphonomic** *adjective* "taffa NOMMIC"
• **taphonomist** *noun*

tapioca *noun*
• "tappy OH kuh"
• a starchy substance in hard white grains obtained from cassava and used for puddings etc.
• [Tupi-Guarani *tipioca* from *tipi* dregs + *og, ok* squeeze out]

tapir *noun*
• "TAPER" or "TAY peer"
• any nocturnal hoofed mammal of the genus *Tapirus*, native to Central and South America and Malaysia, having a short flexible protruding snout used for feeding on vegetation.
• [Tupi *tapira*]
• **tapiroid** *adjective*
HOMOPHONES: *taper*

tappet *noun*
• "TAP it"
• a lever or projecting part used in machinery to give intermittent motion, often in conjunction with a cam.
• [apparently from 'tap' (strike lightly)]

taqueria *noun*
• "tocka REE uh"
• a Mexican restaurant specializing in tacos.
• [Mexican Spanish]

tarabish *noun*
• "TAR bish"
• *Cdn* (*Cape Breton*) a card game based on bridge.
• [origin unknown]

taradiddle *noun*
ALSO SPELLED: **tarradiddle**
• "TERRA did'll"
• a petty lie.
• [origin uncertain]

taramasalata *noun*
• "terra muh suh LATTA"
• a pinkish pâté made from the roe of mullet or other fish with olive oil, seasoning, etc.
• [modern Greek *taramas* roe (from Turkish *tarama*) + *salata* salad]

tarantella *noun*
• "tare 'n TELLA"
• a rapid whirling southern Italian dance in 6/8 time.
• [Italian, from *Taranto* in SE Italy (because the dance was once thought to be a cure for a tarantula bite): compare TARANTULA]

tarantism *noun*
• "TARE 'nt izm"
• dancing mania, esp. that originating in

S Italy among those who had (actually or supposedly) been bitten by a tarantula.
• [Italian *tarantismo* from *Taranto* in SE Italy; compare TARANTULA]

tarantula *noun*
• "tuh RAN choo luh"
• any large hairy tropical spider of the family Theraphosidae, some of which are venomous.
• [Old Italian *tarantola*, from *Taranto* in SE Italy]

tarboosh *noun*
• "tar BOOSH"
• a cap like a fez, sometimes worn as part of a turban.
• [Egyptian Arabic *ṭarbūš*, ultimately from Persian *sar-būš* head covering]

tardigrade *noun*
• "TARDA grade"
• any minute freshwater invertebrate of the phylum Tardigrada, having a short plump body and four pairs of short legs.
• [French *tardigrade* from Latin *tardigradus* from *tardus* slow + *gradi* walk]

tare *noun*
• "TARE"
• the weight of a wrapping, container, or receptacle in which goods are packed.
• [French, = deficiency, tare, from medieval Latin *tara* from Arabic *ṭarḥa* what is rejected, from *ṭaraḥa* reject]
HOMOPHONES: *tear*

tariff *noun*
• "TARE if" or "TA riff"
• a duty on a particular class of imports or exports.
• [French *tarif* from Italian *tariffa* from Turkish *tarife* from Arabic *ta'rīf(a)* from *'arrafa* notify]
HOMOPHONES: *teraph*

tarlatan *noun*
• "TARLA t'n"
• a thin stiff open-weave muslin.
• [French *tarlatane*, prob. of Indian origin]

tarmac *noun*
• "TAR mack"
• = TARMACADAM.
• [abbreviation]

tarmacadam *noun*
• "tarma CAD'm"
• a material of stone or slag bound with tar, used in paving roads etc.
• ['tar' + MACADAM]

taro *noun*
• "TAR oh" or "TARE oh"
• a tropical aroid plant, *Colocasia esculenta*, with tuberous roots used as food.
• [Polynesian]
HOMOPHONES: *tarot*

tarot *noun*
• "TARE oh"
• any of several games played with a pack of cards having five suits, the last of which is a set of permanent trumps.
• [French *tarot*, Italian *tarocchi*, of unknown origin]
HOMOPHONES: *taro*

tarpaulin *noun*
• "tar PAUL'n"
• heavy-duty waterproof cloth esp. of tarred canvas.
• [prob. from 'tar' + PALL]

tarpon *noun*
• "TAR pon"
• a large silvery fish, *Megalops atlanticus*, common in the tropical Atlantic.
• [Dutch *tarpoen*, of unknown origin]

tarragon *noun*
• "TERRA gon" or "TA ruh gon"
• a bushy herb, *Artemisia dracunculus*, with leaves used to flavour salads, stuffings, vinegar, etc.
• [medieval Latin *tarchon* from medieval Greek *tarkhōn*, perhaps through Arabic from Greek *drakōn* dragon]

tarsier *noun*
• "TAR seer"
• any small large-eyed arboreal nocturnal primate of the genus *Tarsius*, native to Borneo, the Philippines, etc., with a long tail and long hind legs used for leaping from tree to tree.
• [French (as TARSUS), from the structure of its foot]

tarsus *noun*
• "TAR suss"
• the group of bones forming the ankle and upper foot.
• [modern Latin from Greek *tarsos* flat of the foot, rim of the eyelid]
• **tarsal** *adjective* "TAR s'll"

tartan *noun*
• "TART'n"
• a pattern of coloured stripes crossing at right angles, esp. a distinctive plaid of a sort orig. worn by the Scottish Highlanders to denote their clan.
• [perhaps from Old French *tertaine*, denoting a kind of cloth; compare with *tartarin*, a rich fabric formerly imported from the east through Tartar territory]

tartar *noun*
• "TARTER"
• a hard deposit of saliva, calcium phosphate, etc., that forms on the teeth.
• [medieval Latin from medieval Greek *tartaron*]
• **tartaric** *adjective* "tar TARRIC"

tartrazine *noun*
• "TAR truh zeen"
• a brilliant yellow dye derived from tartaric acid and used to colour food, drugs, and cosmetics.
• [French *tartre* TARTAR + AZINE]

tartufo *noun*
• "tar TOO foe"
• a ball of ice cream with one flavour in the centre surrounded by another flavour, the whole often coated in cocoa or chopped nuts.
• [Italian, lit. = 'truffle']

Tasmanian *adjective*
• "taz MAINY 'n"
• of or relating to the Australian island of Tasmania.

tassel *noun*
• "TASS'll"
• a tuft of loosely hanging threads or cords etc. attached for decoration to a cushion, scarf, cap, etc.
• [Old French *tas(s)el* clasp, of unknown origin]
• **tasselled** *adjective*

tatami *noun*
• "tuh TOMMY"
• a rush-covered straw mat forming a traditional Japanese floor covering.
• [Japanese]

tatterdemalion *noun*
• "tatter duh MAL y'n" or "tatter duh MALE y'n"
• a person in ragged or tattered clothing.
• [from 'tatter' from Old Norse *tötrar* rags + fanciful ending]

tattersall *noun*
• "TATTER sawl"
• a fabric with a pattern of coloured lines forming squares like a tartan.
• [R. *Tattersall*, English horseman d.1795: from the traditional design of horse blankets]

tattoo *verb*
• "ta TOO"
• mark (the skin) with an indelible design by puncturing it and inserting pigment.
• [Polynesian]
• **tattooer** *noun*
• **tattooist** *noun*

tau *noun*
• "TOW" (rhymes with *COW*) or "TAW"
• the nineteenth letter of the Greek alphabet (Τ, τ).
• [Greek]
HOMOPHONES: *Tao, taw, ta*

taunt *noun*
• "TONT"
• a thing said in order to anger or wound a person.
• [16th c., in phrase *taunt for taunt* from French *tant pour tant* tit for tat, hence a smart rejoinder]
• **taunter** *noun*
• **tauntingly** *adverb*

taupe *noun*
• "TOPE"
• a grey with a tinge of another colour, usu. brown.
• [French, = 'mole']
HOMOPHONES: *tope*

taurine *noun*
• "TORE een"
• a sulphur-containing amino acid important in the metabolism of fats.
• [Greek *tauros* bull (because it was originally obtained from ox bile)]

Taurus *noun*
• "TORE us"
• the second sign of the zodiac.
• [Latin, = bull]
• **Taurean** *adjective*
HOMOPHONES: *torus*

taut *adjective*
• "TOT"
• (of a rope, muscles, etc.) tight; not slack.
• [Middle English *touht*, *togt*, perhaps = 'tough', influenced by *tog-* past participle stem of obsolete *tee* (Old English *tēon*) pull]
• **tauten** *verb*
• **tautly** *adverb*
• **tautness** *noun*
HOMOPHONES: *taught, tot*

tautog *noun*
• "taw TOG"
• a fish, *Tautoga onitis*, found off the Atlantic coast of N America, used as food.
• [Narragansett *tautauog* (pl.)]

tautology *noun*
• "taw TOLLA jee"
• the saying of the same thing twice over in different words, esp. as a fault of style, e.g. *arrived one after the other in succession*.
• [Late Latin *tautologia* from Greek (*tauto, to auto* the same + *logos* word)]
• **tautological** *adjective*
• **tautologically** *adverb*
• **tautologist** *noun*
• **tautologize** *verb* (also esp. *Brit.* **-ise**)
• **tautologous** *adjective* "taw TOLLA guss"

tautomer *noun*
• "TOTTA mur"
• a substance that exists as two mutually convertible isomers in equilibrium.
• [Greek *tauto, to auto* the same + ISOMER]
• **tautomeric** *adjective* "totta MARE ick"
• **tautomerism** *noun* "taw TOMMER izm"

taverna *noun*
• "tuh VARE nuh"
• a Greek café or restaurant.
• [modern Greek from Latin *taberna* hut, tavern]

taw *verb*
• "TAW"
• make (hide) into leather without the use of tannin, esp. by soaking in a solution of alum and salt.
• [Old English *tawian* from Germanic]
• **tawer** *noun*
HOMOPHONES: *ta, tau*

tawdry *adjective*
- "TAW dree"
- showy but worthless.
- [earlier as noun: short for *tawdry lace*, originally *St. Audrey's lace* from *Audrey* = *Etheldrida*, patron saint of Ely, England]
- **tawdrily** *adverb*
- **tawdriness** *noun*

tawny *adjective*
- "TAWNY"
- of an orange- or yellow-brown colour.
- [Anglo-French *tauné*, Old French *tané* from *tan* tan]
- **tawniness** *noun*

taxidermy *noun*
- "TAXA durmy"
- the art of preparing, stuffing, and mounting the skins of animals or birds etc. in lifelike poses.
- [Greek *taxis* arrangement + *derma* skin]
- **taxidermal** *adjective*
- **taxidermic** *adjective*
- **taxidermist** *noun*

taximeter *noun*
- "TAXA meeter"
- an automatic device fitted to a taxi, recording the fare payable.
- [French *taximètre* from *taxe* tariff + Greek *metron* measure]

taxis *noun*
- "TAX iss"
- the restoration of displaced bones or organs by manual pressure.
- [Greek from *tassō* arrange]

taxon *noun*
- "TAX 'n"
- any taxonomic group.
- [back-formation from TAXONOMY]

taxonomy *noun*
- "tax ONNA mee"
- the science of the classification of living and extinct organisms.
- [French *taxonomie* (as TAXIS, Greek *-nomia* distribution)]
- **taxonomic** *adjective* "taxa NOMMIC"
- **taxonomical** *adjective*
- **taxonomically** *adverb*
- **taxonomist** *noun*

tayberry *noun*
- "TAY berry"
- a dark red soft fruit produced by crossing the blackberry and raspberry.
- [*Tay* in Scotland (where introduced in 1977)]

Taylorism *noun*
- "TAY lur izm"
- the principles or practice of scientific management and work efficiency as practised in a system known as the Taylor System, characterized by the division of factory work into the smallest and simplest jobs.
- [from F. W. *Taylor*, US engineer d.1915]
- **Taylorist** *adjective*

tazza *noun*
- "TOTSA"
- a saucer-shaped cup, esp. one mounted on a foot.
- [Italian]

tchotchke *noun*
- "CHOTCH kee"
- a knick-knack.
- [Yiddish *tshatshke* from Polish *czaczko*]

teak *noun*
- "TEEK"
- a large deciduous tree, *Tectona grandis*, native to India and SE Asia.
- [Portuguese *teca* from Malayalam *tēkka*]

teal *noun*
- "TEEL"
- any of various small freshwater ducks of the genus *Anas*, esp. the green-winged teal, *A. crecca*, the male of which has a chestnut head and a green stripe, and the blue-winged teal, *A. discors*, which has a chalky blue forewing and a green speculum.
- [Middle English, related to Middle Dutch *tēling*, of unknown origin]

teammate *noun*
- "TEEM mate"
- a fellow member of a team or group.
- ['team' from Old English *tēam* team of draught animals + 'mate' from Middle Low German *mate* from *gemate* messmate, from West Germanic, related to 'meat']

teapoy *noun*
- "TEE poy"
- a small three- or four-legged table esp. for use in serving tea.
- [Hindi *tīn*, *tir-* three + Persian *pāī* foot: sense and spelling influenced by 'tea']

teasel *noun*
ALSO SPELLED: **teazel**, **teazle**
- "TEEZ'll"
- any plant of the genus *Dipsacus*, with large prickly heads that were formerly dried and used to raise the nap on woven cloth.
- [Old English *tǣs(e)l*, = Old High German *zeisala*]

teat *noun*
- "TEET" or "TIT"
- a mammary nipple, esp. of an animal.
- [Old French *tete*, prob. of Germanic origin]

HOMOPHONES: *tit*

tech *noun*
- "TECK"
- *informal* technology.
- [abbreviation]
- **techy** *adjective*

HOMOPHONES: *techie*

techie *noun*
ALSO SPELLED: **tekkie**
• "TECKY"
• an expert in or enthusiast for technology, esp. computing.
• [abbreviation]
HOMOPHONES: *techy*

technetium *noun*
• "teck NEE shee um" or "teck NEE shum"
• an artificially produced radioactive metallic element occurring in the fission products of uranium.
• [modern Latin from Greek *tekhnētos* artificial, from *tekhnē* art]

technical *adjective*
• "TECKNA k'll"
• of or involving or concerned with the mechanical arts and applied sciences.
• [Latin *technicus* from Greek *tekhnikos* from *tekhnē* art]
• **technically** *adverb*

technicality *noun*
• "teckna CALA tee"
• a technical point or detail.
• [as TECHNICAL]

technician *noun*
• "teck NISH'n"
• a person employed to look after technical equipment and do practical work in a laboratory etc.
• [as TECHNICAL]

technics *noun*
• "TECK nicks"
• technology.
• [Latin *technicus* from Greek *tekhnikos* from *tekhnē* art]

technique *noun*
• "teck NEEK"
• a manner of esp. artistic execution or performance in relation to mechanical or formal details.
• [French (as TECHNICAL)]

techno *noun*
• "TECK no"
• a style of popular dance music making extensive use of electronic instruments and synthesized sound.
• [abbreviation of TECHNOLOGICAL]

technobabble *noun*
• "TECK no babble"
• incomprehensible technical jargon.
• [as TECHNICAL + 'babble' (imitative)]

technocracy *noun*
• "teck NOCKRA see"
• the government or control of society or industry by technical experts.
• [as TECHNICAL + Greek *kratia* from *kratos* strength, power]
• **technocrat** *noun*
• **technocratic** *adjective*

technology *noun*
• "teck NOLLA jee"
• the study or use of the mechanical arts and applied sciences.
• [Greek *tekhnologia* systematic treatment, from *tekhnē* art]
• **technological** *adjective*
• **technologically** *adverb*
• **technologist** *noun*
• **technologize** *verb* (also esp. *Brit.* **-ise**)

technophile *noun*
• "TECKNA file"
• an enthusiast about new technology.
• [as TECHNOLOGY + Greek *philos* dear, loving]
• **technophilia** *noun* "teckna FILLY uh" or "teckna FEELY uh"
• **technophilic** *adjective* "teckna FILLIC"

technophobe *noun*
• "TECKNA fobe"
• a person who fears, dislikes, or avoids new technology.
• [as TECHNOLOGY + PHOBIA]
• **technophobia** *noun*
• **technophobic** *adjective*

technothriller *noun*
• "TECK no thriller"
• a novel or movie in the thriller genre whose plot centres on (usu. military) science and technology.
• [as TECHNOLOGY + 'thrill' from Old English *thyrlian* pierce, from *thȳrel* hole, from *thurh* through]

tectonic *adjective*
• "teck TONNIC"
• of or relating to building or construction.
• [Late Latin *tectonicus* from Greek *tektonikos* from *tektōn -onos* carpenter]
• **tectonically** *adverb*

tectonics *noun*
• "teck TONNIX"
• the art and process of producing practical and aesthetically pleasing buildings.
• [as TECTONIC]

tectorial *adjective*
• "teck TORY 'll"
• designating the membrane covering the organ of Corti in the inner ear.
• [Latin *tectorium* a cover (as TECTRIX)]

tectrix *noun*
• "TECK trix"
• a feather covering the base of a bird's flight feather.
• [modern Latin from Latin *tegere tect-* cover]

tedium *noun*
• "TEEDY um"
• the state of being tiresomely long or boring; boredom.
• [Latin *taedium* from *taedēre* to weary]
• **tedious** *adjective* "TEEDY us"
• **tediously** *adverb*
• **tediousness** *noun*

teem *verb*
• "TEEM"
• be abundant.
• [Old English *tēman* etc. give birth to, from Germanic]
• **teeming** *adjective*
HOMOPHONES: *team*

teepee *noun*
ALSO SPELLED: **tepee, tipi**
• "TEE pee"
• a conical tent used by Plains Aboriginal peoples, made of skins, cloth, or canvas on a frame of poles.
• [Sioux or Dakota *tīpī*]

teethe *verb*
• "TEETHE" (rhymes with *BREATHE*)
• grow or cut baby teeth.
• [Old English *tēth*, pl. of *tōth* from Germanic]
• **teething** *noun*

teetotal *adjective*
• "tee TOTAL"
• advocating or characterized by total abstinence from alcoholic drink.
• [reduplication of 'total']
• **teetotalism** *noun*
• **teetotaller** *noun* (also esp. *US* **teetotaler**)

teetotum *noun*
• "tee TOE tum"
• a spinning top with four sides lettered to determine whether the spinner has won or lost.
• [*T* (the letter on one side) + Latin *totum* the whole (stakes), for which *T* stood]

teff *noun*
• "TEFF"
• an African cereal, *Eragrostis tef.*
• [Amharic *ṭēf*]

tefillin *plural noun*
• "tuh FILLIN"
• Jewish phylacteries.
• [Aramaic *tĕpillī*]

tegument *noun*
• "TEG yoo m'nt"
• an integument, esp. of a flatworm.
• [Latin *tegumentum* from *tegere* cover]

Tejano *noun*
• "tuh HANNO"
• a native or inhabitant of Texas who is of Mexican origin or ancestry.
• [American Spanish, alteration of *Texano* Texan]

tektite *noun*
• "TECK tite"
• a small roundish glassy body of unknown origin occurring in various parts of the earth.
• [German *Tektit* from Greek *tēktos* molten, from *tēkō* melt]

telamon *noun*
• "TELLA m'n" or "TELLA mone"
• a male figure used as a pillar to support an entablature.
• [Latin *telamones* from Greek *telamōnes* pl. of *Telamōn*, the father of Ajax in Greek mythology]

telecine *noun*
• "TELLA sinny"
• the broadcasting of movies on television.
• ['television' + CINEMA]

telecommunication *noun*
• "tella kuh myoona CAY sh'n"
• communication over a distance by telephone, radio, television, etc.
• [Greek *tēle* far off + COMMUNICATION]

telecommute *verb*
• "tella kuh MUTE"
• work from home, communicating electronically.
• [Greek *tēle* far off + COMMUTE]
• **telecommuter** *noun*
• **telecommuting** *noun*

teleconference *noun*
• "tella CONFER ince"
• a conference with participants in different locations linked by telecommunication devices.
• [Greek *tēle* far off + CONFERENCE]
• **teleconferencing** *noun*

telegenic *adjective*
• "tella JENNIC"
• having an appearance or manner that looks pleasing on television.
• ['television' + *-genic* in PHOTOGENIC]
• **telegenically** *adverb*

telegraphese *noun*
• "tella gruh FEEZ"
• abbreviated language; concise elliptical style.
• [from 'telegraph' from Greek *tēle* far off + *graphia* writing]

telekinesis *noun*
• "tella kuh NEE sis"
• movement of objects at a distance supposedly by paranormal means.
• [modern Latin (Greek *tēle* far off, *kinēsis* motion, from *kineō* move)]
• **telekinetic** *adjective*
• **telekinetically** *adverb*

telematics *noun*
• "tella MATTIX"
• the branch of information technology which deals with the long-distance transmission of computerized information.
• [Greek *tēle* far off + 'informatics', translation of Russian *informatika* (from Latin *informare* give shape to, fashion, describe (*in* in, *forma* form))]
• **telematic** *adjective*

telemeter *noun*
• "TELLA meeter" or "tuh LEMMA tur"
• an apparatus for recording the readings of an instrument and transmitting them by radio.
• [Greek *tēle* far off + *metron* measure]

- **telemetric** *adjective* "tella METRIC"
- **telemetry** *noun* "tuh LEMMA tree"

telenovela *noun*
- "tella no VELLA"
- (esp. in Latin America) a Spanish-language or Portuguese-language soap opera.
- [Spanish or Portuguese, from *tele* (in *televisión*) 'television' + *novela* novel]

teleology *noun*
- "telly OLLA jee" or "teely OLLA jee"
- the explanation of phenomena by the purpose they serve rather than by postulated causes.
- [modern Latin *teleologia* from Greek *telos teleos* end + *logos* word]
- **teleologic** *adjective*
- **teleological** *adjective*
- **teleologically** *adverb*
- **teleologism** *noun*
- **teleologist** *noun*

teleoperator *noun*
- "telly OPPER ater"
- any remote-controlled machine which mimics or responds to the actions of a human controller at a distance.
- [Greek *tēle* far off + OPERATOR]
- **teleoperated** *adjective*
- **teleoperation** *noun*

teleost *noun*
- "TELLY awst" or "TEELY awst"
- any fish of the subclass Teleostei, comprising the bony fishes and including most familiar kinds of fish except sharks, rays, sturgeons, and lungfishes.
- [Greek *teleo-* complete + *osteon* bone]

telepath *noun*
- "TELLA path"
- a telepathic person.
- [back-formation from TELEPATHY]

telepathy *noun*
- "tuh LEPPA thee" (with "TH" as in *THIN*)
- the supposed communication or perception of thoughts or ideas by extrasensory means.
- [Greek *tēle* far off + *patheia* feeling]
- **telepathic** *adjective* "tella PATHIC"
- **telepathically** *adverb*
- **telepathist** *noun*

telephone *noun*
- "TELLA fone"
- an apparatus for transmitting sound (esp. speech) over a distance, esp. by converting acoustic vibrations to electrical signals.
- [Greek *tēle* far off + *phōnē* sound]
- **telephoner** *noun*
- **telephonic** *adjective* "tella FONNIC"
- **telephonically** *adverb*

telephonist *noun*
- "tuh LEFFA nist"
- an operator in a telephone exchange or at a switchboard.
- [as TELEPHONE]

televangelist *noun*
- "tella VAN juh list"
- an evangelical preacher who appears regularly on television to promote beliefs and appeal for funds.
- ['television' + EVANGELIST]
- **televangelism** *noun*

telluric *adjective*
- "tel OORIC"
- of the earth as a planet.
- [Latin *tellus -uris* earth]

tellurium *noun*
- "tel URRY um"
- a rare brittle lustrous silver-white element occurring naturally in ores of gold and silver, used in semiconductors.
- [Latin *tellus -uris* earth, prob. named in contrast to *uranium*]
- **telluride** *noun* "TEL yuh ride"
- **tellurite** *noun*

telnet *noun*
- "TEL net"
- a network protocol that allows a user on one computer to log in to another computer that is part of the same network.
- [from 'tel(ecommunication)' + 'net(work)']

telomerase *noun*
- "TELLA meer ace" or "TEELA meer ace"
- the enzyme in a eukaryote that repairs the telomeres of the chromosomes so that they do not become progressively shorter during successive rounds of chromosome replication.
- [as TELOMERE]

telomere *noun*
- "TELLA meer" or "TEELA meer"
- the end of a chromosome, which consists of repeated sequences of DNA that perform the function of ensuring that each cycle of DNA replication has been completed.
- [Greek *telos* end + *meros* part]

telophase *noun*
- "TELLA faze" or "TEELA faze"
- the final stage of cell division, in which the nuclei of the daughter cells are formed.
- [Greek *telos* end + PHASE]

telos *noun*
- "TEL oss" or "TEE loss"
- an ultimate object or aim.
- [Greek = end]

telson *noun*
- "TEL s'n"
- the last segment in the abdomen of crustaceans and arachnids.
- [Greek, = limit]

Telugu *noun*
ALSO SPELLED: **Telegu**
- "TELLA goo"
- a member of a Dravidian people in SE India.
- [Telugu]

temblor *noun*
- "tem BLUR" or "tem BLORE"
- an earthquake.
- [Latin American Spanish]

temerarious *adjective*
- "temma RARE ee us"
- reckless, rash.
- [Latin *temerarius* from *temere* rashly]
- **temerariously** *adverb*

temerity *noun*
- "tuh MERRA tee"
- excessive confidence or boldness; audacity.
- [Latin *temeritas* from *temere* rashly]

Temne *noun*
- "TEM nee"
- a member of a people of Sierra Leone.
- [the name in Temne]

tempeh *noun*
- "TEM pay"
- a fermented soybean product, usu. eaten fried.
- [Indonesian *tempe*]

tempera *noun*
- "TEMPER uh"
- a method of painting using an emulsion of powdered pigment typically held together with egg yolk and water.
- [Italian, in *pingere a tempera* paint in distemper]

temperament *noun*
- "TEMPRA m'nt" or "TEMPER m'nt"
- a person's distinct nature and character, esp. as permanently affecting behaviour; natural disposition, personality.
- [Latin *temperamentum* from *temperare* mingle]

temperamental *adjective*
- "tempra MENT'll" or "temper MENT'll"
- erratic or moody; unreliable, unpredictable.
- [as TEMPERAMENT]
- **temperamentally** *adverb*

temperance *noun*
- "TEMP rince" or "TEMPER ince"
- moderation or self-restraint esp. in eating and drinking.
- [Anglo-French *temperaunce* from Latin *temperantia* (as TEMPERATE)]

temperate *adjective*
- "TEMPER it"
- avoiding excess; self-restrained.
- [Latin *temperatus* past participle of *temperare* mingle]
- **temperately** *adverb*
- **temperateness** *noun*

temperature *noun*
- "TEMPRA chur" or "TEMPER chur"
- the degree or intensity of heat of a substance, the air, etc. in relation to others, esp. as shown by a thermometer or perceived by touch etc.
- [French *température* or Latin *temperatura* (as TEMPERATE)]

tempest *noun*
- "TEM pist"
- a violent windy storm.
- [Old French *tempest(e)*, ultimately from Latin *tempestas* season, storm, from *tempus* time]

tempestuous *adjective*
- "tem PESS choo us"
- stormy.
- [as TEMPEST]
- **tempestuously** *adverb*
- **tempestuousness** *noun*

Templar *noun*
- "TEM plur"
- a member of a religious and military order for the protection of pilgrims to the Holy Land, suppressed in 1312.
- [from 'temple' from Latin *templum* open or consecrated space]

temporal *adjective*
- "TEMPER 'll"
- of worldly as opposed to spiritual affairs; of this life; secular as opposed to ecclesiastical.
- [Old French *temporel*, or from Latin *temporalis* from *tempus -oris* time]
- **temporally** *adverb*

temporality *noun*
- "tempa RALA tee"
- the state of existing within or having some relationship with time.
- [as TEMPORAL]

temporary *adjective*
- "TEMPER airy"
- lasting or meant to last only for a limited time.
- [Latin *temporarius* from *tempus -oris* time]
- **temporarily** *adverb*
- **temporariness** *noun*

temporize *verb*
ALSO SPELLED: esp. *Brit.* **-ise**
- "TEMPER ize"
- avoid committing oneself so as to gain time; employ delaying tactics.
- [French *temporiser* bide one's time, from medieval Latin *temporizare* delay, from *tempus -oris* time]
- **temporization** *noun* (also esp. *Brit.* **-isation**)
- **temporizer** *noun* (also esp. *Brit.* **-iser**)

temporomandibular *adjective*
- "temper oh man DIB yuh lur"
- of or pertaining to the hinge joint between the temporal bone (in the temple) and the lower jaw.
- [Late Latin *temporalis* from *tempora* the temples + MANDIBLE]

Tempranillo *noun*
- "tempra NILLO"
- a type of black grape grown in Spain.

• [Spanish *temprano* early, because the grape ripens early]

tempt *verb*
• "TEMPT"
• entice or incite (a person) to do a wrong or forbidden thing.
• [Old French *tempter* test, from Latin *temptare* handle, test, try]
• **temptable** *adjective*
• **temptation** *noun*
• **tempter** *noun*
• **temptress** *noun*

tempting *adjective*
• "TEMP ting"
• attractive, inviting.
• [as TEMPT]
• **temptingly** *adverb*

tempura *noun*
• "tem POO ruh"
• (in Japanese cuisine) fish, shellfish, or vegetables, fried in batter.
• [Japanese]

tenable *adjective*
• "TENNA bull"
• that can be maintained or defended against attack or objection.
• [French from *tenir* hold, from Latin *tenēre*]
• **tenability** *noun*

tenace *noun*
• "TEN us"
• (in bridge) two cards, one ranking next above, and the other next below, a card held by an opponent.
• [French from Spanish *tenaza*, lit. 'pincers']
HOMOPHONES: *tennis*

tenacious *adjective*
• "tuh NAY sh'ss"
• holding fast.
• [Latin *tenax -acis* from *tenēre* hold]
• **tenaciously** *adverb*
• **tenacity** *noun* "tuh NASSA tee"

tenant *noun*
• "TEN'nt"
• a person, business, etc. who rents a residence, premises, etc. from the owner.
• [Old French, present participle of *tenir* hold, from Latin *tenēre*]
• **tenancy** *noun* "TEN 'n see"
• **tenantless** *adjective*

tenantry *noun*
• "TEN 'n tree"
• the tenants of an estate etc.
• [as TENANT]

tendency *noun*
• "TEN d'n see"
• a leaning or inclination; a way in which a person or thing is likely to behave.
• [Old French *tendre* stretch, from Latin *tendere tens-*]

tendentious *adjective*
• "ten DEN sh'ss"
• *derogatory* (of writing etc.) calculated to promote a particular cause or viewpoint; having an underlying purpose.
• [as TENDENCY]
• **tendentiously** *adverb*
• **tendentiousness** *noun*

tendinitis *noun*
ALSO SPELLED: **tendonitis**
• "tend'n ITE iss"
• inflammation of a tendon, most commonly from overuse but also from infection or rheumatic disease.
• [as TENDON + Greek *-itis*, forming feminine of adjectives in *-itēs* (with *nosos* 'disease' implied)]

tendon *noun*
• "TEND'n"
• a cord or strand of strong fibrous tissue attaching a muscle to a bone etc.
• [French *tendon* or medieval Latin *tendo -dinis* from Greek *tenōn* sinew, from *teinō* stretch]
• **tendinous** *adjective*

tendril *noun*
• "TEN drill"
• each of the slender leafless shoots, often growing in a spiral form, by which some climbing plants cling for support.
• [prob. from obsolete French *tendrillon* diminutive of obsolete *tendron* young shoot, ultimately from Latin *tener* tender]

Tenebrae *noun*
• "TENNA bray"
• (in the Western Church) any of various offices for the last three evenings of Holy Week, at which candles are successively extinguished.
• [Latin, = darkness]

tenebrous *adjective*
• "TENNA bruss"
• dark, gloomy.
• [Old French *tenebrus* from Latin *tenebrosus* (as TENEBRAE)]

tenement *noun*
• "TENNA m'nt"
• a building with apartments or rooms rented cheaply, esp. in a poor area of a city.
• [Old French from medieval Latin *tenementum* from *tenēre* hold]

tenet *noun*
• "TEN it"
• a doctrine, dogma, or principle held by a group or person.
• [Latin, third person singular of *tenēre* hold]

tenge *noun*
• "TENG gay"
• a monetary unit of Kazakhstan, equal to 100 tiyn.
• [Kazakh and Turkmen, lit. = 'coin, ruble']

Tennessean *noun*
• "tenna SEE 'n"
• a person from Tennessee.

tenno *noun*
• "TENNO"
• the Emperor of Japan viewed as a divinity.
• [Japanese]

tenon *noun*
• "TEN'n"
• a projecting piece of wood made for insertion into a corresponding cavity (esp. a mortise) in another piece.
• [French from *tenir* hold, from Latin *tenēre*]

tenor *noun*
• "TENNER"
• a singing voice between baritone and alto or counter-tenor, the highest of the ordinary adult male range.
• [Old French *tenour* from Latin *tenor -oris* from *tenēre* hold]
HOMOPHONES: *tenner*

tenosynovitis *noun*
• "tenno sye no VITE iss" or "tenno sinno VITE iss"
• inflammation and swelling of a tendon sheath, usu. in the wrist, often caused by repetitive movements such as typing.
• [Greek *tenōn* tendon + SYNOVITIS]

tenrec *noun*
• "TEN reck"
• any hedgehog-like tailless insect-eating mammal of the family Tenrecidae, esp. *Tenrec ecaudatus* native to Madagascar.
• [French *tanrec*, from Malagasy *tàndraka*]

tensile *adjective*
• "TEN sile" or "TEN s'll"
• of or relating to tension.
• [medieval Latin *tensilis* from Latin *tensus* past participle of *tendere* stretch]

tension *noun*
• "TEN sh'n"
• the act or an instance of stretching; the state of being stretched; tenseness.
• [French *tension* or Latin *tensio* (as TENSILE)]
• **tensional** *adjective*

tensioner *noun*
• "TEN sh'n ur"
• a device for applying tension to a seat belt, cable, pipeline, etc.
• [as TENSION]

tensor *noun*
• "TENSER"
• a muscle that tightens or stretches a part of the body.
• [modern Latin (as TENSILE)]
• **tensorial** *adjective* "ten SORRY 'll"

tentacle *noun*
• "TENTA k'll"
• a long slender flexible appendage of an (esp. invertebrate) animal, used for feeling, grasping, or moving.
• [modern Latin *tentaculum* from Latin *tentare* = *temptare* (see TENTATIVE) + diminutive *-culum*]
• **tentacled** *adjective*
• **tentacular** *adjective* "ten TACK yuh lur"
• **tentaculate** *adjective* "ten TACK yuh lit"

tentative *adjective*
• "TENTA tiv"
• done by way of trial, experimental, provisional.
• [medieval Latin *tentativus*, from *tentare*, variant of *temptare* handle, try]
• **tentatively** *adverb*
• **tentativeness** *noun*

tenterhook *noun*
• "TENTER hook" ("HOOK" rhymes with *BOOK*)
• any of the hooks to which cloth is fastened on a tenter.
• [medieval Latin *tentorium* (as TENTATIVE) + 'hook' from Old English *hōc*]

tenuous *adjective*
• "TEN yoo us"
• slight, of little substance; insignificant, meagre.
• [Latin *tenuis* thin]
• **tenuity** *noun* "tuh NEW a tee"
• **tenuously** *adverb*
• **tenuousness** *noun*

tenure *noun*
• "TEN yur"
• a condition, or form of right or title, under which (esp. real) property is held.
• [Old French from *tenir* hold, from Latin *tenēre*]

tenured *adjective*
• "TEN yurd"
• (of an official position) carrying a guarantee of permanent employment.
• [as TENURE]

tenuto *adverb*
• "ten OO toe"
• (of a note etc.) sustained, given its full time value.
• [Italian, = held]

teocalli *noun*
• "tee a CAL ee"
• a temple of the Aztecs or other Mexican peoples, usu. on a truncated pyramid.
• [Nahuatl from *teotl* god + *calli* house]

teosinte *noun*
• "tee oh SINTY"
• a subspecies of corn (*Zea mays*) grown as fodder.
• [French from Nahuatl *teocintli*]

tepal *noun*
• "TEEP'll" or "TEP'll"
• a segment of the outer whorl in a flower having no differentiation between petals and sepals.
• [French *tépale*, as blend of PETAL and SEPAL]

tephra *noun*
- "TEFFRA"
- fragmented rock etc. ejected by a volcanic eruption.
- [Greek, = ash]

teppanyaki *noun*
- "TEP 'n yacky"
- a Japanese dish of meat or fish, fried with vegetables on a hot steel plate forming the centre of the dining table.
- [Japanese, from *teppan* steel plate + *yaki* fry]

tequila *noun*
- "tuh KEELA"
- a Mexican spirit made by distilling the fermented sap of an agave.
- [*Tequila*, a town in Mexico where the drink was first produced]

terabyte *noun*
- "TERRA bite"
- 1 099 511 627 776 (i.e. 2^{40}) bytes as a measure of data capacity, or loosely 1 000 000 000 000 bytes.
- [Greek *teras* monster + BYTE]

teraflop *noun*
- "TERRA flop"
- a unit of computing speed equal to 10^{12} floating-point operations per second.
- [Greek *teras* monster + 'flop' from 'floating-point operation']

teraph *noun*
- "TARE if"
- a small image as a domestic deity or oracle of the ancient Hebrews.
- [Late Latin *theraphim*, Greek *theraphin* from Hebrew *t̲rāpîm*]

HOMOPHONES: *tariff*

teratogen *noun*
- "tuh RATTA j'n"
- an agent or factor causing malformation of an embryo.
- [Greek *teras* monster + GENESIS]
- **teratogenic** *adjective* "tare a tuh JENNIC"
- **teratogenicity** *noun* "tuh ratta juh NISSA tee"

teratology *noun*
- "terra TOLLA jee"
- the scientific study of animal or vegetable monstrosities.
- [Greek *teras* monster + *logos* word]
- **teratological** *adjective*

teratoma *noun*
- "terra TOE muh"
- a tumour of heterogeneous tissues, esp. of the gonads.
- [Greek *teras* monster + CARCINOMA]

terawatt *noun*
- "TERRA wot"
- a unit of power equal to 10^{12} watts or a million megawatts.
- [Greek *teras* monster + WATT]

terbium *noun*
- "TURBY um"
- a silvery metallic element of the lanthanide series.
- [modern Latin, named after *Ytterby*, a village in Sweden where it was discovered]

terbutaline *noun*
- "tur BYOO tuh leen"
- a synthetic compound with bronchodilator properties, used especially in the treatment of asthma.
- [Latin *ter* three times + BUTYL]

terce *noun*
- "TURCE"
- the office of the third canonical hour of prayer, originally said at the third hour of the day (i.e. 9 a.m.).
- [var. of TIERCE]

HOMOPHONES: *terse*

tercel *noun*
- "TUR s'll"
- the male of the hawk, esp. a peregrine or goshawk.
- [Old French *tercel*, ultimately a diminutive of Latin *tertius* third, perhaps from a belief that the third egg of a clutch produced a male bird, or that the male was one-third smaller than the female]

tercentenary *noun*
- "tur sen TENNER ee" or "tur sen TEENER ee"
- a tercentennial.
- [Latin *ter* three times + CENTENARY]

tercentennial *noun*
- "tur sen TENNY 'll"
- a three-hundredth anniversary.
- [Latin *ter* three times + CENTENNIAL]

tercet *noun*
- "TURCE it"
- a set or group of three lines rhyming together or connected by rhyme with an adjacent triplet.
- [French from Italian *terzetto* diminutive of *terzo* third, from Latin *tertius*]

terebinth *noun*
- "TERRA binth"
- a small S European tree, *Pistacia terebinthus*, yielding resin formerly used as a source of turpentine.
- [Old French *terebinte* or Latin *terebinthus* from Greek *terebinthos*]

teredo *noun*
- "tuh REE doe"
- any bivalve mollusc of the genus *Teredo*, esp. *Teredo navalis*, that bores into wooden ships, piers, and other submerged wood.
- [Latin from Greek *terēdōn* from *teirō* rub hard, wear away, bore]

terephthalic *adjective*
- "tare if THALIC"
- designating the *para*-isomer of phthalic

acid, used in making plastics and other polymers.
• [*terebic* from TEREBINTH, + PHTHALIC]

terete *adjective*
• "tuh REET"
• smooth and rounded; cylindrical.
• [Latin *teres -etis*]

tergiversate *verb*
• "TURJA vur sate"
• equivocate; make conflicting or evasive statements.
• [Latin *tergiversari* turn one's back, from *tergum* back + *vertere vers-* turn]
• **tergiversation** *noun*
• **tergiversator** *noun*

teriyaki *noun*
• "terry YACKY" or "terry YOCKY"
• (in Japanese cuisine) fish or meat marinated in soy sauce etc. and grilled.
• [Japanese from *teri* gloss, lustre + *yaki* grill]

termagant *noun*
• "TURMA g'nt"
• an overbearing or ill-tempered woman.
• [Middle English *Tervagant* from Old French *Tervagan* from Italian *Trivigante* an imaginary deity of violent and turbulent character, often appearing in morality plays]

terminable *adjective*
• "TURMIN a bull"
• that may be terminated.
• [as TERMINATE]

terminal *adjective*
• "TURMIN'll"
• (of a disease) ending in death, fatal.
• [as TERMINATE]
• **terminally** *adverb*

terminate *verb*
• "TURMIN ate"
• bring or come to an end.
• [as TERMINUS]
• **termination** *noun*
• **terminator** *noun*

terminology *noun*
• "turmin OLLA jee"
• the system of terms used in a particular subject.
• [German *Terminologie* from medieval Latin TERMINUS term]
• **terminological** *adjective*
• **terminologically** *adverb*
• **terminologist** *noun*

terminus *noun*
• "TURMIN us"
• the end of a railway, bus route, etc.
• [Latin, = end, limit, boundary]

termitary *noun*
• "TURMA terry"
• a nest of termites, usu. a large mound of earth.
• [as TERMITE]

termite *noun*
• "TUR mite"
• a small ant-like social insect of the order Isoptera, destructive to timber.
• [Late Latin *termes -mitis*, alteration of Latin *tarmes* after *terere* rub]

tern *noun*
• "TURN"
• a bird of the subfamily Sterninae, like a gull but usu. smaller and with a long forked tail, esp. the common tern *Sterna hirundo* or the arctic tern *S. paradisaea*.
• [of Scandinavian origin: compare Danish *terne*, Swedish *tärna* from Old Norse *therna*]
HOMOPHONES: *terne, turn*

ternary *adjective*
• "TURNER ee"
• composed of three parts or constituents.
• [Latin *ternarius* from *terni* three each]
HOMOPHONES: *turnery*

terne *noun*
• "TURN"
• a lead alloy with about 20 per cent tin and often antimony.
• [prob. from French *terne* dull]
HOMOPHONES: *tern, turn*

terpene *noun*
• "TUR peen"
• any of a large group of unsaturated cyclic hydrocarbons found in the essential oils of plants, esp. conifers and oranges.
• [*terpentin* obsolete var. of TURPENTINE]

terpsichorean *adjective*
• "turp suh CORRY 'n" or "turp sicka REE 'n"
• of or relating to dancing.
• [*Terpsichore*, the Greek Muse of lyric poetry and dance]

terrace *noun*
• "TARE us"
• each of a series of flat areas formed on a slope and used for cultivation.
• [Old French, ultimately from Latin *terra* earth]
• **terracing** *noun*

Terracite *noun*
• "TERRA site"
• a resident of Terrace, BC.

terracotta *noun*
• "terra COTTA"
• unglazed usu. brownish-red earthenware used chiefly as an ornamental building material, in flowerpots etc., and in modelling.
• [Italian, 'baked earth']

terraform *verb*
• "TERRA form"
• (esp. in science fiction) transform (a planet) so as to resemble the earth.
• [Latin *terra* earth + 'transform']
• **terraformed** *adjective*
• **terraformer** *noun*

terrain *noun*
• "tuh RANE"
• ground, a tract of land, esp. with regard to its physical characteristics or their capacity for use by a military tactician, traveller, etc.
• [French, ultimately from Latin *terrenum*, neuter of *terrenus*, from *terra* earth]
HOMOPHONES: *terrane*

Terran *adjective*
• "TARE 'n"
• (in science fiction) of or relating to the planet earth.
• [Latin *terra* earth]

terrane *noun*
• "tuh RANE"
• a fault-bounded area or region with a distinctive stratigraphy, structure, and geological history, which is different from those of adjacent areas, esp. a fragment of a tectonic plate, bounded by strike-slip faults.
• [as TERRAIN]
HOMOPHONES: *terrain*

terrapin *noun*
• "TERRA pin"
• any of various N American edible freshwater turtles of the family Emydidae.
• [Algonquian]

terrarium *noun*
• "tuh RARE ee um"
• a vivarium for small land animals.
• [modern Latin from Latin *terra* earth, after AQUARIUM]

terrazzo *noun*
• "tuh RAT so" or "tuh RAZ oh"
• a flooring material of stone chips set in concrete and given a smooth surface.
• [Italian, = terrace]

terreplein *noun*
• "TARE plane"
• a level space where a battery of guns is mounted.
• [originally a sloping bank behind a rampart: French *terre-plein* from Italian *terrapieno* from *terrapienare* fill with earth, from *terra* earth + *pieno* from Latin *plenus* full]

terrestrial *adjective*
• "tuh RESS tree 'll"
• of or on or relating to the earth; earthly.
• [Latin *terrestris* from *terra* earth]
• **terrestriality** *noun*
• **terrestrially** *adverb*

terret *noun*
• "TARE it"
• each of the loops or rings on a horse harness for the driving reins to pass through.
• [Old French *to(u)ret* diminutive of *to(u)r* from Latin *tornus* from Greek *tornos* lathe]

terrible *adjective*
• "TERRA bull"
• dreadful, awful.
• [French from Latin *terribilis*, from *terrēre* frighten]
• **terribleness** *noun*
HOMOPHONES: *tearable*

terribly *adverb*
• "TERRA blee"
• very, extremely.
• [as TERRIBLE]

terricolous *adjective*
• "tare ICKA luss"
• living on or in the earth.
• [Latin *terricola* earth dweller, from *terra* earth + *colere* inhabit]

terrier *noun*
• "TERRY ur"
• any of various breeds of dog originally used for turning out foxes etc. from their earths.
• [Old French *(chien) terrier* from medieval Latin *terrarius* from Latin *terra* earth]

terrific *adjective*
• "tuh RIFFIC"
• excellent.
• [Latin *terrificus* from *terrēre* frighten]
• **terrifically** *adverb*

terrify *verb*
• "TARE if eye"
• fill with terror; frighten severely.
• [Latin *terrificare* (as TERRIFIC)]
• **terrifying** *adjective*
• **terrifyingly** *adverb*

terrigenous *adjective*
• "tuh RIDGE a nuss"
• derived from the land, esp. (of a marine deposit) made of material eroded from the land.
• [Latin *terrigenus* earth-born]

terrine *noun*
• "tuh REEN"
• a kind of pâté, usu. coarse textured, cooked in and often served from an oval earthenware vessel.
• [original form of TUREEN]
HOMOPHONES: *tureen*

territory *noun*
• "TERRA tory"
• the extent of the land under the jurisdiction of a ruler, country, city, etc.
• [Latin *territorium* from *terra* land]
• **territorial** *adjective*
• **territoriality** *noun*

terroir *noun*
• "tare WARR" ("WARR" rhymes with *CAR*)
• the total natural environment in which a particular wine is produced, including factors such as the soil, topography, and climate, thought to give the wine a distinctive taste.
• [French, lit. 'soil']

terror *noun*
• "TARE ur"
• extreme fear or dread.

• [Old French *terrour* from Latin *terror -oris* from *terrēre* frighten]
• **terrorize** *verb* (also esp. *Brit.* **-ise**)

terrorism *noun*
• "TARE ur izm"
• the systematic employment of violence and intimidation to coerce a government or community, esp. into acceding to specific political demands.
• [as TERROR]
• **terrorist** *noun*
• **terroristic** *adjective*

terse *adjective*
• "TURCE"
• (of language) brief, concise, to the point.
• [Latin *tersus* past participle of *tergēre* wipe, polish]
• **tersely** *adverb*
• **terseness** *noun*
HOMOPHONES: *terce*

tertian *adjective*
• "TUR sh'n"
• (of a fever) recurring every forty-eight hours.
• [Latin *(febris) tertiana*, from *tertius* third (the fever recurring every third day by inclusive reckoning)]

tertiary *adjective*
• "TUR shur ee" or "TUR shee airy"
• third in order or rank etc.
• [Latin *tertiarius* from *tertius* third]

terzetto *noun*
• "turt SETTO"
• a vocal or instrumental trio.
• [Italian: see TERCET]

tesla *noun*
• "TESS luh"
• the SI unit of magnetic flux density, equal to one weber per square metre or 10,000 gauss.
• [N. *Tesla*, Croatian-born US electrical engineer d.1943]

tessellated *adjective*
ALSO SPELLED: **tesselated**
• "TESSA lated"
• (of a floor, wall, etc.) composed of or decorated with small blocks of variously coloured material arranged in a pattern or mosaic.
• [Latin *tessellatus* or Italian *tessellato* from Latin *tessellare* from *tessella* diminutive of TESSERA]
• **tessellate** *verb* (also **tesselate**)

tessellation *noun*
ALSO SPELLED: **tesselation**
• "tessa LAY sh'n"
• an arrangement of shapes, colours, minute parts, etc., closely fitted together.
• [as TESSELLATED]

tessera *noun*
• "TESSER uh"
• a small square block of marble, glass, tile, etc., used in a mosaic.
• [Latin from Greek, neuter of *tesseres, tessares* four]
• **tesseral** *adjective*

tessitura *noun*
• "tessa TURA"
• the range within which most tones of a voice part fall.
• [Italian, = texture, from Latin *textura* weaving]

testaceous *adjective*
• "tess TAY sh'ss"
• having a shell, esp. a hard, calcareous, unarticulated shell.
• [Latin *testa* tile, jug, shell]

testament *noun*
• "TESTA m'nt"
• either of the main divisions of the Christian Bible.
• [Latin *testamentum* will (as TESTATE): in early Christian Latin rendering Greek *diathēkē* covenant]

testamentary *adjective*
• "testa MENTA ree"
• made, bequeathed, or appointed by will.
• [as TESTAMENT]

testate *adjective*
• "TESS tate"
• having left a valid will at death.
• [Latin *testatus* past participle of *testari* testify, make a will, from *testis* witness]

testator *noun*
• "tuh STATER"
• a person who has made a will, esp. one who dies testate.
• [as TESTATE]

testatrix *noun*
• "tuh STAY trix"
• a woman who has made a will, esp. one who dies testate.
• [Latin, feminine of TESTATOR]

testicle *noun*
• "TESTA k'll"
• either of the two glandular organs in male humans and other mammals, which contain the sperm-producing cells and are usu. enclosed in the scrotum.
• [Latin *testiculus* diminutive of *testis* witness (of virility)]
• **testicular** *adjective* "tess TICK yuh lur"

testify *verb*
• "TESTA fie"
• appear as a witness to give evidence in a court of law.
• [Latin *testificari* from *testis* witness]
• **testifier** *noun*

testimonial *noun*
• "testa MOANY 'll"

• a written or oral statement attesting to the quality of esp. a product or service and recommending it to others.
• [as TESTIMONY]

testimony *noun*
• "TESTA moany"
• evidence or the body of evidence presented under oath in a court of law by one or more witnesses.
• [Latin *testimonium* from *testis* witness]

testis *noun*
• "TEST iss"
• a testicle.
• [Latin, = witness: compare TESTICLE]

testosterone *noun*
• "tess TOSS tur own"
• a steroid hormone that stimulates the development of male secondary sexual characteristics, produced in the testicles and, in very much smaller quantities, in the ovaries and adrenal cortex.
• [TESTIS + STEROL + '-one' forming nouns denoting various compounds, from Greek *-onē* feminine patronymic]

testudo *noun*
• "tess TOO doe" or "tess TYOO doe"
• a movable screen with an arched roof used to protect besieging troops.
• [Latin *testudo -dinis*, lit. 'tortoise', from *testa* shell]

tetanus *noun*
• "TET nuss" or "TET a nuss"
• a disease caused by the bacterium *Clostridium tetani*, marked by rigidity and spasms of the voluntary muscles.
• [Latin from Greek *tetanos* muscular spasm, from *teinō* stretch]
• **tetanic** *adjective* "tuh TANNIC"

tetany *noun*
• "TET a nee"
• a disease with intermittent muscular spasms caused by malfunction of the parathyroid glands and a consequent deficiency of calcium.
• [French *tétanie* (as TETANUS)]

tether *noun*
• "TETHER" (with "TH" as in *THIS*)
• a rope etc. by which an animal is tied to confine it to the spot.
• [Old Norse *tjóthr* from Germanic]

tetherball *noun*
• "TETHER ball" (with "TH" as in *THIS*)
• a game in which people use their hands or paddles to hit a ball suspended on a cord from an upright post, the winner being the first person to wind the cord completely around the post.
• [as TETHER + 'ball']

tetra *noun*
• "TETRA"
• any of various small, often brightly coloured tropical fish of the characin family, frequently kept in aquariums.
• [abbreviation of modern Latin *Tetragonopterus* (literally 'tetragonal finned'), former genus name]

tetrachloride *noun*
• "tetra CLORE ide"
• a compound of four atoms of chlorine with some other element or radical.
• [Greek *tetra* from *tettares* four + CHLORIDE]

tetracyclic *adjective*
• "tetra SICK lick"
• (of a compound) having a molecular structure of four fused hydrocarbon rings.
• [Greek *tetra* from *tettares* four + CYCLIC]

tetracycline *noun*
• "tetra SIKE lin"
• a tetracyclic compound which is a broad spectrum antibiotic.
• [as TETRACYCLIC]

tetrad *noun*
• "TET trad"
• a group of four.
• [Greek *tetra* from *tettares* four]

tetragon *noun*
• "TETRA gon"
• a quadrangle.
• [Greek *tetra* from *tettares* four + *-gonos* -angled]

tetragonal *adjective*
• "tuh TRAGGA n'll"
• belonging to or being a crystal system in which there are three mutually perpendicular crystallographic axes, two being equal and the third of a different length.
• [as TETRAGON]

Tetragrammaton *noun*
• "tetra GRAMA tawn"
• the Hebrew name of God transliterated in four letters as YHVH (from 'Yahveh') or JHVH (from 'Jehovah'), often regarded as ineffable and treated as a mysterious symbol of God.
• [Greek (*tetra* from *tettares* four, *gramma, -atos* letter)]

tetrahedrite *noun*
• "tetra HEE drite"
• a metallic grey mineral consisting of native sulphide of antimony, iron, and copper, typically occurring as tetrahedral crystals.
• [as TETRAHEDRON + Greek *lithos* stone]

tetrahedron *noun*
• "tetra HEED r'n"
• a solid figure or object with four plane faces, esp. one with four equal equilateral triangular faces.
• [Greek *tetra* from *tettares* four + *hedra* seat]
• **tetrahedral** *adjective*

tetrahydrocannabinol *noun*
• "tetra hydra kuh NABBIN awl"
• the active principle of cannabis.

• [Greek *tetra* from *tettares* four + HYDROGEN + CANNABIS]

tetralogy *noun*
• "tet TRAL a jee" or "tet TRAWLA jee"
• a group of four related literary or operatic works.
• [Greek *tetra* from *tettares* four + *logos* word]

tetrameter *noun*
• "tet TRAMMA tur"
• a line of four metrical feet.
• [Greek *tetra* from *tettares* four + *metron* measure]

tetraplegia *noun*
• "tetra PLEE juh"
• paralysis of all four limbs; quadriplegia.
• [modern Latin from Greek *tetra* from *tettares* four + *plēgē* blow, strike]
• **tetraplegic** *adjective*

tetraploid *adjective*
• "TETRA ploid"
• (of an organism or cell) having four times the haploid set of chromosomes.
• [Greek *tetra* from *tettares* four + HAPLOID]
• **tetraploidy** *noun*

tetrapod *noun*
• "TETRA pod"
• an animal with four feet or limbs.
• [modern Latin *tetrapodus* from Greek *tetrapous* (*tetra* from *tettares* four, *pous podos* foot)]

tetrarch *noun*
• "TET trark"
• the governor of a fourth part of a country or province.
• [Late Latin *tetrarcha* from Latin *tetrarches* from Greek *tetrarkhēs* (*tetra* from *tettares* four, *arkhō* rule)]

tetravalent *adjective*
• "tetra VALE 'nt"
• having a valence of four; quadrivalent.
• [Greek *tetra* from *tettares* four + VALENCE]

tetri *noun*
• "TET tree"
• a monetary unit of Georgia, equal to one-hundredth of a lari.
• [Georgian]

tetrodotoxin *noun*
• "tettro duh TOXIN"
• a poisonous substance found in the ovaries of certain pufferfishes which affects the action of nerve cells.
• [modern Latin *Tetrodon* former genus name for a variety of pufferfish + TOXIN]

tetroxide *noun*
• "tet TROX ide"
• any oxide containing four atoms of oxygen in its molecule or empirical formula.
• [Greek *tetra* from *tettares* four + OXYGEN]

Teuton *noun*
• "TOO t'n" or "TYOO t'n"
• a German.
• [Latin *Teutones, Teutoni*, from an Indo-European base meaning 'people' or 'country']
• **Teutonic** *adjective* "too TONNIC" or "tyoo TONNIC"

Thai *noun*
• "TIE"
• a native or inhabitant of Thailand in SE Asia.
• [Thai, = free]
HOMOPHONES: *tie*

thalamus *noun*
• "THALLA muss"
• either of two masses of grey matter lying between the cerebral hemispheres on either side of the third ventricle, which relay sensory information and act as a centre for pain perception.
• [Latin from Greek *thalamos* an inner room or woman's apartment]
• **thalamic** *adjective* "thuh LAMMIC" or "THALLA mick"

thalassemia *noun*
ALSO SPELLED: esp. *Brit.* **thalassaemia**
• "thalla SEEMY uh"
• any of a group of hereditary hemolytic diseases caused by faulty hemoglobin synthesis and widespread in Mediterranean, African, and Asian countries.
• [Greek *thalassa* sea (because first known around the Mediterranean) + *aimia* from *haima* blood]

thalassic *adjective*
• "thuh LASSIC"
• of the sea or seas, esp. small or inland seas.
• [French *thalassique* from Greek *thalassa* sea]

thalassotherapy *noun*
• "thuh lasso THERRA pee"
• a therapeutic treatment using sea water.
• [Greek *thalassa* sea + THERAPY]
• **thalassotherapist** *noun*

thaler *noun*
• "TAL ur"
• a German silver coin.
• [German *T(h)aler*, short for *Joachimstaler*, a coin from the silver mine of *Joachimstal*, now *Jáchymov* in the Czech Republic]

thali *noun*
• "TAL ee"
• a metal platter or flat dish on which Indian food is served.
• [Hindi *thālī* from Sanskrit *sthālī*]
HOMOPHONES: *tally*

thalidomide *noun*
• "thuh LIDDA mide"
• a drug formerly used as a sedative but found in 1961 to cause fetal malformation when taken by a mother early in pregnancy.
• [from *(ph)thal(ic acid)* + (im)*ido* + *(i)mide*]

thallium *noun*
- "THALLY um"
- a rare soft white metallic element, occurring naturally in zinc blende and some iron ores.
- [formed as THALLUS, from the green line in its spectrum]
- **thallic** *adjective*

thallus *noun*
- "THAL us"
- a plant body, such as in algae, fungi, lichens, etc., without vascular tissue and not differentiated into root, stem, and leaves.
- [Latin from Greek *thallos* green shoot, from *thallō* bloom]
- **thalloid** *adjective*

thalweg *noun*
- "TAL veg" ("VEG" rhymes with *BEG*)
- the line of fastest descent from any point on land, esp. one connecting the deepest points along a river channel or the lowest points along a valley floor.
- [German from *Thal* valley + *Weg* way]

thanatology *noun*
- "thanna TOLLA jee"
- the branch of science that deals with death, its causes and phenomena, and with the effects of approaching death and the needs of the terminally ill and their families.
- [Greek *thanatos* death + *logos* word]
- **thanatological** *adjective*
- **thanatologist** *noun*

Thanatos *noun*
- "thuh NAT ose" ("OSE" rhymes with *GROSS*)
- (in Freudian psychology) the urge for destruction or self-destruction.
- [Greek, lit. = 'death']

thane *noun*
- "THANE" (with "TH" as in *THIN*)
- (in Anglo-Saxon England) a man who held land from an English king or other superior by military service, ranking between ordinary freemen and hereditary nobles.
- [Old English *theg(e)n* servant, soldier, from Germanic]
- **thanedom** *noun*

thaumaturge *noun*
- "THOMMA turj"
- a person who works wonders or performs miracles.
- [medieval Latin *thaumaturgus* from Greek *thaumatourgos* (adjective) from *thauma -matos* marvel + *-ergos* -working]
- **thaumaturgic** *adjective*
- **thaumaturgical** *adjective*
- **thaumaturgy** *noun*

thebe *noun*
- "THAY bay" (with "TH" as in *THIN*)
- a monetary unit of Botswana, equal to one-hundredth of a pula.
- [Setswana, = shield]

theca *noun*
- "THEE kuh" (with "TH" as in *THIN*)
- a receptacle, sheath, or cell, esp. one enclosing some organ, part, or structure.
- [Latin from Greek *thēkē* case]

theine *noun*
- "THEE een" (with "TH" as in *THIN*)
- caffeine, esp. that obtained from tea and originally thought to be a different substance.
- [modern Latin *Thea* former genus name of the tea plant, from Dutch *thee* tea]

their *possessive adjective*
- "THAIR" (with "TH" as in *THIS*)
- of or belonging to them or themselves.
- [Old Norse *theirra* of them]

HOMOPHONES: *there, they're*

theirs *possessive pronoun*
- "THAIRZ" (with "TH" as in *THIS*)
- the one or ones belonging to or associated with them.
- [as THEIR]

theism *noun*
- "THEE izm" (with "TH" as in *THIN*)
- belief in the existence of gods or a god, esp. one God supernaturally revealed to man, who created and intervenes in the universe.
- [Greek *theos* god]
- **theist** *noun*
- **theistic** *adjective*
- **theistical** *adjective*
- **theistically** *adverb*

thematic *adjective*
- "thee MATTIC" (with "TH" as in *THIN*)
- of or relating to subjects or topics.
- [ultimately from Greek *thema -matos* theme, from *tithēmi* set, place]
- **thematically** *adverb*

thematize *verb*

ALSO SPELLED: esp. *Brit.* **-ise**
- "THEEMA tize" (with "TH" as in *THIN*)
- make thematic; present or select as a theme or topic of discourse.
- [as THEMATIC]
- **thematization** *noun* (also esp. *Brit.* **-isation**)

theobromine *noun*
- "thee a BRO meen" (with "TH" as in *THIN*)
- a bitter white alkaloid obtained from cacao seeds, related to caffeine.
- [*Theobroma* cacao genus: modern Latin from Greek *theos* god + *brōma* food]

theocentric *adjective*
- "thee a SENTRIC" (with "TH" as in *THIN*)
- having God as its centre.
- [Greek *theos* god + CENTRE]
- **theocentrism** *noun*

theocracy *noun*
- "thee OCKRA see" (with "TH" as in *THIN*)
- a form of government by God or a god

directly or by a priestly order etc. claiming divine commission.
• [Greek *theos* god + *kratia* from *kratos* strength, power]
• **theocrat** *noun* "THEE a crat" (with "TH" as in *THIN*)
• **theocratic** *adjective*

theodicy *noun*
• "thee ODDA see" (with "TH" as in *THIN*)
• the vindication or defence of divine providence in view of the existence of evil.
• [Greek *theos* god + *dikē* justice]

theodolite *noun*
• "thee ODDA lite" (with "TH" as in *THIN*)
• a surveying instrument for measuring horizontal and vertical angles with a rotating telescope.
• [16th c. *theodelitus*, of unknown origin]

theogony *noun*
• "thee OGGA nee" (with "TH" as in *THIN*)
• the genealogy of the gods.
• [Greek *theos* god + *-gonia* begetting]

theology *noun*
• "thee OLLA jee" (with "TH" as in *THIN*)
• the branch of knowledge dealing with esp. theistic religion; the study of the nature, attributes, and governance of God.
• [Old French *theologie* from Latin *theologia* from Greek (*theos* god, *logos* word)]
• **theologian** *noun* "thee a LO j'n"
• **theological** *adjective*
• **theologically** *adverb*
• **theologist** *noun*
• **theologize** *verb* (also esp. *Brit.* **-ise**)

theophany *noun*
• "thee OFFA nee" (with "TH" as in *THIN*)
• a visible manifestation of God or a god.
• [ultimately from Greek *theophaneia* (*theos* god, *phainein* show)]

theophylline *noun*
• "thee a FILL een" or "thee a FILL in" (with "TH" as in *THIN*)
• an alkaloid similar to theobromine, found in tea leaves.
• [modern Latin *Thea* tea (see THEINE) + Greek *phullon* leaf]

theorbo *noun*
• "thee ORBO" (with "TH" as in *THIN*)
• a two-necked musical instrument of the lute class much used in the 17th c.
• [Italian *tiorba*, of unknown origin]
• **theorbist** *noun*

theorem *noun*
• "THEER um" or "THEE a rum" (with "TH" as in *THIN*)
• a general proposition not self-evident but proved by a chain of reasoning; a truth established by means of accepted truths.
• [French *théorème* or Late Latin *theorema* from Greek *theōrēma* speculation, proposition, from *theōreō* look at]

theoretic *adjective*
• "thee a RETTIC" (with "TH" as in *THIN*)
• = THEORETICAL.
• [as THEORY]

theoretical *adjective*
• "thee a RETTA k'll" (with "TH" as in *THIN*)
• concerned with knowledge but not with its practical application.
• [as THEORY]
• **theoretically** *adverb*

theoretician *noun*
• "theer a TISH'n"
• a person concerned with the theoretical aspects of a subject.
• [as THEORY]

theory *noun*
• "THEERY" or "THEE a ree" (with "TH" as in *THIN*)
• a supposition or system of ideas explaining something, esp. one based on general principles independent of the particular things to be explained.
• [Greek *theōria* from *theōros* spectator, from *theōreō* look at]
• **theorist** *noun*
• **theorization** *noun* (also esp. *Brit.* **-isation**)
• **theorize** *verb* (also esp. *Brit.* **-ise**)
• **theorizer** *noun* (also esp. *Brit.* **-iser**)

theosophy *noun*
• "thee OSSA fee" (with "TH" as in *THIN*)
• any of various philosophies professing to achieve a knowledge of God by spiritual ecstasy, direct intuition, or special individual relations, esp. a modern movement following Hindu and Buddhist teachings and seeking universal fellowship.
• [medieval Latin *theosophia* from late Greek *theosophia* from *theosophos* wise concerning God (*theos* god, *sophos* wise)]
• **theosophic** *adjective* "thee a SOFFIC" (with "TH" as in *THIN*)
• **theosophical** *adjective*
• **theosophist** *noun* "thee OSSA fist" (with "TH" as in *THIN*)

therapeutics *noun*
• "therra PYOO tix"
• the branch of medicine concerned with the treatment of disease and the action of remedial agents.
• [ultimately from Greek *therapeutika* from *therapeuō* wait on, cure]
• **therapeutic** *adjective*
• **therapeutically** *adverb*

therapsid *noun*
• "thare AP sid" (with "TH" as in *THIN*)
• a fossil reptile of the order Therapsida, related to the ancestors of mammals.
• [modern Latin *Therapsida*, from Greek *thēr*

beast + (*h*)*apsis -idos* arch (referring to the structure of the skull)]

therapy *noun*
- "THERRA pee"
- the treatment of physical or mental disorders, other than by surgery.
- [modern Latin *therapia* from Greek *therapeia* healing]
- **therapist** *noun*
- **therapize** *verb* (also esp. *Brit.* **-ise**)

Theravada *noun*
- "therra VODDA"
- a more conservative form of Buddhism, practised in Sri Lanka, Burma (now Myanmar), Thailand, etc.
- [Pali *theravāda* from *thera* elder, old + *vāda* speech, doctrine]

therefore *adverb*
- "THARE for" (with "TH" as in *THIS*)
- for that reason; accordingly, consequently.
- ['there' + 'for']

theremin *noun*
- "THERRA min"
- an electronic musical instrument in which the tone is generated by two high-frequency oscillators and the pitch controlled by the movement of the performer's hand towards and away from the circuit.
- [L. *Theremin*, Russian inventor d.1993]

thermidor *noun*
- "THURMA dore"
- a mixture of lobster meat, mushrooms, cream, egg yolks, and sherry, cooked in a lobster shell.
- [the name of the 11th month of the French revolutionary calendar]

thermion *noun*
- "THURMY on"
- an ion or electron emitted by a substance at high temperature.
- [Greek *thermē* heat + ION]
- **thermionic** *adjective*
- **thermionics** *noun*

thermistor *noun*
- "thur MISTER"
- a resistor whose resistance is greatly reduced by heating, used for measurement and control.
- [*thermal resistor*]

thermite *noun*
- "THUR mite"
- a mixture of finely powdered aluminum and iron oxide that produces a very high temperature on combustion (used in welding and for incendiary bombs).
- [German *Thermit* from Greek *thermē* heat]

thermobaric *adjective*
- "thurmo BARE ick"
- denoting or relating to a very large fuel-air bomb which ignites into a fireball when detonated, creating a powerful wave of pressure that sucks out oxygen from any confined spaces nearby.
- [Greek *thermē* heat + *barus* heavy]

thermochemistry *noun*
- "thurmo KEMMA stree"
- the branch of chemistry dealing with the quantities of heat evolved or absorbed during chemical reactions.
- [Greek *thermē* heat + CHEMISTRY]
- **thermochemical** *adjective*

thermocline *noun*
- "THURMA cline"
- a temperature gradient, esp. an abrupt one in a body of water.
- [Greek *thermē* heat + *klinō* to slope]

thermocouple *noun*
- "THURMO cup'll"
- a thermoelectric device for measuring temperature, consisting of two wires of different metals connected at two points, a voltage being developed between the two junctions in proportion to the temperature difference.
- [Greek *thermē* heat + COUPLE]

thermodynamics *noun*
- "thurmo die NAMMIX"
- the science of the relations between heat and other (mechanical, electrical, etc.) forms of energy.
- [Greek *thermē* heat + DYNAMIC]
- **thermodynamic** *adjective*
- **thermodynamically** *adverb*
- **thermodynamicist** *noun*

"thurmo die NAMMA sist"

thermoelectric *adjective*
- "thurmo e LECK trick"
- relating to electricity produced by a temperature difference.
- [Greek *thermē* heat + ELECTRIC]
- **thermoelectricity** *noun*

"thurmo e leck TRISSA tee"

thermogenesis *noun*
- "thurmo JENNA sis"
- the production of heat, esp. in a human or animal body.
- [Greek *thermē* heat + GENESIS]
- **thermogenic** *adjective*

thermokarst *noun*
- "THURMO carst"
- topography in which the eventual melting of permafrost has produced hollows, hummocks, etc., reminiscent of karst.
- [Greek *thermē* heat + KARST]

thermolabile *adjective*
- "thurmo LAY bile" or "thurmo LAY bill"
- (of a substance) unstable when heated.
- [Greek *thermē* heat + LABILE]

thermoluminescence *noun*
- "thurmo loomin ESS ince"

• the property of becoming luminescent when pre-treated and subjected to high temperatures, used esp. as a means of dating ancient artifacts.
• [Greek *thermē* heat + LUMINESCENCE]
• **thermoluminescent** *adjective*

thermolysis *noun*
• "thur MOLLA sis"
• decomposition by the action of heat.
• [Greek *thermē* heat + LYSIS]

thermometer *noun*
• "thur MOMMA tur"
• an instrument for measuring temperature, esp. a graduated thin glass tube containing mercury or alcohol which expands when heated.
• [Greek *thermē* heat + *metron* measure]
• **thermometric** *adjective* "thurmo METRIC"
• **thermometry** *noun*

thermonuclear *adjective*
• "thurmo NEW clee ur"
• relating to or using nuclear reactions that occur only at very high temperatures.
• [Greek *thermē* heat + NUCLEAR]

thermophile *noun*
• "THURMO file"
• a bacterium etc. growing optimally at high temperatures.
• [Greek *thermē* heat + *philos* dear, loving]
• **thermophilic** *adjective*

thermosphere *noun*
• "THURMA sfeer"
• the region of the atmosphere beyond the mesosphere, characterized by an increase of temperature with height.
• [Greek *thermē* heat + SPHERE]

theropod *noun*
• "THEERA pod"
• a saurischian dinosaur of the group *Theropoda*, comprising mainly bipedal carnivores, including tyrannosaurs and the possible ancestors of birds.
• [Greek *thēr* beast + *pous podos* foot]

thesaurus *noun*
• "thuh SORE us" (with "TH" as in *THIN*)
• a book that lists words in groups of synonyms and related concepts.
• [Latin from Greek *thēsauros* treasure]

thesis *noun*
• "THEE sis" (with "TH" as in *THIN*)
• a proposition to be maintained or proved.
• [Late Latin from Greek, = putting, placing, a proposition etc., from *the-* root of *tithēmi* place]

thespian *adjective*
• "THESPY 'n" (with "TH" as in *THIN*)
• of or relating to tragedy or drama.
• [*Thespis*, Greek dramatic poet (6th c. BC)]

theta *noun*
• "THAY tuh" (with "TH" as in *THIN*)
• the eighth letter of the Greek alphabet (Θ, ϑ).
• [Greek]

theurgy *noun*
• "THEE ur jee" (with "TH" as in *THIN*)
• supernatural or divine agency esp. in human affairs.
• [Late Latin *theurgia* from Greek *theourgia* from *theos* god + *-ergos* working]
• **theurgic** *adjective*
• **theurgical** *adjective*

thew *noun*
• "THYOO"
• muscular strength.
• [Old English *thēaw* usage, conduct, of unknown origin]
• **thewy** *adjective*

thiamine *noun*
ALSO SPELLED: **thiamin**
• "THYE a min" (with "TH" as in *THIN*)
• a vitamin of the B complex, found in unrefined cereals, beans, and liver, a deficiency of which causes beriberi.
• [Greek *theion* sulphur + *amin* from VITAMIN]

thief *noun*
• "THEEF"
• a person who steals esp. secretly and without violence.
• [Old English *thēof* from Germanic]

thieving *adjective*
• "THEEV ing"
• be a thief.
• [Old English *thēofian* (as THIEF)]
• **thievery** *noun*
• **thievish** *adjective*
• **thievishly** *adverb*
• **thievishness** *noun*

thigh *noun*
• "THYE" (with "TH" as in *THIN*)
• the part of the human leg between the hip and the knee.
• [Old English *thēh*, *thēoh*, *thīoh*, Old High German *dioh*, Old Norse *thjó* from Germanic]

thimerosal *noun*
• "thye MERRA sal" (with "TH" as in *THIN*)
• a crystalline antiseptic.
• [Greek *theion* sulphur + *mer* from MERCURY + *sal* from SALICYLATE]

thiol *noun*
• "THYE awl" (with "TH" as in *THIN*)
• any organic compound containing an alcohol-like group but with sulphur in place of oxygen.
• [Greek *theion* sulphur + ALCOHOL]

thiosulphate *noun*
ALSO SPELLED: **thiosulfate**
• "thye oh SULL fate" (with "TH" as in *THIN*)
• a sulphate in which one oxygen atom is replaced by sulphur.
• [Greek *theion* sulphur + SULPHATE]

thixotropy *noun*
• "thick SOTTRA pee"
• the property displayed by certain gels of

becoming temporarily fluid when shaken or stirred etc., and of reverting back to a gel when left to stand.
• [Greek *thixis* touching + *tropē* turning]
• **thixotropic** *adjective* "thick suh TROPPIC"

thole *noun*
• "THOLE" (with "TH" as in *THIN*)
• a vertical pin or peg in the side or gunwale of a boat which serves as the fulcrum for an oar, esp. either of a pair forming an oarlock.
• [Old English *thol* fir tree, peg]

tholos *noun*
• "THOLL oss"
• a dome-shaped tomb, esp. of the Mycenaean period.
• [Greek]

Thomism *noun*
• "TOME izm"
• the philosophical or theological doctrine developed by St. Thomas Aquinas (1225–74).
• [*Thomas* Aquinas]
• **Thomist** *noun*
• **Thomistic** *adjective*

Thompson *noun*
• "TOM s'n"
• a member of an Aboriginal people living near the Thompson River in the Fraser River Valley of BC; also called Nlaka'pamux.
• [the *Thompson* River in BC]

thorax *noun*
• "THOR ax"
• the part of the body of a mammal between the neck and the abdomen, including the cavity enclosed by the ribs, breastbone, and dorsal vertebrae, and containing the chief organs of circulation and respiration.
• [Latin from Greek *thōrax -akos* breastplate]
• **thoracic** *adjective* "thor ASSIC"

Thoreauvian *adjective*
• "thore OH vee 'n"
• of or relating to the US essayist and poet H.D. Thoreau (d.1862) or his work.

thorium *noun*
• "THORRY um"
• a radioactive metallic element occurring naturally in monazite, used in electronic equipment and as a source of nuclear energy.
• [*Thor*, the Norse god of thunder]

Thoroldite *noun*
• "THOR'ld ite"
• a resident of Thorold, Ont.

thorough *adjective*
• "THURRO" or "THUH roe" (with "TH" as in *THIN*)
• applied to or affecting every part or detail; not superficial.
• [originally as adverb and prep. in the senses of *through*, from Old English *thuruh* var. of *thurh* THROUGH]
• **thoroughly** *adverb*
• **thoroughness** *noun*

thoroughbred *noun*
• "THURRO bred" or "THUH roe bred" (with "TH" as in *THIN*)
• a purebred animal, esp. a horse.
• [THOROUGH + 'bred']

thoroughfare *noun*
• "THURRO fare" or "THUH roe fare" (with "TH" as in *THIN*)
• a road or path open at both ends through which esp. traffic may pass.
• [THOROUGH + FARE]

thoroughgoing *adjective*
• "THURRO go ing" or "THUH roe go ing" (with "TH" as in *THIN*)
• extremely thorough; not superficial.
• [THOROUGH + 'go']

though *conjunction*
• "THO" (with "TH" as in *THIS*)
• despite the fact that.
• [Old Norse *thó* etc., corresponding to Old English *thēah*, from Germanic]

thought *noun*
• "THOT"
• the process or power of thinking; the faculty of reason.
• [Old English *thōht*]

thoughtful *adjective*
• "THOT full"
• showing thought or consideration for others; considerate, kind.
• [as THOUGHT]
• **thoughtfully** *adverb*
• **thoughtfulness** *noun*

thoughtless *adjective*
• "THOT less"
• lacking in consideration for others; inconsiderate, tactless.
• [as THOUGHT]
• **thoughtlessly** *adverb*
• **thoughtlessness** *noun*

Thracian *adjective*
• "THRAY sh'n"
• of or relating to the ancient country of Thrace, now divided between Turkey, Bulgaria, and Greece.

thrall *noun*
• "THRAWL"
• a condition or state of or like slavery or servitude; subjection to a person, power, or influence.
• [Old English *thræl* from Old Norse *thræll*, perhaps from a Germanic root = run]
• **thralldom** *noun* (also **thraldom**)

threnody *noun*
• "THRENNA dee"
• a song of lamentation, esp. for the dead; a dirge.

• [Greek *thrēnōidia* from *thrēnos* wailing + *ōidē* ode]
• **threnodic** *adjective* "thren ODDIC"
• **threnodist** *noun*

threonine *noun*
• "THREE a neen"
• a hydrophilic amino acid widely present in proteins and essential in the human diet.
• [*threose* (name of a sugar), ultimately from Greek *eruthros* red]

threshold *noun*
• "THRESH old" or "THRESH hold"
• a strip of wood or stone forming the bottom of a doorway and crossed upon entering a house or room.
• [Old English *therscold*, *threscold*, etc., related to 'thrash' in the sense 'tread']

throe *noun*
• "THROE"
• a violent pang, esp. of childbirth or death.
• [Middle English *throwe* perhaps from Old English *thrēa*, *thrawu* calamity, alteration perhaps by assoc. with *woe*]
HOMOPHONES: *throw*

thrombin *noun*
• "THROM bin"
• a plasma protein which acts as an enzyme to convert fibrinogen to fibrin and so promote the clotting of blood.
• [as THROMBUS]

thrombocyte *noun*
• "THROM buh site"
• a cell or platelet which circulates in the blood of vertebrates and is responsible for coagulation.
• [as THROMBUS + Greek *kutos* vessel]

thrombocytopenia *noun*
• "thrombo site a PEENY uh"
• deficiency of platelets in the blood.
• [THROMBOCYTE + Greek *penia* poverty]
• **thrombocytopenic** *adjective*

thromboembolism *noun*
• "thrombo EMB'll izm"
• an embolism of a blood vessel caused by a thrombus dislodged from another site.
• [as THROMBUS + EMBOLISM]

thrombosis *noun*
• "throm BO sis"
• a local coagulation or clotting of the blood in a part of the circulatory system.
• [modern Latin from Greek *thrombōsis* curdling (as THROMBUS)]
• **thrombose** *verb* "throm BOZE"
• **thrombotic** *adjective* "throm BOTTIC"

thrombus *noun*
• "THROM buss"
• a blood clot that forms on the wall of a blood vessel or a chamber of the heart, esp. in such a way that it impedes or obstructs the flow of blood.
• [modern Latin from Greek *thrombos* lump, blood clot]

throstle *noun*
• "THROSS'll"
• a song thrush.
• [Old English from Germanic: related to 'thrush']

through *preposition*
• "THROO"
• from one end to the other of.
• [Old English *thurh* from West Germanic]

throughout *preposition*
• "throo OUT"
• through all of; in or to every part of; everywhere in.
• [as THROUGH + 'out']

throughput *noun*
• "THROO put"
• the amount of material put through a process, esp. in manufacturing or computing.
• [as THROUGH + 'put']

throughway *noun*
ALSO SPELLED: esp. *US* **thruway**
• "THROO way"
• an expressway.
• [as THROUGH + 'way']

thuggee *noun*
• "THUGGY"
• the system of robbery and assassination practised by the Thugs, a religious organization of professional robbers and assassins in India, who strangled their victims.
• [Hindi *ṭhagī* from *ṭhag* swindler]

thuja *noun*
• "THOO yuh" or "THOO juh"
• any evergreen coniferous tree of the genus *Thuja*, with small leaves closely pressed to the branches; arborvitae.
• [modern Latin from Greek *thuia*, an African tree]

Thule *noun*
• "TOOLY"
• an Inuit culture widely distributed from Alaska to Greenland AD *c.*100–1400.
• [*Thule*, a country described by the ancient Greek explorer Pytheas (*c.*310 BC) as being six days' sail north of Britain, variously identified with Iceland, the Shetland Islands, and, most plausibly, Norway. It was regarded by the ancients as the northernmost part of the world]

thulium *noun*
• "THOOLY um" or "THYOOLY um"
• a soft metallic element of the lanthanide series, occurring naturally in apatite.
• [modern Latin, as THULE]

thurible *noun*
• "THURRA bull"
• a censer.

• [Old French *thurible* or Latin *t(h)uribulum* from *thus thur-* incense (as THURIFER)]

thurifer *noun*
• "THURRA fur"
• an acolyte carrying a censer.
• [Late Latin from *thus thuris* incense, from Greek *thuos* sacrifice + *-fer* -bearing]

thwart *verb*
• "THWORT"
• successfully oppose (a person or thing); foil, frustrate, block.
• [Old Norse *thvert* neuter of *thverr* transverse = Old English *thwe(o)rh* from Germanic]

thylacine *noun*
• "THYE luh seen" (with "TH" as in *THIN*)
• a Tasmanian doglike carnivorous marsupial with stripes across the rump, now possibly extinct.
• [modern Latin *Thylacinus* from Greek *thulakos* pouch]

thyme *noun*
• "TIME"
• any herb or shrub of the genus *Thymus* with aromatic leaves, esp. *T. vulgare* grown for culinary use.
• [Old French *thym* from *thymum* from Greek *thumon* from *thuō* burn a sacrifice]
HOMOPHONES: *time*

thymidine *noun*
• "THYE muh dine" (with "TH" as in *THIN*)
• a nucleoside of thymine that is found in DNA.
• [as THYMINE]

thymine *noun*
• "THYE meen" (with "TH" as in *THIN*)
• a pyrimidine found in all living tissue as a component base of DNA.
• [*thymic* (as THYMUS)]

thymol *noun*
• "THYE maul" (with "TH" as in *THIN*)
• a white crystalline phenol obtained from oil of thyme and used esp. as an antiseptic, preservative, or flavouring.
• [as THYME]

thymus *noun*
• "THYE muss" (with "TH" as in *THIN*)
• a lymphoid organ situated near the base of the neck of vertebrates which is the site of maturation of T lymphocytes, in humans becoming much smaller at the approach of puberty.
• [modern Latin from Greek *thumos*]
• **thymic** *adjective*

thyristor *noun*
• "thye RISTER" (with "TH" as in *THIN*)
• a semiconductor rectifier in which the current between two electrodes is controlled by a signal applied to a third electrode.
• [Greek *thura* gate + TRANSISTOR]

thyroid *noun*
• "THYE roid" (with "TH" as in *THIN*)
• a large ductless gland in the neck of vertebrates which secretes hormones regulating growth and development through control of the rate of metabolism.
• [obsolete French *thyroide* or modern Latin *thyroides*, from Greek *thureoeidēs* from *thureos* oblong shield]

thyrotoxicosis *noun*
• "thye ro toxa CO sis" (with "TH" as in *THIN*)
• a disorder involving overactivity of the thyroid gland.
• [as THYROID + TOXIN]

thyroxine *noun*
ALSO SPELLED: **thyroxin**
• "thye ROX'n"
• the main hormone produced and secreted by the thyroid gland which increases the metabolic rate and regulates growth and development in animals.
• [THYROID + OXYGEN]

thyrsus *noun*
• "THUR suss"
• a staff or spear tipped with an ornament like a pine cone, carried by Bacchus and his followers.
• [Latin from Greek *thursos*]

ti *noun*
ALSO SPELLED: **te**
• "TEE"
• (in tonic sol-fa) the seventh note of a major scale.
• [earlier *si*: French from Italian, perhaps from Sancte Iohannes: see GAMUT]
HOMOPHONES: *tea, tee*

tiara *noun*
• "tee AIR uh" or "tee ARR uh"
• a woman's jewelled ornamental coronet or headband worn on the front of the hair.
• [Latin from Greek, of unknown origin]
• **tiaraed** *adjective*

Tibetan *noun*
• "tib BET 'n"
• a native or inhabitant of Tibet.

tibia *noun*
• "TIBBY uh"
• the inner and larger of the two bones of the lower leg extending from the knee to the ankle, articulating at its upper end with the fibula.
• [Latin, = shin bone]
• **tibial** *adjective*

tibiotarsus *noun*
• "tibby oh TAR suss"
• the bone in a bird corresponding to the tibia, fused at the lower end with the proximal bones of the tarsus.
• [as TIBIA + TARSUS]

tic *noun*
• "TICK"
• a disorder characterized by a repeated habitual spasmodic twitching of one or more muscles, esp. of the face, largely involuntary and accentuated under stress.
• [French from Italian *ticchio*]
HOMOPHONES: *tick*

tier *noun*
• "TEER"
• each of a series of rows or horizontal units placed one above another in a structure, such as in theatre seating.
• [earlier *tire* from French from *tirer* draw, elongate, from Romanic]
• **tiered** *adjective*
HOMOPHONES: *tear*

tierce *noun*
• "TEERCE"
• an interval of two octaves and a major third.
• [Old French *t(i)erce* from Latin *tertia* feminine of *tertius* third]

tigress *noun*
• "TIE griss"
• a female tiger.
• [Old French *tigresse* from Latin *tigris* tiger, from Greek *tigris*]

tiki *noun*
• "TICKY"
• (in Maori and Polynesian culture) a large wooden or small greenstone image of a human figure, often worn as a neck pendant.
• [Maori]

tikinagan *noun*
• "ticka NOG'n"
• *Cdn* (among some N American Aboriginal peoples) a thin board to which an infant is strapped so that it can be transported on its mother's back or placed on the ground or against a tree; a cradleboard.
• [Cree *tikina:kan*]

tikka *noun*
• "TICKA" or "TEEKA"
• an Indian dish of marinated meat, esp. chicken or lamb, threaded on skewers and grilled.
• [Punjabi *ṭikkā*]

tilapia *noun*
• "til APPY uh" or "til APEY uh"
• a freshwater cichlid fish of the African genus *Tilapia* or a related genus, widely introduced for food.
• [modern Latin]

tilbury *noun*
• "TIL burry"
• a light open two-wheeled carriage.
• [after the inventor's name]

tilde *noun*
• "TILDA"
• a mark (˜), placed over a letter, e.g. over a Spanish *n* when pronounced *ny* (as in *señor*) or a Portuguese *a* or *o* when nasalized (as in *São Paulo*).
• [Spanish, ultimately from Latin *titulus* title]

Tillsonburger *noun*
• "TIL s'n burger"
• a resident of Tillsonburg, Ont.

tilth *noun*
• "TILTH"
• the condition of cultivated soil.
• [Old English *tilth(e)*]

timbale *noun*
• "tam BAL"
• a dish consisting of meat, fish, or vegetables in a creamy sauce, or fruit etc. served in a drum-shaped china or copper mould, a pastry shell, or a similar crust made of rice or pasta.
• [French from Arabic *aṭ-ṭabl* the drum]

timbre *noun*
• "TAM bur" or "TAM bruh"
• the distinctive character or quality of a sound, esp. that of a musical voice or instrument, apart from its pitch and intensity.
• [French from Romanic from medieval Greek *timbanon* from Greek *tumpanon* drum]
• **timbral** *adjective*
HOMOPHONES: *tambour*

Timbuktu *noun*
ALSO SPELLED: **Timbuctoo**
• "tim buck TOO"
• any remote or outlandish place in a faraway country.
• [*Timbuktu*, a town in Mali on the edge of the Sahara Desert, historically a Muslim centre of learning and a major trading centre for gold and salt on the trans-Saharan trade routes]

Timorese *noun*
• "tee more EEZ"
• a native or inhabitant of the island of Timor in the Malay Archipelago.

timorous *adjective*
• "TIMMER us"
• timid; easily alarmed.
• [Old French *temoreus* from medieval Latin *timorosus* from Latin *timor* from *timēre* fear]
• **timorously** *adverb*
• **timorousness** *noun*

timpani *plural noun*
ALSO SPELLED: **tympani**
• "TIMPA nee"
• large drums shaped like a bowl with a membrane adjustable for tension (and so pitch) stretched across; kettledrums.
• [Italian, pl. of *timpano* = TYMPANUM]
• **timpanist** *noun* (also **tympanist**)

tinamou *noun*
• "TINNA moo"

• any S American bird of the family Tinamidae, resembling a grouse but related to the rhea.
• [French from Galibi *tinamu*]

tincture *noun*
• "TINK chur"
• a slight infusion of an element or quality; a tinge, trace, or hint.
• [Latin *tinctura* dyeing, from *tingere tinct-* dye, stain]

tinea *noun*
• "TINNY uh"
• any of various fungous infections of the skin causing circular inflamed patches; ringworm.
• [Latin, = moth, worm]

tinnitus *noun*
• "tin ITE us"
• a ringing in the ears.
• [Latin from *tinnire tinnit-* ring, tinkle, of imitative origin]

tinsel *noun*
• "TIN s'll"
• glittering metallic strands or threads used for decoration, esp. on a Christmas tree.
• [Old French *estincele* spark, from Latin *scintilla*]
• **tinselled** *adjective* (also **tinseled**)
• **tinselly** *adjective* (also **tinsely**)

tintamarre *noun*
• "tanta MAR"
• *Cdn* a noisy parade, esp. the annual celebration on National Acadian Day, August 15, involving a procession, the banging of pots and pans, playing of musical instruments, etc.
• [French, = 'din']

tintinnabulation *noun*
• "tintin ab yoo LAY sh'n"
• a ringing or tinkling of bells.
• [as Latin *tintinnabulum* tinkling bell, from *tintinnare* reduplication of *tinnire* ring]

tintype *noun*
• "TIN tipe"
• a photograph taken as a positive on a thin tin or iron plate coated with enamel.
• ['tin' + TYPE]

tippet *noun*
• "TIP it"
• a length of twisted nylon or hair to which a hook is attached.
• [Middle English, prob. from 'tip']

tirade *noun*
• "TIE rade"
• a long vehement rant or outburst, esp. in denunciation of a particular thing.
• [French, = long speech, from Italian *tirata* volley, from *tirare* pull, from Romanic]

tiramisu *noun*
• "teera mee SOO" or "teera MEE soo"
• an Italian dessert consisting of layers of sponge cake or biscuit soaked in coffee and brandy or liqueur, filled with mascarpone cheese and topped with cocoa powder.
• [Italian, from *tirami sù*, lit. 'pick me up']

tisane *noun*
• "tee ZAN"
• a medicinal infusion formerly made with barley, now usu. made with dried herbs; herbal tea.
• [French from Latin *ptisana* from Greek *ptisanē* peeled barley]

tissue *noun*
• "TISH oo"
• the material of which an animal or plant body, or any of its parts or organs, is composed, consisting of an aggregation of specialized cells.
• [Old French *tissu* rich material, past participle of *tistre* from Latin *texere* weave]
• **tissuey** *adjective*

Titan *noun*
• "TITE 'n"
• a person or organization of very great power, importance, or strength.
• [Middle English from Latin from Greek, = any of the older gods who preceded the Olympians]

titanic *adjective*
• "tie TANNIC"
• huge, gigantic, colossal.
• [as TITAN]
• **titanically** *adverb*

titanium *noun*
• "tie TAINY um" or "tuh TAINY um"
• a grey metallic element occurring naturally in many clays etc., and used to make strong light alloys that are resistant to corrosion.
• [Greek *Titan* a member of a family of early gigantic gods, the offspring of Heaven and Earth, who contended for the sovereignty of heaven and were overthrown by Zeus + *-ium*, after *uranium*]

tithe *noun*
• "TYTHE" (with "TH" as in *BATHE*)
• one-tenth of the annual produce of agriculture, formerly taken as a tax for the support of the Church and clergy.
• [Old English *teogotha* tenth]
• **tithable** *adjective*
• **tithing** *noun*

titi *noun*
• "TEE tee"
• any long-coated S American monkey of the genus *Callicebus*.
• [Tupi]

titian *adjective*
• "TISH'n"
• (of hair) bright golden auburn.
• [from *Titian*, Italian painter d.1576, by association with the auburn hair portrayed in many of his works]

titillate *verb*
- "TITTA late"
- excite, arouse, or stimulate, esp. sexually.
- [Latin *titillare titillat-*]
- **titillating** *adjective*
- **titillatingly** *adverb*
- **titillation** *noun*

titivate *verb*
- "TITTA vate"
- adorn.
- [earlier *tidivate*, perhaps from 'tidy' after *cultivate*]
- **titivation** *noun*

titlist *noun*
- "TITE 'll ist"
- a titleholder.
- [Old French *title* title, from Latin *titulus* placard, title]

titrate *verb*
- "TIE trate"
- ascertain the amount of a constituent in (a solution) by slowly adding measured volumes of a suitable reagent of known concentration until the point when the reaction just begins or ceases to occur.
- [as TITRE]
- **titratable** *adjective*
- **titration** *noun*

titre *noun*
ALSO SPELLED: **titer**
- "TIE tur"
- the concentration of a solution as determined by titration.
- [French, = title, from Latin *titulus* title]

tittup *verb*
- "TIT up"
- (esp. of a horse or rider) gallop, canter, or proceed with a bouncing or bobbing motion.
- [perhaps imitative of hoof beats]

titubation *noun*
- "titch oo BAY sh'n"
- unsteadiness in posture or gait, esp. a rhythmic nodding of the head and trunk due to a cerebellar disease.
- [Latin *titubatio* from *titubare* totter]

titular *adjective*
- "TITCH yuh lur"
- being what is specified in name or title only without having the attributes or exercising the functions implied by it.
- [French *titulaire* or modern Latin *titularis* from *titulus* title]
- **titularly** *adverb*

tiyin *noun*
- "tee YIN"
- a monetary unit of Kyrgyzstan and Uzbekistan equal to one-hundredth of a som.
- [Kirghiz]

HOMOPHONES: *tiyn*

tiyn *noun*
- "tee Y'N"
- a monetary unit in Kazakhstan, equal to one-hundredth of a tenge.
- [Kazakh]

HOMOPHONES: *tiyin*

Tlingit *noun*
- "TLING git"
- a member of an Aboriginal people living on the islands and coast of SE Alaska and northern BC.
- [Tlingit *łi:ngít* person]

tobacco *noun*
- "tuh BACKO"
- a narcotic and addictive preparation of the dried leaves esp. of the plant *Nicotiana tabacum* and hybrids, which is esp. smoked or chewed for its relaxing effects, and used for ceremonial and religious purposes among some N American Aboriginal groups.
- [Spanish *tabaco*, of uncertain origin]

tobacconist *noun*
- "tuh BACKA nist"
- a person who deals in tobacco, esp. the owner of a store selling tobacco, pipes, cigars, cigarettes, and other assorted items.
- [as TOBACCO]

toboggan *noun*
- "tuh BOG'n"
- a long narrow sled without runners, bent or curled upwards at the front, which may be drawn by a rope over compacted snow or ice or used to coast down hills.
- [Canadian French *tabaganne* from Mi'kmaq *topaĝan* sled]
- **tobogganer** *noun*
- **tobogganing** *noun*
- **tobogganist** *noun*

toccata *noun*
- "tuh COTTA"
- a brisk musical composition for a keyboard instrument, having the air of an improvisation and designed to demonstrate the performer's touch and technique.
- [Italian, feminine past participle of *toccare* touch]

Tocharian *noun*
- "tuh KERRY 'n"
- an extinct Indo-European language spoken by a central Asian people that lived in the first millennium AD.
- [French *tocharien* from Latin *Tochari* from Greek *Tokharoi* a Scythian tribe]

tocopherol *noun*
- "toe COFFER awl"
- any of several closely related fat-soluble alcohols that occur in plant oils, wheat germ, egg yolk, and leafy vegetables, which are antioxidants essential in the diets of animals

and humans and collectively constitute vitamin E.
• [Greek *tokos* offspring + *pherō* bear + ALCOHOL]

tocsin *noun*
• "TOXIN"
• an alarm signal sounded by ringing a bell or bells.
• [French from Old French *touquesain*, from Provençal *tocasenh* from *tocar* touch + *senh* signal bell]
HOMOPHONES: *toxin*

tody *noun*
• "TOADY"
• any of several small insect-eating Caribbean birds of the genus *Todus*, which have green backs and red throats and are related to the kingfishers.
• [French *todier* from Latin *todus*, a small bird]
HOMOPHONES: *toady*

toea *noun*
• "TOE ay uh"
• a monetary unit of Papua New Guinea, equal to one-hundredth of a kina.
• [Motu, = 'cone-shaped shell']

tofu *noun*
• "TOE foo"
• a pale curd of varying consistency made from soybean milk and used as a source of protein esp. in vegetarian recipes and Asian cuisine.
• [Japanese *tōfu* from Chinese *dòufu*, from *dòu* beans + *fǔ* rot, turn sour]

Togolese *noun*
• "toe guh LEEZ"
• a native or inhabitant of Togo in W Africa.

toile *noun*
• "TWOLL"
• any of various linen or cotton fabrics.
• [French *toile* cloth, from Latin *tela* web]

toilette *noun*
• "twoll ET"
• the process of washing, dressing, arranging one's hair, etc.
• [French *toilette* cloth, wrapper, diminutive from *toile*: see TOILE]

tokamak *noun*
• "TOE kuh mack"
• a toroidal apparatus for producing controlled fusion reactions in hot plasma.
• [Russian acronym, from *to*roidal'naya *ka*mera s *ma*gnitnym polem 'toroidal chamber with magnetic field']

Tokay *noun*
• "tuh CAY"
• a sweet aromatic wine made near Tokaj in Hungary.

tole *noun*
• "TOLE"
• enamelled or lacquered tin-plated sheet iron used for making decorative metalwork.
• [French *tôle* sheet iron, from dialect *taule* table, from Latin *tabula* a flat board]
HOMOPHONES: *toll*

tolerable *adjective*
• "TOLLER a bull"
• able to be endured; bearable.
• [as TOLERATE]
• **tolerability** *noun*
• **tolerably** *adverb*

tolerate *verb*
• "TOLLER ate"
• allow the existence, practice, or occurrence of without authoritative interference or proscription.
• [Latin *tolerare tolerat-* endure]
• **tolerance** *noun*
• **tolerant** *adjective*
• **tolerantly** *adverb*
• **toleration** *noun*
• **tolerator** *noun*

toll *noun*
• "TOLE"
• a sum of money charged for permission to travel along a road or highway etc., the proceeds of which are used for its maintenance.
• [Old English from medieval Latin *toloneum* from Late Latin *teloneum* from Greek *telōnion* toll house, from *telos* tax]
HOMOPHONES: *tole*

tollgate *noun*
• "TOLE gate"
• a gate preventing passage until a toll is paid.
• [as TOLL + 'gate']

tollgating *noun*
• "TOLE gate ing"
• *Cdn* the illegal practice of paying or extorting a bribe or tribute for the right to do business with or within a province, country, etc.
• [as TOLLGATE]

Toltec *noun*
• "TAWL teck"
• a member of a Nahuatl people that flourished in Mexico before the Aztecs.
• [Spanish *tolteca* from Nahuatl *toltecatl*, lit. 'person from Tula' (ancient Toltec city)]
• **Toltecan** *adjective*

tolu *noun*
• "tuh LOO" or "TOE loo"
• a fragrant brown balsam obtained from either of two S American trees, *Myroxylon balsamum* or *M. toluifera*, and used in perfumery and medicine.
• [Santiago de *Tolu* in Colombia]

toluene *noun*
• "TAWL yoo een"
• a colourless aromatic liquid hydrocarbon derivative of benzene, originally obtained from tolu, now obtained from coal tar and petroleum, and used esp. as a solvent as well as in the manufacture of explosives.

• [TOLU + '-ene' forming names of unsaturated hydrocarbons containing a double bond, from Greek *-ēnos*, adjective suffix denoting origin or source]
• **toluic** *adjective*

tomahawk *noun*
• "TOMMA hock"
• a tool or weapon with a handle and a sharp stone or iron cutting head, formerly used by some N American Indians.
• [Virginia Algonquian]

tomatillo *noun*
• "tomma TILLO"
• a purplish edible fruit.
• [Spanish, diminutive of *tomate* TOMATO]

tomato *noun*
• "tuh MAY toe" or "tuh MAT oh"
• a glossy, usu. bright red and spherical pulpy edible fruit, eaten both raw and cooked as a vegetable.
• [French, Spanish, or Portuguese *tomate*, from Nahuatl *tomatl*]
• **tomatoey** *adjective*

tomb *noun*
• "TOOM"
• a large esp. underground vault for the burial of the dead.
• [Old French *tombe* from Late Latin *tumba* from Greek *tumbos*]

tombola *noun*
• "tom BOLE uh"
• a kind of raffle or draw in which tickets are drawn from a turning drum-shaped container, esp. at a fair or fete.
• [French *tombola* or Italian from *tombolare* tumble]

tombolo *noun*
• "TOMBA lo"
• a spit joining an island to the mainland.
• [Italian, = sand dune]

tombstone *noun*
• "TOOM stone"
• a slab of stone, usu. engraved with an epitaph, placed upright or laid flat over a person's grave as a memorial.
• [as TOMB + 'stone']

tomentum *noun*
• "tuh MEN tum"
• matted woolly down on stems and leaves.
• [Latin, = cushion-stuffing]
• **tomentose** *adjective*
• **tomentous** *adjective*

tomogram *noun*
• "TOMMA gram"
• a visual record obtained by tomography.
• [as TOMOGRAPHY + Greek *gramma* thing written]

tomography *noun*
• "tuh MOGGRA fee"
• any of various techniques which provide images of successive plane sections of the human body or other solid objects using X-rays or ultrasound, now usu. processed by computer to give a three-dimensional image.
• [Greek *tomē* a cutting + *graphia* writing]
• **tomographic** *adjective*

tomorrow *noun*
• "tuh MORE oh" or "tuh MAR oh"
• the day after today.
• ['to' + Middle English *morwe*, *moru* the following day]

ton *noun*
• "TUN"
• a unit of weight equal to 2,000 lb. avoirdupois (907.19 kg).
• [originally the same word as TUN: differentiated in the 17th c.]
HOMOPHONES: *tonne*, *tun*

tondo *noun*
• "TAWN doe"
• a circular painting or relief.
• [Italian, = round (plate), from *rotondo* from Latin *rotundus* round]

tonga *noun*
• "TONG guh"
• a light horse-drawn two-wheeled vehicle used in India.
• [Hindi *tāngā*]

Tongan *adjective*
• "TONG g'n"
• of or relating to the S Pacific country of Tonga or its people or language.

tongue *noun*
• "TUNG"
• the fleshy muscular organ in the mouth used in tasting, licking, and swallowing, and (in humans) for speech.
• [Old English *tunge* from Germanic, related to Latin *lingua*]
• **tongued** *adjective*
• **tongueless** *adjective*
HOMOPHONES: *tung*

tonguing *noun*
• "TUNG ing"
• the technique of playing a wind instrument using the tongue to articulate certain notes.
• [as TONGUE]

tonnage *noun*
• "TUN idge"
• weight in tons.
• [originally in sense 'duty on a tun of wine': Old French *tonnage* from *tonne* TUN: later from TON]

tonne *noun*
• "TUN"
• 1,000 kilograms.
• [French: see TUN]
HOMOPHONES: *ton*, *tun*

tonneau *noun*
• "tuh NO"
• the part of a motor vehicle occupied by the back seats, esp. in an open car.
• [French, lit. cask, tun]

tonsil *noun*
• "TAWN s'll"
• either of two small masses of lymphoid tissue on each side of the root of the tongue.
• [French *tonsilles* or Latin *tonsillae* (pl.)]
• **tonsillar** *adjective*

tonsillectomy *noun*
• "tonsa LECTA mee"
• the surgical removal of the tonsils.
• [as TONSIL + Greek *ektomē* excision, from *ek* out + *temnō* cut]

tonsillitis *noun*
• "tonsa LITE iss"
• inflammation of the tonsils.
• [as TONSIL + Greek *-itis*, forming feminine of adjectives in *-itēs* (with *nosos* 'disease' implied)]

tonsorial *adjective*
• "tawn SORRY 'll"
• of or relating to a hairdresser or hairdressing.
• [Latin *tonsorius* from *tonsor* barber, from *tondēre tons-* shave]
• **tonsorially** *adverb*

tonsure *noun*
• "TAWN shur"
• the shaving of the crown of the head or the entire head, esp. of a person entering a priesthood or monastic order.
• [Old French *tonsure* or Latin *tonsura* (as TONSORIAL)]
• **tonsured** *adjective*

tontine *noun*
• "TAWN teen" or "tawn TEEN"
• an annuity shared by subscribers to a loan, the shares increasing as subscribers die until the last survivor gets all, or until a specified date when the remaining survivors share the proceeds.
• [French, from the name of Lorenzo *Tonti* of Naples, Italy, originator of tontines in France *c.*1653]

toonie *noun*
• "TOONY"
• *Cdn* the Canadian two-dollar coin.
• [after 'two' + 'loonie' (dollar coin)]

toothwort *noun*
• "TOOTH wurt" or "TOOTH wort"
• any of various cruciferous plants of the genus *Dentaria* of eastern N America, esp. *Dentaria diphylla*, with white flowers and an edible root.
• ['tooth' + WORT]

tootsie *noun*
• "TOOT see" (with "OO" as in *FOOT*)
• a toe.
• [jocular diminutive: alteration of 'foot']
HOMOPHONES: *Tutsi*

topaz *noun*
• "TOE paz"
• a transparent or translucent aluminum silicate mineral, usu. yellow, used as a gem.
• [Old French *topaze* from Latin *topazus* from Greek *topazos*]

topgallant *noun*
• "top GAL'nt" or "tuh GAL'nt"
• the mast, sail, yard, or rigging immediately above the topmast and topsail of a sailing ship.
• ['top' + GALLANT, as making a brave or gallant show in comparison with the lower topsails]

topi *noun*
ALSO SPELLED: **topee**
• "TOE pee"
• a pith helmet.
• [Hindi *ṭopī*]

topiary *adjective*
• "TOPE ee airy"
• concerned with or formed by clipping shrubs, trees, etc. into ornamental or animal forms.
• [French *topiaire* from Latin *topiarius* landscape gardener, from *topia opera* fancy gardening, from Greek *topia* pl. diminutive of *topos* place]
• **topiarist** *noun*

topography *noun*
• "tuh POGGRA fee"
• a detailed description, representation on a map, etc., of the natural and artificial features of a town, district, etc.
• [Late Latin *topographia* from Greek from *topos* place]
• **topographer** *noun*
• **topographic** *adjective*
• **topographical** *adjective*
• **topographically** *adverb*

topology *noun*
• "tuh POLLA jee"
• the study of geometrical properties and spatial relations unaffected by the continuous change of shape or size of figures.
• [German *Topologie* from Greek *topos* place + *logos* word]
• **topological** *adjective*
• **topologically** *adverb*
• **topologist** *noun*

toponym *noun*
• "TOPPA nim"
• a place name.
• [Greek *topos* place + *onoma* name]

toponymy *noun*
• "tuh PONNA mee"
• the study of the place names of a region.
• [Greek *topos* place + *onoma* name]
• **toponymic** *adjective* "toppa NIMMIC"

topos *noun*
• "TOP oss" or "TOE poce" or "TOE poss"
• a stock theme in literature etc.
• [Greek, = commonplace]

toque *noun*
ALSO SPELLED: **tuque**
• "TOOK" (rhymes with *DUKE*)
• *Cdn* a close-fitting knitted hat, often with a tassel or pompom on the crown.
• [French, apparently = Italian *tocca*, Spanish *toca*, of unknown origin, assimilated to Canadian French *tuque*, ultimately from a pre-Romance form *tukka* gourd, hill]

tor *noun*
• "TORE"
• a hill or rocky peak, esp. in Devon or Cornwall in SW England.
• [Old English *torr*: compare Gaelic *tòrr* bulging hill]
HOMOPHONES: *torr, tore*

Torah *noun*
• "TORE uh"
• the first five books of the Bible (Genesis, Exodus, Leviticus, Numbers, and Deuteronomy), traditionally ascribed to Moses.
• [Hebrew *tōrāh* instruction]

torc *noun*
ALSO SPELLED: **torque**
• "TORK"
• a necklace of twisted metal, esp. of the ancient Gauls and Britons.
• [French *torque* from Latin *torques* from *torquēre* twist]
HOMOPHONES: *torque*

torchiere *noun*
• "torshy AIR"
• a floor lamp having the light bulb in an upturned saucer-shaped shade at the top of the pole.
• [French *torchère*, from Old French *torche* torch, from Latin *torqua* from *torquēre* twist]

torchon *noun*
• "TOR sh'n" or "tor SHŌH" (with a nasal *OH*)
• coarse bobbin lace with geometrical designs.
• [French, = duster, dishcloth, from *torcher* wipe]
HOMOPHONES: *torsion*

toreador *noun*
• "TORY a dore"
• a bullfighter, esp. one on horseback.
• [Spanish from *torear* fight bulls, from *toro* bull, from Latin *taurus*]

torero *noun*
• "tuh RARE oh"
• a bullfighter, esp. one on foot.
• [Spanish from *toro*: see TOREADOR]

toric *adjective*
• "TORE ick"
• having the form of a torus or part of a torus.
• [as TORUS]

torii *noun*
• "TORY ee"
• the gateway of a Shinto shrine, with two uprights and two crosspieces.
• [Japanese]

torment *noun*
• "TORE ment"
• severe physical or mental suffering; anguish.
• [Old French *torment, tormenter* from Latin *tormentum* instrument of torture, from *torquēre* to twist]
• **tormentingly** *adverb*
• **tormentor** *noun*

tormentil *noun*
• "TORE m'n till"
• a Eurasian plant, *Potentilla erecta*, with bright yellow flowers and a highly astringent rootstock.
• [Old French *tormentille* from medieval Latin *tormentilla*, of unknown origin]

tornado *noun*
• "tore NAY doe"
• a violent storm with very strong circular winds over a small area, often accompanied by a funnel-shaped cloud.
• [apparently assimilation of Spanish *tronada* thunderstorm (from *tronar* to thunder) to Spanish *tornar* to turn]
• **tornadic** *adjective* "tor NADDIC"

toroid *noun*
• "TORE oid"
• a figure resembling a torus.
• [as TORUS]
• **toroidal** *adjective*

Torontonian *noun*
• "tuh ron TONY 'n"
• a resident of Toronto.

torpedo *noun*
• "tore PEE doe"
• a self-propelled underwater missile, usu. cylindrical with a pointed or tapered nose, fired at a ship and exploding on impact.
• [Latin, = numbness, electric ray, from *torpēre* be numb]

torpid *adjective*
• "TORE pid"
• sluggish, inactive.
• [Latin *torpidus* (as TORPOR)]
• **torpidity** *noun*
• **torpidly** *adverb*

torpor *noun*
• "TORE pur"
• a torpid state.
• [Latin from *torpēre* be sluggish]

torque *noun*
• "TORK"
• a twisting or rotating force, esp. in a mechanism.
• [French from Latin *torquēre* to twist]
• **torquey** *adjective*
HOMOPHONES: *torc*

torr *noun*
• "TORE"
• a unit of pressure used in measuring partial vacuums, equal to 133.32 pascals.
• [E. *Torricelli*, Italian physicist d.1647]
HOMOPHONES: *tor*, *tore*

torrent *noun*
• "TORE 'nt"
• a rushing stream of water, lava, etc.
• [French from Italian *torrente* from Latin *torrens -entis* scorching, boiling, roaring, from *torrēre* scorch]
• **torrential** *adjective* "tuh REN sh'll"
• **torrentially** *adverb*

torrid *adjective*
• "TORE id"
• (of the weather) very hot and dry.
• [French *torride* or Latin *torridus*, from *torrēre* parch]
• **torridity** *noun*
• **torridly** *adverb*

torsion *noun*
• "TORE sh'n"
• twisting, esp. of one end of a body while the other is held fixed.
• [Old French from Late Latin *torsio -onis* from Latin *tortio* (as TORT)]
• **torsional** *adjective*
• **torsionally** *adverb*
HOMOPHONES: *torchon*

torso *noun*
• "TORE so"
• the trunk of the human body.
• [Italian, = stalk, stump, torso, from Latin *thyrsus*]

tort *noun*
• "TORT"
• a breach of duty (other than under contract) for which damages can be obtained in a civil court by the person wronged.
• [Old French from medieval Latin *tortum* wrong, neuter past participle of Latin *torquēre tort-* twist]
HOMOPHONES: *torte*

torte *noun*
• "TORT"
• an elaborate rich cake, esp. one with ground nuts as an ingredient and having multiple layers.
• [German]
HOMOPHONES: *tort*

tortellini *noun*
• "torta LEENY"
• small squares of pasta stuffed with meat, cheese, etc., rolled and formed into tight ring-shaped pouches.
• [Italian, pl. of *tortellino*, diminutive of *tortello* small cake, fritter]

tortfeasor *noun*
• "TORT feezer"
• a person guilty of tort.
• [Old French *tort-fesor*, *tort-faiseur*, etc. from *tort* wrong, *-fesor*, *faiseur* doer]

torticollis *noun*
• "torta COLLISS"
• a rheumatic etc. disease of the muscles of the neck, causing twisting and stiffness.
• [modern Latin from Latin *tortus* crooked + *collum* neck]

tortilla *noun*
• "tore TEE uh"
• (esp. in Mexican cooking) a thin round bread made with either cornmeal or wheat flour and usu. filled with meat, cheese, beans, etc.
• [Spanish diminutive of *torta* cake, from Late Latin]

tortious *adjective*
• "TORE sh'ss"
• constituting a tort; wrongful.
• [Anglo-French *torcious* from *torcion* extortion, from Late Latin *tortio* torture: see TORSION]

tortoise *noun*
• "TORT us"
• any slow-moving land or freshwater reptile of the family Testudinidae, encased in a scaly or leathery domed shell, and having a retractile head and elephantine legs.
• [Middle English *tortuce*, Old French *tortue*, from medieval Latin *tortuca*, of uncertain origin]

tortoiseshell *noun*
• "TORT us shell"
• the yellowish-brown mottled or clouded outer shell of some turtles, used for decorative combs, jewellery, etc.
• [as TORTOISE + 'shell']

tortrix *noun*
• "TORE trix"
• any moth of the family Tortricidae, the larvae of which live inside rolled leaves.
• [modern Latin, feminine of Latin *tortor* twister: see TORT]

tortuous *adjective*
• "TORE choo us"
• full of twists and turns.
• [Old French from Latin *tortuosus* from *tortus* a twist (as TORT)]
• **tortuosity** *noun* "tore choo OSSA tee"
• **tortuously** *adverb*

torture *noun*
• "TORCHER"
• the infliction of severe bodily pain esp. as a punishment or a means of interrogation or intimidation.
• [French from Late Latin *tortura* twisting (as TORT)]
• **torturer** *noun*
• **torturous** *adjective*
• **torturously** *adverb*

torus *noun*
• "TORE us"
• a surface or solid formed by rotating a closed curve, esp. a circle, about a line in its plane but not intersecting it, e.g. like a ring doughnut.
• [Latin, = swelling, bulge, cushion, etc.]
HOMOPHONES: *Taurus*

tostada *noun*
• "tuh STODDA"
• a corn tortilla topped with a seasoned mixture of beans, ground meat, and vegetables.
• [Spanish, past participle of *tostar* to toast]

totalitarian *adjective*
• "toe tala TERRY 'n"
• of or relating to a centralized dictatorial form of government requiring complete subservience to the state.
• [Italian *totalitario* complete, absolute, from medieval Latin *totalis* from *totus* entire]
• **totalitarianism** *noun*

tote *verb*
• "TOTE"
• carry.
• [17th-c. US, prob. of dialect origin]
• **toter** *noun*

totem *noun*
• "TOE tum"
• (among some N American Aboriginal peoples) the emblem or symbol of a clan or family, usually the animal or plant that the family claims as its mythical ancestor.
• [Algonquian]
• **totemic** *adjective* "toe TEMMIC"
• **totemism** *noun*
• **totemist** *noun*
• **totemistic** *adjective*

totipotent *adjective*
• "toe TIPPA t'nt"
• (of a cell) capable of differentiating into any other related kind of cell or (in some organisms) a complete individual.
• [from *toti-* combining form of Latin *totus* whole + POTENT]
• **totipotency** *noun*

toucan *noun*
• "TOO can"
• any tropical American fruit-eating bird of the family Ramphastidae, with an immense beak and brightly coloured plumage.
• [Tupi *tucana*, Guarani *tucã*]

touché *interjection*
• "too SHAY"
• the acknowledgement of a hit by a fencing opponent.
• [French, past participle of *toucher* touch, prob. imitative, imitating a knock]

toupée *noun*
• "too PAY"
• a wig or artificial hairpiece to cover a bald spot.
• [French *toupet* hair tuft, diminutive of Old French *toup* tuft]

toupie *noun*
• "TOOPY"
• *Cdn* a round boneless smoked ham.
• [perhaps from French, = spinning top]
HOMOPHONES: *Tupi*

tourmaline *noun*
• "TURMA leen" or "TOORMA leen"
• a boron aluminum silicate mineral of various colours, possessing unusual electrical properties, and used in electrical and optical instruments and as a gemstone.
• [French from Sinhalese *toramalli* porcelain]

tournament *noun*
• "TURNA m'nt" or "TOOR nuh m'nt"
• any contest of skill or series of contests involving a number of competitors.
• [Old French *torneiement* from *torneier* TOURNEY]

tournedos *noun*
• "TOOR nuh doe"
• a small round thick cut from a fillet of beef.
• [French, from *tourner* to turn + *dos* back]

tourney *noun*
• "TURNY" or "TOORNY"
• a tournament.
• [Old French *tornei*, ultimately from Latin *tornus* a turn]

tourniquet *noun*
• "TURNA cay" or "TURNA kit"
• a device for stopping the flow of blood through an artery by twisting a bar etc. in a ligature or bandage so as to tighten it.
• [French prob. from Old French *tournicle* coat of mail, TUNICLE, influenced by *tourner* turn]

tourtière *noun*
• "tore TYARE"
• a French-Canadian meat pie consisting esp. of ground pork and spices with a flaky double crust, traditionally served at Christmas.
• [Canadian French from French dialect, = pie dish]

tousle *verb*
• "TOUSE 'll" ("TOUSE" rhymes either with *HOUSE* or with *COWS*)
• make (esp. the hair) untidy; rumple.
• [frequentative of (now dialect) *touse*, Old English, related to Old High German *zirzuson*, *erzūsen* tear to pieces]

tout *verb*
• "TOUT" (rhymes with *OUT*)
• extol, recommend, advocate.
• [Middle English *tūte* look out = Middle English (now dialect) *toot* (Old English *tōtian*) from Germanic]
• **touted** *adjective*
• **touter** *noun*

touton *noun*
- "TOUT'n" ("TOUT" rhymes with *OUT*)
- *Cdn* (*Nfld*) a deep-fried flat round of bread dough, eaten with molasses.
- [origin unknown]

tovarich *noun*
ALSO SPELLED: **tovarish**
- "tuh VAR ish"
- (in the former USSR) comrade (esp. as a form of address).
- [Russian *tovarishch*]

towelette *noun*
- "towel ET"
- a small moistened tissue for wiping esp. the hands or face, often individually wrapped.
- [Old French *toail(l)e* piece of cloth, from Germanic]

towheaded *adjective*
- "TOE heddid"
- having very light-coloured or unkempt hair.
- ['tow' the coarse and broken part of flax or hemp prepared for spinning, from Middle Low German *touw* from Old Saxon *tou*, related to Old Norse *tó* wool + 'head']
- **towhead** *noun*

towhee *noun*
- "TOW hee" ("TOW" rhymes either with *PLOW* or with *GROW*)
- any of several buntings of the genus *Pipilo*, of brush and woodland in N America, esp. *P. erythrophthalmus*, having a black back, rust sides, and a white breast.
- [imitative of its call]

toxemia *noun*
ALSO SPELLED: esp. *Brit.* **toxaemia**
- "tox EEMY uh"
- blood poisoning.
- [as TOXIC + Greek *aimia* from *haima* blood]
- **toxemic** *adjective* (also esp. *Brit.* **toxaemic**)

toxic *adjective*
- "TOXIC"
- of or relating to poison.
- [medieval Latin *toxicus* poisoned, via Latin *toxicum* from Greek *toxikon* (*pharmakon*) (poison for) arrows, from *toxon* bow, *toxa* arrows]
- **toxically** *adverb*
- **toxicity** *noun* "tox ISSA tee"

toxicant *noun*
- "TOXA k'nt"
- a toxic substance, esp. one used as a pesticide etc.
- [as TOXIC]

toxicology *noun*
- "toxa COLLA jee"
- the scientific study of poisons.
- [as TOXIC + Greek *logos* word]
- **toxicological** *adjective*
- **toxicologist** *noun*

toxin *noun*
- "TOXIN"
- a poison produced by a living organism, esp. one formed in the body and stimulating the production of antibodies.
- [as TOXIC]

HOMOPHONES: *tocsin*

toxoid *noun*
- "TOX oid"
- a chemically modified toxin from a pathogenic micro-organism, which is no longer toxic but is still antigenic and can be used as a vaccine.
- [as TOXIC]

toxoplasmosis *noun*
- "toxo plazz MOE sis"
- a disease caused by infection with the protozoan *Toxoplasma gondii*, transmitted esp. through poorly prepared food or in cat feces and dangerous in unborn children.
- [TOXIC + PLASMA]

trabecula *noun*
- "truh BECK yoo luh"
- a supporting band or bar of connective or bony tissue, esp. dividing an organ into chambers.
- [Latin, diminutive of *trabs* beam]
- **trabecular** *adjective*
- **trabeculate** *adjective*

trachea *noun*
- "TRAY kee uh" or "truh KEE uh"
- the passage reinforced by rings of cartilage, through which air reaches the bronchial tubes from the larynx; the windpipe.
- [medieval Latin *trachia* from Greek *trakheia* (*artēria*) rough (artery), from *trakhus* rough]
- **tracheal** *adjective*
- **tracheate** *adjective*

tracheotomy *noun*
- "tray kee OTTA mee" or "tracky OTTA mee"
- a surgical operation to make an opening in the trachea, esp. so that the patient can breathe through it via a curved tube.
- [TRACHEA + Greek *-tomia* cutting, from *temnō* cut]

trachoma *noun*
- "truh CO muh"
- a contagious disease of the eye with inflamed granulation on the inner surface of the lids.
- [modern Latin from Greek *trakhōma* from *trakhus* rough]

trachyte *noun*
- "TRAY kite" or "TRACK ite"
- a light-coloured volcanic rock rough to the touch.
- [French from Greek *trakhutēs* roughness (as TRACHOMA)]
- **trachytic** *adjective* "truh KITTIC"

tract *noun*
- "TRACT"
- a region or area of indefinite, esp. large, extent.
- [Latin *tractus* drawing, from *trahere tract-* draw, pull]

HOMOPHONES: *tracked*

tractable *adjective*
- "TRACT a bull"
- (of a person) easily handled; manageable; docile.
- [Latin *tractabilis* from *tractare* handle, frequentative of *trahere tract-* draw]
- **tractability** *noun*
- **tractably** *adverb*

Tractarian *noun*
- "track TERRY 'n"
- a member of the Oxford Movement, a 19th-c. movement aimed at restoring traditional teaching and forms of worship in the Anglican Church.
- [after *Tracts for the Times*, published in Oxford 1833–41 and outlining the movement's principles]
- **Tractarianism** *noun*

tractate *noun*
- "TRACK tate"
- a treatise.
- [Latin *tractatus* from *tractare*: see TRACTABLE]

traction *noun*
- "TRACK sh'n"
- the grip of a tire, footwear, etc. on the ground.
- [French *traction* or medieval Latin *tractio* from Latin *trahere tract-* draw]
- **tractive** *adjective*

tractor *noun*
- "TRACK tur"
- a powerful motor vehicle used for hauling etc., esp. one with large treaded rear wheels used to haul farm machinery.
- [Late Latin *tractor* (as TRACTION)]

tradescantia *noun*
- "tradda SKANTY uh"
- any plant of the genus *Tradescantia*, with blue, white, or pink three-petalled flowers, esp. spiderwort, *T. virginiana*, of eastern N America cultivated in gardens, and the trailing wandering Jew frequently grown as a houseplant.
- [modern Latin from J. *Tradescant*, English naturalist d.1638]

traduce *verb*
- "truh DOOCE" or "truh DYOOCE"
- speak ill of; misrepresent.
- [Latin *traducere* disgrace (as Latin *trans* across, *ducere duct-* lead)]
- **traducer** *noun*

tragacanth *noun*
- "TRAGGA canth"
- a white or reddish gum from a plant, *Astragalus gummifer*, used as a vehicle for drugs, dye, etc.
- [French *tragacante* from Latin *tragacantha* from Greek *tragakantha*, name of a shrub, from *tragos* goat + *akantha* thorn]

tragedian *noun*
- "truh JEEDY 'n"
- a writer of tragedies.
- [as TRAGEDY]

tragedienne *noun*
- "truh jeedy EN"
- an actress in tragedy.
- [as TRAGEDY]

tragedy *noun*
- "TRADGE a dee"
- a dramatic representation dealing with tragic events and with an unhappy ending, esp. concerning the downfall of the protagonist.
- [ultimately from Greek *tragōidia*, apparently 'goat song' from *tragos* goat + *ōidē* song]

tragic *adjective*
- "TRADGE ick"
- sad; calamitous; greatly distressing.
- [French *tragique* from Latin *tragicus* from Greek *tragikos* from *tragos* goat: see TRAGEDY]
- **tragical** *adjective*
- **tragically** *adverb*

tragicomedy *noun*
- "tradge a COMMA dee"
- a play having a mixture of comedy and tragedy.
- [as TRAGIC + COMEDY]
- **tragicomic** *adjective*
- **tragicomically** *adverb*

tragopan *noun*
- "TRAGGA pan"
- any Asian pheasant of the genus *Tragopan*, with erect fleshy horns on its head.
- [Latin from Greek from *tragos* goat + *Pan* the god Pan]

traipse *verb*
- "TRAPES"
- tramp or trudge wearily.
- [16th-c. *trapes* (v.), of unknown origin]

trait *noun*
- "TRATE"
- a distinguishing feature or characteristic esp. of a person.
- [French from Latin *tractus* (as TRACT)]

traitor *noun*
- "TRAY tur"
- a person who is treacherous or disloyal, esp. to his or her country.
- [Old French *trait(o)ur* from Latin *traditor -oris* from *tradere* hand on, betray (as *trans* across, *dare* give)]
- **traitorous** *adjective*
- **traitorously** *adverb*

HOMOPHONES: *trader*

trajectory *noun*
• "truh JECTER ee"
• the path described by a projectile flying or an object moving under the action of given forces.
• [(originally adjective) from medieval Latin *trajectorius* from Latin *traicere traject-* (*trans* across, *jacere* throw)]

trammel *verb*
• "TRAM'll"
• impede the free action of; hinder, constrain.
• [in sense 'net' from Old French *tramail* from medieval Latin *tramaculum, tremaculum*, perhaps formed as *tri* three + *macula* link: later history uncertain]

tramontana *noun*
• "truh mon TANNA"
• a cold north wind in the Adriatic Sea.
• [Italian: see TRAMONTANE]

tramontane *adjective*
• "truh MON tane"
• situated or living on the other side of mountains, esp. the Alps as seen from Italy.
• [Italian *tramontano* from Latin *transmontanus* beyond the mountains (*trans* across, *mons montis* mountain)]

trampoline *noun*
• "trampa LEEN" or "TRAMPA leen"
• a strong fabric sheet connected by springs to a horizontal frame, used by gymnasts etc. for somersaults, as a springboard, etc.
• [Italian *trampolino* from *trampoli* stilts]
• **trampoliner** *noun*
• **trampolinist** *noun*

tranche *noun*
• "TRONSH"
• a portion, esp. of income, or of a block of shares.
• [French, = slice, from Old French *trenche* (n.) *trenchier* (v.), ultimately from Latin *truncare* TRUNCATE]

tranquil *adjective*
• "TRANK wull"
• calm, serene, unruffled.
• [French *tranquille* or Latin *tranquillus*]
• **tranquility** *noun*
• **tranquilly** *adverb*

tranquilize *verb*
ALSO SPELLED: **tranquillize**, **tranquillise**
• "TRANK wuh lize"
• make tranquil, esp. by a drug etc.
• [as TRANQUIL]
• **tranquilizer** *noun* (also **tranquillizer**, **tranquilliser**)
• **tranquilizing** *adjective* (also **tranquillizing**, **tranquillising**)

transaminase *noun*
• "tranz AM in ace"
• an enzyme which catalyzes the transfer of an amino group from one molecule to another.
• [Latin *trans* across + AMINO]

transaxle *noun*
• "tranz AX'll"
• an integral driving axle and differential gear in a motor vehicle.
• ['transmission' + AXLE]

transboundary *adjective*
• "tranz BOUND ree" or "tranz BOUND a ree"
• that crosses, or is situated on or pertains to both sides of a boundary.
• [Latin *trans* across + BOUNDARY]

transceiver *noun*
• "tran SEEVER"
• any device which is both a transmitter and receiver of signals, e.g. a radio transceiver, modem, etc.
• ['transmitter' + RECEIVER]

transcend *verb*
• "tran SEND"
• be beyond the range or grasp of (human experience, reason, belief, etc.).
• [Old French *transcendre* or Latin *transcendere* (*trans* across, *scandere* climb)]

transcendent *adjective*
• "tran SEN d'nt"
• excelling, surpassing.
• [as TRANSCEND]
• **transcendence** *noun*
• **transcendency** *noun*
• **transcendental** *adjective*
• **transcendentally** *adverb*
• **transcendently** *adverb*

transcendentalism *noun*
• "tran sen DENT'll izm"
• transcendental philosophy, belief, thought, etc.
• [as TRANSCEND]
• **transcendentalist** *noun*

transcontinental *adjective*
• "tranz conta NENT'll"
• (of a railway etc.) extending across a continent.
• [Latin *trans* across + 'continental']
• **transcontinentally** *adverb*

transcriptase *noun*
• "tran SKRIP tace"
• an enzyme which catalyzes the formation of RNA from a DNA template during transcription or the formation of DNA from an RNA template in reverse transcription.
• [from 'transcript' from Old French *transcrit* from Latin *transcriptum* neuter past participle of *transcribere transcript-* make a copy of (*trans* across, *scribere* write)]

transcutaneous *adjective*
• "tranz kyoo TAINY us"
• through or by the skin.
• [Latin *trans* across + CUTANEOUS]

transdermal *adjective*
• "tranz DURM'll"
• (of a drug) applied through the skin, esp.

from an adhesive patch, and absorbed slowly into the body.
• [Latin *trans* across + DERMAL]

transduce *verb*
• "tranz DOOCE" or "tranz DYOOCE"
• convert (energy, esp. in the form of a signal) into a different medium or form of energy.
• [back-formation from TRANSDUCER]
• **transduction** *noun*

transducer *noun*
• "tranz DOOCE ur" or "tranz DYOOCE ur"
• any device for converting a signal from one medium of transmission to another, esp. a non-electrical signal into an electrical one, e.g. pressure into voltage.
• [Latin *transducere* lead across (*trans* across, *ducere* lead)]

transept *noun*
• "TRAN sept"
• either arm of the part of a cross-shaped church at right angles to the nave.
• [modern Latin *transeptum* (as Latin *trans* across, SEPTUM)]
• **transeptal** *adjective*

transfer *verb*
• "TRAN sfur" or "tranz FUR"
• move (a thing etc.) from one place to another.
• [French *transférer* or Latin *transferre* (as Latin *trans* across, *ferre lat-* bear)]
• **transferability** *noun*
• **transferable** *adjective*
• **transferee** *noun*
• **transference** *noun* "TRAN sfur ince"
• **transferor** *noun*
• **transferral** *noun*

transferase *noun*
• "TRAN sfur ace"
• an enzyme which catalyzes the transfer of a particular group from one molecule to another.
• [as TRANSFER]

transferrin *noun*
• "tranz FARE in"
• a protein transporting iron in blood serum.
• [Latin *trans* across + Latin *ferrum* iron]

transfigure *verb*
• "tranz FIG yur"
• change in form or appearance, esp. so as to elevate or idealize.
• [Latin *trans* across + FIGURE]
• **transfiguration** *noun*

transfinite *adjective*
• "tranz FINE ite"
• beyond or surpassing the finite.
• [Latin *trans* across + FINITE]

transfixion *noun*
• "tranz FICK sh'n"
• the act of piercing with a sharp implement or weapon.
• [Latin *transfixionem* from *transfigēre* (*trans* across, *figēre* fix, set in place)]

transfuse *verb*
• "tranz FYOOZ"
• permeate.
• [Latin *transfundere transfus-* (*trans* across, *fundere* pour)]
• **transfusion** *noun*

transgendered *adjective*
• "tranz JEN durd"
• having an identity which does not conform unambiguously to conventional notions of male or female gender, esp. undergoing, or having undergone, sex change procedures.
• [Latin *trans* across + 'gendered' from Old French *gendre*, ultimately from Latin GENUS]

transgenic *adjective*
• "tranz JENNIC"
• (of an animal or plant) having genetic material introduced from another species.
• [Latin *trans* across + GENE]

transgenics *noun*
• "tranz JENNIX"
• the branch of biology concerned with transgenic organisms.
• [Latin *trans* across + GENE]

transgress *verb*
• "tranz GRESS"
• contravene or go beyond the bounds or limits set by (a commandment, law, etc.).
• [French *transgresser* or Latin *transgredi transgress-* (*trans* across, *gradi* go)]
• **transgression** *noun*
• **transgressive** *adjective*
• **transgressor** *noun*

transhistorical *adjective*
• "tranz hiss TORA k'll"
• having significance that transcends the historical; universal, eternal.
• [Latin *trans* across + 'history' (see HISTORIATED)]

transhumance *noun*
• "tranz HYOO mince"
• the seasonal moving of livestock to a different region.
• [French from *transhumer* from Latin *trans* across + *humus* ground]

transient *adjective*
• "TRANZY 'nt"
• of short duration; momentary; passing; impermanent.
• [Latin *transire* (*trans* across, *ire* go)]
• **transience** *noun*
• **transiency** *noun*
• **transiently** *adverb*

transilluminate *verb*
• "tranza LOOMA nate"
• pass a strong light through for inspection, esp. for medical diagnosis.
• [Latin *trans* across + ILLUMINATE]
• **transillumination** *noun*

transistor *noun*
• "tran ZISTER"
• a semiconductor device with three connections, capable of amplification in addition to rectification.
• [blend of TRANSFER + RESISTOR]

transistorize *verb*
ALSO SPELLED: esp. *Brit.* **-ise**
• "tran ZISTER ize"
• design or equip with, or convert to, transistors.
• [as TRANSISTOR]

transitive *adjective*
• "TRANZA tiv"
• (of a verb or sense of a verb) that takes a direct object (whether expressed or implied), e.g. *saw* in *saw the donkey*, *saw that she was ill*.
• [Late Latin *transitivus* from *transitus* movement, from *transire*]
• **transitively** *adverb*
• **transitiveness** *noun*
• **transitivity** *noun*

transitory *adjective*
• "TRANZA tory"
• not permanent, brief, transient.
• [as TRANSITIVE]
• **transitoriness** *noun*

translate *verb*
• "TRANZ late" or "tranz LATE"
• express the sense of (a word, sentence, speech, book, etc.) in another language.
• [Latin *translatus*, past participle of *transferre*: see TRANSFER]
• **translatability** *noun*
• **translatable** *adjective*
• **translator** *noun*

transliterate *verb*
• "tranz LITTER ate"
• represent (a word etc.) in the closest corresponding letters of a different alphabet or language.
• [Latin *trans* across + Latin *littera* letter]
• **transliteration** *noun*
• **transliterator** *noun*

translucent *adjective*
• "tranz LOO s'nt"
• allowing light to pass through diffusely; semi-transparent.
• [Latin *translucēre* (*trans* across, *lucēre* shine)]
• **translucence** *noun*
• **translucency** *noun*
• **translucently** *adverb*

translunar *adjective*
• "tranz LOONER"
• lying beyond the moon.
• [Latin *trans* across + LUNAR]

transmembrane *adjective*
• "tranz MEM brane"
• existing or occurring across a cell membrane.
• [Latin *trans* across + MEMBRANE]

transmigrant *adjective*
• "tranz MY gr'nt"
• passing through, esp. a country on the way to another.
• [Latin *trans* across + MIGRANT]

transmigrate *verb*
• "tranz MY grate"
• (of the soul) pass into a different body; undergo metempsychosis.
• [Latin *trans* across + MIGRATE]
• **transmigration** *noun*
• **transmigrator** *noun*
• **transmigratory** *adjective*

transmittance *noun*
• "tranz MIT ince"
• the ratio of the light energy falling on a body to that transmitted through it.
• [Latin *transmittere* (*trans* across, *mittere* miss- send)]

transmitter *noun*
• "TRANZ mitter" or "tranz MITTER"
• a person or thing that transmits.
• [as TRANSMITTANCE]

transmogrify *verb*
• "tranz MOGGRA fie"
• transform or be transformed, esp. in a magical or surprising manner.
• [17th c.: origin unknown]
• **transmogrification** *noun*

transmontane *adjective*
• "tranz MON tane" or "tranz mon TANE"
• situated or living on the other side of mountains, esp. the Alps as seen from Italy.
• [Latin *transmontanus*: see TRAMONTANE]

transoceanic *adjective*
• "tranz oh shee ANNIC" or "tranz oh see ANNIC"
• situated beyond the ocean.
• [Latin *trans* across + OCEANIC]

transom *noun*
• "TRAN s'm"
• a horizontal bar of wood or stone across a window or the top of a door.
• [Middle English *traversayn*, *transyn*, *-ing*, from Old French *traversin* from *traverse* TRAVERSE]
• **transomed** *adjective*

transonic *adjective*
• "tran SONNIC"
• relating to speeds close to that of sound.
• [Latin *trans* across + SONIC, after *supersonic* etc.]

transparent *adjective*
• "tranz PARE 'nt"
• allowing light to pass through so that bodies can be distinctly seen.
• [Old French from medieval Latin *transparens* from Latin *transparēre* shine through (*trans* across, *parēre* appear)]
• **transparency** *noun*
• **transparently** *adverb*

transposon *noun*
• "tranz POZE on"
• a chromosomal segment that can undergo transposition, esp. a segment of bacterial DNA that can be translocated as a whole between chromosomal, phage, and plasmid DNA in the absence of a complementary sequence in the host DNA.
• [from 'transpose' from Middle English, = transform, from Old French *transposer* (Latin *trans* across, *ponere* put)]

transputer *noun*
• "tranz PYOO tur"
• a high-performance microprocessor with integral memory designed for parallel processing.
• [TRANSISTOR + COMPUTER]

transracial *adjective*
• "tranz RAY sh'll"
• across or crossing racial boundaries.
• [Latin *trans* across + 'racial' from French *race* from Italian *razza*, of unknown origin]

transubstantiation *noun*
• "tran sub stanshy AY sh'n"
• (in Roman Catholic and Orthodox belief) the conversion in the Eucharist, after consecration, of the whole substance of the bread and wine into the body and blood of Christ, only the appearances of bread and wine remaining.
• [medieval Latin (as Latin *trans* across, SUBSTANCE)]

transude *verb*
• "tran SOOD" or "tran SYOOD"
• (of a fluid) pass through the pores or interstices of a membrane etc.
• [French *transsuder* from Old French *tressuer* (as Latin *trans* across, Latin *sudare* sweat)]
• **transudation** *noun*

transuranic *adjective*
• "tranz yur ANNIC"
• (of an element) having a higher atomic number than uranium.
• [Latin *trans* across + URANIUM]

transvaluation *noun*
• "tranz val yoo AY sh'n"
• an alteration of values; a re-evaluation.
• [Latin *trans* across + 'valuation' from Old French *value*, fem. past participle of *valoir* be worth, from Latin *valēre*]
• **transvalue** *verb*

transvestite *noun*
• "tranz VEST ite"
• a person, esp. a man, who dresses in the clothes of the opposite sex, esp. as a sexual stimulus.
• [German *Transvestismus* from Latin *trans* across + Latin *vestire* clothe]
• **transvestism** *noun*

Transylvanian *adjective*
• "tran s'll VAINY 'n"
• of or relating to the region of Transylvania in NW Romania.

trapeze *noun*
• "truh PEEZ"
• a crossbar or set of crossbars suspended by ropes used as a swing for acrobatics etc.
• [French *trapèze* from Late Latin *trapezium*: see TRAPEZIUM]
• **trapezist** *noun*

trapezium *noun*
• "truh PEEZY um"
• a quadrilateral with no two sides parallel.
• [Late Latin from Greek *trapezion* from *trapeza* table]

trapezius *noun*
• "truh PEEZY us"
• either of a pair of large triangular muscles extending over the back of the neck and shoulders.
• [as TRAPEZIUM]

trapezoid *noun*
• "TRAPPA zoid"
• a quadrilateral with only one pair of sides parallel.
• [modern Latin *trapezoides* from Greek *trapezoeidēs* (as TRAPEZIUM)]
• **trapezoidal** *adjective*

Trappist *noun*
• "TRAPPIST"
• a member of a branch of the Cistercian order of monks founded in 1664 at La Trappe in NW France and noted for an austere rule including a vow of silence.
• [French *trappiste* from *La Trappe*]

trattoria *noun*
• "tratta REE uh"
• an Italian restaurant.
• [Italian]

trauma *noun*
• "TROMMA"
• emotional shock following a stressful event, sometimes leading to long-term neurosis.
• [Greek *trauma traumatos* wound]
• **traumatic** *adjective*
• **traumatically** *adverb*
• **traumatization** *noun* (also esp. *Brit.* **-isation**)
• **traumatize** *verb* (also esp. *Brit.* **-ise**)

traumatism *noun*
• "TROMMA tizm"
• the action of a trauma.
• [as TRAUMA]

travail *noun*
• "truh VALE" or "TRAV ale"
• painful or laborious effort.
• [Old French *travail*, *travaillier*, ultimately from medieval Latin *trepalium* instrument of torture, from Latin *tres* three + *palus* stake]

travelogue *noun*
ALSO SPELLED: esp. *US* **travelog**
• "TRAVVA log"
• a film, book, or illustrated lecture about travel.
• ['travel' (from TRAVAIL), after MONOLOGUE etc.]

traverse *verb*
• "truh VURSE"
• travel or lie across.
• [Old French *traverser* from Late Latin *traversare, transversare* turn across (*trans* across, *vertere* turn)]
• **traversable** *adjective*
• **traversal** *noun*
• **traverser** *noun*

travertine *noun*
• "TRAVVER teen"
• a white or light-coloured calcareous rock deposited from springs.
• [Italian *travertino, tivertino* from Latin *tiburtinus* of Tibur (Tivoli) near Rome]

travesty *noun*
• "TRAVVA stee"
• a grotesque misrepresentation or imitation.
• [(originally adjective) from French *travesti* past participle of *travestir* disguise, change the clothes of, from Italian *travestire* (as Latin *trans* across, Italian *vestire* clothe)]

travois *noun*
• "TRAV wah"
• a V-shaped frame of teepee poles pulled by dogs or horses, used by Plains Aboriginal peoples to carry teepee covers and other possessions.
• [earlier *travail* from French, perhaps the same word as TRAVAIL]

trawl *verb*
• "TRAWL"
• fish with a large wide-mouthed fishing net dragged by a boat along the sea bottom.
• [prob. from Middle Dutch *traghelen* to drag (compare *traghel* dragnet), perhaps from Latin *tragula*]

trawler *noun*
• "TRAWL ur"
• a boat used for trawling.
• [as TRAWL]

treacherous *adjective*
• "TRETCHER us"
• guilty of or involving treachery; disloyal, traitorous.
• [Old French *trecherous* from *trecheor* a cheat, from *trechier, trichier* deceive, of unknown origin]
• **treacherously** *adverb*

treachery *noun*
• "TRETCHER ee"
• violation of faith or trust; betrayal.
• [as TREACHEROUS]

treacle *noun*
• "TREEK'll"
• a syrup produced in refining sugar; golden syrup.
• [Middle English *triacle* from Old French from Latin *theriaca* from Greek *thēriakē* antidote against venom, feminine of *thēriakos* (adjective) from *thērion* wild beast]
• **treacly** *adjective*

treadle *noun*
• "TRED'll"
• a lever worked by the foot and imparting motion to a machine.
• [Old English *tredel* stair]

treason *noun*
• "TREE z'n"
• violation by a subject of allegiance to the sovereign or to the state, esp. by attempting to kill or overthrow the sovereign or to overthrow the government.
• [Old French *traïson*, from Latin *traditio* handing over (see TRAITOR)]
• **treasonable** *adjective*
• **treasonably** *adverb*
• **treasonous** *adjective*

treatise *noun*
• "TREE tiss"
• a written work dealing formally and systematically with a subject.
• [Anglo-French *tretis* from Old French *traitier* treat, from Latin *tractare* handle, frequentative of *trahere tract-* draw, pull]

Trebbiano *noun*
• "treb YANNO"
• a variety of vine and grape widely cultivated in Italy and elsewhere.
• [Italian, from the River *Trebbia* in northern central Italy]

treble *adjective*
• "TREBBLE"
• (of a voice) high-pitched.
• [Old French from Latin *triplus* triple; in the musical sense because it was the highest part in a three-part contrapuntal composition]

trebuchet *noun*
• "TREB yoo shet" or "TREBBA shet"
• a military machine used in siege warfare for throwing stones etc.
• [Old French from *trebucher* overthrow, ultimately from Frankish]

trecento *noun*
• "tray CHENTO"
• the style of Italian art and literature of the 14th c.
• [Italian, = 300, used with reference to the years 1300–99]

trefa *adjective*
• "TRAY fuh"
• not kosher.

• [Hebrew ṭᵉrēpāh 'the flesh of an animal torn', from ṭārap̱ rend]

trefoil *noun*
• "TREFF oil" or "TREE foil"
• any leguminous plant of the genus *Trifolium*, with leaves of three leaflets and flowers of various colours, esp. clover.
• [Anglo-French *trifoil* from Latin *trifolium* (as *tri* three, *folium* leaf)]
• **trefoiled** *adjective*

trek *verb*
• "TRECK"
• travel or make one's way on foot, esp. arduously.
• [South African Dutch *trek* (n.), *trekken* (v.) draw, travel]
• **trekker** *noun*

Trekkie *noun*
• "TRECKY"
• a fan of *Star Trek*, a TV science fiction drama series.

trellis *noun*
• "TRELL iss"
• a lattice or grating of light wooden or metal bars used esp. as a support for fruit trees or creepers and often fastened against a wall.
• [Old French *trelis*, ultimately from Latin *trilix* three-ply (as *tri* three, *licium* warp thread)]

trematode *noun*
• "TREMMA tode"
• any parasitic flatworm of the class Trematoda, esp. a fluke, equipped with hooks or suckers, e.g. a liver fluke.
• [modern Latin *Trematoda* from Greek *trēmatōdēs* perforated, from *trēma* hole]

tremendous *adjective*
• "truh MEND us"
• awe-inspiring, fearful, overpowering.
• [Latin *tremendus*, gerundive of *tremere* tremble]
• **tremendously** *adverb*

tremolo *noun*
• "TREMMA lo"
• a tremulous effect produced on musical instruments or in singing.
• [Italian (as TREMULOUS)]

tremor *noun*
• "TREMMER"
• a shaking or quivering.
• [Old French *tremour* & Latin *tremor* from *tremere* tremble]

tremulous *adjective*
• "TREM yull us"
• trembling or quivering.
• [Latin *tremulus* from *tremere* tremble]
• **tremulously** *adverb*
• **tremulousness** *noun*

trenchant *adjective*
• "TRENCH 'nt"
• (of a style or language etc.) incisive, terse, vigorous.
• [Old French, participle of *trenchier* cut, ultimately from Latin *truncare* TRUNCATE]
• **trenchancy** *noun*
• **trenchantly** *adverb*

Trentonian *noun*
• "tren TONY 'n"
• a resident of Trenton, Ont.

trepan *noun*
• "truh PAN"
• a cylindrical saw formerly used by surgeons for removing part of the bone of the skull.
• [medieval Latin *trepanum* from Greek *trupanon* from *trupaō* bore, from *trupē* hole]
• **trepanation** *noun*
• **trepanning** *noun*

trepang *noun*
• "truh PANG"
• any of several sea cucumbers used to make Chinese soups, usu. cut into long strips and dried.
• [Malay *trīpang*]

trephine *noun*
• "truh FINE" or "truh FEEN"
• an improved form of trepan with a guiding centre pin.
• [originally *trafine*, from Latin *tres fines* three ends, apparently formed after TREPAN]
• **trephination** *noun*

trepidation *noun*
• "treppa DAY sh'n"
• a feeling of fear or alarm; perturbation of the mind.
• [Latin *trepidatio* from *trepidare* be agitated, tremble, from *trepidus* alarmed]
• **trepidatious** *adjective*
• **trepidatiously** *adverb*

très *adverb*
• "TRAY"
• very.
• [French]
HOMOPHONES: *tray*, *trey*

trespass *verb*
• "TRESS pass"
• make an unlawful or unwarrantable intrusion (esp. on land or property).
• [Old French *trespasser* pass over, trespass, *trespas* (n.), from medieval Latin *transpassare* (as Latin *trans* across, *passus* pace)]
• **trespasser** *noun*

trestle *noun*
• "TRESS'll"
• a supporting structure for a table etc., consisting of two frames fixed at an angle or hinged or of a bar supported by two divergent pairs of legs.
• [Old French *trestel*, ultimately from Latin *transtrum* beam]

tretinoin *noun*
• "truh TINNO in"
• retinoic acid, applied topically in the treatment of acne and other skin disorders.
• [*t-* of unknown origin + *retino-* (in RETINOL)]

trevally *noun*
• "truh VAL ee"
• any Australian fish of the genus *Caranx*, used as food.
• [prob. alteration of *cavally*, a kind of fish, from Spanish *caballo* horse, from Latin (as CAVALRY)]

trews *plural noun*
• "TROOZ"
• a pair of pants, esp. close-fitting tartan trousers formerly worn by certain Scottish regiments.
• [Irish *trius*, Gaelic *triubhas* (sing.)]

trey *noun*
• "TRAY"
• a three-point field goal in basketball.
• [Old French *trei*, *treis* three, from Latin *tres*]
HOMOPHONES: *tray*, *très*

triable *adjective*
• "TRY a bull"
• (of a case or person etc.) that may be tried in court; liable to a judicial trial.
• [Middle English *try*, = separate, distinguish, etc., from Old French *trier* sift, of unknown origin]

triacetate *noun*
• "try ASSA tate"
• a cellulose derivative containing three acetate groups.
• [Latin *tri* three + ACETATE]

triactor *noun*
• "TRY acter"
• *Cdn* a bet on the first three finishers in a horse race, specifying their order of finish.
• [blend of *tri* three + EXACTOR]

triad *noun*
• "TRY ad"
• a group of three people or things.
• [ultimately from Greek *trias -ados* from *treis* three]
• **triadic** *adjective*
• **triadically** *adverb*

triage *noun*
• "TREE azh" or "TREE ozh" or "tree AZH" or "tree OZH"
• the process of determining the order in which a large number of injured or ill patients will receive medical treatment, with priority usu. given to those patients with the most severe ailments or the greatest chance of survival.
• [French from *trier*: see TRIABLE]

trial *noun*
• "TRY'll"
• a judicial examination and determination of issues between parties by a judge with or without a jury.
• [Anglo-French *trial*, *triel* from *trier* (see TRIABLE)]

trialist *noun*
• "TRY'll ist"
• a person who takes part in a sports trial or time trial etc.
• [as TRIAL]

triangle *noun*
• "TRY angle"
• a plane closed figure with three sides and angles.
• [ultimately from Latin *triangulus* three-cornered]
• **triangular** *adjective*
• **triangularity** *noun* "try ang gyuh LERRA tee"
• **triangularly** *adverb*

triangulate *verb*
• "try ANG gyoo late"
• arrange in the shape of a triangle.
• [as TRIANGLE]
• **triangulation** *noun*

Triassic *adjective*
• "try ASSIC"
• of or relating to the earliest period of the Mesozoic era, lasting from about 248 to 213 million years ago, during which dinosaurs became numerous and mammals first emerged.
• [Late Latin *trias* (as TRIAD), because the strata are divisible into three groups]

triathlon *noun*
• "try ATH lon"
• an athletic contest in which competitors engage in three different events, usu. swimming, cycling, and long-distance running.
• [*tri* three after DECATHLON]
• **triathlete** *noun*

triatomic *adjective*
• "try a TOMMIC"
• containing three or more atoms in one molecule.
• [*tri* three + ATOMICITY]

triaxial *adjective*
• "try AXY 'll"
• having three axes.
• [*tri* three + AXIS]

triazine *noun*
• "TRY a zeen"
• any of a group of chemical compounds whose molecules contain an unsaturated ring of three carbon and three nitrogen atoms.
• [*tri* three + French *azote* nitrogen, from Greek *azōos* without life]

triboelectric *adjective*
• "trybo e LECK trick" or "tribbo e LECK trick"
• concerning electricity generated by friction.
• [Greek *tribos* rubbing + ELECTRIC]

tribology *noun*
• "try BOLLA jee"
• the branch of science and technology concerned with interacting surfaces in relative motion, and thus with friction, wear, lubrication, and the design of bearings.
• [Greek *tribos* rubbing + *logos* word]
• **tribological** *adjective*

triboluminescence *noun*
• "trybo loomin ESS ince" or "tribbo loomin ESS ince"
• the emission of light from a substance when rubbed, scratched, etc.
• [Greek *tribos* rubbing + LUMINESCENCE]

tribulation *noun*
• "trib yuh LAY sh'n"
• great trouble or suffering.
• [Old French from Church Latin *tribulatio -onis* from Latin *tribulare* press, oppress, from *tribulum* sledge for threshing, from *terere trit-* rub]

tribunal *noun*
• "try BYOO n'll" or "trib YOO n'll"
• a board appointed to adjudicate in some matter, esp. one appointed by a government to investigate a matter of public concern.
• [French *tribunal* or Latin *tribunus* an apse in a basilica containing a bishop's throne]

tribune *noun*
• "TRIB yoon" or "trib YOON"
• a popular leader who attempts to protect the rights and interests of the people, often by demagogic means.
• [Latin *tribunus*, prob. from *tribus* tribe]
• **tribunate** *noun* "TRIB yoon it" or "trib YOON it"
• **tribuneship** *noun*

tributary *noun*
• "TRIB yoo terry"
• a stream or river flowing into a larger river or lake.
• [as TRIBUTE]

tribute *noun*
• "TRIB yoot"
• an act, statement, or gift made or given as a gesture of respect, admiration, or affection for a person.
• [Middle English from Latin *tributum* neuter past participle of *tribuere tribut-* assign, originally divide between tribes (*tribus*)]

tributyltin *noun*
• "try byoot'll TIN"
• an organic radical in which tetravalent tin is covalently linked to three butyl radicals.
• [*tri* three + BUTYL + 'tin']

tricentennial *noun*
• "try sen TENNY 'll"
• a three-hundredth anniversary.
• [*tri* three + CENTENNIAL]

triceps *noun*
• "TRY seps"
• any muscle having three heads or points of attachment at one end, esp. the large extensor muscle at the back of the upper arm.
• [Latin, = three-headed (as *tri* three, *-ceps* from *caput* head)]

triceratops *noun*
• "try SERRA tops"
• a plant-eating dinosaur of the Cretaceous genus *Triceratops*, having a bony horn on the snout, two longer ones above the eyes, and a bony frill around the neck.
• [modern Latin from Greek *trikeratos* three-horned + *ōps* face]

trichina *noun*
• "trick EENA"
• a minute parasitic nematode worm of the genus *Trichinella*, esp. *T. spiralis* which causes trichinosis.
• [modern Latin from Greek *trikhinos* of hair from Greek *thrix trikhos* hair]

trichinosis *noun*
• "tricka NO sis"
• a disease caused by infection with trichinae, often from poorly cooked infected meat, whose larvae penetrate the intestinal wall, migrate around the body, and encyst in muscular tissue, causing fever, pain, and stiffness.
• [as TRICHINA]

trichloroethylene *noun*
• "try cloro ETH'll een"
• a colourless non-flammable volatile liquid, used as a solvent and a cleaner.
• [*tri* three + CHLORINE + ETHYLENE]

trichology *noun*
• "trick OLLA jee" or "try COLLA jee"
• the study of the structure, functions, and diseases of the hair.
• [Greek *thrix trikhos* hair + *logos* word]
• **trichologist** *noun*

trichome *noun*
• "TRIKE ome"
• a hair, scale, prickle, or other outgrowth from the epidermis of a plant.
• [Greek *trikhōma* from *trikhoō* cover with hair, from *thrix trikhos* hair]

trichomonad *noun*
• "tricka MON ad"
• any flagellate protozoan of the genus *Trichomonas*, parasitic in humans, cattle, and fowls.
• [Greek *thrix trikhos* hair + MONAD]

trichomoniasis *noun*
• "tricka muh NIE a sis"
• any of various infections caused by trichomonads parasitic on the urinary tract, vagina, or digestive system.
• [as TRICHOMONAD]

trichotomy *noun*
• "try COTTA mee"

• a division (esp. sharply defined) into three parts, classes, or categories, esp. of human nature into body, soul, and spirit.
• [Greek *trikha* threefold, from *treis* three, after DICHOTOMY]
• **trichotomous** *adjective*

trichromatic *adjective*
• "try crow MATTIC"
• having or using three colours.
• [Latin *tri* three + CHROMATIC]

tricity *noun*
• "TRY sitty"
• a metropolitan area consisting of three adjoining but independent cities.
• [Latin *tri* three + 'city']

triclinic *adjective*
• "try CLINNIC"
• (of a mineral) forming crystals having three unequal axes, all obliquely inclined.
• [*tri* three, from Greek *treis* three + *klinō* incline]

tricolour *noun*
ALSO SPELLED: esp. *US* **tricolor**
• "TRY culler" or "TRICKA lur"
• a flag of three colours, esp. the French national flag of blue, white, and red.
• [Latin *tri* three + 'colour' from Latin *color*]

tricorne *noun*
ALSO SPELLED: **tricorn**
• "TRY corn"
• a hat having three corners or horns.
• [French *tricorne* or Latin *tricornis* (as *tri* three, *cornu* horn)]

tricot *noun*
• "TREE co"
• a fine sheer knitted fabric made of either natural or synthetic fibres, usu. having a ribbed pattern.
• [French, = knitting, from *tricoter* knit, of unknown origin]

tricuspid *noun*
• "try CUSS pid"
• a tooth with three cusps or points.
• [Latin *tri* three + *cuspis -idis* sharp point]

tricycle *noun*
• "TRICE a k'll"
• a vehicle, esp. ridden by children, having three wheels, two on an axle at the back and one at the front, driven by pedals in the same way as a bicycle.
• [Latin *tri* three + CYCLE]
• **tricyclist** *noun*

tricyclic *adjective*
• "try SIKE lick" or "try SICK lick"
• having three rings or circles.
• [as TRICYCLE]

trident *noun*
• "TRY d'nt"
• a three-pronged spear, esp. as an attribute of Poseidon (Neptune) or Britannia.
• [Latin *tridens trident-* (as *tri* three, *dens* tooth)]

tridentate *adjective*
• "try DEN tate"
• having three teeth or prongs.
• [Latin *tri* three + *dentatus* toothed]

Tridentine *adjective*
• "try DEN tine"
• of, relating to, or in accordance with the Council of Trent, held in Trento in Italy 1545–63, esp. as the basis of Roman Catholic doctrine.
• [medieval Latin *Tridentinus* from *Tridentum* Trent]

triduum *noun*
• "TRID yoo um"
• a period of three days of religious observance, esp. Holy Thursday, Good Friday, and Holy Saturday.
• [Latin (as *tri* three, *dies* day)]

triennium *noun*
• "try ENNY um"
• a period of three years.
• [Late Latin *triennis* (*tri* three, *annus* year)]
• **triennial** *adjective*
• **triennially** *adverb*

trifacial *adjective*
• "try FAY sh'll"
• designating or pertaining to the fifth and largest pair of cranial nerves, which divide into three branches, the ophthalmic, maxillary, and mandibular nerves, supplying the front half of the head.
• [Latin *tri* three + FACIAL]

trifecta *noun*
• "try FECTA"
• a bet on the first three finishers in a horse race, specifying their order of finish.
• [Latin *tri* three + 'perfecta' from Latin American Spanish *quiniela perfecta* perfect quinella]

trifid *adjective*
• "TRY fid"
• partly or wholly split into three divisions or lobes.
• [Latin *trifidus* (*tri* three, *findere fid-* split)]

trifocal *noun*
• "try FOKE'll"
• a pair of eyeglasses having lenses with three parts, each with a different focal length.
• [Latin *tri* three + *focus* hearth]

trifoliate *adjective*
• "try FOLEY it"
• (of a compound leaf) having three leaflets.
• [Latin *tri* three + FOLIATE]

triforium *noun*
• "try FORY um"
• a gallery or arcade above the arches of the nave, choir, and transepts of a church.
• [Anglo-Latin, of unknown origin]

trifurcate *adjective*
• "try FUR kit"
• divided into three branches, esp. like the prongs of a fork.
• [Latin *tri-* three + *furca* fork]

trigeminal *adjective*
• "try JEMMIN 'll"
• designating or pertaining to the fifth and largest pair of cranial nerves, which divide into three branches, the ophthalmic, maxillary, and mandibular nerves, supplying the front half of the head.
• [Latin *trigeminus* born as a triplet (*tri* three, *geminus* born at the same birth)]

triglyceride *noun*
• "try GLISSER ide"
• any ester formed from glycerol and three acid radicals, including the main constituents of fats and oils.
• [Latin *tri* three + GLYCERIDE]

triglyph *noun*
• "TRY gliff"
• a block or tablet with three vertical grooves alternating with metopes in a Doric frieze.
• [Latin *triglyphus* from Greek *trigluphos* (*tri* three, *gluphē* carving)]

trigonal *adjective*
• "TRIGGA n'll"
• triangular; of or relating to a triangle.
• [medieval Latin *trigonalis* from Latin *trigonum* from Greek *trigōnon* neuter of *trigōnos* three-cornered (*tri* three, *-gonos* -angled)]

trigonometry *noun*
• "trigga NOMMA tree"
• the branch of mathematics dealing with the relations between the sides and angles of triangles, esp. as expressed by trigonometric functions, and including the theory of triangles, of angles, and of elementary periodic functions.
• [modern Latin *trigonometria* (as TRIGONAL, Greek *metron* measure)]
• **trigonometric** *adjective* "trigga nuh METRIC"
• **trigonometrical** *adjective*

trihalomethane *noun*
• "try hallo METH ane"
• any of the compounds formed by substitution of halogen atoms for three of the hydrogen atoms of methane, certain of which, created as a by-product of the chlorination of drinking water, are considered carcinogenic.
• [Latin *tri* three + HALOGEN + METHANE]

trihedral *adjective*
• "try HEED rull"
• having three surfaces.
• [Greek *tri* three + *hedra* base]

trilateral *adjective*
• "try LATTER'll"
• involving or shared by three countries, esp. as parties to an agreement concerning trade and finance.
• [Latin *tri* three + LATERAL]
• **trilateralism** *noun*
• **trilateralist** *noun*

trilby *noun*
• "TRILL bee"
• a soft felt hat with a narrow brim and indented crown.
• [name of the heroine in G. du Maurier's novel *Trilby* (1894), in the stage version of which such a hat was worn]
• **trilbied** *adjective*

trilight *noun*
• "TRY lite"
• *Cdn* a light bulb that can be adjusted to shine at any of three degrees of brightness.
• [Latin *tri* from *tres* three + 'light' from Old English *lēoht*]

trilinear *adjective*
• "try LINNY ur"
• of or having three lines.
• [Latin *tri* from *tres* three + LINEAR]

trilingual *adjective*
• "try LING gwul" or "try LING gyoo 'll"
• able to speak three languages, esp. fluently.
• [Latin *tri* from *tres* three + *lingua* tongue]
• **trilingualism** *noun*

triliteral *adjective*
• "try LITTER'll"
• consisting of three letters.
• [Latin *tri* from *tres* three + LITERAL]

trilithon *noun*
• "TRY lith on"
• a prehistoric monument consisting of three stones, esp. two uprights surmounted by a lintel.
• [Greek *trilithon* (*tri* three, *lithos* stone)]
• **trilithic** *adjective*

trillium *noun*
• "TRILLY um"
• any of various esp. N American plants of the genus *Trillium*, of the lily family, bearing a whorl of three leaves at the summit of the stem and in the middle a solitary flower with three white or brightly coloured petals. The floral emblem of Ontario.
• [modern Latin, apparently from Swedish *trilling* triplet]

trilobite *noun*
• "TRY luh bite"
• any of numerous extinct marine arthropods of the subphylum Trilobita, which had a body divided into an anterior solid head, a segmented thorax or trunk, and a posterior tail, and which are found abundantly as fossils in Paleozoic rocks.
• [modern Latin *Trilobites* (*tri* three, Greek *lobos* lobe)]

trilogy *noun*
• "TRILLA jee"
• a group or series of three related novels,

theatrical works, etc., often produced by a single author and unified by a common theme or set of characters.
• [Greek *trilogia* (*tri* three, *logos* word)]

trimaran *noun*
• "TRY muh ran"
• a sailing vessel similar to a catamaran, with three hulls side by side.
• [Latin *tri* from *tres* three + CATAMARAN]

trimer *noun*
• "TRY mur"
• a compound whose molecule is composed of three molecules of a monomer.
• [Latin *tri* from *tres* three + MONOMER]
• **trimeric** *adjective* "try MARE ick"

trimester *noun*
• "TRY mester" or "try MESTER"
• a period of three months.
• [French *trimestre* from Latin *trimestris* (*tri* three, *-mestris* from *mensis* month)]

trimeter *noun*
• "TRIMMA tur"
• a verse line of three feet.
• [Latin *trimetrus* from Greek *trimetros* (*tri* three, *metron* measure)]

trimethoprim *noun*
• "try METHA prim"
• an antibiotic often used in conjunction with sulphamethoxazole to treat respiratory and urinary tract infections.
• [*tri* three + METHYL + OXYGEN + PYRIMIDINE]

Trimurti *noun*
• "trim URTY"
• the triad formed by the gods Brahma, Vishnu, and Shiva.
• [Sanskrit from *tri* three + *mūrti* form]

trine *adjective*
• "TRINE"
• designating or pertaining to the aspect of two heavenly bodies 120° (one-third of the zodiac) apart.
• [Old French *trin trine* from Latin *trinus* threefold, from *tres* three]

Trinidadian *noun*
• "trinna DADDY 'n" or "trinna DAY dee 'n"
• a native or inhabitant of Trinidad in the W Indies.

Trinitarian *noun*
• "trinna TERRY 'n"
• a person who believes in the doctrine of the Trinity.
• [as TRINITY]
• **Trinitarianism** *noun*

trinitrotoluene *noun*
• "try nite ruh TAWL yoo een"
• a high explosive that is relatively insensitive to shock and can be conveniently melted, formed from toluene by substitution of three hydrogen atoms with nitro groups; TNT.
• [Latin *tri* from *tres* three + NITRO + TOLUENE]

Trinity *noun*
• "TRINNA tee"
• the three modes of being of the Christian Godhead as conceived in orthodox Christian belief; the Father, Son, and Holy Spirit as constituting one God.
• [Old French *trinité* from Latin *trinitas -tatis* triad (as TRINE)]

trinomial *noun*
• "try NO mee 'll"
• an algebraic expression consisting of three terms connected by a plus or minus sign.
• [Latin *tri* from *tres* three + BINOMIAL]

triode *noun*
• "TRY ode"
• a thermionic valve having three electrodes, usu. an anode, a cathode, and a grid.
• [Latin *tri* from *tres* three + ELECTRODE]

triolet *noun*
• "TRY a lit" or "TREE a lit"
• a poem of eight (usu. eight-syllabled) lines rhyming *abaaabab*, the first line recurring as the fourth and seventh and the second as the eighth.
• [French from Latin *tres* three]

trioxide *noun*
• "try OX ide"
• an oxide containing three oxygen atoms.
• [Latin *tri* from *tres* three + OXYGEN]

tripartite *adjective*
• "try PAR tite"
• divided into or consisting of three parts.
• [Latin *tripartitus* (*tri* three, *partitus* past participle of *partiri* divide)]

triphthong *noun*
• "TRIFF thong" or "TRIP thong"
• a sequence of three vowel sounds pronounced as a single syllable.
• [French *triphtongue* (Latin *tri* three, DIPHTHONG)]

triplane *noun*
• "TRY plane"
• an early type of airplane having three sets of wings, one above the other.
• [Latin *tri* from *tres* three + 'airplane']

triplicate *adjective*
• "TRIP luh kit"
• existing in three examples or copies.
• [Latin *triplicatus* past participle of *triplicare* triple]
• **triplication** *noun*

triplicity *noun*
• "trip LISSA tee"
• the state of being triple.
• [Late Latin *triplicitas* from Latin *triplex* threefold, from *tri* three, *plic-* fold]

triploid *noun*
• "TRIP loid"
• an organism or cell having three times the haploid set of chromosomes.

• [modern Latin *triploides* from Greek *triplous* triple]
• **triploidy** *noun*

tripmeter *noun*
• "TRIP meeter"
• an instrument used to record the distance travelled by a vehicle during a particular trip.
• ['trip' from Old French *triper*, *tripper*, from Middle Dutch *trippen* skip, hop + Greek *metron* measure]

tripod *noun*
• "TRY pod"
• a stand with three usu. adjustable and collapsible legs for supporting a camera or telescope etc.
• [Latin *tripus tripodis* from Greek *tripous* (*tri* three, *pous podos* foot)]
• **tripodal** *adjective*

tripoli *noun*
• "TRIPPA lee"
• decomposed siliceous limestone used as a powder for polishing metals.
• [French from *Tripoli*, either of two cities, one in Libya, one in Lebanon]

tripos *noun*
• "TRY poss"
• the final honours exam that must be written to complete a bachelor's degree at Cambridge University.
• [as TRIPOD, with reference to the stool on which graduates sat to deliver a satirical speech at the degree ceremony]

triptych *noun*
• "TRIP tick"
• a picture or relief carving on three panels, usu. hinged vertically together and often used as an altarpiece.
• [Latin *tri* three, after DIPTYCH]
HOMOPHONES: *tryptic*

trireme *noun*
• "TRY reem"
• a galley with three banks of oars.
• [French *trirème* or Latin *triremis* (*tri* three, *remus* oar)]

trisaccharide *noun*
• "try SACKA ride"
• a sugar consisting of three linked monosaccharides.
• [Latin *tri* from *tres* three + SACCHARIDE]

trisect *verb*
• "try SECT"
• cut or divide into three (usu. equal) parts.
• [Latin *tri* three + *secare sect-* cut]
• **trisection** *noun*
• **trisector** *noun*

trishaw *noun*
• "TRY shaw"
• a light three-wheeled vehicle operated by pedals, used in the Far East as a taxi to chauffeur passengers.
• [*tri* three + 'rickshaw', abbreviation of *jinricksha*, *jinrikshaw* from Japanese *jinrikisha* from *jin* person + *riki* power + *sha* vehicle]

triskaidekaphobia *noun*
• "trisk eye decka FOBEY uh"
• fear or superstition regarding the number thirteen.
• [Greek *treiskaideka* thirteen + PHOBIA]

triskelion *noun*
• "try SKELLY 'n" or "triss KELLY 'n"
• a symbolic figure of three legs or lines radiating from a common centre.
• [Greek *tri* three + *skelos* leg]

trismus *noun*
• "TRIZ muss"
• a variety of tetanus with sustained contractions of the jaw muscles causing the mouth to remain tightly closed; lockjaw.
• [modern Latin from Greek *trismos* = *trigmos* a scream, grinding]

trisomy *noun*
• "TRY suh mee"
• a condition in which an extra copy of a chromosome is present in the cell nuclei, causing developmental abnormalities.
• [Latin *tri* from *tres* three + CHROMOSOME]
• **trisomic** *adjective* "try SO mick"

tristesse *noun*
• "triss TESS"
• sadness, sorrow, melancholy.
• [French, from Latin *tristis* sad]

trisulphide *noun*
• "try SULL fide"
• a compound of an element or radical with three atoms of sulphur.
• [Latin *tri* from *tres* three + SULPHIDE]

trisyllabic *adjective*
• "try suh LABBIC"
• (of a word or metrical foot) having three syllables.
• [Latin *tri* from *tres* three + SYLLABLE]

tritiated *adjective*
• "TRITTY ated"
• containing tritium; having had an atom of ordinary hydrogen replaced by tritium.
• [as TRITIUM]

triticale *noun*
• "tritta CAY lee"
• a high-protein hybrid between wheat, *Triticum aestivum*, and rye, *Secale cereale*, used by the brewing industry, in some baked goods, and as feed for livestock.
• [modern Latin from the genus names *Triti(cum)* wheat + *(Se)cale* rye]

tritium *noun*
• "TRITTY um"
• a radioactive isotope of hydrogen with a mass

about three times that of ordinary hydrogen, which occurs naturally in minute amounts and is produced artificially, esp. for use in fusion reactors.
• [modern Latin from Greek *tritos* third]

triton *noun*
• "TRITE 'n"
• any marine gastropod mollusc of the family Cymatiidae, with a long conical shell.
• [Latin from Greek *Tritōn*, a minor sea god]

tritone *noun*
• "TRY tone"
• an interval of an augmented fourth, comprising three whole tones.
• [Latin *tri* from *tres* three + 'tone']

triturate *verb*
• "TRITCH ur ate"
• reduce to fine particles or a powder by rubbing, crushing, or grinding; pulverize.
• [Latin *triturare* thresh grain, from *tritura* rubbing, from *tritus* past participle of *terere* rub, wear down]
• **trituration** *noun*

triumph *noun*
• "TRY umf"
• a great success, achievement, or victory; a major accomplishment.
• [Old French *triumphe* from Latin *triump(h)us* prob. from Greek *thriambos* hymn to Bacchus]
• **triumphant** *adjective*
• **triumphantly** *adverb*

triumphal *adjective*
• "try UM full"
• done, used, or made to celebrate or commemorate a success or victory.
• [as TRIUMPH]

triumphalism *noun*
• "try UM full izm"
• extreme or ostentatious pride or excessive exultation over one's achievements or those of one's country, party, etc.
• [as TRIUMPH]
• **triumphalist** *adjective*

triumvir *noun*
• "try UM vur"
• a member of a triumvirate.
• [Latin, originally in pl. *triumviri*, back-formation from *trium virorum* genitive of *tres viri* three men]

triumvirate *noun*
• "try UM vur it"
• a group of three people in a joint position of power or authority.
• [as TRIUMVIR]

triune *adjective*
• "TRY yoon"
• (esp. with reference to the Trinity) that is three in one; that constitutes or consists of three persons or things in unity.
• [Latin *tri* three + *unus* one]

trivalent *adjective*
• "try VALE 'nt"
• having a valence of three.
• [Latin *tri* from *tres* three + VALENCE]
• **trivalence** *noun*

trivet *noun*
• "TRIVVIT"
• a low, flat, usu. three-legged cast iron or ceramic stand placed under a hot kettle, pot, or serving dish to protect the surface of a table.
• [Middle English *trevet*, apparently from Latin *tripes* (*tri* three, *pes pedis* foot)]

trivium *noun*
• "TRIVVY um"
• (in the Middle Ages) the lower division of a university course of study, comprising grammar, rhetoric, and logic.
• [Latin, = place where three roads meet (*tri* three, *via* road)]

trocar *noun*
• "TRO car"
• a surgical instrument used for withdrawing fluid from a body cavity, consisting of a shaft with a three-sided cutting point enclosed in a cannula.
• [French *trois-quarts*, *trocart* from *trois* three + *carre* (Latin *quadra*) side, face, from the triangular appearance of this device]

trochanter *noun*
• "tro CANTER"
• any of several bony protuberances by which muscles are attached to the upper part of the femur or thigh bone.
• [French from Greek *trokhantēr* from *trekhō* run]
• **trochanteric** *adjective* "tro can TERRIC"

trochee *noun*
• "TRO kee"
• a metrical foot consisting of one long or stressed syllable followed by one short or unstressed syllable.
• [Latin *trochaeus* from Greek *trokhaios* (*pous*) running (foot), from *trekhō* run]
• **trochaic** *adjective* "tro KAY ick"

trochlea *noun*
• "TROCK lee uh"
• a structure or arrangement of parts resembling a pulley, with a smooth surface over which some other part slides, e.g. the groove at the lower end of the humerus, with which the ulna articulates at the elbow.
• [Latin, = pulley, from Greek *trokhilia*]
• **trochlear** *adjective*

trochoid *adjective*
• "TRO coid"
• (of a joint) in which one bone rotates freely around a central axis.
• [Greek *trokhoeidēs* wheel-like, from *trokhos* wheel]

troglodyte *noun*
- "TROGLA dite"
- a cave dweller, esp. of prehistoric times.
- [Latin *troglodyta* from Greek *trōglodutēs* from the name of an Ethiopian people, after *trōglē* hole]
- **troglodytic** *adjective* "trogla DITTIC"

trogon *noun*
- "TRO gon"
- any tropical bird of the genus *Trogon* or the family Trogonidae, widely distributed in tropical and subtropical forests, having a short thick bill and soft plumage of varied and often brilliant colour.
- [modern Latin from Greek *trōgōn* from *trōgō* gnaw]

troika *noun*
- "TROY kuh"
- a Russian carriage or sleigh drawn by a team of three horses.
- [Russian from *troe* three]

Trojan *adjective*
- "TRO j'n"
- of or relating to ancient Troy or its inhabitants.
- [Latin *Troianus* from *Troia* Troy]

trommel *noun*
- "TROM'll"
- a rotating cylindrical screen or sieve used for washing and sizing ores, coal, gravel, etc.
- [German, = drum]

trophic *adjective*
- "TROFFIC"
- of or concerned with nutrition.
- [Greek *trophikos* from *trophē* nourishment, from *trephō* nourish]

trophoblast *noun*
- "TROFFO blast"
- a layer of cells or a membrane surrounding an embryo, which supplies it with nourishment and later forms most of the placenta.
- [as TROPHIC + Greek *blastos* sprout]
- **trophoblastic** *adjective*

trophy *noun*
- "TRO fee"
- an ornamental commemorative object, such as a gold or silver cup, awarded as a prize for excellence or an outstanding achievement, such as in sports or academics.
- [French *trophée* from Latin *trophaeum* from Greek *tropaion* from *tropē* rout, from *trepō* turn]

tropism *noun*
- "TROPE izm"
- the turning of all or part of an organism in a particular direction by growth, bending, or locomotion, in response to an external stimulus.
- [Greek *tropos* turning, from *trepō* turn]

tropological *adjective*
- "troppa LODGE a k'll"
- of, pertaining to, or involving the figurative use of words.
- [Late Latin *tropologia* from Greek *tropologia* (as TROPISM)]
- **tropology** *noun*

tropopause *noun*
- "TROPPA pozz" or "TROPE a pozz"
- the upper limit of the troposphere, separating it from the stratosphere, at which temperature ceases decreasing with height.
- [TROPOSPHERE + Latin *pausa* from Greek *pausis*, from *pauō* stop]

troposphere *noun*
- "TROPPA sfeer" or "TROPE a sfeer"
- the lowest region of the atmosphere, extending to a height of between 8 and 18 km and marked by convection and a general decrease of temperature with height.
- [Greek *tropos* turning + SPHERE]
- **tropospheric** *adjective* "troppa SFEER ick" or "trope a SFEER ick" or "troppa SFARE ick" or "trope a SFARE ick"

troppo *adverb*
- "TROPPO"
- too much (qualifying a tempo indication).
- [Italian]

Trotskyism *noun*
- "TROT skee izm"
- the political or economic principles of the Russian revolutionary L. Trotsky (d.1940), which called for a worldwide socialist revolution.
- **Trotskyist** *noun*
- **Trotskyite** *noun*

troubadour *noun*
- "TROOBA dore"
- any of a number of French medieval lyric poets composing and singing in Provençal esp. on the themes of chivalry and courtly love, living in S France, E Spain, and N Italy between the 11th and 13th c.
- [French from Provençal *trobador* from *trobar* find, invent, compose in verse]

trough *noun*
- "TROFF"
- a long narrow open receptacle for water, animal feed, etc.
- [Old English *trog* from Germanic]

troupe *noun*
- "TROOP"
- a company of actors or dancers etc.
- [French, back-formation from *troupeau* diminutive of medieval Latin *troppus* flock, prob. of Germanic origin]

HOMOPHONES: *troop*

trouper *noun*
- "TROOPER"
- a member of esp. a theatrical troupe; a performer, esp. an experienced one.
- [as TROUPE]

HOMOPHONES: *trooper*

trousseau *noun*
- "TROO so" or "troo SO"
- the clothes collected by a bride for her marriage.
- [French, lit. = 'bundle', diminutive of *trousse*, of unknown origin]

trouvaille *noun*
- "troo VIE"
- a lucky find or discovery.
- [French from *trouver* find]

trouvère *noun*
- "troo VARE"
- any of a group of French medieval poets composing *chansons de geste* and fabliaux, living in N France between the 11th and 14th c.
- [Old French *trovere* from *trover* find: compare TROUBADOUR]

trowel *noun*
- "TROW'll" ("TROW" rhymes with *COW*)
- a small hand-held tool with a flat metal blade, used to apply and spread mortar, cement, plaster, etc.
- [Old French *truele* from Latin *trulla* scoop, diminutive of *trua* ladle etc.]

truant *noun*
- "TROO 'nt"
- a student who stays away from school without leave or explanation.
- [Old French, prob. ultimately from Celtic: compare Welsh *truan*, Gaelic *truaghan* wretched]
- **truancy** *noun*

truculent *adjective*
- "TRUCK yoo l'nt"
- vehemently defiant.
- [Latin *truculentus* from *trux trucis* fierce]
- **truculence** *noun*
- **truculently** *adverb*

Trudeaumania *noun*
- "troo doe MAINY uh"
- *Cdn* widespread popularity of, and fascination with, the politician Pierre Elliott Trudeau (d.2000) among the Canadian public, esp. during the election campaign of 1968.
- [*Trudeau* + MANIA]

truism *noun*
- "TROO izm"
- a self-evident or indisputable truth, esp. a trivial or hackneyed one, e.g. *nothing lasts forever*.
- [from 'true' from Old English *trēowe*]
- **truistic** *adjective*

truly *adverb*
- "TROO lee"
- sincerely, genuinely.
- [from 'true' from Old English *trēowe*]

truncate *verb*
- "TRUNK ate" or "trunk ATE"
- shorten or diminish by cutting off the top or end part of; cut short, mutilate.
- [Latin *truncare truncat-* maim]
- **truncated** *adjective*
- **truncation** *noun*

truncheon *noun*
- "TRUN chin"
- a short club or cudgel, esp. carried by a police officer.
- [Old French *tronchon* stump, ultimately from Latin *truncus* trunk]

trunnel *noun*
- "TRUN'll"
- a hard wooden pin for securing timbers etc.
- [pronunciation of 'tree nail']

trunnion *noun*
- "TRUN y'n"
- either of a pair of cylindrical projections on opposite sides of a cannon or mortar, by which it is pivoted on its carriage.
- [French *trognon* core, tree trunk, of unknown origin]

Truronian *noun*
- "trur OH nee 'n"
- a resident of Truro, NS.

trustafarian *noun*
- "trusta FERRY 'n"
- a wealthy young (white) person (esp. one living off a trust fund) with a bohemian lifestyle.
- [blend of 'trust' and RASTAFARIAN]

trustful *adjective*
- "TRUST full"
- inclined to trust; not feeling or showing suspicion.
- [Old Norse *traust* trust, from *traustr* strong]
- **trustfully** *adverb*
- **trustfulness** *noun*

truthful *adjective*
- "TROOTH full"
- habitually speaking the truth; sincere, honest.
- [as TRUISM]
- **truthfully** *adverb*
- **truthfulness** *noun*

trypanosome *noun*
- "TRIPPA nuh soam" or "trip ANNA soam"
- any protozoan parasite of the genus *Trypanosoma* having a long trailing flagellum and infesting the blood etc.
- [Greek *trupanon* borer + *sōma* body]

trypanosomiasis *noun*
- "trippa nuh suh MY a sis" or "trip ANNA suh my a sis"
- any of several diseases caused by a trypanosome and usu. transmitted by biting insects, including sleeping sickness and Chagas' disease.
- [as TRYPANOSOME]

trypsin *noun*
- "TRIP sin"
- a digestive enzyme which hydrolyzes proteins, and is secreted by the pancreas.

• [Greek *tripsis* friction, from *tribō* rub (because it was first obtained by rubbing down the pancreas with glycerine)]
• **tryptic** *adjective*
HOMOPHONES: *triptych*

tryptophan *noun*
• "TRIP tuh fan"
• an amino acid essential in the diet of vertebrates.
• [as TRYPSIN + *-phan* from Greek *phainō* appear]

tryst *noun*
• "TRIST"
• an esp. secret meeting between lovers.
• [Middle English, variant of obsolete *trist* an appointed station in hunting, from French *triste* or medieval Latin *trista*, *tristra*]

tsetse *noun*
• "TSEET see" or "TEET see"
• any fly of the genus *Glossina* native to Africa, that feeds on human and animal blood with a needle-like proboscis and transmits trypanosomiasis (sleeping sickness).
• [Setswana]

Tsimshian *noun*
• "TSIMSHY 'n" or "TSIM sh'n"
• a member of a group of Aboriginal peoples living in coastal and interior northern BC.
• [Tsimshian *ĉamsián*, lit. 'inside the Skeena River']

Tsonga *noun*
• "TSONG guh"
• a member of a people living in Transvaal, southern Mozambique, and southern Zimbabwe.
• [a local name, from either Tsonga or Zulu]

tsunami *noun*
• "tsoo NOMMY" or "tsoo NAMMY"
• a long high sea wave caused by underwater earthquakes or other disturbances.
• [Japanese from *tsu* harbour + *nami* wave]

tsuris *noun*
• "TSOO reece"
• trouble, woe.
• [Yiddish *tsores*, pl. of *tsore* trouble]

Tswana *noun*
• "TSWONNA"
• a southern African people living in Botswana and neighbouring areas.
• [Bantu (compare SETSWANA)]

Tuareg *noun*
• "TWAR egg"
• a member of a Berber group of nomads of the western and central Sahara, now concentrated mainly in Algeria, Mali, Niger, and western Libya.
• [Berber]

tuatara *noun*
• "too a TAR uh"
• a large lizard-like reptile, *Sphenodon punctatus*, unique to certain small islands of New Zealand, having a crest of soft spines extending along its back.
• [Maori from *tua* on the back + *tara* spine]

tubercle *noun*
• "TUBE ur k'll"
• a small rounded protuberance esp. on a bone.
• [Latin *tuberculum*, diminutive of *tuber* hump, swelling]

tubercular *adjective*
• "too BURK yuh lur"
• of or having tubercles or tuberculosis.
• [from Latin *tuberculum* (as TUBERCLE)]

tuberculation *noun*
• "too burk yuh LAY sh'n"
• the formation of tubercles.
• [as TUBERCLE]

tuberculin *noun*
• "too BURK yuh lin"
• a sterile protein extract from cultures of tubercle bacillus, used in the diagnosis and (formerly) the treatment of tuberculosis.
• [as TUBERCLE]

tuberculosis *noun*
• "too burk yuh LO sis"
• an infectious disease caused by the bacillus *Mycobacterium tuberculosis*, characterized by tubercles, esp. in the lungs.
• [as TUBERCLE]

tuberose *noun*
• "TUBE uh roze" or "TUBE roze"
• a plant, *Polianthes tuberosa*, native to Mexico, having heavily scented white funnel-like flowers and strap-shaped leaves.
• [Latin *tuberosa*, the specific name of the plant, feminine of *tuberosus* from *tuber* hump, swelling; corrupted by popular etymology into a disyllable, as if from 'tube' + 'rose']

tuberous *adjective*
• "TUBE ur us"
• covered with tubers; knobby.
• [Latin *tuberosus* from *tuber* hump, swelling]

tubifex *noun*
• "TUBE uh fex"
• any red annelid worm of the genus *Tubifex*, found in mud at the bottom of rivers and lakes and used as food for aquarium fish.
• [modern Latin from Latin *tubus* tube + *-fex* from *facere* make]

tubular *adjective*
• "TUBE yuh lur"
• tube-shaped.
• [as TUBULE]

tubule *noun*
• "TUBE yool"
• a small tube in a plant or an animal body.
• [Latin *tubulus*, diminutive of *tubus* tube]

tubulin *noun*
- "TUBE yoo lin"
- a protein that is the main constituent of the microtubules of living cells.
- [as TUBULE]

tuchus *noun*
ALSO SPELLED: **tuchis**
- "TOOK us" (with "OO" as in *BOOK*)
- the buttocks.
- [Yiddish *tokhes* from Hebrew *taḥaṯ* beneath]

tuckamore *noun*
- "TUCKA more"
- *Cdn* (*Nfld*) a stunted tree or bush, esp. a spruce or juniper, with creeping roots and interlacing branches.
- [obsolete sense of 'tuck' = 'tug' + Middle English *more* tree root]

Tudor *adjective*
- "TOODER" or "TYOODER"
- of, characteristic of, or associated with the royal family of England ruling 1485–1603 or this period.
- [Owen *Tudor* of Wales, grandfather of Henry VI]

HOMOPHONES: *tutor*

Tudorbethan *adjective*
- "tooder BEETH 'n" or "tyooder BEETH 'n"
- (of a house etc.) imitating Tudor and Elizabethan styles in design.
- [blend of TUDOR and ELIZABETHAN]

Tuesday *noun*
- "TEWS day" or "TEWS dee"
- the third day of the week, following Monday.
- [Old English *Tīwesdæg* from *Tīw* = *Tiu* the Germanic god of war and the sky]

tufa *noun*
- "TOO fuh" or "TYOO fuh"
- a porous rock composed of calcium carbonate and formed around mineral springs.
- [Italian, var. of *tufo*: see TUFF]
- **tufaceous** *adjective* "too FAY sh'ss" or "tyoo FAY sh'ss"

tuff *noun*
- "TUFF"
- rock formed by the consolidation of volcanic ash.
- [French *tuf*, *tuffe* from Italian *tufo* from Late Latin *tofus*]
- **tuffaceous** *adjective* "tuh FAY sh'ss"

HOMOPHONES: *tough*

tugrik *noun*
- "TOO greek"
- the basic monetary unit of Mongolia, equal to 100 mongos.
- [Mongolian]

tuile *noun*
- "TWEEL"
- a thin curved cookie, usu. made with almonds.
- [French, = 'tile']

tuition *noun*
- "too ISH'n" or "tyoo ISH'n"
- a fee paid for education or instruction.
- [Old French from Latin *tuitio -onis* from *tuēri tuit-* watch, guard]
- **tuitional** *adjective*

tularemia *noun*
ALSO SPELLED: esp. *Brit.* **tularaemia**
- "toola REEMY uh"
- a severe infectious disease of animals transmissible to humans, caused by the bacterium *Pasteurella tularense* and characterized by ulcers at the site of infection, fever, and loss of weight.
- [modern Latin from *Tulare* County in California, where it was first observed]
- **tularemic** *adjective* (also esp. *Brit.* **tularaemic**)

tulle *noun*
- "TOOL"
- a soft fine net used in veils, tutus, etc.
- [*Tulle* in SW France, where it was first made]

HOMOPHONES: *tool*

tullibee *noun*
- "TULLA bee"
- any of various N American whitefishes of the genus *Coregonus*.
- [Canadian French *toulibi*, ultimately from Ojibwa]

tulsi *noun*
- "TULL see" ("TULL" rhymes with *PULL*)
- a kind of basil, *Ocimum sanctum*, which is cultivated by Hindus as a sacred plant.
- [Hindi]

tumbrel *noun*
ALSO SPELLED: **tumbril**
- "TUM brull"
- an open cart in which condemned persons were conveyed to their execution, esp. to the guillotine during the French Revolution.
- [Old French *tumberel*, *tomberel* from *tomber* fall]

tumefy *verb*
- "TOOMA fie" or "TYOOMA fie"
- swell, inflate; be inflated.
- [French *tuméfier* from Latin *tumefacere* from *tumēre* swell]

tumescent *adjective*
- "too MESS'nt" or "tyoo MESS'nt"
- becoming tumid; swelling.
- [Latin *tumescere* (as TUMEFY)]
- **tumescence** *noun*

tumid *adjective*
- "TOO mid" or "TYOO mid"
- (of parts of the body etc.) swollen, inflated.
- [Latin *tumidus* from *tumēre* swell]

tumorigenic *adjective*
- "toomer a JENNIC" or "tyoomer a JENNIC"
- capable of causing tumours.

• [as TUMOUR + GENESIS]
• **tumorigenicity** *noun* "toomer a jen ISSA tee" or "tyoomer a jen ISSA tee"

tumour *noun*
ALSO SPELLED: **tumor**
• "TOOMER" or "TYOOMER"
• an abnormal swelling or enlargement in any part of the body, esp. a permanent swelling without inflammation, caused by excessive continued growth and proliferation of cells in a tissue, which may be either benign or malignant.
• [Latin *tumor* from *tumēre* swell]
• **tumorous** *adjective*

tumult *noun*
• "TYOO mult" or "TOO mult" or "TUM ult"
• an uproar or din, esp. of a disorderly crowd.
• [Old French *tumulte* or Latin *tumultus*]
• **tumultuous** *adjective* "tuh MUL choo us"
• **tumultuously** *adverb*

tumulus *noun*
• "TOOM yoo luss" or "TYOOM yoo luss"
• an ancient burial mound or barrow.
• [Latin from *tumēre* swell]

tun *noun*
• "TUN"
• a large beer or wine cask.
• [Old English *tunne* from medieval Latin *tunna*, prob. of Gaulish origin]
HOMOPHONES: *ton*, *tonne*

tunable *adjective*
• "TOONA bull" or "TYOONA bull"
• that may be tuned.
• [from 'tune' unexplained variant of 'tone']
• **tunability** *noun*

tung *noun*
• "TUNG"
• a tree, *Aleurites fordii*, native to China, bearing poisonous fruits containing seeds that yield oil.
• [Chinese *tong*]
HOMOPHONES: *tongue*

tungstate *noun*
• "TUNG state"
• a salt in which the anion contains both tungsten and oxygen.
• [as TUNGSTEN]

tungsten *noun*
• "TUNG stin"
• a steel-grey dense metallic element with a very high melting point, occurring naturally in scheelite and used for the filaments of electric lamps and for alloying steel etc.
• [Swedish from *tung* heavy + *sten* stone]

Tungus *noun*
• "tung GOOSE" (with "U" as in *PUT*)
• a member of a people of E Siberia.
• [Yakut]

tunicate *noun*
• "TOONA kit" or "TYOONA kit" or "TOONA cate" or "TYOONA cate"
• any marine animal of the subphylum Urochordata having a rubbery or hard outer coat, including sea squirts.
• [Latin *tunicatus* past participle of *tunicare* clothe with a tunic]

tunicle *noun*
• "TOONA k'll" or "TYOONA k'll"
• a short vestment worn over an alb, esp. by an Anglican subdeacon.
• [Old French *tunicle* or Latin *tunicula* diminutive of *tunica* tunic]

Tunisian *noun*
• "too NEE zh'n"
• a native or inhabitant of Tunisia in N Africa.

tupelo *noun*
• "TOOPA lo" or "TYOOPA lo"
• any of various Asian and N American deciduous trees of the genus *Nyssa*, with colourful foliage and growing in swampy conditions.
• [Creek from *ito* tree + *opilwa* swamp]

Tupi *noun*
• "TOOPY"
• a member of an Aboriginal people native to the Amazon valley.
• [S American Aboriginal name]
HOMOPHONES: *toupie*

tupik *noun*
• "TOO pick"
• a traditional skin tent used by Inuit groups during the summer.
• [Inuktitut *tupiq*]

turaco *noun*
ALSO SPELLED: **touraco**
• "TOORA co"
• any African bird of the family Musophagidae, with crimson and green plumage and a prominent crest.
• [French from native West African name]

turban *noun*
• "TUR b'n"
• a man's headdress, consisting of a length of cotton or silk wound around a cap or the head, worn esp. by Muslims and Sikhs.
• [16th c. (also *tulbant* etc.), ultimately from Turkish *tülbent* from Persian *dulband*]
• **turbaned** *adjective*

turbellarian *noun*
• "turba LERRY 'n"
• any usu. free-living flatworm of the class Turbellaria of fresh or salt water or damp earth, having a ciliated surface.
• [modern Latin *Turbellaria* from Latin *turbella* diminutive of *turba* crowd: see TURBID]

turbid *adjective*
• "TUR bid"
• (of a liquid or colour) muddy, thick; not clear.

• [Latin *turbidus* from *turba* a crowd, a disturbance]
• **turbidity** *noun*
• **turbidly** *adverb*

turbinate *adjective*
• "TURBA nit"
• shaped like a spinning top or inverted cone.
• [as TURBINE]

turbine *noun*
• "TUR bine"
• a rotary motor or engine driven by a flow of water, steam, gas, wind, etc., esp. to produce electrical power.
• [French from Latin *turbo -binis* spinning top, whirlwind]

turbit *noun*
• "TUR bit"
• a breed of domestic pigeon of stout build with a neck frill and short beak.
• [apparently from Latin *turbo* top, from its figure]
HOMOPHONES: *turbot*

turbodiesel *noun*
• "TURBO deez'll"
• a turbocharged diesel engine.
• [as TURBINE + DIESEL]

turbot *noun*
• "TUR bit"
• the Greenland halibut.
• [Old French from Old Swedish *törnbut* from *törn* thorn + *but* the thicker end, esp. of a tool or a weapon, from Dutch *bot* stumpy]
HOMOPHONES: *turbit*

turbulent *adjective*
• "TUR byoo l'nt"
• disturbed; in commotion.
• [Latin *turbulentus* from *turba* crowd]
• **turbulence** *noun*
• **turbulently** *adverb*

tureen *noun*
• "tuh REEN" or "tyur EEN"
• a deep covered dish for serving soup etc.
• [earlier *terrine*, *-ene* from French *terrine* large circular earthenware dish, feminine of Old French *terrin* earthen, ultimately from Latin *terra* earth]
HOMOPHONES: *terrine*

turgescent *adjective*
• "tur JESS'nt"
• becoming turgid; swelling.
• [as TURGID]

turgid *adjective*
• "TUR jid"
• swollen, inflated, enlarged.
• [Latin *turgidus* from *turgēre* swell]
• **turgidity** *noun*

turgor *noun*
• "TUR gur"
• the rigidity of cells due to the absorption of water.
• [Late Latin (as TURGID)]

turista *noun*
• "too REESTA"
• a tourist in a Spanish-speaking country.
• [Spanish, = 'tourist']

Turkana *noun*
• "tur CONNA"
• a member of an East African people living between Lake Turkana and the Nile.
• [Nilotic]

turkey *noun*
• "TURKY"
• a large mainly domesticated game bird, *Meleagris gallopavo*, originally of N America, having dark plumage with a green or bronze sheen, prized as food esp. on festive occasions including Christmas and Thanksgiving.
• [16th c.: short for *turkeycock* or *turkeyhen*, originally applied to the guinea fowl which was imported through Turkey, and then erroneously to the N American bird]
HOMOPHONES: *Turki*

Turki *noun*
• "TURKY"
• the Turkic languages, esp. those of central Asia, collectively.
• [Persian *turki*]
HOMOPHONES: *turkey*

Turkic *adjective*
• "TURK ick"
• of or relating to a large group of Altaic languages including Turkish, Azerbaijani, and Kyrgyz, or the peoples speaking them.
• [as TURKI]

Turkish *adjective*
• "TURK ish"
• of or relating to Turkey, or to the Turks or their language.

Turkmen *noun*
• "TURK m'n"
• a member of any of various Turkic peoples inhabiting the region east of the Caspian Sea and south of the Aral Sea, comprising Turkmenistan and parts of Iran and Afghanistan.
• [Persian *turkmān* from Turkish *türkmen*; also influenced by Russian *turkmen*]

turmeric *noun*
• "TURMER ick"
• a tropical Asian plant, *Curcuma longa*, of the ginger family, yielding aromatic rhizomes used as a spice and for yellow dye.
• [16th-c. forms *tarmaret* etc. perhaps from French *terre mérite* and modern Latin *terra merita*, of unknown origin]

turmoil *noun*
• "TUR moil"
• violent confusion; agitation.
• [16th c.: origin unknown]

turnstile *noun*
• "TURN stile"
• a mechanical gate consisting of usu. four revolving arms fixed to a vertical post allowing people through singly, and usu. functioning in one direction only.
• ['turn' + STILE]

turpentine *noun*
• "TURP 'n tine"
• a volatile essential oil with a pungent odour, obtained by distilling gum turpentine or pine wood, used esp. as a solvent and thinner for paints and stains, and in medical liniments.
• [Old French *ter(e)bentine* from Latin *ter(e)binthina* (*resina* resin) (as TEREBINTH)]

turpitude *noun*
• "TURPA tude"
• baseness, depravity, wickedness.
• [French *turpitude* or Latin *turpitudo* from *turpis* disgraceful, base]

turquoise *noun*
• "TUR koyz" or "TUR kwoyz"
• a semi-precious stone, usu. opaque and of a sky-blue to blue-green colour, consisting of hydrated copper aluminum phosphate.
• [Old French *turqueise* (later *-oise*) Turkish (stone)]

turr *noun*
• "TUR"
• *Cdn* (*Nfld*) an auk or guillemot.
• [prob. imitative of MURRE and the sound made by this bird]

turret *noun*
• "TURRIT"
• a small tower, usu. projecting from the wall of a building, such as a castle, as a decorative addition.
• [Old French *to(u)rete* diminutive of *to(u)r* tower]
• **turreted** *adjective*

Tuscan *noun*
• "TUSK'n"
• an inhabitant of Tuscany in west central Italy.

Tuscarora *noun*
• "TUSKA rora"
• a member of an Iroquois people living in southern Ontario and western New York, the last member to join the Iroquoian confederacy.
• [Iroquois, from Tuscarora *skaroo'ren* hemp gatherers, their self-designation]

tush *noun*
• "TUSH" (rhymes with *PUSH*)
• a long pointed tooth, esp. a canine tooth of a horse.
• [Old English *tusc* tusk]

tussah *noun*
• "TUSSA"
• an Indian or Chinese silkworm, *Anthereae mylitta*, yielding strong but coarse brown silk.
• [Urdu from Hindi *tasar* from Sanskrit *tasara* shuttle]

tussive *adjective*
• "TUSSIV"
• of, relating to, or producing a cough.
• [Latin *tussis* cough]

tussle *noun*
• "TUSS'll"
• a struggle, scuffle, or conflict, esp. a minor or playful one.
• [originally Scots & Northern English, perhaps diminutive of *touse*: see TOUSLE]

tussock *noun*
• "TUSS ick"
• a tuft or clump of grass etc. forming a small hill.
• [16th c.: perhaps alteration of dialect *tusk* tuft]
• **tussocky** *adjective*

Tutchone *noun*
• "too CHONE ee"
• a member of an Aboriginal people living in the area of the Yukon River.
• [from Tutchone *dechän* wood]

tutelage *noun*
• "TOOTA lidge" or "TYOOTA lidge"
• instruction, teaching, education.
• [Latin *tutela* from *tuēri tuit-* or *tut-* watch]

tutelary *adjective*
• "TOOTA lerry" or "TYOOTA lerry"
• serving as a guardian, protector, or patron.
• [Late Latin *tutelaris*, Latin *-arius* from *tutela*: see TUTELAGE]

tutor *noun*
• "TOOTER" or "TYOOTER"
• a private teacher, either one in general charge of a person's education or employed to give a student additional instruction in a particular subject or subjects.
• [Latin, from *tuēri tut-* watch]
• **tutorship** *noun*
HOMOPHONES: *Tudor*

tutorial *adjective*
• "too TORY 'll" or "tyoo TORY 'll"
• of or relating to a tutor or tuition.
• [as TUTOR]

Tutsi *noun*
• "TOOT see" ("TOOT" rhymes with *FOOT*)
• a member of a Bantu-speaking people forming a minority of the population of Rwanda.
• [Bantu]
HOMOPHONES: *tootsie*

tutti *adverb*
• "TOOTY"

• with all voices or instruments together.
• [Italian, pl. of *tutto* all]

tutu *noun*
• "TOO too"
• a female ballet dancer's costume with a long, flowing bell-shaped skirt of layered tulle or a short, stiff skirt of layered net standing out from the hips.
• [French, childish alteration of *cucu*, diminutive of *cul* buttocks]

Tuvaluan *noun*
• "toova LOO 'n" or "too VAWL oo 'n"
• a native or inhabitant of Tuvalu in the SW Pacific.

Tuvan *adjective*
• "TOOV 'n"
• of or relating to the Russian autonomous republic of Tuva, bordering Mongolia.

tuxedo *noun*
• "tuck SEE doe"
• a dress suit worn esp. by men on formal occasions, consisting of a usu. black jacket and matching pants, often trimmed in silk, traditionally worn with a black tie, cummerbund, and white dress shirt.
• [after a country club at *Tuxedo* Park, New York where this garment was first worn]
• **tuxedoed** *adjective*

twaddle *noun*
• "TWODDLE"
• useless, senseless, silly, or dull talk, ideas, or writing.
• [alteration of earlier *twattle*, alteration of 'tattle' from Middle Flemish *tatelen*, *tateren* (imitative)]

tweak *verb*
• "TWEEK"
• pinch and twist sharply; pull with a sharp jerk; twitch.
• [prob. alteration of dialect *twick* & 'twitch']

twee *adjective*
• "TWEE"
• affectedly dainty, quaint, or sentimental.
• [childish pronunciation of 'sweet']
• **tweeness** *noun*
HOMOPHONES: *Twi*

twelfth *noun*
• "TWELFTH"
• the position in a sequence corresponding to the number 12.
• [Old English *twelf(e)* twelve]
• **twelfthly** *adverb*

twerp *noun*
• "TWURP"
• a foolish, pathetic, or insignificant person; a pipsqueak, a nobody.
• [20th c.: origin unknown]
• **twerpy** *adjective*

Twi *noun*
• "TWEE"
• one of the two main varieties of Akan spoken in Ghana, the other being the mutually intelligible Fanti.
• [Kwa]
HOMOPHONES: *twee*

twibill *noun*
• "TWY bill"
• a double-bladed battle-axe.
• [Old English from *twi-* double + *bil* a hooked weapon]

twilight *noun*
• "TWY lite"
• the soft glowing light from the sky when the sun is below the horizon, esp. in the evening.
• [Middle English from Old English *twi-* two (in uncertain sense) + 'light']
• **twilit** *adjective*

Twillingater *noun*
• "TWILLING gater"
• a resident of Twillingate, Nfld.

twofer *noun*
• "TOO fur"
• a coupon entitling a person to buy two tickets for a theatrical performance for the price of one.
• [representing a pronunciation of '*two for* one']

tycoon *noun*
• "tie COON"
• a business magnate.
• [Japanese *taikun* great lord, from Chinese *dà* great + *jūn* prince]
• **tycoonery** *noun*

tyee *noun*
• "TIE ee"
• *Cdn (BC)* a chinook salmon, esp. one weighing more than 13.6 kg (30 lb.).
• [Chinook Jargon, from Nuu-chah-nulth *ta:yi:* elder brother, chief]

tyke *noun*
• "TIKE"
• a small child.
• [Old Norse *tík* female dog]

tympanum *noun*
• "TIMPA num"
• the cavity of the central part of the ear behind the drum; the middle ear.
• [Latin from Greek *tumpanon* drum, from *tuptō* strike]
• **tympanic** *adjective*

Tynwald *noun*
• "TIN wold"
• the parliament of the Isle of Man.
• [Old Norse *thing-völlr* place of assembly, from *thing* assembly + *völlr* field]

type *noun*
• "TIPE"
• a class of people or things distinguished by common essential characteristics.
• [French *type* or Latin *typus* from Greek *tupos* impression, figure, type, from *tuptō* strike]
• **typal** *adjective*

typecast *verb*
• "TIPE cast"
• assign (an actor) repeatedly to the same type of role which he or she has often played successfully in previous productions or which seems to fit his or her personality.
• [as TYPE + 'cast' from Old Norse *kasta* throw]
• **typecasting** *noun*

typed *adjective*
• "TIPE'd"
• classified as or having a certain character or type.
• [as TYPE]

typeface *noun*
• "TIPE face"
• the particular style, appearance, size, etc. of a type or set of types.
• [as TYPE + 'face' from Old French, ultimately from Latin *facies* face]

typescript *noun*
• "TIPE script"
• a typewritten document.
• [as TYPE + 'script' from Middle English, = thing written, from Old French *escri(p)t* from Latin *scriptum*, neuter past participle of *scribere* write]

typesetter *noun*
• "TIPE setter"
• a person who composes type.
• [as TYPE + 'set' from Old English *settan*]
• **typeset** *verb*
• **typesetting** *noun*

typewriter *noun*
• "TIPE rite ur"
• a machine for producing characters like those used in printing by means of keys which, when pressed one at a time, cause a type mounted on a bar or ball to strike a sheet of paper inserted around a roller, through an inked ribbon.
• [as TYPE + WRITE]
• **typewriting** *noun*
• **typewritten** *adjective*

typhoid *noun*
• "TIFE oid"
• a severe infectious fever caused by the bacterium *Salmonella typhi*, involving a rash, myalgia, and in some cases delirium and intestinal inflammation.
• [TYPHUS + Greek *-oeidēs* from *eidos* form]
• **typhoidal** *adjective*

typhoon *noun*
• "tie FOON"
• a violent storm occurring in or around the Indian subcontinent, esp. a tropical cyclone occurring in the region of the Indian or W Pacific Oceans.
• [partly from Portuguese *tufão* from Arabic *ṭūfān* (perhaps from Greek *tuphōn* whirlwind); reinforced by Chinese dialect *tai fung* big wind]
• **typhonic** *adjective* "tie FONNIC"

typhus *noun*
• "TIFE us"
• any of a group of acute infectious fevers caused by rickettsiae, often transmitted by lice or fleas, and characterized by a purple rash, headaches, fever, and usu. delirium.
• [modern Latin from Greek *tuphos* smoke, stupor, from *tuphō* to smoke]

typical *adjective*
• "TIPPA k'll"
• serving as a characteristic example; representative.
• [medieval Latin *typicalis* from Latin *typicus* from Greek *tupikos* (as TYPE)]
• **typicality** *noun*
• **typically** *adverb*

typify *verb*
• "TIPPA fie"
• be a representative example of; embody the characteristics of.
• [as TYPE]

typist *noun*
• "TIPE ist"
• a person who types or uses a typewriter, esp. professionally.
• [as TYPE]

typo *noun*
• "TIPE oh"
• an error in typed or printed material, resulting from a mistake in typing or in arranging and setting types etc.
• [abbreviation of 'typographical (error)']

typography *noun*
• "tie POGGRA fee"
• the art or practice of printing.
• [French *typographie* or modern Latin *typographia* (as TYPE, *graphia* writing)]
• **typographer** *noun*
• **typographic** *adjective*
• **typographical** *adjective*
• **typographically** *adverb*

typology *noun*
• "tie POLLA jee"
• the branch of knowledge that deals with classes with common characteristics.
• [as TYPE + Greek *logos* word]
• **typological** *adjective*
• **typologically** *adverb*
• **typologist** *noun*

tyramine *noun*
• "TIE ruh meen"
• a derivative of tyrosine occurring naturally in

cheese and other foods and affecting the sympathetic nervous system.
• [TYROSINE + AMINE]

tyrannical *adjective*
• "tuh RANNA k'll" or "tie RANNA k'll"
• of or pertaining to a tyrant or tyranny.
• [Old French *tyrannique* from Latin *tyrannicus* from Greek *turannikos* (as TYRANT)]
• **tyrannically** *adverb*

tyrannicide *noun*
• "tuh RANNA side" or "tie RANNA side"
• the act or an instance of killing a tyrant.
• [French from Latin *tyrannicida* (as TYRANT + *-cida, -cidium* from *caedere* kill)]
• **tyrannicidal** *adjective*

tyrannize *verb*
ALSO SPELLED: esp. *Brit.* **-ise**
• "TEERA nize"
• rule, control, or behave oppressively or cruelly towards.
• [French *tyranniser* (as TYRANT)]

tyrannosaur *noun*
• "tuh RANNA sore" or "tie RANNA sore" or "tee RANNA sore"
• a huge bipedal carnivorous saurischian dinosaur of the Upper Cretaceous, *Tyrannosaurus rex*, having powerful hind legs and jaws, a large well-developed tail, and small claw-like front legs.
• [Greek *turannos* TYRANT, after *dinosaur*]

tyranny *noun*
• "TEERA nee"
• the arbitrary, cruel, and excessive exercise of power, control, or authority.
• [as TYRANT]
• **tyrannous** *adjective*
• **tyrannously** *adverb*

tyrant *noun*
• "TIE r'nt"
• an oppressive or cruel ruler.
• [Old French from Latin *tyrannus* from Greek *turannos*]

Tyrian *adjective*
• "TEERY 'n"
• of or relating to ancient Tyre in what is now Lebanon.

tyro *noun*
• "TIE roe"
• a beginner or novice.
• [medieval Latin *tyro*, Latin *tiro*, young soldier, recruit]

Tyrolean *noun*
• "tie ROLEY 'n" or "tie ruh LEE 'n"
• a native or inhabitant of the Tyrol in W Austria, or of adjacent areas of N Italy.

tyropita *noun*
• "tuh ROE pee tuh"
• (in Greek cuisine) a savoury pie with a filling of feta and sometimes other cheeses and eggs in phyllo pastry.
• [Greek, from *tyrí* cheese + *pita* pie]

tyrosine *noun*
• "TIE ruh seen"
• a hydrophilic amino acid present in many proteins and important in the synthesis of some hormones etc.
• [formed irregularly from Greek *turos* cheese]

Tzaddik *noun*
• "TSODDIC"
• a person of exemplary righteousness.
• [Hebrew *ṣaddīq* just, righteous]

tzatziki *noun*
• "tsat SEEKY"
• a Greek side dish of yogourt with cucumber, garlic, and sometimes mint.
• [modern Greek from Turkish]

tzedakah *noun*
• "tsed OCKA"
• the obligation to help fellow Jews; charity.
• [Hebrew *ṣědāqāh* righteousness]

tzimmes *noun*
• "TSIM us"
• (in Jewish cuisine) a stew of sweetened vegetables or vegetables and fruit, sometimes with meat.
• [Yiddish *tsimes*, of unknown origin]

Uu

Übermensch *noun*
• "OOBER mensh"
• an ideal superior man of the future who achieves domination through integrity and creativity.
• [German, from *über* over + *Mensch* human being]

ubiquitous *adjective*
• "yoo BICK wit us"
• present everywhere or in several places simultaneously.
• [modern Latin *ubiquitas* from Latin *ubique* everywhere, from *ubi* where]
• **ubiquitously** *adverb*
• **ubiquitousness** *noun*
• **ubiquity** *noun*

udder *noun*
• "UDDER"
• the mammary gland of cattle, sheep, etc., hanging as a bag-like organ with several teats.
• [Old English *ūder* from West Germanic]
• **uddered** *adjective*
HOMOPHONES: *utter*

udon *noun*
• "OO don"
• (in Japanese cooking) a thick noodle made from wheat flour.
• [Japanese]

ufology *noun*
• "yoo FOLLA jee"
• the study of unidentified flying objects.
• [unidentified flying object + Greek *logos* word]
• **ufological** *adjective*
• **ufologist** *noun*

Ugandan *noun*
• "yoo GAN d'n"
• a native or inhabitant of Uganda in E Africa.

Ugrian *adjective*
• "OO gree 'n" or "YOO gree 'n"
• = UGRIC.
• [as UGRIC]

Ugric *adjective*
• "OO grick" or "YOO grick"
• of or relating to the eastern branch of Finnic peoples, esp. the Magyars.
• [Russian *Ugry*, the name of a people dwelling east of the Urals]

uhlan *noun*
• "OO lon" or "YOO l'n"
• a cavalryman armed with a lance in some European armies, esp. the former German army.
• [French & German from Polish *(h)ulan* from Turkish *oğlan* youth, servant]

Uighur *noun*
• "WEE gur"
• a member of a Turkic people prominent in Central Asia from the 8th to the 12th c. and now living mostly in northwestern China.
• [East Turkish *uighur* from *ui* follow, fit, agree + *-gur* adjective suffix]

uillean *adjective*
• "ILL y'n"
• designating a form of Irish bagpipe in which the bag is inflated by bellows worked by the elbow.
• [Irish *uillean*, genitive singular of *uille* elbow]

ukase *noun*
• "yoo CAZE"
• an arbitrary command.
• [Russian *ukaz* ordinance, edict, from *ukazat'* show, decree]

Ukrainian *noun*
• "yoo CRAINY 'n"
• a native of Ukraine in E Europe.

ukulele *noun*
• "yooka LAY lee"
• a small four-stringed Hawaiian (originally Portuguese) guitar.
• [Hawaiian, = jumping flea]

ulcer *noun*
• "ULL sur"
• an open sore on an external or internal surface of the body, often forming pus.
• [Latin *ulcus -eris*, related to Greek *helkos*]
• **ulcerate** *verb*
• **ulcerated** *adjective*
• **ulceration** *noun*
• **ulcerative** *adjective* "ULL sur a tiv"
• **ulcered** *adjective*
• **ulcerous** *adjective*

ulema *noun*
• "OO lim uh"
• a body of Muslim doctors of sacred law and theology.
• [Arabic *'ulamā* pl. of *'ālim* learned, from *'alama* know]

ullage *noun*
• "ULL idge"
• the amount by which a cask, bottle, etc. falls short of being full.
• [Anglo-French *ulliage*, Old French *ouillage* from *ouiller* fill up, ultimately from Latin *oculus* eye, with reference to the bunghole]

ulna *noun*
• "ULL nuh"
• the thinner and longer bone in the forearm, on the side opposite to the thumb.
• [Latin]
• **ulnar** *adjective*

ulster *noun*
• "ULL stur"
• a man's long loose overcoat of rough cloth.
• [*Ulster*, a former province of N Ireland, where it was originally sold]

ulterior *adjective*
• "ull TEERY ur"
• existing in the background, or beyond what is evident or admitted; hidden, secret.
• [Latin, = further, more distant]

ultimate *adjective*
• "ULTA mit"
• last, final.
• [Late Latin *ultimatus*, past participle of *ultimare* come to an end]
• **ultimacy** *noun*
• **ultimately** *adverb*

ultimatum *noun*
• "ulta MATE um"
• a final demand or statement of terms by one party, the rejection of which by another could cause a breakdown in relations, war, or an end of co-operation etc.
• [Latin neuter past participle of *ultimare*: see ULTIMATE]

ultimogeniture *noun*
• "ull tim oh JENNA chur"
• a system in which the youngest son has the right of inheritance.
• [Latin *ultimus* last, after PRIMOGENITURE]

ultracentrifuge *noun*
• "ultra SENTRA fyoodge"
• a high-speed centrifuge used to separate small particles and large molecules in a liquid and to determine their sedimentation rate (and hence their size).
• [Latin *ultra* beyond + CENTRIFUGE]
• **ultracentrifugation** *noun* "ultra sentra fyoo GAY sh'n"

ultrafiltration *noun*
• "ultra fill TRAY sh'n"
• filtration using a filter fine enough to retain large molecules, viruses, and colloidal particles.
• [Latin *ultra* beyond + 'filter' from French *filtre* from medieval Latin *filtrum* felt used as a filter, from West Germanic]

ultraism *noun*
• "ULTRA izm"
• the holding of extreme positions in politics, religion, etc.
• [Latin *ultra* beyond]
• **ultraist** *noun*

ultralight *noun*
• "ULTRA lite"
• a very small, light, low-speed, one- or two-seater aircraft with an open frame.
• [Latin *ultra* beyond + 'light']

ultramontane *adjective*
• "ultra MON tane"
• situated on the other side of the Alps from the point of view of the speaker.
• [medieval Latin *ultramontanus* (Latin *ultra* beyond, *mons montis* mountain)]
• **ultramontanism** *noun* "ultra MON tuh nizm"
• **ultramontanist** *noun*

ultramundane *adjective*
• "ultra MUN dane"
• lying beyond the world or the solar system.
• [Latin *ultramundanus* (*ultra* beyond, *mundanus* from *mundus* world)]

ulu *noun*
• "OO loo"
• an Inuit knife consisting of a semicircular or crescent-shaped blade and a handle centred behind the non-cutting edge, traditionally used by women.
• [Inuktitut]

ululate *verb*
• "ULL yuh late" or "YOOL yuh late"
• howl, wail; make a hooting cry.
• [Latin *ululare ululat-* (imitative)]
• **ululant** *adjective*
• **ululation** *noun*

umbel *noun*
• "UM bull"
• a flower cluster in which stalks nearly equal in length spring from a common centre and form a flat or curved surface, as in parsley.
• [obsolete French *umbelle* or Latin *umbella* sunshade, diminutive of *umbra* shade]
• **umbellate** *adjective*

umbellifer *noun*
• "um BELLA fur"
• any plant of the family Umbelliferae bearing umbels, including parsley and carrot.
• [obsolete French *umbellifère* from Latin (as UMBEL, *-fer* bearing)]
• **umbelliferous** *adjective* "um buh LIFFER us"

umber *noun*
• "UM bur"
• a natural pigment like ochre but darker and browner.
• [French (*terre d'*)*ombre* or Italian (*terra di*) *ombra* = shadow (earth), from Latin *umbra* or *Umbra* feminine of *Umber* Umbrian]

umbilicate *adjective*
• "um BILLA kit"
• shaped like a navel.
• [as UMBILICUS]

umbilicus *noun*
• "um BILLA kuss"
• the navel.
• [Latin]
• **umbilical** *adjective*
• **umbilically** *adverb*

umbles *plural noun*
• "UM bulls"
• the edible offal of deer etc.
• [Middle English var. of Old French *numbles*, *nombles* loin etc., from Latin *lumbulus* diminutive of *lumbus* loin]

umbo *noun*
• "UM bo"
• the boss of a shield, esp. in the centre.
• [Latin *umbo -onis*]
• **umbonal** *adjective*
• **umbonate** *adjective*

umbrage *noun*
• "UM bridge"
• offence; a sense of slight or injury.
• [Old French, ultimately from Latin *umbraticus* from *umbra* shade]
• **umbrageous** *adjective* "um BRAY juss"

umbrella *noun*
• "um BRELLA"
• a light portable device for protection against rain, strong sun, etc., consisting of a usu. circular canopy of cloth mounted by means of a collapsible metal frame on a central stick.
• [Italian *ombrella*, diminutive of *ombra* shade, from Latin *umbra* shade]
• **umbrellaed** *adjective*

Umbrian *adjective*
• "UM bree 'n"
• of or relating to Umbria in central Italy.

umiak *noun*
• "OOMY ack"
• a large, open, flat-bottomed boat made by stretching an animal hide over a wooden frame, traditionally used by Inuit women.
• [Inuktitut *umiaq*]

umlaut *noun*
• "OOM lout"
• a mark (¨) used over a vowel, esp. in Germanic languages, to indicate a vowel change.
• [German from *um* about + *Laut* sound]

umma *noun*
ALSO SPELLED: **ummah**
• "UMMA"
• the whole community of Muslims bound together by ties of religion.
• [Arabic, lit. = 'people, community']

unabated *adjective*
• "un a BATED"
• not abated; undiminished.
• [Old English *un-* not + ABATE]

unaccented *adjective*
• "un ACK sen tid"
• not accented; not emphasized.
• [Old English *un-* not + ACCENT]

unacceptable *adjective*
• "un ack SEPTA bull"
• not acceptable.
• [Old English *un-* not + ACCEPT]
• **unacceptability** *noun*
• **unacceptably** *adverb*

unaccommodating *adjective*
• "un a COMMA date ing"
• not accommodating; disobliging.
• [Old English *un-* not + ACCOMMODATE]

unaccompanied *adjective*
• "un a CUMPA need"
• not accompanied, alone.
• [Old English *un-* not + ACCOMPANY]

unaccountable *adjective*
• "un a COUNT a bull"
• unable to be explained.
• [Old English *un-* not + ACCOUNT]
• **unaccountability** *noun*
• **unaccountably** *adverb*

unaccounted *adjective*
• "un a COUNT id"
• of which no account is given.
• [Old English *un-* not + ACCOUNT]

unaccustomed *adjective*
• "un a CUSS tumd"
• not accustomed.
• [Old English *un-* not + ACCUSTOM]
• **unaccustomedly** *adverb*

unachievable *adjective*
• "un a CHEEVA bull"
• not achievable.
• [Old English *un-* not + ACHIEVE]

unacknowledged *adjective*
• "un ack NOLL idged"
• not acknowledged.
• [Old English *un-* not + ACKNOWLEDGE]

unacquainted *adjective*
• "un a KWAINT id"
• not acquainted.
• [Old English *un-* not + ACQUAINT]

unaddressed *adjective*
• "un a DREST"
• (esp. of a letter etc.) without an address.
• [Old English *un-* not + ADDRESS]

unadjacent *adjective*
- "un a JAY s'nt"
- not adjacent.
- [Old English *un-* not + ADJACENT]

unadulterated *adjective*
- "un a DULTER ated"
- not adulterated; pure; concentrated.
- [Old English *un-* not + ADULTERATE]

unadventurous *adjective*
- "un ad VENCHER us"
- not adventurous.
- [Old English *un-* not + ADVENTURE]

unadvertised *adjective*
- "un AD vur tized"
- not advertised.
- [Old English *un-* not + ADVERTISE]

unaesthetic *adjective*
- "un es THETTIC"
- not aesthetically pleasing.
- [Old English *un-* not + AESTHETIC]
- **unaesthetically** *adverb*

unaffected *adjective*
- "un a FECTED"
- not affected.
- [Old English *un-* not + AFFECT[1]]
- **unaffectedly** *adverb*

unaffectionate *adjective*
- "un a FECK sh'n it"
- lacking or not showing affection.
- [Old English *un-* not + AFFECTION]

unaffiliated *adjective*
- "un a FILLY ated"
- not affiliated.
- [Old English *un-* not + AFFILIATE]

unaggressive *adjective*
- "un a GRESSIV"
- not aggressive.
- [Old English *un-* not + AGGRESSIVE]

unaligned *adjective*
- "un a LINED"
- (of a country etc.) not aligned with another (esp. major) power.
- [Old English *un-* not + ALIGN]

unalleviated *adjective*
- "un a LEEVY ated"
- not alleviated; relentless.
- [Old English *un-* not + ALLEVIATE]

unalloyed *adjective*
- "un a LOID" or "un AL oid"
- not alloyed; pure.
- [Old English *un-* not + ALLOY]

unambiguous *adjective*
- "un am BIG yoo us"
- not ambiguous; clear or definite in meaning.
- [Old English *un-* not + AMBIGUOUS]
- **unambiguously** *adverb*

unambitious *adjective*
- "un am BISH us"
- not ambitious; without ambition.
- [Old English *un-* not + AMBITIOUS]
- **unambitiously** *adverb*

unambivalent *adjective*
- "un am BIVVA l'nt"
- (of feelings etc.) not ambivalent; straightforward.
- [Old English *un-* not + AMBIVALENT]

unamplified *adjective*
- "un AMPLA fide"
- not amplified.
- [Old English *un-* not + AMPLIFY]

unanalyzable *adjective*
ALSO SPELLED: **unanalysable**
- "un anna LIE zuh bull"
- not able to be analyzed.
- [Old English *un-* not + ANALYZE]

unanalyzed *adjective*
ALSO SPELLED: **unanalysed**
- "un ANNA lized"
- not analyzed.
- [Old English *un-* not + ANALYZE]

unanimous *adjective*
- "yoo NANNA muss"
- all in agreement.
- [Late Latin *unanimis*, Latin *unanimus* from *unus* one + *animus* mind]
- **unanimity** *noun* "yoo nuh NIMMA tee"
- **unanimously** *adverb*

unannounced *adjective*
- "un a NOUNST"
- not announced; without warning (of arrival etc.).
- [Old English *un-* not + ANNOUNCE]

unanticipated *adjective*
- "un an TISSA pated"
- not anticipated.
- [Old English *un-* not + ANTICIPATE]

unapologetic *adjective*
- "un a polla JETTIC"
- not apologetic or sorry.
- [Old English *un-* not + APOLOGETIC]
- **unapologetically** *adverb*

unapparent *adjective*
- "un a PARE 'nt"
- not apparent.
- [Old English *un-* not + APPARENT]

unappealable *adjective*
- "un a PEELA bull"
- not able to be appealed against.
- [Old English *un-* not + APPEAL]

unappealing *adjective*
- "un a PEELING"
- not appealing; unattractive.
- [Old English *un-* not + APPEAL]

unappeasable *adjective*
- "un a PEEZA bull"
- that cannot be appeased.
- [Old English *un-* not + APPEASE]

unappeased *adjective*
- "un a PEEZD"
- not appeased.
- [Old English *un-* not + APPEASE]

unappetizing *adjective*
ALSO SPELLED: esp. *Brit.* **-ising**
- "un APPA tize ing"
- not appetizing.
- [Old English *un-* not + APPETIZING]
- **unappetizingly** *adverb* (also esp. *Brit.* **-isingly**)

unappreciated *adjective*
- "un a PREESHY ated"
- not appreciated.
- [Old English *un-* not + APPRECIATE]

unappreciative *adjective*
- "un a PREESHA tiv"
- not appreciative.
- [Old English *un-* not + APPRECIATIVE]

unapprehended *adjective*
- "un ap ree HEN did"
- not perceived by the intellect.
- [Old English *un-* not + APPREHEND]

unapproachable *adjective*
- "un a PROACH a bull"
- not approachable; remote, inaccessible.
- [Old English *un-* not + APPROACHABLE]
- **unapproachability** *noun*
- **unapproachably** *adverb*

unappropriated *adjective*
- "un a PRO pree ated"
- not allocated or assigned.
- [Old English *un-* not + APPROPRIATE[2]]

unapproved *adjective*
- "un a PROOVD"
- not approved or sanctioned.
- [Old English *un-* not + APPROVE]

unarguable *adjective*
- "un ARG yoo a bull"
- not arguable; certain.
- [Old English *un-* not + ARGUABLE]
- **unarguably** *adverb*

unarticulated *adjective*
- "un ar TICK yuh lated"
- not mentioned or coherently expressed.
- [Old English *un-* not + ARTICULATE]

unascertainable *adjective*
- "un asser TANE a bull"
- not ascertainable.
- [Old English *un-* not + ASCERTAIN]

unascertained *adjective*
- "un asser TAIND"
- not ascertained; unknown.
- [Old English *un-* not + ASCERTAIN]

unassailable *adjective*
- "un a SALE a bull"
- unable to be attacked or questioned.
- [Old English *un-* not + ASSAIL]
- **unassailability** *noun*
- **unassailably** *adverb*

unassertive *adjective*
- "un a SURTIV"
- (of a person) not assertive or forthcoming; reticent.
- [Old English *un-* not + ASSERTIVE]
- **unassertively** *adverb*
- **unassertiveness** *noun*

unassigned *adjective*
- "un a SINED" ("SINED" rhymes with *FIND*)
- not assigned.
- [Old English *un-* not + ASSIGN]

unassimilated *adjective*
- "un a SIM'll ated"
- not assimilated.
- [Old English *un-* not + ASSIMILATE]
- **unassimilable** *adjective*

unassociated *adjective*
- "un a SO see ated" or "un a SO shee ated"
- having no connection or association.
- [Old English *un-* not + ASSOCIATE]

unassuaged *adjective*
- "un a SWAGED" ("SWAGED" rhymes with *STAGED*)
- not assuaged.
- [Old English *un-* not + ASSUAGE]
- **unassuageable** *adjective*

unassumed *adjective*
- "un a SOOMD" or "un a SYOOMD"
- *Cdn* (of a road) not taken over for maintenance by a local authority; privately owned.
- [Old English *un-* not + ASSUME]

unassuming *adjective*
- "un a SUME ing"
- not pretentious or arrogant; modest.
- [Old English *un-* not + ASSUME]
- **unassumingly** *adverb*

unathletic *adjective*
- "un ath LETTIC"
- not athletic.
- [Old English *un-* not + ATHLETIC]

unattached *adjective*
- "un a TATCH't"
- not attached, esp. to a particular body, organization, etc.
- [Old English *un-* not + ATTACH]

unattainable *adjective*
- "un a TANE a bull"
- not attainable.
- [Old English *un-* not + ATTAIN]
- **unattainably** *adverb*

unattempted *adjective*
- "un a TEMPTED"
- not attempted.
- [Old English *un-* not + ATTEMPT]

unattended *adjective*
- "un a TENDED"
- unsupervised; alone.
- [Old English *un-* not + ATTEND]

unattractive *adjective*
- "un a TRACTIV"
- not attractive.
- [Old English *un-* not + ATTRACTIVE]
- **unattractively** *adverb*
- **unattractiveness** *noun*

unattributable *adjective*
- "un a TRIB yoot a bull"
- (esp. of information) that cannot or may not be attributed to a source etc.
- [Old English *un-* not + ATTRIBUTE]

unattributed *adjective*
- "un a TRIB yoo tid"
- (of a painting, quotation, etc.) not attributed to a source etc.
- [Old English *un-* not + ATTRIBUTE]

unaudited *adjective*
- "un ODDIT id"
- (of accounts etc.) not audited.
- [Old English *un-* not + AUDIT]

unauthenticated *adjective*
- "un aw THENTA cated" (with "TH" as in *THIN*)
- not authenticated.
- [Old English *un-* not + AUTHENTICATE]

unauthorized *adjective*
ALSO SPELLED: esp. *Brit.* **unauthorised**
- "un OTHA rized"
- not authorized.
- [Old English *un-* not + AUTHORIZE]

unbeautiful *adjective*
- "un BYOOTA full"
- not beautiful; ugly.
- [Old English *un-* not + BEAUTIFUL]
- **unbeautifully** *adverb*

unbefitting *adjective*
- "un be FITTING"
- not befitting; unsuitable.
- [Old English *un-* not + 'befitting' from 'fit' (origin unknown)]

unbelief *noun*
- "un be LEEF"
- lack of belief, esp. in religious matters.
- [Old English *un-* not + BELIEF]
- **unbeliever** *noun*
- **unbelieving** *adjective*
- **unbelievingly** *adverb*

unbelievable *adjective*
- "un buh LEEVA bull"
- not believable; incredible.
- [Old English *un-* not + BELIEVABLE]
- **unbelievability** *noun*
- **unbelievably** *adverb*

unbiased *adjective*
- "un BY ist"
- not biased; impartial.
- [Old English *un-* not + BIAS]

unblemished *adjective*
- "un BLEM isht"
- not damaged or marked in any way.
- [Old English *un-* not + BLEMISH]

unbosom *verb*
- "un BOOZ'm" (with "OO" as in *BOOK*)
- unburden (oneself) of one's thoughts, secrets, etc.
- [Old English *un-* not + BOSOM]

unbreachable *adjective*
- "un BREECH a bull"
- not able to be breached.
- [Old English *un-* not + BREACH]

unbreathable *adjective*
- "un BREETHE a bull" (with "TH" as in *THEE*)
- foul, noxious.
- [Old English *un-* not + BREATHABLE]

unbridgeable *adjective*
- "un BRIDGE a bull"
- unable to be bridged.
- [Old English *un-* not + 'bridge' from Old English *brycg*]

unbridled *adjective*
- "un BRIDE 'ld"
- unconstrained.
- [Old English *un-* not + BRIDLE]

unbudgeable *adjective*
- "un BUDGE a bull"
- that cannot be moved.
- [Old English *un-* not + 'budge' from French *bouger* stir, ultimately from Latin *bullire* boil]

unbusinesslike *adjective*
- "un BIZ niss like"
- not businesslike.
- [Old English *un-* not + BUSINESS]

uncanonical *adjective*
- "un kuh NONNA k'll"
- not canonical.
- [Old English *un-* not + CANONICAL]
- **uncanonically** *adverb*

uncatalogued *adjective*
ALSO SPELLED: *US* **uncataloged**
- "un CATTA logged"
- not catalogued.
- [Old English *un-* not + CATALOGUE]

uncategorizable *adjective*
ALSO SPELLED: esp. *Brit.* **-isable**
- "un catta guh RIZE a bull"
- that cannot be assigned to a category.
- [Old English *un-* not + CATEGORIZE]

unceasing *adjective*
- "un SEE sing"
- not ceasing; continuous.
- [Old English *un-* not + CEASE]
- **unceasingly** *adverb*

unceded *adjective*
• "un SEEDED"
• (of land) that has not been officially ceded to a government by an Aboriginal group by means of a treaty.
• [Old English *un-* not + CEDE]
HOMOPHONES: *unseeded*

uncensored *adjective*
• "un SEN surd"
• not censored.
• [Old English *un-* not + CENSOR]

unceremonious *adjective*
• "un serra MOANY us"
• lacking ceremony or formality.
• [Old English *un-* not + CEREMONIOUS]
• **unceremoniously** *adverb*

uncertain *adjective*
• "un SUR t'n"
• not certainly knowing or known.
• [Old English *un-* not + CERTAIN]
• **uncertainly** *adverb*

uncertainty *noun*
• "un SUR t'n tee"
• the fact or condition of being uncertain.
• [Old English *un-* not + CERTAINTY]

uncertified *adjective*
• "un SURTA fide"
• not attested as certain.
• [Old English *un-* not + CERTIFY]

unchallengeable *adjective*
• "un CHAL 'n juh bull"
• not challengeable; unassailable.
• [Old English *un-* not + CHALLENGE]
• **unchallengeably** *adverb*

unchangeable *adjective*
• "un CHANGE a bull"
• not changeable; immutable, invariable.
• [Old English *un-* not + CHANGEABLE]
• **unchangeability** *noun*
• **unchangeably** *adverb*

unchaperoned *adjective*
• "un SHAPPER owned"
• without a chaperone.
• [Old English *un-* not + CHAPERONE]

uncharacteristic *adjective*
• "un care uck tur ISTIC"
• not characteristic.
• [Old English *un-* not + CHARACTERISTIC]
• **uncharacteristically** *adverb*

uncharismatic *adjective*
• "un care iz MATTIC"
• lacking charisma.
• [Old English *un-* not + CHARISMA]

uncharitable *adjective*
• "un CHAIR it a bull"
• unkind, harsh, and unsympathetic.
• [Old English *un-* not + CHARITABLE]
• **uncharitableness** *noun*
• **uncharitably** *adverb*

unchaste *adjective*
• "un CHAYST" (rhymes with *PASTE*)
• not chaste.
• [Old English *un-* not + CHASTE]
• **unchastity** *noun* "un CHASTA tee"

unchastened *adjective*
• "un CHASE 'nd"
• not sorry.
• [Old English *un-* not + CHASTEN]

unchic *adjective*
• "un SHEEK"
• not chic.
• [Old English *un-* not + CHIC]

unchivalrous *adjective*
• "un SHIV 'll russ"
• not chivalrous; rude.
• [Old English *un-* not + CHIVALRY]
• **unchivalrously** *adverb*

unchristian *adjective*
• "un CRISS ch'n"
• contrary to Christian principles, esp. uncaring or selfish.
• [Old English *un-* not + CHRISTIAN]

uncial *adjective*
• "UN see 'll" or "UN sh'll"
• of or written in majuscule writing with rounded unjoined letters found in manuscripts of the 4th–8th c., from which modern capitals are derived.
• [Latin *uncialis* from *uncia* inch]

uncircumcised *adjective*
• "un SUR k'm sized"
• not circumcised.
• [Old English *un-* not + CIRCUMCISE]

unclassifiable *adjective*
• "un classa FIE a bull"
• not classifiable.
• [Old English *un-* not + CLASSIFY]

unclassified *adjective*
• "un CLASSA fide"
• not classified.
• [Old English *un-* not + CLASSIFY]

unclothe *verb*
• "un CLOTHE" (with "TH" as in *BATHE*)
• remove the clothes from.
• [Old English *un-* not + CLOTHES]
• **unclothed** *adjective*

unco *adjective*
• "UN co"
• strange, unusual; notable.
• [Middle English, var. of UNCOUTH]

uncolonized *adjective*
• "un COLLA nized"
• not colonized.
• [Old English *un-* not + COLONIZE]

uncomfortable *adjective*
• "un CUMF tur bull" or "un CUMFERT a bull"
• not comfortable.

• [Old English *un-* not + COMFORTABLE]
• **uncomfortably** *adverb*

uncommercial *adjective*
• "un kuh MUR sh'll"
• not commercial.
• [Old English *un-* not + COMMERCIAL]

uncommitted *adjective*
• "un kuh MITTID"
• not committed.
• [Old English *un-* not + COMMIT]

uncommunicative *adjective*
• "un kuh MYOONA kuh tiv" or "un kuh MYOONA kay tiv"
• not wanting to communicate; taciturn.
• [Old English *un-* not + COMMUNICATIVE]

uncompensated *adjective*
• "un COMP'n sated"
• not compensated.
• [Old English *un-* not + COMPENSATE]

uncompetitive *adjective*
• "un k'm PETTA tiv"
• not competitive.
• [Old English *un-* not + COMPETITIVE]

uncomplimentary *adjective*
• "un compla MENTA ree"
• not complimentary; insulting.
• [Old English *un-* not + COMPLIMENTARY]

uncomprehending *adjective*
• "un com pree HENDING"
• not comprehending.
• [Old English *un-* not + COMPREHEND]
• **uncomprehendingly** *adverb*

uncompromising *adjective*
• "un COMPRA mize ing"
• unwilling to compromise; stubborn; unyielding.
• [Old English *un-* not + COMPROMISE]
• **uncompromisingly** *adverb*

unconcealed *adjective*
• "un k'n SEELD"
• not concealed; obvious.
• [Old English *un-* not + CONCEAL]

unconditional *adjective*
• "un k'n DISH'n 'll"
• not subject to conditions; complete.
• [Old English *un-* not + CONDITIONAL]
• **unconditionally** *adverb*

unconditioned *adjective*
• "un k'n DISH'nd"
• not subject to conditions or to an antecedent condition.
• [Old English *un-* not + CONDITION]

unconfident *adjective*
• "un CONFA d'nt"
• not confident.
• [Old English *un-* not + 'confident' (as CONFIDENCE)]

unconformity *noun*
• "un k'n FORMA tee"
• a large break in the chronological sequence of layers of rock.
• [Old English *un-* not + CONFORMITY]

uncongenial *adjective*
• "un k'n JEENY 'll"
• not congenial.
• [Old English *un-* not + CONGENIAL]

unconquered *adjective*
• "un CONKERD"
• not conquered or defeated.
• [Old English *un-* not + CONQUER]
• **unconquerable** *adjective*

unconscionable *adjective*
• "un CONSH'n a bull"
• having no conscience.
• [Old English *un-* not + obsolete *conscionable* from *conscions*, obsolete variant of CONSCIENCE]
• **unconscionably** *adverb*

unconscious *adjective*
• "un CON sh'ss"
• not conscious.
• [Old English *un-* not + CONSCIOUS]
• **unconsciously** *adverb*
• **unconsciousness** *noun*

unconsecrated *adjective*
• "un CONSA crated"
• not consecrated.
• [Old English *un-* not + CONSECRATE]

unconsolable *adjective*
• "un k'n SOLE a bull"
• unable to be consoled; inconsolable.
• [Old English *un-* not + CONSOLE[1]]

unconsolidated *adjective*
• "un k'n SOLLA dated"
• not consolidated.
• [Old English *un-* not + CONSOLIDATE]

unconstitutional *adjective*
• "un consta TOO sh'n 'll" or "un consta TYOO sh'n 'll"
• not in accordance with the political constitution or with procedural rules.
• [Old English *un-* not + CONSTITUTION]
• **unconstitutionality** *noun*
• **unconstitutionally** *adverb*

unconsummated *adjective*
• "un CONSA mated"
• not consummated.
• [Old English *un-* not + CONSUMMATE]

uncontaminated *adjective*
• "un k'n TAM'n ated"
• not contaminated; pure, unpolluted.
• [Old English *un-* not + CONTAMINATE]

uncontentious *adjective*
• "un k'n TEN sh'ss"
• not controversial.
• [Old English *un-* not + CONTENTIOUS]

uncontroversial *adjective*
- "un contra VUR sh'll"
- not controversial.
- [Old English *un-* not + CONTROVERSIAL]
- **uncontroversially** *adverb*

unconventional *adjective*
- "un k'n VEN sh'n 'll"
- not bound by convention or custom; unusual; unorthodox.
- [Old English *un-* not + CONVENTIONAL]
- **unconventionality** *noun*
- **unconventionally** *adverb*

uncoordinated *adjective*
- "un co ORD'n ated"
- not coordinated.
- [Old English *un-* not + COORDINATE]

uncorroborated *adjective*
- "un kuh ROBBER ated"
- (esp. of evidence etc.) not corroborated.
- [Old English *un-* not + CORROBORATE]

uncorrupted *adjective*
- "un kuh RUPTED"
- not corrupted.
- [Old English *un-* not + CORRUPT]

uncouth *adjective*
- "un COOTH"
- (of a person, manners, appearance, etc.) lacking in ease and polish; uncultured, rough.
- [Old English *uncūth* unknown (*un-* not + *cūth* past participle of *cunnan* know)]
- **uncouthly** *adverb*
- **uncouthness** *noun*

uncovenanted *adjective*
- "un CUVVA n'nt id"
- not bound by a covenant.
- [Old English *un-* not + COVENANT]

uncritical *adjective*
- "un CRITTA k'll"
- not critical; complacently accepting.
- [Old English *un-* not + CRITICAL]
- **uncritically** *adverb*

unction *noun*
- "UNK sh'n"
- the act of anointing with oil etc. as a religious rite.
- [Latin *unctio* from *ung(u)ere unct-* anoint]

unctuous *adjective*
- "UNK choo us"
- (of behaviour, speech, etc.) unpleasantly flattering.
- [medieval Latin *unctuosus* from Latin *unctus* anointing (as UNCTION)]
- **unctuously** *adverb*
- **unctuousness** *noun*

uncultivated *adjective*
- "un CULTA vated"
- (esp. of land) not cultivated.
- [Old English *un-* not + CULTIVATE]

undaunted *adjective*
- "un DON tid"
- not daunted.
- [Old English *un-* not + DAUNT]
- **undauntable** *adjective*

undecidable *adjective*
- "un de SIDE a bull"
- that cannot be established or refuted; uncertain.
- [Old English *un-* not + DECIDE]
- **undecidability** *noun*

undecipherable *adjective*
- "un de SIFE ur a bull"
- not decipherable.
- [Old English *un-* not + DECIPHER]

undecorated *adjective*
- "un DECKER ated"
- not adorned; plain.
- [Old English *un-* not + DECORATE]

undefiled *adjective*
- "un de FILED" ("FILED" rhymes with *MILD*)
- pure; uncorrupted.
- [Old English *un-* not + 'defile' from Middle English *defoul* from Old French *defouler* trample down, outrage, from *fouler* tread, trample, altered after obsolete *befile* from Old English *befȳlan* make foul]

undelete *verb*
- "un de LEET"
- cancel the deletion of (text or a file).
- [Old English *un-* not + DELETE]

undemocratic *adjective*
- "un demma CRATTIC"
- not democratic.
- [Old English *un-* not + DEMOCRATIC]
- **undemocratically** *adverb*

undemonstrative *adjective*
- "un duh MONSTRA tiv"
- not expressing feelings etc. outwardly; reserved.
- [Old English *un-* not + DEMONSTRATIVE]
- **undemonstratively** *adverb*

undeniable *adjective*
- "un de NIE a bull"
- unable to be denied or disputed; certain.
- [Old English *un-* not + DENIABLE]
- **undeniably** *adverb*

underachieve *verb*
- "under a CHEEVE"
- do less well than might be expected (esp. scholastically).
- ['under' + ACHIEVE]
- **underachievement** *noun*
- **underachiever** *noun*

underappreciated *adjective*
- "under a PREESHY ated"
- not appreciated according to one's merits.
- ['under' + APPRECIATE]

undercarriage *noun*
- "UNDER care idge"
- the supporting frame of a vehicle.
- ['under' + CARRIAGE]

undercroft *noun*
- "UNDER croft"
- a crypt.
- [Middle English from 'under-' + *croft* crypt, from Middle Dutch *crofte* cave, from medieval Latin *crupta* for Latin *crypta*: see CRYPT]

undercurrent *noun*
- "UNDER cur 'nt"
- a current below the surface.
- ['under' + CURRENT]

underdeveloped *adjective*
- "under duh VELL upt"
- not fully developed; immature.
- ['under' + DEVELOP]
- **underdevelopment** *noun*

underemphasize *verb*
ALSO SPELLED: esp. *Brit.* **-ise**
- "under EMFA size"
- place an insufficient degree of emphasis on.
- ['under' + EMPHASIS]
- **underemphasis** *noun* "under EMFA sis"

undergird *verb*
- "under GURD"
- make secure underneath.
- ['under' + GIRD]

undergraduate *noun*
- "under GRADGE oo it"
- a student at a university who has not yet completed a bachelor's degree.
- ['under' + GRADUATE]

undernourished *adjective*
- "under NUR isht"
- insufficiently nourished.
- ['under' + NOURISH]
- **undernourishment** *noun*

underpopulated *adjective*
- "under POP yuh lated"
- having an insufficient or very small population.
- ['under' + POPULATE]
- **underpopulation** *noun*

underprivileged *adjective*
- "under PRIV a lidged" or "under PRIV lidged"
- less privileged than others; deprived.
- ['under' + PRIVILEGE]

underrate *verb*
- "under RATE"
- have too low an opinion of; underestimate.
- ['under' + 'rate' from Old French and medieval Latin *rata* (from Latin *pro rata parte* or *portione* 'according to the proportional share') from *ratus*, past participle of *rēri* reckon]
- **underrated** *adjective*

underripe *adjective*
- "under RIPE"
- not sufficiently ripe.
- ['under' + 'ripe' from Old English *rīpe*]

undersecretary *noun*
- "under SEKRA terry"
- a subordinate official, esp. a junior minister or senior civil servant.
- ['under' + SECRETARY]

underutilized *adjective*
ALSO SPELLED: esp. *Brit.* **-ised**
- "under YOOTA lized"
- underused.
- ['under' + UTILIZE]
- **underutilization** *noun* (also esp. *Brit.* **-isation**)
- **underutilize** *verb* (also esp. *Brit.* **-ise**)

underweight *adjective*
- "under WATE"
- weighing less than is normal or desirable.
- ['under' + WEIGHT]

underwhelm *verb*
- "under WELM"
- fail to impress.
- [after OVERWHELM]
- **underwhelming** *adjective*
- **underwhelmingly** *adverb*

underwrite *verb*
- "UNDER rite"
- sign, issue, and accept liability under (an insurance policy).
- ['under' + WRITE]

underwriter *noun*
- "UNDER rite ur"
- a person who examines a risk, decides whether or not it can be insured, and if it can, works out a premium to be charged, usu. on the basis of the frequency of past claims for similar risks.
- [as UNDERWRITE]

undesirable *adjective*
- "un de ZIRE a bull"
- not desirable; objectionable, unpleasant.
- [Old English *un-* not + DESIRABLE]
- **undesirability** *noun*
- **undesirably** *adverb*

undeterred *adjective*
- "un dee TURD"
- not deterred.
- [Old English *un-* not + DETER]

undeveloped *adjective*
- "un duh VELL upt"
- not developed.
- [Old English *un-* not + DEVELOP]

undeviating *adjective*
- "un DEEVY ate ing"
- not deviating; steady, constant.
- [Old English *un-* not + DEVIATE]
- **undeviatingly** *adverb*

undiagnosed *adjective*
- "un die ug NOAST" or "un die ug NOZED"
- not diagnosed.
- [Old English *un-* not + DIAGNOSE]

undifferentiated *adjective*
- "un diffa REN shee ated"
- not differentiated.
- [Old English *un-* not + DIFFERENTIATE]

undignified *adjective*
- "un DIGNA fide"
- lacking dignity.
- [Old English *un-* not + DIGNIFY]

undiluted *adjective*
- "un die LOOTED" or "un duh LOOTED"
- not diluted.
- [Old English *un-* not + DILUTE]

undiminished *adjective*
- "un duh MIN isht"
- not diminished or lessened.
- [Old English *un-* not + DIMINISH]

undine *noun*
- "UN deen"
- a female water spirit; a nymph.
- [modern Latin *undina* from Latin *unda* wave]

undiplomatic *adjective*
- "un dipla MATTIC"
- tactless.
- [Old English *un-* not + DIPLOMATIC]
- **undiplomatically** *adverb*

undisciplined *adjective*
- "un DISSA plind" ("PLIND" rhymes with *GRINNED*)
- lacking discipline; not disciplined.
- [Old English *un-* not + DISCIPLINE]
- **undiscipline** *noun*

undiscriminating *adjective*
- "un dis CRIM'n ate ing"
- lacking taste or good judgment.
- [Old English *un-* not + DISCRIMINATING]

undiscussed *adjective*
- "un dis CUST"
- not discussed.
- [Old English *un-* not + DISCUSS]
- **undiscussable** *adjective*

undisguised *adjective*
- "un dis GIZED" (with "G" as in *GIVE*)
- not disguised or concealed; open, candid.
- [Old English *un-* not + DISGUISE]
- **undisguisedly** *adverb* "un dis GIZE id lee"

undistinguished *adjective*
- "un dis TING gwisht"
- lacking any distinguishing characteristic or feature.
- [Old English *un-* not + DISTINGUISHED]

undistributed *adjective*
- "un dis TRIB yoo tid" or "un DISTRA byooted"
- not distributed.
- [Old English *un-* not + DISTRIBUTE]

undocumented *adjective*
- "un DOCK yoo m'nt id"
- not having the appropriate legal document or licence.
- [Old English *un-* not + DOCUMENT]

undomesticated *adjective*
- "un duh MESTA cated"
- not domesticated.
- [Old English *un-* not + DOMESTICATE]

undoubted *adjective*
- "un DOUT id"
- certain, not questioned, not regarded as doubtful.
- [Old English *un-* not + DOUBT]
- **undoubtedly** *adverb*

undue *adjective*
- "un DUE"
- excessive, disproportionate; unwarranted.
- [Old English *un-* not + DUE]
- **unduly** *adverb*

HOMOPHONES: *undo*

undulate *verb*
- "UN dyoo late" or "UN joo late"
- have a wavy or rippling outline or appearance.
- [Late Latin *undulatus* from Latin *unda* wave]
- **undulant** *adjective*
- **undulation** *noun*

undyed *adjective*
- "un DIDE"
- not dyed.
- [Old English *un-* not + DYE]

uneconomic *adjective*
- "un ecka NOMMIC" or "un eeka NOMMIC"
- not economic; incapable of being profitably operated etc.
- [Old English *un-* not + ECONOMIC]

uneconomical *adjective*
- "un ecka NOMMA k'll" or "un eeka NOMMA k'll"
- not economical; wasteful.
- [Old English *un-* not + ECONOMICAL]

unedifying *adjective*
- "un EDDA fie ing"
- not edifying, esp. uninstructive or degrading.
- [Old English *un-* not + EDIFY]
- **unedifyingly** *adverb*

unedited *adjective*
- "un EDDA tid"
- not edited.
- [Old English *un-* not + 'edit' (as EDITOR)]

unembarrassed *adjective*
- "un em BARE ust"
- not embarrassed.
- [Old English *un-* not + EMBARRASS]

unembellished *adjective*
- "un em BELL isht"
- not embellished or decorated.
- [Old English *un-* not + EMBELLISH]

unemphatic *adjective*
• "un em FATTIC"
• not emphatic.
• [Old English *un-* not + EMPHATIC]
• **unemphatically** *adverb*

unencumbered *adjective*
• "un en CUMBERD"
• not encumbered; free of any encumbrance.
• [Old English *un-* not + ENCUMBER]

unendurable *adjective*
• "un en DURE a bull"
• that cannot be endured.
• [Old English *un-* not + ENDURE]
• **unendurably** *adverb*

unenforceable *adjective*
• "un en FORCE a bull"
• (of a contract, law, etc.) impossible to enforce.
• [Old English *un-* not + ENFORCE]

unenlightened *adjective*
• "un en LITE 'nd"
• not enlightened.
• [Old English *un-* not + ENLIGHTENED]
• **unenlightening** *adjective*

unenterprising *adjective*
• "un ENTER prize ing"
• not enterprising.
• [Old English *un-* not + ENTERPRISING]

unenthusiastic *adjective*
• "un en thoozy ASTIC" or "un en thyoozy ASTIC"
• not enthusiastic.
• [Old English *un-* not + ENTHUSIASTIC]
• **unenthusiastically** *adverb*

unenviable *adjective*
• "un ENVY a bull"
• unpleasant, undesirable.
• [Old English *un-* not + ENVIABLE]
• **unenviably** *adverb*

unequipped *adjective*
• "un e KWIPT"
• not equipped.
• [Old English *un-* not + French *équiper*, prob. from Old Norse *skipa* to man (a ship) from *skip* ship]

unequivocal *adjective*
• "un e KWIVVA k'll"
• not ambiguous; plain, unmistakable.
• [Old English *un-* not + EQUIVOCAL]
• **unequivocally** *adverb*
• **unequivocalness** *noun*

unerring *adjective*
• "un AIR ing"
• not missing the intended target; certain, sure.
• [Old English *un-* not + ERR]
• **unerringly** *adverb*

unessential *adjective*
• "un e SEN sh'll"
• not essential.
• [Old English *un-* not + ESSENTIAL]

unexceptionable *adjective*
• "un eck SEP sh'n a bull"
• to whom or to which no exception can be taken; perfectly satisfactory or adequate.
• [Old English *un-* not + EXCEPTIONABLE]
• **unexceptionably** *adverb*

unexcitable *adjective*
• "un eck SITE a bull"
• not easily excited.
• [Old English *un-* not + EXCITE]

unexhausted *adjective*
• "un eg ZOSTED"
• not used up, spent, or brought to an end.
• [Old English *un-* not + EXHAUST]

unexpurgated *adjective*
• "un EX purr gated"
• (esp. of a text etc.) complete and containing all the original material; uncensored.
• [Old English *un-* not + EXPURGATE]

unfamiliar *adjective*
• "un fuh MILL yur"
• not familiar.
• [Old English *un-* not + FAMILIAR]
• **unfamiliarity** *noun* "un fuh milly ERRA tee"

unfathomable *adjective*
• "un FA th'm a bull" (with "TH" as in *THEM*)
• incapable of being fathomed.
• [Old English *un-* not + FATHOM]
• **unfathomably** *adverb*

unfathomed *adjective*
• "un FATH umd" (with "TH" as in *BATHE*)
• of unascertained depth.
• [Old English *un-* not + FATHOM]

unfazed *adjective*
• "un FAZED" ("FAZED" rhymes with *PRAISED*)
• untroubled; not disconcerted.
• [Old English *un-* not + FAZE]
• **unfazable** *adjective*

unfeasible *adjective*
• "un FEEZA bull"
• not feasible; impractical.
• [Old English *un-* not + FEASIBLE]
• **unfeasibility** *noun*
• **unfeasibly** *adverb*

unfeigned *adjective*
• "un FAIND"
• genuine, sincere.
• [Old English *un-* not + FEIGN]

unfilial *adjective*
• "un FILLY 'll"
• not befitting a son or daughter.
• [Old English *un-* not + FILIAL]

unforeseeable *adjective*
• "un for SEE a bull"
• not foreseeable.
• [Old English *un-* not + FORESEE]

unforeseen *adjective*
• "un for SEEN"
• not foreseen.
• [Old English *un-* not + FORESEE]

unforgettable *adjective*
• "un for GETTA bull"
• that cannot be forgotten; memorable, wonderful.
• [Old English *un-* not + 'forgettable' from Old English *forgietan* forget]
• **unforgettably** *adverb*

unfortunate *adjective*
• "un FOR chuh nit"
• having bad fortune; unlucky.
• [Old English *un-* not + FORTUNATE]

unfortunately *adverb*
• "un FOR chuh nit lee"
• (qualifying a whole sentence) it is unfortunate that.
• [Old English *un-* not + FORTUNATE]

unfrequented *adjective*
• "un FREE kwin tid"
• not visited habitually.
• [Old English *un-* not + FREQUENT]

unfulfilled *adjective*
• "un full FILD"
• not fulfilled.
• [Old English *un-* not + FULFILL]
• **unfulfillable** *adjective*
• **unfulfilling** *adjective*
• **unfulfillment** *noun*

unfurl *verb*
• "un FURL"
• spread or open out (a sail, flag, etc.) to its greatest length or width.
• [Old English *un-* not + FURL]

ungallant *adjective*
• "un GAL'nt"
• not gallant.
• [Old English *un-* not + GALLANT]
• **ungallantly** *adverb*

ungenerous *adjective*
• "un JENNER us"
• not generous; mean.
• [Old English *un-* not + GENEROUS]
• **ungenerously** *adverb*

unglamorous *adjective*
• "un GLAMMER us"
• lacking glamour or appeal.
• [Old English *un-* not + GLAMOUR]

ungracious *adjective*
• "un GRAY sh'ss"
• not cordial, courteous, or polite; rude or unkind to others.
• [Old English *un-* not + GRACIOUS]
• **ungraciously** *adverb*

ungrammatical *adjective*
• "un gruh MATTA k'll"
• contrary to the rules of grammar.
• [Old English *un-* not + GRAMMATICAL]
• **ungrammaticality** *noun*
• **ungrammatically** *adverb*

unguent *noun*
• "UNG gwint"
• a soft substance, such as a perfumed oil, used esp. as an ointment.
• [Latin *unguentum* from *unguere* anoint]

unguis *noun*
• "UNG gwiss"
• the narrow base of a petal.
• [Latin]

ungulate *adjective*
• "UNG gyoo lit" or "UNG gyoo late"
• hoofed.
• [Late Latin *ungulatus* from Latin *ungula*, diminutive of *unguis* a nail or claw]

unharmonious *adjective*
• "un har MOANY us"
• not harmonious.
• [Old English *un-* not + HARMONIOUS]

unharness *verb*
• "un HAR nuss"
• remove a harness from.
• [Old English *un-* not + HARNESS]
• **unharnessed** *adjective*

unhesitating *adjective*
• "un HEZZA tate ing"
• without pause, uncertainty, or hesitation.
• [Old English *un-* not + HESITATE]
• **unhesitatingly** *adverb*

unhewn *adjective*
• "un HYOON"
• (of stone) not hewn.
• [Old English *un-* not + HEW]

unhittable *adjective*
• "un HITTA bull"
• (esp. of a pitched baseball) that cannot be hit.
• [Old English *un-* not + 'hit' from Old English *hittan* from Old Norse *hitta* meet with]

unholster *verb*
• "un HOLE stur"
• remove from a holster.
• [Old English *un-* not + HOLSTER]

unhygienic *adjective*
• "un hy JEN ick" or "un hy JEEN ick"
• not hygienic.
• [Old English *un-* not + HYGIENIC]
• **unhygienically** *adverb*

unhyphenated *adjective*
• "uh HIFE'n ated"
• not hyphenated.
• [Old English *un-* not + HYPHENATED]

Uniate *adjective*
• "YOONY ut" or "YOONY ate"
• of or relating to any community of Christians

in E Europe or the Near East that acknowledges papal supremacy but retains its own liturgy etc.
• [Russian *uniyat* from *uniya* from Latin *unio* union]

uniaxial *adjective*
• "yoony AXY 'll"
• having a single axis.
• [Latin *uni* from *unus* one + AXIS]
• **uniaxially** *adverb*

unicameral *adjective*
• "yoona CAMMER 'll"
• with a single legislative chamber.
• [Latin *uni* from *unus* one + *camera* room]

unicellular *adjective*
• "yoona SELL yuh lur"
• (of an organism, organ, tissue, etc.) consisting of a single cell.
• [Latin *uni* from *unus* one + CELLULAR]

unicycle *noun*
• "YOONA sike'll"
• a single-wheeled cycle, esp. as used by acrobats.
• [Latin *uni* from *unus* one + CYCLE]
• **unicyclist** *noun*

unidentifiable *adjective*
• "un eye denta FIE a bull"
• unable to be identified.
• [Old English *un-* not + IDENTIFY]

unidimensional *adjective*
• "yoona die MEN sh'n 'll"
• having (only) one dimension; one-dimensional.
• [Latin *uni* from *unus* one + DIMENSION]

unidirectional *adjective*
• "yoona duh RECK sh'n 'll"
• having only one direction of motion, operation, etc.
• [Latin *uni* from *unus* one + 'directional' from Latin *directus* past participle of *dirigere direct-* direct]
• **unidirectionally** *adverb*

unification *noun*
• "yoona fuh CAY sh'n"
• the act or an instance of unifying; the state of being unified.
• [as UNIFY]
• **unificatory** *adjective* "yoo NIFFA kuh tory"

uniformitarian *adjective*
• "yoona forma TERRY 'n"
• of the theory that geological processes are always due to continuously and uniformly operating forces.
• [French *uniforme* or Latin *uniformis* (*uni* from *unus* one, *forma* shape)]
• **uniformitarianism** *noun*

unify *verb*
• "YOONA fie"
• make united or uniform.
• [French *unifier* or Late Latin *unificare* from *uni* from *unus* one]
• **unified** *adjective*
• **unifier** *noun*
• **unifying** *adjective*

unignorable *adjective*
• "un ig NORA bull"
• that cannot be ignored.
• [Old English *un-* not + 'ignorable' from French *ignorer* or Latin *ignorare* not know, ignore (*in-* not, *gno-* know)]
• **unignorably** *adverb*

unilateral *adjective*
• "yoona LATTER'll"
• performed by or affecting only one person or party.
• [Latin *uni* from *unus* one + LATERAL]
• **unilateralism** *noun*
• **unilaterally** *adverb*

unilingual *adjective*
• "yoona LING gwul" or "yoona LING gyoo 'll"
• esp. *Cdn* able to speak only one language.
• [Latin *uni* from *unus* one + LINGUAL]
• **unilingualism** *noun*
• **unilingualist** *adjective*
• **unilingually** *adverb*

unilocular *adjective*
• "yoona LOCK yuh lur"
• single-chambered.
• [Latin *uni* from *unus* one + LOCULUS]

unimaginable *adjective*
• "un im MADGE in a bull"
• impossible to imagine.
• [Old English *un-* not + IMAGINE]
• **unimaginably** *adverb*

unimaginative *adjective*
• "un im MADGE in a tiv"
• lacking imagination; stolid, dull.
• [Old English *un-* not + IMAGINE]
• **unimaginatively** *adverb*
• **unimaginativeness** *noun*

unimagined *adjective*
• "un im MADGE ind"
• not imagined.
• [Old English *un-* not + IMAGINE]

unimpeachable *adjective*
• "un im PEECH a bull"
• giving no opportunity for censure; beyond reproach or question.
• [Old English *un-* not + 'impeach' from Old French *empecher* impede, from Late Latin *impedicare* entangle (*in-* in, *pedica* fetter, from *pes pedis* foot)]
• **unimpeachably** *adverb*

unimpeded *adjective*
• "un im PEEDED"
• not impeded.
• [Old English *un-* not + IMPEDE]

unincorporated *adjective*
• "un in CORPER ated"
• not formed into a corporation.
• [Old English *un-* not + INCORPORATED]

uninfluential *adjective*
• "un in floo EN sh'll"
• having little or no influence.
• [Old English *un-* not + INFLUENTIAL]

uninhabitable *adjective*
• "un in HABBA tuh bull"
• that cannot be lived in.
• [Old English *un-* not + 'inhabit' from Latin *inhabitare* (*in-* in, *habitare* dwell, from *habēre habit-* have, be constituted)]

uninhabited *adjective*
• "un in HABBA tid"
• not lived in.
• [as UNINHABITABLE]

uninhibited *adjective*
• "un in HIBBIT id"
• not inhibited.
• [Old English *un-* not + INHIBIT]
• **uninhibitedly** *adverb*

uninitiated *adjective*
• "un in ISHY ated"
• not initiated; not admitted or instructed.
• [Old English *un-* not + INITIATE]

unintelligible *adjective*
• "un in TELLA juh bull"
• not intelligible.
• [Old English *un-* not + INTELLIGIBLE]
• **unintelligibility** *noun*
• **unintelligibly** *adverb*

unintentional *adjective*
• "un in TEN sh'n 'll"
• not intentional.
• [Old English *un-* not + INTENTION]
• **unintentionally** *adverb*

uninterrupted *adjective*
• "un inter UP tid"
• not interrupted.
• [Old English *un-* not + INTERRUPT]
• **uninterruptedly** *adverb*

uninterruptible *adjective*
• "un inter UPT a bull"
• that cannot be interrupted.
• [Old English *un-* not + INTERRUPT]

uninucleate *adjective*
• "yoona NEW clee it"
• having a single nucleus.
• [Latin *uni* from *unus* one + NUCLEATE]

uniparous *adjective*
• "yoo NIPPER us"
• producing one offspring at a birth.
• [Latin *uni* from *unus* one + *-parus* -bearing, from *parere* bring forth]

unique *adjective*
• "yoo NEEK"
• of which there is only one; unequalled; having no like, equal, or parallel.
• [French from Latin *unicus* from *unus* one]
• **uniquely** *adverb*
• **uniqueness** *noun*

unironic *adjective*
• "un eye RONNIC"
• not ironic; to be taken at face value.
• [Old English *un-* not + IRONY]
• **unironically** *adverb*

uniserial *adjective*
• "yoona SEERY 'll"
• arranged in one row.
• [Latin *uni* from *unus* one + SERIAL]

unison *noun*
• "YOONA s'n"
• identity in pitch of two or more sounds or notes.
• [Old French *unison* or Late Latin *unisonus* (*uni* from *unus* one, *sonus* sound)]

Unitarian *noun*
• "yoona TERRY 'n"
• a person who believes that God is not a Trinity but one person.
• [modern Latin *unitarius* from Latin *unitas* unity]
• **Unitarianism** *noun*

unitary *adjective*
• "YOONA terry"
• of a unit or units.
• [as UNITARIAN]
• **unitarily** *adverb*
• **unitarity** *noun* "yoona TERRA tee"

univalent *adjective*
• "yoona VALE 'nt"
• having a valence of one.
• [Latin *uni* from *unus* one + VALENCE]

univocal *adjective*
• "yoona VOKE'll" or "yoo NIVVA k'll"
• (of a word etc.) having only one proper meaning.
• [Latin *uni* from *unus* one + *vocalis* from *vox vocis* voice]
• **univocality** *noun* "yoona voke ALA tee"
• **univocally** *adverb*

unjustifiable *adjective*
• "un justa FIE a bull"
• not justifiable.
• [Old English *un-* not + JUSTIFY]
• **unjustifiably** *adverb*

unkempt *adjective*
• "un KEMPT"
• untidy, of neglected appearance.
• [Old English *un-* not + archaic *kempt* past participle of *kemb* comb, from Old English *cemban*]

unlaid *adjective*
• "un LADE"
• not laid.

• [Old English *un-* not + 'laid' from Old English *lecgan*]
HOMOPHONES: *unlade*

unleavened *adjective*
• "un LEV 'nd"
• not leavened; made without yeast or other raising agent.
• [Old English *un-* not + LEAVEN]

unlicensed *adjective*
ALSO SPELLED: **unlicenced**
• "un LICE 'nst"
• not licensed, esp. without a licence to sell alcoholic drink.
• [Old English *un-* not + 'license' from Old French from Latin *licentia* from *licēre* be lawful]

unmanageable *adjective*
• "un MAN idge a bull"
• not (easily) managed, manipulated, or controlled.
• [Old English *un-* not + MANAGE]
• **unmanageably** *adverb*

unmanaged *adjective*
• "un MAN idged"
• not handled or directed in a controlled way.
• [Old English *un-* not + MANAGE]

unmeasurable *adjective*
• "un MEZHUR a bull"
• that cannot be measured.
• [Old English *un-* not + MEASURE]
• **unmeasurably** *adverb*

unmeasured *adjective*
• "un MEZH urd"
• not measured.
• [Old English *un-* not + MEASURE]

unmediated *adjective*
• "un MEEDY ated"
• with no intervention; directly perceived.
• [Old English *un-* not + MEDIATE]

unmemorable *adjective*
• "un MEMMER a bull"
• not memorable.
• [Old English *un-* not + MEMORABLE]
• **unmemorably** *adverb*

unmetered *adjective*
• "un MEET 'rd"
• not provided with or measured by a meter.
• [Old English *un-* not + Greek *metron* measure]

unmistakable *adjective*
• "un miss TAKE a bull"
• that cannot be mistaken or doubted, clear.
• [Old English *un-* not + MISTAKE]
• **unmistakability** *noun*
• **unmistakably** *adverb*

unmitigated *adjective*
• "un MITTA gated"
• not mitigated or modified.
• [Old English *un-* not + MITIGATE]
• **unmitigatedly** *adverb*

unmodulated *adjective*
• "un MOD yuh lated" or "un MODGE uh lated"
• not modulated.
• [Old English *un-* not + MODULATE]

unmourned *adjective*
• "un MORND"
• not mourned.
• [Old English *un-* not + MOURN]

unnameable *adjective*
• "un NAME a bull"
• that cannot be named, esp. too bad to be named.
• [Old English *un-* not + 'nameable' from Old English *nama* name]

unnavigable *adjective*
• "un NAVVA guh bull"
• not navigable.
• [Old English *un-* not + NAVIGABLE]

unnecessary *adjective*
• "un NESSA serry"
• not necessary.
• [Old English *un-* not + NECESSARY]
• **unnecessarily** *adverb*
• **unnecessariness** *noun*

unnoticeable *adjective*
• "un NO tiss a bull"
• not easily seen or noticed.
• [Old English *un-* not + NOTICEABLE]
• **unnoticeably** *adverb*

unobjectionable *adjective*
• "un ub JECK sh'n a bull"
• not objectionable; acceptable.
• [Old English *un-* not + OBJECTIONABLE]
• **unobjectionably** *adverb*

unobservant *adjective*
• "un ub ZURV 'nt"
• not observant.
• [Old English *un-* not + OBSERVE]

unobtrusive *adjective*
• "un ub TRUE siv"
• not making oneself or itself noticed.
• [Old English *un-* not + OBTRUSIVE]
• **unobtrusively** *adverb*
• **unobtrusiveness** *noun*

unoccupied *adjective*
• "un OCK yuh pide"
• not occupied.
• [Old English *un-* not + OCCUPY]

unofficial *adjective*
• "un a FISH'll"
• not officially authorized or confirmed.
• [Old English *un-* not + OFFICIAL]
• **unofficially** *adverb*

unopposed *adjective*
• "un a POZED"
• not opposed.
• [Old English *un-* not + OPPOSE]

unordained *adjective*
- "un or DAIND"
- not ordained.
- [Old English *un-* not + ORDAIN]

unornamented *adjective*
- "un ORNA m'nt id"
- not ornamented.
- [Old English *un-* not + ORNAMENT]

unorthodox *adjective*
- "un ORTHA docks"
- not orthodox.
- [Old English *un-* not + ORTHODOX]
- **unorthodoxy** *noun*

unostentatious *adjective*
- "un oss t'n TAY sh'ss"
- not ostentatious.
- [Old English *un-* not + OSTENTATION]
- **unostentatiously** *adverb*

unpalatable *adjective*
- "un PALA tuh bull"
- not pleasant to taste.
- [Old English *un-* not + PALATABLE]
- **unpalatability** *noun*

unparalleled *adjective*
- "un PERRA leld"
- having no parallel or equal.
- [Old English *un-* not + PARALLEL]

unpardonable *adjective*
- "un PARD'n a bull"
- that cannot be pardoned.
- [Old English *un-* not + 'pardonable' from Old French *pardoner* pardon, from medieval Latin *perdonare* concede, remit (*per* through, *donare* give)]
- **unpardonably** *adverb*

unparliamentary *adjective*
- "un parla MENTA ree"
- contrary to proper parliamentary usage.
- [Old English *un-* not + PARLIAMENT]

unpasteurized *adjective*
- "un PASS chur ized"
- not pasteurized.
- [Old English *un-* not + PASTEURIZE]

unpatented *adjective*
- "un PAT 'nt id" or "un PAY t'nt id"
- not patented.
- [Old English *un-* not + PATENT]

unpatriotic *adjective*
- "un pay tree OTTIC"
- not patriotic.
- [Old English *un-* not + PATRIOT]
- **unpatriotically** *adverb*

unperceived *adjective*
- "un purr SEEVD"
- not perceived; unobserved.
- [Old English *un-* not + PERCEIVE]

unperceptive *adjective*
- "un purr SEPTIV"
- not perceptive.
- [Old English *un-* not + PERCEPTIVE]

unperforated *adjective*
- "un PURR fur ated"
- not perforated.
- [Old English *un-* not + PERFORATE]

unpersuadable *adjective*
- "un purr SWADE a bull"
- not able to be persuaded; obstinate.
- [Old English *un-* not + PERSUADE]

unpersuaded *adjective*
- "un purr SWADED"
- not persuaded.
- [Old English *un-* not + PERSUADE]

unpersuasive *adjective*
- "un purr SWAY siv"
- not persuasive.
- [Old English *un-* not + PERSUADE]
- **unpersuasively** *adverb*

unperturbed *adjective*
- "un purr TURBD"
- not perturbed.
- [Old English *un-* not + PERTURB]

unphilosophical *adjective*
- "un filla SOFFA k'll"
- not according to philosophical principles.
- [Old English *un-* not + PHILOSOPHY]

unpicturesque *adjective*
- "un pick chur ESK"
- not picturesque.
- [Old English *un-* not + PICTURESQUE]

unplaceable *adjective*
- "un PLACE a bull"
- that cannot be placed or classified.
- [Old English *un-* not + 'place' from Old French *place* via Latin *platea* from Greek *plateia* (*hodos*) broad (way)]

unpleasantry *noun*
- "un PLEZZ'n tree"
- unkindness.
- [Old English *un-* not + PLEASANTRY]

unplumbed *adjective*
- "un PLUMD"
- not fully explored or understood.
- [Old English *un-* not + PLUMB]
- **unplumbable** *adjective*

unpolitical *adjective*
- "un puh LITTA k'll"
- not concerned with politics.
- [Old English *un-* not + POLITICAL]
- **unpolitically** *adverb*

unpolluted *adjective*
- "un puh LOOTED"
- not polluted.
- [Old English *un-* not + POLLUTE]

unpopular *adjective*
- "un POP yuh lur"

• not popular; not liked by the public or by people in general.
• [Old English *un-* not + POPULAR]
• **unpopularity** *noun* "un pop yuh LERRA tee"

unpopulated *adjective*
• "un POP yuh lated"
• not populated.
• [Old English *un-* not + POPULATE]

unpossessed *adjective*
• "un puh ZEST"
• not in possession of.
• [Old English *un-* not + POSSESS]

unprecedented *adjective*
• "un PRESSA dent id"
• having no precedent; unparalleled.
• [Old English *un-* not + PRECEDENT]
• **unprecedentedly** *adverb*

unprejudiced *adjective*
• "un PREDGE a dist"
• not prejudiced.
• [Old English *un-* not + PREJUDICED]

unpremeditated *adjective*
• "un pre MEDDA tated"
• not previously thought over, not deliberately planned; unintentional.
• [Old English *un-* not + PREMEDITATE]

unprepossessing *adjective*
• "un pree puh ZESSING"
• not prepossessing; unattractive.
• [Old English *un-* not + PREPOSSESSING]

unprescribed *adjective*
• "un pre SCRIBED"
• (esp. of drugs) not prescribed.
• [Old English *un-* not + PRESCRIBE]

unpressurized *adjective*
ALSO SPELLED: esp. *Brit.* **-ised**
• "un PRESH ur ized"
• not pressurized.
• [Old English *un-* not + PRESSURIZE]

unpretentious *adjective*
• "un pre TEN sh'ss"
• not making a great display; simple, modest.
• [Old English *un-* not + PRETENTIOUS]
• **unpretentiously** *adverb*
• **unpretentiousness** *noun*

unprincipled *adjective*
• "un PRINCE a puld"
• lacking or not based on good moral principles.
• [Old English *un-* not + PRINCIPLED]

unprocessed *adjective*
• "un PROSS est"
• (esp. of food, raw materials) not processed.
• [Old English *un-* not + PROCESS[1]]

unprofessional *adjective*
• "un pruh FESH'n 'll"
• contrary to professional standards of behaviour etc.
• [Old English *un-* not + PROFESSIONAL]
• **unprofessionally** *adverb*

unprompted *adjective*
• "un PROMP tid"
• spontaneous.
• [Old English *un-* not + PROMPT]

unpronounceable *adjective*
• "un pruh NOUNCE a bull"
• that cannot be pronounced.
• [Old English *un-* not + 'pronounce' (as PRONUNCIATION)]

unpropitious *adjective*
• "un pruh PISH us"
• not propitious.
• [Old English *un-* not + PROPITIOUS]

unprovable *adjective*
• "un PROOVA bull"
• that cannot be proven.
• [Old English *un-* not + PROVE]
• **unprovability** *noun*

unproven *adjective*
• "un PROOV'n"
• not proven.
• [Old English *un-* not + PROVEN]

unprovoked *adjective*
• "un pruh VOKED"
• (of a person or act) without provocation.
• [Old English *un-* not + PROVOKE]

unpublicized *adjective*
ALSO SPELLED: esp. *Brit.* **-ised**
• "un PUB luh sized"
• not publicized.
• [Old English *un-* not + PUBLICIZE]

unpunctual *adjective*
• "un PUNK choo 'll"
• not punctual.
• [Old English *un-* not + PUNCTUAL]

unpunctuated *adjective*
• "un PUNK choo ated"
• not punctuated.
• [Old English *un-* not + PUNCTUATE]

unquantifiable *adjective*
• "un kwonta FIE a bull"
• impossible to quantify.
• [Old English *un-* not + QUANTIFY]
• **unquantified** *adjective*

unquenchable *adjective*
• "un KWENCH a bull"
• that cannot be quenched.
• [Old English *un-* not + QUENCH]

unquenched *adjective*
• "un KWENCH't"
• not quenched.
• [Old English *un-* not + QUENCH]

unravel *verb*
• "un RAV 'll"
• cause to be no longer ravelled, tangled, or intertwined.
• [Old English *un-* not + RAVEL]

unreactive *adjective*
- "un re ACTIV"
- having little tendency to react chemically.
- [Old English *un-* not + REACTIVE]

unreceptive *adjective*
- "un re SEPTIV"
- not receptive.
- [Old English *un-* not + RECEPTIVE]

unreciprocated *adjective*
- "un re SIPPRA cated"
- not reciprocated.
- [Old English *un-* not + RECIPROCATE]

unrecognizable *adjective*
ALSO SPELLED: esp. *Brit.* **-isable**
- "un reck ig NIZE a bull"
- that cannot be recognized.
- [Old English *un-* not + RECOGNIZE]
- **unrecognizably** *adverb* (also esp. *Brit.* **-isably**)

unrecognized *adjective*
ALSO SPELLED: esp. *Brit.* **-ised**
- "un RECK ug nized"
- not recognized.
- [Old English *un-* not + RECOGNIZE]

unreconciled *adjective*
- "un RECK'n siled" ("SILED" rhymes with *MILD*)
- not reconciled.
- [Old English *un-* not + RECONCILE]

unrecyclable *adjective*
- "un re SIKE luh bull"
- not recyclable.
- [Old English *un-* not + RECYCLE]

unredeemable *adjective*
- "un re DEEMA bull"
- that cannot be redeemed.
- [Old English *un-* not + REDEEM]

unrefereed *adjective*
- "un reffer EED"
- not refereed.
- [Old English *un-* not + REFEREE]

unregenerate *adjective*
- "un re JENNER it"
- obstinately wrong or bad.
- [Old English *un-* not + REGENERATE]
- **unregenerately** *adverb*

unregistered *adjective*
- "un REDGE iss turd"
- not registered.
- [Old English *un-* not + REGISTERED]

unrehearsed *adjective*
- "un re HURST"
- not rehearsed.
- [Old English *un-* not + REHEARSE]

unreliable *adjective*
- "un re LIE a bull"
- not reliable; erratic.
- [Old English *un-* not + RELY]
- **unreliability** *noun*
- **unreliably** *adverb*

unrelieved *adjective*
- "un re LEEVD"
- lacking the relief given by contrast or variation.
- [Old English *un-* not + RELIEVED]
- **unrelievedly** *adverb*

unremitting *adjective*
- "un re MITTING"
- never relaxing or slackening, incessant.
- [Old English *un-* not + REMIT]
- **unremittingly** *adverb*

unremunerative *adjective*
- "un re MYOONER a tiv"
- bringing no, or not enough, profit or income.
- [Old English *un-* not + REMUNERATE]

unrepentant *adjective*
- "un re PENT'nt"
- not repentant, impenitent.
- [Old English *un-* not + REPENT[1]]
- **unrepentantly** *adverb*

unrequited *adjective*
- "un re KWITE id"
- (of love etc.) not reciprocated.
- [Old English *un-* not + REQUITE]

unresolvable *adjective*
- "un re ZOLVA bull"
- (of a problem, conflict, etc.) that cannot be resolved.
- [Old English *un-* not + RESOLVE]

unrhymed *adjective*
- "un RIMED"
- not rhymed.
- [Old English *un-* not + RHYME]

unrighteous *adjective*
- "un RYE ch'ss"
- not righteous; unjust, wicked, dishonest.
- [Old English *un-* not + RIGHTEOUS]
- **unrighteousness** *noun*

unruly *adjective*
- "un RUE lee"
- not easily controlled or disciplined, disorderly.
- [Old English *un-* not + *ruly* from 'rule' from Old French *reule* from Late Latin *regulare* from Latin *regula* straight stick]
- **unruliness** *noun*

unsalvageable *adjective*
- "un SAL vidge a bull"
- not salvageable.
- [Old English *un-* not + SALVAGE]

unsanctified *adjective*
- "un SANCTA fide"
- not sanctified.
- [Old English *un-* not + SANCTIFY]

unsanctioned *adjective*
- "un SANK sh'nd"
- not sanctioned.
- [Old English *un-* not + SANCTION]

unsanitary *adjective*
• "un SANNA terry"
• not sanitary.
• [Old English *un-* not + SANITARY]

unsatisfactory *adjective*
• "un sat iss FACTER ee"
• not satisfactory; poor, unacceptable.
• [Old English *un-* not + SATISFY]

unsatisfying *adjective*
• "un SAT iss fie ing"
• not satisfying.
• [Old English *un-* not + SATISFY]

unsaturated *adjective*
• "un SATCHER ated"
• (of a compound, esp. a fat or oil) having double or triple bonds in its molecule and therefore capable of further reaction.
• [Old English *un-* not + SATURATE]
• **unsaturation** *noun*

unsavoury *adjective*
ALSO SPELLED: **unsavory**
• "un SAVER ee"
• disagreeable to the taste, smell, or feelings; disgusting.
• [Old English *un-* not + SAVOURY]
• **unsavouriness** *noun* (also **unsavoriness**)

unscalable *adjective*
• "un SCALE a bull"
• that cannot be scaled.
• [Old English *un-* not + SCALABLE]

unscathed *adjective*
• "un SCAYTHD" (with "TH" as in *THIS*)
• without suffering any injury.
• [Old English *un-* not + SCATHE]

unscented *adjective*
• "un SENT id"
• not scented.
• [Old English *un-* not + SCENT]

unscheduled *adjective*
• "un SKED joo uld" or "un SKED joold" or "un SHED joold" or "un SHED yoold"
• not scheduled.
• [Old English *un-* not + SCHEDULE]

unscholarly *adjective*
• "un SKAWLER lee"
• not scholarly.
• [Old English *un-* not + SCHOLAR]

unscientific *adjective*
• "un sye 'n TIFFIC"
• not in accordance with scientific principles.
• [Old English *un-* not + SCIENTIFIC]
• **unscientifically** *adverb*

unscriptural *adjective*
• "un SCRIP chur 'll"
• against or not in accordance with Scripture.
• [Old English *un-* not + SCRIPTURE]

unscrupulous *adjective*
• "un SCREW pyoo luss"
• having no scruples, unprincipled.
• [Old English *un-* not + SCRUPULOUS]
• **unscrupulously** *adverb*
• **unscrupulousness** *noun*

unsegregated *adjective*
• "un SEGGRA gated"
• not segregated.
• [Old English *un-* not + SEGREGATE]

unseizable *adjective*
• "un SEEZA bull"
• that cannot be seized or grasped.
• [Old English *un-* not + SEIZE]

unselfconscious *adjective*
• "un self CON sh'ss"
• not self-conscious.
• [Old English *un-* not + 'self' + CONSCIOUS]
• **unselfconsciously** *adverb*
• **unselfconsciousness** *noun*

unsentimental *adjective*
• "un senta MENT'll"
• not sentimental.
• [Old English *un-* not + SENTIMENTAL]
• **unsentimentality** *noun*
• **unsentimentally** *adverb*

unseparated *adjective*
• "un SEPPER ated"
• not separated.
• [Old English *un-* not + SEPARATE]

unserviceable *adjective*
• "un SURVISS a bull"
• not serviceable; unfit for use.
• [Old English *un-* not + SERVICEABLE]

unshapely *adjective*
• "un SHAPE lee"
• not shapely.
• [Old English *un-* not + SHAPELY]

unsheathe *verb*
• "un SHEETHE" (with "TH" as in *BATHE*)
• remove (a knife etc.) from a sheath.
• [Old English *un-* not + SHEATHE]

unshielded *adjective*
• "un SHEELD id"
• not shielded or protected.
• [Old English *un-* not + SHIELD]

unsightly *adjective*
• "un SITE lee"
• unpleasant to look at, ugly.
• [Old English *un-* not + obsolete *sightly* pleasant to look at]
• **unsightliness** *noun*

unsociable *adjective*
• "un SO shuh bull"
• not sociable, disliking the company of others.
• [Old English *un-* not + SOCIABLE]
• **unsociability** *noun*

unsocial *adjective*
• "un SO sh'll"
• not social; not suitable for, seeking, or conforming to society.
• [Old English *un-* not + SOCIAL]

unsolicited *adjective*
• "un suh LISSA tid"
• not asked for.
• [Old English *un-* not + SOLICIT]

unsolvable *adjective*
• "un SOLVA bull"
• that cannot be solved, insoluble.
• [Old English *un-* not + 'solvable' from Middle English 'solve', = loosen, from Latin *solvere solut-* unfasten, release]
• **unsolvability** *noun*

unsophisticated *adjective*
• "un suh FISTA cated"
• not having or showing much experience of the world and social situations.
• [Old English *un-* not + SOPHISTICATED]

unsought *adjective*
• "un SOT"
• not searched out or sought for.
• [Old English *un-* not + 'sought', past of 'seek']

unspecialized *adjective*
ALSO SPELLED: *Brit.* **-ised**
• "un SPESH'll ized"
• not specialized.
• [Old English *un-* not + SPECIALIZE]

unspecific *adjective*
• "un spuh SIFFIC"
• not specific; general, inexact.
• [Old English *un-* not + SPECIFIC]

unspecified *adjective*
• "un SPESSA fide"
• not specified.
• [Old English *un-* not + SPECIFY]

unspectacular *adjective*
• "un speck TACK yuh lur"
• not spectacular; dull.
• [Old English *un-* not + SPECTACULAR]

unspiritual *adjective*
• "un SPEER itch oo 'll"
• not spiritual; earthly, worldly.
• [Old English *un-* not + SPIRITUAL]

unsponsored *adjective*
• "un SPON surd"
• not supported or promoted by a sponsor.
• [Old English *un-* not + SPONSOR]

unsterile *adjective*
• "un STARE ile" or "un STARE ill"
• (of a syringe etc.) not sterile.
• [Old English *un-* not + STERILE]

unstimulating *adjective*
• "un STIM yuh late ing"
• not stimulating.
• [Old English *un-* not + STIMULATE]

unstoppable *adjective*
• "un STOPPA bull"
• that cannot be stopped or prevented.
• [Old English *un-* not + 'stoppable' from 'stop' from Old English *(for)stoppian* from W Germanic, from Late Latin *stuppare* stuff]
• **unstoppability** *noun*
• **unstoppably** *adverb*

unstylish *adjective*
• "un STILE ish"
• lacking style.
• [Old English *un-* not + STYLISH]

unsubstantial *adjective*
• "un sub STAN sh'll"
• having little or no solidity, reality, or factual basis.
• [Old English *un-* not + SUBSTANTIAL]

unsubstantiated *adjective*
• "un sub STAN shee ated"
• not substantiated.
• [Old English *un-* not + SUBSTANTIATE]

unsubtle *adjective*
• "un SUTTLE"
• not subtle; obvious, clumsy.
• [Old English *un-* not + SUBTLE]
• **unsubtly** *adverb*

unsuccessful *adjective*
• "un suck SESS full"
• not successful.
• [Old English *un-* not + SUCCESS]
• **unsuccessfully** *adverb*

unsullied *adjective*
• "un SUH leed"
• not sullied.
• [Old English *un-* not + SULLY]

unsupervised *adjective*
• "un SOOPER vized"
• not supervised.
• [Old English *un-* not + SUPERVISE]

unsupportable *adjective*
• "un suh PORTA bull"
• that cannot be endured.
• [Old English *un-* not + SUPPORT]

unsupported *adjective*
• "un suh PORTED"
• not supported.
• [Old English *un-* not + SUPPORT]

unsupportive *adjective*
• "un suh PORTIV"
• not giving support.
• [Old English *un-* not + SUPPORTIVE]

unsurpassable *adjective*
• "un sur PASSA bull"
• that cannot be surpassed.
• [Old English *un-* not + SURPASS]

unsurpassed *adjective*
• "un sur PAST"
• not surpassed.
• [Old English *un-* not + SURPASS]

unsurveyed *adjective*
• "un SUR vade"

• (of land) not having had its boundaries, extent, and ownership determined.
• [Old English *un-* not + SURVEY]

unsuspicious *adjective*
• "un suh SPISH us"
• not suspicious.
• [Old English *un-* not + SUSPICION]

unsustainable *adjective*
• "un suh STANE a bull"
• not sustainable.
• [Old English *un-* not + SUSTAINABLE]
• **unsustainably** *adverb*

unsustained *adjective*
• "un suh STAIND"
• not sustained.
• [Old English *un-* not + SUSTAIN]

unswerving *adjective*
• "un SWURVING"
• steady, constant.
• [Old English *un-* not + 'swerve' from Old English *sweorfan* scour]
• **unswervingly** *adverb*

unsymmetrical *adjective*
• "un suh METRIC 'll"
• not symmetrical.
• [Old English *un-* not + SYMMETRY]

unsympathetic *adjective*
• "un simpa THETTIC"
• not sympathetic.
• [Old English *un-* not + SYMPATHY]
• **unsympathetically** *adverb*

unsystematic *adjective*
• "un sista MATTIC"
• not systematic.
• [Old English *un-* not + SYSTEMATIC]
• **unsystematically** *adverb*

untenable *adjective*
• "un TENNA bull"
• (of an argument, position, etc.) not tenable; that cannot be defended.
• [Old English *un-* not + TENABLE]
• **untenability** *noun*

untenanted *adjective*
• "un TEN'nt id"
• not occupied by a tenant.
• [Old English *un-* not + TENANT]

untenured *adjective*
• "un TEN yurd"
• (of a teacher, lecturer, etc.) not having guaranteed tenure of office.
• [Old English *un-* not + TENURE]

Untermensch *noun*
• "OONTER mensh" (with "OO" as in *BOOK*)
• a person considered racially or socially inferior.
• [German]

untethered *adjective*
• "un TETH'rd" (with "TH" as in *THIS*)
• not tethered.
• [Old English *un-* not + TETHER]

unthreatening *adjective*
• "un THRET'n ing"
• not threatening or aggressive; safe.
• [Old English *un-* not + 'threatening' from Old English *thrēat* affliction]

untraceable *adjective*
• "un TRACE a bull"
• that cannot be traced.
• [Old English *un-* not + 'traceable' from Old French *tracier* from Latin *tractus* drawing]

untrammelled *adjective*
ALSO SPELLED: esp. *US* **untrammeled**
• "un TRAM 'ld"
• not deprived of freedom of action or expression; not restricted or hampered.
• [Old English *un-* not + TRAMMEL]

untranslatable *adjective*
• "un tranz LATE a bull"
• that cannot be translated (satisfactorily).
• [Old English *un-* not + TRANSLATE]
• **untranslatability** *noun*
• **untranslated** *adjective*

untutored *adjective*
• "un TOO turd" or "un TYOO turd"
• uneducated, untaught.
• [Old English *un-* not + TUTOR]

untypical *adjective*
• "un TIPPA k'll"
• not typical; unusual.
• [Old English *un-* not + TYPICAL]
• **untypically** *adverb*

unvaccinated *adjective*
• "un VACK sin ated"
• not vaccinated.
• [Old English *un-* not + VACCINE]

unvanquished *adjective*
• "un VANG kwisht"
• not vanquished.
• [Old English *un-* not + VANQUISH]

unvarying *adjective*
• "un VERRY ing"
• not varying.
• [Old English *un-* not + VARY]
• **unvaryingly** *adverb*

unveil *verb*
• "un VALE"
• remove a veil from.
• [Old English *un-* not + VEIL]
• **unveiling** *noun*

unventilated *adjective*
• "un VENT'll ated"
• not provided with a means of ventilation.
• [Old English *un-* not + VENTILATE]

unverifiable *adjective*
• "un verra FIE a bull"
• that cannot be verified.
• [Old English *un-* not + VERIFY]

unverified *adjective*
• "un VERRA fide"
• not verified.
• [Old English *un-* not + VERIFY]

unwarrantable *adjective*
• "un WORE 'nt a bull"
• indefensible, unjustifiable.
• [Old English *un-* not + WARRANTABLE]
• **unwarrantably** *adverb*

unwarranted *adjective*
• "un WORE 'nt id"
• unauthorized.
• [Old English *un-* not + WARRANT]

unwary *adjective*
• "un WARE ee"
• not cautious.
• [Old English *un-* not + WARY]
• **unwarily** *adverb*

unwavering *adjective*
• "un WAIVER ing"
• not wavering.
• [Old English *un-* not + WAVER]
• **unwaveringly** *adverb*

unweaned *adjective*
• "un WEEND"
• not weaned.
• [Old English *un-* not + WEAN]

unweighted *adjective*
• "un WATE id"
• having had the weight removed.
• [Old English *un-* not + WEIGHT]

unwholesome *adjective*
• "un HOLE sum"
• not promoting, or detrimental to, physical or moral health; unhealthy, insalubrious.
• [Old English *un-* not + WHOLESOME]
• **unwholesomely** *adverb*

unwieldy *adjective*
• "un WEELDY"
• cumbersome, clumsy, or hard to manage, owing to size, shape, weight, etc.
• [Middle English from Old English *un-* not + *wieldy* active (now dialect) from WIELD]
• **unwieldiness** *noun*

unwinnable *adjective*
• "un WINNA bull"
• that cannot be won.
• [Old English *un-* not + 'winnable' from Old English *winnan* toil, endure]

unwonted *adjective*
• "un WAHN tid" or "un WONE tid"
• not customary or usual.
• [Old English *un-* not + WONTED]
• **unwontedly** *adverb*
HOMOPHONES: *unwanted*

unwrinkled *adjective*
• "un RINK'ld"
• free from wrinkles, smooth.
• [Old English *un-* not + WRINKLE]

unwritable *adjective*
• "un RITE a bull"
• that cannot be written.
• [Old English *un-* not + WRITE]

unyielding *adjective*
• "un YEELD ing"
• not yielding to pressure etc.
• [Old English *un-* not + YIELD]
• **unyieldingly** *adverb*
• **unyieldingness** *noun*

Upanishad *noun*
• "oo PANNA shad"
• each of a series of philosophical compositions concluding the exposition of the Vedas.
• [Sanskrit from *upa* near + *ni-ṣad* sit down]
• **Upanishadic** *adjective*

upas *noun*
• "YOOP us"
• a Javanese tree, *Antiaris toxicaria*, yielding a milky sap used as arrow poison.
• [Malay *ūpas* poison]

upheaval *noun*
• "up HEEV'll"
• a violent or sudden change or disruption.
• ['up' + HEAVE]

upholster *verb*
• "up HOLE stur" or "up OLE stur"
• provide furniture with a textile covering, padding, springs, etc.
• [obsolete *upholster* (n.) from 'uphold' (in obsolete sense 'keep in repair')]
• **upholsterer** *verb*
• **upholstery** *noun*

uproarious *adjective*
• "up ROAR ee us"
• very noisy.
• [Dutch *oproer* from *op* up + *roer* confusion, assoc. with 'roar']
• **uproariously** *adverb*
• **uproariousness** *noun*

upsilon *noun*
• "YOOP sill on" or "up SYE l'n"
• the twentieth letter of the Greek alphabet (Υ, υ).
• [Greek, = slender U, from *psilos* 'slender', with reference to the need to distinguish upsilon from the diphthong *oi*: in late Greek the two had the same pronunciation]

uracil *noun*
• "YURA sill"
• a pyrimidine derivative found in living tissue as a component base of RNA.
• [UREA + ACETIC]

uraeus *noun*
• "yur EE us"
• a representation of the sacred asp or snake, symbolizing supreme power, esp. worn on the headdresses of ancient Egyptian divinities and sovereigns.

• [modern Latin from Greek *ouraios*, representing the Egyptian word for 'cobra']

Uralic *adjective*
• "yur AL ick"
• of, relating to, or denoting a family of languages spoken from northern Scandinavia to western Siberia, comprising the Finno-Ugric and Samoyedic groups.
• [from the *Ural* Mountains]

Uranian *adjective*
• "yur AY nee 'n"
• of or relating to the planet Uranus.

uranium *noun*
• "yur AY nee um"
• a heavy radioactive metallic chemical element of the actinide series occurring naturally in pitchblende and other ores, which is capable of nuclear fission and therefore used as a source of nuclear energy.
• [modern Latin, from the planet *Uranus*]
• **uranic** *adjective* "yur ANNIC"

urbane *adjective*
• "ur BANE"
• elegant and refined in manner and style; courteous, sophisticated, suave.
• [French *urbain* or Latin *urbanus* from *urbs urbis* city]
• **urbanely** *adverb*
• **urbanity** *noun* "ur BANNA tee"

urceolate *adjective*
• "URCY a lit"
• having the shape of a pitcher, with a large body and small mouth.
• [Latin *urceolus* diminutive of *urceus* pitcher]

urchin *noun*
• "UR chin"
• a poor, dirty, and ill-clothed child, esp. in an urban area.
• [Middle English *hirchon*, *urcheon* from Old Northern French *herichon*, Old French *heriçon*, ultimately from Latin *(h)ericius* hedgehog]

Urdu *noun*
• "UR doo"
• an Indo-Aryan language closely related to Hindi with an admixture of Persian and Arabic words, now the official language of Pakistan and also used in India.
• [Persian *(zabān i) urdū* '(language of the) camp' (because it developed as a lingua franca after the Muslim invasions between the occupying armies and the local people of the region around Delhi), *urdū* being from Turkic *ordū*: see HORDE]

urea *noun*
• "yur EE uh"
• a soluble crystalline compound which is the main nitrogenous breakdown product of protein metabolism in mammals, is excreted in their urine, and is used esp. as a fertilizer, de-icing agent, and in the manufacture of synthetic resins.
• [modern Latin from French *urée* from Greek *ouron* urine]

uremia *noun*
ALSO SPELLED: esp. *Brit.* **uraemia**
• "yur EEMY uh"
• a raised level in the blood of urea and other waste compounds that are normally eliminated by the kidneys.
• [Greek *ouron* urine + *haima* blood]
• **uremic** *adjective* (also esp. *Brit.* **uraemic**)

ureter *noun*
• "yur EETER"
• either of two tubes which convey urine from the kidney to the bladder or cloaca.
• [French *uretère* or modern Latin *ureter* from Greek *ourētēr* from *oureō* urinate]
• **ureteral** *adjective*
• **ureteric** *adjective* "yura TARE ick"

urethane *noun*
• "YURA thane"
• a polymer used in adhesives, paints, plastics, rubbers, foams, etc.
• [French *uréthane* (as UREA, ETHANE)]

urethra *noun*
• "yur EETH ruh"
• the tube or canal through which urine is carried out of the body from the bladder, and which in the male also conveys semen.
• [Late Latin from Greek *ourēthra* (as URETER)]
• **urethral** *adjective*
• **urethritis** *noun* "yur eeth RITE iss"

uric *adjective*
• "YURIC"
• of or relating to urine.
• [as URINE]

urinal *noun*
• "YURA n'll"
• a ceramic plumbing fixture for men to urinate into, usu. equipped with a flushing mechanism.
• [as URINE]

urinalysis *noun*
• "yurin ALA sis"
• the analysis of urine by physical, chemical, and microscopical means to test for the presence of disease or drugs etc.
• [as URINE + ANALYSIS]

urinate *verb*
• "YURA nate"
• discharge urine.
• [as URINE]
• **urination** *noun*

urine *noun*
• "YUR in"
• the pale yellow fluid containing waste products filtered from the blood by the kidneys,

stored in the bladder, and discharged at intervals through the urethra.
• [Old French from Latin *urina*]
• **urinary** *adjective*
• **urinous** *adjective*

urn *noun*
• "URN"
• a large decorative vase or container with a rounded usu. egg-shaped body and a pedestal.
• [Latin *urna*, related to *urceus* pitcher]
HOMOPHONES: *earn*

urogenital *adjective*
• "yuro JENNIT'll"
• of, pertaining to, or affecting both the urinary and genital organs.
• [as URINE + GENITAL]

urology *noun*
• "yur OLLA jee"
• the branch of medicine that deals with disorders of the kidney and urinary tract.
• [as URINE + Greek *logos* word]
• **urologic** *adjective*
• **urological** *adjective*
• **urologist** *noun*

uropygium *noun*
• "yuro PIDGE ee um"
• the rump of a bird, supporting the tail feathers.
• [medieval Latin from Greek *ouropugion*]

ursine *adjective*
• "UR sine"
• of or like a bear.
• [Latin *ursinus* from *ursus* bear]

Ursuline *noun*
• "URSA lin" or "URSE yuh lin"
• a nun of an Augustinian order founded by St. Angela in 1535 for nursing the sick and teaching girls.
• [St. *Ursula*, the founder's patron saint]

urticaria *noun*
• "urta KERRY uh"
• any of various skin conditions characterized by itchy red weals caused by allergic reaction, emotional stress, etc.; hives.
• [modern Latin from Latin *urtica* nettle, from *urere* burn]

Uruguayan *noun*
• "yoora GWAY 'n"
• a native or inhabitant of Uruguay in S America.

urus *noun*
• "YUR us"
• an extinct wild ox, *Bos primigenius*, ancestor of domestic cattle and formerly native to many parts of the world; an aurochs.
• [Latin from Germanic]

usance *noun*
• "YOOZ ince"
• the time allowed by commercial usage or law for the payment of foreign bills of exchange.
• [as 'use' from Old French *us*, *user*, ultimately from Latin *uti us-* use]

usquebaugh *noun*
• "US kwuh baw"
• whisky.
• [Irish & Scots Gaelic *uisge beatha* water of life]

usufruct *noun*
• "YOO zoo fruct" or "YOO zyoo fruct"
• (in Roman and Scots law) the right of enjoying the use and income from another's property without destroying, damaging, or diminishing the property.
• [medieval Latin *usufructus* from Latin *usus* (*et*) *fructus* from *usus* use + *fructus* fruit]
• **usufructuary** *adjective* "yoo zoo FRUCK choo airy" or "yoo zyoo FRUCK choo airy"

usurp *verb*
• "yoo SURP" or "yoo ZURP"
• seize or assume (another's position or authority) by force.
• [Old French *usurper* from Latin *usurpare* seize for use]
• **usurpation** *noun*
• **usurper** *noun*

usury *noun*
• "YOO zur ee" or "YOO zhur ee"
• the act or practice of lending money at interest, esp. at an exorbitant, excessive, or illegal rate.
• [medieval Latin *usuria* from Latin *usura*]
• **usurious** *adjective* "yoo ZURY us" or "yoo ZHURY us"
• **usuriously** *adverb*

Ute *noun*
• "YOOT"
• a member of a Shoshone Aboriginal people inhabiting parts of Colorado, Utah, and New Mexico.
• [Spanish *Yuta* an unidentified Aboriginal language]

utensil *noun*
• "yoo TEN s'll"
• a tool or implement for domestic use, esp. any of those objects found in a kitchen and used for eating or preparing food.
• [Old French *utensile* from medieval Latin, neuter of Latin *utensilis* usable]

uterus *noun*
• "YOOTER us"
• the womb.
• [Latin]
• **uterine** *adjective* "YOOTER 'n" or "YOOTER ine"

utilidor *noun*
• "yoo TILLA dore"
• *Cdn* (*North*) an enclosed insulated conduit running above ground and carrying water,

sewerage, and electricity between houses in settlements built on permafrost.
• [blend of UTILITY + CORRIDOR]

utilitarian *adjective*
• "yoo tilla TERRY 'n"
• designed to be practically useful rather than attractive; functional.
• [as UTILITY]

utilitarianism *noun*
• "yoo tilla TERRY 'n izm"
• the doctrine that an action is right in so far as it promotes happiness, and that the guiding principle of conduct should be to achieve the greatest benefit or happiness for the greatest number of people.
• [as UTILITY]

utility *noun*
• "yoo TILLA tee"
• the condition or quality of being useful or beneficial.
• [Old French *utilité* from Latin *utilitas -tatis* from *uti* use]

utilize *verb*
ALSO SPELLED: esp. *Brit.* **-ise**
• "YOOTA lize"
• make use of; use effectively for a practical purpose.
• [French *utiliser* from Italian *utilizzare* from Latin *utilis* from *uti* use]
• **utilizable** *adjective* (also esp. *Brit.* **-isable**)
• **utilization** *noun* (also esp. *Brit.* **-isation**)

utopia *noun*
• "yoo TOPEY uh"
• an imaginary or hypothetical place or state of things considered to be perfect; a condition of social or political perfection.
• [modern Latin, lit. 'no place', from Greek *ou* not + *topos* place, title of a book (1516) by T. More, English scholar and statesman d.1535]
• **utopian** *adjective*
• **utopianism** *noun*

utricle *noun*
• "YOOTRA k'll"
• any of various small cells or sacs found in animals and plants.
• [French *utricule* or Latin *utriculus* diminutive of *uter* leather bag]
• **utricular** *adjective* "yoo TRICK yuh lur"

uvea *noun*
• "YOOVY uh"
• a pigmented layer which is the middle vascular coat of the eye, composed of the choroid, iris, and ciliary body of the eye, lying beneath the outer layer.
• [medieval Latin from Latin *uva* grape]

uvula *noun*
• "YOO vyoo luh" or "UV yoo luh"
• a fleshy extension of the soft palate hanging above the throat.
• [Late Latin, diminutive of Latin *uva* grape]
• **uvular** *adjective*

uxorial *adjective*
• "uck SORRY 'll" or "ug ZORRY 'll"
• of or relating to a wife.
• [Latin *uxor* wife]

uxoricide *noun*
• "uck SORRA side" or "ug ZORRA side"
• the act of killing one's wife.
• [Latin *uxor* wife + *-cida, -cidium* from *caedere* kill]

uxorious *adjective*
• "uck SORRY us" or "ug ZORRY us"
• greatly or excessively fond of one's wife; doting.
• [Latin *uxoriosus* from *uxor* wife]
• **uxoriousness** *noun*

Uzbek *noun*
• "OOZ beck" (with "OO" as in *FOOT*)
• a member of a Turkic people living mainly in Uzbekistan in central Asia.
• [Uzbek]

Uzi *noun*
• "OOZY"
• a type of submachine gun of Israeli design.
• [from *Uziel* Gal, the name of the Israeli army officer who designed it]
HOMOPHONES: *oozy*

Vv

vacant *adjective*
• "VAY k'nt"
• containing no objects; empty.
• [Old French *vacant* or Latin *vacare* (as VACATE)]
• **vacancy** *noun*
• **vacantly** *adverb*

vacate *verb*
• "VAY cate" or "vuh CATE"
• leave or cease to occupy (a house, room, etc.).
• [Latin *vacare vacat-* be empty]

vacation *noun*
• "vay CAY sh'n" or "vuh CAY sh'n"
• a period of several days or weeks spent away from work or school etc., used esp. for recreation and travel; a holiday.
• [as VACATE]
• **vacationer** *noun*
• **vacationist** *noun*

vaccine *noun*
• "vack SEEN" or "VACK seen"
• an antigenic preparation used to stimulate the production of antibodies and procure immunity from one or several diseases.
• [Latin *vaccinus* from *vacca* cow]
• **vaccinate** *verb* "VACK sin ate"
• **vaccination** *noun*
• **vaccinator** *noun*

vaccinia *noun*
• "vack SINNY uh"
• a contagious disease of cows, of which the virus was formerly used in vaccination against smallpox.
• [modern Latin (as VACCINE)]

vacillate *verb*
• "VASS'll ate"
• fluctuate in opinion or resolution; waver between different opinions, options, actions, etc.
• [Latin *vacillare vacillat-* sway]
• **vacillating** *adjective*
• **vacillation** *noun*

vacuity *noun*
• "vuh KYOO it ee"
• absolute emptiness.
• [as VACUOUS]

vacuole *noun*
• "VACK yoo 'll" or "VACK yoo ole"
• a small cavity or vesicle in organic tissue, esp. a tiny space within the cytoplasm of a cell containing air, fluid, food particles, etc.
• [French, diminutive of Latin *vacuus* empty]
• **vacuolar** *adjective* "vack yoo OH lur" or "VACK yuh lur"
• **vacuolated** *adjective*
• **vacuolation** *noun*

vacuous *adjective*
• "VACK yoo us"
• unintelligent, expressionless.
• [Latin *vacuus* empty (as VACATE)]
• **vacuously** *adverb*
• **vacuousness** *noun*

vacuum *noun*
• "VACK yoom"
• a space entirely devoid of matter.
• [modern Latin, neuter of Latin *vacuus* empty]

vagabond *noun*
• "VAGGA bond"
• a person who roams or wanders from place to place with no settled habitation and no visible means of support; a tramp or hobo, esp. an idle or dishonest one.
• [Old French *vagabond* or Latin *vagabundus* from *vagari* wander]
• **vagabondage** *noun*

vagary *noun*
• "VAY guh ree"
• a capricious, outlandish, or eccentric act or notion; a caprice or whim.
• [Latin *vagari* wander]
• **vagarious** *adjective* "vuh GERRY us" (with "G" as in *GET*)

vagrant *noun*
• "VAY gr'nt"
• a person with no settled home or regular work.
• [Anglo-French *vag(a)raunt*, perhaps alteration of Anglo-French *wakerant* etc. by assoc. with Latin *vagari* wander]
• **vagrancy** *noun*

vague *adjective*
• "VAIG"

• (of a statement etc.) couched in general, indefinite, or imprecise terms; lacking in details or particulars.
• [French *vague* or Latin *vagus* wandering, uncertain]
• **vaguely** *adverb*
• **vagueness** *noun*

vagus *noun*
• "VAY guss"
• either of the tenth pair of cranial nerves, which supply the upper digestive tract and the organs of the chest cavity and abdomen.
• [Latin: see VAGUE]
• **vagal** *adjective*

vain *adjective*
• "VANE"
• having an excessively high opinion of one's own appearance, abilities, worth, etc.; conceited.
• [Old French from Latin *vanus* empty, without substance]
• **vainly** *adverb*
• **vainness** *noun*
HOMOPHONES: *vein, vane*

vainglory *noun*
• "VANE glory"
• boastfulness; extreme vanity.
• [Middle English, after Old French *vaine gloire*, Latin *vana gloria*]
• **vainglorious** *adjective*
• **vaingloriously** *adverb*
• **vaingloriousness** *noun*

Vaishnava *noun*
• "VIE shna vuh"
• a devotee of the god Vishnu.
• [Sanskrit *vaiṣṇavá*]

Vaisya *noun*
• "VICE yuh"
• the third of the four great Hindu castes, comprising the merchants and agriculturalists.
• [Sanskrit *vaiśya* peasant, labourer]

valance *noun*
• "VAL ince" or "VALE ince"
• a short ornamental curtain hung around a bedstead or above a window etc. in order to conceal the frame or supporting hardware.
• [Middle English, ultimately from Old French *avaler* descend]
• **valanced** *adjective*
HOMOPHONES: *valence*

vale *noun*
• "VALE"
• a valley.
• [Old French *val* from Latin *vallis, valles*]
HOMOPHONES: *veil*

valediction *noun*
• "valla DICK sh'n"
• the act or an instance of bidding farewell.
• [Latin *valedicere valedict-* (from *vale* imperative of *valēre* be well or strong + *dicere* say), after *benediction*]

valedictory *noun*
• "valla DICTER ee"
• a speech or address given by a student of a graduating class at a school or university as a part of the graduation exercises.
• [as VALEDICTION]
• **valedictorian** *noun* "valla dick TORY 'n"

valence *noun*
• "VALE ince"
• the power or capacity of an atom or group to combine with or displace other atoms or groups in the formation of compounds, equivalent to the number of hydrogen atoms that it could combine with or displace.
• [Late Latin *valentia* power, competence, from *valēre* be well or strong]
HOMOPHONES: *valance*

Valenciennes *noun*
• "va loncy EN"
• a variety of fine bobbin lace.
• [*Valenciennes* in NE France, where it was made in the 17th and 18th c.]

valerian *noun*
• "vuh LEERY 'n"
• any of various flowering plants of the family Valerianaceae, esp. the common valerian, *Valerian officinalis*, with pink or white flowers and a strong smell liked by cats.
• [Old French *valeriane* from medieval Latin *valeriana (herba)*, apparently feminine of *Valerianus* of Valerius]

valet *noun*
• "val AY" or "VAL ay"
• a male servant who attends to a gentleman's clothes, etc.
• [French, = Old French *valet, vaslet*: related to VASSAL]

valetudinarian *noun*
• "valla tude 'n AIRY 'n"
• a person who is chronically in poor health; an invalid.
• [Latin *valetudinarius* in ill health, from *valetudo -dinis* health, from *valēre* be well]

valgus *noun*
• "VAL guss"
• a deformity involving the outward displacement of the foot or hand.
• [Latin, = knock-kneed]

Valhalla *noun*
• "val HAL uh"
• (in Norse mythology) the hall in which the souls of those who have died in battle feast with Odin for eternity.
• [modern Latin from Old Norse *Valhöll* from *valr* the slain + *höll* hall]

valiant *adjective*
• "VAL y'nt"
• (of a person or conduct) brave, courageous, heroic.

• [Anglo-French *valiaunt*, Old French *vailant*, ultimately from Latin *valēre* be strong]
• **valiantly** *adverb*

valine *noun*
• "VAL een" or "VALE een"
• an amino acid that is an essential nutrient for vertebrates and a general constituent of proteins.
• [as VAL(ERIAN)]

valise *noun*
• "vuh LEECE"
• a small piece of luggage similar to a suitcase or portmanteau.
• [French from Italian *valigia* corresponding to medieval Latin *valisia*, of unknown origin]

Valkyrie *noun*
• "VAL keer ee" or "val KEERY"
• each of the maidens who hovered over battlefields and conducted the fallen warriors of their choice to Valhalla.
• [Old Norse *Valkyrja*, lit. 'chooser of the slain' from *valr* the slain + (unrecorded) *kur-*, *kuz-* related to 'choose']

vallecula *noun*
• "vuh LECK yoo luh"
• a groove or furrow.
• [Late Latin, diminutive of Latin *vallis* valley]

vallum *noun*
• "VAL um"
• a defensive wall or rampart of earth, sods, and stone.
• [Latin, collective noun from *vallus* stake]

valorize *verb*
ALSO SPELLED: esp. *Brit.* **-ise**
• "VALLER ize"
• raise or fix the price or value of (a commodity etc.) by artificial means, esp. by government intervention.
• [back-formation from *valorization* from French *valorisation* (as VALOUR)]
• **valorization** *noun* (also esp. *Brit.* **-isation**)

valour *noun*
ALSO SPELLED: **valor**
• "VALLER"
• personal courage, esp. in battle.
• [Old French from Late Latin *valor -oris* from *valēre* be strong]
• **valorous** *adjective*

Valpolicella *noun*
• "val polla CHELLA"
• a red Italian wine made in the Valpolicella region NW of Verona.

valuable *adjective*
• "VAL yuh bull" or "VAL yoo a bull"
• of material or monetary value; precious.
• [from 'value' from Old French, fem. past participle of *valoir* be worth, from Latin *valēre*]
• **valuably** *adverb*

valvular *adjective*
• "VAL vyoo lur"
• of, relating to, or affecting a valve or valves, esp. the valves of the heart.
• [modern Latin *valvula*, diminutive of Latin *valva*]

valvulitis *noun*
• "val vyoo LITE iss"
• inflammation of the valves of the heart.
• [as VALVULAR + Greek *-itis*, forming feminine of adjectives in *-itēs* (with *nosos* 'disease' implied)]

vambrace *noun*
• "VAM brace"
• a piece of armour for the forearm.
• [Old French *avant-bras* from *avant* before + *bras* arm]

vampire *noun*
• "VAM pire"
• a ghost or reanimated corpse supposed to leave its grave at night to suck the blood of sleeping people, often represented as a human figure with long pointed canine teeth.
• [French *vampire* or German *Vampir* from Hungarian *vampir* perhaps from Turkish *uber* witch]
• **vampiric** *adjective* "vam PEERIC"

vanadium *noun*
• "vuh NAY dee um"
• a hard grey metallic transition element occurring naturally in several ores, used in small quantities to strengthen some steels.
• [modern Latin from Old Norse *Vanadís* a name of Freya, the Scandinavian goddess of love and of the night]
• **vanadate** *noun* "VANNA date"

vancomycin *noun*
• "vanco MICE in"
• a bacterial antibiotic used against resistant strains of streptococcus and staphylococcus.
• [*vanco-* (of unknown origin) + *-mycin* suffix for antibiotics, from Greek *mukēs* fungus, mushroom]

Vancouverite *noun*
• "van COOVER ite"
• a resident of Vancouver.

vandal *noun*
• "VAN d'll"
• a person who wilfully or maliciously destroys or damages property.
• [Latin *Vandalus* from Germanic]
• **Vandalic** *adjective* "van DAL ick"
• **vandalism** *noun*
• **vandalize** *verb* (also esp. *Brit.* **-ise**)

Vandyke *noun*
• "van DIKE"
• each of a series of large points forming a border on lace or cloth etc.
• [Sir A. *Van Dyck*, anglicized *Vandyke*, Flemish painter d.1641]

vane *noun*
• "VANE"
• a revolving pointer mounted on a spire or other high place to show the direction of the wind.
• [Middle English, southern & western var. of obsolete *fane* from Old English *fana* banner, from Germanic]
• **vaned** *adjective*
HOMOPHONES: *vain*, *vein*

vanguard *noun*
• "VAN gard"
• the foremost part of an army or fleet advancing or ready to advance.
• [earlier *vandgard*, *(a)vantgard*, from Old French *avan(t)garde* from *avant* before (see AVAUNT) + *garde* GUARD]

vanilla *noun*
• "vuh NILLA"
• any tropical climbing orchid of the genus *Vanilla*, esp. *V. planifolia*, with fragrant flowers.
• [Spanish *vainilla* pod, diminutive of *vaina* sheath, pod, from Latin *vagina*]

vanillin *noun*
• "vuh NILLIN"
• a sweet-smelling crystalline aldehyde which is the chief essential constituent of vanilla.
• [as VANILLA]

vanish *verb*
• "VANNISH"
• disappear suddenly.
• [Old French *e(s)vaniss-* stem of *e(s)vanir* ultimately from Latin *evanescere* (*ex* out of, *vanus* empty)]

vanitas *noun*
• "VANNA tass"
• a still-life painting of a 17th-century Dutch genre containing symbols of death or change as a reminder of their inevitability.
• [Latin, = 'vanity']

vanity *noun*
• "VANNA tee"
• conceit and desire for admiration of one's personal attainments or attractions.
• [Old French *vanité* from Latin *vanitas -tatis* (as VAIN)]

vanquish *verb*
• "VANG kwish"
• conquer or overcome.
• [Old French *vencus* past participle and *venquis* past tense of *veintre*, from Latin *vincere*]
• **vanquisher** *noun*

vantage *noun*
• "VAN tidge"
• a place affording a good view or prospect.
• [Anglo-French from Old French *avantage* ADVANTAGE]

Vanuatuan *noun*
• "van oo AT oo 'n"
• a native or inhabitant of Vanuatu in the S Pacific.

vapid *adjective*
• "VAP id"
• insipid; lacking interest; flat, dull.
• [Latin *vapidus*]
• **vapidity** *noun* "vuh PIDDA tee"
• **vapidly** *adverb*

vaporetto *noun*
• "vappa RETTO"
• (in Venice) a canal boat (originally a steamboat, now a motorboat) used for public transport.
• [Italian, = small steamboat, diminutive of *vapore* from Latin *vapor* steam]

vaporize *verb*
ALSO SPELLED: esp. *Brit.* **-ise**
• "VAY purr ize"
• convert or be converted into vapour.
• [as VAPOUR]
• **vaporization** *noun* (also esp. *Brit.* **-isation**)
• **vaporizer** *noun* (also esp. *Brit.* **-iser**)

vapour *noun*
ALSO SPELLED: **vapor**
• "VAY pur"
• moisture or another substance diffused or suspended in air, e.g. mist or smoke.
• [Old French *vapour* or Latin *vapor* steam, heat]
• **vaporous** *adjective*

vapourware *noun*
ALSO SPELLED: **vaporware**
• "VAY purr ware"
• software that as yet exists only in the plans or publicity material of its developers.
• [VAPOUR + WARE]

vaquero *noun*
• "vuh CARE oh"
• a cowherd or cattle driver, esp. in Spanish-speaking areas.
• [Spanish, from *vaca* cow: compare Portuguese *vaqueiro*]

varactor *noun*
• "vuh RACTER"
• a semiconductor diode with a capacitance dependent on the applied voltage.
• [*var*ying re*actor*]

Varangian *noun*
• "vuh RAN jee 'n"
• any of the Scandinavian rovers who penetrated into Russia in the 9th–10th c. AD, establishing the Rurik dynasty and reaching Constantinople.
• [medieval Latin *Varangus*, ultimately from Old Norse, = confederate]

varec *noun*
• "VARE eck"
• seaweed.
• [French *varec(h)* from Old Norse: related to WRECK]

varenyky *plural noun*
• "var ENNA kee" or "verra NEEKY"
• dough dumplings stuffed with mashed potato, cheese, etc., boiled and then optionally fried, and usu. served with onions, sour cream, etc.; perogies.
• [Ukrainian]

variance *noun*
• "VERRY ince"
• difference of opinion; dispute, disagreement; lack of harmony.
• [as VARIOUS]

variant *adjective*
• "VERRY 'nt"
• differing in form or details from the main one.
• [as VARIOUS]

variate *noun*
• "VERRY it"
• a quantity having a numerical value for each member of a group.
• [as VARIOUS]

varicella *noun*
• "verra SELLA"
• an infectious disease, esp. of children, with a rash of small blisters; chicken pox.
• [modern Latin, diminutive of VARIOLA]

varicocele *noun*
• "VERRA kuh seel"
• a mass of varicose veins in the spermatic cord.
• [formed as VARIX + Greek *kēlē* tumour]

varicoloured *adjective*
ALSO SPELLED: **varicolored**
• "VERRA kull'rd"
• variegated in colour.
• [Latin *varius* VARIOUS + 'colour' from Latin *color*]

varicose *adjective*
• "VARE a cose" (rhymes with *GROSS*)
• (esp. of the veins of the legs) affected by a condition causing them to become dilated and swollen.
• [Latin *varicosus* from VARIX]
• **varicosed** *adjective*
• **varicosity** *noun* "verra COSSA tee".
HOMOPHONES: *verrucose*

variegate *verb*
• "VERRA gate" or "VERRY a gate"
• mark with irregular patches of different colours.
• [Latin *variegare variegat-* from *varius* various]
• **variegation** *noun*

variegated *adjective*
• "VERRA gated" or "VERRY a gated"
• (of plants) having leaves containing two or more colours.
• [as VARIEGATE]

varietal *adjective*
• "vuh RYE a t'll"
• of, forming, or designating a variety.
• [as VARIETY]
• **varietally** *adverb*

variety *noun*
• "vuh RYE a tee"
• diversity; absence of uniformity; many-sidedness; the condition of being various.
• [French *variété* or Latin *varietas* (as VARIOUS)]

variform *adjective*
• "VERRA form"
• having various forms.
• [Latin *varius* + *forma* shape]

variola *noun*
• "vuh RYE a luh"
• smallpox.
• [medieval Latin, = pustule, pock (as VARIOUS)]

variometer *noun*
• "verry OMMA tur"
• a device for varying the inductance in an electric circuit.
• [as VARIOUS + Greek *metron* measure]

variorum *adjective*
• "verry OR um"
• (of an edition of a text) having notes by various editors or commentators.
• [Latin from *editio cum notis variorum* edition with notes by various (commentators): genitive pl. of *varius* VARIOUS]

various *adjective*
• "VERRY us"
• different, diverse.
• [Latin *varius* changing, diverse]
• **variously** *adverb*
• **variousness** *noun*

varistor *noun*
• "vuh RISTER"
• a semiconductor diode with resistance dependent on the applied voltage.
• [*varying resistor*]

varix *noun*
• "VARE ix"
• a permanent abnormal dilation of a vein or artery.
• [Latin *varix -icis*]

varmint *noun*
• "VAR mint"
• a destructive or undesirable wild animal.
• [var. of *varmin*, Old French *vermin* destructive pest, ultimately from Latin *vermis* worm]

varroa *noun*
• "VERRO uh"
• a microscopic mite, *Varroa jacobsoni*, which is a debilitating parasite of the honeybee, causing loss of honey production.
• [Marcus *Varro*, Roman scholar d.27 BC]

varve *noun*
• "VARV"
• annually deposited layers of clay and silt in a lake used to determine the chronology of glacial sediments.
• [Swedish *varv* layer]

vary *verb*
• "VERRY"
• make different; modify, diversify.
• [Old French *varier* or Latin *variare* (as VARIOUS)]
• **variability** *noun*
• **variable** *adjective*
• **variably** *adverb*
• **variation** *noun*
• **variational** *adjective*
• **varied** *adjective*
• **varying** *adjective*
• **varyingly** *adverb*
HOMOPHONES: *very*

vas *noun*
• "VASS"
• a vessel or duct.
• [Latin, = vessel]

vascular *adjective*
• "VASS kyuh lur"
• of, made up of, or containing vessels for conveying blood or sap etc.
• [modern Latin *vascularis* from Latin *vasculum* diminutive of VAS]
• **vascularity** *noun* "vass kyuh LERRA tee"

vascularize *verb*
ALSO SPELLED: esp. *Brit.* **-ise**
• "VASS kyuh lur ize"
• make vascular, develop (esp. blood) vessels in.
• [as VASCULAR]
• **vascularization** *noun* (also esp. *Brit.* **-isation**)

vasculitis *noun*
• "vass kyuh LITE iss"
• inflammation of a blood vessel or blood vessels.
• [as VASCULAR + Greek *-itis*, forming feminine of adjectives in *-itēs* (with *nosos* 'disease' implied)]

vasculum *noun*
• "VASS kyuh lum"
• a botanist's (usu. metal) collecting case with a lengthwise opening.
• [Latin, diminutive of VAS]

vasectomy *noun*
• "vuh SECTA mee"
• the surgical removal of part of each vas deferens (sperm duct) esp. as a means of sterilization.
• [as VAS + Greek *ektomē* excision, from *ek* out + *temnō* cut]
• **vasectomize** *verb* (also esp. *Brit.* **-ise**)

vasoactive *adjective*
• "vay zo ACTIV"
• causing constriction or dilatation of blood vessels.
• [VAS + 'active']

vasoconstriction *noun*
• "vay zo k'n STRICK sh'n"
• the constriction of blood vessels.
• [VAS + 'constriction' (as CONSTRICTOR)]
• **vasoconstricting** *adjective*
• **vasoconstrictive** *adjective*
• **vasoconstrictor** *noun*

vasodilation *noun*
• "vay zo die LAY sh'n"
• the dilation of blood vessels.
• [VAS + DILATE]
• **vasodilator** *noun*
• **vasodilatory** *adjective*

vasomotor *adjective*
• "VAY zo moter"
• causing constriction or dilatation of blood vessels.
• [VAS + 'motor']

vasopressin *noun*
• "vay zo PRESSIN"
• a pituitary hormone acting to reduce diuresis and increase blood pressure.
• [VAS + 'press']

vassal *noun*
• "VASS'll"
• a holder of land by feudal tenure on conditions of homage and allegiance.
• [Old French from medieval Latin *vassallus* retainer, of Celtic origin]
• **vassalage** *noun* "VASS'll idge"

vatic *adjective*
• "VATTIC"
• prophetic or inspired.
• [Latin *vates* prophet]

vaticinate *verb*
• "va TISS'n ate"
• prophesy.
• [Latin *vaticinari* from *vates* prophet]
• **vaticination** *noun*

vatu *noun*
• "VAT oo"
• the basic monetary unit of Vanuatu.
• [Bislama]

vaudeville *noun*
• "VOD vill" or "VODDA vill"
• a form of variety entertainment popular esp. in the US from about 1880 until the early 1930s, featuring a mixture of specialty acts such as burlesque comedy and song and dance.
• [French, originally of convivial song esp. any of those composed by O. Basselin, 15th-c. poet born at *Vau de Vire* in Normandy]
• **vaudevillian** *adjective* "vod VILLY 'n" or "vodda VILLY 'n"

vault *noun*
• "VAULT" (rhymes with *SALT*)
• an arched roof.

• [Old French *voute, vaute*, ultimately from Latin *volvere* roll]
• **vaulter** *noun*

vaulting *noun*
• "VAULT ing"
• arched work in a vaulted roof or ceiling.
• [as VAULT]

vaunt *verb*
• "VONT"
• boast, brag.
• [Anglo-French *vaunter*, Old French *vanter* from Late Latin *vantare* from Latin *vanus* VAIN]

vaunted *adjective*
• "VON tid"
• highly praised, esp. to excess.
• [as VAUNT]

vavasour *noun*
• "VAVVA sur"
• a vassal owing allegiance to a great lord and having other vassals under him.
• [Old French *vavas(s)our* from medieval Latin *vavassor*, perhaps from *vassus vassorum* VASSAL of vassals]

vector *noun*
• "VECTER"
• a quantity having direction as well as magnitude, esp. as determining the position of one point in space relative to another.
• [Latin, = carrier, from *vehere vect-* convey]
• **vectorial** *adjective* "veck TORY 'll"
• **vectorize** *verb* (also esp. *Brit.* **-ise**)

Veda *noun*
• "VAY duh" or "VEE duh"
• the most ancient Hindu scriptures, esp. four collections called Rig-Veda, Sāma-Veda, Yajur-Veda, and Atharva-Veda.
• [Sanskrit *vēda*, lit. (sacred) knowledge]

Vedanta *noun*
• "vuh DANTA" or "vuh DONTA"
• the Upanishads.
• [Sanskrit *vedānta* (as VEDA, *anta* end)]
• **Vedantic** *adjective*
• **Vedantist** *noun*

Vedda *noun*
• "VEDDA"
• a Sri Lankan aboriginal.
• [Sinhalese *veddā* hunter]

vedette *noun*
• "vuh DET"
• a leading star of stage or screen.
• [French, = scout, from Italian *vedetta, veletta* from Spanish *velar* watch, from Latin *vigilare*]

Vedic *adjective*
• "VAY dick" or "VEE dick"
• of or relating to the Veda or Vedas.
• [as VEDA]

veena *noun*
• "VEENA"
• an Indian stringed musical instrument with a fretted fingerboard and a gourd at either end.
• [Sanskrit & Hindi *viṇā*]

veery *noun*
• "VEERY"
• a N American woodland thrush, *Catharus fuscescens*.
• [perhaps imitative]

vegan *noun*
• "VEE g'n" or "VAY g'n" or "VEDGE 'n"
• a person who does not eat or use animal products.
• [contraction of VEGETARIAN]
• **veganism** *noun*

vegetable *noun*
• "VEDGE tuh bull" or "VEDGE a tuh bull"
• any plant or edible fungus whose leaves, roots, tubers, fruit, seeds, or flowers are used for food, e.g. lettuce, potatoes, carrots, tomatoes, and mushrooms.
• [Old French *vegetable* or Late Latin *vegetabilis* animating (as VEGETATE)]

vegetal *adjective*
• "VEDGE a t'll"
• of or having the nature of plants.
• [as VEGETATE]

vegetarian *noun*
• "vedge a TERRY 'n"
• a person who abstains from animal food, esp. that from slaughtered animals, though often not eggs and dairy products.
• [as VEGETATE]
• **vegetarianism** *noun*

vegetate *verb*
• "VEDGE a tate"
• live an uneventful or monotonous life.
• [Latin *vegetare* animate, from *vegetus* from *vegēre* be active]

vegetation *noun*
• "vedge a TAY sh'n"
• plants collectively; plant life.
• [as VEGETATE]
• **vegetational** *adjective*

vegetative *adjective*
• "VEDGE a tay tiv"
• of, relating to, or concerned with growth and development as distinct from reproduction.
• [as VEGETATE]
• **vegetatively** *adverb*

veggie *noun*
ALSO SPELLED: **vegie**
• "VEDGE ee"
• a vegetable.
• [abbreviation]

vehement *adjective*
• "VEE a m'nt"
• showing or caused by strong feeling; forceful, ardent.
• [French *véhément* or Latin *vehemens -entis*,

perhaps from *vemens* (unrecorded) deprived of mind, assoc. with *vehere* carry]
- **vehemence** *noun*
- **vehemently** *adverb*

vehicle *noun*
- "VEE a k'll"
- any conveyance for transporting people, goods, etc., esp. on land.
- [French *véhicule* or Latin *vehiculum* from *vehere* carry]
- **vehicular** *adjective* "vee HICK yuh lur"

veil *noun*
- "VALE"
- a piece of fabric worn, esp. by women, over the head or face for concealment, to protect the face from the sun, dust, etc., or traditionally as part of a bride's attire.
- [Anglo-French *veil(e)* from Latin *vela* pl. of VELUM]
- **veiled** *adjective*

HOMOPHONES: *vale*

veiling *noun*
- "VALE ing"
- light fabric used for veils etc.
- [as VEIL]

vein *noun*
- "VANE"
- any of the anatomical tubes by which blood is conveyed to the heart.
- [Old French *veine* from Latin *vena*]
- **veined** *adjective*
- **veinlike** *adjective*
- **veiny** *adjective*

HOMOPHONES: *vain, vane*

veining *noun*
- "VANE ing"
- a pattern of streaks or veins.
- [as VEIN]

velamen *noun*
- "vill AY m'n"
- an enveloping membrane esp. of an aerial root of an orchid.
- [Latin from *velare* cover]

velar *adjective*
- "VEELER"
- of a veil or velum.
- [Latin *velaris* from *velum*: see VELUM]

veld *noun*

ALSO SPELLED: **veldt**
- "VELT"
- open country; grassland.
- [Afrikaans from Dutch, = 'field']

veliger *noun*
- "VEELA jur"
- the free-swimming larva of a mollusc, with a ciliated velum.
- [VELUM + Latin *-ger* bearing]

velleity *noun*
- "vel EE a tee"
- a wish or inclination not strong enough to lead to action.
- [medieval Latin *velleitas*, from Latin *velle* to wish]

vellum *noun*
- "VELL um"
- fine parchment originally from the skin of a calf.
- [Old French *velin* from *veiaus veel* calf, from Latin *vitellus* diminutive of *vitulus* calf]

velocimeter *noun*
- "vella SIMMA tur"
- an instrument for measuring velocity.
- [as VELOCITY + Greek *metron* measure]

velocipede *noun*
- "vuh LOSSA peed"
- an early form of bicycle propelled by pressure from the rider's feet on the ground.
- [French *vélocipède* from Latin *velox -ocis* swift + *pes pedis* foot]

velociraptor *noun*
- "vuh LOSSA rapter"
- a small bipedal carnivorous dinosaur of the genus *Velociraptor*, of the Cretaceous period, with an enlarged curved claw on each hind foot.
- [modern Latin, from Latin *velox -ocis* swift + RAPTOR]

velocity *noun*
- "vuh LOSSA tee"
- the measure of the rate of movement of a usu. inanimate object in a given direction.
- [French *vélocité* or Latin *velocitas* from *velox -ocis* swift]

velodrome *noun*
- "VELLA drome"
- an arena with a usu. banked track for cycle racing.
- [French *vélodrome* from *vélo* bicycle, VELOCIPEDE + Greek *dromos* course, running]

velour *noun*
- "vuh LOOR"
- any of various fabrics with a velvet-like finish, used for clothing, upholstery, etc.
- [French *velours* velvet, from Old French *velour*, *velous* from Latin *villosus* hairy, from *villus* tuft, down]

velouté *noun*
- "vuh loo TAY"
- a sauce made from chicken stock and cream thickened with a mixture of butter and flour.
- [French, = velvety]

velum *noun*
- "VEE lum"
- a membrane, membranous covering, or flap.
- [Latin, = sail, curtain, covering, veil]

venal *adjective*
- "VEEN 'll"
- (of a person) willing to act dishonestly or immorally, or to sacrifice principles, for money.

• [Latin *venalis* from *venum* thing for sale]
• **venality** *noun* "vee NALA tee"

venation *noun*
• "vuh NAY sh'n"
• the arrangement of veins in a leaf or an insect's wing etc., or the system of venous blood vessels in an organism.
• [Latin *vena* vein]

vendetta *noun*
• "ven DETTA"
• a blood feud in which the family of a murdered person seeks vengeance on the murderer or the murderer's family, orig. as prevalent in Corsica and Sicily.
• [Italian from Latin *vindicta*: see VINDICTIVE]

vendor *noun*
• "VENDER"
• the seller in a sale, esp. of property.
• [French *vendre* or Latin *vendere* sell]

vendu *noun*
• "von DOO"
• *Cdn derogatory* a Québécois who is viewed as having sold out or become assimilated to English-Canadian society.
• [French, lit. = 'sold' (as VENDOR)]

veneer *noun*
• "vuh NEER"
• a thin covering of fine wood or other surface material applied to a coarser wood.
• [earlier *fineer* from German *furni(e)ren* from Old French *fournir* furnish]

venerable *adjective*
• "VENNER a bull"
• entitled to veneration on account of character, age, associations, etc.
• [as VENERATE]
• **venerability** *noun*
• **venerably** *adverb*

venerate *verb*
• "VENNER ate"
• regard with deep respect.
• [Latin *venerari* adore, revere]
• **veneration** *noun*

venereal *adjective*
• "ven EERY 'll"
• of or relating to sexual desire or intercourse.
• [Latin *venereus* from *venus veneris* sexual love]

Venetian *noun*
• "ven EE sh'n"
• a native or citizen of Venice, Italy.
• [Old French *Venicien*, assimilated to medieval Latin *Venetianus* from *Venetia* Venice]

Venezuelan *noun*
• "ven iz WALE 'n"
• a native or inhabitant of Venezuela in northern S America.

vengeance *noun*
• "VEN jince"
• punishment inflicted or retribution exacted for wrong to oneself or to a person etc. whose cause one supports.
• [Old French from *venger* avenge, from Latin (as VINDICATE)]

venial *adjective*
• "VEENY 'll"
• (of a sin or fault) pardonable, excusable; not mortal.
• [Old French from Late Latin *venialis* from *venia* forgiveness]
• **veniality** *noun*
• **venially** *adverb*

venipuncture *noun*
ALSO SPELLED: **venepuncture**
• "VEENA punk chur"
• the puncture of a vein esp. with a hypodermic needle to withdraw blood or for an intravenous injection.
• [Latin *vena* vein + PUNCTURE]

venison *noun*
• "VEN iss 'n" or "VEN iz 'n"
• a deer's flesh as food.
• [Old French *veneso(u)n* from Latin *venatio -onis* hunting, from *venari* to hunt]

Venite *noun*
• "ven ITE ee"
• Psalm 95 used as a canticle.
• [Latin, = 'come ye', its first word]

venom *noun*
• "VEN'm"
• a poisonous fluid secreted by snakes, scorpions, etc., usu. transmitted by a bite or sting.
• [Old French *venim*, var. of *venin* ultimately from Latin *venenum* poison]
• **venomed** *adjective*
• **venomous** *adjective*
• **venomously** *adverb*

venous *adjective*
• "VEE nuss"
• of or full of veins.
• [Latin *vena* vein]

ventifact *noun*
• "VENTA fact"
• a stone shaped by windblown sand.
• [Latin *ventus* wind + *factum* neuter past participle of *facere* make]

ventilate *verb*
• "VENT'll ate"
• cause air to circulate freely in (a room etc.).
• [Latin *ventilare ventilat-* blow, winnow, from *ventus* wind]
• **ventilation** *noun*
• **ventilator** *noun*

ventricle *noun*
• "VEN trickle"
• either of the two muscular lower chambers of the heart (in some animals, a single chamber),

which pump the blood to the arteries and through the body.
• [Latin *ventriculus* diminutive of *venter* belly]
• **ventricular** *adjective* "ven TRICK yuh lur"

ventriloquism *noun*
• "ven TRILLA kwiz'm"
• the skill of speaking or uttering sounds so that they seem to come from the speaker's dummy or a source other than the speaker.
• [ultimately from Latin *ventriloquus* ventriloquist, from *venter* belly + *loqui* speak]
• **ventriloquial** *adjective* "ventra LO kwee 'll"
• **ventriloquist** *noun*
• **ventriloquize** *verb* (also esp. *Brit.* **-ise**)

venturi *noun*
• "ven CHOORY"
• a tube with a narrower middle section for measuring flow rate or exerting suction.
• [G. B. *Venturi*, Italian physicist d.1822]

venule *noun*
• "VEN yool"
• a small vein adjoining the capillaries.
• [Latin *venula* diminutive of *vena* vein]

veracious *adjective*
• "vuh RAY sh'ss"
• speaking or disposed to speak the truth.
• [Latin *verax veracis* from *verus* true]
HOMOPHONES: *voracious*

veracity *noun*
• "vuh RASSA tee"
• truthfulness, honesty.
• [French *veracité* or medieval Latin *veracitas* (as VERACIOUS)]
HOMOPHONES: *voracity*

veranda *noun*
ALSO SPELLED: **verandah**
• "vuh RANDA"
• a usu. roofed porch or external gallery along one or more sides of a house, esp. the front.
• [Hindi *varandā* from Portuguese *varanda* railing, balustrade]

verapamil *noun*
• "vuh RAPPA mill"
• a synthetic compound which acts as a calcium antagonist and is used to treat angina pectoris and cardiac arrhythmias.
• [from *v(al)er(onitr)il(e)* (from VALERIAN + NITRILE), with the insertion of *-apam-* (of unknown origin)]

verbatim *adverb*
• "vur BATE im"
• in exactly the same words; word for word.
• [medieval Latin (adverb), from Latin *verbum* word]

verbena *noun*
• "vur BEENA"
• any plant of the genus *Verbena*, bearing clusters of fragrant flowers.
• [Latin, = sacred bough of olive etc., in medieval Latin, = vervain]

verbiage *noun*
• "VURBY idge"
• needless accumulation of words; verbosity.
• [French from obsolete *verbeier* chatter, from *verbe* word, from Latin *verbum* word, verb]

verboten *adjective*
• "vur BOTE 'n" or "vare BOTE 'n"
• forbidden, esp. by an authority.
• [German]

verdant *adjective*
• "VUR d'nt"
• (of grass etc.) green, fresh-coloured.
• [perhaps from Old French *verdeant* participle of *verdoier* be green, ultimately from Latin *viridis* green]
• **verdancy** *noun*
• **verdantly** *adverb*

verderer *noun*
• "VUR dur ur"
• a judicial officer of royal forests.
• [Anglo-French (earlier *verder*), Old French *verdier*, ultimately from Latin *viridis* green]

Verdian *adjective*
• "VARE dee 'n"
• of or characteristic of the work G. Verdi, Italian operatic composer d.1901.

verdigris *noun*
• "VUR duh griss" or "VUR duh greece"
• a bright bluish-green incrustation formed on copper or brass by atmospheric oxidation, consisting of basic copper carbonate.
• [Old French *verte-gres*, *vert de Grece* green of Greece]

verdure *noun*
• "VUR dyur" or "VUR jur"
• green vegetation.
• [Old French from *verd* green, from Latin *viridis*]
HOMOPHONES: *verger*

verger *noun*
ALSO SPELLED: **virger**
• "VUR jur"
• an official in a church who acts as caretaker and attendant.
• [Anglo-French from Latin *virga* rod]
HOMOPHONES: *verdure*

veridical *adjective*
• "vuh RIDDA k'll"
• truthful.
• [Latin *veridicus* from *verus* true + *dicere* say]
• **veridically** *adverb*

verify *verb*
• "VERRA fie"
• establish the truth or correctness of by examination or demonstration.
• [Old French *verifier* from medieval Latin *verificare* from *verus* true]

- **verifiable** *adjective*
- **verifiably** *adverb*
- **verification** *noun* "verra fuh CAY sh'n"
- **verifier** *noun*

verisimilitude *noun*
- "verra suh MILLA tude"
- the appearance or semblance of being true or real.
- [Latin *verisimilitudo* from *verisimilis* probable, from *veri* genitive of *verus* true + *similis* like]
- **verisimilar** *adjective*

verism *noun*
- "VEER izm"
- realism in literature or art.
- [Latin *verus* or Italian *vero* true]
- **verist** *noun*
- **veristic** *adjective*

verismo *noun*
- "vare IZ moe"
- (esp. of opera) realism.
- [Italian (as VERISM)]

veritable *adjective*
- "VERRA tuh bull"
- real; rightly so called.
- [Old French (as VERITY)]
- **veritably** *adverb*

vérité *noun*
- "verry TAY"
- realism or naturalism in the arts, esp. in film.
- [French, = truth (as VERITY)]

verity *noun*
- "VARE it ee"
- a true statement, esp. one of fundamental import.
- [Old French *verité*, *verté* from Latin *veritas -tatis* from *verus* true]

verjus *noun*
ALSO SPELLED: **verjuice**
- "VUR jooce"
- an acidic juice obtained from crabapples, sour grapes, etc., and formerly used in cooking and medicine.
- [Old French *vertjus* from *vert* green + *jus* juice]

vermeil *noun*
- "VUR male" or "VUR mill"
- silver gilt.
- [Old French: see VERMILION]

vermicelli *noun*
- "vurma CHELLY"
- pasta made in long slender threads.
- [Italian, pl. of *vermicello* diminutive of *verme* from Latin *vermis* worm]

vermicide *noun*
- "VURMA side"
- a substance that kills worms.
- [Latin *vermis* worm +*-cida*, *-cidium* from *caedere* kill]

vermicomposting *noun*
- "vurma COM post ing"
- composting using earthworms to convert organic waste into fertilizer.
- [Latin *vermis* worm + Old French *composte* from Latin *compos(i)tum* (as COMPOSITE)]
- **vermicomposter** *noun*

vermicular *adjective*
- "vur MICK yuh lur"
- like a worm in form or movement; vermiform.
- [medieval Latin *vermicularis* from Latin *vermiculus* diminutive of *vermis* worm]

vermiculate *adjective*
- "vur MICK yuh lit"
- like a worm in form or movement.
- [Latin *vermiculatus* past participle of *vermiculari* be full of worms (as VERMICULAR)]
- **vermiculation** *noun*

vermiculite *noun*
- "vur MICK yoo lite"
- a hydrated silicate resulting from the alteration of mica etc., esp. an aluminosilicate of magnesium.
- [as VERMICULATE]

vermiculture *noun*
- "VURMA cull chur"
- the cultivation of earthworms, esp. in vermicomposting.
- [Latin *vermis* worm + CULTURE]

vermiform *adjective*
- "VURMA form"
- worm-shaped.
- [Latin *vermis* worm + *forma* shape]

vermifuge *adjective*
- "VERMA fyoodge"
- that expels intestinal worms.
- [Latin *vermis* worm + modern Latin *-fugus* from Latin *fugare* put to flight]

vermilion *noun*
- "vur MILL y'n"
- a brilliant red pigment made by grinding a bright red mineral form of mercuric sulphide.
- [Old French *vermeillon* from *vermeil* from Latin *vermiculus* diminutive of *vermis* worm]

vermouth *noun*
- "vur MOOTH"
- a fortified wine flavoured with aromatic herbs.
- [French *vermout* from German *Wermut* a plant used in its preparation]

vernacular *noun*
- "vur NACK yuh lur"
- the language or dialect of a particular country.
- [Latin *vernaculus* domestic, native, from *verna* slave born in the master's home]
- **vernacularly** *adverb*

vernal *adjective*
• "VURN'll"
• of, in, or appropriate to spring.
• [Latin *vernalis* from *vernus* from *ver* spring]

vernier *noun*
• "VURNY ur"
• a small movable graduated scale for obtaining fractional parts of subdivisions on a fixed main scale of a barometer, sextant, calipers, etc.
• [P. *Vernier*, French mathematician d.1637]

vernissage *noun*
• "vare nuh SOZH"
• a private view of an exhibit of paintings etc. before public exhibition.
• [French, = varnishing]

veronal *noun*
• "VARE 'n 'll"
• a sedative drug, a derivative of barbituric acid.
• [German, from *Verona* in N Italy]

verruca *noun*
• "vuh ROO kuh"
• a wart or similar growth.
• [Latin]
• **verrucose** *adjective* "VERRA coze"
• **verrucous** *adjective* "VERRA kuss"
HOMOPHONES: *varicose*

versant *noun*
• "VURSE 'nt"
• the extent of land sloping in one direction.
• [French from *verser* from Latin *versare* frequentative of *vertere vers-* turn]

versicle *noun*
• "VURSA k'll"
• each of the short sentences in a liturgy said or sung by a priest etc. and alternating with responses.
• [Latin *versiculus*, diminutive of *versus* a turn of the plow, a furrow, a line of writing, from *vertere vers-* turn]

versicolour *adjective*
ALSO SPELLED: **versicolor**
• "VURSA culler"
• changing or varying in colour; iridescent.
• [Latin from *versus* past participle of *vertere* turn + *color* colour]

verst *noun*
• "VURST"
• a Russian measure of length, about 1.07 km (0.66 mile).
• [Russian *versta*]
HOMOPHONES: *versed*, *wurst*

vertebra *noun*
• "VURTA bruh"
• each segment of the backbone.
• [Latin from *vertere* turn]
• **vertebral** *adjective*

vertebrate *noun*
• "VURTA brate" or "VURTA brit"
• any animal of the subphylum Vertebrata, having a spinal column, including mammals, birds, reptiles, amphibians, and fishes.
• [as VERTEBRA]

vertex *noun*
• "VUR tex"
• the highest point; the top or apex.
• [Latin *vertex -ticis* whirlpool, crown of a head, vertex, from *vertere* turn]

verticil *noun*
• "VURTA sill"
• a whorl; a set of parts arranged in a circle around an axis.
• [Latin *verticillus* whorl of a spindle, diminutive of VERTEX]

vertigo *noun*
• "VURTA go"
• a condition with a sensation of whirling and a tendency to lose balance; dizziness, giddiness.
• [Latin *vertigo -ginis* whirling, from *vertere* turn]
• **vertiginous** *adjective* "vur TIDGE in us"
• **vertiginously** *adverb*

vervain *noun*
• "VUR vane"
• any of various herbaceous plants of the genus *Verbena*, esp. *V. officinalis* with small blue, white, or purple flowers.
• [Old French *verveine* from Latin VERBENA]

vervet *noun*
• "VUR vit"
• a small grey African monkey, *Cercopithecus aethiops*.
• [French]

vesica *noun*
• "VESSA kuh"
• a bladder, esp. the urinary bladder.
• [Latin]
• **vesical** *adjective*
HOMOPHONES: *vesicle*

vesicle *noun*
• "VESSA k'll"
• a small fluid-filled bladder, sac, or vacuole.
• [French *vésicule* or Latin *vesicula*, diminutive of VESICA]
• **vesicular** *adjective* "vuh SICK yuh lur"
• **vesiculation** *noun*
HOMOPHONES: *vesical*

vespertine *adjective*
• "VESPER tine" or "VESPER tin"
• (of a flower) opening in the evening.
• [Latin *vespertinus* from *vesper* evening]

vespiary *noun*
• "VESPY airy"
• a nest of wasps.
• [Latin *vespa* wasp, after *apiary*]

vespine *adjective*
• "VESS pine"
• of or relating to wasps.
• [Latin *vespa* wasp]

vestal *adjective*
• "VEST'll"
• chaste, pure.
• [*Vesta*, Roman goddess of the hearth, whose attendants were virgins]

vestibular *adjective*
• "vess TIB yuh lur"
• relating to the central cavity of the labyrinth of the inner ear.
• [as VESTIBULE]

vestibule *noun*
• "VESTA byool"
• an antechamber, hall, or lobby just inside the outer door of a building, e.g. where coats may be left.
• [French *vestibule* or Latin *vestibulum* entrance court]

vestige *noun*
• "VESS tidge"
• a trace or piece of evidence; a sign.
• [French from Latin *vestigium* footprint]
• **vestigial** *adjective* "ves TIDGE ee 'll" or "ves TIDGE 'll"
• **vestigially** *adverb*

vestment *noun*
• "VEST m'nt"
• any of the official robes of clergy, choristers, etc., worn during divine service, e.g. a chasuble.
• [Old French *vestiment*, *vestement* from Latin *vestimentum* from *vestis* garment]

vestry *noun*
• "VESS tree"
• a room or building attached to a church for keeping vestments in.
• [Old French *vestiaire*, *vestiarie*, from Latin *vestiarium* from *vestis* garment]

vesture *noun*
• "VESS chur"
• garments, dress.
• [Old French from medieval Latin *vestitura* from *vestis* garment]

veteran *noun*
• "VETTER 'n" or "VET rin"
• a person who has grown old in or had long experience of esp. military service or an occupation.
• [French *vétéran* or Latin *veteranus* from *vetus -eris* old]

veterinarian *noun*
• "vettrin AIRY 'n" or "vetter in AIRY 'n"
• a person qualified to treat diseased or injured animals.
• [as VETERINARY]

veterinary *adjective*
• "VETTRIN airy" or "VETTER in airy"
• of or for diseases and injuries of esp. farm and domestic animals, or their treatment.
• [Latin *veterinarius* from *veterinae* cattle]

vetiver *noun*
• "VET iv ur"
• the aromatic fibrous root of an Indian grass, *Vetiveria zizanioides*, used for making fans etc.
• [French *vétiver* from Tamil *veṭṭivēru* from *vēr* root]

veto *noun*
• "VEETO"
• a constitutional right to reject a legislative enactment.
• [Latin, = I forbid, with reference to its use by Roman tribunes of the people in opposing measures of the Senate]

vexation *noun*
• "vex AY sh'n"
• the act or an instance of vexing; the state of being vexed.
• [Old French, from *vexer* from Latin *vexare* shake, disturb]
• **vexatious** *adjective*
• **vexatiously** *adverb*

vexillology *noun*
• "vex'll OLLA jee"
• the study of flags.
• [Latin *vexillum* flag + Greek *logos* word]
• **vexillologist** *noun*

vexillum *noun*
• "veck SILLUM"
• a military standard, esp. of a maniple.
• [Latin from *vehere vect-* carry]

vial *noun*
• "VIE 'll"
• a small (usu. cylindrical glass) vessel esp. for holding liquid medicines.
• [Middle English, var. of *fiole* etc.: see PHIAL]
HOMOPHONES: *vile*, *viol*

viand *noun*
• "VIE 'nd"
• an article of food.
• [Old French *viande* food, ultimately from Latin *vivenda*, neuter pl. gerundive of *vivere* to live]

viatical *adjective*
• "vie ATTA k'll"
• designating or relating to an arrangement whereby a person having a terminal illness (esp. AIDS) sells his or her life insurance policy to a third party for less than its mature value so that he or she can benefit from the proceeds while alive.
• [as VIATICUM]

viaticum *noun*
• "vie ATTA k'm"
• the Eucharist as given to a person near or in danger of death.
• [Latin, neuter of *viaticus* from *via* road]

vibraculum *noun*
• "vie BRACK yuh lum"
• a whip-like structure of bryozoans used to bring food within reach by lashing movements.
• [modern Latin from Latin *vibrare vibrat-* shake, swing]

vibrant *adjective*
• "VIE br'nt"
• full of life and energy; exciting.
• [Latin *vibrare vibrat-* shake, swing]
• **vibrancy** *noun*
• **vibrantly** *adverb*

vibraphone *noun*
• "VIE bruh fone"
• a percussion instrument of tuned metal bars with motor-driven resonators and metal tubes giving a vibrato effect.
• [VIBRATO + Greek *phōne* sound]
• **vibraphonist** *noun*

vibrato *noun*
• "vib ROTTO"
• a rapid slight variation in pitch in singing or playing a stringed or wind instrument, producing a tremulous effect.
• [Italian, past participle of *vibrare* vibrate from Latin *vibrare vibrat-* shake, swing]

vibrator *noun*
• "VIE brate ur"
• a device that vibrates or causes vibration.
• [Latin *vibrare vibrat-* shake, swing]
• **vibratory** *adjective* "VIE bruh tory"

vibrio *noun*
• "VIB ree oh"
• a water-borne bacterium of the genus *Vibrio* etc., typically shaped like a curved rod with a flagellum, and including the cholera bacterium.
• [modern Latin, from Latin *vibrare* shake]

vibrissae *plural noun*
• "vie BRISSY"
• the stiff coarse sensitive hairs growing on the face, esp. around the mouth, of most mammals, such as a cat's whiskers.
• [Latin from *vibrare* shake]

viburnum *noun*
• "vie BURN um"
• any shrub of the genus *Viburnum*, usu. with white flowers, e.g. the guelder rose and wayfaring tree.
• [Latin, = wayfaring tree]

vicar *noun*
• "VICKER"
• (in the Church of England) an incumbent of a parish where tithes formerly passed to a chapter or religious house or layman.
• [Old French *vicaire* from Latin *vicarius* substitute, from *vicis* change]
• **vicariate** *noun* "vick AIRY it"

vicarage *noun*
• "VICKER idge"
• the residence or benefice of a vicar.
• [as VICAR]

vicarious *adjective*
• "vick AIRY us" or "vie CARE ee us"
• experienced, enjoyed, or undergone second-hand by imagining one's own participation in the experiences of another.
• [Latin *vicarius*: see VICAR]
• **vicariously** *adverb*
• **vicariousness** *noun*

vicegerent *adjective*
• "vice JARE 'nt"
• exercising delegated power.
• [medieval Latin *vicegerens* (*vix* change, Latin *gerere* carry on)]
• **vicegerency** *noun*

vicereine *noun*
• "VICE rane"
• the wife of a viceroy.
• [French (*vice* from Latin *vice* in place of, *reine* from Latin *regina* queen)]

viceroy *noun*
• "VICE roy"
• a person who exercises authority over a colony or province etc. on behalf of a sovereign.
• [French (*vice* from Latin *vice* in place of, *roy* from Latin *rex* king)]
• **viceroyalty** *noun*

vichyssoise *noun*
• "vishy SWOZZ"
• a thick soup made of puréed leeks and potatoes with cream, usu. served chilled.
• [French *crème vichyssoise glacée*, lit. 'iced cream soup of Vichy']

vicinage *noun*
• "VISSIN idge"
• a neighbourhood; a surrounding district or vicinity.
• [Old French *vis(e)nage*, ultimately from Latin *vicinus* neighbour]

vicinal *adjective*
• "VISSIN 'll" or "vuh SINE 'll"
• neighbouring, adjacent.
• [French *vicinal* or Latin *vicinalis* from *vicinus* neighbour]

vicinity *noun*
• "vuh SINNA tee"
• the area within a limited distance of a place.
• [Latin *vicinitas* (as VICINAL)]

vicious *adjective*
• "VISH us"
• malevolent, spiteful, wicked.
• [Old French *vicious* or Latin *vitiosus* from *vitium* vice]
• **viciously** *adverb*
• **viciousness** *noun*

vicissitude *noun*
• "vuh SISSA tude"
• changes in circumstance; uncertainties or variations of fortune or outcome.

• [French *vicissitude* or Latin *vicissitudo -dinis* from *vicissim* by turns from *vix* change]
• **vicissitudinous** *adjective*
"vuh sissa TUDE in us"

victim *noun*
• "VICK t'm"
• a person who suffers or dies as a result of an event or circumstance.
• [Latin *victima*]
• **victimhood** *noun*
• **victimization** *noun* (also esp. *Brit.* **-isation**)
• **victimize** *verb* (also esp. *Brit.* **-ise**)
• **victimizer** *noun* (also esp. *Brit.* **-iser**)

victimology *noun*
• "vick t'm OLLA jee"
• the study of the victims of crime or discrimination, the psychological effects on them of their experience, and methods of recovery.
• [as VICTIM + Greek *logos* word]

Victoriana *plural noun*
• "vick tory ANNA"
• articles, esp. collectors' items and furniture, of the Victorian period.
• [Queen *Victoria*, reigned 1837–1901]

victual *noun*
• "VICK choo 'll" or "VIT'll"
• food, provisions.
• [Old French *vitaille* from Late Latin *victualia*, neuter pl. of Latin *victualis* from *victus* food]

victualler *noun*
ALSO SPELLED: *US* **victualer**
• "VICK choo a lur" or "VIT lur"
• a person who serves food and drink for a living.
• [as VICTUAL]

vicuña *noun*
• "vuh KYOONYA"
• a S American mammal, *Vicugna vicugna*, related to the llama, with fine silky wool.
• [Spanish from Quechua]

Vidal *noun*
• "vid AWL"
• a hybrid variety of white wine grape widely grown in Ontario, used. esp. in icewines.
• [Jean-Louis *Vidal*, 20th-c. French winemaker]

vidalia *noun*
• "vie DAILY uh"
• a sweet onion of the southern US.
• [the city of *Vidalia*, Georgia]

vide *verb*
• "VEE day"
• (as an instruction in a reference to a passage in a book etc.) see, consult.
• [Latin, imperative of *vidēre* see]

videlicet *adverb*
• "vuh DELLA set"
• (usu. introducing a gloss or explanation) namely; that is to say; in other words.
• [Latin from *vidēre* see + *licet* it is permissible]

videodisc *noun*
• "VIDDY oh disk"
• an optical disk on which visual material is recorded for reproduction on a television screen.
• ['video' from Latin *vidēre* see + 'disc' (as DISCUS)]

videography *noun*
• "viddy OGGRA fee"
• the process or art of making videos.
• ['video' from Latin *vidēre* see + Greek *graphia* writing]
• **videographer** *noun*

videophile *noun*
• "VIDDY oh file"
• an enthusiast for videos or video technology.
• ['video' from Latin *vidēre* see + Greek *philos* dear, loving]

vie *verb*
• "VIE"
• compete, contend.
• [prob. from Middle English from Old French *envie* envy, desire, from Latin *invidia* from *invidēre* envy (*in* not, *vidēre* see)]

vielle *noun*
• "vee EL"
• a hurdy-gurdy.
• [French from Old French *viel(l)e*: see VIOL]

Viennese *adjective*
• "vee a NEEZ"
• of or relating to Vienna, Austria.

Vietnamese *adjective*
• "vee etna MEEZ" or "VEE etna meez"
• of or relating to Vietnam, its inhabitants, or language.

vigesimal *adjective*
• "vuh JESSIM 'll" or "vie JESSIM 'll"
• of twentieths or twenty.
• [Latin *vigesimus* from *viginti* twenty]

vigil *noun*
• "VIDGE 'll"
• a stationary and peaceful demonstration in support of a particular cause, usu. without speeches or other explicit advocacy of the cause, and often with some suggestion of mourning.
• [Old French *vigile* from Latin *vigilia* from *vigil* awake]

vigilance *noun*
• "VIDGE a lince"
• the quality of being alert to harm or danger; watchfulness, circumspection, caution.
• [French *vigilance* or Latin *vigilantia* from *vigilare* keep awake (as VIGIL)]
• **vigilant** *adjective*
• **vigilantly** *adverb*

vigilante *noun*
• "vidge a LANTY"
• a person, often a member of a group, who undertakes law enforcement and executes

summary justice in the absence or perceived inadequacy of legally constituted law enforcement bodies.
• [Spanish, = vigilant]
• **vigilantism** *noun*

vigneron *noun*
• "vee nyuh RÕH" (with a nasal *OH*)
• a person who cultivates grapevines for winemaking.
• [French from *vigne* vine, from Latin *vinea* vineyard, from *vinum* wine]

vignette *noun*
• "vin YET"
• a brief descriptive account, anecdote, essay, or character sketch.
• [French, diminutive of *vigne* vine (originally a decoration on a page representing vines)]

vignetting *noun*
• "vin YETTING"
• the technique of producing photographs or portraits showing only the head and shoulders with the edges gradually shaded off into the background, esp. in photography.
• [as VIGNETTE]

vigorish *noun*
• "VIGGER ish"
• the percentage deducted by a bookie from a gambler's winnings.
• [prob. from Yiddish, from Russian *vyigrysh* profit, winnings]

vigour *noun*
ALSO SPELLED: **vigor**
• "VIGGER"
• active physical strength or energy.
• [Old French *vigour* from Latin *vigor -oris* from *vigēre* be lively]
• **vigorous** *adjective*
• **vigorously** *adverb*
• **vigorousness** *noun*

vile *adjective*
• "VILE"
• disgusting.
• [Old French *vil vile* from Latin *vilis* cheap, base]
• **vilely** *adverb*
• **vileness** *noun*
HOMOPHONES: *vial, viol*

vilify *verb*
• "VILLA fie"
• speak or write about in an abusively disparaging manner.
• [Middle English in sense 'lower in value', from Late Latin *vilificare* (as VILE)]
• **vilification** *noun*
• **vilifier** *noun*

villain *noun*
• "VILL 'n"
• a person guilty or capable of great wickedness.
• [Old French *vilain* from Latin *villanus* person living on a country estate (Latin *villa*)]
• **villainess** *noun*
• **villainize** *verb* (also esp. *Brit.* **-ise**)
• **villainous** *adjective*
• **villainously** *adverb*
• **villainy** *noun*
HOMOPHONES: *villein*

villanelle *noun*
• "villa NELL"
• a usu. pastoral or lyric poem consisting normally of five three-line stanzas and a final quatrain, with only two rhymes throughout, and some lines repeated.
• [French from Italian *villanella* feminine of *villanello* rural, diminutive of *villano* (as VILLAIN)]

villein *noun*
• "VILL 'n"
• a feudal tenant entirely subject to a lord or attached to a manor.
• [Middle English, var. of VILLAIN]
• **villeinage** *noun*
HOMOPHONES: *villain*

villous *adjective*
• "VILL us"
• of or pertaining to villi.
• [as VILLUS]
HOMOPHONES: *villus*

villus *noun*
• "VILL us"
• any of numerous short slender hairlike projections on some membranes, esp. in the mucous membrane of the chorion or small intestines.
• [Latin, = shaggy hair]
HOMOPHONES: *villous*

vinaigrette *noun*
• "vinna GRET"
• a dressing served with salads and cold meats, made with oil, vinegar, and various seasonings.
• [French, diminutive of *vinaigre* VINEGAR]

vinarterta *noun*
• "VEENA tare tuh"
• *Cdn* an Icelandic dessert consisting of several layers of white cake with a prune filling.
• [Icelandic]

vinblastine *noun*
• "vin BLAST een"
• a cytotoxic alkaloid obtained from the Madagascar periwinkle, *Catharanthus roseus*, used to treat lymphomas and other cancers.
• [modern Latin *Vinca* former genus name of the periwinkle + Greek *blastos* sprout]

Vincentian *noun*
• "vin SEN sh'n"
• a member of a religious body, the Congregation of the Mission, established at the priory of St. Lazare in Paris in 1625 by St. Vincent de Paul.
• [St. *Vincent*]

vincristine *noun*
• "vin CRISS teen"
• a cytotoxic alkaloid obtained from the Madagascar periwinkle, *Catharanthus roseus*, used to treat acute leukemia and other cancers.
• [as VINBLASTINE, second element prob. from CRISTA]

vinculum *noun*
• "VINK yuh lum"
• a bond or tie.
• [Latin, = bond, from *vincire* bind]

vindaloo *noun*
• "vinda LOO"
• a heavily spiced hot Indian curry dish made with meat, fish, or poultry.
• [prob. from Portuguese *vin d'alho* wine and garlic (sauce), from *vinho* wine + *alho* garlic]

vindicate *verb*
• "VINDA cate"
• clear (a person, oneself, etc.) of blame, suspicion, or criticism by evidence or demonstration.
• [Latin *vindicare* claim, avenge, from *vindex -dicis* claimant, avenger]
• **vindication** *noun*
• **vindicator** *noun*

vindictive *adjective*
• "vin DICTIV"
• tending to seek revenge.
• [Latin *vindicta* vengeance (as VINDICATE)]
• **vindictively** *adverb*
• **vindictiveness** *noun*

vinegar *noun*
• "VINNA gur"
• a sour liquid consisting mainly of dilute acetic acid, produced by the oxidation of the alcohol in wine or cider etc., and used as a condiment or food preservative.
• [Old French *vyn egre*, ultimately from Latin *vinum* wine + *acer, acre* sour]
• **vinegared** *adjective*
• **vinegary** *adjective*

vineyard *noun*
• "VIN yurd"
• a plantation of grapevines, esp. one cultivated for winemaking.
• ['vine' from French *vigne* vine, from Latin *vinea* vineyard, from *vinum* wine + 'yard' from Old English]
• **vineyardist** *noun*

viniculture *noun*
• "VINNA cull chur"
• the cultivation of grapes for the production of wine.
• [Latin *vinum* wine + CULTURE]
• **viniculturist** *noun*

vinifera *adjective*
• "vie NIFFER uh"
• of, derived from, or designating the vine *Vitis vinifera* or its grape, native to Europe and also widely cultivated in N America.
• [modern Latin]

vinification *noun*
• "vin iffa CAY sh'n"
• the conversion of grape juice etc. into wine by fermentation.
• [Latin *vinum* wine]
• **vinify** *verb*

vino *noun*
• "VEENO"
• wine.
• [Spanish & Italian, = wine, from Latin *vinum* wine]

vinous *adjective*
• "VIE nuss"
• of, like, or associated with wine.
• [Latin *vinum* wine]

vintage *noun*
• "VIN tidge"
• the year in which the grapes are picked for the production of a particular wine.
• [alteration (influenced by VINTNER) of Middle English *vendage, vindage* from Old French *vendange* from Latin *vindemia* from *vinum* wine + *demere* remove]

vintner *noun*
• "VINT nur"
• a person who makes or sells wine.
• [Old French *vinetier* from medieval Latin *vinetarius* from Latin *vinetum* vineyard, from *vinum* wine]

vinyl *noun*
• "VINE 'll"
• the radical $-CH{:}CH_2$, derived from ethylene by removal of a hydrogen atom.
• [Latin *vinum* wine]

Viognier *noun*
• "vee ON yay"
• a variety of white wine grape, grown traditionally in the northern Rhone region of France, but also elsewhere since the 1980s, noted for producing wine with a floral, fruity aroma and for its relative scarcity.
• [French]

viol *noun*
• "VIE 'll"
• a musical instrument of the Renaissance and Baroque periods, having five, six, or seven strings, often with frets, played with a bow and held vertically on the knees or between the legs.
• [Old French *viole* from Provençal *viola, viula*, prob. ultimately from Latin *vitulari* be joyful]
HOMOPHONES: *vial, vile*

viola[1] *noun*
• "vee OH luh"
• a four-stringed musical instrument of the violin family, larger than the violin and of lower pitch.

• [Italian & Spanish, prob. from Provençal: see VIOL]

viola² *noun*
• "vie OH luh" or "vee OH luh"
• any plant of the genus *Viola*, including the pansy and violet.
• [Latin, = violet]

violaceous *adjective*
• "vie a LAY sh'ss"
• of a violet colour; purplish blue.
• [VIOLA² + Latin adjective suffix *-aceus* of the nature of]

violate *verb*
• "VIE a late"
• fail to observe or comply with.
• [Latin *violare* treat violently]
• **violation** *noun*
• **violator** *noun*

violent *adjective*
• "VIE a l'nt"
• involving or characterized by the use of great physical force, esp. in order to cause injury.
• [Old French from Latin *violentus*]
• **violence** *noun*
• **violently** *adverb*

violin *noun*
• "vie a LIN"
• a musical instrument with four strings of treble pitch, rested on the shoulder beneath the chin and played with a bow.
• [Italian *violino* diminutive of VIOLA¹]
• **violinist** *noun*
• **violinistic** *adjective*

violist *noun*
• "vee OLE ist"
• a person who plays a viola.
• [as VIOLA¹]

violoncello *noun*
• "vee a l'n CHELLO" or "vie a l'n CHELLO"
• the second-largest instrument of the violin family, held upright on the floor between the knees of the seated player.
• [Italian, diminutive of *violone* (as VIOLIN)]
• **violoncellist** *noun*

vipassana *noun*
• "vuh PASSA nuh"
• (in Buddhism) meditation involving concentration on the body or its sensations, or the insight which this provides.
• [Pali, lit. 'inward vision']

virago *noun*
• "vuh ROGGO" or "vuh RAY go"
• a domineering, abusive, or ill-tempered woman.
• [Old English from Latin, = female warrior, from *vir* man]

virelay *noun*
• "VEERA lay"
• a song or short lyric poem, originating in 14th-c. France, usu. consisting of stanzas composed of short lines and rhymes variously arranged.
• [Old French *virelai*]

vireo *noun*
• "VEERY oh"
• any small plain songbird of the family Vireonidae, inhabiting woodlands throughout the western hemisphere.
• [Latin, perhaps = greenfinch]

virescence *noun*
• "veer ESS ince"
• greenness.
• [Latin *virescere*, inceptive of *virēre* be green]
• **virescent** *adjective*

Virgilian *adjective*
• "vur JILLY 'n"
• of or characteristic of the work of Roman poet Virgil (d.19 BC).

virgule *noun*
• "VUR gyool"
• a slanting line used to mark a pause in a line of medieval manuscripts or a division of lines in poetry; a solidus.
• [French, = comma, from Latin *virgula* diminutive of *virga* rod]

viridescent *adjective*
• "veera DESS'nt"
• approaching green in colour; greenish.
• [Late Latin *viridescere* from Latin *viridis* green]
• **viridescence** *noun*

viridian *noun*
• "vuh RIDDY 'n"
• a bright bluish-green chromium oxide pigment.
• [Latin *viridis* green]

virile *adjective*
• "VEER ile" or "VEER 'll"
• of, belonging to, or characteristic of a man; manly, masculine.
• [French *viril* or Latin *virilis* from *vir* man]
• **virility** *noun* "vuh RILLA tee"

virilization *noun*
ALSO SPELLED: esp. *Brit.* **virilisation**
• "veer'll ize AY sh'n"
• the abnormal development of secondary male characteristics in a female, usu. as a result of excess androgen production.
• [as VIRILE]
• **virilize** *verb* (also esp. *Brit.* **-ise**)

virion *noun*
• "VIE ree 'n"
• the complete infective form of a virus outside a host cell, with a core and a capsid.
• [as VIRUS]

viroid *noun*
• "VIE roid"
• an infectious entity affecting plants, similar

to a virus but smaller and consisting only of nucleic acid without a protein coat.
• [as VIRUS]

virology *noun*
• "vie RAWLA jee"
• the branch of science that deals with the study of viruses.
• [as VIRUS + Greek *logos* word]
• **virological** *adjective*
• **virologically** *adverb*
• **virologist** *noun*

virtu *noun*
ALSO SPELLED: **vertu**
• "vur TOO"
• an interest or expertise in the fine arts.
• [Italian *virtù* virtue, virtu, from Latin *virtus -tutis* from *vir* man]

virtuoso *noun*
• "vur choo OH so" or "vur tyoo OH so" or "vur choo OH zo" or "vur tyoo OH zo"
• a person who has mastered the technique of a fine art, esp. music.
• [Italian, = learned, skilful, from Late Latin (as VIRTU)]
• **virtuosic** *adjective* "vur choo OSSIC" or "vur tyoo OSSIC"
• **virtuosity** *noun*

virtuous *adjective*
• "VUR choo us" or "VUR tyoo us"
• possessing or displaying moral rectitude.
• [as VIRTU]
• **virtuously** *adverb*
• **virtuousness** *noun*

virulent *adjective*
• "VEER oo l'nt" or "VEER yoo l'nt"
• violently bitter or rancorous; full of acrimony or hostility.
• [Latin *virulentus* (as VIRUS)]
• **virulence** *noun*
• **virulently** *adverb*

virus *noun*
• "VIE russ"
• a submicroscopic organism that can multiply only inside living host cells, has a non-cellular structure lacking any intrinsic metabolism and usu. comprising a single DNA or RNA molecule inside a protein coat, and is usu. pathogenic.
• [Latin, = slimy liquid, poison]
• **viral** *adjective*
• **virally** *adverb*

visage *noun*
• "VIZ idge"
• a face, a countenance.
• [Old French from Latin *visus* sight, past participle of *vidēre* see]
• **visaged** *adjective*

viscacha *noun*
• "vis CATCHA"
• any S American burrowing rodent of the genus *Lagidium* of the chinchilla family, having valuable fur.
• [Spanish from Quechua *(h)uiscacha*]

viscera *plural noun*
• "VISSER uh"
• the interior organs in the great cavities of the body, e.g. heart, liver, esp. in the abdomen, e.g. the intestines.
• [Latin, pl. of *viscus*: see VISCUS]

visceral *adjective*
• "VISSER 'll"
• relating to inward feelings or instinct rather than conscious reasoning.
• [as VISCERA]
• **viscerally** *adverb*

viscid *adjective*
• "VISS id"
• glutinous, sticky.
• [Late Latin *viscidus* from Latin *viscum* birdlime]

viscoelastic *adjective*
• "visko a LASTIC"
• (of a substance) exhibiting both elastic and viscous behaviour.
• [as VISCID + ELASTIC]
• **viscoelasticity** *noun*
"visko e lass TISSA tee"

viscometer *noun*
• "viss COMMA tur"
• an instrument for measuring the viscosity of liquids.
• [as VISCID + Greek *metron* measure]
• **viscometric** *adjective* "visko METRIC"
• **viscometry** *noun*

viscose *noun*
• "VISS cose" (rhymes with *GROSS*)
• a form of cellulose in a highly viscous state suitable for drawing into yarn.
• [Late Latin *viscosus* (as VISCOUS)]

viscount *noun*
• "VIE count"
• a nobleman ranking between an earl or count and a baron.
• [Anglo-French *viscounte*, Old French *vi(s)conte* from medieval Latin *vicecomes -mitis* (*vice* 'in place of', *comes comitis* companion)]
• **viscountcy** *noun*

viscountess *noun*
• "VIE count ess"
• a viscount's wife or widow.
• [as VISCOUNT]

viscous *adjective*
• "VISS cuss"
• glutinous, sticky.
• [Anglo-French *viscous* or Late Latin *viscosus* (as VISCID)]
• **viscosity** *noun* "viss COSSA tee"
HOMOPHONES: *viscus*

viscus *noun*
• "VISS cuss"
• any of the soft internal organs of the body.
• [Latin]
HOMOPHONES: *viscous*

vise *noun*
ALSO SPELLED: esp. *Brit.* **vice**
• "VICE"
• an instrument, esp. attached to a workbench, with two movable jaws between which an object may be clamped so as to leave the hands free to work on it.
• [Middle English, = winding stair, screw, from Old French *vis* from Latin *vitis* vine]
• **viselike** *adjective* (also esp. *Brit.* **vicelike**)
HOMOPHONES: *vice*

visible *adjective*
• "VIZZA bull"
• that can be seen by the eye.
• [Old French *visible* or Latin *visibilis* from *vidēre vis-* see]
• **visibility** *noun*
• **visibly** *adverb*

Visigoth *noun*
• "VIZZA goth"
• a West Goth, a member of the branch of the Goths who settled in France and Spain in the 5th c. and ruled much of Spain until 711.
• [Late Latin *Visigothus*]
• **Visigothic** *adjective*

vision *noun*
• "VIZH'n"
• the act or faculty of seeing, sight.
• [Old French from Latin *visio -onis* (as VISIBLE)]
• **visionless** *adjective*

visionary *adjective*
• "VIZH'n airy"
• having vision or foresight.
• [as VISION]

visitant *noun*
• "VIZZA t'nt"
• a visitor, esp. a supposedly supernatural one.
• [Old French, present participle of *visiter*, from Latin *visitare* go to see, frequentative of *visare* view, from *vidēre vis-* see]

visitor *noun*
• "VIZZA tur"
• a person who visits a person or place.
• [as VISITANT]
• **visitorial** *adjective*

visor *noun*
• "VIE zur"
• a movable part of a helmet covering the face.
• [Anglo-French *viser*, Old French *visiere* from *vis* face, from Latin *visus*: see VISAGE]
• **visored** *adjective*

visual *adjective*
• "VIZH oo 'll" or "VIZH yoo 'll"
• of, concerned with, or used in seeing.
• [Late Latin *visualis* from Latin *visus* sight, from *vidēre* see]
• **visuality** *noun*
• **visually** *adverb*

visualize *verb*
ALSO SPELLED: esp. *Brit.* **-ise**
• "VIZH oo 'll ize" or "VIZH yoo 'll ize"
• make visible esp. to one's mind (a thing not visible to the eye).
• [as VISUAL]
• **visualizable** *adjective* (also esp. *Brit.* **-isable**)
• **visualization** *noun* (also esp. *Brit.* **-isation**)

vitamin *noun*
• "VITE a min"
• any of a group of organic compounds essential in small amounts for many living organisms to maintain normal health and development.
• [originally *vitamine* from Latin *vita* life + AMINE, because originally thought to contain an amino acid]
• **vitaminize** *verb* (also esp. *Brit.* **-ise**)

vitellin *noun*
• "vuh TELL in" or "vie TELL in"
• the chief protein constituent of the yolk of an egg.
• [as VITELLUS]
HOMOPHONES: *vitelline*

vitelline *adjective*
• "vuh TELL ine" or "vie TELL ine" or "vuh TELL in" or "vie TELL in"
• of or relating to the yolk of an egg or the contents of the ovum.
• [medieval Latin *vitellinus* (as VITELLUS)]
HOMOPHONES: *vitellin*

vitellus *noun*
• "vuh TELL us" or "vie TELL us"
• the yolk of an egg.
• [Latin, = yolk]

vitiate *verb*
• "VISHY ate"
• impair the quality or efficiency of; corrupt, debase, contaminate.
• [Latin *vitiare* from *vitium* vice]
• **vitiation** *noun*

viticulture *noun*
• "VITTA cull chur"
• the cultivation of grapevines; the science or study of this.
• [Latin *vitis* vine + CULTURE]
• **viticultural** *adjective*
• **viticulturist** *noun*

vitiligo *noun*
• "vitta LIE go"
• a condition in which the pigment is lost from areas of the skin, causing whitish patches.
• [Latin]

vitreous *adjective*
- "VIT tree us"
- of, or of the nature of, glass.
- [Latin *vitreus* from *vitrum* glass]

vitrify *verb*
- "VITTRA fie"
- convert or be converted into glass or a glasslike substance esp. by heat.
- [French *vitrifier* or medieval Latin *vitrificare* (as VITREOUS)]
- **vitrification** *noun*

vitrine *noun*
- "vit TREEN"
- a glass display case.
- [French from *vitre* glass]

vitriol *noun*
- "VIT tree awl" or "VIT tree 'll"
- caustic or hostile speech, criticism, or feeling.
- [Old French *vitriol* or medieval Latin *vitriolum* sulphuric acid, from Latin *vitrum* glass (originally designating an acid with a glassy appearance)]
- **vitriolic** *adjective* "vit tree OLLIC"

vitta *noun*
- "VITTA"
- a resin canal in the fruit of some plants.
- [Latin, = band, chaplet]

vituperate *verb*
- "vuh TEW per ate"
- revile, abuse; find fault with in strong or violent language.
- [Latin *vituperare* from *vitium* vice]
- **vituperation** *noun*
- **vituperative** *adjective*
- **vituperator** *noun*

vivace *adverb*
- "viv OTCH ay"
- in a lively and brisk manner.
- [Italian from Latin (as VIVACIOUS)]

vivacious *adjective*
- "viv AY sh'ss" or "vie VAY sh'ss"
- lively, sprightly, animated.
- [Latin *vivax -acis* from *vivere* live]
- **vivaciously** *adverb*
- **vivaciousness** *noun*
- **vivacity** *noun* "viv ASSA tee"

vivarium *noun*
- "vie VERRY um" or "viv AIRY um"
- a place artificially prepared for keeping animals in (nearly) their natural state; an aquarium or terrarium.
- [Latin, = warren, fish pond, from *vivus* living, from *vivere* live]

viverrid *noun*
- "vuh VERRID" or "vie VERRID"
- any mammal of the family Viverridae, including civets, mongooses, and genets.
- [Latin *viverra* ferret]

vivid *adjective*
- "VIVVID"
- (of light or colour) strong, intense, glaring.
- [Latin *vividus* from *vivere* live]
- **vividly** *adverb*
- **vividness** *noun*

vivify *verb*
- "VIVVA fie"
- enliven, animate, make lively or living.
- [French *vivifier* from Late Latin *vivificare* from Latin *vivus* living, from *vivere* live]
- **vivification** *noun*

viviparous *adjective*
- "viv IPPER us"
- bringing forth young alive, not hatching them by means of eggs.
- [Latin *viviparus* from *vivus* living, from *vivere* live + *-parus* -bearing, from *parere* bring forth]
- **viviparity** *noun* "vivva PERRA tee"
- **viviparously** *adverb*

vivisect *verb*
- "VIVVA sect"
- perform vivisection on.
- [back-formation from VIVISECTION]

vivisection *noun*
- "VIVVA seck sh'n"
- dissection or other painful treatment of living animals for purposes of scientific research.
- [Latin *vivus* living, from *vivere* live, after DISSECTION (as DISSECT)]
- **vivisectional** *adjective*
- **vivisectionist** *noun*
- **vivisector** *noun*

vixen *noun*
- "VIX'n"
- a female fox.
- [Middle English *fixen* from Old English, feminine of 'fox']
- **vixenish** *adjective*

vizier *noun*
- "VIZZY ur" or "viz EER"
- a high official in some Muslim countries, esp. in Turkey under Ottoman rule.
- [ultimately from Arabic *wazīr* caliph's chief counsellor]
- **viziership** *noun*

Vlach *noun*
- "VLACK"
- a member of a Romanic people inhabiting Romania and parts of the former Soviet Union.
- [Bulgarian from Old Slavic *Vlachŭ* Romanian etc. from Germanic, = foreigner]

vlei *noun*
- "FLAY"
- (in South Africa) a hollow in which water collects during the rainy season.
- [Dutch dialect from Dutch *vallei* valley]

HOMOPHONES: *flay*

vocable *noun*
- "VOKE a bull"
- a word, esp. with reference to form rather than meaning.
- [French *vocable* or Latin *vocabulum* from *vocare* call]

vocabulary *noun*
- "voe CAB yoo lerry"
- the (principal) words used in a language or a particular book or branch of science etc. or by a particular author.
- [medieval Latin *vocabularius*, *-um* (as VOCABLE)]

vocalic *adjective*
- "voe CALIC"
- of or consisting of a vowel or vowels.
- [Latin *vocalis (littera)* vowel (*vocalis* vocal, from *vox vocis* voice, *littera* letter)]

vocalise *noun*
- "voke a LEEZ"
- a singing exercise using individual syllables or vowel sounds.
- [French, from *vocaliser* vocalize (as VOCALIC)]

vocation *noun*
- "voe CAY sh'n"
- a strong feeling of fitness for a particular career or occupation.
- [Old French *vocation* or Latin *vocatio* from *vocare* call]

vocational *adjective*
- "voe CAY sh'n 'll"
- of or relating to an occupation or employment.
- [as VOCATION]
- **vocationalism** *noun*
- **vocationalize** *verb* (also esp. *Brit.* **-ise**)
- **vocationally** *adverb*

vocative *noun*
- "VOCKA tiv"
- the case of nouns, pronouns, and adjectives used in addressing or invoking a person or thing.
- [Old French *vocatif -ive* or Latin *vocativus* from *vocare* call]

vociferate *verb*
- "vuh SIFFER ate"
- utter (words etc.) noisily.
- [Latin *vociferari* from *vox* voice + *ferre* bear]
- **vociferation** *noun*

vociferous *adjective*
- "voe SIFFER us"
- (of a person, speech, etc.) noisy, clamorous.
- [as VOCIFERATE]
- **vociferously** *adverb*
- **vociferousness** *noun*

vogue *noun*
- "VOE'g"
- the prevailing fashion.
- [French from Italian *voga* rowing, fashion, from *vogare* row, go well]
- **voguish** *adjective*

voguing *noun*
- "VOE ging" (with "G" as in *GIVE*)
- solo dancing with movements reminiscent of a fashion model's posing and posturing.
- [from the fashion magazine *Vogue*]

voila *interjection*
- "vwah LAH"
- expressing satisfaction or ease of accomplishment.
- [French from imperative of *voir* see + *là* there]

voile *noun*
- "VOIL" or "VWOL"
- a thin semi-transparent material.
- [French, = VEIL]

volant *adjective*
- "VOE l'nt"
- flying, able to fly.
- [French from *voler* from Latin *volare* fly]

volar *adjective*
- "VOE lur"
- of the palm or sole.
- [Latin *vola* hollow of hand or foot]

volatile *adjective*
- "VOLLA tile" or "VOLLA t'll"
- evaporating rapidly.
- [Old French *volatil* or Latin *volatilis* from *volare volat-* fly]
- **volatileness** *noun*
- **volatility** *noun* "volla TILLA tee"

volatilize *verb*
ALSO SPELLED: esp. *Brit.* **-ise**
- "vuh LATTA lize"
- cause to evaporate.
- [as VOLATILE]
- **volatilization** *noun* (also esp. *Brit.* **-isation**)

volcano *noun*
- "voll CAY no"
- a mountain or hill having an opening or openings in the earth's crust through which lava, cinders, steam, gases, etc., are or have been expelled continuously or at intervals.
- [Italian from Latin *Volcanus* Vulcan, the god of fire]

volition *noun*
- "vuh LISH'n"
- the exercise of the will.
- [French *volition* or medieval Latin *volitio* from *volo* I wish]
- **volitional** *adjective*

volk *noun*
- "FAWLK"
- the Afrikaner people.
- [Afrikaans (from Dutch), German = nation, people]

völkisch *adjective*
- "FULL kish"
- populist, nationalist, racist.
- [German]

volley *noun*
- "VOLLY"
- the simultaneous discharge of a number of weapons.
- [French *volée*, ultimately from Latin *volare* fly]
- **volleyer** *noun*

Volscian *noun*
- "VOL sh'n"
- a member of an ancient people formerly inhabiting eastern Latium in central Italy, in conflict with Rome from the 5th c. BC until finally defeated in 304 BC.
- [Latin *Volsci*]

voltaic *adjective*
- "vole TAY ick"
- of electricity from a primary battery; galvanic.
- [A. *Volta*, Italian physicist d.1824]

voltameter *noun*
- "vole TAMMA tur"
- an instrument for measuring an electric charge.
- [A. *Volta*, Italian physicist d.1824 + Greek *metron* measure]

voltammetry *noun*
- "vole TAMMA tree"
- a technique for identifying and finding the concentrations of various ions in solution by plotting the relation of current and voltage in a micro-electrode.
- [A. *Volta*, Italian physicist d.1824 + AMPERE + Greek *metron* measure]
- **voltammetric** *adjective* "vole tuh METRIC"

volte *noun*
ALSO SPELLED: **volt**
- "VOLT" (rhymes with *BOLT*)
- a sideways circular movement of a horse.
- [French from Italian *volta* turn, feminine past participle of *volgere* turn, from Latin *volvere* roll]

HOMOPHONES: *volt*

voluble *adjective*
- "VOL yoo bull"
- speaking or spoken vehemently, incessantly, or fluently.
- [French *voluble* or Latin *volubilis* from *volvere* roll]
- **volubility** *noun*
- **volubleness** *noun*
- **volubly** *adverb*

volumetric *adjective*
- "vol yoo METRIC"
- of or relating to measurement by volume.
- [VOLUMINOUS + METRIC]
- **volumetrically** *adverb*

voluminous *adjective*
- "vuh LOOMIN us"
- large in volume; bulky.
- [Old French *volum(e)* from Latin *volumen -minis* roll, from *volvere* to roll]
- **voluminously** *adverb*
- **voluminousness** *noun*

voluntarism *noun*
- "VOL 'n tuh rizm"
- the principle of relying on voluntary action rather than compulsion, esp. as regards social welfare.
- [as VOLUNTARY]
- **voluntarist** *noun*

voluntary *adjective*
- "VOL 'n terry"
- done, acting, or able to act of one's own free will; not constrained or compulsory, intentional.
- [Old French *volontaire* or Latin *voluntarius* from *voluntas* will]
- **voluntarily** *adverb*
- **voluntariness** *noun*

volunteer *noun*
- "vol 'n TEER"
- a person who voluntarily takes part in an enterprise or offers to undertake a task.
- [French *volontaire* (as VOLUNTARY)]
- **volunteering** *noun*

volunteerism *noun*
- "vol 'n TEER izm"
- the involvement of volunteers, esp. in community service.
- [as VOLUNTEER]

voluptuary *noun*
- "vuh LUP choo airy"
- a person given up to luxury and sensual pleasure.
- [Latin *volupt(u)arius* (as VOLUPTUOUS)]

voluptuous *adjective*
- "vuh LUP choo us" or "vuh LUP tyoo us"
- of, tending to, occupied with, or derived from, sensuous or sensual pleasure.
- [Old French *voluptueux* or Latin *voluptuosus* from *voluptas* pleasure]
- **voluptuously** *adverb*
- **voluptuousness** *noun*

volute *noun*
- "VOL yoot" or "vuh LYOOT" or "vuh LOOT"
- a spiral scroll characteristic of Ionic capitals and also used in Corinthian and composite capitals.
- [French *volute* or Latin *voluta* feminine past participle of *volvere* roll]
- **voluted** *adjective*

vomer *noun*
- "VOE mur"
- the small thin bone separating the nostrils in humans and most vertebrates.
- [Latin, = ploughshare]

voodoo *noun*
- "VOO doo"
- a religion practised in the W Indies (esp. Haiti) and the southern US, characterized by sorcery and spirit possession, and combining elements of traditional African religious rites with Roman Catholic ritual.

• [Louisiana French *voudou* from Fon *vodu* tutelary deity, fetish]
• **voodooism** *noun*
• **voodooist** *noun*

voracious *adjective*
• "vuh RAY sh'ss"
• greedy in eating, ravenous.
• [Latin *vorax* from *vorare* devour]
• **voraciously** *adverb*
• **voraciousness** *noun*
• **voracity** *noun* "vuh RASSA tee"
HOMOPHONES: *veracious*, *veracity*

vortex *noun*
• "VORE tex"
• a mass of whirling fluid, esp. a whirlpool or whirlwind.
• [Latin *vortex -icis* eddy, var. of VERTEX]
• **vortical** *adjective*
• **vorticity** *noun* "vore TISSA tee"

vorticella *noun*
• "vorta SELLA"
• any sedentary protozoan of the family Vorticellidae, consisting of a tubular stalk with a bell-shaped ciliated opening.
• [modern Latin, diminutive of VORTEX]

vorticist *noun*
• "VORTA sist"
• an artist of a British movement *c.*1914–15 influenced by futurism and cubism and characterized by harsh machine-like forms.
• [as VORTEX]
• **vorticism** *noun* "VORTA sizm"

votary *noun*
• "VOTE a ree"
• a devoted follower of a religion, deity, or cult, esp. one who is bound, by vow, to the worship of God.
• [Latin *vot-* from *vovēre* vow]

votive *adjective*
• "VOE tiv"
• offered or undertaken in fulfillment of a vow or as a thanksgiving.
• [Latin *votivus* (as VOTARY)]

voussoir *noun*
• "VOO swarr"
• each of the wedge-shaped or tapered stones or bricks forming an arch or vaulting.
• [Old French *vossoir* etc., from popular Latin *volsorium*, ultimately from Latin *volvere* roll]

voxel *noun*
• "VOX'll"
• each of an array of discrete elements into which a representation of a three-dimensional object is divided; a three-dimensional pixel.
• [blend of 'volume' + 'element', with *-x* inserted for ease of pronunciation]

voyageur *noun*
• "voy a ZHUR" or "vwah ya ZHUR"
• esp. *Cdn* (historically) a usu. French-speaking or Metis canoeman employed by merchants in Montreal to transport goods to and from trading posts in the interior.
• [French, lit. 'voyager' from Old French *voiage* from Latin *viaticum* voyage, from *via* road]

voyeur *noun*
• "voy UR"
• a person who derives sexual gratification from the covert observation of others as they undress or engage in sexual activities.
• [French, from *voir* see]
• **voyeurism** *noun*
• **voyeuristic** *adjective*
• **voyeuristically** *adverb*

vulcanite *noun*
• "VULL k'n ite"
• a hard black vulcanized rubber, ebonite.
• [as VULCANIZE]

vulcanize *verb*
ALSO SPELLED: esp. *Brit.* **-ise**
• "VULL k'n ize"
• treat (rubber or rubber-like material) with sulphur at a high temperature to increase its durability and elasticity.
• [*Vulcan* Roman god of fire (original meaning 'throw into a fire')]
• **vulcanization** *noun* (also esp. *Brit.* **-isation**)
• **vulcanizer** *noun* (also esp. *Brit.* **-iser**)

vulgar *adjective*
• "VULL gur"
• likely to offend; indecent, rude, obscene.
• [Latin *vulgaris* from *vulgus* common people]
• **vulgarity** *noun* "vull GARE it ee"
• **vulgarization** *noun* (also esp. *Brit.* **-isation**)
• **vulgarize** *verb* (also esp. *Brit.* **-ise**)
• **vulgarly** *adverb*

vulgarian *noun*
• "vull GARE ee 'n"
• a vulgar person.
• [as VULGAR]

vulgarism *noun*
• "VULL gur izm"
• a coarse or obscene word or expression.
• [as VULGAR]

vulnerable *adjective*
• "VULL nur a bull"
• able to be physically or emotionally hurt.
• [Late Latin *vulnerabilis* from Latin *vulnerare* to wound, from *vulnus -eris* wound]
• **vulnerability** *noun*
• **vulnerably** *adverb*

vulpine *adjective*
• "VULL pine"
• resembling or characteristic of a fox.
• [Latin *vulpinus* from *vulpes* fox]

Ww

wacke *noun*
- "WACKA"
- a greyish-green or brownish rock resulting from the decomposition of basaltic rock.
- [German from Middle High German *wacke* large stone, Old High German *wacko* pebble]

wadi *noun*
ALSO SPELLED: **wady**
- "WODDY"
- a rocky watercourse in North Africa etc., dry except in the rainy season.
- [Arabic *wādī*]

waggery *noun*
- "WAGGER ee"
- waggish behaviour, joking.
- [prob. from obsolete *waghalter* one likely to be hanged (Old English *wagian* sway, *hælftre* halter)]

waggish *adjective*
- "WAG ish"
- amusing, witty, facetious, tongue-in-cheek.
- [as WAGGERY]
- **waggishly** *adverb*
- **waggishness** *noun*

Wagnerian *adjective*
- "vog NERRY 'n"
- of, relating to, or characteristic of the German operatic composer Richard Wagner (d.1883) or his music and theories of musical and dramatic composition.

Wahhabi *noun*
ALSO SPELLED: **Wahabi**
- "wuh HOBBY"
- a member of a strictly orthodox Sunni Muslim sect founded in the 18th c. by Muhammad ibn Abd al-Wahhab, who called for a return to the earliest doctrines and practices of Islam as embodied in the Quran and Sunna.
- [Abd al-*Wahhab*]
- **Wahhabism** *noun* (also **Wahabism**)

wahoo *noun*
- "wa HOO"
- a large marine fish of the Scombridae family, *Acanthocybium solanderi*, which is a streamlined and fast-swimming predator and is found in all tropical seas.
- [20th c.: origin unknown]

wainscot *noun*
- "WAYNE scott"
- panelling of oak or other wood lining, esp. covering the lower part of a wall of a room.
- [Middle Low German *wagenschot*, apparently from *wagen* wagon + *schot* of uncertain meaning]

wainwright *noun*
- "WAYNE rite"
- a person who makes wagons.
- [Old English *wǣn* wagon, WRIGHT]

waive *verb*
- "WAVE"
- decline to take advantage of (a right, claim, opportunity, etc.); relinquish.
- [Anglo-French *weyver*, Old French *gaiver* allow to become a waif, abandon]

HOMOPHONES: *wave*

waiver *noun*
- "WAIVER"
- the act or an instance of waiving a right, claim, etc.
- [as WAIVE]

HOMOPHONES: *waver*

wakame *noun*
- "WACKA may"
- an edible brown seaweed, typically in dried form, used in Chinese and Japanese cookery.
- [Japanese]

Wakashan *noun*
- "WOCKA shan"
- an Aboriginal language family of the west coast of N America, including such languages as Haisla, Heiltsuk, Kwakwala, and Nuu-chah-nulth.
- [*Wakash*, a former name for the Nuu-chah-nulth, from Nuu-chah-nulth *wa·kaš* 'bravo!']

Waldenses *plural noun*
- "wall DEN seez"
- a puritan religious sect originally in S France, now chiefly in Italy and the US, founded *c.*1170 and much persecuted.
- [medieval Latin from Peter *Waldo* of Lyons, founder]
- **Waldensian** *adjective*

wale *noun*
- "WALE"

• a ridge or raised line of threads on a woven fabric, such as corduroy.
• [Old English *walu* stripe, ridge]
HOMOPHONES: *whale, wail*

wallaby *noun*
• "WOLLA bee"
• any of various marsupials of the family Macropodidae, smaller than kangaroos, and having large hind feet and long tails.
• [Dharuk *walabi* or *waliba*]

Wallaceburger *noun*
• "WALL us burger"
• a resident of Wallaceburg, Ont.

wallah *noun*
• "WOLLA"
• a person concerned with or in charge of a usu. specified thing, business, etc.
• [Hindi *-wālā* agent suffix]

wallaroo *noun*
• "wolla ROO"
• a large brownish-black kangaroo, *Macropus robustus*.
• [Dharuk *wolarū*]

walley *noun*
• "WOLLY"
• a figure skating jump taking off from the back inside edge of the skating foot, completing one complete reverse rotation in the air, and landing on the back outside edge of the same foot.
• [origin unknown]

Walloon *noun*
• "wah LOON"
• a member of a French-speaking people inhabiting S and E Belgium and neighbouring parts of France.
• [French *Wallon* from medieval Latin *Wallo -onis* from Germanic]

wallow *verb*
• "WALL oh"
• (esp. of an animal) lie or roll around in mud, sand, water, etc.
• [Old English *walwian* roll, from Germanic]
• **wallower** *noun*

wallyball *noun*
• "WOLLY ball"
• a game resembling volleyball played in an indoor court like that used for squash or racquetball.
• [blend of 'wall' + 'volleyball']

walnut *noun*
• "WALL nut"
• any tree of the genus *Juglans*, having aromatic leaves and drooping catkins, e.g. the N American black walnut, *J. nigra*.
• [Old English *walh-hnutu* foreign nut]

walrus *noun*
• "WALL russ"
• a large amphibious long-tusked Arctic mammal, *Odobenus rosmarus*, related to the seal and sea lion.
• [prob. from Dutch *walrus, -ros*, perhaps by metathesis after *walvisch* 'whale-fish' from word represented by Old English *horschwæl* 'horse-whale']

waltz *noun*
• "WALTS"
• a dance in triple time performed by couples who rotate and progress around the floor.
• [German *Walzer* from *walzen* revolve]
• **waltzer** *noun*

Wampanoag *noun*
• "wompa NO ug"
• a member of a N American Aboriginal people of southeastern Massachusetts and the eastern shore of Narragansett Bay.
• [Narragansett, lit. = 'easterners']

wampum *noun*
• "WOM pum"
• small, cylindrical blue and white beads cut from the shell of the quahog and woven into strings or belts by Aboriginal peoples of the eastern woodlands and Atlantic coast of N America to be used as a medium of exchange or to record treaties.
• [Algonquian *wampumpeag* from *wap* white + *umpe* string + *-ag* pl. suffix]

wan *adjective*
• "WONN" (rhymes with *DON*)
• (of a person's complexion or appearance) pale, pallid, sickly; exhausted; worn.
• [Old English *wann* dark, black, of unknown origin]
• **wanly** *adverb*
HOMOPHONES: *won*

Wanderjahr *noun*
• "VONDER yar"
• a year spent travelling abroad, typically immediately before or after a university or college course.
• [German, lit. 'wander year']

wanderoo *noun*
• "wonda ROO"
• a langur, *Semnopithecus vetulus*, of Sri Lanka.
• [Sinhalese *wanderu* monkey]

wane *verb*
• "WANE"
• (of the moon) decrease in apparent size after the full moon.
• [Old English *wanian* lessen, from Germanic]
HOMOPHONES: *wain*

wanigan *noun*
• "WAN a g'n" ("WAN" rhymes with *VAN*)
• a watertight box or receptacle for cooking supplies and food, as used by canoeists or at a lumber camp.
• [Algonquian]

wannabe *noun*
• "WONNA bee"
• a person who tries to emulate a particular celebrity, follow the lifestyle of a particular group, etc.; an aspirant.
• [representing informal pronunciation of *want to be*]

wanton *adjective*
• "WON t'n"
• capricious; random; arbitrary; motiveless.
• [Middle English *wantowen* (*wan-* not + *towen* from Old English *togen* past participle of *tēon* discipline, related to 'team')]
• **wantonly** *adverb*
• **wantonness** *noun*

wapentake *noun*
• "WOP 'n take"
• (in areas of England with a large Viking population) a division of a shire.
• [Old English *wǣpen(ge)tæc* from Old Norse *vápnatak* from *vápn* weapon + *tak* taking, from *taka* take: perhaps with reference to voting in assembly by show of weapons]

wapiti *noun*
• "WOP it ee" or "WAP it ee"
• an elk.
• [Cree *wapitik* white deer]

ware *verb*
• "WARE"
• manufactured articles of a specified type.
• [Old English *waru* from Germanic, perhaps originally = 'object of care']
HOMOPHONES: *wear*, *where*

warehouse *noun*
• "WARE house"
• a building in which esp. retail goods are stored and from which they are distributed to retailers etc.; a repository.
• [as WARE + 'house']
• **warehouseman** *noun*
• **warehouser** *noun*

warfare *noun*
• "WORE fare"
• the activity of fighting a war, esp. of a particular type.
• ['war' from Anglo-French, Old Northern French var. of Old French *guerre* from Germanic *werra* + FARE]

warfarin *noun*
• "WORFER in"
• a water-soluble anticoagulant derived from coumarin used esp. as a rat poison and in the treatment of thrombosis.
• [Wisconsin Alumni Research Foundation + *-arin*, after COUMARIN]

warmonger *noun*
• "WORE mong gur" or "WORE mung gur"
• a person who seeks to bring about or promote war.
• ['war' from Anglo-French, Old Northern French var. of Old French *guerre* from Germanic *werra* + MONGER]
• **warmongering** *noun*

warrant *noun*
• "WORE 'nt"
• anything that authorizes a person or an action.
• [Old Northern French *warant*, var. of Old French *guarant*, *-and* from Frankish *werēnd* from *giwerēn* be surety for]

warrantable *adjective*
• "WORE 'nt a bull"
• (of an action or statement) able to be authorized or sanctioned; justifiable.
• [as WARRANT]
• **warrantability** *noun*

warrantee *noun*
• wore 'n TEE"
• a person to whom a warranty is given.
• [as WARRANT]
HOMOPHONES: *warranty*

warranty *noun*
• "WORE 'n tee"
• a manufacturer's written promise as to the extent to which defective goods will be repaired, replaced, etc.
• [as WARRANT]
HOMOPHONES: *warrantee*

warrior *noun*
• "WORE ee ur"
• a person experienced or distinguished in fighting in an armed force etc.
• [Old Northern French *werreior* etc., Old French *guerreior* etc. from *werreier*, *guerreier* make war]

wary *adjective*
• "WARE ee"
• on one's guard; given to caution; circumspect.
• [Old English *wær* aware, from Germanic]
• **warily** *adverb*
• **wariness** *noun*
HOMOPHONES: *wherry*

wasabi *noun*
• "wuh SOBBY"
• a cruciferous plant, *Eutrema wasabi*, with a thick green root which tastes like strong horseradish and is used in Japanese cooking, usu. ground as an accompaniment to raw fish.
• [Japanese]

Washingtonian *noun*
• "washing TONY 'n"
• a resident of Washington D.C. or Washington state.

wassail *noun*
• "woss ALE" or "WOSS'll"
• a festive occasion, esp. during the Christmas season.
• [Middle English *wæs hæil* etc. from Old Norse

ves heill, corresponding to Old English *wes hāl* 'be in health', a form of salutation]
• **wassailer** *noun*

waste *verb*
• "WAIST"
• use to no purpose or for inadequate result or extravagantly.
• [Old Northern French *wast(e)*, var. of Old French *g(u)ast(e)*, from Latin *vastus* unoccupied, uncultivated]
• **wasted** *adjective*
• **wasteful** *adjective*
• **wastefully** *adverb*
• **wastefulness** *noun*
• **waster** *noun*
HOMOPHONES: *waist, waisted*

wastebasket *noun*
• "WAIST basket"
• a receptacle for waste paper.
• [WASTE + 'basket' from Anglo-French *basket*, Anglo-Latin *baskettum*, of unknown origin]

wasteland *noun*
• "WAIST land"
• an unproductive or useless or devastated area of land.
• [as WASTE + 'land']

wastrel *noun*
• "WAIST rull"
• a wasteful or good-for-nothing person.
• [as WASTE]

wat *noun*
• "WOT"
• a Buddhist monastery or temple in Thailand or Cambodia.
• [Thai from Sanskrit *vāṭa* enclosure]
HOMOPHONES: *watt, what*

waterfowl *noun*
• "WATER foul"
• birds frequenting water, esp. swimming game birds.
• ['water' + FOWL]

waterfowling *noun*
• "WATER fouling"
• the hunting of waterfowl for sport or food.
• [as WATERFOWL]
• **waterfowler** *noun*

watt *noun*
• "WOT"
• the SI unit of power, equivalent to one joule per second, corresponding to the rate of energy in an electric circuit where the potential difference is one volt and the current one ampere.
• [J. *Watt*, Scottish engineer d.1819]
HOMOPHONES: *wat, what*

wattage *noun*
• "WOT idge"
• an amount of electrical power expressed in watts, esp. the operating power of an appliance etc.
• [as WATT]

wattle *noun*
• "WOT'll"
• a loose fleshy appendage on the head or throat of a turkey or other birds.
• [16th c.: origin unknown]
• **wattled** *adjective*
HOMOPHONES: *waddle*

waver *verb*
• "WAIVER"
• be or become unsteady; falter; begin to give way.
• [Old Norse *vafra* flicker, from Germanic, related to 'wave']
• **waverer** *noun*
• **waveringly** *adverb*
• **wavery** *adjective*
HOMOPHONES: *waiver*

wayfarer *noun*
• "WAY fare ur"
• a traveller, esp. on foot.
• ['way' from Old English *weg* + FARE]
• **wayfaring** *noun*

wayward *adjective*
• "WAY wurd"
• childishly self-willed or perverse; capricious.
• [obsolete *awayward* turned away, from 'away' + '-ward' indicating direction]
• **waywardly** *adverb*
• **waywardness** *noun*

weal *noun*
• "WEEL"
• welfare, prosperity; good fortune.
• [Old English *wela* from West Germanic (related to 'well')]
HOMOPHONES: *wheel*

wean *verb*
• "WEEN"
• accustom (an infant or other young mammal) to food other than (esp. its mother's) milk.
• [Old English *wenian* accustom, from Germanic: compare WONT]
HOMOPHONES: *ween*

weaner *noun*
• "WEENER"
• a young animal recently weaned.
• [as WEAN]
HOMOPHONES: *wiener*

weanling *noun*
• "WEEN ling"
• a newly-weaned animal etc.
• [as WEAN]

wearisome *adjective*
• "WEER ee sum"
• tedious; tiring by monotony or length.
• [Old English *wērig*, *wǣrig* weary, from West Germanic]

• **wearisomely** *adverb*
• **wearisomeness** *noun*

weasel *noun*
• "WEEZ'll"
• any of various small carnivorous mammals of the family Mustelidae, with a slender body, including ermines, minks, and ferrets, and noted for their ferocity, esp. the long-tailed weasel of N America, *Mustela frenata*, having a brown and yellow coat, or the least weasel of N America and Eurasia, *M. nivalis*, with a very short tail and brown and white coat.
• [Old English *wesle, wesule* from West Germanic]
• **weaselly** *adjective*

weber *noun*
• "VAY bur"
• the SI unit of magnetic flux, causing the electromotive force of one volt in a circuit of one turn when generated or removed in one second.
• [W. E. *Weber*, German physicist d.1891]

Wednesday *noun*
• "WENZ day" or "WENZ dee"
• the fourth day of the week, following Tuesday.
• [Middle English *wednesdei*, Old English *wōdnesdæg* day of (the god) Odin]

weevil *noun*
• "WEEV 'll"
• any destructive beetle of the family Curculionidae, with its head extended into a beak or rostrum and feeding esp. on grain.
• [Middle Low German *wevel* from Germanic]
• **weevily** *adjective*

Wehrmacht *noun*
• "VARE moct"
• the German armed forces, esp. the army, from 1921–1945.
• [German, = defensive force]

weigela *noun*
• "wye GEELA" or "WYE guh luh" (with "G" as in *GUEST*) or "wye JEELA"
• any of various Asian shrubs of the genus *Weigela*, of the honeysuckle family, with pink, white or red flowers, grown as an ornamental.
• [modern Latin, from C. E. *Weigel*, German physician d.1831]

weigh *verb*
• "WAY"
• determine the heaviness of (a body or substance), esp. using scales.
• [Old English *wegan* from Germanic, related to 'way']
• **weigher** *noun*
HOMOPHONES: *whey, way*

weight *noun*
• "WAIT"
• the force experienced by a body as a result of the earth's gravitational pull.
• [Old English *(ge)wiht*: compare WEIGH]
• **weighted** *adjective*
• **weightily** *adverb*
• **weightiness** *noun*
• **weightless** *adjective*
• **weightlessly** *adverb*
• **weightlessness** *noun*
• **weighty** *adjective*
HOMOPHONES: *wait*

weighting *noun*
• "WAITING"
• emphasis or priority.
• [as WEIGHT]
HOMOPHONES: *waiting*

weightlifting *noun*
• "WAIT lifting"
• the sport or exercise of lifting heavy weights.
• [as WEIGHT + 'lift' from Old Norse *lypta*]
• **weightlifter** *noun*

Weimaraner *noun*
• "wye muh RANNER" or "vye muh RANNER"
• a breed of pointer, with a short usu. grey coat and drooping ears, originally bred as a hunting dog in the Weimar region.
• [German, from the city of *Weimar*]

weir *noun*
• "WEER"
• a dam built across a river to raise the level of water upstream or regulate its flow.
• [Old English *wer* from *werian* dam up]

weird *adjective*
• "WEERD"
• strange, unusual, out of the ordinary, bizarre.
• [(earlier as noun) from Old English *wyrd* destiny, from Germanic]
• **weirdly** *adverb*
• **weirdness** *noun*

weirdo *noun*
• "WEER doe"
• a strange or abnormal person.
• [as WEIRD]

welcome *noun*
• "WELL k'm"
• a kind or hospitable reception given to a visitor or stranger upon arriving.
• [originally Old English *wilcuma* one whose coming is pleasing, from *wil-* desire, pleasure + *cuma* comer, with later change to *wel-* well, after Old French *bien venu* or Old Norse *velkominn*]
• **welcomer** *noun*
• **welcoming** *adjective*
• **welcomingly** *adverb*

welfare *noun*
• "WELL fair"
• well-being, happiness; health and prosperity of a person or a community etc.
• ['well' + FARE]

welkin *noun*
• "WELL kin"

• sky; the upper air.
• [Old English *wolcen* cloud, sky]

Wellander *noun*
• "WELL'n dur"
• a resident of Welland, Ont.

wellington *noun*
• "WELLING t'n"
• a waterproof rubber or plastic boot usu. reaching the knee, worn in wet or muddy conditions.
• [the Duke of *Wellington*, British general and statesman d.1852]

Weltanschauung *noun*
• "vell tan SHOU 'ng" ("SHOU" rhymes with *HOW*)
• a comprehensive view or philosophy of life, the world, and the universe; a world view.
• [German from *Welt* world + *Anschauung* perception]

welterweight *noun*
• "WELTER wate"
• a weight class in certain sports intermediate between lightweight and middleweight, in the amateur boxing scale 63.5–67 kg but differing for professionals and wrestlers.
• ['welter' (of unknown origin) + WEIGHT]

Weltschmerz *noun*
• "VELT shmairts"
• a feeling of pessimism; an apathetic or vaguely yearning outlook on life.
• [German from *Welt* world + *Schmerz* pain]

wen *noun*
• "WEN"
• a sebaceous cyst on or under the skin, esp. on the head.
• [Old English *wen*, *wenn*, of unknown origin: compare Dutch *wen*, Middle Low German *wene*, Low German *wehne* tumour, wart]
HOMOPHONES: *when*

Wensleydale *noun*
• "WENZ lee dale"
• a variety of hard flaky white or blue veined cheese made from cow's milk.
• [*Wensleydale* in Yorkshire]

wentletrap *noun*
• "WENT'll trap"
• any marine snail of the genus *Clathrus*, with a spiral shell of many whorls.
• [Dutch *wenteltrap* winding stair, spiral shell]

werewolf *noun*
• "WARE wolf" or "WEER wolf"
• a mythical being who at times changes from a person to a wolf.
• [Old English *werewulf*: first element perhaps from Old English *wer* man = Latin *vir*]

wergild *noun*
• "WARE gild"
• (in Germanic and Anglo-Saxon law) the price put on a person according to his or her rank, payable as a fine or compensation by a person guilty of homicide or certain other crimes.
• [Old English *wergeld*, Anglo-Latin *weregildum*, from *wer* man + *gield* yield]

Wesleyan *adjective*
• "WEZZLY 'n" or "WESSLY 'n"
• of or relating to the English evangelist John Wesley (d.1791) or to Methodism.

Westphalian *adjective*
• "west FAILY 'n"
• of or relating to Westphalia in NW Germany.

wether *noun*
• "WETHER"
• a castrated ram.
• [Old English]
HOMOPHONES: *weather*, *whether*

whale *verb*
• "WALE"
• beat, thrash.
• [var. of WALE]
HOMOPHONES: *wail*, *wale*

whang *verb*
• "WANG"
• produce a loud resonating or ringing sound under or as if under a forceful blow.
• [imitative]

whangee *noun*
• "wang GEE" (with "G" as in *GEEK*)
• a Chinese or Japanese bamboo of the genus *Phyllostachys*.
• [Chinese *huang* old bamboo sprouts]

wharf *noun*
• "WORF"
• a level quayside structure to which a ship may be moored to load and unload.
• [Old English *hwearf*]

wharfage *noun*
• "WORF idge"
• the provision of accommodation or storage at a wharf.
• [as WHARF]

wharfinger *noun*
• "WORF 'n jur"
• an owner or keeper of a wharf.
• [prob. ultimately from WHARFAGE]

whatchamacallit *noun*
• "WUTCHA muh call it" or "WOTCHA muh call it"
• a thing the proper name of which one cannot recall, does not know, or does not wish to mention.
• [representing a pronunciation of *what you may call it*]

wheatear *noun*
• "WEET eer"
• any small migratory bird of the mainly Old World genus *Oenanthe*, esp. with a white belly and rump.

• [apparently from *wheatears* white rump, from Old English *hwīt* white, *ærs* rump]

wheedle *verb*
• "WEED'll"
• attempt to coax or persuade (a person) by flattery or endearments.
• [perhaps from German *wedeln* fawn, cringe, from *Wedel* tail]
• **wheedler** *noun*
• **wheedling** *adjective*
• **wheedlingly** *adverb*

wheelwright *noun*
• "WEEL rite"
• a person who makes or repairs esp. wooden wheels.
• ['wheel' + WRIGHT]

wheeze *verb*
• "WEEZ"
• breathe with an audible congested whistling sound, due to dryness or obstruction of the air passages.
• [prob. from Old Norse *hvæsa* to hiss]
• **wheezer** *noun*
• **wheezily** *adverb*
• **wheeziness** *noun*
• **wheezy** *adjective*

whelk *noun*
• "WELK"
• any predatory marine gastropod mollusc of the family Buccinidae, esp. the edible kind of the genus *Baccinum*, having a spiral shell.
• [Old English *wioloc*, *weoloc*, of unknown origin]

whelp *noun*
• "WELP"
• a young dog; a puppy.
• [Old English *hwelp*]

wherewithal *noun*
• "WARE with all" (with "TH" as in *BATH* or *BATHE*)
• the means by which to do something.
• ['where' + 'with' + 'all']

wherry *noun*
• "WERRY"
• a light rowboat usu. for carrying passengers.
• [Middle English: origin unknown]
HOMOPHONES: *wary*

whet *verb*
• "WET"
• sharpen (a tool or weapon).
• [Old English *hwettan* from Germanic]
• **whetter** *noun*
HOMOPHONES: *wet*, *wetter*

whether *conjunction*
• "WETHER"
• introducing an indirect question or an expression of doubt or choice between alternatives, in which the final alternative is introduced by *or* or *or whether*.
• [Old English *hwæther*, *hwether*]
HOMOPHONES: *wether*, *weather*

whetstone *noun*
• "WET stone"
• a shaped fine-grained stone used to sharpen tools and cutlery etc. by grinding.
• [WHET + 'stone']

whey *noun*
• "WAY"
• the watery liquid that remains when milk forms curds.
• [Old English *hwæg*, *hweg* from Low German]
HOMOPHONES: *weigh*, *way*

whicker *verb*
• "WICKER"
• (of a horse) give a soft breathy whinny.
• [imitative]
HOMOPHONES: *wicker*

whiff *noun*
• "WIFF"
• a puff or breath of air, smoke, etc.
• [imitative]

whiffle *verb*
• "WIFF'll"
• (of the wind) blow gently.
• [as WHIFF]

whiffletree *noun*
• "WIFF'll tree"
• a crossbar pivoted in the middle, to which the traces are attached in a cart, plow, etc.
• [var. of WHIPPLETREE]

whiffy *adjective*
• "WIFFY"
• having an unpleasant smell.
• [as WHIFF]

Whig *noun*
• "WIG"
• a member of the English (later British) reforming and constitutional party that after 1688 sought the supremacy of Parliament and was eventually succeeded in the 19th c. by the Liberal Party.
• [prob. a shortening of Scots *whiggamer*, *-more*, nickname of 17th-c. Scottish rebels, from *whig* to drive + 'mare']
• **Whiggery** *noun*
• **Whiggish** *adjective*
HOMOPHONES: *wig*

whim *noun*
• "WIM"
• a spontaneous and unaccountable idea or decision; a fanciful or capricious notion.
• [17th c.: origin unknown]

whimbrel *noun*
• "WIM brull"
• a small curlew, esp. *Numenius phaeopus*, with a striped head and a trilling call.
• [as WHIMPER (imitative)]

whimper *verb*
• "WIM pur"
• make feeble, querulous, or plaintive sounds expressive of fear, pain, or distress; cry and whine softly.
• [imitative, from dialect *whimp* to whimper, of imitative origin]
• **whimperingly** *adverb*

whimsical *adjective*
• "WIMZA k'll"
• spontaneous; inspired by whim.
• [as WHIM]
• **whimsicality** *noun* "wimza CALA tee"
• **whimsically** *adverb*

whimsy *noun*
• "WIM zee"
• an unpredictable, fanciful, or playful quality or condition.
• [as WHIM]

whin *noun*
• "WIN"
• gorse.
• [prob. Scandinavian: compare Norwegian *hvine*, Swedish *hven*]
HOMOPHONES: *win*

whinchat *noun*
• "WIN chat"
• a small brownish songbird, *Saxicola rubetra*, of Eurasia and N Africa.
• [WHIN + 'chat' imitative of its cry]

whine *noun*
• "WINE"
• a subdued, prolonged, plaintive cry or wail suggesting pain, distress, or complaint.
• [Old English *hwīnan*]
• **whiner** *noun*
• **whiningly** *adverb*
• **whiny** *adjective* (also **whiney**)
HOMOPHONES: *wine, winey*

whinge *verb*
• "WINDGE" (rhymes with *HINGE*)
• whine or grumble in a peevish complaining manner; gripe.
• [Old English *hwinsian* from Germanic]
• **whinger** *noun*

whinny *noun*
• "WIN ee"
• a gentle high-pitched neigh, usu. expressing pleasure.
• [imitative: compare WHINE]

whippersnapper *noun*
• "WIPPER snapper"
• a presumptuous or intrusive young person.
• [perhaps for *whipsnapper*, implying noise and unimportance]

whippet *noun*
• "WIP it"
• a dog of a breed that is a cross between a greyhound and a terrier or spaniel, used for racing.
• [prob. from obsolete *whippet* move briskly, from *whip it*]

whippletree *noun*
• "WIPP'll tree"
• a crossbar pivoted in the middle, to which the traces are attached in a cart, plow, etc.
• [apparently from 'whip' + 'tree']

whippoorwill *noun*
• "WIPPER will"
• a N American bird of the goatsucker family, *Caprimulgus vociferus*, with a loud cry uttered repeatedly at dusk and during the night.
• [imitative of its cry]

whir *noun*
ALSO SPELLED: **whirr**
• "WUR"
• a continuous droning, humming, or buzzing sound like that of machinery or the fluttering of a bird's wings.
• [Middle English, prob. Scandinavian: compare Danish *hvirre*, Norwegian *kvirra*, perhaps related to WHIRL]

whirl *verb*
• "WURL"
• turn around rapidly, esp. repeatedly.
• [Middle English: (v.) from Old Norse *hvirfla*: (n.) from Middle Low German & Middle Dutch *wervel* spindle & Old Norse *hvirfill* circle, from Germanic]
• **whirler** *noun*
• **whirling** *adjective*
HOMOPHONES: *whorl*

whirligig *noun*
• "WURLY gig" (with "G" as in *GIVE*)
• anything having a rapid circling movement.
• [WHIRL + obsolete *gig* a spinning top]

whirlpool *noun*
• "WURL pool"
• a powerful circular eddy in a body of water that draws or sucks objects to its centre, usu. caused by the meeting of adverse currents.
• [WHIRL + 'pool' from Old English *pōl*]

whirlwind *noun*
• "WURL wind"
• a small rotating storm of wind in which a vertical usu. funnel-shaped column of air whirls rapidly around a core of low pressure and moves progressively over land or water.
• [WHIRL + 'wind' from Old English]

whirlybird *noun*
• "WURLY bird"
• a helicopter.
• [WHIRL + 'bird' from Old English *brid*]

whisht *verb*
• "HWISHT"
• be quiet; hush.
• [imitative]

whisk *verb*
- "WISK"
- brush lightly with a sweeping movement.
- [Middle English *wisk*, prob. Scandinavian: compare Old Norse *visk* wisp]

whisker *noun*
- "WISKER"
- any of the hairs growing on a person's face.
- [as WHISK]
- **whiskered** *adjective*
- **whiskery** *adjective*

whisky *noun*
ALSO SPELLED: **whiskey**
- "WISKY"
- an alcoholic liquor distilled esp. from rye, malted barley, or corn.
- [abbreviation of obsolete *whiskybae*, var. of USQUEBAUGH]

whisper *verb*
- "WISS pur"
- say or speak in a soft breathy voice without vibration of the vocal cords, esp. for the sake of secrecy or intimacy.
- [Old English *hwisprian*]
- **whisperer** *noun*
- **whispering** *noun*

whist *noun*
- "WIST"
- a card game for four players grouped into pairs, in which points are scored according to the number of tricks won and, in some forms, by the highest trumps or honours held by each pair.
- [earlier *whisk*, perhaps from WHISK (with reference to whisking away the tricks)]

whistle *noun*
- "WISS'll"
- a clear shrill sound made by forcing breath through the narrow opening made by contracting the lips or through a space between the teeth constricted by the tip of the tongue.
- [Old English *(h)wistle*, of imitative origin: compare Old Norse *hvísla* whisper, Middle Swedish *hvisla* whistle]
- **whistler** *noun*

whistlepunk *noun*
- "WISS'll punk"
- esp. *Cdn* (*BC*) a member of a logging crew who relays to the donkeyman the hooktender's signal that the logs have been secured with chokers and may be hauled away.
- [as WHISTLE + 'punk' of unknown origin]

Whistlerite *noun*
- "WISSLER ite"
- a resident of Whistler, BC.

whit *noun*
- "WIT"
- the least possible amount.
- [earlier *w(h)yt* apparently alteration of WIGHT in phrase *no wight* etc.]

HOMOPHONES: *wit*

whitebait *noun*
- "WITE bate"
- a small silvery-white fish caught in large numbers and eaten whole, comprising the young of herrings and sprats.
- ['white' + BAIT]

whitlow *noun*
- "WIT lo"
- an inflammation near a fingernail or toenail.
- [Middle English *whitflaw*, *-flow*, apparently = 'white' + 'flaw' in the sense 'crack', but perhaps of Low German origin: compare Dutch *fijt*, Low German *fit* whitlow]

Whitsun *noun*
- "WIT sun"
- a Christian festival observed on the seventh Sunday after Easter, commemorating the descent of the Holy Spirit on the disciples; Pentecost.
- [Middle English, from *Whitsun Day* from 'white' (the newly baptized wearing white robes)]

Whitsuntide *noun*
- "WIT sun tide"
- the weekend or week including Pentecost.
- [as WHITSUN]

whittle *verb*
- "WIT'll"
- cut, shape, or pare (wood, a stick, etc.) by carving thin shavings from the surface with a knife.
- [var. of Middle English *thwitel* long knife, from Old English *thwītan* to cut off]

whiz *noun*
ALSO SPELLED: **whizz**
- "WIZZ"
- the sibilant humming or buzzing sound made by the friction of a body moving through the air at great speed.
- [imitative]
- **whizzer** *noun*

HOMOPHONES: *wiz*

whodunit *noun*
ALSO SPELLED: **whodunnit**
- "hoo DUN it"
- a story about the detection of a crime, esp. murder; a mystery.
- [= *who done* (illiterate for *did*) *it?*]

wholesome *adjective*
- "HOLE sum"
- promoting physical health or well-being.
- [Middle English, prob. from Old English (unrecorded) *hālsum*]
- **wholesomely** *adverb*
- **wholesomeness** *noun*

wholly *adverb*
- "HOLE ee"
- entirely, completely; without limitation.
- [from 'whole' from Old English *hāl*]

HOMOPHONES: *holy, holey, Holi*

whomp *noun*
• "WOMP"
• a loud dull heavy sound.
• [imitative]

whoop *noun*
• "WOOP" (with "OO" either as in *HOOT* or in *HOOD*) or "HOOP"
• a loud cry of or as of excitement etc.
• [Middle English: imitative]
HOMOPHONES: *hoop*

whoopee *interjection*
• "woo PEE" (with "OO" as in *HOOD*)
• expressing exuberant joy.
• [as WHOOP]

whooper *noun*
• "WOOP ur" or "HOOP ur" (with "OO" as in *LOOP*)
• a whooping crane, a large endangered N American crane, *Grus americana*, with mainly white plumage, which passes through the Prairie provinces in migration between N Alberta and Texas.
• [as WHOOP]

whoops *interjection*
• "WOOPS" (with "OO" as in *HOOD*)
• expressing surprise or apology, esp. on making an obvious mistake.
• [var. of 'oops']

whorl *noun*
• "WORL" or "WURL"
• a ring of leaves or other organs round a stem of a plant.
• [Middle English *wharwyl*, *whorwil*, apparently var. of WHIRL: influenced by *wharve* (n.) = whorl of a spindle]
• **whorled** *adjective*
HOMOPHONES: *whirl*

whortleberry *noun*
• "WURT'll berry"
• a bilberry.
• [16th c.: dialect form of *hurtleberry*, Middle English, of unknown origin]

whose *pronoun*
• "HOOZ"
• of or belonging to which person.
• [Old English genitive *hwæs* from *hwā* who, from Germanic]

whump *verb*
• "WUMP"
• make or move or knock with a dull thudding sound.
• [imitative]

whup *verb*
• "WUP"
• whip, beat.
• [Scots var. of 'whip' (from Middle English *(h)wippen*, prob. from Middle Low German & Middle Dutch *wippen* swing, leap, dance)]

whydah *noun*
ALSO SPELLED: **whidah**
• "WIDDA"
• any small African weaver bird of the genus *Vidua*, the male having mainly black plumage and tail feathers of great length.
• [originally *widow bird*, altered from assoc. with *Whidah* (now Ouidah) in Benin]

Wiartonian *noun*
• "wire TONY 'n"
• a resident of Wiarton, Ont.

Wicca *noun*
• "WICKA"
• the religious cult of modern witchcraft, a goddess-worshipping, shamanistic nature religion.
• [Old English *wicca* witch]
• **Wiccan** *adjective*

wickiup *noun*
• "WICKY up"
• a hut used by some N American Aboriginal peoples, consisting of a frame covered with grass etc.
• [Fox *wikiyap*]

widgeon *noun*
ALSO SPELLED: **wigeon**
• "WIDGE 'n"
• a species of dabbling duck, esp. the baldpate of N America or *Anas penelope* of Europe.
• [16th c.: origin uncertain]

wield *verb*
• "WEELD"
• hold and use (a weapon or tool).
• [Old English *wealdan*, *wieldan* from Germanic]
• **wielder** *noun*

wieldy *adjective*
• "WEELDY"
• easily wielded, controlled, or handled.
• [as WIELD]

wiener *noun*
• "WEENER"
• a frankfurter.
• [German, abbreviation of *Wienerwurst*, lit. 'Vienna sausage']
HOMOPHONES: *weaner*

wight *noun*
• "WITE"
• a person.
• [Old English *wiht* = thing, creature, of unknown origin]
HOMOPHONES: *white*

wigwam *noun*
• "WIG wom"
• (among some N American Aboriginal peoples) a house consisting of bent saplings stuck in the ground in a dome shape and covered with birch bark.
• [Ojibwa *wigwaum*, Algonquin *wikiwam* their house]

Wildean *adjective*
• "WILE dee 'n"
• of or relating to the Irish writer Oscar Wilde (d.1900).

wildebeest *noun*
• "WILL duh beest" or "VILL duh beest"
• any antelope of the genus *Connochaetes*, native to S Africa, with a large erect head and brown stripes on the neck and shoulders; a gnu.
• [Afrikaans]

wilderness *noun*
• "WILL dur niss"
• a wild, uncultivated, and uninhabited region.
• [Old English *wildēornes* from *wild dēor* wild deer]

wildfowl *noun*
• "WILD foul"
• a game bird, esp. an aquatic one.
• ['wild' + FOWL]

wile *noun*
• "WILE"
• a stratagem; a trick or cunning procedure.
• [Middle English *wīl*, perhaps from Scandinavian (Old Norse *vél* craft)]
HOMOPHONES: *while*

willet *noun*
• "WILL it"
• a large grey and white N American shorebird, *Catoptrophorus semipalmatus*, with a loud call.
• [*pill-will-willet*, imitative of its call]

Wilsonian *adjective*
• "will SO nee 'n"
• of or relating to the policies of W. Wilson, US president 1913–21.

wily *adjective*
• "WILE ee"
• full of wiles; crafty, cunning.
• [as WILE]
• **wiliness** *noun*

wimple *noun*
• "WIMP'll"
• a linen or silk headdress covering the neck and the sides of the face, formerly worn by women and still worn by some nuns.
• [Old English *wimpel*]

windage *noun*
• "WIND idge" ("WIND" rhymes with *FINNED*)
• the friction of air against the moving part of a machine.
• [Old English *wind* wind]

windbreak *noun*
• "WIND brake"
• an obstacle, such as a row of trees, a fence, wall, etc. serving to break the force of the wind and shelter houses, crops, or animals.
• [Old English *wind* wind + 'break' from Old English *brecan*]

windbreaker *noun*
• "WIND braker"
• a kind of wind-resistant outer jacket with close-fitting neck, cuffs, and hip band.
• [as WINDBREAK]

windhover *noun*
• "WIND huvver" ("WIND" rhymes with *FINNED*)
• any of several falcons distinguished by the habit of hunting by sustained hovering; a kestrel.
• [Old English *wind* wind + HOVER]

Windigo *noun*
• "WIN dig oh"
• (in the folklore of Northern Algonquian peoples) a cannibalistic giant; a person who has been transformed into a monster by the consumption of human flesh.
• [Ojibwa *wintiko*]

windlass *noun*
• "WIND luss" ("WIND" rhymes with *FINNED*)
• a machine with a horizontal axle for hauling or hoisting.
• [alteration of (perhaps by assoc. with dialect *windle* to wind) of obsolete *windas* from Old French *guindas* from Old Norse *vindáss* from *vinda* wind (v.) + *áss* pole]

windrow *noun*
• "WIN droe"
• a line of raked hay, sheaves, etc., laid out for drying by the wind.
• [Old English *wind* wind + 'row' from Old English *rōwan*]

Winnipegger *noun*
• "WINNA pegger"
• a resident of Winnipeg.

winnow *verb*
• "WIN oh"
• expose (grain) to the wind or to a current of air so that unwanted lighter particles of chaff are separated or blown away.
• [Old English *windwian*, from *wind* wind]
• **winnower** *noun*

winsome *adjective*
• "WIN sum"
• (of a person, looks, or manner) winning, attractive, engaging.
• [Old English *wynsum* from *wyn* joy]
• **winsomely** *adverb*
• **winsomeness** *noun*

Wiradhuri *noun*
• "wur ADGER ee"
• an Aboriginal language of SE Australia, now extinct.
• [Wiradhuri]

wiry *adjective*
• "WIRE ee"
• resembling wire in texture or appearance, esp. stiff and flexible.
• [Old English *wīr* wire]
• **wiriness** *noun*

wiseacre *noun*
• "WIZE ake ur"
• a foolish person with an air or affectation of wisdom.
• [Middle Dutch *wijsseggher* soothsayer, prob. from Old High German *wīssago, wīzago*, assimilated to 'wise', 'acre']

wisent *noun*
• "WEEZ 'nt"
• the European bison, *Bison bonasus*.
• [German]

wisteria *noun*
• "wiss TEERY uh"
• any climbing plant of the genus *Wisteria*, with hanging racemes of blue, purple, or white flowers.
• [C. *Wistar* (or *Wister*), US anatomist d.1818]

wistful *adjective*
• "WIST full"
• (of a person, looks, etc.) yearningly or mournfully expectant or wishful.
• [apparently assimilation of obsolete *wistly* (adverb) intently (compare WHISHT) to *wishful*, with corresponding change of sense]
• **wistfully** *adverb*
• **wistfulness** *noun*

witchetty *noun*
• "WITCHA tee"
• a large white larva of an Australian beetle or moth, eaten as food by Aborigines.
• [Adnyamahanha, an Aboriginal language]

withdrawal *noun*
• "with DRAWL" or "with DRAW 'll" (with "TH" either as in *BATH* or as in *BATHE*)
• the act or an instance of withdrawing.
• [Middle English from *with-* away + 'draw']

withe *noun*
• "WITH" (with "TH" either as in *BATH* or as in *BATHE*) or "WYTHE" (with "TH" as in *BATHE*)
• a strong flexible shoot esp. of willow or osier, or several of these twisted together, used for tying a bundle of wood, binding planks of a raft, etc.
• [Old English *withthe, withig* from Germanic, related to 'wire']
HOMOPHONES: *with*

withers *plural noun*
• "WITHERZ" (with "TH" as in *BATHE*)
• the highest part of the back of a horse, sheep, ox, etc., lying between the shoulder blades.
• [shortening of (16th-c.) *widersome* (or *-sone*) from *wider-, wither-* against, as the part that resists the strain of the collar: second element obscure]

withershins *adverb*
• "WITHER shinz" (with "TH" as in *BATHE*)
• in a direction contrary to the sun's course (considered as unlucky).
• [Middle Low German *weddersins* from Middle High German *widdersinnes* from *wider* against + *sin* direction]

withhold *verb*
• "with HOLD"
• restrain or hold back from action.
• [Middle English from *with-* away + 'hold']
• **withholder** *noun*

withy *noun*
• "WITHY" (with "TH" as in *BATHE*)
• a willow of any species.
• [as WITHE]

witticism *noun*
• "WITTA sizm"
• a witty remark.
• [coined by English writer John Dryden (d.1700) from 'witty', after *criticism*]

wizard *noun*
• "WIZZ'rd"
• a man who practises magic; a sorcerer.
• [Middle English from 'wise' from Old English *wīs*]
• **wizardly** *adjective*
• **wizardry** *noun*

wizened *adjective*
• "WIZZ'nd"
• shrivelled or wrinkled, esp. with age.
• [past participle of *wizen* shrivel, from Old English *wisnian* from Germanic]

woad *noun*
• "WODE"
• a cruciferous plant, *Isatis tinctoria*, yielding a blue dye now superseded by indigo.
• [Old English *wād* from Germanic]

woebegone *adjective*
• "WOE buh gon"
• sad, miserable, or dismal in appearance.
• [Old English *wā, wǣ* sorrow + *begone* = surrounded, from Old English *begān*]

woeful *adjective*
• "WOE full"
• afflicted with sorrow, distress, or misfortune.
• [Old English *wā, wǣ* sorrow]
• **woefully** *adverb*
• **woefulness** *noun*

wok *noun*
• "WOCK"
• a large bowl-shaped frying pan used in esp. Chinese cooking.
• [Cantonese]
HOMOPHONES: *walk*

wold *noun*
• "WOLD" (rhymes with *BOLD*)
• a tract of high open uncultivated land or moor.
• [Old English *wald* from Germanic, perhaps related to 'wild']

wolffish *noun*
• "WOOLF fish"
• any of various aggressive large deepwater

marine fishes of the family Anarhichadidae which have long bodies and large doglike teeth.
- ['wolf' + 'fish']

HOMOPHONES: *wolfish*

wolfram *noun*
- "WOOL frum"
- tungsten.
- [German: perhaps from *Wolf* wolf + *Rahm* cream, or Middle High German *rām* dirt, soot]

wolframite *noun*
- "WOOL frum ite"
- a monoclinic tungstate of iron and manganese, which occurs as black to brown crystals, blades, granules, and masses, and is the chief ore of tungsten.
- [as WOLFRAM]

wolfsbane *noun*
- "WOOLFS bane"
- an aconite, esp. *Aconitum lycoctonum*.
- ['wolf' + BANE]

Wolof *noun*
- "wall OFF"
- a member of an African people of Senegal and Gambia.
- [Wolof]

wolverine *noun*
- "wool vur EEN"
- a carnivorous animal, *Gulo luscus* of N America or *Gulo gulo* of Europe, of the weasel family, resembling a small bear, with dark brown fur and a long bushy tail.
- [16th-c. *wolvering*, formed obscurely from *wolv-*, stem of 'wolf']

womb *noun*
- "WOOM"
- the organ in the body of a woman or female mammal in which offspring are carried, protected, and nourished before birth; the uterus.
- [Old English *wamb*, *womb*]
- **womblike** *adjective*

won *noun*
- "WONN" (rhymes with *DON*)
- the basic monetary unit of North and South Korea, equal to 100 chon.
- [Korean]

HOMOPHONES: *wan*

wondrous *adjective*
- "WUN druss"
- wonderful.
- [alteration of obsolete *wonders* (adjective), = genitive of 'wonder' after *marvellous*]
- **wondrously** *adverb*

wont *predicative adjective*
- "WONT" (rhymes either with *HAUNT* or with *DON'T*)
- accustomed.
- [Old English *gewunod* past participle of *gewunian* from *wunian* dwell]

HOMOPHONES: *want*

wonted *adjective*
- "WAHN tid" or "WONE tid"
- habitual, accustomed, usual.
- [as WONT]

HOMOPHONES: *wanted*

woodruff *noun*
- "WOOD ruff"
- a white-flowered plant of the genus *Galium*, esp. *G. odoratum* grown for the fragrance of its whorled leaves when dried or crushed.
- [Old English *wudurofe*, from *wudu* wood + an element of unknown meaning]

woodsia *noun*
- "WOODZY uh"
- any of various woodland ferns of the genus *Woodsia*, with lacy fronds.
- [J. *Woods*, English architect and botanist d.1864]

Woodstonian *noun*
- "wood STONEY 'n"
- a resident of Woodstock, Ont.

woolly *adjective*
- "WOOLY"
- bearing or naturally covered with wool or wool-like hair; downy.
- [Old English *wull* wool]
- **woolliness** *noun*

woomera *noun*
- "WOOMER uh"
- an Australian Aboriginal stick for throwing a dart or spear more forcibly.
- [Dharuk *wamara*]

Wordsworthian *adjective*
- "wurdz WURTHY 'n" (with "TH" as in *THICK*)
- of or relating to the English poet William Wordsworth (d.1850).

worriment *noun*
- "WURRY m'nt"
- the act of worrying or state of being worried.
- [Old English *wyrgan* strangle, worry, from West Germanic]

worrisome *adjective*
- "WURRY sum"
- causing or apt to cause worry or distress.
- [as WORRIMENT]
- **worrisomely** *adverb*

worrywart *noun*
- "WURRY wort"
- a person who habitually worries unduly.
- [as WORRIMENT]

worshipful *adjective*
- "WUR ship full"
- a title given to officers of certain organizations.
- [Old English *weorthscipe* worship (related to 'worth')]
- **worshipfully** *adverb*

worsted *noun*
• "WUR stid"
• a fine smooth yarn spun from combed long staple wool.
• [*Worste(a)d* in Norfolk, England]

wort *noun*
• "WURT" or "WORT"
• a plant or herb.
• [Old English *wyrt*: related to 'root']
HOMOPHONES: *wart*

woundwort *noun*
• "WOOND wurt" or "WOOND wort"
• any of various plants esp. of the genus *Stachys*, formerly supposed to have healing properties.
• [Old English *wund* wound + WORT]

wowser *noun*
• "WOW zur"
• a puritanical fanatic.
• [20th c.: origin uncertain]

wrack *noun*
• "RACK"
• seaweed cast up or growing on the shore.
• [Middle Dutch *wrak* or Middle Low German *wra(c)k*, a parallel formation to Old English *wræc*, related to *wrecan* WREAK]
HOMOPHONES: *rack*

wraith *noun*
• "RAITH"
• a ghost or apparition.
• [16th-c. Scots: origin unknown]
• **wraithlike** *adjective*

wrangle *noun*
• "RANGLE"
• a heated or prolonged argument, altercation, or dispute.
• [Middle English, prob. from Low German or Dutch: compare Low German *wrangelen*, frequentative of *wrangen* to struggle, related to WRING]
• **wrangling** *noun*

wrangler *noun*
• "RANG glur"
• a cowboy.
• [as WRANGLE]

wrasse *noun*
• "RASS"
• any bright-coloured marine fish of the family Labridae with thick lips and strong teeth.
• [Cornish *wrach*, var. of *gwrach*, = Welsh *gwrach*, lit. 'old woman']

wrath *noun*
• "RATH"
• extreme anger.
• [Old English *wrǣththu* from *wrāth* angry]
• **wrathful** *adjective*
• **wrathfully** *adverb*
• **wrathfulness** *noun*

wreak *verb*
• "REEK"
• give vent or expression to (vengeance, anger, etc.).
• [Old English *wrecan* drive, avenge, etc., from Germanic]
• **wreaker** *noun*
HOMOPHONES: *reek*

wreath *noun*
• "REETH"
• flowers or leaves fastened in a ring esp. as an ornament for a person's head or a building or for laying on a grave etc. as a mark of honour or respect.
• [Old English *writha* from *wrīthan* WRITHE]

wreathe *verb*
• "REETHE" (with "TH" as in *BATHE*)
• encircle as, with, or like a wreath.
• [partly back-formation from archaic *wrethen* past participle of WRITHE; partly from WREATH]

wreck *noun*
• "RECK"
• the destruction or disablement esp. of a ship.
• [Anglo-French *wrec* etc. (compare VAREC) from a Germanic root meaning 'to drive']
• **wrecked** *adjective*
• **wrecker** *noun*
HOMOPHONES: *reck, rec*

wreckage *noun*
• "RECK idge"
• wrecked material.
• [as WRECK]

wrecking *noun*
• "RECK ing"
• the demolition of old cars, buildings, etc., often to obtain usable scrap.
• [as WRECK]

wren *noun*
• "REN"
• any small usu. brown short-winged songbird of the family Troglodytidae, esp. *Troglodytes troglodytes* of N America and Eurasia, having an erect tail.
• [Old English *wrenna*]

wrench *noun*
• "RENCH"
• a violent twist or oblique pull or act of tearing off.
• [Old English *wrencan* twist]

wrenching *adjective*
• "RENCH ing"
• painfully traumatic.
• [as WRENCH]

wrest *verb*
• "REST"
• force or wrench away from a person's grasp.
• [Old English *wrǣstan* from Germanic, related to 'wrist']
HOMOPHONES: *rest*

wrestle *verb*
• "RESS'll"
• take part in a fight, either as sport or in

earnest, that involves grappling with one's opponent and trying to throw or force him to the ground.

- [Old English (unrecorded) *wrǣstlian*: compare Middle Low German *wrostelen*, Old English *wraxlian*]
- **wrestler** *noun*
- **wrestling** *noun*

wretch *noun*
- "RETCH"
- an unfortunate or unhappy person.
- [Old English *wrecca* from Germanic]
- **wretched** *adjective* "RETCH id"
- **wretchedly** *adverb*
- **wretchedness** *noun*

HOMOPHONES: *retch*

wriggle *verb*
- "RIG'll"
- (of a worm etc.) twist or turn its body with short writhing movements.
- [Middle Low German *wriggelen* frequentative of *wriggen*]
- **wriggler** *noun*
- **wriggly** *adjective*

wright *noun*
- "RITE"
- a maker or builder.
- [Old English *wryhta*, *wyrhta* from West Germanic]

HOMOPHONES: *right*, *write*, *rite*

wring *verb*
- "RING"
- squeeze tightly.
- [Old English *wringan*, related to 'wrong']

HOMOPHONES: *ring*

wringer *noun*
- "RING ur"
- a device for wringing water from washed clothes etc.
- [as WRING]

HOMOPHONES: *ringer*

wringing *adjective*
- "RING ing"
- so wet that water can be wrung out.
- [as WRING]

HOMOPHONES: *ringing*

wrinkle *noun*
- "RINKLE"
- a slight crease or depression in the skin such as is produced by age.
- [originally representing Old English *gewrinclod* sinuous]
- **wrinkled** *adjective*
- **wrinkly** *adjective*

writ *noun*
- "RIT"
- a form of written command in the name of a sovereign, court, government, etc., to act or abstain from acting in some way.
- [Old English (as WRITE)]

write *verb*
- "RITE"
- mark paper or some other surface by means of a pen, pencil, etc., with symbols, letters, or words.
- [Old English *wrītan* scratch, score, write, from Germanic: originally used of symbols inscribed with sharp tools on stone or wood]
- **writable** *adjective*
- **writer** *noun*
- **writing** *noun*

HOMOPHONES: *right*, *rite*, *wright*

writedown *noun*
- "RITE down"
- a reduction in the estimated or nominal value of stock, assets, etc.
- [as WRITE + 'down']

writeoff *noun*
- "RITE off"
- a thing written off, esp. a vehicle too badly damaged to be repaired.
- [as WRITE + 'off']

writerly *adjective*
- "RITER lee"
- characteristic of a professional author.
- [as WRITE]

writhe *verb*
- "RYTHE" (with "TH" as in *BATHE*)
- twist or roll oneself about in or as if in acute pain.
- [Old English *wrīthan*, related to WREATHE]

wrongdoer *noun*
- "RONG doo ur"
- a person who behaves immorally or illegally.
- [Old English *wrang* from Old Norse *rangr* awry, unjust + 'doer']
- **wrongdoing** *noun*

wrongful *adjective*
- "RONG full"
- characterized by unfairness or injustice.
- [Old English *wrang* from Old Norse *rangr* awry, unjust]
- **wrongfully** *adverb*
- **wrongfulness** *noun*

wry *adjective*
- "RYE"
- (of humour) dry and mocking.
- [*wry* (v.) from Old English *wrigian* tend, incline, in Middle English deviate, swerve, contort]
- **wryly** *adverb*
- **wryness** *noun*

HOMOPHONES: *rai*, *rye*

wryneck *noun*
- "RYE neck"
- a rheumatic etc. disease of the muscles of the neck, causing twisting and stiffness.
- [as WRY + 'neck']

Wu *noun*

- "WOO"
- a dialect of Chinese spoken in the Jiangsu and Zhejiang Provinces of E China.
- [Chinese]

HOMOPHONES: *woo*

Wunderkammer *noun*

- "VOONDER cammer"
- a place where a collection of curiosities and rarities is exhibited.
- [German, literally 'wonder chamber']

wunderkind *noun*

- "VOONDER kint"
- a person who achieves great success while relatively young.
- [German from *Wunder* wonder + *Kind* child]

wurst *noun*

- "VOORST" or "VURST" or "WURST"
- sausage, esp. of a German or Austrian type.
- [German]

HOMOPHONES: *versed, verst, worst*

wuss *noun*

- "WOOSS" (with "OO" as in *WOOL*)
- an inept, feeble, or cowardly person.
- [20th c.: origin unknown]
- **wussy** *noun*

Wyandot *noun*

- "WYE 'n dot"
- a member of a N American Aboriginal people originally of Ontario, now living esp. in Oklahoma.
- [French *Ouendat* from the Aboriginal name *Wendat*]

wye *noun*

- "WYE" (rhymes with *WHY*)
- a triangular arrangement of three sections of railway track, used for turning locomotives around.
- [reproducing the pronunciation of the letter *y*]

HOMOPHONES: *why*

WYSIWYG *adjective*

- "WIZZY wig"
- denoting the representation of text onscreen in a form exactly corresponding to its appearance on a printout.
- [acronym from *what you see is what you get*]

wyvern *noun*

ALSO SPELLED: **wivern**

- "WYE vurn"
- a winged two-legged dragon with a barbed tail.
- [Old French *wivre, guivre* from Latin *vipera*]

Xanadu *noun*
- “ZANNA doo”
- used to convey an impression of a place as almost unattainably luxurious or beautiful.
- [alteration of *Shang-tu*, the name of an ancient city in SE Mongolia, as portrayed in the poem *Kubla Khan* (1816) by English poet S. T. Coleridge (d.1834)]

xanthan *noun*
- “ZANTH'n”
- designating a gum which is a polysaccharide produced by fermentation and used in foods as a gelling agent, thickener, etc.
- [modern Latin, from *Xanthomonas campestris* bacteria that produces it]

xanthate *noun*
- “ZANTH ate”
- any salt or ester of xanthic acid.
- [as XANTHIC]

xanthic *adjective*
- “ZAN thick”
- yellowish.
- [Greek *xanthos* yellow]

xanthine *noun*
- “ZANTH een”
- a purine derivative found in blood and urine which is a breakdown product of nucleic acids and is the parent compound of caffeine and other alkaloids.
- [Greek *xanthos* yellow]

xanthoma *noun*
- “zanth OH muh”
- a skin disease characterized by irregular yellow patches.
- [as XANTHIC]

xanthophyll *noun*
- “ZANTH a fill”
- any of various oxygen-containing carotenoids associated with chlorophyll, some of which cause the yellow colour of leaves in autumn.
- [as XANTHIC + Greek *phullon* leaf]

xebec *noun*
ALSO SPELLED: **zebec**, **zebeck**
- “ZEE beck”
- a small three-masted Mediterranean vessel with lateen and usu. some square sails.
- [alteration (influenced by Spanish *xabeque*) of French *chebec*, via Italian *sciabecco* from Arabic *šabāk*]

xenobiology *noun*
- “zenno by OLLA jee” or “zeeno by OLLA jee”
- (esp. in science fiction) the investigation of extraterrestrial life forms.
- [Greek *xenos* strange, foreign, stranger + BIOLOGY]
- **xenobiologist** *noun*

xenobiotic *adjective*
- “zenno by OTTIC” or “zeeno by OTTIC”
- relating to or denoting a substance, typically a synthetic chemical, that is foreign to the body or to an ecological system.
- [Greek *xenos* strange, foreign, stranger + BIOTIC]

xenograft *noun*
- “ZENNO graft” or “ZEENO graft”
- a tissue graft from a donor of a different species from the recipient.
- [Greek *xenos* strange, foreign, stranger + ‘graft’ from Old French *grafe*, *grefe* from Latin *graphium* from Greek *graphion* stylus, from *graphō* write]

xenolith *noun*
- “ZENNA lith” or “ZEENA lith”
- an inclusion within an igneous rock mass, usu. derived from the immediately surrounding rock.
- [Greek *xenos* strange, foreign, stranger + *lithos* stone]
- **xenolithic** *adjective*

xenon *noun*
- “ZEN on” or “ZEEN on”
- a heavy colourless odourless inert gaseous element occurring in traces in the atmosphere and used in fluorescent lamps.
- [Greek, neuter of *xenos* strange]

xenophobia *noun*
- “zenna FOBEY uh” or “zeena FOBEY uh”
- a deep dislike of foreigners.
- [Greek *xenos* strange, foreign, stranger + PHOBIA]
- **xenophobe** *noun*

• **xenophobic** *adjective*
• **xenophobically** *adverb*

xenotransplantation *noun*
• "zeeno tranz plan TAY sh'n" or "zenno tranz plan TAY sh'n"
• the transplantation of organs or tissues from a member of one species to a member of another, esp. the transplantation of animal organs into humans.
• [Greek *xenos* strange, foreign, stranger + 'transplantation' (Latin *trans* across, *planta* sprout, cutting)]
• **xenotransplant** *noun*

xeranthemum *noun*
• "zee RANTHA mum"
• a composite plant of the genus *Xeranthemum*, with dry everlasting composite flowers.
• [modern Latin from Greek *xēros* dry + *anthemon* flower]

xeric *adjective*
• "ZEER ick"
• having or characterized by dry conditions.
• [Greek *xēros* dry]

xeriscaping *noun*
• "ZERRA scape ing"
• environmental design of park or residential land utilizing a variety of methods to minimize the need for water, fertilizer, and labour.
• [Greek *xēros* dry + 'landscaping']
• **xeriscape** *noun*

xeroderma *noun*
• "zeera DURMA"
• any of various diseases characterized by extreme dryness of the skin.
• [modern Latin (Greek *xēros* dry, *derma* skin)]

xerography *noun*
• "zeer OGGRA fee" or "zuh ROGGRA fee"
• a dry copying process in which black or coloured powder adheres to parts of a surface remaining electrically charged after exposure of the surface to light from an image of the document to be copied.
• [Greek *xēros* dry, *graphia* writing]
• **xerographic** *adjective*
• **xerographically** *adverb*

xerophilous *adjective*
• "zee ROFFA luss" or "zuh ROFFA luss"
• (of a plant) adapted to extremely dry conditions.
• [Greek *xēros* dry, *philos* dear, loving]

xerophyte *noun*
• "ZEERA fite" or "ZERRA fite"
• a plant able to grow in very dry conditions, e.g. in a desert.
• [Greek *xēros* dry, *phuton* plant, from *phuō* come into being]
• **xerophytic** *adjective* "zeera FITTIC" or "zerra FITTIC"

Xhosa *noun*
• "KO suh" or "KOSSA"
• a member of a Bantu-speaking people forming the second largest ethnic group in South Africa after the Zulus.
• [Nguni]

xi *noun*
• "SYE" or "g'ZYE" or "ZYE"
• the fourteenth letter of the Greek alphabet (Ξ, ξ).
• [Greek]
HOMOPHONES: *sigh*, *psi*

xiphoid *adjective*
• "ZIFF oid"
• sword-shaped.
• [Greek *xiphoeidēs* from *xiphos* sword]

xu *noun*
• "SOO"
• a monetary unit of Vietnam, equal to one-hundredth of a dong.
• [Vietnamese from French *sou*]
HOMOPHONES: *sue*, *Sioux*, *sou*

xylem *noun*
• "ZYE lem"
• woody tissue.
• [Greek *xulon* wood]

xylene *noun*
• "ZYE leen"
• one of three isomeric hydrocarbons formed from benzene by the substitution of two methyl groups, obtained from wood etc.
• [formed as XYLEM + '-ene' forming names of unsaturated hydrocarbons containing a double bond, from Greek *-ēnos*, adjective suffix denoting origin or source]

xylitol *noun*
• "ZYE lit awl"
• a sweet-tasting crystalline alcohol, present in some plant tissues and used as an artificial sweetener in foods.
• [Greek *xulon* wood + ALCOHOL]

xylophone *noun*
• "ZYE luh fone"
• a musical instrument of wooden or metal bars graduated in length and struck with a small wooden hammer or hammers.
• [Greek *xulon* wood + *phōnē* sound]
• **xylophonist** *noun*

yacht *noun*
• "YOT"
• a light sailing vessel, esp. equipped for racing.
• [early modern Dutch *jaghte* = *jaghtschip* fast pirate ship, from *jag(h)t* chase, from *jagen* to hunt + *schip* ship]
• **yachting** *noun*
• **yachtsman** *noun*

yachtie *noun*
• "YOTTY"
• a yachtsman.
• [as YACHT]

Yagara *noun*
• "YOGGER uh"
• an Aboriginal language of the area around Brisbane, Australia, now extinct.
• [Yagara]

yage *noun*
• "YAW hay"
• a tropical vine of the Amazon region, noted for its hallucinogenic properties.
• [American Spanish]

yahrzeit *noun*
• "YART site"
• (among Jews) the anniversary of someone's death, esp. a parent's.
• [Yiddish, lit. 'anniversary time']

Yahwist *noun*
• "YAW wist"
• the postulated author or authors of parts of the Hexateuch in which God is regularly named *Yahweh*.
• **Yahwistic** *adjective*

yak *noun*
• "YACK"
• a long-haired humped Tibetan ox, *Bos grunniens*.
• [Tibetan *gyag*]
HOMOPHONES: *yack*

yakitori *noun*
• "yacky TORY"
• a Japanese dish of skewered grilled chicken pieces.
• [Japanese, from *yaki* grilling, toasting + *tori* bird]

Yakut *noun*
• "ya KOOT" ("KOOT" rhymes with *FOOT*)
• a member of an indigenous people living in scattered settlements in northern Siberia.
• [via Russian from Yakut]

yakuza *noun*
• "yuh KOOZA"
• a Japanese gangster or racketeer; a member of a Japanese organized crime gang.
• [Japanese *ya* eight + *ku* nine + *za* three, with reference to the worst kind of hand in a gambling game]

Yanomami *noun*
• "YANNA maw mee"
• a member of an indigenous people living in the forests of S Venezuela and N Brazil.
• [the name in Yanomami, literally 'people']

yapok *noun*
• "YAP ock"
• a semi-aquatic Central and South American opossum, *Chironectes minimus*, which has grey fur with dark bands.
• [*Oyapok*, *Oiapoque*, N Brazilian river]

Yarmouthian *noun*
• "yar MUTHY 'n" (with "TH" as in *THIN*)
• a resident of Yarmouth, NS.

yarmulke *noun*
ALSO SPELLED: **yarmulka**
• "YAR m'll kuh"
• a skullcap worn by Jewish men.
• [Yiddish]

yarrow *noun*
• "YERRO"
• any perennial herb of the genus *Achillea*, esp. milfoil.
• [Old English *gearwe*, of unknown origin]

yashmak *noun*
• "YASH mack"
• a veil concealing the face except the eyes, worn by some Muslim women when in public.
• [Arabic *yašmaķ*, Turkish *yaşmak*]

yawl *noun*
• "YAWL"
• a two-masted fore-and-aft sailing boat with the mizzen-mast stepped far aft.

• [Middle Low German *jolle* or Dutch *jol*, of unknown origin]

yawp *noun*
• "YAWP"
• a harsh or hoarse cry.
• [Middle English (imitative)]
• **yawper** *noun*

yaws *plural noun*
• "YAWZ"
• a contagious tropical skin disease with large red swellings.
• [17th c.: origin unknown]

yearn *verb*
• "YURN"
• have a strong emotional longing.
• [Old English *giernan* from a Germanic root meaning 'eager']
• **yearner** *noun*
• **yearning** *noun*
• **yearningly** *adverb*

yegg *noun*
• "YEG"
• a travelling burglar or safecracker.
• [20th c.: perhaps a surname]

yellowwood *noun*
• "YELLO wood"
• a small leguminous tree of eastern N America, *Cladarastis lutea*, with yellow wood which yields a yellow dye, planted as an ornamental.
• ['yellow' + 'wood']

Yemeni *noun*
• "YEM'n ee"
• a native or inhabitant of Yemen in the S Arabian peninsula.

Yemenite *noun*
• "YEM'n ite"
• a native or inhabitant of Yemen in the S Arabian peninsula.

yeoman *noun*
• "YO m'n"
• a man holding and cultivating a small landed estate.
• [Middle English *yoman*, *yeman*, etc., prob. from 'young' + 'man']
• **yeomanly** *adjective*

yeomanry *noun*
• "YO m'n ree"
• a body of yeomen.
• [as YEOMAN]

yeshiva *noun*
ALSO SPELLED: **yeshivah**
• "yuh SHEEVA"
• an Orthodox Jewish college or seminary.
• [Hebrew *yĕšîḇāh*, from *yāšaḇ* sit]

yeti *noun*
• "YETTY"
• an unidentified manlike or bearlike animal said to exist in the Himalayas; the abominable snowman.
• [Tibetan]

yew *noun*
• "YOO"
• any dark-leaved evergreen coniferous tree or shrub of the genus *Taxus*, having seeds enclosed in a fleshy red aril, and historically often planted in churchyards.
• [Old English *īw*, *ēow* from Germanic]
HOMOPHONES: *ewe*, *you*

Yiddish *noun*
• "YIDDISH"
• a vernacular used by Jews in or from central and eastern Europe, originally a German dialect with words from Hebrew and several modern languages, and written using Hebrew characters.
• [German *jüdisch* Jewish]

Yiddisher *noun*
• "YIDDISH ur"
• a person speaking Yiddish.
• [as YIDDISH]

Yiddishism *noun*
• "YIDDISH izm"
• a Yiddish word, idiom, etc., esp. one adopted into another language.
• [as YIDDISH]

Yiddishkeit *noun*
• "YIDDISH kite"
• the quality of being Jewish; the Jewish way of life or its customs or practices.
• [Yiddish *yidishkeyt*]

yield *verb*
• "YEELD"
• produce or return as a fruit, profit, or result.
• [Old English *g(i)eldan* pay, from Germanic]
• **yielder** *noun*

yielding *adjective*
• "YEELD ing"
• compliant, submissive.
• [as YIELD]
• **yieldingness** *noun*

yod *noun*
• "YOD"
• the tenth and smallest letter of the Hebrew alphabet.
• [Hebrew *yōḏ* from *yaḏ* hand]

yodel *verb*
• "YODE 'll"
• sing with melodious inarticulate sounds and frequent changes between falsetto and the normal voice, in the manner of Swiss and Tyrolean mountaineers.
• [German *jodeln*]
• **yodeller** *noun* (also **yodeler**)

yogh *noun*
- "YOG"
- a Middle English letter used for certain values of *g* and *y*.
- [Middle English]

yogi *noun*
- "YO gee" (with "G" as in *GEEK*)
- a person proficient in yoga.
- [Sanskrit from *yoga* = union]
- **yogism** *noun*

yogourt *noun*
ALSO SPELLED: **yogurt**, **yoghurt**
- "YO gurt"
- a semi-solid slightly tart food prepared from milk fermented by added bacteria, usu. sweetened or flavoured with fruit etc.
- [French from Turkish *yoğurt*]

yokel *noun*
- "YOKE 'll"
- a country bumpkin.
- [perhaps from dialect *yokel* green woodpecker]

yolk *noun*
- "YOKE"
- the yellow inner part of an egg that nourishes the young before it hatches.
- [Old English *geol(o)ca* from *geolu* yellow]
- **yolked** *adjective*
- **yolkless** *adjective*
- **yolky** *adjective*

HOMOPHONES: *yoke*

yoni *noun*
- "YO nee"
- a figure or representation of the female genitals as a sacred symbol or object in Hinduism.
- [Sanskrit, = source, womb, female genitals]

Yorkshireman *noun*
- "YORK shur m'n"
- a native of Yorkshire in N England.

Yoruba *noun*
- "YORRA buh"
- a member of an African people inhabiting the west coast, esp. Nigeria.
- [Yoruba]

ytterbium *noun*
- "it TURBY um"
- a silvery metallic element of the lanthanide series occurring naturally as various isotopes.
- [modern Latin from *Ytterby* in Sweden]

yttrium *noun*
- "IT ree um"
- a greyish metallic element resembling the lanthanides, occurring naturally in uranium ores and used in making superconductors.
- [formed as YTTERBIUM]

yuan *noun*
- "yoo ON"
- the chief monetary unit of China.
- [Chinese, = round, dollar]

yucca *noun*
- "YUCKA"
- any N American white-flowered liliaceous plant of the genus *Yucca*, with sword-like leaves.
- [Carib]

Yugoslav *noun*
- "YOOGA slov" or "YOOGA slav"
- a native or national of the former Balkan federation of Yugoslavia.
- [Austrian German *Jugoslav* from Serbian *jugo-* from *jug* south + 'Slav' from medieval Latin *Sclavus*, late Greek *Sklabos*, & from medieval Latin *Slavus*]

yukata *noun*
- "yook ATTA" ("YOOK" rhymes with *BOOK*)
- a light cotton kimono, frequently with stencil designs, worn after a bath or as a housecoat.
- [Japanese *yu* hot water + *kata(bira)* light kimono]

yule *noun*
- "YOOL"
- the Christmas festival.
- [Old English *gēol(a)*: compare Old Norse *jól*]

Yupik *noun*
- "YOO pick"
- a member of a group of Aboriginal peoples living in coastal areas of Alaska and NE Siberia.
- [Yupik *Yup'ik* real person]

yurt *noun*
- "YOORT" or "YURT"
- a circular tent of felt, skins, etc., on a collapsible framework, used by nomads in Mongolia and Siberia.
- [Russian *yurta* via French *yourte* or German *Jurte* from Turkish *jurt*]

Zz

zabaglione *noun*
• "zabble YO nay"
• a dessert consisting of egg yolks, sugar, and (esp. Marsala) wine, whipped to a frothy texture over gentle heat and served warm or cold.
• [Italian]

zaftig *adjective*
• "ZAFF tig"
• (of a woman) plump; having a full, rounded figure.
• [Yiddish, from German *saftig* juicy]

zaibatsu *noun*
• "zye BAT soo"
• a Japanese business cartel or conglomerate.
• [Japanese, from *zai* wealth + *batsu* clique]

zaire *noun*
• "zaw EER"
• the basic monetary unit of Congo (formerly Zaire), equal to 100 makuta.
• [from *Zaire*, local name of the Congo River]

Zairean *noun*
ALSO SPELLED: **Zairian**
• "zye EERY 'n"
• a native or inhabitant of Zaire (the Democratic Republic of the Congo).

zakat *noun*
• "zuh KOT"
• obligatory payment made annually under Islamic law on certain kinds of property and used for charitable and religious purposes.
• [Arabic, = 'almsgiving']

Zambian *noun*
• "ZAMBY 'n"
• a native or inhabitant of Zambia in central Africa.

zamindar *noun*
ALSO SPELLED: **zemindar**
• "zuh MEAN dur"
• (in India) the owner of a large agricultural estate.
• [Urdu, from Persian *zamīndār*, from *zamīn* land + *dār* holder]

zany *adjective*
• "ZAY nee"
• comically idiotic; crazily ridiculous.
• [French *zani* or Italian *zan(n)i*, Venetian form of *Gianni*, *Giovanni* John]
• **zanily** *adverb*
• **zaniness** *noun*

zapateado *noun*
• "zoppa tee ODDO"
• a flamenco dance with rhythmic stamping of the feet.
• [Spanish from *zapato* shoe]

Zapatista *noun*
• "zappa TEESTA"
• a supporter of Mexican revolutionary Emiliano Zapata (d.1919).

Zapf *noun*
• "ZAPF"
• the name of several typefaces designed by Hermann Zapf, German type designer b.1918.

Zapotec *noun*
• "ZAPPA teck"
• a member of an Aboriginal people inhabiting the region around Oaxaca in SW Mexico.
• [Spanish from Nahuatl]

Zarathustrian *noun*
• "zerra THOOSS tree 'n"
• of or relating to Zoroaster or Zarathustra (d. *c.*551 BC) or the dualistic religious system taught by him or his followers in the Zend-Avesta, based on the concept of a conflict between a spirit of light and good and a spirit of darkness and evil.

zareba *noun*
ALSO SPELLED: **zariba**
• "zuh REEBA"
• a hedged or palisaded enclosure for the protection of a camp or village in Sudan etc.
• [Arabic *zarība* cattle pen]

zarzuela *noun*
• "zar ZWAY luh"
• a Spanish traditional form of musical comedy.
• [Spanish: apparently from a place name]

zax *noun*
• "ZAX"
• a slater's chopper, with a point for making nail holes.
• [Old English *seax* knife, from Germanic]

zazen *noun*
- "zaw ZEN"
- Zen meditation, usu. conducted in the lotus position.
- [Japanese, from *za* sitting + *zen* meditation]

zeal *noun*
- "ZEEL"
- earnestness or fervour in advancing a cause or rendering service.
- [Church Latin *zelus* from Greek *zēlos*]
- **zealous** *adjective* "ZELL us"
- **zealously** *adverb*
- **zealousness** *noun*

zealot *noun*
- "ZELL it"
- an uncompromising or extreme partisan; a fanatic.
- [Church Latin *zelotes* from Greek *zēlōtēs* (as ZEAL)]
- **zealotry** *noun*

zeaxanthin *noun*
- "zee a ZAN thin"
- a carotenoid pigment found in corn and egg yolk, used as a colouring.
- [*Zea*, genus name for corn + XANTHIC]

zebu *noun*
- "ZEE boo"
- a humped ox, *Bos indicus*, of India, E Asia, and Africa.
- [French *zébu*, of unknown origin]

zeda *noun*
- "ZAY duh"
- (among Jewish people) grandfather.
- [Yiddish *zeide*]

zedoary *noun*
- "ZEDDO airy"
- an aromatic ginger-like substance made from the rootstock of E Indian plants of the genus *Curcuma* and used in medicine, perfumery, and dyeing.
- [medieval Latin *zedoarium* from Persian *zidwār*]

zein *noun*
- "ZEE in"
- the principal protein of corn.
- [modern Latin *Zea*, genus name of corn]

zeitgeist *noun*
- "TSITE geist" or "ZITE geist" ("GEIST" rhymes with *PRICED*)
- the spirit of the times.
- [German from *Zeit* time + *Geist* spirit]
- **zeitgeisty** *adjective*

zenana *noun*
- "zen ONNA"
- the part of a house for the seclusion of women of high-caste families in India and Iran.
- [Urdu *zenāna* from Persian *zanāna* from *zan* woman]

zendo *noun*
- "ZEN doe"
- a place for Zen Buddhist meditation and study.
- [Japanese, from *zen* meditation + *dō* hall]

zenith *noun*
- "ZEE nith" or "ZEN ith"
- the part of the celestial sphere directly above an observer.
- [Old French *cenit* or medieval Latin *cenit*, ultimately from Arabic *samt* (*ar-ra's*) path (over the head)]
- **zenithal** *adjective*

zeolite *noun*
- "ZEE a lite"
- each of a number of minerals consisting mainly of hydrous silicates of calcium, sodium, and aluminum, able to act as cation exchangers.
- [Swedish & German *zeolit* from Greek *zeō* boil + *lithos* stone (from their characteristic swelling and fusing under the blowpipe)]
- **zeolitic** *adjective* "zee a LITTIC"

zephyr *noun*
- "ZEFFER"
- a mild gentle wind or breeze.
- [Latin *Zephyrus* from Greek *Zephuros*, personification of the west wind]

Zeppelin *noun*
- "ZEP lin"
- a large dirigible airship of the early 20th c., originally for military use.
- [Count F. von *Zeppelin*, German aviation pioneer d.1917]

zeroth *adjective*
- "ZEER oath"
- immediately preceding what is regarded as 'first' in a series.
- [French *zéro* or Italian *zero* from Old Spanish from Arabic *ṣifr* cipher, zero]

zeta *noun*
- "ZEE tuh"
- the sixth letter of the Greek alphabet (Z, ζ).
- [Greek *zēta*]

zeugma *noun*
- "ZOOG muh" or "ZYOOG muh"
- a rhetorical figure by which a single word is made to refer to two or more words in a sentence, esp. when applying to them in different senses.
- [Latin from Greek *zeugma -atos* from *zeugnumi* to yoke, *zugon* yoke]
- **zeugmatic** *adjective*

zidovudine *noun*
- "zye DOV yoo deen"
- an antiviral drug used to treat HIV infection and AIDS.
- [arbitrary alteration of chemical name *azidothymidine*]

ziggurat *noun*
• "ZIGGA rat"
• a rectangular stepped tower in ancient Mesopotamia, surmounted by a temple.
• [Assyrian *ziqquratu* pinnacle]

Zimbabwean *noun*
• "zim BOB wee 'n" or "zim BOB way 'n"
• a native or inhabitant of Zimbabwe in southern Africa.

zinc *noun*
• "ZINK"
• a white metallic element occurring naturally as zinc blende, and used as a component of brass, in galvanizing sheet iron, and in electric batteries.
• [German *Zink*, of unknown origin]

zine *noun*
• "ZEEN"
• a magazine, esp. a fanzine.
• [abbreviation]

Zinfandel *noun*
• "ZIN f'n dell"
• a red, white, or rosé wine made esp. in California.
• [origin unknown]

zinnia *noun*
• "ZIN yuh"
• a composite plant of the chiefly Mexican genus *Zinnia*, often grown for their showy flowers.
• [J. G. *Zinn*, German physician and botanist d.1759]

zircon *noun*
• "ZUR con"
• a zirconium silicate of which some translucent varieties are cut into gems.
• [German *Zirkon*]

zirconia *noun*
• "zur CONEY uh"
• zirconium dioxide, used in ceramics, refractory coatings, etc., and in fused form as a synthetic substitute for diamonds in jewellery.
• [as ZIRCON]

zirconium *noun*
• "zur CONEY um"
• a grey metallic element occurring naturally in zircon and used in various industrial applications.
• [as ZIRCON]

ziti *plural noun*
• "ZEE tee"
• pasta in the form of tubes resembling large macaroni.
• [Italian, prob. from dialect *zito* bridegroom, because traditionally served at weddings]

zloty *noun*
• "ZLOTTY"
• the chief monetary unit of Poland, equal to 100 groszy.
• [Polish, lit. 'golden']

zodiac *noun*
• "ZO dee ack"
• a belt of the heavens within about 8° of the ecliptic, including all apparent positions of the sun, moon, and most familiar planets, and divided into twelve parts (signs) named after constellations (Aries, Taurus, Gemini, Cancer, Leo, Virgo, Libra, Scorpio, Sagittarius, Capricorn, Aquarius, Pisces) and used in astrology.
• [Old French *zodiaque* from Latin *zodiacus* from Greek *zōidiakos* from *zōidion* sculptured animal figure, diminutive of *zōion* animal]

zodiacal *adjective*
• "zuh DIE a k'll"
• of or in the zodiac.
• [as ZODIAC]

zoetrope *noun*
• "ZOA trope"
• a 19th-c. optical toy consisting of a cylinder with a series of pictures on the inner surface that, when viewed through slits with the cylinder rotating, give an impression of continuous motion.
• [formed irregularly from Greek *zōē* life + *-tropos* turning]

Zohar *noun*
• "ZO har"
• the chief text of the Jewish Kabbalah, presented as an allegorical or mystical interpretation of the Pentateuch.
• [Hebrew, lit. = 'light, splendour']

zollverein *noun*
• "TSAWL fuh rine"
• a customs union, esp. of German states in the 19th c.
• [German]

zombie *noun*
• "ZOMBY"
• a dull, apathetic, or exceedingly tired person.
• [Kikongo *zumbi* fetish]
• **zombielike** *adjective*
• **zombification** *noun*
• **zombified** *adjective*
• **zombify** *verb*

zonation *noun*
• "zo NAY sh'n"
• distribution in zones, esp. of plants into zones characterized by the dominant species.
• [French *zone* or Latin *zona* girdle, from Greek *zōnē*]

zoogeography *noun*
• "zoo a jee OGGRA fee" or "zo a jee OGGRA fee"
• the branch of zoology dealing with the geographical distribution of animals.
• [Greek *zōio-* from *zōion* animal + GEOGRAPHY]
• **zoogeographic** *adjective*
• **zoogeographical** *adjective*

zooid *noun*
• "ZOO oid" or "ZO oid"
• a more or less independent invertebrate organism arising by budding or fission.
• [Greek *zōio-* from *zōion* animal]
• **zooidal** *adjective*

zoology *noun*
• "zoo OLLA jee" or "zo OLLA jee"
• the scientific study of animals, esp. with reference to their structure, physiology, classification, and distribution.
• [Greek *zōio-* from *zōion* animal + *logos* word]
• **zoological** *adjective* "zoo a LODGE a k'll" or "zo a LODGE a k'll"
• **zoologically** *adverb*
• **zoologist** *noun*

zoomorphic *adjective*
• "zoo a MORFIC" or "zo a MORFIC" or "zoo MORFIC"
• dealing with or represented in animal forms.
• [Greek *zōio-* from *zōion* animal + *morphē* form]
• **zoomorphism** *noun*

zoonosis *noun*
• "zoo a NO sis" or "zo a NO sis"
• any of various diseases which can be transmitted to humans from animals.
• [Greek *zōio-* from *zōion* animal + *nosos* disease]
• **zoonotic** *adjective*

zoophyte *noun*
• "ZOO a fite" or "ZO a fite"
• any of various sessile invertebrate animals that resemble plants or flowers, such as a coral, sea anemone, or sponge.
• [Greek *zōio-* from *zōion* animal + *phuton* plant, from *phuō* come into being]
• **zoophytic** *adjective* "zoo a FITTIC" or "zo a FITTIC"

zooplankton *noun*
• "zoo a PLANK t'n" or "zo a PLANK t'n"
• the animal component of plankton, consisting of small animals and the immature stages of larger animals.
• [Greek *zōio-* from *zōion* animal + PLANKTON]

zoospore *noun*
• "ZOO a spore" or "ZO a spore"
• a spore of fungi, algae, etc. capable of motion.
• [Greek *zōio-* from *zōion* animal + SPORE]

zooxanthella *noun*
• "zo a zan THELLA"
• a yellowish-brown symbiotic dinoflagellate present in large numbers in the cytoplasm of many marine invertebrates.
• [modern Latin *zoo-* of animals, from Greek *zōio-* from *zōion* animal + Greek *xanthos* yellow + diminutive *ella*]

zori *noun*
• "ZORY"
• a Japanese sandal, having a simple thong between the toes and a flat sole originally of straw but now often of rubber or felt etc.
• [Japanese]

zoril *noun*
ALSO SPELLED: **zorille**
• "ZORE ill"
• a flesh-eating African mammal, *Ictonyx striatus*, of the skunk and the weasel family.
• [French *zorille* from Spanish *zorrilla* diminutive of *zorro* fox]

Zoroastrian *adjective*
• "zoro ASS tree 'n"
• of or relating to Zoroaster or Zarathustra (d. *c.*551 BC) or the dualistic religious system taught by him or his followers in the Zend-Avesta, based on the concept of a conflict between a spirit of light and good and a spirit of darkness and evil.
• **Zoroastrianism** *noun*

Zouave *noun*
• "zoo OV" or "ZWOV"
• a member of a French light-infantry corps originally formed of Algerians and long retaining their original oriental uniform.
• [French from *Zouaoua*, name of a tribe]

zouk *noun*
• "ZOOK" (rhymes with *SPOOK*)
• an exuberant style of popular music, originating in the W Indies, combining Caribbean and Western elements and characterized by a strong fast beat.
• [French Creole, lit. 'to party']

zucchetto *noun*
• "zoo KETTO" or "tsoo KETTO"
• a Roman Catholic ecclesiastic's skullcap, black for a priest, purple for a bishop, red for a cardinal, and white for a pope.
• [Italian *zucchetta* diminutive of *zucca* gourd, head]

zucchini *noun*
• "zoo KEENY"
• a green-skinned summer squash, similar in appearance to a cucumber.
• [Italian, pl. of *zucchino* diminutive of *zucca* gourd]

zugzwang *noun*
• "TSOOK svong" (with "OO" as in *BOOK*)
• (in chess) an obligation to move in one's turn even when this must be disadvantageous.
• [German from *Zug* move + *Zwang* compulsion]

Zulu *noun*
• "ZOO loo"
• a member of a Bantu-speaking people forming the largest ethnic group in South Africa.
• [Zulu *umzulu*, pl. *amazulu*]

Zuni *noun*
• "ZOO nee" or "ZOON yee"
• a member of a Pueblo people of New Mexico.
• [a river in New Mexico]

zuppa *noun*
• "TSOOPA" or "ZOOPA"

• fish soup.
• [Italian, lit. 'soup']

zwieback ***noun***
• "ZWEE back"
• a sweet rich egg bread, sliced and baked again until crisp.
• [German, = twice baked]

zwitterion ***noun***
• "ZWITTER eye 'n"
• a molecule or ion having separate positively and negatively charged groups.
• [German from *Zwitter* a hybrid + ION]
• **zwitterionic** ***adjective***

zydeco ***noun***
• "ZYE duh co"
• a kind of dance music originally from southern Louisiana, combining blues and Cajun influences and often performed on guitar, violin, and accordion.
• [Louisiana Creole, possibly from French *les haricots* in a dance tune title]

zygodactyl ***adjective***
• "zye go DACK t'll"
• (of a bird) having two toes pointing forward and two backward.
• [Greek *zugon* yoke + DACTYL]
• **zygodactylous** ***adjective***

zygoma ***noun***
• "zye GO muh" or "zig OH muh"
• the bony arch of the cheek formed by connection of the zygomatic and temporal bones at the edge of the eye socket.
• [Greek *zugōma -atos* from *zugon* yoke]
• **zygomatic** ***adjective*** "zye go MATTIC" or "zig oh MATTIC"

zygote ***noun***
• "ZYE gote"
• a cell formed by the union of two gametes; a fertilized ovum.
• [Greek *zugōtos* yoked, from *zugoō* to yoke]
• **zygotic** ***adjective*** "zye GOTTIC"
• **zygotically** ***adverb***

zymase ***noun***
• "ZYE mace"
• a mixture of enzymes obtained from yeast which catalyze the breakdown of sugars in alcoholic fermentation.
• [French from Greek *zumē* leaven]

zymotic ***adjective***
• "zye MOTTIC" or "zim OTTIC"
• of, relating to, or denoting an infectious disease.
• [Greek *zumōtikos* (as ZYMASE)]

zymurgy ***noun***
• "ZYE mur jee"
• the branch of applied chemistry dealing with the use of fermentation in brewing etc.
• [Greek *zumē* leaven, after *metallurgy*]